ELIZABETHAN
AND
STUART PLAYS

ELIZABETHAN AND STUART PLAYS

EDITED BY

CHARLES READ BASKERVILL
LATE PROFESSOR OF ENGLISH
UNIVERSITY OF CHICAGO

VIRGIL B. HELTZEL
PROFESSOR OF ENGLISH
NORTHWESTERN UNIVERSITY

ARTHUR H. NETHERCOT
PROFESSOR OF ENGLISH
NORTHWESTERN UNIVERSITY

HOLT, RINEHART AND WINSTON
New York · Chicago · San Francisco
Toronto · London

PREFACE

This collection of Elizabethan and Stuart plays exclusive of Shakespeare has the advantage of a larger compass than similar anthologies for students. It opens with such plays as *Roister Doister*, *Gammer Gurton's Needle*, and *Gorboduc*, in which, through imitation of the classics, English drama broke with medieval tradition as represented in the hybrid moralities, and it extends to the closing of the theaters in 1642, when the tone of the drama was already foreshadowing the Restoration period. Enough plays are included, moreover, to show the richness and variety of the great dramatic art of the era without neglecting the various phases of its historical development. It has been possible, for example, to print five plays and a masque as representative of Jonson's work, and at the same time to give specimens of popular romantic drama like *Mucedorus* or of a hitherto neglected form like the jig. All the significant types of drama in the period are illustrated here.

The plays have been arranged in two groups as Elizabethan and Stuart for the purpose of emphasizing what is distinctive in each period. In this way the Elizabethan group may more readily be studied in connection with medieval drama or Shakespeare, and the Stuart group as a background for Restoration drama. The division is useful even when the two eras are studied together. In Shakespeare's immediate predecessors and contemporaries, the Elizabethan characteristics of boldness of conception and execution are obvious, resulting in an imaginative and emotional power which is frequently accompanied by a disregard for restraint, structure, and form. This distinctive quality survives in the final work of Shakespeare and in the two great tragedies of Webster, so that *The Duchess of Malfi*, in spite of its late date, is included with the Elizabethan plays. Already, however, Jonson had written his chief works that represent the Stuart reaction in drama, following classical ideals of restraint and unity in design; and a change of attitude, with a more searching study of manners, resulted. The centering of interest on form and technique, even in romantic plays, gives a sufficiently distinct character to the plays of the Stuart period as a whole.

The text used as a basis of the editing is indicated in the introduction to each play. For about half the plays, original early editions, photostatic copies of them, reproductions in the Farmer Facsimile Texts, or facsimile reprints of the Malone Society have been used. The rest are based on standard modern editions, in most cases recent critical editions. These have also been checked with other modern editions, or where possible with Farmer Facsimiles or the Malone Society reproductions. In whatever affects the actual content of the play, including stage directions, the principle followed has been one of strict fidelity to the original. Emendations have been avoided when any logical interpretation of the reading given seemed possible, and those adopted are duly recorded in the footnotes. Added material has been enclosed in square brackets. When no source of an emendation is stated, it has been made on the authority of the basic text, except that in stage directions the bracketed material has usually been added by the present editors. Plays with no act and scene division have been divided simply into scenes, with bracketed numbers. Likewise few liberties have been taken with the verse arrangement found in the sixteenth and seventeenth century originals, unless by a simple change in the division of lines a whole passage could be made to fall into pattern. Footnotes call attention to such revision in the plays in which it occurs. In *George a Greene* and the additions to *The Spanish Tragedy*, there are so many doubtful cases or cases in which no satisfactory arrangement of the lines is possible that no attempt has been made to change the original arrangement even in the passages where the dramatist's intention seems fairly clear.

In matters of less fundamental importance, the editing has been done with a view to aiding the student who is interested primarily in the literary and dramatic qualities of the plays. Hence spelling, punctuation, and capitalization have been modernized. Where differences in spelling, however, suggest significant differences in pronunciation resulting from the survival in Elizabethan times of variant forms now obsolete (as in *hunderd, renowm, accompt,* for example), the original has been followed, at times even in doubtful cases. On the other hand, in certain very common words where the vowel varies so frequently as to suggest that perhaps to an Elizabethan there was little distinction in sound, the modern spelling has been adopted. Examples include the use of *than* for *then* (in the modern sense of *than*), *whither* and *hither* for *whether* and *hether* (except in dialect or consciously archaic passages or for rime), *devil* for *divel, show* for *shew, ambassador* for *embassador,* and many *in-* combinations for *en-* combinations (for instance, *increase* for *encrease*). In such original forms as *marchant* and *clark, -er-* has regularly been substituted for *-ar-*. The spellings *dost* and *doth,* rather than *doest* and *doeth,* are regularly used for the words as auxiliaries. *Wive's* as a possessive singular is printed *wife's,* but in general such voicings have been retained whenever any modern justification for them could be found. Again, obvious misprints have been silently corrected throughout. Numerals also are written out, and a compound form like *24* is expanded into the common Elizabethan form *four-and-twenty.* In many of the plays, speech heads vary so irrationally that they have been frankly reduced to some consistency. The prevalent or the most logical form of each speaker's name, usually an abbreviation, has been adopted throughout a play, except that, where there are two or three different names for the same speaker, they are retained, with explanation in the notes. As the original speech heads in *Cambises* are printed in full consistently, however, they have been left unchanged. It is perhaps unnecessary to mention the omission of imprints, colophons, titles repeated at the head of the text proper, and running heads, or the occasional disregard of certain unusual arrangements of the material on the page of the original.

As an aid in the matter of meter, an accent has been placed over *e* in the verbal suffix *-ed* when it is pronounced as an additional syllable contrary to ordinary usage, and an apostrophe marks the omission of a vowel when a shortening in pronunciation seems to be indicated by the spelling of the original (as in *wav'ring,* for example). For the rest, it is felt that with a little attention to Elizabethan practice, the reader will quickly fall into the rhythm of the various dramatists, representing various periods. Especially after playwrights learned to give verse some of the flexibility of speech, blank verse was handled very freely. Occasionally the line is as short as one foot, or as long as six. The foot may have an extra syllable, or a syllable may be omitted, usually at the beginning of a line or after a pause. Inverted stress is frequent in the first foot and occasionally occurs elsewhere, especially after a pause. It is to be noted also that some Elizabethan words differ from modern usage in the position of the accent, and a much larger number seems to have been very flexible as to accent, at least in verse. *Ácademy, revénue, infámous, envý, cómplete, canónize, obdúrate, pórtray, déprive,* and *aspéct* are a few examples taken from the plays printed here. Another large group of words, especially those with endings in *-ion, -ian, -ia, -ience, -ier,* etc., are often to be scanned as having a syllable more than is normal in modern pronunciation (as in *motion, ocean, Christian, Persia, Delia, soldier, marriage*). Not infrequently, too, an extra syllable is developed, especially in connection with *l* and *r* (as in *fair, fire, hour, mild, sure, sworn*).

Webster's *Collegiate Dictionary* has been taken as the standard of what the reader might properly be expected to know in the matter of current vocabulary. Old forms that are not obvious, and words and phrases that are obsolete, or have shifted meaning, or for any other reason might not be understood, have been explained in the notes for each play, but as a rule only in the first occurrence in a given play.

The editors wish to thank Professor J. C. Murley, Professor J. G. Fucilla, and Dr. N. A. Bennetton for help in translating a few difficult or corrupt passages from Latin, Italian, and Spanish, and Professor F. H. Heidbrink, Professor M. E. Prior, Dr. L. S. Wright, and Dr. Z. S. Fink for help in proof-reading the second part.

CONTENTS

PART ONE: ELIZABETHAN PLAYS

PAGE

Roister Doister, *by Nicholas Udall* 1

Gammer Gurton's Needle, *by "Mr. [William] S [tevenson?]"* 47

Gorboduc, *by Thomas Norton and Thomas Sackville* 77

Supposes, *by George Gascoigne* 111

Cambises, *by Thomas Preston* 143

Endymion, *by John Lyly* 171

The Arraignment of Paris, *by George Peele* 205

The Old Wives' Tale, *by George Peele* 231

Friar Bacon and Friar Bungay, *by Robert Greene* 247

George a Greene, *by Robert Greene* (?) 285

Tamburlaine, Part I, *by Christopher Marlowe* 307

Doctor Faustus, *by Christopher Marlowe* 349

Edward II, *by Christopher Marlowe* 375

The Spanish Tragedy, *by Thomas Kyd* 421

Arden of Feversham 475

Attowell's Jig (Francis' New Jig) 519

Mucedorus 525

The Shoemakers' Holiday, *by Thomas Dekker* 553

The Honest Whore, Part I, *by Thomas Dekker* 593

A Woman Killed with Kindness, *by Thomas Heywood* 641

The Malcontent, *by John Marston and John Webster* 679

Bussy d'Ambois, *by George Chapman* 723

The Duchess of Malfi, *by John Webster* 771

PART TWO: STUART PLAYS

Every Man in His Humor, *by Ben Jonson* 827

Sejanus His Fall, *by Ben Jonson* 881

Volpone, or The Fox, *by Ben Jonson* 941

The Alchemist, *by Ben Jonson* 1003

The Hue and Cry after Cupid, *by Ben Jonson* 1067

The Sad Shepherd, *by Ben Jonson* 1075

The Knight of the Burning Pestle, *by Francis Beaumont and John Fletcher* 1099

PAGE

The Faithful Shepherdess, *by John Fletcher* 1147

Philaster, *by Francis Beaumont and John Fletcher* 1189

The Maid's Tragedy, *by Francis Beaumont and John Fletcher* 1233

A Trick to Catch the Old One, *by Thomas Middleton* 1279

The Changeling, *by Thomas Middleton and William Rowley* 1317

A New Way to Pay Old Debts, *by Philip Massinger* 1355

The Maid of Honor, *by Philip Massinger* 1401

The Witch of Edmonton, *by John Ford, Thomas Dekker, and William Rowley* 1443

The Broken Heart, *by John Ford* 1485

Perkin Warbeck, *by John Ford* 1531

The Lady of Pleasure, *by James Shirley* 1577

The Cardinal, *by James Shirley* 1625

ELIZABETHAN PLAYS

EDITED BY

CHARLES READ BASKERVILL
VIRGIL B. HELTZEL
ARTHUR H. NETHERCOT

NICHOLAS UDALL

Nicholas Udall, born about 1505 or 1506, was educated at Winchester College and at Corpus Christi College, Oxford, where he proceeded M.A. in 1534. In 1533 he prepared, with the help of John Leland, the great antiquary, a verse pageant for the coronation of Anne Boleyn, in which Paris bestowed the golden apple on the queen instead of on Venus, and about the same time he brought out *Flowers for Latin Speaking*, selections from Terence, with an English translation. Both enterprises illustrate the increasing influence of humanism, of which the most important early monument in the field of drama is his *Roister Doister*. Udall was Vicar of Braintree, Essex, from 1533 to 1537, and Master of Eton from 1534 to 1541, when charges against him and a confession of misconduct caused his dismissal. In the succeeding years he enjoyed the patronage of different noblemen, wrote or translated several works, and took some part in Protestant propaganda. Nevertheless he retained the favor of the Catholic Mary on her accession in 1553. He was appointed Master of Westminster School in 1555 and died in 1556.

Though Bishop Bale states in his *Catalogus* that Udall wrote several plays ("*Comœdias plures*"), it was not known that any had survived until the unique copy of *Roister Doister*, now at Eton, was discovered early in the nineteenth century. The copy lacks a title-page, and the authorship of the play was established by the fact that the ambiguous letter of III, iv, was quoted as Udall's in Thomas Wilson's *The Rule of Reason* in 1553. Though *Roister Doister* was clearly written for acting by boys, the school, the date, and the occasion are uncertain. The traditional view is that it was written for the boys of Eton, and it has been conjectured that this was the play performed when they played before Cromwell in 1538. Arguments have been advanced, however, for its composition shortly before Wilson's use of the letter. The extant copy is usually dated 1566/7 because the play was licensed by the Stationers' Company for printing in that year, and because the prayer for the queen at the end is obviously for Elizabeth. The edition is possibly a revised form, however.

Roister Doister seems to be the earliest of a small group of extant plays which represent a change in the style of English comedy through the imitation of the classics. The formal act and scene structure, the simple setting of a town street, and the observation of the unities of action, time, and place belong to a new technique, which the humanists developed through a study of classical comedy and criticism. The characters and the incidents are also modeled on Roman comedy. For the group of characters and their relations centering in the household of Dame Custance, parallels are found in the plays of both Plautus and Terence, but especially in Terence's *Eunuchus*. Roister Doister, the braggart, and Merrygreek, a combination of parasite and intriguer, are drawn from the stock figures of Roman comedy. Udall's use of the *Miles gloriosus* of Plautus, in which the portrayal of the braggart soldier is perfected, is especially obvious, though perhaps modified by Terence's portrait of Thraso. Udall, however, blends his classical material rather skillfully with details of English life to give an English atmosphere to the play. The whole is also handled in a spirit of burlesque and extravagance which harmonizes perfectly with the spirit of revelry and misrule that prevailed in the games and pastimes of the holiday seasons in English institutional life of all types. Particularly the boys in schools connected with cathedrals and chapels, led by a boy bishop, celebrated Christmas with parodies of the regular services of the church, a tradition which is preserved in the mock liturgical material woven into *Roister Doister*.

Of the several modern reprints of the play, the best is that of Flügel in Gayley's *Representative English Comedies*, and it has been followed here even to the extent of beginning a new line for each speech, though in the original the speeches, if short or irregular in length, are run along on the same line until a rime word is reached.

1

ROISTER DOISTER[1]

BY

NICHOLAS UDALL

[DRAMATIS PERSONÆ

RALPH ROISTER DOISTER, *a braggart.*
MATTHEW MERRYGREEK, *a parasite.*
GAWIN GOODLUCK, *betrothed to Dame Custance.*
TRISTRAM TRUSTY, *his friend.*
DOBINET DOUGHTY, *a boy* ⎫ *servants to Roister Doister.*
HARPAX ⎭
TOM TRUEPENNY, *a boy, servant to Dame Custance.*

SIM SURESBY, *servant to Goodluck.*
SCRIVENER.
MUSICIANS *and* OTHERS.

DAME CHRISTIAN CUSTANCE, *a widow.*
MARGERY, *or* MADGE, MUMBLECRUST, *her old nurse.*

TIBET TALKAPACE ⎫ *her maids.*
ANNOT ALYFACE [2] ⎭

SCENE: *A street, probably in London.*

TIME: *Contemporary.*]

THE PROLOGUE

What creature is in health, either young or old,
But some mirth with modesty will be glad to use,
As[3] we in this interlude shall now unfold,
Wherein all scurrility we utterly refuse,
Avoiding such mirth wherein is abuse,
Knowing nothing more commendable for a man's recreation
Than mirth which is used in an honest fashion?

For mirth prolongeth life and causeth health;
Mirth recreates our spirits and voideth pensiveness;
Mirth increaseth amity, not hind'ring our wealth; 10
Mirth is to be used both of more and less,[4]
Being mixed with virtue in decent comeliness,
As we trust no good nature can gainsay the same—
Which mirth we intend to use, avoiding all blame.

The wise poets long time heretofore,
Under merry comedies secrets did declare,
Wherein was contained very virtuous lore,
With mysteries and forewarnings very rare.
Such to write neither Plautus nor Terence did spare,
Which among the learned at this day bears the bell; 20
These with such other therein did excel.

Our comedy or interlude which we intend to play
Is naméd *Roister Doister* indeed,
Which against the vainglorious doth inveigh,
Whose humor the roisting[5] sort continually doth feed.
Thus by your patience we intend to proceed
In this our interlude by God's leave and grace,
And here I take my leave for a certain space.

---

[1] Since the title-page is missing from the only copy of the play in existence, this title has been supplied from the prologue.

[2] *I.e.*, beery face.

[3] Such as.   [4] By great and small.

[5] Blustering.

FINIS.

Actus I. Scena i.[1]

Matthew Merrygreek. He ent'reth singing.

[M. Merry.] As long liveth the merry man,
    they say,
As doth the sorry man, and longer by a
    day.
Yet the grasshopper, for all his summer
    piping,
Starveth in winter with hungry griping;
Therefore another sayd [2] saw doth men
    advise
That they be together both merry and
    wise.
This lesson must I practice, or else ere
    long,
With me, Matthew Merrygreek, it will
    be wrong.
Indeed men so call me, for by Him that
    us bought,
Whatever chance betide, I can take no
    thought;   10
Yet wisdom would that I did myself
    bethink
Where to be provided this day of meat
    and drink;
For know ye that, for all this merry
    note of mine,
He might appose [3] me now that should
    ask where I dine.
My living lieth here and there, of God's
    grace:
Sometime with this good man, sometime
    in that place;
Sometime Lewis Loit'rer biddeth me
    come near;
Somewhiles Watkin Waster maketh us
    good cheer;
Sometime Davy Diceplayer, when he
    hath well cast,
Keepeth revel rout as long as it will
    last;   20
Sometime Tom Titivile maketh us a
    feast;
Sometime with Sir Hugh Pie I am a
    bidden guest;
Sometime at Nichol Neverthrive's I get
    a sop;
Sometime I am feasted with Bryan
    Blinkinsop;

Sometime I hang on Hankin Hoddy-
    doddy's sleeve,
But this day on Ralph Roister Doister's
    by his leave.
For truly of all men he is my chief
    banker
Both for meat and money, and my chief
    shoot-anchor.[4]
For, sooth [5] Roister Doister in that he
    doth say,
And, require what ye will, ye shall have
    no nay.   30
But now of Roister Doister somewhat to
    express,
That ye may esteem him after his
    worthiness,
In these twenty towns and seek them
    throughout,
Is not the like stock, whereon to graff [6]
    a lout.
All the day long is he facing and craking [7]
Of his great acts in fighting and fray-
    making;
But when Roister Doister is put to his
    proof,
To keep the queen's peace is more for
    his behoof.
If any woman smile or cast on him an
    eye,
Up is he to the hard ears in love by-and-
    by,[8]   40
And in all the hot haste must she be his
    wife,
Else farewell his good days, and farewell
    his life.
Master Rafe [9] Roister Doister is but
    dead and gone
Except she on him take some compas-
    sion;
Then chief of counsel must be Matthew
    Merrygreek.
"What if I for marriage to such an one
    seek?"
Then must I sooth it, whatever it is;
For what he saith or doth cannot be
    amiss.
Hold up his yea and nay, be his nown
    white son,[10]
Praise and rouse him well, and ye have
    his heart won,   50

For so well liketh he his own fond [1] fashions

That he taketh pride of false commendations.

But such sport have I with him as I
would not leese,[2]

Though I should be bound to live with
bread and cheese.

For exalt him, and have him as ye lust [3]
indeed—

Yea, to hold his finger in a hole for a
need.

I can with a word make him fain or loath;

I can with as much make him pleased or
wroth;

I can when I will make him merry and
glad;

I can when me lust make him sorry and
sad;   60

I can set him in hope and eke in despair;

I can make him speak rough and make
him speak fair.

But I marvel I see him not all this same
day.

I will seek him out.—But lo, he cometh
this way!

I have yond espied him sadly coming,

And in love for twenty pound, by his
glomming.[4]

Actus I. Scena ii.

Rafe Roister Doister, Matthew Merrygreek.

R. Roister. Come, death, when thou wilt!
I am weary of my life!

M. Merry. [*Aside.*] I told you, I, we
should woo another wife.

R. Roister. Why did God make me such
a goodly person?

M. Merry. [*Aside.*] He is in by the
week; [5] we shall have sport anon.[6]

R. Roister. And where is my trusty
friend, Matthew Merrygreek?

M. Merry. [*Aside.*] I will make as I saw
him not; he doth me seek.

R. Roister. I have him espied, methinketh; yond is he.

Ho! Matthew Merrygreek, my friend,
a word with thee.

M. Merry. [*Aside.*] I will not hear him,
but make as I had haste.—

[*To the audience.*] Farewell, all my good
friends; the time away doth waste.   10

And the tide, they say, tarrieth for no
man.

R. Roister. Thou must with thy good
counsel help me if thou can.

M. Merry. God keep thee, worshipful
Master Roister Doister,

And fare well thee, lusty Master Roister
Doister.

R. Roister. I must needs speak with thee
a word or twain.

M. Merry. Within a month or two I will
be here again.

Negligence in great affairs, ye know, may
mar all.

R. Roister. Attend upon me now, and
well reward thee I shall.

M. Merry. I have take my leave, and the
tide is well spent.

R. Roister. I die except thou help; I pray
thee, be content.   20

Do thy part well now, and ask what thou
wilt,

For without thy aid my matter is all
spilt.

M. Merry. Then to serve your turn I will
some pains take,

And let all mine own affairs alone for your
sake.

R. Roister. My whole hope and trust
resteth only in thee.

M. Merry. Then can ye not do amiss,
whatever it be.

R. Roister. Gramercies, Merrygreek, most
bound to thee I am.

M. Merry. But up with that heart, and
speak out like a ram.

Ye speak like a capon that had the cough
now.

Be of good cheer; anon ye shall do well
enow.   30

R. Roister. Upon thy comfort, I will all
things well handle.

M. Merry. So, lo! that is a breast [7] to
blow out a candle!

But what is this great matter, I would
fain know?

We shall find remedy therefore, I trow.

Do ye lack money? Ye know mine old
offers;

Ye have always a key to my purse and
coffers.

[1] Foolish.
[2] Lose.
[3] Desire.
[4] Sullenness.
[5] Trapped.
[6] At once.
[7] Pair of lungs.

R. Roister. I thank thee. Had ever man
  such a friend?
M. Merry. Ye give unto me; I must needs
  to you lend.
R. Roister. Nay, I have money plenty
  all things to discharge.
M. Merry. [*Aside*.] That knew I right
  well when I made offer so large. 40
R. Roister. But it is no such matter.
M. Merry. What is it then?
  Are ye in danger of debt to any man?
  If ye be, take no thought nor be not
  afraid.
  Let them hardly [1] take thought how they
  shall be paid.
R. Roister. Tut, I owe naught.
M. Merry. What
  then? Fear ye imprisonment?
R. Roister. No.
M. Merry. No, I wist [2] ye offend
  not, so to be shent.[3]
  But if ye had, the Tower could not you
  so hold,
  But to break out at all times ye would
  be bold.
  What is it? Hath any man threatened
  you to beat?
R. Roister. What is he that durst have
  put me in that heat? 50
  He that beateth me, by His arms, shall
  well find
  That I will not be far from him nor run
  behind.
M. Merry. That thing know all men ever
  since ye overthrew
  The fellow of the lion which Hercules
  slew.
  But what is it then?
R. Roister. Of love I make my
  moan.
M. Merry. Ah, this foolish a[h]-love, wilt
  ne'er let us alone?
  But, because ye were refused the last day,
  Ye said ye would ne'er more be entangled
  that way.
  I would meddle no more, since I find all
  so unkind.
R. Roister. Yea, but I cannot so put love
  out of my mind. 60
M. Merry. But is your love, tell me first,
  in any wise,
  In the way of marriage, or of merchan-
  dise?

[1] Assuredly.   [2] Knew.   [3] Shamed.

If it may otherwise than lawful be found,
Ye get none of my help for a hundred
  pound.
R. Roister. No, by my troth, I would
  have her to my wife.
M. Merry. Then are ye a good man, and
  God save your life!
  And what or who is she with whom ye
  are in love?
R. Roister. A woman whom I know not
  by what means to move.
M. Merry. Who is it?
R. Roister. A woman yond.
M. Merry. What is her name?
R. Roister. Her yonder.
M. Merry. Whom?
R. Roister. Mistress—ah—
M. Merry. Fie, fie,
  for shame! 70
  Love ye, and know not whom but "her
  yond," "a woman"?
  We shall then get you a wife—I cannot
  tell when.
R. Roister. The fair woman that supped
  with us yesternight;
  And I heard her name twice or thrice,
  and had it right.
M. Merry. Yea, ye may see ye ne'er take
  me to good cheer with you;
  If ye had, I could have told you her name
  now.
R. Roister. I was to blame indeed, but
  the next time perchance—
  And she dwelleth in this house.
M. Merry. What,
  Christian Custance?
R. Roister. Except I have her to my wife,
  I shall run mad.
M. Merry. [*Aside*.] Nay, unwise perhaps,
  but I warrant you for mad. 80
R. Roister. I am utterly dead unless I
  have my desire.
M. Merry. Where be the bellows that
  blew this sudden fire?
R. Roister. I hear she is worth a thou-
  sand pound and more.
M. Merry. Yea, but learn this one lesson
  of me afore:
  An hundred pound of marriage-money,
  doubtless,
  Is ever thirty pound sterling, or some-
  what less,
  So that her thousand pound, if she be
  thrifty,

Is much near [1] about two hundred and
    fifty,
Howbeit wooers and widows are never
    poor.
R. Roister. Is she a widow? I love her
    better therefore.   90
M. Merry. But I hear she hath made
    promise to another.
R. Roister. He shall go without her, and [2]
    he were my brother.
M. Merry. I have heard say—I am right
    well advised—
That she hath to Gawin Goodluck prom-
    ised.
R. Roister. What is that Gawin Good-
    luck?
M. Merry.   A merchant man.
R. Roister. Shall he speed afore me?
    Nay, sir, by sweet Saint Anne.
Ah, sir, "'*Backare*,' [3] quod [4] Mortimer to
    his sow." [5]
I will have her mine own self, I make
    God avow.
For, I tell thee, she is worth a thousand
    pound.
M. Merry. Yet a fitter wife for your
    ma'ship might be found: 100
Such a goodly man as you might get one
    with land,
Besides pounds of gold a thousand, and a
    thousand,
And a thousand, and a thousand, and a
    thousand,
And so to the sum of twenty hundred
    thousand.
Your most goodly personage is worthy of
    no less.
R. Roister. I am sorry God made me so
    comely, doubtless.
For that maketh me each where so highly
    favored,
And all women on me so enamored.
M. Merry. "Enamored," quod you?
    Have ye spied out that?
Ah sir, marry, now I see you know what
    is what.   110
"Enamored," ka? [6] Marry, sir, say that
    again!
But I thought not ye had marked it so
    plain.
R. Roister. Yes, each where they gaze
    all upon me and stare.

M. Merry. Yea, Malkin! [7] I warrant you
    as much as they dare!
And ye will not believe what they say
    in the street,
When your ma'ship passeth by, all such
    as I meet,
That sometimes I can scarce find what
    answer to make.
"Who is this?" saith one. "Sir Launcelot
    du Lake?"
"Who is this? Great Guy of Warwick?"
    saith another.
"No," say I, "it is the thirteenth
    Hercules, brother."   120
"Who is this? Noble Hector of Troy?"
    saith the third.
"No, but of the same nest," say I, "it is
    a bird."
"Who is this? Great Goliah, Sampson,
    or Colbrand?"
"No," say I, "but it is a Brute [8] of the
    Alie [9] land."
"Who is this? Great Alexander or
    Charles le Maigne?"
"No, it is the tenth Worthy," say I to
    them again.
I know not if I said well?
R. Roister.   Yes, for so I am.
M. Merry. Yea, for there were but nine
    Worthies before ye came.
To some others, the third Cato I do you
    call.   129
And so, as well as I can, I answer them all.
"Sir, I pray you, what lord or great
    gentleman is this?"
"Master Ralph Roister Doister, dame,"
    say I, "iwis." [10]
"O Lord," saith she then, "what a
    goodly man it is!
Would Christ I had such a husband as
    he is!"
"O Lord," say some, "that the sight
    of his face we lack!"
"It is enough for you," say I, "to see
    his back.
His face is for ladies of high and noble
    parages, [11]
With whom he hardly scapeth great
    marriages."—
With much more than this, and much
    otherwise.

[7] Probably *by Malkin*.
[8] A Brutus, an exemplary hero; with a pun on
brute.   [9] Holy(?).   [10] Certainly.   [11] Lineage

[1] Nearer.   [3] Keep back.   [5] An old proverb.
[2] An, if.   [4] Quoth, said.   [6] Quoth he.

R. Roister. I can thee thank that thou
    canst such answers devise;   140
But I perceive thou dost me throughly
    know.
M. Merry. I mark your manners for mine
    own learning, I trow.
But such is your beauty, and such are
    your acts,
Such is your personage, and such are
    your facts,[1]
That all women fair and foul, more and
    less,
They eye you, they "lub you," they talk
    of you doubtless.
Your p[l]easant look maketh them all
    merry,
Ye pass not by, but they laugh till they
    be weary;
Yea, and money could I have, the truth
    to tell,
Of many, to bring you that way where
    they dwell.   150
R. Roister. Merrygreek, for this thy re-
    porting well of me—
M. Merry. What should I else, sir? It
    is my duty, pardee.[2]
R. Roister. I promise thou shalt not lack,
    while I have a groat.
M. Merry. Faith, sir, and I ne'er had
    more need of a new coat.
R. Roister. Thou shalt have one to-
    morrow, and gold for to spend.
M. Merry. Then I trust to bring the day
    to a good end.
For, as for mine own part having money
    enow,
I could live only with the remembrance
    of you.
But now to your widow whom you love
    so hot.
R. Roister. By Cock,[3] thou sayest truth.
    I had almost forgot.   160
M. Merry. What if Christian Custance
    will not have you, what?
R. Roister. Have me? Yes, I warrant
    you, never doubt of that;
I know she loveth me, but she dare not
    speak.
M. Merry. Indeed, meet it were some-
    body should it break.[4]

R. Roister. She looked on me twenty
    times yesternight,
And laughed so.
M. Merry.   That she could not sit
    upright.
R. Roister. No, faith, could she not.
M. Merry.   No, even
    such a thing I cast.[5]
R. Roister. But for wooing, thou know-
    est, women are shamefast.[6]
But, and she knew my mind, I know
    she would be glad,
And think it the best chance that ever
    she had.   170
M. Merry. To her then like a man, and
    be bold forth to start.
Wooers never speed well that have a
    false heart.
R. Roister. What may I best do?
M. Merry.   Sir, re-
    main ye awhile [here].[7]
Ere long one or other of her house will
    appear.
Ye know my mind.
R. Roister.   Yea, now hardly let
    me alone.
M. Merry. In the meantime, sir, if you
    please, I will home,
And call your musicians, for in this your
    case
It would set you forth, and all your
    wooing grace.
Ye may not lack your instruments to
    play and sing.
R. Roister. Thou knowest I can do that.
M. Merry.   As well as anything.   180
Shall I go call your folks, that ye may
    show a cast?[8]
R. Roister. Yea, run, I beseech thee, in
    all possible haste.
M. Merry. I go.   *Exeat.*[9]
R. Roister.   Yea, for I love singing
    out of measure,
It comforteth my spirits and doth me
    great pleasure.
But who cometh forth yond from my
    sweetheart Custance?
My matter frameth well; this is a lucky
    chance.

---

[1] Deeds.
[2] From *par Dieu* (by God), an oath that had
become innocuous.
[3] Corruption of *By God*.   [4] Reveal.
[5] Forecast, expected.
[6] Shamefaced, bashful.
[7] Added by Cooper.
[8] Specimen.
[9] Let him go out.

Actus I. Scena iii.

*Madge Mumblecrust, spinning on the distaff.
Tibet Talkapace, sewing. Annot Alyface,[1] knitting. R[alph] Roister.*

M. Mumbl. If this distaff were spun,
Margery Mumblecrust—

Tib. Talk. Where good stale ale is, will
drink no water, I trust.

M. Mumbl. Dame Custance hath promised us good ale and white bread.

Tib. Talk. If she keep not promise, I will
beshrew [2] her head!

But it will be stark night before I shall
have done.

R. Roister. [*Aside.*] I will stand here
awhile, and talk with them anon.

I hear them speak of Custance, which
doth my heart good.

To hear her name spoken doth even
comfort my blood.

M. Mumbl. Sit down to your work, Tibet,
like a good girl.

Tib. Talk. Nurse, meddle you with your
spindle and your whirl.[3]　　　　10

No haste but good, Madge Mumblecrust;
for "Whip and whir," [4]

The old proverb doth say, "never made
good fur."

M. Mumbl. Well, ye will sit down to your
work anon, I trust.

Tib. Talk. "Soft fire maketh sweet malt,"
good Madge Mumblecrust.

M. Mumbl. And sweet malt maketh jolly
good ale for the nonce.

Tib. Talk. Which will slide down the lane
without any bones.　　　　*Cantet.*[5]

Oid brown bread crusts must have much
good mumbling,

But good ale down your throat hath
good easy tumbling.

R. Roister. [*Aside.*] The jolliest wench
that e'er I heard, little mouse!

May I not rejoice that she shall dwell in
my house?　　　　20

Tib. Talk. So, sirrah, now this gear [6] beginneth for to frame.

M. Mumbl. Thanks to God, though your
work stand still, your tongue is not
lame.

Tib. Talk. And though your teeth be
gone, both so sharp and so fine,

Yet your tongue can renne on pattens [7]
as well as mine.

M. Mumbl. Ye were not for naught named
Tib Talkapace.

Tib. Talk. Doth my talk grieve you?
Alack, God save your grace.

M. Mumbl. I hold [8] a groat, ye will drink
anon for this gear.

Tib. Talk. And I will pray you the stripes
for me to bear.

M. Mumbl. I hold a penny, ye will drink
without a cup.

Tib. Talk. Whereinsoe'er ye drink, I wot [9]
ye drink all up.　　　　30

[*Enter Annot.*]

An. Alyface. By Cock, and well sewed,
my good Tibet Talkapace.

Tib. Talk. And e'en as well knit, my
nown Annot Alyface.

R. Roister. [*Aside.*] See what a sort [10] she
keepeth that must be my wife!

Shall not I, when I have her, lead a merry
life?

Tib. Talk. Welcome, my good wench, and
sit here by me just.

An. Alyface. And how doth our old beldame here, Madge Mumblecrust?

Tib. Talk. Chide, and find faults, and
threaten to complain.

An. Alyface. To make us poor girls shent,
to her is small gain.

M. Mumbl. I did neither chide, nor complain, nor threaten.

R. Roister. [*Aside.*] It would grieve my
heart to see one of them beaten.　　40

M. Mumbl. I did nothing but bid her
work and hold her peace.

Tib. Talk. So would I, if you could your
clattering cease;

But the devil cannot make old trot [11] hold
her tongue.

An. Alyface. Let all these matters pass,
and we three sing a song.

So shall we pleasantly both the time
beguile now,

And eke despatch all our works ere we
can tell how.

---

[1] Enters later.
[2] Curse.
[3] Small flywheel on the spindle.
[4] Sound of a whip.
[5] Let her sing.
[6] Affair.
[7] Run on wooden shoes, *i.e.*, clatter.
[8] Wager.　[9] Know.　[10] Company.　[11] Hag.

Tib. Talk. I shrew [1] them that say nay,
and that shall not be I.

M. Mumbl. And I am well content.

Tib. Talk.   Sing on then by-and-by.

R. Roister. [Aside.] And I will not away,
but listen to their song.

Yet Merrygreek and my folks tarry very
long.   50

Tib[et], An[not], and Margery do sing here.
    Pipe, merry Annot, etc.
Trilla, trilla, trillarie.
Work, Tibet; work, Annot; work, Margery.
Sew, Tibet; knit, Annot; spin, Margery.
Let us see who shall win the victory.

Tib. Talk. This sleeve is not willing to be
sewed, I trow.

A small thing might make me all in [2] the
ground to throw.

                Then they sing again.
    Pipe, merry Annot, etc.
Trilla, trilla, trillarie.
What, Tibet! what, Annot! what, Marg-
ery!   60
Ye sleep, but we do not; that shall we try.
Your fingers be numbed; our work will not
lie.

Tib. Talk. If ye do so again, well I would
advise you nay.

In good sooth, one stop [3] more, and I
make holiday.

                They sing the third time.
    Pipe, merry Annot, etc.
Trilla, trilla, trillarie.
Now, Tibet; now, Annot; now, Margery.
Now whippet [4] apace for the mast'ry;
But it will not be, our mouth is so dry.

Tib. Talk. Ah, each finger is a thumb
today, methink;   70
I care not to let all alone, choose it swim
or sink.

                They sing the fourth time.
    Pipe, merry Annot, etc.
Trilla, trilla, trillarie.
When, [5] Tibet! When, Annot! When, Mar-
gery!
I will not, I cannot, no more can I.
Then give we all over, and there let it lie.
    Let her cast down her work.

Tib. Talk. There it lieth! The worst is
but a curried coat. [6]

Tut, I am used thereto; I care not a
groat.

An. Alyface. Have we done singing since?
Then will I in again.

Here I found you, and here I leave both
twain.   *Exeat.* 80

M. Mumbl. And I will not be long after.
[*She sees Roister Doister.*] Tib Talkapace!

Tib. Talk. What is the matter?

M. Mumbl.   Yond
stood a man all this space

And hath heard all that ever we spake
togither.

Tib. Talk. Marry, the more lout he for
his coming hither.

And the less good he can to listen maidens
talk.

I care not and I go bid him hence for to
walk.

It were well done to know what he maketh hereaway.

R. Roister. [*Aside.*] Now might I speak
to them, if I wist what to say.

M. Mumbl. Nay, we will go both off, and
see what he is.

R. Roister. One that hath heard all your
talk and singing, iwis.   90

Tib. Talk. The more to blame you; a good
thrifty husband [7]

Would elsewhere have had some better
matters in hand.

R. Roister. I did it for no harm, but for
good love I bear

To your dame, Mistress Custance, I did
your talk hear.

And, mistress nurse, I will kiss you for
acquaintance.

M. Mumbl. I come anon, sir.

Tib. Talk.   Faith, I
would our Dame Custance

Saw this gear.

M. Mumbl.   I must first wipe all
clean, yea, I must.

Tib. Talk. Ill chieve it, [8] doting fool, but
it must be cust. [9]

        [*He kisses Madge Mumblecrust.*]

---

[1] Beshrew, curse.   [2] On.   [3] Hindrance.
[4] Whip it (?) *i.e.*, move briskly.
[5] An exclamation of impatience.
[6] A whipping.
[7] Manager of a household.
[8] Achieve, succeed.
[9] Kost, kissed.

M. Mumbl. God yeld [1] you, sir; chad not
so much, ichotte not when,
Ne'er since chwas bore, chwine, of such
a gay gentleman.[2]   100
R. Roister. I will kiss you too, maiden,
for the good will I bear you.
Tib. Talk. No, forsooth, by your leave,
ye shall not kiss me.
R. Roister. Yes, be not afeard; I do not
disdain you a whit.
Tib. Talk. Why should I fear you? I have
not so little wit.
Ye are but a man, I know very well.
R. Roister.   Why then?
Tib. Talk. Forsooth, for I will not; I use
not to kiss men.
R. Roister. I would fain kiss you too,
good maiden, if I might.
Tib. Talk. What should that need?
R. Roister.   But to honor you,
by this light.
I use to kiss all them that I love, to God
I vow.
Tib. Talk. Yea, sir? I pray you, when
did ye last kiss your cow?   110
R. Roister. Ye might be proud to kiss
me, if ye were wise.
Tib. Talk. What promotion were therein?
R. Roister.   Nurse is not so nice.[3]
Tib. Talk. Well, I have not been taught
to kissing and licking.
R. Roister. Yet I thank you, mistress
nurse; ye made no sticking.
M. Mumbl. I will not stick for a koss [4]
with such a man as you.
Tib. Talk. They that lust. I will again to
my sewing now.

[Enter Annot Alyface.]

An. Alyface. Tidings, ho! tidings! Dame
Custance greeteth you well.
R. Roister. Whom? me?
An. Alyface.   You, sir? No,
sir! I do no such tale tell.
R. Roister. But, and she knew me here—
An. Alyface.   Tibet Talkapace,
Your mistress, Custance, and mine must
speak with your grace.   120

Tib. Talk. With me?
An. Alyface.   Ye must come in
to her, out of all doubts.
Tib. Talk. And my work not half done?
A mischief on all louts.
          Ex[eant] am[bæ].[5]
R. Roister. Ah, good sweet nurse!
M. Mumbl.   A
good sweet gentleman.
R. Roister.   What?
M. Mumbl. Nay, I cannot tell, sir, but
what thing would you?
R. Roister. How doth sweet Custance,
my heart of gold, tell me how?
M. Mumbl. She doth very well, sir, and
command me to you.
R. Roister. To me?
M. Mumbl.   Yea, to you, sir.
R. Roister.   To me? Nurse,
tell me plain,
To me?
M. Mumbl.   Ye.
R. Roister.   That word maketh
me alive again.
M. Mumbl. She command me to one last
day,[6] whoe'er it was.
R. Roister. That was e'en to me and
none other, by the Mass.   130
M. Mumbl. I cannot tell you surely, but
one it was.
R. Roister. It was I and none other; this
cometh to good pass.
I promise thee, nurse, I favor her.
M. Mumbl.   E'en so, sir.
R. Roister. Bid her sue to me for mar-
riage.
M. Mumbl.   E'en so, sir.
R. Roister. And surely for thy sake she
shall speed.
M. Mumbl.   E'en so, sir.
R. Roister. I shall be contented to take
her.
M. Mumbl.   E'en so, sir.
R. Roister. But at thy request and for
thy sake.
M. Mumbl.   E'en so, sir.
R. Roister. And, come, hark in thine ear
what to say.
M. Mumbl.   E'en so, sir.

*Here let him tell her a great long tale in
          her ear.*

---

[1] Reward.
[2] Madge speaks an artificial Southern dialect,
regularly used by stage rustics. Chad = ich
had = I had; ichotte = ich wot = I know; chwas =
I was; chwine = I ween = I think; etc.
[3] Fastidious.   [4] Kiss.

[5] Let both go out.
[6] Yesterday.

Actus I. Scena iv.

Matthew Merrygreek, Dobinet Doughty, Harpax, [Musicians,] Ralph Roister, Margery Mumblecrust.

M. Merry. Come on, sirs, apace, and quit
yourselves like men.
Your pains shall be rewarded.

D. Dough.   But I
wot not when.

M. Merry. Do your master worship as ye
have done in time past.

D. Dough. Speak to them; of mine office
he shall have a cast.

M. Merry. Harpax, look that thou do
well too, and thy fellow.

Harpax. I warrant, if he will mine example
follow.

M. Merry. Curtsy, whoresons, duck you
and crouch at every word.

D. Dough. Yes, whether our master speak
earnest or bord.[1]

M. Merry. For this lieth upon [2] his preferment,
indeed.

D. Dough. Oft is he a wooer, but never
doth he speed.   10

M. Merry. But with whom is he now so
sadly rounding [3] yond?

D. Dough. With *Nobs nicebecetur miserere* [4] fond.

[M.] Merry. God be at your wedding! Be
ye sped already?

                    [*Approaches Roister Doister.*]

I did not suppose that your love was so
greedy.
I perceive now ye have chose of devotion,
And joy have ye, lady, of your promotion.

R. Roister. Tush, fool, thou art deceived;
this is not she.

M. Merry. Well, mock [5] much of her, and
keep her well, I vise [6] ye.
I will take no charge of such a fair piece
keeping.

M. Mumbl. What aileth this fellow? He
driveth me to weeping.   20

M. Merry. What, weep on the wedding
day? Be merry, woman.
Though I say it, ye have chose a good
gentleman.

R. Roister. Kock's nowns,[7] what meanest
thou, man? Tut, a whistle!

[M. Merry.] [8] Ah, sir, be good to her; she
is but a gristle.[9]
Ah, sweet lamb and cony! [10]

R. Roister.   Tut, thou
art deceived.

M. Merry. Weep no more, lady; ye shall
be well received.—
      [*To Musicians.*] Up with some merry
noise, sirs, to bring home the bride.

R. Roister. Gog's [11] arms, knave, art thou
mad? I tell thee thou art wide.

M. Merry. Then ye intend by night to
have her home brought.

R. Roister. I tell thee no.

M. Merry.   How then?

R. Roister.   'Tis neither
meant ne [12] thought.   30

M. Merry. What shall we then do with
her?

R. Roister.   Ah, foolish harebrain,
This is not she.

M. Merry.   No, is? Why then, unsaid
again!
And what young girl is this with your
ma'ship so bold?

R. Roister. A girl?

M. Merry.   Yea. I dare say,
scarce yet three score year old.

R. Roister. This same is the fair widow's
nurse, of whom ye wot.

M. Merry. Is she but a nurse of a house?
Hence home, old trot,
Hence at once!

R. Roister. No, no.

M. Merry.   What, an please
your ma'ship,
A nurse talk so homely [13] with one of your
worship?

R. Roister. I will have it so; it is my
pleasure and will.

M. Merry. Then I am content. Nurse,
come again; tarry still.   40

R. Roister. What! She will help forward
this my suit for her part.

M. Merry. Then is't mine own pigsnie,[14]
and blessing on my heart.

---

[1] Jest.   [2] Is necessary to.   [3] Whispering.
[4] The meaning of the burlesque Latin is uncertain.
[5] Hazlitt suggests *make*   [6] Advise.
[7] God's wounds.
[8] This speech is assigned to Roister Doister
in the original.
[9] A delicate person; with a pun on the meaning
tough. [10] Rabbit, a term of endearment. [11] God's.
[12] Nor. [13] Familiarly. [14] Pig's eye, darling.

R. Roister. This is our best friend, man.

M. Merry. Then teach her what to say.

M. Mumbl. I am taught already.

M. Merry. Then go; make no delay.

R. Roister. Yet hark, one word in thine ear.

M. Merry. Back, sirs, from his tail.

R. Roister. Back, villains, will ye be privy of my counsel?

M. Merry. Back, sirs, so. I told you afore ye would be shent.

R. Roister. She shall have the first day a whole peck of argent.[1]

M. Mumbl. A peck? *Nomine patris*,[2] have ye so much spare?

R. Roister. Yea, and a cart-load thereto, or else were it bare,　　50
Besides other movables, household stuff, and land.

M. Mumbl. Have ye lands too?

R. Roister. An hundred marks.

M. Merry. Yea, a thousand.

M. Mumbl. And have ye cattle too, and sheep too?

R. Roister. Yea, a few.

M. Merry. He is ashamed the number of them to shew.
E'en round about him, as many thousand sheep goes,
As he and thou, and I too, have fingers and toes.

M. Mumbl. And how many years old be you?

R. Roister. Forty at least.

M. Merry. Yea, and thrice forty to them.

R. Roister. Nay, now thou dost jest.
I am not so old; thou misreckonest my years.

M. Merry. I know that; but my mind was on bullocks and steers.　　60

M. Mumbl. And what shall I show her your mastership's name is?

R. Roister. Nay, she shall make suit ere she know that, iwis.

M. Mumbl. Yet let me somewhat know.

M. Merry. This is he, understand,
That killed the blue spider in Blanchepowder land.

M. Mumbl. Yea, Jesus! William! Zee, law! Did he zo? Law![3]

M. Merry. Yea, and the last elephant that ever he saw,
As the beast passed by, he start out of a busk,[4]
And e'en with pure strength of arms plucked out his great tusk.

M. Mumbl. Jesus, *nomine patris*, what a thing was that?

R. Roister. Yea, but, Merrygreek, one thing thou hast forgot.

M. Merry. What?　　70

R. Roister. Of th' other elephant.

M. Merry. O, him that fled away.

R. Roister. Yea.

M. Merry. Yea, he knew that his match was in place that day.
Tut, he bet [5] the king of crickets on Christmas day,
That he crept in a hole, and not a word to say.

M. Mumbl. A sore [6] man, by zembletee.[7]

M. Merry. Why, he wrong [8] a club
Once in a fray out of the hand of Belzebub.

R. Roister. And how when Mumfision—

M. Merry. O, your coustreling [9]
Bore the lantern afield so before the gozeling [10]—
Nay, that is too long a matter now to be told.
Never ask his name, nurse; I warrant thee, be bold.　　80
He conquered in one day from Rome to Naples,
And won towns, nurse, as fast as thou canst make apples.

M. Mumbl. O Lord, my heart quaketh for fear! He is too sore!

R. Roister. Thou makest her too much afeard, Merrygreek; no more.
This tale would fear my sweetheart Custance right evil.

M. Merry. Nay, let her take him, nurse, and fear not the devil.
But thus is our song dashed. [*To Musicians.*] Sirs, ye may home again.

R. Roister. No, shall they not. I charge you all here to remain.
The villain slaves, a whole day ere they can be found!

---

[1] Silver, money.
[2] In the name of the Father.
[3] Madge relapses into dialect.
[4] Bush.　　[5] Beat.　　[6] Terrible.
[7] Sembletty, semblance—a rustic oath.
[8] Wrung.　　[9] Servant.
[10] Gosling, *i.e.*, a foolish person(?).

M. MERRY. Couch on your marybones,[1] whoresons, down to the ground! 90
Was it meet he should tarry so long in one place
Without harmony of music, or some solace?
Whoso hath such bees as your master in his head,
Had need to have his spirits with music to be fed.
By your mastership's license—
[*Picks something from Roister Doister's coat.*]
R. ROISTER.   What is that? A mote?
M. MERRY. No, it was a fool's[2] feather had light on your coat.
R. ROISTER. I was nigh no feathers since I came from my bed.
M. MERRY. No, sir, it was a hair that was fall from your head.
R. ROISTER. My men come when it please them.
M. MERRY.   By your leave—
R. ROISTER.   What is that?
M. MERRY. Your gown was foul spotted with the foot of a gnat. 100
R. ROISTER. Their master to offend they are nothing afeard.
What now?
M. MERRY.   A lousy hair from your mastership's beard.
OMNES FAMULÆ.[3] And, sir, for nurse's sake, pardon this one offense.
We shall not after this show the like negligence.
R. ROISTER. I pardon you this once, and come, sing ne'er the worse.
M. MERRY. How like you the goodness of this gentleman, nurse?
M. MUMBL. God save his mastership that so can his men forgive!
And I will hear them sing ere I go, by his leave.
R. ROISTER. Marry and thou shalt, wench. Come, we two will dance.
M. MUMBL. Nay, I will by mine own self foot the song perchance. 110
R. ROISTER. Go to it, sirs, lustily.

M. MUMBL.   Pipe up a merry note.
Let me hear it played; I will foot it for a groat.   *Cantent.*[4]
R. ROISTER. Now, nurse, take this same letter here to thy mistress;
And, as my trust is in thee, ply my business.
M. MUMBL. It shall be done.
M. MERRY.   Who made it?
R. ROISTER.   I wrote it each whit.
M. MERRY. Then needs it no mending.
R. ROISTER.   No. no.
M. MERRY.   No, I know your wit.
I warrant it well.
M. MUMBL.   It shall be delivered.
But, if ye speed, shall I be considered?
M. MERRY. Whough! Dost thou doubt of that?
MADGE [MUMBL.] What shall I have? 120
M. MERRY. An hundred times more than thou canst devise to crave.
M. MUMBL. Shall I have some new gear? For my old is all spent.
M. MERRY. The worst kitchen wench shall go in ladies' raiment.
M. MUMBL. Yea?
M. MERRY.   And the worst drudge in the house shall go better
Than your mistress doth now.
MAR. [MUMBL.]   Then I trudge with your letter.   [*Exeat.*]
R. ROISTER. Now may I repose me. Custance is mine own.
Let us sing and play homeward that it may be known.
M. MERRY. But are you sure that your letter is well enough?
R. ROISTER. I wrote it myself.
M. MERRY.   Then sing we to dinner.
Here they sing, and go out singing.

ACTUS I. SCENA v.

Christian Custance, Margery Mumblecrust.

C. CUSTANCE. Who took[5] thee this letter, Margery Mumblecrust?

---

[1] Marrowbones.
[2] With a pun on *fowl's*.
[3] All the servants.

[4] Let them sing (probably "The Second Song," printed at the end of the play).   [5] Gave.

M. Mumbl. A lusty gay bachelor took it me of trust,
And, if ye seek to him, he will low [1] your doing.
C. Custance. Yea, but where learned he that manner of wooing?
M. Mumbl. If to sue to him you will any pains take,
He will have you to his wife, he saith, for my sake.
C. Custance. Some wise gentleman, belike. I am bespoken; [2]
And I thought verily this had been some token
From my dear spouse Gawin Goodluck, whom, when him please,
God luckily send home to both our hearts' ease.   10
M. Mumbl. A joyly [3] man it is, I wot well by report,
And would have you to him for marriage resort.
Best open the writing, and see what it doth speak.
C. Custance. At this time, nurse, I will neither read ne break. [4]
M. Mumbl. He promised to give you a whole peck of gold.
C. Custance. Perchance, lack of a pint when it shall be all told.
M. Mumbl. I would take a gay rich husband, and I were you.
C. Custance. In good sooth, Madge, e'en so would I, if I were thou.
But no more of this fond talk now; let us go in,
And see thou no more move me folly to begin,   20
Nor bring me no mo [5] letters for no man's pleasure,
But thou know from whom.
M. Mumbl.   I warrant ye shall be sure.

Actus II. Scena i.

Dobinet Doughty.

D. Dough. Where is the house I go to, before or behind?
I know not where nor when nor how I shall it find.

If I had ten men's bodies and legs and strength,
This trotting that I have must needs lame me at length.
And now that my master is new set on wooing,
I trust there shall none of us find lack of doing.
Two pair of shoes a day will now be too little
To serve me, I must trot to and fro so mickle. [6]
"Go bear me this token!" "Carry me this letter!"
Now, "This is the best way;" now, "That way is better!"   10
"Up before day, sirs, I charge you, an hour or twain!"
"Trudge! Do me this message, and bring word quick again!"
If one miss but a minute, then, "His arms and wounds,
I would not have slacked for ten thousand pounds.
Nay, see, I beseech you, if my most trusty page
Go not now about to hinder my marriage."
So fervent hot wooing, and so far from wiving,
I trow, never was any creature living.
With every woman is he in some love's pang,
Then up to our lute at midnight, twangledom twang;   20
Then twang with our sonnets, and twang with our dumps, [7]
And heigh-ho from our heart, as heavy as lead lumps;
Then to our recorder [8] with toodle-loodle poop,
As the howlet out of an ivy bush should hoop. [9]
Anon to our gittern, thrumpledum, thrumpledum thrum,
Thrumpledum, thrumpledum, thrumpledum, thrumpledum thrum.
Of songs and ballads also he is a maker,
And that can he as finely do as Jack Raker;
Yea, and extempore will he ditties compose—

---

[1] Allow, approve.
[2] Promised, betrothed.
[3] Pretty, elegant.
[4] Break the seal.
[5] More.
[6] Much.
[7] Melancholy music.
[8] Flute.
[9] Whoop.

Foolish Marsyas ne'er made the like, I
  suppose.   30
Yet must we sing them; as good stuff, I
  undertake,
As for such a penman is well fitting to
  make.
"Ah, for these long nights! Heigh-ho!
  When will it be day?
I fear ere I come she will be wooed
  away."
Then when answer is made that it may
  not be,
"O death, why comest thou not?" by-
  and-by saith he.
But then, from his heart to put away
  sorrow,
He is as far in with some new love next
  morrow.
But in the mean season we trudge and
  we trot;
From dayspring to midnight I sit not
  nor rest not.   40
And now am I sent to Dame Christian
  Custance,
But I fear it will end with a mock for
  pastance.[1]
I bring her a ring, with a token in a
  clout [2]—
And by all guess this same is her house
  out of doubt.
I know it now perfect; I am in my right
  way.
And lo! yond the old nurse that was with
  us last day.

Actus II. Scena ii.

Madge Mumblecrust, Dobinet Doughty.

M. Mumbl. I was ne'er so shoke up [3] afore
  since I was born.
  That our mistress could not have chid,
    I would have sworn;
  And I pray God I die if I meant any
    harm,
  But for my lifetime this shall be to me
    a charm.
D. Dough. God you save and see,[4] nurse,
  and how is it with you?
M. Mumbl. Marry, a great deal the worse
  it is for such as thou.
D. Dough. For me? Why so?

M. Mumbl.   Why, were not thou
  one of them, say,
  That song and played here with the
    gentleman last day?
D. Dough. Yes, and he would know if
  you have for him spoken,
  And prays you to deliver this ring and
    token.   10
M. Mumbl. Now by the token that God
  tokened, brother,
  I will deliver no token, one nor other.
  I have once been so shent for your mas-
    ter's pleasure,
  As I will not be again for all his trea-
    sure.
D. Dough. He will thank you, woman.
M. Mumbl.   I will none of his
  thank.   *Ex[eat].*
D. Dough. I ween I am a prophet! This
  gear will prove blank.[5]
  But what! should I home again without
    answer go?
  It were better go to Rome on my head
    than so.
  I will tarry here this month, but some of
    the house
  Shall take it of me, and then I care not
    a louse.   20
  But yonder cometh forth a wench or a
    lad;
  If he have not one Lombard's [6] touch,
    my luck is bad.

Actus II. Scena iii.

*Truepenny, D[obinet] Dough[ty], Tibet T[alk-
apace], Annot Al[yface].[7]*

Truepenny. I am clean lost for lack of
  merry company;
  We gree [8] not half well within, our wenches
    and I.
  They will command like mistresses; they
    will forbid;
  If they be not served, Truepenny must
    be chid.
  Let them be as merry now as ye can
    desire,
  With turning of a hand, our mirth lieth
    in the mire.

---

[1] Pastime.
[2] Cloth.
[3] Scolded.
[4] Watch over.
[5] Unsuccessful.
[6] The Lombard was proverbially a money
changer. Here, one who likes to handle gold.
[7] Last two enter later.
[8] Agree.

I cannot skill of [1] such changeable
mettle;
There is nothing with them but "in
dock, out nettle." [2]

D. DOUGH. Whether is it better that I
speak to him first,
Or he first to me? It is good to cast the
worst.   10
If I begin first, he will smell all my purpose;
Otherwise I shall not need anything to
disclose.

TRUEPENNY. What boy have we yonder?
I will see what he is.

D. DOUGH. He cometh to me.—It is hereabout, iwis.

TRUEPENNY. Wouldest thou aught, friend,
that thou lookest so about?

D. DOUGH. Yea, but whether ye can help
me or no, I doubt.
I seek to one Mistress Custance' house,
here dwelling.

TRUEPENNY. It is my mistress ye seek to,
by your telling.

D. DOUGH. Is there any of that name here
but she?

TRUEPENNY. Not one in all the whole
town that I know, pardee.   20

D. DOUGH. A widow she is, I trow.

TRUEPENNY.   And what
and she be?

D. DOUGH. But insured to an husband.

TRUEPENNY.   Yea, so think we.

D. DOUGH. And I dwell with her husband
that trusteth to be.

TRUEPENNY. In faith, then must thou
needs be welcome to me.
Let us for acquaintance shake hands
togither,
And whate'er thou be, heartily welcome
hither.

[*Enter Tibet and Annot.*]

TIB. TALK. Well, Truepenny, never but
flinging? [3]

AN. ALYFACE.   And frisking?

TRUEPENNY. Well, Tibet and Annot, still
swinging and whisking?

TIB. TALK. But ye roil [4] abroad.

AN. ALYFACE.   In the street
everywhere.

TRUEPENNY. Where are ye twain, in
chambers when ye meet me there?   30
But come hither, fools; I have one now
by the hand,
Servant to him that must be our mistress'
husband.
Bid him welcome.

AN. ALYFACE.   To me truly is he
welcome.

TIB. TALK. Forsooth, and as I may say,
heartily welcome.

D. DOUGH. I thank you, mistress maids.

AN. ALYFACE.   I hope we shall
better know.

TIB. TALK. And when will our new master
come?

D. DOUGH.   Shortly, I trow.

TIB. TALK. I would it were tomorrow; for
till he resort,
Our mistress, being a widow, hath small
comfort,
And I heard our nurse speak of an husband today
Ready for our mistress, a rich man and
a gay.   40
And we shall go in our French hoods
every day,
In our silk cassocks, I warrant you,
fresh and gay,
In our trick ferdegews [5] and billiments [6]
of gold;
Brave [7] in our suits of change, seven
double fold.
Then shall ye see Tibet, sirs, tread the
moss so trim—
Nay, why said I tread? Ye shall see her
glide and swim,
Not lumperdee clumperdee like our spaniel Rig.

TRUEPENNY. Marry, then, prick-me-dain-
ty, [8] come toast me a fig!
Who shall then know our Tib Talkapace,
trow ye?

AN. ALYFACE. And why not Annot Aly-
face as fine as she?   50

TRUEPENNY. And what had Tom Truepenny, a father or none?

AN. ALYFACE. Then our pretty new-come
man will look to be one.

---

[1] Understand.
[2] Proverbial phrase for inconstancy, referring
to the curing of nettle stings by dock leaves.
[3] Running about.   [4] Gad.
[5] Neat farthingales.
[6] Habiliments, perhaps headdresses.
[7] Gay.   [8] Finical person.

TRUEPENNY. We four, I trust, shall be a
joyly merry knot.
Shall we sing a fit [1] to welcome our friend,
Annot?
AN. ALYFACE. Perchance he cannot sing.
D. DOUGH.   I am at all essays.[2]
TIB. TALK. By Cock, and the better wel-
come to us always.

Here they sing.

A thing very fit
For them that have wit
And are fellows knit,
          Servants in one house to be,   60
Is fast, fast for to sit,
And not oft to flit,
Nor vary a whit,
          But lovingly to agree.

No man complaining,
No other disdaining,
For loss or for gaining,
          But fellows or friends to be.
No grudge remaining,
No work refraining,   70
Nor help restraining,
          But lovingly to agree.

No man for despite,
By word or by write
His fellow to twite,[3]
          But further in honesty;
No good turns entwite,[3]
Nor old sores recite,
But let all go quite,
          And lovingly to agree.   80

After drudgery,
When they be weary,
Then to be merry,
          To laugh and sing they be free;
With chip and cherry,[4]
Heigh derry derry,
Trill on the bery,[5]
          And lovingly to agree.
                    FINIS.

TIB. TALK. Will you now in with us unto
our mistress go?
D. DOUGH. I have first for my master an
errand or two.   90
But I have here from him a token and a
ring;
They shall have most thank of her that
first doth it bring.

---

[1] Song.   [4] Chirp and coo.
[2] Ready for all contingencies.
[3] Twit, blame.   [5] Dance on the hill.

TIB. TALK. Marry, that will I.
TRUEPENNY.   See, and Tibet
snatch not now!
TIB. TALK. And why may not I, sir, get
thanks as well as you?   *Exeat.*
AN. ALYFACE. Yet get ye not all; we will
go with you both
And have part of your thanks, be ye
never so loath.
          [*Exeant all but Doughty.*]
D. DOUGH. So my hands are rid of it; I
care for no more.
I may now return home; so durst I not
afore.   *Exeat.*

ACTUS II. SCENA iv.

C[hristian] Custance, Tibet, Annot Alyface,
          Truepenny.

C. CUSTANCE. Nay, come forth all three;
and come hither, pretty maid.
Will not so many forewarnings make you
afraid?
TIB. TALK. Yes, forsooth.
C. CUSTANCE.   But still be a
runner up and down,
Still be a bringer of tidings and tokens
to town.
TIB. TALK. No, forsooth, mistress.
C. CUSTANCE.   Is all your
delight and joy
In whisking and ramping abroad like a
tomboy?
TIB. TALK. Forsooth, these were there too,
Annot and Truepenny.
TRUEPENNY. Yea, but ye alone took it, ye
cannot deny.
AN. ALYFACE. Yea, that ye did.
TIB. TALK.   But if I had
not, ye twain would.
C. CUSTANCE. You great calf, ye should
have more wit, so ye should.   10
But why should any of you take such
things in hand?
TIB. TALK. Because it came from him that
must be your husband.
C. CUSTANCE. How do ye know that?
TIB. TALK.   Forsooth, the
boy did say so.
C. CUSTANCE. What was his name?
AN. ALYFACE.   We asked not.
C. CUSTANCE.   No, did?[6]

---

[6] This word might be omitted for the sake
of the rime.

An. Alyface. He is not far gone, of likelihood.

Truepenny.   I will see.

C. Custance. If thou canst find him in
the street, bring him to me.

Truepenny. Yes.   *Exeat.*

C. Custance.   Well, ye naughty girls,
if ever I perceive

That henceforth you do letters or tokens
receive,

To bring unto me from any person or
place,

Except ye first show me the party face
to face,   20

Either thou or thou, full truly aby [1] thou
shalt.

Tib. Talk. Pardon this, and the next time
powder me in salt.

C. Custance. I shall make all girls by
you twain to beware.

Tib. Talk. If ever I offend again, do not
me spare.

But if ever I see that false boy any more,

By your mistress-ship's license, I tell you
afore,

I will rather have my coat twenty times
swinged [2]

Than on the naughty wag not to be
avenged.

C. Custance. Good wenches would not so
ramp abroad idly,

But keep within doors, and ply their work
earnestly.   30

If one would speak with me that is a
man likely,

Ye shall have right good thank to bring
me word quickly.

But otherwise with messages to come in
post

From henceforth, I promise you, shall
be to your cost.

Get you in to your work.

Tib. [Talk.]   ⎫ Yes, forsooth.
An. [Alyface.] ⎭

C. Custance.   Hence, both twain.

And let me see you play me such a part
again!   [*Exeant Tibet and Annot.*]

[*Enter Truepenny.*]

Truepenny. Mistress, I have run past the
far end of the street,

Yet can I not yonder crafty boy see nor
meet.

C. Custance. No?

Truepenny.   Yet I looked as far
beyond the people

As one may see out of the top of Paul's
steeple.   40

C. Custance. Hence, in at doors, and let
me no more be vexed.

Truepenny. Forgive me this one fault,
and lay on for the next.   [*Exeat.*]

C. Custance. Now will I in too, for I
think, so God me mend,

This will prove some foolish matter in
the end.   *Exeat.*

ACTUS II[I]. SCENA i.

Matthew Merrygreek.

M. Merry. Now say this again: he hath
somewhat to doing

Which followeth the trace of one that is
wooing,

Specially that hath no more wit in his
head

Than my cousin Roister Doister withal
is led.

I am sent in all haste to espy and to mark

How our letters and tokens are likely to
wark.[3]

Master Roister Doister must have answer
in haste,

For he loveth not to spend much labor
in waste.

Now as for Christian Custance, by this
light,

Though she had not her troth to Gawin
Goodluck plight,   10

Yet rather than with such a loutish dolt
to marry,

I dare say would live a poor life solitary.

But fain would I speak with Custance,
if I wist how,

To laugh at the matter.—Yond cometh
one forth now.

ACTUS III. SCENA ii.

*Tibet, M[atthew] Merrygreek, Christian Cus-
tance.*[4]

Tib. Talk. Ah, that I might but once in
my life have a sight

Of him that made us all so ill shent! By
this light,

He should never escape if I had him by
the ear,

---

[1] Pay the penalty.   [2] Beaten.

[3] Work.   [4] Enters later.

But even from his head I would it bite or
  tear!
Yea, and if one of them were not enow,
I would bite them both off, I make God
  avow.[1]
M. Merry. [*Aside.*] What is he whom
  this little mouse doth so threaten?
Tib. Talk. I would teach him, I trow, to
  make girls shent or beaten.
M. Merry. [*Aside.*] I will call her.—Maid,
  with whom are ye so hasty?
Tib. Talk. Not with you, sir, but with a
  little wagpasty,[2]   10
A deceiver of folks by subtle craft and
  guile.
M. Merry. [*Aside.*] I know where she is:[3]
Dobinet hath wrought some wile.
Tib. Talk. He brought a ring and token
  which he said was sent
From our dame's husband, but I wot
  well I was shent;
For it liked her as well, to tell you no lies,
As water in her ship, or salt cast in her
  eyes.
And yet whence it came neither we nor
  she can tell.
M. Merry. [*Aside.*] We shall have sport
  anon; I like this very well.—
And dwell ye here with Mistress Cus-
  tance, fair maid?
Tib. Talk. Yea, marry, do I, sir. What
  would ye have said?   20
M. Merry. A little message unto her by
  word of mouth.
Tib. Talk. No messages, by your leave,
  nor tokens forsooth.
M. Merry. Then help me to speak with
  her.
Tib. Talk.   With a good will that.
Here she cometh forth.   Now speak ye
  know best what.

[*Enter Custance.*]

C. Custance. None other life with you,
  maid, but abroad to skip?
Tib. Talk. Forsooth, here is one would
  speak with your mistress-ship.
C. Custance. Ah, have ye been learning
  of mo messages now?
Tib. Talk. I would not hear his mind, but
  bade him show it to you.

C. Custance. In at doors!
Tib. Talk.   I am gone.   *Ex[eat.]*
M. Merry.   Dame Custance,
  God ye save.
C. Custance. Welcome, friend Merry-
  greek, and what thing would ye
  have?   30
M. Merry. I am come to you a little
  matter to break.
C. Custance. But see it be honest; else
  better not to speak.
M. Merry. How feel ye yourself affected
  here of late?
C. Custance. I feel no manner change but
  after the old rate.
But whereby do ye mean?
M. Merry.   Concerning
  marriage.
Doth not love lade you?
C. Custance.   I feel no such
  carriage.[4]
M. Merry. Do ye feel no pangs of dotage?
  Answer me right.
C. Custance. I dote so that I make but
  one sleep all the night.
But what need all these words?
M. Merry.   O Jesus,
  will ye see
What dissembling creatures these same
  women be?   40
The gentleman ye wot of, whom ye do so
  love
That ye would fain marry him, if ye
  durst it move,
Among other rich widows, which are of
  him glad,
Lest ye for leesing of him perchance
  might run mad,
Is now contented that, upon your suit
  making,
Ye be as one in election of taking.
C. Custance. What a tale is this! That I
  wot of? Whom I love?
M. Merry. Yea, and he is as loving a
  worm,[5] again, as a dove.
E'en of very pity he is willing you to take,
Because ye shall not destroy yourself for
  his sake.   50
C. Custance. Marry, God yeld his ma'-
  ship whatever he be.
It is gentmanly[6] spoken.

---

[1] An oath, a promise.   [2] Rogue.
[3] I know what's the matter with her.

[4] Burden.
[5] Little creature; a term of endearment.
[6] Colloquial for *gentlemanly*.

irreverant and pugnacious

M. MERRY.　　　　　　　　Is it not,
　trow ye?
If ye have the grace now to offer your-
　self, ye speed.
C. CUSTANCE. As much as though I did,
　this time it shall not need.
But what gentman is it, I pray you tell
　me plain,
That wooeth so finely?
M. MERRY.　　　　　　　Lo, where ye be
　again,
As though ye knew him not.
C. CUSTANCE.　　　　　　Tush, ye
　speak in jest.
M. MERRY. Nay, sure, the party is in
　good knacking [1] earnest,
And have you he will, he saith, and have
　you he must.
C. CUSTANCE. I am promised during my
　life; that is just.　　　　　　　60
M. MERRY. Marry, so thinketh he, unto
　him alone.
C. CUSTANCE. No creature hath my faith
　and troth but one—
That is Gawin Goodluck; and, if it be
　not he,
He hath no title this way whatever he be,
Nor I know none to whom I have such
　word spoken.
M. MERRY. Yea, know him not you by his
　letter and token?
C. CUSTANCE. Indeed, true it is that a
　letter I have,
But I never read it yet, as God me
　save.
M. MERRY. Ye a woman, and your letter
　so long unread?
C. CUSTANCE. Ye may thereby know what
　haste I have to wed.　　　　　70
But now, who it is for my hand I know
　by guess.
M. MERRY. Ah, well I say.
C. CUSTANCE.　　　　　It is Roister
　Doister, doubtless.
M. MERRY. Will ye never leave this dis-
　simulation?
Ye know him not?
C. CUSTANCE.　　　　But by imagination,
For no man there is but a very dolt and
　lout
That to woo a widow would so go about.
He shall never have me his wife while
　he do live.

[1] Downright.

M. MERRY. Then will he have you if he
　may, so mote [2] I thrive,
And he biddeth you send him word by me,
That ye humbly beseech him, ye may his
　wife be,　　　　　　　　　　　　80
And that there shall be no let [3] in you
　nor mistrust,
But to be wedded on Sunday next if he
　lust,
And biddeth you to look for him.
C. CUSTANCE.　　　　　　　Doth
　he bid so?
M. MERRY. When he cometh, ask him
　whether he did or no.
C. CUSTANCE. Go, say that I bid him keep
　him warm at home,
For, if he come abroad, he shall cough
　me a mome. [4]
My mind was vexed; I shrew his head,
　sottish dolt!
M. MERRY. He hath in his head—
C. CUSTANCE.　　　　　　As much
　brain as a burbolt. [5]
M. MERRY. Well, Dame Custance, if he
　hear you thus play choploge [6]—
C. CUSTANCE. What will he?
M. MERRY.　　　　　　　Play the
　devil in the horologe. [7]　　　　90
C. CUSTANCE. I defy him, lout!
M. MERRY.　　　　　　　Shall I
　tell him what ye say?
C. CUSTANCE. Yea, and add whatsoever
　thou canst, I thee pray,
And I will avouch it, whatsoever it be.
M. MERRY. Then let me alone; we will
　laugh well, ye shall see.
It will not be long ere he will hither resort.
C. CUSTANCE. Let him come when him
　lust; I wish no better sport.
Fare ye well. I will in, and read my
　great letter.
I shall to my wooer make answer the
　better.　　　　　　　　　　　*Exeat.*

ACTUS III. SCENA iii.

Matthew Merrygreek, Roister Doister.

M. MERRY. Now that the whole answer
　in my devise doth rest,
I shall paint out our wooer in colors of
　the best.

[2] May.　　　　　　　　　　[3] Hindrance.
[4] Show what a blockhead he is.
[5] Birdbolt, sometimes carried by jesters;
hence, a fool.　　[6] Choplogic.　　[7] Clock.

And all that I say shall be on Custance's
   mouth;
She is author of all that I shall speak
   forsooth.
But yond cometh Roister Doister now
   in a trance.
R. Roister. Juno send me this day good
   luck and good chance.
I cannot but come see how Merrygreek
   doth speed.
M. Merry. [*Aside.*] I will not see him, but
   give him a jut [1] indeed.—
                 [*Runs into him.*]
I cry your mastership mercy!
R. Roister.   And
   whither now?
M. Merry. As fast as I could run, sir, in
   post against you.   10
But why speak ye so faintly, or why are
   ye so sad?
R. Roister. Thou knowest the proverb—
   "Because I cannot be had."
Hast thou spoken with this woman?
M. Merry.   Yea, that I have.
R. Roister. And what will this gear be?
M. Merry.   No, so God me save.
R. Roister. Hast thou a flat answer?
M. Merry.   Nay, a sharp answer.
R. Roister.   What?
M. Merry. Ye shall not, she saith, by her
   will, marry her cat.
Ye are such a calf, such an ass, such a
   block,
Such a lilburn,[2] such a hoball,[3] such a
   lobcock,[4]
And because ye should come to her at
   no season,
She despised your ma'ship out of all
   reason.   20
"Bawawe [5] what ye say," ko [6] I, "of such
   a gentman!"
"Nay, I fear him not," ko she, "do the
   best he can.
He vaunteth himself for a man of prowess
   great,
Whereas a good gander, I dare say, may
   him beat.
And where he is louted [7] and laughed to
   scorn,
For the veriest dolt that ever was born,
And veriest lover,[8] sloven, and beast,

Living in this world from the west to the
   east,
Yet of himself hath he such opinion,
That in all the world is not the like
   minion.[9]   30
He thinketh each woman to be brought
   in dotage
With the only sight of his goodly per-
   sonage;
Yet none that will have him. We do him
   lout and flock,[10]
And make him among us our common
   sporting stock,
And so would I now," ko she, "save only
   because—"
"Better nay," ko I; "I lust not meddle
   with daws.[11]
Ye are happy," ko I, "that ye are a
   woman;
This would cost you your life in case ye
   were a man."
R. Roister. Yea, an hundred thousand
   pound should not save her life.
M. Merry. No, but that ye woo her to
   have her to your wife.   40
But I could not stop her mouth.
R. Roister.   Heigh-
   ho, alas!
M. Merry. Be of good cheer, man, and
   let the world pass.
R. Roister. What shall I do or say now
   that it will not be?
M. Merry. Ye shall have choice of a
   thousand as good as she,
And ye must pardon her; it is for lack of
   wit.
R. Roister. Yea, for were not I an hus-
   band for her fit?
Well, what should I now do?
M. Merry.   In faith, I
   cannot tell.
R. Roister. I will go home and die.
M. Merry.   Then shall
   I bid toll the bell?
R. Roister. No.
M. Merry.   God have mercy on
   your soul! Ah, good gentleman,
That e'er ye should thus die for an un-
   kind woman!   50
Will ye drink once ere ye go?
R. Roister.   No, no,
   I will none.

[1] Jolt.   [4] Lubber.   [7] Ridiculed.
[2] Dolt.   [5] Beware(?).   [8] Lubber(?).
[3] Clodhopper.   [6] Quoth, said.

[9] Darling, favorite.   [11] Fools.
[10] Treat contemptuously.

M. Merry. How feel your soul to God? [1]
R. Roister.   I am nigh gone.
M. Merry. And shall we hence straight?
R. Roister.   Yea.
M. Merry.   *Placebo*.[2] *Dilexi*.[3]
Master Roister Doister will straight go
home and die.   *Ut infra*.[4]
R. Roister. Heigh-ho, alas, the pangs of
death my heart do break!
M. Merry. Hold your peace! For shame,
sir, a dead man may not speak!
    Nequando.[5] What mourners and what
torches shall we have?
R. Roister. None.
M. Merry.   *Dirige*.[6] He will go
darkling to his grave—
Neque lux, neque crux, neque mourners,
neque clink.[7]
He will steal to heaven, unknowing to
God, I think.   60
A porta inferi.[8] Who shall your goods
possess?
R. Roister. Thou shalt be my sector,[9]
and have all, more and less.
M. Merry. *Requiem æternam*.[10] Now, God
reward your mastership.
And I will cry halfpenny-dole for your
worship.
Come forth, sirs, hear the doleful news
I shall you tell. *Evocat servos militis*.[11]

[*Enter four Servants*.]

Our good master here will no longer with
us dwell.
But, in spite of Custance, which hath
him wearied,
Let us see his ma'ship solemnly buried.
And while some piece of his soul is yet
him within,   69
Some part of his funerals let us here begin.
Audivi vocem.[12] All men take heed by
this one gentleman,

How you set your love upon an unkind
woman.
For these women be all such mad peevish
elves,
They will not be won except it please
themselves.
But in faith, Custance, if ever ye come
in hell,
Master Roister Doister shall serve you
as well.
And will ye needs go from us thus in
very deed?
R. Roister. Yea, in good sadness.
M. Merry.   Now,
Jesus Christ be your speed.
Good night, Roger, old knave; farewell,
Roger, old knave!
Good night, Roger, old knave; knave,
knap! [13]   *Ut infra*. 80
Pray for the late Master Roister Dois-
ter's soul,
And come forth, parish clerk, let the
passing bell toll.   *Ad servos militis*.[14]

[*Enter Parish Clerk*.]

Pray for your master, sirs, and for him
ring a peal.[15]
He was your right good master while he
was in heal.[16]
Qui Lazarum.[17]
R. Roister.   Heigh-ho!
M. Merry.   Dead men go
not so fast
In paradisum.[18]
R. Roister.   Heigh-ho!
M. Merry.   Soft, hear what
I have cast.
R. Roister. I will hear nothing; I am
past.
M. Merry.   Whough, wellaway!
Ye may tarry one hour, and hear what
I shall say.
Ye were best, sir, for a while to revive
again,
And quite [19] them ere ye go.
R. Roister.   Trowest thou so?

---

[1] From the service for the visitation of the sick.
[2] I shall be acceptable(?). This word begins
a parody on the Catholic service for the dead.
[3] I have loved(?).
[4] As below. (See "Psalmody" at end of play.)
[5] Never.
[6] Direct [my way].
[7] Neither light nor cross nor mourners nor bell.
[8] From the gate of hell.
[9] Executor.
[10] Eternal rest.
[11] He calls the soldier's [Roister Doister's]
servants.
[12] I have heard a voice.

[13] This word may mean either *knave* or *nap* or
strike (the bell).
[14] To the servants of the soldier.
[15] See "Peal of Bells" at the end of play.
[16] Health.
[17] Thou who [didst raise] Lazarus.
[18] Into paradise.
[19] Requite, get even with.

M. Merry.   Yea, plain.   90

R. Roister. How may I revive, being now
so far past?

M. Merry. I will rub your temples, and
fet [1] you again at last.

R. Roister. It will not be possible.

M. Merry.   Yes,
for twenty pound.

R. Roister. Arms! [2] what dost thou?

M. Merry.   Fet
you again out of your sound. [3]

By this cross, ye were nigh gone indeed;
I might feel
Your soul departing within an inch of
your heel.
Now follow my counsel.

R. Roister.   What is it?

M. Merry.   If I were you,
Custance should eft [4] seek to me, ere I
would bow.

R. Roister. Well, as thou wilt have me,
even so will I do.

M. Merry. Then shall ye revive again for
an hour or two.   100

R. Roister. As thou wilt; I am content
for a little space.

M. Merry. "Good hap is not hasty;"
yet "In space com[e]th grace."
To speak with Custance yourself should
be very well;
What good thereof may come, nor I
nor you can tell.
But now the matter standeth upon your
marriage,
Ye must now take unto you a lusty cour-
age;
Ye may not speak with a faint heart to
Custance,
But with a lusty breast and countenance,
That she may know she hath to answer
to a man.

R. Roister. Yes, I can do that as well
as any can.   110

M. Merry. Then because ye must Custance face to face woo,
Let us see how to behave yourself ye
can do.
Ye must have a portly brag after your
estate. [5]

R. Roister. Tush, I can handle that after
the best rate.

M. Merry. Well done! so, lo! up, man,
with your head and chin,
Up with that snout, man! so, lo! now ye
begin!
So, that is somewhat like! But, pranky-
coat, [6] nay, whan? [7]
That is a lusty brute; hands under your
side, man.
So, lo! now is it even as it should be;
That is somewhat like, for a man of your
degree.   120
Then must ye stately go, jetting [8] up
and down.
Tut, can ye no better shake the tail of
your gown?
There, lo, such a lusty brag it is ye must
make.

R. Roister. To come behind, and make
curtsy, thou must some pains take.

M. Merry. Else were I much to blame, I
thank your mastership.
The Lord one day all-to [9] begrime you
with worship.
"Back, sir sauce, let gentlefolks have
elbow room.
[Shoves imaginary persons out of the way.]
Void, [10] sirs, see ye not Master Roister
Doister come?
Make place, my masters."
                    [Jostles Roister Doister.]

R. Roister.   Thou justlest
now too nigh.   129

M. Merry. "Back, all rude louts!"

R. Roister.   Tush!

M. Merry.   I cry your ma'ship mercy!
Hoiday, if fair fine Mistress Custance
saw ye now,
Ralph Roister Doister were her own, I
warrant you!

R. Roister. Ne'er an M [11] by your girdle? [12]

M. Merry.   Your good mastership's
Mastership were her own mistress-ship's
mistress-ship's! [13]
Ye were take up for hawks [14]— ye were
gone, ye were gone.
But now one other thing more yet I
think upon.

[1] Fetch.   [3] Swoon.
[2] By God's arms.   [4] Again.
[5] Pompous bearing befitting your rank.

[6] Frolicsome fellow.   [9] Completely.
[7] When.   [10] Make room.
[8] Strutting.
[11] Abbreviation for *master* or *mistress*.
[12] *I.e.*, Can't you speak respectfully—address
me as master?   [13] Supply *property, husband*.
[14] Farmer suggests: "You would be snapped
up for a husband like hawks' meat."

R. Roister. Show what it is.

M. Merry.   A wooer, be
he never so poor,
Must play and sing before his best-
belove's door;
How much more, then, you?

R. Roister.   Thou
speakest well, out of doubt.

M. Merry. And perchance that would
make her the sooner come out.   140

R. Roister. Go, call my musicians; bid
them hie apace.

M. Merry. I will be here with them ere
ye can say "trey ace."   *Exeat.*

R. Roister. This was well said of Merrygreek; I low his wit.
Before my sweetheart's door we will have
a fit,
That if my love come forth, that I may
with her talk,
I doubt not but this gear shall on my
side walk.
But lo, how well Merrygreek is returned
sence.[1]

[*Enter Merrygreek with Musicians.*]

M. Merry. There hath grown no grass on
my heel since I went hence;
Lo, here have I brought that shall make
you pastance.

R. Roister. Come, sirs, let us sing to win
my dear love Custance.   150
                Cantent.[2]

M. Merry. Lo, where she cometh! Some
countenance to her make,
And ye shall hear me be plain with her
for your sake.

Actus III. Scena iv.

Custance, Merrygreek, Roister Doister.

C. Custance. What gauding[3] and fooling is this afore my door?

M. Merry. May not folks be honest,
pray you, though they be poor?

C. Custance. As that thing may be true,
so rich folks may be fools.

R. Roister. Her talk is as fine as she
had learned in schools.

[1] Since.
[2] Probably "The Fourth Song," printed at the
end of the play.   [3] Jesting.

M. Merry. Look partly toward her, and
draw a little near.

C. Custance. Get ye home, idle folks.

M. Merry.   Why may not we be here?
Nay, and ye will ha's,[4] ha's; otherwise,
I tell you plain,
And ye will not ha's, then give us our
gear again.

C. Custance. Indeed, I have of yours
much gay things, God save all.

R. Roister. Speak gently unto her, and
let her take all.   10

M. Merry. Ye are too tender-hearted.
Shall she make us daws?
Nay, dame, I will be plain with you in
my friend's cause.

R. Roister. Let all this pass, sweetheart,
and accept my service.

C. Custance. I will not be served with a
fool in no wise;
When I choose an husband, I hope to
take a man.

M. Merry. And where will ye find one
which can do that he can?
Now this man toward you being so kind,
You not to make him an answer somewhat to his mind!

C. Custance. I sent him a full answer by
you, did I not?

M. Merry. And I reported it.

C. Custance.   Nay, I
must speak it again.   20

R. Roister. No, no, he told it all.

M. Merry.   Was
I not metely[5] plain?

R. Roister. Yes.

M. Merry.   But I would not tell
all; for faith, if I had,
With you, Dame Custance, ere this hour
it had been bad,
And not without cause; for this goodly
personage
Meant no less than to join with you in
marriage.

C. Custance. Let him waste no more labor nor suit about me.

M. Merry. Ye know not where your preferment lieth, I see,
He sending you such a token, ring,
and letter.

C. Custance. Marry, here it is; ye never
saw a better.

M. Merry. Let us see your letter.

[4] Have us.   [5] Tolerably.

C. CUSTANCE.   Hold,
    read it if ye can.   30
And see what letter it is to win a woman.
M. MERRY. "To mine own dear cony,
    bird, sweetheart, and pigsnie,
Good Mistress Custance, present these
    by-and-by."
Of this superscription do ye blame the
    style?
C. CUSTANCE. With the rest, as good stuff
    as ye read a great while.
M. MERRY. "Sweet mistress, whereas I
    love you nothing at all,
Regarding your substance and richesse
    chief of all,
For your personage, beauty, demeanor,
    and wit,
I commend me unto you never a whit;
Sorry to hear report of your good wel-
    fare,   40
For, as I hear say, such your conditions
    are,
That ye be worthy favor of no living
    man;
To be abhorred of every honest man;
To be taken for a woman inclined to
    vice;
Nothing at all to virtue giving her due
    price.
Wherefore, concerning marriage, ye are
    thought
Such a fine paragon as ne'er honest
    man bought.
And now by these presents I do you
    advertise
That I am minded to marry you in no
    wise.
For your goods and substance, I could
    be content   50
To take you as ye are. If ye mind to be
    my wife,
Ye shall be assured for the time of my
    life,
I will keep ye right well from good rai-
    ment and fare;
Ye shall not be kept but in sorrow and
    care.
Ye shall in no wise live at your own
    liberty;
Do and say what ye lust, ye shall never
    please me;
But, when ye are merry, I will be all
    sad;
When ye are sorry, I will be very glad

When ye seek your heart's ease, I will
    be unkind.
At no time in me shall ye much gentle-
    ness find.   60
But all things contrary to your will and
    mind
Shall be done; otherwise I will not be
    behind
To speak. And, as for all them that
    would do you wrong,
I will so help and maintain, ye shall not
    live long.
Nor any foolish dolt shall cumber you
    but I.
I, whoe'er say nay, will stick by you
    till I die.
Thus, good Mistress Custance, the Lord
    you save and keep
From me, Roister Doister, whether I
    wake or sleep.
Who favoreth you no less (ye may be
    bold)
Than this letter purporteth, which ye
    have unfold."   70
C. CUSTANCE. How by this letter of love?
    Is it not fine?
R. ROISTER. By the arms of Calais, it is
    none of mine.
M. MERRY. Fie, you are foul to blame;
    this is your own hand!
C. CUSTANCE. Might not a woman be
    proud of such an husband?
M. MERRY. Ah, that ye would in a letter
    show such despite!
R. ROISTER. O, I would I had him here,
    the which did it indite.
M. MERRY. Why, ye made it yourself, ye
    told me by this light.
R. ROISTER. Yea, I meant I wrote it mine
    own self yesternight.
C. CUSTANCE. Iwis, sir, I would not have
    sent you such a mock.
R. ROISTER. Ye may so take it, but I
    meant it not so, by Cock.   80
M. MERRY. Who can blame this woman to
    fume and fret and rage?
Tut, tut! yourself now have marred your
    own marriage.
Well, yet, Mistress Custance, if ye can
    this remit,
This gentleman otherwise may your love
    requit.
C. CUSTANCE. No, God be with you both,
    and seek no more to me.   *Exeat.*

R. Roister. Wough! she is gone forever;
  I shall her no more see.
M. Merry. What, weep? Fie, for shame!
  And blubber? For manhood's sake,
  Never let your foe so much pleasure of
  you take.
  Rather play the man's part, and do love
  refrain.[1]
  If she despise you, e'en despise ye her
  again.   90
R. Roister. By Goss,[2] and for thy sake I
  defy her indeed.
M. Merry. Yea, and perchance that way
  ye shall much sooner speed,
  For one mad property these women have,
  in fay:[3]
  When ye will, they will not; will not ye,
  then will they.
  Ah, foolish woman! ah, most unlucky
  Custance!
  Ah, unfortunate woman! ah, peevish
  Custance!
  Art thou to thine harms so obstinately
  bent
  That thou canst not see where lieth thine
  high preferment?
  Canst thou not lub dis man, which could
  lub dee so well?
  Art thou so much thine own foe?
R. Roister.   Thou
  dost the truth tell.   100
M. Merry. Well, I lament.
R. Roister.   So do I.
M. Merry.   Wherefore?
R. Roister.   For this
  thing:
  Because she is gone.
M. Merry.   I mourn for an-
  other thing.
R. Roister. What is it, Merrygreek, where-
  fore thou dost grief take?
M. Merry. That I am not a woman my-
  self for your sake;
  I would have you myself—and a straw
  for yond Gill[4]—
  And mock[5] much of you though it were
  against my will.
  I would not, I warrant you, fall in such a
  rage[6]
  As so to refuse such a goodly person-
  age.

R. Roister. In faith, I heartily thank
  thee, Merrygreek.
M. Merry. And I were a woman——
R. Roister.   Thou wouldest
  to me seek.   110
M. Merry. For, though I say it, a goodly
  person ye be.
R. Roister. No, no.
M. Merry.   Yes, a goodly man
  as e'er I did see.
R. Roister. No, I am a poor homely man,
  as God made me.
M. Merry. By the faith that I owe to
  God, sir, but ye be.
  Would I might, for your sake, spend a
  thousand pound land.
R. Roister. I dare say thou wouldest have
  me to thy husband.
M. Merry. Yea; and I were the fairest
  lady in the shire,
  And knew you as I know you, and see
  you now here—
  Well, I say no more.
R. Roister.   Gramercies, with
  all my heart.
M. Merry. But since that cannot be, will
  ye play a wise part?   120
R. Roister. How should I?
M. Merry.   Refrain from
  Custance a while now,
  And I warrant her soon right glad to seek
  to you.
  Ye shall see her anon come on her knees
  creeping,
  And pray you to be good to her, salt
  tears weeping.
R. Roister. But what and she come not?
M. Merry. In faith, then, farewell she.
  Or else, if ye be wroth, ye may avengéd
  be.
R. Roister. By Cock's precious potstick,[7]
  and e'en so I shall.
  I will utterly destroy her, and house and
  all!
  But I would be avenged in the mean
  space
  On that vile scribbler that did my wooing
  disgrace.   130
M. Merry. "Scribbler," ko you? Indeed,
  he is worthy no less.
  I will call him to you, and ye bid me
  doubtless.

[1] Desist from.
[2] By God (a mild oath).
[3] Faith.
[4] Wench.
[5] Make (?).
[6] Madness.
[7] Farmer suggests the stick used to extend the sponge to Christ on the cross.

R. ROISTER. Yes, for although he had as
  many lives
As a thousand widows, and a thousand
  wives,
As a thousand lions, and a thousand
  rats,
A thousand wolves, and a thousand
  cats,
A thousand bulls, and a thousand calves,
And a thousand legions divided in halves,
He shall never scape death on my sword's
  point,
Though I should be torn therefor joint
  by joint.   140
M. MERRY. Nay, if ye will kill him, I will
  not fet him;
I will not in so much extremity set
  him.
He may yet amend, sir, and be an honest
  man;
Therefore pardon him, good soul, as
  much as ye can.
R. ROISTER. Well, for thy sake, this once
  with his life he shall pass,
But I will hew him all to pieces, by the
  Mass.
M. MERRY. Nay, faith, ye shall promise
  that he shall no harm have,
Else I will not fet him.
R. ROISTER.   I shall, so God
  me save.
But I may chide him agood.[1]
M. MERRY.   Yea, that
  do hardly.[2]
R. ROISTER. Go, then.
M. MERRY.   I return, and bring
  him to you by-and-by.   Ex[eat].   150

ACTUS III. SCENA v.

*Roister Doister, Matthew Merrygreek, Scriv-
                                   ener.*[3]

R. ROISTER. What is a gentleman but his
  word and his promise?
I must now save this villain's life in any
  wise,
And yet at him already my hands do
  tickle;
I shall uneath[4] hold them, they will be
  so fickle.
But lo, and Merrygreek have not brought
  him sence.

---

[1] In earnest.   [3] Last two enter later.
[2] Hardily, boldly.   [4] With difficulty.

[*Enter Merrygreek and Scrivener.*]

M. MERRY. Nay, I would I had of my
  purse paid forty pence.
SCRIVENER. So would I too; but it needed
  not that stound.[5]
M. MERRY. But the gentman had rather
  spent five thousand pound,
For it disgraced him at least five times
  so much.
SCRIVENER. He disgraced himself, his lout-
  ishness is such.   10
R. ROISTER. [*Aside.*] How long they stand
  prating!—Why com'st thou not away?
M. MERRY. Come now to himself, and
  hark what he will say.
SCRIVENER. I am not afraid in his presence
  to appear.
R. ROISTER. Art thou come, fellow?
SCRIVENER.   How
  think you? Am I not here?
R. ROISTER. What hindrance hast thou
  done me, and what villainy!
SCRIVENER. It hath come of thyself, if
  thou hast had any.
R. ROISTER. All the stock thou comest of,
  later or rather,[6]
From thy first father's grandfather's
  father's father,
Nor all that shall come of thee to the
  world's end,
Though to threescore generations they
  descend,   20
Can be able to make me a just recom-
  pense
For this trespass of thine and this one
  offense.
SCRIVENER. Wherein?
R. ROISTER.   Did not you make
  me a letter, brother?
SCRIVENER. Pay the like hire, I will make
  you such another.
R. ROISTER. Nay, see and these whoreson[7]
  Pharisees and Scribes
Do not get their living by polling and
  bribes![8]
If it were not for shame——
SCRIVENER.   Nay, hold
  thy hands still!
M. MERRY. Why, did ye not promise that
  ye would not him spill?[9]

---

[5] Amazement; *i.e.*, the shock of the letter was
unnecessary (?).   [6] Sooner.   [7] Rascally.
[8] Swindling and robbery.   [9] Destroy.

SCRIVENER. Let him not spare me.

R. ROISTER.   Why,
wilt thou strike me again?

SCRIVENER. Ye shall have as good as ye
bring of me, that is plain.   30

M. MERRY. I cannot blame him, sir,
though your blows would him grieve,
For he knoweth present death to ensue
of all ye give.

R. ROISTER. Well, this man for once hath
purchased thy pardon.

SCRIVENER. And what say ye to me? Or
else I will be gone.

R. ROISTER. I say the letter thou madest
me was not good.

SCRIVENER. Then did ye wrong copy it,
of likelihood.

R. ROISTER. Yes, out of thy copy word
for word I wrote.

SCRIVENER. Then was it as ye prayed to
have it, I wot,
But in reading and pointing [1] there was
made some fault.

R. ROISTER. I wot not, but it made all
my matter to halt.   40

SCRIVENER. How say you, is this mine
original or no?

R. ROISTER. The selfsame that I wrote
out of, so mote I go.[2]

SCRIVENER. Look you on your own fist,
and I will look on this,
And let this man be judge whether I
read amiss.
"To mine own dear cony, bird, sweetheart, and pigsnie,
Good Mistress Custance, present these
by-and-by."
How now? Doth not this superscription
agree?

R. ROISTER. Read that is within, and
there ye shall the fault see.

SCRIVENER. "Sweet mistress, whereas I
love you—nothing at all
Regarding your richesse and substance,
chief of all   50
For your personage, beauty, demeanor,
and wit—
I commend me unto you; never a whit
Sorry to hear report of your good welfare.
For, as I hear say, such your conditions
are
That ye be worthy favor; of no living
man

To be abhorred; of every honest man
To be taken for a woman inclined to vice
Nothing at all; to virtue giving her due
price.
Wherefore concerning marriage, ye are
thought
Such a fine paragon as ne'er honest man
bought.   60
And now by these presents I do you
advertise
That I am minded to marry you—in no
wise
For your goods and substance. I can be
content
To take you as you are. If ye will be my
wife,
Ye shall be assured for the time of my
life,
I will keep you right well. From good
raiment and fare
Ye shall not be kept; but in sorrow and
care
Ye shall in no wise live; at your own
liberty
Do and say what ye lust. Ye shall never
please me
But when ye are merry; I will be all sad 70
When ye are sorry; I will be very glad
When ye seek your heart's ease; I will
be unkind
At no time; in me shall ye much gentle-
ness find.
But all things contrary to your will and
mind
Shall be done otherwise. I will not be
behind
To speak. And as for all them that
would do you wrong
(I will so help and maintain ye) shall
not live long.
Nor any foolish dolt shall cumber you,
but I,
I, whoe'er say nay, will stick by you till
I die.
Thus, good Mistress Custance, the Lord
you save and keep.   80
From me, Roister Doister, whether I
wake or sleep,
Who favoreth you no less (ye may be
bold)
Than this letter purporteth, which ye
have unfold."
Now, sir, what default can ye find in this
letter?

[1] Punctuating.   [2] *I.e.*, so may I live.

R. ROISTER. Of truth, in my mind there
  cannot be a better.
SCRIVENER. Then was the fault in reading,
  and not in writing;
No, nor I dare say in the form of inditing.
But who read this letter, that it sounded
  so naught?
M. MERRY. I read it, indeed.
SCRIVENER.   Ye read it
  not as ye ought.
R. ROISTER. Why, thou wretched villain,
  was all this same fault in thee?   90
M. MERRY. I knock your costard[1] if ye
  offer to strike me.
R. ROISTER. Strikest thou, indeed, and I
  offer but in jest?
M. MERRY. Yea, and rap you again ex-
  cept ye can sit in rest.
And I will no longer tarry here, me be-
  lieve.
R. ROISTER. What, wilt thou be angry,
  and I do thee forgive?
Fare thou well, scribbler; I cry thee
  mercy indeed.
SCRIVENER. Fare ye well, bibbler, and
  worthily may ye speed.
R. ROISTER. If it were another but thou,
  it were a knave.
M. MERRY. Ye are another yourself, sir,
  the Lord us both save,
Albeit in this matter I must your pardon
  crave.   100
Alas, would ye wish in me the wit that
  ye have?
But as for my fault I can quickly amend;
I will show Custance it was I that did
  offend.
R. ROISTER. By so doing her anger may
  be reformed.
M. MERRY. But, if by no entreaty she will
  be turned,
Then set light by her and be as testy as
  she,
And do your force upon her with ex-
  tremity.
R. ROISTER. Come on, therefore, let us go
  home in sadness.
M. MERRY. That if force shall need, all
  may be in a readiness.   109
And, as for this letter, hardly let all go.
We will know whe'er[2] she refuse you for
  that or no.   *Exeant am[bo].*

---

[1] Apple, *i.e.*, head.   [2] Whether.

ACTUS IV. SCENA i.

Sim Suresby.

SIM SURE. Is there any man but I, Sim
  Suresby alone,
That would have taken such an enter-
  prise him upon,
In such an outrageous tempest as this
  was,
Such a dangerous gulf of the sea to
  pass?
I think, verily, Neptune's mighty god-
  ship
Was angry with some that was in our
  ship,
And, but for the honesty which in me
  he found,
I think for the others' sake we had been
  drowned.
But fie on that servant which for his
  master's wealth[3]
Will stick for to hazard both his life and
  his health.   10
My master, Gawin Goodluck, after me
  a day,
Because of the weather, thought best his
  ship to stay;
And now that I have the rough surges so
  well passed,
God grant I may find all things safe here
  at last.
Then will I think all my travail well
  spent.
Now the first point wherefore my master
  hath me sent
Is to salute Dame Christian Custance,
  his wife
Espoused, whom he tend'reth no less
  than his life.
I must see how it is with her, well or
  wrong,
And whether for him she doth not now
  think long.   20
Then to other friends I have a message
  or tway,[4]
And then so to return and meet him on
  the way.
Now will I go knock that I may despatch
  with speed,
But lo, forth cometh herself happily,[5]
  indeed.

---

[3] Welfare.
[4] Two.
[5] Fortunately.

ACTUS IV. SCENA ii.

Christian Custance, Sim Suresby.

C. CUSTANCE. [*Aside.*] I come to see if any
　　more stirring be here.
　But what stranger is this which doth to
　　me appear?
SIM SURE. [*Aside.*] I will speak to her.—
　　Dame, the Lord you save and see.
C. CUSTANCE. What, friend Sim Suresby?
　　Forsooth, right welcome ye be!
　How doth mine own Gawin Goodluck?
　　I pray thee tell.
SIM SURE. When he knoweth of your
　　health, he will be perfect well.
C. CUSTANCE. If he have perfect health,
　　I am as I would be.
SIM SURE. Such news will please him well;
　　this is as it should be.
C. CUSTANCE. I think now long for him.
SIM SURE.　　　　And he as long for you.
C. CUSTANCE. When will he be at home?
SIM SURE.　　　His heart is here e'en now;
　　His body cometh after.
C. CUSTANCE.　　　　I would see that
　　fain.　　　　　　　　　　　　　11
SIM SURE. As fast as wind and sail can
　　carry it amain.
　But what two men are yond coming
　　hitherward?
C. CUSTANCE. Now I shrew their best
　　Christmas cheeks,[1] both togetherward!

ACTUS IV. SCENA iii.

*Christian Custance, Sim Suresby, Ralph
　Roister, Matthew Merrygreek, True-
　　　　　　　　　　　penny.*[2]

C. CUSTANCE. [*Aside.*] What mean these
　　lewd fellows thus to trouble me still?
　Sim Suresby here perchance shall thereof
　　deem some ill,
　And shall suspect in me some point of
　　naughtiness,
　And [3] they come hitherward.
SIM SURE.　　　　　　　　What is
　　their business?
C. CUSTANCE. I have naught to them, nor
　　they to me, in sadness.[4]
SIM SURE. Let us hearken them.—[*Aside.*]
　　Somewhat there is, I fear it.

R. ROISTER. I will speak out aloud best,
　　that she may hear it.
M. MERRY. Nay, alas, ye may so fear [5]
　　her out of her wit.
R. ROISTER. By the cross of my sword, I
　　will hurt her no whit.
M. MERRY. Will ye do no harm indeed?
　　Shall I trust your word?　　　　10
R. ROISTER. By Roister Doister's faith, I
　　will speak but in bord.
SIM SURE. Let us hearken them.—[*Aside.*]
　　Somewhat there is, I fear it.
R. ROISTER. I will speak out aloud; I care
　　not who hear it.
　　　[*Pretends to call to his servants within.*]
　Sirs, see that my harness, my target,
　　and my shield
　Be made as bright now as when I was
　　last in field,
　As white as I should to war again to-
　　morrow;
　For sick shall I be, but I work some folk
　　sorrow.
　Therefore see that all shine as bright as
　　Saint George,
　Or as doth a key newly come from the
　　smith's forge.
　I would have my sword and harness to
　　shine so bright [6]　　　　20
　That I might therewith dim mine
　　enemies' sight.
　I would have it cast beams as fast, I tell
　　you plain,
　As doth the glittering grass after a shower
　　of rain.
　And see that, in case I should need to
　　come to arming,
　All things may be ready at a minute's
　　warning.
　For such chance may chance in an hour—
　　do ye hear?
M. MERRY. As perchance shall not chance
　　again in seven year.
R. ROISTER. Now draw we near to her,
　　and hear what shall be said.
M. MERRY. But I would not have you
　　make her too much afraid.
R. ROISTER. Well found, sweet wife (I
　　trust), for all this your sour look.　30
C. CUSTANCE. Wife? Why call ye me
　　wife?

---

[1] A defiant curse (*N.E.D.*); *i.e.*, I curse their
unrestrained effrontery.
[2] Enters later.　　[3] If.　　[4] Seriousness.

[5] Frighten.
[6] This passage is based on Plautus, *Miles
gloriosus*, I, i.

SIM SURE. [*Aside.*]   Wife? This gear
go'th acrook.

M. MERRY. Nay, Mistress Custance, I
warrant you, our letter
Is not as we read e'en now, but much
better,
And, where ye half stomached this gentleman afore,
For this same letter, ye will love him now
therefor;
Nor it is not this letter, though ye were a
queen,
That should break marriage between
you twain, I ween.[1]

C. CUSTANCE. I did not refuse him for the
letter's sake.

R. ROISTER. Then ye are content me for
your husband to take.

C. CUSTANCE. You for my husband to
take? Nothing less truly.   40

R. ROISTER. Yea, say so, sweet spouse,
afore strangers hardly.

M. MERRY. And, though I have here his
letter of love with me,
Yet his ring and tokens he sent, keep
safe with ye.

C. CUSTANCE. A mischief take his tokens,
and him and thee too.
But what prate I with fools? Have I
nought else to do?
Come in with me, Sim Suresby, to take
some repast.

SIM SURE. I must, ere I drink, by your
leave, go in all haste
To a place or two with earnest letters of
his.

C. CUSTANCE. Then come drink here with
me.

SIM SURE.   I thank you!

C. CUSTANCE.   Do not miss.
You shall have a token to your master
with you.   50

SIM SURE. No tokens this time, gramercies!
God be with you.   *Exeat.*

C. CUSTANCE. Surely this fellow misdeemeth some ill in me—
Which thing, but God help, will go near
to spill me.

R. ROISTER. Yea, farewell, fellow, and tell
thy master Goodluck
That he cometh too late of this blossom
to pluck.

Let him keep him there still, or at least-
wise make no haste,
As for his labor hither he shall spend in
waste.
His betters be in place now.

M. MERRY. [*Aside.*]   As long as it
will hold.

C. CUSTANCE. I will be even with thee,
thou beast, thou mayst be bold.[2]

R. ROISTER. Will ye have us then?

C. CUSTANCE.   I will
never have thee.   60

R. ROISTER. Then will I have you!

C. CUSTANCE.   No,
the devil shall have thee.
I have gotten this hour more shame and
harm by thee
Than all thy life-days thou canst do me
honesty.

M. MERRY. [*To Roister Doister.*] Why, now
may ye see what it com'th to, in the
end,
To make a deadly foe of your most loving friend.—
And iwis this letter, if ye would hear it
now——

C. CUSTANCE. I will hear none of it.

M. MERRY.   In
faith, would ravish you.

C. CUSTANCE. He hath stained my name
forever, this is clear.

R. ROISTER. I can make all as well in an
hour—

M. MERRY. [*Aside.*]   As ten year.—
How say ye, will ye have him?

C. CUSTANCE. No.

M. MERRY.   Will ye take him? 70

C. CUSTANCE. I defy him.

M. MERRY.   At my word?

C. CUSTANCE.   A shame take him.
Waste no more wind, for it will never
be.

M. MERRY. This one fault with twain shall
be mended, ye shall see.
Gentle Mistress Custance now, good
Mistress Custance!
Honey Mistress Custance now, sweet
Mistress Custance!
Golden Mistress Custance now, white [3]
Mistress Custance!
Silken Mistress Custance now, fair Mis-
tress Custance!

---

[1] Imagine.   [2] Certain.   [3] Dear.

C. CUSTANCE. Faith, rather than to marry
with such a doltish lout
I would match myself with a beggar, out
of doubt.
M. MERRY. Then I can say no more; to
speed we are not like, 80
Except ye rap out a rag of your rhetoric.[1]
C. CUSTANCE. Speak not of winning me,
for it shall never be so.
R. ROISTER. Yes, dame, I will have you,
whether ye will or no.
I command you to love me! Wherefore
should ye not?
Is not my love to you chafing and burning
hot?
M. MERRY. To her! That is well said!
R. ROISTER. Shall I so break my brain
To dote upon you, and ye not love us
again?
M. MERRY. Well said yet.
C. CUSTANCE. Go to, you goose.
R. ROISTER. I say, Kit Custance,
In case ye will not ha's—well, better yes,
perchance.
C. CUSTANCE. Avaunt, losel;[2] pick thee
hence![3]
M. MERRY. Well, sir, ye perceive, 90
For all your kind offer, she will not you
receive.
R. ROISTER. Then a straw for her, and a
straw for her again;
She shall not be my wife, would she never
so fain;
No, and though she would be at ten
thousand pound cost.
M. MERRY. Lo, dame, ye may see what
an husband ye have lost.
C. CUSTANCE. Yea, no force;[4] a jewel
much better lost than found.
M. MERRY. Ah, ye will not believe how
this doth my heart wound.
How should a marriage between you be
toward,
If both parties draw back, and become
so froward?
R. ROISTER. Nay, dame, I will fire thee
out of thy house, 100
And destroy thee and all thine, and that
by-and-by.
M. MERRY. Nay, for the passion of God,
sir, do not so.

R. ROISTER. Yes, except she will say yea
to that she said no.
C. CUSTANCE. And what! be there no
officers, trow we, in town
To check idle loiterers, bragging up and
down?
Where be they by whom vacabunds[5]
should be repressed,
That poor silly[6] widows might live in
peace and rest?
Shall I never rid thee out of my company?
I will call for help. What ho! come forth,
Truepenny!
TRUEPENNY. [Within.] Anon.[7]

[Enters.]
What is your will, mistress?
Did ye call me? 110
C. CUSTANCE. Yea; go run apace, and, as
fast as may be,
Pray Tristram Trusty, my most assured
friend,
To be here by-and-by, that he may me
defend.
TRUEPENNY. That message so quickly
shall be done, by God's grace,
That at my return ye shall say I went
apace. Exeat.
C. CUSTANCE. Then shall we see, I trow,
whether ye shall do me harm.
R. ROISTER. Yes, in faith, Kit, I shall
thee and thine so charm
That all women incarnate by thee may
beware.
C. CUSTANCE. Nay, as for charming me,
come hither if thou dare;
I shall clout thee till thou stink, both
thee and thy train, 120
And coil thee[8] mine own hands, and
send thee home again.
R. ROISTER. Yea, sayest thou me that,
dame? Dost thou me threaten?
Go we; I still[9] see whether I shall be
beaten.
M. MERRY. Nay, for the pashe[10] of God,
let me now treat peace,
For bloodshed will there be in case this
strife increase.
Ah, good Dame Custance, take better
way with you.

[1] *I.e.*, unless you spout a bit of your rhetoric.
[2] Rascal.
[3] Away with you! [4] No matter.
[5] Vagabonds. [8] Beat thee [with].
[6] Simple. [9] Cooper suggests *will*.
[7] The usual answer of servants. [10] Passion.

C. CUSTANCE. Let him do his worst!

M. MERRY. Yield in time!

R. ROISTER. Come hence, thou!

Exeant Roister et Merry[greek].

ACTUS IV. SCENA iv.

Christian Custance, Annot Alyface, Tibet T[alkapace], M[adge] Mumblecrust.[1]

C. CUSTANCE. So, sirrah, if I should not with him take this way,

I should not be rid of him, I think, till doomsday.

I will call forth my folks, that, without any mocks,[2]

If he come again, we may give him raps and knocks.

Madge Mumblecrust, come forth, and Tibet Talkapace.

Yea, and come forth too, Mistress Annot Alyface.

[Enter the three Maids.]

AN. ALYFACE. I come.

TIB. TALK. And I am here.

M. MUMBL. And I am here too, at length.

C. CUSTANCE. Like warriors, if need be, ye must show your strength.

The man that this day hath thus beguiled you,

Is Ralph Roister Doister, whom ye know well inowe,[3] 10

The most lout and dastard that ever on ground trod.

TIB. TALK. I see all folk mock him when he go'th abroad.

C. CUSTANCE. What, pretty maid, will ye talk when I speak?

TIB. TALK. No, forsooth, good mistress.

C. CUSTANCE. Will ye my tale break?

He threat'neth to come hither with all his force to fight.

I charge you, if he come, on him with all your might!

M. MUMBL. I with my distaff will reach him one rap!

TIB. TALK. And I with my new broom will sweep him one swap,

And then with our great club I will reach him one rap!

AN. ALYFACE. And I with our skimmer will fling him one flap! 20

TIB. TALK. Then Truepenny's firefork[4] will him shrewdly fray,[5]

And you with the spit may drive him quite away.

C. CUSTANCE. Go, make all ready, that it may be e'en so.

TIB. TALK. For my part, I shrew them that last about it go. *Exeant.*

ACTUS IV. SCENA v.

Christian Custance, Truepenny, Tristram Trusty.[6]

C. CUSTANCE. Truepenny did promise me to run a great pace,

My friend Tristram Trusty to fet into this place.

Indeed he dwelleth hence a good start,[7] I confess;

But yet a quick messenger might twice since, as I guess,

Have gone and come again. Ah, yond I spy him now.

[Enter Truepenny, followed by Tristram Trusty.]

TRUEPENNY. Ye are a slow goer, sir, I make God avow.

My mistress Custance will in me put all the blame.

Your legs be longer than mine; come apace for shame.

C. CUSTANCE. I can thee thank, Truepenny; thou hast done right well.

TRUEPENNY. Mistress, since I went, no grass hath grown on my heel, 10

But Master Tristram Trusty here maketh no speed.

C. CUSTANCE. That he came at all, I thank him in very deed,

For now have I need of the help of some wise man.

T. TRUSTY. Then may I be gone again, for none such I [a]m.

TRUEPENNY. Ye may be, by your going,[8] for no alderman

Can go, I dare say, a sadder[9] pace than ye can.

---

[1] The last three enter later. [2] Pretenses.
[3] *I.e.*, enow. Emendation suggested by Cooper, original reads *mowe*.

[4] Poker.
[5] Frighten.
[6] Last two enter later.
[7] Distance.
[8] Gait.
[9] Soberer.

C, Custance. Truepenny, get thee in;
thou shalt among them know
How to use thyself like a proper man, I
trow.
Truepenny. I go.   [*Exeat.*]
C. Custance.   Now, Tristram Trusty,
I thank you right much,
For, at my first sending, to come ye
never grutch.[1]   20
T. Trusty. Dame Custance, God ye save,
and while my life shall last,
For my friend Goodluck's sake ye shall
not send in waste.
C. Custance. He shall give you thanks.
T. Trusty.   I will do much for his sake.
C. Custance. But, alack, I fear great dis-
pleasure shall be take.
T. Trusty. Wherefore?
C. Custance.   For a foolish matter.
T. Trusty.   What is your cause?
C. Custance. I am ill accumbered with a
couple of daws.
T. Trusty. Nay, weep not, woman, but
tell me what your cause is.
As concerning my friend, is anything
amiss?
C. Custance. No, not on my part. But
here was Sim Suresby—
T. Trusty. He was with me and told me so.
C. Custance.   And he stood by   30
While Ralph Roister Doister with help
of Merrygreek
For promise of marriage did unto me
seek.
T. Trusty. And had ye made any promise
before them twain?
C. Custance. No, I had rather be torn in
pieces and slain.
No man hath my faith and troth but
Gawin Goodluck,
And that before Suresby did I say, and
there stuck.
But of certain letters there were such
words spoken—
T. Trusty. He told me that too.
C. Custance.   And of
a ring and token,
That Suresby, I spied, did more than
half suspect
That I my faith to Gawin Goodluck did
reject.   40
T. Trusty. But there was no such matter,
Dame Custance, indeed?

C. Custance. If ever my head thought it,
God send me ill speed.
Wherefore, I beseech you, with me to be
a witness,
That in all my life I never intended thing
less;
And what a brainsick fool Ralph Roister
Doister is,
Yourself know well enough.
T. Trusty.   Ye say full
true, iwis.
C. Custance. Because to be his wife I ne
grant nor apply,[2]
Hither will he come, he sweareth, by-
and-by,
To kill both me and mine, and beat
down my house flat.
Therefore I pray your aid.
T. Trusty.   I warrant
you that.   50
C. Custance. Have I so many years lived
a sober life,
And showed myself honest, maid, widow,
and wife,
And now to be abused in such a vile sort?
Ye see how poor widows live all void of
comfort.
T. Trusty. I warrant him do you no harm
nor wrong at all.
C. Custance. No, but Matthew Merry-
greek doth me most appall,
That he would join himself with such a
wretched lout.
T. Trusty. He doth it for a jest; I know
him out of doubt.—
And here cometh Merrygreek.
C. Custance.   Then
shall we hear his mind.

Actus IV. Scena vi.

Merrygreek, Christian Custance, Trist[ram]
Trusty.

M. Merry. Custance and Trusty both, I
do you here well find.
C. Custance. Ah, Matthew Merrygreek,
ye have used me well!
M. Merry. Now for altogether[3] ye must
your answer tell.
Will ye have this man, woman, or else
will ye not?
Else will he come never boar so brim
nor toast so hot.

---

[1] Grumble.   [2] Incline.   [3] Once for all.   [4] Fierce

TRIS. AND CUS. But why join ye with him?

T. TRUSTY.   For mirth?

C. CUSTANCE.   Or else in
   sadness?

M. MERRY. The more fond of you! Both?
   Hardly! The matter guess!

T. TRUSTY. Lo, how say ye, dame?

M. MERRY.   Why,
   do ye think, Dame Custance,

That in this wooing I have meant aught
   but pastance?

C. CUSTANCE. Much things ye spake, I
   wot, to maintain his dotage.   10

M. MERRY. But well might ye judge I
   spake it all in mockage.

For why? Is Roister Doister a fit husband for you?

T. TRUSTY. I dare say ye never thought it.

M. MERRY.   No, to God I vow.

And did not I know afore of the insur-
   ance [1]

Between Gawin Goodluck and Christian
   Custance?

And did not I for the nonce, by my conveyance, [2]

Read his letter in a wrong sense for
   dalliance,

That, if you could have take it up at the
   first bound,

We should thereat such a sport and
   pastime have found,

That all the whole town should have been
   the merrier?   20

C. CUSTANCE. Ill ache your heads both!
   I was never wearier,

Nor never more vexed since the first day
   I was born.

T. TRUSTY. But very well I wist he here
   did all in scorn.

C. CUSTANCE. But I feared thereof to take
   dishonesty. [3]

M. MERRY. This should both have made
   sport and showed your honesty,

And Goodluck, I dare swear, your wit
   therein would low.

T. TRUSTY. Yea, being no worse than we
   know it to be now.

M. MERRY. And nothing yet too late; for
   when I come to him,

Hither will he repair with a sheep's look
   full grim,

By plain force and violence to drive you
   to yield.   30

---

[1] Betrothal, promise.   [2] Trickery.   [3] Dishonor.

C. CUSTANCE. If ye two bid me, we will
   with him pitch a field, [4]

I and my maids together.

M. MERRY.   Let us see;
   be bold.

C. CUSTANCE. Ye shall see women's war.

T. TRUSTY.   That fight will I behold.

M. MERRY. If occasion serve, taking his
   part full brim,

I will strike at you, but the rap shall
   light on him,

When we first appear.

C. CUSTANCE.   Then will I run
   away

As though I were afeard.

T. TRUSTY.   Do you that
   part well play

And I will sue for peace.

M. MERRY.   And I will set
   him on.

Then will he look as fierce as a Cotswold
   lion. [5]

T. TRUSTY. But when goest thou for him?

M. MERRY.   That do I very now.   40

C. CUSTANCE. Ye shall find us here.

M. MERRY.   Well, God have
   mercy on you.   *Ex[eat]*.

T. TRUSTY. There is no cause of fear; the
   least boy in the street——

C. CUSTANCE. Nay, the least girl I have
   will make him take his feet.

But hark! methink they make preparation.

T. TRUSTY. No force, it will be a good
   recreation.

C. CUSTANCE. I will stand within, and
   step forth speedily,

And so make as though I ran away
   dreadfully. [6]   *[Exeant.]*

ACTUS IV. SCENA vii.

R[alph] Roister, M[atthew] Merrygreek, C[hris-
   tian] Custance, [7] *D[obinet] Doughty,* [7]
   Harpax, Tristram Trusty. [7]

R. ROISTER. Now, sirs, keep your ray, [8]
   and see your hearts be stout.

But where be these caitiffs? Methink
   they dare not rout. [9]

How sayest thou, Merrygreek? What
   doth Kit Custance say?

---

[4] Engage in a battle.   [7] Enters later.
[5] *I.e.,* a sheep.   [8] Array, due order.
[6] Full of fear.   [9] Assemble.

M. Merry. I am loath to tell you.

R. Roister.   Tush,
　　speak, man: yea or nay?

M. Merry. Forsooth, sir, I have spoken
　　for you all that I can.

　　But if ye win her, ye must e'en play the
　　man;

　　E'en to fight it out, ye must a man's
　　heart take.

R. Roister. Yes, they shall know, and
　　thou knowest I have a stomach.[1]

[M. Merry.] "A stomach," quod you?
　　Yea, as good as e'er man had.

R. Roister. I trow they shall find and
　　feel that I am a lad.   10

M. Merry. By this cross, I have seen you
　　eat your meat as well

　　As any that e'er I have seen of or heard
　　tell.

　　"A stomach," quod you? He that will
　　that deny

　　I know was never at dinner in your
　　company.

R. Roister. Nay, the stomach of a man
　　it is that I mean.

M. Merry. Nay, the stomach of a horse
　　or a dog, I ween.

R. Roister. Nay, a man's stomach with a
　　weapon, mean I.

M. Merry. Ten men can scarce match
　　you with a spoon in a pie.

R. Roister. Nay, the stomach of a man
　　to try in strife.

M. Merry. I never saw your stomach
　　cloyed yet in my life.   20

R. Roister. Tush, I mean in strife or
　　fighting to try.

M. Merry. We shall see how ye will
　　strike now, being angry.

R. Roister. Have at thy pate then, and
　　save thy head if thou may.
　　　　　　　[They strike at each other.]

M. Merry. Nay, then have at your pate
　　again by this day.

R. Roister. Nay, thou mayst not strike
　　at me again in no wise.

M. Merry. I cannot in fight make to you
　　such warrantize; [2]

　　But as for your foes, here let them the
　　bargain by.[3]

R. Roister. Nay, as for they, shall every
　　mother's child die.

And in this my fume a little thing might
　　make me

To beat down house and all, and else
　　the devil take me.   30

M. Merry. If I were as ye be, by Gog's
　　dear mother,

I would not leave one stone upon an-
　　other,

Though she would redeem it with twenty
　　thousand pounds.

R. Roister. It shall be even so, by his
　　lily wounds.

M. Merry. Be not at one with her, upon
　　any amends.

R. Roister. No, though she make to me
　　never so many friends,

Nor if all the world for her would under-
　　take, [4]

No, not God himself neither shall not her
　　peace make.

On, therefore, march forward—soft, stay
　　a while yet!

M. Merry. On!

R. Roister.   Tarry!

M. Merry.   Forth!

R. Roister.   Back!

M. Merry.   On!

R. Roister.   Soft! Now forward
　　set!   40

[Enter Custance.]

C. Custance. What business have we
　　here? Out! alas, alas!   [Exeat.]

R. Roister. Ha, ha, ha, ha, ha!

Didst thou see that, Merrygreek, how
　　afraid she was?

Didst thou see how she fled apace out of
　　my sight?

Ah, good sweet Custance, I pity her, by
　　this light.

M. Merry. That tender heart of yours
　　will mar altogether;

Thus will ye be turned with wagging of
　　a feather.

R. Roister. On, sirs, keep your ray!

M. Merry.   On,
　　forth, while this gear is hot!

R. Roister. Soft, the arms of Calais! I
　　have one thing forgot.

M. Merry. What lack we now?

R. Roister.   Retire,
　　or else we be all slain.   50

---

[1] Courage.   [3] Aby, pay the penalty for.
[2] Guarantee.

[4] Assume responsibility.

M. Merry. Back, for the pashe of God!
Back, sirs, back again!
What is the great matter?

R. Roister. This hasty
forthgoing
Had almost brought us all to utter undoing;
It made me forget a thing most necessary.

M. Merry. Well remembered of a captain, by Saint Mary.

R. Roister. It is a thing must be had.

M. Merry. Let us have it then.

R. Roister. But I wot not where nor how.

M. Merry. Then wot not I when.
But what is it?

R. Roister. Of a chief thing I am to
seek.

M. Merry. Tut, so will ye be, when ye
have studied a week.
But tell me what it is?

R. Roister. I lack yet an
headpiece. 60

M. Merry. The kitchen collocavit,[1] the
best hens to grease![2]
Run, fet it, Dobinet, and come at once
withal,
And bring with thee my potgun,[3] hanging
by the wall. [Exeat Dobinet.]
I have seen your head with it full many
a time
Covered as safe as it had been with a
skrine;[4]
And I warrant it save your head from
any stroke,
Except perchance to be amazed[5] with
the smoke.
I warrant your head therewith, except
for the mist,
As safe as if it were fast locked up in a
chist.[6]
And lo, here our Dobinet cometh with it
now. 70

[Enter Dobinet.]

D. Dough. It will cover me to the shoulders well enow.

M. Merry. Let me see it on.

R. Roister. In faith,
it doth metely well.

[1] Humorous latinization of *collock*, a large
kitchen pail.
[2] Or, punning, "the best hence to Greece."
[3] Popgun. [5] Stupefied, bewildered.
[4] Box, chest. [6] Chest.

M. Merry. There can be no fitter thing.
Now ye must us tell
What to do.

R. Roister. Now forth in ray, sirs,
and stop no more.

M. Merry. Now, Saint George to borrow,[7] drum dub-a-dub afore.

[Enter Trusty.]

T. Trusty. What mean you to do, sir,
commit manslaughter?

R. Roister. To kill forty such is a matter
of laughter.

T. Trusty. And who is it, sir, whom ye
intend thus to spill?

R. Roister. Foolish Custance here forceth me against my will.

T. Trusty. And is there no mean your
extreme wrath to slake? 80
She shall some amends unto your good
ma'ship make.

R. Roister. I will none amends.

T. Trusty. Is her
offense so sore?

M. Merry. And he were a lout, she could
have done no more.
She hath called him fool, and dressed[8]
him like a fool,
Mocked him like a fool, used him like a
fool.

T. Trusty. Well, yet the sheriff, the justice, or constable,
Her misdemeanor to punish might be able.

R. Roister. No, sir, I mine own self will,
in this present cause,
Be sheriff, and justice, and whole judge
of the laws;
This matter to amend, all officers be I
shall, 90
Constable, bailiff, sergeant—

M. Merry. And hang-
man and all.

T. Trusty. Yet a noble courage, and the
heart of a man,
Should more honor win by bearing with
a woman.
Therefore take the law, and let her
answer thereto.

R. Roister. Merrygreek, the best way
were even so to do.
What honor should it be with a woman to
fight?

[7] Saint George for a pledge; Saint George help
us. [8] Addressed.

M. MERRY. And what then? Will ye thus forgo and leese your right?

R. ROISTER. Nay, I will take the law on her withouten grace.

T. TRUSTY. Or if your ma'ship could pardon this one trespace,[1]
I pray you forgive her.

R. ROISTER.   Hoh!

M. MERRY.   Tush,
tush, sir, do not.   100

[T. TRUSTY.] Be good, master, to her.

R. ROISTER.   Hoh!

M. MERRY.   Tush, I say, do not.
And what! shall your people here return straight home?

T. TRUSTY.[2] Yea; levy the camp,[3] sirs, and hence again each one.

R. ROISTER.[2] But be still in readiness, if I hap to call;
I cannot tell what sudden chance may befall.

M. MERRY. Do not off your harness, sirs, I you advise,
At the least for this fortnight in no manner wise.
Perchance in an hour when all ye think least,
Our master's appetite to fight will be best.
But soft, ere ye go, have once at Custance' house.   110

R. ROISTER. Soft, what wilt thou do?

M. MERRY.   Once discharge my harquebouse,   [Shoots the harquebus.]
And, for my heart's ease, have once more with my potgun.   [Shoots the popgun.]

R. ROISTER. Hold thy hands; else is all our purpose clean fordone!

M. MERRY. And it cost me my life—

R. ROISTER.   I say, thou shalt not.

M. MERRY. By the Matte,[4] but I will. Have once more with hail shot.
I will have some pennyworth! I will not leese all!

ACTUS IV. SCENA viii.[5]

M[atthew] Merrygreek, C[hristian] Custance,
    R[alph] Roister, Tib[et] T[alkapace],[6]
    An[not] Alyface,[6] M[adge] Mumblecrust,[6]

---

[1] Trespass.   [3] Raise the siege.
[2] Speakers are reversed in original.   [4] Mass.
[5] For this scene cf. Plautus, Miles gloriosus, V.
[6] Enters later.

Truepenny, Dobinet Doughty, Harpax,
    two Drums[7] with their ensigns.

C. CUSTANCE. What caitiffs are those that so shake my house wall?

M. MERRY. Ah, sirrah! now Custance, if ye had so much wit,
I would see you ask pardon, and yourselves submit.

C. CUSTANCE. Have I still this ado with a couple of fools?

M. MERRY. Hear ye what she saith?

C. CUSTANCE.   Maidens, come forth with your tools.

[Enter Maids.]

R. ROISTER. In a ray!

M. MERRY.   Dubbadub, sirrah.

R. ROISTER.   In a ray!
They come suddenly on us.

M. MERRY.   Dubbadub.

R. ROISTER.   In a ray!
That ever I was born! We are taken tardy![8]

M. MERRY. Now, sirs, quit ourselves like tall men and hardy!

C. CUSTANCE. On afore, Truepenny! Hold thine own, Annot!   10
On toward them, Tibet! for scape us they cannot.
Come forth, Madge Mumblecrust! So stand fast togither.

M. MERRY. God send us a fair day!

R. ROISTER.   See, they march on hither.

TIB. TALK. But, mistress——

C. CUSTANCE. What sayest you?

TIB. TALK.   Shall I go fet our goose?

C. CUSTANCE. What to do?

TIB. TALK.   To yonder captain I will turn her loose.
And she gape and hiss at him, as she doth at me,
I durst jeopard my hand she will make him flee.

C. CUSTANCE. On! Forward!

R. ROISTER.   They come!

M. MERRY.   Stand!

R. ROISTER.   Hold!

M. MERRY.   Keep![9]

R. ROISTER.   There!

M. MERRY.   Strike!

R. ROISTER.   Take heed!

---

[7] I.e., drummers.   [8] Unprepared.   [9] Take care!

C. Custance. Well said, Truepenny!
Truepenny. Ah, whoresons!
C. Custance. Well done,
indeed! 20
M. Merry. Hold thine own, Harpax;
down with them, Dobinet!
C. Custance. Now, Madge! There, An-
not! Now stick them, Tibet!
Tib. Talk. [To Dobinet.] All my chief
quarrel is to this same little knave
That beguiled me last day; nothing shall
him save.
D. Dough. Down with this little quean [1]
that hath at me such spite;
Save you from her, master; it is a very
sprite.
C. Custance. I myself will *mounsire
graunde captaine* undertake.[2]
R. Roister. They win ground.
M. Merry. Save your-
self, sir, for God's sake!
R. Roister. Out, alas! I am slain, help!
M. Merry. Save yourself!
R. Roister. Alas!
M. Merry. Nay, then, have at you, mis-
tress!
R. Roister. Thou hittest me, alas! 30
M. Merry. I will strike at Custance
here.
R. Roister. Thou hittest me!
M. Merry. [Aside.] So I
will. —
Nay, Mistress Custance!
R. Roister. Alas, thou
hittest me still!
Hold!
M. Merry. Save yourself, sir!
R. Roister. Help!
Out, alas! I am slain!
M. Merry. Truce, hold your hands; truce
for a pissing while or twain.
Nay, how say you, Custance? For saving
of your life,
Will ye yield and grant to be this gent-
man's wife?
C. Custance. Ye told me he loved me.
Call ye this love?
M. Merry. He loved a while even like a
turtledove.
C. Custance. Gay love, God save it!
So soon hot, so soon cold!
M. Merry. I am sorry for you. He could
love you yet, so he could. 40

[1] Wench. [2] Engage with.

R. Roister. Nay, by Cock's precious,[3]
she shall be none of mine.
M. Merry. Why so?
R. Roister. Come away; by the
Matte, she is mankine.[4]
I durst adventure the loss of my right
hand,
If she did not slee [5] her other husband.
And see if she prepare not again to fight!
M. Merry. What then? Saint George to
borrow, our Lady's knight!
R. Roister. Slee else whom she will, by
Gog, she shall not slee me!
M. Merry. How then?
R. Roister. Rather than to be
slain, I will flee.
C. Custance. To it again, my knightesses;
down with them all!
R. Roister. Away, away, away! She will
else kill us all. 50
M. Merry. Nay, stick to it, like an hardy
man and a tall.
R. Roister. O bones, thou hittest me!
Away, or else die we shall!
M. Merry. Away, for the pashe of our
sweet Lord Jesus Christ!
C. Custance. Away, lout and lubber, or
I shall be thy priest!
*Exeant om[nes; i.e., Roister Doister and
his Men].*
So this field is ours; we have driven them
all away.
Tib. Talk. Thanks to God, mistress, ye
have had a fair day.
C. Custance. Well, now go ye in, and
make yourself some good cheer.
Omnes pariter.[6] We go! [Exeant Maids.]
T. Trusty. Ah, sir, what a
field we have had here!
C. Custance. Friend Tristram, I pray
you be a witness with me.
T. Trusty. Dame Custance, I shall de-
pose for your honesty. 60
And now fare ye well, except something
else ye would.
C. Custance. Not now, but when I need
to send I will be bold.
Exeat [Trusty].
I thank you for these pains. And now I
will get me in.
Now Roister Doister will no more wooing
begin. *Ex[eat].*

[3] By God's precious (blood, bones, etc.).
[4] Fierce, Amazonian. [5] Slay. [6] All together.

Actus V. Scena i.

Gawin Goodluck, Sim Suresby.

[G. Good.] Sim Suresby, my trusty man,
    now advise thee well,
And see that no false surmises thou me
    tell.
Was there such ado about Custance, of a
    truth?
Sim Sure. To report that I heard and saw,
    to me is ruth,
But both my duty and name and prop-
    erty [1]
Warneth me to you to show fidelity.
It may be well enough, and I wish it so
    to be;
She may herself discharge [2] and try her
    honesty.
Yet their claim to her methought was
    very large,
For with letters, rings, and tokens, they
    did her charge;   10
Which when I heard and saw I would
    none [3] to you bring.
G. Good. No, by Saint Mary, I allow [4]
    thee in that thing.
Ah, sirrah, now I see truth in the proverb
    old,
"All things that shineth is not by-and-by
    pure gold."
If any do live a woman of honesty,
I would have sworn Christian Custance
    had been she.
Sim Sure. Sir, though I to you be a serv-
    ant true and just,
Yet do not ye therefore your faithful
    spouse mistrust,
But examine the matter, and, if ye shall
    it find
To be all well, be not ye for my words
    unkind.   20
G. Good. I shall do that is right, and as
    I see cause why.
But here cometh Custance forth; we shall
    know by-and-by.

Actus V. Scena ii.

*C[hristian] Custance, Gawin Goodluck, Sim
    Suresby.*

C. Custance. I come forth to see and
    hearken for news good,

For about this hour is the time of likeli-
    hood
That Gawin Goodluck by the sayings of
    Suresby
Would be at home, and lo, yond I see
    him, I.
What! Gawin Goodluck, the only hope
    of my life!
Welcome home, and kiss me, your true
    espoused wife.
G. Good. Nay, soft, Dame Custance! I
    must first, by your license,
See whether all things be clear in your
    conscience.
I hear of your doings to me very strange.
C. Custance. What, fear ye that my faith
    towards you should change?   10
G. Good. I must needs mistrust ye be
    elsewhere entangled;
For I hear that certain men with you
    have wrangled
About the promise of marriage by you
    to them made.
C. Custance. Could any man's report
    your mind therein persuade?
G. Good. Well, ye must therein declare
    yourself to stand clear;
Else I and you, Dame Custance, may
    not join this year.
C. Custance. Then would I were dead,
    and fair laid in my grave.
Ah, Suresby, is this the honesty that ye
    have,
To hurt me with your report, not know-
    ing the thing?
Sim Sure. If ye be honest, my words can
    hurt you nothing.   20
But what I heard and saw, I might not
    but report.
C. Custance. Ah, Lord, help poor widows,
    destitute of comfort!
Truly, most dear spouse, naught was
    done but for pastance.
G. Good. But such kind of sporting is
    homely [5] dalliance.
C. Custance. If ye knew the truth, ye
    would take all in good part.
G. Good. By your leave, I am not half
    well skilled in that art.
C. Custance. It was none but Roister
    Doister, that foolish mome.
G. Good. Yea, Custance, better, they say,
    a bad scuse than none.

---

[1] Character.   [3] *I.e.*, tokens. *Cf.* IV, iii, 50–51.
[3] Clear.   [4] Agree with.
[5] Rude.

C. Custance. Why, Tristram Trusty, sir,
　your true and faithful friend,
Was privy both to the beginning and the
　end.　　　　　　　　　　　　　　30
Let him be the judge, and for me testify.
G. Good. I will the more credit that [1] he
　shall verify,
And because I will the truth know e'en
　as it is,
I will to him myself, and know all without
　miss.
Come on, Sim Suresby, that before my
　friend thou may
Avouch the same words which thou didst
　to me say.　　　　　　　　*Exeant.*

Actus V. Scena iii.
Christian Custance.

C. Custance. O Lord! how necessary it
　is now-of-days
That each body live uprightly all manner
　ways;
For let never so little a gap be open,
And be sure of this—the worst shall be
　spoken.
How innocent stand I in this for deed or
　thought,
And yet see what mistrust towards me
　it hath wrought.
But thou, Lord, knowest all folks'
　thoughts and eke intents,
And thou art the deliverer of all inno-
　cents.
Thou didst help the advoutress,[2] that
　she might be amended;
Much more then help, Lord, that [3] never
　ill intended.　　　　　　　　10
Thou didst help Susanna, wrongfully
　accused,
And no less dost thou see, Lord, how I
　am now abused.
Thou didst help Hester, when she should
　have died;
Help also, good Lord, that my truth may
　be tried.
Yet if Gawin Goodluck with Tristram
　Trusty speak,
I trust of ill report the force shall be but
　weak.
And lo, yond they come, sadly talking
　together.
I will abide, and not shrink for their
　coming hither.

[1] That which.　[2] Adulteress.　[3] One that.

Actus V. Scena iv.
*Gawin Goodluck, Tristram Trusty, C[hris-
tian] Custance, Sim Suresby.*

G. Good. And was it none other than ye
　to me report?
T. Trusty. No, and here were ye wished [4]
　to have seen the sport.
G. Good. Would I had, rather than half
　of that in my purse.
Sim Sure. And I do much rejoice the
　matter was no worse,
And like as to open it I was to you faith-
　ful,
So of Dame Custance' honest truth I am
　joyful.
For God forfend that I should hurt her
　by false report.
G. Good. Well, I will no longer hold her
　in discomfort.
C. Custance. Now come they hitherward;
　I trust all shall be well.
G. Good. Sweet Custance, neither heart
　can think nor tongue tell　　　10
How much I joy in your constant fidel-
　ity.
Come now, kiss me, the pearl of perfect
　honesty.
C. Custance. God let me no longer to
　continue in life
Than I shall towards you continue a true
　wife.
G. Good. Well, now to make you for this
　some part of amends,
I shall desire first you, and then such of
　our friends
As shall to you seem best, to sup at home
　with me,
Where at your fought field we shall
　laugh and merry be.
Sim Sure. And, mistress, I beseech you,
　take with me no grief.
I did a true man's part, not wishing you
　reprief.[5]　　　　　　　　20
C. Custance. Though hasty reports
　through surmises growing
May of poor innocents be utter over-
　throwing,
Yet because to thy master thou hast a
　true heart,
And I know mine own truth, I forgive
　thee for my part.

[4] "By me" is understood.
[5] Reproof, reproach.

G. Good. Go we all to my house, and of
　this gear no more.

　Go, prepare all things, Sim Suresby;
　hence, run afore.

Sim Sure. I go.　　　　　　　*Ex[eat]*.

G. Good.　　　　But who cometh yond,
　M[aster] Merrygreek?

C. Custance. Roister Doister's cham-
　pion, I shrew his best cheek.

T. Trusty. Roister Doister self, your
　wooer, is with him too.

　Surely something there is with us they
　have to do.　　　　　　　　30

Actus V. Scena v.[1]

*M[atthew] Merrygreek, Ralph Roister, Gawin
　Goodluck, Tristram Trusty, C[hristian]
　　　　　　　　　　　　Custance.*

M. Merry. Yond I see Gawin Goodluck,
　to whom lieth my message.

　I will first salute him after his long
　voyage,

　And then make all thing well concerning
　your behalf.

R. Roister. Yea, for the pashe of God!

M. Merry.　　Hence, out of sight, ye calf,
　Till I have spoke with them, and then I
　will you fet.

R. Roister. In God's name.　　[*Exeat.*]

M. Merry.　　　　　What, Mas-
　ter Gawin Goodluck, well met!

　And from your long voyage I bid you
　right welcome home.

G. Good. I thank you.

M. Merry.　　　　　I come to you
　from an honest mome.

G. Good. Who is that?

M. Merry.　　　　Roister Doister,
　that doughty kite.

C. Custance. Fie! I can scarce abide ye
　should his name recite.　　　　10

M. Merry. Ye must take him to favor,
　and pardon all past.—

　He heareth of your return, and is full ill
　aghast.

G. Good. I am right well content he have
　with us some cheer.

C. Custance. Fie upon him, beast! Then
　will not I be there.

G. Good. Why, Custance, do ye hate him
　more than ye love me?

C. Custance. But for your mind,[2] sir,
　where he were would I not be.

T. Trusty. He would make us all laugh.

M. Merry.　　　Ye ne'er had better sport.

G. Good. I pray you, sweet Custance, let
　him to us resort.

C. Custance. To your will I assent.

M. Merry.　　　　Why, such a fool it is,
　As no man for good pastime would forgo
　or miss.　　　　　　　　20

G. Good. Fet him to go with us.

M. Merry.　　　　　　　He will
　be a glad man.　　　　　*Ex[eat]*.

T. Trusty. We must to make us mirth
　maintain him all we can.

　And lo, yond he cometh, and Merry-
　greek with him.

C. Custance. At his first entrance ye
　shall see I will him trim.

　But first let us hearken the gentleman's
　wise talk.

T. Trusty. I pray you, mark if ever ye
　saw crane so stalk.

Actus V. Scena vi.

*R[alph] Roister, M[atthew] Merrygreek,
　C[hristian] Custance, G[awin] Goodluck,
　T[ristram] Trusty, D[obinet] Doughty,
　　　　　　　　　　　　Harpax.*[3]

R. Roister. May I then be bold?

M. Merry.　　　　　　I war-
　rant you on my word,

　They say they shall be sick but ye be at
　their board.

R. Roister. They were not angry then?

M. Merry.　　　　Yes, at first,
　and made strange;[4]

　But, when I said your anger to favor
　should change,

　And therewith had commended you ac-
　cordingly,

　They were all in love with your ma'ship
　by-and-by,

　And cried you mercy that they had done
　you wrong.

R. Roister. Forwhy[5] no man, woman,
　nor child can hate me long.

M. Merry. "We fear," quod they, "he
　will be avenged one day;

　Then for a penny give all our lives we
　may!"　　　　　　　　10

R. Roister. Said they so indeed?

[2] Except for your desire.　　[4] Acted shocked.
[3] Last two enter later.　　　[5] Because.

[1] *Cf.* final scene of Terence, *Eunuchus.*

M. Merry.   Did
they? Yea, even with one voice.
"He will forgive all," quod I. O, how
they did rejoice!
R. Roister. Ha, ha, ha!
M. Merry. "Go fet him," say they,
"while he is in good mood,
For have his anger who lust, we will not,
by the Rood."
R. Roister. I pray God that it be all
true, that thou hast me told,
And that she fight no more.
M. Merry.   I warrant
you, be bold.
To them, and salute them.
R. Roister. [Advancing.]   Sirs, I greet
you all well.
Omnes. Your mastership is welcome.
C. Custance.   Saving my quarrel,
For sure I will put you up into the
Exchequer.[1]   20
M. Merry. Why so? Better nay. Where-
fore?
C. Custance.   For an usurer.
R. Roister. I am no usurer, good mis-
tress, by His arms!
M. Merry. When took he gain of money
to any man's harms?
C. Custance. Yes, a foul usurer he is;
ye shall see; else [2]—
R. Roister. Didst not thou promise she
would pick no mo quarrels?
C. Custance. He will lend no blows but
he have in recompense
Fifteen for one, which is too much, of
conscience.[3]
R. Roister. Ah, dame, by the ancient
law of arms, a man
Hath no honor to foil [4] his hands on a
woman.
C. Custance. And where other usurers
take their gains yearly,   30
This man is angry but he have his by-
and-by.
G. Good. Sir, do not for her sake bear me
your displeasure.
M. Merry. Well, he shall with you talk
thereof more at leisure.
Upon your good usage, he will now shake
your hand.
R. Roister. And much heartily welcome
from a strange land.

M. Merry. Be not afeard, Gawin, to let
him shake your fist.
G. Good. O, the most honest gentleman
that e'er I wist.
I beseech your ma'ship to take pain to
sup with us.
M. Merry. He shall not say you nay,
and I too, by Jesus,
Because ye shall be friends, and let all
quarrels pass.   40
R. Roister. I will be as good friends with
them as ere I was.
M. Merry. Then let me fet your quire
that we may have a song.
R. Roister. Go.

[Merrygreek beckons to the Musicians, who
enter.]

G. Good.   I have heard no melody
all this year long.
M. Merry. Come on, sirs, quickly.
R. Roister.   Sing on,
sirs, for my friends' sake.
D. Dough. Call ye these your friends?
R. Roister.   Sing on,
and no mo words make.
                          Here they sing.[5]
G. Good. The Lord preserve our most
noble queen of renown,
And her virtues reward with the heavenly
crown.
C. Custance. The Lord strengthen her
most excellent majesty,
Long to reign over us in all prosperity.
T. Trusty. That her godly proceedings
the faith to defend,   50
He may stablish and maintain through
to the end.
M. Merry. God grant her, as she doth,
the Gospel to protect,
Learning and virtue to advance, and
vice to correct.
R. Roister. God grant her loving subjects
both the mind and grace,
Her most godly proceedings worthily to
embrace.
Harpax. Her highness' most worthy counselors God prosper,
With honor and love of all men to min-
ister.

[5] Whether the lines following represent the
song sung here, or an epilogue in addition to
the song, is uncertain.

[1] Law court.   [3] A mild oath.
[2] Besides.   [4] Soil.

OMNES. God grant the nobility her to
serve and love,
With all the whole commonty,[1] as doth
them behove.

AMEN.

CERTAIN SONGS TO BE SONG BY THOSE
WHICH SHALL USE THIS COMEDY OR
INTERLUDE

THE SECOND SONG

Whoso to marry a minion wife
Hath had good chance and hap,
Must love her and cherish her all his life,
And dandle her in his lap.

If she will fare well, if she will go gay,
A good husband ever still,
Whatever she lust to do or to say,
Must let her have her own will.

About what affairs soever he go,
He must show her all his mind.   10
None of his counsel she may be kept fro;[2]
Else is he a man unkind.

THE FOURTH SONG

I mun[3] be married a[4] Sunday;
I mun be married a Sunday;
Whosoever shall come that way,
    I mun be married a Sunday.

Roister Doister is my name;
Roister Doister is my name;
A lusty brute I am the same;
    I mun be married a Sunday.

Christian Custance have I found;
Christian Custance have I found;   10
A widow worth a thousand pound;
    I mun be married a Sunday.

Custance is as sweet as honey;
Custance is as sweet as honey;
I her lamb and she my cony;
    I mun be married a Sunday.

When we shall make our wedding feast,
When we shall make our wedding feast,
There shall be cheer for man and beast;
I mun be married a Sunday.   20
    I mun be married a Sunday, etc.

THE PSALMODY

Placebo dilexi,
Master Roister Doister will straight go
home and die;
Our Lord Jesus Christ his soul have mercy
upon.
Thus you see today a man, tomorrow John.[5]
Yet saving for a woman's extreme cru-
elty,
He might have lived yet a month or two
or three,
But in spite of Custance, which hath him
wearied,
His ma'ship shall be worshipfully buried.
And while some piece of his soul is yet
him within,
Some part of his funerals let us here begin.
   Dirige. He will go darkling to his grave. 10
Neque lux, neque crux, nisi solum clink,[6]
Never gentman so went toward heaven, I
think.
Yet, sirs, as ye will the bliss of heaven win,
When he cometh to the grave, lay him
softly in,
And all men take heed by this one gentle-
man,
How you set your love upon an unkind
woman.
For these women be all such mad peevish
elves,
They will not be won except it please
themselves.
But in faith, Custance, if ever ye come in
hell,
Master Roister Doister shall serve you as
well.   20
Good night, Roger, old knave; farewell,
Roger, old knave!
Good night, Roger, old knave; knave, nap!
   *Nequando.   Audivi vocem.   Requiem
    æternam.*

THE PEAL OF BELLS RONG BY THE PARISH
CLERK AND ROISTER DOISTER'S FOUR
MEN

The first bell a triple. When died he? When
died he?
The second. We have him! We have him!
The third. Roister Doister! Roister Doister!
The fourth bell. He cometh! He cometh!
The great bell. Our own! Our own!

FINIS.

---

[1] Commons.   [2] From.   [3] Must.   [4] On.   [5] *I.e.*, anybody.   [6] Except only a bell.

GAMMER GURTON'S NEEDLE

In 1563, according to the Stationers' Register, Thomas Colwell was granted a license to print a play entitled *Dyccon of Bedlam*, probably a provisional title for *Gammer Gurton's Needle*, the earliest extant edition of which was issued by him in 1575. The authorship of the play, in spite of a great deal of discussion, still remains a matter of dispute. According to the title-page the play was "made by Mr. S., Mr. of Art," and had been performed "not long ago in Christ's College in Cambridge." As early as 1782 Isaac Reed attributed it to John Still, Bishop of Bath and Wells, but in 1838 Joseph Hunter set forth the claims of Dr. John Bridges. In 1903 Henry Bradley presented strong evidence in favor of William Stevenson, Fellow of Christ's College, Cambridge, whose claim is now generally favored. Stevenson was born at Hunwick, Durham, matriculated at Christ's College in November, 1546, and proceeded B.A. in 1550, M.A. in 1553, and B.D. in 1560. He may have been the William Stevenson who was Fellow of Christ's from 1551 to 1554, and he was certainly Fellow from 1559 to 1561. He was ordained deacon in London in 1552, and was appointed Prebendary of Durham in January, 1561. He died in 1575.

In *Gammer Gurton's Needle*, as in *Roister Doister*, the influence of classical Latin comedy is to be seen in the five-act division with subdivision into scenes, the simple stage setting, and the narrow limitation of the time and place of the action. The broadly farcical treatment, however, follows a tradition reaching back through John Heywood to *Secunda Pastorum* of the Towneley cycle and to medieval farce in general. As an intriguer and manipulator of the action, Diccon is a figure parallel to the tricky rascals of Roman comedy, but, both as a practical joker and as a rogue and vagabond, he is more clearly a successor of the vices of the morality play. Above all, the characters and the life portrayed are far more distinctly English than in *Roister Doister*. In the words of Bradley, "as the first known attempt to present a picture of contemporary rustic life in the form of a regular comedy, it [*Gammer Gurton's Needle*] may be admitted to represent a distinct advance in the development of English dramatic art."

The language of the play is an inaccurate representation of the dialect of the southwestern counties of England, the language which was to be established as the conventional speech of the stage rustic. In making the first attempt to modernize the play, the editors have sought to preserve all forms which may be regarded as dialectal variations from the normal speech of the period.

The text of the present edition is based upon the 1575 quarto as reprinted by H. F. Brett-Smith.

GAMMER GURTON'S NEEDLE[1]

BY

MR. S.

THE NAMES OF THE SPEAKERS IN THIS COMEDY

DICCON *the bedlam*.[2]
HODGE, *Gammer Gurton's servant.*
TIB, *Gammer Gurton's maid.*
GAMMER GURTON.
COCK,[3] *Gammer Gurton's boy.*
DAME CHAT.

DOCTOR RAT, *the curate.*
MASTER BAILY.[4]
DOLL, *Dame Chat's maid.*
SCAPETHRIFT, *Mast[er] Baily's servant.*
MUTES.

[SCENE: *A village in England.*

TIME: *Contemporary.*]

GOD SAVE THE QUEEN!

THE PROLOGUE

As Gammer Gurton with many a wide stitch
Sat piecing and patching of Hodge her
    man's breech,
By chance or misfortune as she her gear[5]
    tossed,
In Hodge' leather breeches her needle she
    lost.
When Diccon the bedlam had heard by
    report
That good Gammer Gurton was robbed in
    this sort,
He quietly persuaded with her in that
    stound[6]
Dame Chat, her dear gossip,[7] this needle
    had found.
Yet knew she no more of this matter, alas,
Than knoweth Tom, our clerk,[8] what the
    priest saith at Mass!   10
Hereof there ensued so fearful a fray

Mas' Doctor was sent for, these gossips to
    stay,
Because he was curate, and esteemed full
    wise,
Who found that[9] he sought not, by Dic-
    con's device.
When all things were tumbled and clean
    out of fashion,
Whether it were by fortune or some other
    constellation,
Suddenly the neele[10] Hodge found by the
    pricking,
And drew it out of his buttock where he
    felt it sticking.
Their hearts then at rest with perfect
    security,
With a pot of good nale[11] they stroke[12] up
    their plaudity.[13]   20

THE I ACT.   THE i SCENE.[14]

Diccon.

DICCON Many a mile have I walked, di-
    vers and sundry ways,
    And many a good man's house have I
      been at in my days,

---

[1] The complete title runs: "A Right Pithy, Pleasant, and Merry Comedy Entitled Gammer Gurton's Needle, Played on Stage Not Long Ago in Christ's College in Cambridge. Made by Mr. S., Mr. of Art."
[2] A partially cured lunatic discharged from the Hospital of St. Mary of Bethlehem in London; he was licensed to make his living by begging.   [3] Original reads *Docke.*
[4] Bailiff.   [6] Occasion.
[5] *I.e.,* sewing materials.   [7] Crony.
[8] The original spelling, *clarke,* indicates the pronunciation.

[9] That which.   [11] Ale.   [13] Applause.
[10] Needle.   [12] Struck.
[14] The scene for the entire play is a village street with Gammer Gurton's house on one side and Dame Chat's alehouse on the other.

Many a gossip's cup in my time have I
　tasted,
And many a broach and spit have I both
　turned and basted,
Many a piece of bacon have I had out of
　their balks [1]
In running over the country with long
　and weary walks;
Yet came my foot never within those
　doorcheeks,[2]
To seek flesh, or fish, garlic, onions, or
　leeks,
That ever I saw a sort [3] in such a plight
As here within this house appeareth to
　my sight!　　　　　　　　　　10
There is howling and scowling, all cast in
　a dump,
With whewling and puling, as though
　they had lost a trump; [4]
Sighing and sobbing they weep and they
　wail.
I marvel in my mind what the devil they
　ail.
The old trot [5] sits groaning, with "alas!"
　and "alas!"
And Tib wrings her hands, and takes on in
　worse case.
With poor Cock, their boy, they be driven
　in such fits
I fear me the folks be not well in their
　wits.
Ask them what they ail, or who brought
　them in this stay,[6]
They answer not at all but "slack!" and
　"welaway!"　　　　　　　　　　20
When I saw it booted not, out at doors I
　hied me,
And caught a slip of bacon, when I saw
　that none spied me,
Which I intend not far hence, unless my
　purpose fail,
Shall serve for a shoeing-horn to draw on
　two pots of ale.

THE I ACT. THE ii SCENE.

Hodge, Diccon.

HODGE. See!　So cham [7] arrayed with
　dabbling in the dirt!

She that set me to ditching, ich wold [8] she
　had the squirt! [9]
Was never poor soul that such a life had!
Gog's bones,[10] this vilthy glay [11] has
　dressed me too bad!
God's soul, see how this stuff tears!
Ich were better to be a bearward and set
　to keep bears!
By the Mass, here is a gash! A shameful
　hole indeed!
And [12] one stitch tear furder,[13] a man may
　thrust in his head.
DICCON. By my father's soul, Hodge, if I
　shuld now be sworn,
I cannot choose but say thy breech is
　foul be-torn!　　　　　　　　　10
But the next remedy in such a case and
　hap
Is to planch [14] on a piece as broad as thy
　cap.
HODGE. Gog's soul, man, 'tis not yet two
　days fully ended
Since my Dame Gurton, cham sure, these
　breeches amended!
But cham made such a drudge, to trudge
　at every need,
Chwold rend it, though it were stitched
　with sturdy packthread.
DICCON. Hodge, let thy breeches go, and
　speak and tell me soon
What devil aileth Gammer Gurton and
　Tib, her maid, to frown.
HODGE. Tush, man, th'art deceived! 'Tis
　their daily look;
They cower so over the coals, their eyes
　be bleared with smoke.　　　　20
DICCON. Nay, by the Mass, I perfectly
　perceived, as I came hether,[15]

[8] Both *wold* and *would*, *cold* and *could*, *shold*
or *shuld* and *should*, and these words, especially
would, in combination with *ch* for *ich* (*I*)—*chold*
and *chould* with a few other variants—occur in
the play. In part the variations in this series of
words are probably unintentional, but the shorter
forms predominate so decidedly in the aggregate
that they cannot be disregarded as a feature of
dialect. Hence it has seemed best to retain the
spelling of the original with its inconsistencies,
except for dropping the meaningless final *e* wherever it occurs.
[9] Diarrhea.
[10] By God's bones.
[11] In the rustic dialect, initial $v=f$, $g=c$, $z=s$.
[12] If.　　　[13] Further.　　　[14] Plank, clap.
[15] A common form for *hither*, which has been
retained in this play because of the dialect and
rime.

[1] Lofts.　　　[3] Company.　　　[5] Hag.
[2] Doorjambs.　[4] A game of cards.　[6] State.
[7] I am. For use and characteristics of this
conventional stage dialect for rustics, see *Roister
Doister* I, iii, 100, n.

That either Tib and her dame hath been
　by the ears together,
Or else as great a matter, as thou shalt
　shortly see.
HODGE. Now ich beseech our Lord they
　never better agree!
DICCON. By Gog's soul, there they sit as
　still as stones in the street,
　As though they had been taken [1]
　with fairies, or else with some ill
　sprite.[2]
HODGE. Gog's heart, I durst have laid my
　cap to a crown
　Chwould learn of some prancome [3] as
　soon as ich came to town!
DICCON. Why, Hodge, art thou inspired?
　Or didst thou thereof hear?
HODGE. Nay, but ich saw such a wonder
　as ich saw nat this seven year:　　30
　Tom Tankard's cow, by Gog's bones,
　she set me up her sail,
　And flinging about his half-acre, fisking [4]
　with her tail,
　As though there had been in her arse a
　swarm of bees,
　And chad not cried, "Tphrowh, whore!"
　she'd leaped out of his leas. [5]
DICCON. Why, Hodge, lies the cunning [6]
　in Tom Tankard's cow's tail?
HODGE. Well, ich chave hard [7] some say
　such tokens do not fail.
　But canst thou not tell,[8] in faith, Diccon,
　why she frowns, or whereat?
　Hath no man stolen her ducks or hens,
　or gelded Gib, her cat?
DICCON. What devil can I tell, man?　I
　cold not have one word;
　They gave no more heed to my talk than
　thou woldst to a lord.　　40
HODGE. Ich cannot still but muse what
　marvelous thing it is!
　Chill in and know myself what matters
　are amiss.
DICCON. Then farewell, Hodge, awhile,
　since thou dost inward haste,
　For I will into the Goodwife Chat's, to
　feel how the ale doth taste.　　[Exit.]

THE I ACT.　THE iii SCENE.

Hodge, Tib.

HODGE. [*To himself.*] Cham aghast, by the
　Mass! Ich wot [9] not what to do.
　Chad need bless me well before ich go
　them to!
　Perchance some felon sprite may haunt
　our house indeed,
　And then chwere but a [10] noddy to ven-
　ter [11] where cha' [12] no need!
TIB. [*To herself.*] Cham worse than mad,
　by the Mass, to be at this stay!
　Cham chid, cham blamed, and beaten all
　thours [13] on the day,
　Lamed, and hunger-starved, pricked up
　all in jags,[14]
　Having no patch to hide my back save a
　few rotten rags!
HODGE. I say, Tib—if thou be Tib, as
　I trow sure thou be—
　What devil make-ado is this between our
　dame and thee?　　10
TIB. Gog's bread, Hodge, thou had a good
　turn thou wert not here [this while!] [15]
　It had been better for some of us to have
　been hence a mile!
　My gammer is so out of course and fran-
　tic all at once
　That Cock, our boy, and I, poor wench,
　have felt it on our bones.
HODGE. What is the matter—say on, Tib—
　whereat she taketh so on?
TIB. She is undone, she saith; alas, her
　joy and life is gone!
　If she hear not of some comfort, she is,
　saith, but dead;
　Shall never come within her lips one inch
　of meat ne [16] bread!
HODGE. By'r Lady, cham not very glad to
　see her in this dump.
　Chold a noble [17] her stool hath fallen and
　she hath broke her rump!　　20
TIB. Nay, and that were the worst, we
　wold not greatly care,

---

[1] Bewitched.
[2] Probably pronounced *spreet*.
[3] Unusual incident, freak.
[4] Frisking.
[5] Pastures.
[6] *I.e.*, prophetic power.
[7] Heard.
[8] Original reads *till*.

[9] Know.
[10] Original reads *at*.
[11] Venture.
[12] I have.
[13] The hours.
[14] Dressed in tatters.
[15] This line is partially cut away in copies of
early edns., but is completed by Brett-Smith
from 1661 quarto.
[16] Nor.
[17] I hold (*i.e.*, wager) a noble (*i.e.*, a piece of
money). The form *ichold* also appears.

For bursting of her huckle bone,[1] or
breaking of her chair;
But greater, greater, is her grief, as,
Hodge, we shall all feel.

HODGE. Gog's wounds, Tib, my gammer
has never lost her—neele?

TIB. Her neele!

HODGE.   Her neele?

TIB.   Her neele!
By Him that made me, it is true, Hodge,
I tell thee.

HODGE. Gog's sacrament, I would she had
lost thart[2] out of her belly!
The devil, or else his dame, they ought[3]
her, sure, a shame!
How a murrion[4] came this chance—say,
Tib—unto our dame?

TIB. My gammer sat her down on
her pess,[5] and bade me reach thy
breeches;   30
And by-and-by[6]—a vengeance in it!—
or[7] she had take two stitches
To clap a clout[8] upon thine arse, by
chance aside she leers,
And Gib, our cat, in the milk pan she
spied over head and ears.
"Ah, whore! Out, thief!" she cried aloud,
and swapt[9] the breeches down.
Up went her staff, and out leaped Gib at
doors into the town,[10]
And since that time was never wight
cold set their eyes upon it.
Gog's malison chave Cock and I bid
twenty times light on it.

HODGE. And is not then my breeches
sewed up, tomorrow that I shuld
wear?

TIB. No, in faith, Hodge, thy breeches lie,
for all this, never the near.[11]

HODGE. Now a vengeance light on all the
sort, that better shold have kept
it—   40
The cat, the house, and Tib, our maid,
that better shold have swept it!
See where she cometh crawling! Come
on, in twenty devils' way!
Ye have made a fair day's work, have
you not? Pray you, say!

THE I ACT. THE iv SCENE.

Gammer, Hodge, Tib, Cock. [12]

GAMMER. Alas, Hodge, alas, I may well
curse and ban
This day, that ever I saw it, with Gib
and the milk pan!
For these and ill luck together, as knoweth Cock, my boy,
Have stack[13] away my dear neele, and
robbed me of my joy—
My fair, long, straight neele, that was
mine only treasure!
The first day of my sorrow is, and last
end of my pleasure!

HODGE. Might ha' kept it when ye had it,
but fools will be fools still!
Lose that is vast in your hands? Ye
need not, but ye will!

GAMMER. Go hie thee, Tib, and run, thou
whore, to th'end here of the town!
Didst carry out dust in thy lap. Seek
where thou pourest it down;   10
And, as thou sawest me roking[14] in the
ashes where I mourned,
So see in all the heap of dust thou leave
no straw unturned.

TIB. That chall, gammer, swith and
tight,[15] and soon be here again!

GAMMER. Tib, stoop and look down to
the ground to it, and take some
pain!   [*Exit Tib.*]

HODGE. Here is a pretty matter, to see
this gear[16] how it goes!
By Gog's soul, I think you wold lose
your arse and it were loose!
Your neele lost? It is pity you shold
lack care and endless sorrow.
Gog's death, how shall my breeches be
sewed? Shall I go thus tomorrow?

GAMMER. Ah, Hodge, Hodge, if that ich
cold find my neele, by the Reed,[17]
Chould sew thy breeches, ich promise
thee, with full good double thread, 20
And set a patch on either knee, shuld
last this moneths[18] twain.
Now God and good Saint Sith[19] I pray to
send it home again!

HODGE. Whereto served your hands and
eyes but this your neele to keep?

What devil had you else to do? Ye kept,
ich wot, no sheep!
Cham fain abroad to dig and delve, in
water, mire, and clay,
Sossing [1] and possing [2] in the dirt still [3]
from day to day;
A hundred things that be abroad, cham
set to see them weal [4]—
And four of you sit idle at home, and
cannot keep a neele!

GAMMER. My neele, alas! Ich lost it,
Hodge, what time ich me uphasted
To save the milk set up for thee, which
Gib, our cat, hath wasted.   30

HODGE. The devil he burst both Gib and
Tib, with all the rest!
Cham always sure of the worst end,
whoever have the best!
Where ha' you been fidging [5] abroad
since you your neele lost?

GAMMER. Within the house, and at the
door, sitting by this same post,
Where I was looking a long hour before
these folks came here.
But, welaway! All was in vain; my neele
is never the near!

HODGE. Set me a candle; let me seek and
grope wherever it be.
Gog's heart, ye be so foolish, ich think
you know it not when you it see!

GAMMER. Come hether, Cock! What,
Cock, I say!

[Enter Cock.]

COCK.   How, gammer!
GAMMER.   Go hie thee soon,
And grope behind the old brass pan;
which thing when thou hast done,[6]
There shalt thou find an old shoe, where-
in, if thou look well,   41
Thou shalt find lying an inch of a white
tallow candle.
Light it, and bring it tight away.

COCK.   That shall be done anon.[7]
[Exit.]

GAMMER. Nay, tarry, Hodge, till thou
hast light, and then we'll seek each
one.

HODGE. Come away, ye whoreson [8] boy!
Are ye asleep? Ye must have a crier! [9]

COCK. *[Within.]* Ich cannot get the candle
light; here is almost no fire.

HODGE. Chill hold thee a penny chill
make thee come if that ich may catch
thine ears!
Art deaf, thou whoreson boy? Cock, I
say, why canst not hear 's?

GAMMER. Beat him not, Hodge, but help
the boy, and come you two together.
[Exit Hodge.]

THE I ACT. THE V SCENE.

Gammer, Tib, Cock, Hodge.[10]

GAMMER. How now, Tib? Quick, let's hear
what news thou hast brought hether!

[Enter Tib.]

TIB. Chave tossed and tumbled yender [11]
heap over and over again,
And winnowed it through my fingers as
men wold winnow grain;
Not so much as a hen's turd but in
pieces I tare it,
Or whatsoever clod or clay I found, I
did not spare it,
Looking within, and eke without, to
find your neele, alas!
But all in vain, and without help—your
neele is where it was!

GAMMER. Alas, my neele! We shall never
meet! Adieu, adieu, for aye!

TIB. Not so, gammer; we might it find
if we knew where it lay.

[Enter Cock.]

COCK. Gog's Cross, gammer, if ye will
laugh, look in but at the door,   10
And see how Hodge lieth tumbling and
tossing amids the floor.
Raking there some fire to find among
the ashes dead,
Where there is not one spark so big as a
pin's head,
At last in a dark corner two sparks he
thought he sees,
Which were [12] indeed naught else but
Gib our cat's two eyes.
"Puff!" quod [13] Hodge, thinking thereby
to have fire without doubt;

---

[1] Sousing, making oneself muddy.
[2] Pushing, beating out.
[3] Continuously.   [4] Prosper.   [5] Fidgeting.
[6] Line division in this couplet made by Manly.
[7] At once.

[8] Rascally.   [10] Last three enter later.
[9] Town crier.   [11] Yonder.
[12] Original reads *where.*   [13] Quoth, **said.**

With that Gib shut her two eyes, and
  so the fire was out,
And by-and-by them opened, even as
  they were before;
With that the sparks appeared, even
  as they had done of yore.
And, even as Hodge blew the fire, as he
  did think,   20
Gib, as she felt the blast, straightway
  began to wink,[1]
Till Hodge fell of swearing, as came best
  to his turn,
The fire was sure bewitched, and there-
  fore wold not burn.
At last Gib up[2] the stairs among the
  old posts and pins;
And Hodge he hied him after till broke
  were both his shins—
Cursing and swearing oaths, were never
  of his making,
That Gib wold fire the house if that she
  were not taken.
GAMMER. See, here is all the thought that
  the foolish urchin taketh,
And Tib, methink, at his elbow almost
  as merry maketh!
This is all the wit ye have, when others
  make their moan.   30
Come down, Hodge! Where art thou?
  And let the cat alone!
HODGE. [*Within.*] Gog's heart, help and
  come up! Gib in her tail hath fire,
And is like to burn all if she get a little
  higher!
"Come down," quoth you? Nay, then
  you might count me a patch![3]
The house cometh down on your heads
  if it take once the thatch.
GAMMER. It is the cat's eyes, fool, that
  shineth in the dark!
HODGE. [*Within.*] Hath the cat, do you
  think, in every eye a spark?
GAMMER. No, but they shine as like fire
  as ever man see.
HODGE. [*Within.*] By the Mass, and she
  burn all, you sh' bear the blame for
  me!
GAMMER. Come down, and help to seek
  here our neele, that it were found.   40
Down, Tib, on the knees, I say! Down,
  Cock, to the ground!

To God I make avow,[4] and so to good
  Saint Anne,
A candle shall they have apiece, get it
  where I can,
If I may my neele find in one place or in
  other.

[Enter Hodge.]

HODGE. Now a vengeance on Gib light,
  on Gib and Gib's mother,
And all the generation of cats both far
  and near!
Look on the ground, whoreson? Thinks
  then the neele is here?
COCK. By my troth, gammer, methought
  your neele here I saw,
But, when my fingers touched it, I felt
  it was a straw.
TIB. See, Hodge, what's t[h]is? May it
  not be within it?   50
HODGE. Break it, fool, with thy hand,
  and see and thou canst find it.
TIB. Nay, break it you, Hodge, according to your word.
HODGE. Gog's sides, fie, it stinks! It
  is a cat's turd!
It were well done to make thee eat it,
  by the Mass!
GAMMER. This matter amendeth not; my
  neele is still where it was.
Our candle is at an end; let us all in
  quite,
And come another time, when we have
  more light.   *[Exeunt.]*

THE II ACT.

First a song.

Back and side, go bare, go bare;
  Both foot and hand, go cold;
But, belly, God send thee good ale enough,
  Whether it be new or old!

I cannot eat but little meat,
  My stomach is not good;
But sure I think that I can drink
  With him that wears a hood.[5]
Though I go bare, take ye no care,
  I am nothing acold,   10
I stuff my skin so full within
  Of jolly good ale and old.

Back and side, go bare, go bare;
  Both foot and hand, go cold;
But, belly, God send thee good ale enough,
  Whether it be new or old!

---

[1] Close the eyes; not merely to blink.
[2] *I.e.*, ran up.
[3] Fool.
[4] Promise.
[5] *I.e.*, a friar.

I love no roast but a nut-brown toast [1]
　And a crab [2] laid in the fire;
A little bread shall do me stead,
　Much bread I not desire.　　　　20
No frost nor snow, no wind, I trow,
　Can hurt me if I wold,
I am so wrapped and throughly lapped
　Of jolly good ale and old.

Back and side, go bare, etc.

And Tib, my wife, that as her life
　Loveth well good ale to seek,
Full oft drinks she till ye may see
　The tears run down her cheeks;
Then doth she troll [3] to me the bowl,
　Even as a maltworm [4] shuld,　　30
And saith, "Sweetheart, I took my part
　Of this jolly good ale and old."

Back and side, go bare, etc.

Now let them drink till they nod and wink,
　Even as good fellows should do;
They shall not miss to have the bliss
　Good ale doth bring men to.
And all poor souls that have scoured [5] bowls
　Or have them lustily trolled,
God save the lives of them and their wives,
　Whether they be young or old!　　40

Back and side, go bare, etc.[6]

The i Scene.

Diccon, Hodge. [7]

Diccon. Well done, by Gog's malt! Well
　sung, and well said!
Come on, Mother Chat, as thou art true
　maid;
One fresh pot of ale let's see, to make an
　end,
Against this cold weather my naked
　arms to defend!　　　　[*Drinks.*]
This gear it warms the soul! Now, wind,
　blow on the worst,
And let us drink and swill till that our
　bellies burst!
Now were he a wise man, by cunning
　cold define

Which way my journey lieth, or where
　Diccon will dine.
But one good turn ï have: be it by night
　or day,
South, east, north, or west, I am never
　out of my way!　　　　10

[*Enter Hodge.*]

Hodge. Cham goodly rewarded, cham I
　not, do you think?
Chad a goodly dinner for all my sweat
　and swink! [8]
Neither butter, cheese, milk, onions,
　flesh, nor fish,
Save this poor piece of barley bread—
　'tis a pleasant, costly dish!
Diccon. Hail, fellow Hodge, and well [9] to
　fare with thy meat—if thou have
　any!
But by thy words, as I them smelled, thy
　daintrels [10] be not many.
Hodge. Daintrels, Diccon? Gog's soul,
　man, save this piece of dry horse-
　bread,
Cha' bit no bit this livelong day; no
　crumb come in my head;
My guts they yawl, [11] crawl, and all my
　belly rumbleth;
The puddings [12] cannot lie still; each one
　over other tumbleth.　　　　20
By Gog's heart, cham so vexed and in my
　belly penned
Chould one piece were at the spittle-
　house,[13] another at the Castle's End!
Diccon. Why, Hodge, was there none at
　home thy dinner for to set?
Hodge. Gog's bread, Diccon, ich came too
　late; was nothing there to get,
Gib—a foul fiend might on her light—
　licked the milk pan so clean!
See, Diccon, 'twas not so well washed
　this seven year, as ich ween!
A pestilence light on all ill luck! Chad
　thought yet, for all this,
Of a morsel of bacon behind the door at
　worst shuld not miss;
But when ich sought a slip to cut, as ich
　was wont to do,

---

[1] Toast soaked in ale.　　[3] Pass around.
[2] Crab apple.　　　　　　[4] Tippler.
[5] Emptied by drinking healths.
[6] **This is a** shortened version of an earlier
drinking song printed in Dyce's edn. of Skelton.
[7] Enters later.

[8] Labor.
[9] Emended by Dodsley. Original reads *wilt.*
[10] Delicacies.
[11] Howl.
[12] Entrails.
[13] Almshouse.

Gog's soul, Diccon, Gib, our cat, had eat
the bacon too!   30
Which bacon Diccon stole, as is declared before.
DICCON. Ill luck, quod he? Marry, swear
it, Hodge, this day, the truth to tell.
Thou rose not on thy right side, or else
blessed thee not well.
Thy milk slopped up, thy bacon filched—
that was too bad luck, Hodge!
HODGE. Nay, nay, there was a fouler fault:
my gammer ga' me the dodge! [1]
Seest not how cham rent and torn—my
heels, my knees, and my breech?
Chad thought as ich sat by the fire, help
here and there a stitch;
But there ich was pooped [2] indeed!
DICCON.   Why, Hodge?
HODGE.   Boots not, man, to tell.
Cham so dressed [3] amongst a sort of fools,
chad better be in hell!
My gammer, cham ashamed to say, by
God, served me not weel! [4]
DICCON. How so, Hodge?
HODGE.   Has she not gone, trowest
now, and lost her neele?   40
DICCON. Her eel, Hodge? Who fished of
late? That was a dainty dish!
HODGE. Tush, tush, her neele! her neele!
her neele, man! 'Tis neither flesh nor
fish.
A little thing with an hole in the end, as
bright as any siller, [5]
Small, long, sharp at the point, and
straight as any pillar.
DICCON. I know not what a devil thou
meanest. Thou bring'st me more in
doubt.
HODGE. Knowest not with what Tom
Tailor's man sits broaching [6] through
a clout?
A neele! neele! a neele! My gammer's
neele is gone!
DICCON. Her neele, Hodge? Now I smell
thee! That was a chance alone! [7]
By the Mass, thou hadst a shameful
loss, and it were but for thy breeches!
HODGE. Gog's soul, man, should give a
crown chad it but three stitches!   50
DICCON. How sayest thou, Hodge? What
shuld he have, again thy neele got?

HODGE. Bem [8] vather's soul, and chad it,
chould give him a new groat!
DICCON. Canst thou keep counsel in this
case?
HODGE.   Else chwold my tongue were
out.
DICCON. Do thou [9] but then by my advice,
and I will fetch it without doubt.
HODGE. Chill run, chill ride, chill dig,
chill delve, chill toil, chill trudge, shalt
see;
Chill hold, chill draw, chill pull, chill
pinch, chill kneel on my bare knee;
Chill scrape, chill scratch, chill sift, chill
seek, chill bow, chill bend, chill sweat,
Chill stoop, chill stir, chill cap, [10] chill
kneel, chill creep on hands and feet;
Chill be thy bondman, Diccon, ich swear
by sun and moon.
And channot somewhat to stop this gap,
cham utterly undone!   60
    Pointing behind to his torn breeches.
DICCON. Why, is there any special cause
thou takest hereat such sorrow?
HODGE. Kirstian Clack, Tom Simson's
maid, by the Mass, comes hether to-
morrow!
Cham not able to say, between us what
may hap—
She smiled on me the last Sunday when
ich put off my cap.
DICCON. Well, Hodge, this is a matter of
weight, and must be kept close;
It might else turn to both our costs, as
the world now goes.
Shalt swear to be no blab, Hodge?
HODGE.   Chill, Diccon!
DICCON.   Then, go to!
Lay thine hand here; say after me as thou
shalt hear me do.
Hast no book?
HODGE.   Cha' no book, I!
DICCON.   Then needs must force
us both
Upon my breech to lay thine hand, and
there to take thine oath.   70
HODGE. [*Repeating after Diccon.*]   I,
Hodge, breechless,
Swear to Diccon rechless, [11]
By the Cross that I shall kiss,

[1] Deceived me.
[2] Befooled.
[3] Mistreated.
[4] Well.

[5] Silver.
[6] Piercing.
[7] Unique mishap.

[8] By my.
[9] Emended by Dodsley. Original reads *than*.
[10] Doff the cap.
[11] Without reservation.

To keep his counsel close,
And always me to dispose
    To work that his pleasure is.
          Here he kisseth Diccon's breech.
DICCON. Now, Hodge, see thou take heed
And do as I thee bid,
    For so I judge it meet.
This needle again to win   80
There is no shift therein
    But conjure up a sprite.

HODGE. What, the great devil, Diccon, I
    say?
DICCON. Yea, in good faith, that is the
    way—
    Fet [1] with some pretty charm.
        [Begins to draw a magic circle.]
HODGE. Soft, Diccon! Be not too hasty
    yet,
By the Mass, for ich begin to sweat!
    Cham afraid of some harm!

DICCON. Come hether then, and stir thee
    not
One inch out of this circle plot,   90
    But stand as I thee teach.
HODGE. And shall ich be here safe from
    their claws?
DICCON. The master devil with his long
    paws
    Here to thee cannot reach.

Now will I settle me to this gear.
HODGE. I say, Diccon, hear me, hear!
    Go softly to this matter!
DICCON. What devil, man, art afraid of
    naught?
HODGE. Canst not tarry a little thought
    Till ich make a curtsy of water?   100

DICCON. Stand still to it! Why shuldest
    thou fear him?
HODGE. Gog's sides, Diccon, methink ich
    hear him!
    And tarry, chall mar all!
DICCON. The matter is no worse than I
    told it.
HODGE. By the Mass, cham able no longer
    to hold it!
    Too bad ich must bewray [2] the hall!
DICCON. Stand to it, Hodge' Stir not,
    you whoreson!

[1] Fetched.   [2] Befoul.

What devil, be thine arse-strings brus-
    ten? [3]
Thyself awhile but stay;
The devil—I smell him—will be here
    anon.   110
HODGE. Hold him fast, Diccon! Cham
    gone! Cham gone!
    Chill not be at that fray!
          [Exit, running.]

THE II ACT. THE ii SCENE.

Diccon, Chat.[4]

DICCON. Fie, shitten knave, and out upon
    thee!
Above all other louts, fie on thee!
    Is not here a cleanly prank?
But [5] thy matter was no better,
Nor thy presence here no sweeter,
    To fly I can thee thank.

Here is a matter worthy glozing [6]
Of Gammer Gurton's needle losing,
    And a foul piece of wark! [7]
A man, I think, might make a play   10
And need no word to [8] this they say,
    Being but half a clerk.

Soft, let me alone! I will take the charge
This matter further to enlarge
    Within a time short.
If ye will mark my toys,[9] and note,
I will give ye leave to cut my throat
    If I make not good sport.

Dame Chat, I say, where be ye? Within?

[Enter Dame Chat with cards in her hand.]

CHAT. Who have we there maketh such
    a din?   20
DICCON. Here is a good fellow, maketh
    no great danger.[10]
CHAT. What, Diccon? Come near; ye
    be no stranger!
We be fast set at trump, man, hard by
    the fire.
Thou shalt set on the king, if thou come
    a little nigher.

[3] Burst, broken.   [4] Enters later.   [5] Because (?).
[6] Worth glossing, *i.e.*, commenting on.
[7] Work.   [9] Tricks, pranks.
[8] In addition to.   [10] Trouble.

DICCON. Nay, nay, there is no tarrying,
    I must be gone again.
But, first, for you, in counsel I have a
    word or twain.
CHAT. Come hether, Doll!

[Enter Doll.]

Doll, sit down and play this game,
And, as thou sawest me do, see thou do
    even the same.
There is five trumps beside the queen—
    the hindmost thou shalt find her.
Take heed of Sim Glover's wife; she hath
    an eye behind her!   *[Exit Doll.]* 30
Now, Diccon, say your will.
DICCON.   Nay, soft a little yet!
I wold nct tell it my sister, the matter
    is so great.
There I will have you swear by our dear
    Lady of Bullain,[1]
S[aint] Dunstan, and S[aint] Donnick,[2]
    three Kings of Kullain,[3]
That ye shall keep it secret.
CHAT.   Gog's bread, that will I do!
As secret as mine own thought, by God,
    and the devil too!
DICCON. Here is Gammer Gurton, your
    neighbor, a sad and heavy wight—
Her goodly fair red cock at home was
    stole this last night.
CHAT. Gog's soul! Her cock with the
    yellow legs, that nightly crowed so
    just? [4]
DICCON. That cock is stolen.
CHAT.   What, was he fet out of
    the hens' rust? [5]   40
DICCON. I cannot tell where the devil he
    was kept, under key or lock;
But Tib hath tickled [6] in gammer's
    ear that you should steal the cock.
CHAT. Have I? Strong whore! By bread
    and salt—
DICCON.   What, soft, I say! Be still!
Say not one word for all this gear.
CHAT.   By the Mass, that I will!
I will have the young whore by the head
    and the old trot by the throat!
DICCON. Not one word, Dame Chat, I
    say! Not one word, for my coat!
CHAT. Shall such a beggar's brawl [7] as
    that, thinkest thou, make me a thief?

The pox light on her whore's sides, a
    pestilence and a mischief!—
Come out, thou hungry, needy bitch!
    O, that my nails be short!   49
DICCON. Gog's bread, woman, hold your
    peace! This gear will else pass sport!
I wold not for an hundred pound this
    matter shuld be known,
That I am auctor [8] of this tale or have
    abroad it blown!
Did ye not swear ye wold be ruled, be-
    fore the tale I told?
I said ye must all secret keep, and ye
    said sure ye wold.
CHAT. Wold you suffer, yourself, Dic-
    con, such a sort to revile you,
With slanderous words to blot your
    name, and so to defile you?
DICCON. No, Goodwife Chat; I wold be
    loath such drabs shuld blot my
    name;
But yet ye must so order all that Diccon
    bear no blame.
CHAT. Go to, then! What is your rede? [9]
    Say on your mind; ye shall me rule
    herein.
DICCON. God-a-mercy [10] to Dame Chat!
    In faith, thou must the gear begin.   60
It is twenty pound to a goose turd, my
    gammer will not tarry,
But hetherward she comes as fast as her
    legs can her carry,
To brawl with you about her cock. For
    well I heard Tib say
The cock was roasted in your house to
    breakfast yesterday;
And, when ye had the carcass eaten, the
    feathers ye out flung;
And Doll, your maid, the legs she hid a
    foot deep in the dung.
CHAT. O gracious God, my heart it [11]
    bursts!
DICCON.   Well, rule yourself a space!
And Gammer Gurton when she cometh
    anon into this place—
Then to the quean! Let's see! Tell her
    your mind, and spare not,
So [12] shall Diccon blameless be; and then
    go to, I care not!   70
CHAT. Then, whore, beware her throat!
    I can abide no longer!

---

[1] Boulogne.   [2] Dominic.   [3] Cologne.
[4] Regularly.   [5] Roost.   [6] Whispered.   [7] Brat.
[8] Author.   [9] Advice.   [10] Thanks.
[11] Emended by Dodsley. Original reads *is.*
[12] So long as.

In faith, old witch, it shall be seen which
  of us two be stronger!
And, Diccon, but at your request, I
  wold not stay one hour.
DICCON. Well, keep it in till she be here,
  and then—out let it pour!
In the meanwhile get you in, and make
  no words of this.
More of this matter within this hour
  to hear you shall not miss.
Because I know you are my friend, hide
  it I cold not, doubtless.
Ye know your harm; see ye be wise
  about your own business!
So fare ye well! [1]
CHAT.   Nay, soft, Diccon, and drink!
  What, Doll, I say!
Bring here a cup of the best ale; let's
  see! Come quickly away! [*Exeunt.*] 80

THE II ACT. THE iii SCENE.

Hodge,[2] *Diccon.*

DICCON. Ye see, masters, the one end
  tapped of this my short device!
Now must we broach tother [3] too, be-
  fore the smoke arise.
And, by the time they have awhile run,
  I trust ye need not crave it;
But look, what lieth in both their hearts,
  ye are like, sure, to have it.

[*Enter Hodge, wearing his other breeches.*]

HODGE. Yea, Gog's soul, art alive yet?
  What, Diccon, dare ich come?
DICCON. A man is well hied [4] to trust to
  thee! I will say nothing but mum.
But, and ye come any nearer, I pray
  you see all be sweet!
HODGE. Tush, man! Is gammer's neele
  found? That chould gladly weet! [5]
DICCON. She may thank thee it is not found,
  for, if thou had kept thy standing,
The devil he wold have fet it out, even,
  Hodge, at thy commanding.   10
HODGE. Gog's heart! And cold he tell noth-
  ing where the neele might be found?
DICCON. Ye foolish dolt, ye were to seek
  ere we had got our ground;
Therefore his tale so doubtful was that
  I cold not perceive it.

HODGE. Then ich see well something was
  said. Chope [6] one day yet to have it.
But, Diccon, Diccon, did not the devil
  cry "Ho, ho, ho"?
DICCON. If thou hadst tarried where thou
  stood'st, thou woldest have said so.
HODGE. Durst swear of [7] a book, chard [8]
  him roar, straight after ich was gone!
But tell me, Diccon, what said the
  knave? Let me hear it anon.
DICCON. The whoreson talked to me, I
  know not well of what:
One while his tongue it ran and paltered
  of a cat;   20
Another while he stammered still upon
  a rat;
Last of all, there was nothing but every
  word "Chat! Chat!"
But this I well perceived, before I wold
  him rid,
Between "Chat" and the "rat" and
  the "cat," the needle is hid.
Now, whether Gib, our cat, have eat it in
  her maw,
Or Doctor Rat, our curate, have found it
  in the straw,
Or this Dame Chat, your neighbor, have
  stolen it, God he knoweth!
But by the morrow at this time we shall
  learn how the matter goeth.
HODGE. Canst not learn tonight, man?
  Seest not what is here?
  Pointing behind to his torn breeches.
DICCON. 'Tis not possible to make it
  sooner appear.   30
HODGE. Alas, Diccon, then chave no shift
  but, lest ich tarry too long,
Hie me to Sim Glover's shop, there to
  seek for a thong,
Therewith this breech to tatch [9] and tie
  as ich may.
DICCON. Tomorrow, Hodge, if we chance
  to meet, shalt see what I will say.
                          [*Exit Hodge.*]

THE II ACT. THE iv SCENE.

Diccon, Gammer.[10]

DICCON. Now this gear must forward go,
  for here my gammer cometh.
Be still awhile, and say nothing; make
  here a little romth! [11]

---

[1] Dodsley's reading. Original reads *will.*
[2] Enters later.   [4] Sped.
[3] That other.   [5] Know.

[6] I hope.   [7] On.   [8] I heard.   [9] Attach, fasten.
[10] Enters later.   [11] Room.

[Enter Gammer.]

GAMMER. Good Lord, shall never be my
luck my neele again to spy?
Alas the while, 'tis past my help! Where
'tis, still it must lie!
DICCON. Now Jesus, Gammer Gurton,
what driveth you to this sadness?
I fear me, by my conscience, you will sure
fall to madness.
GAMMER. Who is that? What, Diccon?
Cham lost, man. Fie! fie!
DICCON. Marry, fie on them that be
worthy! But what shuld be your
trouble?
GAMMER. Alas, the more ich think on it,
my sorrow it waxeth double!
My goodly tossing [1] spurrier's neele,
chave lost, ich wot not where.   10
DICCON. Your neele! When?
GAMMER.   My neele! Alas, ich might
full ill it spare!
As God himself he knoweth, ne'er one
beside chave.
DICCON. If this be all, good gammer, I
warrant you all is save.
GAMMER. Why, know you any tidings
which way my neele is gone?
DICCON. Yea, that I do, doubtless, as ye
shall hear anon.
A [2] see a thing this matter toucheth,
within these twenty hours,
Even at this gate,[3] before my face, by a
neighbor of yours:
She stooped me down, and up she took a
needle or a pin.
I durst be sworn it was even yours, by all
my mother's kin.
GAMMER. It was my neele, Diccon, ich
wot; for here, even by this post,   20
Ich sat what time as ich upstart, and so
my neele it lost.
Who was it, lief [4] son? Speak, ich pray
thee, and quickly tell me that!
DICCON. A subtle quean as any in this
town, your neighbor here, Dame Chat.
GAMMER. Dame Chat, Diccon? Let me
be gone! Chill thither in posthaste.
DICCON. Take my counsel yet or ye go,
for fear ye walk in waste!
It is a murrion crafty drab, and froward
to be pleaséd;

And ye take not the better way, our
needle yet ye lose [5] it.
For, when she took it up, even here before your doors,
"What, soft, Dame Chat," quoth I,
"that same is none of yours!"
"Avaunt," quoth she, "sir knave! What
pratest thou of that I find?   30
I wold thou hadst kissed me I wot where"
(she meant, I know, behind).
And home she went as brag [6] as it had
been a bodylouse,
And I after as bold as it had been the
goodman of the house.
But there and ye had hard her how she
began to scold—
The tongue it went on pattens,[7] by Him
that Judas sold!
Each other word I was a knave, and you
a whore of whores,
Because I spake in your behalf and said
the neele was yours.
GAMMER. Gog's bread! And thinks the
callet [8] thus to keep my neele me
fro? [9]
DICCON. Let her alone, and she minds none
other but even to dress you so!
GAMMER. By the Mass, chill rather spend
the coat that is on my back!   40
Thinks the false quean by such a sleight [10]
that chill my neele lack?
DICCON. Slepe [11] not you[r] gear, I counsel you, but of this take good heed:
Let not be known I told you of it, how
well soever ye speed.
GAMMER. Chill in, Diccon, a clean apern [12]
to take and set before me;
And ich may my neele once see, chill sure
remember thee!   *[Exit.]*

THE II ACT. THE V SCENE.

Diccon.

DICCON. Here will the sport begin! If
these two once may meet,
Their cheer, durst lay money, will prove
scarcely sweet!
My gammer, sure, intends to be upon her
bones

---

[1] Brett-Smith suggests the movement of the
needle in sewing with a long thread.
[2] I.   [3] Door.   [4] Dear.

[5] Rime would require *leese*.   [6] Briskly.
[7] On wooden shoes, *i.e.*, noisily.
[8] Strumpet.   [9] From.
[10] Dodsley's reading. Original reads *slygh*.
[11] Slip, neglect.   [12] Apron.

With staves or with clubs or else with
cobblestones.
Dame Chat, on the other side, if she be
far behind,
I am right far deceived; she is given to it
of kind.[1]
He that may tarry by it awhile, and that
but short,
I warrant him—trust to it—he shall see
all the sport.
Into the town will I, my friends to visit
there,
And hether straight again to see th'end of
this gear.—[*Turns to musicians.*]   10
In the meantime, fellows, pipe up your
fiddles! I say, take them,
And let your friends hear such mirth as
ye can make them!   [*Exit.*]

The III Act. The i Scene.

Hodge.

Hodge. Sim Glover, yet gramercy! Cham
meetly well sped now.
Th'art even as good a fellow as ever
kissed a cow!
Here is a thing [2] indeed; by the Mass,
though ich speak it,
Tom Tankard's great bald curtal,[3] I
think, could not break it!
And, when he spied my need to be so
straight and hard,
Hais [4] lent me here his nawl [5] to set the
jib forward.[6]
As for my gammer's neele, the flying
fiend go weet! [7]
Chill not now go to the door again with it
to meet.
Chould make shift good enough and chad
a candle's end.
The chief hole in my breech with these
two chill amend.   10

The III Act. The ii Scene.

Gammer, Hodge.

Gammer. How, Hodge! mayst now be
glad! Cha' news to tell thee.
Ich know who hais my neele; ich trust
soon shalt it see.

Hodge. The devil thou does! Hast hard,
gammer, indeed, or dost but jest?
Gammer. 'Tis as true as steel, Hodge.
Hodge.   Why, knowest well where
didst leese it?
Gammer. Ich know who found it, and
took it up; shalt see, or it be long.
Hodge. God's Mother dear, if that be
true, farewell both nawl an' thong!
But who hais it, gammer? Say on!
Chould fain hear it disclosed.
Gammer. That false fixen,[8] that same
Dame Chat, that counts herself so
honest!
Hodge. Who told you so?
Gammer.   That same did Diccon
the bedlam, which saw it done.
Hodge. Diccon? It is a vengeable knave,
gammer! 'Tis a bonable [9] whoreson! 10
Can do mo [10] things than that, else cham
deceived evil.
By the Mass, ich saw him of late call up
a great black devil!
O, the knave cried, "Ho! ho!" He roared,
and he thundered.
And ye'd been here, cham sure you'ld
murrainly ha' wondered!
Gammer. Was not thou afraid, Hodge,
to see him in this place?
Hodge. No!   And chad come to me,
chould have laid him on the face,
Chould have promised him!
Gammer.   But, Hodge, had he no
horns to push?
Hodge. As long as your two arms! Saw
ye never Friar Rush [11]
Painted on a cloth, with a side [12] long
cow's tail,
And crooked cloven feet, and many a
hooked nail?   20
For all the world, if I shuld judge,
chould reckon him his brother.
Look, even what face Friar Rush had,
the devil had such another!
Gammer. Now [13] Jesus' mercy, Hodge, did
Diccon in him bring?
Hodge. Nay, gammer, hear me speak!
Chill tell you a greater thing:

---

[1] By nature.   [4] Has.
[2] *I.e.*, the thong he had gone for.   [5] Awl.
[3] Horse with a docked tail.
[6] *I.e.*, help things on.   [7] Wi' it, with it.

[8] Vixen.
[9] Powerful; Hodge's mispronunciation of *abominable*.   [10] More.
[11] A name assumed by the devil in a popular
German folk tale.
[12] Great (literally, *long*).
[13] Dodsley's reading. Early edns. read *new*.

The devil, when Diccon had him—ich
hard him wondrous weel—
Said plainly, here before us, that Dame
Chat had your neele.
GAMMER. Then let us go and ask her
wherefore she minds to keep it!
Seeing we know so much, 'twere a mad-
ness now to slepe it.
HODGE. Go to her, gammer.

[*Enter Chat.*]

See ye not where she stands in her doors?
Bid her give you the neele. 'Tis none
of hers, but yours!   30

THE III ACT. THE iii SCENE.

Gammer, Chat, Hodge.

GAMMER. Dame Chat, chold pray thee
fair, let me have that is mine!
Chill not this twenty years take one
fart that is thine.
Therefore give me mine own, and let
me live beside thee!
CHAT. Why art thou crept from home
hether to mine own doors to chide me?
Hence, doting drab, avaunt, or I shall
set thee further!
Intends thou and that knave me in my
house to murther?
GAMMER. Tush, gape not so on[1] me,
woman! Shalt not yet eat me!
Nor all the friends thou hast, in this
shall not entreat me!
Mine own goods I will have, and ask
thee on beleve.[2]
What, woman! Poor folks must have
right, though the thing you aggrieve. 10
CHAT. Give thee thy right, and hang thee
up, with all thy bagger's[3] brood!
What, wilt thou make me a thief, and
say I stole thy good?
GAMMER. Chill say nothing, ich warrant
thee, but that ich can prove it well.
Thou fet my good even from my door,
cham able this to tell!
CHAT. Did I, old witch, steal oft[4] was
thine? How should that thing be
known?
GAMMER. Ich cannot tell; but up thou
tookest it, as though it had been thine
own.

¹ Emended by Hazlitt. Original reads *no.*
² Belive, lively, at once.
³ Beggar's (?).   ⁴ Aught.

CHAT. Marry, fie on thee, thou old gib,[5]
with all my very heart!
GAMMER. Nay, fie on thee, thou ramp,[6]
thou rig,[7] with all that take thy
part!
CHAT. A vengeance on those lips that
layeth such things to my charge!
GAMMER. A vengeance on those callet-
ships whose conscience is so large![8] 20
CHAT. Come out, Hodge!
GAMMER.   Come out, Hodge, and
let me have[9] right!
CHAT. Thou arrant witch!
GAMMER.   Thou bawdy bitch, chill
make thee curse this night!
CHAT. A bag and a wallet![10]
GAMMER.   A cart for a callet![11]
CHAT.   Why, weenest thou thus to
prevail?
I hold thee a groat I shall patch thy
coat!
GAMMER.   Thou wart[12] as good
kiss my tail!
Thou slut, thou cut,[13] thou rakes,[14] thou
jakes![15] Will not shame make thee
hide thee?
CHAT. Thou scald,[16] thou bald, thou rot-
ten, thou glutton! I will no longer
chide thee!
But I will teach thee to keep home.
GAMMER.   Wilt thou, drunken beast?
                    [*They fight.*]
HODGE. Stick to her, gammer! Take her by
the head! Chill warrant you this feast!
Smite, I say, gammer! Bite, I say, gammer! I trow ye will be keen!
Where be your nails? Claw her by the
jaws! Pull me out both her eyen![17] 30
                    [*Chat throws Gammer down.*]
Gog's bones, gammer, hold up your head!
CHAT.   I trow, drab, I shall dress thee.—
[*To Hodge.*] Tarry, thou knave! I hold
thee a groat I shall make these hands
bless thee!—

                    [*Hodge retires.*]

⁵ Cat.   ⁷ Wanton woman.
⁶ Shameless woman.   ⁸ Liberal, easy.
⁹ Manly's reading. Original reads *let have me.*
¹⁰ Accouterments of a beggar.
¹¹ A drab was commonly punished by being
whipped at the tail of a cart as it was driven
through the streets.
¹² Wert.   ¹⁵ Privy.
¹³ Docked horse or dog.   ¹⁶ Scabby person.
¹⁴ Dissolute person.   ¹⁷ Old plural of *eye.*

Take thou this, old whore, for amends,
    and learn thy tongue well to tame,
And say thou met at this bickering, not
    thy fellow, but thy dame!

[*Hodge returns with a club.*]

HODGE. Where is the strong stewed
    whore? Chill gear [1] a whore's mark!
Stand out one's way that ich kill none
    in the dark!
Up, gammer, and ye be alive! Chill
    fight now for us both.
Come no near me, thou scald callet! To
    kill thee ich were loath.

CHAT. Art here again, thou hoddypeak! [2]
    What, Doll, bring me out my spit!
HODGE. Chill broach thee with this!
    Bim father soul, chill conjure that
    foul sprite!—   40
Let door stand, Cock! Why comes in-
    deed? Keep door, thou whoreson boy!
CHAT. Stand to it, thou dastard, for thine
    ears! Ise [3] teach thee a sluttish toy!
HODGE. Gog's wounds, whore, chill make
    thee avaunt! [*Flees into the house.*]
    Take heed, Cock, pull in the latch!
CHAT. I' faith, sir loose-breech, had ye
    tarried, ye shold have found your
    match!

[*Gammer attacks Chat from behind.*]

GAMMER. Now ware thy throat, losel! [4]
    Thouse [5] pay [6] for all!

[*Throws Chat down.*]

HODGE.   Well said, gammer,
    by my soul!
Hoise [7] her! Souse her! Bounce her!
    Trounce her! Pull out her throatboll! [8]
CHAT. Com'st behind me, thou withered
    witch? And I get once on foot,
Thouse pay for all, thou old tarleather! [9]
    I'll teach thee what longs [10] to it!
Take thee this to make up thy mouth till
    time thou come by more!

[*Chat beats Gammer and goes out.*]

HODGE. Up, gammer! Stand on your
    feet. Where is the old whore?   50
Faith, would chad her by the face!
    Chould crack her callet crown!
GAMMER. Ah, Hodge, Hodge, where was
    thy help, when fixen had me down?

HODGE. By the Mass, gammer, but for my
    staff, Chat had gone nigh to spill you!
Ich think the harlot had not cared, and
    chad not come, to kill you.
But shall we lose our neele thus?
GAMMER.   No, Hodge, chwar [11] loath
    do so.
Thinkest thou chill take that at her
    hand? No, Hodge, ich tell thee, no!
HODGE. Chold yet this fray were well take
    up, and our own neele at home.
'Twill be my chance else some to kill,
    wherever it be, or whom!
GAMMER. We have a parson, Hodge, thou
    knows, a man esteeméd wise,
Mast' Doctor Rat; chill for him send,
    and let me hear his advice.   60
He will her shrive for all this gear, and
    give her penance straight;
Wese [12] have our neele, else Dame Chat
    comes ne'er within heaven-gate!
HODGE. Yea, marry, gammer, that ich
    think best. Will you now for him send?
The sooner Doctor Rat be here, the
    sooner wese ha' an end.
And here, gammer! Diccon's devil, as
    ich remember well,
Of cat, and Chat, and Doctor Rat a
    felonious tale did tell.
Chold you forty pound that is the way
    your neele to get again!
GAMMER. Chill ha' him straight! Call out
    the boy; wese make him take the pain.
HODGE. What, Cock, I say! Come out!
    What devil, canst not hear?

[Enter Cock.]

COCK.[13] How now, Hodge? How does
    gammer? Is yet the weather clear? 70
What wold chave me to do?
GAMMER.   Come hether, Cock, anon!
Hence swith to Doctor Rat! Hie thee
    that thou were gone!
And pray him come speak with me; cham
    not well at ease.
Shalt have him at his chamber, or [14] else
    at Mother Bee's;
Else seek him at Hob Filcher's shop, for,
    as chard it reported,
There is the best ale in all the town, and
    now is most resorted.

---

[1] Gi' her, give her.
[2] Simpleton.
[3] I shall.
[6] Emended by Dodsley. Original reads *pray.*
[7] Lift.
[8] Adam's apple.   [10] Belongs.
[4] Worthless person.
[5] Thou shalt.
[9] Strip of dried sheepskin.

[11] Ich were, I were. Bradley's emendation for
chwarde.   [12] We shall.
[13] Original assigns this speech to Gammer.
[14] Original reads *of.*

Cock. And shall ich bring him with me, gammer?

Gammer.   Yea, by-and-by, good Cock.

Cock. Shalt see that shall be here anon, else let me have on the dock! [1] [*Exit.*]

Hodge. Now, gammer, shall we two go in, and tarry for his coming?

What devil, woman, pluck up your heart, and leave off all this glumming! [2]   80

Though she were stronger at the first, as ich think ye did find her,

Yet there ye dressed the drunken sow, what time ye came behind her.

Gammer. Nay, nay, cham sure she lost not all; for set th'end to the beginning,

And ich doubt not but she will make small boast of her winning.

[*They start to go in.*]

The III Act. The iv Scene.

Tib [*with a cat*], *Hodge, Gammer, Cock.* [3]

Tib. See, gammer, gammer, Gib, our cat! Cham afraid what she aileth!

She stands me gasping behind the door, as though her wind her faileth.

Now let ich doubt what Gib shuld mean, that now she doth so dote. [4]

Hodge. Hold hether! [5]   Ichold twenty pound your neele is in her throat!

Grope [6] her, ich say! Methinks ich feel it. Does not prick your hand?

Gammer. Ich can feel nothing.

Hodge.   No? Ich know thar's not within this land

A murrainer cat than Gib is, betwixt the Thames and Tyne;

Sh'as as much wit in her head almost as chave in mine!

Tib. Faith, sh'as eaten something that will not easily down.

Whether she gat it at home or abroad in the town   10

Ich cannot tell.

Gammer.   Alas, ich fear it be some crooked pin!

And then, farewell Gib! She is undone and lost—all save the skin.

Hodge. Tib, your neele, woman, I say! Gog's soul, give me a knife,

And chill have it out of her maw, or else chall lose my life!

Gammer. What! Nay, Hodge, fie! Kill not our cat. 'Tis all the cats we ha' now!

Hodge. By the Mass, Dame Chat hais me so moved ich care not what I kill, ma' [7] God avow!

Go to, then, Tib! To this gear! Hold up her tail, and take her!

Chill see what devil is in her guts! Chill take the pains to rake [8] her!

Gammer. Rake a cat, Hodge? What woldst thou do?

Hodge.   What! Think'st that cham not able?

Did not Tom Tankard rake his curtal t'or [9] day, standing in the stable?   20

[*Enter Cock.*]

Gammer. Soft, be content; let's hear what news Cock bringeth from Mast' Rat!

Cock. Gammer, chave been there as you bade, you wot well about what.

'Twill not be long before he come, ich durst swear of a book.

He bids you see ye be at home, and there for him to look.

Gammer. Where didst thou find him, boy? Was he not where I told thee?

Cock. Yes, yes, even at Hob Filcher's house, by him that bought and sold me;

A cup of ale had in his hand, and a crab lay in the fire.

Chad much ado to go and come, all was so full of mire.

And, gammer, one thing I can tell: Hob Filcher's nawl was lost,

And Doctor Rat found it again, hard beside the doorpost.   30

Ichold a penny, can say something your neele again to fet.

Gammer. Cham glad to hear so much, Cock; then trust he will not let [10]

To help us herein best he can; therefore, till time he come,

Let us go in. If there be aught to get, thou shalt have some.   [*Exeunt.*]

The IV Act. The i Scene [11]

Doctor Rat, Gammer Gurton.

D. Rat. [*To himself.*] A man were better twenty times be a bandog and bark,

Than here, among such a sort, be parish priest or clerk,

---

[1] Tail, *i.e.*, a beating.
[2] Sullenness.
[3] Enters later.
[4] Act foolishly.
[5] Give her to me!
[6] Feel.
[7] I make.   [8] Clean.   [9] Tother.   [10] Forbear.
[11] Original reads *The II Act. The iv Scene.*

Where he shall never be at rest one
  pissing-while a day,
But he must trudge about the town, this
  way and that way,
Here to a drab, there to a thief, his shoes
  to tear and rent,
And, that which is worst of all, at every
  knave's commandment!
I had not sit the space to drink two pots
  of ale
But Gammer Gurton's sorry boy was
  straightway at my tail,
And she was sick, and I must come—to
  do I wot not what!
If once her finger's end but ache,
  "Trudge! Call for Doctor Rat!"   10
And, when I come not at their call, I only
  thereby lose;
For I am sure to lack therefore a tithe-
  pig or a goose.
I warrant you, when truth is known, and
  told they have their tale,
The matter whereabout I come is not
  worth a halfpennyworth of ale!
Yet must I talk so sage and smooth as
  though I were a glozier,[1]
Else, or the year come at an end, I shall
  be sure the loser.
  [*He spies Gammer Gurton working.*]
What work ye, Gammer Gurton! How,
  here is your friend M[aster] Rat!
GAMMER. Ah, good M[aster] Doctor, cha'
  troubled, cha' troubled you, chwot
  well that!
D. RAT. How do ye, woman? Be ye lusty,
  or be ye not well at ease?
GAMMER. By Gis,[2] master, cham not
  sick,[3] but yet chave a disease.[4]   20
Chad a foul turn now of late; chill tell it
  you, by Gigs!
D. RAT. Hath your brown cow cast her
  calf, or your sandy sow her pigs?
GAMMER. No, but chad been as good they
  had, as this, ich wot weel.
D. RAT. What is the matter?
GAMMER.   Alas! alas! cha' lost my good
  neele!
My neele, I say! And, wot ye what? A
  drab came by and spied it,
And, when I asked her for the same, the
  filth flatly denied it.

D. RAT. What was she that—
GAMMER.   A dame, ich warrant you!
  She began to scold and brawl—
  Alas, alas! Come hether, Hodge! This
  wr[e]tch can tell you all.

THE IV ACT. THE ii SCENE.[5]

Hodge, Doctor Rat, Gammer, Diccon, Chat.[6]

HODGE. Good morrow, Gaffer Vicar!
D. RAT.   Come on, fellow; let us hear.
  Thy dame hath said to me, thou knowest
  of all this gear;
  Let's see what thou canst say.
HODGE.   Bym fay,[7] sir, that ye shall!
What matter soever here was done, ich
  can tell your ma'ship all.
My Gammer Gurton here, see now, sat
  her down at this door, see now;
And, as she began to stir her, see now, her
  neele fell in the floor, see now;
And, while her staff she took, see now, at
  Gib, her cat, to fling, see now,
Her neele was lost in the floor, see now.
  Is not this a wondrous thing, see now?
Then came the quean, Dame Chat, see
  now, to ask for her black cup, see
  now;
And even here at this gate, see now,
  she took that neele up, see now.   10
My gammer then she yeed,[8] see now,
  her neele again to bring, see now,
And was caught by the head, see now!
  Is not this a wondrous thing, see now?
She tare my gammer's coat, see now,
  and scratched her by the face, see
  now;
Chad thought sh'ad stopped her throat,
  see now. Is not this a wondrous case,
  see now?
When ich saw this, ich was wroth,[9] see
  now, and start between them twain,
  see now;
Else, ich durst take a book oath, see
  now, my gammer had been slain, see
  now.
GAMMER. This is even the whole matter,
  as Hodge has plainly told.
And chould fain be quiet, for my part,
  that chould.

---

[1] Flatterer.   [2] Jesus.
[3] Emended by Dodsley. Original reads *sich*.
[4] Dis-ease, anxiety.

[5] Hazlitt, Manly, and Adams begin a new
scene at l. 52 and again at l. 94.
[6] The last two enter later.
[7] By my faith.   [8] Went.
[9] Original misprints *worth*.

But help us, good master—beseech ye
that ye do—
Else shall we both be beaten, and lose
our neele too. 20
D. RAT. What wold ye have me to do?
Tell me, that I were gone.
I will do the best that I can to set you
both at one.
But be ye sure Dame Chat hath this
your neele found?
GAMMER. Here comes the man that see
her take it up of [1] the ground;
Ask him yourself, Master Rat, if ye be-
lieve not me;
And help me to my neele, for God's sake
and Saint Charity!

[Enter Diccon.]

D. RAT. Come near, Diccon, and let us
hear what thou can express.
Wilt thou be sworn thou seest Dame
Chat this woman's neele have?
DICCON. Nay, by S[aint] Benit,[2] will I not!
Then might ye think me rave.[3]
GAMMER. Why, didst not thou tell me so
even here? Canst thou for shame
deny it? 30
DICCON. Ay, marry, gammer; but I said
I wold not abide by it.
D. RAT. Will you say a thing, and not
stick to it to try it?
DICCON. "Stick to it," quoth you, Master
Rat? Marry, sir, I defy it!
Nay, there is many an honest man,
when he such blasts hath blown
In his friend's ears, he would be loath
the same by him were known.
If such a toy be uséd oft among the
honesty,[4]
It may beseem a simple man of [5] your
and my degree.
D. RAT. Then we be never the nearer,
for all that you can tell?
DICCON. Yes, marry, sir, if ye will do by
mine advice and counsel.
If Mother Chat see all us here, she know-
eth how the matter goes; 40
Therefore I rede [6] you three go hence,
and within keep close;
And I will into Dame Chat's house. and
so the matter use

That, or you cold go twice to church, I
warrant you hear news.
She shall look well about her, but, I
durst lay a pledge,
Ye shall of gammer's neele have shortly
better knowledge.
GAMMER. Now, gentle Diccon. do so; and,
good sir, let us trudge.
D. RAT. By the Mass, I may not tarry so
long to be your judge.
DICCON. 'Tis but a little while, man.
What, take so much pain!
If I hear no news of it, I will come sooner
again.
HODGE. Tarry so much, good Master
Doctor, of your gentleness! 50
D. RAT. Then let us hie us inward; and,
Diccon, speed thy business!
DICCON. Now, sirs, do you no more but
keep my counsel just,
And Doctor Rat shall thus catch some
good, I trust.—
[Exeunt Hodge, Rat, and Gammer.
To himself.] But Mother Chat, my
gossip, talk first withal I must,
For she must be chief captain to lay the
Rat in the dust.

[Enter Dame Chat.]

God deven,[7] Dame Chat, in faith, and
well met in this place!
CHAT. God deven, my friend Diccon.
Whether [8] walk ye this pace?
DICCON. By my truth, even to you, to
learn how the world goeth.
Hard ye no more of the other matter,
say me now, by your troth?
CHAT. O, yes, Diccon. Here the old whore
and Hodge, that great knave— 60
But, in faith, I would thou hadst seen!—
O Lord, I dressed them brave! [9]
She bare me two or three souses [10] be-
hind in the nape of the neck,
Till I made her old wesen [11] to answer
again, "keck"! [12]
And Hodge, that dirty dastard that at
her elbow stands.
If one pair of legs had not been worth
two pair of hands,

---

[1] Off.
[2] Benedict.
[3] To be mad.
[4] Persons of quality.
[5] Original reads *if*.
[6] Advise.
[7] God give you good even.
[8] Whither.
[9] Finely.
[10] Thwacks.
[11] Weasand, throat.
[12] Sound of vomiting.

He had had his beard shaven if my nails
    wold have served!
And not without a cause, for the knave
    it well deserved!

Diccon. By the Mass, I can thee thank,
    wench, thou didst so well acquit
    thee!

Chat. And th'adst seen him, Diccon, it
    wold have made thee beshit thee
For laughter. The whoreson dolt at last
    caught up a club   70
As though he would have slain the
    master devil, Belsabub;
But I set him soon inward.

Diccon.   O Lord, there is the thing
That Hodge is so offended, that makes
    him start and fling!

Chat. Why, makes the knave any moil-
    ing,[1] as ye have seen or hard?

Diccon. Even now I saw him last. Like
    a madman he fared,
And sware by heaven and hell he would
    awreak [2] his sorrow,
And leave you never a hen on-live by
    eight of the clock tomorrow.
Therefore mark what I say, and my
    words see that ye trust:
Your hens be as good as dead if ye leave
    them on the rust!

Chat. The knave dare as well go hang
    himself as go upon my ground! 80

Diccon. Well, yet take heed, I say! I
    must tell you my tale round.[3]
Have you not about your house, behind
    your furnace or lead,[4]
A hole where a crafty knave may creep
    in for need?

Chat. Yes, by the Mass, a hole broke
    down even within these two days.

Diccon. Hodge he intends this same
    night to slip in thereaways.

Chat. O Christ, that I were sure of it!
    In faith, he shuld have his meed!

Diccon. Watch well, for the knave will
    be there as sure as is your creed.
I wold spend myself a shilling to have
    him swingéd well.

Chat. I am as glad as a woman can be of
    this thing to hear tell.
By Gog's bones, when he cometh, now
    that I know the matter,   90

He shall sure at the first skip to leap in
    scalding water—
With a worse turn besides! When he will,
    let him come!

Diccon. I tell you as my sister.   You
    know what meaneth "mum"!—
                        [Exit Chat.]
Now lack I but my doctor to play his
    part again.
And lo, where he cometh towards—per-
    adventure to his pain!

[Enter Rat.]

D. Rat. What good news, Diccon? Fel-
    low, is Mother Chat at home?

Diccon. She is, sir, and she is not, but it
    please her to whom.
Yet did I take her tardy,[5] as subtle as
    she was!

D. Rat. The thing that thou went'st for,
    hast thou brought it to pass?

Diccon. I have done that I have done,
    be it worse, be it better!   100
And Dame Chat at her wit's end I have
    almost set her.

D. Rat. Why, hast thou spied the neele?
    Quickly, I pray thee, tell!

Diccon. I have spied it, in faith, sir, I
    handled myself so well.
And yet the crafty quean had almost
    take my trump.
But, or all came to an end, I set her in
    a dump!

D. Rat. How so, I pray thee, Diccon?

Diccon.   Marry, sir, will ye hear?
She was clapped down on the back side,[6]
    by Cock's Mother dear,
And there she sat sewing a halter, or a band,
With no other thing save gammer's
    needle in her hand.
As soon as any knock, if the filth be in
    doubt,   110
She needs but once puff, and her candle
    is out.
Now I, sir, knowing of every door the pin,
Came nicely,[7] and said no word till
    time I was within;
And there I saw the neele, even with
    these two eyes.
Whoever say the contrary, I will swear
    he lies!

[1] Worry, vexation.   [3] Directly.
[2] Avenge.   [4] Pot.
[5] Unaware.
[6] Seated in the back of the house.
[7] Stealthily.

D. RAT. O Diccon, that I was not there
then in thy stead!

DICCON. Well, if ye will be ordered and
do by my rede,

I will bring you to a place, as the house
stands,

Where ye shall take the drab with the
neele in her hands.

D. RAT. For God's sake, do so, Diccon,
and I will gage [1] my gown   120

To give thee a full pot of the best ale
in the town!

DICCON. Follow me but a little, and mark
what I will say.

Lay down your gown beside you. [*Rat
takes off his gown.*] Go to, come on
your way!

See ye not what is here? A hole wherein
ye may creep

Into the house, and suddenly unwares
among them leap.

There shall ye find the bitch fox and the
neele together.

Do as I bid you, man; come on your
ways hether!

D. RAT. Art thou sure, Diccon, the swill-
tub stands not hereabout?

DICCON. I was within myself, man, even
now, there is no doubt.

Go softly, make no noise. Give me your
foot, Sir John! [2]   130

Here will I wait upon you till you come
out anon.

Rat climbs through the hole and is beaten.]

D. RAT. Help, Diccon! Out, alas! I
shall be slain among them!

DICCON. If they give you not the needle,
tell them that ye will hang them.

Ware that!—How, my wenches, have ye
caught the fox

That used to make revel among your
hens and cocks?

Save his life yet for his order, though he
sustain some pain.—

Gog's bread, I am afraid they will beat
out his brain!   [*Exit Diccon.*

Enter Rat.]

D. RAT. Woe worth the hour that I came
here!

And woe worth him that wrought this
gear!

A sort of drabs and queans have me
blessed! [3]   140

Was ever creature half so evil dressed?

Whoever it wrought and first did invent
it,

He shall, I warrant him, ere long repent
it!

I will spend all I have, without [4] my skin,

But he shall be brought to the plight I
am in!

Master Baily, I trow, and he be worth his
ears,

Will snaffle these murderers and all that
them bears. [5]

I will surely neither bite nor sup

Till I fetch him hether, this matter to
take up.   [*Exit.*]

THE V ACT. THE i SCENE.

*Master Bailey, [attended by Scapethrift,] Doc-
tor Rat.*

BAILY. I can perceive none other, I speak
it from my heart,

But either ye are in all the fault, or else
in the greatest part.

D. RAT. If it be counted his fault, besides
all his grieves, [6]

When a poor man is spoiled and beaten
among thieves,

Then I confess my fault herein at this
season;

But I hope you will not judge so much
against reason.

BAILY. And methinks, by your own tale,
of all that ye name,

If any played the thief, you were the very
same.

The women they did nothing, as your
words make probation,

But stoutly withstood your forcible invasion.   10

If that a thief at your window to enter
should begin,

Wold you hold forth your hand and help
to pull him in?

Or you wold keep him out? I pray you,
answer me.

D. RAT. Marry, keep him out, and a good
cause why!

But I am no thief, sir, but an honest,
learned clerk.

---

[1] Pledge.   [2] Conventional name for a parson.

[3] Wounded.   [4] Except.
[5] Everybody that supports them.   [6] Griefs.

BAILY. Yea, but who knoweth that when
he meets you in the dark?
I am sure your learning shines not out at
your nose.
Was it any marvel though the poor
woman arose
And start up, being afraid of that was in
her purse?
Methink you may be glad that you[r]
luck was no worse.   20

D. RAT. Is not this evil enough, I pray
you, as you think?
Showing his broken head.

BAILY. Yea, but a man in the dark, if [1]
chances do wink,
As soon he smites his father as any other
man,
Because for lack of light discern him he
ne can.
Might it not have been your luck with a
spit to have been slain?

D. RAT. I think I am little better—my
scalp is cloven to the brain!
If there be all the remedy, I know who
bears the k[n]ocks.

BAILY. By my troth, and well worthy besides to kiss the stocks!
To come in on the back side, when ye
might go about!
I know none such, unless they long to
have their brains knocked out.   30

D. RAT. Well, will you be so good, sir, as
talk with Dame Chat,
And know what she intended? I ask no
more but that.

BAILY. [*To Scapethrift.*]   Let her be
called, fellow, because of Master Doctor.   [*Exit Scapethrift.*]
I warrant in this case she will be her own
proctor;
She will tell her own tale, in meter or in
prose,
And bid you seek your remedy, and so go
wipe your nose!

THE V ACT. THE ii SCENE.

*M[aster] Baily, Chat, [led in by Scapethrift,]
D[octor] Rat, Gammer, Hodge, Diccon.* [2]

BAILY. Dame Chat, Master Doctor upon
you here complained
That you and your maids shuld him
much misorder,

And taketh many an oath that no word
he feigned,
Laying to your charge how you thought
him to murder;
And, on his part again, that same man
saith furder
He never offended you in word nor intent.
To hear you answer hereto, we have now
for you sent.

CHAT. That I wold have murdered him?
Fie on him, wretch!
And evil mought he thee [3] for it, our
Lord I beseech.
I will swear on all the books that opens
and shuts,   10
He feigneth this tale out of his own guts!
For this seven weeks with me, I am sure,
he sat not down.
Nay, ye have other minions,[4] in the other
end of the town,
Where ye were liker to catch such a blow
Than anywhere else, as far as I know!

BAILY. Belike then, Master Doctor, yon
stripe there ye got not?

D. RAT. Think you I am so mad that
where I was bet [5] I wot not?
Will ye believe this quean before she
hath tried [6] it?
It is not the first deed she hath done and
afterward denied it.

CHAT. What, man, will you say I broke
your head?   20

D. RAT. How canst thou prove the contrary?

CHAT. Nay, how provest thou that I did
the deed?

D. RAT. Too plainly, by S[aint] Mary!
This proof, I trow, may serve though I no
word spoke!
Showing his broken head.

CHAT. Because thy head is broken, was it
I that it broke?
I saw thee, Rat, I tell thee, not once
within this fortnight.

D. RAT. No, marry, thou sawest me not,
forwhy [7] thou hadst no light;
But I felt thee, for all the dark, beshrew
thy smooth cheeks!
And thou groped me—this will declare,
any day this six weeks.
Showing his head.

---

[1] Original reads *of*.   [2] Last three enter later.
[3] Ill may he thrive.   [5] Beaten.   [7] Because.
[4] Darlings.   [6] Proved.

BAILY. Answer me to this, M[aster] Rat: when caught you this harm of yours? 30

D. RAT. A while ago, sir, God he knoweth; within less than these two hours.

BAILY. Dame Chat, was there none with you—confess, i'faith—about that season?

What, woman! Let it be what it will, 'tis neither felony nor treason.

CHAT. Yes, by my faith, Master Baily, there was a knave not far

Who caught one good fillip on the brow with a door bar,

And well was he worthy, as it seemed to me.

But what is that to this man, since this was not he?

BAILY. Who was it then? Let's hear!

D. RAT.   Alas, sir, ask you that?

Is it not made plain enough by the own mouth of Dame Chat?

The time agreeth, my head is broken, her tongue cannot lie;   40

Only upon a bare "nay" she saith it was not I.

CHAT. No, marry, was it not, indeed. Ye shall hear by this one thing:

This afternoon a friend of mine, for good will, gave me warning,

And bade we [1] well look to my rust and all my capons' pens,

For, if I took not better heed, a knave wold have my hens.

Then I, to save my goods, took so much pains as him to watch;

And, as good fortune served me, it was my chance him for to catch.

What strokes he bare away, or other what was his gains,

I wot not—but sure I am he had something for his pains!

BAILY. Yet tells thou not who it was.

CHAT.   Who it was? A false thief,   50

That came like a false fox my pullen [2] to kill and mischief!

BAILY. But knowest thou not his name?

CHAT.   I know it. But what than? [3]

It was that crafty cullion,[4] Hodge, my Gammer Gurton's man.

BAILY. Call me the knave hether.   He shall sure kiss the stocks.

I shall teach him a lesson for filching hens or cocks!   [Exit Scapethrift.]

D. RAT. I marvel, Master Baily,   so bleared be your eyes!

An egg is not so full of meat as she is full of lies.

When she hath played this prank, to excuse all this gear

She layeth the fault in such a one as I know was not there.

CHAT. Was he not there?   Look on his pate! That shall be his witness!   60

D. RAT. I wold my head were half so whole, I wold seek no redress!

[Enter Gammer.]

BAILY. God bless you, Gammer Gurton!

GAMMER.   God dyld you,[5] master mine!

BAILY. Thou hast a knave within thy house—Hodge, a servant of thine.

They tell me that busy knave is such a filching one

That hen, pig, goose, or capon thy neighbor can have none.

GAMMER. By God, cham much ameved [6] to hear any such report!

Hodge was not wont, ich trow, to b'ave [7] him in that sort.

CHAT. A thievisher knave is not on-live, more filching nor more false!

Many a truer man than he has hanged up by the hals.[8]

And thou, his dame, of all his theft thou art the sole receiver.   70

For Hodge to catch and thou to keep, I never knew none better.

GAMMER. Sir [9] reverence of your masterdom, and you were out-a-door,

Chold be so bold, for all her brags, to call her arrant whore!

And ich knew Hodge so bad as tow,[10] ich wish me endless sorrow

And could not take the pains to hang him up before tomorrow!

CHAT. What have I stolen from thee or thine, thou ill-favored old trot?

---

[1] Me (?).

[2] Poultry.

[3] A common Elizabethan spelling of *then*, retained here for the rime.

[4] Rascal.

[5] God yield you; God reward you.

[6] Moved, disturbed.

[7] Behave.   [8] Neck.

[9] Probably a contraction of *save your*.

[10] Thou.

GAMMER. A great deal more, by God's
    blessed,[1] than chever [2] by thee got!
That thou knowest well. I need not say it.
BAILY.   Stop there, I say!
    And tell me here, I pray you, this matter
    by the way:
    How chance Hodge is not here? Him
    wold [3] I fain have had.   80
GAMMER. Alas, sir, he'll be here anon; ha'
    be handled too bad!
CHAT. Master Baily, sir, ye be not such a
    fool, well I know,
    But ye perceive by this lingering there
    is a pad [4] in the straw.
Thinking that Hodge his head was broke,
    and that Gammer would not let him come
                   before them.
GAMMER. Chill show you his face, ich war-
    rant thee.—Lo now, where he is!

[*Enter Hodge, led in by Scapethrift.*]

BAILY. Come on, fellow! It is told me
    thou art a shrew, iwis.[5]
    Thy neighbors' hens thou takest, and
    plays the two-legged fox;
    Their chickens and their capons too, and
    now and then their cocks.
HODGE. Ich defy them all that dare it say!
    Cham as true as the best!
BAILY. Wart not thou take within this
    hour in Dame Chat's hens' nest?
HODGE. Take there? No, master. Chold
    not do't for a house full of gold!   90
CHAT. Thou, or the devil in thy coat!
    Swear this, I dare be bold.
D. RAT. Swear me no swearing, quean!
    The devil he give thee sorrow!
    All is not worth a gnat thou canst swear
    till tomorrow.
    Where is the harm he hath? Show it, by
    God's bread!
    Ye beat him, with a witness, but the
    stripes light on my head!
HODGE. Bet me? Gog's blessed body,
    chold first, ich trow, have burst thee.
    Ich think, and chad my hands loose, cal-
    let, chould have crust [6] thee!
CHAT. Thou shitten knave, I trow thou
    knowest the full weight of my fist!
    I am foully deceived unless thy head and
    my door bar kissed!

HODGE. Hold thy chat, whore! Thou
    criest so loud, can no man else be
    hard.   100
CHAT. Well, knave, and I had thee alone, I
    wold surely rap thy costard! [7]
BAILY. Sir, answer me to this: is thy head
    whole or broken?
CHAT. Yea, Master Baily, blessed be every
    good token!
HODGE. Is my head whole? Ich warrant
    you 'tis neither scurvy nor scald!
    What, you foul beast, does think 'tis
    either pilled [8] or bald?
    Nay, ich thank God, chill not, for all that
    thou mayst spend,
    That chad one scab on my narse as
    broad as thy finger's end.
BAILY. Come nearer here!
HODGE.   Yes, that ich dare.
BAILY. [*Examining Hodge's head.*] By our
    Lady, here is no harm.
    Hodge's head is whole enough, for all
    Dame Chat's charm.[9]
CHAT. By Gog's blessed, however the
    thing he clocks or smolders,[10]   110
    I know the blows he bare away either
    with head or shoulders.
    Camest thou not, knave, within this
    hour creeping into my pens,
    And there was caught within my house
    groping among my hens?
HODGE. A plague both on thy hens and
    thee! A cart, whore, a cart!
    Chould I were hanged as high as a tree
    and chware as false as thou art!
    Give my gammer again her washical [11]
    thou stole away in thy lap!
GAMMER. Yea, Master Baily, there is a
    thing you know not on, mayhap:
    This drab she keeps away my good—the
    devil he might her snare!
    Ich pray you that ich might have a right
    action on her.
CHAT. Have I thy good, old filth, or any
    such, old sows? [12]   120
    I am as true, I wold thou knew, as skin
    between thy brows!
GAMMER. Many a truer hath been hanged,
    though you escape the danger!
CHAT. Thou shalt answer, by God's pity,
    for this thy foul slander!

---

[1] *Cf.* l. 96.   [2] I ever.   [3] Original reads *wole*.
[4] Toad; a proverbial term for something hid-
den.   [5] Indeed.   [6] Crushed.

[7] Apple, head.   [10] Cloaks or smothers.
[8] Peeled, shorn.   [11] What-you-call-it.
[9] Chatter.   [12] Souse (?).

BAILY. Why, what can ye charge her withal? To say so, ye do not well.

GAMMER. Marry, a vengeance to her heart, that whore has stolen my neele!

CHAT. Thy needle, old witch? How so? It were alms thy skull to knock!
So didst thou say the other day that I had stolen thy cock,
And roasted him to my breakfast—which shall not be forgotten.
The devil pull out thy lying tongue and teeth that be so rotten!

GAMMER. Give me my neele! As for my Cock, chould be very loath   130
That chuld hear tell he shuld hang on thy false faith and troth.

BAILY. Your talk is such I can scarce learn who shuld be most in fault.

GAMMER. Yet shall ye find no other wight save she, by bread and salt!

BAILY. Keep ye content awhile; see that your tongues ye hold;
Methinks you shuld remember this is no place to scold.
How knowest thou, Gammer Gurton, Dame Chat thy needle had?

GAMMER. To name you, sir, the party, chould not be very glad.

BAILY. Yea, but we must needs hear it, and therefore say it boldly.

GAMMER. Such one as told the tale full soberly and coldly;
Even he that looked on—will swear on a book—   140
What time this drunken gossip my fair long neele up took:
Diccon, master, the bedlam. Cham very sure ye know him.

BAILY. A false knave, by God's pity! Ye were but a fool to trow [1] him.
I durst aventure well the price of my best cap
That when the end is known all will turn to a jape. [2]
Told he not you that, besides, she stole your cock that tide? [3]

GAMMER. No, master, no, indeed; for then he shuld have lied!
My cock is, I thank Christ, safe and well, a-fine. [4]

CHAT. Yea, but that ragged colt, that whore, that Tib of thine,

Said plainly thy cock was stolen and in my house was eaten.   150
That lying cut is lost that she is not swinged and beaten,
And yet for all my good name it were a small amends!
I pick not this gear, hear'st thou, out of my fingers' ends;
But he that hard it told me, who thou of late didst name:
Diccon, whom all men knows; it was the very same.

BAILY. This is the case: you lost your needle about the doors,
And she answers again she has no cock of yours;
Thus, in your talk and action, from that you do intend
She is whole five mile wide from that she doth defend. [5]
Will you say she hath your cock?

GAMMER.   No, marry, sir, that chill not!   160

BAILY. Will you confess her neele?

CHAT.   Will I? No, sir, will I not! [6]

BAILY. Then there lieth all the matter.

GAMMER.   Soft, master, by the way!
Ye know she could do little and she cold not say nay.

BAILY. Yea, but he that made one lie about your cock-stealing,
Will not stick to make another what time lies be in dealing.
I ween the end will prove this brawl did first arise
Upon no other ground but only Diccon's lies.

CHAT. Though some be lies, as you belike have espied them,
Yet other some be true—by proof I have well tried them.

BAILY. What other thing beside this, Dame Chat?

CHAT.   Marry, sir, even this: 170
The tale I told before, the selfsame tale it was his;
He gave me, like a friend, warning against my loss,
Else had my hens be stolen, each one, by God's Cross!
He told me Hodge wold come, and in he came indeed;

---

[1] Believe, trust.
[2] Jest.
[3] Time.
[4] Finally.
[5] Deny.
[6] Rime would require "I will not."

But, as the matter chanced, with greater
　　haste than speed.
This truth was said, and true was found,
　　as truly I report.

BAILY. If Doctor Rat be not deceived, it
　　was of another sort.

D. RAT. By God's Mother, thou and he
　　be a couple of subtle foxes!
Between you and Hodge I bear away
　　the boxes.[1]
Did not Diccon appoint the place where
　　thou shuldst stand to meet him?　　180

CHAT. Yes, by the Mass; and, if he came,
　　bade me not stick to speet [2] him.

D. RAT. God's sacrament, the villain
　　knave hath dressed us round about!
He is the cause of all this brawl, that
　　dirty, shitten lout!
When Gammer Gurton here complained,
　　and made a rueful moan,
I heard him swear that you had gotten
　　her needle that was gone;
And this to try, he furder said, he was
　　full loath; howbeit
He was content, with small ado, to
　　bring me where to see it.
And where ye sat, he said full certain,
　　if I wold follow his rede,
Into your house a privy way he wold me
　　guide and lead,
And where ye had it in your hands,
　　sewing about a clout;　　190
And set me in the back hole, thereby to
　　find you out.
And, whiles I sought a quietness, creep-
　　ing upon my knees,
I found the weight of your door bar for
　　my reward and fees.
Such is the luck that some men gets
　　while they begin to mell [3]
In setting at one such as were out,
　　minding to make all well.

HODGE. Was not well blessed, gammer, to
　　scape that scour? [4] And chad been
　　there,
Then chad been dressed, belike, as ill,
　　by the Mass, as Gaffer Vicar.

BAILY. Marry, sir, here is a sport alone.
　　I looked for such an end.
If Diccon had not played the knave,
　　this had been soon amend.

[1] Blows.
[2] Spit, *i.e.*, beat with a spit.
[3] Meddle.　　　　　　[4] Scouring, beating.

My gammer here he made a fool, and
　　dressed her as she was;　　200
And Goodwife Chat he set to scole,[5]
　　till both parts cried "alas";
And D[octor] Rat was not behind, whiles
　　Chat his crown did pare;
I wold the knave had been stark blind,
　　if Hodge had not his share!

HODGE. Cham meetly well sped already
　　amongs; cham dressed like a colt!
And chad not had the better wit, chad
　　been made a dolt.

BAILY. [*To Scapethrift.*] Sir knave, make
　　haste Diccon were here; fetch him
　　wherever he be! 　　[*Exit Scapethrift.*]

CHAT. Fie on the villain, fie, fie, that
　　makes us thus agree!

GAMMER. Fie on him, knave, with all my
　　heart! Now fie! and fie again!

D. RAT. "Now fie on him!" may I best
　　say, whom he hath almost slain.

[Enter Diccon, led in by Scapethrift.]

BAILY. Lo, where he cometh at hand.
　　Belike he was not far!　　210
Diccon, here be two or three thy com-
　　pany cannot spare.

DICCON. God bless you—and you may
　　be blessed, so many all at once!

CHAT. Come, knave, it were a good deed
　　to geld thee, by Cock's bones!
Seest not thy handiwark? Sir Rat, can
　　ye forbear [6] him?
　　　　　[Doctor Rat strikes Diccon.]

DICCON. A vengeance on those hands
　　light, for my hands came not near
　　him!
The whoreson priest hath lift the pot [7]
　　in some of these alewives' chairs
That his head wold not serve him, be-
　　like, to come down the stairs.

BAILY. Nay, soft! Thou mayst not play
　　the knave and have this language
　　too!
If thou thy tongue bridle awhile, the
　　better mayst thou do.
Confess the truth, as I shall ask, and
　　cease awhile to fable;　　220
And for thy fault, I promise thee, thy
　　handling shall be reasonable.
Hast thou not made a lie or two to set
　　these two by the ears?

[5] School.　　[6] Tolerate, spare.　　[7] Tankard.

Diccon. What if I have? Five hundred
     such have I seen within these seven
     years.
  I am sorry for nothing else but that I
     see not the sport
  Which was between them when they
     met, as they themselves report.
Baily. The greatest thing—Master Rat!
     Ye see how he is dressed!
Diccon. What devil need he be groping
     so deep in Goodwife Chat's hens'
     nest?
Baily. Yea, but it was thy drift to bring
     him into the briers.
Diccon. God's bread! hath not such an
     old fool wit to save his ears?
  He showeth himself herein, ye see, so
     very a cox [1]   230
  The cat was not so madly allured by the
     fox
  To run into the snares was set for him,
     doubtless;
  For he leaped in for mice, and this Sir
     John for madness.
D. Rat. Well, and ye shift no better, ye
     losel, lither [2] and lazy,
  I will go near, for this, to make ye leap
     at a daisy. [3]
  In the king's name, Master Baily, I
     charge you set him fast!
Diccon. What, fast at cards, or fast on
     sleep? It is the thing I did last.
D. Rat. Nay, fast in fetters, false varlet,
     according to thy deeds!
Baily. Master Doctor, there is no remedy;
     I must entreat you, needs,
  Some other kind of punishment.
D. Rat.   Nay, by All Hallows,   240
  His punishment, if I may judge, shall
     be naught else but the gallows.
Baily. That were too sore. A spiritual
     man to be so extreme!
D. Rat. Is he worthy any better, sir?
     How do ye judge and deem?
Baily. I grant him worthy punishment,
     but in no wise so great.
Gammer. It is a shame, ich tell you plain,
     for such false knaves entreat!
  He has almost undone us all; that is as
     true as steel.
  And yet for all this great ado cham
     never the near my neele!

[1] Fool.   [2] Worthless, idle.   [3] *I.e.*, be hanged.

Baily. Canst thou not say anything to
     that, Diccon, with least or most?
Diccon. Yea, marry, sir, thus much I
     can say well: the needle is lost!
Baily. Nay, canst not thou tell which
     way that needle may be found?   250
Diccon. No, by my fay, sir, though I
     might have an hundred pound.
Hodge. Thou liar, lickdish,[4] didst not say
     the neele wold be gitten? =
Diccon. No, Hodge, by the same token
     you were [6] that time beshitten
  For fear of Hobgobling—you wot well
     what I mean;
  As long as it is sence,[7] I fear me yet ye
     be scarce clean.
Baily. Well, Master Rat, you must both
     learn and teach us to forgeve.[8]
  Since Diccon hath confession made and
     is so clean shreve,[9]
  If ye to me consent, to amend this heavy
     chance
  I will enjoin him here some open kind of
     penance,
  Of this condition. Where ye know my
     fee is twenty pence   260
  For the bloodshed, [10] I am agreed with
     you here to dispense.
  Ye shall go quite,[11] so that ye grant the
     matter now to run
  To end with mirth among us all, even
     as it was begun.
Chat. Say yea, Master Vicar, and he shall
     sure confess to be your debtor,
  And all we that be here present will
     love you much the better.
D. Rat. My part is the worst; but, since
     you all hereon agree,
  Go even to,[12] Master Baily—let it be so
     for me!
Baily. How sayest thou, Diccon? Art
     content this shall on me depend?
Diccon. Go to, M[aster] Baily, say on
     your mind. I know ye are my friend.
Baily. Then mark ye well to recom-
     pense this thy former action,   270
  Because thou hast offended all, to make
     them satisfaction,

[4] Scullion.   [5] Gotten.
[6] Dodsley's reading. Original reads *where*.
[7] Since, past.
[8] Forgive; a common spelling retained here for
the rime.   [11] Quit, free.
[9] Shriven.   [12] Go ahead then.
[10] Case involving violence.

Before their faces here kneel down, and
as [1] I shall thee teach.
For thou shalt take an [2] oath of Hodge's
leather breech:
First, for Master Doctor, upon pain of
his curse,
Where he will pay for all, thou never
draw thy purse,
And when ye meet at one pot, he shall
have the first pull,
And thou shalt never offer him the cup
but it be full;
To Goodwife Chat thou shalt be sworn,
even on the same wise,
If she refuse thy money once, never to
offer it twice;
Thou shalt be bound by the same, here
as thou dost take it,   280
When thou mayst drink of free cost,
thou never forsake it;
For Gammer Gurton's sake, again sworn
shalt thou be,
To help her to her needle again, if it do
lie in thee;
And likewise be bound, by the virtue of
that,
To be of good abearing [3] to Gib, her
great cat;
Last of all, for Hodge, the oath to scan,
Thou shalt never take him for fine
gentleman.
HODGE. [*Stooping over.*] Come on, fellow
Diccon! Chall be even with thee now!
BAILY. Thou wilt not stick to do this,
Diccon, I trow?
DICCON. No, by my father's skin; my
hand down I lay it!   290
Look! As I have promised, I will not
deny [4] it.
But, Hodge, take good heed now thou
do not beshit me!
And gave him a good blow on the buttock.
HODGE. Gog's heart! Thou false villain,
dost thou bite me?
BAILY. What, Hodge, doth he hurt thee
or ever he begin?
HODGE. He thrust me into the buttock
with a bodkin or a pin!
                    [*He draws out the needle.*]
I say, gammer! gammer!

GAMMER.   How now, Hodge? How
now?
HODGE. God's malt, Gammer Gurton!
GAMMER.   Thou art mad, ich trow!
HODGE. Will you see the devil, gam-
mer?
GAMMER.   The devil, son? God
bless us!
HODGE. Chould ich were hanged, gam-
mer!
GAMMER.   Marry, see, ye might
dress us—
HODGE. Chave it, by the Mass, gammer!
GAMMER.   What, not my neele,
Hodge?   300
HODGE. Your neele, gammer, your neele!
GAMMER.   No, fie, dost but dodge! [5]
HODGE. Cha' found your neele, gammer!
Here in my hand be it!
GAMMER. For all the loves on earth,
Hodge, let me see it!
HODGE. Soft, gammer!
GAMMER.   Good Hodge!
HODGE.   Soft, ich say; tarry awhile!
GAMMER. Nay, sweet Hodge, say truth,
and do not me beguile!
HODGE. Cham sure on it, ich warrant
you it goes no more astray.
GAMMER. Hodge, when I speak so fair,
wilt still say me nay?
HODGE. Go near the light, gammer.
This—well, in faith, good luck!—
Chwas almost undone, 'twas so far in
my buttock!
GAMMER. 'Tis mine own dear neele,
Hodge, sikerly [6] I wot!   310
HODGE. Cham I not a good son, gam-
mer, cham I not?
GAMMER. Christ's blessing light on thee!
Hast made me forever!
HODGE. Ich knew that ich must find it,
else choud 'a' [7] had it never!
CHAT. By my troth, Gossip Gurton, I
am even as glad
As though I mine own self as good a
turn had!
BAILY. And I, by my conscience, to see
it so come forth,
Rejoice so much at it as three needles
be worth!
D. RAT. I am no whit sorry to see you
so rejoice!

[1] In the manner that.
[2] Dodsley's reading. Original reads *on*.
[3] Bearing, behavior.
[4] Deny.

[5] Trick me.   [7] I would have.
[6] Truly.

DICCON. Nor I much the gladder for all
  this noise!
  Yet say, "Gramercy, Diccon," for
  springing of the game.   320
GAMMER. Gramercy, Diccon, twenty
  times! O, how glad cham!
  If that chould do so much, your masterdom to come hether,
  Master Rat, Goodwife Chat, and Diccon, together—
  Cha' but one halfpenny, as far as ich
  know it,
  And chill not rest this night till ich
  bestow it.
  If ever ye love me, let us go in and
  drink!

BAILY. I am content, if the rest think as
  I think.
  Master Rat, it shall be best for you if
  we so do;
  Then shall you warm you and dress your-
  self too.
DICCON. Soft, sirs, take us with you; the
  company shall be the more!   330
  As proud comes behind, they say, as any
  goes before!— [Addresses the audience.]
  But now, my good masters, since we
  must be gone
  And leave you behind us here, all alone—
  Since at our last ending thus merry we be,
  For Gammer Gurton's needle sake let
  us have a plaudity!

FINIS, GURTON. PERUSED AND ALLOWED, ETC.

THOMAS NORTON AND THOMAS SACKVILLE

The Tragedy of Gorboduc, historically significant as the first regular English tragedy and the first English play to be written in blank verse, was acted by the gentlemen of the Inner Temple during their Christmas festival in 1561/2 and again before Queen Elizabeth at Whitehall Palace, January 18, 1561/2. It was surreptitiously printed by William Griffith in 1565, but an authorized edition was issued by John Day in 1570. In 1590 Edward Allde published a reprint of the edition of 1565. The title-page of the edition of 1565 informs us that three acts were by Thomas Norton and the last two by Thomas Sackville.

Thomas Norton, born in 1532, probably attended Cambridge University, was admitted to the Inner Temple in 1555, became a successful lawyer, and served as a member of parliament in 1571, 1572, and 1580. Much of his time was devoted to literature, however. He wrote Latin and English poetry, including versions of twenty-eight Psalms printed in the Psalter of Sternhold and Hopkins. He produced a number of controversial pamphlets against the Catholics and a political tract on a Catholic rebellion under Elizabeth which has some interest in view of the theme of *Gorboduc*. He also translated various works, among them Calvin's *Institution of Christian Religion*. In spite of his share in *Gorboduc*, his Puritan connection led him in later years to open hostility toward the stage. He died in 1584.

Thomas Sackville, born in 1536, was a son of Sir Richard Sackville, a first cousin to Anne Boleyn, mother of Queen Elizabeth. Nothing is known of his academic career. In 1563 he contributed to *The Mirror for Magistrates* his well known "Induction" and "The Complaint of Henry Duke of Buckingham," which gave promise of a brilliant literary future. But he soon forsook literature for a political career. After an extensive tour of Europe he was called home in 1566 by his father's death to become heir to a vast estate. He became a special favorite of the queen and was rapidly advanced to a distinguished career of public service. He was knighted and raised to the peerage June 8, 1567, served later on various diplomatic missions, was elected in 1591 to the chancellorship of the University of Oxford, and in 1603 became a member of the privy council and was made lord treasurer for life. In 1604 he was created Earl of Dorset. He died at the council table at Whitehall, April 19, 1608.

For the main elements of the story the authors follow the account of King Gorboduc in Geoffrey of Monmouth's *Historia Regum Britanniæ*, although their immediate source may have been Grafton's *Chronicle* (1556), which follows Geoffrey's version closely. For their dramatic model they chose the Senecan tragedy, a fact which accounts for the division into five acts, the general rhetorical quality of the style with emphasis on balance of structure, the sententious moralizing, the use of the chorus at the end of each act, and the exclusion of violence from the stage by having it announced by a messenger (*Nuntius*). It is noteworthy, however, that the authors drew their story from English legendary history and that they departed from precedent in disregarding the unities of time and place. Italian adaptations of Seneca may have suggested the use of blank verse, and the *intermedii* (allegorical representations between the acts) in Italian tragedy may have furnished the idea of the dumb show, but blank verse had already appeared in Surrey's translation of the *Æneid*, published in 1557, and the dumb show may have been a native development.

Sackville and Norton, both of them prominent members of Queen Elizabeth's first parliament, were keenly interested in the problem of providing for her successor, and they made this tragic story from the apocryphal history of England the vehicle for a special warning to her of the dangers of civil war in its most terrible aspects if she died without definite provision for the succession (see particularly Act V). The warning is set, however, in a general body of political discussion which reflects ideas common in classical and humanistic treatises. Senecan tragedy, didactic in its nature, readily lent itself to this type of moralizing.

The text of the play is based on the second edition, that of 1570, as reprinted by J. W. Cunliffe in his *Early Classical Tragedies* (Oxford, 1912).

THE TRAGEDY OF [GORBODUC;
OR OF][1] FERREX AND PORREX[2]

BY

THOMAS NORTON AND THOMAS SACKVILLE

THE P[RINTER] TO THE READER

Where this tragedy was for furniture of part of the grand Christmas in the Inner Temple first written about nine years ago by the Right Honorable Thomas, now Lord Buckhurst, and by T. Norton, and after showed before her majesty, and never intended by the authors thereof to be published; yet one W. G., getting a copy thereof at some young man's hand that lacked a little money and much discretion, in [10 the last great plague, an[no] 1565, about five years past, while the said lord was out of England, and T. Norton far out of London, and neither of them both made privy, put it forth exceedingly corrupted—even as if by means of a broker, for hire, he should have enticed into his house a fair maid and done her villainy, and after all-to[3] bescratched her face, torn her apparel, bewrayed and disfigured her, and then [20 thrust her out of doors dishonested. In such plight, after long wandering, she came at length home to the sight of her friends, who scant knew her but by a few tokens and marks remaining. They—the authors, I mean—though they were very much displeased that she so ran abroad without leave, whereby she caught her shame, as many wantons do, yet seeing the case, as it is, remediless, have for common hon- [30 esty and shamefastness new appareled, trimmed, and attired her in such form as she was before. In which better form since she hath come to me, I have harbored her for her friends' sake and her own; and I do not doubt her parents, the authors, will not now be discontent that she go abroad among you, good readers, so it be in honest company. For she is by my encouragement and others' somewhat less ashamed of [40 the dishonesty done to her, because it was by fraud and force. If she be welcome among you, and gently entertained, in favor of the house from whence she is descended and of her own nature courteously disposed to offend no man, her friends will thank you for it. If not, but that she shall be still reproached with her former mishap, or quarreled at by envious persons, she, poor gentlewoman, will surely play [50 Lucrece's part, and of herself die for shame; and I shall wish that she had tarried still at home with me, where she was welcome, for she did never put me to more charge but this one poor black gown lined with white that I have now given her to go abroad among you withal.

THE ARGUMENT OF THE TRAGEDY[4]

Gorboduc, King of Britain, divided his realm in his lifetime to his sons, Ferrex and Porrex. The sons fell to dissension. The younger killed the elder. The mother, that more dearly loved the elder, for revenge killed the younger. The people, moved with the cruelty of the fact,[5] rose

Same Was Showed on Stage before the Queen's Majesty, about Nine Years Past, viz., the xviii Day of January, 1561. By the Gentlemen of the Inner Temple. Seen and Allowed, etc."

[3] Thoroughly.

[4] In the original this argument, or synopsis of plot, is printed on the back of the title-page.

[5] Deed.

---

[1] Added by Adams. The title of the 1565 edn. runs: "The Tragedy of Gorboduc, Whereof Three Acts Were Written by Thomas Norton, and the Two Last by Thomas Sackville."

[2] The title continues: "Set Forth without Addition or Alteration but Altogether As the

in rebellion and slew both father and mother. The nobility assembled and most terribly destroyed the rebels. And [10 afterwards, for want of issue of the prince, whereby the succession of the crown be-came uncertain, they fell to civil war, in which both they and many of their issues were slain, and the land for a long time almost desolate and miserably wasted.

THE NAMES OF THE SPEAKERS

GORBODUC, *King of Great Britain.*
VIDENA, *queen and wife to King Gorboduc.*
FERREX, *elder son to King Gorboduc.*
PORREX, *younger son to King Gorboduc.*
CLOTYN, *Duke of Cornwall.*
FERGUS, *Duke of Albany.*
MANDUD, *Duke of Logris.*
GWENARD, *Duke of Cumberland.*
EUBULUS, *secretary to the king.*
AROSTUS, *a counselor to the king.*
DORDAN, *a counselor assigned by the king to his eldest son, Ferrex.*

PHILANDER, *a counselor assigned by the king to his youngest son, Porrex. Both being of the old king's counsel before.*
HERMON, *a parasite remaining with Ferrex.*
TYNDAR, *a parasite remaining with Porrex.*
NUNTIUS, *a messenger of the elder brother's death.*
NUNTIUS, *a messenger of Duke Fergus' rising in arms.*
MARCELLA, *a lady of the queen's privy-chamber.*
CHORUS, *four ancient and sage men of Britain.*

[SCENE: *Britain.*

TIME: *Legendary.*]

THE ORDER OF THE DUMB SHOW BEFORE THE FIRST ACT, AND THE SIGNIFICA-TION THEREOF

First, the music of violins began to play, during which came in upon the stage six wild men, clothed in leaves. Of whom the first bare in his neck a fagot of small sticks, which they all, both sev-erally and together, assayed with all their strength to break; but it could not be broken by them. At the length one of them pulled out one of the sticks and brake it, and the rest, plucking out all the other sticks one after another, did easily break them, the same being sev-ered which, being conjoined, they had before attempted in vain. After they had this done, they departed the stage, and the music ceased. Hereby was sig-nified that a state knit in unity doth continue strong against all force, but, being divided, is easily destroyed; as befell upon Duke Gorboduc dividing his land to his two sons, which he before held in monarchy, and upon the dis-sension of the brethren, to whom it was divided.

ACTUS PRIMUS. SCENA PRIMA.

[*A room in Gorboduc's palace.*]

Viden[a], Ferrex.

VID. The silent night, that brings the quiet pause
From painful travails of the weary day,
Prolongs my careful [1] thoughts, and makes me blame
The slow Aurore, that so for love or shame
Doth long delay to show her blushing face;
And now the day renews my griefful plaint.

FER. My gracious lady and my mother dear,
Pardon my grief for your so grievéd mind
To ask what cause tormenteth so your heart.

VID. So great a wrong and so unjust de-spite,　　　10
Without all cause against all course of kind! [2]

[1] Full of care.
[2] Nature.

FER. Such causeless wrong and so unjust
despite

May have redress or, at the least, revenge.

VID. Neither, my son; such is the froward
will,

The person such, such my mishap and
thine.

FER. Mine know I none, but grief for
your distress.

VID. Yes, mine for thine, my son.   A
father? No.

In kind a father, not in kindliness.

FER. My father? Why, I know nothing
at all

Wherein I have misdone unto his
grace.   20

VID. Therefore, the more unkind to thee
and me.

For, knowing well, my son, the tender
love

That I have ever borne and bear to thee,

He, grieved thereat, is not content alone

To spoil thee of my sight, my chiefest
joy;

But thee, of thy birthright and heritage,

Causeless, unkindly, and in wrongful
wise,

Against all law and right, he will bereave:

Half of his kingdom he will give away.

FER. To whom?

VID.   Even to Porrex, his younger son; 30

Whose growing pride I do so sore suspect

That, being raised to equal rule with thee,

Methinks I see his envious heart to swell,

Filled with disdain and with ambitious
hope.

The end the gods do know, whose altars I

Full oft have made in vain of cattle slain

To send the sacred smoke to heaven's
throne,

For thee, my son, if things do so succeed,

As now my jealous mind misdeemeth
sore.

FER. Madam, leave care and careful plaint
for me.   40

Just hath my father been to every wight;

His first unjustice he will not extend

To me, I trust, that give no cause thereof;

My brother's pride shall hurt himself,
not me.

VID. So grant the gods!   But yet thy
father so

Hath firmly fixéd his unmovéd mind

That plaints and prayers can no whit
avail;

For those have I assayed, but even this
day

He will endeavor to procure assent

Of all his council to his fond devise.[1] 50

FER. Their ancestors from race to race[2]
have borne

True faith to my forefathers and their
seed;

I trust they eke will bear the like to me.

VID. There resteth all.   But if they fail
thereof,

And if the end bring forth an ill success,

On them and theirs the mischief shall
befall,

And so I pray the gods requite it them;

And so they will, for so is wont to be.

When lords and trusted rulers under
kings,

To please the present fancy of the
prince,   60

With wrong transpose the course of
governance,

Murders, mischief, or civil sword at
length,

Or mutual treason, or a just revenge,

When right succeeding line returns again,

By Jove's just judgment and deservéd
wrath,

Brings them to cruel and reproachful
death,

And roots their names and kindreds from
the earth.

FER. Mother, content you, you shall see
the end.

VID. The end? Thy end, I fear! Jove
end me first!   [Exeunt.]

ACTUS PRIMUS. SCENA SECUNDA.

[The council chamber in Gorboduc's palace.]

Gorboduc, Arostus, Philander, Eubulus.

GORB. My lords, whose grave advice and
faithful aid

Have long upheld my honor and my
realm,

And brought me to this age from tender
years,

Guiding so great estate with great renowm,

_____
[1] Foolish design.
[2] From generation to generation.

Now more importeth me [1] than erst [2] to
   use
Your faith and wisdom, whereby yet I
   reign;
That, when by death my life and rule
   shall cease,
The kingdom yet may with unbroken
   course
Have certain prince, by whose undoubted
   right
Your wealth and peace may stand in
   quiet stay;   10
And eke that they whom nature hath
   prepared
In time to take my place in princely
   seat,
While in their father's time their pliant
   youth
Yields to the frame of skillful governance,
May so be taught and trained in noble
   arts
As what their fathers, which have
   reigned before,
Have with great fame derivéd down to
   them,
With honor they may leave unto their
   seed;
And not be thought, for their unworthy
   life,
And for their lawless swerving out of
   kind,   20
Worthy to lose what law and kind them
   gave;
But that they may preserve the common
   peace,
The cause that first began and still main-
   tains
The lineal course of kings' inheritance,
For me, for mine, for you, and for the
   state
Whereof both I and you have charge and
   care.
Thus do I mean to use your wonted faith
To me and mine and to your native land.
My lords, be plain without all wry [3] re-
   spect
Or poisonous craft to speak in pleasing
   wise,   30
Lest, as the blame of ill-succeeding things
Shall light on you, so light the harms
   also.

AROS. Your good acceptance so, most
   noble king,
Of such our faithfulness as heretofore
We have employed in duties to your
   grace
And to this realm, whose worthy head
   you are,
Well proves that neither you mistrust
   at all,
Nor we shall need in boasting wise to
   show
Our truth to you, nor yet our wakeful
   care
For you, for yours, and for our native
   land.   40
Wherefore, O king—I speak as one for all,
Sith [4] all as one do bear you egal [5] faith—
Doubt not to use our counsels and our
   aids,
Whose honors, goods, and lives are whole
   avowed
To serve, to aid, and to defend your
   grace.
GORB. My lords, I thank you all. This is
   the case:
Ye know, the gods, who have the sov-
   ereign care
For kings, for kingdoms, and for com-
   monweals,
Gave me two sons in my more lusty age,
Who now in my decaying years are
   grown   50
Well towards riper state of mind and
   strength
To take in hand some greater princely
   charge.
As yet they live and spend [their] [6] hope-
   ful days
With me and with their mother here in
   court.
Their age now asketh other place and
   trade,
And mine also doth ask another change—
Theirs to more travail, mine to greater
   ease.
When fatal death shall end my mortal
   life,
My purpose is to leave unto them twain
The realm divided into two sundry
   parts: 60
The one, Ferrex, mine elder son, shall
   have;

---

[1] It is more important for me.
[2] Formerly.   [3] Twisted, dissembled.

[4] Since.   [5] Equal.   [6] From 1565 edn.

The other shall the younger, Porrex, rule.
That both my purpose may more firmly
   stand,
And eke that they may better rule their
   charge,
I mean forthwith to place them in the
   same,
That in my life they may both learn to
   rule,
And I may joy to see their ruling well.
This is, in sum, what I would have ye
   weigh:
First, whether ye allow my whole devise,
And think it good for me, for them, for
   you,   70
And for our country, mother of us all;
And if ye like it and allow it well,
Then for their guiding and their gov-
   ernance
Show forth such means of circumstance
As ye think meet to be both known and
   kept.
Lo, this is all. Now tell me your advice.
AROS. And this is much, and asketh great
   advice.
But for my part, my sovereign lord and
   king,
This do I think: your majesty doth know
How under you, in justice and in
   peace,   80
Great wealth and honor long we have
   enjoyed,
So as we cannot seem with greedy minds
To wish for change of prince or gov-
   ernance;
But, if we like your purpose and devise,
Our liking must be deeméd to proceed
Of rightful reason and of heedful care,
Not for ourselves, but for the common
   state,
Sith our own state doth need no better
   change.
I think in all as erst your grace hath
   said.
First, when you shall unload your aged
   mind   90
Of heavy care and troubles manifold,
And lay the same upon my lords, your
   sons,
Whose growing years may bear the bur-
   den long—
And long I pray the gods to grant it
   so!—
And in your life, while you shall so behold

Their rule, their virtues, and their noble
   deeds,
Such as their kind behighteth [1] to us all,
Great be the profits that shall grow
   thereof.
Your age in quiet shall the longer last;
Your lasting age shall be their longer
   stay;   100
For cares of kings that rule as you have
   ruled,
For public wealth and not for private joy,
Do waste man's life and hasten crooked
   age,
With furrowed face and with enfeebled
   limbs,
To draw on creeping death a swifter pace.
They two, yet young, shall bear the
   parted reign
With greater ease than one, now old,
   alone
Can wield the whole, for whom much
   harder is
With lessened strength the double weight
   to bear.
Your eye, your counsel, and the grave
   regard   110
Of father, yea, of such a father's name,
Now at beginning of their sundered reign,
When is the hazard of their whole success,
Shall bridle so their force of youthful
   heats
And so restrain the rage of insolence,
Which most assails the young and noble
   minds,
And so shall guide and train in tempered
   stay
Their yet green bending wits with rev-
   erend awe,
As—now inured with virtues at the
   first—
Custom, O king, shall bring delightful-
   ness.   120
By use of virtue, vice shall grow in hate.
But, if you so dispose it that the day
Which ends your life shall first begin
   their reign,
Great is the peril what will be the end,
When such beginning of such liberties,
Void of such stays as in your life do lie,
Shall leave them free to randon [2] of their
   will,
An open prey to traitorous flattery,
The greatest pestilence of noble youth;

[1] Promises.   [2] Random. rove.

Which peril shall be past if, in your
    life, 130
Their tempered youth with aged father's
    awe
Be brought in ure [1] of skillful stayédness;
And, in your life, their lives disposéd so
Shall length your noble life in joyfulness.
Thus think I that your grace hath wisely
    thought,
And that your tender care of common
    weal [2]
Hath bred this thought, so to divide
    your land,
And plant your sons to bear the present
    rule,
While you yet live to see their ruling well,
That you may longer live by joy
    therein. 140
What furder [3] means behooveful are and
    meet;
At greater leisure may your grace devise,
When all have said, and when we be
    agreed
If this be best, to part the realm in twain,
And place your sons in present govern-
    ment;
Whereof, as I have plainly said my mind,
So would I hear the rest of all my lords.
PHIL. In part I think as hath been said
    before;
In part, again, my mind is otherwise.
As for dividing of this realm in twain, 150
And lotting out the same in egal parts
To either of my lords, your grace's sons,
That think I best for this your realm's
    behoof,
For profit and advancement of your sons,
And for your comfort and your honor eke.
But so to place them while your life do
    last,
To yield to them your royal governance,
To be above them only in the name
Of father, not in kingly state also,
I think not good for you, for them, nor
    us. 160
This kingdom, since the bloody civil field
Where Morgan slain did yield his con-
    quered part
Unto his cousin's sword in Camberland,
Containeth all that whilom [4] did suffice
Three noble sons of your forefather
    Brute;

So your two sons it may suffice also.
The mo [5] the stronger, if they gree [6] in
    one.
The smaller compass that the realm doth
    hold,
The easier is the sway thereof to weld,[7]
The nearer justice to the wrongéd
    poor, 170
The smaller charge, and yet enough for
    one.
And when the region is divided so
That brethren be the lords of either part,
Such strength doth nature knit between
    them both,
In sundry bodies by conjoinéd love,
That, not as two, but one of doubled
    force,
Each is to other as a sure defense;
The nobleness and glory of the one
Doth sharp the courage of the other's
    mind,
With virtuous envy to contend for
    praise. 180
And such an egalness hath nature made
Between the brethren of one father's
    seed
As an unkindly wrong it seems to be
To throw the brother subject under feet
Of him whose peer he is by course of
    kind;
And nature, that did make this egalness,
Oft so repineth at so great a wrong
That oft she raiseth up a grudging grief
In younger brethren at the elder's state,
Whereby both towns and kingdoms have
    been razed, 190
And famous stocks of royal blood de-
    stroyed.
The brother, that should be the brother's
    aid,
And have a wakeful care for his defense,
Gapes for his death, and blames the
    lingering years
That draw not forth his end with faster
    course;
And, oft impatient of so long delays,
With hateful slaughter he prevents [8] the
    fates,
And heaps a just reward for brother's
    blood,
With endless vengeance, on his stock for
    aye.

[1] Use, practice.   [3] Further.
[2] Welfare.   [4] Formerly.
[5] More.   [7] Wield, govern.
[6] Agree.   [8] Anticipates.

Such mischiefs here are wisely met
 withal, 200
If egal state may nourish egal love,
Where none hath cause to grudge at
 other's good.
But now the head to stoop beneath them
 both,
Ne [1] kind, ne reason, ne good order bears.
And oft it hath been seen, where nature's
 course
Hath been perverted in disordered wise,
When fathers cease to know that they
 should rule,
The children cease to know they should
 obey;
And often over-kindly tenderness
Is mother of unkindly stubbornness. 210
I speak not this in envy or reproach,
As if I grudged the glory of your sons,
Whose honor I beseech the gods increase;
Nor yet as if I thought there did remain
So filthy cankers in their noble breasts,
Whom I esteem—which is their greatest
 praise—
Undoubted children of so good a king.
Only I mean to show by certain rules,
Which kind hath graft within the mind
 of man,
That nature hath her order and her
 course, 220
Which, being broken, doth corrupt the
 state
Of minds and things, even in the best of
 all.
My lords, your sons, may learn to rule
 of you;
Your own example in your noble court
Is fittest guider of their youthful years.
If you desire to see some present joy
By sight of their well ruling in your life,
See them obey—so shall you see them
 rule.
Whoso obeyeth not with humbleness
Will rule with outrage and with inso-
 lence. 230
Long may they rule, I do beseech the
 gods,
But long may they learn, ere they begin
 to rule.
If kind and fates would suffer,[2] I would
 wish
Them aged princes and immortal kings.
Wherefore, most noble king, I well assent

Between your sons that you divide your
 realm,
And, as in kind, so match them in degree.
But, while the gods prolong your royal
 life,
Prolong your reign; for thereto [3] live you
 here,
And therefore have the gods so long
 forborne 240
To join you to themselves, that still you
 might
Be prince and father of our commonweal.
They, when they see your children ripe
 to rule,
Will make them room, and will remove
 you hence,
That yours, in right ensuing of your life,
May rightly honor your immortal name.
Eub. Your wonted true regard of faithful
 hearts
Makes me, O king, the bolder to presume
To speak what I conceive within my
 breast,
Although the same do not agree at all 250
With that which other here my lords
 have said,
Nor which yourself have seeméd best to
 like.
Pardon I crave, and that my words be
 deemed
To flow from hearty zeal unto your grace,
And to the safety of your commonweal.
To part your realm unto my lords, your
 sons,
I think not good for you, ne yet for them,
But worst of all for this our native land.
Within one land one single rule is best:
Divided reigns do make divided
 hearts, 260
But peace preserves the country and the
 prince.
Such is in man the greedy mind to reign,
So great is his desire to climb aloft,
In worldly stage the stateliest parts to
 bear,
That faith and justice and all kindly love
Do yield unto desire of sovereignty,
Where egal state doth raise an egal hope
To win the thing that either would attain.
Your grace rememb'reth how in passéd
 years
The mighty Brute, first prince of all this
 land. 270

---

[1] Not, nor. [2] Allow. [3] For this purpose.

Possessed the same and ruled it well in
  one;
He, thinking that the compass did suf-
  fice
For his three sons three kingdoms eke to
  make,
Cut it in three, as you would now in
  twain.
But how much British blood hath since
  been spilt
To join again the sundered unity,
What princes slain before their timely
  hour,
What waste of towns and people in the
  land,
What treasons heaped on murders and
  on spoils—
Whose just revenge even yet is scarcely
  ceased—   280
Ruthful remembrance is yet raw in mind.
The gods forbid the like to chance again!
And you, O king, give not the cause
  thereof.
My Lord Ferrex, your elder son, per-
  haps—
Whom kind and custom gives a rightful
  hope
To be your heir and to succeed your
  reign—
Shall think that he doth suffer greater
  wrong
Than he perchance will bear, if power
  serve.
Porrex, the younger, so upraised in state,
Perhaps in courage will be raised also. 290
If flattery then, which fails not to assail
The tender minds of yet unskillful youth,
In one shall kindle and increase disdain,
And envy in the other's heart inflame,
This fire shall waste their love, their lives,
  their land,
And ruthful ruin shall destroy them both.
I wish not this, O king, so to befall,
But fear the thing that I do most abhor.
Give no beginning to so dreadful end;
Keep them in order and obedience,   300
And let them both, by now obeying you,
Learn such behavior as beseems their
  state—
The elder, mildness in his governance;
The younger, a yielding contentedness.
And keep them near unto your presence
  still,
That they, restrainéd by the awe of you,

May live in compass of well tempered
  stay,
And pass the perils of their youthful
  years.
Your aged life draws on to feebler time,
Wherein you shall less able be to bear
The travails that in youth you have sus-
  tained,   311
Both in your person's and your realm's
  defense.
If planting now your sons in furder parts,
You send them furder from your present
  reach,
Less shall you know how they them-
  selves demean;
Traitorous corrupters of their pliant
  youth
Shall have unspied a much more free
  access;
And, if ambition and inflamed disdain
Shall arm the one, the other, or them
  both,
To civil war or to usurping pride,   320
Late shall you rue that you ne recked [1]
  before.
Good is, I grant, of all to hope the best,
But not to live still [2] dreadless of the
  worst.
So trust the one that the other be fore-
  seen.
Arm not unskillfulness with princely
  power,
But you that long have wisely ruled the
  reins
Of royalty within your noble realm,
So hold them, while the gods for our
  avails [3]
Shall stretch the thread of your pro-
  longéd days.
Too soon he clamb [4] into the flaming
  car,   330
Whose want of skill did set the earth on
  fire.
Time and example of your noble grace
Shall teach your sons both to obey and
  rule.
When time hath taught them, time shall
  make them place,
The place that now is full; and so I pray
Long it remain to comfort of us all.
GORB. I take your faithful hearts in thank-
  ful part.

[1] Did not heed.   [3] Profit.
[2] Always.   [4] Climbed.

But, sith I see no cause to draw my mind
To fear the nature of my loving sons,
Or to misdeem that envy or disdain   340
Can there work hate where nature plant-
  eth love,
In one self purpose do I still abide.
My love extendeth egally to both;
My land sufficeth for them both also.
Humber shall part the marches [1] of their
  realms:
The southern part the elder shall possess;
The northern shall Porrex, the younger,
  rule.
In quiet I will pass mine aged days,
Free from the travail and the painful
  cares   349
That hasten age upon the worthiest kings.
But, lest the fraud, that ye do seem to
  fear,
Of flattering tongues, corrupt their tender
  youth,
And writhe them to the ways of youthful
  lust,
To climbing pride, or to revenging hate,
Or to neglecting of their careful charge
Lewdly to live in wanton recklessness,
Or to oppressing of the rightful cause,
Or not to wreak the wrongs done to the
  poor,
To tread down truth, or favor false
  deceit,
I mean to join to either of my sons   360
Some one of those whose long approvéd
  faith
And wisdom tried may well assure my
  heart
That mining fraud shall find no way to
  creep
Into their fencéd ears with grave advice.
This is the end; and so I pray you all
To bear my sons the love and loyalty
That I have found within your faithful
  breasts.
Aros. You nor your sons, our sovereign
  lord, shall want
Our faith and service while our lives do
  last.   [*Exeunt.*]

Chorus

When settled stay doth hold the royal
  throne   370
  In steadfast place, by known and
    doubtless [2] right,

And chiefly when descent on one alone
  Makes single and unparted reign to
    light,
Each change of course unjoints the whole
    estate,
And yields it thrall to ruin by debate. [3]

The strength that, knit by fast accord in
  one,
  Against all foreign power of mighty
    foes,
Could of itself defend itself alone,
  Disjoinéd once, the former force doth
    lose.
The sticks, that sundered brake so soon
  in twain,   380
In fagot bound attempted were in vain.

Oft tender mind that leads the partial eye
  Of erring parents in their children's
    love,
Destroys the wrongly lovéd child
    thereby.
  This doth the proud son of Apollo
    prove.
Who, rashly set in chariot of his sire,
Inflamed the parchéd earth with heav-
  en's fire.

And this great king, that doth divide
  his land
  And change the course of his descend-
    ing crown,
And yields the reign into his children's
  hand,   390
  From blissful state of joy and great
    renown,
A mirror shall become to princes all,
To learn to shun the cause of such a fall. [4]

The Order and Signification of the
  Dumb Show before the Second Act

*First, the music of cornets began to play,
during which came in upon the stage a
king accompanied with a number of his
nobility and gentlemen. And, after he
had placed himself in a chair of estate
prepared for him, there came and kneeled
before him a grave and aged gentleman,
and offered up a cup unto him of wine
in a glass, which the king refused. After*

[1] Borders.   [2] Undoubted.

[3] Strife.
[4] None of the choruses are divided into stanzas
in the original.

*him comes a brave and lusty young gentle-
man, and presents the king with a cup
of gold filled with poison, which the king
accepted, and, drinking the same, immediately fell down dead upon the stage,
and so was carried thence away by his
lords and gentlemen, and then the music
ceased. Hereby was signified that, as
glass by nature holdeth no poison, but is
clear and may easily be seen through ne
boweth* [1] *by any art, so a faithful counselor holdeth no treason, but is plain and
open, ne yieldeth to any undiscreet affection, but giveth wholesome counsel, which
the ill-advised prince refuseth. The delightful gold filled with poison betokeneth
flattery, which under fair seeming of
pleasant words beareth deadly poison,
which destroyeth* [2] *the prince that receiveth it. As befell in the two brethren,
Ferrex and Porrex, who, refusing the
wholesome advice of grave counselors,
credited these young parasites and
brought to themselves death and destruction thereby.*

Actus Secundus. Scena Prima.

[*The court of Ferrex.*]

Ferrex, Hermon, Dordan.

Fer. I marvel much what reason led the
    king,
My father, thus, without all my desert,
To reave me [3] half the kingdom, which
    by course
Of law and nature should remain to me.
Her. If you with stubborn and untaméd
    pride
Had stood against him in rebelling wise,
Or if with grudging mind you had envied
So slow a sliding of his aged years,
Or sought before your time to haste the
    course
Of fatal death upon his royal head,   10
Or stained your stock with murder of
    your kin,
Some face of reason might perhaps have
    seemed
To yield some likely cause to spoil ye
    thus.

[1] Bendeth.
[2] From 1565 edn. Original reads *destroyed.*
[3] Bereave me of, rob me of.

Fer. The wreakful [4] gods pour on my
    curséd head
Eternal plagues and never-dying woes,
The hellish prince adjudge my damnéd
    ghost
To Tantale's thirst, or proud Ixion's
    wheel,
Or cruel gripe [5] to gnaw my growing
    heart,
To during [6] torments and unquenchéd
    flames,
If ever I conceived so foul a thought, 20
To wish his end of life or yet of reign.
Dor. Ne yet your father, O most noble
    prince,
Did ever think so foul a thing of you;
For he, with more than father's tender
    love,
While yet the fates do lend him life to
    rule—
Who long might live to see your ruling
    well—
To you, my lord, and to his other son,
Lo, he resigns his realm and royalty;
Which never would so wise a prince have
    done
If he had once misdeemed that in your
    heart   30
There ever lodgéd so unkind a thought.
But tender love, my lord, and settled
    trust
Of your good nature and your noble mind
Made him to place you thus in royal
    throne,
And now to give you half his realm to
    guide;
Yea, and that half which, in abounding
    store
Of things that serve to make a wealthy
    realm,
In stately cities, and in fruitful soil,
In temperate breathing of the milder
    heaven,
In things of needful use, which friendly
    sea   40
Transports by traffic from the foreign
    parts,
In flowing wealth, in honor, and in force,
Doth pass the double value of the part
That Porrex hath allotted to his reign.
Such is your case, such is your father's
    love.

[4] Vengeful.   [5] Griffin.   [6] Enduring.

FER. Ah! love, my friends? Love wrongs
  not whom he loves!
DOR. Ne yet he wrongeth you that giveth
  you
  So large a reign ere that the course of time
  Bring you to kingdom by descended
  right,
  Which time perhaps might end your
  time before.   50
FER. Is this no wrong, say you, to reave
  from me
  My native right of half so great a realm,
  And thus to match his younger son with
  me
  In egal power and in as great degree?
  Yea, and what son? The son whose
  swelling pride
  Would never yield one point of reverence,
  When I, the elder and apparent heir,
  Stood in the likelihood to possess the
  whole;
  Yea, and that son which from his childish
  age
  Envieth mine honor and doth hate my
  life.   60
  What will he now do, when his pride, his
  rage,
  The mindful malice of his grudging heart
  Is armed with force, with wealth, and
  kingly state?
HER. Was this not wrong—yea, ill-advisèd
  wrong—
  To give so mad a man so sharp a sword,
  To so great peril of so great mishap,
  Wide open thus to set so large a way?
DOR. Alas, my lord, what griefful thing is
  this,
  That of your brother you can think so ill?
  I never saw him utter likely sign   70
  Whereby a man might see or once mis-
  deem
  Such hate of you ne such unyielding
  pride.
  Ill is their counsel, shameful be their end,
  That raising such mistrustful fear in you,
  Sowing the seed of such unkindly hate,
  Travail by treason to destroy you both.
  Wise is your brother and of noble hope,
  Worthy to wield a large and mighty
  realm.
  So much a stronger friend have you
  thereby,
  Whose strength is your strength if you
  gree in one.   80

HER. If nature and the gods had pinchèd
  so
  Their flowing bounty and their noble
  gifts
  Of princely qualities, from you, my lord,
  And poured them all at once in wasteful
  wise
  Upon your father's younger son alone,
  Perhaps there be [1] that in your preju-
  dice [2]
  Would say that birth should yield to
  worthiness.
  But sith in each good gift and princely art
  Ye are his match, and, in the chief of
  all,
  In mildness and in sober governance 90
  Ye far surmount; and sith there is in you
  Sufficing skill and hopeful towardness
  To weld the whole and match your
  elder's praise,
  I see no cause why ye should lose the
  half.
  Ne would I wish you yield to such a loss,
  Lest your mild sufferance of so great a
  wrong
  Be deemèd cowardish and simple dread,
  Which shall give courage to the fiery
  head
  Of your young brother to invade the
  whole.
  While yet therefore sticks in the people's
  mind   100
  The loathèd wrong of your disheritance;
  And ere your brother have, by settled
  power,
  By guileful cloak of an alluring show,
  Got him some force and favor in the
  realm;
  And, while the noble queen, your mother,
  lives,
  To work and practice all for your avail,
  Attempt redress by arms, and wreak
  yourself
  Upon his life that gaineth by your loss,
  Who now to shame of you and grief of us
  In your own kingdom triumphs over
  you.   110
  Show now your courage meet for kingly
  state,
  That they which have avowed to spend
  their goods,
  Their lands, their lives and honors in
  your cause,

[1] Supply *those*.   [2] To your damage.

May be the bolder to maintain your part,
When they do see that coward fear in you
Shall not betray ne fail their faithful
hearts.
If once the death of Porrex end the strife,
And pay the price of his usurpéd reign,
Your mother shall persuade [1] the angry
king.
The lords, your friends, eke shall appease
his rage; 120
For they be wise, and well they can
foresee
That ere long time your aged father's
death
Will bring a time when you shall well
requite
Their friendly favor or their hateful spite,
Yea, or their slackness to advance your
cause.
"Wise men do not so hang on passing
state
Of present princes, chiefly in their age,
But they will further cast their reaching
eye,
To view and weigh the times and reigns
to come." [2]
Ne is it likely, though the king be
wroth, 130
That he yet will or that the realm will
bear
Extreme revenge upon his only son;
Or, if he would, what one is he that dare
Be minister to such an enterprise?
And here you be now placéd in your
own,
Amid your friends, your vassals, and your
strength.
We shall defend and keep your person
safe,
Till either counsel turn his tender mind,
Or age or sorrow end his weary days.
But, if the fear of gods and secret
grudge 140
Of nature's law, repining at the fact,
Withhold your courage from so great
attempt,
Know ye that lust of kingdoms hath no
law.
The gods do bear and well allow in kings
The thinges [3] they abhor in rascal routs. [4]

"When kings on slender quarrels run to
wars,
And then in cruel and unkindly wise
Command thefts, rapes, murders of in-
nocents,
The spoil of towns, ruins of mighty
realms,
Think you such princes do suppose them-
selves 150
Subject to laws of kind and fear of gods?"
Murders and violent thefts in private
men
Are heinous crimes and full of foul re-
proach,
Yet none offense, but decked with glo-
rious name
Of noble conquests in the hands of kings.
But, if you like not yet so hot devise,
Ne list to take such vantage of the time,
But, though with peril of your own estate,
You will not be the first that shall invade,
Assemble yet your force for your de-
fense, 160
And for your safety stand upon your
guard.
DOR. O heaven! was there ever heard or
known
So wicked counsel to a noble prince?
Let me, my lord, disclose unto your
grace
This heinous tale, what mischief it con-
tains:
Your father's death, your brother's, and
your own—
Your present murder and eternal shame.
Hear me, O king, and suffer not to sink
So high a treason in your princely breast.
FER. The mighty gods forbid that ever I
Should once conceive such mischief in
my heart. 171
Although my brother hath bereft my
realm,
And bear perhaps to me an hateful mind,
Shall I revenge it with his death there-
fore?
Or shall I so destroy my father's life
That gave me life? The gods forbid, I
say.
Cease you to speak so any more to me;
Ne you, my friend, with answer once
repeat
So foul a tale. In silence let it die.
What lord or subject shall have hope at
all 180

[1] Win over.
[2] Quotation marks were commonly used to
call attention to sententious sayings.
[3] Dissyllabic.   [4] The rabble.

That under me they safely shall enjoy
Their goods, their honors, lands, and
liberties,
With whom neither one only brother
dear
Ne father dearer could enjoy their lives?
But, sith I fear my younger brother's
rage,
And sith perhaps some other man may
give
Some like advice, to move his grudging
head
At mine estate—which counsel may per-
chance
Take greater force with him than this
with me—
I will in secret so prepare myself   190
As, if his malice or his lust to reign
Break forth in arms or sudden violence,
I may withstand his rage and keep mine
own.   [*Exeunt Ferrex and Hermon.*]
Dor. I fear the fatal time now draweth on
When civil hate shall end the noble line
Of famous Brute and of his royal seed.
Great Jove, defend [1] the mischiefs now
at hand!
O, that the secretary's wise advice
Had erst been heard when he besought
the king
Not to divide his land, nor send his
sons   200
To further parts from presence of his
court,
Ne yet to yield to them his governance!
Lo, such are they now in the royal throne
As was rash Phaëton in Phœbus' car;
Ne then the fiery steeds did draw the
flame
With wilder randon [2] through the kindled
skies
Than traitorous counsel now will whirl
about
The youthful heads of these unskillful
kings.
But I hereof their father will inform;
The reverence of him perhaps shall
stay   210
The growing mischiefs while they yet are
green.
If this help not, then woe unto them-
selves,
The prince, the people, the divided land!
[*Exit.*]

---

[1] Prevent.   [2] Impetuosity.

ACTUS SECUNDUS. SCENA SECUNDA.

[*The court of Porrex.*]

Porrex, Tyndar, Philander.

Por. And is it thus? And doth he so
prepare
Against his brother as his mortal foe?
And now while yet his aged father lives?
Neither regards he him, nor fears he me?
War would he have? And he shall have
it so!
Tyn. I saw, myself, the great prepared
store
Of horse, of armor, and of weapons there;
Ne bring I to my lord reported tales
Without the ground of seen and searchéd
truth.
Lo, secret quarrels run about his court 10
To bring the name of you, my lord, in
hate.
Each man, almost, can now debate the
cause,
And ask a reason of so great a wrong—
Why he, so noble and so wise a prince,
Is, as unworthy, reft his heritage,
And why the king, misled by crafty
means,
Divided thus his land from course of
right.
The wiser sort hold down their griefful
heads;
Each man withdraws from talk and
company
Of those that have been known to favor
you.   20
To hide the mischief of their meaning
there,
Rumors are spread of your preparing
here.
The rascal numbers of unskillful sort
Are filled with monstrous tales of you
and yours.
In secret I was counseled by my friends
To haste me thence, and brought you,
as you know,
Letters from those that both can truly
tell
And would not write unless they knew it
well.
Phil. My lord, yet ere you move unkindly
war,
Send to your brother to demand the
cause.   30

Perhaps some traitorous tales have filled
  his ears
With false reports against your noble
  grace;
Which, once disclosed, shall end the
  growing strife
That else, not stayed with wise foresight
  in time,
Shall hazard both your kingdoms and
  your lives.
Send to your father eke; he shall appease
Your kindled minds and rid you of this
  fear.
Por. Rid me of fear? I fear him not at all;
  Ne will to him ne to my father send.
If danger were for one to tarry there,   40
Think ye it safety to return again?
In mischiefs such as Ferrex now intends,
The wonted courteous laws to messengers
Are not observed, which in just war they
  use.
Shall I so hazard any one of mine?
Shall I betray my trusty friends to him,
That have disclosed his treason unto me?
Let him entreat that fears; I fear him nct.
Or shall I to the king, my father, send?
Yea, and send now, while such a mother
  lives,   50
That loves my brother and that hateth
  me?
Shall I give leisure, by my fond [1] delays,
To Ferrex to oppress me all unware?
I will not; but I will invade his realm
And seek the traitor prince within his
  court.
Mischief for mischief is a due reward.
His wretched head shall pay the worthy
  price
Of this his treason and his hate to me.
Shall I abide, and treat, and send, and
  pray,
And hold my yelden [2] throat to traitor's
  knife,   60
While I, with valiant mind and conquer-
  ing force,
Might rid myself of foes and win a realm?
Yet rather, when I have the wretch's
  head,
Then to the king, my father, will I send.
The bootless case may yet appease his
  wrath;
If not, I will defend me as I may.
        [Exeunt Porrex and Tyndar.]

[1] Foolish.   [2] Yielded, submissive.

Phil. Lo, here the end of these two youth-
  ful kings,
The father's death, the ruin of their
  realms!
"O most unhappy state of counselors,
That light on so unhappy lords and times
That neither can their good advice be
  heard,   71
Yet must they bear the blames of ill
  success."
But I will to the king, their father, haste,
Ere this mischief come to the likely end;
That, if the mindful wrath of wreakful
  gods—
Since mighty Ilion's fall not yet appeased
With these poor remnants of the Trojan
  name—
Have not determined by unmovéd fate
Out of this realm to raze the British line,
By good advice, by awe of father's name,
By force of wiser lords, this kindled
  hate   81
May yet be quenched ere it consume us
  all.   *[Exit.]*

Chorus

When youth, not bridled with a guiding
  stay,
  Is left to randon of their own delight,
And welds whole realms by force of
  sovereign sway,
  Great is the danger of unmastered
    might,
Lest skilless rage throw down, with
  headlong fall,
Their lands, their states, their lives,
  themselves and all.

When growing pride doth fill the swelling
  breast,
  And greedy lust [3] doth raise the climb-
    ing mind,   90
O, hardly may the peril be repressed.
  Ne fear of angry gods, ne lawes' [4] kind,
Ne country's care can firéd hearts re-
  strain,
When force hath arméd envy and disdain.

When kings of foresight [5] will neglect the
  rede [6]
  Of best advice, and yield to pleasing
    tales

[3] Desire.   [5] Of set purpose.
[4] Dissyllabic.   [6] Counsel.

That do their fancies' noisome humor
  feed,
Ne reason nor regard of right avails.
Succeeding heaps of plagues shall teach,
  too late,   99
To learn the mischiefs of misguided state.

Foul fall the traitor false that under-
  mines
  The love of brethren to destroy them
    both.
Woe to the prince that pliant ear inclines
  And yields his mind to poisonous tale
    that floweth
From flattering mouth!   And woe to
  wretched land
That wastes itself with civil sword in
  hand!

Lo, thus it is, poison in gold to take,
And wholesome drink in homely cup
  forsake.

THE ORDER AND SIGNIFICATION OF THE
  DUMB SHOW BEFORE THE THIRD ACT

*First, the music of flutes began to play, dur-
  ing which came in upon the stage a
  company of mourners, all clad in black,
  betokening death and sorrow to ensue
  upon the ill-advised misgovernment and
  dissension of brethren, as befell upon the
  murder of Ferrex by his younger brother.
  After the mourners had passed thrice
  about the stage, they departed, and then
  the music ceased.*

ACTUS TERTIUS. SCENA PRIMA.

[*The court of Gorboduc.*]

*Gorboduc, Eubulus, Arostus, Philander,
                    Nuntius.*[1]

GORB. O cruel fates, O mindful wrath of
  gods,
Whose vengeance neither Simois' stainéd
  streams
Flowing with blood of Trojan princes
  slain,
Nor Phrygian fields made rank with
  corpses dead
Of Asian kings and lords, can yet ap-
  pease;
Ne slaughter of unhappy Priam's race,
Nor Ilion's fall, made level with the soil,

[1] Last two enter later.

Can yet suffice; but still continued rage
Pursues our lives, and from the farthest
  seas
Doth chase the issues of destroyéd
  Troy.   10
"O, no man happy till his end be seen."
If any flowing wealth and seeming joy
In present years might make a happy
  wight,
Happy was Hecuba, the woefullest wretch
That ever lived to make a mirror of;
And happy Priam, with his noble sons;
And happy I, till now, alas, I see
And feel my most unhappy wretched-
  ness.
Behold, my lords, read ye this letter
  here.
Lo, it contains the ruin of our realm,   20
If timely speed provide not hasty help.
Yet, O ye gods, if ever woeful king
Might move ye, kings of kings, wreak it
  on me
And on my sons, not on this guiltless
  realm!
Send down your wasting flames from
  wrathful skies,
To reave me and my sons the hateful
  breath.
Read, read, my lords; this is the matter
  why
I called ye now to have your good advice.

*The letter from Dordan, the counselor of the
            elder prince.*

Eubulus readeth the letter.

"My sovereign lord, what I am loath to
  write,
But loathest am to see, that I am
  forced   30
By letters now to make you understand.
My Lord Ferrex, your eldest son, misled
By traitorous fraud of young untempered
  wits,
Assembleth force against your younger
  son,
Ne can my counsel yet withdraw the heat
And furious pangs of his inflaméd head.
Disdain, saith he, of his disheritance
Arms him to wreak the great pretended
  wrong
With civil sword upon his brother's life.
If present help do not restrain this
  rage,   40

This flame will waste your sons, your
land, and you.
Your majesty's faithful and most humble
subject,

Dordan."

Aros. O king, appease your grief and stay
your plaint;
Great is the matter, and a woeful case,
But timely knowledge may bring timely
help.
Send for them both unto your presence
here.
The reverence of your honor, age, and
state,
Your grave advice, the awe of father's
name,
Shall quickly knit again this broken
peace.
And, if in either of my lords, your sons, 50
Be such untaméd and unyielding pride
As will not bend unto your noble hests; [1]
If Ferrex, the elder son, can bear no peer,
Or Porrex, not content, aspires to more
Than you him gave above his native
right,
Join with the juster side; so shall you
force
Them to agree, and hold the land in
stay.
Eub. What meaneth this? Lo, yonder
comes in haste
Philander from my lord, your younger
son.

[*Enter Philander.*]

Gorb. The gods send joyful news!
Phil. The mighty Jove 60
Preserve your majesty, O noble king.
Gorb. Philander, welcome! But how doth
my son?
Phil. Your son, sir, lives, and healthy I
him left.
But yet, O king, the want of lustful
health
Could not be half so griefful to your
grace
As these most wretched tidings that I
bring.
Gorb. O heavens, yet more? Not end of
woes to me?
Phil. Tyndar, O king, came lately from
the court

[1] Behests, commands.

Of Ferrex to my lord, your younger son,
And made report of great preparéd
store 70
For war, and saith that it is wholly meant
Against Porrex, for high disdain that he
Lives now a king, and egal in degree
With him that claimeth to succeed the
whole,
As by due title of descending right.
Porrex is now so set on flaming fire,
Partly with kindled rage of cruel wrath,
Partly with hope to gain a realm thereby,
That he in haste prepareth to invade 79
His brother's land, and with unkindly war
Threatens the murder of your elder son;
Ne could I him persuade that first he
should
Send to his brother to demand the cause,
Nor yet to you to stay this hateful strife.
Wherefore, sith there no more I can be
heard,
I come myself now to inform your grace,
And to beseech you, as you love the life
And safety of your children and your
realm,
Now to employ your wisdom and your
force
To stay this mischief ere it be too late. 90
Gorb. Are they in arms? Would he not
send to me?
Is this the honor of a father's name?
In vain we travail to assuage their minds,
As if their hearts, whom neither brother's
love,
Nor father's awe, nor kingdom's cares
can move,
Our counsels could withdraw from raging
heat.
Jove slay them both, and end the curséd
line.
For, though perhaps fear of such mighty
force
As I, my lords, joined with your noble
aids,
May yet raise, shall repress their present
heat, 100
The secret grudge and malice will remain;
The fire, not quenched, but kept in close
restraint,
Fed still within, breaks forth with double
flame.
Their death and mine must pease [2] the
angry gods.

[2] Appease.

PHIL. Yield not, O king, so much to weak
   despair;
   Your sons yet live, and long, I trust,
     they shall.
   If fates had taken you from earthly life
   Before beginning of this civil strife,
   Perhaps your sons in their unmastered
     youth,
   Loose from regard of any living wight, 110
   Would run on headlong, with unbridled
     race,
   To their own death and ruin of this
     realm.
   But, sith the gods, that have the care for
     kings,
   Of things and times dispose the order so
   That in your life this kindled flame
     breaks forth,
   While yet your life, your wisdom, and
     your power
   May stay the growing mischief, and
     repress
   The fiery blaze of their enkindled heat,
   It seems—and so ye ought to deem
     thereof—
   That loving Jove hath tempered so the
     time   120
   Of this debate to happen in your days,
   That you yet living may the same ap-
     pease,
   And add it to the glory of your latter
     age,
   And they your sons may learn to live in
     peace.
   Beware, O king, the greatest harm of all,
   Lest by your wailful plaints your has-
     tened death
   Yield larger room unto their growing
     rage.
   Preserve your life, the only hope of stay.
   And, if your highness herein list to use
   Wisdom or force, counsel or knightly
     aid,   130
   Lo, we, our persons, powers, and lives
     are yours.
   Use us till death, O king; we are your
     own.
EUB. Lo, here the peril that was erst fore-
   seen,
   When you, O king, did first divide your
     land,
   And yield your present reign unto your
     sons.
   But now, O noble prince, now is no time

To wail and plain,[1] and waste your woeful
   life;
Now is the time for present good advice.
Sorrow doth dark the judgment of the
   wit.
"The heart unbroken and the courage
   free   140
From feeble faintness of bootless despair
Doth either rise to safety or renown
By noble valure [2] of unvanquished mind,
Or yet doth perish in more happy sort."
Your grace may send to either of your
   sons
Some one both wise and noble personage,
Which with good counsel and with
   weighty name
Of father shall present before their eyes
Your hest, your life, your safety, and
   their own,
The present mischief of their deadly
   strife.   150
And, in the while, assemble you the force
Which your commandment and the
   speedy haste
Of all my lords here present can prepare.
The terror of your mighty power shall
   stay
The rage of both, or yet of one at least.

[Enter Nuntius.]

NUN. O king, the greatest grief that ever
   prince did hear,
   That ever woeful messenger did tell,
   That ever wretched land hath seen be-
     fore,
   I bring to you: Porrex, your younger son,
   With sudden force invaded hath the
     land   160
   That you to Ferrex did allot to rule,
   And with his own most bloody hand he
     hath
   His brother slain, and doth possess his
     realm.
GORB. O heavens, send down the flames of
   your revenge!
   Destroy, I say, with flash of wreakful
     fire
   The traitor son, and then the wretched
     sire!
   But let us go, that yet perhaps I may
   Die with revenge and pease the hateful
     gods.   *[Exeunt.]*

—————————————————————
[1] Complain.   [2] Valor, worth.

CHORUS

The lust of kingdom knows no sacred
　　faith,
　　No rule of reason, no regard of
　　　　right,　　　　　　　　　　　　170
No kindly love, no fear of heaven's
　　wrath,
　　But, with contempt of gods and man's
　　　　despite,
Through bloody slaughter doth prepare
　　the ways
　　To fatal scepter and accurséd reign.
The son so loathes the father's lingering
　　days,
　　Ne dreads his hand in brother's blood
　　　　to stain.
O wretched prince, ne dost thou yet
　　record
　　The yet fresh murthers done within
　　　　the land
Of thy forefathers, when the cruel sword
　　Bereft Morgan his life with cousin's
　　　　hand?　　　　　　　　　　　　180
Thus fatal plagues pursue the guilty race
　　Whose murderous hand, imbrued with
　　　　guiltless blood,
Asks vengeance still before the heaven's
　　face,
　　With endless mischiefs on the curséd
　　　　brood.
The wicked child thus brings to woeful
　　sire
　　The mournful plaints to waste his very
　　　　life.
Thus do the cruel flames of civil fire
　　Destroy the parted reign with hateful
　　　　strife;
And hence doth spring the well from
　　which doth flow
　　The dead black streams of mourning,
　　　　plaints, and woe.　　　　　　190

THE ORDER AND SIGNIFICATION OF THE
DUMB SHOW BFFORE THE FOURTH
ACT

*First, the music of hautboys began to play,
during which there came forth from under the stage, as though out of hell,
three Furies, Alecto, Megæra, and Tisiphone, clad in black garments sprinkled
with blood and flames, their bodies girt
with snakes, their heads spread with
serpents instead of hair, the one bear-*
*ing in her hand a snake, the other a
whip, and the third a burning firebrand,
each driving before them a king and a
queen, which, moved by Furies, unnaturally had slain their own children. The
names of the kings and queens were
these: Tantalus, Medea, Athamas, Ino,
Cambises, Althea. After that the Furies
and these had passed about the stage
thrice, they departed, and then the music
ceased. Hereby was signified the unnatural murders to follow; that is to
say, Porrex slain by his own mother,
and of King Gorboduc and Queen
Viden[a], killed by their own subjects.*

ACTUS QUARTUS. SCENA PRIMA.

[*A room in Gorboduc's palace.*]

Viden[a] sola.

VID. Why should I live, and linger forth my
　　time
In longer life to double my distress?
O me, most woeful wight, whom no mishap
Long ere this day could have bereavéd
　　hence!
Mought [1] not these hands, by fortune or by
　　fate,
Have pierced this breast, and life with iron
　　reft?
Or in this palace here, where I so long
Have spent my days, could not that happy
　　hour
Once, once have happed, in which these
　　hugy frames
With death by fall might have oppresséd
　　me?　　　　　　　　　　　　10
Or should not this most hard and cruel soil,
So oft where I have pressed my wretched
　　steps,
Sometime had ruth of mine accurséd life
To rend in twain, [and] [2] swallow me
　　therein?
So had my bones possesséd now in peace
Their happy grave within the closéd
　　ground,
And greedy worms had gnawn this pinéd
　　heart
Without my feeling pain; so should not now
This living breast remain the ruthful tomb
Wherein my heart, yelden to death, is
　　graved; [3]　　　　　　　　20

[1] Might.
[2] Supplied from 1565 edn.　　　　[3] Buried.

Nor dreary thoughts, with pangs of pining
   grief,
My doleful mind had not afflicted thus.
O my beloved son! O my sweet child!
My dear Ferrex, my joy, my life's delight!
Is my beloved son, is my sweet child,
My dear Ferrex, my joy, my life's delight,
Murdered with cruel death?   O hateful
   wretch!
O heinous traitor both to heaven and earth!
Thou, Porrex, thou this damnéd deed hast
   wrought;
Thou, Porrex, thou shalt dearly by [1] the
   same.   30
Traitor to kin and kind, to sire and me,
To thine own flesh, and traitor to thyself!
The gods on thee in hell shall wreak their
   wrath,
And here in earth this hand shall take
   revenge
On thee, Porrex, thou false and caitiff
   wight.
If after blood so eager were thy thirst,
And murderous mind had so poss
éssed thee,
If such hard heart of rock and stony flint
Lived in thy breast that nothing else could
   like [2]
Thy cruel tyrant's thought but death and
   blood,   40
Wild savage beasts, mought not their
   slaughter serve
To feed thy greedy will, and in the midst
Of their entrails to stain thy deadly hands
With blood deserved, and drink thereof
   thy fill?
Or if naught else but death and blood of
   man
Mought please thy lust, could none in
   Britain land—
Whose heart betorn out of his panting
   breast
With thine own hand, or work what death
   thou wouldest—
Suffice to make a sacrifice to pease
That deadly mind and murderous thought
   in thee,   50
But he who in the selfsame womb was
   wrapped,
Where thou in dismal hour receivédst life?
Or if needs, needs thy hand must slaughter
   make,
Moughtest thou not have reached a mortal
   wound,

And with thy sword have pierced this
   curséd womb
That the accurséd Porrex brought to light,
And given me a just reward therefor?
So Ferrex yet sweet life mought have en-
   joyed
And to his aged father comfort brought,
With some young son in whom they both
   might live.   60
But whereunto waste I this ruthful speech,
To thee that hast thy brother's blood thus
   shed?
Shall I still think that from this womb thou
   sprung,
That I thee bare, or take thee for my son?
No, traitor, no; I thee refuse for mine.
Murderer, I thee renounce; thou art not
   mine.
Never, O wretch, this womb conceivéd thee,
Nor never bode [3] I painful throes for thee.
Changeling to me thou art, and not my
   child,   69
Nor to no wight that spark of pity knew.
Ruthless, unkind, monster of nature's
   work,
Thou never sucked the milk of woman's
   breast,
But from thy birth the cruel tiger's teats
Have nurséd thee; nor yet of flesh and
   blood
Formed is thy heart, but of hard iron
   wrought;
And wild and desert woods bred thee to life.
But canst thou hope to scape my just re-
   venge,
Or that these hands will not be wroke [4]
   on thee?
Dost thou not know that Ferrex' mother
   lives,
That lovéd him more dearly than herself? 80
And doth she live, and is not venged on
   thee?   [Exit.]

ACTUS QUARTUS. SCENA SECUNDA.

[The court of Gorboduc.]

Gorboduc, Arostus, Eubulus, Porrex, Mar-
                          cella.[5]
GORB. We marvel much whereto this lin-
   g'ring stay
Falls out so long. Porrex unto our court.
By order of our letters, is returned,

---

[1] Aby; pay the penalty for.   [2] Please.
[3] Suffered.   [5] Wreaked, avenged.
[4] Last three enter later.

And Eubulus received from us behest,[1]
At his arrival here, to give him charge
Before our presence straight to make re-
pair;
And yet we have no word whereof he
stays.
Aros. Lo, where he comes, and Eubulus
with him.

[*Enter Eubulus and Porrex.*]

Eub. According to your highness' hest to
me,
Here have I Porrex brought, even in such
sort   10
As from his wearied horse he did alight,
For that your grace did will such haste
therein.
Gorb. We like and praise this speedy will
in you
To work the thing that to your charge
we gave.
Porrex, if we so far should swerve from
kind,
And from those bounds which law of
nature sets,
As thou hast done by vile and wretched
deed,
In cruel murder of thy brother's life,
Our present hand could stay no longer
time,
But straight should bathe this blade in
blood of thee   20
As just revenge of thy detested crime.
No, we should not offend the law of
kind,
If now this sword of ours did slay thee
here;
For thou hast murdered him whose
heinous death
Even nature's force doth move us to re-
venge
By blood again; and justice forceth us
To measure death for death, thy due
desert.
Yet sithens [2] thou art our child, and sith
as yet
In this hard case what word thou canst
allege
For thy defense by us hath not been
heard,   30
We are content to stay our will for that

Which justice bids us presently to work,
And give thee leave to use thy speech at
full,
If aught thou have to lay for thine excuse.
Por. Neither, O king, I can or will deny
But that this hand from Ferrex life hath
reft—
Which fact how much my doleful heart
doth wail,
O, would it mought as full appear to
sight
As inward grief doth pour it forth to me!
So yet perhaps, if ever ruthful heart, 40
Melting in tears within a manly breast,
Through deep repentance of his bloody
fact,
If ever grief, if ever woeful man
Might move regret with sorrow of his
fault,
I think the torment of my mournful case,
Known to your grace, as I do feel the
same,
Would force even Wrath herself to pity
me.
But as the water, troubled with the mud,
Shows not the face which else the eye
should see,
Even so your ireful mind with stirréd
thought   50
Cannot so perfectly discern my cause.
But this unhap, amongst so many heaps,[3]
I must content me with, most wretched
man,
That to myself I must reserve my woe
In pining thoughts of mine accurséd fact,
Since I may not show here my smallest
grief,
Such as it is, and as my breast endures,
Which I esteem the greatest misery
Of all mishaps that fortune now can send.
Not that I rest in hope with plaint and
tears   60
To purchase life; for to the gods I clepe [4]
For true record of this my faithful
speech:
Never this heart shall have the thought-
ful dread
To die the death that by your grace's
doom,
By just desert, shall be pronounced to me;
Nor never shall this tongue once spend
the speech

---

[1] Suggested by Thorndike; all preceding edns.
have *by hest.*
[2] Since (probably pronounced as one syllable).

[3] Among so many heaps (of unhaps). *Cf.* V,
ii, 109.   [4] Call.

Pardon to crave, or seek by suit to live.
I mean not this as though I were not
  touched
With care of dreadful death, or that I
  held
Life in contempt, but that I know the
  mind   70
Stoops to no dread, although the flesh be
  frail.
And for my guilt, I yield the same so
  great
As in myself I find a fear to sue
For grant of life.

GORB.   In vain, O wretch,
  thou showest
A woeful heart! Ferrex now lies in grave,
Slain by thy hand.

POR.   Yet this, O father,
  hear,
And then I end. Your majesty well
  knows
That when my brother Ferrex and my-
  self
By your own hest were joined in gov-
  ernance
Of this your grace's realm of Britain
  land,   80
I never sought nor travailed for the same;
Nor by myself nor by no friend I
  wrought,
But from your highness' will alone it
  sprung,
Of your most gracious goodness bent to
  me.
But how my brother's heart even then
  repined
With swollen disdain against mine egal
  rule,
Seeing that realm which by descent
  should grow
Wholly to him allotted half to me!
Even in your highness' court he now re-
  mains,
And with my brother then in nearest
  place,   90
Who can record what proof thereof was
  showed,
And how my brother's envious heart ap-
  peared.
Yet I that judgéd it my part to seek
His favor and good will, and loath to
  make
Your highness know the thing which
  should have brought

Grief to your grace and your offense to
  him,
Hoping my earnest suit should soon have
  won
A loving heart within a brother's breast,
Wrought in that sort that for a pledge
  of love
And faithful heart he gave to me his
  hand.   100
This made me think that he had ban-
  ished quite
All rancor from his thought, and bare to
  me
Such hearty love as I did owe to him.
But, after once we left your grace's court,
And from your highness' presence lived
  apart,
This egal rule still, still did grudge him so
That now those envious sparks, which
  erst lay raked
In living cinders of dissembling breast,
Kindled so far within his heart disdain
That longer could he not refrain from
  proof   110
Of secret practice to deprive me life
By poison's force, and had bereft me so,
If mine own servant, hired to this fact
And moved by truth with hate to work
  the same,
In time had not bewrayed [1] it unto me.
When thus I saw the knot of love unknit,
All honest league and faithful promise
  broke,
The law of kind and truth thus rent in
  twain,
His heart on mischief set, and in his
  breast
Black treason hid, then, then did I de-
  spair   120
That ever time could win him friend to
  me;
Then saw I how he smiled with slaying
  knife
Wrapped under cloak; then saw I deep
  deceit
Lurk in his face and death prepared for
  me.
Even nature moved me then to hold my
  life
More dear to me than his, and bade this
  hand—
Since by his life my death must needs
  ensue

[1] Betrayed, divulged.

And by his death my life to be pre-
served—
To shed his blood and seek my safety so.
And wisdom willéd me without pro-
tract [1]   130
In speedy wise to put the same in ure.
Thus have I told the cause that movéd
me
To work my brother's death; and so I
yield
My life, my death, to judgment of your
grace.

GORB. O cruel wight, should any cause
prevail
To make thee stain thy hands with
brother's blood?
But what of thee we will resolve to do
Shall yet remain unknown. Thou in the
mean
Shalt from our royal presence banished be,
Until our princely pleasure furder shall
To thee be showed. Depart therefore
our sight,   141
Accurséd child! [Exit Porrex.] What
cruel destiny,
What froward fate hath sorted us this
chance,
That, even in those where we should
comfort find,
Where our delight now in our aged days
S[h]ould rest and be, even there our only
grief
And deepest sorrows to abridge our life,
Most pining cares, and deadly thoughts
do grow?

AROS. Your grace should now, in these
grave years of yours,
Have found ere this the price of mortal
joys: 150
How short they be, how fading here in
earth,
How full of change, how brittle our es-
tate,
Of nothing sure, save only of the death
To whom both man and all the world
doth owe
Their end at last. Neither should na-
ture's power
In other sort against your heart prevail
Than as the naked hand whose stroke
assays
The arméd breast where force doth light
in vain.

[1] Delay.

GORB. Many can yield right sage and
grave advice
Of patient sprite to others wrapped in
woe,   160
And can in speech both rule and conquer
kind,
Who, if by proof they might feel nature's
force,
Would show themselves men as they are
indeed,
Which now will needs be gods. But what
doth mean
The sorry cheer of her that here doth
come?

[Enter Marcella.]

MAR. O, where is ruth, or where is pity
now?
Whither is gentle heart and mercy fled?
Are they exiled out of our stony breasts,
Never to make return? Is all the world
Drownéd in blood, and sunk in cru-
elty?   170
If not in women mercy may be found,
If not, alas, within the mother's breast,
To her own child, to her own flesh and
blood,
If ruth be banished thence, if pity there
May have no place, if there no gentle
heart
Do live and dwell, where should we seek
it then?

GORB. Madam, alas, what means your
woeful tale?

MAR. O silly [2] woman I, why to this hour
Have kind and fortune thus deferred my
breath,
That I should live to see this doleful
day?   180
Will ever wight believe that such hard
heart
Could rest within the cruel mother's
breast,
With her own hand to slay her only son?
But out, alas! these eyes beheld the
same—
They saw the dreary sight, and are be-
come
Most ruthful records of the bloody fact.
Porrex, alas, is by his mother slain,
And with her hand—a woeful thing to
tell—

[2] Helpless.

While slumb'ring on his careful bed he
  rests,
His heart stabbed in with knife, is reft of
  life.   190

GORB. O Eubulus, O, draw this sword of
  ours,
And pierce this heart with speed! O
  hateful light,
O loathsome life, O sweet and welcome
  death!
Dear Eubulus, work this, we thee beseech!

EUB. Patient [1] your grace; perhaps he liveth yet,
With wound received, but not of certain
  death.

GORB. O, let us then repair unto the place,
And see if Porrex live or thus be slain.
            [*Exeunt Gorboduc and Eubulus.*]

MAR. Alas, he liveth not! It is too true
That, with these eyes, of him a peerless
  prince,   200
Son to a king, and in the flower of youth,
Even with a twink a senseless stock I
  saw.[2]

AROS. O damnéd deed!

MAR.   But hear his ruth-
  ful end:
The noble prince, pierced with the sud-
  den wound,
Out of his wretched slumber hastely
  start,[3]
Whose strength now failing, straight he
  overthrew,[4]
When in the fall his eyes, even new
  unclosed,
Beheld the queen, and cried to her for
  help.
We then, alas, the ladies which that time
Did there attend, seeing that heinous
  deed,   210
And hearing him oft call the wretched
  name
Of mother, and to cry to her for aid
Whose direful hand gave him the mortal
  wound,
Pitying, alas—for nought else could we
  do—
His ruthful end, ran to the woeful bed,

Despoiléd straight his breast, and, all we
  might,
Wipéd in vain with napkins next at hand
The sudden streams of blood that flushéd
  fast
Out of the gaping wound. O, what a look,
O, what a ruthful, steadfast eye me-
  thought   220
He fixed upon my face, which to my
  death
Will never part fro [5] me, when with a
  braid [6]
A deep-fet [7] sigh he gave, and there-
  withal,
Clasping his hands, to heaven he cast his
  sight;
And straight—pale death pressing within
  his face—
The flying ghost his mortal corpse for-
  sook.

AROS. Never did age bring forth so vile a
  fact.

MAR. O hard and cruel hap, that thus as-
  signed
Unto so worthy a wight so wretched end;
But most hard cruel heart, that could
  consent   230
To lend the hateful destinies that hand
By which, alas, so heinous crime was
  wrought!
O queen of adamant! O marble breast!
If not the favor of his comely face,
If not his princely cheer and countenance,
His valiant active arms, his manly breast,
If not his fair and seemly personage,
His noble limbs in such proportion cast
As would have rapt a silly woman's
  thought—
If this mought not have moved thy
  bloody heart   240
And that most cruel hand the wretched
  weapon
Even to let fall, and kissed him in the
  face,
With tears for ruth to reave such one by
  death,
Should nature yet consent to slay her
  son?
O mother, thou to murder thus thy child!
Even Jove with justice must with light-
  ning flames
From heaven send down some strange
  revenge on thee.

---

[1] Used as a reflexive verb.

[2] An awkward passage. The sense seems to be:
"It is too true that with these eyes even in an
instant I saw a senseless corpse made of him," etc.

[3] Hastily started.   [4] Fell over.

[5] From.   [6] A start.   [7] Deep-fetched.

Ah, noble prince, how oft have I beheld
Thee mounted on thy fierce and tram-
    pling steed,
Shining in armor bright before the
    tilt,   250
And with thy mistress' sleeve tied on
    thy helm,
And charge thy staff [1]—to please thy
    lady's eye—
That bowed the headpiece of thy friendly
    foe;
How oft in arms on horse to bend the
    mace,
How oft in arms on foot to break the
    sword,
Which never now these eyes may see
    again!
AROS. Madam, alas, in vain these plaints
    are shed;
Rather with me depart, and help to
    swage [2]
The thoughtful griefs that in the aged
    king
Must needs by nature grow by death of
    this   260
His only son, whom he did hold so
    dear.
MAR. What wight is that which saw that
    I did see,
And could refrain to wail with plaint
    and tears?
Not I, alas! That heart is not in me.—
But let us go, for I am grieved anew
To call to mind the wretched father's
    woe.   [*Exeunt.*]

CHORUS

When greedy lust in royal seat to reign
    Hath reft all care of gods and eke of
    men,
And cruel heart, wrath, treason, and
    disdain,
Within ambitious breast are lodgéd,
    then   270
Behold how mischief wide herself dis-
    plays,
And with the brother's hand the brother
    slays.

When blood thus shed doth stain the
    heaven's face,
    Crying to Jove for vengeance of the
    deed,

The mighty god even moveth from his
    place
    With wrath to wreak. Then sends he
    forth with speed
The dreadful Furies, daughters of the
    night,
    With serpents girt, carrying the whip
    of ire,
With hair of stinging snakes, and shining
    bright
    With flames and blood, and with a
    brand of fire.   280
These, for revenge of wretched murder
    done,
Do make the mother kill her only son.

Blood asketh blood, and death must
    death requite;
    Jove, by his just and everlasting doom,
Justly hath ever so requited it.
    The times before record, and times to
    come
Shall find it true, and so doth present
    proof
Present before our eyes for our behoof.

O happy wight that suffers not the snare
    Of murderous mind to tangle him in
    blood;   290
And happy he that can in time beware
    By other's harms and turn it to his
    good.
But woe to him that, fearing not to
    offend,
Doth serve his lust and will not see the
    end.

THE ORDER AND SIGNIFICATION OF THE DUMB SHOW BEFORE THE FIFTH ACT

*First, the drums and flutes began to sound,
during which there came forth upon the
stage a company of harquebusiers and
of armed men, all in order of battle.
These, after their pieces discharged, and
that the armed men had three times
marched about the stage, departed, and
then the drums and flutes did cease.
Hereby was signified tumults, rebellions,
arms, and civil wars to follow, as fell
in the realm of Great Britain, which,
by the space of fifty years and more,
continued in civil war between the nobility after the death of King Gorboduc*

[1] Level thy lance.   [2] Assuage.

and of his issues, for want of certain
limitation in succession of the crown,
till the time of Dunwallo Molmutius,
who reduced the land to monarchy.

ACTUS QUINTUS. SCENA PRIMA.

[*The court of Gorboduc.*]

Clotyn, Mandud, Gwenard, Fergus, Eubulus.

CLOT. Did ever age bring forth such ty-
    rants' hearts?
The brother hath bereft the brother's life;
The mother, she hath dyed her cruel
    hands
In blood of her own son; and now at last
The people, lo, forgetting truth and love,
Contemning quite both law and loyal
    heart,
Even they have slain their sovereign lord
    and queen.
MAND. Shall this their traitorous crime
    unpunished rest?
Even yet they cease not, carried on with
    rage,
In their rebellious routs, to threaten
    still   10
A new bloodshed unto the prince's kin,
To slay them all, and to uproot the race
Both of the king and queen; so are they
    moved
With Porrex' death, wherein they falsely
    charge
The guiltless king without desert at all,
And traitorously have murdered him
    therefor,
And eke the queen.
GWEN.   Shall subjects dare
    with force
To work revenge upon their prince's fact?
Admit the worst that may—as sure in
    this
The deed was foul, the queen to slay
    her son—   20
Shall yet the subject seek to take the
    sword,
Arise against his lord, and slay his king?
O wretched state where those rebellious
    hearts
Are not rent out even from their living
    breasts,
And with the body thrown unto the
    fowls,
As carrion food, for terror of the rest!

FERG. There can no punishment be
    thought too great
For this so grievous crime. Let speed
    therefore
Be used therein, for it behooveth so.
EUB. Ye all, my lords, I see, consent in
    one,   30
And I as one consent with ye in all.
I hold it more than need, with sharpest
    law
To punish this tumultuous bloody rage.
For nothing more may shake the com-
    mon state
Than sufferance of uproars without re-
    dress,
Whereby how some kingdoms of mighty
    power,
After great conquests made, and flour-
    ishing
In fame and wealth, have been to ruin
    brought.
I pray to Jove that we may rather wail
Such hap in them than witness in our-
    selves.   40
Eke fully with the duke my mind agrees,
Though kings forget to govern as they
    ought,
Yet subjects must obey as they are
    bound.
But now, my lords, before ye farder
    wade,[1]
Or spend your speech, what sharp re-
    venge shall fall
By justice' plague on these rebellious
    wights,
Methinks ye rather should first search
    the way
By which in time the rage of this uproar
Mought be repressed, and these great
    tumults ceased.
Even yet the life of Britain land doth
    hang   50
In traitors' balance of unegal weight.
Think not, my lords, the death of Gor-
    boduc
Nor yet Videna's blood will cease their
    rage.
Even our own lives, our wives, and chil-
    dren dear,
Our country, dearest of all, in danger
    stands,
Now to be spoiled, now, now made des-
    olate,

[1] Proceed.

And by ourselves a conquest to ensue.
For, give once sway unto the people's
  lusts
To rush forth on, and stay them not in
  time,
And, as the stream that rolleth down
  the hill,   60
So will they headlong run with raging
  thoughts
From blood to blood, from mischief
  unto mo,
To ruin of the realm, themselves, and
  all—
So giddy are the common people's minds,
So glad of change, more wavering than
  the sea.
Ye see, my lords, what strength these
  rebels have,
What hugy number is assembled still;
For, though the traitorous fact for which
  they rose
Be wrought and done, yet lodge they
  still in field;
So that, how far their furies yet will
  stretch,   70
Great cause we have to dread. That we
  may seek
By present battle to repress their power,
Speed must we use to levy force there-
  for;
For either they forthwith will mischief
  work,
Or their rebellious roars forthwith will
  cease.
These violent things may have no last-
  ing long.
Let us, therefore, use this for present
  help:
Persuade by gentle speech, and offer
  grace
With gift of pardon, save unto the chief,
And that upon condition that forth-
  with   80
They yield the captains of their enter-
  prise,
To bear such guerdon of their traitorous
  fact
As may be both due vengeance to them-
  selves
And wholesome terror to posterity.
This shall, I think, scatter the greatest
  part,
That now are holden, with desire of
  home,

Wearied in field with cold of winter's
  nights,
And some, no doubt, stricken with dread
  of law.
When this is once proclaiméd, it shall
  make
The captains to mistrust the multi-
  tude,   90
Whose safety bids them to betray their
  heads;
And so much more, because the rascal
  routs
In things of great and perilous attempts
Are never trusty to the noble race.
And, while we treat and stand on terms
  of grace,
We shall both stay their fury's rage the
  while,
And eke gain time, whose only help
  sufficeth
Withouten war to vanquish rebels'
  power.
In the meanwhile, make you in readiness
Such band of horsemen as ye may pre-
  pare.   100
Horsemen, you know, are not the com-
  mons' strength,
But are the force and store of noblemen,
Whereby the unchosen and unarméd sort
Of skilless rebels, whom none other power
But number makes to be of dreadful
  force,
With sudden brunt may quickly be op-
  pressed.
And, if this gentle mean of proffered grace
With stubborn hearts cannot so far avail
As to assuage their desperate courages,
Then do I wish such slaughter to be
  made   110
As present age and eke posterity
May be adrad [1] with horror of revenge
That justly then shall on these rebels
  fall.
This is, my lords, the sum of mine advice.
CLOT. Neither this case admits debate at
  large,
And, though it did, this speech that hath
  been said
Hath well abridged the tale I would
  have told.
Fully with Eubulus do I consent
In all that he hath said; and, if the
  same

_____
[1] Adread, afraid.

To you, my lords, may seem for best
    advice,   120
I wish that it should straight be put in
    ure.
MAND. My lords, then let us presently [1]
    depart,
And follow this that liketh us so well.
[*Exeunt Clotyn, Mandud, Gwenard, and*
                    Eubulus.]
FERG. If ever time to gain a kingdom here
    Were offered man, now it is offered me.
The realm is reft both of their king and
    queen;
The offspring of the prince is slain and
    dead;
No issue now remains, the heir unknown;
The people are in arms and mutinies;
The nobles they are busied how to
    cease   130
These great rebellious tumults and up-
    roars;
And Britain land, now desert, left alone,
Amid these broils uncertain where to
    rest,
Offers herself unto that noble heart
That will or dare pursue to bear her
    crown.
Shall I, that am the Duke of Albany,
Descended from that line of noble blood
Which hath so long flourished in worthy
    fame
Of valiant hearts, such as in noble breasts
Of right should rest above the baser
    sort,   140
Refuse to venture life to win a crown?
Whom shall I find enemies that will
    withstand
My fact herein, if I attempt by arms
To seek the same now in these times of
    broil?
These dukes' [2] power can hardly well
    appease
The people that already are in arms.
But, if perhaps my force be once in
    field,
Is not my strength in power above the
    best
Of all these lords now left in Britain land?
And though they should match me with
    power of men,   150
Yet doubtful is the chance of battles
    joined.
If victors of the field we may depart,

Ours is the scepter then of Great Britain;
If slain amid the plain this body lie,
Mine enemies yet shall not deny me
    this,
But that I died giving the noble charge
To hazard life for conquest of a crown.
Forthwith, therefore, will I in post de-
    part
To Albany, and raise in armor there
All power I can; and here my secret
    friends   160
By secret practice shall solicit still
To seek to win to me the people's hearts.
                    [*Exit.*]

ACTUS QUINTUS. SCENA SECUNDA.

[The same.]

Eubulus, Clotyn, Mandud, Gwenard, Arostus,
                      Nuntius. [3]

EUB. O Jove, how are these people's hearts
    abused!
What blind fury thus headlong carries
    them,
That, though so many books, so many
    rolls
Of ancient time, record what grievous
    plagues
Light on these rebels aye, and though so
    oft
Their ears have heard their aged fathers
    tell
What just reward these traitors still re-
    ceive,
Yea, though themselves have seen deep
    death and blood,
By strangling cord and slaughter of the
    sword,
To such assigned, yet can they not be-
    ware,   10
Yet cannot stay their lewd rebellious
    hands,
But suffering, lo, foul treason to distain
Their wretched minds, forget their loyal
    heart,
Reject all truth, and rise against their
    prince?
A ruthful case, that those whom duty's
    bond,
Whom grafted law, by nature, truth, and
    faith,
Bound to preserve their country and
    their king,

---

[1] At once.   [2] Dissyllabic.   [3] The last five enter later.

Born to defend their commonwealth and
    prince,
Even they should give consent thus to
    subvert
Thee, Britain land, and from thy womb
    should spring,   20
O native soil, those that will needs de-
    stroy
And ruin thee and eke themselves in fine.
For lo, when once the dukes had offered
    grace
Of pardon sweet, the multitude misled
By traitorous fraud of their ungracious
    heads,
One sort that saw the dangerous success
Of stubborn standing in rebellious war,
And knew the difference of prince's power
From headless number of tumultuous
    routs,
Whom common country's care and pri-
    vate fear   30
Taught to repent the error of their rage,
Laid hands upon the captains of their
    band,
And brought them bound unto the
    mighty dukes.
And other sort, not trusting yet so well
The truth of pardon, or mistrusting more
Their own offense than that they could
    conceive
Such hope of pardon for so foul misdeed,
Or for that they their captains could not
    yield,
Who, fearing to be yielded, fled before,
Stale [1] home by silence of the secret
    night.   40
The third unhappy and enragéd sort
Of desperate hearts who, stained in
    princes' blood,
From traitorous furor could not be with-
    drawn
By love, by law, by grace, ne yet by fear,
By proffered life, ne yet by threatened
    death,
With minds hopeless of life, dreadless of
    death,
Careless of country, and aweless of God,
Stood bent to fight, as Furies did them
    move
With violent death to close their traitor-
    ous life.
These all by power of horsemen were op-
    pressed,   50

[1] Stole.

And with revenging sword slain in the
    field,
Or with the strangling cord hanged on
    the trees,
Where yet their carrion carcasses do
    preach
The fruits that rebels reap of their up-
    roars,
And of the murder of their sacred prince.
But lo, where do approach the noble
    dukes
By whom these tumults have been thus
    appeased.

[*Enter Clotyn, Mandud, Gwenard, and
    Arostus.*]

CLOT. I think the world will now at length
    beware
And fear to put on arms against their
    prince.
MAND. If not, those traitorous hearts that
    dare rebel,   60
Let them behold the wide and hugy fields
With blood and bodies spread of rebels
    slain,
The lofty trees clothed with the corpses
    dead,
That, strangled with the cord, do hang
    thereon.
AROS. A just reward, such as all times
    before
Have ever lotted to those wretched folks.
GWEN. But what means he that cometh
    here so fast?

[*Enter Nuntius.*]

NUN. My lords, as duty and my troth doth
    move,
And of my country work a care in me,
That, if the spending of my breath
    availed   70
To do the service that my heart desires,
I would not shun to embrace a present
    death,
So have I now, in that wherein I thought
My travail mought perform some good
    effect,
Ventered [2] my life to bring these tidings
    here.
Fergus, the mighty Duke of Albany,
Is now in arms and lodgeth in the field
With twenty thousand men; hither he
    bends

[2] Ventured.

His speedy march, and minds to invade
  the crown.
Daily he gathereth strength, and spreads
  abroad   80
That to this realm no certain heir re-
  mains,
That Britain land is left without a guide,
That he the scepter seeks for nothing
  else
But to preserve the people and the land,
Which now remain as ship without a
  stern.
Lo, this is that which I have here to say.
CLOT. Is this his faith? And shall he falsely
  thus
Abuse the vantage of unhappy times?
O wretched land, if his outrageous pride,
His cruel and untempered willfulness, 90
His deep dissembling shows of false pre-
  tense,
Should once attain the crown of Britain
  land!
Let us, my lords, with timely force resist
The new attempt of this our common
  foe,
As we would quench the flames of com-
  mon fire.
MAND. Though we remain without a cer-
  tain prince
To weld the realm or guide the wand'ring
  rule,
Yet now the common mother of us all,
Our native land, our country, that con-
  tains
Our wives, children, kindred, ourselves,
  and all   100
That ever is or may be dear to man,
Cries unto us to help ourselves and her.
Let us advance our powers to repress
This growing foe of all our liberties.
GWEN. Yea, let us so, my lords, with hasty
  speed.
And ye, O gods, send us the welcome
  death
To shed our blood in field, and leave us
  not
In loathsome life to linger out our days,
To see the hugy heaps of these unhaps
That now roll down upon the wretched
  land,   110
Where empty place of princely govern-
  ance,
No certain stay now left of doubtless
  heir,

Thus leaves [1] this guideless realm an open
  prey
To endless storms and waste of civil war.
AROS. That ye, my lords, do so agree in
  one,
To save your country from the violent
  reign
And wrongfully usurpéd tyranny
Of him that threatens conquest of you all,
To save your realm, and in this realm
  yourselves,
From foreign thraldom of so proud a
  prince,   120
Much do I praise; and I beseech the gods
With happy honor to requite it you.
But, O my lords, sith now the heaven's
  wrath
Hath reft this land the issue of their
  prince;
Sith of the body of our late sovereign
  lord
Remains no mo since the young kings
  be slain,
And of the title of descended crown
Uncertainly the divers minds do think
Even of the learned sort, and more un-
  certainly
Will partial fancy and affection deem, 130
But most uncertainly will climbing pride
And hope of reign withdraw to sundry
  parts
The doubtful right and hopeful lust to
  reign;
When once this noble service is achieved
For Britain land, the mother of ye all;
When once ye have with arméd force
  repressed
The proud attempts of this Albanian
  prince
That threatens thraldom to your native
  land;
When ye shall vanquishers return from
  field
And find the princely state an open
  prey   140
To greedy lust and to usurping power,
Then, then, my lords, if ever kindly care
Of ancient honor of your ancestors,
Of present wealth and noblesse of your
  stocks,
Yea, of the lives and safety yet to come
Of your dear wives, your children, and
  yourselves,

[1] Original reads *leave.*

Might move your noble hearts with
gentle ruth,
Then, then, have pity on the torn estate;
Then help to salve the well-near hopeless
sore;
Which ye shall do if ye yourselves with-
hold   150
The slaying knife from your own mother's
throat.
Her shall you save, and you, and yours
in her,
If ye shall all with one assent forbear
Once to lay hand or take unto yourselves
The crown, by color of pretended right,
Or by what other means soever it be,
Till first by common counsel of you all
In parliament the regal diadem
Be set in certain place of governance—
In which your parliament, and in your
choice,   160
Prefer the right, my lords, without re-
spect
Of strength or friends or whatsoever
cause
That may set forward any other's part.
For right will last, and wrong cannot en-
dure.
Right mean I his or hers upon whose
name
The people rest by mean of native line,
Or by the virtue of some former law,
Already made their title to advance.
Such one, my lords, let be your chosen
king,
Such one so born within your native
land,   170
Such one prefer, and in no wise admit
The heavy yoke of foreign governance;
Let foreign titles yield to public wealth.
And with that heart wherewith ye now
prepare
Thus to withstand the proud invading
foe,
With that same heart, my lords, keep out
also
Unnatural thralldom of stranger's reign;
Ne suffer you, against the rules of kind,
Your mother land to serve a foreign
prince.
Eub. Lo, here the end of Brutus' royal
line,   180
And lo, the entry to the woeful wreck
And utter ruin of this noble realm!
The royal king and eke his sons are slain;

No ruler rests within the regal seat;
The heir to whom the scepter longs [1] un-
known,
That [2] to each force of foreign princes'
power,
Whom vantage of our wretched state may
move
By sudden arms to gain so rich a realm,
And to the proud and greedy mind at
home,
Whom blinded lust to reign leads to as-
pire,   190
Lo, Britain realm is left an open prey,
A present spoil by conquest to ensue.
Who seeth not now how many rising
minds
Do feed their thoughts with hope to
reach a realm?
And who will not by force attempt to
win
So great a gain, that hope persuades to
have?
A simple color [3] shall for title serve.
Who wins the royal crown will want no
right,
Nor such as shall display by long descent
A lineal race to prove him lawful
king.   200
In the meanwhile these civil arms shall
rage,
And thus a thousand mischiefs shall un-
fold,
And far and near spread [4] thee, O Britain
land.
All right and law shall cease, and he that
had
Nothing today, tomorrow shall enjoy
Great heaps of gold, and he that flowed
in wealth,
Lo, he shall be bereft of life and all;
And happiest he that then possesseth
least.
The wives shall suffer rape; the maids
deflowered
And children fatherless shall weep and
wail;   210
With fire and sword thy native folk shall
perish;
One kinsman shall bereave another's life;
The father shall unwitting slay the son;
The son shall slay the sire and know it
not;

---

[1] Belongs.   [3] Pretense.
[2] So that.   [4] Spread over.

Women and maids the cruel soldier's
sword
Shall pierce to death; and silly children,
lo,
That playing [1] in the streets and fields
are found,
By violent hands shall close their latter
day.
Whom shall the fierce and bloody soldier
Reserve to life? Whom shall he spare
from death?   220
Even thou, O wretched mother, half
alive,
Thou shalt behold thy dear and only child
Slain with the sword while he yet sucks
thy breast.
Lo, guiltless blood shall thus each where
be shed.
Thus shall the wasted soil yield forth no
fruit,
But dearth and famine shall possess the
land.
The towns shall be consumed and burnt
with fire,
The peopled cities shall wax desolate;
And thou, O Britain, whilom in renowm,
Whilom in wealth and fame, shalt thus
be torn,   230
Dismembered thus, and thus be rent in
twain,
Thus wasted and defaced, spoiled and
destroyed.
These be the fruits your civil wars will
bring.
Hereto it comes when kings will not
consent
To grave advice, but follow willful will.
This is the end when in fond princes'
hearts
Flattery prevails and sage rede hath no
place.
These are the plagues when murder is the
mean
To make new heirs unto the royal crown.
Thus wreak the gods when that the
mother's wrath   240
Naught but the blood of her own child
may swage.
These mischiefs spring when rebels will
arise
To work revenge and judge their prince's
fact.

This, this ensues, when noble men do fail
In loyal truth, and subjects will be kings.
And this doth grow, when lo, unto the
prince
Whom death or sudden hap of life be-
reaves,
No certain heir remains—such certain
heir,
As not all-only [2] is the rightful heir,
But to the realm is so made known to be,
And troth thereby vested in subjects'
hearts   251
To owe faith there where right is known
to rest.
Alas, in parliament what hope can be,
When is of parliament no hope at all,
Which, though it be assembled by consent,
Yet is not likely with consent to end?
While each one for himself, or for his
friend,
Against his foe shall travail what he may,
While now the state, left open to the man
That shall with greatest force invade the
same,   260
Shall fill ambitious minds with gaping
hope,
When will they once with yielding hearts
agree?
Or in the while, how shall the realm be
used?
No, no; then parliament should have
been holden,
And certain heirs appointed to the crown,
To stay the title of established right,
And in the people plant obedience,
While yet the prince did live whose name
and power
By lawful summons and authority   269
Might make a parliament to be of force,
And might have set the state in quiet stay.
But now, O happy man whom speedy
death
Deprives of life, ne is enforced to see
These hugy mischiefs and these miseries,
These civil wars, these murders, and
these wrongs
Of justice! Yet must God in fine restore
This noble crown unto the lawful heir:
For right will always live, and rise at
length,
But wrong can never take deep root to
last.   [Exeunt.]

[1] From 1565 edn. Original reads *play*.

[2] Alonely, solely.

THE END OF THE TRAGEDY OF KING GORBODUC.

GEORGE GASCOIGNE

George Gascoigne is an early Elizabethan example of the passionate striving for full-ness of achievement and for fame in the Renaissance. Apparently he was born about 1542 or earlier. His career includes stays at Trinity College, Cambridge, and at Gray's Inn, a wealthy marriage with the widowed mother of Nicholas Breton, elections to parliament and charges that prevented him from sitting in 1572, notorious escapades and disinheritance by his father, the patronage of nobles and bids for the favor of the queen herself, travels on the Continent, and service under William of Orange in the Netherlands in 1573–74. In his motto, "*Tam Marti quam Mercurio*," he claims equal devotion to arms and to wit. His literary activity was very varied. In addition to his dramatic work, which includes what has been called the first regular masque in English—devised for Leicester's entertainment of Elizabeth at Kenilworth in 1575—he wrote lyrics, satire, fiction, and criticism, and distinguished himself in each field. He died in his prime, apparently in 1577, although some evidence has been advanced for 1578.

Gascoigne wrote two plays besides *Supposes*. *Jocasta*, a blank verse tragedy presented at Gray's Inn in 1566, was written in collaboration with Francis Kinwelmarsh. The play is not, as its title-page implies, a direct translation of Euripides' *Phœnissæ*, but rather a fairly close translation of an Italian adaptation, made by Lodovico Dolce and printed in 1549 with the title *Giocasta*. *The Glass of Government*, printed in 1575, belongs to a group of English plays dealing with the Prodigal Son theme, which followed the models furnished by a large body of Continental school plays in Latin, chiefly the work of Dutch humanists. Gascoigne's play was written under the influence of several of these Dutch dramatists.

Like *Jocasta*, *Supposes* was performed at Gray's Inn in 1566 and shows the Italian in-fluence on English drama. It is a somewhat free translation of Ariosto's *I Suppositi*, which was acted in a prose form in 1509 and later put into verse. Gascoigne seems to have used both versions for his play. In addition to its literary interest, *Supposes* has great historical importance, first, because it seems to be the first English translation of Italian adaptations of Roman comedy; second, because it is the first extant English play to be written in prose throughout; and third, because it apparently furnished Shake-speare with his underplot in *The Taming of the Shrew*.

Italian adaptations of Roman comedy, like Italian *novelle*, contributed important ele-ments to English romantic comedy. Much more than the English adaptations, they de-veloped the plot interests of comedy, especially love intrigue, disguise, and mistaken identity. For his foundation Ariosto took the young master's exchange of rôles with his servant from the *Captivi* of Plautus, and his entering in disguise the house of a girl from the *Eunuchus* of Terence, adding various elements adapted from these and other Roman plays—the substitute for the father, the discovery of a long lost son, the parasite, and the rich old wooer who developed into the stock character of Italian comedy called the pantaloon. In his preface Ariosto speaks of his imitation as poetic creation, and his plot is superior to those from which he borrowed, in variety of incident and in the heightening of the love interest through the introduction of the rival wooer, comic though the treat-ment here is.

Supposes was first printed about 1572–73. An improved edition was included in *The Posies* of 1575, a miscellany of different types of work, at least in the main Gascoigne's. A reprint of the text of 1575 by R. W. Bond in his *Early Plays from the Italian* is the basis of the present text. J. W. Cunliffe's edition of the play in his *Works of Gascoigne* has been used for comparison.

SUPPOSES[1]

BY

GEORGE GASCOIGNE

THE NAMES OF THE ACTORS

BALIA, *the nurse.*
POLYNESTA, *the young woman.*
CLEANDER, *the doctor,*[2] *suitor to Polynesta.*
PASIPHILO, *the parasite.*
CARION, *the doctor's man.*
DULIPPO, *feigned servant, and lover of Poly-
nesta.*
EROSTRATO, *feigned master, and suitor to
Polynesta.*
DALIO *and* ⎫
CRAPINO ⎭ *servants to feigned Erostrato.*

SIENESE, *a gentleman stranger.*
PAQUETTO *and* ⎫
PETRUCHIO ⎭ *his servants.*
DAMON, *father to Polynesta.*
NEVOLA *and* TWO OTHER HIS SERVANTS.
PSITERIA, *an old hag in his house.*
PHILOGANO, *a Sicilian gentleman, father to
Erostrato.*
LITIO, *his servant.*
FERRARESE, *an innkeeper of Ferrara.*

The comedy presented as it were in Ferrara.

[TIME: *About 1500.*]

THE PROLOGUE OR ARGUMENT

I suppose you are assembled here supposing to reap the fruit of my travails;[3] and,
to be plain, I mean presently to present
you with a comedy called *Supposes,*[4] the
very name whereof may peradventure drive
into every of your heads a sundry suppose,
to suppose the meaning of our Supposes.
Some, percase,[5] will suppose we mean to
occupy your ears with sophistical handling
of subtile suppositions; some other will [10
suppose we go about to decipher unto you
some quaint conceits,[6] which hitherto have
been only supposed, as it were, in shadows;[7] and some I see smiling as though
they supposed we would trouble you with
the vain suppose of some wanton suppose.[8]
But, understand, this our Suppose is noth-

ing else but a mistaking or imagination of
one thing for another. For you shall see
the master supposed for the servant, the [20
servant for the master; the freeman for a
slave, and the bondslave for a freeman;
the stranger for a well-known friend, and
the familiar for a stranger. But what?
I suppose that even already you suppose
me very fond[9] that have so simply disclosed unto you the subtilties of these
our Supposes; where otherwise, indeed, I
suppose you should have heard almost the
last of our Supposes before you could [30
have supposed any of them aright. Let
this then suffice.

ACTUS I. SCENA i.[10]

*Balia, the nurse, [followed by] Polynesta,
the young woman.*

[BAL.] Here is nobody. Come forth,
Polynesta. Let us look about, to be sure
lest any man hear our talk; for I think
within the house the tables, the planks,

---

[1] The original title continues: "A Comedy
Written in the Italian Tongue by Ariosto, Eng-
lished by George Gascoigne, of Gray's Inn, Esquire, and There Presented. 1566."
[2] Of law. [3] Labors.
[4] Ariosto's title, *I Suppositi,* carried the meaning of "substitutions" rather than of "suppositions."
[5] Perchance.
[6] Ingeniously elaborated conceptions.
[7] Pictures. [8] "Prostitute" (Adams).

[9] Foolish.
[10] The whole action, which occupies only a few
hours, takes place in a street between the houses
of Damon and Erostrato.

the beds, the portals,[1] yea, and the cup-
boards themselves have ears.

POLY. You might as well have said the
windows and the doors. Do you not see
how they hearken?

BAL. Well, you jest fair; but I would [10
advise you take heed! I have bidden you
a thousand times beware. You will be
spied one day talking with Dulippo.

POLY. And why should I not talk with
Dulippo as well as with any other, I pray
you?

BAL. I have given you a wherefore for
this why many times. But go to! Follow
your own advice till you overwhelm us all
with sudden mishap.   20

POLY. A great mishap, I promise you!
Marry, God's blessing on their heart that
set such a brooch on my cap.[2]

BAL. Well, look well about you! A
man would think it were enough for you
secretly to rejoice that by my help you
have passed so many pleasant nights together. And yet, by my troth, I do it
more than half against my will, for I would
rather you had settled your fancy in [30
some noble family. Yea, and it is no small
grief unto me that, rejecting the suits of
so many nobles and gentlemen, you have
chosen for your darling a poor servant
of your father's, by whom shame and infamy is the best dower you can look for
to attain.

POLY. And, I pray you, whom may I
thank but gentle nurse, that continually
praising him, what for his personage,[3] [40
his courtesy, and, above all, the extreme
passions [4] of his mind—in fine, you would
never cease till I accepted him, delighted in
him, and at length desired him with no
less affection than he erst [5] desired me.

BAL. I cannot deny but at the beginning I did recommend him unto you (as,
indeed, I may say that for myself I have
a pitiful heart), seeing the depth of his unbridled affection, and that continually [50
he never ceased to fill mine ears with lamentable complaints.

POLY. Nay, rather that he filled your
purse with bribes and rewards, nurse!

BAL. Well, you may judge of nurse as
you list.[6] Indeed, I have thought it always a deed of charity to help the miserable young men whose tender youth consumeth with the furious flames of love.
But, be you sure, if I had thought you [60
would have passed to the terms you now
stand in, pity nor pension,[7] penny nor paternoster,[8] should ever have made nurse
once to open her mouth in the cause.

POLY. No? Of honesty, I pray you,
who first brought him into my chamber,
who first taught him the way to my bed
but you? Fie, nurse, fie! Never speak of
it for shame! You will make me tell a
wise tale anon.[9]   70

BAL. And have I these thanks for my
good will? Why then, I see well I shall be
counted the cause of all mishap.

POLY. Nay, rather the author of my
good hap, gentle nurse. For I would thou
knewest I love not Dulippo, nor any of
so mean estate, but have bestowed my
love more worthily than thou deemest. But
I will say no more at this time.   79

BAL. Then I am glad you have changed
your mind yet.

POLY. Nay, I neither have changed nor
will change it.

BAL. Then I understand you not. How
said you?

POLY. Marry, I say that I love not
Dulippo, nor any such as he; and yet I
neither have changed nor will change my
mind.

BAL. I cannot tell. You love to lie [90
with Dulippo very well. This gear [10] is
Greek to me. Either it hangs not well together or I am very dull of understanding.
Speak plain, I pray you.

POLY. I can speak no plainer; I have
sworn to the contrary.

BAL. How! Make you so dainty [11] to
tell it nurse, lest she should reveal it? You
have trusted me as far as may be (I may
show to you) in things that touch your [100
honor if they were known, and make you
strange to tell me this? I am sure it is
but a trifle in comparison of those things
whereof heretofore you have made me
privy.

POLY. Well, it is of greater importance

---

[1] Passages.
[2] *I.e.*, "put such a feather in my cap."
[3] Bodily form.
[4] Heroic sentiments.   [5] First.

[6] Please.   [7] Payment.   [8] Prayer.   [9] Soon.
[10] Affair.   [11] Are you so squeamish?

than you think, nurse; yet would I tell it you—under condition and promise that you shall not tell it again, nor give any sign or token to be suspected that you know it. [110

BAL. I promise you, of my honesty. Say on.

POLY. Well, hear you me then. This young man whom you have always taken for Dulippo is a noble-born Sicilian, his right name Erostrato, son to Philogano, one of the worthiest men in that country.

BAL. How, Erostrato? Is it not our neighbor, which ——

POLY. Hold thy talking, nurse, and [120 hearken to me that I may explain the whole case unto thee. The man whom to this day you have supposed to be Dulippo is, as I say, Erostrato, a gentleman that came from Sicilia to study in this city; *The first suppose and ground of all the supposes.* and even at his first arrival met me in the street, fell enamored of me, and of such vehement force were the passions he suffered that immediately he cast aside [130 both long gown and books, and determined on me only to apply his study. And to the end he might the more commodiously both see me and talk with me, he exchanged both name, habit, clothes, and credit with his servant Dulippo, whom only he brought with him out of Sicilia. And so, with the turning of a hand, of Erostrato, a gentleman, he became Dulippo, a serving-man, and soon after [140 sought service of my father and obtained it.

BAL. Are you sure of this?

POLY. Yea, out of doubt. On the other side, Dulippo took upon him the name of Erostrato, his master, the habit, the credit, books, and all things needful to a student, and in short space profited very much, and is now esteemed as you see.

BAL. Are there no other Sicilians here nor none that pass this way, which [150 may discover them?

POLY. Very few that pass this way, and few or none that tarry here any time.

BAL. This hath been a strange adventure! But, I pray you, how hang these things together—that the student, whom you say to be the servant and not the master, is become an earnest suitor to you and requireth you of your father in marriage?　　　　　　160

POLY. That is a policy devised between them to put Doctor Dotipole [1] out of conceit [2]—the old dotard!—he that so instantly doth lie upon [3] my father for me. But look where he comes—as God help me, it is he. Out upon him! What a lusky yonker [4] is this! Yet I had rather be a nun a thousand times than be cumbered with such a coistrel.[5]　　　　　　169

BAL. Daughter, you have reason. But let us go in before he come any nearer.

Polynesta goeth in, and Balia stayeth a little while after, speaking a word or two to the doctor, and then departeth.

SCENA ii.

Cleander, doctor; Pasiphilo, parasite; Balia, nurse.

[CLE.] Were these dames [6] here, or did mine eyes dazzle?

PASI. Nay, sir, here were Polynesta and her nurse.

CLE. Was my Polynesta here? Alas, I knew her not!

BAL. [*Aside.*] He must have better eyesight that should marry your Polynesta— or else he may chance to oversee the best point in his tables [7] sometimes. [*Exit.*] 10

PASI. Sir, it is no marvel; the air is very misty today. I myself knew her better by her apparel than by her face.

CLE. In good faith, and I thank God, I have mine eyesight good and perfit [8]— little worse than when I was but twenty years old.

PASI. How can it be otherwise? You are but young.

CLE. I am fifty years old.　　　　　　20

PASI. [*Aside.*] He tells [9] ten less than he is.

CLE. What sayst thou of ten less?

PASI. I say I would have thought you ten less; you look like one of six-and-thirty, or seven-and-thirty at the most.

CLE. I am no less than I tell.

PASI. You are like enough to live fifty more. Show me your hand.

---

[1] A common name for a blockhead.
[2] *I.e.*, humble his pride.
[3] So insistently urges.　　　[4] Lazy youngster.
[5] Rascal.　　　　　　[6] Great ladies.
[7] "*I.e.*, be made a cuckold; metaphor from backgammon" (Bond).
[8] Perfect.　　　　　　[9] Counts.

CLE. Why, is Pasiphilo a chiro- [30 mancer? [1]

PASI. What is not Pasiphilo? I pray you, show me it a little.

CLE. Here it is.

PASI. O, how straight and infract [2] is this line of life! You will live to the years of Melchisedec.

CLE. Thou wouldest say Methusalem.

PASI. Why, is it not all one?

CLE. I perceive you are no very [40 good Bibler, Pasiphilo.

PASI. Yes, sir, an excellent good bibbler,[3] specially in a bottle. O, what a mount of Venus here is! But this light serveth not very well. I will behold it another day, when the air is clearer, and tell you somewhat, peradventure, to your contentation.[4]

CLE. You shall do me great pleasure. But tell me, I pray thee, Pasiphilo, [50 whom dost thou think Polynesta liketh better, Erostrato or me?

PASI. Why, you, out of doubt! She is a gentlewoman of a noble mind, and maketh greater accompt of the reputation she shall have in marrying your worship, than that poor scholar, whose birth and parentage God knoweth, and very few else.

CLE. Yet he taketh it upon him bravely [5] in this country. 60

PASI. Yea, where no man knoweth the contrary. But let him brave it, boast his birth, and do what he can, the virtue and knowledge that is within this body of yours is worth more than all the country he came from.

CLE. It becometh not a man to praise himself; but indeed I may say, and say truly, that my knowledge hath stood me in better stead at a pinch than could all [70 the goods in the world. I came out of Otranto when the Turks won it, and first I came to Padua, after [6] hither, where, by reading,[7] counseling, and pleading, within twenty years I have gathered and gained as good as ten thousand ducats.

PASI. Yea, marry, this is the right knowledge! Philosophy, Poetry, Logic, and all the rest are but pickling [8] sciences in comparison to this. 80

CLE. But pickling indeed; whereof we have a verse:

The trade of law doth fill the boist'rous bags; [9]
They swim in silk, when others roist [10] in rags.

PASI. O excellent verse! Who made it? Virgil?

CLE. Virgil? Tush, it is written in one of our glosses.[11]

PASI. Sure, whosoever wrote it, the moral is excellent, and worthy to be [90 written in letters of gold. But to the purpose! I think you shall never recover the wealth that you lost at Otranto.

CLE. I think I have doubled it, or rather made it four times as much. *Another sup-* But, indeed, I lost mine only *pose.* son there, a child of five years old.

PASI. O great pity!

CLE. Yea, I had rather have lost all the goods in the world. 100

PASI. Alas! alas! by God! And grafts of such a stock are very gayson [12] in these days.

CLE. I know not whether he were slain, or the Turks took him and kept him as a bondslave.

PASI. Alas, I could weep for compassion! But there is no remedy but patience. You shall get many by this young damsel, with the grace of God. 110

CLE. Yea, if I get her.

PASI. Get her? Why doubt you of that?

CLE. Why? Her father holds me off with delays, so that I must needs doubt.

PASI. Content yourself, sir. He is a wise man and desirous to place his daughter well. He will not be too rash in his determination; he will think well of the matter. And let him think, for the longer he thinketh, the more good of you shall he [120 think. Whose wealth, whose virtue, whose skill, or whose estimation can he compare to yours in this city?

CLE. And hast thou not told him that I would make his daughter a dower of two thousand ducats?

PASI. Why, even now. I came but from thence since.[13]

---

[1] Palmist. [4] Satisfaction. [7] Lecturing.
[2] Unbroken. [5] Lives showily. [8] Trifling.
[3] Tippler. [6] Afterward.

[9] Large pouches to hold the back hair of the wigs worn by judges. [12] Geason, rare.
[10] Bluster. [13] Straightway.
[11] Commentaries on the law.

CLE. What said he?

PASI. Nothing but that Erostrato [130 had proffered the like.

CLE. Erostrato? How can he make any dower, and his father yet alive?

PASI. Think you I did not tell him so? Yes, I warrant you, I forgot nothing that may furder [1] your cause. And doubt you not, Erostrato shall never have her—unless it be in a dream.

CLE. Well, gentle Pasiphilo, go thy ways and tell Damon I require nothing but [140 his daughter; I will none of his goods; I shall enrich her of mine own; and, if this dower of two thousand ducats seem not sufficient, I will make it five hundreth more, yea, a thousand, or whatsoever he will demand, rather than fail. Go to, Pasiphilo! Show thyself friendly in working this feat for me; spare for no cost. Since I have gone thus far, I will be loath to be outbidden. Go! 150

PASI. Where shall I come to you again?

CLE. At my house.

PASI. When?

CLE. When thou wilt.

PASI. Shall I come at dinner time?

CLE. I would bid thee to dinner, but it is a saint's even, which I have ever fasted.

PASI. [Aside.] Fast till thou famish!

CLE. Hark!

PASI. [Aside.] He speaketh of a dead [160 man's fast.[2]

CLE. Thou hearest me not.

PASI. [Aside.] Nor thou understandest me not.

CLE. I dare say thou art angry I bid thee not to dinner, but come if thou wilt; thou shalt take such as thou findest.

PASI. What! think you I know not where to dine?

CLE. Yes, Pasiphilo, thou art not to [170 seek.[3]

PASI. No, be you sure; there are enow will pray me.

CLE. That I know well enough, Pasiphilo. But thou canst not be better welcome in any place than to me. I will tarry for thee.

PASI. Well, since you will needs, I will come.

CLE. Despatch then, and bring no [180 news but good.

PASI. [Aside.] Better than my reward, by the Rood!

Cleander exit; Pasiphilo restat.[4]

SCENA iii.

Pasiphilo, Dulippo.[5]

[PASI.] O miserable, covetous wretch! He findeth an excuse by St. Nicholas' fast, because [6] I should not dine with him— as though I should dine at his own dish! He maketh goodly feasts, I promise you! It is no wonder though he think me bound unto him for my fare; for, over and besides that his provision is as scant as may be, yet there is great difference between his diet and mine. I never so much as [10 sip of the wine that he tasteth; I feed at the board's end with brown bread. Marry, I reach always to his own dish, for there are no more but that only on the table. Yet he thinks that for one such dinner I am bound to do him all the service that I can, and thinks me sufficiently rewarded for all my travail with one such festival promotion! And yet, peradventure, some men think I have great gains under him, [20 but I may say, and swear, that this dozen year I have not gained so much in value as the points at my hose,[7] which are but three, with codpiece-point and all. He thinks that I may feed upon his favor and fair words, but, if I could not otherwise provide for one, Pasiphilo were in a wise case.[8] Pasiphilo hath mo [9] pastures to pass in than one, I warrant you! I am of household with this scholar Eros- [30 trato, his rival, as well as with Domine [10] Cleander—now with the one, and then with the other, according as I see their caters [11] provide good cheer at the market—and I find the means so to handle the matter that I am welcome to both. If the one see me talk with the other, I make him believe it is to hearken news in the furtherance of his cause, and thus I become a broker on both sides. Well, [40 let them both apply the matter as well as

---

[1] Further.
[2] *I.e.*, one which, like Cleander's own, is never broken. [3] Not deficient in that respect.

[4] Remains.
[5] Enters later.
[6] By cause; why.
[7] Laces on my breeches.
[8] In a bad way.
[9] More.
[10] Master.
[11] Caterers.

they can, for indeed I will travail for none of them both, yet will I seem to work wonders on each hand. But is not this one of Damon's servants that cometh forth? It is. Of him I shall understand where his master is. Whither goeth this joyly [1] gallant?

[Enter Dulippo from Damon's house.]

DUL. I come to seek somebody that may accompany my master at dinner. [50 He is alone and would fain have good company.

PASI. Seek no further. You could never have found one better than me.

DUL. I have no commission to bring so many.

PASI. How,[2] many? I will come alone.

DUL. How canst thou come alone that hast continually a legion of ravening wolves within thee?   60

PASI. Thou dost, as servants commonly do, hate all that love to visit their masters.

DUL. And why?

PASI. Because they have too many teeth, as you think.

DUL. Nay, because they have too many tongues.

PASI. Tongues? I pray you, what did my tongue ever hurt you?

DUL. I speak but merrily with you, [70 Pasiphilo. Go in; my master is ready to dine.

PASI. What, dineth he so early?

DUL. He that riseth early, dineth early.

PASI. I would I were his man. Master Doctor never dineth till noon, and how delicately then, God knoweth! I will be bold to go in, for I count myself bidden.

DUL. You were best so.

Pasiphilo intrat; [3] *Dul[ippo] restat.*

Hard hap had I when I first be- [80 gan this unfortunate enterprise! For I supposed the readiest medicine to my miserable affects [4] had been to change name, clothes, and credit with my servant, and to place myself in Damon's service; thinking that, as shivering cold by glowing fire, thirst by drink, hunger by pleasant repasts, and a thousand such like

passions find remedy by their contraries, so my restless desire might have found [90 quiet by continual contemplation. But, alas, I find that only love is unsatiable, for, as the fly playeth with the flame till at last she is cause of her own decay, so the lover that thinketh with kissing and coll-ing [5] to content his unbridled appetite, is commonly seen the only cause of his own consumption. Two years are now past since, under the color [6] of Damon's service, I have been a sworn servant to Cupid [100 —of whom I have received as much favor and grace as ever man found in his service. I have free liberty at all times to behold my desired, to talk with her, to embrace her, yea, be it spoken in secret, to lie with her. I reap the fruits of my desire; yet, as my joys abound, even so my pains in-crease. I fare like the covetous man that, having all the world at will, is never yet content. The more I have, the more I [110 desire. Alas! what wretched estate have I brought myself unto, if in the end of all my far fetches [7] she be given by her father to this old doting doctor, this buzzard, this bribing villain, that by so many means seeketh to obtain her at her father's hands! I know she loveth me best of all others. But what may that prevail when perforce she shall be constrained to marry another? Alas! the pleasant taste of my sugared [120 joys doth yet remain so perfect in my remembrance that the least sop of sorrow seemeth more sour than gall in my mouth. If I had never known delight, with better contentation might I have passed these dreadful dolors. And if this old *mump-simus* [8]—whom the pox consume!—should win her, then may I say, "Farewell the pleasant talk, the kind embracings, yea, farewell the sight of my Polynesta!" [130 For he, like a jealous wretch, will pen her up, that I think the birds of the air shall not win the sight of her. I hoped to have cast a block in his way by the means that my servant, who is supposed to be Eros-trato and with my habit and credit is well esteemed, should proffer himself a suitor—at the least to countervail the doctor's proffers. But my master, knowing the wealth of the one and doubting the [140

---

[1] Elegant, well-dressed.   [3] Goes in.
[2] In what way?   [4] Feelings.

[5] "Necking," embracing.   [7] Clever plots.
[6] Pretense.   [8] Obstinate dolt.

state [1] of the other, is determined to be fed no longer with fair words, but to accept the doctor, whom he right well knoweth, for his son-in-law. Well, my servant promised me yesterday to devise yet again some new conspiracy to drive Master Doctor out of conceit, and to lay a snare that the fox himself might be caught in! What it is, I know not, nor I saw him not since he went about it. I will go see if he be [150 within, that at least if he help me not, he may yet prolong my life for this once. But here cometh his lackey. Ho, Jackpack, where is Erostrato?

Here must Crapine be coming in with a basket and a stick in his hand.

Scena iv.

Crapino, the lackey; Dulippo.

[Cra.] Erostrato? Marry, he is in his skin!

Dul. Ah, whoreson [2] boy! I say, how shall I find Erostrato?

Cra. Find [3] him? How mean you—by the week or by the year?

Dul. You crackhalter! [4] If I catch you by the ears, I shall make you answer me directly.

Cra. Indeed?　　　　　　　　10

Dul. Tarry me a little.

Cra. In faith, sir, I have no leisure.

Dul. Shall we try who can run fastest?

Cra. Your legs be longer than mine; you should have given me the advantage.

Dul. Go to! Tell me where is Erostrato?

Cra. I left him in the street, where he gave me this casket—this basket, I would have said—and bade me bear it to [20 Dalio, and return to him at the duke's palace.

Dul. If thou see him, tell him I must needs speak with him immediately; or abide awhile! I will go seek him myself rather than be suspected by going to his house.

Crapino departeth, and Dulippo also; after, Dulippo cometh in again seeking Erostrato.

Finis Actus i.

[1] Estate.　　　　　　　[4] Gallows bird.
[2] Rascally.
[3] Punning on *find*, to board, support.

Actus II. Scena i.

Dulippo, Erostrato. [5]

[Dul.] I think if I had as many eyes as Argus I could not have sought a man more narrowly in every street and every by-lane. There are not many gentlemen, scholars, nor merchants in the city of Ferrara but I have met with them, except him. Peradventure he is come home another way. But look where he cometh at the last!

[Enter Erostrato.]

Ero. In good time have I spied my good master!　　　　　　　10

Dul. For the love of God, call me "Dulippo," not "master." Maintain the credit that thou hast hitherto kept, and let me alone.

Ero. Yet, sir, let me sometimes do my duty unto you, especially where nobody heareth.

Dul. Yea, but so long the parrot useth to cry "knap" [6] in sport that at the last she calleth her master "knave" in [20 earnest; so long you will use to call me "master," that at the last we shall be heard. What news?

Ero. Good!

Dul. Indeed?

Ero. Yea, excellent. We have as good as won the wager.

Dul. O, how happy were I if this were true!

Ero. Hear you me. Yesternight in [30 the evening I walked out and found Pasiphilo, and with small entreating I had him home to supper; where, by such means as I used, he became my great friend, and told me the whole order of our adversary's determination, yea, and what Damon doth intend to do also; and hath promised me that from time to time, what he can espy he will bring me word of it.

Dul. I cannot tell whether you [40 know him or no. He is not to trust unto—a very flattering and a lying knave.

Ero. I know him very well; he cannot deceive me. And this that he hath told me I know must needs be true.

Dul. And what was it in effect?

Ero. That Damon had purposed to give

[5] Enters later.　　　　[6] Knave, rascal.

his daughter in marriage to this *Another sup-*
doctor upon the dower that he *pose.*
hath proffered.   50

Dul. Are these your good news, your
excellent news?

Ero. Stay awhile; you will understand
me before you hear me.

Dul. Well, say on.

Ero. I answered to that, I was ready to
make her the like dower.

Dul. Well said.

Ero. Abide; you hear not the worst yet.

Dul. O God, is there any worse [60
behind?

Ero. Worse? Why, what assurance could
you suppose that I might make without
some special consent from Philogano, my
father?

Dul. Nay, you can tell; you are better
scholar than I.

Ero. Indeed, you have lost your time,
for the books that you toss [1] nowadays
treat of small science!   70

Dul. Leave thy jesting and proceed.

Ero. I said, further, that I received
letters lately from my father, whereby I
understood that he would be here very
shortly to perform all that I had proffered.
Therefore I required him to request Damon
on my behalf that he would stay his promise to the doctor for a fortnight or more.

Dul. This is somewhat yet, for by this
means I shall be sure to linger and live [80
in hope one fortnight longer. But, at the
fortnight's end when Philogano cometh not,
how shall I then do? Yea, and though he
came, how may I any way hope of his consent, when he shall see that to follow this
amorous enterprise I have set aside all
study, all remembrance of my duty, and
all dread of shame? Alas, alas, I may go
hang myself!

Ero. Comfort yourself, man, and [90
trust in me. There is a salve for every sore,
and doubt you not, to this mischief we
shall find a remedy.

Dul. O, friend, revive me, that hitherto,
since I first attempted this matter, have
been continually dying.

Ero. Well, hearken awhile then. This
morning I took my horse and rode into the
fields to solace myself; and, as I passed the
ford beyond St. Anthony's Gate, I met [100

¹ *Turn the leaves of.*

at the foot of the hill a gentleman riding
with two or three men; and, as methought
by his habit and his looks, he should be
none of the wisest. He saluted me, and I
him. I asked him from whence he came,
and whither he would. He answered that
he had come from Venice, then from Padua,
now was going to Ferrara, and so to his
country, which is Siena. As soon as I
knew him to be a Sienese, suddenly [110
lifting up mine eyes, as it were with an admiration,[2] I said unto him, "Are you a
Sienese, and come to Ferrara?" "Why
not?" said he. Quoth I, half and more
with a trembling voice, "Know you the
danger that should ensue if you be known
in Ferrara to be a Sienese?" He, more than
half amazed, desired me earnestly to tell
him what I meant.

Dul. I understand not whereto this [120
tendeth.

Ero. I believe you. But hearken to me.

Dul. Go to, then.

Ero. I answered him in this sort: "Gentleman, because I have heretofore found
very courteous entertainment in your
country, being a student there, I accompt
myself, as it were, bound to a Sienese, and
therefore if I knew of any mishap towards
any of that country, God forbid but I [130
should disclose it. And I marvel that you
knew not of the injury that your countrymen offered this other day to the ambas-
sadors of County [3] Hercules."

Dul. What tales he telleth me! What
appertain these to me?

Ero. If you will hearken awhile, you
shall find them no tales, but that they appertain to you more than you think for.

Dul. Forth.   140

Ero. I told him further, these ambas-
sadors of County Hercules had divers
mules, wagons, and charettes,[4] laden with
divers costly jewels, gorgeous furniture, and
other things, which they carried as presents,
passing that way, to the King of Naples;
the which were not only stayed in Siene
by the officers whom you call customers,[5]
but searched, ransacked, tossed, and
turned, and in the end exacted for trib- [150
ute, as if they had been the goods of a
mean merchant.

² Wondering look.   ⁴ Carts.
³ Count.   ⁵ Customs officers.

DUL. Whither the devil will he? Is it possible that this gear appertain anything to my cause? I find neither head nor foot in it.

ERO. O, how impatient you are! I pray you, stay awhile.

DUL. Go to yet awhile, then.

ERO. I proceeded that upon these [160 causes the duke sent his chancellor to declare the case unto the senate there, of whom he had the most uncourteous answer that ever was heard; whereupon he was so enraged with all of that country that for revenge he had sworn to spoil as many of them as ever should come to Ferrara, and to send them home in their doublet and their hose.

DUL. And, I pray thee, how could- [170 est thou upon the sudden devise or imagine such a lie, and to what purpose?

ERO. You shall hear by-and-by [1] a thing as fit for our purpose as any could have happened.

DUL. I would fain hear you conclude.

ERO. You would fain leap over the stile before you come at the hedge. I would you had heard me, and seen the gestures that I enforced to make him believe this! [180

DUL. I believe you, for I know you can counterfeit well.

ERO. Further, I said, the duke had charged, upon great penalties, that the innholders and victualers should bring word daily of as many Sieneses as came to their houses. The gentleman, being, as I guessed at the first, a man of small *sapientia*,[2] when he heard these news, would have turned his horse another way. 190

DUL. By likelihood he was not very wise when he would believe that of his country which, if it had been true, every man must needs have known it.

ERO. Why not, when he had not been in his country for a month past, and I told him this had happened within these seven days?

DUL. Belike [3] he was of small experience.

ERO. I think, of as little as may be. [200 But best of all for our purpose, and good adventure it was, that I met with such an one. Now hearken, I pray you.

DUL. Make an end, I pray thee.

ERO. He, as I say, when he heard these

words, would have turned the bridle; and I, feigning a countenance as though I were somewhat pensive and careful for him, paused awhile, and after, with a great sigh, said to him: "Gentleman, for the cour- [210 tesy that, as I said, I have found in your country, and because your affair shall be the better despatched, I will find the means to lodge you in my house, and you shall say to every man that you are a Sicilian of Cathanea, your name Philogano, father to me—that am indeed of that country and city—called here Erostrato. And I, to pleasure you, will during your abode here do you reverence as you were my [220 father."

DUL. Out upon me! What a gross-headed fool am I! Now I perceive whereto this tale tendeth.

ERO. Well, and how like you of it?

DUL. Indifferently.[4] But one thing I doubt.

ERO. What is that?

DUL. Marry, that when he hath been here two or three days, he shall hear of [230 every man that there is no such thing between the duke and the town of Siene.

ERO. As for that, let me alone. I do entertain and will entertain him so well that within these two or three days I will disclose unto him all the whole matter, and doubt not but to bring him in for performance of as much as I have promised to Damon. For what hurt can it be to him, when he shall bind [5] a strange name and [240 not his own?

DUL. What! Think you he will be entreated to stand bound for a dower of two thousand ducats by the year?

ERO. Yea, why not, if it were ten thousand, as long as he is not indeed the man that is bound?

DUL. Well, if it be so, what shall we be the nearer to our purpose?

ERO. Why, when we have done as [250 much as we can, how can we do any more?

DUL. And where have you left him?

ERO. At the inn, because of his horses. He and his men shall lie in my house.

DUL. Why brought you him not with you?

ERO. I thought better to use your advice first.

---

[1] Immediately.   [2] Wisdom.   [3] Perhaps.   [4] Moderately well.   [5] Assume.

DUL. Well, go take him home. Make him all the cheer you can; spare for no [260 cost. I will allow it.

ERO. Content. Look where he cometh.

DUL. Is this he? Go meet him. By my troth, he looks even like a good soul! He that fisheth for him might be sure to catch a cod's head![1] I will rest here awhile to decipher him.

Erostrato espieth the Sienese and goeth towards him; Dulippo standeth aside.

SCENA ii.

The Sienese; Paquetto and Petruchio, his servants; Erostrato.

[SIEN.] He that traveleth in this world passeth by many perils.

PAQ. You say true, sir. If the boat had been a little more laden *Another sup-* this morning at the ferry, we *pose.* had been all drowned, for I think there are none of us that could have swum.

SIEN. I speak not of that.

PAQ. O, you mean the foul way that we had since we came from this Padua. I [10 promise you, I was afraid twice or thrice that your mule would have lien[2] fast in the mire.

SIEN. Jesu, what a blockhead thou art! I speak of the peril we are in presently since we came into this city.

PAQ. A great peril, I promise you, that we were no sooner arrived but you found a friend that brought you from the inn and lodged you in his own house! 20

SIEN. Yea, marry, God reward the gentle young man that we met, for else we had been in a wise case by this time. But have done with these tales. *A doltish* And take you heed, and you *suppose.* also, sirrah, take heed that none of you say we be Sieneses; and remember that you call me Philogano of Cathanea.

PAQ. Sure, I shall never remember these outlandish words! I could well re- [30 member Haccanea.[3]

SIEN. I say, "Cathanea," and not "Haccanea," with a vengeance!

PAQ. Let another name it, then, when **need** is, for I shall never remember it.

SIEN. Then hold thy peace, and take heed thou name not Siene.

PAQ. How say you if I feign myself dumb, as I did once in the house of Crisobolus? 40

SIEN. Do as thou thinkest best. [*Erostrato advances.*] But look where cometh the gentleman whom we are so much bound unto.

ERO. Welcome, my dear father Philogano.

SIEN. Gramercy, my good son Erostrato.

ERO. That is well said. Be mindful of your tongue, for these Ferrareses be [50 as crafty as the devil of hell.

SIEN. No, no; be you sure we will do as you have bidden us!

ERO. For, if you should name Siene, they would spoil you immediately, and turn you out of the town with more shame than I would should befall you for a thousand crowns.

SIEN. I warrant you, I was giving them warning as I came to you; and I doubt [60 not but they will take good heed.

ERO. Yea, and trust not the servants of my household too far, for they are Ferrareses all, and never knew my father, nor came never in Sicilia.—This is my house. Will it please you to go in? I will follow.

They go in. Dulippo tarrieth, and espieth the Doctor coming in with his Man.

SCENA iii.

Dulippo alone.

[DUL.] This gear hath had no evil beginning. If it continue so and fall to happy end! But is not this the silly doctor with the side[4] bonnet—the doting fool that dare presume to become a suitor to such a peerless paragon? O, how covetousness doth blind the common sort of men! Damon, more desirous of the dower than mindful of his gentle and gallant daughter, hath determined to make him his [10 son-in-law, who for his age may be his father-in-law, and hath greater respect to the abundance of goods than to his own natural child. He beareth well in mind **to** fill his own purse, but he little rememb'reth

---

[1] Fool.   [2] Lain.

[3] "Possibly a pun on *hackney* . . . a prostitute" (Adams).

[4] Large.

that his daughter's purse shall be continually empty—unless Master Doctor fill
it with double duck eggs.[1] Alas, I jest,
and have no joy! I will stand here aside
and laugh a little at this lobcock.[2]   20
Dulippo espieth the Doctor and his Man
coming.

SCENA iv.

Carion, the Doctor's Man; Cleander; Dulippo
[, who stands aside].

[CAR.] Master, what the devil mean you
to go seek guests at this time of the day?
The mayor's officers have dined ere this
time, which are alway the last in the
market.

CLE. I come to seek Pasiphilo, to the
end he may dine with me.

CAR. As though six mouths, and the
cat for the seventh, be not sufficient to
eat an harlotry shotterell,[3] a penny- [10
worth of cheese, and half a score spur-
lings![4] This is all the dainties you have
dressed for you and your family.

CLE. Ah, greedy gut, art thou afeard
thou shalt want?

CAR. I am afeard indeed! It is not the
first time I have found it so.

DUL. [*Aside.*] Shall I make some sport
with this gallant? What shall I say to
him?   20

CLE. Thou art afeard, belike, that he
will eat thee and the rest.

CAR. Nay, rather that he will eat your
mule, both hair and hide.

CLE. Hair and hide? And why not
flesh and all?

CAR. Because she hath none! If she
had any flesh, I think you had eaten her
yourself by this time.

CLE. She may thank you, then, for [30
your good attendance.

CAR. Nay, she may thank you for your
small allowance.

DUL. [*Aside.*] In faith, now, let me
alone.

CLE. Hold thy peace, drunken knave,
and espy me Pasiphilo.

DUL. [*Aside.*] Since I can do no better,

I will set such a stance [5] between him and
Pasiphilo that all this town shall not [40
make them friends.

CAR. Could you not have sent to seek
him, but you must come yourself? Surely
you come for some other purpose, for, if
you would have had Pasiphilo to dinner,
I warrant you he would have tarried here
an hour since.[6]

CLE. Hold thy peace! Here is one of
Damon's servants. Of him I *Another sup-*
shall understand where he is. *pose.*
Good fellow, art not thou one of Damon's
servants?   52

DUL. Yes, sir, at your knamandement.[7]

CLE. Gramercy. Tell me, then, hath
Pasiphilo been there this day or no?

DUL. Yes, sir, and I think he be there
still. Ah, ah, ah!

CLE. What [8] laughest thou?

DUL. At a thing that every man may
not laugh at.   60

CLE. What?

DUL. Talk that Pasiphilo had with my
master this day.

CLE. What talk, I pray thee?

DUL. I may not tell it.

CLE. Doth it concern me?

DUL. Nay, I will say nothing.

CLE. Tell me.

DUL. I can say no more.

CLE. I would but know if it concern [70
me. I pray thee tell me.

DUL. I would tell you if I were sure
you would not tell it again.

CLE. Believe me, I will keep it close.
Carion, give us leave a little; go aside.
                        [*Carion stands aside.*]

DUL. If my master should know that
it came by me, I were better die a thousand
deaths.

CLE. He shall never know it. Say on.

DUL. Yea, but what assurance shall [80
I have?

CLE. I lay thee my faith and honesty
in pawn.

DUL. A pretty pawn! The fulkers [9]
will not lend you a farthing on it.

CLE. Yea, but amongst honest men it
is more worth than gold.

---

[1] "Pun on 'duckets,' and also with a further
and coarse meaning" (Adams).
[2] Lubber.   [4] Sparlings, smelts.
[3] Scurvy pike.

[5] Distance, disagreement.
[6] He would have been waiting here an hour ago.
[7] Commandment. So all early edns.
[8] Why.   [9] Pawnbrokers.

Dul. Yea, marry, sir, but where be they? But will you needs have me tell it unto you?   90

Cle. Yea, I pray thee, if it anything appertain to me.

Dul. Yes, it is of you. And I would gladly tell it you, because I would not have such a man of worship so scorned by a villain ribald.[1]

Cle. I pray thee tell me then.

Dul. I will tell you, so that you will swear never to tell it to Pasiphilo, to my master, nor to any other body.   100

Car. [Aside.] Surely it is some toy[2] devised to get some money of him.

Cle. I think I have a book here.

Car. [Aside.] If he knew him as well as I, he would never go about it, for he may as soon get one of his teeth from his jaws with a pair of pinchers as a penny out of his purse with such a conceit.

Cle. Here is a letter will serve the turn. I swear to thee by the contents hereof [110 never to disclose it to any man.

Dul. I will tell you. I am sorry to see how Pasiphilo doth abuse you, persuading you that always he laboreth for you, where, indeed, he lieth on my master continually, as it were with tooth and nail, for a stranger, a scholar, born in Sicilia. They call him Roscus, or Arsekiss—he hath a mad name; I can never hit upon it.

Cle. And thou reckonest it as madly. Is it not Erostrato?   121

Dul. That same. I should never have remembered it. And the villain[3] speaketh all the evil of you that can be devised.

Cle. To whom?

Dul. To my master; yea, and to Polynesta herself sometimes.

Cle. Is it possible? Ah, slave! And what saith he?

Dul. More evil than I can imagine: [130 that you are the miserablest and most niggardly man that ever was.

Cle. Sayeth Pasiphilo so by me?

Dul. And that as often as he cometh to your house he is like to die for hunger, you fare so well.

Cle. That the devil take him else!

Dul. And that you are the testiest man,

and most divers[4] to please, in the whole world, so that he cannot please you un- [140 less he should even kill himself with continual pain.

Cle. O devilish tongue!

Dul. Furthermore, that you cough continually and spit, so that a dog cannot abide it.

Cle. I never spit nor cough more than thus—vho, vho; and that but since I caught this murre.[5] But who is free from it?

Dul. You say true, sir. Yet further, [150 he saith your armholes stink, your feet worse than they, and your breath worst of all.

Cle. If I quite[6] him not for this gear!

Dul. And that you are bursten in the cods.[7]

Cle. O villain! He lieth! And if I were not in the street thou shouldest see them.

Dul. And he saith that you desire [160 this young gentlewoman as much for other men's pleasure as for your own.

Cle. What meaneth he by that?

Dul. Peradventure that by her beauty you would entice many young men to your house.

Cle. Young men? To what purpose?

Dul. Nay, guess you that.

Cle. Is it possible that Pasiphilo speaketh thus of me?   170

Dul. Yea, and much more.

Cle. And doth Damon believe him?

Dul. Yea, more than you would think; in such sort that long ere this he would have given you a flat repulse, but Pasiphilo entreated him to continue you a suitor for his advantage.

Cle. How for his advantage?

Dul. Marry, that during your suit he might still have some reward for his [180 great pains.

Cle. He shall have a rope, and yet that is more than he deserveth. I had thought to have given him these hose when I had worn them a little nearer, but he shall have a &c.[8]

Dul. In good faith, sir, they were but lost on him. Will you anything else with me, sir?

---

[1] Lewd scoundrel.   [2] Trick.
[3] So other edns. than original, which has *villainy*.

[4] Diverse, perverse, difficult.
[5] Catarrh.   [7] Scrotum.
[6] Requite.   [8] To be filled out by the actor.

CLE. Nay, I have heard too much [190 of [1] thee already.

DUL. Then I will take my leave of you.

CLE. Farewell! But tell me, may I not know thy name?

DUL. Sir, they call me Foul-fall-you.

CLE. An ill-favored name, by my troth! Art thou this countryman? [2]

DUL. No, sir, I was born by a castle men call Scab-catch-you. Fare you well, sir!   [*Exit.*] 200

CLE. Farewell! O God, how have I been abused! What a spokesman! What a messenger had I provided!

CAR. Why, sir, will you tarry for Pasiphilo till we die for hunger?

CLE. Trouble me not. That the devil take you both!

CAR. [*Aside.*] These news, whatsoever they be, like him not.

CLE. Art thou so hungry yet? I pray [210 to God thou be never satisfied!

CAR. By the Mass, no more I shall, as long as I am your servant.

CLE. Go, with mischance!

CAR. Yea, and a mischief to you and to all such covetous wretches!   [*Exeunt.*]

FINIS ACTUS II.

ACTUS III. SCENA i.

Dalio, the cook; Crapine, the lackey; Erostrato; Dulippo.[3]

[DAL.] By that time we come to the house I trust that of these twenty eggs in the basket we shall find but very few whole. But it is a folly to talk to him. What the devil! Wilt thou never lay that stick out of thy hand? He fighteth with the dogs, beateth the bears; at everything in the street he findeth occasion to tarry. If he spy a slipstring [4] by the way—such another as himself, a page, a lackey, or a [10 dwarf—the devil of hell cannot hold him in chains but he will be doing with him. I cannot go two steps but I must look back for my yonker. Go to, haltersick! [5] If you break one egg, I may chance break &c.

CRA. What will you break? Your nose in mine, &c.?

DAL. Ah, beast!

CRA. If I be a beast, yet I am no horned [6] beast.   20

DAL. Is it even so? Is the wind in that door? If I were unloaden, I would tell you whether I be a horned beast or no.

CRA. You are alway laden either with wine or with ale.

DAL. Ah, spiteful boy! Shall I suffer him?   [*Strikes him.*]

CRA. Ah, cowardly beast, darest thou strike and say never a word?

DAL. Well, my master shall know of [30 this gear. Either he shall redress it or he shall lose one of us.

CRA. Tell him the worst thou canst by me.

Erostra[to] et Du[lippo] ex improviso.[7]

ERO. What noise, what a rule [8] is this?

CRA. Marry, sir, he striketh me because I tell him of his swearing.

DAL. The villain lieth deadly! He reviles me because I bid him make haste.

ERO. Holla! no more of this. Dalio, [40 do you make in a readiness those pigeons, stock doves, and also the breast of veal; and let your vessel be as clear as glass against I return, that I may tell you which I will have roasted and which boiled. [*Exit Dalio.*] Crapine, lay down that basket and follow me. O, that I could tell where to find Pasiphilo!—But look where he cometh that can tell me of him.

          Dulippo is espied by Erostrato.

DUL. What have you done with [50 Philogano, your father?

ERO. I have left him within. I would fain speak with Pasiphilo. Can you tell me where he is?

DUL. He dined this day with my master, but whither he went from thence I know not. What would you with him?

ERO. I would have him go tell Damon that Philogano, my father, is come, and ready to make assurance of as much as [60 he will require. Now shall I teach Master Doctor a school point. He travaileth to none other end but to catch *cornua*,[9] and he shall have them, for, as old as he is, and

---

[1] From.   [2] A man of this country.
[3] Last two enter later.
[4] Eluder of the gallows.
[5] Haltersack, gallows bird.

[6] Alluding to the horns of a cuckold.
[7] Enter unexpectedly. (But Erostrato does not notice Dulippo immediately.)
[8] Conduct, unruliness.   [9] Horns.

as many subtilties as he hath learned in the law, he cannot go beyond me one ace.

DUL. O dear friend, go thy ways, seek Pasiphilo, find him out, and conclude somewhat to our contentation.

ERO. But where shall I find him?　70

DUL. At the feasts, if there be any, or else in the market with the poulters or the fishmongers.

ERO. What should he do with them?

DUL. Marry, he watcheth whose caters buy the best meat. If any buy a fat capon, a good breast of veal, fresh salmon, or any such good dish, he followeth to the house, and either with some news or some stale jest, he will be sure to make himself [80 a guest.

ERO. In faith, and I will seek there for him.

DUL. Then must you needs find him, and, when you have done, I will make you laugh.

ERO. Whereat?

DUL. At certain sport I made today with Master Doctor.

ERO. And why not now?

DUL. No, it asketh further leisure. [90 I pray thee despatch and find out Pasiphilo, that honest man.

Dulippo tarrieth. Erostrato goeth out [with Crapine].

SCENA ii.

Dulippo alone.

[DUL.] This amorous cause that hangeth in controversy between Domine Doctor and me may be compared to them that play at primero: [1] of whom someone, peradventure, shall leese [2] a great sum of money before he win one stake, and at last, half in anger, shall set up his rest, win it, and after that another, another, and another, till at last he draw the most part of the money to his heap, the other by [10 little and little still diminishing his rest, till at last he be come as near the brink as erst the other was; yet again, peradventure, fortune smiling on him, he shall, as it were by piecemeal, pull out the guts of his fellow's bags, and bring him barer than he himself was tofore; [3] and so in play continue still, fortune favoring now this way, now that way, till at last the one of them

¹ Game of cards.　　² Lose.　　³ Before.

is left with as many crosses [4] as God [20 hath brethren. [5]　O, how often have I thought myself sure of the upper hand herein!—but I triumphed before the victory. And then how oft again have I thought the field lost! Thus have I been tossed, now over, now under, even as fortune list to whirl the wheel, neither sure to win nor certain to lose the wager. And this practice that now my servant hath devised, although hitherto it hath not [30 succeeded amiss, yet can I not count myself assured of it; for I fear still that one mischance or other will come and turn it topsy-turvy. But look where my master cometh.

Damon, coming in, espieth Dulippo and calleth him.

SCENA iii.

Damon, Dulippo, Nevola, and two mo Servants. [6]

[DAM.] Dulippo!

DUL. Here, sir.

DAM. Go in and bid Nevola and his fellows come hither, that I may tell them what they shall go about. And go you into my study; there upon the shelf you shall find a roll of writings which John of the Dean [7] made to my father when he sold him the Grange farm, endorsed with both their names. Bring it hither to me.　10

DUL. It shall be done, sir.　　[*Exit.*]

DAM. Go. I will prepare other manner of writings for you than you are aware of. O fools, that trust any man but themselves nowadays! O spiteful fortune! Thou dost me wrong, I think, that from the depth of hell-pit thou hast sent me this servant to be the subversion of me and all mine!— Come hither, sirs, and hear what I shall say unto you. (*The Servants come in.*) [20 Go into my study, where you shall find Dulippo. Step to him all at once, take him, and, with a cord that I have laid on the table for the nonce, bind him hand and foot, carry him into the dungeon under the stairs, make fast the door, and bring me the key—it hangeth by upon a pin on the wall. Despatch, and do this gear as privily as

⁴ Coins.　　　　　⁶ Last three enter later.
⁵ *I.e.*, none at all.　　⁷ Valley.

you can. And thou, Nevola, come hither
to me again with speed.   30

NEV. Well, I shall. [*Exit with Servants.*]

DAM. Alas, how shall I be revenged of
this extreme despite? If I punish my servant according to his devilish deserts, I
shall heap further cares upon mine own
head. For to such detestable offenses no
punishment can seem sufficient but only
death, and in such cases it is not lawful for
a man to be his own carver. The laws are
ordained, and officers appointed to min- [40
ister justice for the redress of wrongs; and,
if to the potestates [1] I complain me, I shall
publish mine own reproach to the world.
Yea, what should it prevail [2] me to use all
the punishments that can be devised? The
thing, once done, cannot be undone. My
daughter is deflowered, and I utterly dishonested.[3] How can I then wipe that blot
off my brow? And on whom shall I seek
revenge? Alas, alas, I myself have been [50
the cause of all these cares, and have deserved to bear the punishment of all these
mishaps! Alas, I should not have committed my dearest darling in custody to so
careless a creature as this old nurse; for we
see by common proof that these old women
be either peevish [4] or pitiful, either easily
inclined to evil or quickly corrupted with
bribes and rewards. O wife, my good wife,
that now liest cold in the grave, now [60
may I well bewail the want of thee, and,
mourning, now may I bemoan that I miss
thee! If thou hadst lived, such was thy
government of the least things that thou
wouldest prudently have provided for the
preservation of this pearl. A costly jewel
may I well accompt her, that hath been
my chief comfort in youth, and is now become the corrosive of mine age! O Polynesta, full evil hast thou requited the [70
clemency of thy careful father! And yet
to excuse thee guiltless before God and to
condemn thee guilty before the world, I
can count none other but my wretched
self the caitiff [5] and causer of all my cares.
For of all the duties that are requisite in
human life, only obedience is by the parents to be required of the child, where, on
the other side, the parents are bound, first
to beget them, then to bring them forth, [80

after to nourish them, to preserve them
from bodily perils in the cradle, from danger
of soul by godly education, to match them
in consort [6] inclined to virtue, to banish
them all idle and wanton company, to
allow them sufficient for their sustentation,
to cut off excess (the open gate of sin),
seldom or never to smile on them unless it
be to their encouragement in virtue, and
finally to provide them marriages in [90
time convenient, lest, neglected of us, they
learn to set either too much or too little
by themselves. Five years are past since
I might have married her, when by continual excuses I have prolonged it to my
own perdition. Alas, I should have considered she is a collop [7] of my own flesh.
What should I think to make her a princess? Alas, alas, a poor kingdom have
I now caught to endow her with! It is [100
too true that of all sorrows this is the head
source and chief fountain of all furies: the
goods of the world are incertain, the gains
[little] [8] to be rejoiced at, and the loss not
greatly to be lamented; only the children,
cast away, cutteth the parents' throat with
the knife of inward care, which knife will
kill me surely—I make none other accompt.

Damon's Servants come to him again.

SCENA iv.

Nevola, Damon, Pasiphilo.[9]

[NEV.] Sir, we have done as you bade us,
and here is the key.

DAM. Well, go then, Nevola, and seek
Master Casteling, the jailor; he dwelleth by
St. Antony's Gate. Desire him to lend
me a pair of the fetters he useth for his
prisoners; and come again quickly.

NEV. Well, sir.

DAM. Hear you. If he ask what I
would do with them, say you cannot [10
tell. And tell neither him nor any other
what is become of Dulippo.

Damon goeth out.

[NEV.] I warrant you, sir.—Fie upon the
devil! It is a thing almost unpossible
for a man nowadays to handle money but
the metal will stick on his *Another sup-*
fingers. I marveled alway at *pose.*
this fellow of mine, Dulippo, that of the

---

[1] Chief magistrates.   [2] Avail.
[3] Dishonored.   [4] Silly, weak.   [5] Captive.

[6] Companionship.   [8] Suggested by Bond.
[7] Slice, chip.   [9] Enters later.

wages he received he could maintain himself so bravely appareled, but now [20 I perceive the cause. He had the disbursing and receipt of all my master's affairs, the keys of the graner;[1] Dulippo here, Dulippo there; [in] favor with my master, in favor with his daughter—what would you more? He was *magister factotum*.[2] He was as fine as the crusado,[3] and we silly wretches as coarse as canvas. Well, behold what it is come to in the end! He had been better to have done less.   30

Pasi[philo] subito et improviso venit.[4]

PASI. Thou sayst true, Nevola! He hath done too much, indeed.

NEV. From whence comest thou, in the devil's name?

PASI. Out of the same house thou camest from, but not out of the same door.

NEV. We had thought thou hadst been gone long since.

PASI. When I arose from the table, I felt a rumbling in my belly, which [40 made me run to the stable, and there I fell on sleep[5] upon the straw and have lien there ever since. And thou—whither goest thou?

NEV. My master hath sent me on an errand in great haste.

PASI. Whither, I pray thee?

NEV. Nay, I may not tell. Farewell.
    [*Exit.*]

PASI. As though I need any further instructions! O God, what news I heard [50 even now, as I lay in the stable! O good Erostrato, and poor Cleander, that have so earnestly stroven for this *Another suppose.* damsel! Happy is he that can get her, I promise you! He shall be sure of mo than one at a clap that catcheth her—either Adam or Eve within her belly. O God, how men may be deceived in a woman! Who would have believed the contrary but that she had [60 been a virgin? Ask the neighbors, and you shall hear very good report of her. Mark her behaviors, and you would have judged her very maidenly—seldom seen abroad but in place of prayer and there very devout, and no gazer at outward sights, no

blazer of her beauty above in the windows, no stale[6] at the door for the bypassers. You would have thought her a holy young woman. But much good do it Domine [70 Doctor! He shall be sure to lack no CORN[7] in a dear year, whatsoever he have with her else. I beshrew me if I let[8] the marriage any way. But is not this the old scabbed quean[9] that I heard disclosing all this gear to her master as I stood in the stable ere now? It is she. Whither goeth, Psiteria?

Pasiphilo espieth Psiteria coming.

SCENA V.

Psiteria, Pasiphilo.

[PSIT.] To a gossip[10] of mine hereby.

PASI. What, to tattle of the goodly stir that thou kept'st concerning Polynesta?

PSIT. No, no. But how knew you of that gear?

PASI. You told me.

PSIT. I? When did I tell you?

PASI. Even now when you told it to Damon. I both saw you and heard you, though you saw me not me. A good part, [10 I promise you, to accuse the poor wench, kill the old man with care, over and besides the danger you have brought Dulippo and the nurse unto, and many mo! Fie! fie!

PSIT. Indeed, I was to blame, but not so much as you think.

PASI. And how not so much? Did I not hear you tell?

PSIT. Yes, but I will tell you how it [20 came to pass. I have known for a great while that this Dulippo and Polynesta have lien together, and all by the means of the nurse; yet I held my peace and never told it. Now this other day the nurse fell on scolding with me, and twice or thrice called me "drunken old whore" and such names that it was too bad; and I called her "bawd" and told her that I knew well enough how often she had brought [30 Dulippo to Polynesta's bed. Yet all this while I thought not that anybody had heard me; but it befell clean contrary, for my master was on the other side of

---

[1] Granary.   [2] Master Do-all.   [3] A coin.
[4] Pasiphilo enters suddenly and unexpectedly.
[5] Asleep.

[6] Decoy.
[7] Pun on the Latin word for *horn.*
[8] Hinder.   [9] Vile slut.   [10] Crony.

the wall and heard all our talk, whereupon he sent for me and forced me to confess all that you heard.

PASI. And why wouldest thou tell him? I would not for &c.

PSIT. Well, if I had thought my [40 master would have taken it so, he should rather have killed me.

PASI. Why, how could he take it?

PSIT. Alas, it pitieth me to see the poor young woman, how she weeps, wails, and tears her hair, not esteeming her own life half so dear as she doth poor Dulippo's; and her father, he weeps on the other side, that it would pierce an heart of stone with pity. But I must be gone.   50

PASI. Go! That the gunpowder consume thee, old trot![1]   [*Exeunt.*]

FINIS ACTUS III.

ACTUS IV. SCENA i.

Erostrato, feigned [,accompanied by Crapine].

[ERO.] What shall I do? Alas! what remedy shall I find for my rueful estate? What escape or what excuse may I now devise to shift over[2] our subtile supposes? For, though to this day I have usurped the name of my master, and that without check or control of any man, now shall I be openly deciphered, and that in the sight of every man. Now shall it openly be known whether I be Erostrato the [10 gentleman, or Dulippo the servant. We have hitherto played our parts in abusing[3] others, but now cometh the man that will not be abused—the right Philogano, the right father of the right Erostrato. Going to seek Pasiphilo and hearing that he was at the water gate, behold I espied my fellow Litio, and by-and-by my old master Philogano setting forth his first step on land. I to fuge,[4] and away [20 hither as fast as I could to bring word to the right Erostrato of his right father Philogano, that to so sudden a mishap some subtile shift might be upon the sudden devised. But what can be imagined to serve the turn, although we had months' respite to beat our brains about it, since we are commonly known—at the least supposed—in this town, he for Dulippo,

a slave and servant to Damon, and I [30 for Erostrato, a gentleman and a student? But behold, run, Crapine, to yonder old woman before she get within the doors, and desire her to call out Dulippo. But hear you—if she ask who would speak with him, say thyself and none other.

Erostrato espieth Psiteria coming, and sendeth his Lackey to her.

SCENA ii.

Crapine, Psiteria, Erostrato, feigned.

[CRA.] Honest woman! you gossip! thou rotten whore! Hearest thou not, old witch?

PSIT. A rope stretch your young bones! Either you must live to be as old as I or be hanged while you are young.

CRA. I pray thee, look if Dulippo be within.

PSIT. Yes, that he is, I warrant him!

CRA. Desire him, then, to come hither and speak a word with me. He shall [10 not tarry.

PSIT. Content yourself; he is otherwise occupied.

CRA. Yet tell him so, gentle girl.

PSIT. I tell you, he is busy.

CRA. Why, is it such a matter to tell him so, thou crooked crone?

PSIT. A rope stretch you, marry!

CRA. A pox eat you, marry!

PSIT. Thou wilt be hanged, I war- [20 rant thee, if thou live to it.

CRA. And thou wilt be burnt, I warrant thee, if the canker consume thee not.

PSIT. If I come near you, hempstring,[5] I will teach you to sing sol fa![6]

CRA. Come on! and if I get a stone I will scare crows with you.

PSIT. Go, with a mischief! I think thou be some devil that would tempt me. [*Exit.*]

ERO. Crapine! Hear you? Come [30 away. Let her go, with a vengeance! Why come you not? Alas, look where my master Philogano cometh! What shall I do? Where shall I hide me? He shall not see me in these clothes, nor before I have spoken with the right Erostrato.

Erostrato espieth Philogano coming and runneth about to hide him

---

[1] Hag.   [2] Conceal.   [3] Deceiving.   [4] Flight.

[5] Gallows bird.   [6] *I.e.,* scream.

Scena iii.

Philogano; Ferrarese, the innkeeper; Litio,
a servant.

[Phi.] Honest man, it is even so. Be
you sure there is no love to be compared
like the love of the parents towards their
children. It is not long since I thought
that a very weighty matter should not
have made me come out of Sicilia; and yet
now I have taken this tedious toil and
travail upon me, only to see my son and
to have him home with me.

Fer. By my faith, sir, it hath been a [10
great travail indeed, and too much for one
of your age.

Phi. Yea, be you sure. I came in
company with certain gentlemen of my
country, who had affairs to despatch as
far as to Ancona, from thence by water
to Ravenna, and from Ravenna hither,
continually against the tide.

Fer. Yea, and I think that you had but
homely lodging by the way.   20

Phi. The worst that ever man had.
But that was nothing to the stir that the
searchers [1] kept with me when I came
aboard the ship. Jesus, how often they
untrussed my male [2] and ransacked a little
capcase [3] that I had, tossed and turned
all that was within it, searched my bosom,
yea, my breeches, that I assure you I
thought they would have flayed me to
search between the fell [4] and the flesh [30
for fardings. [5]

Fer. Sure, I have heard no less, and
that the merchants bob [6] them sometimes;
but they play the knaves still.

Phi. Yea, be you well assured; such
an office is the inheritance of a knave, and
an honest man will not meddle with it.

Fer. Well, this passage shall seem pleasant unto you when you shall find your child
in health and well. But, I pray you, [40
sir, why did you not rather send for him
into Sicilia than to come yourself, specially
since you had none other business? Peradventure you had rather endanger yourself by this noisome [7] journey than hazard
to draw him from his study.

---

[1] Customs officers.   [3] Bag.
[2] Opened my trunk.   [4] Skin.
[5] Farthings, *i.e.*, taxable goods.
[6] Deceive, cheat.   [7] Annoying.

Phi. Nay, that was not the matter,
for I had rather have him give over his
study altogether and come home.

Fer. Why, if you minded not to [50
make him learned, to what end did you
send him hither at the first?

Phi. I will tell you. When he was at
home, he did as most young men do—he
played many mad pranks and did many
things that liked me not very well; and I,
thinking that by that time he had seen the
world he would learn to know himself
better, exhorted him to study and put in
his election what place he would go to. [60
At the last he came hither, and I think
he was scarce here so soon as I felt the
want of him, in such sort as from that
day to this I have passed few nights without tears. I have written to him very
often that he should come home, but continually he refused, still beseeching me to
continue his study, wherein he doubted
not, as he said, but to profit greatly.

Fer. Indeed, he is very much com- [70
mended of all men, and specially of the
best reputed students.

Phi. I am glad he hath not lost his
time, but I care not greatly for so much
knowledge. I would not be without the
sight of him again so long for all the
learning in the world. I am old now,
and, if God should call me in his absence,
I promise you I think it would drive me
into desperation.   80

Fer. It is commendable in a man to
love his children, but to be so tender over
them is more womanlike.

Phi. Well, I confess it is my fault. And
yet I will tell you another cause of my
coming hither, more weighty than this.
Divers of my country have been here since
he came hither, by whom I have sent unto
him, and some of them have been thrice,
some four or five times at his house, [90
and yet could never speak with him. I
fear he applies his study so that he will
not leese the minute of an hour from his
book. What, alas, he might yet talk with
his countrymen for awhile! He is a young
man, tenderly brought up, and, if he fare
thus continually night and day at his book,
it may be enough to drive him into a
frenzy.

Fer. Indeed, enough were as good [100

as a feast. Lo you, sir, here is your son
Erostrato's house. I will knock.

PHI. Yea, I pray you knock.

[*Knocks on the door.*]

FER. They hear not.

PHI. Knock again.

FER. I think they be on sleep.

LIT. If this gate were your grandfather's soul, you could not knock more
softly. Let me come! [*Knocks violently.*]
Ho, ho! Is there anybody within?   110

Dalio cometh to the window, and there maketh
them answer.

SCENA iv.

Dalio, the cook; Ferrarese, the innholder;
Philogano; Litio, his man.

[DAL.] What devil of hell is there? I
think he will break the gates in pieces!

LIT. Marry, sir, we had thought you had
been on sleep within, and therefore we
thought best to wake you. What doth
Erostrato?

DAL. He is not within.

PHI. Open the door, good fellow, I pray
thee.

DAL. If you think to lodge here, [10
you are deceived, I tell you; for here are
guests enow already.

PHI. A good fellow, and much for thy
master['s] honesty, by our Lady! And
what guests, I pray thee?

DAL. Here is Philogano, my *Another sup-*
master's father, lately come *pose.*
out of Sicilia.

PHI. Thou speakest truer than thou art
aware of. He will be, by that time thou [20
hast opened the door. Open, I pray thee
heartily.

DAL. It is a small matter for me to open
the door, but here is no lodging for you. I
tell you plain, the house is full.

PHI. Of whom?

DAL. I told you. Here is Philogano, my
master's father, come from Cathanea.

PHI. And when came he?

DAL. He came three hours since, or [30
more. He alighted at the Angel and left
his horses there. Afterward my master
brought him hither.

PHI. Good fellow, I think thou hast
good sport to mock me.

DAL. Nay, I think you have good sport

to make me tarry here, as though I have
nothing else to do. I am matched with an
unruly mate in the kitchen. I will go look
to him another while.   40

PHI. I think he be drunken.

FER. Sure he seems so. See you not how
red he is about the gills?

PHI. Abide, fellow. What Philogano
is it whom thou talkest of?

DAL. An honest gentleman, father to
Erostrato, my master.

PHI. And where is he?

DAL. Here within.

PHI. May we see him?   50

DAL. I think you may if you be not
blind.

PHI. Go to! Go tell him here is one
would speak with him.

DAL. Marry, that I will willingly do.

Dalio draweth his head in at the window.[1]

PHI. I cannot tell what I should say to
this gear. Litio, what thinkest thou of it?

LIT. I cannot tell you what I should say,
sir. The world is large and long; there [59
may be mo Philoganos and mo *Another sup-*
Erostratos than one, yea, and *pose.*
mo Ferraras, mo Sicilias, and mo Ca-
thaneas. Peradventure this is not that
Ferrara which you sent your son unto.

PHI. Peradventure thou art a fool, and
he was another that answered us even
now.—But be you sure, honest man, that
you mistake not the house?

FER. Nay, then God help! Think you
I know not Erostrato's house? Yes, and [70
himself also. I saw him here no longer
since than yesterday. But here comes one
that will tell us tidings of him. I like his
countenance better than the other's that
answered at the window erewhile.

The Sienese cometh out.

SCENA v.

Sienese, Philogano, [Ferrarese, Litio,] Dalio.

[SIEN.] Would you speak with me, sir?

PHI. Yea, sir; I would fain know whence
you are.

SIEN. Sir, I am a Sicilian, at your commandment.

PHI. What part of Sicilia?

SIEN. Of Cathanea.

[1] This direction appears at the end of the scene
in all early edns.

PHI. What shall I call your name?
SIEN. My name is Philogano.
PHI. What trade do you occupy?   10
SIEN. Merchandise.
PHI. What merchandise brought you hither?
SIEN. None. I came only to see a son that I have here whom I saw not these two years.
PHI. What call they your son?
SIEN. Erostrato.
PHI. Is Erostrato your son?
SIEN. Yea, verily.
PHI. And are you Philogano?   20
SIEN. The same.
PHI. And a merchant of Cathanea?
SIEN. What need I tell you so often? I will not tell you a lie.
PHI. Yes, you have told me a false lie, and thou art a villain, and no better!
SIEN. Sir, you offer me great wrong with these injurious words.
PHI. Nay, I will do more than I have yet proffered to do, for I will prove thee a [30 liar and a knave to take upon thee that thou art not.
SIEN. Sir, I am Philogano of Cathanea, out of all doubt. If I were not, *A stout suppose.* I would be loath to tell you so.
PHI. O, see the boldness of this brute beast! What a brazen face he setteth on it!
SIEN. Well, you may believe me if you list. What wonder you?
PHI. I wonder at thy impudency; for [40 thou, nor nature that framed thee, can ever counterfeit thee to be me, ribald villain and lying wretch that thou art!
DAL. Shall I suffer a knave to abuse my master's father thus? [*Draws A pleasant his sword.*] Hence, villain! *suppose.* Hence, or I will sheathe this good fawchion [1] in your paunch! If my master Erostrato find you prating here on this fashion to his father, I would not be in [50 your coat for mo cony skins [2] than I gat these twelve months. Come you in again, sir, and let this cur bark here till he burst!

Dalio pulleth the Sienese in at the doors.

SCENA vi.

Philogano, Litio, Ferrarese.

[PHI.] Litio, how likest thou this gear?
LIT. Sir, I like it as evil as may be. But have you not often heard tell of the false-

[1] Falchion.   [2] Rabbit skins.

hood of Ferrara? And now may you see, it falleth out accordingly.
FER. Friend, you do not well to slander the city. These men are no Ferrareses, you may know by their tongue.
LIT. Well, there is never a barrel better herring between you both.[3] But indeed [10 your officers are most to blame, that suffer such faults to escape unpunished.
FER. What know the officers of this? Think you they know of every fault?
LIT. Nay, I think they will know as little as may be, specially when they have no gains by it. But they ought to have their ears as open to hear of such offenses as the inn gates be to receive guests.
PHI. Hold thy peace, fool!   20
LIT. By the Mass, I am afeard that we shall be proved fools, both two.
PHI. Well, what shall we do?
LIT. I would think best we should go seek Erostrato himself.
FER. I will wait upon you willingly, and, either at the schools or at the convocations, we shall find him.
PHI. By our Lady, I am weary. I will run no longer about to seek him. I am [30 sure hither he will come at the last.
LIT. Sure, my mind gives *A true suppose.* me that we shall find a new Erostrato ere it be long.
FER. Look where he is! Whither runs he? Stay you awhile; I will go tell him that you are here. Erostrato! Erostrato! ho, Erostrato! I would speak with you!
Erostrato is espied upon the stage running about.

SCENA vii.

Feigned Erostrato, Ferrarese, Philogano, Litio, Dalio.

[ERO. (*Aside.*)] Now can I hide me no longer. Alas! what shall I do? I will set a good face on, to bear out the matter.
FER. O Erostrato, Philogano, your father, is come out of Sicilia.
ERO. Tell me that I know not. I have been with him, and seen him already.
FER. Is it possible? And it seemeth by him that you know not of his coming.

[3] Proverb meaning, "There is no difference between you two."

Ero. Why, have you spoken with [10 him? When saw you him, I pray you?

Fer. Look you where he stands. Why go you not to him? Look you, Philogano; behold your dear son Erostrato.

Phi. Erostrato? This is not Erostrato. This seemeth rather to be Dulippo—and it is Dulippo indeed.

Lit. Why, doubt you of that?

Ero. What saith this honest man?

Phi. Marry, sir, indeed you are so [20 honorably clad it is no marvel if you look big.

Ero. To whom speaketh he?

Phi. What! God help! Do you not know me?

Ero. As far as I remember, sir, I never saw you before.

Phi. Hark, Litio, here is good gear! This honest man will not know me!

Ero. Gentleman, you take your [30 marks amiss.

Lit. Did I not tell you of the   *A shameless* falsehood of Ferrara, master? *suppose.* Dulippo hath learned to play the knave indifferently well since he came hither.

Phi. Peace, I say.

Ero. Friend, my name is not Dulippo. Ask you thoroughout this town of great and small; they know me. Ask this honest man that is with you, if you will not [40 believe me.

Fer. Indeed, I never knew him otherwise called than Erostrato; and so they call him, as many as know him.

Lit. Master, now you may see the falsehood of these fellows. This *A needless* honest man, your host, is of *suppose.* counsel with him, and would face us down that it is Erostrato. Beware of these mates![1]   50

Fer. Friend, thou doest me wrong to suspect me, for sure I never heard him otherwise called than Erostrato.

Ero. What name could you hear me called by but by my right name? But I am wise enough to stand prating here with this old man! I think he be mad.

[*Enter Dalio and other Servants, armed.*]

Phi. Ah, runagate! Ah, villain traitor! Dost thou use thy master thus? What hast thou done with my son, villain? [60

1 Fellows

Dal. Doth this dog bark here still? And will you suffer him, master, thus to revile you?

Ero. Come in, come in. What wilt thou do with this pestil?[2]

Dal. I will rap the old cackabed[3] on the costard.[4]

Ero. Away with it! And you, sirrah, lay down these stones! Come in at door, every one of you. Bear with him, for [70 his age. I pass not of[5] his evil words.

Erostrato taketh all his Servants in at the doors.

Scena viii.

Philogano, Ferrarese, Litio.

[Phi.] Alas, who shall relieve my miserable estate? To whom shall I complain, since he whom I brought up of a child, yea, and cherished him as if he had been mine own, doth now utterly deny to know me? And you, whom I took for an honest man and he that should have brought me to the sight of my son, are compact[6] with this false wretch, and would face me down that he is Erostrato. Alas, you might have [10 some compassion of mine age, *Another sup-* to the misery I am now in, and *pose.* that I am a stranger desolate of all comfort in this country; or, at the least, you should have feared the vengeance of God, the supreme judge, which knoweth the secrets of all hearts, in bearing this false witness with him whom heaven and earth do know to be Dulippo and not Erostrato.

Lit. If there be many such witnesses [20 in this country, men may go about to prove what they will in controversies here.

Fer. Well, sir, you may judge of me as it pleaseth you; and how the matter cometh to pass I know not, but, truly, ever since he came first hither I have known him by the name of Erostrato, the son of Philogano, a Cathanese. Now, whether he be so indeed or whether he be Dulippo, as you allege, let that be proved by them that knew [30 him before he came hither. But I protest before God that which I have said is neither a matter compact with him nor any

2 Pestle, pig's leg.
3 Vulgar term of abuse.   5 Care not for.
4 Apple, head.   6 In conspiracy.

other, but even as I have heard him called and reputed of all men.

PHI. Out and alas! He whom I sent hither with my son to be his servant and to give attendance on him, hath either cut his throat or by some evil means made [39 him away, and hath not only *A shrewd sup-* taken his garments, his books, *pose.* his money, and that which he brought out of Sicilia with him, but usurpeth his name also, and turneth to his own commodity the bills of exchange that I have always allowed for my son's expenses. O miserable Philogano, O unhappy old man! O eternal God, is there no judge, no officer, no higher powers whom I may complain unto for redress of these wrongs?   50

FER. Yes, sir, we have potestates, we have judges, and, above all, we have a most just prince. Doubt you not but you shall have justice, if your cause be just.

PHI. Bring me then to the judges, to the potestates, or to whom you think best; for I will disclose a pack of the greatest knavery, a fardel [1] of the foulest falsehood, that ever was heard of!

LIT. Sir, he that will go to the law [60 must be sure of four things: first, a right and a just cause; then, a righteous advocate to plead; next, favor *coram judice;* [2] and, above all, a good purse to procure it.

FER. I have not heard that the law hath any respect to favor; what you mean by it I cannot tell.

PHI. Have you no regard to his words; he is but a fool.

FER. I pray you, sir, let him tell me [70 what is favor.

LIT. Favor call I to have a friend near about the judge, who may so solicit thy cause as, if it be right, speedy sentence may ensue without any delays; if it be not good, then to prolong it, till at the last thine adversary, being weary, shall be glad to compound with thee.

FER. Of thus much (although I never heard thus much in this country before) [80 doubt you not, Philogano: I will bring you to an advocate that shall speed you accordingly.

PHI. Then shall I give myself, as it were, a prey to the lawyers, whose insatiable jaws I am not able to feed, although I had here all the goods and lands which I possess in mine own country—much less, being a stranger in this misery. I know their cautels [3] of old. At the first time I come [90 they will so extol my cause as though it were already won; but within a sevennight or ten days, if I do not continually feed them, as the crow doth her brats, twenty times in an hour, they will begin to wax cold and to find cavils in my cause, saying that at the first I did not well instruct them; till, at the last, they will not only draw the stuffing out of my purse but the marrow out of my bones.   100

FER. Yea, sir; but this man that I tell you of is half a saint.

LIT. And the other half a devil, I hold [4] a penny!

PHI. Well said, Litio. Indeed, I have but small confidence in their smooth looks.

FER. Well, sir, I think this whom I mean is no such manner of man. But if he were, there is such hatred and evil- *Another sup-* will between him and this *pose.* gentleman (whether he be Erostrato or [111 Dulippo, whatsoever he be) that I warrant you he will do whatsoever he can do for you, were it but to spite him.

PHI. Why, what hatred is betwixt them?

FER. They are both in love and suitors to one gentlewoman, the daughter of a wealthy man in this city.

PHI. Why, is the villain become of such estimation that he dare presume to be [120 a suitor to any gentlewoman of a good family?

FER. Yea, sir, out of all doubt.

PHI. How call you his adversary?

FER. Cleander, one of the excellentest doctors in our city.

PHI. For God's love, let us go to him!

FER. Go we then.   [*Exeunt.*]

FINIS ACTUS IV.

ACTUS V. SCENA i.

Feigned Erostrato.

[ERO.] What a mishap was this, that before I could meet with Erostrato I have light even full in the lap of Philogano, where I was constrained to deny my name, to deny my master, and to feign that I knew him not, to contend with him, and to

---

[1] Bundle.   [2] Before the judge.   [3] Artifices.   [4] Wager.

revile him in such sort that, hap what hap can, I can never hap well in favor with him again! Therefore, if I could come to speak with the right Erostrato, I will renounce [10 unto him both habit and credit, and away as fast as I can trudge into some strange country where I may never see Philogano again—alas, he that of a little child hath brought me up unto this day and nourished me as if I had been his own, and, indeed, to confess the *Another sup-* truth, I have no father to *pose.* trust unto but him. But look where Pasiphilo cometh, the fittest man in the world [20 to go on my message to Erostrato.

Erostrato espieth Pasiphilo coming towards him.

Scena ii.

Pasiphilo, Erostrato.

[Pasi.] Two good news have I heard to-day already: one, that Erostrato prepared a great feast this night; the other, that he seeketh for me. And I, to ease him of his travail, lest he should run up and down seeking me, and because no man loveth better than I to have an errand where good cheer is, come in posthaste even home to his own house. And look where he is.

Ero. Pasiphilo, thou must do one [10 thing for me, if thou love me.

Pasi. If I love you not, who loves you? Command me.

Ero. Go then a little there, to Damon's house; ask for Dulippo, and tell him—

Pasi. Wot[1] you what? I cannot speak with him. He is in prison.

Ero. In prison! How cometh that to pass? Where is he in prison?

Pasi. In a vile dungeon, there, within [20 his master's house.

Ero. Canst thou tell wherefore?

Pasi. Be you content to know he is in prison. I have told you too much.

Ero. If ever you will do anything for me, tell me.

Pasi. I pray you, desire me not. What were you the better if you knew?

Ero. More than thou thinkest, Pasi-philo, by God.   30

Pasi. Well, and yet it stands me upon,[2] more than you think, to keep it secret.

---

[1] Know.   [2] It is incumbent upon me.

Ero. Why, Pasiphilo, is this the trust I have had in you? Are these the fair promises you have a[l]ways made me?

Pasi. By the Mass, I would I had fasted this night with Master Doctor rather than have come hither.

Ero. Well, Pasiphilo, either tell me, or, at few words, never think to be welcome [40 to this house from henceforth.

Pasi. Nay, yet I had rather leese all the gentlemen in this town. But, if I tell you anything that displease you, blame nobody but yourself now.

Ero. There is nothing can grieve me more than Dulippo's mishap—no, not mine own; and therefore I am sure thou canst tell me no worse tidings.

Pasi. Well, since you would needs [50 have it, I will tell you. He *Another* was taken abed with your *plain and* beloved Polynesta. *homely sup-* *pose.* Ero. Alas, and doth Damon know it?

Pasi. An old trot in the house disclosed it to him; whereupon he took both Dulippo and the nurse, which hath been the broker of all this bargain, and clapped them both in a cage—where, I think, they shall [60 have sour[3] sops to[4] their sweetmeats.

Ero. Pasiphilo, go thy ways into the kitchen; command the cook to boil and roast what liketh thee best. I make thee supervisor of this supper.

Pasi. By the Mass, if you should have studied this sevennight you could not have appointed me an office to please me better! You shall see what dishes I will devise.

Pasiphilo goeth in; Erostrato tarrieth.

Scena iii.

Feigned Erostrato alone.

[Ero.] I was glad to rid him out of the way, lest he should see me burst out of these swelling tears, which hitherto with great pain I have prisoned in my breast, and lest he should hear the echo of my doubled sighs, which bounce from the bottom of my heavy heart. O cursed I! O cruel fortune, that so many dispersed griefs as were sufficient to subvert a legion of lovers hast suddenly assem- [10

---

[3] From 1573 edn. Original has *sorowe.*
[4] In addition to.

bled within my careful carcass to fret this fearful heart in sunder with desperation! Thou that hast kept my master all his youth within the realm of Sicilia, reserving the wind and waves in a temperate calm— as it were at his command—now to convey his aged limbs hither, neither sooner nor later, but even in the worst time that may be! If, at any time before, thou haddest conducted him, this enterprise [20 had been cut off without care in the beginning; and, if never so little longer thou hadst lingered [1] his journey, this happy day might then have fully finished our drifts [2] and devises. But, alas, thou hast brought him even in the very worst time, to plunge us all in the pit of perdition! Neither art thou content to entangle me alone in thy ruinous ropes, but thou must also catch the right Erostrato in thy [30 crooked claws, to reward us both with open shame and rebuke. Two years hast thou kept secret our subtile supposes, even this day to decipher them with a sorrowful success. What shall I do? Alas, what shift shall I make? It is too late now to imagine any further deceit, for every minute seemeth an hour till I find some succor for the miserable captive Erostrato. Well, since there is no other remedy, I [40 will go to my master Philogano, and to him will I tell the whole truth of the matter, that at the least he may provide in time before his son feel the smart of some sharp revenge and punishment. This is the best, and thus will I do. Yet I know that for mine own part I shall do bitter penance for my faults forepassed! But such is the good will and duty that I bear to Erostrato as even with the loss [50 of my life I must not stick to adventure anything which may turn to his commodity. But what shall I do? Shall I go seek my master about the town, or shall I tarry his return hither? If I meet him in the streets, he will cry out upon me, neither will he hearken to anything that I shall say till he have gathered all the people wondering about me as it were at an owl. Therefore I were better to abide here. And yet, [60 if he tarry long, I will go seek him rather than prolong the time to Erostrato's peril.

Pasiphilo returneth to Erostrato.

[1] Delayed.   [2] Plots.

Scena iv.

Pasiphilo, feigned Erostrato.

[Pasi. (*To Dalio within.*)] Yea, dress them, but lay them not to the fire till they will be ready to sit down.—This gear goeth in order, but if I had not gone in, there had fallen a foul fault.

Ero. And what fault, I pray thee?

Pasi. Marry, Dalio would have laid the shoulder of mutton and the capon both to the fire at once, like a fool! He did not consider that the one would have more [10 roasting than the other.

Ero. Alas, I would this were the greatest fault.

Pasi. Why? And either the one should have been burned before the other had been roasted, or else he must have drawn them off the spit, and they would have been served to the board either cold or raw.

Ero. Thou hast reason, Pasiphilo.

Pasi. Now, sir, if it please you, I will [20 go into the town and buy oranges, olives, and caphers; [3] for without such sauce the supper were more than half lost.

Ero. There are [4] within already, doubt you not; there shall lack nothing that is necessary.   *Erostrato exit.*

Pasi. Since I told him these news of Dulippo, he is clean beside himself. He hath so many hammers in his head that his brains are ready to burst. And let them [30 break. So I may sup with him tonight, what care I? But is not this *A knavish Dominus noster Cleandrus* [5] that *suppose.* cometh before? Well said. By my truth, we will teach Master Doctor to wear a cornered cap [6] of a new fashion. By God, Polynesta shall be his! He shall have her, out of doubt; for I have told Erostrato such news of her that he will none of her.

Cleander and Philogano come in, talking of the matter in controversy.

Scena v.

Cleander, Philogano, Litio, Pasiphilo.

[Cle.] Yea, but how will ye prove that he is not Erostrato, having such presumptions to the contrary? Or how shall it be thought that you are Philogano, when another taketh upon him this same name,

[3] Capers.   [5] Our master, Cleander.
[4] Supply *some.*   [6] Horns of the cuckold.

and for proof bringeth him for a witness which hath been ever reputed here for Erostrato?

PHI. I will tell you, sir. Let me be kept here fast in prison, and at my [10 charges let there be some man sent into Sicilia that may bring hither with him two or three of the honestest men in Cathanea, and by them let it be proved if I or this other be Philogano, and whether he be Erostrato or Dulippo my servant; and, if you find me contrary,[1] let me suffer death for it.

PASI. I will go salute Master Doctor.

CLE. It will ask great labor and great [20 expenses to prove it this way, but it is the best remedy that I can see.

PASI. God save you, sir!

CLE. And reward you as you have deserved.

PASI. Then shall he give me your favor continually.

CLE. He shall give you a halter, knave and villain that thou art!

PASI. I know I am a knave, but no [30 villain. I am your servant.

CLE. I neither take thee for my servant nor for my friend.

PASI. Why, wherein have I offended you, sir?

CLE. Hence to the gallows, knave!

PASI. What! Soft and fair, sir, I pray you. "*I præ, sequar;*"[2] you are mine elder.

CLE. I will be even with you, be you sure, honest man.   40

PASI. Why, sir? I never offended you.

CLE. Well, I will teach you. Out of my sight, knave!

PASI. What! I am no dog, I would you wist.[3]

CLE. Pratest thou yet, villain? I will make thee—

PASI. What will you make me? I see well the more a man doth suffer you, the worse you are.   50

CLE. Ah, villain, if it were not for this gentleman, I would tell you what I—

PASI. Villain? Nay, I am as honest a man as you.

CLE. Thou liest in thy throat, knave!

PHI. O, sir, stay your wisdom.

PASI. What! Will you fight? Marry, come on!

CLE. Well, knave, I will meet with you another time. Go your way.   60

PASI. Even when you list, sir, I will be your man.

CLE. And if I be not even with thee, call me cut![4]

PASI. Nay, by the Mass, all is one. I care not, for I have nothing. If I had either lands or goods, peradventure you would pull me into the law.   [*Exit.*]

PHI. Sir, I perceive your patience is moved.   70

CLE. This villain! But let him go. I will see him punished as he hath deserved. Now to the matter. How said you?

PHI. This fellow hath disquieted you, sir. Peradventure you would *Lawyers* be loath to be troubled any *are never* further.   *weary to get*

CLE. Not a whit. Say on, *money.* and let him go—with a vengeance!

PHI. I say, let them send at my [80 charge to Cathanea.

CLE. Yea, I remember that well, and it is the surest way as this case requireth. But tell me, how is he your servant, and how come you by him? Inform me fully in the matter.

PHI. I will tell you, sir. When the Turks won Otranto—

CLE. O, you put me in remembrance of my mishaps!   90

PHI. How, sir?

CLE. For I was driven among the rest out of the town (it is my native country), and there I lost more than ever I shall recover again while I live.

PHI. Alas, a pitiful case, by St. Anne!

CLE. Well, proceed.

PHI. At that time, as I said, there were certain of our country that scoured those coasts upon the seas with a good bark, [100 well appointed for the purpose, and had espial of a Turkey vessel that came laden from thence with great abundance of riches.

CLE. And peradventure most *A gentle* of mine.   *suppose.*

PHI. So they boarded them, and in the end overcame them, and brought the goods to Palermo, from whence they came; and amongst other things that they

[1] Wrong.
[2] Terence, *Andria*, I, i, 144: "Go ahead; I'll follow."   [3] Knew.
[4] Gelded horse.

had was this villain, my servant, a [110 boy at that time, I think not past five years old.

CLE. Alas, I lost one of that same age there!

PHI. And I, being there, and liking the child's favor well, proffered them four and twenty ducats for him, and had him.

CLE. What! was the child a Turk? Or had the Turks brought him from Otranto?

PHI. They said he was a child of [120 Otranto. But what is that to the matter? Once four and twenty ducats he cost me— that I wot well.

CLE. Alas, I speak it not for that, sir. I would it were he whom I mean.

PHI. Why, whom mean you, sir?

LIT. Beware, sir; be not too *A crafty* lavish!   *suppose.*

CLE. Was his name Dulippo then or had he not another name?   130

LIT. Beware what you say, sir!

PHI. What the devil hast thou to do!— Dulippo? No, sir, his name was Carino.

LIT. Yea, well said! Tell all, and more too; do!

CLE. O Lord, if it be as I think, how happy were I! And why did you change his name then?

PHI. We called him Dulippo because when he cried, as children do some- [140 times, he would always cry on that name, Dulippo.

CLE. Well, then I see well it is my own only child, whom I lost when I lost my country! He was named Carino after his grandfather; and this Dulippo, whom he always remembered in his lamenting, was his foster-father that nourished him and brought him up.

LIT. Sir, have I not told you enough [150 of the falsehood of Ferrara? This gentleman will not only pick your purse, but beguile you of your servant also, and make you believe he is his son.

CLE. Well, good fellow, I have not used to lie.

LIT. Sir, no; but everything hath a beginning.

CLE. Fie! Philogano, have you not the least suspect [1] that may be of me.   160

LIT. No, marry; but it were good he had the most suspect that may be.

[1] Suspicion.

CLE. Well, hold thou thy peace a little, good fellow. I pray you tell me, Philogano, had the child any remembrance of his father's name, his mother's name, or the name of his family?

PHI. He did remember them, and could name his mother also, but sure I have forgotten the name.   170

LIT. I remember it well enough!

PHI. Tell it then.

LIT. Nay, that I will not, marry! You have told him too much already.

PHI. Tell it, I say, if thou can.

LIT. Can? Yes, by the Mass, I can well enough! But I will have my tongue pulled out rather than tell it unless he tell it first. Do you not perceive, sir, what he goeth about?   180

CLE. Well, I will tell you then. My name you know already; my wife, his mother's, name was Sophronia; the house that I came of they call Spiagia.

LIT. I never heard him speak of Spiagia, but indeed I have heard him say his mother's name was Sophronia. But what of that? A great matter, I promise you! It is like enough that you two have compact together to deceive my master. [190

CLE. What needeth me more evident tokens? This is my son out of doubt, whom I lost eighteen years since, and a thousand thousand times have I lamented for him. He should have also a mold [2] on his left shoulder.

LIT. He hath a mold there indeed, and an hole in another place, too—I would your nose were in it!

CLE. Fair words, fellow Litio! O, [200 I pray you, let us go talk with him! O fortune, how much am I bound to thee if I find my son!

PHI. Yea, how little am I beholden to fortune, that know not where my son is become; and you, whom I chose to be mine advocate, will now, by the means of this Dulippo, become mine adversary!

CLE. Sir, let us first go find mine, [209 and, I warrant you, yours will *A right sup-* be found also ere it be long. *pose.*

PHI. God grant! Go we then.

CLE. Since the door is open, I will never knock nor call, but we will be bold to go in.

[2] Mole.

Lit. [*To Philogano.*] Sir, take you heed lest he lead you to some mischief.

Phi. Alas, Litio, if my son be lost, what care I what become of me?

Lit. Well, I have told you my mind, sir. Do you as you please. 221

Exeunt. Damon and Psiteria come in.

Scena vi.

Damon, Psiteria.

[Dam.] Come hither, you old callet,[1] you tattling huswife! That the devil cut out your tongue! Tell me, how could Pasiphilo know of this gear but by you?

Psit. Sir, he never knew it of me; he was the first that told me of it.

Dam. Thou liest, old drab! But I would advise you tell me the truth, or I will make those old bones rattle in your skin.

Psit. Sir, if you find me contrary, [10 kill me.

Dam. Why, where should he talk with thee?

Psit. He talked with me of it here in the street.

Dam. What did you here?

Psit. I was going to the weaver's for a web of cloth you have there.

Dam. And what cause could Pasiphilo have to talk of it, unless thou began the [20 matter first?

Psit. Nay, he began with me, sir, reviling me because I had told you of it. I asked him how he knew of it, and he said he was in the stable when you examined me erewhile.

Dam. Alas, alas, what shall I do then? In at doors, old whore! I will pluck that tongue of thine out by the roots one day. [*Exit Psiteria.*] Alas, it grieveth me [30 more that Pasiphilo knoweth it than all the rest. He that will have a thing kept secret, let him tell it to Pasiphilo! The people shall know it, and as many as have ears, and no mo. By this time he hath told it in a hundreth places! Cleander was the first, Erostrato the second; and so from one to another throughout the city. Alas, what dower, what marriage shall I now prepare for my daughter? O poor [40 dolorous Damon, more miserable than misery itself! Would God it were true

that Polynesta told me erewhile—that he who hath deflowered her is of no servile estate, as hitherto he hath been *The first suppose brought to conclusion.* supposed in my service, but that he is a gentleman, born of a good parentage in Sicilia. Alas, small riches should content me if he be but of an honest family! But [50 I fear that he hath devised these toys to allure my daughter's love. Well, I will go examine her again. My mind giveth me that I shall perceive by her tale whether it be true or not. But is not this Pasiphilo that cometh out of my neighbor's house? What the devil aileth him to leap and laugh so like a fool in the highway?

Pasiphilo cometh out of the house laughing.

Scena vii.

Pasiphilo,[2] Damon.

[Pasi. (*To himself.*)] O God, that I might find Damon at home!

Dam. What the devil would he with me?

Pasi. [*To himself.*] That I may be the first that shall bring him these news!

Dam. What will he tell me, in the name of God?

Pasi. [*To himself.*] O Lord, how happy am I!—Look where he is.

Dam. What news, Pasiphilo, that [10 thou art so merry?

Pasi. Sir, I am merry to make you glad. I bring you joyful news!

Dam. And that I have need of, Pasiphilo.

Pasi. I know, sir, that you are a sorrowful man for this mishap that hath chanced in your house. Peradventure you thought I had not known of it. But let it pass! Pluck up your sprites,[3] and rejoice! For [20 he that hath done you this injury is so well born and hath so rich parents that you may be glad to make him your son-in-law.

Dam. How knowest thou?

Pasi. His father, Philogano, one of the worthiest men in all Cathanea, is now come to the city, and is here in your neighbor's house.

Dam. What, in Erostrato's house?

Pasi. Nay, in Dulippo's house. For [30 where you have always supposed this gentleman to be Erostrato, it is not so; but

---

[1] Whore.

[2] Original prints *Philogano*.　　[3] Spirits.

your servant, whom you have imprisoned, hitherto supposed to be Dulippo, he is indeed Erostrato, and that other is Dulippo. And thus they have always, even since their first arrival in this city, exchanged names, to the end that Erostrato, the master, under the name of Dulippo, a servant, might be entertained in your house [40 and so win the love of your daughter.

DAM. Well, then I perceive it is even as Polynesta told me.

PASI. Why, did she tell you so?

DAM. Yea, but I thought it but a tale.

PASI. Well, it is a true tale. And here they will be with you by-and-by—both Philogano, this worthy man, and Master Doctor Cleander.

DAM. Cleander? What to do?   50

PASI. Cleander? Why thereby lies another tale—the most fortunate adventure that ever you heard! Wot you what? This other Dulippo, whom all this while we supposed to be Erostrato, is found to be the son of Cleander, whom he lost at the loss of Otranto, and was after sold in Sicilia to this Philogano. The strangest case that ever you heard! A man might make a comedy of it. They will come even [60 straight and tell you the whole circumstance of it themselves.

DAM. Nay, I will first go hear the story of this Dulippo, be it Dulippo or Erostrato, that I have here within, before I speak with Philogano.

PASI. So shall you do well, sir. I will go tell them that they may stay awhile.— But look where they come.

Damon goeth in; Sienese, Cleander, and Philogano come upon the stage.

SCENA viii.

Sienese, Cleander, [Carino,] [1] Philogano.

[SIEN.] Sir, you shall not need to excuse the matter any further. Since I have received no greater injury than by words, let them pass like wind. I take them well in worth and am rather well pleased than offended. For it shall both be a good warning to me another time how to trust every man at the first sight, yea, and I shall have good game hereafter to tell this pleasant story another day in mine own country. [10

[1] *I.e.*, the real Dulippo.

CLE. Gentleman, you have reason; and be you sure that as many as hear it will take great pleasure in it. And you, Philogano, may think that God in heaven above hath ordained your coming hither at this present to the end I might recover my lost son, whom by no other means I could ever have found out.

PHI. Surely, sir, I think no less; for I think that not so much as a leaf falleth [20 from the tree without the ordinance of God. But let us go seek Damon, for methinketh every day a year, every hour a day, and every minute too much, till I see my Erostrato.

CLE. I cannot blame you. Go we then. Carino, take you that gentleman home in the meantime. The fewer the better to be present at such affairs.

Pasiphilo stayeth their going in.

SCENA ix.

Pasiphilo,[2] Cleander.

[PASI.] Master Doctor, will you not show me this favor, to tell me the cause of your displeasure?

CLE. Gentle Pasiphilo, I must needs confess I have done thee wrong, and that I believed tales of thee, which indeed I find now contrary.

PASI. I am glad, then, that it proceeded rather of ignorance than of malice.

CLE. Yea, believe me, Pasiphilo.   10

PASI. O, sir, but yet you should not have given me such foul words.

CLE. Well, content thyself, Pasiphilo. I am thy friend, as I have always been; for proof whereof, come sup with me tonight, and from day to day this sevennight be thou my guest. But behold, here cometh Damon out of his house.

Here they come all together.

SCENA x.

Cleander, Philogano, Damon, Erostrato, Pasiphilo, Polynesta; Nevola and other Servants.[3]

[CLE. (*To Damon.*)] We are come unto you, sir, to turn your sorrow into joy and gladness—the sorrow, we mean, that of force you have sustained since this mishap

[2] Original has *Philogano*.   [3] Enter later.

of late fallen in your house. But be you of good comfort, sir, and assure yourself that this young man, which youthfully and not maliciously hath committed this amorous offense, is very well able, with consent of this worthy man, his father, to make [10 you sufficient amends, being born in Cathanea of Sicilia, of a noble house, no way inferior unto you, and of wealth, by the report of such as know it, far exceeding that of yours.

PHI. And I here, in proper person, do present unto you, sir, not only my assured friendship and brotherhood, but do earnestly desire you to accept my poor child, though unworthy, as your son-in-law. [20 And for recompense of the injury he hath done you, I proffer my whole lands in dower to your daughter; yea, and more would, if more I might.

CLE. And I, sir, who have hitherto so earnestly desired your daughter in marriage, do now willingly yield up and quit claim to this young man, who, both for his years and for the love he beareth her, is most meetest to be her husband. For [30 where I was desirous of a wife by whom I might have issue, to leave that little which God hath sent me, now have I little need, that, thanks be to God, have found my dearly beloved son, whom I lost of a child at the siege of Otranto.

DAM. Worthy gentleman, your friendship, your alliance, and the nobility of your birth are such as I have much more cause to desire them of you than you to re- [40 quest of me that which is already granted. Therefore I gladly and willingly receive the same, and think myself most happy now

of all my life past that I have gotten so toward [1] a son-in-law to myself and so worthy a father-in-law to my daughter. Yea, and much the greater is my contentation since this worthy gentleman, Master Cleander, doth hold himself satisfied. And now, behold your son!　　　　　50

ERO. O father!

PASI. Behold the natural love of the child to the father. For inward joy he cannot pronounce one word; instead whereof he sendeth sobs and tears to tell the effect of his inward intention.[2] But why do you abide here abroad? Will it please you to go into the house, sir?

DAM. Pasiphilo hath said well. Will it please you to go in, sir?　　　　　60

[Enter Nevola with fetters.]

NEV. Here I have brought you, sir, both fetters and bolts.

DAM. Away with them, now!

NEV. Yea, but what shall I do with them?

DAM. Marry, I will tell thee, Nevola. To make a right end of our supposes, lay one of those bolts in the fire, and make thee a suppository as long as mine arm— God save the sample!—[*Turns to the audience.*] Nobles and gentlemen, if you [71 suppose that our Supposes have given you sufficient cause of delight, show some token whereby we may suppose you are content.

Et plauserunt.[3]

[1] Promising.
[2] From 1573 edn. Original reads *invention.*
[3] And they applauded.

FINIS.

THOMAS PRESTON

The identity of the Thomas Preston named as author at the end of the hybrid morality-tragedy *Cambises* is uncertain. Early students of the stage were inclined to identify him with the Thomas Preston who was Fellow of King's College, Cambridge, took his B.A. and M.A. there—the latter in 1561—and became Master of Trinity Hall in 1584 and Vice-Chancellor in 1587. He won Elizabeth's favor and a pension as her "scholar" in 1564 by disputing before her in Latin and acting in the Latin play *Dido*. It is not probable, however, that a man admired for his Latinity would write a play of such an extremely miscellaneous and popular nature as *Cambises*, one clearly designed for the use of some professional or semi-professional troupe of actors, whose personnel of six men and two boys is indicated by "The Division of the Parts" on the title-page of the published version. A more likely conjecture, as Chambers points out, is that the author was the ballad-writer two of whose ballads have at the end a subscription, "Finis, Quod Thomas Preston," similar to that in *Cambises*. He was publishing ballads at the time *Cambises* appeared in print.

As a tragedy *Cambises* offers a sharp contrast to *Gorboduc* in technique, and especially, in the very nature of great tragedy, through the failure of the catastrophe to develop logically out of the preceding incidents. While the spread of humanism may have had its effect on Preston's choice of a story from ancient history and on his attempt at a tragic treatment of it, the play probably represents more definitely the continuance of medieval literary and dramatic motives in the popular drama of the era. The story of Cambises, derived from Herodotus, was often retold in the Middle Ages and the Renaissance. The form found in the play is akin in spirit to the medieval type of narrative "tragedy" in the emphasis on the fall of a great figure at the height of his arrogant pride. A continued interest in such themes is indicated in the reprint of Lydgate's *Fall of Princes* and the production of *The Mirror for Magistrates*. The brutal character of the hero and the presentation of scenes of horror may reflect also an influence of scenes like the torturing of Christ or of the martyrs in medieval drama. For the rest, the technique is clearly that of the late hybrid moralities, in a number of which historical and farcical material was freely mixed with allegory. The story is carried and explained largely by abstract or generic characters, and the action is manipulated largely by Ambidexter, a brilliant example of the morality vice. Tendencies of later Elizabethan tragedy are foreshadowed in *Cambises* in the loose structure, based on a series of historical incidents, in the mixture of tragic and comic scenes, and in the presentation of crude horror on the stage.

The play was entered in the Stationers' Register in 1569/70 by John Allde, but had probably been performed several years earlier. The first edition, undated, appeared simultaneously with the entry or soon afterward. A second edition, also undated, was issued not earlier than 1584, by Edward Allde, John Allde's son, who succeeded to his father's business in that year. This later text, reproduced photographically by Farmer in his Tudor Facsimile Texts in 1910, has been followed by the present editors. Of critical editions, that in Manly's *Specimens of the Pre-Shaksperean Drama* has been most helpful.

CAMBISES, KING OF PERSIA[1]

BY

THOMAS PRESTON

[*DRAMATIS PERSONÆ*

CAMBISES, *King of Persia.*
SMIRDIS, *his brother.*
SISAMNES, *the judge.*
OTIAN, *his son.*
PRAXASPES, *a courtier.*
YOUNG CHILD, *his son.*
FIRST LORD ⎫
SECOND LORD ⎬ *attendants of the king.*
THIRD LORD ⎭

A LADY, *kinswoman of the king and later*
  QUEEN.
WAITING-MAID, *attending her.*
MOTHER *of Young Child and wife of Prax-*
  aspes.

HUF ⎫
RUF ⎬ *ruffianly soldiers.*
SNUF ⎭

MERETRIX, *a courtesan.*

HOB ⎫
LOB ⎬ *clownish countrymen.*

MARIAN-MAY-BE-GOOD, *Hob's wife.*

LORD.[2]
KNIGHT.[2]
COUNSEL.[2]

SHAME.
ATTENDANCE.
DILIGENCE.
PREPARATION.
SMALL HABILITY.[3]
COMMONS' CRY.
COMMONS' COMPLAINT.
TRIAL.
PROOF.
EXECUTION.
CRUELTY.
MURDER.

AMBIDEXTER, *the Vice.*

VENUS.
CUPID.

SCENE: *Persia.*

TIME: *Sixth century B.C.*]

THE DIVISION OF THE PARTS

COUNSEL ⎫
HUF ⎪
PRAXASPES ⎪
MURDER ⎬ *for one man.*
LOB ⎪
THE THIRD LORD ⎭

LORD ⎫
RUF ⎪
COMMONS' CRY ⎪
COMMONS' COMPLAINT ⎬ *for one man.*
LORD SMIRDIS ⎪
VENUS ⎭

KNIGHT ⎫
SNUF ⎪
SMALL HABILITY ⎪
PROOF ⎬ *for one man.*
EXECUTION ⎪
ATTENDANCE ⎪
SECOND LORD ⎭

[1] The complete title reads as follows: "A Lamentable Tragedy, Mixed Full of Pleasant Mirth, Containing the Life of Cambises, King of Persia, from the Beginning of His Kingdom unto His Death, His One Good Deed of Execution, after That Many Wicked Deeds and Tyrannous Murders Committed by and through Him, and Last of All, His Odious Death by God's Justice Appointed. Done in Such Order as Followeth." The running-title, however, reads: "A Comedy of King Cambises."

[2] The character is generic, representing the entire class.
[3] Ability.

CAMBISES
EPILOGUS } *for one man.*

AMBIDEXTER
TRIAL } *for one man.*

PROLOGUE
SISAMNES
DILIGENCE
CRUELTY } *for one man.*
HOB
PREPARATION
THE FIRST LORD

MERETRIX
SHAME
OTIAN
MOTHER } *for one man.*
LADY
QUEEN

YOUNG CHILD
CUPID } *for one man.*

The Prologue entereth.

Agathon, he whose counsel wise to princes'
   weal [1] extended,
By good advice unto a prince three things
   he hath commended:
First is, that he hath government and rul-
   eth over men;
Secondly, to rule with laws, eke justice,
   saith he, then;
Thirdly, that he must well conceive he may
   not always reign.
Lo, thus the rule unto a prince Agathon
   squaréd plain.
Tully the wise, whose sapience in volumes
   great doth tell,
Who in wisdom in that time did many men
   excel,
"A prince," saith he, "is of himself a plain
   and speaking law;
The law, a schoolmaster divine"—this by
   his rule I draw.   10
The sage and witty Seneca his words
   thereto did frame:
"The honest exercise of kings, men will
   ensue [2] the same;
But, contrariwise, if that a king abuse his
   kingly seat,
His ignomy and bitter shame in fine shall
   be more great."
In Persia there reigned a king, who Cyrus
   hight [3] by name,
Who did deserve, as I do read, the lasting
   blast of fame;
But he, when Sisters Three had wrought to
   shear his vital thread,
As heir due, to take the crown Cambises did
   proceed.

He in his youth was trainéd up by trace [4]
   of virtue's lore;
Yet, being king, did clean forget his perfect
   race before;   20
Then, cleaving more unto his will, such vice
   did imitate
As one of Icarus his kind; forewarning then
   did hate,
Thinking that none could him dismay, ne [5]
   none his fact [6] could see.
Yet at the last a fall he took, like Icarus to
   be;
Else,[7] as the fish, which oft had take the
   pleasant bait from hook,
In safe [8] did spring and pierce the streams
   when fisher fast [9] did look
To hoist up from the wat'ry waves unto
   the driéd land,
Then scaped, at last by subtle bait come to
   the fisher's hand:
Even so this King Cambises here, when he
   had wrought his will,
Taking delight the innocent his guiltless
   blood to spill,   30
Then mighty Jove would not permit to
   prosecute offense;
But, what measure the king did mete, the
   same did Jove commence,
To bring to end with shame his race—two
   years he did not reign.
His cruelty we will delate,[10] and make the
   matter plain.
Craving that this may suffice now your
   patience to win,
I take my way. Behold, I see the players
   coming in.   [*Exit.*]

FINIS.

---

[1] Welfare.
[2] Follow.
[3] Was called.
[4] Track, course.
[5] Nor.
[6] Deed.
[7] Or.
[8] Safety.
[9] Intently.
[10] Describe fully.

First enter [1] *Cambises the King, Knight,*
           [Lord,] and Counselor. [2]

CAMBISES. My counsel grave and sapient,
    with lords of legal train,
Attentive ears towards me bend, and
    mark what shall be sain; [3]
So you likewise, my valiant knight, whose
    manly acts doth fly
By bruit of Fame, that sounding trump
    doth pierce the azure sky—
My sapient words, I say, perpend, [4] and
    so your skill delate!
You know that Mors [5] vanquished hath
    Cyrus, that king of state,
And I, by due inheritance, possess that
    princely crown,
Ruling by sword of mighty force in place
    of great renown.
You know, and often have heard tell, my
    father's worthy facts—
A manly Mars's heart he bare, appearing
    by his acts. 10
And what, shall I to ground let fall my
    father's golden praise?
No, no! I mean for to attempt this same
    more large to raise.
In that, that I, his son, succeed his
    kingly seat, as due,
Extend your counsel unto me in that I
    ask of you.
I am the King of Persia, a large and
    fertile soil;
The Egyptians against us repugn [6] as
    varlets slave and vile;
Therefore I mean with Mars's heart with
    wars them to frequent,
Them to subdue as captives mine—this
    is my heart's intent;
So shall I win honor's delight, and praise
    of me shall go.
My counsel, speak, and, lordings, eke:
    is it not best do so? 20
COUNSEL. O puissant king, your blissful
    words deserves abundant praise,
That you in this do go about your fa-
    ther's fame to raise.

[1] "As this play is not divided into acts and
scenes, and as the events occur apparently in a
place which is now a council-chamber, now a
street, and now a garden, it seems improper to
subdivide the play or to indicate changes of
scene. When necessary for intelligibility, the
location is announced in the text" (Manly).
[2] *I.e.,* Counsel.   [3] Said.   [4] Consider.
[5] Death.   [6] Oppose.

O blissful day, that king so young such
    profit should conceive,
His father's praise and his to win from
    those that would deceive!
Sure, my true and sovereign king, I fall
    before you prest, [7]
Answer to give, as duty mine, in that
    your grace request.
If that your heart addicted be the Egyp-
    tians to convince, [8]
Through Mars's aid the conquest won,
    then deed of happy prince
Shall pierce the skies unto the throne of
    the supernal seat,
And merit there a just reward of Jupiter
    the Great. 30
But then your grace must not turn back
    from this pretenséd [9] will;
For to proceed in virtuous life employ
    endeavor still;
Extinguish vice, and in that cup to drink
    have no delight;
To martial feats and kingly sport fix all
    your whole delight.
KING. My counsel grave, a thousand
    thanks with heart I do you render,
That you my case so prosperous entirely
    do tender.
I will not swerve from those your steps
    whereto you would me train.
But now, my lord and valiant knight,
    with words give answer plain:
Are you content with me to go the
    Mars's games to try?
LORD. Yea, peerless prince! To aid your
    grace myself will live and die! 40
KNIGHT. And I, for my hability, for fear
    will not turn back,
But, as the ship against the rocks, sus-
    tain and bide the wrack.
KING. O willing hearts! A thousand
    thanks I render unto you!
Strike up your drums with courage great;
    we will march forth even now!
COUNSEL. Permit, O king, few words to
    hear—my duty serves no less.
Therefore give leave to counsel thine his
    mind for to express.
KING. Speak on, my counsel; what it be,
    you shall have favor mine.
COUNSEL. Then will I speak unto your
    grace as duty doth me bind.

[7] Quickly.   [8] Overpower.   [9] Intended.

Your grace doth mean for to attempt of
  war the manly art;
Your grace therein may hap receive, with
  others, for your part,   50
The dent of death—in those affairs all
  persons are alike.
The heart courageous oftentimes his det-
  riment doth seek.
It's best therefore for to permit a ruler
  of your land
To sit and judge with equity when things
  of right are scanned.
KING. My grace doth yield to this your
  talk. To be thus now it shall.
My knight, therefore prepare yourself
  Sisamnes for to call.
A judge he is of prudent skill; even he
  shall bear the sway
In absence mine, when from the land I
  do depart my way.
KNIGHT. Your knight before your grace
  even here himself hath ready pressed
With willing heart for to fulfill as your
  grace made request.   *Exit.*   60
COUNSEL. Pleaseth your grace, I judge of
  him to be a man right fit;
For he is learned in the law, having the
  gift of wit.
In your grace's precinct I do not view for
  it a meeter man.
His learning is of good effect—bring
  proof thereof I can.
I do not know what is his life—his conscience hid from me;
I doubt not but the fear of God before
  his eyes to be.
LORD. Report declares he is a man that
  to himself is nigh,[1]
One that favoreth much the world and
  sets too much thereby.
But this I say of certainty: if he your
  grace succeed
In your absence but for awhile, he will be
  warned indeed   70
No injustice for to frequent, no partial
  judge to prove,
But rule all things with equity, to win
  your grace's love.
KING. Of that he shall a warning have my
  hests [2] for to obey;
Great punishment for his offense against
  him will I lay.

[1] *I.e.*, self-seeking.
[2] Behests, commands.

[*Enter Sisamnes.*]

COUNSEL. Behold, I see him now aggress [3]
  and enter into place.
SISAMNES. O puissant prince and mighty
  king, the gods preserve your grace!
Your grace's message came to me, your
  will purporting forth;
With grateful mind I it received according to mine oath,
Erecting then myself with speed before
  your grace's eyes,
The tenor of your princely will from you
  for to agnize.[4]   80
KING. Sisamnes, this the whole effect the
  which for you I sent:
Our mind it is to elevate you to great
  preferment.
My grace, and gracious counsel eke,
  hath chose you for this cause;
In judgment you do office bear, which
  have the skill in laws.
We think that you accordingly by jus-
  tice' rule will deal,
That for offense none shall have cause,
  of wrong you to appeal.[5]
SISAMNES. Abundant thanks unto your
  grace for this benignity!
To you, his counsel, in like case, with
  lords of clemency!
Whatso your grace to me permits, if I
  therein offend,
Such execution then commence (and use
  it to this end)   90
That all other, by that my deed, example
  so may take
To admonish them to flee the same by
  fear it may them make.
KING. Then, according to your words, if
  you therein offend,
I assure you, even from my breast correction shall extend.
From Persia I mean to go into the Egypt
  land,
Them to convince by force of arms and
  win the upper hand.
While I therefor absent shall be, I do
  you full permit,
As governor in this my right, in that
  estate to sit,
For to detect and eke correct those that
  abuse my grace.
This is the total of my will. Give answer
  in this case!   100

[3] Approach.   [4] Learn.   [5] Accuse.

SISAMNES. Unworthy much, O prince, am I, and for this gift unfit;
But, sith [1] that it hath pleased your grace that I in it must sit,
I do avouch, unto my death, according to my skill,
With equity for to observe your grace's mind and will,
And naught from it to swarve,[2] indeed, but sincerely to stay;
Else let me taste the penalty, as I before did say.
KING. Well then, of this authority I give you full possession.
SISAMNES. And I will it fulfill also as I have made profession.
KING. My counsel, then let us depart a final stay to make;
To Egypt land now forth with speed my voyage I will take.   110
Strike up your drums, us to rejoice to hear the warlike sound.
Stay you here, Sisamnes, judge, and look well to your bound! [3]

Exeunt King, Lord, and Counsel.

SISAMNES. Even now the king hath me extolled, and set me up aloft.
Now may I wear the bordered guard,[4] and lie in down-bed soft;
Now may I purchase house and land, and have all at my will;
Now may I build a princely place, my mind for to fulfill;
Now may I abrogate the law as I shall think it good;
If anyone me now offend, I may demand his blood.
According to the proverb old, my mouth I will up-make.[5]
Now it doth lie all in my hand to leave, or else to take,   120
To deal with justice to me bound, and so to live in hope.
But oftentimes the birds be gone while one for nest doth grope.
Do well or ill, I dare avouch some evil on me will speak.
No, truly—yet I do not mean the king's precepts to break;
To place I mean for to return my duty to fulfill.   *Exit.*

Enter the Vice, with an old capcase [6] on his head, an old pail about his hips for harness,[7] a scummer [8] and a potlid by his side, and a rake on his shoulder.

AMBIDEXTER. Stand away, stand away, for the passion of God!
Harnessed I am, prepared to the field!
I would have been content at home to have bode,
But I am sent forth with my spear and shield.
I am appointed to fight against a snail,   130
And Wilkin Wren the ancient [9] shall bear.
I doubt not but against him to prevail—
To be a man my deeds shall declare!
If I overcome him, then a butterfly takes his part.
His weapon must be a blue-specked hen;
But you shall see me overthrow him with a fart.
So, without conquest, he shall go home again.
If I overcome him, I must fight with a fly,
And a black-pudding the fly's weapon must be.
At the first blow on the ground he shall lie;   140
I will be sure to thrust him through the mouth to the knee.
To conquest these fellows the man I will play.
Ha, ha, ha! now ye will make me to smile.
.   .   .   .   [10]
To see if I can all men beguile.
Ha! my name? My name would ye so fain know?
Yea, iwis,[11] shall ye, and that with all speed!—
I have forgot it; therefore I cannot show.
Ah! ah! now I have it! I have it, indeed!
My name is Ambidexter. I signify one   150
That with both hands finely can play:
Now with King Cambises, and by-and-by [12] gone.

---

[1] Since.
[2] Swerve.
[3] Bond, contract.
[4] Trimming.
[5] Please my palate.
[6] Bandbox.   [7] Armor.   [8] Skimmer.   [9] Ensign
[10] The rime indicates that a line is missing here
[11] Certainly.   [12] Immediately.

Thus do I run this way and that way.
For while I mean with a soldier to be;
Then give I a leap to Sisamnes the
judge.
I dare avouch you shall his destruction
see!
To all kind of estates I mean for to
trudge.
Ambidexter? Nay, he is a fellow, if ye
knew all!
Cease for a while; hereafter hear more ye
shall.

*Enter three ruffians, Huf, Ruf, and Snuf,
singing.*

HUF. Gog's [1] flesh and His wounds, these
wars rejoice my heart!   160
By His wounds, I hope to do well, for
my part!
By Gog's heart, the world shall go hard
if I do not shift;
At some old carl's budget [2] I mean for
to lift.
RUF. By His flesh, nose, eyes, and ears,
I will venter,[3] void of all cares!
He is not a soldier that doth fear any
doubt,
If that he would bring his purpose about.
SNUF. Fear that fear list,[4] it shall not be I.
By Gog's wounds, I will make some neck
stand awry!
If I lose my share—I swear by Gog's
heart—   170
Then let another take up my part!
HUF. Yet I hope to come the richest sol-
dier away.
RUF. If a man ask ye, ye may hap to say
nay.
SNUF. Let all men get what they can;
not to leese [5] I hope;
Wheresoever I go, in each corner I will
grope.
AMBIDEXTER. What and [6] ye run in the
corner of some pretty maid?
SNUF. To grope there, good fellow, I will
not be afraid.
HUF. Gog's wounds, what art thou that
with us dost mell? [7]
Thou seemest to be a soldier, the truth
to tell;

Thou seemest to be harnessed—I cannot
tell how;   180
I think he came lately from riding some
cow.
Such a deformed slave did I never see!
Ruf, dost thou know him? I pray thee,
tell me.
RUF. No, by my troth, fellow Huf, I never
see him before.
SNUF. As for me, I care not if I never see
him more.
Come, let us run his arse against the post!
AMBIDEXTER. Ah, ye slaves! I will be
with you at ost! [8]
           Here let him swinge them about.
Ah, ye knaves! I will teach ye how ye
shall me deride!
Out of my sight! I can ye not abide!
Now, goodman pouchmouth, I am a slave
with you?   190
Now have at ye afresh—again—even
now!
Mine arse against the post you will
run?
But I will make you from that saying to
turn!
HUF. I beseech ye heartily to be content.
RUF. I insure you, by mine honesty, no
hurt we meant.
Beside that, again, we do not know what
ye are.
Ye know that soldiers their stoutness will
declare;
Therefore, if we have anything offended,
Pardon our rudeness, and it shall be
amended.
AMBIDEXTER. Yea, God's pity, begin ye to
entreat me?   200
Have at ye once again! By the Mass, I
will beat ye!   *Fight again.*
HUF. Gog's heart, let us kill him! Suffer no
longer!   *Draw their swords.*
SNUF. Thou slave, we will see if thou be
the stronger!
RUF. Strike off his head at one blow!
That we be soldiers, Gog's heart, let him
know!
AMBIDEXTER. O the passion of God, I
have done, by mine honesty!
I will take your part hereafter, verily.
ALL. Then come, let us agree!
AMBIDEXTER. Shake hands with me—I
shake hands with thee.

---

[1] God's.
[2] Countryman's wallet.
[3] Venture.
[4] Pleases.
[5] Lose.
[6] If.
[7] Meddle.
[8] Host; *i.e.*, be intimate with you.

Ye are full of courtesy; that is the best.
And you take great pain; ye are a man-
nerly guest.   211
Why, masters, do you not know me?
The truth to me tell.
ALL. No, trust us, not very well.
AMBIDEXTER. Why, I am Ambidexter,
who [1] many soldiers do love.
HUF. Gog's heart, to have thy company
needs we must prove!
We must play with both hands, with our
hostess and host,
Play with both hands, and score on the
post; [2]
Now and then, with our captain, for
many a delay,
We will not stick with both hands to play.
AMBIDEXTER. The honester man, ye may
me trust!   220

Enter Meretrix, with a staff on her shoulder.

MERETRIX. What! is there no lads here
that hath a lust
To have a passing trull to help at their
need?
HUF. Gog's heart, she is come, indeed!
What, Mistress Meretrix, by His wounds,
welcome to me!
MERETRIX. What will ye give me? I pray
you, let me see.
RUF. By His heart, she looks for gifts
by-and-by!
MERETRIX. What? Master Ruf? I cry
you mercy!
The last time I was with you I got a
broken head,
And lay in the street all night for want
of a bed.
SNUF. Gog's wounds, kiss me, my trull so
white! [3]   230
In thee, I swear, is all my delight!
If thou shouldst have had a broken head
for my sake,
I would have made his head to ache.
MERETRIX. What? Master Ambidexter?
Who looked for you?
AMBIDEXTER. Mistress Meretrix, I thought
not to see you here now.
There is no remedy—at meeting I must
have a kiss!

MERETRIX. What, man, I will not stick
for that, by Gis! [4]   *Kiss.*
AMBIDEXTER. So now, gramercy! I pray
thee be gone!
MERETRIX. Nay, soft, my friend; I mean
to have one!
Nay, soft! I swear, and if ye were my
brother,   240
Before I let go, I will have another!
                              Kiss, kiss, kiss.
RUF. Gog's heart, the whore would not
kiss me yet!
MERETRIX. If I be a whore, thou art a
knave; then it is quit.
HUF. But hear'st thou, Meretrix? With
who this night wilt thou lie?
MERETRIX. With him that giveth the most
money.
HUF. Gog's heart, I have no money in
purse, ne yet in clout! [5]
MERETRIX. Then get thee hence and pack,
like a lout!
HUF. Adieu, like a whore!   *Exit Huf.*
MERETRIX.   Farewell, like
a knave! [6]
RUF. Gog's nails, Mistress Meretrix, now
he is gone,
A match ye shall make straight with
me: 250
I will give thee sixpence to lie one night
with thee.
MERETRIX. Gog's heart, slave, dost think
I am a sixpenny Jug? [7]
No, wis [8] ye, Jack, I look a little more
smug!
SNUF. I will give her eighteenpence to
serve me first.
MERETRIX. Gramercy, Snuf, thou art not
the worst!
RUF. By Gog's heart, she were better be
hanged, to forsake me and take thee!
SNUF. Were she so? That shall we see!
RUF. By Gog's heart, my dagger into her
I will thrust!
SNUF. Ah, ye boy, ye would do it and ye
durst!
AMBIDEXTER. Peace, my masters; ye shall
not fight.   260
He that draws first, I will him smite.
RUF. Gog's wounds, Master Snuf, are ye
so lusty?

---

[1] Whom(?).
[2] *I.e.*, mark the reckonings on the tavern
doorposts.   [3] Dear.

[4] Jesus.   [5] In my clothes.
[6] " The rhyme seems to demand some such word
as *whoreson*" (Manly).   [7] Joan, a whore.   [8] Know.

SNUF. Gog's sides, Master Ruf, are ye so
　crusty?

RUF. You may happen to see!

SNUF. Do what thou darest to me!

*Here draw and fight. Here she must lay on
　and coil ¹ them both; the Vice must run
　his way for fear; Snuf fling down his
　sword and buckler and run his way.*

MERETRIX. Gog's sides, knaves! Seeing to
　fight ye be so rough,

Defend yourselves, for I will give ye both
　enough!

I will teach ye how ye shall fall out for
　me!

Yea, thou slave, Snuf, no more blows wilt
　thou bide?

To take thy heels a time hast thou
　spied?　　　　　　　　　　　　　270

Thou villain, seeing Snuf has gone away,

A little better I mean thee to pay!

*He falleth down; she falleth upon him, and
　beats him, and taketh away his weapons.*

RUF. Alas, good Mistress Meretrix, no
　more!

My legs, sides, and arms with beating be
　sore!

MERETRIX. Thou a soldier, and lose thy
　weapon!

Go hence, sir boy; say a woman hath
　thee beaten!

RUF. Good Mistress Meretrix, my weapon
　let me have;

Take pity on me, mine honesty ² to save.

If it be known this repulse I sustain,

It will redound to my ignomy and
　shame.　　　　　　　　　　　　280

MERETRIX. If thou wilt be my man and
　wait upon me,

This sword and buckler I will give thee.

RUF. I will do all at your commandment;

As servant to you I will be obedient.

MERETRIX. Then let me see how before me
　you can go.

When I speak to you, you shall do so:

Off with your cap at place ³ and at
　board ⁴—

"Forsooth, Mistress Meretrix," at every
　word.

Tut! tut! in the camp such soldiers there
　be,

One good woman would beat away two
　or three!　　　　　　　　　　　290

Well, I am sure customers tarry at home.

Mannerly before, and let us be gone!

　　　　　　　　　　　　　　　Exeunt.

Enter Ambidexter.

[AMBIDEXTER.] O the passion of God! Be
　they here still or no?

I durst not abide to see her beat them so!

I may say to you, iwis, in such a flight,⁵

Body of me, I see the hair of my head
　stand upright!

When I saw her so hard upon them lay
　on,

"O the passion of God!" thought I, "she
　will be with me anon!"

I made no more ⁶ ado, but avoided the
　thrust,

And to my legs began for to trust,　300

And fell a-laughing to myself when I was
　once gone.

"It is wisdom," quoth I, "by the Mass,
　to save one!"

Then into this place I intended to trudge,

Thinking to meet Sisamnes the judge.

Behold where he cometh! I will him
　meet,

And like a gentleman I mean him to
　greet.

Enter Sisamnes.

SISAMNES. Since that the king's grace's
　majesty in office did me set,

What abundance of wealth to me might
　I get!

Now and then some vantage I achieve;
　much more yet may I take,

But that I fear unto the king that some
　complaint will make.　　　　　310

AMBIDEXTER. Jesu, Master Sisamnes, you
　are unwise!

SISAMNES. Why so? I pray thee, let me
　agnize.

What, Master Ambidexter, is it you?

Now welcome to me, I make God avow!

AMBIDEXTER. Jesu, Master Sisamnes, with
　me you are well acquainted.

By me rulers may be trimly painted.⁷

Ye are unwise if ye take not time while
　ye may;

If ye will not now, when ye would ye shall
　have nay.

---

¹ Beat.　　　　　　　　³ House.

² Honor.　　　　　　　⁴ Table.

⁵ Possibly a misprint for *fright.*

⁶ Original reads *mare.*　　　⁷ Cheated.

What is he that of you dare make ex-
clamation,
Of your wrong-dealing to make explica-
tion?   320
Can you not play with both hands, and
turn with the wind?
SISAMNES. Believe me, your words draw
deep in my mind.
In color wise unto this day,[1] to bribes I
have inclinéd;
More the same for to frequent, of truth
I am now minded.
Behold, even now unto me suitors do
proceed.

[*Enter Small Hability.*]

SMALL HABILITY. I beseech you here, good
Master Judge, a poor man's cause to
tender![2]
Condemn me not in wrongful wise that
never was offender.
You know right well my right it is. I
have not for to give.
You take away from me my due, that
should my corpse[3] relieve.
The commons of you do complain from
them you devocate;[4]   330
With anguish great and grievous words
their hearts do penetrate;
The right you sell unto the wrong, your
private gain to win;
You violate the simple man, and count it
for no sin.
SISAMNES. Hold thy tongue, thou prattling knave, and give to me reward;
Else, in this wise, I tell thee truth, thy
tale will not be heard.
Ambidexter, let us go hence, and let the
knave alone.
AMBIDEXTER. Farewell, Small Hability, for
help now get you none;
Bribes hath corrupt him good laws to
pollute.
            Exeunt [Sisamnes and Ambidexter].
SMALL HABILITY. A naughty man, that
will not obey the king's constitute![5]
With heavy heart I will return, till God
redress my pain.   *Exit.* 340

[1] Taking color from the practices of the day (?)
[2] Regard favorably.
[3] Body.
[4] Call away, take away.
[5] Law.

Enter Shame, with a trump, black.

SHAME. From among the grisly ghosts I
come, from tyrants' testy train.
Unseemly Shame, of sooth, I am, pro-
curéd to make plain
The odious facts and shameless deeds
that Cambises king doth use.
All piety and virtuous life he doth in
clean refuse;
Lechery and drunkenness he doth it
much frequent.
The tiger's kind[6] to imitate he hath
given full consent.
He naught esteems his Counsel grave ne
virtuous bringing-up,
But daily still receives the drink of
damnéd Vice's cup.
He can bide no instruction, he takes so
great delight
In working of iniquity for to frequent his
spite.   350
As Fame doth sound the royal trump of
worthy men and trim,
So Shame doth blow with strainéd blast
the trump of shame on him.   *Exit.*

*Enter the King, Lord, Praxaspes, and
Sisamnes.*

KING. My judge, since my departure
hence, have you used judgment right?
If faithful steward I ye find, the same I
will requite.
SISAMNES. No doubt your grace shall not
once hear that I have done amiss.
PRAXASPES. I much rejoice to hear so good
news as this.

*Enter Commons' Cry running in, speak this
verse, and go out again hastily.*

COMMONS' CRY. Alas, alas, how are the
commons oppressed
By that vile judge, Sisamnes by name!
I do not know how it should be redressed.
To amend his life no whit he doth
frame.   360
We are undone and thrown out of door;
His damnable dealing doth us so tor-
ment;
At his hand we can find no relief nor suc-
cor.
God grant him grace for to repent!
                        Run away crying.

[6] Nature.

KING. What doleful cries be these, my
l[ord], that sound do in mine ear?
Intelligence if you can give, unto your
king declare.
To me it seemeth my commons all they
do lament and cry
Out of [1] Sisamnes, judge most chief, even
now standing us by.
PRAXASPES. Even so, O king, it seemed to
me, as you rehearsal made.
I doubt [2] the judge culpable be in some
respect or trade.[3]   370
SISAMNES. Redoubted king, have no mistrust! No whit your mind dismay!
There is not one that can me charge, or
aught against me lay.

*Enter Commons' Complaint, with Proof and
Trial.*

COMMONS' COMPLAINT. Commons' Complaint I represent, with thrall of doleful state.
My urgent cause erected forth my grief
for to dilate.
Unto the king I will prepare my misery
to tell,
To have relief of this my grief and fettered feet so fell.[4]
Redoubted prince and mighty king, myself I prostrate here.
Vouchsafe, O king, with me to bear for
this that I appear.
With humble suit I pardon crave of your
most royal grace
To give me leave my mind to break before you in this place.   380
KING. Commons' Complaint, keep nothing
back! Fear not thy tale to tell.
Whate'er he be within this land that
hath not used thee well,
As prince's mouth shall sentence give, he
shall receive the same.
Unfold the secrets of thy breast, for I
extinguish blame.
COMMONS' COMPLAINT. God preserve your
royal grace, and send you blissful days,
That all your deeds might still accord to
give the God the praise!
My complaint is, O mighty king, against
that judge you by,
Whose careless deeds, gain to receive,
hath made the commons cry.

He, by taking bribes and gifts, the poor
he doth oppress,
Taking relief from infants young, widows,
and fatherless.   390
KING. Untrustful traitor and corrupt
judge, how likest thou this complaint?
Forewarning I to thee did give of this to
make restraint;
And hast thou done this devilish deed
mine ire for to augment?
I sentence give, thou Judas judge. Thou
shalt thy deed repent!
SISAMNES. O pusant [5] prince, it is not so.
His complaint I deny.
COMMONS' COMPLAINT. If it be not so,
most mighty king, in place then let me
die.
Behold that I have brought with me both
Proof and Trial true,
To stand even here, and sentence give
what by him did ensue.
PROOF. I, Proof, do him in this appeal: he
did the commons wrong;
Unjustly he with them hath dealt, his
greedy [6] was so strong.   400
His heart did covet in to get, he caréd
not which way;
The poor did leese their due and right,
because they want [7] to pay
Unto him for bribes. Indeed, this was
his wonted use.
Whereas your grace good laws did make,
he did the same abuse.
TRIAL. I, Trial, here to verify what Proof
doth now unfold,
To stand against him in his wrong, as
now I dare be bold.
KING. How likest thou this, thou caitiff
vile? Canst thou the same deny?
SISAMNES. O noble king, forgive my fact!
I yield to thy mercy.
KING. Complaints and Proof, redress will
I all this your misery.
Depart with speed from whence you
came, and straight command by
me   410
The execution man to come before my
grace with haste.
ALL. For to fulfill this your request no
time we mean to waste.
                        Exeunt they three.

[1] On.
[2] Suspect.
[3] Course, practice.
[4] Cruel, cruelly treated.
[5] Puissant.
[6] Greediness(?); greed it(?).
[7] *I.e.,* lacked the wherewithal.

KING. My lord, before my grace go call
Otian, this judge's son,
And he shall hear and also see what his
father hath done.
The father he shall suffer death, the son
his room succeed;
And, if that he no better prove, so like-
wise shall he speed.

PRAXASPES. As your grace hath commandment given, I mean for to fulfill.
Step aside and fetch him.

KING. Accurséd judge, couldst thou consent to do this curséd ill?
According unto thy demand, thou shalt,
for this thy guilt,
Receive thy death before mine eyes. Thy
blood it shall be spilt. 420

[*Enter Praxaspes with Otian.*]

PRAXASPES. Behold, O king, Sisamnes' son
before you doth appear.

KING. Otian, this is my mind; therefore
to me come near:
Thy father here for judgment wrong pro-
curéd hath his death,
And thou, his son, shalt him succeed
when he hath lost his breath;
And, if that thou dost once offend, as
thou seest thy father have,
In like wise thou shalt suffer death. No
mercy shall thee save!

OTIAN. O mighty king, vouchsafe your
grace my father to remit.
Forgive his fault. His pardon I do ask
of you as yet.
Alas, although my father hath your
princely heart offended,
Amends for miss [1] he will now make, and
faults shall be amended. 430
Instead of his requested life, pleaseth
your grace take mine.
This offer I as tender child, so duty doth
me bind.

KING. Do not entreat my grace no more,
for he shall die the death!
Where is the execution man him to bereave of breath?

Enter Execution.

EXECUTION. At hand, and if it like your
grace, my duty to despatch,
In hope that I, when deed is done, a good
reward shall catch.

[1] Wrongdoing.

KING. Despatch with sword this judge's
life; extinguish fear and cares.
So done, draw thou his curséd skin
straight over both his ears.
I will see the office done, and that before
mine eyes.

EXECUTION. To do the thing my king commands I give the enterprise.[2] 440

SISAMNES. Otian, my son, the king to
death by law hath me condemnéd,
And you in room and office mine his
grace's will hath placéd;
Use justice, therefore, in this case, and
yield unto no wrong,
[Lest thou do purchase the like death ere
ever it be long.][3]

OTIAN. O father dear, these words to hear
—that you must die by force—
Bedews my cheeks with stilléd tears.
The king hath no remorse.
The grievous griefs and strainéd sighs
my heart doth break in twain,
And I deplore, most woeful child, that I
should see you slain.
O false and fickle frowning dame, that
turneth as the wind,
Is this the joy in father's age thou me
assignest to find? 450
O doleful day, unhappy hour, that loving
child should see
His father dear before his face thus put
to death should be!
Yet, father, give me blessing thine, and
let me once embrace
Thy comely corpse in folded arms, and
kiss thy ancient face!

SISAMNES. O child, thou makes my eyes to
run, as rivers do, by stream.
My leave I take of thee, my son. Beware of this my Beam! [4]

KING. Despatch even now, thou man of
death; no longer seem to stay!

EXECUTION. Come, M[aster] Sisamnes,
come on your way.
My office I must pay; forgive therefore
my deed.

SISAMNES. I do forgive it thee, my friend;
despatch therefore with speed! 460
*Smite him in the neck with a sword to signify
his death.*

[2] I readily undertake.
[3] Line supplied from first edn.
[4] Affliction, alluding to the Cross.

PRAXASPES. Behold, O king, how he doth
bleed, being of life bereft!
KING. In this wise he shall not yet be left.
Pull his skin over his eyes to make his
death more vile.
A wretch he was, a cruel thief, my com-
mons to beguile!
                    Flay him with a false skin.
OTIAN. What child [1] is he of nature's mold
could bide the same to see—
His father flayéd in this wise? O, how
it grieveth me!
KING. Otian, thou seest thy father dead,
and thou art in his room;
If thou beest proud, as he hath been,
even thereto shalt thou come.
OTIAN. O king, to me this is a glass; with
grief in it I view
Example that unto your grace I do not
prove untrue.   470
PRAXASPES. Otian, convey your father
hence to tomb where he shall lie.
OTIAN. And if it please your lordship, it
shall be done by-and-by.
Good execution man, for need, help me
with him away.
EXECUTION. I will fulfill, as you to me did
say.   *They take him away.*
KING. My l[ord], now that my grace hath
seen that finished is this deed,
To question mine give tentive [2] ear, and
answer make with speed:
Have not I done a gracious deed, to re-
dress my commons' woe?
PRAXASPES. Yea, truly, if it please your
grace, you have indeed done so.
But now, O king, in friendly wise I
counsel you in this:
Certain vices for to leave that in you
placéd is—   480
The vice of drunkenness, O king, which
doth you sore infect,
With other great abuses, which I wish
you to detect.
KING. Peace, my lord! What needeth
this? Of this I will not hear!
To palace now I will return, and thereto
make good cheer.
God Bacchus he bestows his gifts—we
have good store of wine—
And also that the ladies be both passing
brave and fine.

[1] Suggested by Manly. Original reads *thilde.*
[2] Attentive.

But stay! I see a lord now come, and
eke a valiant knight.
What news, my lord? To see you here
my heart it doth delight.

Enter Lord and Knight to meet the King.

LORD. No news, O king; but of duty come
to wait upon your grace.
KING. I thank you, my l[ord] and loving
knight. I pray you with me trace. [3] 490
My lords and knight, I pray ye tell—I
will not be offended—
Am I worthy of any crime once to be
reprehended?
PRAXASPES. The Persians much do praise
your grace, but one thing discommend,
In that to wine subject you be, wherein
you do offend.
Sith that the might of wine's effect doth
oft subdue your brain,
My counsel is, to please their hearts,
from it you would refrain.
LORD. No, no, my lord, it is not so! For
this of prince they tell,
For virtuous proof and princely facts
Cyrus he doth excel.
By that his grace by conquest great the
Egyptians did convince,
Of him report abroad doth pass to be a
worthy prince.   500
KNIGHT. In person of Crœsus I answer
make: we may not his grace compare
In whole respect for to be like Cyrus, the
king's father,
Insomuch your grace hath yet no child
as Cyrus left behind;
Even you I mean, Cambises King, in
whom I favor find.
KING. Crœsus said well in saying so. But,
Praxaspes, tell me why
That to my mouth in such a sort thou
should avouch a lie,
Of drunkenness me thus to charge. But
thou with speed shalt see
Whether that I a sober king or else a
drunkard be.
I know thou hast a blissful babe, wherein
thou dost delight;
Me to revenge of these thy words I will
go wreak this spite.   510
When I the most have tasted wine, my
bow it shall be bent.

[3] Walk.

At heart of him even then to shoot is
now my whole intent,
And, if that I his heart can hit, the king
no drunkard is;
If heart of his I do not kill, I yield to
thee in this.
Therefore, Praxaspes, fetch to me thy
youngest son with speed.
There is no way, I tell thee plain, but I
will do this deed.

PRAXASPES. Redoubted prince, spare my
sweet child. He is mine only joy!
I trust your grace to infant's heart no
such thing will employ.
If that his mother hear of this, she is so
nigh her flight,
In clay her corpse will soon be shrined
to pass from world's delight.   520

KING. No more ado! Go fetch me him.
It shall be as I say.
And if that I do speak the word, how
dare ye once say nay?

PRAXASPES. I will go fetch him to your
grace; but so, I trust, it shall not be!

KING. For fear of my displeasure great, go
fetch him unto me. [*Exit Praxaspes.*]
Is he gone? Now, by the gods, I will do
as I say!
My lord, therefore fill me some wine, I
heartily you pray;
For I must drink to make my brain
somewhat intoxicate.
When that the wine is in my head, O,
trimly I can prate!

LORD. Here is the cup, with filléd wine,
thereof to take repast.

KING. Give it me to drink it off, and see
no wine be waste.   *Drink.*   530
Once again enlarge this cup, for I must
taste it still.   *Drink.*
By the gods, I think of pleasant wine I
cannot take my fill!
Now drink is in, give me my bow and
arrows from Sir Knight.
At heart of child I mean to shoot, hoping
to cleave it right.

KNIGHT. Behold, O king, where he doth
come, his infant young in hand.

[*Enter Praxaspes with the Child.*]

PRAXASPES. O mighty king, your grace'
behest with sorrow I have scanned,
And brought my child fro mother's knee
before you to appear,

And she thereof no whit doth know that
he in place is here.

KING. Set him up, my mark to be.   I
will shoot at his heart.

PRAXASPES. I beseech your grace not so
to do! Set this pretense apart!— 540
Farewell, my dear and loving babe!
Come, kiss thy father dear!
A grievous sight to me it is to see thee
slain even here.
Is this the gain now from the king for
giving counsel good—
Before my face with such despite to spill
my son's heart-blood?
O heavy day to me this is, and mother
in like case!

YOUNG CHILD. O father, father, wipe your
face;
I see the tears run from your eye.
My mother is at home sewing of a band.
Alas, dear father, why do you cry?

KING. Before me as a mark now let him
stand.   550
I will shoot at him my mind to fulfill.

YOUNG CHILD. Alas, alas, father, will you
me kill?
Good Master King, do not shoot at me;
my mother loves me best of all.   *Shoot.*

KING. I have despatched him! Down he
doth fall!
As right as a line his heart I have hit.
Nay, thou shalt see, Praxaspes, stranger
news yet.
My knight, with speed his heart cut out
and give it unto me.

KNIGHT. It shall be done, O mighty king,
with all celerity.

LORD. My Lord Praxaspes, this had not
been but your tongue must be walking.
To the king of correction you must needs
be talking.   560

PRAXASPES. No correction, my lord, but
counsel for the best.

KNIGHT. Here is the heart, according to
your grace's behest.

KING. Behold, Praxaspes, thy son's own
heart! O, how well the same was hit!
After this wine to do this deed I thought
it very fit.
Esteem thou mayst right well thereby
no drunkard is the king
That in the midst of all his cups could
do this valiant thing.

My lord and knight, on me attend. To
    palace we will go,
And leave him here to take his son when
    we are gone him fro.

ALL. With all our hearts we give consent
    to wait upon your grace.

                [*Exeunt all but Praxaspes.*]

PRAXASPES. A woeful man, O Lord, am I,
    to see him in this case!   570
My days, I deem, desires their end. This
    deed will help me hence.
To have the blossoms of my field de-
    stroyed by violence!

           Enter Mother.

[MOTHER.] Alas, alas, I do hear tell the
    king hath killed my son!
If it be so, woe worth the deed that ever
    it was done!
It is even so! My lord I see, how by him
    he doth weep.
What meant I that from hands of him
    this child I did not keep?
Alas, husband and lord, what did you
    mean to fetch this child away?

PRAXASPES. O lady wife, I little thought
    for to have seen this day.

MOTHER. O blissful babe! O joy of womb!
    Heart's comfort and delight!
For counsel given unto the king is this
    thy just requite?   580
O heavy day and doleful time, these
    mourning tunes to make!
With blubbered eyes, into mine arms
    from earth I will thee take,
And wrap thee in mine apron white.
    But, O my heavy heart!
The spiteful pangs that it sustains would
    make it in two to part,
The death of this my son to see! O
    heavy mother now,
That from thy sweet and sugared joy to
    sorrow so shouldst bow!
What grief in womb did I retain before I
    did thee see!
Yet at the last, when smart was gone,
    what joy wert thou to me!
How tender was I of thy food, for to
    preserve thy state!
How stillèd I thy tender heart at times
    early and late!   590
With velvet paps I gave thee suck with
    issue from my breast,

And dancèd thee upon my knee to bring
    thee unto rest!
Is this the joy of thee I reap? O king of
    tiger's brood!
O tiger's whelp, hadst thou the heart
    to see this child's heart-blood?
Nature enforceth me, alas, in this wise
    to deplore,
To wring my hands. O welaway, that I
    should see this hour!
Thy mother yet will kiss thy lips, silk-
    soft and pleasant white,
With wringing hands lamenting for to see
    thee in this plight!
My lording dear, let us go home our
    mourning to augment.

PRAXASPES. My lady dear, with heavy
    heart to it I do consent,   600
Between us both the child to bear unto
    our lordly place.   *Exeunt.*

          Enter Ambidexter.

[AMBIDEXTER. (*To the audience.*)] Indeed, as
    ye say, I have been absent a long space.
But is not my cousin Cutpurse with you
    in the meantime?
To it, to it, cousin, and do your office
    fine!
How like you Sisamnes for using of me?
He played with both hands, but he sped
    ill-favoredly!
The king himself was godly uptrained;
He professed virtue—but I think it was
    feigned.
He plays with both hands, good deeds
    and ill;
But it was no good deed Praxaspes' son
    for to kill.   610
As he for the good deed on the judge was
    commended,
For all his deeds else he is reprehended.
The most evil-disposed person that ever
    was
All the state of his life he would not let
    pass,
Some [1] good deeds he will do, though they
    be but few.
The like things this tyrant Cambises
    doth shew.
No goodness from him to none is ex-
    hibited,
But still malediction abroad is distrib-
    uted;

[1] *I.e.,* but some.

And yet ye shall see in the rest of his race
What infamy he will work against his
own grace.   620
Whist! No more words! Here comes
the king's brother.

Enter Lord Smirdis with Attendance and
Diligence.

SMIRDIS. The king's brother by birth am
I, issued from Cyrus' loins;
A grief to me it is to hear of this the
king's repines.[1]
I like not well of those his deeds that he
doth still frequent;
I wish to God that other ways his mind
he could content.
Young I am, and next to him; no mo [2] of
us there be.
I would be glad a quiet realm in this his
reign to see.
ATTENDANCE. My lord, your good a[nd] [3]
willing heart the gods will recompense,
In that your mind so pensive is for those
his great offense.
My lord, his grace shall have a time to
pair [4] and to amend.   630
Happy is he that can escape and not his
grace offend.
DILIGENCE. If that wicked vice he could
refrain, from wasting wine forbear,
A moderate life he would frequent,
amending this his square.[5]
AMBIDEXTER. My lord, and if your honor
it shall please,
I can inform you what is best for your
ease:
Let him alone; of his deeds do not talk;
Then by his side ye may quietly walk.
After his death you shall be king;
Then may you reform each kind of thing.
In the meantime live quietly; do not
with him deal;   640
So shall it redound much to your weal.
SMIRDIS. Thou say'st true, my friend; that
is the best.
I know not whether he love me or do me
detest.
ATTENDANCE. Lean from his company all
that you may.
I, faithful Attendance, will your honor
obey;

[1] Dissatisfactions. [4] Repair.
[2] More. [5] Regularity of conduct.
[3] Added by Manly.

If against your honor he take any ire,
His grace is as like to kindle his fire
To your honor's destruction as otherwise.
DILIGENCE. Therefore, my lord, take good
advice,
And I, Diligence, your case will so
tender   650
That to his grace your honor shall be
none offender.
SMIRDIS. I thank you both, entire friends.
With my honor still remain.
AMBIDEXTER. Behold where the king doth
come with his train!

Enter King and a Lord.

KING. O lording dear and brother mine, I
joy your state to see,
Surmising much what is the cause you
absent thus from me.
SMIRDIS. Pleaseth your grace, no absence
I, but ready to fulfill,
At all assays, my prince and king, in that
your grace me will.
What I can do in true defense to you, my
prince, aright,
In readiness I always am to offer forth
my might.
KING. And I the like to you again do here
avouch the same.   660
ALL. For this your good agreement here,
now praiséd be God's name!
AMBIDEXTER. [*To Smirdis.*] But hear ye,
noble prince; hark in your ear:
It is best to do as I did declare.
KING. My lord and brother Smirdis, now
this is my mind and will:
That you to court of mine return, and
there to tarry still
Till my return within short space your
honor for to greet.
SMIRDIS. At your behest so will I do till
time again we meet.
My leave I take from you, O king; even
now I do depart.
Exeunt Smirdis, Attendance, and Diligence.
KING. Farewell, lord and brother mine!
farewell with all my heart!
My lord, my brother Smirdis is of youth
and manly might,   670
And in his sweet and pleasant face my
heart doth take delight.
LORD. Yea, noble prince, if that your
grace before his honor die,

He will succeed, a virtuous king, and rule
  with equity.
KING. As you have said, my lord, he is
  chief heir next my grace,
And, if I die tomorrow, next he shall
  succeed my place.
AMBIDEXTER. And, if it please your grace,
  O king, I heard him say,
For your death unto the God day and
  night he did pray;
He would live so virtuously and get him
  such a praise
That Fame by trump his due deserts in
  honor should upraise;
He said your grace deservéd had the
  cursing of all men,   680
That ye should never after him get any
  praise again.
KING. Did he speak thus of my grace in
  such despiteful wise?
Or else dost thou presume to fill my
  princely ears with lies?
LORD. I cannot think it in my heart that
  he would report so.
KING. How sayst thou? Speak the truth:
  was it so or no?
AMBIDEXTER. I think so, if it please your
  grace, but I cannot tell.
KING. Thou play'st with both hands, now
  I perceive well!
But, for to put all doubts aside and to
  make him leese his hope,
He shall die by dint of sword or else by
  choking rope.
Shall he succeed when I am gone, to have
  more praise than I?   690
Were he father, as brother mine, I swear
  that he shall die!
To palace mine I will therefore, his death
  for to pursue.
          Exit [*King with the Lord*].
AMBIDEXTER. Are ye gone? Straightway
  I will follow you.—
[*To the audience.*] How like ye now, my
  masters? Doth not this gear cotton? [1]
The proverb old is verified: "Soon ripe,
  and soon rotten!"
He will not be quiet till his brother be
  killed;
His delight is wholly to have his blood
  spilled.
Marry, sir, I told him a notable lie!
If it were to do again, I durst [not] do it, I!

[1] Affair succeed.

Marry, when I had done, to it I durst
  not stand;   700
Thereby ye may perceive I use to play
  with each hand.
But how now, cousin Cutpurse, with
  whom play you?
Take heed, for his hand is groping even
  now!
Cousin, take heed, if you do secretly
  grope;
If ye be taken, cousin, ye must look
  through a rope.   *Exit.*

          Enter Lord Smirdis alone.

[SMIRDIS.] I am wandering alone, here and
  there to walk;
The court is so unquiet, in it I take
  no joy.
Solitary to myself now I may talk.
If I could rule, I wist what to say.

Enter Cruelty and Murder with bloody hands.

CRUELTY. My coequal partner, Murder,
  come away;   710
From me long thou mayst not stay.
MURDER. Yes, from thee I may stay, but
  not thou from me;
Therefore I have a prerogative above
  thee.
CRUELTY. But in this case we must to-
  gether abide.
Come, come! Lord Smirdis I have spied.
Lay hands on him with all festination, [2]
That on him we may work our indigna-
  tion!   [*They seize him.*]
SMIRDIS. How now, my friends? What
  have you to do with me?
MURDER. King Cambises hath sent us
  unto thee,
Commanding us straightly, without
  mercy or favor,   720
Upon thee to bestow our behavior,
With cruelty to murder you and make
  you away.
SMIRDIS. Yet pardon me, I heartily you
  pray!
Consider, the king is a tyrant tyran-
  nious,
And all his doings be damnable and per-
  nicious.
Favor me therefore; I did him never
  offend.

[2] Speed.

CRUELTY. No favor at all! Your life is at
an end!
Even now I strike, his body to wound.
Strike him in divers places.[1]
Behold, now his blood springs out on
the ground!
A little bladder of vinegar pricked.[2]
MURDER. Now he is dead, let us present
him to the king. 730
CRUELTY. Lay to your hand, away him to
bring. *Exeunt.*

Enter Ambidexter.

AMBIDEXTER. O the passion of God, yonder
is a heavy court!
Some weeps, some wails—and some make
great sport.
Lord Smirdis by Cruelty and Murder is
slain;
But Jesus! for want of him how some do
complain!
If I should have had a thousand pound I
could not forbear weeping.
Now Jesus have his blessed soul in keep-
ing!
Ah, good lord, to think on him, how it
doth me grieve!
I cannot forbear weeping, ye may me
believe. *Weep.*
O my heart, how my pulses do beat! 740
With sorrowful lamentations I am in
such a heat!
Ah, my heart, how for him it doth sor-
row!
Nay, I have done, in faith, now. And
God give ye good morrow!
Ha, ha! Weep? Nay, laugh, with both
hands to play!
The king through his cruelty hath made
him away;
But hath not he wrought a most wicked
deed,
Because king after him he should not
proceed,
His own natural brother, and having no
more,
To procure his death by violence sore?
In spite, because his brother should never
be king, 750
His heart, being wicked, consented to
this thing.

Now he hath no more brothers nor kinred [3] alive.
If the king use this gear still, he cannot
long thrive.

Enter Hob and Lob.

HOB. God's hat, neighbor, come away!
It's time to market to go!
LOB. God's vast,[4] neighbor, zay ye zo?
The clock hath stricken vive, ich [5] think,
by Lakin! [6]
Bum vay,[7] vrom sleep cham not very well
waken!
But, neighbor Hob, neighbor Hob, what
have ye to zell?
HOB. Bum troth, neighbor Lob, to you I
chill tell:
Chave two goslings and a chine of
pork— 760
There is no vatter between this and York.
Chave a pot of strawberries and a calve's
head;
A zennight zince, tomorrow, it hath been
dead.
LOB. Chave a score of eggs and of butter
a pound:
Yesterday a nest of goodly young rabbits
I vound;
Chave vorty things mo, of more and of
less—
My brain is not very good them to ex-
press.
But, God's hat, neighbor, wot'st [8] what?
HOB. No, not well, neighbor; what's that?
LOB. Bum vay, neighbor, master king is a
zhrode [9] lad! 770
Zo God help me, and halidom, I think the
vool be mad!
Zome zay he deal cruelly: his brother he
did kill,
And also a goodly young lad's heart-
blood he did spill.
HOB. Vorbod of God,[10] neighbor! Has he
played zuch a voolish deed?
AMBIDEXTER. Goodman Hob and Good-
man Lob, God be your speed!
As you two towards market do walk,

[1] In the original this stage direction is printed
in the margin at line 723.
[2] In the original this stage direction is printed
in the margin at line 727.
[3] Kindred.
[4] Fast. In the following rustic dialect, initial
z = *s* and initial *v* = *f*.
[5] I. See *Roister Doister*, I, iii, 100, n.
[6] Ladykin; *i.e.*, the Virgin.
[7] By my faith.   [9] Shrewd.
[8] Knowest.   [10] God forbid!

Of the king's cruelty I did hear you talk.
I insure you he is a king most vile and
   pernicious;
His doings and life are odious and vicious.

LOB. It were a good deed zomebody would
   break his head.   780

HOB. Bum vay, neighbor Lob, I chuld he
   were dead!

AMBIDEXTER. So would I, Lob and Hob,
   with all my heart!—
   [To audience.] Now with both hands will
   you see me play my part.—
Ah, ye whoreson [1] traitorly knaves,
Hob and Lob, out upon you, slaves!

LOB. And thou call'st me knave, thou art
   another!
My name is Lob, and Hob my next
   neighbor.

AMBIDEXTER. Hob and Lob! Ah, ye coun-
   try patches, [2]
Ah, ye fools, ye have made wrong
   matches!
Ye have spoken treason against the
   king's grace!   790
For it I will accuse ye before his face;
Then for the same ye shall be martyred.
At the least ye shall be hanged, drawn,
   and quartered!

HOB. O gentleman, ye shall have two
   pear-pies, and tell not of me!

LOB. By God, a vat goose chill give thee.
I think no hurt, by my vather's soul I
   zwear!

HOB. Chave lived well all my lifetime, my
   neighbors among,
And now chould be loath to come to zuch
   wrong—
To be hanged and quartered, the grief
   would be great!

LOB. A foul evil on thee, Hob! Who bid
   thee on it treat?   800
Vor it was thou that first did him
   name.

HOB. Thou liest like a varlet and thou
   zayst the zame!
It was zuch a foolish Lob as thou.

LOB. Speak many words, and, by Cod's
   nails I vow,
Upon thy pate my staff I will lay!

AMBIDEXTER. [Aside.] By the Mass, I will
   cause them to make a fray.—
Yea, Lob, thou sayst true: all came
   through him.

LOB. Bum vay, thou hod,[3] a little would
   make me ye trim!
Give thee a zwap on thy nose till thy
   heart ache!

HOB. If thou darest, do it! Else, man,
   cry "creak!" [4]   810
I trust, before thou hurt me,
With my staff chill make a Lob of
   thee!

Here let them fight with their staves, not come
   near another by three or four yards; the
   Vice set them on as hard as he can; one
   of their wives come out, and all-to [5] beat
   the Vice; he run away.

Enter Marian-May-Be-Good, Hob's Wife,
running in with a broom, and part them.

MARIAN. O the body of me! Husband
   Hob, what mean ye to fight?
For the passion of God, no more blows
   smite!
Neighbors and friends so long, and now
   to fall out?
What! in your age to seem so stout?
If I had not parted ye, one had killed
   another.

LOB. I had not cared, I swear by God's
   Mother!

MARIAN. Shake hands again at the request of me;
As ye have been friends, so friends still
   be.   820

HOB. Bum troth, cham content and zayst
   word, neighbor Lob.

LOB. I am content; agreed, neighbor
   Hob!

Shake hands and laugh heartily one at
   another.

MARIAN. So, get you to market; no longer
   stay.
And with yonder knave let me make a
   fray.

HOB. Content, wife Marian; chill do as
   thou dost say.
But buss me, ich pray thee, at going
   away!   *Exeunt Hob, Lob.*

MARIAN. Thou whoreson knave and prick-
   eared boy, why didst thou let them
   fight?
If one had killed another here, couldst
   thou their deaths requite?

---

[1] Rascally.   [2] Clowns, bumpkins.
[3] Hob(?).   [4] *I.e.*, confess yourself beaten
[5] Thoroughly.

It bears a sign by this thy deed a cowardly knave thou art,
Else wouldst thou draw that weapon thine, like a man,[1] them to part. 830
AMBIDEXTER. What, Marian-May-Be-Good, are you come prattling?
Ye may hap get a box on the ear with your talking!
If they had killed one another, I had not cared a pease.

Here let her swinge him in her broom; she gets him down, and he her down; thus one on the top of another make pastime.

MARIAN. Ah, villain, myself on thee I must ease!
Give me a box on the ear? That will I try.
Who shall be master, thou shalt see by-and-by!
AMBIDEXTER. O, no more, no more, I beseech you heartily!
Even now I yield, and give you the mast'ry.

Run his way out while she is down.

MARIAN. Ah, thou knave! dost thou throw me down and run thy[2] way?
If he were here again, O, how I would him pay! 840
I will after him, and, if I can him meet,
With these my nails his face I will greet.
[*Exit.*]

Enter Venus leading out her son Cupid, blind. He must have a bow and two shafts, one headed with gold and th' other with lead.

VENUS. Come forth, my son. Unto my words attentive ears resign;
What I pretend,[3] see you frequent, to force this game of mine.
The king a kinswoman hath, adorned with beauty store;[4]
And I wish that Diana's gifts they twain shall keep no more,
But use my silver sugared game their joys for to augment.
When I do speak, to wound his heart, Cupid my son, consent,
And shoot at him the shaft of love that bears the head of gold,
To wound his heart in lover's wise, his grief for to unfold. 850

Though kin she be unto his grace, that nature me expel,
Against the course thereof he may in my game please me well.
Wherefore, my son, do not forget; forthwith pursue the deed!
CUPID. Mother, I mean for to obey as you have whole decreed;
But you must tell me, mother dear, when I shall arrow draw,
Else your request to be attained will not be worth a straw;
I am blind and cannot see, but still do shoot by guess.
The poets well, in places, store[5] of my might do express.
VENUS. Cupid my son, when time shall serve that thou shalt do this deed,
Then warning I to thee will give; but see thou shoot with speed. 860

Enter a Lord, a Lady, and a Waiting-maid.

[FIRST] LORD. Lady dear, to king akin, forthwith let us proceed
To trace abroad the beauty fields, as erst we had decreed.
The blowing buds whose savory scents our sense will much delight,
The sweet smell of musk white-rose to please the appetite,
The chirping birds whose pleasant tunes therein shall here record
That our great joy we shall it find in field to walk abroad,
On lute and cittern there to play a heavenly harmony;
Our ears shall hear, heart to content, our sports to beautify.
LADY. Unto your words, most comely lord, myself submit do I;
To trace with you in field so green I mean not to deny. 870

Here trace up and down, playing.

MAID. And I, your waiting-maid, at hand with diligence will be,
For to fulfill with heart and hand, when you shall command me.

Enter King, Lord, and Knight.

KING. Come on, my lord and knight, abroad; our mirth let us employ.
Since he is dead, this heart of mine in corpse I feel it joy.

---

[1] Suggested by Manly. Original reads *knave*.
[2] Emended by Manly; original has *the*.
[3] Intend.   [4] Store of beauty.
[5] Greatness, abundance.

Should brother mine have reignéd king
   when I had yielded breath?
A thousand brothers I rather had to put
   them all to death.
But, O behold, where I do see a lord and
   lady fair!
For beauty she most worthy is to sit in
   prince's chair.

VENUS. Shoot forth, my son! Now is
   the time that thou must wound his
   heart.

CUPID. Content you, mother; I will do
   my part.   880
Shoot there, and go out Venus and Cupid.

KING. Of truth, my lord, in eye of mine
   all ladies she doth excel.
Can none report what dame she is, and to
   my grace it tell?

LORD. Redoubted prince, pleaseth your
   grace, to you she is akin,
Cousin-german, nigh of birth, by mother's side come in.

KNIGHT. And that her waiting-maiden is,
   attending her upon.
He is a lord of prince's court, and will be
   there anon.
They sport themselves in pleasant field,
   to former uséd use.

KING. My lord and knight, of truth I
   speak. My heart it cannot choose
But with my lady I must speak and so
   express my mind.—
My lord and ladies, walking there, if you
   will favor find,   890
Present yourselves unto my grace, and
   by my side come stand.

FIRST LORD. We will fulfill, most mighty
   king, as your grace doth command.

KING. Lady dear, intelligence my grace
   hath got of late,
You issued out of mother's stock and kin
   unto my state.
According to rule of birth you are cousin-
   german mine;
Yet do I wish that farther off this kinred
   I could find;
For Cupid he, that eyeless boy, my heart
   hath so enflamed
With beauty, you me to content the like
   cannot be named;
For, since I entered in this place and on
   you fixed mine eyes,
Most burning fits about my heart in
   ample wise did rise.   900

The heat of them such force doth yield,
   my corpse they scorch, alas!
And burns the same with wasting heat,
   as Titan doth the grass.
And, sith this heat is kindled so and
   fresh in heart of me,
There is no way but of the same the
   quencher you must be.
My meaning is that beauty yours my
   heart with love doth wound;
To give me love mind [1] to content, my
   heart hath you out found;
And you are she must be my wife, else
   shall I end my days.
Consent to this, and be my queen, to
   wear the crown with praise!

LADY. If it please your grace, O mighty
   king, you shall not this request.
It is a thing that nature's course doth
   utterly detest,   910
And high it would the God displease; of
   all, that is the worst.
To grant your grace to marry so, it is
   not I that durst.
Yet humble thanks I render now unto
   you, mighty king,
That you vouchsafe to great estate so
   gladly would me bring.
Were it not it were offense, I would it
   not deny,
But such great honor to achieve my
   heart I would apply.
Therefore, O king, with humble heart in
   this I pardon crave;
My answer is: in this request your mind
   ye may not have.

KING. May I not? Nay, then, I will, by
   all the gods I vow!
And I will marry thee as wife. This is
   mine answer now!   920
Who dare say nay what I pretend, who
   dare the same withstand,
Shall lose his head, and have report as
   traitor through my land.
There is no nay. I will you have, and
   you my queen shall be!

LADY. Then, mighty king, I crave your
   grace to hear the words of me:
Your counsel take of lordings' wit; the
   laws aright peruse;
If I with safe may grant this deed, I will
   it not refuse.

---

[1] Desire.

KING. No, no! What I have said to you,
    I mean to have it so.
For counsel theirs I mean not, I, in this
    respect to go;
But to my palace let us go, the marriage
    to prepare;
For, to avoid [1] my will in this, I can it
    not forbear.   930
LADY. O God, forgive me, if I do amiss!
The king by compulsion enforceth me
    this.
MAID. Unto the gods for your estate I
    will not cease to pray,
That you may be a happy queen, and see
    most joyful day.
KING. Come on, my lords; with gladsome
    hearts let us rejoice with glee!
Your music show to joy this deed at the
    request of me!
BOTH. For to obey your grace's words our
    honors do agree.   *Exeunt.*

Enter Ambidexter.

AMBIDEXTER. O the passion of me! Marry,
    as ye say, yonder is a royal court!
There is triumphing and sport upon
    sport,
Such loyal lords, with such lordly exer-
    cise,   940
Frequenting such pastime as they can
    devise,
Running at tilt, jousting, with running
    at the ring,
Masking and mumming, with each kind
    of thing,
Such dancing, such singing, with musical
    harmony!
Believe me, I was loath to absent their
    company.
But will you believe? Jesu, what haste
    they made till they were married!
Not for a million of pounds one day
    longer they would have tar[ri]ed!
O, there was a banquet royal and super-
    excellent!
Thousands and thousands at that ban-
    quet was spent.
I muse of nothing but how they can be
    married so soon.   950
I care not if I be married before to-
    morrow at noon,
If marriage be a thing that so may be
    had.

[1] Make void, give up.

[*To a girl in the audience.*] How say you,
    maid? To marry me will ye be glad?
Out of doubt, I believe it is some excellent
    treasure;
Else to the same belongs abundant pleas-
    ure.
Yet with mine ears I have heard some
    say,
"That ever I was married, now cursèd
    be the day!"
Those be they [that] [2] with curst [3] wives
    be matched.
That husband for hawk's meat [4] of [5]
    them is up-snatched,
Head broke with a bedstaff, face all-to
    bescratched—   960
"Knave!" "Slave!" and "Villain!"—a
    coiled coat [6] now and then.
When the wife hath given it, she will say,
    "Alas, good man!"
Such were better unmarried, my masters,
    I trow,
Than all their life after be matched with
    a shrow.[7]

Enter Preparation.

[PREPARATION.] With speed I am sent all
    things to prepare,
My message to do as the king did de-
    clare.
His grace doth mean a banquet to
    make,
Meaning in this place repast for to take.
Well, the cloth shall be laid, and all
    things in readiness,
To court to return when done is my
    business.   970
AMBIDEXTER. A proper man and also fit
For the king's estate to prepare a ban-
    quet!
PREPARATION. What, Ambidexter? Thou
    art not unknown!
A mischief on all good faces, so that I
    curse not mine own!
Now, in the knave's name, shake hands
    with me.
AMBIDEXTER. Well said, goodman pouch-
    mouth; your reverence I see.
I will teach ye, if your manners no better
    be.

[2] Supplied from first edn.
[3] Shrewish.
[4] Something seized greedily.
[5] By.
[6] A beating.
[7] Shrew.

Ah, ye slave, the king doth me a gentleman allow;

Therefore I look that to me ye should
bow.   *Fight.*

PREPARATION. Good Master Ambidexter,
pardon my behavior;   980

For this your deeds you are a knave, for
your labor!

AMBIDEXTER. Why, ye stale counterly [1]
villain, nothing but "knave"? *Fight.*

PREPARATION. I am sorry your mastership
offended I have;

Shake hands, that between us agreement
may be.

I was overshot with myself, I do see.

Let me have your help this furniture to
provide.

The king from this place will not long
abide.   *Set the fruit on the board.*

AMBIDEXTER. Content; it is the thing that
I would wish.

I myself will go fetch one dish.

Let the Vice fetch a dish of nuts, and let them
fall in the bringing of them in.

PREPARATION. Cleanly, Master Ambidexter, for fair on the ground they lie. 990

AMBIDEXTER. I will have them up again
by-and-by.

PREPARATION. To see all in readiness I
will put you in trust;

There is no nay, to the court needs I
must.   *Exit Preparation.*

AMBIDEXTER. Have ye no doubt but all
shall be well.—

Marry, sir, as you say, this gear doth
excel!

All things is in a readiness, when they
come hither,

The king's grace and the queen both togither.—

[*To the audience.*] I beseech ye, my masters, tell me, is it not best

That I be so bold as to bid a guest?

He is as honest a man as ever spurred
cow—   1000

My cousin Cutpurse, I mean; I beseech
ye, judge you.

Believe me, cousin, if to be the king's
guest ye could be taken,

I trust that offer will never be forsaken.

But, cousin, because to that office ye are
not like to come,

Frequent your exercises—a horn [2] on
your thumb,

A quick eye, a sharp knife, at hand a
receiver.[3]

But then take heed, cousin, ye be a
cleanly conveyor.

Content yourself, cousin; for this banquet
you are unfit,

When such as I at the same am unworthy
to sit.

Enter King, Queen, and his Train.

KING. My queen and lords, to take repast, let us attempt the same.   1010

Here is the place; delay no time, but to
our purpose frame.

QUEEN. With willing hearts your whole
behest we mind for to obey.

ALL. And we, the rest of prince's train, will
do as you do say.   *Sit at the banquet.*

KING. Methink mine ears doth wish the
sound of music's harmony;

Here, for to play before my grace, in place
I would them spy. *Play at the banquet.*

AMBIDEXTER. They be at hand, sir, with
stick and fiddle;

They can play a new dance, called " Hey-
diddle-diddle."

KING. My queen, perpend. What I pronounce, I will not violate,

But one thing which my heart makes
glad I mind to explicate.

You know in court uptrainéd is a lion
very young;   1020

Of one litter two whelps [4] beside, as yet
not very strong.

I did request one whelp to see and this
young lion fight;

But lion did the whelp convince by
strength of force and might.

His brother whelp, perceiving that the
lion was too good,

And he by force was like to see the other
whelp his [5] blood,

With force to lion he did run, his brother
for to help.

A wonder great it was to see that friendship in a whelp!

So then the whelps between them both
the lion did convince.

---

[1] Fit for the Counter, a prison.

[2] A thimble of horn, worn by cutpurses.
[3] A confederate to whom stolen goods were
handed.   [4] Dogs, in this case.
[5] *Whelp his* is an old form of the possessive.

Which thing to see before mine eyes did
glad the heart of prince.
At this tale told, let the Queen weep.
QUEEN. These words to hear makes stilling
tears issue from crystal eyes. 1030
KING. What dost thou mean, my spouse,
to weep for loss of any prize? [1]
QUEEN. No, no, O king, but, as you see,
friendship in brother's whelp;
When one was like to have repulse, the
other yielded help.
And was this favor showed in dogs, to
shame of royal king?
Alack, I wish these ears of mine had not
once heard this thing!
Even so should you, O mighty king, to
brother been a stay,
And not, without offense to you, in such
wise him to slay.
In all assays it was your part his cause
to have defended,
And whosoever had him misused to have
them reprehended.
But faithful love was more in dog than it
was in your grace. 1040
KING. O cursèd caitiff, vicious and vile,
I hate thee in this place!
This banquet is at an end; take all these
things away.
Before my face thou shalt repent the
words that thou dost say.
O wretch most vile, didst thou the cause
of brother mine so tender
The loss of him should grieve thy heart,
he being none offender?
It did me good his death to have—so will
it to have thine!
What friendship he had at my hands, the
same even thou shalt find.
I give consent, and make a vow, that
thou shalt die the death!
By Cruel's sword and Murder fell even
thou shalt lose thy breath.
Ambidexter, see with speed to Cruelty
ye go; 1050
Cause him hither to approach, Murder
with him also.
AMBIDEXTER. I ready am for to fulfill if
that it be your grace's will.
KING. Then naught oblite [2] my message
given; absent thyself away.
AMBIDEXTER. Then in this place I will no
longer stay.—

[Aside to the Queen.] If that I durst, I
would mourn your case;
But, alas! I dare not, for fear of his
grace. *Exit Ambidex[ter].*
KING. Thou cursèd Jill! [3] by all the gods I
take an oath and swear
That flesh of thine these hands of mine
in pieces small could tear!
But thou shalt die by dent [4] of sword;
there is no friend ne fee
Shall find remorse at prince's hand to
save the life of thee! 1060
QUEEN. O mighty king and husband mine,
vouchsafe to hear me speak,
And license give to spouse of thine her
patient mind to break.
For tender love unto your grace my
words I did so frame;
For pure love doth heart of king me vio-
late and blame.
And to your grace is this offense that I
should purchase death?
Then cursèd time that I was queen to
shorten this my breath!
Your grace doth know by marriage true
I am your wife and spouse,
And one to save another's health at
troth-plight made our vows.
Therefore, O king, let loving queen at
thy hand find remorse;
Let pity be a mean to quench that cruel
raging force, 1070
And pardon, plight [5] from prince's mouth,
yield grace unto your queen,
That amity with faithful zeal may ever
be us between.
KING. Ah, caitiff vile! to pity thee my
heart it is not bent;
Ne yet to pardon your offense it is not
mine intent.
FIRST LORD. Our mighty prince, with
humble suit of your grace this I crave,
That this request it may take place, your
favor for to have.
Let mercy yet abundantly the life of
queen preserve,
Sith she in most obedient wise your
grace's will doth serve.
As yet your grace but while with her hath
had cohabitation,
And sure this is no desert why to yield
her indignation.[6] 1080

[1] Contest.   [2] Forget.

[3] Wench.   [5] Plighted, pledged.
[4] Dint.   [6] Indignity.

Therefore, O king, her life prolong, to joy
her days in bliss!

SECOND LORD. Your grace shall win immortal fame in granting unto this.

She is a queen whose goodly hue excels
the royal rose,

For beauty bright Dame Nature she a
large gift did dispose.

For comeliness who may compare? Of
all she bears the bell.[1]

This should give cause to move your
grace to love her very well.

Her silver breast in those your arms to
sing the songs of love—

Fine qualities most excellent to be in her
you prove;

A precious pearl of price to prince, a
jewel passing all!

Therefore, O king, to beg remorse on both
my knees I fall;   1090

To grant her grace to have her life, with
heart I do desire.

KING. You villains twain, with raging
force ye set my heart on fire!

If I consent that she shall die, how dare
ye crave her life?

You two to ask this at my hand doth
much enlarge my strife.

Were it not for shame, you two should
die, that for her life do sue.

But favor mine from you is gone, my
lords, I tell you true.

I sent for Cruelty of late; if he would
come away,

I would commit her to his hands his
cruel part to play.

Even now I see where he doth come; it
doth my heart delight.

Enter Cruelty and Murder.

CRUELTY. Come, Murder, come; let us go
forth with might;   1100

Once again the king's commandment we
must fulfill.

MURDER. I am contented [2] to do it with a
good will.

KING. Murder and Cruelty, for both of
you I sent,

With all festination your offices to frequent.

Lay hold on the queen; take her to your
power,

And make her away within this hour!

[1] Wins the prize.   [2] Original reads *contended*.

Spare for no fear; I do you full permit.
So I from this place do mean for to flit.

BOTH. With courageous hearts, O king, we
will obey.

KING. Then come, my lords, let us depart
away.   1110

BOTH THE LORDS. With heavy hearts we
will do all your grace doth say.

Exeunt King and Lord[s].

CRUELTY. Come, lady and queen, now are
you in our handling;

In faith, with you we will use no dandling.

MURDER. With all expedition I, Murder,
will take place;

Though thou be a queen, ye be under my
grace.

QUEEN. With patience I will you both
obey.[3]

CRUELTY. No more words, but go with us
away!

QUEEN. Yet before I die, some psalm to
God let me sing.

BOTH. We be content to permit you that
thing.

QUEEN. Farewell, you ladies of the court,
with all your masking hue!   1120

I do forsake these broidered guards, and
all the fashions new,

The court and all the courtly train,
wherein I had delight;

I banished am from happy sport, and all
by spiteful spite;

Yet with a joyful heart to God a psalm
I mean to sing,

Forgiving all [men] [4] and the king of
each kind of thing. *Sing,[5] and exeunt.*

Enter Ambidexter weeping.

AMBIDEXTER. Ah, ah, ah, ah! I cannot
choose but weep for the queen!

Nothing but mourning now at the court
there is seen.

O, O, my heart, my heart! O, my bum
will break!

Very grief so torments me that scarce I
can speak.

Who could but weep for the loss of such
a lady?   1130

That cannot I do, I swear by mine honesty.

But, Lord! so the ladies mourn, crying
"Alack!"

[3] Original interchanges *obey* and *away* of next
line.   [4] Supplied by Manly.   [5] The song is lost.

Nothing is worn now but only black.
I believe all [the] [1] cloth in Watling
   Street to make gowns would not serve.
If I make a lie, the devil let ye sterve! [2]
All ladies mourn, both young and old;
There is not one that weareth a point's
   worth of gold.
There is a sort for fear for the king do
   pray
That would have him dead, by the Mass,
   I dare say.[3]
What a king was he that hath used such
   tyranny!   1140
He was akin to Bishop Bonner,[4] I think
   verily!
For both their delights was to shed blood,
But never intended to do any good.
Cambises put a judge to death—that was
   a good deed;
But to kill the young child was worse to
   proceed;
To murder his brother, and then his own
   wife—
So help me God and halidom, it is pity
   of his life!
Hear ye? I will lay twenty thousand
   pound
That the king himself doth die by some
   wound;
He hath shed so much blood that his will
   be shed.   1150
If it come to pass, in faith, then he is
   sped.

*Enter the King, without a gown, a sword
      thrust up into his side, bleeding.*

KING. Out, alas! What shall I do? My
   life is finishéd!
Wounded I am by sudden chance; my
   blood is minishéd.
Gog's heart, what means might I make
   my life to preserve?
Is there naught to be my help, nor is
   there naught to serve?
Out upon the court and lords that there
   remain!
To help my grief in this my case will
   none of them take pain?

---

[1] Supplied by Hazlitt.   [2] Die.
[3] *I.e.*, there is a group who pray for the king
out of fear, but wish him dead.
[4] Bishop of London, who was hated because
of his persecution of the Protestants.

Who but I, in such a wise, his death's
   wound could have got?
As I on horseback up did leap, my sword
   from scabbard shot,
And ran me thus into the side, as you
   right well may see.   1160
A marvel's chance unfortunate, that in
   this wise should be!
I feel myself a-dying now; of life bereft
   am I;
And Death hath caught me with his
   dart; for want of blood I spy,[5]
Thus, gasping, here on ground I lie; for
   nothing I do care.
A just reward for my misdeeds my death
   doth plain declare.
            Here let him quake and stir.
AMBIDEXTER. How now, noble king? Pluck
   up your heart!
What, will you die, and from us depart?
Speak to me and ye be alive!
He cannot speak. But behold, how with
   Death he doth strive.   [*King dies.*]
Alas, good king! Alas, he is gone!   1170
The devil take me if for him I make any
   moan.
I did prognosticate of his end, by the
   Mass!
Like as I did say, so is it come to pass.
I will be gone. If I should be found here,
That I should kill him it would appear.
For fear with his death they do me
   charge,
Farewell, my masters, I will go take
   barge.
I mean to be packing; now is the tide;
Farewell, my masters, I will no longer
   abide!   *Exit Ambidexter.*

Enter three Lords.

FIRST LORD. Behold, my lord, it is even
   so as he to us did tell.   1180
His grace is dead, upon the ground, by
   dint of sword most fell.
SECOND LORD. As he in saddle would have
   leaped, his sword from sheath did go,
Goring him up into the side. His life was
   ended so.
THIRD LORD. His blood so fast did issue
   out that naught could him prolong;
Yet, before he yielded up the ghost, his
   heart was very strong.

---

[5] Spyre, 'spire, expire(?).

FIRST LORD. A just reward for his mis-
    deeds the God above hath wrought,
For certainly the life he led was to be
    counted naught.
SECOND LORD. Yet a princely burial he
    shall have, according to his estate;
And more of him here at this time we
    have not to dilate.
THIRD LORD. My lords, let us take him
    up and carry him away.   1190
BOTH. Content we are with one accord to
    do as you do say.   *Exeunt all.*

EPILOGUE

Right gentle audience, here have you pe-
    rused
The tragical history of this wicked king.
According to our duty, we have not refused,
    But to our best intent expressed every-
    thing.
    We trust none is offended for this our
    doing.
Our author craves likewise, if he have
    squared [1] amiss,
By gentle admonition to know where
    the fault is.

His good will shall not be neglected to
    amend the same.

  [1] Shaped, built.

Praying all to bear, therefore, with this
    simple deed
Until the time serve a better he may
    frame;   10
Thus yielding you thanks, to end we
    decreed
That you so gently have suffered us to
    proceed,
In such patient wise as to hear and see,
We can but thank ye therefor; we can do
    no more, we!

As duty binds us, for our noble queen let
    us pray,
    And for her honorable council, the truth
    that they may use,
To practice justice and defend her grace
    each day;
    To maintain God's word they may not
    refuse,
To correct all those that would her grace
    and grace's laws abuse;
Beseeching God over us she may reign
    long,   20
To be guided by truth and defended from
    wrong.

AMEN, QUOD [2] THOMAS PRESTON.

  [2] Quoth, said.

JOHN LYLY

John Lyly was probably born in Canterbury in 1553 or 1554. He took his B.A. at Oxford in 1573 and his M.A. in 1575, and was made an M.A. by Cambridge University also in 1579. Late in 1578 his *Euphues: The Anatomy of Wit* was issued, a work intended to set a pattern for English prose, in which he wove into a thin thread of fiction dissertations on such subjects as education and contemporary manners. A second part, *Euphues and His England*, appeared in 1580. In spite of the vogue of *Euphues*, whose style was imitated in a series of romantic novels for many years to come, Lyly turned from fiction to devote himself to drama, possibly under the influence of the Earl of Oxford. Beginning about 1580 as his secretary, Lyly served the earl at least until about 1585. He was esquire of the body to Elizabeth in 1588, probably wrote a pamphlet and plays for the bishops' party in the Marprelate controversy of 1589–90, and secured election to parliament on four separate occasions. Disappointed of his chief hopes, however, he died in 1606, after a decade marked for us only by some petty records of his family life and some letters complaining of failure and neglect.

Lyly's dramatic work was part of his disappointing effort to advance his fortunes at court, especially in connection with the office of the revels, but it was also designed for the professional theater. The records of the activities and interrelations of the boy companies by whom his plays were acted are complicated and often obscure. *Campaspe* and *Sapho and Phao* were printed in 1584 as having been acted early in the year at court, by the Children of the Chapel and the Boys of St. Paul's Choir School, but official payment for the two performances was made to Oxford's "servants" under Lyly. Possibly the boy company under Oxford's patronage was combined with the other two companies in this year to perform at court plays written by Lyly and Oxford. According to the prologues, however, Lyly's two plays were also publicly acted at the "private" theater of Blackfriars, where the Children of the Chapel had given periodic performances for profit since 1576. Apparently Lyly and Oxford acquired an interest in this playhouse just as it was closed by a suit in 1584. Later Lyly wrote plays for Paul's boys, as the title-pages show, clearly for both court and public performances, until the public acting of the boys came to an end in 1591. These plays, with the dates of publication, are *Endymion* (1591), *Galathea* (1592), *Midas* (1592), *Mother Bombie* (1594), and *Love's Metamorphosis* (1601). *The Woman in the Moon* (1597) has no indication of the company, and may have been the result of some other connection.

It is in keeping with this effort to please the court and the public that Lyly's dramatic work marks the first stage in the development toward the Elizabethan popular drama of superb literary quality which was to follow. In the words of Bond, Lyly struck a "balance between classic precedent and romantic freedom." Titles of lost plays suggest that court taste had turned from the stricter classicism of academic circles to romance, sometimes disguised by the use of classical story. Lyly used as a basis of his plots love stories drawn from ancient history or mythology, most often from Ovid, adding at times pastoral or sylvan settings, and always reflecting the ideals of courtly circles. Indirect effects of classical influence, possibly in part derived from Italian influence, are seen in both structure and style. There is good motivation of action, variety and skillful complication of incidents, and suspense, especially in the love story. A simplified form of the famous euphuistic prose style, with new elements of conceit and wit appropriate to brisk dialogue, makes Lyly's dramatic prose significant for the future of Elizabethan drama. In his pages, with their quotations from the classics and their parody of the forms and devices of logic, Lyly developed rôles appropriate to his actors as school boys, and the amount of singing in the plays gives scope for them as choir boys.   Probably his style and his reflection of court life and taste account for the early printing of his plays, which in turn probably led to the printing of other romantic plays written for the London stage, especially those of the University Wits.

In *Endymion* the main incidents of the long sleep and the kiss of Cynthia, drawn from Ovid and Lucian, furnished a basis for Lyly's best blend of classic story, love intrigue, courtly and sylvan setting, satire, and wit.   A long tradition of interpreting classic myth freely as shadowing historical events or embodying allegory was responsible for popularizing in the Renaissance the use of myths for presentation of contemporary events or figures, either for flattery or for satire, in poetry generally but perhaps chiefly in pageants and plays. Lyly availed himself of the fashion to flatter Elizabeth boldly as Cynthia and possibly to glance at events in the court. Many attempts have been made to read the apparent allegory of the play. In 1843 Halpin argued that Endymion's story represents Leicester's love for Elizabeth and his relations to others at court. Other interpretations of the play as personal allegory have been advanced by various scholars. P. W. Long argues, however, perhaps correctly, that the allegory is primarily one of Platonic love, in which Endymion passes from love of Tellus (Earth), or earthly beauty, to adoration of Cynthia as a symbol of heavenly beauty.

Endymion, probably composed some time between 1585 and 1588, was entered in the Stationers' Register on October 4, 1591, and published anonymously later that year. The play was printed as Lyly's by Blount in *Six Court Comedies* of 1632. The style, however, would leave no doubt as to Lyly's authorship. The text of the present edition is based on Bond's reprint of the quarto of 1591 in his *Works of Lyly*.

ENDYMION, THE MAN IN THE MOON[1]

[BY

JOHN LYLY

DRAMATIS PERSONÆ

ENDYMION, *in love with Cynthia.*
EUMENIDES, *his friend, in love with Semele.*
CORSITES, *a captain, in love with Tellus.*
PANELION }
ZONTES } *lords of Cynthia's court.*
PYTHAGORAS, *a philosopher.*
GYPTES, *an Egyptian soothsayer.*
GERON, *an old man, husband to Dipsas.*
SIR TOPHAS, *a braggart.*
DARES, *page to Endymion.*
SAMIAS, *page to Eumenides.*
EPITON, *page to Sir Tophas.*

MASTER CONSTABLE.
FIRST *and* SECOND WATCHMAN.

CYNTHIA, *the queen.*
TELLUS, *her rival, in love with Endymion.*
FLOSCULA, *her friend.*
SEMELE, *a lady at the court.*
SCINTILLA }
FAVILLA } *maids at the court.*
DIPSAS, *an old enchantress.*
BAGOA, *her servant.*
FAIRIES.
THREE LADIES *and an* OLD MAN *in the dumb show.*

SCENE: *Cynthia's realm.*

TIME: *Mythical.*]

THE PROLOGUE

MOST high and happy princess, we must tell you a tale of the Man in the Moon, which, if it seem ridiculous for the method, or superfluous for the matter, or for the means incredible, for three faults we can make but one excuse: it is a tale of the Man in the Moon.

It was forbidden in old time to dispute of Chimera because it was a fiction. We hope in our times none will apply [10 pastimes,[2] because they are fancies; for there liveth none under the sun that knows what to make of the Man in the Moon. We present neither comedy, nor tragedy, nor story, nor anything but that whosoever heareth may say this: "Why, here is a tale of the Man in the Moon."

ACTUS PRIMUS. SCENA PRIMA.

[*A grove near the cell of Endymion.*]

Endymion, Eumenides.

END. I find, Eumenides, in all things both variety to content and satiety to glut, saving only in my affections, which are so staid, and withal so stately that I can neither satisfy my heart with love, nor mine eyes with wonder. My thoughts, Eumenides, are stitched to the stars, which, being as high as I can see, thou mayst imagine how much higher they are than I can reach. 10

EUM. If you be enamored of anything above the moon, your thoughts are ridiculous, for that [3] things immortal are not subject to affections; if allured or enchanted with these transitory things under the moon, you show yourself senseless to attribute such lofty titles to such low [4] trifles.

---

[1] The title continues: "Played before the Queen's Majesty at Greenwich on Candlemas Day at Night by the Children of Paul's."
[2] Read actual events into the play.

[3] Because. [4] Suggested by Bond. Both early edns. read *loue.*

END. My love is placed neither under the moon nor above.

EUM. I hope you be not sotted[1] [20 upon the Man in the Moon.

END. No; but settled either to die or possess the moon herself.

EUM. Is Endymion mad, or do I mistake? Do you love the moon, Endymion?

END. Eumenides, the moon.

EUM. There was never any so peevish[2] to imagine the moon either capable of affection or shape of a mistress; for as impossible it is to make love fit to her hu- [30 mor, which no man knoweth, as a coat to her form, which continueth not in one bigness whilst she is measuring. Cease off, Endymion, to feed so much upon fancies. That melancholy blood must be purged which draweth you to a dotage no less miserable than monstrous.

END. My thoughts have no veins, and yet, unless they be let blood, I shall perish.   40

EUM. But they have vanities, which being reformed, you may be restored.

END. O fair Cynthia, why do others term thee unconstant whom I have ever found unmovable? Injurious time, corrupt manners, unkind men, who, finding a constancy not to be matched in my sweet mistress, have christened her with the name of wavering, waxing, and waning! Is she inconstant that keepeth a settled [50 course, which, since her first creation, altereth not one minute in her moving? There is nothing thought more admirable or commendable in the sea than the ebbing and flowing; and shall the moon, from whom the sea taketh this virtue, be accounted fickle for increasing and decreasing? Flowers in their buds are nothing worth till they be blown, nor blossoms accounted[3] till they be ripe fruit; [60 and shall we then say they be changeable for that they grow from seeds to leaves, from leaves to buds, from buds to their perfection? Then why be not twigs that become trees, children that become men, and mornings that grow to evenings, termed wavering, for that they continue not at one stay?[4] Ay, but Cynthia, being in her fulness, decayeth, as not delighting

in her greatest beauty, or withering [70 when she should be most honored. When malice cannot object anything, folly will, making that a vice which is the greatest virtue. What thing (my mistress excepted) being in the pride of her beauty and latter minute of her age, that waxeth young again? Tell me, Eumenides, what is he that, having a mistress of ripe years and infinite virtues, great honors, and unspeakable beauty, but would wish that [80 she might grow tender again, getting youth by years, and never-decaying beauty by time; whose fair face neither the summer's blaze can scorch, nor winter's blast chap, nor the numbering of years breed altering of colors? Such is my sweet Cynthia, whom time cannot touch because she is divine, nor will offend because she is delicate. O Cynthia, if thou shouldest always continue at thy fulness, both gods and [90 men would conspire to ravish thee. But thou, to abate the pride of our affections, dost detract from thy perfections, thinking it sufficient if once in a month we enjoy a glimpse of thy majesty; and then, to increase our griefs, thou dost decrease thy gleams, coming out of thy royal robes, wherewith thou dazzlest our eyes, down into thy swathe clouts,[5] beguiling our eyes. And then—   100

EUM. Stay there, Endymion. Thou that committest idolatry wilt straight blaspheme if thou be suffered. Sleep would do thee more good than speech. The moon heareth thee not or, if she do, regardeth thee not.

END. Vain Eumenides, whose thoughts never grow higher than the crown of thy head! Why troublest thou me, having neither head to conceive the cause of [110 my love or a heart to receive the impressions? Follow thou thine own fortunes, which creep on the earth, and suffer me to fly to mine, whose fall, though it be desperate, yet shall it come by daring. Farewell!

[*Exit.*]

EUM. Without doubt Endymion is bewitched; otherwise in a man of such rare virtues there could not harbor a mind of such extreme madness. I will follow him, lest in this fancy of the moon he de- [120 prive himself of the sight of the sun.   *Exit.*

---

[1] Besotted, infatuated.   [3] Computed.
[2] Silly.   [4] State.
                                   [5] Swaddling clothes.

SCENA SECUNDA.

[*The gardens of Cynthia's palace.*]

Tellus, Floscula.

TELLUS. Treacherous and most perjured Endymion, is Cynthia the sweetness
of thy life and the bitterness of my death?
What revenge may be devised so full of
shame as my thoughts are replenished
with malice? Tell me, Floscula, if false-
ness in love can possibly be punished with
extremity of hate. As long as sword, fire,
or poison may be hired, no traitor to my
love shall live unrevenged. Were thy [10
oaths without number, thy kisses without
measure, thy sighs without end, forged to
deceive a poor credulous virgin, whose
simplicity had been worth thy favor and
better fortune? If the gods sit unequal[1]
beholders of injuries, or laughers at lovers' deceits, then let mischief be as well
forgiven in women as perjury winked at
in men.

FLOSC. Madam, if you would com- [20
pare the state of Cynthia with your own,
and the height of Endymion his [2] thoughts
with the meanness of your fortune, you
would rather yield than contend, being
between you and her no comparison; and
rather wonder than rage at the greatness
of his mind, being affected with a thing
more than mortal.

TELLUS. No comparison, Floscula? And
why so? Is not my beauty divine, [30
whose body is decked with fair flowers, and
veins are vines, yielding sweet liquor to
the dullest spirits; whose ears are corn,
to bring strength; and whose hairs are
grass, to bring abundance? Doth not
frankincense and myrrh breathe out of
my nostrils, and all the sacrifice of the
gods breed in my bowels? Infinite are my
creatures, without which neither thou nor
Endymion nor any could love or live.   40

FLOSC. But know you not, fair lady,
that Cynthia governeth all things? Your
grapes would be but dry husks, your corn
but chaff, and all your virtues vain, were
it not Cynthia that preserveth the one in
the bud and nourisheth the other in the
blade, and by her influence both comforteth all things, and by her authority com-

mandeth all creatures. Suffer, then, Endymion to follow his affections, though to [50
obtain her be impossible, and let him
flatter himself in his own imaginations,
because they are immortal.

TELLUS. Loath I am, Endymion, thou
shouldest die, because I love thee well;
and that thou shouldest live, it grieveth
me, because thou lovest Cynthia too well.
In these extremities what shall I do?
Floscula, no more words; I am resolved.
He shall neither live nor die!   60

FLOSC. A strange practice,[3] if it be
possible.

TELLUS. Yes, I will entangle him in
such a sweet net that he shall neither find
the means to come out, nor desire it. All
allurements of pleasure will I cast before
his eyes, insomuch that he shall slake
that love which he now voweth to Cynthia, and burn in mine, of which he seemeth careless. In this languishing, be- [70
tween my amorous devices and his own
loose desires, there shall such dissolute
thoughts take root in his head and over
his heart grow so thick a skin that neither
hope of preferment nor fear of punishment nor counsel of the wisest nor company of the worthiest shall alter his humor
nor make him once to think of his honor.

FLOSC. A revenge incredible, and, if it
may be, unnatural.   80

TELLUS. He shall know the malice of
a woman to have neither mean nor end;
and of a woman deluded in love to have
neither rule nor reason. I can do it; I
must; I will! All his virtues will I shadow
with vices. His person—ah, sweet person!—
shall he deck with such rich robes as he
shall forget it is his own person; his sharp
wit—ah, wit too sharp that hath cut off all
my joys!—shall he use in flattering of [90
my face and devising sonnets in my favor.
The prime of his youth and pride of his
time shall be spent in melancholy passions,
careless behavior, untamed thoughts, and
unbridled affections.

FLOSC. When this is done, what then?
Shall it continue till his death, or shall he
dote forever in this delight?

TELLUS. Ah, Floscula, thou rendest
my heart in sunder in putting me in [100
remembrance of the end.

---

[1] Prejudiced.   [2] *I.e.*, Endymion's.   [3] Stratagem.

FLOSC. Why, if this be not the end, all the rest is to no end.

TELLUS. Yet suffer me to imitate Juno, who would turn Jupiter's lovers to beasts on the earth, though she knew afterwards they should be stars in heaven.

FLOSC. Affection that is bred by enchantment is like a flower that is wrought in silk— in color and form most like, but [110 nothing at all in substance or savor.

TELLUS. It shall suffice me, if the world talk, that I am favored of Endymion.

FLOSC. Well, use your own will; but you shall find that love gotten with witchcraft is as unpleasant as fish taken with medicines [1] unwholesome.

TELLUS. Floscula, they that be so poor that they have neither net nor hook will rather poison dough than pine with [120 hunger; and she that is so oppressed with love that she is neither able with beauty nor wit to obtain her friend, will rather use unlawful means than try untolerable pains. I will do it. *Exit.*

FLOSC. Then about it! Poor Endymion, what traps are laid for thee because thou honorest one that all the world wond'reth at! And what plots are cast to make thee unfortunate that studiest of all men [130 to be the faithfulest! *Exit.*

SCENA TERTIA.

[*The same.*]

Dares, Samias, Sir Tophas, Epiton. [2]

DAR. Now our masters are in love up to the ears, what have we to do but to be in knavery up to the crowns?

SAM. O, that we had Sir Tophas, that brave squire, in the midst of our mirth—*et ecce autem,* [3] "Will you see the devil?"—

Enter Sir Tophas [and Epiton].

TOP. Epi!

EPI. Here, sir!

TOP. I brook not this idle humor of [10 love; it tickleth not my liver, from whence the lovemongers in former ages seemed to infer they should proceed.

EPI. Love, sir, may lie in your lungs— and I think it doth, and that is the cause you blow and are so pursy.

TOP. Tush, boy, I think it but some device of the poet to get money.

EPI. A poet? What's that?

TOP. Dost thou not know what a [20 poet is?

EPI. No.

TOP. Why, fool, a poet is as much as one should say—a poet.—But soft, yonder be two wrens; shall I shoot at them?

EPI. They are two lads!

TOP. Larks or wrens, I will kill them.

EPI. Larks! Are you blind? They are two little boys.

TOP. Birds or boys, they are both [30 but a pittance for my breakfast; therefore have at them, for their brains must as it were embroider my bolts. [4]

SAM. Stay your courage, valiant knight, for your widsom is so weary that it stayeth itself.

DAR. Why, Sir Tophas, have you forgotten your old friends?

TOP. Friends? *Nego argumentum.* [5]

SAM. And why not friends? 40

TOP. Because *amicitia* (as in old annuals [6] we find) is *inter pares.* [7] Now, my pretty companions, you shall see how unequal you be to me. But I will not cut you quite off—you shall be my half-friends for reaching to my middle; so far as from the ground to the waist I will be your friend.

DAR. Learnedly! But what shall become of the rest of your body, from the waist to the crown? 50

TOP. My children, *quod supra vos, nihil ad vos.* [8] You must think the rest immortal, because you cannot reach it.

EPI. Nay, I tell ye my master is more than a man.

DAR. And thou less than a mouse.

TOP. But what be you two?

SAM. I am Samias, page to Eumenides. [9]

DAR. And I Dares, page to Endymion.

TOP. Of what occupation are your [60 masters?

[1] Caught with poisoned bait (here, dough balls).
[2] Last two enter later.
[3] And behold indeed!

[4] Flat-headed arrows.
[5] I deny the proof.
[6] Annals (?).
[7] Friendship is among equals.
[8] What is above you is nothing to you.
[9] Bond correctly transposes the names of the masters, in this and the following line.

DAR. Occupation, you clown! Why, they are honorable, and warriors.

TOP. Then are they my prentices.

DAR. Thine? And why so?

TOP. I was the first that ever devised war, and therefore by Mars himself given me for my arms a whole armory; and thus I go, as you see, clothed with artillery. It is not silks—milksops!—nor [70 tissues, nor the fine wool of Seres,[1] but iron, steel, swords, flame, shot, terror, clamor, blood, and ruin, that rocks asleep my thoughts, which never had any other cradle but cruelty. Let me see, do you not bleed?

DAR. Why so?

TOP. Commonly my words wound.

SAM. What then do your blows?

TOP. Not only wound,[2] but also con- [80 found.

SAM. How dar'st thou come so near thy master, Epi? Sir Tophas, spare us!

TOP. You shall live: you, Samias, because you are little; you, Dares, because you are no bigger; and both of you, because you are but two, for commonly I kill by the dozen, and have for every particular adversary a peculiar weapon.

SAM. May we know the use, for our [90 better skill in war?

TOP. You shall. Here is a burbolt [3] for the ugly beast the blackbird.

DAR. A cruel sight!

TOP. Here is the musket for the untamed or, as the vulgar sort term it, the wild mallard.

SAM. O desperate attempt!

EPI. Nay, my master will match them.

DAR. Ay, if he catch them.   100

TOP. Here is a spear and shield, and both necessary, the one to conquer, the other to subdue or overcome the terrible trout, which, although he be under the water, yet tying a string to the top of my spear and an engine of iron to the end of my line, I overthrow him, and then herein I put him.

SAM. O wonderful war!—[Aside.] Dares, didst thou ever hear such a dolt?   110

DAR. [Aside.] All the better; we shall have good sport hereafter, if we can get leisure.

SAM. [Aside.] Leisure! I will rather lose my master's service than his company! Look how he struts!—But what is this? Call you it your sword?

TOP. No, it is my scimitar, which I, by construction often studying to be compendious, call my smiter.   120

DAR. What, are you also learned, sir?

TOP. Learned? I am all Mars and Ars.[4]

SAM. Nay, you are all mass and ass.

TOP. Mock you me? You shall both suffer, yet with such weapons as you shall make choice of the weapon wherewith you shall perish. Am I all a mass or lump? Is there no proportion in me? Am I all ass? Is there no wit in me? Epi, prepare them to the slaughter.   130

SAM. I pray, sir, hear us speak! We call you mass, which your learning doth well understand is all man, for mas, maris is a man. Then as, as you know, is a weight, and we for your virtues account you a weight.

TOP. The Latin hath saved your lives, the which a world of silver could not have ransomed. I understand you, and pardon you.   140

DAR. Well, Sir Tophas, we bid you farewell, and at our next meeting we will be ready to do you service.

TOP. Samias, I thank you; Dares, I thank you; but especially I thank you both.

SAM. [Aside.] Wisely! Come, next time we'll have some pretty gentlewomen with us to walk, for without doubt with them he will be very dainty.   150

DAR. Come, let us see what our masters do; it is high time.

Exeunt [Samias and Dares].

TOP. Now will I march into the field, where, if I cannot encounter with my foul enemies, I will withdraw myself to the river, and there fortify for fish, for there resteth no minute free from fight.

Exit [Sir Tophas with Epiton].

SCENA QUARTA.

[Another part of the same.]

Tellus, Floscula, Dipsas.

TELLUS. Behold, Floscula, we have met with the woman by chance that we

---

[1] Chinese silk. Original reads *Ceres;* changed by Bond.   [2] Early edns. read *confound.*   [3] Birdbolt.   [4] War and art.

sought for by travel.[1] I will break my
mind to her without ceremony or circumstance, lest we lose that time in advice
that should be spent in execution.

FLOSC. Use your discretion; I will in
this case neither give counsel nor consent,
for there cannot be a thing more monstrous
than to force affection by sorcery, [10
neither do I imagine anything more impossible.

TELLUS. Tush, Floscula, in obtaining
of love, what impossibilities will I not try?
And for the winning of Endymion, what
impieties will I not practice?—Dipsas,
whom as many honor for age as wonder
at for cunning, listen in few words to my
tale, and answer in one word to the purpose,
for that neither my burning desire [20
can afford long speech, nor the short time
I have to stay many delays. Is it possible
by herbs, stones, spells, incantation, enchantment, exorcisms, fire, metals, planets,
or any practice, to plant affection where
it is not, and to supplant it where it is?

DIPSAS. Fair lady, you may imagine
that these hoary hairs are not void of
experience, nor the great name that goeth
of my cunning to be without cause. I [30
can darken the sun by my skill and remove the moon out of her course; I can
restore youth to the aged and make hills
without bottoms; there is nothing that I
cannot do but that only which you would
have me do; and therein I differ from the
gods, that I am not able to rule hearts,
for, were it in my power to place affection
by appointment, I would make such evil
appetites, such inordinate lusts, such [40
cursed desires, as all the world should be
filled both with superstitious heats and extreme love.

TELLUS. Unhappy Tellus, whose desires are so desperate that they are neither
to be conceived of any creature, nor to be
cured by any art!

DIPSAS. This I can: breed slackness
in love, though never root it out. What is
he whom you love, and what she that [50
he honoreth?

TELLUS. Endymion, sweet Endymion,
is he that hath my heart; and Cynthia,
too-too fair Cynthia, the miracle of nature, of time, of fortune, is the lady that

1 Travail (?).

he delights in, and dotes on every day,
and dies for ten thousand times a day.

DIPSAS. Would you have his love either
by absence or sickness aslaked?[2] Would
you that Cynthia should mistrust him, [60
or be jealous of him without color?[3]

TELLUS. It is the only thing I crave
that, seeing my love to Endymion, unspotted, cannot be accepted, his truth to
Cynthia, though it be unspeakable, may
be suspected.

DIPSAS. I will undertake it, and overtake[4] him, that all his love shall be doubted
of, and therefore become desperate. But
this will wear out with time, that [70
treadeth all things down but truth.

TELLUS. Let us go.

DIPSAS. I follow.   Exeunt.

ACTUS SECUNDUS. SCENA PRIMA

[A grove near the cell of Endymion.]

Endymion, Tellus.[5]

END. O fair Cynthia! O unfortunate
Endymion! Why was not thy birth as
high as thy thoughts, or her beauty less
than heavenly; or why are not thine honors
as rare as her beauty, or thy fortunes as
great as thy deserts? Sweet Cynthia, how
wouldst thou be pleased, how possessed?
Will labors, patient of all extremities, obtain thy love? There is no mountain so
steep that I will not climb, no monster [10
so cruel that I will not tame, no action
so desperate that I will not attempt.
Desirest thou the passions of love, the
sad and melancholy moods of perplexed
minds, the not-to-be-expressed torments
of racked thoughts? Behold my sad tears,
my deep sighs, my hollow eyes, my broken
sleeps, my heavy countenance! Wouldst
thou have me vowed only to thy beauty
and consume every minute of time in [20
thy service? Remember my solitary life
almost these seven years. Whom have I
entertained but mine own thoughts and
thy virtues? What company have I used
but contemplation? Whom have I wondered at but thee? Nay, whom have I
not contemned for thee? Have I not crept
to those on whom I might have trodden,

2 Slaked, abated.   4 Overcome.
3 Reason, excuse.   5 Enters later.

only because thou didst shine upon them? Have not injuries been sweet to me if [30 thou vouchsafest I should bear them? Have I not spent my golden years in hopes, waxing old with wishing, yet wishing nothing but thy love? With Tellus, fair Tellus, have I dissembled, using her but as a cloak for mine affections, that others, seeing my mangled and disordered mind, might think it were for one that loveth me, not for Cynthia, whose perfection alloweth no companion nor comparison. [40 In the midst of these distempered thoughts of mine thou art not only jealous of my truth, but careless, suspicious, and secure,[1] which strange humor maketh my mind as desperate as thy conceits [2] are doubtful. I am none of those wolves that bark most when thou shinest brightest, but that fish (thy fish, Cynthia, in the flood Araris) [3] which at thy waxing is as white as the driven snow, and at thy [50 waning as black as deepest darkness. I am that Endymion, sweet Cynthia, that have carried my thoughts in equal balance with my actions, being always as free from imagining ill as enterprising; that Endymion whose eyes never esteemed anything fair but thy face, whose tongue termed nothing rare but thy virtues, and whose heart imagined nothing miraculous but thy government; yea, that Endymion, [60 who, divorcing himself from the amiableness of all ladies, the bravery [4] of all courts, the company of all men, hath chosen in a solitary cell to live, only by feeding on thy favor, accounting in the world—but thyself—nothing excellent, nothing immortal. Thus mayst thou see every vein, sinew, muscle, and artery of my love, in which there is no flattery, nor deceit, error, nor art. But soft, here cometh Tellus. [70 I must turn my other face to her, like Janus, lest she be as suspicious as Juno.

Enter Tellus [,Floscula, and Dipsas].

TELLUS. Yonder I espy Endymion. I will seem to suspect nothing, but soothe him, that, seeing I cannct obtain the depth of his love, I may learn the height of his

[1] Overconfident.
[2] Fancies, imaginings, ideas.
[3] Emended by Baker. Original reads *Aranis.*
[4] Splendor.

dissembling. Floscula and Dipsas, withdraw yourselves out of our sight, yet be within the hearing of our saluting.—   79
[Exeunt Floscula and Dipsas.]
How now, Endymion, always solitary? No company but your own thoughts, no friend but melancholy fancies?

END. You know, fair Tellus, that the sweet remembrance of your love is the only companion of my life, and thy presence, my paradise, so that I am not alone when nobody is with me, and in heaven itself when thou art with me.

TELLUS. Then you love me, Endymion?

END. Or else I live not, Tellus.   90

TELLUS. Is it not possible for you, Endymion, to dissemble?

END. Not, Tellus, unless I could make me a woman.

TELLUS. Why, is dissembling joined to their sex inseparable, as heat to fire, heaviness to earth, moisture to water, thinness to air?

END. No, but found in their sex as common as spots upon doves, moles [100 upon faces, caterpillars upon sweet apples, cobwebs upon fair windows.

TELLUS. Do they all dissemble?

END. All but one.

TELLUS. Who is that?

END. I dare not tell; for, if I should say you, then would you imagine my flattery to be extreme; if another, then would you think my love to be but indifferent.   110

TELLUS. You will be sure I shall take no vantage of your words. But, in sooth, Endymion, without more ceremonies, is it not Cynthia?

END. You know, Tellus, that of the gods we are forbidden to dispute, because their deities come not within the compass of our reasons; and of Cynthia we are allowed not to talk but to wonder, because her virtues are not within the reach [120 of our capacities.

TELLUS. Why, she is but a woman.

END. No more was Venus.

TELLUS. She is but a virgin.

END. No more was Vesta.

TELLUS. She shall have an end.

END. So shall the world.

TELLUS. Is not her beauty subject to time?

END. No more than time is to [130 standing still.

TELLUS. Wilt thou make her immortal?

END. No, but incomparable.

TELLUS. Take heed, Endymion, lest like the wrastler in Olympia, that, striving to lift an impossible weight, catched an incurable strain, thou, by fixing thy thoughts above thy reach, fall into a disease without all recure.[1] But I see thou art now in love with Cynthia.   140

END. No, Tellus; thou knowest that the stately cedar, whose top reacheth unto the clouds, never boweth his head to the shrubs that grow in the valley; nor ivy, that climbeth up by the elm, can ever get hold of the beams of the sun. Cynthia I honor in all humility, whom none ought or dare adventure to love, whose affections are immortal, and virtues infinite. Suffer me, therefore, to gaze on the moon, [150 at whom, were it not for thyself, I would die with wondering.   *Exeunt.*

SCENA SECUNDA.

[The gardens of Cynthia's palace.]

Dares, Samias, Scintilla, Favilla.

DAR. Come, Samias, diddest thou ever hear such a sighing, the one for Cynthia, the other for Semele, and both for moonshine in the water?

SAM. Let them sigh, and let us sing. How say you, gentlewomen, are not our masters too far in love?

SCINT. Their tongues, happily,[2] are dipped to the root in amorous words and sweet discourses, but I think their [10 hearts are scarce tipped on the side with constant desires.

DAR. How say you, Favilla, is not love a lurcher,[3] that taketh men's stomachs away that they cannot eat, their spleen that they cannot laugh, their hearts that they cannot fight, their eyes that they cannot sleep, and leaveth nothing but livers to make nothing but lovers?

FAVIL. Away, peevish boy! A rod [20 were better under thy girdle than love in thy mouth. It will be a forward cock that croweth in the shell.

DAR. Alas, good old gentlewoman, how it becometh you to be grave!

SCINT. Favilla, though she be but a spark,[4] yet is she fire.

FAVIL. And you, Scintilla, be not much more than a spark, though you would be esteemed a flame.   30

SAM. *[Aside to Dares.]* It were good sport to see the fight between two sparks.

DAR. *[Aside to Samias.]* Let them to it, and we will warm us by their words.

SCINT. You are not angry, Favilla?

FAVIL. That is, Scintilla, as you list to take it.

SAM. That, that!

SCINT. This it is to be matched with girls who, coming but yesterday from [40 making of babies,[5] would before tomorrow be accounted matrons.

FAVIL. I cry your matronship mercy. Because your pantables[6] be higher with cork, therefore your feet must needs be higher in the insteps. You will be mine elder because you stand upon a stool and I on the floor.

SAM. Good, good!

DAR. *[To Samias.]* Let them alone, [50 and see with what countenance they will become friends.

SCINT. Nay, you think to be the wiser, because you mean to have the last word.

SAM. *[To Dares.]* Step between them lest they scratch.—In faith, gentlewomen, seeing we came out to be merry, let not your jarring mar our jests; be friends. How say you?

SCINT. I am not angry, but it spited [60 me to see how short she was.

FAVIL. I meant nothing till she would needs cross me.

DAR. Then, so let it rest.

SCINT. I am agreed.

FAVIL. And I. *[Weeping.]* Yet I never took anything so unkindly in my life.

SCINT. *[Weeping.]* 'Tis I have the cause, that never offered the occasion.

DAR. Excellent, and right like a [70 woman!

SAM. A strange sight to see water come out of fire!

---

[1] Recovery.   [3] Lurker, thief.
[2] Haply, perhaps.

[4] Punning on *spark*, a person of gay disposition.
[5] Doils.   [6] Pantofles, slippers.

Dar. It is their property to carry in their eyes fire and water, tears and torches, and in their mouths honey and gall.

Scint. You will be a good one if you live. But what is yonder formal fellow?

Enter Sir Tophas [, followed by Epiton].

Dar. Sir Tophas, Sir Tophas, of whom we told you. If you be good wenches, [80 make as though you love him, and wonder at him.

Favil. We will do our parts.

Dar. But first let us stand aside, and let him use his garb,[1] for all consisteth in his gracing.[2]   [*The four retire.*]

Top. Epi!

Epi. At hand, sir.

Top. How likest thou this martial life, where nothing but blood besprinkleth [90 our bosoms? Let me see, be our enemies [3] fat?

Epi. Passing fat; and I would not change this life to be a lord; and yourself passeth all comparison, for other captains kill and beat, and there is nothing you kill but you also eat.

Top. I will draw out their guts out of their bellies, and tear the flesh with my teeth, so mortal is my hate, and so [100 eager my unstaunched stomach.

Epi. [*Aside.*] My master thinks himself the valiantest man in the world if he kill a wren; so warlike a thing he accompteth to take away life, though it be from a lark.

Top. Epi, I find my thoughts to swell and my spirit to take wings, insomuch that I cannot continue within the compass of so slender combats.   110

Favil. ⎫   This passeth!
Scint. ⎬ [*Aside.*] Why, is he not mad?
Sam. ⎭   No, but a little vain-
glorious.

Top. Epi!

Epi. Sir?

Top. I will encounter that black and cruel enemy that beareth rough and untewed [4] locks upon his body, whose sire throweth down the strongest walls, [120

---

[1] Show his demeanor.
[2] All depends on honoring him.
[3] *I.e.*, the fish Epiton carries.
[4] Uncombed.

whose legs are as many as both ours, on whose head are placed most horrible horns by nature as a defense from all harms.

Epi. What mean you, master, to be so desperate?

Top. Honor inciteth me, and very hunger compelleth me.

Epi. What is that monster?

Top. The monster *Ovis.* I have said; let thy wits work.   130

Epi. I cannot imagine it. Yet let me see: a black enemy with rough locks—it may be a sheep, and *Ovis* is a sheep; his sire so strong—a ram is a sheep's sire, that being also an engine of war; horns he hath, and four legs—so hath a sheep. Without doubt, this monster is a black sheep. Is it not a sheep that you mean?

Top. Thou hast hit it. That monster will I kill and sup with.   140

Sam. [*Aside.*] Come, let us take him off.—[*Samias, Dares, Favilla, and Scintilla advance.*] Sir Tophas, all hail!

Top. Welcome, children. I seldom cast mine eyes so low as to the crowns of your heads, and therefore pardon me that I spake not all this while.

Dar. No harm done. Here be fair ladies come to wonder at your person, your valor, your wit, the report where- [150 of hath made them careless of their own honors, to glut their eyes and hearts upon yours.

Top. Report cannot but injure me, for that, not knowing fully what I am, I fear she hath been a niggard in her praises.

Scint. No, gentle knight, Report hath been prodigal; for she hath left you no equal, nor herself credit, so much hath she told—yet no more than we now see. [160

Dar. [*Aside.*] A good wench!

Favil. If there remain as much pity toward women as there is in you courage against your enemies, then shall we be happy, who, hearing of your person, came to see it, and, seeing it, are now in love with it.

Top. Love me, ladies? I easily believe it, but my tough heart receiveth no impression with sweet words. Mars may [170 pierce it; Venus shall not paint on it.

Favil. A cruel saying.

Sam. [*Aside.*] There's a girl!

DAR. Will you cast these ladies away, and all for a little love? Do but speak kindly!

TOP. There cometh no soft syllable within my lips; custom hath made my words bloody and my heart barbarous. That pelting [1] word love, how wat'rish [180 it is in my mouth; it carrieth no sound. Hate, horror, death are speeches that nourish my spirits. I like honey, but I care not for the bees; I delight in music, but I love not to play on the bagpipes; I can vouchsafe to hear the voice of women, but to touch their bodies, I disdain it as a thing childish and fit for such men as can digest nothing but milk.

SCINT. A hard heart! Shall we die [190 for your love and find no remedy?

TOP. I have already taken a surfeit.

EPI. Good master, pity them.

TOP. Pity them, Epi? No, I do not think that this breast shall be pestered with such a foolish passion.—What is that the gentlewoman carrieth in [2] a chain?

EPI. Why, it is a squirrel.

TOP. A squirrel? O gods, what things are made for money! 200

DAR. [Aside.] Is not this gentleman overwise?

FAVIL. [Aside.] I could stay all day with him, if I feared not to be shent.[3]

SCINT. [Aside.] Is it not possible to meet again?

DAR. [Aside.] Yes, at any time.

FAVIL. [Aside.] Then let us hasten home. 209

SCINT. Sir Tophas, the god of war deal better with you than you do with the god of love.

FAVIL. Our love we may dissemble—digest [4] we cannot; but I doubt not but time will hamper you and help us.

TOP. I defy time, who hath no interest in my heart. Come, Epi, let me to the battle with that hideous beast. Love is pap, and hath no relish in my taste because it is not terrible.— 220

DAR. Indeed, a black sheep is a perilous beast. But let us in till another time.

FAVIL. I shall long for that time.

Exeunt.

[1] Paltry, contemptible.
[2] On.
[3] Scolded. [4] Digest, stomach, put up with.

SCENA TERTIA.

[*A grove near the cell of Endymion.*]

Endymion, Dipsas, Bagoa.[5]

END. No rest, Endymion? Still uncertain how to settle thy steps by day or thy thoughts by night? Thy truth is measured by thy fortune, and thou art judged unfaithful because thou art unhappy. I will see if I can beguile myself with sleep, and, if no slumber will take hold in my eyes, yet will I embrace the golden thoughts in my head, and wish to melt by musing; that, as ebony, which no fire [10 can scorch, is yet consumed with sweet savors, so my heart, which cannot be bent by the hardness of fortune, may be bruised by amorous desires. On yonder bank never grew anything but lunary,[6] and hereafter I will never have any bed but that bank. O Endymion, Tellus was fair, but what availeth beauty without wisdom? Nay, Endymion, she was wise, but what availeth wisdom without honor? She [20 was honorable, Endymion; belie her not. Ay, but how obscure is honor without fortune! Was she not fortunate whom so many followed? Yes, yes, but base is fortune without majesty. Thy majesty, Cynthia, all the world knoweth and wondereth at, but not one in the world that can imitate it or comprehend it. No more. Endymion! Sleep or die! Nay, die, for to sleep, it is impossible.—And yet I [30 know not how it cometh to pass, I feel such a heaviness both in mine eyes and heart that I am suddenly benumbed, yea, in every joint. It may be weariness, for when did I rest? It may be deep melancholy, for when did I not sigh? Cynthia! Ay, so—I say, Cynthia! *He falls asleep.*

[*Enter Dipsas and Bagoa.*]

DIPSAS. Little dost thou know, Endymion, when thou shalt wake, for, hadst thou placed thy heart as low in love as [40 thy head lieth now in sleep, thou mightest have commanded Tellus, whom now, instead of a mistress, thou shalt find a tomb. These eyes must I seal up by art, not nature, which are to be opened neither by art nor nature. Thou that lay'st down with

[5] Last two enter later. [6] Moonwort.

golden locks shalt not awake until they be turned to silver hairs; and that chin on which scarcely appeareth soft down shall be filled with bristles as hard as [50 broom. Thou shalt sleep out thy youth and flowering time, and become dry hay before thou knewest thyself green grass; and ready by age to step into the grave when thou wakest, that was youthful in the court when thou laid'st thee down to sleep. The malice of Tellus hath brought this to pass, which, if she could not have entreated of me by fair means, she would have commanded by menacing, for [60 from her gather we all our simples to maintain our sorceries.—Fan with this hemlock over his face, and sing the enchantment for sleep, whilst I go in and finish those ceremonies that are required in our art. Take heed ye touch not his face, for the fan is so seasoned that whoso it toucheth with a leaf shall presently die, and over whom the wind of it breatheth, he shall sleep forever. *Exit.* [70

BAGOA. Let me alone; I will be careful. What hap hadst thou, Endymion, to come under the hands of Dipsas! O fair Endymion, how it grieveth me that that fair face must be turned to a withered skin and taste the pains of death before it feel the reward of love! I fear Tellus will repent that which the heavens themselves seemed to rue. But I hear Dipsas coming! I dare not repine, lest she make me [80 pine, and rock me into such a deep sleep that I shall not awake to my marriage.

Enter Dipsas.

DIPSAS. How now, have you finished?
BAGOA. Yea.
DIPSAS. Well then, let us in. And see that you do not so much as whisper that I did this, for, if you do, I will turn thy hairs to adders and all thy teeth in thy head to tongues. Come away, come away! *Exeunt.* [90

A DUMB SHOW[1]

Music sounds. Three Ladies enter: one with a knife and a looking-glass, who, by

[1] This scene, representing the dream of Endymion, first appeared in Blount's edition of 1632. *Cf.* Endymion's account of the incident, V, i, 109 ff.

the procurement [2] of one of the other two, offers to stab Endymion as he sleeps; but the third wrings her hands, lamenteth, offering still to prevent it, but dares not.

At last, the first Lady, looking in the glass, casts down the knife. *Exeunt.*

Enters an Ancient Man with books with three leaves; offers the same twice. Endymion refuseth. He rendeth two, and offers the third, where he stands awhile; and then Endymion offers to take it.

Exit [the Old Man].

ACTUS TERTIUS. SCENA PRIMA.

[*The gardens of Cynthia's palace.*]

Cynthia, Three Lords [Eumenides, Zontes, and Panelion], Tellus [,Semele, Corsites].

CYNTH. Is the report true that Endymion is stricken into such a dead sleep that nothing can either wake him or move him?

EUM. Too true, madam, and as much to be pitied as wondered at.

TELLUS. As good sleep and do no harm as wake and do no good.

CYNTH. What maketh you, Tellus, to be so short? The time was, Endymion [10 only was.

EUM. It is an old saying, madam, that a waking dog doth afar off bark at a sleeping lion.

SEM. It were good, Eumenides, that you took a nap with your friend, for your speech beginneth to be heavy.

EUM. Contrary to your nature, Semele, which hath been always accounted light.

CYNTH. What, have we here before [20 my face these unseemly and malapert overthwarts![3] I will tame your tongues and your thoughts, and make your speeches answerable to your duties, and your conceits fit for my dignity, else will I banish you both my person and the world.

EUM. Pardon I humbly ask; but such is my unspotted faith to Endymion that whatsoever seemeth a needle to prick his finger is a dagger to wound my heart. [30

CYNTH. If you be so dear to him, how happeneth it you neither go to see him, nor search for remedy for him?

[2] Instigation, urging.
[3] Impertinent wranglings.

EUM. I have seen him to my grief, and sought recure with despair, for that I cannot imagine who should restore him that is the wonder to all men. Your highness, on whose hands the compass of the earth is at command, though not in possession, may show yourself both worthy [40 your sex, your nature, and your favor, if you redeem that honorable Endymion, whose ripe years foretell rare virtues, and whose unmellowed conceits promise ripe counsel.

CYNTH. I have had trial of Endymion, and conceive greater assurance of his age than I could hope of his youth.

TELLUS. But timely,[1] madam, crooks that tree that will be a cammock,[2] and [50 young it pricks that will be a thorn; and therefore he that began without care to settle his life, it is a sign without amendment he will end it.

CYNTH. Presumptuous girl, I will make thy tongue an example of unrecoverable displeasure. Corsites, carry her to the castle in the desert, there to remain and weave.   59

CORS. Shall she work stories or poetries?

CYNTH. It skilleth [3] not which. Go to! In both, for she shall find examples infinite in either what punishment long tongues have. Eumenides, if either the soothsayers in Egypt, or the enchanters in Thessaly, or the philosophers in Greece, or all the sages of the world can find remedy, I will procure it. Therefore, despatch with all speed: you, Eumenides, into [70 Thessaly; you, Zontes, into Greece, because you are acquainted in Athens; you, Panelion, to Egypt; saying that Cynthia sendeth, and, if you will, commandeth.

EUM. On bowed knee I give thanks, and with wings on my legs I fly for remedy.

ZON. We are ready at your highness' command, and hope to return to your full content.

CYNTH. It shall never be said that [80 Cynthia, whose mercy and goodness filleth the heavens with joys and the world with marvels, will suffer either Endymion or any to perish, if he may be protected.

[1] Early.
[2] Tree artificially bent.
[3] Matters.

EUM. Your majesty's words have been always deeds, and your deeds virtues.

Exeunt.

SCENA SECUNDA.

[Before the castle of Corsites in a desert.]

Corsites, Tellus.

CORS. Here is the castle, fair Tellus, in which you must weave, till either time end your days, or Cynthia her displeasure. I am sorry so fair a face should be subject to so hard a fortune, and that the flower of beauty, which is honored in courts, should here wither in prison.

TELLUS. Corsites, Cynthia may restrain the liberty of my body; of my thoughts she cannot, and therefore do I [10 esteem myself most free, though I am in greatest bondage.

CORS. Can you then feed on fancy, and subdue the malice of envy by the sweetness of imagination?

TELLUS. Corsites, there is no sweeter music to the miserable than despair; and therefore the more bitterness I feel, the more sweetness I find; for so vain were liberty, and so unwelcome the following [20 of higher fortune, that I choose rather to pine in this castle than to be a prince in any other court.

CORS. A humor contrary to your years and nothing agreeable to your sex—the one commonly allured with delights, the other always with sovereignty.

TELLUS. I marvel, Corsites, that you, being a captain, who should sound nothing but terror and suck nothing but blood, [30 can find in your heart to talk such smooth words, for that it agreeth not with your calling to use words so soft as that of love.

CORS. Lady, it were unfit of wars to discourse with women, into whose minds nothing can sink but smoothness; besides, you must not think that soldiers be so rough-hewn, or of such knotty mettle, that beauty cannot allure, and you, [40 being beyond perfection, enchant.

TELLUS. Good Corsites, talk not of love, but let me to my labor. The little beauty I have shall be bestowed on my loom, which I now mean to make my lover.

Cors. Let us in, and what favor Corsites can show, Tellus shall command.

Tellus. The only favor I desire is now
and then to walk.   *Exeunt.*

Scena Tertia.

[*The gardens of Cynthia's palace.*]

Sir Tophas and Epi[*ton*].

Top. Epi!

Epi. Here, sir.

Top. Unrig me. Heigh-ho!

Epi. What's that?

Top. An interjection, whereof some are
of mourning: as *eho, vah.*[1]

Epi. I understand you not.

Top. Thou seest me.

Epi. Ay.

Top. Thou hear'st me.   10

Epi. Ay.

Top. Thou feelest me.

Epi. Ay.

Top. And not understand'st me?

Epi. No.

Top. Then am I but three-quarters of
a noun substantive. But alas, Epi, to tell
thee the troth, I am a noun adjective.

Epi. Why?

Top. Because I cannot stand with-   [20
out another.

Epi. Who is that?

Top. Dipsas.

Epi. Are you in love?

Top. No; but love hath, as it were,
milked my thoughts and drained from my
heart the very substance of my accustomed
courage. It worketh in my head like new
wine, so as I must hoop my sconce with
iron, lest my head break, and so I be-   [30
wray[2] my brains. But, I pray thee, first
discover me in all parts, that I may be
like a lover, and then will I sigh and die.
Take my gun and give me a gown: "*Ce-
dant arma togæ.*"[3]

Epi. Here.

Top. Take my sword and shield and
give me beard-brush and scissors: "*Bella
gerant alii; tu, Pari, semper ama.*"[4]

Epi. Will you be trimmed, sir?   40

Top. Not yet; for I feel a contention
within me whether I shall frame the bodkin beard or the bush.[5] But take my pike
and give me pen: "*Dicere quæ puduit,
scribere jussit amor.*"[6]

Epi. I will furnish you, sir.

Top. Now, for my bow and bolts give
me ink and paper, for my smiter a penknife; for

*Scalpellum, calami, atramentum, charta, li-
      belli,*   50
Sint semper studiis arma parata meis.[7]

Epi. Sir, will you give over wars and play
with that bable[8] called love?

Top. Give over wars? No, Epi, "*Mili-
tat omnis amans, et habet sua castra Cupido.*"[9]

Epi. Love hath made you very eloquent, but your face is nothing fair.

Top. "*Non formosus erat, sed erat facun-
dus Ulysses.*"[10]

Epi. Nay, I must seek a new master   [60
if you can speak nothing but verses.

Top. "*Quicquid conabar dicere, versus
erat.*"[11] Epi, I feel all *Ovid de Arte Amandi*
lie as heavy at my heart as a load of logs.
O, what a fine, thin hair hath Dipsas!
What a pretty, low forehead! What a tall
and stately nose! What little, hollow eyes!
What great and goodly lips! How harmless she is, being toothless! Her fingers
fat and short, adorned with long nails   [70
like a bitter![12] In how sweet a proportion

---

[1] The discussion of grammatical terms in this
and the following lines is modeled upon passages
in William Lilly's famous Latin grammar.

[2] Uncover.

[3] From Cicero, *De officiis*, i, 22, 76: "Let
arms give place to the toga."

[4] Combination of verses from Ovid, *Heroides*,
xiii, 84; xvii, 254: "Let others wage wars; thou,
O Paris, must always love."

[5] Shape the beard like a dagger or leave it
untrimmed.

[6] Ovid, *Heroides*, iv, 10: "Those things which
one has hesitated to say, Love has bidden to
write."

[7] Lines apparently invented by Lyly: A penknife, quills, ink, paper, booklets—let these
weapons [*i.e.*, implements] be always in readiness
for my studies.

[8] Bauble.

[9] Ovid, *Amores*, i, 9, 1: "Every lover goes to
war, and Cupid holds his camp."

[10] Ovid, *Ars amatoria*, ii, 123: "Ulysses was
not handsome, but he was eloquent."

[11] Ovid, *Tristia*, iv, 10, 26: "Whatever I was
trying to express was poetry."

[12] Bittern.

her cheeks hang down to her breasts like dugs and her paps to her waist like bags! What a low stature she is, and yet what a great foot she carrieth! How thrifty must she be in whom there is no waist! How virtuous is she like to be over whom no man can be jealous!

EPI. Stay, master, you forget yourself.

TOP. O Epi, even as a dish melteth [80 by the fire, so doth my wit increase by love.

EPI. Pithily, and to the purpose! But what, begin you to nod?

TOP. Good Epi, let me take a nap; for, as some man may better steal a horse than another look over the hedge, so divers shall be sleepy when they would fainest take rest.   *He sleeps.* [89

EPI. Who ever saw such a woodcock![1] Love Dipsas! Without doubt all the world will now account him valiant, that ventureth on her whom none durst undertake. But here cometh two wags.

Enter Dares and Samias.

SAM. Thy master hath slept his share.

DAR. I think he doth it because he would not pay me my board wages.

SAM. It is a thing most strange, and I think mine will never return, so that we must both seek new masters, for we [100 shall never live by our manners.

EPI. If you want masters, join with me and serve Sir Tophas, who must needs keep more men because he is toward marriage.

SAM. What, Epi, where's thy master?

EPI. Yonder, sleeping in love.

DAR. Is it possible?

EPI. He hath taken his thoughts a hole lower, and saith, seeing it is the fashion of the world, he will vail[2] bonnet to beauty.

SAM. How is he attired?   111

EPI. Lovely.

DAR. Whom loveth this amorous knight?

EPI. Dipsas.

SAM. That ugly creature? Why, she is a fool, a scold, fat, without fashion, and quite without favor.

EPI. Tush, you be simple; my master hath a good marriage.

DAR. Good? As how?   120

EPI. Why, in marrying Dipsas he shall have every day twelve dishes of meat to his dinner, though there be none but Dipsas with him: four of flesh, four of fish, four of fruit.

SAM. As how, Epi?

EPI. For flesh these: woodcock, goose, bitter, and rail.

DAR. Indeed, he shall not miss if Dipsas be there.   130

EPI. For fish these: crab, carp, lump, and pouting.

SAM. Excellent, for of my word she is both crabbish, lumpish, and carping.

EPI. For fruit these: fretters,[3] medlars, hartichokes,[4] and lady-longings. Thus you see he shall fare like a king, though he be but a beggar.

DAR. Well, Epi, dine thou with him, for I had rather fast than see her face.   [140 But, see, thy ma[ster] is asleep; let us have a song to wake this amorous knight.

EPI. Agreed.

SAM. Content.

THE FIRST SONG[5]

EPI. Here snores Tophas,
That amorous ass,
Who loves Dipsas,
With face so sweet,
Nose and chin meet.

ALL THREE. {
At sight of her each Fury
skips   150
And flings into her lap
their whips.
}

DAR. Holla, holla in his ear.

SAM. The witch, sure, thrust her fingers there.

EPI. Cramp him, or wring the fool by th' nose;

DAR. Or clap some burning flax to his toes.

SAM. What music's best to wake him?

EPI. Baw-wow, let bandogs shake him!

DAR. Let adders hiss in 's ear!

SAM. Else earwigs wriggle there!

EPI. No, let him batten! When his tongue   160
Once goes, a cat is not worse strung.

ALL THREE. {
But if he ope nor mouth nor eyes,
He may in time sleep himself wise.
}

[3] An unidentified fruit.   [4] Artichokes.
[5] All the songs in the play appeared first in Blount's edn.

[1] Fool.   [2] Doff.

Top. [*Waking.*] Sleep is a binding of the senses, love a loosing.

Epi. [*Aside.*] Let us hear him awhile.

Top. There appeared in my sleep a goodly owl, who, sitting upon my shoulder, cried, "Twit, twit," and before mine eyes presented herself the express image of [170 Dipsas. I marveled what the owl said, till at the last I perceived "Twit, twit"— "To it, to it," only by contraction—admonished by this vision to make account of my sweet Venus.

Sam. Sir Tophas, you have overslept yourself.

Top. No, youth, I have but slept over my love.   179

Dar. Love? Why, it is impossible that into so noble and unconquered a courage love should creep, having first a head as hard to pierce as steel, then to pass to a heart armed with a shirt of mail.

Epi. Ay, but my master yawning one day in the sun, Love crept into his mouth before he could close it, and there kept such a tumbling in his body that he was glad to untruss the points [1] of his heart and entertain Love as a stranger.   190

Top. If there remain any pity in you, plead for me to Dipsas.

Dar. Plead? Nay, we will press her to it.—[*Aside to Samias.*] Let us go with him to Dipsas, and there shall we have good sport.—But, Sir Tophas, when shall we go? For I find my tongue voluble, and my heart venturous, and all myself like myself.   199

Sam. [*Aside to Dares.*] Come, Dares, let us not lose him till we find our masters, for, as long as he liveth, we shall lack neither mirth nor meat.

Epi. We will travice.[2] Will you go, sir?

Top. "*I præ; sequar.*"[3]   *Exeunt.*

Scena Quarta.

[*Near a fountain in the desert.*]

Eumenides, Geron.

Eum. Father, your sad music, being tuned on the same key that my hard fortune is, hath so melted my mind that I

[1] Untie the laces.   [2] Traverse, proceed.
[3] Terence, *Andria*, I, i, 144: "Go ahead; I'll follow."

wish to hang at your mouth's end till my life end.

Ger. These tunes, gentleman, have I been accustomed with these fifty winters, having no other house to shroud myself but the broad heavens. And so familiar with me hath use made misery that I [10 esteem sorrow my chiefest solace, and welcomest is that guest to me that can rehearse the saddest tale or the bloodiest tragedy.

Eum. A strange humor. Might I inquire the cause?

Ger. You must pardon me if I deny to tell it, for, knowing that the revealing of griefs is, as it were, a renewing of sorrow, I have vowed therefore to conceal them, [20 that I might not only feel the depth of everlasting discontentment, but despair of remedy. But whence are you? What fortune hath thrust you to this distress?

Eum. I am going to Thessaly, to seek remedy for Endymion, my dearest friend, who hath been cast into a dead sleep almost these twenty years, waxing old and ready for the grave, being almost but newly come forth of the cradle.   30

Ger. You need not for recure travel far, for whoso can clearly see the bottom of this fountain shall have remedy for anything.

Eum. That, methinketh, is unpossible. Why, what virtue can there be in water?

Ger. Yes, whosoever can shed the tears of a faithful lover shall obtain anything he would. Read these words engraven about the brim.   40

Eum. Have you known this by experience, or is it placed here of purpose to delude men?

Ger. I only would have experience of it, and then should there be an end of my misery; and then would I tell the strangest discourse that ever yet was heard.

Eum. Ah, Eumenides!

Ger. What lack you, gentleman? Are you not well?   50

Eum. Yes, father, but a qualm that often cometh over my heart doth now take hold of me. But did never any lovers come hither?

Ger. Lusters, but not lovers; for often have I seen them weep, but never could I hear they saw the bottom.

Eum. Came there women also?

Ger. Some.

Eum. What did they see?　　　　60

Ger. They all wept, that the fountain overflowed with tears, but so thick became the water with their tears that I could scarce discern the brim, much less behold the bottom.

Eum. Be faithful lovers so scant?

Ger. It seemeth so, for yet heard I never of any.

Eum. Ah, Eumenides, how art thou perplexed! Call to mind the beauty of [70 thy sweet mistress and the depth of thy never-dying affections. How oft hast thou honored her, not only without spot, but suspicion of falsehood! And how hardly hath she rewarded thee without cause or color of despite.[1] How secret hast thou been these seven years, that hast not, nor once darest not, to name her, for [2] discontenting her. How faithful, that hast offered to die for her, to please her! Un- [80 happy Eumenides!

Ger. Why, gentleman, did you once love?

Eum. Once? Ay, father, and ever shall.

Ger. Was she unkind and you faithful?

Eum. She of all women the most froward, and I of all creatures the most fond.

Ger. You doted then, not loved, for affection is grounded on virtue, and virtue is never peevish; or on beauty, and [90 beauty loveth to be praised.

Eum. Ay, but, if all virtuous ladies should yield to all that be loving, or all amiable gentlewomen entertain all that be amorous, their virtues would be accounted vices, and their beauties deformities; for that love can be but between two, and that not proceeding of [3] him that is most faithful but most fortunate.

Ger. I would you were so faithful [100 that your tears might make you fortunate.

Eum. Yea, father, if that my tears clear not this fountain, then may you swear it is but a mere mockery.

Ger. So saith every one yet that wept.

Eum. Ah, I faint, I die! Ah, sweet Semele, let me alone, and dissolve,[4] by weeping, into water.

[*Gazes into the fountain.*]

[1] With no occasion or reason for ill will.
[2] For fear of.　[3] Caused by.　[4] Let me dissolve.

Ger. This affection [5] seemeth strange. If he see nothing, without doubt this [110 dissembling passeth,[6] for nothing shall draw me from the belief.

Eum. Father, I plainly see the bottom, and there in white marble engraven these words: *Ask one for all, and but one thing at all.*

Ger. O fortunate Eumenides (for so have I heard thee call thyself), let me see.— I cannot discern any such thing. I think thou dreamest.　　　　120

Eum. Ah, father, thou art not a faithful lover, and therefore canst not behold it.

Ger. Then ask, that I may be satisfied by the event, and thyself blessed.

Eum. Ask? So I will. And what shall I do but ask, and whom should I ask but Semele, the possessing of whose person is a pleasure that cannot come within the compass of comparison; whose golden locks seem most curious [7] when they seem [130 most careless; whose sweet looks seem most alluring when they are most chaste; and whose words the more virtuous they are, the more amorous they be accounted? I pray thee, Fortune, when I shall first meet with fair Semele, dash my delight with some light disgrace, lest, embracing sweetness beyond measure, I take a surfeit without recure. Let her practice her accustomed coyness that I may diet myself upon [140 my desires; otherwise the fulness of my joys will diminish the sweetness, and I shall perish by them before I possess them.

Why do I trifle the time in words? The least minute being spent in the getting of Semele is more worth than the whole world; therefore let me ask. What now, Eumenides! Whither art thou drawn? Hast thou forgotten both friendship and duty, care of Endymion, and the com- [150 mandment of Cynthia? Shall he die in a leaden sleep because thou sleepest in a golden dream? Ay, let him sleep ever, so I slumber but one minute with Semele. Love knoweth neither friendship nor kindred.

Shall I not hazard the loss of a friend for the obtaining of her for whom I would often lose myself? Fond [8] Eumenides, shall the enticing beauty of a most disdainful lady be of more force than the [160

[5] Passion.　　　[7] Artfully arranged.
[6] This hypocrisy is excessive.　　[8] Foolish

rare fidelity of a tried friend? The love of
men to women is a thing common and of
course; the friendship of man to man infinite and immortal.—Tush! Semele doth
possess my love.—Ay, but Endymion hath
deserved it. I will help Endymion. I
found Endymion unspotted in his truth.—
Ay, but I shall find Semele constant in her
love. I will have Semele.—What shall I do?
Father, thy gray hairs are ambas- [170
sadors of experience. Which shall I ask?

GER. Eumenides, release Endymion,
for all things, friendship excepted, are subject to fortune. Love is but an eyeworm,
which only tickleth the head with hopes
and wishes; friendship the image of eternity, in which there is nothing movable,
nothing mischievous. As much difference as
there is between beauty and virtue, bodies
and shadows, colors and life, so great [180
odds is there between love and friendship.

Love is a chameleon, which draweth
nothing into the mouth but air, and nourisheth nothing in the body but lungs.
Believe me, Eumenides, desire dies in the
same moment that beauty sickens, and
beauty fadeth in the same instant that it
flourisheth. When adversities flow, then
love ebbs; but friendship standeth stiffly in
storms. Time draweth wrinkles in [190
a fair face, but addeth fresh colors to a fast
friend, which neither heat, nor cold, nor
misery, nor place, nor destiny can alter
or diminish. O friendship, of all things
the most rare, and therefore most rare
because most excellent, whose comforts in
misery is always sweet, and whose counsels in prosperity are ever fortunate! Vain
love, that, only coming near to friendship in name, would seem to be the [200
same or better in nature!

EUM. Father, I allow your reasons, and
will therefore conquer mine own. Virtue
shall subdue affections, wisdom lust, friendship beauty. Mistresses are in every place,
and as common as hares in Athos, bees
in Hybla, fowls in the air; but friends to
be found are like the phœnix in Arabia, but
one; or the philadelphi [1] in Arays, never
above two. I will have Endymion. [210
Sacred fountain, in whose bowels are hidden divine secrets, I have increased your
waters with the tears of unspotted thoughts,

[1] Shrubs on which the flowers grow in pairs.

and therefore let me receive the reward
you promise. Endymion, the truest friend
to me, and faithfulest lover to Cynthia,
is in such a dead sleep that nothing can
wake or move him.

GER. Dost thou see anything?

EUM. I see in the same pillar these [220
words: *When she whose figure of all is the
perfectest, and never to be measured—always
one, yet never the same—still inconstant,
yet never wavering—shall come and kiss
Endymion in his sleep, he shall then rise;
else never.* This is strange.

GER. What see you else?

EUM. There cometh over mine eyes
either a dark mist, or upon the fountain
a deep thickness, for I can perceive [230
nothing. But how am I deluded, or what
difficult—nay, impossible—thing is this?

GER. Methinketh it easy.

EUM. Good father, and how?

GER. Is not a circle of all figures the
perfectest?

EUM. Yes.

GER. And is not Cynthia of all circles
the most absolute?

EUM. Yes.   240

GER. Is it not impossible to measure
her, who still worketh by her influence,
never standing at one stay?

EUM. Yes.

GER. Is she not always Cynthia, yet
seldom in the same bigness; always wavering in her waxing or waning, that our
bodies might the better be governed, our
seasons the dailier give their increase; yet
never to be removed from her course, [250
as long as the heavens continue theirs?

EUM. Yes.

GER. Then who can it be but Cynthia,
whose virtues, being all divine, must needs
bring things to pass that be miraculous?
Go, humble thyself to Cynthia; tell her
the success, of which myself shall be a
witness. And this assure thyself, that
she that sent to find means for his safety
will now work her cunning.   260

EUM. How fortunate am I, if Cynthia
be she that may do it!

GER. How fond art thou, if thou do
not believe it!

EUM. I will hasten thither that I may
entreat on my knees for succor, and embrace in mine arms my friend.

GER. I will go with thee, for unto Cynthia must I discover all my sorrows, who also must work in me a contentment.

EUM. May I now know the cause?   [271

GER. That shall be as we walk, and I doubt not but the strangeness of my tale will take away the tediousness of our journey.

EUM. Let us go.

GER. I follow.   *Exeunt.*

ACTUS QUARTUS. SCENA PRIMA.

[*Before the castle of Corsites in a desert.*]

Tellus, Corsites.[1]

TELLUS. I marvel Corsites giveth me so much liberty—all the world knowing his charge [2] to be so high and his nature to be most strange—who hath so ill entreated ladies of great honor that he hath not suffered them to look out of windows, much less to walk abroad. It may be he is in love with me, for (Endymion, hardhearted Endymion, excepted) what is he that is not enamored of my beauty?   [10 But what respectest thou the love of all the world? Endymion hates thee. Alas, poor Endymion, my malice hath exceeded my love, and thy faith to Cynthia quenched my affections. Quenched, Tellus? Nay, kindled them afresh; insomuch that I find scorching flames for dead embers, and cruel encounters of war in my thoughts instead of sweet parleys. Ah, that I might once again see Endymion! Accursed   [20 girl, what hope hast thou to see Endymion, on whose head already are grown gray hairs, and whose life must yield to nature before Cynthia end her displeasure? Wicked Dipsas and most devilish Tellus, the one for cunning too exquisite, the other for hate too intolerable! Thou wast commanded to weave the stories and poetries wherein were showed both examples and punishments of tattling tongues, and   [30 thou hast only embroidered [3] the sweet face of Endymion, devices of love, melancholy imaginations, and what not, out of thy work, that thou shouldst study to pick out of thy mind. But here cometh Corsites. I must seem yielding and stout;

[1] Enters later.
[2] Military position.   [3] Embroidered.

full of mildness, yet tempered with a majesty, for, if I be too flexible, I shall give him more hope than I mean; if too froward, enjoy less liberty than I would.   [40 Love him I cannot, and therefore will practice that which is most contrary [4] to our sex, to dissemble.

Enter Corsites.

COR. Fair Tellus, I perceive you rise with the lark, and to yourself sing with the nightingale.

TELLUS. My lord, I have no playfellow but fancy. Being barred of all company, I must question with myself, and make my thoughts my friends.   50

COR. I would you would account my thoughts also your friends, for they be such as are only busied in wondering at your beauty and wisdom; and some such as have esteemed your fortune too hard; and divers of that kind that offer to set you free, if you will set them free.

TELLUS. There are no colors so contrary as white and black, nor elements so disagreeing as fire and water, nor   [60 anything so opposite as men's thoughts and their words.

COR. He that gave Cassandra the gift of prophesying, with the curse that, spake she never so true, she should never be believed, hath I think poisoned the fortune of men, that, uttering the extremities of their inward passions, are always suspected of outward perjuries.

TELLUS. Well, Corsites, I will flatter   [70 myself and believe you. What would you do to enjoy my love?

COR. Set all the ladies of the castle free, and make you the pleasure of my life. More I cannot do; less I will not.

TELLUS. These be great words, and fit your calling, for captains must promise things impossible. But will you do one thing for all?

COR. Anything, sweet Tellus, that   [80 am ready for all.

TELLUS. You know that on the lunary bank sleepeth Endymion.

COR. I know it.

TELLUS. If you will remove him from that place by force, and convey him into

[4] Bond suggests *customary.*

some obscure cave by policy, I give you here the faith of an unspotted virgin that you only shall possess me as a lover, and in spite of malice have me for a wife.   90

COR. Remove him, Tellus? Yes, Tellus, he shall be removed, and that so soon as [1] thou shalt as much commend my diligence as my force. I go.

TELLUS. Stay, will yourself attempt it?

COR. Ay, Tellus; as I would have none partaker of my sweet love, so shall none be partners of my labors. But I pray thee go at your best leisure, for Cynthia begin- [100 neth to rise, and, if she discover our love, we both perish, for nothing pleaseth her but the fairness of virginity. All things must be not only without lust but without suspicion of lightness.

TELLUS. I will depart, and go you to Endymion.

COR. I fly, Tellus, being of all men the most fortunate.   *Exit.*

TELLUS. Simple Corsites, I have set thee about a task, being but a man, [110 that the gods themselves cannot perform, for little dost thou know how heavy his head lies, how hard his fortune. But such shifts must women have to deceive men, and, under color of things easy, entreat that which is impossible; otherwise we should be cumbered with importunities, oaths, sighs, letters, and all implements of love, which to one resolved to the contrary are most loathsome. I will in, and laugh [120 with the other ladies at Corsites' sweating.
                    Exit.

SCENA SECUNDA.

[The gardens of Cynthia's palace.]

Samias and Dares; Epiton.[2]

SAM. Will thy master never awake?

DAR. No; I think he sleeps for a wager. But how shall we spend the time? Sir Tophas is so far in love that he pineth in his bed and cometh not abroad.

SAM. But here cometh Epi in a pelting chafe.[3]

[Enter Epiton.]

EPI. A pox of all false proverbs, and were a proverb a page, I would have him by the ears!   10

SAM. Why art thou angry?

EPI. Why? You know it is said, "The tide tarrieth no man."

SAM. True.

EPI. A monstrous lie; for I was tied two hours, and tarried for one to unloose me.

DAR. Alas, poor Epi!

EPI. Poor? No, no, you base, con- ceited slaves, I am a most complete [20 gentleman, although I be in disgrace with Sir Tophas.

DAR. Art thou out with him?

EPI. Ay, because I cannot get him a lodging with Endymion. He would fain take a nap for forty or fifty years.

DAR. A short sleep, considering our long life.

SAM. Is he still in love?

EPI. In love? Why, he doth noth- [30 ing but make sonnets!

SAM. Canst thou remember any one of his poems?

EPI. Ay, this is one:

> The beggar Love, that knows not where
>   to lodge,
>   At last within my heart, when I slept,
>   He crept.
> I waked, and so my fancies began to
>   fodge.[4]

SAM. That's a very long verse.

EPI. Why, the other was short. The [40 first is called from the thumb to the little finger; the second from the little finger to the elbow; and some he hath made to reach to the crown of his head, and down again to the sole of his foot. It is set to the tune of the Black Saunce;[5] *ratio est,*[6] because Dipsas is a black saint.

DAR. Very wisely. But pray thee, Epi, how art thou complete, and, being from thy master, what occupation wilt thou [50 take?

EPI. Know,[7] my hearts, I am an ab- solute *microcosmus,* a petty world of my- self: my library is my head, for I have no other books but my brains; my wardrope [8] on my back, for I have no more apparel

---

[1] That.   [2] Enters later.   [3] Petty rage.

[4] Move.
[5] The Black Sanctus was a hymn to Saint Satan in ridicule of the monks.
[6] The reason is.
[7] Emended by Baker. Early edns. read *No.*
[8] Wardrobe.

than is on my body; my armory at my
fingers' ends, for I use no other artillery
than my nails; my treasure in my purse.
"*Sic omnia mea mecum porto.*" [1] 60

DAR. Good!

EPI. Now, sirs, my palace is paved with
grass and tiled with stars, for "*Cælo tegitur
qui non habet urnam*" [2]—"he that hath no
house must lie in the yard."

SAM. A brave resolution! But how wilt
thou spend thy time?

EPI. Not in any melancholy sort; for
mine exercise I will walk horses.

DAR. Too bad! 70

EPI. Why, is it not said, "It is good
walking when one hath his horse in his
hand"?

SAM. Worse and worse! But how wilt
thou live?

EPI. By angling. O, 'tis a stately occupation to stand four hours in a cold morning, and to have his nose bitten with frost
before his bait be mumbled with a fish.

DAR. A rare attempt! But wilt thou [80
never travel?

EPI. Yes, in a western barge, [3] when,
with a good wind and lusty pugs, [4] one may
go ten miles in two days.

SAM. Thou art excellent at thy choice.
But what pastime wilt thou use? None?

EPI. Yes, the quickest of all.

SAM. What, dice?

EPI. No, when I am in haste, one-and-
twenty games at chess, to pass a few [90
minutes.

DAR. A life for a little lord, and full of
quickness. [5]

EPI. Tush, let me alone! But I must
needs see if I can find where Endymion
lieth, and then go to a certain fountain
hard by, where they say faithful lovers
shall have all things they will ask. If I
can find out any of these, *Ego et magister
meus erimus in tuto*—I and my master [100
shall be friends. He is resolved to weep
some three or four pailfuls to avoid [6] the
rheum of love that wambleth [7] in his stomach.

[1] Quoted by Cicero in *Paradoxa Stoicorum,*
i, 1: "Thus all my possessions I carry with me."
[2] Lucan, vii, 819.
[3] *I.e.*, on the Thames.
[4] Bargemen.
[5] Liveliness.
[6] Empty.　　　　　　　　　[7] Rumbles.

Enter the Watch.

SAM. Shall we never see thy master,
Dares?

DAR. Yes; let us go now, for tomorrow
Cynthia will be there.

EPI. I will go with you. But how shall
we see for the watch? 110

SAM. Tush, let me alone! I'll begin to
them. Masters, God speed you.

1 WATCH. Sir boy, we are all sped already.

EPI. [*Aside.*] So methinks, for they
smell all of drink, like a beggar's beard.

DAR. But I pray, sirs, may we see Endymion?

2 WATCH. No, we are commanded in
Cynthia's name that no man shall see [120
him.

SAM. No man? Why, we are but boys.

1 WATCH. Mass, neighbors, he says
true, for, if I swear I will never drink my
liquor by the quart, and yet call for two
pints, I think with a safe conscience I may
carouse both.

DAR. Pithily, and to the purpose!

2 WATCH. Tush, tush, neighbors, take
me with you. [8] 130

SAM. [*Aside.*] This will grow hot.

DAR. [*Aside.*] Let them alone.

2 WATCH. If I say to my wife, "Wife,
I will have no raisins in my pudding,"
she puts in currants. Small raisins are
raisins, and boys are men; even as my
wife should have put no raisins in my pudding, so shall there no boys see Endymion.

DAR. Learnedly!

EPI. Let Master Constable speak; [140
I think he is the wisest among you.

MA. CONST. You know, neighbors, 'tis
an old said [9] saw, "Children and fools speak
true."

ALL *say:* True.

MA. CONST. Well, there you see the
men be the fools, because it is provided
from the children.

DAR. Good!

MA. CONST. Then say I, neighbors, [150
that children must not see Endymion, because children and fools speak true.

EPI. O wicked application!

SAM. Scurvily brought about!

[8] Let me understand you.
[9] Sad, serious.

1 WATCH. Nay, he says true, and therefore till Cynthia have been here, he shall
not be uncovered. Therefore, away!

DAR. [*Aside to Samias and Epiton.*] A
watch, quoth you! A man may watch
seven years for a wise word, and yet [160
go without it. Their wits are all as rusty as
their bills.[1] But come on, Ma[ster] Const[able], shall we have a song before we go?

MA. CONST. With all my heart.

THE SECOND SONG

WATCH. Stand! Who goes there?
We charge you, appear
Fore our constable here,
In the name of the Man in the Moon.
To us billmen relate
Why you stagger so late,   170
And how you come drunk so soon.
  PAGES. What are ye, scabs?[2]
  WATCH.   The watch;
This the constable.
  PAGES.   A patch![3]
  MA. CONST. Knock 'em down unless
    they all stand!
If any run away,
'Tis the old watchman's play,
To reach him a bill of his hand.
  PAGES. O gentlemen, hold;
Your gowns freeze with cold,   179
And your rotten teeth dance in your head.
  EPI. Wine nothing shall cost ye;
  SAM. Nor huge fires to roast ye;
  DAR. Then soberly let us be led.
  MA. CONST. Come, my brown bills, we'll
    roar,[4]
Bounce loud at tavern door,
  OMNES. And i' th' morning steal all to
    bed!
                                    Exeunt.

SCENA TERTIA.

[*A grove near Endymion's cell.*]

Corsites solus. [*Endymion sleeps on the bank
in the grove.*]

CORS. I am come in sight of the lunary
bank. Without doubt Tellus doteth upon
me, and cunningly, that I might not perceive her love, she hath set me to a task
that is done before it is begun. Endymion,
you must change your pillow, and if you
be not weary of sleep, I will carry you

---

[1] Halberds.
[2] Rascals, sheriff's officers.
[3] Fool.   [4] Revel.

where at ease you shall sleep your fill. It
were good that without more ceremonies
I took him, lest, being espied, I be en- [10
trapped, and so incur the displeasure of
Cynthia, who commonly setteth watch
that Endymion have no wrong. (*He lifts.*)
What now, is your mastership so heavy,
or are you nailed to the ground? Not stir
one whit? Then use all thy force, though
he feel it and wake. What, stone-still?
Turned, I think, to earth with lying so
long on the earth. Didst not thou, Corsites,
before Cynthia, pull up a tree that [20
forty years was fastened with roots and
wreathed in knots to the ground? Didst
not thou with main force pull open the
iron gates which no ram or engine could
move? Have my weak thoughts made
brawn-fallen my strong arms? Or is it the
nature of love or the quintessence of the
mind to breed numbness or litherness,[5] or
I know not what languishing in my joints
and sinews, being but the base strings [30
of my body? Or doth the remembrance of
Tellus so refine my spirits into a matter
so subtle and divine that the other fleshy
parts cannot work whilst they muse?
Rest thyself, rest thyself; nay, rent[6] thyself in pieces, Corsites, and strive, in spite
of love, fortune, and nature, to lift up this
dulled body, heavier than dead and more
senseless than death.

Enter Fairies.

But what are these so fair fiends that [40
cause my hairs to stand upright and spirits to fall down? Hags—out, alas, nymphs,
I crave pardon! Ay me, out! What do I
hear?
*The Fairies dance and with a song pinch
him, and he falleth asleep. They kiss
Endymion and depart.*

THE THIRD SONG BY FAIRIES

OMNES. Pinch him, pinch him, black and
    blue,
Saucy mortals must not view
What the Queen of Stars is doing,
Nor pry into our fairy wooing.
  1 FAIRY. Pinch him blue,
  2 FAIRY. And pinch him black;   50
  3 FAIRY. Let him not lack

---

[5] Flaccidity, sloth.   [6] Rend, tear.

Sharp nails to pinch him blue and red,
Till sleep has rocked his addle head.
   4 FAIRY. For the trespass he hath done,
Spots o'er all his flesh shall run.
Kiss Endymion, kiss his eyes,
Then to our midnight hay-de-guise.[1]

Exeunt.

Cynthia, Floscula, Semele, Panelion, Zontes,
Pythagoras, Gyptes.

CYNTH. You see, Pythagoras, what ridiculous opinions you hold, and I doubt
not but you are now of another mind.   60
   PYTHAG. Madam, I plainly perceive
that the perfection of your brightness hath
pierced through the thickness that covered
my mind; insomuch that I am no less glad
to be reformed than ashamed to remember
my grossness.
   GYPTES. They are thrice fortunate that
live in your palace where truth is not in
colors but life, virtues not in imagination but execution.   70
   CYNTH. I have always studied to have
rather living virtues than painted gods,
the body of truth than the tomb. But let
us walk to Endymion; it may be it lieth
in your arts to deliver him. As for Eumenides, I fear he is dead.
   PYTHAG. I have alleged all the natural
reasons I can for such a long sleep.
   GYPTES. I can do nothing till I see him.
   CYNTH. Come, Floscula; I am sure   [80
you are glad that you shall behold Endymion.
   FLOSC. I were blessed, if I might have
him recovered.
   CYNTH. Are you in love with his person?
   FLOSC. No, but with his virtue.
   CYNTH. What say you, Semele?
   SEM. Madam, I dare say nothing for
fear I offend.
   CYNTH. Belike you cannot speak   [90
except you be spiteful; but as good be silent
as saucy. Panelion, what punishment were
fit for Semele, in whose speech and thoughts
is only contempt and sourness?
   PANEL. I love not, madam, to give any
judgment; yet, sith [2] your highness commandeth, I think to commit her tongue
close prisoner to her mouth.
   CYNTH. Agreed. Semele, if thou speak
this twelvemonth, thou shalt forfeit   [100

thy tongue.—Behold Endymion! Alas,
poor gentleman, hast thou spent thy youth
in sleep, that once vowed all to my service? Hollow eyes, gray hairs, wrinkled
cheeks, and decayed limbs! Is it destiny
or deceit that hath brought this to pass?
If the first, who could prevent thy wretched
stars? If the latter, I would I might know
thy cruel enemy. I favored thee, Endymion, for thy honor, thy virtues, thy af-   [110
fections. But [3] to bring thy thoughts within
the compass of thy fortunes, I have seemed
strange, that I might have thee stayed; [4]
and now are thy days ended before my
favor begin! But whom have we here?
Is it not Corsites?
   ZON. It is, but more like a leopard than
a man.
   CYNTH. Awake him.   [*Zontes wakens*
Corsites.] How now, Corsites, what   [120
make [5] you here? How came you deformed?
Look on thy hands, and then thou seest
the picture of thy face.
   CORS. Miserable wretch, and accursed!
How am I deluded! Madam, I ask pardon
for my offense, and you see my fortune
deserveth pity.
   CYNTH. Speak on; thy offense cannot
deserve greater punishment. But see thou
rehearse the truth, else shalt thou not   [130
find me as thou wishest me.
   CORS. Madam, as it is no offense to be
in love, being a man mortal, so I hope can
it be no shame to tell with whom, my
lady being heavenly. Your majesty committed to my charge fair Tellus, whose
beauty in the same moment took my
heart captive that I undertook to carry
her body prisoner. Since that time have
I found such combats in my thoughts   [140
between love and duty, reverence and
affection, that I could neither endure the
conflict nor hope for the conquest.
   CYNTH. In love? A thing far unfitting
the name of a captain, and, as I thought,
the tough and unsmoothed nature of Corsites. But forth!
   CORS. Feeling this continual war, I
thought rather by parley to yield than by
certain danger to perish. I unfolded   [150
to Tellus the depth of my affections, and
framed my tongue to utter a sweet tale of
love, that was wont to sound nothing but

_____
[1] Rustic dance.   [2] Since.   [3] Only.   [4] Checked (*i.e.*, in his ambitions).   [5] Do.

threats of war. She, too fair to be true and too false for one so fair, after a nice [1] denial, practiced a notable deceit, commanding me to remove Endymion from this cabin,[2] and carry him to some dark cave; which I, seeking to accomplish, found impossible, and so by fairies or fiends [160 have been thus handled.

CYNTH. How say you, my lords, is not Tellus always practicing of some deceits? In sooth, Corsites, thy face is now too foul for a lover, and thine heart too fond for a soldier. You may see when warriors become wantons how their manners alter with their faces. Is it not a shame, Corsites, that, having lived so long in Mars his camp, thou shouldest now be rocked [170 in Venus' cradle? Dost thou wear Cupid's quiver at thy girdle and make lances of looks? Well, Corsites, rouse thyself and be as thou hast been; and let Tellus, who is made all of love, melt herself in her own looseness.

CORS. Madam, I doubt not but to recover my former state, for Tellus' beauty never wrought such love in my mind as now her deceit hath despite; and yet to be [180 revenged of a woman were a thing than love itself more womanish.

GYPTES. These spots, gentleman, are to be worn out, if you rub them over with this lunary, so that in place where you received this main,[3] you shall find a medicine.

CORS. I thank you for that. The gods bless [4] me from love and these pretty ladies that haunt this green.   190

FLOSC. Corsites, I would Tellus saw your amiable face.

ZON. How spitefully Semele laugheth, that dare not speak!

CYNTH. Could you not stir Endymion with that doubled strength of yours?

CORS. Not so much as his finger with all my force.

CYNTH. Pythagoras and Gyptes, what think you of Endymion? What rea- [200 son is to be given, what remedy?

PYTHAG. Madam, it is impossible to yield reason for things that happen not in compass of nature. It is most certain that some strange enchantment hath bound all his senses.

CYNTH. What say you, Gyptes?

GYPTES. With Pythagoras, that it is enchantment, and that so strange that no art can undo it (for that heaviness [210 argueth a malice unremovable in the enchantress) and that no power can end it, till she die that did it, or the heavens show some means more than miraculous.

FLOSC. O Endymion, could spite itself devise a mischief so monstrous as to make thee dead with life, and living being altogether dead? Where others number their years, their hours, their minutes, and step to age by stairs, thou only hast [220 thy years and times in a cluster, being old before thou rememb'rest thou wast young.

CYNTH. No more, Floscula; pity doth him no good. I would anything else might, and I vow by the unspotted honor of a lady he should not miss it. But is this all, Gyptes, that is to be done?

GYPTES. All as yet. It may be that either the enchantress shall die or else be discovered. If either happen, I will [230 then practice the utmost of my art. In the mean season, about this grove would I have a watch, and the first living thing that toucheth Endymion to be taken.

CYNTH. Corsites, what say you? Will you undertake this?

CORS. Good madam, pardon me! I was overtaken [5] too late. I should rather break into the middest of a main battle than again fall into the hands of those [240 fair babies.[6]

CYNTH. Well, I will provide others. Pythagoras and Gyptes, you shall yet remain in my court, till I hear what may be done in this matter.

PYTHAG. We attend.

CYNTH. Let us go in.   *Exeunt.*

ACTUS QUINTUS. SCENA PRIMA.

[*The same.*]

Samias, Dares.

SAM. Eumenides hath told such strange tales as I may well wonder at them, but never believe them.

---

[1] Overscrupulous, fastidious.
[2] Shelter (represented by the overhanging inner stage?).   [3] Maim.   [4] Protect.
[5] Overpowered.   [6] *I.e.*, the fairies.

DAR. The other old man, what a sad speech used he, that caused us almost all to weep. Cynthia is so desirous to know the experiment of her own virtue,[1] and so willing to ease Endymion's hard fortune, that she no sooner heard the discourse but she made herself in a readiness to [10 try the event.

SAM. We will also see the event. But whist, here cometh Cynthia with all her train! Let us sneak in amongst them.

Enter Cynthia, Floscula, Semele, [Eumenides,] Panelion, etc.

CYNTH. Eumenides, it cannot sink into my head that I should be signified by that sacred fountain, for many things are there in the world to which those words may be applied.

EUM. Good madam, vouchsafe but [20 to try; else shall I think myself most unhappy that I asked not my sweet mistress.

CYNTH. Will you not yet tell me her name?

EUM. Pardon me, good madam, for if Endymion awake, he shall; myself have sworn never to reveal it.

CYNTH. Well, let us to Endymion. I will not be so stately, good Endymion, not to stoop to do thee good; and, if thy [30 liberty consist in a kiss from me, thou shalt have it. And, although my mouth hath been heretofore as untouched as my thoughts, yet now to recover thy life, though to restore thy youth it be impossible, I will do that to Endymion which yet never mortal man could boast of heretofore, nor shall ever hope for hereafter. *She kisseth him.*

EUM. Madam, he beginneth to stir!

CYNTH. Soft, Eumenides; stand still! [40

EUM. Ah, I see his eyes almost open!

CYNTH. I command thee once again, stir not! I will stand behind him.

PANEL. What do I see? Endymion almost awake?

EUM. Endymion! Endymion! Art thou deaf or dumb, or hath this long sleep taken away thy memory? Ah, my sweet Endymion, seest thou not Eumenides, thy faithful friend, thy faithful Eumenides, who [50 for thy safety hath been careless of his own content? Speak, Endymion! Endymion! Endymion!

[1] Make trial of her power.

END. Endymion? I call to mind such a name.

EUM. Hast thou forgotten thyself, Endymion? Then do I not marvel thou rememb'rest not thy friend. I tell thee thou art Endymion, and I Eumenides. Behold also Cynthia, by whose favor thou art [60 awaked, and by whose virtue thou shalt continue thy natural course.

CYNTH. Endymion, speak, sweet Endymion! Knowest thou not Cynthia?

END. O heavens, whom do I behold? Fair Cynthia, divine Cynthia?

CYNTH. I am Cynthia, and thou Endymion. 68

END. "Endymion"! What do I hear? What! a gray beard, hollow eyes, withered body, decayed limbs—and all in one night?

EUM. One night! Thou hast here slept forty years—by what enchantress as yet it is not known—and behold, the twig to which thou laid'st thy head is now become a tree. Callest thou not Eumenides to remembrance?

END. Thy name I do remember by the sound, but thy favor [2] I do not yet call to mind; only divine Cynthia, to whom [80 time, fortune, destiny, and death are subject, I see and remember, and in all humility I regard and reverence.

CYNTH. You have good cause to remember Eumenides, who hath for thy safety forsaken his own solace.

END. Am I that Endymion who was wont in court to lead my life, and in jousts, tourneys, and arms, to exercise my youth? Am I that Endymion? 90

EUM. Thou art that Endymion, and I Eumenides. Wilt thou not yet call me to remembrance?

END. Ah, sweet Eumenides, I now perceive thou art he, and that myself have the name of Endymion; but that this should be my body I doubt, for how could my curled locks be turned to gray hairs and my strong body to a dying weakness, having waxed old, and not knowing it? [100

CYNTH. Well, Endymion, arise. [*Endymion attempts to rise, but sinks back.*] A while sit down, for that thy limbs are stiff and not able to stay thee, and tell what hast thou seen in thy sleep all this while, what dreams, visions, thoughts, and for-

[2] Appearance, face.

tunes; for it is impossible but in so long time thou shouldest see things strange.

END. Fair Cynthia, I will rehearse what I have seen, humbly desiring that, [110 when I exceed in length, you give me warning, that I may end; for to utter all I have to speak would be troublesome, although happily the strangeness may somewhat abate the tediousness.

CYNTH. Well, Endymion, begin.

END. Methought I saw a lady passing fair, but very mischievous, who in the one hand carried a knife with which she offered to cut my throat, and in the other a [120 looking-glass, wherein seeing how ill anger became ladies, she refrained from intended violence. She was accompanied with other damsels, one of which, with a stern countenance, and as it were with a settled malice engraven in her eyes, provoked her to execute mischief; another, with visage sad, and constant only in sorrow, with her arms crossed and watery eyes, seemed to lament my fortune, but durst not offer to pre- [130 vent the force. I started in my sleep, feeling my very veins to swell and my sinews to stretch with fear, and such a cold sweat bedewed all my body that death itself could not be so terrible as the vision.

CYNTH. A strange sight! Gyptes, at our better leisure, shall expound it.

END. After long debating with herself, mercy overcame anger, and there appeared in her heavenly face such a divine maj- [140 esty mingled with a sweet mildness that I was ravished with the sight above measure, and wished that I might have enjoyed the sight without end. And so she departed with the other ladies, of which the one retained still an unmovable cruelty, the other a constant pity.

CYNTH. Poor Endymion, how wast thou affrighted! What else?   149

END. After her, immediately appeared an aged man with a beard as white as snow, carrying in his hand a book with three leaves, and speaking, as I remember, these words: "Endymion, receive this book with three leaves, in which are contained counsels, policies, and pictures," and with that he offered me the book, which I rejected; wherewith, moved with a disdainful pity, he rent the first leaf in a thousand shivers. The second time he [160

offered it, which I refused also; at which, bending his brows, and pitching his eyes fast to the ground, as though they were fixed to the earth and not again to be removed, then suddenly casting them up to the heavens, he tore in a rage the second leaf, and offered the book only with one leaf. I know not whether fear to offend or desire to know some strange thing moved me. I took the book, and so the old [170 man vanished.

CYNTH. What diddest thou imagine was in the last leaf?

END. There—ay, portrayed to life— with a cold quaking in every joint, I beheld many wolves barking at thee, Cynthia, who, having ground their teeth to bite, did with striving bleed themselves to death. There might I see Ingratitude with an hundred eyes gazing for benefits, [180 and with a thousand teeth gnawing on the bowels wherein she was bred. Treachery stood all clothed in white, with a smiling countenance, but both her hands bathed in blood. Envy with a pale and meager face (whose body was so lean that one might tell [1] all her bones, and whose garment was so tottered [2] that it was easy to number every thread) stood shooting at stars, whose darts fell down again on [190 her own face. There might I behold drones, or beetles—I know not how to term them— creeping under the wings of a princely eagle, who, being carried into her nest, sought there to suck that vein that would have killed the eagle. I mused that things so base should attempt a fact [3] so barbarous, or durst imagine a thing so bloody. And many other things, madam, the repetition whereof may at your better [200 leisure seem more pleasing, for bees surfeit sometimes with honey, and the gods are glutted with harmony, and your highness may be dulled with delight.

CYNTH. I am content to be dieted; therefore, let us in. Eumenides, see that Endymion be well tended, lest, either eating immoderately or sleeping again too long, he fall into a deadly surfeit or into his former sleep.   210

See this also be proclaimed: that whosoever will discover this practice shall

[1] Count.
[2] Tattered.

[3] Deed, act.

have of Cynthia infinite thanks and no small rewards.

Exit [with all but Floscula, Eumenides, Semele, and Endymion].

FLOSC. Ah, Endymion, none so joyful as Floscula of thy restoring.

EUM. Yes, Floscula, let Eumenides be somewhat gladder, and do not that wrong to the settled friendship of a man as to compare it with the light affection [220 of a woman. Ah, my dear friend Endymion, suffer me to die with gazing at thee!

END. Eumenides, thy friendship is immortal and not to be conceived; and thy good will, Floscula, better than I have deserved. But let us all wait on Cynthia. I marvel Semele speaketh not a word.

EUM. Because if she do, she loseth her tongue!

END. But how prospereth your love?

EUM. I never yet spake word since [231 your sleep.

END. I doubt not but your affection is old and your appetite cold.

EUM. No, Endymion, thine hath made it stronger, and now are my sparks grown to flames and my fancies almost to frenzies. But let us follow, and within we will debate all this matter at large.   *Exeunt.*

SCENA SECUNDA.

[*The gardens of Cynthia's palace.*]

Sir Tophas, Epiton.

TOP. Epi, Love hath justled my liberty from the wall, and taken the upper hand of my reason.

EPI. Let me then trip up the heels of your affection and thrust your good will into the gutter.

TOP. No, Epi, Love is a lord of misrule and keepeth Christmas in my corpse.[1]

EPI. No doubt there is good cheer. What dishes of delight doth his lord-[10 ship feast you withal?

TOP. First, with a great platter of plum porridge of pleasure, wherein is stewed the mutton of mistrust.

EPI. Excellent love lap.[2]

TOP. Then cometh a pie of patience, a hen of honey, a goose of gall, a capon of care, and many other viands, some sweet

and some sour, which proveth love to be, as it was said of in old years, *dulce* [20 *venenum.*[3]

EPI. A brave banquet!

TOP. But, Epi, I pray thee feel on my chin; something pricketh me. What dost thou feel or see?

EPI. There are three or four little hairs.

TOP. I pray thee call it my beard. How shall I be troubled when this young spring [4] shall grow to a great wood!

EPI. O, sir, your chin is but a quiller[5] [30 yet; you will be most majestical when it is full-fledge. But I marvel that you love Dipsas, that old crone.

TOP. "*Agnosco veteris vestigia flammæ*"[6]—"I love the smoke of an old fire."

EPI. Why, she is so cold that no fire can thaw her thoughts.

TOP. It is an old goose, Epi, that will eat no oats; old kine will kick, old rats gnaw cheese, and old sacks will have [40 much patching. I prefer an old cony before a rabbit-sucker,[7] and an ancient hen before a young chicken-peeper.

EPI. [*Aside.*] *Argumentum ab antiquitate;*[8] my master loveth antique work.

TOP. Give me a pippin that is withered like an old wife!

EPI. Good, sir.

TOP. Then—*a contrario sequitur argumentum* [9]—give me a wife that looks [50 like an old pippin.

EPI. [*Aside.*] Nothing hath made my master a fool but flat scholarship.

TOP. Knowest thou not that old wine is best?

EPI. Yes.

TOP. And thou knowest that like will be like?

EPI. Ay.

TOP. And thou knowest that Venus [60 loved the best wine?

EPI. So.

TOP. Then I conclude that Venus was an old woman in an old cup of wine, for "*Est Venus in vinis, ignis in igne fuit.*"[10]

---

[3] Sweet poison.   [5] An unfledged bird.
[4] Sprout.   [6] Virgil, Æneid, iv, 23.
[7] An old rabbit before a sucking one.
[8] Argument from antiquity.
[9] From the contrary follows the proof.
[10] Adapted from Ovid, *Ars amat.*, i, 244, meaning, "Love is in wines as surely as fire is [lit., *was*] in fire."

---

[1] Body.   [2] Love broth.

EPI. "*O lepidum caput*,"[1] O madcap
master! You were worthy to win Dipsas,
were she as old again, for in your love you
have worn the nap of your wit quite off
and made it threadbare. But soft, who [70
comes here?

[*Enter Samias and Dares.*]

TOP. My solicitors.
SAM. All hail, Sir Tophas. How feel
you yourself?
TOP. Stately in every joint, which the
common people term stiffness. Doth Dipsas stoop? Will she yield? Will she bend?
DAR. O, sir, as much as you would
wish, for her chin almost toucheth her
knees.   80
EPI. Master, she is bent, I warrant
you.
TOP. What conditions doth she ask?
SAM. She hath vowed she will never
love any that hath not a tooth in his head
less than she.
TOP. How many hath she?
DAR. One.
EPI. That goeth hard, master, for then
you must have none.   90
TOP. A small request, and agreeable to
the gravity of her years. What should a
wise man do with his mouth full of bones
like a charnel[2]-house? The turtle[3] true
hath ne'er a tooth.
SAM. [*Aside to Epiton.*] Thy master is
in a notable vein, that will lose his teeth
to be like a turtle.
EPI. [*Aside to Samias.*] Let him lose
his tongue, too; I care not!   100
DAR. Nay, you must also have no
nails, for she long since hath cast hers.
TOP. That I yield to. What a quiet
life shall Dipsas and I lead when we can
neither bite nor scratch! You may see,
youths, how age provides for peace.
SAM. [*Aside to Epiton.*] How shall we
do to make him leave his love, for we
never spake to her?
DAR. [*Aside to Samias.*] Let me [110
alone.—[*To Sir Tophas.*] She is a notable
witch, and hath turned her maid Bagoa
to an aspen tree, for bewraying her secrets.

---

[1] Terence, *Adelphi*, v, ix, 9: "O fine head!"
[2] Original reads *channel*.
[3] Turtledove.

TOP. I honor her for her cunning, for
now when I am weary of walking on two
legs, what a pleasure may she do me to
turn me to some goodly ass, and help me
to four.
DAR. Nay, then I must tell you the
troth: her husband, Geron, is come [120
home, who this fifty years hath had her
to wife.
TOP. What do I hear? Hath she an
husband? Go to the sexton and tell him
Desire is dead, and will him to dig his
grave. O heavens, an husband! What
death is agreeable to my fortune?
SAM. Be not desperate, and we will
help you to find a young lady.
TOP. I love no grissels;[4] they are [130
so brittle they will crack like glass, or so
dainty that if they be touched they are
straight of the fashion of wax. "*Animus
majoribus instat*"[5]—"I desire old matrons."
What a sight would it be to embrace one
whose hair were as orient as the pearl,
whose teeth shall be so pure a watchet[6]
that they shall stain the truest turkis,[7]
whose nose shall throw more beams from
it than the fiery carbuncle, whose eyes [140
shall be environed about with redness exceeding the deepest coral, and whose lips
might compare with silver for the paleness! Such a one if you can help me to, I
will by piecemeal curtal[8] my affections
towards Dipsas, and walk my swelling
thoughts till they be cold.
EPI. Wisely provided! How say you,
my friends, will you angle for my master's
cause?   150
SAM. Most willingly.
DAR. If we speed him not shortly, I
will burn my cap. We will serve him of
the spades, and dig an old wife out of the
grave that shall be answerable to his
gravity.
TOP. Youths, adieu. He that bringeth me
first news, shall possess mine inheritance.
[*Exit.*]
DAR. What, is thy master landed?
EPI. Know you not that my master [160
is *liber tenens?*
SAM. What's that?

---

[4] Griseldas, young girls.
[5] Ovid, *Ars Amat.*, ii, 535.
[6] Pale blue.
[7] Turquoise.
[8] Curtail.

EPI. A freeholder. But I will after him.

SAM. And we to hear what news of Endymion for the conclusion.   *Exeunt.*

SCENA TERTIA.

[*The same.*]

Panelion, Zontes.

PANEL. Who would have thought that Tellus, being so fair by nature, so honorable by birth, so wise by education, would have entered into a mischief to the gods so odious, to men so detestable, and to her friend so malicious!

ZON. If Bagoa had not bewrayed it, how then should it have come to light? But we see that gold and fair words are of force to corrupt the strongest men, and [10 therefore able to work silly women like wax.

PANEL. I marvel what Cynthia will determine in this cause.

ZON. I fear, as in all causes: hear of it in justice, and then judge of it in mercy; for how can it be that she that is unwilling to punish her deadliest foes with disgrace will revenge injuries of her train with death?   20

PANEL. That old witch, Dipsas, in a rage, having understood her practice to be discovered, turned poor Bagoa to an aspen tree. But let us make haste and bring Tellus before Cynthia, for she was coming out after us.

ZON. Let us go.   *Exeunt.*

Cynthia, Semele, Floscula, Dipsas, Endymion, Eumenides [,Geron, Pythagoras, Gyptes, Sir Tophas].

CYNTH. Dipsas, thy years are not so many as thy vices, yet more in number than commonly nature doth afford or [30 justice should permit. Hast thou almost these fifty years practiced that detested wickedness of witchcraft? Wast thou so simple as for to know the nature of simples of all creatures to be most sinful?

Thou hast threatened to turn my course awry and alter by thy damnable art the government that I now possess by the eternal gods; but know thou, Dipsas, and let all the enchanters know, that Cyn- [40 thia, being placed for light on earth, is also

protected by the powers of heaven. Breathe out thou mayst words; gather thou mayst herbs; find out thou mayst stones agreeable to thine art; yet of no force to appall my heart, in which courage is so rooted, and constant persuasion of the mercy of the gods so grounded, that all thy witchcraft I esteem as weak as the world doth thy case wretched.   50

This noble gentleman, Geron, once thy husband but now thy mortal hate, didst thou procure to live in a desert, almost desperate; Endymion, the flower of my court and the hope of succeeding time, hast thou bewitched by art, before thou wouldest suffer him to flourish by nature.

DIPSAS. Madam, things past may be repented, not recalled. There is nothing so wicked that I have not done, nor [60 anything so wished for as death; yet among all the things that I committed, there is nothing so much tormenteth my rented and ransacked thoughts as that in the prime of my husband's youth I divorced him by my devilish art; for which if to die might be amends, I would not live till tomorrow; if to live and still be more miserable would better content him, I would wish of all creatures to be oldest and [70 ugliest.

GER. Dipsas, thou hast made this difference between me and Endymion, that being both young, thou hast caused me to wake in melancholy, losing the joys of my youth, and him to sleep, not rememb'ring youth.

CYNTH. Stay, here cometh Tellus; we shall now know all.

[*Enter Panelion and Zontes, with Corsites and Tellus.*]

CORS. I would to Cynthia thou [80 couldest make as good an excuse in truth as to me thou hast done by wit.

TELLUS. Truth shall be mine answer, and therefore I will not study for an excuse.

CYNTH. Is it possible, Tellus, that so few years should harbor so many mischiefs? Thy swelling pride have I borne, because it is a thing that beauty maketh blameless, which the more it exceedeth fairness in measure, the more it stretch- [90 eth itself in disdain. Thy devices against Corsites I smile at, for that wits, the sharper they are, the shrewder [1] they are; but this unacquainted [2] and most unnatural practice with a vile enchantress against so noble a gentleman as Endymion I abhor as a thing most malicious, and will revenge as a deed most monstrous.

And as for you, Dipsas, I will send you into the desert amongst wild beasts, [100 and try whether you can cast lions, tigers, boars, and bears into as dead a sleep as you did Endymion, or turn them to trees, as you have done Bagoa. But tell me, Tellus, what was the cause of this cruel part, far unfitting thy sex, in which nothing should be but simpleness, and much disagreeing from thy face, in which nothing seemed to be but softness?

TELLUS. Divine Cynthia, by whom [110 I receive my life and am content to end it, I can neither excuse my fault without lying, nor confess it without shame; yet were it possible that in so heavenly thoughts as yours there could fall such earthly motions as mine, I would then hope, if not to be pardoned without extreme punishment, yet to be heard without great marvel.

CYNTH. Say on, Tellus; I cannot [120 imagine anything that can color such a cruelty.

TELLUS. Endymion, that Endymion, in the prime of his youth, so ravished my heart with love that to obtain my desires I could not find means, nor to recite them, reason.

What was she that favored not Endymion, being young, wise, honorable, and virtuous? Besides, what metal was she [130 made of (be she mortal) that is not affected with the spice, nay, infected with the poison of that not-to-be-expressed, yet always-to-be-felt love, which breaketh the brains and never bruiseth the brow, consumeth the heart and never toucheth the skin, and maketh a deep scar to be seen before any wound at all be felt? My heart, too tender to withstand such a divine fury, yielded to love. Madam, I, [140 not without blushing, confess [I] yielded to love.

CYNTH. A strange effect of love, to work such an extreme hate. How say you, Endymion? All this was for love?

[1] More mischievous.   [2] Unheard of.

END. I say, madam, then the gods send me a woman's hate.

CYNTH. That were as bad, for then by contrary you should never sleep. But on, Tellus; let us hear the end.   150

TELLUS. Feeling a continual burning in all my bowels, and a bursting almost in every vein, I could not smother the inward fire, but it must needs be perceived by the outward smoke; and, by the flying abroad of divers sparks, divers judged of my scalding flames. Endymion, as full of art as wit, marking mine eyes (in which he might see almost his own), my sighs (by which he might ever hear his [160 name sounded), aimed at my heart, in which he was assured his person was imprinted, and by questions wrung out that which was ready to burst out. When he saw the depth of my affections, he sware that mine in respect of his were as fumes to Ætna, valleys to Alps, ants to eagles, and nothing could be compared to my beauty but his love and eternity. Thus drawing a smooth shoe upon a crooked foot, [170 he made me believe that (which all of our sex willingly acknowledge) I was beautiful, and to wonder (which indeed is a thing miraculous) that any of his sex should be faithful.

CYNTH. Endymion, how will you clear yourself?

END. Madam, by mine own accuser.

CYNTH. Well, Tellus, proceed; but [179 briefly, lest, taking delight in uttering thy love, thou offend us with the length of it.

TELLUS. I will, madam, quickly make an end of my love and my tale. Finding continual increase of my tormenting thoughts, and that the enjoying of my love made deeper wounds than the entering into it, I could find no means to ease my grief but to follow Endymion, and continually to have him in the ob- [190 ject of mine eyes who had me slave and subject to his love.

But in the moment that I feared his falsehood and fried myself most in mine affections, I found—ah, grief, even then I lost myself!—I found him in most melancholy and desperate terms, cursing his stars, his state, the earth, the heavens, the world, and all for the love of—

CYNTH. Of whom? Tellus, speak [200 boldly.

TELLUS. Madam, I dare not utter, for fear to offend.

CYNTH. Speak, I say; who dare take offense, if thou be commanded by Cynthia?

TELLUS. For the love of Cynthia.

CYNTH. For my love, Tellus? That were strange. Endymion, is it true?

END. In all things, madam, Tellus doth not speak false.   210

CYNTH. What will this breed to in the end? Well, Endymion, we shall hear all.

TELLUS. I, seeing my hopes turned to mishaps, and a settled dissembling towards me, and an unmovable desire to Cynthia, forgetting both myself and my sex, fell into this unnatural hate; for, knowing your virtues, Cynthia, to be immortal, I could not have an imagination to withdraw him;[1] and, finding mine [220 own affections unquenchable, I could not carry the mind that any else should possess what I had pursued. For, though in majesty, beauty, virtue, and dignity I always humbled and yielded myself to Cynthia, yet in affections I esteemed myself equal with the goddesses; and all other creatures, according to their states, with myself; for stars to their bigness have their lights, and the sun hath no more; [230 and little pitchers, when they can hold no more, are as full as great vessels that run over. Thus, madam, in all truth have I uttered the unhappiness of my love and the cause of my hate, yielding wholly to that divine judgment which never erred for want of wisdom or envied for too much partiality.

CYNTH. How say you, my lords, to this matter? But what say you, En- [240 dymion? Hath Tellus told troth?

END. Madam, in all things but in that she said I loved her and swore to honor her.

CYNTH. Was there such a time whenas for my love thou didst vow thyself to death, and in respect of it loathed thy life? Speak, Endymion; I will not revenge it with hate.

END. The time was, madam, and is, and ever shall be, that I honored [250 your highness above all the world, but to stretch it so far as to call it love I never

[1] Hope to draw him away.

durst. There hath none pleased mine eye but Cynthia, none delighted mine ears but Cynthia, none possessed my heart but Cynthia. I have forsaken all other fortunes to follow Cynthia, and here I stand ready to die, if it please Cynthia. Such a difference hath the gods set between our states that all must be duty, [260 loyalty, and reverence; nothing (without it vouchsafe your highness) be termed love. My unspotted thoughts, my languishing body, my discontented life, let them obtain by princely favor that which to challenge they must not presume, only wishing of impossibilities; with imagination of which I will spend my spirits, and to myself, that no creature may hear, softly call it love; and, if any urge to utter what I [270 whisper, then will I name it honor. From this sweet contemplation if I be not driven. I shall live of all men the most content, taking more pleasure in mine aged thoughts than ever I did in my youthful actions.

CYNTH. Endymion, this honorable respect of thine shall be christened love in thee, and my reward for it, favor. Persevere, Endymion, in loving me, and I account more strength in a true heart [280 than in a walled city. I have labored to win all, and study to keep such as I have won; but those that neither my favor can move to continue constant, nor my offered benefits get to be faithful, the gods shall either reduce to truth, or revenge their treacheries with justice. Endymion, continue as thou hast begun, and thou shalt find that Cynthia shineth not on thee in vain. [*Endymion regains his youth.*] [290

END. Your highness hath blessed me, and your words have again restored my youth; methinks I feel my joints strong and these moldy hairs to molt, and all by your virtue, Cynthia, into whose hands the balance that weigheth time and fortune are committed.

CYNTH. What, young again! Then it is pity to punish Tellus.

TELLUS. Ah, Endymion, now I [300 know thee and ask pardon of thee; suffer me still to wish thee well.

END. Tellus, Cynthia must command what she will.

FLOSC. Endymion, I rejoice to see thee in thy former estate.

END. Good Floscula, to thee also am I in my former affections.

EUM. Endymion, the comfort of my life, how am I ravished with a joy match- [310 less, saving only the enjoying of my mistress!

CYNTH. Endymion, you must now tell who Eumenides shrineth for his saint.

END. Semele, madam.

CYNTH. Semele, Eumenides? Is it Semele, the very wasp of all women, whose tongue stingeth as much as an adder's tooth?

EUM. It is Semele, Cynthia, the [320 possessing of whose love must only prolong my life.

CYNTH. Nay, sith Endymion is restored, we will have all parties pleased. Semele, are you content after so long trial of his faith, such rare secrecy, such unspotted love, to take Eumenides? Why speak you not? Not a word?

END. Silence, madam, consents; that is most true.   330

CYNTH. It is true, Endymion. Eumenides, take Semele; take her, I say.

EUM. Humble thanks, madam; now only do I begin to live.

SEM. A hard choice, madam, either to be married if I say nothing, or to lose my tongue if I speak a word. Yet do I rather choose to have my tongue cut out than my heart distempered—I will not have him.

CYNTH. Speaks the parrot? She [340 shall nod hereafter with signs. Cut off her tongue, nay, her head, that, having a servant of honorable birth, honest manners, and true love, will not be persuaded!

SEM. He is no faithful lover, madam, for then would he have asked his mistress.

GER. Had he not been faithful, he had never seen into the fountain, and so lost his friend and mistress.

EUM. Thine own thoughts, sweet [350 Semele, witness against thy words, for what hast thou found in my life but love? And as yet what have I found in my love but bitterness? Madam, pardon Semele, and let my tongue ransom hers.

CYNTH. Thy tongue, Eumenides? What, shouldst thou live wanting a tongue to blaze the beauty of Semele? Well, Semele, I will not command love, for it cannot be enforced; let me entreat it.   360

SEM. I am content your highness shall command, for now only do I think Eumenides faithful, that is willing to lose his tongue for my sake; yet loath, because it should do me better service. Madam, I accept of Eumenides.

CYNTH. I thank you, Semele.

EUM. Ah, happy Eumenides, that hast a friend so faithful and a mistress so fair! With what sudden mischief will the [370 gods daunt this excess of joy? Sweet Semele, I live or die as thou wilt.

CYNTH. What shall become of Tellus? Tellus, you know Endymion is vowed to a service from which death cannot remove him. Corsites casteth still a lovely [1] look towards you. How say you, will you have your Corsites, and so receive pardon for all that is past?

TELLUS. Madam, most willingly.   380

CYNTH. But I cannot tell whether Corsites be agreed.

CORS. Ay, madam, more happy to enjoy Tellus than the monarchy of the world.

EUM. Why, she caused you to be pinched with fairies!

CORS. Ay, but her fairness hath pinched my heart more deeply.

CYNTH. Well, enjoy thy love. But what have you wrought in the castle, [390 Tellus?

TELLUS. Only the picture of Endymion.

CYNTH. Then so much of Endymion as his picture cometh to, possess and play withal.

CORS. Ah, my sweet Tellus, my love shall be as thy beauty is, matchless.

CYNTH. Now it resteth, Dipsas, that if thou wilt forswear that vile art of enchanting, Geron hath promised again to re- [400 ceive thee; otherwise, if thou be wedded to that wickedness, I must and will see it punished to the uttermost.

DIPSAS. Madam, I renounce both substance and shadow of that most horrible and hateful trade, vowing to the gods continual penance, and to your highness obedience.

CYNTH. How say you, Geron? Will you admit her to your wife?   410

GER. Ay, with more joy than I did the first day, for nothing could happen to make me happy but only her forsaking

[1] Loving.

that lewd [1] and detestable course. Dipsas, I embrace thee.

DIPSAS. And I thee, Geron, to whom I will hereafter recite the cause of these my first follies.

CYNTH. Well, Endymion, nothing resteth now but that we depart. Thou hast my favor; Tellus her friend; Eumenides [421 in paradise with his Semele; Geron contented with Dipsas.

TOP. Nay, soft; I cannot handsomely go to bed without Bagoa.

CYNTH. Well, Sir Tophas, it may be there are more virtues in me than myself knoweth of, for Endymion I awaked, and at my words he waxed young. I will try whether I can turn this tree again to [430 thy true love.

TOP. Turn her to a true love or false, so she be a wench I care not.

CYNTH. Bagoa, Cynthia putteth an end to thy hard fortunes; for, being turned to a tree for revealing a truth, I will recover thee again, if in my power be the effect of truth.   [Bagoa recovers human shape.]

TOP. Bagoa, a bots [2] upon thee!

CYNTH. Come, my lords, let us in. [440 You, Gyptes and Pythagoras, if you can content yourselves in our court, to fall from vain follies of philosophers to such virtues as are here practiced, you shall be entertained according to your deserts, for Cynthia is no stepmother to strangers.

[1] Base.   [2] Worms.

PYTHAG. I had rather in Cynthia's court spend ten years than in Greece one hour.

GYPTES. And I choose rather to [450 live by the sight of Cynthia than by the possessing of all Egypt.

CYNTH. Then follow.

EUM. We all attend.   Exeunt.

FINIS.

THE EPILOGUE

A MAN walking abroad, the Wind and Sun strove for sovereignty, the one with his blast, the other with his beams. The Wind blew hard; the man wrapped his garment about him harder. It blustered more strongly; he then girt it fast to him. "I cannot prevail," said the Wind. The Sun, casting her crystal beams, began to warm the man; he unloosed his gown. Yet it shined brighter; he then put it [10 off. "I yield," said the Wind, "for, if thou continue shining, he will also put off his coat."

Dread sovereign, the malicious that seek to overthrow us with threats do but stiffen our thoughts and make them sturdier in storms; but, if your highness vouchsafe with your favorable beams to glance upon us, we shall not only stoop, but with all humility lay both our hands and [20 hearts at your majesty's feet.

GEORGE PEELE

George Peele was born about 1558, and was educated at the grammar school of Christ's Hospital, of which his father James Peele, a maker of pageants, was clerk, and at Oxford, where he proceeded B.A. in 1577 and M.A. in 1579. When he returned to Oxford on business in 1583, two years after his departure for London, he was called upon to manage the performance of two Latin plays by William Gager for the entertainment of Alasco, a Polish prince, and in two sets of Latin elegiacs Gager commended Peele as wit and poet. The rest of his life was apparently spent in literary work in London among such friends as Greene, Lodge, Nashe, and Watson. Like other convivial spirits among the literary men of the time, Peele seems to have been given to excesses. These probably hastened his end, and were no doubt responsible for the ascription to him of a series of escapades and sayings, chiefly fabulous in all likelihood, which furnished material for the *Jests of George Peele*, published about 1605. He was buried in the Parish of St. James, Clerkenwell, November 9, 1596.

Peele's extant work is predominantly dramatic. His first play, *The Arraignment of Paris*, was prepared for boys and acted before Elizabeth. Its poetic fancy, like the wit and conceit of Lyly's prose dialogue, made its appeal to courtly taste. Nashe in the preface to Greene's *Menaphon* (1589) declares that it reveals the "pregnant dexterity of wit and manifold variety of invention" of Peele, whom he calls the great maker of phrases ("*primum verborum artifex*"). Peele was soon writing for the companies of professional players, and had his share, with other University Wits, in transforming the crude popular drama of the London stage into literary drama. His great contribution lay in his poetic diction, but with his fellows he experimented in the various types of plays in vogue between 1585 and 1595. In addition to the two plays reprinted here, Peele wrote the crude chronicle play of *King Edward the First*, published in mutilated form in 1593 and 1599; *The Battle of Alcazar*, which, although it was published anonymously in 1594, is generally recognized as Peele's from internal evidence and from the fact that six lines from it were printed as his in *England's Parnassus* (1600); and *The Love of King David and Fair Bethsabe*, published in 1599, regarding the merit of whose ornate verse there is a wide range of opinion. He also wrote several plays now lost and verse for London pageants.

The masque-like pastoral, *The Arraignment of Paris*, often considered Peele's best play, was published anonymously, and apparently without entry in the Stationers' Register, by Henry Marsh in 1584. Its authorship is established by Nashe's allusion in the preface to *Menaphon* and by the attribution of two of its songs to Peele in *England's Parnassus*. From the Greek myth of Paris' award of the golden apple, used by Udall to flatter Anne Boleyn, Peele fashioned an elaborate compliment to her daughter Elizabeth. No specific source has been found for the play, but Peele followed pastoral traditions. He is indebted to Spenser's *Shepherd's Calendar* for the names of the shepherds, and, as Miss Jeffrey has shown, to Paulilli's *Il Giudizio di Paride* for many conventional devices. The present text is based on the Malone Society reprint prepared by Child.

The Old Wives' Tale was entered in the Stationers' Register, April 16, 1595, and printed by John Danter the same year. The identification of the initials "G. P." on the title-page as those of George Peele, which was made by Herbert in *Typographical Antiquities*, has never been challenged. The date of composition is usually thought to lie between 1590 and 1593, but recently Larsen has argued for a date between January, 1593, and May, 1594. The play is essentially a medley of motives and incidents drawn from folk tales. Thus the main incident of the pursuit of Delia and her rescue from the conjuror gives the earliest extant version of a tale found also in a section of Christopher Middleton's *Chinon of England* (1597) and in Milton's *Comus*. All three are modified forms of the folk tale *Childe Rowland*, in which the youngest of three brothers rescues his sister from the elf king after the other two have failed. In the play the successful brother is replaced by a suitor and his helper, who come from a tale of "The Lady and the Monster" type. Peele probably followed some form of it closely, for the main incidents and most of the details of the Eumenides plot appear in one version or another of a modern folk tale which is best known as one of the components of *Jack the Giant Killer*. A stock motive in the tale of this type is that of "The Grateful Dead," which Peele used in its most conventional form—the ghostly helper exacting a promise of half the hero's gains and as a test of loyalty demanding that the rescued lady be cut in two. In this form the motive is found, much earlier than the play, in *Oliver of Castile*, translated from French and printed in England in 1518. Still another folk tale introduced into the play is *The Three Heads of the Well*, with its contrasted sisters, which is linked to the main thread by the marriage of the sisters to two who have failed in the quest for Delia. While Peele possibly found many of these various incidents already combined in some folk tale which he followed, evidently he made modifications in details. For instance, the contrast between the husbands of the two sisters in *The Three Heads of the Well* has been subordinated in the play to the treatment of them as stock comic figures, one a clown and the other a braggart. Though the induction, as in *The Taming of the Shrew* and *The Knight of the Burning Pestle*, satirizes the taste of the audience, its primary purpose here is to indicate the source of the material in folk tale. The name Sacrapant and some of the lines in the play came from Greene's *Orlando Furioso*, derived from Ariosto. The present text is based on W. W. Greg's reprint for the Malone Society.

THE ARRAIGNMENT OF PARIS[1]

[BY

GEORGE PEELE

DRAMATIS PERSONÆ

SATURN	JUNO
JUPITER	PALLAS
NEPTUNE	VENUS
PLUTO	DIANA
APOLLO	POMONA
MARS	FLORA
BACCHUS	RHANIS
MERCURY	ATE
VULCAN	CLOTHO
PAN	LACHESIS
FAUNUS	ATROPOS
SILVANUS	THE MUSES
PARIS	A NYMPH OF DIANA
COLIN	ŒNONE
HOBBINOL	HELEN
DIGGON	THESTYLIS
THENOT	

CUPIDS, CYCLOPS, SHEPHERDS, KNIGHTS, A
CHURL, etc.

SCENE: *A vale in Ida.*

TIME: *Mythical.*]

Ate, Prologus.[2]

Condemnéd soul, Ate, from lowest hell
And deadly rivers of the infernal Jove,
Where bloodless ghosts in pains of endless
    date
Fill ruthless ears with never-ceasing cries,
Behold, I come in place, and bring beside
The bane of Troy! Behold, the fatal fruit,
Raught[3] from the golden tree of Proser-
    pine!
Proud Troy must fall, so bid the gods
    above,
And stately Ilium's lofty towers be razed
By conquering hands of the victorious
    foe;   10
King Priam's palace waste with flaming fire,
Whose thick and foggy smoke, piercing
    the sky,

Must serve for messenger of sacrifice,
T' appease the anger of the angry heav-
    ens;
And Priam's younger son, the shepherd
    swain,
Paris, th' unhappy organ[4] of the Greeks.
So loath and weary of her heavy load,
The Earth complains unto the hellish
    prince,
Surchargéd with the burden that she
    nill[5] sustain.
Th' unpartial daughters of Necessity   20
Bin aides[6] in her suit; and so the twine
That holds old Priam's house, the thread
    of Troy,
Dame Atropos with knife in sunder cuts.
Done be the pleasure of the powers above,

---

[1] The original title continues: "A Pastoral.
Presented before the Queen's Majesty by the
Children of Her Chapel."
[2] *I.e.*, speaking as Prologue.
[3] Reached, taken.

[4] Provocation (?).
[5] Will not.
[6] Are aids. Such archaisms as these plurals
(with the final *-es* here pronounced as a syllable)
are fairly common throughout the play to represent shepherds' speech.

Whose hests [1] men must obey; and I my
   part
Perform in Ida vales. Lordings, adieu;
Imposing silence for your task, I end,
Till just assembly of the goddesses
Make me begin the tragedy of Troy.
        Exit Ate cum aureo pomo. [2]

Act[us] I. Scena i.

[*A vale in Ida.*] [3]

Pan, Faunus, and Silvanus, with their At-
tendants, enter to give welcome to the
Goddesses. Pan's Shepherd hath a lamb,
Faunus' Hunter hath a fawn, Silvanus'
Woodman with an oaken bough laden
with acorns.

Pan incipit. [4]

Pan. Silvanus, either Flora doth us
   wrong
Or Faunus made us tarry all too long,
For by this morning mirth it should
   appear
The Muses or the goddesses be near.
Faun. My fawn was nimble, Pan, and
   whipped apace—
'Twas happy that we caught him up
   at last—
The fattest, fairest fawn in all the chase;
I wonder how the knave could skip so
   fast.
Pan. And I have brought a twagger for
   the nonce, [5]
A bunting [6] lamb; nay, pray, you feel
   no bones.   10
Believe me now, my cunning much I
   miss
If ever Pan felt fatter lamb than this.
Sil. Sirs, you may boast your flocks and
   herds that bin both fresh and fair,
Yet hath Silvanus walks, [7] iwis, [8] that
   stand in wholesome air;
And, lo, the honor of the woods, the
   gallant oaken bough,
Do I bestow, laden with acorns and with
   mast enow! [9]

Pan. Peace, man, for shame! Shalt have
   both lambs and dams and flocks and
   herds and all,
And all my pipes to make the[e] glee;
   we meet not now to brawl.
Faun. There's no such matter, Pan! We
   are all friends assembled hether, [10]
To bid Queen Juno and her feres [11]
   most humbly welcome hether.   20
Diana, mistress of our woods, her presence will not want; [12]
Her courtesy to all her friends, we wot, [13]
   is nothing scant.

Act[us] I. Scena ii.

Pomona entereth with her fruit. Manenti-
bus Pan cum reliquis. [14]

Pom. Yea, Pan, no farther yet, and had
   the start of me?
Why, then, Pomona with her fruit comes
   time enough, I see.
Come on awhile; with country store,
   like friends, we venter [15] forth.
Thinkest, Faunus, that these goddesses
   will take our gifts in worth? [16]
Faun. Yea, doubtless, for shall tell thee,
   dame, 'twere better give a thing,
A sign of love, unto a mighty person or
   a king,
Than to a rude and barbarous swain,
   but bad and basely born;
For gently takes the gentleman that [17]
   oft the clown will scorn.
Pan. Say'st truly, Faunus. I myself
   have given good tidy [18] lambs
To Mercury—may say to thee—to Phœbus, and to Jove,   10
When to a country mops, [19] forsooth,
   chave [20] offered all their dams,
And piped and prayed for little worth.
   and ranged about the grove.
Pom. God Pan, that makes your flock so
   thin, and makes you look so lean,
To kiss in corners.

---

[1] Behests, commands.
[2] Ate goes out with the golden apple.
[3] The setting is the same throughout the play
[4] Pan begins.
[5] A male lamb for the occasion.
[6] With budding horns.   [8] Certainly.
[7] Tracts of forest.   [9] Nuts enough.

[10] Hither.   [12] Be lacking.
[11] Companions.   [13] Know.
[14] Pan with the others remaining.
[15] Venture.
[16] "In good part" (Bullen).
[17] That which.
[18] Plump; fit for sacrifice.
[19] Wench, from Mopsa, a common name for a
shepherdess or a rustic girl.
[20] Dialect for *ich have*, I have.

PAN.   Well said, wench! Some other
thing you mean.

POM. Yea, jest it out till it go alone; but
marvel where we miss
Fair Flora all this merry morn.

FAUN.   Some news; see where she is.

ACT[US] I. SCENA iii.

Flora entereth to the country gods.

PAN. Flora, well met, and for thy taken
pain,
Poor country gods, thy debtors we remain.

FLO. Believe me, Pan, not all thy lambs
and yoes,[1]
Nor, Faunus, all thy lusty bucks and
does
(But that I am instructed well to know
What service to the hills and dales I
owe)
Could have enforced me to so strange a
toil,
Thus to enrich this gaudy, gallant [2] soil.

FAUN. But tell me, wench, hast done't
so trick [3] indeed
That heaven itself may wonder at the
deed?   10

FLO. Not Iris, in her pride and bravery,[4]
Adorns her arch [5] with such variety,
Nor doth the milk-white way in frosty
night
Appear so fair and beautiful in sight
As done [6] these fields and groves and
sweetest bowers,
Bestrewed and decked with parti-colored
flowers.
Along the bubbling brooks and silver
glide [7]
That at the bottom doth in silence
slide,
The watery flowers and lilies on the
banks,
Like blazing comets, burgeon all in
ranks;   20
Under the hawthorn and the poplar
tree,
Where sacred Phœbe may delight to be,
The primrose and the purple hyacinth,
The dainty violet and the wholesome
minth,[8]

The double daisy and the cowslip, queen
Of summer flowers, do overpeer the
green;
And round about the valley as ye pass,
Ye may ne [9] see for peeping flowers the
grass—
That [10] well the mighty Juno and the
rest   29
May boldly think to be a welcome guest
On Ida hills, when to approve the thing
The Queen of Flowers prepares a second
spring.

SIL. Thou gentle nymph, what thanks
shall we repay
To thee that makest our fields and
woods so gay?

FLO. Silvanus, when it is thy hap to see,
My workmanship in portraying all the
three—
First stately Juno with her port and
grace,
Her robes, her lawns, her crownet,[11] and
her mace—
Would make thee muse [12] this picture
to behold
Of yellow oxlips bright as burnished
gold.   40

POM. A rare device; and Flora well, perdy,[13]
Did paint her yellow for her jealousy.

FLO. Pallas in flowers of hue and colors
red,
Her plumes, her helm, her lance, her
Gorgon's head,
Her trailing tresses that hang flaring
round,
Of July flowers so grafféd [14] in the ground
That, trust me, sirs, who did the cun-
ning see,
Would at a blush [15] suppose it to be
she.

PAN. Good Flora, by my flock, 'twere
very good
To dight [16] her all in red resembling
blood.   50

FLO. Fair Venus of sweet violets in blue,
With other flowers infixed for change
of hue;
Her plumes, her pendants, bracelets,
and her rings,
Her dainty fan, and twenty other things,

---

[1] Ewes.   [3] Neatly.
[2] Excellent.   [4] Finery.
[5] Rainbow, personified in Iris.
[6] Do, an archaic plural.   [7] Current.   [8] Mint.

[9] Not.   [13] *Par Dieu.*
[10] So that.   [14] Grafted.
[11] Coronet.   [15] Glance.
[12] Marvel.   [16] Dress.

Her lusty mantle waving in the wind,
And every part in color and in kind;[1]
And for her wreath of roses, she nill
dare
With Flora's cunning counterfeit com-
pare;
So that what living wight shall chance
to see
These goddesses, each placed in her
degree, 60
Portrayed by Flora's workmanship alone,
Must say that art and nature met in
one.

SIL. A dainty draught [2] to lay her down
in blue,
The color commonly betokening "true."

FLO. This piece of work, compact with
many a flower,
And well laid in at entrance of the
bower,
Where Phœbe means to make this meeting royal,
Have I prepared to welcome them
withal.

POM. And are they yet dismounted, Flora,
say,
That we may wend to meet them on
the way? 70

FLO. That shall not need. They are at
hand by this,
And the conductor of the train hight [3]
Rhanis.
Juno hath left her chariot long ago,
And hath returned her peacocks by her
rainbow,
And bravely, as becomes the wife of
Jove,
Doth honor by her presence to our
grove.
Fair Venus she hath let her sparrows
fly,
To tend on her and make her melody;
Her turtles [4] and her swans unyokéd
be,
And flicker near her side for company. 80
Pallas hath set her tigers loose to
feed,
Commanding them to wait when she
hath need.
And hitherward with proud and stately
pace,
To do us honor in the sylvan chase,

They march, like to the pomp of heaven
above,
Juno, the wife and sister of King Jove,
The warlike Pallas, and the Queen of
Love.

PAN. Pipe, Pan, for joy, and let thy shepherds sing;
Shall never age forget this memorable
thing.

FLO. Clio, the sagest of the Sisters Nine, 90
To do observance to this dame divine,
Lady of learning and of chivalry,
Is here arrived in fair assembly;[5]
And, wand'ring up and down th' un-
beaten ways,
Ring through the wood sweet songs of
Pallas' praise.

POM. Hark, Flora, Faunus! Here is melody,
A charm [6] of birds, and more than ordinary.

*An artificial charm of birds being heard
within, Pan speaks.*

PAN. The silly [7] birds make mirth; then
should we do them wrong,
Pomona, if we nill bestow an echo to
their song. *An echo to their song.*

THE SONG

(A choir within and without.)

GODS. O Ida, O Ida, O Ida, happy hill! 100
This honor done to Ida, may it continue
still!

MUSES. [*Within.*] Ye country gods that in
this Ida wone,[8]
Bring down your gifts of welcome,
For honor done to Ida.

GODS. Behold, in sign of joy we sing,
And signs of joyful welcome bring,
For honor done to Ida.

MUSES. [*Within.*] The Muses give you melody to gratulate this chance,[9]
And Phœbe, chief of sylvan chase, commands you all to dance.

GODS. (*Dance.*) Then[10] round in a circle our
sportance must be; 110
Hold hands in a hornpipe, all gallant in
glee.

MUSES. [*Within.*] Reverence, reverence,
most humble reverence!

GODS. Most humble reverence!

---

[1] *I.e.*, suitable and natural.
[2] Rare device in painting.
[3] Is called.
[4] Turtledoves.
[5] Last syllable pronounced as two.
[6] Chorus.
[7] Simple.
[8] Dwell.
[9] To greet this occasion.
[10] Original reads *the.*

Act[us] I. Scena iv.

Pallas, Juno, and Venus enter, Rhanis lead-
ing the way.   Pan alone sings.

The Song

The god of shepherds and his mates
With country cheer salutes your states,
Fair, wise, and worthy as you be,
And thank the gracious ladies three
    For honor done to Ida. *The birds sing.*

The song being done, Juno speaks.

Juno. Venus, what shall I say?   For,
    though I be a dame divine,
This welcome and this melody exceeds
    these wits of mine.
Ven. Believe me, Juno, as I hight the
    Sovereign of Love,
These rare delights in pleasures pass the
    banquets of King Jove.
Pal. Then, Venus, I conclude, it easily
    may be seen   10
That in her chaste and pleasant walks
    fair Phœbe is a queen.
Rha. Divine Pallas, and you sacred
    dames,
Juno and Venus, honored by your
    names,
Juno, the wife and sister of King Jove,
Fair Venus, lady-president of love,
If any entertainment in this place
That can afford but homely, rude, and
    base,
It please your godheads to accept in
    gree,[1]
That gracious thought our happiness
    shall be.
My mistress Dian, this right well I
    know,   20
For love that to this presence she doth
    owe,
Accounts more honor done to her this
    day
Than ever whilom [2] in these woods of
    Ida.
And for our country gods, I dare be
    bold,
They make such cheer, your presence
    to behold,
Such jouissance,[3] such mirth, and merri-
    ment,

As nothing else their mind might more
    content.
And that you do believe it to be so,
Fair goddesses, your lovely looks do
    show.
It rests in fine, for to confirm my talk,   30
Ye deign to pass along to Dian's walk,
Where she among her troop of maids
    attends
The fair arrival of her welcome friends.
Flo. And we will wait with all observ-
    ance due,
And do just honor to this heavenly crew.
Pan. The god of shepherds, Juno, ere thou
    go,
Intends a lamb on thee for to bestow.
Faun. Faunus, high ranger in Diana's
    chase,
Presents a fawn to Lady Venus' grace.
Sil. Silvanus gives to Pallas' deity   40
This gallant bough raught from the
    oaken tree.
Pom. To them that doth this honor to
    our fields
Her mellow apples poor Pomona yields.
Juno. And, gentle gods, these signs of
    your good will
We take in worth, and shall accept them
    still.
Ven. And, Flora, this to thee among the
    rest:
Thy workmanship comparing with the
    best,
Let it suffice thy cunning to have [pow-
    er] [4]
To call King Jove from forth his heavenly
    bower.
Hadst thou a lover, Flora, credit me,   50
I think thou wouldst bedeck him gal-
    lantly.
But wend we on; and, Rhanis, lead the
    way,
That kens the painted paths of pleasant
    Ida.   *Exeunt omnes.*

Act[us] I. Scena v et Ultima.[5]

Paris and Œnone.

Par. Œnone, while [6] we bin disposed to
    walk,
Tell me what shall be subject of our
    talk.

---

[1] With good will.   [2] Formerly.   [3] Jollity.

[4] Suggested by Dyce.   [5] And last.   [6] Until.

Thou hast a sort [1] of pretty tales in
store;
Dare say no nymph in Ida woods hath
more.
Again, beside thy sweet alluring face,
In telling them thou hast a special
grace.
Then, prithee, sweet, afford some pretty
thing,
Some toy that from thy pleasant wit
doth spring.
ŒN. Paris, my heart's contentment and
my choice,
Use thou thy pipe, and I will use my
voice;   10
So shall thy just request not be denied,
And time well spent, and both be satis-
fied.
PAR. Well, gentle nymph, although thou
do me wrong,
That can ne tune my pipe unto a song,
Me list [2] this once, Œnone, for thy sake,
This idle task on me to undertake.
    They sit under a tree together.
ŒN. And whereon, then, shall be my
roundelay?
For thou hast heard my store long since,
dare say: [3]
How Saturn did divide his kingdom
tho [4]
To Jove, to Neptune, and to Dis be-
low;   20
How mighty men made foul successless
war
Against the gods and state of Jupiter;
How Phorcys' imp, that was so trick
and fair,
That tangled Neptune in her golden
hair,
Became a Gorgon for her lewd misdeed—
A pretty fable, Paris, for to read,
A piece of cunning, trust me, for the
nonce,
That wealth and beauty alter men to
stones;
How Salmacis, resembling idleness,
Turns men to women all through wan-
tonness;   30
How Pluto raught Queen Ceres' daughter
thence

And what did follow of that love-offense;
Of Daphne turned into the laurel tree,
That shows a mirror of virginity;
Now fair Narcissus, tooting on his shade, [5]
Reproves disdain, and tells how form
doth vade; [6]
How cunning Philomela's needle tells
What force in love, what wit in sorrow
dwells;
What pains unhappy souls abide in
hell,
They say, because on earth they lived
not well—   40
Ixion's wheel, proud Tantal's pining
woe,
Prometheus' torment, and a many mo; [7]
How Danaus' daughters ply their end-
less task;
What toil the toil of Sisyphus doth
ask.
All these are old and known, I know;
yet if thou wilt have any,
Choose some of these, for, trust me,
else Œnone hath not many.
PAR. Nay, what thou wilt; but, sith [8] my
cunning not compares with thine,
Begin some toy [9] that I can play upon
this pipe of mine.
ŒN. There is a pretty sonnet, [10] then—
we call it "Cupid's Curse:"   49
"They that do change old love for
new, pray gods they change for worse!"
The note is fine and quick withal; the
ditty will agree,
Paris, with that same vow of thine upon
our poplar tree.
PAR. No better thing; begin it then.
Œnone, thou shalt see
Our music figure of [11] the love that grows
twixt thee and me.
They sing, and, while Œnone singeth, he
    pipeth. Incipit Œnone.

ŒN. Fair and fair, and twice so fair,
    As fair as any may be,
The fairest shepherd on our green,
    A love for any lady.
PAR. Fair and fair, and twice so far,
    As fair as any may be,   60
Thy love is fair for thee alone,
    And for no other lady.

---

[1] Collection.   [2] It pleases me.
[3] Original has *Fabula* in margin here, and the
following thirteen stories are numbered.
[4] Then.

[5] Gazing on his reflection.   [7] More.
[6] Fade, vanish.   [8] Since.
[9] Trifle, here a light musical air.
[10] Song.   [11] Portray.

Œn. My love is fair, my love is gay,
　　As fresh as bin the flowers in May,
　　And of my love my roundelay,
　　My merry, merry, merry roundelay,
　　　Concludes with Cupid's curse:
　　They that do change old love for new,
　　　Pray gods they change for worse!
Ambo simul.[1] They that do change, etc. 70
Œn. Fair and fair, etc.
Par. Fair and fair, etc. Thy love is fair,
　　etc.

Œn. My love can pipe, my love can sing,
　　My love can many a pretty thing,
　　And of his lovely praises ring
　　My merry, merry roundelays;
　　　Amen to Cupid's curse:
　　They that do change, etc.
Par. They that do change, etc.
Ambo. Fair and fair, etc. *Finis camenæ.*[2]

*The song being ended, they rise, and Œnone
　　　　　　　　　　　　　　　　　speaks.*

Œn. Sweet shepherd, for Œnone's sake
　　be cunning[3] in this song,　　　　81
　And keep thy love, and love thy choice,
　　or else thou dost her wrong.
Par. My vow is made and witnessèd;
　　the poplar will not start,[4]
　Nor shall the nymph Œnone's love from
　　forth my breathing heart.
　I will go bring thee on thy way, my
　　flock are here behind,
　And I will have a lover's fee; they say,
　　"Unkissed, unkind."　　*Exeunt ambo.*

Act[us] II. Scena i.

Venus, Juno, Pallas.

Ven. (*Ex abrupto.*[5]) But pray you, tell
　　me, Juno, was it so,
　As Pallas told me here the tale of Echo?
Jun. She was a nymph indeed, as Pallas
　　tells,
　A walker,[6] such as in these thickets
　　dwells;
　And as she told what subtle, juggling
　　pranks
　She played with Juno, so she told her
　　thanks:[7]

A tattling trull to come at every call,
And now, forsooth, nor tongue nor life
　　at all.
And, though perhaps she was a help to
　　Jove,
And held me chat[8] while he might court
　　his love,　　　　　　　　　　　　10
Believe me, dames, I am of this opinion,
He took but little pleasure in the minion;
And whatsoe'er his scapes[9] have been
　　beside,
Dare say for him, a[10] never strayed so
　　wide.
A lovely nut-brown lass or lusty trull
Have power perhaps to make a god a
　　bull.
Ven. Gramercy, gentle Juno, for that
　　jest;
　I'faith, that item was worth all the rest.
Pal. No matter, Venus, howsoe'er you
　　scorn,
　My father Jove at that time ware the
　　horn.[11]　　　　　　　　　　　　20
Jun. Had every wanton god above, Venus,
　　not better luck,
　Then heaven would be a pleasant park,
　　and Mars a lusty buck.
Ven. Tut, Mars hath horns to butt withal,
　　although no bull a shows.
　A never needs to mask in nets; a fears
　　no jealous froes.[12]
Jun. Forsooth the better is his turn, for,
　　if a speak too loud,
　Must find some shift to shadow him, a
　　net or else a cloud.
Pal. No more of this, fair goddesses; un-
　　rip not so your shames,
　To stand all naked to the world, that
　　been such heavenly dames.
Jun. Nay, Pallas, that's a common trick
　　with Venus, well we know;
　And all the gods in heaven have seen her
　　naked long ago.　　　　　　　　30
Ven. And then she was so fair and bright,
　　and lovely and so trim,
　As Mars is but for Venus' tooth,[13] and
　　she will sport with him.
　And, but me list not here to make com-
　　parison with Jove,
　Mars is no ranger, Juno, he, in every
　　open grove.

---

[1] Both together.
[2] The end of the song.
[3] Skillful, expert.
[4] *I.e.*, tremble in token of a false vow.
[5] Abruptly.
[6] Forest-dweller.
[7] An ironical phrase for *dismissed her.*

[8] In conversation.　　[9] Escapades.　　[10] He.
[11] Wore the horn—the proverbial sign of the
cuckold.　　[12] Women.　　[13] Taste, pleasure.

Pal. Too much of this! We wander far; the skies begin to scowl.

Retire we to Diana's bower; the weather will be foul.

The storm being past of thunder and lightning, and Ate having trundled the ball into place, crying, "Fatum Trojæ," [1] *Juno taketh the ball up and speaketh.*

Jun. Pallas, the storm is past and gone, and Phœbus clears the skies,

And, lo, behold a ball of gold, a fair and worthy prize!

Ven. [*Reading.*] This posy [2] wills the apple to the fairest given be;

Then is it mine, for Venus hight the fairest of the three.   40

Pal. The fairest here, as fair is meant, am I; ye do me wrong;

And, if the fairest have it must, to me it doth belong.

Jun. Then Juno may it not enjoy, so everyone says no;

But I will prove myself the fairest, ere I lose it so.   *They read the posy.*

The brief [3] is this, *Detur pulcherrimæ*—

Let this unto the fairest given be,

The fairest of the three—and I am she.

Pal. (*Reads.*) *Detur pulcherrimæ*—

Let this unto the fairest given be,

The fairest of the three—and I am she. 50

Ven. (*Reads.*) *Detur pulcherrimæ*—

Let this unto the fairest given be,

The fairest of the three—and I am she.

Jun. My face is fair; but yet the majesty

That all the gods in heaven have seen in me

Have made them choose me of the planets seven

To be the wife of Jove and Queen of Heaven;

If then this prize be but bequeathed to beauty,

The only she that wins this prize am I.

Ven. That Venus is the fairest, this doth prove: 60

That Venus is the lovely Queen of Love.

The name of Venus is indeed but beauty,

And men me fairest call per excellency; [4]

If then this prize be but bequeathed to beauty,

The only she that wins this prize am I.

Pal. To stand on terms of beauty as you take it,

Believe me, ladies, is but to mistake it.

The beauty that this subtle prize must win,

No outward beauty hight, but dwells within;

And sift it as you please, and you shall find   70

This beauty is the beauty of the mind.

This fairness, Virtue hight in general,

That many branches hath in special;

This beauty Wisdom hight, whereof am I

By heaven appointed goddess worthily.

And look, how much the mind, the better part,

Doth overpass the body in desert, [5]

So much the mistress of those gifts divine

Excels thy beauty, and that state of thine.

Then, if this prize be thus bequeathed to beauty,   80

The only she that wins this prize am I.

Ven. Nay, Pallas, by your leave you wander clean.

We must not conster [6] hereof as you mean,

But take the sense as it is plainly meant;

And let the fairest ha't, I am content.

Pal. Our reasons will be infinite, I trow,

Unless unto some other point we grow.

But first here's none, methinks, disposed to yield,

And none but will with words maintain the field.

Jun. Then, if you will, to avoid a tedious grudge,   90

Refer it to the sentence of a judge;

Whoe'er he be that cometh next in place,

Let him bestow the ball and end the case.

Ven. So can it not go wrong with me at all. [7]

Pal. I am agreed, however it befall.

And yet by common doom, [8] so may it be,

I may be said the fairest of the three.

Jun. Then yonder, lo, that shepherd swain is he,

That must be umpire in this controversy!

---

[1] The fate of Troy.   [3] Writing.
[2] Inscription.   [4] Above all.

[5] Pronounced *desart.*   [6] Construe.
[7] Emended by Dyce. Original reads *not at all.*
[8] Judgment.

Act[us] II. Scena ii.

Paris alone. Manentibus Pal[lade], Junone,
Venere.

Ven. Juno, in happy time, I do accept
the man;
　It seemeth by his looks some skill of
　love he can.[1]
Par. [*Aside.*] The nymph is gone, and I,
all solitary,
　Must wend to tend my charge, oppressed
　with melancholy.
　This day (or else me fails my shepherd's
　skill)
　Will tide [2] me passing good or passing ill.
Jun. Shepherd, abash not, though at sud-
den thus
　Thou be arrived by ignorance among us,
　Not earthly but divine, and goddesses
　all three;
　Juno, Pallas, Venus, these our titles be. 10
　Nor fear to speak for reverence of the
　place,
　Chosen to end a hard and doubtful case.
　This apple, lo (nor ask thou whence it
　came),
　Is to be given unto the fairest dame.
　And fairest is, nor she, nor she, but she
　Whom, shepherd, thou shalt fairest name
　to be.
　This is thy charge; fulfill without of-
　fense,
　And she that wins shall give thee recom-
　pense.
Pal. Dread not to speak, for we have
chosen thee,
　Sith in this case we can no judges be.   20
Ven. And, shepherd, say that I the fair-
est am,
　And thou shalt win good guerdon for
　the same.
Jun. Nay, shepherd, look upon my stately
grace,
　Because the pomp that longs [3] to Juno's
　mace
　Thou mayst not see; and think Queen
　Juno's name,
　To whom old shepherds title works of
　fame,[4]
　Is mighty, and may easily suffice,
　At Phœbus' hand, to gain a golden prize.

---

[1] Knows.　　[2] Betide, befall.　　[3] Belongs.
[4] *I.e.*, to whom old poets address famous
works.

And for thy meed, sith I am queen of
riches,
Shepherd, I will reward thee with great
monarchies,   30
Empires, and kingdoms, heaps of massy
gold,
Scepters and diadems curious to behold,
Rich robes, of sumptuous workman-
ship and cost,
And thousand things whereof I make
no boast.
The mold whereon thou treadest shall
be of Tagus' sands,
And Xanthus shall run liquid gold for
thee to wash thy hands;
And, if thou like to tend thy flock, and
not from them to fly,
Their fleeces shall be curléd gold to
please their master's eye.
And last, to set thy heart on fire, give
this one fruit to me,
And, shepherd, lo, this tree of gold will
I bestow on thee!   40

Juno's Show

Hereupon did rise a tree of gold, laden
with diadems and crowns of gold.

The ground whereon it grows, the grass,
the root of gold,
The body and the bark of gold, all
glist'ring to behold,
The leaves of burnished gold, the fruits
that thereon grow
Are diadems set with pearl in gold, in
gorgeous glist'ring show:
And, if this tree of gold in lieu may not
suffice,
Require a grove of golden trees, so Juno
bear the prize.   *The tree sinketh.*
Pal. Me list not tempt thee with decaying
wealth,
Which is embased by want of lusty
health;
But, if thou have a mind to fly above,
Ycrowned [5] with fame, near to the seat
of Jove,   50
If thou aspire to wisdom's worthiness,
Whereof thou mayst not see the bright-
ness,
If thou desire honor of chivalry,
To be renowned for happy victory,
To fight it out, and in the champaign [6]
field

---

[5] Old form of the past participle.　　[6] Open.

To shroud thee under Pallas' warlike
  shield,
To prance on barbéd steeds—this honor,
  lo,
Myself for guerdon shall on thee bestow!
And for encouragement, that thou mayst
  see
What famous knights Dame Pallas'
  warriors be,   60
Behold in Pallas' honor here they come,
Marching along with sound of thund'-
  ring drum.

PALLAS' SHOW

*Hereupon did enter nine Knights in armor,
  treading a warlike almain,[1] by drum and
  fife, and then having marched forth again,
  Venus speaketh.*

VEN. Come, shepherd, come, sweet shep-
  herd, look on me;
These been too hot alarums,[2] these, for
  thee.
But, if thou wilt give me the golden
  ball,
Cupid my boy shall ha't to play withal,
That, whensoe'er this apple he shall see,
The God of Love himself shall think
  on thee,
And bid thee look and choose, and he
  will wound
Whereso thy fancy's [3] object shall be
  found;   70
And lightly when he shoots he doth
  not miss.
And I will give thee many a lovely kiss,
And come and play with thee on Ida
  here;
And, if thou wilt a face that hath no peer,
A gallant girl, a lusty minion trull,
That can give sport to thee thy belly-
  ful,
To ravish all thy beating veins with
  joy,
Here is a lass of Venus' court, my boy,

Helen ent'reth with four Cupids.

Here, gentle shepherd, here's for thee
  a piece,
The fairest face, the flower of gallant
  Greece.   80

---

[1] Dance.   [2] Calls to arms.   [3] Love's.

VENUS' SHOW

*Here Helen ent'reth in her bravery, with four
  Cupids attending on her, each having his
  fan in his hand to fan fresh air in her
  face. She singeth as followeth:*

Se Diana nel cielo è una stella,
Chiara e lucente, piena di splendore,
Che porge luc' all' affanato cuore;

Se Diana nel ferno è una dea,
Che da conforto all' anime dannate
Che per amor son morte desperate;

Se Diana, ch' in terra è delle ninfe
Reina imperativa di dolci fiori,
Tra bosch' e selve da morte a pastori;

Io son un Diana dolce e rara,   90
Che con li guardi io posso far guerra
A Dian' in fern', in cielo, e in terra.[4] *Exit.*

*The song being ended, Helen departeth, and
  Paris speaketh.*

PAR. Most heavenly dames, was never
  man as I,
Poor shepherd swain, so happy and un-
  happy;
The least of these delights that you de-
  vise,
Able to rap [5] and dazzle human eyes.
But, since my silence may not pardoned
  be,
And I appoint which is the fairest she,
Pardon, most sacred dames, sith one,
  not all,
By Paris' doom must have this golden
  ball.   100
Thy beauty, stately Juno, dame divine,
That like to Phœbus' golden beams doth
  shine,

---

[4] If Diana is a star in heaven,
bright and shining, full of splendor,
giving light to the grieving heart;

If Diana is a goddess in hell,
who gives comfort to the tormented souls
who on account of love have died in despair;

If Diana, who on earth is of the nymphs
the reigning queen of sweet flowers,
amid woods and groves gives death to shepherds;

I am a Diana gentle and rare,
for with my glances I can make war
upon Diana in hell, in heaven, and on earth.

[5] Affect with rapture.

Approves itself to be most excellent;
But that fair face that doth me most
    content,
Sith fair, fair dames, is neither she nor she,
But she whom I shall fairest deem to be,
That face is hers that hight the Queen
    of Love,
Whose sweetness doth both gods and
    creatures move.

He giveth the golden ball to Venus.

And, if the fairest face deserve the ball,
Fair Venus, ladies, bears it from ye all.
VEN. And in this ball doth Venus more
    delight   111
Than in her lovely boy fair Cupid's
    sight.
Come, shepherd, come; sweet Venus is
    thy friend,
No matter how thou other gods offend.

Venus taketh Paris with her. Exeunt [ambo].

JUN. But he shall rue and ban the dis-
    mal day
Wherein his Venus bare the ball away;
And heaven and earth just witnesses
    shall be
I will revenge it on his progeny.
PAL. Well, Juno, whether we be lief [1] or
    loath,   119
Venus hath got the apple from us both.

                    Exeunt ambo.

ACT[US] III. SCENA i.

*Colin, th' enamored shepherd, singeth his
                    passion of love.*

THE SONG

O gentle Love, ungentle for thy deed,
    Thou makest my heart
    A bloody mark
With piercing shot to bleed!
Shoot soft, sweet Love, for fear thou shoot
    amiss,
    For fear too keen
    Thy arrows been,
And hit the heart where my beloved is.
Too fair that fortune were, nor never I
    Shall be so blessed,   10
    Among the rest,
That Love shall seize on her by sympathy.
Then since with Love my prayers bear no
    boot,[2]
    This doth remain
    To cease my pain,
I take the wound, and die at Venus' foot.

                    Exit Colin.

[1] Willing.   [2] Profit.

ACT[US] III. SCENA ii.

Hobbinol, Diggon, Thenot.

HOB. Poor Colin, woeful man, thy life
    forespoke [3] by love,
What uncouth [4] fit, what malady, is
    this that thou dost prove? [5]
DIG. Or [6] Love is void of physic clean,
    or Love's our common wrack,
That gives us bane [7] to bring us low,
    and let[s] us medicine lack.
HOB. That ever Love had reverence
    'mong silly shepherd swains!
Belike [8] that humor hurts them most
    that most might be their pains.
THE. Hobbin, it is some other god that
    cherisheth their [9] sheep,
For sure this Love doth nothing else
    but make our herdmen weep.
DIG. And what a hap is this, I pray, when
    all our woods rejoice,
For Colin thus to be denied his young
    and lovely choice!   10
THE. She hight indeed so fresh and fair
    that well it is for thee,
Colin—and kind [10] hath been thy friend—
    that Cupid could not see.
HOB. And whither wends yon thriveless [11]
    swain? Like to the stricken deer,
Seeks he dictamum [12] for his wound with-
    in our forest here?
DIG. He wends to greet the Queen of Love,
    that in these woods doth wone,
With mirthless lays to make complaint
    to Venus of her son.
THE. Ah, Colin, thou art all deceived!
    She dallies with the boy,
And winks at all his wanton pranks,
    and thinks thy love a toy.
HOB. Then leave him to his luckless love;
    let him abide his fate.
The sore is rankled all too far; our com-
    fort comes too late.   20
DIG. Though Thestylis the scorpion be
    that breaks his sweet assault,
Yet will Rhamnusia [13] vengeance take
    on her disdainful fault.

[3] Predetermined.   [6] Either.
[4] Strange.   [7] Poison.
[5] Experience.   [8] Perhaps.
[9] Emended by Dyce. Original reads *her*.
[10] Nature.   [11] Unfortunate.
[12] Dictamnum, a healing herb.
[13] Nemesis.

The. Lo, yonder comes the lovely nymph, that in these Ida vales
Plays with Amyntas' lusty boy and coys [1] him in the dales!

Hob. Thenot, methinks her cheer is changed; her mirthful looks are laid;
She frolics not. Pray God the lad have not beguiled the maid!

Act[us] III. Scena iii.

Œnone ent'reth with a wreath of poplar on her head. Manent Pastores.[2]

Œn. Beguiled, disdained, and out of love! Live long, thou poplar tree,
And let thy letters grow in length, to witness this with me.
Ah, Venus, but for reverence unto thy sacred name,
To steal a silly maiden's love, I might account it blame!
And, if the tales be true I hear, and blush for to recite,
Thou dost me wrong to leave the plains and dally out of sight.
False Paris, this was not thy vow, when thou and I were one,
To range and change old love for new; but now those days be gone.
But I will find the goddess out, that she thy vow may read,
And fill these woods with my laments for thy unhappy deed.   10

Hob. So fair a face, so foul a thought to harbor in his breast!
Thy hope consumed, poor nymph, thy hap is worse than all the rest.

Œn. Ah, shepherds, you bin full of wiles, and whet your wits on books,
And rap poor maids with pipes and songs, and sweet alluring looks!

Dig. Misspeak [3] not all for his amiss; [4] there bin that keepen [5] flocks,
That never chose but once, nor yet beguiléd love with mocks.

Œn. False Paris, he is none of those; his trothless double deed
Will hurt a many shepherds else that might go nigh to speed.[6]

[1] Caresses.
[2] The shepherds remain.
[3] Reproach.
[4] Fault.
[5] Those who keep.
[6] Prosper (in love).

The. Poor Colin, that is ill for thee, that art as true in trust
To thy sweet smart as to his nymph Paris hath been unjust.   20

Œn. Ah, well is she hath Colin won, that nill no other love!
And woe is me. My luck is loss, my pains no pity move.

Hob. Farewell, fair nymph, sith he must heal alone that gave the wound;
There grows no herb of such effect upon Dame Nature's ground.

Exeunt Pastores.

[Actus III. Scena iv.]

Manet Œnone.   Mercu[ry] ent'r[eth] with Vulcan's Cyclops.[7]

Mer. Here is a nymph that sadly sits, and she belike
Can tell some news, Pyracmon, of the jolly swain we seek.
Dare wage my wings, the lass doth love, she looks so bleak and thin;
And 'tis for anger or for grief—but I will talk begin.

Œn. [*Aside.*] Break out, poor heart, and make complaint, the mountain flocks to move,
What proud repulse and thankless scorn thou hast received of love.

Mer. She singeth; sirs, be hushed awhile.
Œnone singeth as she sits.

Œnone's Complaint

Melpomene, the Muse of tragic songs,
With mournful tunes, in stole of dismal hue,
Assist a silly nymph to wail her woe,   10
And leave thy lusty company behind.

Thou luckless wreath! Becomes not me to wear
The poplar tree for triumph of my love.
Then, as my joy, my pride of love, is left,
Be thou unclothéd of thy lovely green;

And in thy leaves my fortune written be,
And them some gentle wind let blow abroad,
That all the world may see how false of love
False Paris hath to his Œnone been.

The song ended, Œnone sitting still, Mercury speaketh.

Mer. Good day, fair maid; weary belike with following of your game,   20
I wish thee cunning at thy will, to spare or strike the same.

[7] Used in this play for both singular and plural.

Œn. I thank you, sir; my game is quick,[1]
  and rids [2] a length of ground,
    And yet I am deceived, or else a had a
      deadly wound.
Mer. Your hand perhaps did swarve [3]
  awry.
Œn.   Or else it was my heart.
Mer. Then sure a plied his footmanship.
Œn.   A played a ranging part.
Mer. You should have given a deeper
  wound.
Œn.   I could not that for pity.
Mer. You should have eyed him better,
  then.
Œn.   Blind Love was not so witty.
Mer. Why, tell me, sweet, are you in love?
Œn.   O,[4] would I were not so!
Mer. Ye mean because a does ye wrong?
Œn.   Perdy, the more my woe.
Mer. Why, mean ye Love, or him ye
  loved?
Œn. Well may I mean them both. 30
Mer. Is Love to blame?
Œn.   The Queen of Love hath
  made him false his troth.[5]
Mer. Mean ye, indeed, the Queen of
  Love?
Œn.   Even wanton Cupid's dame.
Mer. Why, was thy love so lovely then?
Œn.   His beauty hight [6] his shame—
  The fairest shepherd on our green.
Mer.   Is he a shepherd, than? [7]
Œn. And sometime kept a bleating flock.
Mer.   Enough, this is the man.
  Where wones he, then?
Œn.   About these woods, far
  from the poplar tree.
Mer. What poplar mean ye?
Œn.   Witness of the vows
  betwixt him and me.
    And come and wend a little way, and
      you shall see his skill.
Mer. Sirs, tarry you.
Œn.   Nay, let them go.
Mer.   Nay, not unless you will.
  Stay, nymph, and hark what I say of
    him thou blamest so,   40
  And, credit me, I have a sad discourse
    to tell thee ere I go.

[1] Alive.   [2] Traverses.   [3] Swerve.
[4] Suggested by Child. Original reads *or*.
[5] Break his promise.   [6] Promised, assured.
[7] Then, a common Elizabethan spelling here
retained for the rime.

Know then, my pretty mops, that I
  hight Mercury,
The messenger of heaven, and hether
  fly,
To seize upon the man whom thou dost
  love,
To summon him before my father Jove,
To answer matter of great consequence;
And Jove himself will not be long from
  hence.
Œn. Sweet Mercury, and have poor
  Œnon's cries
For Paris' fault ypierced th' unpartial
  skies?
Mer. The same is he, that jolly shep-
  herd's swain.   50
Œn. His flock do graze upon Aurora's
  plain;
  The color of his coat is lusty green;
  That would these eyes of mine had never
    seen
  His ticing [8] curléd hair, his front of
    ivory,
  Then had not I, poor I, bin unhappy.
Mer. No marvel, wench, although we
  cannot find him,
  When all-too late [9] the Queen of Heaven
    doth mind him.
  But, if thou wilt have physic for thy
    sore,
  Mind him who list, remember thou him
    no more;
  And find some other game, and get thee
    gone;   60
  For here will lusty suitors come anon,
  Too hot and lusty for thy dying vein,
  Such as ne'er wont [10] to make their suits
    in vain.
          Exit Mer[cury] cum Cyclop[e].
Œn. I will go sit and pine under the
  poplar tree,
  And write my answer to his vow, that
    every eye may see.   *Exit.*

Act[us] III. Scena v.

Venus, Paris, and a company of Shepherds.

Ven. Shepherds, I am content, for this
  sweet shepherd's sake,
  A strange revenge upon the maid and
    her disdain to take.

[8] Enticing.
[9] Very lately.
[10] Suggested by Dyce; original reads *were monte.*

Let Colin's corpse be brought in place,
   and buried [1] in the plain,
And let this be the verse, "The love
   whom Thestylis hath slain."
And, trust me, I will chide my son for
   partiality,
That gave the swain so deep a wound,
   and let her scape him by.
PASTO[R]. Alas, that ever Love was blind,
   to shoot so far amiss!
VEN. Cupid, my son, was more to blame;
   the fault not mine, but his.
Pastores exeunt. Manet Ven[us] cum Pa-
                              r[ide].
PAR. O madam, if yourself would deign
   the handling of the bow,
Albeit it be a task, yourself more skill,
   more justice know.   10
VEN. Sweet shepherd, didst thou ever
   love?
PAR.   Lady, a little once.
VEN. And art thou changed?
PAR.   Fair Queen of Love,
I loved not all attonce.[2]
VEN. Well, wanton, wert thou wounded
   so deep as some have been,
It were a cunning cure to heal, and rue-
   ful to be seen.
PAR. But tell me, gracious goddess, for
   a start [3] and false offense
Hath Venus or her son the power at
   pleasure to dispense? [4]
VEN. My boy, I will instruct thee in a
   piece of poetry
That haply erst [5] thou hast not heard:
   in hell there is a tree
Where once a day do sleep the souls of
   false forsworen lovers,
With open hearts; and thereabout in
   swarms the number hovers   20
Of poor forsaken ghosts, whose wings
   from off this tree do beat
Round drops of fiery Phlegiton to scorch
   false hearts with heat.
This pain did Venus and her son en-
   treat the Prince of Hell
T' impose to such as faithless were to
   such as loved them well.
And therefore this, my lovely boy, fair
   Venus doth advise thee:

Be true and steadfast in thy love; beware thou do disguise [6] thee,
For he that makes but love a jest, when
   pleaseth him to start,
Shall feel those fiery water drops consume his faithless heart.
PAR. Is Venus and her son so full of
   justice and severity?
VEN. Pity it were that love should not
   be linkéd with indifferency.   30
However lovers can exclaim for hard
   success in love,
Trust me, some more than common
   cause that painful hap doth move;
And Cupid's bow is not alone his tri-
   umph, but his rod.
Nor is he only but a boy—he hight a
   mighty god;
And they that do him reverence have
   reason for the same;
His shafts keep heaven and earth in
   awe, and shape rewards for shame.
PAR. And hath he reason to maintain why
   Colin died for love?
VEN. Yea, reason good, I warrant thee;
   in right it might behove.[7]
PAR. Then be the name of Love adored;
   his bow is full of might,
His wounds are all but for desert, his
   laws are all but right.   40
[VEN.] Well, for this once me list [8] apply
   my speeches to thy sense,[9]
And Thestylis shall feel the pain for
   Love's supposed offense.
The Shepherds bring in Colin's hearse, sing-
                                        ing:

Welladay, welladay, poor Colin, thou art
      going to the ground,
   The love whom Thestylis hath slain—
   Hard heart, fair face, fraught with dis-
      dain,
Disdain in love a deadly wound.
   Wound her, sweet Love, so deep again,
   That she may feel the dying pain
   Of this unhappy shepherd's swain,   49
And die for love as Colin died, as Colin died.
                         Finis camenæ.

VEN. Shepherds, abide; let Colin's corpse
   be witness of the pain
That Thestylis endures in love, a plague
   for her disdain.

---

[1] Emended by Dyce. Original reads *burned.*
[2] At once.
[3] Deviation (from right).
[4] Give dispensation.   [5] Before.

[6] Alter.   [7] It was needful.   [8] It pleases me.
[9] *I.e.,* adapt my commands to thy judgment.

Behold the organ of our wrath, this
　　rusty churl is he;
She dotes on his ill-favored face, so
　　much accursed is she.

She singeth an old song called "The Wooing
　　　　　　　　　　of Colman."

A foul, crooked Churl enters, and Thestylis,
a fair lass, wooeth him. He crabbedly
refuseth her, and goeth out of place. She
　　　　　　　　　　　tarrieth behind.

PAR. Ah, poor unhappy Thestylis, un-
　　pitied is thy pain!
VEN. Her fortune not unlike to hers [1]
　　whom cruel thou hast slain.

Thestylis singeth, and the Shepherds reply.

THE SONG

[THEST.] The strange affects [2] of my tor-
　　mented heart,
　　Whom cruel love hath woeful prisoner
　　　caught,
　　Whom cruel hate hath into bondage
　　　brought,
　　Whom wit no way of safe escape hath
　　　taught,　　　　　　　　　　　　　60
　　Enforce me say, in witness of my smart,
　　There is no pain to [3] foul disdain in
　　　hardy suits of love.
SHEP. There is no pain, etc.
THEST. Cruel, farewell.
SHEP. Cruel, farewell.
THEST. Most cruel thou, of all that nature
　　framed.
SHEP. Most cruel, etc.
THEST. To kill thy love with thy disdain.
SHEP. To kill thy love with thy disdain.
THEST. Cruel Disdain, so live thou named.
SHEP. Cruel Disdain, etc.　　　　　　71
THEST. And let me die of Iphis' pain.
SHEP. A life too good for thy disdain.
THEST. Sith this my stars to me allot,
　　And thou thy love hast all forgot.
　　　　　　　　　　　　Exit Thest[ylis].
SHEP. And thou, etc.

The grace of this song is in the Shepherds'
　　　　　　　echo to her verse.
VEN. Now,　shepherds,　bury　Colin's
　　corpse, perfume his hearse with flowers,
And write what justice Venus did amid
　　these woods of yours.

　　　　The Shepherds carry out Colin. [4]

How now, how cheers my lovely boy
　　after this dump [5] of love?
PAR. Such dumps, sweet lady, as bin
　　these are deadly dumps to prove.　　80
VEN. Cease, shepherd; there [6] are other
　　news after this melancholy.
My mind presumes some tempest to-
　　ward [7] upon the speech of Mercury.

ACT[US] III. SCENA vi.

Mercury with Vulcan's Cyclops enter. Ma-
　　nentibus Ven[ere] cum Par[ide].

MER. Fair Lady Venus, let me pardoned
　　be,
　　That have of long been well-beloved of
　　　thee,
　　If, as my office bids, myself first brings
　　To my sweet madam these unwelcome
　　　tidings.
VEN. What news, what tidings, gentle
　　Mercury,
　　In middest of my delights to trouble
　　me?
MER. At Juno's suit, Pallas assisting her,
　　Sith both did join in suit to Jupiter,
　　Action is entered in the court of heaven;
　　And me, the swiftest of the planets
　　　seven,　　　　　　　　　　　　　10
　　With warrant they have thence des-
　　　patched away
　　To apprehend and find the man, they
　　　say,
　　That gave from them that selfsame ball
　　　of gold,
　　Which, I presume, I do in place behold;
　　Which man, unless my marks be taken
　　　wide, [8]
　　Is he that sits so near thy gracious side.
　　This being so, it rests he go from hence,
　　Before the gods to answer his offense.
VEN. What tale is this? Doth Juno and
　　her mate
　　Pursue this shepherd with such deadly
　　hate,　　　　　　　　　　　　　　20
　　As what was then our general agree-
　　　ment
　　To stand unto, they nill be now content?
　　Let Juno jet, [9] and Pallas play her part;
　　What here I have, I won it by desert;

---

[1] Emended by Dyce. Original reads *his*.
[2] Feelings; original has *effects*.
[3] Comparable to.
[4] In the original this direction appears immediately after the song.

[5] Mournful song.
[6] Original reads *these*.
[7] Near at hand.
[8] Unless I am wide of the mark.
[9] Strut.

And heaven and earth shall both con-
    founded be,
Ere wrong in this be done to him or me.
MER. This little fruit, if Mercury can
    spell,[1]
Will send, I fear, a world of souls to
    hell.
VEN. What mean these Cyclops, Mercury?
    Is Vulcan waxed so fine,
To send his chimney-sweepers forth to
    fetter any friend of mine?—   30
Abash not, shepherd, at the thing; my-
    self thy bail will be.—
He shall be present at the court of
    Jove, I warrant thee.
MER. Venus, give me your pledge.
VEN.   My ceston,[2] or my fan, or both?
MER. (*Taketh her fan.*) Nay, this shall
    serve, your word to me as sure as is
    your oath,
At Diana's bower! And, lady, if my wit
    or policy
May profit him, for Venus' sake let him
    make bold with Mercury.
                    Exit [with the Cyclops].
VEN. Sweet Paris, whereon dost thou
    muse?
PAR. The angry heavens, for this fatal jar,
Name me the instrument of dire and
    deadly war.
*Explicit Actus Tertius. Exeunt Venus et
                                Paris.*

ACT[US] IV. SCENA i.

Vulcan, following one of Diana's Nymphs.

VUL. Why, nymph, what need ye run so
    fast? What though but black I be?
I have more pretty knacks to please
    than every eye doth see;
And though I go not so upright, and
    though I am a smith,
To make me gracious you may have
    some other thing therewith.

ACT[US] IV. SCENA ii.

Bacchus, Vulcan, Nymph.

BAC. Yea, Vulcan, will ye so indeed?—
    Nay, turn and tell him, trull,
He hath a mistress of his own to take
    his bellyful.

VUL. Why, sir, if Phœbe's dainty nymph
    please lusty Vulcan's tooth,
Why may not Vulcan tread awry as well
    as Venus doth?
NYM. Ye shall not taint your troth for
    me. You wot it very well,
All that be Dian's maids are vowed to
    halter apes [3] in hell.[4]
BAC. I' faith, i' faith, my gentle mops, but
    I do know a cast[5]—
Lead apes who list—that we would help
    t'unhalter them as fast.
NYM. Fie, fie, your skill is wondrous great!
    Had thought the God of Wine
Had tended but his tubs and grapes,
    and not been half so fine.   10
VUL. Gramercy for that quirk, my girl.
BAC.   That's one of dainty's frumps.[6]
NYM. I pray, sir, take't with all amiss;
    our cunning comes by lumps.
VUL. Sh'ath capped his answer in the Q.[7]
NYM.   How says a, has she so?
As well as she that capped your head
    to keep you warm below.
VUL. Yea, then you will be curst,[8] I see.
BAC.   Best let her even alone.
NYM. Yea, gentle gods, and find some
    other string to harp upon.
BAC. Some other string! Agreed, i'faith,
    some other pretty thing;
'Twere shame fair maids should idle
    be. How say you, will ye sing?
NYM. Some rounds or merry roundelays;
    we sing no other songs.
Your melancholic notes not to our
    country mirth belongs.   20
VUL. Here comes a crew will help us
    trim.[9]

ACTUS IV. SCENA iii.

Mercury with the Cyclops.

MER. Yea, now our task is done.
BAC. Then, merry Mercury, more than
    time this round were well begun.
They sing "Hey down, down, down," etc.

*The song done, she windeth a horn in Vul-
    can's ear, and runneth out. Manent
    Vulc[an], Bac[chus], Mer[cury], Cyclops.*

---

[3] Emended by Dyce. Original reads *apples*.
[4] Proverbial reward of spinsterhood.
[5] Trick.   [7] Question.
[6] Mocks, sneers.   [8] Shrewish.
[9] Balance the parts (of the song).

[1] Foretell.   [2] Cestus, girdle.

VUL. A harlotry,[1] I warrant her!

BAC.   A peevish, elvish shroe![2]

MER. Have seen as far to come as near,
  for all her ranging so.
  But, Bacchus, time well-spent; I wot
  our sacred father Jove
  With Phœbus and the God of War are
  met in Dian's grove.

VUL. Then we are here before them yet;
  but stay—the earth doth swell!
  God Neptune, too (this hap is good),
  doth meet the Prince of Hell.

Pluto ascendeth from below in his chair;
Neptune ent'reth at another way.

PLU. What jars are these that call the
  gods of heaven and hell below?

NEP. It is a work of wit and toil to rule
  a lusty shroe.   10

ACT[US] IV. SCENA iv.

Enter Jupiter, Saturn, Apollo, Mars, Pluto,
Neptune, Bacchus, Vulcan, Mer[cury],
Juno, Pallas, Diana, Cyclops. Jupiter
speaketh.

JUP. Bring forth the man of Troy, that
  he may hear
  Whereof he is to be arraignéd here.

NEP. Lo, where a comes, prepared to plead
  his case,
  Under conduct of lovely Venus' grace!

[Enter Venus with Paris.]

MER. I have not seen a more alluring boy.

APOL. So beauty hight the wrack of
  Priam's Troy.

The Gods being set in Diana's bower, Juno,
Pallas, Diana, Venus, and Paris stand
*   on sides before them.*

VEN. Lo, sacred Jove, at Juno's proud
  complaint,
  As erst I gave my pledge to Mercury,
  I bring the man whom he did late at-
  taint,[3]
  To answer his indictment orderly;   10
  And crave this grace of this immortal
  senate,
  That ye allow the man his advocate.

PAL. That may not be; the laws of heaven
  deny
  A man to plead or answer by attorney.

VEN. Pallas, thy doom is all too peremptory.

APOL. Venus, that favor is denied him
  flatly:
  He is a man, and therefore by our laws,
  Himself, without his aid, must plead
  his cause.

VEN. Then bash not,[4] shepherd, in so
  good a case;
  And friends thou hast, as well as foes,
  in place.   20

JUN. Why, Mercury, why do ye not in-
  dict him?

VEN. Soft, gentle Juno, I pray you, do
  not bite him.

JUN. Nay, gods, I trow you are like to
  have great silence
  Unless this parrot be commanded hence.

JUP.[5] Venus, forbear, be still.—Speak,
  Mercury.

VEN. If Juno jangle, Venus will reply.

MER. Paris, King Priam's son, thou art
  arraigned of partiality,
  Of sentence partial and unjust, for that
  without indifferency,[6]
  Beyond desert or merit fair, as thine
  accusers say,
  From them to Lady Venus here thou
  gavest the prize away.   30
  What is thine answer?

PARIS' ORATION TO THE COUNCIL OF THE
GODS

[PAR.] Sacred and just, thou great and
  dreadful Jove,
  And you thrice-reverend powers, whom
  love nor hate
  May wrest awry, if this to me, a man,
  This fortune fatal [7] be, that I must plead
  For safe excusal of my guiltless thought,
  The honor more makes my mishap the less
  That I, a man, must plead before the
  gods—
  Gracious forbearers [8] of the world's
  amiss—
  For her, whose beauty how it hath en-
  ticed,   40
  This heavenly senate may with me aver.
  But sith nor that nor this may'do me boot,
  And for myself myself must speaker be,
  A mortal man amidst this heavenly
  presence,

---

[1] "Baggage."   [2] Shrew.   [3] Accuse, arrest.

[4] Be not abashed.   [7] Decreed.
[5] Original reads *Jov.*   [8] Tolerators.
[6] Impartiality.

Let me not shape a long defense to them
That been beholders of my guiltless
   thoughts.
Then for the deed that I may not deny,
Wherein consists the full of mine of-
   fense,
I did upon command; if then I erred,
I did no more than to a man belonged. 50
And if, in verdit [1] of their forms divine,
My dazzled eye did swarve or surfeit
   more
On Venus' face than any face of theirs,
It was no partial fault, but fault of his,
Belike, whose eyesight not so perfect
   was
As might discern the brightness of the
   rest.
And, if it were permitted unto men,
Ye gods, to parley with your secret
   thoughts,
There been that sit upon that sacred
   seat
That would with Paris err in Venus'
   praise.   60
But let me cease to speak of error here,
Sith what my hand, the organ of my
   heart,
Did give with good agreement of mine
   eye,
My tongue is void with process to main-
   tain. [2]
PLU. A jolly shepherd, wise and eloquent!
PAR. First, then, arraigned of partiality,
  Paris replies, "Unguilty of the fact;" [3]
His reason is, because he knew no more
Fair Venus' ceston than Dame Juno's
   mace,
Nor never saw wise Pallas' crystal
   shield.   70
Then, as I looked, I loved and liked
   attonce,
And, as it was referred from them to
   me,
To give the prize to her whose beauty
   best
My fancy did commend, so did I praise
And judge as might my dazzled eye
   discern.
NEP. A piece of art, that cunningly,
  perdy,
Refers the blame to weakness of his eye.

PAR. Now—for I must add reason for
  my deed—
Why Venus rather pleased me of the
  three: 79
First, in the entrails [4] of my mortal ears,
The question standing upon beauty's
  blaze, [5]
The name of her that hight the Queen
  of Love,
Methought [6] in beauty should not be
  excelled.
Had it been destinéd to majesty—
Yet will I not rob Venus of her grace—
Then stately Juno might have borne
  the ball.
Had it to wisdom been intituléd,
My human wit had given it Pallas then.
But, sith unto the fairest of the three
That power that threw it for my far-
  ther ill   90
Did dedicate this ball, and safest durst
My shepherd's skill adventure, as I
  thought,
To judge of form and beauty rather
  than
Of Juno's state or Pallas' worthiness,
That learned to ken the fairest of the
  flock,
And praiséd beauty but by nature's
  aim,
Behold, to Venus Paris gave this fruit,
A daysman [7] chosen there by full consent;
And heavenly powers should not repent
  their deeds.
Where it is said beyond desert of hers 100
I honored Venus with this golden prize,
Ye gods, alas, what can a mortal man
Discern betwixt the sacred gifts of
  heaven?
Or, if I may with reverence reason thus,
Suppose I gave—and judged corruptly
  then,
For hope of that that best did please
  my thought—
This apple, not for beauty's praise alone,
I might offend, sith I was pardonéd, [8]
And tempted more than ever creature
  was
With wealth, with beauty, and with
  chivalry,   110

---

[1] Verdict.
[2] Unable to explain in a detailed story.
[3] Deed.
[4] Turnings.   [5] Blazon, proclamation.
[6] Emended by Dyce. Original reads *my thought.*   [7] Judge.
[8] Released from liability to punishment.

And so preferred beauty before them all,
The thing that hath enchanted heaven
  itself.
And for the one, contentment is my
  wealth;
A shell of salt will serve a shepherd swain,
A slender banquet in a homely scrip,[1]
And water running from the silver
  spring.
For arms, they dread no foes that sit so
  low;
A thorn [2] can keep the wind from off
  my back;
A sheepcote thatched, a shepherd's
  palace hight.
Of tragic muses shepherds con [3] no
  skill;   120
Enough is them, if Cupid been dis-
  pleased,
To sing his praise on slender oaten pipe.
And thus, thrice-reverend, have I told
  my tale,
And crave the torment of my guiltless
  soul
To be measured by my faultless thought.
If warlike Pallas or the Queen of Heaven
Sue to reverse my sentence by appeal,
Be it as please your majesties divine;
The wrong, the hurt, not mine, if any
  be,
But hers whose beauty claimed the prize
  of me.   130
    Paris having ended, Jupiter speaketh.
JUP. Venus, withdraw your shepherd for
  a space,
Till he again be called for into place.
                    Exeunt Venus et Paris.
Juno, what will ye after this reply,
But doom with sentence of indifferency?
And, if you will but justice in the cause,
The man must quited [4] be by heaven's
  laws.
JUN. Yea, gentle Jove, when Juno's suits
  are moved,
Then heaven may see how well she is
  beloved!
APOL. But, madam, fits it majesty divine
In any sort from justice to decline?   140
PAL. Whether the man be guilty, yea or
  no,
That doth not hinder our appeal, I
  trow.

JUN. Phœbus, I wot, amid this heavenly
  crew,
There be that have to say as well as you.
APOL. And, Juno, I with them, and they
  with me,
In law and right must needfully agree.
PAL. I grant ye may agree, but be content
To doubt upon regard of [5] your agree-
  ment.
PLU. And, if ye marked, the man in his
  defense
Said thereof as a might with rever-
  ence.   150
VUL. And did ye very well, I promise ye.
JUN. No doubt, sir, you could note it
  cunningly.
SAT. Well, Juno, if ye will appeal, ye may;
But first despatch the shepherd hence
  away.
MARS. Then Vulcan's dame is like to have
  the wrong.
JUN. And that in passion [6] doth to Mars
  belong!
JUP. Call Venus and the shepherd in
  again.   [*Exit Mercury.*]
BAC. And rid [7] the man that he may
  know his pain.[8]
APOL. His pain, his pain, his never-dying
  pain,   159
A cause to make a many mo complain.

Mercury bringeth in Venus and Paris.

JUP. Shepherd, thou hast been heard with
  equity and law,
And, for [9] thy stars do thee to other call-
  ing draw,
We here dismiss thee hence, by order
  of our senate;
Go take thy way to Troy, and there
  abide thy fate.
VEN. Sweet shepherd, with such luck in
  love, while thou dost live,
As may the Queen of Love to any lover
  give!
PAR. My luck is loss, howe'er my love do
  speed.
I fear me Paris shall but rue his deed.
                              Paris exit.
APOL. From Ida woods now wends the
  shepherd's boy,
That in his bosom carries fire to Troy. 170

----

[1] Wallet.   [3] Know, have.
[2] Thorn tree.   [4] Freed.

[5] Hesitate in respect to.   [8] Sentence, fate.
[6] Sorrow.   [9] Because.
[7] Free.

Jup. Venus, these ladies do appeal, you
    see,
And that they may appeal the gods
    agree.
It resteth, then, that you be well content
To stand in this unto our final judg-
    ment;
And, if King Priam's son did well in
    this,
The law of heaven will not lead amiss.
Ven. But, sacred Jupiter, might thy
    daughter choose,
She might with reason this appeal re-
    fuse;
Yet, if they be unmovéd in their shames,
Be it a stain and blemish to their
    names,   180
A deed too far unworthy of the place,
Unworthy Pallas' lance or Juno's mace;
And, if to beauty it bequeathéd be,
I doubt not but it will return to me.
                    She layeth down the ball.
Pal. Venus, there is no more ado than
    so;
It resteth where the gods do it bestow.
Nep. But, ladies—under favor of your
    rage—
Howe'er it be, you play upon the van-
    tage.[1]
Jup. Then, dames, that we more freely
    may debate,
And hear th' indifferent sentence of
    this senate,   190
Withdraw you from this presence for
    a space,
Till we have throughly questioned of
    the case.
Dian shall be your guide; nor shall you
    need
Yourselves t' inquire how things do
    here succeed;
We will, as we resolve, give you to know,
By general doom how everything doth go.
Dian. Thy will, my wish.—Fair ladies,
    will ye wend?
Jun. Beshrew her whom this sentence
    doth offend.
Ven. Now, Jove, be just; and, gods, you
    that be Venus' friends,
If you have ever done her wrong, then
    may you make amends.   200
Manent dii.[2] *Exeunt Diana, Pallas, Juno,*
                                Venus.

Jup. Venus is fair; Pallas and Juno too.
Vul. But tell me now, without some
    more ado,
Who is the fairest she, and do not
    flatter.
Plu. Vulcan, upon comparison hangs all
    the matter;
That done, the quarrel and the strife
    were ended.
Mars. Because 'tis known the quarrel
    is pretended.
Vul. Mars, you have reason for your
    speech, perdy;
My dame, I trow, is fairest in your
    eye.
Mars. Or, Vulcan, I should do her double
    wrong.
Sat. About a toy we tarry here so long. 210
Give it by voices; voices give the
    odds;
A trifle so to trouble all the gods!
Nep. Believe me, Saturn, be it so for me.
Bac. For me.
Plu.   For me.
Mars.   For me, if Jove agree.
Mer. And, gentle gods, I am indifferent;
But then I know who's likely to be
    shent.[3]
Apol. Thrice-reverend gods, and thou,
    immortal Jove,
If Phœbus may, as him doth much be-
    hove,
Be licenséd, according to our laws,
To speak uprightly in this doubted[4]
    cause   220
(Sith women's wits work men's unceas-
    ing woes)
To make them friends, that now bin
    friendless foes,
And peace to keep with them, with us,
    and all,
That make their title to this golden
    ball—
Nor think, ye gods, my speech doth de-
    rogate
From sacred power of this immortal
    senate—
Refer this sentence where it doth be-
    long.
In this, say I, fair Phœbe hath the
    wrong;
Not that I mean her beauty bears the
    prize,   229

---

[1] Have the advantage.   [2] The gods remain.   [3] Reproved.   [4] Dreaded.

But that the holy law of heaven denies
One god to meddle in another's power;
And this befell so near Diana's bower
As, for th' appeasing this unpleasant
    grudge,
In my conceit [1] she hight the fittest
    judge.
If Jove comptrol [2] not Pluto's hell with
    charms,
If Mars have sovereign power to man-
    age arms,
If Bacchus bear no rule in Neptune['s]
    sea,
Nor Vulcan's fire doth Saturn's scythe
    obey,
Suppress not then, gainst law and equity,
Diana's power in her own territory,   240
Whose regiment,[3] amid her sacred bow-
    ers,
As proper hight as any rule of yours.
Well may we so wipe all the speech away
That Pallas, Juno, Venus hath to say,
And answer that, by justice of our laws,
We were not suffered to conclude the
    cause.
And this to me most egal [4] doom ap-
    pears—
A woman to be judge among her feres.
MER. Apollo hath found out the only
    mean
To rid the blame from us and trouble
    clean.   250
VUL. We are beholding [5] to his sacred wit.
JUP. I can commend and well allow of it;
And so derive [6] the matter from us all,
That Dian have the giving of the ball.
VUL. So Jove may clearly excuse him in
    the case,
Where Juno else would chide and brawl
    apace.   *All they rise to [7] go forth.*
MER. And now it were some cunning to
    divine
To whom Diana will this prize resign.
VUL. Sufficeth me, it shall be none of
    mine!
BAC. Vulcan, though thou be black,
    th'art nothing fine.   260
VUL. Go bathe thee, Bacchus, in a tub
    of wine;
The ball's as likely to be mine as thine!
Exeunt omnes. Explicit Act[us] Quartus.

[1] Opinion.   [3] Rule.   [5] Beholden, indebted.
[2] Control.   [4] Equal.   [6] Divert.
[7] Emended by Bullen. Original reads *and*

ACT[US] V ET ULTIMI SCENA i.[8]

Diana, Pallas, Juno, Venus.

DIAN. Lo, ladies, far beyond my hope
    and will, you see,
This thankless office is imposed to me;
Wherein, if you will rest as well content
As Dian will be judge indifferent,
My egal doom shall none of you offend,
And of this quarrel make a final end.
And therefore, whether you be lief or
    loath,
Confirm your promise with some sacred
    oath.
PAL. Phœbe, chief mistress of this sylvan
    chase,
Whom gods have chosen to conclude
    the case   10
That yet in balance undecided lies,
Touching bestowing of this golden prize,
I give my promise and mine oath withal,
By Styx, by heaven's power imperial,
By all that longs to Pallas' deity,
Her shield, her lance, ensigns of chivalry,
Her sacred wreath of olive and of bay,
Her crested helm, and else what Pallas
    may,
That wheresoe'er this ball of purest gold,
That chaste Diana here in hand doth
    hold,   20
Unpartially her wisdom shall bestow,
Without mislike or quarrel any mo
Pallas shall rest content and satisfied,
And say the best desert doth there abide.
JUN. And here I promise and protest
    withal,
By Styx, by heaven's power imperial,
By all that longs to Juno's deity,
Her crown, her mace, ensigns of maj-
    esty,
Her spotless marriage rites, her league
    divine,
And by that holy name of Proserpine,   30
That wheresoe'er this ball of purest gold,
That chaste Diana here in hand doth
    hold,
Unpartially her wisdom shall bestow,
Without mislike or quarrel any mo
Juno shall rest content and satisfied,
And say the best desert doth there
    abide.
VEN. And, lovely Phœbe, for I know thy
    doom

[8] The first scene of the fifth and last act.

Will be no other than shall thee become,
Behold, I take thy dainty hand to kiss,
And with my solemn oath confirm my
  promise,   40
By Styx, by Jove's immortal empery,
By Cupid's bow, by Venus' myrtle tree,
By Vulcan's gift, my ceston and my
  fan,
By this red rose, whose color first began
When erst my wanton boy (the more
  his blame)
Did draw his bow awry and hurt his
  dame,
By all the honor and the sacrifice
That from Cithæron and from Paphos
  rise,

The con- ⎤ That wheresoe'er, ⎧
clusion ⎬   etc.   ⎨ *ut supra.*[1]
above ⎦ Venus shall rest, ⎩
         etc.

Diana, having taken their oaths, speaketh.
Diana describeth the nymph Eliza, a
        figure of the queen.[2]

DIAN. It is enough, and, goddesses, at·
  tend: 51
There wones within these pleasant
  shady woods,
Where neither storm nor sun's dis-
  temperature
Have power to hurt by cruel heat or
  cold,
Under the climate of the milder heaven,
Where seldom lights Jove's angry thun-
  derbolt,
For favor of that sovereign earthly
  peer,
Where whistling winds make music
  'mong the trees,
Far from disturbance of our country
  gods,
Amids the cypress-springs, a gracious
  nymph,   60
That honor[s] Dian for her chastity,
And likes the labors well of Phœbe's
  groves,
The place Elysium hight, and of the
  place
Her name that governs there Eliza is—
A kingdom that may well compare with
  mine,
An ancient seat of kings, a second Troy,

[1] As above.
[2] Symbol of Queen Elizabeth, who was present at the performance.

Ycompassed round with a commodious
  sea;
Her people are yclepéd [3] *Angeli,*
Or, if I miss, a letter is the most.   69
She giveth laws of justice and of peace;
And on her head, as fits her fortune best,
She wears a wreath of laurel, gold, and
  palm;
Her robes of purple and of scarlet dye;
Her veil of white, as best befits a maid.
Her ancestors live in the House of Fame.
She giveth arms of happy victory,
And flowers to deck her lions crowned
  with gold.
This peerless nymph, whom heaven and
  earth beloves,
This paragon, this only, this is she,   79
In whom do meet so many gifts in one,
On whom our country gods so often
  gaze,
In honor of whose name the Muses
  sing—
In state Queen Juno's peer, for power
  in arms
And virtues of the mind Minerva's mate,
As fair and lovely as the Queen of Love,
As chaste as Dian in her chaste desires.
The same is she, if Phœbe do no wrong,
To whom this ball in merit doth belong.
PAL. If this be she whom some Zabeta
  call,
To whom thy wisdom well bequeaths
  the ball,   90
I can remember, at her day of birth,
How Flora with her flowers strewed the
  earth,
How every power with heavenly maj-
  esty
In person honored that solemnity.
JUN. The lovely Graces were not far
  away;
They threw their balm for triumph [4]
  of the day.
VEN. The Fates, against their kind, be-
  gan a cheerful song,
And vowed her life with favor to prolong.
Then first gan [5] Cupid's eyesight wexen [6]
  dim;
Belike Eliza's beauty blinded him.   100
To this fair nymph, not earthly, but
  divine,
Contents it me my honor to resign.

[3] Called.   [5] Did.
[4] Joy.   [6] Wax, grow.

Pal. To this fair queen, so beautiful and
　　wise,
　Pallas bequeaths her title in the prize.
Jun. To her whom Juno's looks so well
　　become,
　The Queen of Heaven yields at Phœbe's [1]
　　doom;
　And glad I am Diana found the art,
　Without offense so well to please desert.
Dian. Then mark my tale: the usual
　　time is nigh,
　When wont [2] the dames of life and des-
　　tiny,　　　　　　　　　　　　　　110
　In robes of cheerful colors, to repair
　To this renownéd queen so wise and
　　fair,
　With pleasant songs this peerless nymph
　　to greet.
　Clotho lays down her distaff at her
　　feet;
　And Lachesis doth pull the thread at
　　length;
　The third with favor gives it stuff and
　　strength,
　And, for [3] contrary kind, affords her
　　leave,
　As her best likes, her web of life to
　　weave.
　This time we will attend, and in the
　　mean while
　With some sweet song the tediousness
　　beguile.　　　　　　　　　　　　120
*The music sound, and the Nymphs within
　sing or solfa with voices and instruments
　awhile.　Then enter Clotho, Lachesis,
　and Atropos, singing as follows, the
　state [4] being in place:*

The Song

Cloth. *Humanæ vitæ filum sic volvere
　Parcæ.*
Lach. *Humanæ vitæ filum sic tendere
　Parcæ.*
Atro. *Humanæ vitæ filum sic scindere
　Parcæ.*
Cloth. *Clotho colum bajulat.*
Lach.　　　　　　*Lachesis trahit.*
Atro.　　　　　　　　*Atropos occat.*

---

[1] Emended by Dyce. Original reads *Phœbus.*
[2] Are wont, accustomed.
[3] Probably a misprint for *far. Cf.* l. 152 for
the phrase *far indeed contrary kind (i.e.,* nature)
and also l. 144 for the Latin equivalent.
[4] Chair of state.

Tres simul. *Vive diu, felix votis homi-
　numque deumque,
　Corpore, mente, libro, doctissima, candida,
　casta.*[5]

*They lay down their properties at the Queen's
　feet.*
Cloth. *Clotho colum pedibus,*
Lach. *Lachesis tibi pendula fila,*
Atro. *Et fatale tuis manibus ferrum Atro-
　pos offert.*
[Tres simul.] *Vive diu, felix, etc.*[6]　　130
*The song being ended, Clotho speaks to the
　Queen.*
Cloth. Gracious and wise, fair queen of
　　rare renown,
　Whom heaven and earth beloves, amid
　　thy train—
　Noble and lovely peers—to honor thee
　And do thee favor more than may belong
　By nature's law to any earthly wight,[7]
　Behold continuance of our yearly due.
　Th' unpartial dames of destiny, we meet,
　As have the gods and we agreed in one,
　In reverence of Eliza's noble name;
　And humbly, lo, her distaff Clotho
　　yields!　　　　　　　　　　　　140
Lach. Her spindle Lachesis, and her fa-
　　tal reel,
　Lays down in reverence at Eliza's feet.
*Te tamen in terris unam tria numina
　Divam
Invita statuunt naturæ lege sorores,
Et tibi, non aliis, didicerunt parcere
　Parcæ.*[8]

[5] Cloth. Thus the Fates spin the thread of
　human life.
Lach. Thus the Fates measure the thread of
　human life.
Atro. Thus the Fates cut the thread of hu-
　man life.
Cloth. Clotho bears the distaff.
Lach.　　　　　　Lachesis measures.
Atro.　　　　　　　　Atropos cuts.
The three together. Live long, happy in
　the prayers of men and gods,
　Chaste in body, pure in mind, most skilled in
　learning.
[6] Cloth. Clotho [places] the distaff at thy
　feet,
Lach. Lachesis [gives] thee the pendent threads,
Atro. And Atropos puts into your hands the
　fateful shears.
[The three together.] Live long, happy, etc.
[7] Person.
[8] The three divine sisters, despite the law of
nature, appoint thee a goddess unique, though on
earth; and thee and no others have the Fates
learned to spare.

ATRO. Dame Atropos, according as her feres,
To thee, fair queen, resigns her fatal knife.
Live long the noble phœnix of our age,
Our fair Eliza, our Zabeta fair!   149
DIAN. And lo, beside this rare solemnity
And sacrifice these dames are wont to do,
A favor, far indeed contrary kind,
Bequeathéd is unto thy worthiness—
She delivereth the ball of gold to the Queen's own hands.
This prize from heaven and heavenly goddesses!
Accept it, then, thy due by Dian's doom,
Praise of the wisdom, beauty, and the state,

That best becomes thy peerless excellency.
VEN. So, fair Eliza, Venus doth resign
The honor of this honor to be thine.
JUN. So is the Queen of Heaven content likewise   160
To yield to thee her title in the prize.
PAL. So Pallas yields the praise hereof to thee,
For wisdom, princely state, and peerless beauty.

EPILOGUS

OMNES SIMUL. *Vive diu felix, votis hominumque deumque,*
Corpore, mente, libro, doctissima, candida, casta.   *Exeunt omnes.*

FINIS.

THE OLD WIVES' TALE[1]

BY

GEORGE PEELE

[DRAMATIS PERSONÆ

SACRAPANT, *the conjurer.*
FIRST BROTHER, *named* CALYPHA.
SECOND BROTHER, *named* THELEA.
EUMENIDES, *the Wandering Knight.*
OLD MAN, *named* ERESTUS.
LAMPRISCUS.
HUANEBANGO.
COREBUS, *or* BOOBY, *the clown.*
WIGGEN.
CHURCHWARDEN, *named* STEVEN LOACH.
SEXTON.
GHOST OF JACK.
FRIAR, HARVESTMEN, *and* HARVESTWOMEN,
   TWO FURIES, *and* FIDDLERS.

DELIA, *sister to Calypha and Thelea.*
VENELIA, *betrothed to Erestus.*
ZANTIPPA, *the Curst* [2] *Daughter of Lampris-*
   cus.
CELANTA, *the Foul Wench, another daughter.*
HOSTESS.
ANTIC   ⎫
FROLIC   ⎪
FANTASTIC ⎪
A SMITH, *named* ⎬ *Characters of induction*
  CLUNCH   ⎪ *and interscenes.*
OLD WOMAN, *his* ⎪
  wife, named ⎪
  MADGE   ⎭

SCENE: *England.*

TIME: *Mythical.*]

Enter Antic, Frolic, and Fantastic.[3]

ANT. How now, fellow Frolic![4] What, all amort?[5] Doth this sadness become thy madness? What though we have lost our way in the woods, yet never hang the head as though thou hadst no hope to live till tomorrow; for Fantastic and I will warrant thy life tonight for twenty in the hundred.

FROL. Antic and Fantastic, as I am frolic franion,[6] never in all my life was I so dead slain. What, to lose our way in [10 the wood, without either fire or candle, so uncomfortable! *O cælum! O terra!*[7] *O Maria! O Neptune!*

FANT. Why makes thou it so strange, seeing Cupid hath led our young master to the fair lady, and she is the only saint that he hath sworn to serve?

FROL. What resteth[8] then but we commit him to his wench, and each of us take his stand up in a tree, and sing out our [20 ill fortune to the tune of "O man in desperation"?

ANT. Desperately spoken, fellow Frolic, in the dark; but, seeing it falls out thus, let us rehearse the old proverb:

"Three merry men, and three merry men,
  And three merry men be we;
I in the wood, and thou on the ground,
  And Jack sleeps in the tree."

FANT. Hush! A dog in the wood, or [30 a wooden[9] dog! O comfortable hearing! I had even as lief the chamberlain of the White Horse had called me up to bed.

---

[1] The traditional title of the play is retained, although *wives* was a common possessive singular, and although the original entry in the Stationers' Register for April 16, 1595, reads: "A booke or interlude, intituled a pleasant Conceipte called the owlde wifes tale." The title continues: "A Pleasant Conceited Comedy, Played by the Queen's Majesty's Players. Written by G. P."
[2] Peevish.
[3] In the original there is no scene division or indication of setting. The action represents what Madge and her group visualize.
[4] Original has *Franticke.*
[5] Dejected.   [6] An idle, carefree fellow.
[7] O heaven! O earth!
[8] Remaineth.   [9] Punning on *wood*, mad.

231

Frol. Either hath this trotting cur gone out of his circuit, or else are we near some

Enter a Smith, with a lantern and candle.

village, which should not be far off, for I perceive the glimmering of a glowworm, a candle, or a cat's eye, my life for a half-penny! In the name of my own father, be thou ox or ass that appearest, tell us [40 what thou art.

Smith. What am I? Why, I am Clunch the smith. What are you? What make [1] you in my territories at this time of the night?

Ant. What do we make, dost thou ask? Why, we make faces for fear, such as, if thy mortal eyes could behold, would make thee water the long seams of thy side slops,[2] smith.   50

Frol. And, in faith, sir, unless your hospitality do relieve us, we are like to wander, with a sorrowful heigh-ho, among the owlets and hobgoblins of the forest. Good Vulcan, for Cupid's sake that hath cozened us all, befriend us as thou mayst; and command us howsoever, wheresoever, whensoever, in whatsoever, for ever and ever.

Smith. Well, masters, it seems to [60 me you have lost your way in the wood; in consideration whereof, if you will go with Clunch to his cottage, you shall have house-room and a good fire to sit by, although we have no bedding to put you in.

All. O blessed smith, O bountiful Clunch!

Smith. For your further entertainment, it shall be as it may be, so and so.
                                   Hear a dog bark.
Hark! [3] This is Ball, my dog, that [70 bids you all welcome in his own language. Come, take heed for stumbling on the threshold.—Open door, Madge; take in guests.

Enter Old Woman.

Old Wom. Welcome, Clunch, and good fellows all, that come with my goodman. For my goodman's sake, come on, sit down. Here is a piece of cheese and a pudding of my own making.

---

[1] Do.   [2] Loose breeches.
[3] The scene is now at the cottage.

Ant. Thanks, gammer; a good ex- [80 ample for the wives of our town.

Frol. Gammer, thou and thy goodman sit lovingly together. We come to chat, and not to eat.

Smith. Well, masters, if you will eat nothing, take away. Come, what do we to pass away the time? Lay a crab in the fire to roast for lamb's wool.[4] What, shall we have a game at trump or ruff [5] to drive away the time? How say you?   90

Fant. This smith leads a life as merry as a king with Madge his wife. Sirrah Frolic, I am sure thou art not without some round [6] or other; no doubt but Clunch can bear his part.

Frol. Else think you me ill brought up; so set to it when you will.   *They sing.*

Song

Whenas the rye reach to the chin,
And chopcherry, chopcherry ripe [7] within,
Strawberries swimming in the cream,   100
And schoolboys playing in the stream;
Then O, then O, then O, my true love said,
Till that time come again,
She could not live a maid.

Ant. This sport does well, but methinks, gammer, a merry winter's tale would drive away the time trimly. Come, I am sure you are not without a score.

Fant. I' faith, gammer, a tale of an hour long were as good as an hour's sleep.   110

Frol. Look you, gammer, of the giant and the king's daughter, and I know not what. I have seen the day, when I was a little one, you might have drawn me a mile after you with such a discourse.

Old Wom. Well, since you be so importunate, my goodman shall fill the pot and get him to bed. They that ply their work must keep good hours. One of you go lie with him; he is a clean-skinned [120 man, I tell you, without either spavin or windgall. So I am content to drive away the time with an old wives' winter's tale.

Fant. No better hay in Devonshire. O' my word, gammer, I'll be one of your audience.

---

[4] Ale mixed with the pulp of roasted crab-apples.
[5] Card games.   [6] Song.
[7] A game of catching a suspended cherry with the teeth.

FROL. And I another, that's flat.

ANT. Then must I to bed with the goodman.—*Bona nox*,[1] gammer. Good night,
Frolic.   130

SMITH. Come on, my lad, thou shalt
take thy unnatural rest with me.

Exeunt Antic and the Smith.

FROL. Yet this vantage shall we have of
them in the morning, to be ready at the
sight thereof extempore.

OLD WOM. Now this bargain, my masters, must I make with you, that you will
say hum and ha to my tale. So shall I
know you are awake.

BOTH. Content, gammer; that will   [140
we do.

OLD WOM. Once upon a time, there was
a king, or a lord, or a duke, that had a fair
daughter, the fairest that ever was, as white
as snow and as red as blood; and once upon
a time his daughter was stolen away, and
he sent all his men to seek out his daughter,
and he sent so long that he sent all his men
out of his land.

FROL. Who dressed his dinner, then?   [150

OLD WOM. Nay, either hear my tale, or
kiss my tail.

FANT. Well said! On with your tale,
gammer.

OLD WOM. O Lord, I quite forgot!
There was a conjurer, and this conjurer
could do anything, and he turned himself
into a great dragon, and carried the king's
daughter away in his mouth to a castle
that he made of stone, and there he   [160
kept her I know not how long, till at last
all the king's men went out so long that her
two brothers went to seek her. O, I forget!
She—he, I would say—turned a proper
young man to a bear in the night, and a
man in the day, and keeps [2] by a cross that
parts three several ways, and he made his
lady run mad.—God's me bones, who comes
here?

Enter the Two Brothers.

FROL. Soft, gammer, here some   [170
come to tell your tale for you.

FANT. Let them alone; let us hear what
they will say.

1 BRO. Upon these chalky cliffs of Albion
We are arrivéd now with tedious toil,

[1] Good night.
[2] Dwells (referring to the young man).

And compassing the wide world round
   about,
To seek our sister, to seek fair Delia forth,
Yet cannot we so much as hear of her.

2 BRO. O fortune cruel, cruel and unkind!
Unkind in that we cannot find our
   sister,   180
Our sister, hapless in her cruel chance!
Soft! Who have we here?

*Enter Senex [Old Man] at the Cross, stooping
                                    to gather.*

1 BRO. Now, father, God be your speed!
What do you gather there?

OLD MAN. Hips and haws, and sticks
and straws, and things that I gather on the
ground, my son.

1 BRO. Hips and haws, and sticks and
straws! Why, is that all your food, father?

OLD MAN. Yea, son.   190

2 BRO. Father, here is an alms penny
for me; and, if I speed in that I go for, I
will give thee as good a gown of gray as
ever thou diddest wear.

1 BRO. And, father, here is another alms
penny for me; and, if I speed in my journey,
I will give thee a palmer's staff of ivory and
a scallop shell of beaten gold.

OLD MAN. Was she fair?

2 BRO. Ay, the fairest for white,   [200
and the purest for red, as the blood of the
deer or the driven snow.

OLD MAN. Then hark well, and mark well,
   my old spell:
Be not afraid of every stranger;
Start not aside at every danger;
Things that seem are not the same;
Blow a blast at every flame;
For, when one flame of fire goes out,
Then comes your wishes well about.
If any ask who told you this good,   210
Say the white bear of England's wood.

1 BRO. Brother, heard you not what the
   old man said?
"Be not afraid of every stranger;
Start not aside for every danger;
Things that seem are not the same;
Blow a blast at every flame;
[For, when one flame of fire goes out,
Then comes your wishes well about.]
If any ask who told you this good,
Say the white bear of England's
   wood."   220

2 BRO. Well, if this do us any good,

Well fare the white bear of England's
wood!   *Ex[eunt the Two Brothers]*.
OLD MAN. Now sit thee here, and tell a
heavy tale.

Sad in thy mood, and sober in thy cheer,
Here sit thee now, and to thyself relate
The hard mishap of thy most wretched
state.
In Thessaly I lived in sweet content,
Until that fortune wrought my over-
throw;
For there I wedded was unto a dame
That lived in honor, virtue, love, and
fame.   230
But Sacrapant, that curséd sorcerer,
Being besotted with my beauteous love,
My dearest love, my true betrothéd wife,
Did seek the means to rid me of my life.
But, worse than this, he with his chant-
ing spells
Did turn me straight unto an ugly bear;
And, when the sun doth settle in the west,
Then I begin to don my ugly hide.
And all the day I sit, as now you see,
And speak in riddles, all inspired with
rage,   240
Seeming an old and miserable man;
And yet I am in April of my age.

*Enter Venelia his lady, mad, and goes in
again.*

See where Venelia, my betrothéd love,
Runs madding, all enraged, about the
woods,
All by his curséd and enchanting spells.—

Enter Lampriscus with a pot of honey.

But here comes Lampriscus, my discontented neighbor. How now, neighbor! You
look toward the ground as well as I; you
muse on something.
LAMP. Neighbor, on nothing but on [250
the matter I so often moved to you. If you
do anything for charity, help me; if for
neighborhood or brotherhood, help me.
Never was one so cumbered as is poor
Lampriscus. And, to begin, I pray receive
this pot of honey to mend your fare.
OLD MAN. Thanks, neighbor, set it
down. Honey is always welcome to the
bear. And now, neighbor, let me hear the
cause of your coming.   260
LAMP. I am, as you know, neighbor, a

man unmarried, and lived so unquietly
with my two wives that I keep every year
holy the day wherein I buried them both.
The first was on Saint Andrew's day,[1] the
other on Saint Luke's.[2]
OLD MAN. And now, neighbor, you of
this country say your custom is out. But
on with your tale, neighbor.
LAMP. By my first wife, whose [270
tongue wearied me alive, and sounded in
my ears like the clapper of a great bell,
whose talk was a continual torment to all
that dwelt by her or lived nigh her, you
have heard me say I had a handsome
daughter.
OLD MAN. True, neighbor.
LAMP. She it is that afflicts me with her
continual clamors, and hangs on me like a
bur. Poor she is, and proud she is; as [280
poor as a sheep new-shorn, and as proud
of her hopes as a peacock of her tail well
grown.
OLD MAN. Well said, Lampriscus! You
speak it like an Englishman.
LAMP. As curst as a wasp and as froward as a child new-taken from the
mother's teat; she is to my age as smoke
to the eyes or as vinegar to the teeth.
OLD MAN. Holily praised, neighbor. [290
As much for the next.
LAMP. By my other wife I had a daughter so hard-favored, so foul and ill-faced,
that I think a grove full of golden trees,
and the leaves of rubies and diamonds,
would not be a dowry answerable to her
deformity.
OLD MAN. Well, neighbor, now you
have spoke, hear me speak. Send them to
the well for the water of life; there shall [300
they find their fortunes unlooked for.
Neighbor, farewell.   *Exit.*
LAMP. Farewell, and a thousand! And
now goeth poor Lampriscus to put in execution this excellent counsel.   *Exit.*[3]

FROL. Why, this goes round without a
fiddling stick. But, do you hear, gammer,
was this the man that was a bear in the
night and a man in the day?
OLD WOM. Ay, this is he; and this [310

---

[1] Lovers' lucky day.
[2] "St. Luke was jocularly regarded as the
patron saint of cuckolds" (Bullen).
[3] Original reads *Exeunt*.

man that came to him was a beggar, and
dwelt upon a green. But soft! Who comes
here? O, these are the harvestmen. Ten
to one they sing a song of mowing.

*Enter the Harvestmen a-singing, with this
song double repeated.*

All ye that lovely lovers be,
Pray you for me.
Lo, here we come a-sowing, a-sowing,
And sow sweet fruits of love;
In your sweet hearts well may it prove!
Exeunt.

*Enter Huanebango with his two-hand sword,
and Booby, the clown.*

FANT. Gammer, what is he?   320
OLD WOM. O, this is one that is going to
the conjurer. Let him alone; hear what he
says.

HUAN. Now, by Mars and Mercury,
Jupiter and Janus, Sol and Saturnus,
Venus and Vesta, Pallas and Proserpina,
and by the honor of my house, Polimacker-
oeplacidus, it is a wonder to see what this
love will make silly fellows adventure, even
in the wane of their wits and infancy of [330
their discretion. Alas, my friend, what fortune calls thee forth to seek thy fortune
among brazen gates, enchanted towers, fire
and brimstone, thunder and lightning?
Beauty, I tell thee, is peerless, and she
precious whom thou affectest. Do off these
desires, good countryman; good friend, run
away from thyself; and, so soon as thou
canst, forget her, whom none must inherit
but he that can monsters tame, labors [340
achieve, riddles absolve, loose enchantments, murther magic, and kill conjuring—
and that is the great and mighty Huanebango.
BOOBY. Hark you, sir, hark you. First
know I have here the flirting [1] feather, and
have given the parish the start for the long
stock.[2] Now, sir, if it be no more but running
through a little lightning and thunder, and
"riddle me, riddle me what's this?" [350
I'll have the wench from the conjurer, if he
were ten conjurers.

[1] Swaying.
[2] Either *startled the parish with my long stockings* or *started the style for long stockings in the
parish.*

HUAN. I have abandoned the court and
honorable company, to do my devoir
against this sore sorcerer and mighty
magician. If this lady be so fair as she is
said to be, she is mine, she is mine; *meus,
mea, meum, in contemptum omnium gram-
maticorum.*[3]
BOOBY. *O falsum Latinum!* The fair [360
maid is *minum, cum apurtinantibus gib-
letes* [4] and all.
HUAN. If she be mine, as I assure myself the heavens will do somewhat to reward
my worthiness, she shall be allied to none
of the meanest gods, but be invested in the
most famous stock of Huanebango—Poli-
mackeroeplacidus, my grandfather; my
father, Pergopolineo; my mother, Dionora
de Sardinia, famously descended.   370
BOOBY. Do you hear, sir? Had not you
a cousin that was called Gusteceridis?
HUAN. Indeed, I had a cousin that sometime followed the court infortunately, and
his name Bustegusteceridis.
BOOBY. O Lord, I know him well! He
is the knight of the neat's feet.
HUAN. O, he loved no capon better! He
hath oftentimes deceived his boy of his dinner. That was his fault, good Buste- [380
gusteceridis.
BOOBY. Come, shall we go along?

[Enter Old Man.]

Soft! Here is an old man at the cross; let us
ask him the way thither.—Ho, you gaffer!
I pray you tell where the wise man, the
conjurer, dwells.
HUAN. Where that earthly goddess
keepeth her abode, the commander of
my thoughts and fair mistress of my heart.
OLD MAN. Fair enough, and far [390
enough from thy fingering, son.
HUAN. I will follow my fortune after
mine own fancy, and do according to mine
own discretion.
OLD MAN. Yet give something to an old
man before you go.
HUAN. Father, methinks a piece of this
cake might serve your turn.
OLD MAN. Yea, son.
HUAN. Huanebango giveth no [400
cakes for alms; ask of them that give gifts

[3] Mine, mine, mine, in contempt of all gram-
marians.   [4] Mine, with her appurtenant parts.

for poor beggars.—Fair lady, if thou wert once shrined in this bosom, I would buckler [1] thee haratantara.   *Exit.*

BOOBY. Father, do you see this man? You little think he'll run a mile or two for such a cake, or pass [2] for a pudding. I tell you, father, he has kept such a begging of me for a piece of this cake! Whoo! He comes upon me with "a superfantial [410 substance, and the foison [3] of the earth," that I know not what he means. If he came to me thus, and said, "My friend Booby," or so, why, I could spare him a piece with all my heart; but, when he tells me how God hath enriched me above other fellows with a cake, why, he makes me blind and deaf at once. Yet, father, here is a piece of cake for you, as hard as the world goes. [4]   420

OLD MAN. Thanks, son, but list to me:
He shall be deaf when thou shalt not see.
Farewell, my son. Things may so hit,
Thou mayst have wealth to mend thy wit.

BOOBY. Farewell, father, farewell; for I must make haste after my two-hand sword that is gone before.   *Exeunt omnes.*

Enter Sacrapant in his study.

SACR. The day is clear, the welkin bright and gray,
The lark is merry and records her notes;
Each thing rejoiceth underneath the sky   430
But only I, whom heaven hath in hate,
Wretched and miserable Sacrapant.
In Thessaly was I born and brought up;
My mother Meroe hight, [5] a famous witch,
And by her cunning I of her did learn
To change and alter shapes of mortal men.
There did I turn myself into a dragon,
And stole away the daughter to the king,
Fair Delia, the mistress of my heart,
And brought her hither to revive the man   440
That seemeth young and pleasant to behold,
And yet is aged, crooked, weak, and numb.
Thus by enchanting spells I do deceive

Those that behold and look upon my face;
But well may I bid youthful years adieu.

Enter Delia with a pot in her hand.

See where she comes from whence my sorrows grow!
How now, fair Delia, where have you been?

DEL. At the foot of the rock for running water, and gathering roots for your dinner, sir.   450

SACR. Ah, Delia, fairer art thou than the running water, yet harder far than steel or adamant!

DEL. Will it please you to sit down, sir?

SACR. Ay, Delia, sit and ask me what thou wilt,
Thou shalt have it brought into thy lap.

DEL. Then, I pray you, sir, let me have the best meat from the King of England's table, and the best wine in all France, brought in by the veriest knave in all [460 Spain.

SACR. Delia, I am glad to see you so pleasant. Well, sit thee down.—
Spread, table, spread
Meat, drink, and bread!
Ever may I have
What I ever crave,
When I am spread,
For meat for my black cock,
And meat for my red.   470

Enter a Friar with a chine of beef and a pot of wine.

Here, Delia, will ye fall to?

DEL. Is this the best meat in England?

SACR. Yea.

DEL. What is it?

SACR. A chine of English beef, meat for a king and a king's followers.

DEL. Is this the best wine in France?

SACR. Yea.

DEL. What wine is it?

SACR. A cup of neat wine of Or- [480 leans, that never came near the brewers in England.

DEL. Is this the veriest knave in all Spain?

SACR. Yea.

DEL. What is he, a friar?

SACR. Yea, a friar indefinite, and a knave infinite.

---

[1] Protect.   [2] Care.
[3] Plentiful harvest. Booby imitates the stilted language of Huanebango.
[4] Though times are hard.   [5] Was called.

DEL. Then, I pray ye, Sir Friar, tell me before you go which is the most greed- [490 iest Englishman?

FRIAR. The miserable and most covetous usurer.

SACR. Hold thee there, friar. *Exit Friar.* But soft! Who have we here? Delia, away, be gone!

Enter the Two Brothers.

Delia, away, for beset are we!—
But heaven [n]or hell shall rescue her for [1] me.

[*Exeunt Delia and Sacrapant.*]

1 BRO. Brother, was not that Delia did appear?
Or was it but her shadow that was here?

2 BRO. Sister, where art thou? Delia, come again! 500
He calls, that of thy absence doth complain.—
Call out, Calypha, that she may hear,
And cry aloud, for Delia is near.

ECHO. Near.

1 BRO. Near! O, where? Hast thou any tidings?

ECHO. Tidings.

2 BRO. Which way is Delia, then—or that, or this?

ECHO. This.

1 BRO. And may we safely come where Delia is?

ECHO. Yes. 510

2 BRO. Brother, remember you the white bear of England's wood?
"Start not aside for every danger;
Be not afeard of every stranger;
Things that seem are not the same."

1 BRO. Brother, why do we not then courageously enter?

2 BRO. Then, brother, draw thy sword and follow me.

Enter the Conjurer; it lightens and thunders; the 2 Brother falls down.

1 BRO. What, brother, dost thou fall?

SACR. Ay, and thou too, Calypha. 520

Fall 1 Brother. Enter two Furies.

Ádeste, dæmones! [2] Away with them!
Go carry them straight to Sacrapanto's cell,
There in despair and torture for to dwell.

[1] Because of.   [2] Come, spirits!

These are Thenores' sons of Thessaly,
That come to seek Delia, their sister, forth;
But, with a potion I to her have given,
My arts hath made her to forget herself.

He removes a turf and shows a light in a glass.[3]

See here the thing which doth prolong my life.
With this enchantment I do anything;
And, till this fade, my skill shall still endure, 530
And never none shall break this little glass,
But she that's neither wife, widow, nor maid.
Then cheer thyself; this is thy destiny,
Never to die but by a dead man's hand.

Exeunt.

Enter Eumenides, the Wandering Knight, and the Old Man at the Cross.

EUM. Tell me, Time, tell me, just Time,
When shall I Delia see?
When shall I see the lodestar of my life?
When shall my wand'ring course end with her sight,
Or I but view my hope, my heart's delight?—
Father, God speed! If you tell fortunes, [540
I pray, good father, tell me mine.

OLD MAN. Son, I do see in thy face
Thy blessed fortune work apace.
I do perceive that thou hast wit;
Beg of thy fate to govern it,
For wisdom governed by advice
Makes many fortunate and wise.
Bestow thy alms, give more than all,
Till dead men's bones come at thy call.
Farewell, my son! Dream of no rest [550
Till thou repent that thou didst best.

Exit Old M[an].

EUM. This man hath left me in a labyrinth:
He biddeth me give more than all,
"Till dead men's bones come at thy call;"
He biddeth me dream of no rest,
Till I repent that I do best.

[*He lies down and sleeps.*]

[3] "The 'Life-Index,' so called, of popular tales, connected with the equally popular *motif* of the 'Thankful Dead'" (Gummere).

Enter Wiggen, Corebus,[1] *Churchwarden, and Sexton.*

WIG. You may be ashamed, you whoreson [2] scald [3] sexton and churchwarden, if you had any shame in those shameless faces of yours, to let a poor man lie so [560 long above ground unburied. A rot on you all, that have no more compassion of a good fellow when he is gone!

CHURCH.[4] What, would you have us to bury him, and to answer it ourselves to the parish?

SEX. Parish me no parishes! Pay me my fees, and let the rest run on in the quarter's accounts, and put it down for one of your good deeds, o' God's name, for I [570 am not one that curiously [5] stands upon merits.

COR. You whoreson, sodden-headed sheep's-face, shall a good fellow do less service and more honesty to the parish, and will you not, when he is dead, let him have Christmas [6] burial?

WIG. Peace, Corebus! As sure as Jack was Jack, the frolic'st franion amongst you, and I, Wiggen, his sweet sworn [580 brother, Jack shall have his funerals, or some of them shall lie on God's dear earth for it, that's once.[7]

CHURCH. Wiggen, I hope thou wilt do no more than thou dar'st answer.

WIG. Sir, sir, dare or dare not, more or less, answer or not answer, do this, or have this.

Wiggen sets upon the parish [8] *with a pikestaff.*

SEX. Help, help, help!

Eumenides awakes and comes to them.

EUM. Hold thy hands, good fellow. [590

COR. Can you blame him, sir, if he take Jack's part against this shake-rotten parish that will not bury Jack?

EUM. Why, what was that Jack?

COR. Who, Jack, sir? Who, our Jack, sir? As good a fellow as ever trod upon neat's-leather.

WIG. Look you, sir, he gave fourscore and nineteen mourning gowns to the parish

when he died, and, because he would [600 not make them up a full hundred, they would not bury him. Was not this good dealing?

CHURCH. O Lord, sir, how he lies! He was not worth a halfpenny, and drunk out every penny; and now his fellows, his drunken companions, would have us to bury him at the charge of the parish. And [9] we make many such matches, we may pull down the steeple, sell the bells, and [610 thatch the chancel. He shall lie above ground till he dance a galliard about the churchyard, for Steven Loach.

WIG. *Sic argumentaris, Domine* Loach:[10] "and we make many such matches, we may pull down the steeple, sell the bells, and thatch the chancel!"—In good time, sir, and hang yourselves in the bell ropes when you have done. *Domine, opponens præpono tibi hanc quæstionem,*[11] whether [620 will you have the ground broken or your pates broken first? For one of them shall be done presently, and, to begin mine, I'll seal it upon your coxcomb.

EUM. Hold thy hands, I pray thee, good fellow; be not too hasty.

COR. You capon's face, we shall have you turned out of the parish one of these days, with never a tatter to your arse. Then you are in worse taking than [630 Jack.

EUM. Faith, and he is bad enough. This fellow does but the part of a friend, to seek to bury his friend. How much will bury him?

WIG. Faith, about some fifteen or sixteen shillings will bestow him honestly.

SEX. Ay, even thereabouts, sir.

EUM. Here, hold it then. [*Starts to give money; then speaks to himself.*] And [640 I have left me but one poor three halfpence. Now do I remember the words the old man spake at the cross, "Bestow all thou hast," and this is all, "till dead men's bones come at thy call."—Here, hold it. [*Gives money.*] And so farewell.

WIG. God and all good be with you, sir! Nay, you cormorants, I'll bestow one peal of [12] Jack at mine own proper costs and charges.   650

---

[1] Previously, Booby, the clown.
[2] Rascally.   [4] Original has *Simon.*
[3] Scabby.   [5] Carefully.
[6] Corebus' blunder for *Christian.*
[7] "That's settled once for all" (Bullen).
[8] Sexton.

[9] If.   [10] Thus you argue, Master Loach.
[11] Master, responding, I put before you this question.   [12] Peal of bells on.

Cor. You may thank God the long staff and the bilbo-blade crossed not your coxcomb. Well, we'll to the church-stile [1] and have a pot, and so trill-lill.

Both [Churchwarden and Sexton]. Come, let's go.   *Exeunt.*

Fant. But, hark you, gammer, methinks this Jack bore a great sway in the parish.   658
Old Wom. O, this Jack was a marvelous fellow! He was but a poor man, but very well beloved. You shall see anon what this Jack will come to.

Enter the Harvestmen singing, with Women in their hands.

Frol. Soft! Who have we here? Our amorous harvesters.[2]
Fant. Ay, ay, let us sit still, and let them alone.
Here they begin to sing, the song doubled.

Lo, here we come a-reaping, a-reaping,
To reap our harvest fruit,
And thus we pass the year so long,
And never be we mute.   670
                    Exit the Harvestmen.

Enter Huanebango and Corebus, the clown.

Frol. Soft! Who have we here?
Old Wom. O, this is a choleric gentleman! All you that love your lives, keep out of the smell of his two-hand sword. Now goes he to the conjurer.
Fant. Methinks the conjurer should put the fool into a juggling-box.

Huan. Fee, fa, fum, here is the English-man—
    Conquer him that can—
    Came for his lady bright,   680
    To prove himself a knight,
    And win her love in fight.
Cor. Who-haw, Master Bango, are you here? Hear you, you had best sit down here and beg an alms with me.
Huan. Hence, base cullion! Here is he that commandeth ingress and egress with

his weapon, and will enter at his voluntary, whosoever saith no.
A voice and flame of fire; Huanebango falleth down.
Voice. No!   690

Old Wom. So with that they kissed, and spoiled the edge of as good a two-hand sword as ever God put life in. Now goes Corebus in, spite of the conjurer.

Enter the Conjurer [with two Furies] and strike Corebus blind.

Sacr. Away with him into the open fields,
To be a ravening prey to crows and kites.
    [*The Furies carry Huanebango out.*]
And, for this villain, let him wander up and down
In naught but darkness and eternal night.
Cor. Here hast thou slain Huan, a slashing knight,
And robbéd poor Corebus of his sight.
                                        Exit.
Sacr. Hence, villain, hence!—   701
Now I have unto Delia given a potion of forgetfulness,
That, when she comes, she shall not know her brothers.
Lo, where they labor, like to country slaves
With spade and mattock on this enchanted ground!
Now will I call her by another name;
For never shall she know herself again,
Until that Sacrapant hath breathed his last.
See where she comes.

Enter Delia.

Come hither, Delia, take this goad. 710
Here hard at hand two slaves do work and dig for gold;
Gore them with this, and thou shalt have enough.   *He gives her a goad.*
Del. Good sir, I know not what you mean.
Sacr. [*Aside.*] She hath forgotten to be Delia,
But not forgot the same she should forget;
But I will change her name.—
Fair Berecynthia, so this country calls you,
Go ply these strangers, wench; they dig for gold.   *Exit Sacrapant.*
Del. O heavens, how am I beholding [3] to this fair young man!

[1] Gummere quotes Overbury's *Characters:* "For at every church stile commonly ther's an ale-house."
[2] Original has *harvest starres.*
[3] Beholden, indebted.

But I must ply these strangers to their work. 720
See where they come.

*Enter the Two Brothers in their shirts, with
spades, digging.*

1 BRO. O brother, see where Delia is!

2 BRO. O Delia, happy are we to see thee here!

DEL. What tell you me of Delia, prating swains?
I know no Delia, nor know I what you mean.
Ply you your work, or else you're like to smart.

1 BRO. Why, Delia, know'st thou not thy brothers here?
We come from Thessaly to seek thee forth;
And thou deceivest thyself, for thou art Delia. 729

DEL. Yet more of Delia? Then take this, and smart. [*Pricks them with the goad.*]
What, feign you shifts for to defer your labor?
Work, villains, work; it is for gold you dig.

2 BRO. Peace, brother, peace! This vild [1] enchanter
Hath ravished Delia of her senses clean,
And she forgets that she is Delia.

1 BRO. Leave, cruel thou, to hurt the miserable.—
Dig, brother, dig, for she is hard as steel.

*Here they dig, and descry the light under a
little hill.*

2 BRO. Stay, brother; what hast thou descried?

DEL. Away, and touch it not; it is something that my lord hath hidden there.
She covers it again.

Enter Sacrapant.

SACR. Well said! Thou plyest these pioners [2] well.—Go, get you in, you laboring slaves.— 740
Come, Berecynthia, let us in likewise,
And hear the nightingale record her notes. *Exeunt omnes.*

*Enter Zantippa, the Curst Daughter, to the
well, with a pot in her hand.* [3]

ZANT. Now for a husband, house, and home. God send a good one or none, I pray

God! My father hath sent me to the well for the water of life, and tells me, if I give fair words, I shall have a husband.

*Enter [Celanta,] the Foul Wench, to the well
for water with a pot in her hand.*

But here comes Celanta, my sweet sister. I'll stand by and hear what she says. [749

CEL. My father hath sent me to the well for water, and he tells me, if I speak fair, I shall have a husband and none of the worst. Well, though I am black,[4] I am sure all the world will not forsake me; and, as the old proverb is, though I am black, I am not the devil.

ZANT. Marry-gup with a murrain,[5] I know wherefore thou speakest that. But go thy ways home as wise as thou [759 cam'st, or I'll set thee home with a wanion.[6]

*Here she strikes her pitcher against her sis-
ter's, and breaks them both, and goes
her way.*

CEL. I think this be the curstest quean in the world. You see what she is, a little fair but as proud as the devil, and the veriest vixen that lives upon God's earth. Well, I'll let her alone, and go home and get another pitcher, and for all this get me to the well for water. *Exit*

*Enter two Furies out of the Conjurer's cell
and lays Huanebango by the Well of
Life [and then exeunt]. Enter Zantippa
with a pitcher to the well.*

ZANT. Once again for a husband; and in faith, Celanta, I have got the start [769 of you. Belike husbands grow by the well-side. Now my father says I must rule my tongue. Why, alas, what am I then? A woman without a tongue is as a soldier without his weapon. But I'll have my water and be gone.

*Here she offers to dip her pitcher in, and a
Head speaks in the well.*

HEAD. Gently dip, but not too deep;
For fear you make the golden beard [7] to weep,
Fair maiden, white and red,
Stroke me smooth, and comb my head;
And thou shalt have some cockle-bread.[8]

---

[1] Vile.   [2] Diggers.
[3] This scene is a reworking of *The Three Heads
of the Well.*

[4] Ugly.
[5] Plague take you!   [6] Vengeance.
[7] Original has *birde*, but see l. 959.
[8] Bread kneaded in a peculiar fashion and used as a love charm.

ZANT. What is this: "Fair maiden, white
and red, 781
Comb me smooth, and stroke my head,
And thou shalt have some cockle-bread"?
"Cockle," callest thou it, boy? Faith,
I'll give you cockle-bread!

*She breaks her pitcher upon his head; then it
thunders and lightens, and Huanebango
rises up. Huanebango is deaf and cannot hear.*

HUAN. Philida phileridos, Pamphilida flo-
rida flortos,
Dub dub-a-dub, bounce, quoth the guns,
with a sulphurous huff-snuff; [1]
Waked with a wench, pretty peat,[2] pretty
love, and my sweet pretty pigsnie,[3]
Just by thy side shall sit surnamed great
Huanebango;
Safe in my arms will I keep thee, threat
Mars or thunder Olympus. 790
ZANT. [*Aside.*] Foh, what greasy groom
have we here? He looks as though he crept
out of the backside of the well, and speaks
like a drum perished at the west end.[4]
HUAN. O, that I might—but I may not,
woe to my destiny therefore! [5]—
Kiss that I clasp, but I cannot. Tell me,
my destiny, wherefore?
ZANT. [*Aside.*] Whoop! Now I have my
dream. Did you never hear so great a wonder as this? Three blue beans in a blue
bladder—rattle, bladder, rattle. 800
HUAN. [*Aside.*] I'll now set my countenance, and to her in prose. It may be this
rim-ram-ruff [6] is too rude an encounter.—
Let me, fair lady, if you be at leisure, revel
with your sweetness, and rail upon that
cowardly conjurer that hath cast me, or
congealed me rather, into an unkind sleep,
and polluted my carcass.
ZANT. [*Aside.*] Laugh, laugh, Zantippa;
thou hast thy fortune, a fool and a hus- [810
band under one.
HUAN. Truly, sweetheart, as I seem,
about some twenty years, the very April of
mine age.
ZANT. [*Aside.*] Why, what a prating ass
is this!
HUAN. Her coral lips, her crimson chin,
Her silver teeth so white within,

[1] Apparently a parody of Stanyhurst's hexam-
eters. [3] Pig's eye, darling.
[2] Pet. [4] *I.e.*, brokenly.
[5] A quotation from Harvey's *Encomium Lauri.*
[6] Chaucer's phrase for alliteration.

Her golden locks, her rolling eye,
Her pretty parts, let them go by, 820
Heigh-ho, hath wounded me,
That I must die this day to see!
ZANT. By Gog's [7] bones, thou art a
flouting knave. "Her coral lips, her crimson chin"! ka, wilshaw! [8]
HUAN. True, my own, and my own
because mine, and mine because mine, ha,
ha! Above a thousand pounds in possibility, and things fitting thy desire in possession. 830
ZANT. [*Aside.*] The sot thinks I ask of
his lands. Lob be your comfort,[9] and cuckold be your destiny!—Hear you, sir; and,
if you will have us, you had best say so
betime.
HUAN. True, sweetheart, and will royalize thy progeny with my pedigree.
Exeunt omnes.

Enter Eumenides, the Wandering Knight.

EUM. Wretched Eumenides, still unfortu-
nate,
Envied by fortune and forlorn by
fate, 839
Here pine and die, wretched Eumenides!
Die in the spring, the April of my age?
Here sit thee down, repent what thou
hast done.
I would to God that it were ne'er begun.

Enter [the Ghost of] Jack.

JACK. You are well overtaken, sir.
EUM. Who's that?
JACK. You are heartily well met, sir.
EUM. Forbear, I say. Who is that which
pincheth me?
JACK. Trusting in God, good Master
Eumenides, that you are in so good [850
health as all your friends were at the making hereof, God give you good morrow, sir!
Lack you not a neat, handsome, and cleanly
young lad, about the age of fifteen or sixteen years, that can run by your horse,
and, for a need, make your mastership's
shoes as black as ink? How say you, sir?
EUM. Alas, pretty lad, I know not how
to keep myself, and much less a serv-

[7] God's.
[8] Quotha wilta-shalta, *i.e.*, quoth he willy-
nilly.
[9] "May you be brought into 'Lob's pound,'
the thralldom of the hen-pecked married man"
(Bullen).

ant, my pretty boy, my state is so [860 bad.

JACK. Content yourself, you shall not be so ill a master but I'll be as bad a servant. Tut, sir, I know you, though you know not me. Are not you the man, sir, deny it if you can, sir, that came from a strange place in the land of Catita, where Jackanapes flies with his tail in his mouth, to seek out a lady as white as snow and as red as blood? Ha, ha! Have I [870 touched you now?

EUM. [*Aside.*] I think this boy be a spirit.—How know'st thou all this?

JACK. Tut, are not you the man, sir, deny it if you can, sir, that gave all the money you had to the burying of a poor man, and but one three halfpence left in your purse? Content you, sir, I'll serve you, that is flat.　879

EUM. Well, my lad, since thou art so impor[tu]nate, I am content to entertain thee, not as a servant, but a copartner in my journey. But whither shall we go, for I have not any money more than one bare three halfpence?

JACK. Well, master, content yourself, for, if my divination be not out, that shall be spent at the next inn or alehouse we come to, for, master, I know you are passing hungry; therefore I'll go before and [890 provide dinner until that you come. No doubt but you'll come fair and softly after.

EUM. Ay, go before; I'll follow thee.

JACK. But do you hear, master? Do you know my name?

EUM. No, I promise thee, not yet.

JACK. Why, I am Jack. *Exit*[1] *Jack.*

EUM. Jack! Why, be it so then.

Enter the Hostess and Jack, setting meat on the table; and Fiddlers come[2] *to play. Eumenides walketh up and down, and will eat no meat.*

HOST. How say you, sir? Do you please to sit down?　900

EUM. Hostess, I thank you, I have no great stomach.

HOST. Pray, sir, what is the reason your master is so strange? Doth not this meat please him?

JACK. Yes, hostess, but it is my mas-

[1] Original reads *Exeunt.*
[2] Original reads *came.*

ter's fashion to pay before he eats; therefore, a reckoning, good hostess.

HOST. Marry, shall you, sir, presently.
Exit.

EUM. Why, Jack, what dost thou [910 mean? Thou knowest I have not any money; therefore, sweet Jack, tell me, what shall I do?

JACK. Well, master, look in your purse.

EUM. Why, faith, it is a folly, for I have no money.

JACK. Why, look you, master; do so much for me.

EUM. [*Looking into his purse.*] Alas, Jack, my purse is full of money!　920

JACK. "Alas," master! Does that word belong to this accident? Why, methinks I should have seen you cast away your cloak, and in a bravado danced a galliard round about the chamber. Why, master, your man can teach you more wit than this.

[Enter Hostess.]

Come, hostess, cheer up my master.

HOST. You are heartily welcome; and, if it please you to eat of a fat capon, a fairer bird, a finer bird, a sweeter bird, [930 a crisper bird, a neater bird, your worship never eat of.

EUM. Thanks, my fine, eloquent hostess.

JACK. But hear you, master, one word by the way. Are you content I shall be halves in all you get in your journey?

EUM. I am, Jack; here is my hand.

JACK. Enough, master, I ask no more.

EUM. Come, hostess, receive your [939 money; and I thank you for my good entertainment.　[*Gives money.*]

HOST. You are heartily welcome, sir.

EUM. Come, Jack, whither go we now?

JACK. Marry, master, to the conjurer's presently.[3]

EUM. Content, Jack.—Hostess, farewell.　*Exe[unt] om[nes].*

Enter Corebus and Celanta, the Foul Wench, to the well for water.

COR. Come, my duck, come. I have now got a wife. Thou art fair, art thou not?　950

CEL. My Corebus, the fairest alive; make no doubt of that.

COR. Come, wench, are we almost at the well?　[3] At once. ╱

CEL. Ay, Corebus, we are almost at the well now. I'll go fetch some water. Sit down while I dip my pitcher in.

VOICE. Gently dip, but not too deep,
For fear you make the golden beard to weep.

A Head comes up with ears of corn, and she combs them in her lap.

Fair maiden, white and red,   960
Comb me smooth, and stroke my head,
And thou shalt have some cockle-bread.

A Head comes up full of gold; she combs it into her lap.[1]

Gently dip, but not too deep,
For fear thou make the golden beard to weep.
Fair maid, white and red,
Comb me smooth, and stroke my head,
And every hair a sheaf shall be,
And every sheaf a golden tree.

CEL. O, see, Corebus, I have combed a great deal of gold into my lap, [970 and a great deal of corn!

COR. Well said, wench! Now we shall have just enough. God send us coiners to coin our gold. But, come, shall we go home, sweetheart?

CEL. Nay, come, Corebus, I will lead you.

COR. So, Corebus, things have well hit;
Thou hast gotten wealth to mend thy wit.
Exit [Corebus with Celanta].

Enter Jack and the Wandering Knight.

JACK. Come away, master, come.   [980
EUM. Go along, Jack; I'll follow thee. Jack, they say it is good to go cross-legged, and say his prayers backward. How sayest thou?

JACK. Tut, never fear, master; let me alone. Here sit you still; speak not a word. And, because you shall not be enticed with his enchanting speeches, with this same wool I'll stop your ears. And so, master, sit still, for I must to the conjurer. [990
Exit Jack.

Enter the Conjurer to the Wandering Knight.

SACR. How now! What man art thou that sits so sad?
Why dost thou gaze upon these stately trees

Without the leave and will of Sacrapant?
What, not a word but mum?
Then, Sacrapant, thou art betrayed.

Enter Jack, invisible, and taketh off Sacrapant's wreath from his head and his sword out of his hand.

What hand invades the head of Sacrapant?
What hateful Fury doth envy my happy state?
Then, Sacrapant, these are thy latest days.
Alas, my veins are numbed, my sinews shrink,
My blood is pierced, my breath fleeting away,   1000
And now my timeless date is come to end!
He in whose life his actions hath been so foul,
Now in his death to hell descends his soul.   *He dieth.*

JACK. O, sir, are you gone? Now I hope we shall have some other coil.[2]—Now, master, how like you this? The conjurer he is dead, and vows never to trouble us more. Now get you to your fair lady, and see what you can do with her.—Alas, he heareth me not all this while; but [1010 I will help that.
He pulls the wool out of his ears.

EUM. How now, Jack! What news?

JACK. Here, master, take this sword, and dig with it at the foot of this hill.
He digs and spies a light.

EUM. How now, Jack! What is this?

JACK. Master, without this the conjurer could do nothing; and so long as this light lasts, so long doth his art endure, and, this being out, then doth his art decay.   1020

EUM. Why, then, Jack, I will soon put out this light.

JACK. Ay, master, how?

EUM. Why, with a stone I'll break the glass, and then blow it out.

JACK. No, master, you may as soon break the smith's anvil as this little vial; nor the biggest blast that ever Boreas blew cannot blow out this little light but she that is neither maid, wife, nor widow. [1030 Master, wind this horn, and see what will happen.

[1] This stage direction occurs in original after l. 968.

[2] Trouble.

He winds the horn. Here enters Venelia,
and breaks the glass, and blows out the
light, and goeth in again.

So, master, how like you this? This is she
that ran madding in the woods, his betrothed love that keeps the cross. And
now, this light being out, all are restored to
their former liberty. And now, master, to
the lady that you have so long looked for.
He draweth a curtain, and there Delia sitteth
asleep.

EUM. God speed, fair maid, sitting alone—
    there is once;   1039
God speed, fair maid—there is twice;
God speed, fair maid—that is thrice.
DEL. Not so, good sir, for you are by.
JACK. Enough, master, she hath spoke;
now I will leave her with you.   [*Exit.*]
EUM. Thou fairest flower of these western
    parts,
Whose beauty so reflecteth in my sight
As doth a crystal mirror in the sun,
For thy sweet sake I have crossed the
    frozen Rhine; [1]
Leaving fair Po, I sailed up Danuby
As far as Saba, whose enhancing streams
Cuts twixt the Tartars and the Rus-
    sians;   1051
These have I crossed for thee, fair Delia.
Then grant me that which I have sued
    for long.
DEL. Thou gentle knight, whose fortune
    is so good
To find me out and set my brothers free,
My faith, my heart, my hand I give to
    thee.
EUM. Thanks, gentle madam. But here
comes Jack. Thank him, for he is the best
friend that we have.   1059

Enter Jack, with a head in his hand.

How now, Jack! What hast thou there?
JACK. Marry, master, the head of the
conjurer.
EUM. Why, Jack, that is impossible; he
was a young man.
JACK. Ah, master, so he deceived them
that beheld him! But he was a miserable,
old, and crooked man, though to each
man's eye h[e see]med young and fresh;
for, master, this conjurer took the shape

[1] "This and the next three lines are found,
with slight variations, in Greene's *Orlando*
Furioso" (Dyce)

of the old man that kept the cross,   [1070
and that old man was in the likeness of the
conjurer. But now, master, wind your horn.

He winds his horn. Enter Venelia, the Two
Brothers, and [Erestus,] he that was at
the cross.

EUM. Welcome, Erestus! Welcome, fair
    Venelia!
Welcome, Thelea and Calypha both!
Now have I her that I so long have
    sought;
So saith fair Delia, if we have your con-
    sent.
1 BRO. Valiant Eumenides, thou well de-
    servest
To have our favors; so let us rejoice
That by thy means we are at liberty.
Here may we joy each in other's sight,
And this fair lady have her Wand'ring
    Knight.   1081
JACK. So, master, now ye think you
have done, but I must have a saying to
you. You know you and I were partners,
I to have half in all you got.
EUM. Why, so thou shalt, Jack.
JACK. Why, then, master, draw your
sword, part your lady, let me have half
of her presently.
EUM. Why, I hope, Jack, thou dost   [1090
but jest. I promised thee half I got, but
not half my lady.
JACK. But what else, master? Have you
not gotten her? Therefore divide her
straight, for I will have half; there is no
remedy.
EUM. Well, ere I will falsify my word
unto my friend, take her all. Here, Jack,
I'll give her thee.
JACK. Nay, neither more nor less,   [1100
master, but even just half.
EUM. Before I will falsify my faith unto
my friend, I will divide her. Jack, thou
shalt have half.
1 BRO. Be not so cruel unto our sister,
gentle knight.
2 BRO. O, spare fair Delia! She deserves
no death.
EUM. Content yourselves; my word is
passed to him.—Therefore prepare   [1110
thyself, Delia, for thou must die.
DEL. Then farewell, world! Adieu, Eu-
    menides!
He offers to strike, and Jack stays him.

JACK. Stay, master; it is sufficient I have tried your constancy. Do you now remember since you paid for the burying of a poor fellow?

EUM. Ay, very well, Jack.

JACK. Then, master, thank that good deed for this good turn; and so God be with you all! *Jack leaps down in the ground.*

EUM. Jack, what, art thou gone? Then farewell, Jack!— 1121

Come, brothers, and my beauteous Delia,

Erestus, and thy dear Venelia,

We will to Thessaly with joyful hearts.

ALL. Agreed! We follow thee and Delia.
Exeunt omnes.

FANT. What, gammer, asleep?

OLD WOM. By the Mass, son, 'tis almost day, and my windows shuts at the cock's crow. 1129

FROL. Do you hear, gammer, methinks this Jack bore a great sway amongst them.

OLD WOM. O, man, this was the ghost of the poor man that they kept such a coil to bury; and that makes him to help the Wand'ring Knight so much. But come, let us in; we will have a cup of ale and a toast this morning, and so depart.[1]

FANT. Then you have made an end of your tale, gammer? [1140

OLD WOM. Yes, faith. When this was done, I took a piece of bread and cheese, and came my way; and so shall you have, too, before you go, to your breakfast.

[Exeunt.]

[1] Separate.

ROBERT GREENE

Robert Greene, certainly the most picturesque and one of the most important of the University Wits, was born at Norwich in 1558. He took his B.A. in 1578 and his M.A. in 1583 at Cambridge, and became an M.A. of Oxford in 1588. By 1583 he had begun his literary career with the publication of a long euphuistic romance, *Mamillia*, licensed in 1580, and he continued to produce romances written in a highly wrought style under such different influences as *Euphues*, *novella* collections, and pastoral and Greek romance, reaching his highest level in *Pandosto* (1588) and *Menaphon* (1589). Short poems and songs incorporated in some of the romances gave him high rank as a lyric poet also. By rapid production of such works Greene became one of the first authors in England to support himself, however precariously, with his pen. He soon began to capitalize on the bohemian existence which he had led from youth, writing his "repentance" pamphlets from 1590 to 1592, with many facts of his own life thinly veiled as fiction. He pictures his early riotous living, his marriage and desertion of his wife and child for the sister of a notorious character of the London underworld, a meeting with players, and his success in the production of plays for them. During this same period he was writing other journalistic and realistic prose, particularly a series of cony-catching pamphlets portraying the life of London rogues. He died September 3, 1592, from what Nashe called a "banquet of Rhenish wine and pickled herring," having written on his deathbed his famous *Groats-worth of Wit Bought with a Million of Repentance* and having despatched a letter to his wife asking her to forgive him and to settle his debts.

The earliest of Greene's plays is perhaps *The Comical History of Alphonsus, King of Aragon*, printed in 1599, which mentions "mighty Tamburlaine," and seems clearly modeled on Marlowe's conqueror play. Besides *The Honorable History of Friar Bacon and Friar Bungay* Greene's other known plays are *The History of Orlando Furioso*, drawn from Ariosto; *The Scottish History of James the Fourth*, with a plot of a *novella* type; and *A Looking-Glass for London and England*, written with Thomas Lodge, which pictures the wickedness of Nineveh as a warning to London. All of these plays were printed in 1594 or later, apparently from playhouse manuscripts, and give evidence of more or less corruption or even mutilation. It is probable that Greene wrote other plays. Of the several ascribed to him by different scholars, *George a Greene* perhaps has the best claim to be considered.

Nashe, in *Have with You to Saffron Walden*, calls Greene the master of his craft in the plotting of plays. His best work shows also effective characterization, especially in his romantic heroines, and a genuinely poetic style. His limitation is indicated by the charge, which he resents in the preface to *Perimedes the Blacksmith*, that he could not make his verses "jet upon the stage in tragical buskins." Greene defended his style by appeal to his prose romances and by bitter denunciation of players and playwrights for their "bumbast." While the type of sentimental and romantic comedy which represents his best work had to yield around 1590 to the turgid and passionate tragedy in vogue, by the end of the century it was carried to its zenith by Shakespeare, who had been the apparent object of Greene's bitterest attack on actors and dramatists in the *Groatsworth of Wit*.

The first record of *Friar Bacon and Friar Bungay* is Henslowe's note of a performance of it as an old play in 1592. Like *Alphonsus*, the play is supposed to have been written in emulation of Marlowe, and it is usually assigned to about 1589 as a rival to *Doctor Faustus*. If, however, as some scholars suggest, the proper date of Marlowe's play is 1592, then the relationship between the two must be reversed. Except for similar treatment of the marvelous powers of magicians, common in such stories, there is little kin. ship between the two plays. Greene drew his plot from *The Famous History of Friar Bacon*, a tale first known in the form of a chapbook, himself adding the romantic story of Margaret from a very slight hint in the romance. The text is apparently corrupt in several passages, and one or more whole scenes may have been omitted as a result of stage adaptation. In 1594 Henslowe has a second record of performance of the play, and it was entered in the Stationers' Register and printed in that year. The Malone Society reprint of this quarto of 1594, prepared by W. W. Greg, is the basis of the present text.

A Pleasant Conceited Comedy of George a Greene was acted for Henslowe as an old play in 1593. It was entered in the Stationers' Register in 1595, but the earliest extant edition is dated 1599. There is no indication of the authorship, but a copy of this edition, formerly in the Chatsworth Collection, has on the title-page the following two notes in an early seventeenth century script: "Written by .... a minister, who ac[ted] the pinners part in it himself. Teste W. Shakespea[re]," and "Ed. Juby saith that the play was made by Ro. Gree[ne]." Opinion, long divided, is represented at the present by Tannenbaum's claim that the entries are forgeries of Collier, and by Greg's that they are in the hand of Sir George Buc, Master of the Revels from 1608 to 1622. If they are Buc's, the second, perhaps correcting the first or perhaps adding to it, furnishes reliable contemporary evidence, since Juby, as an actor prominent from 1594 to 1618, would have known playhouse traditions. On the internal evidence of verse and style, the play is generally ascribed to Greene. He is supposed to have written it before 1590, basing it on an early version, now lost, of the prose tale *The Famous History of George a Greene*. The superiority of the stalwart hero of some trade to the old woodland outlaw and folk hero, Robin Hood, is a fairly frequent theme of ballad and tale, and *George a Greene* has many suggestions of the style and the conventions of the popular ballad. In its extant form the play has clearly been cut and corrupted in the course of use by a traveling company. The present text is based on the Malone Society reprint of the edition of 1599, prepared by F. W. Clarke.

THE HONORABLE HISTORY OF FRIAR BACON AND FRIAR BUNGAY[1]

BY

ROBERT GREENE

[DRAMATIS PERSONÆ

KING HENRY THE THIRD.
EDWARD, *Prince of Wales, his son.*
EMPEROR OF GERMANY.
KING OF CASTILE.
LACY, *Earl of Lincoln* ⎫
WARREN, *Earl of Sussex* ⎬ Edward's
ERMSBY, *a gentleman* ⎭ friends.
RALPH SIMNELL, *the king's fool.*
FRIAR BACON.
MILES, *his poor scholar.*
FRIAR BUNGAY.
JAQUES VANDERMAST, *a German magician.*
BURDEN ⎫
MASON ⎬ doctors of Oxford.
CLEMENT ⎭
LAMBERT ⎫
SERLSBY ⎬ gentlemen.

TWO SCHOLARS, *their sons.*
THE KEEPER OF FRESSINGFIELD.
HIS FRIEND.
THOMAS ⎫
RICHARD ⎬ rustics.
CONSTABLE.
A POST BOY.
LORDS, COUNTRY CLOWNS, *etc.*

ELINOR, *daughter to the King of Castile*
MARGARET,[2] *the keeper's daughter.*
JOAN, *a country wench.*
HOSTESS OF THE BELL AT HENLEY.

A DEVIL.
A SPEAKER FOR THE BRAZEN HEAD.
A SPIRIT IN THE SHAPE OF HERCULES.

SCENE: *England.*

TIME: *Thirteenth Century.*]

[SCENE i.

Framlingham.]

Enter Edward the First,[3] malcontented, with Lacy, Earl of Lincoln, John Warren, Earl of Sussex, and Ermsby, gentleman; Rafe[4] Simnell, the king's fool.

LACY. Why looks my lord like to a troubled sky
When heaven's bright shine is shadowed with a fog?
Alate[5] we ran the deer, and through the lawns[6]

Stripped[7] with our nags the lofty frolic bucks
That scudded fore the teasers[8] like the wind.
Ne'er was the deer of merry Fressingfield
So lustily pulled down by jolly mates,
Nor shared the farmers such fat venison,
So frankly dealt,[9] this hundred years before;
Nor have I seen my lord more frolic in the chase,   10
And now—changed to a melancholy dump.[10]

WARREN. After the prince got to the keeper's lodge,

---

[1] The original title continues: "As It Was Played by Her Majesty's Servants."
[2] In the original usually spelled *Margret.*
[3] Should be Prince Edward, since Henry III is still king at the end of the play.
[4] Variant of *Ralph.*   [5] Of late, lately.   [6] Glades.
[7] Outstripped.
[8] Hunting dogs.
[9] Generously divided.
[10] Fit of abstraction.

And had been jocund in the house
awhile,
Tossing off ale and milk in country
cans,
Whether it was the country's sweet
content,
Or else the bonny damsel filled us drink,
That seemed so stately in her stammel [1]
red,
Or that a qualm did cross his stomach
then,
But straight he fell into his passions.

ERMSBY. Sirrah Rafe, what say you to
your master?   20
Shall he thus all amort [2] live malcontent?

RAFE. Hearest thou, Ned?—Nay, look if
he will speak to me!

EDWARD. What say'st thou to me, fool?

RAFE. I prithee, tell me, Ned, art thou
in love with the keeper's daughter?

EDWARD. How if I be, what then?

RAFE. Why, then, sirrah, I'll teach thee
how to deceive Love.

EDWARD. How, Rafe?   30

RAFE. Marry, sirrah Ned, thou shalt
put on my cap and my coat and my dagger,
and I will put on thy clothes and thy
sword; and so thou shalt be my fool.

EDWARD. And what of this?

RAFE. Why, so thou shalt beguile Love,
for Love is such a proud scab that he will
never meddle with fools nor children. Is
not Rafe's counsel good, Ned?

EDWARD. Tell me, Ned Lacy, didst thou
mark the maid,   40
How lively in her country weeds she
looked?
A bonnier wench all Suffolk cannot yield.
All Suffolk! Nay, all England holds
none such!

RAFE. Sirrah Will Ermsby, Ned is deceived.

ERMSBY. Why, Rafe?

RAFE. He says all England hath no
such, and I say, and I'll stand to it, there
is one better in Warwickshire.

WARREN. How provest thou that, Rafe?

RAFE. Why, is not the abbot a [51
learned man, and hath read many books,
and thinkest thou he hath not more learning than thou to choose a bonny wench?

[1] Woolen cloth.
[2] À la mort, spiritless.

Yes, I warrant thee, by his whole grammar. [3]

ERMSBY. A good reason, Rafe.

EDWARD. I tell thee, Lacy, that her spar-
kling eyes
Do lighten forth sweet love's alluring
fire;
And in her tresses she doth fold the looks
Of such as gaze upon her golden hair;   61
Her bashful white, mixed with the morn-
ing's red,
Luna doth boast upon her lovely cheeks;
Her front is Beauty's table, where she
paints
The glories of her gorgeous excellence;
Her teeth are shelves of precious mar-
garites, [4]
Richly enclosed with ruddy coral
cleeves. [5]
Tush, Lacy, she is Beauty's overmatch,
If thou survey'st her curious imagery. [6]

LACY. I grant, my lord, the damsel is as
fair   70
As simple Suffolk's homely towns can
yield;
But in the court be quainter [7] dames
than she,
Whose faces are enriched with honor's
taint, [8]
Whose beauties stand upon the stage
of fame,
And vaunt their trophies in the courts
of love.

EDWARD. Ah, Ned, but hadst thou watched
her as myself,
And seen the secret beauties of the
maid,
Their courtly coyness were but foolery.

ERMSBY. Why, how watched you her,
my lord?

EDWARD. Whenas she swept like Venus
through the house,   80
And in her shape fast folded up my
thoughts,
Into the milk house went I with the
maid,
And there amongst the cream bowls
she did shine
As Pallas 'mongst her princely hus-
wifery. [9]

[3] Learning.
[4] Pearls.
[5] Cliffs.
[6] Rare appearance.
[7] Daintier, more fastidious.
[8] Tint.
[9] Housekeeping.

She turned her smock over her lily arms,
And dived them into milk to run her
    cheese;
But, whiter than the milk, her crystal
    skin,
Checked with lines of azure, made her [1]
    blush
That art or nature durst bring for com-
    pare.
Ermsby, if thou hadst seen, as I did
    note it well,   90
How Beauty played the huswife, how
    this girl,
Like Lucrece, laid her fingers to the work,
Thou wouldest with Tarquin hazard
    Rome and all
To win the lovely maid of Fressingfield.

RAFE. Sirrah Ned, wouldst fain have
her?

EDWARD. Ay, Rafe.

RAFE. Why, Ned, I have laid the plot
in my head; thou shalt have her already.

EDWARD. I'll give thee a new coat, and
learn me that.[2]   101

RAFE. Why, sirrah Ned, we'll ride to
Oxford to Friar Bacon. O, he is a brave
scholar, sirrah; they say he is a brave
nigromancer,[3] that he can make women of
devils, and he can juggle cats into costermongers.

EDWARD. And how then, Rafe?

RAFE. Marry, sirrah, thou shalt go to
him, and because [4] thy father Harry [110
shall not miss thee, he shall turn me into
thee; and I'll to the court, and I'll prince it
out; and he shall make thee either a silken
purse full of gold or else a fine-wrought
smock.

EDWARD. But how shall I have the
maid?

RAFE. Marry, sirrah, if thou be'st a
silken purse full of gold, then on Sundays
she'll hang thee by her side, and you [120
must not say a word. Now, sir, when
she comes into a great press of people, for
fear of the cutpurse, on a sudden she'll
swap thee into her plackerd;[5] then, sirrah,
being there, you may plead for yourself.

ERMSBY. Excellent policy!

EDWARD. But how if I be a wrought
smock?

RAFE. Then she'll put thee into her
chest and lay thee into lavender, and [130
upon some good day she'll put thee on;
and at night when you go to bed, then being
turned from a smock to a man, you may
make up the match.

LACY. Wonderfully wisely counseled,
Rafe.

EDWARD. Rafe shall have a new coat.

RAFE. God thank you—when I have
it on my back, Ned.

EDWARD. Lacy, the fool hath laid a per-
fect plot,   140
Forwhy [6] our country Margaret is so
    coy
And stands so much upon her honest
    points
That marriage or no market with the
    maid.
Ermsby, it must be nigroma[n]tic spells
And charms of art that must enchain
    her love,
Or else shall Edward never win the girl.
Therefore, my wags, we'll horse us in
    the morn,
And post to Oxford to this jolly friar.
Bacon shall by his magic do this deed.

WARREN. Content, my lord; and that's
    a speedy way   150
To wean these headstrong puppies from
    the teat.

EDWARD. I am unknown, not taken for
    the prince;
They only deem us frolic courtiers,
That revel thus among our liege's game;
Therefore I have devised a policy.
Lacy, thou know'st next Friday is
    S[aint] James',[7]
And then the country flocks to Harles-
    ton Fair;
Then will the keeper's daughter frolic
    there,
And overshine the troop of all the maids
That come to see and to be seen that
    day.   160
Haunt thee disguised among the coun-
    try swains;
Feign th'art a farmer's son, not far
    from thence;
Espy her loves, and who she liketh best;
Cote [8] him, and court her, to control
    the clown;[9]

---

[1] *I.e.*, any other woman.
[2] If you teach me that.
[3] Necromancer.
[4] In order that.
[5] Placket.
[6] Because.
[7] July 25.
[8] Outstrip.
[9] Overmaster the rustic.

Say that the courtier tired [1] all in green,
That helped her handsomely to run her
    cheese,
And filled her father's lodge with venison,
Commends him, and sends fairings, [2]
    to herself.
Buy something worthy of her parentage,
Not worth her beauty, for, Lacy, then
    the fair   170
Affords no jewel fitting for the maid.
And, when thou talkest of me, note if
    she blush.
O, then she loves! But, if her cheeks
    wax pale,
Disdain it is. Lacy, send [3] how she fares,
And spare no time nor cost to win her loves.
LACY. I will, my lord, so execute this charge
As if that Lacy were in love with her.
EDWARD. Send letters speedily to Ox-
    ford of the news.
RAFE. And, sirrah Lacy, buy me a
thousand thousand million of fine bells.
LACY. What wilt thou do with them,
Rafe?   182
RAFE. Marry, every time that Ned sighs
for the keeper's daughter, I'll tie a bell
about him; and so within three or four
days I will send word to his father Harry
that his son and my master Ned is be-
come Love's morris dance.
EDWARD. Well, Lacy, look with care unto
    thy charge,   189
And I will haste to Oxford to the friar,
That he by art and thou by secret gifts
Mayst make me lord of merry Fressing-
    field.
LACY. God send your honor your heart's
    desire.   *Exeunt.*

[SCENE ii.

*Friar Bacon's study at Brazenose College,
                                    Oxford.*]

*Enter Friar Bacon, with Miles, his poor
scholar, with books under his arm; with
them Burden, Mason, Clement, three
                                    doctors.*

BACON. Miles, where are you?
MILES. *Hic sum, dostissime et reveren-
dissime doctor.* [4]

BACON. *Attulisti nos libros meos de
necromantia?* [5]
MILES. *Ecce quam bonum et quam
jocundum, habitares libros in unum!* [6]
BACON. Now, masters of our academic
    state,
That rule in Oxford, viceroys in your
    place,
Whose heads contain maps of the liberal
    arts,   10
Spending your time in depth of learned
    skill,
Why flock you thus to Bacon's secret
    cell,
A friar newly stalled [7] in Brazen-nose?
Say what's your mind, that I may make
    reply.
BURDEN. Bacon, we hear that long we
    have suspect,
That thou art read in magic's mystery—
In pyromancy, to divine by flames;
To tell, by hydroma[n]tic, ebbs and tides;
By aeromancy to discover doubts,
To plain out [8] questions, as Apollo did. 20
BACON. Well, Master Burden, what of
all this?
MILES. Marry, sir, he doth but fulfill,
by rehearsing of these names, the fable of
the Fox and the Grapes; that which is
above us pertains nothing to us.
BURDEN. I tell thee, Bacon, Oxford makes
    report—
Nay, England and the court of Henry
    says—
Th'art making of a brazen head by art,
Which shall unfold strange doubts and
    aphorisms, [9]   30
And read a lecture in philosophy;
And, by the help of devils and ghastly
    fiends,
Thou mean'st, ere many years or days
    be past,
To compass England with a wall of
    brass.
BACON. And what of this?
MILES. What of this, master? Why,
he doth speak mystically, for he knows,
if your skill fail to make a brazen head, yet
Mother Waters' strong ale will fit his turn
to make him have a copper nose.   40

---

[1] Attired.   [2] Gifts bought at the fair.
[3] Send news of.
[4] Here I am, most learned and venerable doctor. (The Latin throughout the play is corrupt.
Translations are approximate.)

[5] Have you brought us my books on magic?
[6] How good and how pleasant it is to live
together among books!   [7] Installed.   [8] Explain.
[9] Statement of scientific principles.

CLEMENT. Bacon, we come not grieving
  at thy skill,
But joying that our academy yields
A man supposed the wonder of the
  world;
For, if thy cunning work these miracles,
England and Europe shall admire thy
  fame,
And Oxford shall in characters of brass
And statues such as were built up in
  Rome
Eternize Friar Bacon for his art.
MASON. Then, gentle friar, tell us thy
  intent.
BACON. Seeing you come as friends unto
  the friar,   50
Resolve you,[1] doctors, Bacon can by
  books
Make storming Boreas thunder from
  his cave,
And dim fair Luna to a dark eclipse.
The great archruler, potentate of hell,
Trembles when Bacon bids him or his
  fiends
Bow to the force of his pentagoron.[2]
What art can work, the frolic friar
  knows;
And therefore will I turn my magic
  books,
And strain out nigromancy to the deep.[3]
I have contrived and framed a head of
  brass   60
(I made Belcephon hammer out the
  stuff),
And that by art shall read philosophy.
And I will strengthen England by my
  skill,
That, if ten Cæsars lived and reigned
  in Rome,
With all the legions Europe doth con-
  tain,
They should not touch a grass of English
  ground.
The work that Ninus reared at Babylon,
The brazen walls framed by Semiramis,
Carved out like to the portal of the sun,
Shall not be such as rings the English
  strand   70
From Dover to the market place of Rye.
BURDEN. Is this possible?

MILES. I'll bring ye two or three wit-
  nesses.
BURDEN. What be those?
MILES. Marry, sir, three or four as
honest devils and good companions as
any be in hell.
MASON. No doubt but magic may do
  much in this;   79
For he that reads but mathematic rules
Shall find conclusions that avail to
  work
Wonders that pass the common sense
  of men.
BURDEN. But Bacon roves a bow beyond
  his reach,[4]
And tells of more than magic can per-
  form,
Thinking to get a fame by fooleries.
Have I not passed as far in state of
  schools,
And read of many secrets?   Yet to
  think
That heads of brass can utter any voice,
Or more, to tell of deep philosophy—
This is a fable Æsop had forgot.   90
BACON. Burden, thou wrong'st me in
  detracting thus;
Bacon loves not to stuff himself with
  lies.
But tell me fore these doctors, if thou
  dare,
Of certain questions I shall move to
  thee.
BURDEN. I will; ask what thou can.
MILES. Marry, sir, he'll straight be
on your pickpack,[5] to know whether the
feminine or the masculine gender be most
worthy.   99
BACON. Were you not yesterday, Mas-
ter Burden, at Henley upon the Thames?
BURDEN. I was.   What then?
BACON. What book studied you thereon
all night?
BURDEN. I?   None at all; I read not
there a line.
BACON. Then, doctors, Friar Bacon's art
  knows naught.
CLEMENT. What say you to this, Master
Burden?   Doth he not touch you?
BURDEN. I pass not of [6] his frivolous
speeches.   111

---

[1] Understand.
[2] Pentagonon, a five-pointed emblem with magical powers.
[3] Exert my magic to the utmost.

[4] Shoots at a target beyond his range.
[5] Pickaback.
[6] Care not for.

MILES. Nay, Master Burden, my master, ere he hath done with you, will turn you from a doctor to a dunce, and shake you so small that he will leave no more learning in you than is in Balaam's ass.

BACON. Masters, for that learned Burden's skill is deep,

And sore he doubts of Bacon's cabalism,

I'll show you why he haunts to Henley oft:

Not, doctors, for to taste the fragrant air,   120

But there to spend the night in alchemy,

To multiply with secret spells of art.

Thus private steals he learning from us all.

To prove my sayings true, I'll show you straight

The book he keeps at Henley for himself.

MILES. Nay, now my master goes to conjuration, take heed!

BACON. Masters, stand still; fear not, I'll show you but his book. (*Here he conjures.*) *Per omnes deos infernales, Belcephon!* [1]   130

Enter a Woman with a shoulder of mutton on a spit, and a Devil.

MILES. O master, cease your conjuration, or you spoil all, for here's a she-devil come with a shoulder of mutton on a spit. You have marred the devil's supper; but no doubt he thinks our college fare is slender, and so hath sent you his cook with a shoulder of mutton, to make it exceed. [2]

HOSTESS. O, where am I, or what's become of me?

BACON. What art thou?   140

HOSTESS. Hostess at Henley, mistress of the Bell.

BACON. How camest thou here?

HOSTESS. As I was in the kitchen 'mongst the maids,

Spitting the meat against supper for my guess, [3]

A motion [4] moved me to look forth of door.

No sooner had I pried into the yard,

But straight a whirlwind hoisted me from thence,

---

[1] By all the infernal gods, Belcephon!
[2] Become better.   [3] Guests.   [4] Impulse.

And mounted me aloft unto the clouds.

As in a trance, I thought nor feared naught,

Nor know I where or whither I was ta'en,   150

Nor where I am nor what these persons be.

BACON. No?   Know you not Master Burden?

HOSTESS. O, yes, good sir, he is my daily guest.—

What, Master Burden, 't was but yesternight

That you and I at Henley played at cards.

BURDEN. I know not what we did!—A pox of all conjuring friars!

CLEMENT. Now, jolly friar, tell us, is this the book

That Burden is so careful to look on?

BACON. It is.—But, Burden, tell me now,

Thinkest thou that Bacon's nigromantic skill   161

Cannot perform his head and wall of brass,

When he can fetch thine hostess in such post?

MILES. I'll warrant you, master, if Master Burden could conjure as well as you, he would have his book every night from Henley to study on at Oxford.

MASON. Burden, what, are you mated [5] by this frolic friar?—

Look how he droops; his guilty conscience

Drives him to bash, [6] and makes his hostess blush.   170

BACON. Well, mistress, for I will not have you missed,

You shall to Henley to cheer up your guests

Fore supper gin. [7]—Burden, bid her adieu;

Say farewell to your hostess fore she goes.—

Sirrah, away, and set her safe at home.

HOSTESS. Master Burden, when shall we see you at Henley?

Exeunt Hostess and the Devil.

BURDEN. The devil take thee and Henley too!   179

MILES. Master, shall I make a good motion?

---

[5] Confounded.   [6] Be abashed.   [7] Begin.

BACON. What's that?

MILES. Marry, sir, now that my hostess is gone to provide supper, conjure up another spirit, and send Doctor Burden flying after.

BACON. Thus, rulers of our academic state,
You have seen the friar frame his art by proof;
And as the college calléd Brazen-nose
Is under him, and he the master there,
So surely shall this head of brass be framed, 191
And yield forth strange and uncouth [1] aphorisms,
And hell and Hecate shall fail the friar,
But I will circle England round with brass.

MILES. So be it *et nunc et semper*,[2] amen. *Exeunt omnes.*

[SCENE iii.

Harleston Fair.]

Enter Margaret, the Fair Maid of Fressingfield, with Thomas, [Richard,] and Joan, and other clowns; Lacy disguised in country apparel.

THOMAS. By my troth, Margaret, here's a weather is able to make a man call his father whoreson. If this weather hold, we shall have hay good cheap,[3] and butter and cheese at Harleston will bear no price.

MARGARET. Thomas, maids, when they come to see the fair,
Count not to make a cope [4] for dearth of hay.
When we have turned our butter to the salt,
And set our cheese safely upon the racks,
Then let our fathers price it as they please. 10
We country sluts of merry Fressingfield
Come to buy needless naughts to make us fine,
And look that young men should be frank this day,
And court us with such fairings as they can.
Phœbus is blithe, and frolic looks from heaven,

As when he courted lovely Semele,
Swearing the peddlers shall have empty packs,
If that fair weather may make chapmen buy.

LACY. But, lovely Peggy, Semele is dead,
And therefore Phœbus from his palace pries, 20
And, seeing such a sweet and seemly saint,
Shows all his glories for to court yourself.

MARGARET. This is a fairing, gentle sir, indeed,
To soothe me up with such smooth flattery;
But, learn of me, your scoff's too broad before.[5]—
Well, Joan, our beauties must abide their jests;
We serve the turn in jolly Fressingfield.

JOAN. Margaret, a farmer's daughter for a farmer's son!
I warrant you, the meanest of us both
Shall have a mate to lead us from the church. 30
But, Thomas, what's the news? What, in a dump?
Give me your hand; we are near a peddler's shop.
Out with your purse; we must have fairings now.

THOMAS. Faith, Joan, and shall. I'll bestow a fairing on you, and then we will to the tavern, and snap off a pint of wine or two.

All this while Lacy whispers Margaret in the ear.

MARGARET. Whence are you, sir? Of Suffolk? For your terms
Are finer than the common sort of men.

LACY. Faith, lovely girl, I am of Beccles by,[6] 40
Your neighbor, not above six miles from hence,
A farmer's son, that never was so quaint
But that he could do courtesy to such dames.
But trust me, Margaret, I am sent in charge
From him that reveled in your father's house,

---

[1] Unusual.
[2] Now and forever.
[3] At a good price.
[4] Bargain.
[5] *I.e.*, obvious.
[6] From near Beccles.

And filled his lodge with cheer and
    venison,
Tired in green. He sent you this rich
    purse,
His token that he helped you run your
    cheese,
And in the milk house chatted with
    yourself.
Margaret. To me? You forget your-
    self.[1]   50
Lacy. Women are often weak in mem-
    ory.
Margaret. O, pardon, sir, I call to mind
    the man.
    'Twere little manners to refuse his gift,
    And yet I hope he sends it not for love;
    For we have little leisure to debate of
    that.
Joan. What, Margaret, blush not; maids
    must have their loves!
Thomas. Nay, by the Mass, she looks
pale as if she were angry.
    Richard. Sirrah, are you of Beccles?
I pray, how doth Goodman Cob? My [60
father bought a horse of him.—I'll tell
you, Margaret, a[2] were good to be a
gentleman's jade, for of all things the
foul hilding[3] could not abide a dung cart.
Margaret. [Aside.] How different is this
    farmer from the rest
    That erst as yet[4] have pleased my
        wand'ring sight!
    His words are witty, quickened with
        a smile,
    His courtesy gentle, smelling of the
        court;
    Facile and debonair in all his deeds,
    Proportioned as was Paris, when, in
        gray,[5]   70
    He courted Œnon in the vale by Troy.
    Great lords have come and pleaded for
        my love—
    Who but the keeper's lass of Fressing-
        field?
    And yet methinks this farmer's jolly
        son
    Passeth the proudest that hath pleased
        mine eye.
    But, Peg, disclose not that thou art in
        love,
    And show as yet no sign of love to him,

Although thou well wouldst wish him
    for thy love.
Keep that to thee till time doth serve
    thy turn,
To show the grief wherein thy heart
    doth burn.—   80
Come, Joan and Thomas, shall we to
    the fair?
You, Beccles man, will not forsake us
    now?
Lacy. Not whilst I may have such quaint
    girls as you.
Margaret. Well, if you chance to come
    by Fressingfield,
Make but a step into the keeper's lodge,
And such poor fare as woodmen can
    afford,
Butter and cheese, cream and fat veni-
    son,
You shall have store, and welcome
    therewithal.
Lacy. Gramercies, Peggy; look for me
    ere long.   *Exeunt omnes.*

[Scene iv.

Hampton Court.]

*Enter Henry the Third, the Emperor, the
    King of Castile, Elinor, his daughter,
    Jaques Vandermast, a German.*

Henry. Great men of Europe, monarchs
    of the West,
Ringed with the walls of old Oceanus,
Whose lofty surge is[6] like the battle-
    ments
That compassed high-built Babel in
    with towers,
Welcome, my lords, welcome, brave
    western kings,
To England's shore, whose promontory
    cleeves
Shows Albion is another little world.
Welcome says English Henry to you
    all;
Chiefly unto the lovely Elinor,
Who dared for Edward's sake cut
    through the seas,   10
And venture as Agenor's damsel through
    the deep,
To get the love of Henry's wanton son.
Castile. England's rich monarch, brave
    Plantagenet,

---

[1] Surely you mistake.   [3] Good-for-nothing.
[2] He.   [4] Until now.
[5] Traditional garb of shepherds.

[6] Original has *surges*.

The Pyren Mounts swelling above the
  clouds
That ward the wealthy Castile in with
  walls
Could not detain the beauteous Elinor;
But, hearing of the fame of Edward's
  youth,
She dared to brook Neptunus' haughty
  pride,
And bide the brunt of froward Æolus.
Then may fair England welcome her
  the more.   20
ELINOR. After that English Henry by
  his lords
Had sent Prince Edward's lovely coun-
  terfeit,[1]
A present to the Castile Elinor,
The comely portrait of so brave a man,
The virtuous fame discoursèd of his
  deeds,
Edward's courageous resolution,
Done at the Holy Land fore Damas'
  walls,
Led both mine eye and thoughts in
  equal links
To like so of the English monarch's
  son
That I attempted perils for his sake.   30
EMPEROR. Where is the prince, my lord?
HENRY. He posted down, not long since,
  from the court
To Suffolk side, to merry Framlingham,
To sport himself amongst my fallow
  deer;
From thence, by packets sent to Hamp-
  ton House,
We hear the prince is ridden with his
  lords
To Oxford, in the academy there
To hear dispute amongst the learned
  men.
But we will send forth letters for my son,
To will him come from Oxford to the
  court.   40
EMPEROR. Nay, rather, Henry, let us,
  as we be,
Ride for to visit Oxford with our train.
Fain would I see your universities,
And what learned men your academy
  yields.
From Hapsburg have I brought a
  learned clerk
To hold dispute with English orators.

[1] Picture.

This doctor, surnamed Jaques Vander-
  mast,
A German born, passed into Padua,
To Florence and to fair Bolonia,
To Paris, Rheims, and stately Orleans, 50
And, talking there with men of art,
  put down
The chiefest of them all in aphorisms,
In magic, and the mathematic rules.
Now let us, Henry, try him in your
  schools.
HENRY. He shall, my lord; this motion
  likes me well.
We'll progress straight to Oxford with
  our trains,
And see what men our academy brings.—
And, wonder Vandermast, welcome to
  me.
In Oxford shalt thou find a jolly friar
Called Friar Bacon, England's only
  flower.   60
Set him but nonplus in his magic spells,
And make him yield in mathematic
  rules,
And for thy glory I will bind thy brows,
Not with a poet's garland made of bays,
But with a coronet of choicest gold.
Whilst then [2] we f[l]it to Oxford with
  our troops,
Let's in and banquet in our English
  court.   Exit [with his Train].

[SCENE V.

An Oxford street.]

Enter Rafe Simnell in Edward's apparel;
  Edward, Warren, Ermsby, disguised.

RAFE. Where be these vagabond knaves,
that they attend no better on their master?
EDWARD. If it please your honor, we
are all ready at an inch.[3]
RAFE. Sirrah Ned, I'll have no more
post horse to ride on. I'll have another
fetch.[4]
ERMSBY. I pray you, how is that, my
lord?   10
RAFE. Marry, sir, I'll send to the Isle
of Ely for four or five dozen of geese, and
I'll have them tied six and six together
with whipcord. Now upon their backs
will I have a fair field bed [5] with a canopy;

[2] Until the time that. [3] At any instant. [4] Trick.
[5] Portable bed used in campaigns.

and so, when it is my pleasure, I'll flee into what place I please. This will be easy.

WARREN. Your honor hath said well.
But shall we to Brazen-nose College before we pull off our boots?   20

ERMSBY. Warren, well motioned; we will
to the friar

Before we revel it within the town.—

Rafe, see you keep your countenance
like a prince.

RAFE. Wherefore have I such a company of cutting [1] knaves to wait upon me,
but to keep and defend my countenance
against all mine enemies? Have you not
good swords and bucklers?

Enter Bacon and Miles.

ERMSBY. Stay, who comes here?

WARREN. Some scholar; and we'll [30
ask him where Friar Bacon is.

BACON. Why, thou arrant dunce, shall
I never make thee good scholar? Doth
not all the town cry out and say, "Friar
Bacon's subsizer [2] is the greatest blockhead in all Oxford"? Why, thou canst not
speak one word of true Latin.

MILES. No, sir? Yes, what is this else?
Ego sum tuus homo—"I am your man."
I warrant you, sir, as good Tully's [40
phrase as any is in Oxford.

BACON. Come on, sirrah! What part
of speech is *Ego?*

MILES. *Ego,* that is "I"; marry, *nomen
substantivo.*

BACON. How prove you that?

MILES. Why, sir, let him prove himself, and a will; "I" can be heard, felt,
and understood.   49

BACON. O gross dunce! *Here beat him.*

EDWARD. Come, let us break off this
dispute between these two.—Sirrah, where
is Brazen-nose College?

MILES. Not far from Coppersmiths'
Hall.

EDWARD. What, dost thou mock me?

MILES. Not I, sir. But what would
you at Brazen-nose?

ERMSBY. Marry, we would speak with
Friar Bacon.   60

MILES. Whose men be you?

ERMSBY. Marry, scholar, here's our
master.

RAFE. Sirrah, I am the master of these
good fellows. Mayst thou not know me to
be a lord by my reparel?

MILES. Then here's good game for the
hawk; for here's the master fool and a
covey of coxcombs. One wise man, I
think, would spring [3] you all.   70

EDWARD. Gog's [4] wounds! Warren,
kill him!

WARREN. Why, Ned, I think the
devil be in my sheath; I cannot get out
my dagger.

ERMSBY. Nor I mine. 'Swones, [5] Ned,
I think I am bewitched.

MILES. A company of scabs! The
proudest of you all draw your weapon, if he
can.—[*Aside.*] See how boldly I speak, [80
now my master is by.

EDWARD. I strive in vain; but, if my sword
be shut

And conjured fast by magic in my sheath,
Villain, here is my fist!
            Strike him a box on the ear.

MILES. O, I beseech you, conjure his
hands too, that he may not lift his arms
to his head, for he is light-fingered!

RAFE. Ned, strike him; I'll warrant [6]
thee, by mine honor.

BACON. What means the English prince
to wrong my man?   90

EDWARD. To whom speakest thou?

BACON. To thee.

EDWARD. Who art thou?

BACON. Could you not judge when all
your swords grew fast

That Friar Bacon was not far from
hence?

Edward, King Henry's son and Prince
of Wales,

Thy fool disguised cannot conceal thyself.

I know both Ermsby and the Sussex
earl,

Else Friar Bacon had but little skill.

Thou comest in post from merry Fressingfield,   100

Fast-fancied [7] to the keeper's bonny
lass,

To crave some succor of the jolly friar;

[1] Swaggering.
[2] Student who worked for his board and tui-
tion.

[3] Springe, ensnare.   [6] Back, support.
[4] God's.   [7] Bound by love.
[5] Swounds, God's wounds.

And Lacy, Earl of Lincoln, hast thou left
To treat [1] fair Margaret to allow thy
   loves.
But friends are men, and love can baffle
   lords;
The earl both woos and courts her for
   himself.

WARREN. Ned, this is strange; the friar
   knoweth all.

ERMSBY. Apollo could not utter more than
   this.

EDWARD. I stand amazed to hear this
   jolly friar
Tell even the very secrets of my
   thoughts.—   110
But, learned Bacon, since thou knowest
   the cause
Why I did post so fast from Fressing-
   field,
Help, friar, at a pinch, that I may have
The love of lovely Margaret to myself,
And, as I am true Prince of Wales, I'll give
Living and lands to strength thy col-
   lege state.

WARREN. Good friar, help the prince in
   this.

RAFE. Why, servant Ned, will not the
friar do it? Were not my sword glued to
my scabbard by conjuration, I would [120
cut off his head, and make him do it by
force.

MILES. In faith, my lord, your manhood and your sword is all alike; they are
so fast conjured that we shall never see
them.

ERMSBY. What, doctor, in a dump?
   Tush, help the prince,
And thou shalt see how liberal he will
   prove.

BACON. Crave not such actions greater
   dumps than these?
I will, my lord, strain out my magic
   spells;   130
For this day comes the earl to Fressing-
   field,
And fore that night shuts in the day
   with dark,
They'll be betrothéd each to other fast.
But come with me; we'll to my study
   straight,
And in a glass prospective [2] I will show
What's done this day in merry Fres-
   singfield.

[1] Entreat.   [2] Magic mirror.

EDWARD. Gramercies, Bacon; I will
   quite [3] thy pain.

BACON. But send your train, my lord,
   into the town.
My scholar shall go bring them to their
   inn.
Meanwhile we'll see the knavery of
   the earl.   140

EDWARD. Warren, leave me, and, Erms-
   by, take the fool;
Let him be master, and go revel it
Till I and Friar Bacon talk awhile.

WARREN. We will, my lord.

RAFE. Faith, Ned, and I'll lord it out
till thou comest. I'll be Prince of Wales
over all the blackpots [4] in Oxford.   *Exeunt.*

[SCENE vi.

Bacon's study.]

Bacon and Edward goes into the study.

BACON. Now, frolic Edward, welcome
   to my cell.
Here tempers Friar Bacon many toys,
And holds this place his consistory
   court,
Wherein the devils plead homage to
   his words.
Within this glass prospective thou shalt
   see
This day what's done in merry Fressingfield
Twixt lovely Peggy and the Lincoln
   earl.

EDWARD. Friar, thou glad'st me. Now
   shall Edward try
How Lacy meaneth to his sovereign
   lord.

BACON. Stand there and look directly
   in the glass.   10

Enter Margaret and Friar Bungay. [5]

What sees my lord?

EDWARD. I see the keeper's lovely lass
   appear,
As bright-sun [6] as the paramour of
   Mars,
Only attended by a jolly friar.

[3] Requite, reward.
[4] Leather wine jugs.
[5] The persons in the magic glass are seen but
not heard by Edward.
[6] Brightsome (?).

BACON. Sit still, and keep the crystal in your eye.

MARGARET. But tell me, Friar Bungay, is it true
That this fair courteous country swain,
Who says his father is a farmer nigh,
Can be Lord Lacy, Earl of Lincolnshire?

BUNGAY. Peggy, 'tis true; 'tis Lacy for my life, 20
Or else mine art and cunning both doth fail,
Left by Prince Edward to procure his loves;
For he in green, that help you run your cheese,
Is son to Henry, and the Prince of Wales.

MARGARET. Be what he will, his lure is but for lust.
But did Lord Lacy like poor Margaret,
Or would he deign to wed a country lass,
Friar, I would his humble handmaid be,
And for great wealth quite him with courtesy.

BUNGAY. Why, Margaret, dost thou love him? 30

MARGARET. His personage, like the pride of vaunting Troy,
Might well avouch to shadow [1] Helen's scape.[2]
His wit is quick and ready in conceit,
As Greece afforded in her chiefest prime,
Courteous, ah, friar, full of pleasing smiles!
Trust me, I love too much to tell thee more;
Suffice, to me he's England's paramour.[3]

BUNGAY. Hath not each eye that viewed thy pleasing face
Surnaméd thee Fair Maid of Fressing-field?

MARGARET. Yes, Bungay; and would God the lovely earl 40
Had that *in esse* [4] that so many sought.

BUNGAY. Fear not, the friar will not be behind
To show his cunning to entangle love.

EDWARD. I think the friar courts the bonny wench;
Bacon, methinks he is a lusty churl.

BACON. Now look, my lord.

Enter Lacy [disguised as before].

EDWARD. Gog's wounds, Bacon, here comes Lacy!

BACON. Sit still, my lord, and mark the comedy.

BUNGAY. Here's Lacy; Margaret, step aside awhile. [*They withdraw.*]

LACY. Daphne, the damsel that caught Phœbus fast, 50
And locked him in the brightness of her looks,
Was not so beauteous in Apollo's eyes
As is fair Margaret to the Lincoln earl.
Recant thee, Lacy. Thou art put in trust.
Edward, thy sovereign's son, hath chosen thee,
A secret friend, to court her for himself,
And darest thou wrong thy prince with treachery?
Lacy, love makes no exception of a friend,
Nor deems it of a prince but as a man.
Honor bids thee control him in his lust.
His wooing is not for to wed the girl, 61
But to entrap her and beguile the lass.
Lacy, thou lovest; then brook not such abuse,
But wed her, and abide thy prince's frown,
For better die than see her live disgraced.

MARGARET. Come, friar, I will shake him from his dumps.— [*Comes forward.*]
How cheer you, sir? A penny for your thought!
You're early up, pray God it be the near.[5]
What, come from Beccles in a morn so soon?

LACY. Thus watchful are such men as live in love, 70
Whose eyes brook broken slumbers for their sleep.
I tell thee, Peggy, since last Harleston fair
My mind hath felt a heap of passions.

MARGARET. A trusty man, that court it for your friend!
Woo you still for the courtier all in green?
I marvel that he sues not for himself.

---

[1] Excuse.
[2] Original reads *cape*.
[3] Darling.
[4] In actuality.
[5] A common expression meaning *the nearer to your purpose.*

LACY. Peggy, I pleaded first to get your grace for him;
But, when mine eyes surveyed your beauteous looks,
Love, like a wag,[1] straight dived into my heart,
And there did shrine the idea [2] of yourself. 80
Pity me, though I be a farmer's son;
And measure not my riches, but my love.
MARGARET. You are very hasty; for to garden well,
Seeds must have time to sprout before they spring.
Love ought to creep as doth the dial's shade,
For timely [3] ripe is rotten too-too soon.
BUNGAY. [*Coming forward.*] *Deus hic.*[4]
Room for a merry friar!
What, youth of Beccles, with the keeper's lass?
'Tis well. But, tell me, hear you any news?
MARGARET. No, friar. What news? 90
BUNGAY. Hear you not how the pursuivants do post
With proclamations through each country town?
LACY. For what, gentle friar? Tell the news.
BUNGAY. Dwell'st thou in Beccles, and hear'st not of these news?
Lacy, the Earl of Lincoln, is late fled
From Windsor court, disguiséd like a swain,
And lurks about the country here unknown.
Henry suspects him of some treachery,
And therefore doth proclaim in every way
That who can take the Lincoln earl shall have, 100
Paid in the Exchequer, twenty thousand crowns.
LACY. The Earl of Lincoln! Friar, thou art mad!
It was some other; thou mistakest the man.
The Earl of Lincoln! Why, it cannot be!
MARGARET. Yes, very well, my lord, for you are he.

The keeper's daughter took you prisoner.
Lord Lacy, yield; I'll be your jailer once.

EDWARD. How familiar they be, Bacon!
BACON. Sit still, and mark the sequel of their loves.

LACY. Then am I double prisoner to thyself. 110
Peggy, I yield! But are these news in jest?
MARGARET. In jest with you, but earnest unto me,
Forwhy these wrongs do wring me at the heart.
Ah, how these earls and noble men of birth
Flatter and feign, to forge poor women's ill!
LACY. Believe me, lass, I am the Lincoln earl;
I not deny but, tired thus in rags,
I lived disguised to win fair Peggy's love.
MARGARET. What love is there where wedding ends not love?
LACY. I meant, fair girl, to make thee Lacy's wife. 120
MARGARET. I little think that earls will stoop so low.
LACY. Say, shall I make thee countess ere I sleep?
MARGARET. Handmaid unto the earl, so please himself;
A wife in name, but servant in obedience.
LACY. The Lincoln countess, for it shall be so!
I'll plight the bands, and seal it with a kiss.

EDWARD. Gog's wounds, Bacon, they kiss!
I'll stab them!
BACON. O, hold your hands, my lord!
It is the glass!
EDWARD. Choler to see the traitors gree [5] so well 129
Made me think the shadows substances.
BACON. 'Twere a long poinard,[6] my lord, to reach between
Oxford and Fressingfield. But sit still and see more.

[1] Mischievous boy.   [3] Prematurely.
[2] Image.   [4] God here.
[5] Agree.   [6] Poniard.

BUNGAY. Well, Lord of Lincoln, if your
  loves be knit,
And that your tongues and thoughts do
  both agree,
To avoid ensuing jars, I'll hamper up [1]
  the match.
I'll take my portace [2] forth and wed you
  here;
Then go to bed and seal up your desires.
LACY. Friar, content.—Peggy, how like
  you this?
MARGARET. What likes my lord is pleasing unto me.
BUNGAY. Then handfast [3] hand, and I
  will to my book.   140

BACON. What sees my lord now?
EDWARD. Bacon, I see the lovers hand
  in hand,
The friar ready with his portace there
To wed them both. Then am I quite
  undone!
Bacon, help now, if e'er thy magic served;
Help, Bacon! Stop the marriage now,
If devils or nigromancy may suffice,
And I will give thee forty thousand
  crowns.
BACON. Fear not, my lord, I'll stop the
  jolly friar   149
For [4] mumbling up his orisons this day.

LACY. Why speak'st not, Bungay? Friar,
  to thy book!
    Bungay is mute, crying, "Hud, hud."
MARGARET. How lookest thou, friar, as
  a man distraught!
Reft of thy senses, Bungay? Show by
  signs,
If thou be dumb, what passions holdeth
  thee.
LACY. He's dumb indeed. Bacon hath
  with his devils
Enchanted him, or else some strange
  disease
Or apoplexy hath possessed his lungs.
But, Peggy, what he cannot with his
  book,
We'll twixt us both unite it up in heart.
MARGARET. Else let me die, my lord, a
  miscreant.   160

EDWARD. Why stands Friar Bungay [5] so
  amazed?
BACON. I have struck him dumb, my
  lord; and, if your honor please,
I'll fetch this Bungay straightway from
  Fressingfield
And he shall dine with us in Oxford here.
EDWARD. Bacon, do that, and thou con-
  tentest me.

LACY. Of courtesy, Margaret, let us lead
  the friar
Unto thy father's lodge, to comfort him
With broths, to bring him from this
  hapless trance.
MARGARET. Or else, my lord, we were
  passing unkind   169
To leave the friar so in his distress.

*Enter a Devil, and carry Bungay on his
                                    back.*

O, help, my lord! A devil, a devil, my
  lord!
Look how he carries Bungay on his back!
Let's hence, for Bacon's spirits be
  abroad.
              Exeunt [Margaret and Lacy].

EDWARD. Bacon, I laugh to see the jolly
  friar
Mounted upon the devil, and how the
  earl
Flees with his bonny lass for fear.
As soon as Bungay is at Brazen-nose,
And I have chatted with the merry
  friar,
I will in post hie me to Fressingfield,
And quite these wrongs on Lacy ere it
  be long.   180
BACON. So be it, my lord. But let us to
  our dinner,
For, ere we have taken our repast awhile,
We shall have Bungay brought to
  Brazen-nose.   *Exeunt.*

[SCENE vii.

The Regent House at Oxford.]

*Enter three doctors, Burden, Mason,
                              Clement.*

MASON. Now that we are gathered in
  the Regent House,
It fits us talk about the king's repair,[6]

---

[1] Make fast.   [2] Breviary for outdoor use.
[3] Join; used of marriage contracts.   [4] From.
[5] Original reads *Bacon*.   [6] Visit.

For he, troopéd with [1] all the western
    kings
That lie alongst the Danzig seas by
    east,
North by the clime of frosty Germany,
The Almain [2] monarch, and the Saxon
    duke,[3]
Castile and lovely Elinor with him,
Have in their jests resolved for Oxford
    town.
BURDEN. We must lay plots of stately
    tragedies,
Strange comic shows such as proud
    Roscius   10
Vaunted before the Roman emperors—
CLEMENT. To welcome all the western
    potentates.
But more: the king by letters hath fore-
    told
That Frederick, the Almain emperor,
Hath brought with him a German of
    esteem,
Whose surname is Don Jaques Vander-
    mast,
Skillful in magic and those secret arts.
MASON. Then must we all make suit
    unto the friar,
To Friar Bacon, that he vouch [4] this
    task,
And undertake to countervail in skill 20
The German; else there's none in Ox-
    ford can
Match and dispute with learned Vander-
    mast.
BURDEN. Bacon, if he will hold the Ger-
    man play,
We'll teach him what an English friar
    can do.
The devil, I think, dare not dispute
    with him.
CLEMENT. Indeed, Mas' Doctor, he pleas-
    ured you,
In that he brought your hostess with
    her spit
From Henley, posting unto Brazen-nose!
BURDEN. A vengeance on the friar for his
    pains!
But, leaving that, let's hie to Bacon
    straight,   30
To see if he will take this task in hand.

CLEMENT. Stay, what rumor is this?
The town is up in a mutiny. What hurly-
burly is this?

Enter a Constable, with Rafe, Warren,
Ermsby, and Miles.

CONSTABLE. Nay, masters, if you were
ne'er so good, you shall before the doctors
to answer your misdemeanor.
BURDEN. What's the matter, fellow?
CONSTABLE. Marry, sir, here's a com-
pany of rufflers, that, drinking in [40
the tavern, have made a great brawl,
and almost killed the vintner.
MILES. *Salve*,[5] Doctor Burden! This
    lubberly lurden,[6]
Ill-shaped and ill-faced, disdained and
    disgraced,
What he tells unto *vobis mentitur de*
    nobis.[7]
BURDEN. Who is the master and chief
of this crew?
MILES. *Ecce asinum mundi fugura ro-*
    tundi,[8]
Neat, sheat,[9] and fine, as brisk as a cup
    of wine.
BURDEN. What are you?   50
RAFE. I am, father doctor, as a man
would say, the bellwether of this com-
pany; these are my lords, and I the Prince
of Wales.
CLEMENT. Are you Edward, the king's
son?
RAFE. Sirrah Miles, bring hither the
tapster that drew the wine, and, I war-
rant, when they see how soundly I have
broke his head, they'll say 'twas done [60
by no less man than a prince.
MASON. I cannot believe that this is
the Prince of Wales.
WARREN. And why so, sir?
MASON. For they say the prince is a
brave and a wise gentleman.
WARREN. Why, and thinkest thou, doc-
    tor, that he is not so?
Dar'st thou detract and derogate from
    him,
Being so lovely and so brave a youth?
ERMSBY. Whose face, shining with many
    a sugared smile,   70

---

[1] Accompanied by.   [2] German.
[3] Original reads *Scocon duke*. This character
does not actually appear, although again referred
to.   [4] Avouch, make good.

[5] Hail!   [6] Blockhead.
[7] Whatever he tells you, he is lying about us.
[8] Behold the jackass of the round-shaped world.
[9] Trim (?); lively (?).

Bewrays[1] that he is bred of princely race.

MILES. And yet, Master Doctor, to speak like a proctor,

And tell unto you what is veriment[2] and true;

To cease of this quarrel, look but on his apparel;

Then mark but my talis, he is great Prince of Walis,

The chief of our *gregis*, and *filius regis;*[3]

Then ware what is done, for he is Henry's white[4] son.

RAFE. Doctors, whose doting nightcaps are not capable of my ingenious dignity, know that I am Edward Plantage-   [80 net, whom if you displease will make a ship that shall hold all your colleges, and so carry away the Niniversity with a fair wind to the Bankside in Southwark. —How say'st thou, Ned Warren? Shall I not do it?

WARREN. Yes, my good lord; and, if it please your lordship, I will gather up all your old pantofles,[5] and with the cork make you a pinnace of five hundred   [90 ton, that shall serve the turn marvelous well, my lord.

ERMSBY. And I, my lord, will have pioners[6] to undermine the town, that the very gardens and orchards be carried away for your summer walks.

MILES. And I, with *scientia* and great *diligentia,*

Will conjure and charm, to keep you from harm;

That, *utrum horum mavis,*[7] your very great *navis,*[8]

Like Bartlet's[9] ship, from Oxford do skip   100

With colleges and schools, full-loaden with fools.

Quid dices ad hoc,[10] worshipful *Domine* Dawcock?[11]

CLEMENT. Why hare-brained courtiers, are you drunk or mad,

To taunt us up with such scurrility?

Deem you us men of base and light esteem,

To bring us such a fop for Henry's son?—

Call out the beadles and convey them hence

Straight to Bocardo;[12] let the roisters lie

Close clapped in bolts, until their wits be tame.

ERMSBY. Why, shall we to prison,   [110 my lord?

RAFE. What sayst, Miles, shall I honor the prison with my presence?

MILES. No, no! Out with your blades, and hamper these jades;

Have a flirt[13] and a crash, now play revel-dash,[14]

And teach these *sacerdos*[15] that the Bocardos,

Like peasants and elves, are meet for themselves.

MASON. To the prison with them, constable!

WARREN. Well, doctors, seeing I have sported me

With laughing at these mad and merry wags,   120

Know that Prince Edward is at Brazennose,

And this, attiréd like the Prince of Wales,

Is Rafe, King Henry's only lovéd fool,

I, Earl of Sussex,[16] and this Ermsby,

One of the privy chamber to the king,

Who, while the prince with Friar Bacon stays,

Have reveled it in Oxford as you see.

MASON. My lord, pardon us, we knew not what you were.

But courtiers may make greater scapes[17] than these.

Will 't please your honor dine with me today?   130

WARREN. I will, Master Doctor, and satisfy the vintner for his hurt; only I must desire you to imagine him all this forenoon the Prince of Wales.

MASON. I will, sir.

RAFE. And upon that I will lead the way; only I will have Miles go before me,

---

[1] Betrays.   [2] Truth.
[3] The chief of our company and son of the king.   [4] Dear.   [5] Slippers.   [6] Diggers.
[7] Whichever of these you prefer.   [8] Ship.
[9] Miles's mistake for Barclay, the translator of Brandt's *Ship of Fools.*
[10] What do you say to this?
[11] Jackdaw, dolt.

[12] A prison at Oxford.   [15] Priests.
[13] Quick blow.   [16] Original reads *Essex.*
[14] Rowdy game.   [17] Escapades.

because I have heard Henry say that wisdom must go before majesty.

Exeunt omnes.

[SCENE viii.

Fressingfield.]

*Enter Prince Edward with his poinard in
his hand, Lacy, and Margaret.*

EDWARD. Lacy, thou canst not shroud
  thy trait'rous thoughts,
Nor cover, as did Cassius, all his wiles;
For Edward hath an eye that looks as
  far
As Lynceus from the shores of Grecia.
Did not I sit in Oxford by the friar,
And see thee court the maid of Fressing-
  field,
Sealing thy flattering fancies with a
  kiss?
Did not proud Bungay draw his por-
  tace forth,
And, joining hand in hand, had married
  you,
If Friar Bacon had not stroke [1] him
  dumb,   10
And mounted him upon a spirit's back,
That we might chat at Oxford with the
  friar?
Traitor, what answer'st?   Is not all
  this true?
LACY. Truth all, my lord; and thus I
  make reply:
At Harleston Fair, there courting for
  your grace,
Whenas mine eye surveyed her curious
  shape,
And drew the beauteous glory of her
  looks
To dive into the center of my heart,
Love taught me that your honor did
  but jest,   19
That princes were in fancy [2] but as men;
How that the lovely maid of Fressing-
  field
Was fitter to be Lacy's wedded wife
Than concubine unto the Prince of
  Wales.
EDWARD. Injurious Lacy, did I love thee
  more
Than Alexander his Hephestion?
Did I unfold the passion[s] of my love,

And lock them in the closet of thy
  thoughts?
Wert thou to Edward second to himself,
Sole friend, and partner of his secret
  loves?
And could a glance of fading beauty
  break   30
The enchainéd fetters of such private
  friends?
Base coward, false, and too effeminate
To be corrival [3] with a prince in thoughts!
From Oxford have I posted since I
  dined,
To quite a traitor fore that Edward
  sleep.
MARGARET. 'Twas I, my lord, not Lacy
  stepped awry;
For oft he sued and courted for yourself,
And still wooed for the courtier all in
  green.   38
But I, whom fancy made but overfond,
Pleaded myself with looks as if I loved;
I fed mine eye with gazing on his face,
And still bewitched loved Lacy with
  my looks.
My heart with sighs, mine eyes pleaded
  with tears,
My face held pity and content at once,
And more I could not cipher out [4] by
  signs
But that I loved Lord Lacy with my
  heart.
Then, worthy Edward, measure with
  thy mind
If women's favors will not force men
  fall,
If beauty and if darts of piercing love
Are not of force to bury thoughts of
  friends.   50
EDWARD. I tell thee, Peggy, I will have
  thy loves;
Edward or none shall conquer Margaret.
In frigates bottomed with rich Sethin [5]
  planks,
Topped with the lofty firs of Lebanon,
Stemmed and incased with burnished
  ivory,
And overlaid with plates of Persian
  wealth,
Like Thetis shalt thou wanton on the
  waves,
And draw the dolphins to thy lovely
  eyes,

---

[1] Struck.   [2] Love.   [3] Partner.   [4] Express.   [5] Shittim.

To dance lavoltas [1] in the purple streams.
Sirens, with harps and silver psalteries, 60
Shall wait with music at thy frigate's
    stem,
And entertain fair Margaret with their [2]
    lays.
England and England's wealth shall
    wait on thee;
Britain shall bend unto her prince's
    love,
And do due homage to thine excellence,
If thou wilt be but Edward's Margaret.
MARGARET. Pardon, my lord; if Jove's
    great royalty
Sent me such presents as to Danaë,
If Phœbus, tired [3] in Latona's webs,
Come courting from the beauty of his
    lodge,   70
The dulcet tunes of frolic Mercury
Nor [4] all the wealth heaven's treasury
    affords
Should make me leave Lord Lacy or
    his love.
EDWARD. I have learned at Oxford, then,
    this point of schools: [5]
Ablata causa, tollitur effectus.[6]
Lacy, the cause that Margaret cannot
    love
Nor fix her liking on the English prince,
Take him away, and then the effects
    will fail.
Villain, prepare thyself; for I will bathe
My poinard in the bosom of an earl.   80
LACY. Rather than live, and miss fair
    Margaret's love,
Prince Edward, stop not at the fatal
    doom,
But stab it home. End both my loves
    and life.
MARGARET. Brave Prince of Wales, hon-
    ored for royal deeds,
'Twere sin to stain fair Venus' courts
    with blood;
Love's conquests ends, my lord, in
    courtesy.
Spare Lacy, gentle Edward; let me die,
For so both you and he do cease your
    loves.

EDWARD. Lacy shall die as traitor to his
    lord.
LACY. I have deserved it, Edward; act
    it well.   90
MARGARET. What hopes the prince to
    gain by Lacy's death?
EDWARD. To end the loves twixt him
    and Margaret.
MARGARET. Why, thinks King Henry's
    son that Margaret's love
Hangs in the uncertain balance of
    proud time?
That death shall make a discord of our
    thoughts?
No, stab the earl, and, fore the morn-
    ing sun
Shall vaunt him thrice over the lofty
    east,
Margaret will meet her Lacy in the
    heavens.
LACY. If aught betides to lovely Margaret
That wrongs or wrings her honor from
    content,   100
Europe's rich wealth nor England's
    monarchy
Should not allure Lacy to overlive.[7]
Then, Edward, short my life, and end
    her loves.
MARGARET. Rid [8] me, and keep a friend
    worth many loves.
LACY. Nay, Edward, keep a love worth
    many friends.
MARGARET. And, if thy mind be such as
    fame hath blazed,
Then, princely Edward, let us both
    abide
The fatal resolution of thy rage.
Banish thou fancy and embrace re-
    venge,
And in one tomb knit both our car-
    casses,   110
Whose hearts were linkéd in one perfect
    love.
EDWARD. [*Aside.*]   Edward, art thou
    that famous Prince of Wales
Who at Damasco beat the Saracens,
And brought'st home triumph on thy
    lance's point,
And shall thy plumes be pulled by Venus
    down?
Is it princely to dissever lovers' leagues,
To part such friends as glory in their
    loves?

[1] Lively dances.
[2] Original reads *her*.
[3] Attired. Original has *tied*.
[4] Emended by Dyce. Original reads *not*.
[5] Principle of scholastic argument.
[6] The cause being removed, the effect is
taken away.
[7] Outlive, survive.   [8] Get rid of.

Leave, Ned, and make a virtue of this
    fault,
And further Peg and Lacy in their loves.
So in subduing fancy's passion,   120
Conquering thyself, thou gett'st the
    richest spoil.—
Lacy, rise up! Fair Peggy, here's my
    hand!
The Prince of Wales hath conquered
    all his thoughts,
And all his loves he yields unto the earl.
Lacy, enjoy the maid of Fressingfield;
Make her thy Lincoln countess at the
    church,
And Ned, as he is true Plantagenet,
Will give her to thee frankly for thy
    wife.
LACY. Humbly I take her of my sover-
    eign,
As if that Edward gave me England's
    right,   130
And riched me with the Albion diadem.
MARGARET. And doth the English prince
    mean true?
Will he vouchsafe to cease his former
    loves,
And yield the title of a country maid
Unto Lord Lacy?
EDWARD. I will, fair Peggy, as I am true
    lord.
MARGARET. Then, lordly sir, whose con-
    quest is as great
In conquering love as Cæsar's victories,
Margaret, as mild and humble in her
    thoughts
As was Aspasia unto Cyrus' self, 140
Yields thanks, and, next Lord Lacy,
    doth enshrine
Edward the second secret in her heart.[1]
EDWARD. Gramercy, Peggy.   Now that
    vows are passed,
And that your loves are not [to] be
    revolt,[2]
Once, Lacy, friends again, come, we will
    post
To Oxford; for this day the king is
    there,
And brings for Edward Castile Elinor.
Peggy, I must go see and view my wife;
I pray God I like her as I loved thee.
Beside, Lord Lincoln, we shall hear
    dispute   150

[1] *I.e.*, the second (next to Lacy) in her affection.   [2] Withdrawn, overturned.

Twixt Friar Bacon and learned Vander-
    mast.
Peggy, we'll leave you for a week or two.
MARGARET. As it please Lord Lacy; but
    love's foolish looks
Think footsteps miles and minutes to
    be hours.
LACY. I'll hasten, Peggy, to make short
    return.—
But, please your honor, go unto the
    lodge.
We shall have butter, cheese, and veni-
    son;
And yesterday I brought for Margaret
A lusty bottle of neat claret wine.
Thus can we feast and entertain your
    grace.   160
EDWARD. 'Tis cheer, Lord Lacy, for an
    emperor,
If he respect the person and the place.
Come, let us in; for I will all this night
Ride post until I come to Bacon's cell.
                                Exeunt.

[SCENE ix.

Oxford.]

Enter Henry, Emperor, Castile, Elinor,
                    Vandermast, Bungay.

EMPEROR. Trust me, Plantagenet, these
    Oxford schools
Are richly seated near the riverside,
The mountains full of fat and fallow
    deer,
The battling [3] pastures lade [4] with kine
    and flocks,
The town gorgeous with high-built
    colleges,
And scholars seemly in their grave at-
    tire,
Learned in searching principles of art.—
What is thy judgment, Jaques Vander-
    mast?
VANDER. That lordly are the buildings of
    the town,
Spacious the rooms, and full of pleasant
    walks;   10
But for the doctors, how that they be
    learned,
It may be meanly, for aught I can hear.
BUNGAY. I tell thee, German, Hapsburg
    holds none such,
None read so deep as Oxenford contains.

[3] Nourishing.   [4] Laden.

There are within our academic state
Men that may lecture it in Germany
To all the doctors of your Belgic schools.
HENRY. Stand to him, Bungay; charm
   this Vandermast,
And I will use thee as a royal king.
VANDER. Wherein darest thou dispute with
   me?   20
BUNGAY. In what a doctor and a friar
   can.
VANDER. Before rich Europe's worthies
   put thou forth
The doubtful question unto Vander-
   mast.
BUNGAY. Let it be this: Whether the
spirits of pyromancy or geomancy be most
predominant in magic?
VANDER. I say, of pyromancy.
BUNGAY. And I, of geomancy.
VANDER. The cabalists that write of
   magic spells,
As Hermes, Melchie, and Pythagoras, 30
Affirm that, 'mongst the quadruplicity
Of elemental essence, *terra* is but thought
To be a *punctum* squaréd to [1] the rest;
And that the compass of ascending
   elements
Exceed in bigness as they do in height;
Judging the concave circle of the sun
To hold the rest in his circumference.
If, then, as Hermes says, the fire be
   great'st,
Purest, and only giveth shapes to
   spirits,
Then must these *dæmones* [2] that haunt
   that place   40
Be every way superior to the rest.
BUNGAY. I reason not of elemental shapes,
Nor tell I of the concave latitudes,
Noting their essence nor their quality,
But of the spirits that pyromancy calls,
And of the vigor of the geomantic
   fiends.
I tell thee, German, magic haunts the
   grounds,
And those strange necromantic spells,
That work such shows and wondering
   in the world,
Are acted by those geomantic spirits 50
That Hermes calleth *terræ filii*.[3]
The fiery spirits are but transparent
   shades,

That lightly pass as heralds to bear
   news;
But earthly fiends, closed in the lowest
   deep,
Dissever mountains, if they be but
   charged,
Being more gross and massy in their
   power.
VANDER. Rather these earthly geomantic
   spirits
Are dull and like the place where they
   remain;
For, when proud Lucifer fell from the
   heavens,
The spirits and angels that did sin with
   him   60
Retained their local essence as their
   faults,
All subject under Luna's continent.
They which offended less hang in the
   fire,
And second faults did rest within the
   air;
But Lucifer and his proud-hearted
   fiends
Were thrown into the center of the
   earth,
Having less understanding than the
   rest,
As having greater sin and lesser grace.
Therefore such gross and earthly spirits
   do serve
For jugglers, witches, and vild [4] sor-
   cerers;   70
Whereas the pyromantic genii
Are mighty, swift, and of far-reaching
   power.
But, grant that geomancy hath most
   force,
Bungay, to please these mighty poten-
   tates,
Prove by some instance what thy art
   can do.
BUNGAY. I will.
EMPEROR. Now, English Harry, here be-
   gins the game;
We shall see sport between these learned
   men.
VANDER. What wilt thou do?
BUNGAY. Show thee the tree, leaved with
   refinéd gold,   80
Whereon the fearful dragon held his
   seat,

---

[1] An atom compared with.
[2] Spirits.   [3] Sons of the earth.
[4] Vile, low in rank.

That watched the garden called Hesperides,
Subdued and won by conquering Hercules.
VANDER. Well done!

Here Bungay conjures, and the tree appears
with the Dragon shooting fire.

HENRY. What say you, royal lordings,
  to my friar?
  Hath he not done a point of cunning
  skill?
VANDER. Each scholar in the nigromantic
  spells
  Can do as much as Bungay hath performed.
  But as Alcmena's bastard razed this
  tree,
  So will I raise him up as when he lived, 90
  And cause him pull the dragon from
  his seat,
  And tear the branches piecemeal from
  the root.—
  Hercules! *Prodi, prodi,*[1] Hercules!

Hercules appears in his lion's skin.

HERCULES. *Quis me vult?*[2]
VANDER. Jove's bastard son, thou Libyan Hercules,
  Pull off the sprigs from off the Hesperian tree,
  As once thou didst to win the golden
  fruit.
HERCULES. *Fiat.*[3]
  Here he begins to break the branches.
VANDER. Now, Bungay, if thou canst
  by magic charm   99
  The fiend appearing like great Hercules
  From pulling down the branches of the
  tree,
  Then art thou worthy to be counted
  learned.
BUNGAY. I cannot.
VANDER. Cease, Hercules, until I give
  thee charge.—
  Mighty commander of this English isle,
  Henry, come from the stout Plantagenets,
  Bungay is learned enough to be a friar;
  But, to compare with Jaques Vandermast,

Oxford and Cambridge must go seek
  their cells
To find a man to match him in his art. 110
I have given nonplus to the Paduans,
To them of Sien, Florence, and Bologna,
Rheims, Louvain, and fair Rotherdam,
Frankfort, Lutrech,[4] and Orleans.
And now must Henry, if he do me right,
Crown me with laurel, as they all have
  done.

Enter Bacon.

BACON. All hail to this royal company,
  That sit to hear and see this strange
  dispute!—
  Bungay, how stand'st thou as a man
  amazed!
  What, hath the German acted more
  than thou?   120
VANDER. What art thou that questions
  thus?
BACON. Men call me Bacon.
VANDER. Lordly thou look'st, as if that
  thou wert learned;
  Thy countenance as if science held her
  seat
  Between the circled arches of thy brows.
HENRY. Now, monarchs, hath the German
  found his match.
EMPEROR. Bestir thee, Jaques; take not
  now the foil,[5]
  Lest thou dost lose what foretime thou
  didst gain.
VANDER. Bacon, wilt thou dispute?
BACON. No, unless he were more learned
  than Vandermast;   130
  For yet, tell me, what hast thou done?
VANDER. Raised Hercules to ruinate that
  tree
  That Bungay mounted by his magic
  spells.
BACON. Set Hercules to work.
VANDER. Now, Hercules, I charge thee
  to thy task;
  Pull off the golden branches from the
  root.
HERCULES. I dare not. Seest thou not
  great Bacon here,
  Whose frown doth act more than thy
  magic can?
VANDER. By all the thrones and dominations,   139

---

[1] Come forth.   [2] Who wishes me?
[3] Let it be done.

[4] Utrecht, or Lutetia (Paris) (?).
[5] Fall, a wrestling term.

Virtues, powers, and mighty hierarchies,
I charge thee to obey to Vandermast.
HERCULES. Bacon, that bridles head-
strong Belcephon,
And rules Asmenoth, guider of the north,
Binds me from yielding unto Vander-
mast.
HENRY. How now, Vandermast! Have
you met with your match?
VANDER. Never before was't known to
Vandermast
That men held devils in such obedient
awe.
Bacon doth more than art, or else I
fail.
EMPEROR. Why, Vandermast, art thou
overcome?—
Bacon, dispute with him, and try his
skill.   150
BACON. I come not, monarchs, for to
hold dispute
With such a novice as is Vandermast;
I come to have your royalties to dine
With Friar Bacon here in Brazen-nose.
And, for this German troubles but the
place,
And holds this audience with a long
suspense,
I'll send him to his academy hence.—
Thou Hercules, whom Vandermast did
raise,
Transport the German unto Hapsburg
straight,
That he may learn by travail, gainst
the spring,[1]   160
More secret dooms and aphorisms of art.
Vanish the tree, and thou away with
him!
Exit the Spirit with Vandermast and the tree.
EMPEROR. Why, Bacon, whither dost
thou send him?
BACON. To Hapsburg; there your high-
ness at return
Shall find the German in his study safe.
HENRY. Bacon, thou hast honored Eng-
land with thy skill,
And made fair Oxford famous by thine
art;
I will be English Henry to thyself.
But tell me, shall we dine with thee
today?
BACON. With me, my lord. And, while I
fit my cheer,   170

---

[1] Original reads *springs*.

See where Prince Edward comes to wel-
come you,
Gracious as the morning star of heaven.
Exit.

Enter Edward, Lacy, Warren, Ermsby.

EMPEROR. Is this Prince Edward, Henry's
royal son?
How martial is the figure of his face,
Yet lovely and beset with amorets![2]
HENRY. Ned, where hast thou been?
EDWARD. At Framlingham, my lord, to
try your bucks
If they could scape the teasers or the
toil.
But, hearing of these lordly potentates
Landed and progressed up to Oxford
town,   180
I posted to give entertain [3] to them—
Chief, to the Almain monarch; next to
him,
And joint with him, Castile and Saxony
Are welcome as they may be to the
English court.
Thus for the men. But see, Venus ap-
pears,
Or one that overmatcheth Venus in
her shape!—
Sweet Elinor, beauty's high-swelling
pride,
Rich nature's glory and her wealth at
once,
Fair of all fairs, welcome to Albion;
Welcome to me, and welcome to thine
own,   190
If that thou deign'st the welcome from
myself.
ELINOR. Martial Plantagenet, Henry's
high-minded son,
The mark that Elinor did count her aim,
I liked thee fore I saw thee. Now I
love,
And so as in so short a time I may;
Yet so as time shall never break that
so,
And therefore so accept of Elinor.
CASTILE. Fear not, my lord, this couple
will agree,
If love may creep into their wanton
eyes,
And therefore, Edward, I accept thee
here,   200
Without suspense, as my adopted son.

---

[2] Loving looks.   [3] Reception.

HENRY. Let me that joy in these consorting greets,
And glory in these honors done to Ned,
Yield thanks for all these favors to my son,
And rest a true Plantagenet to all.

Enter Miles with a cloth and trenchers and salt.

MILES.[1] *Salvete, omnes reges,*[2] that govern your *greges*[3]
In Saxony and Spain, in England and in Almain!
For all this frolic rable[4] must I cover thee, table,[5]
With trenchers, salt, and cloth; and then look for your broth.   209
EMPEROR. What pleasant fellow is this?
HENRY. 'Tis, my lord, Doctor Bacon's poor scholar.
MILES. [*Aside.*] My master hath made me sewer[6] of these great lords; and, God knows, I am as serviceable at a table as a sow is under an apple tree. 'Tis no matter; their cheer shall not be great, and therefore what skills[7] where the salt stand,[8] before or behind?   [*Exit.*]
CASTILE. These scholars knows more skill in axioms,   220
How to use quips and sleights of sophistry,
Than for to cover[9] courtly for a king.

Enter Miles with a mess of pottage and broth; and, after him, Bacon.

MILES.[10] Spill, sir? Why, do you think I never carried twopenny chop[11] before in my life?—
By your leave, *nobile decus,*[12] for here comes Doctor Bacon's *pecus,*[13]
Being in his full age, to carry a mess of pottage.

---

[1] The following speech appears as prose in the original.
[2] Hail, all you kings.   [5] The table (?).
[3] Peoples.   [6] Butler.
[4] Rabble.   [7] What does it matter?
[8] A large saltcellar usually marked the dividing line between superior and inferior guests.
[9] Set a table.
[10] All of the following speech is printed as prose in the original.
[11] Chopped meat in broth (?).
[12] Your worshipful honor.
[13] Beast of burden.

BACON. Lordings, admire[14] not if your cheer be this,
For we must keep our academic fare;
No riot where philosophy doth reign.
And therefore, Henry, place these potentates,   231
And bid them fall unto their frugal cates.
EMPEROR. Presumptuous friar! What, scoff'st thou at a king?
What, dost thou taunt us with thy peasants' fare,
And give us cates fit for country swains?—
Henry, proceeds this jest of thy consent,
To twit us with such a pittance of such price?
Tell me, and Frederick will not grieve thee long.
HENRY. By Henry's honor, and the royal faith
The English monarch beareth to his friend,   240
I knew not of the friar's feeble fare,
Nor am I pleased he entertains you thus.
BACON. Content thee, Frederick, for I showed the cates
To let thee see how scholars use to feed,
How little meat refines our English wits.—
Miles, take away, and let it be thy dinner.
MILES. Marry, sir, I will. This day shall be a festival day with me,
For I shall exceed in the highest degree.
                                Exit Miles.
BACON. I tell thee, monarch, all the German peers
Could not afford thy entertainment such,   250
So royal and so full of majesty,
As Bacon will present to Frederick.
The basest waiter that attends thy cups
Shall be in honors greater than thyself;
And for thy cates, rich Alexandria drugs,[15]
Fetched by carvels from Egypt's richest straits,
Found in the wealthy strond of Africa,
Shall royalize the table of my king.
Wines richer than the 'Gyptian courtesan

---

[14] Wonder.   [15] Spices.

Quaffed to Augustus' kingly counter-
match,[1]   260
Shall be caroused in English Henry's
feast;
Kandy shall yield the richest of her
canes;
Persia, down her Volga by canoes,
Send down the secrets of her spicery;
The Afric dates, mirabiles [2] of Spain,
Conserves and suckets [3] from Tiberias,
Cates from Judea, choicer than the
lamp [4]
That fired Rome with sparks of glut-
tony,
Shall beautify the board for Frederick.
And therefore grudge not at a friar's
feast.   [*Exeunt.*]

[SCENE x.

Fressingfield.]

Enter two gentlemen, Lambert and Serlsby,
with the Keeper.

LAMBERT. Come, frolic keeper of our
liege's game,
Whose table spread hath ever venison
And jacks [5] of wine to welcome passen-
gers,
Know I am in love with jolly Margaret,
That overshines our damsels as the moon
Dark'neth the brightest sparkles of
the night.
In Laxfield here my land and living
lies.
I'll make thy daughter jointer [6] of it
all,
So thou consent to give her to [7] my wife;
And I can spend five hundreth marks
a year.   10
SERLSBY. I am the lands-lord, keeper, of
thy holds;
By copy [8] all thy living lies in me;
Laxfield did never see me raise my due.
I will enfeoff fair Margaret in all
So she will take her to a lusty squire.
KEEPER. Now, courteous gentles, if the
keeper's girl
Hath pleased the liking fancy of you
both,

And with her beauty hath subdued your
thoughts,
'Tis doubtful to decide the question.
It joys me that such men of great esteem
Should lay their liking on this base
estate,   21
And that her state should grow so for-
tunate
To be a wife to meaner men than you.
But sith [9] such squires will stoop to
keeper's fee,
I will, to avoid displeasure of you both,
Call Margaret forth, and she shall make
her choice.   *Exit.*
LAMBERT. Content, keeper; send her un-
to us.
Why, Serlsby, is thy wife so lately dead,
Are all thy loves so lightly passéd over,
As thou canst wed before the year be
out?   30
SERLSBY. I live not, Lambert, to content
the dead,
Nor was I wedded but for life to her.
The grave [10] ends and begins a married
state.

Enter Margaret.

LAMBERT. Peggy, the lovely flower of
all towns,
Suffolk's fair Helen, and rich England's
star,
Whose beauty, tempered with her hus-
wifery,
Makes England talk of merry Fressing-
field!
SERLSBY. I cannot trick it up with poesies,
Nor paint my passions with compari-
sons,   39
Nor tell a tale of Phœbus and his loves;
But this believe me: Laxfield here is
mine,
Of ancient rent seven hundred pounds
a year,
And, if thou canst but love a country
squire,
I will enfeoff thee, Margaret, in all.
I cannot flatter; try me, if thou please.
MARGARET. Brave neighboring squires,
the stay of Suffolk's clime,
A keeper's daughter is too base in gree [11]
To match with men accompted [12] of
such worth.

---

[1] Rival.
[2] Myrobalans, dried plums.
[3] Sweetmeats.
[4] Ward suggests *lamprey*.
[5] Pitchers.
[6] Joint-possessor.
[7] For.
[8] Copyhold.
[9] Since.
[10] Original reads *graves*.
[11] Degree.
[12] Accounted.

But might I not displease, I would
   reply.
LAMBERT. Say, Peggy; naught shall make
   us discontent.   50
MARGARET. Then, gentles, note that love
   hath little stay,
Nor can the flames that Venus sets on
   fire
Be kindled but by fancy's motion.
Then pardon, gentles, if a maid's reply
Be doubtful, while [1] I have debated
   with myself,
Who, or of whom, love shall constrain
   me like.
SERLSBY. Let it be me; and trust me,
   Margaret,
The meads environed with the silver
   streams,
Whose battling pastures fatt'neth all
   my flocks,
Yielding forth fleeces stapled [2] with
   such wool   60
As Leominster [3] cannot yield more finer
   stuff,
And forty kine with fair and burnished
   heads,
With strouting [4] dugs that paggle [5] to
   the ground,
Shall serve thy dairy, if thou wed with me.
LAMBERT. Let pass the country wealth,
   as flocks and kine,
And lands that wave with Ceres' golden
   sheaves,
Filling my barns with plenty of the fields.
But, Peggy, if thou wed thyself to me,
Thou shalt have garments of embro-
   dered [6] silk,
Lawns, and rich networks for thy head-
   attire.   70
Costly shall be thy fair abiliments,[7]
If thou wilt be but Lambert's loving
   wife.
MARGARET. Content you, gentles; you
   have proffered fair,
And more than fits a country maid's
   degree;
But give me leave to counsel me a time,
For fancy blooms not at the first as-
   sault.

Give me but ten days' respite, and I
   will reply,
Which or to whom myself affectionates.
SERLSBY. Lambert, I tell thee, thou art
   importunate;   79
Such beauty fits not such a base esquire.
It is for Serlsby to have Margaret.
LAMBERT. Think'st thou with wealth to
   overreach me?
Serlsby, I scorn to brook thy country
   braves.[8]
I dare thee, coward, to maintain this
   wrong,
At dint of rapier, single in the field.
SERLSBY. I'll answer, Lambert, what I
   have avouched!—
Margaret, farewell; another time shall
   serve.   *Exit Serlsby.*
LAMBERT. I'll follow!—Peggy, farewell
   to thyself;
Listen how well I'll answer for thy love.
        Exit Lambert.
MARGARET. How Fortune tempers lucky
   haps with frowns,   90
And wrongs me with the sweets of my
   delight!
Love is my bliss, and love is now my bale.
Shall I be Helen in my forward [9] fates,
As I am Helen in my matchless hue,
And set rich Suffolk with my face afire?
If lovely Lacy were but with his Peggy,
The cloudy darkness of his bitter frown
Would check the pride of these aspiring
   squires.
Before the term of ten days be expired,
Whenas they look for answer of their
   loves,   100
My lord will come to merry Fressing-
   field,
And end their fancies and their follies
   both.
Till when, Peggy, be blithe and of good
   cheer.

Enter a Post with a letter and a bag of gold.

POST. Fair lovely damsel, which way
   leads this path?
How might I post me unto Fressingfield?
Which footpath leadeth to the keeper's
   lodge?
MARGARET. Your way is ready, and this
   path is right.

---

[1] Until.   [2] Fibered.
[3] The original spelling, *Lempster*, indicates the
pronunciation.
[4] Swelling.   [6] Embroidered.
[5] Hang loosely down.   [7] Habiliments.
[8] Boasts, insults.   [9] **Froward.**

Myself do dwell hereby in Fressingfield,
And, if the keeper be the man you seek,
I am his daughter. May I know the
cause? 110
Post. Lovely, and once beloved of my
lord—
No marvel if his eye was lodged so
low,
When brighter beauty is not in the
heavens—
The Lincoln earl hath sent you letters
here,
And, with them, just an hundred pounds
in gold.
Sweet, bonny wench, read them and
make reply.
MARGARET. The scrolls that Jove sent
Danaë,
Wrapped in rich closures [1] of fine bur-
nished gold,
Were not more welcome than these
lines to me.
Tell me, whilst that I do unrip the
seals, 120
Lives Lacy well? How fares my lovely
lord?
Post. Well, if that wealth may make men
to live well.

The letter, and Margaret reads it.

" The blooms of the almond tree grow in
a night, and vanish in a morn; the flies
hœmeræ,[2] fair Peggy, take life with the
sun, and die with the dew; fancy, that
slippeth in with a gaze, goeth out with
a wink; and too timely loves have ever
the shortest length. I write this as thy
grief, and my folly, who at Fressing- [130
field loved that which time hath taught
me to be but mean dainties. Eyes are
dissemblers, and fancy is but queasy.
Therefore know, Margaret, I have chosen
a Spanish lady to be my wife, chief waiting-
woman to the Princess Elinor—a lady
fair, and no less fair than thyself, honorable and wealthy. In that I forsake thee,
I leave thee to thine own liking; and for
thy dowry I have sent thee an hundred [140
pounds, and ever assure thee of my favor,
which shall avail thee and thine much.
Farewell. Not thine, nor his own,
EDWARD LACY."

[1] Coverings.
[2] Ephemeræ.

Fond Ate, doomer of bad-boding fates,
That wraps proud Fortune in thy snaky
locks,
Didst thou enchant my birthday with
such stars
As lightened mischief from their in-
fancy?
If heavens had vowed, if stars had made
decree, 149
To show on me their froward influ-
ence,
If Lacy had but loved, heavens, hell,
and all
Could not have wronged the patience
of my mind.
Post. It grieves me, damsel; but the earl
is forced
To love the lady by the king's command.
MARGARET. The wealth combined within
the English shelves,
Europe's commander, nor the English
king
Should not have moved the love of
Peggy from her lord.
Post. What answer shall I return to
my lord?
MARGARET. First, for thou cam'st from
Lacy whom I loved—
Ah, give me leave to sigh at every
thought!— 160
Take thou, my friend, the hundred
pound he sent,
For Margaret's resolution craves no
dower.
The world shall be to her as vanity;
Wealth, trash; love, hate; pleasure,
despair.
For I will straight to stately Framling-
ham,
And in the abbey there be shorn a nun,
And yield my loves and liberty to God.
Fellow, I give thee this, not for the
news,
For those be hateful unto Margaret,
But for th'art Lacy's man, once Mar-
garet's love. 170
Post. What I have heard, what passions
I have seen,
I'll make report of them unto the earl.
Exit Post.
MARGARET. Say that she joys his fancies
be at rest,
And prays that his misfortune may be
hers. *Exit.*

[SCENE xi.

Bacon's study.]

*Enter Friar Bacon, drawing the curtains
with a white stick, a book in his hand,
and a lamp lighted by him; and the
Brazen Head, and Miles with weapons
by him.*

BACON. Miles, where are you?

MILES. Here, sir.

BACON. How chance you tarry so long?

MILES. Think you that the watching
of the Brazen Head craves no furniture?
I warrant you, sir, I have so armed myself that, if all your devils come, I will not
fear them an inch.

BACON. Miles, thou knowest that I have
    dived into hell,
And sought the darkest palaces of
    fiends;   10
That with my magic spells great Belce-
    phon
Hath left his lodge and kneeléd at my
    cell;
The rafters of the earth rent from the
    poles,
And three-formed Luna hid her silver
    looks,
Trembling upon her concave continent,
When Bacon read upon his magic book.
With seven years' tossing nigromantic
    charms,
Poring upon dark Hecat's principles,
I have framed out a monstrous head
    of brass,
That, by the enchanting forces of the
    devil,   20
Shall tell out strange and uncouth apho-
    risms,
And girt fair England with a wall of
    brass.
Bungay and I have watched these three-
    score days,
And now our vital spirits crave some
    rest.
If Argus lived, and had his hundred
    eyes,
They could not overwatch Phobetor's
    night.
Now, Miles, in thee rests Friar Bacon's
    weal;
The honor and renown of all his life
Hangs in the watching of this Brazen
    Head.

Therefore I charge thee by the immortal
    God,   30
That holds the souls of men within his
    fist,
This night thou watch, for, ere the
    morning star
Sends out his glorious glister on the
    north,
The head will speak.   Then, Miles,
    upon thy life,
Wake me; for then by magic art I'll
    work
To end my seven years' task with excel-
    lence.
If that a wink but shut thy watchful
    eye,
Then farewell Bacon's glory and his
    fame!
Draw close the curtains, Miles. Now,
    for thy life,
Be watchful, and—   40
              Here he falleth asleep.

MILES. So! I thought you would talk
yourself asleep anon; and 'tis no marvel,
for Bungay on the days, and he on the
nights, have watched just these ten-and-
fifty days. Now this is the night, and
'tis my task, and no more. Now, Jesus
bless me, what a goodly head it is! And
a nose! You talk of *nos autem glorificare*,[1]
but here's a nose that I warrant may be
called *nos autem popelare* for the people [50
of the parish. Well, I am furnished with
weapons. Now, sir, I will set me down by
a post, and make it as good as a watchman
to wake me if I chance to slumber. I
thought, Goodman Head, I would call
you out of your *memento.*
        Sit down and knock your head.
Passion o' God, I have almost broke my
pate! Up, Miles, to your task; take your
brown bill[2] in your hand. Here's some of
your master's hobgoblins abroad.   60
With this a great noise. The Head speaks.

HEAD. Time is!

MILES. Time is! Why, Master Brazen
Head, have you such a capital nose, and
answer you with syllables, "Time is"?
Is this all my master's cunning, to spend
seven years' study about "Time is"?
Well, sir, it may be we shall have some
better orations of it anon. Well, I'll watch

[1] Miles's impossible Latin pun on a liturgical
phrase.   [2] Halbert.

you as narrowly as ever you were watched, and I'll play with you as the nightingale [70 with the slowworm:[1] I'll set a prick against my breast. [*Places the halbert against his breast.*] Now rest there, Miles. [*He falls over.*] Lord, have mercy upon me! I have almost killed myself! [*A great noise.*] Up, Miles; list how they rumble.

HEAD. Time was!

MILES. Well, Friar Bacon, you spent your seven years' study well, that can make your head speak but two words [80 at once. "Time was"! Yea, marry, time was when my master was a wise man, but that was before he began to make the Brazen Head. You shall lie while your arse ache, and your head speak no better. Well, I will watch, and walk up and down, and be a peripatetian and a philosopher of Aristotle's stamp. [*A great noise.*] What, a fresh noise? Take thy pistols in hand, Miles! 90

Here the Head speaks, and a lightning flasheth forth, and a hand appears that breaketh down the Head with a hammer.

HEAD. Time is past!

MILES. Master, master, up! Hell's broken loose! Your head speaks; and there's such a thunder and lightning that I warrant all Oxford is up in arms. Out of your bed, and take a brown bill in your hand. The latter day is come!

BACON. Miles, I come. O, passing warily watched!

Bacon will make thee next himself in love.

When spake the head? 100

MILES. When spake the head! Did not you say that he should tell strange principles of philosophy? Why, sir, it speaks but two words at a time.

BACON. Why, villain, hath it spoken oft?

MILES. Oft! Ay, marry, hath it, thrice; but in all those three times it hath uttered but seven words.

BACON. As how? 110

MILES. Marry, sir, the first time he said, "Time is," as if Fabius Cumentator[2] should have pronounced a sentence; he said, "Time was;" and the third time,

with thunder and lightning, as in great choler, he said, "Time is past."

BACON. 'Tis past indeed! A villain! Time is past!

My life, my fame, my glory, all are past.—

Bacon, the turrets of thy hope are ruined down; 119

Thy seven years' study lieth in the dust!

Thy Brazen Head lies broken through a slave

That watched, and would not when the head did will.—

What said the head first?

MILES. Even, sir, "Time is."

BACON. Villain, if thou hadst called to Bacon then,

If thou hadst watched, and waked the sleepy friar,

The Brazen Head had uttered aphorisms,

And England had been circled round with brass.

But proud Astmeroth,[3] ruler of the North, 129

And Demogorgon, master of the fates,

Grudge that a mortal man should work so much.

Hell trembled at my deep, commanding spells;

Fiends frowned to see a man their overmatch;

Bacon might boast more than a man might boast.

But now the braves of Bacon hath an end;

Europe's conceit[4] of Bacon hath an end;

His seven years' practice sorteth[5] to ill end;

And, villain, sith my glory hath an end,

I will appoint thee fatal to some end.[6]

Villain, avoid! Get thee from Bacon's sight! 140

Vagrant, go roam and range about the world,

And perish as a vagabond on earth!

MILES. Why, then, sir, you forbid me your service?

BACON. My service, villain, with a fatal curse

That direful plagues and mischief fall on thee!

---

[1] Small snake.
[2] Grosart suggests that Miles confuses *commentator* and *cunctator*.

[3] Same as *Asmenoth*.
[4] Conception, opinion.
[5] Tends. [6] To some fatal end (?).

MILES. 'Tis no matter; I am against you with the old proverb, "The more the fox is cursed, the better he fares."[1] God be with you, sir. I'll take but a book in my hand, a wide-sleeved gown on my [150 back, and a crowned cap on my head, and see if I can want promotion.   [*Exit.*]

BACON. Some fiend or ghost haunt on thy weary steps

Until they do transport thee quick to hell;

For Bacon shall have never merry day,

To lose the fame and honor of his Head.
                                        Exit.

[SCENE xii.

At court.]

*Enter Emperor, Castile, Henry, Elinor,
          Edward, Lacy, Rafe.*

EMPEROR. Now, lovely prince, the prince of Albion's wealth,

How fares the Lady Elinor and you?

What, have you courted and found Castile fit

To answer England in equivalence?

Will 't be a match twixt bonny Nell and thee?

EDWARD. Should Paris enter in the courts of Greece,

And not lie fettered in fair Helen's looks,

Or Phœbus scape those piercing amorets

That Daphne glancéd at his deity?

Can Edward then sit by a flame and freeze,   10

Whose heat puts Helen and fair Daphne down?

Now, monarchs, ask the lady if we gree.

HENRY. What, madam, hath my son found grace or no?

ELINOR. Seeing, my lord, his lovely counterfeit,

And hearing how his mind and shape agreed,

I come not, trooped with all this war-like train,

Doubting of love, but so affectionate

As [2] Edward hath in England what he won in Spain.

[1] With puns on *coursed* (*pursued*) and *fares* (*goes*).   [2] That.

CASTILE. A match, my lord; these wantons needs must love.

Men must have wives, and women will be wed.   20

Let's haste the day to honor up the rites.

RAFE. Sirrah Harry, shall Ned marry Nell?

HENRY. Ay, Rafe; how then?

RAFE. Marry, Harry, follow my counsel: send for Friar Bacon to marry them, for he'll so conjure him and her with his nigromancy that they shall love together like pig and lamb whilst they live.

CASTILE. But hear'st thou, Rafe? [30 Art thou content to have Elinor to thy lady?

RAFE. Ay, so she will promise me two things.

CASTILE. What's that, Rafe?

RAFE. That she will never scold with Ned, nor fight with me.—Sirrah Harry, I have put her down with a thing unpossible.

HENRY. What's that, Rafe?   40

RAFE. Why, Harry, didst thou ever see that a woman could both hold her tongue and her hands? No! But when egg pies grows on apple trees, then will thy gray mare prove a bagpiper.

EMPEROR. What says the Lord of Castile and the Earl of Lincoln, that they are in such earnest and secret talk?

CASTILE. I stand, my lord, amazéd at his talk,

How he discourseth of the constancy

Of one surnamed, for beauty's excellence,   51

The Fair Maid of merry Fressingfield.

HENRY. 'Tis true, my lord, 'tis wondrous for to hear;

Her beauty passing Mars's paramour,

Her virgin's right as rich as Vesta's was.

Lacy and Ned hath told me miracles.

CASTILE. What says Lord Lacy? Shall she be his wife?

LACY. Or else Lord Lacy is unfit to live.

May it please your highness give me leave to post

To Fressingfield, I'll fetch the bonny girl,   60

And prove, in true appearance at the court,
What I have vouchéd often with my tongue.
HENRY. Lacy, go to the querry [1] of my stable,
And take such coursers as shall fit thy turn.
Hie thee to Fressingfield, and bring home the lass;
And, for her fame flies through the English coast,
If it may please the Lady Elinor,
One day shall match your excellence and her.
ELINOR. We Castile ladies are not very coy. [2]
Your highness may command a greater boon;   70
And glad were I to grace the Lincoln earl
With being partner of his marriage day.
EDWARD. Gramercy, Nell, for I do love the lord,
As he that's second to myself in love.
RAFE. You love her?—Madam Nell, never believe him you, though he swears he loves you.
ELINOR. Why, Rafe?
RAFE. Why, his love is like unto a tapster's glass that is broken with every [80 touch; for he loved the Fair Maid of Fressingfield once out of all ho. [3]— Nay, Ned, never wink upon me; I care not, I.
HENRY. Rafe tells all; you shall have a good secretary of him.—
But, Lacy, haste thee post to Fressingfield;
For, ere thou hast fitted all things for her state,
The solemn marriage day will be at hand.
LACY. I go, my lord.   *Exit Lacy.*
EMPEROR. How shall we pass this day, my lord?   90
HENRY. To horse, my lord. The day is passing fair;
We'll fly the partridge or go rouse the deer.
Follow, my lords; you shall not want for sport.   *Exeunt.*

[1] Equerry.
[2] Distant. disdainful.
[3] Out of all bounds.

[SCENE xiii.

Bacon's study.]

Enter Friar Bacon with Friar Bungay to his cell.

BUNGAY. What means the friar that frolicked it of late,
To sit as melancholy in his cell
As if he had neither lost nor won today?
BACON. Ah, Bungay, my Brazen Head is spoiled,
My glory gone, my seven years' study lost!
The fame of Bacon, bruited through the world,
Shall end and perish with this deep disgrace.
BUNGAY. Bacon hath built foundation of [4] his fame
So surely on the wings of true report,
With acting strange and uncouth miracles,   10
As this cannot infringe what he deserves.
BACON. Bungay, sit down, for by prospective skill
I find this day shall fall out ominous:
Some deadly act shall tide [5] me ere I sleep;
But what and wherein little can I guess.
BUNGAY. My mind is heavy, whatsoe'er shall hap.

Enter two Scholars, sons to Lambert and Serlsby. Knock.

BACON. Who's that knocks?
BUNGAY. Two scholars that desires to speak with you.
BACON. Bid them come in.—   19
Now, my youths, what would you have?
1 SCHOLAR. Sir, we are Suffolk men and neighboring friends;
Our fathers in their countries lusty squires;
Their lands adjoin. In Crackfield [6] mine doth dwell,
And his in Laxfield. We are college mates,
Sworn brothers, as our fathers lives as friends.

[4] Original reads *on*.   [6] Now Cratfield.
[5] Betide.

BACON. To what end is all this?

2 SCHOLAR. Hearing your worship kept within your cell

A glass prospective, wherein men might see

Whatso their thoughts or hearts' desire could wish,

We come to know how that our fathers fare. 30

BACON. My glass is free for every honest man.

Sit down, and you shall see ere long how

Or in what state your friendly father lives.

Meanwhile, tell me your names.

1 SCHOLAR.[1] Mine Lambert.

2 SCHOLAR. And mine Serlsby.

BACON. Bungay, I smell there will be a tragedy.

Enter [in the glass] Lambert and Serlsby with rapiers and daggers.

LAMBERT. Serlsby, thou hast kept thine hour like a man.

Th'art worthy of the title of a squire,

That durst, for proof of thy affection 40

And for thy mistress' favor, prize[2] thy blood.

Thou know'st what words did pass at Fressingfield,

Such shameless braves as manhood cannot brook.

Ay, for I scorn to bear such piercing taunts,

Prepare thee, Serlsby; one of us will die.

SERLSBY. Thou see'st I single [meet] thee [in] the field,[3]

And what I spake, I'll maintain with my sword.

Stand on thy guard; I cannot scold it out.

And, if thou kill me, think I have a son

That lives in Oxford in the Broadgates Hall, 50

Who will revenge his father's blood with blood.

LAMBERT. And, Serlsby, I have there a lusty boy

That dares at weapon buckle with thy son,

And lives in Broadgates too, as well as thine.

But draw thy rapier, for we'll have a bout.

BACON. Now, lusty younkers, look within the glass,

And tell me if you can discern your sires.

1 SCHOLAR. Serlsby, 'tis hard; thy father offers wrong,

To combat with my father in the field.

2 SCHOLAR. Lambert, thou liest; my father's is the abuse,[4] 60

And thou shalt find it, if my father harm.[5]

BUNGAY. How goes it, sirs?

1 SCHOLAR. Our fathers are in combat, hard by Fressingfield.

BACON. Sit still, my friends, and see the event.

LAMBERT. Why stand'st thou, Serlsby? Doubt'st thou of thy life?

A veney,[6] man! Fair Margaret craves so much.

SERLSBY. Then this for her!

1 SCHOLAR. Ah, well thrust!

2 SCHOLAR. But mark the ward.[7]

They fight and kill each other.

LAMBERT. O, I am slain! 70

SERLSBY. And I.—Lord, have mercy on me!

1 SCHOLAR. My father slain!—Serlsby, ward that!

2 SCHOLAR. And so is mine!—Lambert, I'll quite thee well.

The two Scholars stab one another.[8]

BUNGAY. O, strange stratagem![9]

BACON. See, friar, where the fathers[10] both lie dead!—

Bacon, thy magic doth effect this massacre.

This glass prospective worketh many woes;

[1] Original reads *Lambert.*
[2] Risk. [3] Insertions by Dyce.

[4] *I.e.*, my father is the offended one. [6] Bout.
[5] Come to harm. [7] Guard.
[8] Stage direction appears before the 2 Scholar's speech in original.
[9] Violent deed. [10] Scholars (?).

And therefore, seeing these brave lusty
    Brutes,[1]
These friendly youths, did perish by
    thine art,
End all thy magic and thine art at
    once.   80
The poniard that did end the fatal[2]
    lives
Shall break the cause efficiat of[3] their
    woes.
So fade the glass, and end with it the
    shows
That nigromancy did infuse the crystal
    with.   *He breaks the glass.*
BUNGAY. What means learned Bacon
    thus to break his glass?
BACON. I tell thee, Bungay, it repents
    me sore
That ever Bacon meddled in this art.
The hours I have spent in pyromantic
    spells,
The fearful tossing in the latest night
Of papers full of nigromantic charms,   90
Conjuring and adjuring devils and
    fiends,
With stole and alb and strange pentag-
    onon;
The wresting[4] of the holy name of God,
As Sother, Eloim, and Adonai,
Alpha, Manoth, and Tetragrammaton,
With praying to the fivefold powers
    of heaven,
Are instances that Bacon must be
    damned
For using devils to countervail his God.—
Yet, Bacon, cheer thee; drown not in
    despair.
Sins have their salves; repentance can
    do much.   100
Think Mercy sits where Justice holds
    her seat,
And from those wounds those bloody
    Jews did pierce,
Which by thy magic oft did bleed afresh,
From thence for thee the dew of mercy
    drops
To wash the wrath of high Jehovah's
    ire,
And make thee as a new-born babe from
    sin.—
Bungay, I'll spend the remnant of my
    life

[1] Britons (or heroes?).
[2] Fated.
[3] Effecting.
[4] Misusing.

In pure devotion, praying to my God
That he would save what Bacon vainly
    lost.   *Exit [with Bungay].*

[SCENE xiv.

Fressingfield.]

*Enter Margaret in nun's apparel; Keeper,
    her father; and their Friend.*

KEEPER. Margaret, be not so headstrong
    in these vows!
O, bury not such beauty in a cell,
That England hath held famous for
    the hue!
Thy father's hair, like to the silver
    blooms
That beautify the shrubs of Africa,
Shall fall before the dated time of death,
Thus to forgo his lovely Margaret.
MARGARET. Ah, father, when the harmony
    of heaven
Soundeth the measures of a lively faith,
The vain illusions of this flattering
    world   10
Seems odious to the thoughts of Mar-
    garet.
I lovéd once—Lord Lacy was my love;
And now I hate myself for that I loved,
And doted more on him than on my God.
For this I scourge myself with sharp
    repents.
But now the touch of such aspiring sins
Tells me all love is lust but love of
    heavens;
That beauty used for love is vanity.
The world contains naught but alluring
    baits,   19
Pride, flattery, and inconstant thoughts.
To shun the pricks of death, I leave the
    world,
And vow to meditate on heavenly bliss,
To live in Framlingham a holy nun,
Holy and pure in conscience and in
    deed;
And for to wish all maids to learn of me
To seek heaven's joy before earth's
    vanity.
FRIEND. And will you then, Margaret,
    be shorn a nun, and so leave us all?
MARGARET. Now farewell, world, the
    engine of all woe!
Farewell to friends and father! Wel-
    come, Christ!   30

Adieu to dainty robes! This base attire
Better befits an humble mind to God
Than all the show of rich abiliments.
Love, O love, and, with fond love, fare-
well,
Sweet Lacy, whom I lovéd once so dear.
Ever be well, but never in my thoughts,
Lest I offend to think on Lacy's love.
But even to that, as to the rest, farewell!

Enter Lacy, Warren, Ermsby, booted and
spurred.

Lacy. Come on, my wags, we're near
the keeper's lodge.
Here have I oft walked in the wat'ry
meads,   40
And chatted with my lovely Margaret.
Warren. Sirrah Ned, is not this the
keeper?
Lacy. 'Tis the same.
Ermsby. The old lecher hath gotten holy
mutton [1] to him—a nun, my lord!
Lacy. Keeper, how farest thou? Holla,
man, what cheer?
How doth Peggy, thy daughter and my
love?
Keeper. Ah, good my lord! O, woe is me
for Peg!
See where she stands clad in her nun's
attire,
Ready for to be shorn in Framling-
ham.   50
She leaves the world because she left
your love.
O, good my lord, persuade her if you
can!
Lacy. Why, how now, Margaret! What,
a malcontent?
A nun? What holy father taught you
this,
To task yourself to such a tedious life
As die a maid? 'Twere injury to me
To smother up such beauty in a cell.
Margaret. Lord Lacy, thinking of thy
former miss, [2]
How fond [3] the prime of wanton years
were spent
In love—O, fie upon that fond con-
ceit,   60
Whose hap and essence hangeth in the
eye!—

I leave both love and love's content
at once,
Betaking me to Him that is true love,
And leaving all the world for love of
Him.
Lacy. Whence, Peggy, comes this meta-
morphosis?
What, shorn a nun, and I have from the
court
Posted with coursers to convey thee
hence
To Windsor, where our marriage shall
be kept?
Thy wedding robes are in the tailor's
hands.
Come, Peggy, leave these peremptory
vows.   70
Margaret. Did not my lord resign his
interest,
And make divorce twixt Margaret and
him?
Lacy. 'Twas but to try sweet Peggy's
constancy.
But will fair Margaret leave her love and
lord?
Margaret. Is not heaven's joy before
earth's fading bliss,
And life above sweeter than life in love?
Lacy. Why, then, Margaret will be shorn
a nun?
Margaret. Margaret hath made a vow
which may not be revoked.
Warren. We cannot stay, my lord; and,
if she be so strict,   79
Our leisure grants us not to woo afresh.
Ermsby. Choose you, fair damsel; yet
the choice is yours,
Either a solemn nunnery or the court,
God or Lord Lacy. Which contents you
best,
To be a nun or else Lord Lacy's wife?
Lacy. A good motion.—Peggy, your an-
swer must be short.
Margaret. The flesh is frail. My lord
doth know it well,
That when he comes with his enchanting
face,
Whatsoe'er betide, I cannot say him
nay.
Off goes the habit of a maiden's heart,
And, seeing fortune will, fair Framling-
ham,   90
And all the show of holy nuns, farewell!
Lacy for me, if he will be my lord.

---

[1] Loose woman.   [2] Error.   [3] Foolishly.

LACY. Peggy, thy lord, thy love, thy
    husband!
  Trust me, by truth of knighthood, that
    the king
  Stays for to marry matchless Elinor,
  Until I bring thee richly to the court,
  That one day may both marry her and
    thee.—
  How sayst thou, keeper? Art thou glad
    of this?
KEEPER. As if the English king had given
  The park and deer of Fressingfield to
    me.   100
ERMSBY. I pray thee, my Lord of Sus-
sex, why art thou in a brown study?
WARREN. To see the nature of women—
that be they never so near God, yet they
love to die in a man's arms.
LACY. What have you fit for breakfast?
    We have hied
  And posted all this night to Fressingfield.
MARGARET. Butter and cheese, and um-
    bles [1] of a deer,
  Such as poor keepers have within their
    lodge.
LACY. And not a bottle of wine?   110
MARGARET. We'll find one for my lord.
LACY. Come, Sussex, let's in; we shall
    have more,
  For she speaks least, to hold her promise
    sure.   *Exeunt.*

[SCENE xv.

Bacon's study.]

Enter a Devil to seek Miles.

DEVIL. How restless are the ghosts of
    hellish spirits,
  When every charmer with his magic
    spells
  Calls us from ninefold-trenchéd Phleg-
    eton,[2]
  To scud and overscour the earth in post
  Upon the speedy wings of swiftest winds!
  Now Bacon hath raised me from the
    darkest deep,
  To search about the world for Miles
    his man,
  For Miles, and to torment his lazy bones
  For careless watching of his Brazen
    Head.
  See where he comes. O, he is mine!   10

[1] Numbles; heart, liver, etc.
[2] Emended by Dyce. Original reads *Blegiton.*

Enter Miles with a gown and a cornercap.

MILES. A scholar, quoth you! Marry,
sir, I would I had been made a bottle
maker when I was made a scholar; for I
can get neither to be a deacon, reader, nor
schoolmaster, no, not the clerk of a parish.
Some call me dunce; another saith my head
is as full of Latin as an egg's full of oatmeal. Thus I am tormented, that the
devil and Friar Bacon haunts me.—
Good Lord, here's one of my master's [20
devils! I'll go speak to him.—What,
Master Plutus, how cheer you?
DEVIL. Dost thou know me?
MILES. Know you, sir! Why, are not
you one of my master's devils that were
wont to come to my master, Doctor Bacon,
at Brazen-nose?
DEVIL. Yes, marry, am I.
MILES. Good Lord, M[aster] Plutus,
I have seen you a thousand times at my [30
master's, and yet I had never the manners
to make you drink. But, sir, I am glad
to see how conformable you are to the
statute.—[*To audience.*] I warrant you,
he's as yeomanly a man as you shall see.
Mark you, masters, here's a plain, honest
man, without welt or guard.[3]—But I pray
you, sir, do you come lately from hell?
DEVIL. Ay, marry; how then?
MILES. Faith, 'tis a place I have de- [40
sired long to see. Have you not good tip-
pling houses there? May not a man have
a lusty fire there, a pot of good ale, a pair [4]
of cards, a swingeing [5] piece of chalk,[6]
and a brown toast that will clap a white
waistcoat [7] on a cup of good drink?
DEVIL. All this you may have there.
MILES. You are for me, friend, and I
am for you. But I pray you, may I not
have an office there?   50
DEVIL. Yes, a thousand! What wouldst
thou be?
MILES. By my troth, sir, in a place
where I may profit myself. I know hell
is a hot place, and men are marvelous dry,
and much drink is spent there. I would be
a tapster.
DEVIL. Thou shalt.
MILES. There's nothing lets [8] me from

[3] Facing or trimming.   [4] Pack.
[5] Striking, huge.
[6] Used in marking up alehouse accounts.
[7] *I.e.*, foam.   [8] Hinders.

going with you, but that 'tis a long [60
journey, and I have never a horse.

DEVIL. Thou shalt ride on my back.

MILES. Now surely here's a courteous
devil, that, for to pleasure his friend, will
not stick to make a jade of himself.—
But I pray you, goodman friend, let me
move a question to you.

DEVIL. What's that?

MILES. I pray you, whether is your pace
a trot or an amble?   70

DEVIL. An amble.

MILES. 'Tis well; but take heed it be
not a trot. But 'tis no matter, I'll prevent
it.   [*Puts on spurs.*]

DEVIL. What dost?

MILES. Marry, friend, I put on my
spurs; for, if I find your pace either a trot
or else uneasy, I'll put you to a false gallop;
I'll make you feel the benefit of my
spurs.   80

DEVIL. Get up upon my back.

MILES. O Lord, here's even a goodly
marvel, when a man rides to hell on the
devil's back!   *Exeunt, roaring.*

[SCENE xvi.

At court.]

*Enter the Emperor with a pointless sword;
   next, the King of Castile, carrying a
   sword with a point; Lacy, carrying the
   globe; Ed[ward]; Warr[en], carrying a rod
   of gold with a dove on it; Ermsby with
   a crown and scepter; the Queen [i.e.,
   Princess Elinor] with the Fair Maid of
   Fressingfield on her left hand; Henry;
   Bacon; with other Lords attending.*

EDWARD. Great potentates, earth's miracles for state,
Think that Prince Edward humbles at
   your feet,
And, for these favors, on his martial
   sword
He vows perpetual homage to yourselves,
Yielding these honors unto Elinor.

HENRY. Gramercies, lordings. Old Plan-
tagenet,
That rules and sways the Albion diadem,
With tears discovers these conceivéd
   joys,
And vows requital, if his men-at-arms,

The wealth of England, or due honors
   done   10
To Elinor, may quite his favorites.
But all this while what say you to the
   dames
That shine like to the crystal lamps of
   heaven?

EMPEROR. If but a third were added to
   these two,
They did surpass those gorgeous images
That gloried Ida with rich beauty's
   wealth.

MARGARET. 'Tis I, my lords, who humbly
   on my knee
Must yield her orisons to mighty Jove
For lifting up his handmaid to this state,
Brought from her homely cottage to
   the court,   20
And graced with kings, princes, and
   emperors;
To whom (next to the noble Lincoln
   earl)
I vow obedience, and such humble love
As may a handmaid to such mighty
   men.

ELINOR. Thou martial man that wears
   the Almain crown,
And you the western potentates of
   might,
The Albion princess, English Edward's
   wife,
Proud that the lovely star of Fressingfield,
Fair Margaret, countess to the Lincoln earl,
Attends on Elinor—gramercies, lord,
   for her—   30
'Tis I give thanks for Margaret to you
   all,
And rest,[1] for her, due bounden to yourselves.

HENRY. Seeing the marriage is solemnizéd,
Let's march in triumph to the royal
   feast.—
But why stands Friar Bacon here so
   mute?

BACON. Repentant for the follies of my
   youth,
That magic's secret mysteries misled,
And joyful that this royal marriage
Portends such bliss unto this matchless
   realm.

[1] Remain.

HENRY. Why, Bacon, what strange event
    shall happen to this land?   40
  Or what shall grow from Edward and
    his queen?
BACON. I find by deep prescience of mine
    art,
  Which once I tempered in my secret cell,
  That here where Brute did build his
    Troynovant,[1]
  From forth the royal garden of a king
  Shall flourish out so rich and fair a bud [2]
  Whose brightness shall deface proud
    Phœbus' flower,
  And overshadow Albion with her leaves.
  Till then Mars shall be master of the
    field,
  But then the stormy threats of wars
    shall cease.   50
  The horse shall stamp as careless of the
    pike;
  Drums shall be turned to timbrels of
    delight;
  With wealthy favors plenty shall enrich
  The strond that gladded wand'ring
    Brute to see,
  And peace from heaven shall harbor in
    these leaves
  That gorgeous beautifies this matchless
    flower.
  Apollo's hellitropian [3] then shall stoop,
  And Venus' hyacinth shall vail [4] her top;

Juno shall shut her gilliflowers up,
And Pallas' bay shall bash her bright-
    est green;   60
Ceres' carnation, in consort with those,
  Shall stoop and wonder at Diana's rose.
HENRY. This prophecy is mystical.—
  But, glorious commanders of Europa's
    love,
  That makes fair England like that
    wealthy isle
  Circled with Gihon and swift [5] Euphrates,
  In royalizing Henry's Albion
  With presence of your princely mighti-
    ness,
  Let's march. The tables all are spread,
  And viands such as England's wealth
    affords   70
  Are ready set to furnish out the boards.
  You shall have welcome, mighty po-
    tentates.
  It rests to furnish up this royal feast.
  Only your hearts be frolic, for the time
  Craves that we taste of naught but
    jouissance.[6]
  Thus glories England over all the West.
                Exeunt omnes.

FINIS FRIAR BACON, MADE BY ROBERT
    GREENE, MASTER OF ARTS.

"Omne tulit punctum qui miscuit utile dulci."[7]

---

[1] London, which according to legend was
founded by Brutus, friend of Æneas.
[2] Referring to Queen Elizabeth.
[3] Heliotrope.   [4] Lower.

[5] Dyce's emendation. Original reads *first.*
[6] Pleasure.
[7] "He has everybody's approval who mingles
the useful with the agreeable" (Horace).

GEORGE A GREENE, THE PINNER OF WAKEFIELD [1]

[DRAMATIS PERSONÆ

EDWARD, *King of England.* [2]
EARL OF WARWICK.
JAMES, *King of Scotland.* [2]
LORD HUMES.
EARL OF KENDAL
LORD BONFIELD
SIR NICHOLAS MANNERING }   *rebels.*
SIR GILBERT ARMSTRONG
MUSGROVE, *keeper of Sandown Castle.*
CUDDY, *his son.*
GEORGE A GREENE, *the pinner* [3] *of Wake-field.*
JENKIN, *a clown* } *servants to*
WILY, *a boy* } *George a Greene.*

GRIME.
WOODROFFE, *the justice of Wakefield.*
ROBIN HOOD.
SCARLET } *Robin Hood's men.*
MUCH }
JOHN TAYLOR, *post of King James.*
NED A BARLEY, *a small boy.*
A SHOEMAKER.

JANE A BARLEY, *mother of Ned.*
BETTRIS, *daughter to Grime.*
MAID MARIAN.
TOWNSMEN, SHOEMAKERS, SOLDIERS, MESSENGER, *etc.*

SCENE: *England.*

TIME: *Indefinite.*]

[SCENE i.

Near Bradford.]

Enter the Earl of Kendal; with him the Lord Bonfield, Sir Gilbert Armstrong, [Sir Nicholas Mannering,] and John [Taylor].

KEND. Welcome to Bradford, martial gentlemen,
  L[ord] Bonfield and Sir Gilbert Armstrong both;
  And all my troops, even to my basest groom,
  Courage and welcome, for the day is ours!
  Our cause is good—it is for the land's avail.
  Then let us fight and die for England's good!
OMNES. We will, my lord!

KEND. As I am Henry Momford, Kendal's earl,
  You honor me with this assent of yours;
  And here upon my sword I make protest
  For to relieve the poor or die myself.   11
  And know, my lords, that James, the King of Scots,
  Wars hard upon the borders of this land.—
  Here is his post.—Say, John Taylor,
  What news with King James?
JOHN. War, my lord!   Tall [4] and good news, I trow;
  For King Jamie vows to meet you the twenty-sixth of this month,
  God willing; marry, doth he, sir.
KEND. My friends, you see what we have to win.—
  Well, John, commend me to King James,   20
  And tell him I will meet him the twenty-sixth of this month
  And all the rest; and so, farewell.
                                    Exit John.

---

[1] The complete title reads: "A Pleasant Conceited Comedy of George a Greene, the Pinner of Wakefield. As It Was Sundry Times Acted by the Servants of the Right Honorable the Earl of Sussex."
[2] Identity not clear.
[3] An officer who impounds stray animals.
[4] Excellent.   Suggested by Adams; original reads *tell.*

Bonfield, why stand'st thou as a man in
  dumps?
Courage! For, if I win, I'll make thee
  duke.
I, Henry Momford, will be king myself;
And I will make thee Duke of Lancaster,
And Gilbert Armstrong Lord of Don-
  caster.
BON. Nothing, my lord, makes me
  amazed [1] at all
But that our soldiers finds our victuals
  scant.
We must make havoc of those country
  swains;   30
For so will the rest tremble and be afraid,
And humbly send provision to your
  camp.
GILB. My Lord Bonfield gives good ad-
  vice.
They make a scorn,[2] and stand upon [3]
  the king;
So what is brought is sent from them per-
  force.
Ask Mannering else.
KEND. What sayest thou, Mannering?
MAN. Whenas [4] I showed your high com-
  mission,
They made this answer,
Only to send provision for your horses. 40
KEND. Well, hie thee to Wakefield, bid the
  town
To send me all provision that I want,
Lest I, like martial Tamburlaine, lay
  waste
Their bordering countries,
And leaving none alive that contradicts
  my commission.
MAN. Let me alone, my lord; I'll make
  them
Vail [5] their plumes; for whatsoe'er he be,
The proudest knight, justice, or other,
  that gainsayeth
Your word, I'll clap him fast,[6] to make
  the rest to fear.
KEND. Do so, Nick. Hie thee thither pres-
  ently,[7]   50
And let us hear of thee again tomorrow.
MAN. Will you not remove, my lord?
KEND. No, I will lie at Bradford all this
  night

And all the next.—Come, Bonfield, let
  us go,
And listen out [8] some bonny lasses here.
                              Exeunt omnes.

[SCENE ii.

Wakefield.]

*Enter the Justice, a Townsman, George a
  Greene, and Sir Nicholas Mannering
                              with his commission.*

JUST. M[aster] Mannering, stand aside,
  whilst we confer
What is best to do.—
Townsmen of Wakefield, the Earl of
  Kendal
Here hath sent for victuals;
And in aiding him we show ourselves
No less than traitors to the king;
Therefore let me hear, townsmen,
What is your consents.[9]
TOWNS. Even as you please, we are all
  content.
JUST. Then, M[aster] Mannering, we are
  resolved.   10
MAN. As how?
JUST. Marry, sir, thus.
We will send the Earl of Kendal no
  victuals,
Because he is a traitor to the king,
And in aiding him we show ourselves no
  less.
MAN. Why, men of Wakefield, are you
  waxen mad,
That present danger cannot whet your
  wits
Wisely to make provision of yourselves?
The earl is thirty thousand men strong
  in power,
And what town soever him resist,   20
He lays it flat and level with the
  ground.
Ye silly men, you seek your own decay;
Therefore send my lord such provision as
  he wants,
So he will spare your town, and come no
  nearer
Wakefield than he is.
JUST. Master Mannering, you have your
  answer;
You may be gone.
MAN. Well, Woodroffe, for so I guess is
  thy name,

---

[1] Perplexed.   [5] Lower.
[2] *I.e.*, they scorn us.   [6] Imprison.
[3] With.   [7] At once.
[4] When.   [8] Get news of.   [9] Opinion.

I'll make thee curse thy overthwart [1]
denial;
And all that sit upon the bench this day
Shall rue the hour they have withstood
my lord's   31
Commission.

JUST. Do thy worst; we fear thee not.

MAN. See you these seals? Before you
pass the town,
I will have all things my lord doth want,
In spite of you.

GEORGE. Proud dapper Jack,[2] vail bonnet
to
The bench
That represents the person of the king,
Or, sirrah, I'll lay thy head before thy
feet!   40

MAN. Why, who art thou?

GEORGE. Why, I am George a Greene,
True liegeman to my king,
Who scorns that men of such esteem as
these
Should brook the braves [3] of any traitor-
ous squire.
You of the bench, and you, my fellow-
friends,
Neighbors, we subjects all unto the
king,
We are English born, and therefore Ed-
ward's friends,
Vowed unto him even in our mothers'
womb,
Our minds to God, our hearts unto our
king.   50
Our wealth, our homage, and our car-
casses
Be all King Edward's. Then, sirrah,
we have
Nothing left for traitors but our swords,
Whetted to bathe them in your bloods,
And die against you, before we send you
any victuals.

JUST. Well spoken, George a Greene!

TOWNS. Pray let George a Greene speak
for us.

GEORGE. Sirrah, you get no victuals here,
Not if a hoof of beef would save your
lives.

MAN. Fellow, I stand amazed at thy presumption.   60
Why, what art thou that darest gainsay
my lord,

Knowing his mighty puissance and his
stroke?
Why, my friend, I come not barely of
myself,
For, see, I have a large commission.

GEORGE. Let me see it, sirrah.
                    [Takes the commission.]
Whose seals be these?

MAN. This is the Earl of Kendal's seal-
at-arms,
This Lord Charnel Bonfield's,
And this Sir Gilbert Armstrong's.

GEORGE. I tell thee, sirrah, did good King
Edward's son   70
Seal a commission against the king his
father,
Thus would I tear it in despite of him,
                    He tears the commission.
Being traitor to my sovereign.

MAN. What, hast thou torn my lord's
commission?
Thou shalt rue it, and so shall all Wakefield.

GEORGE. What, are you in choler? I will
give you pills
To cool your stomach.[4]
Seest thou these seals?
Now, by my father's soul, which was a
yeoman
When he was alive, eat them,   80
Or eat my dagger's point, proud squire.

MAN. But thou dost but jest, I hope.

GEORGE. Sure, that shall you see before
we two part.

MAN. Well, and [5] there be no remedy, so,
George—
                    [Swallows one of the seals.]
One is gone; I pray thee, no more now.

GEORGE. O, sir, if one be good, the others
cannot hurt!
        [Mannering swallows the other seals.]
So, sir; now you may go tell the Earl of
Kendal,
Although I have rent his large com-
mission,
Yet of courtesy I have sent all his seals
Back again by you.   90

MAN. Well, sir, I will do your arrant.[6]
                                        Exit.

GEORGE. Now let him tell his lord that he
hath
Spoke with George a Greene,
Right [7] pinner of merry Wakefield town,

---

[1] Perverse.   [3] Endure the threats.
[2] Knave.
[4] Angry temper.   [5] If.   [6] Errand.   [7] True.

That hath physic for a fool,

Pills for a traitor that doth wrong his
sovereign.

Are you content with this that I have
done?

Just. Aye, content, George;

For highly hast thou honored Wakefield
town   99

In cutting of proud Mannering so short.

Come, thou shalt be my welcome guest
today,

For well thou hast deserved reward and
favor.   *Exeunt omnes.*

[Scene iii.

Before Musgrove's castle.]

*Enter Old Musgrove and Young Cuddy, his
son.*

Cuddy. Now, gentle father, list unto thy
son,

And for my mother's love,

That erst[1] was blithe and bonny in
thine eye,

Grant one petition that I shall demand.

Mus. What is that, my Cuddy?

Cuddy. Father, you know the ancient enmity of late

Between the Musgroves and the wily
Scots,

Whereof they have oath

Not to leave one alive that strides a
lance.[2]

O father, you are old and, waning, age
unto the grave.   10

Old William Musgrove, which whilom[3]
was thought

The bravest horseman in all Westmore-
land,

Is weak, and forced to stay his arm upon
a staff,

That erst could wield a lance.

Then, gentle father, resign the hold[4]
to me;

Give arms to youth, and honor unto age.

Mus. Avaunt, false-hearted boy! My
joints do quake

Even with anguish of thy very words.

Hath William Musgrove seen an hundred
years,

Have I been feared and dreaded of the
Scots,   20

That, when they heard my name in any
road,[5]

They fled away, and posted thence
amain,[6]

And shall I die with shame now in mine
age?

No, Cuddy, no. Thus resolve I:

Here have I lived, and here will Musgrove die.   *Exeunt omnes.*

[Scene iv.

Before Grime's house at Bradford.]

*Enter Lord Bonfield, Sir Gilbert Armstrong,
M[aster] Grime, and Bettris, his daughter.*

Bon. Now, gentle Grime, God-a-mercy[7]
for our good cheer;

Our fare was royal, and our welcome
great;

And, sith[8] so kindly thou hast entertained us,

If we return with happy victory,

We will deal as friendly with thee in
recompense.

Grime. Your welcome was but duty,
gentle lord;

For wherefore have we given us our
wealth

But to make our betters welcome when
they come?

[*Aside.*] O, this goes hard when traitors
must be flattered!

But life is sweet, and I cannot withstand it.   10

God, I hope, will revenge the quarrel
of my king.—

Gilb. What said you, Grime?

Grime. I say, Sir Gilbert, looking on my
daughter,

I curse the hour that e'er I got[9] the girl;

For, sir, she may have many wealthy
suitors,

And yet she disdains them all to have

Poor George a Greene unto her husband.

Bon. On that, good Grime, I am talking
with thy
Daughter;

But she, in quirks and quiddities of
love,   20

Sets me to school, she is so overwise.—

---

[1] Formerly.
[2] *I.e.*, even the children.
[3] Formerly.
[4] Fort, castle.
[5] Raid.
[6] At full speed.
[7] God reward you; thank you.
[8] Since.
[9] Begot.

But, gentle girl, if thou wilt forsake
The pinner and be my love, I will ad-
    vance thee high.
To dignify those hairs of amber hue,
I'll grace them with a chaplet made of
    pearl,
Set with choice rubies, sparks,[1] and dia-
    monds,
Planted upon a velvet hood, to hide
    that head
Wherein two sapphires burn like spar-
    kling fire.
This will I do, fair Bettris, and far more,
If thou wilt love the Lord of Doncaster.
BETTRIS. Heigh-ho! My heart is in a
    higher place,   31
Perhaps on the earl, if that be he.
See where he comes, or [2] angry or in
    love,
Forwhy [3] his color [4] looketh discontent.
KEND. [*Entering.*] Come, Nick, follow me.

*Enter the Earl of Kendal and Nicholas
                Mannering.*

BON. How now, my lord? What news?
KEND. Such news, Bonfield, as will make
    thee laugh,
And fret thy fill, to hear how Nick was
    used.
Why, the justices stand on their terms.
Nick, as you know, is haughty in his
    words;   40
He laid the law unto the justices
With threat'ning braves, that one looked
    on another,
Ready to stoop; but that a churl came
    in,
One George a Greene, the pinner of the
    town,
And with his dagger drawn laid hands
    on Nick,
And by no beggars [5] swore that we were
    traitors,
Rent our commission, and upon a brave
Made Nick to eat the seals or brook the
    stab.
Poor Mannering, afraid, came posting
    hither straight.
BETTRIS. O lovely George, fortune be
    still [6] thy friend!   50

And as thy thoughts be high, so be thy
    mind
In all accords, even to thy heart's de-
    sire!
BON. What says fair Bettris?
GRIME. My lord, she is praying for George
    a Greene.
He is the man, and she will none but him.
BON. But him? Why, look on me, my
    girl!
Thou knowest that yesternight I courted
    thee,
And swore at my return to wed with
    thee.
Then tell me, love, shall I have all thy
    fair? [7]
BETTRIS. I care not for earl, nor yet for
    knight,   60
Nor baron that is so bold;
For George a Greene, the merry pinner,
He hath my heart in hold.
BON. Bootless, my lord, are many vain
    replies.
Let us hie us to Wakefield, and send her
    the pinner's head.
KEND. It shall be so.—Grime, gramercy.
Shut up thy daughter; bridle her af-
    fects.[8]
Let me not miss her when I make return;
Therefore look to her, as to thy life, good
    Grime.
GRIME. I warrant you, my lord.   70
            Ex[eunt] Grime and Bettris.
KEND. And, Bettris, leave a base pinner
    for to love an earl.
Fain would I see this pinner, George a
    Greene.
It shall be thus:
Nick Mannering shall lead on the battle,[9]
And we three will go to Wakefield in
    some disguise.
But howsoever, I'll have his head today.
            Ex[eunt] omnes.

[SCENE V.]

Before Sir John a Barley's castle.]

*Enter the King of Scots, Lord Humes, with
            Soldiers, and Johnny [Taylor].*

JAMES.[10] Why, Johnny, then the Earl of
    Kendal is blithe,

---

[1] Precious stones. [4] Appearance.
[2] Either. [5] By no small oath.
[3] Because. [6] Always.

[7] Beauty. [8] Affections. [9] Army.
[10] In the original *King* is used here and at line
6 to designate the speaker.

And hath brave men that troop along
with him?

JOHNNY. Ay, marry, my liege, and hath
good men
That come along with him,
And vows to meet you at Scrasblesea,
God willing.

JAMES. If good S[aint] Andrew lend King
Jamie leave,
I will be with him at the pointed ¹ day.
But, soft!—Whose pretty boy art thou?

Enter Jane a Barley's Son.

NED. Sir, I am son unto Sir John a Barley,
Eldest, and all that e'er my mother
had;   10
Edward my name.

JAMES. And whither art thou going,
pretty Ned?

NED. To seek some birds, and kill them,
if I can.
And now my schoolmaster is also gone,
So have I liberty to ply my bow;
For, when he comes, I stir not from my
book.

JAMES. Lord Humes, but mark the visage
of this child.
By him I guess the beauty of his mother;
None but Leda could breed Helena.
Tell me, Ned, who is within with thy
mother?   20

NED. Not ² but herself and household
servants, sir.
If you would speak with her, knock at
this gate.

JAMES. Johnny, knock at that gate.
                              [*John knocks.*]

Enter Jane a Barley upon the walls.

JANE. O, I am betrayed! What multitudes
be these?

JAMES. Fear not, fair Jane, for all these
men are mine,
And all thy friends, if thou be friend to
me.
I am thy lover, James the King of Scots,
That oft have sued and wooed with
many letters,
Painting my outward passions with my
pen,
Whenas my inward soul did bleed for
woe.   30

¹Appointed.   ² Naught (?)

Little regard was given to my suit,
But haply thy husband's presence
wrought it.
Therefore, sweet Jane, I fitted me to
time,
And, hearing that thy husband was from
home,
Am come to crave what long I have desired.

NED. Nay, soft you, sir! You get no en-
trance here,
That seek to wrong Sir John a Barley so,
And offer such dishonor to my mother.

JAMES. Why, what dishonor, Ned?

NED. Though young, yet often have I
heard   40
My father say
No greater wrong than to be made
cuckold.
Were I of age, or were my body strong,
Were he ten kings, I would shoot him
to the heart
That should attempt to give Sir John
the horn.³
Mother, let him not come in.
I will go lie at Jockie Miller's house.

JAMES. Stay him!

JANE. Ay, well said; Ned, thou hast given
the king
His answer,   50
For, were the ghost of Cæsar on the
earth,
Wrapped in the wonted glory of his
honor,
He should not make me wrong my hus-
band so.
But good King James is pleasant,⁴ as I
guess,
And means to try what humor I am in;
Else would he never have brought an
host of men
To have them witness of his Scottish lust.

JAMES. Jane, in faith, Jane!

JANE. Never reply, for I protest by the
highest
Holy God,   60
That doometh just revenge for things
amiss,
King James, of all men, shall not have
my love.

JAMES. Then list to me: Saint Andrew
be my boot,⁵

³ Proverbial sign of the cuckold.
⁴ Jocular.   ⁵ Aid.

But I'll raze thy castle to the very ground
Unless thou open the gate, and let me in.
JANE. I fear thee not, King Jamie; do thy
worst.
This castle is too strong for thee to scale;
Besides, tomorrow will Sir John come
home.
JAMES. Well, Jane, since thou disdain'st
King James' love,
I'll draw thee on with sharp and deep
extremes; 70
For, by my father's soul, this brat of
thine
Shall perish here before thine eyes,
Unless thou open the gate, and let me in.
JANE. O deep extremes! My heart begins
to break!
My little Ned looks pale for fear!
Cheer thee, my boy; I will do much for
thee.
NED. But not so much as to dishonor me.
JANE. And if thou diest, I cannot live,
sweet Ned.
NED. Then die with honor, mother, dy-
ing chaste.
JANE. I am armed: 80
My husband's love, his honor, and his
fame
Joins [1] victory by virtue.
Now, King James, if mother's tears can-
not allay thine ire,
Then butcher him, for I will never yield.
The son shall die before I wrong the
father.
JAMES. Why, then, he dies.

Alarum within. Enter a Messenger.

MESSENGER. My lord, Musgrove is at
hand.
JAMES. Who, Musgrove? The devil he
is! Come,
My horse! *Exeunt omnes.*

[SCENE vi.

The same.]

*Enter Old Musgrove with King James
prisoner.*

MUS. Now, King James, thou art my
prisoner.
JAMES. Not thine, but fortune's prisoner!

[1] Enjoins.

Enter Cuddy.

CUDDY. Father, the field is ours. Their
colors we
Have seized,
And Humes is slain—I slew him hand
to hand.
MUS. God and Saint George!
CUDDY. O father, I am sore athirst!
JANE. Come in, young Cuddy, come and
drink thy fill.
Bring in King Jamie with you as a guest;
For all this broil was cause [2] he could
not enter. 10
Exeunt omnes.

[SCENE vii.

Wakefield.]

Enter George a Greene alone.

GEORGE. The sweet content of men that
live in love
Breeds fretting humors in a restless mind;
And fancy,[3] being checked by fortune's
spite,
Grows too impatient in her sweet de-
sires—
Sweet to those men whom love leads on
to bliss,
But sour to me whose hap is still amiss.

Enter [Jenkin,] the clown.

JEN. Marry, amen, sir.
GEORGE. Sir, what do you cry "amen" at?
JEN. Why, did not you talk of love?
GEORGE. How do you know that? 10
JEN. Well, though I say it that should not
say it,
There are few fellows in our parish
So nettled with love as I have been of
late.
GEORGE. Sirrah, I thought no less when
the other morning
You rose so early to go to your wenches.
Sir, I had thought you had gone about
my honest business.
JEN. Trow, you have hit it; for, master,
be it known
To you,
There is some good will betwixt Madge
the sousewife [4]

[2] Because. [4] Seller of souse, or pickled pork.
[3] Love.

And I;　　　　　　　　　　　　　　20
Marry, she hath another lover.

GEORGE. Canst thou brook any rivals
　　in thy love?

JEN. A rider? No, he is a sow-gelder and
　　goes afoot.

But Madge pointed to meet me in your
　　wheat close.[1]

GEORGE. Well, did she meet you there?

JEN. Never make question of that.

And first I saluted her with a green
　　gown,[2]

And after fell as hard a-wooing

As if the priest had been at our backs
　　to have married us.

GEORGE. What, did she grant?　　　3C

JEN. Did she grant? Never make question
　　of that.

And she gave me a shirt collar

Wrought over with no counterfeit stuff.

GEORGE. What, was it gold?

JEN. Nay, 'twas better than gold.

GEORGE. What was it?

JEN. Right Coventry blue.[3]

We[4] had no sooner come there but wot
　　you who came by?

GEORGE. No, who?

JEN. Clim, the sow-gelder.　　　　40

GEORGE. Came he by?

JEN. He spied Madge and I sit together.

He leapt from his horse, laid his hand
　　on his dagger, and

Began to swear.

Now I seeing he had a dagger,

And I nothing but this twig in my
　　hand,

I gave him fair words and said nothing.

He comes to me, and takes me by the
　　bosom.

"You whoreson[5] slave," said he, "hold
　　my horse.

And look he take no cold in his feet."　50

"No, marry, shall he, sir," quoth I;

"I'll lay my cloak underneath him."

I took my cloak, spread it all along,

And his horse on the midst of it.

GEORGE. Thou clown, didst thou set his
　　horse upon

Thy cloak?

JEN. Ay, but mark how I served him:

Madge and he was no sooner gone down
　　into the ditch

But I plucked out my knife,

Cut four holes in my cloak, and made
　　his horse stand　　　　　　　　60

On the bare ground.

GEORGE. 'Twas well done. Now, sir, go
　　and survey my fields.

If you find any cattle in the corn, to
　　pound[6] with them!

JEN. And, if I find any in the pound,
　　I shall turn them out.

　　　　　　　　　　　　　Exit Jenkin.

*Enter the Earl of Kendal, Lord Bonfield,
　　Sir Gilbert, all disguised, with a Train
　　　　　　　　　　　　　of Men.*

KEND. Now we have put the horses in
　　the corn,

Let us stand in some corner for to hear

What braving terms the pinner will
　　breathe

When he spies our horses in the corn.
　　　　　　　　[They conceal themselves.]

Enter Jenkin[7] blowing of his horn.

JEN. O master, where are you? We have
a prize.　　　　　　　　　　　　71

GEORGE. A prize! What is it?

JEN. Three goodly horses in our wheat
close.

GEORGE. Three horses in our wheat
close? Whose be they?

JEN. Marry, that's a riddle to me, but
they are there, velvet horses, and I never
saw such horses before. As my duty was,
I put off my cap, and said as followeth: [80
"My masters, what do you make[8] in
our close?" One of them, hearing me ask
what he made there, held up his head and
neighed, and after his manner laughed as
heartily as if a mare had been tied to his
girdle. "My masters," said I, "it is no
laughing matter; for, if my master take you
here, you go as round as a top to the
pound." Another untoward jade, hearing
me threaten him to the pound and to [90
tell you of them, cast up both his heels, and
let such a monstrous great fart that was
as much as in his language to say, "A fart

---

[1] Field.　　　　[2] Tumbled her in the grass.
[3] Superior blue embroidery thread made at
Coventry, with a pun on *black and blue*.
[4] Original reads *who*.　　　[5] Rascally.

[6] Public enclosure for stray cattle.
[7] Original reads *Jack*, possibly the name of the
actor of the part.　　　　　　　[8] Do.

for the pound, and a fart for George a
Greene!" Now I, hearing this, put on my
cap, blew my horn, called them all jades,
and came to tell you.

GEORGE. Now, sir, go and drive me those
three horses
To the pound.

JEN. Do you hear? I were best take a
constable 100
With me.

GEORGE. Why so?

[JEN.] Why, they, being gentlemen's
horses, may stand on their
Reputation, and will not obey me.

GEORGE. Go, do as I bid you, sir.

JEN. Well, I may go.

*The Earl of Kendal, the Lord Bonfield, and
Sir Gilbert Armstrong meet them.*

KEND. Whither away, sir?

JEN. Whither away? I am going to put
the horses
In the pound.

KEND. Sirrah, those three horses belong
to us, and we put 110
Them in, and they must tarry there and
eat their fill.

JEN. Stay, I will go tell my master.—
Hear you, master? We have another
prize:
Those three horses be in your wheat close
still,
And here be three geldings more.

GEORGE. What be these?

JEN. These are the masters of the horses.

GEORGE. Now, gentlemen—I know not
your degrees,
But more you cannot be, unless you be
kings—
Why wrong you us of Wakefield with
your horses? 120
I am the pinner, and, before you pass,
You shall make good the trespass they
have done.

KEND. Peace, saucy mate, prate not to us!
I tell thee, pinner, we are gentlemen.

GEORGE. Why, sir, so may I, sir, although
I give no arms.[1]

KEND. Thou? How art thou a gentleman?

JEN. And such is my master, and he may
give as good

Arms as ever your great-grandfather
could give.

KEND. Pray thee, let me hear how.

JEN. Marry, my master may give for his
arms 130
The picture of April in a green jerkin,
With a rook on one fist and an horn on
the other;
But my master gives his arms the wrong
way,
For he gives the horn on his fist,
And your grandfather, because he would
not lose his
Arms,
Wears the horn on his own head.

KEND. Well, pinner, sith our horses be in,
In spite of thee they now shall feed their
fill,
And eat until our leisures serve to go. 140

GEORGE. Now, by my father's soul,
Were good King Edward's horses in the
corn,
They shall amend the scath or kiss [2] the
pound;
Much more yours, sir, whatsoe'er you be.

KEND. Why, man, thou knowest not us.
We do belong to Henry Momford, Earl of
Kendal,
Men that, before a month be full expired,
Will be King Edward's betters in the
land.

GEORGE. King Edward's better! Rebel,
thou liest! *George strikes him.*

BON. Villain, what hast thou done? Thou
hast stroke [3] 150
An earl.

GEORGE. Why, what care I? A poor man
that is true
Is better than an earl, if he be false.
Traitors reap no better favors at my
hands.

KEND. Ay, so methinks; but thou shalt
dear aby [4] this blow.—
Now or never lay hold on the pinner!

Enter all the Ambush.

GEORGE. Stay, my lords, let us parley on
these broils.—
[*Aside.*] Not Hercules against two, the
proverb is,
Nor I against so great a multitude.

---

[1] Bear no coat of arms.

[2] Be imprisoned in (slang). [4] Dearly pay for.
[3] Struck.

Had not your troops come marching as
they did,   160
I would have stopped your passage unto
London.
But now I'll fly to secret policy.

KEND. What dost thou murmur, George?

GEORGE. Marry, this, my lord; I muse,[1]
If thou be Henry Momford, Kendal's
earl,
That thou wilt do poor G[eorge] a Greene
this wrong,
Ever to match me with a troop of men.

KEND. Why dost thou strike me then?

GEORGE. Why, my lord, measure me but
by yourself:
Had you a man had served you long,
And heard your foe misuse you behind
your back,   171
And would not draw his sword in your
defense,
You would cashier him.
Much more, King Edward is my king;
And before I'll hear him so wronged,
I'll die within this place,
And maintain good whatsoever I have
said.
And, if I speak not reason in this case,
What I have said I'll maintain in this
place.

BON. A pardon, my lord, for this pinner,
For, trust me, he speaketh like a man of
worth.   181

KEND. Well, George, wilt thou leave
Wakefield and
Wend with me,
I'll freely put up all and pardon thee.

GEORGE. Ay, my lord, considering [2] me one
thing:
You will leave these arms, and follow
your good king.

KEND. Why, George, I rise not against
King Edward,
But for the poor that is oppressed by
wrong;
And, if King Edward will redress the
same,
I will not offer him disparagement,   190
But otherwise; and so let this suffice.
Thou hear'st the reason why I rise in
arms.
Now, wilt thou leave Wakefield and
wend with me,
I'll make thee captain of a hardy band,

---

[1] Marvel.   [2] Granting, noting.

And, when I have my will, dub thee a
knight.

GEORGE. Why, my lord, have you any
hope to win?

KEND. Why, there is a prophecy doth say
That King James and I shall meet at
London,
And make the king vail bonnet to us both.

GEORGE. If this were true, my lord, this
were a mighty reason.   200

KEND. Why, it is a miraculous prophecy,
and cannot fail.

GEORGE. Well, my lord, you have almost
turned me.—
Jenkin, come hither.

JEN. Sir?

GEORGE. Go your ways home, sir,
And drive me those three horses home
unto my house,
And pour them down a bushel of good
oats.

JEN. Well, I will.—[Aside]. Must I give
these scurvy horses
Oats?   Exit Jenkin.

GEORGE. Will it please you to command
your train aside?   210

KEND. Stand aside.   Exit the Train.

GEORGE. Now list to me:
Here in a wood not far from hence,
There dwells an old man in a cave alone,
That can foretell what fortunes shall
befall you,
For he is greatly skillful in magic art.
Go you three to him early in the morning,
And question him. If he says good,
Why, then, my lord, I am the foremost
man!
We will march up with your camp to
London.   220

KEND. George, thou honorest me in this.
But where shall we find him out?

GEORGE. My man shall conduct you to the
place.
But, good my lords, tell me true what the
wise man saith.

KEND. That will I, as I am Earl of Kendal.

GEORGE. Why, then, to honor G[eorge] a
Greene the more,
Vouchsafe a piece of beef at my poor
house.
You shall have wafer cakes your fill,
A piece of beef hung up since Martle-
mas.[3]

---

[3] Martinmas, November 11.

If that like you not, take what you bring,
   for me! [1]   230
KEND. Gramercies, George.
Exeunt omnes.

[SCENE viii.

Before Grime's house at Bradford.]

*Enter George a Greene's boy, Wily, disguised
like a woman, to M[aster] Grime's.*

WILY. O, what is love? It is some mighty
   power,
Else could it never conquer G[eorge] a
   Greene.
Here dwells a churl that keeps away his
   love.
I know the worst, and, if I be espied,
'Tis but a beating; and, if I by this
   means
Can get fair Bettris forth her father's
   door,
It is enough. Venus for me, and all gods
   above [2]
Be aiding to my wily enterprise!
He knocks at the door.

Enter Grime.

GRIME. How now! Who knocks there?
   What would you have?
From whence came you? Where do you
   dwell?   10
WILY. I am, forsooth, a sempster's [3] maid
   hard by,
That hath brought work home to your
   daughter.
GRIME. Nay, are you not some crafty
   quean
That comes from George a Greene, that
   rascal,
With some letters to my daughter?
I will have you searched.
WILY. Alas, sir, it is Hebrew unto me
To tell me of George a Greene or any
   other!
Search me, good sir,
And, if you find a letter about me,   20
Let me have the punishment that is
   due.
GRIME. Why are you muffled? I like you
   the worse
For that.

WILY. I am not, sir, ashamed to show my
   face;
Yet loath I am my cheeks should take the
   air—
Not that I am chary of my beauty's
   hue,
But that I am troubled with the tooth-
   ache sore.   [*Uncovers his face.*]
GRIME. [*Aside.*] A pretty wench, of smil-
   ing countenance!
Old men can like, although they cannot
   love;
Ay, and love, though not so brief [4] as
   young men can.—   30
Well, go in, my wench, and speak with
   my daughter.   *Exit [Wily].*
I wonder much at the Earl of Kendal,
Being a mighty man, as still he is;
Yet for to be a traitor to his king
Is more than God or man will well
   allow.
But what a fool am I to talk of him!
My mind is more here of the pretty
   lass.
Had she brought some forty pounds to
   town,
I could be content to make her my
   wife.
Yet I have heard it in a proverb said,   40
He that is old and marries with a lass,
Lies but at home, and proves himself an
   ass.

Enter Bettris in Wily's apparel, to Grime.

How now, my wench! How is't? What,
   not a word?
Alas, poor soul, the toothache plagues
   her sore!
Well, my wench, here is an angel [5] for to
   buy thee pins,
And I pray thee use mine house,
The oft'ner, the more welcome. Farewell.
                  Exit.
BETTRIS. O blessed love, and blessed for-
   tune both!
But, Bettris, stand not here to talk of
   love,
But hie thee straight unto thy George a
   Greene.   50
Never went roebuck swifter on the downs
Than I will trip it till I see my George.
                  Exit.

---

[1] For all I care.   [3] Seamstress'.
[2] Original reads *all goes alone.*

[4] Readily.   [5] Gold coin.

[SCENE ix.

Before a cave near Wakefield.]

*Enter the Earl of Kendal, L[ord] Bonfield,
Sir Gilbert, and Jenkin, the clown.*

KEND. Come away, Jenkin.

JEN. Come, here is his house.—Where be
you, ho?

GEORGE. [*Within.*] Who knocks there?

KEND. Here are two or three poor men,
father,
Would speak with you.

GEORGE. [*Within.*] Pray, give your man
leave to lead me forth.

KEND. Go, Jenkin, fetch him forth.

JEN. Come, old man.

Enter George a Greene, disguised.

KEND. Father, here is three poor men come
to question
Thee a word in secret that concerns their
lives. 10

GEORGE. Say on, my sons.

KEND. Father, I am sure you hear the
news,
How that the Earl of Kendal wars
against the king.
Now, father, we three are gentlemen by
birth,
But younger brethren that want reven-
ues,
And for the hope we have to be preferred,
If that we knew that we shall win,
We will march with him;
If not, we will not march a foot to
London more.
Therefore, good father, tell us what shall
happen, 20
Whether the king or the Earl of Kendal
shall win.

GEORGE. The king, my son.

KEND. Art thou sure of that?

GEORGE. Ay, as sure as thou art Henry
Momford,
The one L[ord] Bonfield, the other Sir
Gilbert.

KEND. Why, this is wondrous, being blind
of sight,
His deep perseverance [1] should be such to
know us.

GILB. Magic is mighty and foretelleth
great matters.

¹ Perceiverance, perception.

Indeed, father, here is the earl come to
see thee,
And therefore, good father, fable not
with him. 30

GEORGE. Welcome is the earl to my poor
cell,
And so are you, my lords; but let me
counsel you
To leave these wars against your king,
And live in quiet.

KEND. Father, we come not for advice in
war,
But to know whether we shall win or
leese. [2]

GEORGE. Lose, gentle lords, but not by
good King Edward;
A baser man shall give you all the foil. [3]

KEND. Ay, marry, father, what man is
that?

GEORGE. Poor George a Greene, the pinner. 40

KEND. What shall he?

GEORGE. Pull all your plumes, and sore
dishonor you.

KEND. He! As how?

GEORGE. Nay, the end tries all; but so
it will fall out.

KEND. But so it shall not, by my honor!
Christ!
I'll raise my camp, and fire Wakefield
town,
And take that servile pinner, George a
Greene,
And butcher him before King Edward's
face.

GEORGE. Good my lord, be not offended,
For I speak no more than art reveals
to me. 50
And for greater proof
Give your man leave to fetch me my staff.

KEND. Jenkin, fetch him his walking staff.

JEN. Here is your walking staff.

GEORGE. I'll prove it good upon your
carcasses;
A wiser wizard never met you yet,
Nor one that better could foredoom
your fall.
Now I have singled you here alone, [4]
I care not, though you be three to one.
[*Throws off his disguise.*]

KEND. Villain, hast thou betrayed us? 60

² Lose.   ³ Defeat.
⁴ *I.e.*, as an animal is selected from a herd for
hunting.

GEORGE. Momford, thou liest! Never was
    I traitor yet;
Only devised this guile to draw you on
    For to be combatants.
Now conquer me, and then march on
    to London!
But shall go hard but I will hold you
    task.[1]

GILB. Come, my lord, cheerly; I'll kill
    him hand to hand.

KEND. A thousand pound to him that
    strikes that stroke!

GEORGE. Then give it me, for I will have
    the first.

Here they fight; George kills Sir Gilbert and
        takes the other two prisoners.

BON. Stay, George; we do appeal.

GEORGE. To whom?   70

BON. Why, to the king!
For rather had we bide what he appoints,
Than here be murthered by a servile
    groom.

KEND. What wilt thou do with us?

GEORGE. Even as Lord Bonfield wished,[2]
    You shall unto the king;
And, for that purpose, see where the
    justice is placed.

Enter Justice.

JUST. Now, my Lord of Kendal, where be
    all your threats?
Even as the cause, so is the combat
    fallen;
Else one could never have conquered
    three.   80

KEND. I pray thee, Woodroffe, do not
    twit me;
If I have faulted, I must make amends.

GEORGE. Master Woodroffe, here is not a
    place for many
    Words;
I beseech ye, sir, discharge all his sol-
    diers,
That every man may go home unto his
    own house.

JUST. It shall be so. What wilt thou do,
    George?

GEORGE. Master Woodroffe, look to your
    charge;
Leave me to myself.

JUST. Come, my lords.   90
        Exit all but George.

[1] If I do not keep you busy.
[2] Original reads *wist.*

GEORGE. Here sit thou, George, wearing
    a willow wreath,
As one despairing of thy beauteous
    love.
Fie, George, no more!
Pine not away for that which cannot be.
I cannot joy in any earthly bliss
So long as I do want my Bettris.

Enter Jenkin.

JEN. Who see a master of mine?

GEORGE. How now, sirrah! Whither away?

JEN. Whither away? Why, who do you
    take me to be?

GEORGE. Why, Jenkin, my man.   100

JEN. I was so once indeed, but now the
    case is altered.

GEORGE. I pray thee, as how?

JEN. Were not you a fortune teller today?

GEORGE. Well, what of that?

JEN. So sure am I become a juggler.
What will you say if I juggle your sweet-
    heart?

GEORGE. Peace, prating losel! [3] Her jeal-
    ous father
Doth wait over her with such suspicious
    eyes
That, if a man but dally by her feet,
He thinks it straight a witch [4] to charm
    his daughter.   110

JEN. Well, what will you give me if I
    bring her hither?

GEORGE. A suit of green and twenty
    crowns besides.

JEN. Well, by your leave, give me room.
You must give me something that you
    have lately worn.

GEORGE. Here is a gown. Will that serve
    you?   [*Gives his gown.*]

JEN. Ay, this will serve me. Keep out of
    my circle,
Lest you be torn in pieces with she-
    devils.—
Mistress Bettris—once, twice, thrice!

He throws the gown [5] in, and she comes out.

O, is this no cunning?

GEORGE. Is this my love, or is it but her
    shadow?   120

JEN. Ay, this is the shadow, but here is
    the substance.

[3] Worthless fellow.
[4] Spell.
[5] Original reads *ground.*

GEORGE. Tell me, sweet love, what good fortune
Brought thee hither?
For one it was that favored George a Greene.
BETTRIS. Both love and fortune brought me to my George,
In whose sweet sight is all my heart's content.
GEORGE. Tell me, sweet love, how cam'st thou from thy Father's?
BETTRIS. A willing mind hath many slips in love.   129
It was not I, but Wily, thy sweet boy.
GEORGE. And where is Wily now?
BETTRIS. In my apparel, in my chamber still.
GEORGE. Jenkin, come hither.   Go to Bradford,
And listen out your fellow Wily.—
Come, Bettris, let us in,
And in my cottage we will sit and talk.
Exeunt omnes.

[SCENE x.

Edward's court at London.]

Enter King Edward, the King of Scots, Lord Warwick, Young Cuddy, and their Train.

EDWARD. Brother of Scotland, I do hold it hard,
Seeing a league of truce was late confirmed
Twixt you and me, without displeasure offered
You should make such invasion in my land.
The vows of kings should be as oracles,
Not blemished with the stain of any breach,
Chiefly [1] where fealty and homage willeth it.
JAMES. Brother of England, rub not the sore afresh;
My conscience grieves me for my deep misdeed.
I have the worst; of thirty thousand men,   10
There scaped not full five thousand from the field.

EDWARD. [*To Cuddy.*] Gramercy, Musgrove, else it had gone hard.
Cuddy, I'll quite [2] thee well ere we two part.
JAMES. But had not his old father, William Musgrove,
Played twice the man, I had not now been here.
A stronger man I seldom felt before;
But one of more resolute valiance
Treads not, I think, upon the English ground.
EDWARD. I wot well. Musgrove shall not lose his hire.
CUDDY. And it please your grace, my father was   20
Fivescore and three at midsummer last past;
Yet had King Jamie been as good as George a Greene,
Yet Billy Musgrove would have fought with him.
EDWARD. As George a Greene?   I pray thee, Cuddy,
Let me question thee.
Much have I heard, since I came to my crown;
Many in manner of a proverb say,
"Were he as good as G[eorge] a Greene, I would strike him sure."
I pray thee, tell me, Cuddy, canst thou inform me,
What is that George a Greene?   30
CUDDY. Know, my lord, I never saw the man,
But mickle [3] talk is of him in the country.
They say he is the pinner of Wakefield town,
But for his other qualities, I let alone.
WAR. May it please your grace, I know the man too well.
EDWARD. Too well? Why so, Warwick?
WAR. For once he swinged me till my bones did ache.
EDWARD. Why, dares he strike an earl?
WAR. An earl, my lord?   Nay, he will strike a king,
Be it not King Edward.   40
For stature he is framed
Like to the picture of stout Hercules,
And for his carriage passeth Robin Hood.

---

[1] Especially.   [2] Requite, reward.   [3] Much.

The boldest earl or baron of your land
That offereth scath unto the town of
Wakefield,
George will arrest his pledge unto the
pound;[1]
And whoso resisteth bears away the
blows,
For he himself is good enough for three.
EDWARD. Why, this is wondrous, my
L[ord] of Warwick!
Sore do I long to see this George a
Greene.   50
But leaving him, what shall we do, my
lord,
For to subdue the rebels in the north?
They are now marching up to Don-
caster.—

Enter one with the Earl of Kendal prisoner.

Soft! Who have we there?
CUDDY. Here is a traitor, the Earl of
Kendal.
EDWARD. Aspiring traitor, how dar'st
thou once
Cast thine eyes upon thy sovereign
That honored thee with kindness and
with favor?
But I will make thee bye[2] this treason
dear.
KEND. Good my lord—   60
EDWARD. Reply not, traitor![3]—
Tell me, Cuddy, whose deed of honor
Won the victory against this rebel?
CUDDY. George a Greene, the pinner of
Wakefield.
EDWARD. George a Greene! Now shall I
hear news
Certain, what this pinner is.
Discourse it briefly, Cuddy, how it be-
fell.
CUDDY. Kendal and Bonfield, with Sir
Gilbert Armstrong,
Came to Wakefield town disguised,
And there spoke ill of your grace;   70
Which George but hearing, felled them
at his feet,
And, had not rescue come into the place,
George had slain them[4] in his close of
wheat.

EDWARD. But, Cuddy, canst thou not
tell
Where I might give and grant some-
thing
That might please and highly gratify
the pinner's thoughts?
CUDDY. This at their parting George did
say to me:[5]
"If the king vouchsafe of this my serv-
ice,
Then, gentle Cuddy, kneel upon thy
knee,
And humbly crave a boon of him for
me."   80
EDWARD. Cuddy, what is it?
CUDDY. It is his will your grace would
pardon them,
And let them live, although they have
offended.
EDWARD. I think the man striveth to be
glorious.[6]
Well, George hath craved it, and it shall
be granted,
Which none but he in England should
have gotten.—
Live, Kendal, but as prisoner;
So shalt thou end thy days within the
Tower.
KEND. Gracious is Edward to offending
subjects.
JAMES. My Lord of Kend[al], you are
welcome to the court.   90
EDWARD. Nay, but "ill-come" as it falls
out now;
Ay, "ill-come" indeed, were it not for
George a Greene.
But, "gentle king," for so you would
aver,
And, "Edward's betters," I salute you
both,
[*He mockingly vails bonnet to them.*[7]]
And here I vow by good Saint George,
You will gain but little when your sums
are counted!
I sore do long to see this George a
Greene.
And, for because I never saw the north,
I will forthwith go see it;
And, for that to none I will be known, 100

---

[1] *I.e.*, keep him in the pound as a hostage.
[2] Aby, pay for.
[3] In the original this line and the preceding are
printed on one line.
[4] Original reads *him*.

[5] The contradiction between this statement
and l. 31 may be due to the careless rewriting
of the play for use by a touring company.
[6] Vainglorious.
[7] Suggested by Adams as a fulfillment of the
prophecy in sc. vii, ll. 197–99.

We will disguise ourselves and steal down
secretly,
Thou and I, King James, Cuddy, and
two or three,
And make a merry journey for a
month.—
Away, then, conduct him to the Tower.—
Come on, King James, my heart must
needs be merry,
If fortune makes such havoc of our foes.
                      Ex[eunt] omnes.

[Scene xi.

Sherwood Forest.]

*Enter Robin Hood, Maid Marian, Scarlet,
and Much, the miller's son.*

Robin. Why is not lovely Marian blithe
of cheer?
What ails my leman,[1] that she gins[2]
to lour?
Say, good Marian, why art thou so sad?
Marian. Nothing, my Robin, grieves me
to the heart
But, whensoever I do walk abroad,
I hear no songs but all of George a
Greene;
Bettris, his fair leman, passeth me,
And this, my Robin, galls my very soul.
Robin. Content [thee].[3] What wreaks[4]
it us though George a
Greene be stout,   10
So long as he does proffer us no scath?
Envy doth seldom hurt but to itself;
And therefore, Marian, smile upon thy
Robin.
Marian. Never will Marian smile upon
her Robin,
Nor lie with him under the greenwood
shade,
Till that thou go to Wakefield on a green,
And beat the pinner for the love of me.
Robin. Content thee, Marian; I will ease
thy grief.
My merry men and I will thither stray;
And here I vow that, for the love of thee,
I will beat George a Greene, or he shall
beat me.   21
Scarlet. As I am Scarlet, next to Little
John,
One of the boldest yeomen of the crew,

So will I wend with Robin all along,
And try this pinner what he dares do.
Much. As I am Much, the miller's son,
That left my mill to go with thee
(And nill[5] repent that I have done;
This pleasant life contenteth me),
In aught I may, to do thee good,   30
I'll live and die with Robin Hood.
Marian. And, Robin, Marian she will go
with thee
To see fair Bettris how bright she is of
blee.[6]
Robin. Marian, thou shalt go with thy
Robin.—
Bend up your bows, and see your strings
be tight,
The arrows keen, and everything be ready,
And each of you a good bat[7] on his neck,
Able to lay a good man on the ground.
Scarlet. I will have Friar Tuck's.
Much. I will have Little John's.   40
Robin. I will have one made of an ashen
plank,[8]
Able to bear a bout or two.—
Then come on, Marian, let us go,
For, before the sun doth show the morn-
ing day,
I will be at Wakefield to see this pinner,
George a Greene.   *Exeunt omnes.*

[Scene xii.

Bradford.]

*Enter a Shoemaker sitting upon the stage at
work; Jenkin to him [,carrying a staff].*

Jen. My masters, he that hath neither
meat nor money,
And hath lost his credit with the ale-wife,
For anything I know, may go supper-
less to bed.—
But soft! Who is here? Here is a shoe-
maker;
He knows where is the best ale.
Shoemaker, I pray thee tell me,
Where is the best ale in the town?
Shoe. Afore, afore, follow thy nose!
At the sign of the Eggshell.
Jen. Come, shoemaker, if thou wilt,   10
And take thy part of a pot.
Shoe. [*Rising.*]   Sirrah, down with your
staff!
Down with your staff!

---

[1] Sweetheart.   [3] Supplied by Dyce.
[2] Begins.   [4] Recks, matters.
[5] Will not.   [6] Complexion.   [7] Staff.
[8] Emended by Mitford. Original reads *plunk.*

JEN. Why, how now! Is the fellow mad?
  I pray thee tell me, why should I hold
    down my staff?
SHOE. You will down with him, will you
    not, sir?
JEN. Why, tell me wherefore?
SHOE. My friend, this is the town of
    merry Bradford,[1]
  And here is a custom held
  That none shall pass with his staff on
    his shoulders   20
  But he must have a bout with me;
  And so shall you, sir.
JEN. And so will not I, sir!
SHOE. That will I try. Barking dogs bite
    not the sorest.
JEN. [Aside.] I would to God I were once
    well rid of him.
SHOE. Now, what, will you down with
    your staff?
JEN. Why, you are not in earnest, are
    you?
SHOE. If I am not, take that!
                              [Strikes him.]
JEN. You whoreson, cowardly scab,
  It is but the part of a clapperdudgeon [2]
  To strike a man in the street.   31
  But darest thou walk to the town's
    end with me?
SHOE. Ay, that I dare do; but stay till I
    lay in my
  Tools, and I will go with thee to the
    town's end
  Presently.[3]
JEN. [Aside.] I would I knew how to be
    rid of this fellow.
SHOE. Come, sir, will you go to the
    town's end now, sir?
JEN. Ay, sir, come.—
                      [They cross the stage.]
  Now we are at the town's end. What
    say you now?
SHOE. Marry, come, let us even have a
    bout.   40
JEN. Ha, stay a little; hold thy hands,
    I pray thee!
SHOE. Why, what's the matter?
JEN. Faith, I am underpinner of a town,
  And there is an order, which if I do not
    keep,
  I shall be turned out of mine office.
SHOE. What is that, sir?

JEN. Whensoever I go fight with any-
    body,
  I use to flourish my staff thrice about
    my head
  Before I strike, and then show no
    favor.
SHOE. Well, sir, and till then I will not
    strike thee.   50
JEN. Well, sir, here is once, twice—
  Here is my hand; I will never do it the
    third time.
SHOE. Why, then, I see we shall not fight.
JEN. Faith, no! Come, I will give thee
    two pots
  Of the best ale, and be friends.
SHOE. [Aside.] Faith, I see it is as hard
    to get water out of a flint
  As to get him to have a bout with me;
  Therefore I will enter into him for some
    good cheer.—
  My friend, I see thou art a faint-hearted
    fellow;
  Thou hast no stomach [4] to fight;   60
  Therefore let us go to the alehouse and
    drink.
JEN. Well, content! Go thy ways, and
    say thy prayers;
  Thou scap'st my hands today.
                              Exeunt omnes.

[SCENE xiii.

Wakefield.]

Enter George a Greene and Bettris.

GEORGE. Tell me, sweet love, how is thy
    mind content?
  What, canst thou brook to live with
    George a Greene?
BETTRIS. O, George, how little pleasing
    are these words!
  Came I from Bradford for the love of
    thee,
  And left my father for so sweet a friend!
  Here will I live until my life do end.

Enter Robin Hood, and Marian, and his
                                      Train.

GEORGE. Happy am I to have so sweet
    a love.—
  But what are these come tracing [5] here
    along?

---

[1] Original reads Wakefield.
[2] Beggar.   [3] Immediately   [4] Courage.   [5] Walking.

BETTRIS. Three men come striking
through the corn,
My love. 10

GEORGE. Back again, you foolish travelers,
For you are wrong, and may not wend
this way.

ROBIN. That were great shame.
Now, by my soul, proud sir,
We be three tall yeomen, and thou art
but one.—
Come, we will forward in despite of him.

GEORGE. Leap the ditch, or I will make
you skip.
What, cannot the highway serve your
turn,
But you must make a path over the
corn?

ROBIN. Why, art thou mad? Dar'st thou
encounter three? 20
We are no babes, man; look upon our
limbs.

GEORGE. Sirrah, the biggest limbs have
not the stoutest hearts.
Were ye as good as Robin Hood and
his three merry men,
I'll drive you back the same way that
ye came.
Be ye men, ye scorn to encounter me
all at once;
But be ye cowards, set upon me all
three,
And try the pinner what he dares perform.

SCARLET. Were thou as high in deeds
As thou art haughty in words,
Thou well mightest be a champion for
a king. 30
But empty vessels have the loudest
sounds,
And cowards prattle more than men of
worth.

GEORGE. Sirrah, darest thou try me?

SCARLET. Ay, sirrah, that I dare.

They fight, and George a Greene beats him.

MUCH. How now! What, art thou down?—
Come, sir, I am next.

They fight, and George a Greene beats him.

ROBIN. Come, sirrah, now to me! Spare
me not,
For I'll not spare thee.

GEORGE. Make no doubt I will be as
liberal to thee.

They fight. Robin Hood stays.[1]

[1] Desists, rests.

ROBIN. Stay, George, for here I do protest 40
Thou art the stoutest champion that
ever I laid
Hands upon.

GEORGE. Soft you, sir! By your leave,
you lie;
You never yet laid hands on me.

ROBIN. George, wilt thou forsake Wake-
field,
And go with me?
Two liveries will I give thee every year,
And forty crowns shall be thy fee.

GEORGE. Why, who art thou?

ROBIN. Why, Robin Hood! 50
I am come hither with my Marian
And these my yeomen for to visit thee.

GEORGE. Robin Hood! Next to King
Edward
Art thou lief [2] to me.
Welcome, sweet Robin; welcome, Maid
Marian;
And welcome, you, my friends.
Will you to my poor house?
You shall have wafer cakes your fill,
A piece of beef hung up since Martlemas,
Mutton and veal. If this like you not, 60
Take that you find, or that you bring,
for me.

ROBIN. God-a-mercies, good George,
I'll be thy guest today.

GEORGE. Robin, therein thou honorest me.
I'll lead the way. *Exeunt omnes.*

[SCENE xiv.

Bradford.]

*Enter King Edward and King James dis-
guised, with two staves.*

EDWARD. Come on, King James; now we
are
Thus disguised,
There is none, I know, will take us to
be kings.
I think we are now in Bradford,
Where all the merry shoemakers dwell.

Enter a Shoemaker [with his Comrades].

SHOE. Down with your staves, my friends,
Down with them!

EDWARD. Down with our staves? I pray
thee, why so?

[2] Dear.

SHOE. My friend, I see thou art a stranger
here,
Else wouldest thou not have questioned
of the thing. 10
This is the town of merry Bradford,
And here hath been a custom kept of
old,
That none may bear his staff upon his
neck,
But trail it all along throughout the
town,
Unless they mean to have a bout with
me.

EDWARD. But hear you, sir, hath the king
Granted you this custom?

SHOE. King or kaiser, none shall pass
this way,
Except King Edward;
No, not the stoutest groom that haunts
his court. 20
Therefore down with your staves!

EDWARD. [*Aside.*] What were we best to
do?

JAMES. [*Aside.*] Faith, my lord, they are
stout fellows;
And, because we will see some sport,
We will trail our staves.

EDWARD. Hear'st thou, my friend?
Because we are men of peace and travel-
ers,
We are content to trail our staves.

SHOE. The way lies before you; go along.

*Enter Robin Hood and George a Greene,
disguised.*

ROBIN. See, George, two men are passing
Through the town, 31
Two lusty men, and yet they trail their
staves.

GEORGE. Robin, they are some peasants
Tricked in yeoman's weeds.—Hollo,
you two travelers!

EDWARD. Call you us, sir?

GEORGE. Ay, you. Are ye not big enough
to bear
Your bats upon your necks,
But you must trail them along the
streets?

EDWARD. Yes, sir, we are big enough;
but here is a custom
Kept, that none may pass, his staff
upon his neck, 40
Unless he trail it at the weapon's point.

Sir, we are men of peace, and love to
sleep
In our whole skins, and therefore quietness is best.

GEORGE. Base-minded peasants, worthless to be men!
What, have you bones and limbs to
strike a blow,
And be your hearts so faint you cannot
fight?
Were't not for shame, I would shrub [1]
your shoulders well,
And teach you manhood against [2] another time.

SHOE. Well preached, Sir Jack! Down
with your staff!

EDWARD. Do you hear, my friends? And
you be wise, 50
Keep down your staves,
For all the town will rise upon you.

GEORGE. Thou speakest like an honest,
quiet fellow.
But hear you me. In spite of all the
swains
Of Bradford town, bear me your staves
upon your necks,
Or, to begin withal, I'll baste you both
so well,
You were never better basted in your
lives.

EDWARD. We will hold up our staves.

*George a Greene fights with the Shoemakers,
and beats them all down.*

GEORGE. What, have you any more?
Call all your town forth, cut and long-
tail. [3] 60

The Shoemakers spy [4] George a Greene.

SHOE. What, George a Greene, is it you?
A plague found [5] you!
I think you longed to swinge me well.
Come, George, we will crush [6] a pot
before we part.

GEORGE. A pot, you slave! We will have
an hundred.—
Here, Will Perkins, take my purse;
Fetch me a stand [7] of ale, and set in the
market place,
That all may drink that are athirst this
day;

[1] Scrub, beat.   [2] In preparation for.
[3] Docked and undocked (said of dogs and
horses); hence, all classes of people.
[4] Recognize.   [6] Drink.
[5] Confound.   [7] Cask.

For this is for a fee to welcome Robin
Hood
To Bradford town.   70
They bring out the stand of ale and fall
a-drinking.
Here, Robin, sit thou here; for thou art
the best man
At the board this day.
You that are strangers, place yourselves
where you will.
Robin, here's a carouse to good King
Edward's self;
And they that love him not, I would
we had
The basting of them a little.

Enter the Earl of Warwick with other Noble-
men, bringing out the King's garments;
then George a Greene and the rest kneel
down to the King.
EDWARD. Come, masters, all fellows!—
Nay, Robin, you are the best man at
the board today.—
Rise up, George.
GEORGE. Nay, good my liege, ill-nurtured
we were, then.   80
Though we Yorkshire men be blunt of
speech,
And little skilled in court or such quaint
fashions,
Yet nature teacheth us duty to our king;
Therefore I humbly beseech you pardon
George a Greene.
ROBIN. And, good my lord, a pardon for
poor Robin;
And for us all a pardon, good King Ed-
ward.
SHOE. I pray you, a pardon for the shoe-
makers.
EDWARD. I frankly grant a pardon to you
all.   [*They rise.*]
And, George a Greene, give me thy hand;
There's none in England that shall do
thee wrong.   90
Even from my court I came to see thy-
self;
And now I see that fame speaks naught
but truth.
GEORGE. I humbly thank your royal
majesty.
That which I did against the Earl of
Kendal,
It was but a subject's duty to his sov-
ereign.

And therefore little merit such good
words.
EDWARD. But, ere I go, I'll grace thee with
good deeds.
Say what King Edward may perform,
And thou shalt have it, being in Eng-
land's bounds.
GEORGE. I have a lovely leman,   100
As bright of blee as is the silver moon,
And old Grime her father will not let
her match
With me, because I am a pinner,
Although I love her, and she me, dearly.
EDWARD. Where is she?
GEORGE. At home at my poor house,
And vows never to marry unless her
father
Give consent; which is my great grief,
my lord.
EDWARD. If this be all, I will despatch it
straight;
I'll send for Grime and force him give
his grant;   110
He will not deny King Edward such a
suit.

Enter Jenkin and speaks.

[JEN.] Ho, who saw a master of mine?
O, he is gotten into company, and a body
should rake
Hell for company!
GEORGE. Peace, ye slave!   See where
King Edward is.
EDWARD. George, what is he?
GEORGE. I beseech your grace pardon
him; he is my man.
SHOE. Sirrah, the king hath been drink-
ing with us,
And did pledge us too.
JEN. Hath he so?   Kneel!   I dub you
"gentlemen."   120
SHOE. Beg it of the king, Jenkin.
JEN. I will.—I beseech your worship grant
me one thing.
EDWARD. What is that?
JEN. Hark in your ear.
         He whispers the King in the ear.
EDWARD. Go your ways, and do it.
JEN. Come, down on your knees; I have
got it.
SHOE. Let us hear what it is first.
JEN. Marry, because you have drunk
with the king,

And the king hath so graciously pledged
  you,
You shall be no more called shoe-
  makers,   130
But you and yours, to the world's end,
  Shall be called "the trade of the gentle [1]
  craft."
SHOE. I beseech your majesty reform
  this
  Which he hath spoken.
JEN. I beseech your worship consume
  this
  Which he hath spoken.
EDWARD. Confirm it, you would say.—
  Well, he hath done it for you; it is suf-
  ficient.
  Come, George, we will go to Grime,
  And have thy love.   140
JEN. I am sure your worship will
  abide;
  For yonder is coming old Musgrove
  And mad Cuddy, his son.—
  Master, my fellow Wily comes dressed
  like a woman,
  And Master Grime will marry Wily.
  Here they come.

*Enter Musgrove and Cuddy; and Master
Grime, Wily, Maid Marian, and Bettris.*

EDWARD. Which is thy old father, Cuddy?
CUDDY. This, if it please your majesty.
                [*Musgrove kneels.*]
EDWARD. Ah, old Musgrove, stand[2] up;
  It fits not such gray hairs to kneel.
MUS. [*Rising.*] Long live my sovereign!
  Long and happy be his days!   151
  Vouchsafe, my gracious lord, a simple
  gift
  At Billy Musgrove's hand.
  King James at Middleham [3] Castle
  gave me this;
  This won the honor, and this give I
  thee.   [*Gives sword to Edward.*]
EDWARD. God-a-mercy, Musgrove, for
  this friendly gift;
  And, for thou felledst a king with this
  same weapon,
  This blade shall here dub valiant Mus-
  grove knight.

[1] Genteel, elegant.
[2] Original reads *kneel*.
[3] The original form *Meddellom* shows the pronunciation.

MUS. Alas, what hath your highness
  done? I am poor.
EDWARD. To mend thy living take thou
  Middleham Castle,   160
  The hold of both. And if thou want
  living, complain;
  Thou shalt have more to maintain thy
  estate.—
  George, which is thy love?
GEORGE. This, if please your majesty.
EDWARD. Art thou her aged father?
GRIME. I am, and it like your majesty.
EDWARD. And wilt not give thy daughter
  unto George?
GRIME. Yes, my lord, if he will let me
  marry
  With this lovely lass.
EDWARD. What sayst thou, George? 170
GEORGE. With all my heart, my lord, I
  give consent.
GRIME. Then do I give my daughter unto
  George.
WILY. Then shall the marriage soon be
  at an end.
  Witness, my lord, if that I be a woman;
              [*Throws off his disguise.*]
  For I am Wily, boy to George a Greene,
  Who for my master wrought this subtle
  shift.
EDWARD. What, is it a boy?—What sayst
  thou to this, Grime?
GRIME. Marry, my lord, I think this boy
  hath
  More knavery than all the world be-
  sides.
  Yet am I content that George shall
  both have   180
  My daughter and my lands.
EDWARD. Now, George, it rests I gratify
  thy worth;
  And therefore here I do bequeath to
  thee,
  In full possession, half that Kendal
  hath;
  And whatas [4] Bradford holds of me in
  chief,
  I give it frankly unto thee forever.
  Kneel down, George.
GEORGE. What will your majesty do?
EDWARD. Dub thee a knight, George.
GEORGE. I beseech your grace, grant me
  one thing.   190
EDWARD. What is that?

[4] Whatsoever.

GEORGE. Then let me live and die a yeoman still.

So was my father, so must live his son.
For 'tis more credit to men of base degree
To do great deeds than men of dignity.

EDWARD. Well, be it so, George.

JAMES. I beseech your grace, despatch with me,
And set down my ransom.

EDWARD. George a Greene, set down the King of Scots
His ransom.   200

GEORGE. I beseech your grace, pardon me;
It passeth my skill.

EDWARD. Do it; the honor's thine.

GEORGE. Then let King James make good
Those towns which he hath burnt upon the borders;
Give a small pension to the fatherless,
Whose fathers he caused murthered in those wars;

Put in pledge for these things to your grace,
And so return.

[EDWARD.] King James, are you content? [1]

JAMES. I am content, and like [2] your majesty,   211
And will leave good castles in security.

EDWARD. I crave no more.—Now, George a Greene,
I'll to thy house; and when I have supped, I'll go to ask
And see if Jane a Barley be so fair
As good King James reports her for to be.
And for the ancient custom of *Vail staff*, keep it still;
Claim privilege from me.
If any ask a reason why or how,
Say English Edward vailed his staff to you.

[1] In the original this sentence is given to George a Greene, completing the last line of his speech.   [2] If it please.

FINIS.

CHRISTOPHER MARLOWE

Christopher Marlowe—the name is also spelled Marly and Marlin in the records—was born in 1564, the son of a well-to-do shoemaker and a clergyman's daughter. He was educated at King's School in his native Canterbury and at Corpus Christi College, Cambridge, where he proceeded B.A. in 1584 and M.A. in 1587. The privy council intervened to see that his employment on some confidential mission for the government, in which he had proved "orderly and discreet," should not put him at a disadvantage in the matter of his M.A. degree. For the remaining six years of his life there is evidence of exceptional activity. Apparently he continued to serve as a confidential agent for the government; he engaged in the philosophical or theological speculation of a circle centering around Raleigh; he achieved distinction by his non-dramatic verse, of which the unfinished *Hero and Leander* is the most important example; and he became the outstanding dramatist of London, in association chiefly with the Admiral's Company of players. Many details of his life were a source of scandal to some of his contemporaries, and for us are still shrouded in mystery. In May, 1593, a manuscript was discovered in Kyd's possession which he declared to be Marlowe's, left with Kyd in 1591 when he was in the service of a noble lord for whose players Marlowe was writing. The document—merely a copy of part of a theological treatise already published—though unitarian in nature, was atheistic in the eyes of the orthodox. Testimony as to blasphemous conversations on Marlowe's part was also produced. Before the privy council took definite action about the charges, Marlowe was killed. Puritan disapproval of his connection with the stage and of his free-thinking perhaps influenced Meres' statement that he was stabbed "by a bawdy serving-man, a rival of his in his lewd love." Records discovered by Hotson merely show that he was stabbed in a tavern in Deptford by Friser, one of three companions who also were, or had been, in the service of the government. The procedure of the coroner's inquest by which Friser was exonerated is regarded by some modern students as regular, by others as an attempt to cover official secrets or even a political assassination. Marlowe was buried on June 1, 1593.

Tamburlaine, unanimously accepted as Marlowe's first play, was attracting attention by 1588, when Greene in the preface to *Perimedes the Blacksmith* speaks of "atheist Tamburlaine" in what is pretty clearly an attack on Marlowe. Evidence of his authorship is chiefly to be found in the character of the play, however. The two parts were published together anonymously in 1590, with some omissions, as the printer's preface indicates. Perhaps the success of the first part led Marlowe to write the inferior second part—not printed in this anthology—in which Tamburlaine is followed by his boasting and unrepentant end. A Renaissance interest in the oriental conqueror and his barbaric passions and display, surviving no doubt in part from medieval story and drama, and stimulated by new contacts with the East, is reflected by the popularity of the type on the London stage. The story of Tamburlaine apparently held an especial fascination for writers, and had become mythical before Marlowe created his conqueror. Marlowe seems to have consulted a number of historical or pseudo-historical accounts of the East for his material, and even contemporary geographical works for some of his sonorous references to distant places. In this first play Marlowe developed his "mighty line," as Jonson calls it, and made it a fit instrument for the intense and passionate characters created by him. While at times, especially in *Tamburlaine*, his style approaches bombast, his swelling periods and bold figures contributed greatly to the effectiveness of tragic style in his successors.

Doctor Faustus has usually been assigned to the winter of 1588–89, but recent scholars like Tucker Brooke and Boas (in his edition of the play for *The Works and Life of Marlowe* under the general editorship of Case) argue for the date 1592. The German *Faustbuch*, translated into English, seems to have been the source, and there is evidence that this was not published before 1592. The first certain record of the play is of its being acted for Henslowe in 1594. The problem of the text is a difficult one. The earliest known edition was not published until 1604, and it contains some material which bears evidence of composition after Marlowe's death. Some scholars trace Dekker's hand in this version, possibly through revision for acting in 1594. Apparently the serious parts of the play have been cut, with an enlargement of the spectacular and comic scenes of conjuring and dancing, the sort of thing always loved by the London populace. In 1602 Henslowe paid William Bird and Samuel Rowley for "additions" to the play. Presumably these were included in the enlarged edition which came out in 1616. The new material in this version, though added to the poetic scenes, is still primarily of a spectacular nature, and does not often suggest Marlowe. Boas argues that Rowley collaborated with Marlowe from the beginning, contributing most of the original comic prose as well as many of the later verse additions. Accordingly he constructs a composite text for the play, but one based primarily on the edition of 1616. It is, however, in the tragic portrayal of the scholar who, irked by the limitations of academic studies, purchased supreme knowledge and power with his soul, that the play represents Marlowe at his best, in spite of the imperfections of the surviving texts. Hence the present editors have preferred to follow the shorter version of 1604, with sparing use of later editions for corrupt passages.

Edward II was entered in the Stationers' Register on July 6, 1593. The first complete edition known was printed in 1594 with the statement that the play had been acted by the Earl of Pembroke's players. The winter of 1592–93 is suggested as the date of composition by indications of maturity in the play and by the fact that Pembroke's Company was prominent in London only at that time. The source is Holinshed's *Chronicles*. *Edward II* represents a great advance over the known plays on English history that preceded, and is the best of Marlowe's work in construction, in characterization, and in sustained tone. Against a background of the fierce feudal barons, Marlowe has drawn a very effective picture of the sentimental and weak but stubborn king.

Of the three extant plays by Marlowe in addition to those printed here, the most important is *The Jew of Malta*, written possibly around 1590. It was being played for Henslowe early in 1592, and was entered in the Stationers' Register early in 1594. The earliest form to survive, however, is an edition by Thomas Heywood in 1633, which has clearly been revamped. *The Massacre at Paris* was printed without date about 1593. *Dido, Queen of Carthage*, printed in 1594, was written in collaboration with Thomas Nashe. It has been claimed that Marlowe had a hand in several other extant plays, particularly in the two parts of *The Contention of York and Lancaster*, which are versions of Shakespeare's Second and Third Parts of *Henry VI*.

Tucker Brooke's variorum *Works of Marlowe* has furnished the basis for the texts of the three plays printed here, which in each case go back to the earliest edition. *Doctor Faustus* has been checked with the edition of 1604 in Farmer's Tudor Facsimile Texts, and *Edward II* with the Malone Society reprint of the edition of 1594 prepared under the direction of W. W. Greg.

TAMBURLAINE THE GREAT

[BY

CHRISTOPHER MARLOWE

THE FIRST PART

DRAMATIS PERSONÆ

MYCETES, *King of Persia.*
COSROE, *his brother.*
ORTYGIUS
CENEUS
MEANDER } *Persian lords and leaders.*
MENAPHON
THERIDAMAS
TAMBURLAINE, *a Scythian shepherd.*
TECHELLES } *his followers.*
USUMCASANE
BAJAZETH, *Emperor of the Turks.*
KING OF ARABIA.
KING OF FEZ.
KING OF MOROCCO.
KING of ARGIER.[2]

SOLDAN of EGYPT.
GOVERNOR of DAMASCUS.
AGYDAS } *Median lords.*
MAGNETES
CAPOLIN, *an Egyptian captain.*
PHILEMUS, *a messenger.*
BASSOES,[3] LORDS, CITIZENS, MOORS, SOLDIERS, *and* ATTENDANTS.

ZENOCRATE, *daughter of the Soldan of Egypt.*
ANIPPE, *her maid.*
ZABINA, *wife of Bajazeth.*
EBEA, *her maid.*
VIRGINS OF DAMASCUS.

SCENE: *Western Asia.*

TIME: *Fourteenth Century.*]

TO THE GENTLEMEN READERS, AND OTHERS THAT TAKE PLEASURE IN READING HISTORIES.

Gentlemen, and courteous readers whosoever: I have here published in print for your sakes the two tragical discourses of the Scythian shepherd, Tamburlaine, that became so great a conqueror and so mighty a monarch. My hope is that they will be now no less acceptable unto you to read after your serious affairs and studies than they have been, lately, delightful for many of you to see, when the same were [10 showed in London upon stages. I have, purposely, omitted and left out some fond [4] and frivolous gestures, digressing and, in my poor opinion, far unmeet for the matter, which I thought might seem more tedious unto the wise than any way else to be regarded, though haply they have been of some vain, conceited fondlings [5] greatly gaped at, what times they were showed upon the stage in their graced deformities; [20 nevertheless, now, to be mixtured in print with such matter of worth, it would prove a great disgrace to so honorable and stately a history. Great folly were it in me to commend unto your wisdoms either the eloquence of the author that writ them, or the worthiness of the matter itself; I therefore leave unto your learned censures [6] both the one and the other, and myself, the poor

---

[1] The title continues: " Who, from a Scythian Shepherd, by His Rare and Wonderful Conquests Became a Most Puissant and Mighty Monarch, and (for His Tyranny and Terror in War) Was Termed the Scourge of God. Divided into Two Tragical Discourses, as They Were Sundry Times Showed upon Stages in the City of London, by the Right Honorable the Lord Admiral His Servants. Now First and Newly Published."

[2] Algiers.   [3] Bashaws.

[4] Foolish.   [5] Fools.   [6] Judgments.

309

printer of them, unto your most cour- [30
teous and favorable protection, which if you
vouchsafe to accept, you shall evermore
bind me to employ what travail and service
I can to the advancing and pleasuring of
your excellent degree.

Yours, most humble at commandment,
R[ichard] J[ones], Printer.

The Prologue

From jigging veins of riming mother wits
And such conceits as clownage keeps in pay,
We'll lead you to the stately tent of war,
Where you shall hear the Scythian Tam-
burlaine
Threat'ning the world with high astound-
ing terms,
And scourging kingdoms with his conquer-
ing sword.
View but his picture in this tragic glass,
And then applaud his fortunes as you
please.

Actus I. Scena i.

[*The Persian court.*]

*Mycetes, Cosroe, Meander, Theridamas,
Ortygius, Ceneus, [Menaphon,] with
Others.*

Myc. Brother Cosroe, I find myself ag-
grieved,
  Yet insufficient to express the same,
  For it requires a great and thund'ring
speech.
  Good brother, tell the cause unto my
lords;
  I know you have a better wit than I.
Cos. Unhappy Persia, that in former age
  Hast been the seat of mighty conquerors
  That, in their prowess and their policies,
  Have triumphed over Afric and the
bounds
  Of Europe, where the sun dares scarce
appear   10
  For freezing meteors and congealéd cold,
  Now to be ruled and governed by a man
  At whose birthday Cynthia with Saturn
joined,
  And Jove, the Sun, and Mercury denied
  To shed their [1] influence in his fickle
brain!

Now Turks and Tartars shake their
swords at thee,
Meaning to mangle all thy provinces.
Myc. Brother, I see your meaning well
enough,
And thorough [2] your planets I perceive
you think
I am not wise enough to be a king;   20
But I refer me to my noblemen
That know my wit, and can be witnesses.
I might command you to be slain for this.
Meander, might I not?
Mean. Not for so small a fault, my sov-
ereign lord.
Myc. I mean it not, but yet I know I
might.
Yet live; yea, live. Mycetes wills it so.
Meander, thou, my faithful counselor,
Declare the cause of my conceivéd grief,
Which is, God knows, about that Tam-
burlaine,   30
That, like a fox in midst of harvest
time,
Doth prey upon my flocks of passengers, [3]
And, as I hear, doth mean to pull my
plumes;
Therefore 'tis good and meet for to be
wise.
Mean. Oft have I heard your majesty
complain
Of Tamburlaine, that sturdy Scythian
thief,
That robs your merchants of Persepolis,
Treading by land unto the Western Isles,
And in your confines with his lawless
train
Daily commits incivil [4] outrages,   40
Hoping (misled by dreaming prophecies)
To reign in Asia, and with barbarous
arms
To make himself the monarch of the
East.
But, ere he march in Asia, or display
His vagrant ensign in the Persian fields,
Your grace hath taken order by Theri-
damas,
Charged with a thousand horse, to appre-
hend
And bring him captive to your highness'
throne.
Myc. Full true thou speak'st, and like
thyself, my lord,

---

[1] Suggested by Dyce. Original has *his*.

[2] Through.   [4] Barbarous.
[3] Travelers, traders.

Whom I may term a Damon for thy
  love. 50
Therefore 'tis best, if so it like you all,
To send my thousand horse incontinent [1]
To apprehend that paltry Scythian.
How like you this, my honorable lords?
Is it not a kingly resolution?

Cos. It cannot choose, because it comes
  from you.

Myc. Then hear thy charge, valiant Theri-
  damas,
The chiefest captain of Mycetes' host,
The hope of Persia, and the very legs
Whereon our state doth lean, as on a
  staff 60
That holds us up, and foils our neighbor
  foes.
Thou shalt be leader of this thousand
  horse,
Whose foaming gall with rage and high
  disdain
Have sworn the death of wicked Tam-
  burlaine.
Go frowning forth; but come thou smiling
  home,
As did Sir Paris with the Grecian dame.
Return with speed—time passeth swift
  away;
Our life is frail, and we may die today.

Ther. Before the moon renew her borrowed light,
Doubt not, my lord and gracious sovereign, 70
But Tamburlaine and that Tartarian
  rout
Shall either perish by our warlike hands
Or plead for mercy at your highness'
  feet.

Myc. Go, stout Theridamas; thy words
  are swords,
And with thy looks thou conquerest all
  thy foes.
I long to see thee back return from
  thence,
That I may view these milk-white steeds
  of mine,
All loaden with the heads of killéd men,
And from their knees even to their hoofs
  below,
Besmeared with blood that makes a
  dainty [2] show. 80

Ther. Then now, my lord, I humbly take
  my leave.

Myc. Therid[amas], farewell ten thousand
  times! *Exit [Theridamas].*
Ah, Menaphon, why stayest thou thus
  behind,
When other men press forward for re-
  nown?
Go, Menaphon, go into Scythia,
And foot by foot follow Theridamas.

Cos. Nay, pray you let him stay; a greater
  [task] [3]
Fits Menaphon than warring with a
  thief.
Create him prorex [4] of [all] [5] Africa,
That he may win the Babylonians'
  hearts, 90
Which will revolt from Persian govern-
  ment,
Unless they have a wiser king than you.

Myc. "Unless they have a wiser king than
  you"!
These are his words. Meander, set them
  down.

Cos. And add this to them—that all
  Asia
Lament to see the folly of their king.

Myc. Well, here I swear by this my royal
  seat—

Cos. You may do well to kiss it then!

Myc. Embossed with silk as best beseems
  my state,
To be revenged for these contemptuous
  words. 100
O, where is duty and allegiance now?
Fled to the Caspian or the Ocean main?
What, shall I call thee brother? No, a foe.
Monster of nature, shame unto thy
  stock,
That dar'st presume thy sovereign for to
  mock!
Meander, come! I am abused, Meander.
*Exit [with his Train]. Manent [6] Cosroe
  et Menaphon.*

Mena. How now, my lord? What, mated [7]
  and amazed
To hear the king thus threaten like himself?

Cos. Ah, Menaphon, I pass [8] not for his
  threats.
The plot is laid by Persian noblemen 110
And captains of the Median garrisons
To crown me Emperor of Asia.

---

[1] Immediately.   [2] Fine, rare.

[3] Added by Robinson.   [5] From 1605 edn.
[4] Viceroy.   [6] Remain.
[7] Checkmated, confounded.   [8] Care.

But this it is that doth excruciate
The very substance of my vexéd soul—
To see our neighbors, that were wont to
　quake
And tremble at the Persian monarch's
　name,
Now sits and laughs our regiment [1] to
　scorn;
And, that which might resolve [2] me into
　tears,
Men from the farthest equinoctial line
Have swarmed in troops into the Eastern
　India,　　　　　　　　　　　　　120
Lading their ships with gold and precious
　stones,
And made their spoils from all our prov-
　inces.
MENA. This should entreat your highness
　to rejoice,
Since fortune gives you opportunity
To gain the title of a conqueror
By curing of this maiméd empery.
Afric and Europe bordering on your land,
And continent [3] to your dominions,
How easily may you, with a mighty host,
Pass into Grecia, as did Cyrus once,　130
And cause them to withdraw their forces
　home,
Lest you subdue the pride of Christen-
　dom!　　　　　　　[*Trumpet within.*]
Cos. But, Menaph[on], what means this
　trumpet's sound?
MENA. Behold, my lord, Ortygius and the
　rest
Bringing the crown to make you em-
　peror!

*Enter Ortygius and Ceneus [4] bearing a
crown, with Others.*

ORTY. Magnificent and mighty Prince Cos-
　roe,
We, in the name of other Persian states [5]
And commons of this mighty monarchy,
Present thee with th' imperial diadem.
CEN. The warlike soldiers and the gentle-
　men,　　　　　　　　　　　　140
That heretofore have filled Persepolis
With Afric captains taken in the field,
Whose ransom made them march in coats
　of gold,

With costly jewels hanging at their ears,
And shining stones upon their lofty
　crests,
Now living idle in the walléd towns,
Wanting both pay and martial discipline,
Begin in troops to threaten civil war,
And openly exclaim against the king.
Therefore, to stay all sudden muti-
　nies,　　　　　　　　　　　　150
We will invest your highness emperor,
Whereat the soldiers will conceive more
　joy
Than did the Macedonians at the spoil
Of great Darius and his wealthy host.
Cos. Well, since I see the state of Persia
　droop
And languish in my brother's govern-
　ment,
I willingly receive th' imperial crown,
And vow to wear it for my country's
　good,
In spite of them [6] shall malice [7] my es-
　tate.
ORTY. And, in assurance of desired suc-
　cess,　　　　　　　　　　　　160
We here do crown thee Monarch of the
　East,
Emperor of Asia and of Persia,
Great Lord of Media and Armenia,
Duke of Africa and Albania,
Mesopotamia and of Parthia,
East India and the late-discovered isles,
Chief Lord of all the wide, vast Euxine
　sea,
And of the ever-raging Caspian lake!
Long live Cosroe, mighty emperor!
Cos. And Jove may [8] never let me longer
　live　　　　　　　　　　　　170
Than I may seek to gratify your love,
And cause the soldiers that thus honor
　me
To triumph over many provinces!
By whose desires of discipline in arms
I doubt not shortly but to reign sole
　king,
And with the army of Theridamas,
Whither we presently will fly, my lords,
To rest secure against my brother's force.
ORTY. We knew, my lord, before we
　brought the crown,
Intending your invest ion [9] so near　180

---

[1] Rule, government.　　　　[3] Contiguous.
[2] Dissolve.
[4] Emended by Dyce. **Original reads** *Cornerus.*
[5] Persons of state.

[6] Them who.
[7] Bear malice to, seek to injure.
[8] May Jove.　　　　　　[9] Investiture.

The residence of your despiséd brother,
The lord[s] would not be too exasperate [1]
To injure or suppress your worthy title;
Or, if they would, there are in readiness
Ten thousand horse to carry you from hence,
In spite of all suspected enemies.
Cos. I know it well, my lord, and thank you all.
Orty. Sound up the trumpets then. God save the king!   *Exeunt.*

Actus I. Scena ii.

[*Tamburlaine's camp in Scythia.*]

Tamburlaine leading Zenocrate; Techelles, Usumcasane, [Agydas, Magnetes;] other Lords and Soldiers loaden with treasure.

Tam. Come, lady, let not this appall your thoughts.
The jewels and the treasure we have ta'en
Shall be reserved, and you in better state
Than if you were arrived in Syria,
Even in the circle of your father's arms,
The mighty Soldan of Egyptia.
Zen. Ah, shepherd, pity my distresséd plight
(If, as thou seemst, thou art so mean a man)
And seek not to enrich thy followers
By lawless rapine from a silly [2] maid 10
Who, traveling with these Median lords
To Memphis, from my uncle's country of Media,
Where all my youth I have been governéd,
Have passed the army of the mighty Turk,
Bearing his privy signet and his hand
To safe conduct us thorough Africa.
Mag. And, since we have arrived in Scythia,
Besides rich presents from the puissant Cham,
We have his highness' letters to command
Aid and assistance, if we stand in need.   20
Tam. But now you see these letters and commands
Are countermanded by a greater man;

And through my provinces you must expect
Letters of conduct from my mightiness,
If you intend to keep your treasure safe.
But, since I love to live at liberty,
As easily may you get the soldan's crown
As any prizes out of my precinct,
For they are friends that help to wean my state
Till men and kingdoms help to strengthen it,   30
And must maintain my life exempt from servitude.—
But, tell me, madam, is your grace betrothed?
Zen. I am, my lord—for so you do import. [3]
Tam. I am a lord, for so my deeds shall prove,
And yet a shepherd by my parentage.
But, lady, this fair face and heavenly hue
Must grace his bed that conquers Asia,
And means to be a terror to the world,
Measuring the limits of his empery
By east and west, as Phœbus doth his course.   40
Lie here, ye weeds that I disdain to wear!
This complete armor and this curtle-ax [4]
Are adjuncts more beseeming Tamburlaine.
And, madam, whatsoever you esteem
Of this success [5] and loss unvaluéd, [6]
Both may invest you Empress of the East;
And these that seem but silly country swains
May have the leading of so great an host
As with their weight shall make the mountains quake,
Even as when windy exhalations,   50
Fighting for passage, tilt within the earth.
Tech. As princely lions, when they rouse themselves,
Stretching their paws, and threat'ning herds of beasts,
So in his armor looketh Tamburlaine.
Methinks I see kings kneeling at his feet,
And he, with frowning brows and fiery looks,
Spurning their crowns from off their captive heads.

[1] Old form of past participle.
[2] Simple, innocent.
[3] Bear yourself.
[4] Cutlass.
[5] Event.
[6] Invaluable.

Usum. And making thee and me, Techelles, kings,
That even to death will follow Tamburlaine.

Tam. Nobly resolved, sweet friends and
followers! 60
These lords, perhaps, do scorn our estimates,
And think we prattle with distempered
spirits;
But, since they measure our deserts so
mean,
That in conceit [1] bear empires on our
spears,
Affecting thoughts coequal with the
clouds,
They shall be kept our forcéd followers,
Till with their eyes they view us emperors.

Zen. The gods, defenders of the innocent,
Will never prosper your intended drifts, [2]
That thus oppress poor friendless passengers. 70
Therefore at least admit us liberty,
Even as thou hop'st to be eternizéd [3]
By living Asia's mighty emperor.

Agyd. I hope our lady's treasure and our
own
May serve for ransom to our liberties.
Return our mules and empty camels
back,
That we may travel into Syria,
Where her betrothéd lord, Alcidamus,
Expects th' arrival of her highness' person.

Mag. And, wheresoever we repose ourselves, 80
We will report but well of Tamburlaine.

Tam. Disdains Zenocrate to live with me?
Or you, my lords, to be my followers?
Think you I weigh this treasure more
than you?
Not all the gold in India's wealthy arms
Shall buy the meanest soldier in my
train.
Zenocrate, lovelier than the love of Jove,
Brighter than is the silver Rhodope, [4]
Fairer than whitest snow on Scythian
hills,
Thy person is more worth to Tamburlaine 90
Than the possession of the Persian crown,
Which gracious stars have promised at
my birth.
A hundreth Tartars shall attend on thee,
Mounted on steeds swifter than Pegasus.
Thy garments shall be made of Median
silk,
Enchased with precious jewels of mine
own,
More rich and valurous [5] than Zenocrate's.
With milk-white harts upon an ivory
sled
Thou shalt be drawn amidst the frozen
pools,
And scale the icy mountains' lofty
tops, 100
Which with thy beauty will be soon
resolved.
My martial prizes with five hundred men,
Won on the fifty-headed Volga's waves,
Shall all we offer to Zenocrate—
And then myself to fair Zenocrate.

Tech. What now!—In love?

Tam. Techelles, women must be flatteréd,
But this is she with whom I am in love.

Enter a Soldier.

Sold. News! News!

Tam. How now, what's the matter? 110

Sold. A thousand Persian horsemen are at
hand,
Sent from the king to overcome us all.

Tam. How now, my lords of Egypt, and
Zenocrate!
Now must your jewels be restored
again,
And I that triumphed so be overcome?
How say you, lordings? Is not this your
hope?

Agyd. We hope yourself will willingly restore them.

Tam. Such hope, such fortune, have the
thousand horse.
Soft ye, my lords and sweet Zenocrate!
You must be forcéd from me ere you
go. 120
A thousand horsemen? We five hundred
foot?
An odds too great for us to stand against!
But are they rich? And is their armor
good?

[1] Idea, fancy, imagination.   [3] Made immortal.
[2] Plans, schemes.
[4] Suggested by Dyce; original has *Rhodolfe*.

[5] Valuable.

SOLD. Their pluméd helms are wrought
with beaten gold,
Their swords enameled, and about their
necks
Hangs massy chains of gold down to the
waist,
In every part exceeding brave [1] and rich.
TAM. Then shall we fight courageously
with them,
Or look [2] you I should play the orator?
TECH. No; cowards and faint-hearted run-
aways 130
Look for orations when the foe is near.
Our swords shall play the orators for us.
USUM. Come! Let us meet them at the
mountain foot,
And with a sudden and an hot alarum
Drive all their horses headlong down the
hill.
TECH. Come, let us march!
TAM. Stay, Techelles! Ask a parley first.

The Soldiers enter.

Open the mails,[3] yet guard the treasure
sure;
Lay out our golden wedges to the
view
That their reflections may amaze the
Persians; 140
And look we friendly on them when they
come.
But, if they offer word or violence,
We'll fight five hundred men-at-arms to
one
Before we part with our possession.
And gainst the general we will lift our
swords,
And either lanch [4] his greedy, thirsting
throat,
Or take him prisoner, and his chain shall
serve
For manacles till he be ransomed home.
TECH. I hear them come. Shall we en-
counter them?
TAM. Keep all your standings and not stir
a foot; 150
Myself will bide the danger of the brunt.

Enter Theridamas with Others.

THER. Where is this Scythian Tambur-
laine?
TAM. Whom seek'st thou, Persian?—I am
Tamburlaine.

THER. Tamburlaine?—
[*Aside.*] A Scythian shepherd so em-
bellishéd
With nature's pride and richest furni-
ture!
His looks do menace heaven and dare the
gods;
His fiery eyes are fixed upon the earth,
As if he now devised some stratagem,
Or meant to pierce Avernus' darksome
vaults 160
To pull the triple-headed dog from hell.
TAM. [*Aside.*] Noble and mild this Persian
seems to be,
If outward habit judge [5] the inward man.
TECH. [*Aside.*] His deep affections [6] make
him passionate.
TAM. [*Aside.*] With what a majesty he
rears his looks!—
In thee, thou valiant man of Persia,
I see the folly of thy emperor.
Art thou but captain of a thousand horse,
That, by characters graven in thy brows
And by thy martial face and stout as-
pect, 170
Deserv'st to have the leading of an host?
Forsake thy king, and do but join with
me,
And we will triumph over all the world.
I hold the Fates bound fast in iron chains,
And with my hand turn Fortune's
wheel about;
And sooner shall the sun fall from his
sphere
Than Tamburlaine be slain or overcome.
Draw forth thy sword, thou mighty
man-at-arms,
Intending but to race [7] my charméd skin,
And Jove himself will stretch his hand
from heaven 180
To ward the blow and shield me safe
from harm.
See how he rains down heaps of gold in
showers,
As if he meant to give my soldiers pay!
And, as a sure and grounded argument
That I shall be the monarch of the East,
He sends this soldan's daughter, rich
and brave,
To be my queen and portly [8] emperess.
If thou wilt stay with me, renowméd
man,

[1] Fine.   [2] Expect, wish.   [3] Baggage.   [4] Lance, cut.
[5] Indicate.   [6] Feelings.   [7] Rase, scratch.   [8] Stately.

And lead thy thousand horse with my
conduct,
Besides thy share of this Egyptian
prize,   190
Those thousand horse shall sweat with
martial spoil
Of conquered kingdoms and of cities
sacked.
Both we will walk upon the lofty clifts; [1]
And Christian merchants [2] that with
Russian stems
Plow up huge furrows in the Caspian sea
Shall vail [3] to us as lords of all the lake.
Both we will reign as consuls of the earth,
And mighty kings shall be our senators.
Jove sometime maskéd in a shepherd's
weed;
And by those steps that he hath scaled
the heavens   200
May we become immortal like the gods!
Join with me now in this my mean
estate
(I call it mean because, being yet ob-
scure,
The nations far removed admire [4] me
not),
And, when my name and honor shall be
spread
As far as Boreas claps his brazen wings,
Or fair Boötes sends his cheerful light,
Then shalt thou be competitor [5] with
me,
And sit with Tamburlaine in all his maj-
esty.
THER. Not Hermes, prolocutor to the
gods,   210
Could use persuasions more pathetical.[6]
TAM. Nor are Apollo's oracles more true
Than thou shalt find my vaunts sub-
stantial.
TECH. We are his friends, and, if the Per-
sian king
Should offer present dukedoms to our
state,
We think it loss to make exchange for
that
We are assured of by our friend's suc-
cess.
USUM. And kingdoms at the least we all
expect,
Besides the honor in assured conquests,

Where kings shall crouch unto our con-
quering swords,   220
And hosts of soldiers stand amazed at
us,
When with their fearful tongues they
shall confess
These are the men that all the world
admires.
THER. What strong enchantments tice [7]
my yielding soul!
Are these resolvéd noble Scythians?
But shall I prove a traitor to my king?
TAM. No, but the trusty friend of Tam-
burlaine.
THER. Won with thy words, and con-
quered with thy looks,
I yield myself, my men, and horse to
thee,
To be partaker of thy good or ill   230
As long as life maintains Theridamas.
TAM. Theridamas, my friend, take here
my hand,
Which is as much as if I swore by heaven
And called the gods to witness of my
vow!
Thus shall my heart be still combined
with thine
Until our bodies turn to elements,
And both our souls aspire [8] celestial
thrones.
Techelles and Casane, welcome him!
TECH. Welcome, renowméd Persian, to us
all!
USUM. Long may Theridamas remain
with us!   240
TAM. These are my friends, in whom I
more rejoice
Than doth the King of Persia in his
crown,
And by the love of Pylades and Orestes,
Whose statues [9] we adore in Scythia,
Thyself and them shall never part from
me
Before I crown you kings in Asia.
Make much of them, gentle Theridamas,
And they will never leave thee till the
death.
THER. Nor thee nor them, thrice noble
Tamburlaine,
Shall want my heart to be with glad-
ness pierced   250
To do you honor and security.

---

[1] Cliffs.   [4] Wonder at.
[2] Merchantmen.   [5] Partner.
[3] Lower their topsails in salute.   [6] Moving.
[7] Entice.   [9] Probably *statues*
[8] Aspire to.

TAM. A thousand thanks, worthy Ther-
  idamas.—
  And now, fair madam and my noble
    lords,
  If you will willingly remain with me,
  You shall have honors as your merits
    be;
  Or else you shall be forced with slavery.
AGYD. We yield unto thee, happy Tambur-
  laine.
TAM. For you then, madam, I am out
  of doubt.
ZEN. I must be pleased perforce. Wretched
  Zenocrate!   *Exeunt.*

ACTUS II. SCENA i.

[*Cosroe's camp.*]

*Cosroe, Menaphon, Ortygius, Ceneus, with
                        other Soldiers.*

COS. Thus far are we towards Therida-
    mas
  And valiant Tamburlaine, the man of
    fame,
  The man that in the forehead of his
    fortune
  Bears figures of renown and miracle.
  But tell me, that hast seen him, Mena-
    phon,
  What stature wields [1] he, and what
    personage?
MENA. Of stature tall, and straightly fash-
    ionéd,
  Like his desire, lift [2] upwards and di-
    vine;
  So large of limbs, his joints so strongly
    knit,
  Such breadth of shoulders as might
    mainly bear   10
  Old Atlas' burthen. Twixt his manly
    pitch, [3]
  A pearl [4] more worth than all the world
    is placed,
  Wherein by curious sovereignty of art
  Are fixed his piercing instruments of
    sight,
  Whose fiery circles bear encompasséd
  A heaven of heavenly bodies in their
    spheres,
  That guides his steps and actions to
    the throne,

[1] Possesses.   [2] Lifted.
[3] Height (falconry); here, shoulders.
[4] *I.e.,* the head.

Where honor sits invested royally.
Pale of complexion, wrought in him with
    passion,
Thirsting with sovereignty, with love of
    arms,   20
His lofty brows, in folds, do figure [5]
    death
And, in their smoothness, amity and
    life.
About them hangs a knot of amber hair,
Wrappéd in curls, as fierce Achilles' was,
On which the breath of heaven delights
    to play,
Making it dance with wanton majesty.
His arms and fingers, long and sinewy, [6]
Betokening valor and excess of strength—
In every part proportioned like the
    man—
Should make the world subdued to Tam-
    burlaine.   30
COS. Well hast thou portrayed in thy
    terms of life
The face and personage of a wondrous
    man.
Nature doth strive with fortune and
    his stars
To make him famous in accomplished
    worth;
And well his merits show him to be
    made
His fortune's master and the king of
    men,
That could persuade at such a sudden
    pinch,
With reasons of his valor and his life,
A thousand sworn and overmatching
    foes.
Then, when our powers in points of
    swords are joined   40
And closed in compass of the killing
    bullet,
Though strait the passage and the port [7]
    be made
That leads to palace of my brother's life,
Proud is his fortune if we pierce it not.
And, when the princely Persian diadem
Shall overweigh his weary, witless head,
And fall like mellowed fruit with shakes
    of death,
In fair Persia, noble Tamburlaine
Shall be my regent and remain as king.

[5] Foreshadow.
[6] Suggested by Dyce; original has *snowy.*
[7] Portal, gate.

ORTY. In happy hour we have set the crown 50
Upon your kingly head, that seeks our honor
In joining with the man ordained by heaven
To further every action to the best.
CEN. He that with shepherds and a little spoil
Durst, in disdain of wrong and tyranny,
Defend his freedom gainst a monarchy,
What will he do supported by a king,
Leading a troop of gentlemen and lords,
And stuffed with treasure for his highest thoughts!
Cos. And such shall wait on worthy Tamburlaine. 60
Our army will be forty thousand strong,
When Tamburlaine and brave Theridamas
Have met us by the river Araris,
And all conjoined to meet the witless king
That now is marching near to Parthia.
And with unwilling soldiers faintly armed,
To seek revenge on me and Tamburlaine—
To whom, sweet Menaphon, direct me straight.
MEN. I will, my lord. *Exeunt.*

ACTUS II. SCENA ii.

[*Mycetes' camp in the Caucasus.*]

Mycetes, Meander, with other Lords and Soldiers.

MYC. Come, my Meander, let us to this gear.[1]
I tell you true, my heart is swoln with wrath
On this same thievish villain, Tamburlaine,
And of [2] that false Cosroe, my traitorous brother.
Would it not grieve a king to be so abused
And have a thousand horsemen ta'en away,

And, which is worst, to have his diadem
Sought for by such scald [3] knaves as love him not?
I think it would. Well then, by heavens I swear,
Aurora shall not peep out of her doors, 10
But I will have Cosroe by the head,
And kill proud Tamburlaine with point of sword.
Tell you the rest, Meander; I have said.
MEAN. Then having passed Armenian deserts now,
And pitched [4] our tents under the Georgian hills,
Whose tops are covered with Tartarian thieves,
That lie in ambush, waiting for a prey,
What should we do but bid them battle straight,
And rid the world of those detested troops,
Lest, if we let them linger here awhile, 20
They gather strength by power of fresh supplies?
This country swarms with vile, outrageous men
That live by rapine and by lawless spoil,
Fit soldiers for the wicked Tamburlaine;
And he that could with gifts and promises
Inveigle him that led a thousand horse,
And make him false [5] his faith unto his king,
Will quickly win such as are like himself.
Therefore cheer up your minds; prepare to fight.
He that can take or slaughter Tamburlaine 30
Shall rule the province of Albania.
Who brings that traitor's head, Theridamas',
Shall have a government in Media,
Beside the spoil of him and all his train.
But, if Cosroe—as our spials [6] say,
And as we know—remains with Tamburlaine,
His highness' pleasure is that he should live,
And be reclaimed with princely lenity.

---

[1] Business. [2] On.
[3] Scabby, base. [4] Original has *pitch.* [5] Betray. [6] Spies.

[*Enter a Spy.*]

A Spy. An hundred horsemen of my company,
    Scouting abroad upon these champion [1]
      plains,   40
    Have viewed the army of the Scythians,
    Which make reports it far exceeds the
      king's.
Mean. Suppose they be in number infinite,
    Yet, being void of martial discipline,
    All running headlong after greedy spoils,
    And more regarding gain than victory,
    Like to the cruel brothers of the earth,
    Sprung of the teeth of dragons venomous,
    Their careless swords shall lanch their
      fellows' throats,
    And make us triumph in their over-
      throw.   50
Myc. Was there such brethren, sweet
    Meander, say,
    That sprung of teeth of dragons venomous?
Mean. So poets say, my lord.
Myc. And 'tis a pretty toy to be a poet.
    Well, well, Meander, thou art deeply
      read,
    And, having thee, I have a jewel sure.
    Go on, my lord, and give your charge,
      I say;
    Thy wit will make us conquerors today.
Mean. Then, noble soldiers, to entrap
    these thieves,
    That live confounded in disordered
      troops,   60
    If wealth or riches may prevail with
      them,
    We have our camels laden all with gold,
    Which you that be but common soldiers
    Shall fling in every corner of the field;
    And, while the baseborn Tartars take
      it up,
    You, fighting more for honor than for
      gold,
    Shall massacre those greedy-minded
      slaves,
    And, when their scattered army is sub-
      dued,
    And you march on their slaughtered
      carcasses,
    Share equally the gold that bought their
      lives,   70

[1] Champaign, level.

And live like gentlemen in Persia.
    Strike up the drum and march cou-
      rageously!
    Fortune herself doth sit upon our crests.
Myc. He tells you true, my masters; so
    he does.
    Drums, why sound ye not, when Me-
      and[er] speaks?   *Exeunt.*

Actus II. Scena iii.

[*Tamburlaine's camp.*]

*Cosroe, Tamburlaine, Theridamas, Techelles,
    Usumcasane, Ortygius, with Others.*

Cos. Now, worthy Tamburlaine, have I
    reposed
    In thy approvéd fortunes all my hope.
    What think'st thou, man, shall come of
      our attempts?
    For, even as from assuréd oracle,
    I take thy doom [2] for satisfaction.
Tam. And so mistake you not a whit, my
    lord;
    For fates and oracles [of] heaven have
      sworn
    To royalize the deeds of Tamburlaine,
    And make them blessed that share in
      his attempts.
    And doubt you not but, if you favor
      me,   10
    And let my fortunes and my valor sway
    To some direction in your martial deeds,
    The world will strive with hosts of men-
      at-arms,
    To swarm unto the ensign I support.
    The host of Xerxes, which by fame is
      said
    To drink the mighty Parthian Araris,
    Was but a handful to that we will have.
    Our quivering lances, shaking in the
      air,
    And bullets, like Jove's dreadful thun-
      derbolts,
    Enrolled in flames and fiery smoldering
      mists,   20
    Shall threat the gods more than Cy-
      clopian wars;
    And, with our sun-bright armor as we
      march,
    We'll chase the stars from heaven and
      dim their eyes
    That stand and muse at our admiréd
      arms.

[2] Opinion.

THER. You see, my lord, what working
  words he hath;
But, when you see his actions stop his
  speech,
Your speech will stay [1] or so extol his
  worth
As I shall be commended and excused
For turning my poor charge to his di-
  rection.
And these his two renowmèd friends,
  my lord,   30
Would make one thrust and strive to be
  retained
In such a great degree of amity.
TECH. With duty and with amity we
  yield
Our utmost service to the fair Cosroe.
COS. Which I esteem as portion of my
  crown.
Usumcasane and Techelles both,
When she [2] that rules in Rhamnis'
  golden gates,
And makes a passage for all prosperous
  arms,
Shall make me solely Emperor of Asia,
Then shall your meeds and valors be
  advanced   40
To rooms of honor and nobility.
TAM. Then haste, Cosroe, to be king
  alone,
That I with these, my friends, and all
  my men
May triumph in our long-expected
  fate.
The king, your brother, is now hard
  at hand;
Meet with the fool, and rid your royal
  shoulders
Of such a burthen as outweighs the
  sands
And all the craggy rocks of Caspia.

[*Enter a Messenger.*]

MESS. My lord, we have discovered the
  enemy
Ready to charge you with a mighty
  army.   50
COS. Come, Tamburlaine! Now whet thy
  wingèd sword,
And lift thy lofty arm into the clouds

That it may reach the King of Persia's
  crown,
And set it safe on my victorious head.
TAM. See where it is, the keenest cuttle-
  ax [3]
That e'er made passage thorough Per-
  sian arms.
These are the wings shall make it fly
  as swift
As doth the lightning or the breath of
  heaven,
And kill as sure as it swiftly flies.   59
COS. Thy words assure me of kind success.
Go, valiant soldier, go before and charge
The fainting army of that foolish king.
TAM. Usumcasane and Techelles, come!
We are enough to scare the enemy,
And more than needs to make an em-
  peror.   [*Exeunt.*]

[ACTUS II. SCENA iv.

Part of the battlefield.]

*To the battle, and Mycetes comes out alone
  with his crown in his hand, offering
  to hide it.*

MYC. Accursed be he that first invented
  war.
They knew not, ah, they knew not,
  simple men,
How those [4] were hit by pelting cannon
  shot
Stand staggering like a quivering aspen
  leaf
Fearing the force of Boreas' boist'rous
  blasts.
In what a lamentable case were I
If nature had not given me wisdom's
  lore!
For kings are clouts [5] that every man
  shoots at,
Our crown the pin [6] that thousands seek
  to cleave.
Therefore in policy I think it good   10
To hide it close—a goodly stratagem,
And far from any man that is a fool.
So shall I not be known; or, if I be,
They cannot take away my crown from
  me.
Here will I hide it in this simple hole.

---

[1] *I.e.*, you will be speechless.
[2] "Nemesis, who had a temple at Rhamnus"
(Bullen).
[3] Curtle-ax, cutlass.
[4] Those who.
[5] Center of an archer's target.
[6] Peg fastening the clout.

Enter Tamburlaine.

TAM. What, fearful coward, straggling from the camp
When kings themselves are present in the field?

MYC. Thou liest!

TAM.　　　　　Base villain, dar'st thou give the lie?

MYC. Away; I am the king! Go; touch me not!
Thou break'st the law of arms, unless thou kneel　　20
And cry me, "Mercy, noble king!"

TAM. Are you the witty King of Persia?

MYC. Ay, marry am I. Have you any suit to me?

TAM. I would entreat you to speak but three wise words.

MYC. So I can when I see my time.

TAM. Is this your crown?

MYC. Ay, didst thou ever see a fairer?

TAM. You will not sell it, will ye?　　30

MYC. Such another word and I will have thee executed. Come, give it me!

TAM. No; I took it prisoner.

MYC. You lie; I gave it you.

TAM. Then 'tis mine.

MYC. No; I mean I let you keep it.

TAM. Well, I mean you shall have it again.
Here, take it for awhile. I lend it thee
Till I may see thee hemmed with arméd men.
Then shalt thou see me pull it from thy head.　　40
Thou art no match for mighty Tamburlaine.　　　　*[Exit.]*

MYC. O gods! Is this Tamburlaine the thief?
I marvel much he stole it not away.

Sound trumpets to the battle, and he runs in.

[ACTUS II. SCENA V.

Tamburlaine's camp.]

Cosroe, Tamburlaine, Theridamas, Mena-
phon, Meander, Ortygius, Techelles,
Usumcasane, with Others.

TAM. Hold thee, Cosroe! Wear two imperial crowns!
Think thee invested now as royally,
Even by the mighty hand of Tamburlaine,

As if as many kings as could encompass thee
With greatest pomp had crowned thee emperor.

COS. So do I, thrice renowméd man-at-arms,
And none shall keep the crown but Tamburlaine.
Thee do I make my regent of Persia,
And general lieftenant [1] of my armies.
Meander, you that were our brother's guide　　10
And chiefest counselor in all his acts,
Since he is yielded to the stroke of war,
On your submission we with thanks excuse,
And give you equal place in our affairs.

MEAN. Most happy emperor, in humblest terms
I vow my service to your majesty,
With utmost virtue of my faith and duty.

COS. Thanks, good Meander. Then, Cosroe, reign
And govern Persia in her former pomp!
Now send ambassage to thy neighbor kings,　　20
And let them know the Persian king is changed
From one that knew not what a king should do,
To one that can command what longs [2] thereto.
And now we will to fair Persepolis,
With twenty thousand expert soldiers.
The lords and captains of my brother's camp
With little slaughter take Meander's course,
And gladly yield them to my gracious rule.
Ortygius and Menaphon, my trusty friends,
Now will I gratify your former good,　　30
And grace your calling with a greater sway.

ORTY. And, as we ever aimed [3] at your behoof, [4]
And sought your state all honor it deserved,
So will we with our powers and our lives
Endeavor to preserve and prosper it.

---

[1] Lieutenant.　　　　　　　　　[2] Belongs.
[3] From 1605 edn. Original reads *and*.
[4] Advantage.

Cos. I will not thank thee, sweet Ortygius;
Better replies shall prove my purposes.
And now, Lord Tamburlaine, my broth-
er's camp
I leave to thee and to Theridamas,
To follow me to fair Persepolis.   40
Then will we march to all those Indian
mines
My witless brother to the Christians lost,
And ransom[1] them with fame and
usury.[2]
And, till thou overtake me, Tamburlaine,
Staying to order all the scattered troops,
Farewell, lord regent and his happy
friends!
I long to sit upon my brother's throne.
MENA. Your majesty shall shortly have
your wish,
And ride in triumph through Persepolis.
*Exeunt. Manent Tamb[urlaine], Tech[elles],
Ther[idamas], Usum[casane].*
TAM. "And ride in triumph through Per-
sepolis"!   50
Is it not brave to be a king, Techelles?
Usumcasane and Theridamas,
Is it not passing brave to be a king,
"And ride in triumph through Persep-
olis"?
TECH. O, my lord, 'tis sweet and full of
pomp.
USUM. To be a king is half to be a god.
THER. A god is not so glorious as a king.
I think the pleasure they enjoy in heaven
Cannot compare with kingly joys in
earth.
To wear a crown enchased with pearl and
gold,   60
Whose virtues carry with it life and
death;
To ask and have, command and be
obeyed;
When looks breed love, with looks to gain
the prize—
Such power attractive shines in princes'
eyes!
TAM. Why, say, Theridamas, wilt thou be
a king?
THER. Nay, though I praise it, I can live
without it.
TAM. What says my other friends? Will
you be kings?
TECH. Ay, if I could, with all my heart,
my lord.

TAM. Why, that's well said, Techelles.
So would I,
And so would you, my masters, would
you not?   70
USUM. What then, my lord?
TAM. Why then, Casane, shall we wish for
aught
The world affords in greatest novelty,
And rest attemptless, faint, and desti-
tute?
Methinks we should not. I am strongly
moved
That, if I should desire the Persian
crown,
I could attain it with a wondrous ease.
And would not all our soldiers soon con-
sent,
If we should aim at such a dignity?
THER. I know they would with our per-
suasions.   80
TAM. Why then, Theridamas, I'll first
assay
To get the Persian kingdom to myself;
Then thou for Parthia; they for Scythia
and Media;
And, if I prosper, all shall be as sure
As if the Turk, the pope, Afric, and
Greece,
Came creeping to us with their crowns
apace.
TECH. Then shall we send to this triumph-
ing king,
And bid him battle for his novel crown?
USUM. Nay, quickly then, before his room
be hot.
TAM. 'Twill prove a pretty jest, in faith,
my friends.   90
THER. A jest to charge on twenty thou-
sand men?
I judge the purchase[3] more important
far.
TAM. Judge by thyself, Theridamas, not
me,
For presently Techelles here shall haste
To bid him battle ere he pass too far,
And lose more labor than the gain will
quite.[4]
Then shalt thou see the Scythian Tam-
burlaine
Make but a jest to win the Persian
crown.
Techelles, take a thousand horse with
thee,

---

[1] Deliver.   [2] Profit.   [3] Undertaking.   [4] Requite.

And bid him turn his back [1] to war with
    us,   100
That only made him king to make us
    sport.
We will not steal upon him cowardly,
But give him warning and more warriors.
Haste thee, Techelles; we will follow
    thee.—
What saith Theridamas?
THER.   Go on for me. *Exeunt.*

ACTUS II. SCENA vi.

[*Cosroe's camp.*]

*Cosroe, Meander, Ortygius, Menaphon, with
                                other Soldiers.*

Cos. What means this devilish shepherd to
    aspire
With such a giantly presumption
To cast up hills against the face of
    heaven,
And dare the force of angry Jupiter?
But, as he thrust them underneath the
    hills,
And pressed out fire from their burning
    jaws,
So will I send this monstrous slave to hell,
Where flames shall ever feed upon his
    soul.
MEAN. Some powers divine, or else in-
    fernal, mixed
Their angry seeds at his conception,   10
For he was never sprung of human race,
Since with the spirit of his fearful pride
He dare so doubtlessly [2] resolve of [3] rule,
And by profession [4] be ambitious.
ORTY. What god, or fiend, or spirit of the
    earth,
Or monster turnéd to a manly shape,
Or of what mold or mettle he be made,
What star or state soever govern him,
Let us put on our meet, encount'ring [5]
    minds
And, in detesting such a devilish thief,   20
In love of honor and defense of right,
Be armed against the hate of such a foe,
Whether from earth, or hell, or heaven he
    grow.
Cos. Nobly resolved, my good Ortygius!
And, since we all have sucked one whole-
    some air,

And with the same proportion of ele-
    ments
Resolve, I hope we are resembled,[6]
Vowing our loves to equal death and life.
Let's cheer our soldiers to encounter him,
That grievous image of ingratitude,   30
That fiery thirster after sovereignty,
And burn him in the fury of that flame
That none can quench [7] but blood and
    empery.
Resolve, my lords and loving soldiers,
    now
To save your king and country from
    decay.
Then strike up, drum; and all the stars
    that make
The loathsome circle of my dated life,
Direct my weapon to his barbarous heart,
That thus opposeth him against the gods,
And scorns the powers that govern
    Persia!   [*Exeunt.*] 40

[ACTUS II. SCENA vii.

A plain.]

*Enter to the battle, and after the battle enter
    Cosroe, wounded, Theridamas, Tam-
    burlaine, Techelles, Usumcasane, with
                                    Others.*

Cos. Barbarous and bloody Tamburlaine,
Thus to deprive me of my crown and life!
Treacherous and false Theridamas,
Even at the morning of my happy state,
Scarce being seated in my royal throne,
To work my downfall and untimely end!
An uncouth [8] pain torments my grievéd
    soul,
And death arrests the organ of my voice,
Who, ent'ring at the breach thy sword
    hath made,
Sacks every vein and artier [9] of my
    heart.   10
Bloody and insatiate Tamburlaine!
TAM. The thirst of reign and sweetness of a
    crown
That caused the eldest son of heavenly
    Ops
To thrust his doting father from his
    chair,
And place himself in the emperial [10]
    heaven,

---

[1] *I.e.*, turn himself, return.   [4] Open avowal.
[2] Fearlessly.   [5] Warlike.
[3] Upon.

[6] Alike.   [8] Strange.
[7] Quench.   [9] Artery.
[10] Imperial or empyreal?

Moved me to manage arms against thy
state.
What better president [1] than mighty
Jove?
Nature, that framed us of four elements,
Warring within our breasts for regiment,
Doth teach us all to have aspiring
minds.   20
Our souls, whose faculties can compre-
hend
The wondrous architecture of the world,
And measure every wand'ring planet's
course,
Still climbing after knowledge infinite,
And always moving as the restless
spheres,
Wills us to wear ourselves and never rest
Until we reach the ripest fruit of all,
That perfect bliss and sole felicity,
The sweet fruition of an earthly crown.

THER. And that made me to join with
Tamburlaine,   30
For he is gross and like the massy earth,
That moves not upwards, nor by princely
deeds
Doth mean to soar above the highest sort.

TECH. And that made us the friends of
Tamburlaine,
To lift our swords against the Persian
king.

USUM. For, as when Jove did thrust old
Saturn down,
Neptune and Dis gained each of them a
crown,
So do we hope to reign in Asia,
If Tamburlaine be placed in Persia.

COS. The strangest men that ever nature
made!   40
I know not how to take their tyrannies.
My bloodless body waxeth chill and cold,
And with my blood my life slides through
my wound.
My soul begins to take her flight to hell,
And summons all my senses to depart.
The heat and moisture, which did feed
each other,
For want of nourishment to feed them
both,
Is dry and cold; and now doth ghastly
Death,
With greedy talents [2] gripe my bleeding
heart,
And like a harpy tires [3] on my life.   50

[1] Precedent.   [2] Talons.   [3] Preys.

Theridamas and Tamburlaine, I die!
And fearful vengeance light upon you
both!
[Dies.] He [4] takes the crown and puts it on.

TAM. Not all the curses which the Furies
breathe
Shall make me leave so rich a prize as
this.
Theridamas, Techelles, and the rest,
Who think you now is King of Persia?

ALL. Tamburlaine! Tamburlaine

TAM. Though Mars himself, the angry god
of arms,
And all the earthly potentates conspire
To dispossess me of this diadem,   60
Yet will I wear it in despite of them,
As great commander of this eastern
world,
If you but say that Tamburlaine shall
reign.

ALL. Long live Tamburlaine and reign in
Asia!

TAM. So now it is more surer on my head
Than if the gods had held a parliament,
And all pronounced me King of Persia.
[Exeunt.]

FINIS ACTUS SECUNDI.

ACTUS III. SCENA i.

[Before Constantinople.]

Bajazeth, the Kings of Fez, Morocco, and
Argier, with Others, in great pomp.

BAJ. Great kings of Barbary and my
portly bassoes,
We hear the Tartars and the eastern
thieves,
Under the conduct of one Tamburlaine,
Presume a bickering [5] with your emperor,
And thinks to rouse us from our dreadful
siege
Of the famous Grecian Constantinople.
You know our army is invincible;
As many circumciséd Turks we have,
And warlike bands of Christians renied, [6]
As hath the ocean or the Terrene sea [7] [10
Small drops of water when the moon be-
gins
To join in one her semicircled horns.
Yet would we not be braved with foreign
power,

[4] I.e., Tamburlaine.   [6] Apostates.
[5] Battle.   [7] The Mediterranean.

Nor raise our siege before the Grecians
    yield,
Or breathless lie before the city walls.
Fez. Renownèd emperor and mighty
    general,
What if you sent the bassoes of your
    guard
To charge him to remain in Asia,
Or else to threaten death and deadly arms
As from the mouth of mighty Baja-
    zeth?   20
Baj. Hie thee, my basso, fast to Persia.
Tell him thy lord, the Turkish emperor,
Dread lord of Afric, Europe, and Asia,
Great king and conqueror of Grecia,
The ocean, Terrene, and the coal-black
    sea,[1]
The high and highest monarch of the
    world,
Wills and commands—for say not I
    entreat—
Not once to set his foot in Africa,
Or spread his colors in Grecia,
Lest he incur the fury of my wrath.   30
Tell him I am content to take a truce,
Because I hear he bears a valiant mind.
But if, presuming on his silly power,
He be so mad to manage arms with me,
Then stay thou with him. Say I bid thee
    so.
And if, before the sun have measured
    heaven
With triple circuit, thou regreet us not,
We mean to take his morning's next arise
For messenger he will not be reclaimed,
And mean to fetch thee in despite of
    him.   40
Basso. Most great and puissant monarch
    of the earth,
Your basso will accomplish your behest,
And show your pleasure to the Persian,
As fits the legate of the stately Turk.
                          Exit Bass[o].
Arg. They say he is the King of Persia;
But, if he dare attempt to stir your siege,
'Twere requisite he should be ten times
    more,
For all flesh quakes at your magnificence.
Baj. True, Argier, and tremble at my
    looks.
Mor. The spring is hindered by your
    smothering host,   50
For neither rain can fall upon the earth,

Nor sun reflex [2] his virtuous beams
    thereon,
The ground is mantled with such multi-
    tudes.
Baj. All this is true as holy Mahomet;
And all the trees are blasted with our
    breaths.
Fez. What thinks your greatness best to
    be achieved
In pursuit of the city's overthrow?
Baj. I will the captive pioners [3] of Argier
Cut off the water that by leaden pipes
Runs to the city from the mountain
    Carnon.   60
Two thousand horse shall forage up and
    down,
That no relief or succor come by land;
And all the sea my galleys countermand.[4]
Then shall our footmen lie within the
    trench,
And with their cannons, mouthed like
    Orcus' gulf,
Batter the walls, and we will enter in.
And thus the Grecians shall be con-
    queréd.   *Exeunt.*

Actus III. Scena ii.

[Tamburlaine's camp.]

Agydas, Zenocrate, Anippe, with Others.

[Agyd.] Madam Zenocrate, may I presume
To know the cause of these unquiet fits,
That work such trouble to your wonted
    rest?
'Tis more than pity such a heavenly face
Should by heart's sorrow wax so wan and
    pale,
When your offensive rape [5] by Tambur-
    laine—
Which of your whole displeasures should
    be most—
Hath seemed to be digested long ago.
Zen. Although it be digested long ago,
As his exceeding favors have deserved, 10
And might content the Queen of Heaven,
    as well
As it hath changed my first conceived
    disdain,
Yet, since, a farther passion feeds my
    thoughts
With ceaseless and disconsolate conceits,

[1] The Black Sea.   [2] Throw.   [4] Control.
                              [3] Miners.   [5] Capture.

Which dyes my looks so lifeless as they
    are,
And might, if my extremes had full
    events,[1]
Make me the ghastly counterfeit of
    death.
AGYD. Eternal heaven sooner be dissolved,
And all that pierceth Phœbe's silver eye,
Before such hap fall to Zenocrate!   20
ZEN. Ah, life and soul, still hover in his
    breast
And leave my body senseless as the earth,
Or else unite you to his life and soul,
That I may live and die with Tambur-
    laine!

Enter [, unseen,] Tamburlaine with Techelles
*   and Others.*

AGYD. With Tamburlaine? Ah, fair Zeno-
    crate,
Let not a man so vile and barbarous,
That holds you from your father in
    despite,
And keeps you from the honors of a
    queen,
Being supposed his worthless concubine,
Be honored with your love but for neces-
    sity.   30
So, now [2] the mighty soldan hears of you,
Your highness needs not doubt but in
    short time
He will with Tamburlaine's destruction
Redeem you from this deadly servitude.
ZEN. Leave to wound me with these words,
And speak of Tamburlaine as he deserves.
The entertainment we have had of him
Is far from villainy [3] or servitude,
And might in noble minds be counted
    princely.
AGYD. How can you fancy one that looks
    so fierce,   40
Only disposed to martial stratagems,
Who, when he shall embrace you in his
    arms,
Will tell how many thousand men he
    slew,
And, when you look for amorous dis-
    course,
Will rattle forth his facts [4] of war and
    blood,
Too harsh a subject for your dainty
    ears?

ZEN. As looks the Sun through Nilus' flow-
    ing stream,
Or when the Morning holds him in her
    arms,
So looks my lordly love, fair Tambur-
    laine;
His talk much sweeter than the Muses'
    song   50
They sung for honor gainst Pierides,
Or when Minerva did with Neptune
    strive.
And higher would I rear my estimate
Than Juno, sister to the highest god,
If I were matched with mighty Tambur-
    laine.
AGYD. Yet be not so inconstant in your
    love,
But let the young Arabian live in hope
After your rescue to enjoy his choice.
You see, though first the King of Persia,
Being a shepherd, seemed to love you
    much,   60
Now in his majesty he leaves those
    looks,
Those words of favor, and those com-
    fortings,
And gives no more than common cour-
    tesies.
ZEN. Thence rise the tears that so distain [5]
    my cheeks,
Fearing his love through my unworthi-
    ness.—

Tamburlaine goes to her and takes her away
*   lovingly by the hand, looking wrathfully*
*   on Agydas, and says nothing. [Exeunt*
*   all but Agydas.]*

AGYD. Betrayed by fortune and suspicious
    love,
Threatened with frowning wrath and
    jealousy,
Surprised with fear of hideous revenge,
I stand aghast; but most astoniéd [6]   69
To see his choler shut in secret thoughts,
And wrapped in silence of his angry soul.
Upon his brows was portrayed ugly
    death,
And in his eyes the fury of his heart,
That shine as comets, menacing revenge,
And casts a pale complexion on his
    cheeks.
As, when the seaman sees the Hyades
Gather an army of Cimmerian clouds
(Auster and Aquilon with wingéd steeds,

---

[1] If my extremities were carried to their out-
come.   [2] Now that.   [3] Serfdom.   [4] Deeds.   [5] Stain.   [6] Astonished.

All sweating, tilt about the watery heav-
　ens,
With shivering spears enforcing thunder-
　claps,　　　　　　　　　　　　　　80
And from their shields strike flames of
　lightening),
All fearful folds his sails and sounds the
　main,
Lifting his prayers to the heavens for aid
Against the terror of the winds and
　waves,
So fares Agydas for the late-felt frowns
That sent a tempest to my daunted
　thoughts,
And makes my soul divine her over-
　throw.

*Enter [Usumcasane and] Techelles with a
　　　　　　　naked dagger.*

TECH. See you, Agydas, how the king
　salutes you.
He bids you prophesy what it imports.
　　　　　　　　　　　　　　Exit.[1]

AGYD. I prophesied before, and now I
　prove　　　　　　　　　　　　90
The killing frowns of jealousy and love.
He needed not with words confirm my
　fear,
For words are vain where working tools
　present
The naked action of my threatened end.
It says, Agydas, thou shalt surely die,
And of extremities elect the least;
More honor and less pain it may procure
To die by this resolvéd hand of thine
Than stay the torments he and heaven
　have sworn.
Then haste, Agydas, and prevent the
　plagues　　　　　　　　　　　100
Which thy prolongéd fates may draw
　on thee.
Go, wander free from fear of tyrant's
　rage,
Removéd from the torments and the
　hell
Wherewith he may excruciate thy soul;
And let Agydas by Agydas die,
And with this stab slumber eternally.
　　　　　　　　[Stabs himself.][2]
TECH. Usumcasane, see how right the man
Hath hit the meaning of my lord the
　king.

[1] He and Usumcasane stand aside.
[2] Supplied from 1605 edn.

USUM. Faith, and, Techelles, it was manly
　done.
And, since he was so wise and honor-
　able,　　　　　　　　　　　　110
Let us afford him now the bearing
　hence,
And crave his triple-worthy burial.
TECH. Agreed, Casane; we will honor him.
　　　　　[Exeunt, bearing out the body.]

ACTUS III. SCENA iii.

[The same.]

*Tamburlaine, Techelles, Usumcasane, Theri-
　damas, Basso, Zenocrate, [Anippe,] with
　　　　　　　　　　　　　　　Others.*

TAM. Basso, by this thy lord and master
　knows
I mean to meet him in Bithynia.
See how he comes! Tush, Turks are full
　of brags,
And menace more than they can well
　perform.
He meet me in the field, and fetch thee
　hence?
Alas, poor Turk! His fortune is too weak
T' encounter with the strength of Tam-
　burlaine.
View well my camp, and speak indiffer-
　ently.[3]
Do not my captains and my soldiers
　look
As if they meant to conquer Africa?　10
BASSO. Your men are valiant, but their
　number few,
And cannot terrify his mighty host.
My lord, the great commander of the
　world,
Besides fifteen contributory kings,
Hath now in arms ten thousand Janis-
　saries,
Mounted on lusty Mauritanian steeds,
Brought to the war by men of Tripoli;
Two hundred thousand footmen that
　have served
In two set battles fought in Grecia;
And for the expedition of this war,　20
If he think good, can from his garri-
　sons
Withdraw as many more to follow him.
TECH. The more he brings, the greater is
　the spoil,

[3] Impartially.

For, when they perish by our warlike
hands,
We mean to seat our footmen on their
steeds,
And rifle all those stately Janisars.

TAM. But will those kings accompany
your lord?

BASSO. Such as his highness please; but
some must stay
To rule the provinces he late subdued.

TAM. [*To his Captains.*] Then fight courageously; their crowns are yours!   30
This hand shall set them on your conquering heads,
That made me Emperor of Asia.

USUM. Let him bring millions infinite
of men,
Unpeopling Western Africa and Greece,
Yet we assure us of the victory.

THER. Even he that in a trice vanquished
two kings
More mighty than the Turkish emperor,
Shall rouse him out of Europe and pur-
sue
His scattered army till they yield or die.

TAM. Well said, Theridamas. Speak in
that mood;   40
For *will* and *shall* best fitteth Tambur-
laine,
Whose smiling stars gives him assuréd
hope
Of martial triumph ere he meet his foes.
I that am termed the scourge and wrath
of God,
The only fear and terror of the world,
Will first subdue the Turk, and then
enlarge
Those Christian captives, which you
keep as slaves,
Burdening their bodies with your heavy
chains,
And feeding them with thin and slender
fare,
That naked row about the Terrene sea, 50
And, when they chance to breathe and
rest a space,
Are punished with bastones[1] so griev-
ously
That they lie panting on the galley's
side,
And strive for life at every stroke they
give.
These are the cruel pirates of Argier,

That damnéd train, the scum of Africa,
Inhabited with straggling runagates,
That make quick havoc of the Christian
blood.
But, as I live, that town shall curse the
time
That Tamburlaine set foot in Africa.   60

*Enter Bajazeth with his Bassoes and con-
tributory Kings [; Zabina and Ebea].*

BAJ. Bassoes and Janissaries of my guard,
Attend upon the person of your lord,
The greatest potentate of Africa.

TAM. Techelles and the rest, prepare your
swords;
I mean t' encounter with that Bajazeth.

BAJ. Kings of Fez, Moroccus, and Argier,
He calls me Bajazeth, whom you call
lord!
Note the presumption of this Scythian
slave!
I tell thee, villain, those that lead my
horse
Have to their names titles of dignity,   70
And dar'st thou bluntly call me Baja-
zeth?

TAM. And know thou, Turk, that those
which lead my horse
Shall lead thee captive thorough Africa.
And dar'st thou bluntly call me Tamburlaine?

BAJ. By Mahomet my kinsman's sep-
ulcher
And by the holy Alcoran,[2] I swear
He shall be made a chaste and lustless
eunuch,
And in my sarell[3] tend my concubines;
And all his captains that thus stoutly
stand
Shall draw the chariot of my emperess, 80
Whom I have brought to see their over-
throw.

TAM. By this my sword that conquered
Persia,
Thy fall shall make me famous through
the world.
I will not tell thee how I'll handle thee,
But every common soldier of my camp
Shall smile to see thy miserable state.

FEZ. What means the mighty Turkish
emperor,
To talk with one so base as Tamburlaine?

[1] Cudgels.   [2] The Koran.   [3] Seraglio.

Mor. Ye Moors and valiant men of Bar-
    bary,
How can ye suffer these indignities? 90
Arg. Leave words, and let them feel your
    lances' points
Which glided through the bowels of
    the Greeks.
Baj. Well said, my stout contributory
    kings!
Your threefold army and my hugy host
Shall swallow up these baseborn Persians.
Tech. Puissant, renowmed, and mighty
    Tamburlaine,
Why stay we thus prolonging all their
    lives?
Ther. I long to see those crowns won by
    our swords,
That we may reign as kings of Africa.
Usum. What coward would not fight for
    such a prize? 100
Tam. Fight all courageously, and be you
    kings;
I speak it, and my words are oracles.
Baj. Zabina, mother of three braver boys
Than Hercules, that in his infancy
Did pash [1] the jaws of serpents ven-
    omous;
Whose hands are made to gripe a war-
    like lance,
Their shoulders broad for complete
    armor fit,
Their limbs more large and of a bigger
    size
Than all the brats ysprung [2] from Ty-
    phon's loins;
Who, when they come unto their fa-
    ther's age, 110
Will batter turrets with their manly
    fists—
Sit here upon this royal chair of state,
And on thy head wear my imperial
    crown
Until I bring this sturdy Tamburlaine
And all his captains bound in captive
    chains.
Zab. Such good success happen to Ba-
    jazeth!
Tam. Zenocrate, the loveliest maid alive,
Fairer than rocks of pearl and precious
    stone,
The only paragon of Tamburlaine,
Whose eyes are brighter than the lamps
    of heaven 120

[1] Dash to pieces.   [2] Old past participle.

And speech more pleasant than sweet
    harmony;
That with thy looks canst clear the
    darkened sky,
And calm the rage of thund'ring Jupi-
    ter,
Sit down by her, adornéd with my
    crown,
As if thou wert the empress of the world.
Stir not, Zenocrate, until thou see
Me march victoriously with all my men,
Triumphing over him and these his
    kings,
Which I will bring as vassals to thy feet;
Till then take thou my crown, vaunt
    of my worth, 130
And manage words with her, as we will
    arms.
Zen. And may my love, the King of
    Persia,
Return with victory and free from
    wound!
Baj. Now shalt thou feel the force of
    Turkish arms,
Which lately made all Europe quake
    for fear.
I have of Turks, Arabians, Moors, and
    Jews
Enough to cover all Bithynia.
Let thousands die; their slaughtered
    carcasses
Shall serve for walls and bulwarks to
    the rest;
And, as the heads of Hydra, so my
    power, 140
Subdued, shall stand as mighty as be-
    fore.
If they should yield their necks unto
    the sword,
Thy soldiers' arms could not endure to
    strike
So many blows as I have heads for
    thee.
Thou knowest not, foolish-hardy Tam-
    burlaine,
What 'tis to meet me in the open field,
That leave no ground for thee to march
    upon.
Tam. Our conquering swords shall mar-
    shal us the way
We used to march upon the slaughtered
    foe,
Trampling their bowels with our horses'
    hoofs—

Brave horses bred on the white Tar-
    tarian hills.
My camp is like to Julius Cæsar's host,
That never fought but had the victory;
Nor in Pharsalia was there such hot
    war
As these my followers willingly would
    have.
Legions of spirits fleeting [1] in the air
Direct our bullets and our weapons'
    points,
And make our strokes to wound the
    senseless lure, [2]
And, when she sees our bloody colors
    spread,   159
Then Victory begins to take her flight,
Resting herself upon my milk-white
    tent.—
But come, my lords, to weapons let us
    fall;
The field is ours, the Turk, his wife, and
    all.   *Exit with his Followers.*
BAJ. Come, kings and bassoes, let us glut
    our swords,
That thirst to drink the feeble Persians'
    blood.   *Exit with his Followers.*
ZAB. Base concubine, must thou be placed
    by me,
That am the empress of the mighty
    Turk?
ZEN. Disdainful Turkess and unreverend
    boss, [3]
Call'st thou me concubine, that am be-
    trothed
Unto the great and mighty Tambur-
    laine?   170
ZAB. To Tamburlaine, the great Tarta-
    rian thief!
ZEN. Thou wilt repent these lavish words
    of thine,
When thy great basso-master and thy-
    self
Must plead for mercy at his kingly feet,
And sue to me to be your advocates. [4]
ZAB. And sue to thee? I tell thee, shame-
    less girl,
Thou shalt be laundress to my waiting
    maid!—
How lik'st thou her, Ebea? Will she
    serve?

EBEA. Madam, she thinks perhaps she
    is too fine,
But I shall turn her into other weeds,   180
And make her dainty fingers fall to work.
ZEN. Hear'st thou, Anippe, how thy
    drudge doth talk?
And how my slave, her mistress, men-
    aceth?
Both for their sauciness shall be em-
    ployed
To dress the common soldiers' meat
    and drink,
For we will scorn they should come
    near ourselves.
ANIP. Yet sometimes let your highness
    send for them
To do the work my chambermaid dis-
    dains.
    They sound the battle within and stay. [5]
ZEN. Ye gods and powers that govern
    Persia,
And made my lordly love her worthy
    king,   190
Now strengthen him against the Turk-
    ish Bajazeth,
And let his foes, like flocks of fearful
    roes
Pursued by hunters, fly his angry looks,
That I may see him issue conqueror!
ZAB. Now, Mahomet, solicit God him-
    self,
And make him rain down murthering
    shot from heaven
To dash the Scythians' brains, and strike
    them dead,
That dare to manage arms with him
That offered jewels to thy sacred shrine,
When first he warred against the Chris-
    tians!   200
                    To the battle again.
ZEN. By this the Turks lie welt'ring in
    their blood,
And Tamburlaine is Lord of Africa.
ZAB. Thou art deceived. I heard the trum-
    pets sound
As when my emperor overthrew the
    Greeks,
And led them captive into Africa.
Straight will I use thee as thy pride de-
    serves.
Prepare thyself to live and die my slave!
ZEN. If Mahomet should come from
    heaven and swear

[1] Floating.
[2] Dyce suggests: "And make *your* strokes to
wound the senseless *air.*"
[3] Fat woman.   [4] Wagner suggests *advocatess.*
[5] Cease, pause.

My royal lord is slain or conqueréd,
Yet should he not persuade me other-
wise   210
But that he lives and will be conqueror.
Bajazeth flies and he [1] *pursues him. The*
battle short, and they enter. Bajazeth is
                                overcome.
TAM. Now, king of bassoes, who is con-
queror?
BAJ. Thou, by the fortune of this damnéd
soil.
TAM. Where are your stout contributory
kings?

Enter Techelles, Theridamas, Usumcasane.

TECH. We have their crowns; their bodies
strow the field.
TAM. Each man a crown? Why, kingly
fought, i' faith!
Deliver them into my treasury.
ZEN. Now let me offer to my gracious
lord
His royal crown again, so highly won.
TAM. Nay, take the Turkish crown from
her, Zenocrate,   220
And crown me Emperor of Africa.
ZAB. No, Tamburlaine; though now thou
gat the best,
Thou shalt not yet be lord of Africa.
THER. Give her the crown, Turkess; you
were best.
He takes it from her and gives it Zenocrate.
ZAB. Injurious villains, thieves, runa-
gates,
How dare you thus abuse my majesty?
THER. Here, madam, you are empress;
she is none.
TAM. Not now, Theridamas; her time is
past.
The pillars that have bolstered up those
terms
Are fallen in clusters at my conquering
feet.   230
ZAB. Though he be prisoner, he may be
ransomed.
TAM. Not all the world shall ransom Ba-
jazeth.
BAJ. Ah, fair Zabina, we have lost the
field!
And never had the Turkish emperor
So great a foil by any foreign foe.
Now will the Christian miscreants be glad,

[1] *I.e.,* Tamburlaine.

Ringing with joy their superstitious
bells,
And making bonfires for my overthrow.
But, ere I die, those foul idolaters
Shall make me bonfires with their
filthy bones,   240
For, though the glory of this day be
lost,
Afric and Greece have garrisons enough
To make me sovereign of the earth
again.
TAM. Those walléd garrisons will I sub-
due,
And write myself great Lord of Africa.
So from the East unto the furthest
West
Shall Tamburlaine extend his puissant
arm.
The galleys and those pilling [2] brigan-
dines
That yearly sail to the Venetian gulf
And hover in the Straits for Christians'
wrack   250
Shall lie at anchor in the isle Asant,
Until the Persian fleet and men of war,
Sailing along the oriental sea,
Have fetched [3] about the Indian conti-
nent,
Even from Persepolis to Mexico,
And thence unto the straits of Jubal-
ter, [4]
Where they shall meet and join their
force in one,
Keeping in awe the Bay of Portingale, [5]
And all the ocean by the British shore;
And by this means I'll win the world
at last.   260
BAJ. Yet set a ransom on me, Tambur-
laine.
TAM. What, think'st thou Tamburlaine
esteems thy gold?
I'll make the kings of India, ere I die,
Offer their mines to sue for peace to me,
And dig for treasure to appease my
wrath.
Come, bind them both, and one lead
in the Turk;
The Turkess let my love's maid lead
away.   *They bind them.*
BAJ. Ah, villains, dare ye touch my sacred
arms?
O Mahomet!—O sleepy Mahomet!

[2] Pillaging.   [3] Sailed.   [4] Gibraltar.
[5] Bay of Portugal, *i.e.,* Bay of Biscay.

ZAB. O cursèd Mahomet, that makest us
    thus   270
  The slaves to Scythians rude and bar-
    barous!
TAM. Come, bring them in, and for this
    happy conquest
  Triumph and solemnize a martial feast.
            Exeunt.

FINIS ACTUS TERTII.

ACTUS IV. SCENA i.

[The Egyptian court.]

Soldan of Egypt, with three or four Lords,
   Capolin [,*and a Messenger*].

SOLD. Awake, ye men of Memphis! Hear
    the clang
  Of Scythian trumpets! Hear the basi-
    lisks [1]
  That, roaring, shake Damascus' turrets
    down!
  The rogue of Volga holds Zenocrate,
  The soldan's daughter, for his concubine,
  And with a troop of thieves and vaga-
    bonds
  Hath spread his colors to our high dis-
    grace,
  While you, faint-hearted, base Egyp-
    tians,
  Lie slumbering on the flowery banks of
    Nile,
  As crocodiles that unaffrighted rest,   10
  While thund'ring cannons rattle on their
    skins.
MESS. Nay, mighty soldan, did your great-
    ness see
  The frowning looks of fiery Tamburlaine,
  That with his terror and imperious eyes
  Commands the hearts of his associates,
  It might amaze your royal majesty.
SOLD. Villain, I tell thee, were that Tam-
    burlaine
  As monstrous as Gorgon, prince of hell,
  The soldan would not start a foot from
    him.
  But speak, what power hath he?
MESS.   Mighty lord,   20
  Three hundred thousand men in armor
    clad,
  Upon their prancing steeds disdainfully
  With wanton paces trampling on the
    ground;

[1] Cannon.

Five hundred thousand footmen threat'-
    ning shot,
  Shaking their swords, their spears, and
    iron bills,
  Environing their standard round, that
    stood
  As bristle-pointed as a thorny wood.
  Their warlike engines and munition
  Exceed the forces of their martial men.
SOLD. Nay, could their numbers counter-
    vail [2] the stars,   30
  Or ever-drizzling drops of April showers,
  Or withered leaves that autumn shaketh
    down,
  Yet would the soldan by his conquering
    power
  So scatter and consume them in his rage
  That not a man should live to rue their
    fall.
CAP. So might your highness, had you
    time to sort [3]
  Your fighting men, and raise your royal
    host;
  But Tamburlaine, by expedition,
  Advantage takes of your unreadiness.
SOLD. Let him take all th' advantages he
    can.   40
  Were all the world conspired to fight for
    him,
  Nay, were he devil, as he is no man,
  Yet in revenge of fair Zenocrate,
  Whom he detaineth in despite of us,
  This arm should send him down to Ere-
    bus
  To shroud his shame in darkness of the
    night.
MESS. Pleaseth your mightiness to under-
    stand,
  His resolution far exceedeth all.
  The first day when he pitcheth down his
    tents,
  White is their hue, and on his silver
    crest   50
  A snowy feather spangled white he
    bears,
  To signify the mildness of his mind,
  That, satiate with spoil, refuseth blood.
  But, when Aurora mounts the second
    time,
  As red as scarlet is his furniture.
  Then must his kindled wrath be
    quenched with blood,
  Not sparing any that can manage arms

[2] Equal.   [3] Select.

But, if these threats move not submis-
sion,
Black are his colors, black pavilion;
His spear, his shield, his horse, his
armor, plumes,   60
And jetty feathers menace death and
hell.
Without respect of sex, degree, or age,
He razeth all his foes with fire and sword.
ᵻOLD. Merciless villain, peasant, ignorant
Of lawful arms or martial discipline!
Pillage and murder are his usual trades;
The slave usurps the glorious name of
war.
See, Capolin, the fair Arabian king,
That hath been disappointed by this
slave
Of my fair daughter and his princely
love,   70
May have fresh warning to go war with
us,
And be revenged for her disparagement.
                                   [*Exeunt.*]

Actus IV. Scena ii.

[*Tamburlaine's camp outside Damascus.*]

*Tamburlaine, Techelles, Theridamas, Usum-
casane, Zenocrate, Anippe, two Moors
drawing Bajazeth in his cage, and his
Wife following him.*

TAM. Bring out my footstool!
                They take him out of the cage.
BAJ. Ye holy priests of heavenly Ma-
homet,
That, sacrificing, slice and cut your flesh,
Staining his altars with your purple
blood,
Make heaven to frown and every fixéd
star
To suck up poison from the moorish fens,
And pour it in this glorious ¹ tyrant's
throat!
TAM. The chiefest God, first mover of that
sphere,
Enchased with thousands ever-shining
lamps,
Will sooner burn the glorious frame of
heaven   10
Than it should so conspire my over-
throw.
But, villain, thou that wishest this to me,

¹ Vainglorious.

Fall prostrate on the low disdainful
earth,
And be the footstool of great Tambur-
laine,
That I may rise into my royal throne.
BAJ. First shalt thou rip my bowels with
thy sword,
And sacrifice my heart to death and hell,
Before I yield to such a slavery.
TAM. Base villain, vassal, slave to Tam-
burlaine,
Unworthy to embrace or touch the
ground   20
That bears the honor of my royal
weight,
Stoop, villain, stoop! Stoop! For so he
bids
That may command thee piecemeal to be
torn,
Or scattered like the lofty cedar trees
Struck with the voice of thund'ring
Jupiter.
BAJ. Then, as I look down to the damnéd
fiends,
Fiends, look on me! And thou, dread
god of hell,
With ebon scepter strike this hateful
earth,
And make it swallow both of us at once!
        He gets up upon him to his chair.
TAM. Now clear the triple region of the
air,   30
And let the majesty of heaven behold
Their scourge and terror tread on em-
perors.
Smile, stars, that reigned at my nativity,
And dim the brightness of their neighbor
lamps!
Disdain to borrow light of Cynthia!
For I, the chiefest lamp of all the earth,
First rising in the east with mild aspect,
But fixéd now in the meridian line,
Will send up fire to your turning spheres,
And cause the sun to borrow light of
you.   40
My sword stroke ² fire from his coat of
steel,
Even in Bithynia, when I took this Turk,
As when a fiery exhalation,
Wrapped in the bowels of a freezing
cloud,
Fighting for passage, make[s] the welkin
crack,

² Struck.

And casts a flash of lightning to the earth.

But, ere I march to wealthy Persia,
Or leave Damascus and th' Egyptian fields,
As was the fame of Clymene's brainsick son,[1]
That almost brent [2] the axletree of heaven,   50
So shall our swords, our lances, and our shot
Fill all the air with fiery meteors.
Then, when the sky shall wax as red as blood,
It shall be said I made it red myself,
To make me think of naught but blood and war.

ZAB. Unworthy king, that by thy cruelty
Unlawfully usurpest the Persian seat,
Dar'st thou, that never saw an emperor
Before thou met my husband in the field,
Being thy captive, thus abuse his state,   60
Keeping his kingly body in a cage,
That roofs of gold and sun-bright palaces
Should have prepared to entertain his grace,
And treading him beneath thy loathsome feet,
Whose feet the kings of Africa have kissed?

TECH. You must devise some torment worse, my lord,
To make these captives rein their lavish tongues.

TAM. Zenocrate, look better to your slave!

ZEN. She is my handmaid's slave, and she shall look
That these abuses flow not from her tongue.   70
Chide her, Anippe!

ANIP. Let these be warnings for you then, my slave,
How you abuse the person of the king;
Or else I swear to have you whipped, stark-naked.

BAJ. Great Tamburlaine, great in my overthrow,
Ambitious pride shall make thee fall as low
For treading on the back of Bajazeth,

That should be horséd on four mighty kings.

TAM. Thy names and titles and thy dignities
Are fled from Bajazeth and remain with me,   80
That will maintain it against a world of kings.
Put him in again!

[*They put him back into the cage.*]

BAJ. Is this a place for mighty Bajazeth?
Confusion light on him that helps thee thus!

TAM. There, whiles he lives, shall Bajazeth be kept,
And, where I go, be thus in triumph drawn;
And thou, his wife, shalt feed him with the scraps
My servitures [3] shall bring thee from my board,
For he that gives him other food than this
Shall sit by him and starve to death himself.   90
This is my mind and I will have it so.
Not all the kings and emperors of the earth,
If they would lay their crowns before my feet,
Shall ransom him or take him from his cage.
The ages that shall talk of Tamburlaine,
Even from this day to Plato's wondrous year,
Shall talk how I have handled Bajazeth.
These Moors, that drew him from Bithynia
To fair Damascus, where we now remain,
Shall lead him with us wheresoe'er we go.   100
Techelles and my loving followers,
Now may we see Damascus' lofty towers,
Like to the shadows of pyramides,[4]
That with their beauties graced the Memphian fields.
The golden stature [5] of their feathered bird
That spreads her wings upon the city walls
Shall not defend it from our battering shot.
The townsmen mask in silk and cloth of gold,

[1] *I.e.*, Phaëton. Original reads *Clymeus*.
[2] Burnt.

[3] Servitors.   [4] Quadrisyllabic.   [5] Statue.

And every house is as a treasury.
The men, the treasure, and the town is
   ours.   110
THER. Your tents of white now pitched
   before the gates,
And gentle flags of amity displayed,
I doubt not but the governor will yield,
Offering Damascus to your majesty.
TAM. So shall he have his life, and all the
   rest.
But, if he stay until the bloody flag
Be once advanced on my vermilion tent,
He dies, and those that kept us out so
   long.
And, when they see me march in black
   array,
With mournful streamers hanging down
   their heads,   120
Were in that city all the world contained,
Not one should scape, but perish by our
   swords.
ZEN. Yet would you have some pity for
   my sake,
Because it is my country's, and my
   father's!
TAM. Not for the world, Zenocrate, if I
   have sworn.
Come; bring in the Turk!   *Exeunt.*

ACTUS IV. SCENA iii.

[The Egyptian court.]

Soldan, Arabia, Capolin, with steeming [1]
                colors and Soldiers.

SOLD. Methinks we march as Meleager did,
   Environéd with brave Argolian knights,
To chase the savage Cal[y]donian boar,
Or Cephalus with lusty Theban youths
Against the wolf that angry Themis sent
To waste and spoil the sweet Aonian
   fields,
A monster of five hundred thousand
   heads,
Compact of rapine, piracy, and spoil.
The scum of men, the hate and scourge of
   God,
Raves in Egyptia and annoyeth us.   10
My lord, it is the bloody Tamburlaine,
A sturdy felon and a base-bred thief,
By murder raiséd to the Persian crown,
That dares control us in our territories.
To tame the pride of this presumptuous
   beast,

---

[1] Bright, gleaming.

Join your Arabians with the soldan's
   power;
Let us unite our royal bands in one,
And hasten to remove Damascus' siege.
It is a blemish to the majesty
And high estate of mighty emperors   20
That such a base, usurping vagabond
Should brave a king, or wear a princely
   crown.
ARAB. Renowméd soldan, have ye lately
   heard
The overthrow of mighty Bajazeth
About the confines of Bithynia,
The slavery wherewith he persecutes
The noble Turk and his great emperess?
SOLD. I have, and sorrow for his bad
   success.
But, noble lord of great Arabia,
Be so persuaded that the soldan is   30
No more dismayed with tidings of his fall
Than in the haven when the pilot stands
And views a stranger's ship rent in the
   winds,
And shiveréd against a craggy rock.
Yet, in compassion of his wretched state,
A sacred vow to heaven and him I make,
Confirming it with Ibis' holy name,
That Tamburlaine shall rue the day, the
   hour,
Wherein he wrought such ignominious
   wrong
Unto the hallowed person of a prince,   40
Or kept the fair Zenocrate so long
As concubine, I fear, to feed his lust.
ARAB. Let grief and fury hasten on re-
   venge;
Let Tamburlaine for his offenses feel
Such plagues as heaven and we can pour
   on him.
I long to break my spear upon his crest,
And prove the weight of his victorious
   arm,
For fame, I fear, hath been too prodigal
In sounding through the world his partial
   praise.
SOLD. Capolin, hast thou surveyed our
   powers?   50
CAP. Great Emperors of Egypt and
   Arabia,
The number of your hosts united is
A hundred and fifty thousand horse,
Two hundred thousand foot, brave men-
   at-arms,
Courageous, and full of hardiness,

As frolic as the hunters in the chase
Of savage beasts amid the desert woods.
ARAB. My mind presageth fortunate suc-
cess;
And, Tamburlaine, my spirit doth fore-
see
The utter ruin of thy men and thee.   60
SOLD. Then rear your standards; let your
sounding drums
Direct our soldiers to Damascus' walls.
Now, Tamburlaine, the mighty soldan
comes,
And leads with him the great Arabian
king
To dim thy baseness and obscurity,
Famous for nothing but for theft and
spoil;
To raze and scatter thy inglorious crew
Of Scythians and slavish Persians.
Exeunt.

ACTUS IV. SCENA iv.[1]

[*Tamburlaine's camp outside Damascus.*]

*The banquet; and to it cometh Tamburlaine,
all in scarlet, [Zenocrate,] Theridamas,
Techelles, Usumcasane, the Turk [Ba-
jazeth in his cage, Zabina], with Others.*

TAM. Now hang our bloody colors by Da-
mascus,
Reflexing hues of blood upon their heads,
While they walk quivering on their city
walls,
Half dead for fear before they feel my
wrath;
Then let us freely banquet and carouse [2]
Full bowls of wine unto the God of War,
That means to fill your helmets full of
gold,
And make Damascus' spoils as rich to
you
As was to Jason Colchos' golden fleece.—
And now, Bajazeth, hast thou any
stomach?   10
BAJ. Ay, such a stomach, cruel Tamburlaine, as I could willingly feed upon thy
blood-raw heart.
TAM. Nay, thine own is easier to come
by; pluck out that, and 'twill serve thee
and thy wife. Well, Zenocrate, Techelles,
and the rest, fall to your victuals.
BAJ. Fall to, and never may your meat
digest!

Ye Furies, that can mask invisible,
Dive to the bottom of Avernus' pool,   20
And in your hands bring hellish poison
up
And squeeze it in the cup of Tambur-
laine!
Or, wingéd snakes of Lerna, cast your
stings,
And leave your venoms in this tyrant's
dish!
ZAB. And may this banquet prove as
ominous
As Progne's to th' adulterous Thracian
king,
That fed upon the substance of his child!
ZEN. My lord, how can you suffer these
Outrageous curses by these slaves of
yours?
TAM. To let them see, divine Zenocrate,   30
I glory in the curses of my foes,
Having the power from the emperial
heaven
To turn them all upon their proper heads.
TECH. I pray you give them leave,
madam; this speech is a goodly refreshing
to them.
THER. But, if his highness would let
them be fed, it would do them more good.
TAM. Sirrah, why fall you not to? Are
you so daintily brought up you cannot   [40
eat your own flesh?
BAJ. First, legions of devils shall tear
thee in pieces!
USUM. Villain, knowest thou to whom
thou speakest?
TAM. O, let him alone. Here, eat, sir.
Take it from my sword's point, or I'll thrust
it to thy heart.
    He [3] *takes it and stamps upon it.*
THER. He stamps it under his feet, my
lord.   50
TAM. Take it up, villain, and eat it, or I
will make thee slice the brawns of thy arms
into carbonadoes [4] and eat them.
USUM. Nay, 'twere better he killed his
wife, and then she shall be sure not to be
starved, and he be provided for a month's
victual beforehand.
TAM. Here is my dagger. Despatch her
while she is fat, for, if she live but awhile
longer, she will fall into a consumption   [60
with fretting, and then she will not be
worth the eating.

[1] Original has *5.*   [2] Drink.   [3] *I.e.,* Bajazeth.   [4] Steaks.

THER. Dost thou think that Mahomet will suffer this?

TECH. 'Tis like he will, when he cannot let [1] it.

TAM. Go to; fall to your meat!—What, not a bit? Belike he hath not been watered today; give him some drink.

They give him water to drink, and he flings it on the ground.

Fast, and welcome, sir, while [2] hunger [70 make you eat. How now, Zenocrate, doth not the Turk and his wife make a goodly show at a banquet?

ZEN. Yes, my lord.

THER. Methinks 'tis a great deal better than a consort [3] of music.

TAM. Yet music would do well to cheer up Zenocrate. Pray thee, tell why art thou so sad? If thou wilt have a song, the Turk shall strain his voice. But why is it?   80

ZEN. My lord, to see my father's town besieged,

The country wasted where myself was born,

How can it but afflict my very soul?

If any love remain in you, my lord,

Or if my love unto your majesty

May merit favor at your highness' hands,

Then raise your siege from fair Damascus' walls,

And with my father take a friendly truce.

TAM. Zenocrate, were Egypt Jove's own land,

Yet would I with my sword make Jove to stoop.   90

I will confute those blind geographers

That make a triple region in the world,

Excluding regions which I mean to trace, [4]

And with this pen [5] reduce them to a map,

Calling the provinces, cities, and towns,

After my name and thine, Zenocrate.

Here at Damascus will I make the point

That shall begin the perpendicular;

And wouldst thou have me buy thy father's love

With such a loss? Tell me, Zenocrate.   100

ZEN. Honor still wait on happy Tamburlaine!

Yet give me leave to plead for him, my lord.

TAM. Content thyself. His person shall be safe

And all the friends of fair Zenocrate,

If with their lives they will be pleased to yield

Or may be forced to make me emperor;

For Egypt and Arabia must be mine.—

Feed, you slave! Thou mayst think thyself happy to be fed from my trencher.

BAJ. My empty stomach, full of idle heat,   110

Draws bloody humors from my feeble parts,

Preserving life by hasting cruel death.

My veins are pale, my sinews hard and dry,

My joints benumbed; unless I eat, I die.

ZAB. Eat, Bajazeth. Let us live in spite of them, looking [6] some happy power will pity and enlarge [7] us.

TAM. Here, Turk, wilt thou have a clean trencher?

BAJ. Ay, tyrant, and more meat.   120

TAM. Soft, sir; you must be dieted; too much eating will make you surfeit.

THER. So it would, my lord, specially having so small a walk and so little exercise.

Enter a second course of crowns.

TAM. Theridamas, Techelles, and Casane, here are the cates [8] you desire to finger, are they not?

THER. Ay, my lord, but none save kings must feed with these.

TECH. 'Tis enough for us to see [130 them, and for Tamburlaine only to enjoy them.

TAM. Well, here is now to the Soldan of Egypt, the King of Arabia, and the Governor of Damascus. Now take these three crowns, and pledge me, my contributory kings. I crown you here, Theridamas, King of Argier; Techelles, King of Fez; and Usumcasane, King of Moroccus. How say you to this, Turk? These are not your [140 contributory kings.

BAJ. Nor shall they long be thine, I warrant them.

TAM. Kings of Argier, Moroccus, and of Fez,

[1] Prevent.
[2] Until.
[3] Concert.
[4] Travel over.
[5] *I.e.*, sword.
[6] Expecting.   [7] Free.   [8] Delicacies

You that have marched with happy Tam-
burlaine
As far as from the frozen place of heaven
Unto the wat'ry morning's ruddy hour,[1]
And thence by land unto the torrid zone,
Deserve these titles I endow you with
By value [2] and by magnanimity.[3]
Your births shall be no blemish to your
    fame,   150
For virtue is the fount whence honor
springs,
And they are worthy she investeth kings.
THER. And, since your highness hath so
well vouchsafed,
If we deserve them not with higher
meeds [4]
Than erst our states and actions have
retained,
Take them away again and make us
slaves.
TAM. Well said, Theridamas; when holy
fates
Shall stablish me in strong Egyptia,
We mean to travel to th' antartic [5] pole,
Conquering the people underneath our
    feet,   160
And be renowmed as never emperors
were.
Zenocrate, I will not crown thee yet,
Until with greater honors I be graced.
                         [*Exeunt.*]

FINIS ACTUS QUARTI.

ACTUS V. SCENA i.

[*Outside the walls of Damascus.*]

*The Governor of Damasco, with three or four
Citizens, and four Virgins with branches
of laurel in their hands.*

GOV. Still doth this man, or rather god, of
war,
Batter our walls and beat our turrets
down,
And to resist with longer stubbornness
Or hope of rescue from the soldan's
power
Were but to bring our willful overthrow,
And make us desperate of our threatened
lives.
We see his tents have now been alteréd

With terrors to the last and cruelest
hue.
His coal-black colors everywhere ad-
vanced
Threaten our city with a general spoil. 10
And, if we should with common rites of
arms
Offer our safeties to his clemency,
I fear the custom, proper to his sword,
Which he observes as parcel of his fame,
Intending so to terrify the world,
By any innovation or remorse
Will never be dispensed with till our
deaths.
Therefore, for these our harmless vir-
gins' sakes,
Whose honors and whose lives rely on
him,
Let us have hope that their unspotted
    prayers,   20
Their blubbered cheeks, and hearty,
humble moans,
Will melt his fury into some remorse,[6]
And use us like a loving conqueror.
[1] VIRG. If humble suits or imprecations,[7]
Uttered with tears of wretchedness and
blood
Shed from the heads and hearts of all
our sex
(Some made your wives, and some your
children),
Might have entreated your obdurate
breasts
To entertain some care of our securities
Whiles [8] only danger beat upon our
    walls,   30
These more than dangerous warrants
of our death
Had never been erected as they be,
Nor you depend on such weak helps as
we.
GOV. Well, lovely virgins, think our
country's care,
Our love of honor, loath to be enthralled
To foreign powers and rough imperious
yokes,
Would not with too much cowardice
or fear,
Before all hope of rescue were denied,
Submit yourselves and us to servitude.
Therefore, in that your safeties and our
    own,   40

[1] *I.e.,* dawn, the east.   [3] Courage.
[2] Worth, goodness.   [4] Merits.
[5] Antarctic. From 1592 edn. Original reads
ıntatique.
[6] Pity.   [8] During the time that.
[7] Prayers.

Your honors, liberties, and lives were
   weighed
In equal care and balance with our own,
Endure as we the malice of our stars,
The wrath of Tamburlaine, and power
   of wars;
Or be the means the overweighing [1]
   heavens
Have kept to qualify [2] these hot ex-
   tremes,
And bring us pardon in your cheerful
   looks.
2 VIRG. Then here before the majesty of
   heaven
And holy patrons of Egyptia,
With knees and hearts submissive we
   entreat   50
Grace to our words and pity to our looks
That this device may prove propitious,
And through the eyes and ears of Tam-
   burlaine
Convey events [3] of mercy to his heart.
Grant that these signs of victory we
   yield
May bind the temples of his conquering
   head,
To hide the folded furrows of his brows,
And shadow his displeaséd countenance
With happy looks of ruth and lenity.
Leave us, my lord and loving country-
   men;   60
What simple virgins may persuade, we
   will.
Gov. Farewell, sweet virgins, on whose
   safe return
Depends our city, liberty, and lives.
        Exeunt [all but the Virgins].

ACTUS V. SCENA ii.

[*The same.*]

[*The Virgins are approached by*] *Tamburlaine, Techelles, Theridamas, Usumcasan[e], with Others; Tamburlaine all in
   black and very melancholy.*

TAM. What, are the turtles [4] frayed [5] out
   of their nests?
Alas, poor fools! Must you be first
   shall feel
The sworn destruction of Damascus?

They know my custom. Could they
   not as well
Have sent ye out when first my milk-
   white flags,
Through which sweet Mercy threw her
   gentle beams,
Reflexing them on your disdainful eyes,
As now, when fury and incenséd hate
Flings slaughtering terror from my coal-
   black tents,
And tells for truth submissions comes
   too late?   10
1 VIRG. Most happy king and emperor
   of the earth,
Image of honor and nobility,
For whom the powers divine have made
   the world,
And on whose throne the holy Graces
   sit,
In whose sweet person is comprised the
   sum
Of nature's skill and heavenly majesty,
Pity our plights! O, pity poor Damascus!
Pity old age, within whose silver hairs
Honor and reverence evermore have
   reigned!
Pity the marriage bed, where many a
   lord,   20
In prime and glory of his loving joy,
Embraceth now with tears of ruth and
   blood
The jealous body of his fearful wife,
Whose cheeks and hearts, so punished
   with conceit
To think thy puissant, never-stayéd
   arm
Will part their bodies, and prevent their
   souls
From heavens of comfort yet their age
   might bear,
Now wax all pale and withered to the
   death,
As well for grief our ruthless governor
Hath thus refused the mercy of thy
   hand   30
(Whose scepter angels kiss and furies
   dread)
As for their liberties, their loves, or
   lives!
O, then for these, and such as we our-
   selves,
For us, for infants, and for all our bloods,
That never nourished thought against
   thy rule,

---

[1] Overruling.   [4] Turtledoves.
[2] Mollify.   [5] Frightened.
[3] Effects.

Pity, O, pity, sacred emperor,
The prostrate service of this wretched
town,
And take in sign thereof this gilded
wreath,
Whereto each man of rule hath given
his hand,
And wished, as worthy subjects, happy
means   40
To be investers of thy royal brows
Even with the true Egyptian diadem!
TAM. Virgins, in vain ye labor to pre-
vent
That which mine honor swears shall
be performed.
Behold my sword! What see you at
the point?
[1] VIRG. Nothing but fear and fatal
steel, my lord.
TAM. Your fearful minds are thick and
misty then;
For there sits Death, there sits impe-
rious Death,
Keeping his circuit [1] by the slicing
edge.
But I am pleased you shall not see him
there;   50
He now is seated on my horsemen's
spears,
And on their points his fleshless body
feeds.
Techelles, straight go charge a few of
them
To charge these dames, and show my
servant, Death,
Sitting in scarlet on their arméd spears.
OMNES. O, pity us!
TAM. Away with them, I say, and show
them Death!   *They take them away.*
I will not spare these proud Egyp-
tians,
Nor change my martial observations
For all the wealth of Gihon's golden
waves,   60
Or for the love of Venus, would she
leave
The angry god of arms and lie with
me.
They have refused the offer of their
lives,
And know my customs are as peremp-
tory
As wrathful planets, death, or destiny.

[1] Law court.

Enter Techelles.

What, have your horsemen shown the
virgins Death?
TECH. They have, my lord, and on Da-
mascus' walls
Have hoisted up their slaughtered car-
casses.
TAM. A sight as baneful to their souls,
I think,
As are Thessalian drugs or mithri-
date.[2]—   70
But go, my lords, put the rest to the
sword.
            Exeunt [all except Tamburlaine].
Ah, fair Zenocrate, divine Zenocrate,
Fair is too foul an epithet for thee,
That in thy passion [3] for thy country's
love,
And fear to see thy kingly father's harm,
With hair disheveled wip'st thy watery
cheeks,
And, like to Flora in her morning's
pride,
Shaking her silver tresses [4] in the air,
Rain'st on the earth resolvéd pearl in
showers,
And sprinklest sapphires on thy shin-
ing face,   80
Where Beauty, mother to the Muses,
sits
And comments [5] volumes with her ivory
pen,
Taking instructions from thy flowing
eyes,
Eyes, when that Ebena steps to heaven,
In silence of thy solemn evening's walk,
Making the mantle of the richest night,
The moon, the planets, and the meteors,
light!
There angels in their crystal armors
fight
A doubtful battle with my tempted
thoughts
For Egypt's freedom, and the soldan's
life—   90
His life that so consumes Zenocrate,
Whose sorrows lay more siege unto my
soul
Than all my army to Damascus' walls;
And neither Persians' sovereign nor
the Turk

[2] Usually an antidote against poison; here, a
poison.   [4] Tresses.
[3] Suffering.   [5] Writes.

Troubled my senses with conceit of foil [1]
So much by much as doth Zenocrate.
What is beauty, saith my sufferings, then?
If all the pens that ever poets held
Had fed the feeling of their masters' thoughts,
And every sweetness that inspired their hearts,   100
Their minds, and muses on admired themes;
If all the heavenly quintessence they still [2]
From their immortal flowers of poesy,
Wherein, as in a mirror, we perceive
The highest reaches of a human wit;
If these had made one poem's period,[3]
And all combined in beauty's worthiness,
Yet should there hover in their restless heads
One thought, one grace, one wonder, at the least,   109
Which into words no virtue can digest.
But how unseemly is it for my sex,
My discipline of arms and chivalry,
My nature, and the terror of my name,
To harbor thoughts effeminate and faint!
Save only that in beauty's just applause,
With whose instinct the soul of man is touched
(And every warrior that is rapt with love
Of fame, of valor, and of victory
Must needs have beauty beat on his conceits),
I, thus conceiving and subduing both   120
That which hath stopped the tempest of the gods,
Even from the fiery-spangled veil of heaven,
To feel the lovely warmth of shepherds' flames,
And march [4] in cottages of strowéd weeds,
Shall give the world to note, for all my birth,
That virtue solely is the sum of glory,
And fashions men with true nobility.—
Who's within there?

[1] Thought of defeat.   [3] Climax.
[2] Distill.   [4] Move about.

Enter two or three [Attendants].

Hath Bajazeth been fed today?
A[TTE]N. Ay, my lord.   130
TAM. Bring him forth; and let us know the town be ransacked.
     [Exeunt Attendants.]

Enter Techelles, Theridamas, Usumcasan[e], and Others.

TECH. The town is ours, my lord, and fresh supply
Of conquest and of spoil is offered us.
TAM. That's well, Techelles. What's the news?
TECH. The soldan and the Arabian king together
March on us with such eager violence
As if there were no way but one with us.
TAM. No more there is not, I warrant thee, Techelles.
     They bring in the Turk [and Zabina].
THER. We know the victory is ours, my lord;   140
But let us save the reverend soldan's life
For fair Zenocrate, that so laments his state.
TAM. That will we chiefly see unto, Theridamas,
For sweet Zenocrate, whose worthiness
Deserves a conquest over every heart.—
And now, my footstool, if I lose the field,
You hope of liberty and restitution.
Here let him stay, my masters, from the tents,
Till we have made us ready for the field.
Pray for us, Bajazeth; we are going.   150
Exeunt [all except Bajazeth and Zabina].
BAJ. Go, never to return with victory!
Millions of men encompass thee about,
And gore thy body with as many wounds!
Sharp, forkéd arrows light upon thy horse!
Furies from the black Cocytus lake
Break up the earth, and with their firebrands
Enforce thee run upon the baneful pikes!
Volleys of shot pierce through thy charméd skin,

And every bullet dipped in poisoned
  drugs,   159
Or roaring cannons sever all thy joints,
Making thee mount as high as eagles
  soar!
ZAB. Let all the swords and lances in the
  field
Stick in his breast as in their proper
  rooms!
At every pore let blood come dropping
  forth,
That ling'ring pains may massacre his
  heart,
And madness send his damnéd soul to
  hell!
BAJ. Ah, fair Zabina, we may curse his
  power,
The heavens may frown, the earth for
  anger quake,
But such a star hath influence in his
  sword
As rules the skies and countermands
  the gods   170
More than Cimmerian Styx or destiny;
And then shall we in this detested
  guise,
With shame, with hunger, and with
  horror lie,[1]
Griping our bowels with retorquéd [2]
  thoughts,
And have no hope to end our ecstasies.[3]
ZAB. Then is there left no Mahomet, no
  God,
No fiend, no fortune, nor no hope of
  end
To our infamous, monstrous slaveries?
Gape, earth, and let the fiends infernal
  view
A hell as hopeless and as full of fear   180
As are the blasted banks of Erebus,
Where shaking ghosts with ever-howling
  groans
Hover about the ugly ferryman,
To get a passage to Elysian!
Why should we live? O, wretches, beg-
  gars, slaves!
Why live we, Bajazeth, and build up
  nests
So high within the region of the air
By living long in this oppression
That all the world will see and laugh to
  scorn

The former triumphs of our mighti-
  ness   190
In this obscure, infernal servitude?
BAJ. O life, more loathsome to my vexéd
  thoughts
Than noisome parbreak [4] of the Stygian
  snakes,
Which fills the nooks of hell with stand-
  ing air,
Infecting all the ghosts with cureless
  griefs!
O dreary engines [5] of my loathéd sight,
That sees my crown, my honor, and my
  name
Thrust under yoke and thralldom of a
  thief,
Why feed ye still on day's accurséd beams
And sink not quite into my tortured
  soul?   200
You see my wife, my queen and em-
  peress,
Brought up and proppéd by the hand of
  Fame,
Queen of fifteen contributory queens,
Now thrown to rooms [6] of black abjec-
  tion,
Smeared with blots of basest drudgery,
And villainess [7] to shame, disdain, and
  misery.
Accurséd Bajazeth, whose words of
  ruth,
That would with pity cheer Zabina's
  heart,
And make our souls resolve in ceaseless
  tears,
Sharp hunger bites upon, and gripes
  the root   210
From whence the issues of my thoughts
  do break!
O poor Zabina, O my queen, my queen,
Fetch me some water for my burning
  breast,
To cool and comfort me with longer date
That in the shortened sequel of my life
I may pour forth my soul into thine arms
With words of love, whose moaning
  intercourse
Hath hitherto been stayed with wrath
  and hate
Of our expressless banned [8] inflic-
  tions.

---

[1] Original has *aie*.   [3] Frenzies.
[2] Twisted inward.

[4] Vomit.   [7] Slave.
[5] Instruments, *i.e.*, eyes.   [8] Cursed.
[6] Positions.

ZAB. Sweet Bajazeth, I will prolong thy
    life   220
As long as any blood or spark of breath
Can quench or cool the torments of
    my grief.   *She goes out.*
BAJ. Now, Bajazeth, abridge thy bane-
    ful days,
And beat thy brains out of thy conquered
    head,
Since other means are all forbidden me
That may be ministers of my decay.
O highest lamp of ever-living Jove,
Accurséd day, infected with my griefs,
Hide now thy stainéd face in endless
    night,
And shut the windows of the lightsome
    heavens!   230
Let ugly Darkness with her rusty coach,
Engirt with tempests, wrapped in pitchy
    clouds,
Smother the earth with never-fading
    mists,
And let her horses from their nostrils
    breathe
Rebellious winds and dreadful thunder-
    claps,
That in this terror Tamburlaine may
    live,
And my pined soul, resolved in liquid
    air,[1]
May still excruciate his tormented
    thoughts!
Then let the stony dart of senseless
    cold
Pierce through the center of my withered
    heart,   240
And make a passage for my loathéd
    life!
         He brains himself against the cage.

Enter Zabina.

ZAB. What do mine eyes behold?   My
    husband dead!
His skull all riven in twain! His brains
    dashed out,
The brains of Bajazeth, my lord and
    sovereign!
O Bajazeth, my husband and my lord!
O Bajazeth, O Turk, O emperor!
Give him his liquor? Not I. Bring milk
and fire, and my blood I bring him again!—
Tear me in pieces! Give me the sword

with a ball of wildfire upon it!—Down   [250
with him, down with him!—Go to my child!
Away, away, away! Ah, save that infant,
save him, save him!—I, even I, speak to
her.—The sun was down; streamers white,
red, black, here, here, here!—Fling the
meat in his face!—Tamburlaine, Tamburlaine!—Let the soldiers be buried.—Hell!
Death! Tamburlaine! Hell!—Make ready
my coach, my chair, my jewels. I come,
I come, I come!   260
She runs against the cage and brains herself.

[Enter] Zenocrate with Anippe.

[ZEN.] Wretched Zenocrate, that livest
    to see
Damascus' walls dyed with Egyptian
    blood,
Thy father's subjects and thy country-
    men;
Thy streets strowed with dissevered
    joints of men
And wounded bodies gasping yet for
    life!
But most accursed, to see the sun-bright
    troop
Of heavenly virgins and unspotted
    maids,
Whose looks might make the angry god
    of arms
To break his sword and mildly treat
    of love,   269
On horsemen's lances to be hoisted up
And guiltlessly endure a cruel death!
For every fell and stout Tartarian steed,
That stamped on others with their thun-
    d'ring hoofs,
When all their riders charged their
    quivering spears,
Began to check[2] the ground and rein
    themselves,
Gazing upon the beauty of their looks.
Ah, Tamburlaine, wert thou the cause
    of this
That term'st Zenocrate thy dearest
    love,
Whose lives were dearer to Zenocrate
Than her own life, or aught save thine
    own love?—   280
But see another bloody spectacle!
Ah, wretched eyes, the enemies of my
    heart,

---

[1] Original has *ay.*

[2] Push against.

How are ye glutted with these grievous
  objects,
And tell my soul more tales of bleeding
  ruth!
See, see, Anippe, if they breathe or no.
ANIP. No breath, nor sense, nor motion
  in them both.
Ah, madam, this their slavery hath en-
  forced,
And ruthless cruelty of Tamburlaine.
ZEN. Earth, cast up fountains from thy
  entrails,
And wet thy cheeks for their untimely
  deaths!   290
Shake with their weight in sign of fear
  and grief!
Blush, Heaven, that gave them honor
  at their birth
And let them die a death so barbarous!
Those that are proud of fickle empery
And place their chiefest good in earthly
  pomp,
Behold the Turk and his great emperess!
Ah, Tamburlaine, my love, sweet Tam-
  burlaine,
That fights for scepters and for slippery
  crowns,
Behold the Turk and his great emper-
  ess!
Thou, that in conduct of thy happy
  stars   300
Sleep'st every night with conquests on
  thy brows,
And yet wouldst shun the wavering
  turns of war,
In fear and feeling of the like distress
Behold the Turk and his great emperess!
Ah, mighty Jove and holy Mahomet,
Pardon my love!—O, pardon his con-
  tempt
Of earthly fortune and respect of pity,
And let not conquest, ruthlessly pur-
  sued,
Be equally against his life incensed   309
In this great Turk and hapless emper-
  ess!
And pardon me that was not moved
  with ruth
To see them live so long in misery!
Ah, what may chance to thee, Zenocrate?
ANIP. Madam, content yourself, and be
  resolved;
Your love hath Fortune so at his com-
  mand

That she shall stay and turn her wheel
  no more,
As long as life maintains his mighty
  arm
That fights for honor to adorn your
  head.

Enter [Philemus,] a Messenger.

ZEN. What other heavy news now brings
  Philemus?
PHIL. Madam, your father, and the Ara-
  bian king,   320
The first affecter [1] of your excellence,
Comes now, as Turnus gainst Æneas
  did,
Arméd with lance into the Egyptian
  fields,
Ready for battle gainst my lord, the king
ZEN. Now shame and duty, love and fear
  presents
A thousand sorrows to my martyred soul.
Whom should I wish the fatal victory
When my poor pleasures are divided
  thus
And racked by duty from my curséd
  heart?   329
My father and my first-betrothéd love
Must fight against my life and present
  love,
Wherein the change I use condemns my
  faith,
And makes my deeds infamous through
  the world.
But as the gods, to end the Troyans'
  toil,
Prevented [2] Turnus of Lavinia
And fatally enriched Æneas' love,
So, for a final issue to my griefs,
To pacify my country and my love
Must Tamburlaine by their resistless
  powers
With virtue of a gentle victory   340
Conclude a league of honor to my hope;
Then, as the powers divine have pre-
  ordained,
With happy safety of my father's life
Send like defense of fair Arabia.

*They sound to the battle [within], and Tam-
  burlaine enjoys the victory. After,
                  Arabia enters wounded.*

ARAB. What curséd power guides the
  murthering hands

[1] Lover.   [2] Deprived.

Of this infamous tyrant's soldiers
That no escape may save their enemies,
Nor fortune keep themselves from vic-
tory?
Lie down, Arabia, wounded to the death,
And let Zenocrate's fair eyes behold
That, as for her thou bear'st these
wretched arms,   351
Even so for her thou diest in these arms,
Leaving thy blood for witness of thy
love.

ZEN. Too dear a witness for such love, my
lord!
Behold Zenocrate, the curséd object,
Whose fortunes never masteréd her
griefs;
Behold her wounded, in conceit, for
thee,
As much as thy fair body is for me,

ARAB. Then shall I die with full, con-
tented heart,
Having beheld divine Zenocrate,   360
Whose sight with joy would take away
my life
As now it bringeth sweetness to my
wound,
If I had not been wounded as I am.
Ah, that the deadly pangs I suffer now
Would lend an hour's license to my
tongue,
To make discourse of some sweet acci-
dents
Have chanced [1] thy merits in this worth-
less [2] bondage,
And that I might be privy to the state
Of thy deserved contentment, and thy
love.   369
But, making now a virtue of thy sight
To drive all sorrow from my fainting
soul,
Since death denies me further cause of
joy,
Deprived of care, my heart with com-
fort dies,
Since thy desiréd hand shall close mine
eyes.   [Dies.]

*Enter Tamburlaine, leading the Soldan,
Techelles, Theridamas, Usumcasane,
with Others.*

TAM. Come, happy father of Zenocrate,
A title higher than thy soldan's name.

[1] Befallen.   [2] Unworthy.

Though my right hand have thus en-
thralléd thee,
Thy princely daughter here shall set
thee free,
She that hath calmed the fury of my
sword,
Which had ere this been bathed in
streams of blood   380
As vast and deep as Euphrates or Nile.

ZEN. O sight thrice welcome to my joyful soul,
To see the king, my father, issue safe
From dangerous battle of my conquering love!

SOLD. Well met, my only dear Zenocrate,
Though with the loss of Egypt and my
crown.

TAM. 'Twas I, my lord, that gat the vic-
tory,
And therefore grieve not at your over-
throw,
Since I shall render all into your hands,
And add more strength to your domin-
ions   390
Than ever yet confirmed th' Egyptian
crown.
The God of War resigns his room to me,
Meaning to make me general of the
world.
Jove, viewing me in arms, looks pale
and wan,
Fearing my power should pull him from
his throne.
Where'er I come, the Fatal Sisters
sweat
And grisly Death, by running to and
fro,
To do their ceaseless homage to my
sword.
And here in Afric, where it seldom
rains,
Since I arrived with my triumphant
host,   400
Have swelling clouds, drawn from wide-
gasping wounds,
Been oft resolved in bloody, purple
showers,
A meteor that might terrify the earth,
And make it quake at every drop it
drinks.
Millions of souls sit on the banks of
Styx,
Waiting the back return of Charon's
boat;

Hell and Elysian swarm with ghosts
  of men
That I have sent from sundry foughten
  fields,
To spread my fame through hell and up
  to heaven.
And see, my lord, a sight of strange im-
  port: 410
Emperors and kings lie breathless at
  my feet.
The Turk and his great empress, as it
  seems,
Left to themselves while we were at
  the fight,
Have desperately despatched their
  slavish lives;
With them Arabia, too, hath left his
  life—
All sights of power to grace my victory.
And such are objects fit for Tambur-
  laine,
Wherein, as in a mirror, may be seen
His honor, that consists in shedding
  blood,
When men presume to manage arms
  with him. 420
SOLD. Mighty hath God and Mahomet
  made thy hand,
Renowmèd Tamburlaine, to whom all
  kings
Of force [1] must yield their crowns and
  emperies;
And I am pleased with this my over-
  throw,
If, as beseems a person of thy state,
Thou hast with honor used Zenocrate.
TAM. Her state and person wants no
  pomp, you see;
And for all blot of foul inchastity
I record [2] heaven her heavenly self is
  clear.
Then let me find no further time to
  grace 430
Her princely temples with the Persian
  crown,
But here these kings that on my for-
  tunes wait,
And have been crowned for provéd
  worthiness,
Even by this hand that shall establish
  them,
Shall now, adjoining all their hands
  with mine,

[1] Of necessity.   [2] Take to witness.

Invest her here my Queen of Persia.
What saith the noble soldan and Zeno-
  crate?
SOLD. I yield with thanks and protesta-
  tions
Of endless honor to thee for her love.
TAM. Then doubt I not but fair Zeno-
  crate 440
Will soon consent to satisfy us both.
ZEN. Else should I much forget myself,
  my lord.
THER. Then let us set the crown upon
  her head,
That long hath lingered for so high a
  seat.
TECH. My hand is ready to perform the
  deed,
For now her marriage time shall work
  us rest.
USUM. And here's the crown, my lord,
  help set it on.
TAM. Then sit thou down, divine Zeno-
  crate;
And here we crown thee Queen of
  Persia 449
And all the kingdoms and dominions
That late the power of Tamburlaine
  subdued.
As Juno, when the giants were sup-
  pressed,
That darted mountains at her brother
  Jove,
So looks my love, shadowing in her
  brows
Triumphs and trophies for my victories;
Or as Latona's daughter, bent to arms,
Adding more courage to my conquering
  mind.
To gratify the sweet Zenocrate,
Egyptians, Moors, and men of Asia,
From Barbary unto the western Indie,
Shall pay a yearly tribute to thy sire; 461
And from the bounds of Afric to the
  banks
Of Ganges shall his mighty arm extend.
And now, my lords and loving followers
That purchased kingdoms by your mar-
  tial deeds,
Cast off your armor, put on scarlet
  robes,
Mount up your royal places of estate,
Environéd with troops of noblemen,
And there make laws to rule your prov-
  inces.

Hang up your weapons on Alcides'
   post,[1]   470
For Tamburlaine takes truce with all
   the world.
Thy first-betrothéd love, Arabia,
Shall we with honor, as beseems, entomb
With this great Turk and his fair em-
   peress.

[1] Doorpost of the temple.

Then, after all these solemn exequies,
We will our celebrated rites of marriage solemnize.   [*Exeunt.*]

FINIS ACTUS QUINTI ET ULTIMI HUJUS
PRIMÆ PARTIS.[2]

[2] The end of the fifth and last act of this first
part.

THE TRAGICAL HISTORY OF D[OCTOR] FAUSTUS[1]

BY

CHRISTOPHER MARLOWE

[*DRAMATIS PERSONÆ*

THE POPE.
CARDINAL OF LORRAIN.
EMPEROR OF GERMANY.
DUKE OF VANHOLT.
FAUSTUS.
VALDES ⎫
CORNELIUS AGRIPPA ⎬ *friends to Faustus.*
WAGNER, *servant to Faustus.*
CLOWN.
ROBIN.
RAFE.[2]
VINTNER.
HORSE-CORSER.[3]
KNIGHT.
OLD MAN.

SCHOLARS, FRIARS, *and* ATTENDANTS.

DUCHESS OF VANHOLT.

LUCIFER.
BELZEBUB.
MEPHISTOPHILIS.
GOOD ANGEL.
EVIL ANGEL.
THE SEVEN DEADLY SINS.
DEVILS.
SPIRITS *in the shapes of* ALEXANDER ⸱⸱ᴇ GREAT, *of his* PARAMOUR, *and of* HELEN OF TROY.

CHORUS.

PLACE: *Germany and Rome.*

TIME: *Early sixteenth century.*]

Enter Chorus.

Not marching now in fields of Thrasi-
    mene,
Where Mars did mate [4] the Carthagin-
    ians,
Nor sporting in the dalliance of love,
In courts of kings where state is over-
    turned,
Nor in the pomp of proud audacious
    deeds,
Intends our Muse to daunt [5] his heavenly
    verse.
Only this, gentlemen: we must perform
The form [6] of Faustus' fortunes, good or
    bad.

To patient judgments we appeal our
    plaud,[7]
And speak for Faustus in his infancy.   10
Now is he born, his parents base of stock,
In Germany, within a town called
    Rhodes;
Of riper years to Wertenberg [8] he went,
Whereas [9] his kinsmen chiefly brought
    him up.
So soon he profits in divinity,
The fruitful plot of scholarism graced,
That shortly he was graced with doctor's
    name,
Excelling all whose sweet delight disputes
In heavenly matters of theology;
Till swollen with cunning,[10] of a self-
    conceit,   20
His waxen wings did mount above his
    reach,

[1] The title continues: "As It Hath Been Acted by the Right Honorable the Earl of Nottingham His Servants. Written by Ch. Marl."
[2] Variant of *Ralph*.   [4] Join with (?).
[3] Dealer in horses.
[5] Wear out, exhaust. The 1616 edn. has *vaunt*.
[6] Course.

[7] For our applause.   [9] Where.
[8] Wittenberg.   [10] Learning.

349

And, melting, heavens conspired his over-
throw,
For, falling to a devilish exercise,
And glutted more with learning's golden
gifts,
He surfeits upon curséd negromancy.[1]
Nothing so sweet as magic is to him,
Which he prefers before his chiefest
bliss.
And this the man that in his study sits!
　　　　　　　　　　　　　　　　　　Exit.

[SCENE i.]

Enter Faustus in his study.

FAUST. Settle thy studies, Faustus, and
begin
To sound the depth of that thou wilt
profess.
Having commenced,[2] be a divine in
show;
Yet level at the end of [3] every art,
And live and die in Aristotle's works.
Sweet analytics,[4] 'tis thou hast ravished
me!
[*Reads.*] *"Bene disserere est finis logices."*
Is to dispute well logic's chiefest end?
Affords this art no greater miracle?
Then read no more; thou hast attained
the end.　　　　　　　　　　　　　10
A greater subject fitteth Faustus' wit.
Bid *Oncaymæon* [5] farewell. [*Puts down
Aristotle and takes up Galen.*] Galen,
come,
Seeing *"Ubi desinit Philosophus, ibi
incipit Medicus."* [6]
Be a physician, Faustus, heap up gold,
And be eternized [7] for some wondrous
cure.
[*Reads.*] *"Summum bonum medicinæ sa-
nitas:"*
"The end of physic is our body's health."
Why, Faustus, hast thou not attained
that end?
Is not thy common talk sound apho-
risms? [8]

Are not thy bills [9] hung up as monu-
ments　　　　　　　　　　　　　20
Whereby whole cities have escaped the
plague,
And thousand desperate maladies been
eased?
Yet art thou still but Faustus, and a man.
Wouldst thou make man to live eternally,
Or, being dead, raise them to life again,
Then this profession were to be esteemed.
Physic, farewell.—Where is Justinian?
[*Puts down Galen, takes up Justinian, and
reads.*]
*"Si una eademque res legatur duobus, alter
rem, alter valorem rei,"* [10] *etc.*
A pretty case of paltry legacies!
[*Reads.*] *"Exhæreditare filium non potest
pater nisi—"* [11]　　　　　　　30
Such is the subject of the Institute [12]
And universal Body of the Law.[13]
His [14] study fits a mercenary drudge,
Who aims at nothing but external trash,
Too servile [15] and illiberal for me.
When all is done, divinity is best.
Jerome's Bible,[16] Faustus, view it well.
[*Puts down Justinian, takes up the Vulgate,
and reads.*]
"Stipendium peccati mors est."　Ha!
"Stipendium," etc.:
"The reward of sin is death."　That's
hard.
[*Reads.*] *"Si peccasse negamus, fallimur,
et nulla est in nobis veritas:"*　　40
"If we say that we have no sin,
We deceive ourselves, and there's no
truth in us."
Why then, belike,
We must sin and so consequently die.
Ay, we must die an everlasting death.
What doctrine call you this? *Che sera,
sera:*
"What will be, shall be."　Divinity,
adieu!
[*Puts down the Vulgate and takes up his
book of magic.*]

---

[1] Necromancy.　　　　[3] Aim at perfection in.
[2] Proceeded to a degree.　　　　[4] Logic.
[5] Bullen points out that this is a corruption
of Aristotle's phrase for "being and not being."
[6] "Where the philosopher stops, there the
physician begins." This and the following quotation are from Aristotle.
[7] Immortalized.
[8] Maxims of medicine.

[9] Doctor's prescriptions.
[10] "If one and the same thing is willed to two
persons, one gets the thing and the other the
value of the thing."
[11] "A father cannot disinherit the son unless—"
[12] Of Justinian.
[13] From 1616 edn.　Original has *church.*
[14] Its.
[15] From 1616 edn.　Original reads *The devil.*
[16] The Vulgate.

These metaphysics of magicians
And negromantic books are heavenly;
Lines, circles, scenes, letters, and char-
acters,   50
Ay, these are those that Faustus most
desires.
O, what a world of profit and delight,
Of power, of honor, of omnipotence
Is promised to the studious artisan! [1]
All things that move between the quiet
poles
Shall be at my command. Emperors and
kings
Are but obeyed in their several provinces,
Nor can they raise the wind or rend the
clouds;
But his dominion that exceeds[2] in this
Stretcheth as far as doth the mind of
man.   60
A sound magician is a mighty god.
Here, Faustus, try thy brains to gain a
deity.—

Enter Wagner.

Wagner! Commend me to my dearest
friends,
The German Valdes and Cornelius;
Request them earnestly to visit me.
WAG. I will, sir.   *Exit.*
FAUST. Their conference will be a greater
help to me
Than all my labors, plod I ne'er so fast.

Enter the Good Angel and the Evil Angel.

GOOD A. O Faustus, lay that damnéd book
aside,   69
And gaze not on it lest it tempt thy soul,
And heap God's heavy wrath upon thy
head!
Read, read the Scriptures. That is blas-
phemy.
EVIL A. Go forward, Faustus, in that fa-
mous art
Wherein all Nature's treasury[3] is con-
tained.
Be thou on earth, as Jove is in the sky,
Lord and commander of these elements.
                               Exeunt [Angels].
FAUST. How am I glutted with conceit[4]
of this!

Shall I make spirits fetch me what I
please,
Resolve me of all ambiguities,[5]
Perform what desperate enterprise I
will?   80
I'll have them fly to India[6] for gold,
Ransack the ocean for orient pearl,
And search all corners of the new-found
world
For pleasant fruits and princely delicates;
I'll have them read me strange philos-
ophy
And tell the secrets of all foreign kings;
I'll have them wall all Germany with
brass,
And make swift Rhine circle fair Werten-
berg;
I'll have them fill the public schools[7]
with silk,[8]
Wherewith the students shall be bravely
clad;   90
I'll levy soldiers with the coin they
bring,
And chase the Prince of Parma from our
land,
And reign sole king of all our provinces;
Yea, stranger engines[9] for the brunt of
war
Than was the fiery keel at Antwerp's
bridge,
I'll make my servile spirits to invent.
Come, German Valdes and Cornelius,
And make me blessed with your sage con-
ference.

Enter Valdes and Cornelius.

Valdes, sweet Valdes, and Cornelius,
Know that your words have won me at
the last   100
To practice magic and concealéd
arts—
Yet not your words only, but mine own
fantasy,
That will receive no object,[10] for my
head
But ruminates on negromantic skill.
Philosophy is odious and obscure;

---

[1] Student of a liberal art.   [3] Treasure.
[2] Excels.   [4] Thought.
[5] Free me from all uncertainties.
[6] The American Indies.
[7] University lecture rooms.
[8] Emended by Dyce. Original reads *skill.*
[9] Machines.
[10] "Will not be impressed by solid realities"
(Boas).

Both law and physic are for petty wits;
Divinity is basest of the three,
Unpleasant, harsh, contemptible, and
vild.[1]
'Tis magic, magic, that hath ravished
me!
Then, gentle friends, aid me in this
attempt;   110
And I that have with concise syllo-
gisms
Graveled the pastors of the German
church,
And made the flow'ring pride of Werten-
berg
Swarm to my problems,[2] as the infernal
spirits
On sweet Musæus when he came to hell,
Will be as cunning as Agrippa was,
Whose shadows [3] made all Europe honor
him.
VALD. Faustus,
These books, thy wit, and our experi-
ence
Shall make all nations to canonize us.
As Indian Moors [4] obey their Spanish
lords,   121
So shall the subjects [5] of every element
Be always serviceable to us three.
Like lions shall they guard us when we
please;
Like Almain rutters [6] with their horse-
men's staves,
Or Lapland giants, trotting by our
sides;
Sometimes like women or unwedded
maids,
Shadowing more beauty in their airy [7]
brows
Than has the [8] white breasts of the Queen
of Love;
From Venice shall they drag [9] huge
argosies,   130
And from America the golden fleece
That yearly stuffs old Philip's treasury,
If learned Faustus will be resolute.
FAUST. Valdes, as resolute am I in this
As thou to live; therefore object it
not.

¹ Vile.
² Lectures.
³ Spirits, here shown in a mirror.
⁴ American Indians.
⁵ Servants, *i.e.*, spirits.
⁶ German cavalry.
⁷ Ethereal.
⁸ From 1616 edn. Original has *Then in their.*
⁹ From 1609 edn. Original has *For Venice
shall they dregge* (dredge?).

CORN. The miracles that magic will per-
form
Will make thee vow to study nothing
else.
He that is grounded in astrology,
Enriched with tongues, well seen [10] [in] [11]
minerals,
Hath all the principles magic doth re-
quire.   140
Then doubt not, Faustus, but to be
renowmed,
And more frequented for this mystery
Than heretofore the Delphian oracle.
The spirits tell me they can dry the
sea,
And fetch the treasure of all foreign
wracks,
Ay, all the wealth that our forefathers
hid
Within the massy entrails of the earth.
Then tell me, Faustus, what shall we
three want?
FAUST. Nothing, Cornelius! O, this cheers
my soul!
Come, show me some demonstrations
magical,   150
That I may conjure in some lusty
grove,
And have these joys in full posses-
sion.
VALD. Then haste thee to some solitary
grove,
And bear wise Bacon's and Albanus'
works,
The Hebrew Psalter and New Testa-
ment;
And whatsoever else is requisite
We will inform thee ere our conference
cease.
CORN. Valdes, first let him know the words
of art,
And then, all other ceremonies learned,
Faustus may try his cunning by him-
self.
VALD. First I'll instruct thee in the rudi-
ments,   161
And then wilt thou be perfecter than I.
FAUST. Then come and dine with me, and
after meat
We'll canvass every quiddity thereof;
For ere I sleep I'll try what I can do.
This night I'll conjure though I die
therefor.   *Exeunt.*

¹⁰ Versed.   ¹¹ From 1616 edn.

[SCENE ii.

Before Faustus' house.]

Enter two Scholars.

1 Sch. I wonder what's become of Faustus that was wont to make our schools ring with *sic probo?* [1]

2 Sch. That shall we know, for see here comes his boy.

Enter Wagner.

1 Sch. How now, sirrah! Where's thy master?

Wag. God in heaven knows!

2 Sch. Why, dost not thou know?

Wag. Yes, I know. But that fol- [10 lows not.

1 Sch. Go to, sirrah! Leave your jesting, and tell us where he is.

Wag. That follows not necessary by force of argument, that you, being licentiate, should stand upon 't; therefore, acknowledge your error and be attentive.

2 Sch. Why, didst thou not say thou knew'st?

Wag. Have you any witness on 't? [20

1 Sch. Yes, sirrah, I heard you.

Wag. Ask my fellow if I be a thief.

2 Sch. Well, you will not tell us?

Wag. Yes, sir, I will tell you; yet if you were not dunces, you would never ask me such a question, for is not he *corpus naturale,* [2] and is not that *mobile?* [2] Then wherefore should you ask me such a question? But that I am by nature phlegmatic, slow to wrath, and prone to lechery (to [30 love, I would say), it were not for you to come within forty foot of the place of execution, [3] although I do not doubt to see you both hanged the next sessions. Thus having triumphed over you, I will set my countenance like a precisian, [4] and begin to speak thus: "Truly, my dear brethren, my master is within at dinner with Valdes and Cornelius, as this wine, if it could speak, would inform your worships; and so [40 the Lord bless you, preserve you, and keep you, my dear brethren, my dear brethren." *Exit.*

[1] Thus I prove.
[2] Terms used in the physics of the day.
[3] The room within, where Faustus is dining.
[4] Puritan.

1 Sch. Nay, then, I fear he has fallen into that damned art for which they two are infamous through the world.

2 Sch. Were he a stranger, and not allied to me, yet should I grieve for him. But come, let us go and inform the rector, and see if he by his grave counsel can reclaim him.   51

1 Sch. O, but I fear me nothing can reclaim him.

2 Sch. Yet let us try what we can do.
Exeunt.

[SCENE iii.

A grove.]

Enter Faustus to conjure.

Faust. Now that the gloomy shadow of the earth,
Longing to view Orion's drizzling look,
Leaps from th' antartic world unto the sky,
And dims the welkin with her pitchy breath,
Faustus, begin thine incantations,
And try if devils will obey thy hest, [5]
Seeing thou hast prayed and sacrificed to them.
Within this circle is Jehovah's name,
Forward and backward anagrammatized, [6]
The breviated names of holy saints,   10
Figures of every adjunct [7] to the heavens,
And characters of signs and erring stars, [8]
By which the spirits are enforced to rise.
Then fear not, Faustus, but be resolute,
And try the uttermost magic can perform.
Sint mihi Dei Acherontis propitii! Valeat numen triplex Jehovæ! Ignei, aerii, aquatani spiritus, salvete! Orientis Princeps, Belzebub, inferni ardentis monarcha, et Demogorgon, propitiamus vos, ut appareat [20 *et surgat Mephistophilis.* [9] *Quid tu moraris?* [10]

[5] Behest, command.
[6] From 1616 edn. Original has *and Agramithist.*
[7] *I.e.,* star.
[8] Moving stars, *i.e.,* planets.
[9] The spelling of this name varies in the original.
[10] Suggested by Schröer; original has *Quod tumeraris.*

Per Jehovam, Gehennam, et consecratam
aquam quam nunc spargo, signumque crucis
quod nunc facio, et per vota nostra, ipse
nunc surgat nobis dicatus Mephistophilis! [1]

Enter [Mephistophilis,] a Devil.

I charge thee to return and change thy
    shape;
Thou art too ugly to attend on me.
Go, and return an old Franciscan friar;
That holy shape becomes a devil best.
                                Exit Devil.
I see there's virtue in my heavenly
    words.   30
Who would not be proficient in this art?
How pliant is this Mephistophilis,
Full of obedience and humility!
Such is the force of magic and my spells.
No, Faustus, thou art conjuror laureate,
That canst command great Mephis-
    tophilis;
Quin regis, Mephistophilis, fratris ima-
    gine. [2]

Enter Mephistophilis [as a Franciscan
                                friar].

MEPH. Now, Faustus, what wouldst thou
    have me do?
FAUST. I charge thee wait upon me whilst
    I live,
To do whatever Faustus shall com-
    mand,   40
Be it to make the moon drop from her
    sphere,
Or the ocean to overwhelm the world.
MEPH. I am a servant to great Lucifer,
And may not follow thee without his
    leave;
No more than he commands must we
    perform.
FAUST. Did he not charge thee to appear to
    me?

---

[1] May the gods of Acheron be propitious
to me! Away with the threefold godhead of
Jehovah! Spirits of fire, air, water, hail! Belzebub, Prince of the East, monarch of burning
hell, and Demogorgon, we propitiate you, that
Mephistophilis may appear and rise. Why dost
thou delay? By Jehovah, Gehenna, and the
holy water which I now sprinkle, and the sign
of the cross which I now make, and by our
prayers, may Mephistophilis himself, invoked
by us, now rise!
[2] Verily thou rulest in the image of a brother
(*i.e.*, a friar), Mephistophilis.

MEPH. No, I came now hither of mine own
    accord.
FAUST. Did not my conjuring speeches
    raise thee? Speak!
MEPH. That was the cause. but yet per
    accident;
For, when we hear one rack the name of
    God,   56
Abjure the Scriptures and his Savior
    Christ,
We fly in hope to get his glorious soul;
Nor will we come, unless he use such
    means
Whereby he is in danger to be damned.
Therefore the shortest cut for conjur-
    ing
Is stoutly to abjure the Trinity,
And pray devoutly to the Prince of Hell.
FAUST. So Faustus hath
Already done, and holds this principle:
There is no chief but only Belzebub,   60
To whom Faustus doth dedicate him-
    self.
This word "damnation" terrifies not
    him,
For he confounds hell in Elysium. [3]
His ghost be with the old philosophers!
But, leaving these vain trifles of men's
    souls,
Tell me what is that Lucifer, thy lord?
MEPH. Arch-regent and commander of all
    spirits.
FAUST. Was not that Lucifer an angel
    once?
MEPH. Yes, Faustus, and most dearly
    loved of God.
FAUST. How comes it then that he is
    prince of devils?   70
MEPH. O, by aspiring pride and insolence,
For which God threw him from the face
    of heaven.
FAUST. And what are you that live with
    Lucifer?
MEPH. Unhappy spirits that fell with
    Lucifer,
Conspired against our God with Lucifer,
And are forever damned with Lucifer.
FAUST. Where are you damned?
MEPH. In hell.
FAUST. How comes it then that thou art
    out of hell?
MEPH. Why, this is hell, nor am I out of
    it.   80

---

[3] *I.e.*, makes no distinction between them.

Think'st thou that I who saw the face of
   God,
And tasted the eternal joys of heaven,
Am not tormented with ten thousand
   hells,
In being deprived of everlasting bliss?
O Faustus, leave these frivolous de-
   mands,
Which strike a terror to my fainting soul!
FAUST. What, is great Mephistophilis so
   passionate [1]
For being deprived of the joys of heaven?
Learn thou of Faustus manly fortitude,
And scorn those joys thou never shalt
   possess.   90
Go bear those tidings to great Lucifer:
Seeing Faustus hath incurred eternal
   death
By desp'rate thoughts against Jove's
   deity,
Say he surrenders up to him his soul,
So he will spare him four-and-twenty
   years,
Letting him live in all voluptuousness,
Having thee ever to attend on me,
To give me whatsoever I shall ask,
To tell me whatsoever I demand,
To slay mine enemies, and aid my
   friends,   100
And always be obedient to my will.
Go and return to mighty Lucifer,
And meet me in my study at midnight,
And then resolve [2] me of thy master's
   mind.
MEPH. I will, Faustus.   *Exit.*
FAUST. Had I as many souls as there be
   stars,
I'd give them all for Mephistophilis.
By him I'll be great emp'ror of the
   world,
And make a bridge through the moving
   air,
To pass the ocean with a band of men. 110
I'll join the hills that bind the Afric
   shore,
And make that land continent [3] to
   Spain,
And both contributory to my crown.
The emp'ror shall not live but by my
   leave,
Nor any potentate of Germany.
Now that I have obtained what I de-
   sire,

I'll live in speculation [4] of this art
Till Mephistophilis return again.   *Exit.*

[SCENE iv.

A street.]

Enter Wagner and the Clown.

WAG. Sirrah boy, come hither.

CLO. How, "boy"? Swowns,[5] "boy"! I
hope you have seen many boys with such
pickadevaunts [6] as I have. "Boy," quotha!

WAG. Tell me, sirrah, hast thou any
comings-in?

CLO. Ay, and goings-out too. You
may see else.

WAG. Alas, poor slave! See how poverty
jesteth in his nakedness! The villain is [10
bare and out of service, and so hungry
that I know he would give his soul to the
devil for a shoulder of mutton, though it
were blood-raw.

CLO. How? My soul to the devil for
a shoulder of mutton, though 'twere
blood-raw! Not so, good friend. Bur [7]
Lady, I had need have it well roasted and
good sauce to it, if I pay so dear.

WAG. Well, wilt thou serve me, and [20
I'll make thee go like *"Qui mihi discipu-
lus?"* [8]

CLO. How, in verse?

WAG. No, sirrah; in beaten [9] silk and
stavesacre.[10]

CLO. How, how, Knave's Acre! [11] Ay,
I thought that was all the land his father
left him. Do you hear? I would be sorry
to rob you of your living.

WAG. Sirrah, I say in stavesacre.   30

CLO. Oho! Oho! Stavesacre! Why, then,
belike if I were your man I should be full
of vermin.

WAG. So thou shalt, whether thou beest
with me or no. But, sirrah, leave your
jesting, and bind yourself presently [12] unto
me for seven years, or I'll turn all the lice
about thee into familiars,[13] and they shall
tear thee in pieces.

[1] Moved.   [2] Inform.   [3] Contiguous.

[4] Contemplation, study.   [6] Pointed beards.
[5] God's wounds.   [7] By'r, by our.
[8] "You who are my pupil" (Dyce notes that the
source of this phrase is William Lilly's *Ad dis-
cipulos carmen de moribus*).
[9] Stamped with metal and embroidered.
[10] Larkspur, used as lice-killer.
[11] A low street in London.
[12] Immediately.   [13] Familiar spirits.

Clo. Do you hear, sir? You may [40 save that labor; they are too familiar with me already. Swowns! They are as bold with my flesh as if they had paid for my meat and drink.

Wag. Well, do you hear, sirrah? Hold, take these guilders.   [Gives money.]

Clo. Gridirons! What be they?

Wag. Why, French crowns.

Clo. Mass, but for the name of French crowns, a man were as good have as [50 many English counters. And what should I do with these?

Wag. Why, now, sirrah, thou art at an hour's warning, whensoever and where-soever the devil shall fetch thee.

Clo. No, no. Here, take your gridirons again.

Wag. Truly, I'll none of them.

Clo. Truly, but you shall.

Wag. Bear witness I gave them him.

Clo. Bear witness I give them you [61 again.

Wag. Well, I will cause two devils presently to fetch thee away—Baliol and Belcher.

Clo. Let your Balio and your Belcher come here, and I'll knock them, they were never so knocked since they were devils. Say I should kill one of them, what would folks say? "Do you see [70 yonder tall [1] fellow in the round slop? [2]— He has killed the devil." So I should be called Kill-devil all the parish over.

Enter two Devils, and the Clown runs up and down crying.

Wag. Baliol and Belcher!   Spirits, away!   *Exeunt [Devils].*

Clo. What, are they gone? A ven-geance on them, they have vild long nails! There was a he-devil and a she-devil! I'll tell you how you shall know them: all he-devils has horns, and all she-devils has clifts [3] and cloven feet.   81

Wag. Well, sirrah, follow me.

Clo. But, do you hear—if I should serve you, would you teach me to raise up Banios and Belcheos?

Wag. I will teach thee to turn thyself to anything—to a dog, or a cat, or a mouse, or a rat, or anything.

Clo. How?   A Christian fellow to a

dog or a cat, a mouse or a rat? No, [90 no, sir. If you turn me into anything, let it be in the likeness of a little pretty frisk-ing flea, that I may be here and there and everywhere.   O, I'll tickle the pretty wenches' plackets; I'll be amongst them, i' faith.

Wag. Well, sirrah, come.

Clo. But, do you hear, Wagner?

Wag. How!—Baliol and Belcher!

Clo. O Lord! I pray, sir, let Banio and Belcher go sleep.   101

Wag. Villain, call me Master Wagner, and let thy left eye be diametarily [4] fixed upon my right heel, with *quasi vesti-gias nostras insistere.*[5]   *Exit.*

Clo. God forgive me, he speaks Dutch fustian.   Well, I'll follow him; I'll serve him; that's flat.   *Exit.*

[Scene v.]

Enter Faustus in his study.

Faust. Now, Faustus, must thou needs
      be damned,
And canst thou not be saved.
What boots it then to think of God or
      heaven?
Away with such vain fancies, and de-
      spair.[6]
Despair in God, and trust in Belzebub.
Now go not backward; no, Faustus, be
      resolute.
Why waverest thou?   O, something
      soundeth in mine ears:
"Abjure this magic; turn to God again!"
Ay, and Faustus will turn to God again
To God?—He loves thee not.   10
The God thou servest is thine own ap-
      petite,
Wherein is fixed the love of Belzebub.
To him I'll build an altar and a church,
And offer lukewarm blood of newborn
      babes.

Enter Good Angel and Evil.

Good A. Sweet Faustus, leave that exe
      crable art!

Faust. Contrition,   prayer,   repentance!
      What of them?

Good A. O, they are means to bring
      thee unto heaven.

---

[1] Brave.   [2] Wide breeches.   [3] Clefts.

[4] Wagner's blunder for *diametrically.*
[5] As if to walk in my footsteps.
[6] Be without hope.

EVIL A. Rather illusions, fruits of lunacy,
That makes men foolish that do trust
them most.
GOOD A. Sweet Faustus, think of heaven
and heavenly things.   20
EVIL A. No, Faustus, think of honor
and [of] wealth!   *Exeunt [Angels].*
FAUST. Of wealth!
Why, the signiory of Emden shall be
mine.
When Mephistophilis shall stand by me,
What God can hurt thee, Faustus?
Thou art safe;
Cast no more doubts. Come, Mephis-
tophilis,
And bring glad tidings from great Luci-
fer.
Is't not midnight? Come, Mephistoph-
ilis;
Veni,[1] *veni, Mephistophile!*

Enter Meph[istophilis].

Now tell [me],[2] what says Lucifer, thy
lord?   30
MEPH. That I shall wait on Faustus
whilst he lives,[3]
So he will buy my service with his soul.
FAUST. Already Faustus hath hazarded
that for thee.
MEPH. But, Faustus, thou must bequeath
it solemnly,
And write a deed of gift with thine own
blood,
For that security craves great Lucifer.
If thou deny it, I will back to hell.
FAUST. Stay, Mephistophilis, and tell me
what good
Will my soul do thy lord.
MEPH.   Enlarge his kingdom.
FAUST. Is that the reason he tempts us
thus?   40
MEPH. *Solamen miseris socios habuisse
doloris.*[4]
FAUST. Have you any pain that tortures
others?
MEPH. As great as have the human souls
of men.
But tell me, Faustus, shall I have thy
soul?

[1] Come.   [2] From 1616 edn.
[3] From 1616 edn. Original has *I live.*
[4] It is a solace to the wretched to have had
companions in sorrow.

And I will be thy slave, and wait on
thee,
And give thee more than thou hast wit
to ask.
FAUST. Ay, Mephistophilis, I give it
thee.
MEPH. Then stab thine arm courageously,
And bind thy soul that at some certain
day
Great Lucifer may claim it as his own; 50
And then be thou as great as Lucifer.
FAUST. [*Stabbing his arm.*] Lo, Mephis-
tophilis, for love of thee
I cut mine arm, and with my proper [5]
blood
Assure my soul to be great Lucifer's,
Chief lord and regent of perpetual
night!
View here the blood that trickles from
mine arm,
And let it be propitious for my wish.
MEPH. But, Faustus, thou must
Write it in manner of a deed of gift.
FAUST. Ay, so I will. [*Writes.*] But,
Mephistophilis,   60
My blood congeals, and I can write no
more.
MEPH. I'll fetch thee fire to dissolve it
straight.   *Exit.*
FAUST. What might the staying of my
blood portend?
Is it unwilling I should write this bill?
Why streams it not that I may write
afresh?
"Faustus gives to thee his soul." Ah,
there it stayed.
Why shouldst thou not? Is not thy
soul thine own?
Then write again, "Faustus gives to
thee his soul."

Enter Mephistophilis with a chafer [6] *of
coals.*

MEPH. Here's fire. Come, Faustus, set
it on.
FAUST. So now the blood begins to clear
again;   70
Now will I make an end immediately.
                         [*Writes.*]
MEPH. [*Aside.*] O, what will not I do to
obtain his soul?
FAUST. *Consummatum est:*[7] this bill is
ended,

[5] Own.   [6] Portable grate.   [7] It is finished.

And Faustus hath bequeathed his soul
to Lucifer.
But what is this inscription on mine arm?
"Homo, fuge!" [1] Whither should I fly?
If unto God, he'll throw me down to
hell.
My senses are deceived; here's nothing
writ.
I see it plain; here in this place is writ,
"Homo, fuge!" Yet shall not Faustus
fly.   80
MEPH. I'll fetch him somewhat to de-
light his mind.   *Exit.*

*Enter with Devils, giving crowns and rich
apparel to Faustus, and dance, and
then depart.*

FAUST. Speak, Mephistophilis, what means
this show?
MEPH. Nothing, Faustus, but to delight
thy mind withal,
And to show thee what magic can per-
form.
FAUST. But may I raise up spirits when I
please?
MEPH. Ay, Faustus, and do greater
things than these.
FAUST. Then there's enough for a thou-
sand souls.
Here, Mephistophilis, receive this scroll,
A deed of gift of body and of soul—
But yet conditionally that thou perform   90
All articles prescribed between us both.
MEPH. Faustus, I swear by hell and Lucifer
To effect all promises between us made.
FAUST. Then hear me read them: "On
these conditions following:—First, that
Faustus may be a spirit in form and substance; secondly, that Mephistophilis
shall be his servant, and at his command;
thirdly, that Mephistophilis shall do for
him and bring him whatsoever; [2] [100
fourthly, that he shall be in his chamber or
house invisible; lastly, that he shall appear
to the said John Faustus, at all times, in
what form or shape soever he please—I,
John Faustus, of Wertenberg, Doctor, by
these presents do give both body and soul
to Lucifer, Prince of the East, and his
minister, Mephistophilis; and further-

more grant unto them that, four-and-
twenty years being expired, the articles [110
above written inviolate, full power to fetch
or carry the said John Faustus, body and
soul, flesh, blood, or goods, into their
habitation wheresoever.   By me, John
Faustus."
MEPH. Speak, Faustus, do you deliver
this as your deed?
FAUST. Ay, take it, and the devil give
thee good on 't.
MEPH. Now, Faustus, ask what thou
wilt.
FAUST. First will I question with thee
about hell.
Tell me, where is the place that men call
hell?   120
MEPH. Under the heavens.
FAUST.   Ay, but whereabout?
MEPH. Within the bowels of these ele-
ments,
Where we are tortured and remain for-
ever.
Hell hath no limits, nor is circumscribed
In one self [3] place, for where we are is
hell,
And where hell is [there] [4] must we ever
be;
And, to conclude, when all the world
dissolves,
And every creature shall be purified,
All places shall be hell that is not heaven.
FAUST. Come, I think hell's a fable.   130
MEPH. Ay, think so still, till experience
change thy mind.
FAUST. Why, think'st thou then that
Faustus shall be damned?
MEPH. Ay, of necessity, for here's the
scroll
Wherein thou hast given thy soul to
Lucifer.
FAUST. Ay, and body too; but what of
that?
Think'st thou that Faustus is so fond [5]
to imagine
That, after this life, there is any pain?
Tush, these are trifles, and mere old
wives' tales.
MEPH. But, Faustus, I am an instance
to prove the contrary,   139
For I am damnéd, and am now in hell.
FAUST. How? Now in hell? Nay, and [6]

---

[1] "Man, fly!"   [2] Ellipsis for *whatsoever it be.*

[3] One and the same.   [5] Foolish.
[4] Added from 1616 edn.   [6] If

this be hell, I'll willingly be damned
here.   What?   Walking, disputing, etc.?
But, leaving off this, let me have a wife,
the fairest maid in Germany, for I am
wanton and lascivious, and cannot live
without a wife.

MEPH. How? A wife? I prithee, Faustus,
talk not of a wife.

FAUST. Nay,   sweet   Mephistophilis,
fetch me one, for I will have one.   151

MEPH. Well—thou wilt have one. Sit
there till I come. I'll fetch thee a wife in
the devil's name.   [Exit.]

Enter with a Devil dressed like a woman,
with fireworks.

MEPH. Tell, Faustus, how dost thou like
    thy wife?

FAUST. A plague on her for a hot whore!

MEPH.   Tut, Faustus,
    Marriage is but a ceremonial toy;
    If thou lovest me, think [no] [1] more of it.
    I'll cull thee out the fairest courte-
        sans,
    And bring them every morning to thy
        bed.   160
    She whom thine eye shall like, thy heart
        shall have,
    Be she as chaste as was Penelope,
    As wise as Saba,[2] or as beautiful
    As was bright Lucifer before his fall.
    Hold, take this book; peruse it thor-
        oughly.   [Gives a book.]
    The iterating of these lines brings gold;
    The framing of this circle on the ground
    Brings whirlwinds, tempests, thunder,
        and lightning;
    Pronounce this thrice devoutly to thy-
        self,   169
    And men in armor shall appear to thee,
    Ready to execute what thou desir'st.

FAUST. Thanks, Mephistophilis; yet fain
would I have a book wherein I might behold all spells and incantations, that I
might raise up spirits when I please.

MEPH. Here they are, in this book.
                        There turn to them.

FAUST. Now would I have a book where
I might see all characters and planets of
the heavens, that I might know their motions and dispositions.[3]   180

[1] Added from 1609 edn.   [2] Sheba.
[3] Situations in relation to their influence upon
men.

MEPH. Here they are too.
                        Turn to them.

FAUST. Nay, let me have one book
more—and then I have done—wherein I
might see all plants, herbs, and trees that
grow upon the earth.

MEPH. Here they be.

FAUST. O, thou art deceived.

MEPH. Tut, I warrant thee.
                        Turn to them.
                        [*Exeunt.*]

[SCENE vi.

The same.

Enter Faustus in his study and Mephis-
tophilis.] [4]

FAUST. When I behold the heavens, then
    I repent,
    And curse thee, wicked Mephistophilis,
    Because thou hast deprived me of those
        joys.

MEPH. Why, Faustus,
    Think'st thou heaven is such a glorious
        thing?
    I tell thee 'tis not half so fair as thou,
    Or any man that breathes on earth.

FAUST. How provest thou that?

MEPH. It was made for man; therefore
    is man more excellent.

FAUST. If it were made for man, 'twas
    made for me;   10
    I will renounce this magic and repent.

Enter Good Angel and Evil Angel.

GOOD A. Faustus, repent; yet God will
    pity thee.

EVIL A. Thou art a spirit; God cannot
    pity thee.

FAUST. Who buzzeth in mine ears I am a
    spirit?
    Be I a devil, yet God may pity me;
    Ay, God will pity me if I repent.

EVIL A. Ay, but Faustus never shall re-
    pent.   *Exeunt* [*Angels*].

FAUST. My heart's so hardened I cannot
    repent.
    Scarce can I name salvation, faith, or
        heaven,
    But fearful echoes thunders in mine
        ears,   20

[4] Stage direction from 1616 edn.

"Faustus, thou art damned!" Then
swords and knives,
Poison, guns, halters, and envenomed
steel
Are laid before me to despatch myself,
And long ere this I should have slain
myself,
Had not sweet pleasure conquered deep
despair.
Have not I made blind Homer sing to
me
Of Alexander's love and Œnon's death?
And hath not he that built the walls of
Thebes
With ravishing sound of his melodious
harp
Made music with my Mephistophilis? 30
Why should I die then, or basely despair?
I am resolved: Faustus shall ne'er re-
pent.
Come, Mephistophilis, let us dispute
again,
And argue of divine astrology.
Tell me, are there many heavens above
the moon?
Are all celestial bodies but one globe,
As is the substance of this centric earth?
MEPH. As are the elements, such are the
spheres
Mutually folded in each other's orb,
And, Faustus, 40
All jointly move upon one axletree
Whose terminine [1] is termed the world's
wide pole;
Nor are the names of Saturn, Mars, or
Jupiter
Feigned, but are erring stars.
FAUST. But tell me, have they all one
motion, both *situ et tempore?* [2]
MEPH. All jointly move from east to
west in four-and-twenty hours upon the
poles of the world, but differ in their motion
upon the poles of the zodiac. 50
FAUST. Tush, these slender trifles Wagner
can decide.
Hath Mephistophilis no greater skill?
Who knows not the double motion of the
planets?
The first is finished in a natural day;
the second thus: as Saturn in thirty years;
Jupiter in twelve; Mars in four; the sun,
Venus, and Mercury in a year; the moon
in eight-and-twenty days. Tush, these are

freshmen's suppositions. But tell me, hath
every sphere a dominion or *intelligentia?* [3] [60
MEPH. Ay.
FAUST. How many heavens, or spheres,
are there?
MEPH. Nine: the seven planets, the
firmament, and the imperial [4] heaven.
FAUST. Well, resolve me in this ques-
tion: Why have we not conjunctions, oppo-
sitions, aspects, eclipses, all at one time, but
in some years we have more, in some less?
MEPH. *Per inæqualem motum respectu
totius.* [5] 70
FAUST. Well, I am answered. Tell me who
made the world.
MEPH. I will not.
FAUST. Sweet Mephistophilis, tell me.
MEPH. Move me not, for I will not tell
thee.
FAUST. Villain, have I not bound thee to
tell me anything?
MEPH. Ay, that is not against our king-
dom; but this is.
Think thou on hell, Faustus, for thou art
damned.
FAUST. Think, Faustus, upon God that
made the world.
MEPH. Remember this. *Exit.*
FAUST. Ay, go, accursèd spirit, to ugly hell.
'Tis thou hast damned distressèd Faus-
tus' soul. 80
Is't not too late?

Enter Good Angel, and Evil.

EVIL A. Too late.
GOOD A. Never too late, if Faustus can
repent.
EVIL A. If thou repent, devils shall tear
thee in pieces.
GOOD A. Repent, and they shall never
rase [6] thy skin. *Exeunt [Angels].*
FAUST. Ah, Christ, my Savior,
Seek to save distressèd Faustus' soul!

*Enter Lucifer, Belzebub, and Mephis-
tophilis.*

LUC. Christ cannot save thy soul, for he is
just;
There's none but I have int'rest in the
same.

---

[1] Limit. [2] In space and in time.

[3] Intelligence, spirit. From 1616 edn.; original
has *intelligentii.* [4] Empyreal.
[5] Because of their uneven motion in regard to
the whole. [6] Scratch.

FAUST. O, who art thou that look'st so
    terrible?   90
LUC. I am Lucifer,
    And this is my companion prince in hell.
FAUST. O Faustus, they are come to fetch
    away thy soul!
LUC. We come to tell thee thou dost in-
    jure us.
    Thou talk'st of Christ, contrary to thy
        promise;
    Thou shouldst not think of God. Think
        of the devil,
    And of his dame, too.
FAUST. Nor will I henceforth. Pardon me
    in this,
    And Faustus vows never to look to
        heaven,   99
    Never to name God, or to pray to him;
    To burn his Scriptures, slay his ministers,
    And make my spirits pull his churches
        down.
LUC. Do so, and we will highly gratify [1]
thee. Faustus, we are come from hell to
show thee some pastime. Sit down, and
thou shalt see all the Seven Deadly Sins
appear in their proper shapes.
FAUST. That sight will be as pleasing unto
    me
    As paradise was to Adam the first day
    Of his creation.   110
LUC. Talk not of paradise nor creation,
but mark this show. Talk of the devil, and
nothing else.—Come away!

Enter the Seven Deadly Sins.

Now, Faustus, examine them of their several names and dispositions.
    FAUST. What art thou, the first?
    PRIDE. I am Pride. I disdain to have
any parents. I am like to Ovid's flea: I can
creep into every corner of a wench. [119
Sometimes, like a periwig, I sit upon her
brow; or, like a fan of feathers, I kiss her
lips; indeed I do—what do I not? But, fie,
what a scent is here! I'll not speak another
word except the ground were perfumed, and
covered with cloth of arras.
    FAUST. What art thou, the second?
    COVET. I am Covetousness, begotten of
an old churl in an old leathern bag; and,
might I have my wish, I would desire that
this house and all the people in it [130

were turned to gold, that I might lock you
up in my good chest. O, my sweet gold!
    FAUST. What art thou, the third?
    WRATH. I am Wrath. I had neither father
nor mother. I leaped out of a lion's mouth
when I was scarce half an hour old and, ever
since, I have run up and down the world
with this case [2] of rapiers, wounding myself when I had nobody to fight withal.
I was born in hell; and look to it, [140
for some of you shall be my father.
    FAUST. What art thou, the fourth?
    ENVY. I am Envy, begotten of a chim-
ney sweeper and an oyster wife. I cannot
read, and therefore wish all books were
burnt. I am lean with seeing others eat. O,
that there would come a famine through
all the world, that all might die, and I live
alone! Then thou shouldst see how fat I
would be. But must thou sit and I [150
stand? Come down with a vengeance!
    FAUST. Away, envious rascal!—What
art thou, the fifth?
    GLUT. Who, I, sir? I am Gluttony. My
parents are all dead, and the devil a penny
they have left me but a bare pension, and
that is thirty meals a day and ten bevers [3]—
a small trifle to suffice nature. O, I come
of a royal parentage! My grandfather was a
Gammon of Bacon, my grandmother [160
a Hogshead of Claret Wine. My godfathers
were these—Peter Pickleherring and Martin Martlemas-beef. O, but my godmother
she was a jolly gentlewoman, and well beloved in every good town and city. Her
name was Mistress Margery Marchbeer.
Now,[4] Faustus, thou hast heard all my
progeny,[5] wilt thou bid me to supper?
    FAUST. No, I'll see thee hanged; thou
wilt eat up all my victuals.   170
    GLUT. Then the devil choke thee!
    FAUST. Choke thyself, glutton!—What
art thou, the sixth?
    SLOTH. I am Sloth. I was begotten on a
sunny bank, where I have lain ever since;
and you have done me great injury to bring
me from thence. Let me be carried thither
again by Gluttony and Lechery. I'll not
speak another word for a king's ransom.
    FAUST. What are you, Mistress Minx, the
    seventh and last?   180
    LECH. Who, I, sir? I am one that loves

---

[1] Reward.
[2] Pair.   [4] Now that.
[3] Refreshments between meals.   [5] Lineage.

an inch of raw mutton better than an ell of
fried stockfish; and the first letter of my
name begins with Lechery.

Luc.[1] Away to hell, to hell! (*Exeunt the
Sins.*)—Now, Faustus, how dost thou like
this?

Faust. O, this feeds my soul!

Luc. Tut, Faustus, in hell is all manner
of delight.　　　　　　　　　　　　　　190

Faust. O, might I see hell, and return
　　again,
　　How happy were I then!

Luc. Thou shalt; I will send for thee at
　　midnight.
　　In meantime take this book; peruse it
　　throughly,
　　And thou shalt turn thyself into what
　　shape thou wilt.

Faust. Great thanks, mighty Lucifer!
　　This will I keep as chary as my life.

Luc. Farewell, Faustus, and think on the
　　devil.

Faust. Farewell, great Lucifer!　Come,
　　Mephistophilis.　　　　*Exeunt omnes.*

[Chorus]

Enter Wagner solus.[2]

Wag. Learned Faustus,　　　　　　　200
　　To know the secrets of astronomy
　　Graven in the book of Jove's high firma-
　　ment,
　　Did mount himself to scale Olympus' top,
　　Being seated in a chariot burning bright,
　　Drawn by the strength of yoky dragons'
　　necks.
　　He now is gone to prove cosmography,
　　And, as I guess, will first arrive at Rome,
　　To see the pope and manner of his court,
　　And take some part of holy Peter's
　　feast,　　　　　　　　　　　　　209
　　That to this day is highly solemnized.
　　　　　　　　　　　　　　Exit Wagner.

[Scene vii.

The Pope's privy chamber.]

Enter Faustus and Mephistophilis.

Faust. Having now, my good Mephis-
　　tophilis,
　　Passed with delight the stately town of
　　Trier,

---

[1] Placed before *Now, Faustus* in the original.
[2] 1616 edn. reads *Enter the Chorus.*

Environed round with airy mountain tops,
With walls of flint, and deep entrenchéd
　　lakes,[3]
Not to be won by any conquering prince,
From Paris next, coasting[4] the realm of
　　France,
We saw the river Maine fall into Rhine,
Whose banks are set with groves of
　　fruitful vines;
Then up to Naples, rich Campania,
Whose buildings fair and gorgeous to the
　　eye,　　　　　　　　　　　　　10
The streets straight forth, and paved
　　with finest brick,
Quarters the town in four equivalents.
There saw we learned Maro's golden
　　tomb,
The way he cut, an English mile in
　　length,
Thorough a rock of stone in one night's
　　space;[5]
From thence to Venice, Padua, and the
　　rest,
In midst of which a sumptuous temple
　　stands,
That threats the stars with her aspiring
　　top.
Thus hitherto hath Faustus spent his time.
But tell me, now, what resting place is
　　this?　　　　　　　　　　　　20
Hast thou, as erst I did command,
Conducted me within the walls of Rome?

Meph. Faustus, I have; and, because we
will not be unprovided, I have taken up his
holiness' privy chamber for our use.

Faust. I hope his holiness will bid us
welcome.

Meph. Tut, 'tis no matter, man; we'll
　　be bold with his good cheer.
　　And now, my Faustus, that thou mayst
　　perceive
　　What Rome containeth to delight thee
　　with,　　　　　　　　　　　　30
　　Know that this city stands upon seven
　　hills
　　That underprops the groundwork of the
　　same.
　　[Just through the midst runs flowing
　　Tiber's stream,
　　With winding banks that cut it in two
　　parts,][6]

---

[3] Moats.　　　　　　　　　[4] Skirting.
[5] Virgil was regarded as a magician in the
Middle Ages.　　　　　[6] From 1616 edn.

Over the which four stately bridges lean,
That makes safe passage to each part of
   Rome.
Upon the bridge called Ponto Angelo,
Erected is a castle passing strong,
Within whose walls such store of ordo-
   nance are,
And double cannons, framed of carvéd
   brass,   40
As match the days within one complete
   year,
Besides the gates and high pyramides,
Which Julius Cæsar brought from Africa.
FAUST. Now by the kingdoms of infernal
   rule,
Of Styx, Acheron, and the fiery lake
Of ever-burning Phlegeton, I swear
That I do long to see the monuments
And situation of bright, splendent Rome.
Come therefore; let's away.
MEPH. Nay, Faustus, stay; I know you'd
   fain see the pope,   50
And take some part of holy Peter's
   feast,
Where thou shalt see a troop of baldpate
   friars,
Whose *summum bonum* [1] is in belly-cheer.
FAUST. Well, I am content to compass then
   some sport,
And by their folly make us merriment.
Then charm me, that I may be invisible,
   to do what I please,
Unseen of any whilst I stay in Rome.
MEPH. [*Charming him.*] So, Faustus, now
   Do what thou wilt; thou shalt not be
   discerned.

Sound a sennet. [2] *Enter the Pope and the
   Cardinal of Lorrain to the banket,* [3] *with
   Friars attending.*

POPE. My Lord of Lorrain, wilt please you
   draw near?   60
FAUST. Fall to, and the devil choke you,
   and [4] you spare!
POPE. How now! Who's that which spake?
   —Friars, look about.
FRIAR. Here's nobody, if it like your holi-
   ness.
POPE. My lord, here is a dainty dish
was sent me from the Bishop of Milan.
FAUST. I thank you, sir.   *Snatch it.*

POPE. How now! Who's that which
snatched the meat from me? Will no man
look? My lord, this dish was sent me from
the Cardinal of Florence.   70
FAUST. You say true; I'll ha't.
                  [*Snatch it.*]
POPE. What, again? My lord, I'll drink
to your grace.
FAUST. I'll pledge your grace.
              [*Snatch the cup.*]
LOR. My lord, it may be some ghost
newly crept out of purgatory, come to beg a
pardon of your holiness.
POPE. It may be so. Friars, prepare a
dirge to lay the fury of this ghost. Once
again, my lord, fall to.   80
         The Pope crosseth himself.
FAUST. What, are you crossing of your-
   self?
Well, use that trick no more, I would
   advise you.   *Cross again.*
Well, there's the second time. Aware the
   third,
I give you fair warning.
*Cross again, and Faustus hits him a box of
   the ear; and they all run away.*
FAUST. Come on, Mephistophilis, what
   shall we do?
MEPH. Nay, I know not. We shall be
   cursed with bell, book, and candle.
FAUST. How? Bell, book, and candle;
   candle, book, and bell—
Forward and backward to curse Faustus
   to hell!
Anon you shall hear a hog grunt, a calf
   bleat, and an ass bray, because it is
   S[aint] Peter's holiday.

Enter all the Friars to sing the dirge.

FRIAR. Come, brethren, let's about our
business with good devotion.   90
                   Sing this:
Cursed be he that stole away his holi-
   ness' meat from the table! *Maledicat
   Dominus!* [5]
Cursed be he that struck his holiness a
   blow on the face! *Maledicat Dominus!*
Cursed be he that took Friar Sandelo a
   blow on the pate! *Male., etc.*
Cursed be he that disturbeth our holy
   dirge! *Male., etc.*
Cursed be he that took away his holi-

---

[1] Highest good.   [3] Banquet.
[2] Trumpet call. Original has *sonnet.*   [4] If.

[5] The Lord curse him!

ness' wine! *Maledicat Dominus! Et
omnes sancti!* [1] *Amen.*

[*Mephistophilis and Faustus*] *beat the
Friars, and fling fireworks among them,
and so exeunt.*

Enter Chorus.

When Faustus had with pleasure ta'en
　　the view
Of rarest things and royal courts of kings,
He stayed his course, and so returnéd
　　home,
Where such as bear his absence but with
　　grief—　　　　　　　　　　　　　　　100
I mean his friends and nearest compan-
　　ions—
Did gratulate his safety with kind words,
And in their conference of what befell,
Touching his journey through the world
　　and air,
They put forth questions of astrology,
Which Faustus answered with such
　　learned skill,
As they admired and wondered at his wit.
Now is his fame spread forth in every land.
Amongst the rest the emperor is one,　109
Carolus the Fifth, at whose palace now
Faustus is feasted 'mongst his noblemen.
What there he did in trial of his art,
I leave untold—your eyes shall see per-
　　formed.　　　　　　　　　　　　*Exit.*

[SCENE viii.

An innyard.]

*Enter Robin the Ostler with a book in his
hand.*

ROBIN. O, this is admirable! Here I ha'
stolen one of Doctor Faustus' conjuring
books, and i' faith I mean to search some
circles for my own use. [*Draws circles on
the ground.*] Now will I make all the
maidens in our parish dance at my pleasure, stark naked before me; and so by that
means I shall see more than e'er I felt or
saw yet.

Enter Rafe, calling Robin.

RAFE. Robin, prithee come away. [10
There's a gentleman tarries to have his
horse, and he would have his things rubbed
and made clean. He keeps such a chafing
with my mistress about it, and she has

[1] And all the saints.

sent me to look thee out. Prithee come
away.

ROBIN. Keep out, keep out, or else you
are blown up; you are dismembered, Rafe!
Keep out, for I am about a roaring piece
of work.　　　　　　　　　　　　　20

RAFE. Come, what doest thou with
that same book thou canst not read?

ROBIN. Yes, my master and mistress
shall find that I can read, he for his forehead, she for her private study. She's born
to bear with me, or else my art fails.

RAFE. Why, Robin, what book is that?

ROBIN. What book? Why, the most
intolerable book for conjuring that e'er was
invented by any brimstone devil.　　30

RAFE. Canst thou conjure with it?

ROBIN. I can do all these things easily
with it: first, I can make thee drunk with
ippocras [2] at any tabern [3] in Europe for
nothing; that's one of my conjuring works.

RAFE. Our Master Parson says that's
nothing.

ROBIN. True, Rafe. And more, Rafe,
if thou hast any mind to Nan Spit, our
kitchenmaid, then turn her and wind　[40
her to thy own use as often as thou wilt,
and at midnight.

RAFE. O brave Robin, shall I have Nan
Spit, and to mine own use? On that condition I'll feed thy devil with horse bread
as long as he lives, of free cost.

ROBIN. No more, sweet Rafe. Let's go
and make clean our boots, which lie foul
upon our hands, and then to our conjuring
in the devil's name.　　　　*Exeunt.*　50

[SCENE ix.

The same.]

Enter Robin and Rafe with a silver goblet.

ROBIN. Come, Rafe, did not I tell thee
we were forever made by this Doctor
Faustus' book? *Ecce signum.* [4] Here's a
simple purchase [5] for horse keepers; our
horses shall eat no hay as long as this lasts.

Enter the Vintner.

RAFE. But, Robin, here comes the
vintner.

ROBIN. Hush! I'll gull him supernatu-

[2] A sweetened, spiced wine.　　[4] Behold the sign.
[3] Tavern.　　　　　　　　　　　[5] Spoil, plunder.

cally. Drawer, I hope all is paid. God be
with you! Come, Rafe.   10

VINT. Soft, sir; a word with you. I must
yet have a goblet paid from you ere you go.

ROBIN. I a goblet? Rafe, I a goblet? I
scorn you, and you are but a &c.[1] I a
goblet? Search me!

VINT. I mean so, sir, with your favor.
                              [*Searches him.*]

ROBIN. How say you now?

VINT. I must say somewhat to your
fellow. You, sir!

RAFE. Me, sir? Me, sir? Search your [20
fill. [*Vintner searches him.*] Now, sir, you
may be ashamed to burden honest men
with a matter of truth.[2]

VINT. Well, t'one of you hath this
goblet about you.

ROBIN. [*Aside.*] You lie, drawer, 'tis
afore me.—Sirrah you, I'll teach ye to
impeach honest men! Stand by! I'll
scour you for a goblet! Stand aside you
had best, I charge you in the name [30
of Belzebub.—[*Aside to Rafe.*] Look to the
goblet, Rafe.

VINT. What mean you, sirrah?

ROBIN. I'll tell you what I mean. (*He
reads.*) Sanctobulorum Periphrasticon!—
Nay, I'll tickle you, vintner.—[*Aside.*]
Look to the goblet, Rafe.—*Polypragmos
Belseborams framanto pacostiphos tostu,
Mephistophilis, etc.*[3]

*Enter Mephistophilis, sets squibs at their
backs [, and then exit]. They run about.*

VINT. O, nomine Domine![4] What [40
mean'st thou, Robin, thou hast no goblet?

RAFE. Peccatum peccatorum![5] Here's
thy goblet, good vintner.
              [*Gives goblet to Vintner. Exit Vintner.*]

ROBIN. Misericordia pro nobis![6] What
shall I do? Good devil, forgive me now,
and I'll never rob thy library more.

Enter to them Meph[istophilis].

MEPH.[7] Monarch of hell, under whose
    black survey

[1] Here the actor extemporizes.
[2] Question of their honesty.
[3] Latin and Greek gibberish used as an incantation.
[4] Ungrammatical phrase for "O, in the name
ʋf the Lord."   [5] Sin of sins!   [6] Mercy on us!
[7] Here the original inserts two lines of prose
roughly approximating ll. 57–59.

Great potentates do kneel with awful
    fear,
Upon whose altars thousand souls do lie,
How am I vexéd with these villains'
    charms!   50
From Constantinople am I hither come
Only for pleasure of these damnéd slaves.

ROBIN. How, from Constantinople? You
have had a great journey. Will you take
sixpence in your purse to pay for your
supper, and be gone?

MEPH. Well, villains, for your presumption I transform thee into an ape, and thee
into a dog. And so be gone.   *Exit.*

ROBIN. How, into an ape? That's [60
brave! I'll have fine sport with the boys.
I'll get nuts and apples enow.

RAFE. And I must be a dog.

ROBIN. I' faith, thy head will never be
out of the pottage pot.   *Exeunt.*

[SCENE X.

The German Court.]

*Enter Emperor, Faustus, [Mephistophilis,]
    and a Knight, with Attendants.*

EMP. Master Doctor Faustus, I have
heard strange report of thy knowledge in
the black art, how that none in my empire
nor in the whole world can compare with
thee for the rare effects of magic. They say
thou hast a familiar spirit, by whom thou
canst accomplish what thou list.[8] This,
therefore, is my request, that thou let me
see some proof of thy skill, that mine eyes
may be witnesses to confirm what mine [10
ears have heard reported; and here I swear
to thee by the honor of mine imperial
crown that, whatever thou doest, thou
shalt be no ways prejudiced or endamaged.

KNIGHT. (*Aside.*) I' faith, he looks much
like a conjuror.

FAUST. My gracious sovereign, though
I must confess myself far inferior to the
report men have published, and nothing
answerable[9] to the honor of your im- [20
perial majesty, yet for that[10] love and duty
binds me thereunto, I am content to do
whatsoever your majesty shall command
me.

EMP. Then, Doctor Faustus, mark what I
    shall say.

[8] Desirest.   [10] Because.
[9] Not at all corresponding.

As I was sometime solitary set
Within my closet, sundry thoughts arose
About the honor of mine ancestors,
How they had won by prowess such ex-
    ploits,
Got such riches, subdued so many king-
    doms,   30
As we that do succeed, or they that shall
Hereafter possess our throne, shall,
I fear me, never attain to that degree
Of high renown and great authority;
Amongest which kings is Alexander the
    Great,
Chief spectacle of the world's preemi-
    nence,
The bright shining of whose glorious acts
Lightens the world with his reflecting
    beams,
As,[1] when I heard but motion [2] made of
    him,   39
It grieves my soul I never saw the man.
If, therefore, thou by cunning of thine
    art
Canst raise this man from hollow vaults
    below,
Where lies entombed this famous con-
    queror,
And bring with him his beauteous par-
    amour,
Both in their right shapes, gesture, and
    attire
They used to wear during their time of
    life,
Thou shalt both satisfy my just desire,
And give me cause to praise thee whilst
    I live.
FAUST. My gracious lord, I am ready to
accomplish your request so far forth as [50
by art and power of my spirit I am able to
perform.
KNIGHT. (Aside.) I' faith, that's just
nothing at all.
FAUST. But, if it like your grace, it is
not in my ability to present before your
eyes the true substantial bodies of those
two deceased princes, which long since are
consumed to dust.
KNIGHT. (Aside.) Ay, marry, Master [60
Doctor, now there's a sign of grace in you,
when you will confess the truth.
FAUST. But such spirits as can lively [3]
resemble Alexander and his paramour shall

appear before your grace in that manner
that they best lived in, in their most flourishing estate, which I doubt not shall sufficiently content your imperial majesty.
EMP. Go to, Master Doctor, let me see
them presently.   70
KNIGHT. Do you hear, Master Doctor?
You bring Alexander and his paramour
before the emperor!
FAUST. How then, sir?
KNIGHT. I' faith, that's as true as Diana
turned me to a stag!
FAUST. No, sir, but when Actæon died,
he left the horns for you. Mephistophilis,
begone!   Exit Meph[istophilis].
KNIGHT. Nay, and you go to con-   [80
juring, I'll be gone.   Exit Kn[ight].
FAUST. I'll meet with you [4] anon for interrupting me so. Here they are, my gracious lord.

*Enter Meph[istophilis] with Alexander and
                                    his Paramour.*

EMP. Master Doctor, I heard this lady
while she lived had a wart or mole in her
neck. How shall I know whether it be so
or no?
FAUST. Your highness may boldly go
and see.   90

*[Emperor examines her.]   Exit Alex[ander
                                    with his Paramour].*

EMP. Sure, these are no spirits, but the
true substantial bodies of those two deceased princes.
FAUST. Will 't please your highness now
to send for the knight that was so pleasant
with me here of late?
EMP. One of you call him forth.
                              [Attendant calls.]

*Enter the Knight with a pair of horns on his
                                    head.*

EMP. How now, Sir Knight! Why, I had
thought thou hadst been a bachelor, but
now I see thou hast a wife, that not   [100
only gives thee horns, but makes thee wear
them. Feel on thy head!
KNIGHT. Thou damnéd wretch and ex-
    ecrable dog,
Bred in the concave [5] of some monstrous
    rock,

---

[1] So that.   [3] In a lifelike way.
[2] *I.e.*, mention.
[4] Get even with you.   [5] Hollow.

How dar'st thou thus abuse a gentleman?
Villain, I say, undo what thou hast done!

FAUST. O, not so fast, sir; there's no
haste. But, good,[1] are you remembered
how you crossed me in my conference with
the emperor? I think I have met with [110
you for it.

EMP. Good Master Doctor, at my entreaty release him; he hath done penance
sufficient.

FAUST. My gracious lord, not so much
for the injury he offered me here in your
presence, as to delight you with some mirth,
hath Faustus worthily requited this injurious knight, which being all I desire, I
am content to release him of his horns. [120
And, Sir Knight, hereafter speak well of
scholars. Mephistophilis, transform him
straight. [Mephistophilis removes the horns.]
Now, my good lord, having done my duty,
I humbly take my leave.

EMP. Farewell, Master Doctor; yet, ere
you go,
Expect from me a bounteous reward.
　　　　　Exit Emperor [with the Others].

[SCENE xi.

A common.

Enter Faustus and Mephistophilis.]

FAUST. Now, Mephistophilis, the restless
　　course
That Time doth run with calm and silent
　　foot,
Short'ning my days and thread of vital
　　life,
Calls for the payment of my latest years;
Therefore, sweet Mephistophilis, let us
Make haste to Wertenberg.

MEPH. What, will you go on horseback
or on foot?

FAUST. Nay, till I am past this fair and
pleasant green, I'll walk on foot.

Enter a Horse-Corser.[2]

HORSE-C. I have been all this day seeking one Master Fustian. Mass, see [10
where he is! God save you, Master Doctor!

FAUST. What, horse-corser! You are
well met.

HORSE-C. Do you hear, sir? I have
brought you forty dollars for your horse.

FAUST. I cannot sell him so. If thou
lik'st him for fifty, take him.

HORSE-C. Alas, sir, I have no more.—I
pray you speak for me.

MEPH. I pray you let him have him. [20
He is an honest fellow, and he has a great
charge, neither wife nor child.

FAUST. Well, come, give me your money.
　　[Horse-Corser gives Faustus the money.]
My boy will deliver him to you. But I
must tell you one thing before you have him:
ride him not into the water at any hand.[3]

HORSE-C. Why, sir, will he not drink of
all waters?

FAUST. O, yes, he will drink of all
waters, but ride him not into the water. [30
Ride him over hedge or ditch, or where thou
wilt, but not into the water.

HORSE-C. Well, sir.—[Aside.] Now am
I made man forever. I'll not leave my
horse for forty. If he had but the quality
of hey-ding-ding, hey-ding-ding, I'd make
a brave living on him. He has a buttock
as slick as an eel.—Well, God buy,[4] sir.
Your boy will deliver him me. But hark ye,
sir; if my horse be sick or ill at ease, if [40
I bring his water to you, you'll tell me
what it is?　　　　　Exit Horse-Corser.

FAUST. Away, you villain! What, dost
think I am a horse doctor?
　　　　　[Retires into his study.]

[SCENE xii.

Faustus' study.]

FAUST. What art thou, Faustus, but a man
　　condemned to die?
Thy fatal time doth draw to final end;
Despair doth drive distrust into my
　　thoughts;
Confound these passions with a quiet
　　sleep.
Tush, Christ did call the thief upon the
　　Cross;
Then rest thee, Faustus, quiet in conceit.
　　　　　Sleep in his chair.

Enter Horse-Corser, all wet, crying.

HORSE-C. Alas, alas! Doctor Fustian,
quotha? Mass, Doctor Lopus[5] was never

[1] I.e., good man.　　　　[2] Horse dealer.
[3] In any case.　[4] God be with you (good bye).
[5] Dr. Lopez, Queen Elizabeth's physician, who
was hanged in 1594 for a supposed attempt to
poison her. This passage, therefore, could not
have been written by Marlowe.

such a doctor. Has given me a purgation, has purged me of forty dollars; I shall [10 never see them more. But yet, like an ass as I was, I would not be ruled by him, for he bade me I should ride him into no water. Now I, thinking my horse had had some rare quality that he would not have had me known of, I, like a vent'rous youth, rid him into the deep pond at the town's end. I was no sooner in the middle of the pond, but my horse vanished away, and I sat upon a bottle [1] of hay, never so near [20 drowning in my life. But I'll seek out my doctor, and have my forty dollars again, or I'll make it the dearest horse!—

[Enter Mephistophilis.]

O, yonder is his snipper-snapper.—Do you hear? You hey-pass,[2] where's your master?

MEPH. Why, sir, what would you? You cannot speak with him.

HORSE-C. But I will speak with him.

MEPH. Why, he's fast asleep. Come some other time.   30

HORSE-C. I'll speak with him now, or I'll break his glass windows [3] about his ears.

MEPH. I tell thee he has not slept this eight nights.

HORSE-C. And he have not slept this eight weeks, I'll speak with him.

MEPH. See where he is, fast asleep.

HORSE-C. Ay, this is he. God save ye, Master Doctor! Master Doctor, Master Doctor Fustian!—Forty dollars, forty [40 dollars for a bottle of hay!

MEPH. Why, thou seest he hears thee not.

HORSE-C. So ho, ho!—So ho, ho! (*Hallo in his ear.*) No, will you not wake? I'll make you wake ere I go! (*Pull him by the leg, and pull it away.*) Alas, I am undone! What shall I do?   48

FAUST. O, my leg, my leg! Help, Mephistophilis! Call the officers. My leg, my leg!

MEPH. Come, villain, to the constable.

HORSE-C. O Lord, sir, let me go, and I'll give you forty dollars more.

MEPH. Where be they?

HORSE-C. I have none about me. Come to my ostry [4] and I'll give them you.

MEPH. Be gone quickly!

Horse-Corser runs away.

FAUST. What, is he gone? Farewell he Faustus has his leg again, and the horse corser, I take it, a bottle of hay for [6(his labor. Well, this trick shall cost him forty dollars more.

Enter Wagner.

How now, Wagner, what's the news with thee?

WAG. Sir, the Duke of Vanholt doth earnestly entreat your company.

FAUST. The Duke of Vanholt! An honorable gentleman, to whom I must be no niggard of my cunning. Come, [69 Mephistophilis, let's away to him. *Exeunt.*

[SCENE xiii.

The court of the Duke of Vanholt.]

Enter the Duke of Vanholt, the Duchess, Faustus, and Mephistophilis.[5]

DUKE. Believe me, Master Doctor, this merriment hath much pleased me.

FAUST. My gracious lord, I am glad it contents you so well.—But it may be, madam, you take no delight in this. I have heard that great-bellied women do long for some dainties or other. What is it, madam? Tell me, and you shall have it.

DUCH. Thanks, good Master Doctor; [10 and, for I see your courteous intent to pleasure me, I will not hide from you the thing my heart desires. And were it now summer, as it is January and the dead time of the winter, I would desire no better meat than a dish of ripe grapes.

FAUST. Alas, madam, that's nothing! Mephistophilis, begone. (*Exit Meph[is-tophilis].*) Were it a greater thing than this, so it would content you, you should [20 have it.

Enter Mephisto[philis] with the grapes.

Here they be, madam. Wilt please you taste on them?

DUKE. Believe me, Master Doctor, this makes me wonder above the rest, that being in the dead time of winter, and in the month of January, how you should come by these grapes.

FAUST. If it like your grace, the year

---

[1] Load, bundle.   [3] Spectacles (?).
[2] Juggler.   [4] Ostlery, inn.

[5] Original reads: "Enter to them the Duke and the Duchess. The Duke speaks."

is divided into two circles over the whole [30
world, that, when it is here winter with us,
in the contrary circle it is summer with
them, as in India, Saba, and farther countries in the East; and by means of a swift
spirit that I have, I had them brought
hither, as ye see.—How do you like them,
madam; be they good?

DUCH. Believe me, Master Doctor,
they be the best grapes that e'er I tasted
in my life before.   40

FAUST. I am glad they content you so,
madam.

DUKE. Come, madam, let us in, where
you must well reward this learned man for
the great kindness he hath showed to you.

DUCH. And so I will, my lord; and, whilst
I live,
Rest beholding [1] for this courtesy.

FAUST. I humbly thank your grace.

DUKE. Come, Master Doctor, follow us
and receive your reward.   *Exeunt.* 50

[SCENE xiv.

Faustus' study.]

Enter Wagner solus.

WAG. I think my master means to die
shortly,
For he hath given to me all his goods;
And yet methinks, if that death were
near,
He would not banquet and carouse and
swill
Amongst the students, as even now he
doth,
Who are at supper with such belly-
cheer
As Wagner ne'er beheld in all his life.
See where they come! Belike the feast
is ended.

Enter Faustus, with two or three Scholars
                    [*and Mephistophilis*].

1 SCH. Master Doctor Faustus, since
our conference about fair ladies, which [10
was the beautifull'st in all the world, we
have determined with ourselves that Helen
of Greece was the admirablest lady that
ever lived. Therefore, Master Doctor,
if you will do us that favor, as to let us
see that peerless dame of Greece, whom all

the world admires for majesty, we should
think ourselves much beholding unto you.

FAUST.[2] Gentlemen,
For that I know your friendship is un-
feigned,   20
And Faustus' custom is not to deny
The just requests of those that wish
him well,
You shall behold that peerless dame of
Greece,
No otherways for pomp and majesty
Than when Sir Paris crossed the seas
with her,
And brought the spoils to rich Dardania.
Be silent, then, for danger is in words.

*Music sounds, and Helen passeth over the
                                        stage.*

2 SCH. Too simple is my wit to tell her
praise,
Whom all the world admires for majesty.

3 SCH. No marvel though the angry
Greeks pursued   30
With ten years' war the rape [3] of such
a queen,
Whose heavenly beauty passeth all
compare.

1 SCH. Since we have seen the pride of
Nature's works
And only paragon of excellence,

Enter an Old Man.

Let us depart; and for this glorious deed
Happy and blessed be Faustus evermore.

FAUSTUS. Gentlemen, farewell—the same
I wish to you.   *Exeunt Scholars.*

OLD MAN. Ah, Doctor Faustus, that I
might prevail
To guide thy steps unto the way of life,
By which sweet path thou mayst at-
tain the goal   40
That shall conduct thee to celestial rest!
Break heart, drop blood, and mingle
it with tears,
Tears falling from repentant heaviness
Of thy most vild and loathsome filthi-
ness,
The stench whereof corrupts the inward
soul
With such flagitious crimes of heinous
sins
As no commiseration may expel,

[1] Beholden, indebted.

[2] The following speech is printed as prose in
the original, but as verse in the 1616 e**n.

[3] Capture.

But mercy, Faustus, of thy Savior sweet,
Whose blood alone must wash away
thy guilt.

FAUST. Where art thou, Faustus? Wretch,
what hast thou done? 50

Damned art thou, Faustus, damned;
despair and die!

Hell calls for right, and with a roaring
voice

Says, "Faustus, come! Thine hour is
come!"

And Faustus will come to do thee right.
Mephi[stophilis] gives him a dagger.

OLD MAN. Ah, stay, good Faustus, stay
thy desperate steps!

I see an angel hovers o'er thy head,
And, with a vial full of precious grace,
Offers to pour the same into thy soul.
Then call for mercy, and avoid despair.

FAUST. Ah, my sweet friend, I feel 60
Thy words to comfort my distresséd
soul.

Leave me a while to ponder on my sins.

OLD MAN. I go, sweet Faustus, but with
heavy cheer,

Fearing the ruin of thy hopeless soul.
[Exit.]

FAUST. Accurséd Faustus, where is mercy
now?

I do repent, and yet I do despair;
Hell strives with grace for conquest in
my breast.

What shall I do to shun the snares of
death?

MEPH. Thou traitor Faustus, I arrest
thy soul

For disobedience to my sovereign lord; 70
Revolt, or I'll in piecemeal tear thy flesh.

FAUST. Sweet Mephistophilis, entreat thy
lord

To pardon my unjust presumption,
And with my blood again I will confirm
My former vow I made to Lucifer.

MEPH. Do it then quickly, with unfeignéd
heart,

Lest greater danger do attend thy drift.
*[Faustus pricks his arm and signs a paper
with his blood.]*

FAUST. Torment, sweet friend, that base
and crooked age,[1]

That durst dissuade me from thy Lucifer,
With greatest torments that our hell
affords. 80

[1] Old Man.

MEPH. His faith is great; I cannot touch
his soul.

But what I may afflict his body with
I will attempt, which is but little worth.

FAUST. One thing, good servant, let me
crave of thee,

To glut the longing of my heart's desire:
That I might have unto my paramour
That heavenly Helen, which I saw of
late,

Whose sweet embraces may extinguish
clean

These thoughts that do dissuade me
from my vow,

And keep mine oath I made to Lucifer. 90

MEPH. Faustus, this or what else thou
shalt desire

Shall be performed in twinkling of an
eye.

Enter Helen.

FAUST. Was this the face that launched
a thousand ships,

And burnt the topless towers of Ilium?
Sweet Helen, make me immortal with
a kiss. *[Kisses her.]*

Her lips sucks forth my soul; see where
it flies!—

Come, Helen, come, give me my soul
again.

Here will I dwell, for heaven be in these
lips,

And all is dross that is not Helena.

Enter Old Man.

I will be Paris, and for love of thee, 100
Instead of Troy, shall Wertenberg be
sacked;

And I will combat with weak Menelaus,
And wear thy colors on my pluméd
crest;

Yea, I will wound Achilles in the heel,
And then return to Helen for a kiss.
O, thou art fairer than the evening air
Clad in the beauty of a thousand stars;
Brighter art thou than flaming Jupiter
When he appeared to hapless Semele;
More lovely than the monarch of the
sky 110

In wanton Arethusa's azured arms;
And none but thou shalt be my paramour. *Exeunt [all except Old Man].*

OLD MAN. Accurséd Faustus, miserable
man,

That from thy soul exclud'st the grace
of heaven,
And fliest the throne of his tribunal
seat!

Enter the Devils.

Sathan begins to sift me with his pride.
As in this furnace God shall try my
faith,
My faith, vile hell, shall triumph over
thee.
Ambitious fiends, see how the heavens
smiles
At your repulse, and laughs your state
to scorn!   120
Hence, hell; for hence I fly unto my
God!   *Exeunt.*

[SCENE XV.

The same.]

Enter Faustus with the Scholars.

FAUST. Ah, gentlemen!
1 SCH. What ails Faustus?
FAUST. Ah, my sweet chamber-fellow,
had I lived with thee, then had I lived
still, but now I die eternally. Look, comes
he not, comes he not?
2 SCH. What means Faustus?
3 SCH. Belike he is grown into some
sickness by being oversolitary.
1 SCH. If it be so, we'll have physi- [10
cians to cure him. 'Tis but a surfeit.
Never fear, man.
FAUST. A surfeit of deadly sin that
hath damned both body and soul.
2 SCH. Yet, Faustus, look up to
heaven; remember God's mercies are infinite.
FAUST. But Faustus' offense can ne'er
be pardoned. The serpent that tempted
Eve may be saved, but not Faustus. [20
Ah, gentlemen, hear me with patience,
and tremble not at my speeches! Though
my heart pants and quivers to remember
that I have been a student here these
thirty years, O, would I had never seen
Wertenberg, never read book! And what
wonders I have done, all Germany can
witness, yea, all the world; for which
Faustus hath lost both Germany and the
world, yea, heaven itself, heaven, the [30
seat of God, the throne of the blessed, the

kingdom of joy, and must remain in hell
forever, hell, ah, hell, forever! Sweet
friends, what shall become of Faustus,
being in hell forever?
3 SCH. Yet, Faustus, call on God.
FAUST. On God, whom Faustus hath
abjured! On God, whom Faustus hath
blasphemed! Ah, my God, I would weep,
but the devil draws in my tears. Gush [40
forth blood instead of tears! Yea, life
and soul! O, he stays my tongue! I would
lift up my hands, but see, they hold them,
they hold them!
ALL. Who, Faustus?
FAUST. Lucifer and Mephistophilis. Ah,
gentlemen, I gave them my soul for my
cunning!
ALL. God forbid!
FAUST. God forbade it indeed, but [50
Faustus hath done it. For vain pleasure
of four-and-twenty years hath Faustus
lost eternal joy and felicity. I writ them
a bill with mine own blood. The date is
expired; the time will come, and he will
fetch me.
1 SCH. Why did not Faustus tell us of
this before, that divines might have prayed
for thee?
FAUST. Oft have I thought to have [60
done so; but the devil threatened to tear
me in pieces if I named God; to fetch both
body and soul if I once gave ear to divinity. And now 'tis too late. Gentlemen,
away, lest you perish with me!
2 SCH. O, what shall we do to [save][1]
Faustus?
FAUST. Talk not of me, but save yourselves, and depart.
3 SCH. God will strengthen me. I [70
will stay with Faustus.
1 SCH. Tempt not God, sweet friend;
but let us into the next room, and there
pray for him.
FAUST. Ay, pray for me, pray for me,
and what noise soever ye hear, come not
unto me, for nothing can rescue me.
2 SCH. Pray thou, and we will pray
that God may have mercy upon thee.
FAUST. Gentlemen, farewell! If I [80
live till morning, I'll visit you. If not—
Faustus is gone to hell.
ALL. Faustus, farewell!
Exeunt Sch[olars]. The clock strikes eleven.

[1] Added from 1616 edn.

Faust. Ah, Faustus,
Now hast thou but one bare hour to
 live,
And then thou must be damned per-
 petually!
Stand still, you ever-moving spheres of
 heaven,
That time may cease, and midnight
 never come!
Fair Nature's eye, rise, rise again and
 make
Perpetual day; or let this hour be but   90
A year, a month, a week, a natural day,
That Faustus may repent and save his
 soul!
O lente, lente, currite, noctis equi! [1]
The stars move still, [2] time runs, the
 clock will strike,
The devil will come, and Faustus must
 be damned.
O, I'll leap up to my God! Who pulls
 me down?
See, see where Christ's blood streams
 in the firmament!
One drop would save my soul—half a
 drop. Ah, my Christ!
Ah, rend not my heart for naming of
 my Christ!
Yet will I call on him! O, spare me,
 Lucifer!—   100
Where is it now? 'Tis gone; and see
 where God
Stretcheth out his arm, and bends his
 ireful brows!
Mountains and hills, come, come and
 fall on me,
And hide me from the heavy wrath of
 God!
No! No!
Then will I headlong run into the earth.
Earth gape! O, no, it will not harbor
 me!
You stars that reigned at my nativity,
Whose influence hath allotted death
 and hell,
Now draw up Faustus like a foggy
 mist   110
Into the entrails of yon lab'ring clouds,
That, when you vomit forth into the
 air,
My limbs may issue from your smoky
 mouths,

[1] Run slowly, slowly, horses of night.
[2] Continuously.

So that my soul may but ascend to
 heaven.   *The watch strikes.*
Ah, half the hour is past!
'Twill all be past anon!
O God!
If thou wilt not have mercy on my soul,
Yet, for Christ's sake whose blood hath
 ransomed me,
Impose some end to my incessant
 pain.   120
Let Faustus live in hell a thousand years,
A hundred thousand, and at last be
 saved!
O, no end is limited to damnéd souls!
Why wert thou not a creature wanting
 soul?
Or why is this immortal that thou hast?
Ah, Pythagoras' metempsychosis! Were
 that true,
This soul should fly from me, and I
 be changed
Unto some brutish beast! All beasts
 are happy,
For, when they die,
Their souls are soon dissolved in ele-
 ments.   130
But mine must live, still to be plagued
 in hell.
Cursed be the parents that engendered me!
No, Faustus, curse thyself; curse Lucifer
That hath deprived thee of the joys of
 heaven.   *The clock striketh twelve.*
O, it strikes, it strikes! Now, body,
 turn to air,
Or Lucifer will bear thee quick [3] to hell.
                 Thunder and lightning.
O soul, be changed into little water-
 drops,
And fall into the ocean—ne'er be found.
My God, my God, look not so fierce on
 me!

Enter Devils.

Adders and serpents, let me breathe
 awhile!   140
Ugly hell, gape not! Come not, Lucifer!
I'll burn my books!—Ah, Mephistophilis!   *Exeunt with him.*

Enter Chorus.

Cut is the branch that might have grown
 full straight,
And burnéd is Apollo's laurel bough
[3] Alive.

That sometime [1] grew within this learned man.

Faustus is gone; regard his hellish fall,

Whose fiendful fortune may exhort the wise

Only to wonder at unlawful things,

[1] Once.

Whose deepness doth entice such forward wits

To practice more than heavenly power permits.   [*Exit.*] 150

TERMINAT HORA DIEM; TERMINAT
                    AUTHOR OPUS. [2]

[2] The hour (midnight) ends the day; the author ends his work.

THE TROUBLESOME REIGN AND LAMENTABLE DEATH OF EDWARD THE SECOND[1]

BY

CHRISTOPHER MARLOWE

[*DRAMATIS PERSONÆ*

KING EDWARD THE SECOND.

PRINCE EDWARD, *his son, afterwards King Edward the Third.*

EDMUND, *Earl of Kent, brother to King Edward the Second.*

PIERS GAVESTON.

ARCHBISHOP OF CANTERBURY.

BISHOP OF COVENTRY.

BERKELEY, *Bishop of Winchester.*

EARL OF WARWICK.

EARL OF LANCASTER.

EARL OF PEMBROKE.[2]

EARL OF ARUNDEL.

EARL OF LEICESTER.

BEAUMONT.

SIR THOMAS BERKELEY.[3]

MORTIMER, SENIOR.

MORTIMER, JUNIOR, *his nephew.*

SPENCER, THE ELDER.

SPENCER, THE YOUNGER, *his son.*

BALDOCK, *a clerk.*

SIR WILLIAM TRUSSEL,[4] *Proctor of Parlia ment.*

GURNEY } *creatures of young*
MATREVIS[5] } *Mortimer.*

LIGHTBORN, *a murderer.*

SIR JOHN OF HAINAULT.

LEVUNE, *a Frenchman.*

RICE AP HOWELL.

JAMES, *servant to Pembroke.*

AN ABBOT, MONKS, A HERALD, LORDS, POOR MEN, A MOWER, THE KING'S CHAMPION, MESSENGERS, SOLDIERS, *and* ATTENDANTS.

QUEEN ISABELLA, *wife to King Edward the Second.*

A LADY, *niece to King Edward the Second and daughter to the Duke of Gloucester.*

OTHER LADIES.

SCENE: *England and Paris.*

TIME: *Early fourteenth century.*]

[SCENE i.

Near the court in London.]

Enter Gaveston, reading on a letter that was brought him from the King.

[GAV.] "My father is deceased! Come, Gaveston,
And share the kingdom with thy dearest friend."

Ah, words that make me surfeit with delight!
What greater bliss can hap to Gaveston
Than live and be the favorite of a king?
Sweet prince, I come. These, these thy amorous lines
Might have enforced me to have swum from France,

---

[1] The title continues: "King of England, with the Tragical Fall of Proud Mortimer, As It Was Sundry Times Publicly Acted in the Honorable City of London by the Right Honorable the Earl of Pembroke His Servants. Written by Chri. Marlowe, Gent."

[2] This name regularly appears as *Penbrook* in original.

[3] Consistent spelling of this name as *Bartley* indicates the pronunciation in this play.

[4] Dyce suggests that this character is represented in the speech head *Tru.* in Scene **xviii**.

[5] Dyce suggests Sir John Maltravers.

And, like Leander, gasped upon the sand,
So thou wouldst smile, and take me in
   thy arms.
The sight of London to my exiled eyes 10
Is as Elysium to a newcome soul;
Not that I love the city, or the men,
But that it harbors him I hold so dear—
The king, upon whose bosom let me die,
And with the world be still at enmity.
What need the artic people love starlight,
To whom the sun shines both by day
   and night?
Farewell, base stooping to the lordly
   peers!
My knee shall bow to none but to the
   king.
As for the multitude, that are but
   sparks   20
Raked up in embers of their poverty,
Tanti! [1] I'll fawn [2] first on the wind
That glanceth at my lips, and flyeth
   away.
But how now, what are these?

Enter three Poor Men.

POOR MEN. Such as desire your worship's
   service.
GAV. What canst thou do?
1 POOR. I can ride.
GAV. But I have no horses.—What art
   thou?
2 POOR. A traveler.
GAV.   Let me see. Thou wouldst do well
   To wait at my trencher and tell me lies
   at dinner time;   30
   And, as I like your discoursing, I'll have
   you.—
   And what art thou?
3 POOR. A soldier that hath served
   against the Scot.
GAV. Why, there are hospitals for such as
   you.
I have no war, and therefore, sir, begone.
SOLDIER. [3] Farewell, and perish by a soldier's hand,
   That wouldst reward them with an hospital.
GAV. [*Aside.*] Ay, ay, these words of his
   move me as much
As if a goose should play the porpen-
   tine, [4]

And dart her plumes, thinking to pierce
   my breast.   40
But yet it is no pain to speak men fair;
I'll flatter these, and make them live in
   hope.—
You know that I came lately out of
   France,
And yet I have not viewed my lord the
   king;
If I speed well, I'll entertain you all.
OMNES. We thank your worship.
GAV. I have some business; leave me to
   myself.
OMNES. We will wait here about the court.
                    Exeunt.
GAV. Do.—These are not men for me. 49
I must have wanton poets, pleasant wits,
Musicians that with touching of a string
May draw the pliant king which way I
   please.
Music and poetry is his delight;
Therefore I'll have Italian masques by
   night,
Sweet speeches, comedies, and pleasing
   shows;
And in the day, when he shall walk
   abroad,
Like sylvan nymphs my pages shall be
   clad;
My men, like satyrs grazing on the lawns,
Shall with their goat feet dance an antic
   hay. [5]   59
Sometime a lovely boy in Dian's shape
With hair that gilds the water as it glides,
Crownets [6] of pearl about his naked arms,
And in his sportful hands an olive tree,
To hide those parts which men delight
   to see,
Shall bathe him in a spring; and there
   hard by,
One like Acteon peeping through the
   grove
Shall by the angry goddess be trans-
   formed,
And running in the likeness of an hart
By yelping hounds pulled down, and
   seem to die.
Such things as these best please his
   majesty,   70
My lord.—Here comes the king and the
   nobles
From the parliament. I'll stand aside.
                 [*Retires.*]

---

[1] So much for them.   [3] *I.e., 3 Poor.*
[2] Original reads *fanne.*   [4] Porcupine.
[5] Country dance.   [6] Coronets, garlands.

Enter the King; Lancaster; Mortimer, Senior;
  Mortimer, Junior; Edmund, Earl of
  Kent; Guy, Earl of Warwick; etc.

EDW. Lancaster!

LAN. My lord.

GAV. [*Aside.*] That Earl of Lancaster do
  I abhor!

EDW. Will you not grant me this?—[*Aside.*]
  In spite of them
  I'll have my will; and these two Morti-
  mers,
  That cross me thus, shall know I am
  displeased.

MOR. SEN. If you love us, my lord, hate
  Gaveston.

GAV. [*Aside.*] That villain Mortimer! I'll
  be his death.   80

MOR. JUN. Mine uncle here, this earl, and
  I myself
  Were sworn to your father at his death
  That he should ne'er return into the
  realm;
  And know, my lord, ere I will break my
  oath,
  This sword of mine, that should offend
  your foes,
  Shall sleep within the scabbard at thy
  need,
  And underneath thy banners march who
  will,
  For Mortimer will hang his armor up.

GAV. [*Aside.*] *Mort Dieu!* [1]

EDW. Well, Mortimer, I'll make thee rue
  these words.   90
  Beseems it thee to contradict thy king?
  Frown'st thou thereat, aspiring Lan-
  caster?
  The sword shall plane the furrows of thy
  brows,
  And hew these knees that now are grown
  so stiff.
  I will have Gaveston; and you shall know
  What danger 'tis to stand against your
  king.

GAV. [*Aside.*] Well done, Ned!

LAN. My lord, why do you thus incense
  your peers,
  That naturally would love and honor
  you   99
  But for that base and obscure Gaveston?
  Four earldoms have I, besides Lancaster—

[1] God's death!

Derby, Salisbury, Lincoln, Leicester;
These will I sell, to give my soldiers pay,
Ere Gaveston shall stay within the realm.
Therefore, if he be come, expel him
  straight.

EDM.[2] Barons and earls, your pride hath
  made me mute;
  But now I'll speak, and to the proof, I
  hope.
  I do remember, in my father's days,
  Lord Percy of the north, being highly
  moved,
  Braved Mowbery [3] in presence of the
  king,   110
  For which, had not his highness loved
  him well,
  He should have lost his head; but with
  his look
  The undaunted spirit of Percy was ap-
  peased,
  And Mowbery and he were reconciled.
  Yet dare you brave the king unto his
  face!—
  Brother, revenge it, and let these their
  heads
  Preach upon poles, for trespass of their
  tongues.

WAR. O, our heads!

EDW. Ay, yours; and therefore I would
  wish you grant—   119

WAR. Bridle thy anger, gentle Mortimer.

MOR. JUN. I cannot, nor I will not; I must
  speak.—
  Cousin, our hands I hope shall fence our
  heads,
  And strike off his that makes you
  threaten us.
  Come, uncle, let us leave the brainsick
  king,
  And henceforth parley with our naked
  swords.

MOR. SEN. Wiltshire hath men enough to
  save our heads.

WAR. [*Ironically.*] All Warwickshire will
  love him for my sake!

LAN. [*Ironically.*] And northward Gaveston hath many friends!—
  Adieu, my lord; and either change your
  mind,
  Or look to see the throne, where you
  should sit,   130

[2] The name of this character appears interchangeably as *Edmund* or *Kent* in speech heads
throughout the play.   [3] Mowbray.

To float in blood, and at thy wanton
  head
The glozing [1] head of thy base minion
  thrown.
                    Exeunt Nobles [except Kent].
EDW. I cannot brook these haughty men-
  aces.
Am I a king, and must be overruled?—
Brother, display my ensigns in the field;
I'll bandy [2] with the barons and the
  earls,
And either die or live with Gaveston.
GAV. I can no longer keep me from my
  lord.   *[Comes forward.]*
EDW. What, Gaveston! Welcome! Kiss
  not my hand;   139
Embrace me, Gaveston, as I do thee.
Why shouldst thou kneel? Knowest thou
  not who I am? [3]
Thy friend, thyself, another Gaveston!
Not Hylas was more mourned of Hercu-
  les
Than thou hast been of me since thy
  exile.
GAV. And, since I went from hence, no
  soul in hell
Hath felt more torment than poor
  Gaveston.
EDW. I know it.—Brother, welcome home
  my friend.
Now let the treacherous Mortimers con-
  spire,
And that high-minded [4] Earl of Lan-
  caster.   149
I have my wish, in that I joy [5] thy sight;
And sooner shall the sea o'erwhelm my
  land
Than bear the ship that shall transport
  thee hence.
I here create thee lord high chamberlain,
Chief secretary to the state and me,
Earl of Cornwall, King and Lord of
  Man. [6]
GAV. My lord, these titles far exceed my
  worth.
KENT. Brother, the least of these may
  well suffice
For one of greater birth than Gaveston.
EDW. Cease, brother, for I cannot brook
  these words.

Thy worth, sweet friend, is far above
  my gifts.   160
Therefore, to equal it, receive my heart.
If for these dignities thou be envied,
I'll give thee more, for, but to honor
  thee,
Is Edward pleased with kingly regiment. [7]
Fear'st thou [8] thy person? Thou shalt
  have a guard!
Wants thou gold? Go to my treasury!
Wouldst thou be loved and feared? Re-
  ceive my seal;
Save or condemn, and in our name com-
  mand
Whatso thy mind affects, [9] or fancy likes.
GAV. It shall suffice me to enjoy your
  love,   170
Which, whiles I have, I think myself as
  great
As Cæsar riding in the Roman street,
With captive kings at his triumphant
  ear.

Enter the Bishop of Coventry.

EDW. Whither goes my Lord of Coventry
  so fast?
BISH. To celebrate your father's exequies.
But is that wicked Gaveston returned?
EDW. Ay, priest, and lives to be revenged
  on thee,
That wert the only cause of his exile.
GAV. 'Tis true, and, but for reverence of
  these robes,
Thou shouldst not plod one foot beyond
  this place.   180
BISH. I did no more than I was bound to
  do;
And, Gaveston, unless thou be reclaimed,
As then I did incense the parliament,
So will I now, and thou shalt back to
  France.
GAV. Saving your reverence, you must
  pardon me.
EDW. Throw off his golden miter, rend his
  stole,
And in the channel [10] christen him anew.
KENT. Ah, brother, lay not violent hands
  on him,
For he'll complain unto the see of Rome!
GAV. Let him complain unto the see of
  hell;   190
I'll be revenged on him for my exile.

[1] Flattering.   [2] Fight.
[3] Here and in a few other passages the line
division has been regularized.   [5] Enjoy.
[4] Arrogant.   [6] Isle of Man.
[7] Rule.   [9] Desires.
[8] Fear'st thou for.   [10] Gutter.

EDW. No, spare his life, but seize upon
his goods.
Be thou lord bishop and receive his rents,
And make him serve thee as thy chaplain.
I give him thee—here, use him as thou
wilt.

GAV. He shall to prison, and there die in
bolts.

EDW. Ay, to the Tower, the Fleet, or
where thou wilt.

BISH. For this offense, be thou accursed of
God!

EDW. Who's there? Convey this priest to
the Tower.

BISH. True, true.[1]   200

EDW. But in the meantime, Gaveston,
away,
And take possession of his house and
goods.
Come, follow me, and thou shalt have
my guard
To see it done, and bring thee safe again.

GAV. What should a priest do with so fair
a house?
A prison may best beseem his holiness.
                                                 [Exeunt.]

[SCENE ii.

Westminster.]

*Enter [on one side] both the Mortimers; [on
the other,] Warwick and Lancaster.*

WAR. 'Tis true, the bishop is in the Tower,
And goods and body given to Gaveston.

LAN. What, will they tyrannize upon the
church?
Ah, wicked king! Accurséd Gaveston!
This ground, which is corrupted with
their steps,
Shall be their timeless [2] sepulcher or
mine.

MOR. JUN. Well, let that peevish Frenchman guard him sure;
Unless his breast be swordproof, he shall
die.

MOR. SEN. How now! Why droops the
Earl of Lancaster?

MOR. JUN. Wherefore is Guy of Warwick
discontent?   10

LAN. That villain Gaveston is made an
earl.

MOR. SEN. An earl!

WAR. Ay, and besides, lord chamberlain
of the realm,
And secretary too, and Lord of Man.

MOR. SEN. We may not nor we will not
suffer this.

MOR. JUN. Why post we not from hence
to levy men?

LAN. "My Lord of Cornwall" now at ev-
ery word!
And happy is the man whom he vouch-
safes
For vailing [3] of his bonnet one good look.
Thus, arm in arm, the king and he doth
march.   20
Nay, more, the guard upon his lordship
waits,
And all the court begins to flatter him.

WAR. Thus leaning on the shoulder of the
king,
He nods and scorns and smiles at those
that pass.

MOR. SEN. Doth no man take exceptions
at the slave?

LAN. All stomach [4] him, but none dare
speak a word.

MOR. JUN. Ah, that bewrays [5] their baseness, Lancaster!
Were all the earls and barons of my
mind,
We'll hale him from the bosom of the
king,
And at the court gate hang the peasant
up,   30
Who, swoln with venom of ambitious
pride,
Will be the ruin of the realm and us.

*Enter the [Arch]bishop of Canterbury [and
an Attendant].*

WAR. Here comes my Lord of Canterbury's grace.

LAN. His countenance bewrays he is displeased.

[ARCH]BISH. First were his sacred garments
rent and torn;
Then laid they violent hands upon him;
next,
Himself imprisoned, and his goods as-
seized.[6]
This certify the pope.—Away, take
horse!   [Exit Attendant.]

---

[1] Alluding to euphemistic use of *convey*, taking the word in the sense of *steal, carry away
feloniously*.   [2] Untimely.

[3] Lowering, doffing.   [5] Reveals.
[4] Resent.   [6] Seized upon.

LAN. My lord, will you take arms against the king?

[ARCH]BISH. What need I? God himself is up in arms, 40
When violence is offered to the church.

MOR. JUN. Then will you join with us that be his peers,
To banish or behead that Gaveston?

[ARCH]BISH. What else, my lords? For it concerns me near;
The bishopric of Coventry is his.

Enter the Queen.

MOR. JUN. Madam, whither walks your majesty so fast?

QUEEN. Unto the forest, gentle Mortimer,
To live in grief and baleful discontent;
For now my lord the king regards me not,
But dotes upon the love of Gaveston. 50
He claps his cheeks, and hangs about his neck,
Smiles in his face, and whispers in his ears;
And, when I come, he frowns, as who should say,
"Go whither thou wilt, seeing I have Gaveston."

MOR. SEN. Is it not strange that he is thus bewitched?

MOR. JUN. Madam, return unto the court again.
That sly, inveigling Frenchman we'll exile
Or lose our lives; and yet, ere that day come,
The king shall lose his crown, for we have power, 59
And courage too, to be revenged at full.

[ARCH]BISH. But yet lift not your swords against the king.

LAN. No, but we'll lift Gaveston from hence.

WAR. And war must be the means, or he'll stay still.

QUEEN. Then let him stay; for rather than my lord
Shall be oppressed by civil mutinies,
I will endure a melancholy life,
And let him frolic with his minion.

[ARCH]BISH. My lords, to ease all this, but hear me speak:
We and the rest, that are his counselors,
Will meet and with a general consent 70
Confirm his banishment with our hands and seals.

LAN. What we confirm the king will frustrate.

MOR. JUN. Then may we lawfully revolt from him.

WAR. But say, my lord, where shall this meeting be?

[ARCH]BISH. At the New Temple.

MOR. JUN. Content.

[ARCH]BISH. And, in the meantime, I'll entreat you all
To cross to Lambeth, and there stay with me.

LAN. Come then, let's away.

MOR. JUN. Madam, farewell! 80

QUEEN. Farewell, sweet Mortimer, and for my sake
Forbear to levy arms against the king.

MOR. JUN. Ay, if words will serve; if not, I must. [*Exeunt.*]

[SCENE iii.

A street in London.]

Enter Gaveston and the Earl of Kent.

GAV. Edmund, the mighty Prince of Lancaster,
That hath more earldoms than an ass can bear,
And both the Mortimers, two goodly men,
With Guy of Warwick, that redoubted knight,
Are gone towards Lambeth—there let them remain! *Exeunt.*

[SCENE iv.

The New Temple.]

Enter Nobles.

LAN. Here is the form of Gaveston's exile.
May it please your lordship to subscribe your name.

[ARCH]BISH. Give me the paper!
[*He signs, followed by the others.*]

LAN. Quick, quick, my lord! I long to write my name.

WAR. But I long more to see him banished hence.

MOR. JUN. The name of Mortimer shall fright the king,
Unless he be declined [1] from that base peasant.

[1] Turned aside, parted.

Enter the King [, Kent,] and Gaveston.

EDW. What, are you moved that Gaveston
  sits here?
  It is our pleasure; we will have it so.
LAN. Your grace doth well to place him by
  your side,   10
  For nowhere else the new earl is so safe.
MOR. SEN. What man of noble birth can
  brook this sight?
  Quam male conveniunt! [1]
  See what a scornful look the peasant
  casts!
PEM. Can kingly lions fawn on creeping
  ants?
WAR. Ignoble vassal, that like Phaëton
  Aspir'st unto the guidance of the sun!
MOR. JUN. Their downfall is at hand, their
  forces down;
  We will not thus be faced and over-
  peered. [2]   19
EDW. Lay hands on that traitor Mortimer!
MOR. SEN. Lay hands on that traitor Gav-
  eston!
KENT. Is this the duty that you owe your
  king?
WAR. We know our duties—let him know
  his peers.
EDW. Whither will you bear him? Stay,
  or ye shall die.
MOR. SEN. We are no traitors; therefore
  threaten not.
GAV. No, threaten not, my lord, but pay
  them home!
  Were I a king—
MOR. JUN. Thou villain, wherefore talks
  thou of a king,
  That hardly art a gentleman by birth?
EDW. Were he a peasant, being my min-
  ion,   30
  I'll make the proudest of you stoop to
  him.
LAN. My lord, you may not thus disparage
  us.—
  Away, I say, with hateful Gaveston!
MOR. SEN. And with the Earl of Kent that
  favors him!
  [*Attendants remove Kent and Gaveston.*]
EDW. Nay, then, lay violent hands upon
  your king.
  Here, Mortimer, sit thou in Edward's
  throne;

Warwick and Lancaster, wear you my
  crown.
  Was ever king thus overruled as I?
LAN. Learn then to rule us better, and the
  realm.
MOR. JUN. What we have done, our heart
  blood shall maintain.   40
WAR. Think you that we can brook this
  upstart pride?
EDW. Anger and wrathful fury stops my
  speech.
[ARCH]BISH. Why are you moved? Be pa-
  tient, my lord,
  And see what we your counselors have
  done.
MOR. JUN. My lords, now let us all be
  resolute,
  And either have our wills or lose our
  lives.
EDW. Meet you for this, proud, overdaring
  peers?
  Ere my sweet Gaveston shall part from
  me,
  This isle shall fleet [3] upon the ocean,
  And wander to the unfrequented Inde. 50
[ARCH]BISH. You know that I am legate to
  the pope!
  On your allegiance to the see of Rome
  Subscribe, as we have done, to his exile.
MOR. JUN. Curse him, if he refuse; and
  then may we
  Depose him and elect another king.
EDW. Ay, there it goes! But yet I will
  not yield.
  Curse me, depose me, do the worst you
  can.
LAN. Then linger not, my lord, but do it
  straight.
[ARCH]BISH. Remember how the bishop
  was abused!
  Either banish him that was the cause
  thereof,   60
  Or I will presently [4] discharge these lords
  Of duty and allegiance due to thee.
EDW. [*Aside.*] It boots me not to threat; I
  must speak fair.—
  The legate of the pope will be obeyed.
  My lord, you shall be chancellor of the
  realm;
  Thou, Lancaster, high admiral of our
  fleet;
  Young Mortimer and his uncle shall be
  earls;

---

[1] How ill they agree!
[2] Looked down upon, scorned.
[3] Float.   [4] Immediately.

And you, Lord Warwick, President of the North;

And thou, of Wales. If this content you not, 69

Make several kingdoms of this monarchy,

And share it equally amongst you all,

So I may have some nook or corner left

To frolic with my dearest Gaveston.

[ARCH]BISH. Nothing shall alter us; we are resolved.

LAN. Come, come, subscribe.

MOR. JUN. Why should you love him whom the world hates so?

EDW. Because he loves me more than all the world.

Ah, none but rude and savage-minded men

Would seek the ruin of my Gaveston. 79

You that be noble born should pity him.

WAR. You that are princely born should shake him off.

For shame, subscribe, and let the lown [1] depart.

MOR. SEN. Urge him, my lord.

[ARCH]BISH. Are you content to banish him the realm?

EDW. I see I must, and therefore am content.

Instead of ink, I'll write it with my tears.
[Signs.]

MOR. JUN. The king is lovesick for his minion.

EDW. 'Tis done; and now, accursèd hand, fall off!

LAN. Give it me; I'll have it published in the streets.

MOR. JUN. I'll see him presently despatched away. 90

[ARCH]BISH. Now is my heart at ease.

WAR. And so is mine.

PEM. This will be good news to the common sort.

MOR. SEN. Be it or no, he shall not linger here. *Exeunt Nobles.*

EDW. How fast they run to banish him I love!

They would not stir, were it to do me good.

Why should a king be subject to a priest?

Proud Rome, that hatchest such imperial grooms,

For these thy superstitious taper lights,

Wherewith thy antichristian churches blaze, 99

[1] Worthless fellow.

I'll fire thy crazéd buildings, and enforce

The papal towers to kiss the lowly ground!

With slaughtered priests may Tiber's channel swell,

And banks raised higher with their sepulchers!

As for the peers that back the clergy thus,

If I be king, not one of them shall live.

Enter Gaveston.

GAV. My lord, I hear it whispered everywhere

That I am banished, and must fly the land.

EDW. 'Tis true, sweet Gaveston—O, were it false!

The legate of the pope will have it so,

And thou must hence, or I shall be deposed. 110

But I will reign to be revenged of them,

And therefore, sweet friend, take it patiently.

Live where thou wilt, I'll send thee gold enough;

And long thou shalt not stay, or, if thou dost,

I'll come to thee. My love shall ne'er decline.

GAV. Is all my hope turned to this hell of grief?

EDW. Rend not my heart with thy too piercing words.

Thou from this land, I from myself am banished.

GAV. To go from hence grieves not poor Gaveston,

But to forsake you, in whose gracious looks 120

The blessedness of Gaveston remains;

For nowhere else seeks he felicity.

EDW. And only this torments my wretched soul

That, whether I will or no, thou must depart.

Be governor of Ireland in my stead,

And there abide till fortune call thee home.

Here take my picture, and let me wear thine; *[They exchange pictures.]*

O, might I keep thee here as I do this,

Happy were I, but now most miserable!

GAV. 'Tis something to be pitied of a king.

EDW. Thou shalt not hence—I'll hide thee,
  Gaveston.   131
GAV. I shall be found, and then 'twill
  grieve me more.
EDW. Kind words and mutual talk makes
  our grief greater;
  Therefore, with dumb embracement, let
  us part.—
  Stay, Gaveston, I cannot leave thee thus!
GAV. For every look, my lord drops down
  a tear.
  Seeing I must go, do not renew my sor-
  row.
EDW. The time is little that thou hast to
  stay,
  And, therefore, give me leave to look
  my fill.
  But come, sweet friend, I'll bear thee on
  thy way.   140
GAV. The peers will frown.
EDW. I pass [1] not for their anger.—Come,
  let's go;
  O, that we might as well return as go.

Enter Edmund and Queen Isabel.

QUEEN. Whither goes my lord?
EDW. Fawn not on me, French strumpet!
  Get thee gone!
QUEEN. On whom but on my husband
  should I fawn?
GAV. On Mortimer, with whom, ungentle
  queen—
  I say no more. Judge you the rest, my
  lord.
QUEEN. In saying this, thou wrong'st
  me, Gaveston.
  Is't not enough that thou corrupts my
  lord,   150
  And art a bawd to his affections,
  But thou must call mine honor thus in
  question?
GAV. I mean not so; your grace must
  pardon me.
EDW. Thou art too familiar with that
  Mortimer,
  And by thy means is Gaveston exiled.
  But I would wish thee reconcile the lords,
  Or thou shalt ne'er be reconciled to me.
QUEEN. Your highness knows it lies not in
  my power.
EDW. Away then! Touch me not.—Come,
  Gaveston.

[1] Care

QUEEN. Villain, 'tis thou that robb'st me
  of my lord!   160
GAV. Madam, 'tis you that rob me of my
  lord.
EDW. Speak not unto her; let her droop
  and pine.
QUEEN. Wherein, my lord, have I deserved
  these words?
  Witness the tears that Isabella sheds,
  Witness this heart, that, sighing for thee,
  breaks,
  How dear my lord is to poor Isabel!
EDW. And witness heaven how dear thou
  art to me!
  There weep, for till my Gaveston be re-
  pealed,[2]
  Assure thyself thou com'st not in my
  sight.   *Exeunt Edward and Gaveston.*
QUEEN. O miserable and distressèd queen!
  Would, when I left sweet France and
  was embarked,   171
  That charming Circes,[3] walking on the
  waves,
  Had changed my shape, or at the mar-
  riage day
  The cup of Hymen had been full of
  poison,
  Or with those arms that twined about
  my neck
  I had been stifled, and not lived to see
  The king my lord thus to abandon me!
  Like frantic Juno will I fill the earth
  With ghastly murmur of my sighs and
  cries;
  For never doted Jove on Ganymede 180
  So much as he on cursèd Gaveston.
  But that will more exasperate his wrath.
  I must entreat him, I must speak him
  fair,
  And be a means to call home Gaveston.
  And yet he'll ever dote on Gaveston,
  And so am I forever miserable.

Enter the Nobles to the Queen.

LAN. Look where the sister of the King of
  France
  Sits wringing of her hands, and beats
  her breast!
WAR. The king, I fear, hath ill entreated [4]
  her.
PEM. Hard is the heart that injures such
  a saint.   190

[2] Recalled from exile.   [4] Treated, used.
[3] Circe.

MOR. JUN. I know 'tis long [1] of Gaveston
she weeps.

MOR. SEN. Why? He is gone.

MOR. JUN.   Madam, how fares
your grace?

QUEEN. Ah, Mortimer, now breaks the
king's hate forth,

And he confesseth that he loves me
not.

MOR. JUN. Cry quittance, madam, then,
and love not him.

QUEEN. No, rather will I die a thousand
deaths!

And yet I love in vain. He'll ne'er love
me.

LAN. Fear ye not, madam; now his minion's gone,

His wanton humor will be quickly left.

QUEEN. O never, Lancaster! I am enjoined   200

To sue unto you all for his repeal.

This wills my lord, and this must I perform,

Or else be banished from his highness'
presence.

LAN. For his repeal? Madam, he comes
not back,

Unless the sea cast up his shipwrack [2]
body.

WAR. And to behold so sweet a sight as
that,

There's none here but would run his
horse to death.

MOR. JUN. But, madam, would you have
us call him home?

QUEEN. Ay, Mortimer, for till he be restored,

The angry king hath banished me the
court;   210

And, therefore, as thou lovest and ten-
d'rest [3] me,

Be thou my advocate unto these peers.

MOR. JUN. What! Would you have me
plead for Gaveston?

MOR. SEN. Plead for him he that will, I
am resolved.

LAN. And so am I, my lord. Dissuade the
queen.

QUEEN. O Lancaster, let him dissuade the
king,

For 'tis against my will he should return.

WAR. Then speak not for him; let the
peasant go.

QUEEN. 'Tis for myself I speak, and not
for him.

PEM. No speaking will prevail, and therefore cease.   220

MOR. JUN. Fair queen, forbear to angle
for the fish

Which, being caught, strikes him that
takes it dead;

I mean that vile torpedo, Gaveston,

That now, I hope, floats on the Irish
seas. [4]

QUEEN. Sweet Mortimer, sit down by me
awhile,

And I will tell thee reasons of such weight
As thou wilt soon subscribe to his repeal.

MOR. JUN. It is impossible; but speak your
mind.

QUEEN. Then thus—but none shall hear
it but ourselves.   [They stand aside.]

LAN. My lords, albeit the queen win Mortimer,   230

Will you be resolute, and hold with me?

MOR. SEN. Not I, against my nephew.

PEM. Fear not; the queen's words cannot
alter him.

WAR. No? Do but mark how earnestly she
pleads!

LAN. And see how coldly his looks make
denial!

WAR. She smiles. Now for my life his
mind is changed!

LAN. I'll rather lose his friendship, I, than
grant.

MOR. JUN. Well, of necessity it must be so.

My lords, that I abhor base Gaveston,

I hope your honors make no question, 240

And therefore, though I plead for his
repeal,

'Tis not for his sake, but for our avail;

Nay, for the realm's behoof, and for the
king's.

LAN. Fie, Mortimer, dishonor not thyself!

Can this be true, 'twas good to banish
him?

And is this true, to call him home again?

Such reasons make white black, and dark
night day.

MOR. JUN. My Lord of Lancaster, mark
the respect. [5]

LAN. In no respect can contraries be true.

QUEEN. Yet, good my lord, hear what he
can allege.   250

---

[1] Because.   [2] Shipwrecked.   [3] Carest for.
[4] A sample of Marlowe's telescoping of time.
[5] Reason.

WAR. All that he speaks is nothing; we are
　resolved.

MOR. JUN. Do you not wish that Gaveston
　were dead?

PEM. I would he were!

MOR. JUN. Why, then, my lord, give me
　but leave to speak.

MOR. SEN. But, nephew, do not play the
　sophister.

MOR. JUN. This which I urge is of a burn-
　ing zeal

　To mend the king, and do our country
　　good.

　Know you not Gaveston hath store of
　　gold,

　Which may in Ireland purchase him
　　such friends　　　　　　　　　259

　As he will front the mightiest of us all?

　And whereas[1] he shall live and be be-
　　loved,

　'Tis hard for us to work his overthrow.

WAR. Mark you but that, my Lord of
　Lancaster.

MOR. JUN. But were he here, detested as
　he is,

　How easily might some base slave be
　　suborned

　To greet his lordship with a poniard,

　And none so much as blame the mur-
　　therer,

　But rather praise him for that brave
　　attempt,[2]

　And in the chronicle enroll his name

　For purging of the realm of such a
　　plague!　　　　　　　　　　270

PEM. He saith true.

LAN. Ay, but how chance this was not
　done before?

MOR. JUN. Because, my lords, it was not
　thought upon.

　Nay, more, when he shall know it lies in
　　us

　To banish him, and then to call him
　　home,

　'Twill make him vail the top flag of his
　　pride,

　And fear to offend the meanest noble-
　　man.

MOR. SEN. But how if he do not, nephew?

MOR. JUN. Then may we with some color[3]
　rise in arms;

　For, howsoever we have borne it out,　280

　'Tis treason to be up against the king.

So shall we have the people of[4] our side,

Which for his father's sake lean to the
　king,

But cannot brook a night-grown mush-
　rump,[5]

Such a one as my Lord of Cornwall is,

Should bear us down of the nobility.

And when the commons and the nobles
　join,

'Tis not the king can buckler Gaveston;

We'll pull him from the strongest hold
　he hath.

My lords, if to perform this I be slack, 290

Think me as base a groom as Gaveston.

LAN. On that condition, Lancaster will
　grant.

WAR. And so will Pembroke and I.

MOR. SEN. And I.

MOR. JUN. In this I count me highly
　gratified,

　And Mortimer will rest at your com-
　mand.

QUEEN. And when this favor Isabel for-
　gets,

　Then let her live abandoned and for-
　lorn.—

　But see, in happy time,[6] my lord the
　king,

　Having brought the Earl of Cornwall on
　his way,　　　　　　　　　　300

　Is new returned. This news will glad
　him much,

　Yet not so much as me. I love him
　more

　Than he can Gaveston. Would he loved
　me

　But half so much, then were I treble-
　blessed.

Enter King Edward, mourning.

EDW. He's gone, and for his absence thus
　I mourn.

Did never sorrow go so near my heart

As doth the want of my sweet Gaveston;

And could my crown's revenue bring
　him back,

I would freely give it to his enemies,

And think I gained, having bought so
　dear a friend.　　　　　　　　310

QUEEN. [*Aside.*] Hark, how he harps upon
　his minion!

---

[1] Where.　　　[2] Enterprise.　　　[3] Excuse.
[4] On.　　　　[6] At an appropriate moment.
[5] Mushroom.

EDW. My heart is as an anvil unto sorrow,
Which beats upon it like the Cyclops'
hammers,
And with the noise turns up my giddy
brain,
And makes me frantic for my Gaveston.
Ah, had some bloodless Fury rose from
hell,
And with my kingly scepter stroke [1] me
dead,
When I was forced to leave my Gaveston!
LAN. *Diablo!* [2] What passions call you
these?
QUEEN. My gracious lord, I come to
bring you news.   320
EDW. That you have parleyed with your
Mortimer!
QUEEN. That Gaveston, my lord, shall be
repealed.
EDW. Repealed! The news is too sweet to
be true.
QUEEN. But will you love me, if you find
it so?
EDW. If it be so, what will not Edward do?
QUEEN. For Gaveston, but not for Isabel.
EDW. For thee, fair queen, if thou lovest
Gaveston.
I'll hang a golden tongue about thy neck,
Seeing thou hast pleaded with so good
success.
QUEEN. No other jewels hang about my
neck   330
Than these, my lord; nor let me have
more wealth
Than I may fetch from this rich treasury.
O, how a kiss revives poor Isabel!
EDW. Once more receive my hand; and
let this be
A second marriage twixt thyself and me.
QUEEN. And may it prove more happy
than the first!
My gentle lord, bespeak these nobles
fair,
That wait attendance for a gracious look,
And on their knees salute your majesty.
EDW. Courageous Lancaster, embrace thy
king!   340
And, as gross vapors perish by the sun,
Even so let hatred with thy sovereign's [3]
smile.
Live thou with me as my companion.
LAN. This salutation overjoys my heart.

[1] Struck.   [2] The devil.
[3] From 1612 edn. Original reads *sovereign*.

EDW. Warwick shall be my chiefest coun-
selor.
These silver hairs will more adorn my
court
Than gaudy silks, or rich imbrothery. [4]
Chide me, sweet Warwick, if I go astray.
WAR. Slay me, my lord, when I offend
your grace.
EDW. In solemn triumphs and in public
shows,   350
Pembroke shall bear the sword before
the king.
PEM. And with this sword Pembroke will
fight for you.
EDW. But wherefore walks young Morti-
mer aside?
Be thou commander of our royal fleet;
Or, if that lofty office like thee not,
I make thee here lord marshal of the
realm.
MOR. JUN. My lord, I'll marshal so your
enemies
As England shall be quiet, and you safe.
EDW. And as for you, Lord Mortimer of
Chirke,
Whose great achievements in our foreign
war   360
Deserves no common place nor mean
reward,
Be you the general of the levied troops
That now are ready to assail the Scots.
MOR. SEN. In this your grace hath highly
honored me,
For with my nature war doth best agree.
QUEEN. Now is the King of England rich
and strong,
Having the love of his renownéd peers.
EDW. Ay, Isabel, ne'er was my heart so
light.
Clerk of the crown, direct our warrant
forth
For Gaveston to Ireland.—Beaumont,
fly   370
As fast as Iris or Jove's Mercury.
BEAU. It shall be done, my gracious lord.
EDW. Lord Mortimer, we leave you to
your charge.
Now let us in, and feast it royally.
Against our friend the Earl of Corn-
wall comes,
We'll have a general tilt and tournament; [5]

[4] Embroidery.
[5] *I.e.,* in anticipation of his coming, we'll prepare for a general tilt, etc.

And then his marriage shall be solemnized.

For wot you not that I have made him sure [1]
Unto our cousin,[2] the Earl of Gloucester's heir?

LAN. Such news we hear, my lord.   380

EDW. That day, if not for him, yet for my sake,
Who [3] in the triumph [4] will be challenger,
Spare for no cost. We will requite your love.

WAR. In this, or aught, your highness shall command us.

EDW. Thanks, gentle Warwick.   Come, let's in and revel.

    Exeunt. Manent [5] Mortimers.

MOR. SEN. Nephew, I must to Scotland; thou stayest here.
Leave now to oppose thyself against the king.
Thou seest by nature he is mild and calm,
And, seeing his mind so dotes on Gaveston,
Let him without controlment have his will.   390
The mightiest kings have had their minions:
Great Alexander loved Ephestion;
The conquering Hercules [6] for Hylas wept;
And for Patroclus stern Achilles drooped;
And not kings only, but the wisest men:
The Roman Tully loved Octavius;
Grave Socrates, wild Alcibiades.
Then let his grace, whose youth is flexible,
And promiseth as much as we can wish,
Freely enjoy that vain, light-headed earl;
For riper years will wean him from such toys.   401

MOR. JUN. Uncle, his wanton humor grieves not me;
But this I scorn, that one so basely born
Should by his sovereign's favor grow so pert,
And riot it with the treasure of the realm.
While soldiers mutiny for want of pay,
He wears a lord's revenue on his back,

And Midas-like he jets [7] it in the court,
With base, outlandish cullions [8] at his heels,
Whose proud, fantastic liveries make such show   410
As if that Proteus, god of shapes, appeared.
I have not seen a dapper Jack [9] so brisk.
He wears a short Italian-hooded cloak
Larded with pearl, and in his Tuscan cap
A jewel of more value than the crown.
Whiles other walk below, the king and he
From out a window laugh at such as we,
And flout our train, and jest at our attire.
Uncle, 'tis this that makes me impatient.

MOR. SEN. But, nephew, now you see the king is changed.   420

MOR. JUN. Then so am I, and live to do him service.
But, whiles I have a sword, a hand, a heart,
I will not yield to any such upstart.
You know my mind; come, uncle, let's away.   *Exeunt.*

[SCENE V.

A room in Gloucester's castle.]

Enter Spencer [10] and Baldock.

BALD. Spencer, seeing that our lord th' Earl of Gloucester's dead,
Which of the nobles dost thou mean to serve?

SPEN. Not Mortimer, nor any of his side,
Because the king and he are enemies.
Baldock, learn this of me, a factious lord
Shall hardly do himself good, much less us;
But he that hath the favor of a king
May with one word advance us while we live.
The liberal Earl of Cornwall is the man
On whose good fortune Spencer's hope depends.   10

BALD. What, mean you then to be his follower?

SPEN. No, his companion, for he loves me well,
And would have once preferred [11] me to the king.

---

[1] Betrothed him.   [4] Tournament.
[2] Relative; here, niece.   [5] Remain.
[3] Whoever.   [6] Original reads *Hector.*

[7] Struts.   [10] *I.e.,* young Spencer.
[8] Rascals.   [11] Recommended.
[9] Knave.

BALD. But he is banished; there's small
    hope of him.

SPEN. Ay, for a while, but, Baldock, mark
    the end.

A friend of mine told me in secrecy

That he's repealed, and sent for back
    again;

And even now a post came from the
    court

With letters to our lady from the king,

And as she read she smiled, which makes
    me think   20

It is about her lover Gaveston.

BALD. 'Tis like enough, for, since he was
    exiled,

She neither walks abroad, nor comes in
    sight.

But I had thought the match had been
    broke off.

And that his banishment had changed
    her mind.

SPEN. Our lady's first love is not waver-
    ing;

My life for thine, she will have Gaveston.

BALD. Then hope I by her means to be pre-
    ferred,

Having read unto her since she was a
    child.

SPEN. Then, Baldock, you must cast the
    scholar off,   30

And learn to court it like a gentleman.

'Tis not a black coat and a little band,

A velvet-caped coat, faced before with
    serge,

And smelling to a nosegay all the day,

Or holding of a napkin in your hand,

Or saying a long grace at a table's end,

Or making low legs [1] to a nobleman,

Or looking downward with your eyelids
    close,

And saying, "Truly, an't [2] may please
    your honor,"

Can get you any favor with great
    men.   40

You must be proud, bold, pleasant,
    resolute,

And now and then stab, as occasion
    serves.

BALD. Spencer, thou knowest I hate such
    formal toys,

And use them but of mere hypocrisy.

Mine old lord whiles he lived was so
    precise

That he would take exceptions at my
    buttons,

And, being like pin's heads, blame me for
    the bigness,

Which made me curatelike in mine
    attire,

Though inwardly licentious enough

And apt for any kind of villainy.   50

I am none of these common pedants,[3] I,

That cannot speak without *propterea
    quod*.[4]

SPEN. But one of those that saith *quando-
    quidem*,[5]

And hath a special gift to form a verb.

BALD. Leave off this jesting; here my lady
    comes.

Enter the Lady [, Gloucester's daughter].

LADY. The grief for his exile was not so
    much

As is the joy of his returning home.

This letter came from my sweet Gaves-
    ton.

What need'st thou, love, thus to excuse
    thyself?

I know thou couldst not come and visit
    me.   60

[*Reads.*] "I will not long be from thee,
    though I die."

This argues the entire love of my lord.

[*Reads.*] "When I forsake thee, death
    seize on my heart."

But rest thee here where Gaveston shall
    sleep.   [*Puts the letter into her bosom.*]

Now to the letter of my lord the king.—

He wills me to repair unto the court,

And meet my Gaveston. Why do I stay,

Seeing that he talks thus of my marriage
    day?—

Who's there? Baldock!

See that my coach be ready; I must
    hence.   70

BALD. It shall be done, madam.   *Exit.*

LADY. And meet me at the park-pale pres-
    ently.—

Spencer, stay you and bear me company,

For I have joyful news to tell thee of.

My Lord of Cornwall is a-coming over,

And will be at the court as soon as we.

SPEN. I knew the king would have him
    home again.

---

[1] Bows.

[2] If it.

[3] From 1598 edn. Original reads *pendants*.

[4] On account of which.

[5] Seeing that.

LADY. If all things sort out [1] as I hope they will,
Thy service, Spencer, shall be thought upon.
SPEN. I humbly thank your ladyship.   80
LADY. Come, lead the way; I long till I am there.   [*Exeunt.*]

[SCENE vi.

Before Tynemouth Castle.]

Enter Edward, the Queen, Lancaster, Mortimer [, Junior], Warwick, Pembroke, Kent, Attendants.

EDW. The wind is good—I wonder why he stays;
I fear me he is wracked upon the sea.
QUEEN. Look, Lancaster, how passionate [2] he is,
And still [3] his mind runs on his minion!
LAN. My lord—
EDW. How now! What news? Is Gaveston arrived?
MOR. JUN. Nothing but Gaveston! What means your grace?
You have matters of more weight to think upon;
The King of France sets foot in Normandy.
EDW. A trifle! We'll expel him when we please.   10
But tell me, Mortimer, what's thy device
Against the stately triumph we decreed?
MOR. JUN. A homely one, my lord, not worth the telling.
EDW. Prithee, let me know it.
MOR. JUN. But, seeing you are so desirous, thus it is:
A lofty cedar tree, fair flourishing,
On whose top branches kingly eagles perch,
And by the bark a canker creeps me up,
And gets unto the highest bough of all.
The motto: *Æque tandem.* [4]   20
EDW. And what is yours, my Lord of Lancaster?
LAN. My lord, mine's more obscure than Mortimer's.
Pliny reports there is a flying fish
Which all the other fishes deadly hate,
And therefore, being pursued, it takes the air;

No sooner is it up, but there's a fowl
That seizeth it. This fish, my lord, I bear.
The motto this: *Undique mors est.* [5]
EDW. Proud Mortimer, ungentle Lancaster,
Is this the love you bear your sovereign?   30
Is this the fruit your reconcilement bears?
Can you in words make show of amity,
And in your shields display your rancorous minds?
What call you this but private libeling
Against the Earl of Cornwall and my brother?
QUEEN. Sweet husband, be content; they all love you.
EDW. They love me not that hate my Gaveston.
I am that cedar; shake me not too much.
And you, the eagles, soar ye ne'er so high,
I have the jesses [6] that will pull you down;   40
And *Æque tandem* shall that canker cry
Unto the proudest peer of Britainy.
Though thou compar'st him to a flying fish,
And threatenest death whether he rise or fall,
'Tis not the hugest monster of the sea
Nor foulest harpy that shall swallow him.
MOR. JUN. [*Aside.*] If in his absence thus he favors him,
What will he do whenas [7] he shall be present?
LAN. [*Aside.*]   That shall we see; look where his lordship comes.

Enter Gaveston.

EDW. My Gaveston! Welcome to Tynemouth! Welcome to thy friend!   50
Thy absence made me droop and pine away;
For, as the lovers of fair Danaë,
When she was locked up in a brazen tower,
Desired her more, and waxed outrageous,
So did it sure with me; and now thy sight
Is sweeter far than was thy parting hence
Bitter and irksome to my sobbing heart.

[1] Chance, turn out.
[2] Sorrowful.
[3] Always.
[4] Justly at last.
[5] Death is everywhere.
[6] Legstraps fastening a hawk to his leash. Original reads *gresses.*
[7] When.

GAV. Sweet lord and king, your speech
preventeth [1] mine,
Yet have I words left to express my joy.
The shepherd, nipped with biting win-
ter's rage, 60
Frolics not more to see the painted
spring
Than I do to behold your majesty.

EDW. Will none of you salute my Gaveston?

LAN. Salute him? Yes. Welcome, lord
chamberlain!

MOR. JUN. Welcome is the good Earl of
Cornwall!

WAR. Welcome, Lord Governor of the Isle
of Man!

PEM. Welcome, Master Secretary!

EDM. Brother, do you hear them?

EDW. Still will these earls and barons
use me thus?

GAV. My lord, I cannot brook these injuries. 70

QUEEN. [Aside.] Ay me, poor soul, when
these begin to jar.

EDW. Return it to their throats; I'll be
thy warrant.

GAV. Base, leaden earls, that glory in
your birth,
Go sit at home and eat your tenants'
beef;
And come not here to scoff at Gaveston,
Whose mounting thoughts did never
creep so low
As to bestow a look on such as you.

LAN. Yet I disdain not to do this for you!
[Offers to stab Gaveston.]

EDW. Treason! Treason! Where's the
traitor?

PEM. Here! Here!

[EDW.] [2] Convey hence Gaveston; they'll
murder him! 80

GAV. The life of thee shall salve this foul
disgrace.

MOR. JUN. Villain, thy life, unless I miss
mine aim. [Wounds Gaveston.]

QUEEN. Ah, furious Mortimer, what hast
thou done?

MOR. JUN. No more than I would answer,
were he slain.

EDW. Yes, more than thou canst answer,
though he live.

---

[1] Anticipateth.
[2] Original has *King* printed as part of preceding
speech.

Dear shall you both aby [3] this riotous
deed.
Out of my presence! Come not near
the court!

MOR. JUN. I'll not be barred the court
for Gaveston.

LAN. We'll hale him by the ears unto the
block.

EDW. Look to your own heads; his is
sure enough. 90

WAR. Look to your own crown, if you
back him thus.

EDM. Warwick, these words do ill beseem thy years.

EDW. Nay, all of them conspire to cross
me thus;
But, if I live, I'll tread upon their
heads
That think with high looks thus to
tread me down.
Come, Edmund, let's away and levy
men;
'Tis war that must abate these barons'
pride.
Exit the King [with his Train].

WAR. Let's to our castles, for the king
is moved.

MOR. JUN. Moved may he be, and perish
in his wrath! 99

LAN. Cousin, it is no dealing with him now.
He means to make us stoop by force
of arms,
And therefore let us jointly here protest
To prosecute that Gaveston to the
death.

MOR. JUN. By heaven, the abject villain
shall not live!

WAR. I'll have his blood, or die in seeking
it.

PEM. The like oath Pembroke takes.

LAN. And so doth Lancaster.
Now send our heralds to defy the
king;
And make the people swear to put him
down.

Enter a Post.

MOR. JUN. Letters! From whence?

MESS. From Scotland, my lord. 110
[Gives letters to Mortimer.]

LAN. Why, how now, cousin, how fares
all our friends?

---

[3] Pay for.

Mor. Jun. My uncle's taken prisoner
   by the Scots.

Lan. We'll have him ransomed, man; be
   of good cheer.

Mor. Jun. They rate his ransom at five
   thousand pound.

Who should defray the money but the
   king,

Seeing he is taken prisoner in his wars?
I'll to the king.

Lan. Do, cousin, and I'll bear thee company.

War. Meantime, my Lord of Pembroke
   and myself

Will to Newcastle here, and gather
   head.[1]   120

Mor. Jun. About it then, and we will
   follow you.

Lan. Be resolute and full of secrecy.

War. I warrant you.

[Exit with Pembroke.]

Mor. Jun. Cousin, and if [2] he will not
   ransom him,

I'll thunder such a peal into his ears
As never subject did unto his king.

Lan. Content, I'll bear my part.—Holla!
   Who's there?

[Enter Guard.]

Mor. Jun. Ay, marry, such a guard as
   this doth well.

Lan. Lead on the way.

Guard. Whither will your lordships? 129

Mor. Jun. Whither else but to the king?

Guard. His highness is disposed to be
   alone.

Lan. Why, so he may, but we will speak
   to him.

Guard. You may not in, my lord.

Mor. Jun. May we not?

[Enter Edward and Kent.]

Edw. How now! What noise is this?
   Who have we there? Is't you?

Mor. Jun. Nay, stay, my lord; I come
   to bring you news;

Mine uncle's taken prisoner by the
   Scots.

Edw. Then ransom him.

Lan. 'Twas in your wars; you should
   ransom him.   140

Mor. Jun. And you shall ransom him,
   or else——

Edm. What, Mortimer, you will not
   threaten him?

Edw. Quiet yourself; you shall have the
   broad seal

To gather for him thoroughout the
   realm.

Lan. Your minion Gaveston hath taught
   you this.

Mor. Jun. My lord, the family of the
   Mortimers

Are not so poor but, would they sell
   their land,

Would levy men enough to anger you.
We never beg, but use such prayers as
   these.

Edw. Shall I still be haunted thus?   150

Mor. Jun. Nay, now you're here alone,
   I'll speak my mind.

Lan. And so will I, and then, my lord,
   farewell.

Mor. Jun. The idle triumphs, masques,
   lascivious shows,

And prodigal gifts bestowed on Gaveston
Have drawn thy treasury dry, and made
   thee weak,

The murmuring commons overstretchéd
   hath.[3]

Lan. Look for rebellion; look to be deposed.

Thy garrisons are beaten out of France,
And, lame and poor, lie groaning at
   the gates.

The wild O'Neill, with swarms of Irish
   kerns,[4]   160

Lives uncontrolled within the English
   pale.

Unto the walls of York the Scots made
   road,

And unresisted drave away rich spoils.

Mor. Jun. The haughty Dane commands
   the narrow seas,

While in the harbor ride thy ships unrigged.

Lan. What foreign prince sends thee am-
   bassadors?

Mor. Jun. Who loves thee but a sort [5]
   of flatterers?

Lan. Thy gentle queen, sole sister to
   Valois,

Complains that thou hast left her all
   forlorn.

---

[3] *I.e.*, the idle triumphs, etc., have over-
stretched the murmuring commons.

[1] Troops.   [2] Emphatic form of *if*.

[4] Foot soldiers.   [5] Company.

Mor. Jun. Thy court is naked, being
bereft of those   170
That makes a king seem glorious to the
world—
I mean the peers, whom thou shouldst
dearly love.
Libels are cast again [1] thee in the street;
Ballads and rimes made of thy over-
throw.
Lan. The northern borderers, seeing the
houses burnt,
Their wives and children slain, run up
and down,
Cursing the name of thee and Gaveston.
Mor. Jun. When wert thou in the field
with banner spread,
But once? And then thy soldiers marched
like players,
With garish robes, not armor; and thy-
self,   180
Bedaubed with gold, rode laughing at
the rest,
Nodding and shaking of thy spangled
crest,
Where women's favors hung like labels
down.
Lan. And therefore came it that the
fleering Scots,
To England's high disgrace, have made
this jig: [2]

  Maids of England, sore may you mourn
  For your lemans [3] you have lost at Ban-
    nocksbourn.[4]
    With a heave and a ho!
  What, weeneth [5] the King of England
  So soon to have won Scotland?   190
    With a rombelow!

Mor. Jun. Wigmore shall fly [6] to set my
uncle free.
Lan. And, when 'tis gone, our swords
shall purchase more.
If ye be moved, revenge it as you can;
Look next to see us with our ensigns
spread.   *Exeunt Nobles.*
Edw. My swelling heart for very anger
breaks!
How oft have I been baited by these
peers,
And dare not be revenged, for their
power is great!

[1] Against.   [2] Carol.   [3] Lovers.
[4] Bannockburn was not actually fought until
1314.   [5] Imagineth.
[6] *I.e.*, Mortimer will sell his estate.

Yet shall the crowing of these cocker-
els
Affright a lion? Edward, unfold thy
paws,   200
And let their lives' blood slake thy
fury's hunger.
If I be cruel and grow tyrannous,
Now let them thank themselves, and
rue too late.
Kent. My lord, I see your love to Gaveston
Will be the ruin of the realm and you,
For now the wrathful nobles threaten
wars,
And therefore, brother, banish him for-
ever.
Edw. Art thou an enemy to my Gaves-
ton?
Kent. Ay, and it grieves me that I fa-
vored him.
Edw. Traitor, begone! Whine thou with
Mortimer.   210
Kent. So will I, rather than with Gaves-
ton.
Edw. Out of my sight, and trouble me
no more!
Kent. No marvel though thou scorn thy
noble peers,
When I thy brother am rejected thus.
                      Exit.
Edw. Away!—Poor Gaveston, that hast
no friend but me,
Do what they can, we'll live in Tyne-
mouth here,
And, so I walk with him about the walls,
What care I though the earls begirt
us round?—
Here comes she that's cause of all these
jars.

Enter the Queen, Ladies three, [Gaveston,]
             Baldock, and Spencer.

Queen. My lord, 'tis thought the earls
are up in arms.   220
Edw. Ay, and 'tis likewise thought you
favor him.[7]
Queen. Thus do you still suspect me
without cause.
Lady.[8] Sweet uncle, speak more kindly
to the queen.
Gav. [*Aside.*] My lord, dissemble with
her; speak her fair.
Edw. Pardon me, sweet, I forgot myself.

[7] *I.e.*, Mortimer.   [8] Gloucester's daughter.

QUEEN. Your pardon is quickly got of
Isabel.

EDW. The younger Mortimer is grown
so brave
That to my face he threatens civil wars.

GAV. Why do you not commit him to the
Tower?

EDW. I dare not, for the people love him
well.   230

GAV. Why, then we'll have him privily
made away.

EDW. Would Lancaster and he had both
caroused [1]
A bowl of poison to each other's health!
But let them go, and tell me what are
these.

LADY. Two of my father's servants whilst
he lived.
May't please your grace to entertain
them now.

EDW. Tell me, where wast thou born?
What is thine arms?

BALD. My name is Baldock, and my
gentry
I fetched from Oxford, not from heraldry.

EDW. The fitter art thou, Baldock, for
my turn.   240
Wait on me, and I'll see thou shalt not
want.

BALD. I humbly thank your majesty.

EDW. Knowest thou him, Gaveston?

GAV.   Ay, my lord;
His name is Spencer; he is well allied.
For my sake, let him wait upon your
grace;
Scarce shall you find a man of more
desert.

EDW. Then, Spencer, wait upon me; for
his sake
I'll grace thee with a higher style ere long.

SPEN. No greater titles happen unto me
Than to be favored of your majesty.

EDW. Cousin, this day shall be your marriage feast.   251
And, Gaveston, think that I love thee
well
To wed thee to our niece, the only heir
Unto the Earl of Gloucester late deceased.

GAV. I know, my lord, many will stomach
me,
But I respect neither their love nor
hate.

EDW. The headstrong barons shall not
limit me;
He that I list to favor shall be great.
Come, let's away; and, when the mar-
riage ends,   259
Have at the rebels, and their complices! [2]
           Exeunt omnes.

[SCENE vii.

The rebels' camp near Tynemouth Castle.]

*Enter Lancaster, Mortimer, Jun[ior,] War-
wick, Pembroke, Kent.*

KENT. My lords, of love to this our native land
I come to join with you and leave the
king,
And in your quarrel and the realm's
behoof
Will be the first that shall adventure
life.

LAN. I fear me, you are sent of policy,[3]
To undermine us with a show of love.

WAR. He is your brother; therefore have
we cause
To cast [4] the worst, and doubt of your
revolt.

EDM. Mine honor shall be hostage of my
truth;
If that will not suffice, farewell, my
lords!   10

MOR. JUN. Stay, Edmund; never was
Plantagenet
False to his word, and therefore trust
we thee.

PEM. But what's the reason you should
leave him now?

KENT. I have informed the Earl of Lancaster.

LAN. And it sufficeth. Now, my lords,
know this,
That Gaveston is secretly arrived,
And here in Tynemouth frolics with
the king.
Let us with these our followers scale
the walls,
And suddenly surprise them unawares. 19

MOR. JUN. I'll give the onset.

WAR.   And I'll follow thee.

MOR. JUN. This tottered [5] ensign of my
ancestors,

---

[2] Accomplices.   [4] Forecast, suspect
[3] In trickery.   [5] Tattered.
[1] Drunk.

Which swept the desert shore of that
    dead sea
Whereof we got the name of Mortimer,
Will I advance upon this castle walls.
Drums, strike alarum, raise them from
    their sport,
And ring aloud the knell of Gaveston!
LAN. None be so hardy as to touch the
    king;
But neither spare you Gaveston nor
    his friends.   *Exeunt.*

[SCENE viii.

In Tynemouth Castle.]

Enter the King and Spencer; to them
              Gaveston, etc.

EDW. O, tell me, Spencer, where is Gaves-
    ton?
SPEN. I fear me he is slain, my gracious
    lord.
EDW. No, here he comes; now let them
    spoil and kill.—
Fly, fly, my lords; the earls have got
    the hold!
Take shipping and away to Scarborough!
Spencer and I will post away by land.
GAV. O, stay, my lord; they will not in-
    jure you.
EDW. I will not trust them; Gaveston,
    away!
GAV. Farewell, my lord.
EDW. Lady, farewell.   10
LADY. Farewell, sweet uncle, till we meet
    again.
EDW. Farewell, sweet Gaveston, and fare-
    well, niece.
QUEEN. No farewell to poor Isabel, thy
    queen?
EDW. Yes, yes, for Mortimer, your lover's
    sake.   *Exeunt omnes; manet Isabella.*
QUEEN. Heavens can witness I love none
    but you!
From my embracements thus he breaks
    away.
O, that mine arms could close this isle
    about,
That I might pull him to me where I
    would,
Or that these tears that drizzle from mine
    eyes
Had power to mollify his stony heart, 20
That when I had him we might never
    part!

Enter the Barons. Alarums.

LAN. I wonder how he scaped!
MOR. JUN.   Who's this? The queen!
QUEEN. Ay, Mortimer, the miserable
    queen,
Whose pining heart her inward sighs have
    blasted,
And body with continual mourning
    wasted.
These hands are tired with haling of my
    lord
From Gaveston, from wicked Gaveston;
And all in vain, for, when I speak him fair,
He turns away, and smiles upon his
    minion.
MOR. JUN. Cease to lament, and tell us
    where's the king.   30
QUEEN. What would you with the king?
    Is't him you seek?
LAN. No, madam, but that cursèd Gaves-
    ton.
Far be it from the thought of Lancaster
To offer violence to his sovereign.
We would but rid the realm of Gaveston.
Tell us where he remains, and he shall die.
QUEEN. He's gone by water unto Scar-
    borough;
Pursue him quickly, and he cannot scape.
The king hath left him, and his train is
    small.
WAR. Foreslow [1] no time, sweet Lancaster;
    let's march.   40
MOR. JUN. How comes it that the king and
    he is parted?
QUEEN. That this your army, going several
    ways,
Might be of lesser force, and, with the
    power
That he intendeth presently to raise,
Be easily suppressed. And therefore be-
    gone!
MOR. JUN. Here in the river rides a Flem-
    ish hoy; [2]
Let's all aboard, and follow him amain.
LAN. The wind that bears him hence will
    fill our sails.
Come, come aboard; 'tis but an hour's
    sailing.
MOR. JUN. Madam, stay you within this
    castle here.   50
QUEEN. No, Mortimer, I'll to my lord the
    king.

---

[1] Delay, lose.   [2] Small ship.

MOR. JUN. Nay, rather sail with us to
 Scarborough.
QUEEN. You know the king is so suspicious
 As, if he hear I have but talked with you,
 Mine honor will be called in question;
 And therefore, gentle Mortimer, begone.
MOR. JUN. Madam, I cannot stay to an-
 swer you,
 But think of Mortimer as he deserves.
QUEEN. [*Aside.*] So well hast thou de-
 served, sweet Mortimer,
 As Isabel could live with thee forever! 60
 In vain I look for love at Edward's hand,
 Whose eyes are fixed on none but Gaves-
 ton;
 Yet once more I'll importune him with
 prayers.
 If he be strange and not regard my
 words,
 My son and I will over into France,
 And to the king my brother there com-
 plain
 How Gaveston hath robbed me of his
 love.
 But yet I hope my sorrows will have end,
 And Gaveston this blessed day be slain.
 Exeunt.

 [SCENE ix.

A field near Pembroke's castle.]

Enter Gaveston, pursued.

GAV. Yet, lusty lords, I have escaped your
 hands,
 Your threats, your larums, and your hot
 pursuits;
 And, though divorcéd from King Edward's eyes,
 Yet liveth Pierce of Gaveston unsur-
 prised,[1]
 Breathing, in hope (*malgrado*[2] all your
 beards,
 That muster rebels thus against your
 king)
 To see his royal sovereign once again.

Enter the Nobles [with Attendants].

WAR. Upon him, soldiers; take away his
 weapons!
MOR. JUN. Thou proud disturber of thy
 country's peace,
 Corrupter of thy king, cause of these
 broils, 10

Base flatterer, yield! And were it not for
 shame,
 Shame and dishonor to a soldier's name,
 Upon my weapon's point here shouldst
 thou fall,
 And welter in thy gore.
LAN. Monster of men,
 That, like the Greekish strumpet,[3]
 trained[4] to arms
 And bloody wars so many valiant
 knights,
 Look for no other fortune, wretch, than
 death!
 King Edward is not here to buckler thee.
WAR. Lancaster, why talk'st thou to the
 slave?
 Go, soldiers, take him hence, for, by my
 sword, 20
 His head shall off. Gaveston, short warn-
 ing
 Shall serve thy turn; it is our country's
 cause
 That here severely we will execute
 Upon thy person. Hang him at a bough.
GAV. My lord—!
WAR. Soldiers, have him away!—
 But, for[5] thou wert the favorite of a
 king,
 Thou shalt have so much honor at our
 hands—[6]
GAV. I thank you all, my lords. Then I
 perceive
 That heading is one, and hanging is the
 other,
 And death is all.

Enter Earl of Arundel.

LAN. How now, my Lord of Arundel?
ARUN. My lords, King Edward greets you
 all by me. 31
WAR. Arundel, say your message.
ARUN. His majesty,
 Hearing that you had taken Gaveston,
 Entreateth you by me, yet but he may
 See him before he dies; forwhy,[7] he says,
 And sends you word, he knows that die
 he shall;
 And, if you gratify his grace so far,
 He will be mindful of the courtesy.
WAR. How now?

---

[1] Uncaptured.   [2] In spite of.
[3] Helen of Troy   [6] *I.e.*, as to be beheaded.
[4] Lured.   [7] Because.
[5] Since.

GAV.   Renowméd Edward, how
   thy name   39
   Revives poor Gaveston!
WAR.   No, it needeth not;
   Arundel, we will gratify the king
   In other matters; he must pardon us in
   this.
   Soldiers, away with him!
GAV.   Why, my Lord of Warwick,
   Will not these delays beget my hopes?
   I know it, lords, it is this life you aim at;
   Yet grant King Edward this.
MOR. JUN.   Shalt thou appoint
   What we shall grant? Soldiers, away
   with him!
   Thus we'll gratify the king:
   We'll send his head by thee. Let him be-
   stow   49
   His tears on that, for that is all he gets
   Of Gaveston, or else his senseless trunk.
LAN. Not so, my lord, lest he bestow more
   cost
   In burying him than he hath ever earned.
ARUN. My lords, it is his majesty's request,
   And in the honor of a king he swears,
   He will but talk with him, and send him
   back.
WAR. When? Can you tell? Arundel, no!
   We wot
   He that the care of realm remits,
   And drives his nobles to these exigents [1]
   For Gaveston, will, if he sees him once,
   Violate any promise to possess him.   61
ARUN. Then if you will not trust his grace
   in keep,[2]
   My lords, I will be pledge for his return.
MOR. JUN. It is honorable in thee to offer
   this;
   But, for we know thou art a noble gentle-
   man,
   We will not wrong thee so,
   To make away a true man for a thief.
GAV. How mean'st thou, Mortimer? That
   is overbase.
MOR. JUN. Away, base groom, robber of
   king's renowm!
   Question with thy companions and thy
   mates.   70
PEM. My Lord Mortimer, and you, my
   lords, each one,
   To gratify the king's request therein,
   Touching the sending of this Gaveston,
   Because his majesty so earnestly

Desires to see the man before his death,
   I will upon mine honor undertake
   To carry him, and bring him back again;
   Provided this, that you, my Lord of
   Arundel,
   Will join with me.
WAR.   Pembroke, what wilt thou do?
   Cause yet more bloodshed? Is it not
   enough   80
   That we have taken him, but must we
   now
   Leave him on "had I wist," [3] and let
   him go?
PEM. My lords, I will not overwoo your
   honors,
   But, if you dare trust Pembroke with the
   prisoner,
   Upon mine oath, I will return him back.
ARUN. My Lord of Lancaster, what say
   you in this?
LAN. Why, I say, let him go on Pem-
   broke's word.
PEM. And you, Lord Mortimer?
MOR. JUN. How say you, my Lord of War-
   wick?
WAR. Nay, do your pleasures; I know how
   'twill prove.   90
PEM. Then give him me.
GAV.   Sweet sovereign, yet I come
   To see thee ere I die.
WAR. [Aside.]   Yet not perhaps,
   If Warwick's wit and policy prevail.
MOR. JUN. My Lord of Pembroke, we de-
   liver him you;
   Return him on your honor. Sound away!
Exeunt.   Manent Pembroke, Arundel,[4]
   Gavest[on], and Pembroke's Men for
                       soldiers.
PEM. My lord, you shall go with me.
   My house is not far hence, out of the way
   A little; but our men shall go along.
   We that have pretty wenches to our
   wives,
   Sir, must not come so near and balk
   their lips.   100
ARUN.[4] 'Tis very kindly spoke, my Lord
   of Pembroke;
   Your honor hath an adamant [5] of power
   To draw a prince.

---

[3] "Had I known—the exclamation of those
who repent of what they have rashly done"
(Dyce).
[4] Original reads *Mat[revis]*, probably, as Dyce
suggests, because the parts of Arundel and Matrevis were taken by the same actor.   [5] Magnet.

---

[1] Straits.   [2] Custody.

PEM.   So, my lord. Come
  hither, James.
I do commit this Gaveston to thee;
Be thou this night his keeper; in the
  morning
We will discharge thee of thy charge.
  Begone!
GAV. Unhappy Gaveston, whither goest
  thou now?   *Exit cum servis Pem.*[1]
HORSE BOY. My lord, we'll quickly be at
  Cobham.   *Exeunt ambo.*

[SCENE x.

A road to Boroughbridge, Yorkshire.]

*Enter Gaveston, mourning, and the Earl of
        Pembroke's Men.*

GAV. O treacherous Warwick, thus to
  wrong thy friend!
JAMES. I see it is your life these arms pur-
  sue.
GAV. Weaponless must I fall, and die in
  bands?
O, must this day be period of my life?
Center of all my bliss! And ye be men,
Speed to the king!

Enter Warwick and his Company.

WAR.   My Lord of Pembroke's men,
  Strive you no longer—I will have that
  Gaveston.
JAMES. Your lordship doth dishonor to
  yourself,
And wrong our lord, your honorable
  friend.
WAR. No, James, it is my country's cause
  I follow.   10
Go, take the villain; soldiers, come away.
We'll make quick work. Commend me
  to your master,
My friend, and tell him that I watched
  it well.
Come, let thy shadow [2] parley with King
  Edward.
GAV. Treacherous earl, shall I not see the
  king?
WAR. The King of Heaven, perhaps; no
  other king.
Away!
*Exeunt Warwick and his Men with Gavest[on].
        Manet James cum cæteris.*[3]

[1] With Pembroke's servants.   [3] With the rest.
[2] Ghost.

[JAMES.] Come, fellows, it booted not for
  us to strive.
We will in haste go certify our lord.
                        Exeunt.

[SCENE xi.

Near Boroughbridge.]

*Enter King Edward, [Baldock,] and Spencer,
        with drums and fifes.*

EDW. I long to hear an answer from the
  barons
Touching my friend, my dearest Gaves-
  ton.
Ah, Spencer, not the riches of my realm
Can ransom him! Ah, he is marked to
  die!
I know the malice of the younger Mor-
  timer;
Warwick, I know, is rough; and Lan-
  caster
Inexorable; and I shall never see
My lovely Pierce, my Gaveston again!
The barons overbear me with their pride.
SPEN. Were I King Edward, England's
  sovereign,   10
Son to the lovely Eleanor of Spain,
Great Edward Longshanks' issue, would
  I bear
These braves, this rage, and suffer un-
  controlled
These barons thus to beard me in my
  land,
In mine own realm? My lord, pardon my
  speech:
Did you retain your father's magnanim-
  ity,
Did you regard the honor of your name,
You would not suffer thus your majesty
Be counterbuffed of [4] your nobility.
Strike off their heads, and let them
  preach on poles!   20
No doubt, such lessons they will teach
  the rest
As by their preachments they will profit
  much,
And learn obedience to their lawful king.
EDW. Yea, gentle Spencer, we have been
  too mild,
Too kind to them, but now have drawn
  our sword.
And, if they send me not my Gaveston,

[4] Curbed by.

We'll steel it [1] on their crest, and poll [2] their tops.

BALD. This haught [3] resolve becomes your majesty,

Not to be tied to their affection,

As though your highness were a school-boy still,   30

And must be awed and governed like a child.

Enter Hugh Spencer, an old man, father to the young Spencer, with his truncheon, and Soldiers.

SPEN. FA[THER.] Long live my sovereign, the noble Edward,

In peace triumphant, fortunate in wars!

EDW. Welcome, old man; com'st thou in Edward's aid?

Then tell thy prince of whence, and what thou art.

SPEN. FA. Lo, with a band of bowmen and of pikes,

Brown bills and targeteers, four hundred strong,

Sworn to defend King Edward's royal right,

I come in person to your majesty,

Spencer, the father of Hugh Spencer there,   40

Bound to your highness everlastingly,

For favors done, in him, unto us all.

EDW. Thy father, Spencer?

SPEN.   True, and it like your grace,

That pours, in lieu of all your goodness shown,

His life, my lord, before your princely feet.

EDW. Welcome ten thousand times, old man, again.

Spencer, this love, this kindness to thy king,

Argues thy noble mind and disposition.

Spencer, I here create thee Earl of Wilt-shire,

And daily will enrich thee with our favor,   50

That, as the sunshine, shall reflect o'er thee.

Beside, the more to manifest our love,

Because we hear Lord Bruce doth sell his land,

And that the Mortimers are in hand [4] withal,

Thou shalt have crowns of us t' outbid the barons.

And, Spencer, spare them not, but lay it on.

Soldiers, a largess, and thrice welcome all!

SPEN. My lord, here comes the queen.

Enter the Queen and her Son, and Levune, a Frenchman.

EDW.   Madam, what news?

QUEEN. News of dishonor, lord, and discontent.

Our friend Levune, faithful and full of trust,   60

Informeth us, by letters and by words,

That Lord Valois, our brother, King of France,

Because your highness hath been slack in homage,

Hath seizéd Normandy into his hands.

These be the letters, this the messenger.

EDW. Welcome, Levune. Tush, Sib, [5] if this be all,

Valois and I will soon be friends again.—

But to my Gaveston! Shall I never see,

Never behold thee now?—Madam, in this matter   69

We will employ you and your little son;

You shall go parley with the King of France.—

Boy, see you bear you bravely to the king,

And do your message with a majesty.

PRINCE. Commit not to my youth things of more weight

Than fits a prince so young as I to bear,

And fear not, lord and father, heaven's great beams

On Atlas' shoulder shall not lie more safe

Than shall your charge committed to my trust.

QUEEN. Ah, boy, this towardness [6] makes thy mother fear

Thou art not marked to many days on earth.   80

EDW. Madam, we will that you with speed be shipped,

And this our son. Levune shall follow you

---

[1] Use steel(?).   [2] Crop.   [3] Haughty, bold.

[4] In negotiation (to sell their lands).

[5] Either *gossip, dear,* or an abbreviation for *Isabella.*   [6] Aptness.

With all the haste we can despatch him
　　hence.
　Choose of our lords to bear you com-
　　pany,
　And go in peace; leave us in wars at
　　home.
QUEEN. Unnatural wars, where subjects
　　brave their king.
　God end them once! My lord, I take
　　my leave,
　To make my preparation for France.
　　　　　　　　[*Exit with Prince Edward.*]

Enter Lord Arundel.[1]

EDW. What, Lord Arundel, dost thou
　　come alone?
ARUN. Yea, my good lord, for Gaveston is
　　dead.　　　　　　　　　　　　　　90
EDW. Ah, traitors! Have they put my
　　friend to death?
　Tell me, Arundel, died he ere thou
　　cam'st,
　Or didst thou see my friend to take his
　　death?
ARUN. Neither, my lord; for, as he was
　　surprised,
　Begirt with weapons and with enemies
　　round,
　I did your highness' message to them all,
　Demanding him of them, entreating
　　rather,
　And said, upon the honor of my name,
　That I would undertake to carry him
　Unto your highness, and to bring him
　　back.　　　　　　　　　　　　　　100
EDW. And tell me, would the rebels deny
　　me that?
SPEN. Proud recreants!
EDW.　　　　　　Yea, Spencer, traitors all.
ARUN. I found them at the first inexorable.
　The Earl of Warwick would not bide the
　　hearing;
　Mortimer hardly; Pembroke and Lan-
　　caster
　Spake least. And, when they flatly had
　　denied,
　Refusing to receive me pledge for him,
　The Earl of Pembroke mildly thus be-
　　spake:
　"My lords, because our sovereign sends
　　for him,　　　　　　　　　　　　109
　And promiseth he shall be safe returned,

I will this undertake, to have him hence,
　And see him redelivered to your hands."
EDW. Well, and how fortunes that he came
　　not?
SPEN. Some treason, or some villainy, was
　　cause.
ARUN. The Earl of Warwick seized him on
　　his way,
　For, being delivered unto Pembroke's
　　men,
　Their lord rode home, thinking his pris-
　　oner safe.
　But, ere he came, Warwick in ambush
　　lay,
　And bare him to his death, and in a
　　trench
　Strake[2] off his head, and marched unto
　　the camp.　　　　　　　　　　　　120
SPEN. A bloody part, flatly against law of
　　arms!
EDW. O, shall I speak, or shall I sigh and
　　die?
SPEN. My lord, refer your vengeance to
　　the sword
　Upon these barons; hearten up your men;
　Let them not unrevenged murther your
　　friends!
　Advance your standard, Edward, in the
　　field,
　And march to fire them from their start-
　　ing holes.[3]
EDWARD (*Kneels and saith:*)
　By earth, the common mother of us all,
　By heaven and all the moving orbs
　　thereof,
　By this right hand, and by my father's
　　sword,　　　　　　　　　　　　　130
　And all the honors longing[4] to my
　　crown,
　I will have heads and lives for him, as
　　many
　As I have manors, castles, towns, and
　　towers!—　　　　　　　　　　[*Rises.*]
　Treacherous Warwick! Traitorous Mor-
　　timer!
　If I be England's king, in lakes of gore
　Your headless trunks, your bodies will I
　　trail,
　That you may drink your fill, and quaff
　　in blood,
　And stain my royal standard with the
　　same,

---

[1] Original gives Arundel's part to Matrevis
throughout the scene.
[2] Struck.　　　　　　　　　　[4] Belonging.
[3] Refuges taken by hunted animals.

That so my bloody colors may suggest 139
Remembrance of revenge immortally
On your accursèd traitorous progeny,
You villains, that have slain my Gaveston!
And in this place of honor and of trust,
Spencer, sweet Spencer, I adopt thee here;
And merely [1] of our love we do create thee
Earl of Gloucester and lord chamberlain,
Despite of times, despite of enemies.

Spen. My lord, here is a messenger from the barons,
Desires access unto your majesty.

Edw. Admit him near.　　150

Enter the Herald from the Barons with his coat-of-arms.

Mess. Long live King Edward, England's lawful lord!

Edw. So wish not they, iwis,[2] that sent thee hither.
Thou com'st from Mortimer and his complices;
A ranker rout of rebels never was.
Well, say thy message.

Mess. The barons, up in arms, by me salute
Your highness with long life and happiness,
And bid me say, as plainer [3] to your grace,
That, if without effusion of blood
You will this grief have ease and remedy,　　160
That from your princely person you remove
This Spencer, as a putrefying branch,
That deads the royal vine, whose golden leaves
Empale your princely head, your diadem,
Whose brightness such pernicious upstarts dim,
Say they, and lovingly advise your grace
To cherish virtue and nobility,
And have old servitors in high esteem,
And shake off smooth dissembling flatterers.

---

[1] Purely.
[2] Certainly.
[3] Complainer, petitioner.

This granted, they, their honors, and their lives　　170
Are to your highness vowed and consecrate.

Spen. Ah, traitors, will they still display their pride?

Edw. Away, tarry no answer, but begone!
Rebels, will they appoint their sovereign
His sports, his pleasures, and his company?
Yet, ere thou go, see how I do divorce
　　　　　　Embrace Spencer.
Spencer from me.—Now get thee to thy lords,
And tell them I will come to chastise them
For murthering Gaveston. Hie thee, get thee gone!
Edward with fire and sword follows at thy heels.　　180
My lords, perceive you how these rebels swell?
Soldiers, good hearts, defend your sovereign's right,
For now, even now, we march to make them stoop.
Away!　　　　　　　　*Exeunt.*
Alarums, excursions, a great fight, and a retreat.

Enter the King, Spencer the Father, Spencer the Son, and the Noblemen of the King's side.

Edw. Why do we sound retreat? Upon them, lords!
This day I shall pour vengeance with my sword
On those proud rebels that are up in arms
And do confront and countermand [4] their king.

Spen. I doubt it not, my lord, right will prevail.

Spen. Fa. 'Tis not amiss, my liege, for either part　　190
To breathe awhile. Our men, with sweat and dust
All choked well near, begin to faint for heat;
And this retire refresheth horse and man.

Spen. Here come the rebels.

---

[4] Oppose.

Enter the Barons, Mortimer, [Junior,] Lancaster, Warwick, Pembroke, cum cæteris.

MOR. JUN. Look, Lancaster; yonder is
    Edward among his flatterers.

LAN. And there let him be
    Till he pay dearly for their company.

WAR. And shall, or Warwick's sword shall
    smite in vain.

EDW. What, rebels. do you shrink and
    sound retreat?

MOR. JUN. No, Edward, no; thy flatterers
    faint and fly.   200

LAN. Th'ad [1] best betimes forsake them [2]
    and their trains,[3]
    For they'll betray thee, traitors as they
    are.

SPEN. Traitor on thy face, rebellious Lancaster!

PEM. Away, base upstart! Brav'st thou
    nobles thus?

SPEN. FA. A noble attempt and honorable
    deed
    Is it not, trow ye, to assemble aid
    And levy arms against your lawful king!

EDW. For which ere long their heads shall
    satisfy,
    T' appease the wrath of their offended
    king.

MOR. JUN. Then, Edward, thou wilt fight
    it to the last,   210
    And rather bathe thy sword in subjects'
    blood
    Than banish that pernicious company?

EDW. Ay, traitors all, rather than thus be
    braved,
    Make England's civil towns huge heaps
    of stones,
    And plows to go about our palace gates.

WAR. A desperate and unnatural resolution!
    Alarum! To the fight!
    St. George for England, and the barons'
    right!

EDW. Saint George for England, and King
    Edward's right!   [*Alarums. Exeunt.*]

*Enter Edward [and his Followers,] with the
Barons captives.*

EDW. Now, lusty lords, now, not by chance
    of war,   220
    But justice of the quarrel and the cause,

Vailed is your pride. Methinks you hang
    the heads;
    But we'll advance [4] them, traitors.
    Now 'tis time
    To be avenged on you for all your
    braves,[5]
    And for the murther of my dearest friend,
    To whom right well you knew our soul
    was knit,
    Good Pierce of Gaveston, my sweet
    favorite.
    Ah, rebels, recreants, you made him
    away!

EDM. Brother, in regard of thee and of thy
    land
    Did they remove that flatterer from thy
    throne.   230

EDW. So, sir, you have spoke; away, avoid
    our presence!—   [*Exit Kent.*]
    Accurséd wretches, was't in regard of us,
    When we had sent our messenger to request
    He might be spared to come to speak
    with us,
    And Pembroke undertook for his return,
    That thou, proud Warwick, watched the
    prisoner,
    Poor Pierce, and headed [6] him against law
    of arms?
    For which thy head shall overlook the
    rest,
    As much as thou in rage outwent'st the
    rest.

WAR. Tyrant, I scorn thy threats and
    menaces;   240
    'Tis but temporal [7] that thou canst inflict.

LAN. The worst is death, and better die to
    live
    Than live in infamy under such a king.

EDW. Away with them, my Lord of Winchester!
    These lusty leaders, Warwick and Lancaster,
    I charge you roundly, off with both their
    heads!
    Away!

WAR. Farewell, vain world!

LAN.   Sweet Mortimer, farewell.

MOR. JUN. England, unkind to thy nobility,
    Groan for this grief; behold how thou art
    maimed!   250

---

[1] Thou had.   [3] Plots.
[2] Original reads *thee.*

[4] Raise.   [6] Beheaded.
[5] Boasts.   [7] Supply *punisnment.*

Edw. Go take that haughty Mortimer to
the Tower;
There see him safe bestowed. And, for
the rest,
Do speedy execution on them all.
Begone!

Mor. Jun. What, Mortimer, can ragged,
stony walls
Immure thy virtue that aspires to
heaven?
No, Edward, England's scourge, it may
not be;
Mortimer's hope surmounts his fortune
far.   [*The Barons are led away.*]

Edw. Sound drums and trumpets! March
with me, my friends.
Edward this day hath crowned him king
anew.   260
Exit [*with his Train*]. *Manent Spencer
filius,*[1] *Levune, and Baldock.*

Spen. Levune, the trust that we repose in
thee
Begets the quiet of King Edward's
land.
Therefore begone in haste, and with
advice
Bestow that treasure on the lords of
France,
That, therewith all enchanted, like the
guard
That suffered Jove to pass in showers of
gold
To Danaë, all aid may be denied
To Isabel, the queen, that now in France
Makes friends, to cross the seas with her
young son,
And step into his father's regiment. 270

Levune. That's it these barons and the
subtle queen
Long levied [2] at.

Bal.   Yea, but, Levune, thou seest
These barons lay their heads on blocks
together.
What they intend, the hangman frus-
trates clean.

Levune. Have you no doubts, my lords,
I'll clap s' close [3]
Among the lords of France with Eng-
land's gold
That Isabel shall make her plaints in
vain,

And France shall be obdurate with her
tears.

Spen. Then make for France amain;
Levune, away!
Proclaim King Edward's wars and vic-
tories.   *Exeunt omnes.*   280

[Scene xii.

Near the Tower of London.]

Enter Edmund.

Edm. Fair blows the wind for France.
Blow, gentle gale,
Till Edmund be arrived for England's
good!
Nature, yield to my country's cause in
this.
A brother? No, a butcher of thy friends!
Proud Edward, dost thou banish me thy
presence?
But I'll to France, and cheer the wrongéd
queen,
And certify what Edward's looseness is.
Unnatural king, to slaughter noble men
And cherish flatterers! Mortimer, I
stay [4]
Thy sweet escape; stand gracious, gloomy
night,   10
To his device.

Enter Mortimer, [*Junior,*] *disguised.*

Mor. Jun.   Holla! Who walketh there?
Is't you, my lord?

Edm.   Mortimer, 'tis I.
But hath thy potion wrought so happily?

Mor. Jun. It hath, my lord; the warders
all asleep,
I thank them, gave me leave to pass in
peace.
But hath your grace got shipping unto
France?

Edm. Fear it not.   *Exeunt.*

[Scene xiii.

Paris.]

Enter the Queen and her Son.

Queen. Ah, boy, our friends do fail us all
in France.
The lords are cruel, and the king unkind.
What shall we do?

---

[1] Son.
[2] Frequently misused for *leveled* in this period.
[3] Contrive so secretly.

[4] Await.

PRINCE.　　Madam, return to England,
And please my father well, and then a fig
For all my uncle's friendship here in
France.
I warrant you, I'll win his highness
quickly;
A [1] loves me better than a thousand
Spencers.
QUEEN. Ah, boy, thou art deceived, at
least in this,
To think that we can yet be tuned to-
gether.
No, no, we jar too far. Unkind Valois! 10
Unhappy Isabel, when France rejects,
Whither, O, whither dost thou bend thy
steps?

Enter Sir John of Hainault.

SIR J. Madam, what cheer?
QUEEN.　　Ah, good Sir John of Hainault,
Never so cheerless, nor so far distressed.
SIR J. I hear, sweet lady, of the king's un-
kindness.
But droop not, madam; noble minds
contemn
Despair. Will your grace with me to
Hainault,
And there stay time's advantage with
your son?
How say you, my lord, will you go with
your friends,　　　　　　　　19
And shake off all our fortunes equally?
PRINCE. So pleaseth the queen, my mother,
me it likes.
The King of England nor the court of
France
Shall have me from my gracious mother's
side,
Till I be strong enough to break a staff;
And then have at the proudest Spencer's
head.
SIR J. Well said, my lord!
QUEEN. O, my sweet heart, how do I moan
thy wrongs,
Yet triumph in the hope of thee, my joy!
Ah, sweet Sir John, even to the utmost
verge
Of Europe, or the shore of Tanais,　30
Will we with thee to Hainault—so we will.
The marquis is a noble gentleman;
His grace, I dare presume, will welcome
me.
But who are these?

[1] He.

Enter Edmund and Mortimer [, Junior].

EDM.　　Madam, long may you live,
Much happier than your friends in
England do!
QUEEN. Lord Edmund and Lord Morti-
mer alive!
Welcome to France! The news was here,
my lord,
That you were dead, or very near your
death.
MOR. JUN. Lady, the last was truest of the
twain;
But Mortimer, reserved for better hap, 40
Hath shaken off the thralldom of the
Tower,
And lives t' advance your standard, good
my lord.
PRINCE. How mean you, and [2] the king,
my father, lives?
No, my Lord Mortimer, not I, I trow.
QUEEN. Not, son? Why not? I would it
were no worse.
But, gentle lords, friendless we are in
France.
MOR. JUN. Monsieur le Grand, a noble
friend of yours,
Told us at our arrival all the news:
How hard the nobles, how unkind the
king
Hath showed himself. But, madam, right
makes room　　　　　　　　　50
Where weapons want; and, though a
many friends
Are made away, as Warwick, Lancaster,
And others of our party and faction,
Yet have we friends—assure your grace—
in England
Would cast up caps and clap their hands
for joy
To see us there, appointed [3] for our foes.
EDM. Would all were well, and Edward
well reclaimed,
For England's honor, peace, and quiet-
ness.
MOR. JUN. But by the sword, my lord, it
must be deserved; [4]
The king will ne'er forsake his flat-
terers.　　　　　　　　　　60
SIR J. My lords of England, sith [5] the
ungentle king
Of France refuseth to give aid of arms
To this distresséd queen his sister here,

[2] If.　　　　　　　　　[4] Earned.
[3] Equipped.　　　　　 [5] Since.

Go you with her to Hainault. Doubt ye
    not,
We will find comfort, money, men, and
    friends
Ere long, to bid the English king a base.[1]
How say, young prince? What think you
    of the match?
PRINCE. I think King Edward will outrun
    us all.
QUEEN. Nay, son, not so; and you must
    not discourage
Your friends, that are so forward in your
    aid.   70
EDM. Sir John of Hainault, pardon us, I
    pray;
These comforts that you give our woeful
    queen
Bind us in kindness all at your command.
QUEEN. Yea, gentle brother; and the God
    of heaven
Prosper your happy motion,[2] good Sir
    John.
MOR. JUN. This noble gentleman, forward
    in arms,
Was born, I see, to be our anchor-hold.
Sir John of Hainault, be it thy renown,
That England's queen and nobles in
    distress
Have been by thee restored and com-
    forted.   80
SIR J. Madam, along, and you, my lord,
    with me,
That England's peers may Hainault's
    welcome see.   [Exeunt.]

[SCENE xiv.

The King's palace in London.]

*Enter the King, Arundel,[3] the two Spencers,
                with Others.*

EDW. Thus, after many threats of wrathful
    war,
Triumpheth England's Edward with his
    friends.
And triumph, Edward, with his friends
    uncontrolled!
My Lord of Gloucester, do you hear the
    news?
SPEN. What news, my lord?
EDW. Why, man, they say there is great
    execution

[1] To challenge, as in the game of prisoner's
base.   [2] Proposal.
[3] As before, original reads *Matr[evis]*.

Done through the realm. My Lord of
    Arundel,
You have the note, have you not?
ARUN.[3] From the lieutenant of the Tower,
    my lord.
EDW. I pray let us see it. What have we
    there?   10
Read it, Spencer.
           Spencer reads their names.
Why, so; they barked apace a month
    ago.
Now, on my life, they'll neither bark nor
    bite.
Now, sirs, the news from France. Glou-
    cester, I trow
The lords of France love England's gold
    so well
As Isabel gets no aid from thence.
What now remains? Have you pro-
    claimed, my lord,
Reward for them can bring in Morti-
    mer?
SPEN. My lord, we have, and, if he be in
    England,
A will be had ere long, I doubt it not.   20
EDW. "If," dost thou say? Spencer, as
    true as death,
He is in England's ground. Our port
    masters
Are not so careless of their king's com-
    mand.

Enter a Post.

How now, what news with thee? From
    whence come these?
POST. Letters, my lord, and tidings forth
    of France—
To you, my Lord of Gloucester, from
    Levune.   *[Gives letters to Spencer.]*
EDW. Read.
SPEN. (*Reads the letter.*)
"My duty to your honor premised,[4] etc.
I have, according to instructions in that
behalf, dealt with the King of France [30
his lords, and effected that the queen, all
discontented and discomforted, is gone.
Whither, if you ask: with Sir John of
Hainault, brother to the marquis, into
Flanders. With them are gone Lord Ed-
mund and the Lord Mortimer, having in
their company divers of your nation, and
others; and, as constant report goeth, they
intend to give King Edward battle in

[4] From 1598 edn. Original reads *promised*.

England sooner than he can look for [40
them. This is all the news of import.
  Your honor's in all service,
LEVUNE."

EDW. Ah, villains, hath that Mortimer
  escaped?
With him is Edmund gone associate?
And will Sir John of Hainault lead the
  round? [1]
Welcome, a God's name, madam, and
  your son;
England shall welcome you and all your
  rout.
Gallop apace, bright Phœbus, through
  the sky,
And dusky Night, in rusty iron car; 50
Between you both shorten the time, I
  pray,
That I may see that most desiréd day
When we may meet these traitors in the
  field.
Ah, nothing grieves me but my little boy
Is thus misled to countenance their ills.
Come, friends, to Bristow,[2] there to make
  us strong;
And, winds, as equal be to bring them in
As you injurious were to bear them
  forth!   [*Exeunt.*]

[SCENE xv.

Near Harwich.]

Enter the Queen, her Son, Edmund, Morti-
mer, [Junior,] and Sir John.

QUEEN. Now, lords, our loving friends and
  countrymen,
Welcome to England all, with prosperous
  winds!
Our kindest friends in Belgia have we
  left,
To cope with friends at home; a heavy
  case
When force to force is knit, and sword
  and glaive
In civil broils makes kin and countrymen
Slaughter themselves in others, and their
  sides
With their own weapons gored! But
  what's the help?
Misgoverned kings are cause of all this
  wrack;
And, Edward, thou art one among them
  all,   10

[1] Dance.   [2] Bristol.

Whose looseness hath betrayed thy land
  to spoil,
And made the channels overflow with
  blood.
Of thine own people patron shouldst
  thou be,
But thou—
MOR. JUN.   Nay, madam, if you be a
  warrior,
Ye must not grow so passionate in
  speeches.
Lords,
Sith that we are by sufferance of heaven
Arrived and arméd in this prince's right,
Here for our country's cause swear we to
  him
All homage, fealty, and forwardness. 20
And, for the open wrongs and injuries
Edward hath done to us, his queen, and
  land,
We come in arms to wreak it with the
  swords,
That England's queen in peace may re-
  possess
Her dignities and honors, and withal
We may remove these flatterers from
  the king,
That havocs England's wealth and
  treasury.
SIR J. Sound trumpets, my lord, and for-
  ward let us march.
Edward will think we come to flatter
  him.
EDM. I would he never had been flattered
  more.   [*Exeunt.*] 30

[SCENE xvi.

Near Bristol.]

Enter the King, Baldock, and Spencer the
Son, flying about the stage.

SPEN. Fly, fly, my lord! The queen is
  overstrong;
Her friends do multiply, and yours do
  fail.
Shape we our course to Ireland, there to
  breathe.
EDW. What! Was I born to fly and run
  away,
And leave the Mortimers conquerors
  behind?
Give me my horse, and let's r'enforce our
  troops,
And in this bed of honors die with fame.

BALD. O, no, my lord, this princely resolution
Fits not the time. Away! We are
pursued. [*Exeunt.*]

[*Enter*] *Edmund alone with a sword and
target.*[1]

EDM. This way he fled, but I am come too
late. 10
Edward, alas, my heart relents for thee!
Proud traitor, Mortimer, why dost thou
chase
Thy lawful king, thy sovereign, with
thy sword?
Vild[2] wretch, and why hast thou, of all
unkind,[3]
Borne arms against thy brother and thy
king?
Rain showers of vengeance on my curséd
head,
Thou God, to whom in justice it belongs
To punish this unnatural revolt!
Edward, this Mortimer aims at thy
life!
O, fly him, then! But, Edmund, calm
this rage; 20
Dissemble, or thou diest, for Mortimer
And Isabel do kiss while they conspire,
And yet she bears a face of love forsooth.
Fie on that love that hatcheth death and
hate!
Edmund, away! Bristow to Longshanks'
blood
Is false. Be not found single for suspect.[4]
Proud Mortimer pries near into thy
walks.

*Enter the Queen, Mortimer, [Junior,] the
young Prince, and Sir John of Hainault.*

QUEEN. Successful battles gives the God of
kings
To them that fight in right and fear his
wrath.
Since then successfully we have prevailed, 30
Thanks be heaven's great Architect, and
you.
Ere farther we proceed, my noble lords,

We here create our well-belovéd son,
Of love and care unto his royal person,
Lord warden of the realm, and, sith the
fates
Have made his father so infortunate,
Deal you, my lords, in this, my loving
lords,
As to your wisdoms fittest seems in all.
EDM. Madam, without offense, if I may
ask,
How will you deal with Edward in his
fall? 40
PRINCE. Tell me, good uncle, what Edward
do you mean?
EDM. Nephew, your father; I dare not
call him king.
MOR. JUN. My Lord of Kent, what needs
these questions?
'Tis not in her controlment, nor in ours,
But as the realm and parliament shall
please,
So shall your brother be disposéd of.—
[*Aside to the Queen.*] I like not this relenting mood in Edmund.
Madam, 'tis good to look to him betimes.
QUEEN. My lord, the Mayor of Bristow
knows our mind.
MOR. JUN. Yea, madam, and they scape
not easily 50
That fled the field.
QUEEN. Baldock is with the king.
A goodly chancellor, is he not, my
lord?
SIR J. So are the Spencers, the father and
the son.
EDM. This, Edward, is the ruin of the
realm.

*Enter Rice ap Howell and the Mayor of
Bristow, with Spencer the Father [, and
Attendants].*

RICE. God save Queen Isabel and her
princely son!
Madam, the mayor and citizens of
Bristow,
In sign of love and duty to this presence,
Present by me this traitor to the state,
Spencer, the father to that wanton
Spencer, 59
That, like the lawless Catiline of Rome,
Reveled in England's wealth and treasary.

[1] Shield.   [2] Vile.   [3] Most unnatural of all.
[4] Alone for fear of suspicion.

QUEEN. We thank you all.

MOR. JUN. Your loving care in this
Deserveth princely favors and rewards.
But where's the king and the other
Spencer fled?

RICE. Spencer the son, created Earl of
Gloucester,
Is with that smooth-tongued scholar
Baldock gone
And shipped but late for Ireland with
the king.

MOR. JUN. Some whirlwind fetch them
back or sink them all!
They shall be started [1] thence, I doubt it
not.

PRINCE. Shall I not see the king my father
yet?   70

EDM. [Aside.] Unhappy's Edward, chased
from England's bounds!

SIR J. Madam, what resteth? Why stand
ye in a muse?

QUEEN. I rue my lord's ill fortune. But,
alas,
Care of my country called me to this
war!

MOR. JUN. Madam, have done with care
and sad complaint;
Your king hath wronged your country
and himself,
And we must seek to right it as we
may.—
Meanwhile, have hence this rebel to the
block.—
Your lordship cannot privilege [2] your
head.

SPEN. FA. Rebel is he that fights against
his prince;   80
So fought not they that fought in Ed-
ward's right.

MOR. JUN. Take him away; he prates.
[Exeunt Attendants with the Elder
Spencer.]—You, Rice ap Howell,
Shall do good service to her majesty,
Being of countenance [3] in your country
here,
To follow these rebellious runagates.
We in meanwhile, madam, must take
advice
How Baldock, Spencer, and their com-
plices
May in their fall be followed to their end.
                                        Exeunt omnes.

[1] Routed out.   [3] In authority, favor.
[2] Exempt, free.

[SCENE xvii.

The Abbey of Neath.]

*Enter the Abbot, Monks, Edward, Spencer,
and Baldock [, the last three disguised].*

ABBOT. Have you no doubt, my lord; have
you no fear.
As silent and as careful will we be
To keep your royal person safe with us,
Free from suspect and fell invasion
Of such as have your majesty in chase,
Yourself, and those your chosen company,
As danger of this stormy time requires.

EDW. Father, thy face should harbor no
deceit.
O, hadst thou ever been a king, thy heart,
Piercéd deeply with sense of my dis-
tress,   10
Could not but take compassion of my
state.
Stately and proud, in riches and in train,
Whilom [4] I was powerful and full of
pomp.
But what is he whom rule and empery
Have not in life or death made miserable?
Come, Spencer; come, Baldock, come, sit
down by me.
Make trial now of that philosophy
That in our famous nurseries of arts
Thou suckedst from Plato and from
Aristotle.   19
Father, this life contemplative is heaven.
O, that I might this life in quiet lead!
But we, alas, are chased; and you, my
friends,
Your lives, and my dishonor they pursue.
Yet, gentle monks, for treasure, gold,
nor fee,
Do you betray us and our company.

MONKS. Your grace may sit secure, if none
but we
Do wot of your abode.

SPEN. Not one alive; but shrewdly I sus-
pect
A gloomy fellow in a mead below.
A gave a long look after us, my lord,   30
And all the land, I know, is up in arms,
Arms that pursue our lives with deadly
hate.

BALD. We were embarked for Ireland,
wretched we!
With awkward winds and sore tempests
driven

[4] Formerly.

To fall on shore, and here to pine in fear
Of Mortimer and his confederates.
EDW. Mortimer! Who talks of Mortimer?
Who wounds me with the name of
　Mortimer,
That bloody man? Good father, on thy
　lap　　　　　　　　　　　　　　39
Lay I this head, laden with mickle care.
O, might I never open these eyes again,
Never again lift up this drooping head,
O, never more lift up this dying heart!
SPEN. Look up, my lord.—Baldock, this
　drowsiness
Betides no good; here, even, we are
　betrayed!

Enter, with Welsh hooks,[1] *Rice ap Howell, a*
　　　Mower, and the Earl of Leicester.

MOW. Upon my life, those be the men ye
　seek!
RICE. Fellow, enough!—My lord, I pray
　be short;
A fair commission warrants what we do.
LEICES. [*Aside.*] The queen's commission,
　urged by Mortimer.
What cannot gallant Mortimer with the
　queen?　　　　　　　　　　　　50
Alas, see where he sits, and hopes unseen
T' escape their hands that seek to reave[2]
　his life.
Too true it is: "*Quem dies vidit veniens
　superbum,*
Hunc dies vidit fugiens jacentem."[3]
But, Leicester, leave to grow so passion-
　ate.—
Spencer and Baldock, by no other names,
I arrest you of high treason here.
Stand not on titles, but obey th' arrest;
'Tis in the name of Isabel the queen.—
My lord, why droop you thus?　　60
EDW. O day, the last of all my bliss on
　earth!
Center of all misfortune! O my stars,
Why do you lour unkindly on a king?
Comes Leicester, then, in Isabella's name
To take my life, my company, from me?
Here, man, rip up this panting breast of
　mine,
And take my heart in rescue of my
　friends!

---

[1] A kind of weapon.　　[2] Rob, take away.
[3] "Whom the dawning day sees proud, departing day sees prostrate" (Seneca, *Thyestes,*
l. 613).

RICE. Away with them!
SPEN.　　　　　　It may become thee yet
To let us take our farewell of his grace.
ABBOT. [*Aside.*] My heart with pity earns[4]
　to see this sight—　　　　　　70
A king to bear these words and proud
　commands!
EDW. Spencer, ah, sweet Spencer, thus
　then must we part?
SPEN. We must, my lord; so will the angry
　heavens.
EDW. Nay, so will hell and cruel Morti-
　mer;
The gentle heavens have not to do in
　this.
BALD. My lord, it is in vain to grieve or
　storm.
Here humbly of your grace we take our
　leaves;
Our lots are cast; I fear me, so is thine.
EDW. In heaven we may, in earth never
　shall we meet—
And, Leicester, say, what shall become of
　us?　　　　　　　　　　　　80
LEICES. Your majesty must go to Killing-
　worth.[5]
EDW. "Must!" 'Tis somewhat hard when
　kings "must" go.
LEICES. Here is a litter ready for your
　grace,
That waits your pleasure; and the day
　grows old.
RICE. As good be gone as stay and be be-
　nighted.
EDW. A litter hast thou? Lay me in a
　hearse,
And to the gates of hell convey me
　hence.
Let Pluto's bells ring out my fatal knell,
And hags howl for my death at Charon's
　shore,
For friends hath Edward none but these
　and these,　　　　　　　　　90
And these must die under a tyrant's
　sword.
RICE. My lord, be going; care not for
　these,
For we shall see them shorter by the
　heads.
EDW. Well, that shall be, shall be! Part
　we must!
Sweet Spencer, gentle Baldock, part we
　must!

---

[4] Yearns, sorrows.　　　　[5] Kenilworth.

Hence, feignéd weeds! [*Throws off his
    disguise.*] Unfeignéd are my woes!
Father, farewell! Leicester, thou stay'st
    for me,
And go I must. Life, farewell, with my
    friends.
                Exeunt Edward and Leicester.
SPEN. O, is he gone? Is noble Edward
    gone?
Parted from hence, never to see us
    more?   100
Rent,[1] sphere of heaven, and, fire, forsake
    thy orb!
Earth, melt to air! Gone is my sovereign,
Gone, gone, alas, never to make return!
BALD. Spencer, I see our souls are fleeted
    hence;
We are deprived the sunshine of our life.
Make for a new life, man; throw up thy
    eyes,
And heart, and hand to heaven's im-
    mortal throne;
Pay nature's debt with cheerful coun-
    tenance.
Reduce we all our lessons unto this:
To die, sweet Spencer, therefor live we
    all;   110
Spencer, all live to die, and rise to fall.
RICE. Come, come, keep these preach-
ments till you come to the place appointed.
You, and such as you are, have made wise
work in England. Will your lordships
away?
MOW. Your lordship, I trust, will remem-
    ber me?
RICE. Remember thee, fellow! What else?
Follow me to the town.   [*Exeunt.*]

[SCENE xviii.

A room in Killingworth Castle.]

*Enter the King, Leicester, with a Bishop [2] for
        the crown [, and Trussel].*

LEICES. Be patient, good my lord; cease
    to lament,
Imagine Killingworth Castle were your
    court,
And that you lay for pleasure here a
    space,
Not of compulsion or necessity.
EDW. Leicester, if gentle words might com-
    fort me,

[1] Rend, split.
[2] Berkeley, Bishop of Winchester.

Thy speeches long ago had eased my
    sorrows,
For kind and loving hast thou always
    been.
The griefs of private men are soon al-
    layed,
But not of kings. The forest deer, being
    struck,
Runs to an herb that closeth up the
    wounds;   10
But, when the imperial lion's flesh is
    gored,
He rends and tears it with his wrathful
    paw,
[And,] [3] highly scorning that the lowly
    earth
Should drink his blood, mounts up into
    the air.
And so it fares with me, whose dauntless
    mind
The ambitious Mortimer would seek to
    curb,
And that unnatural queen, false Isabel,
That thus hath pent and mewed me in a
    prison;
For such outrageous passions cloy my
    soul,
As with the wings of rancor and dis-
    dain   20
Full often am I soaring up to heaven,
To plain me [4] to the gods against them
    both.
But, when I call to mind I am a king,
Methinks I should revenge me of the
    wrongs
That Mortimer and Isabel have done.
But what are kings, when regiment is
    gone,
But perfect shadows in a sunshine day?
My nobles rule; I bear the name of
    king.
I wear the crown, but am controlled by
    them,   29
By Mortimer, and my unconstant queen,
Who spots my nuptial bed with infamy,
Whilst I am lodged within this cave of
    care,
Where sorrow at my elbow still attends,
To company my heart with sad laments,
That bleeds within me for this strange
    exchange.
But tell me, must I now resign my crown,
To make usurping Mortimer a king?

[3] Supplied by Dodsley.   [4] Complain.

BISH. Your grace mistakes; it is for England's good

And princely Edward's right we crave the crown.

EDW. No, 'tis for Mortimer, not Edward's head;   40

For he's a lamb, encompasséd by wolves,

Which in a moment will abridge his life.

But, if proud Mortimer do wear this crown,

Heavens turn it to a blaze of quenchless fire,

Or, like the snaky wreath of Tisiphon,

Engirt the temples of his hateful head!

So shall not England's vines be perishéd,

But Edward's name survives, though Edward dies.

LEICES. My lord, why waste you thus the time away?

They stay your answer. Will you yield your crown?   50

EDW. Ah, Leicester, weigh how hardly I can brook

To lose my crown and kingdom without cause;

To give ambitious Mortimer my right—

That like a mountain overwhelms my bliss,

In which extreme my mind here murthered is.

But what the heavens appoint, I must obey!

Here, take my crown—the life of Edward too;   [Takes off the crown.]

Two kings in England cannot reign at once.

But stay awhile; let me be king till night,

That I may gaze upon this glittering crown.   60

So shall my eyes receive their last content,

My head, the latest honor due to it,

And jointly both yield up their wishéd right.

Continue ever, thou celestial sun;

Let never silent night possess this clime;

Stand still, you watches of the element; [1]

All times and seasons, rest you at a stay,

That Edward may be still fair England's king!

But day's bright beams doth vanish fast away,

[1] *I.e.*, celestial bodies.

And needs I must resign my wishéd crown.   70

Inhuman creatures, nursed with tiger's milk,

Why gape you for your sovereign's overthrow—

My diadem, I mean, and guiltless life?

See, monsters, see, I'll wear my crown again!   [*Puts on the crown.*]

What, fear you not the fury of your king?

But, hapless Edward, thou art fondly [2] led;

They pass [3] not for thy frowns as late they did,

But seeks to make a new-elected king;

Which fills my mind with strange, despairing thoughts,

Which thoughts are martyréd with endless torments,   80

And, in this torment, comfort find I none,

But that I feel the crown upon my head;

And therefore let me wear it yet awhile.

TRU. My lord, the parliament must have present news,

And therefore say, will you resign or no?   *The King rageth.*

EDW. I'll not resign, but whilst I live—

Traitors, be gone and join you with Mortimer!

Elect, conspire, install, do what you will—

Their blood and yours shall seal these treacheries!

BISH. This answer we'll return, and so farewell.   90

LEICES. Call them again, my lord, and speak them fair;

For, if they go, the prince shall lose his right.

EDW. Call thou them back; I have no power to speak.

LEICES. My lord, the king is willing to resign.

BISH. If he be not, let him choose.

EDW. O, would I might, but heavens and earth conspire

To make me miserable! Here receive my crown;

Receive it? No, these innocent hands of mine

Shall not be guilty of so foul a crime.

He of you all that most desires my blood,

[2] Foolishly.   [3] Care.

And will be called the murtherer of a
 king,   101
Take it. What, are you moved? Pity
 you me?
Then send for unrelenting Mortimer,
And Isabel, whose eyes, being [1] turned
 to steel,
Will sooner sparkle fire than shed a tear.
Yet stay, for rather than I will look on
 them—
Here, here! [*Gives the crown.*] Now,
 sweet God of heaven,
Make me despise this transitory pomp,
And sit for aye enthronizéd in heaven!
Come, death, and with thy fingers close
 my eyes,   110
Or, if I live, let me forget myself.

   Enter [Sir Thomas] Berkeley.

BISH. [2] My lord—
EDW. Call me not lord. Away—out of my
 sight!
Ah, pardon me. Grief makes me lunatic!
Let not that Mortimer protect my son;
More safety is there in a tiger's jaws
Than [3] his embracements. Bear this to
 the queen,
Wet with my tears, and dried again with
 sighs;   [*Gives a handkerchief.*]
If with the sight thereof she be not
 moved,   119
Return it back and dip it in my blood.
Commend me to my son, and bid him
 rule
Better than I. Yet how have I trans-
 gressed,
Unless it be with too much clemency?
TRU. And thus most humbly do we take
 our leave.
EDW. Farewell. [*Exeunt the Bishop of
 Winchester and Trussel.*] I know the
 next news that they bring
Will be my death, and welcome shall it
 be;
To wretched men, death is felicity.
LEICES. [*Noticing Berkeley.*] Another post!
 What news brings he?
EDW. Such news as I expect.—Come,
 Berkeley, come,   129
And tell thy message to my naked breast.

[1] From 1598 edn. Original reads *been*.
[2] Original assigns this speech to Sir Thomas
Berkeley.
[3] From 1598 edn. Original reads *this*.

BERK. My lord, think not a thought so
 villainous
Can harbor in a man of noble birth.
To do your highness service and devoir,
And save you from your foes, Berkeley
 would die.
LEICES. My lord, the council of the queen
 commands
That I resign my charge.
EDW. And who must keep me now? Must
 you, my lord?
BERK. Ay, my most gracious lord; so 'tis
 decreed.
EDW. [*Taking the paper.*] By Mortimer,
 whose name is written here!
Well may I rent his name that rends my
 heart!   [*Tears it.*] 140
This poor revenge hath something eased
 my mind.
So may his limbs be torn, as is this paper!
Hear me, immortal Jove, and grant it
 too!
BERK. Your grace must hence with me to
 Berkeley straight.
EDW. Whither you will; all places are
 alike,
And every earth is fit for burial.
LEICES. Favor him, my lord, as much as
 lieth in you.
BERK. Even so betide my soul as I use
 him.
EDW. Mine enemy hath pitied my estate,
And that's the cause that I am now
 removed.   150
BERK. And thinks your grace that Berk-
 eley will be cruel?
EDW. I know not, but of this am I as-
 sured,
That death ends all, and I can die but
 once.
Leicester, farewell!
LEICES. Not yet, my lord; I'll bear you on
 your way.   *Exeunt omnes.*

     [SCENE xix.

  The King's palace in London.]

Enter Mortimer [, Junior,] and Queen Isabel.

MOR. JUN. Fair Isabel, now have we our
 desire;
The proud corrupters of the light-brained
 king
Have done their homage to the lofty
 gallows,

And he himself lies in captivity.
Be ruled by me, and we will rule the
  realm.
In any case take heed of childish fear,
For now we hold an old wolf by the ears,
That, if he slip, will seize upon us both,
And gripe the sorer, being gripped him-
  self.
Think therefore, madam, that imports
  us [1] much   10
To erect [2] your son with all the speed
  we may,
And that I be protector over him;
For our behoof will bear the greater
  sway
Whenas a king's name shall be under-
  writ.
QUEEN. Sweet Mortimer, the life of Isabel,
Be thou persuaded that I love thee well,
And therefore, so the prince my son be
  safe,
Whom I esteem as dear as these mine
  eyes,
Conclude against his father what thou
  wilt,
And I myself will willingly subscribe. 20
MOR. JUN. First would I hear news that
  he were deposed,
And then let me alone to handle him.

Enter Messenger.

MOR. JUN. Letters! From whence?
MESS.   From Killingworth, my lord.
QUEEN. How fares my lord the king?
MESS. In health, madam, but full of pen-
  siveness.
QUEEN. Alas, poor soul, would I could ease
  his grief!

[*Enter the Bishop of Winchester with the
                                    crown.*]

Thanks, gentle Winchester.—[*To the
  Messenger.*] Sirrah, begone.
                        [*Exit Messenger.*]
WIN.[3] The king hath willingly resigned
  his crown.
QUEEN. O happy news! Send for the
  prince my son.
BISH. Further, or [4] this letter was sealed,
  Lord Berkeley came,   30

---

[1] From 1612 edn. Original reads *as.*   [4] Ere.
[2] Crown.
[3] Regularly *Bish.* in speech heads.

So that he now is gone from Killingworth;
And we have heard that Edmund laid a
  plot
To set his brother free; no more but so.
The Lord of Berkeley is so [5] pitiful
As Leicester, that had charge of him
  before.
QUEEN. Then let some other be his guard-
  ian.
MOR. JUN. Let me alone. Here is the
  privy seal.—
          [*Exit the Bishop of Winchester.*]
[*To Attendants within.*] Who's there?—
Call hither Gurney and Matrevis.
To dash the heavy-headed Edmund's
  drift,[6]
Berkeley shall be discharged, the king
  removed,   40
And none but we shall know where he
  lieth.
QUEEN. But, Mortimer, as long as he sur-
  vives,
What safety rests for us or for my son?
MOR. JUN. Speak, shall he presently be des-
  patched and die?
QUEEN. I would he were, so 'twere not
  by my means.

Enter Matrevis and Gurney.

MOR. JUN. Enough.—Matrevis, write a
  letter presently
Unto the Lord of Berkeley from ourself
That he resign the king to thee and
  Gurney;
And, when 'tis done, we will subscribe
  our name.
MAT. It shall be done, my lord.
MOR. JUN.   Gurney!
GUR.   My lord. 50
MOR. JUN. As thou intendest to rise by
  Mortimer,
Who now makes Fortune's wheel turn as
  he please,
Seek all the means thou canst to make
  him droop,
And neither give him kind word nor
  good look.
GUR. I warrant you, my lord.
MOR. JUN. And this above the rest: be-
  cause we hear
That Edmund casts [7] to work his liberty,
Remove him still from place to place by
  night,

---

[5] As.   [6] Plot.   [7] Plots.

Till at the last he come to Killingworth,
And then from thence to Berkeley back
   again. 60
And by the way, to make him fret the
   more,
Speak curstly [1] to him, and in any case
Let no man comfort him; if he chance
   to weep,
But amplify his grief with bitter words.
MAT. Fear not, my lord, we'll do as you
   command.
MOR. JUN. So now away; post thither-
   wards amain.
QUEEN. Whither goes this letter? To my
   lord the king?
Commend me humbly to his majesty,
And tell him that I labor all in vain
To ease his grief, and work his lib-
   erty; 70
And bear him this as witness of my love.
                      [*Gives a ring.*]
MAT. I will, madam.
*Exeunt Matrevis and Gurney. Manent
   Isabel and Mortimer.*

*Enter the young Prince, and the Earl of
   Kent talking with him.*

MOR. JUN. [*Aside.*] Finely dissembled!
   Do so still, sweet queen.
Here comes the young prince with the
   Earl of Kent.
QUEEN. [*Aside.*] Something he whispers
   in his childish ears.
MOR. JUN. [*Aside.*] If he have such access
   unto the prince,
Our plots and stratagems will soon be
   dashed.
QUEEN. [*Aside.*] Use Edmund friendly, as
   if all were well.—
MOR. JUN. How fares my honorable
   Lord of Kent?
EDM. In health, sweet Mortimer.—How
   fares your grace? 80
QUEEN. Well, if my lord your brother were
   enlarged.[2]
EDM. I hear of late he hath deposed him-
   self.
QUEEN. The more my grief.
MOR. JUN.   And mine.
EDM. [*Aside.*]   Ah, they do dissemble!
QUEEN. Sweet son, come hither; I must
   talk with thee.

MOR. JUN. Thou, being his uncle, and
   the next of blood,
Do look to be protector over the prince.
EDM. Not I, my lord. Who should protect
   the son
But she that gave him life? I mean the
   queen.
PRINCE. Mother, persuade me not to wear
   the crown.
Let him be king—I am too young to
   reign. 90
QUEEN. But be content, seeing it his
   highness' pleasure.
PRINCE. Let me but see him first, and then
   I will.
EDM. Ay, do, sweet nephew.
QUEEN. Brother, you know it is impos-
   sible.
PRINCE. Why, is he dead?
QUEEN. No, God forbid!
EDM. I would those words proceeded from
   your heart.
MOR. JUN. Inconstant Edmund, dost thou
   favor him,
That wast the cause of his imprisonment?
EDM. The more cause have I now to make
   amends. 100
MOR. JUN. [*Aside to queen.*] I tell thee,
   'tis not meet that one so false
Should come about the person of a
   prince.—
My lord, he hath betrayed the king his
   brother,
And therefore trust him not.
PRINCE. But he repents, and sorrows for
   it now.
QUEEN. Come, son, and go with this gentle
   lord and me.
PRINCE. With you I will, but not with
   Mortimer.
MOR. JUN. Why, youngling, 'sdain'st thou
   so of Mortimer?
Then I will carry thee by force away.
PRINCE. Help, uncle Kent! Mortimer will
   wrong me. 110
QUEEN. Brother Edmund, strive not; we
   are his friends;
Isabel is nearer than the Earl of Kent.
EDM. Sister, Edward is my charge; re-
   deem him.
QUEEN. Edward is my son, and I will keep
   him.
EDM. Mortimer shall know that he hath
   wronged me!—

---

[1] Ill-temperedly. [2] Freed.

[*Aside.*] Hence will I haste to Killing-
worth Castle,
And rescue aged Edward from his foes,
To be revenged on Mortimer and thee.
                              Exeunt omnes.

[Scene xx.

An outbuilding at Killingworth Castle.]

Enter Matrevis and Gurney [*and Soldiers,*]
                                   with the King.

MAT. My lord, be not pensive; we are your
friends.
Men are ordained to live in misery;
Therefore come—dalliance dangereth
our lives.

EDW. Friends, whither must unhappy Ed-
ward go?
Will hateful Mortimer appoint no rest?
Must I be vexéd like the nightly bird,
Whose sight is loathsome to all wingéd
fowls?
When will the fury of his mind assuage?
When will his heart be satisfied with
blood?
If mine will serve, unbowel straight this
breast,   10
And give my heart to Isabel and him.
It is the chiefest mark they level at.

GUR. Not so, my liege; the queen hath
given this charge
To keep your grace in safety.
Your passions make your dolors to increase.

EDW. This usage makes my misery in-
crease.
But can my air of life continue long
When all my senses are annoyed with
stench?
Within a dungeon England's king is kept,
Where I am starved for want of suste-
nance.   20
My daily diet is heart-breaking sobs,
That almost rents the closet of my heart.
Thus lives old Edward, not relieved by
any,
And so must die, though pitiéd by many.
O, water, gentle friends, to cool my thirst,
And clear my body from foul excre-
ments!

MAT. Here's channel water, as our charge
is given.
Sit down, for we'll be barbers to your
grace.

EDW. Traitors, away! What, will you
murther me,
Or choke your sovereign with puddle
water?   30

GUR. No, but wash your face, and shave
away your beard,
Lest you be known and so be rescuéd.

MAT. Why strive you thus? Your labor
is in vain!

EDW. The wren may strive against the
lion's strength,
But all in vain; so vainly do I strive
To seek for mercy at a tyrant's hand.

*They wash him with puddle water, and shave
                              his beard away.*
Immortal powers, that knows the pain-
ful cares
That waits upon my poor distresséd
soul,
O, level all your looks upon these daring
men
That wrongs their liege and sovereign,
England's king!   40
O Gaveston, it is for thee that I am
wronged!
For me, both thou and both the Spencers
died,
And for your sakes a thousand wrongs
I'll take.
The Spencers' ghosts, wherever they
remain,
Wish well to mine; then tush—for them
I'll die!

MAT. Twixt theirs and yours shall be no
enmity.
Come, come away; now put the torches
out;
We'll enter in by darkness to Killingworth.

Enter Edmund.

GUR. How now, who comes there?

MAT. Guard the king sure; it is the Earl
of Kent.   50

EDW. O, gentle brother, help to rescue
me!

MAT. Keep them asunder; thrust in the
king.

EDM. Soldiers, let me but talk to him one
word.

GUR. Lay hands upon the earl for this
assault.

EDM. Lay down your weapons, traitors!
Yield the king!

MAT. Edmund, yield thou thyself, or thou shalt die!

EDM. Base villains, wherefore do you gripe me thus?

GUR. Bind him and so convey him to the court.

EDM. Where is the court but here? Here is the king.

And I will visit him; why stay you me?   60

MAT. The court is where Lord Mortimer remains.

Thither shall your honor go; and so farewell.

Exeunt Matr[evis] and Gurney, with the King.   Manent Edmund and the Soldiers.

EDM. O, miserable is that commonweal Where lords keep courts, and kings are locked in prison!

SOL. Wherefore stay we?   On, sirs, to the court!

EDM. Ay, lead me whither you will, even to my death,

Seeing that my brother cannot be released.   *Exeunt omnes.*

[SCENE xxi.

The King's palace in London.]

Enter Mortimer alone.

MOR. JUN. The king must die or Mortimer goes down;

The commons now begin to pity him.

Yet he that is the cause of Edward's death

Is sure to pay for it when his son is of age,

And therefore will I do it cunningly.

This letter, written by a friend of ours,

Contains his death, yet bids them save his life.   [*Reads.*]

"*Edwardum occidere nolite timere bonum est:*"

"Fear not to kill the king; 'tis good he die."

But read it thus, and that's another sense: 10

"*Edwardum occidere nolite timere bonum est:*"

"Kill not the king; 'tis good to fear the worst."

Unpointed as it is, thus shall it go,

That, being dead, if it chance to be found,

Matrevis and the rest may bear the blame,

And we be quit that caused it to be done.

Within this room is locked the messenger

That shall convey it, and perform the rest;

And, by a secret token that he bears,

Shall he be murdered when the deed is done.—   20

Lightborn,

Come forth!

[*Enter Lightborn.*]

Art thou as resolute as thou wast?

LIGHT. What else, my lord?   And far more resolute!

MOR. JUN. And hast thou cast how to accomplish it?

LIGHT. Ay, ay, and none shall know which way he died.

MOR. JUN. But at his looks, Lightborn, thou wilt relent.

LIGHT. Relent!   Ha, ha!   I use much to relent!

MOR. JUN. Well, do it bravely, and be secret.

LIGHT. You shall not need to give instructions;   29

'Tis not the first time I have killed a man.

I learned in Naples how to poison flowers;

To strangle with a lawn [1] thrust through [2] the throat;

To pierce the windpipe with a needle's point;

Or, whilst one is asleep, to take a quill And blow a little powder in his ears;

Or open his mouth and pour quicksilver down.

But yet I have a braver way than these.

MOR. JUN. What's that?

LIGHT. Nay, you shall pardon me; none shall know my tricks.

MOR. JUN. I care not how it is, so it be not spied.   40

Deliver this to Gurney and Matrevis.   [*Gives letter.*]

At every ten miles' end thou hast a horse.

Take this.   [*Gives money.*]   Away, and never see me more!

¹ Handkerchief.   ² Down.

Light. No?

Mor. Jun. No;

Unless you bring me news of Edward's
death.

Light. That will I quickly do. Farewell,
my lord. [*Exit.*]

Mor. Jun. The prince I rule, the queen
do I command,

And with a lowly congé to the ground   49

The proudest lords salute me as I pass.

I seal, I cancel, I do what I will.

Feared am I more than loved; let me
be feared,

And, when I frown, make all the court
look pale.

I view the prince with Aristarchus' eyes,

Whose looks were as a breeching [1] to a
boy.

They thrust upon me the protectorship,

And sue to me for that that I desire.

While at the council table, grave enough,

And not unlike a bashful Puritan,

First I complain of imbecility,   60

Saying it is *onus quam gravissimum*,[2]

Till, being interrupted by my friends,

Suscepi that *provinciam*,[3] as they term
it;

And, to conclude, I am protector now.

Now is all sure. The queen and Mortimer

Shall rule the realm, the king, and none
rule us.

Mine enemies will I plague, my friends
advance;

And what I list command who dare
control?

"*Major sum quam cui possit fortuna no-
cere.*" [4]   69

And that this be the coronation day,

It pleaseth me and Isabel the queen.
[*Trumpets within.*]

The trumpets sound; I must go take my
place.

*Enter the young King, [Arch]bishop, Cham-
pion, Nobles, Queen.*

[Arch]bish. Long live King Edward, by
the grace of God

King of England and Lord of Ireland!

Cham. If any Christian, heathen, Turk,
or Jew

Dares but affirm that Edward's not
true king,

And will avouch his saying with the
sword,

I am the champion that will combat him!

Mor. Jun. None comes; sound trumpets.
[*Trumpets sound.*]

King.[5]   Champion, here's to thee!
[*Gives a purse.*]

Queen. Lord Mortimer, now take him
to your charge.   80

*Enter Soldiers, with the Earl of Kent
prisoner.*

Mor. Jun. What traitor have we there
with blades and bills?

Sol. Edmund, the Earl of Kent.

King.   What hath he done?

Sol. A would have taken the king away
perforce,

As we were bringing him to Killingworth.

Mor. Jun. Did you attempt his rescue,
Edmund? Speak.

Edm. Mortimer, I did; he is our king,

And thou compell'st this prince to wear
the crown.

Mor. Jun. Strike off his head! He shall
have martial law.

Edm. Strike off my head? Base traitor,
I defy thee!

King. My lord, he is my uncle, and shall
live.   90

Mor. Jun. My lord, he is your enemy,
and shall die.

Edm. Stay, villains!

King. Sweet mother, if I cannot pardon
him,

Entreat my lord protector for his life.

Queen. Son, be content; I dare not speak
a word.

King. Nor I, and yet methinks I should
command;

But, seeing I cannot, I'll entreat for
him.—

My lord, if you will let my uncle live,

I will requite it when I come to age.

Mor. Jun. 'Tis for your highness' good,
and for the realm's.—   100

How often shall I bid you bear him
hence?

[1] Flogging.

[2] A very heavy burden.

[3] I have undertaken that office.

[4] "I am too great for fortune to harm me"
(Ovid, *Metamorphoses*, vi, 195).

[5] Formerly the prince, now Edward the Third.

EDM. Art thou king? Must I die at thy command?

MOR. JUN. At our command.—Once more away with him!

EDM. Let me but stay and speak; I will not go.

Either my brother or his son is king,
And none of both [1] then thirst for Edmund's blood.

And, therefore, soldiers, whither will you hale me?

They hale Edmund away, and carry him to be beheaded.

KING. What safety may I look for at his hands,

If that my uncle shall be murthered thus?

QUEEN. Fear not, sweet boy; I'll guard thee from thy foes;   110

Had Edmund lived, he would have sought thy death.

Come, son, we'll ride a-hunting in the park.

KING. And shall my uncle Edmund ride with us?

QUEEN. He is a traitor; think not on him.
Come.   *Exeunt omnes.*

[SCENE xxii.

A subterranean room in Berkeley Castle.]

Enter Matr[evis] and Gurney.

MAT. Gurney, I wonder the king dies not,
Being in a vault up to the knees in water,
To which the channels of the castle run,
From whence a damp continually ariseth,
That were enough to poison any man,
Much more a king brought up so tenderly.

GUR. And so do I, Matrevis. Yesternight
I opened but the door to throw him meat,
And I was almost stifled with the savor.

MAT. He hath a body able to endure   10
More than we can inflict; and therefore now
Let us assail his mind another while.

GUR. Send for him out thence, and I will anger him.

MAT. But stay, who's this?

[1] Neither.

Enter Lightborn.

LIGHT.   My lord protector greets you.
    [*Gives letter.*]

GUR. [*Reads.*] What's here? I know not how to conster [2] it.

MAT. Gurney, it was left unpointed for the nonce; [3]
"Edwardum occidere nolite timere"—
That's his meaning.

LIGHT. Know ye this token? I must have the king.   [*Gives token.*]

MAT. Ay, stay awhile; thou shalt have answer straight.—   20
[*Aside.*] This villain's sent to make away the king.

GUR. [*Aside.*] I thought as much.

MAT. [*Aside.*]   And, when the murder's done,
See how he must be handled for his labor.
Pereat iste! [4] Let him have the king.—
What else? Here is the keys; this is the lake. [5]
Do as you are commanded by my lord.

LIGHT. I know what I must do. Get you away.
Yet be not far off; I shall need your help.
See that in the next room I have a fire,
And get me a spit, and let it be red-hot.   30

MAT. Very well.

GUR.   Need you anything besides?

LIGHT. What else? A table and a feather bed.

GUR. That's all?

LIGHT. Ay, ay; so, when I call you, bring it in.

MAT. Fear not you that.

GUR. Here's a light, to go into the dungeon.

[*Gives a light, and then exit with Matrevis.*]

LIGHT. So now must I about this gear; [6] ne'er was there any
So finely handled as this king shall be.
    [*Opens the door.*]
Foh! Here's a place indeed, with all my heart!

EDW. Who's there? What light is that?
Wherefore comes thou?   40

[2] Construe.   [5] Vault, dungeon.
[3] For the occasion, on purpose.   [6] Affair.
[4] Let this man die.

LIGHT. To comfort you, and bring you
    joyful news.
EDW. Small comfort finds poor Edward
    in thy looks.
  Villain, I know thou com'st to murther
    me.
LIGHT. To murther you, my most gracious
    lord?
  Far is it from my heart to do you harm.
  The queen sent me to see how you were
    used,
  For she relents at this your misery.
  And what eyes can refrain from shedding
    tears,
  To see a king in this most piteous state?
EDW. Weep'st thou already? List awhile
    to me   50
  And then thy heart, were it as Gurney's
    is,
  Or as Matrevis', hewn from the Cauca-
    sus,
  Yet will it melt, ere I have done my tale.
  This dungeon where they keep me is
    the sink
  Wherein the filth of all the castle falls.
LIGHT. O villains!
EDW. And there in mire and puddle have
    I stood
  This ten days' space; and, lest that I
    should sleep,
  One plays continually upon a drum.
  They give me bread and water, being
    a king;   60
  So that, for want of sleep and suste-
    nance,
  My mind's distempered, and my body's
    numbed,
  And whether I have limbs or no I know
    not.
  O, would my blood dropped out from
    every vein
  As doth this water from my tattered
    robes.
  Tell Isabel, the queen, I looked not
    thus
  When for her sake I ran at tilt in France,
  And there unhorsed the Duke of Clere-
    mont.
LIGHT. O, speak no more, my lord! This
    breaks my heart.
  Lie on this bed,[1] and rest yourself
    awhile.   70

[1] Dyce suggests that the feather bed has been
thrust in from the wing.

EDW. These looks of thine can harbor
    naught but death.
  I see my tragedy written in thy brows.
  Yet stay awhile; forbear thy bloody
    hand,
  And let me see the stroke before it
    comes,
  That—and even then when I shall lose
    my life—
  My mind may be more steadfast on
    my God.
LIGHT. What means your highness to
    mistrust me thus?
EDW. What means thou to dissemble
    with me thus?
LIGHT. These hands were never stained
    with innocent blood,
  Nor shall they now be tainted with a
    king's.   80
EDW. Forgive my thought for having
    such a thought.
  One jewel have I left; receive thou this.
                              [Gives jewel.]
  Still fear I, and I know not what's the
    cause,
  But every joint shakes as I give it thee.
  O, if thou harbor'st murther in thy
    heart,
  Let this gift change thy mind, and save
    thy soul!
  Know that I am a king! O, at that
    name
  I feel a hell of grief! Where is my crown?
  Gone, gone! And do I remain alive?
LIGHT. You're overwatched, my lord;
    lie down and rest.   90
EDW. But that grief keeps me waking, I
    should sleep,
  For not these ten days have these eye-
    lids closed.
  Now as I speak, they fall, and yet with
    fear
  Open again.   O, wherefore sits thou
    here?
LIGHT. If you mistrust me, I'll be gone,
    my lord.
EDW. No, no, for if thou mean'st to mur-
    ther me,
  Thou wilt return again; and therefore
    stay.   [Dozes.]
LIGHT. He sleeps.
EDW. O, let me not die yet! Stay, O,
    stay a while!
LIGHT. How now, my lord?   100

EDW. [*Waking.*] Something still buzzeth
      in mine ears,
And tells me if I sleep I never wake;
This fear is that which makes me tremble
      thus.
And therefore tell me, wherefore art
      thou come?
LIGHT. To rid thee of thy life.—Matre-
vis, come!

[*Enter Matrevis and Gurney.*]

EDW. I am too weak and feeble to resist.—
Assist me, sweet God, and receive my
      soul!
LIGHT. Run for the table
EDW. O, spare me, or despatch me in a
      trice.   [*Matrevis brings in a table.*]
LIGHT. So, lay the table down, and stamp
      on it,   110
But not too hard, lest that you bruise
      his body.   [*They murder the King.*]
MAT. I fear me that this cry will raise
      the town,
And therefore let us take horse and away.
LIGHT. Tell me, sirs, was it not bravely
      done?
GUR. Excellent well; take this for thy
      reward!
            Then Gurney stabs Lightborn.
Come, let us cast the body in the moat,
And bear the king's to Mortimer our
      lord.
Away!   *Exeunt omnes.*

[SCENE xxiii.

The royal palace in London.]

Enter Mortimer and Matrevis.

MOR. JUN. Is't done, Matrevis, and the
      murtherer dead?
MAT. Ay, my good lord; I would it were
      undone!
MOR. JUN. Matrevis, if thou now growest
      penitent
I'll be thy ghostly father;[1] therefore
      choose
Whether thou wilt be secret in this,
Or else die by the hand of Mortimer.
MAT. Gurney, my lord, is fled, and will, I
      fear,
Betray us both; therefore let me fly.
MOR. JUN. Fly to the savages!   9
MAT. I humbly thank your honor. [*Exit.*]
----
[1] Father confessor.

MOR. JUN. As for myself, I stand as
      Jove's huge tree,
And others are but shrubs compared to me.
All tremble at my name, and I fear none.
Let's see who dare impeach me for his
      death!

Enter the Queen.

QUEEN. Ah, Mortimer, the king my son
      hath news
His father's dead, and we have murdered
      him!
MOR. JUN. What if he have? The king is
      yet a child.
QUEEN. Ay, ay, but he tears his hair, and
      wrings his hands,
And vows to be revenged upon us both.
Into the council chamber he is gone,   20
To crave the aid and succor of his peers.
Ay me! See where he comes, and they
      with him.
Now, Mortimer, begins our tragedy.

Enter the King with the Lords.

LORDS. Fear not, my lord; know that you
      are a king.—
KING. Villain!
MOR. JUN. How now, my lord?
KING. Think not that I am frighted with
      thy words!
My father's murdered through thy
      treachery;
And thou shalt die, and on his mournful
      hearse   29
Thy hateful and accursèd head shall lie,
To witness to the world that by thy means
His kingly body was too soon interred.
QUEEN. Weep not, sweet son!
KING. Forbid not me to weep; he was my
      father.
And, had you loved him half so well as I,
You could not bear his death thus
      patiently.
But you, I fear, conspired with Mortimer.
LORDS. Why speak you not unto my lord
      the king?
MOR. JUN. Because I think scorn to be
      accused.
Who is the man dares say I murdered
      him?   40
KING. Traitor, in me my loving father
      speaks,
And plainly saith 'twas thou that mur-
      d'redst him

Mor. Jun. But hath your grace no other proof than this?

King. Yes, if this be the hand of Mortimer.   [*Shows letter.*]

Mor. Jun. [*Aside.*] False Gurney hath betrayed me and himself.

Queen. [*Aside.*] I feared as much; murther cannot be hid.

Mor. Jun. 'Tis my hand. What gather you by this?

King. That thither thou didst send a murtherer.

Mor. Jun. What murtherer? Bring forth the man I sent!

King. Ah, Mortimer, thou knowest that he is slain,   50
And so shalt thou be too.—Why stays he here?
Bring him unto a hurdle; drag him forth;
Hang him, I say, and set his quarters up;
But bring his head back presently to me.

Queen. For my sake, sweet son, pity Mortimer!

Mor. Jun. Madam, entreat not; I will rather die
Than sue for life unto a paltry boy.

King. Hence with the traitor, with the murderer!

Mor. Jun. Base Fortune, now I see that in thy wheel
There is a point to which when men aspire,   60
They tumble headlong down. That point I touched,
And, seeing there was no place to mount up higher,
Why should I grieve at my declining fall?—
Farewell, fair queen. Weep not for Mortimer,
That scorns the world, and, as a traveler,
Goes to discover countries yet unknown.

King. What, suffer you the traitor to delay?   [*Mortimer is led away.*]

Queen. As thou receivedst thy life from me,
Spill not the blood of gentle Mortimer!

King. This argues that you spilt my father's blood,   70
Else would you not entreat for Mortimer.

Queen. I spill his blood? No!

King. Ay, madam, you, for so the rumor runs.

Queen. That rumor is untrue; for loving thee
Is this report raised on poor Isabel.

King. I do not think her so unnatural.

Lords. My Lord, I fear me it will prove too true.

King. Mother, you are suspected for his death,
And therefore we commit you to the Tower
Till further trial may be made thereof.   80
If you be guilty, though I be your son,
Think not to find me slack or pitiful.

Queen. Nay, to my death, for too long have I lived
Whenas my son thinks to abridge my days.

King. Away with her! Her words enforce these tears,
And I shall pity her if she speak again.

Queen. Shall I not mourn for my beloved lord,
And with the rest accompany him to his grave?

Lords. Thus, madam, 'tis the king's will you shall hence.

Queen. He hath forgotten me. Stay, I am his mother.   90

Lords. That boots not; therefore, gentle madam, go.

Queen. Then come, sweet death, and rid me of this grief.   [*Exit.*]

[*Enter Lords with the head of Mortimer.*]

Lords. My lord, here is the head of Mortimer.

King. Go fetch my father's hearse where it shall lie,
And bring my funeral robes.   [*Exeunt Attendants.*]—Accursèd head,
Could I have ruled thee then, as I do now,
Thou hadst not hatched this monstrous treachery!—
Here comes the hearse; help me to mourn, my lords.

[*Enter Attendants with the hearse and funeral robes.*]

Sweet father, here unto thy murdered ghost
I offer up this wicked traitor's head;   100
And let these tears, distilling from mine eyes,
Be witness of my grief and innocency.   [*Exeunt.*]

Finis.

THOMAS KYD

Thomas Kyd was born in London in 1558, the son of Francis Kyd, a scrivener. He was educated at the Merchant Tailors' School, of which Richard Mulcaster was head master. Probably he followed his father's calling for a while, but little or nothing more is known of him until he reached his thirties. He seems to have had some acquaintance with French, Italian, Spanish, and Latin, and to have done hack work in translating and in pamphleteering. Certainly with his *Spanish Tragedy* at least, he had a part in the outburst of popular tragedy around 1590. It has been supposed that he afterward capitalized on the popularity of this play by writing what might be called a first part, though the extant *First Part of Jeronimo* (printed in 1605) is probably by another hand. *Soliman and Perseda* is usually assigned to him on the basis of style and of the fact that it has the same plot as the play produced by Hieronimo in *The Spanish Tragedy*. The claim that he wrote *Arden of Feversham* is discussed in connection with that play. Kyd is also credited with an early version of *Hamlet*, now lost, especially by those who regard as aimed at him an allusion to one who "will afford you whole *Hamlets*, I should say handfuls of tragical speeches," in Nashe's preface to Greene's *Menaphon*. Nashe's satire in the same connection on the scrivener born who leaves his trade to write tragedies plundered from Seneca is usually accepted as inspired by the success of Kyd's plays. At any rate Nashe here and Greene in his *Groatsworth of Wit* show resentment at the rise of dramatists without classical training who were proving more effective than the University Wits. Kyd was connected with the coterie around the Countess of Pembroke who were interested in developing a literary tragedy, and he translated from Robert Garnier, called the "French Seneca," the tragedy of *Cornelia*, printed in 1594—the only extant play to bear Kyd's name on the title-page. Arrested in 1593 on suspicion of having posted libels on foreigners, he was found in possession of papers considered heretical or atheistic. He was released on his testimony that the papers had been left among his effects by Marlowe in 1591, when the two of them, in the service of an unidentified lord, had used the same room. Kyd died in 1594.

The authorship of *The Spanish Tragedy* is known only from a chance reference in Thomas Heywood's *Apology for Actors* in 1612. The date assigned to the play varies from 1582 to 1589, with the evidence in favor of the latter date, when the vogue of revenge tragedies—most of them now lost—seems to have begun. The known history of the tragedy opens with Henslowe's record of frequent performances in 1592. License to print was granted in October of that year. What is apparently the earliest extant edition is undated; the earliest with date is that of 1594. Both, however, refer to a "first impression," now lost. In 1597 Henslowe records a number of performances of the play as new, perhaps on account of revision. In September, 1601, and June, 1602, he paid Jonson for additions to "*Jeronimo*," possibly in competition with the closely related *Hamlet*, which Shakespeare was reviving for the Chamberlain's players at the same time, and with several new revenge plays of other companies modeled on these two. In 1602 an edition appeared with "new additions," which develop certain impassioned parts, and which have been assigned to Jonson on the basis of Henslowe's payments. The amounts paid would suggest a more thorough revision, however, and the style of the additions is regarded as against Jonson's authorship, though no real evidence has been adduced in favor of anyone else. The play had an extraordinary popularity. It ran into many editions, at least one of them pirated, was freely imitated, was the subject of numerous allusions, especially by way of stage parody and satire, and finally made its way to Germany. The romantic plot, for which no source has been traced, is strongly colored by the influence of Senecan tragedy—in the chorus, the ghost, the sententious and balanced speeches, the declamation, and the melodramatic treatment of character. The style differs from Marlowe's, with its "high astounding terms," in the emphasis on conceit and on elaborate rhetorical devices of repetition and balance.

The present text is based on the recension of the undated quarto in the British Museum (printed for Allde by White) made by Schick in his variorum edition of *The Spanish Tragedy*, except that the additions have been taken from the Malone Society reprint of the edition of 1602 prepared by Greg. Boas' standard edition of *The Works of Thomas Kyd* has been consulted.

THE SPANISH TRAGEDY[a]

[BY

THOMAS KYD

DRAMATIS PERSONÆ

GHOST OF ANDREA, *a Spanish courtier* } *induction and chorus.*
REVENGE

KING OF SPAIN.
DON CYPRIAN, *Duke of Castile, his brother.*
LORENZO, *Don Cyprian's son.*
PAGE OF LORENZO.
HIERONIMO, *Marshal of Spain.*
HORATIO, *his son.*
SPANISH GENERAL.
DEPUTY.
VICEROY OF PORTUGAL.
BALTHAZAR, *his son.*
SERBERINE, *Balthazar's servant.*
DON PEDRO, *the viceroy's brother.*
ALEXANDRO } *Portuguese noblemen.*
VILLUPPO
PORTUGUESE AMBASSADOR.
TWO PORTUGUESE.
DON BAZULTO, *an old man.*

PEDRINGANO, *Bel-imperia's servant.*
CHRISTOPHIL, *Bel-imperia's custodian.*
THREE CITIZENS.
MESSENGER.
HANGMAN.
ARMY, ROYAL SUITES, NOBLEMEN, OFFICERS, HALBERDIERS, SERVANTS, THREE WATCHMEN, ETC.

BEL-IMPERIA, *Don Cyprian's daughter.*
ISABELLA, *Hieronimo's wife.*
MAID OF ISABELLA.

Three KINGS *and three* KNIGHTS, *in the first dumb show;* HYMEN *and two* TORCHBEARERS *in the second.*

BAZARDO, *a painter* } *in the additions to the*
PEDRO *and* JAQUES, } *play.*
Hieronimo's servants

SCENE: *Spain and Portugal.*

TIME: *Contemporary.*]

ACTUS PRIMUS.

[INDUCTION, *or* CHORUS]

Enter the Ghost of Andrea, and with him Revenge.

GHOST. When this eternal substance of my soul
Did live imprisoned in my wanton flesh,
Each in their function serving other's need,
I was a courtier in the Spanish court.
My name was Don Andrea, my descent,
Though not ignoble, yet inferior far
To gracious fortunes of my tender youth.

For there in prime and pride of all my years,
By duteous service and deserving love,
In secret I possessed a worthy dame, 10
Which hight[2] sweet Bel-imperia by name.
But in the harvest of my summer joys
Death's winter nipped the blossoms of my bliss,
Forcing divorce betwixt my love and me.
For in the late conflict with Portingale
My valor drew me into danger's mouth
Till life to death made passage through my wounds.
When I was slain, my soul descended straight
To pass the flowing stream of Acheron;

---

[1] The title continues: "Containing the Lamentable End of Don Horatio and Bel-imperia, with the Pitiful Death of Old Hieronimo." In the 1615 edn. a sub-title is substituted: "Or Hieronimo Is Mad Again."

[2] Who was called.

But churlish Charon, only boatman
   there,   20
Said that, my rites of burial not per-
   formed,
I might not sit amongst his passengers.
Ere Sol had slept three nights in Thetis'
   lap,
And slaked his smoking chariot in her
   flood,
By Don Horatio, our knight marshal's
   son,
My funerals and obsequies were done.
Then was the ferryman of hell content
To pass me over to the slimy strand
That leads to fell Avernus' ugly waves.
There, pleasing Cerberus with honeyed
   speech,   30
I passed the perils of the foremost porch.
Not far from hence, amidst ten thousand
   souls,
Sat Minos, Æacus, and Rhadamanth,
To whom no sooner gan [1] I make ap-
   proach
To crave a passport for my wand'ring
   ghost,
But Minos, in graven leaves of lottery,
Drew forth the manner of my life and
   death.
"This knight," quoth he, "both lived
   and died in love,
And for his love tried fortune of the wars,
And by war's fortune lost both love and
   life."   40
"Why then," said Æacus, "convey him
   hence,
To walk with lovers in our fields of love,
And spend the course of everlasting time
Under green myrtle trees and cypress
   shades."
"No, no," said Rhadamanth, "it were
   not well
With loving souls to place a martialist.
He died in war, and must to martial
   fields,
Where wounded Hector lives in lasting
   pain,
And Achilles' Myrmidons do scour the
   plain."   49
Then Minos, mildest censor [2] of the three,
Made this device to end the difference:
"Send him," quoth he, "to our infernal
   king,
To doom him as best seems his majesty."

[1] Did.   [2] Judge.

To this effect my passport straight was
   drawn.
In keeping on my way to Pluto's court,
Through dreadful shades of ever-
   glooming night,
I saw more sights than thousand tongues
   can tell,
Or pens can write, or mortal hearts can
   think.
Three ways there were.   That on the
   right-hand side   59
Was ready way unto the foresaid fields,
Where lovers live and bloody martialists,
But either sort contained within his
   bounds.
The left-hand path, declining fearfully,
Was ready downfall to the deepest hell,
Where bloody Furies shakes their whips
   of steel,
And poor Ixion turns an endless wheel;
Where usurers are choked with melting
   gold,
And wantons are embraced with ugly
   snakes,
And murderers groan with never-killing
   wounds,
And perjured wights scalded in boiling
   lead,   70
And all foul sins with torments over-
   whelmed.
Twixt these two ways I trod the middle
   path,
Which brought me to the fair Elysian
   green,
In midst whereof there stands a stately
   tower,
The walls of brass, the gates of adamant.
Here finding Pluto with his Proserpine,
I showed my passport, humbled on my
   knee,
Whereat fair Proserpine began to smile,
And begged that only she might give
   my doom.
Pluto was pleased, and sealed it with a
   kiss.   80
Forthwith, Revenge, she rounded [3] thee
   in th' ear,
And bade thee lead me through the gates
   of horn,
Where dreams have passage in the silent
   night.
No sooner had she spoke, but we were
   here—

[3] Whispered.

I wot [1] not how—in twinkling of an eye.

REVENGE. Then know, Andrea, that thou
art arrived

Where thou shalt see the author of thy
death,

Don Balthazar, the prince of Portingale,

Deprived of life by Bel-imperia.

Here sit we down to see the mystery,[2] 90

And serve for Chorus in this tragedy.

[SCENA PRIMA.

The Spanish court.]

*Enter Spanish King, General, Castile, and
Hieronimo.*

KING. Now say, l[ord] general, how fares
our camp?

GEN. All well, my sovereign liege, except
some few

That are deceased by fortune of the war.

KING. But what portends thy cheerful
countenance,

And posting to our presence thus in
haste?

Speak, man, hath fortune given us victory?

GEN. Victory, my liege, and that with little
loss.

KING. Our Portingales will pay us tribute
then?

GEN. Tribute and wonted homage therewithal.

KING. Then blessed be heaven and guider
of the heavens,　　　　　　　　　　10

From whose fair influence such justice
flows.

CAS. *"O multum dilecte Deo, tibi militat
æther,*

Et conjuratæ curvato poplite gentes

*Succumbunt: recti soror est victoria
juris."* [3]

KING. Thanks to my loving brother of
Castile.—

But, general, unfold in brief discourse

Your form of battle and your war's success,

That, adding all the pleasure of thy news

Unto the height of former happiness,

---

[1] Know.　　　　　　　　　　　　[2] Play.

[3] "O thou much loved of God, for thee heaven
wars, and the peoples of earth, united, submit on bended knee. The triumph of justice
is the sister of righteousness" (adapted from
Claudian's *De Tertio Consulatu Honorii,* ll. 96–
98).

With deeper wage and greater dignity 20

We may reward thy blissful chivalry.

GEN. Where Spain and Portingale do
jointly knit

Their frontiers, leaning on each other's
bound,

There met our armies in their proud
array,

Both furnished well, both full of hope
and fear,

Both menacing alike with daring shows,

Both vaunting sundry colors of device,

Both cheerly sounding trumpets, drums,
and fifes,

Both raising dreadful clamors to the sky

That valleys, hills, and rivers made re-
bound,　　　　　　　　　　　　　　30

And heaven itself was frighted with the
sound.

Our battles both were pitched in squadron form,

Each corner strongly fenced with wings
of shot,

But, ere we joined and came to push of
pike,

I brought a squadron of our readiest shot

From out our rearward [4] to begin the
fight;

They brought another wing t' encounter
us.

Meanwhile, our ordinance played on
either side,

And captains strove to have their valors
tried.

Don Pedro, their chief horsemen's colonel,　　　　　　　　　　　　　　40

Did with his cornet [5] bravely make attempt

To break the order of our battle ranks;

But Don Rogero, worthy man of war,

Marched forth against him with our
musketeers,

And stopped the malice of his fell approach.

While they maintain hot skirmish to and
fro,

Both battles join, and fall to handy-
blows,[6]

Their violent shot resembling th' ocean's
rage,

When, roaring loud and with a swelling
tide,

---

[4] Rear division.　　　[6] Hand-to-hand fighting.
[5] Troop of horse.

It beats upon the rampiers [1] of huge
rocks, 50
And gapes to swallow neighbor-bounding
lands.
Now, while Bellona rageth here and
there,
Thick storms of bullets ran like winter's
hail,
And shivered lances dark the troubled
air.
Pede pes et cuspide cuspis;
Arma sonant armis, vir petiturque viro. [2]
On every side drop captains to the
ground,
And soldiers, some ill maimed, some slain
outright.
Here falls a body sindered [3] from his
head;
There legs and arms lie bleeding on the
grass, 60
Mingled with weapons and unboweled
steeds,
That scattering overspread the purple
plain.
In all this turmoil, three long hours and
more,
The victory to neither part inclined,
Till Don Andrea, with his brave lan-
ciers,
In their main battle made so great a
breach
That, half dismayed, the multitude re-
tired.
But Balthazar, the Portingales' young
prince,
Brought rescue, and encouraged them
to stay.
Herehence [4] the fight was eagerly re-
newed, 70
And in that conflict was Andrea slain—
Brave man at arms, but weak to Baltha-
zar.
Yet while the prince, insulting [5] over
him,
Breathed out proud vaunts, sounding to
our reproach,
Friendship and hardy valor joined in one
Pricked forth Horatio, our knight mar-
shal's son,

To challenge forth that prince in single
fight.
Not long between these twain the fight
endured,
But straight the prince was beaten from
his horse,
And forced to yield him prisoner to his
foe. 80
When he was taken, all the rest they fled,
And our carbines pursued them to the
death,
Till, Phœbus waving [6] to the western
deep,
Our trumpeters were charged to sound
retreat.
KING. Thanks, good l[ord] general, for
these good news;
And, for some argument of more to come,
Take this and wear it for thy sovereign's
sake. *Give him his chain.*
But tell me now, hast thou confirmed a
peace?
GEN. No peace, my liege, but peace con-
ditional,
That, if with homage tribute be well
paid, 90
The fury of your forces will be stayed;
And to this peace their viceroy hath
subscribed, *Give the K[ing] a paper.*
And made a solemn vow that, during
life,
His tribute shall be truly paid to Spain.
KING. These words, these deeds, become
thy person well.
But now, knight marshal, frolic with
thy king,
For 'tis thy son that wins this battle's
prize.
HIER. Long may he live to serve my sov-
ereign liege,
And soon decay, unless he serve my
liege.
KING. Nor thou nor he shall die without
reward. *A tucket* [7] *afar off.* 100
What means this warning of this trump-
et's sound?
GEN. This tells me that your grace's men
of war,
Such as war's fortune hath reserved
from death,
Come marching on towards your royal
seat,
To show themselves before your majesty,

---

[1] Rampires, ramparts, embankments.
[2] Foot against foot and spear against spear,
arms clash on arms, hero is assailed by hero
(a combination of phrases from Statius, Virgil,
and Curtius). [4] From this point.
[3] Sundered. [5] Triumphing scornfully.
[6] 1603 edn. has *waning.* [7] Flourish of trumpets.

For so I gave in charge at my depart,
Whereby by demonstration shall appear
That all, except three hundred or few more,
Are safe returned, and by their foes enriched.

The Army enters, Balthazar, between Lorenzo and Horatio, captive.

KING. A gladsome sight! I long to see them here. *They enter and pass by.* 110
Was that the warlike prince of Portingale
That by our nephew was in triumph led?
GEN. It was, my liege, the prince of Portingale.
KING. But what was he that on the other side
Held him by th' arm as partner of the prize?
HIER. That was my son, my gracious sovereign,
Of whom though from his tender infancy
My loving thoughts did never hope but well,
He never pleased his father's eyes till now,
Nor filled my heart with overcloying joys. 120
KING. Go, let them march once more about these walls,
That, staying them, we may confer and talk
With our brave prisoner and his double guard.   [*Exit a Messenger.*]
Hieronimo, it greatly pleaseth us
That in our victory thou have a share,
By virtue of thy worthy son's exploit.

Enter again.

Bring hither the young prince of Portingale.
The rest march on; but, ere they be dismissed,
We will bestow on every soldier
Two ducats and on every leader ten, 130
That they may know our largess welcomes them.
Exeunt all but [*the King,*] *Bal*[*thazar*], *Lor*[*enzo*], *Hor*[*atio*].
Welcome, Don Balthazar! Welcome, nephew!

And thou, Horatio, thou art welcome too.
Young prince, although thy father's hard misdeeds,
In keeping back the tribute that he owes,
Deserve but evil measure at our hands,
Yet shalt thou know that Spain is honorable.
BAL. The trespass that my father made in peace
Is now controlled [1] by fortune of the wars,
And, cards once dealt, it boots not ask why so. 140
His men are slain—a weakening to his realm;
His colors seized—a blot unto his name;
His son distressed—a corsive [2] to his heart.
These punishments may clear his late offense.
KING. Ay, Balthazar, if he observe this truce,
Our peace will grow the stronger for these wars.
Meanwhile live thou, though not in liberty,
Yet free from bearing any servile yoke,
For in our hearing thy deserts were great,
And in our sight thyself art gracious. 150
BAL. And I shall study to deserve this grace.
KING. But tell me—for their holding makes me doubt—
To which of these twain art thou prisoner?
LOR. To me, my liege.
HOR.   To me, my sovereign.
LOR. This hand first took his courser by the reins.
HOR. But first my lance did put him from his horse.
LOR. I seized his weapon, and enjoyed it first.
HOR. But first I forced him lay his weapons down.
KING. Let go his arm, upon our privilege.
                              Let him go.
Say, worthy prince, to whether [3] didst thou yield? 160
BAL. To him in courtesy; to this perforce.
He spake me fair; this other gave me strokes.

[1] Checked.   [2] Corrosive.   [3] Which one.

He promised life; this other threatened
   death.
He won my love; this other conquered
   me—
And, truth to say, I yield myself to both.
HIER. But that I know your grace for
   just and wise,
And might seem partial in this difference,
Enforced by nature and by law of arms,
My tongue should plead for young
   Horatio's right.   169
He hunted well that was a lion's death,
Not he that in a garment wore his skin;
So hares may pull dead lions by the
   beard.
KING. Content thee, marshal, thou shalt
   have no wrong;
And, for thy sake, thy son shall want no
   right.
Will both abide the censure [1] of my
   doom?
LOR. I crave no better than your grace
   awards.
HOR. Nor I, although I sit beside my
   right.
KING. Then by my judgment thus your
   strife shall end:
You both deserve, and both shall have
   reward.
Nephew, thou took'st his weapon and
   his horse;   180
His weapons and his horse are thy re-
   ward.
Horatio, thou didst force him first to
   yield;
His ransom therefore is thy valor's fee.
Appoint the sum, as you shall both agree.
But, nephew, thou shalt have the prince
   in guard,
For thine estate best fitteth such a guest.
Horatio's house were small for all his
   train.
Yet, in regard thy substance passeth his,
And that just guerdon may befall desert,
To him we yield the armor of the
   prince.   190
How likes Don Balthazar of this device?
BAL. Right well, my liege, if this proviso
   were
That Don Horatio bear us company,
Whom I admire and love for chivalry.
KING. Horatio, leave him not that loves
   thee so.—

1 Judgment.

Now let us hence to see our soldiers paid,
And feast our prisoner as our friendly
   guest.   *Exeunt.*

[SCENA SECUNDA.
The Portuguese court.]

Enter Viceroy, Alexandro, Villuppo.

VIC. Is our ambassador despatched for
   Spain?
ALEX. Two days, my liege, are past since
   his depart.
VIC. And tribute payment gone along with
   him?
ALEX. Ay, my good lord.
VIC. Then rest we here awhile in our un-
   rest,
And feed our sorrows with some inward
   sighs,
For deepest cares break never into tears.
But wherefore sit I in a regal throne?
This better fits a wretch's endless moan.
                         Falls to the ground.
Yet this is higher than my fortunes
   reach,   10
And therefore better than my state de-
   serves.
Ay, ay, this earth, image of melancholy,
Seeks him whom fates adjudge to misery.
Here let me lie; now am I at the lowest.
Qui jacet in terra, non habet unde cadat.
In me consumpsit vires Fortuna nocendo;
Nil superest ut jam possit obesse magis. [2]
Yes, Fortune may bereave me of my
   crown—
Here, take it now. Let Fortune do her
   worst,
She will not rob me of this sable weed. 20
O, no, she envies none but pleasant
   things.
Such is the folly of despiteful chance!
Fortune is blind, and sees not my deserts;
So is she deaf, and hears not my laments;
And could she hear, yet is she willful-mad,
And therefore will not pity my distress.
Suppose that she could pity me, what
   then?
What help can be expected at her hands
Whose foot [is] [3] standing on a rolling
   stone,

2 He who lies upon the ground hath not
whence he may fall. On me hath Fortune exhausted her powers of injury. There remains
no further damage that she can inflict (source
unknown).   3 Added by Dodsley.

And mind more mutable than fickle
winds?   30
Why wail I, then, where's hope of no
redress?
O, yes, complaining makes my grief seem
less.
My late ambition hath distained [1] my
faith;
My breach of faith occasioned bloody
wars;
Those bloody wars have spent my treas-
ure;
And with my treasure my people's blood;
And with their blood, my joy and best
beloved,
My best beloved, my sweet and only son.
O, wherefore went I not to war myself?
The cause was mine; I might have died
for both.   40
My years were mellow; his but young
and green.
My death were natural, but his was
forced.
ALEX. No doubt, my liege, but still the
prince survives.
VIC. Survives! Ay, where?
ALEX. In Spain, a prisoner by mischance
of war.
VIC. Then they have slain him for his
father's fault.
ALEX. That were a breach to common
law of arms.
VIC. They reck no laws that meditate re-
venge.
ALEX. His ransom's worth will stay from
foul revenge.
VIC. No; if he lived, the news would soon
be here.   50
ALEX. Nay, evil news fly faster still than
good.
VIC. Tell me no more of news, for he is
dead.
VIL. My sovereign, pardon the author of
ill news,
And I'll bewray [2] the fortune of thy son.
VIC. Speak on, I'll guerdon thee, whate'er
it be.
Mine ear is ready to receive ill news,
My heart grown hard gainst mischief's
battery.
Stand up, I say, and tell thy tale at large.
VIL. Then hear that truth which these
mine eyes have seen.

When both the armies were in battle
joined,   60
Don Balthazar, amidst the thickest
troops,
To win renown did wondrous feats of
arms.
Amongst the rest, I saw him, hand to
hand,
In single fight with their lord general,
Till Alexandro, that here counterfeits
Under the color of a duteous friend,
Discharged his pistol at the prince's back
As though he would have slain their
general—
But therewithal Don Balthazar fell down,
And, when he fell, then we began to
fly;   70
But, had he lived, the day had sure been
ours.
ALEX. O wicked forgery! O traitorous mis-
creant!
VIC. Hold thou thy peace! But now, Vil-
luppo, say,
Where then became [3] the carcass of my
son?
VIL. I saw them drag it to the Spanish
tents.
VIC. Ay, ay, my nightly dreams have told
me this.—
Thou false, unkind, unthankful, traitor-
ous beast,
Wherein had Balthazar offended thee
That thou shouldst thus betray him to
our foes?
Was't Spanish gold that bleared so
thine eyes   80
That thou couldst see no part of our
deserts?
Perchance, because thou art Terceira's
lord,
Thou hadst some hope to wear this
diadem,
If first my son and then myself were
slain.
But thy ambitious thought shall break
thy neck.
Ay, this was it that made thee spill his
blood,
    Take the crown and put it on again.
But I'll now wear it till thy blood be
spilt.
ALEX. Vouchsafe, dread sovereign, to hear
me speak.

[1] Stained, defiled.   [2] Disclose.   [3] What became of.

Vic. Away with him! His sight is second
  hell.
Keep him till we determine of his
  death.   [*They take him out.*] 90
If Balthazar be dead, he shall not live.
Villuppo, follow us for thy reward.
                        Exit Vice[*roy*].
Vil. Thus have I with an envious, forgéd
  tale
Deceived the king, betrayed mine enemy,
And hope for guerdon of my villainy.
                            Exit.

[Scena Tertia.

Hieronimo's garden.[1]]

Enter Horatio and Bel-imperia.

Bel. Signior Horatio, this is the place and
  hour,
Wherein I must entreat thee to relate
The circumstance of Don Andrea's death,
Who, living, was my garland's sweetest
  flower,
And in his death hath buried my de-
  lights.
Hor. For love of him and service to your-
  self,
I nill [2] refuse this heavy, doleful charge;
Yet tears and sighs, I fear, will hinder
  me.
When both our armies were enjoined in
  fight,
Your worthy chevalier amidst the
  thick'st,   10
For glorious cause still aiming at the
  fairest,
Was at the last by young Don Balthazar
Encountered hand to hand. Their fight
  was long,
Their hearts were great, their clamors
  menacing,
Their strength alike, their strokes both
  dangerous.
But wrathful Nemesis, that wicked
  power,
Envying at Andrea's praise and worth,

Cut short his life to end his praise and
  worth.
She, she herself, disguised in armor's
  mask—
As Pallas was before proud Perga-
  mus—   20
Brought in a fresh supply of halberdiers,
Which paunched [3] his horse, and dinged [4]
  him to the ground.
Then young Don Balthazar with ruthless
  rage,
Taking advantage of his foe's distress,
Did finish what his halberdiers begun,
And left not till Andrea's life was done.
Then, though too late, incensed with just
  remorse,[5]
I with my band set forth against the
  prince
And brought him prisoner from his
  halberdiers.
Bel. Would thou hadst slain him that so
  slew my love!   30
But then was Don Andrea's carcass lost?
Hor. No, that was it for which I chiefly
  strove,
Nor stepped I back till I recovered him.
I took him up, and wound him in mine
  arms;
And, welding [6] him unto my private tent,
There laid him down, and dewed him
  with my tears,
And sighed and sorrowed as became a
  friend.
But neither friendly sorrow, sighs, nor
  tears
Could win pale Death from his usurpéd
  right.
Yet this I did, and less I could not do: 40
I saw him honored with due funeral.
This scarf I plucked from off his lifeless
  arm,
And wear it in remembrance of my
  friend.
Bel. I know the scarf. Would he had kept
  it still!
For, had he lived, he would have kept it
  still,
And worn it for his Bel-imperia's sake,
For 'twas my favor at his last depart.
But now wear thou it both for him and
  me,
For after him thou hast deserved it best.

---

[1] If II, ii, 42–43, refers to I, iii, 48–54, the
scene here is Hieronimo's garden, and, according to ll. 110–15, close to the place of the banquet in I, iv. Possibly, however, I, iii and iv, are
to be regarded as one scene, beginning in some
indefinite locality and shifting to a banqueting
hall.
  [2] Ne will; will not.

[3] Stabbed in the belly.   [5] Sorrow.
[4] Knocked down.   [6] Wielding, carrying.

But, for thy kindness in his life and
  death,   50
Be sure, while Bel-imperia's life endures,
She will be Don Horatio's thankful
  friend.
HOR. And, madam, Don Horatio will not
  slack
Humbly to serve fair Bel-imperia.
But now, if your good liking stand
  thereto,
I'll crave your pardon to go seek the
  prince,
For so the duke, your father, gave me
  charge.   *Exit.*
BEL. Ay, go, Horatio, leave me here
  alone,
For solitude best fits my cheerless mood.
Yet what avails to wail Andrea's
  death,   60
From whence Horatio proves my second
  love?
Had he not loved Andrea as he did,
He could not sit in Bel-imperia's
  thoughts.
But how can love find harbor in my
  breast
Till I revenge the death of my beloved?
Yes, second love shall further my re-
  venge!
I'll love Horatio, my Andrea's friend,
The more to spite the prince that
  wrought his end;
And, where Don Balthazar, that slew
  my love,
Himself now pleads for favor at my
  hands,   70
He shall, in rigor of my just disdain,
Reap long repentance for his murderous
  deed.
For what was't else but murderous
  cowardice,
So many to oppress one valiant knight,
Without respect of honor in the fight?
And here he comes that murdered my
  delight.

Enter Lorenzo and Balthazar.

LOR. Sister, what means this melancholy
  walk?
BEL. That for a while I wish no company.
LOR. But here the prince is come to visit
  you.
BEL. That argues that he lives in liberty.   80

BAL. No, madam, but in pleasing servi-
  tude.
BEL. Your prison then, belike, is your
  conceit.[1]
BAL. Ay, by conceit my freedom is enthralled.
BEL. Then with conceit enlarge [2] yourself
  again.
BAL. What if conceit have laid my heart
  to gage? [3]
BEL. Pay that you borrowed, and recover
  it.
BAL. I die, if it return from whence it lies.
BEL. A heartless man, and live? A mir-
  acle!
BAL. Ay, lady, love can work such mir-
  acles.
LOR. Tush, tush, my lord! Let go these
  ambages,[4]   90
And in plain terms acquaint her with
  your love.
BEL. What boots complaint, when there's
  no remedy?
BAL. Yes, to your gracious self must I com-
  plain,
In whose fair answer lies my remedy;
On whose perfection all my thoughts
  attend;
On whose aspect mine eyes find beauty's
  bower;
In whose translucent breast my heart is
  lodged.
BEL. Alas, my lord, these are but words of
  course,[5]
And but devise[d] to drive me from this
  place.
She in going in lets fall her glove, which
        Horatio, coming out, takes up.
HOR. Madam, your glove.   100
BEL. Thanks, good Horatio; take it for thy
  pains.
BAL. Signior Horatio stooped in happy
  time!
HOR. I reaped more grace than I deserved
  or hoped.
LOR. My lord, be not dismayed for what
  is past;
You know that women oft are humor-
  ous.[6]
These clouds will overblow with little
  wind;

---

[1] Thought, imagination.   [4] Roundabout phrases.
[2] Free.   [5] Formal phrases.
[3] As security.   [6] Variable, capricious.

Let me alone, I'll scatter them myself.
Meanwhile, let us devise to spend the
time
In some delightful sports and reveling.
Hor. The king, my lords, is coming hither
straight   110
To feast the Portingale ambassador;
Things were in readiness before I came.
Bal. Then here it fits us to attend the king,
To welcome hither our ambassador,
And learn my father and my country's
health.

[Scena Quarta.

The banqueting hall in the Spanish court.]

*Enter the banquet, Trumpets, the King, and
Ambassador.*

King. See, lord ambassador, how Spain
entreats [1]
Their prisoner Balthazar, thy viceroy's
son.
We pleasure more in kindness than in
wars.
Amb. Sad is our king, and Portingale la-
ments,
Supposing that Don Balthazar is slain.
Bal. So am I—slain by beauty's tyranny!
You see, my lord, how Balthazar is slain:
I frolic with the Duke of Castile's son,
Wrapped every hour in pleasures of the
court,
And graced with favors of his majesty. 10
King. Put off your greetings till our feast
be done;
Now come and sit with us, and taste our
cheer.   *Sit to the banquet.*
Sit down, young prince; you are our
second guest.
Brother, sit down; and, nephew, take
your place.
Signior Horatio, wait thou upon our cup,
For well thou hast deserved to be hon-
ored.
Now, lordings, fall to. Spain is Portugal,
And Portugal is Spain; we both are
friends;
Tribute is paid, and we enjoy our right.
But where is old Hieronimo, our mar-
shal?   20
He promised us, in honor of our guest,
To grace our banquet with some pom-
pous jest. [2]

<hr>

[1] Treats.   [2] Stately entertainment.

*Enter Hieronimo, with a drum, three
Knights, each [with] his scutcheon; then
he fetches three Kings; they take their
crowns and them captive.*

Hieronimo, this masque contents mine
eye,
Although I sound not well the mystery.
Hier. The first armed knight that hung
his scutcheon up
*He takes the scutcheon and gives it to the
King.*
Was English Robert, Earl of Gloucester,
Who, when King Stephen bore sway in
Albion,
Arrived with five-and-twenty thousand
men
In Portingale, and by success of war
Enforced the king, then but a Saracen, 30
To bear the yoke of the English mon-
archy.
King. My lord of Portingale, by this you
see
That which may comfort both your king
and you,
And make your late discomfort seem the
less.
But say, Hieronimo, what was the next?
Hier. The second knight that hung his
scutcheon up   *He doth as he did before.*
Was Edmund, Earl of Kent in Albion,
When English Richard wore the diadem.
He came likewise, and razéd Lisbon
walls,
And took the King of Portingale in
fight,   40
For which and other suchlike service
done
He after was created Duke of York.
King. This is another special argument
That Portingale may deign to bear our
yoke,
When it by little England hath been
yoked.
But now, Hieronimo, what were the last?
Hier. The third and last, not least, in our
account,   *Doing as before.*
Was, as the rest, a valiant Englishman,
Brave John of Gaunt, the Duke of Lan-
caster,
As by his scutcheon plainly may ap-
pear.   50
He with a puissant army came to Spain
And took our King of Castile prisoner.

AMB. This is an argument for our viceroy
  That Spain may not insult for her suc-
    cess,
  Since English warriors likewise conquered
    Spain,
  And made them bow their knees to
    Albion.
KING. Hieronimo, I drink to thee for this
    device,
  Which hath pleased both the ambassador
    and me.
  Pledge me, Hieronimo, if thou love the
    king.   *Takes the cup of Horatio.*
  My lord, I fear we sit but overlong,   60
  Unless our dainties were more delicate,
  But welcome are you to the best we have.
  Now let us in, that you may be des-
    patched.
  I think our council is already set.
                      Exeunt omnes.

[CHORUS]

ANDREA. Come we for this from depth of
  underground,
  To see him feast that gave me my
    death's wound?
  These pleasant sights are sorrow to my
    soul—
  Nothing but league,[1] and love, and ban-
    queting!
REVENGE. Be still, Andrea; ere we go from
  hence,
  I'll turn their friendship into fell de-
    spite,   70
  Their love to mortal hate, their day to
    night,
  Their hope into despair, their peace to
    war,
  Their joys to pain, their bliss to misery.

ACTUS SECUNDUS. [SCENA PRIMA.

A room in Don Cyprian's palace.]

Enter Lorenzo and Balthazar.

LOR. My lord, though Bel-imperia seem
  thus coy,
  Let reason hold you in your wonted joy.
  In time the savage bull sustains the
    yoke,[2]

[1] Friendship.
[2] Lines 3–6, 9–10, are modeled on Sonnet 47
of Watson's *Hecatompathia.*

In time all haggard [3] hawks will stoop to
  lure,
In time small wedges cleave the hardest
  oak,
In time the flint is pierced with softest
  shower,
And she in time will fall from her dis-
  dain,
And rue the sufferance of your friendly
  pain.
BAL. No, she is wilder and more hard
  withal
  Than beast or bird or tree or stony
    wall.   10
  But wherefore blot I Bel-imperia's name?
  It is my fault, not she, that merits blame.
  My feature is not to content her sight,
  My words are rude and work her no
    delight.
  The lines I send her are but harsh and ill,
  Such as do drop from Pan and Marsyas'
    quill.
  My presents are not of sufficient cost,
  And, being worthless, all my labor's lost.
  Yet might she love me for my valiancy—
  Ay, but that's slandered by captivity. 20
  Yet might she love me to content her
    sire—
  Ay, but her reason masters his desire.
  Yet might she love me as her brother's
    friend—
  Ay, but her hopes aim at some other end.
  Yet might she love me to uprear her
    state—
  Ay, but perhaps she hopes some nobler
    mate.
  Yet might she love me as her beauty's
    thrall—
  Ay, but I fear she cannot love at all.
LOR. My lord, for my sake leave this
  ecstasy,[4]
  And doubt not but we'll find some
    remedy.   30
  Some cause there is that lets you not be
    loved;
  First that must needs be known, and
    then removed.
  What if my sister love some other knight?
BAL. My summer's day will turn to win-
  ter's night.
LOR. I have already found a stratagem
  To sound the bottom of this doubtful
    theme.
[3] Wild.   [4] Frenzy.

My lord, for once you shall be ruled by
   me;
Hinder me not, whate'er you hear or see.
By force or fair means will I cast about
To find the truth of all this question
   out.   40
Ho, Pedringano!
PED.   Signior!
LOR.   *Vien qui presto.*[1]

Enter Pedringano.

PED. Hath your lordship any service to
   command me?
LOR. Ay, Pedringano, service of import,
   And—not to spend the time in trifling
      words—
Thus stands the case: it is not long, thou
   know'st,
Since I did shield thee from my father's
   wrath,
For thy conveyance[2] in Andrea's love,
For which thou wert adjudged to punish-
   ment.
I stood betwixt thee and thy punishment,
And, since, thou knowest how I have
   favored thee.   50
Now to these favors will I add reward,
Not with fair words, but store of golden
   coin,
And lands and living joined with dig-
   nities,
If thou but satisfy my just demand.
Tell truth, and have me for thy lasting
   friend.
PED. Whate'er it be your lordship shall de-
   mand,
My bounden duty bids me tell the truth,
If case[3] it lie in me to tell the truth.
LOR. Then, Pedringano, this is my de-
   mand:
Whom loves my sister Bel-imperia?   60
For she reposeth all her trust in thee.
Speak, man, and gain both friendship and
   reward.
I mean, whom loves she in Andrea's
   place?
PED. Alas, my lord, since Don Andrea's
   death
I have no credit with her as before,
And therefore know not if she love or no.
LOR. Nay, if thou dally, then I am thy foe,
          [Draw his sword.][4]

And fear shall force what friendship
   cannot win.
Thy death shall bury what thy life con-
   ceals;
Thou diest for more esteeming her than
   me.   70
PED. O, stay, my lord!
LOR. Yet speak the truth, and I will
   guerdon thee,
And shield thee from whatever can
   ensue,
And will conceal whate'er proceeds from
   thee.
But, if thou dally once again, thou diest.
PED. If Madam Bel-imperia be in love—
LOR. What, villain! If's and and's?
          [Offer to kill him.][4]
PED. O, stay, my lord! She loves Horatio.
          Balthazar starts back.
LOR. What, Don Horatio, our knight
   marshal's son?
PED. Even him, my lord.   80
LOR. Now say but how know'st thou he
   is her love,
And thou shalt find me kind and lib-
   eral.
Stand up, I say, and fearless tell the
   truth.
PED. She sent him letters, which myself
   perused,
Full fraught with lines and arguments of
   love,
Preferring him before Prince Balthazar.
LOR. Swear on this cross[5] that what thou
   sayst is true,
And that thou wilt conceal what thou
   hast told.
PED. I swear to both, by Him that made
   us all.
LOR. In hope thine oath is true, here's thy
   reward;   90
But, if I prove thee perjured and unjust,
This very sword whereon thou took'st
   thine oath
Shall be the worker of thy tragedy.
PED. What I have said is true, and shall—
   for me—
Be still concealed from Bel-imperia.
Besides, your honor's liberality
Deserves my duteous service, even till
   death.
LOR. Let this be all that thou shalt do for
   me:

---

[1] Come here quickly.
[2] Trickery.
[3] In case.
[4] From 1602 edn.
[5] *I.e.*, sword hilt.

Be watchful when and where these lovers
    meet,
And give me notice in some secret
    sort.   100
PED. I will, my lord.
LOR. Then shalt thou find that I am
    liberal.
Thou know'st that I can more advance
    thy state
Than she. Be therefore wise, and fail me
    not.
Go and attend her, as thy custom is,
Lest absence make her think thou dost
    amiss.   *Exit Pedringano.*
Why, so: *tam armis quam ingenio.*[1]
Where words prevail not, violence pre-
    vails;
But gold doth more than either of them
    both.
How likes Prince Balthazar this strata-
    gem?   110
BAL. Both well and ill. It makes me glad
    and sad:
Glad that I know the hinderer of my
    love—
Sad that I fear she hates me whom I
    love;
Glad that I know on whom to be re-
    venged—
Sad that she'll fly me if I take revenge.
Yet must I take revenge or die myself,
For love resisted grows impatient.
I think Horatio be my destined plague.
First, in his hand he brandishéd a sword,
And with that sword he fiercely wagéd
    war,   120
And in that war he gave me dangerous
    wounds,
And by those wounds he forcéd me to
    yield,
And by my yielding I became his slave.
Now in his mouth he carries pleasing
    words,
Which pleasing words do harbor sweet
    conceits,
Which sweet conceits are limed with sly
    deceits,
Which sly deceits smooth Bel-imperia's
    ears,
And through her ears dive down into her
    heart,
And in her heart set him where I should
    stand.

[1] As much by force as by wisdom.

Thus hath he ta'en my body by his
    force,   130
And now by sleight would captivate my
    soul.
But in his fall I'll tempt the destinies,
And either lose my life or win my love.
LOR. Let's go, my lord; your staying stays
    revenge.
Do you but follow me, and gain your love.
Her favor must be won by his remove.
                        Exeunt.

[SCENA SECUNDA.

The same.]

Enter Horatio and Bel-imperia.

HOR. Now, madam, since by favor of your
    love
Our hidden smoke is turned to open flame,
And that with looks and words we feed
    our thought
(Two chief contents, where more cannot
    be had),
Thus, in the midst of love's fair blandish-
    ments,
Why show you sign of inward languish-
    ments?
*Pedringano showeth all to the Prince and
    Lorenzo, placing them in secret.*
BEL. My heart, sweet friend, is like a ship
    at sea.
She wisheth port, where, riding all at ease,
She may repair what stormy times have
    worn,
And, leaning on the shore, may sing with
    joy   10
That pleasure follows pain, and bliss
    annoy.
Possession of thy love is th' only port
Wherein my heart, with fears and hopes
    long tossed,
Each hour doth wish and long to make
    resort,
There to repair the joys that it hath lost,
And, sitting safe, to sing in Cupid's choir
That sweetest bliss is crown of love's
    desire.

Balthazar [and Lorenzo] above.
BAL. O, sleep, mine eyes; see not my love
    profaned.
Be deaf, my ears; hear not my discontent.
Die, heart; another joys what thou de-
    servest.   20

Lor. Watch still, mine eyes, to see this
  love disjoined;
  Hear still, mine ears, to hear them both
    lament;
  Live, heart, to joy at fond Horatio's fall.

Bel. Why stands Horatio speechless all
  this while?

Hor. The less I speak, the more I meditate.

Bel. But whereon dost thou chiefly meditate?

Hor. On dangers past, and pleasures to
  ensue.

Bal. On pleasures past, and dangers to
  ensue.

Bel. What dangers and what pleasures
  dost thou mean?

Hor. Dangers of war, and pleasures of our
  love.   30

Lor. Dangers of death, but pleasures none
  at all.

Bel. Let dangers go; thy war shall be
  with me,
  But such a war as breaks no bond of
    peace.
  Speak thou fair words, I'll cross them
    with fair words;
  Send thou sweet looks, I'll meet them
    with sweet looks;
  Write loving lines, I'll answer loving lines;
  Give me a kiss, I'll countercheck thy kiss.
  Be this our warring peace, or peaceful
    war.

Hor. But, gracious madam, then appoint
  the field,
  Where trial of this war shall first be
    made.   40

Bal. Ambitious villain, how his boldness
  grows!

Bel. Then be thy father's pleasant bower
  the field,
  Where first we vowed a mutual amity.
  The court were dangerous; that place is
    safe.
  Our hour shall be when Vesper gins to
    rise,
  That summons home distressful trav-
    elers.[1]

[1] The meaning *travailers, workers*, is also possible.

There none shall hear us but the harmless
  birds;
Happily [2] the gentle nightingale
Shall carol us asleep, ere we be ware,
And, singing with the prickle at her
  breast,   50
Tell our delight and mirthful dalliance.
Till then each hour will seem a year and
  more.

Hor. But, honeysweet and honorable love,
  Return we now into your father's sight;
  Dangerous suspicion waits on our de-
    light.

Lor. Ay, danger mixed with jealous despite
  Shall send thy soul into eternal night.
                                    Exeunt.

[Scena Tertia.

The Spanish court.]

*Enter King of Spain, Portingale Ambassa-
  dor, Don Cyprian, etc.*

King. Brother of Castile, to the prince's
  love
  What says your daughter Bel-imperia?

Cyp. Although she coy it,[3] as becomes her
  kind,
  And yet dissemble that she loves the
    prince,
  I doubt not, I, but she will stoop in time.
  And, were she froward, which she will
    not be,
  Yet herein shall she follow my advice,
  Which is to love him, or forgo my love.

King. Then, lord ambassador of Portin-
  gale,
  Advise thy king to make this marriage
    up   10
  For strengthening of our late-confirméd
    league.
  I know no better means to make us
    friends.
  Her dowry shall be large and liberal.
  Besides that she is daughter and half-
    heir
  Unto our brother here, Don Cyprian,
  And shall enjoy the moiety of his land,
  I'll grace her marriage with an uncle's
    gift,
  And this it is: in case the match go for-
    ward,

[2] Haply, perhaps.   [3] Pretend to be shy.

The tribute which you pay shall be re-
leased;
And, if by Balthazar she have a son,   20
He shall enjoy the kingdom after us.
AMB. I'll make the motion to my sovereign
liege,
And work it, if my counsel may prevail.
KING. Do so, my lord, and, if he give
consent,
I hope his presence here will honor us
In celebration of the nuptial day;
And let himself determine of the time.
AMB. Will 't please your grace command
me aught beside?
KING. Commend me to the king, and so
farewell.
But where's Prince Balthazar to take his
leave?   30
AMB. That is performed already, my good
lord.
KING. Amongst the rest of what you have
in charge,
The prince's ransom must not be forgot.
That's none of mine, but his that took
him prisoner,
And well his forwardness deserves re-
ward.
It was Horatio, our knight marshal's son.
AMB. Between us there's a price already
pitched,
And shall be sent with all convenient
speed.
KING. Then once again farewell, my lord.
AMB. Farewell, my Lord of Castile, and the
rest.   *Exit.* 40
KING. Now, brother, you must take some
little pains
To win fair Bel-imperia from her will.
Young virgins must be rulèd by their
friends.
The prince is amiable and loves her well.
If she neglect him and forgo his love,
She both will wrong her own estate and
ours.
Therefore, whiles I do entertain the
prince
With greatest pleasure that our court
affords,
Endeavor you to win your daughter's
thought.
If she give back,[1] all this will come to
naught.   50
                 Exeunt.

---

[1] Decline.

[SCENA QUARTA.

Hieronimo's garden.]

Enter Horatio, Bel-imperia, and Pedringano.

HOR. Now that the night begins with
sable wings
To overcloud the brightness of the sun,
And that in darkness pleasures may be
done,
Come, Bel-imperia, let us to the bower,
And there in safety pass a pleasant hour.
BEL. I follow thee, my love, and will not
back,
Although my fainting heart controls my
soul.
HOR. Why, make you doubt of Pedrin-
gano's faith?
BEL. No, he is as trusty as my second
self.—
Go, Pedringano, watch without the
gate,   10
And let us know if any make approach.
PED. [*Aside.*] Instead of watching, I'll de-
serve more gold
By fetching Don Lorenzo to this match.
              Exit Ped[ringano].
HOR. What means my love?
BEL.   I know not what myself,
And yet my heart foretells me some mis-
chance.
HOR. Sweet, say not so; fair fortune is our
friend,
And heavens have shut up day to pleas-
ure us.
The stars, thou seest, hold back their
twinkling shine,
And Luna hides herself to pleasure us.
BEL. Thou hast prevailed; I'll conquer my
misdoubt,   20
And in thy love and counsel drown my
fear.
I fear no more; love now is all my
thoughts.
Why sit we not, for pleasure asketh ease?
HOR. The more thou sitt'st within these
leafy bowers,
The more will Flora deck it with her
flowers.
BEL. Ay, but, if Flora spy Horatio here,
Her jealous eye will think I sit too near.
HOR. Hark, madam, how the birds record[2]
by night,
For joy that Bel-imperia sits in sight.

---

[2] Sing.

BEL. No, Cupid counterfeits the nightin-
    gale,   30
To frame sweet music to Horatio's tale.
HOR. If Cupid sing, then Venus is not far.
    Ay, thou art Venus, or some fairer star.
BEL. If I be Venus, thou must needs be
    Mars;
    And, where Mars reigneth, there must
    needs be wars.
HOR. Then thus begin our wars. Put forth
    thy hand,
    That it may combat with my ruder hand.
BEL. Set forth thy foot to try the push of
    mine.
HOR. But first my looks shall combat
    against thine.
BEL. Then ward thyself: I dart this kiss
    at thee.   40
HOR. Thus I retort the dart thou threw'st
    at me.
BEL. Nay, then, to gain the glory of the
    field
    My twining arms shall yoke and make
    thee yield.
HOR. Nay, then, my arms are large and
    strong withal.
    Thus elms by vines are compassed, till
    they fall.
BEL. O, let me go, for in my troubled eyes
    Now mayst thou read that life in passion
    dies.
HOR. O, stay awhile, and I will die with
    thee;
    So shalt thou yield, and yet have con-
    quered me.
BEL. Who's there? Pedringano?—We are
    betrayed!   50

Enter Lorenzo, Balthazar, Serberine, Pedrin-
gano, disguised.

LOR. My lord, away with her; take her
    aside.—
    O, sir, forbear! Your valor is already
    tried.—
    Quickly despatch, my masters.
           They hang him in the arbor.
HOR.   What, will you murder me?
LOR. Ay, thus, and thus! These are the
    fruits of love.   *They stab him.*
BEL. O, save his life, and let me die for
    him!
    O, save him, brother! Save him, Baltha-
    zar!
I loved Horatio, but he loved not me.

BAL. But Balthazar loves Bel-imperia.
LOR. Although his life were still ambitious,
    proud,
    Yet is he at the highest now he is dead. 60
BEL. Murder! Murder! Help, Hieronimo,
    help!
LOR. Come, stop her mouth; away with
    her.   *Exeunt.*

Enter Hieronimo in his shirt, etc.

HIER. What outcries pluck me from my
    naked bed,
    And chill my throbbing heart with
    trembling fear,
    Which never danger yet could daunt
    before?
    Who calls Hieronimo? Speak, here I am.
    I did not slumber; therefore 'twas no
    dream.
    No, no, it was some woman cried for help,
    And here within this garden did she cry,
    And in this garden must I rescue her.— 70
    But stay, what murd'rous spectacle is
    this?
    A man hanged up and all the murderers
    gone!
    And in my bower, to lay the guilt on me!
    This place was made for pleasure, not
    for death.   *He cuts him down.*
    Those garments that he wears I oft have
    seen—
    Alas, it is Horatio, my sweet son!
    O, no, but he that whilom [1] was my son!
    O, was it thou that calledst me from my
    bed?
    O, speak, if any spark of life remain.
    I am thy father. Who hath slain my
    son?   80
    What savage monster, not of human
    kind,
    Hath here been glutted with thy harm-
    less blood,
    And left thy bloody corpse dishonored
    here,
    For me, amidst these dark and deathful
    shades,
    To drown thee with an ocean of my tears?
    O heavens, why made you night to cover
    sin?
    By day this deed of darkness had not
    been.
    O earth, why didst thou not in time
    devour

[1] Formerly.

The vild [1] profaner of this sacred bower?
O poor Horatio, what hadst thou mis-
  done,   90
To leese [2] thy life ere life was new begun?
O wicked butcher, whatsoe'er thou wert,
How could thou strangle virtue and
  desert?
Ay me most wretched, that have lost my
  joy,
In leesing my Horatio, my sweet boy!

Enter Isabel[la].

ISAB. My husband's absence makes my
  heart to throb.—
Hieronimo!
HIER. Here, Isabella, help me to lament,
  For sighs are stopped, and all my tears
  are spent.
ISAB. What world of grief!   My son
  Horatio!   100
  O, where's the author of this endless
  woe?
HIER. To know the author were some ease
  of grief,
  For in revenge my heart would find relief.
ISAB. Then is he gone? And is my son gone
  too?
  O, gush out, tears, fountains and floods
  of tears;
  Blow, sighs, and raise an everlasting
  storm,
  For outrage fits our curséd wretchedness! [3]
  Ay me, Hieronimo, sweet husband, speak!
HIER. He supped with us tonight, frolic
  and merry,
  And said he would go visit Balthazar 110
  At the duke's palace—there the prince
  doth lodge.
  He had no custom to stay out so late;
  He may be in his chamber. Some go see.
  Roderigo, ho!

Enter Pedro and Jaques.

ISAB. Ay me, he raves!—Sweet Hier-
  onimo!
HIER. True, all Spain takes note of it.
  Besides, he is so generally beloved;
  His majesty the other day did grace him

With waiting on his cup. These be favors
Which do assure me [he] [4] cannot be
  short-lived.
ISAB. Sweet Hieronimo!   120
HIER. I wonder how this fellow got his
  clothes!—
  Sirrah, sirrah, I'll know the truth of all.
  Jaques, run to the Duke of Castile's
  presently,
  And bid my son Horatio to come home.
  I and his mother have had strange
  dreams tonight.
  Do ye hear me, sir?
JAQUES. Ay, sir.
HIER. Well, sir, be gone. Pedro, come
  hither. Know'st thou who this is?
PED. Too well, sir.
HIER. Too well! Who, who is it? Peace,
  Isabella! Nay, blush not, man.   130
PED. It is my lord Horatio.
HIER. Ha, ha! St. James, but this doth
  make me laugh,
  That there are more deluded than my-
  self.
PED. Deluded?
HIER. Ay, I would have sworn myself,
  within this hour,
  That this had been my son Horatio,
  His garments are so like. Ha! Are they
  not great persuasions?
ISAB. O, would to God it were not so!
HIER. Were not, Isabella?   Dost thou
  dream it is?   139
  Can thy soft bosom entertain a thought
  That such a black deed of mischief should
  be done
  On one so pure and spotless as our son?
  Away, I am ashamed.
ISAB. Dear Hieronimo, cast a more serious
  eye upon thy grief;
  Weak apprehension gives but weak
  belief.
HIER. It was a man, sure, that was hanged
  up here;
  A youth, as I remember. I cut him down.
  If it should prove my son now after all—
  Say you? Say you?—Light! Lend me
  a taper;
  Let me look again.—   150
  O God! Confusion, mischief, torment,
  death, and hell,
  Drop all your stings at once in my cold
  bosom,

---

[1] Vile.   [2] Lose.
[3] The first of the additions begins here and
extends through l. 160. Some modern editors
have attempted without success to improve the
form of the verse in these additions by changing
the division of lines. Here the line division of
the original has been kept in all the additions.
[4] From 1603 edn.

That now is stiff with horror. Kill me
quickly!
Be gracious to me, thou infective [1] night,
And drop this deed of murder down on
me.
Gird in my waste of grief with thy large
darkness,
And let me not survive to see the light
May put me in the mind I had a son.

ISAB. O sweet Horatio! O my dearest
son!

HIER. How strangely had I lost my way
to grief! 160
Sweet, lovely rose, ill-plucked before thy
time,
Fair, worthy son, not conquered, but
betrayed,
I'll kiss thee now, for words with tears
are stayed.

ISAB. And I'll close up the glasses of his
sight,
For once these eyes were only my delight.

HIER. Seest thou this handkercher be-
smeared with blood?
It shall not from me, till I take revenge.
Seest thou those wounds that yet are
bleeding fresh?
I'll not entomb them, till I have revenged.
Then will I joy amidst my discontent; 170
Till then my sorrow never shall be spent.

ISAB. The heavens are just; murder cannot be hid.
Time is the author both of truth and
right,
And time will bring this treachery to
light.

HIER. Meanwhile, good Isabella, cease thy
plaints,
Or, at the least, dissemble them awhile.
So shall we sooner find the practice [2] out,
And learn by whom all this was brought
about.
Come, Isabel, now let us take him up,
They take him up.
And bear him in from out this cursèd
place. 180
I'll say his dirge; singing fits not this case.

O aliquis mihi quas pulchrum ver educat
herbas, Hiero[nimo] sets his
breast unto his sword.
Misceat, et nostro detur medicina dolori;

[1] Infectious. [2] Plot.

Aut, si qui faciunt annorum oblivia,
succos
Præbeat; ipse metam magnum quæcunque
per orbem
Gramina Sol pulchras effert in luminis oras;
Ipse bibam quicquid meditatur saga veneni,
Quicquid et herbarum vi cæca nenia nectit:
Omnia perpetiar, lethum quoque, dum
semel omnis
Noster in extincto moriatur pectore sen-
sus. 190
Ergo tuos oculos nunquam, mea vita,
videbo?
Et tua perpetuus sepelivit lumina somnus?
Emoriar tecum: sic, sic, juvat ire sub
umbras.
At tamen absistam properato cedere letho,
Ne mortem vindicta tuam tam nulla
sequatur. [3]

Here he throws it from him
and bears the body away.

[CHORUS]

ANDREA. Brought'st thou me hither to in-
crease my pain?
I looked that Balthazar should have
been slain,
But 'tis my friend Horatio that is slain,
And they abuse fair Bel-imperia,
On whom I doted more than all the
world, 200
Because she loved me more than all the
world.

REVENGE. Thou talk'st of harvest when
the corn is green.
The end is crown of every work well
done;

[3] O, let some one mingle for me herbs which
beautiful spring brings forth, and let a medicine
be given for my pain. Or let one furnish whatever juices provide forgetfulness of the years.
Myself shall reap whatever grasses throughout
the great world the sun brings forth to the fair
shores of light. Myself shall drink whatever
poison a witch devises and whatever of herbs
the incantation weaves by secret power. All
things shall I suffer patiently, even death, provided once for all all feeling die in my extinguished breast. And so shall I never see your
eyes, my life? And hath perpetual sleep buried
your orbs? I shall die with you: so, so it pleases
me to go down to the shades. But yet I shall
abstain from going in hastened death [*i.e.*, by
suicide], lest by so doing no vengeance should
follow your death (a patchwork of verses from
Virgil, Lucretius, Horace, Tibullus, Catullus,
etc.).

The sickle comes not till the corn be ripe.
Be still, and, ere I lead thee from this
place,
I'll show thee Balthazar in heavy case.

ACTUS TERTIUS. [SCENA PRIMA.

The Portuguese court.]

*Enter Viceroy of Portingale, Nobles, Alex-
andro, Villuppo.*

VIC. Infortunate condition of kings,
   Seated amidst so many helpless doubts!
First we are placed upon extremest
   height,
And oft supplanted with exceeding hate,
But ever subject to the wheel of chance.
And at our highest never joy we so
As we both doubt and dread our over-
   throw.
So striveth not the waves with sundry
   winds
As Fortune toileth in the affairs of kings,
That would be feared, yet fear to be
   beloved,   10
Sith [1] fear or love to kings is flattery. [2]
For instance, lordings, look upon your
   king,
By hate deprivéd of his dearest son,
The only hope of our successive line.
[1] NOB. I had not thought that Alex-
   andro's heart
Had been envenomed with such extreme
   hate;
But now I see that words have several
   works,
And there's no credit in the countenance.
VIL. No; for, my lord, had you beheld the
   train [3]
That feignéd love had colored in his
   looks,   20
When he in camp consorted [4] Balthazar,
Far more inconstant had you thought
   the sun,
That hourly coasts [5] the center of the
   earth,
Than Alexandro's purpose to the prince.
VIC. No more, Villuppo, thou hast said
   enough,
And with thy words thou slayest our
   wounded thoughts.

Nor shall I longer dally with the world,
Procrastinating Alexandro's death.
Go, some of you, and fetch the traitor
   forth
That, as he is condemnéd, he may die. 30

*Enter Alexandro with a Nobleman and
   Halberts.*

NOB. In such extremes will naught but
   patience serve.
ALEX. But in extremes what patience
   shall I use?
Nor discontents it me to leave the world,
With whom there nothing can prevail
   but wrong.
NOB. Yet hope the best.
ALEX.   'Tis heaven is my hope.
   As for the earth, it is too much infect
To yield me hope of any of her mold.
VIC. Why linger ye? Bring forth that
   daring fiend,
And let him die for his acccurséd deed.
ALEX. Not that I fear the extremity of
   death   40
(For nobles cannot stoop to servile fear)
Do I, O king, thus discontented live.
But this, O, this, torments my laboring
   soul,
That thus I die suspected of a sin
Whereof, as heavens have known my
   secret thoughts,
So am I free from this suggestion.
VIC. No more, I say! To the tortures!
   When? [6]
Bind him, and burn his body in those
   flames,   *They bind him to the stake.*
That shall prefigure those unquenchéd
   fires
Of Phlegeton, preparéd for his soul.   50
ALEX. My guiltless death will be avenged
   on thee,
On thee, Villuppo, that hath maliced [7]
   thus,
Or for thy meed hast falsely me accused.
VIL. Nay, Alexandro, if thou menace me,
I'll lend a hand to send thee to the
   lake [8]
Where those thy words shall perish with
   thy works,
Injurious traitor! Monstrous homicide!

---

[1] Since.
[2] The preceding passage is based on Seneca's
Agamemnon, ll. 57–73.   [4] Accompanied.
   [3] Deception.   [5] Moves round.

[6] An expression of impatience.
[7] Entertained malice.
[8] *I.e.,* Avernus.

Enter Ambassador.

[AMB.] Stay, hold awhile;
  And here—with pardon of his maj-
    esty—
  Lay hands upon Villuppo.
VIC.   Ambassador, 60
  What news hath urged this sudden
    entrance?
AMB. Know, sovereign l[ord], that Baltha-
  zar doth live.
VIC. What sayest thou? Liveth Balthazar
  our son?
AMB. Your highness' son, L[ord] Baltha-
  zar, doth live,
  And, well entreated in the court of Spain,
  Humbly commends him to your majesty.
  These eyes beheld, and these my fol-
    lowers';
  With these, the letters of the king's
    commends   *Gives him letters.*
  Are happy witnesses of his highness'
    health.
The King looks on the letters, and proceeds.
VIC. "Thy son doth live; your tribute is
  received.   70
  Thy peace is made, and we are satis-
    fied.
  The rest resolve upon as things proposed
  For both our honors and thy benefit."
AMB. These are his highness' farther
  articles.   *He gives him more letters.*
VIC. Accurséd wretch, to intimate these
  ills
  Against the life and reputation
  Of noble Alexandro! Come, my lord,
  unbind him.—
  Let him unbind thee, that is bound to
    death,
  To make a quital [1] for thy discontent.
                  They unbind him.
ALEX. Dread lord, in kindness [2] you could
  do no less   80
  Upon report of such a damnéd fact.
  But thus we see our innocence hath saved
  The hopeless life which thou, Villuppo,
    sought
  By thy suggestions to have massacred.
VIC. Say, false Villuppo, wherefore didst
  thou thus
  Falsely betray Lord Alexandro's life—
  Him whom thou knowest that no un-
    kindness else

But even the slaughter of our dearest
  son
  Could once have moved us to have mis-
    conceived?
ALEX. Say, treacherous Villuppo, tell the
  king: 90
  Wherein [3] hath Alexandro used thee ill?
VIL. Rent with remembrance of so foul a
  deed,
  My guilty soul submits me to thy doom;
  For not for Alexandro's injuries,
  But for reward and hope to be preferred,
  Thus have I shamelessly hazarded his
    life.
VIC. Which, villain, shall be ransomed
  with thy death,
  And not so mean [4] a torment as we here
  Devised for him who, thou said'st, slew
    our son,
  But with the bitterest torments and ex-
    tremes   100
  That may be yet invented for thine end.
          Alex[andro] seems to entreat.
  Entreat me not.—Go, take the traitor
  hence.—   *Exit Vil[luppo].*
  And, Alexandro, let us honor thee
  With public notice of thy loyalty.—
  To end those things articulated here
  By our great lord, the mighty King of
    Spain,
  We with our council will deliberate.
  Come, Alexandro, keep us company.
                   Exeunt.

[SCENA SECUNDA.

Near the place of Bel-imperia's confinement.]

Enter Hieronimo.

HIER. O eyes! No eyes, but fountains
  fraught with tears!
  O life! No life, but lively form of death!
  O world! No world, but mass of public
    wrongs,
  Confused and filled with murder and
    misdeeds!
  O sacred heavens, if this unhallowed
    deed,
  If this inhuman and barbarous attempt,
  If this incomparable murder thus
  Of mine, but now no more my son,
  Shall unrevealed and unrevengéd pass,

---

[1] Requital.   [2] Nature.

[3] Emended by Hazlitt. Early edns. read *Or
wherein.*   [4] Moderate.

How should we term your dealings to be
just,   10
If you unjustly deal with those that in
your justice trust?
The night, sad secretary to my moans,
With direful visions wake my vexéd soul,
And with the wounds of my distressful
son
Solicit me for notice of his death.
The ugly fiends do sally forth of hell,
And frame my steps to unfrequented
paths,
And fear my heart with fierce inflaméd
thoughts.
The cloudy day my discontents records
Early begins to register my dreams,   20
And drive me forth to seek the murderer.
Eyes, life, world, heavens, hell, night,
and day,
See, search, show, send some man, some
mean, that may—   *A letter falleth.*
What's here? A letter? Tush! It is not
so!—
A letter written to Hieronimo!   *Red ink.*
"For want of ink, receive this bloody
writ.
Me hath my hapless brother hid from
thee.
Revenge thyself on Balthazar and him,
For these were they that murderéd thy
son.
Hieronimo, revenge Horatio's death,   30
And better fare than Bel-imperia doth."
What means this unexpected miracle?
My son slain by Lorenzo and the prince!
What cause had they Horatio to malign?
Or what might move thee, Bel-imperia,
To accuse thy brother, had he been the
mean?
Hieronimo, beware!   Thou art be-
trayed,
And to entrap thy life this train is laid.
Advise thee therefore; be not credulous.
This is deviséd to endanger thee,   40
That thou, by this, Lorenzo shouldst
accuse;
And he, for thy dishonor done, should
draw
Thy life in question and thy name in
hate.
Dear was the life of my beloved son,
And of his death behoves me be revenged;
Then hazard not thine own, Hieronimo,
But live t' effect thy resolution.

I therefore will by circumstances [1] try
What I can gather to confirm this writ;
And, hearkening near the Duke of Cas-
tile's house,   50
Close, if I can, with Bel-imperia,
To listen more, but nothing to bewray.

Enter Pedringano.

Now, Pedringano!
PED.   Now, Hieronimo!
HIER. Where's thy lady?
PED.   I know not. Here's my lord.

Enter Lorenzo.

LOR. How now, who's this? Hieronimo?
HIER.   My lord!
PED. He asketh for my lady Bel-imperia.
LOR. What to do, Hieronimo? The duke,
my father, hath
Upon some disgrace awhile removed her
hence;
But, if it be aught I may inform her of,
Tell me, Hieronimo, and I'll let her know
it.   60
HIER. Nay, nay, my lord, I thank you; it
shall not need.
I had a suit unto her, but too late,
And her disgrace makes me unfortunate.
LOR. Why so, Hieronimo? Use me.[2]
HIER. Who? You, my lord?
I reserve your favor for a greater honor;
This is a very toy,[3] my lord, a toy.
LOR. All's one, Hieronimo; acquaint me
with it.
HIER. I' faith, my lord, 'tis an idle thing,
I must confess;
I ha' been too slack, too tardy, too re-
miss unto your honor.   70
LOR. How now, Hieronimo?
HIER. In troth, my lord, it is a thing of
nothing,
The murder of a son, or so—
A thing of nothing, my lord!
LOR.   Why then, farewell.
HIER. My grief no heart, my thoughts no
tongue can tell.   *Exit.*

[1] Roundabout methods.
[2] The passage from this point through "nothing, my lord!" in l. 74 is substituted in the
1602 edn. for the following speech of Hieronimo
in the original:
      O, no, my lord, I dare not; it must not be.
      I humbly thank your lordship.
[3] Trifle.

Lor. Come hither, Pedringano, seest thou
   this?
Ped. My lord, I see it, and suspect it too.
Lor. This is that damnéd villain Serberine
   That hath, I fear, revealed Horatio's
   death.
Ped. My lord, he could not, 'twas so
   lately done;   80
   And, since, he hath not left my company.
Lor. Admit he have not, his condition's
   such
   As fear or flattering words may make
   him false.
   I know his humor, and therewith re-
   pent
   That e'er I used him in this enterprise.
   But, Pedringano, to prevent the worst,
   And cause I know thee secret as my
   soul,
   Here, for thy further satisfaction, take
   thou this,   *Gives him more gold.*
   And hearken to me. Thus it is devised:
   This night thou must (and, prithee, so
   resolve)   90
   Meet Serberine at S[aint] Luigi's Park—
   Thou know'st 'tis here hard by behind
   the house.
   There take thy stand, and see thou
   strike him sure,
   For die he must, if we do mean to live.
Ped. But how shall Serberine be there,
   my lord?
Lor. Let me alone; I'll send to him to
   meet
   The prince and me, where thou must
   do this deed.
Ped. It shall be done, my l[ord], it shall
   be done;
   And I'll go arm myself to meet him
   there.
Lor. When things shall alter, as I hope
   they will,   100
   Then shalt thou mount for this; thou
   knowest my mind.
               Exit Ped[ringano].
Che le Ieron![1]

        Enter Page.

Page.   My lord?
Lor.   Go, sirrah,
   To Serberine, and bid him forthwith
   meet

[1] Unintelligible. Probably a call to the page.

   The prince and me at S[aint] Luigi's
   Park,
   Behind the house, this evening, boy.
Page.   I go, my lord.
Lor. But, sirrah, let the hour be eight
   a-clock.
   Bid him not fail.
Page.   I fly, my lord. *Exit.*
Lor. Now to confirm the complot thou
   hast cast
   Of all these practices, I'll spread the
   watch,
   Upon precise commandment from the
   king,   110
   Strongly to guard the place where Ped-
   ringano
   This night shall murder hapless Serber-
   ine.
   Thus must we work that will avoid dis-
   trust;
   Thus must we practice to prevent mis-
   hap;
   And thus one ill another must expulse.
   This sly inquiry of Hieronimo
   For Bel-imperia breeds suspicion,
   And this suspicion bodes a further ill.
   As for myself, I know my secret fault,
   And so do they. But I have dealt for
   them.   120
   They that for coin their souls endangeréd,
   To save my life, for coin shall venture
   theirs;
   And better it's that base companions
   die
   Than by their life to hazard our good
   haps.
   Nor shall they live, for me to fear their
   faith.
   I'll trust myself, myself shall be my
   friend;
   For die they shall; slaves are ordained
   to no other end.   *Exit.*

        [Scena Tertia.

     Saint Luigi's Park.]

   Enter Pedringano, with a pistol.

[Ped.] Now, Pedringano, bid thy pistol
   hold;
   And hold on, Fortune; once more favor
   me.
   Give but success to mine attempting
   spirit,
   And let me shift for taking of mine aim.

Here is the gold. This is the gold pro-
posed.
It is no dream that I adventure for,
But Pedringano is possessed thereof.
And he that would not strain his con-
science
For him that thus his liberal purse hath
stretched,
Unworthy such a favor, may he fail, 10
And, wishing, want when such as I pre-
vail.
As for the fear of apprehension,
I know, if need should be, my noble
lord
Will stand between me and ensuing
harms.
Besides, this place is free from all sus-
pect.
Here therefore will I stay and take my
stand.

Enter the Watch.

1 [WATCH.] I wonder much to what intent it is
That we are thus expressly charged to
watch.
2 [WATCH.] 'Tis by commandment in the
king's own name.
3 [WATCH.] But we were never wont to
watch and ward 20
So near the duke his brother's house
before.
2 [WATCH.] Content yourself. Stand close;
there's somewhat in 't.

Enter Serberine.

SER. Here, Serberine, attend and stay
thy pace,
For here did Don Lorenzo's page appoint
That thou by his command shouldst
meet with him.
How fit a place—if one were so disposed—
Methinks this corner is to close with
one.
PED. Here comes the bird that I must
seize upon.
Now, Pedringano, or never, play the
man!
SER. I wonder that his lordship stays
so long, 30
Or wherefore should he send for me so
late?

PED. For this, Serberine!—and thou shalt
ha't. *Shoots the dag.*[1]
So, there he lies; my promise is performed.

The Watch.

1 [WATCH.] Hark, gentlemen, this is a
pistol shot.
2 [WATCH.] And here's one slain! Stay
the murderer.
PED. Now by the sorrows of the souls in
hell, *He strives with the Watch.*
Who first lays hand on me, I'll be his
priest.
3 [WATCH.] Sirrah, confess, and therein
play the priest.
Why hast thou thus unkindly[2] killed
the man?
PED. Why? Because he walked abroad
so late. 40
3 [WATCH.] Come, sir, you had been better kept your bed
Than have committed this misdeed so
late.
2 [WATCH.] Come, to the marshal's with
the murderer!
1 [WATCH.] On to Hieronimo's! Help me
here
To bring the murdered body with us
too.
PED. Hieronimo? Carry me before whom
you will.
Whate'er he be, I'll answer him and
you;
And do your worst, for I defy you all.
Exeunt.

[SCENA QUARTA.

A room in Don Cyprian's palace.]

Enter Lorenzo and Balthazar.

BAL. How now, my lord, what makes
you rise so soon?
LOR. Fear of preventing our mishaps too
late.
BAL. What mischief is it that we not mistrust?[3]
LOR. Our greatest ills we least mistrust,
my lord,
And inexpected harms do hurt us
most.

[1] Pistol.   [3] Suspect.
[2] Unnaturally.

BAL. Why, tell me, Don Lorenzo, tell
  me, man,
If aught concerns our honor and your own.
LOR. Nor you, nor me, my lord, but both
  in one;
  For I suspect—and the presumption's
    great—
  That by those base confederates in our
    fault   10
  Touching the death of Don Horatio,
  We are betrayed to old Hieronimo.
BAL. Betrayed, Lorenzo? Tush! It can-
  not be.
LOR. A guilty conscience, urgéd with the
    thought
  Of former evils, easily cannot err.
  I am persuaded—and dissuade me not—
  That all's revealéd to Hieronimo.
  And therefore know that I have cast it
    thus—

[Enter Page.] [1]

But here's the page. How now? What
    news with thee?
PAGE. My lord, Serberine is slain.
BAL.   Who? Serberine, my man?   20
PAGE. Your highness' man, my lord.
LOR.   Speak, page, who murdered
    him?
PAGE. He that is apprehended for the
    fact. [2]
LOR. Who?
PAGE. Pedringano.
BAL. Is Serberine slain, that loved his
    lord so well?
  Injurious villain, murderer of his friend!
LOR. Hath Pedringano murdered Ser-
  berine?
  My lord, let me entreat you to take the
    pains
  To exasperate and hasten his revenge
  With your complaints unto my l[ord] the
    king.   30
  This their dissension breeds a greater
    doubt.
BAL. Assure thee, Don Lorenzo, he shall
    die,
  Or else his highness hardly shall deny. [3]
  Meanwhile I'll haste the marshal-ses-
    sions,
  For die he shall for this his damnéd deed.
                          Exit Balt[hazar].

---

[1] From 1615 edn.   [2] Deed.
[3] *I.e.*, shall with difficulty deny my demand.

LOR. Why so, this fits our former policy,
  And thus experience bids the wise to
    deal.
  I lay the plot; he prosecutes the point.
  I set the trap; he breaks the worthless
    twigs,
  And sees not that wherewith the bird
    was limed.   40
  Thus hopeful men, that mean to hold
    their own,
  Must look like fowlers to their dearest
    friends.
  He runs to kill whom I have holp [4] to
    catch,
  And no man knows it was my reaching
    fatch. [5]
  'Tis hard to trust unto a multitude,
  Or anyone, in mine opinion,
  When men themselves their secrets
    will reveal.

Enter a Messenger with a letter.

Boy!
PAGE. My lord.
LOR. What's he?
MES.   I have a letter to your lordship.
LOR. From whence?
MES.   From Pedringano that's
    imprisoned.   51
LOR. So he is in prison then?
MES.   Ay, my good lord.
LOR. What would he with us?—He writes
    us here
  To stand good lord, and help him in
    distress.—
  Tell him I have his letters, know his
    mind,
  And what we may, let him assure him
    of.
  Fellow, begone; my boy shall follow
    thee.   *Exit Mes[senger].*
  This works like wax; yet once more try
    thy wits.
  Boy, go, convey this purse to Pedrin-
    gano.
  Thou know'st the prison. Closely [6]
    give it him,   60
  And be advised that none be there
    about.
  Bid him be merry still, but secret;
  And, though the marshal-sessions be
    today,

---

[4] Helped.   [5] Deep-reaching trick.   [6] Secretly.

Bid him not doubt of his delivery.
Tell him his pardon is already signed,
And thereon bid him boldly be re-
solved;
For, were he ready to be turnéd off[1]—
As 'tis my will the uttermost be tried—
Thou with his pardon shalt attend him
still.
Show him this box; tell him his pardon's
in't;   70
But open't not, an if [2] thou lov'st thy
life,
But let him wisely keep his hopes un-
known.
He shall not want while Don Lorenzo
lives.
Away!
PAGE. I go, my lord, I run.
LOR. But, sirrah, see that this be cleanly [3]
done.   *Exit Page.*
Now stands our fortune on a tickle
point,
And now or never ends Lorenzo's doubts.
One only thing is uneffected yet,
And that's to see the executioner.   80
But to what end? I list not trust the
air
With utterance of our pretense [4] therein,
For fear the privy whisp'ring of the
wind
Convey our words amongst unfriendly
ears,
That lie too open to advantages.[5]
E quel che voglio io, nessun lo sa;
Intendo io; quel mi basterà.[6]   *Exit.*

[SCENA QUINTA.

A street.]

Enter Boy with the box.

[BOY.] My master hath forbidden me to
look in this box, and, by my troth, 'tis
likely, if he had not warned me, I should
not have had so much idle time; for we
men's-kind in our minority are like women
in their uncertainty—that they are most
forbidden, they will soonest attempt. So
I now.—By my bare honesty, here's noth-

ing but the bare empty box! Were it not
sin against secrecy, I would say it [10
were a piece of gentlemanlike knavery.
I must go to Pedringano, and tell him his
pardon is in this box; nay, I would have
sworn it, had I not seen the contrary. I
cannot choose but smile to think how the
villain will flout the gallows, scorn the
audience, and descant on the hangman,
and all presuming of his pardon from
hence. Will 't not be an odd jest for me
to stand and grace every jest he makes, [20
pointing my finger at this box, as who
would say, "Mock on, here's thy warrant"? Is 't not a scurvy jest that a man
should jest himself to death? Alas, poor
Pedringano, I am in a sort sorry for thee;
but, if I should be hanged with thee, I
cannot weep.   *Exit.*

[SCENA SEXTA.

The Court of Justice.]

Enter Hieronimo and the Deputy.

HIER. Thus must we toil in other men's
extremes,
That know not how to remedy our
own,
And do them justice, when unjustly
we,
For all our wrongs, can compass no
redress.
But shall I never live to see the day
That I may come, by justice of the
heavens,
To know the cause that may my cares
allay?
This toils [7] my body, this consumeth
age,
That only I to all men just must be,
And neither gods nor men be just to
me.   10
DEP. Worthy Hieronimo, your office asks
A care to punish such as do transgress.
HIER. So is 't my duty to regard his death
Who, when he lived, deserved my
dearest blood.
But come, for that we came for! Let's
begin,
For here lies that which bids me to be
gone.

---

[1] Hanged.   [4] Intention.
[2] An emphatic form of *if.*   [5] Opportunities.
[3] Adroitly.
[6] And what I wish, that no one knows. I
intend it; that will be enough for me (source
unknown).

[7] Taxes.

Enter Officers, [Hangman,] Boy, and Pedringano, with a letter in his hand, bound.

DEP. Bring forth the prisoner, for the court is set.

PED. Gramercy, boy, but it was time to come,
For I had written to my lord anew
A nearer matter that concerneth him, 20
For fear his lordship had forgotten me.
But sith he hath remembered me so well—
Come, come, come on, when shall we to this gear? [1]

HIER. Stand forth, thou monster, murderer of men,
And here, for satisfaction of the world,
Confess thy folly, and repent thy fault;
For there's thy place of execution.

PED. This is short work. Well, to your marshalship
First I confess—nor fear I death therefor—
I am the man; 'twas I slew Serberine. 30
But, sir, then you think this shall be the place
Where we shall satisfy you for this gear?

DEP. Ay, Pedringano.

PED.   Now I think not so.

HIER. Peace, impudent, for thou shalt find it so;
For blood with blood shall, while I sit as judge,
Be satisfiéd, and the law discharged.
And, though myself cannot receive the like,
Yet will I see that others have their right.
Despatch! The fault's approvéd [2] and confessed,
And by our law he is condemned to die. 40

HANG. Come on, sir, are you ready?

PED. To do what, my fine, officious knave?

HANG. To go to this gear.

PED. O, sir, you are too forward. Thou wouldst fain furnish me with a halter, to disfurnish me of my habit. [3] So I should go out of this gear, my raiment, into that gear, the rope. But, hangman, now I spy your knavery, I'll not change without boot; that's flat. 50

¹ Business.   ² Proved.
³ The hangman received the criminal's garments.

HANG. Come, sir.

PED. So, then, I must up?

HANG. No remedy.

PED. Yes, but there shall be for my coming down.

HANG. Indeed, here's a remedy for that.

PED. How? Be turned off?

HANG. Ay, truly. Come, are you ready? I pray, sir, despatch; the day goes away.

PED. What, do you hang by the hour? If you do, I may chance to break your old custom. 62

HANG. Faith, you have reason, for I am like to break your young neck.

PED. Dost thou mock me, hangman? Pray God, I be not preserved to break your knave's pate for this.

HANG. Alas, sir, you are a foot too low to reach it, and I hope you will never grow so high while I am in the office. 70

PED. Sirrah, dost see yonder boy with the box in his hand?

HANG. What, he that points to it with his finger?

PED. Ay, that companion.

HANG. I know him not. But what of him?

PED. Dost thou think to live till his old doublet will make thee a new truss? [4]

HANG. Ay, and many a fair year after, [80 to truss up many an honester man than either thou or he.

PED. What hath he in his box, as thou think'st?

HANG. Faith, I cannot tell, nor I care not greatly. Methinks you should rather hearken to your soul's health.

PED. Why, sirrah hangman, I take it that that is good for the body is likewise good for the soul; and, it may be, in [90 that box is balm for both.

HANG. Well, thou art even the merriest piece of man's flesh that e'er groaned at my office door!

PED. Is your roguery become an office with a knave's name?

HANG. Ay, and that shall all they witness that see you seal it with a thief's name.

PED. I prithee, request this good [100 company to pray with me.

⁴ The term was used both for a close-fitting body garment and for tight, short breeches or drawers.

HANG. Ay, marry, sir, this is a good motion.—My masters, you see here's a good fellow.

PED. Nay, nay, now I remember me, let them alone till some other time, for now I have no great need.

HIER. I have not seen a wretch so impudent.
O monstrous times, where murder's set so light,
And where the soul, that should be shrined in heaven,   110
Solely delights in interdicted things,
Still wand'ring in the thorny passages,
That intercepts itself of [1] happiness.
Murder! O bloody monster! God forbid
A fault so foul should scape unpunishéd.
Despatch, and see this execution done!—
This makes me to remember thee, my son.   *Exit Hiero[nimo].*

PED. Nay, soft, no haste.

DEP. Why, wherefore stay you? Have you hope of life?

PED. Why, ay!   120

HANG. As how?

PED. Why, rascal, by my pardon from the king.

HANG. Stand you on that? Then you shall off with this.   *He turns him off.*

DEP. So, executioner!—Convey him hence, But let his body be unburiéd.
Let not the earth be chokéd or infect
With that which heaven contemns, and men neglect.   *Exeunt.*

[SCENA SEPTIMA.

A room in Hieronimo's house.]

Enter Hieronimo.

[HIER.] Where shall I run to breathe abroad my woes,
My woes, whose weight hath weariéd the earth,
Or mine exclaims,[2] that have surcharged the air
With ceaseless plaints for my deceaséd son?
The blust'ring winds, conspiring with my words,
At my lament have moved the leafless trees,
Disrobed the meadows of their flowered green,

[1] Bars itself from.   [2] Exclamations.

Made mountains marsh with spring tides of my tears,
And broken through the brazen gates of hell.
Yet still tormented is my tortured soul 10
With broken sighs and restless passions,
That, wingéd, mount, and hovering in the air,
Beat at the windows of the brightest heavens,
Soliciting for justice and revenge.
But they are placed in those imperial heights,
Where, countermured [3] with walls of diamond,
I find the place impregnable; and they
Resist my woes, and give my words no way.

Enter Hangman with a letter.

HANG. O Lord, sir! God bless you, sir! The man, sir, Petergade, sir, he that [20 was so full of merry conceits—

HIER. Well, what of him?

HANG. O Lord, sir, he went the wrong way; the fellow had a fair commission to the contrary. Sir, here is his passport. I pray you, sir, we have done him wrong.

HIER. I warrant thee; give it me.

HANG. You will stand between the gallows and me?

HIER. Ay, ay.   30

HANG. I thank your l[ord] worship.
                    Exit Hangman.

HIER. And yet, though somewhat nearer me concerns,
I will, to ease the grief that I sustain,
Take truce with sorrow while I read on this.
"My lord, I write,[4] as mine extremes required,
That you would labor my delivery.
If you neglect, my life is desperate,
And in my death I shall reveal the troth.
You know, my lord, I slew him for your sake,
And was confederate with the prince and you;   40
Won by rewards and hopeful promises,
I holp to murder Don Horatio too."—
Holp he to murder mine Horatio?
And actors in th' accurséd tragedy
Wast thou, Lorenzo, Balthazar and thou,

[3] Doubly walled.   [4] Manly emends to *writ.*

Of whom my son, my son, deserved so
   well?
What have I heard? What have mine
   eyes beheld?
O sacred heavens, may it come to pass
That such a monstrous and detested
   deed,
So closely smothered, and so long con-
   cealed,   50
Shall thus by this be vengéd or revealed?
Now see I what I durst not then sus-
   pect,
That Bel-imperia's letter was not feigned.
Nor feignéd she, though falsely they have
   wronged
Both her, myself, Horatio, and them-
   selves.
Now may I make compare twixt hers
   and this,
Of every accident I ne'er could find
Till now, and now I feelingly perceive
They did what heaven unpunished would
   not leave.
O false Lorenzo! Are these thy flattering
   looks?   60
Is this the honor that thou didst my
   son?
And Balthazar—bane to thy soul and
   me!—
Was this the ransom he reserved thee
   for?
Woe to the cause of these constrainéd
   wars!
Woe to thy baseness and captivity!
Woe to thy birth, thy body, and thy
   soul,
Thy curséd father, and thy conquered
   self!
And banned with bitter execrations be
The day and place where he did pity
   thee!
But wherefore waste I mine unfruitful
   words,   70
When naught but blood will satisfy my
   woes?
I will go plain me [1] to my lord the king,
And cry aloud for justice through the
   court,
Wearing the flints with these my with-
   ered feet;
And either purchase justice by entreats,
Or tire them all with my revenging
   threats.   *Exit.*

[1] Complain.

[SCENA OCTAVA.

The same.]

Enter Isabell[a] and her Maid.

ISAB. So that you say this herb will purge
   the eye,
And this, the head?
Ah, but none of them will purge the
   heart!
No, there's no medicine left for my dis-
   ease,
Nor any physic to recure the dead.
            She runs lunatic.
Horatio! O, where's Horatio?
MAID. Good madam, affright not thus
   yourself
With outrage [2] for your son Horatio.
He sleeps in quiet in the Elysian fields.
ISAB. Why, did I not give you gowns and
   goodly things,   10
Bought you a whistle and a whipstalk [3]
   too,
To be revengéd on their villainies?
MAID. Madam, these humors do torment
   my soul.
ISAB. My soul—poor soul, thou talks of
   things
Thou know'st not what—my soul hath
   silver wings,
That mounts me up unto the highest
   heavens.
To heaven? Ay, there sits my Horatio,
Backed with a troop of fiery cherubins,
Dancing about his newly healéd wounds,
Singing sweet hymns and chanting heav-
   enly notes,   20
Rare harmony to greet his innocence,
That died, ay, died, a mirror in our days.
But say, where shall I find the men, the
   murderers,
That slew Horatio? Whither shall I run
To find them out that murderéd my son?
           Exeunt.

[SCENA NONA.

*Outside the place of Bel-imperia's con-
finement.*]

Bel-imperia at a window.

BEL. What means this outrage that is offered me?
Why am I thus sequestered from the
   court?

[2] Outcry.   [3] Whipstock.

No notice! Shall I not know the cause
Of these my secret and suspicious ills?
Accurséd brother, unkind murderer,
Why bends thou thus thy mind to martyr
  me?
Hieronimo, why writ I of thy wrongs,
Or why art thou so slack in thy revenge?
Andrea, O Andrea! That thou saw'st
Me for thy friend Horatio handled thus,
And him for me thus causeless mur-
  deréd!—   11
Well, force perforce, I must constrain
  myself
To patience, and apply me [1] to the time,
Till heaven, as I have hoped, shall set
  me free.

Enter Christophil.

CHRIS. Come, Madam Bel-imperia, this
  may not be.   *Exeunt.*

Enter Lorenzo, Balthazar, and the Page.[2]

LOR. Boy, talk no further. Thus far things
  go well.
Thou art assuréd that thou sawest him
  dead?
PAGE. Or else, my lord, I live not.
LOR.   That's enough.
As for his resolution in his end,
Leave that to him with whom he so-
  journs now.   20
Here, take my ring and give it Christo-
  phil,
And bid him let my sister be enlarged,
And bring her hither straight.—
                    Exit Page.
This that I did was for a policy,
To smooth and keep the murder secret,
Which, as a nine-days' wonder, being
  o'erblown,
My gentle sister will I now enlarge.
BAL. And time, Lorenzo, for my lord the
  duke,
You heard, inquired for her yesternight.
LOR. Why, and, my lord, I hope you heard
  me say   30
Sufficient reason why she kept away.
But that's all one. My lord, you love her?
BAL.   Ay.

[1] Conform myself.
[2] It is conventional to make a new scene here.
Lorenzo and Balthazar probably enter on the
lower stage, however, as Bel-imperia leaves the
upper.

LOR. Then in your love beware. Deal
  cunningly;
Salve all suspicions; only soothe me up, [3]
And, if she hap to stand on terms [4] with
  us—
As for her sweetheart and concealment
  so—
Jest with her gently. Under feignéd jest
Are things concealed that else would
  breed unrest.
But here she comes.

Enter Bel-imperia.

              Now, sister—
BEL.   Sister? No!
Thou art no brother, but an enemy; 40
Else wouldst thou not have used thy
  sister so:
First, to affright me with thy weapons
  drawn,
And with extremes abuse my company; [5]
And then to hurry me, like whirlwind's
  rage,
Amidst a crew of thy confederates,
And clap me up where none might come
  at me,
Nor I at any to reveal my wrongs.
What madding [6] fury did possess thy
  wits?
Or wherein is 't that I offended thee?
LOR. Advise you better, Bel-imperia, 50
For I have done you no disparagement—
Unless, by more discretion than deserved,
I sought to save your honor and mine own.
BEL. Mine honor? Why, Lorenzo, wherein
  is 't
That I neglect my reputation so
As you, or any, need to rescue it?
LOR. His highness and my father were
  resolved
To come confer with old Hieronimo
Concerning certain matters of estate
That by the viceroy was determinéd. 60
BEL. And wherein was mine honor touched
  in that?
BAL. Have patience, Bel-imperia; hear the
  rest.
LOR. Me, next in sight, as messenger they
  sent
To give him notice that they were so
  nigh.

[3] Support me.   [6] Raving.
[4] Insist on her rights.
[5] Do violence to my companion.

Now when I came, consorted with the
  prince,
And unexpected in an arbor there
Found Bel-imperia with Horatio—
BEL.   How then?
LOR. Why then, remembering that old dis-
  grace,
Which you for Don Andrea had en-
  dured,
And now were likely longer to sustain 70
By being found so meanly accompanied,
Thought rather—for I knew no readier
  mean—
To thrust Horatio forth my father's way.
BAL. And carry you obscurely somewhere
  else,
Lest that his highness should have found
  you there.
BEL. Even so, my lord?   And you are
  witness
That this is true which he entreateth of?
You, gentle brother, forged this for my
  sake,
And you, my lord, were made his instru-
  ment?
A work of worth, worthy the noting
  too!   80
But what's the cause that you concealed
  me since?
LOR. Your melancholy, sister, since the
  news
Of your first favorite Don Andrea's
  death
My father's old wrath hath exasperate.
BAL. And better was 't for you, being in
  disgrace,
To absent yourself, and give his fury
  place.
BEL. But why had I no notice of his ire?
LOR. That were to add more fuel to your
  fire,
Who burnt like Ætna for Andrea's loss.
BEL. Hath not my father then inquired
  for me?   90
LOR. Sister, he hath, and thus excused I
  thee.   *He whispereth in her ear.*
But, Bel-imperia, see the gentle prince;
Look on thy love, behold young Baltha-
  zar,
Whose passions by thy presence are
  increased,
And in whose melancholy thou mayst see
Thy hate, his love; thy flight, his follow-
  ing thee.

BEL. Brother, you are become an orator—
I know not, I, by what experience—
Too politic for me, past all compare,
Since last I saw you. But content your-
  self;   100
The prince is meditating higher things.
BAL. 'Tis of thy beauty, then, that con-
  quers kings;
Of those thy tresses, Ariadne's twines,
Wherewith my liberty thou hast sur-
  prised;
Of that thine ivory front, my sorrow's
  map,
Wherein I see no haven to rest my hope.
BEL. To love and fear, and both at once,
  my lord,
In my conceit, are things of more im-
  port
Than women's wits are to be busied
  with.
BAL. 'Tis I that love.
BEL.   Whom?
BAL.   Bel-imperia. 110
BEL. But I that fear.
BAL.   Whom?
BEL.   Bel-imperia.
LOR. Fear yourself?
BEL.   Ay, brother.
LOR.   How?
BEL.   As those
That what they love are loath and fear
  to lose.
BAL. Then, fair, let Balthazar your keeper
  be.
BEL. No, Balthazar doth fear as well as
  we:
Et [1] *tremulo metui pavidum junxere timo-*
  rem—
Et vanum stolidæ proditionis opus. [2] *Exit.*
LOR. Nay, and you argue things so cun-
  ningly,
We'll go continue this discourse at
  court.
BAL. Led by the lodestar of her heavenly
  looks,   120
Wends poor oppresséd Balthazar,
As o'er the mountains walks the wan-
  derer,
Incertain to effect his pilgrimage.
                           Exeunt.

[1] Emended by Hazlitt. Early edns. read *Est.*
[2] And to quivering fear they added trembling
terror—and the vain task of stupid betrayal
(source unknown).

[Scena Decima.

A street.]

*Enter two Portingales, and Hieronimo
meets them.*

1 [Port.] By your leave, sir.

Hier.[1] 'Tis neither as you think, nor as
you think,
  Nor as you think. You're wide all.
  These slippers are not mine; they were
    my son Horatio's.
  My son? And what's a son?
  A thing begot within a pair of minutes—
    thereabout;
  A lump bred up in darkness, and doth
    serve
  To ballace[2] these light creatures we call
    women;
  And, at nine months' end, creeps forth
    to light.
  What is there yet in a son   10
  To make a father dote, rave, or run mad?
  Being born, it pouts, cries, and breeds
    teeth.
  What is there yet in a son? He must be
    fed,
  Be taught to go, and speak. Ay, or yet
  Why might not a man love a calf as well,
  Or melt in passion o'er a frisking kid,
  As for a son? Methinks a young bacon
  Or a fine little smooth horse colt
  Should move a man as much as doth a
    son,
  For one of these, in very little time,   20
  Will grow to some good use, whereas a
    son,
  The more he grows in stature and in
    years,
  The more unsquared, unbeveled,[3] he
    appears,
  Reckons his parents among the rank of
    fools,
  Strikes care upon their heads with his
    mad riots,
  Makes them look old before they meet
    with age.
  This is a son! And what a loss were this,
    considered truly?—
  O, but my Horatio grew out of reach of
    these
  Insatiate humors. He loved his loving
    parents;

[1] The following speech except the last two
lines is an addition.   [2] Ballast.   [3] Unpolished.

He was my comfort and his mother's
    joy,   30
  The very arm that did hold up our house;
  Our hopes were storéd up in him.
  None but a damnéd murderer could hate
    him.
  He had not seen the back of nineteen
    year,
  When his strong arm unhorsed the proud
    Prince Balthazar,
  And his great mind, too full of honor,
  Took him unto [4] mercy, that valiant but
    ignoble Portingale!
  Well, heaven is heaven still,
  And there is Nemesis, and Furies,
  And things called whips,   40
  And they sometimes do meet with mur-
    derers.
  They do not always scape, that is some
    comfort.
  Ay, ay, ay; and then time steals on, and
    steals, and steals,
  Till violence leaps forth like thunder
  Wrapped in a ball of fire,
  And so doth bring confusion to them all.—
  Good leave have you; nay, I pray you go,
  For I'll leave you, if you can leave me so.

2 [Port.] Pray you, which is the next way
    to my lord the duke's?

Hier. The next way from me.

1 [Port.]   To his house, we mean. 50

Hier. O, hard by; 'tis yon house that you
    see.

2 [Port.] You could not tell us if his son
    were there?

Hier. Who, my Lord Lorenzo?

1 [Port.]   Ay, sir.

*He goeth in at one door and comes out at
    another.*

Hier.   O, forbear!
  For other talk for us far fitter were.
  But, if you be importunate to know
  The way to him, and where to find him
    out,
  Then list to me, and I'll resolve your
    doubt.
  There is a path upon your left-hand side
  That leadeth from a guilty conscience
  Unto a forest of distrust and fear,   60
  A darksome place, and dangerous to pass.
  There shall you meet with melancholy
    thoughts,
  Whose baleful humors if you but uphold,

[4] Early edns. read *us to.*

It will conduct you to despair and death—
Whose rocky cliffs when you have once beheld,
Within a hugy dale of lasting night,
That, kindled with the world's iniquities,
Doth cast up filthy and detested fumes—
Not far from thence, where murderers have built
A habitation for their curséd souls,   70
There, in a brazen caldron, fixed by Jove
In his fell wrath, upon a sulphur flame,
Yourselves shall find Lorenzo bathing him
In boiling lead and blood of innocents.

1 [PORT.] Ha, ha, ha!
HIER. Ha, ha, ha! Why, ha, ha, ha! Farewell, good ha, ha, ha!   *Exit.*
2 [PORT.] Doubtless this man is passing lunatic,
Or imperfection of his age doth make him dote.
Come, let's away to seek my lord the duke.   [*Exeunt.*] [1]

[SCENA UNDECIMA.

The Spanish court.]

*Enter Hieronimo, with a poniard in one
hand and a rope in the other.*

HIER. Now, sir, perhaps I come and see the king;
The king sees me, and fain would hear my suit.
Why, is not this a strange and seld-seen [2] thing,
That standers-by with toys should strike me mute?
Go to, I see their shifts, and say no more.
Hieronimo, 'tis time for thee to trudge.
Down by the dale that flows with purple gore
Standeth a fiery tower. There sits a judge
Upon a seat of steel and molten brass,
And twixt his teeth he holds a firebrand,   10
That leads unto the lake where hell doth stand.
Away, Hieronimo! To him be gone;
He'll do thee justice for Horatio's death.
Turn down this path, [3] thou shalt be with him straight;

Or this [4] and then thou need'st not take thy breath.
This way, or that way?—Soft and fair! Not so!
For, if I hang or kill myself, let's know
Who will revenge Horatio's murder then?
No, no! Fie, no! Pardon me, I'll none of that.
          He flings away the dagger and halter.
This way I'll take; and this way comes the king,   *He takes them up again.* 20
And here I'll have a fling at him, that's flat;
And, Balthazar, I'll be with thee to bring, [5]
And thee, Lorenzo! Here's the king—nay, stay;
And here, ay, here—there goes the hare away.

*Enter King, Ambassador, Castile, and
          Lorenzo.*

KING. Now show, ambassador, what our viceroy saith.
Hath he received the articles we sent?
HIER. Justice, O, justice to Hieronimo!
LOR. Back! Seest thou not the king is busy?
HIER.   O, is he so?
KING. Who is he that interrupts our business?
HIER. Not I. [*Aside.*] Hieronimo, beware!
Go by, go by! [6]   30
AMB. Renowméd king, he hath received and read
Thy kingly proffers and thy promised league;
And, as a man extremely overjoyed
To hear his son so princely entertained,
Whose death he had so solemnly bewailed,
This for thy further satisfaction
And kingly love he kindly lets thee know.
First, for the marriage of his princely son
With Bel-imperia, thy beloved niece,
The news are more delightful to his soul   40
Than myrrh or incense to the offended heavens.

[4] *I.e.*, the rope.   [5] Get the upper hand of thee.
[6] A phrase which was widely quoted in Elizabethan literature; probably used to denote impatience.

[1] From 1602 edn.   [3] *I.e.*, the poniard.
[2] Seldom seen.

In person, therefore, will he come himself,
To see the marriage rites solemnizéd,
And, in the presence of the court of Spain.
To knit a sure inextricable [1] band
Of kingly love and everlasting league
Betwixt the crowns of Spain and Portin-
gale.
There will he give his crown to Balthazar,
And make a queen of Bel-imperia.

KING. Brother, how like you this our viceroy's love?   50

CAS. No doubt, my lord, it is an argu-
ment
Of honorable care to keep his friend,
And wondrous zeal to Balthazar his son;
Nor am I least indebted to his grace
That bends his liking to my daughter
thus.

AMB. Now last, dread lord, here hath his
highness sent
(Although he send not that his son return)
His ransom due to Don Horatio.

HIER. Horatio! Who calls Horatio?

KING. And well remembered, thank his
majesty!   60
Here, see it given to Horatio.

HIER. Justice, O, justice, justice, gentle
king!

KING. Who is that? Hieronimo?

HIER. Justice, O, justice! O my son, my
son!
My son, whom naught can ransom or
redeem!

LOR. Hieronimo, you are not well-advised.

HIER. Away, Lorenzo, hinder me no more,
For thou hast made me bankrupt of my
bliss.
Give me my son! You shall not ransom
him!
Away! I'll rip the bowels of the earth, 70
He diggeth with his dagger.
And ferry over to th' Elysian plains,
And bring my son to show his deadly
wounds.
Stand from about me!
I'll make a pickax of my poniard,
And here surrender up my marshalship,
For I'll go marshal up the fiends in hell
To be avengéd on you all for this.

KING. What means this outrage?
Will none of you restrain his fury?

HIER. Nay, soft and fair! You shall not
need to strive.   80
Needs must he go that the devils drive.
Exit.

KING. What accident hath happed Hieronimo?
I have not seen him to demean him so.

LOR. My gracious lord, he is with extreme
pride,
Conceived of young Horatio his son,
And covetous of having to himself
The ransom of the young prince Balthazar,
Distract, and in a manner lunatic.

KING. Believe me, nephew, we are sorry
for 't.
This is the love that fathers bear their
sons.   90
But, gentle brother, go give to him this
gold,
The prince's ransom; let him have his due.
For what he hath, Horatio shall not want.
Happily Hieronimo hath need thereof.

LOR. But, if he be thus helplessly distract,
'Tis requisite his office be resigned,
And given to one of more discretion.

KING. We shall increase his melancholy so.
'Tis best that we see further in it first,
Till when, ourself will exempt [him] [2] the
place.   100
And, brother, now bring in the ambassa-
dor,
That he may be a witness of the match
Twixt Balthazar and Bel-imperia,
And that we may prefix a certain time
Wherein the marriage shall be solemnized,
That we may have thy lord, the viceroy,
here.

AMB. Therein your highness highly shall
content
His majesty, that longs to hear from
hence.

KING. On, then, and hear you, lord ambassador—   *Exeunt.*

[SCENA DUODECIMA.
Hieronimo's garden.]

[3] *Enter Jaques and Pedro.*

JAQ. I wonder, Pedro, why our master thus
At midnight sends us with our torches
light,

[1] Emended by Hawkins. Original reads *in-
execrable.*

[2] Added by Boas; meaning to excuse him from
his duties.

[3] The following scene through l. 156 is an
addition.

When man and bird and beast are all at
  rest,
Save those that watch for rape and
  bloody murder.
PED. O Jaques, know thou that our mas-
  ter's mind
Is much distraught since his Horatio died,
And—now his aged years should sleep in
  rest,
His heart in quiet—like a desperate man,
Grows lunatic and childish for his son.
Sometimes, as he doth at his table sit, 10
He speaks as if Horatio stood by him;
Then starting in a rage, falls on the
  earth,
Cries out, "Horatio, where is my Hora-
  tio?"
So that with extreme grief and cutting
  sorrow
There is not left in him one inch of
  man.—
See, where he comes.

Enter Hieronimo.

HIER. I pry through every crevice of each
  wall,
Look on each tree, and search through
  every brake,
Beat at the bushes, stamp our grandam
  earth,
Dive in the water, and stare up to
  heaven,   20
Yet cannot I behold my son Horatio.—
How now, who's there? Sprites, sprites?
PED. We are your servants that attend
  you, sir.
HIER. What make you with your torches
  in the dark?
PED. You bid us light them, and attend
  you here.
HIER. No, no, you are deceived! Not I;
  you are deceived!
Was I so mad to bid you light your
  torches now?
Light me your torches at the mid of noon,
Whenas the sun-god rides in all his glory;
Light me your torches then.
PED.   Then we burn daylight. 30
HIER. Let it be burnt! Night is a murder-
  ous slut,
That would not have her treasons to be
  seen;
And yonder pale-faced Hecate there, the
  moon,

Doth give consent to that is done in
  darkness;
And all those stars that gaze upon her
  face
Are aglots [1] on her sleeve, pins on her
  train;
And those that should be powerful and
  divine
Do sleep in darkness when they most
  should shine.
PED. Provoke them not, fair sir, with
  tempting words.
The heavens are gracious, and your mis-
  eries and sorrow   40
Makes you speak you know not what.
HIER. Villain, thou liest! And thou doest
  naught
But tell me I am mad. Thou liest! I am
  not mad!
I know thee to be Pedro, and he Jaques.
I'll prove it to thee; and, were I mad, how
  could I?
Where was she that same night when my
  Hor[atio] was murdered?
She should have shone—search thou the
  book.
Had the moon shone, in my boy's face
  there was a kind of grace,
That I know—nay, I do know—had the
  murderer seen him,
His weapon would have fall'n and cut
  the earth,   50
Had he been framed of naught but blood
  and death.
Alack, when mischief doth it knows not
  what,
What shall we say to mischief?

Enter Isabella.

ISAB. Dear Hieronimo, come in a-doors;
O, seek not means so to increase thy
  sorrow.
HIER. Indeed, Isabella, we do nothing here.
I do not cry—ask Pedro, and ask Jaques.
Not I indeed; we are very merry, very
  merry.
ISAB. How? Be merry here, be merry
  here?
Is not this the place, and this the very
  tree,   60
Where my Horatio died, where he was
  murdered?

[1] Metal ornaments. From 1610 edn. Original
reads *aggots.*

HIER. Was—do not say what. Let her
   weep it out.
This was the tree. I set it of a kernel;
And, when our hot Spain could not let
   it grow,
But that the infant and the human sap
Began to wither, duly twice a morning
Would I be sprinkling it with fountain
   water.
At last it grew and grew, and bore and
   bore,
Till at the length it grew a gallows, and
   did bear our son.
It bore thy fruit and mine—O wicked,
   wicked plant!   70
                One knocks within at the door.
See who knocks there.
PED.   It is a painter, sir.
HIER. Bid him come in, and paint some
   comfort,
For surely there's none lives but painted
   comfort.
Let him come in!—One knows not what
   may chance.
God's will that I should set this tree!
But even so, masters ungrateful servants
   rear from naught,
And then they hate them that did bring
   them up.

               Enter the Painter.

PAIN. God bless you, sir.
HIER. Wherefore?   Why, thou scornful
   villain?
How, where, or by what means should I
   be blessed?   80
ISAB. What wouldst thou have, good fel-
   low?
PAIN.   Justice, madam.
HIER. O ambitious beggar! Wouldst thou
   have that
That lives not in the world?
Why, all the undelved mines cannot buy
An ounce of justice, 'tis a jewel so in-
   estimable.
I tell thee, God hath engrossed all jus-
   tice in his hands,
And there is none but what comes from
   him.
PAIN. O, then I see that God must right
   me for my murdered son.
HIER. How, was thy son murdered?
PAIN. Ay, sir. No man did hold a son so
   dear.   90

HIER. What, not as thine? That's a lie
As massy as the earth. I had a son
Whose least unvalued hair did weigh
A thousand of thy sons; and he was
   murdered.
PAIN. Alas, sir, I had no more but he.
HIER. Nor I, nor I! But this same one of
   mine
Was worth a legion. But all is one.
Pedro, Jaques, go in a-doors; Isabella, go!
And this good fellow here and I
Will range this hideous orchard up and
   down   100
Like to two lions reavéd of their young.
Go in a-doors, I say.
       Exeunt. The Painter and he sits down.
                           Come, let's talk wisely now.
Was thy son murdered?
PAIN.   Ay, sir.
HIER.   So was mine.
How dost take it? Art thou not some-
   times mad?
Is there no tricks [1] that comes before
   thine eyes?
PAIN. O Lord, yes, sir. [2]
HIER. Art a painter? Canst paint me a
   tear, or a wound,
A groan, or a sigh? Canst paint me such
   a tree as this?
PAIN. Sir, I am sure you have heard of
   my painting; my name's Bazardo.
HIER. Bazardo! Afore God, an excellent
   fellow. Look you, sir,   110
Do you see, I'd have you paint me [for]
   my gallery
In your oil colors matted, [3] and draw me
   five
Years younger than I am—do ye see, sir,
   let five
Years go; let them go—like the marshal
   of Spain,
My wife Isabella standing by me,
With a speaking look to my son Horatio,
Which should intend to this or some
   suchlike purpose:
"God bless thee, my sweet son;" and
   my hand leaning upon his head, thus,
   sir, do you see? May it be done?

---

[1] Illusions.
[2] The remainder of the added passage is so
chaotic in form that it has been printed as
prose by some editors.
[3] Meaning doubtful; probably either *set in a
mat* or *a mount*, or *lacking in luster.*

PAIN. Very well, sir.

HIER. Nay, I pray mark me, sir. Then,
sir, would I have you paint me this
tree, this very tree.   120
Canst paint a doleful cry?

PAIN. Seemingly, sir.

HIER. Nay, it should cry; but all is one.
Well, sir, paint me a youth, run thorough and thorough with villains'
swords, hanging upon this tree.
Canst draw a murderer?

PAIN. I'll warrant you, sir;
I have the pattern of the most noto-
rious villains that ever lived in all
Spain.

HIER. O, let them be worse, worse. Stretch
thine art,
And let their beards be of Judas his own
color,[1]
And let their eyebrows jutty over—in
any case observe that.   130
Then, sir, after some violent noise,
Bring me forth in my shirt, and my gown
under mine arm, with my torch in my
hand, and my sword reared up thus,
and with these words:
"What noise is this? Who calls Hieronimo?"
May it be done?

PAIN. Yea, sir.

[HIER.] Well, sir, then bring me forth,
bring me thorough alley and alley,
still with a distracted countenance going along, and let my hair heave up
my nightcap.
Let the clouds scowl, make the moon
dark, the stars extinct, the winds blowing, the bells tolling, the owl shrieking,
the toads croaking, the minutes jer-
ring,[2] and the clock striking twelve.
And then at last, sir, starting, behold a
man hanging, and tottering, and tottering as you know the wind will weave
a man, and I, with a trice[3] to cut
him down,
And, looking upon him by the advantage
of my torch, find it to be my son
Horatio.
There you may [show][4] a passion, there
you may show a passion!   140
Draw me like old Priam of Troy,

___
[1] *I.e.*, red, according to medieval tradition.
[2] Jarring, ticking.
[3] Moment.   [4] Added by Dodsley.

Crying, "The house is afire! The house
is afire!"
As the torch over my head. Make me
curse,
Make me rave, make me cry, make me
mad,
Make me well again, make me curse hell,
Invocate heaven, and, in the end, leave me
In a trance, and so forth.

PAIN. And is this the end?

HIER. O no, there is no end! The end is
death and madness,
As I am never better than when I am
mad.   150
Then methinks I am a brave fellow;
Then I do wonders. But reason abuseth
me,
And there's the torment, there's the hell.
At the last, sir, bring me to one of the
murderers.
Were he as strong as Hector, thus would I
Tear and drag him up and down.

*He beats the Painter in, then comes out again
with a book in his hand.*[5]
"*Vindicta mihi!*"[6]
Ay, heaven will be revenged of every ill,
Nor will they suffer murder unrepaid.
Then stay, Hieronimo; attend their
will,   160
For mortal men may not appoint their
time!—
"*Per scelus semper tutum est sceleribus
iter.*"[7]
Strike, and strike home, where wrong is
offered thee,
For evils unto ills conductors be,
And death's the worst of resolution.
For he that thinks with patience to con-
tend
To quiet life, his life shall easily end.—
"*Fata si miseros juvant, habes salutem;
Fata si vitam negant, habes sepulchrum:*"[8]
If destiny thy miseries do ease,   170
Then hast thou health, and happy shalt
thou be;

___
[5] This stage direction is a substitute for
"Enter Hieronimo, with a book in his hand" in
the earlier editions.
[6] "Vengeance for me" (from Seneca's *Octavia*).
[7] "The path to crimes is always made safe by
crime" (from Seneca's *Agamemnon*, l. 115).
[8] "If the Fates aid the unfortunate, you have
safety; if the Fates deny you life, you have a
tomb" (from Seneca's *Troades*, ll. 511–512).
Paraphrased in the following four lines.

If destiny deny thee life, Hieronimo,
Yet shalt thou be assuréd of a tomb;
If neither, yet let this thy comfort be:
Heaven covereth him that hath no burial.
And, to conclude, I will revenge his death!
But how? Not, as the vulgar wits of men,
With open, but inevitable ills,[1]
As by a secret, yet a certain mean,
Which under kindship [2] will be cloakéd
   best.   180
Wise men will take their opportunity,
Closely and safely fitting things to time.
But in extremes advantage hath no time,
And therefore all times fit not for revenge.
Thus therefore will I rest me in unrest,
Dissembling quiet in unquietness,
Not seeming that I know their villainies,
That my simplicity may make them
   think
That ignorantly I will let all slip,
For ignorance, I wot, and well they
   know,   190
"*Remedium malorum iners est.*" [3]
Nor aught avails it me to menace them
Who, as a wintry storm upon a plain,
Will bear me down with their nobility.
No, no, Hieronimo, thou must enjoin
Thine eyes to observation, and thy
   tongue
To milder speeches than thy spirit
   affords,
Thy heart to patience, and thy hands to
   rest,
Thy cap to courtesy, and thy knee to
   bow,
Till to revenge thou know when, where,
   and how.   *A noise within.* 200
How now, what noise? What coil [4] is that
   you keep?

Enter a Servant.

SER. Here are a sort [5] of poor petitioners
   That are importunate, and [6] it shall
     please you, sir,
   That you should plead their cases to the
     king.
HIER. That I should plead their several
   actions?
   Why, let them enter, and let me see
     them.

[1] Injuries, attacks.   [2] Kindness.
[3] "Ignorance is a cowardly remedy for misfortunes" (from Seneca's *Œdipus*, l. 515).
[4] Disturbance.   [5] Company.   [6] If.

Enter three Citizens and an Old Man.

1 [CIT.] So, I tell you this: for learning and
   for law
   There is not any advocate in Spain
   That can prevail, or will take half the
     pain
   That he will, in pursuit of equity. 210
HIER. Come near, you men, that thus
   importune me.—
[*Aside.*] Now must I bear a face of gravity;
   For thus I used, before my marshalship,
   To plead in causes as corregidor.[7]—
   Come on, sirs, what's the matter?
2 [CIT.]   Sir, an action.
HIER. Of battery?
1 [CIT.]   Mine of debt.
HIER.   Give place.
2 [CIT.] No, sir, mine is an action of the
   case.[8]
3 [CIT.] Mine an *ejectione firmæ* [9] by a
   lease.
HIER. Content you, sirs. Are you
   determinéd   219
   That I should plead your several actions?
1 [CIT.] Ay, sir, and here's my declaration.
2 [CIT.] And here's my band.[10]
3 [CIT.]   And here's my lease.
         They give him papers.
HIER. But wherefore stands yon silly man
   so mute,
   With mournful eyes and hands to heaven
     upreared?
   Come hither, father, let me know thy
     cause.
SENEX.[11] O worthy sir, my cause, but
   slightly known,
   May move the hearts of warlike Myrmi-
     dons,
   And melt the Corsic rocks with ruthful
     tears.
HIER. Say, father, tell me what's thy suit.
SENEX. No, sir, could my woes   230
   Give way unto my most distressful words,
   Then should I not in paper, as you see,
   With ink bewray what blood began in me.
HIER. What's here? "The humble sup-
   plication
   Of Don Bazulto for his murdered son."

[7] Advocate; properly, magistrate.
[8] "A universal remedy given for all personal
wrongs . . . so called because the plaintiff's
whole case . . . is set forth at length in the
original writ" (Blackstone).
[9] A writ to eject a tenant.   [10] Bond.
[11] *I.e.*, Old Man: also *Baz.* in speech heads.

Senex. Ay, sir.

Hier.   No, sir, it was my murdered son.

O, my son, my son; O, my son Horatio!
But mine, or thine, Bazulto, be content.
Here, take my handkercher and wipe thine eyes,
Whiles wretched I in thy mishaps may see   240
The lively portrait of my dying self.
          He draweth out a bloody napkin.
O, no, not this! Horatio, this was thine,
And, when I dyed it in thy dearest blood,
This was a token twixt thy soul and me
That of thy death revengéd I should be.
But here, take this, and this—what, my purse?—
Ay, this, and that, and all of them are thine,
For all as one are our extremities.

1 [Cit.] O, see the kindness of Hieronimo!
2 [Cit.] This gentleness shows him a gentleman.   250

Hier. See, see, O, see thy shame, Hieronimo!
See here a loving father to his son!
Behold the sorrows and the sad laments
That he delivereth for his son's decease!
If love's effects so strives in lesser things,
If love enforce such moods in meaner wits,
If love express such power in poor estates,
Hieronimo, whenas a raging sea,
Tossed with the wind and tide, o'erturnest then
The upper billows, course of waves to keep,   260
Whilst lesser waters labor in the deep,
Then shamest thou not, Hieronimo, to neglect
The sweet revenge of thy Horatio?
Though on this earth justice will not be found,
I'll down to hell, and in this passion
Knock at the dismal gates of Pluto's court,
Getting by force, as once Alcides did,
A troop of furies and tormenting hags
To torture Don Lorenzo and the rest.
Yet lest the triple-headed porter should
Deny my passage to the slimy strand,   271
The Thracian poet thou shalt counterfeit.
Come on, old father, be my Orpheus,

And, if thou canst [1] no notes upon the harp,
Then sound the burden [2] of thy sore heart's grief,
Till we do gain that Proserpine may grant
Revenge on them that murderéd my son.
Then will I rent and tear them, thus and thus,
Shivering their limbs in pieces with my teeth.   *Tear the papers.*

1 [Cit.] O sir, my declaration!
          Exit Hieronimo, and they after.
2 [Cit.]   Save my bond! 280

          Enter Hieronimo.

2 [Cit.] Save my bond!
3 [Cit.] Alas, my lease! It cost me ten pound,
And you, my lord, have torn the same.

Hier. That cannot be; I gave it never a wound.
Show me one drop of blood fall from the same!
How is it possible I should slay it then?
Tush, no; run after, catch me if you can.

Exeunt all but the Old Man. Bazulto remains till Hieronimo enters again, who, staring him in the face, speaks.

Hier. And art thou come, Horatio, from the depth,
To ask for justice in this upper earth,
To tell thy father thou art unrevenged,
To wring more tears from Isabella's eyes,   291
Whose lights are dimmed with overlong laments?
Go back, my son; complain to Æacus,
For here's no justice. Gentle boy, begone,
For justice is exiléd from the earth.
Hieronimo will bear thee company.
Thy mother cries on righteous Rhadamanth
For just revenge against the murderers.

Senex. Alas, my lord, whence springs this troubled speech?

Hier. But let me look on my Horatio. 300
Sweet boy, how art thou changed in death's black shade!
Had Proserpine no pity on thy youth,
But suffered thy fair crimson-colored spring
With withered winter to be blasted thus?

[1] Knowest.   [2] Bass accompaniment.

Horatio, thou art older than thy father.
Ah, ruthless fate,[1] that favor [2] thus
　transforms!

Baz. Ah, my good lord, I am not your
　young son.

Hier. What, not my son? Thou then a
　Fury art,
Sent from the empty kingdom of black
　night
To summon me to make appearance　310
Before grim Minos and just Rhada-
　manth,
To plague Hieronimo that is remiss,
And seeks not vengeance for Horatio's
　death.

Baz. I am a grievéd man, and not a ghost,
That came for justice for my murdered
　son.

Hier. Ay, now I know thee, now thou
　namest my son.
Thou art the lively image of my grief;
Within thy face my sorrows I may see.
Thy eyes are gummed with tears, thy
　cheeks are wan,
Thy forehead troubled, and thy mut-
　t'ring lips　　　　　　　　　320
Murmur sad words abruptly broken off
By force of windy sighs thy spirit
　breathes.
And all this sorrow riseth for thy son,
And selfsame sorrow feel I for my son.
Come in, old man, thou shalt to Isabel.
Lean on my arm; I thee, thou me, shalt
　stay,
And thou, and I, and she will sing a song,
Three parts in one, but all of discords
　framed.—
Talk not of chords, but let us now be
　gone,
For with a cord Horatio was slain.　330
　　　　　　　　　　　　Exeunt.

[Scena Tertia Decima.

The Spanish court.]

Enter King of Spain, the Duke, Viceroy, and
　Lorenzo, Balthazar, Don Pedro, and
　　　　　　　　　　Bel-imperia.

King. Go, brother, it is the Duke of
　Castile's cause;
Salute the viceroy in our name.

Cas.　　　　　　　　　　　I go.

Vic. Go forth, Don Pedro, for thy
　nephew's sake,
And greet the Duke of Castile.

Ped.　　　　　　　　It shall be so.

King. And now to meet these Portuguese,
For as we now are, so sometimes were
　these,
Kings and commanders of the western
　Indies.—
Welcome, brave viceroy, to the court of
　Spain,
And welcome all his honorable train!
'Tis not unknown to us for why you
　come,　　　　　　　　　　10
Or have so kingly crossed the seas.
Sufficeth it, in this we note the troth
And more than common love you lend
　to us.
So is it that mine honorable niece
(For it beseems us now that it be known)
Already is betrothed to Balthazar;
And by appointment and our condescent [3]
Tomorrow are they to be marriéd.
To this intent we entertain thyself,
Thy followers, their pleasure, and our
　peace.　　　　　　　　　　20
Speak, men of Portingale, shall it be so?
If ay, say so; if not, say flatly no.

Vic. Renowméd king, I come not, as thou
　think'st,
With doubtful followers, unresolvéd men,
But such as have upon thine articles
Confirmed thy motion, and contented me.
Know, sovereign, I come to solemnize
The marriage of thy beloved niece,
Fair Bel-imperia, with my Balthazar—
With thee, my son, whom sith I live to
　see,　　　　　　　　　　30
Here take my crown, I give it her and
　thee,
And let me live a solitary life,
In ceaseless prayers,
To think how strangely heaven hath thee
　preserved.

King. See, brother, see, how nature strives
　in him!
Come, worthy viceroy, and accompany
Thy friend with thine extremities.[4]
A place more private fits this princely
　mood.

Vic. Or here, or where your highness
　thinks it good.
　　　Exeunt all but Cas[tile] and Lor[enzo].

---

[1] Emended by Dodsley. Original reads Father.
[2] Appearance.
[3] Consent.　[4] Unrestrained expression of feelings.

CAS. Nay, stay, Lorenzo, let me talk with
   you.   40
   Seest thou this entertainment of these
   kings?
LOR. I do, my lord, and joy to see the
   same.
CAS. And knowest thou why this meeting
   is?
LOR. For her, my lord, whom Balthazar
   doth love,
   And to confirm their promised marriage.
CAS. She is thy sister?
LOR.   Who, Bel-imperia? Ay,
   My gracious lord, and this is the day
   That I have longed so happily to see.
CAS. Thou wouldst be loath that any
   fault of thine   49
   Should intercept her in her happiness?
LOR. Heavens will not let Lorenzo err so
   much.
CAS. Why then, Lorenzo, listen to my
   words.
   It is suspected, and reported too,
   That thou, Lorenzo, wrong'st Hieronimo,
   And in his suits towards his majesty
   Still keep'st him back, and seeks to cross
   his suit.
LOR. That I, my lord—?
CAS. I tell thee, son, myself have heard
   it said,
   When, to my sorrow, I have been
   ashamed
   To answer for thee, though thou art
   my son.   60
   Lorenzo, knowest thou not the common
   love
   And kindness that Hieronimo hath won
   By his deserts within the court of Spain?
   Or seest thou not the k[ing] my brother's
   care
   In his behalf, and to procure his health?
   Lorenzo, shouldst thou thwart his
   passions,
   And he exclaim against thee to the king,
   What honor were 't in this assembly,
   Or what a scandal were't among the
   kings
   To hear Hieronimo exclaim on thee!   70
   Tell me—and look thou tell me truly
   too—
   Whence grows the ground of this report
   in court?
LOR. My l[ord], it lies not in Lorenzo's
   power

To stop the vulgar,[1] liberal of their
   tongues.
   A small advantage makes a water-breach,
   And no man lives that long contenteth
   all.
CAS. Myself have seen thee busy to keep
   back
   Him and his supplications from the king.
LOR. Yourself, my l[ord], hath seen his
   passions   79
   That ill beseemed the presence of a king;
   And, for I pitied him in his distress,
   I held him thence with kind and cour-
   teous words
   As free from malice to Hieronimo
   As to my soul, my lord.
CAS. Hieronimo, my son, mistakes thee
   then.
LOR. My gracious father, believe me, so he
   doth.
   But what's a silly man, distract in mind,
   To think upon the murder of his son?
   Alas, how easy is it for him to err!   89
   But for his satisfaction and the world's,
   'Twere good, my l[ord], that Hieronimo
   and I
   Were reconciled, if he misconster[2] me.
CAS. Lorenzo, thou hast said; it shall be so.
   Go one of you, and call Hieronimo.

   Enter Balthazar and Bel-imperia.

BAL. Come, Bel-imperia, Balthazar's content,
   My sorrow's ease and sovereign of my
   bliss,
   Sith heaven hath ordained thee to be
   mine,
   Disperse those clouds and melancholy
   looks,
   And clear them up with those thy sun-
   bright eyes,
   Wherein my hope and heaven's fair
   beauty lies.   100
BEL. My looks, my lord, are fitting for my
   love,
   Which, new-begun, can show [no][3]
   brighter yet.
BAL. New-kindled flames should burn as
   morning sun.
BEL. But not too fast, lest heat and all be
   done.
   I see my lord my father.

---

[1] Common people.   [3] From 1602 edn.
[2] Misconstrue.

BAL.   Truce, my love;
I will go salute him.
CAS.   Welcome, Balthazar.
Welcome, brave prince, the pledge of
  Castile's peace!
And welcome, Bel-imperia!—How now,
  girl?
Why comest thou sadly to salute us thus?
Content thyself, for I am satisfied.   110
It is not now as when Andrea lived;
We have forgotten and forgiven that,
And thou art gracéd with a happier
  love.—
But, Balthazar, here comes Hieronimo;
I'll have a word with him.

Enter Hieronimo and a Servant.

HIER. And where's the duke?
SER.   Yonder.
HIER.   Even so.—
  [*Aside.*] What new device have they
    deviséd, trow? [1]
  Pocas palabras! [2] Mild as the lamb!
  Is 't I will be revenged? No, I am not
    the man.—
CAS. Welcome, Hieronimo.   120
LOR. Welcome, Hieronimo.
BAL. Welcome, Hieronimo.
HIER. My lords, I thank you for Horatio.
CAS. Hieronimo, the reason that I sent
  To speak with you, is this—
HIER.   What, so short?
  Then I'll be gone; I thank you for 't.
CAS. Nay, stay, Hieronimo!—Go call him,
  son.
[LOR.] Hieronimo, my father craves a word
  with you.
HIER. With me, sir? Why, my l[ord], I
  thought you had done.   129
LOR. [*Aside.*] No. Would he had!
CAS.   Hieronimo, I hear
  You find yourself aggrievéd at my son,
  Because you have not access unto the
    king,
  And say 'tis he that intercepts your suits.
HIER. Why, is not this a miserable thing,
  my lord?
CAS. Hieronimo, I hope you have no cause,
  And would be loath that one of your
    deserts
  Should once have reason to suspect my
    son,
  Considering how I think of you myself.
¹ Think you?   ² Few words.

HIER. Your son Lorenzo? Whom, my
  noble lord?
The hope of Spain, mine honorable
  friend?   140
Grant me the combat of them, if they
  dare.   *Draws out his sword.*
I'll meet him face to face, to tell me so!
These be the scandalous reports of such
As love not me, and hate my lord too
  much.
Should I suspect Lorenzo would prevent
Or cross my suit, that loved my son so
  well?
My lord, I am ashamed it should be
  said.
LOR. Hieronimo, I never gave you cause.
HIER. My good lord, I know you did
  not.
CAS.   There then pause;
  And for the satisfaction of the world, 150
  Hieronimo, frequent my homely house,
  The Duke of Castile, Cyprian's ancient
    seat,
  And, when thou wilt, use me, my son,
    and it.
  But here, before Prince Balthazar and
    me,
  Embrace each other, and be perfect
    friends.
HIER. Ay, marry, my lord, and shall.
  Friends, quoth he? See, I'll be friends
    with you all—
  Specially with you, my lovely lord;
  For divers causes it is fit for us
  That we be friends. The world's sus-
    picious,   160
  And men may think what we imagine
    not.
BAL. Why, this is friendly done, Hiero-
  nimo.
LOR. And that I hope. Old grudges are
  forgot?
HIER. What else? It were a shame it
  should not be so.
CAS. Come on, Hieronimo, at my re-
  quest;
  Let us entreat your company today.
                              Exeunt.
HIER. Your lordship's to command.—Pha[
  keep your way.
  Mi. Chi mi fa? Piu Correzza Che no sule
  Tradito viha otrade vule. [3]   *Exit.* 169
³ A corrupt version of a proverb from *Piovana*
Arlotto.

[CHORUS]

Enter Ghost and Revenge.

GHOST. Awake, Erichtho! Cerberus, awake!
Solicit Pluto, gentle Proserpine!
To combat, Acheron and Erebus!
For ne'er, by Styx and Phlegeton in hell,
O'er-ferried Charon to the fiery lakes
Such fearful sights as poor Andrea sees.[1]
Revenge, awake!
REVENGE.   Awake? For why?
GHOST. Awake, Revenge, for thou art ill-
    advised
To sleep away what thou art warned to
    watch!
REVENGE. Content thyself, and do not
    trouble me.
GHOST. Awake, Revenge, if love—as love
    hath had—   180
Have yet the power or prevalence in hell!
Hieronimo with Lorenzo is joined in
    league,
And intercepts our passage to revenge.
Awake, Revenge, or we are woebegone!
REVENGE. Thus worldlings ground[2] what
    they have dreamed upon.
Content thyself, Andrea.   Though I
    sleep,
Yet is my mood soliciting their souls.
Sufficeth thee that poor Hieronimo
Cannot forget his son Horatio.
Nor dies Revenge, although he sleep
    awhile;   190
For, in unquiet, quietness is feigned,
And slumb'ring is a common worldly
    wile.
Behold, Andrea, for an instance, how
Revenge hath slept, and then imagine
    thou
What 'tis to be subject to destiny.

Enter a Dumb Show.

GHOST. Awake, Revenge; reveal this mys-
    tery.
REVENGE. The two first the nuptial
    torches bore
As brightly burning as the midday's sun;
But after them doth Hymen hie as fast,
Clothéd in sable and a saffron robe, 200
And blows them out, and quencheth
    them with blood,
As discontent that things continue so.

―――――――――
[1] Lines 171–74, corrupt in the original, have
been emended by Schick.   [2] Rely on.

GHOST. Sufficeth me; thy meaning's under-
    stood,
And thanks to thee and those infernal
    powers
That will not tolerate a lover's woe.
Rest thee, for I will sit to see the rest.
REVENGE. Then argue not, for thou hast
    thy request.   *Exeunt.*

ACTUS QUARTUS. [SCENA PRIMA.

A room in Don Cyprian's palace.]

Enter Bel-imperia and Hieronimo.

BEL. Is this the love thou bear'st Horatio?
Is this the kindness that thou counter-
    feits?
Are these the fruits of thine incessant
    tears?
Hieronimo, are these thy passions,
Thy protestations and thy deep laments,
That thou wert wont to weary men
    withal?
O unkind father! O deceitful world!
With what excuses canst thou show thy-
    self—
With what dishonor and the hate of
    men—
From this dishonor and the hate of
    men,   10
Thus to neglect the loss and life of him
Whom both my letters and thine own
    belief
Assures thee to be causeless slaughteréd?
Hieronimo, for shame, Hieronimo,
Be not a history to aftertimes
Of such ingratitude unto thy son.
Unhappy mothers of such children then!
But monstrous fathers to forget so soon
The death of those whom they with care
    and cost
Have tendered so, thus careless should
    be lost.   20
Myself, a stranger in respect of thee,
So loved his life as still I wish their
    deaths.
Nor shall his death be unrevenged by
    me,
Although I bear it out for fashion's sake,
For here I swear, in sight of heaven and
    earth,
Shouldst thou neglect the love thou
    shouldst retain,
And give it over and devise no more,

Myself should send their hateful souls
    to hell
That wrought his downfall with extrem-
    est death.
HIER. But may it be that Bel-imperia 30
    Vows such revenge as she hath deigned
    to say?
Why, then I see that heaven applies our
    drift,[1]
And all the saints do sit soliciting
For vengeance on those cursèd murder-
    ers.
Madam, 'tis true, and now I find it so,
I found a letter, written in your name,
And, in that letter, how Horatio died.
Pardon, O, pardon, Bel-imperia,
My fear and care in not believing it;
Nor think I thoughtless think upon a
    mean   40
To let his death be unrevenged at full.
And here I vow—so you but give consent,
And will conceal my resolution—
I will ere long determine of their deaths
That causeless thus have murder[è]d my
    son.
BEL. Hieronimo, I will consent, conceal,
    And aught that may effect for thine
    avail,
Join with thee to revenge Horatio's
    death.
HIER. On, then; [and] whatsoever I devise,
    Let me entreat you, grace my practices,
    Forwhy[2] the plot's already in mine
    head.   51
Here they are.

Enter Balthazar and Lorenzo.

BAL.   How now, Hieronimo?
    What, courting Bel-imperia?
HIER.   Ay, my lord;
    Such courting as, I promise you,
    She hath my heart, but you, my lord,
    have hers.
LOR. But now, Hieronimo, or never,
    We are to entreat your help.
HIER.   My help?
Why, my good lords, assure yourselves
    of me,
For you have given me cause—ay, by
    my faith, have you!
BAL. It pleased you, at the entertainment
    of the ambassador,   60

To grace the king so much as with a
    show.
Now, were your study so well furnishèd,
As, for the passing of the first night's
    sport,
To entertain my father with the like,
Or any suchlike pleasing motion,
Assure yourself, it would content them
    well.
HIER. Is this all?
BAL.   Ay, this is all.
HIER. Why then, I'll fit you; say no more.
When I was young, I gave my mind
And plied myself to fruitless poetry,   70
Which, though it profit the professor
    naught,
Yet is it passing pleasing to the world.
LOR. And how for that?
HIER.   Marry, my good lord, thus
(And yet methinks, you are too quick
    with us):
When in Toledo there I studièd,
It was my chance to write a tragedy—
See here, my lords—
              He shows them a book.
Which, long forgot, I found this other day.
Now would your lordships favor me so
    much
As but to grace me with your acting
    it—   80
I mean each one of you to play a part—
Assure you it will prove most passing
    strange,
And wondrous plausible[3] to that as-
    sembly.
BAL. What, would you have us play a
    tragedy?
HIER. Why, Nero thought it no dispar-
    agement,
And kings and emperors have ta'en de-
    light
To make experience of their wits in
    plays.[4]
LOR. Nay, be not angry, good Hieronimo;
    The prince but asked a question.
BAL. In faith, Hieronimo, an you be in
    earnest,   90
I'll make one.
LOR.   And I another.
HIER. Now, my good lord, could you en-
    treat

---

[1] Approves our plan.   [2] Because.

[3] Acceptable.

[4] These lines, which are quoted by Heywood,
give the clue to Kyd's authorship.

Your sister Bel-imperia to make one?
For what's a play without a woman in it?
BEL. Little entreaty shall serve me, Hiero-
nimo,
For I must needs be employed in your
play.
HIER. Why, this is well. I tell you, lord-
ings,
It was determinéd to have been acted
By gentlemen and scholars too,
Such as could tell what to speak.
BAL.　　　　　　　　And now 100
It shall be played by princes and court-
iers,
Such as can tell how to speak,
If, as it is our country manner,
You will but let us know the argument.
HIER. That shall I roundly. The chron-
icles of Spain
Record this written of a knight of
Rhodes:
He was betrothed, and wedded at the
length,
To one Perseda, an Italian dame,
Whose beauty ravished all that her be-
held,
Especially the soul of Soliman, 110
Who at the marriage was the chiefest
guest.[1]
By sundry means sought Soliman to
win
Perseda's love, and could not gain the
same.
Then gan he break his passions to a
friend,
One of his bashaws, whom he held full
dear.
Her had this bashaw long solicited,
And saw she was not otherwise to be
won
But by her husband's death, this knight
of Rhodes,
Whom presently by treachery he slew.
She, stirred with an exceeding hate
therefor, 120
As cause of this, slew Soliman
And, to escape the bashaw's tyranny,
Did stab herself. And this the tragedy.
LOR. O excellent!
BEL.　　　　　　　　But say, Hieronimo,
What then became of him that was the
bashaw?

<hr>

[1] Cf. the play Soliman and Perseda, attributed
to Kyd.

HIER. Marry, thus: moved with remorse
of his misdeeds,
Ran to a mountain top, and hung him-
self.
BAL. But which of us is to perform that
part?
HIER. O, that will I, my lords; make no
doubt of it.
I'll play the murderer, I warrant you, 130
For I already have conceited that.
BAL. And what shall I?
HIER. Great Soliman, the Turkish em-
peror.
LOR. And I?
HIER.　　　　Erastus, the knight of Rhodes.
BEL. And I?
HIER.　　　　Perseda, chaste and resolute.
And here, my lords, are several abstracts
drawn,
For each of you to note your parts,
And act it, as occasion's offered you.
You must provide a Turkish cap,
A black mustachio and a falchion; 140
　　　　　Gives a paper to Bal[thazar].
You with a cross, like to a knight of
Rhodes;
　　　　　Gives another to Lor[enzo].
And, madam, you must attire yourself
　　　　　He giveth Bel[-imperia] another.
Like Phœbe, Flora, or the huntress,[2]
Which to your discretion shall seem
best.
And, as for me, my lords, I'll look to
one,
And, with the ransom that the viceroy
sent,
So furnish and perform this tragedy
As all the world shall say Hieronimo
Was liberal in gracing of it so.
BAL. Hieronimo, methinks a comedy were
better. 150
HIER. A comedy?
Fie! Comedies are fit for common wits;
But to present a kingly troop withal,
Give me a stately-written tragedy,
Tragedia cothurnata,[3] fitting kings,
Containing matter, and not common
things.
My lords, all this must be performed,
As fitting for the first night's reveling.
The Italian tragedians were so sharp
of wit

<hr>

[2] I.e., Diana.
[3] Wearing the buskin of the tragic actor.

That in one hour's meditation   160
They would perform anything in action.
Lor. And well it may, for I have seen the like
In Paris 'mongst the French tragedians.
Hier. In Paris? Mass! And well remembered!
There's one thing more that rests for us to do.
Bal. What's that, Hieronimo? Forget not anything.
Hier. Each one of us
Must act his part in unknown languages,
That it may breed the more variety:
As you, my lord, in Latin, I in Greek,   170
You in Italian; and, for because I know
That Bel-imperia hath practicéd the French,
In courtly French shall all her phrases be.
Bel. You mean to try my cunning then, Hieronimo?
Bal. But this will be a mere confusion
And hardly shall we all be understood.
Hier. It must be so, for the conclusion
Shall prove the invention and all was good.
And I myself in an oration,
And with a strange and wondrous show besides,   180
That I will have there behind a curtain,
Assure yourself, shall make the matter known.
And all shall be concluded in one scene,
For there's no pleasure ta'en in tediousness.
Bal. [Aside.] How like you this?
Lor. [Aside.]   Why, thus, my lord:
We must resolve to soothe his humors up.
Bal. On then, Hieronimo. Farewell till soon.
Hier. You'll ply this gear?
Lor.   I warrant you.
       Exeunt all but Hiero[nimo].
Hier.   Why, so!
Now shall I see the fall of Babylon,
Wrought by the heavens in this confusion.   190
And, if the world like not this tragedy,
Hard is the hap of old Hieronimo.   *Exit.*

[Scena Secunda.

Hieronimo's garden.]

Enter Isabella with a weapon.

[Isab.] Tell me no more!—O monstrous homicides!
Since neither piety or pity moves
The king to justice or compassion,
I will revenge myself upon this place,
Where thus they murdered my beloved son.   *She cuts down the arbor.*
Down with these branches and these loathsome boughs
Of this unfortunate and fatal pine!
Down with them, Isabella; rent them up,
And burn the roots from whence the rest is sprung!
I will not leave a root, a stalk, a tree,   10
A bough, a branch, a blossom, nor a leaf,
No, not an herb within this garden plot—
Accurséd complot of my misery!
Fruitless forever may this garden be,
Barren the earth, and blissless whosoever
Imagines not to keep it unmanured![1]
An eastern wind, commixed with noisome airs,
Shall blast the plants and the young saplings;
The earth with serpents shall be pesteréd,
And passengers, for fear to be infect,   20
Shall stand aloof, and, looking at it, tell,
"There, murdered, died the son of Isabel."
Ay, here he died, and here I him embrace.
See, where his ghost solicits with his wounds
Revenge on her that should revenge his death.
Hieronimo, make haste to see thy son,
For sorrow and despair hath cited me
To hear Horatio plead with Rhadamanth.
Make haste, Hieronimo, to hold excused[2]
Thy negligence in pursuit of their deaths   30
Whose hateful wrath bereaved him of his breath.

[1] Uncultivated.   [2] Make excuses for.

Ah, nay, thou dost delay their deaths,
Forgives the murderers of thy noble
    son,
And none but I bestir me—to no end!
And, as I curse this tree from further
    fruit,
So shall my womb be cursèd for his
    sake,
And with this weapon will I wound the
    breast,
The hapless breast, that gave Horatio
suck.   *She stabs herself.*

[SCENA TERTIA.

A room in Don Cyprian's palace.]

*Enter Hieronimo; he knocks up the curtain.
    Enter the Duke of Castile.*

CAS. How now, Hieronimo, where's your
    fellows,
    That you take all this pain?
HIER. O, sir, it is for the author's credit
    To look that all things may go well.
    But, good my lord, let me entreat your
    grace
    To give the king the copy of the play.
    This is the argument of what we show.
CAS. I will, Hieronimo.
HIER. One thing more, my good lord.
CAS. What's that?
HIER.   Let me entreat your grace 10
    That, when the train are passed into the
    gallery,
    You would vouchsafe to throw me down
    the key.
CAS. I will, Hieronimo.   *Exit Cas[tile].*
HIER. What, are you ready, Balthazar?
    Bring a chair and a cushion for the king.

Enter Balthazar, with a chair.

Well done, Balthazar! Hang up the title:
"Our scene is Rhodes." What, is your
    beard on?
BAL. Half on; the other is in my hand.
HIER. Despatch, for shame. Are you so
    long?   *Exit Balthazar.*
Bethink thyself, Hieronimo,   20
Recall thy wits, recount thy former
    wrongs
Thou hast received by murder of thy
    son,
And lastly, not least, how Isabel,
Once his mother and thy dearest wife,
All woebegone for him, hath slain herself.

Behoves thee then, Hieronimo, to be
    revenged!
The plot is laid of dire revenge.
On then, Hieronimo, pursue revenge,
For nothing wants but acting of revenge!
                    Exit Hieronimo.

*Enter Spanish King, Viceroy, the Duke of
    Castile, and their Train [to the gallery].*[1]

KING. Now, viceroy, shall we see the
    tragedy   30
Of Soliman, the Turkish emperor,
Performed of pleasure by your son the
    prince,
My nephew Don Lorenzo, and my niece.
VIC. Who? Bel-imperia?
KING. Ay, and Hieronimo, our marshal,
At whose request they deign to do't
    themselves.
These be our pastimes in the court of
    Spain.
Here, brother, you shall be the book-
    keeper.
This is the argument of that they show.
                    He giveth him a book.
(*Gentlemen, this play of Hieronimo, in* [40
*sundry languages, was thought good to be set
down in English, more largely, for the easier
understanding to every public reader.*)

*Enter Balthazar, Bel-imperia, and Hiero-
                    nimo.*

BAL. Bashaw, that Rhodes is ours, yield
    heavens the honor,
And holy Mahomet, our sacred prophet!
And be thou graced with every excellence
That Soliman can give, or thou desire.
But thy desert in conquering Rhodes is
    less
Than in reserving this fair Christian
    nymph,
Perseda, blissful lamp of excellence, 50
Whose eyes compel, like powerful ada-
    mant,
The warlike heart of Soliman to wait.

KING. See, viceroy, that is Balthazar, your
    son,
That represents the emperor Soliman.
How well he acts his amorous passion!
VIC. Ay, Bel-imperia hath taught him
    that.

[1] Added by Manly.

CAS. That's because his mind runs all on
Bel-imperia.

HIER. Whatever joy earth yields, betide
your majesty.
BAL. Earth yields no joy without Perseda's
love.
HIER. Let then Perseda on your grace
attend.   60
BAL. She shall not wait on me, but I on
her.
Drawn by the influence of her lights, I
yield.
But let my friend, the Rhodian knight,
come forth,
Erasto, dearer than my life to me,
That he may see Perseda, my beloved.

Enter Erasto.

KING. Here comes Lorenzo. Look upon
the plot
And tell me, brother, what part plays he?

BEL. Ah, my Erasto, welcome to Perseda.
LOR. Thrice happy is Erasto that thou
livest;
Rhodes' loss is nothing to Erasto's joy. 70
Sith his Perseda lives, his life survives.
BAL. Ah, bashaw, here is love between
Erasto
And fair Perseda, sovereign of my soul.
HIER. Remove Erasto, mighty Soliman,
And then Perseda will be quickly won.
BAL. Erasto is my friend, and, while he
lives,
Perseda never will remove her love.
HIER. Let not Erasto live to grieve great
Soliman.
BAL. Dear is Erasto in our princely eye.
HIER. But, if he be your rival, let him
die.   80
BAL. Why, let him die!—So love com-
mandeth me;
Yet grieve I that Erasto should so die.
HIER. Erasto, Soliman saluteth thee,
And lets thee wit by me his highness' will,
Which is, thou shouldst be thus em-
ployed.   *Stab him.*
BEL.   Ay me!
Erasto! See, Soliman, Erasto's slain!
BAL. Yet liveth Soliman to comfort thee.
Fair queen of beauty, let not favor die,
But with a gracious eye behold his
grief   89

That with Perseda's beauty is increased,
If by Perseda [hi]s grief be not released.
BEL. Tyrant, desist soliciting vain suits.
Relentless are mine ears to thy laments
As thy butcher is pitiless and base,
Which seized on my Erasto, harmless
knight.
Yet by thy power thou thinkest to
command,
And to thy power Perseda doth obey;
But, were she able, thus she would
revenge
Thy treacheries on thee, ignoble prince;
                              Stab him.
And on herself she would be thus re-
venged.   *Stab herself.*

KING. Well said!—Old marshal, this was
bravely done!   101
HIER. But Bel-imperia plays Perseda
well!
VIC. Were this in earnest, Bel-imperia,
You would be better to my son than so.
KING. But now what follows for Hiero-
nimo?
HIER. Marry, this follows for Hieronimo.
Here break we off our sundry languages,
And thus conclude I in our vulgar tongue.
Happily you think—but bootless are
your thoughts—
That this is fabulously counterfeit,   110
And that we do as all tragedians do—
To die today (for fashioning our scene,
The death of Ajax or some Roman peer),
And, in a minute starting up again,
Revive to please tomorrow's audience.
No, princes; know I am Hieronimo,
The hopeless father of a hapless son,
Whose tongue is tuned to tell his latest
tale,
Not to excuse gross errors in the play.
I see, your looks urge instance of these
words;   120
Behold the reason urging me to this!
                         Shows his dead son.
See here my show; look on this spectacle!
Here lay my hope, and here my hope
hath end;
Here lay my heart, and here my heart
was slain;
Here lay my treasure, here my treasure
lost;
Here lay my bliss, and here my bliss
bereft.

But hope, heart, treasure, joy, and bliss,
All fled, failed, died, yea, all decayed
with this.
From forth these wounds came breath
that gave me life;
They murdered me that made these fatal
marks. 130
The cause was love, whence grew this
mortal hate;
The hate—Lorenzo and young Baltha-
zar;
The love—my son to Bel-imperia.
But night, the coverer of accursèd
crimes,
With pitchy silence hushed these trai-
tors' harms,
And lent them leave, for they had sorted [1]
leisure
To take advantage in my garden plot
Upon my son, my dear Horatio.
There merciless they butchered up my
boy,
In black, dark night, to pale, dim, cruel
death. 140
He shrieks. I heard—and yet, methinks,
I hear—
His dismal outcry echo in the air.
With soonest speed I hasted to the noise,
Where hanging on a tree I found my son,
Through-girt [2] with wounds, and slaugh-
tered as you see.
And grieved I, think you, at this spec-
tacle?
Speak, Portuguese, whose loss resembles
mine.
If thou canst weep upon thy Balthazar,
'Tis like I wailed for my Horatio. 149
And you, my l[ord], whose reconcilèd son
Marched in a net, and thought himself
unseen,
And rated me for brainsick lunacy,
With "God amend that mad Hiero-
nimo!"—
How can you brook our play's catastro-
phe?
And here behold this bloody handker-
cher,
Which at Horatio's death I weeping
dipped
Within the river of his bleeding wounds.
It as propitious, see, I have reserved,
And never hath it left my bloody
heart,

Soliciting remembrance of my vow 160
With these, O, these accursèd murderers,
Which now performed, my heart is
satisfied.
And to this end the bashaw I became
That might revenge me on Lorenzo's life,
Who therefore was appointed to the part,
And was to represent the knight of
Rhodes
That I might kill him more conveniently.
So, viceroy, was this Balthazar, thy son,
That Soliman which Bel-imperia,
In person of Perseda, murderèd, 170
So[le]ly appointed to that tragic part
That she might slay him that offended
her.
Poor Bel-imperia missed her part in this:
For, though the story saith she should
have died,
Yet I of kindness, and of care to her,
Did otherwise determine of her end;
But love of him whom they did hate too
much
Did urge her resolution to be such.
And, princes, now behold Hieronimo,
Author and actor in this tragedy, 180
Bearing his latest fortune in his fist,
And will as resolute conclude his part
As any of the actors gone before.
And, gentles, thus I end my play.
Urge no more words; I have no more to
say. *He runs to hang himself.*
KING. O, hearken, viceroy! Hold, Hiero-
nimo!
Brother, my nephew and thy son are
slain!
VIC. We are betrayed; my Balthazar is
slain!
Break ope the doors; run, save Hiero-
nimo.
[*They break in and hold Hieronimo.*][3]
Hieronimo, do but inform the king of
these events; 190
Upon mine honor, thou shalt have no
harm.
HIER. Viceroy, I will not trust thee with
my life,
Which I this day have offered to my son.
Accursèd wretch!
Why stay'st thou him that was resolved
to die?
KING. Speak, traitor! Damnèd, bloody
murderer, speak!

[1] Selected.   [2] Pierced.   [3] From 1602 edn.

For now I have thee, I will make thee
speak.

Why hast thou done this undeserving
deed?

Vic. Why hast thou murderéd my Balthazar?

Cas. Why hast thou butchered both my
children thus? [1]   200

Hier. But are you sure they are dead?

Cas.   Ay, slave, too sure.

Hier. What, and yours too?

Vic. Ay, all are dead; not one of them
survive.

Hier. Nay, then I care not. Come, and we
shall be friends.

Let us lay our heads together;

See, here's a goodly noose will hold them
all.

Vic. O damnéd devil, how secure [2] he is!

Hier. Secure? Why, dost thou wonder
at it?

I tell thee, viceroy, this day I have seen
revenged,

And in that sight am grown a prouder
monarch   210

Than ever sat under the crown of Spain.

Had I as many lives as there be stars,

As many heavens to go to as those lives,

[1] Lines 201–249 are substituted in the 1602
edn. for the following passage in the original:
Hier. O, good words!
  As dear to me was my Horatio
  As yours, or yours, or yours, my l[ord], to you.
  My guiltless son was by Lorenzo slain,
  And by Lorenzo and that Balthazar
  Am I at last revengéd thoroughly,
  Upon whose souls may heavens be yet avenged
  With greater far than these afflictions.
Cas. But who were thy confederates in this?
Vic. That was thy daughter Bel-imperia,
  For by her hand my Balthazar was slain.
  I saw her stab him.
King.   Why speakest thou not?
Hier. What lesser liberty can kings afford
  Than harmless silence? Then afford it me.
  Sufficeth, I may not, nor I will not tell thee.
King. Fetch forth the tortures. Traitor as
  thou art,
  I'll make thee tell.
Hier. Indeed? Thou mayest torment me as
  his wretched son
  Hath done in murd'ring my Horatio,
  But never shalt thou force me to reveal
  The thing which I have vowed inviolate.
  And therefore, in despite of all thy threats,
  Pleased with their deaths, and eased with their
    revenge,
  First take my tongue, and afterwards my
    heart.
[2] Assured.

I'd give them all, ay, and my soul to boot,

But I would see thee ride in this red pool.

Cas. Speak, who were thy confederates in
this?

Vic. That was thy daughter Bel-imperia,

For by her hand my Balthazar was
slain.

I saw her stab him.

Hier. O, good words! As dear to me was
my Horatio,   220

As yours, or yours, or yours, my lord, to
you.

My guiltless son was by Lorenzo slain,

And by Lorenzo and that Balthazar

Am I at last revengéd thoroughly,

Upon whose souls may heavens be yet
revenged

With greater far than these afflictions.

Methinks, since I grew inward with
revenge,

I cannot look with scorn enough on
death.

King. What, dost thou mock us, slave?—
Bring tortures forth.

Hier. Do, do, do; and meantime I'll tor-
ture you.   230

You had a son, as I take it, and your son

Should ha' been married to your
daughter. Ha, was't not so?—

You had a son too; he was my liege's
nephew.

He was proud and politic. Had he lived,

He might ha' come to wear the crown of
Spain.

I think 'twas so; 'twas I that killed him.

Look you, this same hand, 'twas it that
stabbed

His heart—do you see, this hand?—

For one Horatio, if you ever knew him, a
youth,

One that they hanged up in his father's
garden;   240

One that did force your valiant son to
yield,

While your more valiant son did take him
prisoner.

Vic. Be deaf, my senses; I can hear no
more.

King. Fall, heaven, and cover us with thy
sad ruins.

Cas. Roll all the world within thy pitchy
cloud.

Hier. Now do I applaud what I have
acted.

Nunc mers cadæ manus.[1]

Now to express the rupture of my part—

First take my tongue, and afterward my heart. *He bites out his tongue.* 249

KING. O, monstrous resolution of a wretch! See, viceroy, he hath bitten forth his tongue

Rather than to reveal what we required.

CAS. Yet can he write.

KING. And, if in this he satisfy us not, We will devise th' extremest kind of death

That ever was invented for a wretch.

Then he makes signs for a knife to mend his pen.

CAS. O, he would have a knife to mend his pen.

VIC. Here, and advise thee that thou write the troth.—

Look to my brother! Save Hieronimo!

He with a knife stabs the Duke and himself.

KING. What age hath ever heard such monstrous deeds? 260

My brother, and the whole succeeding hope

That Spain expected after my decease!

Go, bear his body hence, that we may mourn

The loss of our beloved brother's death,

That he may be entombed whate'er befall.

I am the next, the nearest, last of all.

VIC. And thou, Don Pedro, do the like for us.

Take up our hapless son, untimely slain;

Set me with him, and he with woeful me, 269

Upon the mainmast of a ship unmanned,

And let the wind and tide haul me along

To Scylla's barking and untaméd gulf,

Or to the loathsome pool of Acheron,

To weep my want for my sweet Balthazar.

Spain hath no refuge for a Portingale.

The trumpets sound a dead march, the King of Spain mourning after his brother's body, and the King of Portingale bearing the body of his son.

[Chorus]

Enter Ghost and Revenge.

GHOST. Ay, now my hopes have end in their effects,

When blood and sorrow finish my desires:

Horatio murdered in his father's bower;

Vild Serberine by Pedringano slain;

False Pedringano hanged by quaint device;

Fair Isabella by herself misdone;

Prince Balthazar by Bel-imperia stabbed;

The Duke of Castile and his wicked son

Both done to death by old Hieronimo;

My Bel-imperia fall'n as Dido fell; 10

And good Hieronimo slain by himself.

Ay, these were spectacles to please my soul!

Now will I beg at lovely Proserpine

That, by the virtue of her princely doom,[2]

I may consort my friends in pleasing sort,

And on my foes work just and sharp revenge.

I'll lead my friend Horatio through those fields

Where never-dying wars are still inured;[3]

I'll lead fair Isabella to that train[4] 19

Where pity weeps, but never feeleth pain;

I'll lead my Bel-imperia to those joys

That vestal virgins and fair queens possess;

I'll lead Hieronimo where Orpheus plays,

Adding sweet pleasure to eternal days.

But say, Revenge (for thou must help, or none),

Against the rest how shall my hate be shown?

REVENGE. This hand shall hale them down to deepest hell,

Where none but furies, bugs,[5] and tortures dwell.

GHOST. Then, sweet Revenge, do this at my request:

Let me be judge, and doom them to unrest. 30

Let loose poor Tityus from the vulture's gripe,

And let Don Cyprian supply his room;

Place Don Lorenzo on Ixion's wheel,

And let the lover's endless pains surcease

(Juno forgets old wrath, and grants him ease);

---

[1] Reading *iners cadat* for *mers cadæ*, the meaning seems to be, "Now let my hand fall lifeless" (source unknown).

[2] Decree.
[3] Carried on.
[4] Company.
[5] Bugbears, terrors.

Hang Balthazar about Chimera's neck,
And let him there bewail his bloody love,
Repining at our joys that are above;
Let Serberine go roll the fatal stone,
And take from Sisyphus his endless
   moan;   40
False Pedringano, for his treachery,
Let him be dragged through boiling
   Acheron,
And there live, dying still in endless
   flames,

Blaspheming gods and all their holy
   names.
REVENGE. Then haste we down to meet
   thy friends and foes,
To place thy friends in ease, the rest in
   woes,
For here, though death hath[1] end their
   misery,
I'll there begin their endless tragedy.
                     Exeunt.

[1] 1623 edn. has *doth.*

ARDEN OF FEVERSHAM

The authorship of *Arden of Feversham* has been a source of much conjecture. In 1770 Edward Jacob reprinted the play with a brief preface in which, without advancing any evidence of value, he attributed it to Shakespeare. In spite of much able criticism written in support of Shakespearean authorship in the last century, this view is now discredited. Boas, as editor of Kyd's works, holds that the author was an imitator of Kyd, rather than Kyd himself, as Fleay had argued many years earlier. Kyd's claim is supported, however, by Charles Crawford in his *Collectanea* and by H. Dugdale Sykes in his *Sidelights on Shakespeare*. Sykes gives the following recapitulation of his evidence: "The play echoes the phrasing not only of Kyd's earlier dramas, but of his later work as well. It uses his vocabulary and exhibits the characteristic features of his diction even to the least conspicuous of his mannerisms. It was written by a dramatist, who like Kyd, had a technical knowledge of legal documents and legal procedure. It deals with just such a crime as he had chosen for the subject of a prose tract [*The Murder of John Brewen*]. Like *Soliman and Perseda* it borrows from Marlowe's *Edward II*. Like *The Spanish Tragedy* and *Soliman and Perseda* it shows the influence of Seneca and of Garnier. Like them it was published anonymously by Edward White. It is with some confidence that I submit that there is here conclusive proof that it is Kyd's play." Though able scholars have accepted this argument, the case for Kyd is very doubtful. Sykes's impressionistic method of determining authorship has been shown to be fallacious in similar cases. Here the argument from diction is especially questionable, first, because he does not confine himself to Kyd's one authentic original play, *The Spanish Tragedy*, for comparison, but speaks of *Arden of Feversham* as echoing Kyd's "earlier dramas" and "later work"; and, second, because there was extensive borrowing of effective phrases and devices in plays around 1590.

The play is founded on an actual murder committed in 1551, a murder so notorious that Holinshed almost a generation later gave a lengthy account of it in his *Chronicles*. The dramatist apparently used the chronicle, but he may have been acquainted with other accounts or even with local legends. Significant variations from Holinshed are the addition of the confidant Franklin, the omission of Arden's winking at his wife's infidelity, and the use of a fog to frustrate the plans of Shakebag and Will. The free use of chronicle material around 1592, especially for tragedy, may have influenced the selection of this story for dramatization. The author handles it realistically, presenting, as he claims in the epilogue, "a naked tragedy" without embellishments of style. Perhaps the fact that the story deals with characters of the middle and lower classes, rather than with kings and nobles common in tragedy drawn from romance and history, led the author to avoid the pomp and rhetoric prevailing in the tragedy of the period. *Arden of Feversham* is the first extant example of the domestic tragedy, and one of the best. The success of the play, with its dramatic force and its vivid impressions of moods and places, probably had much to do with the vogue of the type.

The play was entered in the Stationers' Register on April 3, 1592, and was printed anonymously for Edward White later in the same year. Other editions appeared in 1599 and 1633. The present text is based on Farmer's reproduction of the quarto of 1592 in Tudor Facsimile Texts and on Tucker Brooke's reprint in his *Shakespeare Apocrypha*.

THE LAMENTABLE AND TRUE TRAG-EDY OF M[ASTER] ARDEN OF FEVERSHAM IN KENT[1]

[*DRAMATIS PERSONÆ*

LORD CHEINY.
THOMAS ARDEN, *a gentleman of Feversham.*
FRANKLIN, *his friend.*
MICHAEL, *Arden's servant.*
MOSBIE, *lover of Arden's wife.*
MAYOR OF FEVERSHAM.
ADAM FOWLE, *landlord of the Flower-de-Luce.*
CLARKE, *a painter.*
GREENE, *a tenant.*

BRADSHAW, *a goldsmith.*
DICK REEDE, *a sailor.*
BLACK WILL }
SHAKEBAG   } *murderers.*

ALICE, *Arden's wife.*
SUSAN, *Mosbie's sister.*

ATTENDANTS OF LORD CHEINY, THE WATCH, A SAILOR, A PRENTICE, A FERRYMAN.

SCENE: *Feversham, London, and the surrounding country.*

TIME: *1551.*]

[SCENE i.

Before and in Arden's house.]

Enter Arden and Franklin.

FRANK. Arden, cheer up thy spirits, and droop no more!
My gracious lord, the Duke of Somerset,
Hath freely given to thee and to thy heirs,
By letters patents from his majesty,
All the lands of the Abbey of Feversham.
Here are the deeds, sealed and subscribed with his name and the king's.
              [*Gives the papers.*]
Read them, and leave this melancholy mood.
ARD. Franklin, thy love prolongs my weary life;

And but for thee how odious were this life,
That shows me nothing, but torments my soul,   10
And those foul objects that offend mine eyes,
Which makes me wish that for this veil of heaven
The earth hung over my head and covered me!
Love letters passed twixt Mosbie and my wife,
And they have privy meetings in the town.
Nay, on his finger did I spy the ring
Which at our marriage day the priest put on.
Can any grief be half so great as this?
FRANK. Comfort thyself, sweet friend. It is not strange   19
That women will be false and wavering.
ARD. Ay, but to dote on such a one as he
Is monstrous, Franklin, and intolerable.
FRANK. Why, what is he?
ARD. A botcher,[2] and no better at the first,

---

[1] The title continues: "Who Was Most Wickedly Murdered by the Means of His Disloyal and Wanton Wife, Who for the Love She Bare to One Mosbie Hired Two Desperate Ruffians, Black Will and Shakebag, to Kill Him. Wherein Is Showed the Great Malice and Dissimulation of a Wicked Woman, the Unsatiable Desire of Filthy Lust, and the Shameful End of All Murderers."

[2] A patcher of old clothes, a tailor.

Who, by base brokage getting some small
    stock,
Crept into service of a nobleman,
And by his servile flattery and fawning
Is now become the steward of his house,
And bravely jets it [1] in his silken gown.
FRANK. No nobleman will count'nance
    such a peasant.   30
ARD. Yes, the Lord Clifford, he that loves
    not me.
But through his favor let him not grow
    proud;
For, were he by the lord protector
    backed,
He should not make me to be pointed at.
I am by birth a gentleman of blood,
And that injurious ribald that attempts
To violate my dear wife's chastity
(For dear I hold her love, as dear as
    heaven)
Shall on the bed which he thinks to defile
See his dissevered joints and sinews torn,
Whilst on the planchers [2] pants his weary
    body,   41
Smeared in the channels of his lustful
    blood.
FRANK. Be patient, gentle friend, and
    learn of me
To ease thy grief and save her chastity.
Entreat her fair; sweet words are fittest
    engines
To race [3] the flint walls of a woman's
    breast.
In any case be not too jealous,[4]
Nor make no question of her love to thee;
But, as securely,[5] presently [6] take horse,
And lie with me at London all this term;
For women, when they may, will not, 51
But, being kept back, straight grow out-
    rageous.
ARD. Though this abhors from [7] reason, yet
    I'll try it,
And call her forth and presently take
    leave.—How! Alice!

Here enters Alice.

ALICE. Husband, what mean you to get
    up so early?
Summer nights are short, and yet you
    rise ere day.

Had I been wake, you had not rise [8] so
    soon.
ARD. Sweet love, thou know'st that we
    two, Ovid-like,
Have often chid the morning when it gan
    to peep,
And often wished that dark Night's pur-
    blind steeds   60
Would pull her by the purple mantle
    back,
And cast her in the ocean to her love.
But this night, sweet Alice, thou hast
    killed my heart:
I heard thee call on Mosbie in thy sleep.
ALICE. 'Tis like I was asleep when I named
    him,
For, being awake, he comes not in my
    thoughts.
ARD. Ay, but you started up and suddenly,
Instead of him, caught me about the
    neck.
ALICE. Instead of him? Why, who was
    there but you?   69
And where but one is, how can I mistake?
FRANK. Arden, leave [9] to urge her overfar.
ARD. Nay, love, there is no credit in a
    dream;
Let it suffice I know thou lovest me well.
ALICE. Now I remember whereupon it
    came:
Had we no talk of Mosbie yesternight?
FRANK. Mistress Alice, I heard you name
    him once or twice.
ALICE. And thereof came it, and therefore
    blame not me.
ARD. I know it did, and therefore let it
    pass.
I must to London, sweet Alice, presently.
ALICE. But, tell me, do you mean to stay
    there long?   80
ARD. No longer there till my affairs be
    done.
FRANK. He will not stay above a month at
    most.
ALICE. A month? Ay me! Sweet Arden,
    come again
Within a day or two, or else I die.
ARD. I cannot long be from thee, gentle
    Alice.
Whilst Michael fetch our horses from the
    field,
Franklin and I will down unto the quay,

---

[1] Struts.
[2] Planks, wooden floor.
[3] Raze.
[4] Common form for *jealous*
[5] As if unsuspicious.
[6] Immediately.
[7] Is at variance with.
[8] An old form of the past participle.
[9] Cease.

For I have certain goods there to unload.
Meanwhile prepare our breakfast, gentle
    Alice,
For yet ere noon we'll take horse and
    away.   90
        Exeunt Arden and Franklin.
ALICE. Ere noon he means to take horse
    and away!
Sweet news is this. O, that some airy
    spirit
Would in the shape and likeness of a
    horse
Gallop with Arden cross the ocean,
And throw him from his back into the
    waves!
Sweet Mosbie is the man that hath my
    heart,
And he usurps it, having naught but this,
That I am tied to him by marriage.
Love is a god, and marriage is but words;
And therefore Mosbie's title is the best.
Tush! whether it be or no, he shall be
    mine,   101
In spite of him, of Hymen, and of rites.

Here enters Adam of the Flower-de-Luce.

And here comes Adam of the Flower-de-
    Luce.
I hope he brings me tidings of my love.—
How now, Adam, what is the news with
    you?
Be not afraid; my husband is now from
    home.
ADAM. He whom you wot [1] of, Mosbie,
    Mistress Alice,
Is come to town, and sends you word by
    me
In any case you may not visit him.
ALICE. Not visit him?   110
ADAM. No, nor take no knowledge of his
    being here.
ALICE. But, tell me, is he angry or dis-
    pleased?
ADAM. Should seem so, for he is wondrous
    sad.
ALICE. Were he as mad as raving Hercules,
I'll see him, I; and, were thy house of
    force,[2]
These hands of mine should race it to
    the ground,
Unless that thou wouldst bring me to
    my love.

ADAM. Nay, and [3] you be so impatient, I'll
    be gone.
ALICE. Stay, Adam, stay; thou wert wont
    to be my friend.
Ask Mosbie how I have incurred his
    wrath;   120
Bear him from me these pair of silver
    dice,
With which we played for kisses many a
    time,
And, when I lost, I won, and so did he
(Such winning and such losing Jove send
    me!);
And bid him, if his love do not decline,
[To] [4] come this morning but along my
    door,
And as a stranger but salute me there.
This may he do without suspect [5] or fear.
ADAM. I'll tell him what you say, and so
    farewell.   *Exit Adam.*
ALICE. Do, and one day I'll make amends
    for all.—   130
I know he loves me well, but dares not
    come,
Because my husband is so jealous,
And these my marrow [6]-prying neigh-
    bors' blab
Hinder our meetings, when we would
    confer.
But, if I live, that block shall be removed,
And, Mosbie, thou that comes to me by
    stealth
Shalt neither fear the biting speech of
    men
Nor Arden's looks. As surely shall he die
As I abhor him and love only thee.

Here enters Michael.

How now, Michael, whither are you go-
    ing?   140
MICH. To fetch my master's nag.
I hope you'll think on me.
ALICE. Ay; but, Michael, see you keep
    your oath,
And be as secret as you are resolute.
MICH. I'll see he shall not live above a
    week.
ALICE. On that condition, Michael, here is
    my hand;
None shall have Mosbie's sister but thy-
    self.

---

[1] Know.   [2] Fortified.
[3] If.   [4] Added in 1633 edn.
[5] Suspicion.   [6] Later quartos have *narrow.*

MICH. I understand the painter here hard by

Hath made report that he and Sue is sure.[1]

ALICE. There's no such matter, Michael; believe it not.   150

MICH. But he hath sent a dagger sticking in a heart,

With a verse or two stolen from a painted cloth,[2]

The which I hear the wench keeps in her chest.

Well, let her keep it! I shall find a fellow

That can both write and read and make rime too.

And if I do—well, I say no more.

I'll send from London such a taunting letter

As[3] [she][4] shall eat the heart he sent with salt

And fling the dagger at the painter's head.

ALICE. What needs all this? I say that Susan's thine.   160

MICH. Why, then I say that I will kill my master,

Or anything that you will have me do.

ALICE. But, Michael, see you do it cunningly.

MICH. Why, say I should be took, I'll ne'er confess

That you know anything; and Susan, being a maid,

May beg me from the gallows of the shrieve.[5]

ALICE. Trust not to that, Michael.

MICH. You cannot tell me; I have seen it, I.

But, mistress, tell her, whether I live or die,

I'll make her more worth than twenty painters can,   170

For I will rid mine elder brother away,

And then the farm of Bolton is mine own.

Who would not venture upon house and land,

When he may have it for a right-down[6] blow?

[1] Betrothed.   [3] That.
[2] Hangings for a room.   [4] Supplied by Delius.
[5] Sheriff. "It was a popular belief that an offer of marriage from a virgin might save a criminal from the gallows" (Oliphant).
[6] Downright.

Here enters Mosbie.

ALICE. Yonder comes Mosbie! Michael, get thee gone,

And let not him nor any know thy drifts.[7]
Exit Michael.

Mosbie, my love!

MOS. Away, I say, and talk not to me now!

ALICE. A word or two, sweetheart, and then I will.

'Tis yet but early days;[8] thou needest not fear.   180

MOS. Where is your husband?

ALICE. 'Tis now high water, and he is at the quay.

MOS. There let him be; henceforward know me not.

ALICE. Is this the end of all thy solemn oaths?

Is this the fruit thy reconcilement buds?

Have I for this given thee so many favors,

Incurred my husband's hate, and, out alas,

Made shipwrack of mine honor for thy sake?

And dost thou say, "Henceforward know me not"?

Remember, when I locked thee in my closet,[9]   190

What were thy words and mine. Did we not both

Decree to murder Arden in the night?

The heavens can witness, and the world can tell,

Before I saw that falsehood look of thine,

Fore I was tangled with thy ticing[10] speech,

Arden to me was dearer than my soul—

And shall be still. Base peasant, get thee gone,

And boast not of thy conquest over me,

Gotten by witchcraft and mere[11] sorcery!

For what hast thou to countenance[12] my love,   200

Being descended of a noble house,

And matched already with a gentleman

Whose servant thou mayst be? And so farewell.

MOS. Ungentle and unkind Alice, now I see

That which I ever feared, and find too true:

[7] Plots.   [10] Enticing.
[8] Early in the day.   [11] Absolute.
[9] Private chamber.   [12] Be in keeping with.

A woman's love is as the lightning-
   flame,
Which even in bursting forth consumes
   itself.
To try thy constancy have I been
   strange.
Would I had never tried, but lived in
   hope!
ALICE. What needs thou try me whom
   thou never found false?   210
Mos. Yet pardon me, for love is jealous.
ALICE. So list [1] the sailor to the mermaid's
   song;
So looks the traveler to the basilisk.
I am content for to be reconciled,
And that, I know, will be mine over-
   throw.
Mos. Thine overthrow? First let the world
   dissolve.
ALICE. Nay, Mosbie, let me still enjoy
   thy love,
And, happen what will, I am resolute.
My saving husband hoards up bags of
   gold   219
To make our children rich, and now is he
Gone to unload the goods that shall be
   thine,
And he and Franklin will to London
   straight.
Mos. To London, Alice? If thou'lt be
   ruled by me,
We'll make him sure enough for coming
   there.
ALICE. Ah, would we could!
Mos. I happened on a painter yesternight,
The only cunning man of Christendom,
For he can temper poison with his oil,
That whoso looks upon the work he
   draws
Shall, with the beams that issue from
   his [2] sight,   230
Suck venom to his breast and slay him-
   self.
Sweet Alice, he shall draw thy counter-
   feit,
That Arden may, by gazing on it, perish.
ALICE. Ay, but, Mosbie, that is dangerous,
For thou, or I, or any other else,
Coming into the chamber where it hangs,
   may die.
Mos. Ay, but we'll have it covered with a
   cloth
And hung up in the study for himself.

[1] Listens.   [2] Its.

ALICE. It may not be, for, when the pic-
   ture's drawn,   239
Arden, I know, will come and show it me.
Mos. Fear not; we'll have that shall serve
   the turn.   [*They cross the stage.*]
This is the painter's house; I'll call him
   forth.
ALICE. But, Mosbie, I'll have no such pic-
   ture, I.
Mos. I pray thee leave it to my discretion.
   How, Clarke!

Here enters Clarke.

O, you are an honest man of your word;
   you served me well.
CLARKE. Why, sir, I'll do it for you at
   any time,
Provided, as you have given your word,
I may have Susan Mosbie to my wife.
For, as sharp-witted poets, whose sweet
   verse
Make heavenly gods break off their nec-
   tar draughts   250
And lay their ears down to the lowly
   earth,
Use humble promise to their sacred muse,
So we that are the poets' favorites
Must have a love.   Ay, Love is the
   painter's muse,
That makes him frame a speaking coun-
   tenance,
A weeping eye that witnesses heart's
   grief.
Then tell me, Master Mosbie, shall I
   have her?
ALICE. 'Tis pity but he should; he'll use
   her well.
Mos. Clarke, here's my hand; my sister
   shall be thine.
CLARKE. Then, brother, to requite this
   courtesy,   260
You shall command my life, my skill,
   and all.
ALICE. Ah, that thou couldst be secret!
Mos. Fear him not. Leave; I have talked
   sufficient.
CLARKE. You know not me that ask such
   questions.
Let it suffice I know you love him well,
And fain would have your husband made
   away;
Wherein, trust me, you show a noble
   mind.

That rather than you'll live with him
   you hate,
You'll venture life, and die with him
   you love.
The like will I do for my Susan's sake. 270
ALICE. Yet nothing could enforce me to
   the deed
But Mosbie's love. Might I without
   control
Enjoy thee still, then Arden should not
   die;
But, seeing I cannot, therefore let him
   die.
Mos. Enough, sweet Alice; thy kind words
   makes me melt.
Your trick of poisoned pictures we dis-
   like;
Some other poison would do better far.
ALICE. Ay, such as might be put into his
   broth,
And yet in taste not to be found at all.
CLARKE. I know your mind, and here I
   have it for you.   280
Put but a dram of this into his drink,
Or any kind of broth that he shall eat,
And he shall die within an hour after.
ALICE. As I am a gentlewoman, Clarke,
   next day
Thou and Susan shall be marriéd.
Mos. And I'll make her dowry more than
   I'll talk of, Clarke.
CLARKE. Yonder's your husband. Mosbie,
   I'll be gone.

Here enters Arden and Franklin.

ALICE. In good time [1] see where my hus-
   band comes.
Master Mosbie, ask him the question
   yourself.   *Exit Clarke.*
Mos. Master Arden, being at London yes-
   ternight,   290
The Abbey lands, whereof you are now
   possessed,
Were offered me on some occasion
By Greene, one of Sir Antony Ager's men.
I pray you, sir, tell me, are not the lands
   yours?
Hath any other interest herein?
ARD. Mosbie, that question we'll decide
   anon.
Alice, make ready my breakfast; I must
   hence.   *Exit Alice.*

[1] At the right moment.

As for the lands, Mosbie, they are mine
By letters patents from his majesty. 299
But I must have a mandate for my wife;
They say you seek to rob me of her love.
Villain, what makes thou in her com-
   pany?
She's no companion for so base a groom.
Mos. Arden, I thought not on her; I came
   to thee;
But rather than I pocket up this wrong—
FRANK. [*Interposing.*] What will you do,
   sir?
Mos. Revenge it on the proudest of you
   both.
Then Arden draws forth Mosbie's sword.
ARD. So, sirrah. You may not wear a
   sword—
The statute makes against artificers. [2]
I warrand that I do. [3] Now use your bod-
   kin,   310
Your Spanish needle, and your pressing
   iron,
For this shall go with me. And mark my
   words—
You goodman botcher, 'tis to you I
   speak—
The next time that I take thee near my
   house,
Instead of legs I'll make thee crawl on
   stumps.
Mos. Ah, Master Arden, you have injured
   me;
I do appeal to God and to the world.
FRANK. Why, canst thou deny thou wert
   a botcher once?
Mos. Measure me what I am, not what I
   was.
ARD. Why, what art thou now but a velvet
   drudge,   320
A cheating steward, and base-minded
   peasant?
Mos. Arden, now thou hast belched and
   vomited
The rancorous venom of thy misswoln
   heart,
Hear me but speak. As I intend to live
With God and his elected saints in
   heaven,
I never meant more to solicit her;
And that she knows, and all the world
   shall see.

[2] Provides against the wearing of swords by
handicraftsmen.
[3] I have warrant for what I do.

I loved her once—sweet Arden, pardon
  me.
I could not choose; her beauty fired my
  heart!
But time hath quenched these over-
  raging coals;   330
And, Arden, though I now frequent thy
  house,
'Tis for my sister's sake, her waiting-
  maid,
And not for hers. Mayest thou enjoy
  her long!
Hell-fire and wrathful vengeance light
  on me,
If I dishonor her or injure thee.
ARD. Mosbie, with these thy protestations
The deadly hatred of my heart is ap-
  peased,
And thou and I'll be friends, if this prove
  true.
As for the base terms I gave thee late,
Forget them, Mosbie; I had cause to
  speak,   340
When all the knights and gentlemen of
  Kent
Make common table talk of her and thee.
MOS. Who lives that is not touched with
  slanderous tongues?
FRANK. Then, Mosbie, to eschew the
  speech of men,
Upon whose general bruit [1] all honor
  hangs,
Forbear his house.
ARD. Forbear it! Nay, rather frequent it
  more.
The world shall see that I distrust her
  not.
To warn him on the sudden from my
  house
Were to confirm the rumor that is
  grown.   350
MOS. By my faith, sir,[2] you say true,
And therefore will I sojourn here awhile,
Until our enemies have talked their fill;
And then, I hope, they'll cease, and at
  last confess
How causeless they have injured her and
  me.
[*They pass to a room on the inner stage.*]
ARD. And I will lie at London all this term
To let them see how light I weigh their
  words.

[1] Report.
[2] All early edns. read *By faith, my sir.*

Here enters Alice.

ALICE. Husband, sit down; your breakfast
  will be cold.
ARD. Come, M[aster] Mosbie, will you sit
  with us?
MOS. I cannot eat, but I'll sit for com-
  pany.   360
ARD. Sirrah Michael, see our horse be
  ready.
ALICE. Husband, why pause ye? Why eat
  you not?
ARD. I am not well. There's something
  in this broth
That is not wholesome. Didst thou make
  it, Alice?
ALICE. I did, and that's the cause it likes
  not you.
Then she throws down the broth on the ground.
There's nothing that I do can please your
  taste.
You were best to say I would have poi-
  soned you.
I cannot speak or cast aside my eye,
But he imagines I have stepped awry.
Here's he that you cast in my teeth so
  oft;   370
Now will I be convinced or purge myself.
I charge thee speak to this mistrustful
  man,
Thou that wouldst see me hang, thou,
  Mosbie, thou.
What favor hast thou had more than a
  kiss
At coming or departing from the town?
MOS. You wrong yourself and me to cast
  these doubts;
Your loving husband is not jealous.
ARD. Why, gentle Mistress Alice, cannot
  I be ill
But you'll accuse yourself?—
Franklin, thou hast a box of mithri-
  date;   380
I'll take a little to prevent the worst.
FRANK. Do so, and let us presently take
  horse;
My life for yours, ye shall do well enough.
ALICE. Give me a spoon; I'll eat of it my-
  self.
Would it were full of poison to the brim,
Then should my cares and troubles have
  an end!
Was ever silly [3] woman so tormented?

[3] Simple.

ARD. Be patient, sweet love; I mistrust
not thee.

ALICE. God will revenge it, Arden, if thou
dost;

For never woman loved her husband
better than I do thee.   390

ARD. I know it, sweet Alice. Cease to
complain,

Lest that in tears I answer thee again.

FRANK. Come, leave this dallying, and let
us away.

ALICE. Forbear to wound me with that
bitter word;

Arden shall go to London in my arms.

ARD. Loath am I to depart, yet I must go.

ALICE. Wilt thou to London, then, and
leave me here?

Ah, if thou love me, gentle Arden, stay.

Yet, if thy business be of great import,   399

Go, if thou wilt; I'll bear it as I may.

But write from London to me every week,

Nay, every day, and stay no longer there

Than thou must needs, lest that I die for
sorrow.

ARD. I'll write unto thee every other tide.

And so farewell, sweet Alice, till we meet
next.

ALICE. Farewell, husband, seeing you'll
have it so;

And, M[aster] Franklin, seeing you take
him hence,

In hope you'll hasten him home, I'll give
you this.   *And then she kisseth him.*

FRANK. And if he stay, the fault shall not
be mine.

Mosbie, farewell, and see you keep your
oath.   410

Mos. I hope he is not jealous of me now.

ARD. No, Mosbie, no; hereafter think of
me

As of your dearest friend, and so farewell.
Exeunt Arden, Franklin, and Michael.

ALICE. I am glad he is gone; he was about
to stay,

But did you mark me then how I brake
off?

Mos. Ay, Alice, and it was cunningly performed.

But what a villain is that painter Clarke!

ALICE. Was it not a goodly poison that he
gave?

Why, he's as well now as he was before.   419

It should have been some fine confection

That might have given the broth some
dainty taste.

This powder was too gross and populous.[1]

Mos. But, had he eaten but three spoonfuls more,

Then had he died and our love continued.

ALICE. Why, so it shall, Mosbie, albeit he
live.

Mos. It is unpossible, for I have sworn

Never hereafter to solicit thee,

Or, whilst he lives, once more importune
thee.

ALICE. Thou shalt not need; I will importune thee.

What? Shall an oath make thee forsake
my love?   430

As if I have not sworn as much myself

And given my hand unto him in the
church!

Tush, Mosbie; oaths are words, and
words is wind,

And wind is mutable. Then, I conclude,

'Tis childishness to stand upon an oath.

Mos. Well proved, Mistress Alice; yet by
your leave

I'll keep mine unbroken whilst he lives.

ALICE. Ay, do, and spare not; his time is
but short;

For, if thou beest as resolute as I,

We'll have him murdered as he walks the
streets.   440

In London, many alehouse ruffians keep,[2]

Which, as I hear, will murther men for
gold.

They shall be soundly feed to pay him
home.

Here enters Greene.

Mos. Alice, what's he that comes yonder?
Knowest thou him?

ALICE. Mosbie, begone! I hope 'tis one
that comes

To put in practice our intended drifts.
Exit Mosbie.

GREENE. Mistress Arden, you are well
met.

I am sorry that your husband is from
home,

Whenas[3] my purposed journey was to
him;   449

Yet all my labor is not spent in vain,

----

[1] Thick.   [2] Lodge.   [3] Since.

For I suppose that you can full dis-
course
And flat resolve [1] me of the thing I
seek.
ALICE. What is it, Master Greene? If that
I may
Or can with safety, I will answer you.
GREENE. I heard your husband had the
grant of late,
Confirmed by letters patents from the
king,
Of all the lands of the Abbey of Fever-
sham,
Generally intitled, [2] so that all former
grants
Are cut off, whereof I myself had one;
But now my interest by that is void. 460
This is all, Mistress Arden. Is it true
or no? [3]
ALICE. True, Master Greene; the lands
are his in state, [4]
And whatsoever leases were before
Are void for term of Master Arden's life.
He hath the grant under the chancery
seal.
GREENE. Pardon me, Mistress Arden, I
must speak,
For I am touched. Your husband doth
me wrong
To wring me from the little land I have.
My living is my life; only that
Resteth remainder of my portion. 470
Desire of wealth is endless in his mind,
And he is greedy-gaping still [5] for gain;
Nor cares he though young gentlemen do
beg,
So he may scrape and hoard up in his
pouch.
But, seeing he hath taken my lands, I'll
value life
As careless as he is careful for to get;
And tell him this from me, I'll be re-
venged,
And so as he shall wish the Abbey lands
Had rested still within their former
state. 479
ALICE. Alas, poor gentleman, I pity you,
And woe is me that any man should
want!
God knows 'tis not my fault. But wonder
not

Though he be hard to others, when to
me—
Ah, Master Greene, God knows how I
am used!
GREENE. Why, Mistress Arden, can the
crabbéd churl
Use you unkindly? Respects he not your
birth,
Your honorable friends, nor what you
brought?
Why, all Kent knows your parentage and
what you are.
ALICE. Ah, M[aster] Greene, be it spoken
in secret here, 489
I never live good day with him alone.
When he is at home, then have I froward
looks,
Hard words, and blows to mend the
match withal;
And, though I might content as good a
man,
Yet doth he keep in every corner trulls;
And, weary with his trugs [6] at home,
Then rides he straight to London; there,
forsooth,
He revels it among such filthy ones
As counsels him to make away his wife.
Thus live I daily in continual fear,
In sorrow, so despairing of redress 500
As every day I wish with hearty prayer
That he or I were taken forth the world.
GREENE. Now trust me, Mistress Alice, it
grieveth me
So fair a creature should be so abused.
Why, who would have thought the civil
sir so sullen?
He looks so smoothly. Now, fie upon
him, churl!
And, if he live a day, he lives too long.
But frolic, woman! I shall be the man
Shall set you free from all this discon-
tent;
And, if the churl deny my interest 510
And will not yield my lease into my hand,
I'll pay him home, whatever hap to
me.
ALICE. But speak you as you think?
GREENE. Ay, God's my witness, I mean
plain dealing,
For I had rather die than lose my land.
ALICE. Then, Master Greene, be coun-
seléd by me.
Endanger not yourself for such a churl,

---

[1] Completely satisfy.   [2] Deeded.
[3] From 1599 edn. Original has *nor*.
[4] By law.   [5] Always.
[6] Wenches.

But hire some cutter [1] for to cut him
short,
And here's ten pound to wager them
withal.
When he is dead, you shall have twenty
more,   520
And the lands whereof my husband is
possessed
Shall be intitled as they were before.
GREENE. Will you keep promise with me?
ALICE. Or count me false and perjured
whilst I live.
GREENE. Then here's my hand; I'll have
him so despatched.
I'll up to London straight; I'll thither
post,
And never rest till I have compassed it.
Till then farewell.
ALICE. Good fortune follow all your for-
ward thoughts,   529
Exit Greene.
And whosoever doth attempt the deed,
A happy hand I wish, and so farewell.—
All this goes well. Mosbie, I long for
thee
To let thee know all that I have con-
trived.

Here enters Mosbie and Clarke.

MOS. How now, Alice, what's the news?
ALICE. Such as will content thee well,
sweetheart.
MOS. Well, let them pass awhile, and tell
me, Alice,
How have you dealt and tempered with [2]
my sister?
What, will she have my neighbor, Clarke,
or no?
ALICE. What, M[aster] Mosbie! Let him
woo himself!
Think you that maids look not for fair
words?   540
Go to her, Clarke; she's all alone within.
Michael, my man, is clean out of her
books.
CLARKE. I thank you, Mistress Arden. I
will in;
And, if fair Susan and I can make a
gree, [3]
You shall command me to the uttermost,
As far as either goods or life may stretch.
Exit Clarke.

MOS. Now, Alice, let's hear thy news.
ALICE. They be so good that I must laugh
for joy
Before I can begin to tell my tale.
MOS. Let's hear them, that I may laugh
for company.   550
ALICE. This morning, M[aster] Greene—
Dick Greene, I mean,
From whom my husband had the Abbey
land—
Came hither, railing, for to know the
truth
Whether my husband had the lands by
grant.
I told him all, whereat he stormed amain
And swore he would cry quittance with [4]
the churl,
And, if he did deny his interest,
Stab him, whatsoever did befall himself.
Whenas [5] I saw his choler thus to rise,
I whetted on the gentleman with words;
And, to conclude, Mosbie, at last we
grew   561
To composition [6] for my husband's death.
I gave him ten pound to hire knaves,
By some device to make away the churl;
When he is dead, he should have twenty
more
And repossess his former lands again.
On this we greed, and he is ridden
straight
To London to bring his death about.
MOS. But call you this good news?
ALICE. Ay, sweetheart, be they not?   570
MOS. 'Twere cheerful news to hear the
churl were dead;
But trust me, Alice, I take it passing ill
You would be so forgetful of our state
To make recount of it to every groom.
What! to acquaint each stranger with our
drifts,
Chiefly in case of murther, why, 'tis the
way
To make it open unto Arden's self
And bring thyself and me to ruin both.
Forewarned, forearmed; who threats his
enemy,
Lends him a sword to guard himself
withal.   580
ALICE. I did it for the best.
MOS. Well, seeing 'tis done, cheerly [7] let
it pass.

---

[1] Cutthroat. [3] Reach an agreement.
[2] Worked upon.

[4] Be even with. [5] When.
[6] Agreement. [7] Cheerfully.

You know this Greene; is he not religious? [1]
A man, I guess, of great devotion?

ALICE. He is.

Mos. Then, sweet Alice, let it pass; I
have a drift
Will quiet all, whatever is amiss.

Here enters Clarke and Susan.

ALICE. How now, Clarke? Have you
found me false?
Did I not plead the matter hard for you?

CLARKE. You did.   590

Mos. And what? Wilt be a match?

CLARKE. A match, i' faith, sir; ay, the
day is mine.
The painter lays his colors to the life;
His pencil draws no shadows in his love.
Susan is mine.

ALICE. You make her blush.

Mos. What, sister, is it Clarke must be
the man?

Sus. It resteth in your grant. Some words
are passed,
And happily [2] we be grown unto a match,
If you be willing that it shall be so. 600

Mos. Ah, Master Clarke, it resteth at my
grant;
You see my sister's yet at my dispose.
But, so you'll grant me one thing I shall
ask,
I am content my sister shall be yours.

CLARKE. What is it, M[aster] Mosbie?

Mos. I do remember once in secret talk
You told me how you could compound
by art
A crucifix impoisoned,
That whoso look upon it should wax
blind
And with the scent be stifled, that ere
long   610
He should die poisoned that did view it
well.
I would have you make me such a
crucifix,
And then I'll grant my sister shall be
yours.

CLARKE. Though I am loath, because it
toucheth life,
Yet, rather or I'll leave sweet Susan's
love,
I'll do it, and with all the haste I may.
But for whom is it?

[1] Conscientious.   [2] Haply, perchance.

ALICE. Leave that to us. Why, Clarke, is
it possible
That you should paint and draw it out
yourself,   619
The colors being baleful and impoisoned,
And no ways prejudice [3] yourself withal?

Mos. Well questioned, Alice.—Clarke,
how answer you that? [4]

CLARKE. Very easily: I'll tell you straight
How I do work of these impoisoned drugs.
I fasten on my spectacles so close
As nothing can any way offend my sight;
Then, as I put a leaf within my nose,
So put I rhubarb to avoid the smell,
And softly as another work I paint.

Mos. 'Tis very well. But against when
shall I have it?   630

CLARKE. Within this ten days.

Mos.   'Twill serve the turn.
Now, Alice, let's in and see what cheer
you keep.
I hope, now M[aster] Arden is from home,
You'll give me leave to play your hus-
band's part.

ALICE. Mosbie, you know, who's master
of my heart,
He well may be the master of the house.
E[x]eunt.

[SCENE ii.
The road between Feversham and London.]

Here enters Greene and Bradshaw.

BRAD. See you them that comes yonder,
M[aster] Greene?

GREENE. Ay, very well. Do you know
them?

Here enters Black Will and Shakebag.

BRAD. The one I know not, but he seems a
knave,
Chiefly for bearing the other company;
For such a slave, so vile a rogue as he,
Lives not again upon the earth.
Black Will is his name. I tell you,
M[aster] Greene,
At Boulogne he and I were fellow soldiers,
Where he played such pranks
As all the camp feared him for his
villainy.   10
I warrant you he bears so bad a mind
That for a crown he'll murther any man.

[3] Endanger.
[4] Here and in a few later passages the line
divisions have been regularized.

GREENE. The fitter is he for my purpose, marry!

WILL. How now, fellow Bradshaw? Whither away so early?

BRAD. O Will, times are changed. No fellows now,

Though we were once together in the field;

Yet thy friend to do thee any good I can.

WILL.[1] Why, Bradshaw, was not thou and I fellow soldiers at Boulogne, [20 where I was a corporal, and thou but a base mercenary groom? No fellows now, because you are a goldsmith and have a little plate in your shop! You were glad to call me "fellow Will," and with a cursy[2] to the earth, "One snatch, good corporal," when I stole the half ox from John the victualer, and domineered[3] with it amongst good fellows in one night.   29

BRAD. Ay, Will, those days are past with me.

WILL. Ay, but they be not past with me, for I keep that same honorable mind still. Good neighbor Bradshaw, you are too proud to be my fellow, but, were it not that I see more company coming down the hill, I would be fellows with you once more, and share crowns with you too. But let that pass, and tell me whither you go.   40

BRAD. To London, Will, about a piece of service

Wherein happily thou mayst pleasure me.

WILL. What is it?

BRAD. Of late Lord Cheiny lost some plate,

Which one did bring and sold it at my shop,

Saying he served Sir Antony Cooke.

A search was made, the plate was found with me,

And I am bound to answer at the size.[4]

Now, Lord Cheiny solemnly vows,

If law will serve him, he'll hang me for his plate.   50

Now I am going to London upon hope

To find the fellow. Now, Will, I know

Thou art acquainted with such companions.

WILL. What manner of man was he?

BRAD. A lean-faced, writhen[5] knave,

Hawk-nosed and very hollow-eyed,

With mighty furrows in his stormy brows;

Long hair down his shoulders curled;

His chin was bare, but on his upper lip A mutchado,[6] which he wound about his ear.   60

WILL. What apparel had he?

BRAD. A watchet[7] satin doublet all-to[8] torn

(The inner side did bear the greater show),

A pair of threadbare velvet hose, seam-rent,

A worsted stocking rent above the shoe,

A livery cloak, but all the lace was off;

'Twas bad, but yet it served to hide the plate.

WILL. Sirrah Shakebag, canst thou remember since we trolled the bowl[9] at Sittingburgh, where I broke the tap- [70 ster's head of the Lion with a cudgel-stick?

SHAKE. Ay, very well, Will.

WILL. Why, it was with the money that the plate was sold for. Sirrah Bradshaw, what wilt thou give him that can tell thee who sold thy plate?

BRAD. Who, I pray thee, good Will?

WILL. Why, 'twas one Jack Fitten. He's now in Newgate for stealing a horse, and shall be arraigned the next size.   80

BRAD. Why, then let Lord Cheiny seek Jack Fitten forth,

For I'll back and tell him who robbed him of his plate.

This cheers my heart. M[aster] Greene, I'll leave you,

For I must to the Isle of Sheppy with speed.

GREENE. Before you go, let me entreat you

To carry this letter to Mistress Arden of Feversham

And humbly recommend me to herself.

BRAD. That will I, M[aster] Greene, and so farewell.—

Here, Will, there's a crown for thy good news.   *Exit Bradshaw.*

WILL. Farewell, Bradshaw; I'll [90

---

[1] The passages printed as prose throughout the play are printed as rough verse in the original (with the exception of the letters).

[2] Curtsey.
[3] Lived like a lord, feasted.
[4] Assizes.

[5] Twisted.
[6] Mustache.
[7] Pale blue.
[8] Completely
[9] Passed the drinking cup.

drink no water for thy sake whilst this lasts.
—Now, gentleman, shall we have your company to London?

GREENE. Nay, stay, sirs.
A little more I needs must use your help,
And in a matter of great consequence,
Wherein if you'll be secret and profound,
I'll give you twenty angels for your pains.

WILL. How? Twenty angels? Give my
fellow George Shakebag and me twenty [100
angels, and, if thou'lt have thy own
father slain, that thou mayst inherit his
land, we'll kill him.

SHAKE. Ay, thy mother, thy sister, thy
brother, or all thy kin.

GREENE. Well, this it is: Arden of Feversham
Hath highly wronged me about the
  Abbey land,
That no revenge but death will serve
  the turn.
Will you two kill him? Here's the
  angels down,
And I will lay the platform [1] of his
  death. 110

WILL. Plat me no platforms. Give me
the money, and I'll stab him as he stands
pissing against a wall, but I'll kill him.

SHAKE. Where is he?

GREENE. He is now at London, in
Aldersgate Street.

SHAKE. He's dead as if he had been condemned by an act of parliament, if once
Black Will and I swear his death.

GREENE. Here is ten pound, and, [120
when he is dead, ye shall have twenty more.

WILL. My fingers itches to be at the
peasant. Ah, that I might be set awork
thus through the year, and that murther
would grow to an occupation, that a man
might, without danger of law—Zounds,
I warrant I should be warden of the company! Come, let us be going, and we'll
bait [2] at Rochester, where I'll give thee
a gallon of sack to hansel [3] the match
withal. *Exeunt.* 131

[SCENE iii.

A street near St. Paul's, London.]

Here enters Michael.

MICH. I have gotten such a letter as
will touch the painter; and thus it is:

[1] Plan.　　　[2] Stop to feed.　　　[3] Confirm.

*Here enters Arden and Franklin and hears
Michael read this letter.*

"My duty remembered, Mistress Susan,
hoping in God you be in good health, as
I Michael was at the making hereof. This
is to certify you that as the turtle [4] true,
when she hath lost her mate, sitteth alone,
so I, mourning for your absence, do walk
up and down Paul's till one day I fell
asleep and lost my master's pantofles. [5] [10
Ah, Mistress Susan, abolish that paltry
painter, cut him off by the shins with a
frowning look of your crabbed countenance, and think upon Michael, who,
drunk with the dregs of your favor, will
cleave as fast to your love as a plaster
of pitch to a galled horseback. Thus hoping you will let my passions penetrate,
or rather impetrate [6] mercy of your meek
hands, I end. 20
　　Yours,
　　　MICHAEL, or else not MICHAEL."

ARD. Why, you paltry knave,
Stand you here loitering, knowing my
  affairs,
What haste my business craves to send
  to Kent?

FRANK. Faith, friend Michael, this is
  very ill,
Knowing your master hath no more but
  you,
And do ye slack his business for your
  own?

ARD. Where is the letter, sirrah? Let me
  see it. *Then he gives him the letter.*
See, Master Franklin, here's proper
  stuff: 30
Susan my maid, the painter, and my
  man,
A crew of harlots,[7] all in love, forsooth.
Sirrah, let me hear no more of this.
Now for thy life once write to her a
  word!

Here enters Greene, Will, and Shakebag.

Wilt thou be married to so base a trull?
'Tis Mosbie's sister. Come I once at
  home,
I'll rouse her from remaining in my
  house.

[4] Turtledove.　　　　　[6] Obtain by entreaty.
[5] Slippers.　　[7] Worthless persons of either sex.

Now, M[aster] Franklin, let us go walk
in Paul's;
Come but a turn or two, and then away.
Exeunt [Arden, Franklin, and Michael].
GREENE. The first is Arden, and that's his
man;   40
The other is Franklin, Arden's dearest
friend.
WILL. Zounds, I'll kill them all three.
GREENE. Nay, sirs, touch not his man in
any case;
But stand close, and take you fittest
standing,
And, at his coming forth, speed [1] him.
To the Nag's Head; there is this coward's
haunt.
But now I'll leave you till the deed be
done.   *Exit Greene.*
SHAKE. If he be not paid his own, ne'er
trust Shakebag.
WILL. Sirrah Shakebag, at his coming
forth
I'll run him through, and then to the
Blackfriars,   50
And there take water and away.
SHAKE. Why, that's the best; but see
thou miss him not.
WILL. How can I miss him, when I
think on the forty angels I must have
more?

Here enters a Prentice.

PREN. [*Aside.*] 'Tis very late; I were best
shut up my stall,
For here will be old filching,[2] when the
press
Comes forth of Paul's.
*Then lets he down his window, and it breaks
Black Will's head.*
WILL. Zounds, draw, Shakebag, draw!
I am almost killed.   60
PREN. We'll tame you, I warrant.
WILL. Zounds, I am tame enough al-
ready.

Here enters Arden, Fran[klin], and Michael.

ARD. What troublesome fray or mutiny
is this?
FRANK. 'Tis nothing but some brabbling
paltry fray,
Devised to pick men's pockets in the
throng.

[1] Despatch.   [2] Abundant stealing.

ARD. Is't nothing else? Come, Franklin,
let us away.   *Exeunt.*
WILL. What mends [3] shall I have for my
broken head?
PREN. Marry, this mends: that, if you
get you not away all the sooner, you [70
shall be well beaten and sent to the
Counter.[4]   *Exit Prentice.*
WILL. Well, I'll be gone, but look to
your signs, for I'll pull them down all.
Shakebag, my broken head grieves me
not so much as by this means Arden hath
escaped.

Here enters Greene.

I had a glimpse of him and his companion.   79
GREENE. Why, sirs, Arden's as well
as I. I met him and Franklin going merrily
to the ordinary. What, dare you not do
it?
WILL. Yes, sir, we dare do it; but,
were my consent to give again, we would
not do it under ten pound more. I value
every drop of my blood at a French crown.
I have had ten pound to steal a dog, and
we have no more here to kill a man. But [89
that a bargain is a bargain, and so forth,
you should do it yourself.
GREENE. I pray thee, how came thy
head broke?
WILL. Why, thou seest it is broke, dost
thou not?
SHAKE. Standing against a stall, watching Arden's coming, a boy let down his
shop window and broke his head, whereupon arose a brawl, and in the tumult
Arden escaped us and passed by un- [100
thought on. But forbearance is no acquittance; another time we'll do it, I warrant
thee.
GREENE. I pray thee, Will, make clean
thy bloody brow,
And let us bethink us on some other
place
Where Arden may be met with handsomely.
Remember how devoutly thou hast
sworn
To kill the villain; think upon thine oath.
WILL. Tush, I have broken five hundred
oaths!

[3] Amends.   [4] A London prison.

But wouldst thou charm me to effect
this deed,   110
Tell me of gold, my resolution's fee;
Say thou seest Mosbie kneeling at my
knees,
Off'ring me service for my high attempt,
And sweet Alice Arden, with a lap of
crowns,
Comes with a lowly cursy to the earth,
Saying, "Take this but for thy quarter-
age;[1]
Such yearly tribute will I answer [2] thee."
Why, this would steel soft-mettled cow-
ardice,
With which Black Will was never tainted
with.
I tell thee, Greene, the forlorn trav-
eler   120
Whose lips are glued with summer's
parching heat
Ne'er longed so much to see a running
brook
As I to finish Arden's tragedy.
Seest thou this gore that cleaveth to
my face?
From hence ne'er will I wash this bloody
stain,
Till Arden's heart be panting in my hand.
GREENE. Why, that's well said; but what
saith Shakebag?
SHAKE. I cannot paint my valor out with
words;
But, give me place and opportunity,
Such mercy as the starven lioness,   130
When she is dry-sucked of her eager
young,
Shows to the prey that next encounters
her,
On Arden so much pity would I take.
GREENE. So should it fare with men of
firm resolve.
And now, sirs, seeing this accident
Of meeting him in Paul's hath no suc-
cess,
Let us bethink us on some other place
Whose earth may swallow up this Ar-
den's blood.

Here enters Michael.

See, yonder comes his man. And wot
you what?
The foolish knave is in love with Mos-
bie's sister,   140

[1] Quarterly payment.   [2] Render.

And for her sake, whose love he cannot
get
Unless Mosbie solicit his suit,
The villain hath sworn the slaughter
of his master.
We'll question him, for he may stead [3]
us much.—
How now, Michael, whither are you
going?
MICH. My master hath new supped,
And I am going to prepare his chamber.
GREENE. Where supped M[aster] Arden?
MICH. At the Nag's Head, at the
eighteenpence ordinary. How now, [150
M[aster] Shakebag? What, Black Will!
God's dear Lady, how chance your face is
so bloody?
WILL. Go to, sirrah, there is a chance
in it; this sauciness in you will make you
be knocked.
MICH. Nay, and you be offended, I'll be
gone.
GREENE. Stay, Michael; you may not
scape us so.
Michael, I know you love your m[aster]
well.
MICH. Why, so I do; but wherefore urge
you that?   160
GREENE. Because I think you love your
mistress better.
[MICH.] So think not I; but say, i' faith,
what if I should?
SHAKE. Come to the purpose, Michael;
we hear
You have a pretty love in Feversham.
MICH. Why, have I two or three, what's
that to thee?
WILL. You deal too mildly with the
peasant. Thus it is:
'Tis known to us you love Mosbie's
sister;
We know besides that you have ta'en
your oath
To further Mosbie to your mistress'
bed,
And kill your m[aster] for his sister's
sake.   170
Now, sir, a poorer coward than yourself
Was never fostered in the coast of Kent.
How comes it then that such a knave as
you
Dare swear a matter of such conse-
quence?

[3] Help.

GREENE. Ah, Will—

WILL. Tush, give me leave; there's no
  more but this:
Sith [1] thou hast sworn, we dare discover
  all;
And, hadst thou or shouldst thou utter
  it,
We have devised a complat [2] under
  hand,
Whatever shall betide to any of us, 180
To send thee roundly to the devil of
  hell.
And therefore thus: I am the very man,
Marked in my birth hour by the desti-
  nies,
To give an end to Arden's life on earth;
Thou but a member [3] but to whet the
  knife
Whose edge must search the closet of his
  breast.
Thy office is but to appoint the place,
And train thy m[aster] to his tragedy;
Mine to perform it when occasion
  serves.   189
Then be not nice,[4] but here devise with us
How and what way we may conclude
  his death.

SHAKE. So shalt thou purchase Mosbie
  for thy friend,
And by his friendship gain his sister's
  love.

GREENE. So shall thy mistress be thy
  favorer,
And thou disburdened of the oath thou
  made.

MICH. Well, gentlemen, I cannot but con-
  fess,
Sith you have urged me so apparently,
That I have vowed my M[aster] Arden's
  death;
And he whose kindly love and liberal
  hand
Doth challenge naught but good deserts
  of me,   200
I will deliver over to your hands.
This night come to his house at Alders-
  gate;
The doors I'll leave unlocked against [5]
  you come.
No sooner shall ye enter through the
  latch,

Over the threshold to the inner court,
But on your left hand shall you see the
  stairs
That leads directly to my m[aster's]
  chamber.
There take him and dispose him as ye
  please.
Now it were good we parted com-
  pany.   209
What I have promiséd, I will perform.

WILL. Should you deceive us, 'twould
  go wrong with you.

MICH. I will accomplish all I have revealed.

WILL. Come, let's go drink; choler makes
  me as dry as a dog.

Exeunt Will, Gre[ene], and Shak[ebag].
                    Manet [6] Michael.

MICH. Thus feeds the lamb securely on
  the down,
Whilst through the thicket of an arbor
  brake
The hunger-bitten wolf o'erpries [7] his
  haunt
And takes advantage to eat him up.
Ah, harmless Arden, how, how hast
  thou misdone,
That thus thy gentle life is leveled at?
The many good turns that thou hast
  done to me,   220
Now must I quittance [8] with betraying
  thee.
I, that should take the weapon in my
  hand
And buckler thee from ill-intending foes,
Do lead thee with a wicked, fraudful
  smile,
As unsuspected, to the slaughterhouse.
So have I sworn to Mosbie and my mis-
  tress;
So have I promised to the slaughter-
  men;
And, should I not deal currently [9] with
  them,
Their lawless rage would take revenge
  on me.
Tush, I will spurn at mercy for this
  once.   230
Let pity lodge where feeble women
  lie;
I am resolved, and Arden needs must
  die.   *Exit Michael.*

---

[1] Since.   [3] Helper.
[2] Complot, plan.   [4] Squeamish.
  In expectation of the time when.
[6] Remains.   [8] Requite.
[7] Looks over.   [9] Genuinely, honestly.

[SCENE iv.

A room in Franklin's house at Aldersgate.]

Here enters Arden and Fran[klin].

ARD. No, Franklin, no. If fear or stormy
    threats,
If love of me or care of womanhood,
If fear of God or common speech of men,
Who mangle credit with their wounding
    words,
And couch dishonor as dishonor buds,
Might join repentance in her wanton
    thoughts,
No question then but she would turn the
    leaf
And sorrow for her dissolution.[1]
But she is rooted in her wickedness,
Perverse and stubborn, not to be re-
    claimed;   10
Good counsel is to her as rain to weeds,
And reprehension makes her vice to grow
As Hydra's head that flourished [2] by
    decay.
Her faults, methink, are painted in my
    face,
For every searching eye to overread;
And Mosbie's name, a scandal unto mine,
Is deeply trenchéd in my blushing brow.
Ah, Franklin, Franklin, when I think on
    this,
My heart's grief rends my other powers
Worse than the conflict at the hour of
    death.   20
FRANK. Gentle Arden, leave this sad la-
    ment.
She will amend, and so your griefs will
    cease;
Or else she'll die, and so your sorrows
    end.
If neither of these two do happily fall,
Yet let your comfort be that others bear
Your woes, twice doubled all, with pa-
    tience.
ARD. My house is irksome; there I cannot
    rest.
FRANK. Then stay with me in London; go
    not home.
ARD. Then that base Mosbie doth usurp
    my room
And makes his triumph of my being
    thence.   30

[1] Degeneration.
[2] Suggested by Delius; early edns. read *perished.*

At home or not at home, where'er I be,
Here, here it lies [*Points to his heart.*], ah,
    Franklin, here it lies
That will not out till wretched Arden
    dies.

Here enters Michael.

FRANK. Forget your griefs awhile. Here
    comes your man.
ARD. What a-clock is 't, sirrah?
MICH. Almost ten.
ARD. See, see, how runs away the weary
    time!
Come, M[aster] Franklin, shall we go to
    bed?
Exeunt Arden and Michael. Manet Franklin.
FRANK. I pray you, go before; I'll follow
    you.—
Ah, what a hell is fretful jealousy!   40
What pity-moaning [3] words, what deep-
    fetched sighs,
What grievous groans and overlading
    woes
Accompanies this gentle gentleman!
Now will he shake his care-oppresséd
    head,
Then fix his sad eyes on the sullen
    earth,
Ashamed to gaze upon the open world.
Now will he cast his eyes up towards the
    heavens,
Looking that ways for redress of wrong;
Sometimes he seeketh to beguile his grief
And tells a story with his careful [4]
    tongue;   50
Then comes his wife's dishonor in his
    thoughts
And in the middle cutteth off his tale,
Pouring fresh sorrow on his weary limbs.
So woebegone, so inly charged with woe,
Was never any lived and bare it so.

Here enters Michael.

MICH. My m[aster] would desire you come
    to bed.
FRANK. Is he himself already in his bed?
        Exit Fran[klin]. Manet Mic[hael].
MICH. He is, and fain would have the light
    away.—
Conflicting thoughts, encampéd in my
    breast,

[3] In the original *moning*, possibly a misprint
for *mouing* (*i.e., moving*).   [4] Full of care.

Awake me with the echo of their
strokes,   60
And I, a judge to censure either side,
Can give to neither wishéd victory.
My master's kindness pleads to me for life
With just demand, and I must grant it
him;
My mistress she hath forced me with an
oath,
For Susan's sake, the which I may not
break,
For that is nearer than a master's love.
That grim-faced fellow, pitiless Black
Will,
And Shakebag, stern in bloody strata-
gem—
Two rougher ruffians never lived in
Kent—   70
Have sworn my death, if I infringe my
vow,
A dreadful thing to be considered of.
Methinks I see them with their bol-
stered [1] hair,
Staring and grinning in thy gentle face,
And in their ruthless hands their daggers
drawn,
Insulting o'er thee [2] with a peck of oaths,
Whilst thou, submissive, pleading for
relief,
Art mangled by their ireful instruments.
Methinks I hear them ask where Michael
is,
And pitiless Black Will cries, "Stab the
slave!   80
The peasant will detect the tragedy!"
The wrinkles in his foul death-threat'ning
face
Gapes open wide, like graves to swallow
men.
My death to him is but a merriment,
And he will murther me to make him
sport.
He comes, he comes!   Ah, M[aster]
Franklin, help!
Call up the neighbors, or we are but dead!

Here enters Fran[klin] and Arden.

FRANK. What dismal outcry calls me from
my rest?
ARD. What hath occasioned such a fearful
cry?   89
Speak, Michael! Hath any injured thee?

MICH. Nothing, sir; but, as I fell asleep,
Upon the threshold leaning to the stairs,
I had a fearful dream that troubled me,
And in my slumber thought I was beset
With murtherer thieves that came to
rifle me.
My trembling joints witness my inward
fear.
I crave your pardons for disturbing you.
ARD. So great a cry for nothing I ne'er
heard.
What? Are the doors fast locked and all
things safe?
MICH. I cannot tell; I think I locked the
doors.   100
ARD. I like not this, but I'll go see my-
self.—   [*He tries the doors.*]
Ne'er trust me but the doors were all un-
locked.
This negligence not half contenteth me.
Get you to bed, and, if you love my favor,
Let me have no more such pranks as
these.
Come, M[aster] Franklin, let us go to bed.
FRANK. Ay, by my faith; the air is very
cold.—
Michael, farewell; I pray thee dream no
more.   *Exeunt.*

[SCENE V.

Before Franklin's house.]

Here enters Will, Gre[ene], and Shak[ebag]. [3]

SHAKE. Black night hath hid the pleasures
of the day,
And sheeting darkness overhangs the
earth,
And with the black fold of her cloudy
robe
Obscures [4] us from the eyesight of the
world,
In which sweet silence such as we tri-
umph.
The lazy minutes linger on their time,
Loath to give due audit to the hour,
Till in the watch [5] our purpose be com-
plete
And Arden sent to everlasting night.
Greene, get you gone, and linger here
about,   10

[1] Disheveled.
[2] From 1633 edn. Original reads *there.*

[3] The stage direction follows l. 1 in the
original.
[4] From 1633 edn. Earlier edns. read *obscure.*
[5] Time division of the night.

And at some hour hence come to us
again,
Where we will give you instance [1] of his
death.
GREENE. Speed to my wish, whose will so-
e'er says no; [2]
And so I'll leave you for an hour or two.
              Exit Gre[ene].
WILL. I tell thee, Shakebag, would this
thing were done.
I am so heavy that I can scarce go;
This drowsiness in me bodes little good.
SHAKE. How now, Will? Become a Preci-
sian? [3]
Nay, then let's go sleep, when bugs [4] and
fears
Shall kill our courages with their fancy's
work.   20
WILL. Why, Shakebag, thou mistakes me
much,
And wrongs me too in telling me of fear.
Were 't not a serious thing we go about,
It should be slipped [5] till I had fought
with thee,
To let thee know I am no coward, I.
I tell thee, Shakebag, thou abusest me.
SHAKE. Why, thy speech bewrayed an
inly kind of fear,
And savored of a weak, relenting spirit.
Go forward now in that we have begun,
And afterwards attempt [6] me when thou
darest.   30
WILL. And, if I do not, heaven cut me
off!
But let that pass, and show me to this
house,
Where thou shalt see I'll do as much as
Shakebag.
SHAKE. This is the door; but, soft, me-
thinks 'tis shut.
The villain Michael hath deceivéd us.
WILL. Soft, let me see, Shakebag; 'tis shut
indeed.
Knock with thy sword; perhaps the slave
will hear.
SHAKE. It will not be. The white-livered
peasant is gone to bed,
And laughs us both to scorn.
WILL. And he shall buy his merriment as
dear   40

As ever coistrel [7] bought so little sport.
Ne'er let this sword assist me when I
need,
But rust and canker after I have sworn,
If I, the next time that I meet the hind,
Lop not away his leg, his arm, or both.
SHAKE. And let me never draw a sword
again,
Nor prosper in the twilight, cockshut
light, [8]
When I would fleece the wealthy pas-
senger, [9]
But lie and languish in a loathsome den,
Hated and spit at by the goers-by,   50
And in that death may die unpitiéd,
If I, the next time that I meet the slave,
Cut not the nose from off the coward's
face
And trample on it for this villainy.
WILL. Come, let's go seek out Greene. I
know he'll swear.
SHAKE. He were a villain, and [10] he would
not swear.
'Twould make a peasant swear amongst
his boys,
That ne'er durst say before but "yea"
and "no,"
To be thus flouted of a coisterel.
WILL. Shakebag, let's seek out Greene, and
in the morning   60
At the alehouse butting [11] Arden's house
Watch the outcoming of that prick-
eared cur,
And then let me alone to handle him.
              Exeunt.

[SCENE vi.

A room in Franklin's house.]

Here enters Ard[en], Fra[nklin], and Michael.

ARD. Sirrah, get you back to Billens-
gate [12]
And learn what time the tide will serve
our turn;
Come to us in Paul's. First go make the
bed,
And afterwards go hearken for the flood. [13]
              Exit Michael.
Come, M[aster] Franklin, you shall go
with me.

---

[1] Evidence.
[2] *I.e.*, no matter who wills the contrary.
[3] Puritan.   [5] Let go, put aside.
[4] Bugaboos.   [6] Make trial of, attack.
[7] Varlet.
[8] Time when woodcocks (*i.e.*, gulls) are caught.
[9] Passer-by. [11] Abutting on. [12] Billingsgate.
[10] If.   [13] Flood tide.

This night I dreamed that, being in a park,
A toil [1] was pitched to overthrow the deer,
And I upon a little rising hill
Stood whistly [2] watching for the herd's approach.
Even there, methoughts, a gentle slumber took me,   10
And summoned all my parts to sweet repose;
But in the pleasure of this golden rest
An ill-thewed foster [3] had removed the toil
And rounded me with that beguiling home [4]
Which late, methought, was pitched to cast [5] the deer.
With that he blew an evil-sounding horn,
And at the noise another herdman came,
With fauchon [6] drawn, and bent it at my breast,
Crying aloud, "Thou art the game we seek!"
With this I waked and trembled every joint,   20
Like one obscuréd in a little bush,
That sees a lion foraging about,
And, when the dreadful forest-king is gone,
He pries about with timorous suspect
Throughout the thorny casements of the brake,
And will not think his person dangerless,
But quakes and shewers,[7] though the cause be gone.
So, trust me, Franklin, when I did awake,
I stood in doubt whether I waked or no—
Such great impression took [8] this fond [9] surprise.   30
God grant this vision bedeem [10] me any good.

FRANK. This fantasy doth rise from Michael's fear,
Who being awakéd with the noise he made,
His troubled senses yet could take no rest;
And this, I warrant you, procured your dream.

ARD. It may be so; God frame it to the best.
But oftentimes my dreams presage too true.

FRANK. To such as note their nightly fantasies,
Some one in twenty may incur belief.
But use it not: [11] 'tis but a mockery.   40

ARD. Come, M[aster] Franklin, we'll now walk in Paul's
And dine together at the ordinary,
And by my man's direction draw to the quay,
And with the tide go down to Feversham.
Say, M[aster] Franklin, shall it not be so?

FRANK. At your good pleasure, sir;
I'll bear you company.   *Exeunt.*

[SCENE vii.

A street in Aldersgate.]

Here enters Michael at one door. Here enters Greene, Will, and Shakebag at another door.

WILL. Draw, Shakebag, for here's that villain Michael.

GREENE. First, Will, let's hear what he can say.

WILL. Speak, milksop slave, and never after speak!

MICH. For God's sake, sirs, let me excuse myself!
For here I swear, by heaven and earth and all,
I did perform the outmost [12] of my task,
And left the doors unbolted and unlocked.
But see the chance: Franklin and my master
Were very late conferring in the porch,
And Franklin left his napkin [13] where he sat   10
With certain gold knit in it, as he said.
Being in bed, he did bethink himself,
And coming down he found the doors unshut.
He locked the gates, and brought away the keys,
For which offense my master rated me.
But now I am going to see what flood it is,

[1] Net.
[2] Silently.   [3] Unmannerly forester.
[4] Surrounded me completely with that snare.
[5] Throw.   [8] Gave.
[6] Falchion, sword.   [9] Foolishly credulous.
[7] Shivers.   [10] Forebode (").

[11] Do not make a practice of it.
[12] Utmost.   [13] Handkerchief.

For with the tide my m[aster] will away,
Where you may front [1] him well on
    Rainham Down,
A place well fitting such a stratagem.

WILL. Your excuse hath somewhat molli-
    fied my choler.   20
Why now, Greene, 'tis better now nor [2]
    e'er it was.

GREENE. But, Michael, is this true?

MICH. As true as I report it to be true.

SHAKE. Then, Michael, this shall be your
    penance:
To feast us all at the Salutation,
Where we will plat [3] our purpose
    throughly.

GREENE. And, Michael, you shall bear no
    news of this tide,
Because [4] they two may be in Rainham
    Down
Before your m[aster].

MICH. Why, I'll agree to anything you'll
    have me,   30
So you will except of my company.[5]
                     Exeunt.

[SCENE viii.

A room in Arden's house at Feversham.]

Here enters Mosbie.

MOS. Disturbéd thoughts drives me from
    company
And dries my marrow with their watch-
    fulness;
Continual trouble of my moody brain
Feebles my body by excess of drink,
And nips me as the bitter northeast
    wind
Doth check the tender blossoms in the
    spring.
Well fares the man, howe'er his cates [6] do
    taste,
That tables not with foul suspicion;
And he but pines amongst his delicates,
Whose troubled mind is stuffed with dis-
    content.   10
My golden time was when I had no
    gold.
Though [7] then I wanted, yet I slept
    secure;
My daily toil begat me night's repose,

My night's repose made daylight fresh
    to me.
But, since I climbed the top bough of the
    tree
And sought to build my nest among the
    clouds,
Each gentle, stary [8] gale doth shake my
    bed,
And makes me dread my downfall to the
    earth.
But whither doth contemplation carry
    me?
The way I seek to find, where pleasure
    dwells,   20
Is hedged behind me that I cannot
    back,
But needs must on, although to danger's
    gate.
Then, Arden, perish thou by that decree;
For Greene doth ear [9] the land and weed
    thee up
To make my harvest nothing but pure
    corn.
And for his pains I'll heave him up
    awhile,
And after smother him to have his
    wax—
Such bees as Greene must never live to
    sting.
Then is there Michael and the painter
    too,
Chief actors to Arden's overthrow,   30
Who, when they shall see me sit in
    Arden's seat,
They will insult upon me for my meed,[10]
Or fright me by detecting [11] of his end.
I'll none of that, for I can cast a bone
To make these curs pluck out each
    other's throat,
And then am I sole ruler of mine own.
Yet Mistress Arden lives; but she's my-
    self,
And holy church rites makes us two but
    one.
But what for that? I may not trust you,
    Alice.
You have supplanted Arden for my
    sake,   40
And will extirpen [12] me to plant another.
'Tis fearful sleeping in a serpent's bed,
And I will cleanly rid my hands of her.

---

[1] From 1633 edn.; original reads *frons.*
[2] Than.   [3] Plot.   [4] In order that.
[5] Excuse me from accompanying you.
[6] Dainties.   [7] Original reads *thought.*

[8] Stirry (?); stirring (?).   [11] Betraying.
[9] Plow.   [12] Extirpate.
[10] Assail me for my bribe (?).

Here enters Alice.

But here she comes, and I must flatter
her.—
How now, Alice? What, sad and pas-
sionate? [1]
Make me partaker of thy pensiveness;
Fire divided burns with lesser force.

ALICE. But I will dam that fire in my
breast
Till by the force thereof my part consume. Ah, Mosbie!

Mos. Such deep pathaires,[2] like to a can-
non's burst   50
Discharged against a ruinated wall,
Breaks my relenting heart in thousand
pieces.
Ungentle Alice, thy sorrow is my sore;
Thou know'st it well, and 'tis thy policy
To forge distressful looks to wound a
breast
Where lies a heart that dies where thou
art sad.
It is not love that loves to anger love.

ALICE. It is not love that loves to murther
love.

Mos. How mean you that?

ALICE. Thou knowest how dearly Arden
lovéd me.   60

Mos. And then?

ALICE. And then—conceal the rest, for
'tis too bad,
Lest that my words be carried with the
wind,
And published in the world to both our
shames.
I pray thee, Mosbie, let our springtime
wither;
Our harvest else will yield but loathsome
weeds.
Forget, I pray thee, what hath passed
betwix us,
For now I blush and tremble at the
thoughts!

Mos. What, are you changed?

ALICE. Ay, to my former happy life
again,   70
From title of an odious strumpet's name
To honest Arden's wife, not Arden's
honest [3] wife.
Ha, Mosbie, 'tis thou hast rifled me of
that
And made me sland[e]rous to all my kin;

[1] Full of emotion.   [2] Sighs (?).   [3] Chaste.

Even in my forehead is thy name en-
graven,
A mean artificer, that low-born name.
I was bewitched; woe worth the hapless
hour
And all the causes that enchanted me!

Mos. Nay, if thou ban,[4] let me breathe
curses forth,
And, if you stand so nicely [5] at your
fame.   80
Let me repent the credit I have lost.
I have neglected matters of import
That would have stated [6] me above thy
state,
Forslowed [7] advantages, and spurned at
time;
Ay, Fortune's right hand Mosbie hath
forsook
To take a wanton giglot [8] by the left.
I left the marriage of an honest maid,
Whose dowry would have weighed down
all thy wealth,
Whose beauty and demeanor far ex-
ceeded thee—
This certain good I lost for changing
bad,   90
And wrapped my credit in thy company.
I was bewitched—that is no theme of
thine!—
And thou unhallowed hast enchanted me.
But I will break thy spells and exorcisms,
And put another sight upon these eyes
That showed my heart a raven for a
dow.[9]
Thou art not fair—I viewed thee not till
now;
Thou art not kind—till now I knew thee
not.
And now the rain hath beaten off thy
gilt,
Thy worthless copper shows thee coun-
terfeit.   100
It grieves me not to see how foul thou
art,
But mads me that ever I thought thee
fair.
Go, get thee gone, a copesmate [10] for thy
hinds;
I am too good to be thy favorite.

ALICE. Ay, now I see, and too soon find it
true,

[4] Curse.   [7] Delayed.   [10] Companion.
[5] Fastidiously.   [8] Wench.
[6] Placed.   [9] Dove.

Which often hath been told me by my
  friends,
That Mosbie loves me not but for my
  wealth,
Which, too incredulous, I ne'er believed.
Nay, hear me speak, Mosbie, a word or
  two;   109
I'll bite my tongue if it speak bitterly.
Look on me, Mosbie, or I'll kill myself;
Nothing shall hide me from thy stormy
  look.
If thou cry war, there is no peace for me.
I will do penance for offending thee,
And burn this prayer book, where I here
  use
The holy word that had converted me.
See, Mosbie, I will tear away the leaves,
And all the leaves, and in this golden
  cover
Shall thy sweet phrases and thy letters
  dwell;
And thereon will I chiefly meditate, 120
And hold no other sect but such devotion.
Wilt thou not look? Is all thy love over-
  whelmed?
Wilt thou not hear? What malice stops
  thine ears?
Why speaks thou not? What silence ties
  thy tongue?
Thou hast been sighted [1] as the eagle is,
And heard [2] as quickly as the fearful hare,
And spoke [3] as smoothly as an orator,
When I have bid thee hear or see or
  speak,
And art thou sensible in none of these?
Weigh all thy good turns with this little
  fault,   130
And I deserve not Mosbie's muddy looks.
A fence of trouble is not thickened still.[4]
Be clear again; I'll ne'er more trouble
  thee.
Mos. O, no, I am a base artificer;
My wings are feathered for a lowly flight.
Mosbie? Fie! No, not for a thousand
  pound.
Make love to you? Why, 'tis unpardon-
  able;
We beggars must not breathe where
  gentles are.

ALICE. Sweet Mosbie is as gentle as a king,
And I too blind to judge him otherwise.
Flowers do sometimes spring in fallow
  lands,   141
Weeds in gardens, roses grow on thorns;
So, whatsoe'er my Mosbie's father was,
Himself [is] [5] valued gentle by his worth.
Mos. Ah, how you women can insinuate,
And clear a trespass with your sweet-set
  tongue!
I will forget this quarrel, gentle Alice,
Provided I'll be tempted so no more.

Here enters Bradshaw.

ALICE. Then with thy lips seal up this
  new-made match.   149
Mos. Soft, Alice, for here comes somebody.
ALICE. How now, Bradshaw, what's the
  news with you?
BRAD. I have little news, but here's a letter
That M[aster] Greene importuned me to
  give you.
ALICE. Go in, Bradshaw; call for a cup of
  beer.   Exit [Bradshaw].
'Tis almost supper time; thou shalt stay
  with us.
                    Then she reads the letter.
"We have missed of our purpose at Lon-
don, but shall perform it by the way. We
thank our neighbor Bradshaw.
              Yours,
                    RICHARD GREENE." 160
How likes my love the tenor of this letter?
Mos. Well, were his date complete and
  expired!
ALICE. Ah, would it were! Then comes
  my happy hour;
Till then my bliss is mixed with bitter
  gall.
Come, let us in to shun suspicion.
Mos.[6] Ay, to the gates of death to follow
  thee.   Exeunt.

[SCENE ix.

The country near Rochester.]

Here enters Greene, Will, and Shakebag.

SHAKE. Come, Will, see thy tools be in a
  readiness!
Is not thy powder dank, or will thy flint
  strike fire?

---

[1] Endowed with sight.
[2] Endowed with hearing.
[3] Endowed with speech.
[4] Meaning not certain. The sense seems to be:
"A troubled pool is not always turbid."

[5] Supplied by Jacob.
[6] From 1633 edn. Original has *Alice*.

WILL. Then ask me if my nose be on my face,
Or whether my tongue be frozen in my mouth.
Zounds, here's a coil! [1]
You were best swear me on the intergatories [2]
How many pistols I have took in hand,
Or whether I love the smell of gunpowder,
Or dare abide the noise the dag [3] will make,
Or will not wink at flashing of the fire. 10
I pray thee, Shakebag, let this answer thee,
That I have took more purses in this down
Than e'er thou handledst pistols in thy life.
SHAKE. Ay, happily thou hast picked more in a throng;
But, should I brag what booties I have took,
I think the overplus that's more than thine
Would mount to a greater sum of money
Than either thou or all thy kin are worth.
Zounds, I hate them (as I hate a toad)
That carry a muscado [4] in their tongue,
And scarce a hurting weapon in their hand. 21
WILL. O Greene, intolerable!
It is not for mine honor to bear this.
Why, Shakebag, I did serve the king at Boulogne,
And thou canst brag of nothing that thou hast done.
SHAKE. Why, so can Jack of Feversham,
That sounded [5] for a fillip on the nose,
When he that gave it him holloed in his ear,
And he supposed a cannon-bullet hit him.
Then they fight.
GREENE. I pray you, sirs, list to Æsop's talk: 30
Whilst two stout dogs were striving for a bone,
There comes a cur and stole it from them both;
So, while you stand striving on these terms of manhood,
Arden escapes us, and deceive[s] us all.

SHAKE. Why, he begun.
WILL. And thou shalt find I'll end;
I do but slip it until better time.
But, if I do forget—
Then he kneels down and holds up his hands to heaven.
GREENE. Well, take your fittest standings, and once more
Lime your twigs to catch this weary [6] bird. 39
I'll leave you, and at your dags' discharge
Make towards, like the longing water dog
That coucheth till the fowling piece be off,
Then seizeth on the prey with eager mood.
Ah, might I see him stretching forth his limbs,
As I have seen them beat their wings ere now!
SHAKE. Why, that thou shalt see, if he come this way.
GREENE. Yes, that he doth, Shakebag, I'll warrant thee.
But brawl not when I am gone in any case.
But, sirs, be sure to speed him when he comes,
And in that hope I'll leave you for an hour. *Exit Gre[ene].* 50

Here enters Arden, Fran[klin], and Mic[hael].

MICH. 'Twere best that I went back to Rochester.
The horse halts downright; it were not good
He traveled in such pain to Feversham.
Removing of a shoe may happily help it.
ARD. Well, get you back to Rochester; but, sirrah, see
Ye overtake us ere we come to Rainham Down,
For it will be very late ere we get home.
MICH. [*Aside.*] Ay, God he knows, and so doth Will and Shakebag,
That thou shalt never go further than that down;
And therefore have I pricked the horse on purpose, 60
Because I would not view the massacre.
Exit Michael.

[1] Bother. [3] Pistol. [5] Swooned.
[2] Interrogatories. [4] Musket.

[6] Troublesome, vexatious. Jacob suggests *wary.*

ARD. Come, M[aster] Franklin, onwards
with your tale.

FRANK. I assure you, sir, you task me
much.

A heavy blood is gathered at my heart,
And on the sudden is my wind so short
As hindereth the passage of my speech;
So fierce a qualm yet ne'er assailéd me.

ARD. Come, M[aster] Franklin, let us go
on softly.

The annoyance of the dust or else some
meat
You eat [1] at dinner cannot brook [2] [with] [3]
you.   70
I have been often so, and soon amended.

FRANK. Do you remember where my tale
did leave?

ARD. Ay, where the gentleman did check [4]
his wife.

FRANK. She being reprehended for the
fact, [5]

Witness produced that took her with the
deed,
Her glove brought in which there she left
behind,
And many other assured arguments,
Her husband asked her whether it were
not so.

ARD. Her answer then? I wonder how she
looked,

Having forsworn it with such vehement
oaths,   80
And at the instant so approved [6] upon her.

FRANK. First did she cast her eyes down
to the earth,

Watching the drops that fell amain from
thence;
Then softly draws she forth her handker-
cher,
And modestly she wipes her tear-stained
face;
Then hemmed she out, to clear her voice
should seem,
And with a majesty addressed herself
To encounter all their accusations.—
Pardon me, M[aster] Arden, I can no
more;
This fighting at my heart makes short
my wind.   90

ARD. Come, we are almost now at Rainham Down.

---

[1] Preterit.
[2] Agree.
[3] Added in 1633 edn.
[4] Reprove.
[5] Deed.
[6] Proved.

Your pretty tale beguiles the weary way;
I would you were in state to tell it out.

SHAKE. [Aside.] Stand close, Will; I hear
them coming.

Here enters Lord Cheiny with his Men.

WILL. [Aside.] Stand to it, Shakebag, and
be resolute.

LORD C. Is it so near night as it seems,
Or will this black-faced evening have a
shower?—
What, M[aster] Arden? You are well
met;
I have longed this fortnight's day to
speak with you.
You are a stranger, man, in the Isle of
Sheppy.   100

ARD. Your honor's always! Bound to do
you service!

LORD C. Come you from London, and
ne'er a man with you?

ARD. My man's coming after, but here's
My honest friend that came along with
me.

LORD C. My lord protector's man I take
you to be.

FRANK. Ay, my good lord, and highly
bound to you.

LORD C. You and your friend come home
and sup with me.

ARD. I beseech your honor, pardon me;
I have made a promise to a gentleman,
My honest friend, to meet him at my
house.   110
The occasion is great, or else would I
wait on you.

LORD C. Will you come tomorrow and dine
with me,
And bring your honest friend along with
you?
I have divers matters to talk with you
about.

ARD. Tomorrow we'll wait upon your
honor.

LORD C. One of you stay my horse at the
top of the hill.—
What! Black Will? For whose purse
wait you?
Thou wilt be hanged in Kent, when all
is done.

WILL. Not hanged, God save your honor;
I am your bedesman, [7] bound to pray for
you.   120

---

[7] One who says prayers for charity received.

LORD C. I think thou ne'er saidest prayer
in all thy life.—
One of you give him a crown.—
And, sirrah, leave this kind of life;
If thou beest tainted [1] for a penny mat-
ter,
And come in question, surely thou wilt
truss.[2]—
Come, M[aster] Arden, let us be going;
Your way and mine lies four mile to-
gether.
Exeunt. Manet Black Will and Shakebag.
WILL. The devil break all your necks at
four miles' end!
Zounds, I could kill myself for very
anger!
His lordship chops me in,[3]   130
Even when my dag was leveled at his
heart.
I would his crown were molten down his
throat.
SHAKE. Arden, thou hast wondrous holy
luck.
Did ever man escape as thou hast done?
Well, I'll discharge my pistol at the
sky,
For by this bullet Arden might not die.

Here enters Greene.

GREENE. What, is he down? Is he des-
patched?
SHAKE. Ay, in health towards Feversham,
to shame us all.
GREENE. The devil he is! Why, sirs, how
escaped he?
SHAKE. When we were ready to shoot, 140
Comes my Lord Cheiny to prevent his
death.
GREENE. The Lord of Heaven hath pre-
served him.
WILL. Preserved a fig! The L[ord] Cheiny
hath preserved him,
And bids him to a feast to his house at
Shorlow.
But by the way once more I'll meet with
him,
And, if all the Cheinies in the world say
no,
I'll have a bullet in his breast tomorrow.
Therefore come, Greene, and let us to
Feversham.

GREENE. Ay, and excuse ourselves to Mistress Arden.
O, how she'll chafe when she hears of
this!   150
SHAKE. Why, I'll warrant you she'll think
we dare not do it.
WILL. Why, then let us go, and tell her
all the matter,
And plat the news [4] to cut him off tomorrow.   *Exeunt.*

[SCENE X.

Arden's house at Feversham.]

*Here enters Arden and his Wife, Franklin,
and Michael.*

ARD. See how the hours, the guardant [5]
of heaven's gate,
Have by their toil removed the darksome
clouds,
That Sol may well discern the trampled
pace [6]
Wherein he wont to guide his golden car.
The season fits; come, Franklin, let's
away.
ALICE. I thought you did pretend some
special hunt
That made you thus cut short the time
of rest.
ARD. It was no chase that made me rise
so early,
But, as I told thee yesternight, to go
To the Isle of Sheppy,   10
There to dine with my Lord Cheiny;
For so his honor late commanded me.
ALICE. Ay, such kind husbands seldom
want excuses;
Home is a wild cat to a wandering wit.
The time hath been—would God it were
not past!—
That honor's title nor a lord's command
Could once have drawn you from these
arms of mine.
But my deserts or your desires [7] decay,
Or both; yet if true love may seem desert,
I merit still to have thy company.   20
FRANK. Why, I pray you, sir, let her go
along with us.
I am sure his honor will welcome her
And us the more for bringing her along.

[1] Accused.   [3] Thrusts in, interrupts.
[2] Hang.
[4] Plot a new means.   [6] Course, path.
[5] Guardian.
[7] Suggested by Warnke. Original reads *deserves.*

ARD. Content; sirrah, saddle your mistress' nag.

ALICE. No, begged favor merits little thanks.

If I should go, our house would run away,
Or else be stolen; therefore I'll stay behind.

ARD. Nay, see how mistaking you are!
I pray thee, go.

ALICE. No, no, not now.

ARD. Then let me leave thee satisfied in this,   30
That time nor place nor persons alter me,
But that I hold thee dearer than my life.

ALICE. That will be seen by your quick return.

ARD. And that shall be ere night, and if I live.
Farewell, sweet Alice; we mind to sup with thee.   *Exit Al[ice].*

FRANK. Come, Michael, are our horses ready?

MICH. Ay, your horse are ready, but I am not ready, for I have lost my purse, with six-and-thirty shillings in it, with taking up of [1] my m[aster's] nag.   40

FRANK. Why, I pray you, let us go before,
Whilst he stays behind to seek his purse.

ARD. Go to, sirrah; see you follow us to the Isle of Sheppy
To my Lord Cheiny's, where we mean to dine.

Exeunt Arden and Franklin. Manet Michael.

MICH. So, fair weather after you, for before you lies Black Will and Shakebag in the broom close,[2] too close for you. They'll be your ferrymen to long home.[3]

Here enters the Painter.

But who is this? The painter, my corrival, that would needs win M[istress]   [50
Susan.

CLARKE. How now, Michael? How doth my mistress and all at home?

MICH. Who? Susan Mosbie? She is your mistress too?

CLARKE. Ay, how doth she and all the rest?

MICH. All's well but Susan; she is sick.

CLARKE. Sick? Of what disease?

MICH. Of a great fear.   6(

CLARKE. A fear of what?

MICH. A great fever.

CLARKE. A fever? God forbid!

MICH. Yes, faith, and of a lordaine,[4] too, as big as yourself.

CLARKE. O, Michael, the spleen prickles you. Go to; you carry an eye over Mistress Susan.

MICH. Ay, faith, to keep her from the painter.   70

CLARKE. Why more from a painter than from a serving creature like yourself?

MICH. Because you painters make but a painting-table of a pretty wench, and spoil her beauty with blotting.

CLARKE. What mean you by that?

MICH. Why, that you painters paint lambs in the lining of wenches' petticoats, and we serving-men put horns to them to make them become sheep.   80

CLARKE. Such another word will cost you a cuff or a knock.

MICH. What, with a dagger made of a pencil? Faith, 'tis too weak, and therefore thou too weak to win Susan.

CLARKE. Would Susan's love lay upon this stroke! *Then he breaks Michael's head.*

Here enters Mosbie, Greene, and Alice.

ALICE. I'll lay my life, this is for Susan's love.
Stayed you behind your m[aster] to this end?   89
Have you no other time to brabble in
But now when serious matters are in hand?—
Say, Clarke, hast thou done the thing thou promised?

CLARKE. Ay, here it is. The very touch is death!

ALICE. Then this, I hope, if all the rest do fail,
Will catch M[aster] Arden,
And make him wise in death that lived a fool.
Why should he thrust his sickle in our corn,
Or what hath he to do with thee, my love,
Or govern me that am to rule myself?

[1] Making gambol.   [3] *I.e.,* the grave.
[2] Field.

[4] Clown, with a play on *lurdan*, meaning "fever of idleness."

Forsooth, for credit sake, I must leave
thee!   100
Nay, he must leave to live that we may
love,
May live, may love; for what is life but
love?
And love shall last as long as life remains,
And life shall end before my love depart.
Mos. Why, what's love without true
constancy?
Like to a pillar built of many stones,
Yet neither with good mortar well com-
pact
Nor cement [1] to fasten it in the joints,
But that it shakes with every blast of
wind,
And, being touched, straight falls unto
the earth,   110
And buries all his [2] haughty pride in dust.
No, let our love be rocks of adamant,
Which time nor place nor tempest can
asunder.[3]
Greene. Mosbie, leave protestations now,
And let us bethink us what we have to do.
Black Will and Shakebag I have placed
In the broom close, watching Arden's
coming.
Let's to them and see what they have
done.   *Exeunt.*

[SCENE xi.

*The Kentish coast opposite the Isle of
Sheppy.*]

Here enters Ard[en] and Fra[nklin].

Ard. O ferryman, where art thou?

Here enters the Ferryman.

Fer. Here, here! Go before to the boat,
and I will follow you.
Arden. We have great haste; I pray
thee, come away.
Fer. Fie, what a mist is here!
Ard. This mist, my friend, is mystical,
Like to a good companion's smoky brain
That was half drowned with new ale
overnight.
Fer. 'Twere pity but his skull were [10]
opened to make more chimney room.
Frank. Friend, what's thy opinion of
this mist?
Fer. I think 'tis like to a curst[4] wife in a

little house, that never leaves her husband
till she have driven him out at doors with
a wet pair of eyes. Then looks he as if his
house were afire, or some of his friends
dead.
Ard. Speaks thou this of thine own [20]
experience?
Fer. Perhaps, ay; perhaps, no; for my
wife is as other women are, that is to say,
governed by the moon.
Frank. By the moon? How, I pray
thee?
Fer. Nay, thereby lies a bargain, and
you shall not have it fresh and fasting.[5]
Ard. Yes, I pray thee, good ferryman.
Fer. Then for this once. Let it be [30]
midsummer moon, but yet my wife has
another moon.
Frank. Another moon?
Fer. Ay, and it hath influences and
eclipses.
Ard. Why, then, by this reckoning you
sometimes play the man in the moon?
Fer. Ay, but you had not best to meddle with that moon, lest I scratch you by
the face with my bramble bush.   40
Ard. I am almost stifled with this fog.
Come, let's away.
Frank. And, sirrah, as we go, let us have
some more of your bold yeomandry.[6]
Fer. Nay, by my troth, sir, but flat
knavery.   *Exeunt.*

[SCENE xii.

Another part of the coast.]

*Here enters Will at one door, and Shakebag
at another.*

Shake. O, Will, where art thou?
Will. Here, Shakebag, almost in hell's
mouth, where I cannot see my way for
smoke.
Shake. I pray thee, speak still that we
may meet by the sound, for I shall fall
into some ditch or other, unless my feet
see better than my eyes.
Will. Didst thou ever see better
weather to run away with another man's [10]
wife, or play with a wench at potfinger?
Shake. No; this were a fine world for
chandlers if this weather would last, for

---

[1] From 1633 edn. Original reads *semell.*
[2] Its.   [3] Part.   [4] Cross, shrewish.

[5] Before eating; in your eagerness; for nothing (?).   [6] Yeoman's talk.

then a man should never dine nor sup
without candlelight. But, sirrah Will, what
horses are those that passed?

WILL. Why, didst thou hear any?

SHAKE. Ay, that I did.

WILL. My life for thine, 'twas Arden
and his companion, and then all our [20
labor's lost.

SHAKE. Nay, say not so, for, if it be they,
they may happily lose their way as we have
done, and then we may chance meet with
them.

WILL. Come, let us go on like a couple
of blind pilgrims.
            Then Shakebag falls into a ditch.

SHAKE. Help, Will, help! I am almost
drowned!

            Here enters the Ferryman.

FER. Who's that that calls for help?   30

WILL. 'Twas none here; 'twas thou thyself.

FER. I came to help him that called for
help. Why, how now? Who is this that's
in the ditch? You are well enough served
to go without a guide such weather as
this.

WILL. Sirrah, what companies hath
passed your ferry this morning?

FER. None but a couple of gentle-   [40
men, that went to dine at my Lord
Cheiny's.

WILL. Shakebag, did not I tell thee as
much?

FER. Why, sir, will you have any letters
carried to them?

WILL. No, sir; get you gone.

FER. Did you ever see such a mist as
this?

WILL. No, nor such a fool as will   [50
rather be hought [1] than get his way.

FER. Why, sir, this is no Hough-Mon-
day; [2] you are deceived.—What's his name,
I pray you, sir?

SHAKE. His name is Black Will.

FER. I hope to see him one day hanged
upon a hill.   *Exit Ferryman.*

SHAKE. See how the sun hath cleared the
foggy mist,
Now we have missed the mark of our
intent.

[1] Hamstrung.
[2] Hock Monday, a festival shortly after
Easter.

Here enters Greene, Mosbie, and Alice.

MOS. Black Will and Shakebag, what
make [3] you here?   60
What, is the deed done? Is Arden dead?

WILL. What could a blinded man perform
in arms?
Saw you not how till now the sky was
dark,
That neither horse nor man could be discerned?
Yet did we hear their horses as they
passed.

GREENE. Have they escaped you, then,
and passed the ferry?

SHAKE. Ay, for awhile; but here we two
will stay,
And at their coming back meet with them
once more.
Zounds, I was ne'er so toiled [4] in all my
life
In following so slight a task as this.   70

MOS. How cam'st thou so berayed? [5]

WILL. With making false footing in the
dark.
He needs would follow them without a
guide.

ALICE. Here's to pay for a fire and good
cheer.
Get you to Feversham to the Flower-de-
Luce,
And rest yourselves until some other
time.

GREENE. Let me alone; it most concerns
my state.

WILL. Ay, Mistress Arden, this will serve
the turn,
In case we fall into a second fog.

Exeunt Greene, Will, and Shake[bag].

MOS. These knaves will never do it; let
us give it over.   80

ALICE. First tell me how you like my new
device:
Soon, when my husband is returning
back,
You and I both marching arm in arm,
Like loving friends, we'll meet him on the
way,
And boldly beard and brave him to his
teeth.
When words grow hot and blows begin to
rise,

[3] Do.   [4] Entangled or fatigued.
[5] Befouled with mud.

I'll call those cutters forth your tenement,
Who, in a manner to take up the fray,
Shall wound my husband Hornsby [1] to
the death.

Mos. Ah, fine device! Why, this deserves
a kiss.　　　　　　　　*Exeunt.* 90

[SCENE xiii.

Near the Flower-de-Luce in Feversham.]

Here enters Dick Reede and a Sailor.

SAIL. Faith, Dick Reede, it is to little end.
His conscience is too liberal, and he too
niggardly
To part from anything may do thee good.

REEDE. He is coming from Shorlow, as I
understand.
Here I'll intercept him, for at his house
He never will vouchsafe to speak with
me.
If prayers and fair entreaties will not
serve,
Or make no batt'ry in his flinty breast,

Here enters Fra[nklin], Ard[en], and Michael.

I'll curse the carl, and see what that will
do.
See where he comes to further my in-
tent!—　　　　　　　　　　10
M[aster] Arden, I am now bound to the
sea.
My coming to you was about the plat of
ground
Which wrongfully you detain from me.
Although the rent of it be very small,
Yet will it help my wife and children,
Which here I leave in Feversham, God
knows,
Needy and bare. For Christ's sake, let
them have it!

ARD. Franklin, hearest thou this fellow
speak?
That which he craves I dearly bought of
him,
Although the rent of it was ever
mine.—　　　　　　　　　　20
Sirrah, you that ask these questions,
If with thy clamorous impeaching [2]
tongue
Thou rail on me, as I have heard thou
dost,

[1] Cuckold.　　　　　[2] Accusing.

I'll lay thee up so close a twelvemonth's
day,
As thou shalt neither see the sun nor
moon.
Look to it, for, as surely as I live,
I'll banish pity if thou use me thus.

REEDE. What, wilt thou do me wrong and
threat me too?
Nay, then, I'll tempt thee, Arden; do thy
worst.
God, I beseech thee, show some mir-
acle　　　　　　　　　　30
On thee or thine, in plaguing thee for this.
That plot of ground which thou detains
from me—
I speak it in an agony of spirit—
Be ruinous and fatal unto thee!
Either there be butchered by thy dearest
friends,
Or else be brought for men to wonder at,
Or thou or thine miscarry in that place,
Or there run mad and end thy curséd
days!

FRANK. Fie, bitter knave, bridle thine
envious [3] tongue;
For curses are like arrows shot upright,　　　　　　　　　　40
Which, falling down, light on the shoot-
er's [4] head.

REEDE. Light where they will! Were I
upon the sea,
As oft I have in many a bitter storm,
And saw a dreadful southern flaw at
hand,
The pilot quaking at the doubtful [5]
storm,
And all the sailors praying on their knees,
Even in that fearful time would I fall
down,
And ask of God, whate'er betide of me,
Vengeance on Arden or some misevent [6]
To show the world what wrong the carl
hath done.　　　　　　　　　50
This charge I'll leave with my distressful
wife;
My children shall be taught such prayers
as these;
And thus I go, but leave my curse with
thee.　　　*Exeunt Reede and Sailor.*

ARD. It is the railingest knave in Christendom,

[3] Spiteful.
[4] From 1633 edn. Original reads *sutors.*
[5] Fearful.　　　　　　　[6] Mischance.

And oftentimes the villain will be mad.
It greatly matters not what he says,
But I assure you I ne'er did him
  wrong.
FRANK. I think so, M[aster] Arden.
ARD. Now that our horses are gone home
  before,
My wife may happily meet me on the
  way.   60
For God knows she is grown passing kind
  of late,
And greatly changéd from the old humor
Of her wonted frowardness,
And seeks by fair means to redeem old
  faults.
FRANK. Happy the change that alters for
  the best!
But see in any case you make no speech
Of the cheer we had at my Lord
  Cheiny's,
Although most bounteous and liberal,
For that will make her think herself more
  wronged,
In that we did not carry her along;   70
For sure she grieved that she was left
  behind.
ARD. Come, Franklin, let us strain to
  mend our pace,
And take her unawares playing the cook;

Here enters Alice and Mosbie.

For I believe she'll strive to mend our
  cheer.
FRANK. Why, there's no better creatures
  in the world
Than women are when they are in good
  humors.
ARD. Who is that? Mosbie? What, so
  familiar?
Injurious strumpet, and thou ribald
  knave,
Untwine those arms.
ALICE. Ay, with a sugared kiss let them
  untwine.   80
ARD. Ah, Mosbie, perjured beast! Bear
  this and all!
MOS. And yet no hornéd beast; the horns
  are thine.
FRANK. O monstrous! Nay, then 'tis time
  to draw.
  [*Arden, Franklin, and Mosbie draw.*]
ALICE. Help, help! They murther my hus-
  band.

Here enters Will and Shak[ebag].

SHAKE. Zounds, who injures M[aster]
Mosbie?   [*He and Mosbie are wounded.*]
—Help, Will! I am hurt.
MOS. I may thank you, Mistress Arden,
  for this wound.
  Exeunt Mosbie, Will, and Shakebag.
ALICE. Ah, Arden, what folly blinded
  thee?
Ah, jealous harebrain man, what hast
  thou done!   90
When we, to welcome thee,[1] intended
  sport,
Came lovingly to meet thee on thy way,
Thou drew'st thy sword, enraged with
  jealousy,
And hurt thy friend whose thoughts were
  free from harm—
All for a worthless kiss and joining arms,
Both done but merrily to try thy pa-
  tience.
And me unhappy that devised the jest,
Which, though begun in sport, yet ends
  in blood!
FRANK. Marry, God defend me from such
  a jest!
ALICE. Couldst thou not see us friendly
  smile on thee,   100
When we joined arms and when I kissed
  his cheek?
Hast thou not lately found me overkind?
Didst thou not hear me cry, they murther
  thee?
Called I not help to set my husband free?
No, ears and all were witched. Ah, me ac-
  cursed,
To link in liking with a frantic man!
Henceforth I'll be thy slave, no more thy
  wife,
For with that name I never shall content
  thee.
If I be merry, thou straightways thinks
  me light;
If sad, thou sayest the sullens [2] trouble
  me;   110
If well attired, thou thinks I will be gad-
  ding;
If homely, I seem sluttish in thine eye.
Thus am I still, and shall be while [3] I die.
Poor wench, abused by thy misgovern-
  ment!

[1] Original reads *thy*.   [3] Until.
[2] Dumps.

ARD. But is it for truth that neither thou
　　nor he
Intendedst malice in your misdemeanor?
ALICE. The heavens can witness of our
　　harmless thoughts.
ARD. Then pardon me, sweet Alice,
　　And forgive this fault!　　　　　　119
Forget but this and never see the like.
Impose me penance, and I will perform it,
For in thy discontent I find a death,
A death tormenting more than death it-
　　self.
ALICE. Nay, hadst thou loved me as thou
　　dost pretend,
Thou wouldst have marked the speeches
　　of thy friend,
Who going wounded from the place, he
　　said
His skin was pierced only through my de-
　　vice.
And, if sad sorrow taint thee for this
　　fault,
Thou wouldst have followed him, and
　　seen him dressed,
And cried him mercy whom thou hast
　　misdone.　　　　　　　　　　　130
Ne'er shall my heart be eased till this
　　be done.
ARD. Content thee, sweet Alice, thou shalt
　　have thy will,
Whate'er it be. For that I injured thee
And wronged my friend, shame scourgeth
　　my offense.
Come thou thyself, and go along with me,
And be a mediator twixt us two.
FRANK. Why, M[aster] Arden, know you
　　what you do?
Will you follow him that hath dishonored
　　you?
ALICE. Why, canst thou prove I have been
　　disloyal?
FRANK. Why, Mosbie taunts your [1] hus-
　　band with the horn.　　　　　　140
ALICE. Ay, after he had reviled him
By the injurious name of perjured beast!
He knew no wrong could spite a jealous
　　man
More than the hateful naming of the horn.
FRANK. Suppose 'tis true; yet is it dan-
　　gerous
To follow him whom he hath lately hurt.
ALICE. A fault confessed is more than half
　　amends;

[1] From 1633 edn. Original reads traunt you.

But men of such ill spirit as yourself
Work crosses and debates twixt man and
　　wife.
ARD. I pray thee, gentle Franklin, hold
　　thy peace.　　　　　　　　　　150
I know my wife counsels me for the best.
I'll seek out Mosbie where his wound is
　　dressed,
And salve his hapless quarrel if I may.
　　　　　　　　　Exeunt Arden and Alice.
FRANK. He whom the devil drives must go
　　perforce.
Poor gentleman, how soon he is be-
　　witched!
And yet, because his wife is the instru-
　　ment,
His friends must not be lavish in their
　　speech.　　　　　　　Exit Fran[klin].

[SCENE xiv.

A room in Arden's house.]

Here enters Will, Shakebag, and Greene.

WILL. Sirrah Greene, when was I so
long in killing a man?
GREENE. I think we shall never do it.
Let us give it over.
SHAKE. Nay, zounds! We'll kill him,
though we be hanged at his door for our
labor.
WILL. Thou knowest, Greene, that I have
lived in London this twelve years, where
I have made some go upon wooden [10
legs for taking the wall on me;[2] divers
with silver noses for saying, "There goes
Black Will!" I have cracked as many
blades as thou hast done nuts.
GREENE. O monstrous lie!
WILL. Faith, in a manner I have. The
bawdyhouses have paid me tribute; there
durst not a whore set up unless she have
agreed with me first for opening her shop
windows. For a cross word of a tapster [20
I have pierced one barrel after another
with my dagger, and held him be [3] the ears
till all his beer hath run out. In Thames
Street a brewer's cart was like to have
run over me. I made no more ado, but
went to the clerk and cut all the natches
off his tails [4] and beat them about his head.
I and my company have taken the constable from his watch, and carried him

[2] For pushing me into the street.　　　[3] By.
[4] Notches off his tallies (sticks on which his
accounts were kept).

about the fields on a coltstaff.[1] I have [30
broken a sergeant's head with his own
mace, and bailed whom I list with my
sword and buckler. All the tenpenny
alehouses would stand every morning with
a quart pot in his hand, saying, "Will it
please your worship drink?" He that had
not done so, had been sure to have had his
sign pulled down and his lattice borne away
the next night. To conclude, what have I
not done? Yet cannot do this. Doubt- [40
less he is preserved by miracle.

Here enters Alice and Michael.

GREENE. Hence, Will! Here comes
M[istress] Arden.
ALICE. Ah, gentle Michael, art thou sure
they're friends?
MICH. Why, I saw them when they both
shook hands.
When Mosbie bled, he even wept for
sorrow,
And railed on Franklin that was cause
of all.
No sooner came the surgeon in at doors,
But my m[aster] took to his purse and
gave him money,
And, to conclude, sent me to bring you
word   50
That Mosbie, Franklin, Bradshaw, Adam
Fowle,
With divers of his neighbors and his
friends,
Will come and sup with you at our house
this night.
ALICE. Ah, gentle Michael, run thou
back again,
And, when my husband walks into the
fair,
Bid Mosbie steal from him and come
to me;
And this night shall thou and Susan be
made sure.
MICH. I'll go tell him.
ALICE. And, as thou goest, tell John cook
of our guests,
And bid him lay it on—spare for no
cost.   *Exit Michael.* 60
WILL. Nay, and there be such cheer, we
will bid ourselves.—
Mistress Arden, Dick Greene and I do
mean to sup with you.

[1] Staff used for carrying tubs.

ALICE. And welcome shall you be. Ah,
gentlemen,
How missed you of your purpose yesternight?
GREENE. 'Twas long of [2] Shakebag, that
unlucky villain.
SHAKE. Thou dost me wrong; I did as
much as any.
WILL. Nay then, M[istress] Alice, I'll
tell you how it was.
When he should have locked with both
his hilts,[3]
He in a bravery [4] flourished over his head;
With that comes Franklin at him lust-
ily,   70
And hurts the slave; with that he slinks
away.
Now his way had been to have come
hand and feet, one and two round, at his
costard; [5] he like a fool bears his sword-
point half a yard out of danger. I lie here
for my life. [*Takes a position of defense.*]
If the devil come, and he have no more
strength than fence,[6] he shall never beat
me from this ward.[7]
I'll stand to it, a buckler in a skillful
hand   80
Is as good as a castle; nay,
'Tis better than a sconce,[8] for I have
tried it.
Mosbie, perceiving this, began to faint.
With that comes Arden with his arming sword,[9]
And thrust him through the shoulder in
a trice.
ALICE. Ay, but I wonder why you both
stood still.
WILL. Faith, I was so amazed, I could
not strike.
ALICE. Ah, sirs, had he yesternight been
slain,
For every drop of his detested blood
I would have crammed [10] in angels [11] in
thy fist,   90
And kissed thee, too, and hugged thee
in my arms.
WILL. Patient yourself; we cannot help
it now.

[2] Because of.
[3] Sword. *Hilts* was often used for singular.
[4] Bravado.   [7] Guard.
[5] Apple, head.   [8] Fort.
[6] Fencing skill.   [9] A two-handed sword.
[10] From 1633 edn.; original reads *would
cramme.*   [11] Coins.

Greene and we two will dog him through
the fair,
And stab him in the crowd, and steal
away.

Here enters Mosbie.

ALICE. It is unpossible; but here comes
he
That will, I hope, invent some surer
means.
Sweet Mosbie, hide thy arm; it kills my
heart.
MOS. Ay, Mistress Arden, this is your
favor.
ALICE. Ah, say not so, for, when I saw
thee hurt,
I could have took the weapon thou
lett'st fall,   100
And run at Arden, for I have sworn
That these mine eyes, offended with
his sight,
Shall never close till Arden's be shut up.
This night I rose and walked about the
chamber,
And twice or thrice I thought to have
murthered him.
MOS. What, in the night? Then had we
been undone.
ALICE. Why, how long shall he live?
MOS. Faith, Alice, no longer than this
night.—
Black Will and Shakebag, will you two
Perform the complot that I have laid? 110
WILL. Ay, or else think me as a villain.
GREENE. And rather than you shall
want,[1] I'll help, myself.
MOS. You, M[aster] Greene, shall single
Franklin forth,
And hold him with a long tale of strange
news,
That he may not come home till supper
time.
I'll fetch M[aster] Arden home, and we,
like friends,
Will play a game or two at tables [2] here.
ALICE. But what of all this? How shall he
be slain?
MOS. Why, Black Will and Shakebag,
locked within the countinghouse,
Shall, at a certain watchword given,
rush forth.   120
WILL. What shall the watchword be?

MOS. "Now I take you"—that shall be
the word.
But come not forth before in any case.
WILL. I warrant you. But who shall
lock me in?
ALICE. That will I do; thou'st keep the
key thyself.
MOS. Come, M[aster] Greene; go you
along with me.
See all things ready, Alice, against we
come.
ALICE. Take no care for that; send you
him home,
              Exeunt Mosbie and Greene.
And, if he e'er go forth again, blame me.
Come, Black Will, that in mine eyes
art fair;   130
Next unto Mosbie do I honor thee.
Instead of fair words and large promises
My hands shall play you golden har-
mony.[3]
How like you this? Say, will you do it,
sirs?
WILL. Ay, and that bravely, too. Mark
my device:
Place Mosbie, being a stranger, in a
chair,
And let your husband sit upon a stool,
That I may come behind him cun-
ningly,   138
And with a towel pull him to the ground,
Then stab him till his flesh be as a sine;[4]
That done, bear him behind the Abbey,
That those that find him murthered
may suppose
Some slave or other killed him for his
gold.
ALICE. A fine device! You shall have
twenty pound,
And, when he is dead, you shall have
forty more,
And, lest you might be suspected stay-
ing here,
Michael shall saddle you two lusty geld-
ings;
Ride whither you will, to Scotland, or
to Wales,
I'll see you shall not lack, where'er you be.
WILL. Such words would make one kill
a thousand [5] men!   150
Give me the key! Which is the countinghouse?

---

[1] Fail.   [2] Backgammon.
[3] *I.e.*, give you money.   [4] Seine, sieve.
[5] Original reads *1000* without the article.

ALICE. Here would I stay and still encourage you,
But that I know how resolute you are.
SHAKE. Tush, you are too faint-hearted;
we must do it.
ALICE. But Mosbie will be there, whose
very looks
Will add unwonted courage to my
thought,
And make me the first that shall adventure on him.
WILL. Tush, get you gone; 'tis we must
do the deed.
When this door opens next, look for
his death.
[*Exeunt Will and Shakebag.*]
ALICE. Ah, would he now were here that
it might open! 160
I shall no more be closed in Arden's
arms,
That like the snakes of black Tisiphone
Sting me with their embracings. Mosbie's arms
Shall compass me, and, were I made a
star,
I would have none other spheres but
those.
There is no nectar but in Mosbie's lips!
Had chaste Diana kissed him, she like
me
Would grow lovesick, and from her
wat'ry bower
Fling down Endymion and snatch[1] him
up.
Then blame not me that slay a silly
man 170
Not half so lovely as Endymion.

Here enters Michael.

MICH. Mistress, my master is coming
hard by.
ALICE. Who comes with him?
MICH. Nobody but Mosbie.
ALICE. That's well, Michael. Fetch in
the tables, and, when thou hast done,
stand before the countinghouse door.
MICH. Why so? 179
ALICE. Black Will is locked within to
do the deed.
MICH. What? Shall he die tonight?
ALICE. Ay, Michael.
MICH. But shall not Susan know it?

ALICE. Yes, for she'll be as secret as
ourselves.
MICH. That's brave.[2] I'll go fetch the
tables.
ALICE. But, Michael, hark to me a word
or two.
When my husband is come in, lock the
street door; 190
He shall be murthered or[3] the guests
come in. *Exit Mic[hael].*

Here enters Arden and Mosbie.

Husband, what mean you to bring
Mosbie home?
Although I wished you to be reconciled,
'Twas more for fear of you than love of
him.
Black Will and Greene are his companions,
And they are cutters, and may cut you
short;
Therefore I thought it good to make you
friends.
But wherefore do you bring him hither
now?
You have given me my supper with his
sight.[4]
MOS. M[aster] Arden, methinks your
wife would have me gone. 200
ARD. No, good M[aster] Mosbie; women
will be prating.
Alice, bid him welcome; he and I are
friends.
ALICE. You may enforce me to it if you
will;
But I had rather die than bid him welcome.
His company hath purchased me ill
friends,
And therefore will I ne'er frequent it
more.
MOS. [*Aside.*] O, how cunningly she can
dissemble!
ARD. Now he is here, you will not serve
me so.
ALICE. I pray you be not angry or displeased;
I'll bid him welcome, seeing you'll have
it so. 210
You are welcome, M[aster] Mosbie; will
you sit down?

[1] Snatch.

[2] Splendid. [4] *I.e.*, taken my appetite away.
[3] Before.

Mos. I know I am welcome to your loving husband;

But for yourself you speak not from your heart.

Alice. And, if I do not, sir, think I have cause.

Mos. Pardon me, M[aster] Arden; I'll away.

Ard. No, good M[aster] Mosbie.

Alice. We shall have guests enough, though you go hence.

Mos. I pray you, M[aster] Arden, let me go.

Ard. I pray thee, Mosbie, let her prate her fill.

Alice. The doors are open, sir; you may be gone.   220

Mich. [Aside.] Nay, that's a lie, for I have locked the doors.

Ard. Sirrah, fetch me a cup of wine; I'll make them friends.

And, gentle M[istress] Alice, seeing you are so stout,[1]

You shall begin. Frown not; I'll have it so.

Alice. I pray you meddle with that you have to do.

Ard. Why, Alice, how can I do too much for him

Whose life I have endangered without cause?

Alice. 'Tis true; and, seeing 'twas partly through my means,

I am content to drink to him for this once.

Here, M[aster] Mosbie—and, I pray you, henceforth   230

Be you as strange to me as I to you.

Your company hath purchased me ill friends,

And I for you, God knows, have undeserved

Been ill spoken of in every place;

Therefore henceforth frequent my house no more.

Mos. I'll see your husband in despite of you.

Yet, Arden, I protest to thee by heaven,

Thou ne'er shalt see me more after this night.

I'll go to Rome rather than be forsworn.

Ard. Tush, I'll have no such vows made in my house.   240

[1] Stubborn, proud.

Alice. Yes, I pray you, husband, let him swear;

And, on that condition, Mosbie, pledge me here.

Mos. Ay, as willingly as I mean to live.

Ard. Come, Alice, is our supper ready yet?

Alice. It will by then you have played a game at tables.

Ard. Come, M[aster] Mosbie, what shall we play for?

Mos. Three games for a French crown, sir, and [2] please you.

Ard. Content.

                    Then they play at the tables.

[Enter Will and Shakebag.]

Will. [Aside.] Can he not take him yet? What a spite is that!

Alice. [Aside.] Not yet, Will. Take heed he see thee not.   250

Will. [Aside.] I fear he will spy me as I am coming.

Mich. [Aside.] To prevent that, creep betwixt my legs.

Mos. One ace, or else I lose the game.

Ard. Marry, sir, there's two for failing.[3]

Mos. Ah, M[aster] Arden, "now I can take you."

                    Then Will pulls him down with a towel.

Ard. Mosbie! Michael! Alice! What will you do?

Will. Nothing but take you up, sir, nothing else.

Mos. There's for the pressing iron you told me of.   [Stabs him.]

Shake. And there's for the ten pound in my sleeve.   [Stabs him.]

Alice. What! Groans thou? Nay, then give me the weapon!   260

Take this for hind'ring Mosbie's love and mine!   [She stabs him.]

Mich. O, mistress!

Will. Ah, that villain will betray us all.

Mos. Tush, fear him not; he will be secret.

Mich. Why, dost thou think I will betray myself?

Shake. In Southwark dwells a bonny northern lass,

The widow Chambley; I'll to her house now,

[2] An't, if it.   [3] If one is not sufficient.

And, if she will not give me harborough,[1]
I'll make booty of the quean even to her
  smock.

WILL. Shift for yourselves; we two will
  leave you now.   270

ALICE. First lay the body in the countinghouse.

Then they lay the body in the countinghouse.

WILL. We have our gold; Mistress Alice,
  adieu;
  Mosbie, farewell, and, Michael, farewell
  too.   *Exeunt.*

Enter Susan.

SUS. Mistress, the guests are at the doors.
  Hearken, they knock. What, shall I let
  them in?

ALICE. Mosbie, go thou, and bear them
  company.   *Exit M[osbie].*
  And, Susan, fetch water and wash away
  this blood.

SUS. The blood cleaveth to the ground
  and will not out.

ALICE. But with my nails I'll scrape away
  the blood.—
  The more I strive, the more the blood
  appears!   280

SUS. What's the reason, m[istress], can you
  tell?

ALICE. Because I blush not at my husband's death.

Here enters Mosbie.

MOS. How now? What's the matter? Is
  all well?

ALICE. Ay, well, if Arden were alive again.
  In vain we strive, for here his blood remains.

MOS. Why, strew rushes on it, can you
  not?
  This wench doth nothing. Fall unto the
  work.

ALICE. 'Twas thou that made me murther
  him.

MOS.   What of that?

ALICE. Nay, nothing, Mosbie, so it be not
  known.

MOS. Keep thou it close, and 'tis unpossible.   290

ALICE. Ah, but I cannot! Was he not slain
  by me?
  My husband's death torments me at the
  heart.

  [1] Harbor.

MOS. It shall not long torment thee, gentle
  Alice.
  I am thy husband; think no more of him.

Here enters Adam Fowle and Brad[shaw].

BRAD. How now, M[istress] Arden? What
  ail you weep? [2]

MOS. Because her husband is abroad so
  late.
  A couple of ruffians threatened him yesternight,
  And she, poor soul, is afraid he should be
  hurt.

ADAM. Is 't nothing else? Tush, he'll be
  here anon.

Here enters Greene.

GREENE. Now, M[istress] Arden, lack you
  any guests?   300

ALICE. Ah, M[aster] Greene, did you see
  my husband lately?

GREENE. I saw him walking behind the
  Abbey even now.

Here enters Franklin.

ALICE. I do not like this being out so
  late.—
  M[aster] Franklin, where did you leave
  my husband?

FRANK. Believe me, I saw him not since
  morning.
  Fear you not; he'll come anon. Meantime
  You may do well to bid his guests sit
  down.

ALICE. Ay, so they shall. M[aster] Bradshaw, sit you there;
  I pray you, be content; I'll have my will.
  M[aster] Mosbie, sit you in my husband's
  seat.   310

MICH. [*Aside.*] Susan, shall thou and I
  wait on them?
  Or, and thou sayst the word, let us sit
  down too.

SUS. [*Aside.*] Peace, we have other matters now in hand.
  I fear me, Michael, all will be bewrayed.

MICH. [*Aside.*] Tush, so it be known
  that I shall marry thee in the morning,
  I care not though I be hanged ere night.
  But to prevent the worst I'll buy some
  ratsbane.   319

  [2] *I.e.,* what ails you that you weep?

Sus. [*Aside.*] Why, Michael, wilt thou poison thyself?

Mich. [*Aside.*] No, but my mistress, for I fear she'll tell.

Sus. [*Aside.*] Tush, Michael, fear not her; she's wise enough.

Mos. S:rrah Michael, give's a cup of beer.—

M[istress] Arden, here's to your husband.

Alice.   My husband!

Frank. What ails you, woman, to cry so suddenly?

Alice. Ah, neighbors, a sudden qualm came over my heart;

My husband's being forth torments my mind.   330

I know something's amiss; he is not well Or else I should have heard of him ere now.

Mos. [*Aside.*] She will undo us through her foolishness.

Greene. Fear not, M[istress] Arden; he's well enough.

Alice. Tell not me; I know he is not well. He was not wont for to stay thus late.

Good M[aster] Franklin, go and seek him forth,

And, if you find him, send him home to me, And tell him what a fear he hath put me in.

Frank. [*Aside.*] I like not this; I pray God all be well.—   340

Exeunt Fra[nklin], Mos[bie], and Gre[ene].

I'll seek him out, and find him if I can.

Alice. [*Aside.*] Michael, how shall I do to rid the rest away?

Mich. [*Aside.*] Leave that to my charge; let me alone.—

'Tis very late, M[aster] Bradshaw,

And there are many false knaves abroad, And you have many narrow lanes to pass.

Brad. Faith, friend Michael, and thou sayest true.

Therefore I pray thee light's forth and lend's a link.[1]

Exeunt Brad[shaw], Adam, and Michael.

Alice. Michael, bring them to the doors, but do not stay;   349

You know I do not love to be alone.—

Go, Susan, and bid thy brother come.

But wherefore should he come? Here is naught but fear;

Stay, Susan, stay, and help to counsel me.

[1] Torch.

Sus. Alas, I counsel! Fear frights away my wits.

Then they open the countinghouse door, and look upon Arden.

Alice. See, Susan, where thy quondam master lies,

Sweet Arden, smeared in blood and filthy gore.

Sus. My brother, you, and I shall rue this deed.

Alice. Come, Susan, help to lift his body forth,

And let our salt tears be his obsequies.

Here enters Mosbie and Greene.

Mos. How now, Alice, whither will you bear him?   360

Alice. Sweet Mosbie, art thou come? Then weep that will;

I have my wish in that I joy thy sight.

Greene. Well, it hoves[2] us to be circumspect.

Mos. Ay, for Franklin thinks that we have murthered him.

Alice. Ay, but he cannot prove it for his life.

We'll spend this night in dalliance and in sport.

Here enters Michael.

Mich. O mistress, the mayor and all the watch

Are coming towards our house with glaives and bills![3]

Alice. Make the door fast; let them not come in.

Mos. Tell me, sweet Alice, how shall I escape?   370

Alice. Out at the back door, over the pile of wood,

And for one night lie at the Flower-de-Luce.

Mos. That is the next way to betray myself.

Greene. Alas, M[istress] Arden, the watch will take me here,

And cause suspicion where else would be none.

Alice. Why, take that way that M[aster] Mosbie doth;

But first convey the body to the fields.

Then they bear the body into the fields.

[2] Behooves.   [3] Swords and halberts.

Mos. Until tomorrow, sweet Alice, now
   farewell.
   And see you confess nothing in any case.
GREENE. Be resolute, M[istress] Alice; be-
   tray us not,   380
   But cleave to us as we will stick to you.
                    Exeunt Mosbie and Greene.
ALICE. Now, let the judge and juries do
   their worst.
   My house is clear, and now I fear them
   not.
SUS. As we went, it snowéd all the way,
   Which makes me fear our footsteps will
   be spied.
ALICE. Peace, fool, the snow will cover
   them again.
SUS. But it had done before we came back
   again.
ALICE. Hark, hark, they knock!   Go,
   Michael, let them in.

Here enters the Mayor and the Watch.

   How now, M[aster] Mayor, have you
   brought my husband home?
MAYOR. I saw him come into your house
   an hour ago.   390
ALICE. You are deceived; it was a Lon-
   doner.
MAYOR. Mistress Arden, know you not
   one that is called Black Will?
ALICE. I know none such.   What mean
   these questions?
MAYOR. I have the council's warrand to
   apprehend him.
ALICE. [*Aside.*] I am glad it is no worse.—
   Why, M[aster] Mayor, think you I har-
   bor any such?
MAYOR. We are informed that here he is;
   And therefore pardon us, for we must
   search.
ALICE. Ay, search, and spare you not,
   through every room.
   Were my husband at home, you would
   not offer this.   400

Here enters Franklin.

   M[aster] Franklin, what mean you come
   so sad?
FRANK. Arden, thy husband and my
   friend, is slain!
ALICE. Ah, by whom?   M[aster] Franklin,
   can you tell?

FRANK. I know not; but behind the Ab-
   bey
   There he lies murthered in most piteous
   case.
MAYOR. But, M[aster] Franklin, are you
   sure 'tis he?
FRANK. I am too sure; would God I were
   deceived.
ALICE. Find out the murtherers; let them
   be known.
FRANK. Ay, so they shall.   Come you along
   with us.
ALICE. Wherefore?
FRANK.   Know you this hand towel
   and this knife?   410
SUS. [*Aside.*] Ah, Michael, through this
   thy negligence
   Thou hast betrayéd and undone us all.
MICH. [*Aside.*] I was so afraid I knew not
   what I did;
   I thought I had thrown them both into
   the well.
ALICE. It is the pig's blood we had to
   supper.
   But wherefore stay you?   Find out the
   murtherers.
MAYOR. I fear me you'll prove one of
   them yourself.
ALICE. I one of them?   What mean such
   questions?
FRANK. I fear me he was murthered in
   this house
   And carried to the fields, for from that
   place   420
   Backwards and forwards may you see
   The print of many feet within the
   snow.
   And look about this chamber where we
   are,
   And you shall find part of his guiltless
   blood,
   For in his slipshoe [1] did I find some
   rushes,
   Which argueth he was murthered in this
   room.
MAYOR. Look in the place where he was
   wont to sit.
   See, see! His blood! It is too manifest.
ALICE. It is a cup of wine that Michael
   shed.
MICH. Ay, truly.   430
FRANK. It is his blood, which, strumpet,
   thou hast shed!
   [1] Slipper.

But, if I live, thou and thy complices
Which have conspired and wrought his
    death shall rue it.
ALICE. Ah, M[aster] Franklin, God and
    heaven can tell
I loved him more than all the world be-
    side.
But bring me to him; let me see his body.
FRANK. Bring that villain and Mosbie's
    sister too;
And one of you go to the Flower-de-Luce,
And seek for Mosbie, and apprehend him
    too.   *Exeunt.*

[SCENE XV.

An obscure street in Southwark.]

Here enters Shakebag solus.

SHAKE. The widow Chambley in her hus-
    band's days I kept;
And, now he's dead, she is grown so stout
She will not know her old companions.
I came thither, thinking to have had
Harbor as I was wont,
And she was ready to thrust me out at
    doors.
But, whether she would or no, I got me up,
And, as she followed me, I spurned her
    down the stairs,
And broke her neck, and cut her tapster's
    throat,
And now I am going to fling them in the
    Thames.   10
I have the gold; what care I though it be
    known!
I'll cross the water and take sanctuary.
                              Exit Shakebag.

[SCENE XVI.

A room in Arden's house.]

*Here enters the Mayor, Mosbie, Alice, Frank-
lin, Michael, and Susan.*

MAYOR. See, M[istress] Arden, where your
    husband lies.
Confess this foul fault and be penitent.
ALICE. Arden, sweet husband, what shall
    I say?
The more I sound his name, the more he
    bleeds;
This blood condemns me, and in gushing
    forth
Speaks as it falls, and asks me why I did it.

Forgive me, Arden; I repent me now,
And, would my death save thine, thou
    shouldst not die.
Rise up, sweet Arden, and enjoy thy love,
And frown not on me when we meet in
    heaven;   10
In heaven I love thee, though on earth
    I did not.
MAYOR. Say, Mosbie, what made thee
    murther him?
FRANK. Study not for an answer; look not
    down.
His purse and girdle found at thy bed's
    head
Witness sufficiently thou didst the deed.
It bootless is to swear thou didst it not.
MOS. I hired Black Will and Shakebag,
    ruffians both,
And they and I have done this mur-
    therous deed.
But wherefore stay we? Come and bear
    me hence.
FRANK. Those ruffians shall not escape; I
    will up to London,   20
And get the council's warrand to appre-
    hend them.   *Exeunt.*

[SCENE XVII.

The Kentish coast.]

Here enters Will.

WILL. Shakebag, I hear, hath taken sanc-
    tuary,
But I am so pursued with hues and cries
For petty robberies that I have done
That I can come unto no sanctuary.
Therefore must I in some oyster boat
At last be fain to go aboard some hoy,[1]
And so to Flushing. There is no staying
    here.
At Sittinburgh the watch was like to take
    me,
And, had not I with my buckler covered
    my head,
And run full blank at all adventures,[2] 10
I am sure I had ne'er gone further than
    that place,
For the constable had twenty warrands
    to apprehend me;
Besides that, I robbed him and his man
    once at Gadshill.
Farewell, England; I'll to Flushing now.
                                 Exit Will.

[1] Small boat.   [2] *I.e.,* taken all risks.

[SCENE xviii.

A courtroom at Feversham.]

Here enters the Mayor, Mosbie, Alice, Michael, Susan, and Bradshaw.

MAYOR. Come, make haste and bring away the prisoners.

BRAD. M[istress] Arden, you are now going to God,
And I am by the law condemned to die
About a letter I brought from M[aster] Greene.
I pray you, M[istress] Arden, speak the truth.
Was I ever privy to your intent or no?

ALICE. What should I say? You brought me such a letter,
But I dare swear thou knewest not the contents.
Leave now to trouble me with worldly things,
And let me meditate upon my Savior Christ,   10
Whose blood must save me for the blood I shed.

MOS. How long shall I live in this hell of grief?
Convey me from the presence of that strumpet.

ALICE. Ah, but for thee I had never been strumpet.
What cannot oaths and protestations do,
When men have opportunity to woo?
I was too young to sound thy villainies,
But now I find it and repent too late.

SUS. Ah, gentle brother, wherefore should I die?   19
I knew not of it till the deed was done.

MOS. For thee I mourn more than for myself;
But let it suffice, I cannot save thee now.

MICH. And, if your brother and my mistress
Had not promised me you in marriage,
I had ne'er given consent to this foul deed.

MAYOR. Leave to accuse each other now,
And listen to the sentence I shall give.
Bear Mosbie and his sister to London straight,
Where they in Smithfield must be executed;   29
Bear M[istress] Arden unto Canterbury,

Where her sentence is she must be burnt,
Michael and Bradshaw in Feversham must suffer death.

ALICE. Let my death make amends for all my sins.

MOS. Fie upon women!—this shall be my song.
But bear me hence, for I have lived too long.

SUS. Seeing no hope on earth, in heaven is my hope.

MICH. Faith, I care not, seeing I die with Susan.

BRAD. My blood be on his head that gave the sentence.

MAYOR. To speedy execution with them all!   *Exeunt.*

[EPILOGUE]

Here enters Franklin.

FRANK. Thus have you seen the truth of Arden's death.
As for the ruffians, Shakebag and Black Will,
The one took sanctuary, and, being sent for out,
Was murthered in Southwark as he passed
To Greenwich, where the lord protector lay.
Black Will was burnt in Flushing on a stage;
Greene was hangéd at Osbridge in Kent;
The painter fled and how he died we know not.
But this above the rest is to be noted:
Arden lay murthered in that plot of ground   10
Which he by force and violence held from Reede,
And in the grass his body's print was seen
Two years and more after the deed was done.
Gentlemen, we hope you'll pardon this naked tragedy,
Wherein no filéd [1] points are foisted in
To make it gracious to the ear or eye;
For simple truth is gracious enough,
And needs no other points of glozing stuff.   [*Exit.*]

FINIS.

[1] Polished.

ATTOWELL'S JIG

Attowell's Jig is one of the most interesting specimens—though perhaps not the most typical—of a dramatic form that achieved a remarkable popularity with London audiences by the end of the sixteenth century. Many satiric allusions go to show that the masses were not satisfied without a jig at the end of every play. About the middle of the century the term jig begins to appear in literary allusions as applied to simple song or dance or to the two combined. During the Elizabethan period, song and dance entertainments under the name jig developed in complexity and were popularized on the stage among the various song and dance specialties of the players. These stage jigs apparently showed considerable variety, but the typical form was that of the ballad, which lent itself to the presentation of jest, tale, and satiric skit, with clowns, fools, vagabonds, and other figures traditional in farce and popular drama. The more formal stage jig was usually a brief ballad farce, sung and accompanied by dance. The chief rôles in the jigs, emphasizing the drollery or rascality of the clown, were taken by outstanding comedians of the various companies. Richard Tarlton, the great clown of the Queen's Company, who died in 1588, was the first to win fame for his jigs, both as author and as performer. In the last decade of the century the most famous exponent of the jig was William Kemp, the leading comedian of Shakespeare's company. In spite of the vogue of the jig until well into the seventeenth century, only six farce jigs are known to have survived in English. A larger number are extant in German, however, for English actors carried the formal jig to the Continent, where it remained popular for nearly a century, especially in Germany. *Rowland*, the most famous of the jigs, is lost in English, but preserved in several German texts. Another favorite was *Singing Simpkin*, almost certainly one of Kemp's successes, which survives in several languages.

Attowell's Jig was entered in the Stationers' Register on October 14, 1595, as "A Pretty New Jig between Francis the Gentleman, Richard the Farmer, and Their Wives." It was published as a broadside ballad in two parts, with the name George Attowell at the end. A manuscript form, published in *Shirburn Ballads*, has the title "Mr. Attowell's Jig between Francis," etc. There is also an early seventeenth century version in German, somewhat freely translated. Probably the name of Attowell is connected with the jig because he popularized it by his performances, not because he wrote it. Little is known of him beyond his connection with the jig. He was associated with Strange's men in 1590–91, and is mentioned, without reference to any company, in a business transaction of Henslowe's in 1595. One interesting feature of the jig is its early use of several scenes with different airs. Of the four tunes, "Walsingham" and "Go from My Window" had an extraordinary vogue. No exact source for the plot is known. Similar intrigue plots with a substitution motive are found in a German jest and in the story from the *Decameron* used by Shakespeare in *All's Well*, but the husband of the faithful wife does not appear. The coarse and farcical handling of characters usual in the dramatic jig is lacking. Instead of the droll, stupid, or crafty country clown and the light, tricky wife common in the jig, the farmer and his wife are presented with sympathy and a measure of dignity. The style is characteristic of the ballad, and, while not distinguished, it is also not without occasional quaintness and charm. The text here is based on that of the only extant copy of the broadside, from the Pepys Collection, as printed by Baskervill in *The Elizabethan Jig*.

ATTOWELL'S JIG[1]

[*DRAMATIS PERSONÆ*

MASTER FRANCIS, *a gentleman.*　MISTRESS FRANCIS.
RICHARD, *a farmer.*　BESS, *Richard's wife.*

SCENE: *The farmer's home.*

TIME: *Contemporary.*]

BESS. [*Singing.*]

As I went to Walsingham,
　To the shrine with speed,
Met I with a jolly palmer
　In a pilgrim's weed.

[*Enter Francis.*]

Now God you save, you jolly palmer!

FRAN. Welcome, lady gay!
Oft have I sued to thee for love.
BESS.[2] Oft have I said you nay.

FRAN. My love is fixed. BESS. And so
　　is mine,
But not on you;　　　　　　　　　10
For to my husband whilst I live
　I will ever be true.
FRAN. I'll give thee gold and rich array—
BESS. Which I shall buy too dear.
FRAN. Naught shalt thou want; then say
　　not nay.
BESS. "Naught" would you make me,
　　I fear!

What though you be a gentleman,
　And have lands great store?
I will be chaste, do what you can,
　Though I live ne'er so poor.　　　20
FRAN. Thy beauty rare hath wounded
　　me,
　And pierced my heart.

BESS. Your foolish love doth trouble me.
　Pray you, sir, depart.

FRAN. Then tell me, sweet, wilt thou con-
　　sent
　Unto my desire?
BESS. And, if I should, then tell me, sir,
　What is it you require?
FRAN. For to enjoy thee as my love.
BESS. Sir, you have a wife;　　　　30
Therefore let your suit have an end.
　FRAN. First will I lose my life!

All that I have thou shalt command.
　BESS. Then my love you have.
FRAN. Your meaning I well understand.
　BESS. I yield to what you crave.
FRAN. But tell me, sweet, when shall I
　　enjoy
　My heart's delight?
I prithee, sweetheart, be not coy.
　BESS. Even soon, at night.　　　40

My husband is rid ten miles from home,
　Money to receive.
In the evening see you come.
　FRAN. Till then, I take my leave.　*Exit.*
BESS. Thus have I rid my hands full well
　Of my amorous love,
And my sweet husband will I tell
　How he doth me move.

*Enter Richard, Bess's husband. To the tune
　　　　　　of the "Jewish Dance."*

RICH. [*Not observing Bess.*] Hey, down a
　　down,
　Hey, down a down, a down!　　　50
There is never a lusty farmer
　In all our town

[1] This is the conventional title. The first part of the broadside on which the present text is based has the title "Francis' New Jig, between Francis, a Gentleman, and Richard, a Farmer. To the Tune of 'Walsingham'."
[2] Except for an initial *Bess*, *Fran.*, and *Rich.*, the speech heads are *B.*, *F.*, and *R.* in the original, with *W.*, that is, *Wife*, for Mistress Francis.

That hath more cause
  To lead a merry life
Than I that am married
  To an honest,[1] faithful wife.
BESS. [*Coming forward.*]   I thank you,
    gentle husband;
  You praise me to my face.
RICH. I cry thee mercy, Bessie;
  I knew thee not in place.   60

BESS. Believe me, gentle husband,
  If you knew as much as I,
The words that you have spoken
  You quickly would deny;
For, since you went from home,
  A suitor I have had,
Who is so far in love with me
  That he is almost mad.
He'll give me gold and silver store,
  And money for to spend,   70
And I have promised him therefore
  To be his loving friend.

RICH. Believe me, gentle wife,
  But this makes me to frown!
There is no gentleman nor knight
  Nor lord of high renown
That shall enjoy thy love, girl,
  Though he were ne'er so good!
Before he wrong my Bessie so,
  I'll spend on him my blood!   80
And therefore tell me who it is
  That doth desire thy love.
BESS. Our neighbor, Master Francis,
  That often did me move;

To whom I gave consent,
  His mind for to fulfill,
And promised him this night
  That he should have his will.
Nay, do not frown, good Dickie,
  But hear me speak my mind;   90
For thou shalt see, I'll warrant thee,
  I'll use him in his kind.
For unto thee I will be true
  So long as I do live;
I'll never change thee for a new,
  Nor once my mind so give.

Go you to Mistress Francis,
  And this to her declare,
And will her with all speed
  To my house to repair,   100

[1] Chaste.

Where she and I'll devise
  Some pretty knavish wile;
For I have laid the plot,
  Her husband to beguile.
Make haste, I pray, and tarry not,
  For long he will not stay.
RICH. Fear not; I'll tell her such a tale
  Shall make her come away!   [*Exit.*]

BESS. Now, Bess, bethink thee
  What thou hast to do.   110
Thy lover will come presently,
  And hardly will he woo.
I will teach my gentleman
  A trick that he may know
I am too crafty and too wise
  To be o'erreachéd so.
But here he comes now! Not a word,
  But fall to work again.
          She sews [*as Francis enters*].
FRAN. How now, sweetheart, at work so
    hard?
BESS. Ay, sir, I must take pains.   120

FRAN. But say, my lovely sweeting,
  Thy promise wilt thou keep?
Shall I enjoy thy love,
  This night with me to sleep?
BESS. My husband rid [2] from home;
  Here safely may you stay.
FRAN. And I have made my wife believe
  I rid another way.
BESS. Go in, good sir, whate'er betide,
  This night and lodge with me.   130
FRAN. The happiest night that ever I
    had!
  Thy friend still will I be.   [*Exit.*]

*Enter Mistress Francis with Richard.   To
      the tune of "Bugle Bow."* [3]

WIFE. I thank you, neighbor Richard,
  For bringing me this news.
RICH. Nay, thank my wife that loves me
    so,
  And will not you abuse.

WIFE. But see whereas [4] she stands
  And waiteth our return.

[2] Rode.
[3] The first sheet ends here with a separate
colophon. The second is headed: "The Second
Part of Attowell's New Jig. To the Tune of 'As
I Went to Walsingham'." There is no division
into stanzas marked in the section sung to the
tune of "Bugle Bow."
[4] Where.

Rich. You must go cool your husband's
    heat,
    That so in love doth burn.   140

Bess. Now, Dickie, welcome home,
    And, mistress, welcome hither.
Grieve not, although you find
    Your husband and I together.

For you shall have your right,
    Nor will I wrong you so.
Then change apparel with me straight,
    And unto him do go.
               [*They exchange clothes.*]

Wife. For this your kind good will
    A thousand thanks I give;   150
And make account I will requite
    This kindness, if I live.

Bess. I hope it shall not need;
    Dick will not serve me so.
I know he loves me not so ill
    A-ranging for to go.

Rich. No, faith, my lovely Bess;
    First will I lose my life
Before I'll break my wedlock bonds
    Or seek to wrong my wife.   160
               [*Exit Mistress Francis.*]

Now thinks good Master Francis
    He hath thee in his bed,
And makes account he is grafting
    Of horns upon my head.

But softly! Stand aside!
    Now shall we know his mind,
And how he would have uséd thee,
    If thou hadst been so kind.
               [*They stand aside.*]

Enter Master Francis with his own Wife,
  having a mask before her face, supposing
  her to be Bess. To the tune of "Go from
            My Window."

Fran. Farewell, my joy and heart's de-
    light,
    Till next we meet again.   170
Thy kindness to requite
For lodging me all night,
    Here's ten pound for thy pain;

And more to show my love to thee
    Wear this ring for my sake.

Wife. Without your gold or fee
    You shall have more of me.
    Fran. No doubt of that I make.

Wife. Then let your love continue still.
    Fran. It shall, till life doth end.   180
Wife. Your wife I greatly fear.
Fran. For her thou need'st not care
    So I remain thy friend.

Wife. But you'll suspect me, without
    cause,
    That I am false to you;
And then you'll cast me off
And make me but a scoff,
    Since that I prove untrue.

Fran. Then never trust man for my sake,
    If I prove so unkind!   190
[Wife.] So often have you sworn,
Sir, since that you were born,
    And soon have changed your mind.

[Fran.] Nor wife nor life, nor goods nor
    lands,
    Shall make me leave my love,
Nor any worldly treasure
Make me forgo my pleasure,
    Nor once my mind remove.

    [*Richard and Bess come forward.*]

Wife. But soft awhile! Who is yonder?
    Do you see
    My husband? Out, alas!   200
Fran. And yonder is my wife!
Now shall we have a life!
    How cometh this to pass?

Rich. Come hither, gentle Bess! I charge
    thee, do confess
    What makes Master Francis here?
Wife.[1] Good husband, pardon me!
I'll tell the troth to thee.
    Rich. Then speak, and do not fear.

Fran. Nay, neighbor Richard, hark to
    me!
    I'll tell the troth to you.   210
Bess. Nay, tell it unto me,
Good sir, that I may see
    What you have here to do.

[1] In this stanza and the next, the names of
the women are reversed in the original, probably
because of the disguise.

But you can make no scuse [1] to color this
   abuse;
   This wrong is too-too great!
RICH. Good sir, I take great scorn
You should proffer me the horn.
   WIFE. Now must I cool this heat. [2]

Nay, neighbor Richard, be content;
   Thou hast no wrong at all.   220
                          [*Discloses herself.*]
Thy wife hath done thee right,
And pleasured me this night!
   FRAN. This frets me to the gall!

Good wife, forgive me this offense;
   I do repent mine ill.
WIFE. I thank you with mine heart
For playing this kind part,
   Though sore against your will.

Nay, gentle husband, frown not so,
   For you have made amends;   230
I think it is good gain
To have ten pound for my pain!
   Then let us both be friends.

FRAN. Ashamed I am, and know not what
   to say.
   Good wife, forgive this crime!
Alas, I do repent!
WIFE. Tut, I could be content
   To be served so many a time!

FRAN. Good neighbor Richard, be content;
   I'll woo thy wife no more—   240
   ¹ Excuse.
   ² In the original, the rest of this speech is assigned to Francis.

I have enough of this.
WIFE. Then all forgiven is.—
   I thank thee, Dick, therefore,

And to thy wife I'll give this gol*···*
   I hope you'll not say no.
Since I have had the pleasure,
Let her enjoy the treasure!
   FRAN. Good wife, let it be so.

BESS. I thank you, gentle mistress,
   RICH. Faith, and so do I,
Sir, learn your own wife to know,   250
And shoot not in the dark
For fear you miss the mark.
   BESS. He hath paid for this, I trow.

All women learn of me. FRAN. All men
   by me take heed
How you a woman trust.
WIFE. Nay, women, trust no men.
FRAN. And, if they do, how then?
   WIFE. There's few of them prove just.

Farewell, neighbor Richard!   Farewell,
   honest Bess!
   I hope we are all friends.   260
[*To Francis.*] ³ And, if you stay at home,
And use not thus to roam,
   Here all our quarrel ends.

FINIS.

GEORGE ATTOWELL.

   ³ In the original, the speech head for "Wife"
is repeated here.

MUCEDORUS

If the evidence of editions may be accepted, *Mucedorus* was the most popular play in all pre-Restoration drama, for after its initial publication in 1598 it went through at least sixteen new editions by 1668. The distribution of the parts suggests, however, that the unusual number of editions may have been called forth by a ready sale to small troupes of actors. The Citizen's Wife in *The Knight of the Burning Pestle* remarks of Ralph, the apprentice with histrionic ambitions, "Nay, gentlemen, he hath played before, my husband says—*Mucedorus* before the wardens of our company." In Cowley's *Guardian* and in his Restoration revision of that play as *The Cutter of Coleman Street,* Jolly's servant Will disclaims having acted the clown, but modestly admits to the bear. *Mucedorus* was surreptitiously presented by strolling players while the theaters were closed during the Commonwealth, and was performed by village actors in the north of England as late as 1666. The reduction of the play to a ballad also emphasizes its popular character. The form printed here shows revision for acting before James I.

The bare outline of the play was derived from Sidney's *Arcadia:* the hero's name, his disguise as a shepherd, his rescue of the heroine from the bear, and the elopement, capture, and happy union of the two. With the action set in the forest, the author of the play has added the wild man, whose offer of rustic gifts to Amadine is an ancient convention of pastoral poetry. The wild man represents, however, the ogre of folk tale rather than the savage of pastoral or of Spenser's *Fairy Queen.* The constantly appearing clown is of the droll and stupid type that popular taste seems to have demanded not only in farces and jigs but in the romantic plays of the University Wits and Shakespeare, and even in chronicle plays and tragedies. Thus the author of *Mucedorus* has shifted the treatment from Sidney's courtly mixture of pastoral and chivalric romance to make a play of the type that Sidney condemns in his *Apology for Poetry,* with its romantic absurdities and its inappropriate clown crowding to the very throne of the king. The induction and the epilogue, which like those of several other sixteenth century plays show the continued interest in debates, or flytings, are here used to emphasize the mixed nature of the play as a "tragi-comedy."

The fact that in spite of its vogue the author of *Mucedorus* is unknown reveals a characteristic attitude of the sixteenth century. The cultured looked upon a play as mere entertainment rather than as literature, and printers were inclined to disregard the playwright unless he had achieved popularity with some class of readers. The author of *Mucedorus* was, however, a man of some literary as well as dramatic gifts, and from the characteristics of the play many attempts have been made to identify him as one of the better known dramatists. The older attribution in part or in whole to Shakespeare is now discarded by virtually all scholars. Claims have been made for Peele, Greene, and more especially Lodge. More likely, Tucker Brooke, who edited the play in his *Shakespeare Apocrypha,* is right in his suggestion that it was written by "an obscure and only moderately gifted disciple" of the University Wits.

The present text is based on the edition of 1610, with its added scenes showing the bear and the court of Mucedorus' father. The editors are indebted to the authorities of the Huntington Library for permission to use photostats of the copy of this quarto in the Library.

MUCEDORUS[1]

THE PROLOGUE[2]

Most sacred majesty, whose great deserts
Thy subject England, nay, the world ad-
   mires—
Which heaven grant still increase—O,
   may your praise,
Multiplying with your hours, your fame
   still raise;
Embrace your council; love, with faith,
   them guide,
That both, as one, bench by each other's
   side.
So may your life pass on and run so even

That your firm zeal plant you a throne
   in heaven,
Where smiling angels shall your guardians be
From blemished traitors, stained with per-
   jury.   10
And, as the night's inferior to the day,
So be all earthly regions to your sway.
Be as the sun to day, the day to night;
For, from your beams, Europe shall borrow
   light.
Mirth drown your bosom, fair delight
   your mind,
And may our pastime your contentment
   find.   *Exit.*

[DRAMATIS PERSONÆ]

Ten persons may easily play it.[3]

THE KING *and*
RUMBELO } *for one.*

KING VALENCIA } *for one.*

MUCEDORUS, *the Prince
of Valencia* } *for one.*

ANSELMO } *for one.*

AMADINE, *the king's
daughter of Aragon* } *for one.*

SEGASTO, *a nobleman* } *for one.*

ENVY; TREMELIO, *a captain;*
BREMO, *a wild man* } *for one.*

COMEDY; A BOY; AN OLD WOMAN;
ARIENA, *Amadine's maid* } *for one.*

COLLEN, *a councilor;* A
MESSENGER } *for one.*

MOUSE, *the clown* } *for one.*

[SCENE: *Valencia and Aragon.*

TIME: *Uncertain.*]

[INDUCTION]

*Enter Comedy, joyfully, with a garland of
bays on her head.*

[COM.] Why, so! Thus do I hope to please.
   Music revives, and mirth is tolerable.
   Comedy, play thy part and please;

Make merry them that comes to joy
   with thee.
Joy, then, good gentles;[4] I hope to make
   you laugh.
Sound forth Bellona's silver-tunéd strings.
Time fits us well; the day and place is ours.

*Enter Envy, his arms naked, besmeared with
blood.*

ENV. Nay, stay, minion; there lies a
   block.
What, all on mirth? I'll interrupt your
   tale
And mix your music with a tragic end. 10
COM. What monstrous, ugly hag is this,
   That dares control the pleasures of our
   will?

---

[1] The complete title of 1610 reads: "A Most
Pleasant Comedy of Mucedorus, the King's Son
of Valencia, and Amadine, the King's Daughter
of Aragon, with the Merry Conceits of Mouse.
Amplified with New Additions, As It Was Acted
before the King's Majesty at Whitehall on Shrove
Sunday Night. By His Highness' Servants, Usually Playing at the Globe. Very Delectable and
Full of Conceited Mirth."

[2] The prologue first appeared in the 1610 edn.

[3] In the following list no provision is made for
Roderigo, Borachius, and the Bear.

[4] Gentlefolk.

Vaunt,[1] churlish cur, besmeared with
gory blood,
That seem'st to check the blossom of
delight,
And stifle [2] the sound of sweet Bellona's
breath.
Blush, monster, blush, and post away
with shame,
That seekest disturbance of a goddess'
deeds.
Env. Post hence thyself, thou counter-
checking trull!
I will possess this habit,[3] spite of thee,
And gain the glory of thy wishéd port.[4] 20
I'll thunder music shall appall the
nymphs,
And make them shiver their clattering
strings,
Flying for succor to their dankish [5]
caves.
Sound drums within and cry, "Stab! Stab!"
Hearken, thou shalt hear a noise
Shall fill the air with a shrilling sound,
And thunder music to [the] [6] gods above;
Mars shall himself breathe down
A peerless crown upon brave Envy's
head,
And raise his chivall [7] with a lasting
fame. 29
In this brave music Envy takes delight,
Where I may see them wallow in their
blood,
To spurn at arms and legs quite shivered
off,
And hear the cries of many thousand
slain.
How lik'st thou this, my trull?   This
sport alone for me!
Com. Vaunt, bloody cur, nursed up with
tiger's sap,
That so dost [seek to] [8] quail a woman's
mind.
Comedy is mild, gentle, willing for to
please,
And seeks to gain the love of all estates,
Delighting in mirth, mixed all with
lovely tales,

And bringeth things with treble joy
to pass. 40
Thou, bloody, envious disdainer of men's
joys,
Whose name is fraught with bloody
stratagems,
Delights in nothing but in spoil and
death,
Where thou mayst trample in their
lukewarm blood,
And grasp their hearts within thy curséd
paws.
Yet vail thy mind;[9] revenge thou not
on me—
A silly woman begs it at thy hands.
Give me the leave to utter out my play.
Forbear this place, I humbly crave thee:
hence,
And mix not death 'mongst pleasing
comedies, 50
That treats naught else but pleasure
and delight!
If any spark of human rests in thee,
Forbear, begone, tender [10] the suit of
me.
Env. Why, so I will; forbearance [11] shall
be such
As treble death shall cross thee with
despite,
And make thee mourn where most thou
joyest,
Turning thy mirth into a deadly dole,
Whirling thy pleasures with a peal of
death,
And drench thy methods [12] in a sea of
blood.
This will I do; thus shall I bear with
thee; 60
And, more to vex thee with a deeper
spite,
I will with threats of blood begin thy
play,
Favoring thee with envy and with hate.
Com. Then, ugly monster, do thy worst;
I will defend them in despite of thee.
And, though thou think'st with tragic
fumes [13]
To prave [14] my play unto my deep dis-
grace,

---

[1] Avaunt, be off.
[2] From 1598 edn. Original reads *stiffe.*
[3] Costume.
[4] Station.
[5] Emended by Collier. Original reads *Danish.*
[6] Supplied from 1598 edn.
[7] 'Chieval, achieval, achievement (?).
[8] From 1598 edn.
[9] Modify thy intention.
[10] Regard favorably.
[11] From 1598 edn. Original reads *forbear.*
[12] Designs, *i.e.*, the plot of her play.
[13] Fits of anger.
[14] Deprave, ruin.

I force it not;[1] I scorn what thou canst
do;
I'll grace it so thyself shall it confess
From tragic stuff to be a pleasant
comedy.   70
Env. Why then, Comedy, send thy actors
forth
And I will cross the first steps of their
trade,
Making them fear the very dart of
death.
Com. And I'll defend them mauger all
thy spite.
So, ugly fiend, farewell, till time shall
serve
That we may meet to parley for the best.
Env. Content, Comedy; I'll go spread
my branch,
And scattered blossoms from mine en-
vious tree
Shall prove to[2] monsters, spoiling of
their joys.   Exit [with Comedy].

[Scene i.[3]

The court of Valencia.]

*Sound. Enter Mucedorus and Anselmo, his
friend.*

Mu. Anselmo!
Ans. My lord and friend!
Mu. True, my Anselmo, both thy lord
and friend
Whose dear affections bosom with my
heart,
And keep their domination in one orb.
Ans. Whence ne'er disloyalty shall root
it forth,
But faith plant firmer in your choice
respect.
Mu. Much blame were mine if I should
other deem,
Nor can coy Fortune contrary allow.
But, my Anselmo, loath I am to say
I must estrange that friendship.   11
Misconster[4] not—'tis from the realm,
not thee;
Though lands part bodies, hearts keep
company.
Thou know'st that I imparted often
have
Private relations with my royal sire,

---

[1] I care not for it.   [2] Become.
[3] This scene appears first in the 1610 edn.
[4] Misconstrue.

Had as concerning beauteous Amadine,
Rich Aragon's bright jewel, whose face
some say
That blooming lilies never shone so gay,
Excelling, not excelled. Yet, lest re-
port
Does mangle verity, boasting of what is
not,   20
Winged with desire, thither I'll straight
repair,
And be my fortunes, as my thoughts
are, fair.
Ans. Will you forsake Valencia, leave
the court,
Absent you from the eye of sovereignty?
Do not, sweet prince, adventure on that
task,
Since danger lurks each where. Be won
from it.
Mu. Desist dissuasion;
My resolution brooks no battery;
Therefore, if thou retain thy wonted
form,
Assist what I intend.   30
Ans. Your miss will breed a blemish in
the court,
And throw a frosty dew upon that
beard
Whose front Valencia stoops to.
Mu. If thou my welfare tender, then no
more;
Let love's strong magic charm thy
trivial phrase,
Wasted as vainly as to gripe[5] the sun.
Augment not then more answers; lock
thy lips,
Unless thy wisdom suit[6] me with dis-
guise
According to my purpose.
Ans. That action craves no counsel,   40
Since what you rightly are will more
command
Than best usurpéd shape.
Mu. Thou still art opposite in disposi-
tion.
A more obscure, servile habiliment
Beseems this enterprise.
Ans. Then like a Florentine or mounte-
bank?
Mu. 'Tis much too tedious; I dislike thy
judgment.
My mind is grafted on an humbler
stock.

---

[5] Seize.   [6] Clothe.

Ans. Within my closet does there hang
   a cassock;
   Though base the weed is, 't was a shep-
      herd's   50
   Which J presented in Lord Julio's
      masque.
Mu. That, my Anselmo, and none else
   but that,
   Mask Mucedorus from the vulgar view!
   That habit suits my mind; fetch me
      that weed.   *Exit Anselmo.*
   Better than kings have not disdained
      that state,
   And much inferior, to obtain their mate!

Enter Anselmo with a shepherd's coat.

So let our respect command thy secrecy.
At once a brief farewell!
Delay to lovers is a second hell!
                  Exit Mucedorus.
Ans. Prosperity forerun thee; awkward
   chance   60
   Never be neighbor to thy wish's ven-
      ture;
   Content and fame advance thee; ever
      thrive,
   And glory thy mortality survive.   *Exit.*

[Scene ii.[1]

A forest in Aragon.]

Enter Mouse with a bottle [2] of hay.

Mouse. O, horrible, terrible! Was ever
poor gentleman so scared out of his seven
senses? A bear? Nay, sure it cannot be
a bear, but some devil in a bear's doublet,
for a bear could never have had that agility
to have frighted me. Well, I'll see my
father hanged before I'll serve his horse
any more. Well, I'll carry home my bottle
of hay, and for once make my father's
horse turn Puritan and observe fasting [10
days, for he gets not a bit. But soft! This
way she followed me; therefore I'll take
the other path; and, because I'll be sure
to have an eye on him, I will take hands
with some foolish creditor, and make
every step backward.
*As he goes backwards the bear comes in,
and he tumbles over her, and runs away and
      leaves his bottle of hay behind him.*

---

[1] This scene appeared first in the 1610 edn.
[2] Bundle.

[Scene iii

The same.]

*Enter Segasto running and Amadine after
      him, being pursued with a bear.*

Seg. O, fly, madam, fly or else we are
   but dead!
Am. Help, Segasto, help! Help, sweet
   Segasto, or else I die!
Seg. Alas, madam, there is no way but
   flight;
   Then haste and save yourself!
            Segasto runs away.[3]
Am. Why, then I die; ah, help me in dis-
   tress!

*Enter Mucedorus like a shepherd, with a
   sword drawn and a bear's head in his
               hand.*

Mu. Stay, lady, stay, and be no more
   dismayed.
   That cruel beast most merciless and fell,
   Which hath bereavéd thousands of their
      lives,
   Affrighted many with his hard pursues,
   Prying from place to place to find his
      prey,   10
   Prolonging thus his life by others'
      death,
   His carcass now lies headless, void of
      breath.
Am. That foul, deforméd monster, is he
   dead?
Mu. Assure yourself thereof: behold his
   head,
   Which, if it please you, lady, to accept,
   With willing heart I yield it to your
      majesty.
Am. Thanks, worthy shepherd, thanks
   a thousand times.
   This gift, assure thyself, contents me more
   Than greatest bounty of a mighty prince,
   Although he were the monarch of the
      world.   20
Mu. Most gracious goddess, more than
   mortal wight—
   Your heavenly hue of right imports
      no less—
   Most glad am I in that it was my chance
   To undertake this enterprise in hand,
   Which doth so greatly glad your princely
      mind.

---

[3] All early edns. place this direction after l. 2.

Am. No goddess, shepherd, but a mortal
  wight,
  A mortal wight distresséd as thou seest.
  My father here is king of Aragon.
  I, Amadine, his only daughter am,   25
  And after him sole heir unto the crown.
  Now, whereas it is my father's will
  To marry me unto Segasto, one [1]
  Whose wealth through father's former
    usury
  Is known to be no less than wonderful,
  We both of custom oftentimes did use,
  Leaving the court, to walk within the
    fields
  For recreation, especially [in][2] the spring,
  In that it yields great store of rare de-
    lights,
  And, passing further than our wonted
    walks,
  Scarce entered were within these luck-
    less woods,   40
  But right before us down a steep-fall
    hill
  A monstrous, ugly bear did hie him fast
  To meet us both. I faint to tell the rest,
  Good shepherd, but suppose the ghastly
    looks,
  The hideous fears, the thousand hun-
    dred woes,
  Which at this instant Amadine sustained.
Mu. Yet, worthy princess, let thy sorrow
    cease,
  And let this sight your former joys re-
    vive.
Am. Believe me, shepherd, so it doth no
    less.
Mu. Long may they last unto your heart's
    content.   50
  But tell me, lady, what is become of
    him,
  Segasto called, what is become of him?
Am. I know not, I; that know the powers
    divine;
  But God grant this, that sweet Segasto
    live.
Mu. Yet hard-hearted he in such a case,
  So cowardly to save himself by flight,
  And leave so brave a princess to the
    spoil.
Am. Well, shepherd, for thy worthy valor
    tried,

[1] Here and in a few other cases line divisions
have been regularized.
[2] Supplied by Hazlitt.

Endangering thyself to set me free,
Unrecompenséd sure thou shalt not be. 60
In court thy courage shall be plainly
  known;
Throughout the kingdom will I spread
  thy name,
To thy renown and never-dying fame.
And, that thy courage may be better
  known,
Bear thou the head of this most mon-
  strous beast
In open sight to every courtier's view.
So will the king my father thee reward.
Come, let's away, and guard me to
  the court.
Mu. With all my heart.   *Exeunt.*

[SCENE iv.

The outskirts of the forest.]

Enter Segasto solus.

Seg. When heaps of harms do hover over-
    head,
  'Tis time as then, some say, to look
    about,
  And of [3] ensuing harms to choose the
    least.
  But hard, yea, hapless, is that wretch's
    chance,
  Luckless his lot and caitiff-like accursed,
  At whose proceedings fortune ever
    frowns—
  Myself I mean, most subject unto
    thrall,
  For I, the more I seek to shun the
    worst,
  The more by proof I find myself accursed.
  Erewhiles assaulted with an ugly bear, 10
  Fair Amadine in company all alone,
  Forthwith by flight I thought to save
    myself,
  Leaving my Amadine unto her shifts;
  For death it was for to resist the bear,
  And death no less of Amadine's harms to
    hear.
  Accurséd I in ling'ring life thus long!
  In living thus, each minute of an hour
  Doth pierce my heart with darts of
    thousand deaths.
  If she by flight her fury do escape,
  What will she think?   20
  Will she not say—yea, flatly to my face,

[3] From 1613 edn. Original reads *so.*

Accusing me of mere [1] disloyalty—
A trusty friend is tried in time of need?
But I, when she in danger was of death
And needed me, and cried, "Segasto,
    help!"
I turned my back and quickly ran away.
Unworthy I to bear this vital breath!
But what! What needs these plaints?
If Amadine do live, then happy I;
She will in time forgive and so forget.   30
Amadine is merciful, not Juno-like,
In harmful heart to harbor hatred long.

*Enter Mouse, the clown, running, crying,
                        "Clubs!"*

MOUSE. Clubs, prongs, pitchforks, bills! [2]
O, help! A bear, a bear, a bear! [3]
SEG. Still bears, and nothing else but
bears! Tell me, sirrah, where she is.
CLO. [4] O, sir, she is run down the woods!
I saw her white head and her white
belly.
SEG. Thou talkest of wonders, to tell me
of white bears.   40
    But, sirrah, didst thou ever see any
    such?
CLO. No, faith, I never saw any such,
but I remember my father's words: he
bade me take heed I was not caught with
a white bear.
SEG. A lamentable tale, no doubt.
CLO. I tell you what, sir, as I was going
afield to serve my father's great horse, and
carried a bottle of hay upon my head—now
do you see, sir—I, fast hoodwinked [5]   [50
that I could see nothing, I perceiving the
bear coming, I threw my hay into the hedge
and ran away.
SEG. What, from nothing?
CLO. I warrant you, yes, I saw something, for there was two load of thorns
besides my bottle of hay, and that made
three.
SEG. But tell me, sirrah, the bear that
    thou didst see,   59
Did she not bear a bucket on her arm?
CLO. Ha, ha, ha! I never saw bear go
a-milking in all my life. But hark you,

sir, I did not look so high as her arm; I
saw nothing but her white head and her
white belly.
SEG. But tell me, sirrah, where dost
thou dwell?
CLO. Why, do you not know me?
SEG. Why, no, how should I know thee?
CLO. Why, then, you know nobody,   [70
and [6] you know not me. I tell you, sir,
I am the Goodman Rat's son of the next
parish over the hill.
SEG. Goodman Rat's son?   Why,
what's thy name?
CLO. Why, I am very near kin unto
him.
SEG. I think so, but what's thy name?
CLO. My name? I have a very pretty
name. I'll tell you what my name is; my
name is Mouse.   81
SEG. What, plain Mouse?
CLO. Ay, plain Mouse without either
welt or guard. [7] But do you hear, sir, I am
but a very young mouse, for my tail is
scarce grown out yet; look you here else.
SEG. But, I pray thee, who gave thee
that name?
CLO. Faith, sir, I know not that, but,
if you would fain know, ask my father's   [90
great horse, for he hath been half a year
longer with my father than I have.
SEG. [*Aside.*] This seems to be a merry
    fellow;
I care not if I take him home with me.
Mirth is a comfort to a troubled mind;
A merry man a merry master makes.—
How sayst thou, sirrah, wilt thou dwell
    with me?
CLO. Nay, soft, sir, two words to a bar-
gain! Pray you, what occupation are
you?   100
SEG. No occupation; I live upon my
lands.
CLO. Your lands! Away, you are no
master for me! Why, do you think that
I am so mad, to go seek my living in the
lands amongst the stones, briers, and
bushes, and tear my holiday apparel? Not
I, by your leave.
SEG. Why, I do not mean thou shalt.
CLO. How then?   110
SEG. Why, thou shalt be my man, and
wait upon me at the court.

[1] Absolute.   [2] Pruning hooks.
[3] Ll. 33–45 and a number of other passages
printed as rough verse in the original are here
printed as prose.
[4] Clown, *i.e.*, Mouse.
[5] Completely blindfolded.

[6] If. The whole expression is proverbial.
[7] *I.e.*, undecorated.

CLO. What's that?

SEG. Where the king lies.

CLO. What's that same king, a man or a woman?

SEG. A man as thou art.

CLO. As I am? Hark you, sir; pray you, what kin is he to Goodman King of our parish, the churchwarden?   120

SEG. No kin to him; he is the king of the whole land.

CLO. King of the land! I never see him.

SEG. If thou wilt dwell with me, thou shalt see him every day.

CLO. Shall I go home again to be torn in pieces with bears? No, not I. I will go home and put on a clean shirt, and then go drown myself.   129

SEG. Thou shalt not need; if thou wilt dwell with me, thou shalt want nothing.

CLO. Shall I not? Then here's my hand; I'll dwell with you. And hark you, sir; now you have entertained me, I will tell you what I can do. I can keep my tongue from picking and stealing, and my hands from lying and slandering, I warrant you, as well as ever you had man in all your life.   140

SEG. Now will I to court with sorrowful heart, rounded [1] with doubts. If Amadine do live, then happy I; yea, happy I, if Amadine do live.   [*Exeunt.*]

[SCENE V.

The camp of the King of Aragon.]

Enter the King with a young Prince prisoner,
  Amadine, Tremelio, [2] *with Collen and*
                         Councilors.

KING. Now, brave lords, our wars are brought to end,

Our foes, the foil, [3] and we in safety rest.

It us behooves to use such clemency in peace

As valor in the wars.

It is as great honor to be bountiful at home

As to be conquerors in the field.

Therefore, my lords, the more to my content,

Your liking, and your country's safeguard,

We are disposed in marriage for to give

Our daughter to Lord Segasto here,   10

Who shall succeed the diadem after me,

And reign hereafter as I tofore [4] have done,

Your sole and lawful King of Aragon.

What say you, lordings? Like you of my advice?

COL. An't [5] please your majesty, we do not only allow of your highness' pleasure, but also vow faithfully in what we may to further it.

KING. Thanks, good my lords; if long Adrostus live,

He will at full requite your courtesies. 20

Tremelio, in recompense of thy late valor done,

Take unto thee the Catalone, [6] a prince,

Lately our prisoner taken in the wars.

Be thou his keeper; his ransom shall be thine;

We'll think of it when leisure shall afford.

Meanwhile, do use him well; his father is a king.

TRE. Thanks to your majesty! His usage shall be such

As he thereat shall think no cause to grutch. [7]

          Exeunt [Tremelio and Prince].

KING. Then march we on to court, and rest our wearied limbs.

But, Collen, I have a tale in secret kept for thee: 30

When thou shalt hear a watchword from thy king,

Think then some weighty matter is at hand

That highly shall concern our state;

Then, Collen, look thou be not far from me.

And, for the service thou tofore hast done,

Thy truth and valor proved in every point,

I shall with bounties thee enlarge therefor.

So guard us to the court.

COL. Whatso my sovereign doth command me do,   39

With willing mind I gladly yield consent.

          Exeunt.

[1] Surrounded.   [3] *I.e.*, to defeat.
[2] Appears first in 1610 edn.

[4] Before.   [6] Man from Catalonia.
[5] If it.   [7] Grudge, murmur.

[SCENE vi.

The same.]

*Enter Segasto and the Clown, with weapons
about him.*

SEG. Tell me, sirrah, how do you like
your weapons?

CLO. O, very well, very well; they keep
my sides warm.

SEG. They keep the dogs from your
shins very well, do they not?

CLO. How, keep the dogs from my
shins? I would scorn but my shins could
keep the dogs from them.

SEG. Well, sirrah, leaving idle talk, [10
tell me dost thou know Captain Tremelio's chamber?

CLO. Ay, very well; it hath a door.

SEG. I think so, for so hath every chamber. But dost thou know the man?

CLO. Ay, forsooth; he hath a nose on
his face.

SEG. Why, so hath everyone.

CLO. That's more than I know.

SEG. But dost thou remember the [20
captain that was here with the king even
now, that brought the young prince prisoner?

CLO. O, very well.

SEG. Go unto him and bid him come
unto me. Tell him I have a matter in
secret to impart to him.

CLO. I will, Master.—Master, what's his
name?

SEG. Why, Captain Tremelio. 30

CLO. O, the mealman! I know him very
well. He brings meal every Saturday. But
hark you, master, must I bid him come to
you or must you come to him?

SEG. No, sirrah, he must come to me.

CLO. Hark you, master, how if he be
not at home? What shall I do then?

SEG. Why, then leave word with some
of his folks.

CLO. O, master, if there be nobody [40
within, I will leave word with his dog.

SEG. Why, can his dog speak?

CLO. I cannot tell; wherefore doth he
keep his chamber else?

SEG. To keep out such knaves as thou
art.

CLO. Nay, by Lady; then go yourself.

SEG. You will go, sir, will you not?

CLO. Yes, marry, will I. O, 'tis come
to my head; and a [1] be not within, I'll [50
bring his chamber to you.

SEG. What, wilt thou pluck down the
king's house?

CLO. Nay, by Lady, I'll know the price
of it first. Master, it is such a hard name
I have forgotten it again. I pray you, tell
me his name.

SEG. I tell thee, Captain Tremelio.

CLO. O, Captain Treble-knave, Captain
Treble-knave. 60

Enter Tremelio.

TRE. How now, sirrah, dost thou call
me?

CLO. You must come to my master,
Captain Treble-knave.

TRE. My Lord Segasto, did you send
for me?

SEG. I did, Tremelio.—Sirrah, about
your business.

CLO. Ay, marry, what's that? Can
you tell? 70

SEG. No, not well.

CLO. Marry, then, I can; straight to
the kitchen-dresser, to John the cook, and
get me a good piece of beef and brewis,[2]
and then to the buttery hatch to Thomas
the butler for a jack [3] of beer, and there
for an hour I'll so belabor myself! And
therefore, I pray you, call me not till you
think I have done, I pray you, good master.

Exit.

SEG. Well, sir, away.—Tremelio, this [80
it is: thou knowest the valor of Segasto
spread through all the kingdom of Aragon, and such as have found triumph
and favors, never daunted at any time;
but now a shepherd [is][4] admired at in
court for worthiness, and Segasto's honor
laid aside. My will, therefore, is this:
that thou dost find some means to work
the shepherd's death. I know thy strength
sufficient to perform my desire, and thy [90
love no otherwise than to revenge my
injuries.

TRE. It is not the frowns of a shepherd
that Tremelio fears. Therefore, account
it accomplished, what I take in hand.

---

[1] He.
[2] Thickened broth.
[3] Leather pitcher.
[4] Added by Hazlitt.

Seg. Thanks, good Tremelio, and assure
 thyself
What I promise that will I perform.
Tre. Thanks, my good lord, and in good
 time see where
He cometh. Stand by awhile, and you
 shall see
Me put in practice your intended
 drift.[1]   100

Enter Mucedorus.[2]

Have at thee, swain, if that I hit thee
 right!
Mu. Vild [3] coward, so without cause to
 strike a man!
Turn, coward, turn; now strike and do
 thy worst! *Mucedorus killeth him.*
Seg. Hold, shepherd, hold; spare him,
 kill him not!
Accursed villain, tell me, what hast
 thou done?
Ah, Tremelio, trusty Tremelio!
I sorrow for thy death, and, since that thou,
Living, didst prove faithful to Segasto,
So Segasto now, living, will honor
The dead corpse of Tremelio with re-
 venge.   110
Bloodthirsty villain, born and bred in
 merciless murther,
Tell me, how durst thou be so bold as
 once
To lay thy hands upon the least of
 mine?
Assure thyself, thou shalt be used ac-
 cording to the law.
Mu. Segasto, cease; these threats are
 needless.
Accuse not me of murther, that have
 done nothing
But in mine own defense.
Seg. Nay, shepherd, reason not with me.
I'll manifest thy fact [4] unto the king,
Whose doom [5] will be thy death, as thou
 deserv'st.   120
What ho, Mouse, come away!

Enter Mouse.

Clo. Why, how now, what's the matter? I thought you would be calling before
I had done.

Seg. Come, help; away with my friend!
Clo. Why, is he drunk? Cannot he
stand on his feet?
Seg. No, he is not drunk; he is slain.
Clo. Flain?[6] No, by Lady; he is not
flain.   130
Seg. He's killed, I tell thee.
Clo. What, do you use to kill your
friends? I will serve you no longer.
Seg. I tell thee, the shepherd killed
him.
Clo. O, did a so? But, master, I will
have all his apparel if I carry him away?
Seg. Why, so thou shalt.
Clo. Come, then, I will help. Mass,[7]
master, I think his mother sung [140
"looby"[8] to him, he is so heavy.
    Exeunt [Segasto and Mouse].
Mu. Behold the fickle state of man, al-
 ways mutable,
Never at one. Sometimes we feed on
 fancies
With the sweet of our desires; some-
 times again
We feel the heat of extreme miseries.
Now am I in favor about the court and
 country;
Tomorrow those favors will turn to
 frowns.
Today I live revengéd on my foe;
Tomorrow I die, my foe revenged on me.
        Exit.

[Scene vii.

The forest.]

Enter Bremo, a wild man.

Bre. No passenger [9] this morning? What,
 not one?
A chance that seldom doth befall.
What, not one? Then lie thou there,
And rest thyself till I have further need.
    [Puts down his club.]
Now, Bremo, sith [10] thy leisure so af-
 fords—
An endless thing. Who knows not
 Bremo's strength,
Who like a king commands [11] within
 these woods?
The bear, the boar, dares not abide my
 sight,

---

[1] Scheme.
[2] All early edns. have stage direction after next
line.   [4] Deed, crime.
 [3] Vile.   [5] Judgment. sentence.

[6] Flayed.   [9] Traveler.
[7] By the Mass. [10] Since.
[8] Lubber.   [11] Original reads *commander.*

But haste away to save themselves by
　flight.
The crystal waters in the bubbling
　brooks,　　　　　　　　　　　　10
When I come by, doth swiftly slide away,
And claps themselves in closets under
　banks,
Afraid to look bold Bremo in the face.
The aged oaks at Bremo's breath doth
　bow,
And all things else are still at my com-
　mand.
Else, what would I?
Rend them in pieces and pluck them
　from the earth,
And each way else I would revenge my-
　self.
Why, who comes here with whom I
　dare not fight?
Who fights with me and doth not die the
　death? Not one.　　　　　　　　20
What favor shows this sturdy stick to
　those
That here within these woods are com-
　batants with me?
Why, death, and nothing else but pres-
　ent death.
With restless rage I wander through
　these woods;
No creature here but feareth Bremo's
　force;
Man, woman, child, beast, and bird,
And everything that doth approach
　my sight,
Are forced to fall if Bremo once do frown.
Come, cudgel, come, my partner in my
　spoils,
For here I see this day it will not be;　30
But, when it falls that I encounter any,
One pat sufficeth for to work my will.
What, comes not one? Then let's begone;
A time will serve when we shall better
　speed.　　　　　　　　　　　　*Exit.*

[SCENE viii.

A room of state at the court of Aragon.]

*Enter the King, Segasto, the Shepherd, and
　　　　　　　the Clown, with Others*

KING. Shepherd, thou hast heard thine
　accusers;
Murther is laid to thy charge.
What canst thou say? Thou hast de-
　servéd death.

MU. Dread sovereign, I must needs con-
　fess
I slew this captain in mine own defense,
Not of any malice, but by chance;
But mine accuser hath a further mean-
　ing.
SEG. Words will not here prevail;
I seek for justice, and justice craves
　his death.
KING. Shepherd, thine own confession
　hath condemned thee.　　　　　　10
Sirrah, take him away, and do him to
　execution straight.
CLO. So he shall, I warrant him. But
do you hear, master king, he is kin to a
monkey; his neck is bigger than his head.
SEG. Come, sirrah, away with him, and
hang him about the middle.
CLO. Yes, forsooth, I warrant you.
Come on, sir. Ah, so like a sheepbiter a
looks! [1]

*Enter Amadine and a Boy with a bear's
　　　　　　　　　　　　　　head.*

AM. Dread sovereign and well-belovéd
　sire,　　　　　　　　　　　　20
On bended knee I crave the life of this
Condemnéd shepherd, which hereto-
　fore preserved
The life of thy sometime distresséd
　daughter.
KING. Preserved the life of my sometime
　distresséd daughter?
How can that be? I never knew the time
Wherein thou wast distressed; I never
　knew the day
But that I have maintainéd thy estate
As best beseemed the daughter of a
　king.
I never saw the shepherd until now.
How comes it, then, that he preserved
　thy life?　　　　　　　　　　30
AM. Once walking with Segasto in the
　woods,
Further than our accustomed manner
　was,
Right before us, down a steep-fall hill,
A monstrous, ugly bear did hie him fast
To meet us both. Now whether this be
　true,
I refer it to the credit of Segasto.
SEG. Most true, an't like your majesty.
KING.　　　　　How then?

[1] *I.e.,* he has a hangdog look.

AM. The bear, being eager to obtain his prey,
Made forward to us with an open mouth,
As if he meant to swallow us both at once,   40
The sight whereof did make us both to dread,
But specially your daughter Amadine,
Who, for I saw no succor incident
But in Segasto's valor, I grew desperate,
And he most cowardlike began to fly—
Left me distressed to be devoured of him.
How say you, Segasto, is it not true?
KING. His silence verifies it to be true. What then?   48
AM. Then I amazed, distresséd, all alone,
Did hie me fast to scape that ugly bear;
But all in vain, forwhy[1] he reachéd after me,
And hardly I did oft escape his paws,
Till at the length this shepherd came,
And brought to me his head. Come hither, boy.
Lo, here it is, which I present unto your majesty.
KING. The slaughter of this bear deserves great fame.
SEG. The slaughter of a man deserves great blame.
KING. Indeed, occasion oftentimes so falls out.
SEG. Tremelio in the wars, O king, preservéd thee.
AM. The shepherd in the woods, O king, preservéd me.   60
SEG. Tremelio fought when many men did yield.
AM. So would the shepherd, had he been in field.
CLO. [Aside.] So would my master, had he not run away.
SEG. Tremelio's force saved thousands from the foe.
AM. The shepherd's force hath[2] savéd thousands mo.[3]
CLO. [Aside.] Ay, shipsticks,[4] nothing else.
KING. Segasto, cease to accuse the shepherd;
His worthiness deserves a recompense;
All we are bound to do the shepherd good.

[1] Because.   [2] Brooke suggests would have.
[3] More.   [4] Sheep's ticks (?).

Shepherd, whereas it was my sentence thou shouldst die,   70
So shall my sentence stand, for thou shalt die.
SEG. Thanks to your majesty.
KING. But soft, Segasto, not for this offense!—
Long mayst thou live, and, when the Sisters shall decree
To cut in twain the twisted thread of life,
Then let him die. For this I set him free.—
And for thy valor I will honor thee.
MU. Thanks to your majesty!
KING. Come, daughter, let us now depart, to honor the worthy valor of the [80
shepherd with our rewards.
    Exeunt [all but Clown and Segasto].
CLO. O master, hear you. You have made a fresh hand now. You would be slow, you! What will you do now? You have lost me a good occupation by the means. Faith, master, now I cannot hang the shepherd, I pray you, let me take the pains to hang you—it is but half an hour's exercise.   89
SEG. You are still in your knavery, but, sith I cannot have his life, I will procure his banishment forever. Come on, sirrah.
CLO. Yes, forsooth, I come.—[To audience.] Laugh at him, I pray you.   Exeunt.

[SCENE ix.

A grove near the court.]

Enter Mucedorus solus.

MU. From Amadine and from her father's court,
With gold and silver and with rich rewards,
Flowing from the banks of golden treasures [5]—
More may I boast and say; but I
Was never shepherd in such dignity.

Enter the Messenger and the Clown.

MESS. All hail, worthy shepherd!
CLO. All rain, lousy shepherd!
MU. Welcome, my friends. From whence come you?   9
MESS. The king and Amadine greet

[5] Treasuries.

thee well, and, after greeting done, bids thee depart the court. Shepherd, begone!

CLO. Shepherd! Take law,[1] legs; fly away, shepherd!

MU. Whose words are these? Came these from Amadine?

MESS. Ay, from Amadine.

CLO. Ay, from Amladine.

MU. Ah, luckless fortune, worse than Phaëton's tale, 19
My former bliss is now become my bale.

CLO. What, wilt thou poison thyself?

MU. My former heaven is now become my hell.

CLO. The worst alehouse that ever I came in, in all my life.

MU. What shall I do?

CLO. Even go hang thyself half an hour.

MU. Can Amadine so churlishly command
To banish the shepherd from her father's court?

MESS. What should shepherds do in [30 the court?

CLO. What should shepherds do amongst us? Have we not lords enough on us in the court?

MU. Why, shepherds are men, and kings are no more.

MESS. Shepherds are men, and masters over their flock.

CLO. That's a lie. Who pays them their wages then? 40

MESS. Well, you are always interrupting of me, but you were best to look to him, lest you hang for him when he is gone. *Exit.*

The Clown sings.

CLO. And you shall hang for company,
For leaving me alone.

Shepherd, stand forth and hear my sentence: Shepherd, begone within three days in pain of my displeasure. Shepherd, begone; shepherd, begone; begone, begone, be- [50 gone, shepherd, shepherd, shepherd. *Exit.*

MU. And must I go, and must I needs depart?
Ye goodly groves, partakers of my songs
In time tofore when fortune did not frown,

Pour forth your plaints and wail awhile with me!
And thou, bright sun, my comfort in the cold,
Hide, hide thy face and leave me comfortless!
Ye wholesome herbs and sweet-smelling savors,
Yea, each thing else prolonging life of man,
Change, change your wonted course, that I, 60
Wanting your aid, in woeful sort may die.

Enter Amadine and Ariena, her maid.

AM. Ariena, if anybody ask for me,
Make some excuse till I return.

ARI. What and Segasto call?

AM. Do thou the like to him; I mean not to stay long. *Exit [Ariena].*[2]

MU. This voice so sweet my pining spirits revives.

AM. Shepherd, well met; tell me how thou doest.

MU. I linger life, yet wish for speedy death.

AM. Shepherd, although thy banishment already 70
Be decreed, and all against my will,
Yet Amadine—

MU. Ah, Amadine, to hear of banishment
Is death, ay, double death to me;
But, since I must depart, one thing I crave.

AM. Say on with all my heart.

MU. That in absence, either far or near,
You honor me, as servant, with your name.

AM. Not so.

MU. And why? 80

AM. I honor thee as sovereign of my heart.

MU. A shepherd and a sovereign? Nothing like.

AM. Yet like enough where there is no dislike.

MU. Yet great dislike, or else no banishment.

AM. Shepherd, it is only
Segasto that procures thy banishment.

---

[1] Take a good lead (a hunting term).

[2] Stage direction appears after l. 63 in 1610 and later edns.

Mu. Unworthy wights are more in jealousy.

Am. Would God they would free thee
from banishment,
Or likewise banish me.

Mu. Amen, say I, to have your company.   90

Am. Well, shepherd, sith thou suff'rest
this for my sake,
With thee in exile also let me live—
On this condition, shepherd, thou canst
love.

Mu. No longer love, no longer let me
live!

Am. Of late I lovéd one indeed; now
love
I none but only thee.

Mu.   Thanks, worthy princess.
I burn likewise, yet smother up the
blast;
I dare not promise what I may perform.

Am. Well, shepherd, hark what I shall
say:
I will return unto my father's court,   100
There for to provide me of such neces-
saries
As for my journey I shall think most
fit;
This being done, I will return to
thee.
Do thou, therefore, appoint the place
Where we may meet.

Mu. Down in the valley where I slew the
bear.
And there doth grow a fair, broad-
branchéd beech
That overshades a well; so who comes
first
Let them abide the happy meeting of
us both.
How like you this?

Am.   I like it very well.   110

Mu. Now, if you please, you may appoint the time.

Am. Full three hours hence, God willing,
I will return.

Mu. The thanks that Paris gave the
Grecian queen
The like doth Mucedorus yield.

Am. Then, Mucedorus, for three hours
farewell.   *Exit.*

Mu. Your departure, lady, breeds a
privy pain.   *Exit.*

[SCENE x.

The court of Aragon.]

Enter Segasto solus.

Seg. 'Tis well, Segasto, that thou hast
thy will.
Should such a shepherd, such a simple
swain
As he, eclipse thy credit famous through
The court? No, ply,[1] Segasto, ply!
Let it not in Aragon be said,
A shepherd hath Segasto's honor won.

Enter Mouse, the clown, calling his master.

Clo. What ho, master, will you come
away?

Seg. Will you come hither? I pray you,
what's the matter?   10

Clo. Why, is it not past eleven a-clock?

Seg. How then, sir?

Clo. I pray you, come away to dinner.

Seg. I pray you, come hither.

Clo. Here's such ado with you! Will
you never come?

Seg. I pray you, sir, what news of the
message I sent you about?

Clo. I tell you all the messes be on the
table already. There wants not so   [20
much as a mess of mustard half an hour
ago.

Seg. Come, sir, your mind is all upon
your belly;
You have forgotten what I bid you do.

Clo. Faith, I know nothing, but you
bade me go to breakfast.

Seg. Was that all?

Clo. Faith, I have forgotten it; the
very scent of the meat hath made me forget[2] it quite.   30

Seg. You have forgotten the errand
I bid you do?

Clo. What arrant? An arrant knave,
or an arrant whore?

Seg. Why, thou knave, did I not bid
thee banish the shepherd?

Clo. O, the shepherd's bastard.

Seg. I tell thee, the shepherd's banishment.

Clo. I tell you, the shepherd's bas-   [40
tard shall be well kept. I'll look to it myself. But, I pray you, come away to dinner.

---

[1] Apply, work.
[2] Original reads *made me hath forgot.*

SEG. Then you will not tell me whether you have banished him or no?

CLO. Why, I cannot say "banishment," and you would give me a thousand pounds to say so.

SEG. Why, you whoreson [1] slave, have you forgotten that I sent you and another to drive away the shepherd?　　　50

CLO. What an ass are you! Here's a stir indeed! Here's "message," "arrant," "banishment," and I cannot tell what.

SEG. I pray you, sir, shall I know whether you have drove him away?

CLO. Faith, I think I have; and you will not believe me, ask my staff.

SEG. Why, can thy staff tell?

CLO. Why, he was with me too.

SEG. Then happy I, that have [60 obtained my will.

CLO. And happier I, if you would go to dinner.

SEG. Come, sirrah, follow me.

CLO. I warrant you, I will not lose an inch of you, now you are going to dinner.— [*To audience.*] I promise you, I thought seven year before I could get him away.
　　　　　　　　　　　　　　Exeunt.

[SCENE xi.

The forest.]

Enter Amadine sola. [2]

AM. God grant my long delay procures no harm
Nor this my tarrying frustrate my pretense. [3]
My Mucedorus surely stays for me,
And thinks me overlong. At length I come,
My present promise to perform.
Ah, what a thing is firm, unfeignéd love!
What is it which true love dares not attempt?
My father he may make, but I must match;
Segasto loves, but Amadine must like
Where likes her best; compulsion is a thrall.　　　10
No, no, the hearty choice is all in all;
The shepherd's virtue Amadine esteems.
But what! Methinks my shepherd is not come.

I muse at that; the hour is at hand.
Well, here I'll rest till Mucedorus come.
　　　　　　　　　　　She sits down.

*Enter Bremo, looking about; hastily takes
　　　　　　　　　　　hold of her.*

BRE. A happy prey! Now, Bremo, feed on flesh!
Dainties, Bremo, dainties, thy hungry panch [4] to fill!
Now glut thy greedy guts with luke-warm blood!
Come, fight with me; I long to see thee dead.

AM. How can she fight that weapons cannot wield?　　　20

BRE. What, canst not fight? Then lie thee down and die.

AM. What, must I die?

BRE. What need these words? I thirst to suck thy blood!

AM. Yet pity me and let me live awhile.

BRE. No pity I; I'll feed upon thy flesh;
I'll tear thy body piecemeal joint from joint.

AM. Ah, how I want my shepherd's company.

BRE. I'll crush thy bones betwixt two oaken trees.

AM. Haste, shepherd, haste, or else thou com'st too late!

BRE. I'll suck the sweetness from thy marrowbones.　　　30

AM. Ah, spare, ah, spare to shed my guiltless blood!

BRE. With this my bat will I beat out thy brains!
Down, down, I say; prostrate thyself upon the ground.

AM. Then, Mucedorus, farewell; my hopéd joys, farewell.
Yea, farewell, life, and welcome, present death!　　　*She kneels.*
To thee, O God, I yield my dying ghost.

BRE. Now, Bremo, play thy part.—
How now, what sudden chance is this?
My limbs do tremble and my sinews shake;
My unweakened arms hath lost their former force.　　　40
Ah, Bremo, Bremo, what a foil [5] hast thou

---

[1] Rascally.
[2] Original reads *solus.*
[3] Intention.
[4] Paunch.
[5] Disgrace.

That yet at no time [ever][1] wast afraid
To dare the greatest gods to fight with
thee,   *He strikes.*
And now wants strength for one down-
driving blow!
Ah, how my courage fails when I should
strike!
Some newcome spirit, abiding in my
breast,
Saith, "Spare her," which never sparéd
any.
Shall I spare her, Bremo? Spare her;
do not kill.[2]
To it, Bremo, to it! Say [3] again.—
I cannot wield my weapons in my hand;
Methinks I should not strike so fair a
one.   51
I think her beauty hath bewitched my
force
Or else within me altered nature's course.
Ay, woman, wilt thou live in woods with
me?
AM. Fain would I live, yet loath to live in
woods.
BRE. Thou shalt not choose; it shall be
as I say,
And, therefore, follow me.   *Exeunt.*

[SCENE xii.

The same.]

Enter Mucedorus solus.

MU. It was my will an hour ago and more,
As was my promise, for to make return,
But other business hindered my pre-
tense.
It is a world [4] to see, when man appoints
And purposely one certain thing de-
crees,
How many things may hinder his intent.
What one would wish, the same is
farthest off.
But yet th'appointed time cannot be
past,
Nor hath her presence yet prevented [5]
me.
Well, here I'll stay, and expect [6] her com-
ing.   10
They cry within, "Hold him, hold him!"
MU. Someone or other is pursued, no
doubt;

Perhaps some search for me. 'Tis good
to doubt the worst;
Therefore I'll be gone.   *Exit.*

*Cry within, "Hold him, hold him!" Enter
Mouse, the clown, with a pot.*

CLO. Hold him, hold him, hold him!
Here's a stir indeed. Here came hue after
the crier; and I was set close at Mother
Nip's house, and there I called for three
pots of ale, as 'tis the manner of us courtiers. Now, sirrah, I had taken the maidenhead of two of them. Now, as I was [20
lifting up the third to my mouth, there
came, "Hold him, hold him!" Now I could
not tell whom to catch hold on, but I am
sure I caught one—perchance a may be in
this pot. Well, I'll see! Mass, I cannot
see him yet. Well, I'll look a little further.
Mass, he is a little slave, if a be here. Why,
here's nobody. All this goes well yet; but
if the old trot should come for her pot—
ay, marry, there's the matter. But I   [30
care not; I'll face her out, and call her old
rusty, dusty, musty, fusty, crusty firebrand, and worse than all that, and so
face her out of her pot. But soft, here
she comes!

Enter the Old Woman.

OLD W. Come, you knave! Where's
my pot, you knave?
CLO. Go, look your pot; come not to
me for your pot, 'twere good for you.
OLD W. Thou liest, thou knave;   [40
thou hast my pot.
CLO. You lie, and you say it. I your
pot? I know what I'll say.
[OLD W.][7] Why, what wilt thou say?
CLO. But say I have him, and thou
dar'st.
OLD W. Why, thou knave, thou hast
not only my pot but my drink unpaid for.
CLO. You lie like an old—I will not
say whore.   50
OLD W. Dost thou call me whore? I'll
cap [8] thee for my pot.
CLO. Cap me and thou darest! Search
me whether I have it or no.
*She searcheth him, and he drinketh over
her head and casteth down the pot; she
stumbleth at it; then they fall together by
the ears; she takes up her pot and goes out.*

---

[1] From 1598 edn.
[2] Ll. 47 and 48 are interchanged in the original.
[3] Essay.   [5] Preceded.
[4] It is wonderful.   [6] Await.
[7] From 1598 edn.   [8] Arrest.

Enter Segasto.

SEG. How now, sirrah, what's the matter?

CLO. O, flies, master, flies.

SEG. Flies? Where are they?

CLO. O, here, master, all about your face.   60

SEG. Why, thou liest; I think thou art mad.

CLO. Why, master, I have killed a dungcartful at the least.

SEG. Go to, sirrah! Leaving this idle talk, give ear to me.

CLO. How? Give you one of my ears? Not and you were ten masters.

SEG. Why, sir, I bid you give ear to my words.   70

CLO. I tell you I will not be made a curtal [1] for no man's pleasure.

SEG. I tell thee, attend what I say. Go thy ways straight and rear the whole town.

CLO. How? Rear the whole town? Even go yourself; it is more than I can do. Why, do you think I can rear a town, that can scarce rear a pot of ale to my head? I should rear a town, should I not! [80

SEG. Go to the constable and make a privy search, for the shepherd is run away with the king's daughter.

CLO. How? Is the shepherd run away with the king's daughter, or is the king's daughter run away with the shepherd?

SEG. I cannot tell, but they are both gone together.

CLO. What a fool is she to run away with the shepherd! Why, I think I am [90 a little handsomer man than the shepherd myself. But tell me, master, must I make a privy search, or search in the privy?

SEG. Why, dost thou think they will be there?

CLO. I cannot tell.

SEG. Well, then, search everywhere; leave no place unsearched for them.   *Exit.*

CLO. O, now am I in office; now will I to that old firebrand's house and [100 will not leave one place unsearched; nay, I'll to the alestand [2] and drink as long as I can stand, and, when I have done, I'll let out all the rest, to see if he be not hid in the barrel. And, if I find him not there, I'll to the cupboard; I'll not leave one

corner of her house unsearched. I' faith, ye old crust, I will be with you now.   *Exit.*

[SCENE xiii. [3]

The court of Valencia.]

Sound music.

Enter the King of Valencia, Anselmo, Roderigo, Lord Borachius, with Others.

KING [OF] VAL. Enough of music; it but adds to torment;

Delights to vexéd spirits are as dates Set to a sickly man, which rather cloy than comfort.

Let me entreat you to entreat no more.

ROD. Let your strings sleep; have done there.   *Let the music cease.*

KING [OF] VAL. Mirth to a soul disturbed are embers turned,

Which sudden gleam with molestation, But sooner lose their sight for't;

'Tis gold bestowed upon a rioter,

Which not relieves, but murders him.   10

'Tis a drug given to the healthful,

Which infects, not cures.

How can a father that hath lost his son,

A prince both wise, virtuous, and valiant,

Take pleasure in the idle acts of time?

No, no; till Mucedorus I shall see again,

All joy is comfortless, all pleasure pain.

ANS. Your son, my lord, is well.

KING [OF] VAL. I prithee, speak that thrice.

ANS. The prince, your son, is safe.   20

KING [OF] VAL. O, where, Anselmo? Surfeit me with that.

ANS. In Aragon, my liege; and at his parture

Bound my secrecy

By his affectious love, not to disclose it.

But care of him and pity of your age Makes my tongue blab what my breast vowed concealment.

KING [OF] VAL. Thou not deceiv'st me?

I ever thought thee what I find thee now,

An upright, loyal man. But what desire,

Or young-fed humor nursed within the brain,   30

Drew him so privately to Aragon?

---

[1] Docked animai.   [2] Barrel.

[3] This scene appeared first in the 1610 edn.

ANS. A forcing adamant:[1]
Love, mixed with fear and doubtful
   jealousy,
Whether report gilded a worthless trunk,
Or Amadine deserved her high extol-
   ment.
KING [OF] VAL. See our provision be in
   readiness;
Collect us followers of the comeliest
   hue
For our chief guardians; we will thither
   wend.
The crystal eye of heaven shall not
   thrice wink,
Nor the green flood six times his shoul-
   ders turn,   40
Till we salute the Aragonian king.
Music, speak loudly now; the season's
   apt,
For former dolors are in pleasure
   wrapped.   *Exeunt omnes.*

[SCENE xiv.

The forest.]

Enter Mucedorus to disguise himself.

MU. Now, Mucedorus, whither wilt thou
   go?
Home to thy father to thy native soil,
Or try some long abode within these
   woods?
Well, I will hence depart and hie me
   home.
What, hie me home, said I? That may
   not be;
In Amadine rests my felicity.
Then, Mucedorus, do as thou didst
   decree:
Attire thee hermit-like within these
   groves,
Walk often to the beech and view the
   well,
Make settles there and seat thyself
   thereon,   10
And, when thou feelest thyself to be
   athirst,
Then drink a hearty draught to Ama-
   dine.
No doubt she thinks on thee,
And will one day come pledge thee at
   this well.
Come, habit, thou art fit for me.
              He disguiseth himself.

[1] Compelling magnet.

No shepherd now, a hermit must I be.
Methinks this fits me very well;
Now must I learn to bear a walking
   staff,
And exercise some gravity withal.

Enter the Clown.

CLO. Here's through the woods, and [20
through the woods, to look out a shepherd
and a stray king's daughter.—But soft,
who have we here? What art thou?
MU. I am an hermit.
CLO. An emmet? I never saw such a
big emmet in all my life before.
MU. I tell you, sir, I am an hermit,
one that leads a solitary life within these
woods.
CLO. O, I know thee now; thou art [30
her that eats up all the hips and haws;
we could not have one piece of fat bacon
for thee all this year.
MU. Thou dost mistake me. But, I
pray thee, tell me who dost thou seek in
these woods.
CLO. What do I seek? For a stray
king's daughter run away with a shepherd.
MU. A stray king's daughter run away
with a shepherd! Wherefore, canst [40
thou tell?
CLO. Yes, that I can; 'tis this: my
master and Amadine, walking one day
abroad, nearer to these woods than they
were used—about what I cannot tell—but
towards them comes running a great
bear. Now my master, he played the man
and ran away, and Amadine crying after
him. Now, sir, comes me a shepherd and
he strikes off the bear's head. Now [50
whether the bear were dead before or no I
cannot tell, for bring twenty bears before
me and bind their hands and feet, and
I'll kill them all. Now, ever since, Amadine
hath been in love with the shepherd, and
for good will she's even run away with the
shepherd.
MU. What manner of man was he?
Canst describe him unto me?
CLO. 'Scribe him? Ay, I warrant [60
you that I can. A was a little, low, broad,
tall, narrow, big, well-favored fellow—a
jerkin of white cloth, and buttons of the
same cloth.
MU. Thou describest him well, but, if

I chance to see any such, pray you, where shall I find you, or what's your name?

CLO. My name is called Master Mouse.

MU. O, Master Mouse, I pray you, what office might you bear in the [70 court?

CLO. Marry, sir, I am a rusher of the stable.

MU. O, usher of the table!

CLO. Nay, I say "rusher," and I'll prove mine office good; for look, sir, when any comes from under the sea or so, and a dog chance to blow his nose backward, then with a whip I give him the good time of the day, and strow rushes presently.[1] [80 Therefore, I am a rusher, a high office, I promise ye.

MU. But where shall I find you in the court?

CLO. Why, where it is best being, either in the kitching a-eating or in the buttery drinking. But, if you come, I will provide for thee a piece of beef and brewis knuckle-deep in fat. Pray you, take pains; remember Master Mouse. *Exit.* [90

MU. Ay, sir, I warrant I will not forget you.—

Ah, Amadine, what should become of thee?

Whither shouldst thou go so long unknown?

With watch and ward each passage is beset,

So that she cannot long escape unknown.

Doubtless she hath lost herself within these woods

And, wand'ring to and fro, she seeks the well,

Which yet she cannot find; therefore will I seek her out. *Exit.*

[SCENE XV.

The same.]

Enter Bremo and Amadine.

BRE. Amadine, how like you Bremo and his woods?

AM. As like the woods of Bremo's cruelty!

Though I were dumb and could not answer him,

The beasts themselves would with relenting tears

Bewail thy savage and unhuman deeds.

BRE. My love, why dost thou murmur to thyself?

Speak louder, for thy Bremo hears thee not.

AM. My Bremo? No, the shepherd is my love.

BRE. Have I not savéd thee from sudden death,

Giving thee leave to live that thou mightst love? 10

And dost thou whet me on to cruelty?

Come, kiss me, sweet, for all my favors past.

AM. I may not, Bremo, and therefore pardon me.

BRE. [*Aside.*] See how she flings away from me; I will follow

And give attend to her.—Deny my love!

Ah, worm of beauty, I will chastise thee!

Come, come, prepare thy head upon the block.

AM. O, spare me, Bremo! Love should limit life,

Not to be made a murderer of himself.

If thou wilt glut thy loving heart with blood, 20

Encounter with the lion or the bear,

And like a wolf prey not upon a lamb.

BRE. Why then dost thou repine at me?

If thou wilt love me, thou shalt be my queen;

I will crown thee with a chaplet[2] made of ivory,

And make the rose and lily wait on thee.

I'll rend the burly branches from the oak,[3]

To shadow thee from burning sun.

The trees shall spread themselves where thou dost go,

And, as they spread, I'll trace[4] along with thee. 30

AM. [*Aside.*] You may, for who but you?

BRE. Thou shalt be fed with quails and partridges,

With blackbirds, larks, thrushes, and nightingales.

Thy drink shall be goat's milk and crystal water,

Distilled from the fountains and the clearest springs.

[1] Strew rushes immediately.

[2] Original reads *complet.*

[3] From 1598 edn. Original reads *oxe.*

[4] Walk.

And all the dainties that the woods
afford
I'll freely give thee to obtain thy love.
AM. [*Aside.*] You may, for who but you?
BRE. The day I'll spend to recreate my
love   39
With all the pleasures that I can devise,
And in the night I'll be thy bedfellow,
And lovingly embrace thee in mine
arms.
AM. [*Aside.*] One may; so may not you.
BRE. The satyrs and the wood-nymphs
shall attend on thee
And lull thee asleep with music's sound,
And in the morning when thou dost
awake,
The lark shall sing good morrow to my
queen,
And, whilst he sings, I'll kiss my Ama-
dine.
AM. [*Aside.*] You may, for who but you?
BRE. When thou art up, the wood lanes
shall be strowed   50
With violets, cowslips, and sweet mari-
golds
For thee to trample and to trace upon,
And I will teach thee how to kill the
deer,
To chase the hart and how to rouse the
roe,
If thou wilt live to love and honor me.
AM. [*Aside.*] You may, for who but you?

Enter Mucedorus.

BRE. Welcome, sir;
An hour ago I looked for such a guest.
Be merry, wench, we'll have a frolic
feast.
Here's flesh enough for to suffice us
both.   60
Say, sirrah, wilt thou fight or dost thou
mean to die?
MU. I want a weapon; how can I fight?
BRE. Thou wants a weapon? Why then,
thou yield'st to die.
MU. I say not so; I do not yield to die.
BRE. Thou shalt not choose. I long to
see thee dead!
AM. Yet spare him, Bremo, spare him!
BRE. Away, I say; I will not spare him.
MU. Yet give me leave to speak.
BRE.   Thou shalt not speak.
AM. Yet give him leave to speak for my
sake.

BRE. Speak on, but be not overlong.   70
MU. In time of yore, when men like
brutish beasts
Did lead their lives in loathsome cells
and woods
And wholly gave themselves to witless
will,
A rude, unruly rout, then man to man
Became a present prey; then might
prevailed;
The weakest went to walls.
Right was unknown, for wrong was all
in all.
As men thus livéd in their great outrage,[1]
Behold, one Orpheus came, as poets tell,
And them from rudeness unto reason
brought,   80
Who, led by reason, some forsook the
woods.
Instead of caves they built them castles
strong;
Cities and towns were founded by them
then.
Glad were they, they found such ease,
and in
The end they grew to perfect amity.
Weighing their former wickedness,
They termed the time wherein they livéd
then
A golden age, a goodly golden age.
Now, Bremo, for so I hear thee called,
If men which lived tofore, as thou dost
now,   90
Wild in wood, addicted all to spoil,
Returnéd were by worthy Orpheus'
means,
Let me like Orpheus cause thee to return
From murther, bloodshed, and like
cruelty.
What, should we fight before we have a
cause?
No, let's live and love together faithfully.
I'll fight for thee.
BRE.   Fight for me or die!
Or fight, or else thou diest!
AM.   Hold, Bremo, hold!
BRE. Away, I say; thou troublest me.
AM. You promised me to make me your
queen.   100
BRE. I did; I mean no less.
AM. You promised that I should hav
my will.
BRE. I did; I mean no less.

----
[1] Violent conduct.

Am. Then save this hermit's life, for he may save us both.

Bre. At thy request I'll spare him, but never any after him. Say, hermit, what canst thou do?

Mu. I'll wait on thee; sometime upon thy queen. Such service shalt thou shortly have as Bremo never had.   *Exeunt.*   [110

[SCENE xvi.

The court of Aragon.]

Enter Segasto, the Clown, and Rumbelo.

Seg. Come, sirs; what, shall I never have you find out Amadine and the shepherd?

Clo. And I have been through the woods, and through the woods, and could see nothing but an emmet.

Ru. Why, I see a thousand emmets. Thou mean'st a little one?

Clo. Nay, that emmet that I saw was bigger than thou art.   10

Ru. Bigger than I?—What a fool have you to your man; I pray you, master, turn him away.

Seg. But dost thou hear? Was he not a man?

Clo. Think he was, for he said he did lead a saltseller's life about the woods.

Seg. Thou wouldest say a solitary life about the woods.

Clo. I think it was so, indeed.   20

Ru. I thought what a fool thou art.

Clo. Thou art a wise man! Why, he did nothing but sleep since he went.

Seg. But tell me, Mouse, how did he go?

Clo. In a white gown, and a white hat on his head, and a staff in his hand.

Seg. I thought so; it was an hermit that walked a solitary life in the woods. Well, get you to dinner, and after, never leave seeking till you bring some news of   [30 them, or I'll hang you both.   *Exit.*

Clo. How now, Rumbelo? What shall we do now?

Ru. Faith, I'll home to dinner, and afterward to sleep.

Clo. Why, then, thou wilt be hanged.

Ru. Faith, I care not, for I know I shall never find them. Well, I'll once more abroad, and, if I cannot find them, I'll never come home again.   40

Clo. I tell thee what, Rumbelo, thou

shalt go in at one end of the wood and I at the other, and we will meet both together in the midst.

Ru. Content! Let's away to dinner.
Exeunt.

[SCENE xvii.

The forest.]

Enter Mucedorus solus.

Mu. Unknown to any here within these woods,
With bloody Bremo do I lead my life.
The monster, he doth murder all he meets;
He spareth none, and none doth him escape.
Who would continue—who but only I—
In such a cruel cutthroat's company?
Yet Amadine is there. How can I choose?
Ah, silly soul, how oftentimes she sits
And sighs, and calls, "Come, shepherd, come;
Sweet Mucedorus, come and set me free,"   10
When Mucedorus present [1] stands her by!—
But here she comes!

Enter Amadine. [2]

What news, fair lady, as you walk these woods?

Am. Ah, hermit, none but bad and such as thou knowest.

Mu. How do you like your Bremo and his woods?

Am. Not my Bremo nor Bremo his [3] woods.

Mu. And why not yours? Methinks he loves you well.

Am. I like not him; his love to me is nothing worth.

Mu. Lady, in this methinks you offer wrong,
To hate the man that ever loves you best.   20

Am. Ah, hermit, I take no pleasure in his love;
Neither doth Bremo like me best.

[1] Suggested by Hazlitt. Original reads *peasant.*
[2] In the original this stage direction follows the next line.
[3] Original reads *his Bremo.*

Mu. Pardon my boldness, fair lady; sith
we both
    May safely talk now out of Bremo's
    sight,
    Unfold to me, if so you please, the full
    discourse
    How, when, and why you came into
    these woods,
    And fell into this bloody butcher's
    hands.
Am. Hermit, I will.
    Of late a worthy shepherd I did love—
Mu. A shepherd, lady? Sure, a man un-
    fit   30
    To match with you.
Am. Hermit, this is true; and, when we
    had—
Mu. Stay there; the wild man comes!
    Refer [1] the rest until another time.

Enter Bremo.

Bre. What secret tale is this? What
    whisp'ring have we here?
    Villain, I charge thee tell thy tale again.
Mu. If needs I must, lo, here it is again:
    Whenas we both had lost the sight of
    thee,
    It grieved us both, but specially thy
    queen,   39
    Who in thy absence ever fears the worst,
    Lest some mischance befall your royal
    grace.
    "Shall my sweet Bremo wander through
    the woods?
    Toil to and fro for to redress my want,
    Hazard his life, and all to cherish me?
    I like not this," quoth she,
    And thereupon cravéd to know of me
    If I could teach her handle weapons
    well.
    My answer was I had small skill therein,
    But gladsome, mighty king, to learn of
    thee.
    And this was all.   50
Bre. Was't so? None can dislike of this.
    I'll teach
    You both to fight; but first, my queen,
    begin.
    Here, take this weapon; see how thou
    canst use it.
Am. This is too big; I cannot wield it in
    my arm.

Bre. Is't so? We'll have a knotty crab-
    tree staff
    For thee.—But, sirrah, tell me, what
    sayest thou?
Mu. With all my heart I willing am to
    learn.
Bre. Then take my staff and see how
    thou canst wield it.
Mu. First teach me how to hold it in my
    hand.
Bre. Thou hold'st it well.   60
    Look how he doth; thou mayst the
    sooner learn.
Mu. Next tell me how and when 'tis best
    to strike.
Bre. 'Tis best to strike when time doth
    serve;
    'Tis best to lose no time.
Mu. [*Aside.*] Then now or never is my
    time to strike.
Bre. And, when thou strikest, be sure to
    hit the head.
Mu. The head?
Bre.   The very head.
Mu.   Then have at thine!
    He strikes him down dead.
    So, lie there and die,
    A death no doubt according to desert,
    Or else a worse as thou deserv'st a
    worse.   70
Am. It glads my heart this tyrant's death
    to see.
Mu. Now, lady, it remains in you
    To end the tale you lately had begun,
    Being interrupted by this wicked wight.
    You said you loved a shepherd?
Am. Ay, so I do, and none but only him,
    And will do still as long as life shall
    last.
Mu. But tell me, lady, sith I set you free,
    What course of life do you intend to
    take?
Am. I will disguiséd wander through the
    world,   80
    Till I have found him out.
Mu. How if you find your shepherd in
    these woods?
Am. Ah, none so happy then as Amadine.
    He discloseth [2] himself.
Mu. In tract of time a man may alter
    much.
    Say, lady, do you know your shepherd
    well?

---

[1] Postpone.

[2] Early edns. read *disguiseth.*

Am. My Mucedorus! Hath he set me free?

Mu. He hath set thee free.

Am. And lived so long unknown to Amadine?

Mu. Ay, that's a question whereof you may not be resolved.

You know that I am banished from the court? 90

I know likewise each passage is beset

So that we cannot long escape unknown;

Therefore my will is this: that we return

Right through the thickets to the wild man's cave,

And there awhile live on his provision,

Until the search and narrow watch be past.

This is my counsel, and I think it best.

Am. I think the very same.

Mu. Come, let's begone.

The Clown [enters and] searcheth, and falls over the Wild Man, and so carries him away.

Clo. Nay, soft, sir; are you here? A bots [1] on you! I was like to be hanged [100 for not finding you. We would borrow a certain stray king's daughter of you—a wench, a wench, sir, we would have.

Mu. A wench of me? I'll make thee eat my sword!

Clo. O Lord! Nay, and you are so lusty, I'll call a cooling card [2] for you. Ho, master, master, ay, come away quickly!

Enter Seg[asto].

Seg. What's the matter? 109

Clo. Look, master, Amadine and the shepherd! O, brave!

Seg. What, minion, have I found you out?

Clo. Nay, that's a lie; I found her out myself.

Seg. Thou gadding huswife, what cause hadst thou to gad abroad,

Whenas thou knowest our wedding day so nigh?

Am. Not so, Segasto; no such thing in hand.

Show your assurance; [3] then I'll answer you.

[1] *I.e.*, plague.
[2] A card that dashes the hopes of the adversary. [3] Pledge of betrothal.

Seg. Thy father's promise my assurance is. 120

Am. But what he promised he hath not performed.

Seg. It rests in thee for to perform the same.

Am. Not I.

Seg. And why?

Am. So is my will, and therefore even so.

Clo. Master, with a nonny, nonny, no! [4]

Seg. Ah, wicked villain, art thou here?

Mu. What needs these words? We weigh them not.

Seg. We weigh them not? Proud shepherd, I scorn thy company.

Clo. We'll not have a corner of thy company. 130

Mu. I scorn not thee, nor yet the least of thine.

Clo. That's a lie; a would have killed me with his pugsnando.

Seg. This stoutness, Amadine, contents me not.

Am. Then seek another that may you better please.

Mu. Well, Amadine, it only rests in thee Without delay to make thy choice of three:

There stands Segasto; here a shepherd stands;

There stands the third. Now make thy choice.

Clo. A lord at the least I am. 140

Am. My choice is made, for I will none but thee.

Seg. A worthy mate, no doubt, for such a wife.

Mu. And, Amadine, why wilt thou none but me?

I cannot keep thee as thy father did;

I have no lands for to maintain thy state.

Moreover, if thou mean to be my wife,

Commonly this must be thy use:

To bed at midnight, up at four,

Drudge all day and trudge from place to place, 149

Whereby our daily victual for to win;

And last of all, which is the worst of all,

No princess then, but plain a shepherd's wife.

Clo. Then, God gi' you good morrow, goody shepherd!

[4] Refrain in popular songs.

AM. It shall not need; if Amadine do
   live,
   Thou shalt be crownéd King of Aragon.
CLO. O, master, laugh!   When he's
   king, then I'll be a queen!
MU. Then know that which ne'er to-
   fore was known:
   I am no shepherd, no Aragonian I,
   But born of royal blood—my father's
   of   160
   Valencia king, my mother, queen—
   who for
   Thy sacred sake took this hard task in
   hand.
AM. Ah, how I joy my fortune is so good!
SEG. Well, now I see Segasto shall not
   speed;
   But, Mucedorus, I as much do joy
   To see thee here within our court of
   Aragon,
   As if a kingdom had befall'n me this
   time.
   I with my heart surrender her to thee,
                He gives her to him.
   And loose [1] what right to Amadine I
   have!   169
CLO. What barn's door, and born
   where my father was constable! A bots
   on thee! How dost thee?
MU. Thanks, Segasto; but yet you leveled
   at the crown.
CLO. Master, bear this and bear all.
SEG. Why so, sir?
CLO. He sees you take a goose by the
   crown.
SEG. Go to, sir! Away, post you to the
   king,
   Whose heart is fraught with careful
   doubts, [2]
   Glad him up and tell him these good
   news,   179
   And we will follow as fast as we may.
CLO. I go, master; I run, master!
                        Exeunt.

[SCENE xviii.

An open place near the court of Aragon.]

Enter the King and Collen.

KING. Break, heart, and end my pallid
   woes!
   My Amadine, the comfort of my life,

[1] Emended by Hazlitt. Original reads *looke.*
[2] Anxious fears.

How can I joy except she were in sight?
Her absence breeds sorrow to my soul
And with a thunder breaks my heart in
   twain.
COL. Forbear those passions, gentle king,
   And you shall see 'twill turn unto the
   best,
   And bring your soul to quiet and to joy.
KING. Such joy as death, I do assure me
   that,
   And naught but death, unless of her
   I hear,   10
   And that with speed; I cannot sigh thus
   long—
   But what a tumult do I hear within?
They cry within, "Joy and happiness!"
COL. I hear a noise of overpassing joy
   Within the court; my lord, be of good
   comfort.—
   And here comes one in haste.

Enter the Clown running.

CLO. A king! a king! a king!
COL. Why, how now, sirrah?   What's
   the matter?
CLO. O, 'tis news for a king; 'tis worth
   money.   20
KING. Why, sirrah, thou shalt have sil-
   ver and gold if it be good.
CLO. O, 'tis good, 'tis good! Amadine—
KING. O, what of her? Tell me, and I
   will make thee a knight.
CLO. How, a sprite? No, by Lady, I
   will not be a sprite. Masters, get you
   away; if I be a sprite, I shall be so lean I
   shall make you all afraid.
COL. Thou sot, the king means to   [30
   make thee a gentleman.
CLO. Why, I shall want parel. [3]
KING. Thou shalt want for nothing.
CLO. Then stand away; strike up thyself. Here they come.

Enter Segasto, Mucedorus, and Amadine.

AM. My gracious father, pardon thy disloyal daughter.
KING. What, do mine eyes behold my
   daughter Amadine?
   Rise up, dear daughter, and let these
   my embracing arms
   Show some token of thy father's joy,
   Which ever since thy departure hath
   languished in sorrow.   40

[3] Apparel.

Am. Dear father, never were your sorrows
Greater than my griefs,
Never you so desolate as I comfortless;
Yet, nevertheless, acknowledging myself
To be the cause of both, on bended knees
I humbly crave your pardon.

King. I'll pardon thee, dear daughter;
but, as for him—

Am. Ah, father, what of him?

King. As sure as I am king and wear the
crown,   49
I will revenge on that accursèd wretch.

Mu. Yet, worthy prince, work not thy
will in wrath;
Show favor.

King.   Ay, such favor as thou
deservest.

Mu. I do deserve the daughter of a king.

King. O, impudent! A shepherd and so
insolent?

Mu. No shepherd I, but a worthy prince.

King. In fair conceit,[1] not princely born.

Mu. Yes, princely born: my father is a
king,
My mother a queen, and of Valencia
both.

King. What, Mucedorus? Welcome to
our court!
What cause hadst thou to come to me
disguised?   60

Mu. No cause to fear; I causèd no of-
fense
But this: desiring thy daughter's virtues
for to see,
Disguised myself from out my father's
court,
Unknown to any. In secret I did rest,
And passèd many troubles near to death;
So hath your daughter my partaker been,
As you shall know hereafter more at
large,
Desiring you, you will give her to me,
Even as mine own and sovereign of
my life;
Then shall I think my travails are well
spent.   70

King. With all my heart, but this—
Segasto claims my promise made tofore,
That he should have her as his only
wife,
Before my council when we came from
war.

[1] Imagination.

Segasto, may I crave thee let it pass,
And give Amadine as wife to Mucedorus?

Seg. With all my heart, were it a far
greater thing;
And what I may to furnish up their rites
With pleasing sports and pastimes you
shall see.

King. Thanks, good Segasto, I will think
of this.   80

Mu. Thanks, good my lord, and, while I
live,
Account of me in what I can or may.

Am. And, good Segasto, these great courtesies
Shall not be forgot.

Clo. Why, hark you, master! Bones,[2]
what have you done? What, given away
the wench you made me take such pains
for? You are wise indeed! Mass, and I
had known of that, I would have had her
myself! Faith, master, now we may go   [90
to breakfast with a woodcock pie!

Seg. Go, sir; you were best leave this
knavery.

King. Come on, my lords, let's now to
court,
Where we may finish up the joyfulest day
That ever happed to a distressèd king.[3]
Were but thy father, the Valencia lord,
Present in view of this combining knot!

A shout within. Enter a Messenger.

What shout was that?   98

Mess. My lord, the great Valencia king,
Newly arrived, entreats your presence.

Mu. My father?

King. Preparèd welcomes give him enter-
tainment.
A happier planet never reigned than that
Which governs at this hour.   *Sound.*

*Enter the King of Valencia, Anselmo,
Roderigo, Borachius, with Others; the
King runs and embraces his Son.*

King [of] Val. Rise, honor of my age,
food to my rest!
Condemn not, mighty King of Aragon,
My rude behavior, so compelled by
nature,
That manners stood unknowledged.

[2] By God's bones.
[3] The rest of the scene is different in the 1598
edn., in which the King of Valencia does not
appear.

KING. What we have to recite would
tedious prove   109
By declaration; therefore, in and feast.
Tomorrow the performance shall ex-
plain
What words conceal; till then, drums,
speak; bells, ring.
Give plausive [1] welcomes to our brother
king.
Sound drums and trumpets. Exeunt omnes.

[EPILOGUE]

Enter Comedy and Envy.

COM. How now, Envy? What, blushest
thou already?
Peep forth; hide not thy head with
shame,
But with a courage praise a woman's
deeds.
Thy threats were vain; thou couldst
do me no hurt.
Although thou seemest to cross me with
despite,
I overwhelmed, and turnéd upside down
thy blocks
And made thyself to stumble at the
same.
ENV. Though stumbled, yet not over-
thrown!
Thou canst not draw my heart to mild-
ness;
Yet must I needs confess thou hast done
well,   10
And played thy part with mirth and
pleasant glee.
Say all this, yet canst thou not conquer
me;
Although this time thou hast got—yet
not the conquest neither.
A double revenge another time I'll have. [2]
COM. Envy, spit thy gall;
Plot, work, contrive; create new fal-
lacies;
Teem from thy womb each minute a
black traitor,
Whose blood and thoughts have twins'
conception;
Study to act deeds yet unchronicled;
Cast native monsters in the molds of
men;   20

Case vicious devils under sancted roch-
ets; [3]
Unhasp the wicket [4] where all perjureds
roost,
And swarm this ball with treasons. Do
thy worst,
Thou canst not, hellhound, cross my
steer [5] tonight,
Nor blind that glory where I wish de-
light.
ENV. I can, I will.
COM.   Nefarious hag, begin,
And let us tug till one the mast'ry win.
ENV. Comedy, thou art a shallow goose;
I'll overthrow thee in thine own intent, 29
And make thy fall my comic merriment.
COM. Thy policy wants gravity; thou art
Too weak. Speak, fiend! As how?
ENV. Why, thus:
From my foul study will I hoist a wretch,
A lean and hungry neger [6] cannibal,
Whose jaws swell to his eyes with chaw-
ing malice;
And him I'll make a poet!
COM.   What's that to th' purpose?
ENV. This scrambling raven, with his
needy beard,
Will I whet on to write a comedy,
Wherein shall be composed dark sen-
tences,   40
Pleasing to factious brains;
And every other where place me a jest,
Whose high abuse shall more torment
than blows.
Then I myself, quicker than lightning,
Will fly me to a puissant magistrate,
And, waiting with a trencher at his
back,
In midst of jollity, rehearse those galls,
With some additions,
So lately vented in your theater.
He, upon this, cannot but make com-
plaint,   50
To your great danger, or at least re-
straint.
COM. Ha, ha, ha! I laugh to hear thy
folly;
This is a trap for boys, not men, nor
such,
Especially desertful in their doings,
Whose staid discretion rules their pur-
poses.

---

[1] Applauding.
[2] In the 1598 edn. the remainder of the epilogue
consists of nineteen lines in honor of Elizabeth.

[3] Holy surplices.   [5] Interfere with my rudder.
[4] Gate (in hell).   [6] Negro.

I and my faction do eschew those vices.
But see, O, see! The weary sun for rest
Hath lain his golden compass to the
    west,
Where he perpetual bide and ever shine,
As David's offspring, in his happy
    clime.   60
Stoop, Envy, stoop; bow to the earth
    with me;
Let's beg our pardons on our bended
    knee.   *They kneel.*[1]
ENV. My power has lost her might;
    Envy's date's expired.
Yon splendent majesty hath felled my
    sting,
And I amazéd am.   *Fall down and quake.*
COM. Glorious and wise Arch-Cæsar on
    this earth,

---

[1] To King James, before whom one performance was given.

At whose appearance Envy's stroken
    dumb,
And all bad things cease operation,
Vouchsafe to pardon our unwilling
    error,   69
So late presented to your gracious view,
And we'll endeavor with excess of pain
To please your senses in a choicer strain.
Thus we commit you to the arms of
    Night,
Whose spangled carcass would, for your
    delight,
Strive to excel the Day; be blessed,
    then.
Who other wishes, let him never speak.
ENV.   Amen!
To Fame and Honor we commend your
    rest;
Live still more happy, every hour more
    blessed.

FINIS.

THOMAS DEKKER

Thomas Dekker the dramatist—there are records of several contemporaries with this name—was born in London about 1572, but no details of his family relations or of his education are known. The first record of his work is a payment to him in January, 1598, as a member of Henslowe's group of dramatists. For the next six years he was actively engaged in playwriting, chiefly under Henslowe, first for the Admiral's men and later for Worcester's, and he continued to write plays sporadically during the remainder of a comparatively long life. From early in the seventeenth century, however, he devoted most of his time to the composition of prose pamphlets, which are among the best records of London life in his day. The most important are *The Bellman of London* (1608) and *The Gull's Hornbook* (1609). In spite of his prolific literary output, Dekker lived a life of hardship as a result of debt. He borrowed money of Henslowe in 1598 to secure his release from prison, and in 1619 he had been in prison some years. He may have been the Thomas Dekker who was buried in 1632; he was certainly dead by 1640 or 1641.

In his connection with Henslowe, Dekker had a hand in over forty plays, only a few of which survive. *The Shoemakers' Holiday* and *Old Fortunatus* he wrote alone, but most of his work was done in collaboration with Henslowe's writers, chiefly with Drayton, Chettle, and Wilson, but not infrequently with Jonson, Day, Haughton, Munday, Heywood, Middleton, and Webster. The group exploited many fields—the classics, romance of many periods, history, especially English chronicles, and, to a considerable extent, contemporary life. Thus the French civil wars of the period were stretched to four plays, at least two plays were domestic tragedies, and several apparently dealt with the lower levels of English life. Of the individual plays extant, *Old Fortunatus*, printed in 1600, is Dekker's best romance. *Patient Grissel*, written with Chettle and Haughton in 1598 in the spirit of the domestic play, inaugurated a vogue of the patient wife. In 1601 Dekker was drawn into the stage quarrel and acquitted himself well in *Satiromastix*, a reply to Jonson's *Poetaster*. *The Honest Whore* of 1604 is the first of a series of dramatic studies in which contact of London gallants with the rising merchant classes is depicted. The more realistic *Westward Ho* and *Northward Ho*, written with Webster, followed soon after, and *The Roaring Girl*, in which he collaborated with Middleton, about 1610. Among the later plays, *The Virgin Martyr*, written with Massinger about 1620, and *The Witch of Edmonton*, with Ford and Rowley about 1621, are masterly tragedies. Appropriately Dekker also made his contributions to the great civic pageants of London.

Dekker is the first of a group of writers included in this anthology who represent the culmination of Elizabethan drama proper. The literary decade extending from the first known publication of work by Lyly and Peele in 1584 to the death of Kyd shows the dramatists utilizing a wide range of story and history and developing not only a variety of characters from both the real and the supernatural world, but also a variety of structural devices and styles. For a period of a little over a decade from the middle of the nineties, the early literary drama continued with even greater imaginative fervor and range of style, as illustrated in the work of Shakespeare. Significant new forces, however, were producing a more searching and realistic interpretation of character and a more critical attitude to structure and style. In these respects the drama of this decade prepares for the early Stuart drama or indeed merges with it, for the later work of most of the men represented here is at times more Jacobean than Elizabethan. In Dekker the reaction is indicated not so much by the loss of the romantic or idealizing tendency of the age as by the centering of it on contemporary life, as a result no doubt of the growing wealth and splendor of courts and cities and of man's new adventures in travel.

exploration, and war. With old elements of romance Dekker blends new ones of commerce in the portrayal of the merchant class. Primarily, however, he reflects the infinite Elizabethan zest of life, even in realistic scenes.

The *Shoemakers' Holiday* is first mentioned by Henslowe under date of July 15, 1599, evidently having been written during the preceding six weeks. A court performance was secured for it on the night of January 1, 1600, and it was printed in the same year by Valentine Sims. Other quartos appeared in 1610, 1618, 1624, 1631, and 1657, each one being a reprint of its immediate predecessor. The plot of *The Shoemakers' Holiday* is derived from the three shoemaker stories that make up the first part of Thomas Deloney's *Gentle Craft* (1598). The last story, "Simon Eyre," which furnished Dekker with most of his material for the play, is Deloney's romanticized account of a historical figure, who rose from the position of upholsterer and draper (in Deloney, shoemaker) to become a wealthy lord mayor of London (1445–46). To the other two stories Dekker is indebted for suggestions for characters. He may also have made use of popular ballads for the incident of Ralph, Jane, and Hammon. The play shows the patriotism and many of the romantic conventions of *George a Greene*, transferred to London tradesmen of 1599. The present text is based on Lange's reprint of the quarto of 1600 in Gayley's *Representative English Comedies*.

The first part of *The Honest Whore* was printed by Valentine Sims in 1604 (other editions appeared in 1605, 1615, 1616, and 1635), and the second part (not reprinted here) by Elizabeth Allde in 1630, with the original subtitle considerably expanded: "With the humors of the patient man, the impatient wife; the honest whore, persuaded by strong arguments to turn courtesan again; her brave refuting those arguments; and lastly, the comical passages of an Italian Bridewell, where the scene ends." Although the title-pages of both plays give Dekker alone as the author, from a passage in Henslowe's Diary it appears that Middleton collaborated with him in the first part. Middleton's exact part in the play cannot be determined, but modern scholars are inclined to agree with Dyce that his "share is comparatively small." The source of the plots and characters has never been discovered. It is probable that the plays are compounded of characters whom Dekker had known in the London streets and of stuff of his own imagination, with the use, however, of some conventional motives, especially in the story of Hippolito. The present text is based on the Pearson reprint of the quarto of 1605.

THE SHOEMAKERS' HOLIDAY[1]

BY

THOMAS DEKKER

[*DRAMATIS PERSONÆ*

THE KING.
THE EARL OF CORNWALL.
SIR HUGH LACY, *Earl of Lincoln.*
ROWLAND LACY,
  otherwise HANS } *his nephews.*
ASKEW
SIR ROGER OTELEY, *Lord Mayor of London.*
MASTER HAMMON[2]
MASTER WARNER } *citizens of London.*
MASTER SCOTT
SIMON EYRE, *a shoemaker.*
ROGER, *commonly*
  called HODGE
FIRK } *Eyre's journeymen.*
RAFE[3] DAMPORT

LOVELL, *a courtier.*
DODGER, *a servant to the Earl of Lincoln.*
A DUTCH SKIPPER.
A BOY.
COURTIERS, ATTENDANTS, OFFICERS,
  SOLDIERS, HUNTERS, SHOEMAKERS,
APPRENTICES, SERVANTS.

ROSE, *daughter of Sir Roger.*
SYBIL, *her maid.*
MARGERY, *wife of Simon Eyre.*
JANE, *wife of Rafe.*

SCENE: *London and Old Ford.*

TIME: *Middle of the fifteenth century.*]

To ALL GOOD FELLOWS, PROFESSORS[4] OF THE GENTLE CRAFT,[5] OF WHAT DEGREE SOEVER.

Kind gentlemen and honest boon companions, I present you here with a merry-conceited[6] comedy, called *The Shoemakers' Holiday,* acted by my Lord Admiral's players this present Christmas before the queen's most excellent majesty, for the mirth and pleasant matter by her highness graciously accepted, being indeed no way offensive. The argument of the play I will set down in this epistle: Sir Hugh [10 Lacy, Earl of Lincoln, had a young gentleman of his own name, his near kinsman, that loved the lord mayor's daughter of London; to prevent and cross which love, the earl caused his kinsman to be sent coronel[7] of a company into France; who resigned his place to another gentleman, his friend, and came disguised like a Dutch shoemaker to the house of Simon Eyre in Tower Street, who served the mayor [20 and his household with shoes; the merriments that passed in Eyre's house, his coming to be mayor of London, Lacy's getting his love, and other accidents,[8] with two merry three-men's songs.[9] Take all in good

---

[1] The title continues: "Or the Gentle Craft. With the Humorous Life of Simon Eyre, Shoemaker and Lord Mayor of London. As It Was Acted before the Queen's Most Excellent Majesty on New Year's Day at Night Last by the Right Honorable the Earl of Nottingham, Lord High Admiral of England, his Servants." The running title is "A Pleasant Comedy of the Gentle Craft."

[2] Sometimes spelled *Hammond* in the play.

[3] Variant of *Ralph.*

[4] Followers, practitioners.

[5] According to Deloney, shoemakers were called "Gentlemen of the Gentle Craft" by Hugh, who became their patron saint.

[6] Amusing and fanciful.

[7] Colonel.   [8] Occurrences.

[9] The two songs, which in the 1600 edn. follow this preface, have been removed to their probable places in the play.

555

worth that is well intended, for nothing is purposed but mirth; mirth length'neth long life, which, with all other blessings, I heartily wish you.

FAREWELL!

THE PROLOGUE

As it was pronounced before the queen's majesty

As wretches in a storm, expecting day,
With trembling hands and eyes cast up to heaven,
Make prayers the anchor of their conquered hopes,
So we, dear goddess, wonder of all eyes,
Your meanest vassals, through mistrust and fear
To sink into the bottom of disgrace
By our imperfit pastimes, prostrate thus
On bended knees, our sails of hope do strike,
Dreading the bitter storms of your dislike.
Since then, unhappy men, our hap is such
That to ourselves ourselves no help can bring,　　11
But needs must perish, if your saintlike ears,
Locking the temple where all mercy sits,
Refuse the tribute of our begging tongues,
O, grant, bright mirror of true chastity,
From those life-breathing stars, your sun-like eyes,
One gracious smile, for your celestial breath
Must send us life, or sentence us to death.

[SCENE i.

A street in London.]

Enter Lord Mayor, Lincoln.

LINC. My lord mayor, you have sundry times
Feasted myself and many courtiers more;
Seldom or never can we be so kind
To make requital of your courtesy.
But, leaving this, I hear my cousin [1] Lacy
Is much affected to [2] your daughter Rose.
L. MAYOR. True, my good lord, and she loves him so well
That I mislike her boldness in the chase.
LINC. Why, my lord mayor, think you it then a shame
To join a Lacy with an Oteley's name? 10

[1] Applied to any collateral relative more distant than brother or sister.　　[2] In love with.

L. MAYOR. Too mean is my poor girl for his high birth;
Poor citizens must not with courtiers wed,
Who will in silks and gay apparel spend
More in one year than I am worth, by far.
Therefore your honor need not doubt [3] my girl.
LINC. Take heed, my lord; advise you what you do!
A verier unthrift lives not in the world
Than is my cousin; for I'll tell you what:
'Tis now almost a year since he requested
To travel countries for experience;　　20
I furnished him with coin, bills of exchange,
Letters of credit, men to wait on him,
Solicited my friends in Italy
Well to respect him. But, to see the end,
Scant had he journeyed through half Germany,
But all his coin was spent, his men cast off,
His bills embezzled, [4] and my jolly coz, [5]
Ashamed to show his bankrupt presence here,
Became a shoemaker in Wittenberg,
A goodly science for a gentleman　　30
Of such descent! Now judge the rest by this:
Suppose your daughter have a thousand pound,
He did consume me more in one half year;
And, make him heir to all the wealth you have,
One twelvemonth's rioting will waste it all.
Then seek, my lord, some honest citizen
To wed your daughter to.
L. MAYOR.　　　　I thank your lordship.
[*Aside.*] Well, fox, I understand your subtilty.—
As for your nephew, let your lordship's eye
But watch his actions, and you need not fear,　　40
For I have [sent][6] my daughter far enough.

[3] Fear.　　　　[5] Cousin.
[4] Wasted.　　　[6] Supplied from 1610 edn.

And yet your cousin Rowland might
  do well,
Now he hath learned an occupation;
And yet I scorn to call him son-in-law.
LINC. Ay, but I have a better trade for
  him.
I thank his grace, he hath appointed
  him
Chief colonel of all those companies
Mustered in London and the shires
  about,
To serve his highness in those wars of
  France.
See where he comes!—Lovell, what news
  with you?   50

Enter Lovell, Lacy, and Askew.

LOV. My Lord of Lincoln, 'tis his high-
  ness' will
That presently [1] your cousin ship for
  France
With all his powers; he would not for a
  million
But they should land at Dieppe within
  four days.
LINC. Go certify his grace it shall be done.
                              Exit Lovell.
Now, cousin Lacy, in what forwardness
Are all your companies?
LACY.   All well prepared.
The men of Hertfordshire lie at Mile
  End;
Suffolk and Essex train in Tothill [2]
  Fields;
The Londoners and those of Middle-
  sex,   60
All gallantly prepared in Finsbury,
With frolic spirits long for their parting
  hour.
L. MAYOR. They have their imprest, [3]
  coats, and furniture; [4]
And, if it please your cousin Lacy come
To the Guildhall, he shall receive his
  pay;
And twenty pounds besides my brethren
Will freely give him, to approve [5] our
  loves
We bear unto my lord, your uncle here.
LACY. I thank your honor.
LINC.   Thanks, my good lord mayor.

[1] At once.
[2] The spelling *Tuttle* in the original indicates
the pronunciation.   [4] Equipment.
[3] Advance pay.   [5] Prove.

L. MAYOR. At the Guildhall we will
  expect [6] your coming.   *Exit.* 70
LINC. To approve your loves to me? No
  subtilty!
Nephew, that twenty pound he doth
  bestow
For joy to rid you from his daughter
  Rose.
But, cousins both, now here are none
  but friends,
I would not have you cast an amorous
  eye
Upon so mean a project as the love
Of a gay, wanton, painted citizen.
I know this churl even in the height of
  scorn
Doth hate the mixture of his blood with
  thine.
I pray thee, do thou so! Remember,
  coz,   80
What honorable fortunes wait on thee.
Increase the king's love, which so
  brightly shines,
And gilds thy hopes. I have no heir but
  thee—
And yet not thee if with a wayward
  spirit
Thou start [7] from the true bias of my
  love.
LACY. My lord, I will for honor, not de-
  sire
Of land or livings, or to be your heir,
So guide my actions in pursuit of
  France
As shall add glory to the Lacys' name.
LINC. Coz, for those words here's thirty
  Portuguese, [8]   90
And, nephew Askew, there's a few for
  you.
Fair Honor, in her loftiest eminence,
Stays in France for you, till you fetch
  her thence.
Then, nephews, clap swift wings on
  your designs.
Begone, begone, make haste to the
  Guildhall;
There presently I'll meet you. Do not
  stay.
Where Honor beckons, [9] Shame at-
  tends delay.   *Exit.*
ASKEW. How gladly would your uncle
  have you gone!

[6] Await.   [7] Turn aside.   [8] Gold coins.
[9] Malone's emendation of *becomes.*

LACY. True, coz, but I'll o'erreach his policies.[1]
I have some serious business for three days,   100
Which nothing but my presence can despatch.
You, therefore, cousin, with the companies
Shall haste to Dover; there I'll meet with you.
Or, if I stay past my prefixéd time,
Away for France; we'll meet in Normandy.
The twenty pounds my lord mayor gives to me
You shall receive, and these ten Portuguese,
Part of mine uncle's thirty. Gentle coz,
Have care to our great charge; I know your wisdom   109
Hath tried itself in higher consequence.
ASKEW. Coz, all myself am yours; yet have this care,
To lodge in London with all secrecy.
Our uncle Lincoln hath, besides his own,
Many a jealous eye, that in your face
Stares only to watch means for your disgrace.
LACY. Stay, cousin. Who be these?

Enter Simon Eyre, his Wife, Hodge, Firk, Jane, and Rafe with a piece.[2]

EYRE. Leave whining, leave whining! Away with this whimp'ring, this puling, these blubbering tears, and these wet eyes! I'll get thy husband discharged, [120 I warrant thee, sweet Jane; go to!
HODGE. Master, here be the captains.
EYRE. Peace, Hodge; husht, ye knave, husht!
FIRK. Here be the cavaliers and the coronels, master.
EYRE. Peace, Firk; peace, my fine Firk! Stand by with your pishery-pashery.[3] Away! I am a man of the best presence; I'll speak to them, and [4] they were [130 popes.—Gentlemen, captains, colonels, commanders! Brave men, brave leaders, may it please you to give me audience. I am Simon Eyre, the mad shoemaker of Tower Street; this wench with the mealy

mouth that will never tire, is my wife, I can tell you; here's Hodge, my man and my foreman; here's Firk, my fine firking [5] journeyman; and this is blubbered Jane. All we come to be suitors for this hon- [140 est Rafe. Keep him at home, and, as I am a true shoemaker and a gentleman of the gentle craft, buy spurs yourself, and I'll find [6] ye boots these seven years.
WIFE. Seven years, husband?
EYRE. Peace, midriff, peace! I know what I do. Peace!
FIRK. Truly, master cormorant,[7] you shall do God good service to let Rafe and his wife stay together. She's a young [150 new-married woman; if you take her husband away from her a-night, you undo her; she may beg in the daytime; for he's as good a workman at a prick and an awl as any is in our trade.
JANE. O, let him stay; else I shall be undone!
FIRK. Ay, truly, she shall be laid at one side like a pair of old shoes else, and be occupied for no use.   160
LACY. Truly, my friends, it lies not in my power.
The Londoners are pressed,[8] paid, and set forth
By the lord mayor; I cannot change a man.
HODGE. Why, then you were as good be a corporal as a colonel, if you cannot discharge one good fellow; and, I tell you true, I think you do more than you can answer, to press a man within a year and a day of his marriage.
EYRE. Well said, melancholy [170 Hodge; gramercy, my fine foreman.
WIFE. Truly, gentlemen, it were ill done for such as you to stand so stiffly against a poor young wife, considering her case, she is new-married; but let that pass. I pray, deal not roughly with her; her husband is a young man, and but newly entered; but let that pass.
EYRE. Away with your pishery-pashery, your pols and your edipols![9] Peace, [180 midriff; [10] silence, Cisly Bumtrinket! Let your head speak.

[5] Frisking.   [6] Provide.
[7] His corruption of *coronel*.
[8] Impressed, drafted.
[9] Forms of *By Pollux*.   [10] Original has *midaffe*.

[1] Tricks.   [3] Trifling talk.
[2] *I.e.*, of leather.   [4] An, if.

Firk. Yea, and the horns too, master.

Eyre. Too soon, my fine Firk, too soon! Peace, scoundrels! See you this man? Captains, you will not release him? Well, let him go. He's a proper shot; let him vanish! Peace, Jane, dry up thy tears; they'll make his powder dankish. Take him, brave men. Hector of Troy was [190 an hackney to him; Hercules and Termagant, scoundrels; Prince Arthur's Round Table—by the Lord of Ludgate—ne'er fed such a tall,[1] such a dapper swordman; by the life of Pharaoh, a brave, resolute swordman! Peace, Jane! I say no more, mad knaves.

Firk. See, see, Hodge, how my master raves in commendation of Rafe!

Hodge. Rafe, th'art a gull,[2] by this [200 hand, and thou goest.[3]

Askew. I am glad, good Master Eyre, it is my hap
To meet so resolute a soldier.
Trust me, for your report and love to him,
A common slight regard shall not respect him.

Lacy. Is thy name Rafe?

Rafe.   Yes, sir.

Lacy.   Give me thy hand.
Thou shalt not want, as I am a gentleman.
Woman, be patient. God, no doubt, will send
Thy husband safe again; but he must go—   209
His country's quarrel says it shall be so.

Hodge. Th'art a gull, by my stirrup,[4] if thou dost not go. I will not have thee strike thy gimlet into these weak vessels; prick thine enemies, Rafe.

Enter Dodger.

Dodger. My lord, your uncle on the Tower Hill
Stays with the lord mayor and the aldermen,
And doth request you, with all speed you may,
To hasten thither.

Askew.   Cousin, let's go.

---

[1] Brave.   [2] Fool.
[3] Lange and other editors add *not*.
[4] A strap for steadying the shoemaker's last on his knee.

Lacy. Dodger, run you before; tell them we come.—   *Exit Dodger.*[5] 219
This Dodger is mine uncle's parasite,
The arrant'st varlet that e'er breathed on earth;
He sets more discord in a noble house
By one day's broaching of his pickthank[6] tales
Than can be salved again in twenty years,
And he, I fear, shall go with us to France
To pry into our actions.

Askew.   Therefore, coz,
It shall behoove you to be circumspect.

Lacy. Fear not, good cousin.—Rafe, hie to your colors.
                    [*Exeunt Lacy and Askew.*]

Rafe. I must, because there's no remedy;   229
But, gentle master and my loving dame,
As you have always been a friend to me,
So in mine absence think upon my wife.

Jane. Alas, my Rafe!

Wife.   She cannot speak for weeping.

Eyre. Peace, you cracked groats, you mustard tokens;[7] disquiet not the brave soldier. Go thy ways, Rafe!

Jane. Ay, ay, you bid him go. What shall I do when he is gone?

Firk. Why, be doing with me or my fellow Hodge; be not idle.   240

Eyre. Let me see thy hand, Jane. This fine hand, this white hand, these pretty fingers must spin, must card, must work; work, you bombast cotton-candle[8] quean; work for your living, with a pox to you![9]— Hold thee, Rafe, here's five sixpences for thee. Fight for the honor of the gentle craft, for the gentlemen shoemakers, the courageous cordwainers, the flower of S[aint] Martin's, the mad knaves of Bedlam, [250 Fleet Street, Tower Street, and Whitechapel; crack me the crowns of the French knaves; a pox on them, crack them; fight, by the Lord of Ludgate; fight, my fine boy!

Firk. Here, Rafe, here's three twopences. Two carry into France; the third

---

[5] This direction follows Dodger's speech in original.   [6] Talebearer's.
[7] Yellow spots from the plague.
[8] "Bombast: cotton-wool; cotton-candle: a candle with a cotton wick. Jane's hands are as white as the wax of a candle, as soft as bombast" (Sutherland).   [9] A plague to you!

shall wash our souls at parting, for sorrow is dry. For my sake, firk the *Basa mon cues*.[1]   259

HODGE. Rafe, I am heavy at parting; but here's a shilling for thee. God send thee to cram thy slops [2] with French crowns, and thy enemies' bellies with bullets.

RAFE. I thank you, master, and I thank you all.

Now, gentle wife, my loving, lovely Jane,

Rich men, at parting, give their wives rich gifts,

Jewels and rings, to grace their lily hands.

Thou know'st our trade makes rings for women's heels.

Here take this pair of shoes, cut out by Hodge,

Stitched by my fellow Firk, seamed by myself,   270

Made up and pinked [3] with letters for thy name.

Wear them, my dear Jane, for thy husband's sake,

And every morning when thou pull'st them on,

Remember me, and pray for my return.

Make much of them, for I have made them so

That I can know them from a thousand mo.[4]

Sound drum. Enter Lord Mayor, Lincoln, Lacy, Askew, Dodger, and Soldiers. They pass over the stage; Rafe falls in amongst them; Firk and the rest cry "Farewell," etc., and so exeunt.

[SCENE ii.

A garden at Old Ford.]

Enter Rose, alone, making a garland.

[ROSE.] Here sit thou down upon this flow'ry bank

And make a garland for thy Lacy's head.

These pinks, these roses, and these violets,

These blushing gilliflowers, these marigolds,

The fair embroidery [5] of his coronet,

Carry not half such beauty in their cheeks

As the sweet count'nance of my Lacy doth.

O my most unkind father! O my stars,

Why lowered you so at my nativity,

To make me love, yet live robbed of my love?   10

Here as a thief am I imprisonéd

For my dear Lacy's sake within those walls

Which by my father's cost were builded up

For better purposes.   Here must I languish

For him that doth as much lament, I know,

Mine absence as for him I pine in woe.

Enter Sybil.

SYB. Good morrow, young mistress. I am sure you make that garland for me, against [6] I shall be Lady of the Harvest.

ROSE. Sybil, what news at London?   [20

SYB. None but good.   My lord mayor, your father, and Master Philpot, your uncle, and Master Scot, your cousin, and Mistress Frigbottom by Doctors' Commons do all, by my troth, send you most hearty commendations.

ROSE. Did Lacy send kind greetings to his love?

SYB. O, yes, out of cry,[7] by my troth. I scant knew him. Here a [8] wore [a] [9]   [30 scarf, and here a scarf; here a bunch of feathers, and here precious stones and jewels, and a pair of garters—O, monstrous! —like one of our yellow silk curtains at home here in Old Ford House, here in Master Bellymount's chamber.   I stood at our door in Cornhill, looked at him, he at me indeed, spake to him, but he not to me, not a word. "Marry gup," [10] thought I, "with a wanion!" [11] He passed by me as proud— [40 "Marry foh! Are you grown humorous?" [12] thought I, and so shut the door, and in I came.

ROSE. O Sybil, how dost thou my Lacy wrong!

---

[1] *I.e.*, the Frenchmen. *Cf.* vulgar French, *baisez mon queue*.
[2] Breeches.
[3] Perforated.
[4] More.
[5] Embroidery.
[6] For the time when.
[7] Beyond all description.
[8] He.
[9] From 1618 edn.
[10] Exclamation of impatience.
[11] With a vengeance.
[12] Capricious.

My Rowland is as gentle as a lamb;
No dove was ever half so mild as he.

Syb. Mild? Yea, as a bushel of stamped
crabs.[1] He looked upon me as sour as
verjuice. "Go thy ways," thought I;
"thou mayst be much in my gaskins,[2] [50
but nothing in my netherstocks."[3]
This is your fault, mistress, to love him
that loves not you; he thinks scorn to
do as he's done to; but, if I were as
you, I'd cry, "Go by, Jeronimo, go
by!"[4]

I'd set mine old debts against my new
    driblets,
And the hare's foot against the goose gib-
    lets,
For, if ever I sigh, when sleep I should take,
Pray God I may lose my maidenhead when
    I wake.[5]   60

Rose. Will my love leave me then, and
    go to France?

Syb. I know not that, but I am sure I
see him stalk before the soldiers. By my
troth, he is a proper[6] man; but he is
proper that proper doth. Let him go
snick-up,[7] young mistress.

Rose. Get thee to London, and learn
    perfectly
Whether my Lacy go to France, or no.
Do this, and I will give thee for thy
    pains
My cambric apron and my Romish
    gloves,   70
My purple stockings and a stomacher.
Say, wilt thou do this, Sybil, for my sake?

Syb. Will I, quotha? At whose suit?
By my troth, yes, I'll go. A cambric
apron, gloves, a pair of purple stockings,
and a stomacher! I'll sweat in purple,
mistress, for you; I'll take anything
that comes a God's name. O, rich! A
cambric apron! Faith, then have at "Up
tails all."[8] I'll go jiggy-joggy to [80

London, and be here in a trice, young
mistress.   *Exit.*

Rose. Do so, good Sybil.—Meantime
    wretched I
Will sit and sigh for his lost company.
                                        Exit.

[Scene iii.

Tower Street, London.]

*Enter Rowland Lacy, like a Dutch shoe-
                                    maker.*

Lacy. How many shapes have gods and
    kings devised
Thereby to compass their desired loves!
It is no shame for Rowland Lacy, then,
To clothe his cunning with the gentle
    craft,
That, thus disguised, I may unknown
    possess
The only happy presence of my Rose.
For her have I forsook my charge in
    France,
Incurred the king's displeasure, and
    stirred up
Rough hatred in mine uncle Lincoln's
    breast.
O love, how powerful art thou, that
    canst change   10
High birth to bareness,[9] and a noble
    mind
To the mean semblance of a shoemaker!
But thus it must be, for her cruel
    father,
Hating the single union of our souls,
Has secretly conveyed my Rose from
    London
To bar me of her presence; but I trust
Fortune and this disguise will furder
    me
Once more to view her beauty, gain her
    sight.
Here in Tower Street with Eyre the
    shoemaker
Mean I a while to work; I know the
    trade;   20
I learnt it when I was in Wittenberg.
Then cheer thy hoping sprites; be not
    dismayed;
Thou canst not want. Do Fortune what
    she can,
The gentle craft is living for a man. *Exit.*

---

[1] Crushed crab apples.   [2] Wide trousers.

[3] Stockings. "The meaning seems to be that,
though we may be acquainted, we are not intimate friends" (Neilson).

[4] This tag from Kyd's *Spanish Tragedy* was a
popular slang phrase.

[5] Lange suggests that these verses mean,
"Off with the old love, on with the new." In
these couplets and a few other passages the line
division has been regularized.

[6] Handsome.   [7] Go and be hanged!

[8] *I.e.*, make speed; the name of a dance tune.

[9] 1631 edn. reads *baseness.*

[SCENE iv.

*n open yard before Eyre's house in Tower
Street.*]

Enter Eyre, making himself ready.

EYRE. Where be these boys, these girls,
these drabs, these scoundrels? They wallow
in the fat brewis [1] of my bounty, and lick
up the crumbs of my table, yet will not rise
to see my walks cleansed. Come out, you
powder-beef [2] queans! What, Nan! What,
Madge Mumblecrust! Come out, you fat
midriff-swag-belly-whores, and sweep me
these kennels [3] that the noisome stench
offend not the nose of my neighbors. [10
What, Firk, I say! What, Hodge! Open my
shop windows! What, Firk, I say!

Enter Firk.

FIRK. O master, is 't you that speak
bandog and bedlam [4] this morning? I was
in a dream, and mused what madman
was got into the street so early. Have
you drunk this morning that your throat is
so clear?

EYRE. Ah, well said, Firk; well said,
Firk. To work, my fine knave, to [20
work! Wash thy face, and thou't be more
blessed.

FIRK. Let them wash my face that will
eat it. Good master, send for a sousewife,[5] if you'll have my face cleaner.

Enter Hodge.

EYRE. Away, sloven! Avaunt, scoundrel!
—Good morrow, Hodge; good morrow, my
fine foreman.

HODGE. O master, good morrow; y'are an
early stirrer. Here's a fair morning.— [30
Good morrow, Firk; I could have slept this
hour. Here's a brave day towards.

EYRE. O, haste to work, my fine foreman, haste to work.

FIRK. Master, I am dry as dust to hear
my fellow Roger talk of fair weather. Let
us pray for good leather, and let clowns
and plowboys and those that work in
the fields pray for brave days. We work in
a dry shop; what care I if it rain?   40

[1] Thickened broth.
[2] Salted beef.   [3] Channels, gutters.
[4] *I.e.*, like a watchdog and a madman.
[5] Pig-pickler.

Enter Eyre's Wife.

EYRE. How now, Dame Margery, can
you see to rise? Trip and go; call up the
drabs, your maids.

WIFE. See to rise? I hope 'tis time
enough; 'tis early enough for any woman
to be seen abroad. I marvel how many
wives in Tower Street are up so soon.
God's me,[6] 'tis not noon! Here's a yawling!

EYRE. Peace, Margery, peace! Where's
Cisly Bumtrinket, your maid? She has a [50
privy fault—she farts in her sleep. Call
the quean up; if my men want shoe thread,
I'll swinge her in a stirrup.

FIRK. Yet that's but a dry beating;
here's still a sign of drought.

Enter Lacy singing.

LACY. *Der was een bore van Gelderland*
        (*Frolick si byen!*);
    He was als dronck he cold nyet stand
        Upsolce se byen.
    Tap eens de canneken;   60
    Drincke, schone mannekin.[7]

FIRK. Master, for my life, yonder's a
brother of the gentle craft; if he bear not
Saint Hugh's bones,[8] I'll forfeit my bones;
he's some uplandish [9] workman. Hire him,
good master, that I may learn some gibble-
gabble; 'twill make us work the faster.

EYRE. Peace, Firk! A hard world! Let
him pass, let him vanish; we have journeymen enow. Peace, my fine Firk!   70

WIFE. Nay, nay, y'are best follow your
man's counsel; you shall see what will come
on 't. We have not men enow, but we must
entertain every butterbox;[10] but let that
pass.

HODGE. Dame, fore God, if my master
follow your counsel, he'll consume little
beef. He shall be glad of men and he can
catch them.

[6] An exclamation of impatience.
[7] Adopting Baugh's emendation, "Op zulke
zeebeenen," in line 4, we may translate the song
thus:
    There was a boor from Gelderland
        (Jolly they be!);
    He was so drunk he could not stand
        On such sea legs.
    Tap once the cannikin;
    Drink, pretty mannikin.
[8] St. Hugh's bones were believed to have been
made into shoemakers' tools.
[9] Up-country; perhaps an error for *outlandish*,
foreign.   [10] Dutchman.

FIRK. Ay, that he shall. 80

HODGE. Fore God, a proper man and, I warrant, a fine workman. Master, farewell; dame, adieu. If such a man as he cannot find work, Hodge is not for you.

Offers to go.

EYRE. Stay, my fine Hodge.

FIRK. Faith, and your foreman go, dame, you must take a journey to seek a new journeyman; if Roger remove, Firk follows. If St. Hugh's bones shall not be set awork, I may prick mine awl in the walls, [90 and go play. Fare ye well, master; goodby, dame.

EYRE. Tarry, my fine Hodge, my brisk foreman! Stay, Firk! Peace, puddingbroth! By the Lord of Ludgate, I love my men as my life. Peace, you gallimaufry! [1] Hodge, if he want work, I'll hire him. One of you to him. Stay—he comes to us.

LACY. *Goeden dach, meester, ende u, vro, oak.*[2] 100

FIRK. Nails,[3] if I should speak after him without drinking, I should choke. And you, friend Oak, are you of the gentle craft?

LACY. *Yaw, yaw, ik bin den skomawker.*[4]

FIRK. "*Den skomaker,*" quotha! And hark you, *skomaker,* have you all your tools, a good rubbing pin, a good stopper, a good dresser, your four sorts of awls, and your two balls of wax, your paring knife, your hand-and-thumb-leathers, and [110 good St. Hugh's bones to smooth up your work?

LACY. *Yaw, yaw; be niet vorveard. Ik hab all de dingen voour mack skoes groot and cleane.*[5]

FIRK. Ha, ha! Good master, hire him; he'll make me laugh so that I shall work more in mirth than I can in earnest.

EYRE. Hear ye, friend, have ye any skill in the mystery[6] of cordwainers? 120

LACY. *Ik weet niet wat yow seg; ich verstaw you niet.*[7]

FIRK. Why, thus, man: [*Imitating a shoemaker at work.*] "*Ich verste u niet,*"[8] quotha.

LACY. *Yaw, yaw, yaw; ick can dat wel doen.*[9]

FIRK. "*Yaw, yaw!*" He speaks yawing like a jackdaw that gapes to be fed with cheese curds. O, he'll give a villainous [130 pull at a can of double beer; but Hodge and I have the vantage—we must drink first because we are the eldest journeymen.

EYRE. What is thy name?

LACY. Hans—Hans Meulter.

EYRE. Give me thy hand; th'art welcome.—Hodge, entertain him; Firk, bid him welcome; come, Hans. Run, wife, bid your maids, your trullibubs,[10] make ready my fine men's breakfasts. To him, Hodge! [140

HODGE. Hans, th'art welcome. Use thyself friendly, for we are good fellows; if not, thou shalt be fought with, wert thou bigger than a giant.

FIRK. Yea, and drunk with, wert thou Gargantua. My master keeps no cowards, I tell thee.—Ho, boy, bring him an heel block;[11] here's a new journeyman.

Enter Boy.

LACY. O, *ich wersto you; ich moet een halve dossen cans betaelen. Here, boy,* [150 *nempt dis skilling; tap eens freelicke.*[12]

Exit Boy.

EYRE. Quick, snippersnapper, away! Firk, scour thy throat; thou shalt wash it with Castilian liquor.

Enter Boy.

Come, my last of the fives,[13] give me a can. Have to thee, Hans; here, Hodge; here, Firk; drink, you mad Greeks, and work like true Trojans, and pray for Simon Eyre, the shoemaker.—Here, Hans, and th'art welcome. 160

FIRK. Lo, dame, you would have lost a good fellow that will teach us to laugh. This beer came hopping in well.

WIFE. Simon, it is almost seven.

EYRE. Is't so, Dame Clapperdudgeon?[14]

---

[1] Ragout of hashed meats.
[2] Good day, master, and you, wife, too.
[3] By God's nails.
[4] Yes, yes, I am the shoemaker.
[5] Yes, yes; be not afraid. I have everything to make shoes big and little. [6] Trade.
[7] I don't know what you say; I don't understand you. [8] "I don't understand you."
[9] Yes, yes, yes, I can do that well.
[10] Tripes, sluts.
[11] A last for making heels.
[12] O, I understand you; I must pay for a half dozen cans. Here, boy, take this shilling; tap once freely.
[13] My smallest last; my little one.
[14] Because her mouth rattles like a beggar's clapdish.

Is't seven a-clock, and my men's breakfast not ready? Trip and go, you soused cunger,[1] away! Come, you mad hyperboreans. Follow me, Hodge; follow me, Hans; come after, my fine Firk; to work, to work [170 awhile, and then to breakfast!　　*Exit.*

FIRK. Soft! *Yaw, yaw,* good Hans, though my master have no more wit but to call you afore me, I am not so foolish to go behind you, I being the elder journeyman.　　　　　　　　　　*Exeunt.*

[SCENE v.

A field near Old Ford.]

Halloaing within.　Enter Warner and Hammon, like hunters.

HAM. Cousin, beat every brake; the game's not far.
  This way with wingèd feet he fled from death,
  Whilst the pursuing hounds, scenting his steps,
  Find out his highway to destruction.
  Besides, the miller's boy told me even now,
  He saw him take soil,[2] and he halloaed him,
  Affirming him so embossed [3]
  That long he could not hold.
WARN.　　　　　　　　　If it be so,
  'Tis best we trace these meadows by Old Ford.

A noise of Hunters within.　Enter a Boy.

HAM. How now, boy? Where's the deer?
  Speak! Saw'st thou him?　　　　　10
BOY. O, yea; I saw him leap through a hedge, and then over a ditch; then, at my lord mayor's pale, over he skipped me, and in he went me, and "Holla" the hunters cried, and "There, boy; there, boy!" But there he is, a mine honesty.
HAM. Boy, God-a-mercy.[4]　Cousin, let's away;
  I hope we shall find better sport today.
　　　　　　　　　　Exeunt.

Hunting within.　Enter Rose and Sybil.

ROSE. Why, Sybil, wilt thou prove a forester?　　　　　　　　　20
SYB. Upon some,[5] no. Forester? Go by; no, faith, mistress. The deer came running into the barn through the orchard and over the pale. I wot [6] well I looked as pale as a new cheese to see him. But whip, says Goodman Pinclose, up with his flail, and our Nick with a prong, and down he fell, and they upon him, and I upon them. By my troth, we had such sport; and in the end we ended him; his throat we cut, flayed [30 him, unhorned him, and my lord mayor shall eat of him anon, when he comes.
　　　　　　　　Horns sound within.
ROSE. Hark, hark, the hunters come.
  Y'are best take heed;
  They'll have a saying to you for this deed.

Enter Hammon, Warner, Huntsmen, and Boy.

HAM. God save you, fair ladies.
SYB.　　　　　　　Ladies! O, gross! [7]
WARN. Came not a buck this way?
ROSE.　　　　　　No, but two does.
HAM. And which way went they? Faith, we'll hunt at those.
SYB. At those? Upon some, no. When, can you tell?
WARN. Upon some, ay!
SYB.　　　　Good Lord!
WARN.　　　　　Wounds! [8] Then farewell!
HAM. Boy, which way went he?
BOY.　　　　　This way, sir, he ran.　40
HAM. This way he ran indeed, fair Mistress Rose;
  Our game was lately in your orchard seen.
WARN. Can you advise which way he took his flight?
SYB. Follow your nose; his horns will guide you right.
WARN. Th' art a mad wench.
SYB.　　　　O, rich!
ROSE.　　　　　Trust me, not I.
  It is not like [that] [9] the wild forest deer
  Would come so near to places of resort.
  You are deceived; he fled some other way.

---

[1] Pickled cucumber, or perhaps a misspelling for *conger*, eel.
[2] Take to water. From 1610 edn. Original reads *saile*.
[3] Foaming at the mouth from exhaustion.
[4] Thanks.

[5] An intensive cant phrase of uncertain origin.
[6] Know.　　　　[8] God's wounds!
[7] Stupid.　　　[9] Supplied from 1610 edn.

WARN. Which way, my sugar candy, can you show? [*Puts his arm about Sybil.*]

SYB. Come up, good honeysops; upon some, no!　　　50

ROSE. Why do you stay, and not pursue your game?

SYB. I'll hold [1] my life, their hunting nags be lame.

HAM. A deer more dear is found within this place.

ROSE. But not the deer, sir, which you had in chase.

HAM. I chased the deer, but this dear chaseth me.

ROSE. The strangest hunting that ever I see.

But where's your park?
　　　　　　　　　She offers to go away.

HAM.　　　　　　　'Tis here. O, stay!

ROSE. Impale me, and then I will not stray.

WARN. They wrangle, wench; we are more kind than they.

SYB. What kind of hart is that dear heart you seek?　　　60

WARN. A hart, dear heart!

SYB.　　　　　　Who ever saw the like?

ROSE. To lose your heart, is 't possible you can?

HAM. My heart is lost.

ROSE.　　　　　Alack, good gentleman!

HAM. This poor lost heart would I wish you might find.

ROSE. You, by such luck, might prove your hart a hind.

HAM. Why, Luck had horns, so have I heard some say.

ROSE. Now, God, and 't be his will, send Luck into your way.

Enter L[ord] Mayor and Servants.

L. MAYOR. What, M[aster] Hammon? Welcome to Old Ford!

SYB. God's pitikins, hands off, sir! Here's my lord.

L. MAYOR. I hear you had ill luck, and lost your game.　　　70

HAM. 'Tis true, my lord.

L. MAYOR.　　　I am sorry for the same. What gentleman is this?

HAM.　　　　　　My brother-in-law.

[1] Wager.

L. MAYOR. Y'are welcome both. Sith [2] Fortune offers you

Into my hands, you shall not part from hence

Until you have refreshed your wearied limbs.

Go, Sybil, cover the board! You shall be guest

To no good cheer, but even a hunter's feast.

HAM. I thank your lordship.—Cousin, on my life,

For our lost venison I shall find a wife.
　　　　　　　Exeunt [all but Mayor].

L. MAYOR. In, gentlemen; I'll not be absent long.—　　　80

This Hammon is a proper gentleman,

A citizen by birth, fairly allied;

How fit an husband were he for my girl!

Well, I will in, and do the best I can

To match my daughter to this gentleman.
　　　　　　　　　　　　Exit.

[SCENE vi.

A room in Eyre's house.]

Enter Lacy, Skipper, Hodge, and Firk.

SKIP. *Ick sal yow wat seggen, Hans; dis skip dat comen from Candy, is al vol,[3] by Got's sacrament, van sugar, civet, almonds, cambrick, end alle dingen—towsand towsand ding. Nempt it, Hans, nempt it vor u meester. Daer be de bils van laden. Your meester Simon Eyre sal hae good copen. Wat seggen yow, Hans?* [4]

FIRK. *Wat seggen de reggen de copen, slopen—Laugh, Hodge, laugh!*　　　10

LACY. *Mine liever broder Firk, bringt Meester Eyre tot [5] det signe un Swannekin; daer sal yow finde dis skipper end me. Wat seggen yow, broder Firk? Doot it, Hodge.[6] Come, skipper.*　　　*Exeunt.*

[2] Since.

[3] From 1610 edn. Original reads *wel.*

[4] I'll tell you what, Hans; this ship that is come from Candia is all full, by God's sacrament, of sugar, civet, almonds, cambric, and all things—a thousand thousand things. Take it, Hans, take it for your master. There are the bills of lading. Your master, Simon Eyre, shall have a good bargain. What say you, Hans?

[5] In early edns. *lot.*

[6] My dear brother Firk, bring Master Eyre to the sign of the Swan; there shall you find this skipper and me. What say you, brother Firk? Do it, Hodge.

FIRK. Bring him, quod you? Here's no knavery, to bring my master to buy a ship worth the lading of two or three hundred thousand pounds. Alas, that's nothing; a trifle, a bable,[1] Hodge.   20

HODGE. The truth is, Firk, that the merchant owner of the ship dares not show his head, and therefore this skipper that deals for him, for the love he bears to Hans, offers my master Eyre a bargain in the commodities. He shall have a reasonable day of payment; he may sell the wares by that time, and be an huge gainer himself.

FIRK. Yea, but can my fellow Hans lend my master twenty porpentines as an   [30 earnest penny?

HODGE. Portuguese, thou wouldst say. Here they be, Firk; hark, they jingle in my pocket like St. Mary Overy's bells.

Enter Eyre and his Wife.

FIRK. Mum, here comes my dame and my master. She'll scold, on my life, for loitering this Monday; but all's one—let them all say what they can, Monday's our holiday.

WIFE. You sing, Sir Sauce, but I beshrew[2] your heart.   40
I fear for this your singing we shall smart.

FIRK. Smart for me, dame? Why, dame, why?

HODGE. Master, I hope you'll not suffer my dame to take down your journeymen.

FIRK. If she take me down, I'll take her up; yea, and take her down too, a buttonhole lower.

EYRE. Peace, Firk; not I, Hodge; by the life of Pharaoh, by the Lord of Ludgate,   [50 by this beard, every hair whereof I value at a king's ransom, she shall not meddle with you.—Peace, you bombast cotton-candle quean; away, queen of clubs! Quarrel not with me and my men, with me and my fine Firk; I'll firk you if you do!

WIFE. Yea, yea, man, you may use me as you please; but let that pass.

EYRE. Let it pass, let it vanish away! Peace! Am I not Simon Eyre? Are not   [60 these my brave men, brave shoemakers, all gentlemen of the gentle craft? Prince am I none, yet am I nobly born, as being the sole son of a shoemaker. Away, rubbish! Vanish; melt, melt like kitchen stuff.

WIFE. Yea, yea, 'tis well; I must be called rubbish, kitchen stuff, for a sort[3] of knaves.

FIRK. Nay, dame, you shall not weep and wail in woe for me. Master, I'll stay   [70 no longer; here's a venentory[4] of my shop tools. Adieu, master; Hodge, farewell.

HODGE. Nay, stay, Firk; thou shalt not go alone.

WIFE. I pray, let them go; there be mo maids than Mawkin, more men than Hodge, and more fools than Firk.

FIRK. Fools? Nails! If I tarry now, I would my guts might be turned to shoe thread.   80

HODGE. And, if I stay, I pray God I may be turned to a Turk, and set in Finsbury for boys to shoot at.—Come, Firk.

EYRE. Stay, my fine knaves, you arms of my trade, you pillars of my profession. What, shall a tittle-tattle's words make you forsake Simon Eyre?—Avaunt, kitchen stuff! Rip, you brown bread Tannikin;[5] out of my sight! Move me not! Have not I ta'en you from selling tripes in East-   [90 cheap, and set you in my shop, and made you hail-fellow with Simon Eyre, the shoemaker? And now do you deal thus with my journeymen? Look, you powder-beef quean, on the face of Hodge; here's a face for a lord.

FIRK. And here's a face for any lady in Christendom.

EYRE. Rip, you chitterling, avaunt! Boy, bid the tapster of the Boar's Head   [100 fill me a dozen cans of beer for my journeymen.

FIRK. A dozen cans? O, brave! Hodge, now I'll stay.

EYRE. [*Aside to the Boy.*]   And the knave fills any more than two, he pays for them.—[*Exit Boy.—Aloud.*] A dozen cans of beer for my journeymen. [*Enter Boy.*] Heave,[6] you mad Mesopotamians; wash your livers with this liquor. Where be   [110 the odd ten?—[*Aside.*] No more, Madge, no more.—Well said.[7] Drink and to work! —What work dost thou, Hodge? What work?

---

[3] Pack.   [4] Firk's corruption of *inventory*.
[5] Dutch nickname for Anne.
[6] *I.e.*, lift your tankards.   [7] Well done.

---

[1] Bauble.   [2] Curse.

Hodge. I am a-making a pair of shoes for my lord mayor's daughter, Mistress Rose.

Firk. And I a pair of shoes for Sybil, my lord's maid. I deal with her.

Eyre. Sybil? Fie, defile not thy [120 fine workmanly fingers with the feet of kitchen stuff and basting ladles. Ladies of the court, fine ladies, my lads, commit their feet to our appareling; put gross work to Hans. Yark [1] and seam, yark and seam!

Firk. For yarking and seaming let me alone, and I come to 't.

Hodge. Well, master, all this is from the bias. Do you remember the ship my fellow Hans told you of? The skipper and [130 he are both drinking at the Swan. Here be the Portuguese to give earnest. If you go through with it, you cannot choose but be a lord at least.

Firk. Nay, dame, if my master prove not a lord, and you a lady, hang me.

Wife. Yea, like enough, if you may loiter and tipple thus.

Firk. Tipple, dame? No, we have been bargaining with Skellum Skanderbag [2] [140 Can-You-Dutch-Spreaken for a ship of silk Cyprus,[3] laden with sugar candy.

Enter the Boy with a velvet coat and an alderman's gown. Eyre puts it on.

Eyre. Peace, Firk; silence, Tittle-tattle! Hodge, I'll go through with it. Here's a seal ring, and I have sent for a garded [4] gown and a damask cassock. See where it comes. Look here, Maggy; help me, Firk; apparel me, Hodge; silk and satin, you mad Philistines, silk and satin!

Firk. Ha, ha, my master will be as [150 proud as a dog in a doublet, all in beaten [5] damask and velvet.

Eyre. Softly, Firk, for rearing of the nap, and wearing threadbare my garments. How dost thou like me, Firk? How do I look, my fine Hodge?

Hodge. Why, now you look like yourself, master. I warrant you, there's few in the city but will give you the wall,[6] and

come upon you with the "right wor- [160 shipful."

Firk. Nails, my master looks like a threadbare cloak new turned and dressed! Lord, Lord, to see what good raiment doth! Dame, dame, are you not enamored?

Eyre. How sayst thou, Maggy, am I not brisk? Am I not fine?

Wife. Fine? By my troth, sweetheart, very fine! By my troth, I never liked thee so well in my life, sweetheart; but let [170 that pass. I warrant there be many women in the city have not such handsome husbands, but only for their apparel; but let that pass too.

Enter Hans and Skipper.

Hans. *Godden day, mester. Dis be de skipper dat heb de skip van marchandice. De commodity ben good; nempt it, master, nempt it.*[7]

Eyre. God-a-mercy, Hans; welcome, skipper. Where lies this ship of merchandise?

Skip. *De skip ben in rouere; dor be* [181 *van sugar, cyvet, almonds, cambrick, and a towsand towsand tings. Gotz sacrament, nempt it, mester; yo sal heb good copen.*[8]

Firk. To him, master! O sweet master! O sweet wares! Prunes, almonds, sugar candy, carrot roots, turnips! O brave, fatting meat![9] Let not a man buy a nutmeg but yourself.

Eyre. Peace, Firk! Come, skipper, [190 I'll go aboard [10] with you.—Hans, have you made him drink?

Skip. *Yaw, yaw, ic heb veale gedrunck.*[11]

Eyre. Come, Hans, follow me. Skipper, thou shalt have my countenance in the city.

Exeunt.

Firk. "*Yaw, heb veale gedrunck,*" quotha. They may well be called butterboxes, when they drink fat veal and thick beer too. But come, dame, I hope you'll chide us no more. 200

Wife. No, faith, Firk; no, perdy,[12]

---

[1] Pull stitches tight.
[2] Equivalent to *Rascal*.   [3] Black lawn.
[4] Edged with an ornamental band.
[5] Stamped.
[6] *I.e.*, yield him the favored position in walking the streets.
[7] Good day, master. This is the skipper that has the ship of merchandise. The commodity is good; take it, master, take it.
[8] The ship is in the river; there are sugar, civet, almonds, cambric, and a thousand thousand things. By God's sacrament, take it, master; you shall have a good bargain.
[9] Fattening food.
[10] First two edns. read *abroade*.
[11] Yes, yes, I have drunk much.
[12] *Par Dieu*, truly.

Hodge. I do feel honor creep upon me, and, which is more, a certain rising in my flesh; but let that pass.

Firk. Rising in your flesh do you feel, say you? Ay, you may be with child, but why should not my master feel a rising in his flesh, having a gown and a gold ring on? But you are such a shrew, you'll soon pull him down.   210

Wife. Ha, ha! Prithee, peace! Thou mak'st my worship laugh; but let that pass. Come, I'll go in. Hodge, prithee, go before me; Firk, follow me.

Firk. Firk doth follow; Hodge, pass out in state.   *Exeunt.*

[Scene vii.

A room in Lincoln's house at London.]

Enter Lincoln and Dodger.

Linc. How now, good Dodger, what's the news in France?

Dodger. My lord, upon the eighteen day of May
The French and English were prepared to fight;
Each side with eager fury gave the sign
Of a most hot encounter. Five long hours
Both armies fought together; at the length
The lot of victory fell on our sides.
Twelve thousand of the Frenchmen that day died,
Four thousand English, and no man of name
But Captain Hyam and young Arding-
ton,   10
Two gallant gentlemen—I knew them well.

Linc. But, Dodger, prithee, tell me, in this fight
How did my cousin Lacy bear himself?

Dodger. My lord, your cousin Lacy was not there.

Linc. Not there?

Dodger.   No, my good lord.

Linc.   Sure, thou mistakest.
I saw him shipped, and a thousand eyes beside
Were witnesses of the farewells which he gave,
When I, with weeping eyes, bid him adieu.
Dodger, take heed.

Dodger.   My lord, I am advised
That what I spake is true. To prove it so,   20
His cousin Askew, that supplied his place,
Sent me for him from France, that se-
cretly
He might convey himself hither.

Linc.   Is 't even so?
Dares he so carelessly venture his life
Upon the indignation of a king?
Hath he despised my love, and spurned those favors
Which I with prodigal hand poured on his head?
He shall repent his rashness with his soul;
Since of my love he makes no estimate,
I'll make him wish he had not known my hate.   30
Thou hast no other news?

Dodger.   None else, my lord.

Linc. None worse I know thou hast.—
Procure the king
To crown his giddy brows with ample honors,
Send him chief colonel—and all my hope
Thus to be dashed! But 'tis in vain to grieve;
One evil cannot a worse relieve.
Upon my life, I have found out his plot;
That old dog, Love, that fawned upon him so,
Love to that puling girl, his fair-cheeked Rose,
The lord mayor's daughter, hath dis-
tracted him,   40
And in the fire of that love's lunacy
Hath he burnt up himself, consumed his credit,
Lost the king's love, yea, and, I fear, his life,
Only to get a wanton to his wife.
Dodger, it is so.

Dodger.   I fear so, my good lord.

Linc. It is so—nay, sure it cannot be!
I am at my wits' end. Dodger!

Dodger.   Yea, my lord.

Linc. Thou art acquainted with my neph-
ew's haunts;
Spend this gold for thy pains; go seek him out.
Watch at my lord mayor's—there if he live,   50
Dodger, thou shalt be sure to meet with him.

Frithee, be diligent.—Lacy, thy name
Lived once in honor, now dead in
　　shame!—
Be circumspect.　　　　　　　　*Exit.*
DODGER.　I warrant you, my lord.　*Exit.*

[SCENE viii.

*A room in the Lord Mayor's house at
London.*]

Enter Lord Mayor and Master Scott.

L. MAYOR. Good Master Scott, I have
　　been bold with you
To be a witness to a wedding knot
Betwixt young Master Hammon and my
　　daughter.
O, stand aside; see where the lovers come.

Enter Hammon and Rose.

ROSE. Can it be possible you love me so?
No, no, within those eyeballs I espy
Apparent likelihoods of flattery.
Pray now, let go my hand.
HAM.　　　　　　　Sweet Mistress Rose,
Misconstrue not my words, nor miscon-
　　ceive
Of my affection, whose devoted soul　10
Swears that I love thee dearer than my
　　heart.
ROSE. As dear as your own heart? I judge
　　it right,
Men love their hearts best when th' are
　　out of sight.
HAM. I love you, by this hand.
ROSE.　　　　　　　Yet hands off now!
If flesh be frail, how weak and frail's
　　your vow!
HAM. Then by my life I swear.
ROSE.　　　　　　Then do not brawl;
One quarrel loseth wife and life and all.
Is not your meaning thus?
HAM.　　　　　　In faith, you jest.
ROSE. Love loves to sport; therefore leave
　　love, y'are best.
L. MAYOR. What? Square[1] they, Master
　　Scott?
SCOTT.　　　　Sir, never doubt,　　20
Lovers are quickly in, and quickly out.
HAM. Sweet Rose, be not so strange in
　　fancying me.
Nay, never turn aside, shun not my
　　sight.

I am not grown so fond,[2] to fond[3] my
　　love
On any that shall quit[4] it with disdain,
If you will love me, so—if not, farewell.
L. MAYOR. Why, how now, lovers, are you
　　both agreed?
HAM. Yes, faith, my lord.
L. MAYOR.　'Tis well; give me your hand.
Give me yours, daughter.—How now,
　　both pull back!
What means this, girl?
ROSE.　　　　I mean to live a maid.　30
HAM. (*Aside.*) But not to die one; pause
　　ere that be said.
L. MAYOR. Will you still cross me, still be
　　obstinate?
HAM. Nay, chide her not, my lord, for
　　doing well;
If she can live an happy virgin's life,
'Tis far more blessed than to be a wife.
ROSE. Say, sir, I cannot. I have made a
　　vow.
Whoever be my husband, 'tis not you.
L. MAYOR. Your tongue is quick; but,
　　Master Hammon, know,
I bade you welcome to another end.
HAM. What, would you have me pule and
　　pine and pray,　　　　　　　40
With "lovely lady," "mistress of my
　　heart,"
"Pardon your servant," and the rimer
　　play,
Railing on Cupid and his tyrant's dart?
Or shall I undertake some martial spoil,
Wearing your glove at tourney and at
　　tilt,
And tell how many gallants I unhorsed?
Sweet, will this pleasure you?
ROSE.　　　　Yea, when wilt begin?
What, love rimes, man? Fie on that
　　deadly sin!
L. MAYOR. If you will have her, I'll make
　　her agree.
HAM. Enforcéd love is worse than hate
　　to me.—　　　　　　　　　　50
[*Aside.*] There is a wench keeps shop in
　　the Old Change;
To her will I. It is not wealth I seek;
I have enough, and will prefer her love
Before the world.—My good lord mayor,
　　adieu.
Old love for me; I have no luck with new.
　　　　　　　　　　　　　　　Exit.

---

[1] Quarrel.　　　　[2] Foolish.　[3] Found, set.　[4] Requite, return.

L. Mayor. Now, mammet,[1] you have well
    behaved yourself,
But you shall curse your coyness if I
    live.—
Who's within there? See you convey
    your mistress
Straight to th' Old Ford! I'll keep you
    straight enough.
Fore God, I would have sworn the puling
    girl   60
Would willingly accepted Hammon's
    love;
But banish him, my thoughts!—Go,
    minion, in!   *Exit Rose.*
Now tell me, Master Scott, would you
    have thought
That Master Simon Eyre, the shoe-
    maker,
Had been of wealth to buy such mer-
    chandise?
Scott. 'Twas well, my lord, your honor
    and myself
Grew partners with him, for your bills of
    lading
Show that Eyre's gains in one commodity
Rise at the least to full three thousand
    pound
Besides like gain in other merchandise. 70
L. Mayor. Well, he shall spend some of
    his thousands now,
For I have sent for him to the Guildhall.

Enter Eyre.

See, where he comes.—Good morrow,
    Master Eyre.
Eyre. Poor Simon Eyre, my lord, your
    shoemaker.
L. Mayor. Well, well, it likes [2] yourself to
    term you so.

Enter Dodger.[3]

Now, M[aster] Dodger, what's the news
    with you?
Dodger. I'd gladly speak in private to
    your honor.
L. Mayor. You shall, you shall.—Master
    Eyre and M[aster] Scott,
I have some business with this gentle-
    man;
I pray, let me entreat you to walk
    before   80

To the Guildhall; I'll follow presently.
Master Eyre, I hope ere noon to call you
    sheriff.
Eyre. I would not care, my lord, if you
might call me King of Spain.—Come, Mas-
ter Scott.   *[Exeunt Eyre and Scott.]*
L. Mayor. Now, Master Dodger, what's
    the news you bring?
Dodger. The Earl of Lincoln by me greets
    your lordship,
And earnestly requests you, if you can,
Inform him where his nephew Lacy keeps.
L. Mayor. Is not his nephew Lacy now in
    France?   90
Dodger. No, I assure your lordship, but
    disguised
Lurks here in London.
L. Mayor.   London? Is 't even so?
It may be; but, upon my faith and soul,
I know not where he lives, or whether
    he lives;
So tell my Lord of Lincoln.—Lurk in
    London?
Well, Master Dodger, you perhaps may
    start him;
Be but the means to rid him into France,
I'll give you a dozen angels [4] for your
    pains,
So much I love his honor, hate his
    nephew.   99
And, prithee, so inform thy lord from me.
Dodger. I take my leave.   *Exit Dodger.*
L. Mayor.   Farewell, good Master
    Dodger.—
Lacy in London? I dare pawn my life
My daughter knows thereof, and for that
    cause
Denied young M[aster] Hammon in his
    love.
Well, I am glad I sent her to Old Ford.
God's Lord, 'tis late! To Guildhall I must
    hie;
I know my brethren stay [5] my company.
                              Exit.

[Scene ix.

A room in Eyre's house.]

Enter Firk, Eyre's Wife, Hans, and Roger.

Wife. Thou goest too fast for me,
Roger. [O, Firk!] [6]
Firk. Ay, forsooth.

---

[1] Puppet, doll.   [2] Pleases.
[3] Early edns. print this direction after the
following line.
[4] Gold coins.   [5] Await.
[6] Supplied from 1618 edn.

WIFE. I pray thee, run—do you hear?—run to Guildhall, and learn if my husband, Master Eyre, will take that worshipful vocation of m[aster] sheriff upon him. Hie thee, good Firk.

FIRK. Take it? Well, I go; and he should not take it, Firk swears to for- [10 swear him. Yes, forsooth, I go to Guildhall.

WIFE. Nay, when? Thou art too compendious and tedious.

FIRK. O, rare! Your excellence is full of eloquence; how like a new cart wheel my dame speaks, and she looks like an old musty ale bottle [1] going to scalding.

WIFE. Nay, when? Thou wilt make me melancholy.

FIRK. God forbid your worship [20 should fall into that humor. I run.   *Exit.*

WIFE. Let me see now, Roger and Hans.

HODGE. Ay, forsooth, dame—mistress, I should say, but the old term so sticks to the roof of my mouth I can hardly lick it off.

WIFE. Even what thou wilt, good Roger; dame is a fair name for any honest Christian; but let that pass. How dost thou, Hans?

HANS. *Mee tanck you, vro.*   30

WIFE. Well, Hans and Roger, you see God hath blessed your master, and, perdy, if ever he comes to be m[aster] sheriff of London—as we are all mortal—you shall see, I will have some odd thing or other in a corner for you; I will not be your back-friend; [2] but let that pass. Hans, pray thee, tie my shoe.

HANS. *Yaw, ic sal, vro.*

WIFE. Roger, thou know'st the [40 length of my foot; as it is none of the biggest, so, I thank God, it is handsome enough. Prithee, let me have a pair of shoes made—cork, [3] good Roger, wooden heel too.

HODGE. You shall.

WIFE. Art thou acquainted with never a fardingale-maker nor a French hood-maker? I must enlarge my bum—ha, ha! How shall I look in a hood, I wonder! [50 Perdy, oddly, I think.

HODGE. [4] [*Aside.*] As a cat out of a

pillory.—Very well, I warrant you, mistress.

WIFE. Indeed, all flesh is grass; and, Roger, canst thou tell where I may buy a good hair?

HODGE. Yes, forsooth, at the poulterer's in Gracious Street.

WIFE. Thou art an ungracious wag; [60 perdy, I mean a false hair for my periwig.

HODGE. Why, mistress, the next time I cut my beard, you shall have the shavings of it; but they are all true hairs.

WIFE. It is very hot; I must get me a fan or else a mask.

HODGE. [*Aside.*] So you had need, to hide your wicked face.

WIFE. Fie upon it, how costly this world's calling is; perdy, but that it is [70 one of the wonderful works of God, I would not deal with it.—Is not Firk come yet? Hans, be not so sad; let it pass and vanish, as my husband's worship says.

HANS. *Ick bin vrolicke; lot see yow soo.* [5]

HODGE. Mistress, will you drink [6] a pipe of tobacco?

WIFE. O, fie upon it, Roger, perdy! These filthy tobacco pipes are the most idle, slavering bables that ever I felt. [80 Out upon it! God bless us, men look not like men that use them.

Enter Rafe, being lame.

HODGE. What, fellow Rafe? Mistress, look here, Jane's husband! Why, how [now], [7] lame? Hans, make much of him; he's a brother of our trade, a good workman, and a tall soldier.

HANS. *You be welcome, broder.*

WIFE. Perdy, I knew him not. How dost thou, good Rafe? I am glad [to] see [90 thee well.

RAFE. I would to God you saw me, dame, as well

As when I went from London into France.

WIFE. Trust me, I am sorry, Rafe, to see thee impotent. Lord, how the wars have made him sunburnt! The left leg is not well; 'twas a fair gift of God the infirmity took not hold a little higher, considering thou camest from France; but let that pass.   100

---

[1] Bottles made of leather.
[2] Reluctant friend.
[3] *I.e.,* with an inner pad of cork.
[4] The name now appears as Roger to the end of this scene.
[5] I am merry; let's see you so.
[6] Smoke.   [7] From 1610 edn.

RAFE. I am glad to see you well, and I rejoice

To hear that God hath blessed my master so

Since my departure.

WIFE. Yea, truly, Rafe, I thank my Maker; but let that pass.

HODGE. And, sirrah Rafe, what news, what news in France?

RAFE. Tell me, good Roger, first, what news in England?

How does my Jane?   When didst thou see my wife?

Where lives my poor heart?   She'll be poor indeed,   110

Now I want limbs to get whereon to feed.

HODGE. Limbs?   Hast thou not hands, man?   Thou shalt never see a shoemaker want bread, though he have but three fingers on a hand.

RAFE. Yet all this while I hear not of my Jane.

WIFE. O Rafe, your wife—perdy, we know not what's become of her.   She was here awhile, and, because she was married, grew more stately than became her; I   [120 checked [1] her, and so forth; away she flung, never returned, nor said bye nor bah; and, Rafe, you know, "ka me, ka thee." [2] And, so as I tell ye—Roger, is not Firk come yet?

HODGE. No, forsooth.

WIFE. And so, indeed, we heard not of her, but I hear she lives in London; but let that pass.   If she had wanted, she might have opened her case to me or my hus- [130 band, or to any of my men; I am sure, there's not any of them, perdy, but would have done her good to his power.   Hans, look if Firk be come.

HANS. *Yaw, ik sal, vro.*   *Exit Hans.*

WIFE. And so, as I said—but, Rafe, why dost thou weep?   Thou knowest that naked we came out of our mother's womb, and naked we must return; and, therefore, thank God for all things.   140

HODGE. No, faith, Jane is a stranger here; but, Rafe, pull up a good heart— I know thou hast one.   Thy wife, man, is in London; one told me he saw her a while ago very brave and neat; we'll ferret her out, and [3] London hold her.

WIFE. Alas, poor soul, he's overcome with sorrow; he does but as I do—weep for the loss of any good thing.   But, Rafe, get thee in, call for some meat and drink; [150 thou shalt find me worshipful towards thee.

RAFE. I thank you, dame; since I want limbs and lands,

I'll trust to God, my good friends, and to my hands. [4]   *Exit.*

Enter Hans and Firk running.

FIRK. Run, good Hans!   O Hodge, O mistress!   Hodge, heave up thine ears; mistress, smug up [5] your looks; on with your best apparel!   My master is chosen, my master is called, nay, condemned by the cry of the country to be sheriff of the city for this famous year now to come.   And, [160 time now being, a great many men in black gowns were asked for their voices and their hands, and my master had all their fists about his ears presently, and they cried, "Ay, ay, ay, ay,"—and so I came away.

Wherefore, without all other grieve, [6]

I do salute you, Mistress Shrieve. [7]

HANS. *Yaw, my mester is de groot man, de shrieve.*

HODGE. Did not I tell you, mistress? [170 Now I may boldly say, "Good morrow to your worship."

WIFE. Good morrow, good Roger.   I thank you, my good people all.—Firk, hold up thy hand; here's a threepenny piece for thy tidings.

FIRK. 'Tis but three halfpence, I think. Yes, 'tis threepence; I smell the rose. [8]

HODGE. But, mistress, be ruled by me, and do not speak so pulingly.   180

FIRK. 'Tis her worship speaks so, and not she.   No, faith, mistress, speak me in the old key: "To it, Firk;" "There, good Firk;" "Ply your business, Hodge;" "Hodge, with a full mouth;" "I'll fill your bellies with good cheer, till they cry twang."

Enter Simon Eyre, wearing a gold chain.

HANS. *See, myn liever broder, heer compt my meester.* [9]

---

[1] Scolded.

[2] "Scratch me and I'll scratch thee."   [3] If.

[4] From 1618 edn.   Original reads *I'll to God, my good friends, and to these my hands.*

[5] Smarten up.   [6] Beyond every other sherif..

[7] Sheriff.   [8] This coin had a rose on it.

[9] See, my dear brothers, here comes my master.

WIFE. Welcome home, Master [190 Shrieve; I pray God continue you in health and wealth.

EYRE. See here, my Maggy, a chain, a gold chain for Simon Eyre! I shall make thee a lady; here's a French hood for thee; on with it, on with it! Dress thy brows with this flap of a shoulder of mutton,[1] to make thee look lovely. Where be my fine men? Roger, I'll make over my shop and tools to thee; Firk, thou shalt be the [200 foreman; Hans, thou shalt have an hundred for twenty.[2] Be as mad knaves as your master Sim Eyre hath been, and you shall live to be sheriffs of London.—How dost thou like me, Margery? Prince am I none, yet am I princely born. Firk, Hodge, and Hans!

ALL THREE. Ay, forsooth, what says your worship, Master [3] Sheriff?

EYRE. Worship and honor, you [210 Babylonian knaves, for the gentle craft. But I forgot myself; I am bidden by my lord mayor to dinner to Old Ford. He's gone before; I must after. Come, Madge, on with your trinkets! Now, my true Trojans, my fine Firk, my dapper Hodge, my honest Hans, some device, some odd crochets, some morris, or suchlike, for the honor of the gentle shoemakers. Meet me at Old Ford; you know my mind. [220 Come, Madge, away. Shut up the shop, knaves, and make holiday. *Exeunt.*

FIRK. O, rare! O, brave! Come, Hodge; follow me, Hans;

We'll be with them for a morris dance. *Exeunt.*

[SCENE X.

A room at Old Ford.]

Enter Lord Mayor, Eyre his Wife in a French hood,[4] [Rose,] Sybil, and other Servants.

L. MAYOR. Trust me, you are as welcome to Old Ford
As I myself.

WIFE. Truly, I thank your lordship.

L. MAYOR. Would our bad cheer were worth the thanks you give.

EYRE. Good cheer, my lord mayor,

---

[1] "The flap of a hood trimmed with fur or sheep's wool" (Rhys).
[2] *I.e.*, the twenty Portuguese already lent.
[3] From 1657 edn. Earlier edns. read *Mistress.*
[4] First two edns. give Sybil the French hood.

fine cheer! A fine house, fine walls, all fine and neat.

L. MAYOR. Now, by my troth, I'll tell thee, Master Eyre,
It does me good, and all my brethren,
That such a madcap fellow as thyself
Is entered into our society. 10

WIFE. Ay, but, my lord, he must learn now to put on gravity.

EYRE. Peace, Maggy, a fig for gravity! When I go to Guildhall in my scarlet gown, I'll look as demurely as a saint, and speak as gravely as a justice of peace; but, now I am here at Old Ford, at my good lord mayor's house, let it go by, vanish, Maggy; I'll be merry. Away with flip-flap, these fooleries, these guller- [20 ies! What, honey? Prince am I none, yet am I princely born. What says my lord mayor?

L. MAYOR. Ha, ha, ha! I had rather than a thousand pound I had an heart but half so light as yours.

EYRE. Why, what should I do, my lord? A pound of care pays not a dram of debt. Hum, let's be merry whiles we are young; old age, sack, and sugar will steal upon us, ere we be aware. 31

THE FIRST THREE-MAN'S SONG [5]

O, the month of May, the merry month of May,
So frolic, so gay, and so green, so green, so green!
O, and then did I unto my true love say:
"Sweet Peg, thou shalt be my summer's queen!

"Now the nightingale, the pretty nightingale,
The sweetest singer in all the forest's choir,
Entreats thee, sweet Peggy, to hear thy true love's tale;
Lo, yonder she sitteth, her breast against a brier.

"But, O, I spy the cuckoo, the cuckoo, the cuckoo; 40
See where she sitteth. Come away, my joy;
Come away, I prithee. I do not like the cuckoo
Should sing where my Peggy and I kiss and toy."

---

[5] This seems the most appropriate place to insert this song.

O, the month of May, the merry month of
　　May,
　So frolic, so gay, and so green, so green,
　　so green!
And then did I unto my true love say:
　"Sweet Peg, thou shalt be my summer's
　　queen!"

L. MAYOR. It's well done.　Mistress
Eyre, pray give good counsel to my
daughter.　　　　　　　　　　　　　50
WIFE. I hope Mistress Rose will have
the grace to take nothing that's bad.
L. MAYOR. Pray God she do; for, i' faith,
　　Mistress Eyre,
I would bestow upon that peevish
　girl
A thousand marks more than I mean
　to give her
Upon condition she'd be ruled by me.
The ape [1] still crosseth me.　There came
　of late
A proper gentleman of fair revenues,
Whom gladly I would call son-in-
　law;
But my fine cockney [1] would have none
　of him.　　　　　　　　　　　　　60
You'll prove a coxcomb [2] for it, ere you
　die;
A courtier, or no man, must please
　your eye.
EYRE. Be ruled, sweet Rose; th' art
ripe for a man.　Marry not with a boy
that has no more hair on his face than thou
hast on thy cheeks.　A courtier!　Wash, go
by, stand not upon pishery-pashery.
Those silken fellows are but painted images, outsides, outsides, Rose; their inner
linings are torn.　No, my fine mouse, [70
marry me with a gentleman grocer like my
lord mayor, your father.　A grocer is a
sweet trade—plums, plums!　Had I a son or
daughter should marry out of the generation and blood of the shoemakers, he should
pack.　What!　The gentle trade is a living
for a man through Europe, through the
world.
　　A noise within of a tabor and a pipe.
MAYOR. What noise is this?
EYRE. O my lord mayor, a crew of [80
good fellows that for love to your honor are
come hither with a morris dance.　Come
in, my Mesopotamians, cheerily.

Enter Hodge, Hans, Rafe, Firk, and other
　Shoemakers in a morris; after a little
　　dancing, the Lord Mayor speaks.

MAYOR. Master Eyre, are all these shoe-
makers?
EYRE. All cordwainers, my good lord
mayor.
ROSE. [Aside.] How like my Lacy looks
yond shoemaker!
HANS. [Aside.] O, that I durst but speak
unto my love!　　　　　　　　　　89
MAYOR. Sybil, go fetch some wine to
make these drink.　You are all welcome.
ALL. We thank your lordship.
Rose takes a cup of wine and goes to Hans.
ROSE. For his sake whose fair shape thou
　represent'st,
Good friend, I drink to thee.
HANS. Ic bedancke, good frister.[3]
EYRE'S WIFE. I see, Mistress Rose,
you do not want judgment; you have drunk
to the properest man I keep.
FIRK. Here be some have done their
parts to be as proper as he.　　　　100
MAYOR. Well, urgent business calls me
　back to London.
Good fellows, first go in and taste our
　cheer,
And, to make merry as you homeward go,
Spend these two angels in beer at Strat-
　ford Bow.
EYRE. To these two, my mad lads,
Sim Eyre adds another; then cheerily,
Firk; tickle it, Hans, and all for the honor
of shoemakers.　　　　All go dancing out.
MAYOR. Come, Master Eyre, let's have
　your company.　　　　　　　Exeunt.
ROSE. Sybil, what shall I do?
SYB.　　　　Why, what's the matter? 110
ROSE. That Hans the shoemaker is my
　love Lacy,
Disguised in that attire to find me out.
How should I find the means to speak
　with him?
SYB. What, mistress, never fear; I
dare venter [4] my maidenhead to nothing,
and that's great odds, that Hans the Dutchman, when we come to London, shall
not only see and speak with you, but in
spite of all your father's policies steal you
away and marry you.　Will not this [120
please you?

---

[1] Pet.　　　　　　　　　　[2] Fool.

[3] I thank you, good maid.　　　[4] Venture.

Rose. Do this, and ever be assured of my love.

Syb. Away, then, and follow your father to London, lest your absence cause him to suspect something.

Tomorrow, if my counsel be obeyed, I'll bind you prentice to the gentle trade.   *Exeunt.*

[Scene xi.

A street in London.]

Enter Jane in a semster's [1] *shop, working; and Hammon, muffled, at another door. He stands aloof.*

Ham. Yonder's the shop, and there my fair love sits.

She's fair and lovely, but she is not mine.

O, would she were!   Thrice have I courted her;

Thrice hath my hand been moistened with her hand,

Whilst my poor famished eyes do feed on that

Which made them famish.   I am infortunate:

I still love one, yet nobody loves me.

I muse [2] in other men what women see

That I so want!   Fine Mistress Rose was coy,

And this too curious! [3] O, no, she is chaste,   10

And, for she thinks me wanton, she denies

To cheer my cold heart with her sunny eyes.

How prettily she works! O pretty hand!

O happy work!   It doth me good to stand

Unseen to see her.   Thus I oft have stood

In frosty evenings, a light burning by her,

Enduring biting cold, only to eye her.

One only look hath seemed as rich to me

As a king's crown; such is love's lunacy.

Muffled I'll pass along, and by that try   20

Whether she know me.—

Jane.   Sir, what is 't you buy?

What is 't you lack, sir, calico, or lawn,

Fine cambric shirts, or bands? What will you buy?

Ham. [*Aside.*] That which thou wilt not sell.   Faith, yet I'll try.—

How do you sell this handkercher?

Jane.   Good cheap. [4]

Ham. And how these ruffs?

Jane.   Cheap too.

Ham.   And how this band?

Jane. Cheap too.

Ham.   All cheap! How sell you then this hand?

Jane. My hands are not to be sold.

Ham.   To be given then!

Nay, faith, I come to buy.

Jane.   But none knows when.

Ham. Good sweet, leave work a little while; let's play.   30

Jane. I cannot live by keeping holiday.

Ham. I'll pay you for the time which shall be lost.

Jane. With me you shall not be at so much cost.

Ham. Look, how you wound this cloth, so you wound me.

Jane. It may be so.

Ham.   'Tis so.

Jane.   What remedy?

Ham. Nay, faith, you are too coy.

Jane.   Let go my hand.

Ham. I will do any task at your command;

I would let go this beauty, were I not

In mind to disobey you by a power

That controls kings. I love you!

Jane.   So, now part. 40

Ham. With hands I may, but never with my heart.

In faith, I love you.

Jane.   I believe you do.

Ham. Shall a true love in me breed hate in you?

Jane. I hate you not.

Ham.   Then you must love?

Jane.   I do.

What, are you better now? I love not you.

Ham. All this, I hope, is but a woman's fray,

That means, "Come to me," when she cries, "Away!"

In earnest, mistress, I do not jest;

---

[1] Seamstress'.   [2] Wonder.   [3] Scrupulous.

[4] At a bargain.

A true, chaste love hath entered in my
   breast.
I love you dearly, as I love my life;   50
I love you as a husband loves a wife;
That, and no other love, my love re-
   quires.
Thy wealth, I know, is little; my de-
   sires
Thirst not for gold. Sweet, beauteous
   Jane, what's mine
Shall, if thou make myself thine, all be
   thine.
Say, judge, what is thy sentence, life
   or death?
Mercy or cruelty lies in thy breath.
JANE. Good sir, I do believe you love me
   well;
For 'tis a silly conquest, silly pride,
For one like you—I mean a gentle-
   man—   60
To boast that by his love tricks he hath
   brought
Such and such women to his amorous
   lure.
I think you do not so, yet many do,
And make it even a very trade to woo.
I could be coy, as many women be,
Feed you with sunshine smiles and
   wanton looks,
But I detest witchcraft; say that I
Do constantly believe you, constant [1]
   have—
HAM. Why dost thou not believe me?
JANE.   I believe you;
But yet, good sir, because I will not
   grieve you   70
With hopes to taste fruit which will
   never fall,
In simple truth this is the sum of all:
My husband lives—at least, I hope he
   lives.
Pressed was he to these bitter wars in
   France;
Bitter they are to me by wanting him.
I have but one heart, and that heart's
   his due.
How can I then bestow the same on you?
Whilst he lives, his I live, be it ne'er
   so poor,
And rather be his wife than a king's
   whore.
HAM. Chaste and dear woman, I will not
   abuse thee,   80
[1] Constantly.

Although it cost my life, if thou refuse
   me.
Thy husband, pressed for France, what
   was his name?
JANE. Rafe Damport.
HAM.   Damport?—Here's a letter sent
From France to me, from a dear friend
   of mine,
A gentleman of place; here he doth
   write
Their names that have been slain in
   every fight.
JANE. I hope death's scroll contains not
   my love's name.
HAM. Cannot you read?
JANE.   I can.
HAM.   Peruse the same.
To my remembrance such a name I read
Amongst the rest. See here!
JANE.   Ay me, he's dead!   90
He's dead! If this be true, my dear
   heart's slain!
HAM. Have patience, dear love.
JANE.   Hence, hence!
HAM.   Nay, sweet Jane,
Make not poor sorrow proud with these
   rich tears.
I mourn thy husband's death because
   thou mourn'st.
JANE. That bill is forged; 'tis signed by
   forgery.
HAM. I'll bring thee letters sent besides
   to many,
Carrying the like report. Jane, 'tis too
   true.
Come, weep not; mourning, though it
   rise from love,
Helps not the mournéd, yet hurts them
   that mourn.
JANE. For God's sake, leave me.
HAM.   Whither dost thou turn? 100
Forget the dead; love them that are
   alive.
His love is faded; try how mine will
   thrive.
JANE. 'Tis now no time for me to think
   on love.
HAM. 'Tis now best time for you to think
   on love,
Because your love lives not.
JANE.   Though he be dead,
My love to him shall not be buriéd.
For God's sake, leave me to myself
   alone.

Ham. 'Twould kill my soul to leave thee
　　drowned in moan.
　　Answer me to my suit, and I am gone;
　　Say to me yea or no.
Jane.　　　　No.
Ham.　　　　　　Then farewell!—　110
　　One farewell will not serve; I come
　　again.
　　Come, dry these wet cheeks; tell me,
　　faith, sweet Jane,
　　Yea or no, once more.
Jane.　　　　　　Once more I say no;
　　Once more be gone, I pray; else will I
　　go.
Ham. Nay, then I will grow rude, by this
　　white hand,
　　Until you change that cold "no"; here
　　I'll stand
　　Till by your hard heart—
Jane.　　　Nay, for God's love, peace!
　　My sorrows by your presence more in-
　　crease.
　　Not that you thus are present, but all
　　grief
　　Desires to be alone; therefore in brief　120
　　Thus much I say, and saying bid adieu:
　　If ever I wed man, it shall be you.
Ham. O blessed voice! Dear Jane, I'll
　　urge no more;
　　Thy breath hath made me rich.
Jane.　　　　Death makes me poor.
　　　　　　　　　　　　　Exeunt.

[Scene xii.

The shop in Tower Street.]

*Enter Hodge, at his shopboard, Rafe, Firk,
　　Hans, and a Boy at work [, singing].*

All. Hey, down a down, down derry!

Hodge. Well said, my hearts. Ply your
work today; we loitered yesterday; to it
pell-mell, that we may live to be lord
mayors, or aldermen at least.

Firk. Hey, down a down, derry!

Hodge. Well said, i' faith! How sayst
thou, Hans, doth not Firk tickle it?[1]

Hans. *Yaw, mester.*

Firk. Not so neither; my organ pipe　[10
squeaks this morning for want of liquoring.

Hey, down a down, derry!

Hans. *Forward, Firk; tow best un jolly
："Go it."*

*yongster. Hort, I, mester, ic bid yo, cut me un
pair vampres vor Mester Jeffre's bootes.*[2]
Hodge. Thou shalt, Hans.
Firk. Master!
Hodge. How now, boy?
Firk. Pray, now you are in the cutting
vein, cut me out a pair of counterfeits,[3]　[20
or else my work will not pass current.

Hey, down a down!

Hodge. Tell me, sirs, are my cousin
M[istress] Priscilla's shoes done?
Firk. Your cousin? No, master; one of
your aunts,[4] hang her; let them alone.
Rafe. I am in hand with them; she
gave charge that none but I should do them
for her.
Firk. Thou do for her? Then 'twill　[30
be a lame doing, and that she loves not.
Rafe, thou mightst have sent her to me,
in faith; I would have yerked and firked
your Priscilla.

Hey, down a down, derry.

This gear [5] will not hold.
Hodge. How sayst thou, Firk, were we
not merry at Old Ford?
Firk. How, merry? Why, our buttocks
went jiggy-joggy like a quagmire. Well, [40
Sir Roger Oatmeal,[6] if I thought all
meal of that nature, I would eat nothing
but bagpuddings.
Rafe. Of all good fortunes my fellow
Hans had the best.
Firk. 'Tis true, because Mistress Rose
drank to him.
Hodge. Well, well, work apace. They
say seven of the aldermen be dead, or very
sick.　　　　　　　　　　　　　　　50
Firk. I care not; I'll be none.
Rafe. No, nor I; but then my M[as-
ter] Eyre will come quickly to be l[ord]
mayor.

Enter Sybil.

Firk. Whoop, yonder comes Sybil.
Hodge. Sybil, welcome, i' faith; and
how dost thou, mad wench?
Firk. Sib [7]-whore, welcome to London.

[2] Go on, Firk, thou art a jolly youngster.
Hark, ay, master, I pray you cut me a pair of
vamps for Master Jeffrey's boots.
[3] With a pun on the sense of *anything made
after a pattern.*
[4] Women.　　　　　　　　　　　[5] Matter.
[6] Punning reference to Sir Roger Oteley.
[7] Punning on the sense of *friend.*

Syb. God-a-mercy, sweet Firk. Good Lord, Hodge, what a delicious shop you [60 have got! You tickle it, i' faith.

Rafe. God-a-mercy, Sybil, for our good cheer at Old Ford.

Syb. That you shall have, Rafe.

Firk. Nay, by the Mass, we had tickling cheer, Sybil. And how the plague dost thou and Mistress Rose and my l[ord] mayor? I put the women in first.

Syb. Well, God-a-mercy. But, God's me, I forget myself; where's Hans the Fleming?

Firk. Hark, butterbox, now you must yelp out some *spreken*.   72

Hans. *Vat begaie gou? Vat vod gou, frister?* [1]

Syb. Marry, you must come to my young mistress, to pull on her shoes you made last.

Hans. *Vare ben your egle fro?* [2] *Vare ben your mistris?*

Syb. Marry, here at our London [80 house in Cornhill.[3]

Firk. Will nobody serve her turn but Hans?

Syb. No, sir. Come, Hans, I stand upon needles.

Hodge. Why then, Sybil, take heed of pricking.

Syb. For that let me alone. I have a trick in my budget. Come, Hans.   89

Hans. *Yaw, yaw, ic sall meete yo gane.*[4]
                            Exit Hans and Sybil.

Hodge. Go, Hans, make haste again. Come, who lacks work?

Firk. I, master, for I lack my break-fast; 'tis munching time, and past.

Hodge. Is't so? Why, then leave work, Rafe. To breakfast! Boy, look to the tools. Come, Rafe; come, Firk.   *Exeunt.*

[Scene xiii.

The same.]

Enter a Serving-man.

Serv. Let me see now, the sign of the Last in Tower Street. Mass, yonder's the house. What, haw! Who's within?

Enter Rafe.

Rafe. Who calls there? What want you, sir?

[1] What do you want? What would you, girl?
[2] Where is your noble lady?
[3] First three edns. read *Cornwall.*
[4] I shall with you go.

Serv. Marry, I would have a pair of shoes made for a gentlewoman against to-morrow morning. What, can you do them?

Rafe. Yes, sir, you shall have them. But what length's her foot?   10

Serv. [*Presenting a shoe.*] Why, you must make them in all parts like this shoe; but, at any hand, fail not to do them, for the gentlewoman is to be married very early in the morning.

Rafe. How? By this shoe must it be made? By this? Are you sure, sir, by this?

Serv. How, by this? Am I sure, by this? Art thou in thy wits? I tell thee, I must have a pair of shoes, dost thou [20 mark me? A pair of shoes, two shoes, made by this very shoe, this same shoe, against tomorrow morning by four a-clock. Dost understand me? Canst thou do 't?

Rafe. Yes, sir, yes—I—I—I can do 't. By this shoe, you say? I should know this shoe. Yes, sir, yes, by this shoe, I can do 't. Four a-clock, well. Whither shall I bring them?

Serv. To the sign of the Golden Ball [30 in Watling Street; inquire for one Master Hammon, a gentleman, my master.

Rafe. Yea, sir; by this shoe, you say?

Serv. I say, Master Hammon at the Golden Ball; he's the bridegroom, and those shoes are for his bride.

Rafe. They shall be done by this shoe. Well, well, Master Hammon at the Golden Shoe—I would say, the Golden Ball; very well, very well. But I pray you, sir, [40 where must Master Hammon be married?

Serv. At Saint Faith's Church, under Paul's. But what's that to thee? Prithee, despatch those shoes, and so farewell. *Exit.*

Rafe. "By this shoe," said he. How am I amazed
    At this strange accident! Upon my life,
    This was the very shoe I gave my wife,
    When I was pressed for France—since when, alas!
    I never could hear of her. It is the same,
    And Hammon's bride no other but my Jane.   50

Enter Firk.

Firk. 'Snails, Rafe, thou hast lost thy part of three pots a countryman of mine gave me to breakfast.

RAFE. I care not; I have found a better thing.

FIRK. A thing? Away! Is it a man's thing, or a woman's thing?

RAFE. Firk, dost thou know this shoe?

FIRK. No, by my troth; neither doth that know me! I have no acquaintance [60 with it; 'tis a mere stranger to me.

RAFE. Why, then I do; this shoe, I durst be sworn,
Once coveréd the instep of my Jane.
This is her size, her breadth; thus trod my love;
These truelove knots I pricked. I hold my life,
By this old shoe I shall find out my wife.

FIRK. Ha, ha! Old shoe, that wert new! How a murrain [1] came this ague fit of fool-ishness upon thee?

RAFE. Thus, Firk: even now here came a serving-man; 70
By this shoe would he have a new pair made
Against tomorrow morning for his mis-tress,
That's to be married to a gentleman.
And why may not this be my sweet Jane?

FIRK. And why mayst not thou be my sweet ass? Ha, ha!

RAFE. Well, laugh and spare not! But the truth is this:
Against tomorrow morning I'll provide
A lusty crew of honest shoemakers 78
To watch the going of the bride to church.
If she prove Jane, I'll take her in despite
From Hammon and the devil, were he by.
If it be not my Jane, what remedy?
Hereof am I sure, I shall live till I die,
Although I never with a woman lie. *Exit.*

FIRK. Thou lie with a woman to build nothing but Cripplegates! Well, God sends fools fortune, and it may be he may light upon his matrimony by such a device, for wedding and hanging goes by destiny. *Exit.*

[SCENE xiv.

A room in the Lord Mayor's house at Lon-don.]

Enter Hans and Rose, arm in arm.

HANS. How happy am I by embracing thee!
O, I did fear such cross mishaps did reign
That I should never see my Rose again.

[1] Plague.

ROSE. Sweet Lacy, since fair opportunity
Offers herself to furder our escape,
Let not too overfond esteem of me
Hinder that happy hour. Invent the means,
And Rose will follow thee through all the world.

HANS. O, how I surfeit with excess of joy,
Made happy by thy rich perfection! 10
But since thou pay'st sweet int'rest to my hopes,
Redoubling love on love, let me once more
Like to a bold-faced debtor crave of thee
This night to steal abroad, and at Eyre's house,
Who now by death of certain aldermen
Is mayor of London,[2] and my master once,
Meet thou thy Lacy, where in spite of change,
Your father's anger, and mine uncle's hate,
Our happy nuptials will we consummate.

Enter Sybil.

SYB. O God, what will you do, mis- [20 tress? Shift for yourself; your father is at hand! He's coming, he's coming! Master Lacy, hide yourself in my mistress! For God's sake, shift for yourselves!

HANS. Your father come! Sweet Rose, what shall I do?
Where shall I hide me? How shall I escape?

ROSE. A man, and want wit in extremity?
Come, come, be Hans still; play the shoe-maker;
Pull on my shoe.

Enter Lord Mayor.

HANS. Mass, and that's well remem-bered.

SYB. Here comes your father. 30

HANS. *Forware, metresse, 'tis un good skow; it sal vel dute, or ye sal neit betallen.*[3]

ROSE. O God, it pincheth me. What will you do?

HANS. [*Aside.*] Your father's presence pincheth, not the shoe.

[2] Sir Roger Oteley, however, is called lord mayor in stage directions and speech heads throughout the play.

[3] Indeed, mistress, 'tis a good shoe; it shall well do it, or you shall not pay.

L. Mayor. Well done; fit my daughter well, and she shall please thee well.

Hans. *Yaw, yaw, ick weit dat well; for ware, 'tis un good skoo; 'tis gimait van neits leither. Se ever, mine here.*[1]

Enter a Prentice.

L. Mayor. I do believe it.—What's the news with you?   40

Pren. Please you, the Earl of Lincoln at the gate

Is newly lighted, and would speak with you.

L. Mayor. The Earl of Lincoln come speak with me?

Well, well, I know his errand.—Daughter Rose,

Send hence your shoemaker, despatch, have done!—

Syb, make things handsome.—Sir boy, follow me.   *Exit [with Prentice].*

Hans. Mine uncle come! O, what may this portend?

Sweet Rose, this of our love threatens an end.

Rose. Be not dismayed at this; whate'er befall,

Rose is thine own. To witness I speak truth,   50

Where thou appoints the place, I'll meet with thee.

I will not fix a day to follow thee,

But presently steal hence. Do not reply.

Love which gave strength to bear my father's hate

Shall now add wings to further our escape.   *Exeunt.*

Enter L[ord] Mayor and Lincoln.

L. Mayor. Believe me, on my credit, I speak truth;

Since first your nephew Lacy went to France,

I have not seen him. It seemed strange to me,

When Dodger told me that he stayed behind,

Neglecting the high charge the king imposed.   60

Linc. Trust me, Sir Roger Oteley, I did think

Your counsel had given head to this attempt,

Drawn to it by the love he bears your child.

Here I did hope to find him in your house;

But now I see mine error, and confess

My judgment wronged you by conceiving so.

L. Mayor. Lodge in my house, say you? Trust me, my lord,

I love your nephew Lacy too-too dearly,

So much to wrong his honor; and he hath done so,

That first gave him advice to stay from France.   70

To witness I speak truth, I let you know

How careful I have been to keep my daughter

Free from all conference or speech of him—

Not that I scorn your nephew, but in love

I bear your honor, lest your noble blood

Should by my mean worth be dishonoréd.

Linc. [*Aside.*] How far the churl's tongue wanders from his heart!—

Well, well, Sir Roger Oteley, I believe you,

With more than many thanks for the kind love

So much you seem to bear me. But, my lord,   80

Let me request your help to seek my nephew,

Whom if I find, I'll straight embark for France.

So shall your Rose be free, my thoughts at rest,[2]

And much care die which now lies[3] in my breast.

Enter Sybil.

Syb. O Lord! Help, for God's sake! My mistress; O, my young mistress!

L. Mayor. Where is thy mistress? What's become of her?

Syb. She's gone, she's fled!

L. Mayor.   Gone! Whither is she fled?

Syb. I know not, forsooth. She's fled

---

[1] Yes, yes, I know that well; indeed, 'tis a good shoe; 'tis made of neat's leather. See here, good sir!

[2] First two edns. have *my Rose . . . your thoughts.*

[3] From 1610 edn. Original reads *dies.*

out of doors with Hans the shoemaker; I saw them scud, scud, scud, apace, apace!

L. MAYOR. Which way? What, John! Where be my men? Which way? 92

SYB. I know not, and it please your worship.

L. MAYOR. Fled with a shoemaker? Can this be true?

SYB. O Lord, sir, as true as God's in heaven.

LINC. [*Aside.*] Her love turned shoemaker? I am glad of this.

L. MAYOR. A Fleming butterbox, a shoemaker!

Will she forget her birth, requite my care 100

With such ingratitude? Scorned she young Hammon

To love a honnikin,[1] a needy knave?

Well, let her fly; I'll not fly after her.

Let her starve, if she will; she's none of mine.

LINC. Be not so cruel, sir.

Enter Firk with shoes.

SYB. I am glad she's scaped.

L. MAYOR. I'll not account of her as of my child.

Was there no better object for her eyes

But a foul drunken lubber, swill-belly,

A shoemaker? That's brave! 109

FIRK. Yea, forsooth; 'tis a very brave shoe, and as fit as a pudding.

L. MAYOR. How now, what knave is this? From whence comest thou?

FIRK. No knave, sir. I am Firk the shoemaker, lusty Roger's chief lusty journeyman, and I come hither to take up the pretty leg of sweet Mistress Rose, and thus hoping your worship is in as good health as I was at the making hereof, I bid you farewell, yours—Firk.

L. MAYOR. Stay, stay, Sir Knave! 120

LINC. Come hither, shoemaker!

FIRK. 'Tis happy the knave is put before the shoemaker, or else I would not have vouchsafed to come back to you. I am moved, for I stir.

L. MAYOR. My lord, this villain calls us knaves by craft.

FIRK. Then 'tis by the gentle craft, and to call one knave gently, is no harm. [129

Sit your worship merry! Syb, your young mistress—I'll so bob[2] them,[3] now my master, M[aster] Eyre, is lord mayor of London.

L. MAYOR. Tell me, sirrah, whose man are you?

FIRK. I am glad to see your worship so merry. I have no maw[4] to this gear, no stomach as yet to a red petticoat.

Pointing to Sybil.

LINC. He means not, sir, to woo you to his maid,

But only doth demand whose man you are. 140

FIRK. I sing now to the tune of "Rogero." Roger, my fellow, is now my master.

LINC. Sirrah, know'st thou one Hans, a shoemaker?

FIRK. Hans, shoemaker? O, yes; stay, yes, I have him. I tell you what (I speak it in secret): Mistress Rose and he are by this time—no, not so, but shortly are to come over one another with "Can [149 you dance the shaking of the sheets?"[5] It is that Hans—[*Aside.*] I'll so gull these diggers![6]

L. MAYOR. Know'st thou, then, where he is?

FIRK. Yes, forsooth; yea, marry!

LINC. Canst thou, in sadness[7]—

FIRK. No, forsooth; no, marry!

L. MAYOR. Tell me, good honest fellow, where he is,

And thou shalt see what I'll bestow of thee.

FIRK. Honest fellow? No, sir; not so, sir; my profession is the gentle craft. I [160 care not for seeing; I love feeling. Let me feel it here; *aurium tenus*, ten pieces of gold; *genuum tenus*,[8] ten pieces of silver; and then Firk is your man—[*Aside.*] in a new pair of stretchers.[9]

L. MAYOR. Here is an angel, part of thy reward,

Which I will give thee; tell me where he is. 167

FIRK. No point![10] Shall I betray my brother? No! Shall I prove Judas to Hans?

[1] Low fellow.
[2] Fool.   [3] From 1610 edn. Original reads *then.*
[4] Appetite.   [6] *I.e.*, for information.
[5] An old dance song.   [7] Seriousness.
[8] Firk's Latin phrases actually mean *up to the ears, up to the knees.*
[9] Shoe stretchers; also lies.
[10] Not at all.

No! Shall I cry treason to my corporation?
No, I shall be firked and yerked then. But
give me your angel; your angel shall tell you.

LINC. Do so, good fellow; 'tis no hurt to
thee.

FIRK. Send simpering Syb away.

L. MAYOR. Huswife, get you in.

Exit Syb[il].

FIRK. Pitchers have ears, and maids
have wide mouths; but for Hans Prans,
upon my word, tomorrow morning he and
young Mistress Rose go to this gear; they
shall be married together, by this rush, [180
or else turn Firk to a firkin of butter, to tan
leather withal.

L. MAYOR. But art thou sure of this?

FIRK. Am I sure that Paul's steeple is a
handful higher than London Stone, or that
the Pissing Conduit leaks nothing but
pure Mother Bunch? [1] Am I sure I am
lusty Firk? God's nails, do you think I
am so base to gull you?

LINC. Where are they married? Dost
thou know the church? 191

FIRK. I never go to church, but I know
the name of it; it is a swearing church—
stay awhile! 'Tis—ay, by the Mass! No,
no! 'Tis—ay, by my troth! No, nor that.
'Tis—ay, by my faith! That, that, 'tis,
ay, by my Faith's Church under Paul's
Cross. There they shall be knit like a pair
of stockings in matrimony; there they'll be
incony. [2] 200

LINC. Upon my life, my nephew Lacy
walks
In the disguise of this Dutch shoemaker.

FIRK. Yes, forsooth.

LINC.   Doth he not, honest fellow?

FIRK. No, forsooth; I think Hans is
nobody but Hans, no spirit.

L. MAYOR. My mind misgives me now,
'tis so, indeed.

LINC. My cousin speaks the language,
knows the trade.

L. MAYOR. Let me request your company,
my lord;
Your honorable presence may, no doubt,
Refrain their headstrong rashness, when
myself, 210
Going alone, perchance may be o'erborne.
Shall I request this favor?

LINC.   This, or what else.

FIRK. Then you must rise betimes, for

they mean to fall to their hey-pass and re-
pass, [3] pindy-pandy, [4] which hand will you
have, very early.

L. MAYOR. My care shall every way equal
their haste.
This night accept your lodging in my
house;
The earlier shall we stir, and at Saint
Faith's 219
Prevent this giddy hare-brained nuptial.
This traffic of hot love shall yield cold
gains;
They ban [5] our loves, and we'll forbid
their banes. [6]   *Exit.* [7]

LINC. At Saint Faith's Church, thou
say'st?

FIRK. Yes, by their troth.

LINC. Be secret, on thy life.   *Exit.*

FIRK. Yes, when I kiss your wife! Ha,
ha, here's no craft in the gentle craft. I
came hither of purpose with shoes to Sir
Roger's worship, whilst Rose, his daughter,
be cony-catched [8] by Hans. Soft now; these
two gulls will be at Saint Faith's [230
Church tomorrow morning, to take Master
Bridegroom and Mistress Bride napping,
and they, in the meantime, shall chop up [9]
the matter at the Savoy. But the best
sport is, Sir Roger Oteley will find my fellow, lame Rafe's, wife going to marry a
gentleman, and then he'll stop her instead
of his daughter. O, brave! There will be fine
tickling sport. Soft now, what have I to
do? O, I know; now a mess of shoe- [240
makers meet at the Woolsack in Ivy Lane,
to cozen my gentleman of lame Rafe's
wife; that's true.

Alack, alack!
Girls, hold out tack! [10]
For now smocks for this jumbling
Shall go to wrack.
Exit.

[SCENE XV.

A room in Eyre's house.]

Enter Eyre, his Wife, Hans, and Rose.

EYRE. This is the morning, then; stay,
my bully, my honest Hans, is it not?

HANS. This is the morning that must

[1] A well-known alewife.   [2] Fine.
[3] Conjuring terms.   [5] Curse.
[4] Game of handy-dandy.   [6] Banns.
[7] From 1618 edn. First two edns. have *Exeunt.*
[8] Tricked. [10] *I.e.*, hold out against attack (?).
[9] Conclude.

make us two happy or miserable; therefore, if you—

EYRE. Away with these if's and and's,
Hans, and these *et cetera's!* By mine honor,
Rowland Lacy, none but the king shall
wrong thee. Come, fear nothing. Am
not I Sim Eyre? Is not Sim Eyre lord [10
mayor of London? Fear nothing, Rose.
Let them all say what they can, "Dainty,
come thou to me." [1]—Laughest thou?

WIFE. Good my lord, stand her friend
in what thing you may.

EYRE. Why, my sweet Lady Madgy,
think you Simon Eyre can forget his fine
Dutch journeyman? No, vah! Fie, I scorn
it; it shall never be cast in my teeth that
I was unthankful. Lady Madgy, thou [20
hadst never covered thy Saracen's head
with this French flap, nor loaden thy bum
with this farthingale ('tis trash, trumpery,
vanity); Simon Eyre had never walked in
a red petticoat, nor wore a chain of gold,
but for my fine journeyman's Portuguese.
—And shall I leave him? No! Prince am I
none, yet near a princely mind.

HANS. My lord, 'tis time for us to part
from hence.   30

EYRE. Lady Madgy, Lady Madgy, take
two or three of my piecrust eaters, my
buff jerkin varlets, that do walk in black
gowns at Simon Eyre's heels; take them,
good Lady Madgy; trip and go, my brown
queen of periwigs, with my delicate Rose
and my jolly Rowland to the Savoy; see
them linked; countenance the marriage;
and, when it is done, cling, cling together,
you Hamborough turtledoves. I'll bear [40
you out; come to Simon Eyre. Come, dwell
with me, Hans; thou shalt eat minced pies
and marchpane.[2] Rose, away, cricket; trip
and go, my Lady Madgy, to the Savoy;
Hans, wed, and to bed; kiss, and away! Go,
vanish!

WIFE. Farewell, my lord.

ROSE. Make haste, sweet love.

WIFE.   She'd fain the deed were done.

HANS. Come, my sweet Rose; faster than
  deer we'll run.   *They go out.*

EYRE. Go, vanish, vanish! Avaunt, [50
I say! By the Lord of Ludgate, it's a mad
life to be a lord mayor; it's a stirring life,
a fine life, a velvet life, a careful life. Well,

---

[1] The opening of a popular song.
[2] A sweetmeat.

Simon Eyre, yet set a good face on it,
in the honor of Saint Hugh. Soft, the king
this day comes to dine with me, to see my
new buildings; his majesty is welcome; he
shall have good cheer, delicate cheer,
princely cheer. This day my fellow prentices
of London come to dine with me too; [60
they shall have fine cheer, gentlemanlike
cheer. I promised the mad Cappadocians,
when we all served at the Conduit together, that, if ever I came to be mayor of
London, I would feast them all, and I'll
do 't, I'll do 't, by the life of Pharaoh; by
this beard, Sim Eyre will be no flincher.
Besides, I have procured that upon every
Shrove Tuesday, at the sound of the pancake bell, my fine dapper Assyrian lads [70
shall clap up their shop windows, and
away. This is the day, and this day they
shall do 't, they shall do 't.

Boys, that day are you free, let masters
    care,
And prentices shall pray for Simon
    Eyre.   *Exit.*

[SCENE xvi.

A street near St. Faith's church.]

*Enter Hodge, Firk, Rafe, and five or six
    Shoemakers, all with cudgels or such
                                    weapons.*

HODGE. Come, Rafe; stand to it, Firk.
My masters, as we are the brave bloods of
the shoemakers, heirs apparent to Saint
Hugh, and perpetual benefactors to all good
fellows, thou shalt have no wrong. Were
Hammon a king of spades, he should not
delve in thy close [3] without thy sufferance. But tell me, Rafe, art thou sure 'tis
thy wife?

RAFE. Am I sure this is Firk? This [10
morning, when I stroked on her shoes, I
looked upon her, and she upon me, and
sighed—asked me if ever I knew one Rafe.
"Yes," said I. "For his sake," said she,
tears standing in her eyes, "and for thou
art somewhat like him, spend this piece of
gold." I took it; my lame leg and my
travel beyond sea made me unknown. All
is one for that; I know she's mine.

FIRK. Did she give thee this gold? O [20
glorious, glittering gold! She's thine own,

---

[3] Field.

'tis thy wife, and she loves thee; for I'll
stand to 't there's no woman will give gold
to any man, but she thinks better of him
than she thinks of them she gives silver to.
And for Hammon, neither Hammon nor
hangman shall wrong thee in London! Is
not our old master Eyre lord mayor?
Speak, my hearts.

ALL. Yes, and Hammon shall know it to
his cost.   31

Enter Hammon, his Man, Jane, and Others.

HODGE. Peace, my bullies; yonder they
come.

RAFE. Stand to 't, my hearts. Firk, let
me speak first.

HODGE. No, Rafe, let me.—Hammon,
whither away so early?

HAM. Unmannerly, rude slave, what's that
to thee?

FIRK. To him, sir? Yes, sir, and to me,
and others. Good morrow, Jane, how   [40
dost thou? Good Lord, how the world is
changed with you! God be thanked!

HAM. Villains, hands off! How dare you
touch my love?

ALL. Villains? Down with them! Cry
clubs [1] for prentices!

HODGE. Hold, my hearts! Touch her,
Hammon? Yea, and, more than that,
we'll carry her away with us. My masters
and gentlemen, never draw your bird-
spits; shoemakers are steel to the back,
men every inch of them, all spirit.   51

ALL OF HAMMON'S SIDE. Well, and what
of all this?

HODGE. I'll show you.—Jane, dost thou
know this man? 'Tis Rafe, I can tell thee;
nay, 'tis he in faith, though he be lamed
by the wars. Yet look not strange, but run
to him, fold him about the neck, and kiss
him.

JANE. Lives then my husband? O God,
let me go;   60
Let me embrace my Rafe.

HAM.   What means my Jane?

JANE. Nay what meant you, to tell me he
was slain?

HAM. Pardon me, dear love, for being
misled.—
[*To Rafe.*] 'Twas rumored here in London thou wert dead.

FIRK. Thou seest he lives. Lass, go, pack
home with him.

Now, M[aster] Hammon, where's your
mistress, your wife?

SERV. 'Swounds,[2] m[aster], fight for her!
Will you thus lose her?

ALL. Down with that creature! Clubs!
Down with him!   70

HODGE. Hold, hold!

HAM.   Hold, fool! Sirs, he shall
do no wrong.
Will my Jane leave me thus, and break
her faith?

FIRK. Yea, sir! She must, sir! She shall,
sir! What then? Mend it!

HODGE. Hark, fellow Rafe, follow my
counsel: set the wench in the midst, and
let her choose her man, and let her be his
woman.

JANE. Whom should I choose? Whom
should my thoughts affect
But him whom heaven hath made to be
my love?   80
Thou art my husband, and these humble
weeds
Makes thee more beautiful than all his
wealth.
Therefore, I will but put off his attire,
Returning it into the owner's hand,
And after ever be thy constant wife.

HODGE. Not a rag, Jane! The law's
on our side; he that sows in another
man's ground, forfeits his harvest. Get thee
home, Rafe; follow him, Jane; he shall not
have so much as a busk point[3] from thee. [90

FIRK. Stand to that, Rafe; the appurte-
nances are thine own. Hammon, look not
at her!

SERV. O, 'swounds, no!

FIRK. Blue coat, be quiet. We'll give
you a new livery else; we'll make Shrove
Tuesday Saint George's Day [4] for you.
Look not, Hammon; leer not! I'll firk
you! For thy head now, one glance, one
sheep's eye, anything, at her! Touch   [100
not a rag, lest I and my brethren beat you
to clouts.

SERV. Come, Master Hammon, there's no
striving here.

HAM. Good fellows, hear me speak; and,
honest Rafe,

---

[1] The rallying cry of the London apprentices.

[2] God's wounds.   [3] Corset lace.
[4] The day on which blue coats were worn.
Firk means, "We'll beat you black and blue."

Whom I have injured most by loving
Jane,
Mark what I offer thee. Here in fair gold
Is twenty pound; I'll give it for thy Jane;
If this content thee not, thou shalt have
more.

HODGE. Sell not thy wife, Rafe; make her
not a whore.

HAM. Say, wilt thou freely cease thy claim
in her,   110
And let her be my wife?

ALL.   No, do not, Rafe.

RAFE. Sirrah Hammon, Hammon, dost
thou think a shoemaker is so base to be a
bawd to his own wife for commodity?
Take thy gold; choke with it! Were I
not lame, I would make thee eat thy words.

FIRK. A shoemaker sell his flesh and
blood? O indignity!

HODGE. Sirrah, take up your pelf, and
be packing.   120

HAM. I will not touch one penny, but in
lieu
Of that great wrong I offeréd thy Jane,
To Jane and thee I give that twenty
pound.
Since I have failed of her, during my
life
I vow no woman else shall be my wife.
Farewell, good fellows of the gentle trade.
Your morning's mirth my mourning day
hath made.   *Exit.*

FIRK. [*To Serving-man.*] Touch the gold,
creature, if you dare! Y'are best be trudg-
ing. Here, Jane, take thou it. Now [130
let's home, my hearts.

HODGE. Stay! Who comes here? Jane,
on again with thy mask!

Enter Lincoln, L[ord] Mayor, and Servants.

LINC. Yonder's the lying varlet mocked
us so.

L. MAYOR. Come hither, sirrah!

FIRK. I, sir? I am "sirrah"? You mean
me, do you not?

LINC. Where is my nephew married?

FIRK. Is he married? God give him joy,
I am glad of it. They have a fair [140
day, and the sign is in a good planet,
Mars in Venus.

L. MAYOR. Villain, thou told'st me that
my daughter Rose
This morning should be married at Saint
Faith's;

We have watched there these three hours
at the least,
Yet see we no such thing.

FIRK. Truly, I am sorry for 't; a bride's
a pretty thing.

HODGE. Come to the purpose. Yonder's
the bride and bridegroom you look for, [150
I hope. Though you be lords, you are not
to bar by your authority men from women,
are you?

L. MAYOR. See, see, my daughter's masked.

LINC.   True, and my nephew,
To hide his guilt, counterfeits him lame.

FIRK. Yea, truly; God help the poor
couple, they are lame and blind.

L. MAYOR. I'll ease her blindness.

LINC.   I'll his lameness cure.

FIRK. [*Aside to his friends.*] Lie down,
sirs, and laugh! My fellow Rafe is [160
taken for Rowland Lacy, and Jane for Mistress Damask Rose. This is all my knavery.

L. MAYOR. What, have I found you,
minion?

LINC.   O base wretch!
Nay, hide thy face; the horror of thy
guilt
Can hardly be washed off. Where are
thy powers?
What battles have you made? O, yes,
I see,
Thou fought'st with Shame, and Shame
hath conquered thee.
This lameness will not serve.

L. MAYOR.   Unmask yourself.

LINC. Lead home your daughter.

L. MAYOR.   Take your nephew hence.

RAFE. Hence! 'Swounds, what mean [170
you? Are you mad? I hope you cannot enforce my wife from me. Where's Hammon?

L. MAYOR. Your wife?

LINC. What, Hammon?

RAFE. Yea, my wife; and, therefore, the
proudest of you that lays hands on her
first, I'll lay my crutch cross his pate.

FIRK. To him, lame Rafe! Here's brave
sport!

RAFE. Rose call you her? Why, [180
her name is Jane. Look here else; do you
know her now?   [*Unmasks Jane.*]

LINC. Is this your daughter?

L. MAYOR.   No, nor this your nephew.
My Lord of Lincoln, we are both abused
By this base, crafty varlet.

FIRK. Yea, forsooth, no varlet; forsooth,

no base; forsooth, I am but mean;[1] no crafty neither, but of the gentle craft.

L. MAYOR. Where is my daughter Rose? Where is my child?   189

LINC. Where is my nephew Lacy marriéd?

FIRK. Why, here is good laced mutton,[2] as I promised you.

LINC. Villain, I'll have thee punished for this wrong.

FIRK. Punish the journeyman villain, but not the journeyman shoemaker.

Enter Dodger.

DODGER. My lord, I come to bring unwelcome news.

Your nephew Lacy and your daughter Rose
Early this morning wedded at the Savoy,
None being present but the lady mayoress.   199
Besides, I learned among the officers
The lord mayor vows to stand in their defense
Gainst any that shall seek to cross the match.

LINC. Dares Eyre the shoemaker uphold the deed?

FIRK. Yes, sir, shoemakers dare stand in a woman's quarrel, I warrant you, as deep as another, and deeper too.

DODGER. Besides, his grace today dines with the mayor,
Who on his knees humbly intends to fall
And beg a pardon for your nephew's fault.

LINC. But I'll prevent him! Come, Sir Roger Oteley;   210
The king will do us justice in this cause.
Howe'er their hands have made them man and wife,
I will disjoin the match, or lose my life.
Exeunt [Lincoln, Mayor, Dodger, and Servants].

FIRK. Adieu, Monsieur Dodger! Farewell, fools! Ha, ha! O, if they had stayed, I would have so lammed them with flouts! O heart, my codpiece point is ready to fly in pieces every time I think upon Mistress Rose. But let that pass, as my lady mayoress says.   220

HODGE. This matter is answered. Come, Rafe; home with thy wife. Come, my fine shoemakers, let's to our master's, the new lord mayor, and there swagger this Shrove Tuesday. I'll promise you wine enough, for Madge keeps the cellar.

ALL. O, rare! Madge is a good wench.

FIRK. And I'll promise you meat enough, for simp'ring Susan keeps the larder. I'll lead you to victuals, my brave sol-   [230 diers; follow your captain. O, brave! Hark, hark!   *Bell rings.*

ALL. The pancake bell rings, the pancake bell! Trilill, my hearts!

FIRK. O, brave! O sweet bell! O delicate pancakes! Open the doors, my hearts, and shut up the windows! Keep in the house; let out the pancakes! O, rare, my hearts! Let's march together for the honor of Saint Hugh to the great new hall   [240 in Gracious Street corner, which our master, the new lord mayor, hath built.

RAFE. O, the crew of good fellows that will dine at my lord mayor's cost today!

HODGE. By the Lord, my lord mayor is a most brave man. How shall prentices be bound to pray for him and the honor of the gentlemen shoemakers! Let's feed and be fat with my lord's bounty.   249

FIRK. O musical bell, still! O Hodge, O my brethren! There's cheer for the heavens.[3] Ven'son pasties [4] walk up and down piping hot, like serjeants; beef and brewis comes marching in dryfats;[5] fritters and pancakes comes trolling in in wheelbarrows; hens and oranges hopping in porters' baskets, collops and eggs in scuttles; and tarts and custards comes quavering in in malt shovels.

Enter more Prentices.

ALL. Whoop, look here, look here!   259

HODGE. How now, mad lads, whither away so fast?

1 PREN. Whither? Why, to the great new hall, know you not why? The lord mayor hath bidden all the prentices in London to breakfast this morning.

ALL. O brave shoemaker, O brave lord of incomprehensible good-fellowship! Whoo! Hark you! The pancake bell rings.
                    Cast up caps.

FIRK. Nay, more, my hearts! Every Shrove Tuesday is our year of jubilee; [270

---

[1] *I.e.*, with a tenor, not "bass" voice.
[2] Loose woman, with a pun on *Lacy*.
[3] Food for the gods.
[4] From 1610 edn. Original has *pastimes*.
[5] Large containers.

and, when the pancake bell rings, we are as
free as my lord mayor; we may shut up our
shops, and make holiday. I'll have it called
Saint Hugh's Holiday.

ALL. Agreed, agreed!   Saint Hugh's
Holiday!

HODGE. And this shall continue forever!

ALL. O, brave! Come, come, my hearts.
Away, away!

FIRK. O, eternal credit to us of the gentle
craft! March fair, my hearts! O rare!   [281
                                        Exeunt.

[SCENE xvii.

A street in London.]

Enter King and his Train over the stage.

KING. Is our lord mayor of London such
    a gallant?

NOBLEMAN. One of the merriest madcaps
    in your land.
Your grace will think, when you behold
    the man,
He's rather a wild ruffian than a mayor.
Yet thus much I'll ensure your majesty,
In all his actions that concern his state
He is as serious, provident, and wise,
As full of gravity amongst the grave,
As any mayor hath been these many
    years.

KING. I am with child [1] till I behold this
    huffcap.[2]   10
But all my doubt is, when we come in
    presence,
His madness will be dashed clean out of
    countenance.

NOBLEMAN. It may be so, my liege.

KING.   Which to prevent,
Let someone give him notice, 'tis our
    pleasure
That he put on his wonted merriment.
Set forward!

ALL.   On afore!   *Exeunt.*

[SCENE xviii.

A great hall.]

*Enter Eyre, Hodge, Firk, Rafe, and other
    Shoemakers, all with napkins on their
                                    shoulders.*

EYRE. Come, my fine Hodge, my jolly
gentlemen shoemakers!   Soft, where be
these cannibals, these varlets, my officers?

[1] Impatient.   [2] Swaggerer.

Let them all walk and wait upon my brethren; for my meaning is that none but shoemakers, none but the livery of my company, shall in their satin hoods wait upon
the trencher of my sovereign.

FIRK. O my lord, it will be rare!

EYRE. No more, Firk; come, lively! [10
Let your fellow prentices want no cheer;
let wine be plentiful as beer, and beer as
water. Hang these penny-pinching fathers,
that cram wealth in innocent lambskins.[3]
Rip, knaves, avaunt! Look to my guests!

HODGE. My lord, we are at our wits'
end for room; those hundred tables will
not feast the fourth part of them.

EYRE. Then cover me those hundred
tables again, and again, till all my jolly [20
prentices be feasted. Avoid, Hodge! Run,
Rafe! Frisk about, my nimble Firk! Carouse me fadom healths [4] to the honor of
the shoemakers.   Do they drink lively,
Hodge?   Do they tickle it, Firk?

FIRK. Tickle it?   Some of them have
taken their liquor standing so long that
they can stand no longer; but, for meat,
they would eat it and they had it.

EYRE. Want they meat? Where's [30
this swagbelly, this greasy kitchen stuff
cook? Call the varlet to me! Want meat?
Firk, Hodge, lame Rafe, run, my tall men,
beleaguer the shambles, beggar all East-
cheap, serve me whole oxen in chargers,[5]
and let sheep whine upon the tables like
pigs for want of good fellows to eat them.
Want meat? Vanish, Firk! Avaunt, Hodge!

HODGE. Your lordship mistakes my man
Firk; he means their bellies want meat, [40
not the boards, for they have drunk so
much, they can eat nothing.

THE SECOND THREE-MAN'S SONG [6]

Cold's the wind, and wet's the rain—
    Saint Hugh be our good speed.
Ill is the weather that bringeth no gain,
    Nor helps good hearts in need.

Troll [7] the bowl, the jolly nut-brown bowl,
    And here, kind mate, to thee.
Let's sing a dirge for Saint Hugh's soul,
    And down it merrily.   50

[3] Purses.   [5] Large platters.
[4] Fathom-deep healths.
[6] A direction, "This is to be sung at the latter
end," suggests the insertion of this song here.
[7] Pass.

Down a down, hey down a down,
     (Close with the tenor boy)
 Hey derry derry, down a down!
Ho, well done; to me let come!
 Ring compass,[1] gentle joy.

Troll the bowl, the nut-brown bowl,
 And here, kind, etc.
    As often as there be men to drink.

 At last, when all have drunk, this verse:

Cold's the wind, and wet's the rain—
 Saint Hugh be our good speed.
Ill is the weather that bringeth no gain,
 Nor helps good hearts in need. 60

  Enter Hans, Rose, and Wife.

WIFE. Where is my lord?
EYRE. How now, Lady Madgy?
WIFE. The king's most excellent majesty is new come; he sends me for thy
honor. One of his most worshipful peers
bade me tell thou must be merry, and so
forth; but let that pass.
EYRE. Is my sovereign come? Vanish,
my tall shoemakers, my nimble brethren;
look to my guests, the prentices. Yet [70
stay a little! How now, Hans? How looks
my little Rose?
HANS. Let me request you to remember
me.
I know your honor easily may obtain
Free pardon of the king for me and Rose,
And reconcile me to my uncle's grace.
EYRE. Have done, my good Hans, my
honest journeyman; look cheerily! I'll fall
upon both my knees, till they be as hard
as horn, but I'll get thy pardon. 80
WIFE. Good my lord, have a care what
you speak to his grace.
EYRE. Away, you Islington whitepot![2]
Hence, you hopper[3]-arse! Hence, you
barley pudding, full of maggots! You
broiled carbonado![4] Avaunt, avaunt,
avoid, Mephostophilus! Shall Sim Eyre
learn to speak of you, Lady Madgy? Vanish, Mother Miniver-cap;[5] vanish, go, trip
and go; meddle with your partlets[6] and [90
your pishery-pashery, your flews[7] and
your whirligigs; go, rub,[8] out of mine alley!

---

1 The fullest range of tones possible.
2 Custard.   5 Fur cap.
3 Shaped like a hopper. 6 Ruffs for the neck.
4 Steak.   7 Flaps.
8 An obstruction in bowling.

Sim Eyre knows how to speak to a pope,
to Sultan Soliman, to Tamburlaine, and
he were here; and shall I melt, shall I
droop before my sovereign? No, come,
my Lady Madgy! Follow me, Hans! About
your business, my frolic freebooters! Firk,
frisk about, and about, and about, for the
honor of mad Simon Eyre, lord mayor [100
of London.
FIRK. Hey, for the honor of the shoemakers!   *Exeunt.*

    [SCENE xix.

  An open yard before the hall.]

*A long flourish or two. Enter King, Nobles,
 Eyre, his Wife, Lacy, Rose. Lacy and
         Rose kneel.*

KING. Well, Lacy, though the fact was
 very foul
Of your revolting from our kingly love
And your own duty, yet we pardon you.
Rise both, and, Mistress Lacy, thank
 my lord mayor
For your young bridegroom here.
EYRE. So, my dear liege, Sim Eyre and
my brethren, the gentlemen shoemakers,
shall set your sweet majesty's image cheek
by jowl by Saint Hugh for this honor you
have done poor Simon Eyre. I beseech [10
your grace, pardon my rude behavior; I
am a handicraftsman, yet my heart is without craft; I would be sorry at my soul
that my boldness should offend my king.
KING. Nay, I pray thee, good lord mayor,
 be even as merry
As if thou wert among thy shoemakers;
It does me good to see thee in this humor.
EYRE. Sayst thou me so, my sweet
Dioclesian? Then, hump! Prince am I
none, yet am I princely born. By the [20
Lord of Ludgate, my liege, I'll be as merry
as a pie.[9]
KING. Tell me, in faith, mad Eyre, how
 old thou art.
EYRE. My liege, a very boy, a stripling,
a younker; you see not a white hair on my
head, not a gray in this beard. Every hair,
I assure thy majesty, that sticks in this
beard, Sim Eyre values at the King of
Babylon's ransom; Tamar Cham's beard
was a rubbing brush to 't. Yet I'll [30

---

9 Magpie.

shave it off, and stuff tennis balls with
it, to please my bully king.

KING. But all this while I do not know
your age.

EYRE. My liege, I am six-and-fifty year
old, yet I can cry "hump!" with a sound
heart for the honor of Saint Hugh. Mark
this old wench, my king; I danced the
shaking of the sheets with her six-and-
thirty years ago, and yet I hope to get two
or three young lord mayors ere I die. [40
I am lusty still, Sim Eyre still. Care and
cold lodging brings white hairs. My sweet
majesty, let care vanish, cast it upon thy
nobles; it will make thee look always young
like Apollo, and cry "hump!" Prince am
I none, yet am I princely born.

KING. Ha, ha!
Say, Cornwall, didst thou ever see his
like?

NOBLEMAN. Not I, my lord.

Enter Lincoln and Lord Mayor.

KING.   Lincoln, what news with you?

LINC. My gracious lord, have care unto
yourself,   50
For there are traitors here.

ALL.   Traitors? Where? Who?

EYRE. Traitors in my house? God forbid! Where be my officers? I'll spend my
soul, ere my king feel harm.

KING. Where is the traitor, Lincoln?

LINC. [*Pointing to Lacy.*] Here he stands.

KING. Cornwall, lay hold on Lacy!—
Lincoln, speak;
What canst thou lay unto thy nephew's
charge?

LINC. This, my dear liege: your grace, to
do me honor,
Heaped on the head of this degenerous [1]
boy   59
Desertless favors; you made choice of him
To be commander over powers in France.
But he—

KING.   Good Lincoln, prithee, pause
awhile!
Even in thine eyes I read what thou
wouldst speak.
I know how Lacy did neglect our love,
Ran himself deeply, in the highest degree,
Into vile treason—

LINC.   Is he not a traitor?

[1] Degenerate.

KING. Lincoln, he was; now have we pardoned him.
'Twas not a base want of true valor's fire
That held him out of France, but love's
desire.

LINC. I will not bear his shame upon my
back.   70

KING. Nor shalt thou, Lincoln; I forgive
you both.

LINC. Then, good my liege, forbid the boy
to wed
One whose mean birth will much disgrace his bed.

KING. Are they not married?

LINC.   No, my liege.

BOTH.   We are.

KING. Shall I divorce them then? O, be
it far
That any hand on earth should dare
untie
The sacred knot, knit by God's majesty;
I would not for my crown disjoin their
hands
That are conjoined in holy nuptial bands.
How say'st thou, Lacy, wouldst thou
lose thy Rose?   80

HANS. Not for all Indians' wealth, my
sovereign.

KING. But Rose, I am sure, her Lacy
would forgo?

ROSE. If Rose were asked that question,
she'd say no!

KING. You hear them, Lincoln?

LINC.   Yea, my liege, I do.

KING. Yet canst thou find i' th' heart to
part these two?
Who seeks, besides you, to divorce these
lovers?

L. MAYOR. I do, my gracious lord; I am
her father.

KING. Sir Roger Oteley, our last mayor, I
think?

NOBLEMAN. The same, my liege.

KING.   Would you offend Love's laws?
Well, you shall have your wills; you sue
to me   90
To prohibit the match. Soft, let me see—
You both are married, Lacy, art thou
not?

HANS. I am, dread sovereign.

KING.   Then, upon thy life,
I charge thee not to call this woman
wife.

L. MAYOR. I thank your grace.

ROSE.   O my most gracious lord!
                                        Kneel.
KING. Nay, Rose, never woo me; I tell you
    true,
  Although as yet I am a bachelor,
  Yet I believe I shall not marry you.
ROSE. Can you divide the body from the
    soul,   99
  Yet make the body live?
KING.   Yea, so profound?
  I cannot, Rose, but you I must divide.
  Fair maid, this bridegroom cannot be
    your bride.[1]—
  Are you pleased, Lincoln? Oteley, are
    you pleased?
BOTH. Yes, my lord.
KING.   Then must my heart be eased;
  For, credit me, my conscience lives in
    pain,
  Till these whom I divorced be joined
    again.
  Lacy, give me thy hand; Rose, lend me
    thine!
  Be what you would be! Kiss now! So,
    that's fine.   108
  At night, lovers, to bed!—Now let me see
  Which of you all mislikes this harmony.
L. MAYOR. Will you then take from me
    my child perforce?
KING. Why, tell me, Oteley, shines not
    Lacy's name
  As bright in the world's eye as the gay
    beams
  Of any citizen?
LINC.   Yea, but, my gracious lord,
  I do mislike the match far more than he;
  Her blood is too-too base.
KING.   Lincoln, no more.
  Dost thou not know that love respects
    no blood,
  Cares not for difference of birth or state?
  The maid is young, well born, fair, virtu-
    ous,
  A worthy bride for any gentleman.   120
  Besides, your nephew for her sake did
    stoop
  To bear necessity, and, as I hear,
  Forgetting honors and all courtly pleas-
    ures,
  To gain her love became a shoemaker.
  As for the honor which he lost in France,
  Thus I redeem it: Lacy, kneel thee
    down!—

[1] Used of both sexes.

  Arise, Sir Rowland Lacy! Tell me now,
  Tell me in earnest, Oteley, canst thou
    chide,
  Seeing thy Rose a lady and a bride?
L. MAYOR. I am content with what your
    grace hath done.   130
LINC. And I, my liege, since there's no
    remedy.
KING. Come on, then, all shake hands.
  I'll have you friends;
  Where there is much love, all discord
    ends.
  What says my mad lord mayor to all
    this love?
EYRE. O my liege, this honor you have
done to my fine journeyman here, Rowland
Lacy, and all these favors which you have
shown to me this day in my poor house
will make Simon Eyre live longer by one
dozen of warm summers more than he
should.   141
KING. Nay, my mad lord mayor, that shall
    be thy name;
  If any grace of mine can length thy life,
  One honor more I'll do thee: that new
    building,
  Which at thy cost in Cornhill is erected,
  Shall take a name from us; we'll have it
    called
  The Leadenhall, because in digging it
  You found the lead that covereth the
    same.
EYRE. I thank your majesty.
WIFE.   God bless your grace!
KING. Lincoln, a word with you!   150

Enter Hodge, Firk, Rafe, and more Shoe-
                                makers.

EYRE. How now, my mad knaves?
Peace, speak softly; yonder is the king.
KING. With the old troop which there we
    keep in pay,
  We will incorporate a new supply.
  Before one summer more pass o'er my
    head,
  France shall repent England was injuréd.
  What are all those?
HANS.   All shoemakers, my liege,
  Sometimes my fellows; in their com-
    panies
  I lived as merry as an emperor.
KING. My mad lord mayor, are all these
    shoemakers?   160
EYRE. All shoemakers, my liege; all

gentlemen of the gentle craft, true Trojans, courageous cordwaïners; they all kneel to the shrine of holy Saint Hugh.

ALL. God save your majesty, all shoe-maker[s]!

KING. Mad Simon, would they anything with us?

EYRE. Mum, mad knaves! Not a word! I'll do 't; I warrant you. They are all beggars, my liege; all for themselves, [170 and I for them all, on both my knees do entreat that, for the honor of poor Simon Eyre and the good of his brethren, these mad knaves, your grace would vouchsafe some privilege to my new Leadenhall, that it may be lawful for us to buy and sell leather there two days a week.

KING. Mad Sim, I grant your suit; you shall have patent
To hold two market days in Leadenhall, Mondays and Fridays—those shall be the times.　　180
Will this content you?

ALL. 　　　　　　Jesus bless your grace!

EYRE. In the name of these my poor brethren shoemakers, I most humbly thank your grace. But, before I rise, seeing you are in the giving vein and we in the begging, grant Sim Eyre one boon more.

KING. What is it, my lord mayor?

EYRE. Vouchsafe to taste of a poor banquet that stands sweetly waiting for your sweet presence.　　190

KING. I shall undo thee, Eyre, only with feasts;
Already have I been too troublesome. Say, have I not?

EYRE. O my dear king, Sim Eyre was taken unawares upon a day of shroving [1] which I promised long ago to the prentices of London.
For, and 't please your highness, in time past,　　198
I bare the water tankard,[2] and my coat Sits not a whit the worse upon my back; And then, upon a morning, some mad boys
(It was Shrove Tuesday, even as 'tis now) gave me my breakfast, and I swore then by the stopple of my tankard, if ever I came to be lord mayor of London, I would feast all the prentices. This day, my liege, I did it, and the slaves had an hundred tables five times covered. They are gone home and vanished.　　209
Yet add more honor to the gentle trade; Taste of Eyre's banquet, Simon's happy made.

KING. Eyre, I will taste of thy banquet, and will say
I have not met more pleasure on a day. Friends of the gentle craft, thanks to you all;
Thanks, my kind lady mayoress, for our cheer.—
Come, lords, awhile let's revel it at home! When all our sports and banquetings are done,
Wars must right wrongs which French-men have begun.　　　　*Exeunt.*

FINIS.

[1] Merrymaking.　　　[2] As an apprentice.

THE HONEST[1] WHORE[2]

[PART 1]

BY

THOMAS DEKKER

[DRAMATIS PERSONÆ

GASPARO TREBAZZI, *Duke of Milan.*
HIPPOLITO, *a count.*
CASTRUCHIO ⎫
SINEZI ⎪
PIORATTO ⎬ *gallants.*
FLUELLO ⎪
MATHEO ⎭
BENEDICT, *a doctor.*
ANSELMO, *a friar.*
FUSTIGO, *brother of Viola.*
CANDIDO, *a linen draper.*
GEORGE, *his servant.*
FIRST PRENTICE.

SECOND PRENTICE.
CRAMBO ⎫
POLI *or* POH ⎬ *ruffians.*
ROGER, *servant of Bellafront.*
PORTER.
SWEEPER.
MADMEN, SERVANTS, ETC.

INFELICE, *daughter of the Duke.*
BELLAFRONT, *a whore.*
VIOLA, *wife of Candido.*
MISTRESS FINGERLOCK, *a bawd.*

SCENE: *Milan and the neighborhood.*

TIME: *Contemporary.*]

SCENA i.[3]

[A street in Milan.]

Enter at one door a funeral (a coronet lying on the hearse, scutcheons and garlands hanging on the sides), attended by Gasparo Trebazzi, Duke of Milan, Castruchio, Sinezi, Pioratto, Fluello, and Others. At another door enter Hippolito, in discontented appearance, Matheo, a gentleman, his friend, laboring to hold him back.

DUKE. Behold, yon comet shows his head again!
Twice hath he thus at cross turns[4] thrown on us

Prodigious[5] looks; twice hath he troubled
The waters of our eyes. See, he's turned wild!
Go on, in God's name.
ALL.   On afore there, ho!
DUKE. Kinsmen and friends, take from your manly sides
Your weapons to keep back the desperate boy
From doing violence to the innocent dead.
HIP. I prithee, dear Matheo—
MAT.   Come, y'are mad!
HIP. I do arrest thee, murderer! Set down,
Villains, set down that sorrow; 'tis all mine. 11
DUKE. I do beseech you all, for my blood's sake
Send hence your milder spirits, and let wrath
Join in confederacy with your weapons' points;

---

[1] Chaste.
[2] The title of the first edn. continues: "With the Humors of the Patient Man and the Longing Wife."
[3] Original reads *Actus Primus, Scena Prima,* but from this point on, the play is not divided into acts, although some scene divisions are indicated.   [4] Street crossings.
[5] Portentous.

593

If he proceed to vex us, let your swords
Seek out his bowels. Funeral grief loathes
  words.

ALL. Set on!

HIP.   Set down the body!

MAT.   O my lord!
Y'are wrong! I' th' open street? You see
  she's dead.

HIP. I know she is not dead.

DUKE.   Frantic young man,
Wilt thou believe these gentlemen? Pray
  speak.   20
Thou dost abuse my child, and mock'st
  the tears
That here are shed for her. If to behold
Those roses withered that set out her
  cheeks;
That pair of stars that gave her body light,
Darkened and dim forever; all those
  rivers
That fed her veins with warm and crim-
  son streams
Frozen and dried up—if these be signs of
  death,
Then is she dead. Thou unreligious
  youth,
Art not ashamed to empty all these eyes
Of funeral tears, a debt due to the
  dead,   30
As mirth is to the living? Sham'st thou
  not
To have them stare on thee? Hark, thou
  art cursed
Even to thy face, by those that scarce
  can speak.

HIP. My lord—

DUKE.   What wouldst thou have?
  Is she not dead?

HIP. O, you ha' killed her by your cruelty!

DUKE. Admit I had, thou kill'st her now
  again,
And art more savage than a barbarous
  Moor.

HIP. Let me but kiss her pale and bloodless
  lip.

DUKE. O fie, fie, fie!

HIP. Or, if not touch her, let me look on
  her.   40

MAT. As you regard your honor—

HIP.   Honor? Smoke!

MAT. Or, if you loved her living, spare her
  now.

DUKE. Ay, well done, sir; you play the
  gentleman.—

Steal hence.—'Tis nobly done.—Away!
  —I'll join
My force to yours to stop this violent
  torment.—
Pass on.

*Exeunt with funeral [all except the Duke,
                    Hippolito, and Matheo].*

HIP.   Matheo, thou dost wound me
  more.

MAT. I give you physic, noble friend, not
  wounds.

DUKE. O, well said, well done, a true
  gentleman!
Alack, I know the sea of lovers' rage
Comes rushing with so strong a tide, it
  beats   50
And bears down all respects of life, of
  honor,
Of friends, of foes. Forget her, gallant
  youth.

HIP. Forget her?

DUKE.   Nay, nay, be but patient,
Forwhy [1] death's hand hath sued a strict
  divorce
Twixt her and thee. What's beauty but a
  corse?
What but fair sand-dust are earth's purest forms?
Queen's bodies are but trunks to put in
  worms.

MAT. Speak no more sentences, [2] my
good lord, but slip hence; you see they are
but fits. I'll rule him, I warrant ye. [60
Ay, so, tread gingerly; your grace is here
somewhat too long already. [*Exit Duke.
Aside.*] 'Sblood, [3] the jest were now, if
having ta'en some knocks o' th' pate already, he should get loose again, and, like
a mad ox, toss my new black cloaks into
the kennel. [4] I must humor his lordship.—
My Lord Hippolito, is it in your stomach
to go to dinner?

HIP. Where is the body?   70

MAT. The body, as the duke spake very
wisely, is gone to be wormed.

HIP. I cannot rest; I'll meet it at next
turn. I'll see how my love looks.

          Matheo holds him in 's arms.

MAT. How your love looks? Worse than

---

[1] Because.   [2] Sententious sayings.
[3] God's blood. *Cf.* other mild oaths in this
play, such as *'Sfoot, 'Swounds, 'Snails, Ud's life,
Godso.*
[4] Channel, gutter.

a scarecrow. Wrastle not with me; the great fellow gives the fall for a ducat.

Hɪᴘ. I shall forget myself.

Mᴀᴛ. Pray, do so; leave yourself behind yourself, and go whither you will. [80 'Sfoot, do you long to have base rogues that maintain a Saint Anthony's fire in their noses by nothing but twopenny ale, make ballads of you? If the duke had but so much mettle in him as is in a cobbler's awl, he would ha' been a vexed thing. He and his train had blown you up but that their powder has taken the wet of cowards. You'll bleed three pottles of Alicant,[1] by this light, if you follow 'em, and then [90 we shall have a hole made in a wrong place, to have surgeons roll thee up like a baby in swaddling clouts.

Hɪᴘ. What day is today, Matheo?

Mᴀᴛ. Yea, marry, this is an easy question. Why, today is—let me see—Thursday.

Hɪᴘ. O, Thursday!

Mᴀᴛ. Here's a coil[2] for a dead commodity. 'Sfoot, women when they are [100 alive are but dead commodities, for you shall have one woman lie upon many men's hands.

Hɪᴘ. She died on Monday then.

Mᴀᴛ. And that's the most villainous day of all the week to die in. And she was well, and eat a mess of water gruel on Monday morning.

Hɪᴘ. Ay? It cannot be
    Such a bright taper should burn out so
        soon.   110

Mᴀᴛ. O yes, my lord. So soon? Why, I ha' known them that at dinner have been as well, and had so much health that they were glad to pledge it, yet before three a-clock have been found dead—drunk.

Hɪᴘ. On Thursday buried! And on Monday died!
    Quick haste, by'r Lady. Sure her winding
        sheet
    Was laid out fore her body, and the
        worms
    That now must feast with her were even
        bespoke,
    And solemnly invited like strange
        guests.   120

Mᴀᴛ. Strange feeders they are indeed,

[1] Six quarts of Spanish wine.
[2] Disturbance.

my lord, and, like your jester or young courtier, will enter upon any man's trencher without bidding.

Hɪᴘ. Cursed be that day forever that
        robbed her
    Of breath, and me of bliss! Henceforth
        let it stand
    Within the wizard's book (the calendar)
    Marked with a marginal finger, to be
        chosen
    By thieves, by villains, and black mur-
        derers,
    As the best day for them to labor in. 130
    If henceforth this adulterous, bawdy
        world
    Be got with child with treason, sacrilege,
    Atheism, rapes, treacherous friendship,
        perjury,
    Slander (the beggar's sin), lies (sin of
        fools),
    Or any other damned impieties,
    On Monday let 'em be deliveréd.
    I swear to thee, Matheo, by my soul,
    Hereafter weekly on that day I'll glue
    Mine eyelids down, because they shall
        not gaze
    On any female cheek. And, being locked
        up   140
    In my close[3] chamber, there I'll meditate
    On nothing but my Infelice's end,
    Or on a dead man's skull draw out mine
        own.

Mᴀᴛ. You'll do all these good works now every Monday, because it is so bad; but I hope upon Tuesday morning I shall take you with a wench.

Hɪᴘ. If ever, whilst frail blood through
        my veins run,
    On woman's beams I throw affection,
    Save her that's dead, or that I loosely
        fly   150
    To th' shore of any other wafting eye,
    Let me not prosper, Heaven! I will be
        true
    Even to her dust and ashes. Could her
        tomb
    Stand whilst I lived, so long that it
        might rot,
    That should fall down, but she be ne'er
        forgot.

Mᴀᴛ. If you have this strange monster, honesty,[4] in your belly, why, so jig-[5] makers and chroniclers shall pick something

[3] Private.   [4] Chastity.   [5] Ballad.

out of you; but, and [1] I smell not you and a bawdyhouse out within these ten [160 days, let my nose be as big as an English bag pudding. I'll follow your lordship, though it be to the place aforenamed.

Exeunt.

[SCENA ii.

Another street.]

Enter Fustigo in some fantastic sea suit at one door; a Porter meets him at another.

FUS. How now, porter, will she come?

POR. If I may trust a woman, sir, she will come.

FUS. There's for thy pains. [*Gives money.*] God-a-mercy,[2] if I ever stand in need of a wench that will come with a wet finger,[3] porter, thou shalt earn my money before any clarissimo[4] in Milan; yet, so God sa' me, she's mine own sister, body and soul, as I am a Christian gentleman. Farewell; I'll ponder till she come. Thou [11 hast been no bawd in fetching this woman, I assure thee.

POR. No matter if I had, sir; better men than porters are bawds.

FUS. O God, sir, many that have borne offices. But, porter, art sure thou went'st into a true[5] house?

POR. I think so, for I met with no thieves. 20

FUS. Nay, but art sure it was my sister Viola?

POR. I am sure, by all superscriptions, it was the party you ciphered.[6]

FUS. Not very tall?

POR. Nor very low; a middling woman.

FUS. 'Twas she, faith, 'twas she. A pretty plump cheek, like mine?

POR. At a blush,[7] a little very much like you. 30

FUS. Godso, I would not for a ducat she had kicked up her heels, for I ha' spent an abomination this voyage; marry, I did it amongst sailors and gentlemen. There's a little modicum more, porter, for making thee stay. [*Gives money.*] Farewell, honest porter.

POR. I am in your debt, sir; God preserve you. *Exit.*

---

[1] If.
[2] Thank you.
[3] Promptly.
[4] Grandee.
[5] Respectable.
[6] Described.
[7] Glance.

Enter Viola.

FUS. Not so neither, good porter. God's lid, yonder she comes.—Sister Viola, I [41 am glad to see you stirring. It's news to have me here, is't not, sister?

VIO. Yes, trust me. I wondered who should be so bold to send for me. You're welcome to Milan, brother.

FUS. Troth, sister, I heard you were married to a very rich chuff,[8] and I was very sorry for it that I had no better clothes, and that made me send; for you know we Milaners love to strut upon Span- [51 ish leather. And how does all our friends?

VIO. Very well. You ha' traveled enough now, I trow, to sow your wild oats.

FUS. A pox on 'em! Wild oats? I ha' not an oat to throw at a horse. Troth, sister, I ha' sowed my oats, and reaped two hundred ducats—if I had 'em here. Marry, I must entreat you to lend me some thirty or forty till the ship come. By this hand, I'll discharge at my day, by [61 this hand.

VIO. These are your old oaths.

FUS. Why, sister, do you think I'll forswear my hand?

VIO. Well, well, you shall have them. Put yourself into better fashion, because I must employ you in a serious matter.

FUS. I'll sweat like a horse if I like the matter. [70

VIO. You ha' cast off all your old swaggering humors?

FUS. I had not sailed a league in that great fishpond, the sea, but I cast up my very gall.

VIO. I am the more sorry, for I must employ a true swaggerer.

FUS. Nay, by this iron, sister, they shall find I am powder and touch-box,[9] if they put fire once into me. 80

VIO. Then lend me your ears.

FUS. Mine ears are yours, dear sister.

VIO. I am married to a man that has wealth enough, and wit enough.

FUS. A linen draper, I was told, sister.

VIO. Very true, a grave citizen; I want nothing that a wife can wish from a husband. But here's the spite[10]—he has not all things belonging to a man.

---

[8] Old miser.
[9] A box containing powder for priming a firearm.
[10] Vexation.

Fus. God's my life, he's a very man-drake,[1] or else, God bless us, one a [2]   [91 these whiblins,[3] and that's worse, and then all the children that he gets lawfully of your body, sister, are bastards by a statute.

Vio. O, you run over me too fast, brother. I have heard it often said that he who cannot be angry is no man. I am sure my husband is a man in print,[4] for all things else save only in this: no tempest can move him.   100

Fus. 'Slid, would he had been at sea with us! He should ha' been moved, and moved again, for I'll be sworn, la, our drunken ship reeled like a Dutchman.

Vio. No loss of goods can increase in him a wrinkle; no crabbed language make his countenance sour; the stubbornness of no servant shake him. He has no more gall in him than a dove, no more sting than an ant. Musician will he never be, yet I find much music in him; but he loves no   [111 frets,[5] and is so free from anger that many times I am ready to bite off my tongue, because it wants that virtue which all women's tongues have, to anger their hus-bands. Brother, mine can by no thunder turn him into a sharpness.

Fus. Belike his blood, sister, is well brewed then.

Vio. I protest to thee, Fustigo, I love him most affectionately; but I know not—   [121 I ha' such a tickling within me—such a strange longing; nay, verily I do long.

Fus. Then y'are with child, sister, by all signs and tokens; nay, I am partly a physician, and partly something else. I ha' read Albertus Magnus and Aristotle's Emblems.

Vio. Y'are wide a th' bow hand [6] still, brother; my longings are not wanton, but wayward. I long to have my patient   [131 husband eat up a whole porcupine, to the intent the bristling quills may stick about his lips like a Flemish mustacho, and be shot at me. I shall be leaner than the new moon unless I can make him horn-mad.[7]

Fus. 'Sfoot, half a quarter of an hour does that: make him a cuckold.

Vio. Pooh, he would count such a cut no unkindness.

Fus. The honester citizen he. Then   [141 make him drunk and cut off his beard.

Vio. Fie, fie, idle,[8] idle! He's no French-man, to fret at the loss of a little scald [9] hair. No, brother, thus it shall be—you must be secret.

Fus. As your midwife, I protest, sister, or a barber-surgeon.

Vio. Repair to the Tortoise here in St. Christopher's Street. I will send you money; turn yourself into a brave [10]   [151 man. Instead of the arms of your mistress, let your sword and your military scarf hang about your neck.

Fus. I must have a great horseman's French feather too, sister.

Vio. O, by any means, to show your light head, else your hat will sit like a coxcomb. To be brief, you must be in all points a most terrible wide-mouthed swag-gerer.   161

Fus. Nay, for swaggering points let me alone.

Vio. Resort then to our shop, and, in my husband's presence, kiss me, snatch rings, jewels, or anything, so you give it back again, brother, in secret.

Fus. By this hand, sister.

Vio. Swear as if you came but new from knighting.   170

Fus. Nay, I'll swear after [11] four hundred a year.

Vio. Swagger worse than a lievetenant [12] among freshwater soldiers; [13] call me your love, your ingle,[14] your cousin, or so—but sister at no hand.

Fus. No, no, it shall be cousin, or rather coz; that's the gulling word between the citizens' wives and their madcaps that man [15] 'em to the Garden.[16] To call you one a mine "aunts," sister, were as good   [181 as call you arrant whore; no, no, let me alone to "cousin" you rarely.

Vio. H'as heard I have a brother, but

---

[1] The root of this plant was supposed to resemble the human figure.

[2] Of.   [3] Weak, impotent creatures.

[4] To the letter, exactly; with a pun.

[5] A common pun with reference to the frets of a stringed instrument.   [6] Wide of the mark.

[7] Stark mad; with a pun on the "horns" of a cuckold.

[8] Foolish.   [11] According to an income of.

[9] Scurfy.   [12] Lieutenant.

[10] Richly dressed.

[13] Soldiers who had never crossed the sea.

[14] Darling.   [16] Presumably Paris Garden.

[15] Accompany.

never saw him; therefore put on a good
face.

Fus. The best in Milan, I warrant.

Vio. Take up wares, but pay nothing;
rifle my bosom, my pocket, my purse, the
boxes for money to dice withal; but,
brother, you must give all back again   [191
in secret.

Fus. By this welkin that here roars I
will, or else let me never know what a secret
is. Why, sister, do you think I'll cunny-
catch [1] you, when you are my cousin?
God's my life, then I were a stark ass. If
I fret not his guts, beg me for a fool. [2]

Vio. Be circumspect, and do so then. Farewell.   200

Fus. The Tortoise, sister? I'll stay there.
Forty ducats!   *Exit.*

Vio. Thither I'll send.—This law can none
deny:

Women must have their longings, or
they die.   *Exit.*

[Scena iii.

A room in the Duke's palace.]

*Gasparo the Duke, Doctor Benedict, two
Servants.*

Duke. Give charge that none do enter;
lock the doors.

And, fellows, what your eyes and ears
receive,

Upon your lives trust not the gadding
air

To carry the least part of it. The glass,
The hourglass!

Doc.   Here, my lord.

Duke.   Ah, 'tis near [3] spent! [4]

But, Doctor Benedict, does your art
speak truth?

Art sure the soporiferous stream will
ebb,

And leave the crystal banks of her white
body

Pure as they were at first, just at the
hour?

---

[1] Cheat.
[2] Beg the king for the custody of me as an
idiot.
[3] Emended by Dyce. Original reads *meere.*
[4] The line division here and in a few later
passages has been regularized. A few passages
printed as prose in the original have also been
changed to verse.

Doc. Just at the hour, my lord.

Duke.   Uncurtain her!   10

[*A curtain is drawn back, revealing Infelice
lying on a couch.*]

Softly!—See, doctor, what a coldish
heat

Spreads over all her body!

Doc.   Now it works.

The vital spirits that by a sleepy charm
Were bound up fast, and threw an icy
rust [5]

On her exterior parts, now gin [6] to
break.

Trouble her not, my lord.

Duke.   Some stools! You called

For music, did you not? O ho, it speaks!
[*Music.*]

It speaks! Watch, sirs, her waking;
note those sands.

Doctor, sit down. A dukedom that
should weigh

Mine own down twice, being put into
one scale,   20

And that fond [7] desperate boy, Hippolito,

Making the weight up, should not at
my hands

Buy her i' th' tother [8] were her state
more light

Than hers who makes a dowry up with
alms.

Doctor, I'll starve her on the Apennine
Ere he shall marry her. I must confess
Hippolito is nobly born, a man—
Did not mine enemies' blood boil in
his veins—

Whom I would court to be my son-in-
law;

But princes, whose high spleens for
empery [9] swell,   30

Are not with easy art made parallel.

2 Ser. She wakes, my lord.

Duke.   Look, Doctor Benedict.—

I charge you, on your lives, maintain
for truth

Whate'er the doctor or myself aver,
For you shall bear her hence to Bergamo.

Inf. [*Waking.*] O God, what fearful
dreams!

Doc.   Lady.

---

[5] Coating.   [8] Other.
[6] Begin.   [9] Sovereignty.
[7] Foolish.

INF.   Ha!

DUKE.   Girl.
Why, Infelice, how is't now, ha? Speak.

INF. I'm well. What makes[1] this doctor
  here? I'm well.

DUKE. Thou wert not so even now; sick-
  ness' pale hand
  Laid hold on thee even in the midst of
    feasting;   40
  And, when a cup crowned with thy
    lover's health
  Had touched thy lips, a sensible, cold
    dew
  Stood on thy cheeks, as if that death
    had wept
  To see such beauty alter.

INF.   I remember
  I sate at banquet, but felt no such
    change.

DUKE. Thou hast forgotten, then, how
  a messenger
  Came wildly in, with this unsavory
    news,
  That he was dead?

INF.   What messenger? Who's dead?

DUKE. Hippolito. Alack, wring not thy
  hands.

INF. I saw no messenger, heard no such
  news.   50

DOC. Trust me, you did, sweet lady.

DUKE.   La you now!

2 SER. Yes, indeed, madam.

DUKE.   La you now!—[Aside.]
  'Tis well, good knaves!

INF. You ha' slain him, and now you'll
  murder me.

DUKE. Good Infelice, vex not thus thy-
  self.
  Of this the bad report before did strike
  So coldly to thy heart that the swift
    currents
  Of life were all frozen up.

INF.   It is untrue,
  'Tis most untrue, O most unnatural
    father!

DUKE. And we had much to do by art's
  best cunning
  To fetch life back again.

DOC.   Most certain, lady.   60

DUKE. Why, la you now, you'll not believe me. Friends,
  Sweat we not all? Had we not much to
    do?

[1] Does.

2 SER. Yes, indeed, my lord, much.

DUKE. Death drew such fearful pictures
  in thy face
  That, were Hippolito alive again,
  I'd kneel and woo the noble gentleman
  To be thy husband. Now I sore repent
  My sharpness to him and his family.
  Nay, do not weep for him; we all must
    die.—
  Doctor, this place where she so oft hath
    seen   70
  His lively presence, hurts her, does it
    not?

DOC. Doubtless, my lord, it does.

DUKE.   It does, it does!
  Therefore, sweet girl, thou shalt to Ber-
    gamo.

INF. Even where you will; in any place
  there's woe.

DUKE. A coach is ready. Bergamo doth
    stand
  In a most wholesome air—sweet walks—
    there's deer.
  Ay, thou shalt hunt and send us venison,
  Which, like some goddess in the Cyp-
    rian groves,
  Thine own fair hand shall strike.—Sirs,
    you shall teach her
  To stand, and how to shoot; ay, she
    shall hunt.   80
  Cast off this sorrow. In, girl, and pre-
    pare
  This night to ride away to Bergamo.

INF. O, most unhappy maid!   Exit.

DUKE.   Follow her close.
  No words that she was buried, on your
    lives,
  Or that her ghost walks now after she's
    dead.
  I'll hang you if you name a funeral.

1 SER. I'll speak Greek, my lord, ere
I speak that deadly word.

2 SER. And I'll speak Welsh, which [89
is harder than Greek.   Exeunt [Servants].

DUKE. Away, look to her.—Doctor Bene-
    dict,
  Did you observe how her complexion
    altered
  Upon his name and death? O, would
    'twere true.

DOC. It may, my lord.

DUKE.   May! How? I wish his death.

DOC. And you may have your wish: say
    but the word,

And 'tis a strong spell to rip up his
grave.

I have good knowledge with Hippolito;
He calls me friend. I'll creep into his
bosom,
And sting him there to death; poison
can do 't.

DUKE. Perform it; I'll create thee half
mine heir. 100

DOC. It shall be done, although the fact [1]
be foul.

DUKE. Greatness hides sin; the guilt upon
my soul! *Exeunt.*

[SCENA iv.

A street.]

Enter Castruchio, Pioratto, and Fluello.

CAS. Signior Pioratto, Signior Fluello,
shall 's be merry? Shall 's play the wags
now?

FLU. Ay, anything that may beget the
child of laughter.

CAS. Truth, I have a pretty sportive
conceit [2] new crept into my brain, will
move excellent mirth.

PIO. Let's ha't, let's ha't. And where
shall the scene of mirth lie? 10

CAS. At Signior Candido's house, the
patient man, nay, the monstrous patient
man. They say his blood is immovable.
that he has taken all patience from a man,
and all constancy from a woman.

FLU. That makes so many whores nowadays.

CAS. Ay, and so many knaves too.

PIO. Well, sir.

CAS. To conclude, the report goes, [20
he's so mild, so affable, so suffering, that
nothing indeed can move him. Now do
but think what sport it will be to make
this fellow, the mirror of patience, as angry,
as vexed, and as mad as an English cuckold.

FLU. O, 'twere admirable mirth, that.
But how will 't be done, signior?

CAS. Let me alone; I have a trick, a
conceit, a thing, a device will sting [30
him, i' faith, if he have but a thimbleful of
blood in 's belly, or a spleen not so big as
a tavern token. [3]

PIO. Thou stir him? Thou move him?
Thou anger him? Alas, I know his approved [4] temper. Thou vex him? Why,
he has a patience above man's injuries.
Thou mayst sooner raise a spleen in an
angel than rough humor in him. Why,
I'll give you instance for it. This won- [40
derfully tempered Signior Candido upon a
time invited home to his house certain
Neapolitan lords, of curious [5] taste and
no mean palates, conjuring his wife, of all
loves, [6] to prepare cheer fitting for such
honorable trenchermen. She—just of a
woman's nature, covetous to try the uttermost of vexation, and thinking at last to
get the start of his humor—willingly neglected the preparation, and became [50
unfurnished not only of dainty but of ordinary dishes. He, according to the mildness of his breast, entertained the lords,
and with courtly discourse beguiled the
time, as much as a citizen might do. To
conclude, they were hungry lords, for
there came no meat in; their stomachs
were plainly gulled, and their teeth deluded, and, if anger could have seized a
man, there was matter enough, i' faith, [60
to vex any citizen in the world, if he were
not too much made a fool by his wife.

FLU. Ay, I'll swear for 't. 'Sfoot, had
it been my case, I should ha' played mad
tricks with my wife and family. First, I
would ha' spitted the men, stewed the
maids, and baked the mistress, and so
served them in.

PIO. Why, 't would ha' tempted any
blood but his.
And thou to vex him? Thou to anger
him 70
With some poor, shallow jest?

CAS. 'Sblood, Signior Pioratto, you that
disparage my conceit, I'll wage a hundred
ducats upon the head on 't that it moves
him, frets him, and galls him.

PIO. Done! 'Tis a lay; [7] join golls [8] on 't.
Witness, Signior Fluello.

CAS. Witness; 'tis done.
Come, follow me. The house is not far off.
I'll thrust him from his humor, vex his
breast, 80
And win a hundred ducats by one
jest. *Exeunt.*

---

[1] Deed.
[2] Idea.
[3] Small metal check.
[4] Proved.
[5] Fastidious.
[6] For love's sake.
[7] Bet.
[8] Hands.

[SCENA v.

Candido's shop.]

Enter Candido's Wife, George, and two
Prentices in the shop.

WIFE.[1] Come, you put up your wares in
good order here, do you not, think you?
One piece cast this way, another that way!
You had need have a patient master indeed.

GEO. [*Aside.*] Ay, I'll be sworn, for
we have a curst [2] mistress.

WIFE. You mumble, do you? Mumble?
I would your master or I could be a note
more angry, for two patient folks in a [10
house spoil all the servants that ever shall
come under them.

1 PREN. [*Aside.*] You patient! Ay, so is
the devil when he is horn-mad.

Enter Castruchio, Fluello, and Pioratto.

ALL THREE.[3] Gentlemen, what do you
lack? What is 't you buy?
See, fine hollands, fine cambrics, fine
lawns.

GEO. What is 't you lack?

2 PREN. What is 't you buy?

CAS. Where's Signior Candido, thy
master? 20

GEO. Faith, signior, he's a little nego-
tiated; he'll appear presently.

CAS. Fellow, let's see a lawn, a choice
one, sirrah.

GEO. The best in all Milan, gentlemen,
and this is the piece. I can fit you gentlemen with fine calicoes too for doublets, the
only sweet fashion now, most delicate and
courtly, a meek gentle calico, cut upon two
double affable taffetas—ah, most neat, [30
feat, and unmatchable!

FLU. A notable, voluble-tongued villain!

PIO. I warrant this fellow was never begot without much prating.

CAS. What, and is this she, say'st thou?

GEO. Ay, and the purest she that ever
you fingered since you were a gentleman.
Look how even she is, look how clean she
is! Ha, as even as the brow of Cynthia,
and as clean as your sons and heirs [40
when they ha' spent all!

[1] From this point Viola appears as *Wife* in
speech heads.
[2] Ill-tempered.
[3] *I.e.*, George and the two prentices.

CAS. Pooh, thou talk'st! Pox on 't,
'tis rough.

GEO. How? Is she rough? But, if you
bid pox on 't, sir, 'twill take away the
roughness presently.

FLU. Ha, signior! Has he fitted your
French curse?

GEO. Look you, gentleman, here's another. Compare them, I pray. *Compara* [50
Virgilium cum Homero: compare virgins
with harlots.

CAS. Pooh, I ha' seen better, and, as
you term them, evener and cleaner.

GEO. You may see further for your
mind, but, trust me, you shall not find
better for your body.

Enter Candido.

CAS. [*Aside.*] O, here he comes; let's make
as though we pass.—
Come, come, we'll try in some other
shop.

CAND. How now? What's the matter? 60

GEO. The gentlemen find fault with this
lawn, fall out with it, and without a cause
too.

CAND. Without a cause?
And that makes you to let 'em pass
away.
Ah, may I crave a word with you,
gentlemen?

FLU. He calls us.

CAS. Makes the better for the jest.

CAND. I pray come near; y'are very wel-
come, gallants.
Pray pardon my man's rudeness, for I
fear me
H'as talked above a prentice with you.
Lawns? [*Shows lawns.*] 70
Look you, kind gentlemen, this—no—
ay—this.
Take this upon my honest-dealing faith
To be a true weave, not too hard nor
slack,
But e'en as far from falsehood as from
black.

CAS. Well, how do you rate it?

CAND. Very conscionably—eighteen shillings a yard.

CAS. That's too dear. How many yards
does the whole piece contain, think you?

CAND. Why, some seventeen yards, I
think, or thereabouts. 80

How much would serve your turn, I pray?

Cas. Why, let me see—would it were better too!

Cand. Truth, 'tis the best in Milan, at few words.

Cas. Well, let me have then—a whole pennyworth.

Cand. Ha, ha! Y'are a merry gentleman.

Cas. A penn'orth, I say.

Cand. Of lawn!

Cas. Of lawn? Ay, of lawn, a penn'orth. 'Sblood, dost not hear? A whole penn'orth! Are you deaf?   90

Cand. Deaf? No, sir; but I must tell you,
Our wares do seldom meet such customers.

Cas. Nay, and you and your lawns be so squeamish, fare you well.

Cand. Pray stay; a word, pray, signior. For what purpose is it, I beseech you?

Cas. 'Sblood, what's that to you? I'll have a pennyworth.

Cand. A pennyworth! Why, you shall. I'll serve you presently.[1]   100

2 Pren. 'Sfoot, a pennyworth, mistress!

Wife.[2] A pennyworth! Call you these gentlemen?

Cas. [To Candido.] No, no. Not there.

Cand.   What then, kind gentleman?
What, at this corner here?

Cas.   No, nor there neither;
I'll have it just in the middle, or else not.

Cand. Just in the middle? Ha, you shall too. What?
Have you a single penny?

Cas.   Yes, here's one.

Cand. Lend it me, I pray.

Flu. An excellent-followed jest!   109

Wife. What, will he spoil the lawn now?

Cand. Patience, good wife.

Wife. Ay, that patience makes a fool of you.—Gentlemen, you might ha' found some other citizen to have made a kind gull on besides my husband.

Cand. Pray, gentlemen, take her to be a woman;
Do not regard her language.—O kind soul,

Such words will drive away my customers.

Wife. Customers with a murrain![3] Call you these customers?   121

Cand. Patience, good wife.

Wife. Pox a your patience.

Geo. 'Sfoot, mistress, I warrant these are some cheating companions.[4]

Cand. Look you, gentleman, there's your ware. I thank you; I have your money here. Pray know my shop; pray let me have your custom.

Wife. Custom, quotha!   130

Cand. Let me take more of your money.

Wife. You had need so.

Pio. Hark in thine ear; th'ast lost an hundred ducats.

Cas. Well, well, I know 't. Is 't possible that homo
Should be nor man nor woman--not once moved—
No, not at such an injury, not at all!
Sure he's a pigeon, for he has no gall.

Flu. Come, come, y'are angry though you smother it.
Y'are vexed, i' faith; confess.

Cand.   Why, gentlemen,
Should you conceit[5] me to be vexed or moved?   140
He has my ware; I have his money for 't,
And that's no argument I'm angry. No,
The best logician cannot prove me so.

Flu. O, but the hateful name of a pennyworth of lawn,
And then cut out i' th' middle of the piece—
Pah, I guess it by myself—would move a lamb
Were he a linen draper; 'twould, i' faith.

Cand. Well, give me leave to answer you for that.
We're set here to please all customers,
Their humors and their fancies—offend none;   150
We get by many, if we leese[6] by one.
May be his mind stood to no more than that;
A pennyworth serves him, and, 'mongst trades 'tis found,
Deny a penn'orth, it may cross a pound.

---

[1] At once.
[2] Original has Mist[ress].
[3] Plague.
[4] Fellows.
[5] Imagine.
[6] Lose.

O, he that means to thrive, with patient
eye
Must please the devil if he come to
buy!

FLU. O wondrous man, patient 'bove
wrong or woe,
How blessed were men, if women could be
so!

CAND. And to express how well my breast
is pleased,
And satisfied in all—George, fill a beaker.
Exit George.
I'll drink unto that gentleman who
lately   161
Bestowed his money with me.

WIFE.   God's my life,
We shall have all our gains drunk out in
beakers
To make amends for pennyworths of
lawn!

Enter Geor[ge with beaker].

CAND. Here, wife, begin you to the gentleman.

WIFE. I begin to him!   [*Spills the wine.*]

CAND.   George, fill 't up again.
'Twas my fault; my hand shook.
Exit George.

PIO.   How strangely this doth show!
A patient man linked with a waspish
shrow.[1]

FLU. [*Aside.*] A silver and gilt beaker! I
have a trick
To work upon that beaker. Sure 'twill
fret him;   170
It cannot choose but vex him. Signior
Castruchio,
In pity to thee I have a conceit
Will save thy hundred ducats yet. 'Twill
do 't,
And work him to impatience.

CAS. [*Aside.*] Sweet Fluello, I should be
bountiful to that conceit.

FLU. [*Aside.*] Well, 'tis enough.

Enter George [with beaker].

CAND.   Here, gentlemen, to you!
I wish your custom; y'are exceeding
welcome.   [*Drinks.*]

CAS. I pledge you, Signior Candido!
[*Drinks.*]

Here, you that must receive a hundred
ducats!

PIO. I'll pledge them deep, i' faith, Castruchio.—   180
Signior Fluello.   [*Drinks.*]

FLU.   Come; play 't off to me;
I am your last man.

CAND.   George, supply the cup

FLU. So, so, good honest George.
Here, Signior Candido, all this to you.

CAND. O, you must pardon me; I use it
not.

FLU. Will you not pledge me then?

CAND.   Yes, but not that;
Great love is shown in little.

FLU.   Blurt on [2] your sentences!
'Sfoot, you shall pledge me all.

CAND.   Indeed, I shall not.

FLU. Not pledge me? 'Sblood, I'll carry
away the beaker then.

CAND. The beaker? O, that at your
pleasure, sir.   190

FLU. Now by this drink I will. [*Drinks.*]

CAS.   Pledge him; he'll do 't else.

FLU. So; I ha' done you right on my thumb
nail.[3]
What, will you pledge me now?

CAND.   You know me, sir!
I am not of that sin.

FLU.   Why, then, farewell!
I'll bear away the beaker, by this light.

CAND. That's as you please; 'tis very good.

FLU. Nay, it doth please me, and, as you
say, 'tis a very good one.
Farewell, Signior Candido.

PIO.   Farewell, Candido.

CAND. Y'are welcome, gentlemen.

CAS.   Heart, not moved yet?
I think his patience is above our wit.

Exeunt [Castruchio, Fluello with the beaker,
*   and Pioratto].*

GEO. I told you before, mistress,   [201
they were all cheaters.

WIFE. Why, fool! Why, husband! Why,
madman! I hope you will not let 'em
sneak away so with a silver and gilt beaker,
the best in the house too.—Go, fellows,
make hue and cry after them.

CAND. Pray let your tongue lie still; all
will be well.—
Come hither, George; hie to the constable,

---

[1] Shrew.

[2] A fig for.

[3] So that only enough to stand on a thumb
nail is left.

And in calm order wish him to attach
them.   210
Make no great stir, because they're
gentlemen,
And a thing partly done in merri-
ment.
'Tis but a size above a jest, thou
know'st;
Therefore pursue it mildly. Go, begone;
The constable's hard by; bring him
along.
Make haste again.

WIFE. O, y'are a goodly, patient woodcock,[1] are you not now? (*Exit George.*)
See what your patience comes to: everyone
saddles you, and rides you; you'll be shortly
the common stone-horse [2] of Milan. [221
A woman's well holped [3] up with such a
meacock.[4] I had rather have a husband
that would swaddle [5] me thrice a day than
such a one that will be gulled twice in half
an hour. O, I could burn all the wares in
my shop for anger.

CAND. Pray wear a peaceful temper; be
my wife,
That is, be patient; for a wife and
husband
Share but one soul between them. This
being known,   230
Why should not one soul then agree in
one?   *Exit.*

WIFE. Hang your agreements! But if
my beaker be gone!

Enter Castruchio, Fluello, Pioratto, and
                    George.

CAND. O, here they come.

GEO. The constable, sir, let 'em come
along with me, because [6] there should be
no wond'ring. He stays at door.

CAS. Constable, Goodman Abram! [7]

FLU. Now, Signior Candido, 'sblood,
why do you attach us?   240

CAS. 'Sheart! Attach us!

CAND.   Nay, swear not, gallants;
Your oaths may move your souls, but
not move me;
You have a silver beaker of my wife's.

FLU. You say not true. 'Tis gilt.

CAND.   Then you say true;
And, being gilt, the guilt lies more on you.

CAS. I hope y'are not angry, sir.

CAND. Then you hope right; for I am
not angry.

FLU. No, but a little moved.

CAND. I moved! 'Twas you were moved—
you were brought hither.

CAS. But you, out of your anger and impatience,   250
Caused us to be attached.

CAND.   Nay, you misplace it.
Out of my quiet sufferance I did that,
And not of any wrath. Had I shown
anger,
I should have then pursued you with the
law,
And hunted you to shame, as many
worldlings
Do build their anger upon feebler
grounds,
The more's the pity. Many lose their lives
For scarce so much coin as will hide their
palm—
Which is most cruel. Those have vexéd
spirits
That pursue lives. In this opinion rest:
The loss of millions could not move my
breast.   261

FLU. Thou art a blessed man, and with
peace dost deal;
Such a meek spirit can bless a commonweal.

CAND. Gentlemen, now 'tis upon eating
time.
Pray, part not hence, but dine with me
today.

CAS. I never heard a carter yet say nay
To such a motion. I'll not be the first.

PIO. Nor I.

FLU. Nor I.

CAND. The constable shall bear you
company.   270
George, call him in. Let the world say
what it can,
Nothing can drive me from a patient
man.   *Exeunt.*

[SCENA vi.
A room in Bellafront's house.]

*Enter Roger with a stool, cushion, looking-
glass, and chafing dish;* [8] *those being
set down, he pulls out of his pocket a*

---

1 Simpleton.   4 Milksop.
2 Stallion.   5 Beat.
3 Helped.   6 In order that.
7 A man who shams madness to gain his ends.
8 Used for heating the poker mentioned below.

vial with white color in it, and two boxes, one with white, another red painting. He places all things in order, and a candle by them, singing with the ends of old ballads as he does it. At last Bella-front, as he rubs his cheek with the colors, whistles within.

ROG. Anon, forsooth.

BELL. [*Within.*] What are you playing the rogue about?

ROG. About you, forsooth; I'm drawing up a hole in your white silk stocking.

BELL. Is my glass there and my boxes of complexion?

ROG. Yes, forsooth. Your boxes of complexion are here, I think; yes, 'tis here. Here's your two complexions—[*Aside.*] 10 and, if I had all the four complexions,[1] I should ne'er set a good face upon 't. Some men, I see, are born under hard-favored planets as well as women. Zounds, I look worse now than I did before, and it makes her face glister most damnably. There's knavery in daubing, I hold my life; or else this is only female pomatum.

Enter Bellafront not full ready,[2] without a gown; she sits down; with her bodkin[3] curls her hair; colors her lips.

BELL. Where's my ruff and poker,[4] you blockhead? 20

ROG. Your ruff, your poker, are en-gend'ring together upon the cupboard of the court, or the court-cupboard.[5]

BELL. Fetch 'em. Is the pox in your hams, you can go no faster? [*Strikes him.*]

ROG. Would the pox were in your fingers, unless you could leave flinging![6] Catch— *Exit.*

BELL. I'll catch you, you dog, by-and-by. Do you grumble? *She sings.* 30

Cupid is a God, as naked as my nail;
I'll whip him with a rod, if he my true love
fail.

[*Enter Roger with ruff and poker.*]

ROG. There's your ruff. Shall I poke it?

BELL. Yes, honest Ro[ger]—no, stay; prithee, good boy, hold here.

[*Sings. Roger holds the glass and candle.*]

Down, down, down, down, I fall down and
arise—down—
I never shall arise.

ROG. Troth, m[istress], then leave the trade if you shall never rise. 40

BELL. What trade, Goodman Abram?

ROG. Why, that of down and arise, or the falling trade.

BELL. I'll fall with you by-and-by.

ROG. If you do, I know who shall smart for 't. Troth, mistress, what do I look like now?

BELL. Like as you are, a panderly sixpenny rascal.

ROG. I may thank you for that; in [50 faith, I look like an old proverb, "Hold the candle before the devil."

BELL. Ud's life, I'll stick my knife in your guts and you prate to me so!— What? *She sings.*

"Well met, pug,[7] the pearl of beauty—
umh, umh."
"How now, Sir Knave? You forget your
duty—umh, umh.
Marry muff,[8] sir!" "Are you grown so
dainty? Fa, la, la, etc."
"Is it you, sir?" "The worst of twenty!
Fa, la, la, leera, la."

Pox on you, how dost thou hold my [60 glass?

ROG. Why, as I hold your door—with my fingers.

BELL. Nay, pray thee, sweet honey Ro[ger], hold up handsomely. [*Sings.*]

Sing, pretty wantons, warble, etc.

We shall ha' guests today, I lay my little maidenhead; my nose itches so.

ROG. I said so too last night, when our fleas twinged me. 70

BELL. So, poke my ruff now. My gown, my gown! Have I my fall?[9] Where's my fall, Roger? *One knocks.*

ROG. Your fall, forsooth, is behind.

BELL. God's my pitikins! Some fool or other knocks.

ROG. Shall I open to the fool, mistress?

BELL. And all these bables[10] lying thus? Away with it quickly.—Ay, ay,

[1] Temperaments constituted by the four humors.
[2] Dressed.
[3] Long hairpin.
[4] Rod for pleating ruffs.
[5] Movable sideboard.
[6] Smiting, striking.
[7] Darling; also harlot.
[8] An expression of contempt.
[9] A flat collar.
[10] Baubles.

knock, and be damned, whosoever you   [80
be!—So; give the fresh salmon line now;
let him come ashore. He shall serve for
my breakfast, though he go against my
stomach.

Roger fetch in Fluello, Castruchio, and
Pioratto.

FLU. Morrow, coz.

CAS. How does my sweet acquaintance?

PIO. Save thee, little marmoset! How
dost thou, good, pretty rogue?

BELL. Well, God-a-mercy, good, pretty
rascal.   90

FLU. Roger, some light, I pray thee.

ROG. You shall, signior, for we that
live here in this vale of misery are as dark
as hell.   *Exit for a candle.*

CAS. Good tobacco, Fluello?

FLU. Smell.

Enter Roger.

PIO. It may be tickling gear, for it
plays with my nose already.

ROG. Here's another light angel,[1] signior.   100

BELL. What, you pied curtal,[2] what's
that you are neighing?

ROG. I say God send us the light of
heaven, or some more angels.

BELL. Go fetch some wine, and drink
half of it.

ROG. I must fetch some wine, gentlemen, and drink half of it.

FLU. Here, Roger.

CAS. No, let me send, prithee.   110

FLU. Hold, you cankerworm.

ROG. You shall send both, if you please,
signiors.

PIO. Stay, what's best to drink a-morn-
ings?

ROG. Hippocras, sir, for my mistress,
if I fetch it, is most dear to her.

FLU. Hippocras? There then, here's a
teston[3] for you, you snake.

ROG. Right, sir, here's three shil-   [120
lings sixpence for a pottle and a manchet.[4]
                                        Ex[it].

CAS. Here's most Herculanean tobacco;
ha' some, acquaintance?

BELL. Faugh, not I—makes your breath
stink like the piss of a fox. Acquaintance,
where supped you last night?

CAS. At a place, sweet acquaintance,
where your health danced the canaries,[5]
i' faith. You should ha' been there.

BELL. I there among your punks![6]   [130
Marry, faugh, hang 'em; I scorn 't! Will
you never leave sucking of eggs in other
folks' hens' nests?

CAS. Why, in good troth, if you'll trust
me, acquaintance, there was not one hen
at the board. Ask Fluello.

FLU. No, faith, coz, none but cocks.
Signior Malavella drunk to thee.

BELL. O, a pure beagle; that horse-
leech there?   140

Flu. And the knight, Sir Oliver Lollio,
swore he would bestow a taffeta petticoat
on thee, but to break his fast with thee.

BELL. With me? I'll choke him then,
hang him, molecatcher! It's the dreaming'st snottynose.

PIO. Well, many took that Lollio for
a fool, but he's a subtle fool.

BELL. Ay, and he has fellows. Of all
filthy, dry-fisted knights, I cannot   [150
abide that he should touch me.

CAS. Why, wench, is he scabbed?

BELL. Hang him, he'll not live to be
so honest, nor to the credit to have scabs
about him; his betters have 'em. But I
hate to wear out any of his coarse knighthood, because he's made like an alderman's
nightgown, faced all with cony[7] before,
and within nothing but fox. This sweet
Oliver will eat mutton[8] till he be ready   [160
to burst, but the lean-jawed slave will
not pay for the scraping of his trencher.

PIO. Plague him! Set him beneath the
salt, and let him not touch a bit till everyone has had his full cut.

FLU. Lord Ello, the gentleman usher,
came in to us too. Marry, 'twas in our
cheese,[9] for he had been to borrow money
for his lord, of a citizen.

CAS. What an ass is that lord to   [170
borrow money of a citizen!

BELL. Nay, God's my pity, what an
ass is that citizen to lend money to a
lord!

---

[1] Also a gold coin.   [3] Sixpence.
[2] A docked horse.   [4] Loaf of fine bread.
[5] A lively dance.   [7] Rabbit skin.
[6] Prostitutes.   [8] Strumpet.
[9] During the cheese course (?).

*Enter Matheo and Hippolito, who, saluting
the company as a stranger, walks off.
Roger comes in sadly behind them, with
a pottle pot, and stands aloof off.*

MAT. Save you, gallants. Signior Fluello, exceedingly well met, as I may say.

FLU. Signior Matheo, exceedingly well
met too, as I may say.

MAT. And how fares my little pretty
mistress?   180

BELL. E'en as my little pretty servant—sees three court dishes before her,
and not one good bit in them.—How now?
Why the devil stand'st thou so? Art in
a trance?

ROG. Yes, forsooth.

BELL. Why dost not fill out their wine?

ROG. Forsooth, 'tis filled out already.
All the wine that the signior has bestowed
upon you is cast away; a porter ran   [190
a little at me, and so faced me down that
I had not a drop.

BELL. I'm accursed to let such a withered, artichoke-faced rascal grow under
my nose. Now you look like an old hecat, going to the gallows. I'll be hanged if
he ha' not put up the money to cony-
catch us all.

ROG. No, truly, forsooth, 'tis not put
up yet.   200

BELL. How many gentlemen hast thou
served thus?

ROG. None but five hundred, besides
prentices and serving-men.

BELL. Dost think I'll pocket it up at
thy hands?

ROG. Yes, forsooth, I fear you will
pocket it up.

BELL. Fie, fie, cut my lace, good servant; I shall ha' the mother [1] presently,   [210
I'm so vexed at this horse-plum. [2]

FLU. Plague, not for a scald [3] pottle
of wine!

MAT. Nay, sweet Bellafront, for a little
pig's wash!

CAS. Here, Roger, fetch more. [*Gives
money.*] A mischance, i' faith, acquaintance.

BELL. Out of my sight, thou ungodly,
puritanical creature.   220

ROG. For the tother pottle?   Yes,
forsooth.   *Exit.*

BELL. Spill that too!—What gentleman
is that, servant? Your friend?

MAT. Godso; a stool, a stool! If you
love me, mistress, entertain this gentleman respectively, [4] and bid him welcome.

BELL. He's very welcome. Pray, sir,
sit.

HIP. Thanks, lady.   230

[*Matheo and Bellafront stand aside conversing.*]

FLU. Count Hippolito, is 't not? Cry
you mercy, signior; you walk here all this
while, and we not heard you? Let me
bestow a stool upon you, beseech you.
You are a stranger here; we know the
fashions a th' house.

CAS. Please you, be here, my lord.
                [*Offers*] *tobacco.*

HIP. No, good Castruchio.

FLU. You have abandoned the court, I
see, my lord, since the death of your   [240
mistress. Well, she was a delicate piece.—
Beseech you, sweet, come let us serve
under the colors of your acquaintance still
for all that.—Please you to meet here at
my lodging of my coz, I shall bestow a banquet upon you.

HIP. I never can deserve this kindness,
sir. What may this lady be, whom you call
coz?   249

FLU. Faith, sir, a poor gentlewoman,
of passing good carriage; one that has
some suits in law, and lies here in an attorney's house.

HIP. Is she married?

FLU. Ha, as all your punks are, a captain's wife, or so. Never saw her before,
my lord?

HIP. Never, trust me! A goodly creature!

FLU. By gad, when you know her   [260
as we do, you'll swear she is the prettiest,
kindest, sweetest, most bewitching, honest
ape under the pole. A skin, your satin is
not more soft, nor lawn whiter.

HIP. Belike, then, she's some sale
courtesan.

FLU. Troth, as all your best faces are.
A good wench!

HIP. Great pity that she's a good
wench.   270

MAT. [*To Bellafront.*] Thou shalt
ha', i' faith, mistress.—How now, signiors?

---

[1] Hysteria.   [2] Wild plum.   [3] Paltry.   [4] Respectfully.

What, whispering? Did not I lay a wager I should take you within seven days in a house of vanity?

HIP. You did; and, I beshrew your heart, you have won.

MAT. How do you like my mistress?

HIP. Well, for such a mistress; better, if your mistress be not your mas- [280 ter.—I must break manners, gentlemen; fare you well.

MAT. 'Sfoot, you shall not leave us.

BELL. The gentleman likes not the taste of our company.

OMNES. Beseech you, stay.

HIP. Trust me, my affairs beckon for me; pardon me.

MAT. Will you call for me half an hour hence here?　　　　　　　　　　290

HIP. Perhaps I shall.

MAT. Perhaps? Faugh! I know you can swear to me you will.

HIP. Since you will press me, on my word, I will.　　　　　　　　　　*Exit.*

BELL. What sullen picture is this, servant?

MAT. It's Count Hippolito, the brave count.

PIO. As gallant a spirit as any in [300 Milan, you sweet Jew.[1]

FLU. O, he's a most essential gentleman, coz!

CAS. Did you never hear of Count Hippolito, acquaintance?

BELL. Marry muff a your counts, and be no more life in 'em!

MAT. He's so malcontent, sirrah Bellafronta.—And you be honest gallants, let's sup together and have the count [310 with us.—Thou shalt sit at the upper end, punk.

BELL. Punk, you soused gurnet?[2]

MAT. King's truce! Come, I'll bestow the supper to have him but laugh.

CAS. He betrays his youth too grossly to that tyrant melancholy.

MAT. All this is for a woman.

BELL. A woman? Some whore! What sweet jewel is 't?　　　　　　　320

PIO. Would she heard you!

FLU. Troth, so would I.

CAS. And I, by heaven.

BELL. Nay, good servant, what woman?

MAT. Pah!

BELL. Prithee, tell me; a buss,[3] and tell me. I warrant he's an honest fellow, if he take on thus for a wench. Good rogue, who?

MAT. By th' Lord, I will not, must not, faith, mistress. Is 't a match, sirs? [330 This night, at th' Antelope. Ay, for there's best wine, and good boys.

OMNES. It's done; at th' Antelope.

BELL. I cannot be there tonight.

MAT. Cannot? By th' Lord, you shall.

BELL. By the Lady, I will not. Shall!

FLU. Why, then, put it off till Friday; woot[4] come then, coz?

BELL. Well.

Enter Roger.

MAT. Y'are the waspishest ape. [340 Roger, put your mistress in mind to sup with us on Friday next. Y'are best come like a madwoman, without a band, in your waistcoat,[5] and the linings of your kirtle outward, like every common hackney[6] that steals out at the back gate of her sweet knight's lodging.

BELL. Go, go, hang yourself!

CAS. It's dinner time, Matheo. Shall 's hence?　　　　　　　　　　350

OMNES. Yes, yes.—Farewell, wench.

Exeunt [all but Bellafront and Roger].

BELL. Farewell, boys.—Roger, what wine sent they for?

ROG. Bastard wine,[7] for, if it had been truly begotten, it would not ha' been ashamed to come in. Here's six shillings to pay for nursing the bastard.

BELL. A company of rooks![8] O good sweet Roger, run to the poulter' s, and buy me some fine larks!　　　　　　360

ROG. No woodcocks?

BELL. Yes, faith, a couple, if they be not dear.

ROG. I'll buy but one; there's one[9] already here.　　　　　　　　　　*Exit.*

Enter Hippolito.

HIP. Is the gentleman, my friend, departed, mistress?

BELL. His back is but new turned, sir.

HIP. Fare you well.

BELL. I can direct you to him.

[1] Term of endearment.　　　[2] Pickled fish.

[3] Kiss.　　　　　　　　　[4] Wilt thou.
[5] I.e., without your upper dress.　[6] Harlot.
[7] Sweet Spanish wine.　　　[8] Simpletons.
[9] I.e., Hippolito, with a play on *woodcock* as simpleton.

HIP.   Can you, pray?

BELL. If you please stay, he'll not be absent long.

HIP. I care not much.

BELL.   Pray sit, forsooth.

HIP.   I'm hot.
If I may use your room, I'll rather
    walk.

BELL. At your best pleasure.—Whew!
    Some rubbers [1] there!   370

HIP. Indeed, I'll none—indeed I will not;
    thanks.
    Pretty fine lodging. I perceive my
       friend
    Is old in your acquaintance.

BELL.   Troth, sir, he comes,
As other gentlemen, to spend spare
    hours.
If yourself like our roof, such as it is,
Your own acquaintance may be as old
    as his.

HIP. Say I did like, what welcome should
    I find?

BELL. Such as my present fortunes can
    afford.

HIP. But would you let me play Matheo's
    part?

BELL. What part?

HIP.   Why, embrace you,
    dally with you, kiss.   380
Faith, tell me, will you leave him and
    love me?

BELL. I am in bonds to no man, sir.

HIP.   Why then,
Y'are free for any man; if any, me.
But I must tell you, lady, were you
    mine,
You should be all mine. I could brook
    no sharers;
I should be covetous, and sweep up all.
I should be pleasure's usurer; faith, I
    should.

BELL. O fate!

HIP.   Why sigh you, lady? May
    I know?

BELL. 'T has never been my fortune yet
    to single
Out that one man whose love could fellow mine,   390
As I have ever wished it. O my stars!
Had I but met with one kind gentleman,
That would have purchased sin alone
    to himself,

[1] Towels.

For his own private use, although scarce
    proper [2]—
Indifferent handsome, meetly legged
    and thighed—
And my allowance reasonable, i' faith,
According to my body, by my troth,
I would have been as true unto his
    pleasures,
Yea, and as loyal to his afternoons,   399
As ever a poor gentlewoman could be.

HIP. This were well now to one but newly
    fledged,
And scarce a day old in this subtle
    world;
'Twere pretty art, good birdlime, cunning net.
But come, come, faith, confess. How
    many men
Have drunk this selfsame protestation,
From that red ticing [3] lip?

BELL.   Indeed, not any.

HIP. "Indeed," and blush not!

BELL.   No, in truth, not any.

HIP. "Indeed!" "In truth!"—how warily you swear!
'Tis well, if ill it be not; yet had I
The ruffian in me, and were drawn before you   410
But in light colors, I do know indeed
You could not swear "Indeed," but
    thunder oaths
That should shake heaven, drown the
    harmonious spheres,
And pierce a soul that loved her Maker's
    honor
With horror and amazement.

BELL.   Shall I swear?
Will you believe me then?

HIP.   Worst then of all;
Our sins by custom seem at last but
    small.
Were I but o'er your threshold, a next
    man,
And after him a next, and then a fourth,
Should have this golden hook and lascivious bait   420
Thrown out to the full length. Why,
    let me tell you,
I ha' seen letters sent from that white
    hand,
Tuning such music to Matheo's ear.

BELL. Matheo! That's true, but, believe
    it, I

[2] Fine-looking.   [3] Enticing.

No sooner had laid hold upon your presence,
But straight mine eye conveyed you to
my heart.

HIP. O, you cannot feign with me! Why,
I know, lady,
This is the common passion of you all,
To hook in a kind gentleman, and then
Abuse his coin, conveying it to your
lover,   430
And in the end you show him a French
trick,
And so you leave him, that a coach may
run
Between his legs for breadth.

BELL.   O, by my soul,
Not I! Therein I'll prove an honest
whore,
In being true to one, and to no more.

HIP. If any be disposed to trust your oath,
Let him; I'll not be he. I know you
feign
All that you speak; ay, for a mingled
harlot
Is true in nothing but in being false.
What! shall I teach you how to loathe
yourself?   440
And mildly too, not without sense or
reason?

BELL. I am content; I would feign loathe
myself
If you not love me.

HIP.   Then, if your gracious blood
Be not all wasted, I shall assay to do 't.
Lend me your silence and attention.
You have no soul;
That makes you weigh so light. Heaven's
treasure bought it,
And half a crown hath sold it. For your
body
Is like the common shore, that still re-
ceives
All the town's filth. The sin of many
men
Is within you; and thus much I sup-
pose   450
That, if all your committers stood in
rank,
They'd make a lane in which your
shame might dwell,
And with their spaces reach from hence
to hell.
Nay, shall I urge it more? There has
been known

As many by one harlot maimed and
dismembered
As would ha' stuffed an hospital. This
I might
Apply to you, and perhaps do you right.
O, y'are as base as any beast that bears;
Your body is e'en hired, and so are
theirs.
For gold and sparkling jewels, if he
can,   460
You'll let a Jew get you with Christian—
Be he a Moor, a Tartar, though his
face
Look uglier than a dead man's skull.
Could the devil put on a human shape,
If his purse shake out crowns, up then
he gets;
Whores will be rid to hell with golden
bits.
So that y'are crueler than Turks, for
they
Sell Christians only; you sell yourselves
away.
Why, those that love you, hate you, and
will term you
Lickerish [1] damnation; wish themselves
half-sunk   470
After the sin is laid out, and e'en curse
Their fruitless riot (for what one begets
Another poisons); lust and murder hit.
A tree being often shook, what fruit
can knit?

BELL. O me unhappy!

HIP.   I can vex you more.
A harlot is like Dunkirk, true to none,
Swallows both English, Spanish, ful-
some Dutch,
Back-doored [2] Italian, last of all, the
French,
And he sticks to you, faith, gives you
your diet,
Brings you acquainted, first, with Mon-
sieur Doctor,   480
And then you know what follows.

BELL.   Misery!
Rank, stinking, and most loathsome
misery!

HIP. Methinks a toad is happier than a
whore.
That, with one poison, swells; with
thousands more
The other stocks her veins. Harlot?
Fie, fie!

[1] Lascivious.   [2] Sneaking.

You are the miserablest creatures breathing,
The very slaves of nature. Mark me
else.
You put on rich attires—others' eyes
wear them;
You eat, but to supply your blood with
sin.
And this strange curse e'en haunts you
to your graves.   490
From fools you get, and spend it upon
slaves.
Like bears and apes, y'are baited and
show tricks
For money; but your bawd the sweet-
ness licks.
Indeed, you are their journeywomen,
and do
All base and damned works they list
set you to,
So that you ne'er are rich; for do but
show me,
In present memory or in ages past,
The fairest and most famous courtesan,
Whose flesh was dear'st; that raised the
price of sin,
And held it up; to whose intemperate
bosom,   500
Princes, earls, lords, the worst has been
a knight,
The mean'st a gentleman, have offered
up
Whole hecatombs of sighs, and rained
in showers
Handfuls of gold; yet, for all this, at
last
Diseases sucked her marrow, then grew
so poor
That she has begged e'en at a beggar's
door.
And (wherein heaven has a finger) when
this idol,
From coast to coast, has leaped on foreign shores,
And had more worship than the outlandish whores;
When several nations have gone over
her;   510
When, for each several city she has
seen,
Her maidenhead has been new, and been
sold dear;
Did live well there, and might have
died unknown

And undefamed—back comes she to
her own,
And there both miserably lives and
dies,
Scorned even of those that once adored
her eyes,
As if her fatal, circled life thus ran:
Her pride should end there where it
first began.
What, do you weep to hear your story
read?
Nay, if you spoil your cheeks, I'll read
no more.   520
BELL. O yes, I pray, proceed.
Indeed, 'twill do me good to weep, in-
deed.
HIP. To give those tears a relish, this I
add—
Y'are like the Jews, scattered, in no
place certain;
Your days are tedious, your hours bur-
densome;
And, were 't not for full suppers, mid-
night revels,
Dancing, wine, riotous meetings, which
do drown
And bury quite in you all virtuous
thoughts,
And on your eyelids hang so heavily
They have no power to look so high as
heaven,   530
You'd sit and muse on nothing but
despair,
Curse that devil Lust, that so burns up
your blood,
And in ten thousand shivers break your
glass
For his temptation. Say you taste de-
light,
To have a golden gull from rise to set,
To mete [1] you in his hot, luxurious [2]
arms,
Yet your nights pay for all. I know you
dream
Of warrants, whips, and beadles, and
then start
At a door's windy creak; think every
weasel
To be a constable, and every rat   540
A long-tailed officer. Are you now not
slaves?
O, you have damnation without pleas-
ure for it!

[1] Measure, embrace.   [2] Lecherous.

Such is the state of harlots. To conclude:
When you are old and can well paint
   no more,
You turn bawd, and are then worse
   than before.
Make use of this. Farewell.

BELL.   O, I pray, stay.

HIP. I see Matheo comes not; time hath
   barred me.
Would all the harlots in the town had
   heard me.   *Exit.*

BELL. Stay yet a little longer! No?
Quite gone!
Cursed be that minute—for it was no
   more,   550
So soon a maid is changed into a whore—
Wherein I first fell! Be it forever black!
Yet why should sweet Hippolito shun
   mine eyes,
For whose true love I would become
   pure-honest,
Hate the world's mixtures, and the
   smiles of gold?
Am I not fair? Why should he fly me
   then?
Fair creatures are desired, not scorned
   of men.
How many gallants have drunk healths
   to me,
Out of their daggered arms, and thought
   them blessed,
Enjoying but mine eyes at prodigal
   feasts!   560
And does Hippolito detest my love?
O, sure their heedless lusts but flattered
   me;
I am not pleasing, beautiful, nor young.
Hippolito hath spied some ugly blemish,
Eclipsing all my beauties. I am foul.
Harlot! Ay, that's the spot that taints
   my soul.
His weapon left here? O fit instrument
To let forth all the poison of my flesh!
Thy master hates me, cause my blood
   hath ranged;
But, when 'tis forth, then he'll believe
   I'm changed.   570

[*As she prepares to stab herself,*] *enter*
                   Hipp[*olito*].

HIP. Mad woman, what art doing?

BELL.   Either love me,
Or cleave my bosom on thy rapier's
   point.

Yet do not neither; for thou then de-
   stroy'st
That which I love thee for—thy virtues.
   Here, here;
            [*Gives sword to Hippolito.*]
Th' art crueler, and kill'st me with dis-
   dain.
To die so, sheds no blood, yet 'tis worse
   pain.   *Exit Hipp*[*olito*].
Not speak to me? Not look? Not bid
   farewell?
Hated! This must not be; some means
   I'll try.
Would all whores were as honest now as
   I!   *Exit.*[1]

SCENA vii.

Enter Candido, his Wife, George, and two
   Prentices in the shop. Fustigo enters,
                    walking by.

GEO. See, gentlemen, what you lack—
a fine holland, a fine cambric! See what you
buy.

1 PREN. Holland for shirts, cambric for
bands! What is 't you lack?

FUS. [*Aside.*] 'Sfoot, I lack 'em all; nay,
more, I lack money to buy 'em. Let me
see, let me look again. Mass, this is the
shop.—What, coz! Sweet coz! How dost,
i' faith, since last night after candle- [10
light? We had good sport, i' faith, had we
not? And when shall 's laugh again?

WIFE. When you will, cousin.

FUS. Spoke like a kind Lacedemonian.
I see yonder's thy husband.

WIFE. Ay, there's the sweet youth, God
bless him!

FUS. And how is 't, cousin? And how,
how is 't, thou squall?[2]

WIFE. Well, cousin. How fare you? [20

FUS. How fare I? Troth, for sixpence a
meal, wench, as well as heart can wish, with
calves' chaldrons[3] and chitterlings;[4] besides, I have a punk after supper, as good
as a roasted apple.

CAND. Are you my wife's cousin?

FUS. I am, sir. What hast thou to do
with that?

CAND. O, nothing, but y'are welcome.

FUS. The devil's dung in thy teeth! [30

---

[1] Original reads *Exeunt.*   [3] Edible entrails.
[2] Minx.   [4] Tripe.

I'll be welcome whether thou wilt or no,
I.—What ring's this, coz? Very pretty and
fantastical, i' faith! Let's see it.

WIFE. Pooh! Nay, you wrench my
finger.

FUS. I ha' sworn I'll ha't, and I hope you
will not let my oaths be cracked in the
ring,[1] will you? [*Seizes the ring.*] I hope, sir,
you are not malicolly [2] at this, for all your
great looks. Are you angry?   40

CAND. Angry? Not I, sir; nay, if she
can part
So easily with her ring, 'tis with my
heart.

GEO. Suffer this, sir, and suffer all. A
whoreson [3] gull, to—

CAND. Peace, George! When she has
reaped what I have sown,
She'll say one grain tastes better of her
own
Than whole sheaves gathered from another's land.
Wit's never good till bought at a dear
hand.[4]

GEO. But in the meantime she makes an
ass of somebody.   50

2 PREN. See, see, see, sir; as you turn
your back, they do nothing but kiss.

CAND. No matter; let 'em. When I touch
her lip,
I shall not feel his kisses, no, nor miss
Any of her lip; no harm in kissing is.
Look to your business, pray; make up
your wares.

FUS. Troth, coz, and well remembered.
I would thou wouldst give me five yards of
lawn, to make my punk some falling bands
a the fashion—three falling one upon [60
another, for that's the new edition [5] now.
She's out of linen horribly, too; troth,
sh'as never a good smock to her back
neither, but one that has a great many
patches in 't, and that I'm fain to wear
myself for want of shift, too. Prithee, put
me into wholesome napery, and bestow
some clean commodities upon us.

WIFE. Reach me those cambrics, and the
lawns hither.   70

CAND. What to do, wife? To lavish out
my goods upon a fool?

FUS. Fool? 'Snails, eat the "fool," or

I'll so batter your crown that it shall
scarce go for five shillings.

2 PREN. Do you hear, sir? Y'are best
be quiet, and say a fool tells you so.

FUS. Nails, I think so, for thou tell'st
me.

CAND. Are you angry, sir, because I
named thee fool?   80
Trust me, you are not wise in my own
house
And to my face to play the antic [6] thus.
If you'll needs play the madman, choose
a stage
Of lesser compass, where few eyes may
note
Your action's error; but, if still you miss,
As here you do, for one clap, ten will
hiss.

FUS. 'Swounds, cousin, he talks to me
as if I were a scurvy tragedian.

2 PREN. [*Aside.*] Sirrah George, I ha'
thought upon a device how to break [90
his pate, beat him soundly, and ship him
away.

GEO. [*Aside.*] Do 't.

2 PREN. [*Aside.*] I'll go in, pass through
the house, give some of our fellow prentices
the watchword when they shall enter, then
come and fetch my master in by a wile, and
place one in the hall to hold him in conference, whilst we cudgel the gull out of his
coxcomb.   100

GEO. [*Aside.*] Do 't; away, do 't.
[*Exit 2 Prentice.*]

WIFE. Must I call twice for these cambrics and lawns?

CAND. Nay, see, you anger her, George:
prithee despatch.

1 PREN. Two of the choicest pieces are
in the warehouse, sir.

CAND. Go fetch them presently.
Exit 1 Prentice.

FUS. Ay, do, make haste, sirrah.

CAND. Why were you such a stran- [110
ger all this while, being my wife's cousin?

FUS. Stranger? No, sir, I'm a natural
Milaner born.

CAND. I perceive still it is your natural
guise to mistake me, but you are welcome,
sir; I much wish your acquaintance.

FUS. My acquaintance? I scorn that,
i' faith; I hope my acquaintance goes in
chains of gold three-and-fifty times double.

---

[1] Invalid, like a damaged coin.
[2] Corruption of *melancholy.*   [4] High price.
[3] Rascally.   [5] Kind, fashion.
[6] Buffoon.

You know who I mean, coz; the posts of
his gate are a-painting too.[1]   121

Enter the 2 Prentice.

2 PREN. Signior Pandulfo, the mer-
chant, desires conference with you.
CAND. Signior Pandulfo? I'll be with him
    straight.
Attend your mistress and the gentleman.
                                        Exit.
WIFE. When do you show those pieces?
FUS. Ay, when do you show those
pieces?
OMNES. [*Within.*] Presently, sir, pres-
ently; we are but charging them.   130
FUS. Come, sirrah. You flatcap,[2] where
be these whites?

[*Enter 1 Prentice with cloth.*]

GEO. [*Whispering.*] Flatcap? Hark in
your ear, sir; y'are a flat fool, an ass, a gull,
and I'll thrum[3] you.—Do you see this
cambric, sir?
FUS. 'Sfoot, coz, a good jest! Did you
hear him? He told me in my ear, I was a
"flat fool, an ass, a gull, and I'll thrum
you.—Do you see this cambric, sir?"   140
WIFE. What, not my men, I hope?
FUS. No, not your men, but one of your
men, i' faith.
1 PREN. I pray, sir, come hither. What
say you to this? Here's an excellent good
one.
FUS. Ay, marry, this likes[4] me well.
Cut me off some half-score yards.
2 PREN. [*Whispering.*] Let your whores
cut. Y'are an impudent coxcomb. [150
You get none, and yet I'll thrum you.—A
very good cambric, sir.
FUS. Again, again, as God judge me!
'Sfoot, coz, they stand thrumming here
with me all day, and yet I get nothing.
2 PREN. [*Whispering.*] A word, I pray,
sir; you must not be angry. Prentices have
hot bloods, young fellows.—What say you
to this piece? Look you, 'tis so delicate,
so soft, so even, so fine a thread, that [160
a lady may wear it.
FUS. 'Sfoot, I think so. If a knight

marry my punk, a lady shall wear it. Cut
me off twenty yards. Th'art an honest lad.
1 PREN. Not without money, gull, and
I'll thrum you too.
OMNES. Gull, we'll thrum you!
FUS. O Lord, sister, did you not hear
something cry "thump"? Zounds, your
men here make a plain ass of me.   170
WIFE. What, to my face so impudent?
GEO. Ay, in a cause so honest, we'll not
    suffer
Our master's goods to vanish moneyless.
WIFE. You will not suffer them?
2 PREN.   No, and you may blush
In going about to vex so mild a breast
As is our master's.
WIFE.   Take away those pieces!
Cousin, I give them freely.
FUS. Mass, and I'll take 'em as freely.
                    [*Other Prentices rush in.*]
OMNES. We'll make you lay 'em down
    again more freely.
            [*They attack Fustigo with their clubs.*]
WIFE. Help, help! My brother will be
    murderéd.   180

Enter Can[dido].

CAND. How now, what coil is here? For-
    bear, I say.
[*Exeunt all the Prentices except the 1 and 2.*]
GEO. He calls us flatcaps, and abuses
    us.
CAND. Why, sirs, do such examples flow
    from me?
WIFE. They are of your keeping, sir. Alas,
    poor brother!
FUS. I' faith, they ha' peppered me,
sister. Look, dost not spin? Call you these
prentices? I'll ne'er play at cards more
when clubs is trump. I have a goodly
coxcomb, sister, have I not?
CAND. Sister and brother? Brother [190
to my wife?
FUS. If you have any skill in heraldry,
you may soon know that; break but her
pate, and you shall see her blood and
mine is all one.
CAND. A surgeon! Run, a surgeon!
[*Exit 1 Prentice.*] Why then wore you that
forged name of cousin?
FUS. Because it's a common thing to
call coz and ningle[5] nowadays all the [200
world over.

---

[1] In reference to the painting of the sheriff's
gateposts for displaying proclamations.
[2] Derisive name for apprentice.
[3] Beat.   [4] Pleases.
[5] Mine ingle, my intimate.

CAND. Cousin! A name of much deceit,
    folly, and sin,
For under that common abuséd word
Many an honest-tempered citizen
Is made a monster, and his wife trained
    out
To foul adulterous action, full of fraud.
I may well call that word a city's bawd.
FUS. Troth, brother, my sister would
needs ha' me take upon me to gull your
patience a little; but it has made [210
double gules ¹ on my coxcomb.
WIFE. What, playing the woman? Blab-
bing now, you fool?
CAND. O, my wife did but exercise a jest
upon your wit.
FUS. 'Sfoot, my wit bleeds for 't, me-
thinks.
CAND. Then let this warning more of sense
    afford;
The name of cousin is a bloody word.
FUS. I'll ne'er call coz again whilst [220
I live, to have such a coil about it. This
should be a coronation day, for my head
runs claret lustily.   *Exit.*

Enter an Officer.

CAND. Go, wish the surgeon to have great
    respect—   *Exit 2 Prentice.*
  How now, my friend? What, do they sit
  today?
OFF. Yes, sir, they expect you at the senate
  house.
CAND. I thank your pains; I'll not be last
  man there.—   *Exit Offi[cer].*
My gown, George, go, my gown.—A
  happy land,
Where grave men meet each cause to
  understand;
Whose consciences are not cut out in
  bribes   230
To gull the poor man's right; but in even
  scales,
Peise ² rich and poor, without corrup-
  tion's vails.³
Come, where's the gown?
GEO.   I cannot find the key, sir.
CAND. Request it of your mistress.
WIFE. Come not to me for any key;
  I'll not be troubled to deliver it.
CAND. Good wife, kind wife, it is a need-
  ful trouble,
  But for my gown!

WIFE.   Moths swallow down your gown!
  You set my teeth on edge with talking
  on 't.
CAND. Nay, prithee, sweet, I cannot meet
  without it.   240
  I should have a great fine set on my
  head.
WIFE. Set on your coxcomb; tush, fine
  me no fines.
CAND. Believe me, sweet, none greets the
  senate house
  Without his robe of reverence—that's his
  gown.
WIFE. Well, then, y'are like to cross that
  custom once;
  You get nor key nor gown. And so
  depart.—
  [*Aside.*] This trick will vex him sure, and
  fret his heart.   *Exit.*
CAND. Stay, let me see; I must have some
  device.
My cloak's too short; fie, fie, no cloak
  will do 't.
It must be something fashioned like a
  gown,   250
With my arms out. O, George, come
  hither, George!
I prithee, lend me thine advice.
GEO. Troth, sir, were it any but you,
they would break open chest.
CAND. O, no! Break open chest! That's a
  thieves' office.
Therein you counsel me against my
  blood;
'Twould show impatience, that. Any
  meek means
I would be glad to embrace. Mass, I have
  got it.
Go, step up, fetch me down one of the
  carpets,⁴
The saddest ⁵-colored carpet, honest
  George;   260
Cut thou a hole i' th' middle for my
  neck,
Two for mine arms. Nay, prithee, look
  not strange.
GEO. I hope you do not think, sir, as you
  mean.
CAND. Prithee, about it quickly; the hour
  chides me.
Warily, George, softly, take heed of eyes.
                    Exit George.
Out of two evils he's accounted wise

¹ Heraldic term for red.   ² Weigh.   ³ Bribes, tips.   ⁴ Table covers.   ⁵ Quietest.

That can pick out the least. The fine
  imposed
For an ungownéd senator is about
Forty crusadoes,[1] the carpet not 'bove
  four.
Thus have I chosen the lesser evil yet,
Preserved my patience, foiled her desper-
  ate wit.   271

Enter George.

GEO. Here, sir, here's the carpet.
CAND. O, well done, George; we'll cut it
  just i' th' midst. [*They cut the carpet.*]
'Tis very well; I thank thee. Help it on.
  GEO. It must come over your head, sir,
like a wench's petticoat.
CAND. Th'art in the right, good George; it
  must indeed.
Fetch me a nightcap, for I'll gird it close,
As if my health were queasy. 'Twill show
  well
For a rude, careless nightgown,[2] will 't
  not, think'st?   280
GEO. Indifferent well, sir, for a night-
gown, being girt and pleated.
CAND. Ay, and a nightcap on my head.
GEO. That's true, sir; I'll run and fetch
one, and a staff.   *Ex[it] Ge[orge].*
CAND. For thus they cannot choose but
  conster[3] it:
One that is out of health takes no delight,
Wears his apparel without appetite,
And puts on heedless raiment without
  form.—

Enter Geo[rge with nightcap and staff].

So, so, kind George. [*Puts on nightcap.*]
  Be secret now; and, prithee,   290
Do not laugh at me till I'm out of
  sight.
GEO. I laugh? Not I, sir.
CAND.   Now to the senate house.
Methinks I'd rather wear, without a
  frown,
A patient carpet than an angry gown.
                        Exit.
GEO. Now looks my m[aster] just like
one of our carpet knights,[4] only he's some-
what the honester of the two.

---

[1] Portuguese coins.
[2] Dressing gown.   [3] Construe.
[4] A contemptuous term for a knight whose
achievements belong rather to the carpet (the
lady's boudoir) than to the field of battle.

Enter Candido's Wife.

WIFE. What, is your master gone?
GEO. Yes, forsooth, his back is but new
  turned.
WIFE. And in his cloak? Did he not vex
  and swear?   300
GEO. [*Aside.*] No, but he'll make you
swear anon.—No, indeed, he went away
like a lamb.
WIFE. Key, sink to hell! Still patient,
  patient still?
I am with child[5] to vex him. Prithee,
  George,
If e'er thou look'st for favor at my
  hands,
Uphold one jest for me.
GEO.   Against my master?
WIFE. 'Tis a mere jest, in faith. Say, wilt
  thou do 't?
GEO. Well, what is 't?
WIFE. Here, take this key; thou know'st
  where all things lie.   310
Put on thy master's best apparel—gown,
Chain, cap, ruff, everything. Be like
  himself,
And, gainst his coming home, walk in the
  shop;
Feign the same carriage and his patient
  look.
'Twill breed but a jest, thou know'st.
  Speak, wilt thou?
GEO. 'Twill wrong my master's patience.
WIFE.   Prithee, George.
GEO. Well, if you'll save me harmless,
and put me under covert-barn,[6] I am con-
tent to please you, provided it may breed
no wrong against him.   320
WIFE. No wrong at all. Here, take the
  key; begone.
If any vex him, this; if not this, none.
                       Exeunt.

SCENA viii.

[*A room in Bellafront's house.*]

Enter a Bawd and Roger.

BAWD. O Roger, Roger, where's your
mistress, where's your mistress? There's
the finest, neatest gentleman at my house,
but newly come over. O, where is she,
where is she, where is she?

---

[5] Filled with longing.
[6] Covert-baron, *i.e.*, under protection.

Rog. My mistress is abroad, but not amongst 'em. My mistress is not the whore now that you take her for.

Bawd. How? Is she not a whore? Do you go about to take away her good [10 name, Roger? You are a fine pander indeed.

Rog. I tell you, Madonna Fingerlock, I am not sad for nothing; I ha' not eaten one good meal this three-and-thirty days. I had wont to get sixteenpence by fetching a pottle of hippocras, but now those days are past. We had as good doings, Madonna Fingerlock, she within doors, and I without, as any poor young couple [20 in Milan.

Bawd. God's my life, and is she changed now?

Rog. I ha' lost by her squeamishness more than would have builded twelve bawdyhouses.

Bawd. And had she no time to turn honest but now? What a vile woman is this! Twenty pound a night, I'll be sworn, Roger, in good gold and no silver. Why, [30 here was a time! If she should ha' picked out a time, it could not be better—gold enough stirring, choice of men, choice of hair, choice of beards, choice of legs, and choice of every, every, everything. It cannot sink into my head that she should be such an ass. Roger, I never believe it.

Rog. Here she comes now.

Enter Bellafront.

Bawd. O sweet madonna, on with your loose gown, your felt,[1] and your feather. [40 There's the sweetest, prop'rest, gallantest gentleman at my house; he smells all of musk and ambergris, his pocket full of crowns, flame-colored doublet, red satin hose, carnation silk stockings, and a leg, and a body—O!

Bell. Hence, thou, our sex's monster, poisonous bawd,
Lust's factor,[2] and damnation's orator!
Gossip of hell! Were all the harlots' sins
Which the whole world contains, num- bered together, 50
Thine far exceeds them all; of all the creatures
That ever were created, thou art basest.

What serpent would beguile thee of thy office?
It is destestable, for thou liv'st
Upon the dregs of harlots, guard'st the door
Whilst couples go to dancing. O coarse devil!
Thou art the bastard's curse—thou brand'st his birth;
The lecher's French disease, for thou dry- suck'st him;
The harlot's poison, and thine own con- fusion.

Bawd. Marry come up, with a pox! [60 Have you nobody to rail against but your bawd now?

Bell. And you, knave pander, kinsman to a bawd!

Rog. You and I, madonna, are cousins.

Bell. Of the same blood and making, near allied.
Thou, that slave to sixpence, base- metaled villain!

Rog. Sixpence? Nay, that's not so. I never took under two shillings fourpence; I hope I know my fee.

Bell. I know not against which most to inveigh, 70
For both of you are damned so equally.
Thou never spar'st for oaths, swear'st anything,
As if thy soul were made of shoe leather:
"God damn me, gentlemen, if she be within!"—
When in the next room she's found dallying.

Rog. If it be my vocation to swear, every man in his vocation. I hope my betters swear and damn themselves, and why should not I?

Bell. Roger, you cheat kind gentle- [80 men.

Rog. The more gulls they.

Bell. Slave, I cashier thee.

Bawd. And you do cashier him, he shall be entertained.

Rog. Shall I? Then blurt a[3] your service!

Bell. As hell would have it, entertained by you! I dare the devil himself to match those two. *Exit.* 90

Bawd. Marry gup,[4] are you grown so holy, so pure, so honest, with a pox?

---

[1] Hat.   [2] Agent.   [3] On.   [4] Go up, get along!

Rog. Scurvy, honest punk! But stay,
madonna, how must our agreement be
now? For you know I am to have all the
comings-in at the hall door, and you at
the chamber door.

Bawd. True, Roger, except my vails.

Rog. Vails? What vails?

Bawd. Why, as thus: if a couple [100
come in a coach, and light to lie down a
little, then, Roger, that's my fee, and you
may walk abroad, for the coachman himself is their pander.

Rog. Is a [1] so? In truth, I have almost forgot for want of exercise. But how
if I fetch this citizen's wife to that gull,
and that madonna to that gallant, how
then?

Bawd. Why then, Roger, you are [110
to have sixpence a lain; [2] so many lains,
so many sixpences.

Rog. Is 't so? Then I see we two shall
agree, and live together.

Bawd. Ay, Roger, so long as there be
any taverns and bawdyhouses in Milan.

Exeunt.

Scena ix.

[*Another room in Bellafront's house.*]

*Enter Bellafront with lute, pen, ink, and
paper being placed before her.*

Song

[Bell.] The courtier's flattering jewels,
    Temptation's only fuels;
The lawyer's ill-got moneys,
    That suck up poor bees' honeys;
The citizen's son's riot,
    The gallant, costly diet;
Silks and velvets, pearls and ambers—
Shall not draw me to their chambers.
    Silks and velvets, etc.

She writes.

O, 'tis in vain to write! It will not
    please.   10
Ink on this paper would ha' but presented
The foul black spots that stick upon my
    soul,
And rather make me loathsomer than
    wrought
My love's impression in Hippolito's
    thought.

[1] He.   [2] Lying down (?).

No, I must turn the chaste leaves of
    my breast,
And pick out some sweet means to breed
    my rest.
Hippolito, believe me, I will be
As true unto thy heart as thy heart to
    thee,
And hate all men, their gifts and com-
    pany!

Enter Matheo, Castruchio, Fluello, Pioratto.

Mat. You, goody punk—*subaudi*,[3] [20
cockatrice—O, y'are a sweet whore of
your promise, are you not, think you? How
well you came to supper to us last night!
Mew, a whore, and break her word! Nay,
you may blush, and hold down your head
at it well enough. 'Sfoot, ask these gallants if we stayed not till we were as
hungry as serjeants.[4]

Flu. Ay, and their yeomen [5] too.

Cas. Nay, faith, acquaintance, let [30
me tell you, you forgat yourself too much.
We had excellent cheer, rare vintage, and
were drunk after supper.

Pio. And, when we were in, our woodcocks, sweet rogue, a brace of gulls, dwelling
here in the city, came in, and paid all the
shot.[6]

Mat. Pox on her! Let her alone.

Bell. O, I pray do, if you be gentlemen;
I pray, depart the house. Beshrew the
    door [7]   40
For being so easily entreated! Faith,
I lent but little ear unto your talk;
My mind was busied otherwise, in troth,
And so your words did unregarded pass.
Let this suffice—I am not as I was.

Flu. I am not what I was? No, I'll
be sworn thou art not, for thou wert honest at five, and now th'art a punk at fifteen.
Thou wert yesterday a simple whore, and
now th'art a cunning, cony-catching baggage today.   51

Bell. I'll say I'm worse; I pray, forsake
    me then.
I do desire you leave me, gentlemen,
And leave yourselves. O, be not what
    you are,
Spendthrifts of soul and body!

[3] Understand.   [6] Reckoning, bill.
[4] Sheriff's officers.   [7] Doorkeeper.
[5] Assistants.

Let me persuade you to forsake all
  harlots,
Worse than the deadliest poisons—they
  are worse,
For o'er their souls hangs an eternal
  curse.
In being slaves to slaves, their labors
  perish;
Th'are seldom blessed with fruit, for,
  ere it blossoms,   60
Many a worm confounds it.
They have no issue but foul, ugly ones,
That run along with them, e'en to their
  graves;
For, stead of children, they breed rank
  diseases,
And all you gallants can bestow on them
Is that French infant, which ne'er acts,
  but speaks.
What shallow son and heir then, foolish
  gallants,
Would waste all his inheritance to purchase
A filthy, loathed disease, and pawn his
  body
To a dry evil? That usury's worst of all,
When th' int'rest will eat out the princi-
  pal.   71
MAT. [*Aside.*] 'Sfoot, she gulls 'em the
best! This is always her fashion, when
she would be rid of any company that she
cares not for, to enjoy mine alone.
FLU. What's here? Instructions, ad-
monitions, and caveats? Come out, you
scabbard of vengeance.
MAT. Fluello, spurn your hounds when
they foist[1]— you shall not spurn my punk,
I can tell you; my blood is vexed.   81
FLU. Pox a your blood! Make it a
quarrel.
MAT. Y'are a slave! Will that serve
turn?
OMNES. 'Sblood, hold, hold!
CAS. Matheo, Fluello, for shame, put up!
BELL. O, how many, thus
Moved with a little folly, have let out
Their souls in brothel houses, fell down
  and died   90
Just at their harlot's foot, as 'twere in
  pride!
FLU. Matheo, we shall meet.
MAT. Ay, ay; anywhere saving at church;
pray take heed we meet not there.

¹ Break wind silently.

FLU. Adieu, damnation!
CAS.   Cockatrice, farewell!
PIO. There's more deceit in women than in
  hell.
Exeunt [Castruchio, Fluello, and Pioratto].
MAT. Ha, ha, thou dost gull 'em so
rarely, so naturally! If I did not think
thou hadst been in earnest! Thou art a
sweet rogue for 't, i' faith.   100
BELL. Why are not you gone too, Signior
  Matheo?
I pray depart my house; you may be-
  lieve me,
In troth, I have no part of harlot in
  me.
MAT. How is this?
BELL. Indeed, I love you not, but hate
  you worse
Than any man, because you were the first
Gave money for my soul. You brake the
  ice,
Which after turned a puddle; I was led
By your temptation to be miserable.
I pray, seek out some other that will
  fall,   110
Or rather, I pray, seek out none at all.
MAT. Is 't possible to be impossible! An
honest whore! I have heard many honest
wenches turn strumpets with a wet finger,
but for a harlot to turn honest is one of
Hercules' labors. It was more easy for
him in one night to make fifty queans ²
than to make one of them honest again in
fifty years. Come, I hope thou dost but
jest.   120
BELL. 'Tis time to leave off jesting; I
  had almost
Jested away salvation. I shall love you
If you will soon forsake me.
MAT.   God be with thee!
BELL. O, tempt no more women! Shun
  their weighty curse!
Women at best are bad; make them not
  worse.
You gladly seek our sex's overthrow,
But not to raise our states. For all your
  wrongs,
Will you vouchsafe me but due recom-
  pense,
To marry with me?
MAT. How! Marry with a punk, a [130
cockatrice, a harlot? Marry, foh, I'll be
burnt thorough the nose first.

² Whores.

BELL. Why, la, these are your oaths!
  You love to undo us,
    To put heaven from us, whilst our best
      hours waste;
  You love to make us lewd, but never
    chaste.
MAT. I'll hear no more of this, this ground
  upon.
  Th'art damned for alt'ring thy religion.
                                    Exit.
BELL. Thy lust and sin speak so much.
  Go thou, my ruin,
  The first fall my soul took! By my ex-
    ample,
  I hope few maidens now will put their
    heads   140
  Under men's girdles; who least trusts is
    most wise.
  Men's oaths do cast a mist before our
    eyes.
  My best of wit, be ready! Now I go
  By some device to greet Hippolito.

SCENA X.

[An apartment in Hippolito's house.]

Enter a Servant, setting out a table, on which
  he places a skull, a picture [of Infelice],
  a book, and a taper.

SER. So, this is Monday morning, and
now must I to my huswif'ry. Would I
had been created a shoemaker, for all the
gentle craft are gentlemen every Monday
by their copy,[1] and scorn then to work one
true stitch. My master means sure to turn
me into a student, for here's my book,
here my desk, here my light, this my close
chamber, and here my punk—so that this
dull, drowsy first day of the week   [10
makes me half a priest, half a chandler, half a
painter, half a sexton, ay, and half a bawd;
for all this day my office is to do nothing but
keep the door. To prove it, look you, this
good face and yonder gentleman, so soon as
ever my back is turned, will be naught together.

Enter Hippolito.

HIP. Are all the windows shut?
SER. Close, sir, as the fist of a courtier
that hath stood [2] in three reigns.   20

---

[1] Membership certificate.
[2] Waited without advancement (?).

HIP. Thou art a faithful servant, and ob-
  serv'st
The calendar both of my solemn vows
And ceremonious sorrow. Get thee gone;
I charge thee on thy life, let not the
  sound
Of any woman's voice pierce through
  that door.
SER. If they do, my lord, I'll pierce some
  of them.
What will your lordship have to break-
  fast?
HIP. Sighs.
SER. What to dinner?
HIP. Tears.   30
SER. The one of them, my lord, will fill
you too full of wind, the other wet you too
much. What to supper?
HIP. That which now thou canst not
get me, the constancy of a woman.
SER. Indeed, that's harder to come by
than ever was Ostend.[3]
HIP. Prithee, away!
SER. I'll make away myself presently,
which few servants will do for their   [40
lords, but rather help to make them away.
Now to my doorkeeping; I hope to pick
something out of it.   *Exit.*
HIP. [*Taking up the picture.*] My In-
  felice's face, her brow, her eye,
  The dimple on her cheek! And such
    sweet skill
  Hath from the cunning workman's
    pencil flown,
  These lips look fresh and lively as her
    own,
  Seeming to move and speak. 'Las, now
    I see
  The reason why fond women love to buy
  Adulterate complexion! Here 'tis
    read: 50
  False colors last after the true be dead.
  Of all the roses grafted on her cheeks,
  Of all the graces dancing in her eyes,
  Of all the music set upon her tongue,
  Of all that was past woman's excellence,
  In her white bosom—look!—a painted
    board
  Circumscribes all. Earth can no bliss
    afford.
  Nothing of her but this? This cannot
    speak,

---

[3] Taken Sept. 8, 1604, after holding out for
more than three years.

It has no lap for me to rest upon,
No lip worth tasting; here the worms
will feed, 60
As in her coffin. Hence, then, idle art!
True love's best pictured in a truelove's
heart.
Here art thou drawn, sweet maid, till
this be dead,
So that thou liv'st twice, twice art buriéd.
Thou figure of my friend, lie there.
What's here? [*Takes up the skull.*]
Perhaps this shrewd [1] pate was mine
enemy's.
'Las, say it were! I need not fear him
now!
For all his braves,[2] his contumelious
breath,
His frowns, though dagger-pointed, all
his plot,
Though ne'er so mischievous, his Italian
pills, 70
His quarrels, and that common fence,
his law,
See, see, they're all eaten out! Here's
not left one!
How clean they're picked away to the
bare bone!
How mad are mortals, then, to rear
great names
On tops of swelling houses, or to wear out
Their fingers' ends in dirt, to scrape up
gold,
Not caring, so that sumpter horse, the
back,
Be hung with gaudy trappings! With
what coarse,
Yea, rags most beggarly, they clothe the
soul!
Yet, after all, their gayness looks thus
foul. 80
What fools are men to build a garish
tomb,
Only to save the carcass whilst it rots,
To maintain 't long in stinking, make
good carrion,
But leave no good deeds to preserve
them sound!
For good deeds keep men sweet, long
above ground.
And must all come to this? Fools, wise,
all hither?
Must all heads thus at last be laid together?

Draw me my picture then, thou grave
neat workman,
After this fashion, not like this. These
colors 89
In time, kissing but air, will be kissed off;
But here's a fellow—that which he lays
on
Till doomsday alters not complexion.
Death's the best painter then; they that
draw shapes
And live by wicked faces are but God's
apes.
They come but near the life, and there
they stay.
This fellow draws life too; his art is
fuller—
The pictures which he makes are with-
out color.

Enter his Servant.

SER. Here's a person would speak with
you, sir.
HIP. Hah! 100
SER. A parson,[3] sir, would speak with
you.
HIP. Vicar?
SER. Vicar? No, sir; h'as too good a
face to be a vicar yet; a youth, a very
youth.
HIP. What youth? Of man or woman?
Lock the doors.
SER. If it be a woman, maribones and
potato pies [4] keep me from meddling with
her, for the thing has got the breeches! [110
'Tis a male-varlet sure, my lord, for a
woman's tailor ne'er measured him.
HIP. Let him give thee his message and be
gone.
SER. He says he's Signior Matheo's
man, but I know he lies.
HIP. How dost thou know it?
SER. Cause h'as ne'er a beard. 'Tis
his boy, I think, sir, whosoe'er paid for his
nursing.
HIP. Send him and keep the door. 120
[*Exit Servant.*]
(*Reads.*) "*Fata si liceat mihi,*
Fingere arbitrio meo,
Temperem zephyro levi vela." [5]

---

[1] Accursed.   [2] Boasts.
[3] Common pronunciation of *person.*
[4] Marrow bones and potato pies were regarded
as aphrodisiacs.
[5] "If I were permitted to determine my fate
according to my wish, I should regulate my sails
by a light breeze" (Seneca, *Œdipus*, l. 882).

I'd sail, were I to choose, not in the
　ocean;
Cedars are shaken when shrubs do feel no
　bruise.

Enter Bellafront, like a Page [*, giving a letter*].

How? From Matheo?
BELL.　　　　　　　Yes, my lord.
HIP.　　　　　　　　　　　Art sick?
BELL. Not all in health, my lord.
HIP.　　　　　　　Keep off!
BELL.　　　　　　　　　　　I do.—
　[*Aside.*] Hard fate when women are com-
　pelled to woo.
HIP. This paper does speak nothing.
BELL.　　　　　　　Yes, my lord,
　Matter of life it speaks, and therefore
　　writ　　　　　　　　　　　130
　In hidden character; to me instruction
　My master gives, and, less you please to
　　stay
　Till you both meet, I can the text dis-
　　play.
HIP. Do so; read out.
BELL.　　　　　　　I am already out.[1]
　　　　　　　　[*Discloses herself.*]
　Look on my face, and read the strangest
　　story!
HIP. What, villain, ho!

Enter his Servant.

SER. Call you, my lord?
HIP. Thou slave, thou hast let in the
devil!
SER. Lord bless us, where? He's　[140
not cloven, my lord, that I can see; besides, the devil goes more like a gentleman
than a page. Good my lord, *buon coraggio.*[2]
HIP. Thou hast let in a woman in man's
shape. And thou art damned for 't.
SER. Not damned, I hope, for putting
in a woman to a lord.
HIP. Fetch me my rapier!—Do not—I
　shall kill thee!
　Purge this infected chamber of that
　　plague
　That runs upon me thus. Slave, thrust
　　her hence!　　　　　　　150
SER. Alas, my lord, I shall never be able
to thrust her hence without help. Come,
mermaid, you must to sea again.

_____
[1] *I.e.,* out of words.　　　[2] Good courage.

BELL. Hear me but speak; my words shall
　be all music;
Hear me but speak.　[*Knocking within.*]
HIP.　　　　　Another beats the door;
Tother she-devil! Look!
SER. Why, then, hell's broke loose. *Exit.*
HIP. Hence; guard the chamber! Let no
　more come on!
　One woman serves for man's damnation.
　Beshrew thee, thou dost make me violate
　The chastest and most sanctimonious
　　vow　　　　　　　　　　160
　That e'er was entered in the court of
　　heaven!
　I was, on meditation's spotless wings,
　Upon my journey thither; like a storm
　Thou beat'st my ripened cogitations
　Flat to the ground, and like a thief dost
　　stand
　To steal devotion from the holy land.
BELL. If woman were thy mother, if thy
　heart
　Be not all marble, or, if 't marble be,
　Let my tears soften it, to pity me.
　I do beseech thee, do not thus with
　　scorn　　　　　　　　　　170
　Destroy a woman!
HIP.　　　　　Woman, I beseech thee,
　Get thee some other suit; this fits thee
　　not.
　I would not grant it to a kneeling queen;
　I cannot love thee, nor I must not. See
　　　　　　[*Points to Infelice's picture.*]
　The copy of that obligation,
　Where my soul's bound in heavy pen-
　　alties.
BELL. She's dead, you told me; she'll let
　fall her suit.
HIP. My vows to her fled after her to
　heaven.
　Were thine eyes clear as mine, thou
　　mightst behold her,　　　179
　Watching upon yon battlements of stars.
　How I observe them! Should I break
　　my bond,
　This board would rive in twain, these
　　wooden lips
　Call me most perjured villain. Let it
　　suffice,
　I ha' set thee in the path; is't not a sign
　I love thee, when with one so most most
　　dear
　I'll have thee fellows? All are fellows
　　there.

BELL. Be greater than a king; save not a
   body,
But from eternal shipwrack keep a
   soul.
If not, and that again sin's path I tread,
The grief be mine, the guilt fall on thy
   head!   190

HIP. Stay, and take physic for it. Read
   this book;
Ask counsel of this head what's to be
   done.
He'll strike it dead [1] that 'tis damnation
If you turn Turk again. O, do it not!
Though heaven cannot allure you to do
   well,
From doing ill let hell fright you; and
   learn this:
The soul whose bosom lust did never
   touch
Is God's fair bride, and maidens' souls
   are such;
The soul that, leaving chastity's white
   shore,
Swims in hot sensual streams, is the
   devil's whore.—   200
How now, who comes?

Enter his Servant [with a letter].

SER. No more knaves, my lord, that
wear smocks! Here's a letter from Doctor
Benedict. I would not enter his man,
though he had hairs at his mouth, for fear
he should be a woman, for some women
have beards; marry, they are half witches.
'Slid, you are a sweet youth to wear a
codpiece, and have no pins to stick upon 't.

HIP. I'll meet the doctor, tell him; yet
   tonight   210
I cannot; but at morrow rising sun
I will not fail.—Go, woman; fare thee
   well.
      Exeunt [Hippolito and Servant].

BELL. The lowest fall can be but into hell.
It does not move him. I must therefore
   fly
From this undoing city, and with
   tears
Wash off all anger from my father's
   brow.
He cannot sure but joy, seeing me new
   born.
A woman honest first, and then turn
   whore,

[1] *I.e.*, state flatly.

Is, as with me, common to thousands
   more;
But from a strumpet to turn chaste, that
   sound   220
Has oft been heard, that woman hardly
   found.   *Exit.*

SCENA xi.[2]

[*A street near Candido's shop.*]

Enter Fustigo, Crambo, and Poli.

FUS. Hold up your hands, gentlemen.
Here's one, two, three. [*Gives money.*] Nay,
I warrant they are sound pistoles, and
without flaws; I had them of my sister and
I know she uses to put [up] nothing that's
cracked—four, five, six, seven, eight, and
nine. By this hand, bring me but a piece of
his blood, and you shall have nine more.
I'll lurk in a tavern not far off, and provide supper to close up the end of the [10
tragedy. The linen draper's, remember.
Stand to 't, I beseech you, and play your
parts perfectly.

CRAM. Look you, signior, 'tis not your
gold that we weigh.

FUS. Nay, nay, weigh it and spare not;
if it lack one grain of corn, I'll give you a
bushel of wheat to make it up.

CRAM. But by your favor, signior, which
of the servants is it? Because we'll [20
punish justly.

FUS. Marry, 'tis the head man; you
shall taste him by his tongue; a pretty, tall,
prating fellow, with a Tuscalonian beard.

POLI. Tuscalonian? Very good.

FUS. God's life, I was ne'er so thrummed
since I was a gentleman. My coxcomb was
dry-beaten, as if my hair had been hemp.

CRAM. We'll dry-beat some of them.

FUS. Nay, it grew so high that my [30
sister cried out murder, very manfully. I
have her consent, in a manner, to have him
peppered; else I'll not do 't, to win more
than ten cheaters do at a rifling.[3] Break
but his pate, or so, only his mazer,[4] because
I'll have his head in a cloth as well as mine.
He's a linen draper, and may take enough.
I could enter mine action of battery against
him, but we may perhaps be both dead and
rotten before the lawyers would end it. [40

CRAM. No more to do, but ensconce

[2] Original reads *11. SCE.*   [4] Mazzard, head.
[3] A game with dice.

yourself i' th' tavern. Provide no great cheer—a couple of capons, some pheasants, plovers, an orangeado [1] pie, or so. But how bloody soe'er the day be, sally you not forth.

Fus. No, no; nay, if I stir, somebody shall stink. I'll not budge; I'll lie like a dog in a manger.

Cram. Well, well, to the tavern; let [50 not our supper be raw, for you shall have blood enough, your belly full.

Fus. That's all (so God sa' me) I thirst after: blood for blood, bump for bump, nose for nose, head for head, plaster for plaster. And so farewell. What shall I call your names? Because I'll leave word, if any such come to the bar.

Cram. My name is Corporal Crambo.
Poh. And mine, Lieutenant Poh. 60
Exit.[2]

Cram. Poli is as tall [3] a man as ever opened oyster; I would not be the devil to meet Poh. Farewell.

Fus. Nor I, by this light, if Poh be such a Poli. Exeunt.

[Scena xii.]

Enter Candido's Wife in her shop, and the two Prentices.

Wife. What's a-clock now?
2 Pren. 'Tis almost twelve.
Wife. That's well.
The Senate will leave wording [4] presently.
But is George ready?
2 Pren. Yes, forsooth, he's furbushed.[5]
Wife. Now, as you ever hope to win my favor,
Throw both your duties and respects on him
With the like awe as if he were your master.
Let not your looks betray it with a smile
Or jeering glance to any customer;
Keep a true settled countenance, and beware
You laugh not, whatsoe'er you hear or see. 10
2 Pren. I warrant you, mistress, let us alone for keeping our countenance; for, if I list, there's never a fool in all Milan shall

make me laugh, let him play the fool never so like an ass, whether it be the fat court fool or the lean city fool.

Wife. Enough then; call down George.
2 Pren. I hear him coming.

Enter George [in Candido's dress].

Wife. Be ready with your legs [6] then; let me see
How court'sy would become him.—Gallantly!
Beshrew my blood, a proper, seemly man, 20
Of a choice carriage, walks with a good port!
Geo. I thank you, mistress, my back's broad enough, now my master's gown's on.
Wife. Sure, I should think 'twere the least of sin
To mistake the master, and to let him in.
Geo. 'Twere a good Comedy of Errors that, i' faith.
2 Pren. Whist, whist! My master!

Enter Candido, and exit presently.

Wife. You all know your tasks.—God's my life,
What's that he has got on 's back? Who can tell? 30
Geo. [Aside.] That can I, but I will not.
Wife. Girt about him like a madman! What, has he lost his cloak too? This is the maddest fashion that e'er I saw. What said he, George, when he passed by thee?
Geo. Troth, mistress, nothing! Not so much as a bee, he did not hum; not so much as a bawd, he did not hem; not so much as a cuckold, he did not ha; neither hum, [40 hem, nor ha; only stared me in the face, passed along, and made haste in, as if my looks had wrought with him to give him a stool.
Wife. Sure he's vexed now; this trick has moved his spleen.
He's angered now, because he uttered nothing;
And wordless wrath breaks out more violent.
May be he'll strive for place when he comes down,
But, if thou lov'st me, George, afford him none.

[1] Candied orange peel.
[2] Original reads Exeunt.
[3] Bold.
[4] Disputing.
[5] Furbished.
[6] Bows.

GEO. Nay, let me alone to play [50 my master's prize,[1] as long as my mistress warrants me. I'm sure I have his best clothes on, and I scorn to give place to any that is inferior in apparel to me; that's an axiom, a principle, and is observed as much as the fashion. Let that persuade you, then, that I'll shoulder with him for the upper hand in the shop as long as this chain [2] will maintain it.

WIFE. Spoke with the spirit of a [60 master, though with the tongue of a prentice.

Enter Candido like a prentice.

Why, how now, madman? What, in your tricksy coats?

CAND. O, peace, good mistress.—

Enter Crambo and Poli.

See, what you lack? What is 't you buy? Pure calicoes, fine hollands, choice cambrics, neat lawns! See what you buy! Pray come near; my master will use you well; he can afford you a pennyworth.

WIFE. Ay, that he can, out of a whole piece of lawn, i' faith.   70

CAND. Pray see your choice here, gentlemen.

WIFE. O fine fool! What a madman, a patient madman! Who ever heard of the like? Well, sir, I'll fit you and your humor presently. What, cross-points? [3] I'll untie 'em all in a trice; I'll vex you, i' faith. Boy, take your cloak; quick, come.

Exit [with 1 Prentice].

CAND. Be covered, George! This chain and welted gown
Bare to this coat? Then the world's up-
      side down!   80

GEO. Umh, umh, hum.

CRAM. That's the shop, and there's the fellow.

POH. Ay, but the master is walking in there.

CRAM. No matter, we'll in.

POH. 'Sblood, dost long to lie in limbo?

CRAM. And limbo be in hell, I care not.

CAND. Look you, gentlemen, your choice. Cambrics?   90

[1] A public contest for a master's degree in fencing.
[2] Symbol of office.
[3] Crossed laces by which garments were fastened.

CRAM. No, sir, some shirting.

CAND. You shall.

CRAM. Have you none of this striped canvas for doublets?

CAND. None striped, sir, but plain.

2 PREN. I think there be one piece striped within.

GEO. Step, sirrah, and fetch it.—Hum, hum, hum.   99

[*Exit 2 Prentice and returns with the canvas.*]

CAND. Look you, gentlemen, I'll make but one spreading; here's a piece of cloth, fine yet shall wear like iron. 'Tis without fault; take this upon my word, 'tis without fault.

CRAM. Then 'tis better than you, sirrah.

CAND. Ay, and a number more. O, that each soul
Were but as spotless as this innocent white,
And had as few breaks in it!

CRAM.   'Twould have some then.
There was a fray here last day in this shop.

CAND. There was, indeed, a little flea-
      biting.   110

POLI. A gentleman had his pate broke; call you that but a flea-biting?

CAND. He had so.

CRAM. Zounds, do you stand to it?
                              He strikes him.

GEO. 'Sfoot, clubs, clubs! Prentices, down with 'em!

[*Enter Prentices, who disarm Crambo and Poli.*]

Ay, you rogues, strike a citizen in 's shop?

CAND. None of you stir, I pray. Forbear, good George.

CRAM. I beseech you, sir, we mistook our marks; deliver us our weapons.   120

GEO. Your head bleeds, sir; cry clubs!

CAND. I say you shall not; pray be patient;
Give them their weapons. Sirs, y'are best be gone;
I tell you here are boys more tough than bears.
Hence, lest more fists do walk about your ears.

BOTH. We thank you, sir.   *Exeunt.*

CAND.   You shall not follow them;
Let them alone, pray. This did me no harm;

Troth, I was cold, and the blow made
  me warm;
I thank 'em for 't.   Besides, I had
  decreed [1]
To have a vein pricked—I did mean to
  bleed,   130
So that there's money saved. They are
  honest men;
Pray use 'em well when they appear
  again.
GEO. Yes, sir, we'll use 'em like honest
men.
CAND. Ay, well said, George, like honest
men, though they be arrant knaves, for
that's the phrase of the city. Help to lay
up these wares.

[*He and the Prentices retire to the back of the
    shop.*] *Enter his Wife with Officers.*

WIFE. Yonder he stands.
[1] OFF.   What, in a prentice's coat?
WIFE. Ay, ay; mad, mad. Pray, take heed.
CAND.   How now,   140
  What news with them? What make they
    with my wife?—
  Officers, is she attached?—Look to your
    wares.
WIFE. He talks to himself. O, he's much
  gone indeed.
[1] OFF. Pray, pluck up a good heart; be
  not so fearful.
  Sirs, hark, we'll gather to him by de-
    grees.
WIFE. Ay, ay, by degrees, I pray. O me!
  What makes he with the lawn in his
    hand?
  He'll tear all the ware in my shop.
[1] OFF. Fear not, we'll catch him on a
  sudden.
WIFE. You had need do so; pray take
  heed of your warrant.   150
[1] OFF. I warrant, mistress. Now, Signior
  Candido.
CAND. Now, sir, what news with you, sir?
WIFE. [*Aside to 1 Officer.*] "What news
  with you?" he says. O, he 's far gone!
[1] OFF. [*Aside to Wife.*] I pray, fear
  nothing; let's alone with him.—
  Signior, you look not like yourself, me-
    thinks.—
  Steal you a tother side.—Y'are changed,
    y'are altered.

[1] Decided.

CAND. Changed, sir? Why, true, sir. Is
  "changed" strange? 'Tis not
The fashion unless it alter. Monarchs
  turn
To beggars, beggars creep into the
  nests
Of princes, masters serve their prentices,
Ladies their serving-men, men turn to
  women.   161
[1] OFF. And women turn to men.
CAND. Ay, and women turn to men, you
say true. Ha, ha, a mad world, a mad
world.   [*Officers seize him.*]
[1] OFF. Have we caught you, sir?
CAND. Caught me? Well, well, you have
caught me.
WIFE. He laughs in your faces.
GEO. A rescue, prentices! My master's
  catchpolled. [2]   170
[1] OFF. I charge you, keep the peace, or
  have your legs
Gartered with irons! We have from the
  duke
A warrant strong enough for what we do.
CAND. I pray, rest quiet; I desire no rescue.
WIFE. La, he desires no rescue! 'Las, poor
  heart,
He talks against himself.
CAND.   Well, what's the matter?
[1] OFF. [*Binding Candido.*] Look to that
  arm.
  Pray, make sure work; double the cord.
CAND.   Why, why?
WIFE. Look how his head goes. Should he
  get but loose,
  O, 'twere as much as all our lives were
    worth!   180
[1] OFF. Fear not; we'll make all sure for
  our own safety.
CAND. Are you at leisure now?   Well,
  what's the matter?
  Why do I enter into bonds thus, ha?
[1] OFF. Because y'are mad, put fear upon
  your wife.
WIFE. O, ay, I went in danger of my life
every minute.
CAND. What, am I mad, say you, and I
  not know it?
[1] OFF. That proves you mad, because
  you know it not.
WIFE. Pray talk to him as little as you
  can;
  You see he's too far spent.

[2] Caught by a bumbailiff.

CAND. Bound with strong cord!
A sister's [1] thread, i' faith, had been
enough 191
To lead me anywhere.—Wife, do you
long?
You are mad too, or else you do me
wrong.
GEO. But are you mad indeed, master?
CAND. My wife says so,
And what she says, George, is all truth,
you know.—
And whither now, to Bethlem Mon-
astery?
Ha! whither?
[1] OFF. Faith, e'en to the mad-
men's pound.
CAND. A God's name! Still I feel my
patience sound. *Exit [with Officers].*
GEO. Come, we'll see whither he goes.
If the master be mad, we are his [200
servants, and must follow his steps; we'll
be madcaps too. Farewell, mistress; you
shall have us all in Bedlam.
Exeunt [George and Prentices].
WIFE. I think I have fitted you now, you
and your clothes.
If this move not his patience, nothing
can;
I'll swear then I have a saint, and not a
man. *[Exit.]*

SCENA xiii.

[A street near an abbey.]

*Enter Duke, Doctor, Fluello, Castruchio,
Pioratto.*

DUKE. Give us a little leave.
[Exeunt Fluello, Castruchio, and Pioratto.]
Doctor, your news.
DOC. I sent for him, my lord. At last he
came,
And did receive all speech that went
from me
As gilded pills made to prolong his health.
My credit with him wrought it, for some
men
Swallow even empty hooks, like fools
that fear
No drowning where 'tis deepest, cause
'tis clear.
In th' end we sat and eat; [2] a health I
drank
To Infelice's sweet, departed soul.

This train [3] I knew would take.
DUKE. 'Twas excellent. 10
DOC. He fell with such devotion on his
knees
To pledge the same—
DUKE. Fond, superstitious fool!
DOC. That had he been inflamed with zeal
of prayer,
He could not pour 't out with more
reverence.
About my neck he hung, wept on my
cheek,
Kissed it, and swore he would adore my
lips,
Because they brought forth Infelice's
name.
DUKE. Ha, ha! Alack, alack!
DOC. The cup he lifts up high, and thus he
said,
"Here, noble maid!"—drinks, and was
poisonéd. 20
DUKE. And died?
DOC. And died, my lord.
DUKE. Thou in that word
Hast pieced mine aged hours out with
more years
Than thou hast taken from Hippolito.
A noble youth he was, but lesser
branches
Hind'ring the greater's growth must be
lopped off,
And feed the fire. Doctor, we're now all
thine,
And use us so; be bold.
DOC. Thanks, gracious lord.
My honored lord—
DUKE. Hum.
DOC. I do beseech your grace to bury deep
This bloody act of mine.
DUKE. Nay, nay, for that, 31
Doctor, look you to 't; me it shall not
move.
They're cursed that ill do, not that ill do
love.
DOC. You throw an angry forehead on my
face;
But, be you pleased backward thus far
to look,
That, for your good, this evil I under-
took—
DUKE. Ay, ay, we conster so.
DOC. And only for your love.
DUKE. Confessed; 'tis true.

---

[1] Sewster's, seamstress'.   [2] Preterit.   [3] Device.

Doc. Nor let it stand against me as a bar
   To thrust me from your presence; nor
      believe,   40
   As princes have quick thoughts, that
      now, my finger
   Being dipped in blood, I will not spare
      the hand,
   But that for gold—as what can gold not
      do?—
   I may be hired to work the like on you.
DUKE. Which to prevent—
Doc.   'Tis from my heart as far—
DUKE. No matter, doctor; cause I'll
      fearless sleep,
   And that you shall stand clear of that
      suspicion,
   I banish thee forever from my court.
   This principle is old, but true as fate:
   Kings may love treason, but the traitor
      hate.   *Exit.*
Doc. Is 't so? Nay then, duke, your stale
      principle,   51
   With one as stale, the doctor thus shall
      quit: [1]
   He falls himself that digs another's
      pit.—
   How now! Where is he? Will he not
      meet me?

      Enter the Doctor's Man.

Do. MAN. Meet you, sir? He might
have met with three fencers in this time,
and have received less hurt than by meeting one doctor of physic. Why, sir, he has
walked under the old abbey wall yonder
this hour, till he's more cold than a [60
citizen's country house in Janivere. You
may smell him behind, sir. La you, yonder he comes.
   Doc. Leave me.

      Enter Hippolito.

Do. MAN. Ich lurch,[2] if you will.   *Exit.*
Doc. O my most noble friend!
HIP.   Few but yourself
   Could have enticed me thus to trust
      the air
   With my close sighs. You sent for me.
      What news?
Doc. Come, you must doff this black,
      dye that pale cheek

   [1] Repay.
   [2] Perhaps dialect for *I lurk* (*i.e.,* wait); or
perhaps a misprint for *i' th' lurch.*

Into his own color, go, attire yourself
   Fresh as a bridegroom when he meets
      his bride.   71
   The duke has done much treason to
      thy love,
   'Tis now revealed; 'tis now to be re-
      venged.
   Be merry, honored friend.   Thy lady
      lives.
HIP. What lady?
Doc.   Infelice; she's revived.
   Revived? Alack, Death never had the
      heart
   To take breath from her.
HIP.   Umh! I thank you, sir;
   Physic prolongs life when it cannot
      save.
   This helps not my hopes; mine are in
      their grave.
   You do some wrong to mock me.
Doc.   By that love
   Which I have ever borne you, what I
      speak   81
   Is truth. The maiden lives; that fun-
      eral,
   Duke's tears, the mourning, was all
      counterfeit.
   A sleepy draught cozened the world and
      you;
   I was his minister, and then chambered
      up
   To stop discovery.
HIP.   O treacherous duke!
Doc. He cannot hope so certainly for
      bliss
   As he believes that I have poisoned you.
   He wooed me to 't; I yielded, and con-
      firmed him
   In his most bloody thoughts.
HIP.   A very devil!
Doc. Her did he closely coach to Ber-
      gamo,   91
   And thither—
HIP.   Will I ride. Stood Bergamo
   In the Low Countries of black hell, I'll
      to her.
Doc. You shall to her, but not to Bergamo.
   How passion makes you fly beyond
      yourself!
   Much of that weary journey I ha' cut
      off,
   For she by letters hath intelligence
   Of your supposéd death, her own inter-
      ment,

And all those plots which that false
   duke, her father,
Has wrought against you; and sh?'ll
   meet you—
HIP.   O, when? 100
Doc. Nay, see how covetous are your
   desires.
Early tomorrow morn.
HIP.   O where, good father?
Doc. At Bethlem Monastery. Are you
   pleased now?
HIP. At Bethlem Monastery! The place
   well fits;
It is the school where those that lose
   their wits
Practice again to get them. I am sick
Of that disease; all love is lunatic.
Doc. We'll steal away this night in some
   disguise.
Father Anselmo, a most reverend friar,
Expects our coming, before whom we'll
   lay   110
Reasons so strong that he shall yield
   in bands
Of holy wedlock to tie both your hands.
HIP. This is such happiness
That, to believe it, 'tis impossible.
Doc. Let all your joys then die in mis-
   belief;
I will reveal no more.
HIP.   O, yes, good father,
I am so well acquainted with despair
I know not how to hope; I believe all.
Doc. We'll hence this night. Much must
   be done, much said;
But, if the doctor fail not in his
   charms,   120
Your lady shall ere morning fill these
   arms.
HIP. Heavenly physician! Far thy fame
   shall spread,
That mak'st two lovers speak when
   they be dead.   *Exeunt.*

[SCENA xiv.

A hall in the Duke's palace.]

*Candido's Wife and George; Pioratto meets
            them.*

WIFE. O, watch, good George, watch
which way the duke comes.
GEO. Here comes one of the butterflies; ask him.

WIFE. Pray, sir, comes the duke this
way?
PIO. He's upon coming, mistress. *Exit.*
WIFE. I thank you, sir. George, are
there many mad folks where thy master
lies?   10
GEO. O, yes, of all countries some, but
especially mad Greeks—they swarm. Troth,
mistress, the world is altered with you;
you had not wont to stand thus with
a paper "humbly complaining."[1] But
you're well enough served; provender
pricked[2] you, as it does many of our city
wives besides.
WIFE. Dost think, George, we shall
get him forth?   20
GEO. Truly, mistress, I cannot tell;
I think you'll hardly[3] get him forth. Why,
'tis strange! 'Sfoot, I have known many
women that have had mad rascals to their
husbands, whom they would belabor by
all means possible to keep 'em in their
right wits; but of a woman to long to turn
a tame man into a madman, why, the
devil himself was never used so by his
dam.   30
WIFE. How does he talk, George?
Ha! Good George, tell me.
GEO. Why, you're best go see.
WIFE. Alas, I am afraid!
GEO. Afraid! You had more need be
ashamed. He may rather be afraid of you.
WIFE. But, George, he's not stark mad,
is he? He does not rave; he is not horn-
mad, George, is he?
GEO. Nay, I know not that, but he [40
talks like a justice of peace, of a thousand
matters, and to no purpose.
WIFE. I'll to the monastery. I shall be
mad till I enjoy him; I shall be sick until
I see him; yet, when I do see him, I shall
weep out mine eyes.
GEO. Ay, I'd fain see a woman weep
out her eyes! That's as true as to say a
man's cloak burns, when it hangs in the
water. I know you'll weep, mistress, but [50
what says the painted cloth?[4]

Trust not a woman when she cries,
For she'll pump water from her eyes
With a wet finger, and in faster showers
Than April when he rains down flowers.

---

[1] The opening phrase of a petition.   [2] Urged.
[3] With difficulty.   [4] Hanging with mottoes on it.

WIFE. Ay, but, George, that painted cloth is worthy to be hanged up for lying. All women have not tears at will, unless they have good cause.

GEO. Ay, but, mistress, how easily [60 will they find a cause, and, as one of our cheese trenchers [1] says very learnedly:

As out of wormwood bees suck honey,
As from poor clients lawyers firk [2] money,
As parsley from a roasted cunny [3]—
So, though the day be ne'er so sunny,
If wives will have it rain, down then it drives;
The calmest husbands make the storm[i]est wives.

WIFE. Tame, George; but I ha' done storming now.   70

GEO. Why, that's well done. Good mistress, throw aside this fashion of your humor; be not so fantastical in wearing it; storm no more, long no more. This longing has made you come short of many a good thing that you might have had from my master. Here comes the duke.

Enter Duke, Fluello, Pioratto, Sinezi.

WIFE. O, I beseech you, pardon my offense,
    In that I durst abuse your grace's warrant;
    Deliver forth my husband, good my lord.   80

DUKE. Who is her husband?

FLU.   Candido, my lord.

DUKE. Where is he?

WIFE.   He's among the lunatics.
He was a man made up without a gall;
Nothing could move him, nothing could convert
His meek blood into fury; yet, like a monster,
I often beat at the most constant rock
Of his unshaken patience, and did long
To vex him.

DUKE.   Did you so?

WIFE.   And for that purpose
Had warrant from your grace to carry him
To Bethlem Monastery, whence they will not free him   90
Without your grace's hand that sent him in.

[1] *I.e.,* inscriptions on cheese trenchers.
[2] Trick.   [3] Cony, rabbit.

DUKE. You have longed fair; 'tis you are mad, I fear.
    It's fit to fetch him thence, and keep you there.
    If he be mad, why would you have him forth?

GEO. And please your grace, he's not stark mad, but only talks like a young gentleman, somewhat fantastically, that's all. There's a thousand about your court, city, and country madder than he.

DUKE. Provide a warrant; you shall have our hand.   100

GEO. Here's a warrant ready drawn, my lord.

DUKE. Get pen and ink, get pen and ink.   [*Exit George.*]

Enter Castruchio.

CAS. Where is my lord the duke?

DUKE.   How now! More madmen?

CAS. I have strange news, my lord.

DUKE.   Of what? Of whom?

CAS. Of Infelice, and a marriage.

DUKE. Ha! Where? With whom?

CAS.   Hippolito.

[*Enter George, with pen and ink.*]

GEO.   Here, my lord.

DUKE. Hence with that woman! Void the room!

FLU.   Away!
    The duke's vexed.

GEO.   Whoop, come, mistress, the duke's mad too.

                    Exeunt [*Wife and George*].

DUKE. Who told me that Hippolito was dead?   109

CAS. He that can make any man dead, the doctor. But, my lord, he's as full of life as wildfire, and as quick. Hippolito, the doctor, and one more rid hence this evening; the inn at which they light is Bethlem Monastery; Infelice comes from Bergamo and meets them there. Hippolito is mad, for he means this day to be married. The afternoon is the hour, and Friar Anselmo is the knitter.

DUKE. From Bergamo?   Is 't possible?
    It cannot be!   120
    It cannot be!

CAS.   I will not swear, my lord,
But this intelligence I took from one
Whose brains work in the plot.

DUKE. What's he?

CAS. Matheo.

FLU. Matheo knows all.

PIO. He's Hippolito's bosom.[1]

DUKE. How far stands Bethlem hence?

OMNES. Six or seven miles.

DUKE. Is 't so? Not married till the after-
noon?
Stay, stay, let's work out some preven-
tion. How?
This is most strange. Can none but
madmen serve
To dress their wedding dinner? All of
you
Get presently to horse, disguise your-
selves 130
Like country gentlemen,
Or riding citizens, or so; and take
Each man a several path, but let us
meet
At Bethlem Monastery, some space of
time
Being spent between the arrival each
of other,
As if we came to see the lunatics.
To horse, away! Be secret, on your
lives.
Love must be punished that unjustly
thrives.
Exeunt [all but Fluello].

FLU. Be secret, on your lives! Castruchio,
Y'are but a scurvy spaniel. Honest
lord, 140
Good lady! Zounds, their love is just,
'tis good,
And I'll prevent you, though I swim in
blood. *Exit.*

[SCENE XV.

A room in Bethlem Monastery.]

*Enter Friar Anselmo, Hippolito, Matheo,
Infelice.*

HIP. Nay, nay, resolve,[2] good father, or
deny.

ANS. You press me to an act both full of
danger
And full of happiness; for I behold
Your father's frowns, his threats, nay,
perhaps death
To him that dare do this. Yet, noble
lord,

Such comfortable beams break through
these clouds
By this blessed marriage, that, your honored word
Being pawned in my defense, I will
tie fast
The holy wedding knot.

HIP. Tush, fear not the duke.

ANS. O son, wisely to fear is to be free
from fear. 10

HIP. You have our words, and you shall
have our lives,
To guard you safe from all ensuing
danger.

MAT. Ay, ay, chop 'em up, and away.

ANS. Stay! When is 't fit for me, and
safest for you,
To entertain this business?

HIP. Not till the evening.

ANS. Be it so. There is a chapel stands
hard by,
Upon the west end of the abbey wall;
Thither convey yourselves, and, when
the sun
Hath turned his back upon this upper
world,
I'll marry you; that done, no thund'ring
voice 20
Can break the sacred bond. Yet, lady,
here
You are most safe.

INF. Father, your love's most dear.

MAT. Ay, well said; lock us into some
little room by ourselves, that we may be
mad for an hour or two.

HIP. O, good Matheo, no; let's make no
noise.

MAT. How! No noise! Do you know
where you are? 'Sfoot, amongst all the
madcaps in Milan; so that to throw the
house out at window will be the better, [30
and no man will suspect that we lurk here
to steal mutton.[3] The more sober we are,
the more scurvy 'tis. And, though the
friar tell us that here we are safest, I am
not of his mind; for, if those lay here that
had lost their money, none would ever look
after them; but here are none but those
that have lost their wits, so that if hue
and cry be made, hither they'll come. And
my reason is, because none goes to be [40
married till he be stark mad.

HIP. Muffle yourselves; yonder's Fluello.

---

[1] Bosom friend.   [2] Agree.   [3] *I.e.,* a wench.

Enter Fluello.

MAT.   Zounds!

FLU. O my lord, these cloaks are not
for this rain. The tempest is too great. I
come sweating to tell you of it, that you
may get out of it.

MAT. Why, what's the matter?

FLU. What's the matter? You have mat-
tered it fair; the duke's at hand.   49

OMNES. The duke?

FLU.   The very duke.

HIP.   Then all our plots
Are turned upon our heads and we're
     blown up
With our own underminings.   'Sfoot,
     how comes he?
What villain durst betray our being
     here?

FLU. Castruchio told the duke, and
Matheo here told Castruchio.

HIP. Would you betray me to Castruchio?

MAT. 'Sfoot, he damned himself to the
pit of hell, if he spake on 't again.

HIP. So did you swear to me; so were you
     damned.   59

MAT. Pox on 'em, and there be no
faith in men, if a man shall not believe
oaths. He took bread and salt,[1] by this
light, that he would never open his lips.

HIP. O God, O God!

ANS.   Son, be not desperate;
Have patience.   You shall trip your
     enemy
Down by his own sleights. How far is
     the duke hence?

FLU. He's but new set out. Castruchio,
Pioratto, and Sinezi come along with him.
You have time enough yet to prevent[2]
them, if you have but courage.   70

ANS. Ye shall steal secretly into the
     chapel,
And presently be married. If the duke
Abide here still, spite of ten thousand
     eyes,
You shall scape hence like friars.

HIP. O blessed disguise! O happy man!

ANS. Talk not of Happiness till your
     closed hand
Have her by th' forehead, like the lock
     of Time.
Be nor too slow, nor hasty, now you
     climb

Up to the tower of bliss; only be wary
And patient, that's all. If you like my
     plot,   80
Build and despatch; if not, farewell;
     then not.

HIP. O, yes, we do applaud it! We'll dis-
     pute
No longer, but will hence and execute.
Fluello, you'll stay here; let us be gone.
The ground that frighted lovers tread
     upon
Is stuck with thorns.

ANS.   Come, then away, 'tis meet,
Exeunt [Anselmo, Hippolito, and Infelice.]
To escape those thorns, to put on wingéd
     feet.

MAT. No words, I pray, Fluello, for
it stands us upon.[3]

FLU. O, sir, let that be your lesson!   90
                         [*Exit Matheo.*]
Alas, poor lovers! On what hopes and
     fears
Men toss themselves for women! When
     she's got,
The best has in her that which pleaseth
     not.

Enter to Fluello, the Duke, Castruchio,
     Pioratto, and Sinezi from several doors,
                              muffled.

DUKE. Who's there?

CAS.   My lord—

DUKE.   Peace;
     send that "lord" away.
A lordship will spoil all; let's be all
     fellows.
What's he?

CAS. Fluello, or else Sinezi, by his little
legs.

OMNES. All friends, all friends.

DUKE. What? Met upon the very point
     of time?   100
Is this the place?

PIO.   This is the place, my lord.

DUKE. Dream you on lordships? Come
     no more "lords," I pray.
You have not seen these lovers yet?

OMNES.   Not yet.

DUKE. Castruchio, art thou sure this
     wedding feat
Is not till afternoon?

CAS.   So it is given out, my lord.

---

[1] To seal the oath.   [2] Anticipate.   [3] It is an important matter to us.

DUKE. Nay, nay, 'tis like. Thieves must
  observe their hours;
Lovers watch minutes like astrono-
  mers.
How shall the interim hours by us be
  spent?
FLU. Let's all go see the madmen.
OMNES.   Mass, content.   109

Enter Towne [1] *like a sweeper.*

DUKE. O, here comes one.   Question
him, question him.
FLU. Now, honest fellow, dost thou belong to the house?
TOWNE. Yes, forsooth, I am one of the
implements; I sweep the madmen's rooms,
and fetch straw for 'em, and buy chains to
tie 'em, and rods to whip 'em.   I was a
mad wag myself here once, but, I thank
Father Anselmo, he lashed me into my
right mind again.   120
DUKE. Anselmo is the friar must marry
  them;
Question him where he is.
CAS. And where is Father Anselmo now?
TOWNE. Marry, he's gone but e'en now.
DUKE. Ay, well done.   Tell me, whither
  is he gone?
TOWNE. Why, to God A'mighty.
FLU. Ha, ha!   This fellow's a fool,
talks idly.
PIO. Sirrah, are all the mad folks in
Milan brought hither?   130
TOWNE. How, all?   There's a question
indeed!   Why, if all the mad folks in Milan
should come hither, there would not be
left ten men in the city.
DUKE. Few gentlemen or courtiers here,
ha?
TOWNE. O, yes, abundance, abundance.
Lands no sooner fall into their hands, but
straight they run out a their wits.   Citizens' sons and heirs are free of the   [140
house by their fathers' copy.   Farmers'
sons come hither like geese, in flocks, and,
when they ha' sold all their cornfields,
here they sit and pick the straws.
SIN. Methinks you should have women
here as well as men.
TOWNE. O, ay, a plague on 'em, there's
no "ho!"[2] with 'em; they're madder than
March hares.   149

<hr>

[1] Thomas Towne, the name of the actor who
took the part.   [2] A cry commanding to stop.

FLU. Are there no lawyers amongst
you?
TOWNE. O, no, not one; never any lawyer.   We dare not let a lawyer come in,
for he'll make 'em mad faster than we can
recover 'em.
DUKE. And how long is 't ere you recover any of these?
TOWNE. Why, according to the quantity of the moon [3] that's got into 'em.   An
alderman's son will be mad a great   [160
while, a very great while, especially if his
friends left him well.   A whore will hardly
come to her wits again.   A Puritan, there's
no hope of him, unless he may pull down the
steeple, and hang himself i' th' bell ropes.
FLU. I perceive all sorts of fish come
to your net.
TOWNE. Yes, in truth, we have blocks
for all heads.   We have good store of wild
oats here; for the courtier is mad   [170
at the citizen, the citizen is mad at the
countryman; the shoemaker is mad at the
cobbler, the cobbler at the carman;[4] the
punk is mad that the merchant's wife is no
whore, the merchant's wife is mad that
the punk is so common a whore.   Godso,
here's Father Anselmo; pray, say nothing
that I tell tales out of the school.   *Exit.*

Enter Anselmo [5] *[and Servants].*

OMNES. God bless you, father.
ANS.   I thank you, gentlemen.
CAS. Pray, may we see some of those
    wretched souls   180
That here are in your keeping?
ANS.   Yes, you shall;
  But, gentlemen, I must disarm you
    then.
There are of mad men, as there are of
    tame,
All humored not alike.   We have here
    some
So apish and fantastic, play with a
    feather,
And, though 'twould grieve a soul to
    see God's image
So blemished and defaced, yet do they
    act
Such antic and such pretty lunacies,

<hr>

[3] Alluding to the superstition that the moon's
rays made lunatics.
[4] Carter.
[5] This direction appears after line 180 in the
original.

That spite of sorrow they will make
you smile;   189
Others again we have like hungry lions,
Fierce as wild bulls, untamable as flies,
And these have oftentimes from stran-
gers' sides
Snatched rapiers suddenly, and done
much harm,
Whom if you'll see, you must be weapon-
less.
OMNES. With all our hearts.
                [They give Anselmo their weapons.]
ANS.   Here, take these weapons in.—
                [Exit Servant with weapons.]
Stand off a little, pray; so, so, 'tis well.
I'll show you here a man that was some-
times
A very grave and wealthy citizen,
Has served a prenticeship to this mis-
fortune,
Been here seven years, and dwelt in
Bergamo.   200
DUKE. How fell he from his wits?
ANS.   By loss at sea.
I'll stand aside; question him you alone,
For, if he spy me, he'll not speak a word,
Unless he's throughly vexed.
        Discovers an Old Man, wrapped in a net.
FLU.   Alas, poor soul!
CAS. A very old man.
DUKE. God speed, father!
1 MAD. God speed the plow; thou
shalt not speed me.
PIO. We see you, old man, for all you
dance in a net.   210
1 MAD. True, but thou wilt dance in
a halter, and I shall not see thee.
ANS. O, do not vex him, pray.
CAS. Are you a fisherman, father?
1 MAD. No, I am neither fish nor flesh.
FLU. What do you with that net then?
1 MAD. Dost not see, fool? There's a
fresh salmon in 't. If you step one foot
furder, you'll be over shoes, for you see I'm
over head and ears in the salt water; [220
and, if you fall into this whirlpool where
I am, y'are drowned—y'are a drowned
rat. I am fishing here for five ships, but
I cannot have a good draught, for my net
breaks still,[1] and breaks; but I'll break
some of your necks and I catch you in my
clutches. Stay, stay, stay, stay, stay,
where's the wind? **Where's** the wind?

[1] Always.

Where's the wind? Where's the wind? Out,
you gulls, you goosecaps,[2] you gud- [230
geon-eaters![3] Do you look for the wind in
the heavens? Ha, ha, ha, ha! No, no!
Look there, look there, look there! The
wind is always at that door; hark how it
blows, puff, puff, puff!
OMNES. Ha, ha, ha!
1 MAD. Do you laugh at God's creatures? Do you mock old age, you rogues?
Is this gray beard and head counterfeit
that you cry, "Ha, ha, ha"? Sirrah, [240
art not thou my eldest son?
PIO. Yes, indeed, father.
1 MAD. Then th'art a fool, for my eldest son had a polt foot,[4] crooked legs, a
verjuice face, and a pear-colored beard.
I made him a scholar, and he made himself a fool.—Sirrah, thou there, hold out
thy hand!
DUKE. My hand? Well, here 'tis.   249
1 MAD. Look, look, look, look! Has
he not long nails and short hair?
FLU. Yes, monstrous short hair, and
abominable long nails.
1 MAD. Tenpenny nails, are they not?
FLU. Yes, tenpenny nails.
1 MAD. Such nails had my second boy.
Kneel down, thou varlet, and ask thy father
blessing. Such nails had my middlemost
son, and I made him a promoter;[5] and
he scraped, and scraped, and scraped, [260
till he got the devil and all; but he scraped
thus, and thus, and thus, and it went
under his legs, till at length a company
of kites, taking him for carrion, swept up
all, all, all, all, all, all, all. If you love
your lives, look to yourselves! See, see, see,
see, the Turks' galleys are fighting with
my ships! "Bounce," goes the guns.
"Oooh!" cry the men. "Rumble, rumble,"
go the waters. Alas, there, 'tis sunk, [270
'tis sunk! I am undone, I am undone! You
are the damned pirates have undone me.
You are, by the Lord, you are, you are!
Stop 'em! You are!
ANS. Why, how now, sirrah! Must I fall
to tame you?
1 MAD. Tame me! No, I'll be madder
than a roasted cat. See, see, I am burnt
with gunpowder. These are our close
fights!   280

[2] Boobies.   [4] Club foot.
[3] Simpletons.   [5] Informer.

Ans. I'll whip you if you grow unruly thus.

1 Mad. Whip me?   Out, you toad! Whip me? What justice is this, to whip me because I am a beggar? Alas, I am a poor man, a very poor man! I am starved, and have had no meat, by this light, ever since the great flood; I am a poor man.

Ans. Well, well, be quiet, and you shall have meat.   290

1 Mad. Ay, ay, pray do; for, look you, here be my guts. These are my ribs—you may look through my ribs—see how my guts come out! These are my red guts, my very guts, O, O!

Ans. Take him in there.
      [*Servants take 1 Madman in.*]
Omnes. A very piteous sight.

Cas. Father, I see you have a busy charge.

Ans. They must be used like children, pleased with toys,   300
And anon whipped for their unruliness.
I'll show you now a pair quite different
From him that's gone. He was all words; and these,
Unless you urge 'em, seldom spend their speech,
But save their tongues. [*Discovers 2 and 3 Madmen.*] La you, this hithermost
Fell from the happy quietness of mind
About a maiden that he loved, and died.
He followed her to church, being full of tears,
And, as her body went into the ground,
He fell stark mad. This is a married man   310
Was jealous of a fair, but, as some say,
A very virtuous wife; and that spoiled him.

2 Mad. All these are whoremongers, and lay with my wife! Whore, whore, whore, whore, whore!

Flu. Observe him.

2 Mad. Gaffer shoemaker, you pulled on my wife's pumps, and then crept into her pantofles.[1] Lie there, lie there!—This was her tailor. You cut out her loose- [320 bodied gown, and put in a yard more than I allowed her. Lie there by the shoemaker.—O Master Doctor, are you here? You gave me a purgation, and then crept

into my wife's chamber to feel her pulses, and you said, and she said, and her maid said, that they went pit-a-pat, pit-a-pat, pit-a-pat. Doctor, I'll put you anon [328 into my wife's urinal.—Heigh, come aloft, Jack![2] This was her schoolmaster, and taught her to play upon the virginals,[3] and still his jacks[4] leapt up, up. You pricked[5] her out nothing but bawdy lessons, but I'll prick you all, fiddler—doctor—tailor—shoemaker—shoemaker—fiddler—doctor—tailor! So, lie with my wife again, now!

Cas. See how he notes the other, now[6] he feeds.

2 Mad. Give me some porridge.   340
3 Mad. I'll give thee none.
2 Mad. Give me some porridge.
3 Mad. I'll not give thee a bit.
2 Mad. Give me that flapdragon.[7]
3 Mad. I'll not give thee a spoonful. Thou liest; it's no dragon—'tis a parrot that I bought for my sweetheart, and I'll keep it.
2 Mad. Here's an almond for parrot.[8]
3 Mad. Hang thyself!   350
2 Mad. Here's a rope for parrot.[8]
3 Mad. Eat it, for I'll eat this.
2 Mad. I'll shoot at thee, and thou't give me none.
3 Mad. Woot thou?
2 Mad. I'll run a tilt at thee, and thou't give me none.
3 Mad. Woot thou? Do, and thou dar'st.
2 Mad. Bounce!   [*Strikes him.*]   360
3 Mad. O, O! I am slain! Murder, murder, murder! I am slain; my brains are beaten out.
Ans. How now, you villains! Bring me whips; I'll whip you.
3 Mad. I am dead! I am slain! Ring out the bell, for I am dead.
Duke. How will you do now, sirrah? You ha' killed him.   368
2 Mad. I'll answer 't at sessions. He was eating of almond butter, and I longed

[1] Slippers.
[2] Command to a performing monkey.
[3] Musical instrument with keys.
[4] Devices which plucked the strings of the virginals.
[5] Wrote in musical notes.
[6] Now that.
[7] A tidbit in a flaming cup of liquor.
[8] Proverbial phrase of uncertain meaning.

for 't. The child had never been delivered out of my belly, if I had not killed
him. I'll answer 't at sessions, so my wife
may be burnt i' th' hand,[1] too.

ANS. Take 'em in both. Bury him, for
he's dead.

3 MAD. Indeed, I am dead; put me,
I pray, into a good pit-hole.

2 MAD. I'll answer 't at sessions. 379

Exeunt [Servants with 2 and 3 Madmen].

Enter Bellafront mad.

ANS. How now, huswife, whither gad
you?

BELL. A-nutting, forsooth. How do
you, gaffer? How do you, gaffer? There's
a French curtsy for you, too.

FLU. 'Tis Bellafront!

PIO. 'Tis the punk, by th' Lord!

DUKE. Father, what's she, I pray?

ANS. As yet I know not.
  She came in but this day, talks little
      idly,
  And therefore has the freedom of the
      house. 389

BELL. Do not you know me?—nor
you?—nor you?—nor you?

OMNES. No, indeed.

BELL. Then you are an ass—and you
an ass—and you are an ass—for I know
you.

ANS. Why, what are they? Come,
tell me, what are they?

BELL. They're fishwives. Will you buy
any gudgeons? God's santy![2] Yonder
come friars; I know them too.—How [400
do you, friar?

Enter Hippolito, Matheo, and Infelice dis-
guised in the habits of friars.

ANS. Nay, nay, away, you must not
    trouble friars.—
[*Aside to Hippolito, etc.*] The duke is
here; speak nothing.

BELL. Nay, indeed, you shall not go.
We'll run at barleybreak first, and you
shall be in hell.[3]

MAT. [*Aside.*] My punk turned mad
whore, as all her fellows are?

---

[1] Punishment for adultery.

[2] Sanctity.

[3] Name of the middle compartment in the
game of barleybreak.

HIP. [*Aside.*] Say nothing, but steal hence,
    when you spy time. 410

ANS. I'll lock you up, if y'are unruly. Fie!

BELL. Fie! Marry, so! They shall not
go indeed, till I ha' told 'em their fortunes.

DUKE. Good father, give her leave.

BELL. Ay, pray, good father, and I'll
give you my blessing.

ANS. Well then, be brief, but, if you are
    thus unruly,
I'll have you locked up fast.

PIO. Come, to their fortunes. 419

BELL. Let me see: one, two, three, and
four. I'll begin with the little friar[4] first.
Here's a fine hand, indeed! I never saw
friar have such a dainty hand. Here's a
hand for a lady! Here's your fortune:—
  You love a friar better than a nun;
  Yet long you'll love no friar, nor no
      friar's son.
  Bow a little; the line of life is out; yet
      I am afraid,
  For all y'are holy, you'll not die a maid.
  God give you joy!—Now to you, Friar
      Tuck.

MAT. God send me good luck! 430

BELL. You love one, and one loves you;
  You are a false knave, and she's a Jew.
  Here is a dial that false ever goes—

MAT. O, your wit drops!

BELL. Troth, so does your nose.—
[*To Hippolito.*] Nay, let's shake hands
with you too. Pray open. Here's a fine
hand!
  Ho, friar, ho! God be here! 438
  So he had need. You'll keep good cheer,
  Here's a free table,[5] but a frozen breast,
  For you'll starve those that love you
      best;
  Yet you have good fortune, for, if I am
      no liar,
  Then you are no friar, nor you, nor you
      no friar!
  Ha, ha, ha, ha! *Discovers them.*

DUKE. Are holy habits cloaks for villainy?
  Draw all your weapons!

HIP. Do; draw all your weapons.

DUKE. Where are your weapons? Draw!

OMNES. The friar has gulled us of 'em.

---

[4] *I.e.*, Infelice.

[5] A quibble on a term in palmistry for a section of the hand.

MAT.	O rare trick!
You ha' learned one mad point of arithmetic.

HIP. Why swells your spleen so high?
Against what bosom	450
Would you your weapons draw? Hers?
'Tis your daughter's.
Mine? 'Tis your son's.

DUKE.	Son?

MAT.	Son, by yonder sun.

HIP. You cannot shed blood here but 'tis
your own;
To spill your own blood were damnation.
Lay smooth that wrinkled brow, and
I will throw
Myself beneath your feet.
Let it be rugged still and flinted ore,
What can come forth but sparkles, that
will burn
Yourself and us? She's mine; my claim's
most good;
She's mine by marriage, though she's
yours by blood.	460

[ANS. (*Kneeling.*)] I have a hand, dear
lord, deep in this act,
For I foresaw this storm, yet willingly
Put forth to meet it. Oft have I seen a
father
Washing the wounds of his dear son in
tears,
A son to curse the sword that struck his
father,
Both slain i' th' quarrel of your fami-
lies.
Those scars are now ta'en off, and I
beseech you
To seal our pardon! All was to this end,
To turn the ancient hates of your two
houses
To fresh green friendship, that your
loves might look	470
Like the Spring's forehead, comfortably
sweet,
And your vexed souls in peaceful union
meet.
Their blood will now be yours, yours
will be theirs,
And happiness shall crown your silver
hairs.

FLU. You see, my lord, there's now no
remedy.

OMNES. Beseech your lordship!

DUKE. You beseech fair; you have me in
place fit

To bridle me.—Rise, friar. You may be
glad
You can make madmen tame, and tame
men mad.
Since Fate hath conquered, I must rest
content;	480
To strive now would but add new pun-
ishment.
I yield unto your happiness; be blessed.
Our families shall henceforth breathe in
rest.

OMNES. O, happy change!

DUKE.	Yours now is my content;
I throw upon your joys my full consent.

BELL. Am not I a good girl, for finding "the friar in the well"?[1] Godso, you
are a brave man! Will not you buy me some
sugarplums, because I am so good a fortune
teller?	490

DUKE. Would thou hadst wit, thou pretty
soul, to ask,
As I have will to give.

BELL. Pretty soul? A pretty soul is
better than a pretty body. Do not you
know my pretty soul? I know you. Is not
your name Matheo?

MAT. Yes, lamb.	497

BELL. Baa, lamb! There you lie, for
I am mutton.—Look, fine man! He was
mad for me once, and I was mad for him
once, and he was mad for her once, and
were you never mad? Yes, I warrant. I had
a fine jewel once, a very fine jewel, and
that naughty man stole it away from me—
a very fine and a rich jewel.

DUKE. What jewel, pretty maid?

BELL. Maid? Nay, that's a lie. O,
'twas a very rich jewel, called a maiden-
head, and had not you it, leerer?	509

MAT. Out, you mad ass! Away!

DUKE.	Had he thy maidenhead?
He shall make thee amends, and marry
thee.

BELL. Shall he? O brave Arthur of
Bradley[2] then!

DUKE. And, if he bear the mind of a
gentleman, I know he will.

MAT. I think I rifled her of some such
paltry jewel.

DUKE. Did you? Then marry her; you
see the wrong
Has led her spirits into a lunacy.	519

[1] The name of a popular ballad.
[2] The opening of a well-known ballad.

MAT. How? Marry her, my lord?
'Sfoot, marry a madwoman? Let a man
get the tamest wife he can come by, she'll
be mad enough afterward, do what he
can.

DUKE. Nay, then, Father Anselmo here
shall do his best
To bring her to her wits. And will you
then?

MAT. I cannot tell; I may choose.

DUKE. Nay, then, law shall compel. I
tell you, sir,
So much her hard fate moves me, you
should not breathe   529
Under this air unless you married her.

MAT. Well, then, when her wits stand
in their right place,
I'll marry her.

BELL. I thank your grace.—Matheo, thou
art mine.—
[*To Hippolito.*] I am not mad, but put
on this disguise,
Only for you, my lord; for you can tell
Much wonder of me; but you are gone.
Farewell.—
Matheo, thou didst first turn my soul
black;
Now make it white again. I do pro-
test,
I'm pure as fire now, chaste as Cynthia's
breast.

HIP. I durst be sworn, Matheo, she's indeed.   540

MAT. Cony-catched, gulled! Must I sail
in your flyboat
Because I helped to rear your main-
mast first?
Plague found [1] you for 't, 'tis well.
The cuckold's stamp goes current in
all nations.
Some men ha' horns giv'n them at their
creations;
If I be one of those, why so. 'Tis better
To take a common wench, and make
her good,
Than one that simpers, and at first will
scarce
Be tempted forth over the threshold
door,
Yet in one sennight, zounds, turns ar-
rant whore.   550
Come, wench, thou shalt be mine. Give
me thy golls;

[1] Confound.

We'll talk of legs hereafter.—See, my
lord,
God give us joy!

OMNES. God give you joy!

Enter Candido's Wife and George.

GEO. Come, mistress, we are in Bedlam
now. Mass, and see, we come in pudding
time,[2] for here's the duke.

WIFE. My husband, good my lord!

DUKE. Have I thy husband?   559

CAS. It's Candido, my lord; he's here
among the lunatics. Father Anselmo, pray
fetch him forth. [*Exit Anselmo.*] This mad
woman is his wife, and, though she were
not with child, yet did she long most spitefully to have her husband mad; and, because she would be sure he should turn
Jew, she placed him here in Bethlem.
Yonder he comes.

Enter Candido with Anselmo.

DUKE. Come hither, signior. Are you
mad?   570

CAND. You are not mad.

DUKE. Why, I know that.

CAND. Then may you know I am not mad,
that know
You are not mad, and that you are the
duke.
None is mad here but one.—How do
you, wife?
What do you long for now?—Pardon,
my lord,
She had lost her child's nose else. I did
cut out
Pennyworths of lawn; the lawn was yet
mine own.
A carpet was my gown, yet 'twas mine
own.
I wore my man's coat, yet the cloth
mine own;   580
Had a cracked crown, the crown was
yet mine own.
She says for this I'm mad. Were her
words true,
I should be mad indeed. O foolish skill![3]
Is patience madness? I'll be a madman
still.

WIFE. [*Kneeling.*] Forgive me, and I'll
vex your spirit no more.

[2] In good time.
[3] Reason.

DUKE. Come, come, we'll have you friends; join hearts, join hands.

CAND. See, my lord, we are even.—
Nay, rise, for ill deeds kneel unto none but heaven.

DUKE. Signior, methinks patience has laid on you
Such heavy weight that you should loathe it—

CAND.   Loathe it?   590

DUKE. For he whose breast is tender, blood so cool,
That no wrongs heat it, is a patient fool.
What comfort do you find in being so calm?

CAND. That which green wounds receive from sovereign balm.
Patience, my lord? Why, 'tis the soul of peace;
Of all the virtues, 'tis near'st kin to heaven;
It makes men look like gods. The best of men
That e'er wore earth about him was a sufferer,
A soft, meek, patient, humble, tranquil spirit,
The first true gentleman that ever breathed.   600
The stock of patience then cannot be poor;
All it desires, it has; what monarch more?
It is the greatest enemy to law
That can be, for it doth embrace all wrongs,

And so chains up lawyers' and women's tongues.
'Tis the perpetual prisoner's liberty,
His walks and orchards. 'Tis the bond-slave's freedom,
And makes him seem proud of each iron chain,
As though he wore it more for state than pain.   609
It is the beggars' music, and thus sings,
Although their bodies beg, their souls are kings.
O my dread liege, It is the sap of bliss
Rears us aloft, makes men and angels kiss.
And last of all, to end a household strife,
It is the honey gainst a waspish wife.

DUKE. Thou giv'st it lively colors. Who dare say
He's mad, whose words march in so good array?
'Twere sin all women should such husbands have,
For every man must then be his wife's slave.
Come, therefore, you shall teach our court to shine;   620
So calm a spirit is worth a golden mine.
Wives with meek husbands that to vex them long,
In Bedlam must they dwell, else dwell they wrong.   *Exeunt.*

FINIS.

THOMAS HEYWOOD

Thomas Heywood, who, though not a genius, at times achieved dramatic work of the finest quality, was for more than forty years an industrious literary journeyman, willing for profit to turn his hand to any respectable job. Born in Lincolnshire about 1573 or 1574 into the family of a country parson who in descent and education seems to have been considerably above his station, Heywood had some pretensions to gentility. He studied at Cambridge and took an active interest in the many dramatic productions there. About 1594 he went to London, and soon afterward his name began to appear in Henslowe's Diary as playwright and actor. By 1598 he had won sufficient distinction to be listed by Meres in *Palladis Tamia* as among the "best for comedy" in England. He wrote and acted at first chiefly for the Admiral's Company and afterwards for Worcester's, which continued as Queen Anne's from 1603 until her death in 1619. In some of his work he collaborated with Wentworth Smith, Chettle, Dekker, Webster, or others. The average pay for an original play was about six pounds—a sum, however, which had in the Elizabethan period several times its present value—and this was sometimes shared with collaborators. Yet Heywood's productivity enabled him to support a wife and several children apparently in some comfort. In 1633 he stated that he had had "either an entire hand or at the least a main finger" in some two hundred and twenty plays. Of these probably not thirty survive. The dramatic work of his later years seems to have been confined to a series of lord mayors' pageants from 1631 to 1639 and the printing of plays that had been written by himself and others, usually long before. Besides *An Apology for Actors* (1612), his non-dramatic works include an epic on London, a history of Elizabeth's early life, and, in his later years, various semi-learned compilations. He died in 1641.

Heywood's university training may have led him to write plays drawn from classical sources, chiefly mythological, as in his series *The Four Ages*, in *The Rape of Lucrece*, and in *Love's Mistress*. The largest part of his extant work, however, and the best, depicts phases of English life, all classes being presented with unusual insight and sympathy. Even his stories from foreign sources, as in the Plautine plot of *The Captives*, are used for the portrayal of English characters. The outburst of national self-glorification that followed the defeat of the Armada is fully reflected in his plays. In one or the other of the double plots common in them, place is frequently found for one or more characters who illustrate the sterling qualities of the yeoman or the citizen—his patriotism, sturdy independence, thrift, generosity. The extreme example is the glorification of the apprentice in *The Four Prentices of London* (an adaptation of the story of Godfrey of Boulogne), which was satirized in *The Knight of the Burning Pestle*. There is the same emphasis, however, in the two chronicle plays, each in two parts—*Edward IV* (printed in 1599) and *If You Know Not Me, You Know Nobody* (printed in 1605 and 1606), which deals with the life of Queen Elizabeth, especially the early part. Romantic tales of English adventure on sea or in far lands are found in *Fortune by Land and Sea*, written with William Rowley, *A Challenge for Beauty*, and *The Fair Maid of the West*, in two parts. *The Fair Maid of the Exchange* and *The Wise Woman of Hogsdon* are more realistic studies of London life. Heywood's most sympathetic vein, however, is found in plays portraying the gentry, as in his *Royal King and Loyal Subject*. Two of these dealing with rural England are *A Woman Killed with Kindness* and *The English Traveler*, both domestic plays written in the restrained style considered appropriate for the type.

A Woman Killed with Kindness, Heywood's undoubted masterpiece, was begun, and probably acted, in 1603 for Henslowe, who squandered thirty-five shillings more on

Mistress Frankford's black velvet gown than he paid for the play. Printed in 1607, it was the first of Heywood's extant plays to carry his name on the title-page. A third edition is dated 1617, but no copy of the second is known. Heywood may have taken from life the basis of his main plot, with its thoroughly English tone, but it has been suggested that he reworked a story one form of which was translated from the *Heptameron* in Painter's *Palace of Pleasure*. The subplot comes from a novella of Illicini, which was translated into English by Fenton in his *Tragical Discourses* as well as by Painter, but the characters are as typically English as is the rest of the play. The basis of the present edition is the reproduction of the text of 1617 by Katherine Lee Bates in the Belles-Lettres Series.

A WOMAN KILLED WITH KINDNESS[1]

BY

THOMAS HEYWOOD

[DRAMATIS PERSONÆ

SIR FRANCIS ACTON, *brother to Mistress Frankford.*
SIR CHARLES MOUNTFORD.
MASTER JOHN FRANKFORD.
MASTER MALBY, *friend to Sir Francis.*
MASTER WENDOLL, *friend to Frankford.*
MASTER CRANWELL.
MASTER SHAFTON, *false friend to Sir Charles.*
OLD MOUNTFORD, *uncle to Sir Charles.*
MASTER SANDY, *former friend to Sir Charles.*
MASTER RODER, *former tenant to Sir Charles.*
MASTER TIDY, *cousin to Sir Charles.*
NICHOLAS ⎫
JENKIN ⎬ *household servants to Frankford.*
SPIGOT ⎭

ROGER BRICKBAT ⎫
JACK SLIME ⎬ *country fellows.*
SHERIFF.
KEEPER OF PRISON.
SHERIFF'S OFFICERS, SERJEANT, HUNTSMEN, FALCONERS, COACHMEN, CARTERS, SERVANTS, MUSICIANS.
FRANKFORD'S CHILDREN.

MISTRESS ANNE FRANKFORD.
SUSAN, *sister to Sir Charles Mountford.*
SISLY,[2] *maid to Mistress Frankford.*
WOMEN SERVANTS *in Master Frankford's household.*
JOAN MINIVER ⎫
JANE TRUBKIN ⎬ *country wenches.*
ISBEL MOTLEY ⎭

SCENE: *Yorkshire.*

TIME: *Contemporary.*]

PROLOGUE

I COME but as a harbinger, being sent
To tell you what these preparations mean.
Look for no glorious state; our Muse is bent
Upon a barren subject, a bare scene.
We could afford this twig a timber tree,
Whose strength might boldly on your favors build;
Our russet, tissue;[3] drone, a honeybee;
Our barren plot, a large and spacious field;
Our coarse fare, banquets; our thin water, wine;
Our brook, a sea; our bat's eyes, eagle's sight; 10
Our poet's dull and earthy Muse, divine;
Our ravens, doves; our crow's black feathers, white.
But gentle thoughts, when they may give the foil,[4]
Save them that yield, and spare where they may spoil.

[SCENE i.

A room in Frankford's house.]

Enter M[aster] John Frankford, Mistress Anne, Sir Francis Acton, Sir Charles Mountford, Master Malby, Master Wendoll, and M[aster] Cranwell.

FRAN. Some music there! None lead the bride a dance?
CHAR. Yes, would she dance "The Shaking of the Sheets";[5]
But that's the dance her husband means to lead her.

---

[1] The title continues: "As It Hath Been Oftentimes Acted by the Queen's Majest. Servants."
[2] Cicely.
[3] Fine cloth interwoven with gold or silver threads.
[4] Repulse, disapproval.
[5] A popular ballad and dance tune, also known as "The Dance of Death."

643

WEN. That's not the dance that every man must dance,
According to the ballet.[1]
FRAN.   Music, ho!
By your leave, sister—by your husband's leave,
I should have said—the hand that but this day
Was given you in the church I'll borrow.—Sound!
This marriage music hoists me from the ground.
FRANK. Ay, you may caper; you are light and free!   10
Marriage hath yoked my heels; pray, pardon me.
FRAN. I'll have you dance too, brother!
CHAR.   Master Frankford,
Y'are a happy man, sir, and much joy
Succeed your marriage mirth, you have a wife
So qualified, and with such ornaments
Both of the mind and body. First, her birth
Is noble, and her education such
As might become the daughter of a prince;
Her own tongue speaks all tongues, and her own hand
Can teach all strings to speak in their best grace,   20
From the shrill'st treble to the hoarsest bass.
To end her many praises in one word,
She's Beauty and Perfection's eldest daughter,
Only found by yours, though many a heart hath sought her.
FRANK. But that I know your virtues and chaste thoughts,
I should be jealous of your praise, Sir Charles.
CRAN. He speaks no more than you approve.
MAL. Nor flatters he that gives to her her due.
ANNE. I would your praise could find a fitter theme
Than my imperfect beauty to speak on.   30
Such as they be, if they my husband please,
They suffice me now I am marriéd.

His sweet content is like a flatt'ring glass,
To make my face seem fairer to mine eye;
But the least wrinkle from his stormy brow
Will blast the roses in my cheeks that grow.
FRAN. A perfect wife already, meek and patient!
How strangely the word husband fits your mouth,
Not married three hours since! Sister, 'tis good;
You that begin betimes thus, must needs prove   40
Pliant and duteous in your husband's love.—
Gramercies,[2] brother! Wrought her to 't already:
"Sweet husband," and a curtsy the first day!
Mark this, mark this, you that are bachelors,
And never took the grace of honest man,[3]
Mark this, against you marry,[4] this one phrase:
"In a good time that man both wins and woos
That takes his wife down in her wedding shoes."[5]
FRANK. Your sister takes not after you, Sir Francis.
All his wild blood your father spent on you;   50
He got her in his age, when he grew civil.
All his mad tricks were to his land entailed,
And you are heir to all; your sister, she
Hath to her dower her mother's modesty.
CHAR. Lord, sir, in what a happy state live you!
This morning, which to many seems a burthen
Too heavy to bear, is unto you a pleasure.
This lady is no clog, as many are;
She doth become you like a well-made suit,

---

[1] Ballad.
[2] Many thanks.
[3] "Assumed the honorable estate of husband", (Bates).
[4] In preparation for your marriage.
[5] *I.e.*, tames her at once.

In which the tailor hath used all his
　art,　　　　　　　　　　　　　　　60
Not like a thick coat of unseasoned
　frieze,
Forced on your back in summer. She's
　no chain
To tie your neck, and curb ye to the yoke;
But she's a chain of gold to adorn your
　neck.
You both adorn each other, and your
　hands,
Methinks, are matches. There's equality
In this fair combination; y'are both
Scholars, both young, both being de-
　scended nobly.
There's music in this sympathy; it
　carries
Consort [1] and expectation of much
　joy,　　　　　　　　　　　　　　70
Which God bestow on you from this
　first day
Until your dissolution—that's for aye!
FRAN. We keep you here too long, good
　brother Frankford.
Into the hall; away! Go cheer your
　guests.
What! Bride and bridegroom both with-
　drawn at once?
If you be missed, the guests will doubt
　their welcome,
And charge you with unkindness.
FRANK.　　　　　　To prevent it,
I'll leave you here, to see the dance
　within.
ANNE. And so will I.
　　　　　　Exeunt [Frankford and Anne].
FRAN.　　　　To part you it were sin.—
Now, gallants, while the town musi-
　cians　　　　　　　　　　　　　80
Finger their frets within, and the mad
　lads
And country lasses, every mother's child,
With nosegays and bride-laces [2] in their
　hats,
Dance all their country measures,
　rounds, and jigs,
What shall we do? Hark! They're all
　on the hoigh; [3]
They toil like mill horses, and turn as
　round;

Marry, not on the toe! Ay, and they
　caper,
Not without cutting; [4] you shall see to-
　morrow
The hall floor pecked and dinted like a
　millstone,
Made with their high shoes. Though
　their skill be small,　　　　　90
Yet they tread heavy where their hob-
　nails fall.
CHAR. Well, leave them to their sports!—
　Sir Francis Acton,
I'll make a match with you. Meet to-
　morrow
At Chevy Chase; I'll fly my hawk with
　yours.
FRAN. For what? For what?
CHAR.　　　　Why, for a hundred pound.
FRAN. Pawn [5] me some gold of that!
CHAR.　　　　　　　Here are ten angels;
I'll make them good a hundred pound
　tomorrow
Upon my hawk's wing.
FRAN.　　　　　　'Tis a match; 'tis done.
Another hundred pound upon your dogs,
Dare ye, Sir Charles?
CHAR.　　　I dare. Were I sure to lose,　100
I durst do more than that; here's my
　hand,
The first course for a hundred pound!
FRAN.　　　　　　　　　A match!
WEN. Ten angels on Sir Francis Acton's
　hawk;
As much upon his dogs!
CRAN. I'm for Sir Charles Mountford; I
　have seen
His hawk and dog both tried. What,
　clap [6] ye hands,
Or is 't no bargain?
WEN.　　　Yes, and stake them down.
Were they five hundred, they were all
　my own.
FRAN. Be stirring early with the lark to-
　morrow;
I'll rise into my saddle ere the sun　　110
Rise from his bed.
CHAR.　　　　　If there you miss me, say
I am no gentleman! I'll hold my day.
FRAN. It holds on all sides.—Come, to-
　night let's dance;
Early tomorrow let's prepare to ride.
We had need be three hours up before
　the bride.　　　　　　*[Exeunt.]*

---

[1] Harmony as well as companionship.
[2] Ribbons used for tying up the rosemary
sprigs carried by wedding guests.
[3] In a state of excitement.
[4] Curveting.　[5] Pledge, "put up."　[6] Shake.

The yard of Frankford's house.]

*Enter Nick and Jenkin, Jack Slime, Roger
Brickbat, with Country Wenches, and
two or three Musicians.*

JENK. Come, Nick, take you Joan Min-
iver, to trace [1] withal; Jack Slime, traverse [1]
you with Sisly Milkpail; I will take Jane
Trubkin, and Roger Brickbat shall have
Isbel Motley. And now that they are
busy in the parlor, come, strike up; we'll
have a crash [2] here in the yard.

NICK. My humor is not compendious.
Dancing I possess not, though I can foot
it; yet, since I am fallen into the hands   [10
of Sisly Milkpail, I consent.

SLIME. [3] Truly, Nick, though we were
never brought up like serving courtiers,
yet we have been brought up with serving creatures, ay, and God's creatures,
too, for we have been brought up to serve
sheep, oxen, horses, hogs, and suchlike;
and, though we be but country fellows,
it may be in the way of dancing we can
do the horse-trick [4] as well as the serv-   [20
ing-men.

ROGER. Ay, and the crosspoint [4] too.

JENK. O Slime! O Brickbat! Do not
you know that comparisons are odious?
Now we are odious ourselves, too; therefore there are no comparisons to be made
betwixt us.

NICK. I am sudden, and not superfluous;
I am quarrelsome, and not seditious;
I am peaceable, and not contentious;   30
I am brief, and not compendious.

SLIME. Foot it quickly! If the music
overcome not my melancholy, I shall
quarrel; and, if they suddenly do not strike
up, I shall presently strike thee down.

JENK. No quarreling, for God's sake!
Truly, if you do, I shall set a knave between ye.

SLIME. I come to dance, not to quarrel.
Come, what shall it be? "Rogero"?   [40

JENK. "Rogero"? No; we will dance
"The Beginning of the World."

SISLY. I love no dance so well as "John,
come kiss me now."

NICK. I, that have ere now deserved
a cushion, call for the "Cushion Dance."

ROGER. For my part, I like nothing
so well as "Tom Tyler."

JENK. No; we'll have "The Hunting
of the Fox."   50

SLIME. The hay,[5] the hay! There's
nothing like the hay.

NICK. I have said, do say, and will say
again—

JENK. Every man agree to have it as
Nick says!

ALL. Content.

NICK. It hath been, it now is, and it
shall be—   5S

SISLY. What, Master Nich'las? What?

NICK. "Put on your Smock a Monday."

JENK. So the dance will come cleanly
off! Come, for God's sake, agree of something; if you like not that, put it to the
musicians; or let me speak for all, and
we'll have "Sellenger's Round."

ALL. That, that, that!

NICK. No, I am resolved thus it shall be;
First take hands, then take ye to your
heels.

JENK. Why, would ye have us run   [70
away?

NICK. No; but I would have you shake
your heels.—Music, strike up!

*They dance; Nick, dancing, speaks stately
and scurvily, the rest after the country
fashion.*

JENK. Hey! Lively, my lasses! Here's
a turn for thee!   [*Exeunt.*]

[SCENE iii.

The open country.]

*Wind horns. Enter Sir Charles, Sir Francis,
Malby, Cranwell, Wendoll, Falconer,
and Huntsmen.*

CHAR. So; well cast off! Aloft, aloft!
Well flown!
O, now she takes her at the souse,[6] and
strikes her
Down to th' earth, like a swift thunder-
clap.[7]

WEN. She hath stroke ten angels out of
my way.

FRAN. A hundred pound from me.

CHAR. What, falc'ner!

FALC. At hand, sir!

---

[1] Dance.   [3] Original reads *Jack.*
[2] Revel.   [4] Vigorous movement of the dance.

[5] A winding country dance.   [6] Swoop.
[7] Here and in a few other passages the line
divisions have been regularized.

CHAR. Now she hath seized the fowl and
　　gins to plume [1] her;
Rebeck her not; [2] rather stand still and
　　check her!　　　　　　　　　　　　10
So, seize her gets, [3] her jesses, [4] and her
　　bells!
Away!
FRAN. My hawk killed, too.
CHAR. 　　　　　Ay, but 'twas at the querre, [5]
　　Not at the mount like mine.
FRAN. 　　　　　　Judgment, my masters!
CRAN. Yours missed her at the ferre. [6]
WEN. Ay, but our merlin first had plumed
　　the fowl,
And twice renewed [7] her from the river
　　too.
Her bells, Sir Francis, had not both one
　　weight,
Nor was one semitune above the other.
Methinks these Milan bells do sound
　　too full,　　　　　　　　　　　　　20
And spoil the mounting of your hawk.
CHAR. 　　　　　　　　　　　　'Tis lost.
FRAN. I grant it not.　Mine likewise
　　seized a fowl
Within her talents, [8] and you saw her
　　paws
Full of the feathers; both her petty
　　singles [9]
And her long singles griped her more
　　than other;
The terrials [10] of her [11] legs were stained
　　with blood,
Not of the fowl only; she did discomfit
Some of her feathers, but she [12] brake
　　away.
Come, come; your hawk is but a rifler. [13]
CHAR. 　　　　　　　　　　　　　How!
FRAN. Ay, and your dogs are trindle-
　　tails [14] and curs.　　　　　　　　30
CHAR. You stir my blood!
　　You keep not one good hound in all
　　your kennel,
Nor one good hawk upon your perch.
FRAN. 　　　　　　　　　How, knight!

---

[1] Begins to pluck.　　[2] Do not call her off.
[3] Part of the hawk's harness.　　[4] Leg straps.
[5] At the quarry, i.e., before the prey rose
from the ground.
　[6] At the far, i.e., at a higher point.　[8] Talons.
　[7] Driven again.　　　　　　[9] Claws.
[10] Perhaps a misprint for terrets, a part of the
jesses.
　[11] Mountford's hawk's.　　[13] Bungler.
　[12] The fowl.　　　　　　[14] Curly-tailed dogs.

CHAR. So, knight! You will not swagger,
　　sir?
FRAN. Why, say I did?
CHAR. 　　　　　　　　　　Why, sir,
　　I say you would gain as much by swag-
　　g'ring
As you have got by wagers on your
　　dogs.
You will come short in all things.
FRAN. 　　　　　　　　　Not in this!
　　Now I'll strike home.
　　　　　　　　　[Strikes Sir Charles.]
CHAR. 　　Thou shalt to thy long home,
　　Or I will want my will.　　　　　40
FRAN. All they that love Sir Francis,
　　follow me!
CHAR. All that affect Sir Charles, draw on
　　my part!
CRAN. On this side heaves my hand.
WEN. 　　　　　　　Here goes my heart.
They divide themselves.　Sir Charles, Cran-
　　well, Falconer, and Huntsman fight
　　against Sir Francis, Wendoll, his Fal-
　　coner, and Huntsman; and Sir Charles
　　hath the better, and beats them away,
　　killing both of Sir Francis his men.
　　　　　　　[Exeunt all but Sir Charles.]
CHAR. My God, what have I done! What
　　have I done!
My rage hath plunged into a sea of
　　blood,
In which my soul lies drowned.　Poor
　　innocents,
For whom we are to answer! Well, 'tis
　　done,
And I remain the victor.　A great con-
　　quest,
When I would give this right hand, nay,
　　this head,
To breathe in them new life whom I
　　have slain!　　　　　　　　　　50
Forgive me, God! 'Twas in the heat of
　　blood,
And anger quite removes me from my-
　　self.
It was not I, but rage, did this vile
　　murther;
Yet I, and not my rage, must answer it.
Sir Francis Acton, he is fled the field;
With him all those that did partake his
　　quarrel;
And I am left alone with sorrow dumb,
And in my heighth of conquest over-
　　come.

Enter Susan.

Sus. O God! My brother wounded 'mong
the dead!
Unhappy jests, that in such earnest
ends!   60
The rumor of this fear stretched to my
ears,
And I am come to know if you be wounded.

CHAR. O, sister, sister, wounded at the
heart!

Sus. My God forbid!

CHAR. In doing that thing which he forbade,
I am wounded, sister.

Sus.   I hope, not at the heart.

CHAR. Yes, at the heart.

Sus.   O God! A surgeon, there!

CHAR. Call me a surgeon, sister, for my
soul!
The sin of murther, it hath pierced my
heart
And made a wide wound there; but for
these scratches,   70
They are nothing, nothing.

Sus.   Charles, what have you done?
Sir Francis hath great friends, and will
pursue you
Unto the utmost danger [1] of the law.

CHAR. My conscience is become mine
enemy,
And will pursue me more than Acton
can.

Sus. O, fly, sweet brother!

CHAR.   Shall I fly from thee?
Why, Sue, art weary of my company?

Sus. Fly from your foe!

CHAR.   You, sister, are my friend,
And, flying you, I shall pursue my end.

Sus. Your company is as my eyeball dear;
Being far from you, no comfort can be
near.   81
Yet fly to save your life! What would I
care
To spend my future age in black despair,
So you were safe? And yet to live one
week
Without my brother Charles, through
every cheek
My streaming tears would downwards
run so rank,

Till they could set on either side a bank,
And in the midst a channel; so my face
For two saltwater brooks shall still
find place.

CHAR. Thou shall not weep so much, for
I will stay,   90
In spite of danger's teeth. I'll live with
thee,
Or I'll not live at all. I will not sell
My country and my father's patrimony,
Nor [2] thy sweet sight, for a vain hope
of life.

Enter Sheriff with Officers.

SHER. Sir Charles, I am made the un-
willing instrument
Of your attach [3] and apprehension.
I'm sorry that the blood of innocent
men
Should be of you exacted.[4] It was told me
That you were guarded with a troop of
friends,
And therefore [I] came thus armed.

CHAR.   O, Master Sheriff, 100
I came into the field with many friends,
But see, they all have left me; only one
Clings to my sad misfortune, my dear
sister.
I know you for an honest gentleman;
I yield my weapons, and submit to you.
Convey me where you please!

SHER.   To prison, then,
To answer for the lives of these dead
men.

Sus. O God! O God!

CHAR.   Sweet sister, every strain
Of sorrow from your heart augments
my pain;
Your grief abounds, and hits against
my breast.   110

SHER. Sir, will you go?

CHAR.   Even where it likes you best.
                              [*Exeunt.*]

[SCENE iv.

A room in Frankford's house.]

Enter Master Frankford in a study.[5]

FRANK. How happy am I amongst other
men,
That in my mean estate embrace content!

[1] Penalty.

[2] Original has *no.*   [3] Arrest.
[4] From 1607 edn. Original reads *enacted.*
[5] Reverie.

I am a gentleman, and by my birth
Companion with a king; a king's no more.
I am possessed of many fair revenues,
Sufficient to maintain a gentleman;
Touching my mind, I am studied in all
  arts,
The riches of my thoughts; and of my
  time
Have been a good proficient; [1] but, the
  chief
Of all the sweet felicities on earth,   10
I have a fair, a chaste, and loving wife—
Perfection all, all truth, all ornament.
If man on earth may truly happy be,
Of these at once possessed, sure I am he.

Enter Nicholas.

NICK. Sir, there's a gentleman attends
  without
To speak with you.
FRANK.   On horseback?
NICK.   Yes, on horseback.
FRANK. Entreat him to alight, and I'll
  attend him.
Know'st thou him, Nick?
NICK.   Know him? Yes; his name's
  Wendoll.
It seems he comes in haste. His horse is
  booted [2]
Up to the flank in mire, himself all
  spotted   20
And stained with plashing. Sure, he rid
  in fear,
Or for a wager. Horse and man both
  sweat;
I ne'er saw two in such a smoking heat.
FRANK. Entreat him in.   About it in-
  stantly!   [*Exit Nick.*]
This Wendoll I have noted, and his car-
  riage
Hath pleased me much; by observation
I have noted many good deserts in
  him.
He's affable, and seen [3] in many things;
Discourses well, a good companion,
And, though of small means, yet a gentle-
  man   30
Of a good house, somewhat pressed by
  want.
I have preferred him to a second place
In my opinion and my best regard.

[1] Have made good use.
[2] Covered.
[3] Skilled, accomplished.

*Enter Wendoll, Mistress Frankford, and
                                  Nick.*

ANNE. O, M[aster] Frankford, Master
  Wendoll here
Brings you the strangest news that e'er
  you heard.
FRANK. What news, sweet wife? What
  news, good M[aster] Wendoll?
WEN. You knew the match made twixt
  Sir Francis Acton
And Sir Charles Mountford?
FRANK.   True; with their hounds
  and hawks.
WEN. The matches were both played.
FRANK.   Ha? And which won?
WEN. Sir Francis, your wife's brother, had
  the worst,   40
And lost the wager.
FRANK.   Why, the worse his chance;
Perhaps the fortune of some other day
Will change his luck.
WEN. [4]   O, but you hear not all.
Sir Francis lost, and yet was loath to
  yield.
At length the two knights grew to dif-
  ference,
From words to blows, and so to banding
  sides,
Where valorous Sir Charles slew, in his
  spleen,
Two of your brother's men—his falc'ner
And his good huntsman whom he loved
  so well.
More men were wounded, no more slain
  outright.   50
FRANK. Now, trust me, I am sorry for the
  knight.
But is my brother safe?
WEN.   All whole and sound,
His body not being blemished with one
  wound.
But poor Sir Charles is to the prison led,
To answer at th' assize for them that's
  dead.
FRANK. I thank your pains, sir. Had the
  news been better,
Your will was to have brought it, M[as-
  ter] Wendoll.
Sir Charles will find hard friends; his case
  is heinous
And will be most severely censured on. [5]
I'm sorry for him. Sir, a word with you!

[4] Original reads *Anne*.   [5] Judged.

I know you, sir, to be a gentleman 61
In all things; your possibility [1] but mean.
Please you to use my table and my purse;
They are yours.
WEN.   O Lord, sir, I shall ne'er
    deserve it!
FRANK. O, sir, disparage not your worth
    too much;
You are full of quality and fair desert.
Choose of my men which shall attend
    you, sir,
And he is yours. I will allow you, sir,
Your man, your gelding, and your
    table,
All at my own charge. Be my compan-
    ion!   70
WEN. M[aster] Frankford, I have oft been
    bound to you
By many favors; this exceeds them all,
That I shall never merit your least favor;
But, when your last remembrance I for-
    get,
Heaven at my soul exact that weighty
    debt!
FRANK. There needs no protestation, for
    I know you
Virtuous, and therefore grateful.—
    Prithee, Nan,
Use him with all thy loving'st courtesy!
ANNE. As far as modesty may well ex-
    tend,
It is my duty to receive your friend. 80
FRANK. To dinner! Come, sir, from this
    present day,
Welcome to me forever! Come, away!
    [*Exeunt Frankford, Anne, and Wendoll.*]
NICK. I do not like this fellow by no
    means.
I never see him but my heart still earns.[2]
Zounds! I could fight with him, yet
    know not why;
The devil and he are all one, in mine eye.

Enter Jenkin.

JENK. O Nick, what gentleman is that
that comes to lie at our house? My master
allows him one to wait on him, and I believe it will fall to thy lot.   90
NICK. I love my master; by these hilts, I
    do;
But rather than I'll ever come to serve
    him,
I'll turn away my master.

[1] Possessions.   [2] Yearns, grieves.

Enter Sisly.

SISLY. Nich'las, where are you, Nich'-
las? You must come in, Nich'las, and
help the gentleman off with his boots.
NICK. If I pluck off his boots, I'll eat the
    spurs,
And they shall stick fast in my throat
    like burrs.
SISLY. Then, Jenkin, come you!   99
JENK. Nay, 'tis no boot [3] for me to
deny it. My master hath given me a coat
here, but he takes pains himself to brush it
once or twice a day with a holly wand.
SISLY. Come, come, make haste, that
you may wash your hands again, and help
to serve in dinner!
JENK. You may see, my masters, though
it be afternoon with you, 'tis but early days [4]
with us, for we have not dined yet. Stay
but a little; I'll but go in and help   [110
to bear up the first course, and come to you
again presently.   *Exeunt.*

[SCENE V.

The jail.]

Enter Malby and Cranwell.

MAL. This is the sessions day. Pray, can
    you tell me
How young Sir Charles hath sped? Is he
    acquit,
Or must he try the law's strict penalty?
CRAN. He's cleared of all, spite of his
    enemies,
Whose earnest labor was to take his life.
But in this suit of pardon he hath spent
All the revenues that his father left him;
And he is now turned a plain country
    man,
Reformed [5] in all things. See, sir, here he
    comes.

Enter Sir Charles and his Keeper.

KEEP. Discharge your fees, and you are
    then at freedom.   10
CHAR. Here, M[aster] Keeper, take the
    poor remainder
Of all the wealth I have! My heavy foes

[3] Use.
[4] Jenkin addresses the audience, for whom the
time is afternoon, although on the stage it is
early morning.
[5] Transformed.

Have made my purse light, but, alas, to me

'Tis wealth enough that you have set me free.

MAL. God give you joy of your delivery!
I am glad to see you abroad, Sir Charles.

CHAR. The poorest knight in England, M[aster] Malby.

My life hath cost me all my patrimony
My father left his son. Well, God forgive them
That are the authors of my penury! 20

Enter Shafton.

SHAFT. Sir Charles! A hand, a hand! At liberty?

Now, by the faith I owe, I am glad to see it.

What want you? Wherein may I pleasure you?

CHAR. O me, O, most unhappy gentleman!
I am not worthy to have friends stirred up,
Whose hands may help me in this plunge of want.

I would I were in heaven, to inherit there
Th' immortal birthright which my Savior keeps,
And by no unthrift [1] can be bought and sold;
For here on earth what pleasures should we trust? 30

SHAFT. To rid you from these contemplations,
Three hundred pounds you shall receive of me;
Nay, five for fail.[2] Come, sir, the sight of gold
Is the most sweet receipt for melancholy,
And will revive your spirits. You shall hold law
With your proud adversaries. Tush!
Let Frank Acton
Wage [3] his knighthood like expense [4] with me,
And a [5] will sink, he will. Nay, good Sir Charles,
Applaud your fortune and your fair escape
From all these perils.

CHAR.   O, sir, they have
undone me! 40

Two thousand and five hundred pound a year
My father at his death possessed me of,
All which the envious [6] Acton made me spend;
And, notwithstanding all this large expense,
I had much ado to gain my liberty;
And I have only now a house of pleasure,
With some five hundred pounds, reserved
Both to maintain me and my loving sister.

SHAFT. [*Aside.*] That must I have; it lies convenient for me.
If I can fasten but one finger on him, 50
With my full hand I'll gripe him to the heart.
'Tis not for love I proffered him this coin,
But for my gain and pleasure.—Come, Sir Charles,
I know you have need of money; take my offer.

CHAR. Sir, I accept it, and remain indebted
Even to the best of my unable power.
Come, gentlemen, and see it tendered down! [*Exeunt.*]

[SCENE vi.

A room in Frankford's house.]

Enter Wendoll, melancholy.

WEN. I am a villain, if I apprehend
But such a thought! Then, to attempt the deed—
Slave, thou art damned without redemption!
I'll drive away this passion with a song.
A song! Ha, ha! A song! As if, fond [7] man,
Thy eyes could swim in laughter when thy soul
Lies drenched and drownéd in red tears of blood!
I'll pray, and see if God within my heart
Plant better thoughts. Why, prayers are meditations,
And when I meditate (O, God forgive me!) 10

---

[1] Spendthrift or unthriftiness.
[2] For fear of failure to give enough.
[3] Hazard.   [4] Expenditure.   [5] He.
[6] Malicious.   [7] Foolish.

It is on her divine perfections.
I will forget her; I will arm myself
Not t' entertain a thought of love to her;
And, when I come by chance into her
    presence,
I'll hale [1] these balls until my eyestrings
    crack
From being pulled and drawn to look
    that way.

*Enter, over the stage, Frankford, his Wife,
               and Nick [, and exeunt].*

O God, O God! With what a violence
I'm hurried to mine own destruction!
There goest thou, the most perfect's[t]
    man
That ever England bred a gentleman, 20
And shall I wrong his bed?—Thou God
    of Thunder,
Stay, in thy thoughts of vengeance and
    of wrath,
Thy great, almighty, and all-judging
    hand
From speedy execution on a villain,
A villain and a traitor to his friend!

Enter Jenkin.

JENK. Did your worship call?
WEN. [*Not noticing Jenkin.*] He doth
    maintain me; he allows me largely
    Money to spend—
JENK. By my faith, so do not you me;
I cannot get a cross [2] of you.   30
WEN. My gelding, and my man—
JENK. That's Sorrel and I.
WEN. This kindness grows of no alliance [3]
    twixt us—
JENK. Nor is my service of any great ac-
    quaintance. [4]
WEN. I never bound him to me by desert.
Of a mere stranger, a poor gentleman,
A man by whom in no kind he could
    gain,
He hath placed me in the height of all
    his thoughts, [5]
Made me companion with the best and
    chiefest   40
In Yorkshire. He cannot eat without
    me,

Nor laugh without me; I am to his body
As necessary as his digestion,
And equally do make him whole or sick.
And shall I wrong this man? Base man!
    Ingrate!
Hast thou the power, straight with thy
    gory hands,
To rip thy image from his bleeding heart,
To scratch thy name from out the holy
    book
Of his remembrance, and to wound his
    name
That holds thy name so dear, or rend his
    heart   50
To whom thy heart was knit and joined
    together?
And yet I must. Then, Wendoll, be con-
    tent!
Thus villains, when they would, cannot
    repent.
JENK. What a strange humor is my new
master in! Pray God he be not mad; if he
should be so, I should never have any mind
to serve him in Bedlam. It may be he's
mad for missing of me.
WEN. [*Seeing Jenkin.*] What, Jenkin!
Where's your mistress?   60
JENK. Is your worship married?
WEN. Why dost thou ask?
JENK. Because you are my master; and,
if I have a mistress, I would be glad, like a
good servant, to do my duty to her.
WEN. I mean Mistress Frankford.
JENK. Marry, sir, her husband is riding
out of town, and she went very lovingly to
bring him on his way to horse. Do you
see, sir? Here she comes, and here I go.
WEN. Vanish!   [*Exit Jenkin.*] 71

Enter Mistress Frankford.

ANNE. Y'are well met, sir. Now, in troth,
    my husband,
Before he took horse, had a great desire
To speak with you; we sought about the
    house,
Hallooed into the fields, sent every way,
But could not meet you. Therefore he
    enjoined me
To do unto you his most kind commends.
Nay, more; he wills you, as you prize his
    love,
Or hold in estimation his kind friendship,
To make bold in his absence, and com-
    mand   80

---

[1] Draw away, turn away.   [3] Kinship.
[2] Coin.   [4] Close relationship.
[5] From 1607 edn. Original reads, *And he
hath placed me in his highest thoughts.*

Even as himself were present in the house;

For you must keep his table, use his servants,

And be a present Frankford in his absence.

WEN. I thank him for his love.—

[*Aside.*] Give me a name, you whose infectious tongues

Are tipped with gall and poison. As you would

Think on a man that had your father slain,

Murdered your children, made your wives base strumpets,

So call me, call me so; print in my face

The most stigmatic title of a villain, 90

For hatching treason to so true a friend!

ANNE. Sir, you are much beholding to my husband;

You are a man most dear in his regard.

WEN. I am bound unto your husband, and you too.—

[*Aside.*] I will not speak to wrong a gentleman

Of that good estimation, my kind friend.

I will not, zounds! I will not. I may choose,

And I will choose. Shall I be so misled?

Or shall I purchase [1] to my father's crest

The motto of a villain? If I say 100

I will not do it, what thing can enforce me?

What can compel me? What sad destiny

Hath such command upon my yielding thoughts?

I will not. Ha! Some fury pricks me on;

The swift Fates drag me at their chariot wheel,

And hurry me to mischief. Speak I must;

Injure myself, wrong her, deceive his trust!—

ANNE. Are you not well, sir, that ye seem thus troubled?

There is sedition in your countenance.

WEN. And in my heart, fair angel, chaste and wise. 110

I love you! Start not, speak not, answer not.

I love you—nay, let me speak the rest.

Bid me to swear, and I will call to record

The host of heaven.

[1] Acquire, add.

ANNE. The host of heaven forbid

Wendoll should hatch such a disloyal thought!

WEN. Such is my fate; to this suit I was born,

To wear rich pleasure's crown, or fortune's scorn.

ANNE. My husband loves you.

WEN. I know it.

ANNE. He esteems you

Even as his brain, his eyeball, or his heart.

WEN. I have tried it. 120

ANNE. His purse is your exchequer, and his table

Doth freely serve you.

WEN. So I have found it.

ANNE. O, with what face of brass, what brow of steel,

Can you, unblushing, speak this to the face

Of the espoused wife of so dear a friend?

It is my husband that maintains your state.

Will you dishonor him—I am his wife—

That in your power hath left his whole affairs?

It is to me you speak?

WEN. O, speak no more,

For more than this I know, and have recorded 130

Within the red-leaved table [2] of my heart.

Fair, and of all beloved, I was not fearful

Bluntly to give my life into your hand,

And at one, [3] hazard all my earthly means.

Go, tell your husband; he will turn me off,

And I am then undone. I care not, I;

'Twas for your sake. Perchance in rage he'll kill me;

I care not, 'twas for you. Say I incur

The general name of villain through the world,

Of traitor to my friend; I care not, I.

Beggary, shame, death, scandal, and reproach— 141

For you I'll hazard all. Why, what care I?

For you I'll love, and in your love I'll die.

ANNE. You move me, sir, to passion and to pity.

[2] Tablet, notebook.   [3] At one throw.

The love I bear my husband is as precious
As my soul's health.

WEN.   I love your husband too,
And for his love I will engage my life.
Mistake me not; the augmentation
Of my sincere affection borne to you
Doth no whit lessen my regard of him.
I will be secret, lady, close as night; 151
And not the light of one small glorious star
Shall shine here in my forehead, to bewray
That act of night.

ANNE.   What shall I say?
My soul is wand'ring, and hath lost her way.
O, Master Wendoll! O!

WEN.   Sigh not, sweet saint,
For every sigh you breathe draws from my heart
A drop of blood.

ANNE.   I ne'er offended yet.
My fault, I fear, will in my brow be writ.
Women that fall, not quite bereft of grace, 160
Have their offenses noted in their face.
I blush, and am ashamed. O, Master Wendoll,
Pray God I be not born to curse your tongue
That hath enchanted me! This maze I am in
I fear will prove the labyrinth of sin.

Enter Nick [behind].

WEN. The path of pleasure and the gate to bliss,
Which on your lips I knock at with a kiss!

NICK. [*Aside.*] I'll kill the rogue.

WEN. Your husband is from home; your bed's no blab.
Nay, look not down and blush!

          [*Exeunt Wendoll and Anne.*]

NICK.   Zounds! I'll stab!
Ay, Nick, was it thy chance to come just in the nick? 171
I love my master, and I hate that slave;
I love my mistress, but these tricks I like not.
My master shall not pocket up this wrong;

I'll eat my fingers first. What sayst thou, metal?
Does not that rascal Wendoll go on legs
That thou must cut off? Hath he not hamstrings
That thou must hock? [1] Nay, metal, thou shalt stand
To all I say. I'll henceforth turn a spy,
And watch them in their close conveyances. [2] 180
I never looked for better of that rascal,
Since he came miching [3] first into our house.
It is that Sathan hath corrupted her,
For she was fair and chaste. I'll have an eye
In all their gestures. Thus I think of them,
If they proceed as they have done before:
Wendoll's a knave, my mistress is a ——.

                  Exit.

[SCENE vii.

Near Mountford's house.]

Enter Charles and Susan.

CHAR. Sister, you see we are driven to hard shift
To keep this poor house we have left unsold.
I am now enforced to follow husbandry,
And you to milk. And do we not live well?
Well, I thank God.

SUS.   O brother, here's a change
Since old Sir Charles died in our father's house.

CHAR. All things on earth thus change, some up, some down;
Content's a kingdom, and I wear that crown.

Enter Shafton, with a Serjeant.

SHAFT. Good morrow, morrow, Sir Charles! What, with your sister,
Plying your husbandry?—Serjeant, stand off!— 10
You have a pretty house here, and a garden,
And goodly ground about it. Since it lies
So near a lordship that I lately bought,

---

[1] Hack, cut.   [2] Secret trickery.   [3] Skulking.

I would fain buy it of you. I will give
you—

CHAR. O, pardon me; this house successively

Hath longed [1] to me and my progenitors

Three hundred years. My great-great-
grandfather,

He in whom first our gentle style [2] began,

Dwelt here, and in this ground increased
this molehill

Unto that mountain which my father
left me. 20

Where he, the first of all our house, begun,

I now, the last, will end, and keep this
house,

This virgin title never yet deflowered

By any unthrift of the Mountfords' line.

In brief, I will not sell it for more gold

Than you could hide or pave the ground
withal.

SHAFT. Ha, ha! A proud mind and a
beggar's purse!

Where's my three hundred pounds, besides the use? [3]

I have brought it to execution

By course of law. What, is my monies
ready? 30

CHAR. An execution, sir, and never tell me

You put my bond in suit? You deal extremely.

SHAFT. Sell me the land, and I'll acquit
you straight.

CHAR. Alas, alas! 'Tis all trouble hath
left me

To cherish me and my poor sister's life.

If this were sold, our names [4] should then
be quite

Raced [5] from the beadroll of gentility.

You see what hard shift we have made
to keep it

Allied still to our own name. This palm
you see,

Labor hath glowed within; her silver
brow, 40

That never tasted a rough winter's blast

Without a mask or fan, doth with a grace

Defy cold winter, and his storms outface.

SUS. Sir, we feed sparing, and we labor
hard;

We lie uneasy, to reserve to us

And our succession this small spot of
ground.

CHAR. I have so bent my thoughts to husbandry

That I protest I scarcely can remember

What a new fashion is, how silk or satin

Feels in my hand. Why, pride is grown
to us 50

A mere, mere stranger. I have quite
forgot

The names of all that ever waited on me.

I cannot name ye any of my hounds,

Once from whose echoing mouths I
heard all music

That e'er my heart desired. What should
I say?

To keep this place, I have changed myself away.

SHAFT. [*To the Serjeant.*] Arrest him at my
suit!—Actions and actions

Shall keep thee in continual bondage fast;

Nay, more, I'll sue thee by a late appeal,

And call thy former life in question. 60

The keeper is my friend; thou shalt have
irons,

And usage such as I'll deny to dogs.—
Away with him!

CHAR. Ye are too timorous.[6] But trouble
is my master,

And I will serve him truly.—My kind
sister,

Thy tears are of no force to mollify

This flinty man. Go to my father's
brother,

My kinsmen, and allies; entreat them for
me,

To ransom me from this injurious man

That seeks my ruin.

SHAFT. Come, irons, irons! Come away!

I'll see thee lodged far from the sight of
day. [*Exeunt all except Susan.*] 70

SUS. My heart's so hardened with the
frost of grief,

Death cannot pierce it through.—Tyrant
too fell!

So lead the fiends condemnéd souls to
hell.

Enter Acton and Malby.

FRAN. Again to prison! Malby, hast thou
seen

A poor slave better tortured? Shall we
hear

[1] Belonged.
[2] Title of gentleman.
[3] Interest.
[4] Old edns. read *means.*
[5] Erased, scraped.
[6] Terrible.

The music of his voice cry from the grate,[1]
"Meat, for the Lord's sake"? No, no; yet I am not
Throughly revenged. They say he hath a pretty wench
To his sister. Shall I, in my mercy sake   79
To him and to his kindred, bribe the fool
To shame herself by lewd, dishonest lust?
I'll proffer largely; but, the deed being done,
I'll smile to see her base confusion.

MAL. Methinks, Sir Francis, you are full revenged
For greater wrongs than he can proffer you.
See where the poor sad gentlewoman stands!

FRAN. Ha, ha! Now will I flout her poverty,
Deride her fortunes, scoff her base estate.
My very soul the name of Mountford hate.
But stay, my heart! O,[2] what a look did fly   90
To strike my soul through with thy piercing eye!
I am enchanted, all my spirits are fled,
And with one glance my envious spleen strook dead.

SUS. Acton, that seeks our blood!
                                   Runs away.
FRAN.   O chaste and fair!
MAL. Sir Francis, why, Sir Francis, in a trance?
Sir Francis, what cheer, man? Come, come, how is 't?

FRAN. Was she not fair? Or else this judging eye
Cannot distinguish beauty.
MAL.   She was fair.
FRAN. She was an angel in a mortal's shape,
And ne'er descended from old Mountford's line.   100
But soft, soft, let me call my wits together!
A poor, poor wench, to my great adversary
Sister, whose very souls denounce stern war

Each against other! How now, Frank? Turned fool
Or madman, whether?[3] But no! Master of
My perfect senses and directest wits.
Then why should I be in this violent humor
Of passion and of love? And with a person
So different every way, and so opposed
In all contractions[4] and still-warring actions?   110
Fie, fie! How I dispute against my soul!
Come, come; I'll gain her, or in her fair quest
Purchase my soul free and immortal rest.
                                   [*Exeunt.*]

[SCENE viii.

A room in Frankford's house.]

Enter three or four Serving-men, one with a voider[5] and a wooden knife, to take away; another the salt and bread; another the tablecloth and napkins; another the carpet;[6] Jenkin with two lights after them.

JENK. So; march in order, and retire in battle array! My master and the guests have supped already; all's taken away. Here, now spread for the serving-men in the hall!—Butler, it belongs to your office.
BUT. I know it, Jenkin. What d' ye call the gentleman that supped there tonight?
JENK. Who? My master?
BUT. No, no; Master Wendoll, he's a daily guest. I mean the gentleman that [10 came but this afternoon.
JENK. His name's M[aster] Cranwell. God's light! Hark, within there; my master calls to lay more billets upon the fire. Come, come! Lord, how we that are in office here in the house are troubled! One spread the carpet in the parlor, and stand ready to snuff the lights; the rest be ready to prepare their stomachs! More lights in the hall there! Come, Nich'las.   20
                         [*Exeunt all but Nick.*]
NICK. I cannot eat, but, had I Wendoll's heart,

[3] Which one?
[4] Lawsuits.
[5] Tray for clearing the remains of the meal.
[6] Heavy covering for a table.

[1] Grating of prison.   [2] Original reads *Or.*

I would eat that. The rogue grows im-
    pudent!
O, I have seen such vild,[1] notorious
    tricks,
Ready to make my eyes dart from my
    head!
I'll tell my master; by this air, I will.
Fall what may fall, I'll tell him. Here
    he comes.

Enter Master Frankford, as it were brushing
    the crumbs from his clothes with a
    napkin, as newly risen from supper.

FRANK. Nich'las, what make [2] you here?
    Why are not you
At supper in the hall, among your
    fellows?
NICK. Master, I stayed [3] your rising from
    the board,   29
To speak with you.
FRANK.   Be brief then, gentle Nich'las;
My wife and guests attend [4] me in the
    parlor.
Why dost thou pause? Now, Nich'las,
    you want money,
And, unthriftlike, would eat into your
    wages
Ere you have earned it. Here, sir, 's
    half a crown;
Play the good husband.[5] And away to
    supper!
NICK. [*Aside.*] By this hand, an honor-
able gentleman! I will not see him
wronged.—Sir, I have served you long;
you entertained me seven years before
your beard; you knew me, sir, before [40
you knew my mistress.
FRANK. What of this, good Nich'las?
NICK. I never was a makebate [6] or a
    knave;
I have no fault but one—I'm given to
    quarrel,
But not with women. I will tell you,
    master,
That which will make your heart leap
    from your breast,
Your hair to startle from your head,
    your ears to tingle,
FRANK. What preparation's this to dismal
    news?

---

[1] Vile.
[2] Do.
[3] Awaited.
[4] Await.
[5] *I.e.*, be thrifty.
[6] Maker of debates, quarrels.

NICK. 'Sblood! [7] Sir, I love you better
    than your wife.
I'll make it good.   50
FRANK. Y'are a knave, and I have much
    ado
With wonted patience to contain my
    rage,
And not to break thy pate. Th' art a
    knave.
I'll turn you, with your base comparisons,
Out of my doors.
NICK.   Do, do!
There is not room for Wendoll and me
    too,
Both in one house. O master, master,
That Wendoll is a villain!
FRANK. [*Striking him.*]   Ay, saucy!
NICK. Strike, strike, do strike; yet hear
    me! I am no fool;
I know a villain, when I see him act 60
Deeds of a villain. Master, master,
    that base slave
Enjoys my mistress, and dishonors you.
FRANK. Thou hast killed me with a weapon
    whose sharp point
Hath pricked quite through and through
    my shiv'ring heart.
Drops of cold sweat sit dangling on my
    hairs,
Like morning's dew upon the golden
    flowers,
And I am plunged into strange agonies.
What didst thou say? If any word that
    touched
His credit or her reputation,
It is as hard to enter my belief   70
As Dives into heaven.
NICK.   I can gain nothing.
They are two that never wronged me. I
    knew before
'Twas but a thankless office, and perhaps
As much as is my service, or my life is
    worth.
All this I know; but this, and more,
More by a thousand dangers, could not
    hire me
To smother such a heinous wrong from
    you.
I saw, and I have said.
FRANK. [*Aside.*] 'Tis probable. Though
    blunt, yet he is honest.
Though I durst pawn my life, and on
    their faith   80

---

[7] God's blood.

Hazard the dear salvation of my soul,
Yet in my trust I may be too secure.
May this be true? O, may it? Can it be?
Is it by any wonder possible?
Man, woman, what thing mortal can we
   trust,
When friends and bosom wives prove so
   unjust?—
What instance [1] hast thou of this strange
   report?

NICK. Eyes, master, eyes.

FRANK. Thy eyes may be deceived, I tell
   thee;
For, should an angel from the heavens
   drop down,   90
And preach this to me that thyself hast
   told,
He should have much ado to win belief,
In both their loves I am so confident.

NICK. Shall I discourse the same by circumstance?

FRANK. No more! To supper, and com-
   mand your fellows
To attend us and the strangers. Not a
   word,
I charge thee, on thy life! Be secret then,
For I know nothing.

NICK. I am dumb; and, now that I have
   eased my stomach,[2]
I will go fill my stomach.   *Exit.*

FRANK.   Away! Begone!—   100
She is well born, descended nobly;
Virtuous her education; her repute
Is in the general voice of all the country
Honest and fair; her carriage, her de-
   meanor,
In all her actions that concern the love
To me her husband, modest, chaste, and
   godly.
Is all this seeming gold plain copper?
But he, that Judas that hath borne my
   purse,
And sold me for a sin! O God! O God!
Shall I put up these wrongs? No! Shall
   I trust   110
The bare report of this suspicious groom
Before the double gilt,[3] the well-hatch[4]
   ore
Of their two hearts? No, I will loose [5]
   these thoughts;

Distraction I will banish from my brow,
And from my looks exile sad discontent.
Their wonted favors in my tongue shall
   flow;
Till I know all, I'll nothing seem to
   know.—
Lights and a table there! Wife, M[aster]
   Wendoll,
And gentle Master Cranwell!

*Enter Mistress Frankford, Master Wendoll,
   Master Cranwell, Nick, and Jenkin
   with cards, carpets, stools, and other
               necessaries.*

FRANK. O, Master Cranwell, you are a
   stranger here,   120
And often balk [6] my house; faith, y'are a
   churl!
Now we have supped, a table and to
   cards!

JENK. A pair [7] of cards, Nich'las, and a
carpet to cover the table! Where's Sisly,
with her counters and her box? Candles
and candlesticks there! Fie! We have
such a household of serving-creatures! Unless it be Nick and I, there's not one
amongst them all can say "bo" to a
goose!—Well said,[8] Nick!   130

*They spread a carpet, set down lights and
                 cards.*

ANNE. Come, M[aster] Frankford, who
shall take my part? [9]

FRANK. Marry, that will I, sweet wife.

WEN. No, by my faith, when you are together, I sit out. It must be Mistress
Frankford and I, or else it is no match.

FRANK. I do not like that match.

NICK. [*Aside.*] You have no reason,
marry, knowing all.   139

FRANK. 'Tis no great matter, neither.—
Come, Master Cranwell, shall you and I
take them up?

CRAN. At your pleasure, sir.

FRANK. I must look to you, Master
Wendoll, for you'll be playing false. Nay,
so will my wife, too.

NICK. [*Aside.*] I will be sworn she will.

ANNE. Let them that are taken false,
forfeit the set!

FRANK. Content; it shall go hard but I'll
   take you.   150

---

[1] Evidence.   [2] Anger.
[3] Gold; with a pun on the meaning *guilt.*
[4] Well-hatched, nobly wrought.
[5] Possibly a spelling of *lose.*

[6] Avoid.   [8] Well done.
[7] Pack.   [9] Be my partner.

CRAN. Gentlemen, what shall our game be?

WEN. Master Frankford, you play best at noddy.[1]

FRANK. You shall not find it so; indeed, you shall not.

ANNE. I can play at nothing so well as double-ruff.[2]

FRANK. If Master Wendoll and my wife be together, there's no playing against them at double-hand.[3]

NICK. I can tell you, sir, the game that Master Wendoll is best at.

WEN. What game is that, Nick?   160

NICK. Marry, sir, knave-out-of-doors.

WEN. She and I will take you at loadum.

ANNE. Husband, shall we play at saint?

FRANK. [Aside.] My saint's turned devil.—No, we'll none of saint.

You are best at new-cut, wife; you'll play at that.

WEN. If you play at new-cut, I'm soonest[4] hitter of any here, for a wager.

FRANK. [Aside.] 'Tis me they play on.—
Well, you may draw out;
For all your cunning, 'twill be to your shame;
I'll teach you, at your new-cut, a new game.   170
Come, come!

CRAN. If you cannot agree upon the game,
To post and pair!

WEN. We shall be soonest pairs, and my good host,
When he comes late home, he must kiss the post.[5]

FRANK. Whoever wins, it shall be to thy cost.

CRAN. Faith, let it be vide-ruff, and let's make honors!

FRANK. If you make honors, one thing let me crave:
Honor the king and queen; except[6] the knave.

WEN. Well, as you please for that.—Lift![7]
Who shall deal?   180

ANNE. The least in sight. What are you, Master Wendoll?

WEN. I am a knave.

NICK. [Aside.] I'll swear it.

ANNE.   I am queen.

FRANK. [Aside.] A quean, thou shouldst say.—Well, the cards are mine;
They are the grossest pair that e'er I felt.

ANNE. Shuffle; I'll cut. Would I had never dealt!

FRANK. [Misdealing]. I have lost my dealing.

WEN.   Sir, the fault's in me;
This queen I have more than mine own, you see.
Give me the stock![8]

FRANK.   My mind's not on my game.
Many a deal I've lost; the more's your shame.
You have served me a bad trick, Master Wendoll.   190

WEN. Sir, you must take your lot. To end this strife,
I know I have dealt better with your wife.

FRANK. Thou hast dealt falsely, then.

ANNE. What's trumps?

WEN. Hearts. Partner, I rub.

FRANK. [Aside.] Thou robb'st me of my soul, of her chaste love;
In thy false dealing thou hast robbed my heart.—
Booty you play;[9] I, like a loser, stand,
Having no heart, or[10] here or in my hand.
I will give o'er the set; I am not well.
Come, who will hold my cards?   201

ANNE. Not well, sweet M[aster] Frankford?
Alas, what ail you? 'Tis some sudden qualm.

WEN. How long have you been so, Master Frankford?

FRANK. Sir, I was lusty, and I had my health,
But I grew ill when you began to deal.—
Take hence this table!—Gentle Master Cranwell,
Y'are welcome; see your chamber at your pleasure!
I am sorry that this megrim takes me so;
I cannot sit and bear you company.—
Jenkin, some lights, and show him to his chamber!   211
[Exeunt Cranwell and Jenkin.]

[1] A game like cribbage; also, a simpleton.
[2] Forerunner of whist; with a double meaning.
[3] The names of this and the following games, the nature of which is not known, are of course used with double meanings.
[4] Quickest, speediest.
[5] I.e., be shut out.
[6] Exclude.
[7] Cut.
[8] Remainder of the pack.
[9] Lose, by arrangement with a confederate, in order to draw the opponent on.
[10] Either.

ANNE. A nightgown [1] for my husband;
quickly there!
It is some rheum or cold.

WEN.   Now, in good faith,
This illness you have got by sitting late
Without your gown.

FRANK.   I know it, M[aster] Wendoll.
Go, go to bed, lest you complain like
me!—
Wife, prithee, wife, into my bedcham-
ber!
The night is raw and cold and rheumatic.
Leave me my gown and light; I'll walk
away my fit.

WEN. Sweet sir, good night!   220

FRANK. Myself, good night!
                              [Exit Wendoll.]

ANNE.   Shall I attend you, husband?

FRANK. No, gentle wife, thou't catch cold
in thy head.
Prithee, begone, sweet; I'll make haste to
bed.

ANNE. No sleep will fasten on mine eyes,
you know,
Until you come.   Exit.

FRANK.   Sweet Nan, I prithee, go!—
I have bethought me. Get me by degrees
The keys of all my doors, which I will
mold
In wax, and take their fair impression,
To have by them new keys. This being
compassed,   229
At a set hour a letter shall be brought me,
And, when they think they may securely
play,
They nearest are to danger. Nick, I must
rely
Upon thy trust and faithful secrecy.

NICK. Build on my faith!

FRANK.   To bed, then, not to rest!
Care lodges in my brain, grief in my
breast.   [Exeunt.]

[SCENE ix.

Near the home of Old Mountford.]

*Enter Sir Charles his [2] Sister, Old Mountford,
Sandy, Roder, and Tidy.*

MOUNT. You say my nephew is in great
distress.
Who brought it to him but his own
lewd life?

[1] Dressing gown.   [2] *I.e.,* Charles's.

I cannot spare a cross. I must confess
He was my brother's son; why, niece,
what then?
This is no world in which to pity men.

SUS. I was not born a beggar, though his
extremes
Enforce this language from me. I pro-
test
No fortune of mine own could lead my
tongue
To this base key. I do beseech you,
uncle,
For the name's sake, for Christianity, 10
Nay, for God's sake, to pity his dis-
tress.
He is denied the freedom of the prison,
And in the hole is laid with men con-
demned.
Plenty he hath of nothing but of irons,
And it remains in you to free him thence.

MOUNT. Money I cannot spare; men
should take heed.
He lost my kindred when he fell to need.
                                  [Exit.]

SUS. Gold is but earth; thou earth enough
shalt have,
When thou hast once took measure of
thy grave.
You know me, Master Sandy, and my
suit.   20

SANDY. I knew you, lady, when the old
man lived;
I knew you ere your brother sold his
land.
Then you were Mistress Sue, tricked up
in jewels;
Then you sung well, played sweetly on
the lute.
But now I neither know you nor your
suit.   [Exit.]

SUS. You, Master Roder, was my brother's
tenant;
Rent-free he placed you in that wealthy
farm
Of which you are possessed.

RODER.   True, he did;
And have I not there dwelt still for his
sake?
I have some business now; but without
doubt   30
They that have hurled him in will help
him out.   Exit.

SUS. Cold comfort still. What say you,
cousin Tidy?

TIDY. I say this comes of roisting,[1] swag-
g'ring.

Call me not cousin. Each man for himself!

Some men are born to mirth, and some
to sorrow;

I am no cousin unto them that borrow.
Exit.

SUS. O Charity, why art thou fled to
heaven,

And left all things on this earth uneven?

Their scoffing answers I will ne'er return, 39

But to myself his grief in silence mourn.

Enter Sir Francis and Malby.

FRAN. She is poor; I'll therefore tempt
her with this gold.

Go, Malby, in my name deliver it,

And I will stay thy answer.

MAL. Fair mistress, as I understand your
grief

Doth grow from want, so I have here
in store

A means to furnish you, a bag of gold,

Which to your hands I freely tender you.

SUS. I thank you, heavens! I thank you,
gentle sir;

God make me able to requite this favor!

MAL. This gold Sir Francis Acton sends
by me, 50

And prays you—

SUS. Acton? O God! That name I'm
born to curse.

Hence, bawd; hence, broker![2] See, I
spurn his gold.

My honor never shall for gain be sold.

FRAN. Stay, lady, stay!

SUS. From you I'll posting hie,

Even as the doves from feathered eagles
fly. *Exit.*

FRAN. She hates my name, my face. How
should I woo?

I am disgraced in everything I do.

The more she hates me, and disdains my
love,

The more I am rapt in admiration 60

Of her divine and chaste perfections.

Woo her with gifts I cannot, for all gifts

Sent in my name she spurns; with looks
I cannot,

For she abhors my sight; nor yet with
letters,

For none she will receive. How then?
How then?

Well, I will fasten such a kindness on
her

As shall o'ercome her hate and conquer it.

Sir Charles, her brother, lies in execution

For a great sum of money; and, besides,

The appeal is sued still for my huntsmen's death, 70

Which only I have power to reverse.

In her I'll bury all my hate of him.—

Go seek the keeper, Malby; bring him
to me!

To save his body, I his debts will pay;

To save his life, I his appeal will stay.
[Exeunt.]

[SCENE X.

A dungeon in York Castle.]

*Enter Sir Charles in prison, with irons, his
feet bare, his garments all ragged and
torn.*

CHAR. Of all on the earth's face most
miserable,

Breathe in this hellish dungeon thy laments,

Thus like a slave ragg'd, like a felon
gyved!

That hurls thee headlong to this base
estate!

O unkind uncle! O my friends ingrate,

Unthankful kinsmen, Mountfords all-
too [3] base,

To let thy name be fettered in disgrace!

A thousand deaths here in this grave I
die!

Fear, hunger, sorrow, cold, all threat
my death, 9

And join together to deprive my breath.

But, that which most torments me, my
dear sister

Hath left [4] to visit me, and from my
friends

Hath brought no hopeful answer; therefore, I

Divine they will not help my misery.

If it be so, shame, scandal, and contempt

Attend their covetous thoughts; need
make their graves!

Usurers they live, and may they die
like slaves!

---

[1] Roistering. rioting.   [2] Go-between.   [3] Entirely.   [4] Ceased.

Enter Keeper.

KEEP. Knight, be of comfort, for I bring
    thee freedom
From all thy troubles.
CHAR.   Then I am doomed to die:
Death is the end of all calamity.   20
KEEP. Live! Your appeal is stayed; the
    execution
Of all your debts discharged; your
    creditors
Even to the utmost penny satisfied;
In sign whereof your shackles I knock
    off.
You are not left so much indebted to us
As for your fees; all is discharged, all
    paid.
Go freely to your house, or where you
    please;
After long miseries, embrace your ease.
CHAR. Thou grumblest out the sweetest
    music to me
That ever organ played.—Is this a
    dream?   30
Or do my waking senses apprehend
The pleasing taste of these applausive [1]
    news?
Slave that I was, to wrong such honest
    friends,
My loving kinsmen, and my near allies!
Tongue, I will bite thee for the scandal
    breath [2]
Against such faithful kinsmen; they are
    all
Composed of pity and compassion,
Of melting charity and of moving ruth.
That which I spake before was in my
    rage;
They are my friends, the mirrors [3] of
    this age,   40
Bounteous and free. The noble Mount-
    fords' race
Ne'er bred a covetous thought, or humor
    base.

Enter Susan.

SUS. [*Aside.*] I can no longer stay from
    visiting
My woeful brother. While I could, I
    kept
My hapless tidings from his hopeful
    ear.

----

[1] Worthy of applause, joyful.   [3] Paragons.
[2] Scandalous talk.

CHAR. Sister, how much am I indebted
    to thee
And to thy travail!
SUS.   What, at liberty?
CHAR. Thou seest I am, thanks to thy
    industry.
O, unto which of all my courteous friends
Am I thus bound? My uncle Mount-
    ford, he   50
Even of an infant loved me. Was it he?
So did my cousin Tidy. Was it he?
So Master Roder, Master Sandy, too.
Which of all these did this high kind-
    ness do?
SUS. Charles, can you mock me in your
    poverty,
Knowing your friends deride your
    misery?
Now, I protest I stand so much amazed,
To see your bonds free, and your irons
    knocked off,
That I am rapt into a maze of wonder;
The rather for I know not by what
    means   60
This happiness hath chanced.
CHAR.   Why, by my uncle,
My cousins, and my friends. Who else,
    I pray,
Would take upon them all my debts to
    pay?
SUS. O brother, they are men all of flint,
Pictures of marble, and as void of pity
As chaséd bears. I begged, I sued, I
    kneeled,
Laid open all your griefs and miseries,
Which they derided; more than that,
    denied us
A part in their alliance, but, in pride,
Said that our kindred with our plenty
    died.   70
CHAR. Drudges too much [4]—what did
    they? O, known evil!
Rich fly the poor as good men shun the
    devil.
Whence should my freedom come? Of
    whom alive,
Saving of those, have I deserved so well?
Guess, sister, call to mind, remember me!
These I have raised, [5] they follow the
    world's guise,
Whom, rich in honor, they in woe despise. [6]

----

[4] Menials too base.   [5] Recalled, named.
[6] *I.e.*, those who are honorable but unfortunate they despise.

Sus. My wits have lost themselves; let's
    ask the keeper!
Char. Jailer!
Keep. At hand, sir.   80
Char. Of courtesy resolve me one de-
    mand! [1]
  What was he took the burthen of my
    debts
  From off my back, stayed my appeal to
    death,
  Discharged my fees, and brought me
    liberty?
Keep. A courteous knight, and called
    Sir Francis Acton.
Char. Ha! Acton! O me, more dis-
    tressed in this
  Than all my troubles! Hale me back,
  Double my irons, and my sparing meals
  Put into halves, and lodge me in a
    dungeon
  More deep, more dark, more cold, more
    comfortless!   90
  By Acton freed! Not all thy manacles
  Could fetter so my heels as this one
    word
  Hath thralled my heart, and it must now
    lie bound
  In more strict prison than thy stony
    jail.
  I am not free; I go but under bail.
Keep. My charge is done, sir, now I have
    my fees.
  As we get little, we will nothing leese.[2]
                      Exit.
Char. By Acton freed, my dangerous op-
    posite!
  Why, to what end? Or what occasion?
    Ha!
  Let me forget the name of enemy,   100
  And with indifference balance [3] this
    high favor! Ha!
Sus. [*Aside.*] His love to me! Upon my
    soul, 'tis so!
  That is the root from whence these
    strange things grow.
Char. Had this proceeded from my fa-
    ther, he
  That by the law of nature is most bound
  In offices of love, it had deserved
  My best employment to requite that
    grace.
  Had it proceeded from my friends, or him,

[1] Answer me one question.
[2] Lose.   [3] Weigh with impartiality.

  From them this action had deserved my
    life,
  And from a stranger more, because
    from such   110
  There is less execution of good deeds.
  But he, nor father, nor ally, nor friend,
  More than a stranger, both remote in
    blood,
  And in his heart opposed my enemy,
  That this high bounty should proceed
    from him—
  O, there I lose myself! What should I say,
  What think, what do, his bounty to re-
    pay?
Sus. You wonder, I am sure, whence this
    strange kindness
  Proceeds in Acton; I will tell you,
    brother.
  He dotes on me, and oft hath sent me
    gifts,   120
  Letters, and tokens; I refused them all.
Char. I have enough, though poor; my
    heart is set
  In one rich gift to pay back all my debt.
                      Exeunt.

[Scene xi.

A room in Frankford's house.]

*Enter Frankford and Nick, with keys and
              a letter in his hand.*

Frank. This is the night that I must play
    my part,
  To try two seeming angels.—Where's
    my keys?
Nick. They are made according to your
    mold in wax.
  I bade the smith be secret, gave him
    money,
  And here they are. The letter, sir!
Frank. [*Giving letter.*] True, take it; there
    it is;
  And, when thou seest me in my pleas-
    ant's[t] vein,
  Ready to sit to supper, bring it me!
Nick. I'll do 't; make no more question
    but I'll do 't.   *Exit.*

*Enter Mistress Frankford, Cranwell, Wen-
              doll, and Jenkin.*

Anne. Sirrah, 'tis six a-clock already
    stroke;   10
  Go bid them spread the cloth, and serve
    in supper.

JENK. It shall be done, forsooth, mistress. Where's Spigot, the butler, to give us our salt and trenchers?   [*Exit.*]

WEN. We that have been a-hunting all the day
Come with preparéd stomachs.—Master Frankford,
We wished you at our sport.

FRANK. My heart was with you, and my mind was on you.—
Fie, Master Cranwell! You are still thus sad?—
A stool, a stool! Where's Jenkin, and where's Nick?   20
'Tis supper time at least an hour ago.
What's the best news abroad?

WEN. I know none good.

FRANK. [*Aside.*]   But I know too much bad.

Enter Butler and Jenkin, with a tablecloth, bread, trenchers, and salt.

CRAN. Methinks, sir, you might have that interest
In [1] your wife's brother, to be more remiss [2]
In his hard dealing against poor Sir Charles,
Who, as I hear, lies in York Castle,
Needy and in great want.
    [*Exeunt Jenkin and Butler.*]

FRANK. Did not more weighty business of mine own
Hold me away, I would have labored peace   30
Betwixt them with all care; indeed I would, sir.

ANNE. I'll write unto my brother earnestly
In that behalf.   .

WEN.   A charitable deed,
And will beget the good opinion
Of all your friends that love you, Mistress Frankford.

FRANK. That's you, for one; I know you love Sir Charles,
And my wife too, well.

WEN.   He deserves the love
Of all true gentlemen; be yourselves judge!

FRANK. But supper, ho!—Now, as thou lov'st me, Wendoll,
Which I am sure thou dost, be merry, pleasant,   40

And frolic it tonight! Sweet Master Cranwell,
Do you the like! Wife, I protest, my heart
Was ne'er more bent on sweet alacrity.
Where be those lazy knaves to serve in supper?

Enter Nick.

NICK. Here's a letter, sir.

FRANK. Whence comes it, and who brought it?

NICK. A stripling that below attends your answer,
And, as he tells me, it is sent from York.

FRANK. Have him into the cellar; let him taste
A cup of our March beer; go, make him drink!   [*Reads the letter.*]   50

NICK. I'll make him drunk, if he be a Trojan. [3]

FRANK. My boots and spurs! Where's Jenkin? God forgive me,
How I neglect my business! Wife, look here!
I have a matter to be tried tomorrow
By eight a-clock, and my attorney writes me
I must be there betimes with evidence,
Or it will go against me. Where's my boots?

Enter Jenkin, with boots and spurs.

ANNE. I hope your business craves no such despatch
That you must ride tonight?

WEN. [*Aside.*]   I hope it doth.

FRANK. God's me! No such despatch!   60
Jenkin, my boots! Where's Nick? Saddle my roan,
And the gray dapple for himself!—Content ye,
It much concerns me.—Gentle Master Cranwell,
And Master Wendoll, in my absence use
The very ripest pleasures of my house!

WEN. Lord, Master Frankford, will you ride tonight?
The ways are dangerous.

FRANK.   Therefore will I ride
Appointed [4] well; and so shall Nick, my man.

---

[1] Influence with.   [2] Lenient.

[3] Good fellow.   [4] Equipped, armed.

ANNE. I'll call you up by five a-clock to-morrow.

FRANK. No, by my faith, wife, I'll not trust to that. 70
'Tis not such easy rising in a morning
From one I love so dearly. No, by my faith,
I shall not leave so sweet a bedfellow
But with much pain. You have made me a sluggard
Since I first knew you.

ANNE.   Then, if you needs will go
This dangerous evening, Master Wendoll,
Let me entreat you bear him company.

WEN. With all my heart, sweet mistress.—
My boots there!

FRANK. Fie, fie, that for my private business 79
I should disease [1] a friend, and be a trouble
To the whole house!—Nick!

NICK.   Anon, sir!

FRANK. Bring forth my gelding! [*Exit Nick.*]—As you love me, sir,
Use no more words. A hand, good Master Cranwell!

CRAN. Sir, God be your good speed!

FRANK. Good night, sweet Nan; nay, nay, a kiss, and part!—
[*Aside.*] Dissembling lips, you suit not with my heart.   *Exit.*

WEN. [*Aside.*] How business, time, and hours all gracious prove,
And are the furtherers to my new-born love!
I am husband now in Master Frankford's place,
And must command the house.—My pleasure is 90
We will not sup abroad so publicly,
But in your private chamber, Mistress Frankford.

ANNE. [*Aside to Wendoll.*] O, sir, you are too public in your love,
And Master Frankford's wife—

CRAN.   Might I crave favor,
I would entreat you I might see my chamber.
I am on the sudden grown exceeding ill,
And would be spared from supper.

WEN.   Light there, ho!—
See you want nothing, sir, for, if you do,
You injure that good man, and wrong me too. 99

[1] Dis-ease, inconvenience.

CRAN. I will make bold. Good night!
                              Exit.

WEN.   How all conspire
To make our bosom [2] sweet, and full entire! [3]
Come, Nan, I prithee let us sup within!

ANNE. O, what a clog unto the soul is sin!
We pale offenders are still full of fear;
Every suspicious eye brings danger near,
When they whose clear heart from offense are free
Despise report, base scandals do outface,
And stand at mere [4] defiance with disgrace.

WEN. Fie, fie! You talk too like a Puritan.

ANNE. You have tempted me to mischief,
M[aster] Wendoll; 110
I have done I know not what. Well, you plead custom;
That which for want of wit I granted erst, [5]
I now must yield through fear. Come, come, let's in;
Once o'er shoes, we are straight o'er head in sin.

WEN. My jocund soul is joyful above measure;
I'll be profuse in Frankford's richest treasure.   *Exeunt.*

[SCENE xii.

Another room in the house.]

Enter Sisly, Jenkin, Butler.

JENK. My mistress and Master Wendoll, my master, sup in her chamber tonight. Sisly, you are preferred [6] from being the cook to be chambermaid. Of all the loves betwixt thee and me, tell me what thou think'st of this.

SISLY. Mum; there's an old proverb, "When the cat's away, the mouse may play."

JENK. Now you talk of a cat, Sisly, I [10] smell a rat.

SISLY. Good words, Jenkin, lest you be called to answer them!

JENK. Why, God make my mistress an honest woman! Are not these good words? Pray God my new master play not the knave with my old master! Is there any

[2] Intimacy.   [5] Formerly.
[3] Very complete.   [6] Promoted.
[4] Absolute.

hurt in this? God send no villainy intended;
and, if they do sup together, pray God they
do not lie together! God make my mis-   [20
tress chaste, and make us all His servants!
What harm is there in all this? Nay, more;
here is my hand; thou shalt never have
my heart unless thou say amen.

SISLY. Amen, I pray God, I say.

Enter Serving-men.

SERVING-MAN. My mistress sends that
you should make less noise, to lock up the
doors, and see the household all got to bed.
You, Jenkin, for this night are made the
porter, to see the gates shut in.   30

JENK. Thus by little and little I creep
into office. Come, to kennel, my masters,
to kennel; 'tis eleven a-clock already.

SERV. When you have locked the gates
in, you must send up the keys to my
mistress.

SISLY. Quickly, for God's sake, Jenkin,
for I must carry them. I am neither pillow
nor bolster, but I know more than both.

JENK. To bed, good Spigot; to bed, [40
good honest serving-creatures; and let us
sleep as snug as pigs in pea straw! *Exeunt.*

[SCENE xiii.

Outside Frankford's house.[1]]

Enter Frankford and Nick.

FRANK. Soft, soft! We have tied our [2]
    geldings to a tree,
Two flight-shot [3] off, lest by their thun-
    dering hoofs
They blab our coming. Hear'st thou no
    noise?

NICK. I hear nothing but the owl and
you.

FRANK. So; now my watch's hand points
    upon twelve,
And it is just midnight. Where are my
    keys?

NICK. Here, sir.

FRANK. This is the key that opes my out-
    ward gate;
This, the hall door; this, the withdraw-
    ing-chamber;   10

But this, that door that's bawd unto my
    shame,
Fountain and spring of all my bleeding
    thoughts,
Where the most hallowed order and true
    knot
Of nuptial sanctity hath been profaned.
It leads to my polluted bedchamber,
Once my terrestrial heaven, now my
    earth's hell,
The place where sins in all their ripeness
    dwell.—
But I forget myself; now to my gate!

NICK. It must ope with far less noise
than Cripplegate, or your plot's dashed. [20

FRANK. So, reach me my dark lanthorn to
    the rest! [4]
Tread softly, softly!

NICK.   I will walk on eggs this pace.
                    [*They enter the house.*]

FRANK. A general silence hath surprised
    the house,
And this is the last door. Astonishment,
Fear, and amazement beat upon my
    heart,
Even as a madman beats upon a drum.
O, keep my eyes, you heavens, before I
    enter,
From any sight that may transfix my
    soul;
Or, if there be so black a spectacle,
O, strike mine eyes stark blind; or, if
    not so,   30
Lend me such patience to digest my
    grief,
That I may keep this white and virgin
    hand
From any violent outrage or red murther!
And with that prayer I enter.
                    [*Peers into the bedchamber.*]

NICK. [*Aside.*] Here's a circumstance,
indeed! A man may be made cuckold in
the time that he's about it. And [5] the
case were mine, as 'tis my master's—'sblood,
that he makes me swear!—I would
have placed his action,[6] entered there; [40
I would, I would!

FRANK. [*Turning away.*] O! O!

NICK. Master! 'Sblood! Master, master!

FRANK. O me unhappy! I have found them
    lying

---

[1] This scene shifts gradually to the hall of the house.

[2] From 1607 edn. Original reads *your*.

[3] Early edns. read *flight shoot;* long bow-shot.

[4] *I.e.*, in addition to the other equipment.

[5] If.

[6] Established his case (Ward).

Close in each other arms, and fast asleep.
But that I would not damn two precious
souls,
Bought with my Savior's blood, and send
them laden
With all their scarlet sins upon their
backs
Unto a fearful judgment, their two lives
Had met upon my rapier.   50
NICK. Master, what, have you left them
sleeping still?
Let me go wake 'em!
FRANK.   Stay, let me pause awhile!—
O God! O God! That it were possible
To undo things done, to call back yester-
day;
That Time could turn up his swift sandy
glass,
To untell the days, and to redeem these
hours;
Or that the sun
Could, rising from the west, draw his
coach backward,
Take from th' account of time so many
minutes,   59
Till he had all these seasons called again,
Those minutes, and those actions done
in them,
Even from her first offense that I might
take her
As spotless as an angel in my arms!
But, O, I talk of things impossible,
And cast beyond the moon.[1] God give
me patience,
For I will in, and wake them.   *Exit.*
NICK.   Here's patience perforce!
He needs must trot afoot that tires his
horse.

*Enter Wendoll, running over the stage in a
nightgown, he [Frankford] after him
with his sword drawn; the Maid in her
smock stays his hand, and clasps hold
on him. He pauses for a while.*

FRANK. I thank thee, maid; thou, like an
angel's hand,
Hast stayed me from a bloody sacrifice.—
Go, villain, and my wrongs sit on thy
soul   70
As heavy as this grief doth upon mine!
When thou record'st my many courtesies,
And shall compare them with thy treach-
erous heart,

[1] *I.e.*, speak wildly.

Lay them together, weigh them equally,
'Twill be revenge enough.   Go, to thy
friend
A Judas; pray, pray, lest I live to see
Thee, Judas-like, hanged on an eldertree!

*Enter Mistress Frankford in her smock,
nightgown, and night attire.*

ANNE. O, by what word, what title, or
what name,
Shall I entreat your pardon? Pardon! O,
I am as far from hoping such sweet grace
As Lucifer from heaven.   To call you
husband—   81
O me, most wretched! I have lost that
name;
I am no more your wife.
NICK.   'Sblood, sir, she sounds.[2]
FRANK. Spare thou thy tears, for I will
weep for thee;
And keep thy count'nance, for I'll blush
for thee.
Now, I protest, I think 'tis I am tainted,
For I am most ashamed; and 'tis more
hard
For me to look upon thy guilty face
Than on the sun's clear brow.   What
wouldst thou speak?
ANNE. I would I had no tongue, no ears,
no eyes,   90
No apprehension, no capacity.
When do you spurn me like a dog? When
tread me
Under feet? When drag me by the hair?
Though I deserve a thousand thousand
fold
More than you can inflict, yet, once my
husband,
For womanhood—to which I am a
shame,[3]
Though once an ornament—even for His
sake
That hath redeemed our souls, mark not
my face,
Nor hack me with your sword, but let
me go   99
Perfect and undeforméd to my tomb!
I am not worthy that I should prevail
In the least suit; no, not to speak to you,
Nor look on you, nor to be in your
presence;
Yet, as an abject, this one suit I crave.
This granted, I am ready for my grave.

[2] Swoons.   [3] Early edns. read *ashamed*.

FRANK. My God, with patience arm me!—
Rise, nay, rise,
And I'll debate with thee. Was it for
want
Thou playedst the strumpet? Wast thou
not supplied
With every pleasure, fashion, and new
toy,
Nay, even beyond my calling? [1]
ANNE.   I was.   110
FRANK. Was it, then, disability in me?
Or in thine eye seemed he a properer [2]
man?
ANNE. O, no!
FRANK.   Did not I lodge thee in
my bosom?
Wear thee in my heart?
ANNE.   You did.
FRANK. I did, indeed; witness my tears, I
did.—
Go, bring my infants hither!—
[*Exit Maid and returns with two Children.*]
                    O Nan! O Nan!
If neither fear of shame, regard of honor,
The blemish of my house, nor my dear love
Could have withheld thee from so lewd
a fact, [3]
Yet for these infants, these young, harm-
less souls,   120
On whose white brows thy shame is
charactered,
And grows in greatness as they wax in
years—
Look but on them, and melt away in
tears!—
Away with them, lest, as her spotted
body
Hath stained their names with stripe of
bastardy,
So her adulterous breath may blast their
spirits
With her infectious thoughts! Away with
them!   [*Exeunt Maid and Children.*]
ANNE. In this one life, I die ten thousand
deaths.
FRANK. Stand up, stand up! I will do
nothing rashly.
I will retire awhile into my study,   130
And thou shalt hear thy sentence pres-
ently. [4]   *Exit.*
ANNE. 'Tis welcome, be it death. O me,
base strumpet,

[1] Estate, station.   [3] Act.
[2] Handsomer.   [4] Immediately.

That, having such a husband, such sweet
children,
Must enjoy neither! O, to redeem mine
honor,
I would have this hand cut off, these my
breasts seared;
Be racked, strappadoed, put to any
torment;
Nay, to whip but this scandal out, I
would hazard
The rich and dear redemption of my soul!
He cannot be so base as to forgive me,
Nor I so shameless to accept his par-
don.   140
O women, women, you that yet have
kept
Your holy matrimonial vow unstained,
Make me your instance; when you tread
awry,
Your sins, like mine, will on your con-
science lie.

*Enter Sisly, Spigot, all the Serving-men, and
     Jenkin, as newly come out of bed.*

ALL. O mistress, mistress! What have you
done, mistress?
NICK. What a caterwauling keep you here!
JENK. O Lord, mistress, how comes this
to pass? My master is run away in his
shirt, and never so much as called me to
bring his clothes after him.   150
ANNE. See what guilt is! Here stand I in
this place,
Ashamed to look my servants in the
face.

*Enter M[aster] Frankford and Cranwell,
     whom seeing, she falls on her knees.*

FRANK. My words are registered in heaven
already.
With patience hear me. I'll not martyr
thee,
Nor mark thee for a strumpet, but with
usage
Of more humility torment thy soul,
And kill thee even with kindness.
CRAN.   M[aster] Frankford—
FRANK. Good M[aster] Cranwell!—Wo-
man, hear thy judgment!
Go make thee ready in thy best attire,
Take with thee all thy gowns, all thy
apparel,   160
Leave nothing that did ever call thee
mistress,

Or by whose sight, being left here in the house,
I may remember such a woman by.
Choose thee a bed and hangings for thy chamber,
Take with thee everything which hath thy mark,
And get thee to my manor seven mile off,
Where live. 'Tis thine; I freely give it thee.
My tenants by [1] shall furnish thee with wains
To carry all thy stuff within two hours;
No longer will I limit [2] thee my sight. 170
Choose which of all my servants thou lik'st best,
And they are thine to attend thee.

ANNE.   A mild sentence.

FRANK. But, as thou hop'st for heaven, as thou believ'st
Thy name's recorded in the Book of Life,
I charge thee never after this sad day
To see me, or to meet me, or to send,
By word or writing, gift or otherwise,
To move me, by thyself or by thy friends,
Nor challenge any part in my two children.
So farewell, Nan; for we will henceforth be 180
As we had never seen, ne'er more shall see.

ANNE. How full my heart is, in mine eyes appears;
What wants in words, I will supply in tears.

FRANK. Come, take your coach, your stuff; all must along.
Servants and all make ready; all begone!
It was thy hand cut two hearts out of one.   *Exeunt.*

[SCENE xiv.

Before Sir Francis Acton's house.]

Enter Sir Charles, gentlemanlike, and his Sister, gentlewomanlike.

SUS. Brother, why have you tricked [3] me like a bride,
Bought me this gay attire, these ornaments?
Forget you our estate, our poverty?

CHAR. Call me not brother, but imagine me
Some barbarous outlaw, or uncivil kern; [4]
For, if thou shutt'st thy eye, and only hear'st
The words that I shall utter, thou shalt judge me
Some staring ruffian, not thy brother Charles.
O sister!—

SUS. O brother, what doth this strange language mean? 10

CHAR. Dost love me, sister? Wouldst thou see me live
A bankrout [5] beggar in the world's disgrace,
And die indebted to mine enemies?
Wouldst thou behold me stand like a huge beam
In the world's eye, a byword and a scorn?
It lies in thee of these to acquit me free,
And all my debt I may outstrip by thee.

SUS. By me? Why, I have nothing, nothing left;
I owe even for the clothes upon my back;
I am not worth—

CHAR.   O sister, say not so! 20
It lies in you my downcast state to raise,
To make me stand on even points with the world.
Come, sister, you are rich; indeed you are,
And in your power you have, without delay,
Acton's five hundred pound back to repay.

SUS. Till now I had thought y' had loved me. By my honor,
Which I have kept as spotless as the moon,
I ne'er was mistress of that single doit [6]
Which I reserved not to supply your wants;
And d' ye think that I would hoard from you? 30
Now, by my hopes in heaven, knew I the means
To buy you from the slavery of your debts
(Especially from Acton, whom I hate),
I would redeem it with my life or blood!

CHAR. I challenge it, and, kindred set apart,

---

[1] Near by.
[2] Allot, permit.
[3] Tricked out, dressed.
[4] Peasant.   [5] Bankrupt.   [6] Half a farthing.

Thus, ruffianlike, I lay siege to thy heart.
What do I owe to Acton?

Sus. Why, some five hundred pounds,
    towards which, I swear,
In all the world I have not one denier.[1]

Char. It will not prove so. Sister, now
    resolve me: 40
What do you think (and speak your con-
    science)
Would Acton give, might he enjoy your
    bed?

Sus. He would not shrink to spend a thou-
    sand pound
To give the Mountfords' name so deep a
    wound.

Char. A thousand pound! I but five hun-
    dred owe;
Grant him your bed; he's paid with
    int'rest so.

Sus. O brother!

Char.   O sister! Only this one way,
With that rich jewel you my debts may
    pay.
In speaking this my cold heart shakes
    with shame;
Nor do I woo you in a brother's name, 50
But in a stranger's. Shall I die in debt
To Acton, my grand foe, and you still wear
The precious jewel that he holds so dear?

Sus. My honor I esteem as dear and precious
As my redemption.

Char.   I esteem you, sister,
As dear, for so dear prizing it.

Sus.   Will Charles
Have me cut off my hands, and send
    them Acton?
Rip up my breast, and with my bleeding
    heart
Present him as a token?

Char.   Neither, sister;
But hear me in my strange assertion! 60
Thy honor and my soul are equal in my
    regard;
Nor will thy brother Charles survive thy
    shame.
His kindness, like a burthen, hath sur-
    charged me,
And under his good deeds I stooping go,
Not with an upright soul. Had I re-
    mained
In prison still, there doubtless I had died.
Then, unto him that freed me from that
    prison,

[1] Penny.

Still do I owe this life. What moved my
    foe
To enfranchise [2] me? 'Twas, sister, for
    your love.
With full five hundred pounds he bought
    your love,   70
And shall he not enjoy it? Shall the
    weight
Of all this heavy burthen lean on me,
And will not you bear part? You did
    partake
The joy of my release; will you not stand
In joint bond bound to satisfy the debt?
Shall I be only charged?

Sus.   But that I know
These arguments come from an honored
    mind,
As in your most extremity of need
Scorning to stand in debt to one you
    hate—
Nay, rather would engage your unstained
    honor   80
Than to be held ingrate—I should con-
    demn you.
I see your resolution, and assent.
So Charles will have me, and I am content.

Char. For this I tricked you up.

Sus.   But here's a knife,
To save mine honor, shall slice out my life.

Char. I know thou pleasest me a thousand
    times
More in thy resolution than thy grant.—
[Aside.] Observe her love; to soothe it to
    my suit,
Her honor she will hazard, though not
    lose;
To bring me out of debt, her rigorous
    hand   90
Will pierce her heart. O wonder, that
    will choose,
Rather than stain her blood, her life to
    lose.—
Come, you sad sister to a woeful brother,
This is the gate. I'll bear him such a
    present,
Such an acquittance for the knight to seal,
As will amaze his senses, and surprise
With admiration [3] all his fantasies.

Enter Acton and Malby.

Sus. Before his unchaste thoughts shall
    seize on me,
'Tis here shall my imprisoned soul set free.

[2] Set free.   [3] Wonder.

FRAN. How! Mountford with his sister,
    hand in hand!   100
  What miracle's afoot?

MAL.   It is a sight
  Begets in me much admiration.

CHAR. Stand not amazed to see me thus
    attended!
  Acton, I owe thee money, and, being
    unable
  To bring thee the full sum in ready coin,
  Lo, for thy more assurance, here's a
    pawn—
  My sister, my dear sister, whose chaste
    honor
  I prize above a million. Here! Nay, take
    her;
  She's worth your money, man; do not
    forsake her.

FRAN. I would he were in earnest!   110

SUS. Impute it not to my immodesty.
  My brother, being rich in nothing else
  But in his interest that he hath in me,
  According to his poverty hath brought
    you
  Me, all his store, whom, howsoe'er you
    prize,
  As forfeit to your hand, he values highly,
  And would not sell, but to acquit your
    debt,
  For any emperor's ransom.

FRAN. [Aside.]   Stern heart, relent;
  Thy former cruelty at length repent!
  Was ever known, in any former age,   120
  Such honorable, wrested [1] courtesy?
  Lands, honors, life, and all the world forgo
  Rather than stand engaged to such a foe!

CHAR. Acton, she is too poor to be thy
    bride,
  And I too much opposed to be thy
    brother.
  There, take her to thee. If thou hast the
    heart
  To seize her as a rape or lustful prey,
  To blur our house, that never yet was
    stained,
  To murther her that never meant thee
    harm,
  To kill me now, whom once thou savedst
    from death,   130
  Do them at once; on her all these rely,
  And perish with her spotted chastity.

FRAN. You overcome me in your love, Sir
    Charles.

  [1] Distorted.

I cannot be so cruel to a lady
I love so dearly. Since you have not
    spared
To engage your reputation to the world,
Your sister's honor, which you prize so
    dear,
Nay, all the comfort which you hold on
    earth,
To grow out of my debt, being your foe,
Your honored thoughts, lo! thus I recom-
    pense.   140
Your metamorphosed foe receives your
    gift
In satisfaction of all former wrongs.
This jewel I will wear here in my heart;
And, where before I thought her, for her
    wants,
Too base to be my bride, to end all strife
I seal you my dear brother, her my wife.

SUS. You still exceed us. I will yield to
    fate,
  And learn to love, where I till now did
    hate.

CHAR. With that enchantment you have
    charmed my soul
  And made me rich even in those very
    words!   150
  I pay no debt, but am indebted more;
  Rich in your love, I never can be poor.

FRAN. All's mine is yours; we are alike in
    state;
  Let's knit in love what was opposed in
    hate!
  Come, for our nuptials we will straight
    provide,
  Blessed only in our brother and fair bride.
                                    Exeunt.

[SCENE XV.

A room in Frankford's house.]

Enter Cranwell, Frankford, and Nick.

CRAN. Why do you search each room
    about your house,
  Now that you have despatched your
    wife away?

FRANK. O, sir, to see that nothing may be
    left
  That ever was my wife's. I loved her
    dearly,
  And, when I do but think of her un-
    kindness,
  My thoughts are all in hell; to avoid
    which torment,

I would not have a bodkin or a cuff,
A bracelet, necklace, or rabato wire,[1]
Nor anything that ever was called hers
Left me, by which I might remember her.
Seek round about.   11

NICK. 'Sblood! Master, here's her lute
    flung in a corner.

FRANK. Her lute! O God! Upon this in-
    strument
Her fingers have rung quick division,[2]
Sweeter than that which now divides our
    hearts.
These frets have made me pleasant, that
    have now
Frets of my heartstrings made. O, Mas-
    ter Cranwell,
Oft hath she made this melancholy wood
(Now mute and dumb for her disastrous
    chance)[3]
Speak sweetly many a note, sound many
    a strain   20
To her own ravishing voice, which being
    well strung,
What pleasant strange airs have they
    jointly rung!—
Post with it after her!—Now nothing's left;
Of her and hers I am at once bereft.

NICK. I'll ride and overtake her, do my
    message,
And come back again.   [Exit.]

CRAN.   Meantime, sir, if you please,
I'll to Sir Francis Acton, and inform him
Of what hath passed betwixt you and
    his sister.

FRANK. Do as you please.—How ill am I
    bestead,   29
To be a widower ere my wife be dead!
                                  [Exeunt.]

[SCENE xvi.

On the road to Frankford's manor.]

*Enter Mistress Frankford, with Jenkin, her
    maid Sisly, her Coachmen, and three
                                    Carters.*

ANNE. Bid my coach stay! Why should I
    ride in state,
Being hurled so low down by the hand
    of fate?
A seat like to my fortunes let me have—
Earth for my chair, and for my bed a
    grave!

[1] Wire to support a ruff.
[2] Variations.   [3] Because of her misfortune.

JEN. Comfort, good mistress; you have
watered your coach with tears already.
You have but two mile now to go to
your manor. A man cannot say by my
old master Frankford as he may say by
me, that he wants manors; for he hath [10
three or four, of which this is one that we
are going to now.

SISLY. Good mistress, be of good cheer!
Sorrow, you see, hurts you, but helps you
not; we all mourn to see you so sad.

CARTER. Mistress, I see some of my land-
    lord's men
Come riding post;[4] 'tis like he brings
    some news.

ANNE. Comes he from M[aster] Frankford,
    he is welcome;
So is his news, because they come from
    him.

Enter Nick.

NICK. [*Presents lute.*] There!   20
ANNE. I know the lute. Oft have I sung
    to thee;
We both are out of tune, both out of
    time.

NICK. Would that had been the worst
instrument that e'er you played on! My
master commends him unto ye. There's
all he can find that was ever yours; he
hath nothing left that ever you could lay
claim to but his own heart—and he could
afford you that! All that I have to deliver you is this: he prays you to [30
forget him, and so he bids you farewell.

ANNE. I thank him; he is kind, and ever
    was.
All you that have true feeling of my grief,
That know my loss, and have relenting
    hearts,
Gird me about, and help me with your
    tears
To wash my spotted sins! My lute shall
    groan;
It cannot weep, but shall lament my
    moan.   [*She plays.*]

Enter Wendoll [behind].

WEN. Pursued with horror of a guilty soul,
And with the sharp scourge of repentance
    lashed,   39
I fly from mine own shadow. O my stars!
[4] Posthaste.

What have my parents in their lives
   deserved,
That you should lay this penance on
   their son?
When I but think of Master Frankford's
   love,
And lay it to my treason, or compare
My murthering him for his relieving
   me,
It strikes a terror like a lightning's flash,
To scorch my blood up. Thus I, like
   the owl,
Ashamed of day, live in these shadowy
   woods,
Afraid of every leaf or murmuring blast.
Yet longing to receive some perfect
   knowledge   50
How he hath dealt with her.   [*Sees
   Anne.*] O my sad fate!
Here, and so far from home, and thus
   attended!
O God! I have divorced the truest
   turtles [1]
That ever lived together, and, being
   divided,
In several places make their several
   moan;
She in the fields laments, and he at home.
So poets write that Orpheus made the
   trees
And stones to dance to his melodious
   harp,
Meaning the rustic and the barbarous
   hinds,   59
That had no understanding part in them;
So she from these rude carters tears
   extracts,
Making their flinty hearts with grief to
   rise,
And draw down rivers from their rocky
   eyes.
ANNE. [*To Nick.*] If you return unto my
   master, say
(Though not from me, for I am all
   unworthy
To blast his name so with a strumpet's
   tongue)
That you have seen me weep, wish myself dead!
Nay, you may say, too (for my vow is
   passed),
Last night you saw me eat and drink
   my last.

[1] Turtledoves.

This to your master you may say and
   swear,   70
For it is writ in heaven, and decreed here.
NICK. I'll say you wept; I'll swear you
   made me sad.
Why, how now, eyes? What now?
   What's here to do?
I'm gone, or I shall straight turn baby too.
WEN. [*Aside.*] I cannot weep; my heart is
   all on fire.
Cursed be the fruits of my unchaste
   desire!
ANNE. Go, break this lute upon my coach's
   wheel,
As the last music that I e'er shall make—
Not as my husband's gift, but my
   farewell
To all earth's joy; and so your master
   tell!   80
NICK. If I can for crying.
WEN. [*Aside.*]   Grief, have done,
Or, like a madman, I shall frantic run.
ANNE. You have beheld the woefull'st
   wretch on earth,
A woman made of tears. Would you
   had words
To express but what you see! My inward
   grief
No tongue can utter, yet unto your power
You may describe my sorrow, and disclose
To thy sad master my abundant woes.
NICK. I'll do your commendations.
ANNE.   O, no!
I dare not so presume; nor to my
   children!   90
I am disclaimed in both; alas, I am!
O, never teach them, when they come to
   speak,
To name the name of mother. Chide
   their tongue,
If they by chance light on that hated
   word;
Tell them 'tis naught, for, when that
   word they name,
Poor, pretty souls, they harp on their
   own shame.
WEN. [*Aside.*] To recompense her wrongs,
   what canst thou do?
Thou hast made her husbandless and
   childless too.
ANNE. I have no more to say.—Speak not
   for me;
Yet you may tell your master what you
   see.   100

NICK. I'll do 't. *Exit.*

WEN. [*Aside.*] I'll speak to her, and comfort her in grief.

O, but her wound cannot be cured with words!

No matter, though; I'll do my best good will

To work a cure on her whom I did kill.

ANNE. So, now unto my coach, then to my home,

So to my deathbed, for from this sad hour

I never will nor eat, nor drink, nor taste

Of any cates[1] that may preserve my life.

I never will nor smile, nor sleep, nor rest;

But, when my tears have washed my black soul white, 111

Sweet Savior, to Thy hands I yield my sprite.

WEN. [*Coming forward.*] O, Mistress Frankford!

ANNE. O, for God's sake, fly!

The devil doth come to tempt me, ere I die.

My coach!—This sin, that with an angel's face

Conjured[2] mine honor, till he sought my wrack,

In my repentant eye seems ugly black.

Exeunt all [except Wendoll and Jenkin], the Carters whistling.

JENK. What, my young master, that fled in his shirt! How come you by your clothes again? You have made our [120 house in a sweet pickle, ha' ye not, think you? What, shall I serve you still, or cleave to the old house?

WEN. Hence, slave! Away with thy unseasoned mirth!

Unless thou canst shed tears, and sigh, and howl,

Curse thy sad fortunes, and exclaim on fate,

Thou art not for my turn.

JENK. Marry, and you will not, another will; farewell, and be hanged! Would you had never come to have kept this [130 quoil[3] within our doors! We shall ha' you run away like a sprite again. [*Exit.*]

WEN. She's gone to death; I live to want and woe,

Her life, her sins, and all upon my head.

[1] Food.
[2] Enchanted, seduced.
[3] Coil, disturbance.

And I must now go wander, like a Cain,

In foreign countries and remoted climes,

Where the report of my ingratitude

Cannot be heard. I'll over first to France,

And so to Germany and Italy,

Where, when I have recovered, and by travel 140

Gotten those perfect tongues,[4] and that these rumors

May in their height abate, I will return;

And I divine (however now dejected),

My worth and parts being by some great man praised,

At my return I may in court be raised.

Exit.

[SCENE xvii.

Before the manor house.[5]]

Enter Sir Francis, Sir Charles, Cranwell, [Malby,] and Susan.

FRAN. Brother, and now my wife, I think these troubles

Fall on my head by justice of the heavens,

For being so strict to you in your extremities;

But we are now atoned.[6] I would my sister

Could with like happiness o'ercome her griefs

As we have ours.

SUS. You tell us, Master Cranwell, wondrous things

Touching the patience of that gentleman,

With what strange virtue he demeans[7] his grief.

CRAN. I told you what I was witness of; 10

It was my fortune to lodge there that night.

FRAN. O, that same villain, Wendoll! 'Twas his tongue

That did corrupt her; she was of herself

Chaste and devoted well.[8] Is this the house?

[4] Learned those languages perfectly.
[5] The scene shifts to the interior of the house during the action.
[6] Reconciled.
[7] Manages.
[8] *I.e.,* true to her marriage vow.

CRAN. Yes, sir; I take it, here your sister lies.

FRAN. My brother Frankford showed too
    mild a spirit
In the revenge of such a loathéd crime.
Less than he did, no man of spirit could
    do.
I am so far from blaming his revenge,
That I commend it. Had it been my
    case,   20
Their souls at once had from their
    breasts been freed;
Death to such deeds of shame is the
    due meed.

Enter Jenkin [and Sisly].

JEN. O my mistress, mistress! My poor
mistress!

SISLY. Alas, that ever I was born!
What shall I do for my poor mistress?

CHAR. Why, what of her?

JENK. O Lord, sir, she no sooner heard
that her brother and her friends were
come to see how she did, but she, for [30
very shame of her guilty conscience, fell
into such a swound that we had much ado
to get life in her.

SUS. Alas, that she should bear so hard
    a fate!
Pity it is repentance comes too late.

FRAN. Is she so weak in body?

JENK. O, sir, I can assure you there's
no hope of life in her, for she will take no
sust'nance. She hath plainly starved herself, and now she's as lean as a lath. She [40
ever looks for the good hour. Many gentlemen and gentlewomen of the country are
come to comfort her.

Enter Mistress Frankford in her bed.[1]

MAL. How fare you, Mistress Frankford?

ANNE. Sick, sick, O, sick! Give me some
    air, I pray!
Tell me, O, tell me, where's Master
    Frankford?
Will not [he] deign to see me ere I die?

MAL. Yes, Mistress Frankford; divers
    gentlemen,
Your loving neighbors, with that just
    request

[1] Either the bed was pushed onto the stage
or the curtains of the inner stage were drawn to
disclose her.

Have moved and told him of your weak
    estate,   50
Who, though with much ado to get belief,
Examining of the general circumstance,
Seeing your sorrow and your peni-
    tence,
And hearing therewithal the great de-
    sire
You have to see him, ere you left the
    world,
He gave to us his faith to follow us,
And sure he will be here immediately.

ANNE. You have half revived me with
    the pleasing news.
Raise me a little higher in my bed.
Blush I not, brother Acton? Blush I
    not, Sir Charles?   60
Can you not read my fault writ in my
    cheek?
Is not my crime there? Tell me, gentle-
    men.

CHAR. Alas, good mistress, sickness hath
    not left you
Blood in your face enough to make
    you blush.

ANNE. Then sickness, like a friend, my
    fault would hide.
Is my husband come? My soul but tar-
    ries
His arrive; then I am fit for heaven.

FRAN. I came to chide you, but my words
    of hate
Are turned to pity and compassionate
    grief.
I came to rate you, but my brawls, you
    see,   70
Melt into tears, and I must weep by
    thee.—
Here's M[aster] Frankford now.

Enter Frankford.

FRANK. Good morrow, brother; morrow,
    gentlemen!
God, that hath laid this cross upon our
    heads,
Might, had He pleased, have made our
    cause of meeting
On a more fair and more contented
    ground;
But He that made us, made us to this
    woe.

ANNE. And is he come? Methinks that
    voice I know.

FRANK. How do you, woman?

ANNE. Well, M[aster] Frankford, well;
but shall be better, 80
I hope, within this hour. Will you vouchsafe,
Out of your grace and your humanity,
To take a spotted strumpet by the
hand?

FRANK. This hand once held my heart
in faster bonds
Than now 'tis griped by me. God pardon
them
That made us first break hold!

ANNE. Amen, amen!
Out of my zeal to heaven, whither I'm
now bound,
I was so impudent to wish you here,
And once more beg your pardon. O,
good man, 89
And father to my children, pardon me.
Pardon, O, pardon me! My fault so
heinous is
That, if you in this world forgive it not,
Heaven will not clear it in the world to
come.
Faintness hath so usurped upon my
knees,
That kneel I cannot; but on my heart's
knees
My prostrate soul lies thrown down at
your feet,
To beg your gracious pardon. Pardon,
O, pardon me!

FRANK. As freely, from the low depth of
my soul,
As my Redeemer hath forgiven His
death,
I pardon thee. I will shed tears for thee,
pray with thee, 100
And, in mere pity of thy weak estate,
I'll wish to die with thee.

ALL. So do we all.

NICK. So will not I;
I'll sigh and sob, but, by my faith, not die.

FRAN. O, Master Frankford, all the near
alliance
I lose by her shall be supplied in thee.
You are my brother by the nearest way;
Her kindred hath fallen off, but yours
doth stay.

FRANK. Even as I hope for pardon at
that day
When the great Judge of Heaven in
scarlet sits,

So be thou pardoned! Though thy rash
offense 110
Divorced our bodies, thy repentant
tears
Unite our souls.

CHAR. Then comfort, Mistress
Frankford!
You see your husband hath forgiven
your fall;
Then rouse your spirits, and cheer your
fainting soul!

SUS. How is it with you?

FRAN. How d' ye feel yourself?

ANNE. Not of this world.

FRANK. I see you are not, and I weep
to see it.
My wife, the mother to my pretty
babes!
Both those lost names I do restore thee
back, 119
And with this kiss I wed thee once again.
Though thou art wounded in thy honored
name,
And with that grief upon thy deathbed
liest,
Honest in heart, upon my soul, thou
diest.

ANNE. Pardoned on earth, soul, thou in
heaven art free;
Once more thy wife dies, thus embracing thee. [Dies.]

FRANK. New-married, and new-widowed!—
O! she's dead,
And a cold grave must be her nuptial
bed.

CHAR. Sir, be of good comfort, and your
heavy sorrow
Part equally amongst us. Storms divided
Abate their force, and with less rage
are guided. 130

CRAN. Do, Master Frankford; he that
hath least part
Will find enough to drown one troubled
heart.

FRAN. Peace with thee, Nan!—Brothers
and gentlemen,
All we that can plead interest in her
grief,
Bestow upon her body funeral tears!
Brother, had you with threats and usage
bad
Punished her sin, the grief of her offense

Had not with such true sorrow touched
  her heart.
FRANK. I see it had not; therefore, on her
  grave
Will I bestow this funeral epitaph,   140
Which on her marble tomb shall be en-
  graved.
In golden letters shall these words be
  filled:
Here lies she whom her husband's kind-
ness killed.

FINIS.

THE EPILOGUE

AN honest crew, disposéd to be merry,
  Came to a tavern by, and called for
  wine.
The drawer brought it, smiling like a
  cherry,
  And told them it was pleasant, neat,[1]
  and fine.
"Taste it," quoth one. He did so. "Fie!"
  quoth he,

[1] Pure.

"This wine was good; now 't runs too near
  the lee."[2]

Another sipped, to give the wine his due,
  And said unto the rest it drunk too
  flat;
The third said it was old; the fourth,
  too new;
  "Nay," quoth the fift, "the sharpness
  likes me not."   10
Thus, gentlemen, you see how, in one hour,
The wine was new, old, flat, sharp, sweet,
  and sour.

Unto this wine we do allude[3] our play,
  Which some will judge too trivial, some
  too grave.
You as our guests we entertain this day,
  And bid you welcome to the best we
  have.
Excuse us, then; good wine may be dis-
  graced
When every several mouth hath sundry
  taste.

[2] Lees.   [3] Compare.

JOHN MARSTON

John Marston was born about 1576, seemingly at Coventry. His father was a lawyer, his mother the daughter of an Italian physician resident in England. Marston took his B.A. at Oxford in 1594 and entered the Middle Temple to study law. Turning to literature, he won a reputation by his satiric verse published in 1598, especially by *The Scourge of Villainy*. The first record of his dramatic work is Henslowe's payment to him in 1599 toward an unnamed play. His chief work, however, was done for the boy companies, for the Children of Paul's apparently from 1599 until 1604, when he acquired an interest in the Children of the Queen's Revels. He was a prominent figure in the stage quarrel, or war of the theaters as it was called because of the several companies at different theaters involved. According to Jonson, it arose from Marston's representing him on the stage, but in spite of much study the early history of the affair remains obscure. It lasted from about 1599 until 1601. In 1601 Marston apparently satirized Jonson in *What You Will*, and possibly aided Dekker in preparing the attack in *Satiromastix*. Marston's eulogistic dedication of *The Malcontent* to Jonson indicates a renewal of friendly relations by 1604, and in the same year the two joined Chapman in writing *Eastward Ho*. Marston escaped the imprisonment which his collaborators suffered for *Eastward Ho*, but he was committed to Newgate by the privy council in 1608—it has been conjectured for satire on King James in a play now lost. After this he apparently abandoned the theater and sold his interest in the Children of the Revels. He took orders before 1616, held a living in Hampshire until the end of 1631, and died in 1634. His misanthropy—or his pose—was carried to the grave, for the inscription on his tombstone read, *Oblivioni sacrum*.

Marston's plays follow many of the romantic conventions of Elizabethan drama, but with a fundamental change in spirit. By the end of the sixteenth century, the growth of conservatism and nationalism in the middle classes had brought a sharp reaction against the Italianate elements in English life and literature. Marston and others, taking as their model the rugged style of the Roman satirists, made bitter attacks on the affected gallants of the day and on the artifices of romance and poetry. But their satire reflects also a reaction of Europe as a whole against the idealism of the earlier Renaissance, for many forces were tending to weaken man's faith in the glory of the world and in his own perfectibility. The mood of disillusion is reflected in the misanthropy and melancholy of many writers, who picture the follies of the age as inordinate, its crimes as monstrous. Marston's satire impressed even his contemporaries by its extravagance, its bitterness, and cynicism. As a vehicle for it, he developed—with an affectation equal to that he satirized—a style both blunt and tumid, which is the chief point of Jonson's ridicule in *The Poetaster*. Both mood and manner were carried over into Marston's plays, with a malcontent character used as a critic or an intriguer to set the tone. In keeping with the current conception of the evil of Italian life, he drew the material for his plots and his characters largely from Italy. Here libertinism and Machiavellian intrigue had indeed produced many sinister figures, which were vividly portrayed by Italian writers in both history and story, and which had already been utilized to some extent in Elizabethan novels and plays. But, where direct sources seem to be lacking, dramatists like Marston and Tourneur were able to outdo their models in creating characters and situations of morbid lust and villainy.

Marston's first acknowledged play was *Antonio and Mellida*, an extravagant tragicomedy with disguises and other conventions of romance. The characters were quickly used as a basis for *Antonio's Revenge*, a form of revenge tragedy in which a malcontent revenger carried the type to new depths of gloom and terror. The double play was printed in 1602. *What You Will* (printed in 1607) and *The Malcontent* in its first form were also probably early. In *The Dutch Courtesan* (printed in 1605), with an English setting instead of the usual Italian scene, Marston has used a modification of the plot found in Bandello's famous story of the Countess of Celant, translated by Painter in *The Palace of Pleasure* and by Fenton in *Tragical Discourses*. The comic plot is drawn from a story of Masuccio translated by Painter. *Parasitaster, or the Fawn* (printed in 1606) is based on a story from Boccaccio's *Decameron*. Incidents from Roman history furnished the plot for *The Wonder of Women, or The Tragedy of Sophonisba* (printed in 1606). In *The Insatiate Countess* (published in 1613), which was apparently completed by William Barksted, Marston has used the story of the Countess of Celant for the main plot and another *novella* of Bandello for the subplot.

The Malcontent, for which no source has been discovered, is a tragi-comedy with the dominating atmosphere of tragedy. It was published in 1604, but an allusion (I, vii) to a "horn . . . growing in the woman's forehead, twelve years since" would seem to carry at least part of the play back to 1600 or 1601. A second edition, which quickly followed in the same year, was provided with "additions" by Webster (apparently consisting of little more than an inferior though topically interesting induction) and "augmented" by many passages, primarily comic, presumably from Marston's own pen. The reference to the woman's horn first occurred in one of these "augmentations." *The Works of Mr. John Marston* published in a single volume in 1633 failed to include *The Malcontent*, as well as *Eastward Ho* and *The Insatiate Countess*, in which others had had a hand. The present text is based directly on a photostatic copy of the second edition (1604) in the possession of the Huntington Library, with the permission of the authorities of the Library. The editions of Bullen in *The Works of Marston* and of Neilson in *The Chief Elizabethan Dramatists* have also been consulted.

THE MALCONTENT[1]

BY

JOHN MARSTON

BENJAMINO [2] JONSONIO, POETÆ ELEGANTISSIMO, GRAVISSIMO, AMICO SUO, CANDIDO ET CORDATO, JOHANNES MARSTON, MUSARUM ALUMNUS, ASPERAM HANC SUAM THALIAM D.D.[3]

TO THE READER

I am an ill orator, and, in truth, use to indite more honestly than eloquently, for it is my custom to speak as I think, and write as I speak.

In plainness, therefore, understand that in some things I have willingly erred, as in supposing a Duke of Genoa, and in taking names different from that city's families, for which some may wittily accuse me; but my defense shall be as honest as many [10 reproofs unto me have been most malicious, since, I heartily protest, it was my care to write so far from reasonable offense that even strangers in whose state I laid my scene should not from thence draw any disgrace to any, dead or living. Yet, in despite of my endeavors, I understand some have been most unadvisedly overcunning in misinterpreting me, and with subtility as deep as hell have maliciously spread [20 ill rumors, which, springing from themselves, might to themselves have heavily returned. Surely I desire to satisfy every firm spirit, who, in all his actions, proposeth to himself no more ends than God and virtue do, whose intentions are always simple. To such I protest that, with my free understanding, I have not glanced at disgrace of any, but of those whose unquiet studies labor [4] innovation, contempt of holy [30 policy, reverent, comely superiority, and established unity. For the rest of my supposed tartness, I fear not but unto every worthy mind it will be approved so general and honest as may modestly pass with the freedom of a satire. I would fain leave the paper; only one thing afflicts me, to think that scenes invented merely to be spoken should be enforcively [5] published to be read, and that the least hurt I [40 can receive is to do myself the wrong. But, since others otherwise would do me more, the least inconvenience is to be accepted. I have myself, therefore, set forth this comedy, but so [6] that my enforced absence must much rely upon the printer's discretion; but I shall entreat slight errors in orthography may be as slightly overpassed, and that the unhandsome shape which this trifle in reading presents, may be par- [50 doned for the pleasure it once afforded you when it was presented with the soul of lively action.

Sine aliqua dementia nullus Phœbus.[7]

---

[1] The title continues: "Augmented by Marston. With the Additions Played by the King's Majesty's Servants. Written by John Webster."

[2] Original reads *Beniamini.*

[3] "To Benjamin Jonson, poet most accomplished and most eminent, his frank and judicious friend—John Marston, follower of the Muses—dedicates this his unpolished comedy."

[4] Work for.

[5] Compulsorily.

[6] In such a manner.

[7] No poet is without some madness.

DRAMATIS PERSONÆ

GIOVANNI ALTOFRONTO,[1] *disguised Male-vole, sometime Duke of Genoa.*

PIETRO JACOMO, *Duke of Genoa.*

MENDOZA, *a minion [2] to the duchess of Pietro Jacomo.*

CELSO, *a friend to Altofront.*

BILIOSO, *an old choleric marshal.*

PREPASSO, *a gentleman usher.*

FERNEZE, *a young courtier, and enamored on the duchess.*

FERRARDO, *a minion to Duke Pietro Jacomo.*

EQUATO }
GUERRINO } *two courtiers.*

AURELIA, *duchess to Duke Pietro Jacomo.*

MARIA, *duchess to Duke Altofront.*

EMILIA } *two ladies attending the*
BIANCHA } *duchess [, Aurelia].*

MAQUERELLE, *an old panderess.*

PASSARELLO, *fool to Bilioso.*

[CAPTAIN *of the citadel.*

SCENE: *Genoa.*

TIME: *Contemporary.*]

THE INDUCTION [3]

TO

THE MALCONTENT, AND THE ADDITIONS [4] ACTED BY THE KING'S MAJESTY'S SERVANTS

WRITTEN BY JOHN WEBSTER

Enter W[illiam] Sly,[5] a Tireman[6] following him with a stool.

TIRE. Sir, the gentlemen will be angry if you sit here.

SLY. Why? We may sit upon the stage at the private house.[7] Thou dost not take me for a country gentleman, dost? Dost think I fear hissing? I'll hold my life thou took'st me for one of the players.

TIRE. No, sir.

SLY. By God's slid,[8] if you had, I would have given you but sixpence for your [10 stool. Let them that have stale suits sit in the galleries. Hiss at me! He that will be laughed out of a tavern or an ordinary shall seldom feed well, or be drunk in good company.—Where's Harry Condell, D[ick]

Burbadge, and W[illiam] Sly? Let me speak with some of them.

TIRE. An't [9] please you to go in, sir, you may.

SLY. I tell you, no. I am one that [20 hath seen this play often, and can give them intelligence for their action. I have most of the jests here in my table-book.[10]

Enter Sinklo.

SINK. Save you, coz! [11]

SLY. O, cousin, come, you shall sit between my legs here.

SINK. No, indeed, cousin; the audience then will take me for a viol-de-gambo, and think that you play upon me.

SLY. Nay, rather that I work upon [30 you, coz.

SINK. We stayed for you at supper last night at my cousin Honeymoon's, the woolen draper. After supper we drew cuts for a score of apricocks,[12] the longest cut still to draw an apricock. By this light, 'twas Mistress Frank Honeymoon's fortune still to have the longest cut; I did measure for the women.—What be these, coz?

---

[1] The significance of many of these names as indicating "humors" or offices is obvious.

[2] Favorite, lover.

[3] The induction does not appear in the first edn.

[4] The significant additions are indicated in footnotes.

[5] William Sly, John Sinklo, Richard Burbadge, etc., were prominent members of the King's Company.

[6] Property man.

[7] The Blackfriars Theater.

[8] Eyelid.

[9] If it.

[10] Notebook.

[11] Cousin, friend.

[12] Apricots.

Enter D[ick] Burbadge, H[arry] Condell,
J[ohn] Lowin.

SLY. The players.—God save you!　40
BUR. You are very welcome.
SLY. I pray you, know this gentleman,
my cousin; 'tis Master Doomsday's son,
the usurer.
CON. I beseech you, sir, be covered.[1]
SLY. No, in good faith, for mine ease.
Look you, my hat's the handle to this fan.
God's so,[2] what a beast was I, I did not
leave my feather at home! Well, but I'll
take an order with you.　　　　　　　50
　　　Puts his feather in his pocket.
BUR. Why do you conceal your feather,
sir?
SLY. Why? Do you think I'll have jests
broken upon me in the play, to be laughed
at? This play hath beaten all your gallants
out of the feathers. Blackfriars hath almost
spoiled Blackfriars for feathers.[3]
SINK. God's so, I thought 'twas for
somewhat our gentlewomen at home counseled me to wear my feather to the　[60
play; yet I am loath to spoil it.
SLY. Why, coz?
SINK. Because I got it in the tiltyard;
there was a herald broke my pate for taking
it up. But I have worn it up and down the
Strand, and met him forty times since, and
yet he dares not challenge it.
SLY. Do you hear, sir? This play is a
bitter play.
CON. Why, sir, 'tis neither satire nor　[70
moral, but the mean[4] passage of a history;
yet there are a sort of discontented creatures that bear a stingless envy to great
ones, and these will wrest the doings of any
man to their base, malicious applyment;
but, should their interpretation come to the
test, like your marmoset they presently
turn their teeth to their tail and eat it.
SLY. I will not go so far with you; but
I say any man that hath wit may cen-　[80
sure,[5] if he sit in the twelvepenny room;[6]
and I say again the play is bitter.
BUR. Sir, you are like a patron that,
presenting a poor scholar to a benefice,
enjoins him not to rail against anything

that stands within compass of his patron's
folly. Why should not we enjoy the ancient freedom of poesy? Shall we protest
to the ladies that their painting makes
them angels, or to my young gallant　[90
that his expense in the brothel shall gain
him reputation? No, sir, such vices as
stand not accountable to law should be
cured as men heal tetters, by casting ink
upon them. Would you be satisfied[7] in
anything else, sir?
SLY. Ay, marry, would I: I would know
how you came by this play.
CON. Faith, sir, the book was lost; and,
because 'twas pity so good a play　[100
should be lost, we found it, and play it.
SLY. I wonder you would play it, another company having interest in it.
CON. Why not Malevole in folio with us,
as Jeronimo in decimo-sexto with them?[8]
They taught us a name for our play; we
call it *One for Another.*
SLY. What are your additions?
BUR. Sooth, not greatly needful; only
as your sallet[9] to your great feast, to　[110
entertain a little more time, and to abridge
the not-received custom of music in our
theater.[10] I must leave you, sir.
　　　　　　　　　　Exit Burbadge.
SINK. Doth he play the Malcontent?
CON. Yes, sir.
SINK. I durst lay four of mine ears the
play is not so well acted as it hath been.
CON. O, no, sir, nothing *ad Parmenonis*
suem.[11]

[7] Answered.
[8] "*I.e.* Why should not the King's Company
of grown up (folio) actors play *The Malcontent*
(which was the property of the children's company playing at Blackfriars), since the children
(16mo actors) have appropriated *The Spanish*
Tragedy, in which the King's Company had
rights?" (Neilson).
[9] Salad.
[10] *I.e.,* fill in the interval ordinarily taken by
music in other theaters.
[11] "'Tis reported that Parmeno, being very
famous for imitating the grunting of a pig, some
endeavoured to rival and outdo him. And when
the hearers, being prejudiced, cried out, 'Very
well, indeed, but nothing comparable to Parmeno's sow,' one took a pig under his arm and
came upon the stage; and when, tho' they heard
the very pig, they still continued, 'This is nothing comparable to Parmeno's sow,' he threw the
pig among them to show that they judged according to opinion and not truth" (Plutarch's
Symposium, V, i, cited by "L. S." and Bullen).

[1] Put your hat on.　　　[2] A mild oath.
[3] This presumably refers to V, ii, 47–48, and
perhaps means that gallants wearing feathers
were so ridiculed that they quit the district.
[4] Common.　　[5] Judge, criticize.　　[6] Box.

Low. Have you lost your ears, sir, [120 that you are so prodigal of laying them?

Sink. Why did you ask that, friend?

Low. Marry, sir, because I have heard of a fellow would offer to lay a hundred pound wager, that was not worth five baubees;[1] and in this kind you might venter[2] four of your elbows; yet God defend[3] your coat should have so many!

Sink. Nay, truly, I am no great censurer; and yet I might have been one of [130 the College of Critics once. My cousin here hath an excellent memory, indeed, sir.

Sly. Who, I? I'll tell you a strange thing of myself; and I can tell you, for one that never studied the art of memory, 'tis very strange too.

Con. What's that, sir?

Sly. Why, I'll lay a hundred pound I'll walk but once down by the Goldsmiths' Row in Cheap, take notice of the signs, [140 and tell you them with a breath instantly.

Low. 'Tis very strange.

Sly. They begin as the world did, with Adam and Eve. There's in all just five-and-fifty. I do use to meditate much when I come to plays too. What do you think might come into a man's head now, seeing all this company?

Con. I know not, sir.

Sly. I have an excellent thought. [150 If some fifty of the Grecians that were crammed in the horse-belly had eaten garlic, do you not think the Trojans might have smelt out their knavery?

Con. Very likely.

Sly. By God, I would he had, for I love Hector horribly.

Sink. O, but, coz, coz!—

"Great Alexander, when he came to the tomb of Achilles,

Spake with a big loud voice, 'O thou thrice blessed and happy!'"[4] [160

Sly. Alexander was an ass to speak so well of a filthy cullion.[5]

Low. Good sir, will you leave the stage? I'll help you to a private room.[6]

Sly. Come, coz, let's take some tobacco.—Have you never a prologue?

Low. Not any, sir.

Sly. Let me see, I will make one extempore.

Come to them, and fencing of a congee[7] with arms and legs, be round[8] with them.[9]

Gentlemen, I could wish for the [170 women's sakes you had all soft cushions; and, gentlewomen, I could wish that for the men's sakes you had all more easy standings.—What would they wish more but the play now? And that they shall have instantly. [*Exeunt.*]

ACTUS PRIMUS.[10] SCENA PRIMA.

[*The palace of the Duke of Genoa.*]

The vilest out-of-tune music being heard, enter Bilioso and Prepasso.

Bil. Why, how now! Are ye mad, or drunk, or both, or what?

Pre. Are ye building Babylon there?

Bil. Here's a noise in court! You think you are in a tavern, do you not?

Pre. You think you are in a brothel house, do you not?—This room is ill-scented.

Enter One with a perfume.

So, perfume, perfume; some upon me, I pray thee.—

The duke is upon instant entrance; so, make place there! 10

SCENA SECUNDA.

[*The same.*]

Enter the Duke Pietro, Ferrardo, Count Equato, Count Celso before, and Guerrino.[11]

Piet. Where breathes that music?

Bil. The discord rather than the music is heard from the malcontent Malevole's chamber.

Fer. [*Calling.*] Malevole!

---

[1] Halfpennies.   [2] Venture.   [3] Forbid.
[4] From John Harvey's translation of Petrarch's 153rd sonnet.
[5] Knave.   [6] Box.
[7] Making a bow.
[8] Plain-spoken.
[9] This stage direction is printed as part of Sly's speech in the original.
[10] The title is repeated before this line, and in the margin appears Juvenal's phrase, *Vexat censura columbas*, "Censorship disturbs the doves" (*i.e.*, the peace).
[11] The characters from the preceding scene remain, as in general they do throughout the play.

MAL. (*Out of his chamber.*) Yaugh, God a [1] man, what dost thou there? Duke's Ganymede, Juno's jealous of thy long stockings. Shadow of a woman, what wouldst, weasel? Thou lamb a court, [10 what dost thou bleat for? Ah, you smooth-chinned catamite! [2]

PIET. Come down, thou ragged cur, and snarl here. I give thy dogged sullenness free liberty; trot about and bespurtle [3] whom thou pleasest.

MAL. I'll come among you, you goatish-blooded toderers,[4] as gum into taffeta, to fret, to fret.[5] I'll fall like a sponge into water, to suck up, to suck up. Howl [20 again! I'll go to church and come to you.   [*Exit above.*]

PIET. This Malevole is one of the most prodigious affections [6] that ever conversed with nature; a man, or rather a monster, more discontent than Lucifer when he was thrust out of the presence. His appetite is unsatiable as the grave, as far from any content as from heaven. His highest delight is to procure others vexation, and therein he thinks he truly serves heaven; [30 for 'tis his position, whosoever in this earth can be contented is a slave and damned; therefore does he afflict all in that to which they are most affected.[7] Th' elements struggle within him; his own soul is at variance within herself; his speech is halter-worthy at all hours. I like him; faith, he gives good intelligence to my spirit, makes me understand those weaknesses which others' flattery palliates.—Hark! They [40 sing.[8]

SCENA TERTIA.

[*The same.*]

Enter Malevole after the song.

[PIET.] See, he comes. Now shall you hear the extremity of a malcontent. He is as free as air; he blows over every man.— And, sir, whence come you now?

MAL. From the public place of much dissimulation, the church.[9]

PIET. What didst there?

---

[1] Of.   [2] Male prostitute.   [3] Besprinkle.
[4] Perhaps dealers in sheep or mutton, *i.e.*, in prostitutes.   [5] *I.e.*, to wear you out quickly.
[6] Passions.   [7] Inclined.   [8] The song is not given.
[9] *The church* does not appear in the first edn. and is erased in some copies of the second.

MAL. Talk with a usurer; take up at interest.

PIET. I wonder what religion thou [10 art of.

MAL. Of a soldier's religion.

PIET. And what dost think makes most infidels now?

MAL. Sects, sects. I have seen seeming Piety change her robe so oft that sure none but some arch-devil can shape her a petticoat.

PIET. O, a religious policy.

MAL. But damnation on a politic re- [20 ligion! I am weary. Would I were one of the duke's hounds now!

PIET. But what's the common news abroad, Malevole? Thou dogg'st rumor still.

MAL. Common news? Why, common words are, "God save ye," "Fare ye well;" common actions, flattery and cozenage; common things, women and cuckolds.— And how does my little Ferrard? Ah, ye [30 lecherous animal! My little ferret, he goes sucking up and down the palace into every hen's nest, like a weasel. And to what dost thou addict thy time to now more than to those antique painted drabs that are still affected of [10] young courtiers, Flattery, Pride, and Venery?

FER. I study languages. Who dost think to be the best linguist of our age?

MAL. Phew, the devil! Let him pos- [40 sess thee; he'll teach thee to speak all languages most readily and strangely; and great reason, marry, he's traveled greatly in the world, and is everywhere.

FER. Save i' th' court.

MAL. Ay, save i' th' court.—(*To Bili-oso.*) And how does my old muckhill, over-spread with fresh snow? Thou half a man, half a goat, all a beast! How does thy young wife, old huddle? [11]   50

BIL. Out, you improvident rascal!

MAL. Do, kick, thou hugely-horned old duke's ox, good Master Make-pleas.

PIET. How dost thou live nowadays, Malevole?

MAL. Why, like the knight, Sir Patrick Penlolians, with killing a spiders for my lady's monkey.

PIET. How dost spend the night? I hear thou never sleep'st.   60

---

[10] Liked by.   [11] Decrepit old man.

MAL. O, no, but dream the most fantastical! O heaven! O fubbery, fubbery![1]

PIET. Dream! What dream'st?

MAL. Why, methinks I see that signior pawn his footcloth,[2] that *metreza*[3] her plate; this madam takes physic that tother[4] *monsieur* may minister to her. Here is a pander jeweled; there's a fellow in shift of satin this day, that could not shift a shirt tother night. Here a Paris [70 supports that Helen; there's a Lady Guinevere bears up that Sir Lancelot. Dreams, dreams, visions, fantasies, chimeras, imaginations, tricks, conceits![5]—(*To Prepasso.*) Sir Tristram Trimtram, come aloft, Jackanapes,[6] with a whim-wham. Here's a knight of the land of Catito shall play at trap[7] with any page in Europe, do the sword dance with any morris dancer in Christendom, ride at the [80 ring[8] till the fin[9] of his eyes look as blue as the welkin, and run the wild goose chase even with Pompey the Huge.

PIET. You run!

MAL. To the devil. Now, Signior Guerrino, that thou from a most pitied prisoner shouldst grow a most loathed flatterer!— Alas, poor Celso, thy star's oppressed: thou art an honest lord. 'Tis pity.

EQU. Is 't pity?   90

MAL. Ay, marry is 't, philosophical Equato; and 'tis pity that thou, being so excellent a scholar by art, shouldst be so ridiculous a fool by nature.—I have a thing to tell you, duke; bid um avaunt, bid um avaunt.

PIET. Leave us, leave us.—Now, sir, what is 't?

Exeunt all saving Pietro and Malevole.

MAL. Duke, thou art a *becco*,[10] a *cornuto*.[11]

PIET. How?   100

MAL. Thou art a cuckold.

PIET. Speak; unshale[12] him quick.

MAL. With most tumblerlike nimbleness.

PIET. Who? By whom? I burst with desire.

MAL. Mendoza is the man makes thee a horned beast; duke, 'tis Mendoza cornutes thee.

PIET. What conformance?[13] Relate; [110 short, short!

MAL. As a lawyer's beard.

There is an old crone in the court-- her name is Maquerelle;

She is my mistress, sooth to say, and she doth ever tell me.

Blurt a rime,[14] blurt a rime! Maquerelle is a cunning bawd; I am an honest villain; thy wife is a close drab;[15] and thou art a notorious cuckold. Farewell, duke.

PIET. Stay, stay.

MAL. Dull, dull duke, can lazy pa- [120 tience make lame revenge? O God, for a woman to make a man that which God never created, never made!

PIET. What did God never make?

MAL. A cuckold! To be made a thing that's hoodwinked with kindness, whilst every rascal fillips his brows; to have a coxcomb with egregious horns pinned to a lord's back, every page sporting himself with delightful laughter, whilst he [130 must be the last must know it! Pistols and poniards! Pistols and poniards!

PIET. Death and damnation!

MAL. Lightning and thunder!

PIET. Vengeance and torture!

MAL. *Catso!*[16]

PIET. O, revenge![17]

MAL. Nay, to select among ten thousand fairs

A lady far inferior to the most,

In fair proportion both of limb and soul;   140

To take her from austerer check of parents,

To make her his by most devoutful rites,

Make her commandress of a better essence

Than is the gorgeous world, even of a man;

To hug her with as raised an appetite

As usurers do their delved-up treasury[18]

---

[1] Deceit.
[2] The housings of a horse.
[3] Mistress.
[4] That other.
[5] Fancies.
[6] The ape-trainer's call to his monkey.
[7] A game played with a bat, a ball, and a trap.
[8] Tilt at a ring.
[9] Lid.
[10] Cuckold.
[11] A horned one.
[12] Unshell.
[13] Confirmance (?), proof.
[14] A fig for rime.
[15] Secret harlot.
[16] A provocative exclamation.
[17] Lines 138–85 are the first significant addition.
[18] Treasure.

(Thinking none tells [1] it but his private
    self);
To meet her spirit in a nimble kiss,
Distilling panting ardor to her heart;
True to her sheets, nay, diets strong his
    blood,   150
To give her height of hymeneal sweets—
PIET. O God!
MAL. Whilst she lisps, and gives him some
    court *quelquechose*,[2]
Made only to provoke, not satiate;
And yet, even then, the thaw of her de-
    light
Flows from lewd heat of apprehension,
Only from strange imagination's rank-
    ness,
That forms the adulterer's presence in
    her soul,
And makes her think she clips [3] the
    foul knave's loins.
    PIET. Affliction to my blood's root! [160
MAL. Nay, think, but think what may
proceed of this; adultery is often the
mother of incest.
    PIET. Incest?
MAL. Yes, incest. Mark! Mendoza of
his wife begets perchance a daughter;
Mendoza dies; his son marries this daughter. Say you? Nay, 'tis frequent, not
only probable, but no question often acted,
whilst ignorance, fearless ignorance, [170
clasps his own seed.
    PIET. Hideous imagination!
MAL. Adultery! Why, next to the sin
of simony, 'tis the most horrid transgres-
sion under the cope of salvation.[4]
    PIET. Next to simony?
MAL. Ay, next to simony, in which our
men in next age shall not sin.
    PIET. Not sin? Why?
MAL. Because (thanks to some [180
churchmen) our age will leave them nothing to sin with. But adultery, O dullness, should show [5] exemplary punishment, that intemperate bloods may freeze
but to think it. I would dam [6] him and
all his generation; my own hands should
do it; ha, I would not trust heaven with
my vengeance anything.
    PIET. Anything, anything, Malevole!
Thou shalt see instantly what temper [190

my spirit holds. Farewell; remember I
forget thee not; farewell.   *Exit Pietro.*
MAL.[7] Farewell.
Lean thoughtfulness, a sallow meditation,
Suck thy veins dry! Distemperance rob
    thy sleep!
The heart's disquiet is revenge most deep;
He that gets blood, the life of flesh but
    spills,[8]
But he that breaks heart's peace, the dear
    soul kills.[9]—
Well, this disguise doth yet afford me
    that
Which kings do seldom hear, or great
    men use,   200
Free speech; and, though my state's
    usurped,
Yet this affected strain gives me a
    tongue
As fetterless as is an emperor's.
I may speak foolishly, ay, knavishly,
Always carelessly, yet no one thinks it
    fashion
To poise [10] my breath, "for he that laughs
    and strikes
Is lightly felt, or seldom struck again."
Duke, I'll torment thee; now my just
    revenge
From thee than crown a richer gem
    shall part.
Beneath God, naught's so dear as a calm
    heart.   210

SCENA QUARTA.

[*The same.*]

Enter Celso.

CEL. My honored lord—
MAL. Peace, speak low; peace! O Celso,
    constant lord,
Thou to whose faith I only rest dis-
    covered,
Thou, one of full ten millions of men,
That lovest virtue only for itself,
Thou in whose hands old Ops [11] may put
    her soul,
Behold forever-banished Altofront,

---

[1] Counts.   [2] Kickshaws, delicacies.   [3] Embraces.
[4] Under the expanse of heaven.
[5] Original reads *show should.*   [6] Stop up, choke.

[7] This speech is an addition.
[8] Destroys.
[9] Italics or quotation marks were often used
to mark sententious passages.
[10] Weigh seriously.
[11] The goddess of plenty.

This Genoa's last year's duke. O truly
noble!
I wanted [1] those old instruments of
state—
Dissemblance and suspect.[2] I could not
time it, [3] Celso;   10
My throne stood like a point in middest
of a circle,
To all of equal nearness; bore with none;
Reined all alike; so slept in fearless virtue,
Suspectless, too suspectless; till the
crowd,
Still lickerous of [4] untried novelties,
Impatient with severer government,
Made strong with Florence, banished
Altofront.
CEL. Strong with Florence! Ay, thence
your mischief rose;
For, when the daughter of the Florentine
Was matched once with this [5] Pietro,
now duke,   20
No stratagem of state untried was left,
Till you of all— [6]
MAL.   Of all was quite bereft.
Alas, Maria too, close prisonéd,
My true-faithed duchess, i' the citadel!
CEL. I'll still adhere; let's mutiny and die.
MAL. O, no, climb not a falling tower,
Celso;
'Tis well held desperation, no zeal,
Hopeless to strive with fate. Peace!
Temporize!
Hope, hope, that never forsak'st the
wretched'st man,
Yet bidd'st me live, and lurk in this
disguise!   30
What, play I well the free-breathed
discontent?
Why, man, we are all philosophical
monarchs
Or natural fools. Celso, the court's afire;
The duchess' sheets will smoke for 't ere
it be long.
Impure Mendoza, that sharp-nosed lord,
that made
The curséd match linked Genoa with
Florence,

Now broad-horns the duke, which he now
knows.
Discord to malcontents is very manna;
When the ranks are burst, then scuffle,
Altofront.
CEL. Ay, but durst—   40
MAL. 'Tis gone; 'tis swallowed like a min-
eral. [7]
Some way 'twill work. Pheut, I'll not
shrink!
"He's resolute who can no lower sink."

[8] *Bilioso entering, Malevole shifteth his*
speech.

MAL. O, the father of Maypoles! Did
you never see a fellow whose strength con-
sisted in his breath, respect in his office,
religion in [9] his lord, and love in himself?
Why, then, behold!
BIL. Signior—
MAL. My right worshipful lord, [50
your court nightcap makes you have a
passing high forehead.
BIL. I can tell you strange news, but I
am sure you know them already: the duke
speaks much good of you.
MAL. Go to, then; and shall you and I
now enter into a strict friendship?
BIL. Second one another?
MAL. Yes.
BIL. Do one another good offices?   60
MAL. Just. What though I called thee
old ox, egregious wittol, [10] broken-bellied
coward, rotten mummy? Yet, since I am
in favor—
BIL. Words, of course, terms of disport.
His grace presents you by me a chain, as
his grateful remembrance for—I am ignorant for what; marry, ye may impart. Yet
howsoever—come, dear friend. Dost know
my son?   70
MAL. Your son?
BIL. He shall eat woodcocks, dance jigs,
make possets, and play at shuttlecock with
any young lord about the court. He has
as sweet a lady, too. Dost know her little
bitch?
MAL. 'Tis a dog, man.
BIL. Believe me, a she-bitch. O, 'tis a

---

[1] Lacked.   [2] Suspicion.
[3] *I.e.*, could not force myself into time with
conditions.
[4] Craving.   [5] Original reads *his*.
[6] Here and in a few other passages the line
division has been regularized.   Some later
passages printed in the original as prose have
been set as verse.

[7] Medicine.
[8] The passage from this point through the
stage direction in l. 103 is an addition.
[9] Original reads *on*.
[10] A man who winks at his own cuckoldry.

good creature! Thou shalt be her servant.
I'll make thee acquainted with my [80
young wife too. What, I keep her not at
court for nothing! 'Tis grown to supper
time; come to my table; that—anything I
have—stands open to thee.

MAL. ([*Aside*] *to Cel*[*so*].) How smooth
    to him that is in state of grace,
How servile is the rugged'st courtier's
    face!
What profit, nay, what nature would keep
    down,
Are heaved [1] *to them are minions to a crown.*
Envious ambition never sates his thirst,
Till, sucking all, he swells and swells,
    and bursts.   90

BIL. I shall now leave you with my
always-best wishes; only let's hold betwixt us a firm correspondence, a mutual
friendly-reciprocal kind of steady-unani-
mous-heartily-leagued—

MAL. Did your signiorship ne'er see
a pigeonhouse that was smooth, round,
and white without, and full of holes and
stink within? Ha' ye not, old courtier?

BIL. O, yes, 'tis the form, the fashion
of them all.   101

MAL. Adieu, my true court friend; farewell, my dear Castilio.[2]   *Exit Bilioso.*

CEL. Yonder's Mendoza.

MAL.   True, the privy-key.
                 Descries Mendoza.

CEL. I take my leave, sweet lord.
                   Exit Celso.

MAL.   'Tis fit; away!

SCENA QUINTA.

[*The same.*]

Enter Mendoza with three or four Suitors.

MEN. Leave your suits with me; I
can and will. Attend my secretary; leave
me.   [*Exeunt Suitors.*]

MAL. Mendoza, hark ye, hark ye. You
are a treacherous villain, God b' wi' ye!

MEN. Out, you baseborn rascal!

MAL. We are all the sons of heaven,
though a tripe-wife were our mother. Ah,
you whoreson,[3] hot-reined[4] he-marmoset!
Ægistus—didst ever hear of one Ægistus?

MEN. Gistus?   11

[1] Lifted.
[2] Alluding to Castiglione, author of *Il Corte-
giano* (*The Courtier*).
[3] Rascally.   [4] Lecherous.

MAL. Ay, Ægistus; he was a filthy, incontinent fleshmonger, such a one as thou
art.

MEN. Out, grumbling rogue!

MAL. Orestes, beware Orestes!

MEN. Out, beggar!

MAL. I once shall rise!

MEN. Thou rise?

MAL. Ay, at the resurrection.   20
"No vulgar seed but once may rise and
    shall;
No king so huge but fore he die may
    fall."   *Exit.*

MEN. Now, good Elysium! What a
delicious heaven is it for a man to be in a
prince's favor! O sweet God! O pleasure!
O fortune! O all thou best of life! What
should I think, what say, what do, to be a
favorite, a minion? To have a general
timorous respect, observe [5] a man, a [29
stateful silence in his presence, solitariness in his absence, a confused hum and
busy murmur of obsequious suitors training [6] him, the cloth held up, and way
proclaimed before him, petitionary vassals
licking the pavement with their slavish
knees, whilst some odd palace-lampreels [7]
that engender with snakes, and are full
of eyes on both sides, with a kind of
insinuated humbleness, fix all their delights upon his brow! O blessed state! [40
What a ravishing prospect doth the Olympus of favor yield! Death, I cornute
the duke! Sweet women, most sweet
ladies, nay, angels! By heaven, he is more
accursed than a devil that hates you, or
is hated by you, and happier than a god
that loves you, or is beloved by you. You
preservers of mankind, lifeblood of society,
who would live, nay, who can live without you? O paradise, how majes- [50
tical is your austerer presence! How
imperiously chaste is your more modest
face! But, O, how full of ravishing attraction is your pretty, petulant, languishing, lasciviously-composed countenance!
These amorous smiles, those soul-warming
sparkling glances, ardent as those flames
that singed the world by heedless Phaëton! In body how delicate, in soul how [59
witty, in discourse how pregnant, in life
how wary, in favors how judicious, in day
how sociable, and in night how—! O

[5] Be obsequious to.   [6] Following.   [7] Lampreys.

pleasure unutterable! Indeed, it is most certain, one man cannot deserve only to enjoy a beauteous woman. But a duchess! In despite of Phœbus, I'll write a sonnet instantly in praise of her. *Exit.*

SCENA SEXTA.

[*The same.*]

Enter Ferneze ushering Aurelia, Emilia and Maquerelle bearing up her train, Biancha attending; all go out but Aurelia, Maquerelle, and Ferneze.

AUR. And is 't possible? Mendoza slight me! Possible?

FER. Possible! What can be strange in him that's drunk with favor,
Grows insolent with grace?—Speak, Maquerelle, speak.

MAQ. To speak feelingly, more, more richly in solid sense than worthless words, give me those jewels of your ears to receive my enforced duty. As for my part, 'tis well known. (*Ferneze privately feeds Maquerelle's hands with jewels during* [10 *this speech.*) I can put [1] anything, can bear patiently with any man. But, when I heard he wronged your precious sweetness, I was enforced to take deep offense. 'Tis most certain he loves Emilia with high appetite; and, as she told me (as you know we women impart our secrets one to another), when she repulsed his suit, in that he was possessed with your endeared grace, Mendoza most ingratefully renounced [20 all faith to you.

FER. Nay, called you—speak, Maquerelle, speak.

MAQ. By heaven, witch, dried bisque, [2] and contested blushlessly he loved you but for a spurt or so.

FER. For maintenance.

MAQ. Advancement and regard.

AUR. O villain! O impudent Mendoza!

MAQ. Nay, he is the rustiest jade, [30 the foulest-mouthed knave in railing against our sex! He will rail against women—

AUR. How? How?

MAQ. I am ashamed to speak 't, I.

AUR. I love to hate him. Speak.

MAQ. Why, when Emilia scorned his base unsteadiness, the black-throated rascal scolded, and said—

AUR. What?

MAQ. Troth, 'tis too shameless. 40

AUR. What said he?

MAQ. Why, that, at four, women were fools; at fourteen, drabs, at forty, bawds; at fourscore, witches; and [at] [3] a hundred, cats.

AUR. O unlimitable impudency!

FER. But, as for poor Ferneze's fixéd heart,
Was never shadeless meadow drier parched
Under the scorching heat of heaven's Dog
Than is my heart with your enforcing [4] eyes. 50

MAQ. A hot simile!

FER. Your smiles have been my heaven, your frowns my hell.
O, pity, then! Grace should with beauty dwell.

MAQ. Reasonable perfect, by 'r Lady.

AUR. I will love thee, be it but in despite
Of that Mendoza. "Witch," Ferneze, "witch"!
Ferneze, thou art the duchess' favorite;
Be faithful, private; but 'tis dangerous.

FER. "His love is liveless that for love fears breath;
The worst that's due to sin, O, would 'twere death!" 60

AUR. Enjoy my favor. I will be sick instantly and take physic; therefore in depth of night visit—

MAQ. Visit her chamber, but conditionally: you shall not offend her bed, by this diamond!

FER. By this diamond.
Gives it to Maquerelle.

MAQ. Nor tarry longer than you please, by this ruby!

FER. By this ruby. *Gives again.* 70

MAQ. And that the door shall not creak.

FER. And that the door shall not creak.

MAQ. Nay, but swear.

FER. By this purse. *Gives her his purse.*

MAQ. Go to, I'll keep your oaths for you. Remember, visit.

Enter Mendoza, reading a sonnet.

AUR. "Dried biscuit"!—Look where the base wretch comes.

MEN. "Beauty's life, heaven's model, love's queen—" 80

---

[1] Endure.　　　　　[2] Biscuit.　　　　　[3] Supplied by Bullen.　　　　　[4] Ravishing.

MAQ. [*Aside.*] That's his Emilia.

MEN. "Nature's triumph, best on earth—"

MAQ. [*Aside.*] Meaning Emilia.

MEN. "Thou only wonder that the world hath seen—"

MAQ. [*Aside.*] That's Emilia.

AUR. [*Aside.*] Must I then hear her praised?—Mendoza!

MEN. Madam, your excellency is [90 graciously encountered; I have been writing passionate flashes in honor of—

                Exit Fer[neze].

AUR. Out, villain, villain! O judgment, where have been my eyes? What bewitched election made me dote on thee? What sorcery made me love thee? But be gone; bury thy head. O, that I could do more than loathe thee! Hence, worst of ill! No reason ask; our reason is our will.

           Exit with Maquerelle.

MEN. Women! Nay, furies; nay, [100 worse, for they torment only the bad, but women good and bad. Damnation of mankind! Breath, hast thou praised them for this? And is't you, Ferneze, are wriggled into smock-grace? Sit sure. O, that I could rail against these monsters in nature, models of hell, curse of the earth, women that dare attempt anything, and what they attempt they care not how they accomplish; without all premeditation or prevention; [110 rash in asking, desperate in working, impatient in suffering, extreme in desiring, slaves unto appetite, mistresses in dissembling, only constant in unconstancy, only perfect in counterfeiting. Their words are feigned, their eyes forged, their sights [1] dissembled, their looks counterfeit, their hair false, their given hopes deceitful, their very breath artificial. *Their blood is their only god; bad clothes and old age are* [120 *only the devils they tremble at.* That I could rail now!

SCENA SEPTA.

[*The same.*]

Enter Pietro, his sword drawn.

PIET. A mischief fill thy throat, thou foul-jawed slave!

Say thy prayers.

MEN.   I ha' forgot um.

    [1] Sighs.

PIET.   Thou shalt die!

MEN. So shalt thou. I am heart-mad.

PIET.   I am horn-mad.[2]

MEN. Extreme mad.

PIET.   Monstrously mad.

MEN.   Why?

PIET. Why? Thou, thou hast dishonoréd my bed.

MEN. I? Come, come, sit; here's my bare heart to thee,

As steady as is this center to the glorious world.

And yet, hark, thou art a cornuto—but by me?

PIET. Yes, slave, by thee.

MEN. Do not, do not with tart and spleen-ful breath   10

Lose him can lose thee. I offend my duke?

Bear record, O ye dumb and raw-aired nights,

How vigilant my sleepless eyes have been

To watch the traitor! Record, thou spirit of truth,

With what debasement I ha' thrown myself

To under offices, only to learn

The truth, the party, time, the means, the place,

By whom, and when, and where thou wert disgraced!

And am I paid with "slave"? Hath my intrusion

To places private and prohibited,   20

Only to observe the closer passages

(Heaven knows with vows of revelation),

Made me suspected, made me deemed a villain?

What rogue hath wronged us?

PIET.   Mendoza, I may err.

MEN. Err? 'Tis too mild a name; but err and err,

Run giddy with suspect fore through me thou know

That which most creatures, save thyself, do know.

Nay, since my service hath so loathed reject,[3]

Fore I'll reveal, shalt find them clipped together.

PIET. Mendoza, thou know'st I am [30 a most plain-breasted [4] man.

   [2] Intensive, with a double meaning.
   [3] Rejection.   [4] Plain-spoken.

MEN. The fitter to make a cuckold!
Would your brows were most plain too!

PIET. Tell me; indeed, I heard thee rail.

MEN. At women, true. Why, what cold
    fleam [1] could choose,
  Knowing a lord so honest, virtuous,
  So boundless-loving, bounteous, fair-
    shaped, sweet,
  To be contemned, abused, defamed,
    made cuckold?
Heart! I hate all women for 't—sweet
sheets, wax lights, antique bedposts, [40
cambric smocks, villainous curtains, arras
pictures, oiled hinges, and all the tongue-
tied lascivious witnesses of great creatures'
wantonness! What salvation can you
expect?

PIET. Wilt thou tell me?

MEN. Why, you may find it yourself;
observe, observe.

PIET. I ha' not the patience. Wilt thou
deserve [2] me? Tell, give it.   50

MEN. Take 't! Why, Ferneze is the
man, Ferneze. I'll prove 't; this night you
shall take him in your sheets. Will 't serve?

PIET. It will; my bosom's in some peace.
    Till night!

MEN. What?

PIET. Farewell.

MEN.   God! How weak a lord are you!
  Why, do you think there is no more but
    so?

PIET. Why?

MEN.   Nay, then will I presume to
    counsel you.
  It should be thus. You with some guard
    upon the sudden
  Break into the princess' chamber; I stay
    behind,
  Without the door through which he needs
    must pass.   60
  Ferneze flies—let him. To me he comes.
    He's killed
  By me—observe—by me. You follow; [3]
    I rail,
  And seem to save the body. Duchess
    comes,
  On whom (respecting her advancéd birth
  And your fair nature) I know, nay, I do
    know,
  No violence must be used. She comes; I
    storm;

I praise, excuse Ferneze, and still main-
    tain
  The duchess' honor; she for this loves me.
  I honor you, shall know her soul, you
    mine.
  Then naught shall she contrive in
    vengeance   70
  (As women are most thoughtful in re-
    venge)
  Of her Ferneze, but you shall sooner
    know' t
  Than she can think 't. Thus shall his
    death come sure;
  Your duchess brain-caught, so your life
    secure.

PIET. It is too well, my bosom and my
    heart!
  "When nothing helps, cut off the rotten
    part."   Exit.

MEN. "Who cannot feign friendship can
ne'er produce the effects of hatred." Honest fool duke, subtile lascivious duchess, silly
novice Ferneze, I do laugh at ye. My [80
brain is in labor till it produce mischief,
and I feel sudden throes, proofs sensible the
issue is at hand.
  "As bears shape young, so I'll form my
    device,
  Which grown proves horrid. Vengeance
    makes men wise."   [Exit.] [4]

Enter Malevole and Passarello.

MAL. Fool, most happily encountered!
Canst sing, fool?

PASS. Yes, I can sing, fool, if you'll bear
the burden; [5] and I can play upon instruments, scurvily, as gentlemen do. O, [90
that I had been gelded! I should then have
been a fat fool for a chamber, a squeaking
fool for a tavern, and a private fool for all
the ladies.

MAL. You are in good case since you
came to court, fool. What, garded, [6]
garded!

PASS. Yes, faith, even as footmen and
bawds wear velvet, not for an ornament
of honor, but for a badge of drudgery; [100
for, now the duke is discontented, I am
fain to fool him asleep every night.

MAL. What are his griefs?

PASS. He hath sore eyes.

MAL. I never observed so much.

---

[1] Phlegm.
[2] Be serviceable to.
[3] Original reads *fellow.*
[4] The remainder of the scene is an addition.
[5] Sing the bass.
[6] Trimmed up.

Pass. Horrible sore eyes; and so hath every cuckold, for the roots of the horns spring in the eyeballs, and that's the reason the horn of a cuckold is as tender as his eye, or as that growing in the woman's [110 forehead, twelve years since, that could not endure to be touched.[1] The duke hangs down his head like a columbine.

Mal. Passarello, why do great men beg fools? [2]

Pass. As the Welshman stole rushes when there was nothing else to filch—only to keep begging in fashion.

Mal. Pooh, thou givest no good reason; thou speakest like a fool. 120

Pass. Faith, I utter small fragments, as your knight courts your city widow with something of his gilt,[3] some advancing his high-colored [4] beard, and taking tobacco. This is all the mirror of their knightly complements.[5] Nay, I shall talk when my tongue is a-going once; 'tis like a citizen on horseback, evermore in a false gallop.

Mal. And how doth Maquerelle fare nowadays? 130

Pass. Faith, I was wont to salute her as our English women are at their first landing in Flushing—I would call her whore. But now that antiquity leaves her as an old piece of plastic [6] t' work by, I only ask her how her rotten teeth fare every morning, and so leave her. She was the first that ever invented perfumed smocks for the gentlewomen, and woolen shoes for fear of creaking for the visitant. She were [140 an excellent lady but that her face peeleth like Muscovy glass.[7]

Mal. And how doth thy old lord, that hath wit enough to be a flatterer, and conscience enough to be a knave?

Pass. O, excellent; he keeps beside me fifteen jesters to instruct him in the art of fooling, and utters their jests in private to the duke and duchess. He'll lie like to your Switzer or lawyer; he'll be of any side [150 for most money.

Mal. I am in haste; be brief.

Pass. As your fiddler when he is paid. He'll thrive, I warrant you, while your young courtier stands like Good Friday in Lent; men long to see it, because more fatting days come after it; else he's the leanest and pitifull'st actor in the whole pageant. Adieu, Malevole.

Mal. [Aside.] O world most vild,[8] when thy loose vanities, 160
Taught by this fool, do make the fool seem wise!

Pass. You'll know me again, Malevole.

Mal. O, ay, by that velvet.

Pass. Ay, as a pettifogger by his buckram bag. I am as common in the court as an hostess's lips in the country; knights, and clowns, and knaves, and all share me; the court cannot possibly be without me. Adieu, Malevole. [Exeunt.]

ACTUS SECUNDUS. SCENA PRIMA.

[A hall outside the Duchess' chamber.]

Enter Mendoza, with a sconce,[9] to observe Ferneze's entrance, who, whilst the act is playing, enter [10] unbraced,[11] two Pages before him with lights; is met by Maquerelle and conveyed in; the Pages are sent away.

Men. He's caught; the woodcock's head is i' th' noose.
Now treads Ferneze in dangerous path of lust,
Swearing his sense is merely [12] deified.
The fool grasps clouds, and shall beget centaurs;
And now, in strength of panting, faint delight,
The goat bids heaven envy him.—Good goose,
I can afford thee nothing but the poor comfort of calamity, pity.
"Lust's like the plummets hanging on clock lines,
Will ne'er ha' done till all is quite undone."
Such is the course salt [13] sallow lust doth run, 10
Which thou shalt try. I'll be revenged. Duke, thy suspect,
Duchess, thy disgrace, Ferneze, thy rivalship

---

[1] A pamphlet describing this monstrosity was printed in 1588.
[2] Seek the custody of idiots to enjoy their estates.
[3] Money (?).
[4] Deeply dyed.
[5] Accomplishments.
[6] Sculpture.
[7] Talc.
[8] Vile.
[9] Lantern.
[10] I.e., should enter.
[11] With garments unfastened.
[12] Absolutely.
[13] Salacious.

Shall have swift vengeance. Nothing so
  holy,
No band of nature so strong,
No law of friendship so sacred,
But I'll profane, burst, violate,
Fore I'll endure disgrace, contempt, and
  poverty.
Shall I, whose very "Hum" strook all
  heads bare,
Whose face made silence, creaking of
  whose shoe
Forced the most private passages fly
  ope,   20
Scrape like a servile dog at some latched
  door;
Learn now to make a leg [1] and cry,
  "Beseech ye,
Pray ye, is such a lord within?"; be
  awed
At some odd usher's scoffed formality?
First sear [2] my brains! "*Unde cadis non
  quo, refert.*" [3]
My heart cries, "Perish all!"   How!
  How! "What fate
Can once avoid revenge, that's desper-
  ate?"
I'll to the duke. If all should ope—If?
  Tush!
"Fortune still dotes on those who cannot
  blush."   [*Exit.*]

SCENA SECUNDA.

[*The same.*]

*Enter Malevole at one door; Biancha,
Emilia, and Maquerelle at the other
              door.*

MAL. Bless ye, cast [4] a ladies!—Ha,
dip-sauce! [5] How dost thou, old coal?
MAQ. Old coal?
MAL. Ay, old coal; methinks thou liest
like a brand under billets of green wood.
He that will inflame a young wench's
heart, let him lay close to her an old coal
that hath first been fired, a panderess, my
half-burnt lint, who, though thou canst
[not] flame thyself, yet art able to set a   [10

----

thousand virgins' tapers afire.—[*Turns
to Biancha.*] And how doth Janivere thy
husband, my little periwinkle?   Is he
troubled with the cough of th' lungs still?
Does he hawk a-nights still? He will not
bite.
BIAN. No, by my troth, I took him with
his mouth empty of old teeth.
MAL. And he took thee with thy belly
full of young bones. Marry, he took   [20
his maim by the stroke of his enemy.
BIAN. And I mine by the stroke of my
friend.
MAL. The close stock! [6]   O mortal
wench! Lady, ha' ye now no restoratives [7]
for your decayed Jasons? Look ye: crabs'
guts baked, distilled ox-pith, the pul-
verized hairs of a lion's upper lip, jelly of
cock sparrows, he-monkeys' marrow, or
pouldre [8] of fox-stones? And whither   [30
are you ambling now?
BIAN. To bed, to bed.
MAL. Do your husbands lie with ye?
BIAN. That were country fashion, i' faith.
MAL. Ha' ye no foregoers [9] about you?
Come, whither in good deed, la now?
BIAN. In good indeed, la now, to eat
the most miraculously, admirably, astonish-
able-composed posset with three curds,   [39
without any drink. Will ye help me with
a he-fox?—Here's the duke.
                The Ladies go out.
MAL. [10] (*To Bian[cha].*) Fried frogs are
very good, and Frenchlike too!

SCENA TERTIA.

[*The same.*]

*Enter Duke Pietro, Count Celso, Count
Equato, Bilioso, Ferrard, and Mendoza.*

PIET. The night grows deep and foul.
What hour is 't?
CEL. Upon the stroke of twelve.
MAL. Save ye, duke!
PIET. From thee! Begone, I do not love
thee!   Let me see thee no more; we are
displeased.
MAL. Why, God be with thee! Heaven
hear my curse—may thy wife and thee
live long together!   10
PIET. Begone, sirrah!

----

[1] Bow.

[2] Emended by Bullen. Original reads *seate*.

[3] "No matter whither, but from whence you
fall" (Seneca, *Thyestes*, l. 929. *Cf. Antonio and
Mellida*, Part I, III, ii, 115).

[4] Pair.

[5] With an allusion to *dipsas*, a fabulous snake,
and perhaps to Lyly's Dipsas.

[6] A thrust in fencing.   [9] Ushers.
[7] Aphrodisiacs.   [10] This speech is an addition.
[8] Powder.

MAL. "When Arthur first in court began"—Agamemnon—Menelaus—was ever
any duke a cornuto?

PIET. Begone hence!

MAL. What religion wilt thou be of
next?

MEN. Out with him!

MAL. With most servile patience time
will come

When wonder of thy error will strike
dumb　　　　　　　　　　　　　　20

Thy bezzled [1] sense.—Slaves! Ay, favor!
Ay, marry, shall he rise?

"Good God! How subtile hell doth
flatter vice,

Mounts him aloft, and makes him seem
to fly,

As fowl the tortoise mocked, who to the
sky

Th' ambitious shellfish raised! Th' end
of all

Is only that from height he might dead
fall." [2]

BIL. Why, when? Out, ye rogue! Begone,
ye rascal!

MAL. I shall now leave ye with all my
best wishes.　　　　　　　　　　　30

BIL. Out, ye cur!

MAL. Only let's hold together a firm
correspondence.

BIL. Out!

MAL. A mutual-friendly-reciprocal-per-
petual kind of steady-unanimous-heartily-
leagued—

BIL. Hence, ye gross-jawed, peasantly
—out, go!

MAL. Adieu, pigeon house; thou burr,
that only stickest to nappy fortunes. [41
The sarpego,[3] the strangury,[4] an eternal,
uneffectual priapism seize thee!

BIL. Out, rogue!

MAL. Mayest thou be a notorious wit-
tolly pander to thine own wife, and yet
get no office, but live to be the utmost
misery of mankind, a beggarly cuckold!
　　　　　　　　　　　　　　Exit.

PIET. It shall be so.

MEN. It must be so, for, where great states
revenge,　　　　　　　　　　　50

'Tis requisite the parts with piety [5]

(And loft [6] respect forbears) be closely
dogged.

Lay one into his breast shall sleep with
him,

Feed in the same dish, run in self-
faction,

Who may discover any shape of danger;

For once disgraced, displayéd in offense,

It makes man blushless, and man is
(all confess)

More prone to vengeance than to grate-
fulness.

Favors are writ in dust; but stripes we feel
Depravéd nature stamps in lasting steel."

PIET. You shall be leagued with the　[61
duchess.

EQU. The plot is very good.

MEN. You shall both kill, and seem the
corse to save.

FER. A most fine brain-trick.

CEL. (*Tacite.*) [7]　　　Of a most cunning
knave.

PIET. My lords, the heavy action we intend

Is death and shame, two of the ugliest
shapes

That can confound a soul. Think, think
of it.

I strike, but yet, like him that gainst
stone walls

Directs his shafts, rebounds in his own
face;　　　　　　　　　　　　70

My lady's shame is mine, O God,
'tis mine!

Therefore I do conjure all secrecy.

Let it be as very little as may be, pray
ye, as may be.

Make frightless entrance, salute her with
soft eyes,

Strain [8] naught with blood.　Only
Ferneze dies,

But not before her brows.　O gentlemen,

God knows I love her!　Nothing else
but this.

I am not well. If grief, that sucks veins
dry,

Rivels [9] the skin, casts ashes in men's
faces,

Bedulls the eye, unstrengthens all the
blood,　　　　　　　　　　　　80

---

[1] Drunken.　　　　　　　　[5] Devotion.

[2] Lines 27–48 are an addition.

[3] Serpigo, a skin eruption.

[4] Disease of the bladder.

[6] Proud.　　　　　　　　[7] Silently, aside.

[8] Do violence to; or perhaps a misprint for
stain.　　　　　　　　　　　[9] Wrinkles

Chance to remove me to another
world,
As sure I once must die, let him succeed.
I have no child; all that my youth begot
Hath been your loves, which shall in-
herit [1] me;
Which as it ever shall, I do conjure it,
Mendoza may succeed; he's noble born,
With me of much desert.

CEL. (*Tacite*.) Much!

PIET. Your silence answers, "Ay."
I thank you. Come on now. O, that I
might die   90
Before her shame's displayed! Would
I were forced
To burn my father's tomb, unheal [2]
his bones,
And dash them in the dirt, rather than
this!
This both the living and the dead of-
fends:
"Sharp surgery where naught but death
amends."   *Exit with the others.*

SCENA QUARTA.

[*The same.*]

*Enter Maquerelle, Emilia, and Biancha
with the posset.*

MAQ. Even here it is, three curds in
three regions individually distinct, most
methodical according to art composed,
without any drink.

BIAN. Without any drink?

MAQ. Upon my honor. Will you sit
and eat?   [*They eat.*]

EM. Good! The composure, the receipt,
how is 't?

MAQ. 'Tis a pretty pearl; by this   [10
pearl (how does it with me?) [3] thus it is:
Seven-and-thirty yelks of Barbary hens'
eggs; eighteen spoonfuls and a half of
the juice of cock sparrow bones; one ounce,
three drams, four scruples, and one quarter
of the syrup of Ethiopian dates; sweetened
with three-quarters of a pound of pure
candied Indian eryngoes; [4] strewed over
with the powder of pearl of America, amber of Cataia, and lamb-stones of   [20
Muscovia.

BIAN. Trust me, the ingredients are
very cordial, and, no question, good, and
most powerful in restoration.

MAQ. I know not what you mean by restoration, but this it doth—it purifieth the
blood, smootheth the skin, enliveneth the
eye, strengtheneth the veins, mundi-
fieth [5] the teeth, comforteth the stomach,
fortifieth the back, and quickeneth the   [30
wit; that's all.

EM. By my troth, I have eaten but two
spoonfuls, and methinks I could discourse
most swiftly and wittily already.

MAQ. Have you the art to seem honest? [6]

BIAN. I thank advice and practice.

MAQ. Why, then, eat me of this posset,
quicken your blood, and preserve your
beauty. Do you know Doctor Plaster-   [40
face? By this curd, he is the most exquisite
in forging of veins, sprightening [7] of eyes,
dyeing of hair, sleeking of skins, blushing
of cheeks, surphling [8] of breasts, blanch-
ing and bleaching of teeth, that ever
made an old lady gracious by torchlight;
by this curd, la!

BIAN. We, we are resolved; what God
has given us we'll cherish.

MAQ. Cherish anything saving your   [50
husband; keep him not too high, lest he
leap the pale. But, for your beauty, let
it be your saint; bequeath two hours to
it every morning in your closet.   I ha'
been young, and yet, in my conscience,
I am not above five-and-twenty; but,
believe me, preserve and use your beauty;
for youth and beauty once gone, we are
like beehives without honey, out-a-fashion,
apparel that no man will wear; there-   [60
fore use me your beauty.

EM. Ay, but men say—

MAQ. Men say! Let men say what they
will. Life a woman! They are ignorant
of your wants. The more in years, the
more in perfection they grow; if they lose
youth and beauty, they gain wisdom and
discretion. But when our beauty fades,
good night with us. There cannot be an
uglier thing to see than an old woman,   [70
from which—O pruning, pinching, and
painting!—deliver all sweet beauties!
                                 [*Music within.*]

BIAN. Hark! Music!

---

[1] Be heir to.
[2] Uncover.
[3] How does it become me?
[4] Candied sea-holly.
[5] Cleanseth.
[6] Virtuous.
[7] Brightening.
[8] Tinting.

MAQ. Peace, 'tis in the duchess' bed-chamber. Good rest, most prosperously-graced ladies.

EM. Good night, sentinel.

BIAN. Night, dear Maquerelle.

　　　　　　　Exeunt all but Maq[uerelle].

MAQ. May my posset's operation send you my wit and honesty; and me, your　[80 youth and beauty. The pleasing'st rest!

　　　　　　　　　Exit Maq[uerelle].

SCENA QUINTA.

[*The same.*]

A song [*within*].

Whilst the song is singing, enter Mendoza with his sword drawn, standing ready to murder Ferneze as he flies from the Duchess' chamber.

ALL. [*Within.*] Strike, strike!

AUR. [*Within.*] Save my Ferneze! O, save my Ferneze!

Enter Ferneze in his shirt, and is received upon Mendoza's sword.

ALL. [*Within.*] Follow, pursue!

AUR. [*Within.*] O, save Ferneze!

MEN. Pierce, pierce!—Thou shallow fool, drop there!

"He that attempts a princess' lawless love

Must have broad hands, close heart, with Argus' eyes,

And back of Hercules, or else he dies."

　　　　　Thrusts his rapier in Fer[neze].

Enter Aurelia, Duke Pietro, Ferrard, Bilioso, Celso, and Equato.

ALL. Follow, follow!

MEN. Stand off, forbear, ye most uncivil lords!　　　　　　　　　　　10

PIET. Strike!

MEN.　Do not; tempt not a man re-solved.

Would you, inhuman murtherers, more than death?

AUR. O poor Ferneze!

MEN. Alas, now all defense too late!

AUR.　　He's dead.

PIET. I am sorry for our shame.—Go to your bed;

Weep not too much, but leave some tears to shed

When I am dead.

AUR. What, weep for thee? My soul no tears shall find.

PIET. Alas, alas, that women's souls are blind!

MEN. Betray such beauty! Murther such youth! Contemn civility!　　　20

He loves him not that rails not at him.

PIET. Thou canst not move us; we have blood enough.—

And please you, lady, we have quite for-got

All your defects; if not, why, then—

AUR. Not.

PIET. Not. The best of rest; good night.

　　　　　Exit Pietro with other Courtiers.

AUR. Despite go with thee!

MEN. Madam, you ha' done me foul disgrace; you have wronged him much, loves [1] you too much. Go to, your soul　[30 knows you have.

AUR. I think I have.

MEN. Do you but think so?

AUR. Nay, sure, I have; my eyes have witnessed thy love. Thou hast stood too firm for me.

MEN. Why, tell me, fair-cheeked lady, who even in tears

Art powerfully beauteous, what unad-vised passion

Strook ye into such a violent heat against me?

Speak, what mischief wronged us? What devil injured us?　　　　　　40

Speak.

AUR. That thing ne'er worthy of the name of man, Ferneze;

Ferneze swore thou lov'st Emilia;

Which to advance, with most reproach-ful breath,

Thou both didst blemish and denounce my love.

MEN. Ignoble villain! Did I for this be-stride

Thy wounded limbs? For this? O God! For this

Sunk all my hopes, and with my hopes my life?

Ripped bare my throat unto the hang-man's ax?—　　　　　　　　49

Thou most dishonored trunk!—Emilia!

_____
[1] *I.e.,* who loves.

By life, I know her not—Emilia—!
Did you believe him?

AUR.   Pardon me, I did.

MEN. Did you? And thereupon you gracéd him?

AUR. I did.

MEN. Took him to favor, nay, even clasped with him?

AUR. Alas, I did!

MEN.   This night?

AUR.   This night.

MEN. And in your lustful twines the duke took you?

AUR. A most sad truth.

MEN. O God, O God! How we dull honest souls,
Heavy-brained men, are swallowed in the bogs   60
Of a deceitful ground, whilst nimble bloods,
Light-jointed spirits, spent,[1] cut good men's throats,
And scape! Alas, I am too honest for this age,
Too full of fleam and heavy steadiness;
Stood still whilst this slave cast a noose about me;
Nay, then to stand in honor of him and her
Who had even sliced my heart!

AUR.   Come, I did err,
And am most sorry I did err.

MEN. Why, we are both but dead; the duke hates us.
"And those whom princes do once groundly[2] hate,   70
Let them provide to die, as sure as fate.
Prevention is the heart of policy."

AUR. Shall we murder him?

MEN. Instantly?

AUR. Instantly! Before he casts a plot,
Or further blaze my honor's much-known blot,
Let's murther him!

MEN. I would do much for you; will ye marry me?

AUR. I'll make thee duke. We are of Medicis;   79
Florence our friend; in court my faction
Not meanly strengthful; the duke then dead;
We well prepared for change; the multitude

Irresolutely reeling; we in force;
Our party seconded; the kingdom mazed—
No doubt of swift success; all shall be graced.

MEN. You do confirm me; we are resolute.
Tomorrow look for change; rest confident.
'Tis now about the immodest waist of night;
The mother of moist dew with pallid light
Spreads gloomy shades about the numbéd earth.   90
Sleep, sleep, whilst we contrive our mischief's birth.
This man I'll get inhumed. Farewell; to bed.
Ay, kiss the pillow; dream the duke is dead.   *Exit Aurelia.*
So, so, good night. How fortune dotes on impudence!
I am in private the adopted son of yon good prince.
I must be duke. Why, if I must, I must!
Most seely[3] lord, name me! O heaven!
I see God made honest fools to maintain crafty knaves.
The duchess is wholly mine too; must kill her husband
To quit her shame. Much![4] Then marry her! Ay.   100
O, I grow proud in prosperous treachery!
As wrastlers clip, so I'll embrace you all,
Not to support, but to procure your fall.

Enter Malevole.

MAL. God arrest thee!

MEN. At whose suit?

MAL. At the devil's. Ah, you treacherous, damnable monster!
How dost? How dost, thou treacherous rogue?
Ah, ye rascal! I am banished the court, sirrah.

MEN. Prithee, let's be acquainted; I do love thee, faith.   110

MAL. At your service, by the Lord, la! Shall's go to supper? Let's be once drunk together, and so unite a most virtuously strengthened friendship. Shall 's, Huguenot? Shall 's?

---

[1] Exhausted, dissolute.   [2] Completely.

[3] Silly, simple.

[4] Great! Excellent!

MEN. Wilt fall upon my chamber tomorrow morn?

MAL. As a raven to a dunghill. They
say there's one dead here—pricked for
the pride of the flesh.   120

MEN. Ferneze. There he is; prithee,
bury him.

MAL. O, most willingly; I mean to turn
pure Rochelle [1] churchman, I.

MEN. Thou churchman! Why, why?

MAL. Because I'll live lazily, rail upon
authority, deny kings' supremacy in things
indifferent, and be a pope in mine own
parish.   129

MEN. Wherefore dost thou think
churches were made?

MAL. To scour plowshares; I have seen
oxen plow up altars; "*et nunc seges ubi
Sion fuit.*" [2]

MEN. Strange!

MAL. Nay, monstrous! I ha' seen a
sumptuous steeple turned to a stinking
privy; more beastly, the sacred'st place
made a dogs' kennel; nay, most inhuman,
the stoned coffins of long-dead Chris-   [140
tians burst up, and made hogs' troughs:
Hic finis Priami. [3] Shall I ha' some sack and
cheese at thy chamber? Good night, good
mischievous incarnate devil; good night,
Mendoza; ah, you inhuman villain, good
night! Night, fub. [4]

MEN. Good night; tomorrow morn.
                                Exit Mendoza.

MAL. Ay, I will come, friendly damnation, I will come. I do descry crosspoints: [5]
honesty and courtship straddle as far   [150
asunder as a true Frenchman's legs.

FER. O!

MAL. Proclamations! More proclamations!

FER. O! A surgeon!

MAL. Hark! Lust cries for a surgeon.
What news from Limbo? How doth the
grand cuckold, Lucifer?

FER. O, help, help! Conceal and save
me.   160

*Ferneze stirs, and Malevole helps him up and
                    conveys him away.*

MAL. Thy shame more than thy wounds
        do grieve me far;

[1] Where persecuted Huguenots took refuge.
[2] Paraphrased from Ovid: "Now the corn
grows where Sion stood."
[3] Here the end of Priam.
[4] Impostor.   [5] A step in dancing.

"Thy wounds but leave upon thy flesh
        some scar;
But fame ne'er heals, still rankles worse
        and worse;
Such is of uncontrollèd lust the curse.
Think what it is in lawless sheets to lie;
But, O, Ferneze, what in lust to die!
Then thou that shame respect's[t], O,
        fly converse
With women's eyes and lisping wanton-
        ness!
Stick candles gainst a virgin wall's
        white back;
If they not burn, yet at the least they'll
        black."   170
Come, I'll convey thee to a private port,
Where thou shalt live (O happy man!)
        from court.
The beauty of the day begins to rise,
From whose bright form night's heavy
        shadow flies.
Now gins [6] close plots to work; the scene
        grows full,
And craves his eyes who hath a solid
        skull.[7]   *Exeunt.*

ACTUS TERTIUS. SCENA PRIMA.

[*A room in the Duke's palace.*]

*Enter Pietro the Duke, Mendoza, Count
                    Equato, and Bilioso.*

PIET. 'Tis grown to youth of day; how
        shall we waste this light?
My heart's more heavy than a tyrant's
        crown.
Shall we go hunt? Prepare for field.
                                Exit Equato.

MEN. Would ye could be merry!

PIET. Would God I could! Mendoza, bid
        um haste.   *Exit Mendoza.*
I would fain shift place; O vain relief!
"Sad souls may well change place, but
        not change grief."
As deer, being struck, fly thorough many
        soils,[8]
Yet still the shaft sticks fast, so—

BIL. A good old simile, my honest
        lord.   10

PIET. I am not much unlike to some
        sick man
That long desired hurtful drink; at
        last

[6] Begins.   [7] Sound head.   [8] Streams.

Swills in and drinks his last, ending at
　once
Both life and thirst.　O, would I ne'er
　had known
My own dishonor!　Good God, that men
　should
Desire to search out that which, being
　found, kills all
Their joy of life!　To taste the tree of
　knowledge,
And then be driven from out paradise!
Canst give me some comfort?

Bil.　My lord, I have some books　[20
which have been dedicated to my honor,
and I ne'er read um, and yet they had
very fine names—*Physic for Fortune,
Lozenges of Sanctified Sincerity*, very pretty
works of curates, scriveners, and school-
masters.　Marry, I remember one Seneca,
Lucius Annæus Seneca—

Piet.　Out upon him!　He writ of temperance and fortitude, yet lived like a
voluptuous epicure, and died like an　[30
effeminate coward.—

Haste thee to Florence.

Here, take our letters; see um sealed;
　away!

Report in private to the honored duke
His daughter's forced disgrace; tell him
　at length
We know too much; due compliments
　advance.

"There's naught that's safe and sweet
　but ignorance."　　　　　*Exit Duke*.[1]

Enter Bilioso [2] *and Bianc[h]a*.[1]

Bil.　Madam, I am going ambassador
for Florence; 'twill be great charges to me.

Bian.　No matter, my lord, you　[40
have the lease of two manors come out next
Christmas; you may lay your tenants on
the greater rack for it; and, when you come
home again, I'll teach you how you shall
get two hundred pounds a year by your
teeth.

Bill.　How, madam?

Bian.　Cut off so much from housekeeping; that which is saved by the teeth,
you know, is got by the teeth.　　　50

Bil.　Fore God, and so I may; I am in
wondrous credit, lady.

Bian.　See the use of flattery; I did
ever counsel you to flatter greatness, and
you have profited well.　Any man that will
do so shall be sure to be like your Scotch
barnacle,[3] now a block, instantly a worm,
and presently a great goose.　This it is to
rot and putrefy in the bosom of greatness.

Bil.　Thou art ever my politician.　[60
O, how happy is that old lord that hath a
politician to his young lady!　I'll have
fifty gentlemen shall attend upon me.
Marry, the most of them shall be farmer's
sons, because they shall bear their own
charges; and they shall go appareled thus—
in sea-water-green suits, ash-color cloaks,
watchet [4] stockings, and popinjay-green
feathers.　Will not the colors do excellent?

Bian.　Out upon 't!　They'll look like　[70
citizens riding to their friends at Whitsuntide, their apparel just so many several
parishes.[5]

Bil.　I'll have it so; and Passarello, my
fool, shall go along with me; marry, he
shall be in velvet.

Bian.　A fool in velvet?

Bil.　Ay, 'tis common for your fool to
wear satin; I'll have mine in velvet.　　79

Bian.　What will you wear, then, my
lord?

Bil.　Velvet too; marry, it shall be embroidered, because I'll differ from the fool
somewhat.　I am horribly troubled with
the gout; nothing grieves me but that my
doctor hath forbidden me wine, and you
know your ambassador must drink.　Didst
thou ask thy doctor what was good for
the gout?　　　　　　　　　　　　89

Bian.　Yes; he said ease, wine, and
women were good for it.

Bil.　Nay, thou hast such a wit!　What
was good to cure it, said he?

Bian.　Why, the rack.　All your em-
pirics could never do the like cure upon
the gout the rack did in England, or your
Scotch boot.[6]　The French harlequin will
instruct you.

Bil.　Surely, I do wonder how thou,
having for the most part of thy life-　[100

---

[1] The rest of this scene is an addition.

[2] Apparently, however, he has really remained
on the stage.

[3] "It was formerly thought that this species of
shell-fish, which is found on timber exposed to
the action of the sea, became, when broken off,
a kind of geese " (Halliwell).

[4] Pale blue.

[5] *I.e.*, mismatched.

[6] Instrument of torture.

time been a country body, shouldst have
so good a wit.

BIAN. Who, I? Why, I have been a
courtier thrice two months.

BIL. So have I this twenty year, and
yet there was a gentleman usher called
me coxcomb tother day, and to my face
too. Was 't not a backbiting rascal? I
would I were better traveled, that I
might have been better acquainted [110
with the fashions of several countrymen;
but my secretary, I think, he hath sufficiently instructed me.

BIAN. How, my lord?

BIL. "Marry, my good lord," quoth
he, "your lordship shall ever find
amongst a hundred Frenchmen forty hot-
shots;[1] amongst a hundred Spaniards,
threescore braggarts; amongst a hundred
Dutchmen, fourscore drunkards; [120
amongst an hundred Englishmen, fourscore and ten madmen; and amongst an
hundred Welshmen"—

BIAN. What, my lord?

BIL. "Fourscore and nineteen gentlemen."

BIAN. But, since you go about a sad
embassy, I would have you go in black,
my lord.   129

BIL. Why, dost think I cannot mourn,
unless I wear my hat in cypress,[2] like an
alderman's heir? That's vile, very old,
in faith.

BIAN. I'll learn of you shortly. O, we
should have a fine gallant of you, should
not I instruct you! How will you bear
yourself when you come into the Duke
of Florence' court?

BIL. Proud enough, and 'twill do well
enough. As I walk up and down the [140
chamber, I'll spit frowns about me, have
a strong perfume in my jerkin, let my
beard grow to make me look terrible,
salute no man beneath[3] the fourth but-
ton; and 'twill do excellent.

BIAN. But there is a very beautiful
lady there; how will you entertain her?

BIL. I'll tell you that when the lady
hath entertained me. But to satisfy thee,
here comes the fool.—Fool, thou shalt [150
stand for the fair lady.

---

[1] Reckless persons.
[2] Crape.
[3] Bow no lower than.

Enter Passarello.

PASS. Your fool will stand for your
lady most willingly and most uprightly.

BIL. I'll salute her in Latin.

PASS. O, your fool can understand no
Latin.

BIL. Ay, but your lady can.

PASS. Why, then, if your lady take
down your fool, your fool will stand no
longer for your lady.   160

BIL. A pestilent fool! Fore God, I
think the world be turned upside down
too.

PASS. O, no, sir; for then your lady
and all the ladies in the palace should go
with their heels upward, and that were a
strange sight, you know.

BIL. There be many will repine at my
preferment.

PASS. O, ay, like the envy of an [170
elder sister, that hath her younger made
a lady before her.

BIL. The duke is wondrous discontented.

PASS. Ay, and more melancholic than
a usurer having all his money out at the
death of a prince.

BIL. Didst thou see Madam Floria
today?

PASS. Yes, I found her repairing her
face today. The red upon the white [180
showed as if her cheeks should have been
served in for two dishes of barberries in
stewed broth, and the flesh to them a woodcock.

BIL. A bitter fowl![4] Come, madam,
this night thou shalt enjoy me freely, and
tomorrow for Florence.

                [Exeunt Bilioso and Biancha.]

PASS. What a natural fool is he that
would be a pair of bodies[5] to a woman's
petticoat, to be trussed and pointed to
them! Well, I'll dog my lord; and the [191
word is proper, for, when I fawn upon him,
he feeds me; when I snap him by the fingers,
he spits in my mouth. If a dog's death
were not strangling, I had rather be one
than a serving-man; for the corruption of
coin is either the generation of a usurer or
a lousy beggar.   *Exit.*[6]

---

[4] With a pun on *fool*.
[5] Bodice, pair of stays.
[6] In the original, this direction appears at the
end of Passarello's preceding speech.

Scena Secunda.

[*Another room in the Duke's palace.*]

*Enter Malevole in some frieze gown, whilst
Bilioso reads his patent.*[1]

Mal. I cannot sleep; my eyes' ill-neigh-
　　boring lids
Will hold no fellowship. O thou pale,
　　sober night,
Thou that in sluggish fumes all sense
　　dost steep;
Thou that gives all the world full leave
　　to play,
Unbend'st the feebled veins of sweaty
　　labor!
The galley slave, that all the toilsome
　　day
Tugs at his oar against the stubborn
　　wave,
Straining his rugged veins, snores fast;
The stooping scythe-man, that doth
　　barb [2] the field,
Thou makest wink [3] sure. In night all
　　creatures sleep;　　　　　　　　10
Only the malcontent, that gainst his
　　fate
Repines and quarrels, alas, he's good-
　　man tell-clock! [4]
His sallow jawbones sink with wasting
　　moan;
Whilst others' beds are down, his pil-
　　low's stone.
Bil. Malevole!
Mal. (*To Bilioso.*) Elder of Israel,
thou honest defect of wicked nature and
obstinate ignorance, when did thy wife let
thee lie with her?　　　　　　　　19
Bil. I am going ambassador to Florence.
Mal. Ambassador? Now, for thy
country's honor, prithee, do not put up
mutton and porridge in thy cloak bag.
Thy young lady wife goes to Florence with
thee too, does she not?
Bil. No, I leave her at the palace.
Mal. At the palace? Now, discretion
shield, man! For God's love, let's ha' no
more cuckolds! Hymen begins to put　[30
off his saffron robe; keep thy wife i' the
state of grace. Heart a truth, I would
sooner leave my lady singled in a bordello [5]
than in the Genoa palace.

---

[1] Commission.　　　[2] Mow.　　　[3] Sleep.
[4] Counter of the clock; idler.　　　[5] Brothel.

Sin, there appearing in her sluttish shape,
Would soon grow loathsome, even to
　　blushes' sense;
Surfeit would cloak [6] intemperate appe-
　　tite,
Make the soul scent the rotten breath of
　　lust.
When in an Italian lascivious palace, a
　　lady guardianless,
Left to the push of all allurement,　40
The strongest incitements to immodesty,
To have her bound, incensed with wan-
　　ton sweets,
Her veins filled high with heating deli-
　　cates,
Soft rest, sweet music, amorous mas-
　　querers,
Lascivious banquets, sin itself gilt o'er,
Strong fantasy tricking up strange de-
　　lights,
Presenting it dressed pleasingly to
　　sense,
Sense leading it unto the soul, con-
　　firmed
With potent example, impudent custom,
Enticed by that great bawd, Oppor-
　　tunity—　　　　　　　　　　　50
Thus being prepared, clap to her easy ear
Youth in good clothes, well-shaped, rich,
Fair-spoken, promising-noble, ardent,
　　blood-full,
Witty, flattering—Ulysses absent,
O Ithaca, can [7] chastest Penelope hold
　　out?
Bil. Mass, I'll think on't. Farewell.
　　　　　　　　　　Exit Bilioso.
Mal. Farewell. Take thy wife with thee.
　　Farewell.—
To Florence; umh! It may prove good,
　　it may!
And we may once unmask our brows.

Scena Tertia.

[*The same.*]

Enter Count Celso.

Cel. My honored lord—
Mal. Celso, peace! How is 't? Speak
low. Pale fears suspect that hedges, walls,
and trees have ears. Speak, how runs all?
Cel. I' faith, my lord, that beast with
　　many heads,

---

[6] Bullen emends to *choke.*
[7] From first edn. Original has *Ithacan chastest.*

The staggering multitude, recoils apace.
Though thorough great men's envy, most
   men's malice,
Their much-intemperate heat hath ban-
   ished you,
Yet now they find envy and malice ne'er
Produce faint reformation.   10
The duke, the too soft duke, lies as a
   block,
For which two tugging factions seem to
   saw;
But still the iron through the ribs they
   draw.
MAL. I tell thee, Celso, I have ever found
Thy breast most far from shifting cow-
   ardice
And fearful baseness; therefore I'll tell
   thee, Celso,
I find the wind begins to come about;
I'll shift my suit of fortune.
I know the Florentine, whose only force,[1]
By marrying his proud daughter to this
   prince,   20
Both banished me and made this weak
   lord duke,
Will now forsake them all; be sure he
   will.
I'll lie in ambush for conveniency,
Upon their severance to confirm myself.
CEL. Is Ferneze interred?
MAL. Of that at leisure; he lives.
CEL. But how stands Mendoza? How
is 't with him?
MAL. Faith, like a pair of snuffers—
snibs [2] filth in other men, and retains   [30
it in itself.
CEL. He does fly from public notice,
methinks, as a hare does from hounds; the
feet whereon he flies betrays him.
MAL. I can track him, Celso.
O, my disguise fools him most power-
   fully!
For that I seem a desperate malcontent,
He fain would clasp with me; he is the
   true slave
That will put on the most affected grace
For some vild second cause.

          Enter Mendoza.

CEL.   He's here.
MAL.   Give place.—   40
Illo, ho, ho, ho! Art there, old truepenny?
                        Exit Celso.

[1] Whose force alone.   [2] Snips off.

Where hast thou spent thyself this morn-
ing? I see flattery in thine eyes, and
damnation in thy soul. Ha, thou huge
rascal!
MEN. Thou art very merry.
MAL. As a scholar, *futuens gratis.*[3] How
doth the devil go with thee now?
MEN. Malevole, thou art an arrant
knave.   50
MAL. Who, I? I have been a sergeant,
man.
MEN. Thou art very poor.
MAL. As Job, an alcumist, [4] or a poet.
MEN. The duke hates thee.
MAL. As Irishmen do bum-cracks.
MEN. Thou hast lost his amity.
MAL. As pleasing as maids lose their
virginity.
MEN. Would thou wert of a lusty   [60
spirit! Would thou wert noble!
MAL. Why, sure my blood gives me I
am noble, sure I am of noble kind; for I
find myself possessed with all their qualities: love dogs, dice, and drabs; scorn
wit in stuff-clothes; [5] have beat my shoemaker, knocked my semsters, [6] cuckold[ed] my potecary, and undone my
tailor. Noble, why not? Since the stoic
said, "*Neminem servum non ex regibus,* [70
*neminem regem non ex servis esse oriun-
dum,*"[7] only busy Fortune touses,[8] and
the provident Chances blends them together. I'll give you a simile. Did you
e'er see a well with two buckets—whilst
one comes up full to be emptied, another
goes down empty to be filled? Such is the
state of all humanity. Why, look you, I
may be the son of some duke; for, believe
me, intemperate lascivious bastardy [80
makes nobility doubtful. I have a lusty,
daring heart, Mendoza.
MEN. Let's grasp; I do like thee infinitely. Wilt enact one thing for me?
MAL. Shall I get by it?   (*[Mendoza]
gives him his purse.*) Command me; I am
thy slave, beyond death and hell.
MEN. Murther the duke.
MAL. My heart's wish, my soul's desire, my fantasy's dream, my blood's [90

[3] Loving freely.   [5] Persons coarsely dressed.
[4] Alchemist.   [6] Seamstresses.
[7] "There is no slave who has not sprung
from kings, and no king who has not sprung
from slaves" (Seneca, *Epist.,* xliv).
[8] Tears apart.

longing, the only height of my hopes! How,
O God, how? O, how my united spirits
throng together! So strengthen my resolve!

MEN. The duke is now a-hunting.

MAL. Excellent, admirable, as the devil
would have it! Lend me, lend me rapier,
pistol, crossbow. So, so, I'll do it.

MEN. Then we agree.

MAL. As Lent and fishmongers. Come,
à cap-a-pie. How? Inform.   100

MEN. Know that this weak-brained duke,
        who only stands
    On Florence' stilts, hath out of witless
        zeal
    Made me his heir, and secretly confirmed
    The wreath to me after his life's full
        point.

MAL. Upon what merit?

MEN.   Merit! By heaven, I horn him.
    Only Ferneze's death gave me state's
        life.
    Tut, we are politic; he must not live now.

MAL. No reason, marry. But how must
        he die now?   108

MEN. My utmost project is to murder
the duke, that I might have his state, because he makes me his heir; to banish the
duchess, that I might be rid of a cunning
Lacedæmonian, because I know Florence
will forsake her; and then to marry Maria,
the banished Duke Altofront's wife, that
her friends might strengthen me and my
faction. This is all, la.

MAL. Do you love Maria?   118

MEN. Faith, no great affection, but as
wise men do love great women, to ennoble
their blood and augment their revenue. To
accomplish this now, thus now: the duke
is in the forest, next the sea; single him,
kill him, hurl him in the main, and proclaim thou sawest wolves eat him.

MAL. Umh! Not so good. Methinks when
        he is slain,
    To get some hypocrite, some dangerous
        wretch
    That's muffled [1] or with [2] feigned holiness,
    To swear he heard the duke on some
        steep cliff
    Lament his wife's dishonor, and, in an
        agony   130
    Of his heart's torture, hurled his groan-
        ing sides
    Into the swoln sea. This circumstance,

---

[1] Disguised.   [2] I.e., one with.

Well made, sounds probable; and here-
        upon
    The duchess—

MEN. May well be banished.
    O unpeerable [3] invention! Rare!
    Thou god of policy, it honeys me.

MAL. Then fear not for the wife of Alto-
        front;
    I'll close to her.

MEN. Thou shalt, thou shalt. Our ex-
        cellency is pleased.   140
    Why wert not thou an emperor? When
        we
    Are duke, I'll make thee some great man,
        sure.

MAL. Nay, make me some rich knave, and
        I'll make myself
    Some great man.

MEN. In thee be all my spirit.
    Retain ten souls; unite thy virtual
        powers.
    Resolve; ha, remember greatness! Heart,
        farewell.

Enter Celso.

"The fate of all my hopes in thee doth
        dwell."   [*Exit.*]

MAL. Celso, didst hear? O heaven, didst
        hear
    Such devilish mischief? Sufferest thou
        the world
    Carouse damnation even with greedy
        swallow,   150
    And still dost wink, still does thy ven-
        geance slumber?
    "If now thy brows are clear, when will
        they thunder?"   *Exit* [*with Celso*].

[*A forest near the sea.*]

*Enter Pietro, Ferrard, Prepasso, and three
                                    Pages.*

FER. The dogs are at a fault.
                    Cornets like horns.

PIET. Would God nothing but the dogs
were at it! Let the deer pursue safety,[4]
the dogs follow the game, and do you follow
the dogs. As for me, 'tis unfit one beast
should hunt another. I ha' one chaseth

---

[3] Peerless.
[4] Emended by Bullen. Original reads *safely*.

me; and 't [1] please you, I would be rid of you a little.

FER. Would your grief would as soon leave you, as we, to quietness.   10

Exeunt [Ferrardo and Prepasso].

PIET. I thank you.—Boy, what dost thou dream of now?

[1] PAGE. Of a dry summer, my lord; for here's a hot world towards.[2] But, my lord, I had a strange dream last night.

PIET. What strange dream?

[1] PAGE. Why, methought I pleased you with singing, and then I dreamt you gave me that short sword.

PIET. Prettily begged. Hold thee, [20 I'll prove thy dream true; take 't.

[Gives sword.]

[1] PAGE. My duty! But still I dreamt on, my lord; and methought, and 't shall please your excellency, you would needs out of your royal bounty give me that jewel in your hat.

PIET. O, thou didst but dream, boy; do not believe it. Dreams prove not always true; they may hold in a short sword, but not in a jewel. But now, sir, you dreamt [30 you had pleased me with singing; make that true, as I have made the other.

[1] PAGE. Faith, my lord, I did but dream, and dreams, you say, prove not always true; they may hold in a good sword, but not in a good song. The truth is, I ha' lost my voice.

PIET. Lost thy voice! How?

[1] PAGE. With dreaming, faith. But here's a couple of sirenical [3] rascals shall [40 enchant ye. What shall they sing, my good lord?

PIET. Sing of the nature of women, and then the song shall be surely full of variety, old crotchets,[4] and most sweet closes; it shall be humorous, grave, fantastic, amorous, melancholy, sprightly, one in all, and all in one.

[1] PAGE. All in one?

PIET. By 'r Lady, too many. Sing! [50 My speech grows culpable of unthrifty idleness.[5] Sing!

Song [by 2 and 3 Pages].

---

[1] If it.
[2] Approaching.
[3] Sirenlike.
[4] Quarter notes, with a pun.
[5] Triviality, folly.

SCENA QUINTA.

[The same.]

Enter Malevole, with crossbow and pistol.

[PIET.] Ah, so, so, sing. I am heavy. Walk off; I shall talk in my sleep. Walk off.

Exeunt Pages.

MAL. *[Aside.]* Brief,[6] brief, who? The duke? Good heaven, that fools
Should stumble upon greatness!—Do not sleep, duke;
Give ye good morrow. You must be brief, duke;
I am feed to murther thee. Start not! Mendoza,
Mendoza hired me; here's his gold, his pistol,
Crossbow, and sword. 'Tis all as firm as earth.
O fool, fool, choked with the common maze
Of easy idiots, credulity!   10
Make him thine heir! What, thy sworn murtherer!

PIET. O, can it be?

MAL.   Can?

PIET.   Discovered he not Ferneze?

MAL. Yes, but why? But why? For love to thee?
Much, much! To be revenged upon his rival,
Who had thrust his jaws awry;
Who being slain, supposed by thine own hands,
Defended by his sword, made thee most loathsome,
Him most gracious with thy loose princess;
Thou, closely [7] yielding egress and regress to her,   19
Madest him heir; whose hot unquiet lust
Straight toused [8] thy sheets, and now would seize thy state.
Politician! Wise man! Death! To be
Led to the stake like a bull by the horns;
To make even kindness cut a gentle throat!
Life, why art thou numbed? Thou foggy dullness, speak!
Lives not more faith in a home-thrusting tongue
Than in these fencing tip-tap [9] courtiers?

---

[6] In short.
[7] Privately.
[8] Disturbed.
[9] Light-thrusting.

Enter Celso, with a hermit's gown and beard.

PIET.[1] Lord Malevole, if this be true—

MAL. If? Come, shade thee with this disguise. If? Thou shalt handle it; he [30 shall thank thee for killing thyself. Come, follow my directions, and thou shalt see strange sleights.

PIET. World, whither wilt thou?

MAL. Why, to the devil. Come, the morn grows late.

A steady quickness is the soul of state.

Exeunt.

ACTUS QUARTUS. SCENA PRIMA.

[*A hall outside the chamber of Biancha and Emilia.*]

Enter Maquerelle, knocking at the Ladies' door.

MAQ. Medam, medam, are you stirring, medam? If you be stirring, medam—if I thought I should disturb ye—

[*Enter Page.*]

PAGE. My lady is up, forsooth.

MAQ. A pretty boy, faith. How old art thou?

PAGE. I think fourteen.

MAQ. Nay, and ye be in the teens—Are ye a gentleman born? Do you know me? My name is Medam Maquerelle; I lie in [10 the old cunnycourt.[2]—See, here the ladies.

Enter Biancha and Emilia.

BIAN. A fair day to ye, Maquerelle.

EM. Is the duchess up yet, sentinel?

MAQ. O ladies, the most abominable mischance! O dear ladies, the most piteous disaster! Ferneze was taken last night in the duchess' chamber. Alas, the duke catched him and killed him!

BIAN. Was he found in bed?

MAQ. O, no; but the villainous cer- [20 tainty is, the door was not bolted; the tongue-tied hatch[3] held his peace. So the naked troth is, he was found in his shirt, whilst I, like an arrand beast, lay in the outward chamber, heard nothing; and yet they came by me in the dark, and yet I felt them not, like a senseless creature as I was. O beauties, look to your busk-points,[4] if

not chastely, yet charily; be sure the door be bolted.—Is your lord gone to Flor- [30 ence?

BIAN. Yes, Maquerelle.

MAQ. I hope you'll find the discretion to purchase a fresh gown for his return.— Now, by my troth, beauties, I would ha' ye once wise. He loves ye; pish! He is witty; bubble! Fair-proportioned; meaw! Nobly-born; wind! Let this be still your fixed position: esteem me every man accord- ing to his good gifts, and so ye shall [40 ever remain most dear and most worthy to be most dear—ladies.

EM. Is the duke returned from hunting yet?

MAQ. They say not yet.

BIAN. 'Tis now in midst of day.

EM. How bears the duchess with this blemish now?

MAQ. Faith, boldly; strongly defies de- fame, as one that has a duke to her father. And there's a note to you: be sure of a stout friend in a corner, that may always awe your husband. Mark the havior of the [50 duchess now. She dares defame; cries, "Duke, do what thou canst, I'll quite[5] mine honor." Nay, as one confirmed in her own virtue against ten thousand mouths that mutter her disgrace, she's presently for dances.

Enter Ferrard.

BIAN. For dances?

MAQ. Most true.

EM. Most strange. [*Aside to Maque-* [59 *relle.*] See, here's my servant,[6] young Fer- rard. How many servants think'st thou I have, Maquerelle?[7]

MAQ. [*Aside to Emilia.*] The more, the merrier. 'Twas well said, use your servants as you do your smocks; have many, use one, and change often, for that's most sweet and courtlike.

FER. Save ye, fair ladies! Is the duke re- turned?

BIAN. Sweet sir, no voice of him as yet in court.

FER. 'Tis very strange. 70

BIAN. [*Aside to Maquerelle.*] And how like you my servant, Maquerelle?

MAQ. [*Aside to Biancha.*] I think he

[1] Original reads *Cel.*
[2] Quarters for women.
[3] Half-door.
[4] Stay-laces.
[5] Quit, acquit.
[6] Lover.
[7] Neilson suggests that this speech should probably be given to Biancha.

could hardly draw Ulysses' bow; but, by my fidelity, were his nose narrower, his eyes broader, his hands thinner, his lips thicker, his legs bigger, his feet lesser, his hair blacker, and his teeth whiter, he were a tolerable sweet youth, i' faith. And he will come to my chamber, I will read him the fortune of his beard. *Cornets sound.* [80

FER. Not yet returned! I fear—But the duchess approacheth.

SCENA SECUNDA.[1]

[*The same.*]

Enter Mendoza supporting the Duchess; Guerrino. The Ladies that are on the stage rise. Ferrard ushers in the Duchess, and then takes a Lady to tread a measure.[2]

AUR. We will dance; music! We will dance.

GUER. "*Les quanto,*" lady, "*Pensez bien,*" "*Passa regis,*" or Bianca's brawl? [3]

AUR. We have forgot the brawl.

FER. So soon? 'Tis wonder.

GUER. Why, 'tis but two singles on the left, two on the right, three doubles forward, a traverse of six round; do this twice, three singles side, galliard trick- [10 of-twenty, coranto-pace; a figure of eight, three singles broken down, come up, meet, two doubles, fall back, and then honor.

AUR. O Dædalus, thy maze! I have quite forgot it.

MAQ. Trust me, so have I, saving the falling-back, and then honor.

Enter Prepasso.

AUR. Music, music!

PREP. Who saw the duke? The duke?

Enter Equato.

AUR. Music!　　　　　　　　　　　20

EQU.[4] The duke? Is the duke returned?

AUR. Music!

Enter Celso.

CEL. The duke is either quite invisible or else is not.

[1] Follows stage direction in the original.
[2] A grave or stately dance.
[3] Names of old dances.
[4] Original reads *Pre.*

AUR. We are not pleased with your intrusion upon our private retirement; we are not pleased. You have forgot yourselves.

Enter a Page.

CEL. Boy, thy master? Where's the [30 duke?

PAGE. Alas, I left him burying the earth with his spread, joyless limbs. He told me he was heavy, would sleep; bid me walk off, for that the strength of fantasy oft made him talk in his dreams. I straight obeyed, nor ever saw him since; but, wheresoe'er he is, he's sad.

AUR. Music, sound high, as is our heart! Sound high!　　　　　　　40

SCENA TERTIA.

[*The same.*]

Enter Malevole, and Pietro disguised like an hermit.

MAL. The duke—peace!—the duke is dead.

AUR. Music!

MAL. Is 't music?

MEN. Give proof.

FER. How?

CEL. Where?

PRE. When?

MAL. Rest in peace, as the duke does; quietly sit! For my own part, I beheld [10 him but dead; that's all. Marry, here's one can give you a more particular account of him.

MEN. Speak, holy father, nor let any brow
Within this presence fright thee from the truth;
Speak confidently and freely.

AUR.　　　　　　　　We attend.

PIET. Now had the mounting sun's all-ripening wings
Swept the cold sweat of night from earth's dank breast,
When I, whom men call Hermit of the Rock,
Forsook my cell, and clambered up a cliff,　　　　　　　20
Against whose base the heady Neptune dashed
His high-curled brows; there 'twas I eased my limbs,

When, lo, my entrails melted with the
  moan
Someone, who far 'bove me was climbed,
  did make—
I shall offend.
MEN. Not.
AUR. On.
PIET. Methinks I hear him yet: "O female
  faith!
*Go sow the ingrateful sand, and love a
woman!*
And do I live to be the scoff of men?
To be the wittol-cuckold, even to hug
  my poison? 31
Thou knowest, O truth,
Sooner hard steel will melt with southern
  wind,
A seaman's whistle calm the ocean,
A town on fire be extinct with tears,
Than women, vowed to blushless im-
  pudence,
With sweet behavior and soft minioning
Will turn from that where appetite is
  fixed.
O powerful blood, how thou dost slave
  their soul!
I washed an Ethiope, who, for recom-
  pense, 40
Sullied my name. And must I, then, be
  forced
To walk, to live thus black? Must!
  Must! Fie!
*He that can bear with 'must,' he cannot
die."*
With that he sighed so [1] passionately
  deep
That the dull air even groaned. At last
  he cries,
"Sink shame in seas, sink deep enough!"
  so dies,
For then I viewed his body fall and souse
Into the foamy main. O, then I saw
That which methinks I see: it was the
  duke
Whom straight the nicer-stomached sea
Belched up, but then— 51
MAL. Then came I in; but, 'las, all was
  too late,
For even straight he sunk!
PIET.   Such was the duke's sad fate.
CEL. A better fortune to our Duke Men-
  doza!
OMNES. Mendoza!

[1] From first edn. Original has *too.*

Cornets flourish. Enter a Guard.

MEN. A guard, a guard! We, full of
  hearty tears,
For our good father's loss—
For so we well may call him
Who did beseech your loves for our
  succession— 59
Cannot so lightly overjump his death
As leave his woes revengeless.—(*To
Aurelia.*) Woman of shame,
We banish thee forever to the place
From whence this good man comes;
Nor permit, on death, unto the body any
  ornament;
But, base as was thy life, depart away!
AUR. Ungrateful!
MEN.   Away!
AUR.   Villain, hear me!
*Prepasso and Guerrino lead away the
Duchess.*
MEN. Begone! My lords, address to [2]
  public council;
'Tis most fit
The train of Fortune is borne up by wit.
Away! Our presence shall be sudden;
  haste. 70
*All depart saving Mendoza, Malevole, and
Pietro.*
MAL. Now, you egregious devil! Ha,
ye murthering politician! [3] How dost,
duke? How dost look now? Brave duke,
i' faith!
MEN. How did you kill him?
MAL. Slatted his brains out, then
soused him in the briny sea.
MEN. Brained him, and drowned him
too?
MAL. O, 'twas best, sure work; *for* [80
*he that strikes a great man, let him strike
home, or else ware he'll prove no man. Shoulder
not a huge fellow, unless you may be sure to
lay him in the kennel.* [4]
MEN. A most sound brainpan!
I'll make you both emperors.
MAL. Make us Christians, make us
Christians!
MEN. I'll hoist ye; ye shall mount. 89
MAL. To the gallows, say ye? Come!
"Præmium incertum petit certum scelus." [5]
How stands the progress? [6]

[2] Prepare for.   [3] Intriguer.   [4] Channel, gutter.
[5] "Uncertain is the reward sought, but certain
the crime" (adapted from Seneca's *Phœnissæ,*
l. 632).   [6] Plan of action.

MEN. [*Gives ring.*] Here, take my ring
　unto the citadel;
Have entrance to Maria, the grave
　duchess
Of banished Altofront. Tell her we love
　her;
Omit no circumstance to grace our per-
　son. Do 't.
MAL. I'll make an excellent pander.
Duke, farewell; 'dieu, adieu, duke.
　　　　　　　　　　　Exit Malevole.
MEN. Take Maquerelle with thee, for
　'tis found　　　　　　　　　　　99
None cuts a diamond but a diamond.
Hermit, thou art a man for me, my con-
　fessor.
O thou selected spirit, born for my good,
Sure thou wouldst make
An excellent elder in a deformed church.
Come, we must be inward,[1] thou and I
　all one.
PIET. I am glad I was ordained for ye.
MEN. Go to, then; thou must know
that Malevole is a strange villain; danger-
ous, very dangerous. You see how broad a[2]
speaks; a gross-jawed rogue. I would　[110
have thee poison him; he's like a corn upon
my great toe, I cannot go for him; he
must be cored out, he must. Wilt do 't, ha?
PIET. Anything, anything.
MEN. Heart of my life! Thus, then, to
　the citadel.
Thou shalt consort with this Malevole;
There being at supper, poison him.
It shall be laid upon Maria, who yields
love or dies.
Scud quick like lightning.
PIET. "Good deeds crawl, but mischief
　flies."　　　　　　　　　　　　120

　　　Enter Malevole. Exit Pietro.

MAL. Your devilship's ring has no
virtue. The buff-captain, the sallow
Westphalian gammon-faced zaza, cries,
"Stand out! Must have a stiffer warrant,
or no pass into the Castle of Comfort."
MEN. Command our sudden letter.—
Not enter! Sh'a't![3] What place is there
in Genoa but thou shalt? Into my heart,
into my very heart! Come, let's love; we
must love, we two, soul and body.　　130
MAL. How didst like the hermit? A
strange hermit, sirrah.

[1] Intimate.　　　[2] He.　　　[3] Shall have it.

MEN. A dangerous fellow, very peril-
ous. He must die.
MAL. Ay, he must die.
MEN. Thou'st[4] kill him. We are wise;
we must be wise.
MAL. And provident.
MEN. Yea, provident. Beware an hypo-
　crite;　　　　　　　　　　　　139
A churchman once corrupted, O, avoid!
A fellow that makes religion his stalking-
　horse,[5]
He breeds a plague. Thou shalt poison
　him.
MAL. Ho, 'tis wondrous necessary! How?
MEN. You both go jointly to the citadel;
There sup, there poison him; and Maria,
Because she is our opposite,[6] shall
　bear
The sad suspect—on which she dies or
　loves us.
MAL. I run.　　　　　　*Exit Malevole.*
MEN. *We that are great, our sole self-good*
　still moves us.
They shall die both, for their deserts
　craves more　　　　　　　　　150
Than we can recompense; their pres-
　ence still
Imbraids[7] our fortunes with beholding-
　ness,
Which we abhor; like deed, not doer.
Then conclude,
They live not to cry out, "Ingratitude!"
One stick burns tother; steel cuts steel
　alone.
'Tis good trust few; but, O, 'tis best trust
　none!
　　　　　　　　　　　Exit Mendoza.

　　　　　SCENA QUARTA.

　　　　　　[*The same.*]

Enter Malevole and Pietro still disguised, at
　　　　　　　　　　　several doors.

MAL. How do you? How dost, duke?
PIET. O, let the last day fall! Drop, drop
　on our cursed heads!

[4] Thou must.
[5] A marginal note for the reader, *Shoots under
his belly,* appears here, meaning, according to
Collier, that "a corrupted churchman makes
religion his *stalking-horse,* viz. by shooting at his
object under its belly."
[6] Opponent.
[7] Upbraids.

Let heaven unclasp itself, vomit forth flames.

MAL. O, do not rand,[1] do not turn player. There's more of them than can well live one by another already. What, art an infidel still?

PIET. I am amazed, struck in a swown with wonder. I am commanded to poison thee.   10

MAL. I am commanded to poison thee at supper.

PIET. At supper?

MAL. In the citadel.

PIET. In the citadel?

MAL. Cross-capers! Tricks! Truth a heaven! He would discharge us as boys do eldern guns,[2] one pellet to strick[3] out another. Of what faith art now?

PIET. All is damnation, wickedness extreme.   20

There is no faith in man.

MAL. In none but usurers and brokers; they deceive no man. Men take um for bloodsuckers, and so they are. Now, God deliver me from my friends!

PIET. Thy friends?

MAL. Yes, from my friends, for from mine enemies I'll deliver myself. O, cutthroat friendship is the rankest villainy! Mark this Mendoza; mark him for a   [30 villain; but heaven will send a plague upon him for a rogue.

PIET. O world!

MAL. World! 'Tis the only region of death, the greatest shop of the devil, the cruelest prison of men, out of the which none pass without paying their dearest breath for a fee. There's nothing perfect in it but extreme, extreme calamity, such as comes yonder.   40

SCENA QUINTA.

[The same.]

Enter Aurelia, two Halberts before and two after, supported by Celso and Ferrard; Aurelia in base mourning attire.

AUR. To banishment! Led on to banishment!

PIET. Lady, the blessedness of repentance to you!

---

[1] Rant, storm.   [3] Strike.
[2] Elderwood guns, *i.e.*, popguns.

AUR. Why? Why? I can desire nothing but death,
Nor deserve anything but hell.
If heaven should give sufficiency of grace
To clear my soul, it would make heaven graceless;
My sins would make the stock of mercy poor.
O, they would tire heaven's goodness to reclaim them!
Judgment is just, yet from that vast villain—
But, sure, he shall not miss sad punishment   10
Fore he shall rule.—On to my cell of shame!

PIET. My cell 'tis, lady, where, instead of masques,
Music, tilts, tourneys, and such courtlike shows,
The hollow murmur of the checkless winds
Shall groan again, whilst the unquiet sea
Shakes the whole rock with foamy battery.
There usherless the air comes in and out;
The rheumy vault will force your eyes to weep,
Whilst you behold true desolation.   19
A rocky barrenness shall pain your eyes,
Where all at once one reaches where he stands,
With brows the roof, both walls with both his hands.

AUR. It is too good.—Blessed spirit of my lord,
O, in what orb soe'er thy soul is throned,
Behold me worthily most miserable!
O, let the anguish of my contrite spirit
Entreat some reconciliation!
If not, O, joy, triumph in my just grief!
Death is the end of woes, and tears' relief.

PIET. Belike your lord not loved you, was unkind.   30

AUR. O heaven!
As the soul loved the body, so loved he.
'Twas death to him to part my presence, heaven
To see me pleased.
Yet I, like to a wretch given o'er to hell,
Brake all the sacred rites of marriage
To clip a base, ungentle, faithless villain.
O God, a very pagan reprobate—

What should I say?—ungrateful, throws
    me out,
For whom I lost soul, body, fame, and
    honor.   40
But 'tis most fit. Why should a better fate
Attend on any who forsake chaste sheets,
Fly the embrace of a devoted heart,
Joined by a solemn vow fore God and
    man,
To taste the brackish blood of beastly
    lust
In an adulterous touch?   O ravenous
    immodesty!
Insatiate impudence of appetite!
Look, here's your end; for mark, what sap
    in dust,
What sin in good, even so much love in lust.
Joy to thy ghost, sweet lord! Pardon to
    me!   50
Cel. 'Tis the duke's pleasure this night
    you rest in court.
Aur. Soul, lurk in shades; run, shame,
    from brightsome skies;
    In night the blind man misseth not his
    eyes.
Exit [with Celso, Ferrardo, and Halberts].
    Mal. Do not weep, kind cuckold; take
comfort, man; thy betters have been bec-
cos. Agamemnon, emperor of all the merry
Greeks, that tickled all the true Troyans,
was a cornuto; Prince Arthur, that cut off
twelve kings' beards, was a cornuto; Hercules, whose back bore up heaven, and [60
got forty wenches with child in one night—
    Piet. Nay, 't was fifty.
    Mal. Faith, forty's enow, a conscience
—yet was a cornuto. Patience; mischief
grows proud; be wise.
    Piet. Thou pinchest too deep, art too
keen upon me.
    Mal. Tut, a pitiful surgeon makes a
dangerous sore; I'll tent [1] thee to the
ground. Thinkest I'll sustain myself by [70
flattering thee, because thou art a prince?
I had rather follow a drunkard, and live by
licking up his vomit, than by servile
flattery.
    Piet. Yet great men ha' done 't.
    Mal. Great slaves fear better than love,
born naturally for a coal basket, though the
common usher of princes' presence, Fortune, hath blindly given them better place.
I am vowed to be thy affliction.   80

[1] Probe.

    Piet. Prithee, be. I love much misery,
and be thou son to me.

Enter Bilioso.

    Mal. Because you are an usurping
duke.—(*To Bilioso.*) Your lordship's well
returned from Florence.
    Bil. Well returned, I praise my horse.
    Mal. What news from the Floren-
tines?   88
    Bil. I will conceal the great duke's
pleasure; only this was his charge. His
pleasure is that his daughter die; Duke
Pietro be banished for banishing his blood's
dishonor; and that Duke Altofront be re-
accepted. This is all. But I hear Duke
Pietro is dead.
    Mal. Ay, and Mendoza is duke. What
will you do?
    Bil. Is Mendoza strongest?
    Mal. Yet he is.
    Bil. Then yet I'll hold with him.   100
    Mal. But if that Altofront should turn
straight again? [2]
    Bil. Why, then, I would turn straight
again.
    'Tis good run still with him that has most
    might;
    I had rather stand with wrong than fall
    with right.
    Mal. What religion will you be of
now?
    Bil. Of the duke's religion, when I know
what it is.   110
    Mal. O Hercules!
    Bil. Hercules? Hercules was the son of
Jupiter and Alcmena.
    Mal. Your lordship is a very wittol.
    Bil. Wittol?
    Mal. Ay, all-wit.
    Bil. Amphitryo was a cuckold.   117
    Mal. Your lordship sweats; your young
lady will get you a cloth for your old worship's brows. (*Exit Bilioso.*) Here's a
fellow to be damned! This is his inviolable
maxim—flatter the greatest and oppress
the least. A whoreson flesh-fly, that still
gnaws upon the lean, galled backs!
    Piet. Why dost, then, salute him?
    Mal. I' faith, as bawds go to church, for
fashion sake. Come, be not confounded;
thou art but in danger to lose a dukedom. Think this: this earth is the only grave

[2] Return straightway.

and Golgotha wherein all things that [130]
live must rot; 'tis but the draught wherein
the heavenly bodies discharge their corruption; the very muck hill on which the
sublunary orbs cast their excrements.
Man is the slime of this dung pit, and
princes are the governors of these men, for,
for our souls, they are as free as emperors,
all of one piece. There goes but a pair of
shears betwixt an emperor and the son of a
bagpiper;[1] only the dyeing, dressing, [140]
pressing, glossing, makes the difference.

Now, what art thou like to lose?
A jailer's office to keep men in bonds,
Whilst toil and treason all life's good con-
founds.

PIET. I here renounce forever regency.
O Altofront, I wrong thee to supplant
thy right,
To trip thy heels up with a devilish
sleight,
For which I now from throne am thrown,
world-tricks abjure;
For vengeance, though 't comes slow, yet it
comes sure.
O, I am changed! For here, fore the
dread power, 150
In true contrition, I do dedicate
My breath to solitary holiness,
My lips to prayer, and my breast's care
shall be
Restoring Altofront to regency.

MAL. Thy vows are heard, and we accept
thy faith. *Undisguiseth himself.*

Enter Ferneze and Celso.[2]

Banish amazement; come, we four must
stand
Full shock of fortune. Be not so wonder-
stricken.

PIET. Doth Ferneze live?
FER. For your pardon.
PIET. Pardon and love. Give leave to
recollect
My thoughts dispersed in wild astonish-
ment. 160
My vows stand fixed in heaven, and from
hence
I crave all love and pardon.

MAL. Who doubts of providence,

That sees this change? A hearty faith to
all!
He needs must rise [who][3] *can no lower*
fall;
For still impetuous vicissitude
Touseth the world; then let no maze
intrude
Upon your spirits. Wonder not I rise,
For who can sink that close can temporize?
The time grows ripe for action. I'll
detect[4]
My privat'st plot, lest ignorance fear
suspect. 170
Let's close to counsel, leave the rest to
fate;
Mature discretion is the life of state.

Exeunt.

ACTUS QUINTUS. SCENA PRIMA.

[Outside the citadel.]

[5] *Enter Bilioso and Passarello.*

BIL. Fool, how dost thou like my calf in
a long stocking?

PASS. An excellent calf, my lord.

BIL. This calf hath been a reveler this
twenty year. When Monsieur Gundi lay
here ambassador, I could have carried a
lady up and down at arm's end in a platter;
and I can tell you, there were those at
that time who, to try the strength of a
man's back and his arm, would be [10]
coistered.[6] I have measured calves with
most of the palace, and they come nothing
near me; besides, I think there be not
many armors in the arsenal will fit me,
especially for the headpiece. I'll tell thee—

PASS. What, my lord?

BIL. I can eat stewed broth as it comes
seething off the fire, or a custard as it
comes reeking out of the oven, and I think
there are not many lords can do it. [20]
[Displaying his pomander.] A good pomander—a little decayed in the scent, but six
grains of musk, ground with rosewater and
tempered with a little civet, shall fetch her
again presently!

PASS. O, ay, as a bawd with aqua vitæ.

BIL. And, what, dost thou rail upon the
ladies as thou wert wont?

[1] *I.e.*, they are cut out of the same cloth.
[2] Here original adds, *Altofront, Ferneze,*
Celso, Pietro.
[3] Supplied from first edn.
[4] Expose.
[5] The following lines to Bilioso's exit are an
addition.
[6] Coiled up (?).

Pass. I were better roast a live cat, and might do it with more safety. I am [30 as secret to [the] [1] thieves as their painting. There's Maquerelle, oldest bawd and a perpetual beggar. Did you never hear of her trick to be known in the city?

Bil. Never.

Pass. Why, she gets all the picter-[2] makers to draw her picture; when they have done, she most courtly finds fault with them one after another, and never fetcheth them. They, in revenge of this, [40 execute her in pictures as they do in Germany, and hang her in their shops. By this means is she better known to the stinkards [3] than if she had been five times carted.[4]

Bil. Fore God, an excellent policy.

Pass. Are there any revels tonight, my lord?

Bil. Yes.

Pass. Good my lord, give me leave to break a fellow's pate that hath abused [50 me.

Bil. Whose pate?

Pass. Young Ferrard, my lord.

Bil. Take heed, he's very valiant; I have known him fight eight quarrels in five days, believe it.

Pass. O, is he so great a quarreler? Why, then, he's an arrant coward.

Bil. How prove you that?

Pass. Why, thus: he that quarrels [60 seeks to fight; and he that seeks to fight seeks to die; and he that seeks to die seeks never to fight more; and he that will quarrel, and seeks means never to answer a man more, I think he's a coward.

Bil. Thou canst prove anything.

Pass. Anything but a rich knave, for I can flatter no man.

Bil. Well, be not drunk, good fool. I shall see you anon[5] in the presence. [70
                              Exit [with Passarello].

Enter Malevole and Maquerelle, at several doors opposite, singing.

Mal. The Dutchman for a drunkard—
Maq. The Dane for golden locks—
Mal. The Irishman for usquebath [6]—
Maq. The Frenchman for the (   ).[7]

Mal. O, thou art a blessed creature! Had I a modest woman to conceal, I would put her to thy custody, for no reasonable creature would ever suspect her to be in thy company. Ha, thou art a melodious Maquerelle, thou picture of a woman, [80 and substance of a beast!

[8] *Enter Passarello.*

Maq. O fool, will ye be ready anon to go with me to the revels? The hall will be so pestered [9] anon.

Pass. Ay, as the country is with attorneys.

Mal. What hast thou there, fool?

Pass. Wine; I have learned to drink since I went with my lord ambassador. I'll drink to the health of Madam [90 Maquerelle.

Mal. Why, thou wast wont to rail upon her.

Pass. Ay; but since I borrowed money of her, I'll drink to her health now, as gentlemen visit brokers, or as knights send venison to the city, either to take up more money, or to procure longer forbearance.

Mal. Give me the bowl. I drink a health to Altofront, our deposed duke. [100
                                        [*Drinks.*]

Pass. I'll take it. [*Drinks.*] So? Now I'll begin a health to Madam Maquerelle.
                                        [*Drinks.*]

Mal. Pugh! I will not pledge her.

Pass. Why, I pledged your lord.

Mal. I care not.

Pass. Not pledge Madam Maquerelle! Why, then will I spew up your lord again with this fool's finger.

Mal. Hold; I'll take it.   [*Drinks.*]

Maq. Now thou hast drunk my health, fool, I am friends with thee.   111

Pass. Art? Art?

When Griffon saw the reconciléd quean
Offering about his neck her arms to cast,
He threw off sword and heart's malignant stream,
And lovely her below the loins embraced.—
Adieu, Madam Maquerelle.
                              Exit Passarello.

Mal. And how dost thou think a this transformation of state now?   119

---

[1] Supplied by Bullen.   [2] Picture.   [3] The mob.
[4] Bawds were punished by being carted through the streets.   [5] Immediately.
[6] Usquebaugh, whiskey.   [7] Pox.
[8] The passage from this point to the exit of Passarello is an addition.
[9] Crowded.

MAQ. Verily, very well; for we women always note, the falling of the one is the rising of the other. Some must be fat, some must be lean; some must be fools, and some must be lords; some must be knaves, and some must be officers; some must be beggars, some must be knights; some must be cuckolds, and some must be citizens. As for example, I have two court dogs, the most fawning curs, the one called Watch, th' other Catch. [130 Now I, like Lady Fortune, sometimes love this dog, sometimes raise that dog, sometimes favor Watch, most commonly fancy Catch. Now, that dog which I favor I feed; and he's so ravenous that what I give he never chaws it, gulps it down whole, without any relish of what he has, but with a greedy expectation of what he shall have. The other dog now—   139

MAL. No more dog, sweet Maquerelle, no more dog. And what hope hast thou of the Duchess Maria? Will she stoop to the duke's lure? Will she cow, [1] think'st?

MAQ. Let me see, where's the sign now? Ha' ye e'er a calendar? Where's the sign, trow you?

MAL. Sign! Why, is there any moment in that?   148

MAQ. O, believe me, a most secret power. Look ye, a Chaldean or an Assyrian, I am sure 'twas a most sweet Jew, told me, court any woman in the right sign, you shall not miss. But you must take her in the right vein then, as, when the sign is in Pisces, a fishmonger's wife is very sociable; in Cancer, a Precisian's [2] wife is very flexible; in Capricorn, a merchant's wife hardly holds out; in Libra, a lawyer's wife is very tractable, especially if her husband be at the term; [3] only in [160 Scorpio 'tis very dangerous meddling. Has the duke sent any jewel, any rich stones?

Enter Captain.

MAL. Ay, I think those are the best signs to take a lady in.—By your favor, signior, I must discourse with the Lady Maria, Altofront's duchess; I must enter for the duke.

CAP. She here shall give you interview. I received the guardship of this citadel

from the good Altofront, and for his [170 use I'll keep 't till I am of no use.

MAL. Wilt thou? O heavens, that a Christian should be found in a buff jerkin! Captain Conscience, I love thee, captain. (*Exit Captain.*) We attend. And what hope hast thou of this duchess' easiness?

MAQ. 'Twill go hard. She was a cold creature ever; she hated monkeys, fools, jesters, and gentlemen ushers ex- [179 tremely; she had the vile trick on 't, not only to be truly modestly honorable in her own conscience, but she would avoid the least wanton carriage that might incur suspect, as, God bless me, she had almost brought bed-pressing out of fashion. I could scarce get a fine [4] for the lease of a lady's favor once in a fortnight.

MAL. Now, in the name of immodesty, how many maidenheads hast thou brought to the block?   190

MAQ. Let me see. Heaven forgive us our misdeeds!—Here's the duchess.

SCENA SECUNDA.

[*The same.*]

Enter Maria and Captain.

MAL. God bless thee, lady!

MAR. Out of thy company!

MAL. We have brought thee tender of a husband.

MAR. I hope I have one already.

MAQ. Nay, by mine honor, madam, as good ha' ne'er a husband as a banished husband; he's in another world now. I'll tell ye, lady, I have heard of a sect that maintained, when the husband was [10 asleep, the wife might lawfully entertain another man, for then her husband was as dead. Much more when he is banished!

MAR. Unhonest creature!

MAQ. Pish, honesty is but an art to seem so.

Pray ye, what's honesty, what's constancy,

But fables feigned, odd old fools' chat, devised

By jealous fools to wrong our liberty?

MAL. Mully,[5] he that loves thee is a duke, Mendoza. He will maintain thee [20 royally, love thee ardently, defend thee

---

[1] Submit.   [3] Court.
[2] Puritan's.

[4] Fee.   [5] Molly.

powerfully, marry thee sumptuously, and
keep thee in despite of Rosicleer or Donzel
del Phebo.[1] There's jewels. [*Gives jewels.*]
If thou wilt, so; if not, so.

MAR. Captain, for God's sake, save poor
　wretchedness
　From tyranny of lustful insolence!
　Enforce me in the deepest dungeon dwell,
　Rather than here; here round about is
　　hell.—
　O my dear'st Altofront, where'er thou
　　breathe,　　　　　　　　　　　　　30
　Let my soul sink into the shades beneath
　Before I stain thine honor! This thou
　　hast,
　And, long as I can die, I will live chaste.

MAL. Gainst him that can enforce, how
　vain is strife!

MAR. She that can be enforced has ne'er a
　　knife;
　*She that through force her limbs with lust
　　enrolls,*
　Wants Cleopatra's asps and Portia's coals.
　God amend you!　　*Exit with Captain.*

MAL. Now, the fear of the devil forever
go with thee!—Maquerelle, I tell thee, [40
I have found an honest woman. Faith, I
perceive, when all is done, there is of
women, as of all other things, some good,
most bad; some saints, some sinners. For
as nowadays no courtier but has his mistress, no captain but has his cockatrice,[2]
no cuckold but has his horns, and no fool
but has his feather, even so, no woman but
has her weakness and feather too, no sex
but has his—I can hunt the letter no [50
farder.—[*Aside.*] O God, how loathsome
this toying is to me! That a duke should
be forced to fool it! Well, "*Stultorum plena
sunt omnia.*"[3] Better play the fool lord
than be the fool lord.—Now, where's your
sleights, Madam Maquerelle?

MAQ. Why, are ye ignorant that 'tis said
a squeamish, affected niceness is natural to
women, and that the excuse of their yielding
is only, forsooth, the difficult obtaining? [60
You must put her to 't. Women are flax,
and will fire in a moment.

MAL. Why, was the flax put into thy
mouth, and yet thou—thou set fire, thou
inflame her?

MAQ. Marry, but I'll tell ye now, you
were too hot.

MAL. The fitter to have inflamed the
flax-woman.

MAQ. You were too boisterous, [70
spleeny, for, indeed—

MAL. Go, go, thou art a weak pandress;
　now I see,
　Sooner earth's fire heaven itself shall waste
　*Than all with heat can melt a mind that's
　　chaste.*
Go thou, the duke's lime-twig![4] I'll make
the duke turn thee out of thine office.
What, not get one touch of hope, and had
her at such advantage!

MAQ. Now, a my conscience, now I
think in my discretion, we did not take [80
her in the right sign; the blood was not in
the true vein, sure.　　　　　　　*Exit.*

[5] *Enter Bilioso.*

BIL. Make way there! The duke returns
from the enthronement.—Malevole—

MAL. Out, rogue!

BIL. Malevole—

MAL. "Hence, ye gross-jawed, peasantly—out, go!"

BIL. Nay, sweet Malevole, since my
return I hear you are become the thing [90
I always prophesied would be—an advanced virtue, a worthily-employed faithfulness, a man a grace, dear friend.

Come, what! *Si quoties peccant homines—*
if as often as courtiers play the knaves,
honest men should be angry—why, look
ye, we must collogue[6] sometimes, forswear
sometimes.

MAL. Be damned sometimes.

BIL. Right.　*Nemo omnibus horis* [100
sapit: No man can be honest at all hours.
Necessity often depraves virtue.

MAL. I will commend thee to the duke.

BIL. Do let us be friends, man.

MAL. And knaves, man.

BIL. Right. Let us prosper and purchase;[7] our lordships shall live, and our
knavery be forgotten.

MAL. He that by any ways gets riches,
his means never shames him.　　　　110

---

[1] Heroes of the Spanish romance translated as
The Mirror of Knighthood.　　　　[2] Courtesan.
[3] "All things are full of fools" (Cicero).

[4] Snare, trap.
[5] The remainder of the scene is another addition.
[6] Confer secretly.
[7] Acquire wealth (by illegitimate means).

BIL. True.

MAL. For impudency and faithlessness are the main stays to greatness.

BIL. By the Lord, thou art a profound lad.

MAL. By the Lord, thou art a perfect knave. Out, ye ancient damnation!

BIL. Peace, peace! And thou wilt not be a friend to me as I am a knave, be not a knave to me as I am thy friend, and [120 disclose me. Peace! Cornets!

SCENA TERTIA.

[*The same.*]

Enter Prepasso and Ferrard, two Pages with lights, Celso and Equato, Mendoza in duke's robes, and Guerrino.[1] *Exeunt all saving Malevole [and Mendoza].*

MEN. On, on; leave us, leave us.— Stay, where is the hermit?

MAL. With Duke Pietro, with Duke Pietro.

MEN. Is he dead? Is he poisoned?

MAL. Dead as the duke is.

MEN. Good, excellent. He will not blab; secureness lives in secrecy. Come hither, come hither.

MAL. Thou hast a certain strong [10 villainous scent about thee my nature cannot endure.

MEN. Scent, man? What returns Maria—what answer to our suit?

MAL. Cold-frosty; she is obstinate.

MEN. Then she's but dead; 'tis resolute she dies.

Black deed only through black deed safely flees.

MAL. Pugh! "*Per scelera semper sceleribus tutum est iter.*"[2] 19

MEN. What, art a scholar? Art a politician? Sure, thou art an arrand knave.

MAL. Who, I? I have been twice an undersheriff, man.[3]

---

[1] Direction reads *Bilioso and Guerrino.*

[2] "The way to wickedness is always made safe by wickedness" (Seneca, *Agamemnon*, l. 115).

[3] Ll. 24–40 are an addition. In the original they are preceded by the passage:

"*Enter Malevole and Mendoza.*

MEN. Hast been with Maria?

MAL. As your scrivener to your usurer, I have dealt about taking of this commodity; but she's cold-frosty,"

The passage just quoted has been omitted here

Well, I will go rail upon some great man, that I may purchase the bastinado, or else go marry some rich Genoan lady, and instantly go travel.

MEN. Travel, when thou art married?

MAL. Ay, 'tis your young lord's fashion to do so, though he was so lazy, being a [30 bachelor, that he would never travel so far as the university; yet, when he married her, tales of—and, catso, for England!

MEN. And why for England?

MAL. Because there is no brothel houses there.

MEN. Nor courtesans?

MAL. Neither; your whore went down with the stews, and your punk came up with your Puritan. 40

MEN. Canst thou empoison? Canst thou empoison?

MAL. Excellently; no Jew, potecary, or politician better. Look ye, here's a box. Whom wouldst thou empoison? Here's a box (*Giving it.*) which, opened and the fume taken up in conduits thorough which the brain purges itself, doth instantly for twelve hours' space bind up all show of life in a deep senseless sleep. Here's an- [50 other (*Giving it.*) which, being opened under the sleeper's nose, chokes all the power of life, kills him suddenly.

MEN. I'll try experiments; 'tis good not to be deceived.—So, so; catso!

Seems to poison Malevole [, who falls].

Who would fear that may destroy?
 Death hath no teeth or tongue;
And he that's great, to him are slaves
 Shame, murder, fame, and wrong.—

Celso! 60

Enter Celso.[4]

CEL. My honored lord?

MEN. The good Malevole, that plain-tongued man, alas, is dead on sudden, wondrous strangely! He held in our esteem good place. Celso, see him buried, see him buried.

CEL. I shall observe ye.

MEN. And, Celso, prithee, let it be thy care tonight

because with its repetition of the earlier part of the scene it was apparently an alternate reading for all or part of the first twenty-three lines.

[4] In the original this direction follows l. 53.

To have some pretty show, to solem-
nize
Our high installment; some music,
masquery.   70
We'll give fair entertain unto Maria,
The duchess to the banished Altofront.
Thou shalt conduct her from the citadel
Unto the palace.   Think on some
masquery.
CEL. Of what shape, sweet lord?
MEN. Why, shape? Why, any quick-done
fiction,
As some brave spirits of the Genoan
dukes
To come out of Elysium, forsooth,
Led in by Mercury, to gratulate   79
Our happy fortune; some such anything,
Some far-fet [1] trick good for ladies, some
stale toy
Or other, no matter, so 't be of our de-
vising.
Do thou prepare 't; 'tis but for a fashion
sake.
Fear not; it shall be graced, man; it shall
take.
CEL. All service.
MEN. All thanks; our hand shall not be
close to thee; farewell.—
[Aside.] Now is my teachery secure, nor
can we fall.
Mischief that prospers, men do virtue call.
I'll trust no man; he that by tricks gets
wreaths
Keeps them with steel; no man securely
breathes   90
Out of deservéd ranks; the crowd will
mutter, "Fool!"
Who cannot bear with spite, he cannot rule.
The chiefest secret for a man of state
Is to live senseless of a strengthless hate.
[Exit.]
MAL. (Starts up and speaks.) Death of
the damned thief! I'll make one i' the
masque; thou shalt ha' some brave spirits
of the antique dukes.   98
CEL. My lord, what strange delusion?
MAL. Most happy, dear Celso! Poisoned
with an empty box! I'll give thee all anon.
My lady comes to court; there is a whirl
of fate comes tumbling on; the castle's
captain stands for me, the people pray for
me, and the great leader of the just stands
for me.   Then courage, Celso.

[1] Far-fetched.

For no disastrous chance can ever move him
That leaveth nothing but a God above him.
[Exeunt.]

SCENA QUARTA.[2]

[The presence chamber.]

Enter Prepasso and Bilioso, two Pages before
them; Maquer[elle], Biancha, and
Emilia.

BIL. Make room there, room for the
ladies! Why, gentlemen, will not ye suffer
the ladies to be entered in the great chamber? Why, gallants! And you, sir, to drop
your torch where the beauties must sit too!
PRE. And there's a great fellow plays
the knave. Why dost not strike him?
BIL. Let him play the knave, a God's
name; think'st thou I have no more wit
than to strike a great fellow?—The [10
music! More lights! Reveling-scaffolds! Do
you hear? Let there be oaths enow ready
at the door; swear out the devil himself.
Let's leave the ladies, and go see if the
lords be ready for them.
All save the Ladies depart.
MAQ. And, by my troth, beauties, why
do you not put you into the fashion? This
is a stale cut; you must come in fashion.
Look ye, you must be all felt, felt and
feather, a felt upon your bare hair. [20
Look ye, these tiring things [3] are justly out of
request now. And, do ye hear, you must
wear falling bands,[4] you must come into
the falling fashion; there is such a deal a
pinning these ruffs, when the fine clean fall
is worth all; and again, if you should chance
to take a nap in the afternoon, your falling
band requires no poting stick [5] to recover
his form. Believe me, no fashion to the
falling, I say.   30
BIAN. And is not Signior St. Andrew a
gallant fellow now?
MAQ. By my maidenhead, la, honor and
he agrees as well together as a satin suit
and woolen stockings.
EM. But is not Marshal Make-room,
my servant in reversion,[6] a proper gentleman?

[2] In the original the new scene begins at the
entry of the duke's procession.
[3] Headdresses.
[4] Flat collars.   [5] Stick for plaiting ruffs.
[6] Upon the death or withdrawal of the present
owner.

MAQ. Yes, in reversion, as he had his office; as, in truth, he hath all things in [40 reversion. He has his mistress in reversion, his clothes in reversion, his wit in reversion, and, indeed, is a suitor to me for my dog in reversion. But, in good verity, la, he is as proper a gentleman in reversion as—and, indeed, as fine a man as may be, having a red beard and a pair of wrapped [1] legs.

BIAN. But, i' faith, I am most monstrously in love with Count Quidlibet-in-quodlibet. Is he not a pretty, dapper, [50 unidle gallant?

MAQ. He is even one of the most busy-fingered lords; he will put the beauties to the squeak most hideously.

Enter Bilioso.

BIL. Room! Make a lane there! The duke is entering. Stand handsomely, for beauty's sake; take up the ladies there! So, cornets, cornets!

Enter Prepasso; joins to Bilioso. Two Pages and lights; Ferrard; Mendoza. At the other door, two Pages with lights, and the Captain leading in Maria. The Duke meets Maria, and closeth with her. The rest fall back.

MEN. Madam, with gentle ear receive my suit;
A kingdom's safety should o'erpeise [2] slight rites;   60
Marriage is merely nature's policy.
Then since, unless our royal beds be joined,
Danger and civil tumult frights the state,
Be wise as you are fair, give way to fate.
MAR. What wouldst thou, thou affliction to our house?
Thou ever-devil, 'twas thou that banishedst
My truly noble lord!
MEN. I?
MAR. Ay, by thy plots, by thy black stratagems.
Twelve moons have suffered change since I beheld   70
The lovéd presence of my dearest lord.
O thou, far worse than Death! He parts but soul

From a weak body; but thou soul from soul
Disseverest, that which God's own hand did knit;
Thou, scant of honor, full of devilish wit!
MEN. We'll check your too-intemperate lavishness.
I can and will.
MAR. What canst?
MEN. Go to; in banishment thy husband dies.   79
MAR. *He ever is at home that's ever wise.*
MEN. You'st [3] never meet more; reason should love control.
MAR. Not meet?
She that dear loves, her love's still in her soul.
MEN. You are but a woman, lady; you must yield.
MAR. O, save me, thou innated [4] bashfulness,
Thou only ornament of woman's modesty!
MEN. Modesty? Death, I'll torment thee.
MAR. Do, urge all torments, all afflictions try;
I'll die my lord's as long as I can die.
MEN. Thou obstinate, thou shalt die.—
Captain, that lady's   90
Life is forfeited [5] to justice. We have examined her,
And we do find she hath empoisonéd
The reverend hermit; therefore we command
Severest custody.—Nay, if you'll do 's no good,
You 'st do 's no harm. A tyrant's peace is blood.
MAR. O, thou art merciful! O gracious devil,
Rather by much let me condemnéd be
For seeming murder than be damned for thee!
I'll mourn no more; come, girt my brows with flowers;
Revel and dance. Soul, now thy wish thou hast;   100
Die like a bride; poor heart, thou shalt die chaste.

Enter Aurelia in mourning habit.

AUR. *Life is a frost of cold felicity,*
And death the thaw of all our vanity.
Was't not an honest priest [6] that wrote so?

---

[1] Padded. Perhaps a misprint for *warped.*
[2] Outweigh.
[3] You must.   [4] Innate.
[5] From first edn. Original reads *forteified.*
[6] Thomas Bastard.

MEN. Who let her in?

BIL.   Forbear!

PRE.   Forbear!

AUR. *Alas, calamity is everywhere.*
Sad misery, despite your double doors,
Will enter even in court.

BIL. Peace!

AUR.   I ha' done. One word—take
heed! I ha' done.

Enter Mercury with loud music.

MER. Cyllenian Mercury, the god of
ghosts,   110
From gloomy shades that spread the
lower coasts,
Calls four high-famed Genoan dukes to
come,
And make this presence their Elysium,
To pass away this high triumphal night
With song and dances, court's more soft
delight.

AUR. Are you god of ghosts? I have a
suit depending in hell betwixt me and my
conscience. I would fain have thee help
me to an advocate.   119

BIL. Mercury shall be your lawyer, lady.

AUR. Nay, faith, Mercury has too good
a face to be a right lawyer.

PRE. Peace, forbear! Mercury presents
the masque.

*Cornets. The song to the cornets, which play-
ing, the masque enters; Malevole,
Pietro, Ferneze, and Celso, in white
robes, with duke's crowns upon laurel
wreaths, pistolets and short swords under
their robes.*

MEN. Celso, Celso, court [1] Maria for our
love.—Lady, be gracious, yet grace—
          Malevole takes his Wife to dance.

MAR. With me, sir?

MAL.   Yes, more lovéd
than my breath;
With you I'll dance.

MAR.   Why, then, you
dance with death.
But, come, sir, I was ne'er more apt to
mirth.   129
*Death gives eternity a glorious breath;
O, to die honored, who would fear to die?*

MAL. *They die in fear who live in villainy.*

[1] From first edn. Original reads *count.*

MEN. Yes, believe him, lady, and be ruled
by him.
          Pietro takes his wife Aurelia to dance.

PIET. Madam, with me?

AUR.   Wouldst then be miserable?

PIET. I need not wish.

AUR. O, yet forbear my hand! Away, fly,
fly!
O, seek not her that only seeks to die!

PIET. Poor lovéd soul!

AUR.   What, wouldst court misery?

PIET. Yes.

AUR.   She'll come too soon. O my
grieved heart!

PIET. Lady, ha' done, ha' done.   140
Come, let's dance; be once from sorrow
free.

AUR. Art a sad man?

PIET.   Yes, sweet.

AUR.   Then we'll agree.

*Ferneze takes Maquerelle, and Celso, Bi-
ancha; then the cornets sound the
measure, one change and rest.*

FER. (*To Biancha.*) Believe it, lady;
shall I swear? Let me enjoy you in private,
and I'll marry you, by my soul.

BIAN. I had rather you would swear by
your body; I think that would prove the
more regarded oath with you.

FER. I'll swear by them both, to please
you.   150

BIAN. O, damn them not both to please
me, for God's sake!

FER. Faith, sweet creature, let me enjoy
you tonight, and I'll marry you tomorrow
fortnight, by my troth, la.

MAQ. On his troth, la! Believe him not;
that kind of cunny-catching [2] is as stale as
Sir Oliver Anchovy's perfumed jerkin.
Promise of matrimony by a young gallant,
to bring a virgin lady into a fool's paradise;
make her a great woman, and then [161
cast her off—'tis as common, as natural, to a
courtier, as jealousy to a citizen, gluttony
to a Puritan, wisdom to an alderman, pride
to a tailor, or an empty hand basket to one
of these sixpenny damnations.[3] Of his
troth, la, believe him not; traps to catch
polecats!

MAL. (*To Maria.*) Keep your face constant; let no sudden passion
Speak in your eyes.   [*Reveals himself.*]

MAR.   O my Altofront!

[2] Cony-catching, deceiving.   [3] Prostitutes.

PIET. [*To Aurelia.*]   A tyrant's jealous-
ies   171
Are very nimble; you receive it all.
AUR.[1] My heart, though not my knees, doth
humbly fall
Low as the earth, to thee.
PIET. Peace! Next change; no words.
MAR. Speech to such, ay, O, what will
affords!

Cornets sound the measure over again; which
danced, they unmask.

MEN. Malevole!

They environ Mendoza, bending their pistols
on him.

MAL. No!
MEN. Altofront! Duke Pietro! Ferneze!
Ha!
ALL. Duke Altofront! Duke Altofront! 180

Cornets, a flourish.—They seize upon
Mendoza.

MEN. Are we surprised? What strange de-
lusions mock
Our senses? Do I dream? Or have I
dreamt
This two days' space? Where am I?
MAL. Where an archvillain is.
MEN. O, lend me breath till I am fit to die!
For peace with heaven, for your own
souls' sake,
Vouchsafe me life!
PIET. Ignoble villain, whom neither heaven
nor hell,
Goodness of God or man, could once
make good!
MAL. Base, treacherous wretch, what
grace canst thou expect,   190
That hast grown impudent in graceless-
ness?
MEN. O, life!
MAL. Slave, take thy life.
Wert thou defenséd,[2] through blood and
wounds,
The sternest horror of a civil fight
Would I achieve thee; but, prostrate at
my feet,
I scorn to hurt thee.   *'Tis the heart of slaves*
That deigns to triumph over peasants'
graves;
For such thou art, since birth doth ne'er enroll
A man 'mong monarchs, but a glorious soul.[3]
O, I have seen strange accidents of
state—   201

The flatterer, like the ivy, clip the oak,
And waste it to the heart; lust so con-
firmed
That the black act of sin itself not
shamed
To be termed courtship.
O, they that are as great as be their sins,
Let them remember that th' inconstant
people
Love many princes merely for their faces
And outward shows; and they do covet
more
To have a sight of these than of their
virtues.   210
Yet thus much let the great ones still
conceal.[4]
When they observe not heaven's imposed
conditions,
They are no kings, but forfeit their commissions.
MAQ. O good my lord, I have lived in
the court this twenty year; they that have
been old courtiers, and come to live in the
city, they are spited at, and thrust to the
walls like apricocks, good my lord.   218
BIL. My lord, I did know your lordship
in this disguise; you heard me ever say, if
Altofront did return, I would stand for
him. Besides, 'twas your lordship's pleasure
to call me wittol and cuckold; you must not
think, but that I knew you, I would have
put it up so patiently.
[MAL.] (*To Pietro and Aurelia.*)   You
o'erjoyed spirits, wipe your long-wet
eyes.—
Hence with this man!   (*Kicks out*
Mendoza.) An eagle takes not flies.—
(*To Pietro and Aurelia.*) You to your
vows—(*To   Maquerelle.*) and thou
unto the suburbs.[5]
You to my worst friend I would hardly
give.—
(*To Bilioso.*) Thou art a perfect old
knave.—(*To Celso and the Captain.*)
All-pleased, live   230
You two unto my breast—(*To Maria.*)
thou to my heart.
The rest of idle actors idly part;
And as for me, I here assume my right,
To which I hope all's pleased. To all,
good night.

Cornets, a flourish. Exeunt omnes.

FINIS.

----

[1] Marginal note: *Aurelia to Pietro.*
[2] Defended.   [3] Lines 201–25 are an addition.
[4] Conceive (?).   [5] The disreputable district.

An Imperfect Ode, Being But One Staff, Spoken by the Prologue

To wrest each hurtless thought to private sense
Is the foul use of ill-bred impudence.
  Immodest censure [1] now grows wild,
    All overrunning.
  Let Innocence be ne'er so chaste,
    Yet at the last
    She is defiled
  With too nice-brainéd cunning.
    O you of fairer soul,
      Control   10
  With an Herculean arm
    This harm;
And once teach all old freedom of a pen,
Which still must write of fools, whilst writes of men!

Epilogus

Your modest silence, full of heedy [2] stillness,
Makes me thus speak: a voluntary illness [3]

---

[1] Immoderate criticism.
[2] Heedful.
[3] Defect.

Is merely [4] senseless; but unwilling error,
Such as proceeds from too rash youthful fervor,
May well be called a fault, but not a sin.
Rivers take names from founts where they begin.
Then let not too severe an eye peruse
The slighter brakes [5] of our reforméd Muse,
Who could herself herself of faults detect,
But that she knows 'tis easy to correct,
Though [6] some men's labor. Troth, to err is fit,   11
As long as wisdom's not professed, but wit.
Then till another's [7] happier Muse appears,
Till his Thalia feast your learned ears,
To whose desertful lamps [8] pleased Fates impart
Art above Nature, Judgment above Art,
  Receive this piece, which hope nor fear yet daunteth:
  He that knows most, knows most how much he wanteth.

Finis.

---

[4] Wholly.
[5] Flaws.
[6] Supply *'tis.*
[7] Ben Jonson's.
[8] Nocturnal studies.

GEORGE CHAPMAN

George Chapman was born near Hitchin about 1559, and, according to Wood, "spent some time in Oxon, where he was observed to be most excellent in the Latin and Greek tongues, but not in logic or philosophy." He is first heard of upon the publication of his poem *The Shadow of Night* in 1594. He is first mentioned as a dramatist in Henslowe's record of the performance of his *Blind Beggar of Alexandria* by the Admiral's Men in February, 1596. In 1598 Meres placed him among the best for both comedy and tragedy. Not long after 1600 he seems to have been writing for the Children of the Chapel—called after 1604 the Children of the Queen's Revels—at Blackfriars Theater. His share in *Eastward Ho*, written for the children in collaboration with Jonson and Marston, caused his imprisonment for a short while because James I was offended by its satire on the Scots. In *Byron*, also written for the boy actors, Chapman offended again by his representation of French royalty on the stage. His major activity as a dramatist probably ceased by 1613. In the meanwhile he had published in 1598 *Seven Books of the Iliads* and a continuation of Marlowe's *Hero and Leander*. Minor poetic works and parts of the famous Homeric translation were published at intervals, the complete edition of the two epics appearing in 1616 and a volume of other Homeric poems about 1624. From Prince Henry, his chief patron, whom he had served as sewer, he received promise of a large reward and a pension for his Homer, but after the death of the prince in 1612 the promise was not fulfilled. Chapman wrote a poem on his death and prepared a court masque the next year, but he did not continue in favor at court. His later life was one of poverty. He died in 1634, and was honored with a monument designed by his friend, the great architect Inigo Jones.

In Chapman's plays the Elizabethan poetic and romantic treatment of life is united with the humanist's interest in classical learning. Early in his career he experimented with elements of the comedy of humors, or manners, which Jonson, the dominant figure of the Stuart era, established in 1598 with his *Every Man in His Humor*, using a classical technique to satirize the follies of contemporary society. After depicting characters warped by humors in *An Humorous Day's Mirth*, apparently written for Henslowe in 1597, Chapman made a still more searching study of follies in *All Fools* of 1599, based on two plays of Terence. But in his comic plots, drawn from various sources including the classics, he seems to be interested primarily in devices of romantic comedy—love story, intrigue, disguise, mistakes of identity, and other features of the complicated action developed under the influence chiefly of Italian comedy and novel. His later comedies with date of publication are *The Gentleman Usher* (1606), *Monsieur D'Olive* (1606), *May Day* (1611), and *The Widow's Tears* (1612). *Sir Giles Goosecap*, printed in 1606, is usually ascribed to Chapman. In tragedy also Chapman showed a kinship to Jonson in his combination of history, philosophic discourse drawn from classic writers, and Senecan technique, but he did not achieve the clarity and sustained tone that made Jonson a model for later writers. Chapman is distinctly Elizabethan in his style, which frequently rises to passionate intensity, with passages lighted by felicitous figures as vivid and elaborate as his Homeric similes, but at times becomes bombastic, strained, or "metaphysical." One of his tragedies, *Cæsar and Pompey*, published in 1631 as written long before, deals with a theme of ancient history popular in drama. With the omission of some tragedies doubtfully ascribed to him, the rest are drawn from contemporary or recent French history: *Bussy D'Ambois* (printed in 1607), the two parts of *The Conspiracy and the Tragedy of Charles, Duke of Byron* (printed in 1608), *The Revenge of Bussy D'Ambois* (printed in 1613), and *The Tragedy of Chabot* (printed in 1639 as written by Chapman and Shirley). The main incidents of *Byron* and *The Revenge of Bussy D'Ambois* Chapman apparently drew from Grimestone's *General Inventory of the History of France*, a translation of Jean de Serres, brought nearer to the date of publication in 1607 by the use of other French works. He modified or supplemented his material, however, to emphasize certain aspects of character or to secure tragic effects. The influence of Seneca on his tragedies is clear in such devices as the ghost and in his fondness for the declamatory and sententious. Ethical or metaphysical discourses are adapted from classical treatises, as F. L. Schoell has shown, often through Renaissance translations or through compilations like Erasmus' *Adagia*. Plutarch's moral treatises furnished Chapman with numerous passages, and the stoic philosophy of Cleremont in *The Revenge of Bussy D'Ambois* is built up from passages in a Latin translation of Epictetus.

Bussy D'Ambois, Chapman's best tragedy, may have been written as early as 1598, to judge from the names of the characters in an inventory of garments to be found in Henslowe's Diary for that year. If so, it was revised before publication in 1607. Possibly the play was inspired by Marlowe's *Massacre at Paris*, for several of the same historical figures appear in the two, and there is a not dissimilar portrayal of bold, arrogant characters. As in other cases, Chapman must have had contemporary accounts for his historical details, but the extant French works of importance covering the field seem to have been printed after the play was written—De Thou's *Historiæ sui temporis*, formerly regarded as a possible source, the memoirs of Brantôme and Marguerite de Valois, and Rosset's *Histoires tragiques*. Whatever his source, he has varied from historical fact, not only in a convention like the introduction of the ghost, but in giving a logical connection to the incidents chosen for plot, and in making Bussy a man of lower social status and more truculent nature than seems warranted. Bussy thus becomes an example of the aspiring spirits produced by the Renaissance, who dared much to win recognition, as other historical characters in the play have taken form as Renaissance types.

After its publication by Aspley in 1607, *Bussy D'Ambois* was reissued in 1608. Robert Lunne brought out another edition in 1641, which according to the title-page had been "much corrected and amended by the Author before his death." The present text is based on Parrott's reprint of this quarto of 1641 in *The Plays and Poems of George Chapman*. The edition of Boas in the Belles-Lettres Series has also been consulted.

BUSSY D'AMBOIS[1]

BY

GEORGE CHAPMAN

[*DRAMATIS PERSONÆ*

HENRY III, *King of France.*
MONSIEUR, *his brother.*
MAFFÉ, *steward to Monsieur.*
THE DUKE OF GUISE.
MONTSURRY, *a count.*
BUSSY D'AMBOIS.
BARRISOR ⎫ *courtiers; enemies*
L'ANOU ⎬ *of D'Ambois.*
PYRRHOT ⎭
BRISAC ⎫ *courtiers; friends*
MELYNELL ⎭ *of D'Ambois.*
FRIAR COMOLET.
NUNTIUS, *a messenger.*

MURDERERS.
BEHEMOTH ⎫ *spirits.*
CARTOPHYLAX ⎭
UMBRA of FRIAR.

ELENOR, *Duchess of Guise.*
ANNABELLE, *maid to Elenor.*
BEAUPRÉ, *niece to Elenor.*
CHARLOTTE, *maid to Beaupré.*
TAMYRA, *Countess of Montsurry.*
PERO, *maid to Tamyra.*
PYRA, *a court lady.*
LORDS, LADIES, PAGES, etc.

SCENE: *Paris.*

TIME: *Later sixteenth century.*]

PROLOGUE

NOT out of confidence that none but we [2]
Are able to present this tragedy,
Nor out of envy at the grace of late
It did receive, nor yet to derogate
From their deserts who [3] give out boldly
     that
They move with equal feet on the same
     flat; [4]
Neither for all nor any of such ends
We offer it, gracious and noble friends,
To your review. We, far from emulation
And (charitably judge) from imitation,   10
With this work entertain you, a piece
     known
And still believed in court to be our own.
To quit our claim, doubting our right or
     merit,

Would argue in us poverty of spirit
Which we must not subscribe to. Field [5]
     is gone,
Whose action first did give it name, and
     one
Who came the nearest to him,[6] is denied
By his gray beard to show the height and
     pride
Of D'Ambois' youth and bravery. Yet,
     to hold
Our title still afoot, and not grow cold   20
By giving it o'er, a third man [7] with his
     best
Of care and pains defends our interest;
As Richard he was liked, nor do we
     fear
In personating D'Ambois he'll appear
To faint, or go less, so [8] your free con-
     sent,
As heretofore, give him encouragement.

---

[1] The title continues: "A Tragedy, As It Hath Been Often Acted with Great Applause, Being Much Corrected and Amended by the Author before his Death."
[2] *I.e.*, the King's Men.
[3] A rival company which had given the play.
[4] Over the same ground.
[5] Nathan Field, one of the company when the play was acted about 1616.
[6] Unidentified.
[7] Probably Elliard Swanston.
[8] If.

ACTUS PRIMI SCENA PRIMA.[1]

[*A forest near Paris.*]

Enter Bussy D'Ambois, poor.

[BUS.] Fortune, not Reason, rules the
  state of things;
Reward goes backwards, Honor on his
  head; [2]
Who is not poor, is monstrous; only
  Need
Gives form and worth to every human
  seed.
As cedars beaten with continual storms,
So great men flourish, and do imitate
Unskillful statuaries, who suppose,
In forming a colossus, if they make him
Straddle enough, strut, and look big,
  and gape,
Their work is goodly. So men merely
  great   10
In their affected gravity of voice,
Sourness of countenance, manners' cru-
  elty,
Authority, wealth, and all the spawn of
  fortune,
Think they bear all the kingdom's
  worth before them,
Yet differ not from those colossic statues,
Which, with heroic forms without o'er-
  spread,
Within are naught but mortar, flint,
  and lead.
Man is a torch borne in the wind; a
  dream
But of a shadow, summed [3] with all
  his substance;
And, as great seamen, using all their
  wealth   20
And skills in Neptune's deep invisible
  paths,
In tall ships richly built and ribbed with
  brass,
To put a girdle round about the world,
When they have done it, coming near
  their haven,
Are fain to give a warning-piece,[4] and
  call
A poor, staid fisherman, that never
  passed
His country's sight, to waft and guide
  them in;

So, when we wander furthest through
  the waves
Of glassy glory, and the gulfs of state,
Topped with all titles, spreading all our
  reaches,   30
As if each private arm would sphere the
  earth,
We must to Virtue for her guide resort,
Or we shall shipwrack in our safest port.
                    Procumbit.[5]

[*Enter*] *Monsieur, with two Pages.*

[MON.] There is no second place in nu-
  merous state
That holds more than a cipher; in a
  king
All places are contained. His words and
  looks
Are like the flashes and the bolts of
  Jove;
His deeds inimitable, like the sea
That shuts still as it opes, and leaves
  no tracts
Nor prints of precedent for mean men's
  facts.[6]   40
There's but a thread betwixt me and a
  crown;
I would not wish it cut, unless by na-
  ture;
Yet to prepare me for that possible
  fortune,
'Tis good to get resolvéd spirits about
  me.
I followed D'Ambois to this green re-
  treat,
A man of spirit beyond the reach of
  fear,
Who, discontent with his neglected
  worth,
Neglects the light, and loves obscure
  abodes;
But he is young and haughty, apt to
  take
Fire at advancement, to bear state, and
  flourish;   50
In his rise therefore shall my bounties
  shine.
None loathes the world so much, nor
  loves to scoff it,
But gold and grace will make him sur-
  feit of it.—
What, D'Ambois?
BUS.   He, sir.

---

[1] The first scene of the first act.   [3] Clothed.
[2] *I.e.*, upside down.   [4] Signal shot.
[5] He falls forward.   [6] Deeds.

Mon.   Turned to earth, alive?
Up, man; the sun shines on thee.
Bus.   Let it shine.
I am no mote to play in 't, as great men
    are.
Mon. Callest thou men great in state,
    motes in the sun?
They say so that would have thee
    freeze in shades,
That, like the gross Sicilian gourmandist,
Empty their noses in the cates they
    love,   60
That none may eat but they. Do thou
    but bring
Light to the banquet Fortune sets be-
    fore thee,
And thou wilt loathe lean darkness like
    thy death.
Who would believe thy mettle could
    let sloth
Rust and consume it? If Themistocles
Had lived obscured thus in th' Athe-
    nian state,
Xerxes had made both him and it his
    slaves.
If brave Camillus had lurked so in
    Rome,
He had not five times been dictator
    there,
Nor four times triumphed. If Epami-
    nondas,   70
Who lived twice twenty years obscured
    in Thebes,
Had lived so still, he had been still un-
    named,
And paid his country nor himself their
    right;
But, putting forth his strength, he res-
    cued both
From imminent ruin, and, like bur-
    nished steel,
After long use he shined; for, as the
    light
Not only serves to show, but renders us
Mutually profitable, so our lives
In acts exemplary not only win
Ourselves good names, but do to others
    give   80
Matter for virtuous deeds, by which we
    live.
Bus. What would you wish me?
Mon.   Leave the troubled streams,
    And live, where thrivers do, at the well-
    head.

Bus. At the wellhead? Alas, what should
    I do
With that enchanted glass? See devils
    there;
Or, like a strumpet, learn to set my
    looks
In an eternal brake [1] or practice jug-
    gling,
To keep my face still fast, my heart
    still loose;
Or bear, like dame's schoolmistresses
    their riddles,
Two tongues, and be good only for a
    shift; [2]   90
Flatter great lords, to put them still in
    mind
Why they were made lords; or please
    humorous [3] ladies
With a good carriage, tell them idle
    tales
To make their physic work; spend a
    man's life
In sights and visitations that will make
His eyes as hollow as his mistress'
    heart;
To do none good but those that have no
    need;
To gain being forward, though you
    break for haste
All the commandments ere you break
    your fast;
But believe backwards, make your
    period   100
And creed's last article, "I believe in
    God;"
And, hearing villainies preached, t'un-
    fold their art,
Learn to commit them? 'Tis a great
    man's part.
Shall I learn this there?
Mon.   No, thou need'st not learn;
Thou hast the theory; now go there and
    practice.
Bus. Ay, in a thridbare suit. When men
    come there,
They must have high naps,[4] and go
    from thence bare.
A man may drown the parts [5] of ten
    rich men
In one poor suit. Brave barks [6] and out-
    ward gloss

[1] Vise.
[2] Deception.
[3] Capricious.

[4] Rich clothes.
[5] Abilities.
[6] Fine coverings.

Attract court loves, be in-parts ne'er
so gross.   110
Mon. Thou shalt have gloss enough, and
all things fit
T'enchase in all show thy long-smothered
spirit.
Be ruled by me then. The old Scythians
Painted blind Fortune's powerful hands
with wings.
To show her gifts come swift and sud-
denly,
Which, if her favorite be not swift to
take,
He loses them forever. Then be wise;
Stay but awhile here, and I'll send to
thee.
Exit Mon[sieur with Pages].   Manet[1]
Buss[y].
Bus. What will he send? Some crowns?
It is to sow them
Upon my spirit, and make them spring
a crown   120
Worth millions of the seed-crowns he
will send.
Like to disparking[2] noble husbandmen,
He'll put his plow into me, plow me up.
But his unsweating thrift is policy,
And learning-hating policy is ignorant
To fit his seed-land soil; a smooth plain
ground
Will never nourish any politic seed.
I am for honest actions, not for great.
If I may bring up a new fashion,
And rise in court for virtue, speed his
plow!   130
The king hath known me long as well
as he,
Yet could my fortune never fit the
length
Of both their understandings till this
hour.
There is a deep nick in Time's restless
wheel
For each man's good; when which nick
comes, it strikes;
As rhetoric yet works not persuasion,
But only is a mean to make it work,
So no man riseth by his real merit,
But when it cries "Clink"[3] in his rais-
er's spirit.
Many will say, that cannot rise at all, 140

Man's first hour's rise is first step to his
fall.
I'll venture that; men that fall low must
die,
As well as men cast headlong from the sky.

Ent[er] Maffé.

[Maf. (*Aside.*)] Humor of princes! Is this
wretch indued
With any merit worth a thousand
crowns?
Will my lord have me be so ill a steward
Of his revenue, to dispose a sum
So great with so small cause as shows in
him?
I must examine this.—Is your name
D'Ambois?
Bus. Sir?
Maf.   Is your name D'Ambois?
Bus.   Who have we here?   150
Serve you the Monsieur?
Maf.   How?
Bus.   Serve you the Monsieur?
Maf. Sir, y'are very hot. I do serve the
Monsieur,
But in such place as gives me the com-
mand[4]
Of all his other servants. And, because
His grace's pleasure is to give your good
His pass[5] through my command, me-
thinks you might
Use me with more respect.
Bus.   Cry you mercy![6]
Now you have opened my dull eyes, I
see you,
And would be glad to see the good you
speak of.
What might I call your name?
Maf.   Monsieur Maffé. 160
Bus. Monsieur Maffé? Then, good Mon-
sieur Maffé,
Pray let me know you better.
Maf.   Pray do so,
That you may use me better. For your-
self,
By your no better outside, I would judge
you
To be some poet. Have you given my
lord
Some pamphlet?

---

[1] Remains.
[2] Changing parks into open fields.
[3] "Now is the hour."

[4] At this point the original has the stage direction, "*Table, chessboard, and tapers behind the
arras,*" in preparation for the following scene.
[5] Passage.   [6] I beg your pardon!

Bus.   Pamphlet?

Maf.   Pamphlet, sir, I say.

Bus. Did your great master's goodness leave the good
That is to pass your charge to my poor use,
To your discretion?

Maf.   Though he did not, sir,
I hope 'tis no rude office to ask reason   170
How that [1] his grace gives me in charge, goes from me?

Bus. That's very perfect, sir.

Maf.   Why, very good, sir.
I pray then give me leave; if for no pamphlet,
May I not know what other merit in you
Makes his compunction willing to relieve you?

Bus. No merit in the world, sir.

Maf.   That is strange.
Y'are a poor soldier, are you?

Bus.   That I am, sir.

Maf. And have commanded?

Bus.   Ay, and gone without, sir.

Maf. [Aside.] I see the man; a hundred crowns will make him
Swagger and drink healths to his grace's bounty,   180
And swear he could not be more bountiful;
So there's nine hundred crowns saved.—
Here, tall [2] soldier,
His grace hath sent you a whole hundred crowns.

Bus. A hundred, sir? Nay, do his highness right;
I know his hand is larger, and perhaps
I may deserve more than my outside shows.
I am a poet, as I am a soldier,
And I can poetize; and, being well encouraged,
May sing his fame for giving, yours for delivering—
Like a most faithful steward—what he gives.   190

Maf. What shall your subject be?

Bus.   I care not much,
If to his bounteous grace I sing the praise
Of fair great noses, and to you of long ones. [3]

---

[1] That which.   [2] Brave.
[3] Monsieur's large nose was the object of much satire.

What qualities have you, sir, beside your chain
And velvet jacket? [4] Can your worship dance?

Maf. [Aside.] A pleasant fellow, faith.
It seems my lord
Will have him for his jester, and, by'r Lady,
Such men are now no fools; 'tis a knight's place.
If I, to save his grace some crowns, should urge him
T'abate his bounty, I should not be heard;   200
I would to heaven I were an arrant ass,
For then I should be sure to have the ears
Of these great men, where now their jesters have them.
'Tis good to please him, yet I'll take no notice
Of his preferment, but in policy
Will still be grave and serious, lest he think
I fear his wooden dagger.[5]—Here, Sir Ambo!

Bus. How, Ambo, sir?

Maf.   Ay, is not your name Ambo?

Bus. You called me lately D'Ambois.
Has your worship
So short a head?

Maf. I cry thee mercy, D'Ambois.   210
A thousand crowns I bring you from my lord.
If you be thrifty and [6] play the good husband,[7] you may make
This a good standing living. 'Tis a bounty
His highness might perhaps have bestowed better.

Bus. Go, y'are a rascal; hence, away, you rogue!

Maf. What mean you, sir?

Bus.   Hence! Prate no more,

---

[4] Emblems of a steward's office.
[5] Emblem of the jester.
[6] As Parrott points out, *If you be thrifty and* has been substituted for the better reading *Serve God* of the 1607 edn. "to avoid the penalty fixed by the law of 1606 for the abuse of the name of God in stage-plays." *Cf.* II, i, 207, for the omission of *Mort Dieu*, and V, i, 41, 61, where *Heaven* replaces *God* of the 1607 edn.
[7] *I.e.*, be economical.

Or, by thy villain's blood, thou prat'st
   thy last!
A barbarous groom grudge at his master's bounty!
But, since I know he would as much abhor
His hind should argue what he gives his
   friend,   220
Take that, sir, [*Strikes him.*] for your
   aptness to dispute.   *Exit.*
MAF. These crowns are set in blood; blood
   be their fruit!   *Exit.*

[SCENA SECUNDA.

A room in the court.]

Henry, Guise, Montsurry, Elenor, Tamyra,
  Beaupré, Pero, Charlotte, Pyra, Anna-
  belle. [*Henry and Guise are playing*
                chess.]

HEN. Duchess of Guise, your grace is much
   enriched
In the attendance of that English virgin,
That will initiate her prime of youth
(Disposed to court conditions) under the
   hand
Of your preferred instructions and com-
   mand,
Rather than any in the English court,
Whose ladies are not matched in Chris-
   tendom
For graceful and confirmed behaviors,
More than the court, where they are
   bred, is equaled.
GUISE. I like not their court fashion; it is
   too crestfallen   10
In all observance, making demigods
Of their great nobles, and of their old
   queen
An ever young and most immortal god-
   dess.
MONT. No question she's the rarest queen
   in Europe.
GUISE. But what's that to her immortal-
   ity?
HEN. Assure you, cousin Guise, so great a
   courtier,
So full of majesty and royal parts,
No queen in Christendom may vaunt
   herself.
Her court approves it, that's a court
   indeed,
Not mixed with clowneries used in com-
   mon houses,   20

But, as courts should be th' abstracts of
   their kingdoms
In all the beauty, state, and worth they
   hold,
So is hers, amply, and by her informed.[1]
The world is not contracted in a man
With more proportion and expression
Than in her court, her kingdom. Our
   French court
Is a mere mirror of confusion to it.
The king and subject, lord and every
   slave,
Dance a continual hay;[2] our rooms of
   state
Kept like our stables; no place more ob-
   served[3]   30
Than a rude market place; and, though
   our custom
Keep this assured confusion from our eyes,
'Tis ne'er the less essentially unsightly,
Which they would soon see, would they
   change their form
To this of ours, and then compare them
   both,
Which we must not affect, because in
   kingdoms
Where the king's change doth breed the
   subject's terror,
Pure innovation is more gross than error.
MONT. No question we shall see them im-
   itate,
Though afar off, the fashions of our
   courts,   40
As they have ever aped us in attire.
Never were men so weary of their skins,
And apt to leap out of themselves as
   they,
Who, when they travel[4] to bring forth
   rare men,
Come home, delivered of a fine French
   suit.
Their brains lie with their tailors, and
   get babies
For their most complete issue; he's sole
   heir
To all the moral virtues that first greets
The light with a new fashion, which be-
   comes them
Like apes, disfigured with the attires of
   men.   50
HEN. No question they much wrong their
   real worth

[1] Molded, fashioned.   [3] Respected.
[2] Country dance.   [4] With a pun on *travail.*

In affectation of outlandish scum;
But they have faults, and we more; they
foolish-proud
To jet [1] in others' plumes so haughtily;
We proud that they are proud of foolery,
Holding our worths more complete for
their vaunts.

Enter Monsieur, D'Ambois.

MON. Come, mine own sweetheart, [2] I will
enter [3] thee.—
Sir, I have brought a gentleman to court,
And pray you would vouchsafe to do him
grace.
HEN. D'Ambois, I think?
BUS.   That's still my name, my lord, 60
Though I be something altered in attire.
HEN. We like your alteration, and must
tell you
We have expected th' offer of your serv-
ice;
For we, in fear to make mild virtue
proud,
Use not to seek her out in any man.
BUS. Nor doth she use to seek out any
man.
They that will win must woo her [; she's
not shameless]. [4]
MON. [5] I urged her modesty in him, my
lord,
And gave her those rites that he says
she merits.
HEN. If you have wooed and won, then,
brother, wear him. 70
MON. Th' art mine, sweetheart. See, here's
the Guise's duchess,
The Countess of Montsurreau, Beaupré.
Come, I'll enseam [6] thee.—Ladies, y'are
too many
To be in council; I have here a friend
That I would gladly enter in your graces.
BUS. Save you, [7] ladies.
DUCH. If you enter him in our graces,
my lord, methinks by his blunt behavior he
should come out of himself.
TAM. Has he never been courtier, [80
my lord?

MON. Never, my lady.
BEAU. And why did the toy [8] take him
in th' head now?
BUS. 'Tis leap year, lady, and therefore
very good to enter a courtier.
HEN. Mark, Duchess of Guise, there is
one is not bashful.
DUCH. No, my lord, he is much guilty of
the bold extremity. 90
TAM. The man's a courtier at first sight.
BUS. I can sing pricksong, [9] lady, at
first sight; and why not be a courtier as
suddenly?
BEAU. Here's a courtier rotten before
he be ripe.
BUS. Think me not impudent, lady. I
am yet no courtier; I desire to be one, and
would gladly take entrance, [*To the Duchess.*] madam, under your princely colors.

Enter Barrisor, L'Anou, Pyrrhot.

DUCH. Soft, sir, you must rise by [101
degrees, first being the servant [10] of some
common lady or knight's wife; then a little
higher to a lord's wife; next a little higher
to a countess; yet a little higher to a duchess, and then turn the ladder. [11]
BUS. Do you allow a man, then, four
mistresses when the greatest mistress is
allowed but three servants? 109
DUCH. Where find you that statute, sir?
BUS. Why, be judged by the groom
porters. [12]
DUCH. The groom porters?
BUS. Ay, madam; must not they judge
of all gamings i' th' court?
DUCH. You talk like a gamester.
GUISE. [*Rising from the chess table.*] Sir,
know you me?
BUS. My lord?
GUISE. I know not you. Whom do [120
you serve?
BUS. Serve, my lord!
GUISE. Go to, companion, [13] your court-
ship's too saucy.
BUS. [*Aside.*] Saucy! Companion! 'Tis
the Guise, but yet those terms might have

---

[1] Strut.
[2] Merely a term of affectionate address.
[3] Introduce, be sponsor for.
[4] From 1607 edn.
[5] The following eight lines are printed as prose
in the original.
[6] Introduce.   [7] God save you.

[8] Whim.
[9] Music pricked or noted down as distinguished from extemporaneous music.
[10] Lover.
[11] *I.e.*, be hanged.
[12] Minor court officials in charge of gaming.
[13] Fellow.

been spared of the Guisard.[1] Companion!
He's jealous, by this light. Are you blind
of that side, duke? I'll to her again for
that.—Forth, princely mistress, for [130
the honor of courtship. Another riddle!

GUISE. Cease your courtship, or by
heaven I'll cut your throat.

BUS. Cut my throat? Cut a whetstone,
young Accius Nævius! Do as much with
your tongue as he did with a razor. Cut
my throat!

BAR. [Aside.] What newcome gallant
have we here, that dares mate[2] the Guise
thus?   140

L'AN. [Aside.] 'Sfoot,[3] 'tis D'Ambois.
The duke mistakes him, on my life, for
some knight of the new edition.[4]

BUS. Cut my throat! I would the king
feared thy cutting of his throat no more
than I fear thy cutting of mine.

GUISE. I'll do 't, by this hand.

BUS.[5] That hand dares not do 't. Y'ave
cut too many throats already, Guise, and
robbed the realm of many thousand [150
souls, more precious than thine own.—
Come, madam, talk on. 'Sfoot, can you not
talk? Talk on, I say. Another riddle!

PYR. Here's some strange distemper.

BAR. Here's a sudden transmigration
with D'Ambois—out of the Knight's
Ward[6] into the duchess' bed.

L'AN. See what a metamorphosis a
brave suit can work.

PYR. 'Slight, step to the Guise and [160
discover him.

BAR. By no means! Let the new suit
work; we'll see the issue.

GUISE. Leave your courting!

BUS. I will not.—I say, mistress, and I
will stand unto it, that, if a woman may
have three servants, a man may have three
score mistresses.

GUISE. Sirrah, I'll have you whipped
out of the court for this insolence.   170

BUS. Whipped? Such another syllable

---

[1] Follower of the Guise, with a probable pun
on gizzard, the throat.
[2] Checkmate, defy.
[3] God's foot.
[4] A reference to the recent creation of a number of knights by James I.
[5] Lines 148–53 and 241–44 are set as verse in
the original.
[6] Part of the Counter, a London prison for
debtors.

out o' th' presence,[7] if thou dar'st, for thy
dukedom!

GUISE. Remember, poltroon!
          [He returns to his game.]

MON. Pray thee, forbear.

BUS. Passion of death! Were not the
king here, he should strow the chamber
like a rush.

MON. But leave courting his wife, then.

BUS. I will not. I'll court her in [180
despite of him. Not court her!—Come,
madam, talk on, fear me nothing.—[To
Guise.] Well mayst thou drive thy master
from the court, but never D'Ambois.

MON. [Aside.] His great heart will not
          down. 'Tis like the sea,
That, partly by his own internal heat,
Partly the stars' daily and nightly mo-
          tion,
Their heat and light, and partly of the
          place,
The divers frames,[8] but chiefly by the
          moon,
Bristled with surges, never will be won
(No, not when th' hearts of all those
          powers are burst)   191
To make retreat into his settled home,
Till he be crowned with his own quiet
          foam.

HEN. You have the mate. Another?

GUISE. No more.   Flourish short.[9]
Exit Guise, after him the King, Mons[ieur]
          whispering.

BAR. Why, here's the lion, scared with
the throat of a dunghill cock, a fellow that
has newly shaked off his shackles; now
does he crow for that victory.

L'AN. 'Tis one of the best jigs that [200
ever was acted.

PYR. Whom does the Guise suppose him
to be, trow?[10]

L'AN. Out of doubt, some new deni-
zened[11] lord, and thinks that suit newly
drawn out a[12] th' mercer's books.

BAR. I have heard of a fellow that, by
a fixed imagination looking upon a bull-
baiting, had a visible pair of horns grew
out of his forehead; and I believe [210
this gallant, overjoyed with the conceit of

---

[7] Out of the king's presence. [9] Trumpet call.
[8] Perhaps the bed of the sea. [10] Think you.
[11] Naturalized, referring to James's new Scottish nobility.
[12] Of.

Monsieur's cast suit, imagines himself to be the Monsieur.

L'AN. And why not, as well as the ass, stalking in the lion's case,[1] bare himself like a lion, braying all the huger beasts out of the forest?

PYR. Peace, he looks this way.

BAR. Marry, let him look, sir. What will you say now if the Guise be gone to [220 fetch a blanket [2] for him?

L'AN. Faith, I believe it for his honor sake.

PYR. But, if D'Ambois carry it clean? [3]
Exeunt Ladies.

BAR. True, when he curvets in the blanket.

PYR. Ay, marry, sir.

L'AN. 'Sfoot, see how he stares on 's.

BAR. Lord bless us, let's away.

BUS. Now, sir, take your full view. [230 How does the object please ye?

BAR. If you ask my opinion, sir, I think your suit sits as well as if 't had been made for you.

BUS. So, sir, and was that the subject of your ridiculous jollity?

L'AN. What's that to you, sir?

BUS. Sir, I have observed all your fleer-ings, and resolve yourselves ye shall give a strict account for 't.   240

Enter Brisac, Melynell.

BAR. O, miraculous jealousy! [4] Do you think yourself such a singular subject for laughter that none can fall into the matter of our merriment but you?

L'AN. This jealousy of yours, sir, con-fesses some close defect in yourself that we never dreamed of.

PYR. We held discourse of a perfumed ass that, being disguised in a lion's case, im-agined himself a lion. I hope that [250 touched not you.

BUS. So, sir; your descants do mar-velous well fit this ground.[5]   We shall meet where your buffoonly laughters will cost ye the best blood in your bodies.

BAR. For life's sake let's be gone; he'll kill 's outright else.

BUS. Go, at your pleasures. I'll be your

ghost to haunt you; and ye sleep an 't,[6] hang me.   260

L'AN. Go, go, sir; court your mistress.

PYR. And, be advised, we shall have odds against you.

BUS. Tush! Valor stands not in num-ber; I'll maintain it that one man may beat three boys.

BRIS. Nay, you shall have no odds of him in number, sir; he's a gentleman as good as the proudest of you, and ye shall not wrong him.   270

BAR. Not, sir?

MEL. Not, sir. Though he be not so rich, he's a better man than the best of you, and I will not endure it.

L'AN. Not you, sir?

BRIS. No, sir, nor I.

BUS. I should thank you for this kind-ness, if I thought these perfumed musk cats, being out of this privilege, durst but once mew at us.   280

BAR. Does your confident spirit doubt that, sir?   Follow us and try.

L'AN. Come, sir, we'll lead you a dance.
Exeunt.

FINIS ACTUS PRIMI.

ACTUS SECUND[I]   SCENA PRIMA.

[A room in the court.]

*Henry, Guise, Montsurry, [Beaumond,]
and Attendants.*

HEN. This desperate quarrel sprung out of their envies
To D'Ambois' sudden bravery [7] and great spirit.

GUISE. Neither is worth their envy.

HEN.   Less than either
Will make the gall of Envy overflow.
She feeds on outcast entrails like a kite,
In which foul heap, if any ill lies hid,
She sticks her beak into it, shakes it up,
And hurls it all abroad, that all may view it.
Corruption is her nutriment; but touch her
With any precious ointment, and you kill her.   10
Where she finds any filth in men, she feasts,

---

[1] Skin.   [3] *I.e.*, get the better of him.
[2] To toss him.   [4] Suspicion.
[5] With an additional reference to music, mean-ing variations on a theme.

[6] If you sleep on it.
[7] Presumably here in the common sense of *finery*.

And with her black throat bruits it
   through the world,
Being sound and healthful; but, if she
   but taste
The slenderest pittance of commended
   virtue,
She surfeits of it, and is like a fly
That passes all the body's soundest parts,
And dwells upon the sores; or, if her
   squint eye
Have power to find none there, she forges
   some.
She makes that crooked ever which is
   straight;
Calls valor giddiness, justice tyranny. 20
A wise man may shun her, she not her-
   self;
Whithersoever she flies from her harms,
She bears her foes still clasped in her own
   arms.
And therefore, cousin Guise, let us avoid
   her.

Enter Nuntius.

Nun. What Atlas or Olympus lifts his
   head
So far past covert that with air enough
My words may be informed, and from
   their height
I may be seen and heard through all the
   world?
A tale so worthy and so fraught with
   wonder   29
Sticks in my jaws, and labors with event.
Hen. Com'st thou from D'Ambois?
Nun.   From him, and the rest,
   His friends and enemies, whose stern
   fight I saw,
And heard their words before and in the
   fray.
Hen. Relate at large what thou hast seen
   and heard.
Nun. I saw fierce D'Ambois and his two
   brave friends
Enter the field, and at their heels their
   foes,
Which were the famous soldiers, Bar-
   risor,
L'Anou, and Pyrrhot, great in deeds of
   arms;
All which arrived at the evenest piece of
   earth
The field afforded, the three challeng-
   ers   40

Turned head, drew all their rapiers, and
   stood ranked,
When face to face the three defendants
   met them,
Alike prepared, and resolute alike.
Like bonfires of contributory wood
Every man's look showed, fed with
   either's spirit,
As one had been a mirror to another,
Like forms of life and death, each took
   from other;
And so were life and death mixed at
   their heights
That you could see no fear of death, for
   life,
Nor love of life, for death; but in their
   brows   50
Pyrrho's opinion in great letters shone:
That life and death in all respects are one.
Hen. Passed there no sort of words at
   their encounter?
Nun. As Hector, twixt the hosts of Greece
   and Troy,
When Paris and the Spartan king should
   end
The nine years' war, held up his brazen
   lance
For signal that both hosts should cease
   from arms,
And hear him speak, so Barrisor, ad-
   vised,[1]
Advanced his naked rapier twixt both
   sides,
Ripped up[2] the quarrel, and compared
   six lives   60
Then laid in balance with six idle words;
Offered remission and contrition too;
Or else that he and D'Ambois might
   conclude
The others' dangers. D'Ambois liked the
   last;
But Barrisor's friends, being equally
   engaged
In the main quarrel, never would expose
His life alone to that they all deserved.
And, for the other offer of remission,
D'Ambois, that like a laurel put in fire
Sparkled and spit, did much, much more
   than scorn   70
That his wrong should incense him so like
   chaff
To go so soon out, and like lighted paper

---

[1] Cautious.
[2] Recalled the causes of.

Approve [1] his spirit at once both fire and ashes.

So drew they lots and in them Fates appointed

That Barrisor should fight with fiery D'Ambois,

Pyrrhot with Melynell, with Brisac, L'Anou.

And then like flame and powder they commixed

So spritely that I wished they had been spirits,

That the ne'er-shutting wounds they needs must open

Might, as they opened, shut and never kill.   80

But D'Ambois' sword, that lightened as it flew,

Shot like a pointed comet at the face

Of manly Barrisor; and there it stuck.

Thrice plucked he at it, and thrice drew on thrusts

From him that of himself was free as fire;

Who thrust still as he plucked, yet, past belief,

He with his subtle eye, hand, body, scaped.

At last, the deadly-bitten point tugged off,

On fell his yet undaunted foe so fiercely

That, only made more horrid with his wound,   90

Great D'Ambois shrunk, and gave a little ground;

But soon returned, redoubled in [2] his danger,

And at the heart of Barrisor sealed his anger.

Then, as in Arden I have seen an oak

Long shook with tempests, and his lofty top

Bent to his root, which being at length made loose,

Even groaning with his weight, he gan to nod

This way and that, as loath his curléd brows,

Which he had oft wrapped in the sky with storms,

Should stoop; and yet, his radical fibers burst,   100

Stormlike he fell, and hid the fear-cold earth,

So fell stout Barrisor, that had stood the shocks

Of ten set battles in your highness' war

Gainst the sole soldier of the world, Navarre.

GUISE. O, piteous and horrid murther!

BEAUM.   Such a life

Methinks had metal in it to survive

An age of men.

HEN.   Such often soonest end.—

Thy felt report calls on; [3] we long to know

On what events the other have arrived.

NUN. Sorrow and fury, like two opposite fumes   110

Met in the upper region of a cloud,

At the report made by this worthy's fall,

Brake from the earth, and with them rose Revenge,

Ent'ring with fresh powers his two noble friends;

And under that odds fell surcharged [4] Brisac,

The friend of D'Ambois, before fierce L'Anou;

Which D'Ambois seeing, as I once did see

In my young travels through Armenia

An angry unicorn in his full career

Charge with too swift a foot a jeweler   120

That watched him for the treasure of his brow, [5]

And, ere he could get shelter of a tree,

Nail him with his rich antler to the earth,

So D'Ambois ran upon revenged L'Anou,

Who, eying th' eager point borne in his face,

And giving back, fell back, and in his fall

His foe's uncurbéd sword stopped in his heart;

By which time all the lifestrings of the tw' other

Were cut, and both fell as their spirit[s] flew

Upwards, and still hunt honor at the view. [6]   130

And now, of all the six, sole D'Ambois stood

[1] Prove.   [2] Coming a second time into.

[3] Thy affecting report calls for more.
[4] Overpowered.
[5] *I.e.*, his horn.
[6] Like dogs that have sighted the quarry.

Untouched, save only with the others'
    blood.

HEN. All slain outright but he?

NUN.   All slain outright but he,
Who, kneeling in the warm life of his
    friends,
All freckled with the blood his rapier
    rained,
He kissed their pale lips, and bade both
    farewell—
And see the bravest man the French
    earth bears!

Enter Monsieur, D'Amb[ois] bare.

BUS. Now is the time. Y'are princely
    vowed my friend;
Perform it princely, and obtain my
    pardon.

MON. Else heaven forgive not me! Come
    on, brave friend!— [*They kneel.*] 140
If ever nature held herself her own,
When the great trial of a king and sub-
    ject
Met in one blood, both from one belly
    springing,
Now prove her virtue and her greatness
    one,
Or make the t' one the greater with the
    tother,
As true kings should, and for your
    brother's love,
Which is a special species of true virtue,
Do that you could not do, not being a
    king.

HEN. Brother, I know your suit; these
    willful murthers
Are ever past our pardon.

MON.   Manly slaughter 150
Should never bear th' account of willful
    murther,
It being a spice ¹ of justice, where with life
Offending past law, equal life is laid
In equal balance, to scourge that offense
By law of reputation, which to men
Exceeds all positive law; and what that
    leaves
To true men's valors, not prefixing rights
Of satisfaction, suited to their wrongs,
A free man's eminence may supply and
    take.

HEN. This would make every man that
    thinks him wronged   160
Or is offended, or in wrong or right,

¹ Sort.

Lay on this violence, and all vaunt them-
    selves
Law-menders and suppliers, though mere
    butchers.
Should this fact, though of justice, be
    forgiven?

MON. O, no, my lord; it would make
    cowards fear
To touch the reputations of true men
When only they are left to imp ² the law.
Justice will soon distinguish murtherous
    minds
From just revengers.   Had my friend
    been slain,
His enemy surviving, he should die,   170
Since he had added to a murthered
    fame,
Which was in his intent, a murthered
    man,
And this had worthily been willful mur-
    ther.
But my friend only saved his fame's dear
    life,
Which is above life, taking th' under
    value,
Which, in the wrong it did, was forfeit
    to him;
And in this fact only preserves a man
In his uprightness, worthy to survive
Millions of such as murther men alive.

HEN. Well, brother, rise, and raise your
    friend withal   180
From death to life. And, D'Ambois, let
    your life,
Refined by passing through this merited
    death,
Be purged from more such foul pollution,
Nor on your scape nor valor more pre-
    suming
To be again so daring.

BUS.   My lord,
I loathe as much a deed of unjust death
As law itself doth, and to tyrannize,
Because I have a little spirit to dare
And power to do, as to be tyrannized.
This is a grace that, on my knees re-
    doubled, ³   190
I crave to double this, my short life's gift,
And shall your royal bounty centuple,
That I may so make good what law and
    nature
Have given me for my good; since I am
    free,

² Piece out.   ³ Rekneeling.

Offending no just law, let no law make,
By any wrong it does, my life her slave.
When I am wronged, and that law fails
　to right me,
Let me be king myself, as man was made,
And do a justice that exceeds the law;
If my wrong pass the power of single
　valor　　　　　　　　　　　　　　　200
To right and expiate, then be you my
　king,
And do a right, exceeding law and nature.
Who to himself is law, no law doth need,
Offends no law, and is a king indeed.

HEN. Enjoy what thou entreat'st; we give
　but ours.

BUS. What you have given, my lord, is
　ever yours.

Exit Rex [1] *cum Beau[mond, Attendants,
　　　Nuntius, and Montsurry].*

GUISE. [*Mort Dieu!*] [2]　Who would have
　pardoned such a murther?　　　*Exit.*

MON. Now vanish horrors into court at-
　tractions,
For which let this balm make thee fresh
　and fair.
And now forth with thy service to the
　duchess,　　　　　　　　　　　　210
As my long love will to Montsurry's
　countess.　　　　　　　　　　　　*Exit.*

BUS. To whom my love hath long been
　vowed in heart,
Although in hand for show I held the
　duchess.
And now through blood and vengeance,
　deeds of height
And hard to be achieved, 'tis fit I make
Attempt of her perfection. I need fear
No check in his rivality,[3] since her virtues
Are so renowned, and he of all dames
　hated.　　　　　　　　　　　　　*Exit.*

[SCENA SECUNDA.

A room in Montsurry's house.]

*Enter Monsieur, Tamyra, and Pero with a
　　　　book.*

MON. Pray thee regard thine own good, if
　not mine,
And cheer my love for that. You do not
　know

───
[1] King.
[2] God's death! From 1607 edn.; omitted in
the original.
[3] Rivalry.

What you may be by me, nor what with-
　out me;
I may have power t' advance and pull
　down any.

TAM. That's not my study. One way I am
　sure
You shall not pull down me; my hus-
　band's height
Is crown to all my hopes, and his retiring
To any mean state shall be my aspiring.
Mine honor's in mine own hands, spite
　of kings.

MON. Honor, what's that? Your second
　maidenhead!　　　　　　　　　10
And what is that? A word. The word is
　gone;
The thing remains. The rose is plucked;
　the stalk
Abides. An easy loss where no lack's
　found!
Believe it, there's as small lack in the loss
As there is pain i' th' losing. Archers ever
Have two strings to a bow, and shall
　great Cupid,
Archer of archers both in men and
　women,
Be worse provided than a common
　archer?
A husband and a friend all wise wives
　have.

TAM. Wise wives they are that on such
　strings depend,　　　　　　　　20
With a firm husband joining a loose
　friend!

MON. Still you stand on your husband; so
　do all
The common sex of you, when y'are
　encountered
With one ye cannot fancy. All men know
You live in court here by your own
　election,
Frequenting all our common sports and
　triumphs,
All the most youthful company of men.
And wherefore do you this? To please
　your husband?
'Tis gross and fulsome. If your husband's
　pleasure
Be all your object, and you aim at
　honor　　　　　　　　　　　　30
In living close to him, get you from
　court;
You may have him at home. These
　common put-offs

For common women serve: "My honor!
  Husband!"
Dames maritorious [1] ne'er were meri-
  torious.
Speak plain and say, "I do not like you,
  sir;
Y'are an ill-favored fellow in my eye,"
And I am answered.

TAM.   Then, I pray, be answered;
For in good faith, my lord, I do not like
  you
In that sort you like.

MON.   Then have at you, here!
Take, with a politic hand, this rope
  of pearl,   40
And, though you be not amorous, yet be
  wise.
Take me for wisdom; he that you can love
Is ne'er the further from you.

TAM.   Now it comes
So ill prepared that I may take a poison
Under a medicine as good cheap [2] as it;
I will not have it were it worth the world.

MON. Horror of death! Could I but please
  your eye,
You would give me the like ere you
  would lose [3] me.
"Honor and husband!"

TAM.   By this light, my lord,
Y'are a vile fellow, and I'll tell the
  king   50
Your occupation of dishonoring ladies
And of his court. A lady cannot live
As she was born, and with that sort of
  pleasure
That fits her state, but she must be
  defamed
With an infamous lord's detraction.
Who would endure the court if these
  attempts
Of open and professed lust must be
  borne?—
Who's there? Come on, dame; you are
  at your book
When men are at your mistress. Have I
  taught you
Any such waiting-woman's quality?   60

MON. Farewell, good "husband."
                      Exit Mons[ieur].

TAM.   Farewell, wicked lord.

---

[1] Excessively fond of their husbands.
[2] Cheaply, readily.
[3] The original spelling *loose* carries a possible
meaning.

Enter Mont[surry].

MONT. Was not the Monsieur here?

TAM.   Yes, to good purpose;
And your cause is as good to seek him too,
And haunt his company.

MONT.   Why, what's the matter?

TAM. Matter of death, were I some hus-
  bands' wife.
I cannot live at quiet in my chamber
For opportunities [4] almost to rapes
Offered me by him.

MONT.   Pray thee bear with him.
Thou know'st he is a bachelor and a
  courtier,
Ay, and a prince; and their preroga-
  tives   70
Are to their laws as to their pardons are
Their reservations, after parliaments—
One quits another; form gives all their
  essence.
That prince doth high in virtue's reck-
  oning stand
That will entreat a vice, and not com-
  mand.
So far bear with him; should another man
Trust to his privilege, he should trust
  to death.
Take comfort, then, my comfort; nay,
  triumph
And crown thyself; thou part'st [5] with
  victory.
My presence is so only dear to thee   80
That other men's appear worse than
  they be.
For this night yet, bear with my forcéd
  absence;
Thou know'st my business, and with
  how much weight
My vow hath charged it.

TAM.   True, my lord, and never
My fruitless love shall let [6] your serious
  honor;
Yet, sweet lord, do not stay; you know
  my soul
Is so long time without me, and I dead,
As you are absent.

MONT.   By this kiss, receive
My soul for hostage till I see my love.

TAM. The morn shall let me see you?

MONT.   With the sun 90
I'll visit thy more comfortable beauties.

---

[4] Importunities.
[5] Depart'st, com'st off.
[6] Hinder.

TAM. This is my comfort, that the sun hath left

The whole world's beauty ere my sun leaves me.

MONT. 'Tis late night now indeed; farewell, my light!   *Exit.*

TAM. Farewell, my light and life!—[*Aside.*] But not in him,

In mine own dark love and light bent to another.

Alas, that in the wave [1] of our affections

We should supply it with a full dissembling,

In which each youngest maid is grown a mother.

Frailty is fruitful; one sin gets another.   100

Our loves like sparkles are that brightest shine

When they go out; most vice shows most divine.—

Go, maid, to bed; lend me your book, I pray—

Not, like yourself, for form; I'll this night trouble

None of your services. Make sure the doors,

And call your other fellows to their rest.

PER. I will.—[*Aside.*] Yet I will watch to know why you watch.   *Exit.*

TAM. Now all ye peaceful regents of the night,

Silently gliding exhalations,

Languishing winds and murmuring falls of waters,   110

Sadness of heart and ominous secureness,

Enchantments, dead sleeps, all the friends of rest,

That ever wrought upon the life of man,

Extend your utmost strengths, and this charmed hour

Fix like the center.[2] Make the violent wheels

Of Time and Fortune stand, and great Existence,

The Maker's treasury, now not seem to be,

To all but my approaching friends and me!

They come, alas, they come! Fear, fear and hope

Of one thing, at one instant fight in me;   120

I love what most I loathe, and cannot live

Unless I compass that which holds my death;

For life's mere death, loving one that loathes me,

And he I love will loathe me, when he sees

I fly my sex, my virtue, my renown,

To run so madly on a man unknown.

                              The vault opens.[3]

See, see, a vault is opening that was never

Known to my lord and husband, nor to any

But him that brings the man I love, and me.

How shall I look on him? How shall I live,   130

And not consume in blushes? I will in,

And cast myself off, as I ne'er had been.[4]

                                            Exit.

Ascendit Friar and D'Ambois.

FRI. Come, worthiest son, I am past measure glad

That you, whose worth I have approved so long,

Should be the object of her fearful love,

Since both your wit and spirit can adapt

Their full force to supply her utmost weakness.

You know her worths and virtues, for report

Of all that know is to a man a knowledge;

You know, besides, that our affections' storm,   140

Raised in our blood, no reason can reform.

Though she seek then their satisfaction,

Which she must needs, or rest unsatisfied,

Your judgment will esteem her peace thus wrought,

Nothing less dear than if yourself had sought;

---

[1] Wavering. Dilke suggests *wane*.
[2] Center of the earth.
[3] This direction follows l. 123 in the original.
[4] Undress as if I had never been here (?); completely cast off my old self (?).

And with another color,[1] which my art
Shall teach you to lay on, yourself must
    seem
The only agent, and the first orb [2] move
In this our set and cunning world of
    love.
Bus. Give me the color, my most hon-
    ored father,   150
And trust my cunning then to lay it on.
Fri. 'Tis this, good son.   Lord Barrisor,
    whom you slew,
Did love her dearly, and with all fit
    means
Hath urged his acceptation, of all which
She keeps one letter written in his blood.
You must say thus, then, that you
    heard from me
How much herself was touched in con-
    science
With a report, which is in truth dis-
    persed,
That your main quarrel grew about her
    love,   159
Lord Barrisor imagining your courtship
Of the great Guise's duchess in the pres-
    ence
Was by you made to his elected mistress;
And so made me your mean now to re-
    solve her,[3]
Choosing, by my direction, this night's
    depth
For the more clear avoiding of all note
Of your presuméd presence; and with
    this,
To clear her hands of such a lover's blood,
She will so kindly thank and entertain
    you—
Methinks I see how—ay, and ten to one,
Show you the confirmation in his blood,
Lest you should think report and she
    did feign,   171
That you shall so have circumstantial
    means
To come to the direct, which must be
    used;
For the direct is crooked; love comes
    flying;
The height of love is still won with deny-
    ing.
Bus. Thanks, honored father.

¹ Pretense.
² *Primum mobile*, the sphere which, according
to the Ptolemaic system, set the other spheres
in motion.   ³ Explain to her.

Fri.   She must never know
That you know anything of any love
Sustained on her part; for, learn this of
    me,
In anything a woman does alone,
If she dissemble, she thinks 'tis not
    done;   180
If not dissemble, nor a little chide,
Give her her wish, she is not satisfied.
To have a man think that she never
    seeks,
Does her more good than to have all she
    likes.
This frailty sticks in them beyond their
    sex,
Which to reform, reason is too perplex.[4]
Urge reason to them, it will do no good;
Humor, that is the chariot of our food
In everybody, must in them be fed,
To carry their affections by it bred. 190
Stand close.   [*They withdraw.*]

            Enter Tamyra with a book.

Tam. Alas, I fear my strangeness will re-
    tire him.
If he go back, I die; I must prevent it,
And cheer his onset with my sight at
    least,
And that's the most.   Though every step
    he takes
Goes to my heart, I'll rather die than
    seem
Not to be strange to that I most esteem.
Fri. [*Advancing.*] Madam!
Tam.   Ah!
Fri.   You will
    pardon me, I hope,
That so beyond your expectation,
And at a time for visitants so unfit, 200
I, with my noble friend here, visit you.
You know that my access at any time
Hath ever been admitted; and that friend
That my care will presume to bring with
    me
Shall have all circumstance of worth in
    him
To merit as free welcome as myself.
Tam. O father!   But at this suspicious
    hour
You know how apt best men are to sus-
    pect us
In any cause that makes suspicious
    shadow

⁴ Intricate.

No greater than the shadow of a hair; 210
And y'are to blame. What though my
　　lord and husband
Lie forth tonight, and, since I cannot
　　sleep
When he is absent, I sit up tonight;
Though all the doors are sure, and all
　　our servants
As sure bound with their sleeps, yet
　　there is One
That wakes above, whose eye no sleep
　　can bind.
He sees through doors, and darkness, and
　　our thoughts;
And therefore, as we should avoid with
　　fear
To think amiss ourselves before his
　　search,
So should we be as curious [1] to shun　220
All cause that other think not ill of us.
Bus. Madam, 'tis far from that; I only
　　heard
By this my honored father that your
　　conscience
Made some deep scruple with a false
　　report
That Barrisor's blood should something
　　touch your honor,
Since he imagined I was courting you
When I was bold to change words with
　　the duchess,
And therefore made his quarrel, his long
　　love
And service, as I hear, being deeply
　　vowed
To your perfections, which my ready
　　presence,　　　　　　　　　　230
Presumed on with my father at this
　　season
For the more care of your so curious
　　honor,
Can well resolve [2] your conscience is most
　　false.
Tam. And is it therefore that you come,
　　good sir?
Then crave I now your pardon and my
　　father's,
And swear your presence does me so
　　much good
That all I have it binds to your requital.
Indeed, sir, 'tis most true that a report
Is spread, alleging that his love to me
Was reason of your quarrel, and, because

You shall not think I feign it for my
　　glory　　　　　　　　　　　　241
That he importuned me for his court
　　service,[3]
I'll show you his own hand, set down in
　　blood
To that vain purpose. Good sir, then
　　come in.
Father, I thank you now a thousandfold.
　　　　　Exit Tamyra and D'Amb[ois].
Fri. May it be worth it to you, honored
　　daughter.　　　　*Descendit Friar*.

FINIS ACTUS SECUNDI.

ACTUS TERTII　SCENA PRIMA.

[*A room in Montsurry's house*.]

*Enter D'Ambois, Tamyra, with a chain of
　　　　　　　　　　　　　　pearl*.

Bus. Sweet mistress, cease! Your con-
　　science is too nice,[4]
And bites too hotly of the Puritan spice.
Tam. O, my dear servant, in thy close
　　embraces
I have set open all the doors of danger
To my encompassed honor and my life.
Before, I was secure against death and
　　hell,
But now am subject to the heartless fear
Of every shadow and of every breath,
And would change firmness with an as-
　　pen leaf;
So confident a spotless conscience is,　10
So weak a guilty. O, the dangerous siege
Sin lays about us, and the tyranny
He exercises when he hath expunged! [5]
Like to the horror of a winter's thunder,
Mixed with a gushing storm, that suffer
　　nothing
To stir abroad on earth but their own
　　rages,
Is Sin, when it hath gathered head above
　　us.
No roof, no shelter can secure us so,
But he will drown our cheeks in fear or
　　woe.　　　　　　　　　　　　19
Bus. Sin is a coward, madam, and insults
But on [6] our weakness, in his truest valor;

---

[1] Careful.　　　　　　　　　[2] Assure.
[3] *I.e.*, to accept him as courtly lover.
[4] Scrupulous, squeamish.
[5] Attacked successfully, been victorious.
[6] Merely exults scornfully over.

And so our ignorance tames us, that we let

His shadows fright us; and like empty clouds,

In which our faulty apprehensions forge

The forms of dragons, lions, elephants,

When they hold no proportion,[1] the sly charms

Of the witch, Policy, makes him like a monster

Kept only to show men for servile money.

That false hag often paints him in her cloth

Ten times more monstrous than he is in troth.   30

In three of us, the secret of our meeting

Is only guarded, and three friends as one

Have ever been esteemed, as our three powers

That in one soul are as one united.

Why should we fear then? For myself I swear

Sooner shall torture be the sire to pleasure,

And health be grievous to one long-time sick,

Than the dear jewel of your fame in me

Be made an outcast to your infamy;

Nor shall my value (sacred to your virtues)   40

Only give free course to it, from myself,

But make it fly out of the mouths of kings

In golden vapors and with awful wings.

TAM. It rests as all kings' seals were set in thee.[2]

Now let us call my father, whom I swear

I could extremely chide, but that I fear

To make him so suspicious of my love,

Of which, sweet servant, do not let him know

For all the world.

BUS.   Alas, he will not think it!

TAM. Come, then.—Ho, father, ope, and take your friend.   50

Ascendit Friar.

FRI. Now, honored daughter, is your doubt resolved?

TAM. Ay, father, but you went away too soon.

FRI. Too soon?

---

[1] Resemblance.

[2] *I.e.*, it remains inviolable.

TAM.   Indeed you did; you should have stayed.

Had not your worthy friend been of your bringing—

And that contains all laws to temper me—

Not all the fearful danger that besieged us

Had awed my throat from exclamation.

FRI. I know your serious disposition well.

Come, son, the morn comes on.

BUS.   Now, honored mistress,

Till farther service call, all bliss supply you!   60

TAM. And you this chain of pearl, and my love only!

          Descendit Friar and D'Amb[ois].

It is not I, but urgent destiny,

That (as great statesmen for their general end,

In politic justice, make poor men offend)

Enforceth my offense to make it just.

What shall weak dames do, when th' whole work of nature

Hath a strong finger in each one of us?

Needs must that sweep away the silly cobweb

Of our still undone labors, that lays still

Our powers to it; as to the line, the stone,   70

Not to the stone, the line should be opposed.

We cannot keep our constant course in virtue.

What is alike at all parts? Every day

Differs from other—every hour and minute,

Ay, every thought in our false clock of life

Ofttimes inverts the whole circumference.

We must be sometimes one, sometimes another.

Our bodies are but thick clouds to our souls,

Through which they cannot shine when they desire.

When all the stars, and even the sun himself,   80

Must stay the vapors' times that he exhales

Before he can make good his beams to us,

O, how can we, that are but motes to him,

Wand'ring at random in his ordered rays,

Disperse our passions' fumes, with our
weak labors,
That are more thick and black than all
earth's vapors?

Enter Mont[surry].

Mont. Good day, my love! What, up and
ready [1] too?
Tam. Both, my dear lord; not all this
night made I
Myself unready, or could sleep a wink.
Mont. Alas, what troubled my true love,
my peace,   90
From being at peace within her better
self?
Or how could sleep forbear to seize thine
eyes
When he might challenge them as his just
prize?
Tam. I am in no power earthly, but in
yours.
To what end should I go to bed, my lord,
That wholly missed the comfort of my
bed?
Or how should sleep possess my faculties,
Wanting the proper closer of mine eyes?
Mont. Then will I never more sleep night
from thee.
All mine own business, all the king's
affairs,   100
Shall take the day to serve them; every
night
I'll ever dedicate to thy delight.
Tam. Nay, good my lord, esteem not my
desires
Such doters on their humors that my
judgment
Cannot subdue them to your worthier
pleasure;
A wife's pleased husband must her object
be
In all her acts, not her soothed fantasy.
Mont. Then come, my love, now pay
those rites to sleep
Thy fair eyes owe him. Shall we now to
bed?   109
Tam. O, no, my lord; your holy friar says
All couplings in the day that touch the
bed
Adulterous are, even in the marriéd;
Whose grave and worthy doctrine, well
I know,
Your faith in him will liberally allow.

[1] Dressed.

Mont. He's a most learned and religious
man.
Come to the presence then, and see great
D'Ambois
(Fortune's proud mushroom shot up in
a night)
Stand like an Atlas under our king's arm;
Which greatness with him Monsieur
now envies
As bitterly and deadly as the Guise. 120
Tam. What, he that was but yesterday
his maker,
His raiser and preserver?
Mont.   Even the same.
Each natural agent works but to this end,
To render that it works on like itself;
Which, since the Monsieur in his act
on D'Ambois
Cannot to his ambitious end effect,
But that, quite opposite, the king hath
power,
In his love borne to D'Ambois, to convert
The point of Monsieur's aim on his own
breast,
He turns his outward love to inward
hate.   130
A prince's love is like the lightning's
fume,
Which no man can embrace, but must
consume.   *Exeunt.*

[Scena Secunda.

A room in the court.]

*Henry, D'Ambois, Monsieur, Guise, Duchess,
Annabelle, Charlotte, Attendants.*

Hen. Speak home, Bussy! Thy impartial
words
Are like brave falcons that dare truss [2]
a fowl
Much greater than themselves. Flatterers are kites
That check at [3] sparrows; thou shalt be
my eagle,
And bear my thunder underneath thy
wings.
Truth's words like jewels hang in th'
ears of kings.
Bus. Would I might live to see no Jews
hang there
Instead of jewels—sycophants, I mean,
Who use Truth like the devil, his true
foe,

[2] Seize.   [3] Pursue.

Cast by the angel to the pit of fears,   10
And bound in chains; Truth seldom decks
     kings' ears.
Slave Flattery (like a rippier's [1] legs
     rolled up
In boots of hay ropes) with kings' soothéd
     guts
Swaddled and strappled,[2] now lives only
     free.
O, 'tis a subtle knave; how like the
     plague
Unfelt he strikes into the brain of man,
And rageth in his entrails, when he can,
Worse than the poison of a red-haired
     man! [3]
HEN. Fly at him and his brood! I cast
     thee off,[4]
And once more give thee surname of
     mine eagle.   20
BUS. I'll make you sport enough, then;
     let me have
My lucerns [5] too, or dogs inured to hunt
Beasts of most rapine, but to put them
     up,[6]
And, if I truss not, let me not be trusted.
Show me a great man (by the people's
     voice,
Which is the voice of God) that by his
     greatness
Bombasts [7] his private roofs with public
     riches;
That affects royalty, rising from a clap-
     dish; [8]
That rules so much more by his suffering
     king [9]
That he makes kings of his subordinate
     slaves;   30
Himself and them graduate [10] (like wood-
     mongers,
Piling a stack of billets) from the earth,
Raising each other into steeples' heights;
Let him convey this on the turning
     props
Of Protean law, and, his own counsel
     keeping,[11]

[1] Fishmonger's.
[2] Strapped.
[3] Judas was supposed to have had red hair;
hence, a traitor.
[4] Release thee for flight.
[5] Properly lynxes; here, hunting dogs.
[6] Start them from cover.
[7] Stuffs out.   [9] By his king's sufferance.
[8] Beggar's dish.   [10] Rise by steps.
[11] Perhaps referring to the keeping of a private
lawyer.

Keep all upright—let me but hawk at
     him,
I'll play the vulture, and so thump his
     liver
That, like a huge, unlading argosy,
He shall confess all, and you then may
     hang him.
Show me a clergyman that is in voice   40
A lark of heaven, in heart a mole of
     earth;
That hath good living, and a wicked life;
A temperate look, and a luxurious gut;
Turning the rents of his superfluous
     cures [12]
Into your pheasants and your partridges;
Venting their quintessence as men read
     Hebrew[13]—
Let me but hawk at him, and, like the
     other,
He shall confess all, and you then may
     hang him.
Show me a lawyer that turns sacred law
(The equal rend'rer of each man his
     own,   50
The scourge of rapine and extortion,
The sanctuary and impregnable defense
Of retired learning and besiegéd virtue)
Into a harpy, that eats all but 's own,
Into the damnéd sins it punisheth,
Into the synagogue of thieves and athe-
     ists,
Blood into gold, and justice into lust—
Let me but hawk at him as at the rest,
He shall confess all, and you then may
     hang him.

Enter Montsurry, Tamyra, and Pero.

GUISE. Where will you find such game as
     you would hawk at?   60
BUS. I'll hawk about your house for one
     of them.
GUISE. Come, y'are a glorious [14] ruffian,
     and run proud
Of [15] the king's headlong graces. Hold
     your breath,
Or, by that poisoned vapor, not the king
Shall back your murtherous valor against
     me.
BUS. I would the king would make his
     presence free

[12] Income of his supplementary parishes.
[13] *I.e.*, backwards.
[14] Boastful.
[15] On account of.

But for one bout betwixt us; by the
　reverence
Due to the sacred space twixt kings
　and subjects,
Here would I make thee cast that
　popular purple,
In which thy proud soul sits and braves
　thy sovereign.　　　　　　　　70
Mon. Peace, peace, I pray thee, peace!
Bus.　　　　　　　Let him peace first
That made the first war.
Mon.　　　　　　He's the better man.
Bus. And therefore may do worst?
Mon.　　　　　　He has more titles.
Bus. So Hydra had more heads.
Mon.　　　　　　He's greater known.
Bus. His greatness is the people's; mine's
　mine own.
Mon. He's nobly [1] born.
Bus.　　　　　He is not; I am noble.
And noblesse in his [2] blood hath no
　gradation
But in his merit.
Guise.　　　　Th' art not nobly born,
But bastard to the Cardinal of Ambois.
Bus. Thou liest, proud Guisard. Let me
　fly, my lord!　　　　　　　80
Hen. Not in my face, my eagle; violence
　flies
The sanctuaries of a prince's eyes.
Bus. Still shall we chide and foam upon
　this bit?
Is the Guise only great in faction?
Stands he not by himself? Proves he
　th' opinion
That men's souls are without them? Be
　a duke,
And lead me to the field.
Guise.　　　　　　　Come, follow me
Hen. Stay them! Stay, D'Ambois! Cousin
　Guise, I wonder
Your honored disposition brooks so ill
A man so good, that only would uphold
Man in his native noblesse, from whose
　fall　　　　　　　　　　91
All our dissensions rise; that in himself
(Without the outward patches of our
　frailty,
Riches and honor) knows he compre-
　hends
Worth with the greatest. Kings had
　never borne
Such boundless empire over other men,

Had all maintained the spirit and state
　of D'Ambois;
Nor had the full impartial hand of
　Nature,
That all things gave in her original [3]
Without these definite terms of "mine"
　and "thine,"　　　　　　　100
Been turned unjustly to the hand of
　Fortune,
Had all preserved her in her prime, like
　D'Ambois.
No envy, no disjunction had dissolved,
Or plucked one stick out of the golden
　faggot
In which the world of Saturn [4] bound
　our lives,
Had all been held together with the
　nerves,
The genius, and th' ingenious soul of
　D'Ambois.
Let my hand therefore be the Hermean
　rod [5]
To part and reconcile, and so conserve
　you,
As my combined embracers and sup-
　porters.　　　　　　　　110
Bus. 'Tis our king's motion,[6] and we shall
　not seem
To worst eyes womanish, though we
　change thus soon
Never so great grudge for his greater
　pleasure.
Guise. I seal to that; and, so the manly
　freedom
That you so much profess, hereafter
　prove not
A bold and glorious license to deprave,[7]
To me his hand shall hold the Hermean
　virtue
His grace affects, in which submissive
　sign
On this his sacred right hand I lay mine.
Bus. 'Tis well, my lord, and, so your
　worthy greatness　　　　　120
Decline not to the greater insolence,
Nor make you think it a prerogative
To rack men's freedoms with the ruder
　wrongs,
My hand (stuck full of laurel, in true
　sign
'Tis wholly dedicate to righteous peace)

[1] Boas emends to *noblier*.　　　　　[2] Its.

[3] In the beginning.　　　　[6] Desire, proposal.
[4] The fabled Golden Age.　　[7] Vilify.
[5] Caduceus.

In all submission kisseth th' other side.
Hen. Thanks to ye both; and kindly I
    invite ye
Both to a banquet, where we'll sacrifice
Full cups to confirmation of your loves—
At which, fair ladies, I entreat your
    presence,   130
And hope you, madam, will take one
    carouse
For reconcilement of your lord and
    servant.
Duch. If I should fail, my lord, some
    other lady
Would be found there to do that for
    my servant.
Mon. Any of these here?
Duch.   Nay, I know not that.
Bus. [To Tamyra.] Think your thoughts
    like my mistress', honored lady?
Tam. I think not on you, sir; y'are one I
    know not.
Bus. Cry you mercy, madam!
Mont.   O, sir, has she met you?
    Exeunt Henry, D'Amb[ois], Ladies.
Mon. What had my bounty drunk when
    it raised him?
Guise. Y'ave stuck us up a very worthy
    flag,   140
That takes more wind than we with all
    our sails.
Mon. O, so he spreads and flourishes.
Guise.   He must down;
Upstarts should never perch too near
    a crown.
Mon. 'Tis true, my lord; and as this dot-
    ing hand,
Even out of earth, like Juno, struck
    this giant,
So Jove's great ordinance [1] shall be here
    implied
To strike him under th' Etna of his pride,
To which work lend your hands, and
    let us cast
Where we may set snares for his ranging
    greatness.
I think it best amongst our greatest
    women;   150
For there is no such trap to catch an up-
    start
As a loose downfall, for you know their
    falls
Are th' ends of all men's rising. If
    great men

[1] Ordnance, thunderbolt.

And wise make scapes to please ad-
    vantage,[2]
'Tis with a woman. Women, that worst
    may,
Still hold men's candles:[3] they direct
    and know
All things amiss in all men; and their
    women,[4]
All things amiss in them, through whose
    charmed mouths
We may see all the close [5] scapes of the
    court.
When the most royal beast of chase,
    the hart,   160
Being old and cunning in his lairs and
    haunts,
Can never be discovered to the bow,
The piece,[6] or hound, yet where, behind
    some queach,[7]
He breaks his gall, and rutteth with his
    hind,
The place is marked, and by his venery
He still is taken. Shall we then attempt
The chiefest mean to that discovery
    here,
And court our greatest ladies' chiefest
    women
With shows of love and liberal promises?
'Tis but our breath. If something given
    in hand   170
Sharpen their hopes of more, 'twill be
    well ventured.
Guise. No doubt of that; and 'tis the
    cunning'st point
Of your devised investigation.
Mon.   I have broken
The ice to it already with the woman
Of your chaste lady, and conceive good
    hope
I shall wade thorough to some wishéd
    shore
At our next meeting.
Mont.   Nay, there's small hope there.
Guise. Take say of [8] her, my lord; she
    comes most fitly.

[2] "Commit escapades, and thereby give points
against themselves" (Boas).
[3] This passage is based on an old proverb.
"Women, who hold the candles because of their
inferiority to men, none the less know well how
the game is going" (Parrott).
[4] Waiting-women.
[5] Secret.
[6] Gun.
[7] Thicket.
[8] Assay, make trial of.

Enter Charlotte, Annabelle, Pero.

Mon. Starting back?

Guise. Y'are engaged, indeed.　　　180

Ann. Nay, pray, my lord, forbear.

Mont. What, skittish, servant?

Ann. No, my lord, I am not so fit for your service.

Char. Pray pardon me now, my lord; my lady expects me.

Guise. I'll satisfy her expectation, as far as an uncle may.

Mon. Well said; a spirit of courtship of
　　　all hands.　　　　　*[Takes Pero aside.]*
Now, mine own Pero, hast thou remem-
　　　bered me　　　　　　　190
For the discovery I entreated thee to
　　　make of thy mistress?
Speak boldly, and be sure of all things
　　　I have sworn to thee.

Per. Building on that assurance, my lord, I may speak, and much the rather because my lady hath not trusted me with that I can tell you, for now I cannot be said to betray her.

Mon. That's all one, so we reach our objects. Forth, I beseech thee.

Per. To tell you truth, my lord, I [200 have made a strange discovery.

Mon. Excellent, Pero, thou reviv'st me. May I sink quick to perdition if my tongue discover it.

Per. 'Tis thus, then: this last night my lord lay forth, and I, watching my lady's sitting up, stole up at midnight from my pallet, and, having before made a hole both through the wall and arras to her inmost chamber, I saw D'Ambois and [210 herself reading a letter.

Mon. D'Ambois?

Per. Even he, my lord.

Mon. Dost thou not dream, wench?

Per. I swear he is the man.

Mon. The devil he is, and thy lady his dam! Why, this was the happiest shot that ever flew! The just plague of hypocrisy leveled it. O, the infinite regions betwixt a woman's tongue and her [220 heart! Is this our goddess of chastity? I thought I could not be so slighted if she had not her fraught[1] besides, and therefore plotted this with her woman, never dreaming of D'Ambois. Dear Pero, I will advance thee forever. But tell me

now—God's precious, it transforms me with admiration [2]—sweet Pero, whom should she trust with this conveyance? [3] Or, all the doors being made sure, how [230 should his conveyance be made?

Per. Nay, my lord, that amazes me; I cannot by any study so much as guess at it.

Mon. Well, let's favor our apprehensions with forbearing that a little; for, if my heart were not hooped with adamant, the conceit[4] of this would have burst it. But hark thee!—　　　　　*Whispers.*

Mont. *[Aside to Annabelle.]* I pray [240 thee, resolve me; the duke will never imagine that I am busy about 's wife. Hath D'Ambois any privy access to her?

Ann. No, my lord, D'Ambois neglects her, as she takes it, and is therefore suspicious that either your lady or the Lady Beaupré hath closely entertained him.

Mont. By'r Lady, a likely suspi- [250 cion, and very near the life, especially of my wife.—

Mon. *[Aside to Pero.]* Come, we'll disguise all with seeming only to have courted.—Away, dry palm! [5] Sh'as a liver as hard as a biscuit; a man may go a whole voyage with her, and get nothing but tempests from her windpipe.

Guise. Here's one, I think, has swallowed a porcupine, she casts pricks [260 from her tongue so.

Mont. And here's a peacock seems to have devoured one of the Alps, she has so swelling a spirit, and is so cold of her kindness.

Char. We are no windfalls, my lord; ye must gather us with the ladder of matrimony, or we'll hang till we be rotten.

Mon. Indeed, that's the way to make ye right openarses.[6] But, alas, ye have [270 no portions fit for such husbands as we wish you.

Per. Portions, my lord? Yes, and such portions as your principality cannot purchase.

Mon. What, woman! What are those portions?

---

[1] Freight.

[2] Wonder.
[3] *I.e.*, of Bussy to her room.
[4] Thought.
[5] Sign of chastity.
[6] Medlars.

PER. Riddle my riddle, my lord.

MON. Ay, marry, wench, I think thy portion is a right riddle; a man shall [280 never find it out. But let's hear it.

PER. You shall, my lord.

What's that, that being most rare's most
* cheap?*
That when you sow, you never reap?
That when it grows most, most you in [1] *it?*
And still you lose it when you win it;
That, when 'tis commonest, 'tis dearest,
And, when 'tis farthest off, 'tis nearest?

MON. Is this your great portion?

PER. Even this, my lord.   290

MON. Believe me, I cannot riddle it.

PER. No, my lord; 'tis my chastity, which you shall neither riddle nor fiddle.

MON. Your chastity? Let me begin with the end of it; how is a woman's chastity nearest a man when 'tis furthest off?

PER. Why, my lord, when you cannot get it, it goes to th' heart on you; and that, I think, comes most near [300 you; and I am sure it shall be far enough off. And so we leave you to our mercies.

Exeunt Women.

MON. Farewell, riddle!

GUISE. Farewell, medlar!

MONT. Farewell, winter plum!

MON. Now, my lords, what fruit of our inquisition? Feel you nothing budding yet? Speak, good my Lord Montsurry.

MONT. Nothing but this: D'Ambois is thought negligent in observing the [310 duchess, and therefore she is suspicious that your niece or my wife closely entertains him.

MON. Your wife, my lord? Think you that possible?

MONT. Alas, I know she flies him like her last hour.

MON. Her last hour? Why, that comes upon her the more she flies it. Does D'Ambois so, think you?   320

MONT. That's not worth the answering. 'Tis miraculous to think with what monsters women's imaginations engross them when they are once enamored, and what wonders they will work for their satisfaction. They will make a sheep valiant, a lion fearful.

MON. [*Aside.*] And an ass confident.—

[1] Boas suggests *thin.*

Well, my lord, more will come forth shortly; get you to the banquet.   330

GUISE. Come, my lord; I have the blind side of one of them.

Exit Guise cum Mont[surry].

MON. O, the unsounded sea of women's bloods,
That, when 'tis calmest, is most dangerous;
Not any wrinkle creaming in their faces
When in their hearts are Scylla and Charybdis,
Which still are hid in dark and standing fogs,
Where never day shines, nothing never grows
But weeds and poisons that no statesman knows;
Not Cerberus ever saw the damnéd nooks   340
Hid with the veils of women's virtuous looks!
But what a cloud of sulphur have I drawn
Up to my bosom in this dangerous secret!
Which if my haste with any spark should light,
Ere D'Ambois were engaged in some sure plot,
I were blown up; he would be sure my death.
Would I had never known it, for before
I shall persuade th' importance to Montsurry,
And make him with some studied stratagem
Train D'Ambois to his wreak,[2] his maid may tell it,   350
Or I (out of my fiery thirst to play
With the fell tiger, up in darkness tied,
And give it some light) make it quite break loose.
I fear it, afore heaven, and will not see
D'Ambois again till I have told Montsurry
And set a snare with him to free my fears.
Who's there?

Enter Maffé.[3]

MAF.   My lord?

MON.   Go call the Count Montsurry,

[2] *I.e.,* to Montsurry's vengeance.
[3] The scene apparently shifts to Monsieur's chamber.

And make the doors fast; I will speak
with none
Till he come to me.

MAF.   Well, my lord.   *Exiturus.*[1]

MON.   Or else
Send you some other, and see all the
doors   360
Made safe yourself, I pray; haste, fly
about it.

MAF. You'll speak with none but with
the Count Montsurry?

MON. With none but he, except it be the
Guise.

MAF. See even by this, there's one excep-
tion more!
Your grace must be more firm in the
command,
Or else shall I as weakly execute.
The Guise shall speak with you?

MON.   He shall, I say.

MAF. And Count Montsurry?

MON.   Ay, and Count Montsurry.

MAF. Your grace must pardon me, that I
am bold
To urge the clear and full sense of your
pleasure;   370
Which whensoever I have known, I hope
Your grace will say, I hit it to a hair.

MON. You have.

MAF.   I hope so, or I would be glad—

MON. I pray thee get thee gone; thou art
so tedious
In the strict form of all thy services
That I had better have one negligent.
You hit my pleasure well when D'Ambois
hit you;
Did you not, think you?

MAF.   D'Ambois? Why, my lord—

MON. I pray thee talk no more, but shut
the doors.
Do what I charge thee.

MAF.   I will, my lord, and yet   380
I would be glad the wrong I had of
D'Ambois—

MON. Precious! Then it is a fate that
plagues me
In this man's foolery! I may be mur-
thered
While he stands on protection of his folly.
Avaunt about thy charge!

MAF.   I go, my lord.—
[*Aside.*] I had my head broke in his
faithful service;

[1] About to go out.

I had no suit the more, nor any thanks,
And yet my teeth must still be hit with
D'Ambois.—
D'Ambois, my lord, shall know—

MON.   The devil and D'Ambois!
Exit Maffé.
How am I tortured with this trusty fool!
Never was any curious [2] in his place   391
To do things justly, but he was an ass;
We cannot find one trusty that is witty,[3]
And therefore bear their disproportion.
Grant thou, great star and angel of my
life,[4]
A sure lease of it but for some few days,
That I may clear my bosom of the snake
I cherished there, and I will then defy
All check to it but Nature's, and her
altars
Shall crack with vessels crowned with
every liquor   400
Drawn from her highest and most bloody
humors.
I fear him strangely; his advancéd valor
Is like a spirit raised without a circle,
Endangering him that ignorantly raised
him,
And for whose fury he hath learnt no
limit.

Enter Maffé hastily.

MAF. I cannot help it; what should I do
more?
As I was gathering a fit guard to make
My passage to the doors, and the doors
sure,
The man of blood is entered.

MON.   Rage of death!   409
If I had told the secret, and he knew it,
Thus had I been endangered.

Enter D'Ambois.[5]

                       My sweetheart!
How now, what leap'st thou at?

BUS.   O royal object!

MON. Thou dream'st, awake; object in
th' empty air?

BUS. Worthy the brows of Titan, worth
his chair.

MON. Pray thee, what mean'st thou?

BUS.   See you not a crown

[2] Careful.   [3] Sensible.   [4] Guardian angel.
[5] In the original this direction comes at the
end of the speech.

Impale the forehead of the great King
    Monsieur?
Mon. O, fie upon thee!
Bus.   Prince, that is the subject
    Of all these your retired and sole dis-
    courses.
Mon. Wilt thou not leave that wrongful
    supposition?
Bus. Why wrongful, to suppose the doubt-
    less right   420
    To the succession worth the thinking
    on?
Mon. Well, leave these jests. How I am
    overjoyed
    With thy wished presence, and how fit
    thou com'st,
    For, of mine honor, I was sending for thee.
Bus. To what end?
Mon.   Only for thy company,
    Which I have still in thought; but that's
    no payment
    On thy part made with personal ap-
    pearance.
    Thy absence, so long suffered, often-
    times
    Put me in some little doubt thou dost
    not love me.
    Wilt thou do one thing therefore now
    sincerely?   430
Bus. Ay, anything but killing of the king.
Mon. Still in that discord and ill-taken
    note?
    How most unseasonable thou playest
    the cuckoo,
    In this thy fall of friendship! [1]
Bus.   Then do not doubt
    That there is any act within my nerves [2]
    But killing of the king, that is not yours.
Mon. I will not, then; to prove which
    by my love
    Shown to thy virtues, and by all fruits
    else
    Already sprung from that still flourish-
    ing tree,
    With whatsoever may hereafter spring,
    I charge thee utter (even with all the
    freedom   441
    Both of thy noble nature and thy friend-
    ship)
    The full and plain state of me in thy
    thoughts.

Bus. What, utter plainly what I think of
    you?
Mon. Plain as truth!
Bus. Why, this swims quite against the
    stream of greatness;
    Great men would rather hear their flat-
    teries,
    And, if they be not made fools, are not
    wise.
Mon. I am no such great fool, and there-
    fore charge thee,
    Even from the root of thy free heart,
    display me.   450
Bus. Since you affect [3] it in such serious
    terms,
    If yourself first will tell me what you think.
    As freely and as heartily of me,
    I'll be as open in my thoughts of you.
Mon. A bargain, of mine honor! And
    make this,
    That, prove we in our full dissection
    Never so foul, live still the sounder
    friends.
Bus. What else, sir? Come, pay me home;
    I'll bide it bravely.
Mon. I will, I swear. I think thee then
    a man
    That dares as much as a wild horse or
    tiger;   460
    As headstrong and as bloody; and to
    feed
    The ravenous wolf of thy most cannibal
    valor,
    Rather than not employ it, thou wouldst
    turn
    Hackster to any whore, [4] slave to a Jew
    Or English usurer, to force possessions
    (And cut men's throats) of mortgagéd
    estates;
    Or thou wouldst tire [5] thee like a tinker's
    strumpet,
    And murther market folks, quarrel with
    sheep,
    And run as mad as Ajax, serve a
    butcher—
    Do anything but killing of the king; 470
    That in thy valor th' art like other
    naturals [6]
    That have strange gifts in nature, but
    no soul
    Diffused quite through, to make them
    of a piece,

---

[1] The cuckoo, known for its monotonous song, sings in spring rather than in autumn.
[2] Strength, power.

[3] Desire.   [4] Ruffian serving her as bodyguard.
[5] Attire, dress.   [6] Idiots.

But stop at humors that are more ab-
  surd,
Childish, and villainous than that hack-
  ster, whore,
Slave, cutthroat, tinker's bitch, com-
  pared before;
And in those humors wouldst envy, be-
  tray,
Slander, blaspheme, change each hour
  a religion—
Do anything but killing of the king;
That in thy valor (which is still the
  dunghill,   480
To which hath reference all filth in thy
  house)
Th' art more ridiculous and vainglori-
  ous
Than any mountebank, and impudent
Than any painted bawd; which, not to
  soothe
And glorify thee like a Jupiter Hammon,
Thou eat'st thy heart in vinegar; and
  thy gall
Turns all thy blood to poison, which is
  cause
Of that toad pool that stands in thy
  complexion,
And makes thee (with a cold and earthy
  moisture,
Which is the dam of putrefaction,   490
As plague to thy damned pride) rot as
  thou liv'st;
To study calumnies and treacheries;
To thy friends' slaughters like a screech
  owl sing,
And to all mischiefs—but to kill the
  king.
Bus. So! Have you said?
Mon.   How think'st thou? Do I
  flatter?
Speak I not like a trusty friend to thee?
Bus. That ever any man was blessed
  withal!
So here's for me! I think you are, at
  worst,
No devil, since y'are like to be no king;
Of which, with any friend of yours, I'll
  lay   500
This poor stillado [1] here gainst all the
  stars,
Ay, and gainst all your treacheries, which
  are more,
That you did never good, but to do ill;

But ill of all sorts, free and for itself,
That (like a murthering piece, making
  lanes in armies,
The first man of a rank, the whole rank
  falling),
If you have wronged one man, you are
  so far
From making him amends that all his
  race,
Friends, and associates fall into your
  chase;   508
That y'are for perjuries the very prince
Of all intelligencers; [2] and your voice
Is like an eastern wind, that where it
  flies
Knits nets of caterpillars, with which
  you catch
The prime of all the fruits the kingdom
  yields;
That your political head is the cursed
  fount
Of all the violence, rapine, cruelty,
Tyranny, and atheism flowing through
  the realm;
That y'ave a tongue so scandalous, 'twill
  cut
The purest crystal, and a breath that
  will
Kill to [3] that wall a spider; you will
  jest   520
With God, and your soul to the devil
  tender
For lust; kiss horror, and with death
  engender;
That your foul body is a Lernean fen
Of all the maladies breeding in all men
That you are utterly without a soul;
And, for your life, the thread of that
  was spun
When Clotho slept, and let her breath-
  ing rock [4]
Fall in the dirt; and Lachesis still draws
  it,
Dipping her twisting fingers in a bowl
Defiled, and crowned with virtue's
  forcéd soul;   530
And lastly, which I must for gratitude
Ever remember, that of all my height
And dearest life, you are the only spring,
Only in royal hope to kill the king.

[1] Stiletto.
[2] Spies.
[3] At the distance of.
[4] "The distaff from whence she draws the
breath of life" (Dilke).

Mon. Why, now I see thou lovest me.
  Come to the banquet.   *Exeunt.*

FINIS ACTUS TERTII.

ACTUS QUARTI   SCENA PRIMA.

[*A room in the court.*]

*Henry, Monsieur with a letter, Guise,
  Montsurry, Bussy, Elenor, Tamyra,
  Beaupré, Pero, Charlotte, Annabelle,
    Pyra, with four Pages.*

HEN. Ladies, ye have not done our ban-
    quet right,
  Nor looked upon it with those cheerful
    rays
  That lately turned your breaths to
    floods of gold.
  Your looks, methinks, are not drawn
    out with thoughts
  So clear and free as heretofore, but foul,
  As if the thick complexions [1] of men
  Governed within them.
BUS.   'Tis not like, my lord,
  That men in women rule, but contrary;
  For, as the moon, of all things God
    created,
  Not only is the most appropriate im-
    age   10
  Or glass to show them how they wax
    and wane,
  But in her height and motion likewise
    bears
  Imperial influences that command
  In all their powers, and make them wax
    and wane;
  So women, that, of all things made of
    nothing,
  Are the most perfect idols of the moon,
  Or still-unweaned, sweet mooncalves [2]
    with white faces,
  Not only are patterns of change to men,
  But, as the tender moonshine of their
    beauties
  Clears or is cloudy, make men glad or
    sad;   20
  So then they rule in men, not men in
    them.
MON. But here the moons are changed,
    as the king notes,
  And either men rule in them, or some
    power

Beyond their voluntary faculty,
  For nothing can recover their lost faces.
MONT. None can be always one. Our
    griefs and joys
  Hold several scepters in us, and have
    times
  For their divided empires; which grief
    now in them
  Doth prove as proper to his diadem.
BUS. And grief's a natural sickness of
    the blood,   30
  That time to part asks, as his coming
    had;
  Only slight fools, grieved, suddenly are
    glad.
  A man may say t' a dead man, "Be re-
    vived,"
  As well as to one sorrowful, "Be not
    grieved."
  [*To the Duchess.*] And therefore, princely
    mistress, in all wars
  Against these base foes that insult on
    weakness,
  And still fight housed behind the shield
    of nature,
  Of privilege, law, treachery, or beastly
    need,
  Your servant cannot help; authority
    here
  Goes with corruption, something like
    some states,   40
  That back worst men. Valor to them
    must creep
  That, to themselves left, would fear him
    asleep.
DUCH. Ye all take that for granted that
    doth rest
  Yet to be proved; we all are as we were,
  As merry and as free in thought as ever.
GUISE. And why then can ye not disclose
    your thoughts?
TAM. Methinks the man hath answered
    for us well.
MON. The man? Why, madam, d' ye
    not know his name?
TAM. Man is a name of honor for a king;
  Additions [3] take away from each chief
    thing.   50
  The school of modesty not to learn
    learns dames;
  They sit in high forms [4] there, that know
    men's names.

---

[1] Humors, bodily fluids.
[2] Deformed creatures, monstrosities.
[3] Titles.
[4] "On the stools of disgrace" (Boas).

Mon. [*To Bussy.*] Hark, sweetheart, here's
  a bar set to your valor!
It cannot enter here; no, not to notice
Of what your name is. Your great eagle's
  beak,
Should you fly at her, had as good en-
  counter
An Albion cliff as her more craggy liver.[1]
Bus. I'll not attempt her, sir; her sight
  and name,
By which I only know her, doth deter me.
Hen. So they do all men else.
Mon.   You would say so   60
  If you knew all.
Tam.   Knew all, my lord? What
  mean you?
Mon. All that I know, madam.
Tam.   That you know? Speak it.
Mon. No, 'tis enough I feel it.
Hen.   But, methinks
  Her courtship is more pure than here-
  tofore;
True courtiers should be modest, and
  not nice;
Bold, but not impudent; pleasure love,
  not vice.
Mon. Sweetheart, come hither! What if
  one should make
Horns at Montsurry? Would it not
  strike him jealous
Through all the proofs of his chaste
  lady's virtues?
Bus. If he be wise, not.   70
Mon. What? Not if I should name the
  gardener
That I would have him think hath
  grafted him?
Bus. So the large license that your great-
  ness uses
To jest that all men may be taught in-
  deed
To make a difference of the grounds you
  play on,
Both in the men you scandal, and the
  matter.
Mon. As how? As how?
Bus.   Perhaps led with a train,[2]
Where you may have your nose made
  less and slit,
Your eyes thrust out.
Mon.   Peace, peace, I pray thee peace!
  Who dares do that? The brother of his
  king?   80

---

[1] Supposed to be the seat of love.   [2] Trick.

Bus. Were your king brother in you; all
  your powers,
Stretched in the arms of great men and
  their bawds,
Set close down by you; all your stormy
  laws
Spouted with lawyers' mouths and gush-
  ing blood
Like to so many torrents; all your glo-
  ries
(Making you terrible, like enchanted
  flames)
Fed with bare coxcombs and with crooked
  hams; [3]
All your prerogatives, your shames, and
  tortures;
All daring heaven, and opening hell
  about you—
Were I the man ye wronged so and pro-
  voked,   90
Though ne'er so much beneath you, like
  a box tree
I would, out of the roughness of my root,
Ram hardness in my lowness, and, like
  Death
Mounted on earthquakes, I would trot
  through all
Honors and horrors, thorough foul and
  fair,
And from your whole strength toss you
  into the air.
Mon. Go, th' art a devil! Such another
  spirit
Could not be stilled [4] from all th' Arme-
  nian dragons.
O my love's glory, heir to all I have
(That's all I can say, and that all I
  swear)   100
If thou outlive me, as I know thou must,
Or else hath Nature no proportioned
  end
To her great labors, she hath breathed
  a mind
Into thy entrails, of desert to swell
Into another great Augustus Cæsar,
Organs and faculties fitted to her great-
  ness;
And, should that perish like a common
  spirit,
Nature's a courtier and regards no merit.
Hen. Here's naught but whispering with
  us, like a calm

---

[3] The bare heads and bent knees of sycophants.
[4] Distilled.

Before a tempest, when the silent air   110
Lays her soft ear close to the earth to
   hearken
For that she fears steals on to ravish
   her,
Some fate doth join [1] our ears to hear
   it coming.
Come, my brave eagle, let's to covert
   fly;
I see almighty Æther in the smoke
Of all his clouds descending, and the
   sky
Hid in the dim ostents [2] of tragedy.

Exit Henr[y] with D'Amb[ois] and Ladies.

GUISE. [*Aside to Monsieur.*]   Now stir
   the humor, and begin the brawl.
MONT. The king and D'Ambois now are
   grown all one.
MON. [*Making horns at Montsurry.*] Nay,
   they are two, my lord.
MONT.   How's that?
MON.   No more.   120
MONT. I must have more, my lord.
MON.   What, more than two?
MONT. How monstrous is this!
MON.   Why?
MONT.   You make me horns!
MON. Not I; it is a work without my
   power.
Married men's ensigns are not made
   with fingers;
Of divine fabric they are, not men's
   hands.
Your wife, you know, is a mere [3] Cyn-
   thia,
And she must fashion horns out of her
   nature.
MONT. But doth she—dare you charge
   her? Speak, false prince!
MON. I must not speak, my lord; but, if
   you'll use
The learning of a nobleman and read,   130
Here's something to those points. Soft,
   you must pawn [4]
Your honor, having read it, to return
   it.

Enter Tamyra, Pero.

MONT. Not I! I pawn my honor for a
   paper?
MON. You must not buy it under.

Exeunt Guise and Monsieur.

[1] Enjoin.   [3] Absolute.
[2] Manifestations, omens.   [4] Pledge.

MONT.   Keep it then,
And keep fire in your bosom.
TAM.   What says he?
MONT. You must make good the rest.
TAM.   How fares my lord?
Takes my love anything to heart he
   says?
MONT. Come, y'are a—
TAM.   What, my lord?
MONT.   The plague of Herod
Feast in his rotten entrails.
TAM.   Will you wreak
Your anger's just cause given by him,
   on me?   140
MONT. By him?
TAM.   By him, my lord. I have
   admired [5]
You could all this time be at concord
   with him,
That still hath played such discords on
   your honor.
MONT. Perhaps 'tis with some proud
   string of my wife's.
TAM. How's that, my lord?
MONT.   Your tongue will still admire,
Till my head be the miracle of the world.
TAM. O, woe is me!   *She seems to sound.* [6]
PER.   What does your lordship
   mean?—
Madam, be comforted; my lord but
   tries you.
Madam!—Help, good my lord, are you
   not moved?
Do your set looks print in your words
   your thoughts?   150
Sweet lord, clear up those eyes, unbend
   that masking forehead.
Whence is it you rush upon her with
   these Irish wars,
More full of sound than hurt? But it
   is enough.
You have shot home; your words are
   in her heart.
She has not lived to bear a trial now.
MONT. Look up, my love, and by this
   kiss receive
My soul amongst thy spirits for supply
To thine, chased with my fury.
TAM.   O, my lord,
I have too long lived to hear this from
   you.
MONT. 'Twas from my troubled blood,
   and not from me.—   160

[5] Wondered.   [6] Swound, swoon.

[*Aside.*] I know not how I fare; a sudden night
Flows through my entrails, and a headlong chaos
Murmurs within me, which I must digest,
And not drown her in my confusions,
That was my life's joy, being best informed.—
Sweet, you must needs forgive me, that my love,
Like to a fire disdaining his suppression,
Raged, being discouraged; my whole heart is wounded
When any least thought in you is but touched,
And shall be till I know your former merits;   170
Your name and memory altogether crave
In just oblivion their eternal grave;
And then, you must hear from me, there's no mean
In any passion I shall feel for you.
Love is a razor, cleansing, being well used,
But fetcheth blood still, being the least abused.
To tell you briefly all, the man that left me
When you appeared, did turn me worse than woman,
And stabbed me to the heart thus, with his fingers.
TAM. O, happy woman! Comes my stain from him?   180
It is my beauty, and that innocence proves
That slew Chimera, rescued Peleus
From all the savage beasts in Pelion,
And raised the chaste Athenian prince from hell;
All suffering with me, they for women's lusts,
I for a man's, that the Augean stable
Of his foul sin would empty in my lap.
How his guilt shunned me! Sacred Innocence
That where thou fear'st, art dreadful, and his face
Turned in flight from thee, that had thee in chase!   190
Come, bring me to him; I will tell the serpent

Even to his venomed teeth, from whose cursed seed
A pitched field [1] starts up twixt my lord and me,
That his throat lies, and he shall curse his fingers
For being so governed by his filthy soul.
MONT. I know not if himself will vaunt t' have been
The princely author of the slavish sin,
Or any other; he would have resolved me,
Had you not come, not by his word, but writing,
Would I have sworn to give it him again,   200
And pawned mine honor to him for a paper.
TAM. See how he flies me still; 'tis a foul heart
That fears his own hand. Good my lord, make haste
To see the dangerous paper; papers hold
Ofttimes the forms and copies of our souls,
And, though the world despise them, are the prizes
Of all our honors. Make your honor then
A hostage for it, and with it confer [2]
My nearest woman here, in all she knows,
Who, if the sun or Cerberus could have seen   210
Any stain in me, might as well as they.
And, Pero, here I charge thee by my love,
And all proofs of it, which I might call bounties,
By all that thou hast seen seem good in me,
And all the ill which thou shouldst spit from thee,
By pity of the wound this touch hath given me,
Not as thy mistress now, but a poor woman,
To death given over, rid me of my pains;
Pour on thy powder; clear thy breast of me.
My lord is only here. Here speak thy worst;   220
Thy best will do me mischief. If thou spar'st me,

[1] Battle.   [2] Consult.

Never shine good tnought on thy mem-
ory!
Resolve my lord, and leave me desper-
ate.
Per. My lord! My lord hath played a
prodigal's part,
To break his stock for nothing; and an
insolent,
To cut a Gordian [1] when he could not
loose it.
What violence is this, to put true fire
To a false train, to blow up long-crowned
peace
With sudden outrage, and believe a
man
Sworn to the shame of women, gainst
a woman, 230
Born to their honors? But I will to him.
Tam. No, I will write (for I shall never
more
Meet with the fugitive) where I will
defy him,
Were he ten times the brother of my
king.
To him, my lord, and I'll to cursing
him. *Exeunt.*

[Scena Secunda.

A room in Montsurry's house.]

Enter D'Ambois and Friar.

Bus. I am suspicious, my most honored
father,
By some of Monsieur's cunning passages,
That his still ranging and contentious
nostrils,
To scent the haunts of Mischief, have
so used
The vicious virtue of his busy sense
That he trails hotly of him, and will
rouse him,
Driving him all enraged and foaming on
us,
And therefore have entreated your deep
skill
In the command of good aërial spirits,
To assume these magic rites, and call
up one 10
To know if any have revealed unto him
Anything touching my dear love and me.
Fri. Good son, you have amazed me but
to make

[1] Gordian knot.

The least doubt of it, it concerns so
nearly
The faith and reverence of my name and
order.
Yet will I justify, upon my soul,
All I have done; if any spirit i' th' earth
or air
Can give you the resolve, do not despair.

*Music; and Tamyra enters with Pero, her
maid,* [2] *bearing a letter.*

Tam. Away, deliver it! (*Exit Pero.*) O,
may my lines
Filled with the poison of a woman's
hate, 20
When he shall open them, shrink up
his cursed eyes
With torturous darkness, such as stands
in hell,
Stuck full of inward horrors, never
lighted,
With which are all things to be feared,
affrighted.
Bus. [*Advancing.*] How is it with my
honored mistress?
Tam. O servant, help, and save me from
the gripes
Of shame and infamy. Our love is known;
Your Monsieur hath a paper where is writ
Some secret tokens that decipher it.
Bus. What cold dull northern brain, what
fool but he 30
Durst take into his Epimethean breast
A box of such plagues as the danger
yields
Incurred in this discovery? He had
better
Ventured his breast in the consuming
reach
Of the hot surfeits cast out of the clouds,
Or stood the bullets that, to wreak the
sky,
The Cyclops ram in Jove's artillery.
Fri. We soon will take the darkness from
his face
That did that deed of darkness; we will
know
What now the Monsieur and your hus-
band do, 40
What is contained within the secret
paper
Offered by Monsieur, and your love's
events;

[2] Original reads *and her maid.*

To which ends, honored daughter, at
your motion,
I have put on these exorcising rites,
And, by my power of learned holiness
Vouchsafed me from above, I will com-
mand
Our resolution of [1] a raiséd spirit.

TAM. Good father, raise him in some
beauteous form
That with least terror I may brook
his sight.

FRI. Stand sure together, then, whate'er
you see,   50
And stir not, as ye tender all our lives.
                    He puts on his robes.
Occidentalium legionum spiritualium im-
perator, magnus ille Behemoth, veni, veni,
comitatus cum Astaroth locotenente invicto!
Adjuro te per Stygis inscrutabilia arcana,
per ipsos irremeabiles anfractus Averni:
Adesto, O Behemoth, tu cui pervia sunt
Magnatum scrinia; veni, per Noctis et tene-
brarum abdita profundissima; per labentia
sidera; per ipsos motus horarum furtivos, [60
Hecatesque altum silentium! Appare in
forma spiritali, lucente, splendida, et ama-
bili! [2]

Thunder. Ascendit [Behemoth with Carto-
phylax and other Spirits].

BEH. What would the holy friar?

FRI.   I would see
What now the Monsieur and Montsurry
do,
And see the secret paper that the Mon-
sieur
Offered to Count Montsurry, longing
much
To know on what events the secret loves
Of these two honored persons shall
arrive.

BEH. Why calledst thou me to this accursed light,   70

[1] From.
[2] O ruler of the legions of western spirits, that
mighty Behemoth, come, come, accompanied by
Astaroth, unconquered lieutenant! I command
thee by the hidden mysteries of the Styx, by the
unretraceable labyrinths of Avernus themselves:
Appear, O Behemoth, thou to whom the cabinets of the Mighty are accessible; come, by the
deepest caves of Night and the shades; by the
wandering stars; by the stealthy motions of the
hours themselves, and the deep silence of Hecate!
Appear in spirit form, shining, brilliant, and
lovely!

To these light purposes? I am emperor
Of that inscrutable darkness where are
hid
All deepest truths and secrets never seen,
All which I know, and command legions
Of knowing spirits that can do more than
these.
Any of this my guard that circle me
In these blue fires, and out of whose
dim fumes
Vast murmurs use to break, and from
their sounds
Articulate voices, can do ten parts
more
Than open such slight truths as you
require.   80

FRI. From the last night's black depth I
called up one
Of the inferior ablest ministers,
And he could not resolve me. Send one
then
Out of thine own command, to fetch the
paper
That Monsieur hath to show to Count
Montsurry.

BEH. I will. Cartophylax, thou that properly
Hast in thy power all papers so inscribed,
Glide through all bars to it and fetch
that paper.

CART. I will.   *A torch* [3] *removes.*

FRI. Till he returns, great Prince of Darkness,   90
Tell me if Monsieur and the Count Montsurry
Are yet encountered?

BEH.   Both them and the Guise
Are now together.

FRI.   Show us all their persons,
And represent the place, with all their
actions.

BEH. The spirit will straight return, and
then I'll show thee.

[Enter Cartophylax.]

See, he is come; why brought'st thou
not the paper?

CART. He hath prevented me, and got a
spirit
Raised by another, great in our command,
To take the guard of it before I came.

[3] *I.e.,* a torchbearer (Cartophylax).

BEH. This is your slackness, not t' invoke
    our powers   100
    When first your acts set forth to their
      effects;
    Yet shall you see it and themselves.
      Behold,
    They come here, and the earl now holds
      the paper.

Ent[er] Mons[ieur], Gui[se], Mont[surry]
                  with a paper.

BUS. May we not hear them?
[FRI.][1]   No, be still and see.
BUS. I will go fetch the paper.
FRI.   Do not stir;
    There's too much distance and too many
      locks
    Twixt you and them, how near soe'er
      they seem,
    For any man to interrupt their secrets.
TAM. O honored spirit, fly into the fancy
    Of my offended lord, and do not let him
    Believe what there the wicked man
      hath written.   111
BEH.[2] Persuasion hath already entered
    him
    Beyond reflection.[3] Peace till their de-
      parture!—

MON. There is a glass of ink [4] where you
    may see
    How to make ready black-faced tragedy.
    You now discern, I hope, through all
      her paintings,
    Her gasping wrinkles and fame's sepul-
      chers.
GUISE. Think you he feigns, my lord?
    What hold you now?
    Do we malign your wife, or honor you?
MON. What, stricken dumb! Nay, fie,
    lord, be not daunted;   120
    Your case is common; were it ne'er so
      rare,
    Bear it as rarely. Now to laugh were
      manly.
    A worthy man should imitate the
      weather
    That sings in tempests, and, being clear,
      is silent.

GUISE. Go home, my lord, and force your
    wife to write
    Such loving lines to D'Ambois as she
      used
    When she desired his presence.
MON.   Do, my lord,
    And make her name her concealed mes-
      senger,
    That close and most inennerable [5]
      pander,   129
    That passeth all our studies to exquire; [6]
    By whom convey the letter to her love;
    And so you shall be sure to have him
      come
    Within the thirsty reach of your revenge;
    Before which, lodge an ambush in her
      chamber
    Behind the arras, of your stoutest men
    All close and soundly armed, and let
      them share
    A spirit amongst them that would serve
      a thousand.

Enter Pero with a letter.

GUISE. Yet stay a little; see, she sends
    for you.
MON. Poor, loving lady; she'll make all
    good yet.
    Think you not so, my lord?
      Exit Mont[surry] and stabs Pero.[7]
GUISE.   Alas, poor soul!   140
MON. This was cruelly done, i' faith.
PER.   'Twas nobly done.
    And I forgive his lordship from my soul.
MON. Then much good do 't thee, Pero!
    Hast a letter?
PER. I hope it rather be a bitter volume
    Of worthy curses for your perjury.
GUISE. To you, my lord.
MON.   To me? Now, out upon her.
GUISE. Let me see, my lord.
MON. You shall presently.   How fares
    my Pero?
    Who's there?

Enter Servant.

          Take in this maid—sh' as
    caught a clap—
    And fetch my surgeon to her.   Come,
    my lord,   150

---

[1] Original reads *Mon.*
[2] Original reads *Pre.*
[3] Turning back, return.
[4] *I.e.*, the letter is a mirror.

[5] Inenarrable, indescribable, unknown.
[6] Discover.
[7] Boas emends: *Mont[surry] stabs Pero, and exit.*

We'll now peruse our letter.
Exeunt Mons[ieur], Guise. Lead her out.
PER.   Furies rise
Out of the black lines, and torment his
    soul!—

TAM. Hath my lord slain my woman?
BEH.   No, she lives.
FRI. What shall become of us?
BEH.   All I can say,
    Being called thus late, is brief, and darkly
    this:
    If D'Ambois' mistress dye not her[1]
        white hand
    In her forced blood, he shall remain un-
        touched;
    So, father, shall yourself, but by your-
        self.
    To make this augury plainer, when the
        voice
    Of D'Ambois shall invoke me, I will
        rise,   160
    Shining in greater light, and show him
        all
    That will betide ye all. Meantime be
        wise,
    And curb his valor with your policies.
                        Descendit cum suis.[2]
BUS. Will he appear to me when I invoke
        him?
FRI. He will, be sure.
BUS.   It must be shortly then;
    For his dark words have tied my
        thoughts on knots,
    Till he dissolve and free them.
TAM.   In meantime,
    Dear servant, till your powerful voice
        revoke him,
    Be sure to use the policy he advised;
    Lest fury in your too quick knowledge
        taken   170
    Of our abuse, and your defense of me,
    Accuse me more than any enemy.
    And, father, you must on my lord im-
        pose
    Your holiest charges and the church's
        power
    To temper his hot spirit and disperse
    The cruelty and the blood I know his
        hand
    Will shower upon our heads, if you put
        not

Your finger to the storm, and hold it up,
As my dear servant here must do with
    Monsieur.
BUS. I'll soothe his plots, and strow my
    hate with smiles,   180
    Till all at once the close mines of my
        heart
    Rise at full date, and rush into his
        blood.
    I'll bind his arm in silk, and rub his
        flesh,
    To make the vein swell, that his soul
        may gush
    Into some kennel,[3] where it longs to lie,
    And policy shall be flanked[4] with policy.
    Yet shall the feeling center[5] where we
        meet
    Groan with the weight of my approach-
        ing feet;
    I'll make th' inspired[6] thresholds of his
        court
    Sweat with the weather of my horrid
        steps,[7]   190
    Before I enter; yet will I appear
    Like calm security before a ruin.
    A politician must, like lightning, melt
    The very marrow, and not taint the
        skin;
    His ways must not be seen; the super-
        ficies
    Of the green center must not taste his
        feet,
    When hell is plowed up with his wound-
        ing tracts,[8]
    And all his harvest reaped by hellish
        facts.   *Exeunt.*

FINIS ACTUS QUARTI.

ACTUS QUINTI SCENA PRIMA.

[A room in Montsurry's house.]

*Montsurry, bare, unbraced,[9] pulling Ta-
myra in by the hair; Friar; One bearing
light, a standish,[10] and paper, which[11]
                sets a table [and exit].*

TAM. O, help me, father!
FRI.   Impious earl, forbear!

---

[1] Original has *his*.
[2] He descends with his attendants.
[3] Channel, gutter.   [4] Outflanked.
[5] The conscious earth, considered the center
of the universe.
[6] Blown upon.   [7] Storm of my terrifying steps.
[8] Tracks.   [9] With his garments unfastened.
[10] Receptacle for pen and ink.   [11] Who

Take violent hand from her, or by mine
   order
The king shall force thee.

MONT.   'Tis not violent.—
   Come you not willingly?

TAM.   Yes, good my lord.

FRI. My lord, remember that your soul
   must seek
Her peace, as well as your revengeful
   blood.
You ever to this hour have proved your-
   self
A noble, zealous, and obedient son
T' our Holy Mother; be not an apostate.
Your wife's offense serves not, were it the
   worst   10
You can imagine, without greater proofs,
To sever your eternal bonds and hearts,
Much less to touch her with a bloody
   hand;
Nor is it manly, much less husbandly,
To expiate any frailty in your wife
With churlish strokes or beastly odds of
   strength.
The stony birth of clouds [1] will touch no
   laurel,
Nor any sleeper; your wife is your laurel,
And sweetest sleeper. Do not touch her
   then;
Be not more rude than the wild seed of
   vapor,   20
To her that is more gentle than that rude,
In whom kind nature suffered one offense
But to set off her other excellence.

MONT. Good father, leave us; interrupt no
   more
The course I must run for mine honor
   sake.
Rely on my love to her, which her fault
Cannot extinguish. Will she but disclose
Who was the secret minister of her love,
And through what maze he served it, we
   are friends.

FRI. It is a damned work to pursue those
   secrets   30
That would ope more sin, and prove
   springs of slaughter;
Nor is't a path for Christian feet to tread,
But out of all way to the health of souls,
A sin impossible to be forgiven;
Which he that dares commit—

MONT. Good father, cease your terrors;
   Tempt not a man distracted; I am apt

[1] *I.e.*, the thunderbolt.

To outrages that I shall ever rue!
I will not pass the verge that bounds a
   Christian,
Nor break the limits of a man nor hus-
   band.   40

FRI. Then Heaven inspire you both with
   thoughts and deeds
Worthy His high respect and your own
   souls.

TAM. Father!

FRI.   I warrant thee, my dearest
   daughter,
He will not touch thee. Think'st thou
   him a pagan?
His honor and his soul lies for thy safety.
                      Exit.

MONT. Who shall remove the mountain
   from my breast,
Stand the opening furnace of my
   thoughts,
And set fit outcries for a soul in hell?
              Mont[surry] turns a key.
For now it nothing fits my woes to speak
But thunder, or to take into my throat 50
The trump of heaven, with whose deter-
   minate [2] blasts
The winds shall burst, and the devouring
   seas
Be drunk up in his sounds; that my hot
   woes,
Vented enough, I might convert to vapor,
Ascending from my infamy unseen,
Shorten the world, preventing [3] the last
   breath
That kills the living and regenerates
   death.

TAM. My lord, my fault (as you may censure it
With too strong arguments) is past your
   pardon.
But how the circumstances may excuse
   me   60
Heaven knows, and your more temperate
   mind hereafter
May let my penitent miseries make you
   know.

MONT. Hereafter? 'Tis a supposed infinite,
That from this point will rise eternally.
Fame grows in going; in the scapes of
   virtue
Excuses damn her: they be fires in cities
Enraged with those winds that less lights
   extinguish.

[2] Final.   [3] Anticipating.

Come, siren, sing, and dash against my
rocks
Thy ruffian galley, rigged with quench
for lust; [1]
Sing, and put all the nets into thy
voice   70
With which thou drew'st into thy strum-
pet's lap
The spawn of Venus, and in which ye
danced,
That, in thy lap's stead, I may dig his
tomb,
And quit [2] his manhood with a woman's
sleight,
Who never is deceived in her deceit.
Sing (that is, write), and then take from
mine eyes
The mists that hide the most inscrutable
pander
That ever lapped up an adulterous
vomit,
That I may see the devil, and survive
To be a devil, and then learn to wive;   80
That I may hang him, and then cut him
down,
Then cut him up, and with my soul's
beams search
The cranks [3] and caverns of his brain, and
study
The errant wilderness of a woman's face,
Where men cannot get out, for all the
comets
That have been lighted at it. Though
they know
That adders lie a-sunning in their smiles,
That basilisks drink their poison from
their eyes,
And no way there to coast out to their
hearts,
Yet still they wander there, and are not
stayed   90
Till they be fettered, nor secure before
All cares devour them, nor in human
consort
Till they embrace within their wife's two
breasts
All Pelion and Cytheron with their
beasts.
Why write you not?
TAM.   O, good my lord, forbear
In wreak of great faults to engender
greater,

And make my love's corruption generate
murther.
MONT. It follows needfully as child and
parent;
The chain shot of thy lust is yet aloft,
And it must murther; 'tis thine own dear
twin.   100
No man can add height to a woman's sin.
Vice never doth her just hate so provoke
As when she rageth under virtue's cloak.
Write! For it must be—by this ruthless
steel,
By this impartial torture, and the death
Thy tyrannies have invented in my en-
trails,
To quicken life in dying, and hold up
The spirits in fainting, teaching to pre-
serve
Torments in ashes, that will ever last.
Speak! Will you write?
TAM.   Sweet lord, enjoin my sin
Some other penance than what makes it
worse.   111
Hide in some gloomy dungeon my
loathed face,
And let condemnéd murtherers let me
down
(Stopping their noses) my abhorréd food.
Hang me in chains, and let me eat these
arms
That have offended; bind me face to face
To some dead woman, taken from the
cart
Of execution, till death and time
In grains of dust dissolve me; I'll endure;
Or any torture that your wrath's in-
vention   120
Can fright all pity from the world withal;
But to betray a friend with show of
friendship,
That is too common for the rare revenge
Your rage affecteth. Here then are my
breasts,
Last night your pillows; here my
wretched arms,
As late the wishéd confines of your life;
Now break them as you please, and all
the bounds
Of manhood, noblesse, and religion.
MONT. Where all these have been broken,
they are kept,   129
In doing their justice there with any show
Of the like cruel cruelty; thine arms have
lost

---

[1] *I.e.*, D'Ambois is to be lured with the desire to
quench his lust.   [2] Requite.   [3] Winding paths.

Their privilege in lust, and in their
    torture
Thus they must pay it.   *Stabs her.*
TAM.   O Lord!
MONT.   Till thou writ'st,
    I'll write in wounds (my wrong's fit
      characters)
    Thy right of sufferance. Write!
TAM.   O, kill me, kill me!
    Dear husband, be not crueler than death.
    You have beheld some Gorgon; feel, O,
      feel
    How you are turned to stone. With my
      heartblood
    Dissolve yourself again, or you will grow
    Into the image of all tyranny.   140
MONT. As thou art of adultery; I will ever
    Prove thee my parallel, being most a
      monster;
    Thus I express thee yet.[1] *Stabs her again.*
TAM.   And yet I live.
MONT. Ay, for thy monstrous idol is not
      done yet;
    This tool hath wrought enough; now,
      torture, use

Ent[er] Servants.

This other engine [2] on th' habituate
      powers
Of her thrice-damned and whorish forti-
    tude.
Use the most madding pains in her that
      ever
Thy venoms soaked through, making
      most of death,
That she may weigh her wrongs with
    them, and then   150
Stand Vengeance on thy steepest rock, a
    victor.
TAM. O, who is turned into my lord and
      husband?
    Husband! My lord! None but my lord
      and husband!
    Heaven, I ask thee remission of my sins,
    Not of my pains. Husband, O, help me,
      husband!

Ascendit Friar with a sword drawn.

FRI. What rape of honor and religion—
    O, wrack of nature!   *Falls and dies.*
TAM.   Poor man! O, my father!

[1] "Thus I give a further stroke to my delinea-
:on of thee" (Boas).   [2] Rack.

Father, look up; O, let me down, my lord.
    And I will write.
MONT.   Author of prodigies!
    What new flame breaks out of the fir-
      mament,   160
    That turns up counsels never known
      before?
    Now is it true earth moves, and heaven
      stands still;
    Even heaven itself must see and suffer
      ill.
    The too huge bias [3] of the world hath
      swayed
    Her backpart upwards, and with that
      she braves
    This hemisphere, that long her mouth
      hath mocked.
    The gravity of her religious face,
    Now grown too weighty with her sacri-
      lege,
    And here discerned sophisticate enough,
    Turns to th' antipodes; and all the
      forms   170
    That her illusions have impressed in her
    Have eaten through her back; and now
      all see
    How she is riveted with hypocrisy.
    Was this the way? Was he the mean be-
      twixt you?
TAM. He was, he was; kind worthy man,
      he was!
MONT. Write, write a word or two.
TAM.   I will, I will.
    I'll write, but with my blood, that he may
      see
    These lines come from my wounds, and
      not from me.   *Writes.*
MONT. Well might he die for thought;
      methinks the frame
    And shaken joints of the whole world
      should crack   180
    To see her parts so disproportionate,
    And that his general beauty cannot
      stand
    Without these stains in the particular
      man.
    Why wander I so far? Here, here was she
    That was a whole world without spot to
      me,
    Though now a world of spots. O, what a
      lightning
    Is man's delight in women! What a
      bubble
[3] Slant.

He builds his state, fame, life on, when
    he marries!
Since all earth's pleasures are so short
    and small,
The way t' enjoy it, is t' abjure it all. 190
Enough! I must be messenger myself,
Disguised like this strange creature. In!
    I'll after,
To see what guilty light gives this cave
    eyes,
And to the world sing new impieties.
Exeunt [Servants]. He puts the Friar in the
    vault and follows. She wraps herself in
                     the arras.

[SCENA SECUNDA.

Another room in Montsurry's house.]

Enter Monsieur and Guise.

MON. Now shall we see that Nature hath
    no end
In her great works responsive to their
    worths,
That she, that makes so many eyes and
    souls
To see and foresee, is stark blind herself;
And, as illiterate men say Latin prayers
By rote of heart and daily iteration,
Not knowing what they say, so Nature
    lays
A deal of stuff together, and by use,
Or by the mere necessity of matter,
Ends such a work, fills it, or leaves it
    empty   10
Of strength or virtue, error or clear
    truth,
Not knowing what she does; but usually
Gives that which she calls merit to a man,
And belief must arrive [1] him on huge
    riches,
Honor, and happiness, that effects his
    ruin,
Even as in ships of war, whole lasts [2] of
    powder
Are laid, methinks, to make them last
    and guard,[3]
When a disordered spark, that powder
    taking,

[1] Bring.
[2] Measures, in this case of twenty-four barrels.
[3] In ll. 13–17 the 1607 edition reads *wee call*
for *she calls*, *believe* for *beliefe*, *should* for *must*,
Right for *Even*, *men thinke* for *me thinks*, *gard*
them for *guard*. Parrott accepts all the readings
of 1607 as preferable.

Blows up with sudden violence and horror
Ships that, kept empty, had sailed long
    with terror.[4]   20
GUISE. He that observes but like a worldly
    man
That which doth oft succeed, and by th'
    events
Values the worth of things, will think it
    true
That Nature works at random, just with
    you;
But with as much proportion she may
    make
A thing that from the feet up to the
    throat
Hath all the wondrous fabric man should
    have,
And leave it headless, for a perfect man,
As give a full man valor, virtue, learning,
Without an end more excellent than
    those   30
On whom she no such worthy part be-
    stows.
MON. Yet shall you see it here; here will
    be one
Young, learned, valiant, virtuous, and
    full manned—
One on whom Nature spent so rich a
    hand
That with an ominous eye she wept to see
So much consumed her virtuous treas-
    ury.[5]
Yet, as the winds sing through a hollow
    tree
And (since it lets them pass through) lets
    it stand,
But a tree solid (since it gives no way
To their wild rage) they rend up by the
    root,   40
So this whole man
(That will not wind with every crooked
    way,
Trod by the servile world) shall reel and
    fall
Before the frantic puffs of blind-born
    chance,
That pipes through empty men, and
    makes them dance.[6]
Not so the sea raves on the Lybian
    sands,

[4] "Inspiring terror in their enemies" (Boas).
[5] Store of virtues.
[6] Lines 46–53 are adapted from Seneca's
Agamemnon.

Tumbling her billows in each other's
　　neck;
Not so the surges of the Euxine sea
(Near to the frosty pole, where free
　　Boötes
From those dark deep waves turns his
　　radiant team)　　　　　　　　　　50
Swell, being enraged, even from their
　　inmost drop,
As Fortune swings about the restless
　　state
Of virtue, now thrown into all men's
　　hate.

*Enter Montsurry disguised [as the Friar,]
　　　　　　　　with the Murtherers.*

Away, my lord; you are perfectly dis-
　　guised;
Leave us to lodge your ambush.
Mont.　　　　Speed me, vengeance! *Exit.*
Mon.　Resolve, my masters, you shall meet
　　with one
Will try what proofs your privy coats[1]
　　are made on.
When he is entered, and you hear us
　　stamp,
Approach, and make all sure.　　　　59
Murtherers.　We will, my lord. *Exeunt.*

[Scena Tertia.

A room in Bussy's house.]

D'Ambois with two Pages with tapers.

Bus.　Sit up tonight, and watch; I'll speak
　　with none
But the old friar, who bring to me.
Pages.　　　　　We will, sir.　*Exeunt.*
Bus.　What violent heat is this?　Methinks
　　the fire
Of twenty lives doth on a sudden flash
Through all my faculties; the air goes
　　high
In this close chamber, and the frighted
　　earth　　　　　　　　　*Thunder.*
Trembles, and shrinks beneath me; the
　　whole house
Nods with his shaken burthen.

Enter Umb[ra][2] Friar.

　　　　　　　　　Bless me, heaven!
Umb. [Fri.]　Note what I want,[3] dear son,
　　and be forewarned;

O, there are bloody deeds past and to
　　come.　　　　　　　　　　　　　10
I cannot stay; a fate doth ravish me;
I'll meet thee in the chamber of thy
　　love.　　　　　　　　　　*Exit.*
Bus.　What dismal change is here; the good
　　old friar
Is murthered, being made known to serve
　　my love;
And now his restless spirit would fore-
　　warn me
Of some plot dangerous and imminent.
Note what he wants?　He wants his upper
　　weed;
He wants his life and body.　Which of
　　these
Should be the want he means, and may
　　supply me
With any fit forewarning?　This strange
　　vision　　　　　　　　　　　　20
(Together with the dark prediction
Used by the Prince of Darkness that was
　　raised
By this embodied shadow) stir my
　　thoughts
With reminiscion[4] of the spirit's promise,
Who told me that by any invocation
I should have power to raise him, though
　　it wanted
The powerful words and decent rites of
　　art.
Never had my set brain such need of
　　spirit
T' instruct and cheer it; now, then, I will
　　claim　　　　　　　　　　　　29
Performance of his free and gentle vow
T' appear in greater light, and make
　　more plain
His rugged[5] oracle.　I long to know
How my dear mistress fares, and be
　　informed
What hand she now holds on the troubled
　　blood
Of her incenséd lord.　Methought the
　　spirit,
When he had uttered his perplexed
　　presage,
Threw his changed countenance headlong
　　into clouds;
His forehead bent, as it would hide his
　　face,
He knocked his chin against his dark-
　　ened breast,

----

[1] Secret coats of mail.　[2] Shade, ghost.　[3] Lack.　　　[4] Remembrance.　　[5] Unpolished, unfinished.

And struck a churlish silence through his
    powers.   40
Terror of Darkness!   O thou King of
    Flames,
That with thy music-footed horse dost
    strike
The clear light out of crystal on dark
    earth,
And hurl'st instructive fire [1] about the
    world,
Wake, wake the drowsy and enchanted
    Night
That sleeps with dead eyes in this heavy
    riddle!
Or, thou great Prince of Shades, where
    never sun
Sticks his far-darted beams, whose eyes
    are made
To shine in darkness, and see ever best
Where men are blindest, open now the
    heart   50
Of thy abashéd oracle, that, for fear
Of some ill it includes, would fain lie hid,
And rise thou with it in thy greater light.

Thunders. Surgit spiritus cum suis. [2]

BEH. [3] Thus to observe my vow of appari-
    tion
In greater light, and explicate thy fate,
I come, and tell thee that, if thou obey
The summons that thy mistress next will
    send thee,
Her hand shall be thy death.
BUS.   When will she send?
BEH.   Soon as I set again, where late I rose.
BUS.   Is the old friar slain?
BEH.   No, and yet lives not. 60
BUS.   Died he a natural death?
BEH.   He did.
BUS.   Who then
Will my dear mistress send?
BEH.   I must not tell thee.
BUS.   Who lets [4] thee?
BEH.   Fate.
BUS.   Who are Fate's ministers?
BEH.   The Guise and Monsieur.
BUS.   A fit pair of shears
    To cut the threads of kings and kingly
    spirits,

And consorts [5] fit to sound forth har-
    mony,
Set to the falls of kingdoms! Shall the
    hand
Of my kind mistress kill me?
BEH.   If thou yield
To her next summons.   Y'are fair-
    warned. Farewell!   *Thunders. Exit.*
BUS.   I must fare well, however, though I
    die,   70
My death consenting [6] with his augury.
Should not my powers obey when she
    commands,
My motion must be rebel to my will,
My will to life. If, when I have obeyed,
Her hand should so reward me, they must
    arm it,
Bind me, or force it; or, I lay my life,
She rather would convert it many times
On her own bosom, even to many deaths.
But, were there danger of such violence,
I know 'tis far from her intent to
    send,   80
And who she should send is as far from
    thought,
Since he is dead whose only mean she
    used.   *Knocks.*
Who's there? Look to the door, and let
    him in,
Though politic Monsieur or the violent
    Guise.

*Enter Montsurry, like the Friar, with a
                letter written in blood.*

MONT.   Hail to my worthy son!
BUS.   O lying spirit,
To say the friar was dead! I'll now
    believe
Nothing of all his forged predictions.
My kind and honored father, well re-
    vived!
I have been frighted with your death and
    mine,
And told my mistress' hand should be my
    death   90
If I obeyed this summons.
MONT.   I believed
Your love had been much clearer than
    to give
Any such doubt a thought, for she is
    clear,
And, having freed her husband's jealousy

---

[1] *I.e.*, the sun's rays.
[2] The spirit rises with his attendants.
[3] In the original this speaker is *Sp.* (for
Spirit), clearly Behemoth, come to fulfill his
promise of IV, ii, 159–62.
[4] Prevents.
[5] Companions, with a pun on the meaning
concerts.   [6] Agreeing.

(Of which her much abused hand here is
witness),

She prays, for urgent cause, your instant
presence.

Bus. Why, then your Prince of Spirits may
be called

The prince of liars.

MONT. Holy Writ so calls him.

Bus. [*Opening the letter.*] What, writ in
blood?

MONT. Ay, 'tis the ink of lovers.

Bus. O, 'tis a sacred witness of her
love. 100

So much elixir of her blood as this,

Dropped in the lightest dame, would
make her firm

As heat to fire, and, like to all the signs,[1]

Commands the life confined in all my
veins.

O, how it multiplies my blood with spirit,

And makes me apt t' encounter death
and hell.

But come, kind father, you fetch me to
heaven,

And to that end your holy weed was
given. *Exeunt.*

[SCENA QUARTA.

Same as Scena Prima.]

Thunder. Intrat[2] *Umbra Friar, and discovers*[3] *Tamyra.*

[UMB.] FRI. Up with these stupid thoughts,
still lovéd daughter,

And strike away this heartless trance of
anguish.

Be like the sun, and labor in eclipses;[4]

Look to the end of woes! O, can you sit

Mustering the horrors of your servant's
slaughter

Before your contemplation, and not
study

How to prevent it? Watch when he shall
rise,

And, with a sudden outcry of his murther,

Blow[5] his retreat before he be revenged.[6]

[1] Signs of the heavens, the stars.
[2] Enters.
[3] Reveals, unwraps from the arras.
[4] *I.e.*, to throw them off.
[5] Give a signal for.
[6] *I.e.*, before your husband's vengeance overtake him.

TAM. O father, have my dumb woes
waked your death? 10

When will our human griefs be at their
height?

Man is a tree that hath no top in cares,

No root in comforts; all his power to live

Is given to no end, but t' have power to
grieve.

UMB. FRI. It is the misery of our creation.
Your true friend,

Led by your husband, shadowed in my
weed,

Now enters the dark vault.

TAM. But, my dearest father,

Why will not you appear to him yourself,

And see that none of these deceits annoy
him? 20

UMB. FRI. My power is limited; alas! I
cannot.

All that I can do—See, the cave opens!
Exit. D'Ambois at the gulf.[7]

TAM. Away, my love, away! Thou wilt be
murthered!

Enter Monsieur and Guise above.

Bus. Murthered? I know not what that
Hebrew means.

That word had ne'er been named had all
been D'Ambois.

Murthered? By heaven, he is my murtherer

That shows me not a murtherer; what
such bug[8]

Abhorreth not the very sleep of D'Ambois?

Murthered? Who dares give all the room
I see

To D'Ambois' reach, or look with any
odds 30

His fight i' th' face, upon whose hand sits
death,

Whose sword hath wings, and every
feather pierceth?

If I scape Monsieur's pothecary shops,

Foutre[9] for Guise's shambles! 'Twas ill
plotted;

They should have mauled me here

When I was rising. I am up and ready.

Let in my politic visitants; let them in,

Though ent'ring like so many moving
armors.

[7] Cave, vault.
[8] Object of terror, bogey.
[9] A fig (an expression of contempt).

Fate is more strong than arms and sly
   than treason,   39
And I at all parts buckled [1] in my fate.
Mon. ⎱ Why enter not the coward vil-
Guise. ⎰   lains?
Bus. Dare they not come?

*Enter Murtherers with [Umbra] Friar at the
                                    other door.*
Tam.   They come!
First Mur.   Come all at once!
[Umb.] Fri. Back, coward murtherers,
   back!
Omnes.   Defend us, heaven!
   Exeunt all but the First [Murtherer].
First Mur. Come ye not on?
Bus.   No, slave, nor goest thou off!
Stand you so firm? [*Strikes at him.*] Will
   it not enter here?
You have a face yet. [*Kills him.*] So!
In thy life's flame
I burn the first rites to my mistress' fame.
Umb. Fri. Breathe thee, brave son, against
   the other charge.
Bus. O, is it true then that my sense first
   told me?
Is my kind father dead?
Tam.   He is, my love. 50
'Twas the earl, my husband, in his weed,
   that brought thee.
Bus. That was a speeding sleight,[2] and
   well resembled.
Where is that angry earl? My lord, come
   forth
And show your own face in your own
   affair;
Take not into your noble veins the blood
Of these base villains, nor the light re-
   ports
Of blistered tongues for clear and weighty
   truth,
But me against the world, in pure defense
Of your rare lady, to whose spotless name
I stand here as a bulwark, and project 60
A life to her renown, that ever yet
Hath been untainted, even in Envy's eye.
And, where it would protect, a sanctuary,
Brave earl, come forth, and keep your
   scandal in;
'Tis not our fault if you enforce the spot,[3]
Nor the wreak [4] yours, if you perform it
   not.

---

[1] Armored.   [3] Emphasize the dishonor.
[2] Successful trick.   [4] Vengeance.

Enter Mont[surry], with all the Murtherers.

Mont. Cowards, a fiend or spirit beat ye
   off?
They are your own faint spirits that have
   forged
The fearful shadows that your eyes
   deluded.
The fiend was in you; cast him out then,
   thus.   70
[*They fight.*]   D'Ambois hath Montsurry
                                    down.
Tam. Favor my lord, my love, O, favor
   him!
Bus. I will not touch him; take your life,
   my lord,
And be appeased.
Pistols shot within.[5]   [*Bussy is wounded.*]
              O, then the coward Fates
Have maimed themselves, and ever lost
   their honor.
Umb. Fri. What have ye done, slaves?
   Irreligious lord!
Bus. Forbear them, father; 'tis enough for
   me
That Guise and Monsieur, death and
   destiny,
Come behind D'Ambois. Is my body,
   then,
But penetrable flesh? And must my
   mind   79
Follow my blood? Can my divine part
   add
No aid to th' earthly in extremity?
Then these divines are but for form, not
   fact.
Man is of two sweet courtly friends com-
   pact,
A mistress and a servant; let my death
Define life nothing but a courtier's
   breath.
Nothing is made of naught, of all things
   made,
Their abstract being a dream but of a
   shade.
I'll not complain to earth yet, but to
   heaven,
And, like a man, look upwards even in
   death.
And, if Vespasian thought in majesty 90
An emperor might die standing, why not
   I?   *She offers to help him.*[6]

---

[5] In the original this direction follows l. 71.
[6] In the original this direction follows l. 93.

Nay, without help, in which I will exceed
him;
For he died splinted with [1] his chamber
grooms.
Prop me, true sword, as thou hast ever
done!
The equal thought I bear of life and death
Shall make me faint on no side; I am up.
Here like a Roman statue I will stand
Till death hath made me marble. O my
fame,
Live in despite of murther! Take thy
wings
And haste thee where the gray-eyed
Morn perfumes   100
Her rosy chariot with Sabean spices;
Fly where the Evening from th' Iberian
vales
Takes on her swarthy shoulders Hecate,
Crowned with a grove of oaks; fly where
men feel
The burning axletree, and those that
suffer
Beneath the chariot of the snowy Bear; [2]
And tell them all that D'Ambois now is
hasting
To the eternal dwellers; that a thunder
Of all their sighs together (for their
frailties
Beheld in me) may quit my worthless [3]
fall   110
With a fit volley for my funeral.
UMB. FRI. Forgive thy murtherers.
BUS.   I forgive them all,
And you, my lord, their fautor; [4] for true
sign
Of which unfeigned remission, take my
sword;
Take it, and only give it motion,
And it shall find the way to victory
By his own brightness, and th' inherent
valor
My fight hath stilled [5] into 't, with
charms of spirit.
Now let me pray you that my weighty
blood,
Laid in one scale of your impartial
spleen,   120
May sway the forfeit of my worthy love
Weighed in the other; and be reconciled

With all forgiveness to your matchless
wife.
TAM. Forgive thou me, dear servant, and
this hand
That led thy life to this unworthy end;
Forgive it, for the blood with which 'tis
stained,
In which I writ the summons of thy
death
(The forcéd summons) by this bleeding
wound,
By this here in my bosom, and by this
That makes me hold up both my hands
imbrued   130
For thy dear pardon.
BUS.   O, my heart is broken!
Fate nor these murtherers, Monsieur nor
the Guise,
Have any glory in my death, but this,
This killing spectacle, this prodigy.
My sun is turned to blood, in whose red
beams
Pindus and Ossa, hid in drifts of snow
Laid on my heart and liver, from their
veins
Melt like two hungry torrents, eating
rocks,
Into the ocean of all human life,
And make it bitter, only with my
blood.   140
O frail condition of strength, valor, vir-
tue,
In me (like warning fire upon the top
Of some steep beacon on a steeper hill)
Made to express it, like a falling star
Silently glanced [6] that like a thunderbolt
Looked to have stuck [7] and shook the
firmament.   Moritur.[8]
UMB. FRI. Farewell, brave relics of a com-
plete man!
Look up and see thy spirit made a star;
Join flames with Hercules,[9] and, when
thou sett'st
Thy radiant forehead in the firma-
ment,   150
Make the vast crystal [10] crack with thy
receipt;
Spread to a world of fire, and the aged sky
Cheer with new sparks of old humanity.

---

[1] Supported by.
[2] *I.e.*, equatorial and arctic regions. This
passage is adapted from Seneca, *Hercules Œtæus.*
[3] Unworthy.   [4] Patron.   [5] Instilled.

[6] Glimpsed.
[7] Pierced. Boas conjectures *struck.*
[8] He dies.
[9] From 1607 edn. 1641 edn. has *Jove flames
with her rules.*   [10] Crystalline sphere.

[*To Montsurry*.] Son of the earth, whom my
 unrested soul
 Rues t' have begotten in the faith of
  heaven,
 Assay to gratulate ¹ and pacify
 The soul fled from this worthy by per-
  forming
 The Christian reconcilement he besought
 Betwixt thee and thy lady. Let her
  wounds
 Manlessly ² digged in her, be eased and
  cured   160
 With balm of thine own tears, or be
  assured
 Never to rest free from my haunt and
  horror.
Mont. See how she merits this, still kneel-
  ing by,
 And mourning his fall more than her own
  fault.
Umb. Fri. Remove, dear daughter, and
  content thy husband;
 So piety wills thee, and thy servant's
  peace.
Tam. O wretched piety, that art so distract
 In thine own constancy, and in thy right
 Must be unrighteous! If I right my
  friend,
 I wrong my husband; if his wrong I
  shun,   170
 The duty of my friend I leave undone.
 Ill plays on both sides; here and there it
  riseth;
 No place, no good, so good but ill com-
  priseth.
 O, had I never married but for form,
 Never vowed faith but purposed to de-
  ceive,
 Never made conscience of any sin,
 But cloaked it privately and made it
  common,
 Nor never honored been in blood or
  mind,
 Happy had I been then, as others are
 Of the like license. I had then been
  honored;   180
 Lived without envy; custom had be-
  numbed
 All sense of scruple, and all note of
  frailty;
 My fame had been untouched, my heart
  unbroken;
 But, shunning all, I strike on all offense.

¹ Repay, please. ² In an unmanly fashion.

O husband! Dear friend! O my con-
 science!
Mon. Come, let's away; my senses are not
 proof
 Against those plaints.
*Exeunt Guise, Mon[sieur]. D'Ambois is
         borne off.*
Mont. I must not yield to pity, nor to
 love
 So servile and so traitorous. Cease, my
  blood,
 To wrastle with my honor, fame, and
  judgment.—   190
 Away! Forsake my house; forbear com-
  plaints
 Where thou hast bred them. Here all
  things [are] ³ full
 Of their own shame and sorrow; leave my
  house.
Tam. Sweet lord, forgive me, and I will be
  gone,
 And till these wounds—that never balm
  shall close
 Till death hath entered at them, so I love
  them,
 Being opened by your hands—by death
  be cured,
 I never more will grieve you with my
  sight,
 Never endure that any roof shall part
 Mine eyes and heaven; but to the open
  deserts,   200
 Like to a hunted tigress, I will fly,
 Eating my heart, shunning the steps of
  men,
 And look on no side till I be arrived.
Mont. I do forgive thee, and upon my
  knees,
 With hands held up to heaven, wish that
  mine honor
 Would suffer reconcilement to my love;
 But, since it will not, honor never serve
 My love with flourishing object till it
  sterve! ⁴
 And, as this taper, though it upwards
  look,
 Downwards must needs consume, so let
  our love!   210
 As having lost his honey, the sweet taste
 Runs into savor, and will needs retain
 A spice of his first parents, till, like life,
 It sees and dies, so let our love! And
  lastly,

³ Added by Dilke.   ⁴ Perish.

As, when the flame is suffered to look up,
It keeps his luster, but, being thus turned
  down,
His natural course of useful light in-
  verted,
His own stuff puts it out, so let our
  love!
Now turn from me, as here I turn from
  thee,
And may both points of heaven's straight
  axletree   220
Conjoin in one, before thyself and me.
                                  Exeunt severally.

FINIS ACTUS QUINTI ET ULTIMI.

EPILOGUE

WITH many hands you have seen D'Ambois
  slain,
Yet by your grace he may revive again,
And every day grow stronger in his skill
To please, as we presume he is in will.
The best deserving actors of the time
Had their ascents, and by degrees did climb
To their full height, a place to study due.
To make him tread in their path lies in you;
He'll not forget his makers, but still prove
His thankfulness as you increase your
  love.

                        FINIS.

JOHN WEBSTER

No one has discovered when John Webster was born or when he died. He tells us himself that he was born "free" of the Merchant Tailors' Company, but there is no evidence that he ever followed in his father's footsteps or even attended the Merchant Tailors' School. In fact, his education is as obscure as his birth. Chambers has pointed out that a John Webster acted with an English company in Germany in 1596, and Lucas has tried to identify the dramatist with the John Webster who entered the Middle Temple in 1598 to study law. No certain record of him appears before 1602, however, when Henslowe's Diary shows that he had a part that year in several plays, now lost under the titles given, in which he collaborated in different combinations with Dekker, Drayton, Middleton, Heywood, and others. *Sir Thomas Wyatt*, published in 1607 as by Webster and Dekker, was probably a revised form of one of these plays. It is possible that Webster had only a secondary part in the later plays *Westward Ho* and *Northward Ho*, written with Dekker and probably acted in 1604 and 1605. He merely made slight "additions" to *The Malcontent*. The tragedy *Appius and Virginia*, about the date of which there is a wide difference of opinion, was published in 1654 as Webster's, but critics are now inclined to give Heywood a share in it. There is in all this work nothing to prepare one for the two great tragedies, *The White Devil*, printed in 1612, and *The Duchess of Malfi*, probably produced in 1613–14. After them Webster wrote *The Devil's Law Case*, a tragicomedy in the Fletcherian manner; he mentions a play of *Guise*, now lost; a share in *A Cure for a Cuckold* is doubtfully assigned to him; and in 1624 there is record of a new play by Ford and Webster, which from its title must have been a domestic tragedy. Besides some minor verse, he composed the lord mayor's pageant for 1624. Nothing specific is heard of him after that date. He may have been the John Webster who was buried in 1638.

Critics prefer *The White Devil* or *The Duchess of Malfi* according as they are impressed by the greater plausibility and dramatic effectiveness of the first or the greater poetry and pathos of the second. Both plays are concerned with actual events that occurred in Italy. *The White Devil*, which dramatizes a murder committed in 1585, may have been based on oral reports or on some lost news sheet. At least no printed source is known. *The Duchess of Malfi* came ultimately from a story of Bandello, translated into French by Belleforest in *Histoires tragiques*, and from the French version into English in Painter's *Palace of Pleasure*, which was Webster's direct source. Bandello claimed to have known intimately those involved in the tragedy, and he may even have been the original of the character Delio. To some extent, facts have been altered in both plays to meet the needs of drama, and have been overlaid with conventions of the Elizabethan tragedy of blood. In the treatment of revenge for honor, features of the older revenge plays have been used, but the tool-villain in each case is of the malcontent type, and the Italian characters breathe a spirit only less fraught with deadly passions than those of Marston and Tourneur. *The Duchess of Malfi* has a loosely constructed plot, whose dragging action leads to a climax at the end of the fourth act, only to be prolonged through a fifth. It is chiefly on the characters and the appropriateness and poetic power of their speech that Webster fixed his attention. His interest in humanizing his characters is suggested in a note printed at the end of *The White Devil* praising the actors for their "true imitation of life, without striving to make nature a monster." No doubt some of his power to give appropriate utterances to his characters and to illuminate them with an imaginative flash results from a study of sententious and pictorial language, indicated by his admiration for Seneca and, among his contemporaries, for Chapman, with his "full and heightened style." Occasionally one of his sentientious passages can be traced to a classical writer or to a contemporary like Montaigne. Many of the vivid phrases in the scene in which the Duchess of Malfi is tortured and slain are borrowed from Sidney's *Arcadia*. The attention to effective lines is also suggested by the frequency with which Webster repeats the more vivid ones in different plays. In the poetic quality of his style, in his moving reflection on the mysteries of life, and in his understanding of character, Webster is most often compared to Shakespeare. Certainly the full imaginative and creative sweep of Elizabethan drama ends with *The Duchess of Malfi*.

The play was first published in 1623. Other editions followed in 1640, 1678, 1708. The present text is based on the critical edition of the quarto of 1623 printed by Sampson in the Belles-Lettres Series. The edition of the play published by Lucas in *The Complete Works of John Webster* has also been consulted.

THE DUCHESS OF MALFI[1]

BY

JOHN WEBSTER

THE ACTORS' NAMES

[DANIEL DE] BOSOLA [, *gentleman of the horse to the Duchess*]: *J. Lowin.*
FERDINAND [, *Duke of Calabria*]: 1. *R. Burbadge;* 2. *J. Taylor.*
CARDINAL [, *his brother*]: 1. *H. Condell;* 2. *R. Robinson.*
ANTONIO [BOLOGNA, *the Duchess' steward*]: 1. *W. Ostler;* 2. *R. Benfield.*
DELIO [, *his friend*]: *J. Underwood.*
FOROBOSCO[2] [, *an attendant*]: *N. Tooley.*
MALATESTE [, *a count*].
THE MARQUIS OF PESCARA: *J. Rice.*
SILVIO [, *a lord*]: *T. Pollard.*
[CASTRUCHIO, *an old lord*.]

[RODERIGO, *a lord.*]
[GRISOLAN, *a lord.*]
THE SEVERAL MADMEN: *N. Tooley, J. Underwood, etc.*
THE DUCHESS: *R. Sharp.*
[JULIA, *Castruchio's wife and*] the Cardinal's mis[*tress*]: *J. Thompson.*
DOCTOR ⎰
CARIOLA ⎱ : *R. Pallant.*
COURT OFFICERS ⎰
[OLD LADY.]
THREE YOUNG CHILDREN.
TWO PILGRIMS.
[LADIES, EXECUTIONERS, *and* ATTENDANTS.]

[SCENE: *Italy.*

TIME: *Early sixteenth century.*][3]

ACTUS I. SCENA i.

[*The presence chamber of the Duchess' palace at Amalfi.*]

Antonio and Delio; Bosola, Cardinal.[4]

DEL. You are welcome to your country, dear Antonio;
You have been long in France, and you return

A very formal Frenchman in your habit.
How do you like the French court?
ANT.   I admire it.
In seeking to reduce both state and people
To a fixed order, their judicious king
Begins at home, quits[5] first his royal palace
Of flatt'ring sycophants, of dissolute
And infamous persons, which he sweetly terms
His master's masterpiece, the work of heaven,   10
Consid'ring duly that a prince's court
Is like a common fountain, whence should flow
Pure silver drops in general,[6] but, if 't chance
Some cursed example poison 't near the head,

---

[1] The complete title reads: "The Tragedy of the Duchess of Malfi. As It Was Presented Privately at the Blackfriars, and Publicly at the Globe, by the King's Majesty's Servants. The Perfect and Exact Copy, with Divers Things Printed That the Length of the Play Would not Bear in the Presentment. Written by John Webster."
[2] In the printed version of the play this character does not speak.
[3] A dedication to George Harding, Baron Berkeley, and commendatory verses by Thomas Middleton, William Rowley, and John Ford are omitted in the present edition.
[4] Last two enter later.

[5] Clears.   [6] Without exception.

"Death and diseases through the whole
  land spread." [1]
And what is 't makes this blessed govern-
  ment
But a most provident council, who dare
  freely
Inform him the corruption of the times?
Though some o' th' court hold it pre-
  sumption
To instruct princes what they ought to
  do,   20
It is a noble duty to inform them
What they ought to foresee.—Here
  comes Bosola,
The only court-gall.

[Enter Bosola.]

                Yet I observe his railing
Is not for simple love of piety.
Indeed, he rails at those things which he
  wants,
Would be as lecherous, covetous, or
  proud,
Bloody, or envious as any man,
If he had means to be so.—Here's the
  cardinal.

[Enter Cardinal.]

Bos. I do haunt you still.
Card. So.   30
Bos.[2] I have done you better service
than to be slighted thus. Miserable age,
where only the reward of doing well is the
doing of it!
Card. You enforce your merit too much.
Bos. I fell into the galleys in your service, where, for two years together, I wore
two towels instead of a shirt, with a knot on
the shoulder, after the fashion of a Roman
mantle. Slighted thus! I will thrive   [40
some way. Blackbirds fatten best in
hard weather; why not I in these dog
days?
Card. Would you could become honest!
Bos. With all your divinity, do but
direct me the way to it. I have known many
travel far for it, and yet return as arrant
knaves as they went forth, because they

carried themselves always along with them.
[*Exit Cardinal.*] Are you gone? Some [50
fellows, they say, are possessed with the
devil, but this great fellow were able to
possess the greatest devil, and make him
worse.
Ant. He hath denied thee some suit?
Bos. He and his brother are like plum
trees that grow crooked over standing
pools; they are rich and o'erladen with
fruit, but none but crows, pies, and caterpillars feed on them. Could I be one [60
of their flatt'ring panders, I would hang
on their ears like a horseleech, till I were
full, and then drop off. I pray, leave me.
Who would rely upon these miserable
dependences, in expectation to be advanced tomorrow? What creature ever
fed worse than hoping Tantalus? Nor
ever died [3] any man more fearfully than
he that hoped for a pardon.[3] There are
rewards for hawks and dogs when [4] [70
they have done us service; but, for a soldier
that hazards his limbs in a battle, nothing
but a kind of geometry is his last supporta-
tion.
Del. Geometry?
Bos. Ay, to hang in a fair pair of slings,
take his latter swing in the world upon
an honorable pair of crutches, from hospital to hospital. Fare ye well, sir. And
yet do not you scorn us, for places in [80
the court are but like beds in the hospital,
where this man's head lies at that man's
foot, and so lower and lower.   [*Exit.*]
Del. I knew this fellow seven years in
  the galleys
For a notorious murther; and 'twas
  thought
The cardinal suborned it. He was released
By the French general, Gaston de Foix,[5]
When he recovered Naples.
Ant.   'Tis great pity
He should be thus neglected. I have
  heard
He's very valiant. This foul melancholy   90
Will poison all his goodness; for, I'll
  tell you,

---

[1] Sententious passages set off in the original
with quotation marks or italics are here indicated throughout by quotation marks.
[2] All prose passages in the play were originally
printed as irregular verse.

[3] Readings from 1640 edn. Original reads *did*
and *pleadon*.
[4] From 1640 edn. Earlier edns. read *and when*.
[5] Original reads *Foux*.

If too immoderate sleep be truly said
To be an inward rust unto the soul,
It then doth follow want of action
Breeds all black malcontents; and their
　close rearing,
Like moths in cloth, do hurt for want of
　wearing.[1]

Scena ii.

[*The same.*]

Antonio, Delio, Ferdinand,[2] *Cardinal,*[2]
Duchess,[2] *Castruchio, Silvio, Roderigo,
Grisolan, Bosola, Julia,*[2] *Cariola.*[2]

DEL. The presence gins [3] to fill. You prom-
　ised me
To make me the partaker of the natures
Of some of your great courtiers.

ANT.　　　　　　The lord cardinal's
And other strangers' that are now in
　court?
I shall.—Here comes the great Calabrian
　duke.

[*Enter Ferdinand and Attendants.*]

FERD. Who took the ring oft'nest? [4]

SIL. Antonio Bologna, my lord.

FERD. Our sister duchess' great master
of her household?　Give him the jewel.—
When shall we leave this sportive ac-　[10
tion, and fall to action indeed?

CAST. Methinks, my lord, you should
not desire to go to war in person.

FERD. [*Aside.*] Now for some gravity.—
Why, my lord?

CAST. It is fitting a soldier arise to be a
prince, but not necessary a prince descend
to be a captain.

FERD. No?

CAST. No, my lord; he were far bet-　[20
ter do it by a deputy.

FERD. Why should he not as well sleep
or eat by a deputy?　This might take idle,
offensive, and base office from him, whereas
the other deprives him of honor.

CAST. Believe my experience: that realm
is never long in quiet where the ruler is a
soldier.

FERD. Thou told'st me thy wife could
not endure fighting—　　　　　　　30

CAST. True, my lord.

FERD. And of a jest she broke [5] of a captain she met full of wounds—I have forgot
it.

CAST. She told him, my lord, he was a
pitiful fellow, to lie, like the children of
Ismael, all in tents.[6]

FERD. Why, there's a wit were able to
undo all the chirurgeons [7] o' the city, for,
although gallants should quarrel, and　[40
had drawn their weapons, and were ready
to go to it, yet her persuasions would make
them put up.

CAST. That she would, my lord.—How
do you like my Spanish jennet?

ROD. He is all fire.

FERD. I am of Pliny's opinion; I think
he was begot by the wind; he runs as if he
were ballast with quicksilver.

SIL. True, my lord, he reels from　[50
the tilt often.

ROD. }
GRIS. } Ha, ha, ha!

FERD. Why do you laugh? Methinks you
that are courtiers should be my touchwood—
take fire when I give fire; that is, laugh when
I laugh, were the subject never so witty.

CAST. True, my lord; I myself have
heard a very good jest, and have scorned to
seem to have so silly a wit as to understand
it.　　　　　　　　　　　　　　60

FERD. But I can laugh at your fool, my
lord.

CAST. He cannot speak, you know, but
he makes faces. My lady cannot abide him.

FERD. No?

CAST. Nor endure to be in merry company; for she says too much laughing and
too much company fills her too full of the
wrinkle.

FERD. I would, then, have a mathe-　[70
matical instrument made for her face, that
she might not laugh out of compass.—I
shall shortly visit you at Milan, Lord
Silvio.

SIL. Your grace shall arrive most welcome.

FERD. You are a good horseman, Antonio; you have excellent riders in France.
What do you think of good horsemanship?

ANT. Nobly, my lord. As out of　[80

---

[1] The scene division throughout appears to be
purely artificial, since the action continues without pause.　　[3] Begins.
[2] Enters later.　[4] *I.e.,* in the tilting at the ring.

[5] Told.
[6] With a pun on the meaning *lint,* for dressing
wounds.　　　　　　　　[7] Surgeons.

the Grecian horse issued many famous princes, so out of brave horsemanship arise the first sparks of growing resolution, that raise the mind to noble action.

FERD. You have bespoke it worthily.

SIL. Your brother, the lord cardinal, and sister duchess.

[*Enter Cardinal, Duchess, Cariola, and Julia.*]

CARD. Are the galleys come about?

GRIS. They are, my lord.

FERD. Here's the Lord Silvio, is come to take his leave.

DEL. [*Aside to Antonio.*] Now, sir, your promise. What's that cardinal? 90
I mean his temper. They say he's a brave fellow,
Will play his five thousand crowns at tennis, dance,
Court ladies, and one that hath fought single combats.

ANT. Some such flashes superficially hang on him for form, but, observe his inward character, he is a melancholy churchman. The spring in his face is nothing but the engend'ring of toads; where he is jealous of any man, he lays worse plots for them than ever was imposed [100 on Hercules, for he strews in his way flatter[er]s, panders, intelligencers,[1] atheists, and a thousand such political monsters. He should have been pope; but, instead of coming to it by the primitive decency of the church, he did bestow bribes so largely and so impudently as if he would have carried it away without heaven's knowledge. Some good he hath done—

DEL. You have given too much of him. What's his brother? 110

ANT. The duke there? A most perverse and turbulent nature.
What appears in him mirth is merely outside;
If he laugh heartily, it is to laugh
All honesty out of fashion.

DEL. Twins?

ANT. In quality.
He speaks with others' tongues, and hears men's suits
With others' ears; will seem to sleep o' th' bench
Only to entrap offenders in their answers;

Dooms men to death by information;[2]
Rewards by hearsay.

DEL. Then the law to him
Is like a foul, black cobweb to a spider— 120
He makes it his dwelling and a prison
To entangle those shall feed him.

ANT. Most true.
He never pays debts unless they be shrewd[3] turns,
And those he will confess that he doth owe.
Last, for his brother there, the cardinal,
They that do flatter him most say oracles
Hang at his lips; and verily I believe them,
For the devil speaks in them.
But for their sister, the right noble duchess,
You never fixed your eye on three fair medals 130
Cast in one figure,[4] of so different temper.
For her discourse, it is so full of rapture,
You only will begin then to be sorry
When she doth end her speech, and wish, in wonder,
She held it less vainglory to talk much
Than your penance to hear her. Whilst she speaks,
She throws upon a man so sweet a look
That it were able raise one to a galliard
That lay in a dead palsy, and to dote
On that sweet countenance; but in that look 140
There speaketh so divine a continence
As cuts off all lascivious and vain hope.
Her days are practiced in such noble virtue
That sure her nights, nay, more, her very sleeps,
Are more in heaven than other ladies' shrifts.
Let all sweet ladies break their flatt'ring glasses,
And dress themselves in her.

DEL. Fie, Antonio,
You play the wire-drawer with her commendations.[5]

ANT. I'll case the picture up only thus much—

---

[1] Spies.

[2] Informer's evidence.
[3] From 1640 edn. Original has *shewed.*
[4] Mold.
[5] You draw her praises out at great length.

All her particular worth grows to this
   sum: 150
She stains [1] the time past, lights the time
   to come.
CARI. You must attend my lady in the gal-
   lery
Some half an hour hence.
ANT. I shall.
              [Exeunt Antonio and Delio.]
FERD. Sister, I have a suit to you.
DUCH.   To me, sir?
FERD. A gentlemen here, Daniel de
   Bosola,
One that was in the galleys—
DUCH.   Yes, I know him.
FERD. A worthy fellow h' is; pray, let me
   entreat for
The provisorship [2] of your horse.
DUCH.   Your knowledge of him
Commends him and prefers him.
FERD.   Call him hither.
               [Exeunt Attendants.]
We now upon [3] parting, good Lord
   Silvio,   161
Do us commend to all our noble friends
At the leaguer. [4]
SIL.   Sir, I shall.
FERD. [5]   You are for Milan?
SIL. I am.
DUCH. Bring the caroches. [6]—We'll bring
   you down to the haven.

[Exeunt all except Cardinal and Ferdinand.]

CARD. Be sure you entertain that Bosola
For your intelligence. [7] I would not be
   seen in 't;
And therefore many times I have slighted
   him
When he did court our furtherance, as
   this morning.
FERD. Antonio, the great master of her
   household,   170
Had been far fitter.
CARD.   You are deceived in him.
His nature is too honest for such busi-
   ness.—
He comes; I'll leave you.   [Exit.]

<hr />

[1] "Deprives of luster" (Lucas).
[2] Office of purveyor.
[3] At the point of.
[4] Camp. From 1640 edn.; original reads
   leagues.
[5] Sampson assigns this speech to the Duchess.
[6] Coaches.
[7] Information from spies.

[Enter Bosola.]

BOS.   I was lured [8] to you.
FERD. My brother here, the cardinal,
   could never
Abide you.
BOS.   Never since he was in my debt.
FERD. May be some oblique character in
   your face
Made him suspect you.
BOS.   Doth he study physiognomy?
There's no more credit to be given to th'
   face
Than to a sick man's urine, which some
   call
The physician's whore, because she
   cozens him.   180
He did suspect me wrongfully.
FERD.   For that
You must give great men leave to take
   their times.
Distrust doth cause us seldom be de-
   ceived.
You see, the oft shaking of the cedar tree
Fastens it more at root.
BOS.   Yet take heed,
For to suspect a friend unworthily
Instructs him the next way to suspect
   you,
And prompts him to deceive you.
FERD.   There's gold.
BOS.   So!
What follows? Never rained such
   showers as these
Without thunderbolts i' th' tail of
   them. Whose throat must I cut?
FERD. Your inclination to shed blood rides
   post [9]   191
Before my occasion to use you. I give
   you that
To live i' th' court here, and observe the
   duchess;
To note all the particulars of her havior,
What suitors do solicit her for marriage,
And whom she best affects. [10] She's a
   young widow;
I would not have her marry again.
BOS.   No, sir?
FERD. Do not you ask the reason, but be
   satisfied.
I say I would not.
BOS.   It seems you would create me
One of your familiars.

<hr />

[8] Called.   [9] At full speed.   [10] Likes.

FERD.   Familiar! What's that?

Bos. Why, a very quaint invisible devil in
   flesh—   201
   An intelligencer.

FERD.   Such a kind of thriving thing
   I would wish thee; and ere long thou
   mayst arrive
   At a higher place by 't.

Bos.   Take your devils,
   Which hell calls angels![1] These cursed
   gifts would make
   You a corrupter, me an impudent traitor;
   And, should I take these, they'ld take
   me [to][2] hell.

FERD. Sir, I'll take nothing from you that
   I have given.
   There is a place that I procured for you
   This morning, the provisorship o' th'
   horse.   210
   Have you heard on 't?

Bos.   No.

FERD.   'Tis yours. Is 't not
   worth thanks?

Bos. I would have you curse yourself now,
   that your bounty
   (Which makes men truly noble) e'er
   should make me
   A villain. O, that to avoid ingratitude
   For the good deed you have done me, I
   must do
   All the ill man can invent! Thus the
   devil
   Candies all sins o'er;[3] and what heaven
   terms vild,[4]
   That names he complimental.

FERD.   Be yourself;
   Keep your old garb of melancholy. 'Twill
   express
   You envy those that stand above your
   reach,   220
   Yet strive not to come near 'em. This
   will gain
   Access to private lodgings, where yourself
   May, like a politic dormouse—

Bos.   As I have seen some
   Feed in a lord's dish, half asleep, not
   seeming
   To listen to any talk; and yet these
   rogues
   Have cut his throat in a dream. What's
   my place?

The provisorship o' th' horse? Say, then,
   my corruption
Grew out of horse dung. I am your
   creature.

FERD.   Away!

Bos. [*Aside.*] Let good men, for good
   deeds, covet good fame,
   Since place and riches oft are bribes of
   shame.   230
   Sometimes the devil doth preach.
                      Exit Bosola.[5]

[*Enter Duchess, Cardinal, and Cariola.*]

CARD. We are to part from you, and your
   own discretion
   Must now be your director.

FERD.   You are a widow:
   You know already what man is; and
   therefore
   Let not youth, high promotion, eloquence—

CARD. No, nor anything without the addition,[6] Honor,
   Sway your high blood.

FERD.   Marry! They
   are most luxurious[7]
   Will wed twice.

CARD.   O, fie!

FERD.   Their livers[8] are
   more spotted
   Than Laban's sheep.

DUCH.   Diamonds are of most value,
   They say, that have passed through most
   jewelers' hands.   240

FERD. Whores by that rule are precious.

DUCH.   Will you hear me?
   I'll never marry.

CARD.   So most widows say;
   But commonly that motion[9] lasts no
   longer
   Than the turning of an hourglass—the
   funeral sermon
   And it end both together.

FERD.   Now hear me:
   You live in a rank pasture, here, i' th'
   court.
   There is a kind of honeydew that's
   deadly;

---

[5] With no indication of scene division the
scene apparently shifts slowly to the gallery of
the palace.

[1] Gold coins.   [2] From 1708 edn.
[3] From 1640 edn. Original reads *are.*
[4] Vile.
[6] Title.   [8] Seat of love.
[7] Lecherous.   [9] Intention.

'Twill poison your fame; look to 't. Be
  not cunning,
For they whose faces do belie their
  hearts
Are witches ere they arrive at twenty
  years—   250
Ay, and give the devil suck.
DUCH. This is terrible good counsel.
FERD. Hypocrisy is woven of a fine, small
  thread,
Subtler than Vulcan's engine; [1] yet, be-
  lieve 't,
Your darkest actions, nay, your privat'st
  thoughts,
Will come to light.
CARD.   You may flatter yourself,
And take your own choice; privately be
  married
Under the eaves of night—
FERD.   Think 't the best voyage
That e'er you made, like the irregular
  crab,
Which, though 't goes backward, thinks
  that it goes right   260
Because it goes its own way. But ob-
  serve,
Such weddings may more properly be
  said
To be executed than celebrated.
CARD.   The marriage night
Is the entrance into some prison.
FERD.   And those joys,
Those lustful pleasures, are like heavy
  sleeps
Which do forerun man's mischief.
CARD.   Fare you well.
Wisdom begins at the end; remember it.
                        [Exit.]
DUCH. I think this speech between you
  both was studied,
It came so roundly off.
FERD.   You are my sister.
This was my father's poniard, do you
  see?   270
I'ld be loath to see 't look rusty, cause
  'twas his.
I would have you to give o'er these
  chargeable [2] revels;
A visor and a mask are whispering-
  rooms [3]
That were never built for goodness—
  fare ye well—

And women like that part which, like the
  lamprey,
Hath never a bone in 't.
DUCH.   Fie, sir!
FERD.   Nay,
I mean the tongue—variety of courtship.
What cannot a neat knave with a smooth
  tale
Make a woman believe? Farewell, lusty
  widow.   [Exit.]
DUCH. Shall this move me? If all my royal
  kindred   280
Lay in my way unto this marriage,
I'ld make them my low footsteps. [4] And
  even now,
Even in this hate, as men in some great
  battles,
By apprehending [5] danger, have achieved
Almost impossible actions (I have heard
  soldiers say so),
So I through frights and threat'nings will
  assay
This dangerous venture. Let old wives
  report
I winked [6] and chose a husband.—
  Cariola,
To thy known secrecy I have given up
More than my life—my fame.
CARI.   Both shall be safe, 290
For I'll conceal this secret from the world
As warily as those that trade in poison
Keep poison from their children.
DUCH.   Thy protestation
Is ingenious and hearty; [7] I believe it.
Is Antonio come?
CARI.   He attends [8] you.
DUCH.   Good dear soul,
Leave me, but place thyself behind the
  arras,
Where thou mayst overhear us. Wish
  me good speed,
      [Cariola hides behind the arras.]
For I am going into a wilderness
Where I shall find nor path nor friendly
  clew   299
To be my guide.—

        [Enter Antonio.]

            I sent for you; sit down.
Take pen and ink, and write. Are you
  ready?

[1] Device; here, a net.   [2] Costly.
[3] Private chambers.

[4] Rungs of a ladder.
[5] Grasping.   [6] Shut my eyes.
[7] Ingenuous and from the heart.   [8] Awaits.

ANT.   Yes.

DUCH. What did I say?

ANT. That I should write somewhat.

DUCH.   O, I remember.

After these triumphs [1] and this large expense

It's fit, like thrifty husbands,[2] we inquire

What's laid up for tomorrow.

ANT. So please your beauteous excellence.

DUCH. Beauteous? Indeed, I thank you.

I look young for your sake;

You have ta'en my cares upon you.

ANT.   I'll fetch your grace [3]

The particulars of your revenue and expense.   310

DUCH. O, you are an upright treasurer, but you mistook;

For, when I said I meant to make inquiry

What's laid up for tomorrow, I did mean

What's laid up yonder for me.

ANT.   Where?

DUCH.   In heaven.

I am making my will (as 'tis fit princes should,

In perfect memory), and, I pray, sir, tell me,

Were not one better make it smiling, thus,

Than in deep groans and terrible ghastly looks,

As if the gifts we parted with procured [4]

That violent destruction? [5]

ANT.   O, much better.

DUCH. If I had a husband now, this care were quit.   321

But I intend to make you overseer.[6]

What good deed shall we first remember? Say.

ANT. Begin with that first good deed began i' th' world

After man's creation, the sacrament of marriage.

I'ld have you first provide for a good husband;

Give him all.

DUCH.   All?

ANT.   Yes, your excellent self.

DUCH. In a winding sheet?

ANT.   In a couple.

DUCH. Saint Winfrid, that were a strange will!

ANT.   'Twere strange

If there were no will in you to marry again.   330

DUCH. What do you think of marriage?

ANT. I take 't, as those that deny purgatory,

It locally contains or heaven or hell;

There's no third place in 't.

DUCH.   How do you affect it?

ANT. My banishment, feeding my melancholy,

Would often reason thus:—

DUCH.   Pray, let's hear it.

ANT. Say a man never marry nor have children,

What takes that from him? Only the bare name

Of being a father, or the weak delight

To see the little wanton ride a cockhorse

Upon a painted stick, or hear him chatter   341

Like a taught starling.

DUCH.   Fie, fie, what's all this?

One of your eyes is bloodshot. Use my ring to 't;

They say 'tis very sovereign. 'Twas my wedding ring,

And I did vow never to part with it

But to my second husband.

ANT. You have parted with it now.

DUCH. Yes, to help your eyesight.

ANT. You have made me stark blind.

DUCH. How?   350

ANT. There is a saucy and ambitious devil

Is dancing in this circle.

DUCH.   Remove him.

ANT.   How?

DUCH. There needs small conjuration when your finger

May do it: thus. [She puts the ring upon his finger.] Is it fit?

ANT.   What said you? He kneels.

DUCH.   Sir,

This goodly roof of yours is too low built;

I cannot stand upright in 't nor discourse,

Without I raise it higher. Raise yourself;

Or, if you please, my hand to help you—so.

                                        [Raises him.]

Ant. Ambition, madam, is a great man's madness,
That is not kept in chains and close-pent rooms, 360
But in fair, lightsome lodgings, and is girt
With the wild noise of prattling visitants,
Which makes it lunatic beyond all cure.
Conceive not I am so stupid but I aim [1]
Whereto your favors tend; but he's a fool
That, being acold, would thrust his hands i' th' fire
To warm them.
Duch. So, now the ground's broke,
You may discover what a wealthy mine
I make you lord of.
Ant. O, my unworthiness!
Duch. You were ill to sell yourself. 370
This dark'ning of your worth is not like that
Which tradesmen use i' th' city; their false lights
Are to rid bad wares off; and I must tell you,
If you will know where breathes a complete man
(I speak it without flattery), turn your eyes,
And progress through yourself.
Ant. Were there nor heaven nor hell,
I should be honest. I have long served virtue,
And never ta'en wages of her.
Duch. Now she pays it.
The misery of us that are born great!
We are forced to woo,[2] because none dare woo [2] us; 381
And, as a tyrant doubles with his words
And fearfully equivocates, so we
Are forced to express our violent passions
In riddles and in dreams, and leave the path
Of simple virtue, which was never made
To seem the thing it is not. Go, go brag
You have left me heartless; mine is in your bosom.
I hope 'twill multiply love there. You do tremble.
Make not your heart so dead a piece of flesh, 390

To fear more than to love me. Sir, be confident.
What is 't distracts you? This is flesh and blood, sir;
'Tis not the figure cut in alablaster [3]
Kneels at my husband's tomb. Awake, awake, man!
I do here put off all vain ceremony,
And only do appear to you a young widow
That claims you for her husband, and, like a widow,
I use but half a blush in 't.
Ant. Truth speak for me;
I will remain the constant sanctuary
Of your good name.
Duch. I thank you, gentle love, 400
And, cause you shall not come to me in debt,
Being now my steward, here upon your lips
I sign your *Quietus est.*[4] This you should have begged now.
I have seen children oft eat sweetmeats thus,
As fearful to devour them too soon.
Ant. But for your brothers?
Duch. Do not think of them.
All discord without this circumference
　　　　　　　　　　[*Puts her arms about him.*]
Is only to be pitied, and not feared.
Yet, should they know it, time will easily
Scatter the tempest.
Ant. These words should be mine,
And all the parts you have spoke, if some part of it 411
Would not have savored flattery.
Duch. Kneel!
　　　　　　　[*Cariola discloses herself.*]
Ant. Ha!
Duch. Be not amazed. This woman's of my counsel.
I have heard lawyers say a contract in a chamber
Per verba [*de*] *presenti* [5] is absolute marriage. [*She and Antonio kneel.*]
Bless, heaven, this sacred Gordian,[6] which let violence
Never untwine. [*They rise.*]

[1] Guess.
[2] Original spelling is *woe* with double meaning.
[3] Common corrupt pronunciation of *alabaster*.
[4] He is acquitted of his obligations (an accountant's term).
[5] Using words (*i.e.*, vows) in the present tense: I take thee. etc.
[6] Knot.

ANT. And may our sweet affections, like the spheres,
Be still [1] in motion!
DUCH.　　　　　Quick'ning, and make
The like soft music!　　　　　　420
ANT. That we may imitate the loving palms,
Best emblem of a peaceful marriage,
That never bore fruit, divided!
DUCH. What can the church force more?
ANT. That fortune may not know an accident,
Either of joy or sorrow, to divide
Our fixéd wishes!
DUCH.　　How can the church build faster?[2]
We now are man and wife, and 'tis the church
That must but echo this.[3]—Maid, stand apart.—
I now am blind.
ANT.　　　What's your conceit [4] in this?
DUCH. I would have you lead your fortune by the hand　　　　431
Unto your marriage bed.
(You speak in me this, for we now are one.)
We'll only lie and talk together, and plot
T' appease my humorous [5] kindred; and, if you please,
Like the old tale in *Alexander and Lodowick*,
Lay a naked sword between us, keep us chaste.
O, let me shroud my blushes in your bosom,
Since 'tis the treasury of all my secrets!
CARI. [*Aside.*] Whether the spirit of greatness or of woman　　　　440
Reign most in her, I know not; but it shows
A fearful madness. I owe her much of pity.　　　　　　　　*Exeunt.*

ACTUS II. SCENA i.

[*An apartment in the Duchess' palace.*]

Bosola, Castruchio, an Old Lady, Antonio, Delio, Duchess, Roderigo, Grisolan.[6]

BOS. You say you would fain be taken for an eminent courtier? [7]

---

[1] Always.　　　　　　[2] More firmly.
[3] Ordinarily it was expected that the church ceremony should follow such a marriage.
[4] Idea.　　　　　　　[5] Temperamental.
[6] All but the first two enter later.
[7] Member of a law court.

CAST. 'Tis the very main [8] of my ambition.
BOS. Let me see. You have a reasonable good face for 't already, and your nightcap [9] expresses your ears sufficient largely. I would have you learn to twirl the strings of your band with a good grace, and in a set speech, at th' end of every sentence, to hum three or four times, [11 or blow your nose till it smart again, to recover your memory. When you come to be a president in criminal causes, if you smile upon a prisoner, hang him; but, if you frown upon him and threaten him, let him be sure to scape the gallows.
CAST. I would be a very merry president.　　　　　　　20
BOS. Do not sup a-nights; 'twill beget you an admirable wit.
CAST. Rather it would make me have a good stomach to quarrel; for they say your roaring boys [10] eat meat seldom, and that makes them so valiant. But how shall I know whether the people take me for an eminent fellow?　　　　28
BOS. I will teach a trick to know it. Give out you lie a-dying, and, if you hear the common people curse you, be sure you are taken for one of the prime nightcaps.—

[*Enter an Old Lady.*]

You come from painting now?
OLD LADY. From what?
BOS. Why, from your scurvy face-physic. To behold thee not painted inclines somewhat near a miracle. These in thy face here were deep ruts and foul sloughs the last progress.[11] There was a lady in France that, having had the [40 small-pox, flayed the skin off her face to make it more level; and, whereas before she looked like a nutmeg-grater, after she resembled an abortive hedgehog.
OLD LADY. Do you call this painting?
BOS. No, no, but you call [it] [12] careening [13] of an old morphewed [14] lady, to make her disembogue [15] again. There's rough-cast phrase to your plastic.[16]

---

[8] Goal.
[9] Lawyer's coif.　　[11] Royal journey.
[10] Rowdies.　　　　[12] Supplied from 1678 edn.
[13] Turning a boat on its side for repairs.
[14] Scabbed.　　[15] Put to sea.　　[16] Modeling.

OLD LADY. It seems you are well ac- [50 quainted with my closet.

BOS. One would suspect it for a shop of witchcraft, to find in it the fat of serpents, spawn of snakes, Jews' spittle, and their young children['s] ordures; and all these for the face. I would sooner eat a dead pigeon taken from the soles of the feet of one sick of the plague than kiss one of you fasting. Here are two of you whose sin of your youth is the very patrimony [60 of the physician; makes him renew his footcloth with the spring, and change his high-priced courtesan with the fall of the leaf. I do wonder you do not loathe yourselves. Observe my meditation now.

What thing is in this outward form of man
To be beloved? We account it ominous
If nature do produce a colt, or lamb,
A fawn, or goat, in any limb resembling
A man, and fly from 't as a prodigy.
Man stands amazed to see his deformity
In any other creature but himself. 72
But in our own flesh, though we bear diseases
Which have their true names only ta'en from beasts,
As the most ulcerous wolf [1] and swinish measle;
Though we are eaten up of lice and worms;
And though continually we bear about us
A rotten and dead body, we delight
To hide it in rich tissue. All our fear,
Nay, all our terror, is lest our physician
Should put us in the ground to be made sweet.— 81
Your wife's gone to Rome; you two couple; and get you
To the wells at Lucca to recover your aches.
I have other work on foot.
　　[Exeunt Castruchio and Old Lady.]
I observe our duchess
Is sick a-days. She pukes, her stomach seethes,
The fins [2] of her eyelids look most teeming blue,[3]

[1] Lupus (Lat. for *wolf*) is a medical term for ulcer.
[2] Rims.
[3] Blue like those of a pregnant woman.

She wanes i' th' cheek, and waxes fat i' th' flank,
And, contrary to our Italian fashion,
Wears a loose-bodied gown. There's somewhat in 't. 90
I have a trick may chance discover it,
A pretty one; I have bought some apricocks,
The first our spring yields.

[*Enter Antonio and Delio.*]

DEL. [*Aside to Antonio.*] 　　　And so long since married?
You amaze me.

ANT. [*Aside to Delio.*] 　　　Let me seal your lips forever,
For, did I think that anything but th' air
Could carry these words from you, I should wish
You had no breath at all.—[*To Bosola.*] Now, sir, in your contemplation?
You are studying to become a great wise fellow?

BOS. O, sir, the opinion of wisdom is a foul tetter that runs all over a man's [100 body. If simplicity direct us to have no evil, it directs us to a happy being, for the subtlest folly proceeds from the subtlest wisdom. Let me be simply honest.

ANT. I do understand your inside.

BOS. 　　　　　　　Do you so?

ANT. Because you would not seem to appear to th' world
Puffed up with your preferment, you continue
This out-of-fashion melancholy. Leave it, leave it!

BOS. Give me leave to be honest in any phrase, in any compliment whatsoever. [110 Shall I confess myself to you? I look no higher than I can reach. They are the gods that must ride on winged horses; a lawyer's mule of a slow pace will both suit my disposition and business; for, mark me, when a man's mind rides faster than his horse can gallop, they quickly both tire.

ANT. You would look up to heaven, but I think
The devil, that rules i' th' air, stands in your light. 119

BOS. O, sir, you are lord of the ascendant,[4] chief man with the duchess; a duke was

[4] Person of the highest influence (an astrological term).

your cousin-german removed. Say you
were lineally descended from King Pepin,
or he himself, what of this? Search the
heads of the greatest rivers in the world,
you shall find them but bubbles of water.
Some would think the souls of princes
were brought forth by some more weighty
cause than those of meaner persons. They
are deceived; there's the same hand to [130
them. The like passions sway them; the
same reason that makes a vicar go to law
for a tithe-pig and undo his neighbors,
makes them spoil a whole province, and
batter down goodly cities with the cannon.

[Enter Duchess and Ladies.]

DUCH. Your arm, Antonio. Do I not grow
  fat?
I am exceeding short-winded.—Bosola,
  I would have you, sir, provide for me a
  litter,
Such a one as the Duchess of Florence
  rode in.
BOS. The duchess used one when she was
  great with child.   140
DUCH. I think she did.—Come hither;
  mend my ruff.
Here, when? Thou art such a tedious
  lady, and
Thy breath smells of lemon pills.[1]
  Would thou hadst done!
Shall I sound [2] under thy fingers? I am
So troubled with the mother![3]
BOS. [*Aside.*]   I fear, too much.
DUCH. I have heard you say that the
  French courtiers
Wear their hats on fore the king.
ANT. I have seen it.
DUCH.   In the presence?
ANT.   Yes.
[DUCH.] Why should not we bring up that
  fashion?
'Tis ceremony more than duty that con-
  sists   150
In the removing of a piece of felt.
Be you the example to the rest o' th'
  court;
Put on your hat first.
ANT.   You must pardon me.
I have seen, in colder countries than in
  France,

Nobles stand bare to th' prince; and the
  distinction
Methought showed reverently.
BOS. I have a present for your grace.
DUCH.   For me, sir?
BOS. Apricocks, madam.
DUCH.   O, sir, where are they?
I have heard of none to-year.[4]
BOS. [*Aside.*]   Good; her color rises!
DUCH. Indeed, I thank you; they are won-
  drous fair ones.   160
What an unskillful fellow is our gardener!
We shall have none this month.
BOS. Will not your grace pare them?
DUCH. No. They taste of musk, methinks;
  indeed they do.
BOS. I know not; yet I wish your grace
  had pared 'em.
DUCH. Why?
BOS.   I forgot to tell you, the
  knave gard'ner,
Only to raise his profit by them the sooner,
Did ripen them in horse dung.
DUCH.   O, you jest!—
You shall judge. Pray, taste one.
ANT.   Indeed, madam,
I do not love the fruit.
DUCH.   Sir, you are loath
To rob us of our dainties. 'Tis a delicate
  fruit;   171
They say they are restorative.
BOS.   'Tis a pretty
Art, this grafting.
DUCH.   'Tis so; a bett'ring of nature.
BOS. To make a pippin grow upon a crab,
A damson on a blackthorn.—[*Aside.*]
  How greedily she eats them!
A whirlwind strike off these bawd-
  farthingales!
For, but for that and the loose-bodied
  gown,
I should have discovered apparently [5]
The young springal [6] cutting a caper in
  her belly.
DUCH. I thank you, Bosola. They were
  right good ones,   180
If they do not make me sick.
ANT.   How now, madam?
DUCH. This green fruit and my stomach
  are not friends.
How they swell me!
BOS. [*Aside.*] Nay, you are too much
  swelled already.

---

[1] Lemon peels.   [2] Swoon.
[3] Hysteria, with a double meaning.
[4] This year.   [5] Clearly.   [6] Youngster.

Duch. O, I am in an extreme cold sweat!

Bos. I am very sorry.   [*Exit.*]

Duch. Lights to my chamber!—O good Antonio,
I fear I am undone!
        Exit Duchess [with Ladies].

Del.   Lights there, lights!

Ant. O my most trusty Delio, we are lost!
I fear she's fall'n in labor; and there's left
No time for her remove.

Del.   Have you prepared   191
Those ladies to attend her, and procured
That politic safe conveyance for the midwife
Your duchess plotted?

Ant. I have.

Del. Make use, then, of this forced occasion.
Give out that Bosola hath poisoned her
With these apricocks; that will give some color
For her keeping close.

Ant.   Fie, fie, the physicians
Will then flock to her.

Del.   For that you may pretend   200
She'll use some prepared antidote of her own,
Lest the physicians should repoison her.

Ant. I am lost in amazement. I know not
what to think on 't.   *Ex[eunt].*

Scena ii.

[*A hall in the palace.*]

Bosola, Old Lady, Antonio, Roderigo, Grisolan, Servants, Delio, Cariola.[1]

Bos. So, so, there's no question but her techiness and most vulturous eating of the apricocks are apparent signs of breeding.—

[*Enter Old Lady.*]

Now?

Old Lady. I am in haste, sir.

Bos. There was a young waiting-woman had a monstrous desire to see the Glass House [2]—

Old Lady. Nay, pray, let me go.

Bos. And it was only to know what   [10
strange instrument it was should swell up a glass to the fashion of a woman's belly.

Old Lady. I will hear no more of the Glass House. You are still abusing women!

---

[1] All except the first enter later.

[2] A London glass factory.

Bos. Who? I? No, only, by the way now and then, mention your frailties. The orange tree bear[s] ripe and green fruit and blossoms all together; and some of you give entertainment for pure love, but more for more precious reward. The   [20
lusty spring smells well, but drooping autumn tastes well. If we have the same golden showers that rained in the time of Jupiter the thunderer, you have the same Dan[ä]es [3] still, to hold up their laps to receive them. Didst thou never study the mathematics?

Old Lady. What's that, sir?

Bos. Why, to know the trick how to make a many lines meet in one center.   [30
Go, go, give your foster daughters good counsel. Tell them that the devil takes delight to hang at a woman's girdle, like a false, rusty watch, that she cannot discern how the time passes. [*Exit Old Lady.*

Enter Antonio, Delio, Roderigo, and Grisolan.]

Ant. Shut up the court gates!

Rod.   Why, sir? What's the danger?

Ant. Shut up the posterns presently,[4] and call
All the officers o' th' court.

Gris.   I shall instantly. [*Exit.*]

Ant. Who keeps the key o' th' park gate?

Rod.   Forobosco.

Ant. Let him bring 't presently.   40

[*Enter Grisolan with Servants.*]

[1] Ser. O, gentleman o' th' court, the foulest treason!

Bos. [*Aside.*] If that these apricocks should be poisoned now,
Without my knowledge!

[1] Ser. There was taken even now a Switzer
In the duchess' bedchamber—

2 Ser.   A Switzer?

[1] Ser. With a pistol in his great codpiece.

Bos. Ha, ha, ha!

[1] Ser. The codpiece was the case for 't.

2 Ser. There was a cunning traitor.   [50
Who would have searched his codpiece?

[1] Ser. True, if he had kept out of the ladies' chambers. And all the molds of his buttons were leaden bullets.

---

[3] Correction from 1708 edn.   [4] At once.

2 Ser. O wicked cannibal! A firelock in 's codpiece?

[1] Ser. 'Twas a French plot, upon my life.

2 Ser. To see what the devil can do!

Ant. All the officers[1] here?   60

[1] Ser. We are.

Ant. Gentlemen,
We have lost much plate, you know; and but this evening
Jewels, to the value of four thousand ducats,
Are missing in the duchess' cabinet.
Are the gates shut?

[1] Ser.   Yes.

Ant.   'Tis the duchess' pleasure
Each officer be locked into his chamber
Till the sun-rising, and to send the keys
Of all their chests and of their outward doors   69
Into her bedchamber. She is very sick.

Rod. At her pleasure.

Ant. She entreats you take 't not ill. The innocent
Shall be the more approved[2] by it.

Bos. Gentlemen o' th' woodyard, where's your Switzer now?

[1] Ser. By this hand, 'twas credibly reported by one o' th' black guard.[3]

          [Exeunt all except Antonio and Delio.]

Del. How fares it with the duchess?

Ant.   She's exposed
Unto the worst of torture—pain and fear.

Del. Speak to her all happy comfort.   80

Ant. How I do play the fool with mine own danger!
You are this night, dear friend, to post to Rome.
My life lies in your service.

Del.   Do not doubt me.

Ant. O, 'tis far from me; and yet fear presents me
Somewhat that look[s] like danger.

Del.   Believe it,
'Tis but the shadow of your fear, no more.
How superstitiously we mind our evils!
The throwing down salt, or crossing of a hare,
Bleeding at nose, the stumbling of a horse,

Or singing of a cricket are of power   90
To daunt whole man in us. Sir, fare you well.
I wish you all the joys of a blessed father;
And, for my faith, lay this unto your breast:
Old friends, like old swords, still are trusted best.   [Exit.]

          [Enter Cariola with a Child.][4]

Cari. Sir, you are the happy father of a son.
Your wife commends him to you.

Ant.   Blessed comfort!—
For heaven sake, tend her well. I'll presently
Go set a figure for 's nativity.[5]   Exeunt.

          Scena iii.

          [The courtyard of the palace.]

          Bosola, Antonio.[6]

Bos. Sure I did hear a woman shriek. List, ha!
And the sound came, if I received it right,
From the duchess' lodgings. There's some stratagem
In the confining all our courtiers
To their several wards. I must have part of it;
My intelligence will freeze else. List, again!
It may be 'twas the melancholy bird,
Best friend of silence and of solitariness,
The owl, that screamed so.—Ha! Antonio?

[Enter Antonio with a candle, his sword drawn.][7]

Ant. I heard some noise.—Who's there? What art thou? Speak.   10

Bos. Antonio, put not your face nor body
To such a forced expression of fear;
I am Bosola, your friend.

Ant.   Bosola!—
[Aside.] This mole does undermine me.—
Heard you not
A noise even now?

---

[1] From 1640 edn. Original reads *offices*.
[2] Proved.   [3] Scullions.
[4] From 1708 edn.   [5] Cast his horoscope.
[6] Antonio enters later. 1708 edn. reads *Enter Bosola with a dark lanthorn*.
[7] From 1708 edn.

Bos.　　　From whence?

Ant.　　　　From the duchess' lodging.

Bos. Not I. Did you?

Ant.　　　　I did, or else I dreamed.

Bos. Let's walk towards it.

Ant.　　　　No; it may be 'twas
But the rising of the wind.

Bos.　　　　Very likely.
Methinks 'tis very cold, and yet you
　sweat.
You look wildly.

Ant.　　I have been setting a figure　20
For the duchess' jewels.

Bos.　　Ah, and how falls your question?
Do you find it radical? [1]

Ant.　　　　What's that to you?
'Tis rather to be questioned what design,
When all men were commanded to their
　lodgings,
Makes you a night-walker.

Bos.　　　　In sooth, I'll tell you.
Now all the court's asleep, I thought the
　devil
Had least to do here; I came to say my
　prayers;
And, if it do offend you I do so,
You are a fine courtier.

Ant. [Aside.]　　　This fellow will undo
　me.—
You gave the duchess apricocks to-
　day.　　　　　　　　　　　　30
Pray heaven they were not poisoned!

Bos.　　　Poisoned? A Spanish fig
For the imputation!

Ant.　　　Traitors are ever confident
Till they are discovered. There were
　jewels stol'n too—
In my conceit, none are to be suspected
More than yourself.

Bos.　　　　You are a false steward!

Ant. Saucy slave, I'll pull thee up by the
　roots!

Bos. May be the ruin will crush you to
　pieces.

Ant. You are an impudent snake indeed,
　sir.
Are you scarce warm, and do you show
　your sting?

[Bos.] [2] . . . .　　　　　　　40

Ant. You libel [3] well, sir?

Bos.　　　No, sir; copy it out,
And I will set my hand to 't.

Ant.　　　　My nose bleeds.—
[Aside, taking out his handkerchief and care-
　lessly dropping a paper.] One that were
　superstitious would count
This ominous, when it merely comes by
　chance.
Two letters, that are wrought here for
　my name,
Are drowned in blood!
Mere accident!—For you, sir, I'll take
　order;
I' th' morn you shall be safe.—[Aside.]
　'Tis that must color
Her lying-in.—Sir, this door you pass not.
I do not hold it fit that you come near
The duchess' lodgings till you have
　quite [4] yourself.—　　　　　51
[Aside.] "The great are like the base,
　nay, they are the same,
When they seek shameful ways to avoid
　shame."　　　　　　　Ex[it].

Bos. Antonio hereabout did drop a paper.
Some of your help, false friend. [5]—O,
　here it is.
What's here? A child's nativity cal-
　culated!　　　　　　　　[Reads.]
"The duchess was delivered of a son,
tween the hours twelve and one in the
night, Anno Dom. 1504"—that's this
year—"decimo nono Decembris" [6]—that's
this night—"taken according to the　[61
meridian of Malfi"—that's our duchess.
Happy discovery!—"The lord of the first
house being combust in the ascendant
signifies short life; and Mars being in a
human sign, joined to the tail of the
Dragon, in the eight house, doth threaten a
violent death. Cætera non scrutantur." [7]
Why, now 'tis most apparent; this pre-
　cise fellow
Is the duchess' bawd. I have it to my
　wish!　　　　　　　　　70
This is a parcel of intelligency [8]
Our courtiers were cased up for! It needs
　must follow
That I must be committed on pretense
Of poisoning her, which I'll endure, and
　laugh at.

---

[1] Fit to be decided (astrological term).

[2] The passage is obscure. Lucas suggests that
a speech by Bosola seems to have been omitted.

[3] Draw up a document, with a double meaning.

[4] Acquitted.　　　　　　　[8] News.

[5] I.e., his dark lantern.

[6] December 19.

[7] Other things are not investigated.

If one could find the father now! But
   that
Time will discover. Old Castruchio
I' th' morning posts to Rome; by him
   I'll send
A letter that shall make her brothers'
   galls
O'erflow their livers. This was a thrifty
   way!
"Though Lust do mask in ne'er so
   strange disguise.   80
She's oft found witty, but is never
   wise."   [*Exit.*]

SCENA iv.

[*An apartment in the Cardinal's palace at
Rome.*]

Cardinal and Julia; Servant and Delio.[1]

CARD. Sit; thou art my best of wishes.
   Prithee, tell me
What trick didst thou invent to come
   to Rome
Without thy husband?
JUL.   Why, my lord, I told him
I came to visit an old anchorite
Here, for devotion.
CARD.   Thou art a witty false one—
I mean, to him.
JUL.   You have prevailed with me
Beyond my strongest thoughts; I would
   not now
Find you inconstant.
CARD.   Do not put thyself
To such a voluntary torture, which pro-
   ceeds
Out of your own guilt.
JUL.   How, my lord!
CARD.   You fear   10
My constancy, because you have ap-
   proved[2]
Those giddy and wild turning[s] in
   yourself.
JUL. Did you e'er find them?
CARD.   Sooth, generally for women;
A man might strive to make glass mal-
   leable
Ere he should make them fixéd.
JUL.   So, my lord!
CARD. We had need go borrow that fan-
   tastic glass
Invented by Galileo the Florentine

[1] Last two enter later.   [2] Experienced.

To view another spacious world i' th'
   moon,
And look to find a constant woman
   there.
JUL. [*Weeping.*] This is very well, my lord.
CARD.   Why do you weep?   20
Are tears your justification? The self-
   same tears
Will fall into your husband's bosom,
   lady,
With a loud protestation that you love
   him
Above the world. Come, I'll love you
   wisely—
That's jealously, since I am very cer-
   tain
You cannot me make cuckold.
JUL.   I'll go home
To my husband.
CARD.   You may thank me, lady,
I have taken you off your melancholy
   perch,
Bore you upon my fist, and showed you
   game,
And let you fly at it. I pray thee, kiss
   me.   30
When thou wast with thy husband, thou
   wast watched
Like a tame elephant. (Still you are to
   thank me.)
Thou hadst only kisses from him, and
   high feeding;
But what delight was that? 'Twas just
   like one
That hath a little fing'ring on the lute,
Yet cannot tune it. (Still you are to
   thank me.)
JUL. You told me of a piteous wound i'
   th' heart
And a sick liver when you wooed me
   first,
And spake like one in physic.[3]
CARD.   Who's that?—

[*Enter Servant.*]

Rest firm; for my affection to thee,   40
Lightning moves slow to 't.
SER.   Madam, a gentleman
That's comes post from Malfi desires
   to see you.
CARD. Let him enter; I'll withdraw.   *Exit.*
SER.   He says

[3] *I.e.,* sick.

Your husband, old Castruchio, is come to Rome,
Most pitifully tired with riding post.
                                        [*Exit.*

Enter Delio.]

JUL. Signior Delio?—[*Aside.*] 'Tis one of my old suitors.
DEL. I was bold to come and see you.
JUL.   Sir, you are welcome.
DEL. Do you lie here?
JUL.   Sure, your own experience
Will satisfy you no—our Roman prelates
Do not keep lodging for ladies.
DEL.   Very well. 50
I have brought you no commendations from your husband,
For I know none by him.
JUL.   I hear he's come to Rome.
DEL. I never knew man and beast, of a horse and a knight,
So weary of each other. If he had had a good back,
He would have undertook to have borne his horse,
His breech was so pitifully sore.
JUL.   Your laughter
Is my pity.
DEL.   Lady, I know not whether
You want money, but I have brought you some.
JUL. From my husband?
DEL.   No, from mine own allowance.
JUL. I must hear the condition, ere I be bound to take it.   60
DEL. Look on 't; 'tis gold. Hath it not a fine color?
JUL. I have a bird more beautiful.
DEL.   Try the sound on 't.
JUL. A lutestring far exceeds it.
It hath no smell, like cassia or civet;
Nor is it physical,[1] though some fond [2] doctors
Persuade us seethe 't [3] in cullises.[4] I'll tell you,
This is a creature bred by—

[*Enter Servant.*]

SER.   Your husband's come,
Hath delivered a letter to the Duke of Calabria

---

[1] Medicinal.   [2] Foolish.
[3] Boil it. Dyce's emendation. Original reads *seeth's*.   [4] Strong broths.

That, to my thinking, hath put him out of his wits.   [*Exit.*]
JUL. Sir, you hear.   70
Pray, let me know your business and your suit
As briefly as can be.
DEL.   With good speed.
I would wish you
(At such time as you are non-resident
With your husband) my mistress.
JUL. Sir, I'll go ask my husband if I shall,
And straight return your answer.   *Exit.*
DEL.   Very fine!
Is this her wit, or honesty, that speaks thus?
I heard one say the duke was highly moved
With a letter sent from Malfi. I do fear
Antonio is betrayed. How fearfully   80
Shows his ambition now! Unfortunate fortune!
"They pass through whirlpools, and deep woes do shun,
Who the event weigh ere the action's done."   *Exit.*

SCENA V.

[*The same.*]

Cardinal and Ferdinand, with a letter.

FERD. I have this night digged up a mandrake.[5]
CARD.   Say you?
FERD. And I am grown mad with 't.
CARD.   What's the prodigy?
FERD. Read there—a sister damned! She's loose i' th' hilts,
Grown a notorious strumpet.
CARD.   Speak lower.
FERD.   Lower?
Rogues do not whisper 't now, but seek to publish 't
(As servants do the bounty of their lords)
Aloud, and with a covetous, searching eye,
To mark who note them. O, confusion seize her!
She hath had most cunning bawds to serve her turn,   9
And more secure conveyances for lust
Than towns of garrison for service.

---

[5] The mandrake, when dug up, supposedly gave forth shrieks which drove the hearer mad.

CARD.   Is 't possible?
Can this be certain?
FERD.   Rhubarb, O, for rhubarb
To purge this choler! [*Points to the
    horoscope.*] Here's the cursed day
To prompt my memory; and here 't
    shall stick
Till of her bleeding heart I make a
    sponge
To wipe it out.
CARD.   Why do you make yourself
So wild a tempest?
FERD.   Would I could be one,
That I might toss her palace 'bout her ears,
Root up her goodly forests, blast her
    meads,
And lay her general territory as waste   20
As she hath done her honors.
CARD.   Shall our blood,
The royal blood of Aragon and Castile,
Be thus attainted?
FERD.   Apply desperate physic.
We must not now use balsamum, but
    fire—
The smarting cupping glass, for that's
    the mean
To purge infected blood, such blood as
    hers.
There is a kind of pity in mine eye;
I'll give it to my handkercher, and, now
    'tis here,
I'll bequeath this to her bastard.
CARD.   What to do?
FERD. Why, to make soft lint for his
    mother's [1] wounds,   30
When I have hewed her to pieces.
CARD.   Cursed creature!
Unequal nature, to place women's
    hearts
So far upon the left side! [2]
FERD.   Foolish men,
That e'er will trust their honor in a bark
Made of so slight, weak bulrush as is
    woman,
Apt every minute to sink it!
CARD.   Thus
Ignorance, when it hath purchased
    honor,
It cannot wield it.
FERD.   Methinks I see her laughing—
Excellent hyena! Talk to me some-
    what, quickly,

Or my imagination will carry me   40
To see her in the shameful act of sin.
CARD. With whom?
FERD.   Happily [3] with some
    strong-thighed bargeman,
Or one [o'] [4] th' woodyard that can quoit
    the sledge [5]
Or toss the bar, or else some lovely
    squire
That carries coals up to her privy lodg-
    ings.
CARD. You fly beyond your reason.
FERD.   Go to, mistress!
'Tis not your whore's milk that shall
    quench my wildfire,
But your whore's blood.
CARD. How idly [6] shows this rage, which
    carries you,
As men conveyed by witches through
    the air,   50
On violent whirlwinds! This intemper-
    ate noise
Fitly resembles deaf men's shrill dis-
    course,
Who talk aloud, thinking all other
    men
To have their imperfection.
FERD.   Have not you
My palsy?
CARD.   Yes. I can be angry
Without this rupture. There is not in
    nature
A thing that makes man so deformed,
    so beastly,
As doth intemperate anger. Chide your-
    self.
You have divers men who never yet
    expressed
Their strong desire of rest but by un-
    rest,   60
By vexing of themselves. Come, put
    yourself
In tune.
FERD.   So! I will only study to seem
The thing I am not. I could kill her
    now,
In you, or in myself; for I do think
It is some sin in us heaven doth re-
    venge
By her.
CARD.   Are you stark mad?
FERD.   I would have their bodies

---

[1] From 1640 edn. Original reads *mother*.
[2] *I.e.*, to make women so perverse.

[3] Haply, perhaps.   [5] Throw the hammer.
[4] From 1678 edn.   [6] Madly.

Burnt in a coalpit with the ventage
  stopped,
That their cursed smoke might not as-
  cend to heaven;
Or dip the sheets they lie in in pitch or
  sulphur,
Wrap them in 't, and then light them
  like a match;   70
Or else to boil their bastard to a cullis,
And give 't his lecherous father to re-
  new
The sin of his back.
CARD.   I'll leave you.
FERD.   Nay, I have done.
I am confident, had I been damned in
  hell,
And should have heard of this, it would
  have put me
Into a cold sweat. In, in! I'll go sleep.
Till I know who leaps my sister, I'll not
  stir.
That known, I'll find scorpions to string
  my whips,
And fix her in a general eclipse. *Exeunt.*

ACTUS III. SCENA i.

[An apartment in the Duchess' palace.]

Antonio and Delio; Duchess, Ferdinand,
                    Bosola.[1]

ANT. Our noble friend, my most beloved
  Delio!
O, you have been a stranger long at
  court.
Came you along with the Lord Ferdi-
  nand?
DEL. I did, sir. And how fares your noble
  duchess?
ANT. Right fortunately well. She's an
  excellent
Feeder of pedigrees; since you last saw
  her,
She hath had two children more, a son
  and daughter.
DEL. Methinks 'twas yesterday. Let me
  but wink,
And not behold your face, which to mine
  eye
Is somewhat leaner, verily I should
  dream   10
It were within this half hour.
ANT. You have not been in law, friend
  Delio,

[1] Last three enter later.

Nor in prison, nor a suitor at the court,
Nor begged the reversion of some great
  man's place,
Nor troubled with an old wife, which
  doth make
Your time so insensibly hasten.
DEL.   Pray, sir, tell me,
Hath not this news arrived yet to the ear
Of the lord cardinal?
ANT.   I fear it hath.
The Lord Ferdinand, that's newly come
  to court,
Doth bear himself right dangerously.
DEL.   Pray, why? 20
ANT. He is so quiet that he seems to sleep
The tempest out, as dormice do in winter.
Those houses that are haunted are most
  still
Till the devil be up.
DEL.   What say the common people?
ANT. The common rabble do directly say
She is a strumpet.
DEL.   And your graver heads
Which would be politic, what censure[2]
  they?
ANT. They do observe I grow to infinite
  purchase[3]
The left-hand way; and all suppose the
  duchess
Would amend it, if she could; for, say
  they,   30
Great princes, though they grudge their
  officers
Should have such large and unconfinéd
  means
To get wealth under them, will not com-
  plain,
Lest thereby they should make them
  odious
Unto the people. For other obligation
Of love or marriage between her and me,
They never dream of.

[Enter Duchess, Ferdinand, Bosola, and
                   Attendants.]

DEL. *[Aside.]*   The Lord Ferdinand
Is going to bed.
FERD.   I'll instantly to bed,
For I am weary.—I am to bespeak
A husband for you.
DUCH. For me, sir? Pray, who is 't? 40
FERD. The great Count Malateste.
DUCH.   Fie upon him!

[2] Judge.   [3] Wealth.

A count? He's a mere stick of sugar candy;
You may look quite thorough him. When I choose
A husband, I will marry for your honor.
FERD. You shall do well in 't.—How is 't, worthy Antonio?
DUCH. But, sir, I am to have private conference with you
About a scandalous report is spread
Touching mine honor.
FERD.   Let me be ever deaf to 't—
One of Pasquil's paper bullets,[1] court calumny,
A pestilent air which princes' palaces   50
Are seldom purged of. Yet, say that it were true,
I pour it in your bosom, my fixed love
Would strongly excuse, extenuate, nay, deny
Faults, were they apparent in you. Go, be safe
In your own innocency.
DUCH. [Aside.]   O blessed comfort!
This deadly air is purged.
Exeunt [all except Ferdinand and Bosola].
FERD.   Her guilt treads on
Hot, burning cultures.[2] Now, Bosola,
How thrives our intelligence?
BOS.   Sir, uncertainly.
'Tis rumored she hath had three bastards, but
By whom we may go read i' th' stars.
FERD.   Why, some   60
Hold opinion all things are written there.
BOS. Yes, if we could find spectacles to read them.
I do suspect there hath been some sorcery
Used on the duchess.
FERD.   Sorcery! To what purpose?
BOS. To make her dote on some desertless fellow
She shames to acknowledge.
FERD.   Can your faith give way
To think there's power in potions or in charms,
To make us love whether we will or no?
BOS. Most certainly.
FERD. Away! These are mere gulleries,[3] horrid things,   70
Invented by some cheating mountebanks
To abuse us. Do you think that herbs or charms

[1] Lampoons.   [2] Plowshares.   [3] Deceptions.

Can force the will? Some trials have been made
In this foolish practice, but the ingredients
Were lenitive poisons, such as are of force
To make the patient mad; and straight the witch
Swears by equivocation they are in love.
The witchcraft lies in her rank blood. This night
I will force confession from her. You told me
You had got, within these two days, a false key   80
Into her bedchamber.
BOS.   I have.
FERD.   As I would wish.
BOS. What do you intend to do?
FERD.   Can you guess?
BOS.   No.
FERD. Do not ask, then.
He that can compass me, and know my drifts,
May say he hath put a girdle 'bout the world,
And sounded all her quicksands.
BOS.   I do not
Think so.
FERD.   What do you think, then, pray?
BOS.   That you are
Your own chronicle too much, and grossly
Flatter yourself.
FERD.   Give me thy hand; I thank thee.
I never gave pension but to flatterers   90
Till I entertainéd thee. Farewell.
"That friend a great man's ruin strongly checks,
Who rails into his belief all his defects."
                Exeunt.

SCENA ii.

[*The Duchess' bedchamber.*]

*Duchess, Antonio, Cariola, Ferdinand,
        Bosola, Officers.*[4]

DUCH. Bring me the casket hither, and the glass.—
You get no lodging here tonight, my lord.
ANT. Indeed, I must persuade one.
DUCH.   Very good!
I hope in time 'twill grow into a custom

[4] Ferdinand, Bosola, and Officers enter later.

That noblemen shall come with cap and
   knee
To purchase a night's lodging of their
   wives.
ANT. I must lie here.
DUCH.   Must? You are a lord of misrule.
ANT. Indeed, my rule is only in the night.
DUCH. To what use will you put me?
ANT.   We'll sleep together.
DUCH. Alas, what pleasure can two lovers
   find in sleep?   10
CARI. My lord, I lie with her often, and I
   know
She'll much disquiet you.
ANT.   See, you are complained of.
CARI. For she's the sprawling'st bedfellow.
ANT. I shall like her the better for that.
CARI. Sir, shall I ask you a question?
ANT. I pray thee, Cariola.
CARI. Wherefore still when you lie with my
   lady
Do you rise so early?
ANT.   Laboring men
Count the clock oft'nest, Cariola,
Are glad when their task's ended.
DUCH.   I'll stop your mouth. 20
                    [Kisses him.]
ANT. Nay, that's but one; Venus had two
   soft doves
To draw her chariot; I must have
   another.—   [Another kiss.]
When wilt thou marry, Cariola?
CARI.   Never, my lord.
ANT. O, fie upon this single life! Forgo it.
We read how Daphne, for her peevish
   slight,[1]
Became a fruitless bay tree, Syrinx
   turned
To the pale, empty reed, Anaxarete
Was frozen into marble; whereas those
Which married or proved kind unto their
   friends
Were by a gracious influence trans-
   shaped   30
Into the olive, pomegranate, mulberry,
Became flowers, precious stones, or
   eminent stars.
CARI. This is a vain poetry   But I pray
   you, tell me,
If there were proposed me wisdom,
   riches, and beauty,
In three several young men, which should
   I choose?

[1] I.e., of Apollo. Mod. edns. print flight.

ANT. 'Tis a hard question. This was Paris'
   case,
And he was blind in 't, and there was a
   great cause.
For how was 't possible he could judge
   right,
Having three amorous goddesses in view,
And they stark naked? 'Twas a motion [2]
Were able to benight the apprehension
Of the severest counselor of Europe. 42
Now I look on both your faces so well
   formed,
It puts me in mind of a question I would
   ask.
CARI. What is 't?
ANT.   I do wonder why hard-
   favored ladies
For the most part keep worse-favored
   waiting-women
To attend them, and cannot endure fair
   ones.
DUCH. O, that's soon answered.
Did you ever in your life know an ill
   painter
Desire to have his dwelling next door to
   the shop   50
Of an excellent picture maker? 'Twould
   disgrace
His face-making, and undo him. I prithee,
When were we so merry?—My hair
   tangles.
ANT. [Aside.] Pray thee, Cariola, let's
   steal forth the room,
And let her talk to herself. I have divers
   times
Served her the like, when she hath
   chafed extremely.
I love to see her angry. Softly, Cariola.
          Exeunt [Antonio and Cariola].
DUCH. Doth not the color of my hair gin
   to change?
When I wax gray, I shall have all the
   court
Powder their hair with arras,[3] to be like
   me.   60
You have cause to love me; I entered you
   into my heart

[Enter Ferdinand unseen.] [4]

Before you would vouchsafe to call for
   the keys.

[2] Spectacle, show.   [3] Powder of orris-root.
[4] Stage direction from 1708 edn.

We shall one day have my brothers take
you napping.
Methinks his presence, being now in court,
Should make you keep your own bed;
but you'll say
Love mixed with fear is sweetest. I'll
assure you,
You shall get no more children till my
brothers
Consent to be your gossips.[1] Have you
lost your tongue?—[*Sees Ferdinand
with a poniard.*] 'Tis welcome;
For know, whether I am doomed to live
or die,
I can do both like a prince.
Ferdinand gives her a poniard.

FERD.   Die, then, quickly. 70
Virtue, where art thou hid? What hideous
thing
Is it that doth eclipse[2] thee?

DUCH.   Pray, sir, hear me!

FERD. Or is it true thou art but a bare
name,
And no essential thing?

DUCH.   Sir—

FERD.   Do not speak.

DUCH. No, sir!
I will plant my soul in mine ears, to hear
you.

FERD. O most imperfect light of human
reason,
That mak'st [us][3] so unhappy to foresee
What we can least prevent! Pursue thy
wishes,
And glory in them; there's in shame no
comfort   80
But to be past all bounds and sense of
shame.

DUCH. I pray, sir, hear me. I am married!

FERD.   So!

DUCH. Happily, not to your liking. But
for that,
Alas, your shears do come untimely now
To clip the bird's wings that's already
flown!
Will you see my husband?

FERD.   Yes, if I
Could change eyes with a basilisk.

DUCH.   Sure, you came hither
By his confederacy.[4]

---

[1] Godparents to your children.

[2] Perhaps with a pun on *clip*, to embrace.

[3] From 1708 edn.

[4] Confederacy. It is not clear in the original
whether the word is *consideracy* or *confideracy*.

FERD.   The howling of a wolf
Is music to thee, screech owl! Prithee,
peace!—
Whate'er thou art that hast enjoyed my
sister,   90
For I am sure thou hear'st me, for thine
own sake
Let me not know thee. I came hither
prepared
To work thy discovery, yet am now persuaded
It would beget such violent effects
As would damn us both. I would not for
ten millions
I had beheld thee; therefore use all
means
I never may have knowledge of thy
name;
Enjoy thy lust still, and a wretched life,
On that condition.—And for thee, vild
woman,
If thou do wish thy lecher may grow
old   100
In thy embracements, I would have thee
build
Such a room for him as our anchorites
To holier use inhabit. Let not the sun
Shine on him till he's dead; let dogs and
monkeys
Only converse with him, and such dumb
things
To whom nature denies use to sound his
name;
Do not keep a paraquito, lest she learn it;
If thou do love him, cut out thine own
tongue,
Lest it bewray him.

DUCH.   Why might not I marry? 109
I have not gone about in this to create
Any new world or custom.

FERD.   Thou art undone;
And thou hast ta'en that massy sheet of
lead
That hid thy husband's bones, and folded
it
About my heart.

DUCH.   Mine bleeds for 't.

FERD.   Thine? Thy heart?
What should I name 't, unless a hollow
bullet
Filled with unquenchable wildfire?

DUCH.   You are in this
Too strict, and, were you not my princely
brother.

I would say, too willful. My reputation
Is safe.
FERD.   Dost thou know what reputa-
    tion is?
I'll tell thee—to small purpose, since th'
    instruction   120
Comes now too late.
Upon a time Reputation, Love, and
    Death
Would travel o'er the world; and it was
    concluded
That they should part, and take three
    several ways.
Death told them they should find him in
    great battles,
Or cities plagued with plagues. Love
    gives them counsel
To inquire for him 'mongst unambitious
    shepherds,
Where dowries were not talked of and
    sometimes
'Mongst quiet kindred that had nothing
    left
By their dead parents. "Stay," quoth
    Reputation,   130
"Do not forsake me; for it is my nature,
If once I part from any man I meet,
I am never found again." And so, for
    you.
You have shook hands with Reputation,
And made him invisible. So, fare you
    well;
I will never see you more.
DUCH.   Why should only I,
Of all the other princes of the world,
Be cased up, like a holy relic? I have
    youth
And a little beauty.
FERD.   So you have some virgins
That are witches. I will never see thee
    more.   *Exit.* 140

Enter Antonio with a pistol [*, and Cariola*].[1]

DUCH. You saw this apparition?
ANT.   Yes; we are
Betrayed. How came he hither? [*Points
    the pistol at Cariola.*] I should turn
This to thee, for that.
CARI.   Pray, sir, do; and, when
That you have cleft my heart, you shall
    read there
Mine innocence.
DUCH.   That gallery gave him entrance.
_____
[1] Direction in original follows next speech.

ANT. I would this terrible thing would
    come again
That, standing on my guard, I might
    relate
My warrantable love.—Ha! what means
    this?   *She shows the poniard.*
DUCH. He left this with me.
ANT.   And it seems did wish
You would use it on yourself?
DUCH.   His action seemed   150
To intend so much.
ANT.   This hath a handle to 't,
As well as a point—turn it towards him,
    and
So fasten the keen edge in his rank gall.
                    [*Knocking within.*]
How now! Who knocks? More earth-
    quakes?
DUCH.   I stand
As if a mine beneath my feet were ready
To be blown up.
CARI.   'Tis Bosola.
DUCH.   Away!
O misery! Methinks unjust actions
Should wear these masks and curtains,
    and not we.
You must instantly part hence; I have
    fashioned it already. *Ex*[*it*] *Ant*[*onio*].

                [Enter Bosola.]

BOS. The duke your brother is ta'en up
    in a whirlwind,   160
Hath took horse, and 's rid post to
    Rome.
DUCH.   So late?
BOS. He told me, as he mounted into th'
    saddle,
You were undone.
DUCH.   Indeed I am very near it.
BOS. What's the matter?
DUCH. Antonio, the master of our house-
    hold,
Hath dealt so falsely with me in 's
    accounts.
My brother stood engaged with me for
    money
Ta'en up of certain Neapolitan Jews,
And Antonio lets the bonds be forfeit.
BOS. Strange!—[*Aside.*] This is cunning.
DUCH.   And hereupon 170
My brother's bills at Naples are pro-
    tested
Against.—Call up our officers.
BOS.   I shall. *Exit.*

[*Enter Antonio.*]

DUCH. The place that you must fly to is
     Ancona.
Hire a house there; I'll send after you
My treasure and my jewels. Our weak
     safety
Runs upon enginous [1] wheels; short
     syllables
Must stand for periods. I must now
     accuse you
Of such a feignéd crime as Tasso calls
Magnanima menzogna, "a noble lie,"
Cause it must shield our honors.—Hark!
     they are coming.   180

[*Enter Bosola and Officers.*]

ANT. Will your grace hear me?
DUCH. I have got well by you; you have
     yielded me
A million of loss. I am like to inherit
The people's curses for your stewardship.
You had the trick in audit-time to be
     sick,
Till I had signed your *Quietus;* and that
     cured you
Without help of a doctor.—Gentlemen,
I would have this man be an example to
     you all;
So shall you hold my favor. I pray, let
     him, [2]
For h'as done that, alas, you would not
     think of,   190
And, because I intend to be rid of him,
I mean not to publish.—Use your fortune
     elsewhere.
ANT. I am strongly armed to brook my
     overthrow,
As commonly men bear with a hard year.
I will not blame the cause on 't; but do
     think
The necessity of my malevolent star
Procures this, not her humor. O, the
     inconstant
And rotten ground of service! You may
     see,
'Tis even like him that in a winter night
Takes a long slumber o'er a dying
     fire,   200
As loath [3] to part from 't, yet parts
     thence as cold
As when he first sat down.

[1] Ingenious, intricate.   [2] Let him go.
[3] Some apparently uncorrected copies of 1623
edn. read *a-loth.*

DUCH.   We do confiscate,
Towards the satisfying of your accounts,
All that you have.
ANT.   I am all yours; and 'tis very fit
All mine should be so.
DUCH.   So, sir, you have your pass.
ANT. You may see, gentlemen, what 'tis
     to serve
A prince with body and soul.   *Exit.*
BOS. Here's an example for extortion;
what moisture is drawn out of the sea, when
foul weather comes, pours down, and   [210
runs into the sea again.
DUCH. I would know what are your
opinions of this Antonio.
2 OFF. He could not abide to see a pig's
head gaping; [4] I thought your grace would
find him a Jew.
3 OFF. I would you had been his officer,
for your own sake.
4 OFF. You would have had more
money.   220
1 OFF. He stopped his ears with black
wool, and to those came to him for money
said he was thick of hearing.
2 OFF. Some said he was an hermaphrodite, for he could not abide a woman.
4 OFF. How scurvy proud he would look
when the treasury was full! Well, let him
go.
1 OFF. Yes, and the chippings of the
butt'ry fly after him, to scour his gold [230
chain. [5]
DUCH. Leave us.—   (*Exeunt* [*Officers*].)
What do you think of these?
BOS. That these are rogues that, in 's
     prosperity,
But to have waited on his fortune could
     have wished
His dirty stirrup riveted through their
     noses,
And followed after 's mule, like a bear in
     a ring;
Would have prostituted their daughters
     to his lust;
Made their first-born intelligencers;
     thought none happy
But such as were born under his blessed
     planet,   240
And wore his livery—and do these lice
     drop off now?
Well, never look to have the like again.

[4] A roasted pig with an apple in its mouth.
[5] Symbol of a steward's office.

He hath left a sort [1] of flatt'ring rogues
behind him;
Their doom must follow. Princes pay
flatterers
In their own money; flatterers dissemble
their vices,
And they dissemble their lies. That's
justice.
Alas, poor gentleman!

DUCH. Poor? He hath amply filled his
coffers.

BOS. Sure, he was too honest. Pluto, the
god of riches,
When he's sent by Jupiter to any
man,   250
He goes limping, to signify that wealth
That comes on God's name comes slowly;
but, when he's sent
On the devil's errand, he rides post and
comes in by scuttles.[2]
Let me show you what a most unvalued
jewel
You have in a wanton humor thrown
away,
To bless the man shall find him. He was
an excellent
Courtier and most faithful; a soldier that
thought it
As beastly to know his own value too
little
As devilish to acknowledge it too much.
Both his virtue and form deserved a far
better fortune;   260
His discourse rather delighted to judge
itself than show itself;
His breast was filled with all perfec-
tion,
And yet it seemed a private whisp'ring-
room,
It made so little noise of 't.

DUCH. But he was basely descended.

BOS. Will you make yourself a mercenary
herald,
Rather to examine men's pedigrees than
virtues?
You shall want him;
For know an honest statesman to a
prince
Is like a cedar planted by a spring;   270
The spring bathes the tree's root; the
grateful tree
Rewards it with his shadow. You have
not done so.

I would sooner swim to the Bermoothes [3]
on two politicians'[4]
Rotten bladders, tied together with an
intelligencer's heartstring,
Than depend on so changeable a prince's
favor.
Fare thee well, Antonio! Since the malice
of the world
Would needs down with thee, it cannot
be said yet
That any ill happened unto thee, considering thy fall
Was accompanied with virtue.

DUCH. O, you render me excellent music!

BOS.   Say you?   280

DUCH. This good one that you speak of is
my husband.

BOS. Do I not dream? Can this ambitious
age
Have so much goodness in 't as to prefer
A man merely for worth, without these
shadows
Of wealth and painted honors? Possible?

DUCH. I have had three children by him.

BOS.   Fortunate lady!
For you have made your private nuptial
bed
The humble and fair seminary of peace—
No question but. Many an unbeneficed
scholar
Shall pray for you for this deed, and
rejoice   290
That some preferment in the world can
yet
Arise from merit. The virgins of your
land
That have no dowries shall hope your
example
Will raise them to rich husbands. Should
you want
Soldiers, 'twould make the very Turks
and Moors
Turn Christians, and serve you for this
act.
Last, the neglected poets of your time,
In honor of this trophy of a man,
Raised by that curious engine, your white
hand,
Shall thank you in your grave for 't, and
make that   300
More reverend than all the cabinets [5]
Of living princes. For Antonio,

[1] Crowd.   [2] Quick steps.

[3] Bermudas.   [5] Museums.
[4] Intriguers'.

His fame shall likewise flow from many a pen,
When heralds shall want coats to sell to men.

Duch. As I taste comfort in this friendly speech,
So would I find concealment.

Bos.   O, the secret of my prince,
Which I will wear on th' inside of my heart!

Duch. You shall take charge of all my coin and jewels,
And follow him, for he retires himself   310
To Ancona.

Bos.   So!

Duch.   Whither, within few days,
I mean to follow thee.

Bos.   Let me think.
I would wish your grace to feign a pilgrimage
To our Lady of Loretto, scarce seven leagues
From fair Ancona; so may you depart
Your country with more honor, and your flight
Will seem a princely progress, retaining
Your usual train about you.

Duch.   Sir, your direction
Shall lead me by the hand.

Cari.   In my opinion,
She were better progress to the baths   320
At Lucca, or go visit the Spa
In Germany, for, if you will believe me,
I do not like this jesting with religion,
This feignéd pilgrimage.

Duch. Thou art a superstitious fool!
Prepare us instantly for our departure.
Past sorrows, let us moderately lament them,
For those to come, seek wisely to prevent them.

        Exit [Duchess with Cariola].

Bos. A politician is the devil's quilted anvil;
He fashions all sins on him, and the blows   330
Are never heard. He may work in a lady's chamber,
As here for proof. What rests[1] but I reveal
All to my lord? O, this base quality[2]
Of intelligencer! Why, every quality i' th' world

---

[1] Remains.   [2] Profession.

Prefers but gain or commendation.
Now, for this act I am certain to be raised,
"And men that paint weeds to the life are praised."   *Exit.*

SCENA iii.

[An apartment in the Cardinal's palace at Rome.]

Cardinal, Ferdinand, Malateste, Pescara, Silvio, Delio, Bosola.[3]

Card. Must we turn soldier, then?

Mal.   The emperor,
Hearing your worth that way ere you attained
This reverend garment, joins you in commission
With the right fortunate soldier, the Marquis of Pescara,
And the famous Lannoy.

Card.   He that had the honor
Of taking the French king prisoner?

Mal.   The same.
Here's a plot drawn for a new fortification
At Naples.

[Cardinal and Malateste stand aside conversing.]

Ferd.   This great Count Malateste, I perceive,
Hath got employment?

Del.   No employment, my lord;
A marginal note in the muster book that he is   10
A voluntary[4] lord.

Ferd.   He's no soldier?

Del. He has worn gunpowder in 's hollow tooth for the toothache.

Sil. He comes to the leaguer with a full intent
To eat fresh beef and garlic, means to stay
Till the scent be gone, and straight return to court.

Del. He hath read all the late service
As the city chronicle relates it;
And keep[s] two painters[5] going, only to express
Battles in model.

---

[3] Enters later.   [4] *I.e.*, a volunteer.
[5] Some apparently uncorrected copies of 1623 edn. read *pewterers*.

Sil.   Then he'll fight by the book.

Del. By the almanac, I think,   20
To choose good days and shun the critical.

That's his mistress' scarf.

Sil.   Yes, he protests
He would do much for that taffeta.

Del. I think he would run away from a battle
To save it from taking prisoner.

Sil.   He is horribly afraid
Gunpowder will spoil the perfume on 't.

Del. I saw a Dutchman break his pate once
For calling him potgun;[1] he made his head
Have a bore in 't like a musket.

Sil. I would he had made a touchhole to 't.   30
He is indeed a garded sumpter cloth,[2]
Only for the remove of the court.[3]

[Enter Bosola.]

Pes. Bosola arrived? What should be the business?
Some falling out amongst the cardinals.
These factions amongst great men, they are like
Foxes; when their heads are divided,
They carry fire in their tails, and all the country
About them goes to wrack for 't.

Sil.   What's that Bosola?

Del. I knew him in Padua—a fantastical scholar, like such who study to [40 know how many knots was in Hercules' club, of what color Achilles' beard was, or whether Hector were not troubled with the toothache. He hath studied himself half blear-eyed to know the true symmetry of Cæsar's nose by a shoeinghorn; and this he did to gain the name of a speculative man.

Pes. Mark Prince Ferdinand.
A very salamander lives in 's eye,   50
To mock the eager violence of fire.

Sil. That cardinal hath made more bad faces with his oppression than ever Michael Angelo made good ones. He lifts up 's nose like a foul porpoise before a storm.

Pes. The Lord Ferdinand laughs.

Del.   Like a deadly cannon
That lightens ere it smokes.

Pes. These are your true pangs of death,
The pangs of life, that struggle with great statesmen.

Del. In such a deformed silence, witches whisper their charms.   60

[Silvio, Pescara, and Delio stand aside.]

Card. Doth she make religion her riding hood
To keep her from the sun and tempest?

Ferd. That, that damns her. Methinks her fault and beauty,
Blended together, show like leprosy—
The whiter the fouler. I make it a question
Whether her beggarly brats were ever christened.

Card. I will instantly solicit the state of Ancona
To have them banished.

Ferd.   You are for Loretto?
I shall not be at your ceremony. Fare you well.—
Write to the Duke of Malfi, my young nephew   70
She had by her first husband, and acquaint him
With 's mother's honesty.[4]

Bos.   I will.

Ferd.   Antonio!
A slave that only smelled of ink and compters,[5]
And never in 's life looked like a gentleman
But in the audit-time.—Go, go presently;
Draw me out an hundreth and fifty of our horse,
And meet me at the fort-bridge.

                    Exeunt.

Scena iv.

Two Pilgrims to the Shrine of Our Lady of Loretto.

1 Pil. I have not seen a goodlier shrine than this;
Yet I have visited many.

2 Pil.   The Cardinal of Aragon
Is this day to resign his cardinal's hat;
His sister duchess likewise is arrived

---

[1] Popgun.
[2] Ornamented horse cloth.
[3] When the court moves from place to place.

[4] Chastity.   [5] Counters.

To pay her vow of pilgrimage. I expect
A noble ceremony.

1 PIL.   No question.—They come.

Here the ceremony of the Cardinal's in-
stallment in the habit [of] [1] *a soldier,*
performed in delivering up his cross, hat,
robes, and ring at the shrine, and in-
vesting him with sword, helmet, shield,
and spurs. Then Antonio, the Duch-
ess, and their Children, having presented
themselves at the shrine, are, by a form
of banishment in dumb show, expressed
towards them by the Cardinal and the
state of Ancona, banished. During all
which ceremony, this ditty is sung, to
very solemn music, by divers Church-
men; and then exeunt.

Arms and honors deck thy story
To thy fame's eternal glory!
Adverse fortune ever fly thee;
No disastrous fate come nigh
    thee!
I alone will sing thy praises, ⌈ *The author*
Whom to honor virtue raises, | *disclaims this*
                      ⌊ *ditty to be his.*
And thy study, that divine is,
Bent to martial discipline is,
Lay aside all those robes lie by thee.
Crown thy arts with arms; they'll beautify
    thee.

O worthy of worthiest name, adorned in
    this manner,
Lead bravely thy forces on under war's
    warlike banner!
O, mayst thou prove fortunate in all mar-
    tial courses!   19
Guide thou still by skill in arts and forces!
Victory attend thee nigh, whilst fame sings
    loud thy powers;
Triumphant conquest crown thy head, and
    blessings pour down showers!

1 PIL. Here's a strange turn of state! Who
    would have thought
So great a lady would have matched
    herself
Unto so mean a person? Yet the cardinal
Bears himself much too cruel.

2 PIL.   They are banished.

1 PIL. But I would ask what power hath
    this state
Of Ancona to determine of a free prince?

2 PIL. They are a free state, sir, and her
    brother showed

[1] Supplied from 1640 edn.

How that the pope, forehearing of her
    looseness,   30
Hath seized into th' protection of the
    church
The dukedom which she held as dowager.

1 PIL. But by what justice?

2 PIL.   Sure, I think by none,
Only her brother's instigation.

1 PIL. What was it with such violence he
    took
Off from her finger?

2 PIL.   'Twas her wedding ring,
Which he vowed shortly he would
    sacrifice
To his revenge.

1 PIL.   Alas, Antonio!
If that a man be thrust into a well,
No matter who sets hand to 't, his own
    weight   40
Will bring him sooner to th' bottom.
Come, let's hence.
Fortune makes this conclusion general,
"All things do help th' unhappy man to
    fall."   *Exeunt.*

SCENA V.

[A road near Loretto.]

Antonio, Duchess, Children, Cariola, Serv-
ants; Bosola, Soldiers with vizards. [2]

DUCH. Banished Ancona!

ANT.   Yes, you see what power
Lightens in great men's breath.

DUCH.   Is all our train
Shrunk to this poor remainder?

ANT.   These poor men,
Which have got little in your service,
    vow
To take your fortune. But your wiser
    buntings,
Now they are fledged, are gone.

DUCH.   They have done wisely.
This puts me in mind of death; physi-
    cians thus,
With their hands full of money, use to
    give o'er
Their patients.

ANT.   Right the fashion of the world—
From decayed fortunes every flatterer
    shrinks;   10
Men cease to build where the founda-
    tion sinks.

[2] Bosola and Soldiers enter later.

Duch. I had a very strange dream tonight.
Ant.   What was 't?
Duch. Methought I wore my coronet of
   state,
And on a sudden all the diamonds
Were changed to pearls.
Ant.   My interpretation
Is, you'll weep shortly, for to me the
   pearls
Do signify your tears.
Duch.   The birds, that live i' th' field
On the wild benefit of nature, live
Happier than we, for they may choose
   their mates,
And carol their sweet pleasures to the
   spring.   20

[*Enter Bosola with a letter.*]

Bos. You are happily o'erta'en.
Duch.   From my brother?
Bos. Yes, from the Lord Ferdinand your
   brother
All love and safety.
Duch.   Thou dost blanch mischief,
Wouldst make it white. See, see, like to
   calm weather
At sea before a tempest, false hearts
   speak fair
To those they intend most mischief.

A Letter:

"Send Antonio to me; I want his head in
   a business."
A politic equivocation!
He doth not want your counsel, but your
   head;
That is, he cannot sleep till you be
   dead.   30
And here's another pitfall that's strewed
   o'er
With roses. Mark it; 'tis a cunning one:
"I stand engaged for your husband
for several debts at Naples. Let not
that trouble him; I had rather have his
heart than his money."
And I believe so too.
Bos.   What do you believe?
Duch. That he so much distrusts my
   husband's love,
He will by no means believe his heart
   is with him
Until he see it. The devil is not cunning
   enough   40
To circumvent us in riddles.

Bos. Will you reject that noble and free
   league
Of amity and love which I present you?
Duch. Their league is like that of some
   politic kings,
Only to make themselves of strength and
   power
To be our after-ruin. Tell them so.
Bos. And what from you?
Ant.   Thus tell him: I will not come.
Bos. And what of this?
Ant.   My brothers have dispersed
Bloodhounds abroad, which till I hear
   are muzzled,
No truce, though hatched with ne'er
   such politic skill,   50
Is safe, that hangs upon our enemies'
   will.
I'll not come at them.
Bos.   This proclaims your breeding.
Every small thing draws a base mind to
   fear
As the adamant [1] draws iron. Fare you
   well, sir;
You shall shortly hear from 's. *Exit.*
Duch.   I suspect some ambush;
Therefore by all my love I do conjure
   you
To take your eldest son, and fly to-
   wards Milan.
Let us not venture all this poor re-
   mainder
In one unlucky bottom.
Ant.   You counsel safely.
Best of my life, farewell. Since we must
   part,   60
Heaven hath a hand in 't; but no other-
   wise
Than as some curious artist takes in
   sunder
A clock or watch, when it is out of
   frame,
To bring 't in better order.
Duch. I know not which is best,
To see you dead or part with you.
   Farewell, boy.
Thou art happy that thou hast not
   understanding
To know thy misery, for all our wit
And reading brings us to a truer sense
Of sorrow.—In the eternal church, sir,
I do hope we shall not part thus.
Ant.   O, be of comfort!   71

----

[1] Magnet.

Make patience a noble fortitude,
And think not how unkindly we are
used.
"Man, like to cassia, is proved best,
being bruised."

DUCH. Must I, like to a slave-born
Russian,
Account it praise to suffer tyranny?
And yet, O heaven, thy heavy hand is
in 't!
I have seen my little boy oft scourge [1]
his top,
And compared myself to 't. Naught
made me e'er
Go right but heaven's scourge-stick.

ANT. Do not weep. 80
Heaven fashioned us of nothing, and
we strive
To bring ourselves to nothing.—Fare-
well, Cariola,
And thy sweet armful.—If I do never see
thee more,
Be a good mother to your little ones,
And save them from the tiger. Fare
you well.

DUCH. Let me look upon you once more,
for that speech
Came from a dying father. Your kiss is
colder
Than that I have seen an holy anchorite
Give to a dead man's skull.

ANT. My heart is turned to a heavy lump
of lead, 90
With which I sound my danger. Fare
you well. *Exit [with his Son].*

DUCH. My laurel is all withered.

CARI. Look, madam, what a troop of
arméd men
Make toward us!

Enter Bosola with a Guard.

DUCH. O, they are very welcome.
When Fortune's wheel is overcharged
with princes,
The weight makes it move swift. I
would have my ruin
Be sudden.—I am your adventure,[2] am
I not?

BOS. You are. You must see your husband no more.

DUCH. What devil art thou that counterfeits heaven's thunder?

BOS. Is that terrible? I would have you
tell me whether 100
Is that note worse that frights the silly
birds
Out of the corn, or that which doth allure them
To the nets? You have hearkened to
the last too much.

DUCH. O misery! Like to a rusty o'ercharged [3] cannon,
Shall I never fly in pieces? Come, to
what prison?

BOS. To none.

DUCH. Whither, then?

BOS. To your palace.

DUCH. I have heard
That Charon's boat serves to convey
all o'er
The dismal lake, but brings none back
again.

BOS. Your brothers mean you safety and
pity.

DUCH. Pity! With such a pity men preserve alive 110
Pheasants and quails, when they are
not fat enough
To be eaten.

BOS. These are your children?

DUCH. Yes.

BOS. Can they prattle?

DUCH. No.
But I intend, since they were born ac-
cursed,
Curses shall be their first language.

BOS. Fie, madam!
Forget this base, low fellow!

DUCH. Were I a man,
I'ld beat that counterfeit face [4] into thy
other.

BOS. One of no birth.

DUCH. Say that he was born mean,
Man is most happy when 's own actions
Be arguments and examples of his vir-
tue. 120

BOS. A barren, beggarly virtue!

DUCH. I prithee, who is greatest? Can
you tell?
Sad tales befit my woe; I'll tell you one.
A salmon, as she swam unto the sea,
Met with a dogfish, who encounters her
With this rough language, "Why art
thou so bold

___

[1] Whip, to keep in motion.
[2] Object of your quest.

[3] From 1640 edn. Original reads *o'erchar'd.*
[4] His vizard.

To mix thyself with our high state of
floods,
Being no eminent courtier, but one
That for the calmest and fresh time o' th'
year
Dost live in shallow rivers, rank'st thy-
self   130
With silly smelts and shrimps?   And
darest thou
Pass by our dogship without reverence?"
"O," quoth the salmon, "sister, be at
peace.
Thank Jupiter we both have passed the
net!
Our value never can be truly known
Till in the fisher's basket we be shown;
I' th' market then my price may be the
higher,
Even when I am nearest to the cook and
fire."
So to great men the moral may be
stretched,
"Men oft are valued high, when they're
most wretch'd."   140
But come, whither you please.   I am
armed gainst misery,
Bent to all sways of the oppressor's will.
"There's no deep valley but near some
great hill."   *Ex[eunt]*.

Actus IV. Scena i.

[*The place of the Duchess' imprisonment.*]

*Ferdinand,   Bosola,   Duchess,   Cariola,
                                        Servants.*[1]

FERD. How doth our sister duchess bear
herself
In her imprisonment?
Bos.   Nobly. I'll describe her.
She's sad, as one long used to 't, and
she seems
Rather to welcome the end of misery
Than shun it, a behavior so noble
As gives a majesty to adversity;
You may discern the shape of loveli-
ness
More perfect in her tears than in her
smiles.
She will muse four hours together, and
her silence,
Methinks, expresseth more than if she
spake.   10

[1] All but first two enter later.

FERD. Her melancholy seems to be forti-
fied
With a strange disdain.
Bos.   'Tis so; and this restraint,
Like English mastiffs that grow fierce
with tying,
Makes her too passionately apprehend
Those pleasures she's kept from.
FERD.   Curse upon her!
I will no longer study in the book
Of another's heart. Inform her what I
told you.   *Exit*.

[*Enter Duchess and Attendants.*]

Bos. All comfort to your grace!
DUCH.   I will have none.
Pray thee, why dost thou wrap thy
poisoned pills
In gold and sugar?   20
Bos. Your elder brother, the Lord Ferdi-
nand,
Is come to visit you, and sends you
word,
Cause once he rashly made a solemn
vow
Never to see you more, he comes i' th'
night;
And prays you gently neither torch nor
taper
Shine in your chamber. He will kiss
your hand,
And reconcile himself; but for his vow
He dares not see you.
DUCH.   At his pleasure.—
Take hence the lights.—He's come.
                    [*Exeunt Attendants with lights.*

Enter Ferdinand.]

FERD.   Where are you?
DUCH.   Here, sir.
FERD. This darkness suits you well.
DUCH.   I would ask you pardon.   30
FERD. You have it;
For I account it the honorabl'st revenge,
Where I may kill, to pardon.—Where
are your cubs?
DUCH. Whom?
FERD. Call them your children;
For, though our national law distinguish
bastards
From true legitimate issue, compassion-
ate nature
Makes them all equal.

Duch.   Do you visit me for this?
You violate a sacrament o' th' church
Shall make you howl in hell for 't.
Ferd.   It had been well
Could you have lived thus always; for
    indeed   41
You were too much i' th' light. But
    no more;
I come to seal my peace with you. Here's
    a hand   *Gives her a dead man's hand.*
To which you have vowed much love;
    the ring upon 't
You gave.   I affectionately kiss it.
Duch.
Ferd. Pray do, and bury the print of it
    in your heart.
I will leave this ring with you for a love
    token;
And the hand as sure as the ring; and
    do not doubt
But you shall have the heart too. When
    you need a friend,
Send it to him that owed [1] it; you shall
    see   50
Whether he can aid you.
Duch.   You are very cold.
I fear you are not well after your
    travel.—
Ha! Lights!—O, horrible!
Ferd.   Let her have lights enough.
                                            Exit.
Duch. What witchcraft doth he practice,
    that he hath left
A dead man's hand here?

[*By Servants who enter,*] *here is discovered,
behind a traverse,* [2] *the artificial figures
of Antonio and his Children, appearing as if they were dead.*

Bos. Look you, here's the piece from
    which 'twas ta'en.
He doth present you this sad spectacle,
That, now you know directly they are
    dead,
Hereafter you may wisely cease to
    grieve
For that which cannot be recoveréd.
Duch. There is not between heaven and
    earth one wish   61
I stay for after this. It wastes me more
Than were 't my picture, fashioned out
    of wax,

Stuck with a magical needle, and then
    buried
In some foul dunghill; and yon's an ex-
    cellent property
For a tyrant, which I would account
    mercy.
Bos.   What's that?
Duch. If they would bind me to that
    lifeless trunk,
And let me freeze to death.
Bos.   Come, you must live.
Duch. That's the greatest torture souls
    feel in hell—
In hell, that they must live, and cannot
    die.   70
Portia, I'll new kindle thy coals again,
And revive the rare and almost dead
    example
Of a loving wife.
Bos.   O, fie! Despair? Remember
You are a Christian.
Duch.   The church enjoins fasting.
I'll starve myself to death.
Bos.   Leave this vain sorrow.
Things being at the worst begin to mend.
The bee, when he hath shot his sting
    into your hand,
May then play with your eyelid.
Duch.   Good comfortable fellow,
Persuade a wretch that's broke upon
    the wheel
To have all his bones new set; entreat
    him live   80
To be executed again! Who must des-
    patch me?
I account this world a tedious theater,
For I do play a part in 't gainst my
    will.
Bos. Come, be of comfort; I will save
    your life.
Duch. Indeed, I have not leisure to tend
    so small a business.
Bos. Now, by my life, I pity you.
Duch.   Thou art a fool, then,
To waste thy pity on a thing so wretched
As cannot pity it. [3] I am full of daggers.
Puff, let me blow these vipers from me.—
[*To a Servant.*] What are you?
Ser.   One that wishes you long life.
Duch. I would thou wert hanged for the
    horrible curse   91
Thou hast given me. I shall shortly
    grow one

_____
[1] Owned.   [2] Curtain.   [3] *I.e.,* itself.

Of the miracles of pity. I'll go pray.—
No,
I'll go curse.
Bos.   O, fie!
Duch.   I could curse the stars—
Bos.   O, fearful!
Duch. And those three smiling seasons
of the year
Into a Russian winter; nay, the world
To its first chaos.
Bos.   Look you, the stars shine still.
Duch. O, but you must remember my
curse hath a great way to go.—
Plagues, that make lanes through larg-
est families,
Consume them!
Bos.   Fie, lady!
Duch.   Let them, like tyrants, 100
Never be remembered but for the ill
they have done;
Let all the zealous prayers of mortified
Churchmen forget them!
Bos.   O, uncharitable!
Duch. Let heaven a little while cease
crowning martyrs, to punish them!
Go, howl them this, and say I long to
bleed:
"It is some mercy when men kill with
speed."   *Exit [with Servants.*

Enter Ferdinand.]

Ferd. Excellent, as I would wish; she's
plagued in art.
These presentations are but framed in
wax
By the curious master in that quality,
Vincentio Lauriola, and she takes
them   110
For true substantial bodies.
Bos.   Why do you do this?
Ferd. To bring her to despair.
Bos.   Faith, end here,
And go no farther in your cruelty.
Send her a penitential garment to put on
Next to her delicate skin, and furnish
her
With beads and prayer books.
Ferd.   Damn her! That body of hers,
While that my blood ran pure in 't, was
more worth
Than that which thou wouldst comfort,
called a soul.
I will send her masques of common
courtesans,

Have her meat served up by bawds and
ruffians,   120
And, cause she'll needs be mad, I am
resolved
To remove forth [1] the common hospital
All the mad folk, and place them near
her lodging;
There let them practice together, sing
and dance,
And act their gambols to the full o' th'
moon.
If she can sleep the better for it, let her.
Your work is almost ended.
Bos.   Must I see her again?
Ferd. Yes.
Bos.   Never.
Ferd.   You must.
Bos.   Never in mine own shape;
That's forfeited by my intelligence
And this last cruel lie. When you send
me next,   130
The business shall be comfort.
Ferd.   Very likely!
Thy pity is nothing of kin to thee. An-
tonio
Lurks about Milan; thou shalt shortly
thither
To feed a fire as great as my revenge,
Which never will slack till it hath
spent his fuel.
"Intemperate agues make physicians
cruel."   *Exeunt*

SCENA ii.

[*The same.*]

*Duchess, Cariola, Servant, Madmen, Bosola,
Executioners, Ferdinand.* [2]

Duch. What hideous noise was that?
Cari.   'Tis the wild consort [3]
Of madmen, lady, which your tyrant
brother
Hath placed about your lodging. This
tyranny,
I think, was never practiced till this hour.
Duch. Indeed, I thank him. Nothing
but noise and folly
Can keep me in my right wits, whereas
reason
And silence make me stark mad. Sit
down;
Discourse to me some dismal tragedy.

[1] From.   [2] All but the first two enter later.
[3] Company, especially of musicians

CARI. O, 'twill increase your melancholy!

DUCH.   Thou art deceived;
To hear of greater grief would lessen
  mine.   10
This is a prison?

CARI.   Yes, but you shall live
To shake this durance off.

DUCH.   Thou art a fool.
The robin redbreast and the nightin-
  gale
Never live long in cages.

CARI.   Pray, dry your eyes.—
What think you of, madam?

DUCH.   Of nothing;
When I muse thus, I sleep.

CARI. Like a madman, with your eyes
  open?

DUCH. Dost thou think we shall know
  one another
In th' other world?

CARI.   Yes, out of question.   19

DUCH. O, that it were possible we might
But hold some two days' conference with
  the dead!
From them I should learn somewhat, I
  am sure,
I never shall know here. I'll tell thee a
  miracle:
I am not mad yet, to my cause of sorrow.
Th' heaven o'er my head seems made of
  molten brass,
The earth of flaming sulphur, yet I am
  not mad.
I am acquainted with sad misery
As the tanned galley slave is with his
  oar.
Necessity makes me suffer constantly,
And custom makes it easy. Who do I
  look like now?   30

CARI. Like to your picture in the gallery,
A deal of life in show, but none in prac-
  tice;
Or rather like some reverend monument
Whose ruins are even pitied.

DUCH.   Very proper;
And Fortune seems only to have her
  eyesight
To behold my tragedy.—How now!
What noise is that?

[Enter Servant.]

SER.   I am come to tell you
Your brother hath intended you some
  sport.

A great physician, when the pope was
  sick
Of a deep melancholy, presented him   40
With several sorts of madmen, which
  wild object,
Being full of change and sport, forced
  him to laugh,
And so th' imposthume [1] broke. The
  selfsame cure
The duke intends on you.

DUCH.   Let them come in.

SER. There's a mad lawyer and a secular
  priest;
A doctor that hath forfeited his wits
By jealousy; an astrologian
That in his works said such a day o' th'
  month
Should be the day of doom, and, failing
  of 't,
Ran mad; an English tailor crazed i' th'
  brain   50
With the study of new fashion; a gentle-
  man usher
Quite beside himself with care to keep
  in mind
The number of his lady's salutations
(Or "How do you") she employed him
  in each morning;
A farmer, too, an excellent knave in
  grain,[2]
Mad cause he was hindered transporta-
  tion.[3]
And let one broker [4] that's mad loose to
  these,
You'ld think the devil were among them.

DUCH. Sit, Cariola.—Let them loose when
  you please,
For I am chained to endure all your tyranny.   60

[Enter Madmen.]

*Here by a Madman this song is sung to a
                    dismal kind of music.*

  O, let us howl some heavy note,
    Some deadly dogged howl,
  Sounding as from the threat'ning throat
    Of beasts and fatal fowl!
  As ravens, scritch owls, bulls, and bears,
    We'll bill [5] and bawl our parts,

---

[1] Abscess.
[2] A pun on (1) in dye, *i.e.*, incorrigible, and
(2) in the grain trade.
[3] *I.e.*, forbidden to export his produce.
[4] Pawnbroker.
[5] Bell, bellow.

Till yerksome [1] noise have cloyed your ears
  And corrasived [2] your hearts.
At last, whenas our choir wants breath,
  Our bodies being blessed,   70
We'll sing, like swans, to welcome death,
  And die in love and rest.

1 Mad. Doomsday not come yet? I'll
draw it nearer by a perspective,[3] or
make a glass that shall set all the world
on fire upon an instant. I cannot sleep; my
pillow is stuffed with a litter of porcupines.

2 Mad. Hell is a mere glass house,
where the devils are continually blowing
up women's souls on hollow irons, and [80
the fire never goes out.

3 Mad. I will lie with every woman in
my parish the tenth night. I will tithe
them over like haycocks.

4 Mad. Shall my pothecary outgo me,
because I am a cuckold? I have found out
his roguery: he makes alum of his wife's
urine, and sells it to Puritans that have
sore throats with overstraining.

1 [Mad.] I have skill in heraldry.   90
2 [Mad.] Hast?
1 [Mad.] You do give for your crest
a woodcock's head with the brains picked
out on 't; you are a very ancient gentleman.

3 [Mad.] Greek is turned Turk; we
are only to be saved by the Helvetian
translation.[4]

1 [Mad.] Come on, sir, I will lay [5] the
law to you.

2 [Mad.] O, rather lay a corrasive; [100
the law will eat to the bone.

3 [Mad.] He that drinks but to satisfy
nature is damned.

4 [Mad.] If I had my glass here, I
would show a sight should make all the
women here call me mad doctor.

1 [Mad. (Pointing at 3 Madman.)]
What's he? A rope maker?

2 [Mad.] No, no, no; a snuffling knave
that, while he shows the tombs, will [110
have his hand in a wench's placket.[6]

3 [Mad.] Woe to the caroche that
brought home my wife from the masque
at three a-clock in the morning! It had a
large feather bed in it.

4 [Mad.] I have pared the devil's nails

forty times, roasted them in raven's eggs,
and cured agues with them.

3 [Mad.] Get me three hundred milch-
bats, to make possets to procure sleep. [120

4 [Mad.] All the college may throw
their caps at me—I have made a soap
boiler costive; it was my masterpiece.

*Here the dance, consisting of eight Madmen,
  with music answerable thereunto, after
  which Bosola, like an old man, enters.*

Duch. Is he mad too?
Ser. Pray, question him. I'll leave you.
            [*Exeunt Servant and Madmen.*]
Bos. I am come to make thy tomb.
Duch.   Ha! My tomb?
  Thou speak'st as if I lay upon my death-
      bed,
  Gasping for breath. Dost thou perceive
      me sick?
Bos. Yes, and the more dangerously
since thy sickness is insensible.   130
Duch. Thou art not mad, sure. Dost
      know me?
Bos.   Yes.
Duch.   Who am I?
Bos. Thou art a box of worm-seed, at
best but a salvatory of green mummy.[7]
What's this flesh? A little crudded [8] milk,
fantastical puff paste. Our bodies are
weaker than those paper prisons boys use
to keep flies in; more contemptible, since
ours is to preserve earthworms. Didst
thou ever see a lark in a cage? Such is the
soul in the body; this world is like [140
her little turf of grass, and the heaven o'er
our heads, like her looking-glass, only
gives us a miserable knowledge of the small
compass of our prison.
  Duch. Am not I thy duchess?
  Bos. Thou art some great woman, sure,
for riot begins to sit on thy forehead (clad
in gray hairs) twenty years sooner than on
a merry milkmaid's. Thou sleep'st worse
than if a mouse should be forced to [150
take up her lodging in a cat's ear; a little infant that breeds its teeth, should it lie with
thee, would cry out, as if thou wert the
more unquiet bedfellow.
  Duch. I am Duchess of Malfi still!
  Bos. That makes thy sleep so broken,

---

[1] Irksome.   [2] Corroded.   [3] Telescope.
[4] The Geneva Bible, prohibited in England
because of its Puritan tone.
[5] Expound.   [6] Opening in petticoat.
[7] Ointment box filled with dried flesh, widely
used as a medicine.
[8] Curdled.

Glories, like glowworms, afar off shine
bright,
But, looked to near, have neither heat
nor light.

DUCH. Thou art very plain. 159

Bos. My trade is to flatter the dead,
not the living; I am a tomb-maker.

DUCH. And thou com'st to make my
tomb?

Bos. Yes.

DUCH. Let me be a little merry. Of
what stuff wilt thou make it?

Bos. Nay, resolve [1] me first, of what
fashion?

DUCH. Why, do we grow fantastical in
our deathbed?
Do we affect fashion in the grave? 170

Bos. Most ambitiously. Princes' images
on their tombs
Do not lie, as they were wont, seeming
to pray
Up to heaven, but with their hands under
their cheeks,
As if they died of the toothache. They
are not carved
With their eyes fixed upon the stars,
but, as their
Minds were wholly bent upon the world,
The selfsame way they seem to turn
their faces.

DUCH. Let me know fully therefore the
effect
Of this thy dismal preparation,
This talk fit for a charnel.

Bos. Now I shall.—

[Enter Executioners, with] a coffin, cords,
and a bell.

Here is a present from your princely
brothers; 181
And may it arrive welcome, for it brings
Last benefit, last sorrow.

DUCH. Let me see it.
I have so much obedience in my blood,
I wish it in their veins to do them good.

Bos. This is your last presence chamber.

CARI. O, my sweet lady!

DUCH. Peace; it affrights not me.

Bos. I am the common bellman
That usually is sent to condemned per-
sons
The night before they suffer.

[1] Satisfy.

DUCH. Even now thou said'st 190
Thou wast a tomb-maker.

Bos. 'Twas to bring you
By degrees to mortification. Listen.
[Rings his bell.] [2]

Hark, now everything is still;
The scritch owl and the whistler shrill
Call upon our dame aloud,
And bid her quickly don her shroud!
Much you had of land and rent;
Your length in clay's now competent.
A long war disturbed your mind;
Here your perfect peace is signed. 200
Of what is 't fools make such vain keeping?
Sin their conception, their birth weeping,
Their life a general mist of error,
Their death a hideous storm of terror.
Strew your hair with powders sweet,
Don clean linen, bathe your feet,
And (the foul fiend more to check)
A crucifix let bless your neck.
'Tis now full tide tween night and day;
End your groan, and come away. 210

CARI. Hence, villains, tyrants, murderers!
Alas!
What will you do with my lady?—Call
for help!

DUCH. To whom? To our next neighbors?
They are madfolks.

Bos. Remove that noise!

DUCH. Farewell, Cariola.
In my last will I have not much to give—
A many hungry guests have fed upon
me;
Thine will be a poor reversion. [3]

CARI. I will die with her.

DUCH. I pray thee, look thou giv'st my
little boy
Some syrup for his cold, and let the girl
Say her prayers ere she sleep.
[Cariola is forced off.] [4]
Now what you please—
What death?

Bos. Strangling; here are your
executioners. 221

DUCH. I forgive them.
The apoplexy, cathar, [5] or cough o' th'
lungs
Would do as much as they do.

Bos. Doth not death fright you?

[2] From 1708 edn.
[3] Right of future possession.
[4] From 1708 edn.
[5] Catarrh; here, cerebral hemorrhage.

DUCH.   Who would be afraid on 't,
Knowing to meet such excellent company
In th' other world?
BOS. Yet, methinks,
The manner of your death should much afflict you—
This cord should terrify you!
DUCH.   Not a whit.
What would it pleasure me to have my throat cut   231
With diamonds? Or to be smotheréd
With cassia? Or to be shot to death with pearls?
I know death hath ten thousand several doors
For men to take their exits; and 'tis found
They go on such strange geometrical hinges,
You may open them both ways. Any way, for heaven sake,
So I were out of your whispering. Tell my brothers
That I perceive death, now I am well awake,
Best gift is they can give or I can take.   240
I would fain put off my last woman's fault:
I'ld not be tedious to you.
[1] EXEC.   We are ready.
DUCH. Dispose my breath how please you; but my body
Bestow upon my women, will you?
[1] EXEC.   Yes.
DUCH. Pull, and pull strongly, for your able strength
Must pull down heaven upon me.—
Yet stay. Heaven-gates are not so highly arched
As princes' palaces; they that enter there
Must go upon their knees.—[Kneels.]
Come, violent death;
Serve for mandragora to make me sleep!—   250
Go tell my brothers, when I am laid out,
They then may feed in quiet.
        They strangle her.
BOS. Where's the waiting-woman?
Fetch her. [Exeunt Executioners.] Some other strangle the children.

[Enter Cariola.]

Look you, there sleeps your mistress.
CARI.   O, you are damned
Perpetually for this! My turn is next.
Is 't not so ordered?
BOS.   Yes, and I am glad
You are so well prepared for 't.
CARI.   You are deceived, sir;
I am not prepared for 't. I will not die;
I will first come to my answer,[1] and know   260
How I have offended.
        BOS.   Come, despatch her.—
You kept her counsel; now you shall keep ours.
CARI. I will not die; I must not! I am contracted
To a young gentleman.
[1] EXEC.   Here's your wedding ring.
CARI. Let me but speak with the duke. I'll discover
Treason to his person.
BOS.   Delays!—Throttle her!
[1] EXEC. She bites and scratches.
CARI.   If you kill me now,
I am damned; I have not been at confession
This two years.
BOS. [To Executioners.]   When![2]
CARI.   I am quick with child.
BOS.   Why, then,
Your credit's saved. [Executioners strangle Cariola.] Bear her into th' next room;   270
Let this lie still.
[Exeunt Executioners with body of Cariola.

Enter Ferdinand.]

FERD.   Is she dead?
BOS.   She is what
You'ld have her. But here begin your pity! Shows the Children strangled.
Alas, how have these offended?
FERD.   The death
Of young wolves is never to be pitied.
BOS. Fix your eye here.
FERD.   Constantly.
BOS.   Do you not weep?
Other sins only speak; murther shrieks out.
The element of water moistens the earth,

---

[1] Opportunity for defense.
[2] Exclamation of impatience.

But blood flies upwards and bedews the
  heavens.

FERD. Cover her face! Mine eyes dazzle;
  she died young.

Bos. I think not so; her infelicity   280
Seemed to have years too many.

FERD. She and I were twins;
  And, should I die this instant, I had
    lived
  Her time to a minute.

Bos.   It seems she was born first.
You have bloodily approved the ancient
  truth
That kindred commonly do worse agree
Than remote strangers.

FERD.   Let me see her face
Again. Why didst thou not pity her?
  What
An excellent, honest man mightst thou
  have been,
If thou hadst borne her to some sanc-
  tuary,   290
Or, bold in a good cause, opposed thy-
  self
With thy advancéd sword above thy
  head
Between her innocence and my revenge!
I bade thee, when I was distracted of my
  wits,
Go kill my dearest friend, and thou hast
  done 't.
For let me but examine well the cause.
What was the meanness of her match
  to me?
Only I must confess I had a hope,
Had she continued widow, to have
  gained
An infinite mass of treasure by her
  death,   300
And that was the main cause. Her mar-
  riage—
That drew a stream of gall quite through
  my heart.
For thee (as we observe in tragedies
That a good actor many times is cursed
For playing a villain's part), I hate thee
  for 't.
And, for my sake, say thou hast done
  much ill well.

Bos. Let me quicken your memory, for
  I perceive
You are falling into ingratitude. I chal-
  lenge
The reward due to my service.

FERD.   I'll tell thee
What I'll give thee.

Bos.   Do.

FERD.   I'll give thee a pardon   310
For this murther.

Bos.   Ha!

FERD.   Yes, and 'tis
The largest bounty I can study to do
  thee.
By what authority didst thou execute
This bloody sentence?

Bos. By yours.

FERD. Mine? Was I her judge?
Did any ceremonial form of law
Doom her to not-being? Did a complete
  jury
Deliver her conviction up i' th' court?
Where shalt thou find this judgment
  registered,   320
Unless in hell? See, like a bloody fool,
Th' hast forfeited thy life, and thou shalt
  die for 't.

Bos. The office of justice is perverted quite
When one thief hangs another. Who
  shall dare
To reveal this?

FERD.   O, I'll tell thee;
The wolf shall find her grave, and scrape
  it up,
Not to devour the corpse, but to dis-
  cover
The horrid murther.

Bos.   You, not I, shall quake for 't.

FERD. Leave me.

Bos.   I will first receive my pension.

FERD. You are a villain!

Bos.   When your ingratitude   330
Is judge, I am so.

FERD. O horror,
That not the fear of him which binds
  the devils
Can prescribe man obedience!—
Never look upon me more.

Bos.   Why, fare thee well.
Your brother and yourself are worthy
  men!
You have a pair of hearts are hollow
  graves,
Rotten, and rotting others; and your
  vengeance,
Like two chained-bullets, still goes arm
  in arm.
You may be brothers, for treason, like
  the plague,   340

Doth take much in a blood. I stand like one
That long hath ta'en a sweet and golden dream.
I am angry with myself, now that I wake.
FERD. Get thee into some unknown part o' th' world,
That I may never see thee.
Bos.   Let me know
Wherefore I should be thus neglected. Sir,
I served your tyranny, and rather strove
To satisfy yourself than all the world;
And, though I loathed the evil, yet I loved
You that did counsel it, and rather sought   350
To appear a true servant than an honest man.
FERD. I'll go hunt the badger by owl-light;
'Tis a deed of darkness.   *Exit.*
Bos. He's much distracted. Off, my painted honor!
While with vain hopes our faculties we tire,
We seem to sweat in ice and freeze in fire.
What would I do, were this to do again?
I would not change my peace of conscience
For all the wealth of Europe. She stirs; here's life!
Return, fair soul, from darkness, and lead mine   360
Out of this sensible hell! She's warm; she breathes!
Upon thy pale lips I will melt my heart,
To store them with fresh color.—Who's there?
Some cordial drink!—Alas! I dare not call.
So pity would destroy pity. Her eye opes,
And heaven in it seems to ope, that late was shut,
To take me up to mercy.
DUCH. Antonio!
Bos.   Yes, madam, he is living;
The dead bodies you saw were but feigned statues.
He's reconciled to your brothers; the pope hath wrought   370

The atonement.[1]
DUCH. Mercy!   *She dies.*
Bos. O, she's gone again! There the cords of life broke.
O sacred Innocence, that sweetly sleeps
On turtles'[2] feathers, whilst a guilty conscience
Is a black register wherein is writ
All our good deeds and bad, a perspective
That shows us hell! That we cannot be suffered
To do good when we have a mind to it!
This is manly sorrow;   380
These tears, I am very certain, never grew
In my mother's milk. My estate is sunk
Below the degree of fear. Where were
These penitent fountains while she was living?
O, they were frozen up! Here is a sight
As direful to my soul as is the sword
Unto a wretch hath slain his father.
Come, I'll bear thee hence,
And execute thy last will—that's deliver
Thy body to the reverend dispose
Of some good women. That the cruel tyrant   390
Shall not deny me. Then I'll post to Milan,
Where somewhat I will speedily enact
Worth my dejection.
             Exit [with the body].[3]

ACTUS V. SCENA i.

[A public place in Milan.]

Antonio, Delio, Pescara, Julia.[4]

ANT. What think you of my hope of reconcilement
To the Aragonian brethren?
DELIO.   I misdoubt it;
For, though they have sent their letters of safe-conduct
For your repair to Milan, they appear
But nets to entrap you. The Marquis of Pescara,
Under whom you hold certain land in cheat,[5]

[1] Reconciliation.
[2] Turtledoves'.
[3] From 1708 edn.

[4] Last two enter later.
[5] Escheat.

Much gainst his noble nature hath been
  moved
To seize those lands; and some of his
  dependants
Are at this instant making it their suit
To be invested in your revenues.   10
I cannot think they mean well to your
  life
That do deprive you of your means of
  life,
Your living.   ANT.   You are still an heretic
To any safety I can shape myself.
DEL. Here comes the marquis. I will make
  myself
Petitioner for some part of your land,
To know whither it is flying.
ANT.   I pray, do. [*Withdraws.*

Enter Pescara.]

DEL. Sir, I have a suit to you.
PES.   To me?
DEL.   An easy one.
There is the Citadel of Saint Bennet,
With some demesnes, of late in the
  possession   20
Of Antonio Bologna—please you bestow
  them on me.
PES. You are my friend; but this is such a
  suit
Nor fit for me to give nor you to take.
DEL. No, sir?
PES.   I will give you ample reason for 't
Soon in private.—Here's the cardinal's
  mistress.

[*Enter Julia.*]

JUL. My lord, I am grown your poor peti-
  tioner,
And should be an ill beggar, had I not
A great man's letter here, the cardinal's,
To court you in my favor. [*Gives a letter.*]
PES. [*After reading.*]   He entreats
  for you
The Citadel of Saint Bennet, that be-
  longed   30
To the banishéd Bologna.
JUL.   Yes.
PES. I could not have thought of a friend I
  could
Rather pleasure with it. 'Tis yours.
JUL.   Sir, I thank you;
And he shall know how doubly I am
  engaged

Both in your gift and speediness o
  giving,
Which makes your grant the greater.
                       Exit.
ANT. [*Aside.*]   How they fortify
Themselves with my ruin!
DEL.   Sir, I am
  Little bound to you.
PES. Why?
DEL. Because you denied this suit to me,
  and gave 't   40
To such a creature.
PES.   Do you know what it was?
It was Antonio's land, not forfeited
By course of law, but ravished from his
  throat
By the cardinal's entreaty. It were not
  fit
I should bestow so main a piece of wrong
Upon my friend; 'tis a gratification
Only due to a strumpet, for it is injustice.
Shall I sprinkle the pure blood of in-
  nocents
To make those followers I call my friends
Look ruddier [1] upon me? I am glad   50
This land, ta'en from the owner by such
  wrong,
Returns again unto so foul an use
As salary for his lust. Learn, good Delio,
To ask noble things of me, and you shall
  find
I'll be a noble giver.
DEL.   You instruct me well.
ANT. [*Aside.*] Why, here's a man now
  would fright impudence
From sauciest beggars.
PES.   Prince Ferdi-
  nand's come to Milan,
Sick, as they give out, of an apoplexy;
But some say 'tis a frenzy. I am going
To visit him.   *Exit.*
ANT.   'Tis a noble old fellow!
DEL. What course do you mean to take,
  Antonio?   61
ANT. This night I mean to venture all my
  fortune,
Which is no more than a poor ling'ring
  life,
To the cardinal's worst of malice. I have
  got
Private access to his chamber, and in-
  tend
To visit him about the mid of night,

---

[1] More favorably.

As once his brother did our noble
duchess.

It may be that the sudden apprehension
Of danger (for I'll go in mine own shape),
When he shall see it fraught [1] with love
and duty,　　　　　　　　　70
May draw the poison out of him, and
work
A friendly reconcilement. If it fail,
Yet it shall rid me of this infamous
calling;
For better fall once than be ever falling.
DEL. I'll second you in all danger; and,
howe'er,
My life keeps rank with yours.
ANT. You are still my lovéd and best
friend.　　　　　　　　*Exeunt.*

SCENA ii.

[*A gallery in the palace of the Cardinal and
Ferdinand at Milan.*]

*Pescara, a Doctor, Ferdinand, Cardinal,
Malateste, Bosola, Julia.* [2]

PES. Now, doctor, may I visit your pa-
tient?
DOC. If 't please your lordship; but he's
instantly
To take the air here in the gallery
By my direction.
PES.　　　　Pray thee, what's his disease?
DOC. A very pestilent disease, my lord,
They call lycanthropia.
PES.　　　　　　　　What's that?
I need a dictionary to 't.
DOC.　　　　　　　　I'll tell you.
In those that are possessed with 't there
o'erflows
Such melancholy humor they imagine
Themselves to be transforméd into
wolves,　　　　　　　　10
Steal forth to churchyards in the dead
of night,
And dig dead bodies up; as two nights
since
One met the duke 'bout midnight in a
lane
Behind Saint Mark's Church, with the
leg of a man
Upon his shoulder; and he howled fear-
fully;
Said he was a wolf, only the difference

[1] Fraught.　　　[2] Last five enter later.

Was, a wolf's skin was hairy on the out-
side,
His on the inside; bade them take their
swords,
Rip up his flesh, and try. Straight I was
sent for,
And, having ministered to him, found his
grace　　　　　　　　20
Very well recovered.
PES. I am glad on 't.
DOC.　　　　Yet not without some fear
Of a relapse. If he grow to his fit again,
I'll go a nearer way to work with him
Than ever Paracelsus dreamed of. If
They'll give me leave, I'll buffet his
madness out of him.
Stand aside; he comes.

[*Enter Ferdinand, Cardinal, Malateste,
and Bosola.*]

FERD. Leave me.
MAL. Why doth your lordship love this
solitariness?　　　　　　　　30
FERD. Eagles commonly fly alone; they
are crows, daws, and starlings that flock
together.　　　Look, what's that follows
me?
MAL. Nothing, my lord.
FERD. Yes.
MAL. 'Tis your shadow.
FERD. Stay it; let it not haunt me.
MAL. Impossible, if you move, and the
sun shine.　　　　　　　　40
FERD. I will throttle it.
[*Throws himself down on his shadow.*]
MAL. O, my lord, you are angry with
nothing.
FERD. You are a fool. How is 't possible
I should catch my shadow unless I fall
upon 't? When I go to hell, I mean to carry
a bribe, for, look you, good gifts evermore
make way for the worst persons.
PES. Rise, good my lord.　　　49
FERD. I am studying the art of patience.
PES. 'Tis a noble virtue.
FERD. To drive six snails before me
from this town to Moscow; neither use
goad nor whip to them, but let them take
their own time (the patient'st man i' th'
world match me for an experiment!), and
I'll crawl after like a sheepbiter.
CARD. Force him up. [*They raise him.*]
FERD. Use me well, you were best.

What I have done, I have done; I'll [60
confess nothing.

Doc. Now let me come to him.—Are you
mad, my lord?

Are you out of your princely wits?

FERD.   What's he?

PES.   Your doctor.

FERD. Let me have his beard sawed off,
and his eyebrows filed more civil.

Doc. I must do mad tricks with him, for
that's the only way on 't.—I have brought
your grace a salamander's skin to keep you
from sunburning.

FERD. I have cruel sore eyes.   70

Doc. The white of a cockatrix's egg is
present remedy.

FERD. Let it be a new-laid one, you were
best.

Hide me from him! Physicians are like
kings—

They brook no contradiction.

Doc. Now he begins to fear me; now let
me alone with him.

[*Puts off his four cloaks one after another.*][1]

CARD. How now! Put off your gown?

Doc. Let me have some forty urinals
filled with rose water. He and I'll go [80
pelt one another with them.—Now he begins
to fear me.—Can you fetch a frisk,[2] sir?—
Let him go, let him go, upon my peril!
I find by his eye he stands in awe of me;
I'll make him as tame as a dormouse.

FERD. Can you fetch your frisks, sir?—
I will stamp him into a cullis, flay off his
skin to cover one of the anatomies [3] this
rogue hath set i' th' cold yonder in Barber-
Chirurgeons'[4] Hall.—Hence, hence! [90
You are all of you like beasts for sacrifice.
[*Throws the Doctor down and beats him.*][5]
There's nothing left of you but tongue
and belly, flattery and lechery.   [*Exit.*]

PES. Doctor, he did not fear you
throughly!

Doc. True; I was somewhat too forward.

BOS. Mercy upon me, what a fatal judgment
Hath fall'n upon this Ferdinand!

PES.   Knows your grace
What accident hath brought unto the
prince

This strange distraction?   100

CARD. [*Aside.*] I must feign somewhat.—
Thus they say it grew:
You have heard it rumored, for these
many years,
None of our family dies but there is seen
The shape of an old woman, which is
given
By tradition to us to have been mur-
thered
By her nephews for her riches. Such a
figure
One night, as the prince sat up late at 's
book,
Appeared to him, when, crying out for
help,
The gentleman of 's chamber found his
grace   109
All on a cold sweat, altered much in face
And language; since which apparition,
He hath grown worse and worse, and I
much fear
He cannot live.

BOS.   Sir, I would speak with you.

PES. We'll leave your grace,
Wishing to the sick prince, our noble
lord,
All health of mind and body.

CARD.   You are most welcome.
[*Exeunt. Manent*[6] *Cardinal and Bosola.*][7]
Are you come? So.—[*Aside.*] This fellow
must not know
By any means I had intelligence
In our duchess' death; for, though I
counseled it,
The full of all th' engagement seemed to
grow   120
From Ferdinand.—Now, sir, how fares
our sister?
I do not think but sorrow makes her
look
Like to an oft-dyed garment. She shall
now
Taste comfort from me. Why do you
look so wildly?
O, the fortune of your master here, the
prince,
Dejects you; but be you of happy com-
fort.
If you'll do one thing for me I'll entreat,
Though he had a cold tombstone o'er his
bones,
I'ld make you what you would be.

---

[1] From 1708 edn.   [2] Cut a caper.   [3] Skeletons.
[4] Barber-Surgeons'.   Barbers often performed
some of the duties of the physician.
[5] From 1708 edn.

[6] Remain.   [7] From 1708 edn.

Bos.   Anything;
  Give it me in a breath, and let me fly
    to 't.   130
  They that think long, small expedition
    win,
  For musing much o' th' end, cannot
    begin.

[Enter Julia.]

Jul. Sir, will you come in to supper?
Card. I am busy; leave me.
Jul. [*Aside.*]   What an excellent shape
  hath that fellow!   *Exit.*
Card. 'Tis thus. Antonio lurks here in
  Milan;
  Inquire him out, and kill him. While he
    lives,
  Our sister cannot marry; and I have
    thought
  Of an excellent match for her. Do this,
    and style me
  Thy advancement.   140
Bos. But by what means shall I find him
  out?
Card. There is a gentleman called Delio
  Here in the camp, that hath been long
    approved
  His loyal friend.   Set eye upon that
    fellow;
  Follow him to mass; may be Antonio,
  Although he do account religion
  But a school-name, for fashion of the
    world
  May accompany him; or else go inquire
    out
  Delio's confessor, and see if you can bribe
  Him to reveal it. There are a thousand
    ways   150
  A man might find to trace him—as to
    know
  What fellows haunt the Jews for taking up
  Great sums of money, for sure he's in
    want;
  Or else to go to th' picture makers, and
    learn
  Who bought [1] her picture lately. Some
    of these
  Happily may take.
Bos.   Well, I'll not freeze i' th' business;
  I would see that wretched thing, An-
    tonio,
  Above all sights i' th' world.
Card.   Do, and be happy. *Exit.*

[1] Dyce's emendation for *brought.*

Bos. This fellow doth breed basilisks in 's
  eyes;
  He's nothing else but murder; yet he
    seems   160
  Not to have notice of the duchess' death.
  'Tis his cunning; I must follow his
    example.
  There cannot be a surer way to trace
  Than that of an old fox.

[Enter Julia, with a pistol.]

Jul. So, sir, you are well met.
Bos. How now!
Jul. Nay, the doors are fast enough.
Now, sir, I will make you confess your
treachery.
  Bos. Treachery?   170
Jul. Yes, confess to me
  Which of my women 'twas you hired to
    put
  Love powder into my drink.
Bos. Love powder!
Jul.   Yes, when I was at Malfi.
  Why should I fall in love with such a
    face else?
  I have already suffered for thee so much
    pain,
  The only remedy to do me good
  Is to kill my longing.
Bos.   Sure, your pistol holds
  Nothing but perfumes or kissing-comfits.[2]
  Excellent lady,   179
  You have a pretty way on 't to discover
  Your longing. Come, come, I'll disarm
    you,
  And arm [3] you thus. Yet this is wondrous
    strange.
Jul. Compare thy form and my eyes to-
    gether,
  You'll find my love no such great miracle.
  Now you'll say
  I am wanton. This nice modesty in ladies
  Is but a troublesome familiar [4]
  That haunts them.
Bos. Know you me; I am a blunt soldier.
Jul.   The better.
  Sure, there wants fire where there are no
    lively sparks
  Of roughness.   190
Bos. And I want compliment.
Jul.   Why, ignorance

[2] Sweetmeats for the breath.
[3] Embrace.   [4] Spirit.

In courtship cannot make you do amiss,
If you have a heart to do well.
Bos.   You are very fair.
Jul. Nay, if you lay beauty to my charge,
I must plead unguilty.
Bos.   Your bright eyes
Carry a quiver of darts in them, sharper
Than sunbeams.
Jul.   You will mar me with
commendation;
Put yourself to the charge of courting me,
Whereas now I woo you.
Bos. [*Aside.*] I have it; I will work upon
this creature.—   200
Let us grow most amorously familiar.
If the great cardinal now should see me
thus,
Would he not count me a villain?
Jul. No; he might count me a wanton,
Not lay a scruple of offense on you;
For, if I see and steal a diamond,
The fault is not i' th' stone, but in me,
the thief
That purloins it. I am sudden with you.
We that are great women of pleasure use
to cut off
These uncertain wishes and unquiet long-
ings,   210
And in an instant join the sweet delight
And the pretty excuse together. Had you
been i' th' street,
Under my chamber window, even
there
I should have courted you.
Bos. O, you are an excellent lady!
Jul. Bid me do somewhat for you pres-
ently
To express I love you.
Bos. I will; and, if you love me, fail not to
effect it.
The cardinal is grown wondrous melan-
choly;
Demand the cause; let him not put you
off   220
With feigned excuse; discover the main
ground on 't.
Jul. Why would you know this?
Bos.   I have depended on him,
And I hear that he is fall'n in some dis-
grace
With the emperor. If he be, like the
mice
That forsake falling houses, I would shift
To other dependence.

Jul.   You shall not need follow the
wars—
I'll be your maintenance.
Bos.   And I your loyal servant;
But I cannot leave my calling.
Jul.   Not leave an
Ungrateful general for the love of a sweet
lady!
You are like some cannot sleep in feather
beds,   230
But must have blocks for their pillows.
Bos.   Will you do this?
Jul. Cunningly.
Bos. Tomorrow I'll expect th' intelli-
gence.
Jul. Tomorrow! Get you into my cabinet;
You shall have it with you. Do not delay
me,
No more than I do you. I am like one
That is condemned; I have my pardon
promised,
But I would see it sealed. Go, get you in;
You shall see me wind my tongue about
his heart
Like a skein of silk.   [*Exit Bosola.*

Enter Cardinal.]

Card.   Where are you?

[*Enter Servants.*]

Servants.   Here.
Card. Let none, upon your lives,   241
Have conference with the Prince Fer-
dinand,
Unless I know it. [*Exeunt Servants.*]—
[*Aside.*] In this distraction
He may reveal the murther.
Yond's my lingering consumption.
I am weary of her, and by any means
Would be quit of.
Jul. How now, my lord! What ails you?
Card. Nothing.
Jul.   O, you are much alteréd.
Come, I must be your secretary,[1] and
remove
This lead from off your bosom. What's
the matter?   250
Card. I may not tell you.
Jul. Are you so far in love with sorrow
You cannot part with part of it? Or
think you

---

[1] Sharer of secrets.

I cannot love your grace when you are
    sad
As well as merry? Or do you suspect
I, that have been a secret to your heart
These many winters, cannot be the same
Unto your tongue?

CARD.   Satisfy thy longing—
The only way to make thee keep my
    counsel   259
Is not to tell thee.

JUL.   Tell your echo this,
Or flatterers, that like echoes still re-
    port
What they hear, though most imperfect,
    and not me;
For, if that you be true unto yourself,
    I'll know.

CARD.   Will you rack me?

JUL.   No, judgment shall
Draw it from you. It is an equal fault
To tell one's secrets unto all or none.

CARD. The first argues folly.

JUL. But the last tyranny.

CARD. Very well; why, imagine I have
    committed
Some secret deed which I desire the
    world   270
May never hear of.

JUL.   Therefore may not I know it?
You have concealed for me as great a sin
As adultery. Sir, never was occasion
For perfect trial of my constancy
Till now. Sir, I beseech you—

CARD.   You'll repent it.

JUL. Never.

CARD. It hurries thee to ruin. I'll not tell
    thee.
Be well advised, and think what danger
    'tis
To receive a prince's secrets. They that
    do,
Had need have their breasts hooped with
    adamant   280
To contain them. I pray thee, yet be
    satisfied;
Examine thine own frailty; 'tis more easy
To tie knots than unloose them. 'Tis a
    secret
That, like a ling'ring poison, may chance
    lie
Spread in thy veins, and kill thee seven
    year hence.

JUL. Now you dally with me.

CARD. No more; thou shalt know it.

By my appointment, the great Duchess
    of Malfi
And two of her young children, four
    nights since,
Were strangled.

JUL.   O heaven! Sir, what
have you done?   290

CARD. How now? How settles this? Think
    you your
Bosom will be a grave, dark and obscure
    enough
For such a secret?

JUL.   You have undone yourself, sir.

CARD. Why?

JUL.   It lies not in me to conceal it.

CARD. No? Come, I will swear you to 't
    upon this book.

JUL. Most religiously.

CARD. Kiss it.   [*She kisses the book.*]
Now you shall never utter it; thy curios-
    ity
Hath undone thee; thou'rt poisoned with
    that book.
Because I knew thou couldst not keep
    my counsel,   300
I have bound thee to 't by death.

[*Enter Bosola.*]

BOS. For pity sake, hold!

CARD.   Ha, Bosola?

JUL.   I forgive you
This equal piece of justice you have done;
For I betrayed your counsel to that
    fellow.
He overheard it; that was the cause I
    said
It lay not in me to conceal it.

BOS. O foolish woman,
Couldst not thou have poisoned him?

JUL.   'Tis weakness
Too much to think what should have
    been done.   309
I go, I know not whither.   [*Dies.*]

CARD. Wherefore com'st thou hither?

BOS. That I might find a great man like
    yourself,
Not out of his wits, as the Lord Ferdi-
    nand,
To remember my service.

CARD.   I'll have thee hewed in pieces.

BOS. Make not yourself such a promise of
    that life
Which is not yours to dispose of.

CARD.   Who placed thee here?

Bos. Her lust, as she intended.

Card.   Very well;
Now you know me for your fellow-
murderer.

Bos. And wherefore should you lay fair
marble colors
Upon your rotten purposes to me,   320
Unless you imitate some that do plot
great treasons,
And, when they have done, go hide them-
selves i' th' graves
Of those were actors in 't?

Card.   No more; there is
A fortune attends thee.

Bos. Shall I go sue to Fortune any longer?
'Tis the fool's pilgrimage.

Card. I have honors in store for thee.

Bos. There are a many ways that conduct
to seeming
Honor, and some of them very dirty ones.

Card. Throw to the devil   330
Thy melancholy. The fire burns well;
What need we keep a-stirring of 't, and
make
A greater smoother? [1]   Thou wilt kill
Antonio?

Bos. Yes.

Card.   Take up that body.

Bos.   I think I shall
Shortly grow the common bier for
churchyards!

Card. I will allow thee some dozen of
attendants
To aid thee in the murther.

Bos. O, by no means. Physicians that
apply horseleeches to any rank swelling use
to cut off their tails, that the blood [340
may run through them the faster, let
me have no train when I go to shed blood,
lest it make me have a greater when I
ride to the gallows.

Card. Come to me after midnight, to help
to remove
That body to her own lodging. I'll give out
She died o' th' plague;
'Twill breed the less inquiry after her
death.

Bos. Where's Castruchio her husband?

Card. He's rode to Naples, to take possession   350
Of Antonio's citadel.

Bos. Believe me, you have done a very
happy turn.

[1] Smother, smoke.

Card. Fail not to come. There is the
master key
Of our lodgings; and by that you may
conceive
What trust I plant in you.   Exit.

Bos.   You shall find me ready.—
O poor Antonio, though nothing be so
needful
To thy estate as pity, yet I find
Nothing so dangerous! I must look to my
footing;
In such slippery ice-pavements men had
need
To be frost-nailed well—they may break
their necks else.   360
The precedent's here afore me. How this
man
Bears up in blood, seems fearless! Why,
'tis well.
Security some men call the suburbs of
hell,
Only a dead wall between. Well, good
Antonio,
I'll seek thee out; and all my care shall be
To put thee into safety from the reach
Of these most cruel biters that have got
Some of thy blood already. It may be,
I'll join with thee in a most just revenge.
The weakest arm is strong enough that
strikes   370
With the sword of justice. Still methinks
the duchess
Haunts me. There, there!—'Tis nothing
but my melancholy.
O Penitence, let me truly taste thy cup,
That throws men down only to raise
them up!   Exit.

Scena iii.

[A fortification in Milan.]

Antonio, Delio.   Echo (from the Duchess'
grave).

Del. Yond's the cardinal's window. This
fortification
Grew from the ruins of an ancient abbey;
And to yond side o' th' river lies a wall,
Piece of a cloister, which in my opinion
Gives the best echo that you ever heard,
So hollow and so dismal, and withal
So plain in the distinction of our words
That many have supposed it is a spirit
That answers.

ANT.   I do love these ancient ruins.
We never tread upon them but we set   10
Our foot upon some reverend history;
And, questionless, here in this open
    court,
Which now lies naked to the injuries
Of stormy weather, some men lie interred
Loved the church so well, and gave so
    largely to 't,
They thought it should have canopied
    their bones
Till doomsday. But all things have their
    end;
Churches and cities, which have diseases
    like to men,
Must have like death that we have.
ECHO.   *Like death that we have.*
DEL. Now the echo hath caught you.   20
ANT. It groaned, methought, and gave
A very deadly accent.
ECHO.   *Deadly accent.*
DEL. I told you 'twas a pretty one. You
    may make it
A huntsman, or a falconer, a musician,
Or a thing of sorrow.
ECHO.   *A thing of sorrow.*
ANT. Ay, sure, that suits it best.
ECHO.   *That suits it best.*
ANT. 'Tis very like my wife's voice.
ECHO.   *Ay, wife's voice.*
DEL. Come, let's us walk farther from 't.
I would not have you go to th' cardinal's
    tonight.
Do not.   30
ECHO. *Do not.*
DEL. Wisdom doth not more moderate
    wasting sorrow
Than time. Take time for 't; be mindful
    of thy safety.
ECHO. *Be mindful of thy safety.*
ANT. Necessity compels me.
Make scrutiny throughout the passes
Of your own life, you'll find it impossible
To fly your fate.
[ECHO.] *O, fly your fate!*
DEL. Hark! The dead stones seem to
    have pity on you,   40
And give you good counsel.
ANT. Echo, I will not talk with thee,
For thou art a dead thing.
ECHO. *Thou art a dead thing.*
ANT. My duchess is asleep now,
And her little ones, I hope sweetly. O
    heaven,

Shall I never see her more?
ECHO. *Never see her more.*
ANT. I marked not one repetition of the
    echo
But that; and on the sudden a clear
    light   50
Presented me a face folded in sorrow.
DEL. Your fancy merely.
ANT.   Come, I'll be out of this ague.
For to live thus is not indeed to live;
It is a mockery and abuse of life.
I will not henceforth save myself by
    halves;
Lose all, or nothing.
DEL.   Your own virtue save you!
I'll fetch your eldest son, and second you.
It may be that the sight of his own blood
Spread in so sweet a figure may beget
The more compassion. However, fare
    you well.   60
Though in our miseries Fortune have a
    part,
Yet in our noble suff'rings she hath none.
Contempt of pain, that we may call our
    own.   *Exe[unt].*

SCENA iv.

[*An apartment in the palace of the Cardinal
and Ferdinand at Milan.*]

*Cardinal, Pescara, Malateste, Roderigo,
Grisolan, Bosola, Ferdinand, Antonio,
Servant.*[1]

CARD. You shall not watch tonight by the
    sick prince;
His grace is very well recovered.
MAL. Good my lord, suffer us.
CARD.   O, by no means;
The noise, and change of object in his
    eye,
Doth more distract him. I pray, all to
    bed;
And, though you hear him in his violent
    fit,
Do not rise, I entreat you.
PES. So, sir; we shall not.
CARD.   Nay, I must have you promise
Upon your honors, for I was enjoined
    to 't
By himself; and he seemed to urge it
    sensibly.   10
PES. Let our honors bind this trifle.
CARD. Nor any of your followers.

    [1] Last four enter later.

MAL. Neither.

CARD. It may be, to make trial of your
promise,
When he's asleep, myself will rise and
feign
Some of his mad tricks, and cry out for
help,
And feign myself in danger.

MAL. If your throat were cutting,
I'd not come at you, now I have protested against it.

CARD. Why, I thank you.

GRIS. 'Twas a foul storm tonight. 20

ROD. The Lord Ferdinand's chamber
shook like an osier.

MAL. [Aside.] 'Twas nothing but pure
kindness in the devil
To rock his own child.

Exeunt [all except the Cardinal].

CARD. The reason why I would not suffer
these
About my brother is because at midnight
I may with better privacy convey
Julia's body to her own lodging. O, my
conscience!
I would pray now, but the devil takes
away my heart
For having any confidence in prayer.
About this hour I appointed Bosola 30
To fetch the body. When he hath served
my turn,
He dies. Exit.

[Enter Bosola.]

BOS. Ha! 'Twas the cardinal's voice; I
heard him name
Bosola and my death. Listen; I hear
one's footing.

[Enter Ferdinand.]

FERD. Strangling is a very quiet death.

BOS. [Aside.] Nay, then, I see I must stand
upon my guard.

FERD. What say to that? Whisper
softly. Do you agree to 't? So; it must be
done i' th' dark; the cardinal would not for
a thousand pounds the doctor should [40
see it. Exit.

BOS. My death is plotted; here's the consequence of murther.
"We value not desert nor Christian
breath,
When we know black deeds must be
cured with death."

[Enter Antonio and Servant.]

SER. Here stay, sir, and be confident, I
pray;
I'll fetch you a dark lanthorn. Exit.

ANT. Could I take
Him at his prayers, there were hope of
pardon.

BOS. Fall right, my sword! [Stabs him.]—
I'll not give thee so much leisure as to
pray.

ANT. O, I am gone! Thou hast ended a
long suit 50
In a minute.

BOS. What art thou?

ANT. A most wretched thing,
That only have thy benefit [1] in death,
To appear myself.

[Enter Servant with a lantern.]

SER. Where are you, sir?

ANT. Very near my home!—Bosola!

SER. O, misfortune!

BOS. [To Servant.] Smother thy pity; thou
art dead else.—Antonio!
The man I would have saved 'bove
mine own life!
We are merely the stars' tennis balls,
strook [2] and banded [3]
Which way please them.—O good
Antonio,
I'll whisper one thing in thy dying
ear 60
Shall make thy heart break quickly!
Thy fair duchess
And two sweet children—

ANT. Their very names
Kindle a little life in me.

BOS. Are murdered!

ANT. Some men have wished to die
At the hearing of sad tidings; I am glad
That I shall do 't in sadness.[4] I would
not now
Wish my wounds balmed nor healed,
for I have no use
To put my life to. In all our quest of
greatness,
Like wanton boys whose pastime is
their care,
We follow after bubbles blown in th'
air. 70
Pleasure of life, what is 't? Only the
good hours

1 Assistance. 2 Bandied.
2 Struck. 4 Seriousness, reality.

Of an ague; merely a preparative to rest,
To endure vexation. I do not ask
The process [1] of my death; only com-
　mend me
To Delio.
Bos. Break, heart!
Ant. And let my son fly the courts of
　princes.　　　　　　　　　　[*Dies.*]
Bos. Thou seem'st to have loved An-
　tonio?
Ser. I brought him hither,　　　　79
To have reconciled him to the cardinal.
Bos. I do not ask thee that.
　Take him up, if thou tender thine own
　　life,
And bear him where the lady Julia
Was wont to lodge.—O, my fate moves
　swift!
I have this cardinal in the forge al-
　ready;
Now I'll bring him to th' hammer. O
　direful misprision! [2]
I will not imitate things glorious,
No more than base; I'll be mine own
　example.—
On, on, and look thou represent, for
　silence,
The thing thou bear'st.　　*Exeunt.*　90

SCENA V.

[*A hall and gallery of the same.*]

*Cardinal, with a book. Bosola, Pescara,
Malateste, Roderigo, Ferdinand, Delio,
Servant with Antonio's body.*[3]

Card. I am puzzled in a question about
　hell.
He says in hell there's one material fire,
And yet it shall not burn all men alike.
Lay him by. How tedious is a guilty
　conscience!
When I look into the fish ponds in my
　garden,
Methinks I see a thing armed with a
　rake,
That seems to strike at me.

[*Enter Bosola, and Servant bearing Antonio's
body.*]

Now, art thou come?　　Thou look'st
　ghastly;

[1] Account, story.　　　　　[2] Mistake.
[3] All but the first enter later.

There sits in thy face some great deter-
　mination,
Mixed with some fear.
Bos.　　　Thus it lightens into action;　10
I am come to kill thee.
Card.　　　　　Ha!—Help! Our guard!
Bos. Thou art deceived; they are out of
　thy howling.
Card. Hold, and I will faithfully divide
Revenues with thee.
Bos.　　　　　Thy prayers and proffers
Are both unseasonable.
Card.　　　　　Raise the watch!
We are betrayed!
Bos.　　　I have confined your flight.
I'll suffer your retreat to Julia's chamber,
But no further.
Card.　　　Help! We are betrayed!

[*Enter, above, Pescara, Malateste, Roderigo,
and Grisolan.*]

Mal. Listen!
Card. My dukedom for rescue!　　20
Rod. Fie upon his counterfeiting!
Mal. Why, 'tis not the cardinal.
Rod. Yes, yes, 'tis he.
But I'll see him hanged ere I'll go down
　to him.
Card. Here's a plot upon me. I am as-
　saulted! I am lost,
Unless some rescue!
Gris.　　　He doth this pretty well;
But it will not serve to laugh me out of
　mine honor.
Card. The sword's at my throat!
Rod.　　　You would not bawl so loud then.
Mal. Come, come, lets's go to bed. He
told us this much aforehand.　　30
Pes. He wished you should not come at
　him; but, believe 't,
The accent of the voice sounds not in
　jest.
I'll down to him, howsoever, and with
　engines
Force ope the doors.　　[*Exit above.*]
Rod.　　　Let's follow him aloof,
And note how the cardinal will laugh
　at him.
[*Exeunt, above, Malateste, Roderigo, and
Grisolan.*]
Bos. There's for you first, cause you shall
　not unbarricade the door
To let in rescue.　　*He kills the Servant.*

CARD. What cause hast thou to pursue
my life?

Bos.   Look there.

CARD. Antonio?

Bos.   Slain by my hand unwittingly.
Pray, and be sudden. When thou
    killedst thy sister,   40
Thou took'st from Justice her most
    equal balance,
And left her naught but her sword.

CARD.   O, mercy!

Bos. Now it seems thy greatness was
    only outward;
For thou fall'st faster of thyself than
    calamity
Can drive thee. I'll not waste longer
    time. There!   [*Wounds him.*]

CARD. Thou hast hurt me!

Bos.   Again!

CARD.   Shall I die like a leveret,
Without any resistance?—Help, help,
    help!
I am slain!

[Enter Ferdinand.]

FERD.   Th' alarum! Give me a fresh
    horse;
Rally the vaunt-guard,[1] or the day is
    lost.
Yield, yield! I give you the honor of
    arms,   50
Shake my sword over you. Will you
    yield?

CARD. Help me; I am your brother!

FERD. The devil!
My brother fight upon the adverse
    party?

He wounds the Cardinal, and, in the scuffle,
    gives Bosola his death wound.

There flies your ransom.

CARD. O justice!
I suffer now for what hath former been.
"Sorrow is held the eldest child of sin."

FERD. Now you're brave fellows. Cæsar's
fortune was harder than Pompey's; [60
Cæsar died in the arms of prosperity,
Pompey at the feet of disgrace. You both
died in the field. The pain's nothing;
pain many times is taken away with the
apprehension of greater, as the toothache
with the sight of a barber that comes to
pull it out. There's philosophy for you.

    [1] Vanguard.

Bos. Now my revenge is perfect.—Sink,
    thou main cause
Of my undoing!—The last part of my
    life
Hath done me best service.   70
          He kills Ferdinand.

FERD. Give me some wet hay; I am broken-
    winded.
I do account this world but a dog
    kennel.
I will vault credit [2] and affect [3] high
    pleasures
Beyond death.

Bos. He seems to come to himself, now
    he's so near the bottom.

FERD. My sister, O my sister! There's
    the cause on 't.
"Whether we fall by ambition, blood, or
    lust,
Like diamonds, we are cut with our own
    dust."   [*Dies.*]

CARD. Thou hast thy payment too.

Bos. Yes, I hold my weary soul in my
    teeth;   80
'Tis ready to part from me. I do glory
That thou, which stood'st like a huge
    pyramid
Begun upon a large and ample base,
Shalt end in a little point, a kind of
    nothing.

[Enter, below, Pescara, Malateste, Roderigo,
    and Grisolan.]

PES. How now, my lord!

MAL.   O sad disaster!

ROD.   How comes this?

Bos. Revenge for the Duchess of Malfi,
    murderéd
By th' Aragonian brethren; for Antonio
Slain by this [4] hand; for lustful Julia
Poisoned by this man; and lastly for
    myself,
That was an actor in the main of all   90
Much gainst mine own good nature, yet
    i' th' end
Neglected.

PES.   How now, my lord!

CARD.   Look to my brother.
He gave us these large wounds, as we
    were struggling

    [2] "Overleap rational expectation" (Lucas).
    [3] Aspire to.
    [4] From 1708 edn. Original has *his.*

Here i' th' rushes. And now, I pray, let
　me
Be laid by and never thought of. [*Dies.*]
Pes. How fatally, it seems, he did with-
　stand
His own rescue!
Mal. 　　　Thou wretched thing of blood,
How came Antonio by his death?
Bos. In a mist; I know not how;
Such a mistake as I have often seen　100
In a play. O, I am gone!
We are only like dead walls or vaulted
　graves,
That, ruined, yields no echo. Fare you
　well!
It may be pain, but no harm, to me to
　die
In so good a quarrel. O, this gloomy
　world!
In what a shadow, or deep pit of dark-
　ness,
Doth womanish and fearful mankind
　live!
Let worthy minds ne'er stagger in dis-
　trust
To suffer death or shame for what is
　just.
Mine is another voyage. 　[*Dies.*]　110
Pes. The noble Delio, as I came to th'
　palace.

Told me of Antonio's being here, and
　showed me
A pretty gentleman, his son and heir.

[*Enter Delio, and Antonio's Son.*]

Mal. O, sir, you come too late!
Del. 　　　　　　I heard so, and
Was armed for 't, ere I came. Let us
　make noble use
Of this great ruin, and join all our force
To establish this young hopeful gentle-
　man
In 's mother's right. These wretched
　eminent things
Leave no more fame behind 'em than
　should one
Fall in a frost, and leave his print in
　snow.　　　　　　　　　120
As soon as the sun shines, it ever melts,
Both form and matter. I have ever
　thought
Nature doth nothing so great for great
　men
As when she's pleased to make them
　lords of truth.
"Integrity of life is fame's best friend,
Which nobly, beyond death, shall crown
　the end." 　　　　　　*Exeunt.*

Finis.

STUART PLAYS

EDITED BY

VIRGIL B. HELTZEL
ARTHUR H. NETHERCOT

BEN JONSON

Intimately acquainted with the Greek and Roman classics, critically observant of life about him, and endowed beyond any other writer of his day with the satirist's gifts Ben Jonson with his originality, his clearly defined principles of art, and his impatience with anything but the best, brought to the business of play-writing an equipment which enabled him to infuse into his work elements which profoundly influenced English drama for generations after his time. He was born in London or its environs in the year 1572, the posthumous son of a clergyman, and, according to Fuller, was sent to a private school in St. Martin's Church, and later to Westminster, where his tutor, the eminent antiquary, William Camden, probably instilled into him that taste for the classics which was to influence strongly the subsequent work of the dramatist. About 1589, probably because of his poverty, instead of pursuing a university education he left Westminster to follow his stepfather's trade of bricklaying. Except that he saw service as a soldier in the Netherlands, was married to one whom he later characterized as "a shrew, yet honest," was a member of a strolling company of actors in which he may have played the hero of Kyd's *Spanish Tragedy*, very little is known of his career until July 28, 1597, when Henslowe's Diary records a loan of £4 made to him as an actor at Paris Garden. On the same day the privy council ordered all London theaters suppressed as a result of the performance of a play now lost, *The Isle of Dogs*. Probably for his share with Nashe in the writing of this play, Jonson was imprisoned in the Marshalsea until an order was signed on October 3 for his release. In the same year he is thought to have composed *The Case Is Altered*, a comedy in the manner of Chapman. By September, 1598, he had acquired sufficient reputation to be accounted by Francis Meres one of the best for tragedy, but Meres' basis for such a pronouncement can now be but a subject of conjecture. About the middle of September, however, Jonson's reputation as a writer of comedy was definitely established when *Every Man in His Humor* was played by the Lord Chamberlain's Company at the Curtain, a performance in which Shakespeare acted a part, possibly that of the elder Knowell. On September 22, 1598, Jonson killed his fellow-actor, Gabriel Spencer, in a duel. When brought to trial, he confessed and claimed right of clergy; his property was confiscated and his thumb branded. The following year he collaborated with Dekker in two plays now lost, *The Page of Plymouth* and *Robert the Second, King of Scots*, and wrote *Every Man out of His Humor*, performed and published in 1600. By caricaturing Marston in this play he definitely committed himself to a part in the stage quarrel, in which his next two plays, *Cynthia's Revels* and *The Poetaster*, were to figure prominently. With the performance of *Sejanus* in 1603 Jonson appeared as a writer of a tragedy which not only was unpopular on the boards but which, because of political attacks made upon it, caused him to be questioned by the privy council. Late in 1604 he collaborated with Chapman and Marston in writing *Eastward Ho!* and, when they were sent to prison "for writing something against the Scots," Jonson voluntarily accompanied them. On January 6, 1605, he began his great career of masque-writing with the production of *The Masque of Blackness* at Whitehall, and during the reign of James he furnished twenty of the thirty-seven masques presented at court. Early in 1606 he composed *Volpone;* toward the close of 1609, *Epicoene;* in 1610, *The Alchemist;* and in 1611, another tragedy, *Catiline His Conspiracy*, which was as little of a success as *Sejanus* had been. During the first years of the century Jonson formed friendships with some of the greatest wits of the day and with such eminent patrons as the Countess of Bedford, the Countess of Rutland, Lady Wroth, and the Earl of Pembroke. About 1612 he had the first of several quarrels with Inigo Jones, the noted architect who designed costumes and scenery for masques at court, and in the autumn he accompanied Raleigh's son to France in the capacity of tutor, returning before the end of June the following year. About this time he began the task of preparing his works for publication in the folio of 1616. Following the performance of *Bartholomew Fair* in October, 1614, and the rather unsuccessful, loosely constructed play, *The Devil Is an Ass*, in 1616, Jonson produced no plays for about nine years, although he wrote a few masques. In the summer of 1618 he set out for Scotland, where he visited William Drummond of Hawthornden, whose notes on Ben's conversations are invaluable for biographical details and for their criticisms upon contemporaries. On July 19, 1619, Jonson was made M.A. of Oxford. He now stood at the head of English men of letters, a past master about whom the wits of London gathered in tavern meetings, especially at the Devil's Head, where the upper chamber, known as the Apollo, was set aside for meetings of "The Tribe of Ben." The performance of *The Staple of News* in 1626 marks the dramatist's return to the stage, and by 1634 he had produced *The New Inn*, *The Magnetic Lady*, and *A Tale of a Tub*, probably, though not certainly, an old play revised. *The Sad Shepherd* he left unfinished at his death. Although in 1628 a paralytic stroke confined him to his chamber, he succeeded Thomas Middleton as city chronologer, and in the following year he was granted a pension of £100 by King Charles. From November, 1635, when his son died, until his own death, no biographical information is available. He died on August 6, 1637, and was buried three days later in Westminster Abbey. The following year saw the appearance of *Jonsonus Virbius*, a collection of thirty-three pieces of verse contributed to his memory by his admirers. In 1640 appeared a reprint of the 1616 folio, and a second volume of Jonson's works, printed 1631–41, was issued 1640–41 under the supervision of Sir Kenelm Digby.

Every Man in His Humor, not Jonson's greatest but probably his most influential play, first acted by the Lord Chamberlain's Men in 1598, was entered in the Stationers' Register August 4, 1600, and was printed the following year. This version, with its scene laid in Florence and its chief characters bearing Italian names, was later carefully revised by Jonson for publication in the 1616 folio. The scene was shifted to London, the characters were given English names and were more individualized, and the expression in general was much altered, the most notable change being the excision of Lorenzo's (Knowell's) defense of poetry at the end of the play, a passage which delayed the action and to Jonson's mind probably violated the principle of decorum because it was unsuited to such a gathering. The plot is of Jonson's own invention, but from Chapman's *An Humorous Day's Mirth* (1599) he drew hints for the gull, and from Plautine comedy he derived the suggestion of a pair of elderly persons deceived and outwitted by a pair of clever young men, as well as the shrewd serving-man and the braggart soldier. In its preservation of unity of tone, its observance of the unities of time, place, and action, and its truth to what is typical or normal in action and character, the play shows a definite adherence to the requirements of classical comedy as formulated by Renaissance criticism, notably by Sidney in his *Defense of Poesy*, published in 1595. The prologue to the later version of the play presents Jonson's essential dramatic theory for all his comedies. He here expresses condemnation of the wildly romantic tendencies in the drama and declares his purpose to "show the image of the times" by employing "deeds and language such as men do use," and to make follies, not crimes, his chief consideration. During the last twenty years of the sixteenth century, Lyly, Greene, Nashe, and Lodge in their didactic writings and, at the end of the century, Chapman in his *Blind Beggar of Alexandria* (1598) and *An Humorous Day's Mirth* (1599) had created characters dominated by humors. To exhibit the follies of men Jonson created the comedy of humors which, though illustrated by the present play, is fully developed in *Every Man out of His Humor* and *Cynthia's Revels*. The present text is based on Herford and Simpson's reprint of the 1616 folio checked by the original in the Newberry Library.

Perhaps prompted by the success of Shakespeare's *Julius Cæsar* and by the popularity of the tragedy of political adventure about the time of the conspiracy and trial of Essex, Jonson turned from the Comic Muse, who, as he says, had proved "so ominous" to him, and tried his hand at Roman tragedy. *Sejanus,* performed before the end of 1603 by the King's Men at the Globe, with Shakespeare among the actors, was entered in the Stationers' Register November 2, 1604, and published in 1605. In his address to the reader Jonson says "a second pen" had a good share in the original version of the play, but, since Jonson rewrote the parts of his collaborator, neither these passages nor their original author can be identified, though Chapman has been suggested with some probability. For the story of *Sejanus,* Jonson relied mainly upon Tacitus' *Annals* and Dion's *Roman History,* but he drew details from Suetonius' life of Tiberius, Juvenal's tenth satire, and Seneca's *De Tranquillitate.* Although he departs but little from his sources, the play is far more than a mosaic of translated passages, for he has thoroughly re-created and quickened his materials by the imaginative treatment required of the dramatist. He does not adhere nearly so closely to classical technique as in his earlier plays, but he achieves greater coherence and displays more constructive skill. In stressing the arrogance and fall of Sejanus, Jonson was influenced by the medieval conception of tragedy still surviving in the popular *Mirror for Magistrates.* The play was not and never can be popular. The characters are too numerous, too little individualized, and too imperfectly grouped. Moreover, the play is lacking in pity. As Herford says, "Jonsonian tragedy suffers from an inner poverty in the humanities of the heart." The present text is based on Herford and Simpson's reprint of the 1616 folio checked by the original in the Newberry Library.

Volpone, "fully penned" in five weeks early in 1606, was presented shortly after by the King's Men at the Globe and in the summer and autumn of the same year at both universities, and was published in 1607/8. The play is not confined merely to follies, as were the earlier comedies, but includes crimes, so that, as Coleridge remarks, "there is no goodness of heart in any of the prominent characters." Nevertheless, the production of *Volpone* restored Jonson's popularity, which had been temporarily dimmed by the poor reception accorded *Sejanus.* The latter play had taught him the necessity of a closely knit plot and the value of Roman history as a source. Legacy-hunting, so frequent in Roman literature, had impressed him as fertile soil for imposture and fraud, and for the materials of the play he drew suggestions from numerous classical sources, among which may be mentioned Lucian's dialogues, Horace's satires, and Libanius. Professor J. D. Rea in his edition of the play has stressed Jonson's debt to Erasmus' *Praise of Folly.* The scene of the action is quite appropriately laid in Italy, to the Elizabethan mind the land of villainy, and only in the sub-plot (which, although it affords some effective comic episodes, does not advance the action) does Jonson introduce a bit of his own England in the persons of Sir Politic and his lady. The play observes the unities carefully, and the arrangement of scenes is according to classical precedent. The present text is based on the Newberry Library copy of the 1616 folio.

Jonson's most popular and, in the light of his theory, most perfect play, *The Alchemist,* entered in the Stationers' Register October 3, 1610, and published in 1612, was written during the plague season of 1610 for performance before Londoners who, like Lovewit, would return to their homes after all danger of infection had passed. The practice of alchemy was as common to the life of the time as it had been in the Middle Ages, and exposures of impostures such as Jonson portrays were so frequent in life as well as in literature that it has been impossible to discover any source for this aspect of the play. From Plautus' *Mostellaria* he may have derived the quarrel scene at the opening of the play and the idea of the unexpected return of the owner of a house in which rogues are carrying on their practices; and he may have taken certain minor suggestions from Plautus' *Pœnulus* and Erasmus' colloquy on the alchemist. Professor Child's suggestion of Giordano Bruno's *Il Candelaio* (1582) as a source has not won general acceptance. The construction of the play reveals the hand of the master. All the unities are rigidly observed. The action takes place in a single day at a house in the Blackfriars district of London, and, while the three intrigues remain distinct, each being a unit in itself, they are actuated by similar motives, are pervaded by one comic tone, and are related to the general plan. Suspense as to the outcome of the action constantly increases to the very end of the play. The present text is based on Hathaway's reprint of the 1616 folio checked with the original in the Newberry Library. Occasional reference has also been made to Noel Douglas' replica of the 1612 quarto in the British Museum.

Lord Haddington's Masque or, as it is appropriately named by Gifford, *The Hue and Cry after Cupid*, was printed, probably in 1608, in an undated quarto, and in the folio of 1616. The classical legend upon which it was founded is as old at least as Moschus, and had been often retold in Italy and in France. None of these versions, however, can be designated as a source for Jonson's masque. The piece occupies an important place in the evolution of the masque, not only because in the rôles of Cupid and his twelve boys "most anticly attired" it offers a good example of the antimasque or foil, intended by its grotesqueness and drollery to set off the beauty of the main masque, but because in its brevity, simplicity, and high poetical quality it avoids the excesses which often characterized its successors. The present text is based on the 1616 folio in the Newberry Library.

Jonson's one extant attempt at pastoral drama, *The Sad Shepherd*, was found as a fragment among his papers after his death, and was published by Sir Kenelm Digby in the second folio with the date 1641 on its title-page. The circumstances and exact date of its composition are still to be ascertained, but there is some reason for regarding it as the work of the author's last years. Jonson here turns aside from examples set by his predecessors in the type, and boldly strikes out to produce a truly English pastoral play. He suppresses satire and symbolism, and for Arcadia with its shadowy shepherds as main characters he substitutes Sherwood Forest with Maid Marian and Robin Hood and his merry men; instead of the satyr of conventional pastoral tradition he introduces Maudlin the Witch and Puck-Hairy. In thus subordinating or ignoring many of the time-worn conventions of the pastoral and introducing freshness and real life, Jonson was reverting to the practice of the first pastoral poet, Theocritus. The present text is based on the second folio in the Newberry Library.

EVERY MAN IN HIS HUMOR [1]

BY

BEN JONSON

To the Most Learned, and My Honored Friend, Mr.[2] Camden, Clarencieux [3]

Sir:

There are, no doubt, a supercilious race in the world who will esteem all office done you in this kind an injury, so solemn a vice it is with them to use the authority of their ignorance to the crying down of poetry or the professors.[4] But my gratitude must not leave [5] to correct their error, since I am none of those that can suffer the benefits conferred upon my youth to perish with my age. It is a frail memory that remembers [10 but present things, and had the favor of the times so conspired with my disposition, as it could have brought forth other or better, you had had the same proportion and number of the fruits, the first. Now I pray you to accept this, such wherein neither the confession of my manners shall make you blush, nor of my studies repent you [6] to have been the instructor; and for the profession of my thankfulness, I am sure [20 it will, with good men, find either praise or excuse.

Your true lover,
BEN. JONSON.

THE PERSONS OF THE PLAY

KNOWELL,[7] an old gentleman.
ED[WARD] KNOWELL, his son.
BRAINWORM, the father's man.
MR. STEPHEN, a country gull.
[GEORGE] DOWNRIGHT, a plain squire.
WELLBRED, his half-brother.
JUST[ICE] CLEMENT, an old, merry magistrate.
ROGER FORMAL, his clerk.

KITELY, a merchant.
DAME KITELY, his wife.
MRS.[8] BRIDGET, his sister.
MR. MATTHEW, the town gull.
[THOMAS] CASH, Kitely's man.
[OLIVER] COB, a water bearer.
TIB, his wife.
CAP[TAIN] BOBADILL, a Paul's man.[9]
[SERVANTS, etc.]

THE SCENE: London.

[TIME: Contemporary.]

PROLOGUE

Though need make many poets, and some such
As art and nature have not bettered much,
Yet ours for want hath not so loved the stage
As he dare serve th' ill customs of the age,
Or purchase your delight at such a rate,
As, for it, he himself must justly hate:
To make a child, now swaddled, to proceed
Man, and then shoot up, in one beard and weed,
Past threescore years; or, with three rusty swords,
And help of some few foot-and-half-foot words,   10
Fight over York and Lancaster's long jars,

---

[1] The title continues: "A Comedy. Acted in the Year 1598 by the Then Lord Chamberlain His Servants. The Author B. J."
[2] Master.
[3] One of the kings-at-arms in the Heralds' College.   [5] Omit.
[4] Supporters of poetry.   [6] Make you repent.
[7] Printed Kno'well throughout.
[8] Mistress.
[9] A lounger in the middle aisle of St. Paul's Cathedral, a social and business center.

And in the tiring-house [1] bring wounds to
    scars.
He rather prays you will be pleased to see
One such today, as other plays should be,
Where neither chorus wafts you o'er the
    seas,
Nor creaking throne comes down, the boys
    to please,
Nor nimble squib is seen, to make afeard
The gentlewomen, nor rolled bullet heard,
To say it thunders, nor tempestuous drum
Rumbles, to tell you when the storm doth
    come,   20
But deeds and language such as men do use,
And persons such as comedy would choose,
When she would show an image of the
    times,
And sport with human follies, not with
    crimes—
Except we make hem [2] such, by loving still
Our popular errors, when we know th' are
    ill.
I mean such errors as you'll all confess,
By laughing at them, they deserve no less—
Which when you heartily do, there's hope
    left then,
You, that have so graced [3] monsters, may
    like men.   30

ACT I. SCENE i.

[A street.]

Knowell, Brainworm, Mr. Stephen. [4]

[KNOW.] A goodly day toward, and a fresh
    morning!—Brainworm,

[Enter Brainworm.]

Call up your young master; bid him rise,
    sir.
Tell him I have some business to employ
    him.
BRA. I will, sir, presently. [5]
KNOW.   But hear you, sirrah,
If he be at [6] his book, disturb him not.
BRA. Well, sir.   [*Exit.*]
KNOW. How happy yet should I esteem
    myself,

[1] Dressing room.
[2] Them.   [4] Enters later.
[3] Approved.   [5] At once.
[6] Original reads *be 'at.* Jonson and other poets
often use the apostrophe thus to indicate elision,
but in deference to modern practice it has been
omitted in this anthology.

Could I, by any practice, [7] wean the boy
From one vain course of study he affects.
He is a scholar, if a man may trust   10
The liberal voice of fame, in her report
Of good accompt in both our universities,
Either of which hath favored him with
    graces.
But their indulgence must not spring in
    me
A fond [8] opinion that he cannot err.
Myself was once a student, and, indeed,
Fed with the selfsame humor [9] he is now,
Dreaming on naught but idle poetry,
That fruitless and unprofitable art,
Good unto none, but least to the pro-
    fessors,   20
Which then I thought the mistress of all
    knowledge;
But, since, time and the truth have
    waked my judgment,
And reason taught me better to distin-
    guish
The vain from th' useful learnings.—

[Enter Stephen.]

                    Cousin [10] Stephen,
What news with you, that you are here
    so early?
STE. Nothing, but e'en come to see how
you do, uncle.
KNOW. That's kindly done; you are
welcome, coz.
STE. Ay, I know that, sir; I would not ha'
    come else.   30
How do my cousin Edward, uncle?
KNOW. O, well, coz; go in and see; I
doubt he be scarce stirring yet.
STE. Uncle, afore I go in, can you tell
me, an [11] he have e'er a book of the sciences
of hawking and hunting? I would fain
borrow it.
KNOW. Why, I hope you will not a-hawk-
ing now, will you?
STE. No, wusse; [12] but I'll practice   [40
against [13] next year, uncle. I have bought
me a hawk, and a hood, and bells, and all;
I lack nothing but a book to keep it by.
KNOW. O, most ridiculous!

[7] Artifice.   [8] Foolish.
[9] A dominating quality or caprice in a person's
temperament.
[10] A general term of relationship or intimacy.
[11] If.
[12] I wis, certainly.   [13] In preparation for.

STE. Nay, look you now, you are angry, uncle. Why, you know, an a man have not skill in the hawking and hunting languages nowadays, I'll not give a rush for him. They are more studied than the Greek or the Latin. He is for no gallant's company [50 without hem; and, by Gad's lid,[1] I scorn it, I, so I do, to be a consort for every humdrum;[2] hang hem, scroyles![3] There's nothing in hem i' the world. What[4] do you talk on it? Because I dwell at Hogsden, I shall keep company with none but the archers of Finsbury or the citizens that come a-ducking to Islington ponds? A fine jest, i' faith! 'Slid,[1] a gentleman mun[5] show himself like a gentleman. Uncle, [60 I pray you be not angry; I know what I have to do, I trow; I am no novice.

KNOW. You are a prodigal, absurd coxcomb; go to!

Nay, never look at me. It's I that speak.
Take 't as you will, sir, I'll not flatter you.
Ha' you not yet found means enow to waste
That which your friends have left you, but you must
Go cast away your money on a kite,
And know not how to keep it, when you ha' done?
O, it's comely! This will make you a gentleman! 70
Well, cousin, well, I see you are e'en past hope
Of all reclaim.—Ay, so, now you are told on it,
You look another way.

STE. What would you ha' me do?

KNOW. What would I have you do? I'll tell you, kinsman;
Learn to be wise, and practice how to thrive.
That would I have you do, and not to spend
Your coin on every bable[6] that you fancy,
Or every foolish brain that humors you.
I would not have you to invade each place,
Nor thrust yourself on all societies, 80
Till men's affections, or your own desert,
Should worthily invite you to your rank.

He that is so respectless[7] in his courses
Oft sells his reputation at cheap market.
Nor would I you should melt away yourself
In flashing bravery,[8] lest, while you affect
To make a blaze of gentry to the world,
A little puff of scorn extinguish it,
And you be left like an unsavory snuff,
Whose property is only to offend. 90
I'ld ha' you sober, and contain yourself
Not that your sail be bigger than your boat;
But moderate your expenses now, at first,
As[9] you may keep the same proportion still;[10]
Nor stand so much on your gentility,
Which is an airy and mere borrowed thing
From dead men's dust and bones, and none of yours
Except you make or hold it. Who comes here?

ACT I. SCENE ii.

[*The same.*]

Servant, Mr. Stephen, Knowell, Brainworm.[11]

[SERV.] Save you, gentlemen!

STE. Nay, we do not stand much on our gentility, friend; yet you are welcome; and I assure you mine uncle here is a man of a thousand a year, Middlesex land. He has but one son in all the world; I am his next heir, at the common law, Master Stephen, as simple as I stand here, if my cousin die, as there's hope he will. I have a pretty living o' mine own too, beside, hard [10 by here.

SERV. In good time,[12] sir.

STE. In good time, sir? Why, and in very good time, sir! You do not flout, friend, do you?

SERV. Not I, sir.

STE. Not you, sir? You were not best, sir; an you should, here be them can perceive it, and that quickly too. Go to! And they can give it again soundly too, [20 and[13] need be.

---

[7] Lacking in self-respect.
[8] Finery.
[9] So that.
[10] Always.
[11] Enters later.
[12] Certainly.
[13] If.

[1] God's eyelid.
[2] Commonplace person.
[3] Mangy fellows.
[4] Why.
[5] Must.
[6] Bauble.

SERV. Why, sir, let this satisfy you; good faith, I had no such intent.

STE. Sir, an I thought you had, I would talk with you, and that presently.

SERV. Good Master Stephen, so you may, sir, at your pleasure.

STE. And so I would, sir, good my saucy companion! An you were out o' mine uncle's ground, I can tell you, [30 though I do not stand upon my gentility neither in 't.

KNOW. Cousin, cousin, will this ne'er be left?

STE. Whoreson,[1] base fellow! A mechanical[2] serving-man! By this cudgel, and 'twere not for shame, I would—

KNOW. What would you do, you peremptory gull?[3]
If you cannot be quiet, get you hence.
You see the honest man demeans himself   40
Modestly towards you, giving no reply
To your unseasoned, quarreling, rude fashion;
And still you huff it,[4] with a kind of carriage
As void of wit as of humanity.
Go, get you in; fore[5] heaven, I am ashamed
Thou hast a kinsman's interest in me.
                              [*Exit Stephen.*]

SERV. I pray you, sir, is this Master Knowell's house?

KNOW. Yes, marry, is it, sir.

SERV. I should inquire for a gentle- [50 man here, one Master Edward Knowell. Do you know any such, sir, I pray you?

KNOW. I should forget myself else, sir.

SERV. Are you the gentleman? Cry you mercy,[6] sir! I was required by a gentleman i' the city, as I rode out at this end o' the town, to deliver you this letter, sir.

KNOW. To me, sir! What do you mean? Pray you, remember your court'sy.[7] [*Reads.*] "To his most selected friend, [60 Master Edward Knowell." What might the gentleman's name be, sir, that sent it? Nay, pray you be covered.

SERV. One Master Wellbred, sir.

---
[1] Rascally.   [2] Menial.
[3] Absolute, complete fool.
[4] Swagger.   [6] I beg your pardon.
[5] Before.   [7] *I.e.*, put on your hat.

KNOW. Master Wellbred! A young gentleman, is he not?

SERV. The same, sir. Master Kitely married his sister; the rich merchant i' the Old Jewry.   69

KNOW. You say very true.—Brainworm!

[*Enter Brainworm.*]

BRA. Sir?

KNOW. Make this honest friend drink here.
Pray you, go in.—
                    [*Exeunt Brainworm and Servant.*]
This letter is directed to my son;
Yet I am Edward Knowell too, and may,
With the safe conscience of good manners, use
The fellow's error to my satisfaction.
Well, I will break it ope (old men are curious),
Be it but for the style's sake and the phrase,
To see if both do answer my son's praises,
Who is almost grown the idolater   80
Of this young Wellbred. What have we here? What's this?

THE LETTER

"Why, Ned, I beseech thee, hast thou forsworn all thy friends i' the Old Jewry? Or dost thou think us all Jews that inhabit there yet? If thou dost, come over, and but see our frippery;[8] change an old shirt for a whole smock[9] with us. Do not conceive that antipathy between us and Hogsden, as was between Jews and [89 hog's flesh. Leave thy vigilant father alone, to number over his green apricots, evening and morning, o' the northwest wall. An I had been his son, I had saved him the labor long since, if taking in all the young wenches that pass by at the backdoor, and coddling[10] every kernel of the fruit for hem, would ha' served. But, prithee, come over to me quickly this morning; I have such a present for thee! Our Turkey company never sent the like to the Grand [100 Signior. One is a rimer, sir, o' your own batch, your own leaven, but doth think himself poet-major o' the town, willing to be shown, and worthy to be seen. The

---
[8] Old clothes shop.
[9] *I.e.*, wench.   [10] Stewing.

other—I will not venter [1] his description
with you till you come, because I would ha'
you make hither with an appetite. If the
worst of hem be not worth your journey, draw your bill of charges, as unconscionable as any Guildhall verdict [110
will give it you, and you shall be allowed
your viaticum. [2]

             From the Windmill." [3]
From the Burdello [4] it might come as
     well,
The Spittle, [5] or Pict-hatch. [6] Is this the
     man
My son hath sung so, for the happiest
     wit,
The choicest brain the times hath sent
     us forth?
I know not what he may be in the arts,
Nor what in schools; [7] but, surely, for
     his manners
I judge him a profane and dissolute
     wretch,
Worse by possession of such great good
     gifts,   120
Being the master of so loose a spirit.
Why, what unhallowed ruffian would
     have writ
In such a scurrilous manner to a friend!
Why should he think I tell [8] my apricots,
Or play th' Hesperian dragon with my
     fruit,
To watch it? Well, my son, I had thought
Y' had had more judgment t' have made
     election
Of your companions than t' have ta'en
     on trust
Such petulant, jeering gamesters, that
     can spare   129
No argument or subject from their jest.
But I perceive affection makes a fool
Of any man too much the father.—
     Brainworm!

             [Enter Brainworm.]

BRA. Sir?
KNOW.   Is the fellow gone that brought
     this letter?
BRA. Yes, sir, a pretty while since.
KNOW. And where's your young master?

[1] Venture.   [2] Traveling expenses.
[3] A tavern, formerly a synagogue.
[4] Bordello, a brothel.   [7] Lecture rooms.
[5] Hospital.   [8] Count.
[6] A low district of London.

BRA. In his chamber, sir.
KNOW. He spake not with the fellow, did
he?
BRA. No, sir, he saw him not.   139
KNOW. [9] Take you this letter, and deliver
it my son, but with no notice that I have
opened it, on your life.
BRA. O Lord, sir, that were a jest indeed!
                           [Exit.]
KNOW. I am resolved I will not stop his
     journey,
Nor practice any violent mean to stay
The unbridled course of youth in him,
     for that,
Restrained, grows more impatient, and
     in kind [10]
Like to the eager, but the generous, [11]
     grayhound,
Who, ne'er so little from his game with-
     held,
Turns head, and leaps up at his holder's
     throat.   150
There is a way of winning more by
     love
And urging of the modesty than fear;
Force works on servile natures, not the
     free.
He that's compelled to goodness may be
     good,
But 'tis but for that fit; [12] where others,
     drawn
By softness and example, get a habit.
Then, if they stray, but warn hem, and
     the same
They should for virtue have done, they'll
     do foɪ shame.   [Exit.]

            ACT I. SCENE ii[i].

       [A room in Knowell's house.]

Edw[ard]   Knowell,   Brainworm,   Mr.
                          Stephen. [13]
[E. KNOW. (With a letter in his hand.)]
Did he open it, sayest thou?
BRA. Yes, o' my word, sir, and read
the contents.
E. KNOW. That scarce contents me.
What countenance, prithee, made he i'
the reading of it? Was he angry or pleased?

     [9] Here and in two or three other passages the
original verse has been changed to prose.
     [10] Nature.   [12] Moment.
     [11] Well-bred.   [13] Enters later.

Bra. Nay, sir, I saw him not read it, nor open it, I assure your worship.

E. Know. No! How know'st thou [10 then that he did either?

Bra. Marry, sir, because he charged me, on my life, to tell nobody that he opened it, which unless he had done, he would never fear to have it revealed.

E. Know. That's true; well, I thank thee, Brainworm.

[*Enter Stephen.*]

Ste. O, Brainworm, didst thou not see a fellow here in a what-sha'-call-him doublet? He brought mine uncle a letter [20 e'en now.

Bra. Yes, Master Stephen. What of him?

Ste. O, I ha' such a mind to beat him—where is he, canst thou tell?

Bra. Faith, he is not of that mind; he is gone, Master Stephen.

Ste. Gone! Which way? When went he? How long since?

Bra. He is rid hence; he took horse [30 at the street door.

Ste. And I stayed i' the fields! Whoreson Scanderbag[1] rogue! O, that I had but a horse to fetch him back again!

Bra. Why, you may ha' my m[aste]r's gelding, to save your longing, sir.

Ste. But I ha' no boots—that's the spite on 't.

Bra. Why, a fine wisp of hay, rolled hard, Master Stephen.　　40

Ste. No, faith, it's no boot[2] to follow him now; let him e'en go and hang. Pray thee, help to truss me[3] a little. He does so vex me—

Bra. You'll be worse vexed when you are trussed,[4] Master Stephen. Best keep unbraced,[5] and walk yourself till you be cold; your choler may founder you else.

Ste. By my faith, and so I will, now thou tell'st me on 't. How dost thou [50 like my leg, Brainworm?

Bra. A very good leg, Master Stephen; but the woolen stocking does not commend it so well.

Ste. Foh! The stockings be good

enough, now summer is coming on, for the dust; I'll have a pair of silk again' winter, that[6] I go to dwell i' the town. I think my leg would show in a silk hose—

Bra. Believe me, Master Stephen, [60 rarely well.

Ste. In sadness,[7] I think it would; I have a reasonable good leg.

Bra. You have an excellent good leg, Master Stephen; but I cannot stay to praise it longer now, and I am very sorry for 't.

Ste. Another time will serve, Brainworm; gramercy for this.

[*Exit Brainworm.*]

E. Know. Ha, ha, ha!　　70

Knowell laughs, having read the letter.

Ste. [*Aside.*] 'Slid, I hope he laughs not at me; and he do—

E. Know. Here was a letter indeed, to be intercepted by a man's father, and do him good with him! He cannot but think most virtuously both of me and the sender, sure, that make the careful costermonger of him in our familiar epistles. Well, if he read this with patience I'll be gelt,[8] and troll ballads for Mr. John Trundle[9] [80 yonder the rest of my mortality.[10] It is true, and likely, my father may have as much patience as another man, for he takes much physic; and oft taking physic makes a man very patient. But would your packet, Master Wellbred, had arrived at him in such a minute of his patience! Then we had known the end of it, which now is doubtful, and threatens—[*Notices Stephen. Aside.*] What, my wise [90 cousin! Nay, then I'll furnish our feast with one gull more toward the mess.[11] He writes to me of a brace, and here's one—that's three. O, for a fourth! Fortune, if ever thou'lt use thine eyes, I entreat thee—

Ste. [*Aside.*] O, now I see who he laughed at. He laughed at somebody in that letter. By this good light, and he had laughed at me—　　100

E. Know. How now, cousin Stephen, melancholy?

Ste. Yes, a little. I thought you had laughed at me, cousin.

---

[1] *I.e.*, mighty, in reference to Iskender-beg, fifteenth century Albanian leader against the Turks.

[2] Use.
[3] Lace me up.

[4] Beaten.
[5] Unlaced.

[6] When.
[7] Seriously.
[8] Gelded.

[9] An actual publisher.
[10] Life.
[11] A group of four.

E. Know. Why, what an I had, coz? What would you ha' done?

Ste. By this light, I would ha' told mine uncle.

E. Know. Nay, if you would ha' told your uncle, I did laugh at you, coz.   110

Ste. Did you, indeed?

E. Know. Yes, indeed.

Ste. Why then—

E. Know. What then?

Ste. I am satisfied; it is sufficient.

E. Know. Why, be so, gentle coz. And, I pray you, let me entreat a courtesy of you. I am sent for this morning by a friend i' the Old Jewry to come to him; it's but crossing over the fields to Moor- [120 gate. Will you bear me company? I protest it is not to draw you into bond or any plot against the state, coz.

Ste. Sir, that's all one and 'twere; you shall command me twice so far as Moorgate, to do you good in such a matter. Do you think I would leave you? I protest—

E. Know. No, no, you shall not protest, coz.

Ste. By my fackins,[1] but I will, [130 by your leave; I'll protest more to my friend than I'll speak of at this time.

E. Know. You speak very well, coz.

Ste. Nay, not so neither; you shall pardon me. But I speak to serve my turn.

E. Know. Your turn, coz? Do you know what you say? A gentleman of your sort,[2] parts, carriage, and estimation, to talk o' your "turn"[3] i' this company, and to me alone, like a tankard bearer at [140 a conduit! Fie! A wight that, hitherto, his every step hath left the stamp of a great foot behind him, as every word the savor of a strong spirit, and he, this man, so graced, gilded, or, to use a more fit metaphor, so tin-foiled by nature, as not ten housewives' pewter again' a good time shows more bright to the world than he! And he (as I said last, so I say again, and still shall say it), this man, to conceal [150 such real ornaments as these, and shadow their glory, as a milliner's wife does her wrought stomacher, with a smoky lawn or a black cyprus![4] O, coz, it cannot be answered; go not about it! Drake's old

ship at Detford[5] may sooner circle the world again. Come, wrong not the quality of your desert, with looking downward, coz; but hold up your head, so; and let the idea of what you are be portrayed i' [160 your face, that men may read i' your physnomy,[6] "Here within this place is to be seen the true, rare, and accomplished monster, or miracle of nature," which is all one. What think you of this, coz?

Ste. Why, I do think of it; and I will be more proud, and melancholy, and gentlemanlike than I have been, I'll insure you.

E. Know. Why, that's resolute,[7] [170 Master Stephen!—[Aside.] Now, if I can but hold him up to his height, as it is happily begun, it will do well for a suburb[8] humor: we may hap have a match with the city, and play him for forty pound.— Come, coz.

Ste. I'll follow you.

E. Know. Follow me! You must go before.[9]

Ste. Nay, an I must, I will. Pray [180 you, show me, good cousin.   [Exeunt.]

Act I. Scene iv.

[The lane before Cob's house.]

Mr. Matthew, Cob.[10]

[Mat.] I think this be the house. What, ho!

[Enter Cob.]

Cob. Who's there? O, Master Matthew! Gi' your worship good morrow.

Mat. What, Cob! How dost thou, good Cob? Dost thou inhabit here, Cob?

Cob. Ay, sir, I and my linage[11] ha' kept a poor house here in our days.

Mat. Thy linage, Monsieur Cob! What linage? What linage?   10

Cob. Why, sir, an ancient linage, and a princely. Mine ance'try came from a king's belly, no worse man; and yet no man neither (by your worship's leave, I did lie in that), but herring,[12] the king of

---

[1] Faith.   [2] Station.
[3] A trip, according to which water-carriers were paid.   [4] Transparent cloth.

[5] Deptford, where the *Golden Hind* was laid up.
[6] Physiognomy.   [10] Enters later.
[7] Decided.   [11] Lineage, family.
[8] Rustic.   [12] A cob is a young herring.
[9] *I.e.*, like a servant.

fish (from his belly I proceed), one o' the monarchs o' the world, I assure you. The first red herring that was broiled in Adam and Eve's kitchen do I fetch my pedigree from, by the harrot's [1] books. His cob [20 was my great-great-mighty-great grand-father.

MAT. Why mighty, why mighty, I pray thee?

COB. O, it was a mighty while ago, sir, and a mighty great cob.

MAT. How know'st thou that?

COB. How know I? Why, I smell his ghost ever and anon.

MAT. Smell a ghost? O unsavory [30 jest! And the ghost of a herring cob? [2]

COB. Ay, sir. With favor of your worship's nose, Mr. Matthew, why not the ghost of a herring cob as well as the ghost of Rasher Bacon?

MAT. Roger Bacon, thou wouldst say?

COB. I say Rasher Bacon. They were both broiled o' the coals; and a man may smell broiled meat, I hope? You are a scholar; upsolve me that now.   40

MAT. O raw ignorance!—Cob, canst thou show me of a gentleman, one Captain Bobadill, where his lodging is?

COB. O, my guest, sir, you mean.

MAT. Thy guest! Alas! Ha, ha!

COB. Why do you laugh, sir? Do you not mean Captain Bobadill?

MAT. Cob, pray thee, advise thyself well; do not wrong the gentleman, and thyself too. I dare be sworn he scorns [50 thy house. He! He lodge in such a base, obscure place as thy house! Tut, I know his disposition so well he would not lie in thy bed if thou'ldst gi' it him.

COB. I will not give it him though, sir. Mass, I thought somewhat was in 't—we could not get him to bed all night! Well, sir, though he lie not o' my bed, he lies o' my bench; an 't please you to go up, sir, you shall find him with two cushions [60 under his head, and his cloak wrapped about him, as though he had neither won nor lost, and yet, I warrant, he ne'er cast [3] better in his life than he has done tonight. [4]

MAT. Why, was he drunk?

COB. Drunk, sir? You hear not me say

so. Perhaps he swallowed a tavern token, [5] or some such device, sir; I have nothing to do withal. I deal with water and not with wine.—Gi' me my tankard there, ho!— [70 God b' w' you, sir. It's six a-clock; I should ha' carried two turns by this. What ho! My stopple! [6] Come.

MAT. Lie in a water bearer's house! A gentleman of his havings! [7] Well, I'll tell him my mind.

[Enter Tib with a water tankard.]

COB. What, Tib; show this gentleman up to the captain.—[Exit Tib with Master Matthew.] O, an my house were the Brazen Head now, faith, it would e'en speak, [80 "Mo [8] fools yet." [9] You should ha' some now would take this Mr. Matthew to be a gentleman, at the least. His father's an honest man, a worshipful fishmonger, and so forth; and now does he creep and wriggle into acquaintance with all the brave gallants about the town, such as my guest is (O, my guest is a fine man!), and they flout him invincibly. [10] He useth [11] every day to a merchant's house where I serve [90 water, one Master Kitely's, i' the Old Jewry; and here's the jest: he is in love with my master's sister, Mistress Bridget, and calls her "Mistress"; and there he will sit you a whole afternoon some-times, reading o' these same abominable, vile (a pox on hem, I cannot abide them), rascally verses, "poyetry," "poyetry," and speaking of "interludes"; 'twill make a man burst to hear him. And the [100 wenches, they do so jeer, and tee-hee at him. Well, should they do so much to me, I'ld forswear them all, by the foot of Pharaoh! There's an oath! How many water bearers shall you hear swear such an oath? O, I have a guest—he teaches me—he does swear the legiblest of any man chris-tened: "By St. George! The foot of Pharaoh! The body of me! As I am [a] [109 gentleman and a soldier!" Such dainty oaths! And withal he does take this same filthy, roguish tabacco, [12] the finest and cleanliest! It would do a man good to see

[5] Slang term for got drunk.   [7] Possessions.
[6] Stopper.   [8] More.
[9] Cf. Greene's Friar Bacon and Friar Bungay.
[10] Exceedingly.   [11] Is accustomed to go.
[12] Tobacco.

[1] Herald's.   [2] Here, herring's head.
[3] Pun on cast, to throw dice, and to vomit.
[4] I.e., last night.

the fume come forth at 's tonnels.[1] Well, he owes me forty shillings my wife lent him out of her purse, by sixpence a time, besides his lodging; I would I had it! I shall ha' it, he says, the next action.[2] Helter-skelter, hang sorrow, care 'll kill a cat, up-tails all, and a louse for the [120 hangman!   [*Exit.*]

Act I. Scene v.

[*A room in Cob's house.*]

Bobadill, Tib, Matthew.[3] *Bobad[ill] is discovered lying on his bench.*

[Bob.] Hostess, hostess!

[*Enter Tib.*]

Tib. What say you, sir?

Bob. A cup o' thy small beer, sweet hostess.

Tib. Sir, there's a gentleman below would speak with you.

Bob. A gentleman! 'Odso,[4] I am not within.

Tib. My husband told him you were, sir.   10

Bob. What a plague—what meant he?

Mat. [*Below.*] Captain Bobadill?

Bob. Who's there?—(Take away the basin, good hostess!) Come up, sir.

Tib. He would desire you to come up, sir.

[*Enter Matthew.*]

You come into a cleanly house, here!

Mat. Save you, sir; save you, captain!

Bob. Gentle Master Matthew! Is it you, sir? Please you, sit down.   20

Mat. Thank you, good captain; you may see I am somewhat audacious.

Bob. Not so, sir. I was requested to supper last night by a sort[5] of gallants, where you were wished for and drunk to, I assure you.

Mat. Vouchsafe me, by whom, good captain?

Bob. Marry, by young Wellbred and others.—Why, hostess, a stool here [30 for this gentleman!

Mat. No haste, sir; 'tis very well.

Bob. Body of me! It was so late ere we parted last night I can scarce open my eyes yet; I was but new risen, as you came. How passes the day abroad, sir? You can tell.

Mat. Faith, some half hour to seven. Now, trust me, you have an exceeding fine lodging here, very neat and pri- [40 vate.

Bob. Ay, sir; sit down, I pray you. Master Matthew, in any case possess no gentlemen of our acquaintance with notice of my lodging.

Mat. Who? I, sir? No.

Bob. Not that I need to care who know it, for the cabin[6] is convenient; but in regard I would not be too popular, and generally visited, as some are.   50

Mat. True, captain, I conceive you.

Bob. For, do you see, sir, by the heart of valor in me, except it be to some peculiar and choice spirits, to whom I am extraordinarily engaged, as yourself or so, I could not extend thus far.

Mat. O Lord, sir! I resolve so.[7]

Bob. I confess I love a cleanly and quiet privacy, above all the tumult and roar of fortune. What new book [60 ha' you there? What! "Go by, Hieronymo"?[8]

Mat. Ay; did you ever see it acted? Is 't not well penned?

Bob. Well penned? I would fain see all the poets of these times pen such another play as that was! They'll prate and swagger, and keep a stir of art and devices, when, as I am a gentleman, read hem, they are the most shallow, pitiful, bar- [70 ren fellows that live upon the face of the earth again.

Mat. Indeed, here are a number of fine speeches in this book. "O eyes, no eyes, but fountains fraught with tears!" There's a conceit! "Fountains fraught with tears!"—"O life, no life, but lively form of death!" Another—"O world, no world, but mass of public wrongs!" A third—"Confused and filled with mur- [80 der and misdeeds!" A fourth—O, the muses! Is 't not excellent? Is 't not simply the best that ever you heard, captain? Ha! How do you like it?

---

[1] Tunnels, nostrils.
[2] *I.e.,* court action.
[3] Last two enter later.
[4] A mild oath.
[5] Company.
[6] Room.
[7] I am sure of it.
[8] *I.e.,* Kyd's *Spanish Tragedy.*

Bob. 'Tis good.

Mat. "To thee, the purest object to my sense,

The most refinéd essence heaven covers,

Send I these lines, wherein I do commence

The happy state of turtle-billing lovers.

If they prove rough, unpolished, harsh, and rude,   90

Haste made the waste: thus mildly I conclude." [1]

Bob. Nay, proceed, proceed. Where's this?

Bobadill is making him ready all this while.

Mat. This, sir? A toy o' mine own, in my nonage, the infancy of my muses. But when will you come and see my study? Good faith, I can show you some very good things I have done of late.—That boot becomes your leg passing well, captain, methinks.   100

Bob. So, so; it's the fashion gentlemen now use.

Mat. Troth, captain, and now you speak o' the fashion, Master Wellbred's elder brother and I are fall'n out exceedingly. This other day I happened to enter into some discourse of a hanger,[2] which, I assure you, both for fashion and workmanship, was most peremptory[3]-beautiful and gentlemanlike! Yet he con- [110 demned and cried it down for the most pied[4] and ridiculous that ever he saw.

Bob. Squire Downright, the half brother, was 't not?

Mat. Ay, sir, he.

Bob. Hang him, rook![5] He! Why, he has no more judgment than a malt horse.[6] By S[t]. George, I wonder you'ld loose a thought upon such an animal; the most peremptory-absurd clown of Chris- [120 tendom this day he is holden. I protest to you, as I am a gentleman and a soldier, I ne'er changed words with his like. By his discourse, he should eat nothing but hay; he was born for the manger, pannier, or pack-saddle. He has not so much as a good phrase in his belly, but all old iron

and rusty proverbs! A good commodity for some smith to make hobnails of!

Mat. Ay, and he thinks to carry [130 it away with his manhood still, where he comes. He brags he will gi' me the *bastinado*, as I hear.

Bob. How! He the *bastinado*! How came he by that word, trow?

Mat. Nay, indeed, he said "cudgel me"; I termed it so, for my more grace.

Bob. That may be, for I was sure it was none of his word. But when? When said he so?   140

Mat. Faith, yesterday, they say; a young gallant, a friend of mine, told me so.

Bob. By the foot of Pharaoh, and 'twere my case now, I should send him a *chartel* [7] presently. The *bastinado*! A most proper and sufficient *dependence*,[8] warranted by the great Caranza.[9] Come hither; you shall *chartel* him; I'll show you a trick or two you shall kill him with at pleasure; the first *stoccata*,[10] if you [150 will, by this air.

Mat. Indeed, you have absolute knowledge i' the mystery,[11] I have heard, sir.

Bob. Of whom? Of whom? Ha' you heard it, I beseech you?

Mat. Troth, I have heard it spoken of divers[12] that you have very rare and un-in-one-breath-utterable skill, sir.

Bob. By heaven, no, not I; no skill i' the earth; some small rudiments i' [160 the science, as to know my time, distance, or so. I have professed it more for noblemen and gentlemen's use than mine own practice, I assure you.—Hostess, accommodate us with another bedstaff [13] here quickly. Lend us another bedstaff.—The woman does not understand the words of action.—[*Takes the position of a fencer.*] Look you, sir; exalt not your point above this state, at any hand, and let your [170 poinard [14] maintain your defense, thus. (Give it the gentleman, and leave us.)— [*Exit Tib.*] So, sir. Come on. O, twine your body more about, that you may fall to a more sweet, comely, gentlemanlike guard; so, indifferent![15]   Hollow your

---

[1] The source of these lines is unknown, although Matthew usually pilfers other poets.

[2] A belt by which a weapon was hung from the girdle.

[3] Exceedingly.   [5] Simpleton.

[4] Variegated.   [6] Drunkard.

[7] Challenge.   [8] Ground for a duel.

[9] Author of a Spanish book on fencing.

[10] Thrust.   [11] Art, profession.   [12] By many.

[13] For preparing a feather bed.   [14] Poniard.

[15] Fairly well.

body more, sir, thus. Now, stand fast o'
your left leg, note your distance, keep
your due proportion of time. O, you disorder your point most irregularly!   180

MAT. How is the bearing of it now, sir?

BOB. O, out of measure ill. A well-
experienced hand would pass upon you
at pleasure.

MAT. How mean you, sir, pass upon
me?

BOB. Why, thus, sir: make a thrust at
me, come in upon the answer, control
your point, and make a full career[1] at the
body. The best-practiced gallants [190
of the time name it the *passada*. A most
desperate thrust, believe it!

MAT. Well, come, sir.

BOB. Why, you do not manage your
weapon with any facility or grace to invite
me. I have no spirit to play with you;
your dearth of judgment renders you
tedious.

MAT. But one *venue*,[2] sir.

BOB. "*Venue*"! Fie! Most gross [200
denomination as ever I heard. O, the
"*stoccata*," while you live, sir; note that.—
Come, put on your cloak, and we'll go
to some private place where you are acquainted—some tavern or so—and have
a bit. I'll send for one of these fencers,
and he shall breathe[3] you, by my direction; and then I will teach you your trick.
You shall kill him with it at the first, if
you please. Why, I will learn you, by [210
the true judgment of the eye, hand, and
foot, to control any enemy's point i' the
world. Should your adversary confront
you with a pistol, 'twere nothing, by this
hand! You should, by the same rule, control his bullet, in a line, except it were hail
shot, and spread. What money ha' you
about you, Mr. Matthew?

MAT. Faith, I ha' not past a two shillings or so.   220

BOB. 'Tis somewhat with the least.
But come; we will have a bunch of reddish[4] and salt to taste our wine, and a
pipe of tabacco to close the orifice of the
stomach; and then we'll call upon young
Wellbred. Perhaps we shall meet the
Corydon[5] his brother there, and put him
to the question.   [*Exeunt.*]

---

[1] Lunge.   [2] Thrust.   [3] Exercise.
[4] Radish.   [5] Rustic.

ACT II. SCENE i.

[A room in Kitely's house in the Old Jewry.]

Kitely, Cash, Downright.

[KITE.] Thomas, come hither.
There lies a note within upon my desk.
Here, take my key. It is no matter
neither.
Where is the boy?

CASH.   Within, sir, i' the warehouse.

KITE. Let him tell over straight that
Spanish gold,
And weigh it, with th' pieces of eight.
Do you
See the delivery of those silver stuffs
To Mr. Lucre; tell him, if he will,
He shall ha' the grograns[6] at the rate
I told him,
And I will meet him on the Exchange
anon.   10

CASH. Good, sir.   [*Exit.*]

KITE. Do you see that fellow, brother
Downright?

DOW. Ay, what of him?

KITE.   He is a jewel, brother.
I took him of[7] a child up at my door,
And christened him, gave him mine own
name, Thomas;
Since, bred him at the Hospital,[8] where
proving
A toward imp,[9] I called him home, and
taught him
So much as I have made him my cashier,
And given him who had none, a surname,
Cash,
And find him in his place so full of
faith   20
That I durst trust my life into his hands.

DOW. So would not I in any bastard's,
brother,
As it is like he is, although I knew
Myself his father. But you said yo' had
somewhat
To tell me, gentle brother. What is 't?
What is 't?

KITE. Faith, I am very loath to utter it,
As fearing it may hurt your patience;
But that I know your judgment is of
strength,
Against the nearness of affection—

---

[6] Coarse silk cloth.   [7] As.
[8] Christ's Hospital, where foundlings and
others were educated.   [9] Apt lad.

Dow. What need this circumstance? [1]
Pray you, be direct.   30
Kite. I will not say how much I do ascribe
Unto your friendship, nor in what regard
I hold your love; but let my past be-
havior
And usage of your sister but confirm
How well I've been affected to your—
Dow. You are too tedious; come to the
matter, the matter.
Kite. Then, without further ceremony,
thus.
My brother Wellbred, sir, I know not how,
Of late is much declined in what he was,
And greatly altered in his disposi-
tion.   40
When he came first to lodge here in my
house,
Ne'er trust me if I were not proud of him;
Methought he bare himself in such a
fashion,
So full of man [2] and sweetness in his car-
riage,
And, what was chief, it showed not bor-
rowed in him,
But all he did became him as his own,
And seemed as perfect, proper, and pos-
sessed
As breath with life, or color with the
blood.
But now, his course is so irregular,   49
So loose, affected, and deprived of grace,
And he himself withal so far fall'n off
From that first place as scarce no note
remains
To tell men's judgments where he lately
stood.
He's grown a stranger to all due respect,
Forgetful of his friends; and, not content
To stale himself in all societies,
He makes my house here common as a
mart,
A theater, a public receptacle
For giddy humor and diseaséd riot;
And here, as in a tavern or a stews,   60
He and his wild associates spend their
hours
In repetition of lascivious jests,
Swear, leap, drink, dance, and revel
night by night,
Control my servants, and, indeed, what
not?

Dow. 'Sdeynes,[3] I know not what I
should say to him, i' the whole world! He
values me at a cracked three farthings, for
aught I see. It will never out o' the flesh
that's bred i' the bone. I have told him
enough, one would think, if that would [70
serve; but counsel to him is as good as a
shoulder of mutton to a sick horse. Well,
he knows what to trust to, for George.[4]
Let him spend and spend and domineer,
till his heart ache; an he think to be relieved by me, when he is got into one o'
your city pounds, the counters,[5] he has
the wrong sow by the ear, i' faith, and claps
his dish [6] at the wrong man's door. I'll
lay my hand o' my halfpenny, ere I [80
part with 't to fetch him out, I'll assure
him.
Kite. Nay, good brother, let it not trouble
you thus.
Dow. 'Sdeath, he mads me! I could eat
my very spur-leathers for anger! But why
are you so tame? Why do you not speak
to him, and tell him how he disquiets your
house?
Kite. O, there are divers reasons to dissuade, brother.
But, would yourself vouchsafe to travail
in it   90
(Though but with plain and easy circum-
stance),
It would both come much better to his
sense,
And savor less of stomach [7] or of passion.
You are his elder brother, and that title
Both gives and warrants you authority,
Which, by your presence seconded, must
breed
A kind of duty in him, and regard;
Whereas, if I should intimate the least,
It would but add contempt to his neglect,
Heap worse on ill, make up a pile of
hatred,   100
That in the rearing would come tott'ring
down,
And in the ruin bury all our love.
Nay, more than this, brother; if I should
speak,
He would be ready, from his heat of
humor [8]

---

[1] Circuitous narration.   [2] Manliness.

[3] By God's dignesse, i.e., dignity(?).
[4] I.e., for all I care.   [6] I.e., like a beggar.
[5] Debtors' prisons.   [7] Anger.
[8] From his temper.

And overflowing of the vapor in him,
To blow the ears of his familiars
With the false breath of telling what dis-
graces
And low disparagements I had put upon
him,
Whilst they, sir, to relieve him in the
fable,[1]
Make their loose comments upon every
word,   110
Gesture, or look I use; mock me all over,
From my flat cap[2] unto my shining
shoes;[2]
And, out of their impetuous, rioting
fant'sies,
Beget some slander that shall dwell with
me.
And what would that be, think you?
Marry, this:
They would give out, because my wife is
fair,
Myself but lately married, and my sister
Here sojourning a virgin in my house,
That I were jealous—nay, as sure as
death,
That they would say—and how that I
had quarreled[3]   120
My brother purposely, thereby to find
An apt pretext to banish them my
house.
Dow. Mass, perhaps so; they are like
enough to do it.
Kite. Brother, they would, believe it; so
should I,
Like one of these penurious quack-
salvers,
But set the bills[4] up to mine own dis-
grace,
And try experiments upon myself;
Lend scorn and envy opportunity
To stab my reputation and good
name—

Act II. Scene ii.

[*The same.*]

Matthew, Bobadill, Downright, Kitely.

[Mat. (*Enters, struggling with Bobadill.*)]
I will speak to him.
Bob. Speak to him? Away! By the foot
of Pharaoh, you shall not! You shall not
do him that grace.—The time of day to
you, gentleman o' the house. Is Mr. Well-
bred stirring?
Dow. How then? What should he do?
Bob. Gentleman of the house, it[5] is to
you. Is he within, sir?   10
Kite. He came not to his lodging to-
night, sir, I assure you.
Dow. Why, do you hear? You!
Bob. The gentleman-citizen hath satis-
fied me; I'll talk to no scavenger.
          [*Exeunt Bobadill and Matthew.*]
Dow. How! Scavenger? Stay, sir, stay!
Kite. Nay, brother Downright—
Dow. Heart! Stand you away, and you
love me.
Kite. You shall not follow him now,   [20
I pray you, brother; good faith, you shall
not. I will overrule you.
Dow. Ha! Scavenger? Well, go to, I say
little; but, by this good day (God forgive
me I should swear), if I put it up[6] so, say
I am the rankest cow that ever pissed.
'Sdeynes, and I swallow this, I'll ne'er draw
my sword in the sight of Fleet Street again
while I live; I'll sit in a barn with madge-
howlet,[7] and catch mice first. Scaven- [30
ger, heart!—and I'll go near to fill that
huge tumbrel-slop[8] of yours with somewhat, and I have good luck; your Gara-
gantua breech cannot carry it away so.
Kite. O, do not fret yourself thus; never
think on 't.
Dow. These are my brother's consorts,
these! These are his cam'rades, his walking
mates! He's a gallant, a *cavaliero* too, right
hangman cut![9] Let me not live, and I
could not find in my heart to swinge   [40
the whole ging[10] of hem, one after another,
and begin with him first. I am grieved it
should be said he is my brother, and take
these courses. Well, as he brews, so shall
he drink, for George, again. Yet he shall
hear on 't, and that tightly[11] too, and I
live, i' faith.
Kite. But, brother, let your reprehension,
then,
Run in an easy current, not o'erhigh
Carried with rashness or devouring
choler;   50
But rather use the soft, persuading way,

---

[1] Narrating.   [3] Quarreled with.
[2] Marks of the citizen.   [4] Advertisements.
[5] *I.e.*, my question.   [7] The barn owl.
[6] Endure it.   [8] Loose breeches.
[9] In the exact form of a hangman.
[10] Gang, crowd.   [11] Quickly.

Whose powers will work more gently,
and compose
Th' imperfect thoughts you labor to re-
claim,
More winning than enforcing the consent.
Dow. Ay, ay, let me alone for that, I war-
rant you.   *Bell rings.*
Kite. How now! O, the bell rings to
breakfast.
Brother, I pray you go in, and bear my
wife
Company till I come; I'll but give order
For some despatch of business to my
servants—   [*Exit Downright.*]

Act II. Scene iii.

[*The same.*]

¹ *Kitely, Cob, Dame Kitely.*²

[Kite.] What, Cob! Our maids will have
you by the back, i' faith,
For coming so late this morning.
Cob. Perhaps so, sir; take heed some-
body have not them by the belly for walk-
ing so late in the evening.
                      He passes by with his tankard.
Kite. Well, yet my troubled spirit's some-
what eased,
Though not reposed in that security
As I could wish; but I must be content,
Howe'er I set a face on 't to the world.
Would I had lost this finger at a venter,
So Wellbred had ne'er lodged within my
house.   11
Why, 't cannot be, where there is such
resort
Of wanton gallants and young revelers,
That any woman should be honest ³
long.
Is 't like that factious beauty will pre-
serve
The public weal of chastity unshaken,
When such strong motives muster and
make head ⁴
Against her single peace? No, no. Be-
ware.
When mutual appetite doth meet to
treat,
And spirits of one kind and quality 20
Come once to parley in the pride of blood,
It is no slow conspiracy that follows.

Well, to be plain, if I but thought the
time
Had answered their affections,⁵ all the
world
Should not persuade me but I were a
cuckold.
Marry, I hope they ha' not got that
start,
For opportunity hath balked hem yet,
And shall do still, while I have eyes and
ears
To attend the impositions ⁶ of my heart.
My presence shall be as an iron bar   30
Twixt the conspiring motions of desire;
Yea, every look or glance mine eye ejects
Shall check occasion, as one doth his
slave,
When he forgets the limits of prescrip-
tion.

[*Enter Dame Kitely.*]

Dame. [*Calling.*] Sister Bridget, pray
you, fetch down the rose water above in the
closet.—Sweetheart, will you come in to
breakfast?
Kite. An she have overheard me
now—!   40
Dame. I pray thee, good muss,⁷ we stay
for you.
Kite. By heaven, I would not for a
thousand angels.⁸
Dame. What ail you, sweetheart? Are
you not well? Speak, good muss.
Kite. Troth, my head aches extremely
on a sudden.
Dame. [*Putting her hand to his forehead.*]
O, the Lord!   50
Kite. How now! What?
Dame. Alas, how it burns! Muss, keep
you warm; good truth, it is this new
disease; ⁹ there's a number are troubled
withal. For love's sake, sweetheart, come
in out of the air.
Kite. [*Aside.*] How simple and how subtle
are her answers!
A new disease, and many troubled with
it?
Why, true; she heard me, all ¹⁰ the world
to nothing.
Dame. I pray thee, good sweet- [60

---

¹ The marginal direction *"To them"* is erroneously printed here.   ³ Virtuous.
² Enters later.   ⁴ Gather their forces.
⁵ Suited their inclinations.   ⁷ Mouse.
⁶ Promptings.   ⁸ Gold coins.
⁹ A form of fever, probably typhoid.
¹⁰ *I.e.,* I wager all.

heart, come in; the air will do you harm, in
troth.

Kite. [*Aside.*] The air! She has me i' the
wind.[1]—Sweetheart,
  I'll come to you presently; 'twill away,
    I hope.

Dame. Pray heaven it do.   [*Exit.*]

Kite. A new disease? I know not, new or
  old,
But it may well be called poor mortals'
  plague,
For, like a pestilence, it doth infect
The houses of the brain. First it begins
Solely to work upon the fantasy,   70
Filling her seat with such pestiferous air
As soon corrupts the judgment; and from
  thence
Sends like contagion to the memory,
Still each to other giving the infection,
Which as a subtle vapor spreads itself
Confusedly through every sensive [2] part,
Till not a thought or motion in the mind
Be free from the black poison of suspect.[3]
Ah, but what misery is it to know this!
Or, knowing it, to want the mind's erec-
  tion [4]   80
In such extremes? Well, I will once more
  strive,
In spite of this black cloud, myself to be,
And shake the fever off that thus shakes
  me.   [*Exit.*]

Act II. Scene iv.

[*Moorfields.*]

Brainworm, Ed[ward] Knowell, Mr. Ste-
phen.[5]

Bra. [*Disguised like a maimed soldier.*]
'Slid, I cannot choose but laugh to see myself translated thus from a poor creature to
a creator; for now must I create an intolerable sort of lies, or my present profession
loses the grace. And yet the lie, to a man
of my coat, is as ominous a fruit as the
fico.[6] O, sir, it holds for good polity ever,
to have that outwardly in vilest estimation,
that inwardly is most dear to us. So [10
much for my borrowed shape. Well, the
troth is, my old master intends to follow

my young, dry-foot,[7] over Moorfields to
London this morning; now I, knowing of
this hunting match, or rather conspiracy,
and to insinuate with my young master
(for so must we that are blue waiters [8] and
men of hope and service do, or perhaps we
may wear motley at the year's end, and
who wears motley,[9] you know—), [20
have got me afore in this disguise, determining here to lie in *ambuscado*, and intercept him in the midway. If I can but get
his cloak, his purse, his hat, nay, any thing
to cut him off, that is, to stay his journey,
"*Veni, vidi, vici,*" [10] I may say, with Captain
Cæsar, I am made forever, i' faith. Well,
now must I practice to get the true garb
of one of these lance-knights,[11] my arm
here, and my—young master, and his [30
cousin, Mr. Stephen, as I am true counterfeit man of war, and no soldier! [*Retires.*]

[*Enter Edward Knowell and Stephen.*]

E. Know. So, sir! And how then, coz?

Ste. 'Sfoot, I have lost my purse, I
think.

E. Know. How?   Lost your purse?
Where? When had you it?

Ste. I cannot tell. Stay.

Bra. 'Slid, I am afeard they will know
me. Would I could get by them!   40

E. Know. What, ha' you it?

Ste. No; I think I was bewitched, I—
                        [*Weeps.*]

E. Know. Nay, do not weep the loss;
hang it, let it go.

Ste. [*Finding his purse.*] O, it's here.
No, and it had been lost, I had not cared,
but for a jet ring Mistress Mary sent me.

E. Know. A jet ring? O, the poesy,[12]
the poesy?

Ste. Fine, i' faith.—   50
    "Though Fancy [13] sleep,
      My love is deep—"
meaning that, though I did not fancy her,
yet she loved me dearly.

E. Know. Most excellent!

Ste. And then I sent her another, and
my poesy was,

---

[1] She's on my scent.
[2] Sensitive.   [4] To lack elevation of mind.
[3] Suspicion.   [5] The last two enter later.
[6] Fig, an insulting gesture.

[7] By the scent.   [8] Blue-liveried servants.
[9] The fool's coat.
[10] "I came, I saw, I conquered."
[11] Mercenary footsoldiers.
[12] Posy, motto.   [13] Affection.

"The deeper, the sweeter,
　I'll be judged by St. Peter."

E. Know. How, by St. Peter? I do　[60
not conceive that.

Ste. Marry, St. Peter, to make up the
meter.

E. Know. Well, there the saint was
your good patron; he helped you at your
need. Thank him, thank him.

Bra. (*He is come back.*)[1] [*Aside.*] I cannot take leave on hem so; I will venture,
come what will.—Gentlemen, please you
change a few crowns for a very excel-　[70
lent good blade here? I am a poor gentleman, a soldier, one that, in the better state
of my fortunes, scorned so mean a refuge;
but now it is the humor of necessity to
have it so. You seem to be gentlemen well
affected to martial men, else I should rather
die with silence than live with shame.
However, vouchsafe to remember it is my
want speaks, not myself; this condition
agrees not with my spirit—　　　80

E. Know. Where hast thou served?

Bra. May it please you, sir, in all the
late wars of Bohemia, Hungaria, Dalmatia,
Poland—where not, sir? I have been a poor
servitor by sea and land any time this fourteen years, and followed the fortunes of the
best commanders in Christendom. I was
twice shot at the taking of Aleppo, once
at the relief of Vienna; I have been at
Marseilles, Naples, and the Adriatic　[90
gulf, a gentleman slave in the galleys thrice,
where I was most dangerously shot in the
head, through both the thighs; and yet,
being thus maimed, I am void of maintenance, nothing left me but my scars, the
noted marks of my resolution.

Ste. How will you sell this rapier,
friend?

Bra. Generous sir, I refer it to your
own judgment. You are a gentle-　[100
man; give me what you please.

Ste. True, I am a gentleman, I know
that, friend; but what though? I pray you
say, what would you ask?

Bra. I assure you, the blade may become the side or thigh of the best prince
in Europe.

E. Know. Ay, with a velvet scabbard,
I think.

Ste. Nay, and 't be mine, it shall　[110
have a velvet scabbard, coz, that's flat; I'd
not wear it as 'tis, and you would give me
an angel.

Bra. At your worship's pleasure, sir.
[*Stephen examines the blade.*] Nay, 'tis a
most pure Toledo.

Ste. I had rather it were a Spaniard.
But tell me, what shall I give you for it?
An it had a silver hilt—

E. Know. Come, come, you shall　[120
not buy it. Hold, there's a shilling, fellow;
take thy rapier.

Ste. Why, but I will buy it now, because you say so; and there's another shilling, fellow; I scorn to be outbidden. What,
shall I walk with a cudgel, like Higgin-
bottom,[2] and may have a rapier for money?

E. Know. You may buy one in the city.

Ste. Tut! I'll buy this i' the field, so
I will; I have a mind to 't, because 'tis　[130
a field rapier. Tell me your lowest price.

E. Know. You shall not buy it, I say.

Ste. By this money, but I will, though
I give more than 'tis worth.

E. Know. Come away; you are a fool.

Ste. Friend, I am a fool, that's granted;
but I'll have it, for that word's sake. Follow me for your money.

Bra. At your service, sir.　[*Exeunt.*]

Act II. Scene v.

[*Another part of Moorfields.*]

Knowell, Brainworm.[3]

[Know.] I cannot lose the thought yet of
　　this letter
Sent to my son; nor leave t' admire[4] the
　　change
Of manners and the breeding of our
　　youth
Within the kingdom, since myself was one.
When I was young, he lived not in the
　　stews
Durst have conceived a scorn and ut-
　　tered it
On a gray head; age was authority
Against a buffon,[5] and a man had then
A certain reverence paid unto his years,
That had none due unto his life. So much

---

[1] This direction appears opposite the preceding
line in the original.
[2] Unidentified; probably any rustic.
[3] Enters later.
[4] Wonder at.　　　　　　　　　[5] Buffoon.

The sanctity of some prevailed for others.
But now we all are fall'n, youth from
    their fear,   12
And age from that which bred it, good
    example.[1]
Nay, would ourselves were not the first
    even parents
That did destroy the hopes in our own
    children,
Or they not learned our vices in their
    cradles,
And sucked in our ill customs with their
    milk!
Ere all their teeth be born, or they can
    speak,
We make their palates cunning; the first
    words
We form their tongues with are licentious
    jests!   20
Can it call "whore"? Cry "bastard"?
    O, then, kiss it!
A witty child! Can't swear? The father's
    dearling![2]
Give it two plums. Nay, rather than 't
    shall learn
No bawdy song, the mother herself will
    teach it!
But this is in the infancy, the days
Of the long coat; when it puts on the
    breeches,
It will put off all this. Ay, it is like,
When it is gone into the bone already!
No, no; this dye goes deeper than the
    coat,   29
Or shirt, or skin; it stains unto the liver [3]
And heart [4] in some. And, rather than it
    should not,
Note what we fathers do! Look how we
    live,
What mistresses we keep, at what ex-
    pense!
In our sons' eyes, where they may handle
    our gifts,
Hear our lascivious courtships, see our
    dalliance,
Taste of the same provoking meats with
    us,
To ruin of our states! Nay, when our own
Portion [5] is fled, to prey on their re-
    mainder,[5]

We call them into fellowship of vice;
Bait hem with the young chambermaid,
    to seal,[6]   40
And teach hem all bad ways to buy af-
    fiction.[7]
This is one path; but there are millions
    more,
In which we spoil our own with leading
    them.
Well, I thank heaven, I never yet was he
That traveled with my son, before six-
    teen,
To show him the Venetian courtesans;
Nor read the grammar of cheating I had
    made,
To my sharp boy, at twelve, repeating
    still
The rule,[8] "Get money;" still, "Get
    money, boy,   49
No matter by what means; money will do
More, boy, than my lord's letter." Nei-
    ther have I
Dressed snails or mushrooms curiously
    before him,
Perfumed my sauces, and taught him to
    make hem;
Preceding still, with my gray gluttony,
At all the ordinaries, and only feared
His palate should degenerate, not his
    manners.
These are the trade of fathers now; how-
    ever,
My son, I hope, hath met within my
    threshold
None of these household precedents,
    which are strong
And swift to rape youth to their preci-
    pice.[9]   60
But let the house at home be ne'er so
    clean-
Swept, or kept sweet from filth, nay,
    dust and cobwebs,
If he will live abroad with his compan-
    ions
In dung and leystalls,[10] it is worth a fear;
Nor is the danger of conversing less
Than all that I have mentioned of ex-
    ample.

[1] The following twenty lines are taken from Quintilian.
[2] Darling.
[3] Seat of the passions.
[4] Seat of knowledge.
[5] Inheritance.
[6] "Probably, to agree to the sale of family estates" (Neilson).
[7] Affliction, from Lat. *afficio*.
[8] The following lines are based on passages from Horace and Juvenal.
[9] Carry youth off to their downfall
[10] Laystalls. rubbish heaps.

[*Enter Brainworm.*]

BRA. [*Aside.*] My master! Nay, faith,
have at you; I am fleshed [1] now, I have
sped so well.—Worshipful sir, I beseech
you, respect the estate of a poor sol-   [70
dier; I am ashamed of this base course of
life—God's my comfort [2]—but extremity
provokes me to 't. What remedy?

KNOW. I have not for you now.

BRA. By the faith I bear unto truth,
gentleman, it is no ordinary custom in me,
but only to preserve manhood. I protest
to you, a man I have been; a man I may be,
by your sweet bounty.

KNOW. Pray thee, good friend, be   [80
satisfied.

BRA. Good sir, by that hand, you may
do the part of a kind gentleman in lending
a poor soldier the price of two cans of beer,
a matter of small value; the king of heaven
shall pay you, and I shall rest thankful.
Sweet worship—

KNOW. Nay, and you be so importunate—

BRA. O, tender sir, need will have   [90
his course; I was not made to this vile use!
Well, the edge of the enemy could not have
abated me so much. It's hard when a man
hath served in his prince's cause, and
be thus—(*He weeps.*) Honorable worship,
let me derive a small piece of silver from
you; it shall not be given in the course of
time.[3] By this good ground, I was fain to
pawn my rapier last night for a poor supper;
I had sucked the hilts long before, I   [100
am a pagan else. Sweet honor—

KNOW. Believe me, I am taken with some
      wonder
To think a fellow of thy outward pres-
      ence
Should, in the frame and fashion of his
      mind,
Be so degenerate and sordid-base.
Art thou a man, and sham'st thou not to
      beg?
To practice such a servile kind of life?
Why, were thy education ne'er so mean,
Having thy limbs, a thousand fairer
      courses
Offer themselves to thy election.   110

[1] Encouraged by success.
[2] Confirmation, witness.
[3] Not forever; *i.e.*, it will be repaid.

Either the wars might still supply thy
      wants,
Or service of some virtuous gentleman,
Or honest labor; nay, what can I name
But would become thee better than to
      beg?
But men of thy condition feed on sloth,
As doth the beetle on the dung she breeds
      in,
Not caring how the metal of your minds
Is eaten with the rust of idleness.
Now, afore me, whate'er he be that
      should
Relieve a person of thy quality,   120
While thou insists in this loose, desperate
      course,
I would esteem the sin not thine, but
      his.

BRA. Faith, sir, I would gladly find some
other course, if so—

KNOW. Ay, you'ld gladly find it, but you
will not seek it.

BRA. Alas, sir, where should a man seek?
In the wars there's no ascent by desert in
these days; but—and, for service, would
it were as soon purchased [4] as wished   [130
for! The air's my comfort, I know. What
I would say—

KNOW. What's thy name?

BRA.   Please you, Fitzsword, sir.

KNOW.   Fitzsword?
Say that a man should entertain thee
      now,
Wouldst thou be honest, humble, just,
      and true?

BRA. Sir, by the place and honor of a
      soldier—

KNOW. Nay, nay, I like not those affected
      oaths.
Speak plainly, man, what think'st thou
      of my words?

BRA. Nothing, sir, but wish my fortunes were as happy as my service   [140
should be honest.

KNOW. Well, follow me; I'll prove [5] thee,
      if thy deeds
Will carry a proportion to thy words.

BRA. Yes, sir, straight; I'll but garter
my hose.—[*Exit Knowell.*] O, that my belly
were hooped now, for I am ready to burst
with laughing! Never was bottle or bagpipe fuller. 'Slid, was there ever seen a fox
in years to betray himself thus? Now shall

[4] Acquired.   [5] Test.

I be possessed of all his counsels, and, [150 by that conduit, my young master. Well, he is resolved to prove my honesty; faith, and I'm resolved to prove his patience. O, I shall abuse [1] him intolerably. This small piece of service will bring him clean out of love with the soldier forever. He will never come within the sign of it, the sight of a cassock,[2] or a musket rest again. He will hate the musters at Mile End for it, to his dying day. It's no matter; let the [160 world think me a bad counterfeit, if I cannot give him the slip [3] at an instant. Why, this is better than to have stayed [4] his journey. Well, I'll follow him. O, how I long to be employed!   [*Exit.*]

Act III. Scene i.

[*A room in the Windmill Tavern.*]

Matthew, Wellbred, Bobadill, Ed[ward] Knowell, Stephen.[5]

[MAT.] Yes, faith, sir, we were at your lodging to seek you too.

WELL. O, I came not there tonight.

BOB. Your brother delivered us as much.

WELL. Who, my brother Downright?

BOB. He. Mr. Wellbred, I know not in what kind [6] you hold me, but let me say to you this: as sure as honor, I esteem it so much out of the sunshine of reputation to throw the least beam of regard upon [10 such a——

WELL. Sir, I must hear no ill words of my brother.

BOB. I protest to you, as [7] I have a thing to be saved about me, I never saw any gentlemanlike part—

WELL. Good captain, "faces about" [8] to some other discourse.

BOB. With your leave, sir, and there were no more men living upon the face [20 of the earth, I should not fancy him, by St. George!

MAT. Troth, nor I; he is of a rustical cut, I know not how, he doth not carry himself like a gentleman of fashion.

WELL. O, Mr. Matthew, that's a grace peculiar but to a few, "*quos æquus amavit Jupiter.*" [9]

MAT. I understand you, sir.

WELL. No question, you do—[*Aside.*] [30 or you do not, sir.—

Young Knowell enters [with Stephen].

Ned Knowell! By my soul, welcome! How doest thou, sweet spirit, my genius? 'Slid, I shall love Apollo and the mad Thespian girls [10] the better, while I live, for this, my dear Fury; now I see there's some love in thee! Sirrah, these be the two I writ to thee of. Nay, what a drowsy humor is this now! Why dost thou not speak?

E. KNOW. O, you are a fine gallant; [40 you sent me a rare letter!

WELL. Why, was 't not rare?

E. KNOW. Yes, I'll be sworn, I was ne'er guilty of reading the like; match it in all Pliny, or Symmachus' epistles, and I'll have my judgment burned in the ear for a rogue.[11] Make much of thy vein, for it is inimitable. But I mar'l [12] what camel it was that had the carriage of it, for, doubtless, he was no ordinary beast that [50 brought it.

WELL. Why?

E. KNOW. "Why?" say'st thou! Why, dost thou think that any reasonable creature, especially in the morning, the sober time of the day too, could have mista'en my father for me?

WELL. 'Slid, you jest, I hope?

E. KNOW. Indeed, the best use we can turn it to is to make a jest on't now; [60 but, I'll assure you, my father had the full view o' your flourishing style some hour before I saw it.

WELL. What a dull slave was this! But, sirrah, what said he to it, i' faith?

E. KNOW. Nay, I know not what he said; but I have a shrewd guess what he thought.

WELL. What? What?

E. KNOW. Marry, that thou art [70 some strange, dissolute young fellow, and

---

[1] Deceive.   [2] A soldier's cloak.
[3] With a pun on *counterfeit coin.*
[4] Prevented.   [5] The last two enter later.
[6] Fashion, relationship.
[7] As surely as.   [8] About face.

[9] "Whom friendly Jupiter has loved" (Virgil, *Æneid*, VI, 129).
[10] The Muses.
[11] Common method of punishing criminals.
[12] Marvel.

I—a grain or two better for keeping thee company.

WELL. Tut! That thought is like the moon in her last quarter—'twill change shortly. But, sirrah, I pray thee be acquainted with my two hang-bys here; thou wilt take exceeding pleasure in hem if thou hear'st hem once go: my wind instruments. I'll wind hem up— [80 But what strange piece of silence is this? The Sign of the Dumb Man?

E. KNOW. O, sir, a kinsman of mine, one that may make your music the fuller, and he please; he has his humor, sir.

WELL. O, what is 't? What is 't?

E. KNOW. Nay, I'll neither do your judgment nor his folly that wrong as to prepare your apprehension; I'll leave him to the mercy o' your search. If you [90 can take him, so!

WELL. Well, Captain Bobadill, Mr. Matthew, pray you, know this gentleman here; he is a friend of mine, and one that will deserve your affection.—(*To Master Stephen.*) I know not your name, sir, but I shall be glad of any occasion to render me more familiar to you.

STE. My name is Mr. Stephen, sir; I am this gentleman's own cousin, sir; [100 his father is mine uncle, sir. I am somewhat melancholy, but you shall command me, sir, in whatsoever is incident to a gentleman.

BOB. (*To [E.] Knowell.*) Sir, I must tell you this, I am no general[1] man; but, for Mr. Wellbred's sake (you may embrace it at what height of favor you please), I do communicate with you, and conceive you to be a gentleman of some parts; I love [110 few words.

E. KNOW. And I fewer, sir; I have scarce enow to thank you.

MAT. (*To Master Stephen.*) But are you, indeed, sir, so given to it?

STE. Ay, truly, sir, I am mightily given to melancholy.

MAT. O, it's your only fine humor, sir; your true melancholy breeds your perfect, fine wit, sir. I am melancholy [120 myself, diver times, sir, and then do I no more but take pen and paper presently, and overflow you half a score or a dozen of sonnets at a sitting.

[1] Open to general acquaintance.

(²E. KNOW. Sure he utters³ them then by the gross.)

STE. Truly, sir, and I love such things out of measure.

E. KNOW. I' faith, better than in measure, I'll undertake. 130

MAT. Why, I pray you, sir, make use of my study; it's at your service.

STE. I thank you, sir; I shall be bold, I warrant you. Have you a stool there to be melancholy upon?

MAT. That I have, sir, and some papers there of mine own doing, at idle hours, that you'll say there's some sparks of wit in hem, when you see them.

WELL. [*Aside.*] Would the sparks [140 would kindle once, and become a fire amongst hem! I might see self-love burnt for her heresy.

STE. Cousin, is it well? Am I melancholy enough?

E. KNOW. O, ay, excellent.

WELL. Captain Bobadill, why muse you so?

E. KNOW. He is melancholy too. [149

BOB. Faith, sir, I was thinking of a most honorable piece of service, was performed tomorrow, being St. Mark's Day, shall be some ten years now.

E. KNOW. In what place, captain?

BOB. Why, at the beleag'ring of Strigonium, where, in less than two hours, seven hundred resolute gentlemen as any were in Europe lost their lives upon the breach. I'll tell you, gentlemen, it was the first, but the best leaguer that [160 ever I beheld with these eyes, except the taking-in of—what do you call it?—last year, by the Genoways;⁴ but that, of all other, was the most fatal and dangerous exploit that ever I was ranged in, since I first bore arms before the face of the enemy, as I am a gentleman and soldier.

STE. So! I had as lief as an angel I could swear as well as that gentleman. [169

E. KNOW. Then you were a servitor at both, it seems; at Strigonium, and what do you call 't?

BOB. O Lord, sir! By S[t]. George, I was the first man that entered the breach;

² Jonson frequently encloses speeches in parenthesis to indicate an aside or a passage incidental to the main action.
³ Puts into circulation.   ⁴ Genoese.

and, had I not effected it with resolution, I had been slain if I had had a million of lives.

E. Know. 'Twas pity you had not ten— a cat's and your own, i' faith. But—was it possible? 180

(Mat. Pray you, mark this discourse, sir!

Ste. So I do.)

Bob. I assure you, upon my reputation, 'tis true, and yourself shall confess.

E. Know. [*Aside.*] You must bring me to the rack first.

Bob. Observe me judicially, sweet sir: they had planted me three demi-culverings[1] just in the mouth of the breach; [190 now, sir, as we were to give on,[2] their master gunner (a man of no mean skill and mark, you must think) confronts me with his linstock,[3] ready to give fire; I, spying his intendment, discharged my petronel[4] in his bosom, and with these single arms, my poor rapier, ran violently upon the Moors that guarded the ordinance, and put hem pellmell to the sword. 199

Well. To the sword? To the rapier, captain?

E. Know. O, it was a good figure observed, sir. But did you all this, captain, without hurting your blade?

Bob. Without any impeach[5] o' the earth. You shall perceive, sir. [*Shows his rapier.*] It is the most fortunate weapon that ever rid on poor gentleman's thigh. Shall I tell you, sir? You talk of Morglay, Excalibur, Durindana, or so. Tut! [210 I lend no credit to that is fabled of hem. I know the virtue of mine own, and therefore I dare the boldlier maintain it.

Ste. I mar'l whether it be a Toledo or no?

Bob. A most perfect Toledo, I assure you, sir.

Ste. I have a countryman of his here.

Mat. Pray you, let's see, sir; yes, faith, it is! 220

Bob. This a Toledo? Pish!

Ste. Why do you pish, captain?

Bob. A Fleming, by heaven! I'll buy them for a guilder[6] apiece, an I would have a thousand of them.

E. Know. How say you, cousin? I told you thus much!

Well. Where bought you it, Mr. Stephen? 229

Ste. Of a scurvy rogue soldier. A hundred of lice go with him! He swore it was a Toledo.

Bob. A poor provant[7] rapier, no better.

Mat. Mass, I think it be indeed, now I look on 't better.

E. Know. Nay, the longer you look on 't, the worse. Put it up, put it up.

Ste. Well, I will put it up; but by— I ha' forgot the captain's oath; I [239 thought to ha' sworn by it—an e'er I meet him—

Well. O, it is past help now, sir; you must have patience.

Ste. Whoreson, cony-catching[8] rascal! I could eat the very hilts for anger.

E. Know. A sign of good digestion; you have an ostrich stomach, cousin!

Ste. A stomach? Would I had him here, you should see an I had a stomach.[9] 250

Well. It's better as 'tis.—Come, gentlemen, shall we go?

Act III. Scene ii.

[*The same.*]

E[*dward*] *Knowell, Brainworm, Stephen, Wellbred, Bobadill, Matthew.*

[*Enter Brainworm.*]

[E. Know.] A miracle, cousin; look here, look here!

Ste. O!—God's lid! By your leave, do you know me, sir?

Bra. Ay, sir, I know you by sight.

Ste. You sold me a rapier, did you not?

Bra. Yes, marry, did I, sir.

Ste. You said it was a Toledo, ha?

Bra. True, I did so.

Ste. But it is none? 10

Bra. No, sir, I confess it; it is none.

Ste. Do you confess it? Gentlemen, bear witness, he has confessed it.—By God's will, and you had not confessed it—

E. Know. O, cousin, forbear, forbear!

Ste. Nay, I have done, cousin.

---

[1] Small cannon.
[2] Charge.
[3] A lighted match.
[4] Petronel, a large pistol.
[5] Question.
[6] A Dutch coin.
[7] Supplied by the government.
[8] Swindling.
[9] Courage.

WELL. Why, you have done like a gentleman; he has confessed it; what would you more?   20

STE. Yet, by his leave, he is a rascal, under his favor, do you see?

E. KNOW. [Aside.] Ay, by his leave, he is, and under favor—a pretty piece of civility! Sirrah, how dost thou like him?

WELL. [Aside.] O, it's a most precious fool; make much on him. I can compare him to nothing more happily than a drum, for everyone may play upon him.

E. KNOW. [Aside.] No, no, a child's whistle were far the fitter.   31

BRA. Sir, shall I entreat a word with you?

E. KNOW. With me, sir? You have not another Toledo to sell, ha' you?

BRA. You are conceited,[1] sir. Your name is Mr. Knowell, as I take it?

E. KNOW. You are i' the right; you mean not to proceed in the catechism, do you?   40

BRA. No, sir; I am none of that coat.[2]

E. KNOW. Of as bare a coat, though. Well, say, sir.

BRA. [Taking Edward Knowell aside.] Faith, sir, I am but servant to the drum extraordinary, and, indeed, this smoky varnish being washed off, and three or four patches removed, I appear your worship's in reversion, after the decease of your good father.—Brainworm!   50

E. KNOW. Brainworm! 'Slight, what breath of a conjurer hath blown thee hither in this shape?

BRA. The breath o' your letter, sir, this morning, the same that blew you to the Windmill, and your father after you.

E. KNOW. My father?

BRA. Nay, never start; 'tis true. He has followed you over the fields by the foot, as you would do a hare i' the [60 snow.

E. KNOW. Sirrah, Wellbred, what shall we do, sirrah? My father is come over after me.

WELL. Thy father? Where is he?

BRA. At Justice Clement's house here, in Coleman Street, where he but stays my return; and then—

WELL. Who's this? Brainworm?

BRA. The same, sir.   70

WELL. Why, how, i' the name of wit, com'st thou transmuted thus?

BRA. Faith, a device, a device; nay, for the love of reason, gentlemen, and avoiding the danger, stand not here; withdraw, and I'll tell you all.

WELL. But art thou sure he will stay thy return?

BRA. Do I live, sir? What a question is that!   80

WELL. We'll prorogue his expectation, then, a little. Brainworm, thou shalt go with us.—Come on, gentlemen. Nay, I pray thee, sweet Ned, droop not; heart, and our wits be so wretchedly dull that one old plodding brain can outstrip us all, would we were e'en pressed[3] to make porters of, and serve out the remnant of our days in Thames Street, or at Customhouse quay, in a civil war against [90 the carmen![4]

BRA. Amen, amen, amen, say I.

                              [Exeunt.]

ACT III. SCENE iii.

[Kitely's shop.]

Kitely, Cash.

[KITE.] What says he, Thomas? Did you speak with him?

CASH. He will expect you, sir, within this half hour.

KITE. Has he the money ready, can you tell?

CASH. Yes, sir, the money was brought in last night.

KITE. O, that's well; fetch me my cloak, my cloak!—   [Exit Cash.]
Stay, let me see. An hour to go and come—
Ay, that will be the least; and then 'twill be
An hour before I can despatch with him,
Or very near; well, I will say two hours.
Two hours? Ha! Things never dreamt of yet   10
May be contrived, ay, and effected too,
In two hours' absence; well, I will not go.
Two hours! No, fleering Opportunity,
I will not give your subtilty that scope.
Who will not judge him worthy to be robbed
That sets his doors wide open to a thief,

---

[1] Witty.   [2] *I.e.,* not a clergyman.   [3] Impressed.   [4] Carters.

And shows the felon where his treasure
  lies?
Again, what earthy spirit but will
  attempt
To taste the fruit of Beauty's golden
  tree,
When leaden sleep seals up the dragon's
  eyes?   20
I will not go. Business, go by for once.
No, beauty, no; you are of too good
  caract [1]
To be left so, without a guard, or open.
Your luster, too, 'll inflame at any dis-
  tance,
Draw courtship to you, as a jet doth
  straws,
Put motion in a stone, strike fire from
  ice,
Nay, make a porter leap you with his
  burden.
You must be then kept up, close, and
  well watched,
For, give you opportunity, no quicksand
Devours or swallows swifter! He that
  lends   30
His wife, if she be fair, or [2] time or place,
Compels her to be false. I will not go!
The dangers are too many—and then the
  dressing
Is a most main attractive! [3] Our great
  heads
Within the city never were in safety
Since our wives wore these little caps.
I'll change hem;
I'll change hem straight in mine. Mine
  shall no more
Wear three-piled acorns [4] to make my
  horns ache.
Nor will I go; I am resolved for that.—

        [Enter Cash with a cloak.]

Carry in my cloak again. Yet stay. Yet
  do, too.   40
I will defer going, on all occasions.
CASH. Sir, Snare, your scrivener, will be
  there with th' bonds.
KITE. That's true! "Fool" on me! I had
  clean forgot it;
I must go. What's a-clock?
CASH.   Exchange time,[5] sir.

[1] Carat, worth.   [2] Either.
[3] Mighty attraction.
[4] Fine velvet tags for hat cords.
[5] Time for opening the Exchange, *i.e.*, about
ten.

KITE. Heart, then will Wellbred presently
  be here too,
With one or other of his loose consorts.
I am a knave if I know what to say,
What course to take, or which way to
  resolve.
My brain, methinks, is like an hour-
  glass,
Wherein my imaginations run like sands,
Filling up time, but then are turned and
  turned,   51
So that I know not what to stay upon,
And less, to put in act. It shall be so.
Nay, I dare build upon his secrecy.
He knows not to deceive me.—Thomas!
CASH.   Sir.
KITE. Yet now I have bethought me, too,
  I will not.—
Thomas, is Cob within?
CASH.   I think he be, sir.
KITE. [*Aside.*] But he'll prate too; there's
  no speech of him.
No, there were no man o' the earth to [6]
  Thomas,
If I durst trust him; there is all the
  doubt.   60
But should he have a chink in him, I were
  gone,
Lost i' my fame forever, talk for th'
  Exchange!
The manner he hath stood with, till this
  present,
Doth promise no such change. What
  should I fear then?
Well, come what will, I'll tempt my
  fortune once.—
Thomas—you may deceive me, but, I
  hope—
Your love to me is more—
CASH.   Sir, if a servant's
Duty, with faith, may be called love,
  you are
More than in hope—you are possessed
  of it.
KITE. I thank you heartily, Thomas; gi'
  me your hand.   70
With all my heart, good Thomas. I have,
  Thomas,
A secret to impart unto you—but,
When once you have it, I must seal your
  lips up;
So far I tell you, Thomas.
CASH.   Sir, for that—

[6] Compared to.

KITE. Nay, hear me out. Think I esteem
　you, Thomas,
When I will let you in thus to my pri-
　vate.[1]
It is a thing sits nearer to my crest
Than thou art ware of, Thomas; if thou
　shouldst
Reveal it, but—

CASH. 　　　　　　　How? I reveal it?

KITE. 　　　　　　　　　　　　Nay,
I do not think thou wouldst; but, if
　thou shouldst, 　　　　　　　　　80
'Twere a great weakness.

CASH. 　　　　　　A great treachery:
Give it no other name.

KITE. 　　　Thou wilt not do 't, then?

CASH. Sir, if I do, mankind disclaim me
　ever!

KITE. [Aside.] He will not swear; he has
　some reservation,
Some concealed purpose, and close mean-
　ing, sure;
Else, being urged so much, how should
　he choose
But lend an oath to all this protestation?
H'is no Precisian [2] that I am certain of—
Nor rigid Roman Catholic. He'll play
At fayles and ticktack; [3] I have heard
　him swear. 　　　　　　　　　90
What should I think of it? Urge him
　again,
And by some other way? I will do so.—
Well, Thomas, thou hast sworn not to
　disclose.
Yes, you did swear?

CASH. 　　　　　　Not yet, sir, but I will,
　Please you—

KITE. 　　No, Thomas, I dare take thy word.
But, if thou wilt swear, do as thou
　think'st good;
I am resolved [4] without it; at thy pleas-
　ure.

CASH. By my soul's safety then, sir, I
　protest,
My tongue shall ne'er take knowledge of
　a word 　　　　　　　　　　　99
Delivered me in nature of your trust.

KITE. It's too much; these ceremonies
　need not;
I know thy faith to be as firm as rock.
Thomas, come hither, near; [5] we cannot be

Too private in this business. So it is—
[Aside.] Now he has sworn, I dare the
　safelier venter.—
I have of late, by divers observations—
[Aside.] But whether his oath can bind
　him, yea, or no,
Being not taken lawfully? [6] Ha! Say you?
I will ask counsel ere I do proceed.—
Thomas, it will be now too long to
　stay; 　　　　　　　　　　　110
I'll spy some fitter time soon, or to-
　morrow.

CASH. Sir, at your pleasure.

KITE. 　　　I will think—and, Thomas,
I pray you, search the books gainst my
　return
For the receipts twixt me and Traps.

CASH. 　　　　　　　　　　I will, sir.

KITE. And hear you, if your mistress'
　brother, Wellbred,
Chance to bring hither any gentlemen
Ere I come back, let one straight bring
　me word.

CASH. Very well, sir.

KITE. 　　To the Exchange, do you hear?
Or here in Coleman Street, to Justice
　Clement's.
Forget it not, nor be not out of the
　way. 　　　　　　　　　　　120

CASH. I will not, sir.

KITE. 　　I pray you have a care on 't.
Or, whether he come or no, if any other,
Stranger or else, fail not to send me word.

CASH. I shall not, sir.

KITE. 　　Be 't your special business
Now to remember it.

CASH. 　　　　　Sir, I warrant you.

KITE. But, Thomas, this is not the secret,
　Thomas,
I told you of.

CASH. 　　　No, sir; I do suppose it.

KITE. Believe me, it is not.

CASH. 　　　　　Sir, I do believe you.

KITE. By heaven, it is not; that's enough.
　But, Thomas,
I would not you should utter it, do you
　see, 　　　　　　　　　　　130
To any creature living; yet I care not.
Well, I must hence. Thomas, conceive
　thus much;
It was a trial of you, when I meant
So deep a secret to you; I mean not
　this,

[1] Privacy.
[2] Puritan.
[3] Varieties of backgammon.
[4] Convinced.
[5] Nearer.
[6] I.e., before an officer.

But that [1] I have to tell you; this is nothing, this.

But, Thomas, keep this from my wife, I charge you—

Locked up in silence, midnight, buried here.—

[*Aside.*] No greater hell than to be slave to fear. 　　　　[*Exit.*]

CASH. "Locked up in silence, midnight, buried here!"

Whence should this flood of passion, trow, take head? Ha!　　　　140

Best dream no longer of this running humor,

For fear I sink; the violence of the stream Already hath transported me so far That I can feel no ground at all. But soft—

O, 'tis our water bearer; somewhat has crossed him now.

ACT III. SCENE iv.

[*The same.*]

Cob, Cash.

[COB. (*To himself.*)] Fasting days! What tell you me of fasting days? 'Slid, would they were all on a light fire [2] for me! They say the whole world shall be consumed with fire one day, but would I had these ember weeks and villainous Fridays burnt in the meantime, and then—

CASH. Why, how now, Cob? What moves thee to this choler, ha?

COB. Collar, Master Thomas? I [10 scorn your collar, I, sir; I am none o' your cart horse, though I carry and draw water. An you offer to ride me with your collar, or halter either, I may hap show you a jade's trick, sir.

CASH. O, you'll slip your head out of the collar? Why, Goodman Cob, you mistake me.

COB. Nay, I have my rheum, and I can be angry as well as another, sir.　　　20

CASH. Thy rheum, Cob! Thy humor, thy humor—thou mistak'st.[3]

COB. Humor? Mack,[4] I think it be so indeed. What is that humor? Some rare thing, I warrant.

CASH. Marry, I'll tell thee, Cob: it is a

gentlemanlike monster, bred in the special gallantry of our time, by affectation, and fed by folly.

COB. How? Must it be fed?　　　30

CASH. O, ay, humor is nothing if it be not fed; didst thou never hear that? It's a common phrase, "Feed my humor."

COB. I'll none on it. Humor, avaunt! I know you not; begone! Let who will, make hungry meals for your monstership, it shall not be I. Feed you, quoth he? 'Slid, I ha' much ado to feed myself, especially on these lean rascally days too; and 't had been any other day but a [40 fasting day—a plague on them all for me— by this light, one might have done the commonwealth good service, and have drowned them all i' the flood, two or three hundred thousand years ago. O, I do stomach [5] them hugely. I have a maw [6] now, and 'twere for S[i]r Bevis his horse, against hem.

CASH. I pray thee, good Cob, what makes thee so out of love with fasting [50 days?

COB. Marry, that which will make any man out of love with hem, I think—their bad conditions, and you will needs know. First, they are of a Flemish breed, I am sure on 't, for they raven up [7] more butter than all the days of the week beside; next, they stink of fish and leek porridge miserably; thirdly, they'll keep a man devoutly hungry all day, and at night send him [60 supperless to bed.

CASH. Indeed, these are faults, Cob.

COB. Nay, and this were all, 'twere something; but they are the only known enemies to my generation. A fasting day no sooner comes but my lineage goes to wrack. Poor cobs, they smoke for it, they are made martyrs o' the gridiron, they melt in passion; and your maids too know this, and yet would have me turn Han- [70 nibal,[8] and eat my own fish and blood. (*He pulls out a red herring.*) My princely coz, fear nothing; I have not the heart to devour you, and I might be made as rich as King Cophetua. O, that I had room for my tears! I could weep salt water enough now to preserve the lives of ten thousand of my kin! But I may curse none but these

[1] That which.　　　　[2] Ablaze.
[3] *Humor* had superseded *rheum* as a fashionable term.　　　　[4] Corruption of *Mass.*

[5] Resent.　　　　[7] Devour.
[6] Stomach, appetite.　　　　[8] *I.e.*, cannibal.

filthy almanacs; for, an 'twere not for them, these days of persecution would ne'er [80 be known. I'll be hanged an some fish-monger's son do not make of [1] hem, and puts in more fasting days than he should do, because he would utter [2] his father's dried stockfish and stinking conger.[3]

CASH. 'Slight, peace! Thou'lt be beaten like a stockfish else. Here is Mr. Matthew. Now must I look out for a messenger to my master.   [*Exeunt.*]

ACT III. SCENE v.

[*The same.*]

Wellbred, Ed[ward] Knowell, Brainworm, Bobadill, Matthew, Stephen, Thomas,[4] Cob.[5]

[WELL.] Beshrew me, but it was an ab-solute good jest, and exceedingly well carried!

E. KNOW. Ay, and our ignorance main-tained it as well, did it not?

WELL. Yes, faith; but was 't possible thou shouldst not know him? I forgive Mr. Stephen, for he is stupidity itself.

E. KNOW. Fore God, not I, and I might have been joined patten [6] with one of [10 the seven wise masters for knowing him. He had so writhen [7] himself into the habit of one of your poor *infanterie*,[8] your decayed, ruinous, worm-eaten gentlemen of the round,[9] such as have vowed to sit on the skirts of the city—let your provost and his half dozen of halberdiers do what they can—and have translated begging out of the old hackney pace to a fine easy amble, and made it run as smooth off [20 the tongue as a shovegroat shilling.[10] Into the likeness of one of these *reformados* [11] had he molded himself so perfectly, ob-serving every trick of their action, as varying the accent, swearing with an em-phasis, indeed, all with so special and exquisite a grace, that, hadst thou seen

[1] Make.   [2] Vend.
[3] "Wednesday and Friday were fast days legally enforced for the benefit of the fisheries" (Smithson).
[4] *I.e.*, Cash.   [7] Twisted.
[5] Last two enter later.   [8] Infantry.
[6] By letters patent.   [9] Military patrol.
[10] A smooth shilling used in the game of shovel-board.
[11] "Officers of a re-formed or disbanded com-pany" (Simpson).

him, thou wouldst have sworn he might have been sergeant major,[12] if not lieutenant coronel,[13] to the regiment.   30

WELL. Why, Brainworm, who would have thought thou hadst been such an artificer?

E. KNOW. An artificer! An architect! Except a man had studied begging all his lifetime, and been a weaver of language from his infancy for the clothing of it, I never saw his rival.

WELL. Where got'st thou this coat, I mar'l?   40

BRA. Of a Houndsditch man, sir, one of the devil's near kinsmen, a broker.[14]

WELL. That cannot be, if the proverb hold; for "A crafty knave needs no broker."

BRA. True, sir; but I did need a broker; ergo—

WELL. Well put off—no "crafty knave," you'll say.

E. KNOW. Tut, he has more of these shifts.   50

BRA. And yet, where I have one, the broker has ten,[15] sir.

[*Enter Cash.*]

CASH. Francis! Martin! Ne'er a one to be found now? What a spite's this?

WELL. How now, Thomas? Is my brother Kitely within?

CASH. No, sir, my master went forth e'en now; but Master Downright is with-in.—Cob! What, Cob! Is he gone too?

WELL. Whither went your master? [60 Thomas, canst thou tell?

CASH. I know not. To Justice Clem-ent's, I think, sir.—Cob!

E. KNOW. Justice Clement! What's he?

WELL. Why, dost thou not know him? He is a city magistrate, a justice here, an excellent good lawyer, and a great scholar, but the only mad, merry old fellow in Europe. I showed him you the other day.   70

E. KNOW. O, is that he? I remember him now. Good faith, and he has a very strange presence, methinks; it shows as if he stood out of the rank from other men. I have heard many of his jests i' univer-

[12] A rank corresponding to the modern major.
[13] Colonel.   [14] Pawnbroker.
[15] Punning on the meaning of *changes of cloth-ing*.

sity. They say he will commit a man for taking the wall [1] of his horse.

WELL. Ay, or wearing his cloak of [2] one shoulder, or serving of God; anything, indeed, if it come in the way of his humor.

Cash goes in and out calling.

CASH. Gasper! Martin! Cob! Heart, where should they be, trow?   82

BOB. Master Kitely's man, pray thee vouchsafe us the lighting of this match.

CASH. Fire on your match! No time but now to vouchsafe?—Francis! Cob!
[Exit.]

BOB. Body of me! Here's the remainder of seven pound since yesterday was seven-night. 'Tis your right *Trinidado!* [3] Did you never take any, Master Stephen? [90

STE. No, truly, sir; but I'll learn to take it now, since you commend it so.

BOB. Sir, believe me upon my relation, for what I tell you the world shall not reprove. [4] I have been in the Indies, where this herb grows, where neither myself nor a dozen gentlemen more, of my knowledge, have received the taste of any other nutriment in the world for the space of one-and-twenty weeks but the fume of this simple [5] only; therefore it cannot be but 'tis [101 most divine. Further, take it in the nature, in the true kind; so, it makes an antidote, that, had you taken the most deadly poisonous plant in all Italy, it should expel it, and clarify you, with as much ease as I speak. And for your green wound, your balsamum and your St. John's wort are all mere gulleries and trash to it, especially your *Trinidado;* [110 your *Nicotian* [6] is good too. I could say what I know of the virtue of it, for the expulsion of rheums, raw humors, crudities, obstructions, with a thousand of this kind; but I profess myself no quacksalver. Only thus much: by Hercules, I do hold it, and will affirm it before any prince in Europe, to be the most sovereign and precious weed that ever the earth tendered to the use of man.   120

E. KNOW. This speech would ha' done decently in a tobacco trader's mouth.

[Enter Cash with Cob.]

CASH. At Justice Clement's he is, in the middle of Coleman Street.

COB. O! O!

BOB. Where's the match I gave thee, Master Kitely's man?

CASH. Would his match and he, and pipe and all, were at Sancto Domingo! I had forgot it.   *[Exit.]*

COB. By God's me,[7] I mar'l [131 what pleasure or felicity they have in taking this roguish tobacco! It's good for nothing but to choke a man, and fill him full of smoke and embers. There were four died out of one house last week with taking of it, and two more the bell [8] went for yesternight; one of them, they say, will ne'er scape it; he voided a bushel of soot yesterday, upward and downward. [140 By the stocks, an there were no wiser men than I, I'ld have it present whipping, man or woman, that should but deal with a tabacco pipe. Why, it will stifle them all in the end, as many as use it; it's little better than ratsbane or rosaker.[9]

Bobadill beats him with a cudgel.

ALL. O, good captain, hold, hold!

BOB. You base cullion, you!

[Enter Cash.]

CASH. Sir, here's your match.—Come, thou must needs be talking too; thou'rt [150 well enough served.

COB. Nay, he will not meddle with his match, I warrant you. Well, it shall be a dear beating, and I live.

BOB. Do you prate? Do you murmur?

E. KNOW. Nay, good captain, will you regard the humor of a fool? Away, knave!

WELL. Thomas, get him away.
[Exeunt Cash and Cob.]

BOB. A whoreson filthy slave, a dung worm, an excrement! Body o' Cæsar, [160 but that I scorn to let forth so mean a spirit, I'ld ha' stabbed him to the earth.

WELL. Marry, the law forbid, sir!

BOB. By Pharaoh's foot, I would have done it.

STE. *[Aside.]* O, he swears admirably! "By Pharaoh's foot!" "Body of Cæsar!"

---

[1] The cleanest part of the street was nearest the wall.

[2] On.

[3] The best tobacco.

[4] Disprove.

[5] Herb.

[6] A tobacco named from Jacques Nicot.

[7] A mild oath.

[8] Rung for one in mortal extremity.

[9] Poisons.

—I shall never do it, sure. Upon mine
honor, and by Saint George! No, I ha' not
the right grace.   170
MAT. Master Stephen, will you any?
By this air, the most divine tabacco that
ever I drunk.[1]
STE. None, I thank you, sir. O, this
gentleman does it rarely too; but nothing
like the other. "By this air!" "As I am
a gentleman!" "By—"
Master Stephen is practicing to the post.
    [*Exeunt Bobadill and Matthew.*]
BRA. Master, glance, glance! Master
Wellbred!
STE. As I have somewhat to be saved, I
protest—   181
WELL. You are a fool; it needs no
affidavit.
E. KNOW. Cousin, will you any ta-
bacco?
STE. I, sir! Upon my reputation—
E. KNOW. How now, cousin!
STE. I protest, as I am a gentleman, but
no soldier, indeed—
WELL. No, Master Stephen! As [190
I remember, your name is entered in the
artillery garden.[2]
STE. Ay, sir, that's true. Cousin, may
I swear "as I am a soldier" by that?
E. KNOW. O, yes, that you may; it's all
you have for your money.
STE. Then, as I am a gentleman and a
soldier, it is "divine tabacco"!
WELL. But soft, where's Mr. Matthew?
Gone?   200
BRA. No, sir; they went in here.
WELL. O, let's follow them. Mas-
ter Matthew is gone to salute his mis-
tress in verse; we shall ha' the happiness
to hear some of his poetry now; he never
comes unfurnished.—Brainworm?
STE. Brainworm? Where? Is this
Brainworm?
E. KNOW. Ay, cousin; no words of it,
upon your gentility.   210
STE. Not I, "body of me"! "By this
air"! "S[t]. George"! And "the foot of
Pharaoh"!
WELL. Rare! Your cousin's discourse
is simply drawn out with oaths.
E. KNOW. 'Tis larded with hem—a kind
of French dressing, if you love it. [*Exeunt.*]

[1] Smoked.
[2] Practice grounds.

ACT III. SCENE vi.

[*A room in Justice Clement's house in
Coleman Street.*]

Kitely, Cob.

[KITE.] Ha! How many are there, say-
est thou?
COB. Marry, sir, your brother, Master
Wellbred—
KITE. Tut, beside him? What strangers
are there, man?
COB. Strangers? Let me see, one, two;
Mass,
I know not well, there are so many.
KITE. How? So many?
COB. Ay, there's some five or six of them
at the most.
KITE. [*Aside.*] A swarm, a swarm!
Spite of the devil, how they sting my
head
With forkéd stings, thus wide and
large!—But, Cob,   10
How long hast thou been coming hither,
Cob?
COB. A little while, sir.
KITE. Didst thou come running?
COB. No, sir.
KITE. [*Aside.*] Nay, then I am familiar
with thy haste.
Bane to my fortunes! What meant I
to marry?
I, that before was ranked in such content,
My mind at rest too, in so soft a peace,
Being free master of mine own free
thoughts,
And now become a slave? What? Never
sigh;   20
Be of good cheer, man, for thou art a
cuckold.
'Tis done, 'tis done! Nay, when such
flowing store,
Plenty itself, falls in my wife's lap,
The *cornu-copiæ* [3] will be mine, I
know.—But, Cob,
What entertainment had they? I am
sure
My sister and my wife would bid them
welcome! Ha?
COB. Like enough, sir; yet I heard not a
word of it.
KITE. [*Aside.*] No; their lips were sealed
with kisses, and the voice,
Drowned in a flood of joy at their arrival,

[3] Horns of plenty, with an allusion to cuckoldry.

Had lost her motion, state. and faculty.—
Cob, which of them was 't that first
  kissed my wife,   31
My sister, I should say? My wife, alas,
I fear not her. Ha! Who was it, say'st
  thou?

Cob. By my troth, sir, will you have the
  truth of it?

Kite. O, ay, good Cob, I pray thee heartily.

Cob. Then I am a vagabond, and fitter
for Bridewell than your worship's company,
if I saw anybody to be kissed, unless they
would have kissed the post in the middle
of the warehouse,[1] for there I left them [40
all at their tabacco, with a pox!

Kite. How? Were they not gone in
then ere thou cam'st?

Cob. O, no, sir.

Kite. Spite of the devil! What do I
stay here then? Cob, follow me.   [Exit.]

Cob. Nay, soft and fair, I have eggs
on the spit; I cannot go yet, sir. Now am
I, for some five-and-fifty reasons, hammering, hammering revenge. O, for three [50
or four gallons of vinegar to sharpen my
wits! Revenge, vinegar revenge, vinegar
and mustard revenge! Nay, and he had
not lyen[2] in my house, 'twould never have
grieved me; but being my guest, one that,
I'll be sworn, my wife has lent him her
smock off her back, while his one shirt
has been at washing; pawned her necker-
chers[3] for clean bands for him; sold almost all my platters to buy him ta- [60
bacco; and he to turn monster of ingratitude, and strike his lawful host! Well, I
hope to raise up an host of fury for 't! Here
comes Justice Clement.

Act III. Scene vii.

[The same.]

Clement, Knowell, Formal, Cob.

[Clem.] What, 's Master Kitely gone,
Roger?

For. Ay, sir.

Clem. Heart of me! What made him
leave us so abruptly?—How now, sirrah!
What make[4] you here? What would you
have, ha?

Cob. And 't please your worship, I am
a poor neighbor of your worship's—

Clem. A poor neighbor of mine? [10
Why, speak, poor neighbor.

Cob. I dwell, sir, at the sign of the
Water Tankard, hard by the Green Lattice;[5] I have paid scot and lot[6] there any
time this eighteen years.

Clem. To the Green Lattice?

Cob. No, sir, to the parish. Marry, I
have seldom scaped scot-free[7] at the Lattice.

Clem. O, well; what business has [20
my poor neighbor with me?

Cob. And 't like your worship, I am
come to crave the peace of your worship.

Clem. Of me, knave? Peace of me,
knave? Did I e'er hurt thee? Or threaten
thee? Or wrong thee, ha?

Cob. No, sir; but your worship's warrant for one that has wronged me, sir. His
arms are at too much liberty; I would fain
have them bound to a treaty of peace, [30
an my credit could compass it with your
worship.

Clem. Thou goest far enough about
for 't, I am sure.

Know. Why, dost thou go in danger of
thy life for him, friend?

Cob. No, sir; but I go in danger of my
death every hour, by his means; an I die
within a twelvemonth and a day,[8] I may
swear by the law of the land that he [40
killed me.

Clem. How? How, knave? Swear he
killed thee? And by the law? What pretense? What color[9] hast thou for that?

Cob. Marry, and 't please your worship, both black and blue; color enough,
I warrant you. I have it here to show your
worship.   [Shows his bruises.]

Clem. What is he that gave you this,
sirrah?   50

Cob. A gentleman and a soldier, he
says he is, o' the city here.

Clem. A soldier o' the city? What call
you him?

Cob. Captain Bobadill.

Clem. Bobadill? And why did he bob[10]

---

[1] Shop.   [3] Neckerchiefs.
[2] Lain.   [4] Do.

[5] A tavern.   [7] Without paying a tavern bill.
[6] Parish taxes.
[8] A twelvemonth and a day was the legal time
for determining the cause of death from bodily
injury.
[9] Reason.   [10] Strike.

and beat you, sirrah? How began the quarrel betwixt you, ha? Speak truly, knave, I advise you.

Cob. Marry, indeed, and please [60 your worship, only because I spake against their vagrant tabacco, as I came by hem when they were taking on 't; for nothing else.

Clem. Ha! You speak against tabacco?— Formal, his name.

For. What's your name, sirrah?

Cob. Oliver, sir; Oliver Cob, sir.

Clem. Tell Oliver Cob he shall go to the jail, Formal. 70

For. Oliver Cob, my master, Justice Clement, says you shall go to the jail.

Cob. O, I beseech your worship, for God's sake, dear master justice!

Clem. Nay, God's precious![1] And such drunkards and tankards as you are come to dispute of tabacco once, I have done. Away with him!

Cob. O, good master justice!—[To Knowell.] Sweet old gentleman! 80

Know. Sweet Oliver, would I could do thee any good!—Justice Clement, let me entreat you, sir.

Clem. What? A threadbare rascal, a beggar, a slave that never drunk out of better than pisspot metal[2] in his life! And he to deprave[3] and abuse the virtue of an herb so generally received in the courts of princes, the chambers of nobles, the bowers of sweet ladies, the cabins[4] [90 of soldiers!—Roger, away with him! By God's precious—I say, go to.

Cob. Dear master justice, let me be beaten again; I have deserved it; but not the prison, I beseech you.

Know. Alas, poor Oliver!

Clem. Roger, make him a warrant.— [Aside.] He shall not go; I but fear[5] the knave.

For. [Aside.] Do not stink, sweet [100 Oliver; you shall not go.—My master will give you a warrant.

Cob. O, the Lord maintain his worship, his worthy worship!

Clem. Away, despatch him.—[Exeunt Formal and Cob.] How now, Master Knowell, in dumps? In dumps? Come, this becomes not.

Know. Sir, would I could not feel my cares. 110

Clem. Your cares are nothing; they are like my cap, soon put on, and as soon put off. What? Your son is old enough to govern himself. Let him run his course; it's the only way to make him a staid man. If he were an unthrift,[6] a ruffian, a drunkard, or a licentious liver, then you had reason; you had reason to take care; but, being none of these, mirth's my witness, an I had twice so [120 many cares as you have, I'd drown them all in a cup of sack. Come, come, let's try it. I muse[7] your parcel[8] of a soldier returns not all this while. [Exeunt].

Act IV. Scene i.

[A room in Kitely's house.]

Downright, Dame Kitely.

[Dow.] Well, sister, I tell you true; and you'll find it so in the end.

Dame. Alas, brother, what would you have me to do? I cannot help it; you see my brother brings hem in here; they are his friends.

Dow. His friends? His fiends! 'Slud,[9] they do nothing but haunt him up and down like a sort of unlucky sprites, and tempt him to all manner of villainy [10 that can be thought of. Well, by this light, a little thing would make me play the devil with some of hem; and 'twere not more for your husband's sake than anything else, I'ld make the house too hot for the best on hem; they should say, and swear, hell were broken loose, ere they went hence. But, by God's will, 'tis nobody's fault but yours; for, an you had done as you might have done, they should have been [20 purboiled[10] and baked too, every mother's son, ere they should ha' come in, e'er a one of hem.

Dame. God's my life! Did you ever hear the like? What a strange man is this! Could I keep out all them, think you? I should put myself against half a dozen men, should I? Good faith, you'ld mad the patient'st body in the world, to hear you talk so, without any sense [30 or reason.

---

[1] God's precious body.   [2] Pewter.
[3] Disparage.   [4] Tents.   [5] Frighten.
[6] Prodigal.   [8] Portion.
[7] Wonder.   [9] God's Lord.
[10] Parboiled, boiled thoroughly.

Act IV. Scene ii.

[*The same.*]

*Mrs. Bridget, Mr. Matthew, [observed by]
Dame Kitely, Downright, Wellbred,
Stephen, Ed[ward] Knowell, Bobadill,
Brainworm, Cash.*[1]

[Brid.] Servant,[2] in troth you are too
    prodigal
Of your wit's treasure, thus to pour it
    forth
Upon so mean a subject as my worth.
Mat. You say well, mistress, and I mean
    as well.
Dow. Hoyday,[3] here is stuff!
Well. O, now stand close;[4] pray heaven,
she can get him to read! He should do it
of his own natural impudency.
Brid. Servant, what is this same, I
pray you?   10
Mat. Marry, an elegy, an elegy, an
odd toy—
Dow. To mock an ape withal![5] O, I
could sew up his mouth now.
Dame. Sister, I pray you let's hear it.
Dow. Are you rime-given too?
Mat. Mistress, I'll read it, if you please.
Brid. Pray you do, servant.
Dow. O, here's no foppery![6] Death,
I can endure the stocks better. [*Exit.*]   20
E. Know. What ails thy brother? Can
he not hold his water at reading of a ballad?
Well. O, no; a rime to him is worse than
cheese or a bagpipe. But mark, you lose
the protestation.
Mat. Faith, I did it in an humor; I
know not how it is. But please you come
near, sir. This gentleman has judgment; he
knows how to censure of a—pray you, sir,
you can judge?   30
Ste. Not I, sir; upon my reputation,
and by the foot of Pharaoh!
Well. O, chide your cousin for swearing.
E. Know. Not I, so long as he does
not forswear himself.
Bob. Master Matthew, you abuse the
expectation of your dear mistress and her
fair sister. Fie! While you live, avoid this
prolixity.   40

Mat. I shall, sir; well, *incipere dulce.*[7]
E. Know. How, *insipere dulce!* "A
sweet thing to be a fool," indeed!
Well. What, do you take *incipere* in
that sense?
E. Know. You do not, you? This was
your villainy, to gull him with a motte,[8]
Well. O, the benchers'[9] phrase! *Pauca
verba, pauca verba!*[10]
Mat. [*Reading.*] "Rare creature, let me
    speak without offense;   50
Would God my rude words had the in-
    fluence
To rule thy thoughts, as thy fair looks
    do mine;
Then shouldst thou be his prisoner, who
    is thine."
E. Know. [*Aside.*] This is in *Hero and
Leander!*
Well. [*Aside.*] O, ay! Peace, we shall
have more of this.
Mat. "Be not unkind and fair; mis-
    shapen stuff
Is of behavior boisterous and rough."
Well. [*Aside.*] How like you that, sir?
*Master Stephen answers with shaking his
    head.*
E. Know. [*Aside.*] 'Slight, he shakes [61
his head like a bottle, to feel and there be
any brain in it!
Mat. But observe the catastrophe now:
"And I in duty will exceed all other,
As you in beauty do excel Love's
    mother."
E. Know. [*Aside.*] Well, I'll have him
free of[11] the wit brokers, for he utters noth-
ing but stol'n remnants.
Well. [*Aside.*] O, forgive it him.   70
E. Know. A filching rogue, hang him!
And from the dead? It's worse than sacri-
lege.
Well. [*Coming forward.*] Sister, what ha'
you here? Verses? Pray you, let's see.
Who made these verses? They are ex-
cellent good.
Mat. O, Master Wellbred, 'tis your
disposition to say so, sir. They were good
i' the morning; I made hem *ex tem-* [80
pore this morning.
Well. How? *Ex tempore?*
Mat. Ay, would I might be hanged

---

[1] Enters later.   [3] Exclamation of surprise.
[2] Lover.   [4] Aside.
[5] To dupe a simpleton with.   [6] Deceit.

[7] It is sweet to begin.   [8] *Mot*, word.
[9] Justices', or alehouse loafers'.
[10] Few words.   [11] Made a member of.

else. Ask Captain Bobadill; he saw me write them, at the—pox on it!—the Star yonder.

Bra. [*Aside.*] Can he find in his heart to curse the stars so?

E. Know. [*Aside.*] Faith, his are even with him; they ha' cursed him enough [90 already.

Ste. Cousin, how do you like this gentleman's verses?

E. Know. O, admirable! The best that ever I heard, coz.

Ste. Body o' Cæsar, they are admirable! The best that ever I heard, as I am a soldier!

[*Enter Downright.*]

Dow. [*Aside.*] I am vexed; I can hold ne'er a bone of me still! Heart, I think they mean to build and breed here. 100

Well. Sister, you have a simple servant here, that crowns your beauty with such *encomions* [1] and devices; you may see what it is to be the mistress of a wit that can make your perfections so transparent that every blear eye may look through them, and see him drowned over head and ears in the deep well of desire. Sister Kitely, I marvel you get you not a servant that can rime, and do tricks too. 110

Dow. [*Aside.*] O monster! Impudence itself! Tricks? [2]

Dame. Tricks, brother? What tricks?

Brid. Nay, speak, I pray you, what tricks?

Dame. Ay, never spare anybody here; but say, what tricks?

Brid. Passion of my heart, do tricks?

Well. 'Slight, here's a trick vied and revied! [3] Why, you monkeys, you, [120 what a caterwauling do you keep! Has he not given you rimes and verses and tricks?

Dow. [*Aside.*] O, the fiend!

Well. Nay, you lamp of virginity, that take it in snuff [4] so, come, and cherish this tame poetical fury in your servant; you'll be begged else shortly for a concealment. [5]

[1] Encomiums.
[2] Punning on the sense of *wantonness*.
[3] A bet made and raised.　[4] Take offense at.
[5] "This is a reference to the unauthorized holding of sequestered lands, such as those which had belonged to the monasteries. Elizabeth had appointed commissions to search such holdings or 'concealments,' which her courtiers often 'begged'" (Neilson).

Go to, reward his muse. You cannot give him less than a shilling, in conscience, for the book he had it out of cost him a [130 teston [6] at least. How now, gallants? Mr. Matthew? Captain? What, all sons of silence? No spirit?

Dow. Come, you might practice your ruffian tricks somewhere else, and not here, I wusse; this is no tavern nor drinking school to vent your exploits in.

Well. How now! Whose cow has calved? [7]

Dow. Marry, that has mine, sir. [140 Nay, boy, never look askance at me for the matter; I'll tell you of it, I, sir. You and your companions mend yourselves when I ha' done.

Well. My companions!

Dow. Yes, sir, your companions, so I say; I am not afraid of you, nor them neither; your hang-bys here. You must have your poets and your potlings, [8] your *soldados* and *foolados* to follow you up [150 and down the city; and here they must come to domineer and swagger.—Sirrah, you ballad singer, and slops, [9] your fellow there, get you out; get you home; or, by this steel, I'll cut off your ears, and that presently.

Well. 'Slight, stay, let's see what he dare do! Cut off his ears? Cut a whetstone! You are an ass, do you see? Touch any man here, and, by this hand, I'll [160 run my rapier to the hilts in you.

Dow. Yea, that would I fain see, boy.
They all draw, and they of the house make
out to part them.

Dame. O Jesu! Murder! Thomas! Gasper!

Brid. Help, help! Thomas!

[*Enter Cash and Servants.*]

E. Know. Gentlemen, forbear, I pray you.

Bob. Well, sirrah, you Holofernes; by my hand, I will pink your flesh full of holes with my rapier for this; I will, by this [170 good heaven!—
They offer to fight again and are parted.
Nay, let him come, let him come, gentle-

[6] Sixpence.
[7] *I.e.*, what's the matter?
[8] Tipplers.　　　　[9] *I.e.*, Bobadill.

men; by the body of Saint George, I'll
not kill him.

CASH. Hold, hold, good gentlemen.

Dow. You whoreson, bragging cois-
tril! [1]

ACT IV. SCENE iii.

[The same.]

To them, Kitely.

[KITE.] Why, how now? What's the mat-
  ter? What's the stir here?
Whence springs the quarrel? Thomas!
  Where is he?
Put up your weapons, and put off this
  rage.
My wife and sister, they are the cause of
  this.
What, Thomas! Where is this knave?

CASH. Here, sir.

WELL. Come, let's go; this is one of my
brother's ancient humors, this.

STE. I am glad nobody was hurt by his
ancient humor.   10

*[Exeunt Wellbred, Stephen, Edward Know-
    ell, Bobadill, Brainworm, and Serv-
    ants.]*

KITE. Why, how now, brother, who enforced this brawl?

Dow. A sort of lewd rakehells that
care neither for God nor the devil. And
they must come here to read ballads, and
roguery, and trash! I'll mar the knot of
hem ere I sleep, perhaps—especially Bob
there, he that's all manner of shapes—and
Songs and Sonnets, his fellow.

BRID. Brother, indeed you are too violent,
Too sudden in your humor; and you
  know   20
My brother Wellbred's temper will not
  bear
Any reproof, chiefly in such a presence,
Where every slight disgrace he should
  receive
Might wound him in opinion and respect.

Dow. Respect? What talk you of
respect 'mong such as ha' nor spark of
manhood nor good manners? 'Sdeynes,
I am ashamed to hear you! Respect! *[Exit.]*

BRID. Yes, there was one, a civil gentleman,
And very worthily demeaned himself.   30

KITE. O, that was some love of yours,
  sister.

———
[1] Knave.

BRID. A love of mine? I would it were no
  worse, brother;
You'ld pay my portion sooner than you
  think for.

DAME. Indeed he seemed to be a gentleman of an exceeding fair disposition, and
of very excellent good parts.

[Exeunt Dame Kitely and Bridget.]

KITE. *[Aside.]* Her love, by heaven! My
  wife's minion!
"Fair disposition"? "Excellent good
  parts"?
Death, these phrases are intolerable!
Good parts? How should she know his
  parts?   40
His parts? Well, well, well, well, well, well!
It is too plain, too clear.—Thomas, come
  hither.
What, are they gone?

CASH.   Ay, sir, they went in.
My mistress and your sister—

KITE. Are any of the gallants within?

CASH. No, sir, they are all gone.

KITE.   Art thou sure of it?

CASH. I can assure you, sir.

KITE. What gentleman was that they
praised so, Thomas?

CASH. One, they call him Master   [50
Knowell, a handsome young gentleman, sir.

KITE. Ay, I thought so; my mind gave me
  as much.
I'll die, but they have hid him i' the house
Somewhere; I'll go and search; go with
  me, Thomas.
Be true to me, and thou shalt find me a
  master.   *[Exeunt.]*

ACT IV. SCENE iv.

[The lane before Cob's house.]

Cob, Tib. [2]

COB. *[Knocking.]* What, Tib! Tib, I
say!

TIB. *[Within.]* How now, what cuckold
is that knocks so hard? *[Enters.]* O husband, is 't you? What's the news?

COB. Nay, you have stonned [3] me, i'
faith; you ha' giv'n me a knock o' the
forehead will stick by me. Cuckold? 'Slid,
cuckold?

TIB. Away, you fool! Did I know it   [10
was you that knocked? Come, come, you
may call me as bad when you list. [4]

———
[2] Enters later.   [3] Stunned.   [4] Please.

Cob. May I? Tib, you are a whore.

Tib. You lie in your throat, husband.

Cob. How, the lie? And in my throat too? Do you long to be stabbed, ha?

Tib. Why, you are no soldier, I hope?

Cob. O, must you be stabbed by a soldier? Mass, that's true! When was Bobadill here, your captain? That [20 rogue, that foist,[1] that fencing Burgullion? [2] I'll tickle him, i' faith.

Tib. Why, what's the matter, trow?

Cob. O, he has basted me rarely, sumptiously! But I have it here in black and white. [*Pulls out the warrant.*] For his black and blue, shall [3] pay him. O, the justice, the honestest old brave Trojan in London; I do honor the very flea of his dog. A plague on him, though, [30 he put me once in a villainous filthy fear; marry, it vanished away like the smoke of tabacco; but I was smoked [4] soundly first. I thank the devil and his good angel, my guest. Well, wife, or Tib, which you will, get you in and lock the door; I charge you let nobody in to you, wife; nobody in to you; those are my words. Not Captain Bob himself, nor the fiend in his likeness. You are a woman; you have [40 flesh and blood enough in you to be tempted; therefore keep the door shut upon all comers.

Tib. I warrant you, there shall nobody enter here without my consent.

Cob. Nor with your consent, sweet Tib; and so I leave you.

Tib. It's more than you know, whether you leave me so.

Cob. How?　　　　　　　　　50

Tib. Why, "sweet."

Cob. Tut, sweet or sour, thou art a flower. Keep close thy door; I ask no more.
　　　　　　　　　　　　[*Exeunt.*]

Act IV. Scene v.

[*A room in the Windmill.*]

Ed[ward] Knowell, Wellbred, Stephen, Brainworm.

[E. Know.] Well, Brainworm, perform this business happily, and thou makest a purchase of my love forever.

Well. I' faith, now let thy spirits use their best faculties. But, at any hand,[5]

---

remember the message to my brother, for there's no other means to start him.

Bra. I warrant you, sir; fear nothing; I have a nimble soul has waked all forces of my fant'sy by this time, and put [10 hem in true motion. What you have possessed me withal,[6] I'll discharge it amply, sir; make it no question.

Well. Forth, and prosper, Brainworm.— [*Exit Brainworm.*] Faith, Ned, how dost thou approve of my abilities in this device?

E. Know. Troth, well, howsoever; but it will come excellent if it take.

Well. Take, man? Why, it cannot [20 choose but take, if the circumstances miscarry not. But tell me ingenuously, dost thou affect my sister Bridget as thou pretend'st?

E. Know. Friend, am I worth belief?

Well. Come, do not protest. In faith, she is a maid of good ornament and much modesty; and, except I conceived very worthily of her, thou shouldest not have her.　　　　　　　　　30

E. Know. Nay, that, I am afraid, will be a question yet, whether I shall have her or no.

Well. 'Slid, thou shalt have her; by this light, thou shalt.

E. Know. Nay, do not swear.

Well. By this hand, thou shalt have her; I'll go fetch her presently. Point [7] but where to meet, and as I am an honest man I'll bring her.　　　　　　40

E. Know. Hold, hold, be temperate.

Well. Why, by—what shall I swear by? Thou shalt have her, as I am—

E. Know. Pray thee, be at peace; I am satisfied, and do believe thou wilt omit no offered occasion to make my desires complete.

Well. Thou shalt see and know I will not.　　　　　　　　　[*Exeunt.*]

Act IV. Scene vi.

[*A street in the Old Jewry.*]

Formal, Knowell, Brainworm.[8]

[For.] Was your man a soldier, sir?

Know. Ay, a knave; I took him begging o' the way,
This morning as I came over Moorfields.

---

[1] Pickpocket.　　　　　　[3] *I.e.*, I shall.
[2] Bully.　　　[4] Beaten.　　[5] Rate.

[6] Informed me of.　[7] Appoint.　[8] Enters later.

[*Enter Brainworm.*]

O, here he is!—Yo' have made fair speed,
　believe me.
Where, i' the name of sloth, could you
　be thus—
Bra. Marry, peace be my comfort,
where I thought I should have had little
comfort of your worship's service.
Know. How so?
Bra. O, sir, your coming to the [10
city, your entertainment of me, and your
sending me to watch—indeed all the circumstances either of your charge or my
employment are as open to your son as to
yourself.
Know. How should that be, unless that
　villain, Brainworm,
Have told him of the letter, and dis-
　covered [1]
All that I strictly charged him to con-
　ceal? 'Tis so.
Bra. I am partly o' the faith, 'tis so,
　indeed.
Know. But how should he know thee
to be my man?　　　　　　　　　　21
Bra. Nay, sir, I cannot tell, unless it
be by the black art. Is not your son a
scholar, sir?
Know. Yes, but I hope his soul is not
　allied
Unto such hellish practice; if it were,
I had just cause to weep my part in him,
And curse the time of his creation.
But where didst thou find them, Fitz-
　sword?
Bra. You should rather ask where [30
they found me, sir, for, I'll be sworn, I
was going along in the street, thinking
nothing, when, of a sudden, a voice calls,
"Mr. Knowell's man!" another cries,
"Soldier!" and thus half a dozen of them,
till they had called me within a house,
where I no sooner came but they seemed
men, and out flew all their rapiers at my
bosom, with some three or four score
oaths to accompany hem; and all to [40
tell me I was but a dead man if I did not
confess where you were, and how I was
employed, and about what; which when
they could not get out of me (as, I protest,
they must ha' dissected and made an
anatomy [2] o' me first, and so I told hem),

they locked me up into a room i' the top
of a high house, whence by great miracle
(having a light heart) I slid down by a
bottom [3] of packthread into the [50
street, and so scaped. But, sir, thus much
I can assure you, for I heard it while I
was locked up: there were a great many
rich merchants and brave [4] citizens' wives
with hem at a feast; and your son, Mr. Edward, withdrew with one of hem, and has
pointed to meet her anon at one Cob's
house, a water bearer that dwells by the
Wall. Now there your worship shall be sure
to take him, for there he preys, and fail
he will not.　　　　　　　　　　61
Know. Nor will I fail to break his match,
　I doubt not.
Go thou along with Justice Clement's
　man,
And stay there for me. At one Cob's
　house, say'st thou?
Bra. Ay, sir, there you shall have him.—
[*Exit Knowell.—Aside.*]　Yes—invisible!
Much wench, or much son! 'Slight, when he
has stayed there three or four hours, travail-
ing with the expectation of wonders, and
at length be delivered of air, O, the [70
sport that I should then take to look on him,
if I durst! But now I mean to appear no
more afore him in this shape. I have another trick to act yet. O, that I were so
happy as to light on a nupson [5] now of [6]
this justice's novice!—Sir, I make you
stay somewhat long.
For. Not a whit, sir. Pray you, what
do you mean, sir?
Bra. I was putting up some papers—
For. You ha' been lately in the [81
wars, sir, it seems.
Bra. Marry, have I, sir, to my loss, and
expense of all, almost—
For. Troth, sir, I would be glad to bestow a pottle [7] of wine o' you, if it please
you to accept it—
Bra. O, sir—
For. But to hear the manner of your
services, and your devices in the wars, [90
they say they be very strange, and not like
those a man reads in the Roman histories,
or sees at Mile End.
Bra. No, I assure you, sir; why, at any

---

[1] Revealed.　　　　　　　　　　[2] Skeleton.

[3] Ball.
[4] Finely dressed.　　　　　　　　[6] In.
[5] Simpleton.　　　　　　　　　　[7] Bottle.

time when it please you, I shall be ready to discourse to you all I know.—[*Aside.*] And more too somewhat.

FOR. No better time than now, sir. We'll go to the Windmill; there we shall have a cup of neat grist,[1] we call it. [100 I pray you, sir, let me request you to the Windmill.

BRA. I'll follow you, sir.—[*Aside.*] And make grist o' you, if I have good luck.

[*Exeunt.*]

ACT IV. SCENE vii.

[*The same.*]

[2] *Matthew, Ed[ward] Knowell, Bobadill, Stephen, Downright.*[3]

[MAT.] Sir, did your eyes ever taste the like clown of him where we were to-day, Mr. Wellbred's half brother? I think the whole earth cannot show his parallel, by this daylight.

E. KNOW. We were now speaking of him; Captain Bobadill tells me he is fall'n foul o' you too.

MAT. O, ay, sir, he threatened me with the *bastinado.* 10

BOB. Ay, but I think I taught you prevention this morning for that. You shall kill him beyond question, if you be so generously[4] minded.

MAT. Indeed, it is a most excellent trick. [*Fences.*]

BOB. O, you do not give spirit enough to your motion; you are too tardy, too heavy! O, it must be done like lightning. Hay![5]

He practices at a post.

MAT. Rare, captain! 20

BOB. Tut! 'Tis nothing, and 't be not done in a—*punto.*[6]

E. KNOW. Captain, did you ever prove yourself upon any of our masters of defense here?

MAT. O good sir! Yes, I hope he has.

BOB. I will tell you, sir. Upon my first coming to the city, after my long travel[7]

---

[1] Liquor sold at the Windmill.
[2] The marginal direction *To them* is erroneously printed here.
[3] Enters later. 　　[4] Gentlemanly.
[5] A fencer's cry, meaning "a hit!"—"you have it!"
[6] Instant, with a pun on *thrust with a point.*
[7] With a pun on *travail.*

for knowledge in that mystery only, there came three or four of hem to me, at [30 a gentleman's house where it was my chance to be resident at that time, to entreat my presence at their schools, and withal so much importuned me that, I protest to you as I am a gentleman, I was ashamed of their rude demeanor out of all measure. Well, I told hem that to come to a public school, they should pardon me, it was opposite, in diameter,[8] to my humor; but, if so they would [40 give their attendance at my lodging, I protested to do them what right or favor I could, as I was a gentleman, and so forth.

E. KNOW. So, sir, then you tried their skill?

BOB. Alas, soon tried! You shall hear, sir. Within two or three days after, they came; and, by honesty, fair sir, believe me, I graced them exceedingly, showed them some two or three tricks of pre- [50 vention have purchased hem, since, a credit—to admiration. They cannot deny this; and yet now they hate me; and why? Because I am excellent; and for no other vile reason on the earth.

E. KNOW. This is strange and barbarous, as ever I heard.

BOB. Nay, for a more instance of their preposterous natures, but note, sir. They have assaulted me some three, four, [60 five, six of them together, as I have walked alone in divers skirts i' the town, as Turnbull, Whitechapel, Shoreditch,[9] which were then my quarters, and since, upon the Exchange, at my lodging, and at my ordinary, where I have driven them afore me the whole length of a street, in the open view of all our gallants, pitying to hurt them, believe me. Yet all this lenity will not o'ercome their spleen; they [70 will be doing with the pismire,[10] raising a hill a man may spurn abroad with his foot at pleasure. By myself, I could have slain them all, but I delight not in murder. I am loath to bear any other than this *bastinado* for hem; yet I hold it good polity not to go disarmed, for, though I be skillful, I may be oppressed with multitudes.

E. KNOW. Ay, believe me, may you, sir; and, in my conceit,[11] our whole [80

---

[8] *I.e.,* diametrically. 　　[10] Ant.
[9] Disreputable districts of London. 　[11] Opinion.

nation should sustain the loss by it, if it were so.

Bob. Alas, no! What's a peculiar [1] man to a nation? Not seen.

E. Know. O, but your skill, sir!

Bob. Indeed, that might be some loss; but who respects it? I will tell you, sir, by the way of private, and under seal; I am a gentleman, and live here obscure, and to myself; but were I known to her [90 majesty and the lords, observe me, I would undertake, upon this poor head and life, for the public benefit of the state, not only to spare the entire lives of her subjects in general, but to save the one half, nay, three parts of her yearly charge in holding war, and against what enemy soever. And how would I do it, think you?

E. Know. Nay, I know not, nor [100 can I conceive.

Bob. Why thus, sir. I would select nineteen more to [2] myself throughout the land; gentlemen they should be of good spirit, strong and able constitution; I would choose them by an instinct, a character, that I have; and I would teach these nineteen the special rules, as your *punto*, your *reverso*, your *stoccata*, your *imbroccata*, your *passada*, your *mon-* [110 *tanto* [3]—till they could all play very near, or altogether, as well as myself. This done, say the enemy were forty thousand strong, we twenty would come into the field the tenth of March, or thereabouts; and we would challenge twenty of the enemy; they could not in their honor refuse us. Well, we would kill them; challenge twenty more, kill them; twenty more, kill them; twenty more, kill them too; and thus [120 would we kill every man his twenty a day—that's twenty score; twenty score, that's two hundreth; two hundreth a day, five days a thousand; forty thousand; forty times five, five times forty, two hundreth days kills them all up, by computation. And this will I venture my poor gentlemanlike carcass to perform, provided there be no treason practiced upon us, by fair and discreet manhood; [130 that is, civilly by the sword.

E. Know. Why, are you so sure of your hand, captain, at all times?

Bob. Tut! Never miss [4] thrust, upon my reputation with you.

E. Know. I would not stand in Downright's state then, an you meet him, for the wealth of any one street in London.

Bob. Why, sir, you mistake me. If he were here now, by this welkin, I would [140 not draw my weapon on him. Let this gentleman do his mind; but I will *bastinado* him, by the bright sun, wherever I meet him.

Mat. Faith, and I'll have a fling at him, at my distance.

Downright walks over the stage.

E. Know. God's so, look where he is! Yonder he goes.

Dow. What peevish luck have I, I cannot meet with these bragging [150 rascals?

Bob. It's not he, is it?

E. Know. Yes, faith, it is he.

Mat. I'll be hanged, then, if that were he.

E. Know. Sir, keep your hanging good for some greater matter, for I assure you that was he.

Ste. Upon my reputation, it was he.

Bob. Had I thought it had been [160 he, he must not have gone so; but I can hardly be induced to believe it was he yet.

E. Know. That I think, sir.

[Enter Downright.]

But see, he is come again!

Dow. O, Pharaoh's foot, have I found you? Come, draw, to your tools; draw, gipsy, or I'll thresh you.

Bob. Gentleman of valor, I do believe in thee; hear me—   170

Dow. Draw your weapon then.

Bob. Tall [5] man, I never thought on it till now: body of me, I had a warrant of the peace served on me, even now as I came along, by a water bearer; this gentleman saw it, Mr. Matthew.

Dow. 'Sdeath, you will not draw then?

*He beats him and disarms him; Matthew
runs away.*

Bob. Hold, hold! Under thy favor, forbear!

---

[1] Individual.
[2] In addition to.
[3] Italian fencing terms.

[4] *I.e.,* I never miss.   [5] Bold.

Dow. Prate again, as you like [180 this, you whoreson foist, you! You'll "control [1] the point," you! Your consort is gone; had he stayed, he had shared with you, sir. [*Exit.*]

Bob. Well, gentlemen, bear witness I was bound to the peace, by this good day.

E. Know. No, faith, it's an ill day, captain—never reckon it other; but, say you were bound to the peace, the law allows you to defend yourself. That'll prove [190 but a poor excuse.

Bob. I cannot tell, sir; I desire good construction in fair sort. I never sustained the like disgrace, by heaven! Sure I was strook [2] with a planet thence, for I had no power to touch my weapon.

E. Know. Ay, like enough; I have heard of many that have been beaten under a planet; go, get you to a surgeon. 'Slid, an these be your tricks, your *pas-* [200 *sadas* and your *montantos*, I'll none of them.—[*Exit Bobadill.*] O, manners! That this age should bring forth such creatures! That nature should be at leisure to make hem! Come, coz.

Ste. Mass, I'll ha' this cloak.

E. Know. God's will, 'tis Downright's.

Ste. Nay, it's mine now. Another might have ta'en up as well as I. I'll wear it, so I will. 210

E. Know. How an he see it? He'll challenge it, assure yourself.

Ste. Ay, but he shall not ha' it; I'll say I bought it.

E. Know. Take heed you buy it not too dear, coz. [*Exeunt.*]

Act IV. Scene viii.

[*A room in Kitely's house.*]

Kitely, Wellbred, Dame Kit[ely], Bridget, Brainworm, Cash.[3]

[Kite.] Now, trust me, brother, you were much to blame,

T' incense his anger, and disturb the peace

Of my poor house, where there are sentinels

That every minute watch to give alarms

Of civil war, without adjection [4]

Of your assistance or occasion.

---

[1] Beat down. [3] Last two enter later.
[2] Struck, bewitched. [4] Addition.

Well. No harm done, brother, I warrant you. Since there is no harm done, anger costs a man nothing; and a tall man is never his own man till he be angry. [10 To keep his valure [5] in obscurity is to keep himself as it were in a cloak bag. What's a musician, unless he play? What's a tall man, unless he fight? For, indeed, all this my wise brother stands upon absolutely; and that made me fall in with him so resolutely.

Dame. Ay, but what harm might have come of it, brother?

Well. "Might," sister? So might [20 the good warm clothes your husband wears be poisoned, for anything he knows; or the wholesome wine he drunk, even now at the table—

Kite. [*Aside.*] Now, God forbid! O me! Now I remember

My wife drunk to me last, and changed the cup,

And bade me wear this curséd suit today.

See, if heaven suffer murder undiscovered!—

I feel me ill; give me some mithridate; [6]

Some mithridate and oil, good sister, fetch me. 30

O, I am sick at heart; I burn, I burn.

If you will save my life, go fetch it me.

Well. O strange humor! My very breath has poisoned him.

Brid. Good brother, be content. What do you mean?

The strength of these extreme conceits [7] will kill you.

Dame. Beshrew your heart-blood, brother Wellbred, now, for putting such a toy [8] into his head!

Well. Is a fit simile a "toy"? Will [40 he be poisoned with a simile? Brother Kitely, what a strange and idle [9] imagination is this! For shame, be wiser. O' my soul, there's no such matter.

Kite. Am I not sick? How am I then not poisoned?

Am I not poisoned? How am I then so sick?

Dame. If you be sick, your own thoughts make you sick.

---

[5] Worth; 1640 edn. has *valor*.
[6] Antidote to poisons. [8] Whim.
[7] Fancies. [9] Foolish.

WELL. [*Aside.*] His jealousy is the poison
he has taken.

BRA. (*He comes disguised like Justice
Clement's man.*) Mr. Kitely, my master, [50
Justice Clement, salutes you, and desires to
speak with you with all possible speed.

KITE. No time but now? When I think
I am sick? Very sick! Well, I will wait
upon his worship. Thomas! Cob! I must
seek them out, and set hem sentinels till I
return. Thomas! Cob! Thomas! [*Exit.*]

WELL. This is perfectly rare, Brainworm. [*Takes him aside.*] But how got'st
thou this apparel of the justice's man?   60

BRA. [*Aside.*] Marry, sir, my proper
fine penman would needs bestow the
grist o' me at the Windmill, to hear some
martial discourse, where so I marshaled
him that I made him drunk—with admiration—and, because too much heat was the
cause of his distemper, I stripped him
stark naked as he lay along asleep, and
borrowed his suit to deliver this counterfeit
message in, leaving a rusty armor and   [70
an old brown bill[1] to watch him till my
return—which shall be when I ha'
pawned his apparel, and spent the better
part o' the money, perhaps.

WELL. [*Aside.*] Well, thou art a successful, merry knave, Brainworm; his absence
will be a good subject for more mirth. I
pray thee, return to thy young master, and
will him to meet me and my sister Bridget
at the Tower[2] instantly, for here, tell   [80
him, the house is so stored with jealousy
there is no room for love to stand upright in.
We must get our fortunes committed to
some larger prison, say, and than the
Tower I know no better air, nor where the
liberty of the house may do us more present
service. Away!

[*Exit Brainworm.   Enter Kitely, talking
aside to Cash.*]

KITE. Come hither, Thomas. Now my
secret's ripe,

And thou shalt have it; lay to both thine
ears.

Hark what I say to thee. I must go
forth, Thomas;   90

Be careful of thy promise, keep good
watch,

Note every gallant, and observe him
well,

That enters in my absence to thy mistress.

If she would show him rooms—the jest
is stale[3]—

Follow hem, Thomas, or else hang on
him,

And let him not go after. Mark their
looks;

Note if she offer but to see his band,

Or any other amorous toy about him;

But praise his leg, or foot; or if she say

The day is hot, and bid him feel her hand,

How hot it is—O, that's a monstrous
thing!   101

Note me all this, good Thomas; mark
their sighs,

And, if they do but whisper, break hem
off.

I'll bear thee out in it. Wilt thou do this?

Wilt thou be true, my Thomas?

CASH.   As truth's self, sir.

KITE. Why, I believe thee. Where is Cob,
now? Cob!   [*Exit.*]

DAME. He's ever calling for Cob! I
wonder how he employs Cob so.

WELL. Indeed, sister, to ask how he employs Cob is a necessary question for   [110
you that are his wife, and a thing not very
easy for you to be satisfied in; but this
I'll assure you, Cob's wife is an excellent
bawd, sister, and oftentimes your husband
haunts her house—marry, to what end
I cannot altogether accuse him; imagine
you what you think convenient. But I have
known fair hides have foul hearts ere now,
sister.

DAME. Never said you truer than   [120
that, brother; so much I can tell you for
your learning. Thomas, fetch your cloak
and go with me. I'll after him presently;
I would to fortune I could take him there,
i' faith. I'ld return him his own, I warrant
him!   [*Exeunt Dame and Cash.*]

WELL. So, let hem go; this may make
sport anon. Now, my fair sister-in-law,
that you knew but how happy a thing it
were to be fair and beautiful!   130

BRID. That touches not me, brother.

WELL. That's true; that's even the
fault of it; for, indeed, beauty stands a
woman in no stead, unless it procure her

---

[1] Pike.
[2] Since the Tower was in no parish, a marriage
might be performed there immediately.
[3] With a pun on the meaning *harlot.*

touching. But, sister, whether it touch you
or no, it touches your beauties; and I am
sure they will abide the touch. An they
do not, a plague of all ceruse,[1] say I! And
it touches me too in part, though not in
the—Well, there's a dear and re- [140
spected friend of mine, sister, stands very
strongly and worthily affected toward you,
and hath vowed to inflame whole bonefires [2]
of zeal at his heart, in honor of your perfections. I have already engaged my
promise to bring you where you shall hear
him confirm much more. Ned Knowell is
the man, sister; there's no exception
against the party. You are ripe for a husband; and a minute's loss to such an [150
occasion is a great trespass in a wise beauty.
What say you, sister? On my soul, he
loves you. Will you give him the meeting?

BRID. Faith, I had very little confidence
in mine own constancy, brother, if I durst
not meet a man; but this motion of yours
savors of an old knight-adventurer's servant a little too much, methinks.

WELL. What's that, sister?

BRID. Marry, of the squire.[3]   160

WELL. No matter if it did, I would be
such an one for my friend. But see who
is returned to hinder us.

[*Enter Kitely.*]

KITE. What villainy is this? Called out on
a false message?
This was some plot; I was not sent for.—
Bridget,
Where's your sister?

BRID.   I think she be gone forth, sir.

KITE. How! Is my wife gone forth?
Whither, for God's sake?

BRID. She's gone abroad with Thomas.

KITE. Abroad with Thomas? O, that
villain dors [4] me.   169
He hath discovered all unto my wife.
Beast that I was, to trust him! Whither,
I pray you,
Went she?

BRID.   I know not, sir.

WELL.   I'll tell you, brother,
Whither I suspect she's gone.

KITE.   Whither, good brother?

WELL. To Cob's house, I believe; but keep
my counsel.

---

[1] Cosmetic of white lead.   [2] Bonfires.
[3] Implying the meaning *pander*.   [4] Cheats.

KITE. I will, I will. To Cob's house? Doth
she haunt Cob's?
She's gone a purpose now to cuckold me
With that lewd rascal, who, to win her
favor,
Hath told her all.   [*Exit.*]

WELL.   Come, he's once more gone;
Sister, let's lose no time; th' affair is
worth it.   [*Exeunt.*]

ACT IV. SCENE ix.

[*Another street in the Old Jewry.*]

[5] *Matthew, Bobadill, Brainworm.*

[MAT.] I wonder, captain, what they
will say of my going away, ha?

BOB. Why, what should they say, but as
of a discreet gentleman, quick, wary, respectful of nature's fair lineaments? And
that's all.

MAT. Why, so! But what can they say
of your beating?

BOB. A rude part, a touch with soft
wood, a kind of gross battery used, [10
laid on strongly, borne most patiently; and
that's all.

MAT. Ay, but would any man have
offered it in Venice, as you say?

BOB. Tut! I assure you, no; you shall
have there your *nobilis*,[6] your *gentilezza*,[7]
come in bravely upon your *reverse*, stand
you close, stand you firm, stand you fair,
save your *retricato* with his left leg, come
to the *assalto* with the right, thrust [20
with brave steel, defy your base wood!
But wherefore do I awake this remembrance? I was fascinated,[8] by Jupiter—
fascinated. But I will be unwitched and
revenged by law.

MAT. Do you hear? Is 't not best to get
a warrant, and have him arrested and
brought before Justice Clement?

BOB. It were not amiss. Would we had
it!   30

[*Enter Brainworm, disguised as Formal.*]

MAT. Why, here comes his man; let's
speak to him.

BOB. Agreed, do you speak.

MAT. Save you, sir.

---

[5] The marginal direction *To them* is erroneously printed here. The name of Downright also
appears by mistake in the list of characters.
[6] Nobility.   [7] Gentility.   [8] Bewitched.

Bra. With all my heart, sir.

Mat. Sir, there is one Downright hath abused this gentleman and myself, and we determine to make our amends by law. Now, if you would do us the favor to procure a warrant to bring him afore your [40 master, you shall be well considered, I assure you, sir.

Bra. Sir, you know my service is my living; such favors as these, gotten of my master, is his only preferment,[1] and therefore you must consider me as I may make benefit of my place.

Mat. How is that, sir?

Bra. Faith, sir, the thing is extraordinary, and the gentleman may be of [50 great accompt; yet, be what he will, if you will lay me down a brace of angels in my hand, you shall have it; otherwise not.

Mat. How shall we do, captain? He asks a brace of angels; you have no money?

Bob. Not a cross,[2] by Fortune.

Mat. Nor I, as I am a gentleman, but twopence left of my two shillings in the morning for wine and reddish. Let's find him some pawn.   60

Bob. Pawn? We have none to the value of his demand.

Mat. O, yes. I'll pawn this jewel in my ear, and you may pawn your silk stockings, and pull up your boots; they will ne'er be missed.

Bob. Well, an there be no remedy, I'll step aside and pull hem off. [Withdraws.]

Mat. Do you hear, sir? We have no store of money at this time, but you [70 shall have good pawns. Look you, sir, this jewel, and that gentleman's silk stockings, because we would have it despatched ere we went to our chambers.

Bra. I am content, sir; I will get you the warrant presently. What's his name, say you? Downright?

Mat. Ay, ay, George Downright.

Bra. What manner of man is he?

Mat. A tall, big man, sir; he goes in [80 a cloak most commonly of silk russet, laid about with russet lace.

Bra. 'Tis very good, sir.

Mat. Here, sir, here's my jewel.

Bob. [Returning.] And here are stockings.

Bra. Well, gentlemen, I'll procure you this warrant presently. But who will you have to serve it?

Mat. That's true, captain; that [90 must be considered.

Bob. Body o' me, I know not; 'tis service of danger.

Bra. Why, you were best get one o' the varlets o' the city,[3] a serjeant. I'll appoint you one, if you please.

Mat. Will you, sir? Why, we can wish no better.

Bob. We'll leave it to you, sir.

[Exeunt Bobadill and Matthew.]

Bra. This is rare! Now will I go [100 pawn this cloak of the justice's man's at the broker's for a varlet's suit, and be the varlet myself, and get either more pawns, or more money of Downright, for the arrest.   [Exit.]

Act IV. Scene x.

[The lane before Cob's house.]

Knowell, Tib, Cash, Dame Kitely, Kitely, Cob.[4]

[Know.] O, here it is; I am glad. I have found it now.
Ho! Who is within here?

Tib. [Within.] I am within, sir. What's your pleasure?

Know. To know who is within besides yourself.

Tib. Why, sir, you are no constable, I hope?

Know. O, fear you the constable? Then I doubt not
You have some guests within deserve that fear.
I'll fetch him straight.

[Enter Tib.]

Tib.   O' God's name, sir!

Know. Go to; come tell me, is not young Knowell here?

Tib. Young Knowell? I know none such, sir, o' mine honesty.   10

Know. Your honesty? Dame, it flies too lightly from you.
There is no way but fetch the constable.

Tib. The constable? The man is mad, I think.   [Exit.]

[1] I.e., the only reward he gives me.
[2] A small coin.
[3] Bailiffs.   [4] The last five enter later.

[Enter Dame Kitely and Cash.]

CASH. Ho! Who keeps house here?

KNOW. O, this is the female copesmate [1]
of my son?

Now shall I meet him straight.

DAME.   Knock, Thomas, hard.

CASH. Ho, goodwife!

[Enter Tib.]

TIB.   Why, what's the matter with you?

DAME. Why, woman, grieves it you to ope
your door?

Belike you get something to keep it shut.

TIB. What mean these questions, pray
ye?   20

DAME. So strange you make it? Is not my
husband here?

KNOW. Her husband!

DAME.   My tried husband, Master
Kitely.

TIB. I hope he needs not to be triéd here.

DAME. No, dame, he does it not for need,
but pleasure.

TIB. Neither for need nor pleasure is he
here.

KNOW. This is but a device to balk me
withal—

[Enter Kitely with his face covered.]

Soft, who is this? 'Tis not my son disguised?

DAME. (*She spies her husband come, and
runs to him.*) O, sir, have I forestalled
your honest market?

Found your close [2] walks? You stand
amazed now, do you?

I' faith, I am glad I have smoked [3] you
yet at last.   30

What is your jewel, trow? In, come, let's
see her.

Fetch forth your huswife, dame; if she
be fairer,

In any honest judgment, than myself,

I'll be content with it; but she is change,

She feeds you fat, she soothes your appetite,

And you are well? Your wife, an honest
woman,

Is meat twice sod [4] to you, sir? O, you
treachor! [5]

KNOW. [*Aside.*] She cannot counterfeit
thus palpably.

KITE. Out on thy more than strumpet's
impudence!

Steal'st thou thus to thy haunts? And
have I taken   40

Thy bawd and thee, and thy companion,
          (*Pointing to old Knoweli.*)

This hoary-headed lecher, this old goat,

Close at your villainy, and wouldst thou
scuse [6] it

With this stale harlot's jest, accusing
me?—

(*To him.*) O, old incontinent, dost not
thou shame,

When all thy powers in chastity is spent,

To have a mind so hot, and to entice,

And feed th' enticements of a lustful
woman?

DAME. Out, I defy thee, I, dissembling
wretch!

KITE. Defy me, strumpet? (*By [7] Thomas.*)
Ask thy pander here,   50

Can he deny it? Or that wicked elder?

KNOW. Why, hear you, sir—

KITE.   Tut, tut, tut; never speak.

Thy guilty conscience will discover thee.

KNOW. What lunacy is this that haunts
this man?

KITE. Well, good wife Bad,[8] Cob's wife,
and you,

That make your husband such a hoddy-
doddy; [9]

And you, young apple-squire; [10] and old
cuckold-maker—

I'll ha' you every one before a justice.

Nay, you shall answer it; I charge you
go.

KNOW. Marry, with all my heart, sir, I go
willingly,   60

Though I do taste this as a trick put on
me,

To punish my impertinent search, and
justly,

And half forgive my son for the device.

KITE. Come, will you go?

DAME.   Go? To thy shame, believe it.

[Enter Cob.]

COB. Why, what's the matter here?
What's here to do?

---

[1] Companion.
[2] Secret.
[3] Found.
[4] Boiled.
[5] Traitor.
[6] Excuse.
[7] *I. e.*, referring to.
[8] With a pun on *bawd.*
[9] Dupe, cuckold.
[10] Pimp.

KITE. O, Cob, art thou come? I have been
 abused,
And i' thy house; never was man so
 wronged!
COB. 'Slid, in my house? My master,
Kitely? Who wrongs you in my house? [70
KITE. Marry, young lust in old, and old in
 young here;
Thy wife's their bawd; here have I
 taken hem.
COB. How? Bawd? (*He falls upon his
Wife and beats her.*) Is my house come to
that? Am I preferred thither? Did I
charge you to keep your doors shut, Isbel?
And do you let hem lie open for all comers?
KNOW. Friend, know some cause before
 thou beat'st thy wife.
This's madness in thee.
COB.   Why, is there no cause?
KITE. Yes, I'll show cause before the jus-
 tice, Cob.   80
Come, let her go with me.
COB.   Nay, she shall go.
TIB. Nay, I will go. I'll see an you may
be allowed to make a bundle o' hemp o' [1]
your right and lawful wife thus at every
cuckoldly knave's pleasure. Why do you
not go?
KITE A bitter quean! Come, we'll ha' you
 tamed.   [*Exeunt*.]

ACT IV. SCENE xi.

[*A street near Justice Clement's house.*]

*Brainworm, Matthew, Bobadill, Stephen,
                              Downright.*[2]

[BRA.] Well, of all my disguises yet,
now am I most like myself, being in this
serjeant's gown. A man of my present profession never counterfeits, till he lays hold
upon a debtor and says he rests [3] him; for
then he brings him to all manner of unrest.
A kind of little kings we are, bearing the
diminutive of a mace, made like a young
artichock,[4] that always carries pepper
and salt in itself.[5] Well, I know not [10
what danger I undergo by this exploit;
pray heaven I come well off!

[*Enter Matthew and Bobadill.*]

MAT. See, I think, yonder is the varlet,
by his gown.

---

[1] *I. e.*, beat.   [2] Last four enter later.   [3] Arrests.
[4] Artichoke.   [5] Punning on *mace*, the spice.

BOB. Let's go in quest of him.
MAT. Save you, friend! Are not you
here by appointment of Justice Clement's
man?
BRA. Yes, an 't please you, sir; he told
me two gentlemen had willed him to [20
procure a warrant from his master, which
I have about me, to be served on one Downright.
MAT. It is honestly done of you both;
and see where the party comes you must
arrest. Serve it upon him quickly, afore
he be aware.
BOB. Bear back, Master Matthew.

[*Enter Stephen, in Downright's cloak.*]

BRA. Master Downright, I arrest you
i' the queen's name, and must carry [30
you afore a justice by virtue of this warrant.
STE. Me, friend? I am no Downright,
I; I am Master Stephen. You do not well
to arrest me, I tell you truly; I am in nobody's bonds nor books, I would you should
know it. A plague on you heartily, for
making me thus afraid afore my time!
BRA. Why, now are you deceived,
gentlemen?
BOB. He wears such a cloak, and [40
that deceived us. But see, here a [6] comes
indeed; this is he, officer.

[*Enter Downright.*]

DOW. Why, how now, signior gull! Are
you turned filcher of late? Come, deliver
my cloak.
STE. Your cloak, sir? I bought it even
now in open market.
BRA. Master Downright, I have a warrant I must serve upon you, procured by
these two gentlemen.   50
DOW. These gentlemen? These ras-
cals?   [*Offers to beat them.*]
BRA. Keep the peace, I charge you in
her majesty's name.
DOW. I obey thee. What must I do,
officer?
BRA. Go before Master Justice Clement,
to answer what they can object against
you, sir. I will use you kindly, sir.   59
MAT. Come, let's before, and make [7]
the justice, captain.

---

[6] He.   [7] Prepare.

Bob. The varlet's a tall man, afore heaven! [*Exeunt Bobadill and Matthew.*]

Dow. Gull, you'll gi' me my cloak?

Ste. Sir, I bought it, and I'll keep it.

Dow. You will?

Ste. Ay, that I will.

Dow. Officer, there's thy fee; arrest him.

Bra. Master Stephen, I must arrest you.

Ste. Arrest me? I scorn it. There, take your cloak; I'll none on 't.   71

Dow. Nay, that shall not serve your turn now, sir. Officer, I'll go with thee to the justice's; bring him along.

Ste. Why, is not here your cloak? What would you have?

Dow. I'll ha' you answer it, sir.

Bra. Sir, I'll take your word, and this gentleman's too, for his appearance.   79

Dow. I'll ha' no words taken. Bring him along.

Bra. Sir, I may choose to do that; I may take bail.

Dow. 'Tis true, you may take bail, and choose at another time; but you shall not now, varlet. Bring him along, or I'll swinge you.

Bra. Sir, I pity the gentleman's case; here's your money again.   89

Dow. 'Sdeynes, tell not me of my money; bring him away, I say.

Bra. I warrant you he will go with you of himself, sir.

Dow. Yet more ado?

Bra. [*Aside.*] I have made a fair mash on 't.

Ste. Must I go?

Bra. I know no remedy, Master Stephen.   99

Dow. Come along afore me here; I do not love your hanging look behind.

Ste. Why, sir, I hope you cannot hang me for it. Can he, fellow?

Bra. I think not, sir; it is but a whipping matter, sure!

Ste. Why, then let him do his worst; I am resolute.   [*Exeunt.*]

Act V. Scene i.

[*A hall in Justice Clement's house.*]

Clement, Knowell, Kitely, Dame Kitely,
        Tib, Cash, Cob, Servants.

[Clem.] Nay, but stay, stay, give me leave. My chair, sirrah.—You, Master Knowell, say you went thither to meet your son?

Know. Ay, sir.

Clem. But who directed you thither?

Know. That did mine own man, sir.

Clem. Where is he?

Know. Nay, I know not now; I left him with your clerk and appointed [10 him to stay here for me.

Clem. My clerk? About what time was this?

Know. Marry, between one and two, as I take it.

Clem. And what time came my man with the false message to you, Master Kitely?

Kite. After two, sir.

Clem. Very good; but, Mistress [20 Kitely, how that you were at Cob's, ha?

Dame. An please you, sir, I'll tell you: my brother Wellbred told me that Cob's house was a suspected place—

Clem. So it appears, methinks; but on.

Dame. And that my husband used thither daily.

Clem. No matter, so he used himself well, mistress.   30

Dame. True, sir, but you know what grows by such haunts oftentimes.

Clem. I see rank fruits of a jealous brain, Mistress Kitely; but did you find your husband there in that case as you suspected?

Kite. I found her there, sir.

Clem. Did you so? That alters the case. Who gave you knowledge of your wife's being there?   40

Kite. Marry, that did my brother Wellbred.

Clem. How? Wellbred first tell her? Then tell you after? Where is Wellbred?

Kite. Gone with my sister, sir, I know not whither.

Clem. Why, this is a mere trick, a device; you are gulled in this most grossly, all. Alas, poor wench, wert thou beaten for this?   50

Tib. Yes, most pitifully, and 't please you.

Cob. And worthily, I hope, if it shall prove so.

Clem. Ay, that's like, and a piece of a sentence.—

[*Enter a Servant.*]

How now, sir? What's the matter?

SER. Sir, there's a gentleman i' the court without, desires to speak with your worship.　　　　　60

CLEM. A gentleman? What's he?

SER. A soldier, sir, he says.

CLEM. A soldier? Take down my armor, my sword, quickly. A soldier speak with me! Why, when, knaves? Come on, come on. (*He arms himself.*) Hold my cap there, so; give me my gorget, my sword. Stand by. I will end your matters anon. Let the soldier enter. [*Exit Servant.*]— Now, sir,[1] what ha' you to say to me?

ACT V. SCENE ii.

[*The same.*]

[*To them,*] *Bobadill, Matthew.*

[BOB.] By your worship's favor—

CLEM. Nay, keep out, sir; I know not your pretense.[2] You send me word, sir, you are a soldier. Why, sir, you shall be answered here; here be them have been amongst soldiers. Sir, your pleasure.

BOB. Faith, sir, so it is, this gentleman and myself have been most uncivilly wronged and beaten by one Downright, a coarse fellow about the town here; [10 and, for mine own part, I protest, being a man in no sort given to this filthy humor of quarreling, he hath assaulted me in the way of my peace, despoiled me of mine honor, disarmed me of my weapons, and rudely laid me along in the open streets, when I not so much as once offered to resist him.

CLEM. O, God's precious! Is this the soldier? Here, take my armor off [20 quickly. 'Twill make him swoon, I fear; he is not fit to look on 't, that will put up [3] a blow.

MAT. An 't please your worship, he was bound to the peace.

CLEM. Why, and he were, sir, his hands were not bound, were they?

[*Enter Servant.*]

SER. There's one of the varlets of the city, sir, has brought two gentlemen here, one, upon your worship's warrant.　　　30

[1] Notice that here and in the rest of the act Jonson does not indicate a formal scene division until the new characters actually speak.

[2] Intention.　　　　　[3] Put up with.

CLEM. My warrant!

SER. Yes, sir; the officer says, procured by these two.

CLEM. Bid him come in. [*Exit Servant.*] Set by this picture.[4]—What, Mr. Downright! Are you brought at Mr. Freshwater's [5] suit here?

ACT V. SCENE iii.

[*The same.*]

[*To them,*] *Downright, Stephen, Brainworm.*

[DOW.] I' faith, sir, and here's another brought at my suit.

CLEM. What are you, sir?

STE. A gentleman, sir—O, uncle!

CLEM. Uncle? Who? Master Knowell?

KNOW. Ay, sir; this is a wise kinsman of mine.

STE. God's my witness, uncle, I am wronged here monstrously; he charges me with stealing of his cloak, and would [10 I might never stir, if I did not find it in the street by chance.

DOW. O, did you find it now? You said you bought it erewhile.

STE. And you said I stole it. Nay, now my uncle is here, I'll do well enough with you.

CLEM. Well, let this breathe awhile. You that have cause to complain there, stand forth. Had you my warrant for [20 this gentleman's apprehension?

BOB. Ay, an 't please your worship.

CLEM. Nay, do not speak in passion [6] so. Where had you it?

BOB. Of your clerk, sir.

CLEM. That's well! An my clerk can make warrants, and my hand not at hem! Where is the warrant—officer, have you it?

BRA. No, sir. Your worship's man, Master Formal, bid me do it for these [30 gentlemen, and he would be my discharge.[7]

CLEM. Why, Master Downright, are you such a novice, to be served and never see the warrant?

DOW. Sir, he did not serve it on me.

CLEM. No? How then?

DOW. Marry, sir, he came to me, and said he must serve it, and he would use me kindly, and so—

[4] Put aside this imitation of a soldier.

[5] A soldier who had seen no service abroad.

[6] Feeling.　　　　　[7] Guarantee.

CLEM. O, God's pity, was it so, sir? [40 "He must serve it"? Give me my long sword there, and help me off. So, come on, Sir Varlet. (*He flourishes over him with his long sword.*) I "must" cut off your legs, sirrah. [*Brainworm kneels.*] Nay, stand up! I'll "use you kindly"; I *must* cut off your legs, I say.

BRA. O, good sir; I beseech you; nay, good Master Justice!

CLEM. I "must" do it; there is no [50 remedy. I "must" cut off your legs, sirrah; I "must" cut off your ears, you rascal; I "must" do it. I "must" cut off your nose; I "must" cut off your head.

BRA. O, good your worship!

CLEM. Well, rise; how dost thou do now? Dost thou feel thyself well? Hast thou no harm?

BRA. No, I thank your good worship, sir. 60

CLEM. Why, so! I said I must cut off thy legs, and I must cut off thy arms, and I must cut off thy head; but I did not do it. So you said you must serve this gentleman with my warrant, but you did not serve him. You knave, you slave, you rogue, do you say you "must," sirrah! Away with him to the jail; I'll teach you a trick for your "must," sir.

BRA. Good sir, I beseech you, be [70 good to me.

CLEM. Tell him he shall to the jail; away with him, I say.

BRA. Nay, sir, if you will commit me, it shall be for committing more than this; I will not lose, by my travail, any grain of my fame, certain. [*Reveals himself.*]

CLEM. How is this?

KNOW. My man Brainworm!

STE. O, yes, uncle; Brainworm has [80 been with my cousin Edward and I all this day.

CLEM. I told you all there was some device.

BRA. Nay, excellent justice, since I have laid myself thus open to you, now stand strong for me—both with your sword and your balance.

CLEM. Body o' me, a merry knave! Give me a bowl of sack. If he belong [90 to you, Master Knowell, I bespeak your patience.

BRA. That is it I have most need of.

Sir, if you'll pardon me only, I'll glory in all the rest of my exploits.

KNOW. Sir, you know I love not to have my favors come hard from me. You have your pardon, though I suspect you shrewdly for being of counsel with my son against me. 100

BRA. Yes, faith, I have, sir, though you retained me doubly this morning for yourself: first, as Brainworm; after, as Fitzsword. I was your reformed soldier, sir. 'Twas I sent you to Cob's upon the errand without end.

KNOW. Is it possible? Or that thou shouldst disguise thy language so as I should not know thee?

BRA. O, sir, this has been the day [110 of my metamorphosis. It is not that shape alone that I have run through today. I brought this gentleman, Master Kitely, a message too, in the form of Master Justice's man here, to draw him out o' the way, as well as your worship, while Master Wellbred might make a conveyance of Mistress Bridget to my young master.

KITE. How! My sister stol'n away?

KNOW. My son is not married, I [120 hope.

BRA. Faith, sir, they are both as sure as love, a priest, and three thousand pound, which is her portion, can make hem, and by this time are ready to bespeak their wedding supper at the Windmill, except some friend here prevent [1] hem, and invite hem home.

CLEM. Marry, that will I; I thank thee for putting me in mind on 't.—Sirrah, [130 go you and fetch hem hither upon my warrant.—[*Exit Servant.*] Neither's friends have cause to be sorry, if I know the young couple aright. Here, I drink to thee for thy good news. But, I pray thee, what hast thou done with my man Formal?

BRA. Faith, sir, after some ceremony past, as making him drunk, first with story, and then with wine (but all in kindness), and stripping him to his shirt, I left [140 him in that cool vein, departed, sold your worship's warrant to these two, pawned his livery for that varlet's gown to serve it in, and thus have brought myself by my activity to your worship's consideration.

[1] Forestall.

CLEM. And I will consider thee in another cup of sack. Here's to thee, which having drunk off, this is my sentence: Pledge me. Thou hast done, or assisted to, nothing, in my judgment, but de- [151 serves to be pardoned for the wit o' the offense. If thy master, or any man here, be angry with thee, I shall suspect his ingine,[1] while I know him, for 't. How now, what noise is that?

[Enter Servant.]

SER. Sir, it is Roger is come home.

CLEM. Bring him in, bring him in.— What! Drunk in arms against me? Your reason, your reason for this?   160

ACT V. SCENE iv.

[The same.]

To them, Formal [in armor].

[FOR.] I beseech your worship to pardon me; I happened into ill company by chance, that cast me into a sleep, and stripped me of all my clothes.

CLEM. Well, tell him I am Justice Clement, and do pardon him. But what is this to your armor? What may that signify?

FOR. And 't please you, sir, it hung up i' the room where I was stripped, and I borrowed it of one o' the drawers to [10 come home in, because I was loath to do penance through the street i' my shirt.

CLEM. Well, stand by a while.—Who be these? O, the young company; welcome, welcome! Gi' you joy. Nay, Mistress Bridget, blush not, you are not so fresh a bride, but the news of it is come hither afore you. Master Bridegroom, I ha' made your peace, give me your hand. So will I for all the rest ere you forsake [20 my roof.

ACT V. SCENE v.

[The same.]

To them Ed[ward] Knowell, Wellbred, Bridget.

[E. KNOW.] We are the more bound to your humanity, sir.

CLEM. Only these two have so little

[1] Ingenuity, wit.

of man in hem, they are no part of my care.

WELL. Yes, sir, let me pray you for this gentleman; he belongs to my sister, the bride.

CLEM. In what place, sir?   9

WELL. Of her delight, sir, below the stairs, and in public: her poet, sir.

CLEM. A poet? I will challenge him myself presently at extempore.

> Mount up thy Phlegon,[2] Muse, and testify
>   How Saturn, sitting in an ebon cloud,
> Disrobed his podex,[3] white as ivory,
>   And through the welkin thundered all
>   aloud.[4]

WELL. He is not for extempore, sir; he is all for the pocket muse. Please you command a sight of it.   20

CLEM. Yes, yes, search him for a taste of his vein.   *[They search Matthew.]*

WELL. You must not deny the queen's justice, sir, under a writ o' rebellion.

CLEM. What! All this verse? Body o' me, he carries a whole realm,[5] a commonwealth of paper, in 's hose. Let's see some of his subjects.   *[Reads.]*

> Unto the boundless ocean of thy face,
> Runs this poor river, charged with streams
>   of eyes.   30

How? This is stol'n!

E. KNOW. A parody![6] A parody! With a kind of miraculous gift to make it absurder than it was!

CLEM. Is all the rest of this batch? Bring me a torch, lay it together, and give fire. Cleanse the air. *[Sets the papers on fire.]* Here was enough to have infected the whole city, if it had not been taken in time. See, see how our poet's glory shines! Brighter and brighter! Still it increases! [41 O, now it's at the highest; and now it declines as fast. You may see, *sic transit gloria mundi!*[7]

KNOW. There's an emblem[8] for you, son, and your studies.

[2] One of the Sun's horses.   [3] Fundament.
[4] These verses parody Marston.
[5] Pronounced *ream.*
[6] Of the opening lines of Daniel's *Delia.*
[7] Thus passes the glory of the world.
[8] Motto.

CLEM. Nay, no speech or act of mine be drawn against such as profess it worthily. They are not born every year, as an alderman. There goes more to the making of a good poet than a sheriff, Master [51 Kitely. You look upon me! Though I live i' the city here amongst you, I will do more reverence to him, when I meet him, than I will to the mayor out of his year.[1] But these paper-peddlers! These ink-dabblers! They cannot expect reprehension or reproach; they have it with the fact.[2]   59

E. KNOW. Sir, you have saved me the labor of a defense.[3]

CLEM. It shall be discourse for supper between your father and me, if he dare undertake me. But to despatch away these: you sign o' the soldier, and picture o' the poet (but both so false I will not ha' you hanged out at my door till midnight), while we are at supper, you two shall penitently fast it out in my court

---

[1] When his term is expired.   [2] Deed, crime.

[3] At approximately this point in the Italian version the following passage, based on Sidney's *Defense of Poesy*, occurs:

If it may stand with your most wished content,
I can refel [a] opinion and approve
The state of poesy, such as it is,
Blessed, eternal, and most true divine.
Indeed, if you will look on poesy
As she appears in many, poor and lame,
Patched up in remnants and old worn rags,
Half starved for want of her peculiar food,
Sacred invention, then I must confirm
Both your conceit and censure of her merit.
But view her in her glorious ornaments,
Attired in the majesty of art,
Set high in spirit with the precious taste
Of sweet philosophy, and, which is most,
Crowned with the rich traditions of a soul
That hates to have her dignity profaned
With any relish of an earthly thought—
O, then how proud a presence doth she bear!
Then is she like herself, fit to be seen
Of none but grave and consecrated eyes.
Nor is it any blemish to her fame
That such lean, ignorant, and blasted wits,
Such brainless gulls, should utter their stol'n wares
With such applauses in our vulgar ears,
Or that their slubbered lines have current pass
From the fat judgments of the multitude.
But that this barren and infected age
Should set no difference twixt these empty spirits
And a true poet, than which reverend name
Nothing can more adorn humanity!

---

[a] Refute.

without; and, if you will, you may [70 pray there that we may be so merry within as to forgive or forget you when we come out. Here's a third,[4] because we tender your safety, shall watch you; he is provided for the purpose.—Look to your charge, sir.

STE. And what shall I do?

CLEM. O! I had lost a sheep an he had not bleated. Why, sir, you shall give Mr. Downright his cloak; and I will entreat him to take it. A trencher and a nap- [81 kin you shall have i' the butt'ry, and keep Cob and his wife company here, whom I will entreat first to be reconciled, and you to endeavor with your wit to keep hem so.

STE. I'll do my best.

COB. Why, now I see thou art honest, Tib, I receive thee as my dear and mortal wife again.   90

TIB. And I you, as my loving and obedient husband.

CLEM. Good complement! It will be their bridal night too. They are married anew. Come, I conjure the rest to put off all discontent. You, Mr. Downright, your anger; you, Master Knowell, your cares; Master Kitely and his wife, their jealousy.

For, I must tell you both, while that is fed,
Horns i' the mind are worse than o' the head.   100

KITE. Sir, thus they go from me; kiss me, sweetheart.

See what a drove of horns fly in the air,
Winged with my cleansèd and my credulous breath!
Watch hem, suspicious eyes, watch where they fall.
See, see! On heads that think th' have none at all!
O, what a plenteous world of this will come!
When air rains horns, all may be sure of some.[5]

I ha' learned so much verse out of a jealous man's part in a play.   110

CLEM. 'Tis well, 'tis well! This night we'll dedicate to friendship, love, and laughter. Master Bridegroom, take your bride and lead, everyone, a fellow. Here

---

[4] *I.e.*, Formal in his armor.

[5] From 1601 edn. Original has *fame*.

is my mistress, Brainworm, to whom all my addresses of courtship shall have their reference—whose adventures this day, when our grandchildren shall hear to be made a fable, I doubt not but it shall find both spectators and applause.   [*Exeunt.*]

THE END.

This comedy was first acted in the year 1598 by the then L[ord] Chamberlain his Servants. The principal comedians were:

Will. Shakespeare	*Ric. Burbadge*
Aug. Philips	*Joh. Hemings*
Hen. Condell	*Tho. Pope*
Will. Sly	*Chr. Beeston*
Will. Kemp	*Joh. Duke*

With the allowance of the Master of Revels.

SEJANUS HIS FALL[1]

BY

BEN JONSON

To the No Less Noble by Virtue Than
Blood, Esme, L[ord] Aubigny

My Lord:

If ever any ruin were so great as to
survive, I think this be one I send you,
The Fall of Sejanus. It is a poem, that,
if I well remember, in your lo[rdship's]
sight, suffered no less violence from our
people here than the subject of it did from
the rage of the people of Rome—but with
a different fate as, I hope, merit; for this
hath outlived their malice, and begot [10
itself a greater favor than he lost, the love
of good men. Amongst whom, if I make
your lo[rdship] the first it thanks, it is
not without a just confession of the bond
your benefits have, and ever shall hold,
upon me.

Your lo[rdship's] most faithful honorer,

BEN. JONSON.

[2] To the Readers

The following and voluntary labors[3]
of my friends, prefixed to my book, have
relieved me in much whereat, without them,
I should necessarily have touched. Now I
will only use three or four short and needful
notes, and so rest.

First, if it be objected that what I publish is no true poem, in the strict laws of
time, I confess it, as also in the want of a
proper chorus, whose habit and moods [10
are such and so difficult as not any whom I
have seen since the ancients—no, not they
who have most presently affected laws[4]
—have yet come in the way of. Nor is
it needful, or almost possible in these our
times, and to such auditors as commonly
things are presented, to observe the old
state and splendor of dramatic poems,
with preservation of any popular delight.
But of this I shall take more seasonable [20
cause to speak, in my observations upon
Horace his *Art of Poetry*, which, with the
text translated, I intend shortly to publish.[5] In the meantime, if in truth of argument, dignity of persons, gravity and
height of elocution, fullness and frequency
of sentence,[6] I have discharged the other
offices of a tragic writer, let not the absence of these forms be imputed to[7] me,
wherein I shall give you occasion here- [30
after, and without my boast, to think I
could better prescribe than omit the due
use for want of a convenient knowledge.

The next is, lest in some nice nostril
the quotations might savor affected, I
do let you know that I abhor nothing more,
and have only done it to show my integrity
in the story, and save myself in those
common torturers that bring all wit to the
rack, whose noses are ever like swine [40
spoiling and rooting up the Muses' gardens, and their whole bodies like moles,
as blindly working under earth to cast any,
the least, hills upon virtue.

Whereas they are in Latin, and the work
in English, it was presupposed none but
the learned would take the pains to confer[8]
them, the authors themselves being all in
the learned tongues, save one,[9] with whose

---

[1] The title continues: "A Tragedy, Acted in
the Year 1603 by the K. Majesty's Servants.
The Author, B. J. Mart[ial]. *Non hic centauros,
non Gorgonas, Harpyiasque invenies; hominem
pagina nostra sapit.*" ("You will not find centaurs, nor Gorgons, nor Harpies here; our page
deals with man.")

[2] This address occurs only in the 1605 edn.

[3] Commendatory verses by George Chapman,
Hugh Holland, John Marston, etc., printed in
the 1605 edn.

[4] Most recently favored the rules of dramatic
composition.

[5] This commentary, but not the translation,
was destroyed in the burning of his library.

[6] Sententious statement.

[7] Charged against.

[8] Compare.

[9] Tacitus, translated by Richard Greenwey
in 1598.

English side I have had little to do. [50
To which it may be required, since I have
quoted the page, to name what edition
I followed: *Tacit. Lips. in 4.⁰, Antverp. edit.*
[1]600. *Dio. folio Hen. Step.* [15]92. For
the rest, as *Sueton., Seneca, etc.,* the chap-
ter doth sufficiently direct, or the edition
is not varied.¹

Lastly, I would inform you that this
book, in all numbers, ² is not the same with
that which was acted on the public [60
stage, wherein a second pen ³ had good share,
in place of which I have rather chosen to
put weaker, and, no doubt, less pleasing,
of mine own than to defraud so happy a
genius of his right by my loathed usurpa-
tion.

Fare you well. And if you read farder ⁴
of me, and like, I shall not be afraid of it,
though you praise me out.   69

*Neque enim mihi cornea fibra est.*⁵

But that I should plant my felicity in
your general saying, "good," or "well," etc.,
were a weakness which the better sort of
you might worthily contemn, if not absolutely hate me for.

BEN. JONSON, and no such,

Quem
Palma negata macrum, donata reducit
*opimum.*⁶

THE ARGUMENT

Ælius Sejanus, son to Sejus Strabo, a
gentleman of Rome, and born at Vul-
sinium, after his long service in court—
first under Augustus, afterward, Tiberius—
grew into that favor with the latter, and
won him by those arts, as there wanted
nothing but the name to make him a copartner of the empire. Which greatness
of his, Drusus, the emperor's son, not brook-
ing, after many smothered dislikes, [10
it one day breaking out, the prince strook ⁷

¹ The hundreds of marginal notes referring to
Jonson's sources appeared only in the 1605 edn.
² Verses.
³ The identity of this writer is unknown.
⁴ Farther.
⁵ "For my fiber is not of cornel wood"
(Persius' *Satires*, I, 47); *i.e.,* I am not hardened
to praise.
⁶ "Whom denied applause makes lean, but
bestowed applause makes happy" (Horace,
Epist., II, i, 181).
⁷ Struck.

him publicly on the face. To revenge
which disgrace, Livia, the wife of Drusus
(being before corrupted by him to her dishonor, and the discovery of her husband's
counsels), Sejanus practiceth⁸ with, together with her physician, called Eudemus,
and one Lygdus, an eunuch, to poison
Drusus. This their inhuman act having
successful and unsuspected passage,⁹ [20
it emboldeneth Sejanus to farther and more
insolent projects, even the ambition of
the empire; where finding the lets ¹⁰ he
must encounter to be many and hard, in respect of the issue of Germanicus, who
were next in hope for the succession, he
deviseth to make Tiberius' self his means,
and instills into his ears many doubts and
suspicions, both against the princes, and
their mother Agrippina, which Cæsar [30
jealously heark'ning to, as covetously
consenteth to their ruin, and their friends'.
In this time, the better to mature and
strengthen his design, Sejanus labors to
marry Livia, and worketh with all his
ingine ¹¹ to remove Tiberius from the
knowledge of public business, with allurements of a quiet and retired life; the
latter of which, Tiberius, out of a proneness to lust, and a desire to hide those [40
unnatural pleasures which he could not
so publicly practice, embraceth; the former
enkindleth his fears, and there gives him
first cause of doubt or suspect towards
Sejanus. Against whom he raiseth in
private a new instrument, one Sertorius
Macro, and by him underworketh, discovers the other's counsels, his means, his
ends, sounds the affections of the senators,
divides, distracts them; at last, when [50
Sejanus least looketh, and is most secure,
with pretext of doing him an unwonted
honor in the senate, he trains ¹² him from
his guards, and with a long doubtful letter
in one day hath him suspected, accused,
condemned, and torn in pieces by the rage
of the people.¹³

⁸ Conspires.   ¹¹ Ingenuity.
⁹ Outcome.   ¹² Tricks.
¹⁰ Obstacles.

¹³ The following passage, apparently alluding
to the Gunpowder Plot, occurs only in the 1605
edn.: "This do we advance as a mark of terror
to all traitors and treasons, to show how just
the heavens are in pouring and thund'ring down
a weighty vengeance on their unnatural intents.

THE PERSONS OF THE PLAY

TIBERIUS [, *the emperor*].	HATERIUS.
DRUSUS SE[NIOR, *his son*].	SANQUINIUS.
NERO ⎫ [, *sons of Germanicus*	POMPONIUS.
DRUSUS JU[NIOR] ⎬ *and grandnephews*	[JULIUS] POSTHUMUS.
CALIGULA ⎭ *of Tiberius*].	[FULCINUS] TRIO, *consul*.
[LUCIUS] ARRUNTIUS ⎫	MINUTIUS.
[CAIUS] SILIUS ⎪ [, *gentlemen*	SATRIUS [SECUNDUS].
[TITIUS] SABINUS ⎪ *opposed*	[PINNARIUS] NATTA.
[MARCUS] LEPIDUS ⎬ *to*	OPSIUS.
[CREMUTIUS] CORDUS ⎪ *Sejanus*].	
[ASINIUS] GALLUS ⎭	AGRIPPINA [, *widow of Germanicus*].
REGULUS [, *consul*].	LIVIA [, *wife of Drusus Senior*].
TERENTIUS.	SOSIA [, *wife of Caius Silius*].
[GRACINUS] LACO.	TRIBUNI.
EUDEMUS [, *a physician*].	PRÆCONES.
RUFUS.	FLAMEN.
SEJANUS.	TUBICINES.
LATIARIS.	NUNTIUS.
VARRO [, *consul*].	LICTORES.
[SERTORIUS] MACRO.	MINISTRI.
COTTA.	TIBICINES.
[DOMITIUS] AFER.	SERVUS [, *etc.*]

THE SCENE: *Rome.*

[TIME: *23–31 A.D.*]

ACT I. [SCENE i.

A room of state in the palace.]

Sabinus, Silius, Natta, Latiaris, Cordus,
Satrius, Arruntius, Eudemus, Haterius, etc.

[SAB.] Hail, Caius Silius!
SIL.   Titius Sabinus, hail!
   Yo' are rarely met in court!
SAB.   Therefore, well met.
SIL. 'Tis true; indeed, this place is not our
     sphere.
SAB. No, Silius, we are no good inginers.[1]
   We want the fine arts, and their thriving
     use
   Should make us graced or favored of the
     times;
   We have no shift of faces, no cleft
     tongues,
   No soft and glutinous bodies that can
     stick

even to the worst princes—much more to those,
for guard of whose piety and virtue the angels
are in continual watch, and God himself miraculously working."
   [1] Plotters.

Like snails on painted walls, or on our
     breasts
Creep up, to fall from that proud height
     to which   10
We did by slavery, not by service, climb.
We are no guilty men, and then no great;
We have nor place in court, office in state,
That we can say we owe unto our crimes;
We burn with no black secrets, which
     can make
Us dear to the [pale] [2] authors; or live
     feared
Of their still waking jealousies, to raise
Ourselves a fortune by subverting theirs.
We stand not in the lines that do advance
To that so courted point.
SIL. [*Pointing to Satrius and Natta.*]   But
     yonder lean   20
   A pair that do.
([3]SAB.   Good cousin Latiaris.)

   [2] Supplied from the Newberry Library copy
of the 1616 folio.
   [3] Jonson frequently encloses speeches in parenthesis to indicate an aside or a passage incidental to the main action.

Sil. Satrius Secundus and Pinnarius Natta,
The great Sejanus' clients.[1] There be two
Know more than honest counsels, whose close [2] breasts,
Were they ripped up to light, it would be found
A poor and idle [3] sin to which their trunks
Had not been made fit organs. These can lie,
Flatter, and swear, forswear, deprave, inform,
Smile, and betray; make guilty men; then beg
The forfeit lives, to get the livings; cut   30
Men's throats with whisp'rings; sell to gaping suitors
The empty smoke that flies about the palace;
Laugh when their patron laughs; sweat when he sweats;
Be hot and cold with him; change every mood,
Habit, and garb as often as he varies;
Observe him, as his watch observes [4] his clock;
And, true as turkis [5] in the dear lord's ring,
Look well or ill with him; [6] ready to praise
His lordship, if he spit, or but piss fair,
Have an indifferent stool, or break wind well;   40
Nothing can scape their catch.
Sab.   Alas! These things
Deserve no note, conferred with other vile
And filthier flatteries that corrupt the times,
When, not alone our gentries chief are fain
To make their safety from such sordid acts,
But all our consuls, and no little part
Of such as have been prætors, yea, the most

Of senators, that else not use their voices,[7]
Start up in public senate, and there strive
Who shall propound most abject things and base,   50
So much as oft Tiberius hath been heard,
Leaving the court, to cry, "O race of men,
Prepared for servitude!"—which showed that he,
Who least the public liberty could like,
As loathly brooked their flat servility.
Sil. Well, all is worthy of us, were it more,
Who with our riots, pride, and civil hate
Have so provoked the justice of the gods—
We, that within these fourscore years were born
Free, equal lords of the triumphéd world,   60
And knew no masters but affections,
To which, betraying first our liberties,
We since became the slaves to one man's lusts,
And now to many; every minist'ring spy
That will accuse and swear is lord of you,
Of me, of all, our fortunes and our lives.
Our looks are called to question, and our words,
How innocent soever, are made crimes;
We shall not shortly dare to tell our dreams,
Or think, but 'twill be treason.
Sab.   "Tyrans' [8] arts   70
Are to give flatterers grace, accusers power,
That those may seem to kill whom they devour." [9]—
[Turns to Cordus.]   Now, good Cremutius Cordus.
Cor.   Hail to your lordship!
Nat. [To Latiaris.]   Who's that salutes your cousin?
          They whisper. [Exeunt Satrius and Eudemus.]
Lat.   'Tis one Cordus,
A gentleman of Rome, one that has writ
Annals of late, they say, and very well.

---

[1] Dependents of a patrician family.
[2] Secret.   [4] Is set by.
[3] Empty.   [5] Turquoise.
[6] A common superstition.

[7] Jonson's marginal note reads Pedarii (i.e., senators who could speak only when called upon by the presiding officer).
[8] Tyrants'.
[9] Sententious passages were commonly set in quotation marks.

NAT. Annals? Of what times?

LAT.   I think of Pompey's
And Caius Cæsar's; and so down to
these.

NAT. How stands h' affected to the pres-
ent state?
Is he or [1] Drusian or Germanican?   80
Or ours or neutral?

LAT.   I know him not so far.

NAT. Those times are somewhat queasy to
be touched.
Have you or seen or heard part of his
work?

LAT. Not I; he means they shall be public shortly.

NAT. O, Cordus do you call him?

LAT.   Ay.

SAB.   But these our times
Are not the same, Arruntius.

ARR.   Times? The men,
The men are not the same! 'Tis we are
base,
Poor, and degenerate from th' exalted
strain
Of our great fathers. Where is now the
soul
Of godlike Cato—he that durst be
good   90
When Cæsar durst be evil, and had
power,
As not to live his slave, to die his master?
Or where the constant Brutus, that,
being proof
Against all charm of benefits, did strike
So brave a blow into the monster's heart
That sought unkindly to captive [2] his
country?
O, they are fled the light! Those mighty
spirits
Lie raked up with their ashes in their
urns,
And not a spark of their eternal fire
Glows in a present bosom. All's but
blaze,   100
Flashes, and smoke, wherewith we
labor so;
There's nothing Roman in us, nothing
good,
Gallant, or great. 'Tis true that Cordus
says,
"Brave Cassius was the last of all that
race."

[1] Either.
[2] Unnaturally to capture.

Drusus [Senior] passeth by.

SAB. Stand by! Lord Drusus!

HAT.   Th' emp'ror's son! Give place.

SIL. I like the prince well.

ARR.   A riotous youth;
There's little hope of him.

SAB.   That fault his age
Will, as it grows, correct. Methinks he
bears
Himself each day more nobly than other,
And wins no less on men's affections   110
Than doth his father lose. Believe me, I
love him,
And chiefly for opposing to Sejanus.

SIL. And I, for gracing his young kinsmen
so,
The sons of Prince Germanicus; it shows
A gallant clearness in him, a straight
mind
That envies not, in them, their father's
name.

ARR. His name was, while he lived, above
all envy,
And, being dead, without it. O, that man!
If there were seeds of the old virtue left,
They lived in him.

SIL.   He had the fruits, Arruntius,   120
More than the seeds; Sabinus and my-
self
Had means to know him within, and
can report him.
We were his followers (he would call us
friends).
He was a man most like to virtue; in all,
And every action, nearer to the gods
Than men, in nature; of a body as fair
As was his mind; and no less reverend
In face than fame. He could so use his
state,
Temp'ring his greatness with his gravity,
As it avoided all self-love in him   130
And spite in others. What his funerals
lacked
In images and pomp, they had supplied
With honorable sorrow, soldiers' sad-
ness,
A kind of silent mourning, such as men,
Who know no tears but from their cap-
tives, use
To show in so great losses.

COR.   I thought once,
Considering their forms, age, manner of
deaths,

The nearness of the places where they
　　fell,
T' have paralleled him with great Alex-
　　ander;
For both were of best feature, of high
　　race,　　　　　　　　　　　　　　140
Yeared [1] but to thirty, and, in foreign
　　lands,
By their own people alike made away.
SAB. I know not, for his death, how you
　　might wrest [2] it;
But, for his life, it did as much disdain
Comparison with that voluptuous, rash,
Giddy, and drunken Macedon's as mine
Doth with my bondman's. All the good
　　in him,
His valor, and his fortune, he made his;
But he had other touches of late Romans,
That more did speak [3] him: Pompey's
　　dignity,　　　　　　　　　　　　150
The innocence of Cato, Cæsar's spirit,
Wise Brutus' temperance, and every
　　virtue,
Which, parted unto others, gave them
　　name,
Flowed mixed in him. He was the soul
　　of goodness;
And all our praises of him are like
　　streams
Drawn from a spring, that still rise
　　full, and leave
The part remaining greatest.
ARR.　　　　　　　　　　　I am sure
He was too great for us, and that they
　　knew
Who did remove him hence.
SAB.　　　　　　When men grow fast [4]
Honored and loved, there is a trick in
　　state　　　　　　　　　　　　160
(Which jealous princes never fail to use)
How to decline [5] that growth, with fair
　　pretext,
And honorable colors [6] of employment,
Either by embassy, the war, or such,
To shift them forth into another air
Where they may purge and lessen. So
　　was he,
And had his seconds there, sent by
　　Tiberius
And his more subtile dam, to discontent
　　him,

To breed and cherish mutinies, detract
His greatest actions, give audacious
　　check　　　　　　　　　　　　170
To his commands, and work to put him
　　out
In open act of treason. All which
　　snares
When his wise cares prevented, a fine
　　poison
Was thought on to mature their prac-
　　tices.
COR. Here comes Sejanus.
SIL.　　　　　　　Now observe the stoops,
The bendings, and the falls.
ARR.　　　　　　　　Most creeping base!

[*Enter*] *Sejanus, Satrius, Terentius, etc.*
　　　　　　　　　　They pass over the stage.

[SEJ.] I note hem [7] well; no more. Say
　　you?
SAT.　　　　　My lord,
There is a gentleman of Rome would
　　buy—
SEJ. How call you him you talked with?
SAT.　　　　　　　Please your lordship,
It is Eudemus, the physician　　　180
To Livia, Drusus' wife.
SEJ.　　　　　　　On with your suit.
Would buy, you said—
SAT.　　　　　A tribune's place, my lord.
SEJ. What will he give?
SAT.　　　　　　　　Fifty sestertia.
SEJ. Livia's physician, say you, is that
　　fellow?
SAT. It is, my lord. Your lordship's
　　answer?
SEJ.　　　　　To what?
SAT. The place, my lord. 'Tis for a gen-
　　tleman
Your lordship will well like of, when
　　you see him,
And one you may make yours by the
　　grant.
SEJ. Well, let him bring his money, and his
　　name.
SAT. Thank your lordship. He shall, my
　　lord.
SEJ.　　　　　Come hither.　　　　　190
Know you this same Eudemus? Is he
　　learned?
SAT. Reputed so, my lord, and of deep
　　practice.
SEJ. Bring him in to me in the gallery,

---

[1] Aged.
[2] Interpret.
[3] Celebrate.
[4] Greatly.
[5] Lower.
[6] Pretenses.
[7] Them.

And take you cause to leave us there
  together;
I would confer with him, about a
  grief.—On!
[*Exit Sejanus with Satrius, Terentius, and*
                    Attendants.]
ARR. So, yet! Another? Yet? O desperate
  state
Of grov'ling honor! Seest thou this, O
  sun,
And do we see thee after? Methinks,
  day
Should lose his light when men do lose
  their shames,
And for the empty circumstance of
  life   200
Betray their cause of living.
SIL.   Nothing so.
Sejanus can repair, if Jove should ruin.
He is the now court-god; and, well ap-
  plied
With sacrifice of knees, of crooks, and
  cringe,
He will do more than all the house of
  heav'n
Can for a thousand hecatombs. 'Tis
  he
Makes us our day or night; hell and
  Elysium
Are in his look. We talk of Radamanth,
Furies, and firebrands; but 'tis his frown
That is all these, where, on the adverse
  part,   210
His smile is more than e'er yet poets
  feigned
Of bliss, and shades, nectar—
ARR.   A serving boy!
I knew him at Caius' trencher, when for
  hire
He prostituted his abuséd body
To that great gourmand, fat Apicius,
And was the noted pathic [1] of the time.
SAB. And, now, the second face of the
  whole world,
The partner of the empire—hath his
  image
Reared equal with Tiberius, borne in
  ensigns;
Commands, disposes every dignity. 220
Centurions, tribunes, heads of prov-
  inces,
Prætors, and consuls, all that hereto-
  fore

[1] A male prostitute.

Rome's general suffrage gave, is now his
  sale. [2]
The gain, or rather spoil of all the earth,
One, and his house, receives.
SIL.   He hath of late
Made him a strength too, strangely, by
  reducing
All the prætorian bands into one camp,
Which he commands, pretending that
  the soldier,
By living loose and scattered, fell to riot;
And that, if any sudden enterprise 230
Should be attempted, their united
  strength
Would be far more than severed; and
  their life
More strict, if from the city more re-
  moved—
SAB. Where now he builds what kind of
  forts he please,
Is heard to court the soldier by his name,
Woos, feasts the chiefest men of action,
Whose wants, not loves, compel them
  to be his.
And, though he ne'er were liberal by
  kind, [3]
Yet, to his own dark ends, he's most
  profuse,
Lavish, and letting fly he cares not
  what   240
To his ambition.
ARR.   Yet hath he ambition?
Is there that step in state can make
  him higher,
Or more, or anything he is, but less?
SIL. Nothing but emp'ror.
ARR.   The name Tiberius,
I hope, will keep, howe'er he hath for-
  gone
The dignity and power.
SIL.   Sure, while he lives.
ARR. And dead, it comes to Drusus. [4]
  Should he fail,
To the brave issue of Germanicus;
And they are three: too many—ha?—for
  him
To have a plot upon?
SAB.   I do not know 250
The heart of his designs, but sure their
  face
Looks farther than the present.

[2] At his disposal for sale.
[3] Nature.
[4] *I.e.*, Drusus Senior.

ARR.   By the gods,
  If I could guess he had but such a
    thought,
  My sword should cleave him down from
    head to heart
  But I would find it out; and with my
    hand
  I'ld hurl his panting brain about the
    air
  In mites as small as *atomi* [1] to undo
  The knotted bed—
SAB.   You are observed, Arruntius!
ARR. (*He turns to Sejanus' Clients.*) Death!
  I dare tell him so, and all his spies.
  You, sir, I would—do you look?—and
    you.
SAB.   Forbear!   260

[*Enter*] *Satrius, Eudemus, Sejanus* [2] [*in the
                              gallery above*].

SAT. Here he will instant be; let's walk a
    turn;
  Yo' are in a muse, Eudemus?
EUD.   Not I, sir.—
  [*Aside.*] I wonder he should mark me
    out so. Well,
  Jove and Apollo form it for the best!
SAT. Your fortune's made unto you now,
    Eudemus,
  If you can but lay hold upon the means;
  Do but observe his humor, and—believe
    it—
  He's the noblest Roman, where he
    takes—
  Here comes his lordship.

[*Enter Sejanus.*]

SEJ.   Now, good Satrius.
SAT. This is the gentleman, my lord.
SEJ.   Is this?   270
  Give me your hand; we must be more ac-
    quainted.
  Report, sir, hath spoke out your art and
    learning,
  And I am glad I have so needful cause,
  However in itself painful and hard,
  To make me known to so great virtue.
    Look,
  Who's that? Satrius—[*He motions and
    Satrius leaves.*] I have a grief, sir,
  That will desire your help. Your name's
    Eudemus?

EUD. Yes.
SEJ.   Sir?
EUD.   It is, my lord.
SEJ.   I hear you are
  Physician to Livia, the princess.   279
EUD. I minister unto her, my good lord.
SEJ. You minister to a royal lady, then.
EUD. She is, my lord, and fair.
SEJ.   That's understood
  Of all their sex, who are or would be so;
  And those that would be, physic soon
    can make hem;
  For those that are, their beauties fear
    no colors. [3]
EUD. Your lordship is conceited. [4]
SEJ.   Sir, you know it,
  And can, if need be, read a learned lec-
    ture
  On this, and other secrets. Pray you,
    tell me,
  What more of ladies, besides Livia,
  Have you your patients?
EUD.   Many, my good lord: 290
  The great Augusta, Urgulania,
  Mutilia Prisca, and Plancina; divers—
SEJ. And all these tell you the particulars
  Of every several grief: how first it grew,
  And then increased; what action caused
    that;
  What passion that; and answer to each
    point
  That you will put hem?
EUD.   Else, my lord, we know not
  How to prescribe the remedies.
SEJ.   Go to,
  Yo' are a subtile nation, you physicians,
  And grown the only cabinets in court 300
  To ladies' privacies! Faith, which of
    these
  Is the most pleasant lady in her physic?
  Come, you are modest now.
EUD.   'Tis fit, my lord.
SEJ. Why, sir, I do not ask you of their
    urines,
  Whose smell's most violet, or whose
    siege [5] is best,
  Or who makes hardest faces on her
    stool,
  Which lady sleeps with her own face
    a-nights,
  Which puts her teeth off, with her
    clothes, in court,

---

[1] Atoms.   [2] Actually enters later.
[3] With a punning reference to *fear no enemy.*
[4] Witty.   [5] Defecation.

Or which her hair, which her com-
plexion,
And in which box she puts it.   These
were questions   310
That might, perhaps, have put your
gravity
To some defense of blush.   But I in-
quired
Which was the wittiest, merriest, wan-
tonest?
Harmless intergatories,[1] but conceits.[2]
Methinks Augusta should be most per-
verse,
And froward in her fit?
EUD.   She's so, my lord.
SEJ. I knew it; and Mutilia the most
jocund?
EUD. 'Tis very true, my lord.
SEJ.   And why would you
Conceal this from me, now?   Come,
what's Livia?
I know she's quick and quaintly spir-
ited,   320
And will have strange thoughts, when
she's at leisure.
She tells hem all to you?
EUD.   My noblest lord,
He breathes not in the empire, or on
earth,
Whom I would be ambitious to serve
(In any act that may preserve mine
honor)
Before your lordship.
SEJ.   Sir, you can lose no honor
By trusting aught to me.   The coarsest
act
Done to my service I can so requite
As all the world shall style it honorable.
"Your idle, virtuous definitions   330
Keep honor poor, and are as scorned as
vain;
Those deeds breathe honor that do suck
in gain."[3]
EUD. But, good my lord, if I should thus
betray
The counsels of my patient, and a lady's
Of her high place and worth, what might
your lordship
(Who presently are to trust me with
your own)
Judge of my faith?

SEJ.   Only the best, I swear.
Say now that I should utter you my
grief—
And with it the true cause—that it were
love,
And love to Livia—you should tell her
this?   340
Should she suspect your faith?   I would
you could
Tell me as much from her; see if my
brain
Could be turned jealous.[4]
EUD.   Happily,[5] my lord,
I could in time tell you as much and
more,
So I might safely promise but the first
To her from you.
SEJ.   As safely, my Eudemus
(I now dare call thee so), as I have put
The secret into thee.
EUD.   My lord—
SEJ.   Protest not;
Thy looks are vows to me; use only
speed;   349
And but affect her with Sejanus' love,
Thou art a man made to make consuls.
Go!
EUD. My lord, I'll promise you a private
meeting
This day together.
SEJ.   Canst thou?
EUD.   Yes.
SEJ.   The place?
EUD. My gardens, whither I shall fetch
your lordship.
SEJ. Let me adore my Æsculapius![6]
Why, this indeed is physic, and out-
speaks
The knowledge of cheap drugs, or any
use
Can be made out of it!   More comfort-
ing
Than all your opiates, *julebes*,[7] *apozems*,[8]
Magistral[9]   syrups, or—begone, my
friend,   360
Not barely styléd, but created so;
Expect things greater than thy largest
hopes
To overtake thee.   Fortune shall be
taught

---

[1] Interrogatories.   [2] Merely fancies.
[3] As usual, quotation marks indicate sententious passages.

[4] Suspicious.   [5] Haply, perhaps.
[6] God of medicine, used here in reference to
Venus.   [8] Decoctions.
[7] Juleps.   [9] Sovereign.

To know how ill she hath deserved thus
    long,
To come behind thy wishes. Go, and
    speed.   [*Exit Eudemus.*]
"Ambition makes more trusty slaves
    than need."
These fellows, by the favor of their art,
Have still the means to tempt, ofttimes
    the power.
If Livia will be now corrupted, then
Thou hast the way, Sejanus, to work
    out   370
His secrets, who, thou knowest, endures
    thee not,
Her husband, Drusus; and to work
    against them.
Prosper it, Pallas, thou that better'st
    wit;
For Venus hath the smallest share in it.

[*Enter*] *Tiberius; Sejanus* [*from the gallery*];
           Drusus [*Senior*].

[TIB.] (*One kneels to him.*) We not endure
    these flatteries; let him stand.
Our empire, ensigns, axes, rods, and state
Take not away our human nature from
    us.
Look up on us, and fall before the gods.
SEJ. How like a god speaks Cæsar!
ARR. [*Aside to Cordus.*]   There,
    observe!
He can endure that second [1]—that's no
    flattery.   380
O, what is it proud slime will not believe
Of his own worth, to hear it equal
    praised
Thus with the gods?
COR. [*Aside.*]   He did not hear it, sir.
ARR. [*Aside.*] He did not? Tut, he must
    not; we think meanly.
'Tis your most courtly known confed-
    eracy,
To have your private parasite redeem
What he, in public subtilty, will lose
To making him a name.
HAT.   Right mighty lord—
                   [*Gives him letters.*]
TIB. We must make up our ears gainst
    these assaults
Of charming tongues. We pray you use
    no more   390
These contumelies to us; style not us

[1] Support.

Or "lord" or "mighty," who profess
    ourself
The servant of the senate, and are proud
T' enjoy them our good, just, and favor-
    ing lords.
COR. [*Aside.*] Rarely dissembled!
ARR. [*Aside.*]   Princelike to the life.
SAB. "When power that may command,
    so much descends,
Their bondage, whom it stoops to, it
    intends."
TIB. Whence are these letters?
HAT.   From the senate.
TIB.   So.
         [*Latiaris gives him letters.*]
Whence these?
LAT.   From thence too.
        [*Tiberius reads the letters.*]
TIB.   Are they sitting now?
LAT. They stay [2] thy answer, Cæsar.
SIL. [*Aside.*]   If this man   400
Had but a mind allied unto his words,
How blessed a fate were it to us, and
    Rome!
We could not think [3] that state for
    which to change,[4]
Although the aim were our old liberty;
The ghosts of those that fell for that
    would grieve
Their bodies lived not now, again to
    serve.
"Men are deceived, who think there can
    be thrall
Beneath a virtuous prince. Wished
    liberty
Ne'er lovelier looks than under such a
    crown."
But, when his grace is merely but lip-
    good,   410
And that no longer than he airs himself
Abroad in public, there to seem to shun
The strokes and stripes of flatterers,
    which within
Are lechery unto him, and so feed
His brutish sense with their afflicting
    sound,
As, dead to virtue, he permits himself
Be carried like a pitcher by the ears,
To every act of vice—this is a case
Deserves our fear, and doth presage the
    nigh
And close approach of blood and tyr-
    anny.   420

[2] Await.   [3] Imagine.   [4] Exchange.

"Flattery is midwife unto prince's rage;
And nothing sooner doth help forth a
  tyran
Than that and whisperers' grace, who
  have the time,
The place, the power to make all men
  offenders."
ARR. [*Aside*.] He should be told this; and
  be bid dissemble
With fools and blind men. We that know
  the evil
Should hunt the palace rats, or give them
  bane;
Fright hence these worse than ravens,
  that devour
The quick, where they but prey upon
  the dead.
He shall be told it.
SAB. [*Aside*.]   Stay, Arruntius, 430
We must abide our opportunity,
And practice what is fit, as what is
  needful.
"It is not safe t' enforce a sovereign's
  ear;
Princes hear well, if they at all will
  hear."
ARR. [*Aside*.] Ha, say you so? Well!
  In the meantime, Jove
(Say not but I do call upon thee now),
Of all wild beasts preserve me from a
  tyran;
And of all tame, a flatterer.
SIL. [*Aside*.]   'Tis well prayed.
TIB. Return the lords this voice: We are
  their creature,
And it is fit a good and honest prince, 440
Whom they, out of their bounty, have
  instructed
With so dilate [1] and absolute a power,
Should owe the office of it to their service
And good of all and every citizen.
Nor shall it e'er repent us to have
  wished
The senate just and fav'ring lords unto
  us,
"Since their free loves do yield no less
  defense
T' a prince's state than his own inno-
  cence."
Say then, there can be nothing in their
  thought
Shall want to please us, that hath
  pleaséd them;   450
[1] Extended.

Our suffrage rather shall prevent [2] than
  stay
Behind their wills; 'tis empire to obey,
Where such, so great, so grave, so good,
  determine.
Yet, for the suit of Spain t' erect a
  temple
In honor of our mother and ourself,
We must, with pardon of the senate, not
Assent thereto. Their lordships may ob-
  ject
Our not denying the same late request
Unto the Asian cities. We desire
That our defense for suffering that be
  known   460
In these brief reasons, with our after-
  purpose.
Since deified Augustus hindered not
A temple to be built at Pergamum,
In honor of himself and sacred Rome,
We, that have all his deeds and words
  observed
Ever, in place of laws, the rather followed
That pleasing precedent, because with
  ours
The senate's reverence, also, there was
  joined.
But as,[3] t' have once received it, may
  deserve
The gain of pardon, so to be adored 470
With the continued style and note [4]
  of gods,
Through all the provinces, were wild am-
  bition,
And no less pride. Yea, ev'n Augustus'
  name
Would early vanish, should it be pro-
  faned
With such promiscuous flatteries. For
  our part,
We here protest it, and are covetous
Posterity should know it: we are mortal,
And can [5] but deeds of men. 'Twere
  glory enough,
Could we be truly a prince. And they
  shall add
Abounding grace unto our memory, 480
That shall report us worthy our fore-
  fathers,
Careful of your affairs, constant in
  dangers,
And not afraid of any private frown

[2] Anticipate.   [4] Manner of address.
[3] *I.e.*, as one.   [5] Can do.

For public good. These things shall be to
us
Temples and statues, reared in your
minds,
The fairest and most during imag'ry;
For those of stone or brass, if they be-
come
Odious in judgment of posterity,
Are more contemned as dying sepulchers
Than ta'en for living monuments. We
then   490
Make here our suit alike to gods and men:
The one, until the period of our race,
T' inspire us with a free and quiet mind,
Discerning both divine and human laws;
The other, to vouchsafe us after death
An honorable mention and fair praise
T' accompany our actions and our name.
The rest of greatness princes may com-
mand,
And, therefore, may neglect; only, a long,
A lasting, high, and happy memory   500
They should, without being satisfied,
pursue.
Contempt of fame begets contempt of
virtue.
NAT. Rare!
SAT.   Most divine!
SEJ.   The oracles are ceased
That only Cæsar, with their tongue,
might speak.
ARR. [*Aside.*] Let me be gone! Most
felt and open this!
COR. [*Aside.*] Stay.
ARR. [*Aside.*]   What? To hear more
cunning and fine words,
With their sound flattered, ere their
sense be meant?
TIB. Their choice of Antium, there to
place the gift,[1]
Vowed to the goddess for our mother's
health,
We will the senate know we fairly
like,   510
As also of their grant [2] to Lepidus
For his repairing the Æmilian place
And restoration of those monuments.
Their grace, too, in confining of Silanus
To th' other isle Cithera, at the suit
Of his religious sister, much commends
Their policy, so tempered with their
mercy.

[1] Jonson's marginal note reads: "*Fortuna
equestris.*"   [2] Permission.

But for the honors which they have
decreed
To our Sejanus, to advance [3] his statue
In Pompey's theater (whose ruining
fire   520
His vigilance and labor kept restrained
In that one loss), they have therein
outgone
Their own great wisdoms, by their
skillful choice
And placing of their bounties on a man
Whose merit more adorns the dignity
Than that can him, and gives a benefit
In taking greater than it can receive.
Blush not, Sejanus, thou great aid of
Rome,
Associate of our labors, our chief helper;
Let us not force thy simple modesty 530
With off'ring at [4] thy praise, for more
we cannot,
Since there's no voice can take [5] it. No
man here
Receive our speeches as hyperboles,
For we are far from flattering our
friend,
Let envy know, as from the need to
flatter.
Nor let them ask the causes of our
praise;
Princes have still their grounds reared
with themselves,
Above the poor low flats of common men;
And who will search the reasons of their
acts,
Must stand on equal bases. Lead,
away.   540
Our loves unto the senate.
ARR.   Cæsar!—
SAB.   Peace!—
[*Exeunt Tiberius, Sejanus, and Attendants.*]
COR. Great Pompey's theater was never
ruined
Till now that proud Sejanus hath a
statue
Reared on his ashes.
ARR.   Place the shame of soldiers
Above the best of generals? Crack the
world,
And bruise the name of Romans into
dust,
Ere we behold it!
SIL.   Check your passion;
Lord Drusus tarries.

[3] Set up.   [4] Attempting.   [5] Accomplish.

Dru.   Is my father mad,
   Weary of life and rule, lords, thus to
     heave
   An idol up with praise? Make him his
     mate,   550
   His rival in the empire?
Arr.   O, good prince!
Dru. Allow him statues, titles, honors,
     such
   As he himself refuseth?
Arr.   Brave, brave Drusus!
Dru. The first ascents to sovereignty are
     hard;
   But, entered once, there never wants or
     means
   Or ministers to help th' aspirer on.
Arr. True, gallant Drusus.
Dru.   We must shortly pray
   To Modesty, that he will rest con-
     tented—
Arr. Ay, where he is, and not write em-
     p'ror.

Sejanus,[1] *etc.; he enters, followed with Clients.*

[Sej.] There is your bill, and yours.—[*To*
     Satrius.] Bring you your man.   560
   I have moved for you, too, Latiaris.
Dru.   What?
   Is your vast greatness grown so blindly
     bold
   That you will over us?
Sej.   Why, then give way!
Dru. Give way, Colossus? Do you lift?
     Advance you?
   Take that!   *Drusus strikes him.*
Arr.   Good! Brave! Excellent
     brave prince!
Dru. Nay, come, approach. [*Draws his
     sword.*] What, stand you off? At
     gaze?
   It looks too full of death for thy cold
     spirits.
   Avoid mine eye, dull camel, or my sword
   Shall make thy brav'ry fitter for a grave
   Than for a triumph. I'll advance a
     statue   570
   O' your own bulk; but 't shall be on the
     cross,
   Where I will nail your pride at breadth
     and length,

---

[1] The fact that the names, *Drusus, Arruntius,*
are repeated at this point in the original would
perhaps indicate that Jonson conceived of his
act as being divided into scenes in classical fashion.

   And crack those sinews, which are yet
     but stretched
   With your swol'n fortune's rage.
Arr.   A noble prince!
All. A Castor, a Castor, a Castor, a
     Castor!   [*Exeunt All but Sejanus.*]
Sej. He that, with such wrong moved,
     can bear it through
   With patience and an even mind, knows
     how
   To turn it back. Wrath, covered, carries
     fate;
   Revenge is lost if I profess my hate.
   What was my practice [2] late, I'll now
     pursue   580
   As my fell justice. This hath styled it
     new.   [*Exit.*]
        Chorus—*of Musicians.*

      Act II. [Scene i.

     The garden of Eudemus.]

     Sejanus, Livia, Eudemus.

[Sej.] Physician, thou art worthy of a
     province
   For the great favors done unto our loves,
   And, but that greatest Livia bears a
     part
   In the requital of thy services,
   I should alone despair of aught like
     means
   To give them worthy satisfaction.
Liv. Eudemus, I will see it, shall receive
   A fit and full reward for his large merit.
   But for this potion we intend to Drusus
   (No more our husband now), whom
     shall we choose   10
   As the most apt and abled instrument
   To minister it to him?
Eud.   I say, Lygdus.
Sej. Lygdus? What's he?
Liv.   An eunuch Drusus loves.
Eud. Ay, and his cupbearer.
Sej.   Name not a second.
   If Drusus love him, and he have that
     place,
   We cannot think a fitter.
Eud.   True, my lord;
   For free access and trust are two main
     aids.
Sej. Skillful physician!
Liv.   But he must be wrought
   To th' undertaking with some labored art.

---

[2] Trickery.

Sej. Is he ambitious?
Liv.   No.
Sej.   Or covetous? 20
Liv. Neither.
Eud.   Yet gold is a good general charm.
Sej. What is he, then?
Liv.   Faith, only wanton, light.
Sej. How! Is he young and fair?
Eud.   A delicate youth.
Sej. Send him to me; I'll work him.—
    Royal lady,
Though I have loved you long, and with
    that height
Of zeal and duty, like the fire, which
    more
It mounts it trembles, thinking naught
    could add
Unto the fervor which your eye had
    kindled,
Yet, now I see your wisdom, judgment,
    strength,
Quickness, and will to apprehend the
    means   30
To your own good and greatness, I
    protest
Myself through rarefied, and turned all
    flame
In your affection. Such a spirit as yours
Was not created for the idle second
To a poor flash, as Drusus, but to shine
Bright as the moon among the lesser
    lights,
And share the sov'reignty of all the
    world.
Then Livia triumphs in her proper
    sphere,
When she and her Sejanus shall divide
The name of Cæsar, and Augusta's star
Be dimmed with glory of a brighter
    beam,   41
When Agrippina's fires are quite ex-
    tinct,
And the scarce-seen Tiberius borrows
    all
As little light from us, whose folded
    arms
Shall make one perfect orb! [*Knocking
    within.*] Who's that? Eudemus,
Look 'tis not Drusus.—[*Exit Eudemus.*]
    Lady, do not fear.
Liv. Not I, my lord. My fear and love
    of him
Left me at once.[1]

[1] Simultaneously.

Sej.   Illustr'ous lady, stay—
Eud. [*Within.*] I'll tell his lordship.

          [*Enter Eudemus.*]

Sej.   Who is 't, Eudemus?
Eud. One of your lordship's servants
    brings you word   50
The emp'ror hath sent for you.
Sej.   O! Where is he?—
With your fair leave, dear princess, I'll
    but ask
A question, and return.   *He goes out.*
Eud.   Fortunate princess!
How are you blessed in the fruition
Of this unequaled man, this soul of
    Rome,
The empire's life, and voice of Cæsar's
    world!
Liv. So blessed, my Eudemus, as to know
The bliss I have, with what I ought to
    owe
The means that wrought it. How do I
    look today?
Eud. Excellent clear, believe it.   This
    same fucus [2]   60
Was well laid on.
Liv.   Methinks 'tis here not white.
Eud. Lend me your scarlet, lady. 'Tis
    the sun
Hath giv'n some little taint unto the
    ceruse; [3]
You should have used of the white oil
    I gave you.
Sejanus for your love! His very name
Commandeth above Cupid or his shafts—
          [*Paints her cheek.*]
(Liv. Nay, now yo' have made it worse.
Eud.   I'll help it straight.)
—And, but pronounced, is a sufficient
    charm
Against all rumor, and of absolute power
To satisfy for any lady's honor.   70
(Liv. What do you now, Eudemus?
Eud.   Make a light fucus,
To touch you o'er withal.) Honored
    Sejanus!
What act, though ne'er so strange and
    insolent,
But that addition [4] will at least bear out,
If 't do not expiate?
Liv.   Here, good physician.

[2] Cosmetic.
[3] Cosmetic containing white lead.
[4] Title.

Eud. I like this study to preserve the love
　Of such a man, that comes not every
　　hour
　To greet the world. ('Tis now well, lady;
　　you should
　Use of the dentifrice I prescribed you,
　　too,
　To clear your teeth, and the prepared
　　pomatum,   80
　To smooth the skin.) A lady cannot be
　Too curious [1] of her form, that still
　　would hold
　The heart of such a person, made her
　　captive,
　As you have his; who, to endear him
　　more
　In your clear eye, hath put away his
　　wife,
　The trouble of his bed and your delights,
　Fair Apicata, and made spacious room
　To your new pleasures.
Liv.　　　　　　Have not we returned
　That with our hate of Drusus, and dis-
　　covery
　Of all his counsels?
Eud.　　　　Yes, and wisely, lady.　90
　The ages that succeed, and stand far off
　To gaze at your high prudence, shall
　　admire,
　And reckon it an act without [2] your sex;
　It hath that rare appearance. Some will
　　think
　Your fortune could not yield a deeper
　　sound
　Than mixed with Drusus'; but, when
　　they shall hear
　That and the thunder of Sejanus meet,
　Sejanus, whose high name doth strike
　　the stars,
　And rings about the concave—great
　　Sejanus,
　Whose glories, style, and titles are him-
　　self,   100
　The often iterating of Sejanus—
　They then will lose their thoughts, and
　　be ashamed
　To take acquaintance of them.

　　　　　　[Enter Sejanus.]
Sej.　　　　　　　　I must make
　A rude departure, lady; Cæsar sends
　With all his haste both of command and
　　prayer.

[1] Careful.　　　　　　　[2] Beyond.

Be resolute in our plot; you have my
　　soul,
　As certain yours as it is my body's.
　And, wise physician, so prepare the
　　poison
　As you may lay the subtile operation
　Upon some natural disease of his.　110
　Your eunuch send to me. I kiss your
　　hands,
　Glory of ladies, and commend my love
　To your best faith and memory.
Liv.　　　　　　　　My lord,
　I shall but change [3] your words. Fare-
　　well. Yet, this
　Remember for your heed, he loves you
　　not;
　You know what I have told you. His
　　designs
　Are full of grudge and danger; we must
　　use
　More than a common speed.
Sej.　　　　　　Excellent lady,
　How you do fire my blood!
Liv.　　　　　Well, you must go?
　The thoughts be best, are least set forth
　　to show.　　　　[Exit Sejanus.]　120
Eud. When will you take some physic,
　　lady?
Liv.　　　　When
　I shall, Eudemus; but let Drusus' drug
　Be first prepared.
Eud.　　Were Lygdus made, [4] that's done;
　I have it ready. And tomorrow morning
　I'll send you a perfume, first to resolve
　And procure sweat, and then prepare
　　a bath
　To cleanse and clear the cutis; against
　　when
　I'll have an excellent new fucus made,
　Resistive gainst the sun, the rain, or
　　wind,
　Which you shall lay on with a breath,
　　or oil,   130
　As you best like, and last some fourteen
　　hours.
　This change came timely, lady, for your
　　health,
　And the restoring your complexion,
　Which Drusus' choler had almost burnt
　　up,
　Wherein your fortune hath prescribed
　　you better
　Than art could do.

[3] Reciprocate.　　[4] Won to our purpose.

LIV. Thanks, good physician;
I'll use my fortune, you shall see, with
reverence.
Is my coach ready?
EUD. It attends your highness.
[*Exeunt.*]

[SCENE ii.

A room in the palace.]

Sejanus.

[SEJ.] If this be not revenge, when I have
done
And made it perfect, let Egyptian slaves,
Parthians, and barefoot Hebrews brand
my face,
And print my body full of injuries.
Thou lost thyself, childe [1] Drusus, when
thou thought'st
Thou couldst outskip my vengeance,
or outstand [2]
The power I had to crush thee into air.
Thy follies now shall taste what kind
of man
They have provoked, and this thy
father's house 9
Crack in the flame of my incenséd rage,
Whose fury shall admit no shame or
mean.
Adultery? It is the lightest ill
I will commit. A race of wicked acts
Shall flow out of my anger, and o'er-
spread
The world's wide face, which no pos-
terity
Shall e'er approve, nor yet keep silent—
things
That, for their cunning, close, and cruel
mark,
Thy father would wish his, and shall,
perhaps,
Carry the empty name, but we the prize.
On, then, my soul, and start not in thy
course; 20
Though heav'n drop sulphur, and hell
belch out fire,
Laugh at the idle terrors. Tell proud
Jove,
Between his power and thine there is
no odds.
'Twas only fear first in the world made
gods.

[Enter] *Tiberius* [*with Attendants*].[3]

[TIB.] Is yet Sejanus come?
SEJ. He's here, dread Cæsar.
TIB. Let all depart that chamber, and the
next.— [*Exeunt Attendants.*]
Sit down, my comfort. When the master-
prince
Of all the world, Sejanus, saith he fears,
Is it not fatal?
SEJ. Yes, to those are feared.
TIB. And not to him?
SEJ. Not if he wisely turn 30
That part of fate he holdeth, first on
them.
TIB. That nature, blood, and laws of
kind forbid.
SEJ. Do policy and state forbid it?
TIB. No.
SEJ. The rest of poor respects, then, let
go by;
State [4] is enough to make th' act just,
them guilty.
TIB. Long hate pursues such acts.
SEJ. Whom hatred frights,
Let him not dream on sov'reignty.
TIB. Are rites
Of faith, love, piety, to be trod down,
Forgotten, and made vain?
SEJ. All for a crown.
The prince who shames a tyran's name
to bear 40
Shall never dare do anything but fear;
All the command of scepters quite doth
perish,
If it begin religious thoughts to cherish;
Whole empires fall, swayed by those
nice respects;
It is the license of dark deeds protects
Ev'n states most hated, when no laws
resist
The sword, but that it acteth what it
list.
TIB. Yet so, we may do all things cruelly,
Not safely.
SEJ. Yes, and do them thoroughly.
TIB. Knows yet Sejanus whom we point
at?
SEJ. Ay, 50
Or else my thought, my sense, or both
do err:
'Tis Agrippina?
TIB. She, and her proud race.

[1] A youth of noble birth. [2] Withstand.

[3] The name *Sejanus* is repeated here.
[4] Reasons of state.

SEJ. Proud? Dangerous, Cæsar; for in
   them apace
The father's spirit shoots up. Germani-
   cus
Lives in their looks, their gait, their
   form, t' upbraid us
With his close death, if not revenge the
   same.
TIB. The act's not known.
SEJ.   Not proved; but whisp'ring Fame [1]
Knowledge and proof doth to the jeal-
   ous give,
Who, than to fail, would their own
   thought believe.
It is not safe the children draw long
   breath,   60
That are provokéd by a parent's death.
TIB. It is as dangerous to make them
   hence,
If nothing but their birth be their of-
   fense.
SEJ. Stay till they strike at Cæsar; then
   their crime
Will be enough; but late and out of time
For him to punish.
TIB.   Do they purpose it?
SEJ. You know, sir, thunder speaks not
   till it hit.
Be not secure; [2] none swiftlier are op-
   pressed
Than they whom confidence betrays to
   rest.
Let not your daring make your danger
   such;   70
All power's to be feared, where 'tis too
   much.
The youths are of themselves hot, vi-
   olent,
Full of great thought; and that male-
   spirited dame,
Their mother, slacks no means to put
   them on,
By large allowance, popular presentings,
Increase of train and state, suing for
   titles;
Hath them commended with like prayers,
   like vows,
To the same gods, with Caesar; days
   and nights
She spends in banquets and ambitious
   feasts
For the nobility, where Caius Silius,   80
Titius Sabinus, old Arruntius,

Asinius Gallus, Furnius, Regulus,
And others of that discontented list
Are the prime guests. There, and to
   these, she tells
Whose niece she was, whose daughter,
   and whose wife.
And then must they compare her with
   Augusta,
Ay, and prefer her too, commend her
   form,
Extol her fruitfulness, at which a
   shower
Falls for the memory of Germanicus,
Which they blow over straight with
   windy praise   90
And puffing hopes of her aspiring sons,
Who, with these hourly ticklings, grow
   so pleased
And wantonly conceited of themselves
As now they stick not to believe they're
   such
As these do give hem out, and would
   be thought
More than competitors, [3] immediate
   heirs,
Whilest to their thirst of rule they win
   the rout
(That's still the friend of novelty) with
   hope
Of future freedom, which on every
   change   99
That greedily, though emptily, expects. [4]
Cæsar, 'tis age in all things breeds neg-
   lects,
And princes that will keep old dignity
Must not admit too youthful heirs
   stand by—
Not their own issue—but so darkly set
As shadows are in picture, to give
   height
And luster to themselves.
TIB.   We will command
Their rank thoughts down, and with a
   stricter hand
Than we have yet put forth; their trains
   must bate,
Their titles, feasts, and factions.
SEJ.   Or your state.
But how, sir, will you work?
TIB.   Confine hem.
SEJ.   No.   110
They are too great, and that too faint
   a blow

---

[1] Rumor.   [2] Overconfident.

[3] Partners.   [4] Awaits.

To give them now; it would have served
   at first,
When with the weakest touch their
   knot had burst.
But now your care must be, not to de-
   tect
The smallest cord or line of your suspect,
For such, who know the weight of
   princes' fear,
Will, when they find themselves dis-
   covered, rear
Their forces, like seen snakes, that else
   would lie
Rolled in their circles, close. Naught is
   more high,
Daring, or desperate than offenders
   found;   120
Where guilt is, rage and courage doth
   abound.
The course must be, to let hem still
   swell up,
Riot, and surfeit on blind Fortune's cup;
Give hem more place, more dignities,
   more style,
Call hem to court, to senate; in the while,
Take from their strength some one or
   twain or more
Of the main fautors [1] (it will fright the
   store [2]),
And by some by-occasion. Thus, with
   sleight
You shall disarm first, and they, in
   night   129
Of their ambition, not perceive the train,
Till in the ingine [3] they are caught and
   slain.
TIB. We would not kill, if we knew how
   to save;
Yet, than a throne, 'tis cheaper give a
   grave.
Is there no way to bind them by deserts?
SEJ. Sir, wolves do change their hair, but
   not their hearts.
While thus your thought unto a mean
   is tied,
You neither dare enough, nor do provide.
All modesty is fond,[4] and chiefly where
The subject is no less compelled to bear,
Than praise, his sov'reign's acts.
TIB.   We can no longer   140
Keep on our mask to thee, our dear
   Sejanus;

[1] Adherents.   [2] Many.   [3] Trap.
[4] All moderation is foolish.

Thy thoughts are ours, in all, and we
   but proved
Their voice, in our designs, which by as-
   senting
Hath more confirmed us than if heart'n-
   ing Jove
Had, from his hundred statues, bid us
   strike,
And at the stroke clicked all his marble
   thumbs.
But who shall first be strook?
SEJ.   First, Caius Silius;
He is the most of mark, and most of
   danger—
In power and reputation equal strong,
Having commanded an imperial army
Seven years together, vanquished Sa-
   crovir   151
In Germany, and thence obtained to
   wear
The ornaments triumphal. His steep
   fall,
By how much it doth give the weightier
   crack,
Will send more wounding terror to the
   rest,
Command them stand aloof, and give
   more way
To our surprising of the principal.
TIB. But what, Sabinus?
SEJ.   Let him grow awhile;
His fate is not yet ripe. We must not
   pluck   159
At all together, lest we catch ourselves.
And there's Arruntius too; he only talks.
But Sosia, Silius' wife, would be wound
   in
Now, for she hath a fury in her breast
More than hell ever knew, and would
   be sent
Thither in time. Then is there one Cre-
   mutius
Cordus, a writing fellow, they have got
To gather notes of the precedent times,
And make them into annals—a most
   tart
And bitter spirit, I hear, who, under
   color
Of praising those, doth tax [5] the present
   state,   170
Censures [6] the men, the actions, leaves
   no trick,
No practice unexamined, parallels

[5] Accuse.   [6] Judges.

The times, the governments—a professed champion
For the old liberty—
TIB.   A perishing wretch!
As if there were that chaos bred in things,
That laws and liberty would not rather choose
To be quite broken and ta'en hence by us
Than have the stain to be preserved by such.
Have we the means to make these guilty first?
SEJ. Trust that to me. Let Cæsar, by his power,   180
But cause a formal meeting of the senate,
I will have matter and accusers ready.
TIB. But how? Let us consult.
SEJ.   We shall misspend
The time of action. Counsels are unfit
In business where all rest is more pernicious
Than rashness can be. Acts of this close kind
Thrive more by execution than advice.
There is no ling'ring in that work begun,
Which cannot praiséd be, until through done.
TIB. Our edict shall forthwith command a court.   190
While I can live, I will prevent earth's fury:
Ἐμοῦ θανόντος γαῖα μιχθήτω πυρί.[1]
                                        [*Exit.*]

[*Enter*] *Posthumus.*[2]

[Pos.] My Lord Sejanus—
SEJ.   Julius Posthumus,
Come with my wish! What news from Agrippina's?
Pos. Faith, none. They all lock up themselves alate,
Or talk in character;[3] I have not seen
A company so changed. Except they had
Intelligence by augury of our practice—
SEJ. When were you there?
Pos.   Last night.
SEJ.   And what guests found you?

Pos. Sabinus, Silius (the old list), Arruntius,   200
Furnius, and Gallus.
SEJ.   Would not these talk?
Pos.   Little.
And yet we offered choice of argument.[4]
Satrius was with me.
SEJ.   Well. 'Tis guilt enough,
Their often meeting. You forgot t' extol
The hospitable lady?
Pos.   No; that trick
Was well put home, and had succeeded too,
But that Sabinus coughed a caution out;
For she began to swell—
SEJ.   And may she burst!
Julius, I would have you go instantly
Unto the palace of the great Augusta,   210
And, by your kindest friend,[5] get swift access;
Acquaint her with these meetings. Tell the words
You brought me, th' other day, of Silius;
Add somewhat to hem. Make her understand
The danger of Sabinus, and the times,
Out of his closeness. Give Arruntius' words
Of malice against Cæsar; so, to Gallus;
But, above all, to Agrippina. Say,
As you may truly, that her infinite pride,
Propped with the hopes of her too fruitful womb,   220
With popular studies [6] gapes for sovereignty,
And threatens Cæsar. Pray Augusta then
That for her own, great Cæsar's, and the pub-
Lic safety, she be pleased to urge these dangers.
Cæsar is too secure; he must be told,
And best he'll take it from a mother's tongue.
Alas! What is 't for us to sound, t' explore,

---

[1] When I am dead, let the earth be overwhelmed with fire.
[2] The name *Sejanus* is repeated here.
[3] Cipher.

[4] Subject.
[5] Marginal note reads "Mutilia Prisca."
[6] Jonson's questionable rendering of *popularibus studiis, i.e.,* "The zeal and devotion of the people" (Briggs).

To watch, oppose, plot, practice, or pre-
    vent,
If he, for whom it is so strongly labored,
Shall, out of greatness and free spirit,
    be   230
Supinely negligent?   Our city's now
Divided as in time o' th' civil war,
And men forbear not to declare them-
    selves
Of Agrippina's party.   Every day
The faction multiplies, and will do more
If not resisted; you can best enlarge it,
As you find audience.   Noble Posthumus,
Commend me to your Prisca, and pray
    her
She will solicit this great business
To earnest and most present execu-
    tion,   240
With all her utmost credit with Augusta.
Pos. I shall not fail in my instructions.
                                       [*Exit.*]
SEJ. This second, from his mother, will
    well urge
Our late design, and spur on Cæsar's
    rage,
Which else might grow remiss.   The way
    to put
A prince in blood [1] is to present the
    shapes
Of dangers greater than they are, like
    late
Or early shadows, and, sometimes, to
    feign
Where there are none, only to make him
    fear.
His fear will make him cruel, and, once
    entered,   250
He doth not easily learn to stop, or
    spare
Where he may doubt.   This have I
    made my rule
To thrust Tiberius into tyranny,
And make him toil to turn aside those
    blocks
Which I alone could not remove with
    safety.
Drusus once gone, Germanicus' three
    sons
Would clog my way, whose guards have
    too much faith
To be corrupted, and their mother known
Of too-too unreproved [2] a chastity

---

[1] *I.e.*, make him angry.
[2] Too completely blameless.

To be attempted as light Livia was.   260
Work then, my art, on Cæsar's fears,
    as they
On those they fear, till all my lets [3] be
    cleared,
And he in ruins of his house, and hate
Of all his subjects, bury his own state,
When with my peace and safety I will
    rise
By making him the public sacrifice.
                                   [*Exit.*]

[SCENE iii.

A room in Agrippina's house.]

Satrius, Natta.

[SAT.] They are grown exceeding circum-
    spect and wary.
NAT. They have us in the wind; [4] and yet
    Arruntius
Cannot contain himself.
SAT.   Tut, he's not yet
Looked after; there are others more
    desired
That are more silent.
NAT.   Here he comes. Away! [*Exeunt.*]

[*Enter*] *Sabinus, Arruntius, Cordus.*

[SAB.] How is it that these beagles haunt
    the house
Of Agrippina?
ARR.   O, they hunt, they hunt!
There is some game here lodged, which
    they must rouse,
To make the great ones sport.
COR.   Did you observe
How they inveighed gainst Cæsar?
ARR.   Ay, baits, baits
For us to bite at; would I have my
    flesh   11
Torn by the public hook, these qualified
    hangmen
Should be my company.
COR.   Here comes another.

[*Afer passes by.*]

ARR. Ay, there's a man, Afer the orator!
One that hath phrases, figures, and fine
    flowers
To strew his rethoric [5] with, and doth
    make haste

---

[3] From 1605 edn.; original reads *betts.*
[4] They are on our scent.
[5] Rhetoric.

To get him note or name by any offer
Where blood or gain be objects; steeps
    his words,
When he would kill, in artificial tears—
The crocodile of Tiber! Him I love, 20
That man is mine. He hath my heart
    and voice
When I would curse—he, he.

SAB.   Contemn the slaves;
Their present lives will be their future
    graves.   [*Exeunt.*]

[*Enter*] *Silius, Agrippina, Nero, Sosia.*

[SIL.] May 't please your highness not
    forget yourself;
I dare not, with my manners, to attempt
Your trouble farder.

AGR.   Farewell, noble Silius!
SIL. Most royal princess!
AGR.   Sosia stays with us?
SIL. She is your servant, and doth owe
    your grace
An honest, but unprofitable love.
AGR. How can that be, when there's no
    gain but virtue's?   30
SIL. You take the moral, not the politic
    sense.
I meant, as she is bold, and free of
    speech,
Earnest to utter what her zealous
    thought
Travails withal, in honor of your house—
Which act, as it is simply borne in her,
Partakes of love and honesty, but may,
By th' over-often and unseasoned use,
Turn to your loss and danger; for your
    state
Is waited on by envies, as by eyes;
And every second guest your tables take
Is a fee'd spy, t' observe who goes, who
    comes,   41
What conference you have, with whom,
    where, when,
What the discourse is, what the looks,
    the thoughts
Of ev'ry person there, they do extract
And make into a substance.

AGR.   Hear me, Silius.
Were all Tiberius' body stuck with
    eyes,
And ev'ry wall and hanging in my house
Transparent, as this lawn I wear, or air,
Yea, had Sejanus both his ears as long
As to my inmost closet, I would hate 50

To whisper any thought, or change an
    act,
To be made Juno's rival. Virtue's forces
Show ever noblest in conspicuous
    courses.

SIL. 'Tis great, and bravely spoken, like
    the spirit
Of Agrippina; yet, your highness knows,
There is nor loss nor shame in provi-
    dence;[1]
Few can, what all should do, beware
    enough.
You may perceive with what officious
    face
Satrius and Natta, Afer and the rest
Visit your house of late, t' inquire the
    secrets,   60
And with what bold and privileged art
    they rail
Against Augusta, yea, and at Tiberius;
Tell tricks of Livia, and Sejanus—all
T' excite, and call your indignation on,
That they might hear it at more liberty.

AGR. Yo' are too suspicious, Silius.
SIL.   Pray the gods
I be so, Agrippina; but I fear
Some subtile practice. They that durst
    to strike
At so examples [2] and unblamed a life
As that of the renowned Germanicus, 70
Will not sit down with that exploit alone.
"He threatens many that hath injured
    one."

NERO. 'Twere best rip forth their tongues,
    sear out their eyes,
When next they come.

SOS.   A fit reward for spies.

[*Enter*] *Drusus Ju[nior].*[3]

DRU. Hear you the rumor?
AGR.   What?
DRU.   Drusus is dying.
AGR. Dying?
NERO.   That's strange!
AGR.   Yo' were with him yesternight.
DRU. One met Eudemus the physician,
Sent for but now, who thinks he can-
    not live.
SIL. Thinks? If 't be arrived at that, he
    knows,
Or none.

_____

[1] Prudence.   [2] Example-less, unexampled.
[3] The names *Agrippina, Nero,* and *Silius* are
here repeated.

AGR.　　　This 's quick! What should
　be his disease?　　　　　　　　　　80
SIL. Poison, poison—
AGR.　　　　　　How, Silius!
NERO.　　　　　　　　What's that?
SIL. Nay, nothing.　There was late a
　certain blow
　Giv'n o' the face.
NERO.　　　　　Ay, to Sejanus?
SIL.　　　　　　　　　　　True.
DRU. And what of that?
SIL.　　　　I am glad I gave it not.
NERO. But there is somewhat else?
SIL.　　　　Yes, private meetings,
　With a great lady at a physician's,
　And a wife turned away—
NERO.　　　Ha!
SIL.　　　　　　　Toys, mere toys!
　What wisdom's now i' th' streets? I'
　th' common mouth?
DRU. Fears, whisp'rings, tumults, noise,
　I know not what;
　They say the senate sit.
SIL.　　　　　I'll thither straight,　90
　And see what's in the forge.
AGR.　　　　　　　Good Silius, do;
　Sosia and I will in.
SIL.　　　　　　Haste you, my lords,
　To visit the sick prince; tender your
　loves
　And sorrows to the people. This Sejanus,
　Trust my divining soul, hath plots on
　all;
　No tree that stops his prospect but must
　fall.　　　　　　　　　　　[Exeunt.]
　　　CHORUS—of Musicians.

ACT III. [SCENE i.]

The Senate.

Sejanus, Varro, Latiaris. Cotta, Afer.
[Sabinus,] Gallus, Lepidus, Arruntius.
　　　　　Præcones,[1] Lictores.
[SEJ.] 'Tis only you must urge against him,
　Varro;
　Nor I nor Cæsar may appear therein,
　Except in your defense, who are the
　consul,
　And, under color of late enmity
　Between your father and his, may better
　do it,
　As free from all suspicion of a practice.

[1] Public criers.

Here be your notes, what points to touch
　at. Read;
　Be cunning in them. Afer has them too.
VAR. But is he summoned?
SEJ.　　　　　No. It was debated
　By Cæsar, and concluded as most fit　10
　To take him unprepared.
AFER.　　　　　And prosecute
　All under name of treason.
VAR.　　　　　　　I conceive.
SAB. Drusus being dead, Cæsar will not be
　here.
GAL. What should the business of this
　senate be?
ARR. That can my subtile whisperers tell
　you: we
　That are the good-dull-noble lookers-on
　Are only called to keep the marble
　warm.
　What should we do with those deep
　mysteries,
　Proper to these fine heads? Let them
　alone.
　Our ignorance may, perchance, help us
　be saved　　　　　　　　　　　　20
　From whips and Furies.
GAL.　　　See, see, see their action!
ARR. Ay, now their heads do travail, now
　they work;
　Their faces run like shittles;[2] they are
　weaving
　Some curious cobweb to catch flies.
SAB.　　　　　　　　　Observe,
　They take their places.
ARR.　　　　What, so low?
GAL.　　　　　　　　　O, yes,
　They must be seen to flatter Cæsar's
　grief,
　Though but in sitting.
VAR.　　　　Bid us silence.
PRÆ.　　　　　　　　Silence!
VAR. "Fathers conscript, may this our
　present meeting
　Turn fair and fortunate to the common-
　wealth!"

[Enter] Silius.[3]

SEJ. See, Silius enters.
SIL.　　　　　Hail, grave fathers!
LIC.　　　　　　　Stand.　30
　Silius, forbear thy place!
SEN[ATE].　　　　　　How!

[2] Shuttles.
[3] The word Senate is repeated here.

PRÆ.   Silius, stand forth;
The consul hath to charge thee.
LIC.   Room for Cæsar!
ARR. Is he come too? Nay, then, expect a
    trick.
SAB. Silius accused? Sure he will answer
    nobly.

[Enter] Tiberius [1] *[with Attendants].*

[TIB.] We stand amazéd, fathers, to be-
    hold
This general dejection. Wherefore sit
Rome's consuls thus dissolved,[2] as they
    had lost
All the remembrance both of style and
    place?
It not becomes. No woes are of fit weight
To make the honor of the empire stoop,
Though I, in my peculiar self, may
    meet   41
Just reprehension, that so suddenly,
And in so fresh a grief, would greet the
    senate,
When private tongues of kinsmen and
    allies,
Inspired with comforts, loathly are en-
    dured,
The face of men not seen, and scarce the
    day,
To thousands that communicate [3] our
    loss.
Nor can I argue these of weakness, since
They take but natural ways; yet I must
    seek
For stronger aids, and those fair helps
    draw out   50
From warm embraces of the common-
    wealth.
Our mother, great Augusta, is strook
    with time,
Our self impressed with aged characters,
Drusus is gone, his children young and
    babes.
Our aims must now reflect on those that
    may
Give timely succor to these present ills,
And are our only glad-surviving hopes,
The noble issue of Germanicus,
Nero and Drusus. Might it please the
    consul
Honor them in; they both attend with-
    out.   60

[1] The word *Senate* is repeated here.
[2] Discomposed.   [3] Share.

I would present them to the senate's
    care,
And raise those suns of joy that should
    drink up
These floods of sorrow in your drownéd
    eyes.
ARR. By Jove, I am not Œdipus enough
To understand this Sphinx.
SAB.   The princes come.

[Enter] [4] *Nero, Drusus Junior.*

[TIB.] Approach you, noble Nero, noble
    Drusus.
These princes, fathers, when their parent
    died,
I gave unto their uncle, with this prayer,
That though h' had proper issue of his
    own,
He would no less bring up and foster
    these   70
Than that self-blood, and by that act
    confirm
Their worths to him and to posterity.
Drusus ta'en hence, I turn my prayers to
    you,
And, fore [5] our country and our gods, be-
    seech
You take and rule Augustus' nephew's
    sons,
Sprung of the noblest ancestors, and so
Accomplish both my duty and your own.
Nero and Drusus, these shall be to you
In place of parents, these your fathers,
    these;
And not unfitly, for you are so born   80
As all your good or ill's the common-
    wealth's.
Receive them, you strong guardians, and,
    blessed gods,
Make all their actions answer to their
    bloods;
Let their great titles find increase by
    them,
Not they by titles. Set them, as in place,
So in example, above all the Romans;
And may they know no rivals but them-
    selves.
Let Fortune give them nothing, but
    attend
Upon their virtue, and that still come
    forth

[4] The name of *Tiberius* is repeated here.
[5] Before.

Greater than hope, and better than their
   fame.,   90
Relieve me, fathers, with your general
   voice.

SEN. "May all the gods consent to Cæsar's
   wish,
And add to any honors that may crown
The hopeful issue of Germanicus!" [1]

TIB. We thank you, reverend fathers, in
   their right.

ARR. [*Aside.*] If this were true now! But
   the space, the space
Between the breast and lips! Tiberius'
   heart
Lies a thought farder than another
   man's.

TIB. My comforts are so flowing in my
   joys,
As, in them, all my streams of grief are
   lost,   100
No less than are land-waters in the sea,
Or showers in rivers, though their cause
   was such
As might have sprinkled ev'n the gods
   with tears;
Yet, since the greater doth embrace the
   less,
We covetously obey.

(ARR.   Well acted, Cæsar.)

TIB. And, now I am the happy witness
   made
Of your so much desired affections
To this great issue, I could wish the
   Fates
Would here set peaceful period to my
   days;
However, to my labors I entreat—   110
And beg it of this senate—some fit ease.

(ARR. Laugh, fathers, laugh! Ha' you no
   spleens [2] about you?)

TIB. The burden is too heavy I sustain
On my unwilling shoulders; and I pray
It may be taken off, and reconferred
Upon the consuls, or some other Roman,
More able and more worthy.

(ARR.   Laugh on still!

SAB. Why, this doth render all the rest
   suspected!

GAL. It poisons all.

ARR.   O, do you taste it then?

SAB. It takes away my faith to anything
He shall hereafter speak.

ARR.   Ay, to pray that,   121
Which would be to his head as hot as
   thunder,
Gainst which he wears that charm,[3]
   should but the court
Receive him at his word.

GAL.   Hear!)

TIB.   For myself
I know my weakness, and so little covet,
Like some gone past, the weight that will
   oppress me,
As my ambition is the counterpoint.[4]

(ARR. Finely maintained; good still!)

SEJ.   But Rome, whose blood,
Whose nerves, whose life, whose very
   frame relies
On Cæsar's strength, no less than heaven
   on Atlas,   130
Cannot admit it but with general ruin.

(ARR. Ah, are you there to bring him off?)

SEJ.   Let Cæsar
No more then urge a point so contrary
To Cæsar's greatness, the grieved sen-
   ate's vows,
Or Rome's necessity.

(GAL.   He comes about.

ARR. More nimbly than Vertumnus.)

TIB.   For the public,
I may be drawn to show I can neglect
All private aims, though I affect my
   rest;
But, if the senate still command me
   serve,
I must be glad to practice my obedience.

(ARR. You must and will, sir. We do
   know it.)

SEN.   "Cæsar,   141
Live long and happy, great and royal
   Cæsar;
The gods preserve thee and thy modesty,
Thy wisdom and thy innocence!" [5]

(ARR.   Where is 't?
The prayer is made before the subject.)

SEN.   "Guard
His meekness, Jove, his piety, his care,
His bounty—"

ARR. [*Aside.*]   And his subtilty, I'll put
   in;

---

[1] Jonson's marginal note reads, "A form of
speaking they had."
[2] Supposed seat of the emotions such as
laughter.

[3] Jonson's marginal note reads, "A wreath
of laurel."   [4] Opposite.
[5] Jonson's marginal note reads, "Another
form."

Yet he'll keep that himself, without the gods.
All prayers are vain for him.

TIB.   We will not hold
Your patience, fathers, with long answer, but   150
Shall still contend [1] to be what you desire,
And work to satisfy so great a hope.
Proceed to your affairs.

ARR. [*Aside.*]   Now, Silius, guard thee;
The curtain's drawing. Afer advanceth.

PRÆ.   Silence!

AFER. Cite Caius Silius.

PRÆ.   Caius Silius!

SIL.   Here.

AFER. The triumph that thou hadst in Germany
For thy late victory on Sacrovir,
Thou hast enjoyed so freely, Caius Silius,
As no man it envied thee; nor would Cæsar
Or Rome admit that thou wert then defrauded   160
Of any honors thy deserts could claim
In the fair service of the commonwealth;
But now, if after all their loves and graces
(Thy actions and their courses being discovered)
It shall appear to Cæsar and this senate,
Thou hast defiled those glories with thy crimes—

SIL. Crimes?

AFER.   Patience, Silius.

SIL.   Tell thy moil [2] of patience;
I am a Roman. What are my crimes?
Proclaim them.
Am I too rich, too honest for the times?
Have I or treasure, jewels, land, or houses   170
That some informer gapes for? Is my strength
Too much to be admitted, or my knowledge?
These now are crimes.

AFER.   Nay, Silius, if the name
Of crime so touch thee, with what impotence
Wilt thou endure the matter to be searched?

SIL. I tell thee, Afer, with more scorn than fear:

[1] Strive.   [2] Mule.

Employ your mercenary tongue and art.
Where's my accuser?

VAR.   Here.

ARR. [*Aside.*]   Varro? The consul?
Is he thrust in?

VAR.   'Tis I accuse thee, Silius.
Against the majesty of Rome and Cæsar,   180
I do pronounce thee here a guilty cause,
First, of beginning and occasioning,
Next, drawing out the war in Gallia,
For which thou late triumph'st; dissembling long
That Sacrovir to be an enemy,
Only to make thy entertainment [3] more,
Whilst thou and thy wife Sosia polled [4] the province—
Wherein, with sordid-base desire of gain,
Thou hast discredited thy actions' worth,
And been a traitor to the state.

SIL.   Thou liest! 190

ARR. [*Aside.*] I thank thee, Silius; speak so still and often.

VAR. If I not prove it, Cæsar, but injustly
Have called him into trial, here I bind
Myself to suffer what I claim gainst him,
And yield to have what I have spoke, confirmed
By judgment of the court and all good men.

SIL. Cæsar, I crave to have my cause deferred,
Till this man's consulship be out.

TIB.   We cannot,
Nor may we grant it.

SIL.   Why? Shall he design [5]
My day of trial? Is he my accuser? 200
And must he be my judge?

TIB.   It hath been usual,
And is a right that custom hath allowed
The magistrate, to call forth private men
And to appoint their day, which privilege
We may not in the consul see infringed,
By whose deep watches and industrious care
It is so labored, as the commonwealth
Receive no loss, by any oblique course.

SIL. Cæsar, thy fraud is worse than violence.

TIB. Silius, mistake us not; we dare not use   210

[3] Reward, proceeds.
[4] Plundered by extortion.
[5] Designate.

The credit of the consul to thy wrong,
But only do preserve his place and power
So far as it concerns the dignity
And honor of the state.
ARR.   Believe him, Silius.
COT. Why, so he may, Arruntius.
ARR.   I say so;
And he may choose too.
TIB.   By the Capitol
And all our gods, but that the dear
    republic,
Our sacred laws, and just authority
Are interessed [1] therein, I should be
    silent.
AFER. Please Cæsar to give way unto his
    trial.   220
He shall have justice.
SIL.   Nay, I shall have law;
Shall I not, Afer? Speak!
AFER.   Would you have mo[re?] [2]
SIL. No, my well-spoken man, I would no
    more;
Nor less, might I enjoy it natural,
Not taught to speak unto your present
    ends,
Free from thine, his, and all your unkind
    handling,
Furious enforcing, most unjust pre-
    suming,
Malicious and manifold applying,
Foul wresting, and impossible construc-
    tion.
AFER. He raves, he raves!
SIL.   Thou durst not tell me so,   230
Hadst thou not Cæsar's warrant. I can
    see
Whose power condemns me.
VAR.   This betrays his spirit;
This doth enough declare him what he is.
SIL. What am I? Speak.
VAR.   An enemy to the state.
SIL. Because I am an enemy to thee,
And such corrupted ministers o' the
    state,
That here art made a present instru-
    ment
To gratify it with thine own disgrace.
SEJ. This, to the consul, is most insolent,
And impious!
SIL.   Ay, take part. Reveal yourselves.
Alas! I scent not your confed'racies,   241

Your plots, and combinations? I not
    know
Minion Sejanus hates me, and that all
This boast of law and law is but a form,
A net of Vulcan's filing, a mere ingine
To take that life by a pretext of justice,
Which you pursue in malice? I want
    brain
Or nostril to persuade me that your ends
And purposes are made to what they are,
Before my answer? O, you equal gods,
Whose justice not a world of wolf-turned
    men   251
Shall make me to accuse (howe'er pro-
    voke[d]),
Have I for this so oft engaged myself?
Stood in the heat and fervor of a fight,
When Phœbus sooner hath forsook the
    day
Than I the field, against the blue-eyed
    Gauls,
And crispéd [3] Germans, when our Roman
    eagles
Have fanned the fire with their laboring
    wings,
And no blow dealt that left not death
    behind it;
When I have charged, alone, into the
    troops   260
Of curled Sicambrians, routed them, and
    came
Not off with backward ensigns of a slave,
But forward marks, wounds on my breast
    and face,
Were meant to thee, O Cæsar, and thy
    Rome?
And have I this return? Did I, for this,
Perform so noble and so brave defeat
On Sacrovir? O Jove, let it become me
To boast my deeds, when he whom they
    concern
Shall thus forget them.
AFER.   Silius, Silius,
These are the common customs of thy
    blood   270
When it is high with wine, as now with
    rage.
This well agrees with that intemperate
    vaunt
Thou lately mad'st at Agrippina's table
That, when all other of the troops were
    prone
To fall into rebellion, only yours

Remained in their obedience. You were he
That saved the empire, which had then been lost
Had but your legions there rebelled or mutined; [1]
Your virtue met and fronted every peril.
You gave to Cæsar and to Rome their surety.   280
Their name, their strength, their spirit, and their state,
Their being was a donative from you.

ARR. [*Aside.*] Well worded, and most like an orator.

TIB. Is this true, Silius?

SIL.   Save thy question, Cæsar;
Thy spy of famous credit hath affirmed it.

ARR. [*Aside.*] Excellent Roman!

SAB. [*Aside.*]   He doth answer stoutly.

SEJ. If this be so, there needs no farder cause
Of crime against him.

VAR.   What can more impeach
The royal dignity and state of Cæsar
Than to be urgéd with a benefit   290
He cannot pay.

COT.   In this, all Cæsar's fortune
Is made unequal to the courtesy.

LAT. His means are clean destroyed that should requite.

GAL. [*Ironically.*] Nothing is great enough for Silius' merit.

ARR. [*Aside.*] Gallus on that side too?

SIL.   Come, do not hunt
And labor so about for circumstance
To make him guilty whom you have foredoomed.
Take shorter ways; I'll meet your purposes.
The words were mine, and more I now will say:
Since I have done thee that great service, Cæsar,   300
Thou still hast feared me, and, in place of grace,
Returned me hatred; so soon all best turns,
With doubtful [2] princes, turn deep injuries
In estimation, when they greater rise
Than can be answered. Benefits, with you,

Are of no longer pleasure than you can
With ease restore them; that transcended once,
Your studies are not how to thank, but kill.
It is your nature to have all men slaves
To you, but you acknowledging to none.
The means that makes your greatness must not come   311
In mention of it; if it do, it takes
So much away, you think; and that which helped
Shall soonest perish, if it stand in eye,
Where it may front [3] or but upbraid the high.

COT. Suffer him speak no more.

VAR.   Note but his spirit.

AFER. This shows him in the rest.

LAT.   Let him be censured.[4]

SEJ. He hath spoke enough to prove him Cæsar's foe.

COT. His thoughts look through his words.

SEJ.   A censure!

SIL.   Stay,
Stay, most officious senate, I shall straight   320
Delude thy fury. Silius hath not placed
His guards within him, against Fortune's spite,
So weakly but he can escape your gripe
That are but hands of Fortune. She herself,
When Virtue doth oppose, must lose her threats.
All that can happen in humanity,
The frown of Cæsar, proud Sejanus' hatred,
Base Varro's spleen, and Afer's bloodying tongue,
The senate's servile flattery, and these
Mustered to kill, I am fortified against,
And can look down upon; they are beneath me.   331
It is not life whereof I stand enamored,
Nor shall my end make me accuse my fate.
The coward and the valiant man must fall;
Only the cause, and manner how, discerns them[5]—
Which then are gladdest, when they cost us dearest.

[1] Mutinied.   [2] Suspicious.

[3] Affront.   [4] Judged.
[5] Distinguishes them from each other.

Romans, if any here be in this senate,
Would know to mock Tiberius' tyranny,
Look upon Silius, and so learn to die.

                      [*Stabs himself.*] [1]

VAR. O desperate act!
ARR. [*Aside.*]   An honorable hand! 340
TIB. Look, is he dead?
SAB. [*Aside.*]   'Twas nobly strook, and
  home.
ARR. [*Aside.*] My thought did prompt him
  to it. Farewell, Silius!
  Be famous ever for thy great example.
TIB. We are not pleased in this sad acci-
  dent,
  That thus hath stalléd,[2] and abused our
    mercy,
  Intended to preserve thee, noble Roman,
  And to prevent thy hopes.
ARR. [*Aside.*]   Excellent wolf!
  Now he is full, he howls.
SEJ.   Cæsar doth wrong
  His dignity and safety thus to mourn
  The deserved end of so professed a
    traitor,   350
  And doth, by this his lenity, instruct
  Others as factious to the like offense.
TIB. The confiscation merely of his state
  Had been enough.
ARR. [*Aside.*]   O, that was gaped for
  then?
VAR. Remove the body.
SEJ.   Let citation
  Go out for Sosia.
GAL.   Let her be proscribed;
  And for the goods, I think it fit that half
  Go to the treasure,[3] half unto the chil-
  dren.
LEP. With leave of Cæsar, I would think
  that fourth
  Part, which the law doth cast on the
    informers,   360
  Should be enough; the rest go to the
  children—
  Wherein the prince shall show humanity
  And bounty, not to force them by their
    want,
  Which in their parent's trespass they
    deserved,
  To take ill courses.
TIB.   It shall please us.
ARR. [*Aside.*]   Ay,
  Out of necessity. This Lepidus

Is grave and honest, and I have observed
A moderation still in all his censures.
SAB. [*Aside.*] And bending to the better.—
  Stay, who's this?
  Cremutius Cordus? What? Is he brought
  in?   370
ARR. [*Aside.*] More blood unto the ban-
  quet? Noble Cordus,
  I wish thee good; be as thy writings, free
  And honest.
TIB.   What is he?
SEJ.   For th' annals, Cæsar.

[*Enter*] *Præco[nes], Cordus* [*with Guards*],
                     Satrius, Natta.

[PRÆ.] Cremutius Cordus!
COR.   Here.
PRÆ.   Satrius Secundus,
  Pinnarius Natta, you are his accusers.
ARR. [*Aside.*] Two of Sejanus' blood-
  hounds, whom he breeds
  With human flesh, to bay at citizens.
AFER. Stand forth before the senate, and
  confront him.
SAT. I do accuse thee here, Cremutius
  Cordus,
  To be a man factious and dangerous, 380
  A sower of sedition in the state,
  A turbulent and discontented spirit,
  Which I will prove from thine own writ-
    ings here,
  The annals thou hast published, where
    thou bit'st
  The present age, and with a viper's
    tooth,
  Being a member of it, dar'st that ill
  Which never yet degenerous [4] bastard
    did
  Upon his parent.
NAT.   To this I subscribe,
  And, forth [5] a world of more particu-
    lars,
  Instance in only one: comparing men
  And times, thou praisest Brutus, and
    affirm'st   391
  That Cassius was the last of all the
  Romans.
COT. How! What are we then?
VAR.   What is Cæsar? Nothing?
AFER. My lords, this strikes at every
  Roman's private,[6]

---

[1] From 1692 edn.   [3] Treasury.
[2] Forestalled.

[4] Degenerate.   [6] Private interest.
[5] From.

In whom reigns gentry and estate of
    spirit,[1]
To have a Brutus brought in parallel,
A parricide, an enemy of his country,
Ranked, and preferred to any real worth
That Rome now holds. This is most
    strangely invective,
Most full of spite, and insolent up-
    braiding.   400
Nor is 't the time alone is here disprized,[2]
But the whole man of time, yea, Cæsar's
    self,
Brought in disvalue; and he aimed at
    most
By oblique glance of his licentious pen.
Cæsar, if Cassius were the last of Ro-
    mans,
Thou hast no name.
TIB.   Let's hear him answer. Silence!
COR. So innocent I am of fact,[3] my lords,
As but my words are argued, yet those
    words
Not reaching either prince or prince's
    parent—
The which your law of treason compre-
    hends.   410
Brutus and Cassius I am charged t' have
    praised,
Whose deeds, when many more besides
    myself
Have writ, not one hath mentioned with-
    out honor.
Great Titus Livius, great for eloquence
And faith amongst us, in his history
With so great praises Pompey did extol,
As oft Augustus called him a Pompeian:
Yet this not hurt their friendship. In his
    book
He often names Scipio, Afranius,
Yea, the same Cassius, and this Brutus
    too,   420
As worthi'st men—not thieves and par-
    ricides,
Which notes upon their fames are now
    imposed.
Asinius Pollio's writings quite throughout
Give them a noble memory; so Messala
Renowned his general, Cassius; yet both
    these
Lived with Augustus, full of wealth and
    honors.

To Cicero's book, where Cato was heaved
    up
Equal with heaven, what else did Cæsar
    answer,
Being then dictator, but with a penned
    oration,
As if before the judges? Do but see   430
Antonius' letters; read but Brutus'
    pleadings—
What vile reproach they hold against
    Augustus,
False, I confess, but with much bitter-
    ness.
The epigrams of Bibaculus and Catullus
Are read, full stuffed with spite of both
    the Cæsars;
Yet deified Julius, and no less Augustus,
Both bore them, and contemned them.
    I not know,
Promptly to speak it, whether done with
    more
Temper, or wisdom; for such obloquies
If they despiséd be, they die suppressed;
But, if with rage acknowledged, they are
    confessed.   441
The Greeks I slip,[4] whose license not
    alone
But also lust did scape unpunishéd,
Or where someone, by chance, exception
    took,
He words with words revenged. But in
    my work
What could be aimed more free,[5] or
    farder off
From the time's scandal, than to write of
    those
Whom death from grace or hatred had
    exempted?
Did I, with Brutus and with Cassius,
Armed and possessed of the Philippi
    fields,   450
Incense the people in the civil cause,
With dangerous speeches? Or do they,
    being slain
Seventy years since, as by their images,
Which not the conqueror hath defaced,
    appears,
Retain that guilty memory with writers?
Posterity pays every man his honor.
Nor shall there want, though I con-
    demnéd am,
That [6] will not only Cassius well approve,

[1] Gentle blood and spirit befitting one of rank.
[2] Contemptuously depreciated.
[3] Deed.
[4] Pass over.   [6] Those who.
[5] Innocently.

And of great Brutus' honor mindful be,
But that will also mention make of
   me.   460

ARR. [*Aside.*] Freely and nobly spoken!

SAB. [*Aside.*]   With good temper;
   I like him, that he is not moved with
   passion.

ARR. [*Aside.*] He puts hem to their whisper.

TIB.   Take him hence;
   We shall determine of him at next sitting.
           [*Exeunt Guards with Cordus.*]

COT. Meantime, give order that his books
   be burnt,
   To the ædiles.

SEJ.   You have well advised.

AFER. It fits not such licentious things
   should live
   T' upbraid the age.

ARR.   If th' age were good, they might.

LAT. Let hem be burnt.

GAL.   All sought and burnt today.

PRÆ. The court is up; lictors, resume the
   fasces.   470
[*Exeunt All but*] *Arruntius, Sabinus, Lepidus.*

[ARR.] Let hem be burnt! O, how ridic-
   ulous
   Appears the senate's brainless diligence,
   Who think they can, with present power,
      extinguish
   The memory of all succeeding times!

SAB. 'Tis true, when, contrary, the punish-
   ment
   Of wit doth make th' authority in-
      crease.
   Nor do they aught, that use this cruelty
   Of interdiction, and this rage of burn-
      ing,
   But purchase to themselves rebuke and
      shame,
   And to the writers an eternal name. 480

LEP. It is an argument the times are
   sore,
   When virtue cannot safely be advanced,
   Nor vice reproved.

ARR.   Ay, noble Lepidus;
   Augustus well foresaw what we should
      suffer
   Under Tiberius, when he did pronounce
   The Roman race most wretched, that
      should live
   Between so slow jaws, and so long
   a-bruising.   [*Exeunt.*]

[SCENE ii.

A room in the palace.]

Tiberius, Sejanus.

[TIB.] This business hath succeeded well,
   Sejanus,
   And quite removed all jealousy of prac-
      tice
   Gainst Agrippina and our nephews. Now
   We must bethink us how to plant our in-
      gines
   For th' other pair, Sabinus and Arrun-
      tius,
   And Gallus too; howe'er he flatter us,
   His heart we know.

SEJ.   Give it some respite, Cæsar.
   Time shall mature and bring to perfect
      crown
   What we, with so good vultures,[1] have
      begun;
   Sabinus shall be next.

TIB.   Rather Arruntius. 10

SEJ. By any means, preserve him. His
   frank tongue,
   Being lent the reins, will take away all
      thought
   Of malice, in your course against the
      rest.
   We must keep him to stalk with.

TIB.   Dearest head,
   To thy most fortunate design I yield it.

SEJ. Sir, I have been so long trained up
   in grace,
   First with your father, great Augustus,
      since
   With your most happy bounties so
      familiar,
   As I not sooner would commit my
      hopes
   Or wishes to the gods than to your
      ears.   20
   Nor have I ever yet been covetous
   Of overbright and dazzling honors—
      rather
   To watch and travail in great Cæsar's
      safety,
   With the most common soldier.

TIB.   'Tis confessed.

SEJ. The only gain, and which I count
   most fair
   Of all my fortunes, is that mighty Cæsar

---

[1] *I.e.,* auspiciously, with reference to augury
by means of birds.

Hath thought me worthy his alliance.[1]
Hence
Begin my hopes.

TIB.　　　H'mh?

SEJ.　　　　　I have heard Augustus,
In the bestowing of his daughter, thought
But even [2] of gentlemen of Rome; if
so—　　　　　　　　　　　　　　　30
I know not how to hope so great a favor—
But, if a husband should be sought for
Livia,
And I be had in mind, as Cæsar's friend,
I would but use the glory of the kindred.
It should not make me slothful, or less
caring
For Cæsar's state; it were enough to me
It did confirm and strengthen my weak
house
Against the now-unequal opposition
Of Agrippina; and for dear regard
Unto my children, this I wish. Myself　40
Have no ambition farder than to end
My days in service of so dear a master.

TIB. We cannot but commend thy piety,
Most loved Sejanus, in acknowledging
Those bounties, which we, faintly, such
remember.
But to thy suit. The rest of mortal men,
In all their drifts and counsels, pursue
profit;
Princes alone are of a different sort,
Directing their main actions still to
fame.
We therefore will take time to think and
answer.　　　　　　　　　　　　50
For Livia she can best, herself, resolve
If she will marry, after Drusus, or
Continue in the family; besides,
She hath a mother, and a grandame yet,
Whose nearer counsels she may guide
her by;
But I will simply deal. That enmity
Thou fear'st in Agrippina would burn
more,
If Livia's marriage should, as 'twere in
parts,
Divide th' imperial house; an emulation
Between the women might break forth,
and discord　　　　　　　　　　60
Ruin the sons and nephews on both
hands.

What if it cause some present difference?
Thou art not safe, Sejanus, if thou
prove [3] it.
Canst thou believe that Livia, first the
wife
To Caius Cæsar, then my Drusus, now
Will be contented to grow old with thee,
Born but a private gentleman of Rome,
And raise thee with her loss, if not her
shame?
Or, say that I should wish it, cans't
thou think
The senate or the people (who have
seen　　　　　　　　　　　　　70
Her brother, father, and our ancestors
In highest place of empire) will endure it?
The state thou hold'st already, is in
talk;
Men murmur at thy greatness; and the
nobles
Stick not, in public, to upbraid thy
climbing
Above our father's favors, or thy scale,
And dare accuse me, from their hate to
thee.
Be wise, dear friend. We would not hide
these things,
For friendship's dear respect. Nor will
we stand
Adverse to thine or Livia's design-
ments.　　　　　　　　　　　　80
What we have purposed to thee, in our
thought,
And with what near degrees of love to
bind thee,
And make thee equal to us, for the pres-
ent
We will forbear to speak. Only, thus
much
Believe, our loved Sejanus, we not know
That height in blood or honor, which
thy virtue
And mind to us may not aspire [4] with
merit.
And this we'll publish on all watched
occasion
The senate or the people shall present.

SEJ. I am restored, and to my sense
again,　　　　　　　　　　　　90
Which I had lost in this so blinding suit.
Cæsar hath taught me better to refuse
Than I knew how to ask. How pleaseth
Cæsar

T' embrace my late advice for leaving
    Rome?

TIB. We are resolved.

SEJ.   Here are some motives more,
               [*Gives him a paper.*]
    Which I have thought on since, may
    more confirm.

TIB. Careful Sejanus!   We will straight
    peruse them.
    Go forward in our main design, and
    prosper.   [*Exit.*]

SEJ. If those but take, I shall. Dull, heavy
    Cæsar!
    Wouldst thou tell me thy favors were
    made crimes,   100
    And that my fortunes were esteemed thy
    faults,
    That thou for me wert hated, and not
    think
    I would with wingéd haste prevent that
    change,
    When thou might'st win all to thyself
    again
    By forfeiture of me?   Did those fond
    words
    Fly swifter from thy lips than this my
    brain,
    This sparkling forge, created me an
    armor
    T' encounter chance and thee?   Well,
    read my charms,
    And may they lay that hold upon thy
    senses,
    As thou hadst snuffed up hemlock, or
    ta'en down   110
    The juice of poppy and of mandrakes.
    Sleep,
    Voluptuous Cæsar, and security
    Seize on thy stupid powers, and leave
    them dead
    To public cares; awake but to thy
    lusts,
    The strength of which makes thy li-
    bidinous soul
    Itch to leave Rome—and I have thrust
    it on,
    With blaming of the city business,
    The multitude of suits, the confluence
    Of suitors, then their importunacies,
    The manifold distractions he must
    suffer,   120
    Besides ill-rumors, envies, and re-
    proaches,
    All which a quiet and retiréd life,

    Larded with ease and pleasure, did
    avoid,
    And yet for any weighty and great
    affair,
    The fittest place to give the soundest
    counsels.
    By this shall I remove him both from
    thought
    And knowledge of his own most dear
    affairs;
    Draw all despatches through my private
    hands;
    Know his designments, and pursue mine
    own;
    Make mine own strengths by giving suits
    and places,   130
    Conferring dignities and offices;
    And these that hate me now, wanting
    access
    To him, will make their envy none, or
    less;
    For, when they see me arbiter of all,
    They must observe, or else with Cæsar
    fall.   [*Exit.*]

[SCENE iii.

Another room in the palace.]

Tiberius, Servus.[1]

[TIB.] To marry Livia?   Will no less,
    Sejanus,
    Content thy aims?   No lower object?
    Well!
    Thou know'st how thou art wrought into
    our trust,
    Woven in our design, and think'st we
    must
    Now use thee, whatso'er thy projects
    are.
    'Tis true—but yet with caution and fit
    care.
    And, now we better think—who's there
    within?

[*Enter Servus.*]

SER. Cæsar?

TIB. [*Aside.*]   To leave our journey off
    were sin
    Gainst our decreed delights, and would
    appear
    Doubt, or, what less becomes a prince,
    low fear.   20

_____
[1] *I.e.*, a servant, who enters later.

Yet doubt hath law, and fears have their
　　excuse,
Where princes' states plead necessary
　　use,
As ours doth now more in Sejanus'
　　pride,
Than all fell [1] Agrippina's hates beside.
Those are the dreadful enemies we raise
With favors and make dangerous with
　　praise;
The injured by us may have will alike,
But 'tis the favorite hath the power to
　　strike;
And fury ever boils more high and
　　strong,
Heat' [2] with ambition, than revenge of
　　wrong.　　　　　　　　　　　　　20
'Tis then a part of supreme skill, to
　　grace
No man too much, but hold a certain
　　space
Between th' ascender's rise and thine
　　own flat, [3]
Lest, when all rounds [4] be reached, his
　　aim be that.
'Tis thought—[To Servus.]　Is Macro in
　　the palace?　See.
If not, go seek him, to come to us.—[Exit
　　Servus.]　He
Must be the organ we must work by
　　now,
Though none less apt for trust; need
　　doth allow
What choice would not.　I have heard
　　that aconite,
Being timely taken, hath a healing
　　might　　　　　　　　　　　　30
Against the scorpion's stroke; the proof
　　we'll give,
That, while two poisons wrastle, we may
　　live.
He hath a spirit too working [5] to be
　　used
But to th' encounter of his like; ex-
　　cused
Are wiser sov'reigns then, that raise
　　one ill
Against another, and both safely kill.
The prince that feeds great natures,
　　they will sway him;
Who nourisheth a lion, must obey him.—

[Enter Servus with] Macro. [6]

Macro, we sent for you.
MAC.　　　　　　I heard so, Cæsar.　39
TIB. Leave us awhile.—　　[Exit Servus.]
　　When you shall know, good Macro,
The causes of our sending and the ends,
You will then hearken nearer, and be
　　pleased
You stand so high both in our choice and
　　trust.
MAC. The humblest place in Cæsar's
　　choice or trust
May make glad Macro proud, with-
　　out ambition
Save to do Cæsar service.
TIB.　　　　　　Leave our courtings.
We are in purpose, Macro, to depart
The city for a time, and see Campania,
Not for our pleasures, but to dedicate
A pair of temples, one to Jupiter　　50
At Capua, th' other at Nola to Augustus,
In which great work, perhaps, our stay
　　will be
Beyond our will produced. [7]　Now, since
　　we are
Not ignorant what danger may be born
Out of our shortest absence, in a state
So subject unto envy, and embroiled
With hate and faction, we have thought
　　on thee,
Amongst a field of Romans, worthiest
　　Macro,
To be our eye and ear, to keep strict
　　watch
On Agrippina, Nero, Drusus, ay,　　60
And on Sejanus—not that we distrust
His loyalty, or do repent one grace
Of all that heap we have conferred on
　　him
(For that were to disparage our elec-
　　tion, [8]
And call that judgment now in doubt,
　　which then
Seemed as unquestioned as an oracle);
But greatness hath his cankers.　Worms
　　and moths
Breed out of too fit matter, in the things
Which after they consume, transferring
　　quite
The substance of their makers int'
　　themselves.　　　　　　　　70

---

[1] Fierce.
[2] Heated.
[3] Level.
[4] I.e., of the ladder.
[5] Active.

[6] The name Tiberius is repeated here.
[7] Prolonged.　　　　　　　　[8] Selection.

Macro is sharp, and apprehends. Besides,
I know him subtile, close, wise, and well-read
In man, and his large nature; he hath studied
Affections, passions, knows their springs, their ends,
Which way and whether they will work; 'tis proof
Enough of his great merit that we trust him.
Then to a point (because our conference
Cannot be long without suspicion):
Here, Macro, we assign thee both to spy,
Inform, and chastise; think, and use thy means,   80
Thy ministers, what, where, on whom thou wilt;
Explore, plot, practice. All thou dost in this
Shall be, as if the senate or the laws
Had giv'n it privilege, and thou thence styled
The savior both of Cæsar and of Rome,
We will not take thy answer but in act,
Whereto, as thou proceed'st, we hope to hear
By trusted messengers. If 't be inquired
Wherefore we called you, say you have in charge
To see our chariots ready, and our horse.   90
Be still our loved and, shortly, honored Macro.   [*Exit.*]
MAC. I will not ask why Cæsar bids do this,
But joy that he bids me. It is the bliss
Of courts to be employed, no matter how;
A prince's power makes all his actions virtue.
We whom he works by are dumb instruments,
To do, but not inquire; his great intents
Are to be served, not searched. Yet, as that bow
Is most in hand whose owner best doth know
T' affect [1] his aims, so let that statesman hope   100
Most use, most price, can hit his prince's scope.[2]

[1] Know how to effect.   [2] Mark.

Nor must he look at what or whom to strike,
But loose [3] at all; each mark must be alike.
Were it to plot against the fame, the life
Of one with whom I twinned; remove a wife
From my warm side, as loved as is the air;
Practice away each parent; draw mine heir
In compass,[4] though but one; work all my kin
To swift perdition; leave no untrained engine [5]
For friendship, or for innocence; nay, make   110
The gods all guilty; I would undertake
This, being imposed me, both with gain and ease.
The way to rise is to obey and please.
He that will thrive in state, he must neglect
The trodden paths that truth and right respect,
And prove new, wilder ways; for virtue there
Is not that narrow thing she is elsewhere.
Men's fortune there is virtue; reason, their will;
Their license, law; and their observance, skill.
Occasion is their foil; conscience, their stain;   120
Profit, their luster; and what else is, vain.
If then it be the lust of Cæsar's power
T' have raised Sejanus up, and in an hour
O'erturn him, tumbling, down from height of all,
We are his ready engine, and his fall
May be our rise. It is no uncouth [6] thing
To see fresh buildings from old ruins spring.   [*Exit.*]

CHORUS—*of Musicians.*

[3] Shoot.
[4] Into a trap.
[5] Instrument.
[6] Unknown.

Act IV. [Scene i.

A room in Agrippina's house.]

Gallus, Agrippina, Nero, Drusus, Caligula.[1]

[Gal.] You must have patience, royal Agrippina.

Agr. I must have vengeance first; and that were nectar
Unto my famished spirits. O, my fortune,
Let it be sudden thou prepar'st against me;
Strike all my powers of understanding blind,
And ignorant of destiny to come!
Let me not fear, that cannot hope.

Gal.   Dear princess,
These tyrannies[2] on yourself are worse than Cæsar's.

Agr. Is this the happiness of being born great?
Still to be aimed at? Still to be suspected?   10
To live the subject of all jealousies?
At least the color[3] made, if not the ground,
To every painted danger? Who would not
Choose once to fall than thus to hang forever?

Gal. You might be safe if you would—

Agr.   What, my Gallus?
Be lewd Sejanus' strumpet? Or the bawd
To Cæsar's lusts he now is gone to practice?
Not these are safe, where nothing is. Yourself,
While thus you stand but by me, are not safe.
Was Silius safe? Or the good Sosia safe?   20
Or was my niece, dear Claudia Pulchra, safe?
Or innocent Furnius? They that latest have
(By being made guilty) added reputation
To Afer's eloquence? O, foolish friends,
Could not so fresh example warn your loves,
But you must buy my favors with that loss

Unto yourselves, and when you might perceive
That Cæsar's cause of raging must forsake him
Before his will? Away, good Gallus, leave me.
Here to be seen is danger; to speak, treason;   30
To do me least observance is called faction.
You are unhappy in me, and I in all.
Where are my sons, Nero and Drusus? We
Are they be shot at; let us fall apart,
Not in our ruins sepulcher our friends.
Or shall we do some action, like offense,[4]
To mock their studies that would make us faulty,
And frustrate practice by preventing[5] it?
The danger's like; for what they can contrive
They will make good. No innocence is safe   40
When power contests; nor can they trespass more,
Whose only being was all crime before.

[*Enter Nero, Drusus, and Caligula.*]

Nero. You hear Sejanus is come back from Cæsar?

Gal. No. How? Disgraced?

Dru.   More gracéd now than ever.

Gal. By what mischance?

Cal.   A fortune like enough
Once to be bad.

Dru.   But turned too good to both.

Gal. What was 't?

Nero.   Tiberius sitting at his meat,
In a farmhouse they call Spelunca, sited
By the seaside, among the Fundane hills,
Within a natural cave, part of the grot 50
About the entry fell and overwhelmed
Some of the waiters; others ran away;
Only Sejanus with his knees, hands, face,
O'erhanging Cæsar, did oppose himself
To the remaining ruins, and was found
In that so laboring posture by the soldiers
That came to succor him. With which adventure

---

[1] Last three enter later.   [2] Cruelties.
[3] Pretext, although double meanings run through the sentence.

[4] Like what we are charged with.
[5] Anticipating.

He hath so fixed himself in Cæsar's trust
As thunder cannot move him, and is come
With all the height of Cæsar's praise to Rome.   60
AGR. And power to turn those ruins all on us,
And bury whole posterities beneath them.
Nero and Drusus and Caligula,
Your places are the next, and therefore most
In their offense. Think on your birth and blood,
Awake your spirits, meet their violence;
'Tis princely when a tyran doth oppose,
And is a fortune sent to exercise
Your virtue, as the wind doth try strong trees,
Who by vexation [1] grow more sound and firm.   70
After your father's fall, and uncle's fate,
What can you hope, but all the change of stroke
That force or sleight can give? Then stand upright;
And, though you do not act, yet suffer nobly.
Be worthy of my womb, and take strong cheer;
What we do know will come, we should not fear.   [Exeunt.]

[SCENE ii.

A room in the palace.]

Macro.

[MAC.] Returned so soon? Renewed in trust and grace?
Is Cæsar then so weak, or hath the place
But wrought this alteration with the air,
And he, on next remove, will all repair?
Macro, thou art engaged,[2] and what before
Was public, now must be thy private more.
The weal of Cæsar, fitness did imply;
But thine own fate confers necessity
On thy employment; and the thoughts borne nearest

Unto ourselves, move swiftest still and dearest.   10
If he recover, thou art lost; yea, all
The weight of preparation to his fall
Will turn on thee, and crush thee. Therefore strike
Before he settle, to prevent the like
Upon thyself. He doth his vantage know,
That makes [3] it home, and gives the foremost blow.   [Exit.]

[SCENE iii.

An upper room in Agrippina's house.]

Latiaris, Rufus, Opsius.

[LAT.] It is a service great Sejanus will
See well requited, and accept of nobly.
Here place yourselves between the roof and ceiling,
And, when I bring him to his words of danger,
Reveal yourselves, and take him.
RUF.   Is he come?
LAT. I'll now go fetch him.   [Exit.]
OPS.   With good speed.—I long
To merit from the state in such an action.
RUF. I hope it will obtain the consulship
For one of us.
OPS.   We cannot think of less,
To bring in one so dangerous as Sabinus.   10
RUF. He was a follower of Germanicus,
And still is an observer of [4] his wife
And children, though they be declined in grace—
A daily visitant, keeps them company
In private and in public, and is noted
To be the only client of the house.
Pray Jove, he will be free [5] to Latiaris.
OPS. H' is allied to him, and doth trust him well.
RUF. And he'll requite his trust?
OPS.   To do an office   19
So grateful to the state, I know no man
But would strain nearer bands than kindred—
RUF.   List!
I hear them come.
OPS.   Shift to our holes with silence.
                                            [They retire.]

___

[1] Shaking.   [2] Entangled.
[3] Strikes.
[4] One who shows respectful attentions to.
[5] Outspoken.

[Enter] Latiaris, Sabinus.

[LAT.] It is a noble constancy you show
　To this afflicted house, that not like
　　others,
The friends of season, you do follow
　fortune,
And, in the winter of their fate, forsake
The place whose glories warmed you.
　You are just,
And worthy such a princely patron's
　love,
As was the world's-renowned Germani-
　cus,
Whose ample merit when I call to
　thought,　　　　　　　　　　　30
And see his wife and issue objects made
To so much envy, jealousy, and hate,
It makes me ready to accuse the gods
Of negligence, as men of tyranny.
SAB. They must be patient; so must we.
LAT.　　　　　　　　　　　O Jove,
　What will become of us or of the times,
When to be high or noble are made
　crimes,
When land and treasure are most dan-
　gerous faults?
SAB. Nay, when our table, yea, our bed
　assaults
Our peace and safety? When our writ-
　ings are,　　　　　　　　　　　40
By any envious instruments that dare
Apply them to the guilty, made to speak
What they will have to fit their tyran-
　nous wreak? [1]
When ignorance is scarcely innocence,
And knowledge made a capital offense?
When not so much but the bare empty
　shade
Of liberty is reft us, and we made
The prey to greedy vultures and vile
　spies,
That first transfix us with their murder-
　ing eyes?
LAT. Methinks the genius of the Roman
　race　　　　　　　　　　　50
Should not be so extinct, but that bright
　flame
Of liberty might be revived again
(Which no good man but with his life
　should lose)
And we not sit like spent and patient
　fools,

[1] Vengeance.

Still puffing in the dark at one poor coal,
Held on by hope, till the last spark is
　out.
The cause is public, and the honor,
　name,
The immortality of every soul
That is not bastard or a slave in Rome
Therein concerned; whereto, if men
　would change　　　　　　　　60
The wearied arm, and for the weighty
　shield
So long sustained employ the ready
　sword,
We might have some assurance of our
　vows.
This ass's fortitude doth tire us all;
It must be active valor must redeem
Our loss, or none. The rock and our hard
　steel
Should meet t' enforce those glorious
　fires again,
Whose splendor cheered the world, and
　heat gave life
No less than doth the sun's.
SAB.　　　　　　　'Twere better stay
In lasting darkness and despair of day. 70
No ill should force the subject undertake
Against the sovereign, more than hell
　should make
The gods do wrong. A good man should
　and must
Sit rather down with loss than rise un-
　just,
Though, when the Romans first did yield
　themselves
To one man's power, they did not mean
　their lives,
Their fortunes, and their liberties should
　be
His absolute spoil, as purchased by the
　sword.
LAT. Why, we are worse, if to be slaves,
　and bond
To Cæsar's slave, be such, the proud
　Sejanus!　　　　　　　　　　80
He that is all, does all, gives Cæsar leave
To hide his ulcerous and anointed face,
With his bald crown at Rhodes, while
　he here stalks
Upon the heads of Romans and their
　princes,
Familiarly to empire. [2]

[2] *I.e.*, as if accustomed to the state of an
emperor.

SAB.   Now you touch
A point indeed, wherein he shows his art
As well as power.
LAT.   And villainy in both.
Do you observe where Livia lodges?
   How
Drusus came dead?   What men have
   been cut off?
SAB. Yes, those are things removed. I
   nearer looked   90
Into his later practice, where he stands
Declared a master in his mystery.[1]
First, ere Tiberius went, he wrought
   his fear
To think that Agrippina sought his
   death;
Then put those doubts in her; sent her
   oft word,
Under the show of friendship, to beware
Of Cæsar, for he laid to poison her;
Drave them to frowns, to mutual jeal-
   ousies,
Which now in visible hatred are burst
   out.
Since, he hath had his hired instru-
   ments   100
To work on Nero, and to heave him up;
To tell him Cæsar's old, that all the
   people,
Yea, all the army have their eyes on him;
That both do long to have him under-
   take
Something of worth, to give the world
   a hope;
Bids him to court their grace. The easy
   youth
Perhaps gives ear, which straight he
   writes to Cæsar,
And with this comment: "See yon
   dangerous boy;
Note but the practice of the mother
   there;
She's tying him for purposes at hand,   110
With men of sword."   Here's Cæsar put
   in fright
Gainst son and mother. Yet he leaves
   not thus.
The second brother, Drusus, a fierce
   nature
And fitter for his snares, because ambitious
And full of envy, him he clasps and
   hugs,

[1] Profession. art.

Poisons with praise, tells him what
   hearts he wears,
How bright he stands in popular ex-
   pectance,
That Rome doth suffer with him in the
   wrong
His mother does him, by preferring
   Nero.
Thus sets he them asunder, each gainst
   other,   120
Projects the course that serves him to
   condemn,
Keeps in opinion of a friend to all,
And all drives on to ruin.
LAT.   Cæsar sleeps,
And nods at this?
SAB.   Would he might ever sleep,
Bogged in his filthy lusts!
             [*Opsius and Rufus rush in.*]
OPS.   Treason to Cæsar!
RUF. Lay hands upon the traitor, Latiaris,
Or take the name thyself.
LAT.   I am for Cæsar.
SAB. Am I then catched?
RUF.   How think you, sir? You are.
SAB. Spies of this head, so white, so full
   of years!
Well, my most reverend monsters, you
   may live   130
To see yourselves thus snared.
OPS.   Away with him!
LAT. Hale him away!
RUF.   To be a spy for traitors
Is honorable vigilance.
SAB.   You do well,
My most officious instruments of state,
Men of all uses. Drag me hence, away.
The year is well begun, and I fall fit
To be an off'ring to Sejanus. Go!
OPS. Cover him with his garments; hide
   his face.
SAB. It shall not need. Forbear your rude
   assault.
The fault's not shameful, villainy makes
   a fault.   [*Exeunt.*]   140

[SCENE iv.

A street before Agrippina's house.]

Macro, Caligula.

[MAC.] Sir, but observe how thick your
   dangers meet
In his clear drifts! Your mother and
   your brothers,

Now cited to the senate; their friend
　Gallus,
Feasted today by Cæsar, since com-
　mitted!
Sabinus here we met, hurried to fetters!
The senators all strook with fear and
　silence,
Save those whose hopes depend not on
　good means,
But force their private prey from public
　spoil.
And you must know, if here you stay,
　your state
Is sure to be the subject of his hate,　10
As now the object.
CAL.　　　　　What would you advise me?
MAC. To go for Capreæ presently,[1] and
　there
Give up yourself entirely to your uncle.
Tell Cæsar (since your mother is accused
To fly for succors [2] to Augustus' statue,
And to the army, with your brethren)
　you
Have rather chose to place your aids in
　him
Than live suspected, or in hourly fear
To be thrust out by bold Sejanus' plots—
Which you shall confidently urge to be　20
Most full of peril to the state and Cæsar,
As being laid to his peculiar ends,
And not to be let run with common
　safety.
All which, upon the second, I'll make
　plain,
So both shall love and trust with Cæsar
　gain.
CAL. Away then; let's prepare us for our
　journey.　　　　　　　　　　［*Exeunt.*］

［SCENE v.

Another street.］

Arruntius.

'[ARR.] Still dost thou suffer, heaven?
　Will no flame,
No heat of sin, make thy just wrath to
　boil
In thy distempered bosom, and o'er-
　flow
The pitchy blazes of impiety,
Kindled beneath thy throne? Still canst
　thou sleep,

[1] At once.
[2] Accused of flying for the right of asylum.

Patient, while vice doth make an antic
　face
At thy drad [3] power, and blow dust and
　smoke
Into thy nostrils? Jove, will nothing
　wake thee?
Must vile Sejanus pull thee by the beard
Ere thou wilt open thy black-lidded
　eye　　　　　　　　　　　　　10
And look him dead? Well! Snore on,
　dreaming gods,
And let this last of that proud giant race
Heave mountain upon mountain gainst
　your state.
Be good unto me, Fortune, and you
　powers
Whom I, expostulating, have profaned;
I see (what's equal with a prodigy)
A great, a noble Roman, and an honest,
Live an old man!—O Marcus Lepidus,
When is our turn to bleed? Thyself
　and I,
Without our boast, are a'most all the
　few　　　　　　　　　　　　20
Left to be honest in these impious times.

［Enter］ Lepidus.[4]

［LEP.］ What we are left to be, we will be,
　Lucius,
Though tyranny did stare as wide as
　death
To fright us from it.
ARR.　　　　　　'T hath so on Sabinus.
LEP. I saw him now drawn from the Gem-
　onies,[5]
And, what increased the direness of
　the fact,
His faithful dog, upbraiding all us Ro-
　mans,
Never forsook the corpse, but, seeing it
　thrown
Into the stream, leaped in, and drowned
　with it.　　　　　　　　　　29
ARR. O act, to be envied him of [6] us men!
We are the next the hook lays hold on,
　Marcus.
What are thy arts (good patriot, teach
　them me)

[3] Dread.
[4] The name *Arruntius* is repeated here.
[5] Steps on the Aventine, down which corpses
of criminals were dragged by the executioner's
hook and thrown into the river.
[6] By.

That have preserved thy hairs to this
    white dye,
And kept so reverend and so dear a head
Safe on his comely shoulders?
LEP.   Arts, Arruntius?
None but the plain and passive fortitude
To suffer and be silent, never stretch
These arms against the torrent, live at
    home
With my own thoughts and innocence
    about me,
Not tempting the wolves' jaws—these
    are my arts.   40
ARR. I would begin to study hem, if I
    thought
They would secure me. May I pray to
    Jove
In secret and be safe? Ay, or aloud?
With open wishes? So I do not mention
Tiberius or Sejanus? Yes, I must,
If I speak out. 'Tis hard, that. May I
    think,
And not be racked? What danger is 't
    to dream?
Talk in one's sleep, or cough? Who
    knows the law?
May I shake my head without a com-
    ment? Say
It rains, or it holds up, and not be
    thrown   50
Upon the Gemonies? These now are
    things
Whereon men's fortune, yea, their fate
    depends.
Nothing hath privilege gainst the violent
    ear.
No place, no day, no hour, we see, is
    free
(Not our religious and most sacred
    times)
From some one kind of cruelty; all
    matter,
Nay, all occasion pleaseth. Madmen's
    rage,
The idleness of drunkards, women's
    nothing,
Jester's simplicity, all, all is good
That can be catched at. Nor is now th'
    event [1]   60
Of any person, or for any crime,
To be expected,[2] for 'tis always one:
Death, with some little difference of
    place,

[1] Fate.   [2] Dreaded.

Or time—what's this?   Prince Nero?
    Guarded?

[*Enter*] *Laco, Nero* [*, with Guards*].[3]

[LAC.] On, lictors, keep your way. My
    lords, forbear.
On pain of Cæsar's wrath, no man at-
    tempt
Speech with the prisoner.
NERO.   Noble friends, be safe;
To lose yourselves for words were as
    vain hazard
As unto me small comfort. Fare you
    well!
Would all Rome's suff'rings in my fate
    did dwell!   70
LAC. Lictors, away!
LEP.   Where goes he, Laco?
LAC.   Sir,
H' is banished into Pontia by the
    senate.
ARR. Do I see, and hear, and feel? May
    I trust sense?
Or doth my phant'sy form it?
LEP.   Where's his brother?
LAC. Drusus is prisoner in the palace.
ARR.   Ha!
I smell it now; 'tis rank. Where's Agrip-
    pina?
LAC. The princess is confined to Panda-
    taria.
ARR. Bolts, Vulcan, bolts for Jove! Phœ-
    bus, thy bow;
Stern Mars, thy sword; and, blue-eyed
    Maid, thy spear;
Thy club, Alcides—all the armory   80
Of heaven is too little!—Ha! To guard
The gods, I meant. Fine, rare despatch!
    This same
Was swiftly borne! Confined? Im-
    prisoned? Banished?
Most tripartite! The cause, sir?
LAC.   Treason.
ARR.   O!
The complement of all accusings? That
Will hit, when all else fails.
LEP.   This turn is strange!
But yesterday the people would not
    hear,
Far less objected, but cried Cæsar's
    letters

[3] The names *Lepidus* and *Arruntius* are repeated here.

Were false and forged, that all these
plots were malice,
And that the ruin of the prince's house 90
Was practiced gainst his knowledge.
Where are now
Their voices, now that they behold his
heirs
Locked up, disgraced, led into exile?
ARR.   Hushed.
Drowned in their bellies. Wild Sejanus'
breath
Hath, like a whirlwind, scattered that
poor dust
With this rude blast.—(*He turns to Laco
and the Rest.*) We'll talk no treason, sir,
If that be it you stand for. Fare you well.
We have no need of horse-leeches. Good
spy,
Now you are spied, begone.
          [*Exeunt Laco, Nero, and Guards.*]
LEP.   I fear you wrong him.
He has the voice to be an honest Ro-
man.   100
ARR. And trusted to this office? Lepidus,
I'ld sooner trust Greek Sinon than a
man
Our state employs. He's gone; and be-
ing gone,
I dare tell you, whom I dare better
trust,
That our night-eyed Tiberius doth not
see
His minion's drifts; or, if he do, h' is not
So arrant subtile as we fools do take
him.
To breed a mungrel [1] up in his own house,
With his own blood, and, if the good
gods please,
At his own throat flesh [2] him to take a
leap!   110
I do not beg it, heav'n; but, if the fates
Grant it these eyes, they must not wink.
LEP.   They must
Not see it, Lucius.
ARR.   Who should let [3] hem?
LEP.   Zeal
And duty; with the thought he is our
prince.
ARR. He is our monster, forfeited to vice
So far as no racked virtue can redeem
him;
His loathéd person fouler than all crimes;
An emp'ror only in his lusts. Retired,

[1] Mongrel.   [2] Incite.   [3] Hinder.

From all regard of his own fame or
Rome's,
Into an obscure island, where he lives, 120
Acting his tragedies with a comic face,
Amidst his rout of Chaldees,[4] spending
hours,
Days, weeks, and months in the unkind [5]
abuse
Of grave astrology, to the bane of men,
Casting the scope of men's nativities,
And, having found aught worthy in
their fortune,
Kill, or precipitate them in the sea,
And boast he can mock fate. Nay,
muse not; these
Are far from ends of evil, scarce de-
grees.
He hath his slaughterhouse at Capreæ,
Where he doth study murder as an art;
And they are dearest in his grace that
can   132
Devise the deepest tortures. Thither,
too,
He hath his boys and beauteous girls
ta'en up
Out of our noblest houses, the best
formed,
Best nurtured, and most modest; what's
their good
Serves to provoke his bad. Some are
allured,
Some threatened; others, by their friends
detained,
Are ravished hence like captives, and,
in sight
Of their most grievéd parents, dealt
away   140
Unto his spintries,[6] sellaries,[7] and slaves,
Masters of strange and new-com-
mented [8] lusts,
For which wise nature hath not left a
name.
To this (what most strikes us and bleed-
ing Rome)
He is, with all his craft, become the
ward
To his own vassal, a stale catamite [9]
Whom he, upon our low and suffering
necks,

[4] Chaldeans, astrologers.
[5] Unnatural.
[6] Male prostitutes.
[7] Lewd persons.
[8] New-invented.
[9] Male prostitute.

Hath raised from excrement to side [1]
    the gods
And have his proper sacrifice in Rome,
Which Jove beholds, and yet will sooner
    rive   150
A senseless oak with thunder than his
    trunk!

Laco, Pomponius, Minutius, Terentius, to
                                    them.

[LAC.] These letters make men doubtful
    what t' expect,
Whether his coming or his death.
POM.   Troth, both;
And which comes soonest, thank the
    gods for.
(ARR.   List!
    Their talk is Cæsar; I would hear all
    voices.)
        [*Arruntius and Lepidus withdraw.*]
MIN. One day he's well and will return
    to Rome;
The next day, sick, and knows not when
    to hope it.
LAC. True; and today one of Sejanus'
    friends
Honored by special writ, and on the
    morrow
Another punished—
POM.   By more special writ. 160
MIN. This man receives his praises of
    Sejanus;
A second, but slight mention; a third,
    none;
A fourth, rebukes. And thus he leaves
    the senate
Divided and suspended, all uncertain.
LAC. These forkèd tricks, I understand
    hem not;
Would he would tell us whom he loves
    or hates,
That we might follow, without fear or
    doubt.
(ARR. Good Heliotrope! [2] Is this your
    honest man?
Let him be yours so still; he is my knave.)
POM. I cannot tell; Sejanus still goes
    on,   170
And mounts, we see; new statues are
    advanced,
Fresh leaves of titles, large inscriptions
    read,

¹ Match.
² Because he keeps turning toward the sun.

His fortune sworn by, himself new gone
    out
Cæsar's colleague in the fifth consulship;
More altars smoke to him than all the
    gods.
What would we more?
(ARR.   That the dear smoke would
    choke him,
That would I more!
LEP.   Peace, good Arruntius.)
LAC. But there are letters come, they
    say, ev'n now,
Which do forbid that last.
MIN.   Do you hear so?
LAC.   Yes.
POM. By Pollux, that's the worst.
(ARR.   By Hercules, best.)
MIN. I did not like the sign, when Regu-
    lus,   181
Whom all we know no friend unto Se-
    janus,
Did, by Tiberius' so precise command,
Succeed a fellow in the consulship;
It boded somewhat.
POM.   Not a mote. His partner,
Fulcinius Trio, is his own, and sure.—
Here comes Terentius. He can give us
    more.

[*Enter Terentius.*]   *They whisper with*
                                    Terentius.

LEP. I'll ne'er believe but Cæsar hath
    some scent
Of bold Sejanus' footing. These cross-
    points
Of varying letters and opposing con-
    suls,   190
Mingling his honors and his punish-
    ments,
Feigning now ill, now well, raising Se-
    janus,
And then depressing him, as now of late
In all reports we have it, cannot be
Empty of practice; 'tis Tiberius' art,
For (having found his favorite grown
    too great,
And with his greatness strong, that all
    the soldiers
Are, with their leaders, made at his de-
    votion,
That almost all the senate are his crea-
    tures,
Or hold on him their main dependen-
    cies,   200

Either for benefit, or hope, or fear,
And that himself hath lost much of his
  own,
By parting unto him, and, by th' in-
  crease
Of his rank lusts and rages, quite dis-
  armed
Himself of love or other public means
To dare an open contestation)
His subtilty hath chose this doubling
  line,
To hold him even in, not so to fear him,
As wholly put him out, and yet give
  check   209
Unto his farder boldness; in meantime,
By his employments, makes him odious
Unto the staggering rout, whose aid,
  in fine,
He hopes to use, as sure, who, when
  they sway,
Bear down, o'erturn all objects in their
  way.
ARR. You may be a Lynceus, Lepidus;
  yet I
See no such cause but that a politic
  tyran,
Who can so well disguise it, should
  have ta'en
A nearer way: feigned honest, and come
  home
To cut his throat, by law.
LEP.   Ay, but his fear
Would ne'er be masked, allbe [1] his vices
  were.   220
POM. His lordship then is still in grace?
TER.   Assure you,
Never in more, either of grace or power.
POM. The gods are wise and just.
(ARR.   The fiends they are,
To suffer thee belie hem!)
TER.   I have here
His last and present letters, where he
  writes him,
The "partner of his cares," and "his
  Sejanus"—
LAC. But is that true, it is [2] prohibited
To sacrifice unto him?
TER.   Some such thing
Cæsar makes scruple of, but forbids it
  not,
No more than to himself; says he could
  wish   230

It were forborne to all.
LAC.   Is it no other?
TER. No other, on my trust. For your
  more surety,
Here is that letter too.
(ARR.   How easily
Do wretched men believe what they
  would have!
Looks this like plot?
LEP.   Noble Arruntius, stay.)
LAC. He names him here without his
  titles.
(LEP.   Note!
ARR. Yes, and come off [3] your notable
  fool. I will.)
LAC. No other than Sejanus.
POM.   That's but haste
In him that writes. Here he gives large
  amends.   239
MIN. And with his own hand written?
POM.   Yes.
LAC.   Indeed?
TER. Believe it, gentlemen, Sejanus'
  breast
Never received more full contentments
  in
Than at this present.
POM.   Takes he well th' escape
Of young Caligula with Macro?
TER.   Faith,
At the first air it somewhat troubled
  him.
(LEP. Observe you?
ARR.   Nothing; riddles. Till I see
Sejanus strook, no sound thereof strikes
  me.)
POM. I like it not. I muse h' would not
  attempt
Somewhat against him in the consul-
  ship,
Seeing the people gin [4] to favor him.   250
TER. He doth repent it now; but h' has
  employed
Pagonianus after him; and he holds
That correspondence there, with all
  that are
Near about Cæsar, [5] as no thought can
  pass
Without his knowledge thence, in act
  to front [6] him.
POM. I gratulate [7] the news.

---

[1] Although.
[2] From 1640 edn. Original reads 'tis.
[3] Turn out to be.
[4] Begin.
[5] I.e., Caligula.
[6] Oppose.
[7] Welcome.

LAC.   But how comes Macro
So in trust and favor with Caligula?
POM. O, sir, he has a wife, and the young
prince
An appetite. He can look up and spy
Flies in the roof, when there are fleas
i' bed,   260
And hath a learned nose to assure his
sleeps.
Who, to be favored of the rising sun,
Would not lend little of his waning moon?
'Tis the saf'st ambition. Noble Teren-
tius!
TER. The night grows fast upon us. At
your service.   [*Exeunt.*]

CHORUS—*of Musicians.*

ACT V. [SCENE i.

An apartment in Sejanus' house.]

Sejanus.

[SEJ.] Swell, swell, my joys, and faint not
to declare
Yourselves as ample as your causes are.
I did not live till now—this my first
hour,
Wherein I see my thoughts reached by
my power.
But this, and gripe my wishes.[1] Great
and high,
The world knows only two, that's Rome
and I.
My roof receives me not; 'tis air I
tread;
And at each step I feel my advancéd
head
Knock out a star in heaven! Reared to
this height,
All my desires seem modest, poor, and
slight,   10
That did before sound impudent; 'tis
place,
Not blood, discerns the noble and the
base.
Is there not something more than to
be Cæsar?
Must we rest there? It irks t' have come
so far,
To be so near a stay. Caligula,
Would thou stood'st stiff and many in
our way!

Winds lose their strength, when they
do empty fly,
Unmet of woods or buildings; great
fires die,
That want their matter to withstand
them; so,
It is our grief, and will be our loss, to
know   20
Our power shall want opposites, unless
The gods, by mixing in the cause, would
bless
Our fortune with their conquest. That
were worth
Sejanus' strife, durst fates but bring it
forth.

[Enter] Terentius.[2]

[TER.] Safety to great Sejanus!
SEJ.   Now, Terentius?
TER. Hears not my lord the wonder?
SEJ.   Speak it; no.
TER. I meet it violent in the people's
mouths,
Who run in routs to Pompey's theater
To view your statue, which, they say,
sends forth
A smoke, as from a fornace,[3] black and
dreadful.   30
SEJ. Some traitor hath put fire in; you
go see,
And let the head be taken off, to look
What 'tis. Some slave hath practiced
an imposture
To stir the people.—[*Terentius starts to
go.*] How now! Why return you?

Satrius, Natta, to them.

SAT. The head, my lord, already is ta'en
off;
I saw it; and, at op'ning, there leaped
out
A great and monstrous serpent.
SEJ.   Monstrous! Why?
Had it a beard and horns, no heart, a
tongue
Forkéd as flattery? Looked it of the
hue
To such as live in great men's bosoms?
Was   40
The spirit of it Macro's?
NAT.   May it please

---

[1] Only this obstacle (Caligula), and I shall
obtain my wishes.

[2] The name *Sejanus* is repeated here.
[3] Furnace.

The most divine Sejanus, in my days
(And by his sacred fortune I affirm it)
I have not seen a more extended, grown,
Foul, spotted, venomous, ugly—
SEJ.   O, the Fates!
What a wild muster's here of attributes
T' express a worm, a snake?
TER.   But how that should
Come there, my lord?
SEJ.   What, and you too, Terentius?
I think you mean to make 't a prodigy
In your reporting!
TER.   Can the wise Sejanus   50
Think heav'n hath meant it less?
SEJ.   O, superstition!
Why, then the falling of our bed, that
  brake
This morning, burdened with the popu-
  lous weight
Of our expecting clients, to salute us,
Or running of the cat bewixt our legs,
As we set forth unto the Capitol,
Were prodigies.
TER.   I think them ominous,
And would they had not happened—
  as, today,
The fate of some your servants, who,
  declining
Their way, not able, for the throng, to
  follow,   60
Slipped down the Gemonies, and brake
  their necks!
Besides, in taking your last augury,
No prosperous bird appeared, but croak-
  ing ravens
Flagged up and down, and from the
  sacrifice
Flew to the prison, where they sat all
  night,
Beating the air with their obstreperous
  beaks!
I dare not counsel, but I could entreat
That great Sejanus would attempt the
  gods
Once more with sacrifice.
SEJ.   What excellent fools
Religion makes of men!   Believes
  Terentius,   70
If these were dangers, as I shame to
  think them,
The gods could change the certain
  course of fate?
Or, if they could, they would, now in a
  moment,

For a beeve's fat, or less, be bribed t'
  invert
Those long decrees?   Then think the
  gods, like flies,
Are to be taken with the steam of flesh,
Or blood, diffused about their altars;
  think
Their power as cheap as I esteem it
  small.
Of all the throng that fill th' Olympian
  hall,
And, without pity, lade poor Atlas'
  back,   80
I know not that one deity, but Fortune,
To whom I would throw up, in begging
  smoke,
One grain of incense, or whose ear I'ld
  buy
With thus much oil. Her I indeed adore,
And keep her grateful image in my
  house,
Sometimes belonging to a Roman king,
But now called mine, as by the better
  style;
To her I care not, if, for satisfying
Your scrupulous phant'sies, I go offer.
  Bid
Our priest prepare us honey, milk, and
  poppy,   90
His masculine odors and night vest-
  ments; say
Our rites are instant, which performed,
  you'll see
How vain, and worthy laughter, your
  fears be.   [Exeunt.]

[SCENE ii.

A street.]

Cotta, Pomponius.

[COT.] Pomponius, whither in such speed?
POM.   I go
To give my lord Sejanus notice—
COT.   What?
POM. Of Macro.
COT.   Is he come?
POM.   Entered but now
The house of Regulus.
COT.   The opposite consul?
POM. Some half hour since.
COT.   And by night too! Stay, sir;
I'll bear you company.
POM.   Along then. [Exeunt.]

[SCENE iii.

A room in Regulus' house.]

Macro, Regulus, Laco[1] [*, and Attendant*].

[MAC.] 'Tis Cæsar's will to have a fre-
quent [2] senate;
And therefore must your edict lay deep
mulct
On such as shall be absent.
REG.   So it doth.
Bear it my fellow consul to adscribe.[3]
MAC. And tell him it must early be pro-
claimed;
The place Apollo's temple.
                              [*Exit Attendant.*]
REG.   That's remembered.
MAC. And at what hour?
REG.   Yes.
MAC.   You do forget
To send one for the provost of the
watch?
REG. I have not; here he comes.

[*Enter Laco.*]

MAC.   Gracinus Laco,
You are a friend most welcome; by-and-
by   10
I'll speak with you.—[*Aside.*] You must
procure this list
Of the prætorian cohorts, with the
names
Of the centurions and the tribunes.
REG. [*Aside.*]   Ay.
MAC. I bring you letters, and a health
from Cæsar.
LAC. Sir, both come well.
(MAC.   And, hear you, with your note,
Which are the eminent men, and most
of action.
REG. That shall be done you too.)
                    The Consul goes out.
MAC.   Most worthy Laco,
Cæsar salutes you.—[*Aside.*] Consul!
Death and furies!
Gone now?—The argument will please
you, sir.—
[*Aside.*] Ho! Regulus? The anger of
the gods   20
Follow his diligent legs, and overtake
hem,
In likeness of the gout!—

---

[1] Enters later.   [2] Full.   [3] Sign.

[*Regulus*] *returns.*

                    O, good my lord,
We lacked you present; I would pray
you send
Another to Fulcinius Trio straight,
To tell him you will come and speak
with him;
The matter we'll devise, to stay him
there,
While I with Laco do survey the watch.—
                    [*Regulus*] *goes out again.*
What are your strengths, Gracinus?
LAC.   Seven cohorts.
MAC. You see what Cæsar writes; and
—[*Aside.*] Gone again?
H' has sure a vein of mercury in his
feet.—   30
Knew you what store of the prætorian
soldiers
Sejanus holds about him for his
guard?
LAC. I cannot the just number, but I
think
Three centuries.
MAC.   Three? Good.
LAC.   At most not four.
MAC. And who be those centurions?
LAC.   That the consul
Can best deliver you.
(MAC.   When h' is away?
Spite on his nimble industry!)—Graci-
nus,
You find what place you hold, there, in
the trust
Of royal Cæsar?
LAC.   Ay, and I am—
MAC.   Sir,
The honors there proposed are but
beginnings   40
Of his great favors.
LAC.   They are more—
MAC.   I heard him
When he did study what to add.
LAC.   My life,
And all I hold—
MAC.   You were his own first choice,
Which doth confirm as much as you can
speak,
And will, if we succeed, make more—
Your guards
Are seven cohorts, you say?
LAC.   Yes.
MAC.   Those we must

Hold still in readiness and undis-
charged.

Lac. I understand so much. But how it
can—

Mac. Be done without suspicion, you'll
object?

[Regulus] returns.

Reg. What's that?

Lac.　　　The keeping of the watch in
arms,　　　　　　　　　　　　　50
When morning comes.

Mac.　　　　The senate shall be met, and
set
So early in the temple, as all mark
Of that will be avoided.

Reg.　　　　　　　　If we need,
We have commission to possess the palace,
Enlarge [1] Prince Drusus, and make him
our chief.

(Mac. That secret would have burnt his
reverend mouth,
Had he not spit it out now.)—By the
gods,
You carry things too. Let me borrow a
man
Or two to bear these. That of freeing
Drusus,
Cæsar projected as the last and ut-
most—　　　　　　　　　　　　60
Not else to be remembered.

Reg. [*Beckoning to Servants.*]　Here are
servants.

Mac. These to Arruntius, these to Lepi-
dus.
This bear to Cotta, this to Latiaris.
If they demand you of me, say I have
ta'en
Fresh horse and am departed.—[*Exeunt
Servants.*] You, my lord,
To your colleague, and be you sure to
hold him
With long narration of the new fresh
favors,
Meant to Sejanus, his great patron; I,
With trusted Laco here, are for the
guards;
Then, to divide. For night hath many
eyes,　　　　　　　　　　　　　70
Whereof, though most do sleep, yet some
are spies.　　　　　　　　[*Exeunt.*]

[1] Free.

[Scene iv.

A chapel in Sejanus' house.]

Præcones, Flamen,[2] *Ministri,*[3] *Sejanus, Terentius, Satrius, [Natta,] etc.*

[Præ.] *Be all profane far hence; fly, fly far
off.*
　Be absent far; far hence be all profane!
Tub[icines], Tib[icines] [4] *sound while the
　　　　　Flamen washeth.*
Fla. *We have been faulty, but repent us
now,*
　*And bring pure hands, pure vestments, and
　pure minds.*
[1] Min. *Pure vessels.*
[2] Min.　　　　*And pure off'rings.*
[3] Min.　　　　　*Garlands pure.*
Fla. *Bestow your garlands; and, with reverence, place*
　The vervine [5] *on the altar.*
Præ.　　　　*Favor* [6] *your tongues.*
While they sound again, the Flamen takes
　of the honey with his finger, and tastes,
　then ministers to all the rest; so of the
　milk, in an earthen vessel, he deals
　about; which done, he sprinkleth upon
　the altar, milk; then imposeth the
　honey, and kindleth his gums, and
　after censing about the altar, placeth
　his censer thereon, into which they
　put several branches of poppy, and,
　　　　　the music ceasing, proceed.
Fla. *Great mother Fortune, queen of human
state,*
　Rectress [7] *of action, arbitress of fate,*
　*To whom all sway, all power, all empire
　bows,*　　　　　　　　　　　10
　Be present, and propitious to our vows!
Præ. *Favor it with your tongues.*[8]
Min. *Be present, and propitious to our
vows!*
　*Accept our off'ring, and be pleased, great
goddess.*
Ter. *See, see, the image stirs!*
Sat.　　　　　　　*And turns away!*
Nat. *Fortune averts her face!*
Fla.　　　　　　　*Avert, you gods,*
　*The prodigy! Still! Still! Some pious rite
　We have neglected. Yet, heav'n, be
　appeased,*

[2] Priest.　　　　　　　　[3] Servitors.
[4] Trumpeters, flute-players.
[5] Vervain, verbena.　　　　　[7] Governess.
[6] Silence.　　　　　[8] Speak the good words.

And be all tokens false or void that speak
Thy present wrath!

SEJ.   Be thou dumb, scrupulous[1] priest,
And gather up thyself, with these thy
 wares,   21
Which I, in spite of thy blind mistress, or
Thy juggling mystery, religion, throw
Thus scornéd on the earth.
   [*Overturns the statue and the altar.*]
       Nay, hold thy look
Averted till I woo thee turn again;
And thou shalt stand, to all posterity,
Th' eternal game and laughter, with thy
 neck
Writhed to thy tail, like a ridiculous cat.
Avoid[2] these fumes, these superstitious
 lights,   29
And all these coz'ning ceremonies—you,
Your pure and spicéd[3] conscience!
  [*Exit Flamen with his Attendants.*]
        I, the slave
And mock of fools (scorn on my worthy
 head!),
That have been titled and adored a god,
Yea, sacrificed unto, myself, in Rome,
No less than Jove—and I be brought
 to do
A peevish giglot rites![4] Perhaps the
 thought
And shame of that made Fortune turn
 her face,
Knowing herself the lesser deity,
And but my servant.—Bashful queen,
 if so,
Sejanus thanks thy modesty.—Who's
 that?   40

   [*Enter*] *Pomponius*,[5] *Minutius, etc.*

[POM.] His fortune suffers till he hears my
 news;
 I have waited here too long. Macro, my
  lord—
SEJ.   Speak lower and withdraw.
      [*Draws him aside.*]
TER.   Are these things true?
MIN.   Thousands are gazing at it in the
 streets.
SEJ.   What's that?
TER. Minutius tells us here, my lord,

[1] Doubtful, untrustworthy.
[2] Remove.
[3] Overscrupulous.
[4] Do rites to a crazy wanton (*i.e.*, to Fortune).
[5] The name *Sejanus* is repeated here.

That, a new head being set upon your
 statue,
A rope is since found wreathed about it,
 and
But now a fiery meteor in the form
Of a great ball was seen to roll along
The troubled air, where yet it hangs un-
 perfect,   50
The amazing wonder of the multitude!
SEJ.   No more. That Macro's come, is more
 than all!
TER.   Is Macro come?
POM.   I saw him.
TER.   Where?   With whom?
POM. With Regulus.
SEJ.   Terentius!
TER.   My lord?
SEJ.   Send for the tribunes; we will straight
 have up
More of the soldiers for our guard.—[*Exit
 Terentius.*] Minutius,
We pray you go for Cotta, Latiaris,
Trio the consul, or what senators
You know are sure, and ours.—[*Exit
 Minutius.*] You, my good Natta,
For Laco, provost of the watch.—[*Exit
 Natta.*] Now, Satrius,   60
The time of proof comes on; arm all our
 servants,
And without tumult.—[*Exit Satrius.*]
 You, Pomponius,
Hold some good correspondence with the
 consul;
Attempt him, noble friend.—[*Exit Pom-
 ponius.*] These things begin
To look like dangers, now, worthy my
 fates.
Fortune, I see thy worst. Let doubtful
 states
And things uncertain hang upon thy will;
Me surest death shall render certain still.
Yet why is now my thought turned
 toward death,
Whom fates have let go on so far in
 breath,   70
Unchecked or unreproved? I, that did
 help
To fell the lofty cedar of the world,
Germanicus; that at one stroke cut down
Drusus, that upright elm; withered his
 vine;
Laid Silius and Sabinus, two strong oaks,
Flat on the earth; besides those other
 shrubs,

Cordus and Sosia, Claudia Pulchra,
Furnius and Gallus, which I have
　grubbed up;
And since, have set my ax so strong
　and deep
Into the root of spreading Agrippine;　80
Lopped off and scattered her proud
　branches, Nero,
Drusus, and Caius too, although re-
　planted;
If you will, Destinies, that, after all,
I faint now ere I touch my period,
You are but cruel; and I already have
　done
Things great enough.　All Rome hath
　been my slave;
The senate sate an idle looker-on
And witness of my power, when I have
　blushed
More to command than it to suffer;　¹ all
The fathers have sat ready and pre-
　pared　　　　　　　　　　　　90
To give me empire, temples, or their
　throats,
When I would ask hem; and, what crowns
　the top,
Rome, senate, people, all the world have
　seen
Jove but my equal, Cæsar but my second.
'Tis then your malice, Fates, who, but
　your own,
Envy and fear t' have any power long
　known.　　　　　　　　　　[Exit.]

[SCENE V.

A room in the same.]

Terentius, Tribunes.

[TER.]　Stay here; I'll give ² his lordship you
　are come.

[Enter] Minutius, Cotta, Latiaris.

[MIN.]　Marcus Terentius, pray you, tell
　my lord
Here's Cotta and Latiaris.
TER.　　　　　　　　　　Sir, I shall.
　　　　[Exit.]　They confer their letters.
COT.　My letter is the very same with
　yours,
Only requires me to be present there,
And give my voice to strengthen his
　design.

¹ I.e., than it has blushed to permit me to
command.　　　　　² I.e., tell.

LAT.　Names he not what it is?
COT.　　　　　　　　No, nor to you.
LAT.　'Tis strange and singular doubtful!
COT.　　　　　　　　So it is.
　It may be all is left to Lord Sejanus.

Natta, Laco, to them.

[NAT.]　Gentlemen, where's my lord?
TRI.　　　　　We wait him here.　　10
COT.　The provost Laco?　What's the
　news?
LAT.　　My lord—

Sejanus, to them.

[SEJ.]　Now, my right dear, noble, and
　trusted friends,
How much I am a captive to your kind-
　ness!
Most worthy Cotta, Latiaris, Laco,
Your valiant hand; and, gentlemen, your
　loves.
I wish I could divide myself unto you,
Or that it lay within our narrow powers
To satisfy for so enlargéd bounty.
Gracinus, we must pray you, hold your
　guards
Unquit when morning comes.　Saw you
　the consul?　　　　　　　　　20
MIN.　Trio will presently be here, my lord.
COT.　They are but giving order for the
　edict,
To warn the senate?
SEJ.　　　　　How! The senate?
LAT.　　　　　　　　Yes.
This morning in Apollo's temple—
COT.　　　　　　　　We
Are charged by letter to be there, my
　lord.
SEJ.　By letter?　Pray you, let's see.
LAT.　　　　　Knows not his lordship?
COT.　It seems so!
SEJ.　　　　　A senate warned?　Without
　my knowledge?
And on this sudden?　Senators by letters
Required to be there!　Who brought
　these?
COT.　　　　　Macro.
SEJ.　Mine enemy!　And when?
COT.　　　　　　　This midnight.
SEJ.　　　　　　　　Time,　30
With ev'ry other circumstance, doth give
It hath some strain of ingine in 't!—How
　now?

[*Enter*] *Satrius*.[1]

[SAT.] My lord, Sertorius Macro is without,
    Alone, and prays t' have private conference
    In business of high nature with your lordship,
    He says to me, and which regards you much.

SEJ. Let him come here.

SAT.   Better, my lord, withdraw;
    You will betray what store and strength of friends
    Are now about you, which he comes to spy.

SEJ. Is he not armed?

SAT.   We'll search him.

SEJ.   No; but take   40
    And lead him to some room, where you concealed
    May keep a guard upon us.—[*Exit Satrius.*] Noble Laco,
    You are our trust; and, till our own cohorts
    Can be brought up, your strengths must be our guard.
    Now, good Minutius, honored Latiaris.
                He salutes them humbly.
    Most worthy and my most unwearied friends,
    I return instantly.   [*Exit.*]

LAT.   Most worthy lord!

COT. His lordship is turned instant kind, methinks;
    I have not observed it in him heretofore.

TRI. 1. 'Tis true, and it becomes him nobly.

MIN.   I   50
    Am rapt withal.

TRI. 2.   By Mars, he has my lives,
    Were they a million, for this only grace.

LAC. Ay, and to name a man!

LAT.   As he did me!

MIN. And me!

LAT.   Who would not spend his life and fortunes
    To purchase but the look of such a lord?

LAC. [*Aside.*] He that would nor be lord's fool nor the world's.   [*Exeunt.*]

---

[1] The words *Sejanus, etc.*, are repeated here.

[SCENE vi.

Another room in the same.]

Sejanus, Macro [, *Satrius*].

[SEJ.] Macro, most welcome as most coveted friend!
    Let me enjoy my longings. When arrived you?

MAC. About the noon of night.

SEJ.   Satrius, give leave. [*Exit Satrius.*]

MAC. I have been, since I came, with both the consuls,
    On a particular design from Cæsar.

SEJ. How fares it with our great and royal master?

MAC. Right plentifully well, as with a prince
    That still holds out the great proportion
    Of his large favors, where his judgment hath   9
    Made once divine election, like the god
    That wants not, nor is wearied to bestow
    Where merit meets his bounty, as it doth
    In you, already the most happy, and, ere
    The sun shall climb the south, most high Sejanus.
    Let not my lord be amused.[2] For to this end
    Was I by Cæsar sent for to the isle,
    With special caution to conceal my journey,
    And thence had my despatch as privately
    Again to Rome, charged to come here by night,   19
    And only to the consuls make narration
    Of his great purpose, that the benefit
    Might come more full and striking, by how much
    It was less looked for, or aspired by you,
    Or least informéd to the common thought.

SEJ. What may this be? Part of myself, dear Macro,
    If good, speak out, and share with your Sejanus.

MAC. If bad, I should forever loathe myself
    To be the messenger to so good a lord.
    I do exceed m' instructions to acquaint
    Your lordship with thus much; but 'tis my venture   30

---

[2] Amazed.

On your retentive wisdom, and because
I would no jealous scruple should molest
Or rack your peace of thought. For I
  assure
My noble lord, no senator yet knows
The business meant, though all by sev-
  eral letters
Are warnéd to be there, and give their
  voices,
Only to add unto the state and grace
Of what is purposed.
SEJ.   You take pleasure, Macro,
Like a coy wench, in torturing your
  lover.
What can be worth this suffering?
MAC.   That which follows, 40
The tribunitial dignity and power—
Both which Sejanus is to have this day
Conferred upon him, and by public
  senate.
SEJ. [*Aside.*] Fortune, be mine again! Thou
  hast satisfied
For thy suspected loyalty.
MAC.   My lord,
I have no longer time; the day approach-
  eth,
And I must back to Cæsar.
SEJ.   Where's Caligula?
MAC. That I forgot to tell your lordship.
  Why,
He lingers yonder about Capreæ,
Disgraced; Tiberius hath not seen him
  yet.   50
He needs would thrust himself to go with
  me,
Against my wish or will; but I have
  quitted
His forward trouble,[1] with as tardy note
As my neglect or silence could afford
  him.
Your lordship cannot now command me
  aught,
Because I take no knowledge that I saw
  you;
But I shall boast to live to serve your
  lordship;
And so take leave.
SEJ.   Honest and worthy Macro,
Your love and friendship.—[*Exit Macro.*]
  Who's there? Satrius,   59
Attend my honorable friend forth.—O!
How vain and vile a passion is this
  fear!

[1] Troublesome forwardness.

What base uncomely things it makes
  men do:
Suspect their noblest friends, as I did
  this,
Flatter poor enemies, entreat their ser-
  vants,
Stoop, court, and catch at the benevo-
  lence
Of creatures unto whom, within this hour,
I would not have vouchsafed a quarter-
  look,
Or piece of face! By you that fools call
  gods,
Hang all the sky with your prodigious
  signs,
Fill earth with monsters, drop the scor-
  pion down   70
Out of the zodiac, or the fiercer lion,
Shake off the loosened globe from her
  long henge, [2]
Roll all the world in darkness, and let
  loose
Th' enragéd winds to turn up groves and
  towns!
When I do fear again, let me be strook
With forked fire, and unpitied die;
Who fears, is worthy of calamity. [*Exit.*]

[SCENE vii.

Another room in the same.]

Pomponius, Regulus, Trio, to the Rest.[3]

P[OM.] Is not my lord here?
TER.   Sir, he will be straight.
COT. What news, Fulcinius Trio?
TRIO.   Good, good tidings;
But keep it to yourself. My lord Sejanus
Is to receive this day in open senate
The tribunitial dignity.
COT.   Is 't true?
TRIO. No words, not to your thought; but,
  sir, believe it.
LAT. What says the consul?
COT. [*Aside.*]   Speak it not again.—
He tells me that today my lord Seja-
  nus—
(TRIO. I must entreat you, Cotta, on your
  honor
Not to reveal it.
COT.   On my life, sir.)
LAT.   Say. 10

[2] Hinge, axis.
[3] *I.e.,* Terentius, Minutius, Laco, Cotta,
Latiaris, and Tribunes.

Cot. Is to receive the tribunitial power.
But, as you are an honorable man,
Let me conjure you not to utter it;
For it is trusted to me with that bond.
Lat. I am Harpocrates.
Ter.   Can you assure it?
Pom. The consul told it me; but keep it
close.
Min. Lord Latiaris, what's the news?
Lat.   I'll tell you;
But you must swear to keep it secret.

To them, Sejanus.

[Sej.] I knew the Fates had on their distaff
left
More of our thread than so.
Reg.   Hail, great Sejanus! 20
Trio. Hail, the most honored—!
Cot.   Happy—!
Lat.   High Sejanus!
Sej. Do you bring prodigies too?
Trio.   May all presage
Turn to those fair effects whereof we
bring
Your lordship news.
Reg.   May 't please my lord withdraw.
Sej. Yes.—(*To Some that stand by.*)   I
will speak with you anon.
Ter.   My lord,
What is your pleasure for the tribunes?
Sej.   Why,
Let hem be thanked and sent away.
Min.   My lord—
Lac. Will 't please your lordship to
command me—
Sej.   No.
You are troublesome.
Min.   The mood is changed.
Tri.[1.]   Not speak?
Tri.[2.] Nor look?
Lac.   Ay, he is wise, will
make him friends   30
Of such who never love but for their
ends.   [*Exeunt.*]

[Scene viii.

Before the Temple of Apollo.]

*Arruntius, Lepidus, divers other Senators
passing by them.*

[Arr.] Ay, go, make haste; take heed you
be not last
To tender your "All hail" in the wide
hall

Of huge Sejanus; run a lictor's pace;
Stay not to put your robes on, but
away
With the pale troubled ensigns of great
friendship
Stamped i' your face! Now, Marcus
Lepidus,
You still believe your former augury?
Sejanus must go downward? You per-
ceive
His wane approaching fast?
Lep.   Believe me, Lucius,
I wonder at this rising.
Arr.   Ay, and that we   10
Must give our suffrage to it? You will
say,
It is to make his fall more steep and
grievous?
It may be so. But think it, they that
can
With idle wishes 'ssay to bring back
time;
In cases desperate, all hope is crime.
See, see! What troops of his officious
friends
Flock to salute my lord, and start before
My great proud lord, to get a lordlike
nod!
Attend my lord unto the Senate House!
Bring back my lord! Like servile
huishers,[1] make   20
Way for my lord! Proclaim his idol
lordship,
More than ten criers, or six noise of
trumpets![2]
Make legs,[3] kiss hands, and take a scat-
tered hair
From my lord's eminent shoulder! See,
Sanquinius,
With his slow belly, and his dropsy!
Look,
What toiling haste he makes! Yet here's
another
Retarded with the gout, will be afore
him.
Get thee Liburnian porters, thou gross
fool,
To bear thy obsequious fatness, like
thy peers.
They are met! The gout returns, and
his great carriage.   30

[1] Ushers.
[2] Companies of trumpeters.
[3] *I.e.*, bow.

Lictors, Consuls, Sejanus, etc., pass over the stage.

Lic. Give way, make place, room for the consul!

San.   Hail,
Hail, great Sejanus!

Hat.   Hail, my honored lord!

Arr. [*Aside.*] We shall be marked anon
for our not "Hail."

Lep. [*Aside.*] That is already done.

Arr. [*Aside.*]   It is a note
Of upstart greatness to observe and
watch
For these poor trifles, which the noble
mind
Neglects and scorns.

Lep. [*Aside.*]   Ay, and they think them-
selves
Deeply dishonored where they are
omitted,
As if they were necessities that helped
To the perfection of their dignities,   40
And hate the men that but refrain hem.

Arr. [*Aside.*]   O!
There is a farder cause of hate. Their
breasts
Are guilty that we know their obscure
springs
And base beginnings; thence the anger
grows.   On! Follow!   [*Exeunt.*]

[Scene ix.

The same.]

Macro, Laco.

[Mac.] When all are entered, shut the
temple doors,
And bring your guards up to the gate.

Lac.   I will.

Mac. If you shall hear commotion in the
senate,
Present yourself, and charge on any man
Shall offer to come forth.

Lac.   I am instructed.   [*Exeunt.*]

[Scene x.

The Temple of Apollo.]   *The Senate.*

*Haterius, Trio, Sanquinius, Cotta, Regulus,
Sejanus, Pomponius, Latiaris, Lepidus,
Arruntius, Præcones, Lictores, [etc.]*

[Hat.] How well his lordship looks today!

Trio.   As if
He had been born or made for this
hour's state.

Cot. Your fellow consul's come about,
methinks?

Trio. Ay, he is wise.

San.   Sejanus trusts him well.

Trio. Sejanus is a noble, bounteous lord.

Hat. He is so, and most valiant.

Lat.   And most wise.

[1] Sen. He's everything.

Lat.   Worthy of all, and more
Than bounty can bestow.

Trio.   This dignity
Will make him worthy.

Pom.   Above Cæsar.

San.   Tut,
Cæsar is but the rector of an isle,   10
He of the empire.

Trio.   Now he will have power
More to reward than ever.

Cot.   Let us look
We be not slack in giving him our
voices.

Lat. Not I.

San.   Nor I.

Cot.   The readier we seem
To propagate his honors, will more bind
His thought to ours.

Hat.   I think right with your lordship;
It is the way to have us hold our places.

San. Ay, and get more.

Lat.   More office and more titles.

Pom. I will not lose the part I hope to
share
In these his fortunes, for my patrimony.   20

Lat. See how Arruntius sits, and Lepidus!

Trio. Let hem alone; they will be marked
anon.

[1] Sen. I'll do with others.

[2] Sen.   So will I.

[3] Sen.   And I.
Men grow not in the state but as they
are planted
Warm in his favors.

Cot.   Noble Sejanus!

Hat. Honored Sejanus!

Lat.   Worthy and great Sejanus!

Arr. [*Aside.*] Gods! How the sponges
open and take in
And shut again! Look, look! Is not he
blessed
That gets a seat in eye-reach of him?
More
That comes in ear- or tongue-reach? O,
but most   30

Can claw his subtile elbow, or with a
buzz
Flyblow his ears?

PRÆT[OR].   Proclaim the senate's peace,
And give last summons by the edict.

PRÆ.   Silence!
In name of Cæsar and the senate! Si-
lence!

"Memmius Regulus, and Fulcinius Trio,
consuls, these present kalends of June, with
the first light, shall hold a senate in the
Temple of Apollo Palatine; all that are
fathers, and are registered fathers,[1] that
have right of ent'ring the senate, we   [40
warn or command you be frequently present; take knowledge the business is the
commonwealth's.   Whosoever is absent,
his fine or mulct will be taken, his excuse
will not be taken."

TRIO. Note who are absent, and record
their names.

REG. Fathers conscript, may what I am
to utter
Turn good and happy for the common-
wealth!
And thou, Apollo, in whose holy house
We here are met, inspire us all with
truth,   50
And liberty of censure to our thought!
The majesty of great Tiberius Cæsar
Propounds to this grave senate the
bestowing
Upon the man he loves, honored Sejanus,
The tribunitial dignity and power.
Here are his letters, signéd with his
signet.
What pleaseth now the fathers to be
done?

SEN. Read, read hem, open, publicly read
hem.

COT. Cæsar hath honored his own greatness much
In thinking of this act.

TRIO.   It was a thought   60
Happy, and worthy Cæsar.

LAT.   And the lord
As worthy it, on whom it is directed!

HAT. Most worthy!

SAN.   Rome did never boast the virtue
That could give envy bounds, but his;
Sejanus—

[1] SEN. Honored and noble!

[2] SEN.   Good and great Sejanus!

----
[1] I.e., conscript fathers.

ARR. [Aside.] O, most tame slavery, and
fierce flattery!

PRÆ.   Silence!   The epistle is read.
"Tiberius Cæsar to the senate, greeting.
If you, conscript fathers, with your children, be in health, it is abundantly well;
we with our friends here are so.   The   [70
care of the commonwealth, howsoever we
are removed in person, cannot be absent
to our thought, although oftentimes, even
to princes most present, the truth of their
own affairs is hid; than which nothing
falls out more miserable to a state, or
makes the art of governing more difficult.
But, since it hath been our easeful happiness to enjoy both the aids and industry
of so vigilant a senate, we profess to   [80
have been the more indulgent to our
pleasures, not as being careless of our office,
but rather secure of the necessity. Neither
do these common rumors of many and infamous libels published against our retirement, at all afflict us, being born more
out of men's ignorance than their malice,
and will, neglected, find their own grave
quickly; whereas, too sensibly acknowledged, it would make their obloquy   [90
ours.   Nor do we desire their authors,
though found, be censured, since in a free
state, as ours, all men ought to enjoy their
minds and tongues free."
(ARR. The lapwing, the lapwing!)
"Yet in things which shall worthily and
more near concern the majesty of a prince,
we shall fear to be so unnaturally cruel
to our own fame, as to neglect them. True
it is, conscript fathers, that we have   [100
raised Sejanus from obscure and almost
unknown gentry"—
(SEN. How, how!)
"to the highest and most conspicuous
point of greatness, and, we hope, deserv-
ingly; yet not without danger, it being a
most bold hazard in that sov'reign who,
by his particular love to one, dares adventure the hatred of all his other subjects."
(ARR. This touches; the blood turns.)
"But we affy [2] in your loves and un-   [111
derstandings, and do no way suspect the
merit of our Sejanus to make our favors
offensive to any."
(SEN. O, good, good!)
"Though we could have wished his zeal

----
[2] Trust.

had run a calmer course against Agrippina
and our nephews, howsoever the openness
of their actions declared them delinquents,
and that he would have remembered [120
no innocence is so safe but it rejoiceth
to stand in the sight of mercy—the use
of which in us he hath so quite taken away
toward them, by his loyal fury, as now our
clemency would be thought but wearied
cruelty, if we should offer to exercise it."
(Arr. I thank him; there I looked for 't.
    A good fox!)
"Some there be that would interpret this
his public severity to be particular ambition, and that, under a pretext of [130
service to us, he doth but remove his own
lets, alleging the strengths he hath made to
himself, by the prætorian soldiers, by his
faction in court and senate, by the offices
he holds himself, and confers on others,
his popularity and dependents, his urging
and almost driving us to this our unwilling
retirement, and, lastly, his aspiring to be
our son-in-law."
(Sen. This 's strange!   140
Arr. I shall anon believe your vultures,
    Marcus.)
"Your wisdoms, conscript fathers, are
able to examine and censure these suggestions. But were they left to our absolving
voice, we durst pronounce them, as we
think them, most malicious."
(Sen. O, he has restored all; list!)
"Yet are they offered to be averred, and
on the lives of the informers. What we
should say, or rather what we should [150
not say, lords of the senate, if this be
true, our gods and goddesses confound
us if we know! Only we must think,
we have placed our benefits ill, and conclude that, in our choice, either we were
wanting to the gods, or the gods to us."
    The Senators shift their places.
(Arr. The place grows hot; they shift.)
"We have not been covetous, honorable
fathers, to change; neither is it now any
new lust that alters our affection, [160
or old loathing, but those needful jealousies
of state, that warn wiser princes hourly
to provide their safety, and do teach them
how learned a thing it is to beware of the
humblest enemy—much more of those
great ones whom their own employed
favors have made fit for their fears."

([1] Sen. Away!
[2] Sen.   Sit farder.
Cot.   Let's remove—
Arr. Gods! How the leaves drop off,
    this little wind!)
"We therefore desire that the offices [170
he holds be first seized by the senate, and
himself suspended from all exercise of
place or power—"
(Sen. How!
San. [*Pushing through.*] By your leave!
Arr. Come, porcpisce.[1]—Where's Hate-
    rius?
    His gout keeps him most miserably
        constant!—
    Your dancing shows a tempest.)
Sej.   Read no more!
Reg. Lords of the senate, hold your
        seats; read on.
Sej. These letters, they are forged.
Reg.   A guard! Sit still. 180

    Laco enters with the Guards.

Arr. There's change!
Reg.   Bid silence, and read forward.
    Præ. Silence!—"and himself suspended
from all exercise of place or power but
till due and mature trial be made of his
innocency, which yet we can faintly apprehend the necessity to doubt. If, conscript fathers, to your more searching wisdoms there shall appear farther cause
—or of farder proceeding, either to seizure
of lands, goods, or more—it is not our [190
power that shall limit your authority, or
our favor that must corrupt your justice;
either were dishonorable in you, and
both uncharitable to ourself. We would
willingly be present with your counsels in
this business; but the danger of so potent
a faction, if it should prove so, forbids
our attempting it, except one of the consuls
would be entreated for our safety, to undertake the guard of us home; then we [200
should most readily adventure. In the
meantime, it shall not be fit for us to importune so judicious a senate, who know
how much they hurt the innocent that
spare the guilty, and how grateful a
sacrifice to the gods is the life of an ingrateful person. We reflect not in this on Sejanus (notwithstanding, if you keep an

---

[1] Porpoise.

eye upon him—and there is Latiaris, a
senator, and Pinnarius Natta, two [210
of his most trusted ministers, and so professed, whom we desire not to have apprehended) but as the necessity of the cause
exacts it."

REG. A guard on Latiaris!

ARR.   O, the spy,
  The reverend spy is caught! Who pities
    him?
  Reward, sir, for your service.   Now
    you ha' done
  Your property,[1] you see what use is
    made?
    [*Exeunt Latiaris and Natta, guarded.*]
  Hang up the instrument.

SEJ.   Give leave.

LAC.   Stand, stand!
  He comes upon his death, that doth
    advance   220
  An inch toward my point.

SEJ.   Have we no friends here?

ARR. Hush't!   Where now are all the
  hails and acclamations?

[*Enter*] *Macro.*[2]

[MAC.] Hail to the consuls, and this noble
  senate!

SEJ. [*Aside.*] Is Macro here? O, thou art
  lost, Sejanus!

MAC. Sit still and unaffrighted, reverend
  fathers;
  Macro, by Cæsar's grace the new-made
    provost,
  And now possessed of the prætorian
    bands,
  An honor late belonged to that proud
    man,
  Bids you be safe, and, to your constant
    doom [3]   229
  Of his deservings, offers you the surety
  Of all the soldiers, tribunes, and cen-
    turions
  Received in our command.

REG.   Sejanus, Sejanus,
  Stand forth, Sejanus!

SEJ.   Am I called?

MAC.   Ay, thou,
  Thou insolent monster, art bid stand.

SEJ.   Why, Macro,

[1] Performed your office.
[2] The word *Senate* is repeated here.
[3] Firm judgment.

It hath been otherwise between you
  and I;
This court, that knows us both, hath
  seen a difference,
And can, if it be pleased to speak, confirm
Whose insolence is most.

MAC.   Come down, Typhœus!
If mine be most, lo, thus I make it more;
Kick up thy heels in air, tear off thy
  robe,   240
Play with thy beard and nostrils. Thus
  'tis fit
(And no man take compassion of thy
  state)
To use th' ingrateful viper, tread his
  brains
Into the earth.

REG.   Forbear!

MAC.   If I could lose
All my humanity now, 'twere well to
  torture
So meriting a traitor.—Wherefore, fa-
  thers,
Sit you amazed and silent, and not
  censure
This wretch, who, in the hour he first
  rebelled
Gainst Cæsar's bounty, did condemn
  himself?
Phlegra, the field where all the sons of
  earth   250
Mustered against the gods, did ne'er
  acknowledge
So proud and huge a monster.

REG.   Take him hence;
And all the gods guard Cæsar!

TRIO.   Take him hence.

HAT. Hence.

COT.   To the dungeon with him.

SAN.   He deserves it.

SEN. Crown all our doors with bays.

SAN.   And let an ox,
With gilded horns and garlands, straight
  be led
Unto the Capitol.

HAT.   And sacrificed
To Jove, for Cæsar's safety.

TRIO.   All our gods
Be present still to Cæsar!

COT.   Phœbus.

SAN.   Mars.

HAT. Diana.

SAN.   Pallas.

SEN.   Juno, Mercury,   260
All guard him!
MAC.   Forth, thou prodigy of men.
                    [*Exit Sejanus, guarded.*]
COT. Let all the traitor's titles be de-
    faced.
TRIO. His images and statues be pulled
    down.
HAT. His chariot-wheels be broken.
ARR.   And the legs
Of the poor horses, that deserved naught,
Let them be broken too!
LEP.   O violent change,
And whirl of men's affections!
ARR.   Like as both
    Their bulks and souls were bound on
        Fortune's wheel,
    And must act only with her motion.
        [*Exeunt All but*] *Lepidus, Arruntius.*
[LEP.] Who would depend upon the popu-
    lar air,   270
    Or voice of men, that have today
        beheld
    (That which, if all the gods had fore-
        declared,
    Would not have been believed) Sejanus'
        fall?
He that this morn rose proudly as the
    sun,
And, breaking through a mist of clients'
    breath,
Came on as gazed at and admired as
    he
When superstitious Moors salute his
    light!
That had our servile nobles waiting
    him
As common grooms, and hanging on
    his look   279
No less than human life on destiny!
That had men's knees as frequent as the
    gods,
And sacrifices more than Rome had
    altars!
And this man fall! Fall? Ay, without
    a look
That durst appear his friend, or lend
    so much
Of vain relief, to his changed state, as
    pity!
ARR. They that before, like gnats, played
    in his beams,
And thronged to circumscribe him, now
    not seen,

Nor deign to hold a common seat with
    him!
Others, that waited him unto the
    senate,   289
Now inhumanely ravish him to prison,
Whom but this morn they followed as
    their lord;
Guard through the streets, bound like
    a fugitive;
Instead of wreaths give fetters, strokes
    for stoops,
Blind shame for honors, and black taunts
    for titles!
Who would trust slippery Chance?
LEP.   They that would make
    Themselves her spoil, and foolishly
        forget,
    When she doth flatter, that she comes
        to prey.
    Fortune, thou hadst no deity, if men
    Had wisdom; we have placéd thee so
        high
    By fond belief in thy felicity.   300
SEN. (*Shout within.*) The gods guard Cæ-
    sar! All the gods guard Cæsar!

    [*Enter*] *Macro, Regulus, Senators.*

[MAC.] Now, great Sejanus, you that awed
    the state,
And sought to bring the nobles to your
    whip;
That would be Cæsar's tutor, and dis-
    pose
Of dignities and offices; that had
The public head still bare to your de-
    signs,
And made the general voice to echo
    yours;
That looked for salutations twelve
    score off,
And would have pyramids, yea, temples,
    reared
To your huge greatness—now you lie
    as flat   310
As was your pride advanced!
REG.   Thanks to the gods!
SEN. And praise to Macro, that hath
    savéd Rome!
Liberty, liberty, liberty! Lead on,
And praise to Macro, that hath savéd
    Rome!
[*Exeunt All but*] *Arruntius, Lepidus.* [*Enter*]
                    Terentius.

[ARR.] I prophesy, out of this senate's
　　flattery,
　That this new fellow, Macro, will be-
　　come
　A greater prodigy in Rome than he
　That now is fall'n.
TER.　　　　O you whose minds are good,
　And have not forced all mankind from
　　your breasts,
　That yet have so much stock of virtue
　　left　　　　　　　　　　　　　　　320
　To pity guilty states, when they are
　　wretched,
　Lend your soft ears to hear, and eyes to
　　weep,
　Deeds done by men beyond the acts of
　　Furies.
　The eager multitude (who never yet
　Knew why to love or hate, but only
　　pleased
　T' express their rage of power) no sooner
　　heard
　The murmur of Sejanus in decline,
　But with that speed and heat of appe-
　　tite,
　With which they greedily devour the
　　way
　To some great sports or a new thea-
　　ter,　　　　　　　　　　　　　　330
　They filled the Capitol and Pompey's
　　Cirque [1]
　Where, like so many mastives [2] biting
　　stones,
　As if his statues now were sensive [3]
　　grown
　Of their wild fury, first, they tear them
　　down,
　Then, fast'ning ropes, drag them along
　　the streets,
　Crying in scorn, "This, this was that
　　rich head
　Was crowned with girlands [4] and with
　　odors, this
　That was in Rome so reverencéd! Now
　The fornace and the bellows shall to
　　work,
　The great Sejanus crack, and piece by
　　piece　　　　　　　　　　　　　340
　Drop in the founder's pit."
LEP.　　　　　　　O popular rage!
TER.　The whilst the senate at the Temple
　　of Concord

Make haste to meet again, and throng-
　　ing cry,
　"Let us condemn him, tread him down
　　in water,
　While he doth lie upon the bank. Away!"
　Where some, more tardy, cry unto their
　　bearers,
　"He will be censured ere we come; run,
　　knaves,"
　And use that furious diligence, for fear
　Their bondmen should inform against
　　their slackness,
　And bring their quaking flesh unto the
　　hook.　　　　　　　　　　　　350
　The rout, they follow with confuséd
　　voice,
　Crying they are glad; say they could
　　ne'er abide him;
　Inquire what man he was, what kind
　　of face,
　What beard he had, what nose, what
　　lips; protest
　They ever did presage h' would come to
　　this,
　They never thought him wise, nor val-
　　iant, ask
　After his garments, when he dies; what
　　death.
　And not a beast of all the herd demands
　What was his crime, or who were his
　　accusers,　　　　　　　　　　359
　Under what proof or testimony he fell.
　There came, says one, a huge long-
　　worded letter
　From Capreæ against him. Did there
　　so?
　O, they are satisfied; no more.
LEP.　　　　　　　　　　　　　Alas!
　They follow Fortune, and hate men
　　condemned,
　Guilty or not.
ARR.　　　　　But had Sejanus thrived
　In his design, and prosperously oppressed
　The old Tiberius, then, in that same
　　minute,
　These very rascals, that now rage like
　　Furies,
　Would have proclaimed Sejanus emperor.
LEP.　But what hath followed?
TER.　　　　　　Sentence by the senate,
　To lose his head, which was no sooner
　　off　　　　　　　　　　　　　371
　But that and th' unfortunate trunk
　　were seized

---

[1] Circus, stadium.　　　　[3] Sensitive.
[2] Mastiffs.　　　　　　　　[4] Garlands.

By the rude multitude, who, not content
With what the forward justice of the
  state
Officiously had done, with violent rage
Have rent it limb from limb. A thousand
  heads,
A thousand hands, ten thousand tongues
  and voices,
Employed at once in several acts of
  malice!
Old men not staid with age, virgins with
  shame,
Late wives with loss of husbands, moth-
  ers of children,   380
Losing all grief in joy of his sad fall,
Run quite transported with their cruelty!
These mounting at his head, these at
  his face,
These digging out his eyes, those with
  his brain
Sprinkling themselves, their houses, and
  their friends;
Others are met, have ravished thence
  an arm,
And deal small pieces of the flesh for
  favors;
These with a thigh, this hath cut off
  his hands,
And this his feet; these fingers, and
  these toes;
That hath his liver, he his heart; there
  wants   390
Nothing but room for wrath, and place
  for hatred!
What cannot oft be done, is now o'er-
  done.
The whole, and all of what was great
  Sejanus,
And, next to Cæsar, did possess the world,
Now torn and scattered, as he needs
  no grave;
Each little dust covers a little part.
So lies he nowhere, and yet often buried!

[*Enter*] *Nuntius.*[1]

[ARR.] More of Sejanus?
NUN.   Yes.
LEP.   What can be added?
  We know him dead.
NUN.   Then there begin your pity.
  There is enough behind to melt ev'n
    Rome   400

[1] The names *Arruntius, Lepidus,* and *Terentius*
are repeated here.

And Cæsar into tears; since never
  slave
Could yet so highly offend, but tyranny,
In torturing him, would make him worth
  lamenting.
A son and daughter to the dead Se-
  janus
(Of whom there is not now so much
  remaining
As would give fast'ning to the hang-
  man's hook)
Have they drawn forth for farder sac-
  rifice;
Whose tenderness of knowledge, unripe
  years,
And childish silly [2] innocence was such
As scarce would lend them feeling of
  their danger;   410
The girl so simple, as she often asked
Where they would lead her, for what
  cause they dragged her,
Cried she would do no more, that she
  could take
Warning with beating. And, because
  our laws
Admit no virgin immature to die,
The wittily and strangely cruel Macro
Delivered her to be deflowered and
  spoiled
By the rude lust of the licentious hang-
  man,
Then to be strangled with her harmless
  brother.
LEP. O, act most worthy hell and lasting
  night   420
  To hide it from the world!
NUN.   Their bodies thrown
  Into the Gemonies (I know not how,
  Or by what accident returned), the
    mother,
Th' expulséd Apicata, finds them there,
Whom when she saw lie spread on the
  degrees,[3]
After a world of fury on herself,
Tearing her hair, defacing of her face,
Beating her breasts and womb, kneeling
  amazed,
Crying to heaven, then to them, at
  last
Her drownéd voice gat up above her
  woes,   430
And with such black and bitter execra-
  tions

[2] Simple.   [3] Steps.

As might affright the gods, and force
the sun
Run backward to the east, nay, make the
old
Deforméd chaos rise again, t' o'erwhelm
Them, us, and all the world, she fills
the air,
Upbraids the heavens with their partial
dooms,[1]
Defies their tyrannous powers, and de-
mands
What she and those poor innocents have
transgressed,
That they must suffer such a share in
vengeance,
Whilst Livia, Lygdus, and Eudemus
live,   440
Who, as she says, and firmly vows to
prove it
To Cæsar and the senate, poisoned
Drusus?
LEP. Confederates with her husband?
NUN.   Ay.
LEP.   Strange act!
ARR. And strangely opened. What says
now my monster,
The multitude? They reel now, do they
not?
NUN. Their gall is gone, and now they
gin to weep
The mischief they have done.
ARR.   I thank hem, rogues.
NUN. Part are so stupid, or so flexible,
As they believe him innocent; all
grieve;

[1] Unfair judgments.

And some whose hands yet reek with
his warm blood,   450
And gripe the part which they did tear
of him,
Wish him collected and created new.
LEP. How Fortune plies her sports, when
she begins
To practice hem! Pursues, continues,
adds,
Confounds with varying her impassioned
moods!
ARR. Dost thou hope, Fortune, to redeem
thy crimes,
To make amends for thy ill-placéd
favors
With these strange punishments? For-
bear, you things
That stand upon the pinnacles of state,
To boast your slippery height; when you
do fall,   460
You pash [2] yourselves in pieces, ne'er to
rise;
And he that lends you pity is not wise.
TER. Let this example move th' insolent
man
Not to grow proud and careless of the
gods.
It is an odious wisdom to blaspheme,
Much more to slighten or deny their
powers;
For whom the morning saw so great
and high,
Thus low and little, fore the even doth
lie.   [Exeunt.]

[2] Dash.

THE END.

This tragedy was first acted in the year 1603 by the King's Majesty's Servants. The
principal tragedians were:

Ric. Burbadge	Will. Shakespeare
Aug. Philips	Joh. Hemings
Will. Sly	Hen. Condell
Joh. Lowin	Alex. Cooke

With the allowance of the Master of Revels.

VOLPONE, OR THE FOX[1]

BY

BEN JONSON

To the most noble and most equal sisters, the two famous universities, for their love and acceptance shown to his poem in the presentation, Ben Jonson, the grateful acknowledger, dedicates both it and himself.

Never, most equal sisters, had any man a wit so presently[2] excellent as that it could raise itself, but there must come both matter, occasion, commenders, and favorers to it. If this be true, and that [10 the fortune of all writers doth daily prove it, it behooves the careful to provide well toward these accidents, and, having acquired them, to preserve that part of reputation most tenderly wherein the benefit of a friend is also defended. Hence it is that I now render myself grateful and am studious to justify the bounty of your act, to which, though your mere authority were satisfying, yet, it being an [20 age wherein poetry and the professors[3] of it hear so ill[4] on all sides, there will a reason be looked for in the subject. It is certain, nor can it with any forehead be opposed, that the too much license of poetasters in this time hath much deformed their mistress, that every day their manifold and manifest ignorance doth stick unnatural reproaches upon her. But for their petulancy it were an act of the [30 greatest injustice either to let the learned suffer, or so divine a skill, which indeed should not be attempted with unclean hands, to fall under the least contempt. For, if men will impartially and not asquint look toward the offices and function of a poet, they will easily conclude to themselves the impossibility of any man's being the good poet without first being a good man. He that is said [40

to be able to inform young men to all good disciplines, inflame grown men to all great virtues, keep old men in their best and supreme state or, as they decline to childhood, recover them to their first strength; that comes forth the interpreter and arbiter of nature, a teacher of things divine no less than human, a master in manners, and can alone, or with a few, effect the business of mankind— [50 this, I take him, is no subject for pride and ignorance to exercise their railing rhetoric upon. But it will here be hastily answered that the writers of these days are other things; that not only their manners but their natures are inverted, and nothing remaining with them of the dignity of poet but the abused name, which every scribe usurps; that now, especially in dramatic or, as they term it, stage [60 poetry, nothing but ribaldry, profanation, blasphemy, all license of offense to God and man is practiced. I dare not deny a great part of this, and am sorry I dare not, because in some men's abortive features (and would they had never boasted the light) it is overtrue; but that all are embarked in this bold adventure for hell is a most uncharitable thought and, uttered, a more malicious slander. For my par- [70 ticular[5] I can, and from a most clear conscience, affirm that I have ever trembled to think toward the least profaneness, have loathed the use of such foul and unwashed bawdry as is now made the food of the scene;[6] and, howsoever I cannot escape from some the imputation of sharpness but that they will say I have taken a pride or lust to be bitter, and not my youngest infant but hath come [80 into the world with all his teeth, I would ask of these supercilious politics[7] what

---

[1] The title continues: "A Comedy, Acted in the Year 1605, by the K[ing's] Majesty's Servants."   [3] Practitioners.
[2] Actually.   [4] Are so ill spoken of.
[5] In my own case.   [7] Politicians, intriguers.
[6] Stage.

nation, society, or general order or state I have provoked?—what public person?—whether I have not in all these preserved their dignity, as mine own person, safe? My works are read, allowed [1] (I speak of those that are entirely mine); look into them. What broad reproofs have I used? Where have I been particular, where [90 personal, except to a mimic, cheater, bawd, or buffoon—creatures for their insolencies worthy to be taxed? Yet to which of these so pointingly as he might not either ingenuously have confessed or wisely dissembled his disease? But it is not rumor can make men guilty, much less entitle me to other men's crimes. I know that nothing can be so innocently writ or carried but may be made obnoxious to con- [100 struction; [2] marry, whilst I bear mine innocence about me I fear it not. Application [3] is now grown a trade with many; and there are that profess to have a key for the deciphering of everything. But let wise and noble persons take heed how they be too credulous or give leave to these invading interpreters to be overfamiliar with their fames, who cunningly and often utter their own virulent malice under [110 other men's simplest meanings. As for those that will (by faults which charity hath raked [4] up or common honesty concealed) make themselves a name with the multitude, or, to draw their rude and beastly claps, care not whose living faces they intrench with their petulant styles, may they do it without a rival, for me! I choose rather to live graved [5] in obscurity than share with them in so prepos- [120 terous a fame. Nor can I blame the wishes of those severe and wiser patriots, who, providing [6] the hurts these licentious spirits may do in a state, desire rather to see fools and devils and those antique relics of barbarism retrieved, with all other ridiculous and exploded follies, than behold the wounds of private men, of princes and nations, for, as Horace makes Trebatius speak among these,   130

Sibi quisque timet, quanquam est intactus, et odit. [7]

And men may justly impute such rages, if continued, to the writer as his sports. The increase of which lust in liberty, together with the present trade of the stage in all their misc'line [8] interludes, what learned or liberal soul doth not already abhor, where nothing but the filth of the time is uttered, and that with such impropriety of phrase, such [140 plenty of solecisms, such dearth of sense, so bold prolepses, so racked metaphors, with brothelry able to violate the ear of a pagan, and blasphemy to turn the blood of a Christian to water? I cannot but be serious in a cause of this nature, wherein my fame and the reputations of divers honest and learned are the question, when a name so full of authority, antiquity, and all great mark is through [150 their insolence become the lowest scorn of the age, and those men subject to the petulancy of every vernaculous [9] orator, that were wont to be the care of kings and happiest monarchs. This it is that hath not only rapt [10] me to present indignation, but made me studious heretofore, and, by all my actions, to stand off from them, which may most appear in this my latest work, which you, most [160 learned arbitresses, have seen, judged, and to my crown approved, wherein I have labored for their instruction and amendment, to reduce not only the ancient forms but manners of the scene, the easiness, the propriety, the innocence, and, last, the doctrine, which is the principal end of poesy, to inform men in the best reason of living. And, though my catastrophe may, in the strict rigor of comic law, [170 meet with censure, as turning back to my promise, I desire the learned and charitable critic to have so much faith in me to think it was done of industry, for with what ease I could have varied it nearer his scale (but that I fear to boast my own faculty) I could here insert. But my special aim being to put the snaffle in their mouths that cry out, "We never

---

[1] *I.e.*, passed by the censor.
[2] Through interpretation.
[3] Reading of cloaked allusions.
[4] Covered.
[5] Buried.
[6] Foreseeing.

[7] " Everybody fears for himself and is vexed, although he is untouched " (*Sermones*, II, i, 23).
[8] Miscelline, miscellaneous.
[9] Scurrilous.   [10] Transported.

punish vice in our interludes," etc., [180
I took the more liberty, though not without some lines of example, drawn even
in the ancients themselves, the goings out [1]
of whose comedies are not always joyful,
but ofttimes the bawds, the servants,
the rivals, yea, and the masters are mulcted
—and fitly, it being the office of a comic
poet to imitate justice and instruct to
life as well as purity of language, or stir
up gentle affections,[2] to which I shall [190
take the occasion elsewhere to speak.

For the present, most reverenced sisters, as I have cared to be thankful for
your affections past, and here made the
understanding acquainted with some ground
of your favors, let me not despair their continuance to the maturing of some worthier
fruits, wherein, if my muses be true to
me, I shall raise the despised head of
poetry again, and, stripping her out [200
of those rotten and base rags wherewith the times have adulterated her form,
restore her to her primitive habit, feature,
and majesty, and render her worthy to
be embraced and kissed of all the great
and master spirits of our world. As for
the vile and slothful, who never affected
an act worthy of celebration, or are so
inward [3] with their own vicious natures as
they worthily fear her and think it [210
a high point of policy to keep her in contempt with their declamatory and windy
invectives, she shall out of just rage incite
her servants (who are "*genus irritabile*" [4])
to spout ink in their faces, that shall eat
farder [5] than their marrow, into their fames;
and not Cinnamus the barber,[6] with his
art, shall be able to take out the brands;
but they shall live and be read till the
wretches die, as things worst deserving [220
of themselves in chief and then of all mankind.

[From my house in the Blackfriars,
    this 11th day of February, 1607.] [7]

THE PERSONS OF THE PLAY

VOLPONE [*the Fox*], *a magnifico.*
MOSCA [*the Gadfly*], *his parasite.*
VOLTORE [*the Vulture*], *an advocate.*
CORBACCIO [*the Crow*], *an old gentleman.*
CORVINO [*the Raven*], *a merchant.*
AVOCATORI, *four magistrates.*
NOTARIO, *the register.*
NANO, *a dwarf.*
CASTRONE, *an eunuch.*
GREGE [*or* MOB].

POLITIC WOULD-BE, *a knight.*
PEREGRINE, *a gent[leman] traveler.*
BONARIO, *a young gentleman.*

FINE MADAME WOULD-BE, *the knight's wife.*
CELIA, *the merchant's wife.*

COMMANDADORI, *officers [of justice].*
MERCATORI, *three merchants.*
ANDROGYNO, *a hermaphrodite.*
SERVITORE, *a servant;* WOMEN [SERVANTS].

THE SCENE: *Venice.*

[TIME: *Contemporary.*]

THE ARGUMENT

V OLPONE, childless, rich, feigns sick, de-
    spairs,
O ffers his state to hopes of several heirs,
L ies languishing; his parasite receives
P resents of all, assures, deludes, then
    weaves
O ther cross plots, which ope themselves,
    are told.
N ew tricks for safety are sought; they
    thrive, when, bold,
E ach tempts th' other again, and all are
    sold.

PROLOGUE

Now, luck yet send us, and a little wit
    Will serve to make our play hit;
According to the palates of the season,
    Here is rime, not empty of reason.
This we were bid to credit from our poet,
    Whose true scope, if you would know it,
In all his poems still hath been this measure:
    To mix profit with your pleasure;

[3] Familiar.
[4] "*Genus irritabile vatum*" (Horace, *Epistles*, II,
2, 102): "The excitable race of poets."
[5] Farther.
[6] The barber was also a surgeon.

[1] Conclusions.   [2] Feelings.   [7] From 1607 edn.

And not as some, whose throats their envy
    failing,   9
Cry hoarsely, "All he writes is railing,"
And, when his plays come forth, think
    they can flout them,
With saying he was a year about them.
To these there needs no lie, but this his
    creature,[1]
Which was two months since no feature;
And, though he dares give them five lives
    to mend it,
'Tis known five weeks fully penned it,
From his own hand, without a coadjutor,
    Novice, journeyman, or tutor.
Yet thus much I can give you as a token
    Of his play's worth: no eggs are broken,
Nor quaking custards [2] with fierce teeth
    affrighted,   21
Wherewith your rout are so delighted;
Nor hales he in a gull, old ends reciting,
    To stop gaps in his loose writing;
With such a deal of monstrous and forced
    action,
As might make Bet'lem a faction; [3]
Nor made he his play for jests stol'n from
    each table,
But makes jests to fit his fable;
And so presents quick [4] comedy refined
    As best critics have designed.   30
The laws of time, place, persons he observ-
    eth;
From no needful rule he swerveth.
All gall and copp'ras from his ink he drain-
    eth;
Only a little salt remaineth,
Wherewith he'll rub your cheeks till, red
    with laughter,
They shall look fresh a week after.

ACT I. SCENE i.

[*A room in Volpone's house.*][5]

Volpone, Mosca.

VOLP. Good morning to the day; and next
    my gold!
Open the shrine that I may see my saint.

---

[1] Creation, *i.e.*, the play.
[2] An allusion to the tricks sometimes played
with immense custards at the lord mayors' and
other official feasts, and apparently later transferred to the theater (Gifford).
[3] Make Bedlam, the madhouse, more confused.
[4] Living, lively.
[5] The scene remains the same throughout the
act, and the action is continuous.

[*Mosca opens the curtain, revealing Vol-*
pone's treasure.]

Hail, the world's soul and mine! More
    glad than is
The teeming earth to see the longed-for
    sun
Peep through the horns of the celestial
    Ram,
Am I, to view thy splendor darkening
    his,
That, lying here amongst my other
    hoards,
Show'st like a flame by night, or like
    the day
Strook [6] out of chaos, when all darkness
    fled
Unto the center.[7] O, thou son of Sol,   10
But brighter than thy father, let me
    kiss
With adoration thee and every relic
Of sacred treasure in this blessed room.
Well did wise poets, by thy glorious
    name,
Title that age which they would have
    the best,
Thou being the best of things, and far
    transcending
All style of joy in children, parents,
    friends,
Or any other waking dream on earth.
Thy looks when they to Venus did as-
    cribe,
They should have given her twenty
    thousand Cupids;   20
Such are thy beauties and our loves!
    Dear saint,
Riches, the dumb god, that giv'st all
    men tongues,
That canst do naught, and yet mak'st
    men do all things,
The price of souls, even hell, with thee
    to boot,
Is made worth heaven! Thou art virtue,
    fame,
Honor, and all things else. Who can
    get thee,
He shall be noble, valiant, honest, wise—
MOS. And what he will, sir. Riches are
    in fortune
A greater good than wisdom is in na-
    ture.
VOLP. True, my beloved Mosca. Yet I
    glory   30

---

[6] Struck.   [7] *I.e.*, of the earth.

More in the cunning purchase [1] of my
  wealth
Than in the glad possession, since I gain
No common way: I use no trade, no
  venter; [2]
I wound no earth with plowshares; I
  fat no beasts
To feed the shambles, have no mills
  for iron,
Oil, corn, or men to grind hem [3] into
  poulder; [4]
I blow no subtle glass, expose no ships
To threat'nings of the furrow-facéd sea;
I turn no moneys in the public bank,
Nor usure [5] private.

Mos.   No, sir, nor devour   40
Soft prodigals. You shall ha' some will
  swallow
A melting heir as glibly as your Dutch
Will pills of butter, and ne'er purge for 't;
Tear forth the fathers of poor families
Out of their beds, and coffin them alive
In some kind, clasping prison, where
  their bones
May be forthcoming when the flesh is
  rotten.
But your sweet nature doth abhor these
  courses;
You loathe the widow's or the orphan's
  tears
Should wash your pavements, or their
  piteous cries   50
Ring in your roofs, and beat the air for
  vengeance.

Volp. Right, Mosca; I do loathe it.

Mos.   And besides, sir,
You are not like a thresher that doth
  stand
With a huge flail, watching a heap of corn,
And, hungry, dares not taste the small-
  est grain,
But feeds on mallows and such bitter
  herbs,
Nor like the merchant, who hath filled
  his vaults
With Romagnia and rich Candian wines,
Yet drinks the lees of Lombard's vinegar.
You will not lie in straw, whilst moths
  and worms   60
Feed on your sumptuous hangings and
  soft beds;

You know the use of riches, and dare
  give now
From that bright heap, to me, your
  poor observer, [6]
Or to your dwarf, or your hermaphrodite,
Your eunuch, or what other household
  trifle
Your pleasure allows maint'nance—

Volp.   Hold thee, Mosca;
Take of my hand; thou strik'st on truth
  in all,
And they are envious term thee parasite.
Call forth my dwarf, my eunuch, and
  my fool,
And let hem make me sport.   [Exit
  Mosca.] What should I do   70
But cocker up [7] my genius, and live free
To all delights my fortune calls me to?
I have no wife, no parent, child, ally,
To give my substance to; but whom I
  make
Must be my heir; and this makes men
  observe [8] me.
This draws new clients daily to my
  house,
Women and men of every sex and age,
That bring me presents, send me plate,
  coin, jewels,
With hope that when I die (which they
  expect
Each greedy minute) it shall then re-
  turn   80
Tenfold upon them, whilst some, cov-
  etous
Above the rest, seek to engross [9] me
  whole,
And counterwork the one unto the other,
Contend in gifts, as they would seem in
  love—
All which I suffer, playing with their
  hopes,
And am content to coin hem into profit,
And look upon their kindness, and take
  more,
And look on that, still bearing them in
  hand, [10]
Letting the cherry knock against their
  lips,
And draw it by their mouths, and back
  again.—   90
How now!

---

[1] Gain by underhand methods.   [4] Powder.
[2] Venture.   [5] Usury.
[3] Them.

[6] Dutiful attendant.   [8] Take notice of.
[7] Indulge.   [9] Absorb.
[10] Deceiving them.

ACT I. SCENE ii.

Nano, Androgyno, Castrone, Volpone, Mosca.

[NAN.] Now, room for fresh gamesters,
   who do will you to know
They do bring you neither play nor
   university show,
And therefore do entreat you that whatsoever they rehearse
May not fare a whit the worse for the
   false pace of the verse.[1]
If you wonder at this, you will wonder
   more ere we pass,
For know, here [*Points to Androgyno.*]
   is enclosed the soul of Pythagoras,
That juggler divine, as hereafter shall
   follow—
Which soul, fast and loose, sir, came
   first from Apollo,
And was breathed into Æthalides, Mer-
   curius his son,
Where it had the gift to remember all
   that ever was done.   10
From thence it fled forth, and made
   quick transmigration
To goldilocked Euphorbus, who was
   killed in good fashion
At the siege of old Troy, by the cuck-
   old of Sparta.
Hermotimus was next (I find it in my
   charta [2]),
To whom it did pass, where no sooner
   it was missing
But with one Pyrrhus of Delos it learned
   to go a-fishing;
And thence did it enter the sophist of
   Greece.
From Pythagore, she went into a beauti-
   ful piece,
Hight [3] Aspasia, the meretrix; [4] and the
   next toss of her
Was again of [5] a whore she became a
   philosopher,   20
Crates the Cynic, as itself doth relate it.
Since, kings, knights, and beggars,
   knaves, lords, and fools gat it,
Besides ox and ass, camel, mule, goat,
   and brock,[6]

In all which it hath spoke, as in the cob-
   bler's cock.
But I come not here to discourse of that
   matter,
Or his "one," "two," or "three," or his
   great oath, "by quater," [7]
His musics, his trigon,[8] his golden thigh,[9]
Or his telling how elements shift; but I
Would ask how of late thou hast suffered
   translation,
And shifted thy coat in these days of
   reformation.   30
AND. Like one of the reformed, a fool, as
   you see,
Counting all old doctrine heresy.
NAN. But not on thine own forbid meats [10]
   hast thou ventered?
AND. On fish, when first a Carthusian I
   entered.
NAN. Why, then thy dogmatical silence
   hath left thee?
AND. Of that an obstreperous lawyer be-
   reft me.
NAN. O wonderful change, when Sir
   Lawyer forsook thee!
For Pythagore's sake, what body then
   took thee?
AND. A good dull moil.[11]
NAN.   And how! By that means
Thou wert brought to allow of the eat-
   ing of beans?   40
AND. Yes.
NAN.   But from the moil into whom
   didst thou pass?
AND. Into a very strange beast, by some
   writers called an ass;
By others, a precise, pure, illuminate
   brother [12]
Of those devour flesh, and sometimes
   one another,
And will drop you forth a libel or a
   sanctified lie
Betwixt every spoonful of a Nativity pie.
NAN. Now quit thee, for heaven, of that
   profane nation,
And gently report thy next transmigra-
   tion.
AND. To the same that I am.

---

[1] The verse of this interlude or debate based
on Lucian's dialogue of a cobbler and a cock is
in the old-fashioned tumbling meter. In the
original the sixty-two lines of the passage are
printed in italics.   [4] Hetaira.
[2] Paper.   [5] From being.
[3] Called.   [6] Badger.

[7] By four.
[8] Triangular harp.
[9] According to legend, Pythagoras actually
showed his golden thigh to Abaris, priest of the
Hyperboreans, and also exhibited it once at the
Olympic games.   [11] Mule.
[10] Forbidden foods.   [12] *I.e.,* Puritan.

NAN.   A creature of delight?
And, what is more than a fool, an her-
  maphrodite?   50
Now, pray thee, sweet soul, in all thy
  variation,
Which body wouldst thou choose to
  take up thy station?
AND. Troth, this I am in; even here would
  I tarry.
NAN. Cause [1] here the delight of each sex
  thou canst vary?
AND. Alas, those pleasures be stale and
  forsaken;
No, 'tis your fool wherewith I am so
  taken,
The only one creature that I can call
  blessed,
For all other forms I have proved most
  distressed.
NAN. Spoke true, as thou wert in Pythag-
  oras still.
This learned opinion we celebrate will, 60
Fellow eunuch, as behooves us, with all
  our wit and art,
To dignify that whereof ourselves are
  so great and special a part.—

VOLP. Now, very, very pretty! Mosca,
  this
Was thy invention?
MOS.   If it please my patron;
  Not else.
VOLP.   It doth, good Mosca.
MOS.   Then it was, sir.

SONG

Fools, they are the only nation
Worth men's envy or admiration,
Free from care or sorrow-taking,
Selves and others merry making;
All they speak or do is sterling.   70
Your fool he is your great man's dearling [2]
And your ladies' sport and pleasure;
Tongue and bable [3] are his treasure.
E'en his face begetteth laughter,
And he speaks truth free from slaughter; [4]
He's the grace of every feast,
And sometimes the chiefest guest,
Hath his trencher and his stool,
When wit waits upon the fool.
  O, who would not be   80
  He, he, he?

[1] Because.
[2] Darling.
[3] Babble.
[4] I.e., with safety.

One knocks without.
VOLP. Who's that? Away! Look, Mosca.
MOS.   Fool, begone!—
[*Exeunt Nano, Castrone, and Androgyno.*]
'Tis Signior Voltore, the advocate;
I know him by his knock.
VOLP.   Fetch me my gown,
My furs, and nightcaps. Say my couch
  is changing,
And let him entertain himself awhile
Without i' th' gallery.—[*Exit Mosca.*]
  Now, now, my clients
Begin their visitation! Vulture, kite,
Raven, and gorcrow, [5] all my birds of
  prey,
That think me turning carcass, now they
  come.   90
I am not for hem yet.—

[*Enter Mosca, with the gown, etc.*]
                How now! The news?
MOS. A piece of plate, sir.
VOLP.   Of what bigness?
MOS.   Huge,
Massy, and antique, with your name
  inscribed
And arms engraven.
VOLP.   Good! And not a fox
Stretched on the earth, with fine delusive
  sleights
Mocking a gaping crow? Ha, Mosca?
MOS.   Sharp, sir.
VOLP. Give me my furs. [*Puts on his dress-
  ing gown.*] Why dost thou laugh so,
  man?
MOS. I cannot choose, sir, when I appre-
  hend
What thoughts he has without now, as he
  walks:
That this might be the last gift he should
  give;   100
That this would fetch you; if you died
  today,
And gave him all, what he should be
  tomorrow;
What large return would come of all
  his venters;
How he should worshiped be and reverenced,
Ride with his furs and footcloths, [6]
  waited on
By herds of fools and clients, have clear
  way

[5] Carrion crow.
[6] A caparison of a horse.

Made for his moil, as lettered as himself,
Be called the great and learned advocate,
And then concludes there's naught impossible.

Volp. Yes, to be learned, Mosca.

Mos.   O, no. Rich 110
Implies it. Hood an ass with reverend purple,
So you can hide his two ambitious [1] ears,
And he shall pass for a cathedral doctor.[2]

Volp. My caps, my caps, good Mosca.
Fetch him in.

Mos. Stay, sir; your ointment for your eyes.

Volp.   That's true;
Despatch, despatch! I long to have possession
Of my new present.

Mos.   That, and thousands more,
I hope to see you lord of.

Volp.   Thanks, kind Mosca.

Mos. And that, when I am lost in blended dust,
And hundred such as I am, in succession—   120

Volp. Nay, that were too much, Mosca.

Mos.   You shall live
Still to delude these harpies.

Volp.   Loving Mosca,
'Tis well! My pillow now, and let him enter.—   [Exit Mosca.]
Now, my feigned cough, my phthisic, and my gout,
My apoplexy, palsy, and catarrhs,
Help, with your forcéd functions, this my posture,
Wherein this three year I have milked their hopes.
He comes; I hear him—Uh! uh! uh! uh!
O—

Act I. Scene iii.

Mosca, Voltore, Volpone.

[Mos. (*To Voltore.*)] You still are what you were, sir. Only you,
Of all the rest, are he commands his love,
And you do wisely to preserve it thus,
With early visitation and kind notes
Of your good meaning to him, which I know

[1] Moving, flapping.
[2] One who holds a university chair.

Cannot but come most grateful.—Patron! Sir!
Here's Signior Voltore is come—

Volp.   What say you?

Mos. Sir, Signior Voltore is come this morning
To visit you.

Volp.   I thank him.

Mos.   And hath brought
A piece of antique plate, bought of S[t]. Mark,[3]   10
With which he here presents you.

Volp.   He is welcome.
Pray him to come more often.

Mos.   Yes.

Volt.   What says he?

Mos. He thanks you, and desires you see him often.

Volp. Mosca!

Mos.   My patron?

Volp.   Bring him near. Where is he?
I long to feel his hand.

Mos.   The plate is here, sir.

Volt. How fare you, sir?

Volp.   I thank you, Signior Voltore.
Where is the plate? Mine eyes are bad.

Volt. [*Giving the plate to him.*]   I'm sorry
To see you still thus weak.

Mos. [*Aside.*]   That he is not weaker.

Volp. You are too munificent.

Volt.   No, sir; would to heaven
I could as well give health to you as that plate!   20

Volp. You give, sir, what you can; I thank you. Your love
Hath taste in this, and shall not be unanswered.
I pray you see me often.

Volt.   Yes, I shall, sir.

Volp. Be not far from me.

Mos.   Do you observe that, sir?

Volp. Hearken unto me still; it will concern you.

Mos. You are a happy man, sir; know your good.

Volp. I cannot now last long—

[4] (Mos.   You are his heir, sir.

Volt. Am I?)

Volp.   I feel me going. Uh! uh! uh! uh!
I am sailing to my port. Uh! uh! uh! uh!

[3] *I.e.*, at a shop in St. Mark's Place.
[4] Jonson frequently uses parentheses to indicate asides and other passages incidental to the main action.

And I am glad I am so near my haven. 30

Mos. Alas, kind gentleman! Well, we
must all go—

Volt. But, Mosca—

Mos.　　　　　　　　Age will conquer.

Volt.　　　　　　　Pray thee, hear me.
Am I inscribed his heir for certain?

Mos.　　　　　　　　　Are you?
I do beseech you, sir, you will vouchsafe
To write me i' your family. All my hopes
Depend upon your worship. I am lost
Except the rising sun do shine on me.

Volt. It shall both shine and warm thee,
Mosca.

Mos.　　Sir,
I am a man that hath not done your
love
All the worst offices; here I wear your
keys,　　　　　　　　　40
See all your coffers and your caskets
locked,
Keep the poor inventory of your jewels,
Your plate, and moneys, am your stew-
ard, sir,
Husband your goods here.

Volt.　　　　　　　But am I sole heir?

Mos. Without a partner, sir—confirmed
this morning.
The wax is warm yet, and the ink scarce
dry
Upon the parchment.

Volt.　　　　　　　Happy, happy me!
By what good chance, sweet Mosca?

Mos.　　　　　　　Your desert, sir;
I know no second cause.

Volt.　　　　　　　Thy modesty
Is loath to know it; well, we shall requite
it.　　　　　　　　　50

Mos. He ever liked your course, sir; that
first took him.
I oft have heard him say how he admired
Men of your large profession, that could
speak
To every cause, and things mere con-
traries,
Till they were hoarse again, yet all be
law;
That with most quick agility could turn,
And re-turn, make knots and undo them,
Give forkéd counsel, take provoking gold
On either hand, and put it up—these
men,
He knew, would thrive with their hu-
mility.　　　　　　　　60

And, for his part, he thought he should
be blessed
To have his heir of such a suffering spirit,
So wise, so grave, of so perplexed a
tongue,
And loud withal, that would not wag,
nor scarce
Lie still, without a fee, when every word
Your worship but lets fall is a cecchine![1]—
　　　　　　　　　Another knocks.
Who's that? One knocks; I would not
have you seen, sir.
And yet—pretend you came and went
in haste;
I'll fashion an excuse. And, gentle sir,
When you do come to swim in golden
lard,　　　　　　　　　70
Up to the arms in honey, that your chin
Is borne up stiff with fatness of the flood,
Think on your vassal; but remember me.
I ha' not been your worst of clients.

Volt.　　　　　　　Mosca!—

Mos. When will you have your inventory
brought, sir?
Or see a copy of the will? (Anon!)
I'll bring hem to you, sir. Away, begone;
Put business i' your face. [*Exit Voltore.*]

Volp.　　　　　　　Excellent Mosca!
Come hither; let me kiss thee.

Mos.　　　　　　　Keep you still, sir.
Here is Corbaccio.

Volp.　　　　　　　Set the plate away. 80
The vulture's gone, and the old raven's
come.

Act I. Scene iv.

Mosca, Corbaccio,[2] Volpone.

[Mos.] Betake you to your silence and
your sleep.—
　　　[*Puts the plate among the treasures.*]
Stand there and multiply.—Now we
shall see
A wretch who is indeed more impotent
Than this can feign to be, yet hopes to
hop
Over his grave.

　　　　　[*Enter Corbaccio.*]
　　　　　　　Signior Corbaccio!
Yo' are very welcome, sir.

Corb.　　　　　　How does your patron?

Mos. Troth, as he did, sir; no amends.

[1] Sequin, a gold coin.　　　[2] Enters later.

CORB.   What? Mends he?
MOS. No, sir; he is rather worse.
CORB.   That's well. Where is he?
MOS. Upon his couch, sir, newly fall'n
    asleep.
CORB. Does he sleep well?
MOS.   No wink, sir, all this night, 10
    Nor yesterday; but slumbers.
CORB.   Good! He should take
    Some counsel of physicians. I have
    brought him
An opiate here from mine own doctor—
MOS. He will not hear of drugs.
CORB.   Why? I myself
    Stood by while 'twas made, saw all th'
    ingredients,
    And know it cannot but most gently
    work.
    My life for his, 'tis but to make him
    sleep.
VOLP. [Aside.] Ay, his last sleep, if he
    would take it.
MOS.   Sir,
    He has no faith in physic.
CORB.   Say you, say you?
MOS. He has no faith in physic. He does
    think   20
    Most of your doctors are the greater
    danger,
    And worse disease, t' escape. I often
    have
    Heard him protest that your physician
    Should never be his heir.
CORB.   Not I his heir?
MOS. Not your physician, sir.
CORB.   O, no, no, no,
    I do not mean it.
MOS.   No, sir, nor their fees
    He cannot brook; he says they flay a
    man
    Before they kill him.
CORB.   Right, I do conceive you.
MOS. And then they do it by experiment,
    For which the law not only doth absolve
    hem,   30
    But gives them great reward; and he is
    loath
    To hire his death so.
CORB.   It is true, they kill
    With as much license as a judge.
MOS.   Nay, more,
    For he but kills, sir, where the law con-
    demns,
    And these can kill him too.

CORB.   Ay, or me,
    Or any man. How does his apoplex?[1]
    Is that strong on him still?
MOS.   Most violent.
    His speech is broken, and his eyes are
    set,
    His face drawn longer than 'twas wont—
CORB.   How? How?
    Stronger than he was wont?
MOS.   No, sir; his face 40
    Drawn longer than 'twas wont.
CORB.   O, good!
MOS.   His mouth
    Is ever gaping, and his eyelids hang.
CORB.   Good.
MOS. A freezing numbness stiffens all his
    joints,
    And makes the color of his flesh like lead.
CORB.   'Tis good.
MOS. His pulse beats slow and dull.
CORB.   Good symptoms still.
MOS. And from his brain—
CORB.   Ha? How? Not from his brain?
MOS. Yes, sir, and from his brain—
(CORB.   I conceive you; good.)
MOS. Flows a cold sweat, with a continual
    rheum,[2]
    Forth the resolvéd[3] corners of his eyes.
CORB. Is 't possible? Yet I am better, ha!
    How does he with the swimming of his
    head?   51
MOS. O, sir, 'tis past the scotomy;[4] he
    now
    Hath lost his feeling, and hath left[5] to
    snort;
    You hardly can perceive him, that he
    breathes.
CORB. Excellent, excellent! Sure I shall
    outlast him.
    This makes me young again, a score of
    years.
MOS. I was a-coming for you, sir.
CORB.   Has he made his will?
    What has he given me?
MOS.   No, sir.
CORB.   Nothing? Ha?
MOS. He has not made his will, sir.
CORB.   O, O, O! 59
    What then did Voltore, the lawyer, here?
MOS. He smelt a carcass, sir, when he
    but heard

---

[1] Apoplexy.   [2] Discharge.   [3] Loosened.
[4] Dizziness, with dimness of sight.
[5] Ceased.

My master was about his testament;
As I did urge him to it for your good—
CORB. He came unto him, did he?   I
   thought so.
MOS. Yes, and presented him this piece
   of plate.
CORB. To be his heir?
MOS.   I do not know, sir.
CORB.   True;
   I know it too.
MOS. [*Aside.*]   By your own scale, sir.
CORB.   Well,
   I shall prevent him yet. See, Mosca,
   look!
   Here I have brought a bag of bright
   cecchines
   Will quite weigh down his plate.
MOS.   Yea, marry, sir.   70
   This is true physic, this your sacred
   medicine;
   No talk of opiates to this great elixir!
CORB. 'Tis *aurum palpabile*, if not *pota-
   bile*.[1]
MOS. It shall be ministered to him in his
   bowl?
CORB. Ay, do, do, do.
MOS.   Most blessed cordial!
   This will recover him.
CORB.   Yes, do, do, do.
MOS. I think it were not best, sir.
CORB.   What?
MOS.   To recover him.
CORB. O, no, no, no; by no means.
MOS.   Why, sir, this
   Will work some strange effect, if he but
   feel it.
CORB. 'Tis true; therefore forbear.   I'll
   take my venter;   80
   Give me 't again.
MOS.   At no hand;[2] pardon me.
   You shall not do yourself that wrong,
   sir. I
   Will so advise you, you shall have it all.
CORB. How?
MOS.   All, sir; 'tis your right, your
   own; no man
   Can claim a part. 'Tis yours without a
   rival,
   Decreed by destiny.
CORB.   How, how, good Mosca?
MOS. I'll tell you, sir. This fit he shall
   recover—

---

[1] Palpable gold, if not potable.—"Potable
gold" was a medicine.   [2] By no means.

CORB. I do conceive you.
MOS.   And, on first advantage
   Of his gained sense, will I reimportune
   him
   Unto the making of his testament,   90
   And show him this.
CORB.   Good, good.
MOS.   'Tis better yet,
   If you will hear, sir.
CORB.   Yes, with all my heart.
MOS. Now would I counsel you, make
   home with speed;
   There, frame a will, whereto you shall
   inscribe
   My master your sole heir.
CORB.   And disinherit
   My son?
MOS. O, sir, the better, for that color[3]
   Shall make it much more taking.
CORB.   O, but [4] color?
MOS. This will, sir, you shall send it unto
   me.
   Now, when I come to enforce, as I will
   do,
   Your cares, your watchings, and your
   many prayers,   100
   Your more than many gifts, your this
   day's present,
   And, last, produce your will, where
   without thought
   Or least regard unto your proper issue,
   A son so brave and highly meriting,
   The stream of your diverted love hath
   thrown you
   Upon my master, and made him your
   heir,
   He cannot be so stupid or stone dead
   But out of conscience and mere grati-
   tude—
CORB. He must pronounce me his?
MOS.   'Tis true.
CORB.   This plot
   Did I think on before.
MOS.   I do believe it.   110
CORB. Do you not believe it?
MOS.   Yes, sir.
CORB.   Mine own project.
MOS. Which when he hath done, sir—
CORB.   Published me his heir?
MOS. And you so certain to survive him—
CORB.   Ay.
MOS. Being so lusty a man—
CORB.   'Tis true.

---

[3] Pretense.   [4] Merely.

Mos. Yes, sir—

Corb. I thought on that too. See, how he should be
The very organ to express my thoughts!

Mos. You have not only done yourself a good—

Corb. But multiplied it on my son?

Mos. 'Tis right, sir.

Corb. Still, my invention.

Mos. 'Las, sir! Heaven knows
It hath been all my study, all my care 120
(I e'en grow gray withal) how to work things—

Corb. I do conceive, sweet Mosca.

Mos. You are he
For whom I labor here.

Corb. Ay, do, do, do.
I'll straight about it.

Mos. [Aside.] Rook go with you,[1] raven!

Corb. I know thee honest.

Mos. [Aside.] You do lie, sir!

Corb. And—

Mos. [Aside.] Your knowledge is no better than your ears, sir.

Corb. I do not doubt to be a father to thee.

Mos. [Aside.] Nor I to gull my brother of his blessing.

Corb. I may ha' my youth restored to me; why not?

Mos. [Aside.] Your worship is a precious ass!

Corb. What say'st thou? 130

Mos. I do desire your worship to make haste, sir.

Corb. 'Tis done, 'tis done; I go. [Exit.]

Volp. [Springing from his bed.] O, I shall burst!
Let out my sides, let out my sides—

Mos. Contain
Your flux of laughter, sir. You know this hope
Is such a bait it covers any hook.

Volp. O, but thy working, and thy placing it!
I cannot hold; good rascal, let me kiss thee.
I never knew thee in so rare a humor.

Mos. Alas, sir, I but do as I am taught—
Follow your grave instructions, give hem words, 140
Pour oil into their ears, and send them hence.

[1] May you be rooked.

Volp. 'Tis true, 'tis true. What a rare punishment
Is avarice to itself!

Mos. Ay, with our help, sir.

Volp. So many cares, so many maladies,
So many fears attending on old age,
Yea, death so often called on, as no wish
Can be more frequent with hem, their limbs faint,
Their senses dull, their seeing, hearing, going,
All dead before them, yea, their very teeth,
Their instruments of eating, failing them— 150
Yet this is reckoned life! Nay, here was one,
Is now gone home, that wishes to live longer—
Feels not his gout nor palsy, feigns himself
Younger by scores of years, flatters his age
With confident belying it, hopes he may
With charms like Æson have his youth restored,
And with these thoughts so battens, as if fate
Would be as easily cheated on as he,
And all turns air! Who's that there, now? A third? Another knocks.

Mos. Close, to your couch again; I hear his voice. 160
It is Corvino, our spruce merchant.

Volp. [Lying on his bed.] Dead!

Mos. Another bout, sir, with your eyes.—Who's there?

Act I. Scene v.

Mosca, Corvino, Volpone.

[Mos.] Signior Corvino! Come most wished for! O,
How happy were you, if you knew it, now!

Corv. Why? What? Wherein?

Mos. The tardy hour is come, sir.

Corv. He is not dead?

Mos. Not dead, sir, but as good;
He knows no man.

Corv. How shall I do then?

Mos. Why, sir?

Corv. I have brought him here a pearl.

Mos. Perhaps he has

So much remembrance left as to know
　　you, sir;
He still [1] calls on you; nothing but your
　　name
Is in his mouth. Is your pearl orient,[2]
　　sir?
CORV. Venice was never owner of the
　　like.　　　　　　　　　　　　　　10
VOLP. Signior Corvino!
MOS.　　　　　　Hark!
VOLP.　　　　　　　　Signior Corvino!
MOS. He calls you; step and give it him.—
　　H' is here, sir,
And he has brought you a rich pearl.
CORV.　　　　　　How do you, sir?—
Tell him it doubles the twelve caract.[3]
MOS.　　　　　　　　　　　Sir,
He cannot understand; his hearing's
　　gone;
And yet it comforts him to see you—
CORV.　　　　　　　　　　　Say
I have a diamant [4] for him, too.
MOS.　　　　　　Best show 't, sir;
Put it into his hand—'tis only there
He apprehends. He has his feeling yet.
See how he grasps it!
CORV.　　　　　'Las, good gentleman!　20
How pitiful the sight is!
MOS.　　　　　　　Tut, forget, sir.
The weeping of an heir should still be
　　laughter
Under a visor.[5]
CORV.　　　　　　Why, am I his heir?
MOS. Sir, I am sworn; I may not show
　　the will
Till he be dead. But here has been Cor-
　　baccio,
Here has been Voltore, here were others
　　too;
I cannot number hem, they were so
　　many,
All gaping here for legacies; but I,
Taking the vantage of his naming you,
"Signior Corvino, Signior Corvino,"
　　took　　　　　　　　　　　　　30
Paper and pen and ink and there I
　　asked him
Whom he would have his heir. "Cor-
　　vino." Who
Should be executor? "Corvino." And

To any question he was silent to,
I still interpreted the nods he made,
Through weakness, for consent, and
　　sent home th' others,
Nothing bequeathed them, but to cry
　　and curse.
CORV. O, my dear Mosca! (*They embrace.*)
　　Does he not perceive us?
MOS. No more than a blind harper. He
　　knows no man,
No face of friend, nor name of any serv-
　　ant,　　　　　　　　　　　　　40
Who 'twas that fed him last, or gave
　　him drink—
Not those he hath begotten or brought up
Can he remember.
CORV.　　　　　Has he children?
MOS.　　　　　　　　Bastards,
Some dozen or more, that he begot on
　　beggars,
Gypsies and Jews and blackmoors,
　　when he was drunk.
Knew you not that, sir? 'Tis the com-
　　mon fable.
The dwarf, the fool, the eunuch are all
　　his;
H' is the true father of his family,
In all save me; but he has given hem
　　nothing.
CORV. That's well, that's well! Art sure
　　he does not hear us?　　　　　　50
MOS. Sure, sir? Why, look you, credit
　　your own sense.—[*Shouts at Volpone.*]
The pox approach, and add to your
　　diseases,
If it would send you hence the sooner, sir.
For your incontinence, it hath deserved
　　it
Throughly [6] and throughly, and the
　　plague to boot!—
(You may come near, sir.) Would you
　　would once close
Those filthy eyes of yours, that flow
　　with slime
Like two frog-pits; [7] and those same
　　hanging cheeks,
Covered with hide instead of skin—
　　(Nay, help, sir!)
That look like frozen dishclouts set on
　　end!　　　　　　　　　　　　60
CORV. Or like an old smoked wall, on
　　which the rain
Ran down in streaks!

---

[1] Continually.　　　　　[3] Carat.
[2] Lustrous.　　　　　　[4] Diamond.
[5] *I.e.,* an heir's sorrow is actually disguised
happiness.
[6] Thoroughly.　　　　　[7] Frog's eyes (?).

Mos.   Excellent, sir! Speak out.
You may be louder yet. A culvering [1]
Dischargéd in his ear would hardly bore
it.
Corv. His nose is like a common sewer,
still running.
Mos. 'Tis good! And what his mouth?
Corv.   A very draught.
Mos. O, stop it up—
Corv.   By no means.
Mos.   Pray you, let me.
Faith, I could stifle him rarely with a
pillow
As well as any woman that should keep [2]
him.
Corv. Do as you will; but I'll be gone.
Mos.   Be so; 70
It is your presence makes him last so
long.
Corv. I pray you use no violence.
Mos.   No, sir? Why?
Why should you be thus scrupulous,
pray you, sir?
Corv. Nay, at your discretion.
Mos.   Well, good sir, begone.
Corv. I will not trouble him now to take [3]
my pearl?
Mos. Pooh! Nor your diamant? What
a needless care
Is this afflicts you? Is not all here yours?
Am not I here, whom you have made?
Your creature
That owe my being to you?
Corv.   Grateful Mosca!
Thou art my friend, my fellow, my com-
panion,   80
My partner, and shalt share in all my
fortunes.
Mos. Excepting one.
Corv.   What's that?
Mos.   Your gallant wife,
sir.—   [Exit Corvino precipitately.]
Now is he gone. We had no other means
To shoot him hence but this.
Volp.   My divine Mosca!
Thou hast today outgone thyself.—
(Another knocks.)   Who's there?
I will be troubled with no more. Pre-
pare
Me music, dances, banquets, all delights;
The Turk is not more sensual in his
pleasures

Than will Volpone. [Exit Mosca.] Let
me see. A pearl?
A diamant? Plate? Cecchines? Good
morning's purchase.   90
Why, this is better than rob churches,
yet;
Or fat by eating once a month a man—

[Enter Mosca.]

Who is 't?
Mos.   The beauteous Lady Would-be,
sir,
Wife to the English knight, Sir Politic
Would-be
(This is the style, sir, is directed me),
Hath sent to know how you have slept
tonight,
And if you would be visited.
Volp.   Not now.
Some three hours hence—
Mos.   I told the squire [4] so much.
Volp. When I am high with mirth and
wine, then, then!
Fore heaven, I wonder at the desperate
valure [5]   100
Of the bold English, that they dare
let loose
Their wives to all encounters!
Mos.   Sir, this knight
Had not his name for nothing; he is
politic,
And knows, howe'er his wife affect
strange airs,
She hath not yet the face to be dishonest.[6]
But, had she Signior Corvino's wife's
face—
Volp. Has she so rare a face?
Mos.   O, sir, the wonder,
The blazing star of Italy! A wench
O' the first year, a beauty ripe as har-
vest!
Whose skin is whiter than a swan all
over,   110
Than silver, snow, or lilies! A soft lip
Would tempt you to eternity of kissing!
And flesh that melteth in the touch to
blood!
Bright as your gold, and lovely as your
gold!
Volp. Why had not I known this before?
Mos.   Alas, sir,
Myself but yesterday discovered it.

[1] Culverin, a small cannon.
[2] Care for.   [3] Take away (from Volpone).
[4] Messenger.   [5] Valor.   [6] Unchaste.

Volp. How might I see her?

Mos.　　　　　　　　　O, not possible;
She's kept as warily as is your gold;
Never does come abroad, never takes
　air
But at a windore.[1] All her looks are
　sweet,　　　　　　　　　　　120
As the first grapes or cherries, and are
　watched
As near as they are.

Volp.　　　　　I must see her—

Mos.　　　　　　　　　　　Sir,
There is a guard of ten spies thick upon
　her,
All his whole household, each of which
　is set
Upon his fellow, and have all their
　charge,
When he goes out, when he comes in,
　examined.

Volp. I will go see her, though but at her
　windore.

Mos. In some disguise then.

Volp.　　　　　That is true; I must
Maintain mine own shape still the same.
We'll think.　　　　　　　　[Exeunt.]

Act II. Scene i.

[Before Corvino's house on St. Mark's
　　　　　　　　　　　　　Place.]

Politic Would-be, Peregrine.

[Pol.] Sir, to a wise man all the world's his
　soil:
It is not Italy nor France nor Europe
That must bound me, if my fates call me
　forth.
Yet I protest it is no salt [2] desire
Of seeing countries, shifting a religion,
Nor any disaffection to the state
Where I was bred, and unto which I owe
My dearest plots,[3] hath brought me out,
　much less
That idle, antique, stale, gray-headed
　project
Of knowing men's minds and manners,
　with Ulysses,　　　　　　　10
But a peculiar humor of my wife's,
Laid for this height [4] of Venice, to ob-
　serve,

To quote,[5] to learn the language, and so
　forth—
I hope you travel, sir, with license?[6]

Per.　　　　　　　　　　　Yes.

Pol. I dare the safelier converse. How
　long, sir,
Since you left England?

Per.　　　　　　Seven weeks.

Pol.　　　　　　　　　So lately!
You ha' not been with my lord ambassa-
　dor?

Per. Not yet, sir.

Pol.　　　　Pray you, what news, sir, vents
　our climate?[7]
I heard last night a most strange thing
　reported
By some of my lord's followers, and I
　long　　　　　　　　　　　20
To hear how 'twill be seconded.[8]

Per.　　　　　　　What was 't, sir?

Pol. Marry, sir, of a raven that should
　build
In a ship royal of the king's.[9]

Per. [Aside.]　　　　　　This fellow,
Does he gull me, trow?[10] Or is gulled?—
　Your name, sir?

Pol. My name is Politic Would-be.

Per. [Aside.]　　　O, that speaks him.—
A knight, sir?

Pol.　　　　A poor knight, sir.

Per.　　　　　　　　　Your lady
Lies here in Venice, for intelligence
Of tires [11] and fashions and behavior
Among the courtesans? The fine Lady
　Would-be?

Pol. Yes, sir; the spider and the bee oft-
　times　　　　　　　　　　30
Suck from one flower.

Per.　　　　　　　Good Sir Politic,
I cry you mercy; I have heard much of
　you.
'Tis true, sir, of your raven.

Pol.　　　　　　　On your knowledge?

Per. Yes, and your lion's whelping in the
　Tower.

[5] Make notes.
[6] Required of men of rank by the English
government.
[7] *I.e.*, does our country give forth?
[8] Followed up.
[9] Probably a reference to an actual event of
the day. like the following allusions to the lion's
whelping, the Woolwich whale, etc.
[10] Do you suppose?
[11] Attires.

[1] Window.　　　　　[3] Plans.
[2] Wanton.　　　　　[4] Latitude.

Pol. Another whelp!

Per. 　　　　　　　Another, sir.

Pol. 　　　　　　　　　　Now, heaven!
What prodigies be these?　The fires at
　Berwick!
And the new star!　These things concur-
　ring, strange,
And full of omen!　Saw you those
　meteors?

Per. I did, sir.

Pol. 　Fearful!　Pray you, sir, confirm me.
Were there three porcpisces [1] seen above
　the bridge, 　　　　　　　　　　40
As they give out?

Per. 　　　　　　Six, and a sturgeon, sir.

Pol. I am astonished.

Per. 　　　　　Nay, sir, be not so;
I'll tell you a greater prodigy than these.

Pol. What should these things portend!

Per. 　　　　　　　　The very day
(Let me be sure) that I put forth from
　London,
There was a whale discovered in the
　river,
As high as Woolwich, that had waited
　there,
Few know how many months, for the
　subversion
Of the Stode fleet.

Pol. 　　　　Is 't possible?　Believe it,
'Twas either sent from Spain, or the
　archduke's— 　　　　　　　　　　50
Spinola's whale, upon my life, my credit!
Will they not leave these projects?
　Worthy sir,
Some other news.

Per. 　　　Faith, Stone the fool is dead,
And they do lack a tavern fool extremely.

Pol. Is Mas' Stone dead?

Per. 　　　　H' is dead, sir; why, I hope
You thought him not immortal?—
　[Aside.] O, this knight,
Were he well-known, would be a precious
　thing
To fit our English stage; he that should
　write
But such a fellow, should be thought to
　feign
Extremely, if not maliciously.

Pol. 　　　　　　　Stone dead!　60

Per. Dead.　Lord!　How deeply, sir, you
　apprehend it!
He was no kinsman to you?

1 Porpoises.

Pol. 　　　　　　　　That I know of.
Well, that same fellow was an unknown
　fool.

Per. And yet you knew him, it seems?

Pol. 　　　　　　　I did so.　Sir,
I knew him one of the most dangerous
　heads
Living within the state, and so I held
　him.

Per. Indeed, sir?

Pol. 　　　　While he lived, in action,
He has received weekly intelligence,
Upon my knowledge, out of the Low
　Countries, 　　　　　　　　　　69
For all parts of the world, in cabbages,
And those dispensed again to ambas-
　sadors,
In oranges, muskmelons, apricots,
Limons,[2] pome-citrons,[3] and suchlike—
　sometimes
In Colchester oysters, and your Selsey
　cockles.

Per. You make me wonder.

Pol. 　　　　Sir, upon my knowledge.
Nay, I've observed him, at your public
　ordinary,
Take his advertisement [4] from a traveler,
A concealed statesman, in a trencher of
　meat,
And instantly, before the meal was done,
Convey an answer in a toothpick.

Per. 　　　　　　　Strange!　80
How could this be, sir?

Pol. 　　　　　Why, the meat was cut
So like his character, and so laid as he
Must easily read the cipher.

Per. 　　　　　　　I have heard
He could not read, sir.

Pol. 　　　　　So 'twas given out,
In polity, by those that did employ him;
But he could read, and had your lan-
　guages,
And to 't as sound a noddle—

Per. 　　　　　　I have heard, sir,
That your babions [5] were spies, and that
　they were
A kind of subtle nation near to China.

Pol. Ay, ay, your Mamuluchi.[6]　Faith,
　they had 　　　　　　　　　　90
Their hand in a French plot or two; but
　they

2 Lemons. 　　　　　　　4 Information.
3 Citrons. 　　　　　　　5 Baboons.
6 Mamelukes, a kind of Islamite soldier.

Were so extremely given to women as
They made discovery of all; yet I
Had my advices here, on Wednesday
    last,
From one of their own coat, they were
    returned,
Made their relations,[1] as the fashion is,
And now stand fair for fresh employ-
    ment.
Per. [*Aside.*]   Heart!
This Sir Pol will be ignorant of noth-
    ing.—
It seems, sir, you know all.
Pol.   Not all, sir; but
I have some general notions.   I do
    love   100
To note and to observe.   Though I live
    out,
Free from the active torrent, yet I'ld
    mark
The currents and the passages of things
For mine own private use, and know the
    ebbs
And flows of state.
Per.   Believe it, sir, I hold
Myself in no small tie [2] unto my fortunes
For casting me thus luckily upon you,
Whose knowledge, if your bounty equal it,
May do me great assistance in instruction
For my behavior and my bearing,
    which   110
Is yet so rude and raw—
Pol.   Why? Came you forth
Empty of rules for travel?
Per.   Faith, I had
Some common ones, from out that vulgar
    grammar,
Which he that cried Italian to me taught
    me.
Pol. Why, this it is that spoils all our
    brave bloods,
Trusting our hopeful gentry unto ped-
    ants,
Fellows of outside, and mere bark. You
    seem
To be a gentleman of ingenuous race—
I not profess it, but my fate hath been
To be where I have been consulted
    with,   120
In this high kind, touching some great
    men's sons,
Persons of blood and honor.
Per.   Who be these, sir?

Act II. Scene ii.

[*The same.*]

*Mosca [with Assistants carrying material for
a platform], Politic, Peregrine, Volpone,
Nano, Grege.*[3]

[Mos.] Under that windore, there 't must
    be. The same.
Pol. Fellows, to mount a bank.[4] Did your
    instructor
In the dear tongues [5] never discourse to
    you
Of the Italian mountebanks?
Per.   Yes, sir.
Pol.   Why,
Here shall you see one.
Per.   They are quacksalvers,
Fellows that live by venting [6] oils and
    drugs.
Pol. Was that the character he gave you
    of them?
Per. As I remember.
Pol.   Pity his ignorance.
They are the only knowing men of
    Europe!
Great general scholars, excellent physi-
    cians,   10
Most admired statesmen, professed fa-
    vorites
And cabinet counselors to the greatest
    princes—
The only languaged men of all the world!
Per. And, I have heard, they are most
    lewd [7] impostors,
Made all of terms and shreds, no less be-
    liers
Of great men's favors than their own vile
    med'cines,
Which they will utter[8] upon monstrous
    oaths,
Selling that drug for twopence ere they
    part,
Which they have valued at twelve crowns
    before.
Pol. Sir, calumnies are answered best with
    silence.   20
Yourself shall judge.—Who is it mounts,
    my friends?
Mos. Scoto of Mantua,[9] sir.

---

[1] Reports.   [2] Obligation.

[3] Last three enter later.   [6] Vending.
[4] Bench, platform.   [7] Ignorant.
[5] Modern languages.   [8] Vend.
[9] An actual Italian juggler who was then in
England.

Pol. Is 't he? Nay, then I'll proudly promise, sir, you shall behold Another man than has been fant'sied [1] to you.

I wonder yet that he should mount his bank

Here in this nook, that has been wont t' appear

In face of the Piazza!—Here he comes.

[*Enter Volpone, disguised as a mountebank, followed by Nano, also disguised, and Grege.*]

Volp. Mount, zany.[2]

Gre. Follow, follow, follow, follow, follow!

Pol. See how the people follow him! H' is a man 30

May write ten thousand crowns in bank here. Note,

[*Volpone mounts the platform.*]

Mark but his gesture; I do use to observe The state he keeps in getting up.

Per. 'Tis worth it, sir.

Volp. Most noble gentlemen and my worthy patrons! It may seem strange that I, your Scoto Mantuano, who was ever wont to fix my bank in face of the public Piazza, near the shelter of the Portico to the Procuratia, should now, after eight months' absence from this illustrous city of [40 Venice, humbly retire myself into an obscure nook of the Piazza.

Pol. [*Aside.*] Did not I now object the same?

Per. [*Aside.*] Peace, sir.

Volp. Let me tell you I am not, as your Lombard proverb saith, cold on my feet, or content to part with my commodities at a cheaper rate than I accustomed—look not for it; nor that the calumnious reports of that impudent detractor and shame to our profession (Alessandro Buttone, I [50 mean), who gave out, in public, I was condemned *a' sforzato* [3] to the galleys for poisoning the Cardinal Bembo's—cook, hath at all attached,[4] much less dejected me. No, no, worthy gentlemen! To tell you true, I cannot endure to see the rabble of these ground *ciarlitani*,[5] that spread their cloaks on the pavement as if they meant to do feats of activity, and then come in

lamely with their moldy tales out of [60 Boccaccio, like stale Tabarine,[6] the fabulist,[7] some of them discoursing their travels, and of their tedious captivity in the Turks' galleys, when indeed, were the truth known, they were the Christians' galleys, where very temperately they eat bread and drunk water as a wholesome penance, enjoined them by their confessors, for base pilferies.

Pol. [*Aside.*] Note but his bearing, and contempt of these.

Volp. These turdy-facey-nasty- [70 patey-lousy-fartical rogues, with one poor groatsworth of unprepared antimony, finely wrapped up in several *scartoccios*,[8] are able, very well, to kill their twenty a week, and play; yet these meager, starved spirits, who have half stopped the organs of their minds with earthy oppilations, [9] want not their favorers among your shriveled, salad-eating artisans, who are overjoyed that they may have their half-pe'rth of physic; [80 though it purge hem into another world, 't makes no matter.

Pol. [*Aside.*] Excellent! Ha' you heard better language, sir?

Volp. Well, let hem go. And, gentlemen, honorable gentlemen, know that for this time our bank, being thus removed from the clamors of the *canaglia*,[10] shall be the scene of pleasure and delight, for I have nothing to sell, little or nothing to sell. 90

Pol. [*Aside.*] I told you, sir, his end.

Per. [*Aside.*] You did so, sir.

Volp. I protest I and my six servants are not able to make of this precious liquor so fast as it is fetched away from my lodging by gentlemen of your city, strangers of the *terrafirma*,[11] worshipful merchants, ay, and senators too, who ever since my arrival have detained me to their uses by their splendidous liberalities—and worthily. For what avails your rich man to have his [100 magazines stuffed with *moscadelli*,[12] or of the purest grape, when his physicians prescribe him, on pain of death, to drink nothing but water cocted [13] with anis seeds? O health, health! The blessing of the rich! The riches

---

[1] Represented.
[2] A subordinate buffoon.
[3] To hard labor.
[4] Attacked.
[5] Trivial charlatans.
[6] Tabarin, a popular French mountebank.
[7] A professional teller of tales.
[8] Twists of paper.
[9] Obstructions.
[10] Canaille, mob.
[11] Mainland.
[12] Muscatel.
[13] Boiled.

of the poor! Who can buy thee at too dear a rate, since there is no enjoying this world without thee? Be not then so sparing of your purses, honorable gentlemen, as to abridge the natural course of life— [110

PER. [*Aside.*] You see his end?

POL. [*Aside.*]   Ay, is 't not good?

VOLP. For, when a humid flux, or catarrh, by the mutability of air, falls from your head into an arm or shoulder, or any other part, take you a ducat, or your cecchine of gold, and apply to the place affected; see what good effect it can work. No, no, 'tis this blessed *unguento*,[1] this rare extraction, that hath only power to disperse all malignant humors [2] that [120 proceed either of hot, cold, moist, or windy causes—

PER. [*Aside.*] I would he had put in dry too.

POL. [*Aside.*]   Pray you, observe.

VOLP. To fortify the most indigest [3] and crude stomach, ay, were it of one that, through extreme weakness, vomited blood, applying only a warm napkin to the place, after the unction and fricace; [4] for the *vertigine* [5] in the head, putting but a drop into your nostrils, likewise behind the [130 ears, a most sovereign and approved remedy, the *mal caduco*,[6] cramps, convulsions, paralyses, epilepsies, *tremorcordia*,[7] retired [8] nerves, ill vapors of the spleen, stoppings of the liver, the stone, the strangury, *hernia ventosa, iliaca passio;* [9] stops a *dysenteria* immediately; easeth the torsion of the small guts; and cures *melancholia hypocondriaca*, being taken and applied according to my printed receipt. [140 (*Pointing to his bill and his glass.*) For this is the physician, this the medicine; this counsels, this cures; this gives the direction, this works the effect; and, in sum, both together may be termed an abstract of the theoric and practic in the Æsculapian art.[10] 'Twill cost you eight crowns. And, Zan Fritada, pray thee, sing a verse extempore in honor of it.   149

POL. [*Aside.*] How do you like him, sir?

PER. [*Aside.*]   Most strangely, I!

POL. [*Aside.*] Is not his language rare?

PER. [*Aside.*]   But [11] alchemy, I never heard the like—or Broughton's [12] books.

SONG

Had old Hippocrates or Galen,
That to their books put med'cines all in,
But known this secret, they had never
(Of which they will be guilty ever)
Been murderers of so much paper,
Or wasted many a hurtless taper;
No Indian drug had e'er been famed,
Tabacco,[13] sassafras not named;   160
Ne [14] yet of guacum [15] one small stick, sir,
Nor Raymond Lully's [16] great elixir;
Ne had been known the Danish Gonswart,[17]
Or Paracelsus, with his long sword.[18]

PER. [*Aside.*] All this, yet, will not do; eight crowns is high.

VOLP. No more.—Gentlemen, if I had but time to discourse to you the miraculous effects of this my oil, surnamed Oglio del Scoto, with the countless catalogue of those I have cured of th' aforesaid and [170 many more diseases, the patents and privileges of all the princes and commonwealths of Christendom, or but the depositions of those that appeared on my part before the signiory of the Sanita and most learned College of Physicians, where I was authorized, upon notice taken of the admirable virtues of my medicaments, and mine own excellency in matter of rare and unknown secrets, not only to disperse them [180 publicly in this famous city, but in all the territories that happily joy under the government of the most pious and magnificent states of Italy! But may some other gallant fellow say, "O, there be divers that make profession to have as good and as experimented receipts as yours." Indeed, very many have assayed, like apes, in imitation of that which is really and essentially in me, to make of this oil, [190 bestowed great cost in furnaces, stills, alembics, continual fires, and preparation

[11] Except for.
[12] Hugh Broughton was a fanatical commentator on the Old Testament.
[13] Tobacco.   [15] Guaiacum, a kind of resin.
[14] Nor.   [16] Fourteenth century alchemist.
[17] Johan Gansfort, or Wessel, a fifteenth century scholar.
[18] In the hollow handle of which his familiar spirit was supposed to reside.

[1] Ointment.   [6] Epilepsy.
[2] Fluids.   [7] Palpitating heart.
[3] Disordered.   [8] Overtired.
[4] Salve.   [9] Varieties of colic.
[5] Vertigo.
[10] The theory and practice of medicine.

of the ingredients (as indeed there goes to it six hundred several simples, besides some quantity of human fat, for the conglutination, which we buy of the anatomists), but, when these practitioners come to the last decoction, blow, blow, puff, puff, and all flies *in fumo*.[1] Ha, ha, ha! Poor wretches! I rather pity their folly and in- [200 discretion than their loss of time and money, for those may be recovered by industry, but to be a fool born is a disease incurable. For myself I always from my youth have endeavored to get the rarest secrets, and book them, either in exchange or for money; I spared nor cost nor labor, where anything was worthy to be learned. And, gentlemen, honorable gentlemen, I will undertake, by virtue of chymi- [210 cal[2] art, out of the honorable hat that covers your head, to extract the four elements; that is to say, the fire, air, water, and earth, and return you your felt without burn or stain. For, whilst others have been at the balloo,[3] I have been at my book, and am now past the craggy paths of study, and come to the flowery plains of honor and reputation.

POL. [*Aside.*] I do assure you, sir, that is
 his aim.   220

VOLP. But to our price—

PER. [*Aside.*]   And that withal, Sir Pol.

VOLP. You all know, honorable gentlemen, I never valued this *ampulla*, or vial, at less than eight crowns; but for this time I am content to be deprived of it for six; six crowns is the price, and less in courtesy I know you cannot offer me. Take it or leave it; howsoever, both it and I am at your service. I ask you not as the value of the thing, for then I should de- [230 mand of you a thousand crowns; so the Cardinals Montalto, Fernese, the great Duke of Tuscany, my gossip,[4] with divers other princes, have given me; but I despise money. Only to show my affection to you, honorable gentlemen, and your illustrous state here, I have neglected the messages of these princes, mine own offices, framed my journey hither, only to present you with the fruits of my travels.—Tune [240 your voices once more to the touch of your

instruments, and give the honorable assembly some delightful recreation.

PER. What monstrous and most painful circumstance
Is here, to get some three or four gazettes,[5]
Some threepence i' th' whole, for that 'twill come to.

SONG

You that would last long, list to my song;
Make no more coil,[6] but buy of this oil.
Would you be ever fair and young?
Stout of teeth, and strong of tongue?   250
Tart of palate? Quick of ear?
Sharp of sight? Of nostril clear?
Moist of hand? And light of foot?
Or, I will come nearer to 't,
Would you live free from all diseases?
Do the act your mistress pleases?
Yet fright all aches[7] from your bones?
Here's a med'cine for the nones.[8]

VOLP. Well, I am in a humor at this time to make a present of the small [260 quantity my coffer contains—to the rich in courtesy, and to the poor for God's sake. Wherefore now mark: I asked you six crowns; and six crowns at other times you have paid me; you shall not give me six crowns, nor five, nor four, nor three, nor two, nor one; nor half a ducat; no, nor a muccinigo.[9] Six—pence it will cost you, or six hundred pound—expect no lower price, for, by the banner of my front, I will [270 not bate a bagatine[10]—that I will have, only, a pledge of your loves, to carry something from amongst you, to show I am not contemned by you. Therefore, now, toss your handkerchiefs cheerfully, cheerfully; and be advertised that the first heroic spirit that deigns to grace me with a handkerchief, I will give it a little remembrance of something beside, shall please it better than if I had presented it with a [280 double pistolet.[11]

PER. [*Aside.*]   Will you be that heroic spark, Sir Pol?

Celia, at the windo', throws down her handkerchief.

O, see! The windore has prevented[12] you.

---

[1] In smoke.   [2] Chemical.
[3] Probably a misprint for *balloon*, a game of ball.   [4] Intimate friend.

[5] Small Italian coins.   [7] Pronounced *aitches.*
[6] Fuss.   [8] Occasion.
[9] Moccinigo, an Italian coin.
[10] An Italian coin.
[11] A Spanish gold coin.   [12] Anticipated.

VOLP. Lady, I kiss your bounty; and for this timely grace you have done your poor Scoto of Mantua I will return you, over and above my oil, a secret of that high and inestimable nature shall make you forever enamored on that minute wherein your eye first descended on so mean, [290 yet not altogether to be despised, an object. Here is a poulder concealed in this paper, of which, if I should speak to the worth, nine thousand volumes were but as one page, that page as a line, that line as a word, so short is this pilgrimage of man (which some call life) to the expressing of it. Would I reflect on the price? Why, the whole world were but as an empire, that empire as a province, that province as [300 a bank, that bank as a private purse to the purchase of it. I will only tell you it is the poulder that made Venus a goddess (given her by Apollo), that kept her perpetually young, cleared her wrinkles, firmed her gums, filled her skin, colored her hair; from her derived[1] to Helen, and at the sack of Troy unfortunately lost; till now, in this our age, it was as happily recovered, by a studious antiquary, out of some ruins [310 of Asia, who sent a moiety of it to the court of France (but much sophisticated[2]), wherewith the ladies there now color their hair. The rest, at this present, remains with me, extracted to a quintessence, so that, wherever it but touches, in youth it perpetually preserves, in age restores, the complexion; seats your teeth, did they dance like virginal jacks,[3] firm as a wall; makes them white as ivory, that were black as— [320

Act II. Scene iii.

[The same.]

Corvino, Politic, Peregrine.

[CORV.] Spite o' the devil, and my shame! Come down here;
Come down! No house but mine to make your scene?
Signior Flaminio,[4] will you down, sir? Down?

---

[1] Transmitted.
[2] Adulterated.
[3] Attachments to the keys of a virginal.
[4] This name, like the following ones, is associated with the Italian *commedia dell' arte* of the day.

What, is my wife your Franciscina, sir? No windores on the whole Piazza here To make your properties but mine? But mine?
He beats away the Mountebank, etc.[5]
Heart! Ere tomorrow I shall be new christened,
And called the Pantalone di Besogniosi[6]
About the town.
PER.   What should this mean, Sir Pol?
POL. Some trick of state, believe it; I will home.   10
PER. It may be some design on you.
POL.   I know not.
I'll stand upon my guard.
PER.   It is your best, sir.
POL. This three weeks, all my advices, all my letters,
They have been intercepted.
PER.   Indeed, sir?
Best have a care.
POL.   Nay, so I will.
PER.   This knight,
I may not lose him, for my mirth, till night.   [*Exeunt.*]

Act II. Scene iv.

[A room in Volpone's house.]

Volpone, Mosca.

VOLP. O, I am wounded!
MOS.   Where, sir?
VOLP.   Not without;
Those blows were nothing—I could bear them ever.
But angry Cupid, bolting from her eyes, Hath shot himself into me like a flame, Where now he flings about his burning heat,
As in a fornace[7] an ambitious fire, Whose vent is stopped. The fight is all within me.
I cannot live except thou help me, Mosca;
My liver melts, and I, without the hope Of some soft air from her refreshing breath,   10
Am but a heap of cinders.
MOS.   'Las, good sir,

---

[5] This stage direction appears as a marginal note opposite the first line of the scene.
[6] Fool of Beggars.
[7] Furnace.

Would you had never seen her!

VOLP.   Nay, would thou
Hadst never told me of her!

Mos.   Sir, 'tis true;
I do confess I was unfortunate,
And you unhappy; but I'm bound in
   conscience,
No less than duty, to effect my best
To your release of torment, and I will,
   sir.

VOLP. Dear Mosca, shall I hope?

Mos.   Sir, more than dear,
I will not bid you to despair of aught
Within a human compass.

VOLP.   O, there spoke   20
My better angel. Mosca, take my
   keys,
Gold, plate, and jewels—all 's at thy de-
   votion;
Employ them how thou wilt. Nay, coin
   me too,
So thou in this but crown my longings,
   Mosca.

Mos. Use but your patience.

VOLP.   So I have.

Mos.   I doubt not
To bring success to your desires.

VOLP.   Nay, then,
I not repent me of my late disguise.

Mos. If you can horn [1] him, sir, you need
   not.

VOLP.   True.
Besides, I never meant him for my heir.
Is not the color o' my beard and eye-
   brows   30
To make me known?

Mos.   No jot.

VOLP.   I did it well.

Mos. So well, would I could follow you
   in mine
With half the happiness! And yet I
   would
Escape your epilogue. [2]

VOLP.   But were they gulled
With a belief that I was Scoto?

Mos.   Sir,
Scoto himself could hardly have dis-
   tinguished!
I have not time to flatter you now; we'll
   part,
And, as I prosper, so applaud my art.
                              [Exeunt.]

---

[1] Cuckold.
[2] I.e., a similar beating from Corvino.

ACT II. SCENE v.

[A room in Corvino's house.]

Corvino, Celia, Servatore.[3]

[CORV.] Death of mine honor, with the
   city's fool?
A juggling, tooth-drawing, prating
   mountebank?
And at a public windore? Where, whilst
   he,
With his strained action and his dole of
   faces,[4]
To his drug-lecture draws your itching
   ears,
A crew of old, unmarried, noted lechers
Stood leering up like satyrs; and you
   smile
Most graciously, and fan your favors
   forth,
To give your hot spectators satisfaction!
What, was your mountebank their call?
   Their whistle?   10
Or were you enamored on his copper
   rings,
His saffron jewel, with the toadstone [5]
   in 't,
Or his embroidered suit, with the cope
   stitch,
Made of a hearse cloth? Or his old tilt [6]
   feather?
Or his starched beard? Well, you shall
   have him, yes!
He shall come home, and minister unto
   you
The fricace for the mother.[7] Or, let me
   see,
I think you had rather mount; would
   you not mount?
Why, if you'll mount, you may; yes,
   truly, you may!
And so you may be seen, down to th'
   foot.   20
Get you a cittern, Lady Vanity,
And be a dealer with the virtuous man;
Make one. I'll but protest myself a cuck-
   old,
And save your dowry. I'm a Dutch-
   man, I!
For, if you thought me an Italian,

---

[3] Enters later.   [4] Grimaces.
[5] A fossil or semi-precious stone, popularly
supposed to have come from the head of a toad.
[6] Tilted.   [7] Hysteria.

You would be damned ere you did this,
    you whore!
Thou'ldst tremble to imagine that the
    murder
Of father, mother, brother, all thy race,
Should follow as the subject of my jus-
    tice.
CEL. Good sir, have patience.
CORV. [*Drawing his dagger*.]   What
    couldst thou propose [1]   30
Less to thyself than, in this heat of wrath
And stung with my dishonor, I should
    strike
This steel unto thee, with as many stabs
As thou wert gazed upon with goatish
    eyes?
CEL. Alas, sir, be appeased! I could not
    think
My being at the windore should more now
Move your impatience than at other
    times.
CORV. No? Not to seek and entertain a
    parley
With a known knave, before a multi-
    tude?
You were an actor with your handker-
    chief,   40
Which he most sweetly kissed in the re-
    ceipt,
And might, no doubt, return it with a
    letter,
And point the place where you might
    meet; your sister's,
Your mother's, or your aunt's might
    serve the turn.
CEL. Why, dear sir, when do I make these
    excuses,
Or ever stir abroad but to the church?
And that so seldom—
CORV.   Well, it shall be less;
And thy restraint before was liberty
To what I now decree; and therefore
    mark me.
First, I will have this bawdy light
    dammed up,   50
And, till 't be done, some two or three
    yards off
I'll chalk a line, o'er which if thou but
    chance
To set thy desp'rate foot, more hell,
    more horror,
More wild, remorseless rage shall seize
    on thee

[1] Expect.

Than on a conjuror that had heedless
    left
His circle's safety ere his devil was laid.
Then here's a lock which I will hang upon
    thee,
And, now I think on 't, I will keep thee
    backwards; [2]
Thy lodging shall be backwards; thy
    walks backwards;
Thy prospect, all be backwards; and no
    pleasure   60
That thou shalt know but backwards.
    Nay, since you force
My honest nature, know it is your own,
Being too open, makes me use you thus.
Since you will not contain your subtle
    nostrils
In a sweet room, but they must snuff
    the air
Of rank and sweaty passengers—(*Knock
    within.*) One knocks.
Away, and be not seen, pain of thy life;
Not look toward the windore; if thou
    dost—
Nay, stay, hear this—let me not pros-
    per, whore,
But I will make thee an anatomy, [3]   70
Dissect thee mine own self, and read a
    lecture
Upon thee to the city, and in public.
Away!—   [*Exit Celia.*

Enter Servitore.]

              Who's there?
SER.   'Tis Signior Mosca, sir.

ACT II. SCENE vi.

[The same.]

Corvino, Mosca.

[CORV.] Let him come in. His master's
    dead; there's yet
Some good to help the bad.—My Mosca,
    welcome!
I guess your news.
MOS.   I fear you cannot, sir.
CORV. Is 't not his death?
MOS.   Rather the contrary.
CORV. Not his recovery?
MOS.   Yes, sir.
CORV.   I am cursed,

[2] In the rear of the house.   [3] Cadaver.

I am bewitched, my crosses meet to
    vex me.
How? How? How? How?
Mos.   Why, sir, with Scoto's oil;
    Corbaccio and Voltore brought of it,
    Whilst I was busy in an inner room—
Corv. Death!   That damned mounte-
    bank! But for the law   10
Now, I could kill the rascal. 'T cannot be
His oil should have that virtue. Ha'
    not I
Known him a common rogue, come fid-
    dling in
To th' osteria,[1] with a tumbling whore,
And, when he has done all his forced
    tricks, been glad
Of a poor spoonful of dead wine, with
    flies in 't?
It cannot be. All his ingredients
Are a sheep's gall, a roasted bitch's
    marrow,
Some few sod [2] earwigs, pounded cater-
    pillars,
A little capon's grease, and fasting
    spittle—   20
I know hem to a dram.
Mos.   I know not, sir;
But some on 't, there, they poured into
    his ears,
Some in his nostrils, and recovered him,
Applying but the fricace.
Corv.   Pox o' that fricace!
Mos. And since, to seem the more officious
And flatt'ring of his health, there they
    have had,
At extreme fees, the College of Physicians
Consulting on him, how they might
    restore him,
Where one would have a cataplasm [3]
    of spices,
Another a flayed ape clapped to his
    breast,   30
A third would ha' it a dog, a fourth an
    oil,
With wild cats' skins. At last, they all
    resolved
That to preserve him was no other means
But some young woman must be straight
    sought out,
Lusty, and full of juice, to sleep by him;
And to this service most unhappily,
And most unwillingly, am I now em-
    ployed,

Which here I thought to preacquaint
    you with,
For your advice, since it concerns you
    most,
Because I would not do that thing might
    cross   40
Your ends, on whom I have my whole
    dependence, sir.
Yet, if I do it not, they may delate [4]
My slackness to my patron, work me
    out
Of his opinion, and there all your hopes,
Venters, or whatsoever are all frustrate!
I do but tell you, sir. Besides, they are
    all
Now striving who shall first present him;
    therefore,
I could entreat you, briefly conclude
    somewhat;
Prevent hem if you can.
Corv.   Death to my hopes!
This is my villainous fortune! Best to
    hire   50
Some common courtesan.
Mos.   Ay, I thought on that, sir;
But they are all so subtle, full of art—
And age again doting and flexible,
So as—I cannot tell—we may, per-
    chance,
Light on a quean may cheat us all.
Corv.   'Tis true.
Mos. No, no. It must be one that has no
    tricks, sir,
Some simple thing, a creature made [5]
    unto it—
Some wench you may command. Ha'
    you no kinswoman?
Godso [6]—think, think, think, think,
    think, think, think, sir.
One o' the doctors offered there his
    daughter.   60
Corv. How!
Mos.   Yes, Signior Lupo, the physician.
Corv. His daughter?
Mos.   And a virgin, sir. Why, alas,
He knows the state of 's body, what it is—
That naught can warm his blood, sir,
    but a fever,
Nor any incantation raise his spirit.
A long forgetfulness hath seized that
    part.

[4] Blame, denounce.
[5] Prepared beforehand.
[6] Gadso, catso, a term of impatience.

[1] Hostelry.   [2] Sodden, boiled.   [3] Poultice.

Besides, sir, who shall know it? Some
  one or two—
CORV. I pray thee give me leave. [*Walks
  aside.*] If any man
But I had had this luck—the thing in
  'tself,
I know, is nothing.—Wherefore should
  not I   70
As well command my blood and my af-
  fections
As this dull doctor? In the point of
  honor,
The cases are all one of wife and daugh-
  ter.
MOS. [*Aside.*] I hear him coming.[1]
CORV.   She shall do 't; 'tis done.
'Slight! If this doctor, who is not en-
  gaged,
Unless 't be for his counsel, which is
  nothing,
Offer his daughter, what should I, that
  am
So deeply in? I will prevent him. Wretch!
Covetous wretch!—Mosca, I have de-
  termined.
MOS. How, sir?
CORV. We 'll make all sure. The party
  you wot [2] of   80
Shall be mine own wife, Mosca.
MOS.   Sir, the thing,
But that I would not seem to counsel
  you,
I should have motioned [3] to you at the
  first;
And, make your count,[4] you have cut
  all their throats.[5]
Why, 'tis directly taking a possession!
And in his next fit we may let him go.
'Tis but to pull the pillow from his
  head,
And he is thratled.[6] 'T had been done
  before
But for your scrupulous doubts.
CORV.   Ay, a plague on 't,
My conscience fools my wit! Well, I'll
  be brief,   90
And so be thou, lest they should be be-
  fore us.
Go home, prepare him, tell him with
  what zeal
And willingness I do it; swear it was

On the first hearing, as thou mayst do
  truly,
Mine own free motion.
MOS.   Sir, I warrant you,
I'll so possess him with it that the rest
Of his starved clients shall be banished
  all,
And only you received. But come not,
  sir,
Until I send, for I have something else
To ripen for your good—you must not
  know 't.   100
CORV. But do not you forget to send now.
MOS.   Fear not. [*Exit.*]

ACT II. SCENE vii.

[*The same.*]

Corvino, Celia.

CORV. Where are you, wife? My Celia!
  Wife!

[*Enter Celia.*]

          What, blubbering?
Come, dry those tears. I think thou
  thought'st me in earnest?
Ha! By this light, I talked so but to
  try thee.
Methinks the lightness of the occasion
Should ha' confirmed thee. Come, I am
  not jealous.
CEL. No?
CORV.   Faith, I am not, I, nor never was;
It is a poor, unprofitable humor.
Do not I know, if women have a will,
They'll do gainst all the watches o' the
  world,
And that the fiercest spies are tamed
  with gold?   10
Tut, I am confident in thee; thou shalt
  see 't.
And see I'll give thee cause, too, to
  believe it.
Come, kiss me. Go, and make thee ready
  straight,
In all thy best attire, thy choicest jewels;
Put them all on, and with hem thy best
  looks;
We are invited to a solemn feast,
At old Volpone's, where it shall appear
How far I am free from jealousy or fear.
                [*Exeunt.*]

[1] *I.e.*, into my trap.   [4] Count on it.
[2] Know.   [5] Worsted them all.
[3] Suggested.   [6] Throttled.

Act III. Scene i.

[A street.]

Mosca.

[Mos.] I fear I shall begin to grow in love
  With my dear self and my most pros-
    p'rous parts,
They do so spring and burgeon; I can feel
A whimsy i' my blood. I know not how,
Success hath made me wanton. I could
  skip
Out of my skin now, like a subtle snake,
I am so limber. O! Your parasite
Is a most precious thing, dropped from
  above,
Not bred 'mongst clods and clotpolls [1]
  here on earth.
I muse the mystery [2] was not made a
  science,   10
It is so liberally professed! Almost
All the wise world is little else, in nature,
But parasites or sub-parasites. And yet
I mean not those that have your bare
  town-art,
To know who's fit to feed hem, have no
  house,
No family, no care, and therefore mold
Tales for men's ears to bait that sense,
  or get
Kitchen invention and some stale re-
  ceipts
To please the belly and the groin, nor
  those,
With their court-dog tricks, that can
  fawn and fleer,   20
Make their revenue out of legs and
  faces,[3]
Echo my lord, and lick [4] away a moth—
But your fine, elegant rascal, that can
  rise
And stoop, almost together, like an ar-
  row,
Shoot through the air as nimbly as a
  star,
Turn short as doth a swallow, and be
  here,
And there, and here, and yonder, all
  at once,
Present to any humor, all occasion,
And change a visor [5] swifter than a
  thought!

[1] Clodpolls, blockheads.   [4] Flick.
[2] I wonder that the profession.
[3] Bows and smiles.   [5] Facial expression.

This is the creature had the art born
  with him,   30
Toils not to learn it, but doth practice it
Out of most excellent nature, and such
  sparks
Are the true parasites, others but their
  zanies.

Act III. Scene ii.

[The same.]

Mosca, Bonario.

[Mos. (Aside.)] Who's this? Bonario, old
  Corbaccio's son?
The person I was bound to seek.—Fair
  sir,
You are happ'ly met.
Bon.   That cannot be by thee.
Mos. Why, sir?
Bon.   Nay, pray thee, know thy way,
  and leave me;
I would be loath to interchange discourse
With such a mate [6] as thou art.
Mos.   Courteous sir,
  Scorn not my poverty.
Bon.   Not I, by heaven;
But thou shalt give me leave to hate thy
  baseness.
Mos. Baseness?
Bon.   Ay; answer me, is not thy sloth
  Sufficient argument? Thy flattery?   10
Thy means of feeding?
Mos.   Heaven be good to me!
These imputations are too common, sir,
And easily stuck on virtue when she's
  poor.
You are unequal [7] to me, and howe'er
Your sentence may be righteous, yet you
  are not,
That, ere you know me, thus proceed in
  censure.
St. Mark bear witness gainst you, 'tis
  inhuman.   [Weeps.]
Bon. [Aside.] What! Does he weep? The
  sign is soft and good!
I do repent me that I was so harsh.
Mos. 'Tis true that, swayed by strong
  necessity,   20
I am enforced to eat my careful bread
With too much obsequy; [8] 'tis true, be-
  side,
That I am fain to spin mine own poor
  raiment

[6] Fellow.   [7] Unfair.   [8] Obsequiousness.

Out of my mere observance,[1] being not
  born
To a free fortune; but that I have done
Base offices, in rending friends asunder,
Dividing families, betraying counsels,
Whispering false lies, or mining men
  with praises,
Trained [2] their credulity with perjuries,
Corrupted chastity, or am in love   30
With mine own tender ease, but would
  not rather
Prove the most rugged and laborious
  course,
That might redeem my present estima-
  tion,
Let me here perish, in all hope of good-
  ness.
Bon. [*Aside.*] This cannot be a personated
  passion.—
I was to blame, so to mistake thy nature;
Pray thee, forgive me, and speak out thy
  business.
Mos. Sir, it concerns you; and, though I
  may seem
At first to make a main offense in man-
  ners,
And in my gratitude unto my master,   40
Yet for the pure love which I bear all
  right,
And hatred of the wrong, I must reveal
  it.
This very hour your father is in purpose
To disinherit you—
Bon.   How!
Mos.   And thrust you forth
As a mere stranger to his blood; 'tis true,
  sir.
The work no way engageth me but as
I claim an interest in the general state
Of goodness and true virtue, which I hear
T' abound in you, and for which mere
  respect,
Without a second aim, sir, I have done
  it.   50
Bon. This tale hath lost thee much of the
  late trust
Thou hadst with me; it is impossible.
I know not how to lend it any thought
My father should be so unnatural.
Mos. It is a confidence that well becomes
  Your piety;[3] and formed, no doubt, it is
From your own simple innocence, which
  makes

Your wrong more monstrous and ab-
  horred. But, sir,
I now will tell you more. This very
  minute
It is or will be doing; and, if you   60
Shall be but pleased to go with me, I'll
  bring you,
I dare not say where you shall see, but
  where
Your ear shall be a witness of the deed,
Hear yourself written bastard, and pro-
  fessed
The common issue of the earth.
Bon.   I'm mazed!
Mos. Sir, if I do it not, draw your just
  sword,
And score your vengeance on my front
  and face;
Mark me your villain. You have too
  much wrong,
And I do suffer for you, sir. My heart   69
Weeps blood in anguish—
Bon.   Lead; I follow thee. [*Exeunt.*]

Act III. Scene iii.

[*A room in Volpone's house.*] [4]

Volpone, Nano, Androgyno, Castrone.

[Volp.] [5] Mosca stays long, methinks.—
  Bring forth your sports,
And help to make the wretched time
  more sweet.
Nan. Dwarf, fool, and eunuch, well met
  here we be.
A question it were now, whether [6] of us
  three,
Being all the known delicates of a rich
  man,
In pleasing him, claim the precedency
  can?
Cas. I claim for myself.
And.   And so doth the fool.
Nan. 'Tis foolish indeed; let me set you
  both to school.
First, for your dwarf, he's little and
  witty,   9
And everything, as it is little, is pretty;
Else why do men say to a creature of my
  shape,

---

[1] Service.   [2] Enticed, led on.   [3] Filial love.

[4] The scene remains the same to the end of the
act.
[5] The following short debate through line 20
is printed in italics in the original.
[6] Which.

So soon as they see him, "It's a pretty
　little ape"?
And why a pretty ape but for pleasing
　imitation
Of greater men's action in a ridiculous
　fashion?
Beside, this feat [1] body of mine doth not
　crave
Half the meat, drink, and cloth one of
　your bulks will have.
Admit your fool's face be the mother of
　laughter,
Yet, for his brain, it must always come
　after;
And, though that do feed him, it's a
　pitiful case,
His body is beholding [2] to such a bad
　face.　　　　　　　　*One knocks.*　20
VOLP. Who's there? My couch! Away!
　Look, Nano, see!
　　　　[Exeunt Androgyno and Castrone.]
Give me my caps first—go, inquire. *[Exit
　Nano.]* Now, Cupid
Send it be Mosca, and with fair return!
NAN. *[Within.]* It is the beauteous Mad-
　am—
VOLP.　　　　　Would-be—is it?
NAN. The same.
VOLP. Now torment on me! Squire her in,
　For she will enter, or dwell here forever.
　Nay, quickly. *[Lies down on his couch.]*
　That my fit were past! I fear
A second hell too, that my loathing this
Will quite expel my appetite to the other.
Would she were taking now her tedious
　leave.　　　　　　　　　　30
Lord, how it threats me what I am to
　suffer!

ACT III. SCENE iv.

*Lady [Politic Would-be], Volpone, Nano,
　　　　　　　　　Women 2.[3]*

[LADY.] I thank you, good sir. Pray you
　signify
Unto your patron I am here.—This band
Shows not my neck enough.—(I trouble
　you, sir;
Let me request you bid one of my women
Come hither to me.) In good faith, I am
　dressed
Most favorably today! It is no matter;
　'Tis well enough.

---

[1] Delicate, dainty.　　　[2] Beholden.
[3] The waiting-women enter later.

　　　[Enter 1 Waiting-woman.]
　　　Look, see these petulant things,
How they have done this!
VOLP. *[Aside.]*　　　I do feel the fever
Ent'ring in at mine ears. O, for a
　charm　　　　　　　　　9
To fright it hence!
LADY.　　　Come nearer. Is this curl
In his right place, or this? Why is this
　higher
Than all the rest? You ha' not washed
　your eyes yet?
Or do they not stand even i' your head?
Where's your fellow? Call her.
　　　　　　　　[Exit 1 Woman.]
NAN. *[Aside.]*　　　Now St. Mark
Deliver us! Anon she'll beat her women
Because her nose is red.

　　　[Enter 1 and 2 Women.]

LADY.　　　　I pray you view
This tire,[4] forsooth. Are all things apt,
　or no?
[1] WOM. One hair a little here sticks out,
　forsooth.
LADY. Does 't so, forsooth? And where was
　your dear sight
When it did so, forsooth? What now!
　Bird-eyed? [5]　　　　　　　20
And you, too? Pray you, both approach
　and mend it.
Now, by that light, I muse yo' are not
　ashamed!
I, that have preached these things so oft
　unto you,
Read you the principles, argued all the
　grounds,
Disputed every fitness, every grace,
Called you to counsel of so frequent
　dressings—
(NAN. More carefully than of your fame
　or honor.)
LADY. Made you acquainted what an
　ample dowry
The knowledge of these things would be
　unto you,
Able alone to get you noble husbands　30
At your return—and you thus to neglect
　it!
Besides, you seeing what a curious [6]
　nation

---

[4] Headdress.　　　[6] Fastidious.
[5] Sharp-eyed.

Th' Italians are, what will they say of
me?
"The English lady cannot dress herself."
Here's a fine imputation to our country!
Well, go your ways, and stay i' the next
room.
This fucus [1] was too coarse too; it's no
matter.—
Good sir, you 'll give hem entertainment?
    [*Exeunt Nano and Waiting-women.*]
VOLP. [*Aside.*] The storm comes toward
me.
LADY.   How does my Volp[one]?
VOLP. Troubled with noise, I cannot sleep;
I dreamt   40
That a strange fury entered now my
house,
And with the dreadful tempest of her
breath
Did cleave my roof asunder.
LADY.   Believe me, and I
Had the most fearful dream, could I
remember 't—
VOLP. [*Aside.*] Out on my fate! I ha'
given her the occasion
How to torment me; she will tell me hers.
LADY. Methought the golden mediocrity,[2]
Polite and delicate—
VOLP.   O, if you do love me,
No more! I sweat and suffer at the
mention   49
Of any dream; feel how I tremble yet.
LADY. Alas, good soul! The passion of the
heart.
Seed pearl were good now, boiled with
syrup of apples,
Tincture of gold, and coral, citron pills,[3]
Your elecampane [4] root, myrobalans [5]—
VOLP. Ay me, I have ta'en a grasshopper
by the wing!
LADY. Burnt silk and amber. You have
muscadel
Good i' the house—
VOLP.   You will not drink, and part?
LADY. No, fear not that. I doubt we shall
not get
Some English saffron (half a dram would
serve),
Your sixteen cloves, a little musk, dried
mints,   60
Bugloss, and barley meal—

[1] Cosmetic.   [3] Peels.
[2] Golden mean.   [4] A herb used as a tonic.
[5] A dried fruit, once used as a medicine.

VOLP. [*Aside.*]   She's in again!
Before, I feigned diseases; now I have
one.
LADY. And these applied with a right
scarlet cloth—
VOLP. [*Aside.*] Another flood of words! A
very torrent!
LADY. Shall I, sir, make you a poultice?
VOLP.   No, no, no!
I am very well; you need prescribe no
more.
LADY. I have a little studied physic; but
now
I am all for music, save, i' the forenoons,
An hour or two for painting. I would
have
A lady, indeed, t' have all—letters and
arts,   70
Be able to discourse, to write, to paint,
But principal, as Plato holds, your music
(And so does wise Pythagoras, I take it)
Is your true rapture, when there is con-
cent [6]
In face, in voice, and clothes, and is,
indeed,
Our sex's chiefest ornament.
VOLP.   The poet
As old in time as Plato, and as knowing,
Says that your highest female grace is
silence.
LADY. Which of your poets? Petrarch?
Or Tasso? Or Dante?
Guarini? Ariosto? Aretine?   80
Cieco di Hadria? I have read them all.
VOLP. [*Aside.*] Is everything a cause to
my destruction?
LADY. I think I ha' two or three of hem
about me.
VOLP. [*Aside.*] The sun, the sea will sooner
both stand still
Than her eternal tongue! Nothing can
scape it.
LADY. Here's *Pastor Fido*—
VOLP. [*Aside.*]   Profess obstinate silence;
That's now my safest.
LADY.   All our English writers,
I mean such as are happy in th' Italian,
Will deign to steal out of this author,
mainly,
Almost as much as from Montagnié.   90
He has so modern and facile a vein,
Fitting the time, and catching the court
ear!

[6] Harmony, agreement.

Your Petrarch is more passionate, yet he,
In days of sonneting, trusted hem with much;
Dante is hard, and few can understand him.
But for a desperate wit there's Aretine;
Only his pictures are a little obscene—
You mark me not?
VOLP.　　　　Alas, my mind's perturbed.
LADY. Why, in such cases, we must cure ourselves,
Make use of our philosophy—
VOLP.　　　　　　Oi me!　100
LADY. And, as we find our passions do rebel,
Encounter hem with reason, or divert hem
By giving scope unto some other humor
Of lesser danger, as, in politic bodies,
There's nothing more doth overwhelm the judgment
And cloud the understanding than too much
Settling and fixing, and, as 'twere, subsiding
Upon one object. For the incorporating
Of these same outward things into that part
Which we call mental, leaves some certain fæces　110
That stop the organs, and, as Plato says,
Assassinates our knowledge.
VOLP. [Aside.]　　　Now, the spirit
Of patience help me!
LADY.　　　　Come, in faith, I must
Visit you more a-days, and make you well.
Laugh and be lusty.
VOLP. [Aside.]　My good angel save me!
LADY. There was but one sole man in all the world
With whom I e'er could sympathize, and he
Would lie you, often, three, four hours together
To hear me speak, and be sometime so rapt
As he would answer me quite from the purpose,　120
Like you; and you are like him, just. I'll discourse,
And 't be but only, sir, to bring you asleep,

How we did spend our time and loves together
For some six years.
VOLP.　　　　O, O, O, O, O, O!
LADY. For we were coætanei,[1] and brought up—
VOLP. [Aside.] Some power, some fate, some fortune rescue me!

ACT III. SCENE v.

Mosca, Lady, Volpone.

[MOS.] God save you, madam!
LADY.　　　　Good sir.
VOLP.　　　　Mosca, welcome,
Welcome to my redemption!
MOS.　　　　　　Why, sir?
VOLP. [Aside.]　　　　　　O,
Rid me of this my torture, quickly, there—
My madam with the everlasting voice.
The bells, in time of pestilence, ne'er made
Like noise, or were in that perpetual motion!
The Cockpit[2] comes not near it. All my house,
But now, steamed like a bath with her thick breath;
A lawyer could not have been heard, nor scarce
Another woman, such a hail of words　10
She has let fall. For hell's sake, rid her hence.
MOS. [Aside.] Has she presented?
VOLP. [Aside.]　　　O, I do not care;
I'll take her absence upon any price,
With any loss.
MOS.　　　Madam—
LADY.　　　　I ha' brought your patron
A toy, a cap here, of mine own work.
MOS.　　　　　　'Tis well.
I had forgot to tell you I saw your knight
Where you'ld little think it.
LADY.　　　　　　Where?
MOS.　　　　　　Marry,
Where yet, if you make haste, you may apprehend him,
Rowing upon the water in a gondole,
With the most cunning courtesan of Venice.　20
LADY. Is 't true?

[1] Of the same age.
[2] Where cockfighting and other noisy entertainments were held.

Mos.   Pursue hem, and believe your eyes;
Leave me to make your gift.—
              [*Exit Lady.*]
             I knew 'twould take,
For, lightly,[1] they that use themselves most license
Are still most jealous.
Volp.   Mosca, hearty thanks
For thy quick fiction and delivery of me.
Now to my hopes, what say'st thou?

[*Enter Lady.*]

Lady.   But do you hear, sir?
Volp. [*Aside.*] Again! I fear a paroxysm.
Lady.   Which way
Rowed they together?
Mos.   Toward the Rialto.
Lady. I pray you lend me your dwarf.
Mos.   I pray you take him.—[*Exit Lady.*]
Your hopes, sir, are like happy blossoms, fair,   30
And promise timely fruit, if you will stay
But the maturing; keep you at your couch.
Corbaccio will arrive straight with the will;
When he is gone, I'll tell you more.
                [*Exit.*]
Volp.   My blood,
My spirits are returned; I am alive,
And, like your wanton gamester at primero,[2]
Whose thought had whispered to him, "Not go less,"
Methinks I lie, and draw [3]—[*Draws the curtains across his bed.*] for an encounter.[3]

Act III. Scene vi.

Mosca, Bonario.

[Mos.] Sir, here concealed you may hear all. [*Shows Bonario the hiding place.*]
But, pray you,
Have patience, sir. (*One knocks.*) The same's your father knocks;
I am compelled to leave you.   [*Exit.*]
Bon.   Do so.—Yet
Cannot my thought imagine this a truth.
             [*Hides himself.*]

[1] Generally.   [2] A card game.
[3] Terms in primero, used punningly.

Act III. Scene vii.

Mosca, Corvino, Celia, Bonario, Volpone.

[Mos.] Death on me! You are come too soon. What meant you?
Did not I say I would send?
Corv.   Yes, but I feared
You might forget it, and then they prevent us.
Mos. Prevent?—[*Aside.*]   Did e'er man haste so for his horns?
A courtier would not ply it so for a place.—
Well, now there's no helping it, stay here;
I'll presently return.   [*Exit.*]
Corv.   Where are you, Celia?
You know not wherefore I have brought you hither?
Cel. Not well, except you told me.
Corv.   Now I will:
Hark hither.   [*They step aside.*

Enter Mosca.

Mos. (*To Bonario.*)   Sir, your father hath sent word   10
It will be half an hour ere he come;
And therefore, if you please to walk the while
Into that gallery—at the upper end,
There are some books to entertain the time;
And I'll take care no man shall come unto you, sir.
Bon. Yes, I will stay there.—[*Aside.*]   I do doubt this fellow.   [*Exit.*]
Mos. There! He is far enough; he can hear nothing.
And, for his father, I can keep him off.
          [*Draws Volpone's curtains.*]
Corv. Nay, now, there is no starting back, and therefore
Resolve upon it. I have so decreed.   20
It must be done. Nor would I move 't afore,
Because I would avoid all shifts and tricks
That might deny me.
Cel.   Sir, let me beseech you,
Affect not these strange trials; if you doubt
My chastity, why, lock me up forever;
Make me the heir of darkness. Let me live

Where I may please your fears, if not
  your trust.
Corv. Believe it, I have no such humor, I.
All that I speak I mean; yet I am not
  mad—
Not horn-mad,[1] see you? Go to, show
  yourself   30
Obedient, and a wife.
Cel.   O heaven!
Corv.   I say it,
Do so.
Cel.   Was this the train?[2]
Corv.   I have told you reasons:
What the physicians have set down,
  how much
It may concern me, what my engage-
  ments are,
My means, and the necessity of those
  means
For my recovery; wherefore, if you be
Loyal and mine, be won; respect my
  venture.
Cel. Before your honor?
Corv.   Honor? Tut, a breath!
There's no such thing in nature—a mere
  term   39
Invented to awe fools. What is my gold
The worse for touching, clothes for be-
  ing looked on?
Why, this 's no more. An old decrepit
  wretch
That has no sense, no sinew; takes his
  meat
With others' fingers; only knows to gape
When you do scald his gums; a voice, a
  shadow;
And what can this man hurt you?
Cel. [Aside.]   Lord! What spirit
Is this hath entered him?
Corv.   And, for your fame,
That's such a jig.[3] As if I would go tell it,
Cry it on the Piazza! Who shall know it
But he that cannot speak it, and this
  fellow,   50
Whose lips are i' my pocket? Save
  yourself
(If you'll proclaim 't, you may), I know
  no other
Should come to know it.
Cel.   Are heaven and saints then
  nothing?
Will they be blind or stupid?

[1] Raving mad, with a reference to cuckoldry.
[2] Trick.   [3] Trifle.

Corv.   How!
Cel.   Good sir,
Be jealous still, emulate them, and think
What hate they burn with toward every
  sin.
Corv. I grant you; if I thought it were a
  sin,
I would not urge you. Should I offer
  this
To some young Frenchman, or hot
  Tuscan blood
That had read Aretine, conned all his
  prints,   60
Knew every quirk within lust's laby-
  rinth,
And were professed critic in lechery,
And I would look upon him and applaud
  him,
This were a sin; but here, 'tis contrary,
A pious work, mere charity for physic,
And honest polity to assure mine own.
Cel. O heaven! Canst thou suffer such
  a change?
Volp. [Aside.] Thou art mine honor,
  Mosca, and my pride,
My joy, my tickling, my delight! Go
  bring hem.
Mos. Please you draw near, sir.
Corv.   Come on! What? 70
You will not be rebellious? By that
  light—
Mos. Sir, Signior Corvino, here, is come
  to see you.
Volp. O!
Mos.   And, hearing of the consultation
  had
So lately for your health, is come to
  offer,
Or rather, sir, to prostitute—
Corv.   Thanks, sweet Mosca.
Mos. Freely, unasked, or unentreated—
Corv.   Well.
Mos. As the true, fervent instance of his
  love,
His own most fair and proper wife, the
  beauty
Only of price in Venice—
Corv.   'Tis well urged.
Mos. To be your comfortress, and to pre-
  serve you.   80
Volp. Alas, I am past already! Pray you,
  thank him
For his good care and promptness; but
  for that,

'Tis a vain labor e'en to fight gainst
   heaven—
Applying fire to a stone—uh, uh, uh,
   uh!—
Making a dead leaf grow again. I take
His wishes gently, though; and you may
   tell him
What I have done for him. Marry, my
   state is hopeless.
Will him to pray for me, and t' use his
   fortune
With reverence when he comes to 't.

Mos.   Do you hear, sir?
   Go to him with your wife.

Corv.   Heart of my father! 90
   Wilt thou persist thus? Come, I pray
   thee, come.
Thou seest 'tis nothing, Celia. By this
   hand,
I shall grow violent. Come, do 't, I say.

Cel. Sir, kill me rather; I will take down
   poison,
Eat burning coals, do anything—

Corv.   Be damned!
   Heart, I will drag thee hence home by
   the hair;
Cry thee a strumpet through the streets;
   rip up
Thy mouth unto thine ears; and slit
   thy nose,
Like a raw rochet![1] Do not tempt me;
   come.
Yield, I am loath—Death! I will buy
   some slave   100
Whom I will kill, and bind thee to him
   alive,
And at my windore hang you forth,
   devising
Some monstrous crime, which I, in cap-
   ital letters,
Will eat into thy flesh with aqua fortis
And burning corsives[2] on this stubborn
   breast.
Now, by the blood thou hast incensed,
   I'll do 't!

Cel. Sir, what you please, you may; I
   am your martyr.

Corv. Be not thus obstinate; I ha' not
   deserved it.
Think who it is entreats you. Pray thee,
   sweet—
Good faith, thou shalt have jewels,
   gowns, attires,   110

What thou wilt think and ask. Do but
   go kiss him.
Or touch him but. For my sake. At my
   suit—
This once. No? Not? I shall remember
   this.
Will you disgrace me thus? Do you
   thirst my undoing?

Mos. Nay, gentle lady, be advised.

Corv.   No, no.
   She has watched her time. God's pre-
   cious, this is scurvy,
'Tis very scurvy; and you are—

Mos.   Nay, good sir.

Corv. An arrant locust—by heaven, a
   locust!—
Whore, crocodile, that hast thy tears
   prepared,
Expecting how thou'lt bid hem flow—

Mos.   Nay, pray you, sir! 120
   She will consider.

Cel.   Would my life would serve
   To satisfy.

Corv.   'Sdeath! If she would but
   speak to him,
And save my reputation, 'twere somewhat;
But spitefully to affect my utter ruin—

Mos. Ay, now you have put your fortune
   in her hands.
Why, i' faith, it is her modesty; I must
   quit [3] her.
If you were absent, she would be more
   coming;
I know it, and dare undertake for her.
What woman can before her husband?
   Pray you,
Let us depart and leave her here.

Corv.   Sweet Celia, 130
   Thou mayst redeem all yet; I'll say no
   more.
If not, esteem yourself as lost. Nay,
   stay there.
            [Exeunt Corvino and Mosca.]

Cel. O God and his good angels! Whither,
   whither
Is shame fled human breasts, that with
   such ease
Men dare put off your honors and their
   own?
Is that, which ever was a cause of life,[4]
Now placed beneath the basest circumstance,

---

[1] A fish.   [2] Corrosives.   [3] Acquit, excuse.   [4] I.e., wedlock.

And modesty an exile made for money?
VOLP. (*He leaps off from his couch.*) Ay,
  in Corvino, and such earth-fed minds,
That never tasted the true heaven of
  love.   140
Assure thee, Celia, he that would sell
  thee
Only for hope of gain, and that uncertain,
He would have sold his part of Paradise
For ready money, had he met a cope-
  man.[1]
Why art thou mazed to see me thus re-
  vived?
Rather applaud thy beauty's miracle;
'Tis thy great work, that hath, not now
  alone,
But sundry times, raised me in several
  shapes,
And but this morning, like a mounte-
  bank,   149
To see thee at thy windore. Ay, before
I would have left my practice,[2] for thy
  love,
In varying figures I would have con-
  tended
With the blue Proteus or the hornéd
  flood.[3]
Now art thou welcome.
CEL.   Sir!
VOLP.   Nay, fly me not,
  Nor let thy false imagination
That I was bedrid make thee think I
  am so;
Thou shalt not find it. I am now as
  fresh,
As hot, as high, and in as jovial plight
As when, in that so celebrated scene
At recitation of our comedy   160
For entertainment of the great Valois,[4]
I acted young Antinous, and attracted
The eyes and ears of all the ladies pres-
  ent
To admire each graceful gesture, note,
  and footing.

SONG

Come, my Celia, let us prove,
While we can, the sports of love.
Time will not be ours forever;
He, at length, our good will sever.

Spend not then his gifts in vain.
Suns that set may rise again;   170
But, if once we lose this light,
'Tis with us perpetual night.
Why should we defer our joys?
Fame and rumor are but toys.
Cannot we delude the eyes
Of a few poor household spies,
Or his easier ears beguile,
Thus removéd by our wile?
'Tis no sin love's fruits to steal,
But the sweet thefts to reveal.   180
To be taken, to be seen,
These have crimes accounted been.

CEL. Some serene [5] blast me, or dire light-
  ning strike
  This my offending face!
VOLP.   Why droops my Celia?
Thou hast in place of a base husband
  found
A worthy lover; use thy fortune well,
With secrecy and pleasure. See, behold,
What thou art queen of—not in expec-
  tation,
As I feed others, but possessed and
  crowned.
See here a rope of pearl, and each more
  orient   190
Than that the brave Egyptian queen
  caroused;[6]
Dissolve and drink hem. See, a car-
  buncle,
May put out both the eyes of our St.
  Mark;
A diamant, would have bought Lollia
  Paulina,[7]
When she came in like starlight, hid
  with jewels
That were the spoils of provinces. Take
  these,
And wear and lose hem; yet remains
  an earring
To purchase them again, and this whole
  state.
A gem but worth a private patrimony
Is nothing; we will eat such at a meal. 200
The heads of parrots, tongues of night-
  ingales,
The brains of peacocks and of estriches[8]
Shall be our food, and, could we get the
  phœnix,

---

[1] Chapman, dealer.   [2] Plotting.
[3] A reference to the story of Acheloüs, god of the Grecian river.
[4] Henry VI was entertained at Venice in 1574.

[5] The damp evening air.
[6] *I.e.*, Cleopatra drank.
[7] Mistress of Emperor Claudius.
[8] Ostriches.

Though nature lost her kind, she were
   our dish.
CEL. Good sir, these things might move a
   mind affected
With such delights; but I, whose inno-
   cence
Is all I can think wealthy, or worth th'
   enjoying,
And which, once lost, I have naught to
   lose beyond it,
Cannot be taken with these sensual
   baits.   209
If you have conscience—
VOLP.   'Tis the beggar's virtue;
If thou hast wisdom, hear me, Celia.
Thy baths shall be the juice of July-
   flowers,[1]
Spirit of roses and of violets,
The milk of unicorns, and panthers'
   breath [2]
Gathered in bags and mixed with Cre-
   tan wines.
Our drink shall be prepared gold and
   amber,
Which we will take until my roof whirl
   round
With the vertigo, and my dwarf shall
   dance,
My eunuch sing, my fool make up the
   antic,[3]
Whilst we, in changéd shapes, act Ovid's
   tales,   220
Thou, like Europa now, and I like Jove,
Then I like Mars, and thou like Erycine;
So of the rest, till we have quite run
   through
And wearied all the fables of the gods.
Then will I have thee in more modern
   forms,
Attired like some sprightly dame of
   France,
Brave Tuscan lady, or proud Spanish
   beauty,
Sometimes unto the Persian sophy's
   wife,
Or the grand signior's mistress, and,
   for change,
To one of our most artful courtesans, 230
Or some quick Negro, or cold Russian;

And I will meet thee in as many shapes,
Where we may so transfuse our wan-
   d'ring souls
Out at our lips, and score up sums of
   pleasures,

> That the curious shall not know
> How to tell [4] them as they flow,
> And the envious, when they find
> What their number is, be pined.[5]

CEL. If you have ears that will be pierced,
   or eyes
That can be opened, a heart may be
   touched,   240
Or any part that yet sounds man about
   you,
If you have touch of holy saints or
   heaven,
Do me the grace to let me scape. If not,
Be bountiful and kill me. You do know
I am a creature, hither ill betrayed,
By one whose shame I would forget it
   were;
If you will deign me neither of these
   graces,
Yet feed your wrath, sir, rather than
   your lust
(It is a vice comes nearer manliness),
And punish that unhappy crime of
   nature,   250
Which you miscall my beauty. Flay my
   face,
Or poison it with ointments, for seducing
Your blood to this rebellion. Rub these
   hands
With what may cause an eating leprosy,
E'en to my bones and marrow—anything
That may disfavor me, save in my honor.
And I will kneel to you, pray for you,
   pay down
A thousand hourly vows, sir, for your
   health,
Report and think you virtuous—
VOLP.   Think me cold,
Frozen, and impotent, and so report
   me?   260
That I had Nestor's hernia, thou wouldst
   think.
I do degenerate, and abuse my nation,
To play with opportunity thus long;
I should have done the act, and then
   have parleyed.
Yield, or I'll force thee.   [Seizes her.]

---

[1] Gillyflowers.
[2] It was a common belief that panthers had
fragrant breaths. Panther was also the name
of a sweet-smelling drug.
[3] Pageant.

[4] Count.   [5] Pained.

Cel.　　　　　　O! Just God!
Volp.　　　　　　　In vain—
Bon. (*He leaps out from where Mosca had placed him.*) Forbear, foul ravisher!
Libidinous swine!
Free the forced lady, or thou di'st, impostor.
But that I am loath to snatch thy punishment
Out of the hand of justice, thou shouldst yet
Be made the timely sacrifice of vengeance　　　　　　　　　　　　270
Before this altar and this dross, thy idol.—
Lady, let's quit the place; it is the den
Of villainy. Fear naught; you have a guard.
And he ere long shall meet his just reward.　　[*Exeunt Bonario and Celia.*]
Volp. Fall on me, roof, and bury me in ruin!
Become my grave, that wert my shelter! O!
I am unmasked, unspirited, undone,
Betrayed to beggary, to infamy—

Act III. Scene viii.

Mosca, Volpone.

[Mos.] Where shall I run, most wretched shame of men,
To beat out my unlucky brains?
Volp.　　　　　　　Here, here.
What! Dost thou bleed?
Mos.　　　O, that his well-driv'n sword
Had been so courteous to have cleft me down
Unto the navel, ere I lived to see
My life, my hopes, my spirits, my patron, all
Thus desperately engagéd by my error!
Volp. Woe on thy fortune!
Mos.　　　　　　And my follies, sir.
Volp. Th' hast made me miserable.
Mos.　　　　　　And myself, sir.
Who would have thought he would have hearkened so?　　　　　　　10
Volp. What shall we do?
Mos.　　　　I know not; if my heart
Could expiate the mischance, I'ld pluck it out.
Will you be pleased to hang me, or cut my throat?

And I'll requite you, sir. Let's die like Romans,[1]
Since we have lived like Grecians.[2]
　　　　　　　　They knock without.
Volp.　　　　　　Hark! Who's there?
I hear some footing; officers, the *saffi*,[3]
Come to apprehend us! I do feel the brand
Hissing already at my forehead; now
Mine ears are boring.
Mos.　　　　To your couch, sir; you
Make that place good, however. [*Volpone lies down.*] Guilty men　20
Suspect what they deserve still.—Signior Corbaccio!

Act III. Scene ix.

Corbaccio, Mosca, Voltore,[4] Volpone.

[Corb.] Why, how now, Mosca?
Mos.　　　O, undone, amazed, sir.
Your son, I know not by what accident,
Acquainted with your purpose to my patron,
Touching your will and making him your heir,
Entered our house with violence, his sword drawn,
Sought for you, called you wretch, unnatural,
Vowed he would kill you.
Corb.　　　　　　　Me?
Mos.　　　　Yes, and my patron.
Corb. This act shall disinherit him indeed;
Here is the will.
Mos.　　　　　'Tis well, sir.
Corb.　　　　　　　Right and well.
Be you as careful now for me.

[*Enter Voltore behind.*]

Mos.　　　　　My life, sir,　10
Is not more tendered;[5] I am only yours.
Corb. How does he? Will he die shortly, think'st thou?
Mos.　　　　　I fear
He'll outlast May.
Corb.　　　　Today?
Mos.　　　　　No, last out May, sir.
Corb. Couldst thou not gi' him a dram?
Mos.　　　　O, by no means, sir.
Corb. Nay, I'll not bid you.

---

[1] *I.e.*, commit suicide.
[2] Greeks, roisterers.
[3] Police.
[4] Enters later.
[5] Attended to.

Volt. [*Coming forward.*] This is a
knave, I see.
Mos. [*Aside.*] How! Signior Voltore! Did
he hear me?
Volt. Parasite!
Mos. Who's that?—O, sir, most timely
welcome—
Volt. Scarce
To the discovery of your tricks, I fear.
You are his, "only"? And mine also,
are you not?
Mos. Who? I, sir!
Volt. You, sir. What devise is this 20
About a will?
Mos. A plot for you, sir.
Volt. Come,
Put not your foists [1] upon me; I shall
scent hem.
Mos. Did you not hear it?
Volt. Yes, I hear Corbaccio
Hath made your patron there his heir.
Mos. 'Tis true,
By my device, drawn to it by my plot,
With hope—
Volt. Your patron should reciprocate?
And you have promised?
Mos. For your good I did, sir.
Nay, more, I told his son, brought, hid
him here,
Where he might hear his father pass the
deed,
Being persuaded to it by this thought,
sir, 30
That the unnaturalness, first, of the act,
And then his father's oft disclaiming in
him
(Which I did mean t' help on), would
sure enrage him
To do some violence upon his parent,
On which the law should take sufficient
hold,
And you be stated in a double hope.
Truth be my comfort and my conscience,
My only aim was to dig you a fortune
Out of these two old rotten sepulchers—
Volt. I cry thee mercy, Mosca.
Mos. Worth your patience 40
And your great merit, sir. And see the
change!
Volt. Why, what success?
Mos. Most hapless! You must help, sir.
Whilst we expected th' old raven, in
comes

[1] Tricks.

Corvino's wife, sent hither by her
husband—
Volt. What, with a present?
Mos. No, sir, on visitation
(I'll tell you how anon), and, staying long,
The youth he grows impatient, rushes
forth,
Seizeth the lady, wounds me, makes her
swear
(Or he would murder her, that was his
vow)
T' affirm my patron to have done her
rape— 50
Which how unlike it is, you see!—and
hence,
With that pretext he's gone, t' accuse his
father,
Defame my patron, defeat you—
Volt. Where's her husband?
Let him be sent for straight.
Mos. Sir, I'll go fetch him.
Volt. Bring him to the Scrutineo.[2]
Mos. Sir, I will.
Volt. This must be stopped.
Mos. O, you do nobly, sir.
Alas, 'twas labored all, sir, for your good;
Nor was there want of counsel in the
plot;
But Fortune can at any time o'erthrow
The projects of a hundred learned clerks,
sir. 60
Corb. [*Cupping his ear.*] What's that?
Volt. Wilt please you, sir, to go along?
[*Exit with Corbaccio.*]
Mos. Patron, go in, and pray for our suc-
cess.
Volp. [*Rising.*] Need makes devotion;
heaven your labor bless! [*Exeunt.*]

Act IV. Scene i.

[A street.]

Politic, Peregrine.

[Pol.] I told you, sir, it was a plot; you see
What observation is! You mentioned me
For some instructions; I will tell you, sir
(Since we are met here in this height of
Venice),
Some few particulars I have set down,
Only for this meridian,[3] fit to be known
Of your crude [4] traveler; and they are
these.

[2] Senate House. [4] Inexperienced.
[3] Special locality.

I will not touch, sir, at your phrase, or
   clothes,
For they are old.
PER.   Sir, I have better.
POL.   Pardon;
   I meant, as they are themes.
PER.   O, sir, proceed.   10
   I'll slander you no more of wit, good sir.
POL. First, for your garb,[1] it must be
   grave and serious,
Very reserved and locked; not tell a secret
On any terms, not to your father; scarce
A fable, but with caution; make sure
   choice
Both of your company and discourse;
   beware
You never speak[2] a truth—
PER.   How!
POL.   Not to strangers,
   For those be they you must converse[3]
   with most;
Others I would not know, sir, but at
   distance,
So as I still might be a saver in hem;[4]   20
You shall have tricks else passed upon
   you hourly.
And then, for your religion, profess none,
But wonder at the diversity of all;
And, for your part, protest, were there
   no other
But simply the laws o' th' land, you
   could content you.
Nic. Machiavel and Monsieur Bodine[5]
   both
Were of this mind. Then must you learn
   the use
And handling of your silver fork at meals,
The metal of your glass (these are main
   matters
With your Italian), and to know the
   hour   30
When you must eat your melons and
   your figs.
PER. Is that a point of state too?
POL.   Here it is.
  For your Venetian, if he see a man
Preposterous in the least, he has him
   straight;

He has; he strips him. I'll acquaint you,
   sir.
I now have lived here 'tis some fourteen
   months.
Within the first week of my landing here
All took me for a citizen of Venice,
I knew the forms so well.
PER. [Aside.]   And nothing else.
POL. I had read Contarene,[6] took me a
   house,   40
Dealt with my Jews to furnish it with
   movables—
Well, if I could but find one man, one
   man
To mine own heart, whom I durst trust,
   I would—
PER. What, what, sir?
POL.   Make him rich, make him a
   fortune.
He should not think again. I would
   command it.
PER. As how?
POL.   With certain projects that I have,
   Which I may not discover.
PER. [Aside.]   If I had
   But one to wager with, I would lay odds
   now
He tells me instantly.
POL.   One is, and that
I care not greatly who knows, to serve
   the state   50
Of Venice with red herrings for three
   years,
And at a certain rate from Rotterdam,
Where I have correspondence. There's
   a letter,
Sent me from one o' th' states, and to
   that purpose.
He cannot write his name, but that's his
   mark.
PER. He is a chaundler?[7]
POL.   No, a cheesemonger.
There are some other too with whom I
   treat
About the same negotiation;
And I will undertake it. For 'tis thus
(I'll do 't with ease; I have cast[8] it all):
   your hoy[9]   60
Carries but three men in her, and a boy;

---

[1] Demeanor.
[2] Original reads *spake*.
[3] Associate.
[4] *I.e.*, so that I might not lose any money
through them.
[5] Jean Bodin, a sixteenth century French political philosopher.

[6] Cardinal Gasparo Contraini, author of a
work on Venice.
[7] Chandler, dealer in provisions.
[8] Calculated.
[9] A small coasting vessel.

And she shall make me three returns a
　　year;
So, if there come but one of three, I save;
If two, I can defalk.[1] But this is, now,
If my main project fail.
PER.　　　　　　　Then you have others?
POL. I should be loath to draw the subtle
　　air
Of such a place without my thousand
　　aims.
I'll not dissemble, sir; where'er I come,
I love to be considerative; and, 'tis true,
I have at my free hours thought upon　70
Some certain goods unto the state of
　　Venice,
Which I do call my cautions, and, sir,
　　which
I mean, in hope of pension, to propound
To the Great Council, then unto the
　　Forty,
So to the Ten. My means are made al-
　　ready—
PER. By whom?
POL.　　　　Sir, one that, though his place
　　b' obscure,
Yet he can sway, and they will hear him.
　　H'is
A *commandadore*.
PER.　　　　What! A common sergeant?
POL. Sir, such as they are, put it in their
　　mouths,
What they should say, sometimes; as
　　well as greater.　　　　　　　　　80
I think I have my notes to show you—
PER.　　　　　　　　　　Good sir.
POL. But you shall swear unto me, on your
　　gentry,
Not to anticipate—
PER.　　　　　　I, sir?
POL.　　　　　　　　　Nor reveal
A circumstance—My paper is not with
　　me.
PER. O, but you can remember, sir.
POL.　　　　　　　　　My first is
Concerning tinder boxes. You must
　　know
No family is here without its box.
Now, sir, it being so portable a thing,
Put case that you or I were ill affected
Unto the state, sir; with it in our pockets,
Might not I go into the Arsenal,　　91
Or you come out again, and none the
　　wiser?

[1] Cut off, reduce.

PER. Except yourself, sir.
POL.　　　　　　Go to, then. I therefore
Advertise to the state how fit it were
That none but such as were known
　　patriots,
Sound lovers of their country, should be
　　suffered
T' enjoy them in their houses, and even
　　those
Sealed at some office, and at such a
　　bigness
As might not lurk in pockets.
PER.　　　　　　　　　　Admirable!
POL. My next is, how t' inquire, and be re-
　　solved　　　　　　　　　　　　　100
By present demonstration, whether a
　　ship,
Newly arrived from Soria [2] or from
Any suspected part of all the Levant,
Be guilty of the plague; and, where they
　　use
To lie out forty, fifty days sometimes,
About the Lazaretto, for their trial,
I'll save that charge and loss unto the
　　merchant,
And in an hour clear the doubt.
PER.　　　　　　　　　Indeed, sir?
POL. Or—I will lose my labor.
PER.　　　　　　My faith, that's much.
POL. Nay, sir, conceive [3] me. 'Twill cost
　　me, in onions,　　　　　　　　110
Some thirty livres—
PER.　　　　Which is one pound sterling.
POL. Beside my waterworks; for this I do,
　　sir:
First, I bring in your ship twixt two brick
　　walls
(But those the state shall venter); on the
　　one
I strain me a fair tarpauling, and in that
I stick my onions, cut in halves; the
　　other
Is full of loopholes, out at which I thrust
The noses of my bellows; and those
　　bellows
I keep, with waterworks, in perpetual
　　motion,　　　　　　　　　　　119
Which is the easi'st matter of a hundred.
Now, sir, your onion, which doth nat-
　　urally
Attract th' infection, and your bellows
　　blowing
The air upon him, will show instantly,

[2] Syria.　　　　　　　　　[3] Understand.

By his changed color, if there be con-
tagion,
Or else remain as fair as at the first.
Now 'tis known, 'tis nothing.

PER. You are right, sir.

POL. I would I had my note.

PER. Faith, so would I;
But you ha' done well for once, sir.

POL. Were I false,
Or would be made so, I could show you
reasons
How I could sell this state now to the
Turk, 130
Spite of their galleys or their—
[*Examines his notes.*]

PER. Pray you, Sir Pol.

POL. I have hem not about me.

PER. [*Aside.*] That I feared.—
They are there, sir?

POL. No, this is my diary,
Wherein I note my actions of the day.

PER. Pray you, let's see, sir. What is here?
Notandum,[1] [*Reads.*]
"A rat had gnawn my spur leathers;
notwithstanding,
I put on new, and did go forth; but first
I threw three beans over the threshold.
Item,
I went and bought two toothpicks,
whereof one
I burst immediately, in a discourse 140
With a Dutch merchant, 'bout *ragion'*
del stato.[2]
From him I went and paid a moccinigo
For piecing my silk stockings; by the way
I cheapened[3] sprats; and at St. Mark's I
urined."
Faith, these are politic notes!

POL. Sir, I do slip
No action of my life, thus but I quote it.

PER. Believe me, it is wise!

POL. Nay, sir, read forth.

Act IV. Scene ii.

[*The same.*]

[*Enter, at a distance,*] *Lady, Nano, Women,*
Politic, Peregrine.

[LADY.] Where should this loose knight be,
trow? Sure, h' is housed.

NAN. Why, then he's fast.

[1] Let it be noted; take notice.
[2] Politics.   [3] Bargained for.

LADY. Ay, he plays both[4] with me.
I pray you stay. This heat will do more
harm
To my complexion than his heart is
worth.
(I do not care to hinder, but to take
him.) [*Rubs her cheeks.*]
How it comes off!

[1] WOM. My master's yonder.

LADY. Where?

[2] WOM. With a young gentleman.

LADY. That same's the party—
In man's apparel! Pray you, sir, jog my
knight;
I will be tender to his reputation,
However he demerit.

POL. [*Spying his Wife at a distance.*] My
lady!

PER. Where? 10

POL. 'Tis she indeed, sir; you shall know
her. She is,
Were she not mine, a lady of that merit,
For fashion and behavior; and for beauty
I durst compare—

PER. It seems you are not jealous,
That dare commend her.

POL. Nay, and for discourse—

PER. Being your wife, she cannot miss
that.

POL. [*Approaching his Wife.*] Madam,
Here is a gentleman; pray you, use him
fairly;
He seems a youth, but he is—

LADY. None?

POL. Yes, one
Has put his face as soon into the
world—

LADY. You mean, as early? But today?

POL. How's this? 20

LADY. Why, in this habit, sir; you appre-
hend me.
Well, Master Would-be, this doth not
become you;
I had thought the odor, sir, of your good
name
Had been more precious to you; that you
would not
Have done this dire massacre on your
honor.
One of your gravity and rank besides!
But knights, I see, care little for the oath
They make to ladies—chiefly their own
ladies.

[4] *I.e.,* both fast and loose.

Pol. Now, by my spurs, the symbol of my
    knighthood—
(Per. Lord, how his brain is humbled for
    an oath!)   30
Pol. I reach [1] you not.
Lady.   Right, sir, your polity
    May bear it through thus.—[*To Pere-
    grine.*] Sir, a word with you.
I would be loath to contest publicly
With any gentlewoman, or to seem
Froward or violent, as the courtier says;
It comes too near rusticity in a lady,
Which I would shun by all means. And
    however
I may deserve from Master Would-be,
    yet
T' have one fair gentlewoman thus be
    made
Th' unkind instrument to wrong an-
    other,   40
And one she knows not, ay, and to
    persever, [2]
In my poor judgment, is not warranted
From being a solecism in [3] our sex,
If not in manners.
Per.   How is this!
Pol.   Sweet madam,
Come nearer to your aim.
Lady.   Marry, and will, sir.
    Since you provoke me with your im-
    pudence
And laughter of your light land-siren
    here,
Your Sporus, your hermaphrodite—
Per.   What's here?
Poetic fury and historic storms! [4]
Pol. The gentleman, believe it, is of
    worth   50
And of our nation.
Lady.   Ay, your Whitefriars [5] nation.
    Come, I blush for you, Master Would-be,
    I,
And am ashamed you should ha' no more
    forehead [6]
Than thus to be the patron, or St.
    George,
To a lewd harlot, a base fricatrice, [7]
A female devil, in a male outside.
Pol.   Nay,

And you be such a one, I must bid adieu
To your delights. The case appears too
    liquid. [8]   [*Exit.*]
Lady. Ay, you may carry 't clear, with
    your state face!   59
But, for your carnival concupiscence, [9]
Who here is fled for liberty of con-
    science,
From furious persecution of the marshal,
Her will I disc'ple. [10]
Per.   This is fine, i' faith!
And do you use this often? Is this part
Of your wit's exercise gainst you have
    occasion?
Madam—
Lady.   Go to, sir.
Per.   Do you hear me, lady?
Why, if your knight have set you to beg
    shirts,
Or to invite me home, you might have
    done it
A nearer way by far.
Lady.   This cannot work you
Out of my snare.
Per.   Why, am I in it, then?   70
Indeed, your husband told me you were
    fair,
And so you are, only your nose inclines,
That side that's next the sun, to the
    queenapple. [11]
Lady. This cannot be endured by any
    patience.

Act IV. Scene iii.

[*The same.*]

Mosca, Lady, Peregrine [, Nano, Women].

[Mos.] What's the matter, madam?
Lady.   If the senate
    Right not my quest in this, I will protest
    hem
To all the world no aristocracy.
Mos. What is the injury, lady?
Lady.   Why, the callet [12]
    You told me of, here I have ta'en dis-
    guised.
Mos. Who? This? What means your
    ladyship? The creature

---

[1] Comprehend.   [3] Crime against.
[2] Persevere.   [4] Dramatic stormings.
[5] Disreputable district in London where evil-
doers were not followed by the law.
[6] Modesty.   [7] Prostitute.

[8] Clear.
[9] The object of your carnal desire.
[10] Disciple, discipline.
[11] A particularly red apple.
[12] Wench.

I mentioned to you is apprehended now
Before the senate; you shall see her—
LADY. Where?
Mos. I'll bring you to her. This young
  gentleman,
I saw him land this morning at the
  port. 10
LADY. Is 't possible! How has my judg-
  ment wandered!
Sir, I must, blushing, say to you I have
  erred
And plead your pardon.
PER. What, more changes yet?
LADY. I hope yo' ha' not the malice to
  remember
A gentlewoman's passion. If you stay
In Venice here, please you to use me,
  sir—
Mos. Will you go, madam?
LADY. Pray you, sir, use me; in faith,
The more you see me, the more I shall
  conceive
You have forgot our quarrel.
         [Exeunt All but Peregrine.]
PER. This is rare!
Sir Politic Would-be? No, Sir Politic
  Bawd, 20
To bring me thus acquainted with his
  wife!
Well, wise Sir Pol, since you have prac-
  ticed thus
Upon my freshmanship, I'll try your
  salthead,[1]
What proof it is against a counterplot.
           [Exit.]

ACT IV. SCENE iv.

[The Senate.]

Voltore, Corbaccio, Corvino, Mosca.

[VOLT.] Well, now you know the carriage
  of the business,
Your constancy is all that is required
Unto the safety of it.
Mos. Is the lie
Safely conveyed[2] amongst us? Is that
  sure?
Knows every man his burden?[3]
CORV. Yes.
Mos. Then shrink not.
CORV. But knows the advocate the truth?
Mos. O, sir,

By no means; I devised a formal tale
That salved your reputation. But be
  valiant, sir.
CORV. I fear no one but him, that this his
  pleading
Should make him stand for a co-heir—
Mos. Co-halter! 10
Hang him; we will but use his tongue,
  his noise,
As we do Croaker's[4] here.
CORV. Ay, what shall he do?
Mos. When we ha' done, you mean?
CORV. Yes.
Mos. Why, we'll think—
Sell him for mummia![5] He's half dust
  already.—
(*To Voltore.*) Do not you smile to see
  this buffalo,[6]
How he doth sport it with his head?—
  [*Aside.*] I should,
If all were well and past.—(*To Corbaccio.*)
  Sir, only you
Are he that shall enjoy the crop of all,
And these not know for whom they toil.
CORB. Ay, peace.
Mos. (*To Corvino.*) But you shall eat it.—
  [*Aside.*] Much!—(*Then to Voltore
  again.*) Worshipful sir, 20
Mercury sit upon your thund'ring tongue,
Or the French Hercules,[7] and make your
  language
As conquering as his club, to beat along,
As with a tempest, flat, our adversaries;
But much more yours, sir.
VOLT. Here they come; ha' done.
Mos. I have another witness, if you need,
  sir,
I can produce.
VOLT. Who is it?
Mos. Sir, I have her.

ACT IV. SCENE v.

[The same.]

*Avocatori 4, Bonario, Celia, Voltore, Cor-
baccio, Corvino, Mosca, Notario, Commandadori.*

[AVOC. 1.] The like of this the senate
  never heard of.

---

[1] Salthood, lechery.
[2] Arranged.   [3] Refrain of a song; part.
[4] Corbaccio's.
[5] Mummy, a medicine.
[6] A horned animal; *i.e.*, a cuckold.
[7] *I.e.*, Ognius, regarded as the symbol of eloquence. See Lucian.

Avoc. 2. 'Twill come most strange to them when we report it.

Avoc. 4. The gentlewoman has been ever held
Of unreprovéd name.

Avoc. 3.   So the young man.

Avoc. 4. The more unnatural part, that of his father.

Avoc. 2. More of the husband.

Avoc. 1.   I not know to give
His act a name, it is so monstrous!

Avoc. 4. But the impostor, he is a thing created
T' exceed example!

Avoc. [1.]   And all aftertimes! 9

Avoc. 2. I never heard a true voluptuary
Described but him.

Avoc. 3.   Appear yet those were cited?

Not. All but the old magnifico, Volpone.

Avoc. 1. Why is not he here?

Mos.   Please your fatherhoods,
Here is his advocate. Himself's so weak,
So feeble—

Avoc. 4.   What are you?

Bon.   His parasite,
His knave, his pander. I beseech the court
He may be forced to come, that your grave eyes
May bear strong witness of his strange impostures.

Volt. Upon my faith and credit with your virtues,
He is not able to endure the air.   20

Avoc. 2. Bring him, however.

Avoc. 3.   We will see him.

Avoc. 4.   Fetch him.

Volt. Your fatherhoods' fit pleasures be
obeyed;   [Exeunt Commandadori.]
But sure, the sight will rather move your pities
Than indignation. May it please the court,
In the meantime, he may be heard in me.
I know this place most void of preju-dice,
And therefore crave it, since we have no reason
To fear our truth should hurt our cause.

Avoc. 3.   Speak free.

Volt. Then know, most honored fathers,
I must now   29
Discover to your strangely abuséd ears,

The most prodigious and most frontless [1]
piece
Of solid impudence and treachery
That ever vicious nature yet brought forth
To shame the state of Venice. This lewd woman,
That wants no artificial looks or tears
To help the visor she has now put on,
Hath long been known a close [2] adulter-ess
To that lascivious youth there; not sus-pected,
I say, but known, and taken in the act
With him, and by this man, the easy husband,   40
Pardoned, whose timeless [3] bounty makes him now
Stand here, the most unhappy, innocent person
That ever man's own goodness made accused.
For these not knowing how to owe [4] a gift
Of that dear grace, but with their shame, being placed
So above all powers of their gratitude,
Began to hate the benefit, and, in place
Of thanks, devise t'extirp [5] the mem-ory
Of such an act, wherein I pray your fatherhoods
To observe the malice, yea, the rage of creatures   50
Discovered in their evils, and what heart
Such take, even from their crimes. But that anon
Will more appear. This gentleman, the father,
Hearing of this foul fact,[6] with many others,
Which daily strook at his too tender ears,
And, grieved in nothing more than that he could not
Preserve himself a parent (his son's ills
Growing to that strange flood), at last decreed
To disinherit him.

Avoc. 1.   These be strange turns!

[1] Shameless.   [4] Own.
[2] Secret.   [5] Extirpate.
[3] Untimely.   [6] Deed.

Avoc. 2. The young man's fame was ever
   fair and honest.   60
Volt. So much more full of danger is his
   vice,
   That can beguile so, under shade of
     virtue.
   But, as I said, my honored sires, his
     father
   Having this settled purpose, by what
     means
   To him betrayed we know not, and this
     day
   Appointed for the deed, that parricide—
   I cannot style him better—by confeder-
     acy
   Preparing this his paramour to be there,
   Entered Volpone's house (who was the
     man,
   Your fatherhoods must understand,
     designed   70
   For the inheritance), there sought his
     father—
   But with what purpose sought he him,
     my lords?
   I tremble to pronounce it, that a son
   Unto a father, and to such a father,
   Should have so foul, felonious intent!
   It was to murder him—when, being pre-
     vented
   By his more happy absence, what then
     did he?
   Not check his wicked thoughts; no, now
     new deeds!
   (Mischief doth ever end where it begins.)
   An act of horror, fathers! He dragged
     forth   80
   The aged gentleman that had there
     lyen [1] bedrid
   Three years and more, out of his inno-
     cent couch,
   Naked upon the floor; there left him;
     wounded
   His servant in the face; and with this
     strumpet,
   The stale to his forged practice,[2] who
     was glad
   To be so active (I shall here desire
   Your fatherhoods to note but my col-
     lections [3]
   As most remarkable), thought at once
     to stop

[1] Lain.
[2] Decoy to his invented plot.
[3] Inferences, conclusions.

His father's ends, discredit his free choice
   In the old gentleman, redeem them-
     selves   90
   By laying infamy upon this man,
   To whom, with blushing, they should
     owe their lives.
Avoc. 1. What proofs have you of this?
Bon.   Most honored fathers,
   I humbly crave there be no credit given
   To this man's mercenary tongue.
Avoc. 2.   Forbear.
Bon. His soul moves in his fee.
Avoc. 3.   O, sir!
Bon.   This fellow
   For six sols [4] more would plead against
     his Maker.
Avoc. 1. You do forget yourself.
Volt.   Nay, nay, grave fathers,
   Let him have scope. Can any man im-
     agine
   That he will spare his accuser, that
     would not   100
   Have spared his parent?
Avoc. 1.   Well, produce your proofs.
Cel. I would I could forget I were a
     creature.
Volt. Signior Corbaccio!
               [Corbaccio advances.]
Avoc. 4.   What is he?
Volt.   The father.
Avoc. 2. Has he had an oath?
Not.   Yes.
Corb.   What must I do now?
Not. Your testimony's craved.
Corb.   Speak to the knave?
   I'll ha' my mouth first stopped with
     earth; my heart
   Abhors his knowledge. I disclaim in [5]
     him.
Avoc. 1. But for what cause?
Corb.   The mere portent of nature!
   He is an utter stranger to my loins.
Bon. Have they made [6] you to this?
Corb.   I will not hear thee,
   Monster of men, swine, goat, wolf, par-
     ricide!   111
   Speak not, thou viper.
Bon.   Sir, I will sit down,
   And rather wish my innocence should
     suffer
   Than I resist the authority of a father.
Volt. Signior Corvino!
             [Corvino advances.]

[4] Small coins.   [5] Disown.   [6] Worked, wrought.

Avoc. 2.　　　　This is strange.

Avoc. 1.　　　　　　　　Who's this?

Not. The husband.

Avoc. 4.　　　　Is he sworn?

Not.　　　　　　　　He is.

Avoc. 3.　　　　　　　Speak then.

Corv. This woman, please your fatherhoods, is a whore,

Of most hot exercise, more than a partrich,[1]

Upon record—

Avoc. 1.　　　　No more.

Corv.　　　　　Neighs like a jennet.

Not. Preserve the honor of the court.

Corv.　　　　　　　I shall,　120

And modesty of your most reverend
ears.

And yet I hope that I may say these
eyes

Have seen her glued unto that piece of
cedar,

That fine, well-timbered gallant, and
that here　　[*Points to Celia's face.*]

The letters may be read, thorough [2] the
horn,[3]

That make the story perfect.

Mos.　　　　　　　Excellent, sir!

Corv. [*Aside to Mosca.*] There is no shame
in this now, is there?

Mos. [*Aside.*]　　　　None.

Corv. Or, if I said I hoped that she were
onward

To her damnation, if there be a hell

Greater than whore and woman, a good
Catholic　　　　　　　　130

May make the doubt.

Avoc. 3.　　　His grief hath made him
frantic.

Avoc. 1. Remove him hence. *She swoons.*

Avoc. 2.　　　　Look to the woman!

Corv.　　　　　　　　Rare!
Prettily feigned again!

Avoc. 4.　　　　Stand from about her!

Avoc. 1. Give her the air.

Avoc. 3. [*To Mosca.*]　What can you say?

Mos.　　　　　　My wound,

May 't please your wisdoms, speaks for
me, received

In aid of my good patron, when he
missed

---

[1] Partridge.　　　　　　　[2] Through.
[3] The child's A B C card, or hornbook, had a
thin covering of horn. The inevitable allusion
to cuckoldry is also present.

His sought-for father, when that well-
taught dame

Had her cue given her to cry out a rape.

Bon. O most laid [4] impudence! Fathers—

Avoc. 3.　　　　　Sir, be silent.
You had your hearing free; so must they
theirs.　　　　　　　　140

Avoc. 2. I do begin to doubt th' imposture
here.

Avoc. 4. This woman has too many
moods.

Volt.　　　　Grave fathers,
She is a creature of a most professed
And prostituted lewdness.

Corv.　　　　　　Most impetuous,
Unsatisfied—grave fathers!

Volt.　　　　　　May her feignings
Not take your wisdoms; but this day
she baited

A stranger, a grave knight, with her
loose eyes

And more lascivious kisses. This man
saw hem

Together on the water in a gondola.

Mos. Here is the lady herself that saw
hem too,　　　　　　　150

Without, who then had in the open
streets

Pursued them but for saving her knight's
honor.

Avoc. 1. Produce that lady.

Avoc. 2.　　Let her come. [*Exit Mosca.*]

Avoc. 4.　　　　　　These things,
They strike with wonder.

Avoc. 3.　　　I am turned a stone.

ACT IV.　SCENE vi.

[*The same.*]

Mosca, Lady, Avocatori, etc.

[Mos.] Be resolute, madam.

Lady.　　　　Ay, this same is she.
Out, thou chameleon harlot! Now thine
eyes

Vie tears with the hyena. Dar'st thou
look

Upon my wrongéd face? I cry your
pardons.

I fear I have forgettingly transgressed

Against the dignity of the court—

Avoc. 2.　　　　　　No, madam.

Lady. And been exorbitant—

---

[4] Carefully plotted.

Avoc. 2.   You have not, lady.
Avoc. 4. These proofs are strong.
Lady.   Surely, I had no purpose
To scandalize your honors or my sex's.
Avoc. 3. We do believe it.
Lady.   Surely you may believe it.   10
Avoc. 2. Madam, we do.
Lady.   Indeed you may; my breeding
Is not so coarse—
Avoc. 4.   We know it.
Lady.   To offend
With pertinacy[1]—
Avoc. 3.   Lady—
Lady.   Such a presence!
No, surely.
Avoc. 1.   We well think it.
Lady.   You may think it.
Avoc. 1. Let her o'ercome.—What wit-
nesses have you,
To make good your report?
Bon.   Our consciences.
Cel. And heaven, that never fails the
innocent.
Avoc. 4. These are no testimonies.
Bon.   Not in your courts,
Where multitude and clamor overcomes.
Avoc. 1. Nay, then you do wax insolent.

*Volpone is brought in, as impotent. [Lady
Would-be kisses him.]*

Volt.   Here, here,   20
The testimony comes that will convince
And put to utter dumbness their bold
tongues!
See here, grave fathers, here's the rav-
isher,
The rider on men's wives, the great im-
postor,
The grand voluptuary! Do you not think
These limbs should affect venery? Or
these eyes
Covet a concubine? Pray you, mark
these hands.
Are they not fit to stroke a lady's breasts?
Perhaps he doth dissemble?
Bon.   So he does.
Volt. Would you ha' him tortured?
Bon.   I would have him proved.   30
Volt. Best try him then with goads, or
burning irons;
Put him to the strappado.[2] I have heard

The rack hath cured the gout; faith,
give it him,
And help him of a malady. Be courteous.
I'll undertake, before these honored
fathers,
He shall have yet as many left diseases
As she has known adulterers, or thou
strumpets.
O, my most equal [3] hearers, if these deeds,
Acts of this bold and most exorbitant
strain,   39
May pass with suffrance, what one citizen
But owes the forfeit of his life, yea, fame,
To him that dares traduce him? Which
of you
Are safe, my honored fathers? I would
ask,
With leave of your grave fatherhoods, if
their plot
Have any face or color like to truth?
Or if, unto the dullest nostril here,
It smell not rank, and most abhorréd
slander?
I crave your care of this good gentleman,
Whose life is much endangered by their
fable;
And, as for them, I will conclude with
this,   50
That vicious persons, when they are
hot and fleshed
In impious acts, their constancy abounds.
Damned deeds are done with greatest
confidence.
Avoc. 1. Take hem to custody, and sever
them.
Avoc. 2. 'Tis pity two such prodigies
should live.
Avoc. 1. Let the old gentleman be re-
turned with care.
        [*Exeunt Commandadori with Volpone.*]
I am sorry our credulity wronged him.
Avoc. 4. These are two creatures!
Avoc. 3.   I have an earthquake in me.
Avoc. 2. Their shame, even in their
cradles, fled their faces.
Avoc. 4. [*To Voltore.*] You have done a
worthy service to the state, sir,   60
In their discovery.
Avoc. 1.   You shall hear, ere night,
What punishment the court decrees
upon hem.
[*Exeunt Avocatori, Notario, and Command-
adori with Bonario and Celia.*]

---

[1] Pertinacity.   [2] A kind of torture.   [3] Impartial.

Volt. We thank your fatherhoods. How
  like you it?
Mos.   Rare!
  I'ld ha' your tongue, sir, tipped with
    gold for this;
  I'ld ha' you be the heir to the whole city;
  The earth I'ld have want men ere you
    want living.
  They are bound to erect your statue in
    St. Mark's.
  Signior Corvino, I would have you go
  And show yourself, that you have con-
    quered.
Corv.   Yes.
Mos. It was much better that you should
    profess   70
  Yourself a cuckold thus than that the
    other
  Should have been proved.
Corv.   Nay, I considered that;
  Now it is her fault.
Mos.   Then it had been yours.
Corv. True. I do doubt this advocate
    still.
Mos.   I' faith,
  You need not; I dare ease you of that
    care.
Corv. I trust thee, Mosca.
Mos.   As your own soul, sir.
                    [Exit Corvino.]
Corb.   Mosca!
Mos. Now for your business, sir.
Corb.   How! Ha' you business?
Mos. Yes, yours, sir.
Corb.   O, none else?
Mos.   None else, not I.
Corb. Be careful then.
Mos.   Rest you with both your eyes, sir.
Corb. Despatch it.
Mos.   Instantly.
Corb.   And look that all, 80
  Whatever, be put in, jewels, plate,
    moneys,
  Household stuff, bedding, cortines.[1]
Mos.   Cortine rings, sir;
  Only the advocate's fee must be de-
    ducted.
Corb. I'll pay him now; you'll be too
    prodigal.
Mos. Sir, I must tender it.
Corb.   Two cecchines is well?
Mos. No, six, sir.
Corb.   'Tis too much.

---

¹ Curtains.

Mos.   He talked a great while;
  You must consider that, sir.
Corb.   Well, there's three—
Mos. I'll give it him.
Corb. Do so, and there's for thee. [Exit.]
Mos. [Aside.] Bountiful bones!   What
  horrid, strange offense
  Did he commit gainst nature, in his
    youth,   90
  Worthy this age?—You see, sir, how I
    work
  Unto your ends; take you no notice.
Volt.   No;
  I'll leave you.
Mos.   All is yours, the devil and all,
  Good advocate!—[Exit Voltore.] Mad-
    am, I'll bring you home.
Lady. No, I'll go see your patron.
Mos.   That you shall not;
  I'll tell you why. My purpose is to urge
  My patron to reform his will, and for
  The zeal you have shown today, where-
    as before
  You were but third or fourth, you shall
    be now
  Put in the first, which would appear as
    begged   100
  If you were present. Therefore—
Lady.   You shall sway me. [Exeunt.]

ACT V. SCENE i.

[A room in Volpone's house.]

Volpone.

[Volp.] Well, I am here, and all this brunt
  is past.
  I ne'er was in dislike with my disguise
  Till this fled moment; here 'twas good,
    in private;
  But in your public—cave ² whilst I
    breathe.
  Fore God, my left leg gan ³ to have the
    cramp,
  And I apprehended straight some power
    had strook me
  With a dead palsy. Well, I must be
    merry,
  And shake it off. A many of these fears
  Would put me into some villainous
    disease,
  Should they come thick upon me; I'll
    prevent hem.   10

---

² Beware.   ³ Began.

Give me a bowl of lusty wine to fright
This humor from my heart. (*He drinks.*)
Hum, hum, hum!
'Tis almost gone already; I shall con-
quer.
Any device now of rare, ingenious knav-
ery,
That would possess me with a violent
laughter,
Would make me up again. (*Drinks
again.*) So, so, so, so!
This heat is life; 'tis blood by this time.—
Mosca!

ACT V. SCENE ii.

[*The same.*]

Mosca, Volpone, Nano, Castrone.[1]

[MOS.] How now, sir? Does the day look
clear again?
Are we recovered, and wrought out of
error,
Into our way, to see our path before us?
Is our trade free once more?
VOLP.   Exquisite Mosca!
MOS. Was it not carried learnedly?
VOLP.   And stoutly.
Good wits are greatest in extremities.
MOS. It were a folly beyond thought to
trust
Any grand act unto a cowardly spirit.
You are not taken with it enough, me-
thinks?
VOLP. O, more than if I had enjoyed the
wench;   10
The pleasure of all womankind's not like
it.
MOS. Why, now you speak, sir. We must
here be fixed;
Here we must rest. This is our master-
piece;
We cannot think to go beyond this.
VOLP.   True,
Thou hast played thy prize, my precious
Mosca.
MOS.   Nay, sir,
To gull the court—
VOLP.   And quite divert the torrent
Upon the innocent.
MOS.   Yes, and to make
So rare a music out of discords—
VOLP.   Right.

¹ Last two enter later.

That yet to me 's the strangest (how th'
hast borne it!),
That these, being so divided mongst
themselves,   20
Should not scent somewhat or ² in me or
thee,
Or doubt their own side.
MOS.   True, they will not see 't.
Too much light blinds hem, I think.
Each of hem
Is so possessed and stuffed with his own
hopes
That anything unto the contrary,
Never so true, or never so apparent,
Never so palpable, they will resist it—
VOLP. Like a temptation of the devil.
MOS.   Right, sir.
Merchants may talk of trade, and your
great signiors
Of land that yields well; but, if Italy   30
Have any glebe ³ more fruitful than these
fellows,
I am deceived. Did not your advocate
rare?
VOLP. O—"My most honored fathers, my
grave fathers,
Under correction of your fatherhoods,
What face of truth is here? If these
strange deeds
May pass, most honored fathers"—I had
much ado
To forbear laughing.
MOS.   'T seemed to me you sweat, sir.
VOLP. In troth, I did a little.
MOS.   But confess, sir,
Were you not daunted?
VOLP.   In good faith, I was
A little in a mist, but not dejected;   40
Never but still myself.
MOS.   I think it, sir.
Now, so truth help me, I must needs
say this, sir,
And out of conscience for your advocate,
He has taken pains, in faith, sir, and
deserved,
In my poor judgment, I speak it under
favor,
Not to contrary you, sir, very richly—
Well—to be cozened.
VOLP.   Troth, and I think so too,
By that I heard him in the latter end.
MOS. O, but before, sir. Had you heard
him first

² Either.   ³ Cultivated ground.

Draw it to certain heads, then ag-
gravate,[1]   50
Then use his vehement figures—I looked
still
When he would shift a shirt; and doing
this
Out of pure love, no hope of gain—
VOLP.   'Tis right.
I cannot answer him, Mosca, as I would,
Not yet; but for thy sake, at thy en-
treaty,
I will begin even now—to vex hem all,
This very instant.
MOS.   Good sir.
VOLP.   Call the dwarf
And eunuch forth.
MOS.   Castrone, Nano!

[Enter Castrone and Nano.]

NANO.   Here.
VOLP. Shall we have a jig[2] now?
MOS.   What you please, sir.
VOLP.   Go,
Straight give out about the streets, you
two,   60
That I am dead. Do it with constancy,
Sadly,[3] do you hear? Impute it to the
grief
Of this late slander.
                    [Exeunt Castrone and Nano.]
MOS.   What do you mean, sir?
VOLP.   O,
I shall have instantly my vulture, crow,
Raven, come flying hither, on the news,
To peck for carrion, my she-wolf, and all,
Greedy, and full of expectation—
MOS. And then to have it ravished from
their mouths?
VOLP. 'Tis true. I will ha' thee put on a
gown,
And take upon thee, as thou wert mine
heir;   70
Show hem a will. Open that chest, and
reach
Forth one of those that has the blanks;
I'll straight
Put in thy name.
MOS.   It will be rare, sir.
                              [Gives him a paper.]
VOLP.   Ay,
When they e'en gape, and find themselves
deluded—

MOS. Yes.
VOLP.   And thou use them scurvily!
Despatch;
Get on thy gown.
MOS. *[Putting on a gown.]*   But what,
sir, if they ask
After the body?
VOLP.   Say it was corrupted.
MOS. I'll say it stunk, sir, and was fain t'
have it
Coffined up instantly, and sent away.
VOLP. Anything; what thou wilt. Hold,
here's my will.   80
Get thee a cap, a count-book, pen and
ink,
Papers afore thee; sit as thou wert taking
An inventory of parcels. I'll get up
Behind the cortine, on a stool, and
harken;
Sometime peep over; see how they do
look,
With what degrees their blood doth leave
their faces.
O, 'twill afford me a rare meal of laugh-
ter!
MOS. *[Following Volpone's directions.]* Your
advocate will turn stark dull upon it.
VOLP. It will take off his oratory's edge.
MOS. But your clarissimo,[4] old round-
back, he   90
Will crump you like a hog louse, with
the touch.
VOLP. And what Corvino?
MOS.   O, sir, look for him
Tomorrow morning with a rope and a
dagger
To visit all the streets; he must run mad.
My lady, too, that came into the court
To bear false witness for your wor-
ship—
VOLP.   Yes,
And kissed me fore the fathers, when my
face
Flowed all with oils—
MOS.   And sweat, sir. Why, your gold
Is such another med'cine, it dries up
All those offensive savors; it trans-
forms   100
The most deforméd, and restores hem
lovely,
As 'twere the strange poetical girdle.[5]
Jove

---

[1] Make his accusations.
[2] Entertainment, jest.   [3] Seriously.
[4] Grandee.
[5] Jonson's marginal note reads: "Cestus."

Could not invent t' himself a shroud more
  subtile
To pass Acrisius' [1] guards. It is the thing
Makes all the world her grace, her youth,
  her beauty.
VOLP. I think she loves me.
MOS.   Who? The lady, sir?
  She's jealous of you.
VOLP.   Dost thou say so?
               [Knocking within.]
MOS.   Hark!
  There's some already.
VOLP.   Look.
MOS.   It is the vulture;
  He has the quickest scent.
VOLP.   I'll to my place;
  Thou to thy posture.
         [Goes behind the curtain.]
MOS.   I am set.
VOLP.   But, Mosca, 110
  Play the artificer now; torture hem
  rarely.

ACT V. SCENE iii.

[The same.]

Voltore, Mosca, Corbaccio,[2] *Corvino,*[2] *Lady,*[2]
                Volpone.

[VOLT.] How now, my Mosca?
MOS. [*Writing.*]   "Turkey carpets,
  nine—"
VOLT. Taking an inventory? That is well.
MOS. "Two suits of bedding, tissue—"
VOLT.   Where's the will?
  Let me read that the while.

[Enter Servants with Corbaccio in a chair.]

CORB.   So, set me down,
  And get you home.   [Exeunt Servants.]
VOLT.   Is he come now to trouble us?
MOS. "Of cloth of gold, two more—"
CORB.   Is it done, Mosca?
MOS. "Of several vellets,[3] eight—"
VOLT.   I like his care.
CORB. Dost thou not hear?

[Enter Corvino.]

CORV.   Ha! Is the hour come, Mosca?
  Volpone peeps from behind a traverse.
VOLP. [*Aside.*] Ay, now they muster.

<hr>

[1] Danaë's father's.
[2] Enters later.   [3] Velvets.

CORV.   What does the advocate here,
  Or this Corbaccio?
CORB.   What do these here?

[Enter Lady Would-be.]

LADY.   Mosca! 10
  Is his thread spun?
MOS.   "Eight chests of linen—"
VOLP. [*Aside.*]   O,
  My fine Dame Would-be, too!
CORV.   Mosca, the will,
  That I may show it these, and rid hem
  hence.
MOS. "Six chests of diaper,[4] four of dam-
  ask."—There! [*Gives them the will.*]
CORB. Is that the will?
MOS.   "Down beds, and bolsters—"
VOLP. [*Aside.*]   Rare!
  Be busy still. Now they begin to flut-
  ter;
  They never think of me. Look, see, see,
  see!
  How their swift eyes run over the long
  deed,
  Unto the name, and to the legacies, 19
  What is bequeathed them there—
MOS.   "Ten suits of hangings—"
VOLP. [*Aside.*] Ay, i' their garters, Mosca.
  Now their hopes
  Are at the gasp.
VOLT.   Mosca the heir!
CORB.   What's that?
VOLP. [*Aside.*] My advocate is dumb.
  Look to my merchant;
  He has heard of some strange storm—
  a ship is lost;
  He faints. My lady will swoon. Old
  glazen-eyes,
  He hath not reached his despair yet.
CORB.   All these
  Are out of hope; I am, sure, the man.
                [*Takes the will.*]
CORV.   But, Mosca—
MOS. "Two cabinets—"
CORV.   Is this in earnest?
MOS.   "One
  Of ebony—"
CORV.   Or do you but delude me?
MOS. "The other, mother of pearl."—I'm
  very busy.   30
  Good faith, it is a fortune thrown upon
  me—

<hr>

[4] Fine linen.

"Item, one salt [1] of agate"—not my seeking.

LADY. Do you hear, sir?

MOS.   "A perfumed box"—pray you, forbear;

You see I am troubled—"made of an onyx—"

LADY.   How!

MOS. Tomorrow or next day, I shall be at leisure

To talk with you all.

CORV.   Is this my large hope's issue?

LADY. Sir, I must have a fairer answer.

MOS.   Madam!

Marry, and shall. Pray you, fairly quit my house.

Nay, raise no tempest with your looks; but, hark you,   39

Remember what your ladyship offered me

To put you in an heir; go to, think on 't,

And what you said e'en your best madams did

For maintenance; and why not you? Enough.

Go home, and use the poor Sir Pol, your knight, well,

For fear I tell some riddles. Go, be melancholic.   [*Exit Lady Would-be.*]

VOLP. [*Aside.*] O, my fine devil!

CORV.   Mosca, pray you a word.

MOS. Lord! Will not you take your despatch hence yet?

Methinks, of all, you should have been th' example.

Why should you stay here? With what thought, what promise?

Hear you! Do not you know I know you an ass?   50

And that you would most fain have been a wittol [2]

If fortune would have let you? That you are

A declared cuckold, on good terms? This pearl,

You'll say, was yours? Right. This diamant?

I'll not deny 't, but thank you. Much here else?

It may be so. Why, think that these good works

May help to hide your [3] bad. I'll not betray you;

[1] Saltcellar.
[2] A passive cuckold.   [3] Original reads *you.*

Although you be but extraordinary,

And have it only in title, it sufficeth.

Go home; be melancholy too, or mad.   60

             [*Exit Corvino.*]

VOLP. [*Aside.*] Rare Mosca! How his villainy becomes him!

VOLT. Certain he doth delude all these for me.

CORB. Mosca the heir?

VOLP. [*Aside.*]   O, his four eyes have found it.

CORB. I am cozened, cheated, by a parasite-slave;

Harlot, [4] t' hast gulled me.

MOS.   Yes, sir. Stop your mouth,

Or I shall draw the only tooth is left.

Are not you he, that filthy, covetous wretch,

With the three legs, [5] that here, in hope of prey,

Have, any time this three year, snuffed about

With your most grov'ling nose, and would have hired   70

Me to the pois'ning of my patron, sir?

Are not you he that have today in court

Professed the disinheriting of your son?

Perjured yourself? Go home, and die, and stink;

If you but croak a syllable, all comes out.

Away, and call your porters! Go, go, stink!   [*Exit Corbaccio.*]

VOLP. [*Aside.*] Excellent varlet!

VOLT.   Now, my faithful Mosca,

I find thy constancy—

MOS.   Sir?

VOLT.   Sincere.

MOS. [*Writing.*]   "A table

Of porphyry"—I marl [6] you'll be thus troublesome.

VOLT. Nay, leave off now; they are gone.

MOS.   Why, who are you?   80

What? Who did send for you? O, cry you mercy,

Reverend sir! Good faith, I am grieved for you,

That any chance of mine should thus defeat

Your (I must needs say) most deserving travails;

But I protest, sir, it was cast upon me,

And I could almost wish to be without it,

[4] Knave.
[5] In reference to his cane.   [6] Marvel.

But that the will o' th' dead must be
  observed.
Marry, my joy is that you need it not;
You have a gift, sir (thank your educa-
  tion),
Will never let you want, while there are
  men   90
And malice to breed causes.[1] Would I
  had
But half the like, for all my fortune, sir!
If I have any suits (as I do hope,
Things being so easy and direct, I shall
  not),
I will make bold with your obstreperous
  aid,
Conceive me—for your fee, sir. In mean-
  time,
You that have so much law, I know ha'
  the conscience
Not to be covetous of what is mine.
Good sir, I thank you for my plate;
  'twill help
To set up a young man. Good faith, you
  look   100
As you were costive; best go home and
  purge, sir.   [Exit Voltore.]
Volp. [Coming from behind the curtain.]
  Bid him eat lettuce well.[2] My witty
  mischief,
Let me embrace thee. O, that I could
  now
Transform thee to a Venus!—Mosca, go,
Straight take my habit of clarissimo,
And walk the streets. Be seen; torment
  hem more.
We must pursue as well as plot. Who
  would
Have lost this feast?
Mos.   I doubt it will lose them.
Volp. O, my recovery shall recover all.
  That I could now but think on some dis-
  guise   110
To meet hem in, and ask hem questions!
How I would vex hem still at every turn!
Mos. Sir, I can fit you.
Volp.   Canst thou?
Mos.   Yes, I know
One o' the commandadori,[3] sir, so like
  you;
Him will I straight make drunk, and
  bring you his habit.

[1] Lawsuits.
[2] I.e., as a soporific.
[3] Original has commandatori.

Volp. A rare disguise, and answering thy
  brain!
O, I will be a sharp disease unto hem.
Mos. Sir, you must look for curses—
Volp.   Till they burst;
The fox fares ever best when he is curst.
                                    [Exeunt.]

ACT V. SCENE iv.

[A room in Politic's house.]

Peregrine, [disguised,] Mercatori 3, Woman,
                                    Politic.[4]

[Per.] Am I enough disguised?
Mer. 1.   I warrant you.
Per. All my ambition is to fright him
  only.
Mer. 2. If you could ship him away,
  'twere excellent.
Mer. 3. To Zant or to Aleppo!
Per.   Yes, and ha' his
  Adventures put i' th' Book of Voyages,[5]
And his gulled story registered for truth.
Well, gentlemen, when I am in a while,
And that you think us warm in our dis-
  course,
Know your approaches.
Mer. 1.   Trust it to our care.
                          [Exeunt Mercatori.

Enter Woman.]

Per. Save you, fair lady! Is Sir Pol
  within?   10
Wom. I do not know, sir.
Per.   Pray you, say unto him
Here is a merchant, upon earnest busi-
  ness,
Desires to speak with him.
Wom.   I will see, sir. [Exit.]
Per.   Pray you.
I see the family is all female here.

[Enter Woman.]

Wom. He says, sir, he has weighty affairs
  of state
That now require him whole; some other
  time
You may possess him.
Per.   Pray you, say again,
If those require him whole, these will
  exact[6] him,

[4] Last two enter later.
[5] By Hakluyt.   [6] Finish off.

Whereof I bring him tidings.— [*Exit
Woman.*] What might be
His grave affair of state now? How to
make　　　　　　　　　　　20
Bolognian sausages here in Venice, spar-
ing
One o' th' ingredients!

[*Enter Woman.*]

Wom.　　　　Sir, he says he knows
By your word "tidings" that you are
no statesman,
And therefore wills you stay.
Per.　　Sweet, pray you, return [1] him:
I have not read so many proclamations,
And studied them for words as he has
done,
But—here he deigns to come.
　　　　　　　　　[*Exit Woman.*

Enter Sir Politic.]

Pol.　　　　　Sir, I must crave
Your courteous pardon. There hath
chanced today
Unkind disaster twixt my lady and me;
And I was penning my apology　　30
To give her satisfaction, as you came
now.
Per. Sir, I am grieved I bring you worse
disaster.
The gentleman you met at th' port to-
day,
That told you he was newly arrived—
Pol.　　　　　　　　Ay, was
A fugitive punk? [2]
Per.　　No, sir, a spy set on you;
And he has made relation to the senate
That you professed to him to have a
plot
To sell the state of Venice to the Turk.
Pol. O me!
Per. For which warrants are signed by
this time,
To apprehend you, and to search your
study　　　　　　　　　40
For papers—
Pol.　Alas, sir, I have none but notes
Drawn out of playbooks—
Per.　　　All the better, sir.
Pol. And some essays. What shall I do?
Per.　　　　　　　Sir, best
Convey yourself into a sugar chest,

Or, if you could lie round, a frail [3] were
rare,
And I could send you aboard.
Pol.　　　　Sir, I but talked so
For discourse' sake merely.
　　　　　　　　They knock without.
Per.　　　　Hark! They are there.
Pol. I am a wretch, a wretch!
Per.　　　　What will you do, sir?
Ha' you ne'er a curran-butt [4] to leap
into?
They'll put you to the rack; you must
be sudden.　　　　　　　50
Pol. Sir, I have an engine [5]—
Mer. 3. [*Within.*]　Sir Politic Would-be?
Mer. 2. [*Within.*]　Where is he?
Pol.　　　　　That I have
thought upon before time.
Per. What is it?
Pol.　(I shall ne'er endure the torture.)
Marry, it is, sir, of a tortoise shell,
Fitted for these extremities; pray you,
sir, help me. [*Brings out his contrivance.*]
Here I have a place, sir, to put back my
legs
(Please you to lay it on, sir), with this cap
And my black gloves. I'll lie, sir, like
a tortoise,
Till they are gone.
Per.　　And call you this an engine?
Pol. Mine own device.—Good sir, bid my
wife's women
To burn my papers.　　[*Exit Peregrine.*]

They rush in.

Mer. 1.　　　Where's he hid?
Mer. 3.　　　　　　We must
And will sure find him.
Mer. 2.　　Which is his study?

[*Enter Peregrine.*]

Mer. 1.　　　　　　　What
Are you, sir?
Per.　I am a merchant that came here
To look upon this tortoise.
Mer. 3.　　　　　How?
Mer. 1.　　　　　　St. Mark!
What beast is this?
Per.　　　It is a fish.
Mer. 2.　　　Come out here!

---

[3] A basket made of rushes.
[4] Wine cask.
[5] Contrivance.

[1] Answer.　　　　　　[2] Prostitute.

PER. Nay, you may strike him, sir, and
    tread upon him;
    He'll bear a cart.
MER. 1.   What, to run over him?
PER.   Yes.
MER. 3. Let's jump upon him.
MER. 2.   Can he not go?
PER.   He creeps, sir.
MER. 1. [*Drawing a weapon.*] Let's see him
    creep.
PER.   No, good sir, you will hurt him.
MER. 2. Heart, I'll see him creep, or prick
    his guts.   70
MER. 3. Come out here!
PER.   Pray you, sir.—(Creep a little!)
MER. 1.   Forth.
MER. 2. Yet furder.
PER.   Good sir!—(Creep!)
MER. 2.   We'll see his legs.
    They pull off the shell and discover him.
MER. 3. Godso, he has garters!
MER. 1.   Ay, and gloves!
MER. 2.   Is this
    Your fearful tortoise?
PER. [*Discovering himself.*]   Now, Sir
    Pol, we're even;
For your next project I shall be pre-
    pared.
I am sorry for the funeral of your notes,
    sir.
MER. 1. 'Twere a rare motion [1] to be seen
    in Fleet Street.
MER. 2. Ay, i' the term.
MER. 1.   Or Smithfield, in the fair.
MER. 3. Methinks 'tis but a melancholic
    sight.
PER.   Farewell, most politic tortoise!
    [*Exeunt Peregrine and Merchants.*

Enter Woman.]

POL.   Where's my lady?   80
    Knows she of this?
WOM.   I know not, sir.
POL.   Inquire.—
O, I shall be the fable of all feasts,
The freight of the *gazetti*,[2] ship boys'
    tale,
And, which is worst, even talk for ordi-
    naries.
WOM. My lady's come most melancholic
    home,

[1] Puppet show.
[2] The theme of the newspapers.

And says, sir, she will straight to sea
    for physic.
POL. And I, to shun this place and clime
    forever,
Creeping with house on back, and think
    it well
To shrink my poor head in my politic
    shell.   [*Exeunt*]

ACT V. SCENE v.

[*A room in Volpone's house.*]

*Volpone, Mosca, the first in the habit of a
commandadore, the other of a clarissimo.*

[VOLP.] Am I then like him?
MOS.   O, sir, you are he;
    No man can sever you.
VOLP.   Good.
MOS.   But what am I?
VOLP. Fore heaven, a brave clarissimo;
    thou becom'st it!
    Pity thou wert not born one.
MOS. [*Aside.*]   If I hold
    My made one, 'twill be well.
VOLP.   I'll go and see
    What news first at the court.   [*Exit.*
MOS.   Do so. My fox
Is out on his hole, and, ere he shall re-
    enter,
I'll make him languish in his borrowed
    case,[3]
Except he come to composition [4] with
    me.—
Androgyno, Castrone, Nano!

[*Enter Androgyno, Castrone, and Nano.*]

ALL.   Here!   10
MOS. Go, recreate yourselves abroad; go,
    sport.—   [*Exeunt.*
So, now I have the keys, and am pos-
    sessed.
Since he will needs be dead afore his
    time,
I'll bury him, or gain by him. I am his
    heir,
And so will keep me till he share at
    least.
To cozen him of all were but a cheat
Well placed; no man would construe it
    a sin.
Let his sport pay for 't. This is called
    the Fox Trap.   [*Exit.*]

[3] Disguise.   [4] Agreement, terms.

Act V. Scene vi.

[*A street.*]

Corbaccio, Corvino, Volpone.[1]

[Corb.] They say the court is set.

Corv.   We must maintain
Our first tale good, for both our reputations.

Corb. Why, mine's no tale; my son would
there have killed me.

Corv. That's true; I had forgot. Mine is,
I am sure.
But for your will, sir—

Corb.   Ay, I'll come upon him
For that hereafter, now his patron's dead.

[*Enter Volpone.*]

Volp. Signior Corvino! And Corbaccio!
Sir,
Much joy unto you.

Corv.   Of what?

Volp.   The sudden good
Dropped down upon you—

Corb.   Where?

Volp.   (And none knows how.)
From old Volpone, sir.

Corb.   Out, arrant knave! 10

Volp. Let not your too much wealth, sir,
make you furious.

Corb. Away, thou varlet!

Volp.   Why, sir?

Corb.   Dost thou mock me?

Volp. You mock the world, sir. Did you
not change wills?

Corb. Out, harlot!

Volp.   O! Belike you are the man,
Signior Corvino? Faith, you carry it
well;
You grow not mad withal. I love your
spirit.
You are not overleavened with your
fortune.
You should ha' some would swell now,
like a wine fat,[2]
With such an autumn.—Did he gi' you
all, sir?

Corv. Avoid, you rascal!

Volp.   Troth, your wife has shown 20
Herself a very woman; but you are
well.
You need not care; you have a good
estate

1 Enters later.   2 Vat.

To bear it out, sir, better by this
chance—
Except Corbaccio have a share?

Corb.   Hence, varlet!

Volp. You will not be a'known,[3] sir; why,
'tis wise.
Thus do all gamesters, at all games, dissemble;
No man will seem to win.—[*Exeunt Corvino and Corbaccio.*] Here comes my
vulture,
Heaving his beak up i' the air, and snuff-
ing.

Act V. Scene vii.

[*The same.*]

Voltore, Volpone.

[Volt.] Outstripped thus by a parasite?
A slave?
Would run on errands? And make legs [4]
for crumbs?
Well, what I'll do—

Volp.   The court stays for your [5]
worship.
I e'en rejoice, sir, at your worship's
happiness,
And that it fell into so learned hands,
That understand the fingering.

Volt.   What do you mean?

Volp. I mean to be a suitor to your wor-
ship,
For the small tenement out of repara-
tions [6]—
That at the end of your long row of
houses,
By the Piscaria. It was, in Volpone's
time,   10
Your predecessor, ere he grew diseased,
A handsome, pretty, customed [7] bawdy-
house
As any was in Venice, none dispraised,
But fell with him; his body and that
house
Decayed together.

Volt.   Come, sir, leave your prating.

Volp. Why, if your worship give me but
your hand
That I may ha' the refusal, I have done.
'Tis a mere toy to you, sir—candle-
rents.[8]

3 Acknown, recognized.   6 Out of repair.
4 Bows.   7 Well patronized.
5 Original reads *you*.   8 Pin money.

As your learned worship knows—
VOLT.   What do I know?
VOLP. Marry, no end of your wealth, sir;
   God decrease it!   20
VOLT. Mistaking knave! What, mock'st
   thou my misfortune?
VOLP. His blessing on your heart, sir;
   would 'twere more!—   [*Exit Voltore.*]
Now to my first again, at the next corner.
                                    [*Exit.*]

ACT V. SCENE viii.

[*The Senate.*]

Corbaccio, Corvino,   (Mosca   passant,)[1]
                               Volpone.

[CORB.] See, in our habit![2] See the impudent varlet!
CORV. That I could shoot mine eyes at
   him, like gunstones![3]

[*Enter Volpone.*]

VOLP. But is this true, sir, of the parasite?
CORB. Again, t' afflict us? Monster!
VOLP.   In good faith, sir,
   I am heartily grieved a beard of your
      grave length
   Should be so overreached.   I never
      brooked[4]
   That parasite's hair; methought his nose
      should cozen;
   There still was somewhat in his look
      did promise
   The bane of a clarissimo.
CORB.   Knave—
VOLP. [*To Corvino.*]   Methinks   9
   Yet you, that are so traded i' the world,
   A witty merchant, the fine bird, Corvino,
   That have such moral emblems[5] on
      your name,
   Should not have sung your[6] shame,
      and dropped your cheese
   To let the fox laugh at your emptiness.
CORV. Sirrah, you think the privilege of
   the place
   And your red, saucy cap, that seems to
      me

[1] *I.e.,* passing over the stage.
[2] *I.e.,* of a clarissimo.
[3] Cannon balls.
[4] Could endure.
[5] Allegorical pictures with mottoes.
[6] Original reads *you.*

Nailed to your jolthead[7] with those
   two cecchines,[8]
Can warrant your abuses.   Come you
   hither;
You shall perceive, sir, I dare beat you.
   Approach!
VOLP. No haste, sir; I do know your valure
   well,   20
Since you durst publish what you are,
   sir.
CORV.   Tarry;
   I'ld speak with you.
VOLP.   Sir, sir, another time—
CORV. Nay, now.
VOLP.   O God, sir! I were a wise man,
   Would stand the fury of a distracted
   cuckold.   *Mosca walks by hem.*
CORB. What, come again?
VOLP. [*Aside.*]   Upon hem, Mosca;
   save me.
CORB. The   air's   infected   where   he
   breathes.
CORV.   Let's fly him.
         [*Exeunt Corvino and Corbaccio.*]
VOLP. Excellent basilisk! Turn upon the
   vulture.

ACT V. SCENE ix.

[*The same.*]

Voltore, Mosca, Volpone.

[VOLT.] Well, flesh fly, it is summer with
   you now;
   Your winter will come on.
MOS.   Good advocate,
   Pray thee not rail, nor threaten out of
      place thus;
   Thou'lt make a solecism, as madam
      says.
   Get you a biggin[9] more; your brain
      breaks loose.   [*Exit.*]
VOLT. Well, sir.
VOLP.   Would you ha' me beat the inso-
   lent slave?
   Throw dirt upon his first good clothes?
VOLT.   This same
   Is doubtless some familiar.[10]
VOLP.   Sir, the court,
   In troth, stays for you.   I am mad, a
      mule
   That never read Justinian should get
      up   10

[7] Blockhead.   [9] Lawyer's coif.
[8] *I.e.,* gold buttons.   [10] Familiar spirit.

And ride an advocate. Had you no quirk
To avoid gullage, sir, by such a creature?
I hope you do but jest; he has not done 't.
This 's but confederacy to blind the rest.
You are the heir?
VOLT.　　　　　　A strange, officious,
Troublesome knave! Thou dost torment me.
VOLP.　　I know—
It cannot be, sir, that you should be cozened.
'Tis not within the wit of man to do it;
You are so wise, so prudent; and 'tis fit
That wealth and wisdom still should go together.　　　　[Exeunt.]　20

ACT V. SCENE x.

[The same.]

Avocatori 4, Notario, Commandadore, Bonario, Celia, Corbaccio, Corvino, Voltore, Volpone.

[AVOC. 1.] Are all the parties here ?
NOT.　　　　　　All but the advocate.
AVOC. 2. And here he comes.

[Enter Voltore and Volpone.]

AVOC. [1.]　　Then bring hem forth to sentence.
VOLT. O, my most honored fathers, let your mercy
Once win upon your justice, to forgive—
I am distracted—
(VOLP.　　　What will he do now?)
VOLT.[1]　　　　　　　　　O,
I know not which t' address myself to first,
Whether your fatherhoods or these innocents—
(CORV. Will he betray himself?)
VOLT.　　　　　　Whom equally
I have abused, out of most covetous ends—
(CORV. The man is mad!
CORB.　　　　What's that?
CORV.　　　　　He is possessed.)　10
VOLT. For which, now strook in conscience, here I prostrate
Myself at your offended feet for pardon.
AVOC. 1, 2. Arise.

[1] Original reads Volp.

CEL.　　　　O heaven, how just thou art!
VOLP. [Aside.]　　　　　I am caught
I' mine own noose—
CORV. [To Corbaccio.]　　Be constant, sir; naught now
Can help but impudence.
AVOC. 1.　　　　Speak forward.
COM.　　　　　　　Silence!
VOLT. It is not passion in me, reverend fathers,
But only conscience, conscience, my good sires,
That makes me now tell truth. That parasite,
That knave, hath been the instrument of all.
AVOC. [1.] Where is that knave? Fetch him.
VOLP.　　I go.　　　　　　[Exit.]
CORV.　　　　Grave fathers,　20
This man's distracted; he confessed it now;
For, hoping to be old Volpone's heir,
Who now is dead—
AVOC. 3.　　　　How?
AVOC. 2.　　　　Is Volpone dead?
CORV. Dead since, grave fathers—
BON.　　　　O sure vengeance!
AVOC. 1.　　　　　　Stay!
Then he was no deceiver?
VOLT.　　　　　O, no, none;
The parasite, grave fathers.
CORV.　　　　　He does speak
Out of mere envy, cause the servant's made
The thing he gaped for. Please your fatherhoods,
This is the truth, though I'll not justify
The other, but he may be somedeal[2] faulty.　30
VOLT. Ay, to your hopes as well as mine, Corvino;
But I'll use modesty.[3] Pleaseth your wisdoms
To view these certain notes, and but confer[4] them;
As I hope favor, they shall speak clear truth.
CORV. The devil has entered him!
BON.　　　　　Or bides in you.
AVOC. 4. We have done ill, by a public officer
To send for him, if he be heir.

[2] Somewhat.　　[3] Moderation.　　[4] Compare.

Avoc. 2.　　　　　　　For whom?

Avoc. 4. Him that they call the parasite.

Avoc. 3.　　　　　　　　　'Tis true;
He is a man of great estate, now left.

Avoc. 4. Go you, and learn his name, and
　　say the court　　　　　　　　40
　　Entreats his presence here, but to the
　　clearing
　　Of some few doubts.　　[*Exit Notario.*]

Avoc. 2.　　　　This same's a labyrinth!

Avoc. 1. Stand you unto your first report?

Corv.　　　　　　　　　　My state,
　　My life, my fame—

(Bon.　　　　　Where is 't?)

Corv.　　　　　　　Are at the stake.

Avoc. 1. Is yours so too?

Corb.　　　　　The advocate's a knave,
　　And has a forkéd tongue—

Avoc. 2.　　　　　Speak to the point.[1]

Corb. So is the parasite too.

Avoc. 1.　　　　　　This is confusion.

Volt. I do beseech your fatherhoods,
　　read but those—　[*Gives them papers.*]

Corv. And credit nothing the false spirit
　　hath writ.
　　It cannot be but he is possessed, grave
　　fathers. [*Exeunt.*]　　　　　50

Act V. Scene xi.

[*A street.*]

Volpone, Nano, Androgyno, Castrone.[2]

[Volp.] To make a snare for mine own
　　neck, and run
My head into it willfully, with laughter,
When I had newly scaped, was free and
　　clear!
Out of mere wantonness! O, the dull
　　devil
Was in this brain of mine when I de-
　　vised it,
And Mosca gave it second; he must now
Help to sear up this vein, or we bleed
　　dead.—

[*Enter Nano, Androgyno, and Castrone.*]

How now! Who let you loose? Whither
　　go you now?
What, to buy gingerbread, or to drown
　　kittlings?[3]

[1] This speech is printed in parenthesis in the
original.
[2] Last three enter later.　　　[3] Kittens.

Nan. Sir, Master Mosca called us out of
　　doors,　　　　　　　　　　10
And bid us all go play, and took the keys.

And. Yes.

Volp.　　Did Master Mosca take the keys?
Why, so!
I am farder in. These are my fine con-
　　ceits!
I must be merry, with a mischief to me!
What a vile wretch was I, that could
　　not bear
My fortune soberly? I must ha' my
　　crotchets
And my conundrums! Well, go you,
　　and seek him;
His meaning may be truer than my fear.
Bid him, he straight come to me to the
　　court;
Thither will I, and, if 't be possible,　20
Unscrew my advocate, upon new hopes.
When I provoked him, then I lost my-
　　self.　　　　　　　　　[*Exeunt.*]

Act V. Scene xii.

[*The Senate.*]

Avocatori, etc.

[Avoc. 1.] These things can ne'er be
　　reconciled. He here
　　　　　　　[*Points to the papers.*]
Professeth that the gentleman was
　　wronged,
And that the gentlewoman was brought
　　thither,
Forced by her husband, and there left.

Volt.　　　　　　　　　Most true.

Cel. How ready is heaven to those that
　　pray!

Avoc. 1.　　　　But that
Volpone would have ravished her, he
　　holds
Utterly false, knowing his impotence.

Corv. Grave fathers, he is possessed;
　　again, I say,
Possessed; nay, if there be possession
And obsession, he has both.

Avoc. 3.　　　Here comes our officer.　10

[*Enter Volpone.*]

Volp. The parasite will straight be here,
　　grave fathers.

Avoc. 4. You might invent some other
　　name, Sir Varlet.

Avoc. 3. Did not the notary meet him?

Volp.   Not that I know.

Avoc. 4. His coming will clear all.

Avoc. 2.   Yet it is misty.

Volt. May 't please your fatherhoods—
Volpone whispers the Advocate.

Volp.   Sir, the parasite
Willed me to tell you that his master
lives;
That you are still the man; your hopes
the same;
And this was only a jest—

Volt.   How?

Volp.   Sir, to try
If you were firm, and how you stood
affected.

Volt. Art sure he lives?

Volp.   Do I live, sir?

Volt.   O me! 20
I was too violent.

Volp.   Sir, you may redeem it.
They said you were possessed; fall
down, and seem so.
I'll help to make it good.—(*Voltore falls.*)
God bless the man!—
(Stop your wind hard, and swell.) See,
see, see, see!
He vomits crooked pins! His eyes are
set,
Like a dead hare's hung in a poulter's
shop!
His mouth's running away! Do you
see, signior?
Now 'tis in his belly.

(Corv.   Ay, the devil!)

Volp. Now in his throat.

(Corv.   Ay, I perceive it plain.)

Volp. 'Twill out, 'twill out! Stand clear.
See where it flies,   30
In shape of a blue toad, with a bat's
wings!
Do not you see it, sir?

Corb.   What? I think I do.

Corv. 'Tis too manifest.

Volp.   Look! He comes t' himself!

Volt. Where am I?

Volp.   Take good heart; the worst
is past, sir.
You're dispossessed.

Avoc. 1.   What accident is
this?

Avoc. [2.] Sudden and full of wonder!

Avoc. 3.   If he were
Possessed, as it appears, all this is
nothing.

Corv. He has been often subject to
these fits.

Avoc. 1. Show him that writing.—Do
you know it, sir?

Volp. [*Whispering to Voltore.*] Deny it,
sir; forswear it; know it not.   40

Volt. Yes, I do know it well; it is my hand.
But all that it contains is false.

Bon.   O, practice! [1]

Avoc. 2. What maze is this!

Avoc. 1.   Is he not guilty then
Whom you there name the parasite?

Volt.   Grave fathers,
No more than his good patron, old
Volpone.

Avoc. 4. Why, he is dead.

Volt.   O, no, my honored fathers,
He lives—

Avoc. 1.   How! Lives?

Volt.   Lives.

Avoc. 2.   This is subtler yet!

Avoc. 3. You said he was dead.

Volt.   Never.

Avoc. 3.   You said so.

Corv.   I heard so.

Avoc. 4. Here comes the gentleman; make
him way.

[*Enter Mosca.*]

Avoc. 3.   A stool!

Avoc. 4. [*Aside.*] A proper man; and,
were Volpone dead,   50
A fit match for my daughter.

Avoc. 3.   Give him way.

Volp. [*Aside to Mosca.*] Mosca, I was
a'most lost; the advocate
Had betrayed all; but now it is recovered.
All's o' the hinge again.—Say I am
living.

Mos. What busy knave is this!—Most
reverend fathers,
I sooner had attended your grave pleas-
ures,
But that my order for the funeral
Of my dear patron did require me—

(Volp.   Mosca!)

Mos. Whom I intend to bury like a
gentleman.

Volp. [*Aside.*] Ay, quick,[2] and cozen me
of all.

Avoc. 2. Still stranger!   60
More intricate!

---

[1] Deceit.   [2] Alive.

AVOC. 1.　　　　　And come about again!

AVOC. 4. [*Aside.*] It is a match; my daughter is bestowed.

(MOS. Will you gi' me half?

VOLP.　　　　　First I'll be hanged.

MOS.　　　　　I know Your voice is good; cry not so loud.)

AVOC. 1.　　　　　Demand The advocate.—Sir, did you not affirm Volpone was alive?

VOLP.　　　　　Yes, and he is; This gent'man told me so.—(Thou shalt have half.)

MOS. Whose drunkard is this same? Speak, some that know him; I never saw his face.—(I cannot now Afford it you so cheap.

VOLP.　　　No?)

AVOC. 1.　　　　　What say you?　　70

VOLT. The officer told me.

VOLP.　　　　　I did, grave fathers, And will maintain he lives, with mine own life, And that this creature [*Points to Mosca.*] told me.—(I was born With all good stars my enemies.)

MOS.　　　　　Most grave fathers, If such an insolence as this must pass Upon me, I am silent; 'twas not this For which you sent, I hope.

AVOC. 2.　　　　　Take him away.

(VOLP. Mosca!)

AVOC. 3.　　　Let him be whipped.

(VOLP.　　　　　Wilt thou betray me? Cozen me?)

AVOC. 3.　　　And taught to bear himself Toward a person of his rank.

AVOC. 4.　　　　　Away!　80 [*Commendadore seizes Volpone.*]

MOS. I humbly thank your fatherhoods.

VOLP.　　　　　Soft, soft!— [*Aside.*] Whipped? And lose all that I have? If I confess, It cannot be much more.

AVOC. 4.　　　Sir, are you married?

VOLP. They'll be allied anon; I must be resolute. The fox shall here uncase.

　　　　　He puts off his disguise.

(MOS.　　　　　Patron!)

VOLP.　　　　　Nay, now

My ruins shall not come alone; your match I'll hinder sure. My substance shall not glue you, Nor screw you, into a family.

(MOS.　　　　　Why, patron!)

VOLP. I am Volpone, and this is my knave;　　　[*Points to Mosca.*] This [*To Voltore.*] his own knave; this [*To Corbaccio.*] avarice's fool;　90 This [*To Corvino.*] a chimera of wittol, fool, and knave; And, reverend fathers, since we all can hope Naught but a sentence, let's not now despair it. You hear me brief.

CORV.　May it please your fatherhoods—

COM.　　　　　Silence!

AVOC. 1. The knot is now undone by miracle.

AVOC. 2. Nothing can be more clear.

AVOC. 3.　　　Or can more prove These innocent.

AVOC. 1.　　　Give hem their liberty. [*Bonario and Celia are released.*]

BON. Heaven could not long let such gross crimes be hid.

AVOC. 1. If this be held the highway to get riches, May I be poor!

AVOC. 3.　This 's not the gain, but torment.　　　100

AVOC. 1. These possess wealth, as sick men possess fevers, Which trulier may be said to possess them.

AVOC. 2. Disrobe that parasite.

CORV. }
MOS. }　　　Most honored fathers—

AVOC. 1. Can you plead aught to stay the course of justice? If you can, speak.

CORV. }
VOLT. }　　　We beg favor.

CEL.　　　　　And mercy.

AVOC. 1. You hurt your innocence, suing for the guilty. Stand forth; and first the parasite. You appear T' have been the chiefest minister, if not plotter, In all these lewd impostures, and now, lastly,

Have with your impudence abused [1]
the court,   110
And habit of a gentleman of Venice,
Being a fellow of no birth or blood—
For which our sentence is, first, thou be
whipped,
Then live perpetual prisoner in our
galleys.

VOLP. I thank you for him.

MOS.   Bane to thy wolvish nature!

AVOC. 1. Deliver him to the saffi.— [*Mosca
is led away.*] Thou, Volpone,
By blood and rank a gentleman, canst
not fall
Under like censure; but our judgment
on thee
Is that thy substance all be straight
confiscate
To the hospital of the Incurabili;   120
And, since the most was gotten by
imposture,
By feigning lame, gout, palsy, and
such diseases,
Thou art to lie in prison, cramped with
irons,
Till thou beest sick and lame indeed.
Remove him!
     [*Volpone is removed from the bar.*]

VOLP. This is called mortifying of a
fox.

AVOC. 1. Thou, Voltore, to take away the
scandal
Thou hast giv'n all worthy men of thy
profession,
Art banished from their fellowship and
our state.—
Corbaccio!—Bring him near.—We here
possess   129
Thy son of all thy state,[2] and confine
thee
To the monastery of San Spirito,
Where, since thou knew'st not how to
live well here,
Thou shalt be learned to die well.

CORB.   Ha! What said he?

COM. You shall know anon, sir.

AVOC. [1.]   Thou, Corvino, shalt

[1] Imposed on.   [2] Estate.

Be straight embarked from thine own
house, and rowed
Round about Venice, through the Grand
Canal,
Wearing a cap, with fair, long ass's ears,
Instead of horns, and so to mount, a
paper
Pinned on thy breast, to the *berlino!*[3]

CORV.   Yes,
And have mine eyes beat out with stink-
ing fish,   140
Bruised fruit, and rotten eggs—'tis well.
I am glad
I shall not see my shame yet.

AVOC. 1.   And, to expiate
Thy wrongs done to thy wife, thou art
to send her
Home to her father, with her dowry
trebled.
And these are all your judgments—

(ALL.   Honored fathers—)

AVOC. 1. Which may not be revoked.
Now you begin,
When crimes are done and past, and
to be punished,
To think what your crimes are. Away
with them!
Let all that see these vices thus re-
warded,
Take heart, and love to study hem.
Mischiefs feed   150
Like beasts, till they be fat, and then
they bleed.   [*Exeunt.*]

Volpone [*comes forward*].

The seasoning of a play is the applause.
Now, though the fox be punished by
the laws,
He yet doth hope there is no suff'ring due
For any fact which he hath done gainst
you.
If there be, censure him; here he doubt-
ful stands.
If not, fare jovially, and clap your
hands.   [*Exit.*]

THE END.

[3] Pillory.

This comedy was first acted in the year 1605 by the King's Majesty's Servants.
The principal comedians were:

Ric. Burbadge	*Will. Sly*	*Joh. Lowin*
Hen. Condell	*Joh. Hemings*	*Alex. Cooke*

With the allowance of the Master of Revels.

THE ALCHEMIST[1]

BY

BEN JONSON

[TO THE READER [2]

If thou beest more, thou art an understander, and then I trust thee. If thou art one that tak'st up,[3] and but a pretender, beware at what hands thou receiv'st thy commodity, for thou wert never more fair in the way to be cozened than in this age in poetry, especially in plays—wherein now the concupiscence of jigs and dances[4] so reigneth, as to run away from nature and be afraid of her is the only point of art [10 that tickles the spectators. But how out of purpose and place do I name art, when the professors[5] are grown so obstinate contemners of it, and presumers on their own naturals,[6] as they are deriders of all diligence that way, and, by simple mocking at the terms when they understand not the things, think to get off wittily with their ignorance? Nay, they are esteemed the more learned and sufficient for this by [20 the multitude,[7] through their excellent vice[8] of judgment, for they commend writers as they do fencers or wrastlers, who, if they come in robustuously[9] and put for it with a great deal of violence, are received for the braver fellows, when many times their own rudeness is the cause of their disgrace, and a little touch of their adversary gives all that boisterous force the foil.[10] I deny not but that these men who always seek to [30 do more than enough may sometime happen on something that is good and great, but very seldom. And, when it comes, it doth not recompense the rest of their ill. It sticks out, perhaps, and is more eminent, because all is sordid and vile about it, as lights are more discerned in a thick darkness than a faint shadow. I speak not this out of a hope to do good on any man against his will, for I know, if it were put to the question of [40 theirs and mine, the worse would find more suffrages, because the most favor common errors. But I give thee this warning, that there is a great difference between those that (to gain the opinion of copy[11]) utter[12] all they can, however unfitly, and those that use election and a mean.[13] For it is only the disease of the unskillful to think rude things greater than polished, or scattered more numerous than composed.] 50

THE PERSONS OF THE PLAY

SUBTLE, *the alchemist.*
FACE, *the housekeeper.*
DOLL COMMON, *their colleague.*
DAPPER, *a [lawyer's] clerk.*

DRUGGER, *a tabacco-man.*[14]
LOVEWIT, *master of the house.*
EPICURE MAMMON, *a knight.*
[PERTINAX] SURLY, *a gamester.*
TRIBULATION [WHOLESOME], *a pastor of Amsterdam.*
ANANIAS, *a deacon there.*
KASTRIL, *the angry boy.*
DA[ME] PLIANT, *his sister, a widow.*
NEIGHBORS.
OFFICERS.
MUTES.

[1] The title continues: "A Comedy, Acted in the Year 1610 by the King's Majesty's Servants." After the title-page appears a dedication to Mary, Lady Wroth.
[2] This address appears in the 1612 edn. only.
[3] *I.e.,* a person who accepts other peoples' judgments on faith.
[4] The Hoe copy reads *dances and antics.*
[5] Practitioners.
[6] Natural endowments.
[7] The Hoe copy reads *many.*
[8] Surpassing deficiency.
[9] Robustiously.

[10] An incomplete fall in wrestling.
[11] Copious supply, abundance of wit.
[12] Publish.
[13] Selection and moderation.   [14] Tobacconist.

THE SCENE: [*A house in the Blackfriars district,*] *London.*

[TIME: *A single day in the autumn of 1610.*]

THE ARGUMENT [1]

T he sickness [2] hot, a master quit, for fear,
H is house in town and left one servant
     there.
E ase him corrupted, and gave means to
     know
A cheater and his punk,[3] who, now brought
     low,
L eaving their narrow practice, were be-
     come
C oz'ners at large, and, only wanting some
H ouse to set up, with him they here con-
     tract
E ach for a share, and all begin to act.
M uch company they draw and much
     abuse,[4]   9
I n casting figures,[5] telling fortunes, news,
S elling of flies,[6] flat bawdry, with the
     stone,[7]
T ill it and they and all in fume are gone.

PROLOGUE

Fortune, that favors fools, these two short
     hours
   We wish away, both for your sakes and
     ours,
Judging spectators; and desire in place,
   To th' author justice, to ourselves but
     grace.
Our scene is London, cause we would make
     known
   No country's mirth is better than our
     own;
No clime breeds better matter for your
     whore,
   Bawd, squire, impostor, many persons
     more,
Whose manners, now called humors, feed
     the stage,
   And which have still [8] been subject for
     the rage   10
Or spleen of comic writers. Though, this
     pen
   Did never aim to grieve, but better, men,
Howe'er the age he lives in doth endure

The vices that she breeds, above their
     cure.
But, when the wholesome remedies are
     sweet
And in their working gain and profit
     meet,
He hopes to find no spirit so much diseased
   But will with such fair correctives be
     pleased;
For here he doth not fear who can apply.
   If there be any that will sit so nigh   20
Unto the stream, to look what it doth run,
   They shall find things they'ld think or
     wish were done;
They are so natural follies, but so shown,
   As even the doers may see, and yet not
     own.

ACT I. SCENE i.

[*A room in Lovewit's house.*] [9]

Face, Subtle, Doll Common.

[FACE.] Believe 't, I will.
SUB.   Thy worst. I fart at thee!
DOLL. Ha' you your wits? Why, gentle-
     men! For love—
FACE. Sirrah, I'll strip you—
SUB.   What to do? Lick figs [10]
   Out at my—
FACE.   Rogue, rogue, out of all your
     sleights! [11]
DOLL. Nay, look ye! Sovereign, general,
     are you madmen?
SUB. O, let the wild sheep loose. I'll gum
     your silks
   With good strong water,[12] an [13] you come.
DOLL.   Will you have
   The neighbors hear you? Will you betray
     all?
   Hark! I hear somebody.
FACE.   Sirrah—
SUB.   I shall mar
   All that the tailor has made, if you
     approach.   10

[9] The scene and the action are continuous
throughout the act.
[10] For this vulgar allusion, *cf.* Rabelais, bk. IV,
ch. 45.
[11] Cease your tricks!
[12] *I.e.,* some chemical preparation which he
carries in his hand.   [13] If.

---

[1] Summary of the plot.   [5] Horoscopes.
[2] The plague.   [6] Familiar spirits.
[3] Mistress.   [7] Philosophers' stone.
[1] Deceive.   [8] Always

FACE. You most notorious whelp, you insolent slave,
Dare you do this?

SUB.   Yes. faith; yes, faith.

FACE.   Why, who
Am I, my mungril? [1] Who am I?

SUB.   I'll tell you,
Since you know not yourself.

FACE.   Speak lower, rogue.

SUB. Yes. You were once (time's not long
past) the good,
Honest, plain, livery-three-pound-thrum [2]
that kept
Your master's worship's house here in the
Friars [3]
For the vacations [4]—

FACE.   Will you be so loud?

SUB. Since, by my means, translated sub-
urb-captain. [5]

FACE. By your means, Doctor Dog?

SUB.   Within man's memory,   20
All this I speak of.

FACE.   Why, I pray you, have I
Been countenanced by you, or you by
me?
Do but collect, [6] sir, where I met you
first.

SUB. I do not hear well.

FACE.   Not of this, I think it.
But I shall put you in mind, sir—at Pie
Corner,
Taking your meal of steam in from cooks'
stalls,
Where, like the father of hunger, you did
walk
Piteously costive, with your pinched
horn-nose
And your complexion of the Roman
wash, [7]
Stuck full of black and melancholic
worms,   30
Like poulder corns [8] shot at th' artillery
yard.

SUB. I wish you could advance your voice
a little.

FACE. When you went pinned up in the
several rags
Yo' had raked and picked from dunghills
before day,
Your feet in moldy slippers for your
kibes, [9]
A felt of rug, [10] and a thin-threaden cloak
That scarce would cover your no-
buttocks—

SUB.   So, sir!

FACE. When all your *alchemy* and your
algebra,
Your *minerals, vegetals,* and *animals*, [11]
Your conjuring, coz'ning, and your dozen
of trades   40
Could not relieve your corpse with so
much linen
Would make you tinder but to see a
fire, [12]
I ga' you count'nance, credit for your
coals,
Your stills, your glasses, your *materials*,
Built you a fornace, [13] drew you cus-
tomers,
Advanced all your black arts, lent you,
beside,
A house to practice in—

SUB.   Your master's house?

FACE. Where you have studied the more
thriving skill
Of bawdry since.

SUB.   Yes, in your master's house.
You and the rats here kept possession.
Make it not strange. [14] I know yo' were
one could keep   51
The butt'ry-hatch still locked and save
the chippings, [15]
Sell the dole-beer [16] to aqua-vitæ-men, [17]
The which, together with your Christ-
mas vails [18]
At post-and-pair, [19] your letting out of
counters, [20]
Made you a pretty stock, some twenty
marks,

[9] Chilblains.   [10] A hat of coarse cloth.
[11] Throughout the play Jonson italicizes terms
associated with alchemy. The present editors
have not glossed these except where intelligibility demands.
[12] *I.e.*, as would make you sufficient tinder to
provide a fire.   [13] Furnace.
[14] Do not counterfeit ignorance.
[15] Scraps of bread.
[16] Beer intended to be given to the poor.
[17] Liquor-dealers.   [19] A game of cards.
[18] Tips.   [20] *I.e.*, to the gamesters.

[1] Mongrel.
[2] An inferior servant wearing a livery made out
of weaver's warp.
[3] The Blackfriars, a district in London.
[4] *I.e.*, between the terms of court.
[5] Pander, since the stews were generally located in the suburbs.
[6] Recollect.
[7] *I.e.*, swarthy (?).
[8] Powder corns, grains of powder.

And gave you credit to converse with
cobwebs
Here since your mistress' death hath
broke up house.
FACE. You might talk softlier, rascal.
SUB.   No, you scarab,
I'll thunder you in pieces. I will teach
you   60
How to beware to tempt a Fury again
That carries tempest in his hand and
voice.
FACE. The place has made you valiant.
SUB.   No, your clothes.
Thou vermin, have I ta'en thee out of
dung,
So poor, so wretched, when no living
thing
Would keep thee company but a spider
or worse?
Raised thee from brooms, and dust, and
wat'ring-pots,
Sublimed thee, and *exalted* thee, and
fixed thee
I' the *third region*, called our *state of
grace?*
Wrought thee to *spirit*, to *quintessence*,
with pains   70
Would twice have won me the *philos-
ophers' work?*
Put thee in words and fashion? Made
thee fit
For more than ordinary fellowships?
Giv'n thee thy oaths, thy quarreling
dimensions?
Thy rules to cheat at horse race, cockpit,
cards,
Dice, or whatever gallant tincture [1] else?
Made thee a second in mine own great
art?
And have I this for thank? Do you
rebel?
Do you fly out i' the *projection?* [2]
Would you be gone now?
DOLL.   Gentlemen, what mean you?   80
Will you mar all?
SUB.   Slave, thou hadst had no name—
DOLL. Will you undo yourselves with
civil war?
SUB. Never been known, past *equi cliba-
num*,
The heat of horse dung, under ground,
in cellars,

[1] Inclination to gallantry.
[2] On the completion of the experiment.

Or an alehouse darker than deaf John's—
been lost
To all mankind but laundresses and
tapsters,
Had not I been.
DOLL.   Do you know who hears you,
sovereign?
FACE. Sirrah—
DOLL.   Nay, general, I thought you
were civil.
FACE. I shall turn desperate, if you grow
thus loud.
SUB. And hang thyself, I care not.
FACE.   Hang thee, collier,   90
And all thy pots and pans! In picture
I will,
Since thou hast moved me—
[3] (DOLL.   O, this'll o'erthrow all.)
FACE. Write thee up bawd in Paul's, [4] have
all thy tricks
Of coz'ning with a hollow coal, dust,
scrapings,
Searching for things lost, with a sieve and
shears,
Erecting *figures* in your rows of *houses*,
And taking in of shadows with a glass, [5]
Told [6] in red letters, and a face cut for
thee
Worse than Gamaliel Ratsey's. [7]
DOLL.   Are you sound?
Ha' you your senses, masters?
FACE.   I will have   100
A book, but barely reckoning thy im-
postures,
Shall prove a true *philosophers' stone* to
printers.
SUB. Away, you trencher-rascal!
FACE.   Out, you dog leech!
The vomit of all prisons—
DOLL.   Will you be
Your own destructions, gentlemen?
FACE.   Still spewed out
For lying too heavy o' the basket. [8]
SUB.   Cheater!
FACE. Bawd!

[3] Jonson frequently encloses in parenthesis
passages that are aside or are incidental to the
main action.
[4] St. Paul's Cathedral, a common meeting
place for all London.
[5] A method of divination.
[6] Written.
[7] A highwayman hanged in 1605.
[8] Taking more than his share of the prisoners'
food.

SUB.   Cowherd!
FACE.   Conjurer!
SUB.   Cutpurse!
FACE.   Witch!
DOLL.   O me!
We are ruined, lost! Ha' you no more
    regard
To your reputations? Where's your
    judgment? 'Slight,[1]
Have yet some care of me, o' your
    republic—   110
FACE. Away, this brach![2] I'll bring thee,
    rogue, within
The statute of sorcery, tricesimo tertio
Of Harry the Eight,[3] ay, and perhaps
    thy neck
Within a noose, for laund'ring [4] gold and
    barbing [5] it.
DOLL. You'll bring your head within a
    coxcomb,[6] will you?

She catcheth out Face his sword, and breaks
                     Subtle's glass.

And you, sir, with your *menstrue!* [7]
    Gather it up.
'Sdeath, you abominable pair of stink-
    ards,
Leave off your barking, and grow one
    again,
Or, by the light that shines, I'll cut your
    throats.
I'll not be made a prey unto the mar-
    shal [8]   120
For ne'er a snarling dogbolt [9] o' you both.
Ha' you together cozened all this while
And all the world, and shall it now be
    said
Yo' have made most courteous shift to
    cozen yourselves?—
[*To Face.*] You will accuse him? You
    will bring him in
Within the statute? Who shall take your
    word—
A whoreson, upstart, apocryphal cap-
    tain,
Whom not a Puritan in Blackfriars will
    trust

---

[1] By God's light, a mild oath. *Cf.* also *Od's
precious*, *'Slid*, etc.   [2] Bitch.
[3] In the thirty-third year of Henry the
Eighth, *i.e.*, 1541.
[4] "Sweating," *i.e.*, washing in acid.
[5] Clipping.   [7] Solvent.
[6] Fool's cap.   [8] Prison warden.
[9] Useless arrow; hence, a worthless thing.

So much as for a feather?—[*To Subtle.*]
    And you too
Will give the cause, forsooth? You will
    insult,[10]   130
And claim a primacy in the divisions?
You must be chief, as if you only had
The poulder to project [11] with, and the
    work
Were not begun out of equality?
The venter [12] tripartite? All things in
    common?
Without priority? 'Sdeath, you per-
    petual curs,
Fall to your couples again, and cozen
    kindly
And heartily and lovingly, as you should,
And lose not the beginning of a term,[13]
Or, by this hand, I shall grow factious
    too   140
And take my part and quit you.
FACE.   'Tis his fault;
He ever murmurs, and objects his pains,
And says the weight of all lies upon
    him.
SUB. Why, so it does.
DOLL.   How does it? Do not we
    Sustain our parts?
SUB.   Yes, but they are not equal.
DOLL. Why, if your part exceed today, I
    hope
Ours may tomorrow match it.
SUB.   Ay, they *may*.
DOLL. "May," murmuring mastiff? Ay,
    and do. Death on me!
Help me to thrattle [14] him.
               [*Strives to choke him.*]
SUB.   Dorothy! Mistress Dorothy!
Od's precious, I'll do anything. What
    do you mean?   150
DOLL. Because o' your *fermentation* and
    cibation?
SUB. Not I, by heaven—
DOLL.   Your *Sol* and *Luna*—[*To Face.*]
    Help me!
SUB. Would I were hanged then! I'll
    conform myself.
DOLL. Will you, sir? Do so then, and
    quickly. Swear.
SUB. What should I swear?

---

[10] Behave insolently.
[11] Apply the elixir to the metal to be transmuted.   [12] Venture.
[13] A term of court, when London was crowded
with visitors.   [14] Throttle.

Doll.   To leave your faction, sir,
And labor kindly in the commune [1] work.
Sub. Let me not breathe if I meant aught
  beside.
  I only used those speeches as a spur
  To him.
Doll.   I hope we need no spurs, sir.
  Do we?
Face. 'Slid, prove today who shall shark [2]
  best.
Sub.   Agreed.   160
Doll. Yes, and work close and friendly.
Sub.   'Slight, the knot
  Shall grow the stronger for this breach,
    with me.   [They shake hands.]
Doll. Why, so, my good baboons! Shall
    we go make
  A sort [3] of sober, scurvy, precise neigh-
    bors, [4]
  That scarce have smiled twice sin' the
    king came in, [5]
  A feast of laughter at our follies? Rascals,
  Would run themselves from breath to see
    me ride, [6]
  Or you t' have but a hole to thrust your
    heads in,
  For which you should pay ear-rent. [7] No,
    agree.
  And may Don Provost [8] ride a-feasting [9]
    long   170
  In his old velvet jerkin and stained
    scarfs,
  My noble sovereign and worthy general,
  Ere we contribute a new crewel [10] garter
  To his most worsted worship.
Sub.   Royal Doll!
  Spoken like Claridiana, [11] and thyself.
Face. For which at supper thou shalt sit
    in triumph,
  And not be styled Doll Common, but
    Doll Proper,
  Doll Singular. The longest cut at
    night
  Shall draw thee for his Doll Particular.
                              [A bell rings.]

---

¹ Common.   ⁴ I.e., the Puritans.
² Swindle, cozen.   ⁵ In 1603.
³ Crowd.   ⁶ I.e., carted as a bawd.
⁷ I.e., lose your ears in the pillory.
⁸ I.e. the hangman, part of whose perquisites
was the clothes of the criminal.
⁹ Thriving.
¹⁰ A worsted yarn, with a pun on cruel.
¹¹ Heroine of the romance, The Mirror of
Knighthood.

Sub. Who's that? One rings. To the
  window, Doll. Pray heaven   180
  The master do not trouble us this
  quarter.
Face. O, fear not him. While there dies
    one a week
  O' the plague, he's safe from thinking
    toward London.
  Beside, he's busy at his hopyards now;
  I had a letter from him. If he do,
  He'll send such word for airing o' the
    house
  As you shall have sufficient time to quit
    it.
  Though we break up a fortnight, 'tis no
    matter.
Sub. Who is it, Doll?
Doll.   A fine young quodling. [12]
Face.   O,
  My lawyer's clerk I lighted on last
    night   190
  In Holborn at the Dagger. He would
    have
  (I told you of him) a familiar, [13]
  To rifle [14] with at horses and win cups.
Doll. O, let him in.
Sub.   Stay. Who shall do 't?
Face.   Get you
  Your robes on; I will meet him, as [15]
  going out.
Doll. And what shall I do?
Face.   Not be seen; away!—[Exit Doll]
  Seem you very reserved.
Sub.   Enough. [Exit.]
Face. [Shouting to Subtle.]   God be
  w' you, sir.
  I pray you let him know that I was here.
  His name is Dapper.—[Pretends to leave.]
  I would gladly have stayed, but—

ACT I. SCENE ii.

Dapper, Face, Subtle.

[Dap.] Captain, I am here.
Face.   Who's that?—He's come, I think,
    doctor.—
  Good faith, sir, I was going away.
Dap.   In truth,
  I am very sorry, captain.
Face.   But I thought
  Sure I should meet you.

---

¹² Codling, a green apple; here an immature
young man.   ¹⁴ Raffle, hold a lottery
¹³ Familiar spirit.   ¹⁵ As if.

DAP.   Ay, I am very glad.
I had a scurvy writ or two to make,
And I had lent my watch last night to
    one
That dines today at the shrief's,[1] and
    so was robbed
Of my pass-time.

[*Enter Subtle in his robes.*]

                    Is this the cunning [2] man?
FACE. This is his worship.
DAP.   Is he a doctor?
FACE.   Yes.
DAP. And ha' you broke [3] with him, cap-
    tain?
FACE.   Ay.
DAP.   And how?   10
FACE. Faith, he does make the matter,
    sir, so dainty [4]
I know not what to say.
DAP.   Not so, good captain.
FACE. Would I were fairly rid on 't, be-
    lieve me.
DAP. Nay, now you grieve me, sir. Why
    should you wish so?
I dare assure you, I'll not be ungrate-
    ful.
FACE. I cannot think you will, sir. But
    the law
Is such a thing—and then he says Read's
    matter
Falling so lately [5]—
DAP.   Read? He was an ass,
And dealt, sir, with a fool.
FACE.   It was a clerk, sir.
DAP. A clerk?
FACE.   Nay, hear me, sir. You know the
    law   20
Better, I think—
DAP.   I should, sir, and the danger.
You know I showed the statute to
    you?
FACE.   You did so.
DAP. And will I tell then? By this hand
    of flesh,
Would it might never write good court-
    hand [6] more,

[1] Sheriff's.
[2] Learned, especially in magic.
[3] Broached the question.
[4] *I.e.*, he has so many scruples.
[5] Dr. Simon Read had been recently convicted
as a magician.
[6] Handwriting of the law courts.

If I discover.[7] What do you think of me,
    That I am a chiaus? [8]
FACE.   What's that?
DAP.   The Turk was here.
As one would say, do you think I am a
    Turk?
FACE. I'll tell the doctor so.
DAP.   Do, good sweet captain.
FACE. Come, noble doctor, pray thee, let's
    prevail;
This is the gentleman, and he is no
    chiaus.   30
SUB. Captain, I have returned you all my
    answer.
I would do much, sir, for your love—
    but this
I neither may, nor can.
FACE.   Tut, do not say so.
You deal now with a noble fellow, doctor,
One that will thank you richly; and
    h' is no chiaus.
Let that, sir, move you.
SUB.   Pray you, forbear.
FACE.   He has
Four angels [9] here.
SUB.   You do me wrong, good sir.
FACE. Doctor, wherein? To tempt you
    with these spirits?
SUB. To tempt my art and love, sir, to my
    peril.
Fore [10] heav'n, I scarce can think you
    are my friend,   40
That so would draw me to apparent
    danger.
FACE. I draw you? A horse draw you,
    and a halter,
You and your flies together—
DAP.   Nay, good captain.
FACE. That know no difference of men.
SUB.   Good words, sir.
FACE. Good deeds, sir, Doctor Dogs'-
    meat. 'Slight, I bring you
No cheating Clim o' the Cloughs or
    Claribels,[11]
That look as big as five-and-fifty and
    flush,[12]
And spit out secrets like hot custard—
DAP.   Captain!

[7] Reveal.
[8] Chouse, a Turkish messenger, like the one
who had recently cheated some London merchants.
[9] Gold coins.   [10] Before.
[11] Heroes of romantic tales.
[12] The highest hand at primero, a card game.

FACE. Nor any melancholic underscribe,
Shall tell the vicar; but a special gentle,[1]
That is the heir to forty marks a year, 51
Consorts with the small poets of the time,
Is the sole hope of his old grandmother;
That knows the law and writes you six fair hands,
Is a fine clerk and has his ciph'ring perfect,
Will take his oath o' the Greek Xenophon,
If need be, in his pocket, and can court
His mistress out of Ovid.

DAP. Nay, dear captain—

FACE. Did you not tell me so?

DAP. Yes; but I'ld ha' you
Use Master Doctor with some more respect. 60

FACE. Hang him, proud stag, with his broad velvet head!
But for your sake I'ld choke ere I would change
An article of breath with such a puck-fist![2]
Come, let's be gone.

SUB. Pray you, le' me speak with you.

DAP. His worship calls you, captain.

FACE. I am sorry
I e'er embarked myself in such a business.

DAP. Nay, good sir; he did call you.

FACE. Will he take then?

SUB. First, hear me—

FACE. Not a syllable, 'less you take.

SUB. Pray ye, sir—

FACE. Upon no terms but an *assumpsit*.[3]

SUB. Your humor must be law.

He takes the money.

FACE. Why now, sir, talk 70
Now I dare hear you with mine honor. Speak.
So may this gentleman too.

SUB. [*Pretending to whisper to Face.*] Why, sir—

FACE. No whisp'ring.

SUB. Fore heav'n, you do not apprehend the loss
You do yourself in this.

FACE. Wherein? For what?

SUB. Marry, to be so importunate for one
That, when he has it, will undo you all;
He'll win up all the money i' the town.

FACE. How!

SUB. Yes, and blow up gamester after gamester,
As they do crackers in a puppet play.
If I do give him a familiar, 80
Give you him all you play for; never set[4] him,
For he will have it.

FACE. Y' are mistaken, doctor.
Why, he does ask one but for cups and horses,
A rifling fly—none o' your great familiars.

DAP. Yes, captain, I would have it for all games.

SUB. I told you so.

FACE. [*Drawing Dapper aside.*] 'Slight,
that's a new business!
I understood you, a tame bird,[5] to fly
Twice in a term or so, on Friday nights
When you had left the office, for a nag
Of forty or fifty shillings.

DAP. Ay, 'tis true, sir; 90
But I do think now I shall leave the law,
And therefore—

FACE. Why, this changes quite the case.
Do you think that I dare move him?

DAP. If you please, sir;
All's one to him, I see.

FACE. What? For that money?
I cannot with my conscience, nor should you
Make the request, methinks.

DAP. No, sir, I mean
To add consideration.

FACE. Why, then, sir,
I'll try.—[*To Subtle.*] Say that it were
for all games, doctor?

SUB. I say then not a mouth shall eat
for[6] him
At any ordinary but o' the score;[7] 100
That is a gaming mouth, conceive me.

FACE. Indeed!

SUB. He'll draw you all the treasure of the realm,
If it be set him.

FACE. Speak you this from art?

SUB. Ay, sir, and reason too, the ground of art.

---

[1] Gentleman.
[2] Puffball, a worthless person.
[3] Legal term for a contract involving an initial payment.
[4] Stake against.
[5] A familiar spirit.
[6] On account of.
[7] On credit.

H' is o' the only best complexion
The Queen of Fairy loves.
FACE.　　　　　　　What! Is he?
SUB.　　　　　　　　　　　Peace!
He'll overhear you. Sir, should she but
　see him—
FACE. What?
SUB.　　　　Do not you tell him.
FACE.　　　　　　Will he win at cards too?
SUB. The spirits of dead Holland, living
　Isaac,[1]
You'ld swear, were in him—such a
　vigorous luck　　　　　　　　　110
As cannot be resisted. 'Slight, he'll put
Six o' your gallants to a cloak,[2] indeed.
FACE. A strange success, that some man
　shall be born to!
SUB. He hears you, man—
DAP.　　　　　Sir, I'll not be ingrateful.
FACE. Faith, I have a confidence in his
　good nature.
You hear, he says he will not be ingrate-
　ful.
SUB. Why, as you please; my venture
　follows yours.
FACE. Troth, do it, doctor; think him
　trusty, and make him.
He may make us both happy in an
　hour—
Win some five thousand pound, and send
　us two on 't.　　　　　　　　　120
DAI. Believe it, and I will, sir.
FACE.　　　　　And you shall, sir.
You have heard all?
　　　　　　　　　Face takes him aside.
DAP.　No, what was 't? Nothing, I, sir.
FACE. Nothing?
DAP.　　　　A little, sir.
FACE.　　　　　Well, a rare star
Reigned at your birth.
DAP.　　　　At mine, sir? No!
FACE.　　　　　The doctor
Swears that you are—
SUB.　Nay, captain, yo'll tell all now.
FACE. Allied to the Queen of Fairy.
DAP.　　　　Who? That I am?
Believe it, no such matter.
FACE.　　　　　Yes, and that
Yo' were born with a caul o' your head.[3]

---

[1] Whalley suggests these are the names of
well-known gamblers of the period.
[2] *I.e.*, strip them to a single cloak for all.
[3] An old superstition connected with good
luck.

DAP.　　　　　Who says so?
FACE.　　　　　　　　Come,
You know it well enough, though you
　dissemble it.
DAP. I' fac,[4] I do not; you are mistaken.
FACE.　　　　　　How! 130
Swear by your fac, and in a thing so
　known
Unto the doctor? How shall we, sir,
　trust you
I' the other matter? Can we ever think,
When you have won five or six thousand
　pound,
You'll send us shares in 't, by this rate?
DAP.　　　　　By Jove, sir,
I'll win ten thousand pound, and send
　you half.
I' fac 's no oath.
SUB.　　　　No, no, he did but jest.
FACE. Go to. Go thank the doctor. He's
　your friend,
To take it so.
DAP.　　　I thank his worship.
FACE.　　　　　　　So?
Another angel.
DAP.　　　Must I?
FACE.　　　　Must you? 'Slight, 140
What else is thanks? Will you be triv-
　ial?—[*Dapper gives Subtle money.*]
　Doctor,
When must he come for his familiar?
DAP. Shall I not ha' it with me?
SUB.　　　　　O, good sir,
There must a world of ceremonies pass;
You must be bathed and fumigated
　first;
Besides, the Queen of Fairy does not
　rise
Till it be noon.
FACE.　　　Not if she danced tonight.[5]
SUB. And she must bless it.
FACE.　　　　　Did you never see
Her royal grace yet?
DAP.　　　　Whom?
FACE.　　　　　Your aunt of Fairy?
SUB. Not since she kissed him in the cra-
　dle, captain;　　　　　　　　　150
I can resolve[6] you that.
FACE.　　　　　Well, see her grace,
Whate'er it cost you, for a thing that I
　know.
It will be somewhat hard to compass;
　but,

---

[4] In faith.　　　[5] Last night.　　　[6] Tell.

However, see her. You are made, believe it,
If you can see her. Her grace is a lone woman,
And very rich; and, if she take a fancy,
She will do strange things. See her, at any hand.[1]
'Slid, she may hap to leave you all she has!
It is the doctor's fear.

DAP.   How will 't be done, then?

FACE. Let me alone; take you no thought. Do you   160
But say to me, "Captain, I'll see her grace."

DAP. Captain, I'll see her grace.

FACE.   Enough.   *One knocks without.*

SUB.   Who's there?
Anon.—(Conduct him forth by the back way.)
Sir, against one a-clock prepare yourself;
Till when, you must be fasting; only take
Three drops of vinegar in at your nose,
Two at your mouth, and one at either ear;
Then bath[2] your fingers' ends and wash your eyes,
To sharpen your five senses, and cry "hum"
Thrice, and then "buzz" as often; and then come.   *[Exit.]*   170

FACE. Can you remember this?

DAP.   I warrant you.

FACE. Well then, away. 'Tis but your bestowing
Some twenty nobles 'mong her grace's servants,
And put on a clean shirt. You do not know
What grace her grace may do you in clean linen.   *[Exeunt.]*

ACT I. SCENE iii.

Subtile, Drugger, Face.[3]

[SUB. (*Within.*)] Come in! (Good wives, I pray you forbear me now;
Troth, I can do you no good till afternoon.)

[1] Rate.   [3] All actually enter later.
[2] Bathe.

[Enter Subtle and Drugger.]

SUB. What is your name, say you? Abel Drugger?

DRUG.   Yes, sir.

SUB. A seller of tabacco?

DRUG.   Yes, sir.

SUB.   Umh!
Free of the Grocers?[4]

DRUG.   Ay, and[5] 't please you.

SUB.   Well.
Your business, Abel?

DRUG.   This, and 't please your worship:
I am a young beginner, and am building
Of a new shop, and 't like your worship, just
At corner of a street.   (Here's the plot[6] on 't.)
And I would know by art, sir, of your worship,   10
Which way I should make my door, by necromancy,
And where my shelves, and which should be for boxes,
And which for pots. I would be glad to thrive, sir.
And I was wished[7] to your worship by a gentleman,
One Captain Face, that says you know men's planets,
And their good angels, and their bad.

SUB.   I do,
If I do see hem.[8]—

[Enter Face.]

FACE.   What! My honest Abel?
Thou art well met here.

DRUG.   Troth, sir, I was speaking,
Just as your worship came here, of your worship.
I pray you speak for me to Master Doctor.   20

FACE. He shall do anything. Doctor, do you hear?
This is my friend, Abel, an honest fellow;
He lets me have good tabacco, and he does not
Sophisticate[9] it with sack lees or oil,
Nor washes it in muscadel and grains,[10]

[4] *I.e.*, a member of the Grocers' Guild.
[5] If it.   [7] Recommended.
[6] Plat, diagram.   [8] Them.
[9] Adulterate.
[10] Grains of paradise, a spice.

Nor buries it in gravel under ground,
Wrapped up in greasy leather or pissed
    clouts,
But keeps it in fine lily pots,[1] that,
    opened,
Smell like conserve of roses, or French
    beans.   29
He has his maple block,[2] his silver tongs,
Winchester pipes, and fire of juniper [3]—
A neat, spruce, honest fellow, and no
    goldsmith.[4]
SUB. H' is a fortunate fellow; that I am
    sure on.
FACE. Already, sir, ha' you found it?
    Lo thee,[5] Abel!
SUB. And in right way toward riches.
FACE.   Sir!
SUB.   This summer
He will be of the clothing [6] of his com-
    pany,
And next spring called to the scarlet;[7]
    spend what he can—
FACE. What, and so little beard?
SUB.   Sir, you must think
He may have a receipt to make hair
    come.
But he'll be wise, preserve his youth,
    and fine [8] for 't;   40
His fortune looks for him another way.
FACE. 'Slid, doctor, how canst thou know
    this so soon?
I am amused [9] at that.
SUB.   By a rule, captain,
In metoposcopy,[10] which I do work by—
A certain star i' the forehead, which
    you see not.
Your chestnut- or your olive-colored
    face
Does never fail, and your long ear doth
    promise.
I knew 't by certain spots too in his
    teeth
And on the nail of his mercurial finger.
FACE. Which finger's that?
SUB.   His little finger. Look. 50
Yo' were born upon a Wednesday?
DRUG.   Yes, indeed, sir.

---

[1] Ornamental jars.
[2] For shredding tobacco.
[3] At which customers could light their pipes.
[4] Usurer.   [7] Become alderman.
[5] Behold thyself.   [8] Pay a fine.
[6] Wear the livery.   [9] Amazed.
[10] Divination by observing the forehead.
Original reads *metaposcopy*.

SUB. The thumb, in chiromanty [11] we give
    Venus,
The forefinger to Jove, the midst to
    Saturn,
The ring to Sol, the least to Mercury,
Who was the lord, sir, of his horoscope,
His house of life being Libra, which for-
    showed
He should be a merchant, and should
    trade with balance.
FACE. Why, this is strange! Is 't not,
    honest Nab?
SUB. There is a ship now coming from
    Ormus,
That shall yield him such a commodity 60
Of drugs—[*Points to the plan.*] This
    is the west, and this the south?
DRUG. Yes, sir.
SUB.   And those are your two sides?
DRUG.   Ay, sir.
SUB. Make me your door then, south;
    your broad side, west;
And on the east side of your shop, aloft,
Write Mathlai, Tarmiel, and Baraborat;
Upon the north part, Rael, Velel, Thiel.
They are the names of those Mercurial
    spirits
That do fright flies from boxes.
DRUG.   Yes, sir.
SUB.   And
Beneath your threshold bury me a load-
    stone
To draw in gallants that wear spurs;
    the rest,   70
They'll seem [12] to follow.
FACE.   That's a secret, Nab!
SUB. And on your stall a puppet, with a
    vise [13]
And a court-fucus,[14] to call city dames;
You shall deal much with minerals.
DRUG.   Sir, I have,
At home, already—
SUB.   Ay, I know you have ars'nic,
    Vitriol, sal tartar, argaile,[15] alkali,
Cinoper.[16] I know all.—This fellow, cap-
    tain,
Will come, in time, to be a great distiller,
And give a say [17]—I will not say directly,
But very fair—at the philosophers'
    stone.   80

---

[11] Chiromancy.   [13] Screw, clamp.
[12] Be seen.   [14] A cosmetic used at court.
[15] Argol, tartar deposited by wine.
[16] Cinnabar.   [17] An assay, attempt.

FACE. Why, how now, Abel! Is this true?

DRUG. [*Drawing Face aside.*] Good captain,
What must I give?

FACE. Nay, I'll not counsel thee.
Thou hear'st what wealth (he says, spend what thou canst)
Thou 'rt like to come to.

DRUG. I would gi' him a crown.

FACE. A crown? And toward such a fortune? Heart,
Thou shalt rather gi' him thy shop. No gold about thee?

DRUG. Yes, I have a portague [1] I ha' kept this half year.

FACE. Out on thee, Nab! 'Slight, there was such an offer.
Shalt keep 't no longer. I'll gi' it him for thee?—Doctor,
Nab prays your worship to drink this, and swears   90
He will appear more grateful, as your skill
Does raise him in the world.

DRUG. I would entreat
Another favor of his worship.

FACE. What is 't, Nab?

DRUG. But to look over, sir, my almanac,
And cross out my ill-days, that I may neither
Bargain, nor trust upon them.

FACE. That he shall, Nab.
Leave it; it shall be done gainst afternoon.

SUB. And a direction for his shelves.

FACE. Now, Nab,
Art thou well pleased, Nab?

DRUG. Thank, sir, both your worships.

FACE. Away! [*Exit Drugger.*]
Why, now, you smoky persecutor of nature!   100
Now do you see that something's to be done
Beside your beech-coal and your corsive [2] waters,
Your crosslets, [3] crucibles, and cucurbites? [4]
You must have stuff brought home to you, to work on?
And yet you think I am at no expense
In searching out these veins, then following hem,

Then trying hem out. Fore God, my intelligence
Costs me more money than my share oft comes to
In these rare works.

SUB. You are pleasant, sir.—How now?

ACT I. SCENE iv.

Face, Doll, Subtle.

[SUB.] What says my dainty Dolkin?

DOLL. Yonder fishwife
Will not away. And there's your giantess,
The bawd of Lambeth.

SUB. Heart, I cannot speak with hem.

DOLL. Not afore night, I have told hem in a voice
Thorough the trunk, [5] like one of your familiars.
But I have spied Sir Epicure Mammon.

SUB. Where?

DOLL. Coming along, at far end of the lane,
Slow of his feet, but earnest of his tongue
To one that's with him.

SUB. Face, go you and shift. [6]—
[*Exit Face.*]
Doll, you must presently [7] make ready too.   10

DOLL. Why, what's the matter?

SUB. O, I did look for him
With the sun's rising. Marvel, he could sleep!
This is the day I am to perfect for him
The *magisterium*, our *great work*, the *stone*,
And yield it, made, into his hands—of which
He has this month talked as he were possessed. [8]
And now he's dealing pieces on 't away.
Methinks I see him ent'ring ordinaries,
Dispensing for the pox, and plaguy houses, [9]
Reaching [10] his dose, walking Moorfields for lepers,   20
And off'ring citizens' wives pomander bracelets [11]

---

[1] A gold coin.
[2] Corrosive.
[3] Vessels.
[4] Retorts.
[5] Through the speaking tube.
[6] Change your clothes.
[7] At once.
[8] *I.e.*, as if he owned it.
[9] Houses infested with the plague.
[10] Offering.
[11] As a protection against disease.

As his preservative, made of the *elixir;*
Searching the spital [1] to make old bawds
  young,
And the highways for beggars to make
  rich.
I see no end of his labors. He will make
Nature ashamed of her long sleep,
  when art,
Who's but a stepdame, shall do more
  than she
In her best love to mankind ever could.
If his dream last, he'll turn the age to
  gold.   [*Exeunt.*]

ACT II. SCENE i.

[*The same.*] [2]

Mammon, Surly.

[MAM.] Come on, sir. Now you set your
  foot on shore
In *Novo Orbe;* [3] here's the rich Peru,
And there within, sir, are the golden
  mines,
Great Salomon's [4] Ophir! He was
  sailing to 't
Three years, but we have reached it in
  ten months.
This is the day wherein to all my
  friends
I will pronounce the happy word, "Be
  rich;
This day you shall be *spectatissimi.*" [5]
You shall no more deal with the hollow [6]
  die
Or the frail card; no more be at charge
  of keeping   10
The livery-punk [7] for the young heir
  that must
Seal at all hours in his shirt; no more,
If he deny, ha' him beaten to 't, as he is
That brings him the commodity. No
  more
Shall thirst of satin, or the covetous
  hunger
Of velvet entrails [8] for [9] a rude-spun cloak,

To be displayed at Madam Augusta's, [10]
  make
The sons of sword and hazard fall
  before
The golden calf, and on their knees,
  whole nights,
Commit idolatry with wine and trump-
  ets,   20
Or go a-feasting after drum and en-
  sign.
No more of this. You shall start up
  young viceroys,
And have your punks and punkettees, [11]
  my Surly.
And unto thee I speak it first, "Be
  rich."
Where is my Subtle there? Within, ho!
[FACE.] (*Within.*)   Sir,
He'll come to you by-and-by.
MAM.   That's his firedrake, [12]
His lungs, [13] his Zephyrus, he that puffs
  his coals
Till he firk [14] nature up in her own cen-
  ter.
You are not faithful, [15] sir. This night
  I'll change
All that is metal in my [16] house to
  gold,   30
And early in the morning will I send
To all the plumbers and the pewter-
  ers,
And buy their tin and lead up, and to
  Lothbury
For all the copper.
SUR.   What, and turn that too?
MAM. Yes, and I'll purchase Devonshire
  and Cornwall,
And make them perfect Indies! You
  admire [17] now?
SUR. No, faith.
MAM.   But, when you see th' effects
  of the great med'cine,
Of which one part projected on a hun
  dred
Of Mercury, or Venus, or the Moon   3
Shall turn it to as many of the Sun [18]—
Nay, to a thousand, so *ad infinitum*—
You will believe me.

---

[1] Hospital.
[2] The setting and action are continuous
throughout the act.
[3] The New World.   [5] Highly esteemed.
[4] Solomon's.   [6] *I.e.*, loaded.
[7] A prostitute used as an accomplice in effecting the commodity swindle in which a young
heir was tricked to lend money on the security
of valueless goods.
[8] Lining.   [9] In exchange for.

[10] Probably a brothel.   [13] Bellows
[11] Young prostitutes.   [14] Stir.
[12] Dragon.   [15] Believing.
[16] From 1612 edn. Original reads *thy.*
[17] Wonder.
[18] Transmute quicksilver, copper, or silver
into gold.

SUR.   Yes, when I see 't, I
will.
But, if my eyes do cozen me so, and I
Giving hem no occasion, sure I'll have
A whore shall piss hem out next day.

MAM.   Ha! Why?
Do you think I fable with you?   I
assure you,
He that has once the *Flower of the
Sun*,
The perfect *ruby*, which we call *elixir*,
Not only can do that, but by its vir-
tue
Can confer honor, love, respect, long
life;   50
Give safety, valure, [1] yea, and victory
To whom he will. In eight-and-twenty
days
I'll make an old man of fourscore a
child.

SUR. No doubt; he's that already.

MAM.   Nay, I mean,
Restore his years, renew him, like an
eagle,
To the fifth age,[2] make him get sons and
daughters,
Young giants (as our philosophers have
done,
The ancient patriarchs afore the flood),
But, taking once a week on a knife's
point
The quantity of a grain of mustard of
it,   60
Become stout Marses and beget young
Cupids.

SUR. The decayed vestals of Pickt-hatch[3]
would thank you,
That keep the fire alive there.

MAM.   'Tis the secret
Of nature naturized gainst all infec-
tions,
Cures all diseases coming of all causes,
A month's grief in a day, a year's in
twelve,
And, of what age soever, in a month,
Past all the doses of your drugging
doctors.
I'll undertake, withal, to fright the
plague
Out o' the kingdom in three months.

SUR.   And I'll   70

Be bound, the players shall sing your
praises then,
Without their poets.[4]

MAM.   Sir, I'll do 't. Meantime,
I'll give away so much unto my man,
Shall serve th' whole city with preserva-
tive
Weekly, each house his dose, and at the
rate—

SUR. As he that built the Waterwork
does with water?

MAM. You are incredulous.

SUR.   Faith, I have a humor;
I would not willingly be gulled. Your
stone
Cannot transmute me.

MAM.   Pertinax Surly,
Will you believe antiquity? Records?   80
I'll show you a book where Moses and
his sister
And Salomon have written of the art;
Ay, and a treatise penned by Adam—

SUR.   How!

MAM. O' the *philosophers' stone*, and in
High Dutch.

SUR. Did Adam write, sir, in High Dutch?

MAM.   He did,
Which proves it was the primitive
tongue.

SUR.   What paper?

MAM. On cedar board.

SUR.   O, that, indeed, they say,
Will last gainst worms.

MAM.   'Tis like your Irish wood
Gainst cobwebs.   I have a piece of
Jason's fleece too,
Which was no other than a book of
alchemy,   90
Writ in large sheepskin, a good fat ram-
vellam.[5]
Such was Pythagoras' thigh,[6] Pandora's
tub,
And all that fable of Medea's charms.
The manner of our work: the bulls,
our fornace,
Still breathing fire; our *argent-vive*,[7] the
dragon;
The dragon's teeth, *mercury sublimate*,
That keeps the whiteness, hardness,
and the biting;

---

[1] Valor.

[2] *I.e.*, of the seven ages of man.

[3] A low district in London.

[4] Plays were not given when the plague was
raging.   [7] Quicksilver.

[5] Vellum made of ram skin.

[6] *Cf.* note on *Volpone*, I, ii, 27.

And they are gathered into Jason's
    helm,
Th' *alembic*, and then sowed in Mars his
    field,
And thence sublimed so often, till they
    are fixed.   100
Both this, th' Hesperian garden, Cad-
    mus' story,
Jove's shower, the boon of Midas, Ar-
    gus' eyes,
Boccace his Demogorgon, thousands
    more,
All abstract riddles of our *stone.*—How
    now?

ACT II. SCENE ii.

Mammon, Face, Surly.

MAM.] Do we succeed? Is our day come?
    And holds it?
FACE. The evening will set red upon you,
    sir;
You have color for it, crimson; the red
    ferment
Has done his office; three hours hence
    prepare you
To see projection.
MAM.   Pertinax, my Surly,
Again I say to thee, aloud, "Be rich."
This day thou shalt have ingots, and
    tomorrow
Give lords th' affront.—Is it, my
    Zephyrus, right?
Blushes the bolt's-head? [1]
FACE.   Like a wench with child, sir,
That were but now discovered to her
    master.   10
MAM. Excellent witty Lungs!—My only
    care is
Where to get stuff enough now to pro-
    ject on;
This town will not half serve me.
FACE.   No, sir? Buy
The covering off o' churches.
MAM.   That's true.
FACE.   Yes.
Let hem stand bare, as do their audi-
    tory, [2]
Or cap hem new with shingles.
MAM.   No, good thatch;
Thatch will lie light upo' the rafters,
    Lungs.

Lungs, I will manumit thee from the
    fornace;
I will restore thee thy complexion,
    Puff,
Lost in the embers, and repair this
    brain,   20
Hurt wi' the fume o' the metals.
FACE.   I have blown, sir,
Hard for your worship, thrown by many
    a coal,
When 'twas not beech, weighed those
    I put in, just, [3]
To keep your heat still even. These
    bleared eyes
Have waked to read your several colors,
    sir,
Of the *pale citron*, the *green lion*, the
    crow,
The *peacock's tail*, the *plumed swan*.
MAM.   And lastly
Thou hast descried the *flower*, the
    sanguis agni? [4]
FACE. Yes, sir.
MAM.   Where's master?
FACE.   At 's prayers, sir, he;
Good man, he's doing his devotions   30
For the success.
MAM.   Lungs, I will set a period
To all thy labors; thou shalt be the
    master
Of my seraglia. [5]
FACE.   Good, sir.
MAM.   But do you hear?
I'll geld you, Lungs.
FACE.   Yes, sir.
MAM.   For I do mean
To have a list of wives and concubines
Equal with Salomon, who had the *stone*
Alike with me; and I will make me a
    back
With the *elixir*, that shall be as tough
As Hercules, to encounter fifty a night.—
Thou'rt sure thou saw'st it *blood?*
FACE.   Both *blood and spirit*, sir.   40
MAM. I will have all my beds blown up,
    not stuffed;
Down is too hard. And then, mine
    oval room
Filled with such pictures as Tiberius
    took
From Elephantis, and dull Aretine
But coldly imitated. Then, my glasses

---

[1] Flask.   [2] Auditors, congregation.   [3] Exactly.   [5] Seraglio.
[4] Blood of the Lamb.

Cut in more subtle angles to disperse
And multiply the figures, as I walk
Naked between my *succubæ*.[1] My mists
I'll have of perfume, vapored 'bout the room,
To lose ourselves in, and my baths like pits   50
To fall into, from whence we will come forth,
And roll us dry in gossamer and roses.—
Is it arrived at *ruby?*—Where I spy
A wealthy citizen or rich lawyer
Have a sublimed pure wife, unto that fellow
I'll send a thousand pound to be my cuckold.

FACE. And I shall carry it?

MAM.   No. I'll ha' no bawds
But fathers and mothers. They will do it best,
Best of all others. And my flatterers
Shall be the pure and gravest of divines   60
That I can get for money; my mere fools
Eloquent burgesses; and then my poets
The same that writ so subtly of the fart,
Whom I will entertain still for that subject.
The few that would give out themselves to be
Court- and town-stallions, and, each-where, belie
Ladies who are known most innocent, for them,
Those will I beg to make me eunuchs of;
And they shall fan me with ten es-trich[2] tails
Apiece, made in a plume to gather wind.   70
We will be brave, Puff, now we ha' the *med'cine*.
My meat shall all come in, in Indian shells,
Dishes of agate set in gold, and studded
With emeralds, sapphires, hyacinths,[3] and rubies.
The tongues of carps, dormice, and camels' heels,
Boiled i' the spirit of *Sol*, and dissolved pearl

(Apicius' diet gainst the epilepsy)—
And I will eat these broths with spoons of amber,
Headed with diamant[4] and carbuncle.
My footboy shall eat pheasants, calvered salmons,[5]   80
Knots,[6] godwits,[7] lampreys; I myself will have
The beards of barbels[8] served instead of salads;
Oiled mushrooms; and the swelling unctuous paps
Of a fat pregnant sow, newly cut off,
Dressed with an exquisite and poignant sauce,
For which I'll say unto my cook, "There's gold;
Go forth, and be a knight."

FACE.   Sir, I'll go look
A little how it heightens.

MAM.   Do.—[*Exit Face.*] My shirts
I'll have of taffeta-sarsnet,[9] soft and light
As cobwebs; and for all my other rai-ment,   90
It shall be such as might provoke the Persian,
Were he to teach the world riot anew.
My gloves of fishes' and birds' skins, perfumed
With gums of Paradise, and Eastern air—

SUR. And do you think to have the *stone* with this?

MAM. No, I do think t' have all this with the *stone*.

SUR. Why, I have heard he must be *homo frugi*,
A pious, holy, and religious man,
One free from mortal sin, a very virgin.

MAM. That makes it, sir; he is so. But I buy it;   100
My venter brings it me. He, honest wretch,
A notable, superstitious, good soul,
Has worn his knees bare, and his slip-pers bald,
With prayer and fasting for it. And, sir, let him

---

[1] Paramours.   [3] An ancient precious stone.
[2] Ostrich.

[4] Diamond.
[5] Specially prepared salmon, perhaps pickled
[6] Robin-snipes, a kind of sandpiper.
[7] Wading birds of the snipe family.
[8] A fresh-water fish.
[9] Fine silk.

Do it alone, for me, still. Here he comes.
Not a profane word afore him; 'tis
  poison.—

Act II. Scene iii.

Mammon, Subtle, Surly, Face.[1]

[MAM.] Good morrow, father.
SUB.   Gentle son, good morrow,
  And to your friend there. What is he
  is with you?
MAM. An heretic that I did bring along
  In hope, sir, to convert him.
SUB.   Son, I doubt[2]
  Yo' are covetous, that thus you meet
  your time
  I' the just point, prevent your day[3] at
  morning.
  This argues something worthy of a fear
  Of importune and carnal appetite.
  Take heed you do not cause the blessing
  leave you,
  With your ungoverned haste. I should
  be sorry   10
  To see my labors, now e'en at perfection,
  Got by long watching and large patience,
  Not prosper where my love and zeal
  hath placed hem—
  Which[4] (heaven I call to witness, with
  yourself,
  To whom I have poured my thoughts),
  in all my ends,
  Have looked no way but unto public
  good,
  To pious uses and dear charity,
  Now[5] grown a prodigy with men;
  wherein
  If you, my son, should now prevaricate,
  And to your own particular lusts em-
  ploy   20
  So great and catholic a bliss, be sure
  A curse will follow, yea, and overtake
  Your subtle and most secret ways.
MAM.   I know, sir;
  You shall not need to fear me; I but
  come
  To ha' you confute this gentleman.
SUR.   Who is,
  Indeed, sir, somewhat costive of belief
  Toward your *stone*—would not be gulled.

SUB.   Well, son,
  All that I can convince him in is this:
  The work is done; bright *Sol* is in his
  robe.
  We have a *med'cine of the triple soul*, 30
  The *glorified spirit.* Thanks be to heaven,
  And make us worthy of it!—Ulen
     Spiegel![6]
FACE. [*Within.*] Anon, sir.
SUB.   Look well to the register,
  And let your heat still lessen by degrees
  To the *aludels.*[7]
FACE. [*Within.*] Yes, sir.
SUB.   Did you look
  O' the *bolt's-head* yet?
FACE. [*Within.*] Which? On *D*, sir?
SUB.   Ay.
  What's the complexion?
FACE. [*Within.*] Whitish.
SUB.   Infuse vinegar, 40
  To draw his *volatile substance* and his
  tincture;
  And let the water in *glass E* be feltered,[8]
  And put into the *gripe's egg.* Lute[9]
  him well,
  And leave him closed *in balneo.*[10]
FACE. [*Within.*]   I will, sir.
SUR. What a brave language here is!
  Next to canting.[11]
SUB. I have another work you never saw,
  son,
  That three days since passed the *philos-
  ophers' wheel,*
  In the lent[12] heat of *Athanor*,[13] and 's
  become
  Sulphur o' nature.
MAM.   But 'tis for me?
SUB.   What need you?
  You have enough, in that is perfect.
MAM.   O, but— 50
SUB. Why, this is covetise![14]
MAM.   No, I assure you,
  I shall employ it all in pious uses,
  Founding of colleges and grammar
  schools,
  Marrying young virgins, building hos-
  pitals,
  And now and then a church.

---

[1] Enters later.   [2] Fear.
[3] Come before your time.
[4] *I.e.*, I who.
[5] From 1640 edn. Original has *no.*

[6] Owl Glass, the hero of a popular German
jest book.
[7] Alchemical vessels.   [12] Mild.
[8] Filtered.   [13] Furnace.
[9] Seal.   [14] Covetousness.
[10] In a pan of warm water.
[11] Cant, rogues' jargon.

[*Enter Face.*]

Sub.   How now?
Face.   Sir, please you,
  Shall I not change the felter?
Sub.   Marry, yes;
  And bring me the complexion of *glass B*.
                                  [*Exit Face.*]
Mam. Ha' you another?
Sub.   Yes, son; were I assured
  Your piety were firm, we would not
    want
  The means to glorify it. But I hope the
    best.   60
  I mean to tinct *C* in *sand-heat* tomorrow,
  And give him *imbibition*.
Mam.   Of white oil?
Sub. No, sir, of red. *F* is come over the
    helm too,
  I thank my Maker, in *S[t]*. *Mary's
    bath*,
  And shows *lac virginis*.[1] Blessed be
    heaven!
  I sent you of his *fæces* there *calcined;*
  Out of that *calx* I ha' won the *salt of
    mercury*.
Mam. By pouring on your *rectified water?*
Sub. Yes, and *reverberating* in *Athanor*.—

[*Enter Face.*]

  How now? What color says it?
Face.   The ground black, sir.   70
Mam. That's your *crow's head?*
Sur. [*Aside.*]   Your coxcomb's, is 't
    not?
Sub. No, 'tis not perfect. Would it were
    the *crow!*
  That work wants something.
Sur. [*Aside.*]   O, I looked for this;
  The hay [2] is a-pitching.
Sub.   Are you sure you loosed hem
  I' their own *menstrue?*
Face.   Yes, sir, and then married hem,
  And put hem in a *bolt's-head* nipped to
    digestion,
  According as you bade me, when I set
  The *liquor of Mars* to *circulation*
  In the same heat.
Sub.   The process then was right.
Face. Yes, by the token, sir, the *retort*
    brake,   80

And what was saved was put into the
    pelican,
  And signed with *Hermes' seal*.[3]
Sub.   I think 'twas so.
  We should have a new *amalgama*.
Sur. [*Aside.*]   O, this ferret
  Is rank as any polecat.
Sub.   But I care not;
  Let him e'en die; we have enough be-
    side,
  In *embryon*. *H* has his *white shirt* on?
Face.   Yes, sir,
  He's ripe for *inceration;* he stands warm
  In his *ash-fire*. I would not you should
    let
  Any die now, if I might counsel, sir,
  For luck's sake to the rest. It is not
    good.   90
Mam. He says right.
Sur. [*Aside.*]   Ay, are you bolted? [4]
Face.   Nay, I know 't, sir;
  I have seen th' ill fortune. What is
    some three ounces
  Of fresh *materials?*
Mam.   Is 't no more?
Face.   No more, sir,
  Of gold, t' *amalgam* with some six of
    mercury.
Mam. Away, here's money. What will
    serve?
Face.   Ask him, sir.
Mam. How much?
Sub.   Give him nine pound;
  you may gi' him ten.
Sur. [*Aside.*] Yes, twenty, and be cozened,
    do.
Mam.   There 'tis. [*Gives Face the money.*]
Sub. This needs not, but that you will
    have it so,
  To see conclusions of all. For two
  Of our inferior works are at *fixation;*   100
  A third is in *ascension*. Go your ways.
  Ha' you set the *oil of Luna* in *kemia?*
Face. Yes, sir.
Sub.   And the *philosophers' vinegar?*
Face.   Ay. [*Exit.*]
Sur. [*Aside.*] We shall have a salad!
Mam.   When do you make *projection?*
Sub. Son, be not hasty. I *exalt* our
    med'cine
  By hanging him *in balneo vaporoso,*
  And giving him solution; then *congeal*
    him,

And then *dissolve* him; then again *congeal* him;
For look, how oft I iterate the work,
So many times I add unto his virtue.   110
As, if at first one ounce convert a hundred,
After his second loose, he'll turn a thousand;
His third solution, ten; his fourth, a hundred;
After his fifth, a thousand thousand ounces
Of any imperfect metal, into pure
Silver or gold, in all examinations,
As good as any of the natural mine.
Get you your stuff here against afternoon,
Your brass, your pewter, and your andirons.
MAM. Not those of iron?
SUB.   Yes, you may bring them too; 120
We'll change all metals.
SUR. [*Aside.*]   I believe you in that.
MAM. Then I may send my spits?
SUB.   Yes, and your racks.
SUR. And dripping pans, and pothangers, and hooks?
    Shall he not?
SUB.   If he please.
SUR.   To be an ass.
SUB. How, sir!
MAM.   This gent'man you must bear withal.
    I told you he had no faith.
SUR.   And little hope, sir;
But much less charity, should I gull myself.
SUB. Why, what have you observed, sir, in our art
    Seems so impossible?
SUR.   But your whole work; no more.
That you should hatch gold in a fornace, sir,   130
    As they do eggs in Egypt!
SUB.   Sir, do you
Believe that eggs are hatched so?
SUR.   If I should?
SUB. Why, I think that the greater miracle.
    No egg but differs from a chicken more
    Than metals in themselves.
SUR.   That cannot be.

The egg's ordained by nature to that end,
And is a chicken *in potentia*.[1]
SUB. The same we say of lead and other metals,
Which would be gold if they had time.
MAM.   And that
Our art doth furder.[2]
SUB.   Ay, for 't were absurd 140
To think that nature in the earth bred gold
Perfect i' the instant; something went before.
There must be *remote matter*.
SUR.   Ay, what is that?
SUB. Marry, we say—
MAM.   Ay, now it heats. Stand, father;
Pound him to dust.
SUB.   It is, of the one part,
A humid exhalation, which we call
Materia liquida, or the *unctuous water;*
On th' other part, a certain crass and viscous
Portion of earth; both which, concorporate,
Do make the *elementary matter* of gold,   150
Which is not yet *propria materia*,
But commune to all metals and all stones;
For, where it is forsaken of that moisture,
And hath more dryness, it becomes a stone;
Where it retains more of the humid fatness,
It turns to *sulphur* or to *quicksilver*,
Who are the parents of all other metals.
Nor can this *remote matter* suddenly
Progress so from extreme unto extreme
As to grow gold, and leap o'er all the means.[3]   160
Nature doth first beget th' imperfect; then
Proceeds she to the perfect. Of that airy
And oily water, *mercury* is engendered;
Sulphur o' the fat and earthy part; the one,
Which is the last, supplying the place of male,
The other of the female, in all metals.
Some do believe hermaphrodeity,

[1] Potentially.
[2] Further.
[3] Intermediate stages.

That both do act and suffer. But these
two
Make the rest ductile, malleable, extensive.
And even in gold they are; for we do
find   170
Seeds of them by our fire, and gold in
them,
And can produce the *species* of each
metal
More perfect thence than nature doth in
earth.
Beside, who doth not see in daily practice
Art can beget bees, hornets, beetles,
wasps
Out of the carcasses and dung of creatures—
Yea, scorpions of an herb, being rightly
placed?
And these are living creatures, far more
perfect
And excellent than metals.

MAM.   Well said, father!
Nay, if he take you in hand, sir, with
an argument,   180
He'll bray [1] you in a mortar.

SUR.   Pray you, sir, stay.
Rather than I'll be brayed, sir, I'll be-
lieve
That alchemy is a pretty kind of game,
Somewhat like tricks o' the cards, to
cheat a man
With charming.

SUB.   Sir?

SUR.   What else are all your terms,
Whereon no one o' your writers grees
with other?
Of your *elixir*, your *lac virginis*,
Your *stone*, your *med'cine*, and your
chrysosperm,
Your *sal*, your *sulphur*, and your *mer-
cury*,
Your *oil of height*, your *tree of life*, your
blood,   190
Your *marchesite*, your *tutie*, your
magnesia,
Your *toad*, your *crow*, your *dragon*, and
your *panther*,
Your *sun*, your *moon*, your *firmament*,
your *adrop*,
Your *lato, azoch, zernich, chibrit, heau-
tarit*,

[1] Pulverize.

And then your *red man* and your
white woman,
With all your broths, your *menstrues*, and
materials
Of piss and eggshells, women's terms,
man's blood,
Hair o' the head, burnt clouts, chalk,
merds, [2] and clay,
Poulder of bones, scalings of iron, glass,
And worlds of other strange *ingredi-
ents*   200
Would burst a man to name?

SUB.   And all these, named,
Intending but one thing, which art our
writers
Used to obscure their art.

MAM.   Sir, so I told him—
Because [3] the simple idiot should not
learn it,
And make it vulgar.

SUB.   Was not all the knowledge
Of the Egyptians writ in mystic sym-
bols?
Speak not the Scriptures oft in parables?
Are not the choicest fables of the poets,
That were the fountains and first springs
of wisdom,
Wrapped in perplexéd allegories?

MAM.   I urged that, 210
And cleared to him that Sisyphus was
damned
To roll the ceaseless stone, only because
He would have made ours common.—
(*Doll is seen.*) Who is this?

SUB. God's precious!—What do you mean?
Go in, good lady,
Let me entreat you.—[*Exit Doll.*]
Where's this varlet?

[*Enter Face.*]

FACE.   Sir?

SUB. You very knave! Do you use me
thus?

FACE.   Wherein, sir?

SUB. Go in and see, you traitor. Go!
                              [*Exit Face.*]

MAM.   Who is it, sir?

SUB. Nothing, sir; nothing.

MAM.   What's the matter, good sir?
I have not seen you thus distempered.
Who is 't?

[2] Fæces.
[3] In order that.

Sub. All arts have still had, sir, their
     adversaries;   220
But ours the most ignorant.—

Face returns.

                                What now?
Face. 'Twas not my fault, sir; she would
     speak with you.
Sub. Would she, sir? Follow me. [*Exit.*]
Mam.   Stay, Lungs!
Face.   I dare not, sir.
Mam. How! Pray thee, stay.
Face.   She's mad, sir, and
     sent hither—
Mam. Stay, man; what is she?
Face.   A lord's sister, sir.—
     (He'll be mad too.
Mam.   I warrant thee.[1]) Why sent
     hither?
Face. Sir, to be cured.
Sub. [*Within.*]   Why, rascal!
Face.   Lo you!—Here, sir!
                        He goes out.
Mam. Fore God, a Bradamante,[2] a brave
     piece.
Sur. Heart, this is a bawdyhouse! I'll be
     burnt else.
Mam. O, by this light, no. Do not wrong
     him. H' is   230
Too scrupulous that way; it is his vice.
No, h' is a rare physician (do him right),
An excellent Paracelsian, and has done
Strange cures with mineral physic. He
     deals all
With spirits, he; he will not hear a word
Of Galen or his tedious recipes.—

Face again.

                        How now, Lungs?
Face. Softly, sir; speak softly. I meant
     To ha' told your worship all. This[3]
     must not hear.
Mam. No, he will not be gulled; let him
     alone.
Face. Y' are very right, sir; she is a most
     rare scholar,   240
And is gone mad with studying Brough-
     ton's[4] works.
If you but name a word touching the
     Hebrew,

[1] *I.e.,* I guarantee to protect you against
Subtle.
[2] Heroine in Ariosto's *Orlando Furioso.*
[3] *I.e.,* Surly.   [4] A rabbinical scholar.

She falls into her fit, and will discourse
So learnedly of genealogies
As you would run mad, too, to hear her,
     sir.
Mam. How might one do t' have confer-
     ence with her, Lungs?
Face. O, divers have run mad upon the
     conference.
I do not know, sir. I am sent in haste
To fetch a vial.
Sur.   Be not gulled, Sir Mammon.
Mam. Wherein? Pray ye, be patient.
Sur.   Yes, as you are,   250
And trust confederate knaves and bawds
     and whores.
Mam. You are too foul, believe it.—
     Come here, Ulen.
One word.
Face.   I dare not, in good faith.
Mam.   Stay, knave.
Face. H' is extreme angry that you saw
     her, sir.
Mam. Drink that. [*Gives him money.*]
     What is she when she's out of her
     fit?
Face. O, the most affablest creature, sir!
     So merry!
So pleasant! She'll mount you up, like
     quicksilver,
Over the helm, and *circulate* like *oil;*
A very *vegetal;* discourse of state,   259
Of mathematics, bawdry, anything—
Mam. Is she no way accessible? No means,
No trick to give a man a taste of her—
     wit—
Or so?—Ulen!
Face.   I'll come to you again, sir. [*Exit.*]
Mam. Surly, I did not think one o' your
     breeding
Would traduce personages of worth.
Sur.   Sir Epicure,
Your friend to use, yet still loath to be
     gulled.
I do not like your philosophical bawds.
Their *stone* is lechery enough to pay
     for,
Without this bait.
Mam.   Heart, you abuse yourself.
I know the lady, and her friends, and
     means,   270
The original of this disaster. Her brother
Has told me all.
Sur.   And yet you ne'er saw her
     Till now?

Mam. O, yes, but I forgot. I have, believe it,
One o' the treacherous'st memories, I do think,
Of all mankind.
Sur. What call you her brother?
Mam. My lord—
He wi' not have his name known, now I think on 't.
Sur. A very treacherous memory!
Mam. O' my faith—
Sur. Tut, if you ha' it not about you, pass it
Till we meet next.
Mam. Nay, by this hand, 'tis true.
He's one I honor, and my noble friend;
And I respect his house.
Sur. Heart! Can it be 281
That a grave sir, a rich, that has no need,
A wise sir, too, at other times, should thus
With his own oaths and arguments make hard means
To gull himself? And this be your *elixir*,
Your *lapis mineralis*, and your *lunary*,
Give me your honest trick yet at primero
Or gleek,[1] and take your *lutum sapientis*,
Your *menstruum simplex!* I'll have gold before you, 289
And with less danger of the *quicksilver*,
Or the hot *sulphur*.

[*Enter Face.*]

Face. (*To Surly.*) Here's one from Captain Face, sir,
Desires you meet him i' the Temple Church
Some half hour hence, and upon earnest business.—
(*He whispers Mammon.*) Sir, if you please to quit us now, and come
Again within two hours, you shall have
My master busy examining o' the works;
And I will steal you in unto the party,
That you may see her converse.—Sir, shall I say
You'll meet the captain's worship?
Sur. Sir, I will.—
[*Aside.*] But by attorney, and to a second purpose. 300

Now I am sure it is a bawdyhouse;
I'll swear it, were the marshal here to thank me.
The naming this commander doth confirm it.
Don Face! Why, h' is the most autentic [2] dealer
I' these commodities, the superintendent
To all the quainter [3] traffickers in town!
He is their visitor, and does appoint
Who lies with whom, and at what hour, what price,
Which gown, and in what smock, what fall,[4] what tire.[5]
Him will I prove, by a third person, to find 310
The subtleties of this dark labyrinth,
Which if I do discover, dear Sir Mammon,
You'll give your poor friend leave, though no *philosopher*,
To laugh; for you that are, 't is thought, shall weep.
Face. Sir, he does pray you'll not forget.
Sur. I will not, sir.
Sir Epicure, I shall leave you. [*Exit.*]
Mam. I follow you straight.
Face. But do so, good sir, to avoid suspicion.
This gent'man has a parlous head.
Mam. But wilt thou, Ulen,
Be constant to thy promise?
Face. As my life, sir.
Mam. And wilt thou insinuate what I am, and praise me, 320
And say I am a noble fellow?
Face. O, what else, sir?
And that you'll make her royal with the *stone*,
An empress, and yourself King of Bantam.
Mam. Wilt thou do this?
Face. Will I, sir?
Mam. Lungs, my Lungs, I love thee!
Face. Send your stuff, sir, that my master
May busy himself about projection.
Mam. Th' hast witched me, rogue. Take, go. [*Gives him money.*]

---

[1] Card games.
[2] Authentic.
[3] More crafty.
[4] Collar, ruff.
[5] Headdress.

FACE.   Your jack [1] and all, sir.

MAM. Thou art a villain! I will send my jack,

And the weights too. Slave, I could bite thine ear.

Away, thou dost not care for me.

FACE.   Not I, sir?   330

MAM. Come, I was born to make thee, my good weasel,

Set thee on a bench, and ha' thee twirl a chain

With the best lord's vermin of hem all.

FACE.   Away, sir.

MAM. A count, nay, a count palatine—

FACE.   Good sir, go.

MAM. Shall not advance thee better; no, nor faster.   [*Exit.*]

ACT II. SCENE iv.

Subtle, Face, Doll.

[SUB.] Has he bit? Has he bit?

FACE.   And swallowed too, my Subtle.

I ha' given him line, and now he plays, i' faith.

SUB. And shall we twitch him?

FACE.   Thorough both the gills.

A wench is a rare bait, with which a man

No sooner 's taken, but he straight firks [2] mad.

SUB. Doll, my Lord What's-hum's sister, you must now

Bear yourself ſtatelich.[3]

DOLL.   O, let me alone,

I'll not forget my race, I warrant you.

I'll keep my distance, laugh and talk aloud,

Have all the tricks of a proud, scurvy lady,   10

And be as rude as her woman.

FACE.   Well said, sanguine! [4]

SUB. But will he send his andirons?

FACE.   His jack too,

And 's iron shoeing-horn; I ha' spoke to him. Well,

I must not lose my wary gamester yonder.

SUB. O, Monsieur Caution, that will not be gulled?

FACE. Ay, if I can strike a fine hook into him now!

The Temple Church, there I have cast mine angle.

Well, pray for me. I'll about it.

           (*One knocks.*)

SUB.   What, more gudgeons!

Doll, scout, scout!—[*Doll goes to the window.*] Stay, Face, you must go to the door.

Pray God it be my Anabaptist.—Who is 't, Doll?   20

DOLL. I know him not. He looks like a gold-end man.[5]

SUB. God's so! [6] 'Tis he, he said he would send—what call you him?—

The sanctified elder, that should deal

For Mammon's jack and andirons. Let him in.

Stay, help me off first with my gown.—[*Exit Face with the gown.*] Away,

Madam, to your withdrawing chamber.—[*Exit Doll.*] Now,

In a new tune, new gesture, but old language.—

This fellow is sent from one negotiates with me

About the *stone* too, for the holy Brethren

Of Amsterdam, the exiled Saints, that hope   30

To raise their discipline [7] by it. I must use him

In some strange fashion now, to make him admire me.

ACT II. SCENE v.

Subtle, Face, Ananias.

[SUB.] Where is my drudge?

FACE. [*Entering.*]   Sir!

SUB.   Take away the *recipient*,

And rectify your *menstrue* from the *phlegma*.

Then pour it o' the *Sol* in the *cucurbite*,

And let hem macerate together.

FACE.   Yes, sir.

And save the ground?

SUB.   No; *terra damnata*

Must not have entrance in the *work*.—Who are you?

ANA. A faithful Brother,[8] if it please you.

---

[1] A turnspit moved by weights.

[2] Runs.   [3] Stately.   [4] Red face.

[5] One who buys odds and ends of gold.

[6] A mild oath.

[7] Form of church government.

[8] *I.e.*, a Puritan.

Sub. What's that?
A Lullianist? A Ripley? [1] *Filius artis?* [2]
Can you *sublime* and *dulcify? Calcine?*
Know you the *sapor pontic? Sapor
stiptic?* 10
Or what is *homogene* or *heterogene?*
Ana. I understand no heathen language,
truly.
Sub. Heathen, you Knipperdolling? [3] Is
ars sacra,
Or *chrysopœia,* or *spagyrica,*
Or the *pamphysic* or *panarchic* knowledge
A heathen language?
Ana. Heathen Greek, I take it.
Sub. How? Heathen Greek?
Ana. All's heathen but the Hebrew.
Sub. Sirrah, my varlet, stand you forth
and speak to him
Like a *philosopher;* answer i' the lan-
guage.
Name the vexations and the martyriza-
tions 20
Of metals in the *work.*
Face. Sir, *putrefaction,*
Solution, ablution, sublimation,
Cohobation, calcination, ceration, and
Fixation.
Sub. This is heathen Greek to you
now?—
And when comes *vivification?*
Face. After *mortification.*
Sub. What's *cohobation?*
Face. 'Tis the pouring on
Your *aqua regis,* and then drawing him
off,
To the *trine circle* of the *seven spheres.*
Sub. What's the proper passion of metals?
Face. *Malleation.*
Sub. What's your *ultimum supplicium
auri?*
Face. *Antimonium.* 30
Sub. This 's heathen Greek to you?—And
what's your *mercury?*
Face. A very *fugitive,* he will be gone, sir.
Sub. How know you him?
Face. By his *viscosity,*
His *oleosity,* and his *suscitability.*
Sub. How do you *sublime* him?
Face. With the *calce of eggshells,*
White *marble, talc.*

[1] Followers of Lully and Ripley, two earlier
alchemists.
[2] Son of the art?
[3] An Anabaptist leader.

Sub. Your *magisterium* now,
What's that?
Face. Shifting, sir, your *elements,*
Dry into cold, cold into moist, moist in-
To hot, hot into dry.
Sub. This is heathen Greek to you
still?—
Your *lapis philosophicus?*
Face. 'Tis a *stone,* 40
And not a *stone;* a *spirit,* a *soul,* and a
body;
Which if you do *dissolve,* it is *dissolved;*
If you *coagulate,* it is *coagulated;*
If you make it to *fly,* it *flieth.*
Sub. Enough.—[*Exit Face.*]
This 's heathen Greek to you? What are
you, sir?
Ana. Please you, a servant of the exiled
Brethren,
That deal with widows' and with or-
phans' goods,
And make a just account unto the
Saints—
A deacon.
Sub. O, you are sent from Master
Wholesome,
Your teacher?
Ana. From Tribulation Wholesome, 50
Our very zealous pastor.
Sub. Good! I have
Some orphans' goods to come here.
Ana. Of what kind, sir?
Sub. Pewter and brass, andirons and
kitchenware,
Metals that we must use our *med'cine*
on,
Wherein the Brethren may have a penn'-
orth
For ready money.
Ana. Were the orphans' parents
Sincere professors?
Sub. Why do you ask?
Ana. Because
We then are to deal justly, and give, in
truth,
Their utmost value.
Sub. 'Slid, you'ld cozen else,
And if their parents were not of the
faithful? 60
I will not trust you, now I think on 't,
Till I ha' talked with your pastor. Ha'
you brought money
To buy more coals?
Ana. No, surely

Sub.   No? How so?

Ana. The Brethren bid me say unto you,
    sir,
    Surely they will not venter any more
    Till they may see *projection.*

Sub.   How!

Ana.   Yo' have had
    For the *instruments,* as bricks and lome,[1]
    and glasses,
    Already thirty pound, and for *materials,*
    They say, some ninety more; and they
    have heard since
    That one at Heidelberg made it of an
    egg   70
    And a small paper of pin dust.[2]

Sub.   What's your name?

Ana. My name is Ananias.

Sub.   Out, the varlet
    That cozened the apostles! Hence, away!
    Flee, mischief! Had your holy consistory
    No name to send me of another sound
    Than wicked Ananias? Send your elders
    Hither, to make atonement for you,
    quickly,
    And gi' me satisfaction; or out goes
    The fire, and down th' *alembics,* and the
    fornace,
    Piger Henricus, or what not. Thou
    wretch!   80
    Both *sericon* and *bufo* shall be lost,
    Tell hem. All hope of rooting out the
    bishops
    Or th' antichristian hierarchy shall per-
    ish,
    If they stay threescore minutes; the
    aqueity,
    Terreity, and *sulphureity*
    Shall run together again, and all be
    annulled,
    Thou wicked Ananias!—[*Exit Ananias.*]
    This will fetch hem,
    And make hem haste towards their
    gulling more.
    A man must deal like a rough nurse, and
    fright   89
    Those that are froward, to an appetite.

Act II. Scene vi.

Face [in his uniform], Subtle, Drugger.

[Face.] H' is busy with his spirits, but
    we'll upon him.

[1] A vessel.
[2] Dust from the manufacture of pins.

Sub. How now! What mates,[3] what
    Bayards [4] ha' we here?

Face. I told you he would be furious.—
    Sir, here's Nab
    Has brought yo' another piece of gold to
    look on
    (We must appease him. Give it me.)
    and prays you
    You would devise—(What is it, Nab?)

Drug.   A sign, sir.

Face. Ay, a good lucky one, a thriving
    sign, doctor.

Sub. I was devising now.

Face. [*Aside to Subtle.*]   'Slight, do not
    say so;
    He will repent he ga' you any more.—
    What say you to his constellation, doctor,
    The Balance?

Sub.   No, that way is stale and com-
    mon.   11
    A townsman born in Taurus gives the
    Bull,
    Or the bull's head; in Aries, the Ram—
    A poor device! No, I will have his name
    Formed in some mystic character, whose
    radii,
    Striking the senses of the passers-by,
    Shall, by a virtual influence,[5] breed affec-
    tions [6]
    That may result upon the party owns it,
    As thus—

Face. Nab!

Sub.   He first shall have *a bell*—
    that's *Abel;*
    And by it standing one whose name is
    Dee,[7]   20
    In a *rug* [8] gown; there's D, and *rug*—
    that's *Drug;*
    And right anenst [9] him a dog snarling
    "er"—
    There's Drugger, Abel Drugger. That's
    his sign.
    And here's now mystery and hiero-
    glyphic!

Face. Abel, thou art made.

[3] Wretches.
[4] Blind fools—named from a legendary blind
horse of Charlemagne.
[5] *I.e.,* an influence deriving from the virtue or
power of the symbol.
[6] Inclinations.
[7] Referring to the mathematician and astrolo-
ger, Dr. John Dee, popularly regarded as a
magician, who had recently died.
[8] Coarse cloth.
[9] Beside.

Drug. [*Bowing*.]   Sir, I do thank his
  worship.
Face. Six o' thy legs [1] more will not do it,
  Nab.—
  He has brought you a pipe of tabacco,
  doctor.
Drug.   Yes, sir.
I have another thing I would impart—
Face. Out with it, Nab.
Drug.   Sir, there is lodged hard by me
  A rich young widow—
Face.   Good! A *bona roba?* [2]   31
Drug. But nineteen at the most.
Face.   Very good, Abel.
Drug. Marry, sh' is not in fashion yet· she
  wears
  A hood, but 't stands acop.[3]
Face.   No matter, Abel.
Drug. And I do now and then give her a
  fucus—
Face. What! Dost thou deal, Nab?
Sub.   I did tell you, captain.
Drug. And physic too sometime, sir, for
  which she trusts me
  With all her mind. She's come up here
  of purpose
  To learn the fashion.
Face.   Good! (His match too!)
  On, Nab.
Drug. And she does strangely long to
  know her fortune.   40
Face. God's lid, Nab, send her to the
  doctor, hither.
Drug. Yes, I have spoke to her of his
  worship already;
  But she's afraid it will be blown abroad,
  And hurt her marriage.
Face.   Hurt it? 'Tis the way
  To heal it, if 'twere hurt—to make it
  more
  Followed and sought. Nab, thou shalt
  tell her this.
  She'll be more known, more talked of;
  and your widows
  Are ne'er of any price till they be famous;
  Their honor is their multitude of suitors.
  Send her; it may be thy good fortune.
  What?   50
  Thou dost not know?
Drug.   No, sir, she'll never marry
  Under a knight; her brother has made
  a vow.

Face. What, and dost thou despair, my
  little Nab,
  Knowing what the doctor has set down
  for thee,
  And seeing so many o' the city dubbed?
  One glass o' thy water, with a madam I
  know,
  Will have it done, Nab. What's her
  brother? A knight?
Drug. No, sir, a gentleman newly warm
  in his land, sir,
  Scarce cold in his one-and-twenty, that
  does govern
  His sister here, and is a man himself   60
  Of some three thousand a year, and is
  come up
  To learn to quarrel, and to live by his
  wits,
  And will go down again, and die i' the
  country.
Face. How! To quarrel?
Drug.   Yes, sir, to carry quarrels
  As gallants do, and manage hem by line.[4]
Face. 'Slid, Nab, the doctor is the only
  man
  In Christendom for him. He has made
  a table,
  With mathematical demonstrations,
  Touching the art of quarrels. He will
  give him
  An instrument to quarrel by. Go, bring
  hem both,   76
  Him and his sister. And, for thee, with
  her
  The doctor haply may persuade.[5] Go to!
  Shalt give his worship a new damask suit
  Upon the premises.
Sub.   O, good captain!
Face.   He shall;
  He is the honestest fellow, doctor. Stay
  not,
  No offers; bring the damask and the
  parties.
Drug. I'll try my power, sir.
Face.   And thy will too, Nab.
Sub. 'Tis good tabacco, this! What is 't an
  ounce?
Face. He'll send you a pound, doctor.
Sub.   O, no.
Face.   He will do 't.
  It is the goodest soul!—Abel, about it.
  (Thou shalt know more anon. Away, be-
  gone.)—   [*Exit Abel.*] 81

---

[1] Bows.   [2] Fine wench.
[3] On the top of her head, not tilted.
[4] Rule.   [5] Plead.

A miserable rogue, and lives with cheese,
And has the worms. That was the cause,
    indeed,
Why he came now; he dealt with me in
    private,
To get a med'cine for hem.
SUB.   And shall, sir. This works.
FACE. A wife, a wife for one on us, my dear
    Subtle!
We'll e'en draw lots, and he that fails
    shall have
The more in goods, the other has in tail.
SUB. Rather the less, for she may be so
    light
She may want grains.[1]
FACE.   Ay; or be such a burden 90
A man would scarce endure her for the
    whole.
SUB. Faith, best let's see her first, and
    then determine.
FACE. Content, but Doll must ha' no
    breath on 't.
SUB.   Mum!
    Away, you, to your Surly yonder; catch
    him.
FACE. Pray God I ha' not stayed too long.
SUB.   I fear it. [*Exeunt.*]

ACT III. SCENE i.

[*The street before Lovewit's house.*]

Tribulation, Ananias.

[TRI.] These chastisements are common
    to the Saints,
And such rebukes we of the separation [2]
Must bear with willing shoulders as the
    trials
Sent forth to tempt our frailties.
ANA.   In pure zeal,
I do not like the man; he is a heathen,
And speaks the language of Canaan,
    truly.
TRI. I think him a profane person indeed.
ANA.   He bears
The visible mark of the beast in his
    forehead.
And, for his *stone*, it is a work of darkness,
And with *philosophy* blinds the eyes of
    man. 10
TRI. Good brother, we must bend unto all
    means
That may give furtherance to the holy
    cause.

[1] Groins, with a pun on the measure of weight.
[2] Dissenting sect.

ANA. Which his cannot. The sanctified
    cause
Should have a sanctified course.
TRI.   Not always necessary.
The children of perdition are ofttimes
Made instruments even of the greatest
    works.
Beside, we should give somewhat to [3]
    man's nature,
The place he lives in, still about the fire
And fume of metals, that intoxicate
The brain of man and make him prone
    to passion. 20
Where have you greater atheists than
    your cooks?
Or more profane or choleric than your
    glassmen?
More antichristian than your bell-
    founders?
What makes the devil so devilish, I
    would ask you,
Sathan, our common enemy, but his
    being
Perpetually about the fire, and boiling
Brimstone and arsenic? We must give,
    I say,
Unto the motives and the stirrers-up
Of humors in the blood. It may be so.
Whenas [4] the *work* is done, the *stone* is
    made, 30
This heat of his may turn into a zeal,
And stand up for the beauteous discipline
Against the menstruous cloth and rag of
    Rome.
We must await his calling and the com-
    ing
Of the good spirit. You did fault t' up-
    braid him
With the Brethren's blessing of Heidel-
    berg, weighing
What need we have to hasten on the work
For the restoring of the silenced Saints,[5]
Which ne'er will be but by the *philos-*
    ophers' stone. 39
And so a learned elder, one of Scotland,
Assured me, *aurum potabile* [6] being
The only med'cine for the civil magistrate
T' incline him to a feeling of the cause,
And must be daily used in the disease.

[3] Make allowance for.
[4] When.
[5] Non-conformist clergy not permitted to
preach.
[6] Drinkable gold, an elixir; here a bribe.

Ana. I have not edified [1] more, truly, by man,
Not since the beautiful light first shone on me;
And I am sad my zeal hath so offended.
Tri. Let us call on him then.
Ana.　　　　　　The motion's good,
And of the spirit. I will knock first.—
[*Knocks.*] Peace be within!
　　　　　　　　[*Exeunt into the house.*] [2]

Act III. Scene ii.

[*A room in Lovewit's house.*] [3]

Subtle, Tribulation, Ananias.

[Sub.] O, are you come? 'Twas time. Your threescore minutes
Were at the last thread, you see; and down had gone
Furnus acediæ, turris circulatorius;
Lembec, [4] *bolt's-head, retort,* and *pelican*
Had all been cinders. Wicked Ananias!
Art thou returned? Nay, then it goes down yet.
Tri. Sir, be appeased; he is come to humble
Himself in spirit, and to ask your patience,
If too much zeal hath carried him aside
From the due path.
Sub.　　　　Why, this doth qualify! [5] 10
Tri. The Brethren had no purpose, verily,
To give you the least grievance, but are ready
To lend their willing hands to any project
The spirit and you direct.
Sub.　　　　　　This qualifies more!
Tri. And, for the orphans' goods, let them be valued,
Or what is needful else to the holy work,
It shall be numbered; here, by me, the Saints
Throw down their purse before you.
Sub.　　　　　　This qualifies most!
Why, thus it should be, now you understand.
Have I discoursed so unto you of our *stone,* 20

And of the good that it shall bring your cause?
Showed you (beside the main [6] of hiring forces
Abroad, drawing the Hollanders, your friends,
From th' Indies to serve you with all their fleet)
That even the med'cinal use shall make you a faction
And party in the realm? As, put the case
That some great man in state, he have the gout,
Why, you but send three drops of your *elixir,*
You help him straight; there you have made a friend.
Another has the palsy or the dropsy; 30
He takes of your incombustible stuff,
He's young again; there you have made a friend.
A lady that is past the feat of body,
Though not of mind, and hath her face decayed
Beyond all cure of paintings, you restore
With the *oil of talc;* there you have made a friend—
And all her friends. A lord that is a leper,
A knight that has the boneache, or a squire
That hath both these, you make hem smooth and sound
With a bare *fricace* [7] of your *med'cine;* still 40
You increase your friends.
Tri.　　　　　Ay, 'tis very pregnant.
Sub. And then the turning of this lawyer's pewter
To plate at Christmas—
Ana.　　　　　Christ-tide, I pray you.
Sub. Yet, [8] Ananias!
Ana.　　　　I have done.
Sub.　　　　　　Or changing
His parcel [9] gilt to massy gold. You cannot
But raise you friends. Withal, to be of power
To pay an army in the field, to buy

---

[1] Been edified.
[2] They perhaps simply pass from the outer to the inner stage by the drawing of the traverse.
[3] The scene and action are continuous through the remainder of the act.　　　[5] Mollify.
[4] Alembic.

[6] Important matter.
[7] Rubbing.
[8] An exclamation of impatience.
[9] Partly.

The King of France out of his realms,
　or Spain
Out of his Indies—what can you not do
Against lords spiritual or temporal　50
That shall oppone [1] you?
Tri.　　　　　　　　　Verily, 'tis true.
We may be temporal lords ourselves, I
　take it.
Sub. You may be anything, and leave off
　to make
Long-winded exercises, or suck up
Your "ha!" and "hum!" in a tune. I
　not deny,
But such as are not gracéd in a state,
May, for their ends, be adverse in re-
　ligion,
And get a tune to call the flock together,
For, to say sooth, a tune does much with
　women
And other phlegmatic people; it is your
　bell.　　　　　　　　　　　　　　60
Ana. Bells are profane; a tune may be
　religious.
Sub. No warning with you? Then fare-
　well my patience.
'Slight, it shall down; I will not be thus
　tortured.
Tri. I pray you, sir.
Sub.　　　All shall perish. I have spoke it.
Tri. Let me find grace, sir, in your eyes;
　the man,
He stands corrected. Neither did his
　zeal,
But as yourself, allow a tune somewhere,
Which now, being toward [2] the *stone*,
　we shall not need.
Sub. No, nor your holy vizard,[3] to win
　widows
To give you legacies; or make zealous
　wives　　　　　　　　　　　　　70
To rob their husbands for the common
　cause;
Nor take the start of bonds broke but
　one day,[4]
And say they were forfeited by provi-
　dence.
Nor shall you need o'er night to eat huge
　meals,
To celebrate your next day's fast the
　better,

The whilst the Brethren and the Sisters,
　humbled,
Abate the stiffness of the flesh. Nor cast
Before your hungry hearers scrupulous
　bones,[5]
As whether a Christian may hawk or
　hunt,　　　　　　　　　　　　　79
Or whether matrons of the holy assembly
May lay their hair out, or wear doublets,
Or have that idol, starch, about their
　linen.
Ana. It is indeed an idol.
Tri.　　　　　　　　Mind him not, sir.
I do command thee, spirit (of zeal, but
　trouble),
To peace within him! Pray you, sir, go
　on.
Sub. Nor shall you need to libel gainst
　the prelates,
And shorten so your ears [6] against the
　hearing
Of the next wiredrawn grace; nor of
　necessity
Rail against plays, to please the alder-
　man
Whose daily custard you devour; nor
　lie　　　　　　　　　　　　　90
With zealous rage till you are hoarse.
　Not one
Of these so singular arts! Nor call your-
　selves
By names of Tribulation, Persecution,
Restraint, Long-patience, and suchlike,
　affected
By the whole family or wood [7] of you,
Only for glory, and to catch the ear
Of the disciple.
Tri.　　　　　　　　Truly, sir, they are
Ways that the godly Brethren have in-
　vented
For propagation of the glorious cause,
As very notable means, and whereby
　also　　　　　　　　　　　　　100
Themselves grow soon and profitably
　famous.
Sub. O, but the *stone*, all's idle to it! Noth-
　ing!
The art of angels, nature's miracle,
The *divine secret* that doth fly in clouds
From east to west, and whose tradition
Is not from men, but *spirits*.

---

[1] Oppose.
[2] Near to owning.
[3] Mask, sanctimonious expression.
[4] *I.e.*, foreclose obligations just expired.
[5] Dry bones of discussion on small points.
[6] Lose your ears in a pillory.
[7] Crowd.

ANA.   I hate traditions;
I do not trust them——
TRI.   Peace!
ANA.   They are popish all.
I will not peace. I will not——
TRI.   Ananias!
ANA. Please the profane, to grieve the
godly; I may not.   109
SUB. Well, Ananias, thou shalt overcome.
TRI. It is an ignorant zeal that haunts
him, sir—
But truly else a very faithful Brother,
A botcher,[1] and a man by revelation
That hath a competent knowledge of
the truth.
SUB. Has he a competent sum there i'
the bag
To buy the goods within? I am made
guardian,
And must, for charity and conscience'
sake,
Now see the most be made for my poor
orphan,
Though I desire the Brethren, too, good
gainers.
There they are within. When you have
viewed and bought hem,   120
And ta'en the inventory of what they
are,
They are ready for *projection;* there's no
more
To do. Cast on the *med'cine,* so much
silver
As there is tin there, so much gold as
brass,
I'll gi' it you in by weight.
TRI.   But how long time,
Sir, must the Saints expect[2] yet?
SUB.   Let me see,
How's the moon now? Eight, nine, ten
days hence,
He will be *silver potate;* then three days
Before he *citronize;* some fifteen days,
The *magisterium* will be perfected.   130
ANA. About the second day of the third
week
In the ninth month?
SUB.   Yes, my good Ananias.
TRI. What will the orphans' goods arise
to, think you?
SUB. Some hundred marks, as much as
filled three cars,[3]

---

[1] Tailor, a cant term for Puritan.
[2] Wait.   [3] Carts.

Unladed now; you'll make six millions
of hem.
But I must ha' more coals laid in.
TRI.   How!
SUB.   Another load,
And then we ha' finished. We must
now increase
Our fire to *ignis ardens;* we are past
Fimus equinus, balnei, cineris,
And all those lenter heats. If the holy
purse   140
Should with this draught fall low, and
that the Saints
Do need a present sum, I have [a][4] trick
To melt the pewter you shall buy now
instantly,
And with a *tincture* make you as good
Dutch dollars
As any are in Holland.
TRI.   Can you so?
SUB. Ay, and shall bide the third exami-
nation.
ANA. It will be joyful tidings to the
Brethren.
SUB. But you must carry it secret.
TRI.   Ay; but stay—
This act of coining, is it lawful?
ANA.   Lawful?
We know[5] no magistrate; or, if we did,
This's foreign coin.
SUB.   It is no coining, sir.   151
It is but casting.
TRI.   Ha! You distinguish well.
Casting of money may be lawful.
ANA.   'Tis, sir.
TRI. Truly, I take it so.
SUB.   There is no scruple,
Sir, to be made of it; believe Ananias;
This case of conscience he is studied in.
TRI. I'll make a question of it to the Breth·
ren.
ANA. The Brethren shall approve it law-
ful, doubt not.
Where shall 't be done?
SUB.   For that we'll talk anon.
                    Knock without.
There's some to speak with me. Go in,
I pray you,   160
And view the parcels. That's the in-
ventory.
I'll come to you straight.—[*Exeunt Trib-
ulation and Ananias.*] Who is it?—
Face, appear!

---

[4] From 1640 edn.   [5] Acknowledge.

Act III. Scene iii.

Subtle, Face, Doll.[1]

[Sub.] How now? Good prize?

Face.　　　Good pox! Yond' costive cheater
Never came on.

Sub.　　　How then?

Face.　　　　　　I ha' walked the round
Till now, and no such thing.

Sub.　　　　　　And ha' you quit him?

Face. Quit him? And hell would quit
　　him too, he were happy.

'Slight! Would you have me stalk like
　　a mill jade,

All day, for one that will not yield us
　　grains?

I know him of old.

Sub.　　　　　O, but to ha' gulled him
Had been a maistry.[2]

Face.　　　　　　Let him go, black boy!
And turn thee, that some fresh news
　　may possess thee.

A noble count, a don of Spain (my
　　dear　　　　　　　　　　　　　　10

Delicious compeer, and my party-[3]
　　bawd),

Who is come hither private for his con-
　　science

And brought munition with him, six
　　great slops,[4]

Bigger than three Dutch hoys,[5] beside
　　round trunks,[6]

Furnished with pistolets[7] and pieces of
　　eight,[7]

Will straight be here, my rogue, to have
　　thy bath

(That is the color[8]) and to make his
　　batt'ry

Upon our Doll, our castle, our Cinque
　　Port,[9]

Our Dover pier, our what thou wilt.
　　Where is she?

She must prepare perfumes, delicate
　　linen,　　　　　　　　　　　　　20

The bath in chief, a banquet, and her
　　wit,

For she must milk his epididymis—
Where is the doxy?

Sub.　　　　　　I'll send her to thee,

And but despatch my brace of little
　　John Leydens[10]
And come again myself.

Face.　　　　　　Are they within then?

Sub. Numb'ring the sum.

Face. How much?

Sub.　　　A hundred marks, boy. [*Exit.*]

Face. Why, this 's a lucky day. Ten
　　pounds of Mammon!

Three o' my clerk! A portague o' my
　　grocer!

This o' the Brethren! Beside rever-
　　sions

And states to come i' the widow and
　　my count!　　　　　　　　　　30

My share today will not be bought for
　　forty—

[Enter Doll.]

Doll.　　　What?

Face. Pounds, dainty Dorothy! Art
　　thou so near?

Doll. Yes. Say, lord general, how fares
　　our camp?

Face. As with the few that had entrenched
　　themselves

Safe, by their discipline, against a world,
　　Doll,

And laughed within those trenches, and
　　grew fat

With thinking on the booties, Doll,
　　brought in

Daily by their small parties. This dear
　　hour

A doughty don is taken with my Doll;

And thou mayst make his ransom what
　　thou wilt,　　　　　　　　　　40

My dowsabel;[11] he shall be brought here,
　　fettered

With thy fair looks, before he sees thee,
　　and thrown

In a down bed as dark as any dun-
　　geon,

Where thou shalt keep him waking with
　　thy drum—

Thy drum, my Doll, thy drum—till he
　　be tame

As the poor blackbirds were i' the great
　　frost,[12]

Or bees are with a basin, and so hive
　　him

---

[1] Enters later.
[2] Mastery, achievement.
[3] Partner.
[4] Loose breeches.
[5] Ships.
[6] Trunk hose.
[7] Gold coins.
[8] Pretext.
[9] One of five strategic Channel towns.
[10] Puritans, so called from their leader, John
Bockholdt, or John of Leyden.
[11] Sweetheart.
[12] Of 1608.

I' the swan-skin coverlid and cambric sheets,
Till he work honey and wax, my little God's-gift.[1]

DOLL. What is he, general?

FACE. An adalantado,[2] 50
A grandee, girl. Was not my Dapper here yet?

DOLL. No.

FACE. Nor my Drugger?

DOLL. Neither.

FACE. A pox on hem,
They are so long a-furnishing! Such stinkards
Would not be seen upon these festival days.—

[Enter Subtle.]

How now! Ha' you done?

SUB. Done. They are gone; the sum
Is here in bank, my Face. I would we knew
Another chapman[3] now would buy hem outright.

FACE. 'Slid, Nab shall do 't against he ha' the widow,
To furnish household.

SUB. Excellent, well thought on.
Pray God he come.

FACE. I pray he keep away 60
Till our new business be o'erpast.

SUB. But, Face,
How cam'st thou by this secret don?

[FACE.][4] A spirit
Brought me th' intelligence in a paper here,
As I was conjuring yonder in my circle
For Surly; I ha' my flies abroad. Your bath
Is famous, Subtle, by my means. Sweet Doll,
You must go tune your virginal, no losing
O' the least time. And—do you hear?— good action!
Firk like a flounder; kiss like a scallop, close;
And tickle him with thy mother-tongue. His great 70

Verdugoship[5] has not a jot of language[6]—
So much the easier to be cozened, my Dolly.
He will come here in a hired coach, obscure,
And our own coachman, whom I have sent, as guide,
No creature else. (*One knocks.*) Who's that? *[Exit Doll.]*

SUB. It i' not he?

FACE. O, no, not yet this hour.

[Enter Doll.]

SUB. Who is 't?

DOLL. Dapper,
Your clerk.

FACE. God's will then, Queen of Fairy,
On with your tire[7]—*[Exit Doll.]* and, doctor, with your robes.
Let's despatch him for God's sake.

SUB. 'Twill be long.

FACE. I warrant you, take but the cues I give you, 80
It shall be brief enough. [*Goes to the window.*] 'Slight, here are more!
Abel and, I think, the angry boy, the heir
That fain would quarrel.

SUB. And the widow?

FACE. No,
Not that I see. Away!—[*Exit Subtle.*]
O, sir, you are welcome.

ACT III. SCENE iv.

Face, Dapper, Drugger, Kastril.[8]

[FACE.] The doctor is within, a-moving for you.
(I have had the most ado to win him to it!)
He swears you'll be the dearling o' the dice;
He never heard her highness dote till now, he says.
Your aunt has giv'n you the most gracious words
That can be thought on.

DAP. Shall I see her grace?

FACE. See her, and kiss her too.—

---

[1] Alluding to the etymological meaning of *Dorothea*.
[2] Adelantado, a Spanish governor.
[3] Dealer. [4] From 1612 edn.
[5] Hangmanship; a word coined from the Spanish.
[6] *I.e.*, he cannot speak English.
[7] Attire. [8] The last two enter later.

[*Enter Drugger and Kastril.*]

                 What, honest Nab!
Hast brought the damask?

NAB.   No, sir; here's tabacco.

FACE. 'Tis well done, Nab. Thou'lt bring
    the damask too?

DRUG. Yes. Here's the gentleman, cap-
    tain, Master Kastril,   10
I have brought to see the doctor.

FACE.   Where's the widow?

DRUG. Sir, as he likes, his sister, he says,
    shall come.

FACE. O, is it so? Good time. Is your
    name Kastril, sir?

KAS. Ay, and the best o' the Kastrils—
    I'ld be sorry else—
By fifteen hundred a year. Where is this
    doctor?
My mad tabacco-boy here tells me of
    one
That can do things. Has he any skill?

FACE.   Wherein, sir?

KAS. To carry a business, manage a
    quarrel fairly,
Upon fit terms.

FACE   It seems, sir, yo' are but young
About the town, that can make that a
    question.   20

KAS. Sir, not so young but I have heard
    some speech
Of the angry boys,[1] and seen hem take
    tabacco,
And in his shop; and I can take it too.
And I would fain be one of hem, and go
    down
And practice i' the country.

FACE.   Sir, for the duello,
The doctor, I assure you, shall inform
    you
To the least shadow of a hair, and show
    you
An instrument he has of his own making,
Wherewith, no sooner shall you make
    report
Of any quarrel, but he will take the
    height on 't   30
Most instantly, and tell in what degree
Of safety it lies in, or mortality,
And how it may be borne, whether in a
    right line
Or a half circle, or may else be cast
Into an angle blunt, if not acute—

[1] Roisterers.

All this he will demonstrate; and then,
    rules
To give and take the lie by.

KAS.   How? To take it?

FACE. Yes, in oblique[2] he'll show you, or
    in circle;[2]
But ne'er in diameter.[3] The whole
    town
Study his theorems, and dispute them
    ordinarily   40
At the eating academies.

KAS.   But does he teach
Living by the wits too?

FACE.   Anything whatever.
You cannot think that subtlety but he
    reads it.
He made me a captain. I was a stark
    pimp,
Just o' your standing, fore I met with
    him;
It i' not two months since. I'll tell you
    his method:
First, he will enter you at some ordi-
    nary.

KAS. No, I'll not come there. You shall
    pardon me.

FACE.   For why, sir?

KAS. There's gaming there, and tricks.

FACE.   Why, would you be
A gallant, and not game?

KAS.   Ay, 'twill spend a man. 50

FACE. Spend you? It will repair you when
    you are spent.
How do they live by their wits there,
    that have vented
Six times your fortunes?

KAS.   What, three thousand a year!

FACE. Ay, forty thousand.

KAS.   Are there such?

FACE.   Ay, sir,
And gallants yet. Here's a young gentle-
    man
Is born to nothing—[*Indicates Dapper.*]
    forty marks a year,
Which I count nothing. H' is to be
    initiated,
And have a fly o' the doctor. He will win
    you
By unresistible luck, within this fort-
    night,
Enough to buy a barony. They will set
    him   60

[2] *I.e.*, the lie circumstantial.
[3] *I.e.*, the lie direct.

Upmost, at the groom porter's,[1] all the
　　Christmas,
And, for the whole year through at every
　　place
Where there is play, present him with the
　　chair,
The best attendance, the best drink,
　　sometimes
Two glasses of Canary—and pay noth-
　　ing—
The purest linen and the sharpest knife,
The partrich [2] next his trencher, and
　　somewhere
The dainty bed, in private, with the
　　dainty.
You shall ha' your ordinaries bid for
　　him,
As playhouses for a poet, and the mas-
　　ter　　　　　　　　　　　　　　　　70
Pray him aloud to name what dish he
　　affects,
Which must be buttered shrimps; and
　　those that drink
To no mouth else will drink to his, as
　　being
The goodly president mouth of all the
　　board.
KAS. Do you not gull one?
FACE. 　　'Od's my life! Do you think it?
You shall have a cast [3] commander (can
　　but get
In credit with a glover or a spurrier
For some two pair of either's ware afore-
　　hand)
Will, by most swift posts, dealing with
　　him,
Arrive at competent means to keep
　　himself,　　　　　　　　　　　　80
His punk, and naked boy in excellent
　　fashion,
And be admired for 't.
KAS. 　　　　　Will the doctor teach this?
FACE. He will do more, sir: when your
　　land is gone
(As men of spirit hate to keep earth
　　long),
In a vacation,[4] when small money is
　　stirring,
And ordinaries suspended till the term,

He'll show a perspective [5] where on one
　　side
You shall behold the faces and the per-
　　sons
Of all sufficient young heirs in town,　89
Whose bonds are current for commodity;
On th' other side, the merchants' forms,
　　and others
That, without help of any second broker,
Who would expect a share, will trust such
　　parcels;
In the third square, the very street and
　　sign
Where the commodity dwells, and does
　　but wait
To be delivered, be it pepper. soap,
Hops, or tabacco, oatmeal, woad,[6] or
　　cheeses—
All which you may so handle, to enjoy
To your own use, and never stand
　　obliged.
KAS. I' faith, is he such a fellow?
FACE. 　　Why, Nab here knows him.　100
And then for making matches for rich
　　widows,
Young gentlewomen, heirs, the for-
　　tunat'st man!
He's sent to, far and near, all over
　　England,
To have his counsel and to know their
　　fortunes.
KAS. God's will, my suster [7] shall see him.
FACE. 　　　　　　　　　I'll tell you, sir,
What he did tell me of Nab. It's a
　　strange thing!
(By the way, you must eat no cheese,
　　Nab; it breeds melancholy,
And that same melancholy breeds worms
　　—but pass it.)
He told me, honest Nab here was ne'er
　　at tavern　　　　　　　　　　　109
But once in 's life.
DRUG. 　　Truth, and no more I was not.
FACE. And then he was so sick—
DRUG. 　　　　Could he tell you that too?
FACE. How should I know it?
DRUG. 　In troth, we had been a-shooting,
And had a piece of fat ram-mutton to
　　supper,
That lay so heavy o' my stomach—

---

[1] An officer of the court who superintended
gaming.
　[2] Partridge.
　[3] Cassed, cashiered, dismissed.
　[4] Of the law courts.

[5] A picture the appearance of which changes
according to the angle of vision.
　[6] A plant which produced blue dye.
　[7] Provincial form for *sister*.

FACE.   And he has no head
To bear any wine; for what with the
noise o' the fiddlers
And care of his shop, for he dares keep
no servants—
DRUG. My head did so ache—
FACE.   As he was fain to be brought
home,
The doctor told me. And then a good
old woman—
DRUG. Yes, faith, she dwells in Seacoal
Lane—did cure me
With sodden [1] ale and pellitory o' the
wall [2]—   120
Cost me but twopence. I had another
sickness
Was worse than that.
FACE.   Ay, that was with the grief
Thou took'st for being cessed [3] at eigh-
teenpence
For the waterwork.
DRUG.   In truth, and it was like
T' have cost me almost my life.
FACE.   Thy hair went off?
DRUG. Yes, sir; 'twas done for spite.
FACE.   Nay, so says the doctor.
KAS. Pray thee, tabacco-boy, go fetch my
suster;
I'll see this learned boy before I go;
And so shall she.
FACE.   Sir, he is busy now;
But, if you have a sister to fetch
hither,   130
Perhaps your own pains may command
her sooner,
And he by that time will be free.
KAS.   I go. [Exit.]
FACE. Drugger, she's thine. The damask!
—[Exit Abel.] (Subtle and I
Must wrastle for her.) Come on, Master
Dapper;
You see how I turn clients here
away,
To give your cause despatch; ha' you
performed
The ceremonies were enjoined you?
DAP.   Yes, o' the vinegar
And the clean shirt.
FACE. 'Tis well. That shirt may do you
More worship than you think. Your
aunt's afire,

[1] Heated.
[2] Wall-pellitory, a herb.
[3] Assessed.

But that she will not show it, t' have a
sight on you.   140
Ha' you provided for her grace's serv-
ants?
DAP. Yes, here are sixscore Edward shil-
lings—
FACE.   Good!
DAP. And an old Harry's sovereign—
FACE.   Very good!
DAP. And three James shillings, and an
Elizabeth groat—
Just twenty nobles.
FACE.   O, you are too just.
I would you had had the other noble in
Marys.
DAP. I have some Philip and Marys.
FACE.   Ay, those same
Are best of all. Where are they? Hark,
the doctor.

ACT III. SCENE v.

*Subtle, Face, Dapper, Doll.[4] Subtle disguised
like a Priest of Fairy.*

[SUB.] Is yet her grace's cousin come?
FACE.   He is come.
SUB. And is he fasting?
FACE.   Yes.
SUB.   And hath cried "hum"?
FACE. Thrice, you must answer.
DAP.   Thrice.
SUB.   And as oft "buzz"?
FACE. If you have, say.
DAP.   I have.
SUB.   Then, to her coz,
Hoping that he hath vinegared his senses,
As he was bid, the Fairy Queen dispenses,
By me, this robe, the petticoat of For-
tune,
Which that he straight put on, she doth
importune.
And though to Fortune near be her
petticoat,
Yet nearer is her smock, the queen doth
note;   10
And therefore even of that a piece she
hath sent,
Which, being a child, to wrap him in was
rent,
And prays him for a scarf he now will
wear it
(With as much love as then her grace
did tear it)

[4] Enters later.

About his eyes (*They blind him with a
rag.*) to show he is fortunate.
And, trusting unto her to make his state,
He'll throw away all worldly pelf about
him;
Which that he will perform, she doth not
doubt him.

FACE. She need not doubt him, sir. Alas,
he has nothing
But what he will part withal as will-
ingly,   20
Upon her grace's word (throw away your
purse),
As she would ask it. (Handkerchiefs and
all!)
She cannot bid that thing but he'll obey.
(If you have a ring about you, cast it off,
Or a silver seal at your wrist; her grace
will send
        He throws away, as they bid him.
Her fairies here to search you; therefore
deal
Directly [1] with her highness. If they find
That you conceal a mite, you are un-
done.)

DAP. Truly, there's all.

FACE.   All what?

DAP.   My money; truly.

FACE. Keep nothing that is transitory
about you.   30
(Bid Doll play music.)

Doll enters with a cittern. They pinch him.

                     Look, the elves are come
To pinch you, if you tell not truth. Advise you.

DAP. O! I have a paper with a spur ryal [2]
in 't.

FACE.   *Ti, ti.*
They knew 't, they say.

SUB.   *Ti, ti, ti, ti.* He has more yet.

FACE. *Ti, ti-ti-ti.* I' the tother [3] pocket?

SUB.   *Titi, titi, titi, titi.*
They must pinch him or he will never
confess, they say.
                     [*They pinch him again.*]

DAP. O, O!

FACE.   Nay, pray you, hold. He is her
grace's nephew.—
Ti, ti, ti? What care you? Good faith,
you shall care.—

---

[1] Honestly.   [3] Other.
[2] Spur royal, a gold coin.

Deal plainly, sir, and shame the fairies.
Show   39
You are an innocent.

DAP.   By this good light, I ha' nothing.

SUB. *Titi, tititota.* He does equivocate, she
says—
Ti, ti do ti, ti ti do, ti da—and swears by
the light when he is blinded.

DAP. By this good dark, I ha' nothing but
a half crown
Of gold about my wrist, that my love
gave me;
And a leaden heart I wore sin' she forsook
me.

FACE. I thought 'twas something. And
would you incur
Your aunt's displeasure for these trifles?
Come,
I had rather you had thrown away
twenty half crowns. [*Removes the coin.*]
You may wear your leaden heart still.—
How now?

SUB. [*Aside.*] What news, Doll?

DOLL. [*Aside.*]   Yonder's your knight,
Sir Mammon.   50

FACE. [*Aside.*] God's lid, we never thought
of him till now!
Where is he?

DOLL. [*Aside.*]   Here hard by. H' is at
the door.

SUB. [*Aside.*] And you are not ready now?
Doll, get his suit.—   [*Exit Doll.*]
He must not be sent back.

FACE. [*Aside.*]   O, by no means.
What shall we do with this same puffin
here,
Now he's o' the spit?

SUB. [*Aside.*]   Why, lay him back
awhile
With some device.—

[*Enter Doll with Face's clothes.*]

                     Ti, titi, tititi. Would her grace
speak with me?
I come.—Help, Doll!

FACE. (*He speaks through the keyhole, the
Other knocking.*)   Who's there?
Sir Epicure,
My master's i' the way. Please you to
walk
Three or four turns but till his back be
turned,   60
And I am for you.—Quickly, Doll!

Sub.　　　　　　　　　　　Her grace
　Commends her kindly to you, Master
　　Dapper.

Dap. I long to see her grace.

Sub.　　　　　　　　　She now is set
　At dinner in her bed, and she has sent you
　From her own private trencher a dead
　　mouse
　And a piece of gingerbread, to be merry
　　withal
　And stay your stomach, lest you faint
　　with fasting;
　Yet if you could hold out till she saw
　　you, she says,
　It would be better for you.

Face.　　　　　　　　Sir, he shall
　Hold out, and 'twere this two hours, for
　　her highness;　　　　　　　　　　70
　I can assure you that. We will not lose
　All we ha' done.—

Sub.　　　　He must not see nor speak
　To anybody till then.

Face.　　　　　　For that we'll put, sir,
　A stay in 'is mouth.

Sub.　　　　　　　　Of what?

Face.　　　　　　　　Of gingerbread.
　Make you it fit. He that hath pleased
　　her grace
　Thus far, shall not now crinkle [1] for a
　　little.—
　Gape, sir, and let him fit you.
　　　　　　　　　　　　　　[They gag him.]

Sub. [Aside.]　　　　Where shall we now
　Bestow him?

Doll. [Aside.]　　　　　I' the privy.

Sub.　　　　　　　　Come along, sir;
　I must now show you Fortune's privy
　　lodgings.

Face. Are they perfumed, and his bath
　　ready?

Sub.　　All.　　　　　　　　　　　　80
　Only the fumigation's somewhat strong.

Face. [Through the keyhole.] Sir Epicure,
　I am yours, sir, by-and-by.[2]
　　[Exeunt Subtle and Doll with Dapper.]

Act IV. Scene i.

[The same.]

Face, Mammon, Doll.[3]

[Face.] O, sir, yo' are come i' the only
　finest time!

Mam. Where's master?

[1] Turn aside.　　[2] Immediately.　　[3] Enters later.

Face.　Now preparing for projection, sir.
　Your stuff will b' all changed shortly.

Mam.　　　　　　　　　　Into gold?

Face. To gold and silver, sir.

Mam.　　　　　　　Silver I care not for.

Face. Yes, sir, a little to give beggars.

Mam.　　　　　　　Where's the lady?

Face. At hand here. I ha' told her such
　brave things o' you,
　Touching your bounty and your noble
　　spirit—

Mam.　　　　　　　　Hast thou?

Face. As she is almost in her fit to see
　　you.
　But, good sir, no divinity i' your confer-
　　ence,
　For fear of putting her in rage.[4]

Mam.　　　　　　　I warrant thee. 10

Face. Six men will not hold her down.
　　And then,
　If the old man should hear or see you—

Mam.　　　　　　　　　　Fear not.

Face. The very house, sir, would run
　　mad. You know it,
　How scrupulous he is and violent
　Gainst the least act of sin. Physic or
　　mathematics,
　Poetry, state,[5] or bawdry, as I told you,
　She will endure, and never startle; but
　No word of controversy.

Mam.　　　　　I am schooled, good Ulen.

Face. And you must praise her house,
　　remember that,
　And her nobility.

Mam.　　　　　　　Let me alone;　　20
　No herald, no, nor antiquary, Lungs,
　Shall do it better. Go.

Face. [Aside.]　　　　　Why, this is yet
　A kind of modern[7] happiness,[8] to have
　Doll Common for a great lady. [Exit.]

Mam.　　　　　　　　　Now, Epicure.
　Heighten thyself; talk to her all in gold;
　Rain her as many showers as Jove did
　　drops
　Unto his Danaë; show the god a miser,
　Compared with Mammon. What! The
　　stone will do 't.
　She shall feel gold, taste gold, hear gold,
　　sleep gold;

[4] Insanity.
[5] Matters of state; politics.
[6] Family.
[7] With a pun on the meaning common.
[8] Fitness, appropriateness.

Nay, we will *concumbere* [1] gold. I will be
puissant   30
And mighty in my talk to her.—

[Enter Face with Doll.]

                 Here she comes.
FACE. *[Aside.]* To him, Doll; suckle him.—
This is the noble knight
I told your ladyship—
MAM.   Madam, with your pardon,
I kiss your vesture.
DOLL.   Sir, I were uncivil
If I would suffer that; my lip to you,
sir.
MAM. I hope my lord your brother be in
health, lady.
DOLL. My lord my brother is, though I
no lady, sir.
(FACE. Well said, my Guinea bird.[2])
MAM.   Right noble madam—
(FACE. O, we shall have most fierce idola-
try.)
MAM. 'Tis your prerogative.
DOLL.   Rather your courtesy. 40
MAM. Were there naught else t' enlarge
your virtues to me,
These answers speak your breeding and
your blood.
DOLL. Blood we boast none, sir; a poor
baron's daughter.
MAM. "Poor"!—and gat you? Profane
not. Had your father
Slept all the happy remnant of his life
After that act, lyen [3] but there still, and
panted,
H' had done enough to make himself,
his issue,
And his posterity noble.
DOLL.   Sir, although
We may be said to want the gilt and
trappings,
The dress of honor, yet we strive to
keep   50
The seeds and the materials.
MAM.   I do see
The old ingredient, virtue, was not lost,
Nor the drug, money, used to make your
compound.
There is a strange nobility i' your eye,
This lip, that chin! Methinks you do
resemble
One o' the Austriac [4] princes.

FACE. *[Aside.]*   Very like!
Her father was an Irish costermonger.[5]
MAM. The house of Valois, just, had
such a nose,
And such a forehead yet the Medici
Of Florence boast.
DOLL.   Troth, and I have been likened 60
To all these princes.
FACE. *[Aside.]*   I'll be sworn, I heard it.
MAM. I know not how! It is not any one,
But e'en the very choice of all their
features.
FACE. *[Aside.]* I'll in, and laugh. *[Exit.]*
MAM.   A certain touch, or air,
That sparkles a divinity beyond
An earthly beauty!
DOLL.   O, you play the courtier.
MAM. Good lady, gi' me leave—
DOLL.   In faith, I may not,
To mock me, sir.
MAM.   To burn i' this sweet flame;
The phœnix never knew a nobler death.
DOLL. Nay, now you court the courtier,
and destroy   70
What you would build. This art, sir,
i' your words,
Calls your whole faith in question.
MAM.   By my soul—
DOLL. Nay, oaths are made o' the same
air, sir.
MAM.   Nature
Never bestowed upon mortality
A more unblamed,[6] a more harmonious
feature;
She played the stepdame in all faces else.
Sweet madam, le' me be particular—
DOLL. Particular,[7] sir? I pray you, know
your distance.
MAM. In no ill sense, sweet lady, but to
ask
How your fair graces pass the hours.
I see   80
Yo' are lodged here i' the house of a rare
man,
An excellent artist—but what's that
to you?
DOLL. Yes, sir; I study here the mathe-
matics,
And distillation.
MAM.   O, I cry your pardon.
H' is a divine instructor, can extract
The souls of all things by his art, call all

---

[1] Lie with.   [3] Lain.
[2] Prostitute.   [4] Austrian.

[5] Apple seller.   [7] Personal.
[6] Unblemished.

The virtues and the miracles of the sun
Into a temperate fornace, teach dull na-
　　ture
What her own forces are—a man the
　　emp'ror
Has courted above Kelly,[1] sent his
　　medals　　　　　　　　　　　　　　90
And chains t' invite him.

DOLL.　　　　　　Ay, and for his physic, sir—

MAM. Above the art of Esculapius,
　　That drew the envy of the Thunderer!
　　I know all this, and more.

DOLL.　　　　　　Troth, I am taken, sir,
　　Whole with these studies that con-
　　template nature.

MAM. It is a noble humor; but this form
　　Was not intended to so dark a use.
　　Had you been crooked, foul, of some
　　　　coarse mold,
　　A cloister had done well; but such a
　　　　feature,
　　That might stand up the glory of a
　　　　kingdom,　　　　　　　　　　　100
　　To live recluse is a mere solecism,
　　Though in a nunnery. It must not be.
　　I muse [2] my lord your brother will per-
　　　　mit it!
　　You should spend half my land first,
　　　　were I he.
　　Does not this diamant better on my
　　　　finger
　　Than i' the quarry?

DOLL.　　　　　Yes.

MAM.　　　　　　　Why, you are like it.
　　You were created, lady, for the light.
　　Here, you shall wear it; take it, the first
　　　　pledge
　　Of what I speak, to bind you to believe
　　　　me.

DOLL. In chains of adamant?

MAM.　　　　Yes, the strongest bands.　110
　　And take a secret too—here, by your
　　　　side,
　　Doth stand this hour the happiest man
　　　　in Europe.

DOLL. You are contented, sir?

MAM.　　　　　　　Nay, in true being,
　　The envy of princes and the fear of
　　　　states.

DOLL. Say you so, Sir Epicure?

MAM.　　　　Yes, and thou shalt prove it,
　　Daughter of honor. I have cast mine
　　　　eye

Upon thy form, and I will rear this
　　beauty
Above all styles.

DOLL.　　　　　　You mean no treason, sir?

MAM. No, I will take away that jealousy.[3]
　　I am the lord of the *philosophers' stone,*
　　And thou the lady.

DOLL.　　　　How, sir! Ha' you that?　121

MAM. I am the master of the *maistry.*
　　This day the good old wretch here o'
　　　　the house
　　Has made it for us; now he's at *projec-
　　　　tion.*
　　Think therefore thy first wish now; let
　　　　me hear it,
　　And it shall rain into thy lap—no shower,
　　But floods of gold, whole cataracts, a
　　　　deluge,
　　To get a nation on thee.

DOLL.　　　　　　　　You are pleased, sir,
　　To work on the ambition of our sex.

MAM. I am pleased the glory of her sex
　　　　should know　　　　　　　　　130
　　This nook here of the Friars is no climate
　　For her to live obscurely in, to learn
　　Physic and surgery for the constable's
　　　　wife
　　Of some odd hundred [4] in Essex; but
　　　　come forth,
　　And taste the air of palaces; eat, drink
　　The toils of emp'rics,[5] and their boasted
　　　　practice—
　　Tincture of pearl and coral, gold and
　　　　amber;
　　Be seen at feasts and triumphs;[6] have
　　　　it asked
　　What miracle she is; set all the eyes
　　Of court afire, like a burning glass,　140
　　And work hem into cinders, when the
　　　　jewels
　　Of twenty states adorn thee, and the
　　　　light
　　Strikes out the stars that,[7] when thy
　　　　name is mentioned,
　　Queens may look pale, and, we but show-
　　　　ing our love,
　　Nero's Poppæa may be lost in story!
　　Thus will we have it.

DOLL.　　　　　　I could well consent, sir.
　　But in a monarchy how will this be?

---

[1] The partner of Dee.　　[2] Am astonished.

[3] Suspicion.
[4] A division of a county.
[5] The results of the toil of experimenters.
[6] Festivities.　　　　　　[7] So that.

The prince will soon take notice, and
　　both seize
You and your *stone*, it being a wealth
　　unfit
For any private subject.

MAM.　　　　　　　　If he knew it.　　150

DOLL. Yourself do boast it, sir.

MAM.　　　　　　　　To thee, my life.

DOLL. O, but beware, sir! You may come
　　to end
The remnant of your days in a loathed
　　prison
By speaking of it.

MAM.　　　　　　　'Tis no idle fear.
We'll therefore go with all, my girl, and
　　live
In a free state, where we will eat our
　　mullets,
Soused in high-country wines, sup pheas-
　　ants' eggs,
And have our cockles boiled in silver
　　shells,
Our shrimps to swim again, as when
　　they lived,
In a rare butter made of dolphins'
　　milk,　　　　　　　　　　　　160
Whose cream does look like opals, and
　　with these
Delicate meats set ourselves high for
　　pleasure,
And take us down again, and then renew
Our youth and strength with drinking
　　the *elixir*,
And so enjoy a perpetuity
Of life and lust! And thou shalt ha'
　　thy wardrobe
Richer than Nature's, still to change
　　thyself,
And vary oft'ner, for thy pride, than
　　she,
Or Art, her wise and almost equal serv-
　　ant.

[Enter Face.]

FACE. Sir, you are too loud. I hear you
　　every word　　　　　　　　　　170
Into the laboratory. Some fitter place;
The garden, or great chamber above.—
　　[Aside.] How like you her?

MAM. *[Aside.]* Excellent, Lungs. There's
　　for thee.　　　　*[Gives him money.]*

FACE. *[Aside.]*　　　But do you hear?
Good sir, beware, no mention of the
　　rabbins.

MAM. *[Aside.]* We think not on hem.

FACE.　　　　O, it is well, sir.—*[Exeunt
Mammon and Doll.]* Subtle!

ACT IV. SCENE ii.

[The same.]

Face, Subtle, Kastril, Dame Pliant.[1]

[FACE.] Dost thou not laugh?

SUB.　　　　　　Yes. Are they gone?

FACE.　　　　　　　　All's clear.

SUB. The widow is come.

FACE.　　　And your quarreling disciple?

SUB. Ay.

FACE.　　I must to my captainship again
　　then.

SUB. Stay, bring hem in first.

FACE.　　　　So I meant. What is she?
A bonnibel?[2]

SUB.　　　　　I know not.

FACE.　　　　　　　We'll draw lots.
You'll stand to that?

SUB.　　　　What else?

FACE.　　　　　　O, for a suit,
To fall now like a cortine[3]— flap!

SUB.　　　　　To th' door, man.

FACE　You'll ha' the first kiss, cause[4] I
　　am not ready.　　　　　*[Exit.]*

SUB. Yes, and perhaps hit you through
　　both the nostrils.[5]

FACE. *[Within.]* Who would you speak
　　with?

KAS. *[Within.]*　　Where's the captain?

FACE. *[Within.]*　　　　Gone, sir,　10
About some business.

KAS. *[Within.]*　　Gone?

FACE. *[Within.]*　　　He'll return straight.
But Master Doctor, his lieutenant, is
　　here.

[Enter Kastril and Dame Pliant.]

SUB. Come near, my worshipful boy, my
　　terræ fili,
That is, my boy of land; make thy ap-
　　proaches.
Welcome. I know thy lusts and thy de-
　　sires,
And I will serve and satisfy hem. Begin;

---

[1] Last two enter later.　　　　[3] Curtain.
[2] Fair lass.　　　　　　　　　[4] Because
[5] "Put your nose out of joint."

Charge me from thence, or thence, or
    in this line.
Here is my center; ground thy quarrel.
KAS.   You lie!
SUB. How, child of wrath and anger! The
    loud lie?
For what, my sudden boy?
KAS.   Nay, that look you to; 20
I am aforehand.
SUB.   O, this 's no true grammar,
    And as ill logic! You must render causes,[1]
      child,
    Your first and second intentions, know
      your canons
    And your divisions, moods, degrees, and
      differences,
    Your predicaments, substance, and ac-
      cident,
    Series extern and intern, with their
      causes,
    Efficient, material, formal, final,
    And ha' your elements perfect.
KAS.   What is this?
    The angry [2] tongue he talks in?
SUB.   That false precept
    Of being aforehand has deceived a
      number,   30
    And made hem enter quarrels often-
      times
    Before they were aware, and afterward
    Against their wills.
KAS.   How must I do then, sir?
SUB. I cry this lady mercy; she should
    first
    Have been saluted. I do call you lady,
    Because you are to be one ere 't be long,
                 He kisses her.
    My soft and buxom widow.
KAS.   Is she, i' faith?
SUB. Yes, or my art is an egregious liar.
KAS. How know you?
SUB.   By inspection on her forehead,
    And subtlety of her lip, which must be
      tasted   40
    Often to make a judgment. (*He kisses
    her again.*)—[*Aside.*] 'Slight, she melts
    Like a myrobalan! [3]— Here is yet a line
    In *rivo frontis* [4] tells me he is no knight.
PLI. What is he then, sir?
SUB.   Let me see your hand.

[1] The following terms are from scholastic logic.
[2] Quarrel-provoking.
[3] A kind of dried plum.
[4] The vein of the forehead.

O, your *linea Fortunæ* [5] makes it plain,
And *stella* [6] here in *monte Veneris*,[7]
But, most of all, *junctura annularis*.[8]
He is a soldier, or a man of art, lady,
But shall have some great honor shortly.
PLI.   Brother,
    He's a rare man, believe me!

        [*Enter Face, in his uniform.*]

KAS.   Hold your peace! 50
Here comes the tother rare man.—Save
    you, captain.
FACE. Good Master Kastril! Is this your
    sister?
KAS.   Ay, sir.
Please you to kuss [9] her, and be proud
    to know her?
FACE. I shall be proud to know you, lady.
                 [*Kisses her.*]
PLI.   Brother,
    He calls me lady, too.
KAS.   Ay, peace. I heard it.
FACE. [*Taking Subtle aside.*] The count is
    come.
SUB.   Where is he?
FACE.   At the door.
SUB. Why, you must entertain him.
FACE.   What 'll you do
    With these the while?
SUB. Why, have hem up, and show hem
    Some fustian book, or the dark glass.[10]
FACE.   Fore God,
    She is a delicate dabchick! [11] I must have
    her.   [*Exit.*] 60
SUB. [*Aside.*] Must you? Ay, if your
    fortune will, you must.—
Come, sir, the captain will come to us
    presently.
I'll ha' you to my chamber of demon-
    strations,
Where I'll show you both the grammar
    and logic
And rhetoric of quarreling; my whole
    method
Drawn out in tables; and my instrument
That hath the several scale upon 't
    shall make you
Able to quarrel at a straw's breadth by
    moonlight

[5] Line of Fortune.
[6] The star.
[7] Mount of Venus.
[8] The ring joint.
[9] Kiss.
[10] Polished black stone into which astrologers
gazed.
[11] Water hen.

And, lady, I'll have you look in a glass,
Some half an hour, but to clear your
   eyesight 70
Against you see [1] your fortune, which
   is greater
Than I may judge upon the sudden,
   trust me.   [*Exeunt.*]

Act IV. Scene iii.

[*The same.*]

Face, Subtle, Surly.[2]

[Face.] Where are you, doctor?
Sub. [*Within.*]   I'll come to you
   presently.
Face. I will ha' this same widow, now I
   ha' seen her,
On any composition.[3]

[*Enter Subtle.*]

Sub.   What do you say?
Face. Ha' you disposed of them?
Sub.   I ha' sent hem up.
Face. Subtle, in troth, I needs must have
   this widow.
Sub. Is that the matter?
Face.   Nay, but hear me.
Sub.   Go to!
  If you rebel once, Doll shall know it
   all;
  Therefore be quiet, and obey your
   chance.
Face. Nay, thou art so violent now. Do
  but conceive:
Thou art old, and canst not serve—
Sub.   Who cannot? I? 10
'Slight, I will serve her with thee, for a—
Face.   Nay,
But understand; I'll gi' you composi-
  tion.
Sub. I will not treat with thee. What!
  Sell my fortune?
'Tis better than my birthright. Do not
  murmur.
Win her, and carry her. If you grumble,
  Doll
Knows it directly.
Face.   Well, sir, I am silent.
Will you go help to fetch in Don in state?

Sub. I follow you, sir.—[*Exit Face.*] We
  must keep Face in awe,
Or he will overlook [4] us like a tyran.[5]

[*Enter Face with*] *Surly like a Spaniard.*

Brain of a tailor! Who comes here?
  Don John!   20
Sur. *Senores, beso las manos á vuestras
  mercedes.*[6]
Sub. Would you had stooped a little, and
  kissed our *anos.*
Face. Peace, Subtle!
Sub.   Stab me; I shall never hold, man.
He looks in that deep ruff like a head in
  a platter,
Served in by a short cloak upon two
  trestles.[7]
Face. Or what do you say to a collar of
  brawn,[8] cut down
Beneath the souse,[9] and wriggled [10]
  with a knife?
Sub. 'Slud,[11] he does look too fat to be a
  Spaniard.
Face. Perhaps some Fleming or some
  Hollander got him
In d'Alva's time—Count Egmont's bas-
  tard.
Sub.   Don,   30
Your scurvy, yellow, Madrid face is
  welcome.
Sur. *Gratia.*[12]
Sub.   He speaks out of a fortification.
Pray God he ha' no squibs in those deep
  sets.[13]
Sur. *Por dios, senores, muy linda casa!* [14]
Sub. What says he?
Face.   Praises the house, I think;
I know no more but's action.
Sub.   Yes, the *casa*,
My precious Diego, will prove fair
  enough
To cozen you in. Do you mark? You
  shall
Be cozened, Diego.

---

[1] In preparation for seeing.
[2] Last two enter later.
[3] Terms.
[4] Look down upon, despise.
[5] Tyrant.
[6] Gentlemen, I kiss your worships' hands.
[7] Stilts.
[8] Roll of boar's flesh.
[9] Ear.
[10] Cut into wrinkles, like a ruff.
[11] God's Lord, a mild oath.
[12] Thanks.
[13] Plaits of the ruff.
[14] By Jove, sirs, a very fine house!

FACE.   Cozened, do you see,
My worthy Donzel,[1] cozened.

SUR.   *Entiendo.*[2]   40

SUB. Do you intend it? So do we, dear
Don.
Have you brought pistolets or porta-
gues,[3]
My solemn Don?—(*He* [, *i.e., Face,*] *feels
his pockets.*) Dost thou feel any?

FACE.   Full.

SUB. You shall be emptied, Don, pumped
and drawn
Dry, as they say.

FACE.   Milked, in troth, sweet Don.

SUB. See all the monsters [4]—the great
lion of all, Don.

SUR. *Con licencia, se puede ver á esta senora?* [5]

SUB. What talks he now?

FACE.   O' the *senora.*

SUB.   O, Don,
That is the lioness, which you shall see
Also, my Don.

FACE.   'Slid, Subtle, how shall we do?   50

SUB. For what?

FACE. Why, Doll's employed, you know.

SUB.   That's true.
Fore heav'n, I know not. He must stay,
that's all.

FACE. Stay? That he must not, by no
means.

SUB.   No? Why?

FACE. Unless you'll mar all. 'Slight, he'll
suspect it;
And then he will not pay, not half so
well.
This is a traveled punk-master, and
does know
All the delays—a notable hot rascal,
And looks already rampant.

SUB.   'Sdeath, and Mammon
Must not be troubled.

FACE.   Mammon, in no case!

SUB. What shall we do then?

FACE.   Think; you must be sudden.   60

SUR. *Entiendo que la senora es tan hermosa,
que codicio tan
Á verla como la bien aventuranza de mi
vida.* [6]

---

1 Little Don.   3 Gold coins.
2 I understand.   4 *I.e.*, see the sights.
5 By your leave, may I see this lady?
6 I understand that the lady is so beautiful
that I desire to see her as much as the good
fortune of my life.

FACE. *Mi vida?* 'Slid, Subtle, he puts me
in mind o' the widow.
What dost thou say to draw her to 't—
ha!—
And tell her it is her fortune? All our
venter
Now lies upon 't. It is but one man
more,
Which on 's chance [7] to have her; and
beside,
There is no maidenhead to be feared
or lost.
What dost thou think on 't, Subtle?

SUB.   Who, I? Why—

FACE. The credit of our house too is engaged.   70

SUB. You made me an offer for my share
erewhile.
What wilt thou gi' me, i' faith?

FACE.   O, by that light,
I'll not buy now. You know your doom [8]
to me.
E'en take your lot; obey your chance,
sir; win her,
And wear her—out for me.

SUB.   'Slight, I'll not work her then.

FACE. It is the common cause; therefore
bethink you.
Doll else must know it, as you said.

SUB.   I care not.

SUR. *Senores, porque se tarda tanta?* [9]

SUB. Faith, I am not fit; I am old.

FACE.   That's now no reason, sir.

SUR. *Puede ser de hazer burla de mi
amor?* [10]   80

FACE. You hear the Don too? By this air
I call,
And loose the hinges—Doll!

SUB.   A plague of hell—

FACE. Will you then do?

SUB.   Yo' are a terrible rogue!
I'll think of this. Will you, sir, call the
widow?

FACE. Yes, and I'll take her too with all
her faults,
Now I do think on 't better.

SUB.   With all my heart, sir.
Am I discharged o' the lot?

FACE.   As you please.

SUB.   Hands. [*They shake hands.*]

---

7 Whichever of us should chance.
8 Decision.
9 Sirs, why so much delay?
10 Can it be you are making a jest of my love?

FACE. Remember now, that upon any change
    You never claim her.
SUB.   Much good joy and health to you, sir.
    Marry a whore? Fate, let me wed a witch first.   90
SUR. *Por estas honradas barbas* [1]—
SUB.   He swears by his beard.
    Despatch, and call the brother too.
                             [Exit Face.]
SUR. *Tengo duda, senores, que no me hagan alguna traycion.* [2]
SUB. How, *issue on?* Yes, *præsto, senor.* [3]
    Please you
    Enthratha the *chambratha*, worthy Don,
    Where, if it please the Fates, in your *bathada,*
    You shall be soaked, and stroked, and tubbed, and rubbed,
    And scrubbed, and fubbed,[4] dear Don, before you go.
    You shall, in faith, my scurvy babion [5] Don,
    Be curried, clawed, and flawed,[6] and tawed,[7] indeed.   100
    I will the heartlier go about it now,
    And make the widow a punk so much the sooner,
    To be revenged on this impetuous Face;
    The quickly doing of it is the grace.
                             [Exeunt.]

ACT IV. SCENE iv.

[Another room in the same.]

Face, Kastril, Da[me] *Pliant, Subtle, Surly.*[8]

[FACE.] Come, lady. I knew the doctor would not leave
    Till he had found the very nick of her fortune.
KAS. To be a countess, say you?
[FACE.] [9]   A Spanish countess, sir.
PLI. Why, is that better than an English countess?
FACE. Better? 'Slight, make you that a question, lady?

[1] By these honored hairs—
[2] I fear, sirs, that you are playing me some trick.
[3] Quickly, sir.   [5] Baboon.
[4] Cheated.   [6] Flayed.
[7] Soaked in preparation for tanning.
[8] Last two enter later.
[9] From 1612 edn.

KAS. Nay, she is a fool, captain; you must pardon her.
FACE. Ask from your courtier to your Inns of Court man,
    To your mere milaner; [10] they will tell you all
    Your Spanish jennet is the best horse; your Spanish
    Stoop is the best garb; [11] your Spanish beard   10
    Is the best cut; your Spanish ruffs are the best
    Wear; your Spanish pavin the best dance;
    Your Spanish titillation in a glove
    The best perfume; and for your Spanish pike,
    And Spanish blade, let your poor captain speak.—
    Here comes the doctor.

[Enter Subtle with a paper.]

SUB.   My most honored lady,
    For so I am now to style you, having found,
    By this my scheme,[12] you are to undergo
    An honorable fortune very shortly,
    What will you say now, if some—
FACE.   I ha' told her all, sir,   20
    And her right worshipful brother here, that she shall be
    A countess; do not delay hem, sir. A Spanish countess!
SUB. Still, my scarce-worshipful captain, you can keep
    No secret! Well, since he has told you, madam,
    Do you forgive him, and I do.
KAS.   She shall do that, sir.
    I'll look to 't; 'tis my charge.
SUB.   Well then, naught rests
    But that she fit her love now to her fortune.
PLI. Truly, I shall never brook a Spaniard.
SUB.   No?
PLI. Never sin' eighty-eight [13] could I abide hem,
    And that was some three year afore I was born, in truth.   30

[10] Milliner, dealer in fancy articles.
[11] Bearing.
[12] Horoscope.
[13] 1588, the date of the destruction of the Armada.

Sub. Come, you must love him, or be miserable;
Choose which you will.

Face.   By this good rush, persuade her,
She will cry [1] strawberries else within this twelvemonth.

Sub. Nay, shads and mack'rel, which is worse.

Face.   Indeed, sir?

Kas. God's lid, you shall love him, or I'll kick you.

Pli.   Why,
I'll do as you will ha' me, brother.

Kas.   Do,
Or by this hand I'll maul you.

Face.   Nay, good sir,
Be not so fierce.

Sub.   No, my enragéd child;
She will be ruled. What, when she comes to taste
The pleasures of a countess! To be courted—   40

Face. And kissed and ruffled!

Sub.   Ay, behind the hangings.

Face. And then come forth in pomp!

Sub.   And know her state!

Face. Of keeping all th' idolators o' the chamber
Barer to her than at their prayers!

Sub.   Is served
Upon the knee!

Face.   And has her pages, huishers,[2]
Footmen, and coaches—

Sub.   Her six mares—

Face.   Nay, eight!

Sub. To hurry her through London to th' Exchange,[3]
Bet'lem,[4] the China-houses [5]—

Face.   Yes, and have
The citizens gape at her, and praise her tires,
And my lord's goose-turd bands,[6] that rides with her!   50

Kas. Most brave![7] By this hand, you are not my suster
If you refuse.

Pli.   I will not refuse, brother.

[1] Hawk on the street.
[2] Ushers.
[3] Where shops were located.
[4] Bethlehem Hospital, where people visited the insane for amusement.
[5] Where ware from China was shown.
[6] Green-colored collars.
[7] Fine.

[Enter Surly.]

Sur. *Que es esto, senores, que non se venga? Esta tardanza me mata!* [8]

Face.   It is the count come;
The doctor knew he would be here, by his art.

Sub. *En gallanta madama, Don, gallantissima!*

Sur. *Por todos los dioses, la mas acabada Hermosura, que he visto en mi vida!* [9]

Face. Is 't not a gallant language that they speak?

Kas. An admirable language! Is 't not French?   60

Face. No, Spanish, sir.

Kas.   It goes like law French,
And that, they say, is the court-liest language.

Face.   List, sir.

Sur. *El sol ha perdido su lumbre, con el Resplandor que træ esta dama! Valgame dios!* [10]

Face. He admires your sister.

Kas.   Must not she make court'sy?

Sub. 'Od's will, she must go to him, man, and kiss him!
It is the Spanish fashion for the women
To make first court.

Face.   'Tis true he tells you, sir;
His art knows all.

Sur.   *Porque no se acude?* [11]

Kas. He speaks to her, I think?

Face.   That he does, sir.   70

Sur. *Por el amor de dios, que es esto que se tarda?* [12]

Kas. Nay, see; she will not understand him!—Gull!
Noddy!

Pli.   What say you, brother?

Kas.   Ass, my suster,
Go kuss him, as the cunning man would ha' you;
I'll thrust a pin i' your buttocks else.

Face.   O, no, sir.

[8] What's the matter, sirs, that nobody comes? This delay is killing me.
[9] By all the gods, the most finished beauty that I have seen in my life.
[10] The sun has lost his light in comparison with the splendor which this lady brings! God bless me!
[11] Why don't you draw near?
[12] For the love of God, why this delay?

SUR. *Senora mia, mi persona muy indigna*
    esta
Á llegar á tanta hermosura.[1] [*Kisses her.*]
FACE. Does he not use her bravely?
KAS.   Bravely, i' faith!
FACE. Nay, he will use her better.
KAS.   Do you think so?
SUR. *Senora, si sera servida, entremos.*[2]   80
           [*Exit with Dame Pliant.*]
KAS. Where does he carry her?
FACE.   Into the garden, sir.
    Take you no thought; I must interpret
    for her.
SUB. [*Aside to Face.*] Give Doll the word.—
                 [*Exit Face*].
    Come, my fierce child, advance;
    We'll to our quarreling lesson again.
KAS.   Agreed.
    I love a Spanish boy with all my heart.
SUB. Nay, and by this means, sir, you shall
    be brother
    To a great count.
KAS.   Ay, I knew that at first.
    This match will advance the house of
    the Kastrils.
SUB. Pray God your sister prove but
    pliant!
KAS.   Why,
    Her name is so, by her other husband.
SUB.   How! 90
KAS. The Widow Pliant. Knew you not
    that?
SUB.   No, faith, sir;
    Yet, by erection of her figure,[3] I guessed it.
    Come, let's go practice.
KAS.   Yes, but do you think, doctor,
    I e'er shall quarrel well?
SUB.   I warrant you. [*Exeunt.*]

ACT IV. SCENE v.

[*Another room in the same.*]

Doll, Mammon, Face, Subtle.[4]

[DOLL.] (*In her fit of talking.*) For after
    Alexander's death [5]—
MAM.   Good lady—

---

[1] Madam, my person is entirely unworthy to
come near to such beauty.
[2] Madam, if you will, let us go in.
[3] Casting of her horoscope, with an obvious
double meaning.
[4] Last two enter later.
[5] The following speeches by Doll are inco-
herent extracts from Hugh Broughton's *Concent
of Scripture.*

DOLL. That Perdiccas and Antigonus were
    slain,
    The two that stood, Seleuc' and Ptol-
    omy—
MAM. Madam—
DOLL.   Made up the two legs, and the
    fourth beast,
    That was Gog-north and Egypt-south,
    which after
    Was called Gog-iron-leg and South-iron-
    leg—
MAM.   Lady—
DOLL. And then Gog-horned. So was
    Egypt, too.
    Then Egypt-clay-leg, and Gog-clay-leg—
MAM.   Sweet madam –
DOLL. And last Gog-dust, and Egypt-dust,
    which fall
    In the last link of the fourth chain. And
    these   10
    Be stars in story, which none see, or look
    at—
MAM. What shall I do?
DOLL.   For, as he says, except
    We call the rabbins and the heathen
    Greeks—
MAM. Dear lady—
DOLL.   To come from Salem, and from
    Athens,
    And teach the people of Great Britain—

[*Enter Face, in his livery.*]

FACE.   What's the matter, sir?
DOLL. To speak the tongue of Eber and
    Javan [6]—
MAM.   O,
    Sh' is in her fit.
DOLL.   We shall know nothing—
FACE.   Death, sir,
    We are undone!
DOLL.   Where then a learned linguist
    Shall see the ancient used communion
    Of vowels and consonants—
FACE.   My master will hear! 20
DOLL. A wisdom which Pythagoras held
    most high—
MAM. Sweet honorable lady!
DOLL.   To comprise
    All sounds of voices, in few marks of
    letters—
FACE. Nay, you must never hope to lay
    her now.   *They* [*all*] *speak together.*

---

[6] *I.e.*, of the Hebrews and the Greeks.

Doll. And so we may arrive by Talmud
　　skill [1]
And profane Greek to raise the building
　　up
Of Helen's house against the Ismaelite,
King of Thogarma, and his habergeons
Brimstony, blue, and fiery; and the force
Of King Abaddon, and the beast of
　　Cittim,　　　　　　　　　　　30
Which Rabbi David Kimchi, Onkelos,
And Aben Ezra do interpret Rome.
Face. How did you put her into 't?
Mam.　　　　　　Alas, I talked
Of a fift [2] monarchy I would erect
With the *philosophers' stone,* by chance,
　　and she
Falls on the other four straight.
Face.　　　　　Out of Broughton!
I told you so. 'Slid, stop her mouth.
Mam.　　　　　　　　Is 't best?
Face. She'll never leave else. If the old
　　man hear her,
We are but fæces, ashes.
Sub. [*Within.*]　　What's to do there?
Face. O, we are lost! Now she hears him,
　　she is quiet.　　　　　　　　40
Mam. Where shall I hide me?
Sub.　　　　How! What sight is here?
　　　Upon Subtle's entry they disperse.
Close [3] deeds of darkness, and that shun
　　the light!
Bring him again. Who is he? What, my
　　son!
O, I have lived too long.
Mam.　　　　　Nay, good, dear father,
There was no unchaste purpose.
Sub.　　　　　Not? And flee me
When I come in?
Mam.　　　　That was my error.
Sub.　　　　　　　　　Error?
Guilt, guilt, my son; give it the right
　　name. No marvel
If I found check in our *great work* within,
When such affairs as these were managing!
Mam. Why, have you so?
Sub.　　　It has stood still this half hour,
And all the rest of our *less works* gone
　　back.　　　　　　　　　　51
Where is the instrument of wickedness,
My lewd, false drudge?

Mam.　　　Nay, good sir, blame not him;
Believe me, 'twas against his will or
　　knowledge.
I saw her by chance.
Sub.　　　　Will you commit more sin,
T' excuse a varlet?
Mam.　　　　By my hope, 'tis true, sir.
Sub. Nay, then I wonder less, if you, for
　　whom
The blessing was prepared, would so
　　tempt heaven,
And lose your fortunes.
Mam.　　　　　Why, sir?
Sub.　　　　　This 'll retard
The *work* a month at least.
Mam.　　　　　Why, if it do,　　60
What remedy? But think it not, good
　　father.
Our purposes were honest. [4]
Sub.　　　　As they were,
So the reward will prove. (*A great crack
　　and noise within.*)—How now! Ay me!
God and all saints be good to us.—

　　　　　　[*Enter Face.*]

　　　　　　　　　　　What's that?
Face. O, sir, we are defeated! All the
　　works
Are flown *in fumo;* every glass is burst;
Fornace and all rent down, as if a bolt
Of thunder had been driven through the
　　house.
Retorts, receivers, pelicans, boltheads,
All strook [5] in shivers!
　　　　　Subtle falls down as in a swoon.
　　　　　　Help, good sir! Alas,　　70
Coldness and death invades him. Nay,
　　Sir Mammon,
Do the fair offices of a man! You stand,
As you were readier to depart than he.—
　　　　　　　　　　One knocks.
Who's there?—My lord her brother is
　　come.
Mam.　　　Ha, Lungs?
Face. His coach is at the door. Avoid his
　　sight,
For he's as furious as his sister is mad.
Mam. Alas!
Face.　　My brain is quite undone with
　　the fume, sir;
I ne'er must hope to be mine own man
　　again.

----

[1] In the original this speech and the following
dialogue including Face's final speech are
printed in parallel columns.
[2] Fifth.　　　　　　　　[3] Secret.
[4] Chaste.　　　　　　　[5] Struck.

MAM. Is all lost, Lungs? Will nothing be preserved
Of all our cost?
FACE.   Faith, very little, sir; 80
A peck of coals or so, which is cold comfort, sir.
MAM. O, my voluptuous mind! I am justly punished.
FACE. And so am I, sir.
MAM.   Cast from all my hopes—
FACE. Nay, certainties, sir.
MAM.   By mine own base affections.
          Subtle seems come to himself.
SUB. O, the cursed fruits of vice and lust!
MAM.   Good father,
It was my sin. Forgive it.
SUB.   Hangs my roof
Over us still, and will not fall, O justice,
Upon us for this wicked man?
FACE.   Nay, look, sir;
You grieve him now with staying in his sight.
Good sir, the nobleman will come too, and take you,   90
And that may breed a tragedy.
MAM.   I'll go.
FACE. Ay, and repent at home, sir. It may be
For some good penance you may ha' it yet;
A hundred pound to the box at Bet'lem—
MAM.   Yes.
FACE. For the restoring such as—ha' their wits.
MAM.   I'll do 't.
FACE. I'll send one to you to receive it.
MAM.   Do.
Is no *projection* left?
FACE.   All flown, or stinks, sir.
MAM. Will naught be saved that's good for *med'cine*, think'st thou?
FACE. I cannot tell, sir. There will be perhaps
Something about the scraping of the shards   100
Will cure the itch—[*Aside.*] though not your itch of mind, sir.—
It shall be saved for you, and sent home. Good sir,
This way, for fear the lord should meet you.   [*Exit Mammon.*]
SUB.   Face!
FACE. Ay.
SUB.   Is he gone?

FACE.   Yes, and as heavily
As all the gold he hoped for were in his blood.
Let us be light though.
SUB.   Ay, as balls, and bound
And hit our heads against the roof for joy;
There's so much of our care now cast away.
FACE. Now to our Don.
SUB.   Yes, your young widow by this time
Is made a countess, Face; sh' has been in travail   110
Of a young heir for you.
FACE.   Good, sir.
SUB.   Off with your case,[1]
And greet her kindly, as a bridegroom should,
After these common hazards.
FACE.   Very well, sir.
Will you go fetch Don Diego off the while?
SUB. And fetch him over too, if you'll be pleased, sir.
Would Doll were in her place, to pick his pockets now!
FACE. Why, you can do it as well, if you would set to 't.
I pray you, prove your virtue.[2]
SUB.   For your sake, sir.   [*Exeunt.*]

ACT IV. SCENE vi.

[*Another room in the same.*]

Surly, Da[me] Pliant, Subtle, Face.[3]

[SUR.] Lady, you see into what hands you are fall'n,
'Mongst what a nest of villains, and how near
Your honor was t' have catched a certain clap,
Through your credulity, had I but been
So punctually forward, as place, time,
And other circumstance would ha' made a man;
For yo' are a handsome woman—would yo' were wise too!
I am a gentleman come here disguised,
Only to find the knaveries of this citadel·

---

[1] *I.e.,* his present costume.
[2] Power.
[3] Last two enter later.

And where I might have wronged your
    honor, and have not,   10
I claim some interest in your love. You
    are,
They say, a widow, rich; and I'm a
    bachelor,
Worth naught; your fortunes may make
    me a man,
As mine ha' preserved you a woman.
    Think upon it,
And whether I have deserved you or no.
PLI.   I will, sir.
SUR. And for these household-rogues, let
    me alone
To treat with them.

[*Enter Subtle.*]

SUB.   How doth my noble Diego,
And my dear madam countess? Hath the
    count   18
Been courteous, lady, liberal and open?
Donzel, methinks you look melancholic
After your *coitum*,[1] and scurvy! Truly,
I do not like the dullness of your eye;
It hath a heavy cast—'tis upsee Dutch,[2]
And says you are a lumpish whoremaster.
Be lighter; I will make your pockets so.
    He falls to picking of them.
SUR. [*Disclosing himself.*] Will you, Don
    bawd and pickpurse? [*Beats him.*]
    How now? Reel you?
Stand up, sir; you shall find, since I am
    so heavy,
I'll gi' you equal weight.
SUB.   Help! Murder!
SUR.   No, sir,
There's no such thing intended. A good
    cart [3]
And a clean whip shall ease you of that
    fear.   30
I am the Spanish Don that should be
    cozened,
Do you see? Cozened? Where's your
    Captain Face,
That parcel [4] broker, and whole bawd,
    all rascal?

[*Enter Face in his uniform.*]

FACE. How, Surly!
SUR.   O, make your approach,
    good captain.

I have found from whence your copper
    rings and spoons
Come now, wherewith you cheat abroad
    in taverns.
'Twas here you learned t' anoint your
    boot with brimstone,
Then rub men's gold on 't for a kind of
    touch,
And say, 'twas naught, when you had
    changed the color,
That you might ha't for nothing? And
    this doctor,   40
Your sooty, smoky-bearded compeer,
    he
Will close you so much gold, in a *bolt's-
    head,*
And, on a turn, convey i' the stead an-
    other
With *sublimed mercury,* that shall burst
    i' the heat,
And fly out all *in fumo!* Then weeps
    Mammon;
Then swoons his worship. [*Exit Face.*]
    Or he is the Faustus,
That casteth figures and can conjure,
    cures
Plague, piles, and pox, by the ephemer-
    ides,[5]
And holds intelligence with all the bawds
And midwives of three shires, while you
    send in   50
(Captain!—What! Is he gone?) damsels
    with child,
Wives that are barren, or the waiting-
    maid
With the green sickness? [*Seizes Subtle
    as he attempts to escape.*] Nay, sir,
    you must tarry,
Though he be scaped, and answer by the
    ears,[6] sir.

ACT IV. SCENE vii.

[*The same.*]

*Face, Kastril, Surly, Subtle, Drugger,[7]
    Ananias,[7] Da[me] Pliant, Doll.[7]*

[FACE. (*To Kastril.*)] Why, now's the
    time, if ever you will quarrel
Well, as they say, and be a true-born
    child.
The doctor and your sister both are
    abused.

---

[1] Coition.   [2] In the Dutch fashion.
[3] Bawds were "carted" through the city as a
punishment.   [4] Partial. part.
[5] Astrological almanacs.   [7] Enters later.
[6] Referring to punishment in the pillory.

KAS. Where is he? Which is he? He is a slave,
Whate'er he is, and the son of a whore.—
Are you
The man, sir, I would know?
SUR.   I should be loath, sir,
To confess so much.
KAS.   Then you lie i' your throat.
SUR.   How!
FACE. [*To Kastril.*] A very arrant rogue, sir, and a cheater,
Employed here by another con-jurer
That does not love the doctor, and would cross him   10
If he knew how.
SUR.   Sir, you are abused.
KAS.   You lie—
And 'tis no matter.
FACE.   Well said, sir! He is
The impudent'st rascal—
SUR.   You are indeed. Will you hear me, sir?
FACE. By no means. Bid him be gone.
KAS.   Begone, sir, quickly!
SUR. This 's strange!—Lady, do you in-form your brother.
          [*Dame Pliant whispers to Kastril.*]
FACE. There is not such a foist[1] in all the town.
The doctor had him[2] presently,[3] and finds yet
The Spanish count will come here.—
          [*Aside.*] Bear up, Subtle.
SUB. Yes, sir, he must appear within this hour.
FACE. And yet this rogue would come in a disguise,   20
By the temptation of another spirit,
To trouble our art, though he could not hurt it!
KAS.   Ay,
I know.—[*To Pliant.*] Away, you talk like a foolish mauther.[4]
SUR. Sir, all is truth she says.
FACE.   Do not believe him, sir.
He is the lying'st swabber! Come your ways, sir.
SUR. You are valiant out of company!
KAS.   Yes, how then, sir?

[*Enter Drugger with a piece of cloth.*]

FACE. Nay, here's an honest fellow too that knows him
And all his tricks. (Make good what I say, Abel.
This cheater would ha' cozened thee o' the widow.)
He owes this honest Drugger here seven pound   30
He has had[5] on him in twopenny'orths of tabacco.
DRUG. Yes, sir. And h' has damned him-self[6] three terms to pay me.
FACE. And what does he owe for lotium?[7]
DRUG.   Thirty shillings, sir;
And for six syringes.
SUR.   Hydra of villainy!
FACE. [*To Kastril.*] Nay, sir, you must quarrel him out o' the house.
KAS.   I will.—
Sir, if you get not out o' doors, you lie;
And you are a pimp.
SUR.   Why, this is madness, sir,
Not valure in you; I must laugh at this.
KAS. It is my humor; you are a pimp and a trig,[8]
And an Amadis de Gaul, or a Don Quixote.   40
DRUG. Or a Knight o' the Curious Cox-comb, do you see?

[*Enter Ananias.*]

ANA. Peace to the household!
KAS.   I'll keep peace for no man.
ANA. Casting of dollars is concluded lawful.
KAS. Is he the constable?
SUB.   Peace, Ananias.
FACE.   No, sir.
KAS. Then you are an otter, and a shad, a whit,
A very tim.[9]
SUR.   You'll hear me, sir?
KAS.   I will not.
ANA. What is the motive?
SUB.   Zeal in the young gentleman
Against his Spanish slops—
ANA.   They are profane,
Lewd, superstitious, and idolatrous breeches.

---

[1] Rogue.   [3] In actual presence.
[2] *I.e.*, the count(?).   [4] Wench.
[5] Charged.   [7] Lotion.
[6] *I.e.*, sworn.   [8] Coxcomb.
[9] A term of abuse which has baffled the editors.

Sur. New rascals!

Kas.   Will you be gone, sir?

Ana.   Avoid, Sathan! 50
Thou art not of the light! That ruff of
   pride
About thy neck betrays thee, and is
   the same
With that which the unclean birds, in
   seventy-seven,[1]
Were seen to prank it with on divers
   coasts.
Thou look'st like antichrist, in that lewd
   hat.

Sur. I must give way.

Kas.   Begone, sir.

Sur.   But I'll take
A course with you—

Ana.   Depart, proud Spanish fiend!

Sur. Captain and doctor—

Ana.   Child of perdition!

Kas.   Hence, sir!—[*Exit Surly.*]
Did I not quarrel bravely?

Face.   Yes, indeed, sir.

Kas. Nay, and I give my mind to 't, I
   shall do 't.   60

Face. O, you must follow, sir, and
   threaten him tame.
He'll turn again else.

Kas.   I'll re-turn him then. [*Exit.*]

Face. Drugger, this rogue prevented[2] us
   for thee;
We had determined that thou shouldst
   ha' come
In a Spanish suit, and ha' carried her so;
   and he,
A brokerly slave, goes, puts it on himself.
Hast brought the damask?

Drug.   Yes, sir.

Face.   Thou must borrow
A Spanish suit. Hast thou no credit
   with the players?

Drug. Yes, sir; did you never see me play
   the Fool?

Face. I know not, Nab.—[*Aside.*] Thou
   shalt, if I can help it.—   70
Hieronimo's[3] old cloak, ruff, and hat
   will serve;
I'll tell thee more when thou bring'st
   hem.   [*Exit Drugger.*]

---

[1] An occurrence in 1577 which has not been explained.

[2] Forestalled.

[3] Referring to Kyd's *Spanish Tragedy*.

Ana. (*Subtle hath whispered with him this
   while.*)   Sir, I know
The Spaniard hates the Brethren, and
   hath spies
Upon their actions; and that this was
   one
I make no scruple.—But the holy Synod
Have been in prayer and meditation
   for it;
And 'tis revealed no less to them than me
That casting of money is most lawful.

Sub.   True.
But here I cannot do it; if the house
Should chance to be suspected, all
   would out,   80
And we be locked up in the Tower for-
   ever,
To make gold there for th' state, never
   come out;
And then are you defeated.

Ana.   I will tell
This to the elders and the weaker
   Brethren,
That the whole company of the sepa-
   ration
May join in humble prayer again.

(Sub.   And fasting.)

Ana. Yea, for some fitter place. The peace
   of mind
Rest with these walls!

Sub.   Thanks, courteous Ananias.
              [*Exit Ananias.*]

Face. What did he come for?

Sub.   About casting dollars,
Presently out of hand. And so I told
   him   90
A Spanish minister came here to spy
Against the faithful—

Face.   I conceive. Come, Subtle,
Thou art so down upon the least disaster!
How wouldst thou ha' done, if I had not
   helped thee out?

Sub. I thank thee, Face, for the angry
   boy, i' faith.

Face. Who would ha' looked[4] it should
   ha' been that rascal
Surly? He had dyed his beard and all.
   Well, sir,
Here's damask come to make you a suit.

Sub.   Where's Drugger?

Face. He is gone to borrow me a Spanish
   habit;
I'll be the count now.

---

[4] Expected.

SUB. But where's the widow? 100

FACE. Within, with my lord's sister;
Madam Doll
Is entertaining her.

SUB. By your favor, Face,
Now she is honest, I will stand again.

FACE. You will not offer it?

SUB. Why?

FACE. Stand to your word,
Or—here comes Doll. She knows—

SUB. Yo' are tyrannous still.

FACE. Strict for my right.—

[*Enter Doll.*]

How now, Doll? Hast told her
The Spanish count will come?

DOLL. Yes; but another is come
You little looked for!

FACE. Who's that?

DOLL. Your master;
The master of the house.

SUB. How, Doll!

FACE. She lies.
This is some trick. Come, leave your
quiblins,[1] Dorothy. 110

DOLL. Look out and see.

[*Face goes to the window.*]

SUB. Art thou in earnest?

DOLL. 'Slight,
Forty o' the neighbors are about him,
talking.

FACE. 'Tis he, by this good day.

DOLL. 'Twill prove ill day
For some on us.

FACE. We are undone, and taken.

DOLL. Lost, I am afraid.

SUB. You said he would not come,
While there died one a week within the
liberties.[2]

FACE. No; 'twas within the walls.

SUB. Was 't so? Cry you mercy.
I thought the liberties. What shall we
do now, Face?

FACE. Be silent; not a word, if he call or
knock.
I'll into mine old shape again, and meet
him, 120
Of Jeremy, the butler. I' the meantime,
Do you two pack up all the goods and
purchase[3]

---

[1] Quibbles, equivocations.
[2] Slum district just outside the walls of the
city.
[3] Plunder, booty.

That we can carry i' the two trunks
I'll keep him
Off for today, if I cannot longer; and
then
At night I'll ship you both away to
Ratcliff,
Where we'll meet tomorrow, and there
we'll share.
Let Mammon's brass and pewter keep
the cellar;
We'll have another time for that. But,
Doll,
Pray thee, go heat a little water quickly;
Subtle must shave me. All my captain's
beard 130
Must off, to make me appear smooth
Jeremy.
You'll do 't?

SUB. Yes, I'll shave you as well as
I can.

FACE. And not cut my throat, but trim
me?

SUB. You shall see, sir. [*Exeunt.*]

ACT V. SCENE i.

[*The street before Lovewit's house.*]
Lovewit, Neighbors.

[LOVE.] Has there been such resort, say
you?

NEI. 1. Daily, sir.

NEI. 2. And nightly, too.

NEI. 3. Ay, some as brave as lords.

NEI. 4. Ladies and gentlewomen.

NEI. 5. Citizens' wives.

NEI. 1. And knights.

NEI. 6. In coaches.

NEI. 2. Yes, and oyster women.

NEI. 1. Beside other gallants.

NEI. 3. Sailors' wives.

NEI. 4. Tabacco men.

NEI. 5. Another Pimlico![4]

LOVE. What should my knave advance
To draw this company? He hung out
no banners
Of a strange calf with five legs to be seen,
Or a huge lobster with six claws?

NEI. 6. No, sir.

NEI. 3. We had gone in then, sir.

LOVE. He has no gift 10
Of teaching i' the nose[5] that e'er I
knew of.

---

[4] A popular summer resort.
[5] *I.e.*, like a Puritan.

You saw no bills set up that promised
　cure
Of agues or the toothache?

NEI. 2.　　　　　　　No such thing, sir!

LOVE. Nor heard a drum strook for
　babions or puppets?

NEI. 5. Neither, sir.

LOVE.　　　What device should he bring
　forth now?
I love a teeming wit as I love my nour-
　ishment.
Pray God he ha' not kept such open
　house
That he hath sold my hangings and my
　bedding!
I left him nothing else. If he have
　eat hem,
A plague o' the moth, say I! Sure he
　has got　　　　　　　　　　　　20
Some bawdy pictures to call all this
　ging: [1]
The Friar and the Nun; or the new
　motion [2]
Of the knight's courser covering the
　parson's mare;
The boy of six year old with the great
　thing.
Or 't may be he has the fleas that run
　at tilt
Upon a table, or some dog to dance?
When saw you him?

NEI. 1.　　　　　　Who, sir, Jeremy?

NEI. 2.　　　　　　　Jeremy butler?
We saw him not this month.

LOVE.　　　How!

NEI. 4.　　　　　Not these five weeks, sir.

NEI. [6.] [3] These six weeks, at the least.

LOVE.　　　　　Yo' amaze me, neighbors!

NEI. 5. Sure, if your worship know not
　where he is,　　　　　　　　　30
He's slipped away.

NEI. 6.　Pray God he be not made away.
　　　　　　　　　　　　He knocks.

LOVE. Ha! It's no time to question, then.

NEI. 6.　　　　　　　　　　About
Some three weeks since I heard a dole-
　ful cry,
As I sat up a-mending my wife's stock-
　ings.

LOVE. This 's strange that none will
　answer! Didst thou hear
A cry, say'st thou?

[1] Gang.
[2] Puppet show.
[3] From 1640 edn.

NEI. 6.　　　　　Yes, sir, like unto a man
That had been strangled an hour, and
　could not speak.

NEI. 2. I heard it, too, just this day three
　weeks, at two a-clock
Next morning.

LOVE.　　　These be miracles, or you make
　hem so!
A man an hour strangled, and could
　not speak,　　　　　　　　　40
And both you heard him cry?

NEI. 3.　　　　　　Yes, downward,[4] sir.

LOVE. Thou art a wise fellow. Give me
　thy hand, I pray thee.
What trade art thou on?

NEI. 3.　　　A smith and 't please your
　worship.

LOVE. A smith? Then lend me thy help
　to get this door open.

NEI. 3. That I will presently, sir; but
　fetch my tools—　　　　　　[Exit.]

NEI. 1. Sir, best to knock again afore
　you break it.

ACT V. SCENE ii.

[The same.]

Lovewit, Face, Neighbors.

[LOVE. (*Knocking again.*)] I will.

[*Enter Face dressed as a butler.*]

FACE.　　　　　　What mean you, sir?

NEI. 1, 2, 4.　　　　　O, here's Jeremy!

FACE. Good sir, come from the door.

LOVE.　　　　　Why, what's the matter?

FACE. Yet farder; [5] you are too near yet.

LOVE.　　　　I' the name of wonder,
What means the fellow?

FACE.　　　The house, sir, has been visited.

LOVE. What, with the plague? Stand thou
　then farder.

FACE.　　　No, sir,
I had it not.

LOVE.　　　Who had it then? I left
None else but thee i' the house.

FACE.　　　Yes, sir, my fellow,
The cat that kept [6] the butt'ry, had it
　on her
A week before I spied it; but I got her

[4] Hathaway suggests that this is a slang term
of negation.
[5] Farther.　　　　　　[6] Guarded.

Conveyed away i' the night. And so I shut 10
The house up for a month—

LOVE. How!

FACE. Purposing then, sir,
T' have burnt rose-vinegar, treacle, and tar,
And ha' made it sweet, that you should ne'er ha' known it,
Because I knew the news would but afflict you, sir.

LOVE. Breathe less, and farder off! Why, this is stranger!
The neighbors tell me all here that the doors
Have still been open—

FACE. How, sir!

LOVE. Gallants, men and women,
And of all sorts, tag-rag, been seen to flock here
In threaves [1] these ten weeks, as to a second Hogsden,
In days of Pimlico and Eye-bright. [2]

FACE. Sir, 20
Their wisdoms will not say so.

LOVE. Today they speak
Of coaches and gallants; one in a French hood
Went in, they tell me; and another was seen
In a velvet gown at the windore; [3] divers more
Pass in and out.

FACE. They did pass through the doors then,
Or walls, I assure their eyesights and their spectacles;
For here, sir, are the keys, and here have been,
In this my pocket, now above twenty days!
And for before, I kept the fort alone there.
But that 'tis yet not deep i' the afternoon, 30
I should believe my neighbors had seen double
Through the black pot, and made these apparitions!
For, on my faith to your worship, for these three weeks
And upwards, the door has not been opened.

[1] Droves.   [2] A tavern.   [3] Window.

LOVE. Strange!

NEI. 1. Good faith, I think I saw a coach.

NEI. 2. And I too,
I'ld ha' been sworn.

LOVE. Do you but think it now?
And but one coach?

NEI. 4. We cannot tell, sir; Jeremy
Is a very honest fellow.

FACE. Did you see me at all?

NEI. 1. No; that we are sure on.

NEI. 2. I'll be sworn o' that.

LOVE. Fine rogues to have your testimonies built on! 40

[*Enter Third Neighbor, with his tools.*]

NEI. 3. Is Jeremy come?

NEI. 1. O, yes; you may leave your tools;
We were deceived, he says.

NEI. 2. He has had the keys,
And the door has been shut these three weeks.

NEI. 3. Like enough!

LOVE. Peace, and get hence, you changelings.

[*Enter Surly and Mammon.*]

FACE. [*Aside.*] Surly come!
And Mammon made acquainted! They'll tell all.
How shall I beat them off? What shall I do?
Nothing's more wretched than a guilty conscience.

ACT V. SCENE iii.

[*The same.*]

Surly, Mammon, Lovewit, Face, Neighbors, Kastril, Ananias, Tribulation, Dapper, Subtle. [4]

[SUR.] No, sir, he was a great physician. This,
It was no bawdyhouse, but a mere chancel!
You knew the lord and his sister.

MAM. Nay, good Surly—

SUR. The happy word, "Be rich"—

MAM. Play not the tyran—

SUR. Should be today pronounced to all your friends.

[4] The last five enter later.

And where be your andirons now, and
    your brass pots,
That should ha' been golden flagons
    and great wedges?
MAM. Let me but breathe. What, they
    ha' shut their doors,
Methinks!   *Mammon and Surly knock.*
SUR.   Ay, now 'tis holiday with them.
MAM.   Rogues,
Cozeners, impostors, bawds!
FACE.   What mean you, sir?   10
MAM. To enter if we can.
FACE.   Another man's house?
  Here is the owner, sir; turn you to
    him,
And speak your business.
MAM.   Are you, sir, the owner?
LOVE. Yes, sir.
MAM.   And are those knaves within,
    your cheaters?
LOVE. What knaves? What cheaters?
MAM.   Subtle and his Lungs.
FACE. The gentleman is distracted, sir!
  No lungs
  Nor lights ha' been seen here these
    three weeks, sir,
  Within these doors, upon my word.
SUR.   Your word,
  Groom arrogant?
FACE.   Yes, sir, I am the housekeeper,
  And know the keys ha' not been out o'
    my hands.   20
SUR. This 's a new Face?
FACE.   You do mistake the
  house, sir.
  What sign was 't at?
SUR.   You rascal! This is one
  O' the confederacy. Come, let's get
    officers,
  And force the door.
LOVE.   Pray you, stay, gentle-
  men.
SUR. No, sir, we'll come with warrant.
MAM.   Ay, and then
  We shall ha' your doors open.
        [Exeunt Mammon and Surly.]
LOVE.   What means this?
FACE. I cannot tell, sir.
NEI. 1.   These are two o' the gallants
  That we do think we saw.
FACE.   Two o' the fools?
  You talk as idly as they. Good faith,
    sir,
  I think the moon has crazed hem all.

[Enter Kastril.]

(O me,   30
The angry boy come too? He'll make a
  noise,
And ne'er away till he have betrayed us
  all.)   *Kastril knocks.*
KAS. What, rogues, bawds, slaves, you'll
  open the door anon!
Punk, cockatrice,[1] my suster! By this
  light,
I'll fetch the marshal to you. You are
  a whore
To keep your castle—
FACE.   Who would you speak with, sir?
KAS. The bawdy doctor, and the cozen-
  ing captain,
And Puss, my suster.
LOVE.   This is something, sure.
FACE. Upon my trust, the doors were
  never open, sir.
KAS. I have heard all their tricks told me
  twice over   40
By the fat knight and the lean gentle-
  man.
LOVE. Here comes another.

[Enter Ananias and Tribulation.]

FACE. *[Aside.]*   Ananias too?
  And his pastor?
TRI.   The doors are shut against us.
        They beat, too, at the door.
ANA. Come forth, you seed of sulphur,
  sons of fire!
  Your stench, it is broke forth; abomina-
    tion
  Is in the house.
KAS.   Ay, my suster's there.
ANA.   The place,
  It is become a cage of unclean birds.
KAS. Yes, I will fetch the scavenger and
  the constable.
TRI. You shall do well.
ANA.   We'll join to weed them out.
KAS. You will not come then, punk de-
  vice,[2] my suster!   50
ANA. Call her not sister; she is a harlot
  verily.
KAS. I'll raise the street.
LOVE.   Good gentlemen, a word.
ANA. Sathan avoid, and hinder not our
  zeal!

[1] Here, a prostitute.
[2] Perfect harlot, possibly with a pun on *point-device.*

[Exeunt Ananias, Tribulation, and Kastril.]

LOVE. The world's turned Bet'lem.

FACE.   These are all broke loose
Out of S[t]. Kather'ne's, where they use
to keep
The better sort of madfolks.

NEI. 1.   All these persons
We saw go in and out here.

NEI. 2.   Yes, indeed, sir.

NEI. 3. These were the parties.

FACE.   Peace, you drunkards! Sir,
I wonder at it. Please you to give me
leave
To touch the door; I'll try an the lock
be changed.   60

LOVE. It mazes me!

FACE. [*Going to the door.*]   Good faith, sir,
I believe
There's no such thing. 'Tis all *deceptio
visus.*[1]—
[*Aside.*] Would I could get him away.
          Dapper cries out within.

DAP.   Master Captain! Master Doctor!

LOVE. Who's that?

FACE.   (Our clerk within, that I
forgot!)—I know not, sir.

DAP. For God's sake, when will her grace
be at leisure?

FACE.   Ha!
Illusions, some spirit o' the air!—(His
gag is melted,
And now he sets out the throat.[2])

DAP.   I am almost stifled—
(FACE. Would you were altogether.)

LOVE.   'Tis i' the house.
Ha! List!

FACE.   Believe it, sir, i' the air.

LOVE.   Peace, you—

DAP. Mine aunt's grace does not use me
well.

SUB. [*Within.*]   You fool,   70
Peace; you'll mar all.

FACE. [*Through the keyhole, but is overheard
by Lovewit.*]   Or you will else,
you rogue.

LOVE. O, is it so? Then you converse
with spirits!—
Come, sir. No more o' your tricks, good
Jeremy.
The truth, the shortest way.

[1] Optical illusion.
[2] "Lets off his mouth."

FACE.   Dismiss this rabble, sir.—
[*Aside.*] What shall I do? I am catched.

LOVE.   Good neighbors,
I thank you all. You may depart.—
[*Exeunt Neighbors.*] Come, sir,
You know that I am an indulgent
master;
And therefore conceal nothing. What's
your med'cine,
To draw so many several sorts of wild
fowl?

FACE. Sir, you were wont to affect mirth
and wit—   80
But here's no place to talk on 't i' the
street.
Give me but leave to make the best of
my fortune,
And only pardon me th' abuse of your
house;
It's all I beg. I'll help you to a widow,
In recompense, that you shall gi' me
thanks for,
Will make you seven years younger,
and a rich one.
'Tis but your putting on a Spanish cloak.
I have her within. You need not fear
the house;
It was not visited.

LOVE.   But by me, who came
Sooner than you expected.

FACE.   It is true, sir.   90
Pray you, forgive me.

LOVE.   Well; let's see your widow.
                              [*Exeunt.*]

ACT V. SCENE iv.

[*A room in Lovewit's house.*]

Subtle, Dapper [blindfolded], Face, Doll.[3]

[SUB.] How! Ha' you eaten your gag?

DAP.   Yes, faith, it crumbled
Away i' my mouth.

SUB.   You ha' spoiled all then.

DAP.   No!
I hope my aunt of Fairy will forgive me.

SUB. Your aunt's a gracious lady; but in
truth
You were to blame.

DAP.   The fume did overcome me,
And I did do 't to stay my stomach.
    Pray you
So satisfy her grace.

[3] Last two enter later.

[*Enter Face in his uniform.*]

               Here comes the captain.

FACE. How now! Is his mouth down?

SUB.   Ay, he has spoken!

FACE. (A pox, I heard him, and you too.)
  He's undone then.—
  (I have been fain to say the house is
    haunted   10
  With spirits, to keep churl back.

SUB.   And hast thou done it?

FACE. Sure, for this night.

SUB.   Why, then triumph and sing
  Of Face so famous, the precious king
  Of present wits.

FACE.   Did you not hear the coil [1]
  About the door?

SUB.   Yes, and I dwindled with it.)

FACE. Show him his aunt, and let him be
    despatched;
  I'll send her to you.   [*Exit.*]

SUB.   Well, sir, your aunt her
    grace
  Will give you audience presently, on
    my suit,
  And the captain's word that you did
    not eat your gag
  In any contempt of her highness.
      [*Removes the blindfold from his eyes.*]

DAP.   Not I, in troth, sir.   20

[*Enter*] *Doll like the Queen of Fairy.*

SUB. Here she is come. Down o' your
  knees and wriggle;
  She has a stately presence.
               [*Dapper kneels.*]
          Good! Yet nearer,
  And bid, "God save you!"

DAP.   Madam!

SUB.   And your aunt.

DAP. And my most gracious aunt, God
  save your grace.

DOLL. Nephew, we thought to have been
  angry with you;
  But that sweet face of yours hath
    turned the tide,
  And made it flow with joy, that ebbed
    of love.
  Arise, and touch our velvet gown.

SUB.   The skirts,
  And kiss hem. So!

DOLL.   Let me now stroke that head.

[1] Disturbance.

---

*Much, nephew, shalt thou win; much shalt
  thou spend.*   30
*Much shalt thou give away; much shalt
  thou lend.*

SUB. (Ay, much, indeed.)—Why do you
  not thank her grace?

DAP. I cannot speak for joy.

SUB.   See, the kind wretch!
  Your grace's kinsman right.

DOLL.   Give me the bird.—
  Here is your fly in a purse, about your
    neck, cousin;
  Wear it, and feed it about this day
    sev'night,
  On your right wrist—

SUB.   Open a vein with a pin
  And let it suck but once a week; till then,
  You must not look on 't.

DOLL.   No. And, kinsman,
  Bear yourself worthy of the blood you
    come on.   40

SUB. Her grace would ha' you eat no
  more Woolsack [2] pies
  Nor Dagger [2] frume'ty.[3]

DOLL.   Nor break his fast
  In Heaven [2] and Hell.[2]

SUB.   She's with you everywhere!
  Nor play with costermongers, at mum-
    chance,[4] traytrip,[4]
  God-make-you-rich [4] (whenas your aunt
    has done it); but keep
  The gallant'st company and the best
    games—

DAP.   Yes, sir.

SUB. Gleek [4] and primero; [4] and what you
  get, be true to us.

DAP. By this hand, I will.

SUB.   You may bring 's a thousand pound
  Before tomorrow night, if but three
    thousand
  Be stirring, an you will.

DAP.   I swear I will then.   50

SUB. Your fly will learn you all games.

FACE. [*Within.*]   Ha' you done there?

SUB. Your grace will command him no
  more duties?

DOLL.   No;
  But come and see me often. I may
    chance
  To leave him three or four hundred
    chests of treasure,

[2] Name of a tavern.
[3] Frumenty, wheat boiled in milk, etc.
[4] A game of chance.

And some twelve thousand acres of
  fairy land,
If he game well and comely with good
  gamesters.
SUB. There's a kind aunt! Kiss her de-
  parting part.—
But you must sell your forty mark a
  year now.
DAP. Ay, sir, I mean.
SUB.   Or gi't away; pox on 't!
DAP. I'll gi't mine aunt. I'll go and fetch
  the writings.   60
SUB. 'Tis well; away.   [Exit Dapper.

                Enter Face.]

FACE.   Where's Subtle?
SUB.   Here. What news?
FACE. Drugger is at the door; go take his
  suit,
And bid him fetch a parson presently.
Say he shall marry the widow. Thou
  shalt spend
A hundred pound by the service!—
                        [Exit Subtle.]
              Now, Queen Doll,
Ha' you packed up all?
DOLL.   Yes.
FACE.   And how do you like
The Lady Pliant?
DOLL.   A good, dull innocent.

              [*Enter Subtle.*]

SUB. Here's your Hieronimo's cloak and
  hat.
FACE.   Give me hem.
SUB. And the ruff too?
FACE.   Yes; I'll come to you presently.
                          [Exit.]
SUB. Now he is gone about his project,
  Doll,   70
I told you of, for the widow.
DOLL.   'Tis direct
Against our articles.
SUB.   Well, we'll fit him, wench.
Hast thou gulled her of her jewels or
  her bracelets?
DOLL. No; but I will do 't.
SUB.   Soon at night, my Dolly,
When we are shipped, and all our goods
  aboard,
Eastward for Ratcliff, we will turn our
  course

To Brainford, westward, if thou say'st
  the word,
And take our leaves of this o'erweening
  rascal,
This peremptory Face.
DOLL.   Content; I am weary of him.
SUB. Thou hast cause, when the slave
  will run a-wiving, Doll,   80
Against the instrument that was drawn
  between us.
DOLL. I'll pluck his bird as bare as I can.
SUB.   Yes, tell her
She must by any means address some
  present
To th' cunning man, make him amends
  for wronging
His art with her suspicion, send a ring,
Or chain of pearl; she will be tortured
  else
Extremely in her sleep, say, and ha'
  strange things
Come to her. Wilt thou?
DOLL.   Yes.
SUB.   My fine flittermouse,[1]
My bird o' the night! We'll tickle it at
  the Pigeons,[2]
When we have all, and may unlock the
  trunks,   *They kiss.*   90
And say this 's mine and thine, and thine
  and mine—

                [*Enter Face.*]

FACE. What now! A-billing?
SUB.   Yes, a little exalted
In the good passage of our stock-affairs.
FACE. Drugger has brought his parson;
  take him in, Subtle,
And send Nab back again to wash his
  face.
SUB. I will—and shave himself?
FACE.   If you can get him.
                        [Exit Subtle.]
DOLL. You are hot upon it, Face, what-
  e'er it is!
FACE. A trick that Doll shall spend ten
  pound a month by.

                [*Enter Subtle.*]

Is he gone?
SUB.   The chaplain waits you i' the hall,
  sir.   99

[1] Bat.
[2] An inn at Brainford, or Brentford.

FACE. I'll go bestow him.   [*Exit.*]

DOLL.   He'll now marry her instantly.

SUB. He cannot yet; he is not ready. Dear Doll,

Cozen her of all thou canst. To deceive him

Is no deceit, but justice, that would break

Such an inextricable tie as ours was.

DOLL. Let me alone to fit him.

[*Enter Face.*]

FACE.   Come, my venturers;
You ha' packed up all? Where be the trunks? Bring forth.

SUB. Here.

FACE.   Let 's see hem. Where's the money?

SUB.   Here.
In this.

FACE.   Mammon's ten pound; eight score before;

The Brethren's money this; Drugger's and Dapper's.   109
What paper's that?

DOLL.   The jewel of the waiting-maid's,
That stole it from her lady, to know certain—

FACE. If she should have precedence of her mistress?

DOLL.   Yes.

FACE. What box is that?

SUB.   The fishwife's rings, I think,
And th' alewife's single money.[1] Is 't not, Doll?

DOLL. Yes; and the whistle that the sail-or's wife

Brought you, to know and her husband were with Ward.[2]

FACE. We'll wet it tomorrow; and our silver beakers

And tavern cups. Where be the French petticoats

And girdles and hangers?[3]

SUB.   Here, i' the trunk,
And the bolts of lawn.

FACE.   Is Drugger's damask there,   120
And the tabacco?

SUB.   Yes.

FACE.   Give me the keys.

DOLL. Why you the keys?

[1] Small change.
[2] A notorious pirate.
[3] Loops from which swords were hung.

SUB.   No matter, Doll; because
We shall not open hem before he comes.

FACE. 'TIS true, you shall not open them, indeed;

Nor have hem forth. Do you see? Not forth, Doll.

DOLL.   No!

FACE. No, my smock-rampant. The right is, my master

Knows all, has pardoned me, and he will keep them.

Doctor, 'tis true—you look [4]—for [5] all your figures;

I sent for him, indeed. Wherefore, good partners,

Both he and she, be satisfied, for here 130

Determines [6] the indenture tripartite

Twixt Subtle, Doll, and Face. All I can do

Is to help you over the wall, o' the back side,

Or lend you a sheet to save your velvet gown, Doll.

Here will be officers presently; bethink you

Of some course suddenly to scape the dock,

For thither you'll come else. (*Some knock.*) Hark you, thunder!

SUB. You are a precious fiend!

OFFICERS. [*Without.*]   Open the door!

FACE. Doll, I am sorry for thee, i' faith; but hear'st thou?

It shall go hard but I will place thee somewhere;   140

Thou shalt ha' my letter to Mistress Amo—

DOLL.   Hang you—

FACE. Or Madam Cæsarean.

DOLL.   Pox upon you, rogue!
Would I had but time to beat thee!

FACE.   Subtle,
Let 's know where you set up next; I'll send you

A customer now and then, for old acquaintance.

What new course ha' you?

SUB.   Rogue, I'll hang myself,
That I may walk a greater devil than thou,

And haunt thee i' the flockbed [7] and the buttery.   [*Exeunt.*]

[4] Stare.   [5] In spite of.   [6] Terminates.
[7] A bed stuffed with pieces of wool or cloth.

Act V. Scene v.

[*Another room in the same.*]

Lovewit [*in Spanish costume, Parson*], *Officers, Mammon, Surly, Face, Kastril, Ananias, Tribulation, Drugger, Da*[*me*] *Pliant.*[1]

[Love.] What do you mean, my masters?

Mam. [*Without.*]   Open your door,
Cheaters, bawds, conjurers.

Off. [*Without.*]   Or we'll break it open.

Love. What warrant have you?

Off. [*Without.*]   Warrant enough, sir,
doubt not,
If you'll not open it.

Love.   Is there an officer there?

Off. [*Without.*]   Yes, two or three for[2]
failing.

Love.   Have but patience,
And I will open it straight.

[*Enter Face, as butler.*]

Face.   Sir, ha' you done?
Is it a marriage? Perfect?

Love.   Yes, my brain.

Face. Off with your ruff and cloak then;
be yourself, sir.
            [*Lovewit takes off his disguise.*]

Sur. [*Without.*] Down with the door!

Kas. [*Without.*]   'Slight, ding[3] it open.

Love. [*Opening the door.*]   Hold,
Hold, gentlemen, what means this violence?   10

[*Enter Mammon, Surly, Kastril, Ananias,
Tribulation, and Officers.*]

Mam. Where is this collier?

Sur.   And my Captain Face?

Mam. These day-owls.

Sur.   That are birding[4] in men's purses.

Mam. Madam Suppository.

Kas.   Doxy, my sister.

Ana.   Locusts
Of the foul pit.

Tri.   Profane as Bel and the Dragon.

Ana. Worse than the grasshoppers, or the
lice of Egypt.

---

[1] All except Lovewit and the Parson are without or enter later.
[2] For fear of.   [3] Break.   [4] Thieving.

Love. Good gentlemen, hear me. Are you
officers,
And cannot stay this violence?

Off. [1.]   Keep the peace.

Love. Gentlemen, what is the matter?
Whom do you seek?

Mam. The chymical[5] cozener.

Sur.   And the captain pander.

Kas. The nun my suster.

Mam.   Madam Rabbi.

Ana.   Scorpions 20
And caterpillars.

Love.   Fewer at once, I pray you.

Off. [1.] One after another, gentlemen, I
charge you,
By virtue of my staff—

Ana.   They are the vessels
Of pride, lust, and the cart.

Love.   Good zeal, lie still
A little while.

Tri.   Peace, Deacon Ananias.

Love. The house is mine here, and the
doors are open;
If there be any such persons as you seek
for,
Use your authority; search on, o' God's
name.
I am but newly come to town, and, find-
ing
This tumult 'bout my door, to tell you
true,   30
It somewhat mazed me, till my man here,
fearing
My more displeasure, told me he had
done
Somewhat an insolent part, let out my
house
(Belike presuming on my known aversion
From any air o' the town while there was
sickness)
To a doctor and a captain, who, what
they are
Or where they be, he knows not.

They enter.[6]

Mam.   Are they gone?

Love. You may go in and search, sir.—
[*Exit Mammon.*] Here I find
The empty walls worse than I left hem,
smoked,

---

[5] Chemical.
[6] *I.e.*, the Officers, Tribulation, and Ananias
start their search.

A few cracked pots, and glasses, and a
  fornace;   40
The ceiling filled with poesies of the
  candle,
And "Madam with a dildo" [1] writ o' the
  walls.
Only one gentlewoman I met here,
That is within, that said she was a
  widow—

KAS. Ay, that's my suster; I'll go thump
  her. Where is she?   [Exit.]

LOVE. And should ha' married a Spanish
  count, but he,
When he came to 't, neglected her so
  grossly
That I, a widower, am gone through with
  her.

SUR. How! Have I lost her then?

LOVE.   Were you the Don, sir?
Good faith, now she does blame yo'
  extremely, and says   50
You swore and told her you had ta'en the
  pains
To dye your beard, and umber o'er your
  face,
Borrowed a suit and ruff, all for her
  love—
And then did nothing. What an over-
  sight
And want of putting forward, sir, was
  this!
Well tare an old hargubuzier [2] yet,
Could prime his poulder, and give fire,
  and hit,
All in a twinkling!

Mammon comes forth.

MAM.   The whole nest are fled!

LOVE. What sort of birds were they?

MAM.   A kind of choughs,
Or thievish daws, sir, that have picked
  my purse   60
Of eight score and ten pounds within
  these five weeks,
Beside my first materials, and my goods
That lie i' the cellar, which I am glad
  they ha' left,
I may have home yet.

LOVE.   Think you so, sir?

MAM.   Ay.

LOVE. By order of law, sir, but not otherwise.

[1] Fragment of a ballad.
[2] Harquebusier, musketeer.

MAM. Not mine own stuff?

LOVE.   Sir, I can take no knowledge
That they are yours, but by public
  means.
If you can bring certificate that you were
  gulled of hem,
Or any formal writ out of a court
That you did cozen yourself, I will not
  hold them.   70

MAM. I'll rather lose hem.

LOVE.   That you shall not, sir,
By me, in troth; upon these terms, they
  are yours.
What, should they ha' been, sir, turned
  into gold, all?

MAM.   No.
I cannot tell. It may be they should.
  What then?

LOVE. What a great loss in hope have you
  sustained!

MAM. Not I; the commonwealth has.

FACE.   Ay, he would ha' built
The city new, and made a ditch about it
Of silver, should have run with cream
  from Hogsden,
That every Sunday in Moorfields the
  younkers [3]
And tits [4] and tomboys should have fed
  on, gratis.   80

MAM. I will go mount a turnip-cart, and
  preach
The end o' the world within these two
  months.—Surly,
What! In a dream?

SUR.   Must I needs cheat myself
With that same foolish vice of honesty?
Come, let us go and hearken [5] out the
  rogues.
That Face I'll mark for mine, if e'er I
  meet him.

FACE. If I can hear of him, sir, I'll bring
  you word
Unto your lodging; for, in troth, they
  were strangers
To me. I thought hem honest as myself,
  sir.

They come forth.

TRI. 'Tis well, the Saints shall not lose all
  yet. Go   90
And get some carts—

LOVE.   For what, my zealous friends?

[3] Youths.
[4] Wenches.
[5] Inquire, search.

ANA. To bear away the portion of the righteous
Out of this den of thieves.

LOVE. What is that portion?

ANA. The goods sometimes the orphans', that the Brethren
Bought with their silver pence.

LOVE. What, those i' the cellar
The knight Sir Mammon claims?

ANA. I do defy
The wicked Mammon; so do all the Brethren,
Thou profane man! I ask thee with what conscience
Thou canst advance that idol against us,
That have the seal? [1] Were not the shillings numbered 100
That made the pounds? Were not the pounds told out
Upon the second day of the fourth week
In the eighth month, upon the table dormant,[2]
The year of the last patience of the Saints,
Six hundred and ten?

LOVE. Mine earnest, vehement botcher,
And deacon also, I cannot dispute with you;
But, if you get you not away the sooner,
I shall confute you with a cudgel.

ANA. Sir!

TRI. Be patient, Ananias.

ANA. I am strong,
And will stand up, well girt, against an host 110
That threaten Gad in exile.

LOVE. I shall send you
To Amsterdam, to your cellar.

ANA. I will pray there,
Against thy house. May dogs defile thy walls,
And wasps and hornets breed beneath thy roof,
This seat of falsehood, and this cave of coz'nage!

[Exeunt Ananias and Tribulation.]

Drugger enters, and he beats him away.

LOVE. Another too?

DRUG. Not I, sir; I am no Brother.

LOVE. Away, you Harry Nicholas! [3] Do you talk? [Exit Drugger.]

[1] *I.e.*, of the chosen of God.
[2] Fixed, stationary.   [3] A notorious fanatic.

FACE. No, this was Abel Drugger.—(*To the Parson.*) Good sir, go,
And satisfy him; tell him all is done.
He stayed too long a-washing of his face. 120
The doctor, he shall hear of him at Westchester,
And of the captain, tell him, at Yarmouth, or
Some good port-town else, lying for a wind.— [Exit Parson.]
If you [can] [4] get off the angry child now, sir—

[*Enter Kastril and Dame Pliant.*]

KAS. (*To his sister.*) Come on, you ewe; you have matched most sweetly, ha' you not?
Did not I say I would never ha' you tupped
But by a dubbed boy,[5] to make you a lady-tom?
'Slight, you are a mammet! [6] O, I could touse you now.
Death, mun [7] you marry, with a pox!

LOVE. You lie, boy;
As sound as you; and I'm aforehand with you.

KAS. [*To Pliant.*] Anon! 130

LOVE. Come, will you quarrel? I will feeze [8] you, sirrah;
Why do you not buckle to your tools?

KAS. God's light,
This is a fine old boy as e'er I saw!

LOVE. What, do you change your copy [9] now? Proceed;
Here stands my dove. Stoop [10] at her if you dare.

KAS. 'Slight, I must love him! I cannot choose, i' faith,
And I should be hanged for 't! Suster, I protest
I honor thee for this match.

LOVE. O, do you so, sir?

KAS. Yes, and thou canst take tabacco and drink, old boy,
I'll give her five hundred pound more to her marriage 140
Than her own state.

[4] From 1612 edn.   [7] Must.
[5] *I.e.*, a knight.   [8] Flog.
[6] Puppet.   [9] Theme, "tune."
[10] Swoop (a term of falconry). The name Kastril meant a hawk.

Love.　　　　　　Fill a pipeful, Jeremy.

Face. Yes; but go in and take it, sir.

Love.　　　　　　　　　We will.
　　I will be ruled by thee in anything,
　　　Jeremy.

Kas. 'Slight, thou art not hidebound; thou
　　art a jovy [1] boy!
　　Come, let 's in, I pray thee, and take our
　　whiffs.

Love. Whiff in with your sister, brother
　　boy.—[*Exeunt Kastril and Dame
　　　　　　　　　　　　　　　Pliant.*]
　　　　　　　　　　　　　　That master
　　That had received such happiness by a
　　　servant,
　　In such a widow, and with so much
　　　wealth,
　　Were very ungrateful if he would not
　　　be
　　A little indulgent to that servant's
　　　wit,　　　　　　　　　　　　　150
　　And help his fortune, though with some
　　　small strain
　　Of his own candor.[2]—[*To the audience.*]
　　Therefore, gentlemen

And kind spectators, if I have out-
　　stripped
An old man's gravity or strict canon,
　　think
What a young wife and a good brain may
　　do—
Stretch age's truth sometimes, and crack
　　it too.—
Speak for thyself, knave.

Face.　　　　　So I will, sir.—Gentlemen,
　　My part a little fell in this last scene,
　　Yet 'twas decorum.[3]　And though I am
　　　clean
　　Got off from Subtle, Surly, Mammon,
　　　Doll,　　　　　　　　　　　　　160
　　Hot Ananias, Dapper, Drugger, all
　　With whom I traded, yet I put myself
　　On you, that are my country; [4] and this
　　　pelf
　　Which I have got, if you do quit [5] me,
　　　rests
　　To feast you often and invite new guests.
　　　　　　　　　　　　　　　[*Exeunt.*]
　　　　　　　　　The End.

[1] Jovial.　　　　　　[2] Integrity.　　　　[3] Dramatic propriety.　　　[4] Jury.　　　　　[5] Acquit.

This comedy was first acted in the year 1610 by the King's Majesty's Servants.　The
principal comedians were:

Ric. Burbadge	*Joh. Hemings*
Joh. Lowin	*Will. Ostler*
Hen. Condell	*Joh. Underwood*
Alex. Cooke	*Nic. Tooly*
Rob. Armin	*Will. Eglestone*

　　　With the allowance of the Master of Revels.

THE HUE AND CRY AFTER CUPID[1]

BY

BEN JONSON

[*DRAMATIS PERSONÆ*

Cupid.

Vulcan.

Hymen.

Venus.

Pyracmon
Brontes } *Cyclopes.*
Steropes

Graces 1, 2, and 3.

Scene: *Imaginary.*

Time: *Contemporary.*]

The worthy custom of honoring worthy marriages with these noble solemnities hath of late years advanced itself frequently with us, to the reputation no less of our court than nobles, expressing besides (through the difficulties of expense and travel, with the cheerfulness of undertaking) a most real affection in the personators, to those for whose sake they would sustain these persons. It behoves then us, that are trusted with a part of their honor in these celebrations, to do nothing in them beneath the dignity of either. With this proposed part of judgment, I adventure to give that abroad, which in my first conception I intended honorably fit; and, though it hath labored since, under censure, I, that know truth to be always of one stature and so like a rule as [2] who bends it the least way must needs do an injury to the right, cannot but smile at their tyrannous ignorance, that will offer to slight me (in these things being an artificer) and give themselves a peremptory license to judge, who have never touched so much as to the bark or utter [3] shell of any knowl-

edge. But their daring dwell with them. They have found a place to pour out their follies, and I a seat to sleep out the passage.

The scene to this masque was a high, steep, red cliff, advancing itself into the clouds, figuring the place from whence (as I have been, not fabulously, informed) the honorable family of the Radcliffes first took their name, a clivo rubro,[4] and is to be written with that orthography, as I have observed out of M[aster] Camden in his mention of the Earls of Sussex. This cliff was also a note of height, greatness, and antiquity, before which, on the two sides, were erected two pilasters, charged with spoils and trophies of Love and his mother, consecrate to marriage; amongst which were old and young persons figured, bound with roses, the wedding garments, rocks and spindles, hearts transfixed with arrows, others flaming, virgins' girdles, girlonds,[5] and worlds of suchlike, all wrought round and bold; and overhead two personages, Triumph and Victory, in flying postures, and twice so big as the life, in place of the arch, and holding a girlond of myrtle for the key— all which, with the pillars, seemed to be of burnished gold, and embossed out of the metal. Beyond the cliff was seen nothing but clouds, thick and obscure, till on the sudden, with a solemn music, a bright sky breaking forth, there were discovered first two doves,

[1] This title was assigned to the masque by Gifford. The title in the 1616 folio reads: "The Description of the Masque, with the Nuptial Songs, at the Lord Viscount Haddington's Marriage at Court on the Shrove Tuesday at Night. 1608." On this occasion the bride was Lady Elizabeth Ratcliffe, or Radcliffe, daughter of Robert Earl of Sussex.

[2] That.

[3] Outer.

[4] From a red cliff.

[5] Garlands.

*then two swans,[1] with silver gears,[2] drawing
forth a triumphant chariot, in which Venus
sat, crowned with her star, and beneath her
the three Graces, or* Charites, *Aglaia,
Thalia, Euphrosyne, all attired according
to their antique figures. These from their
chariot alighted on the top of the cliff, and,
descending by certain abrupt and winding
passages, Venus having left her star only
flaming in her seat, came to the earth, the
Graces throwing girlonds all the way, and
began to speak.*

VENUS. It is no common cause, ye will
    conceive,
My lovely Graces, makes your goddess
    leave
Her state in heaven, tonight to visit
    earth.
Love late is fled away, my eldest birth,
Cupid, whom I did joy to call my son;
And, whom long absent, Venus is un-
    done.
Spy, if you can, his footsteps on this
    green,
For here, as I am told, he late hath
    been,
With divers of his brethren,[3] lending
    light
From their best flames to gild a glorious
    night,   10
Which I not grudge at, being done for
    her
Whose honors to mine own I still prefer.
But he not yet returning, I am in fear
Some gentle Grace or innocent Beauty
    here
Be taken with him, or he hath surprised
A second Psyche, and lives here dis-
    guised.
Find ye no tract [4] of his strayed feet?
1 GRACE.   Not I.
2 GRACE. Nor I.
3 GRACE.   Nor I.

[1] Jonson's note runs: "Both doves and swans
were sacred to this goddess, and as well with the
one as the other; her chariot is induced by
Ovid, L. x and xi, *Metamor.*" The editors of the
present text omit most of Jonson's notes on this
masque and a small amount of similar material
incorporated in the stage directions.
[2] Trappings.
[3] "Alluding to the Loves in the Queen's
Masque before" (Jonson's note referring to his
Masque of Beauty).
[4] Track, trace.

VENUS.   Stay, nymphs,
    we then will try
A nearer way. Look [5] all these ladies'
    eyes,
And see if there he not concealéd lies, 20
Or in their bosoms twixt their swelling
    breasts
(The wag affects to make himself such
    nests).
Perchance he hath got some simple
    heart to hide
His subtle shape in. I will have him
    cried,[6]
And all his virtues told, that, when
    they know
What sprite he is, she soon may let
    him go,
That guards him now, and think her-
    self right blessed
To be so timely rid of such a guest.
Begin, soft Graces, and proclaim reward
To her that brings him in. Speak to
    be heard.   30
1 GRACE. Beauties, have ye seen this toy,
Calléd Love, a little boy,
Almost naked, wanton, blind,
Cruel now, and then as kind?
If he be amongst ye, say.
He is Venus' runaway.
2 GRACE. She that will but now discover
Where the wingéd wag doth hover,
Shall tonight receive a kiss,
How or where herself would wish;   40
But who brings him to his mother,
Shall have that kiss, and another.
3 GRACE. H' hath of marks about him
    plenty;
You shall know him among twenty.
All his body is a fire,
And his breath a flame entire,
That being shot, like lightning, in,
Wounds the heart, but not the skin.
1 GRACE. At his sight, the sun hath turned;
Neptune in the waters burned;   50
Hell hath felt a greater heat;
Jove himself forsook his seat.
From the center [7] to the sky
Are his trophies rearéd high.
2 GRACE. Wings he hath, which though
    ye clip,
He will leap from lip to lip,

[5] Look at, examine.
[6] Proclaimed by the public crier.
[7] Center of the world.

Over liver, lights, and heart,
But not stay in any part;
And, if chance his arrow misses,
He will shoot himself in kisses.   60
3 Grace. He doth bear a golden bow,
And a quiver, hanging low,
Full of arrows that outbrave
Dian's shafts, where, if he have
Any head more sharp than other,
With that first he strikes his mother.
1 Grace. Still the fairest are his fuel.
When his days are to be cruel,
Lovers' hearts are all his food,
And his baths their warmest blood.   70
Naught but wounds his hand doth
    season,
And he hates none like to Reason.
2 Grace. Trust him not; his words, though
    sweet,
Seldom with his heart do meet.
All his practice is deceit,
Every gift it is a bait,
Not a kiss but poison bears,
And most treason in his tears.
3 Grace. Idle minutes are his reign;
Then the straggler makes his gain   80
By presenting maids with toys,
And would have ye think hem joys;
'Tis the ambition of the elf
To have all childish as himself.
1 Grace. If by these ye please to know
    him,
Beauties, be not nice,[1] but show him.
2 Grace. Though ye had a will to hide
    him,
Now, we hope, ye'll not abide him—
3 Grace. Since ye hear his falser play,
And that he is Venus' runaway.   90

*At this, from behind the trophies, Cupid
    discovered himself and came forth
    armed, attended with twelve Boys, most
    anticly attired, that represented the
    Sports and pretty Lightnesses that ac-
    company Love, under the titles of* Joci
    and Risus, *and are said to wait on*
    Venus, *as she is Prefect of Marriage.*

Cupid. Come, my little jocund Sports,
Come away; the time now sorts [2]
With your pastime. This same night
Is Cupid's day. Advance your light.
With your revel fill the room,
That our triumphs be not dumb.

---

[1] Scrupulous.   [2] Agrees.

*Wherewith they fell into a subtle, capricious
    dance, to as odd a music, each of them
    bearing two torches, and nodding with
    their antic faces, with other variety of
    ridiculous gesture, which gave much
    occasion of mirth and delight to the
    spectators.   The dance ended, Cupid
                                went forward.*

Cupid. Well done, antics! Now my bow
And my quiver bear to show
That these Beauties here may know
By what arms this feat was done,   100
That hath so much honor won
Unto Venus and her son.

*At which his Mother apprehended him and,
    circling him in with the Graces, began
                                to demand.*

Venus. What feat, what honor is it that
    you boast,
My little straggler? I had given you
    lost,
With all your games here.
Cupid.   Mother?
Venus.   Yes, sir, she.
What might your glorious cause of
    triumph be?
Ha' you shot Minerva or the Thespian
    dames?
Heat [3] aged Ops again with youthful
    flames?
Or have you made the colder Moon to
    visit
Once more a sheepcote? Say, what con-
    quest is it   110
Can make you hope such a renown to
    win?
Is there a second Hercules brought to
    spin?
Or, for some new disguise, leaves Jove
    his thunder?
Cupid. Nor that, nor those, and yet no
    less a wonder—
Which to tell, I may not stay.
                And there slips from her.

*Here Hymen, the God of Marriage, entered,
    and was so induced here as you have
        him described in my* Hymenæi.

Hymen's presence bids away;
'Tis already at his night;

---

[3] Heated.

He can give you farther light.
You, my Sports, may here abide
Till I call to light the bride.　　120
HYMEN. Venus, is this a time to quit your car?
To stoop to earth, to leave alone your star,
Without your influence, and, on such a night,
Which should be crowned with your most cheering sight,
As [1] you were ignorant of what were done
By Cupid's hand, your all-triumphing son?
Look on this state, [2] and, if you yet not know
What crown there shines, whose scepter here doth grow,
Think on thy loved Æneas; and what name
Maro, the golden trumpet [3] of his fame,　　130
Gave him, read thou in this: a prince that draws
By example more than others do by laws,
That is so just to his great act and thought,
To do, not what kings may, but what kings ought;
Who, out of piety, unto peace is vowed,
To spare his subjects, yet to quell the proud,
And dares esteem it the first fortitude
To have his passions, foes at home, subdued;
That was reserved, until the Parcæ spun
Their whitest wool and then his thread begun,　　140
Which thread, when treason would have burst, [4] a soul
(Today renowned and added to my roll)
Opposed; and, by that act, to his name did bring
The honor to be saver of his king—
This king, whose worth, if gods for virtue love,
Should Venus with the same affections move

¹ As if.　² Canopied throne.　³ Trumpeter.
⁴ Jonson's note runs: "In that monstrous conspiracy of E[arl] Gowry." Haddington aided the future James I to put down the conspiracy in 1600.

As her Æneas, and no less endear
Her love to his safety than when she did cheer,
After a tempest, long-afflicted Troy,
Upon the Lybian shore, and brought them joy.　　150
VENUS. I love, and know his virtues, and do boast
Mine own renown when I renown him most.
My Cupid's absence I forgive and praise,
That me to such a present grace could raise.
His champion shall hereafter be my care.
But speak his bride, and what her virtues are.
HYMEN. She is a noble virgin, styled the Maid
Of the Red Cliff, and hath her dowry weighed
No less in virtue, blood, and form than gold;
Thence, where my pillar's reared (you may behold)　　160
Filled with Love's trophies, doth she take her name.
Those pillars did uxorious Vulcan frame
Against [5] this day; and underneath that hill
He and his Cyclopes are forging still
Some strange and curious piece t' adorn the night,
And give these gracéd nuptials greater light.

Here Vulcan presented himself, as overhearing Hymen, attired in a cassock girt to him, with bare arms, his hair and beard rough, his hat of blue and ending in a cone, in his hand a hammer and tongs, as coming from the forge.

VULCAN. Which I have done—the best of all my life—
And have my end, if it but please my wife,
And she commend it, to the labored worth.
Cleave, solid rock, and bring the wonder forth!　　170

At which, with a loud and full music, the cliff parted in the midst and dis-

⁵ In preparation for.

*covered an illustrious ¹ concave, filled
with an ample and glistering light, in
which an artificial sphere was made of
silver, eighteen foot in the diameter,
that turned perpetually; the* coluri ²
*were heightened with gold; so were the
arctic and antarctic circles, the tropics,
the equinoctial, the meridian and hori-
zon; only the zodiac was of pure gold,
in which the Masquers, under the characters of the twelve signs, were placed,
answering them in number, whose offices, with the whole frame, as it turned,
Vulcan went forward to describe.*

VULCAN. It is a sphere I have formed
round and even,
In due proportion to the sphere of
heaven,
With all his ³ lines and circles that compose
The perfect'st form, and aptly do disclose
The heaven of marriage (which I title it),
Within whose zodiac I have made to sit,
In order of the signs, twelve sacred
powers
That are presiding at all nuptial hours:
1. The first, in Aries' place, respecteth
pride
Of youth and beauty, graces in
the bride.   180
2. In Taurus, he loves strength and
manliness,
The virtues which the bridegroom
should profess.
3. In Gemini, that noble power is
shown,
That twins their hearts, and doth
of two make one.
4. In Cancer, he that bids the wife
give way
With backward yielding to her
husband's sway.
5. In Leo, he that doth instill the heat
Into the man, which from the following seat
6. Is tempered so as he that looks
from thence
Sees yet they keep a Virgin innocence.   190

7. In Libra's room, rules he that doth
supply
All happy beds with sweet equality.
8. The Scorpion's place he fills, that
makes the jars,
And stings in wedlock little strifes
and wars,
9. Which he in th' Archer's throne
doth soon remove
By making with his shafts new
wounds of love.
10. And those the follower with more
heat inspires,
As in the Goat the sun renews his
fires.
11. In wet Aquarius' stead, reigns he
that showers
Fertility upon the genial bowers. 200
12. Last, in the Fishes' place, sits he
doth say,
"In married joys all should be dumb
as they."
And this hath Vulcan for his Venus done,
To grace the chaster triumph of her
son.
VENUS. And for this gift will I to heaven
return,
And vow forever that my lamp shall
burn
With pure and chastest fire, or never
shine
But when it mixeth with thy sphere and
mine.

*Here Venus returned to her chariot with
the Graces, while Vulcan, calling out
the Priests of Hymen, who were the
musicians, was interrupted by Pyracmon (one of the Cyclopes), . . .
Brontes, and Steropes. . . .*

VULCAN. Sing then, ye priests.
PYRACMON.   Stay, Vulcan, shall not
these   209
Come forth and dance?
VULCAN.   Yes, my Pyracmon, please
The eyes of these spectators with our
art.
PYRACMON. Come here, then, Brontes;
bear a Cyclop's part,
And Steropes; both with your sledges
stand,
And strike a time unto them as they
land,

¹ Brilliantly lighted.
² The great circles of the celestial sphere in-
tersecting at the poles.   ³ Its.

And, as they forwards come, still guide
their paces
In musical and sweet proportioned
graces,
While I upon the work and frame attend,
And Hymen's priests forth, at their
seasons, send
To chaunt their hymns, and make this
square admire
Our great artificer, the god of fire.   220

*Here the Musicians, attired in yellow,
with wreaths of marjoram, and veils like
Hymen's priests, sung the first staff of the
following epithalamion, which, because it
was sung in pieces between the dances,
showed to be so many several songs, but
was made to be read an entire poem. After
the song, they came forth (descending in
an oblique motion) from the zodiac, and
danced their first dance; then, music inter-
posed (but varied with voices, only keeping
the same chorus), they danced their second
dance. So after, their third and fourth
dances, which were all full of elegancy and
curious device. The two latter were made
by M[aster] Tho. Giles,[1] the two first by
M[aster] Hie. Herne,[2] who, in the persons
of the two Cyclopes, beat a time to them with
their hammers. The tunes were M[aster]
Alphonso Ferrabosco's.[3] The device and act
of the scene M[aster] Inigo Jones[4] his, with
addition of the trophies. For the invention
of the whole and the verses, Assertor qui
dicat esse meos, imponet plagiario pu-
dorem.[5]*

*The attire of the Masquers throughout
was most graceful and noble, partaking of
the best both ancient and later figure; the
colors carnation and silver, enriched both
with embroidery[6] and lace; the dressing of
their heads, feathers and jewels; and so*

excellently ordered to the rest of the habit
as all would suffer under any description
after the show. Their performance of all, so
magnificent and illustrous that nothing can
add to the seal of it but the subscription of
their names:[7]

The Duke of Lennox	*Lord Hay*
Earl of Arundel	*Lord Sankre*
Earl of Pembroke	*Sir Ro. Riche*
Earl of Montgomery	*Sir Jo. Kennethie*
Lord D'Aubigny	*[Master of Mar][8]*
Lord of Walden	*Mr. Ersskins*

EPITHALAMION

Up, youths and virgins, up, and praise
The god whose nights outshine his days—
Hymen, whose hallowed rites
Could never boast of brighter lights;
Whose bands pass liberty.
Two of your troop, that with the morn were
free,
Are now waged to his war.
And what they are,
If you'll perfection see,
Yourselves must be.   10
Shine, Hesperus, shine forth, thou wishéd
star!

What joy or honors can compare
With holy nuptials, when they are
Made out of equal parts
Of years, of states, of hands, of hearts,
When, in the happy choice,
The spouse and spouséd have the fore-
most voice?
Such, glad of Hymen's war,
Live what they are,
And long perfection see;   20
And such ours be.
Shine, Hesperus, shine forth, thou wishéd
star!

The solemn state of this one night
Were fit to last an age's light;

---

[1] Formerly Master of the Children of Paul's
and later instructor in music to the princes
royal.

[2] Hierome Herne, a minor musician and
dancing master.

[3] A well-known Italian dancing master.

[4] The most famous architect of the day and
inventor of scenery and costumes for court
masques. He was on constantly shifting terms
of enmity and friendship with Jonson.

[5] The declarer who calls them mine will bring
shame upon the plagiarist.

[6] Embroidery.

[7] Gifford in his 1816 edn. of Jonson, VII, 94,
quotes a letter from Rowland White to the Earl
of Shrewsbury: "The great masque intended for
my L. Haddington's marriage is now *the only
thing thought upon* at court, by 5 English: L.
Arundel, L. Pemb., L. Montgomery, L. Theoph.
Howard, and Sir Robt. Rich; and by 7 Scots:
D. Lennox, D'Aubigny, Hay, Mr. of Mar, young
Erskine, Sankier, and Kennedy. It will cost
them about 300 *l.* a man."

[8] Supplied from White's letter above.

But there are rites behind
Have less of state, but more of kind: [1]
Love's wealthy crop of kisses,
And fruitful harvest of his mother's blisses.
Sound then to Hymen's war—
That what these are,   30
Who will perfection see,
May haste to be.
Shine, Hesperus, shine forth, thou wishéd
    star!

Love's commonwealth consists of toys;
His council are those antic boys,
Games, Laughter, Sports, Delights,
That triumph with him on these nights,
To whom we must give way,
For now their reign begins, and lasts till
    day.
They sweeten Hymen's war,   40
And, in that jar,
Make all that married be,
Perfection see.
Shine, Hesperus, shine forth, thou wishéd
    star!

Why stays the bridegroom to invade
Her that would be a matron made?
Good night, whilst yet we may
Good night, to you a virgin, say;
Tomorrow rise the same   49
Your mother is, and use a nobler name.
Speed well in Hymen's war

  [1] Nature.

That what you are,
By your perfection we
And all may see.
Shine, Hesperus, shine forth, thou wishéd
    star!

Tonight is Venus' vigil kept.
This night no bridegroom ever slept;
And, if the fair bride do,
The married say, 'tis his fault, too.
Wake then, and let your lights   60
Wake too; for they'll tell nothing of your
    nights
But that in Hymen's war
You perfect are.
And such perfection we
Do pray should be.
Shine, Hesperus, shine forth, thou wishéd
    star!

That, ere the rosy-fingered morn
Behold nine moons, there may be born
A babe, t' uphold the fame   69
Of Radcliffe's blood and Ramsey's [2] name,
That may, in his great seed,
Wear the long honors of his father's deed.
Such fruits of Hymen's war
Most perfect are;
And all perfection we
Wish you should see.
Shine, Hesperus, shine forth, thou wishéd
    star!

  [2] The family name of Viscount Haddington.

THE SAD SHEPHERD
OR
A TALE OF ROBIN HOOD

BY

BEN JONSON

THE PERSONS OF THE PLAY

ROBIN HOOD, *the chief woodman,*[1] *master of the feast.*
MARIAN, *his lady, the mistress.*

MELLIFLEUR, *the sweet*
AMIE, *the gentle* } *shepherdesses.*
EARINE, *the beautiful*

THEIR FAMILY [2]

FRIAR TUCK, *the chaplain and steward.*
LITTLE JOHN, *bow bearer.*[3]
SCARLET
SCATHLOCK } *two brothers, huntsmen.*
GEORGE A GREENE, *huisher*[4] *of the bower.*[5]
MUCH, *Robin Hood's bailiff or acater.*[6]

THE TROUBLES UNEXPECTED

MAUDLIN, *the envious, the Witch of Papple-wick.*
DOUCE, *the proud, her daughter.*
LOREL, *the rude, a swine'ard,*[7] *the witch's son.*
PUCK-HAIRY, *or Robin Goodfellow, their hine.*[8]

THE GUESTS INVITED

CLARION, *the rich*
LIONEL, *the courteous*
ALKEN, *the sage* } *shepherds.*
EGLAMOUR, *the sat*
KAROLIN, *the kind*

THE RECONCILER

REUBEN, *a devout hermit.*

The scene is Sherwood, consisting of a landtshape[9] *of forest, hills, valleys, cottages, a castle, a river, pastures, herds, flocks, all full of country simplicity. Robin Hood's bower; his well; the witch's dimble;*[10] *the swine'ard's oak; the hermit's cell.*

[TIME: *Late Middle Ages.*]

PROLOGUE [11]

He that hath feasted you these forty years,
And fitted fables for your finer ears,
Although at first he scarce could hit the bore,[12]

Yet you, with patience heark'ning more and more,
At length have grown up to him, and made known
The working of his pen is now your own.
He prays you would vouchsafe, for your own sake,
To hear him this once more, but sit awake.
And, though he now present you with such wool
As from mere [13] English flocks his muse can pull,   10
He hopes when it is made up into cloth,

---

[1] Huntsman.   [2] Followers.
[3] An under officer charged with the prevention of trespassing.
[4] Usher, doorkeeper.   [5] Rustic cottage.
[6] Caterer, purchaser of provisions.
[7] Swineherd.   [9] Landscape.
[8] Hind, servant.   [10] Dingle, narrow valley.
[11] In the original the prologue follows the argument of the first act.
[12] *I.e.,* suit the caliber of your intelligence.
[13] Pure.

Not the most curious head here will be
   loath
To wear a hood of it, it being a fleece
To match or [1] those of Sicily or Greece.
His scene is Sherwood, and his play a tale
Of Robin Hood's inviting from the Vale
Of Be'voir [2] all the shepherds to a feast,
Where by the casual absence of one guest
The mirth is troubled much, and in one
   man   19
As much of sadness shown as passion can—
The sad young shepherd, whom we here
   present,

The Sad Shepherd passeth silently over the
                         stage.

Like his woes' figure, dark and discontent
For his lost love, who in the Trent is said
To have miscarried. 'Las! What knows the
   head
Of a calm river whom the feet have
   drowned?
Hear what his sorrows are, and, if they
   wound
Your gentle breasts, so that the end crown
   all,
Which in the scope of one day's chance
   may fall,
Old Trent will send you more such tales
   as these,
And shall grow young again as one doth
   please.   30

Here the Prologue, thinking to end, returns
   upon a new purpose and speaks on.

But here's an heresy of late let fall,
That mirth by no means fits a pastoral.
Such say so, who can make none, he pre-
   sumes;
Else there's no scene more properly as-
   sumes
The sock. [3] For whence can sport in kind [4]
   arise
But from the rural routs and families?
Safe on this ground then, we not fear today
To tempt your laughter by our rustic play;
Wherein if we distaste, [5] or be cried down,
We think we therefore shall not leave the
   town,   40

   [1] Either.
   [2] Belvoir, the seat of the Earls of Rutland.
   [3] Shoe worn by actors of classical comedy.
   [4] In nature, naturally.   [5] Disgust, displease.

Nor that the forewits, [6] that would draw
   the rest
Unto their liking, always like the best.
The wise and knowing critic will not say,
This worst, or better is, before he weigh
Where [7] every piece be perfect in the kind, [8]
And then, though in themselves he differ-
   ence find,
Yet, if the place require it where they stood,
The equal fitting makes them equal good.
You shall have love and hate and jealousy,
As well as mirth and rage and melancholy,
Or whatsoever else may either move   51
Or stir affections, [9] and your likings prove.
But that no style for pastoral should go
Current but what is stamped with "Ah"
   and "O,"
Who judgeth so, may singularly err,
As if all poesy had one character
In which what were not written, were not
   right,
Or that the man who made such one poor
   flight
In his whole life, had with his wingéd skill
Advanced him upmost on the muses' hill, 60
When he like poet yet remains, as those
Are painters who can only make a rose.
From such your wits redeem you, or your
   chance,
Lest to a greater height you do advance
Of folly, to contemn those that are known
Artificers, and trust such as are none.

THE ARGUMENT OF THE FIRST ACT

   Robin Hood, having invited all the
shepherds and shepherdesses of the Vale
of Be'voir to a feast in the Forest of Sherwood, and, trusting to his mistress, Maid
Marian, with her woodmen, to kill him
venison against [10] the day, having left the
like charge with Friar Tuck, his chaplain
and steward, to command the rest of his
merry men to see the bower made ready
and all things in order for the enter- [10
tainment, meeting with his guests at their
entrance into the wood, welcomes and
conducts them to his bower, where, by
the way, he receives the relation of the
Sad Shepherd, Eglamour, who is fallen
into a deep melancholy for the loss of his
beloved Earine, reported to have been
drowned in passing over the Trent some

   [6] Critics.   [7] Whether.   [8] Type.
   [9] Emotions.   [10] In preparation for.

few days before. They endeavor in what
they can to comfort him, but, his dis- [20
ease having taken so strong root, all is in
vain, and they are forced to leave him.
In the meantime Marian is come from
hunting with the huntsmen, where the
lovers interchangeably express their loves.
Robin Hood inquires if she hunted the
deer at force [1] and what sport he made,
how long he stood, and what head [2] he
bore; all which is briefly answered with a
relation of breaking him up,[3] and the [30
raven and her bone, the suspect [4] had of
that raven to be Maudlin, the Witch of
Papplewick, whom one of the huntsmen
met i' the morning at the rousing of the
deer, and is confirmed by her, being then
in Robin Hood's kitchen, i' the chimney
corner broiling the same bit which was
thrown to the raven at the quarry [5] or fall
of the deer. Marian, being gone in to show
the deer to some of the shepherdesses, [40
returns instantly to the scene discontented,
sends away the venison she had killed to
her they call the Witch, quarrels with
her love, Robin Hood, abuseth him and
his guests, the shepherds, and so departs,
leaving them all in wonder and perplexity.

Act I. Scene i.

[Robin Hood's bower.] [6]

Eglamour.

EG. Here she was wont to go, and here,
   and here—
Just where those daisies, pinks, and
   violets grow!
The world may find the spring by following her,
For other print her airy steps ne'er
   left.
Her treading would not bend a blade
   of grass,
Or shake the downy blowball [7] from his
   stalk!
But like the soft west wind she shot
   along,

And, where she went, the flowers took
   thickest root,
As she had sowed hem [8] with her odorous
   foot.

Act I. Scene ii.

[To him,] Marian, Tuck, John, Woodmen,
                         etc.

MAR. Know you, or can you guess, my
   merry men,
What 'tis that keeps your master Robin
   Hood
So long both from his Marian and the
   wood?
TUCK. Forsooth, madam, he will be here
   by noon,
And prays it of your bounty, as a boon,
That you by then have killed him veni-
   son some
To feast his jolly friends, who hither
   come
In threaves [9] to frolic with him and make
   cheer.
Here's Little John hath harbored [10] you
   a deer,
I see by his tackling.[11]
JOHN.   And a hart of ten,[12]   10
I trow he be, madam, or blame your
   men,
For by his slot,[13] his entries,[14] and his
   port,[15]
His frayings,[16] fewmets [17] he doth prom-
   ise sport
And standing fore [18] the dogs; he bears
   a head
Large and well-beamed, with all rights
   summed [19] and spread.
MAR. Let's rouse him quickly, and lay
   on the hounds.
JOHN. Scathlock is ready with them on
   the grounds;
So is his brother Scarlet. Now they
   'ave found
His lair, they have him sure within the
   pound.[20]

---

[1] Ran the deer down with dogs instead of
slaying it with weapons.
[2] Horns.   [4] Suspicion.
[3] *I.e.*, cutting up the deer.   [5] Cutting up.
[6] The scene remains the same throughout the
act.
[7] Dandelion's head gone to seed.

[8] Them.   [11] Equipment.
[9] Numbers.   [12] *I.e.*, ten-pronged horns.
[10] Tracked down. [13] Track.
[14] Openings made in the thickets by the deer.
[15] Weight indicated by the depth of his foot-
prints.
[16] Velvet rubbed from his antlers.
[17] Dung of a deer.   [18] Before.
[19] With all tines completed.
[20] *I.e.*, in a hopeless position.

MAR. Away then! When my Robin bids
a feast,   20
'Twere sin in Marian to defraud a guest.
[*Exeunt Marian and John with the Woodmen.*]

ACT I. SCENE iii.

Tuck, George a Greene, Much, Eglamour.[1]

TUCK. And I, the chaplain, here am left
to be
Steward today, and charge you all in fee [2]
To don your liveries, see the bower
dressed,
And fit the fine devices for the feast.
You, George, must care to make the
baldric [3] trim,
And garland that must crown or her or
him
Whose flock this year hath brought the
earliest lamb.
GEORGE. Good Father Tuck, at your com-
mands I am
To cut the table out o' the greensward,
Or any other service for my lord,   10
To carve the guests large seats and these
laid in
With turf as soft and smooth as the
mole's skin,
And hang the bulléd [4] nosegays 'bove
their heads . . . .[5]
The piper's bank whereon to sit and
play,
And a fair dial to mete out the day.
Our master's feast shall want no just
delights;
His entertainments must have all the
rites.
MUCH. Ay, and all choice that plenty
can send in—
Bread, wine, acates,[6] fowl, feather, fish,
or fin,
For which my father's nets have swept
the Trent.   20

Eglamour falls in with them.

EG. And ha' you found her?
MUCH.   Whom?
EG.   My drownéd love,
Earine! The sweet Earine!

The bright and beautiful Earine!
Have you not heard of my Earine?
Just by your father's mills (I think I am
right—
Are not you Much the Miller's son?)—
MUCH.   I am.
EG. And baily [7] to brave Robin Hood?
MUCH.   The same.
EG. Close by your father's mills, Earine,
Earine was drowned! O my Earine!
(Old Maudlin tells me so, and Douce, her
daughter.)   30
Ha' you swept the river, say you, and
not found her?
MUCH. For fowl and fish we have.
EG.   O, not for her?
You are goodly friends, right charita-
ble men!
Nay, keep your way and leave me; make
your toys,
Your tales, your poesies, that you talked
of—all
Your entertainments. You not injure me.
Only if I may enjoy my cypress wreath,
And you will let me weep, 'tis all I ask,
Till I be turned to water as was she!
And, troth, what less suit can you grant
a man?   40
TUCK. His fantasy [8] is hurt; let us now
leave him;
The wound is yet too fresh to admit
searching.   [*Exit.*]
EG. Searching? Where should I search,
or on what track?
Can my slow drop of tears or this dark
shade
About my brows enough describe her
loss?
Earine! O, my Earine's loss!
No, no, no, no; this heart will break first.
GEORGE. How will this sad disaster strike
the ears
Of bounteous Robin Hood, our gentle
master!   [*Exit.*]
MUCH. How will it mar his mirth, abate
his feast,   50
And strike a horror into every guest!
                                        [*Exit.*]
EG. If I could knit whole clouds about
my brows,
And weep like Swithin [9] or those wat'ry
signs,

---

[1] Enters later   [3] Belt.
[2] Fealty.   [4] Swollen, budding.
[5] The rime and sense indicate that at least one
line has here dropped out.   [6] Cates, dainties.

[7] Bailiff.   [8] Imagination.
[9] Patron saint of rainy weather.

The Kids [1] that rise then, and drown all
 the flocks
Of those rich shepherds dwelling in this
 vale,
Those careless shepherds that did let
 her drown,
Then I did something; or could make old
 Trent
Drunk with my sorrow, to start out in
 breaches
To drown their herds, their cattle, and
 their corn,
Break down their mills, their dams, o'er-
 turn their weirs,   60
And see their houses and whole liveli-
 hood
Wrought into water with her, all were
 good—
I'ld kiss the torrent and those whirls of
 Trent
That sucked her in, my sweet Earine!
When they have cast their body [2] on
 the shore,
And it comes up as tainted as them-
 selves,
All pale and bloodless, I will love it still,
For all that they can do, and make hem
 mad
To see how I will hug it in mine arms,
And hang upon the looks, dwell on her
 eyes,   70
Feed round about her lips, and eat her
 kisses,
Suck of her drownéd flesh!—and where's
 their malice? [3]
Not all their envious sousing can change
 that.
But I will study some revenge past this!
I pray you, give me leave, for I will study,
Though all the bells, pipes, tabors, tim-
 burines [4] ring,
That you can plant about me; I will study.

Act I. Scene iv.

To him, Robin Hood, Clarion, Mellifleur,
 Lionel, Amie, Alken, Tuck, Servants,
 with music of all sorts.

Rob. Welcome, bright Clarion and sweet
 Mellifleur,
 The courteous Lionel, fair Amie, all

My friends and neighbors, to the jolly
 bower
Of Robin Hood and to the greenwood
 walks!
Now that the shearing of your sheep is
 done,
And the washed flocks are lighted [5] of
 their wool,
The smoother ewes are ready to receive
The mounting rams again; and both do
 feed,
As either promised, to increase your
 breed
At eaning [6] time, and bring you lusty
 twins.   10
Why should or you or we so much forget
The season in ourselves as not to make
Use of our youth and spirits to awake
The nimble hornpipe [7] and the timbu-
 rine,
And mix our songs and dances in the
 wood,
And each of us cut down a triumph
 bough?
Such were the rites the youthful June
 allow.
Cla. They were, gay Robin; but the sourer
 sort
Of shepherds [8] now disclaim in [9] all such
 sport,
And say our flocks the while are poorly
 fed,   20
When with such vanities the swains are
 led.
Tuck. Would they, wise Clarion, were
 not hurried more
With covetise [10] and rage, when to their
 store
They add the poor man's eanling,[11] and
 dare sell
Both fleece and carcass, not gi'ing him
 the fell,
When to one goat they reach that prickly
 weed,
Which maketh all the rest forbear to
 feed,
Or strew tods' [12] hairs, or with their tails
 do sweep
The dewy grass, to doff the simpler
 sheep,

---

[1] A group of stars supposed to influence hur-
ricanes.
[2] *I.e.*, the body held by the waters.
[3] Power to harm.   [4] Tambourines.

[5] Lightened.   [7] A musical instrument.
[6] Yeaning, lambing.
[8] Satirical allusion to the Puritans.
[9] Declaim against.   [11] Yeanling, lamb.
[10] Covetousness.   [12] Foxes'.

Or dig deep pits their neighbor's neat [1]
   to vex,   30
To drown the calves and crack the heif-
   ers' necks,
Or with pretense of chasing thence the
   brock [2]
Send in a cur to worry the whole flock!
Lio. O friar, those are faults that are not
   seen;
Ours open and of worst example been. [3]
They call ours pagan pastimes, that in-
   fect
Our blood with ease, our youth with all
   neglect,
Our tongues with wantonness, our
   thoughts with lust;
And what they censure [4] ill, all others
   must.
Rob. I do not know what their sharp sight
   may see   40
Of late, but I should think it still might
   be,
As 'twas, a happy age, when on the
   plains
The woodmen met the damsels, and the
   swains,
The neat'ards, [5] plowmen, and the pipers
   loud,
And each did dance, some to the kit or
   crowd, [6]
Some to the bagpipe; some the tabret [7]
   moved,
And all did either love or were beloved.
Lio. The dextrous shepherd then would
   try his sling,
Then dart his hook at daisies, then
   would sing,
Sometimes would wrastle.
Cla.   Ay, and with a lass,   50
And give her a new garment on the
   grass [8]
After a course [9] at barleybreak or base. [10]
Lio. And all these deeds were seen with-
   out offense,
Or the least hazard o' their innocence.
Rob. Those charitable times had no mis-
   trust;
Shepherds knew how to love and not
   to lust.

Cla. Each minute that we lose thus, I
   confess,
Deserves a censure on us, more or less,
But that a sadder chance hath given
   allay [11]
Both to the mirth and music of this
   day.   60
Our fairest shepherdess we had of late,
Here upon Trent, is drowned, for whom
   her mate,
Young Eglamour, a swain, who best
   could tread
Our country dances, and our games did
   lead,
Lives like the melancholy turtle, [12]
   drowned
Deeper in woe than she in water, crowned
With yew and cypress, and will scarce
   admit
The physic of our presence to his fit.
Lio. Sometimes he sits, and thinks all
   day, then walks,
Then thinks again, and sighs, weeps,
   laughs, and talks,   70
And twixt his pleasing frenzy [13] and sad
   grief
Is so distracted as [14] no sought relief
By all our studies can procure his peace.
Cla. The passion finds in him that [15] large
   increase
As we doubt hourly we shall lose him too.
Rob. You should not cross him then,
   whate'er you do,
For fant'sy stopped will soon take fire
   and burn
Into an anger, or to a frenzy turn.
Cla. Nay, so we are advised by Alken
   here,
A good sage shepherd, who, although he
   wear   80
An old worn hat and cloak, can tell us
   more
Than all the forward fry that boast their
   lore.
Lio. See, yonder comes the brother of
   the maid,
Young Karolin! How curious and
   afraid
He is at once, willing to find him out,
And loath to offend him.
Alk.   Sure he's here about.

---

[1] Cattle.
[2] Badger.
[3] Are.
[4] Judge.
[5] Neatherds.
[6] Two varieties of fiddle.
[7] Taboret, a small drum.
[8] Stain her dress green.
[9] Round.
[10] Varieties of boys' games.

[11] Abatement, check.
[12] Turtledove.
[13] Happy delirium.
[14] That.
[15] Such.

ACT I. SCENE v.

Robin Hood, Clarion, Mellifleur, Lionel,
Amie, Alken, Karolin; Eglamour, sit-
ting upon a bank by.

CLA. See where he sits.

EG.   It will be rare, rare, rare!
An exquisite revenge! But peace, no
    words—
Not for the fairest fleece of all the flock!
If it be known afore, 'tis all worth noth-
    ing.
I'll carve it on the trees and in the turf,
On every greensworth [1] and in every path,
Just to the margin of the cruel Trent.
There will I knock the story in the
    ground,
In smooth great pebble and moss fill it
    round,
Till the whole country read how she
    was drowned,   10
And with the plenty of salt tears there
    shed
Quite alter the complexion of the spring.
Or I will get some old, old grandam
    thither,
Whose rigid foot, but dipped into the
    water,
Shall strike that sharp and sudden cold
    throughout
As it shall lose all virtue; and those
    nymphs,
Those treacherous nymphs, pulled in
    Earine,
Shall stand curled up like images of ice,
And never thaw. Mark, never! A sharp
    justice!
Or, stay, a better! When the year's at
    hottest,   20
And that the Dog Star foams, and the
    streams boils
And curls and works and swells ready
    to sparkle,
To fling a fellow with a fever in,
To set it all on fire till it burn
Blue as Scamander fore the walls of Troy
When Vulcan leaped into him to con-
    sume him!

ROB. A deep-hurt fant'sy!

                        [*They approach him.*]

EG.   Do you not approve it?

ROB. Yes, gentle Eglamour, we all ap-
    prove,

And come to gratulate your just revenge,
Which, since it is so perfect, we now
    hope   30
You'll leave all care thereof and mix
    with us
In all the proffered solace of the spring.

EG. A spring, now she is dead! Of what?
    Of thorns?
Briars and brambles? Thistles? Burs
    and docks?
Cold hemlock? Yew? The mandrake
    or the box?
These may grow still; but what can
    spring beside?
Did not the whole earth sicken when she
    died?
As if there since did fall one drop of dew
But what was wept for her, or any stalk
Did bear a flower, or any branch a
    bloom,   40
After her wreath was made! In faith, in
    faith,
You do not fair to put these things upon
    me,
Which can in no sort be. Earine,
Who had her very being and her name
With the first knots [2] or buddings of
    the spring,
Born with the primrose and the violet,
Or earliest roses blown, when Cupid
    smiled,
And Venus led the Graces out to dance,
And all the flowers and sweets in na-
    ture's lap
Leaped out, and made their solemn con-
    juration   50
To last but while she lived! Do not I
    know
How the vale withered the same day,
    how Dove,
Dean, Eye, and Erwash, Idel, Snite,
    and Soare
Each broke his urn, [3] and twenty waters
    more
That swelled proud Trent shrunk them-
    selves dry? That, since,
No sun or moon or other cheerful star
Looked out of heaven, but all the cope [4]
    was dark,
As it were hung so for her exequies!
And not a voice or sound to ring her
    knell

[1] Greensward.

[2] Swellings.

[3] Flow(?).   [4] Vault of the sky.

But of that dismal pair, the scritching
owl [1]   60
And buzzing hornet! Hark, hark, hark,
the foul
Bird! How she flutters with her wicker [2]
wings!
Peace! You shall hear her scritch.
CLA.   Good Karolin, sing.
Help to divert this fant'sy.
KAR.   All I can.

The Song, which while Karolin sings, Egla-
mour reads.

Though I am young and cannot tell
Either what Death or Love is well,
Yet I have heard they both bear darts,
And both do aim at human hearts.
And then again I have been told,
Love wounds with heat,[3] as Death with
cold,   70
So that I fear they do but bring
Extremes to touch, and mean one thing.

As in a ruin we it call
One thing to be blown up or fall,
Or to our end like way may have
By a flash of lightning or a wave,
So Love's inflaméd shaft or brand
May kill as soon as Death's cold hand,
Except Love's fires the virtue have
To fright the frost out of the grave.   80

EG. Do you think so? Are you in that
good heresy,
I mean opinion? If you be, say nothing.
I'll study it as a new philosophy,
But by myself alone. Now you shall
leave me.
Some of these nymphs here will reward
you—this,
This pretty maid, although but with a
kiss. *He forces Amie to kiss him.*[4]
Lived my Earine, you should have
twenty;
For every line here, one I would allow
hem
From mine own store, the treasure I
had in her.
Now I am as poor as you.
KAR.   And I a wretch!   90
CLA. Yet keep an eye upon him, Karolin.
Eglamour goes out and Karolin follows him.

MEL. Alas, that ever such a generous spirit
As Eglamour's should sink by such a loss!
CLA. The truest lovers are least fortunate:
Look 't [5] all their lives and legends, what
they call
The lovers' scriptures, Heliodore's or
Tatii,
Longi, Eustathii, Prodomi,[6] you'll find it!
What think you, father?
ALK.   I have known some few,
And read of more, wh' have had their
dose, and deep,
Of these sharp bittersweets.
LIO.   But what is this   100
To jolly Robin, who the story [7] is
Of all beatitude in love?
CLA.   And told
Here every day with wonder on the
wold.[8]
LIO. And with Fame's voice.
ALK.   Save that some folk delight
To blend all good of others with some
spite.
CLA. He and his Marian are the sum and
talk
Of all that breathe here in the green-
wood walk.
MEL. Or Be'voir Vale.
LIO.   The turtles of the wood.
CLA. The billing pair.
ALK.   And so are understood
For simple loves, and sampled [9] lives
beside.   110
MEL. Faith, so much virtue should not
be envied.
ALK. Better be so than pitied, Mellifleur,
For gainst all envy virtue is a cure,
But wretched pity ever calls on scorns.—
                            [*Horns within.*]
The deer's brought home; I hear it by
their horns.

ACT I. SCENE vi.

To Robin, etc., Marian, John, Scarlet,
                          Scathlock.[10]

ROB. My Marian, and my mistress!
MAR.   My loved Robin!
MEL. The moon's at full; the happy pair
are met.

---

[1] Screech owl.   [4] *I.e.*, Karolin, the singer.
[2] Pliant(?), ominous(?).
[3] Original reads *heart.*

[5] Original reads *looks.*
[6] Authors of late Greek romances, the last four
names being Latin genitives.
[7] Example.   [9] Exemplary.
[8] Original reads *world.*   [10] Enters later.

MAR. How hath this morning paid me for
my rising—
First, with my sports, but most with
meeting you.
I did not half so well reward my hounds
As she hath me today, although I gave
them
All the sweet morsels called tongue, ears,
and dowcets! [1]

ROB. What, and the inchpin? [2]

MAR.   Yes.

ROB.   Your sports then pleased you?

MAR. You are a wanton.

ROB.   *One*, I do confess,
I *want*ed till you came; but now I have
you   10
I'll grow to your embraces, till two souls,
Distilléd into kisses through our lips,
Do make one spirit of love. [*Kisses her.*]

MAR.   O Robin, Robin!

ROB. Breathe, breathe awhile. What says
my gentle Marian?

MAR. Could you so long be absent?

ROB.   What, a week?
Was that so long?

MAR.   How long are lovers' weeks,
Do you think, Robin, when they are
asunder?
Are they not pris'ners' years?

ROB.   To some they seem so,
But, being met again, they are schoolboys' hours—

MAR. That have got leave to play, and
so we use them.   20

ROB. Had you good sport i' your chase
today?

JOHN.   O, prime!

MAR. A lusty stag.

ROB.   And hunted ye at force?

MAR. In a full cry.

JOHN.   And never hunted change! [3]

ROB. You had stanch hounds then?

MAR.   Old and sure; I love
No young rash dogs, no more than changing friends.

ROB. What relays set you?

JOHN.   None at all; we laid not
In one fresh dog.

ROB.   He stood not long then?

SCAR.   Yes,
Five hours and more. A great, large deer!

ROB.   What head?

JOHN. Forkéd! A hart of ten.

MAR.   He is good venison,
According to the season i' the blood,   30
I'll promise all your friends for whom he
fell.

JOHN. But at his fall there happed a
chance.

MAR.   Worth mark.

ROB. Ay, what was that, sweet Marian?
                 He kisses her.

MAR.   You'll not hear?

ROB. I love these interruptions in a story;
                He kisses her again.
They make it sweeter.

MAR.   You do know as soon
As the assay [4] is taken.
                He kisses her again.

ROB.   On, my Marian.
I did but take the assay.

MAR.   You stop one's mouth,
And yet you bid hem speak!—When the
arbor's [5] made—

ROB. Pulled down, and paunch turned
out—

MAR.   He that undoes him [6]
Doth cleave the brisket bone, upon the
spoon   40
Of which a little gristle grows; you call
it—

ROB. The raven's bone. [7]

MAR.   Now o'erhead sat a raven
On a sere bough—a grown, great bird,
and hoarse,
Who, all the while the deer was breaking
up,
So croaked and cried for 't as all the
huntsmen,
Especially old Scathlock, thought it omi-
nous,
Swore it was mother Maudlin, whom he
met
At the day-dawn just as he roused the deer
Out of his lair; but we made shift to run
him
Off his four legs, and sunk him ere we
left.   50

[*Enter Scathlock.*]

Is the deer come?

SCATH.   He lies within o' the dresser. [8]

MAR. Will you go see him, Mellifleur?

---

[1] Doucets.
[2] Sweetbread.   [3] Followed a cross scent.
[4] Test of quality.   [6] Cuts him up.
[5] Disemboweling is.
[7] Because it was given to the ravens.
[8] Block on which meat is dressed.

Mel.　　　　　　　I attend you.
Mar. Come, Amie, you'll go with us?
Amie.　　　　　　I am not well.
Lio. She's sick o' the young shepherd that
　bekissed her.
Mar. Friend, cheer your friends up; we
　will eat him merrily.
　　[*Exeunt Marian, Mellifleur, and Amie.*]
Alk. Saw you the raven, friend?
Scath.　　　　Ay, quha suld let me? [1]
　I suld be afraid o' you, sir, suld I?
Clar.　　　　　　　　Huntsman,
　A dram more of civility would not hurt
　you.
Rob. Nay, you must give [2] them all their
　rudenesses;
　They are not else themselves without
　their language.　　　　　　　　60
Alk. And what do you think of her?
Scath.　　　　　　　As of a witch.
　They call her a wise woman, but I think
　her
　An arrant witch.
Clar.　　　And wherefore think you so?
Scath. Because I saw her since, broiling
　the bone
　Was cast her at the quarry.
Alk.　　　　　　Where saw you her?
Scath. I' the chimley nuik,[3] within; she's
　there now.
Rob.　　　　　Marian!

Act I. Scene vii.

To them, Marian.

[Rob.] Your hunt holds in [4] his tale still,
　and tells more.
Mar. My hunt? What tale?
Rob.　　　　　　How! Cloudy, Marian!
　What look is this?
Mar.　　　　　A fit one, sir, for you.
　Hand off, rude ranger!—(*To Scathlock.*)
　Sirrah, get you in,
　And bear the venison hence. It is too
　good
　For these coarse, rustic mouths that
　cannot open,
　Or spend a thank for 't. A starved mut-
　ton's carcass
　Would better fit their palates. See it
　carried

To mother Maudlin's, whom you call
　the witch, sir.
Tell her I sent it to make merry with.　10
She'll turn [5] us thanks at least! Why
　stand'st thou, groom?
Rob. I wonder he can move, that he's not
　fixed,
　If that his feeling be the same with
　mine!
　I dare not trust the faith of mine own
　senses;
　I fear [6] mine eyes and ears. This is not
　Marian!
　Nor am I Robin Hood! I pray you ask
　her,
　Ask her, good shepherds, ask her all for
　me—
　Or rather ask yourselves—if she be she,
　Or I be I.
Mar.　　　　Yes, and you are the spy,
　And the spied spy that watch upon my
　walks　　　　　　　　　20
　To inform what deer I kill or give away!
　Where! When! To whom! But spy your
　worst, good spy.
　I will dispose of this where least you like!
　Fall to your cheesecakes, curds, and
　clawted [7] cream,
　Your fools,[8] your flauns,[9] and of ale a
　stream
　To wash it from your livers. Strain ewes'
　milk
　Into your cider sillabubs, and be drunk
　To [10] him whose fleece hath brought the
　earliest lamb
　This year, and wears the baudric [11] at your
　board,
　Where you may all go whistle, and
　record　　　　　　　　30
　This i' your dance, and foot it lustily.
　　　　　　　　　　She leaves them.
Rob. I pray you, friends, do you hear and
　see as I do?
　Did the same accents strike your ears,
　and objects
　Your eyes, as mine?
Alk.　　　　We taste the same reproaches.
Lio. Have seen the changes.
Rob.　　　　Are we not all changed,
　Transforméd from ourselves?

---

[1] Who should stop me?　　[3] Chimney nook.
[2] Grant, allow.　　　　　[4] Huntsman holds to.

[5] Return.　　　　　　[9] Pancakes.
[6] Doubt.　　　　　　[10] In honor of.
[7] Clouted, clotted.　　[11] Baldric.
[8] Custards.

LIO.   I do not know.
  The best is silence.
ALK.   And to await the issue.
ROB. The dead or lazy wait for 't! I will
  find it.   [*Exeunt.*]

THE ARGUMENT OF THE SECOND ACT

The Witch Maudlin, having taken the
shape of Marian to abuse Robin Hood and
perplex his guests, cometh forth with her
daughter, Douce, reporting in what confusion she hath left them, defrauded them
of their venison, made them suspicious each
of the other, but most of all Robin Hood so
jealous of his Marian as she hopes no effect
of love would ever reconcile them, glorying
so far in the extent of her mischief as   [10
she confesseth to have surprised Earine,
stripped her of her garments to make her
daughter appear fine at this feast in them,
and to have shut the maiden up in a tree
as her son's prize, if he could win her, or his
prey, if he would force her. Her son, a rude,
bragging swine'ard, comes to the tree to
woo her (his mother and sister stepping
aside to overhear him) and first boasts his
wealth to her and his possessions—   [20
which move not. Then he presents her
gifts such as himself is taken with, but she
utterly shows a scorn and loathing both of
him and them. His mother is angry, rates
him, instructs him what to do the next time,
and persuades her daughter to show herself
about the bower, tells how she shall know
her mother, when she is transformed, by
her broidered belt. Meanwhile the young
shepherdess Amie, being kissed by   [30
Karolin, Earine's brother, before, falls in
love, but knows not what love is, but de-
scribes her disease so innocently that
Marian pities her. When Robin Hood and
the rest of his guests, invited, enter to
Marian, upbraiding her with sending away
their venison to mother Maudlin by Scathlock, which she denies, Scathlock affirms
it, but, seeing his mistress weep and to
forswear it, begins to doubt his own   [40
understanding rather than affront her
farder,[1] which makes Robin Hood and
the rest to examine themselves better. But
Maudlin, entering like herself, the witch,
comes to thank her for her bounty, at

[1] Farther.

which Marian is more angry, and more
denies the deed. Scathlock enters, tells he
has brought it again, and delivered it to the
cook. The witch is inwardly vexed the
venison is so recovered from her by   [50
the rude huntsman, and murmurs and
curses, bewitches the cook, mocks poor
Amie and the rest, discovereth her ill nature, and is a mean of reconciling them all.
For the Sage Shepherd suspecteth her mischief, if she be not prevented,[2] and so
persuadeth to seize on her. Whereupon
Robin Hood despatcheth out his woodmen
to hunt and take her, which ends the act.

ACT II. SCENE i.

[*The witch's dimble, with the swineherd's
oak at one side.*]

Maudlin, Douce [*dressed in Earine's clothes*].

MAUD. Have I not left 'em in a brave
  confusion,
  Amazed their expectation, got their veni-
    son,
  Troubled their mirth and meeting, made
    them doubtful
  And jealous of each other, all distracted,
  And, i' the close, uncertain of themselves?
  This can your mother do, my dainty
    Douce:
  Take any shape upon her, and delude
  The senses best acquainted with their
    owners!
  The jolly Robin, who hath bid this feast,
  And made this solemn invitation,   10
  I ha' possesséd so with syke[3] dislikes
  Of his own Marian that, albee[4] he know
    her
  As doth the vauting[5] hart his venting[6]
    hind,
  He ne'er fra hence sall nase[7] her i' the
    wind,
  To his first liking.
DOUCE.   Did you so distaste him?
MAUD. As far as her proud scorning him
  could bate,
  Or blunt the edge of any lover's temper.
DOUCE. But were ye like her, mother?
MAUD.   So like, Douce,
  As, had she seen me her sel', her sel' had
    doubted   19

[2] Anticipated.   [5] Vaulting.
[3] Sic, such.   [6] Scenting, smelling.
[4] Albeit, although.
[7] From hence shall nose (smell).

Whether had been the liker of the twa!
This can your mother do, I tell you,
    daughter!
I ha' but dight [1] ye yet i' the outdress [2]
And parel [3] of Earine; but this raiment,
These very weeds, sall make ye as, but
    coming
In view or ken of Eglamour, your form
Shall show too slippery [4] to be looked
    upon,
And all the forests swear you to be she!
They shall rin [5] after ye, and wage the
    odds,
Upo' their own deceivéd sights, ye are
    her,
Whilst she, poor lass, is stocked up [6] in a
    tree—   30
Your brother Lorel's prize! For so my
    largess
Hath lotted her to be your brother's mis-
    tress,
Gif [7] she can be reclaimed [8]—gif not, his
    prey!
And here he comes new claithéd, [9] like a
    prince
Of swine'ards. Syke he seems, dight i'
    the spoils
Of those he feeds—a mighty lord of
    swine!
He is comand [10] now to woo. Let's step
    aside,
And hear his lovecraft. See, he opes the
    door,
And takes her by the hand, and helps her
    forth.
This is true courtship, and becomes his
    ray. [11]   40

Act II. Scene ii.

[*The same.*]

Lorel, Earine, Maudlin, Douce.

Lor. Ye kind to others, but ye coy to me,
Deft mistress, whiter than the cheese new
    pressed,
Smoother than cream, and softer than
    the curds,

[1] Dressed.
[2] Outer dress.
[3] Apparel.
[4] Uncertain.
[5] Run.
[6] Imprisoned.
[7] If.
[8] Tamed, as a hawk.
[9] Clothed.
[10] Coming. In many later words in this play
the northern ending *-and* is used for participles
in *-ing.*   [11] Array, dress.

Why start ye from me ere ye hear me tell
My wooing errand and what rents I
    have?
Large herds and pastures! Swine and
    ky [12] mine own!
And though my nase be camused, [13] my
    lips thick,
And my chin bristled, Pan, great Pan,
    was such,
Who was the chief of herdsmen, and our
    sire!   9
I am na [14] fay, na incubus, na changelin',
But a good man that lives o' my awn
    gear. [15]
This house, these grounds, this stock is
    all mine awn.
Ear. How better 'twere to me, this were
    not known!
Maud. [*Aside.*] She likes it not; but it is
    boasted well.
Lor. An hundred udders for the pail I
    have,
That gi' me milk and curds, that make
    me cheese
To cloy the markets! Twenty swarm of
    bees,
Whilk [16] all the summer hum about the
    hive,
And bring me wax and honey in bilive. [17]
An aged oak, the king of all the field,   20
With a broad beech there grows afore my
    dur, [18]
That mickle mast [19] unto the farm doth
    yield.
A chestnut, whilk hath larded mony [20] a
    swine,
Whose skins I wear to fend [21] me fra the
    cold;
A poplar green, and with a carvéd seat,
Under whose shade I solace in the heat,
And thence can see gang [22] out and in my
    neat.
Twa trilland [23] brooks each from his
    spring doth meet
And make a river to refresh my feet,
In which each morning, ere the sun doth
    rise,   30
I look myself, and clear my pleasant eyes,
Before I pipe, for therein I have skill

[12] Kine.
[13] Flat.
[14] No.
[15] Own property.
[16] Which.
[17] Belive, quickly.
[18] Before my door.
[19] Much food (nuts).
[20] Fattened many.
[21] Defend, protect.
[22] Go.
[23] Trickling.

'Bove other swine'ards. Bid me, and I
will
Straight play to you, and make you
melody.
EAR. By no means. Ah, to me all min-
strelsy
Is irksome, as are you.
LOR.   Why scorn you me?
Because I am a herdsman, and feed
swine!   *He draws out other presents.*
I am a lord of other gear. This fine,
Smooth bauson's [1] cub, the young grice
of a gray,[2]   39
Twa tiny urshins,[3] and this ferret gay.
EAR. Out on hem! What are these?
LOR.   I give hem ye
As presents, Mrs.[4]—
EAR.   O, the fiend and thee!
Gar [5] take them hence; they fewmand [6]
all the claithes,
And prick my coats.[7] Hence with hem,
limmer lown,[8]
Thy vermin and thyself; thyself art one!
Ay, lock me up—all's well when thou art
gone.
        [*Lorel shuts her in the tree again.*]

ACT II. SCENE iii.

[*The same.*]

Lorel, Maudlin, Douce.

LOR. Did you hear this? She wished me at
the fiend
With all my presents!
MAUD.   A too lucky end
She wishend [9] thee, foul limmer, dritty [10]
lown!
Gude [11] faith, it dules [12] me that I am thy
mother.
And see, thy sister scorns thee for her
brother.
Thou woo thy love, thy mistress, with
twa hedgehogs,
A stinkand brock, a polecat? Out, thou
howlet! [13]
Thou shouldst ha' given her a madge-
owl,[14] and then

Tho' hadst made a present o' thyself,
owlspiegle! [15]
DOUCE. Why, mother, I have heard ye bid
to give,   10
And often as the cause calls.
MAUD.   I know well,
It is a witty [16] part sometimes to give;
But what? To wham? [17] No monsters,
nor to maidens.
He suld present them with mare [18]
pleasand things,
Things natural, and what all women
covet
To see: the common parent of us all,
Which maids will twire [19] at tween their
fingers thus;
With which [20] his sire gat him, he s' [21]
get another,
And so beget posterity upon her.
This he should do! False gelden,[22] gang
thy gait,   20
And do thy turns betimes; or I s' gar
take
Thy new breikes [23] fra thee, and thy
duiblet [24] too.
The talleur [25] and the souter [26] sall
undo
All they ha' made, except thou manlier
woo!   *Lorel goes out.*
DOUCE. Gud mother, gif you chide him,
he'll do wairs.[27]
MAUD. Hang him! I geif [28] him to the
devil's erse.[29]
But ye, my Douce, I charge ye, show
yoursel'
To all the shepherds baudly.[30] Gang
amang hem,
Be mickel i' their eye, frequent and
fugeand,[31]
And, gif they ask ye of Earine,   30
Or of these claithes, say that I ga' hem
ye,
And say no more. I ha' that wark [32] in
hand,

[15] Mirror of an owl, a term of contempt derived
from *Eulenspiegel*, the hero of certain medieval
German jest books.   [18] More.
[16] Clever.   [19] Peer.
[17] Whom.   [20] That which.
[21] Shall. Put later in the original the first person
of this form reads *'is.*   [27] Worse.
[22] Gelding.   [28] Give.
[23] Breeks, breeches.   [29] Arse.
[24] Doublet.   [30] Joyously.
[25] Tailor.   [31] Figent, lively.
[26] Cobbler.   [32] Work.

[1] Badger's.   [4] *I.e.*, mistress.
[2] Cub of a badger.   [5] Cause to.
[3] Hedgehogs.
[6] Soil—a form perhaps invented by Jonson.
[7] Make holes in my petticoats. [11] Good.
[8] Rascally loon.   [12] Grieves.
[9] Wished.   [13] Owl.
[10] Dirty.   [14] Barn owl.

That web upo' the luime,[1] shall gar hem think

By then, they feelin' their own frights and fears,

I s' pu'[2] the world or nature 'bout their ears.

But hear ye, Douce, bycause[3] ye may meet me

In mony shapes today, where'er you spy

This brodered[4] belt with characters, 'tis I.

A Gypsan[5] lady, and a right beldame,

Wrought it by moonshine for me, and starlight,   40

Upo' your grannam's[6] grave, that very night

We earthed her in the shades, when our dame Hecate

Made it her gang-night[7] over the kirk-yard,

With all the barkand parish-tikes set at her,

While I sat whirland of my brazen spindle.

At every twisted thrid[8] my rock[9] let fly

Unto the sewster,[10] who did sit me nigh,

Under the town turnpike, which ran each spell

She stitchéd in the work, and knit it well.

See ye take tent[11] to this, and ken your mother.   [*Exeunt.*] 50

Act II. Scene iv.

[*Before Robin Hood's bower.*]

Marian, Mellifleur, Amie.

MAR. How do you, sweet Amie? Yet?

MEL.   She cannot tell;

If she could sleep, she says, she should do well.

She feels a hurt, but where, she cannot show

Any least sign that she is hurt or no.

Her pain's not doubtful to her, but the seat

Of her pain is. Her thoughts, too, work and beat,

Oppressed with cares, but why she cannot say.

All matter of her care is quite away.

MAR. Hath any vermin[12] broke into your fold?

Or any rot seized on your flock, or cold?   10

Or hath your feighting[13] ram burst his hard horn,

Or any ewe her fleece or bag hath torn,

My gentle Amie?

AMIE.   Marian, none of these.

MAR. Ha' you been stung by wasps or angry bees,

Or rased[14] with some rude bramble or rough brier?

AMIE. No, Marian, my disease is some-what nigher.

I weep, and boil away myself in tears;

And then my panting heart would dry those fears.

I burn, though all the forest lend a shade,

And freeze, though the whole wood one fire were made.

MAR.   Alas!   20

AMIE. I often have been torn with thorn and brier,

Both in the leg and foot, and somewhat higher,

Yet gave not then such fearful shrieks as these. Ah!

I often have been stung too with curst[15] bees,

Yet not remember that I then did quit

Either my company or mirth for it. Ah!

And therefore what it is that I feel now,

And know no cause of it, nor where, nor how

It entered in me, nor least print can see,

I feel, afflicts me more than brier or bee. O!   30

How often when the sun, heaven's brightest birth,

Hath with his burning fervor cleft the earth,

Under a spreading elm or oak hard by

A cool, clear fountain could I sleeping lie,

Safe from the heat! But now no shady tree

Nor purling brook can my refreshing be.

---

[1] Loom.
[2] Pull.
[3] Because.
[4] Embroidered.
[5] Egyptian, gipsy.
[6] Grandam's, grandmother's.
[7] Night when spirits walk.
[8] Thread.
[9] Spindle.
[10] Sempstress.
[11] Attention.
[12] Obnoxious animal.
[13] Fighting.
[14] Scratched
[15] Angry.

Oft when the meadows were grown rough
  with frost,
The rivers ice-bound, and their currents
  lost,
My thick, warm fleece I wore was my
  defense;
Or large, good fires I made drave [1]
  winter thence.   40
But now my whole flock's fells, nor this
  thick grove,
Enflamed to ashes, can my cold remove.
It is a cold and heat that doth outgo
All sense of winter's and of summer's
  so.

Act II. Scene v.

[*The same.*]

[*To them,*] *Robin Hood, Clarion, Lionel,*
             Alken.

Rob. O, are you here, my mistress?
Mar.   Ay, my love!
She, seeing him, runs to embrace him. He
           puts her back.
  Where should I be but in my Robin's
    arms,
  The sphere which I delight in so to
    move?
Rob. What, "the rude ranger" and "spied
  spy"? Hand off!
You are "for no such rustics."
Mar.   What means this?
Thrice worthy Clarion, or wise Alken,
  know ye?
Rob. 'Las, no, not they! "A poor, starved
  mutton's carcass
Would better fit their palates than your
  venison."
Mar. What riddle is this? Unfold your-
  self, dear Robin.
Rob. You ha' not sent your venison hence
  by Scathlock   10
To mother Maudlin?
Mar.   I to mother Maudlin!
Will Scathlock say so?
Rob.   Nay, we will all swear so.
For all did hear it when you gave the
  charge so,
Both Clarion, Alken, Lionel, myself.
Mar. Good honest shepherds, masters of
  your flocks,
Simple and virtuous men, no others'
  hirelings,

[1] Drove.

Be not you made to speak against your
  conscience
That which may soil the truth. I send
  the venison
Away? By Scathlock, and to mother
  Maudlin?
I came to show it here to Mellifleur,   20
I do confess; but Amie's falling ill
Did put us off it. Since, we employed
  ourselves
In comforting of her.

Scathlock enters.

             O, here he is!—
Did I, sir, bid you bear away the venison
To mother Maudlin?
Scath.   Ay, gude faith, madam,
Did you, and I ha' done it.
Mar.   What ha' you done?
Scath. Obeyed your hests,[2] madam, done
  your commands.
Mar. Done my commands, dull groom?
  Fetch it again,
Or kennel with the hounds.—Are these
  the arts,
Robin, you rede [3] your rude ones o'
  the wood   30
To countenance your quarrels and mis-
  takings?
Or are the sports to entertain your
  friends
Those forméd jealousies? [4]   Ask of
  Mellifleur
If I were ever from her here, or Amie,
Since I came in with them, or saw this
  Scathlock
Since I related to you his tale o' the
  raven.
Scath. Ay, say you so? *Scathlock goes out.*
Mel.   She never left my side
Since I came in here, nor I hers.
Cla.   This 's strange!
Our best of senses were deceived, our
  eyes, then!
Lio. And ears too.
Mar. What you have concluded on,   40
Make good, I pray you.
Amie.   O my heart, my heart!
Mar. My heart it is, is wounded, pretty
  Amie.
Report not you your griefs; I'll tell
  for all.

[2] Behests.   [4] *I.e.*, suspicions of those kinds.
[3] Counsel.

MEL. Somebody is to blame there is a fault.
MAR. Try if you can take rest. A little slumber
Will much refresh you, Amie.

                        [Amie sleeps.]
ALK.   What's her grief?
MAR. She does not know, and therein she is happy.

ACT II. SCENE vi.

[The same.]

To them, John, Maudlin, and Scathlock
after.

JOHN. Here's mother Maudlin come to give you thanks,
Madam, for some late gift she hath received—
Which she's not worthy of, she says, but crakes [1]
And wonders of it, hops about the house,
Transported with the joy.
MAUD.   Send me a stag,
                  (She danceth.)
A whole stag, madam, and so fat a deer!
So fairly hunted, and at such a time too,
When all your friends were here!
ROB.   Do you mark this, Clarion?
Her own acknowledgment?
MAUD.   'Twas such a bounty
And honor done to your poor beadswoman,   10
I know not how to owe [2] it but to thank you;
And that I come to do. I shall go round
And giddy with the toy [3] of the good turn.

	Look out, look out,
	Gay folk about,
She	And see me spin
turns	The ring I am in
round	Of mirth and glee,
	With thanks for fee
	The heart puts on, 20
	For th' venison
	My lady sent,
	Which shall be spent
	In draughts of wine,
	To fume up fine
	Into the brain,
till	And down again
she	Fall in a swoun,[4]
falls.	Upo' the groun'. 29

[1] Cracks, chatters.   [3] Surprising thought.
[2] Own, acknowledge.   [4] Swoon.

ROB. Look to her; she is mad.
MAUD. [*Rising.*]   My son hath sent you
A pot of strawberries gathered i' the wood
(His hogs would else have rooted up or trod);
With a choice dish of wildings [5] here to scald
And mingle with your cream.
MAR.   Thank you, good Maudlin,
And thank your son. Go, bear hem in to Much,
Th' acater; let him thank her. Surely, mother,
Your were mistaken, or my woodmen more,
Or most myself, to send you all our store
Of venison, hunted for ourselves this day.
You will not take it, mother, I dare say,   40
If we'ld entreat you, when you know our guests;
Red deer is head still of the forest feasts.
MAUD. But I knaw [6] ye, a right freehearted lady,
Can spare it out of superfluity.
I have departit [7] it 'mong my poor neighbors,
To speak your largess.
MAR.   I not gave it, mother;
You have done wrong then. I know how to place
My gifts, and where; and when to find my seasons
To give, not throw away my courtesies.
MAUD. Count you this thrown away?
MAR.   What's ravished from me 50
I count it worse, as stolen; I lose my thanks.
But leave this quest. They fit not you nor me,
Maudlin, contentions of this quality.—

Scathlock enters.

                     How now?
SCATH. Your stag's returned upon my shoulders;
He has found his way into the kitchen again
With his two legs, if now your cook can dress him.

[5] Crab apples.   [6] Know.   [7] Divided.

'Slid,[1] I thought the swine'ard would ha'
    beat me,
He looks so big,[2] the sturdy karl,[3]
    lewd [4] Lorel!
MAR. There, Scathlock, for thy pains;
    thou hast deserved it.
              Marian gives him gold.
MAUD. Do you give a thing, and take a
    thing, madam?   60
MAR. No, Maudlin, "you had imparted
    to your neighbors;"
As much good do 't them! I ha' done
    no wrong.

THE FIRST CHARM

MAUD.
    The spit stand still, no broaches turn
    Before the fire, but let it burn
    Both sides and haunches till the whole
    Converted be into one coal!

CLA. What devil's paternoster mumbles
    she?
ALK. Stay, you will hear more of her
    witchery.

MAUD.
    The swilland [5] dropsy enter in
    The lazy cuke [6] and swell his skin;   70
    And the old mortmal [7] on his shin
    Now prick and itch withouten blin.[8]

CLA. Speak out, hag, we may hear your
    devil's matins.

MAUD.
    The pain we call S[t]. Anton's fire,
    The gout, or what we can desire,
    To cramp a cuke in every limb,
    Before they dine yet, seize on him.

ALK. A foul, ill spirit hath posséssed
    her.
AMIE. [*From her sleep.*] O Karol, Karol,
    call him back again!
LIO. Her thoughts do work upon her in
    her slumber,   80
And may express some part of her
    disease.
ROB. Observe and mark, but trouble not
    her ease.

[1] By God's lid, a mild oath.
[2] Menacing.   [6] Cuckold(?).
[3] Churl, fellow.   [7] Mormal, ulcer.
[4] Rude.   [8] Without stopping.
[5] Swelling.

AMIE. O, O!
MAR.   How is 't, Amie?
MEL.   Wherefore start you?
AMIE. [*Awakening.*] O Karol! He is fair
    and sweet.
MAUD.   What then?
Are there not flowers as sweet and fair
    as men?
The lily is fair, and rose is sweet.
AMIE.   Ay, so!
Let all the roses and the lilies go.
Karol is only fair to me.
MAR.   And why?
AMIE. Alas, for Karol, Marian, I could
    die!
Karol, he singeth sweetly too.
MAUD.   What then?   90
Are there not birds sing sweeter far than
    men?
AMIE. I grant the linnet, lark, and bull-
    finch sing,
But best the dear, good angel [9] of the
    spring,
The nightingale.
MAUD.   Then why, then why, alone,
Should his notes please you?
AMIE.   I not long agone [10]
Took a delight with wanton kids to
    play,
And sport with little lambs a summer's
    day,
And view their frisks. Methought it
    was a sight
Of joy to see my two brave rams to
    fight!   99
Now Karol only all delight doth move;
All that is Karol, Karol I approve!
This very morning but,[11] I did bestow
(It was a little gainst my will, I know)
A single kiss upon the seely [12] swain,
And now I wish that very kiss again.
His lip is softer, sweeter than the rose;
His mouth and tongue with dropping
    honey flows;
The relish of it was a pleasing thing.
MAUD. Yet, like the bees, it had a little
    sting.
AMIE. And sunk, and sticks yet in my
    marrow deep;   110
And what doth hurt me I now wish to
    keep.
MAR. Alas, how innocent her story is!

[9] Messenger.   [11] Just this morning.
[10] Ago.   [12] Simple.

AMIE. I do remember, Marian, I have
  oft
With pleasure kissed my lambs and
  puppies soft;
And once a dainty, fine roe-fawn I
  had,
Of whose outskipping bounds I was as
  glad
As of my health, and him I oft would
  kiss;
Yet had his no such sting or pain as
  this.
They never pricked or hurt my heart;
  and, for
They were so blunt and dull, I wish no
  more.   120
But this, that hurts and pricks, doth
  please; this sweet
Mingled with sour I wish again to
  meet;
And that delay, methinks, most tedious
  is
That keeps or hinders me of Karol's
  kiss.
MAR. We'll send for him, sweet Amie, to
  come to you.
MAUD. But I will keep him off, if charms
  will do it.   *She goes murmuring out.*
CLA. Do you mark the murmuring hag,
  how she doth mutter?
ROB. I like her not; and less her manners
  now.
ALK. She is a shrewd, deforméd piece, I
  vow.
LIO. As crooked as her body.
ROB.   I believe   130
She can take any shape, as Scathlock
  says.
ALK. She may deceive the sense, but
  really
She cannot change herself.
ROB.   Would I could see her
Once more in Marian's form, for I am
  certain
Now it was she abused us, as I think
My Marian, and my love, now in-
  nocent—
Which faith I seal unto her with this
  kiss,
And call you all to witness of my pen-
  ance.   [*Kisses Marian.*]
ALK. It was believed before, but now
  confirmed,
That we have seen the monster.   140

ACT II. SCENE vii.

[*The same.*]

To them, Tuck, John, Much, Scarlet.

TUCK.   Hear you how
Poor Tom, the cook, is taken! [1] All his
  joints
Do crack, as if his limbs were tied with
  points; [2]
His whole frame slackens; and a kind of
  rack
Runs down along the spondils [3] of his
  back;
A gout or cramp now seizeth on his
  head,
Then falls into his feet; his knees are
  lead;
And he can stir his either hand no
  more
Than a dead stump, to his office, as
  before.
ALK. He is bewitched.
CLA.   This is an argument   10
Both of her malice and her power, we
  see.
ALK. She must by some device restrainéd
  be,
Or she'll go far in mischief.
ROB.   Advise how,
Sage Shepherd, we shall put it straight
  in practice.
ALK. Send forth your woodmen then
  into the walks,
Or let 'em prick [4] her footing hence; a
  witch
Is sure a creature of melancholy,
And will be found or sitting in her
  fourm, [5]
Or else at relief, [6] like a hare.
CLA.   You speak,
Alken, as if you knew the sport of witch-
  hunting,   20
Or starting of a hag.

*Enter George to the Huntsmen, who by
  themselves continue the scene, the Rest
  going off.*

ROB.   Go, sirs, about it.
Take George here with you; he can help
  to find her.

[1] Bewitched.   [4] Track.
[2] Laces.   [5] Form, bed of a hare.
[3] Vertebræ.   [6] Feeding.

Leave Tuck and Much behind to dress
the dinner
I' the cook's stead.
MUCH.   We'll care to get that done.
ROB. Come, Marian, let's withdraw into
the bower.

ACT II. SCENE viii.

[The same.]

John, Scarlet, Scathlock, George, Alken.[1]

JOHN. Rare sport, I swear, this hunting
of the witch
Will make us.
SCAR.   Let's advise upon 't like
huntsmen.
GEORGE. And [2] we can spy her once, she
is our own.
SCATH. First, think which way she four-
meth,[3] on what wind—
Or north or south.
GEORGE.   For, as the shepherd said,
A witch is a kind of hare.
SCATH.   And marks the weather,
As the hare does.
JOHN.   Where shall we hope to find her?
                          Alken returns.
ALK. I have asked leave to assist you,
jolly huntsmen,
If an old shepherd may be heard among
you,
Not jeered or laughed at.
JOHN.   Father, you will see   10
Robin Hood's household know more
courtesy.
SCATH. Who scorns at eld,[4] peels off his
own young hairs.
ALK. Ye say right well. Know ye the
Witch's Dell?
SCATH. No more than I do know the walks
of hell.
ALK. Within a gloomy dimble she doth
dwell
Down in a pit, o'ergrown with brakes
and briers,
Close by the ruins of a shaken abbey,
Torn with an earthquake down unto the
ground,
'Mongst graves and grots, near an old
charnel house,
Where you shall find her sitting in her
fourm   20

[1] Enters later.   [3] Crouches.
[2] If.   [4] Age.

As fearful and melancholic as that
She is about, with caterpillars' kells [5]
And knotty cobwebs, rounded in with
spells.
Thence she steals forth to relief, in the
fogs
And rotten mists, upon the fens and
bogs,
Down to the drownéd lands of Lincoln-
shire,
To make ewes cast their lambs, swine
eat their farrow,
The housewife's tun not work,[6] nor the
milk churn!
Writhe children's wrists, and suck their
breath in sleep,
Get vials of their blood! And, where
the sea   30
Casts up his slimy owze,[7] search for a
weed
To open locks with, and to rivet charms,
Planted about her in the wicked feat [8]
Of all her mischiefs, which are mani-
fold.
JOHN. I wonder such a story could be
told
Of her dire deeds.
GEORGE.   I thought a witch's banks [9]
Had enclosed nothing but the merry
pranks
Of some old woman.
SCAR.   Yes, her malice more.
SCATH. As it would quickly appear had
we the store
Of his collects.[10]
GEORGE.   Ay, this gude, learned man   40
Can speak her right.
SCAR.   He knows her shifts and haunts.
ALK. And all her wiles and turns; the
venomed plants
Wherewith she kills; where the sad man-
drake grows,
Whose groans are deathful; the dead-
numbing nightshade,
The stupefying hemlock, adder's tongue,
And martagan; [11] the shrieks of luckless [12]
owls
We hear, and croaking night crows in
the air;

[5] Cauls, cocoons.   [7] Ooze.
[6] Ferment.   [8] Performance.
[9] *I.e.*, the banks of the dimble.
[10] Collections of information.
[11] Martagon, a kind of lily.
[12] Ominous of ill luck.

Green-bellied snakes; blue firedrakes [1]
in the sky,
And giddy flittermice [2] with leather wings;
The scaly beetles, with their haber-
geons, 50
That make a humming murmur as they fly!
There in the stocks [3] of trees white fays
do dwell,
And span-long elves that dance about
a pool,
With each a little changeling in their
arms!
The airy spirits play with falling stars,
And mount the sphere of fire to kiss the
moon,
While she sits reading by the glowworm's
light
Or rotten wood, o'er which the worm
hath crept,
The baneful schedule of her nocent [4]
charms,
And binding characters through which
she wounds 60
Her puppets, [5] the sigilla [6] of her witch-
craft.
All this I know, and I will find her for you,
And show you her sitting in her fourm.
I'll lay
My hand upon her, make her throw her
scut
Along her back, when she doth start be-
fore us.
But you must give her law; [7] and you
shall see her
Make twenty leaps and doubles, cross
the paths,
And then squat down beside us.
JOHN. Crafty crone!
I long to be at the sport, and to report it.
SCAR. We'll make this hunting of the witch
as famous 70
As any other blast of venery. [8]
SCATH. Hang her, foul hag! She'll be a
stinking chase.
I had rather ha' the hunting of her heir.
GEORGE. If we could come to see her, cry
"so haw" [9] once.
ALK. That I do promise, or I am no good
hag-finder. [*Exeunt.*]

---

[1] Firedragons. [5] *I.e.*, images in wax or cloth.
[2] Bats. [6] Signatures.
[3] Trunks. [7] A fair start.
[4] Hurtful. [8] Famous story of hunting.
[9] A huntsman's cry of discovery.

THE ARGUMENT OF THE THIRD ACT

Puck-Hairy discovers himself in the
forest, and discourseth his offices, with
their necessities, briefly; after which,
Douce, entering in the habit of Earine, is
pursued by Karol, who, mistaking her at
first to be his sister, questions her how she
came by those garments. She answers, by
her mother's gift. The Sad Shepherd coming in the while, she runs away affrighted,
and leaves Karol suddenly; Eglamour, [10
thinking it to be Earine's ghost he saw, falls
into a melancholic expression of his fant'sy
to Karol, and questions him sadly about
that point, which moves compassion in
Karol of his mistake still. When Clarion
and Lionel enter to call Karol to Amie,
Karol reports to them Eglamour's passion with much regret. Clarion resolves
to seek him, Karol to return with Lionel.
By the way, Douce and her mother, [20
in the shape of Marian, meet them, and
would divert them, affirming Amie to be
recovered, which Lionel wondered at to
be so soon. Robin Hood enters; they tell
him the relation of the witch, thinking
her to be Marian; Robin, suspecting her
to be Maudlin, lays hold of her girdle
suddenly, but, she striving to get free,
they both run out, and he returns with
the belt broken. She, following in her [30
own shape, demanding it, but at a distance, as fearing to be seized upon again,
and seeing she cannot recover it, falls into
a rage and cursing, resolving to trust to
her old arts, which she calls her daughter
to assist in. The shepherds, content with
this discovery, go home triumphing, make
the relation to Marian. Amie is gladded [10]
with the sight of Karol, etc. In the meantime, enters Lorel, with purpose to [40
ravish Earine, and, calling her forth to
that lewd end, he, by the hearing of Clarion's footing, [11] is stayed and forced to commit her hastily to the tree again, where
Clarion, coming by and hearing a voice
singing, draws near unto it; but Eglamour,
hearing it also and knowing it to be Earine's, falls into a superstitious commendation of it, as being an angel's, and in the
air; when Clarion espies a hand put [50
forth from the tree, and makes towards it,

leaving Eglamour to his wild fant'sy, who quitteth the place; and, Clarion beginning to court the hand and make love to it, there ariseth a mist suddenly, which darkening all the place, Clarion loseth himself and the tree where Earine is enclosed, lamenting his misfortune, with the unknown nymph's misery. The air clearing, enters the witch with her son and [60 daughter, tells them how she had caused that late darkness, to free Lorel from surprisal, and his prey from being rescued from him, bids him look to her, and lock her up more carefully, and follow her to assist a work she hath in hand of recovering her lost girdle, which she laments the loss of, with cursings, execrations, wishing confusion to their feast and meeting; sends her son and daughter to gather [70 certain simples for her purpose, and bring them to her dell. This Puck, hearing, prevents, and shows her error still. The huntsmen, having found her footing, follow the tract,[1] and prick after her. She gets to her dell, and takes her form.[2] Enter [the huntsmen]. Alken has spied her sitting with her spindle, threads, and images. They are eager to seize her presently,[3] but Alken persuades them to let her begin [80 her charms, which they do. Her son and daughter come to her; the huntsmen are affrighted as they see her work go forward; and, overhasty to apprehend her, she escapeth them all by the help and delusions of Puck.

Act III. Scene i.

[*The forest.*][4]

Puck-Hairy.

[Puck.] The fiend hath much to do that keeps a school,
Or is the father of a family,
Or governs but a country academy.
His labors must be great, as are his cares,
To watch all turns, and cast [5] how to
  prevent hem.
This dame of mine here, Maud, grows
  high in evil,
And thinks she does all, when 'tis I,
  her devil,

---

[1] Track.
[2] *I.e.* her human figure.   [3] Immediately.
[4] The scene remains the same through the act.
[5] Plan.

That both delude her and must yet protect her.
She's confident in mischief, and presumes
The changing of her shape will still [6]
secure her;   10
But that may fail, and divers hazards
  meet
Of other consequence, which I must
  look to—
Not let her be surprised on the first
  catch.
I must go dance about the forest now,
And firk [7] it like a goblin till I find her.
Then will my service come worth acceptation,
When not expected of her; when the
  help
Meets the necessity, and both do kiss,
'Tis called the timing of a duty, this.
                                  [*Exit.*]

Act III. Scene ii.

*Karol, Douce [in the dress of Earine]. To
                    them, Eglamour.*

Kar. Sure, you are very like her! I conceived
You had been she, seeing you run afore
  me,
For such a suit she made her gainst this
  feast,
In all resemblance, or the very same;
I saw her in it. Had she lived t' enjoy it,
She had been there an acceptable guest
To Marian and the gentle Robin Hood,
Who are the crown and girlond [8] of the
  wood.
Douce. I cannot tell; my mother gave it
  me,
And bade me wear it.
Kar.   Who, the wise, good woman,   10
Old Maud of Papplewick?
Douce.   Yes.—[*Aside.*] This sullen man,
I cannot like him.—I must take my
  leave.

Eglamour enters and Douce goes out.

Eg. What said she to you?
Kar.   Who?
Eg.   Earine.
I saw her talking with you, or her ghost,

---

[6] Always.   [7] Frisk.   [8] Garland.

For she indeed is drowned in old Trent's
  bottom.
Did she not tell who would ha' pulled her
  in,
And had her maidenhead upon the place,
The river's brim, the margin of the
  flood?
No ground is holy enough (you know my
  meaning);
Lust is committed in kings' palaces,   20
And yet their majesty's not violated!
No words!
KAR.   How sad and wild his thoughts
  are! Gone?
  Eglamour goes out, but comes in again.
EG. But she, as chaste as was her name,
  Earine,
Died undeflowered; and now her sweet
  soul hovers
Here in the air above us, and doth haste
To get up to the moon and Mercury,
And whisper Venus in her orb; then
  spring
Up to old Saturn, and come down by
  Mars,
Consulting Jupiter, and seat herself
Just in the midst with Phœbus, temp'ring
  all   30
The jarring spheres, and giving to the
  world
Again his first and tuneful planeting.[1]
O, what an age will here be of new con-
  cords!
Delightful harmony, to rock old sages,
Twice infants, in the cradle o' specula-
  tion,
And throw a silence upon all the crea-
  tures!
He goes out again but returns as soon as
  before.
KAR. A cogitation of the highest rapture!
EG. The loudest seas and most enragéd
  winds
Shall lose their clangor; tempest shall
  grow hoarse,
Loud thunder dumb, and every spece [2] of
  storm,   40
Laid in the lap of list'ning nature, hushed
To hear the changéd chime of this eighth
  sphere.
Take tent, and hearken for it; lose it not.
            Eglamour departs.

[1] An allusion to the music of the spheres.
[2] Species.

ACT III. SCENE iii.

Clarion, Lionel, Karol.

CLA. O, here is Karol! Was not that the
  Sad
Shepherd slipped from him?
LIO.   Yes, I guess it was.—
Who was that left you, Karol?
KAR.   The lost [3] man,
Whom we shall never see himself again,
Or ours, I fear; he starts away from hand
  so,
And all the touches or soft stroke of rea-
  son
Ye can apply! No colt is so unbroken,
Or hawk yet half so haggard or un-
  manned! [4]
He takes all toys that his wild fant'sy
  proffers,
And flies away with them. He now con-
  ceives   10
That my lost sister, his Earine,
Is lately turned a sphere amid the seven,
And reads a music lecture to the planets!
And with this thought he's run to call
  hem hearers.
CLA. Alas, this is a strained but innocent
  fant'sy!
I'll follow him. and find him if I can.
Meantime, go you with Lionel, sweet
  Karol;
He will acquaint you with an accident,[5]
Which much desires your presence on the
  place.   [*Exit.*]

ACT III. SCENE iv.

Karol, Lionel.

KAR. What is it, Lionel, wherein I may
  serve you?
Why do you so survey and circumscribe
  me,
As if you stuck one eye into my breast,
And with the other took my whole dimen-
  sions?
LIO. I wish you had a window i' your
  bosom,
Or i' your back, I might look thorough
  you,
And see your in-parts, Karol, liver, heart;
For there the seat of Love is, whence the
  boy,

[3] Original reads *last.*
[4] Untamed or unmastered.   [5] Happening.

The wingéd archer, hath shot home a
  shaft
Into my sister's breast, the innocent
  Amie,   10
Who now cries out, upon her bed, on
  Karol,
Sweet-singing Karol, the delicious Karol,
That kissed her like a Cupid! In your
  eyes,
She says, his stand is, and between your
  lips
He runs forth his divisions [1] to her ears,
But will not bide there, 'less yourself do
  bring him.
Go with me, Karol, and bestow a visit
In charity upon the afflicted maid,
Who pineth with the languor of your
  love.

To them, Maud and Douce, but Maud ap-
  pearing like Marian.

MAR.[2] Whither intend you? Amie is recovered,   20
  Feels no such grief as she complained of
  lately.
This maiden hath been with her from her
  mother
Maudlin, the cunning woman, who hath
  sent her
Herbs for her head, and simples of that
  nature
Have wrought upon her a miraculous
  cure,
Settled her brain to all our wish and
  wonder.
LIO. So instantly? You know I now but
  left her,
Possessed with such a fit almost to a
  frenzy;
Yourself, too, feared her,[3] Marian, and
  did urge
My haste to seek out Karol and to bring
  him.   30
MAR. I did so. But the skill of that wise
  woman,
And her great charity of doing good,
Hath by the ready hand of this deft
  lass,
Her daughter, wrought effects beyond
  belief,

And to astonishment; we can but thank,
And praise, and be amazed, while we tell
  it.   *They go out.*
LIO. 'Tis strange that any art should so
  help nature
In her extremes.
KAR.   Then it appears most real,
When th' other is deficient.

Enter Robin Hood.

ROB.   Wherefore stay you
  Discoursing here, and haste not with
  your succors   40
To poor afflicted Amie, that so needs
  them?
LIO. She is recovered well, your Marian
  told us
But now here. See, she is returned t' affirm it!

Enter Maudl[in] like Marian. Maudl[in],
  espying Robin Hood, would run out,
  but he stays her by the girdle, and runs
  in with her.

ROB. My Marian?
MAR.   Robin Hood! Is he here?
ROB.   Stay;
What was 't you ha' told my friend?
He returns with the girdle broken and she in
  her own shape.
MAUD.   Help, murder, help!
  You will not rob me, outlaw? Thief,
  restore
My belt that ye have broken!
ROB.   Yes, come near.
MAUD. Not i' your gripe.
ROB.   Was this the charméd circle,[4]
The copy [5] that so cozened and deceived
  us?
I'll carry hence the trophy of your
  spoils.   50
My men shall hunt you too upon the
  start,[6]
And course [7] you soundly.
MAUD.   I shall make hem sport,
And send some home without their legs
  or arms.
I'll teach hem to climb stiles, leap ditches,
  ponds,
And lie i' the waters, if they follow me.

[1] Melodies.
[2] While Maudlin is still undiscovered she is
referred to as Marian.   [3] For her.
[4] Spell.
[5] Disguise, assumed shape.
[6] Without a fair start.   [7] Pursue.

Rob. Out, murmuring hag!

              [Exeunt All but Maudlin.]

Maud.   I must use all my powers,
Lay all my wits to piecing of this loss.
Things run unluckily.   Where's my
  Puck-Hairy?

Act III. Scene v.

Maud, Puck.

[Maud.] Hath he forsook me?

Puck.   At your beck, madam.

Maud. O Puck, my goblin! I have lost
  my belt;
The strong thief, Robin Outlaw, forced
  it from me.

Puck. They are other clouds and blacker
  threat you, dame;
You must be wary, and pull in your
  sails,
And yield unto the weather of the tempest.
You think your power's infinite as your
  malice,
And would do all your anger prompts you
  to;
But you must wait occasions, and obey
  them.

Sail in an eggshell, make a straw your
  mast,   10
A cobweb all your cloth,[1] and pass unseen,
Till you have scaped the rocks that are
  about you.

Maud. What rocks about me?

Puck.   I do love, madam,
To show you all your dangers, when you
  are past hem!
Come, follow me; I'll once more be your
  pilot,
And you shall thank me.   *[Exit.]*

Maud.   Lucky, my loved goblin!

Lorel meets her.

Where are you gaang [2] now?

Lor.   Unto my tree,
To see my maistress.

Maud.   Gang thy gait, and try
Thy turns with better luck, or hang
  thysel'.

The End.[3]

[1] Sail.   [2] Going(?).
[3] The play, of course, is actually unfinished,
but F. G. Waldron published a completion of it
in 1783, reprinted by W. W. Greg in his edition
of the play (Bang's *Materialen*, 1905).

FRANCIS BEAUMONT AND
JOHN FLETCHER

When the first collected folio of Beaumont and Fletcher, containing a masque and some thirty-four plays, none of the latter having previously been printed, was published in 1647, long after the deaths of its authors, no attempt was made to discriminate between the parts of the famous collaborators; nor did the 1679 folio, in spite of its eighteen additional plays, suggest that a separation was desirable or feasible. But recent investigation has tended more and more strongly toward such a distinction, until, for instance, C. M. Gayley in his *Beaumont the Dramatist* is sure of only six plays as the joint product of Swinburne's Castor and Pollux of the English drama—although E. H. C. Oliphant in his *The Plays of Beaumont and Fletcher* prefers eight and allows the two men three more with the assistance of Massinger. Moreover, contrary to the older impression growing out of the longer dramatic career and larger output of Fletcher, virtually all modern critics insist that Beaumont was the greater dramatist. But the disentangling of the web has not ended here, since the hands of Massinger and Field, not to mention those of William Rowley, Shirley, Shakespeare, and others have been identified in a considerable part of the work which for many years masqueraded under the label of "Beaumont and Fletcher." The whole situation provides a striking commentary on the conditions of Elizabethan dramatic publication and authorship.

Both Beaumont and Fletcher brought a new respectability to the Stuart drama, for both came from excellent families and were able to picture the life of the upper classes, especially in comedies of manners and "fashion," with ease and authenticity. Fletcher's father eventually became Bishop of London, and his uncle, Giles Fletcher, himself an author, was the parent of the two Spenserian poets, Phineas and Giles the Younger. Beaumont (born about 1584) was the youngest son of a prominent judge, and his brother John early became recognized as a poet. Fletcher entered Cambridge about 1591, when he was some twelve years of age, and perhaps intended to take orders like his father, but the latter's loss of Elizabeth's favor soon afterward may account for the lack of any record of the boy's graduation; Beaumont went to Oxford in 1597, but by 1600 had transferred himself to the Inner Temple, though not necessarily because of any particular ambition to follow his father's profession of the law. The date at which the two men began to write, and even the date of their first collaboration, cannot be exactly established, but Beaumont published his first poetry about 1602, and seems soon to have become a friend of Jonson and a member of his circle—Dryden, in fact, preserving the story that Jonson had such a regard for the other's judgment that he submitted all his plays to him for criticism, especially as regarded plot. Probably both of the future collaborators had independently written a play or two apiece before their intimacy began, sometime between 1604 and 1606; but they rapidly became such friends that a tradition runs to the effect that they shared rooms on the Bankside and owned all things in common. Since almost no one holds to a date much earlier than 1606 for their first significant collaboration, and since Beaumont's marriage in 1613 and his non-professional attitude toward the drama led to an almost complete cessation of activity in literary creation after that date, the partnership was not actually very long in duration. After the year 1616 had seen the deaths of both Beaumont and his twenty-year senior, Shakespeare, Fletcher continued to write so prolifically and successfully, both alone and in his favorite collaboration, as to become the leading English dramatist, easily overshadowing Jonson in popularity. Fletcher died of the plague in 1625.

The Knight of the Burning Pestle is generally considered to have been written about 1607–8, although Oliphant, on the evidence of the printer's epistle, etc., prefers 1610. Some critics also believe it to have been written entirely by Beaumont, at least in its initial composition, but Oliphant, saying that none of Beaumont's unaided work is extant, agrees with earlier critics in attributing a small portion of it to Fletcher. According to the frank admission of the publisher in the prefatory epistle to the anonymous first quarto edition in 1613, the play was composed in little more than a week, and, upon being produced at the Blackfriars by the Children of the Queen's Revels, was promptly rejected by its audience, which obviously must have been restless under its satire as well as bored by its form. For, in addition to poking fun at the taste and manners of the London tradesman, the play is a burlesque not only of such popular romantic dramas as *Mucedorus* and Heywood's *The Four Prentices of London* but also of such fictional romances, in both verse and prose, as Rafe's own favorite *Palmerin of England*. The question of Beaumont's debt to *Don Quixote* has likewise produced much controversy, since no English translation of Cervantes' work has definitely been shown to have been printed before 1612, although the manuscript was apparently circulated before this date; moreover, though Fletcher used much Spanish material in later plays, Beaumont never did, and there is no evidence to show that either could read Spanish. French or English translations were usually available in some form or other. Scholarly opinion today inclines toward the rejection of the Spanish influence on the play and toward the stressing of the English motives, conventions, and tendencies of the time. The present text is based on the 1613 quarto as reprinted by R. M. Alden in the Belles-Lettres Series (New York, 1912), but these readings have been checked by reference to those given by H. S. Murch in his critical edition for the Yale Series in English in 1908, and by A. R. Waller in the Cambridge edition of the plays of Beaumont and Fletcher.

No serious question has ever been raised as to Fletcher's complete authorship of *The Faithful Shepherdess*, since the first quarto (undated, but probably issued about 1609–10, a year or two after the production by the Children of the Queen's Revels) bears his name, as do the four other editions preceding the second folio, in which there was no distinction of authors. This pastoral drama, or rather pastoral "tragi-comedy," which Fletcher carefully defines in his preface, is in the Italian tradition of Guarini's *Il Pastor Fido*, itself modeled after Tasso's *Aminta;* but these authors, as well as Spenser, merely furnished some general suggestions and a few incidental details without in any way detracting from Fletcher's originality. The plot, largely because of the several pairings of lovers necessitated by the author's desire to illustrate all the gradations of love from the most sensual to the most chaste, is rather complicated, but the poetry is fresh and graceful. Though the play was not a stage success, it has retained the enthusiasm of readers, and its influence is shown in Milton's *Comus*, both in theme and in versification. The present text follows the first quarto as given by Greg in the third volume of the Variorum edition, but, since different copies of the quarto vary, in rare cases Waller's readings in the Cambridge edition have been adopted.

Philaster, or Love Lies a-Bleeding, produced about 1609 and first printed in an imperfect quarto in 1620, was the earliest play of its authors, either singly or together, to achieve a popular success; it was the first important play to spring from their collaboration; and it was their first play to be acted by Shakespeare's company. It belongs to the type of romantic drama or tragi-comedy which was then coming into vogue, with its rapidity of action, its spectacular scenes, its contrast of love and lust, its mingling of humor and seriousness, its sentimentalities, its glittering but shallow characters drawn from the nobility, and its poetical passages. In spite of Thorndike's opinion, expressed in 1901, that these tragi-comedies of Beaumont and Fletcher influenced Shakespeare in *Cymbeline* and *The Winter's Tale*, the general view today is that the influence was in the opposite direction. *Philaster*, although held by Oliphant to be mostly by Beaumont, has given scholars an excellent opportunity to apply their tests of authorship to its various parts. These tests, after eliminating the negligible external evidence, depend upon the following internal elements: versification, especially Fletcher's free approximation of conversational prose effects by the use of weak (*i.e.*, double, triple, or even quadruple) endings for his lines, with a general avoidance of rime (*The Faithful Shepherdess* is an obvious exception), and a favoring of the end-stop; diction and recurring rhetorical devices, such as repetition of words, constructions, and ideas; and mental attitude, shown in the use of certain types of material, such as Fletcher's greater fondness for questionable moral situations and furtive innuendo, and Beaumont's more truly philosophical and speculative outlook. No source for *Philaster* has been discovered, though resemblances to parts of Sidney's *Arcadia* and Montemayor's *Diana* have been noted. The basis of the present text is the 1622 quarto ("second impression, corrected and amended") as reproduced by A. H. Thorndike in the Belles-Lettres Series (New York, 1906), but these readings have been checked with those of the same quarto as given in the Variorum edition by P. A. Daniel and in the Cambridge by Waller.

The Maid's Tragedy was apparently produced about 1611, and was printed anonymously in 1619. A revised edition was brought out in 1622, and another in 1630, containing the authors' names. Both the record of publications and the stage history of the play attest its extreme popularity, for it went through many editions, and leading actors appeared in it, or adaptations of it, on into the nineteenth century. Although Beaumont, famed for his plotting ability, is usually given credit for the major part of the tragedy, there are still some rather unnatural and unplausible aspects of both plot and motivation, but these are almost overlooked in the intensity and interest of the action. The tragedy of blood, lust, and revenge reaches one of its highest points in this play. No source for the plot is known, but the character and some of the acts of Aspatia are not unlike those of Sidney's deserted Parthenia. The present text follows Thorndike's reprint of the 1622 quarto in the Belles-Lettres Series (New York, 1906), checked by the readings of the same quarto given in the Variorum edition by Daniel and in the Cambridge by Waller.

THE KNIGHT OF THE BURNING PESTLE [1]

[BY

FRANCIS BEAUMONT AND JOHN FLETCHER][2]

To His Many Ways Endeared Friend,
Master Robert Keysar [3]

Sir:

This unfortunate child, who in eight days, as lately I have learned, was begot and born, soon after was by his parents (perhaps because he was so unlike his brethren) exposed to the wide world, who, for want of judgment or not understanding the privy mark of irony about it (which showed it was no offspring of any vulgar brain), utterly rejected it, so that for want of acceptance it was even [10 ready to give up the ghost and was in danger to have been smothered in perpetual oblivion, if you out of your direct antipathy to ingratitude had not been moved both to relieve and cherish it, wherein I must needs commend both your judgment, understanding, and singular love to good wits. You afterwards sent it to me, yet being an infant and somewhat ragged. I have fostered it privately [20 in my bosom these two years, and now to show my love return it to you, clad in good, lasting clothes which scarce memory will wear out, and able to speak for itself, and withal, as it telleth me, desirous to try his fortune in the world, where, if yet it be welcome, father, foster-father, nurse, and child—all have their desired end. If it be slighted or traduced, it hopes his father will beget him a younger [30 brother who shall revenge his quarrel and challenge the world either of fond [4

and merely literal interpretation or illiterate misprision.[5] Perhaps it will be thought to be of the race of *Don Quixote.* We both may confidently swear it is his elder above a year, and therefore may by virtue of his birthright challenge the wall of [6] him. I doubt not but they will meet in their adventures, and I hope [40 the breaking of one staff will make them friends; and perhaps they will combine themselves and travel through the world to seek their adventures. So I commit him to his good fortune, and myself to your love.

Your assured friend,
W. B.[7]

[To the Readers of This Comedy [8]

Gentlemen:

The world is so nice [9] in these our times that for apparel there is no fashion; for music (which is a rare art, though now slighted), no instrument; for diet, none but the French kickshews [10] that are delicate; and, for plays, no invention but that which now runneth an invective way, touching some particular person, or else it is contemned before it is thoroughly understood. This is all that I have to say: [10 that the author had no intent to wrong anyone in this comedy, but, as a merry passage, here and there interlaced it with delight, which he hopes will please all, and be hurtful to none.

---

[1] The title at the head of the text is *The Famous History of the Knight of the Burning Pestle.*

[2] The names of the authors do not appear until the second quarto (1635).

[3] Concerning Keysar nothing is known.

[4] Foolish.

[5] Misapprehension.

[6] *I.e.,* take precedence of.

[7] Walter Burre, the publisher.

[8] The address "To the Readers," the prologue, and the dramatis personæ are all from the 1635 edn.

[9] Fastidious.

[10] Kickshaws.

Prologue [1]

Where the bee can suck no honey, she leaves her sting behind; and, where the bear cannot find origanum [2] to heal his grief, he blasteth all other leaves with his breath. We fear it is like to fare so with us—that, seeing you cannot draw from our labors sweet content, you leave behind you a sour mislike, and with open reproach blame our good meanings, because you cannot reap the wonted mirth. Our intent was at this time to move [11 inward delight, not outward lightness, and to breed (if it might be) soft smiling, not loud laughing, knowing it to the wise to be a great pleasure to hear counsel mixed with wit, as to the foolish to have sport mingled with rudeness. They were banished the theater of Athens, and from Rome hissed, that brought parasites on the stage with apish actions, or fools [20 with uncivil habits, or courtesans with immodest words. We have endeavored to be as far from unseemly speeches to make your ears glow as we hope you will be free from unkind reports or mistaking the author's intention (who never aimed at any one particular in this play) to make our cheeks blush. And thus I leave it, and thee to thine own censure, to like or dislike.—*Vale.*[3]] 30

THE SPEAKERS' NAMES

THE PROLOGUE.
Then A CITIZEN.
THE CITIZEN'S WIFE, *and* RAFE,[4] *her man, sitting below amidst the spectators.*
[VENTUREWELL,] *a rich merchant.*
JASPER, *his apprentice.*
MASTER HUMPHREY, *a friend to the merchant.*
LUCE, *merchant's daughter.*
MISTRESS MERRYTHOUGHT, *Jasper's mother.*
MICHAEL, *a second son of Mistress Merrythought.*
OLD MASTER MERRYTHOUGHT.

[TIM,] *a squire.*
[GEORGE,] *a dwarf.*
A TAPSTER.
A BOY *that danceth and singeth.*
AN HOST.
A BARBER.
[THREE CAPTIVE] KNIGHTS.[5]
[CAPTIVE WOMAN.]
A CAPTAIN.
A SERGEANT.
SOLDIERS.
[BOYS.
POMPIONA, *daughter of the King of Moldavia.*

SCENE: *London, Moldavia, etc.*

TIME: *Indefinite.*

INDUCTION

Several Gentlemen sitting on stools on the stage; the Citizen, his Wife, and Rafe standing below among the audience.]

Enter Prologue.

[PRO.] From all that's near the court, from all that's great,
Within the compass of the city [6] walls,
We now have brought our scene—

Enter Citizen [, climbing onto the stage].

CIT. Hold your peace, Goodman [7] Boy!
PRO. What do you mean, sir?
CIT. That you have no good meaning. This seven years there hath been plays at this house,[8] I have observed it, you have still girds [9] at citizens; and now you call your play *The London Merchant*. Down with your title,[10] boy! Down with [11 your title!
PRO. Are you a member of the noble city?
CIT. I am.

---

[1] This prologue is an almost exact reproduction of "The Prologue at the Blackfriars" prefixed to Lyly's *Sappho and Phao.*
[2] Marjoram.
[3] Farewell.
[4] Colloquial for *Ralph.*
[5] Early edns. read *Two Knights.*
[6] The business district of London, as opposed to Westminster, the court.
[7] Master.
[8] Probably Whitefriars, a private theater.
[9] Sneers.
[10] A sign hung or set on the stage to announce the name of the play.

Pro. And a freeman? [1]

Cit. Yea, and a grocer.

Pro. So, grocer, then, by your sweet favor, we intend no abuse to the city.

Cit. [2] No, sir! Yes, sir! If you were [20 not resolved to play the Jacks,[3] what need you study for new subjects, purposely to abuse your betters? Why could not you be contented, as well as others, with the legend of Whittington, or the life and death of Sir Thomas Gresham, with the building of the Royal Exchange, or the story of Queen Eleanor, with the rearing of London Bridge upon woolsacks? [4]   29

Pro. You seem to be an understanding man. What would you have us do, sir?

Cit. Why, present something notably in honor of the commons of the city.

Pro. Why, what do you say to the life and death of fat Drake, or the repairing of Fleet privies?

Cit. I do not like that; but I will have a citizen, and he shall be of my own trade.

Pro. O, you should have told us your mind a month since; our play is ready [40 to begin now.

Cit. 'Tis all one for that; I will have a grocer, and he shall do admirable [5] things.

Pro. What will you have him do?

Cit. Marry, I will have him—

Wife. (Below.[6]) Husband, husband!

Rafe. (Below.[7]) Peace, mistress!

Wife. Hold thy peace, Rafe; I know what I do, I warrant tee.[8] —Husband, [50 husband!

Cit. What sayst thou, cunny? [9]

Wife. Let him kill a lion with a pestle, husband! Let him kill a lion with a pestle!

Cit. So he shall.—I'll have him kill a lion with a pestle.

Wife. Husband! Shall I come up, husband?

Cit. Ay, cunny.—Rafe, help your mistress this way.—Pray, gentlemen, [60

make her a little room.—I pray you, sir, lend me your hand to help up my wife. I thank you, sir.—So.

[Wife is pulled onto the stage.]

Wife. By your leave, gentlemen all; I'm something troublesome. I'm a stranger here; I was ne'er at one of these plays, as they say, before; but I should have seen [10 Jane Shore once; and my husband hath promised me, any time this twelvemonth, to carry me to the Bold Beauchamps, [70 but in truth he did not. I pray you, bear with me.

Cit. Boy, let my wife and I have a couple stools and then begin; and let the grocer do rare things. [Stools are brought.]

Pro. But, sir, we have never a boy [11] to play him; everyone hath a part already.

Wife. Husband, husband, for God's sake, let Rafe play him! Beshrew me, if I do not think he will go beyond them all. [80

Cit. Well remembered, wife.—Come up, Rafe.—I'll tell you, gentlemen; let them but lend him a suit of reparel [12] and necessaries, and, by Gad, if any of them all blow wind in the tail on him.[13] I'll be hanged.

[Rafe leaps onto the stage.]

Wife. I pray you, youth, let him have a suit of reparel!—I'll be sworn, gentlemen, my husband tells you true. He will act you sometimes at our house that [90 all the neighbors cry out on him; he will fetch you up a couraging part so in the garret that we are all as feared, I warrant you, that we quake again. We'll fear [14 our children with him; if they be never so unruly, do but cry, "Rafe comes, Rafe comes!" to them, and they'll be as quiet as lambs.—Hold up thy head, Rafe; show the gentlemen what thou canst do. Speak a huffing [15] part; I warrant you, [100 the gentlemen will accept of it.

Cit. Do, Rafe, do.

Rafe. "By heaven, methinks, it were an easy leap

---

[1] In this case, a member of one of the great tradesmen's guilds.

[2] The original prints the remainder of this scene in extremely irregular verse.

[3] Act like low fellows.

[4] Allusions to actual plays of the period.

[5] Wonderful.

[6] Marginal note in the original reads *Wife below.*

[7] Marginal note in the original reads *Rafe below.*

[8] Thee.

[9] Cony, pet.

[10] Was to have seen.

[11] The play was first performed by the Children of Her Majesty's Revels.

[12] Apparel.

[13] A vulgar expression for *find fault with him.*

[14] Frighten.

[15] Blustering.

To pluck bright honor from the pale-
faced moon,
Or dive into the bottom of the sea,
Where never fathom line touched any
ground,
And pluck up drownéd honor from the
lake of hell." [1]

CIT. How say you, gentlemen, is it not
as I told you?

WIFE. Nay, gentlemen, he hath [110
played before, my husband says, *Mucedorus*, before the wardens of our Company.

CIT. Ay, and he should have played
Jeronimo [2] with a shoemaker for a wager.

PRO. He shall have a suit of apparel,
if he will go in.

CIT. In, Rafe, in, Rafe, and set out the
grocery [3] in their kind,[4] if thou lov'st me.
[*Exit Rafe.*]

WIFE. I warrant, our Rafe will look
finely when he's dressed.　　120

PRO. But what will you have it called?

CIT. *The Grocer's Honor.*

PRO. Methinks *The Knight of the Burning Pestle* were better.

WIFE. I'll be sworn, husband, that's
as good a name as can be.

CIT. Let it be so.—Begin, begin; my
wife and I will sit down.

PRO. I pray you, do.　　129

CIT. What stately music have you?
You have shawms? [5]

PRO. Shawms? No.

CIT. No? I'm a thief if my mind did
not give [6] me so. Rafe plays a stately part,
and he must needs have shawns. I'll be
at the charge of them myself rather than
we'll be without them.

PRO. So you are like to be.

CIT. Why, and so I will be; there's
two shillings. [*Gives money.*] Let's [140
have the waits [7] of Southwark; they are
as rare fellows as any are in England;
and that will fetch them all o'er the water
with a vengeance, as if they were mad.

PRO. You shall have them. Will you
sit down then?

CIT. Ay.—Come, wife.

WIFE. Sit you merry all, gentlemen;

I'm bold to sit amongst you for my ease.
[*Citizen and Wife sit down.*]

PRO. From all that's near the court,
from all that's great,　　150
Within the compass of the city walls,
We now have brought our scene. Fly
far from hence
All private taxes,[8] immodest phrases,
Whatever may but show like vicious!
For wicked mirth never true pleasure
brings,
But honest minds are pleased with hon-
est things.—
Thus much for that we do; but for
Rafe's part you must answer for yourself.

CIT. Take you no care for Rafe; he'll
discharge himself, I warrant you.　　160
[*Exit Prologue.*]

WIFE. I' faith, gentlemen, I'll give my
word for Rafe.

ACTUS PRIMI SCENA PRIMA.[9]

[*A room in Venturewell's house.*]

*Enter Merchant [Venturewell] and Jasper,
his prentice.*

MERCH. Sirrah, I'll make you know you
are my prentice,
And whom my charitable love redeemed
Even from the fall of fortune; gave
thee heat
And growth, to be what now thou art;
new-cast [10] thee,
Adding the trust of all I have at home,
In foreign staples,[11] or upon the sea,
To thy direction; tied the good opinions
Both of myself and friends to thy en-
deavors.
So fair were thy beginnings. But with
these,
As I remember, you had never charge 10
To love your master's daughter, and
even then
When I had found a wealthy husband
for her.
I take it, sir, you had not. But, however,
I'll break the neck of that commission,
And make you know you are but a
merchant's factor.

JASP. Sir, I do liberally confess I am yours,
Bound both by love and duty to your
service,

---

[1] A slightly inaccurate quotation from Shakespeare's *I Henry IV*, I, iii.
[2] The conventional allusion to *The Spanish
Tragedy*.
[3] Grocers.
[4] In their proper livery.
[5] Wind instruments.
[6] Misgive.
[7] Musicians.
[8] Criticisms of individuals.
[9] Scene one of act one.
[10] Remade.
[11] Markets.

In which my labor hath been all my
profit;
I have not lost in bargain, nor delighted
To wear your honest gains upon my
back;   20
Nor have I given a pension to my blood,[1]
Or lavishly in play consumed your stock;
These, and the miseries that do attend
them,
I dare with innocence proclaim are
strangers
To all my temperate actions. For your
daughter,
If there be any love to my deservings
Borne by her virtuous self, I cannot
stop it;
Nor am I able to refrain [2] her wishes.
She's private to herself and best of
knowledge [3]
Whom she'll make so happy as to sigh
for;   30
Besides, I cannot think you mean to
match her
Unto a fellow of so lame a presence,
One that hath little left of nature in
him.
MERCH. 'Tis very well, sir; I can tell
your wisdom
How all this shall be cured.
JASP.   Your care becomes you.
MERCH. And thus it must be, sir: I here
discharge you
My house and service; take your liberty;
And, when I want a son, I'll send for
you.   *Exit.*
JASP. These be the fair rewards of them
that love!   39
O, you that live in freedom, never prove
The travail of a mind led by desire!

Enter Luce.

LUCE. Why, how now, friend?   Struck
with my father's thunder?
JASP. Struck, and struck dead, unless the
remedy
Be full of speed and virtue; I am now,
What I expected long, no more your
father's.
LUCE. But mine.
JASP.   But yours, and only yours, I am;

That's all I have to keep me from the
statute.[4]
You dare be constant still?
LUCE.   O, fear me not!
In this I dare be better than a woman.
Nor shall his anger nor his offers move me,
Were they both equal to a prince's
power.   51
JASP. You know my rival?
LUCE.   Yes, and love him dearly,
Even as I love an ague or foul weather.
I prithee, Jasper, fear him not.
JASP.   O, no!
I do not mean to do him so much kind-
ness.
But to our own desires: you know the plot
We both agreed on?
LUCE.   Yes, and will perform
My part exactly.
JASP.   I desire no more.
Farewell, and keep my heart; 'tis yours.
LUCE.   I take it;
He must do miracles makes me forsake
it.   *Exeunt.* 60

CIT. Fie upon 'em, little infidels! What
a matter's here now? Well, I'll be hanged
for a halfpenny, if there be not some
abomination knavery in this play. Well,
let 'em look to 't; Rafe must come, and if
there be any tricks a-brewing—
WIFE. Let 'em brew, and bake too,
husband, a [5] God's name; Rafe will find
all out, I warrant you, and [6] they were
older than they are.—   70

[*Enter Boy.*]

I pray, my pretty youth, is Rafe ready?
BOY. He will be presently.
WIFE. Now, I pray you, make my commendations unto him, and withal carry
him this stick of licoras.[7] Tell him his
mistress sent it him, and bid him bite a
piece; 'twill open his pipes the better, say.
[*Exit Boy.*]

[SCENA SECUNDA.

The same.]

Enter Merchant and Master Humphrey.

MERCH. Come, sir, she's yours; upon my
faith, she's yours.

---

[1] A license to my passion.
[2] Restrain.
[3] *I.e.*, she is secret and knows best.
[4] Against masterless men.   [6] If.
[5] In.   [7] Licorice.

You have my hand. For other idle lets [1]
Between your hopes and her, thus with
    a wind
They are scattered and no more. My
    wanton prentice,
That like a bladder blew himself with
    love,
I have let out, and sent him to discover
New masters yet unknown.

HUM.   I thank you, sir;
Indeed, I thank you, sir; and, ere I stir,
It shall be known, however you do deem,
I am of gentle blood and gentle seem. 10

MERCH. O, sir, I know it certain.

HUM.   Sir, my friend,
Although, as writers say, all things have
    end,
And that we call a pudding hath his two,
O, let it not seem strange, I pray, to you,
If in this bloody simile I put
My love, more endless than frail things
    or gut!

WIFE. Husband, I prithee, sweet lamb,
tell me one thing, but tell me truly.—
Stay, youths, I beseech you, till I question
my husband.   20

CIT. What is it, mouse?

WIFE. Sirrah, didst thou ever see a
prettier child? How it behaves itself, I
warrant ye, and speaks and looks and
perts [2] up the head!—I pray you, brother,
with your favor, were you never none of
M[aster] Monkester's [3] scholars?

CIT. Chicken, I prithee heartily, contain thyself; the childer [4] are pretty childer;
but, when Rafe comes, lamb—   30

WIFE. Ay, when Rafe comes, conny!—
Well, my youth, you may proceed.

MERCH. Well, sir, you know my love, and
    rest, I hope,
Assured of my consent; get but my
    daughter's,
And wed her when you please. You must
    be bold,
And clap in close unto her; come, I know
You have language good enough to win
    a wench.

[1] Obstacles.
[2] Cocks.
[3] Richard Mulcaster, until 1608 Headmaster
of St. Paul's School, encouraged the acting of
plays among his pupils.
[4] Children.

WIFE. A whoreson [5] tyrant! H'as been
an old stringer [6] in 's days, I warrant him.

HUM. I take your gentle offer, and withal
Yield love again for love reciprocal. [41

MERCH. What, Luce! Within there!

Enter Luce.

LUCE.   Called you, sir?

MERCH.   I did.
Give entertainment to this gentleman,
And see you be not froward.—To her,
    sir;
My presence will but be an eyesore to
    you.   *Exit.*

HUM. Fair Mistress Luce, how do you do?
    Are you well?
Give me your hand, and then I pray
    you tell
How doth your little sister and your
    brother,
And whether you love me or any other.

LUCE. Sir, these are quickly answered.

HUM.   So they are, 50
Where women are not cruel. But how
    far
Is it now distant from this place we are
    in,
Unto that blessed place, your father's
    warren?

LUCE. What makes you think of that, sir?

HUM.   Even that face;
For, stealing rabbits whilom [7] in that
    place,
God Cupid, or the keeper, I know not
    whether,[8]
Unto my cost and charges brought you
    thither,
And there began—

LUCE.   Your game, sir.

HUM.   Let no game,
Or anything that tendeth to the same,
Be evermore remembered, thou fair
    killer,   60
For whom I sat me down, and brake my
    tiller.[9]

WIFE. There's a kind gentleman, I
warrant you; when will you do as much for
me, George?

[5] Rascally.
[6] Libertine.
[7] Formerly.
[8] Which.
[9] Crossbow.

Luce. Beshrew me, sir, I am sorry for
   your losses,
   But, as the proverb says, I cannot cry.
   I would you had not seen me!
Hum.   So would I,
   Unless you had more maw [1] to do me
   good.
Luce. Why, cannot this strange passion
   be withstood?   69
   Send for a constable, and raise the town.
Hum. O, no! My valiant love will batter
   down
   Millions of constables, and put to flight
   Even that great watch of Midsummer
   Day at night. [2]
Luce. Beshrew me, sir, 'twere good I
   yielded then;
   Weak women cannot hope, where vai-
   iant men
   Have no resistance.
Hum.   Yield, then; I am full
   Of pity, though I say it, and can pull
   Out of my pocket thus a pair of gloves.
   Look, Lucy, look; the dog's tooth nor
   the dove's
   Are not so white as these; and sweet
   they be,   80
   And whipped [3] about with silk, as you
   may see.
   If you desire the price, shoot [4] from your
   eye
   A beam to this place, and you shall espy
   "F S," [5] which is to say, my sweetest
   honey,
   They cost me three and twopence, or
   no money.
Luce. Well, sir, I take them kindly, and
   I thank you.
   What would you more?
Hum.   Nothing.
Luce.   Why, then, farewell.
Hum. Nor so, nor so; for, lady, I must
   tell,
   Before we part, for what we met to-
   gether.
   God grant me time and patience and
   fair weather!   90
Luce. Speak, and declare your mind in
   terms so brief.

Hum. I shall. Then, first and foremost,
   for relief
   I call to you, I, if that you can afford it;
   I care not at what price, for, on my word,
   it
   Shall be repaid again, although it cost me
   More than I'll speak of now, for love
   hath tossed me
   In furious blanket like a tennis ball,
   And now I rise aloft, and now I fall.
Luce. Alas, good gentleman, alas the
   day!
Hum. I thank you heart[i]ly; and, as I
   say,   100
   Thus do I still continue without rest,
   I' th' morning like a man, at night a
   beast,
   Roaring and bellowing mine own dis-
   quiet,
   That much I fear forsaking of my diet
   Will bring me presently to that quan-
   dary
   I shall bid all adieu.
Luce.   Now, by S[t]. Mary,
   That were great pity!
Hum.   So it were, beshrew me;
   Then, ease me, lusty [6] Luce, and pity
   show me.
Luce. Why, sir, you know my will is
   nothing worth
   Without my father's grant; get his
   consent,   110
   And then you may with assurance try me.
Hum. The worshipful your sire will not
   deny me;
   For I have asked him, and he hath
   replied,
   "Sweet Master Humphrey, Luce shall
   be thy bride."
Luce. Sweet Master Humphrey, then
   I am content.
Hum. And so am I, in truth.
Luce.   Yet take me with you; [7]
   There is another clause must be annexed,
   And this it is (I swore, and will perform
   it):
   No man shall ever joy [8] me as his wife
   But he that stole me hence. If you dare
   venter, [9]   120
   I am yours (you need not fear; my
   father loves you);
   If not, farewell forever!

[1] Appetite, desire.
[2] The annual military muster of the guilds.
[3] Embroidered.
[4] From 1711 edn. Original reads *sute*.
[5] Evidently the trade-mark or price mark.

[6] Jolly.
[7] Understand me fully.
[8] Enjoy.
[9] Venture.

Hum.   Stay, nymph, stay.
I have a double gelding, colored bay,
Sprung by his father from Barbarian [1]
  kind;
Another for myself, though somewhat
  blind,
Yet true as trusty tree.
Luce.   I am satisfied;
And so I give my hand.   Our course
  must lie
Through Waltham Forest, where I have
  a friend
Will entertain us. So, farewell, Sir Hum-
  phrey,
And think upon your business.
                              Exit Luce.
Hum.   Though I die,   130
I am resolved to venter life and limb
For one so young, so fair, so kind, so
  trim.   *Exit Humphrey.*

Wife. By my faith and troth, George,
and as I am virtuous, it is e'en the kindest
young man that ever trod on shoe leather.
—Well, go thy ways; if thou hast her not,
'tis not thy fault, faith.
Cit. I prithee, mouse, be patient; a [2]
shall have her, or I'll make some [of] [3] 'em
smoke [4] for 't.   140
Wife. That's my good lamb, George.—
Fie, this stinking tobacco kills men! [5]
Would there were none in England!—Now,
I pray, gentlemen, what good does this
stinking tobacco do you? Nothing, I war-
rant. You make chimneys a [6] your faces!—
O, husband, husband, now, now! There's
Rafe, there's Rafe.

[SCENA TERTIA.]

Enter Rafe, like a grocer in 's shop with
two Prentices, [Tim and George,] read-
ing Palmerin of England.

Cit. Peace, fool! Let Rafe alone.—
Hark you, Rafe; do not strain yourself
too much at the first.—Peace!—Begin,
Rafe.

Rafe. [*Reading.*] [7] "Then Palmerin and
Trineus, snatching their launces from

their dwarfs, and clasping their helmets,
galloped amain after the giant; and Palmerin, having gotten a sight of him, came
posting amain, saying, 'Stay, traitor- [10
ous thief! For thou mayst not so carry
away her that is worth the greatest lord
in the world;' and with these words gave
him a blow on the shoulder that he
stroke [8] him besides [9] his elephant. And
Trineus, coming to the knight that had
Agricola behind him, set him soon besides
his horse, with his neck broken in the
fall, so that the princess, getting out of
the throng, between joy and grief, [20
said, 'All happy knight, the mirror of all
such as follow arms, now may I be well
assured of the love thou bearest me.' "—
I wonder why the kings do not raise an
army of fourteen or fifteen hundred thousand men, as big as the army that the
Prince of Portigo brought against Rosicleer, and destroy these giants; they do
much hurt to wandering damsels that
go in quest of their knights.   30

Wife. Faith, husband, and Rafe says
true; for they say the King of Portugal
cannot sit at his meat but the giants and
the ettins [10] will come and snatch it from
him.
Cit. Hold thy tongue!—On, Rafe!

Rafe. And certainly those knights are
much to be commended, who, neglecting
their possessions, wander with a squire
and a dwarf through the deserts to [40
relieve poor ladies.
Wife. Ay, by faith, are they, Rafe;
let 'em say what they will, they are indeed. Our knights neglect their possessions well enough, but they do not the rest.

Rafe. There are no such courteous
and fair well-spoken knights in this age;
they will call one "the son of a whore "
that Palmerin of England would have
called "fair sir"; and one that Rosi- [50
cleer would have called "right beauteous
damsel " they will call "damned bitch."

Wife. I'll be sworn will they, Rafe;
they have called me so an hundred times
about a scurvy pipe of tobacco.

---

[1] *I.e.*, Barbary.
[2] He.
[3] From 1635 edn.
[4] Suffer.
[5] Me(?).
[6] Of.
[7] The following passage is actually a con-
densed quotation from Munday's translation
of *Palmerin de Oliva*
[8] Struck.
[9] Off.
[10] Another word for *giants*.

RAFE. But what brave spirit could be content to sit in his shop, with a flappet [1] of wood and a blue apron before him, selling mithridatum and dragon's-water [2] to visited [3] houses, that might pursue [60 feats of arms, and, through his noble achievements, procure such a famous history to be written of his heroic prowess?

CIT. Well said, Rafe; some more of those words, Rafe!

WIFE. They go finely, by my troth.

RAFE. Why should not I then pursue this course, both for the credit of myself and our company? For, amongst all the worthy books of achievements, I do [70 not call to mind that I yet read of a grocer-errant. I will be the said knight.—Have you heard of any that hath wandered unfurnished of his squire and dwarf? My elder prentice Tim shall be my trusty squire, and little George my dwarf. Hence, my blue aporn! [4] Yet, in remembrance of my former trade, upon my shield shall be portrayed a burning pestle, and I will be called the Knight o' th' Burning Pestle.

WIFE. Nay, I dare swear thou wilt [81 not forget thy old trade; thou wert ever meek.

RAFE. Tim!

TIM. Anon.

RAFE. My beloved squire, and George my dwarf, I charge you that from henceforth you never call me by any other name but "the right courteous and valiant Knight of the Burning Pestle," and [90 that you never call any female by the name of a woman or wench, but "fair lady," if she have her desires; if not, "distressed damsel;" that you call all forests and heaths "deserts," and all horses "palfreys."

WIFE. This is very fine, faith.—Do the gentlemen like Rafe, think you, husband?

CIT. Ay, I warrant thee; the players would give all the shoes in their shop [100 for him.

RAFE. My beloved squire Tim, stand out. Admit this were a desert, and over it a knight-errant pricking,[5] and I should bid you inquire of his intents, what would you say?

TIM. Sir, my master sent me to know whither you are riding?

RAFE. No, thus: "Fair sir, the right courteous and valiant Knight of the [110 Burning Pestle commanded me to inquire upon what adventure you are bound, whether to relieve some distressed damsels, or otherwise."

CIT. Whoresome [6] blockhead, cannot remember!

WIFE. I' faith, and Rafe told him on 't before; all the gentlemen heard him.—Did he not, gentlemen? Did not Rafe tell him on 't?

GEORGE. Right courteous and valiant Knight of the Burning Pestle, here is a distressed damsel to have a halfpennyworth of pepper.

WIFE. That's a good boy! See, the little boy can hit it; by my troth, it's a fine child.

RAFE. Relieve her, with all courteous language. Now shut up shop; no more my prentice, but my trusty squire [130 and dwarf. I must bespeak my shield and arming [7] pestle. [*Exeunt Tim and George.*]

CIT. Go thy ways, Rafe! As I'm a true man, thou art the best on 'em all.

WIFE. Rafe, Rafe!

RAFE. What say you, mistress?

WIFE. I prithee, come again quickly, sweet Rafe.

RAFE. By-and-by.[8]   *Exit Rafe.*

[SCENA QUARTA.

A room in Merrythought's house.]

Enter Jasper and his mother, Mistress Merrythought.

MIST. MER. Give thee my blessing? No, I'll ne'er give thee my blessing; I'll

---

[1] Ledge, *i.e.*, of the counter.
[2] Medicines used against the plague.
[3] I e., by the plague.   [4] Apron.

[5] Spurring.   [7] Heraldic
[6] Whoreson.   [8] At once

see thee hanged first; it shall ne'er be said I gave thee my blessing. Th' art thy father's own son, of the right blood of the Merrythoughts. I may curse the time that e'er I knew thy father; he hath spent all his own and mine too; and, when I tell him of it, he laughs, and dances, and sings, and cries, "A merry heart lives [10 long-a." And thou art a wastethrift, and art run away from thy master that loved thee well, and art come to me; and I have laid up a little for my younger son Michael, and thou think'st to bezzle[1] that, but thou shalt never be able to do it.—Come hither, Michael! Come, Michael.

Enter Michael.

Down on thy knees; thou shalt have my blessing.   19
MICH. [*Kneeling.*] I pray you, mother, pray to God to bless me.
MIST. MER. God bless thee! [*Michael rises.*] But Jasper shall never have my blessing; he shall be hanged first; shall he not, Michael? How say'st thou?
MICH. Yes, forsooth, mother, and grace of God.
MIST. MER. That's a good boy!

WIFE. Ay, faith, it's a fine-spoken child.

JASP. Mother, though you forget a parent's love,   30
I must preserve the duty of a child.
I ran not from my master, nor return
To have your stock maintain my idleness.

WIFE. Ungracious child, I warrant him; hark, how he chops logic[2] with his mother!—Thou hadst best tell her she lies; do tell her she lies.
CIT. If he were my son, I would hang him up by the heels, and flay him, and salt him, whoreson haltersack.[3]   40

JASP. My coming only is to beg your love,
Which I must ever, though I never gain it;
And, howsoever you esteem of me,

There is no drop of blood hid in these veins
But, I remember well, belongs to you
That brought me forth, and would be glad for you
To rip them all again, and let it out.
MIST. MER. Ay, faith, I had sorrow enough for thee, God knows; but I'll hamper thee well enough. Get thee [50 in, thou vagabond, get thee in, and learn of thy brother Michael.
    [*Exeunt Jasper and Michael.*]
OLD MER. ([*Singing*] *within.*)

Nose, nose, jolly red nose,
And who gave thee this jolly red nose?

MIST. MER. Hark, my husband! He's singing and hoiting,[4] and I'm fain to cark and care, and all little enough.—Husband! Charles! Charles Merrythought!

Enter Old Merrythought.

OLD MER. [*Singing.*]

Nutmegs and ginger, cinnamon and cloves—
And they gave me this jolly red nose.   60

MIST. MER. If you would consider your state, you would have little list[5] to sing, iwis.[6]
OLD MER. It should never be considered, while it were an estate, if I thought it would spoil my singing.
MIST MER. But how wilt thou do, Charles? Thou art an old man, and thou canst not work, and thou hast not forty shillings left, and thou eatest good [70 meat, and drinkest good drink, and laughest.
OLD MER. And will do.
MIST. MER. But how wilt thou come by it, Charles?
OLD MER. How? Why, how have I done hitherto this forty years? I never came into my dining room but at eleven and six a-clock I found excellent meat and drink a th' table; my clothes were [80 never worn out but next morning a tailor brought me a new suit; and without question it will be so ever; use makes perfectness. If all should fail, it is but a little

---

[1] Embezzle, squander.
[2] Argues.   [3] Gallows bird.
[4] Making merry.   [5] Desire.   [6] Certainly.

straining myself extraordinary and laugh myself to death.

WIFE. It's a foolish old man this, is not he, George?

CIT. Yes, cunny.

WIFE. Give me a penny i' th' purse [90 while I live, George.

CIT. Ay, by Lady, cunny; hold thee there.[1]

MIST. MER. Well, Charles, you promised to provide for Jasper, and I have laid up for Michael. I pray you, pay Jasper his portion. He's come home, and he shall not consume Michael's stock; he says his master turned him away, but, I promise you truly, I think he ran away. 100

WIFE. No, indeed, Mistress Merrythought; though he be a notable gallows,[2] yet I'll assure you his master did turn him away, even in this place. 'Twas, i' faith, within this half hour, about his daughter; my husband was by.

CIT. Hang him, rogue! He served him well enough. Love his master's daughter! By my troth, cunny, if there were a thousand boys, thou wouldst spoil them [110 all with taking their parts. Let his mother alone with him.

WIFE. Ay, George; but yet truth is truth.

OLD MER. Where is Jasper? He's welcome, however. Call him in; he shall have his portion. Is he merry?

Enter Jasper and Michael.

MIST. MER. Ay, foul chive[3] him, he is too merry!—Jasper! Michael!

OLD MER. Welcome, Jasper! Though [120 thou runn'st away, welcome! God bless thee! 'Tis thy mother's mind thou shouldst receive thy portion. Thou hast been abroad, and I hope hast learned experience enough to govern it; thou art of sufficient years. Hold thy hand—one, two, three, four, five, six, seven, eight, nine, there's ten shillings for thee. [*Gives money.*] Thrust thyself into the world with that,

and take some settled course. If [130 fortune cross thee, thou hast a retiring place. Come home to me; I have twenty shillings left. Be a good husband,[4] that is, wear ordinary clothes, eat the best meat, and drink the best drink; be merry, and give to the poor; and, believe me, thou hast no end of thy goods.

JASP. Long may you live free from all thought of ill,
And long have cause to be thus merry still!
But, father— 140

OLD MER. No more words, Jasper; get thee gone. Thou hast my blessing; thy father's spirit upon thee! Farewell, Jasper! [*Sings.*]

But yet, or ere you part (O, cruel!),
Kiss me, kiss me, sweeting, mine own dear jewel!

So, now begone; no words. *Exit Jasper.*

MIST. MER. So, Michael, now get thee gone too.

MICH. Yes, forsooth, mother; but I'll have my father's blessing first. 150

MIST. MER. No, Michael; 'tis no[5] matter for his blessing. Thou hast my blessing; begone. I'll fetch my money and jewels, and follow thee; I'll stay no longer with him, I warrant thee.—[*Exit Michael.*] Truly, Charles, I'll be gone too.

OLD MER. What, you will not?

MIST. MER. Yes, indeed will I.

OLD MER. [*Singing.*]

Heigh-ho, farewell, Nan! 159
I'll never trust wench more again, if I can.

MIST. MER. You shall not think, when all your own is gone, to spend that I have been scraping up for Michael.

OLD MER. Farewell, good wife; I expect it not. All I have to do in this world is to be merry, which I shall, if the ground be not taken from me; and, if it be, [*Sings.*]

When earth and seas from me are reft,
The skies aloft for me are left. 169
Exeunt.

Boy danceth. Music.

FINIS ACTUS PRIMI.

---

1 Stand by your belief.
2 Gallows bird.
3 Ill befall.
4 Be economical.
5 From 1635 edn. Original has *now.*

WIFE. I'll be sworn he's a merry old gentleman for all that. Hark, hark, husband, hark! Fiddles, fiddles! Now surely they go finely. They say 'tis present death for these fiddlers to tune their rebecks before the great Turk's grace, is 't not, George? But look, look! Here's a youth dances!—Now, good youth, do a turn a th' toe.—Sweetheart, i' faith, I'll have Rafe come and do some of his gambols.— He'll ride the wild mare,[1] gentle- [180 men, 'twould do your hearts good to see him.—I thank you, kind youth; pray, bid Rafe come.

CIT. Peace, cunny!—Sirrah, you scurvy boy, bid the players send Rafe; or, by God's——,[2] and they do not, I'll tear some of their periwigs beside their heads; this is all riffraff.   [Exit Boy.]

ACTUS SECUNDI SCENA PRIMA.

[A room in Venturewell's house.]

Enter Merchant and Humphrey.

MERCH. And how, faith, how goes it now, son Humphrey?

HUM. Right worshipful, and my beloved friend
And father dear, this matter's at an end.

MERCH. 'Tis well; it should be so. I'm glad the girl
Is found so tractable.

HUM.   Nay, she must whirl
From hence (and you must wink, for so, I say,
The story [3] tells) tomorrow before day.

WIFE. George, dost thou think in thy conscience now 'twill be a match? Tell me but what thou think'st, sweet [10 rogue. Thou seest the poor gentleman, dear heart, how it labors and throbs, I warrant you, to be at rest! I'll go move the father for 't.

CIT. No, no; I prithee, sit still, honeysuckle; thou'lt spoil all. If he deny him, I'll bring half a dozen good fellows myself, and in the shutting of an evening knock 't up, and there's an end.

WIFE. I'll buss thee for that, i' [20 faith, boy. Well, George, well, you have

been a wag in your days, I warrant you; but God forgive you, and I do with all my heart.

MERCH. How was it, son? You told me that tomorrow
Before daybreak you must convey her hence.

HUM. I must, I must; and thus it is agreed.
Your daughter rides upon a brown-bay steed,
I on a sorrel, which I bought of Brian,   29
The honest host of the red roaring Lion,
In Waltham situate. Then, if you may,
Consent in seemly sort, lest, by delay,
The Fatal Sisters come, and do the office,
And then you'll sing another song.

MERCH.   Alas,
Why should you be thus full of grief to me,
That do as willing as yourself agree
To anything, so it be good and fair?
Then, steal her when you will, if such a pleasure
Content you both; I'll sleep and never see it,
To make your joys more full. But tell me why   40
You may not here perform your marriage?

WIFE. God's blessing a thy soul, old man! I' faith, thou art loath to part true hearts. I see a has her, George; and I'm as glad on 't!—Well, go thy ways, Humphrey; for a fair-spoken man, I believe thou hast not thy fellow within the walls of London; and I should say the suburbs too, I should not lie.—Why dost not rejoice with me, George?   50

CIT. If I could but see Rafe again, I were as merry as mine host, i' faith.

HUM. The cause you seem to ask, I thus declare—
Help me, O Muses nine! Your daughter sware
A foolish oath, and more it was the pity;
Yet none but myself within this city
Shall dare to say so, but a bold defiance
Shall meet him, were he of the noble science;[4]

---

[1] Play at seesaw.
[2] To be filled in by the actor.
[3] I.e., the plan of eloping.
[4] I.e., a fencer.

And yet she sware, and yet why did
she swear?
Truly, I cannot tell, unless it were 60
For her own ease, for, sure, sometimes
an oath,
Being sworn thereafter, is like cordial
broth;
And thus it was she swore, never to
marry
But such a one whose mighty arm could
carry
(As meaning me, for I am such a one)
Her bodily away, through stick and
stone,
Till both of us arrive, at her request,
Some ten miles off, in the wild Wal-
tham Forest.
MERCH. If this be all, you shall not need
to fear
Any denial in your love. Proceed; 70
I'll neither follow, nor repent the deed.
HUM. Good night, twenty good nights,
and twenty more,
And twenty more good nights—that
makes threescore!   *Exeunt.*

[SCENA SECUNDA.

Waltham Forest.]

*Enter Mistress Merrythought and her son
Michael.*

MIST. MER. Come, Michael; art thou
not weary, boy?
MICH. No, forsooth, mother, not I.
MIST. MER. Where be we now, child?
MICH. Indeed, forsooth, mother, I cannot tell, unless we be at Mile End. Is not
all the world Mile End, mother?
MIST. MER. No, Michael, not all the
world, boy; but I can assure thee, Michael,
Mile End is a goodly matter. There [10
has been a pitchfield,[1] my child, between
the naughty Spaniels and the Englishmen; and the Spaniels ran away, Michael,
and the Englishmen followed. My neighbor Coxstone was there, boy, and killed
them all with a birding piece.
MICH. Mother, forsooth—
MIST. MER. What says my white[2] boy?
MICH. Shall not my father go with us
too?   20

MIST. MER. No, Michael, let thy father
go snick up;[3] he shall never come between
a pair of sheets with me again while he
lives. Let him stay at home, and sing for
his supper, boy. Come, child, sit down,
and I'll show my boy fine knacks, indeed.
[*They sit down; and she opens a casket.*]
Look here, Michael; here's a ring, and
here's a brooch, and here's a bracelet, and
here's two rings more, and here's money
and gold by th' eye,[4] my boy.   30
MICH. Shall I have all this, mother?
MIST. MER. Ay, Michael, thou shalt
have all, Michael.

CIT. How lik'st thou this, wench?
WIFE. I cannot tell; I would have Rafe,
George; I'll see no more else, indeed-law;[5]
and, I pray you, let the youths understand so much by word of mouth; for, I
tell you truly, I'm afraid a my boy. Come,
come, George, let's be merry and [40
wise; the child's a fatherless child; and
say they should put him into a strait pair
of gaskins,[6] 'twere worse than knotgrass;[7]
he would never grow after it.

Enter Rafe, Squire, and Dwarf.

CIT. Here's Rafe, here's Rafe!
WIFE. How do you do, Rafe? You are
welcome, Rafe, as I may say. It's a good
boy; hold up thy head, and be not afraid.
We are thy friends, Rafe; the gentlemen
will praise thee, Rafe, if thou play'st [50
thy part with audacity. Begin, Rafe, a
God's name!

RAFE. My trusty squire, unlace my
helm; give me my hat. Where are we, or
what desert may this be?
DWARF. Mirror of knighthood, this
is, as I take it, the perilous Waltham
Down, in whose bottom stands the enchanted valley.
MIST. MER. O, Michael, we are be- [60
trayed, we are betrayed! Here be giants!
Fly, boy! Fly, boy, fly!
Exeunt Mother and Michael [, *leaving the
casket*].

[1] Perhaps an allusion to a sham battle fought
on this drill ground by the trained bands.
[2] Dear.
[3] Go hang.
[4] In unlimited quantity.
[5] An exclamation of annoyance.
[6] Tight breeches.
[7] A concoction of this was supposed to retard
growth.

RAFE. Lace on my helm again. What
  noise is this?
A gentle lady, flying the embrace
Of some uncourteous knight! I will re-
  lieve her.
Go, squire, and say the knight that
  wears this pestle
In honor of all ladies swears revenge
Upon that recreant coward that pur-
  sues her.
Go, comfort her, and that same gentle
  squire
That bears her company.
SQUIRE.   I go, brave knight. [*Exit*.] 70
RAFE. My trusty dwarf and friend, reach
  me my shield,
And hold it while I swear. First, by my
  knighthood;
Then by the soul of Amadis de Gaul,
My famous ancestor; then by my sword
The beauteous Brionella girt about me;
By this bright burning pestle, of mine
  honor
The living trophy; and by all respect
Due to distressèd damsels, here I vow
Never to end the quest of this fair
  lady
And that forsaken squire till by my
  valor   80
I gain their liberty!
DWARF.   Heaven bless the knight
That thus relieves poor errant gentle-
  women!   *Exit* [*with Rafe*].

WIFE. Ay, marry, Rafe, this has some
savor in 't; I would see the proudest of
them all offer to carry his books after him.
But, George, I will not have him go away
so soon; I shall be sick if he go away, that
I shall. Call Rafe again, George, call Rafe
again; I prithee, sweetheart, let him come
fight before me, and let's ha' some [90
drums and some trumpets, and let him kill
all that comes near him, and thou lov'st
me, George!
CIT. Peace a little, bird; he shall kill
them all, and they were twenty more on
'em than there are.

Enter Jasper.

JASP. Now, Fortune, if thou beest not
  only ill,
Show me thy better face, and bring
  about

Thy desperate wheel, that I may climb
  at length,   99
And stand. This is our place of meeting,
If love have any constancy. O age
Where only wealthy men are counted
  happy!
How shall I please thee, how deserve
  thy smiles,
When I am only rich in misery?
My father's blessing and this little coin
Is my inheritance—a strong revenue!
From earth thou art, and to the earth I
  give thee.   [*Throws away the money*.]
There grow and multiply, whilst fresher
  air
Breeds me a fresher fortune.—(*Spies the
  casket*.) How! Illusion?
What, hath the devil coined himself
  before me?   110
'Tis metal good; it rings well. I am wak-
  ing,
And taking too, I hope. Now, God's dear
  blessing
Upon his heart that left it here! 'Tis
  mine;
These pearls, I take it, were not left
  for swine.   *Exit* [*with the casket*].

WIFE. I do not like that this unthrifty
youth should embezzle away the money;
the poor gentlewoman his mother will
have a heavy heart for it, God knows.
CIT. And reason good, sweetheart. 119
WIFE. But let him go; I'll tell Rafe a
tale in 's ear shall fetch him again with a
wanion,[1] I warrant him, if he be above
ground; and besides, George, here are a
number of sufficient gentlemen can witness, and myself, and yourself, and the
musicians, if we be called in question.
But here comes Rafe, George; thou shalt
hear him speak as [2] he were an emperal.[3]

[SCENA TERTIA.

Another part of the forest.]

Enter Rafe and Dwarf.

RAFE. Comes not Sir Squire again?
DWARF.   Right courteous knight,
Your squire doth come, and with him
  comes the lady,

---

[1] Vengeance.
[2] From 1635 edn.; original reads *an*.
[3] Imperial, *i.e.*, emperor.

Enter Mistress Merr[ythought] and Michael and Squire.

For and [1] the Squire of Damsels, as I take it.

RAFE. Madam, if any service or devoir
Of a poor errant knight may right your wrongs,
Command it; I am prest [2] to give you succor,
For to that holy end I bear my armor.

MIST. MER. Alas, sir, I am a poor gentlewoman, and I have lost my money in this forest!   10

RAFE. Desert, you would say, lady; and not lost
Whilst I have sword and lance. Dry up your tears,
Which ill befits the beauty of that face,
And tell the story, if I may request it,
Of your disastrous fortune.

MIST. MER. Out, alas! I left a thousand pound, a thousand pound, e'en all the money I had laid up for this youth, upon the sight of your mastership—you looked so grim, and, as I may say it,   [20
saving your presence, more like a giant than a mortal man.

RAFE. I am as you are, lady; so are they
All mortal. But why weeps this gentle squire?

MIST. MER. Has he not cause to weep, do you think, when he hath lost his inheritance?

RAFE. Young hope of valor, weep not;
I am here
That will confound thy foe, and pay it dear   29
Upon his coward head that dares deny
Distresséd squires and ladies equity.
I have but one horse, on which shall ride
This lady fair behind me, and, before,
This courteous squire. Fortune will give us more
Upon our next adventure. Fairly speed
Beside us, squire and dwarf, to do us need!   *Exeunt.*

CIT. Did not I tell you, Nell, what your man would do? By the faith of my body, wench, for clean action and good delivery they may all cast their caps   [40 at him.[3]

WIFE. And so they may, i' faith, for I dare speak it boldly, the twelve companies of London cannot match him, timber for timber.[4] Well, George, and he be not inveigled by some of these paltry players, I ha' much marvel. But, George, we ha' done our parts, if the boy have any grace to be thankful.

CIT. Yes, I warrant thee, duckling.   50

[SCENA QUARTA.

Another part of the forest.]

Enter Humphrey and Luce.

HUM. Good Mistress Luce, however I in fault am
For your lame horse, you're welcome unto Waltham;
But which way now to go, or what to say,
I know not truly, till it be broad day.

LUCE. O, fear not, Master Humphrey; I am guide
For this place good enough.

HUM.   Then up and ride;
Or, if it please you, walk, for your repose;
Or sit, or, if you will, go pluck a rose [5]—
Either of which shall be indifferent
To your good friend and Humphrey, whose consent   10
Is so entangled ever to your will
As the poor harmless horse is to the mill.

LUCE. Faith, and you say the word, we'll e'en sit down,
And take a nap.

HUM.   'Tis better in the town,
Where we may nap together, for, believe me,
To sleep without a snatch would mickle grieve me.

LUCE. You're merry, Master Humphrey.

HUM.   So I am,
And have been ever merry from my dam.

LUCE. Your nurse had the less labor.

HUM.   Faith, it may be,
Unless it were by chance I did beray [6]
me.   20

Enter Jasper.

JASP. Luce! Dear friend Luce!

LUCE.   Here, Jasper.

---

[1] And also.
[2] Ready.   [3] Take off their hats to him.
[4] Man for man.
[5] A vulgar euphemism.   [6] Befoul.

JASP.   You are mine.

HUM. If it be so, my friend, you use me
fine.

What do you think I am?

JASP.   An arrant noddy.

HUM. A word of obloquy! Now, by God's
body,

I'll tell thy master, for I know thee well.

JASP. Nay, and you be so forward for to
tell,

Take that, and that! [*Beats him.*] And
tell him, sir, I gave it,

And say I paid you well.

HUM.   O, sir, I have it,

And do confess the payment! Pray, be
quiet.

JASP. Go, get you to your nightcap
and the diet   30

To cure your beaten bones.

LUCE.   Alas, poor Humphrey!

Get thee some wholesome broth, with
sage and comfrey,[1]

A little oil of roses and a feather

To noint [2] thy back withal.

HUM.   When I came hether,[3]

Would I had gone to Paris with John
Dory! [4]

LUCE. Farewell, my pretty nump; [5] I am
very sorry

I cannot bear thee company.

HUM.   Farewell!

The devil's dam was ne'er so banged in
hell.   *Exeunt. Manet [6] Humphrey.*

WIFE. This young Jasper will prove me
anotherthings,[7] a my conscience, and   [40
he may be suffered. George, dost not see,
George, how a swaggers, and flies at the
very heads a folks, as he were a dragon?
Well, if I do not do his lesson [8] for wronging the poor gentleman, I am no true
woman. His friends that brought him
up might have been better occupied, iwis,
than ha' taught him these fegaries; [9] he's
e'en in the high way to the gallows, God
bless him!   50

CIT. You're too bitter, cunny; the
young man may do well enough for all
this.

---

[1] A herb used to cure wounds.   [3] Hither.
[2] Anoint.   [4] The subject of a popular song.
[5] Blockhead, or, perhaps, a nickname for
Humphrey.
[6] Remains.   [8] Teach him.
[7] Otherwise.   [9] Vagaries, pranks.

WIFE. Come hither, Master Humphrey;
has he hurt you? Now, beshrew his fingers
for 't! Here, sweetheart, here's some green
ginger for thee. Now, beshrew my heart,
but a has peppernel [10] in 's head as big as
a pullet's egg! Alas, sweet lamb, how thy
temples beat! Take the peace on him,[11] [60
sweetheart, take the peace on him.

Enter a Boy.

CIT. No, no; you talk like a foolish
woman. I'll ha' Rafe fight with him, and
swinge him up well-favoredly.—Sirrah
Boy, come hither. Let Rafe come in and
fight with Jasper.

WIFE. Ay, and beat him well; he's an
unhappy [12] boy.

BOY. Sir, you must pardon us; the plot
of our play lies contrary, and 'twill   [70
hazard the spoiling of our play.

CIT. Plot me no plots! I'll ha' Rafe
come out; I'll make your house too hot
for you else.

BOY. Why, sir, he shall; but, if anything fall out of order, the gentlemen must
pardon us.

CIT. Go your ways, Goodman Boy!—
[*Exit Boy.*] I'll hold [13] him a penny he shall
have his bellyful of fighting now. Ho, [80
here comes Rafe! No more! [14]

*Enter Rafe, Mistress Mer y[thought], Mi-
chael, Squire, and Dwarf.*

RAFE. What knight is that, squire? Ask
him if he keep

The passage, bound by love of lady fair,

Or else but prickant.[15]

HUM.   Sir, I am no knight,

But a poor gentleman, that this same
night

Had stolen from me, on yonder green,

My lovely wife, and suffered (to be seen

Yet extant on my shoulders) such a
greeting

That whilst I live I shall think of that
meeting.

WIFE. Ay, Rafe, he beat him un- [90
mercifully, Rafe; and thou spar'st him,
Rafe, I would thou wert hanged.

CIT. No more, wife, no more.

---

[10] A lump.
[11] Have him bound to keep the peace.
[12] Mischievous.   [14] *I.e.*, Silence!
[13] Wager.   [15] Pricking, traveling.

RAFE. Where is the caitiff wretch hath
    done this deed?
Lady, your pardon, that I may proceed
Upon the quest of this injurious knight.—
And thou, fair squire, repute me not
    the worse
In leaving the great venture of the purse
And the rich casket, till some better
    leisure.

Enter Jasper and Luce.

HUM. Here comes the broker [1] hath pur-
    loined my treasure.   100
RAFE. Go, squire, and tell him I am here,
An errant knight-at-arms, to crave de-
    livery
Of that fair lady to her own knight's
    arms.
If he deny, bid him take choice of
    ground,
And so defy him.
SQUIRE.   From the knight that bears
The golden pestle, I defy thee, knight,
Unless thou make fair restitution
Of that bright lady.
JASP.   Tell the knight that sent thee
He is an ass; and I will keep the wench,
And knock his headpiece.
RAFE.   Knight, thou art but dead,   110
If thou recall not thy uncourteous terms.

WIFE. Break 's pate, Rafe; break 's pate,
Rafe, soundly!

JASP. Come, knight; I am ready for you.
    Now your pestle
        (*Snatches away his pestle.*)
Shall try what temper, sir, your mor-
    tar 's of.
"With that he stood upright in his
    stirrups,
And gave the Knight of the Calfskin
    such a knock   [*Knocks Rafe down.*]
That he forsook his horse and down he
    fell;
And then he leaped upon him, and,
    plucking off his helmet—"
HUM. Nay, and my noble knight be down
    so soon,   120
Though I can scarcely go,[2] I needs must
    run.   *Exeunt* [3] *Humphrey and Rafe.*

[1] With a pun on the meaning of *pander.*
[2] Walk.
[3] Original reads *Exit.*

WIFE. Run, Rafe; run, Rafe! Run for
thy life, boy! Jasper comes, Jasper comes!

JASP. Come, Luce, we must have other
    arms for you;
Humphrey and golden pestle, both
    adieu!   *Exeunt.*

WIFE. Sure the devil (God bless us!)
is in this springald![4] Why, George, didst
ever see such a firedrake? [5] I am afraid my
boy's miscarried; [6] if he be, though he were
Master Merrythought's son a thou-   [130
sand times, if there be any law in England,
I'll make some of them smart for 't.
CIT. No, no; I have found out the matter, sweetheart. Jasper is enchanted; as
sure as we are here, he is enchanted. He
could no more have stood in Rafe's hands
than I can stand in my lord mayor's. I'll
have a ring to discover all enchantments,
and Rafe shall beat him yet. Be no more
vexed, for it shall be so.   140

[SCENA QUINTA.

Before the Bell Inn at Waltham.]

*Enter Rafe, Squire, Dwarf, Mistress Merry-
                thought, and Michael.*

WIFE. O, husband, here's Rafe again!—
Stay, Rafe, let me speak with thee. How
dost thou, Rafe? Art thou not shrowdly [7]
hurt?—The foul great lungis [8] laid un-
mercifully on thee; there's some sugar
candy for thee. Proceed; thou shalt have
another bout with him.
CIT. If Rafe had him at the fencing
school, if he did not make a puppy of him,
and drive him up and down the school,   [10
he should ne'er come in my shop more.

MIST. MER. Truly, Master Knight of
the Burning Pestle, I am weary.
MICH. Indeed-law, mother, and I am
very hungry.
RAFE. Take comfort, gentle dame, and
    you, fair squire;
For in this desert there must needs be
    placed
Many strong castles held by courteous
    knights;

[4] Young man.   [7] Shrowdly, severely.
[5] Fiery dragon.   [8] Lout.
[6] Ruined.

And, till I bring you safe to one of those,
I swear by this my order ne'er to leave
you.   20

WIFE. Well said, Rafe!—George, Rafe
was ever comfortable,[1] was he not?
CIT. Yes, duck.
WIFE. I shall ne'er forget him. When
we had lost our child (you know it was
strayed almost, alone, to Puddle Wharf,
and the criers were abroad for it, and there
it had drowned itself but for a sculler),
Rafe was the most comfortablest to me.
"Peace, mistress," says he, "let it go;   [30
I'll get you another as good." Did he not,
George, did he not say so?
CIT. Yes, indeed did he, mouse.

DWARF. I would we had a mess of
pottage and a pot of drink, squire, and
were going to bed!
SQUIRE. Why, we are at Waltham
town's end, and that's the Bell Inn.
DWARF. Take courage, valiant knight,
damsel, and squire!
I have discovered, not a stonecast off, 40
An ancient castle, held by the old knight
Of the most holy Order of the Bell,
Who gives to all knights-errant enter-
tain.[2]
There plenty is of food, and all pre-
pared
By the white hands of his own lady
dear.
He hath three squires that welcome
all his guests:
The first, high[t][3] Chamberlino, who
will see
Our beds prepared, and bring us snowy
sheets,
Where never footman stretched his
buttered hams;[4]
The second, hight Ta[p]stero, who will
see   50
Our pots full filléd, and no froth therein;
The third, a gentle squire, Ostlero hight,
Who will our palfreys slick with wisps
of straw,
And in the maunger[5] put them oats
enough,

And never grease their teeth with candle
snuff.[6]

WIFE. That same dwarf's a pretty
boy, but the squire's a groutnole.[7]

RAFE. Knock at the gates, my squire,
with stately lance.   [Squire knocks.]

Enter Tapster.

TAP. Who's there?—You're welcome,
gentlemen. Will you see a room?   60
DWARF. Right courteous and valiant
Knight of the Burning Pestle, this is the
Squire Tapstero.
RAFE. Fair Squire Tapstero, I a wander-
ing knight,
Hight of the Burning Pestle, in the
quest
Of this fair lady's casket and wrought
purse,
Losing myself in this vast wilderness,
Am to this castle well by fortune
brought,
Where, hearing of the goodly entertain
Your knight of holy Order of the Bell   70
Gives to all damsels and all errant
knights,
I thought to knock, and now am bold
to enter.
TAP. An 't please you see a chamber,
you are very welcome.   *Exeunt.*

WIFE. George, I would have something
done, and I cannot tell what it is.
CIT. What is it, Nell?
WIFE. Why, George, shall Rafe beat
nobody again? Prithee, sweetheart, let
him.   80
CIT. So he shall, Nell; and, if I join with
him, we'll knock them all.

[SCENA SEXTA.

A room in Venturewell's house.]

Enter Humphrey and Merchant.

WIFE. O, George, here's Master Humphrey again now, that lost Mistress Luce,
and Mistress Lucy's father. Master Hum-

---

[1] Comforting.   [3] Called.
[2] Entertainment.
[4] The calves of running footmen were greased
to prevent cramps.   [5] Manger.

[6] An ostler's trick to keep horses from eating
their feed.
[7] Blockhead.

phrey will do somebody's errant,[1] I'll warrant him.

Hum. Father, it's true in arms I ne'er shall clasp her,
For she is stol'n away by your man Jasper.

Wife. I thought he would tell him.

Merch. Unhappy that I am, to lose my child!　9
Now I begin to think on Jasper's words,
Who oft hath urged to me thy foolishness.
Why didst thou let her go? Thou lov'st her not,
That wouldst bring home thy life, and not bring her.

Hum. Father, forgive me. Shall I tell you true?
Look on my shoulders; they are black and blue.
Whilst to and fro fair Luce and I were winding,
He came and basted me with a hedge binding.

Merch. Get men and horses straight; we will be there
Within this hour. You know the place again?

Hum. I know the place where he my loins did swaddle;　20
I'll get six horses, and to each a saddle.

Merch. Meantime I'll go talk with Jasper's father.　*Exeunt.*

Wife. George, what wilt thou lay with me now, that Master Humphrey has not Mistress Luce yet? Speak, George, what wilt thou lay with me?

Cit. No, Nell; I warrant thee Jasper is at Puckeridge with her by this.

Wife. Nay, George, you must consider Mistress Lucy's feet are tender; and [30 besides 'tis dark; and, I promise you truly, I do not see how he should get out of Waltham Forest with her yet.

Cit. Nay, cunny, what wilt thou lay with me that Rafe has her not yet?

Wife. I will not lay against Rafe, honey, because I have not spoken with him. But look, George; peace! Here comes the merry old gentleman again.

[1] Errand, expedition.

[Scena Septima.

A room in Merrythought's house.]

Enter Old Merrythought.

Old. Mer. [*Singing.*]

When it was grown to dark midnight,
　And all were fast asleep,
In came Margaret's grimely [2] ghost,
　And stood at William's feet.

I have money, and meat and drink beforehand, till tomorrow at noon; why should I be sad? Methinks I have half a dozen jovial spirits within me! [*Sings.*]

I am three merry men, and three merry men!

To what end should any man be sad [10 in this world? Give me a man that, when he goes to hanging, cries, "Troll [3] the black bowl to me!"—and a woman that will sing a catch in her travail! I have seen a man come by my door with a serious face, in a black cloak, without a hatband, carrying his head as if he looked for pins in the street; I have looked out of my window half a year after, and have spied that man's head upon London Bridge. [4] [20 'Tis vile. Never trust a tailor that does not sing at his work; his mind is of nothing but filching.

Wife. Mark this, George; 'tis worth noting: Godfrey my tailor, you know, never sings, and he had fourteen yards to make this gown; and, I'll be sworn, Mistress Pennistone the draper's wife had one made with twelve.　29

Old Mer. [*Singing.*]

'Tis mirth that fills the veins with blood,
More than wine, or sleep, or food.
Let each man keep his heart at ease;
No man dies of that disease.
He that would his body keep
From diseases, must not weep;
But whoever laughs and sings,
Never he his body brings
Into fevers, gouts, or rheums,

[2] Grim-looking.　　[3] Pass.
[4] The heads of traitors and heretics were here displayed upon poles.

Or ling'ringly his lungs consumes,
Or meets with achës in the bone,   40
Or catarrhs or griping stone,
But contented lives for aye.
The more he laughs, the more he may.

WIFE. Look, George; how say'st thou
by this, George? Is 't not a fine old man?—
Now, God's blessing a thy sweet lips!—
When wilt thou be so merry, George?
Faith, thou art the frowning'st little thing,
when thou art angry, in a country.

Enter Merchant.

CIT. Peace, cony; thou shalt see [50
him taken down too, I warrant thee. Here's
Luce's father come now.

OLD MER. [*Singing.*]

As you came from Walsingham,
   From that holy land,
There met you not with my true love
   By the way as you came?

MERCH. O, Master Merrythought, my
   daughter's gone!
This mirth becomes you not; my daughter's gone!
OLD. MER. [*Singing.*]

Why, an if she be, what care I?
   Or let her come, or go, or tarry.   60

MERCH. Mock not my misery; it is your
   son
(Whom I have made my own, when all
   forsook him)
Has stol'n my only joy, my child, away.
OLD. MER. [*Singing.*]

He set her on a milk-white steed,
   And himself upon a gray;
He never turned his face again,
   But he bore her quite away.

MERCH. Unworthy of the kindness I have
   shown
To thee and thine! Too late I well perceive
Thou art consenting to my daughter's
   loss.   70
OLD MER. Your daughter! What a
stir 's here wi' your daughter? Let her go,
think no more on her, but sing loud. If

both my sons were on the gallows, I would
sing,

Down, down, down—they fall
Down, and arise they never shall.

MERCH. O, might I behold her once again,
   And she once more embrace her aged
      sire!
OLD MER. Fie, how scurvily this goes! [80
"And she once more embrace her aged
sire"? You'll make a dog on her, will
ye? She cares much for her aged sire, I
warrant you.   [*Sings.*]

She cares not for her daddy,
   Nor she cares not for her mammy,
For she is, she is, she is, she is
   My Lord of Lowgave's lassy.

MERCH. For this thy scorn I will pursue
   That son of thine to death.   90
OLD MER. Do; and when you ha' killed
him,   [*Sings.*]

Give him flowers enow, palmer, give him
   flowers enow;
Give him red and white, and blue, green,
   and yellow.

MERCH. I'll fetch my daughter—
OLD MER. I'll hear no more a your
daughter; it spoils my mirth.
MERCH. I say, I'll fetch my daughter.
OLD MER. [*Singing.*]

Was never man for lady's sake—
   Down, down—   100
Tormented as I, poor Sir Guy—
   De derry down—
For Lucy's sake, that lady bright—
   Down, down—
As ever men beheld with eye—
   De derry down.

MERCH. I'll be revenged, by heaven!
      Exeunt.

Music.

FINIS ACTUS SECUNDI.

WIFE. How dost thou like this, George?
CIT. Why, this is well, cony; but, if
Rafe were hot once, thou shouldst see
more.   111
WIFE. The fiddlers go again, husband.

CIT. Ay, Nell; but this is scurvy music. I gave the whoreson gallows money, and I think he has not got me the waits of Southwark. If I hear 'em [1] not anan,[2] I'll twinge him by the ears.—You musicians, play "Baloo"! [3]

WIFE. No, good George, let's ha' "Lachrymæ"!   120

CIT. Why, this is it, cony.

WIFE. It's all the better, George. Now, sweet lamb, what story is that painted upon the cloth? The Confutation[4] of St. Paul?

CIT. No, lamb; that's [5] Rafe and Lucrece.

WIFE. Rafe and Lucrece? Which Rafe? Our Rafe?   129

CIT. No, mouse; that was a Tartarian.[6]

WIFE. A Tartarian? Well, I would the fiddlers had done, that we might see our Rafe again!

ACTUS TERTIUS. SCENA PRIMA.

[Waltham Forest.]

Enter Jasper and Luce.

JASP. Come, my dear dear; though we have lost our way,
We have not lost ourselves. Are you not weary
With this night's wand'ring, broken from your rest,
And frighted with the terror that attends
The darkness of this [7] wild unpeopled place?

LUCE. No, my best friend; I cannot either fear,
Or entertain a weary thought, whilst you
(The end of all my full desires) stand by me.
Let them that lose their hopes, and live to languish   9
Amongst the number of forsaken lovers,
Tell the long, weary steps, and number time,

[1] Original reads *him.*
[2] Anon, at once.
[3] A ballad tune.
[4] Her blunder for *Conversion.*
[5] From 1635 edn. Original reads *that.*
[6] His blunder for *Tarquin. Tartarian* was also a cant term for *thief.*
[7] From 1635 edn. Original has *these.*

Start at a shadow, and shrink up their blood,
Whilst I, possessed with all content and quiet,
Thus take my pretty love, and thus embrace him.   *[Embraces him.]*

JASP. You have caught me, Luce, so fast that, whilst I live,
I shall become your faithful prisoner,
And wear these chains forever. Come, sit down,
And rest your body, too-too delicate
For these disturbances.   *[They sit down.]*
So, will you sleep?
Come, do not be more able [8] than you are;   20
I know you are not skillful in these watches,
For women are no soliders. Be not nice,[9]
But take it;[10] sleep, I say.

LUCE.   I cannot sleep;
Indeed, I cannot, friend.

JASP.   Why, then we'll sing,
And try how that will work upon our senses.

LUCE. I'll sing, or say, or anything but sleep.

JASP. Come, little mermaid, rob me of my heart
With that enchanting voice.

LUCE.   You mock me, Jasper.

SONG

JASP. Tell me, dearest, what is love?
LUCE. 'Tis a lightning from above;   30
     'Tis an arrow; 'tis a fire;
     'Tis a boy they call Desire;
          'Tis a smile
          Doth beguile
JASP. The poor hearts of men that prove.

Tell me more, are women true?
LUCE. Some love change, and so do you.
JASP. Are they fair and never kind?
LUCE. Yes, when men turn with the wind.
JASP.   Are they froward?   40
LUCE.   Ever toward,[11]
     Those that love, to love anew.

JASP. Dissemble it no more; I see the god
Of heavy sleep lay on his heavy mace
Upon your eyelids.

LUCE.   I am very heavy.   *[Sleeps.]*

[8] Capable of endurance.   [10] Acquiesce, agree.
[9] Foolish.   [11] Apt.

JASP. Sleep, sleep; and quiet rest crown
    thy sweet thoughts!
Keep from her fair blood distempers,
    startings,
Horrors, and fearful shapes! Let all her
    dreams
Be joys and chaste delights, embraces,
    wishes,
And such new pleasures as the ravished
    soul   50
Gives to the senses!—So; my charms
    have took.—
Keep her, you powers divine, whilst I
    contemplate
Upon the wealth and beauty of her mind!
She is only fair and constant, only kind,
And only to thee, Jasper. O, my joys!
Whither will you transport me? Let
    not fullness
Of my poor buried hopes come up to-
    gether
And overcharge my spirits! I am weak.
Some say (however ill) the sea and
    women
Are governed by the moon; both ebb
    and flow,   60
Both full of changes; yet to them that
    know,
And truly judge, these but opinions are,
And heresies, to bring on pleasing war
Between our tempers, that without
    these were
Both void of after-love and present
    fear,
Which are the best of Cupid. O, thou
    child
Bred from despair, I dare not enter-
    tain thee,
Having a love without the faults of
    women,
And greater in her perfect goods than
    men—
Which to make good, and please my-
    self the stronger, .   70
Though certainly I am certain of her
    love,
I'll try her, that the world and memory
May sing to aftertimes her constancy.—
        [Draws his sword.]
    Luce! Luce! Awake!
LUCE.   Why do you fright me, friend,
With those distempered looks? What
    makes [1] your sword

[1] Does.

Drawn in your hand? Who hath of-
    fended you?
I prithee, Jasper, sleep; thou art wild
    with watching.
JASP. Come, make your way to heaven,
    and bid the world,
With all the villainies that stick upon it,
Farewell; you're for another life.
LUCE.   O, Jasper, 80
How have my tender years committed
    evil,
Especially against the man I love,
Thus to be cropped untimely?
JASP.   Foolish girl,
Canst thou imagine I could love his
    daughter
That flung me from my fortune into
    nothing?
Dischargéd me his service, shut the
    doors
Upon my poverty, and scorned my
    prayers,
Sending me, like a boat without a mast,
To sink or swim? Come; by this hand
    you die.
I must have life and blood to satisfy 90
Your father's wrongs.

WIFE. Away, George, away! Raise
the watch at Ludgate, and bring a mittimus from the justice for this desperate
villain!—Now, I charge you, gentlemen,
see the king's peace kept!—O, my heart,
what a varlet's this to offer manslaughter
upon the harmless gentlewoman!
    CIT. I warrant thee, sweetheart, we'll
have him hampered.   100

LUCE. O, Jasper, be not cruel!
If thou wilt kill me, smile, and do it
    quickly,
And let not many deaths appear before
    me.
I am a woman, made of fear and love,
A weak, weak woman; kill not with
    thy eyes;
They shoot me through and through.
    Strike, I am ready;
And, dying, still I love thee.

Enter Merchant, Humphrey, and his Men.
MERCH.   Whereabouts?
JASP. [*Aside.*] No more of this; now to
    myself again.

Hum. There, there he stands, with sword, like martial knight,
Drawn in his hand; therefore beware the fight,   110
You that be wise, for, were I good Sir Bevis,
I would not stay his coming, by your leaves.
Merch. Sirrah, restore my daughter!
Jasp.   Sirrah, no.
Merch. Upon him, then!
[*They set upon Jasper and take Luce from him.*]

Wife. So; down with him, down with him, down with him! Cut him i' th' leg, boys, cut him i' th' leg!

Merch. Come your ways, minion; I'll provide a cage
For you, you're grown so tame.—Horse her away.   119
Hum. Truly, I'm glad your forces have the day.   *Exeunt. Manet Jasper.*
Jasp. They are gone, and I am hurt; my love is lost,
Never to get again. O, me unhappy!
Bleed, bleed and die! I cannot. O, my folly,
Thou hast betrayed me! Hope, where art thou fled?
Tell me, if thou beest anywhere remaining.
Shall I but see my love again? O, no!
She will not deign to look upon her butcher,
Nor is it fit she should; yet I must venter.
O, Chance, or Fortune, or whate'er thou art
That men adore for powerful, hear my cry,   130
And let me loving live, or losing die!
                                                      Exit.

Wife. Is a gone, George?
Cit. Ay, cony.
Wife. Marry, and let him go, sweetheart. By the faith a my body, a has put me into such a fright that I tremble (as they say) as 'twere an aspine leaf. Look a my little finger, George, how it shakes. Now, i' truth, every member of my body is the worse for 't.   140

Cit. Come, hug in mine arms, sweet mouse; he shall not fright thee any more. Alas, mine own dear heart, how it quivers!

[Scena Secunda.

Before the Bell Inn at Waltham.]

Enter Mistress Merrythought, Rafe, Michael, Squire, Dwarf, Host, and a Tapster.

Wife. O, Rafe! How dost thou, Rafe? How hast thou slept tonight?[1] Has the knight used thee well?
Cit. Peace, Nell; let Rafe alone.

Tap. Master, the reckoning is not paid.
Rafe. Right courteous knight, who, for the order's sake
Which thou hast ta'en, hang'st out the holy Bell,
As I this flaming pestle bear about,
We render thanks to your puissant self,
Your beauteous lady, and your gentle squires   10
For thus refreshing of our wearied limbs,
Stiffened with hard achievements in wild desert.
Tap. Sir, there is twelve shillings to pay.
Rafe. Thou merry Squire Tapstero, thanks to thee
For comforting our souls with double jug;
And, if advent'rous fortune prick thee forth,
Thou jovial squire, to follow feats of arms,
Take heed thou tender[2] every lady's cause,
Every true knight, and every damsel fair;
But spill the blood of treacherous Saracens,   20
And false enchanters that with magic spells
Have done to death full many a noble knight.
Host. Thou valiant Knight of the Burning Pestle, give ear to me. There is twelve shillings to pay, and, as I am a true knight, I will not bate a penny.

Wife. George, I pray thee, tell me, must Rafe pay twelve shillings now?

_____
[1] Last night.   [2] Treat with care.

CIT. No, Nell, no; nothing but the old
knight is merry with Rafe.   30

WIFE. O, is 't nothing else? Rafe will be
as merry as he.

RAFE. Sir Knight, this mirth of yours
  becomes you well;
But, to requite this liberal courtesy,
If any of your squires will follow arms,
He shall receive from my heroic hand
A knighthood, by the virtue of this
  pestle.

HOST. Fair knight, I thank you for your
  noble offer;
Therefore, gentle knight,
Twelve shillings you must pay, or I
  must cap [1] you.   40

WIFE. Look, George! Did not I tell
thee as much? The Knight of the Bell is
in earnest. Rafe shall not be beholding [2]
to him; give him his money, George, and
let him go snick up.

CIT. Cap Rafe? No.—Hold your hand,
Sir Knight of the Bell; there's your money.
[Gives money.] Have you anything to say
to Rafe now? Cap Rafe?

WIFE. I would you should know it, [50
Rafe has friends that will not suffer him
to be capped for ten times so much, and
ten times to the end of that.—Now take
thy course, Rafe.

MIST. MER. Come, Michael; thou and
I will go home to thy father. He hath
enough left to keep us a day or two, and
we'll set fellows abroad to cry [3] our purse
and our casket. Shall we, Michael?

MICH. Ay, I pray, mother; in truth [60
my feet are full of chilblains with traveling.

WIFE. Faith, and those chilblains are
a foul trouble. Mistress Merrythought,
when your youth comes home, let him rub
all the soles of his feet, and the heels, and
his ankles, with a mouse skin; or, if none
of your people can catch a mouse, when
he goes to bed, let him roll his feet in the
warm embers, and, I warrant you, he [70
shall be well; and you may make him put
his fingers between his toes, and smell to

them; it's very sovereign for his head, if
he be costive.

MIST. MER. Master Knight of the
Burning Pestle, my son Michael and I bid
you farewell. I thank your worship heartily for your kindness.

RAFE. Farewell, fair lady, and your tender
  squire.
If, pricking through these deserts, I do
  hear   80
Of any traitorous knight, who through
  his guile
Hath light [4] upon your casket and your
  purse,
I will despoil him of them, and restore
  them.

MIST. MER. I thank your worship.
                          Exit with Michael.

RAFE. Dwarf, bear my shield; squire,
  elevate my lance.
And now farewell, you Knight of holy
  Bell.

CIT. Ay, ay, Rafe, all is paid.

RAFE. But yet, before I go, speak, worthy
  knight,
If aught you do of sad [5] adventures
  know,
Where errant knight [6] may through his
  prowess win   90
Eternal fame, and free some gentle souls
From endless bonds of steel and ling'ring
  pain.

HOST. Sirrah, go to Nick the barber,
and bid him prepare himself, as I told you
before, quickly.

TAP. I am gone, sir.   Exit Tapster.

HOST. Sir Knight, this wilderness afford-
  eth none
But the great venter, where full many
  a knight
Hath tried his prowess, and come off
  with shame,
And where I would not have you lose
  your life   100
Against no man, but furious fiend of
  hell.

RAFE. Speak on, Sir Knight; tell what he
  is and where,
For here I vow, upon my blazing badge,

---

[1] Arrest.   [2] Beholden.
[3] I.e., have public criers announce the loss of.
[4] Lit.
[5] Important.   [6] Original reads Knights.

Never to blaze a day in quietness,
But bread and water will I only eat,
And the green herb and rock shall be
my couch,
Till I have quelled [1] that man, or beast,
or fiend
That works such damage to all errant
knights.

HOST. Not far from hence, near to a
craggy cliff,   109
At the north end of this distresséd town,
There doth stand a lowly house,
Ruggedly builded, and in it a cave
In which an ugly giant now doth wone,[2]
Yclepéd [3] Barbaroso; in his hand
He shakes a naked lance of purest steel,
With sleeves turned up; and him be-
fore he wears
A motley garment, to preserve his
clothes
From blood of those knights which he
massacres,
And ladies gent; [4] without his door doth
hang
A copper basin on a prickant [5] spear,[6] 120
At which no sooner gentle knights can
knock
But the shrill sound fierce Barbaroso
hears,
And, rushing forth, brings in the errant
knight
And sets him down in an enchanted
chair;
Then with an engine,[7] which he hath
prepared
With forty teeth, he claws his courtly
crown,
Next makes him wink,[8] and underneath
his chin
He plants a brazen piece of mighty
bord,[9]
And knocks his bullets [10] round about
his cheeks,
Whilst with his fingers and an instrument   130

[1] Killed.
[2] Dwell.
[3] Called.
[4] Gentle, noble.
[5] With point upward.
[6] The basin and spear advertised the barber-
surgeon.   [7] Instrument, i.e., comb.
[8] I.e., close his eyes to anoint them with perfume.
[9] Circumference. The barber's basin, which
was held up by the customer, had a semicircular
opening to fit around his neck.
[10] Balls of soap.

With which he snaps his hair off he
doth fill
The wretch's ears with a most hideous
noise.
Thus every knight adventurer he doth
trim,
And now no creature dares encounter
him.

RAFE. In God's name, I will fight him.
Kind sir,
Go but before me to this dismal cave,
Where this huge giant Barbaroso dwells,
And, by that virtue that [11] brave Rosi-
cleer
That damnéd brood of ugly giants slew,
And Palmerin Frannarco overthrew, 140
I doubt not but to curb this traitor
foul,
And to the devil send his guilty soul.

HOST. Brave-sprighted [12] knight, thus far
I will perform
This your request: I'll bring you within
sight
Of this most loathsome place, inhabited
By a more loathsome man, but dare
not stay,
For his main force soops [13] all he sees
away.

RAFE. Saint George, set on before!
March, squire and page!   *Exeunt.*

WIFE. George, dost think Rafe will
confound the giant?   150
CIT. I hold my cap to a farthing he
does. Why, Nell, I saw him wrastle with
the great Dutchman, and hurl him.
WIFE. Faith, and that Dutchman was
a goodly man, if all things were answerable to his bigness. And yet they say there
was a Scotchman higher than he, and that
they two and a knight met, and saw one
another for nothing. But of all the sights
that ever were in London, since I was [160
married, methinks the little child that was
so fair grown about the members was the
prettiest; that and the hermaphrodite.
CIT. Nay, by your leave, Nell, Ninivy [14]
was better.
WIFE. Ninivy! O, that was the story
of Jone and the wall,[15] was it not, George?
CIT. Yes, lamb.

[11] By which.   [12] Brave-spirited.   [13] Sweeps.
[14] A popular puppet show about Ninevah.
[15] I.e., Jonah and the whale.

[SCENA TERTIA.

Before Merrythought's house.]

Enter Mistress Merrythought.

WIFE. Look, George, here comes Mistress Merrythought again! And I would have Rafe come and fight with the giant; I tell you true, I long to see 't.

CIT. Good Mistress Merrythought, begone, I pray you, for my sake; I pray you, forbear a little; you shall have audience presently. I have a little business.

WIFE. Mistress Merrythought, if it please you to refrain your passion a [10 little, till Rafe have despatched the giant out of the way, we shall think ourselves much bound to you. I thank you, good Mistress Merrythought.

Exit Mist[ress] Merrythou[ght].

Enter a Boy.

CIT. Boy, come hither. Send away Rafe and this whoreson giant quickly.

BOY. In good faith, sir, we cannot; you'll utterly spoil our play, and make it to be hissed; and it cost money; you will not suffer us to go on with our plot.— [20 I pray, gentlemen, rule him.

CIT. Let him come now and despatch this, and I'll trouble you no more.

BOY. Will you give me your hand of that?

WIFE. Give him thy hand, George, do; and I'll kiss him. I warrant thee, the youth means plainly.[1]

BOY. I'll send him to you presently.

WIFE. [*Kissing him.*] I thank you, [30 little youth.—(*Exit Boy.*) Faith, the child hath a sweet breath, George; but I think it be troubled with the worms. *Carduus Benedictus* [2] and mare's milk were the only thing in the world for 't.—O, Rafe's here, George!—God send thee good luck, Rafe!

[SCENA QUARTA.

Before a barber's shop.]

Enter Rafe, Host, Squire, and Dwarf.

HOST. Puissant knight, yonder his mansion is.

Lo, where the spear and copper basin are!

[1] Sincerely.

[2] The Blessed Thistle, regarded as a panacea.

Behold that string, on which hangs many a tooth,

Drawn from the gentle jaw of wand'ring knights!

I dare not stay to sound; [3] he will appear.   *Exit Host.*

RAFE. O, faint not, heart! Susan, my lady dear,

The cobbler's maid in Milk Street, for whose sake

I take these arms, O, let the thought of thee

Carry thy knight through all adventerous deeds;

And, in the honor of thy beauteous self,   10

May I destroy this monster Barbaroso!—

Knock, squire, upon the basin till it break

With the shrill strokes, or till the giant speak. [*Squire knocks upon the basin.*]

Enter Barber.

WIFE. O, George, the giant, the giant!—Now, Rafe, for thy life!

BARBER. What fond unknowing wight is this that dares

So rudely knock at Barbaroso's cell,

Where no man comes but leaves his fleece behind?

RAFE. I, traitorous caitiff, who am sent by fate

To punish all the sad enormities   20

Thou hast committed against ladies gent

And errant knights. Traitor to God and men,

Prepare thyself! This is the dismal hour

Appointed for thee to give strict account

Of all thy beastly, treacherous villainies

BARBER. Foolhardy knight, full soon thou shalt aby [4]

This fond reproach; thy body will I bang;   *He takes down his pole.*

And, lo, upon that string thy teeth shall hang!

Prepare thyself, for dead soon shalt thou be.

RAFE. Saint George for me! *They fight.*

BARBER.   Gargantua for me!   30

[3] Blow horn.   [4] Pay for.

WIFE. To him, Rafe, to him! Hold up the giant; set out thy leg before, Rafe!

CIT. Falsify [1] a blow, Rafe, falsify a blow! The giant lies open on the left side.

WIFE. Bear 't off, bear 't off still! There, boy!—O, Rafe's almost down, Rafe's almost down!

RAFE. Susan, inspire me! Now have up again.

WIFE. Up, up, up, up, up! So, Rafe! Down with him, down with him, Rafe!

CIT. Fetch him o'er the hip, boy!   41
[*Rafe knocks the Barber down.*]

WIFE. There, boy! Kill, kill, kill, kill, kill, Rafe!

CIT. No, Rafe; get all out of him first.

RAFE. Presumptuous man, see to what desperate end
Thy treachery hath brought thee! The just gods,
Who never prosper those that do despise them,
For all the villainies which thou hast done
To knights and ladies, now have paid thee home
By my stiff arm, a knight adventurous.   50
But say, vile wretch, before I send thy soul
To sad Avernus, whither it must go,
What captives hold'st thou in thy sable cave?

BARBER. Go in, and free them all; thou hast the day.

RAFE. Go, squire and dwarf, search in this dreadful cave,
And free the wretched prisoners from their bonds.
Exeunt [2] *Squire and Dwarf.*

BARBER. I crave for mercy, as thou art a knight,
And scorn'st to spill the blood of those that beg.

RAFE. Thou showed'st no mercy, nor shalt thou have any;
Prepare thyself, for thou shalt surely die.   60

Enter Squire, leading One winking, with a basin under his chin.

SQUIRE. Behold, brave knight, here is one prisoner,
Whom this wild man hath uséd as you see.

WIFE. This is the first wise word I heard the squire speak.

RAFE. Speak what thou art, and how thou hast been used,
That I may give [him] [3] condign punishment.

1 KNI. I am a knight that took my journey post
Northward from London; and in courteous wise
This giant trained me to his loathsome den   69
Under pretense of killing of the itch;
And all my body with a powder strewed,
That smarts and stings, and cut away my beard,
And my curled locks wherein were ribands tied,
And with a water washed my tender eyes
(Whilst up and down about me still he skipped),
Whose virtue is that, till my eyes be wiped
With a dry cloth, for this my foul disgrace
I shall not dare to look a dog i' th' face.

WIFE. Alas, poor knight!—Relieve him, Rafe; relieve poor knights, whilst you live.

RAFE. My trusty squire, convey him to the town,   81
Where he may find relief.—Adieu, fair knight.   *Exit* [1] *Knight.*

Enter Dwarf, leading One with a patch o'er his nose.

DWARF. Puissant knight, of the Burning Pestle hight,
See here another wretch, whom this foul beast

---

[1] Counterfeit.
[2] Original reads *Exit.*

[3] From 1635 edn. Original reads *That that I may give.*

Hath scorched [1] and scored in this inhuman wise.

RAFE. Speak me thy name, and eke thy
place of birth,
And what hath been thy usage in this
cave.

2 KNI. I am a knight, Sir Pockhole is
my name,
And by my birth I am a Londoner,
Free by my copy,[2] but my ancestors   90
Were Frenchmen [3] all; and, riding hard
this way
Upon a trotting horse, my bones did
ache,
And I, faint knight, to ease my weary
limbs,
Light at this cave, when straight this
furious fiend
With sharpest instrument of purest
steel
Did cut the gristle of my nose away,
And in the place this velvet plaster
stands.
Relieve me, gentle knight, out of his
hands!

WIFE. Good Rafe, relieve Sir Pockhole, and send him away, for in truth his
breath stinks.   101

RAFE. Convey him straight after the
other knight.—
Sir Pockhole, fare you well.

2 KNI.   Kind sir, good night. *Exit.*
                                Cries within.

MAN. Deliver us!
WOMAN. Deliver us!

WIFE. Hark, George, what a woeful
cry there is! I think some woman lies-in
there.

MAN. Deliver us!
WOMAN. Deliver us!   110

RAFE. What ghastly noise is this? Speak,
Barbaroso,
Or, by this blazing steel, thy head goes
off!

BARBER. Prisoners of mine, whom I in
diet keep.
Send lower down into the cave,

[1] Scotched, cut.
[2] Certificate of citizenship.
[3] In allusion to the "French disease," a common name for the pox or syphilis.

And in a tub that's heated smoking hot
There may they find them, and deliver
them.

RAFE. Run, squire and dwarf; deliver
them with speed.
                Exeunt Squire and Dwarf.

WIFE. But will not Rafe kill this giant?
Surely I am afeard, if he let him go, he
will do as much hurt as ever he did.   120

CIT. Not so, mouse, neither, if he could
convert him.

WIFE. Ay, George, if he could convert
him; but a giant is not so soon converted
as one of us ordinary people. There's a
pretty tale of a witch that had the devil's
mark about her (God bless us!), that had
a giant to her son, that was called Lob-lie-
by-the-fire; didst never hear it, George?

*Enter Squire, leading a Man, with a glass
of lotion in his hand, and the Dwarf,
leading a Woman, with diet bread [4] and
                                        drink.*

CIT. Peace, Nell, here comes the prisoners.

DWARF. Here be these pinéd wretches,
manful knight,   131
That for these six weeks have not seen
a wight.

RAFE. Deliver what you are, and how
you came
To this sad cave, and what your usage
was.

MAN. I am an errant knight that followed
arms
With spear and shield; and in my tender
years
I stricken was with Cupid's fiery shaft,
And fell in love with this my lady dear,
And stole her from her friends in Turn-
bull Street,[5]
And bore her up and down from town
to town,   140
Where we did eat and drink, and music
hear,
Till at the length at this unhappy town
We did arrive, and, coming to this cave,
This beast us caught and put us in a
tub,
Where we this two months sweat, and
should have done

[4] Special bread prepared for invalids.
[5] A disreputable district.

Another month, if you had not relieved
us.

WOMAN. This bread and water hath our
diet been,
Together with a rib cut from a neck
Of burnéd mutton; hard hath been our
fare.   149
Release us from this ugly giant's snare!

MAN. This hath been all the food we have
received;
But only twice a day, for novelty,
He gave a spoonful of this hearty broth
                    Pulls out a syringe.
To each of us, through this same slender
quill.

RAFE. From this infernal monster you
shall go,
That useth knights and gentle ladies
so!—
Convey them hence.
                    Exeunt Man and Woman.

CIT. Cony, I can tell thee, the gentlemen like Rafe.

WIFE. Ay, George, I see it well   [160
enough.—Gentlemen, I thank you all
heartily for gracing my man Rafe; and,
I promise you, you shall see him oft'ner.

BARBER. Mercy, great knight! I do recant my ill,
And henceforth never gentle blood will
spill.

RAFE. I give thee mercy; but yet shalt
thou swear
Upon my burning pestle, to perform
Thy promise uttered.

BARBER. I swear and kiss.
                    [Kisses the pestle.]

RAFE.   Depart then, and amend.—
                    [Exit Barber.]
Come, squire and dwarf; the sun grows
towards his set,   170
And we have many more adventures
yet.   *Exeunt.*

CIT. Now Rafe is in this humor I know
he would ha' beaten all the boys in the
house, if they had been set on him.

WIFE. Ay, George, but it is well as it
is. I warrant you, the gentlemen do consider what it is to overthrow a giant. But
look, George; here comes Mistress Merrythought and her son Michael.—Now you

are welcome, Mistress Merrythought;   [180
now Rafe has done, you may go on.

[SCENA QUINTA.

Before Merrythought's house.]

Enter Mistress Merrythought and Michael.

MIST. MER. Mick, my boy—

MICH. Ay, forsooth, mother.

MIST. MER. Be merry, Mick; we are
at home now, where, I warrant you, you
shall find the house flung out at the windows. *[Music within.]* Hark! Hey, dogs,
hey! This is the old world,[1] i' faith, with
my husband. If I get in among 'em, I'll
play 'em such a lesson that they shall
have little list to come scraping hither   [10
again.—Why, Master Merrythought! Husband! Charles Merrythought!

OLD MER. *(Within.)*

If you will sing, and dance, and laugh,
   And hollo, and laugh again,
And then cry, "There, boys, there!" why,
      then,
   One, two, three, and four,
We shall be merry within this hour.

MIST. MER. Why, Charles, do you not
know your own natural wife? I say, open
the door, and turn me out those mangy   [20
companions; 'tis more than time that they
were fellow and fellowlike with you. You
are a gentleman, Charles, and an old man,
and father of two children; and I myself
(though I say it) by my mother's side
niece to a worshipful gentleman and a
conductor;[2] ha[3] has been three times
in his majesty's service at Chester, and
is now the fourth time, God bless him and
his charge, upon his journey.   30

OLD MER. *[Singing.]*

Go from my window, love, go;
   Go from my window, my dear!
The wind and the rain will drive you back
      again;
   You cannot be lodgéd here.

Hark you, Mistress Merrythought, you
that walk upon adventures, and forsake
your husband, because he sings with never

---
[1] Way.
[2] Military leader.   [3] He.

a penny in his purse, what shall I think myself the worse? Faith, no; I'll be merry.

You come not here; here's none but [40 lads of mettle, lives of a hundred years and upwards; care never drunk their bloods, nor want made 'em warble, "Heigh-ho, my heart is heavy."

MIST. MER. Why, Mr.[1] Merrythought, what am I that you should laugh me to scorn thus abruptly? Am I not your fellow-feeler, as we may say, in all our miseries? Your comforter in health and sickness? Have I not brought you [50 children? Are they not like you, Charles? Look upon thine own image, hard-hearted man! And yet for all this—

OLD MER. (*Within.*)

> Begone, begone, my juggy,[2] my puggy, [3]
> Begone, my love, my dear!
> The weather is warm, 'twill do thee no harm;
> Thou canst not be lodgéd here.—

Be merry, boys! Some light music, and more wine!

WIFE. He's not in earnest, I hope, [60 George, is he?

CIT. What if he be, sweetheart?

WIFE. Marry, if he be, George, I'll make bold to tell him he's an ingrant [4] old man to use his bedfellow so scurvily.

CIT. What! How does he use her, honey?

WIFE. Marry, come up, Sir Saucebox! I think you'll take his part, will you not? Lord, how hot you are grown! You [70 are a fine man, an you had a fine dog; [5] it becomes you sweetly!

CIT. Nay, prithee, Nell, chide not, for, as I am an honest man and a true Christian grocer, I do not like his doings.

WIFE. I cry you mercy, then, George! You know we are all frail and full of infirmities.—D'e hear, Mr. Merrythought? May I crave a word with you?

OLD MER. (*Within.*) Strike up [80 lively, lads!

---

[1] Master.
[2] Diminutive of Joan.
[3] Term of endearment.
[4] Wife's confusion of *ignorant* and *ingrate*.
[5] A mark of gentility.

WIFE. I had not thought, in truth, Mr. Merrythought, that a man of your age and discretion (as I may say), being a gentleman, and therefore known by your gentle conditions,[6] could have used so little respect to the weakness of his wife, for your wife is your own flesh, the staff of your age, your yokefellow, with whose help you draw through the mire of [90 this transitory world; nay, she's your own rib! And again—

OLD MER. [*Singing.*]

> I come not hither for thee to teach;
> I have no pulpit for thee to preach;
> I would thou hadst kissed me under the breech,
> As thou art a lady gay.

WIFE. Marry, with a vengeance! I am heartily sorry for the poor gentlewoman, but, if I were thy wife, i' faith, graybeard, i' faith— 100

CIT. I prithee, sweet honeysuckle, be content.

WIFE. Give me such words, that am a gentlewoman born! Hang him, hoary rascal! Get me some drink, George; I am almost molten with fretting. Now, beshrew his knave's heart for it!

[*Exit Citizen.*]

OLD MER. Play me a light lavalto.[7] Come, be frolic. Fill the good fellows wine. 110

MIST. MER. Why, Mr. Merrythought, are you disposed to make me wait here? You'll open, I hope; I'll fetch them that shall open else.

OLD MER. Good woman, if you will sing, I'll give you something; if not—

SONG

> You are no love for me, Margret;
> I am no love for you.—

Come aloft,[8] boys, aloft!

MIST. MER. Now a churl's fart in [120 your teeth, sir!—Come, Mick, we'll not trouble him; a shall not ding us i' th' teeth

---

[6] Qualities.
[7] Lavolta, a lively dance.
[8] Be merry.

with his bread and his broth, that he shall
not. Come, boy; I'll provide for thee, I
warrant thee. We'll go to Master Venter-
well's, the merchant; I'll get his letter to
mine host of the Bell in Waltham; there
I'll place thee with the tapster. Will not
that do well for thee, Mick? And let me
alone for that old cuckoldly knave   [130
your father; I'll use him in his kind,[1] I warrant ye.   [*Exeunt.*

Enter Citizen with beer.]

WIFE. Come, George, where's the beer?
CIT. Here, love.
WIFE. This old fornicating fellow will
not out of my mind yet.—Gentlemen, I'll
begin to you all; and I desire more of your
acquaintance with all my heart.—[*Drinks.*]
Fill the gentlemen some beer, George.

FINIS ACTUS TERTII.

Music.

ACTUS QUARTUS. SCENA PRIMA.

[*A street.*]
Boy danceth.

WIFE. Look, George, the little boy 's
come again; methinks he looks something
like the Prince of Orange in his long stocking, if he had a little harness[2] about his
neck. George, I will have him dance "Fading."—"Fading" is a fine jig, I'll assure
you, gentlemen.—Begin, brother.—Now a
capers, sweetheart!—Now a turn a th'
toe, and then tumble! Cannot you tumble,
youth?   10
BOY. No, indeed, forsooth.
WIFE. Nor eat fire?
BOY. Neither.
WIFE. Why, then, I thank you heartily;
there's twopence to buy you points[3] withal.
                                   [*Exit Boy.*]

Enter Jasper and Boy.

JASP. There, boy, deliver this. [*Gives a
letter.*] But do it well.
Hast thou provided me four lusty fellows,
Able to carry me? And art thou perfect
In all thy business?

[1] According to his own nature.
[2] Armor.
[3] Laces for fastening clothes.

BOY.   Sir, you need not fear;   19
I have my lesson here, and cannot miss it.
The men are ready for you and what else
Pertains to this employment.
JASP.   There, my boy. [*Gives money.*]
Take it, but buy no land.
BOY.   Faith, sir, 'twere rare
To see so young a purchaser. I fly,
And on my wings carry your destiny.
                                         Exit.
JASP. Go and be happy!—Now, my latest
     hope,
Forsake me not, but fling thy anchor
     out,
And let it hold! Stand fixed, thou roll-
     ing stone,   28
Till I enjoy my dearest! Hear me, all
You powers, that rule in men, celestial!
                                         Exit.

WIFE. Go thy ways; thou art as crooked
a sprig as ever grew in London. I warrant
him, he'll come to some naughty end or
other, for his looks say no less. Besides,
his father (you know, George) is none of
the best; you heard him take me up like
a flirt-gill,[4] and sing bawdy songs upon
me; but, i' faith, if I live, George—
CIT. Let me alone, sweetheart; I have a
trick in my head shall lodge him in the   [40
Arches[5] for one year, and make him sing
peccavi[6] ere I leave him; and yet he shall
never know who hurt him neither.
WIFE. Do, my good George, do!
CIT. What shall we have Rafe do now,
boy?
BOY. You shall have what you will, sir.
CIT. Why, so, sir, go and fetch me him
then, and let the Sophy of Persia come and
christen him a child.[7]   50
BOY. Believe me, sir, that will not do
so well; 'tis stale; it has been had before
at the Red Bull.[8]
WIFE. George, let Rafe travel over
great hills, and let him be very weary, and
come to the King of Cracovia's house,
covered with velvet; and there let the
king's daughter stand in her window, all
in beaten gold, combing her golden locks

[4] Loose woman.   [5] A prison.   [6] I have sinned.
[7] *I. e.*, a member of his nation. (The passage al-
ludes to *The Travels of the Three English Brothers*,
a play by Day, Rowley, and Wilkins.)
[8] A rival theater.

with a comb of ivory; and let her spy [60
Rafe, and fall in love with him, and come
down to him, and carry him into her
father's house; and then let Rafe talk
with her.

CIT. Well said, Nell; it shall be so.—
Boy, let's ha't done quickly.

BOY. Sir, if you will imagine all this
to be done already, you shall hear them
talk together; but we cannot present a
house covered with black velvet, and [70
a lady in beaten gold.

CIT. Sir Boy, let's ha't as you can, then.

BOY. Besides, it will show ill-favoredly
to have a grocer's prentice to court a
king's daughter.

CIT. Will it so, sir? You are well read
in histories![1] I pray you, what was Sir
Dagonet? Was not he prentice to a grocer
in London? Read the play of *The Four
Prentices of London*,[2] where they toss [80
their pikes so. I pray you, fetch him in, sir,
fetch him in.

BOY. It shall be done.—[*To audience.*]
It is not our fault, gentlemen.   *Exit.*

WIFE. Now we shall see fine doings, I
warrant tee, George. O, here they come;
how prettily the King of Cracovia's
daughter is dressed!

[SCENA SECUNDA.

A hall in the palace of the King of Moldavia.]

Enter Rafe and the Lady, Squire, and Dwarf.

CIT. Ay, Nell, it is the fashion of that
country, I warrant tee.

LADY. Welcome, Sir Knight, unto my
       father's court,
King of Moldavia, unto me, Pompiona,
His daughter dear! But, sure, you do
       not like
Your entertainment, that will stay with
       us
No longer but a night.
RAFE.   Damsel right fair,
I am on many sad adventures bound,
That call me forth into the wilderness;
Besides, my horse's back is something
       galled,   10
Which will enforce me ride a sober pace.
But many thanks, fair lady, be to you

For using errant knight with courtesy!
LADY. But say, brave knight, what is your
       name and birth?
RAFE. My name is Rafe; I am an
       Englishman,
As true as steel, a hearty Englishman,
And prentice to a grocer in the Strond[3]
By deed indent,[4] of which I have one
       part;
But, Fortune calling me to follow arms,
On me this holy order I did take   20
Of Burning Pestle, which in all men's
       eyes
I bear, confounding ladies' enemies.
LADY. Oft have I heard of your brave
       countrymen,
And fertile soil, and store of wholesome
       food;
My father oft will tell me of a drink
In England found, and nippitato[5] called,
Which driveth all the sorrow from your
       hearts.
RAFE. Lady, 'tis true; you need not lay
       your lips
To better nippitato than there is.
LADY. And of a wild fowl he will often
       speak,   30
Which   poudered[6]-beef-and-mustard
       calléd is;
For there have been great wars twixt us
       and you.
But truly, Rafe, it was not long[7] of me.
Tell me then, Rafe, could you contented
       be
To wear lady's favor in your shield?
RAFE. I am a knight of religious order,
And will not wear a favor of a lady's
That   trusts   in   Antichrist   and   false
       traditions.

CIT. Well said, Rafe! Convert her, if
thou canst.   40

RAFE. Besides, I have a lady of my own
In merry England, for whose virtuous
       sake
I took these arms; and Susan is her name,
A cobbler's maid in Milk Street, whom I
       vow
Ne'er to forsake whilst life and pestle last.
LADY. Happy that cobbling dame, whoe'er
       she be,

---

[1] Fiction.   [2] By Thomas Heywood.

[3] Strand.   [6] Salted.
[4] Indenture.   [7] Because.
[5] Strong liquor.

That for her own, dear Rafe, hath got-
    ten thee!
Unhappy I, that ne'er shall see the day
To see thee more, that bear'st my heart
    away!
RAFE. Lady, farewell; I needs must take
    my leave.   50
LADY. Hard-hearted Rafe, that ladies dost
    deceive!

CIT. Hark thee, Rafe; there's money
for thee. [*Gives money.*] Give something
in the King of Cracovia's house; be not
beholding to him.

RAFE. Lady, before I go, I must remember
Your father's officers, who, truth to tell,
Have been about me very diligent.
Hold up thy snowy hand, thou princely
    maid!
There's twelvepence for your father's
    chamberlain;   60
And another shilling for his cook,
For, by my troth, the goose was roasted
    well;
And twelvepence for your father's
    horse keeper,
For nointing my horse' back, and for
    his butter [1]
There is another shilling; to the maid
That washed my boothose [2] there's an
    English groat,
And twopence to the boy that wiped my
    boots;
And last, fair lady, there is for yourself
Threepence to buy you pins at Bumbo
    Fair.
LADY. Full many thanks; and I will keep
    them safe   70
Till all the heads be off, for thy sake,
    Rafe.
RAFE. Advance, my squire and dwarf! I
    cannot stay.
LADY. Thou kill'st my heart in parting
    thus away.   *Exeunt.*

WIFE. I commend Rafe yet, that he
will not stoop to a Cracovian; there's
properer [3] women in London than any are
there, iwis. But here comes Master Humphrey and his love again now, George.
CIT. Ay, cony; peace.

[1] Used to rub the horse's back.
[2] Leggings.   [3] Handsomer.

[SCENA TERTIA.

A room in Venturewell's house.]

*Enter Merchant, Humphrey, Luce, and a
                    Boy.*

MERCH. Go, get you up; [4] I will not be
    entreated;
And, gossip [5] mine, I'll keep you sure
    hereafter
From gadding out again with boys and
    unthrifts.[6]
Come, they are women's tears; I know
    your fashion.—
Go, sirrah, lock her in, and keep the key
Safe as you love your life.—
            Exeunt [7] Luce and Boy.
          Now, my son Humphrey,
You may both rest assuréd of my love
In this, and reap your own desire.
HUM. I see this love you speak of, through
    your daughter,
Although the hole be little, and here-
    after   10
Will yield the like in all I may or can,
Fitting a Christian and a gentleman.
MERCH. I do believe you, my good son,
    and thank you,
For 'twere an impudence to think you
    flattered.
HUM. It were, indeed; but shall I tell you
    why?
I have been beaten twice about the
    lie.
MERCH. Well, son, no more of compliment.
    My daughter
Is yours again; appoint the time and
    take her.
We'll have no stealing for it; I myself
And some few of our friends will see
    you married.   20
HUM. I would you would, i' faith, for, be
    it known,
I ever was afraid to lie alone.
MERCH. Some three days hence, then.
HUM.   Three days! Let me see;
'Tis somewhat of the most; [8] yet I
    agree,
Because I mean against [9] the appointed
    day
To visit all my friends in new array.

[4] Upstairs.   [7] Original reads *Exit.*
[5] Relative.   [8] Rather long.
[6] Prodigals.   [9] In preparation for.

Enter Servant.

SER. Sir, there's a gentlewoman without would speak with your worship.

MERCH. What is she?

SER. Sir, I asked her not.   30

MERCH. Bid her come in. [*Exit Servant.*]

Enter Mistress Merrythought and Michael.

MIST. MER. Peace be to your worship! I come as a poor suitor to you, sir, in the behalf of this child.

MERCH. Are you not wife to Merrythought?

MIST. MER. Yes, truly. Would I had ne'er seen his eyes! Ha has undone me and himself and his children; and there he lives at home, and sings and hoits [40 and revels among his drunken companions! But, I warrant you, where to get a penny to put bread in his mouth he knows not; and therefore, if it like your worship, I would entreat your letter to the honest host of the Bell in Waltham that I may place my child under the protection of his tapster, in some settled course of life.

MERCH. I'm glad the heavens have heard my prayers. Thy husband,
  When I was ripe in sorrows, laughed at me;   50
  Thy son, like an unthankful wretch, I having
  Redeemed him from his fall, and made him mine,
  To show his love again first stole my daughter,
  Then wronged this gentleman, and, last of all,
  Gave me that grief had almost brought me down
  Unto my grave, had not a stronger hand
  Relieved my sorrows. Go, and weep as I did,
  And be unpitied, for I here profess
  An everlasting hate to all thy name.

MIST. MER. Will you so, sir? How [60 say you by that? —Come, Mick; let him keep his wind to cool his porridge. We'll go to thy nurse's, Mick; she knits silk stockings, boy; and we'll knit too, boy, and be beholding to none of them all.

Exeunt Michael and Mother.

Enter a Boy with a letter.

BOY. Sir, I take it you are the master of this house.

MERCH. How then, boy?

BOY. Then to yourself, sir, comes this letter.   70

MERCH. From whom, my pretty boy?

BOY. From him that was your servant; but no more
  Shall that name ever be, for he is dead.
  Grief of your purchased [1] anger broke his heart.
  I saw him die, and from his hand received
  This paper, with a charge to bring it hither.
  Read it, and satisfy yourself in all.

LETTER

MERCH. "Sir, that I have wronged your love I must confess, in which I have purchased to myself, besides mine [80 own undoing, the ill opinion of my friends. Let not your anger, good sir, outlive me, but suffer me to rest in peace with your forgiveness. Let my body (if a dying man may so much prevail with you) be brought to your daughter, that she may truly know my hot flames are now buried, and withal receive a testimony of the zeal I bore her virtue. Farewell forever, and be ever happy!   JASPER."

God's hand is great in this. I do forgive him;   91
  Yet I am glad he's quiet, where I hope
  He will not bite again.—Boy, bring the body,
  And let him have his will, if that be all.

BOY. 'Tis here without, sir.

MERCH.   So, sir; if you please,
  You may conduct it in; I do not fear it.

HUM. I'll be your usher, boy, for, though I say it,
  He owed me something once, and well did pay it.   *Exeunt.*

Enter Luce, alone.

LUCE. If there be any punishment inflicted
  Upon the miserable more than yet I feel,   100

[1] Acquired.

Let it together seize me, and at once
Press down my soul! I cannot bear the
    pain
Of these delaying tortures.—Thou that
    art
The end of all, and the sweet rest of all,
Come, come, O Death! Bring me to
    thy peace,
And blot out all the memory I nourish
Both of my father and my cruel friend!—
O, wretched maid, still living to be
    wretched,
To be a say [1] to Fortune in her changes,
And grow to number times and woes
    together.   110
How happy had I been, if, being born,
My grave had been my cradle!

Enter Servant.

SER.   By your leave,
    Young mistress, here's a boy hath
    brought a coffin.
What a would say, I know not; but your
    father
Charged me to give you notice. Here
    they come.   [*Exit.*]

Enter Two bearing a coffin, Jasper in it.

LUCE. For me I hope 'tis come, and 'tis
    most welcome.
BOY. Fair mistress, let me not add greater
    grief
To that great store you have already.
    Jasper
(That whilst he lived was yours, now dead
And here enclosed) commanded me to
    bring   120
His body hither, and to crave a tear
From those fair eyes (though he deserved
    not pity)
To deck his funeral, for so he bid me
Tell her for whom he died.
LUCE.   He shall have many.—
    Good friends, depart a little, whilst I
    take
My leave of this dead man that once I
    loved. *Exeunt Coffin Carrier and Boy.*
Hold yet a little, life, and then I give thee
To thy first heavenly being. O, my
    friend!
Hast thou deceived me thus, and got
    before me?

[1] Subject for experiment.

I shall not long be after. But, believe
    me,   130
Thou wert too cruel, Jasper, gainst
    thyself,
In punishing the fault I could have par-
    doned,
With so untimely death. Thou didst
    not wrong me,
But ever wert most kind, most true,
    most loving,
And I the most unkind, most false, most
    cruel!
Didst thou but ask a tear? I'll give thee
    all,
Even all my eyes can pour down, all my
    sighs,
And all myself. Before thou goest from
    me
There are but sparing rites; but, if thy
    soul   139
Be yet about this place, and can behold
And see what I prepare to deck thee
    with,
It shall go up, borne on the wings of
    peace,
And satisfied. First will I sing thy dirge,
Then kiss thy pale lips, and then die
    myself,
And fill one coffin and one grave to-
    gether.

SONG

Come, you whose loves are dead,
    And, whiles I sing,
      Weep and wring
Every hand, and every head
Bind with cypress and sad yew;   150
Ribands black and candles blue
For him that was of men most true!

Come with heavy mourning, [2]
    And on his grave
      Let him have
Sacrifice of sighs and groaning;
Let him have fair flowers enow,
White and purple, green and yellow,
For him that was of men most true!

Thou sable cloth, sad cover of my joys,
I lift thee up, and thus I meet with
    death.   161
[*Removes the cloth, and Jasper rises out of
            the coffin.*]
JASP. And thus you meet the living!
LUCE.   Save me, heaven!

[2] Moaning(?).

JASP. Nay, do not fly me, fair; I am no
　　spirit.
　　Look better on me; do you know me yet?
LUCE. O, thou dear shadow of my friend!
JASP. 　　　　　　　　Dear substance,
　　I swear I am no shadow. Feel my hand;
　　It is the same it was. I am your Jasper,
　　Your Jasper that's yet living, and yet
　　　loving.
　　Pardon my rash attempt, my foolish
　　　proof 　　　　　　　　　　　169
　　I put in practice of your constancy,
　　For sooner should my sword have drunk
　　　my blood,
　　And set my soul at liberty than drawn
　　The least drop from that body, for
　　　which boldness
　　Doom me to anything; if death, I take it,
　　And willingly.
LUCE. 　　This death I'll give you for it.
　　　　　　　　　　　　　[*Kisses him.*]
　　So, now I am satisfied you are no spirit,
　　But my own truest, truest, truest friend.
　　Why do you come thus to me?
JASP. 　　　　　　　　First, to see you;
　　Then to convey you hence.
LUCE. 　　　　　　　　It cannot be;
　　For I am locked up here, and watched
　　　at all hours, 　　　　　　　　180
　　That 'tis impossible for me to scape.
JASP. Nothing more possible. Within
　　this coffin
　　Do you convey yourself. Let me alone;
　　I have the wits of twenty men about me;
　　Only I crave the shelter of your closet [1]
　　A little, and then fear me [2] not. Creep
　　　in,
　　That they may presently convey you
　　　hence.
　　Fear nothing, dearest love; I'll be your
　　　second.
[*Luce places herself in the coffin and Jasper
　　　puts the cloth over her.*]
　　Lie close. So; all goes well yet.—Boy!

　　　　[*Enter Coffin Carrier and Boy.*]

BOY. 　　　　　　　　At hand, sir.
JASP. Convey away the coffin, and be wary.
BOY. 'Tis done already.
[*Exeunt Coffin Carrier and Boy with the
　　　　　　　　　　　　coffin.*]
JASP. 　　　Now must I go conjure. 191
　　　　　　　　　　　　　　Exit.

[1] Private room. 　　　　[2] *I.e.,* for me.

　　　　　　Enter Merchant.

MERCH. Boy, boy!

　　　　　　[*Enter Boy.*]

BOY. Your servant, sir.
MERCH. Do me this kindness, boy.
Hold, here's a crown. Before thou bury
the body of this fellow, carry it to his
old merry father, and salute him from me,
and bid him sing; he hath cause.
BOY. I will, sir. 　　　　　　　192
MERCH. And then bring me word what
tune he is in, and have another crown; but
do it truly. I have fitted him a bargain now
will vex him.
BOY. God bless your worship's health,
sir!
MERCH. Farewell, boy. 　　　*Exeunt.*

　　　　[SCENA QUARTA.

　　Before Merrythought's house.]

　　Enter Master Merrythought.

WIFE. Ah, old Merrythought, art thou
there again? Let's hear some of thy songs.
OLD MER. [*Singing.*]

　　Who can sing a merrier note
　　Than he that cannot change a groat?

Not a denier [3] left, and yet my heart leaps!
I do wonder yet, as old as I am, that any
man will follow a trade, or serve, that may
sing and laugh, and walk the streets. My
wife and both my sons are I know not
where; I have nothing left, nor know I　[10
how to come by meat to supper; yet am
I merry still, for I know I shall find it upon
the table at six a-clock; therefore, hang
thought! 　　　　　　　　　[*Sings.*]

　　I would not be a serving-man
　　　To carry the cloak bag still,
　　Nor would I be a falconer
　　　The greedy hawks to fill;
　　But I would be in a good house,
　　　And have a good master too; 　　20
　　But I would eat and drink of the best,
　　　And no work would I do.

This is it that keeps life and soul together—
mirth; this is the philosophers' stone that
they write so much on, that keeps a man
ever young.

[3] Penny.

Enter a Boy.

BOY. Sir, they say they know all your money is gone, and they will trust you for no more drink.

OLD MER. Will they not? Let [30 am [1] choose! The best is, I have mirth at home, and need not send abroad for that. Let them keep their drink to themselves. [*Sings.*]

For Jillian of Berry, she dwells on a hill,
And she hath good beer and ale to sell,
And of good fellows she thinks no ill;
　And thither will we go now, now, now, now,
　And thither will we go now.

And, when you have made a little stay,
You need not ask what is to pay, 40
But kiss your hostess, and go your way;
　And thither, etc.

Enter another Boy.

2 BOY. Sir, I can get no bread for supper.

OLD MER. Hang bread and supper! Let's preserve our mirth, and we shall never feel hunger, I'll warrant you. Let's have a catch. Boy, follow me; come, sing this catch.

　Ho, ho, nobody at home! 50
Meat, nor drink, nor money ha' we none.
　Fill the pot, Eedy,
　Never more need I.

OLD MER. So, boys, enough. Follow me. Let's change our place, and we shall laugh afresh. *Exeunt.*

WIFE. Let him go, George; a shall not have any countenance from us, nor a good word from any i' th' company, if I may strike stroke in 't.[2] 60

CIT. No more a sha' not, love. But, Nell, I will have Rafe do a very notable matter now, to the eternal honor and glory of all grocers.—Sirrah! You there, boy! Can none of you hear?

[*Enter Boy.*]

BOY. Sir, your pleasure?

CIT. Let Rafe come out on May Day in the morning, and speak upon a conduit, with all his scarfs about him, and his feathers, and his rings, and his knacks. 70

[1] 'Em. [2] *I.e.,* have anything to do with it.

BOY. Why, sir, you do not think of our plot; what will become of that, then?

CIT. Why, sir, I care not what become on 't. I'll have him come out, or I'll fetch him out myself; I'll have something done in honor of the city. Besides, he hath been long enough upon adventures. Bring him out quickly; or, if I come in amongst you—

BOY. Well, sir, he shall come out, but if our play miscarry, sir, you are like [80 to pay for 't. *Exit Boy.*

CIT. Bring him away then!

WIFE. This will be brave, i' faith! George, shall not he dance the morris too, for the credit of the Strand?

CIT. No, sweetheart, it will be too much for the boy. O, there he is, Nell! He's reasonable well in reparel; but he has not rings enough.

Enter Rafe [dressed as the Lord of the May].

RAFE. London, to thee I do present the merry month of May; 90
Let each true subject be content to hear me what I say.
For from the top of conduit head, as plainly may appear,
I will both tell my name to you, and wherefore I came here.
My name is Rafe, by due descent though not ignoble I,
Yet far inferior to the flock of gracious grocery;[3]
And by the common counsel of my fellows in the Strand,
With gilded staff and crosséd scarf, the May Lord here I stand.
Rejoice, O English hearts, rejoice! Rejoice, O lovers dear!
Rejoice, O city, town, and country! Rejoice, eke every shire!
For now the fragrant flowers do spring and sprout in seemly sort, 100
The little birds do sit and sing, the lambs do make fine sport;
And now the birchen tree doth bud, that makes the schoolboy cry;
The morris rings, while hobbyhorse doth foot it featously;[4]
The lords and ladies now abroad, for their disport and play,

[3] A parody of part of the Ghost's opening speech in *The Spanish Tragedy.*
[4] Neatly, expertly.

Do kiss sometimes upon the grass, and
    sometimes in the hay;
Now butter with a leaf of sage is good
    to purge the blood;
Fly Venus and phlebotomy, for they
    are neither good;
Now little fish on tender stone begin
    to cast their bellies,[1]
And sluggish snails, that erst were mute,[2]
    do creep out of their shellës;
The rumbling rivers now do warm, for
    little boys to paddle;   110
The sturdy steed now goes to grass,
    and up they hang his saddle;
The heavy hart, the bellowing buck,
    the rascal,[3] and the pricket [4]
Are now among the yeoman's peas,
    and leave the fearful thicket.
And be like them, O you, I say, of this
    same noble town,
And lift aloft your velvet heads, and,
    slipping off your gown,
With bells on legs, and napkins [5] clean
    unto your shoulders tied,
With scarfs and garters as you please,
    and "Hey for our town!" cried,
March out, and show your willing minds,
    by twenty and by twenty,
To Hogsdon or to Newington, where ale
    and cakes are plenty;
And let it ne'er be said for shame that
    we, the youths of London,   120
Lay thrumming of [6] our caps at home,
    and left our custom undone.
Up, then, I say, both young and old,
    both man and maid a-maying,
With drums and guns that bounce [7]
    aloud, and merry tabor playing!
Which to prolong, God save our king,
    and send his country peace,
And root out treason from the land!
And so, my friends, I cease. [*Exit.*]

FINIS ACTUS QUARTI.

ACTUS QUINTUS. SCENA PRIMA.

[*A room in Venturewell's house.*]

Enter Merchant, solus.[8]

MERCH. I will have no great store of
company at the wedding—a couple of neigh-

bors and their wives; and we will have a
capon in stewed broth, with marrow, and
a good piece of beef stuck with rosemary.

Enter Jasper, his face mealed.[9]

JASP. Forbear thy pains, fond man! It
    is too late.
MERCH. Heaven bless me! Jasper?
JASP.   Ay, I am his ghost,
    Whom thou hast injured for his con-
        stant love,
Fond worldly wretch, who dost not
    understand
In death that true hearts cannot parted
    be!   10
First, know thy daughter is quite borne
    away
On wings of angels, through the liquid
    air,
To far out of thy reach, and never more
Shalt thou behold her face; but she
    and I
Will in another world enjoy our loves,
Where neither father's anger, poverty,
Nor any cross that troubles earthly
    men
Shall make us sever our united hearts.
And never shalt thou sit or be alone
In any place, but I will visit thee   20
With ghastly looks, and put into thy
    mind
The great offenses which thou didst to
    me.
When thou art at thy table with thy
    friends,
Merry in heart, and filled with swelling
    wine,
I'll come in midst of all thy pride and
    mirth,
Invisible to all men but thyself,
And whisper such a sad tale in thine
    ear
Shall make thee let the cup fall from
    thy hand,
And stand as mute and pale as Death
    itself.
MERCH. Forgive me, Jasper! O, what
    might I do,   30
Tell me, to satisfy thy troubled ghost?
JASP. There is no means; too late thou
    think'st of this.
MERCH. But tell me what were best for
    me to do?

---

[1] Spawn.
[2] Mewed (?).
[3] A lean young deer.
[4] A yearling buck.
[5] Handkerchiefs.
[6] Setting tufts on.
[7] Boom, bang.
[8] Alone.
[9] Whitened with flour.

Jasp. Repent thy deed, and satisfy my
    father,
And beat fond Humphrey out of thy
    doors.   *Exit Jasper.*

Enter Humphrey.

Wife. Look, George; his very ghost
would have folks beaten.

Hum. Father, my bride is gone, fair Mis-
    tress Luce;
    My soul's the fount of vengeance, mis-
    chief's sluice.
Merch. Hence, fool, out of my sight;
    with thy fond passion   40
    Thou hast undone me.   [*Beats him.*]
Hum.   Hold, my father dear,
    For Luce thy daughter's sake, that had
    no peer!
Merch. Thy father, fool? There's some
    blows more; begone.—   [*Beats him.*]
    Jasper, I hope thy ghost be well appeased
    To see thy will performed. Now will
    I go
    To satisfy thy father for thy wrongs.
                                  Exit.
Hum. What shall I do? I have been beaten
    twice,
    And Mistress Luce is gone. Help me,
    device!
    Since my true love is gone, I never more,
    Whilst I do live, upon the sky will pore,
    But in the dark will wear out my shoe
    soles   51
    In passion in Saint Faith's Church under
    Paul's.[1]   *Exit.*

Wife. George, call Rafe hither; if you
love me, call Rafe hither. I have the
bravest[2] thing for him to do, George;
prithee, call him quickly.
Cit. Rafe! Why, Rafe, boy!

Enter Rafe.

Rafe. Here, sir.
Cit. Come hither, Rafe; come to thy
mistress, boy.   60
Wife. Rafe, I would have thee call
all the youths together in battle ray,[3] with
drums, and guns, and flags, and march
to Mile End in pompous fashion, and

there exhort your soldiers to be merry and
wise, and to keep their beards from burning, Rafe; and then skirmish, and let your
flags fly, and cry, "Kill, kill, kill!" My
husband shall lend you his jerkin, Rafe,
and there's a scarf; for the rest, the [70
house shall furnish you, and we'll pay
for 't. Do it bravely, Rafe; and think before whom you perform, and what person
you represent.
Rafe. I warrant you, mistress; if I do
it not for the honor of the city and the
credit of my master, let me never hope for
freedom![4]
Wife. 'Tis well spoken, i' faith. Go
thy ways; thou art a spark indeed.   80
Cit. Rafe, Rafe, double your files
bravely, Rafe!
Rafe. I warrant you, sir.   *Exit Rafe.*
Cit. Let him look narrowly to his service;[5] I shall take him else. I was there myself a pikeman once, in the hottest of the
day, wench, had my feather shot sheer
away, the fringe of my pike burnt off with
powder, my pate broken with a scouring
stick,[6] and yet, I thank God, I am here.   90
                              Drum within.
Wife. Hark, George, the drums!
Cit. Ran, tan, tan, tan; ran, tan! O,
wench, an thou hadst but seen little Ned
of Algate, Drum[7] Ned, how he made it
roar again, and laid on like a tyrant, and
then stroke softly till the ward[8] came up,
and then thundered again, and together
we go! "Sa, sa, sa, bounce!" quoth the
guns; "Courage, my hearts!" quoth the
captains; "Saint George!" quoth the [100
pikemen; and withal, here they lay, and
there they lay. And yet for all this I am
here, wench.
Wife. Be thankful for it, George, for
indeed 'tis wonderful.

[Scena Secunda.

A street in London.]

*Enter Rafe and his Company with drums
                              and colors.*

Rafe. March fair, my hearts! Lieutenant, beat the rear up.—Ancient,[9] let
your colors fly; but have a great care of

---

[1] Near St. Paul's Cathedral.
[2] Finest.   [3] Array.
[4] *I.e.*, full membership in his company.
[5] Equipment.
[6] Ramrod.   [8] Guard.
[7] Drummer.   [9] Standard bearer.

the butchers' hooks at Whitechapel; they have been the death of many a fair ancient.[1]—Open your files that I may take a view both of your persons and munition.—Sergeant, call a muster.

SERG. A stand![2]—William Hammerton, pewterer? 10

HAM. Here, captain.

RAFE. A corselet and a Spanish pike; 'tis well. Can you shake it with a terror?

HAM. I hope so, captain.

RAFE. Charge upon me. [*He charges on Rafe.*] 'Tis with the weakest; put more strength, William Hammerton, more strength. As you were, again!—Proceed, sergeant. 19

SERG. George Greengoose, poulterer?

GREEN. Here.

RAFE. Let me see your piece, Neighbor Greengoose. When was she shot in?

GREEN. And 't[3] like you, Master Captain, I made a shot even now, partly to scour her, and partly for audacity.

RAFE. It should seem so certainly, for her breath is yet inflamed; besides, there is a main[4] fault in the touchhole—it runs and stinketh; and I tell you, moreover, [30 and believe it, ten such touchholes would breed the pox in the army. Get you a feather,[5] neighbor, get you a feather, sweet oil, and paper, and your piece may do well enough yet. Where's your powder?

GREEN. Here.

RAFE. What, in a paper? As I am a soldier and a gentleman, it craves a martial court! You ought to die for 't. Where's your horn? Answer me to that. 40

GREEN. An 't like you, sir, I was oblivious.

RAFE. It likes me not you should be so; 'tis a shame for you, and a scandal to all our neighbors, being a man of worth and estimation, to leave your horn behind you; I am afraid 'twill breed example. But let me tell you no more on 't.—Stand, till I view you all. What's become o' th' nose of your flask? 50

1 SOLD. Indeed-law, captain, 'twas blown away with powder.

RAFE. Put on a new one at the city's charge.—Where's the stone of this piece?

2 SOLD. The drummer took it out to light tobacco.

RAFE. 'Tis a fault, my friend; put it in again.—You want a nose, and you a stone.—Sergeant, take a note on 't, for I mean to stop it in the pay.—Remove, [60 and march! [*They march.*] Soft and fair, gentlemen, soft and fair! Double your files! As you were! Faces about! Now, you with the sodden face, keep in there! Look to your match, sirrah; it will be in your fellow's flask anon! So; make a crescent now! Advance your pikes! Stand and give ear!—Gentlemen, countrymen, friends, and my fellow soldiers, I have brought you this day from the shops [70 of security and the counters of content to measure out in these furious fields honor by the ell and prowess by the pound. Let it not, O, let it not, I say, be told hereafter, the noble issue of this city fainted; but bear yourselves in this fair action like men, valiant men, and free men! Fear not the face of the enemy, nor the noise of the guns, for, believe me, brethren, the rude rumbling of a brewer's car is far [80 more terrible, of which you have a daily experience; neither let the stink of powder offend you, since a more valiant stink is nightly with you. To a resolved mind his home is everywhere. I speak not this to take away the hope of your return, for you shall see (I do not doubt it), and that very shortly, your loving wives again and your sweet children, whose care doth bear you company in baskets.[6] Remember, [90 then, whose cause you have in hand, and, like a sort[7] of true-born scavengers, scour me this famous realm of enemies. I have no more to say but this: stand to your tacklings,[8] lads, and show to the world you can as well brandish a sword as shake an apron. Saint George, and on, my hearts!

OMNES. St. George, St. George!

Exeunt.

WIFE. 'Twas well done, Rafe! I'll [100 send thee a cold capon afield and a bottle

---

[1] Flag.
[2] Halt!
[3] If it. Emended by Dyce. Original reads *And.*
[4] Serious.
[5] A sharp blade placed in the musket rest.
[6] Lunch baskets(?).
[7] Company.
[8] Tackle, equipment.

of March beer, and, it may be, come myself to see thee.

CIT. Nell, the boy has deceived me
much; I did not think it had been in him.
He has performed such a matter, wench,
that, if I live, next year I'll have him captain of the galley foist [1] or I'll want my will.

[SCENA TERTIA.

A room in Merrythought's house.]

Enter Old Merrythought.

OLD MER. Yet, I thank God, I break
not a wrinkle more than I had, not a stoop,
boys! Care, live with cats; I defy thee!
My heart is as sound as an oak; and, though
I want drink to wet my whistle, I can sing.
[*Sings.*]

Come no more there, boys, come no more
there,
For we shall never whilst we live come any
more there.

*Enter a Boy [and a Coffin Carrier] with a
coffin.*

BOY. God save you, sir!
OLD MER. It's a brave boy. Canst
thou sing? 10
BOY. Yes, sir, I can sing; but 'tis not
so necessary at this time.
OLD MER. [*Singing.*]

Sing we, and chant it,
Whilst love doth grant it.

BOY. Sir, sir, if you knew what I have
brought you, you would have little list
to sing.
OLD MER. [*Singing.*]

O, the Mimon round,
Full long, long I have thee sought,
And now I have thee found, 20
And what hast thou here brought?

BOY. A coffin, sir, and your dead son
Jasper in it. [*Exit with Coffin Carrier.*]
OLD MER. Dead? Why, farewell he!
[*Sings.*]

Thou wast a bonny boy, and I did love thee.

Enter Jasper.

JASP. Then, I pray you, sir, do so still.

[1] Barge used in the Lord Mayors' pageants.

OLD MER. Jasper's ghost? [*Sings.*]

Thou art welcome from Stygian lake so
soon;
Declare to me what wondrous things in
Pluto's court are done.

JASP. By my troth, sir, I ne'er came [30
there; 'tis too hot for me, sir.
OLD MER. A merry ghost, a very merry
ghost! [*Sings.*]

And where is your true love? O, where is
yours?

JASP. Marry, look you, sir!
Heaves up the coffin [, and Luce steps forth].
OLD MER. Ah, ha! Art thou good at
that, i' faith? [*Sings.*]

With hey, trixy, terlery-whiskin,
The world it runs on wheels;
When the young man's ——, 40
Up goes the maiden's heels.

Mistress Merrythought and Michael within.

MIST. MER. What, Mr. Merrythought,
will you not let 's in? What do you think
shall become of us?
OLD MER. [*Singing.*]

What voice is that, that calleth at our door?

MIST. MER. You know me well enough;
I am sure I have not been such a stranger
to you.
OLD MER. [*Singing.*]

And some they whistled, and some they
sung,
"Hey, down, down!" 50
And some did loudly say,
Ever as the Lord Barnet's horn blew,
"Away, Musgrave, away!"

MIST. MER. You will not have us
starve here, will you, Mr. Merrythought?
JASP. Nay, good sir, be persuaded; she
is my mother. If her offenses have been
great against you, let your own love remember she is yours, and so forgive her.
LUCE. Good Mr. Merrythought, let [60
me entreat you; I will not be denied.
MIST. MER. Why, Mr. Merrythought,
will you be a vext [2] thing still?
OLD MER. Woman, I take you to my

[2] Ill-tempered.

love again; but you shall sing before you enter; therefore despatch your song and so come in.

MIST. MER. Well, you must have your will, when all's done.—Mick, what song canst thou sing, boy? 70

MICH. I can sing none, forsooth, but "A lady's daughter of Paris properly."

{ MIST. MER.
{ [MICH.]

SONG

It was a lady's daughter, etc.

[*Merrythought opens the door and Mistress Merrythought and Michael enter.*]

OLD MER. Come, you're welcome home again. [*Sings.*]

    If such danger be in playing,
      And jest must to earnest turn,
    You shall go no more a-maying—

MERCH. (*Within.*) Are you within, sir, Master Merrythought? 80

JASP. It is my master's voice! Good sir, go hold him in talk, whilst we convey ourselves into some inward room.
[*Exit with Luce.*]

OLD MER. What are you? Are you merry? You must be very merry, if you enter.

MERCH. I am, sir.

OLD MER. Sing, then.

MERCH. Nay, good sir, open to me.

OLD MER. Sing, I say, or, by the merry heart, you come not in! 91

MERCH. Well, sir, I'll sing. [*Sings.*]

Fortune, my foe, etc.

[*Merrythought opens the door and Venture-well enters.*]

OLD MER. You are welcome, sir; you are welcome. You see your entertainment; pray you, be merry.

MERCH. O, Mr. Merrythought, I'm come to ask you
Forgiveness for the wrongs I offered you
And your most virtuous son! They're infinite;
Yet my contrition shall be more than they. 100

I do confess my hardness broke his heart,
For which just heaven hath given me punishment
More than my age can carry. His wand'ring spirit,
Not yet at rest, pursues me everywhere,
Crying, "I'll haunt thee for thy cruelty."
My daughter, she is gone, I know not how,
Taken invisible, and whether living
Or in grave, 'tis yet uncertain to me.
O, Master Merrythought, these are the weights
Will sink me to my grave! Forgive me, sir. 110

OLD MER. Why, sir, I do forgive you; and be merry.
And, if the wag in 's lifetime played the knave,
Can you forgive him too?

MERCH.   With all my heart, sir.

OLD MER. Speak it again, and heartly.

MERCH.   I do, sir.
Now, by my soul, I do.

OLD MER. [*Singing.*]

    With that came out his paramour;
    She was as white as the lily flower.
      Hey, troll, trolly, lolly!

Enter Luce and Jasper.

    With that came out her own dear knight;
    He was as true as ever did fight, etc. 120

Sir, if you will forgive him, clap their hands together; there's no more to be said [1] i' th' matter.

MERCH. I do, I do.

CIT. I do not like this! Peace, boys! Hear me, one of you! Everybody's part is come to an end but Rafe's, and he's left out.

BOY. 'Tis long of yourself, sir; we have nothing to do with his part. 130

CIT. Rafe, come away!—Make on him, as you have done of the rest, boys; come.

WIFE. Now, good husband, let him come out and die.

CIT. He shall, Nell.—Rafe, come away quickly, and die, boy!

BOY. 'Twill be very unfit he should die

---

[1] From 1635 edn. Original reads *sad*.

sir, upon no occasion—and in a comedy
too.   139
    CIT. Take you no care of that, Sir Boy;
is not his part at an end, think you, when
he's dead?—Come away, Rafe!

*Enter Rafe, with a forked arrow through
his head.*

RAFE.[1] When I was mortal, this my cos-
    tive corpse
Did lap up figs and raisins in the Strand,
Where, sitting, I espied a lovely dame,
Whose master wrought with lingel [2]
    and with awl,
And underground he vampied [3] many
    a boot.
Straight did her love prick forth me,
    tender sprig,
To follow feats of arms in warlike wise
Through Waltham Desert, where I did
    perform   150
Many achievements, and did lay on
    ground
Huge Barbaroso, that insulting giant,
And all his captives soon set at liberty.
Then honor pricked me from my native
    soil
Into Moldavia, where I gained the love
Of Pompiona, his beloved daughter,
But yet proved constant to the black-
    thumbed maid,
Susan, and scornéd Pompiona's love;
Yet liberal I was, and gave her pins,
And money for her father's officers.   160
I then returnéd home, and thrust my-
    self
In action, and by all men chosen was
Lord of the May, where I did flourish
    it,
With scarfs and rings, and posy in my
    hand.
After this action I preferréd was,
And chosen city captain at Mile End,
With hat and feather, and with leading
    staff,
And trained my men, and brought them
    all off clear,
Save one man that berayed him with
    the noise.

But all these things I Rafe did under-
    take   170
Only for my beloved Susan's sake.
Then coming home, and sitting in my
    shop
With apron blue, Death came into my
    stall
To cheapen [4] *aqua vitæ;* but ere I
Could take the bottle down and fill a
    taste,
Death caught a pound of pepper in his
    hand,
And sprinkled all my face and body o'er,
And in an instant vanishéd away.

    CIT. 'Tis a pretty fiction, i' faith.

RAFE. Then took I up my bow and shaft
    in hand,   180
And walked into Moorfields to cool
    myself;
But there grim cruel Death met me
    again,
And shot this forkéd arrow through
    my head.
And now I faint. Therefore be warned
    by me,
My fellows every one, of forkéd heads!
Farewell, all you good boys in merry
    London!
Ne'er shall we more upon Shrove Tues-
    day meet,
And pluck down houses of iniquity.[5]—
My pain increaseth—I shall never more
Hold open, whilst another pumps both
    legs,   190
Nor daub a satin gown with rotten eggs;
Set up a stake,[6] O, never more I shall!
I die! Fly, fly, my soul, to Grocers'
    Hall!
O, O, O, etc.

    WIFE. Well said, Rafe! Do your obei-
sance to the gentlemen, and go your ways.
Well said, Rafe!   *Exit Rafe.*

    OLD MER. Methinks all we, thus kindly
and unexpectedly reconciled, should not
depart without a song.   200

---

[1] Many parts of the following passage are a
parody of the opening speech of Andrea's Ghost
in *The Spanish Tragedy.*
[2] Waxed thread.
[3] Patched.

[4] Bargain for.
[5] An annual custom of the London apprentices.
[6] To which cocks were tied for targets to be
thrown at.

MERCH. A good motion.

OLD MER. Strike up, then!

SONG

Better music ne'er was known
Than a choir of hearts in one.
Let each other that hath been
Troubled with the gall or spleen
Learn of us to keep his brow
Smooth and plain, as ours are now.
Sing, though before the hour of dying;
He shall rise, and then be crying,   210
"Hey, ho, 'tis naught but mirth
That keeps the body from the earth!"

Exeunt omnes.

EPILOGUS

CIT. Come, Nell, shall we go? The play's done.

WIFE. Nay, by my faith, George, I have more manners than so; I'll speak to these gentlemen first.—I thank you all, gentlemen, for your patience and countenance to Rafe, a poor fatherless child; and, if I might see you at my house, [220 it should go hard but I would have a pottle [1] of wine and a pipe of tabacco for you, for, truly, I hope you do like the youth, but I would be glad to know the truth. I refer it to your own discretions, whether you will applaud him or no, for I will wink, and whilst [2] you shall do what you will. I thank you with all my heart. God give you good night!—Come, George.

[Exeunt.]

FINIS.

[1] Bottle.   [2] In the meantime.

THE FAITHFUL SHEPHERDESS

BY

JOHN FLETCHER [1]

[DRAMATIS PERSONÆ

PERIGOT.
THENOT.
DAPHNIS.
ALEXIS.
SULLEN SHEPHERD.
OLD SHEPHERD.
PRIEST OF PAN.
GOD OF THE RIVER.

SATYR.
SHEPHERDS.

CLORIN.
AMORET.
AMARILLIS.
CLOE.
SHEPHERDESSES.

SCENE: *Thessaly.*

TIME: *Mythical.*]

TO THE READER

If you be not reasonably assured of your knowledge in this kind of poem, lay down the book, or read this, which I would wish had been the prologue. It is a pastoral tragi-comedy, which the people, seeing when it was played, having ever had a singular gift in defining, concluded to be a play of country hired shepherds in gray cloaks, with curtailed dogs in strings, some- [10 times laughing together, and some- times killing one another; and, missing Whitsun ales, cream, wassail, and mor-ris dances, began to be angry. In their error I would not have you fall, lest you incur their censure.[2] Understand, there-fore, a pastoral to be a representation of shepherds and shepherdesses with their actions and passions, which must be such as may agree with their natures, at least not exceeding former fictions and vul- [20 gar traditions; they are not to be adorned with any art but such improper [3] ones as nature is said to bestow, as singing and poetry, or such as experience may teach them, as the virtues of herbs and foun-tains, the ordinary course of the sun, moon, and stars, and suchlike. But you are ever to remember shepherds to be such as all the ancient poets, and modern of under-standing, have received them; that [30 is, the owners of flocks, and not hirelings. A tragi-comedy is not so called in respect of mirth and killing, but in respect it wants deaths, which is enough to make it no tragedy, yet brings some near it, which is enough to make it no comedy, which must be a representation of familiar people, with such kind of trouble as no life be ques-tioned,[4] so that a god is as lawful in this as in a tragedy, and mean people as in a [40 comedy. Thus much I hope will serve to justify my poem, and make you understand it; to teach you more for nothing, I do not know that I am in conscience bound.

JOHN FLETCHER.

[1] Commendatory verses by Nathan Field, Francis Beaumont, Ben Jonson, and George Chapman, and dedicatory verses to Sir Walter Aston, Sir William Skipwith, and Sir Robert Townshend follow here.
[2] *I.e.,* the criticism which they received.

[3] *I.e.,* common to all men.
[4] *I.e.,* be put in danger.

1147

ACTUS PRIMI SCENA PRIMA.[1]

[*A glade in a wood.*][2]

Enter Clorin, a shepherdess, having buried
her love in an arbor.

[CLORIN.] Hail, holy earth, whose cold
  arms do embrace
The truest man that ever fed his flocks
By the fat plains of fruitful Thessaly!
Thus I salute thy grave; thus do I pay
My early vows and tribute of mine eyes
To thy still-lovéd ashes; thus I free
Myself from all ensuing heats and fires
Of love; all sports, delights, and games
That shepherds hold full dear, thus put
  I off.
Now no more shall these smooth brows
  be girt   10
With youthful coronals, and lead the
  dance;
No more the company of fresh fair
  maids
And wanton shepherds be to me de-
  lightful,
Nor the shrill, pleasing sound of merry
  pipes
Under some shady dell, when the cool
  wind
Plays on the leaves—all be far away,
Since thou art far away, by whose dear
  side
How often have I sat crowned with fresh
  flowers
For summer's queen, whilst every shep-
  herd's boy
Puts on his lusty green, with gaudy
  hook[3]   20
And hanging scrip of finest cordevan.[4]
But thou art gone, and these are gone
  with thee,
And all are dead but thy dear memory.
That shall outlive thee, and shall ever
  spring,
Whilst there are pipes, or jolly shep-
  herds sing.
And here will I, in honor of thy love,

Dwell by thy grave, forgetting all those
  joys
That former times made precious to
  mine eyes,
Only rememb'ring what my youth did
  gain
In the dark, hidden, virtuous[5] use of
  herbs.   30
That will I practice, and as freely give
All my endeavors, as I gained them free.
Of all green wounds I know the remedies
In men or cattle, be they stung with
  snakes,
Or charmed with powerful words of
  wicked art,
Or be they lovesick, or, through too
  much heat
Grown wild or lunatic, their eyes or ears
Thickened with misty film of dulling
  rheum;
These I can cure, such secret virtue lies
In herbs appliéd by a virgin's hand. 40
My meat shall be what these wild woods
  afford,
Berries and chestnuts, plantains, on
  whose cheeks
The sun sits smiling, and the lofty fruit
Pulled from the fair head of the
  straight-grown pine.
On these I'll feed with free content, and
  rest,
When night shall blind the world, by
  thy side blessed.

Enter a Satyr [with a basket of fruit].

SAT. Through[6] yon same bending plain,
That flings his arms down to the main,
And through these thick woods have I
  run,
Whose bottom never kissed the sun 50
Since the lusty spring began;
All to please my master Pan,
Have I trotted without rest
To get him fruit, for at a feast
He entertains this coming night
His paramour, the Syrinx bright.—
But, behold, a fairer sight!
      He stands amazed.
By that heavenly form of thine,
Brightest fair, thou art divine,
Sprong[7] from great immortal race 60

---

[1] The first scene of the first act.
[2] The setting, which apparently remains unchanged throughout the play, consists of
Clorin's bower (or cottage) in the inner stage,
a wood on one side of the main stage, and a hill
with a well on the other.
[3] Crook.
[4] Cordovan leather.

[5] Efficacious.   [7] Sprung.
[6] Perhaps pronounced *thorough*.

Of the gods; for in thy face
Shines more awful majesty
Than dull weak mortality
Dare with misty eyes behold,
And live. Therefore on this mold
Lowly do I bend my knee
In worship of thy deity.
Deign it, goddess, from my hand
To receive whate'er this land
From her fertile womb doth send   70
Of her choice fruits, and but lend
Belief to that the satyr tells:
Fairer by the famous wells
To this present day ne'er grew,
Never better nor more true.
Here be grapes, whose lusty blood
Is the learned poets' good,
Sweeter yet did never crown
The head of Bacchus; nuts more brown
Than the squirrel's teeth that crack
   them.   80
Deign, O fairest fair, to take them!
For these black-eyed Dryope
Hath oftentimes commanded me
With my claspéd knee to climb—
See how well the lusty time
Hath decked their rising cheeks in
   red,
Such as on your lips is spread!
Here be berries for a queen—
Some be red, some be green;
These are of that luscious meat   90
The great god Pan himself doth eat;
All these, and what the woods can yield,
The hanging mountain, or the field,
I freely offer, and ere long
Will bring you more, more sweet and
   strong,
Till when, humbly leave I take,
Lest the great Pan do awake,
That sleeping lies in a deep glade
Under a broad beech's shade.
I must go, I must run   100
Swifter than the fiery sun.   *Exit.*
Clo. And all my fears go with thee!
What greatness, or what private hidden
   power,
Is there in me, to draw submission
From this rude man and beast? Sure
   I am mortal,
The daughter of a shepherd; he was
   mortal,
And she that bore me mortal; prick my
   hand,

And it will bleed; a fever shakes me, and
The selfsame wind that makes the young
   lambs shrink
Makes me acold; my fear says I am
   mortal.   110
Yet I have heard (my mother told it
   me,
And now I do believe it), if I keep
My virgin-flower uncropped, pure, chaste,
   and fair,
No goblin, wood god, fairy, elf, or fiend,
Satyr, or other power that haunts these
   groves
Shall hurt my body, or by vain illusion
Draw me to wander after idle fires,
Or voices calling me in dead of night
To make me follow, and so toll me on
Through mires and standing pools.   120
Else why should this rough thing, who
   never knew
Manners nor smooth humanity, whose
   heats [1]
Are rougher than himself and more mis-
   shapen,
Thus mildly kneel to me? Sure there is
   a power
In that great name of virgin that binds
   fast
All rude, uncivil bloods, all appetites
That break their confines. Then, strong
   chastity,
Be thou my strongest guard, for here
   I'll dwell
In opposition against fate and hell!
                                      [Exit.]

*Enter an Old Shepherd, with four couple of
   Shepherds and Shepherdesses [, among
   whom are Perigot and Amoret].* [2]

Old Shep. Now we have done this holy
   festival   130
In honor of our great god, and his rites
Performed, prepare yourselves for chaste
And uncorrupted fires, that, as the priest
With powerful hand shall sprinkle on
   your brows
His pure and holy water, ye may be
From all hot flames of lust and loose
   thoughts free.
Kneel, shepherds, kneel; here comes the
   priest of Pan.   *[They kneel.]*

[1] Passions.
[2] Added by Dyce.

Enter Priest.

PRIEST. [*Sprinkling them with water.*] Shep-
herds, thus I purge away
Whatsoever this great day
Or the past hours gave not good   140
To corrupt your maiden blood.
From the high rebellious heat
Of the grapes, and strength of meat,
From the wanton quick desires
They do kindle by their fires
I do wash you with this water.
Be you pure and fair hereafter.
From your livers [1] and your veins
Thus I take away the stains;
All your thoughts be smooth and fair;   150
Be ye fresh and free as air.
Never more let lustful heat
Through your purgéd conduits [2] beat,
Or a plighted troth be broken,
Or a wanton verse be spoken
In a shepherdess's ear.
Go your ways; ye are all clear.
        They rise and sing in praise of Pan.

THE SONG

Sing his praises that doth keep
    Our flocks from harm,
Pan, the father of our sheep;   160
    And arm in arm
Tread we softly in a round,
Whilst the hollow neighboring ground
Fills the music with her sound.

Pan, O great god Pan, to thee
    Thus do we sing,
Thou that keep'st us chaste and free
    As the young spring!
Ever be thy honor spoke,
From that place the Morn is broke   170
To that place Day doth unyoke!

Exeunt omnes but Perigot and Amoret.
PERI. Stay, gentle Amoret, thou fair-
browed maid;
Thy shepherd prays thee stay, that holds
thee dear,
Equal with his soul's good.
AMO.   Speak; I give
Thee freedom, shepherd, and [3] thy
tongue be still [4]
The same it ever was, as free from ill
As he whose conversation never knew
The court or city; be thou ever true!

[1] The supposed seat of desire.   [3] If.
[2] Veins.   [4] Always.

PERI. When I fall off from my affection,
Or mingle my clean thoughts with foul
desires,   180
First, let our great god cease to keep
my flocks,
That, being left alone without a guard,
The wolf, or winter's rage, summer's
great heat
And want of water, rots, or what to us
Of ill is yet unknown, fall speedily,
And in their general ruin let me go!
AMO. I pray thee, gentle shepherd, wish
not so.
I do believe thee; 'tis as hard for me
To think thee false, and harder, than
for thee
To hold me foul.
PERI.   O, you are fairer far 190
Than the chaste blushing morn, or that
fair star
That guides the wand'ring seaman
through the deep,
Straighter than the straightest pine
upon the steep
Head of an aged mountain, and more
white
Than the new milk we strip before day-
light
From the full-freighted bags of our fair
flocks;
Your hair more beauteous than those
hanging locks
Of young Apollo!
AMO.   Shepherd, be not lost;
Y' are sailed too far already from the
coast
Of our discourse.
PERI.   Did you not tell me once 200
I should not love alone, I should not
lose
Those many passions, vows, and holy
oaths
I've sent to heaven? Did you not give
your hand,
Even that fair hand, in hostage? Do
not, then,
Give back again those sweets to other
men
You yourself vowed were mine.
AMO. Shepherd, so far as maiden's mod-
esty
May give assurance, I am once more
thine;
Once more I give my hand. Be ever free

From that great foe to faith, foul jeal-
  ousy!   210
PERI. I take it as my best good, and de-
  sire,
For stronger confirmation of our love,
To meet this happy night in that fair
  grove
Where all true shepherds have rewarded
  been
For their long service. Say, sweet, shall
  it hold?
AMO. Dear friend, you must not blame
  me if I make
A doubt of what the silent night may do,
Coupled with this day's heat, to move
  your blood.
Maids must be fearful. Sure you have
  not been
Washed white enough, for yet I see a
  stain   220
Stick in your liver; go and purge again.
PERI. O, do not wrong my honest, simple
  truth!
Myself and my affections are as pure
As those chaste flames that burn be-
  fore the shrine
Of the great Dian; only my intent
To draw you thither was to plight our
  troths,
With interchange of mutual chaste em-
  braces
And ceremonious tying of our souls.
For to that holy wood is consecrate
A virtuous well, about whose flowery
  banks   230
The nimble-footed fairies dance their
  rounds
By the pale moonshine, dipping often-
  times
Their stolen children, so to make them
  free
From dying flesh and dull mortality.
By this fair fount hath many a shep-
  herd sworn,
And given away his freedom, many a
  troth
Been plight, which neither envy nor old
  time
Could ever break, with many a chaste
  kiss given
In hope of coming happiness. By this
Fresh fountain many a blushing maid 240
Hath crowned the head of her long-
  lovéd shepherd

With gaudy flowers, whilst he happy sung
Lays of his love and dear captivity.
There grows all herbs fit to cool looser
  flames
Our sensual parts provoke, chiding our
  bloods,
And quenching by their power those
  hidden sparks
That else would break out, and provoke
  our sense
To open fires; so virtuous is that place.
Then, gentle shepherdess, believe, and
  grant.
In troth, it fits not with that face to
  scant   250
Your faithful shepherd of those chaste
  desires
He ever aimed at, and—
AMO. Thou hast prevailed; farewell. This
  coming night
Shall crown thy chaste hopes with long-
  wished delight.
PERI. Our great god Pan reward thee for
  that good
Thou hast given thy poor shepherd!
  Fairest bud
Of maiden virtues, when I leave to be
The true admirer of thy chastity,
Let me deserve the hot polluted name
Of a wild woodman, or affect some dame
Whose often prostitution hath begot 261
More foul diseases than ever yet the hot
Sun bred through his burnings, whilst
  the Dog [1]
Pursues the raging Lion,[1] throwing fog
And deadly vapor from his angry breath,
Filling the lower world with plague and
  death!   *Ex[it] Am[oret].*

*Enter [Amarillis,] another shepherdess that
          is in love with Perigot.*

AMAR. Shepherd, may I desire to be be-
  lieved,
What I shall blushing tell?
PERI.   Fair maid, you may.
AMAR. Then, softly thus: I love thee, Peri-
  got,
And would be gladder to be loved
  again   270
Than the cold earth is in his frozen arms
To clip [2] the wanton spring. Nay, do
  not start,

---

[1] Sign of the zodiac.   [2] Embrace.

Nor wonder that I woo thee, thou that art
The prime of our young grooms, even the top
Of all our lusty shepherds. What dull eye,
That never was acquainted with desire,
Hath seen thee wrastle, run, or cast the stone
With nimble strength and fair delivery,
And hath not sparkled fire, and speedily
Sent secret heat to all the neighboring veins? 280
Who ever heard thee sing, that brought again
That freedom back was lent unto thy voice?
Then, do not blame me, shepherd, if I be
One to be numbered in this company,
Since none that ever saw thee yet were free.

PERI. Fair shepherdess, much pity I can lend
To your complaints; but sure I shall not love.
All that is mine, myself and my best hopes,
Are given already. Do not love him, then,
That cannot love again; on other men 290
Bestow those heats, more free, that may return
You fire for fire, and in one flame equal burn.

AMAR. Shall I rewarded be so slenderly
For my affection, most unkind of men?
If I were old, or had agreed with art
To give another nature to my cheeks,
Or were I common mistress to the love
Of every swain, or could I with such ease
Call back my love as many a wanton doth,
Thou mightst refuse me, shepherd, but to thee 300
I am only fixed and set. Let it not be
A sport, thou gentle shepherd, to abuse
The love of silly [1] maid.

PERI.   Fair soul, you use
These words to little end; for, know, I may
Better call back that time was yesterday,

[1] Weak.

Or stay the coming night, than bring my love
Home to myself again, or recreant prove.
I will no longer hold you with delays.
This present night I have appointed been
To meet that chaste fair that enjoys my soul, 310
In yonder grove, there to make up our loves.
Be not deceived no longer; choose again.
These neighboring plains have many a comely swain,
Fresher and freer [2] far than I e'er was;
Bestow that love on them, and let me pass.
Farewell; be happy in a better choice!
                                    Exit.

AMAR. Cruel, thou hast struck me deader with thy voice
Than if the angry heavens with their quick flames
Had shot me through. I must not leave to love;
I cannot; no, I must enjoy thee, boy, 320
Though the great dangers twixt my hopes and that
Be infinite. There is a shepherd dwells
Down by the moor, whose life hath ever shown
More sullen discontent than Saturn's brow
When he sits frowning on the births of men—
One that doth wear himself away in loneness,
And never joys, unless it be in breaking
The holy plighted troths of mutual souls;
One that lusts after every several beauty,
But never yet was known to love or like, 330
Were the face fairer or more full of truth
Than Phœbe in her fullness, or the youth
Of smooth Lyæus, whose nigh-starvéd flocks
Are always scabby, and infect all sheep
They feed withal, whose lambs are ever last,
And die before their weaning, and whose dog
Looks, like his master, lean and full of scurf,

[2] More liberal.

Not caring for the pipe or whistle. This
  man may,
If he be well wrought, do a deed of won-
  der,   339
Forcing me passage to my long desires.
And here he comes, as fitly to my pur-
  pose
As my quick thoughts could wish for.

Enter Sullen [Shepherd].

SULL. Fresh beauty, let me not be thought
  uncivil,
  Thus to be partner of your loneness;
    'twas
My love (that ever-working passion)
  drew
Me to this place to seek some remedy
For my sick soul. Be not unkind and
  fair,
For such the mighty Cupid in his doom
Hath sworn to be avenged on. Then
  give room
To my consuming fires that so I may   350
Enjoy my long desires, and so allay
Those flames that else would burn my
  life away.
AMAR. Shepherd, were I but sure thy
  heart were sound
As thy words seem to be, means might
  be found
To cure thee of thy long pains; for to me
That heavy, youth-consuming misery
The lovesick soul endures never was
  pleasing.
I could be well content with the quick
  easing
Of thee and thy hot fires, might it
  procure
Thy faith and farther service to be
  sure.   360
[SULL.] [1] Name but that work, danger, or
  what can
Be compassed by the wit or art of man,
And, if I fail in my performance, may
I never more kneel to the rising day!
AMAR. Then thus I try thee, shepherd.
  This same night
That now comes stealing on, a gentle pair
Have promised equal love, and do
  appoint
To make yon wood the place where
  hands and hearts

[1] From 1634 edn.

Are to be tied forever. Break their
  meeting
And their strong faith, and I am ever
  thine.   370
SULL. Tell me their names, and, if I do
  not move,
By my great power, the center of their
  love
From his fixed being, let me never more
Warm me by those fair eyes I thus adore.
AMAR. Come; as we go, I'll tell thee what
  they are,
And give thee fit directions for thy work.
                             Exeunt.

Enter Cloe.

CLOE. How have I wronged the times or
  men, that thus
After this holy feast I pass unknown
And unsaluted? 'Twas not wont to be
Thus frozen with the younger com-
  pany   380
Of jolly shepherds; 'twas not then held
  good
For lusty grooms [2] to mix their quicker
  blood
With that dull humor, most unfit to be
The friend of man, cold and dull chastity.
Sure I am held not fair, or am too old,
Or else not free enough, or from my
  fold
Drive not a flock sufficient great to
  gain
The greedy eyes of wealth-alluring
  swain.
Yet, if I may believe what others say,
My face has foil [3] enough; nor can they
  lay   390
Justly too strict a coyness to my charge;
My flocks are many, and the downs as
  large
They feed upon. Then, let it ever be
Their coldness, not my virgin-modesty,
Makes me complain.

Enter Thenot.

THE.   Was ever man but I
Thus truly taken with uncertainty? [4]
Where shall that man be found that
  loves a mind

[2] Merry fellows.
[3] Beauty.
[4] Bewitched with "the desire of things in-
compatible" (Greg).

Made up in constancy, and dares not find
His love rewarded? Here, let all men know,
A wretch that lives to love his mistress so.   400
CLOE. Shepherd, I pray thee stay. Where hast thou been?
Or whither go'st thou? Here be woods as green
As any; air as fresh and sweet
As where smooth Zephyrus plays on the fleet
Face of the curléd streams, with flowers as many
As the young spring gives, and as choice as any;
Here be all new delights, cool streams and wells,
Arbors o'ergrown with woodbines, caves, and dells.
Choose where thou wilt, whilst I sit by and sing,
Or gather rushes, to make many a ring   410
For thy long fingers; tell thee tales of love—
How the pale Phoebe, hunting in a grove,
First saw the boy Endymion, from whose eyes
She took eternal fire that never dies,
How she conveyed him softly in a sleep,
His temples bound with poppy, to the steep
Head of old Latmus, where she stoops each night,
Gilding the mountain with her brother's light,
To kiss her sweetest.
THE.   Far from me are these
Hot flashes, bred from wanton heat and ease;   420
I have forgot what love and loving meant;
Rimes, songs, and merry rounds,[1] that oft are sent
To the soft ear of maid, are strange to me.
Only I live t' admire a chastity
That neither pleasing age,[2] smooth tongue, or gold
Could ever break upon, so sure a mold

Is that her mind was cast in. 'Tis to her
I only am reserved; she is my form I stir
By, breathe, and move; 'tis she, and only she,   429
Can make me happy, or give misery.
CLOE. Good shepherd, may a stranger crave to know
To whom this dear observance [3] you do owe?
THE. You may, and by her virtue learn to square
And level out your life; for to be fair,
And nothing virtuous, only fits the eye
Of gaudy youth and swelling vanity.
Then, know, she's called the Virgin of the Grove,
She that hath long since buried her chaste love,
And now lives by his grave, for whose dear soul
She hath vowed herself into the holy roll   440
Of strict virginity. 'Tis her I so admire,
Not any looser blood or new desire.
                              [Exit.]
CLOE. Farewell, poor swain! Thou art not for my bend; [4]
I must have quicker souls, whose words may tend
To some free action. Give me him dare love
At first encounter, and as soon dare prove!

THE SONG

Come, shepherds, come!
Come away without delay,
Whilst the gentle time doth stay.
    Green woods are dumb,   450
And will never tell to any
Those dear kisses and those many
Sweet embraces that are given—
Dainty pleasures that would even
Raise in coldest age a fire,
And give virgin-blood desire.
    Then, if ever,
    Now or never,
    Come and have it;
    Think not I   460
    Dare deny,
    If you crave it.

[1] Roundelays.   [2] Youth.   [3] Homage.   [4] Bent, purpose.

Enter Daphnis.

[CLOE. (*Aside.*)] Here comes another.
  Better be my speed,
Thou god of blood! But certain, if I
    read
Not false, this is that modest shepherd,
    he
That only dare salute, but ne'er could
    be
Brought to kiss any, hold discourse, or
    sing,
Whisper, or boldly ask that wishéd thing
We all are born for—one that makes
    loving faces,
And could be well content to covet
    graces,   470
Were they not got by boldness. In
    this thing
My hopes are frozen; and, but fate doth
    bring
Him hither, I would sooner choose
A man made out of snow, and freer use
An eunuch to my ends. But since he
    is here,
Thus I attempt him.—Thou, of men
    most dear,
Welcome to her that only for thy sake
Hath been content to live! Here, boldly
    take
My hand in pledge, this hand that
    never yet
Was given away to any, and but sit   480
Down on this rushy bank whilst I go
    pull
Fresh blossoms from the boughs, or
    quickly cull
The choicest delicates from yonder
    mead,
To make thee chains or chaplets, or
    to spread
Under our fainting bodies, when delight
Shall lock up all our senses. How the
    sight
Of those smooth rising cheeks renew
    the story
Of young Adonis, when in pride and glory
He lay infolded twixt the beating arms
Of willing Venus! Methinks stronger
    charms   490
Dwell in those speaking eyes, and on
    that brow
More sweetness than the painters can
    allow

To their best pieces. Not Narcissus, he
That wept himself away in memory
Of his own beauty, nor Silvanus' boy,
Nor the twice-ravished maid, for whom
    old Troy
Fell by the hand of Pyrrhus, may to
    thee
Be otherwise compared than some dead
    tree
To a young fruitful olive.
DAPH.   I can love,   499
  But I am loath to say so, lest I prove
Too soon unhappy.
CLOE.   Happy, thou wouldst say.
  My dearest Daphnis, blush not. If the
    day
To thee and thy soft heats be enemy,
Then take the coming night. Fair
    youth, 'tis free
To all the world. Shepherd, I'll meet
    thee, then,
When darkness hath shut up the eyes of
    men,
In yonder grove. Speak, shall our
    meeting hold?
Indeed ye are too bashful; be more bold,
And tell me ay.
DAPH.   I am content to say so,
  And would be glad to meet, might I
    but pray so   510
Much from your fairness, that you
    would be true.
CLOE. Shepherd, thou hast thy wish.
DAPH.   Fresh maid, adieu.
  Yet one word more. Since you have
    drawn me on
To come this night, fear not to meet
    alone
That man that will not offer to be ill,
Though your bright self would ask it,
    for his fill
Of this world's goodness. Do not fear
    him, then,
But keep your pointed [1] time. Let
    other men
Set up their bloods to sale; mine shall
    be ever
Fair as the soul it carries, and un-
    chaste never.   *Exit.*   520
CLOE. Yet am I poorer than I was before.
  Is it not strange, among so many a score
  Of lusty bloods, I should pick out these
    things
_____
[1] Appointed.

Whose veins, like a dull river far from
  springs,
Is still the same, slow, heavy, and unfit
For stream or motion, though the strong
  winds hit
With their continual power upon his
  sides?
O, happy be your names that have been
  brides,
And tasted those rare sweets for which
  I pine!
And far more heavy be thy grief and
  tine,[1]   530
Thou lazy swain, that mayst relieve
  my needs,
Than his upon whose liver always feeds
A hungry vulture!

Enter Alexis.

ALEX.   Can such beauty be
Safe in his [2] own guard, and not draw
  the eye
Of him that passeth on, to greedy gaze
Or covetous desire, whilst in a maze
The better part contemplates, giving
  rein
And wishéd freedom to the laboring
  vein? [3]
Fairest and whitest, may I crave to
  know
The cause of your retirement, why ye
  go   540
Thus all alone? Methinks the downs are
  sweeter,
And the young company of swains more
  meeter,
Than these forsaken and untrodden
  places.
Give not yourself to loneness, and those
  graces
Hide from the eyes of men, that were
  intended
To live amongst us swains.
CLOE.   Thou art befriended,
Shepherd; in all my life I have not seen
A man in whom greater contents hath
  been
Than thou thyself art. I could tell thee
  more,
Were there but any hope left to re-
  store   550
My freedom lost. O, lend me all thy red,

Thou shamefast [4] Morning, when from
  Tithon's bed
Thou risest ever maiden!
ALEX.   If for me,
Thou sweetest of all sweets, these flashes
  be,
Speak, and be satisfied. O, guide her
  tongue,
My better angel; force my name among
Her modest thoughts, that the first
  word may be—
CLOE. Alexis, when the sun shall kiss the
  sea,
Taking his rest by the white Thetis'
  side,
Meet me in the holy wood, where I'll
  abide   560
Thy coming, shepherd.
ALEX.   If I stay behind,
An everlasting dullness, and the wind,
That as he passeth by shuts up the
  stream
Of Rhine or Volga, whilst the sun's
  hot beam
Beats back again, seize me, and let me
  turn
To coldness more than ice! O, how I
  burn
And rise in youth and fire! I dare not
  stay.
CLOE. My name shall be your word.
ALEX.   Fly, fly, thou day! *Exit.*
CLOE. My grief is great, if both these
  boys should fail;
He that will use all winds must shift
  his sail.   *Exit.*   570

ACTUS SECUNDUS. SCENA PRIMA.

[*The same.*]

*Enter an Old Shepherd, with a bell ringing,
    and the Priest of Pan following.*

PRIEST. Shepherds all, and maidens fair,
Fold your flocks up, for the air
Gins [5] to thicken, and the sun
Already his great course hath run.
See the dewdrops, how they kiss
Every little flower that is,
Hanging on their velvet heads,
Like a rope of crystal beads.
See the heavy clouds low [6] falling,

---

[1] Teen, sorrow.   [2] Its.   [3] *I.e.*, pulsing blood.

[4] Modest.
[5] Begins.
[6] From 1656 edn. Original reads *lowde*.

And bright Hesperus down calling　10
The dead Night from underground,
At whose rising mists unsound,[1]
Damps and vapors fly apace,
Hovering o'er the wanton face
Of these pastures, where they come,
Striking dead both bud and bloom.
Therefore, from such danger lock
Every one his lovéd flock;
And let your dogs lie loose without,
Lest the wolf come as a scout　20
From the mountain, and, ere day,
Bear a lamb or kid away;
Or the crafty thievish fox
Break upon your simple flocks.
To secure yourselves from these,
Be not too secure in ease.
Let one eye his watches keep,
Whilst the tother [2] eye doth sleep;
So you shall good shepherds prove,
And forever hold the love　30
Of our great god. Sweetest slumbers
And soft silence fall in numbers
On your eyelids! So, farewell.
Thus I end my evening's knell. *Exeunt.*

*Enter Clorin, the shepherdess, sorting of
　herbs, and telling the natures of them.*

CLO. Now let me know what my best
　art hath done,
Helped by the great power of the vir-
　tuous moon
In her full light. O, you sons of earth,
You only brood, unto whose happy birth
Virtue was given, holding more of nature
Than man, her first-born and most
　perfect creature,　40
Let me adore you! You, that only can
Help or kill nature, drawing out that
　span
Of life and breath even to the end of
　time;
You, that these hands did crop long
　before prime
Of day, give me your names, and, next,
　your hidden power.
This is the clote,[3] bearing a yellow
　flower;
And this, black horehound. Both are
　very good

[1] Unwholesome.
[2] That other.
[3] The name is applied to both the burdock and
the yellow water lily.

For sheep or shepherd bitten by a wood [4]
Dog's venomed tooth. These rhamnus [5]
　branches are,
Which, stuck in entries or about the
　bar　50
That holds the door fast, kill all enchant-
　ments, charms
(Were they Medea's verses) that do
　harms
To men or cattle. These for frenzy be
A speedy and a sovereign remedy—
The bitter wormwood, sage, and mari-
　gold—
Such sympathy with man's good they do
　hold.
This tormentil, whose virtue is to part
All deadly killing poison from the heart.
And here, narcissus root, for swellings
　best;
Yellow lysimachus,[6] to give sweet rest　60
To the faint shepherd, killing, where it
　comes,
All busy gnats and every fly that hums.
For leprosy, darnel and celandine,
With calamint, whose virtues do refine
The blood of man, making it free and
　fair
As the first hour it breathed, or the best
　air.
Here, other two; but your rebellious use
Is not for me, whose goodness is abuse.
Therefore, foul standergrass,[7] from me
　and mine
I banish thee, with lustful turpentine—70
You that entice the veins and stir the
　heat
To civil mutiny, scaling the seat
Our reason moves in, and deluding it
With dreams and wanton fancies till
　the fit
Of burning lust be quenched, by ap-
　petite
Robbing the soul of blessedness and
　light.
And thou, light varvin [8] too, thou must
　go after,
Provoking easy souls to mirth and
　laughter;
No more shall I dip thee in water now,

[4] Mad.
[5] A thorny shrub. Dyce's emendation for
Ramuus.
[6] Loosestrife.
[7] A variety of orchid.
[8] Vervain.

And sprinkle every post and every
   bough   80
With thy well-pleasing juice, to make
   the grooms
Swell with high mirth, as with joy all
   the rooms.

Enter Thenot.[1]

THE. This is the cabin where the best of
   all
Her sex that ever breathed, or ever
   shall
Give heat or happiness to the shep-
   herd's side,
Doth only to her worthy self abide.
Thou blessed star, I thank thee for thy
   light,
Thou by whose power the darkness of
   sad night
Is banished from the earth, in whose
   dull place
Thy chaster beams play on the heavy
   face   90
Of all the world, making the blue sea
   smile
To see how cunningly thou dost be-
   guile
Thy brother of his brightness, giving
   day
Again from chaos; whiter than that way
That leads to Jove's high court, and
   chaster far
Than chastity itself, yon blessed star
That nightly shines; thou, all the con-
   stancy
That in all women was or e'er shall be,
From whose fair eyeballs flies that holy
   fire
That poets[2] style the mother of de-
   sire,   100
Infusing into every gentle breast
A soul of greater price, and far more
   blessed
Than that quick power which gives a
   difference
Twixt man and creatures of a lower
   sense!
CLO. Shepherd, how cam'st thou hither
   to this place?
No way is trodden; all the verdant grass

The spring shot up stands yet unbruiséd
   here
Of any foot; only the dappled deer,
Far from the fearéd sound of crooked
   horn,
Dwells in this fastness.
THE.   Chaster than the morn,   110
I have not wandered, or by strong
   illusion
Into this virtuous place have made in-
   trusion;
But hither am I come (believe me, fair)
To seek you out, of whose great good
   the air
Is full, and strongly labors, whilst the
   sound
Breaks against heaven, and drives into
   a stound[3]
The amazéd shepherd, that such virtue
   can
Be resident in lesser than a man.
CLO. If any art I have, or hidden skill,
May cure thee of disease or festered
   ill   120
Whose grief or greenness to another's
   eye
May seem unpossible of remedy,
I dare yet undertake it.
THE.   'Tis no pain
I suffer through disease, no beating vein
Conveys infection dangerous to the heart,
No part impostumed, to be cured by art,
This body holds, and yet a feller[4] grief
Than ever skillful hand did give relief,
Dwells on my soul, and may be healed
   by you,
Fair, beauteous virgin.
CLO.   Then, shepherd, let me sue   130
To know thy grief; that man yet never
   knew
The way to health that durst not show
   his sore.
THE. Then, fairest, know, I love you.
CLO.   Swain, no more!
Thou hast abused the strictness of this
   place,
And offered sacrilegious foul disgrace
To the sweet rest of these interréd
   bones,
For fear of whose ascending, fly at
   once,

---

[1] From 1629 edn. Original reads *Shepherd.*
The following speech heads also read *Shep.* in
the original.
[2] From 1629 edn. Original reads *ports.*

[3] Astonishment. From 1634 edn. Original has
stround.
[4] Crueler.

Thou and thy idle passions, that the
    sight
Of death and speedy vengeance may
    not fright
Thy very soul with horror.
[THE.] [1]   Let me not, 140
Thou all perfection, merit such a blot
For my true, zealous faith.
CLO.   Dar'st thou abide
To see this holy earth at once divide,
And give her body up? For sure it will,
If thou pursu'st with wanton flames
    to fill
This hallowed place; therefore repent
    and go,
Whilst I with praye[r]s appease his
    ghost below,
That else would tell thee what it were
    to be
A rival in that virtuous love that he
Embraces yet.
THE.   'Tis not the white or red 150
Inhabits in your cheek that thus can
    wed
My mind to adoration; nor your eye,
Though it be full and fair; your fore-
    head high
And smooth as Pelops' shoulder; not
    the smile
Lies watching in those dimples to be-
    guile
The easy soul; your hands and fingers
    long,
With veins enameled richly, nor your
    tongue,
Though it spoke sweeter than Arion's
    harp;
Your hair woven into many a curious
    warp,
Able in endless error to infold [2] 160
The wand'ring soul; not the true, per-
    fect mold
Of all your body, which as pure doth
    show
In maiden whiteness as the Alpsian
    snow—
All these, were but your constancy
    away,
Would please me less than a black,
    stormy day
The wretched seaman toiling through
    the deep.

[1] From 1629 edn.
[2] From 1634 edn. Original has *unfold*.

But, whilst this honored strictness you
    dare keep,
Though all the plagues that e'er be-
    gotten were
In the great womb of air were settled
    here,
In opposition, I would, like the tree, 170
Shake off those drops of weakness, and
    be free
Even in the arm of danger.
CLO.   Wouldst thou have
Me raise again, fond [3] man, from silent
    grave
Those sparks that long ago were buried
    here
With my dead friend's cold ashes?
THE.   Dearest dear,
I dare not ask it, nor you must not
    grant;
Stand strongly to your vow, and do
    not faint.
Remember how he loved ye, and be
    still
The same opinion speaks ye. Let not
    will,
And that great god of women, ap-
    petite,   180
Set up your blood again; do not invite
Desire and fancy from their long exile,
To seat them once more in a pleasing
    smile.
Be, like a rock, made firmly up gainst
    all
The power of angry heaven or the
    strong fall
Of Neptune's battery. If ye yield, I
    die
To all affection; 'tis that loyalty
Ye tie unto this grave I so admire.
And yet there's something else I would
    desire,   189
If you would hear me, but withal deny.
O, Pan, what an uncertain destiny
Hangs over all my hopes! I will retire,
For, if I longer stay, this double fire
Will lick my life up.
CLO.   Do; and let time wear out
What art and nature cannot bring about.
THE. Farewell, thou soul of virtue, and be
    blessed
Forever, whilst I wretched rest
Thus to myself! Yet grant me leave to
    dwell

[3] Foolish.

In kenning [1] of this arbor; yon same dell,
O'ertopped with mourning cypress and
    sad yew,   200
Shall be my cabin, where I'll early rue,
Before the sun hath kissed this dew
    away,
The hard uncertain chance which faith
    doth lay
Upon this head.
CLO.   The gods give quick release
And happy cure unto thy hard disease! [2]
                Exeunt.

Enter Sullen Shepherd.

SULL. I do not love this wench that I
    should meet,
For never did my unconstant eye yet
    greet
That beauty, were it sweeter or more fair
Than the new blossoms when the morn-
    ing air
Blows gently on them, or the breaking
    light   210
When many maiden blushes to our
    sight
Shoot from his early face—were all
    these set
In some neat form before me, 'twould
    not get
The least love from me. Some desire it
    might,
And present burning. All to me in sight
Are equal; be they fair or black or
    brown,
Virgin or careless wanton, I can crown
My appetite with any; swear as oft,
And weep, as any; melt my words as
    soft   219
Into a maiden's ears, and tell how long
My heart has been her servant, and
    how strong
My passions are; call her unkind and
    cruel;
Offer her all I have to gain the jewel
Maidens so highly praise; then loathe,
    and fly.
This do I hold a blessed destiny.

Enter Amarillis.

AMAR. Hail, shepherd! Pan bless both
    thy flock and thee
For being mindful of thy word to me!

SULL. Welcome, fair shepherdess! Thy
    loving swain
Gives thee the selfsame wishes back
    again,
Who till this present hour ne'er knew
    that eye   230
Could make me cross mine arms, or
    daily die
With fresh consumings. Boldly tell
    me, then,
How shall we part their faithful loves,
    and when?
Shall I belie him to her? Shall I swear
His faith is false and he loves every-
    where?
I'll say he mocked her the other day to
    you,
Which will by your confirming show as
    true,
For she [3] is of so pure an honesty,
To think, because she [3] will not, none
    will lie.
Or else to him I'll slander Amoret,   240
And say she but seems chaste. I'll
    swear she met
Me mongst the shady sycamores last
    night,
And loosely offered up her flame and
    sprite
Into my bosom, made a wanton bed
Of leaves and many flowers, where she
    spread
Her willing body to be pressed by me.
There have I carved her name on many
    a tree,
Together with mine own. To make this
    show
More full of seeming—Hobinal, you
    know,
Son to the aged shepherd of the glen,   250
Him I have sorted out of many men,
To say he found us at our private sport,
And roused us fore our time by his re-
    sort.
This to confirm, I've promised to the
    boy
Many a pretty knack and many a toy,
As gren [4] to catch him birds, with bow
    and bolt
To shoot at nimble squirrels in the holt,
A pair of painted buskins, and a lamb
Soft as his own locks or the down of
    swan.

---

[1] View.   [2] Dis-ease, discomfort.   [3] Early edns. read *he.*   [4] Snare.

This I have done to win ye, which doth
  give   260
Me double pleasure. Discord makes me
  live.

AMAR. Loved swain, I thank ye. These
  tricks might prevail
With other rustic shepherds, but will
  fail
Even once to stir, much more to overthrow,
His fixéd love from judgment, who doth
  know
Your nature, my end, and his chosen's
  merit.
Therefore some stronger way must force
  his spirit,
Which I have found: give second, and
  my love
Is everlasting thine.

SULL.   Try me, and prove.

AMAR. These happy pair of lovers meet
  straightway,   270
Soon as they fold their flocks up with
  the day,
In the thick grove bordering upon yon
  hill,
In whose hard side nature hath carved a
  well,
And, but that matchless spring which
  poets know,
Was ne'er the like to this. By it doth
  grow
About the sides all herbs which witches
  use,
All simples good for medicine or abuse,
All sweets that crown the happy nup-
  tial day
With all their colors. There the month
  of May   279
Is ever dwelling; all is young and green:
There's not a grass on which was ever
  seen
The falling autumn or cold winter's hand,
So full of heat and virtue is the land
About this fountain, which doth slowly
  break,
Below yon mountain's foot, into a creek
That waters all the valley, giving fish
Of many sorts to fill the shepherd's
  dish.
This holy well, my grandam that is
  dead,
Right wise in charms, hath often to me
  said,

Hath power to change the form of any
  creature,   290
Being thrice dipped over the head, into
  what feature
Or shape 'twould please the letter-down
  to crave,
Who must pronounce this charm too,
  which she gave   [Shows a scroll.]
Me on her deathbed, told me what, and
  how,
I should apply unto the patients' brow
That would be changed, casting them
  thrice asleep,
Before I trusted them into this deep.
All this she showed me, and did charge
  me prove
This secret of her art, if crossed in
  love.
I'll this attempt now, shepherd. I
  have here   300
All her prescriptions, and I will not
  fear
To be myself dipped. Come, my temples
  bind
With these sad herbs, and, when I sleep
  you find,
As you do speak your charm, thrice
  down me let,
And bid the water raise me Amoret;
Which being done, leave me to my af-
  fair,
And, ere the day shall quite itself out-
  wear,
I will return unto my shepherd's arm.
Dip me again, and then repeat this
  charm,
And pluck me up myself, whom freely
  take,   310
And the hott'st fire of thine affection
  slake.

SULL. And, if I fit thee not, then fit not
  me.
I long the truth of this well's power to
  see.   Exeunt.[1]

Enter Daphnis.

DAPH. Here will I stay, for this the covert is
Where I appointed Cloe. Do not miss,
Thou bright-eyed virgin; come, O, come,
  my fair!

[1] In the first quarto only here follows: "ACTUS
SECUNDUS. SCENA QUARTA"—the only attempt in
the play to divide acts into shorter scenes.

Be not abused [1] with fear, or let cold care
Of honor stay thee from thy shepherd's arm,
Who would as hard be won to offer harm
To thy chaste thoughts, as whiteness from the day,   320
Or yon great round [2] to move another way.
My language shall be honest, full of truth;
My flame, as smooth and spotless as my youth.
I will not entertain that wand'ring thought,
Whose easy current may at length be brought
To a loose vastness.

ALEX. (*Within.*)   Cloe!
DAPH.   'Tis her voice,
And I must answer.—Cloe!—O, the choice
Of dear embraces, chaste and holy strains
Our hands shall give! I charge you, all my veins,
Through which the blood and spirit take their way,   330
Lock up your disobedient heats, and stay
Those mutinous desires that else would grow
To strong rebellion; do not wilder show
Than blushing modesty may entertain.
ALEX. (*Within.*) Cloe!
DAPH.   There sounds that blessed name again,
And I will meet it. Let me not mistake.

Enter Alexis.

This is some shepherd. Sure, I am awake.
What may this riddle mean? I will retire,
To give myself more knowledge.
                              [*Retires.*]
ALEX.   O, my fire,
How thou consum'st me!—Cloe, answer me!   340
Alexis, strong Alexis, high and free,
Calls upon Cloe. See, mine arms are full
Of entertainment, ready for to pull
That golden fruit which too-too long hath hung

[1] Cheated.   [2] *I.e.*, the moon.

Tempting the greedy eye. Thou stayest too long;
I am impatient of these mad delays;
I must not leave unsought those many ways
That lead into this center, till I find
Quench for my burning lust. I come, unkind!   *Exit Alexis.*
DAPH. [*Coming forward.*] Can my imagination work me so much ill   350
That I may credit this for truth and still
Believe mine eyes? Or shall I firmly hold
Her yet untainted, and these sights but bold
Illusion? Sure, such fancies oft have been
Sent to abuse true love, and yet are seen
Daring to blind the virtuous thought [3] with error.
But be they far from me with their fond terror!
I am resolved my Cloe yet is true.
CLOE. (*Within.*) Cloe!
[DAPH.]   Hark! Cloe! Sure, this voice is new,
Whose shrillness, like the sounding of a bell,   360
Tells me it is a woman.—Cloe, tell
Thy blessed name again.
CLOE. (*Within.*)   Here!
[DAPH.] O, what a grief is this, to be so near
And not encounter!

Enter Cloe.

CLOE.   Shepherd, we are met;
Draw close into the covert, lest the wet,
Which falls like lazy mists upon the ground,
Soak through your startups.[4]
DAPH.   Fairest, are you found?
How have we wandered, that the better part
Of this good night is perished? O, my heart!
How have I longed to meet ye, how to kiss   370
Those lily hands, how to receive the bliss
That charming tongue gives to the happy ear

[3] From 1634 edn. Original reads *though.*
[4] Rustic shoes.

Of him that drinks your language! But
　I fear
I am too much unmannered, far too
　rude,
And almost grown lascivious, to intrude
These hot behaviors, where regard of
　fame,
Honor, and modesty, a virtuous name,
And such discourse as one fair sister
　may
Without offense unto the brother say,
Should rather have been tendered. But,
　believe,　　　　　　　　　　　380
Here dwells a better temper. Do not
　grieve,
Then, ever-kindest, that my first salute
Seasons so much of fancy.[1] I am mute
Henceforth to all discourses but shall be
Suiting to your sweet thoughts and
　modesty.
Indeed, I will not ask a kiss of you,
No, not to wring your fingers, nor to sue
To those blessed pair of fixéd stars for
　smiles.
All a young lover's cunning, all his
　wiles,　　　　　　　　　　　　389
And pretty wanton dyings shall to me
Be strangers; only to your chastity
I am devoted ever.
CLOE.　　　　　　　Honest swain,
　First let me thank you, then return
　　again
As much of my love.—[Aside.] No,
　thou art too cold,
Unhappy boy, not tempered to my
　mold;
Thy blood falls heavy downward. 'Tis
　not fear
To offend in boldness wins; they never
　wear
Deservéd favors that deny to take
When they are offered freely. Do I
　wake,
To see a man of his youth, years, and
　feature,　　　　　　　　　　　400
And such a one as we call goodly crea-
　ture,
Thus backward? What a world of
　precious art
Were merely[2] lost, to make him do his
　part!
But I will shake him off, that dares not
　hold.

Let men that hope to be beloved be
　bold.—
Daphnis, I do desire, since we are met
So happily, our lives and fortunes set
Upon one stake, to give assurance now,
By interchange of hands and holy vow,
Never to break again. Walk you that
　way,　　　　　　　　　　　　410
Whilst I in zealous meditation stray
A little this way. When we both have
　ended
These rites and duties, by the woods be-
　friended
And secrecy of night, retire and find
An aged oak, whose hollowness may bind
Us both within his body. Thither go.
It stands within yon bottom.
DAPH.　　　　　Be it so. Ex[it] Daph[nis].
CLOE. And I will meet there never more
　with thee,
Thou idle shamefastness!
ALEX. [Within.]　　　　　Cloe!
CLOE.　　　　　　　　　　'Tis he
That dare, I hope, be bolder.
ALEX. [Within.]　　　　　Cloe!
CLOE.　　　　　　　　Now,　420
Great Pan, for Syrinx' sake, bid speed
　our plow!　　　　　　Exit Cloe.

ACTUS TERTIUS. SCENA PRIMA.

[The same.]

Enter the Sullen Shepherd, with Amarillis
　　　　　　　　　in a sleep.

SULL. From thy forehead thus I take
These herbs, and charge thee not awake
Till in yonder holy well
Thrice, with powerful magic spell
Filled with many a baleful word,
Thou hast been dipped. Thus, with my
　cord
Of blasted hemp, by moonlight twined,
I do thy sleepy body bind.
I turn thy head into the east,
And thy feet into the west,　　　　10
Thy left arm to the south put forth,
And thy right unto the north.
I take thy body from the ground,
In this deep and deadly sound,[3]
And into this holy spring
I let thee slide down by my string.—
　　　[Lowers her into the well.]
Take this maid, thou holy pit,

---

[1] Amorousness.　　　　[2] Wholly.　　　　[3] Swound, swoon.

To thy bottom; nearer yet.
In thy water pure and sweet,
By thy leave I dip her feet.   20
Thus I let her lower yet,
That her ankles may be wet.
Yet down lower, let her knee
In thy waters washéd be.
There stop. Fly away,
Everything that loves the day!
Truth, that hath but one face,
Thus I charm thee from this place.
Snakes that cast your coats for new,
Chameleons that alter hue,   30
Hares that yearly sexes change,
Proteus alt'ring oft and strange,
Hecate with shapës three,
Let this maiden changéd be,
With this holy water wet,
To the shape of Amoret!
Cynthia, work thou with my charm!—
Thus I draw thee, free from harm,
[*Draws her from the well, in the shape of
                              Amoret.*]
Up out of this blessed lake.
Rise both like her and awake!   40
                              She awaketh.
AMAR. Speak, shepherd, am I Amoret to
     sight?
  Or hast thou missed in any magic
     rite,
  For want of which any defect in me
  May make our practices discovered be?
SULL. By yonder moon, but that I here
     do stand,
  Whose breath hath thus re-formed thee,
     and whose hand
  Let thee down dry, and plucked thee up
     thus wet,
  I should myself take thee for Amoret!
  Thou art in clothes, in feature, voice,
     and hue
  So like that sense cannot distinguish
     you.   50
AMAR. Then this deceit, which cannot
     crosséd be,
  At once [1] shall lose her him, and gain
     thee me.
  Hither she needs must come, by promise
     made;
  And, sure, his nature never was so bad,
  To bid a virgin meet him in the wood
  When night and fear are up, but under-
     stood

---

[1] Simultaneously.

'Twas his part to come first. Being come,
     I'll say
  My constant love made me come first
     and stay;
  Then will I lead him further to the
     grove.
  But stay you here, and, if his own true
     love   60
  Shall seek him here, set her in some wrong
     path,
  Which say her lover lately trodden hath.
  I'll not be far from hence. If need there
     be,
  Here is another charm [*Gives a scroll.*],
     whose power will free
  The dazzled sense, read by the moon-
     beams clear,
  And in my own true shape make me
     appear.

                Enter Perigot.

SULL. Stand close; here's Perigot, whose
     constant heart
  Longs to behold her in whose shape thou
     art.   [*Retires with Amarillis.*]
PERI. This is the place.—Fair Amoret!—
     The hour
  Is yet scarce come. Here every sylvan
     power   70
  Delights to be about yon sacred well,
  Which they have blessed with many a
     powerful spell;
  For never traveler in dead of night,
  Nor strayéd beasts have fall'n in; but,
     when sight
  Hath failed them, then their right way
     they have found
  By help of them, so holy is the ground.
  But I will farther seek, lest Amoret
  Should be first come, and so stray long
     unmet.—
  My Amoret, Amoret!   *Exit.*[2]
AMAR.   Perigot!
PERI. [*Within.*] My love!
AMAR.   I come, my love!   *Exit.*
SULL.   Now she hath got   80
  Her own desires, and I shall gainer be
  Of my long-looked-for hopes as well as
     she.
  How bright the moon shines here, as if
     she strove
  To show her glory in this little grove

---

[2] Original reads *Ex. Amarillis. Perigot.*

Enter Amoret.

To some new-lovéd shepherd!—[*Aside.*]
    Yonder is
Another Amoret. Where differs this
From that? But that she Perigot hath
    met,
I should have ta'en this for the counter-
    feit.
Herbs, woods, and springs, the power
    that in you lies,
If mortal men could know your prop-
    erties!   89
Amo. Methinks it is not night; I have no
    fear,
Walking this wood, of lion or of bear,
Whose names at other times have made
    me quake,
When any shepherdess in her tale spake
Of some of them that underneath a wood
Have torn true lovers that together
    stood.
Methinks there are no goblins, and men's
    talk,
That in these woods the nimble fairies
    walk,
Are fables—such a strong heart I have
    got
Because I come to meet with Peri-
    got.—   100
My Perigot! Who's that? My Perigot?
Sull. Fair maid!
Amo.   Aye me, thou art not Perigot?
Sull. But I can tell ye news of Perigot.
An hour together under yonder tree
He sat with wreathéd arms, and called
    on thee
And said, "Why, Amoret, stayest thou
    so long?"
Then starting up, down yonder path he
    flung,
Lest thou hadst missed thy way. Were
    it daylight,
He could not yet have borne him out of
    sight.
Amo. Thanks, gentle shepherd; and be-
    shrew [1] my stay,   110
That made me fearful I had lost my way.
As fast as my weak legs (that cannot be
Weary with seeking him) will carry me,
I'll follow; and, for this thy care of me,
Pray Pan thy love may ever follow thee!
                                         Exit.

[1] Curse.

Sull. How bright she was, how lovely
    did she show!
Was it not pity to deceive her so?
She plucked her garments up, and tripped
    away,
And with a virgin innocence did pray
For me that perjured [2] her.   Whilst
    she was here   120
Methought the beams of light that did
    appear
Were shot from her; methought the
    moon gave none
But what it had from her. She was
    alone
With me; if then her presence did so
    move,
Why did not I essay to win her love?
She would (not sure) [3] have yielded
    unto me.
Women love only opportunity,
And not the man; or, if she had denied,
Alone, I might have forced her to have
    tried
Who had been stronger. O, vain fool,
    to let   130
Such blessed occasion pass! I'll follow yet.
My blood is up; I cannot now forbear.

Enter Alex[is] and Cloe.

I come, sweet Amoret!—[*Aside.*] Soft,
    who is here?
A pair of lovers? He shall yield her me;
Now lust is up, alike all women be.
                                    [*Retires.*]
Alex. Where shall we rest? But for the
    love of me,
Cloe, I know, ere this would weary be.
Cloe. Alexis, let us rest here, if the place
Be private, and out of the common
    trace [4]   139
Of every shepherd; for, I understood,
This night a number are about the
    wood.
Then let us choose some place, where,
    out of sight,
We freely may enjoy our stol'n delight.
Alex. Then boldly here, where we shall
    ne'er be found.
No shepherd's way lies here; 'tis hallowed
    ground.
No maid seeks here her strayéd cow
    or sheep.

[2] Swore falsely to.   [4] Track, path.
[3] *I.e.*, perhaps (?)

Fairies and fauns and satyrs do it keep.
Then, carelessly rest here, and clip and
  kiss,
And let no fear make us our pleasures
  miss.
CLOE. Then, lie by me; the sooner we
  begin,   150
The longer ere the day descry our sin.
                              [*They lie down.*]
SULL. [*Coming forward.*] Forbear to touch
  my love; or, by yon flame,
The greatest power that shepherds
  dare to name,
Here where thou sit'st, under this holy
  tree,
Her to dishonor, thou shalt buried be!
ALEX. If Pan himself should come out
  of the lawns,[1]
With all his troops of satyrs and of
  fauns,
And bid me leave, I swear by her two
  eyes
(A greater oath than thine), I would not
  rise!
SULL. Then, from the cold earth never
  thou shalt move,   160
But lose at one stroke both thy life and
  love.   [*Wounds him.*]
CLOE. Hold, gentle shepherd!
SULL.   Fairest shepherdess,
Come you with me; I do not love ye
  less
Than that fond man that would have
  kept you there
From me of more desert.
ALEX.   O, yet forbear
To take her from me! Give me leave to
  die
By her!

*The Satyr enters; he[2] runs one way and
                              she another.*

SAT.   Now, whilst the moon doth rule
  the sky,
And the stars, whose feeble light
Gives a pale shadow to the night,
Are up, great Pan commanded me   170
To walk this grove about, whilst he,
In a corner of the wood,
Where never mortal foot hath stood,
Keeps dancing, music, and a feast,
To entertain a lovely guest;
Where he gives her many a rose—

Sweeter than the breath that blows
The leaves—grapes, berries of the best.
I never saw so great a feast.   179
But to my charge. Here must I stay,
To see what mortals lose their way,
And by a false fire, seeming bright,
Train them in and leave them right.
Then must I watch if any be
Forcing of a chastity.
If I find it, then in haste
Give my wreathéd horn a blast,
And the fairies all will run,
Wildly dancing by the moon,
And will pinch him to the bone   190
Till his lustful thoughts be gone.
ALEX. O, death!
SAT. Back again about this ground;
Sure, I hear a mortal sound.—
I bind thee by this powerful spell,
By the waters of this well,
By the glimmering moonbeams bright,
Speak again, thou mortal wight!
ALEX. O!
SAT.[3] Here the foolish mortal lies,   200
Sleeping on the ground.—Arise!—
The poor wight is almost dead;
On the ground his wounds have bled,
And his clothes fouled with his blood.
To my goddess in the wood
Will I lead him, whose hands pure
Will help this mortal wight to cure.
                    [*Exit, supporting Alexis.*]

            Enter Cloe again.

CLOE. Since I beheld yon[4] shaggy man,
  my breast
Doth pant; each bush, methinks, should
  hide a beast.
Yet my desire keeps still above my
  fear.   210
I would fain meet some shepherd, knew I
  where,
For from one cause of fear I am most
  free:
It is impossible to ravish me,
I am so willing. Here upon this ground
I left my love, all bloody with his wound;
Yet, till that fearful shape made me
  be gone,
Though he were hurt, I furnished was
  of one;

[3] Original here repeats *Speak again, thou
mortal wight.*
[4] From 1634 edn. Original has *you.*

[1] Glades.   [2] *I.e.*, Sullen Shepherd.

But now both lost.—Alexis, speak or
move,
If thou hast any life; thou art yet my
love!—
He's dead, or else is with his little
    might   220
Crept from the bank for fear of that ill
    sprite.—
Then, where art thou that struck'st my
love? O, stay!
Bring me thyself in change, and then
I'll say
Thou hast some justice. I will make
thee trim
With flowers and garlands that were
meant for him;
I'll clip thee round with both mine arms,
as fast
As I did mean he should have been em-
braced.
But thou art fled.—What hope is left
for me?
I'll run to Daphnis in the hollow tree,
Who I did mean to mock; though hope
    be small   230
To make him bold, rather than none at
all,
I'll try him; his heart, and my behavior
too,
Perhaps may teach him what he ought
to do.   *Exit.*

Enter the Sullen Shepherd.

SULL. This was the place. 'Twas but my
feeble sight,
Mixed with the horror of my deed, and
night,
That shaped these fears, and made me
run away,
And lose my beauteous, hardly-gotten
prey.—
Speak, gentle shepherdess! I am alone,
And tender love for love.—But she is gone
From me, that, having struck her lover
    dead,   240
For silly fear left her alone and fled.
And see, the wounded body is removed
By her of whom it was so well beloved.

*Enter Perigot, and Amarillis in the shape of
Amoret.*

But all these fancies must be quite
forgot.

I must lie close; here comes young Peri-
got,
With subtle Amarillis in the shape
Of Amoret. Pray, love, he may not
    scape!   *[Retires.]*
AMAR. Beloved Perigot, show me some
place
Where I may rest my limbs weak with
the chase
Of thee, an hour before thou cam'st
    at least.   250
PERI. Beshrew my tardy steps! Here
shalt thou rest
Upon this holy bank. No deadly snake
Upon this turf herself in folds doth make;
Here is no poison for the toad to feed.
Here boldly spread thy hands—no
venomed weed
Dares blister them; no slimy snail dare
creep
Over thy face when thou art fast asleep;
Here never durst the babbling cuckoo
    spit; [1]
No slough [2] of falling star did ever hit
Upon this bank. Let this thy cabin be;
This other, set with violets, for me.   261
                         [They lie down.]
AMAR. Thou dost not love me, Perigot.
PERI.   Fair maid,
You only love to hear it often said;
You do not doubt.
AMAR.   Believe me, but I do.
PERI. What, shall we now begin again to
woo?
'Tis the best way to make your lover
last,
To play with him when you have caught
him fast.
AMAR. By Pan I swear, beloved Perigot,
And by yon moon, I think thou lov'st
me not.
PERI. By Pan I swear—and, if I falsely
    swear,   270
Let him not guard my flocks. Let
foxes tear
My earliest lambs, and wolves, whilst
I do sleep,
Fall on the rest—a rot among my sheep.
I love thee better than the careful ewe
The new-yeaned lamb that is of her own
hue.

[1] An allusion to cuckoo-spit, a frothy secre-
tion exuded by the larvæ of certain insects.
[2] Shell.

I dote upon thee more than that young
    lamb
Doth on the bag that feeds him from
    his dam!
Were there a sort [1] of wolves got in
    my fold,
And one ran after thee, both young and
    old
Should be devoured, and it should be
    my strife   280
To save thee whom I love above my
    life.
Amar. How should I trust thee, when I
    see thee choose
Another bed, and dost my side refuse?
Peri. 'Twas only that the chaste thoughts
    might be shown
'Twixt thee and me, although we were
    alone.
Amar. Come, Perigot will show his power,
    that he
Can make his Amoret, though she
    weary be,
Rise nimbly from her couch and come
    to his.
Here, take thy Amoret; embrace and
    kiss.   [Comes to him.]
Peri. What means my love?
Amar.   To do as lovers should,   290
That are to be enjoyed, not to be wooed.
There's ne'er a shepherdess in all the
    plain
Can kiss thee with more art; there's
    none can feign
More wanton tricks.
Peri.   Forbear, dear soul, to try
Whether my heart be pure; I'll rather
    die
Than nourish one thought to dishonor
    thee.
Amar. Still think'st thou such a thing
    as chastity
Is amongst women? Perigot, there's
    none
That with her love is in a wood alone,
And would come home a maid; be not
    abused   300
With thy fond first belief; let time be
    used.   [Perigot rises.]
Why dost thou rise?
Peri.   My true heart thou hast slain!
Amar. Faith, Perigot, I'll pluck thee
    down again.

[1] Pack.

Peri. Let go, thou serpent, that into
    my breast
Hast with thy cunning dived!—Art not
    in jest?
Amar. Sweet love, lie down.
Peri.   Since this I live to see,
Some bitter north wind blast my flocks
    and me!
Amar. You swore you loved, yet will not
    do my will.
Peri. O, be as thou wert once, I'll love
    thee still!
Amar. I am as still I was, and all my
    kind,   310
Though other shows we have, poor
    men to blind.
Peri. Then, here I end all love; and,
    lest my vain
Belief should ever draw me in again,
Before thy face, that hast my youth
    misled,
I end my life! My blood be on thy
    head!   [Offers to kill himself.]
Amar. [Rising.] O, hold thy hands, thy
    Amoret doth cry!
Peri. Thou counsel'st well; first, Amoret
    shall die,
That is the cause of my eternal smart!
          He runs after her.
Amar. O, hold!
Peri.   This steel shall pierce thy lustful
    heart!   [Exeunt.]

The Sullen Shepherd steps out and uncharms
*   her.*

Sull. Up and down, everywhere,   320
I strew the herbs to purge the air.
Let your odor drive hence
All mists that dazzle sense.
Herbs and springs, whose hidden might
Alters shapes, and mocks the sight,
Thus I charge ye to undo
All before I brought ye to!
Let her fly, let her scape;
Give again her own shape!   [Retires.]

Enter Amarillis [in her own shape] [2] [, fol-
*   lowed by Perigot].*

Amar. Forbear, thou gentle swain! Thou
    dost mistake;   330
She whom thou follow'dst fled into the
    brake,

[2] From 1629 edn.

And, as I crossed thy way, I met thy
　　wrath,
The only fear of which near slain me hath.
PERI. Pardon, fair shepherdess; my rage
　　and night
Were both upon me, and beguiled my
　　sight.
But far be it from me to spill the blood
Of harmless maids that wander in the
　　wood! 　　　　　　　*Ex[it Amarillis].*

Enter Amoret.

AMO. Many a weary step, in yonder path,
Poor hopeless Amoret twice trodden
　　hath, 　　　　　　　　　　　339
To seek her Perigot, yet cannot hear
His voice.—My Perigot! She loves thee
　　dear
That calls.
PERI. 　　　　　See yonder where she is!
　　How fair
She shows, and yet her breath infests
　　the air!
AMO. My Perigot!
PERI. 　　　　　　　Here.
AMO. 　　　　　　　　　Happy!
PERI. 　　　　　　　　　　Hapless! First
It lights on thee; the next blow is the
　　worst. 　　　　　　　　*[Wounds her.]*
AMO. Stay, Perigot! My love, thou art un-
　　just. 　　　　　　　　　　*[Falls.]*
PERI. Death is the best reward that's
　　due to lust. 　　　　　*Exit Perigot.*
SULL. *[Aside.]* Now shall their love be
　　crossed, for, being struck,
I'll throw her in the fount, lest being
　　took
By some night-traveler, whose honest
　　care 　　　　　　　　　　　350
May help to cure her—
　　　　　　　　　　　[Comes forward.]
　　　　　　　Shepherdess, prepare
Yourself to die!
AMO. 　　　　　　　No mercy I do crave.
　　Thou canst not give a worse blow than
　　　I have.
Tell him that gave me this, who loved
　　him too,
He struck my soul, and not my body
　　through;
Tell him, when I am dead, my soul
　　shall be
At peace, if he but think he injured
　　me.

SULL. In this fount be thy grave. Thou
　　wert not meant
Sure for a woman, thou art so innocent.—
　　　　　　　He flings her into the well.
She cannot scape, for, underneath the
　　ground, 　　　　　　　　　360
In a long hollow the clear spring is bound,
Till on yon side, where the morn's sun
　　doth look,
The struggling water breaks out in a
　　brook. 　　　　　　　　　*Exit.*

*The God of the River riseth with Amoret in
　　　　　　　his arms.*

GOD. What powerful charms my streams
　　do bring
Back again unto their spring,
With such force that I their god,
Three times striking with my rod,
Could not keep them in their ranks?
My fishes shoot into the banks;
There's not one that stays and feeds; 370
All have hid them in the weeds.
Here's a mortal almost dead,
Fall'n into my riverhead,
Hallowed so with many a spell,
That till now none ever fell.
'Tis a female young and clear,
Cast in by some ravisher.
See, upon her breast a wound,
On which there is no plaster bound.
Yet, she's warm; her pulses beat; 380
'Tis a sign of life and heat.—
If thou be'st a virgin pure,
I can give a present cure.
Take a drop into thy wound,
From my watery lock[s], [1] more round
Than orient pearl, and far more pure
Than unchaste flesh may endure.—
See, she pants, and from her flesh
The warm blood gusheth out afresh.
She is an unpolluted maid; 　　　390
I must have this bleeding stayed.
From my banks I pluck this flower
With holy hand, whose virtuous power
Is at once to heal and draw.
The blood returns. I never saw
A fairer mortal. Now doth break
Her deadly slumber.—Virgin, speak.
AMO. Who hath restored my sense, given
　　me new breath,
And brought me back out of the arms of
　　death?

[1] From 1629 edn.

God. I have healed thy wounds.
Amo. 　　　　　　　　　Ay me! 　400
God. Fear not him that succored thee.
　I am this fountain's god; below,
　My waters to a river grow,
　And twixt two banks with osiers set,
　That only prosper in the wet,
　Through the meadows do they glide,
　Wheeling still on every side,
　Sometimes winding round about,
　To find the evenest channel out.
　And, if thou wilt go with me, 　　410
　Leaving mortal company,
　In the cool streams shalt thou lie,
　Free from harm as well as I.
　I will give thee for thy food
　No fish that useth [1] in the mud,
　But trout and pike, that love to swim
　Where the gravel from the brim
　Through the pure streams may be seen;
　Orient pearl fit for a queen
　Will I give, thy love to win, 　　420
　And a shell to keep them in;
　Not a fish in all my brook
　That shall disobey thy look,
　But, when thou wilt, come sliding by,
　And from thy white hand take a fly;
　And, to make thee understand
　How I can my waves command,
　They shall bubble, whilst I sing,
　Sweeter than the silver string.

The Song

　Do not fear to put thy feet 　　430
　Naked in the river sweet;
　Think not leech or newt or toad
　Will bite thy foot when thou hast trod;
　Nor let the water rising high,
　As thou wad'st in, make thee cry
　And sob; but ever live with me,
　And not a wave shall trouble thee.

Amo. Immortal power, that rul'st this
　　holy flood,
I know myself unworthy to be wooed
By thee, a god, for ere this, but for
　　thee, 　　　　　　　　　　440
I should have shown my weak mortality.
Besides, by holy oath betwixt us twain,
I am betrothed unto a shepherd swain,
Whose comely face, I know, the gods
　　above
May make me leave to see, but not to
　　love.

[1] Lives.

God. May he prove to thee as true!
　Fairest virgin, now adieu.
　I must make my waters fly,
　Lest they leave their channels dry, 449
　And beasts that come unto the spring
　Miss their morning's watering,
　Which I would not; for of late
　All the neighbor people sate
　On my banks, and from the fold
　Two white lambs of three weeks old
　Offered to my deity;
　For which this year they shall be free
　From raging floods that, as they pass,
　Leave their gravel in the grass;
　Nor shall their meads be overflown 　460
　When their grass is newly mown.
Amo. For thy kindness to me shown,
　Never from thy banks be blown
　Any tree, with windy force,
　Cross [2] thy streams, to stop thy course;
　May no beast that comes to drink,
　With his horns cast down thy brink;
　May none that for thy fish do look,
　Cut thy banks to dam thy brook;
　Barefoot may no neighbor wade 　470
　In thy cool streams, wife nor maid,
　When the spawns on stones do lie,
　To wash their hemp, and spoil the fry!
God. Thanks, virgin. I must down again.
　Thy wound will put thee to no pain.
　Wonder not so soon 'tis gone;
　A holy hand was laid upon. 　　Exit.
Amo. And I, unhappy born to be,
　Must follow him that flies from me.
　　　　　　　　　　　　[Exit.]

[Actus Quartus. Scena Prima.[3]

The same.]

Enter Perigot.

Peri. She is untrue, unconstant, and
　　unkind.
　She's gone, she's gone! Blow high, thou
　　northwest wind,
　And raise the sea to mountains; let the
　　trees
　That dare oppose thy raging fury leese [4]
　Their firm foundation, creep into the
　　earth,

[2] Across.
[3] From 1629 edn. The act division in the
original is indicated merely by *Finis actus
terti[u]s.*
[4] Lose.

And shake the world as at the monstrous
    birth
Of some new prodigy, whilst I constant
    stand,
Holding this trusty boar spear in my
    hand,
And falling thus upon it.

Enter to Perigot,[1] *Amarillis running.*

AMAR. Stay thy dead-doing hand! Thou
    art too hot   10
Against thyself.   Believe me, comely
    swain,
If that thou diest, not all the showers of
    rain
The heavy clouds send down can wash
    away
That foul unmanly guilt the world will
    lay
Upon thee.   Yet thy love untainted
    stands.
Believe me, she is constant; not the
    sands
Can be so hardly numbered as she won.
I do not trifle, shepherd; by the moon
And all those lesser lights our eyes do
    view,
All that I told thee, Perigot, is true.   20
Then be a free man; put away despair
And will to die; smooth gently up that
    fair,
Dejected forehead; be as when those eyes
Took the first heat.
PERI.   Alas, he double dies
That would believe, but cannot! 'Tis
    not well
Ye keep me thus from dying, here to
    dwell
With many worse companions. But, O,
    death!
I am not yet enamored of this[2] breath
So much but I dare leave it; 'tis not pain
In forcing of a wound, nor after-gain   30
Of many days, can hold me from my
    will.
'Tis not myself, but Amoret, bids kill.
AMAR. Stay but a little, little—but one
    hour—
And, if I do not show thee, through the
    power
Of herbs and words I have, as dark as
    night,

Myself turned to thy Amoret, in sight,
Her very figure, and the robe she wears,
With tawny buskins, and the hook she
    bears
Of thine own carving, where your names
    are set,
Wrought underneath with many a
    curious fret,   40
The primrose-chaplet, tawdry-lace,[3] and
    ring,
Thou gav'st her for her singing, with
    each thing
Else that she wears about her, let me
    feel
The first fell stroke of that revenging
    steel!
PERI. I am contented, if there be a hope,
To give it entertainment for the scope
Of one poor hour. Go; you shall find
    me next
Under yon shady beech, even thus per-
    plexed,
And thus believing.
AMAR.   Bind, before I go,
Thy soul by Pan unto me, not to do   50
Harm or outrageous wrong upon thy
    life
Till my return.
PERI.   By Pan, and by the strife
He had with Phœbus for the mastery,
When golden Midas judged their min-
    strelsy,
I will not!   *Exeunt.*

Enter Satyr with Alexis, hurt.

SAT. Softly gliding as I go,
With this burthen full of woe,
Through still silence of the night
Guided by the glowworm's light,
Hither am I come at last.   60
Many a thicket have I passed;
Not a twig that durst deny me,
Not a bush that durst descry[4] me
To the little bird that sleeps
On the tender spray; nor creeps
That hardy worm with pointed tail,
But if[5] I be under sail,
Flying faster than the wind,
Leaving all the clouds behind,
But doth hide her tender head   70
In some hollow tree, or bed

---

1 Original reads *Perigot to enter.*
2 From 1634 edn. Original reads *his.*
3 Lace bought at the fair of St. Audrey at Ely.
4 Reveal.   5 Unless.

Of seeded nettles; not a hare
Can be started from his fare
By my footing; nor a wish
Is more sudden, nor a fish
Can be found with greater ease
Cut the vast unbounded seas,
Leaving neither print nor sound,
Than I, when nimbly on the ground
I measure many a league an hour.   80
But, behold, the happy bower
That must ease me of my charge,
And by holy hand enlarge [1]
The soul of this sad man that yet
Lies fast bound in deadly fit.
Heaven and great Pan succor it!—
Hail, thou beauty of the bower,
Whiter than the paramour
Of my master! Let me crave   89
Thy virtuous help, to keep from grave
This poor mortal that here lies,
Waiting when the Destinies
Will undo his thread of life.
View the wound, by cruel knife
Trenched into him.

[*Enter Clorin.*]

CLO. What art thou call'st me from my
          holy rites,
And with the feared name of death
          affrights
My tender ears? Speak me thy name
          and will.
SAT. I am the satyr that did fill
Your lap with early fruit, and will,   100
When I hap to gather more,
Bring ye better and more store.
Yet I come not empty now:
See, a blossom from the bough;
But beshrew his heart that pulled it,
And his perfect sight that culled it
From the other springing blooms!
For a sweeter youth the grooms
Cannot show me, nor the downs,
Nor the many neighboring towns.   110
Low in yonder glade I found him;
Softly in mine arms I bound him;
Hither have I brought him sleeping
In a trance, his wounds fresh weeping,
In remembrance such youth may
Spring and perish in a day.
CLO. Satyr, they wrong thee that do
          term thee rude;

[1] *Free.*

Though thou be'st outward-rough and
          tawny-hued,
Thy manners are as gentle and as fair
As his who brags himself born only
          heir   120
To all humanity.—Let me see thy wound.
This herb will stay the current, being
          bound
Fast to the orifice, and this restrain
Ulcers and swellings, and such inward
          pain
As the cold air hath forced into the sore;
This to draw out such putrefying gore
As inward falls.
SAT.   Heaven grant it may do good!
CLO. Fairly wipe away the blood.
Hold him gently, till I fling
Water of a virtuous spring   130
On his temples; turn him twice
To the moonbeams; pinch him thrice,
That the laboring soul may draw
From his great eclipse.
SAT.   I saw
His eyelids moving.
CLO.   Give him breath;
All the danger of cold death
Now is vanished! With this plaster
And this unction do I master
All the festered ill that may
Give him grief another day.   140
SAT. See, he gathers up his sprite,
And begins to hunt for light;
Now a [2] gaps and breathes again.
How the blood runs to the vein
That erst was empty!
ALEX.   O my heart!
My dearest, dearest Cloe! O, the smart
Runs through my side! I feel some
          pointed thing
Pass through my bowels, sharper than
          the sting
Of scorpion.—
Pan, preserve me!—What are you?   150
Do not hurt me; I am true
To my Cloe, though she fly,
And leave me to this destiny.
There she stands, and will not lend
Her smooth white hand to help her
          friend.
But I am much mistaken, for that face
Bears more austerity and modest grace,
More reproving and more awe,
Than these eyes yet ever saw

[2] *He.*

In my Cloe. O, my pain   160
Eagerly renews again!
Give me your help for his sake you love
  best.
CLO. Shepherd, thou canst not possible
  take rest,
Till thou hast laid aside all heats, desires,
Provoking thoughts that stir up lusty
  fires,
Commerce with wanton eyes, strong
  blood, and will
To execute. These must be purged until
The vein grow whiter; then repent, and
  pray
Great Pan to keep you from the like
  decay,
And I shall undertake your cure with
  ease;   170
Till when, this virtuous plaster [1] will
  displease [2]
Your tender sides. Give me your hand,
  and rise!
Help him a little, satyr, for his thighs
Yet are feeble.
ALEX. [*Rising.*]   Sure, I have lost much
  blood.
SAT. 'Tis no matter; 'twas not good.
Mortal, you must leave your wooing;
Though there be a joy in doing,
Yet it brings much grief behind it.
They best feel it that do find it.
CLO. Come, bring him in; I will attend his
  sore.—   180
When you are well, take heed you lust
  no more.   [*They retire.*]
SAT. Shepherd, see what comes of kissing;
By my head, 'twere better missing.—
Brightest, if there be remaining
Any service, without feigning
I will do it. Were I set
To catch the nimble wind, or get
Shadows gliding on the green,
Or to steal from the great queen
Of fairies all her beauty,   190
I would do it, so much duty
Do I owe those precious eyes.
CLO. I thank thee, honest satyr. If the
  cries
Of any other that be hurt or ill
Draw thee unto them, prithee, do thy
  will
To bring them hether.

[1] From 1629 edn. Original reads *Playsters.*
[2] Discomfort.

SAT. I will; and, when the weather
Serves to angle in the brook,
I will bring a silver hook,
With a line of finest silk,   200
And a rod as white as milk,
To deceive the little fish.
So I take my leave, and wish
On this bower may ever dwell
Spring and summer!
CLO.   Friend, farewell.
        Exit [with Alexis and Satyr].

Enter Amoret, seeking her Love.

AMO. This place is ominous; for here I lost
My love and almost life, and since have
  crossed
All these woods over; never a nook or
  dell,
Where any little bird or beast doth dwell,
But I have sought it; never a bending
  brow   210
Of any hill, or glade the wind sings
  through,
Nor a green bank or shade where shep-
  herds use
To sit and riddle, sweetly pipe, or
  choose
Their valentines, but I have missed [3] to
  find
My love in. Perigot! O, too unkind,
Why hast thou fled me? Whither art
  thou gone?
How have I wronged thee? Was my
  love alone
To thee worthy this scorned recompense?
  'Tis well;
I am content to feel it. But I tell
Thee, shepherd, and these lusty woods
  shall hear,   220
Forsaken Amoret is yet as clear
Of any stranger fire as heaven is
From foul corruption, or the deep abyss
From light and happiness; and thou
  mayst know
All this for truth, and how that fatal
  blow
Thou gav'st me, never from desert of
  mine
Fell on my life, but from suspect [4] of
  thine,
Or fury more than madness. There-
  fore here,

[3] Failed.   [4] Suspicion.

Since I have lost my life, my love, my
    dear,
Upon this curséd place, and on this
    green   230
That first divorced us, shortly shall be
    seen
A sight of so great pity that each eye
Shall daily spend his spring in memory
Of my untimely fall.

Enter Amarillis.

AMAR. [*Aside.*]   I am not blind,
    Nor is it through the working of my
    mind
That this shows Amoret. Forsake me, all
That dwell upon the soul, but what
    men call
Wonder, or, more than wonder, miracle!
For, sure, so strange as this, the oracle
Never gave answer of; it passeth dreams,
Or madmen's fancy, when the many
    streams   241
Of new imagination rise and fall.
'Tis but an hour since these ears heard
    her call
For pity to young Perigot, whilst he,
Directed by his fury, bloodily
Lanched [1] up her breast, which bloodless
    fell and cold;
And, if belief may credit what was told,
After all this, the melancholy swain
Took her into his arms, being almost
    slain,
And to the bottom of the holy well   250
Flung her, forever with the waves to
    dwell.
'Tis she, the very same, 'tis Amoret,
And living yet! The great powers will
    not let
Their virtuous love be crossed.—Maid,
    wipe away
Those heavy drops of sorrow, and allay
The storm that yet goes high, which,
    not depressed,
Breaks heart and life and all before it
    rest.
Thy Perigot—
AMO.   Where, which is Perigot?
AMAR. Sits there below, lamenting much,
    God wot,
Thee and thy fortune. Go and comfort
    him: 260

[1] Lanced.

And thou shalt find him underneath a
    brim
Of sailing [2] pines that edge yon moun-
    tain in.
AMO. I go, I run. Heaven grant me I may
    win
His soul again!   [*Exit Amoret.*] [3]

Enter Sullen.

SULL.   Stay, Amarillis, stay!
You are too fleet; 'tis two hours yet to
    day.
I have performed my promise; let us sit
And warm our bloods together, till the
    fit
Come lively on us.
AMAR.   Friend, you are too keen;
The morning riseth, and we shall be seen.
Forbear a little.
SULL.   I can stay no longer.   270
AMAR. Hold, shepherd, hold! Learn not
    to be a wronger
Of your word. Was not your promise
    laid,
To break their loves first?
SULL.   I have done it, maid.
AMAR. No; they are yet unbroken, met
    again,
And are as hard to part yet as the stain
Is from the finest lawn.
SULL.   I say they are
Now at this present parted, and so far
That they shall never meet.
AMAR.   Swain, 'tis not so;
For do but to yon hanging mountain go,
And there believe your eyes.
SULL.   You do but hold   280
Off with delays and trifles.—Farewell,
    cold
And frozen bashfulness, unfit for men!—
Thus I salute thee, virgin!
               [*Attempts to seize her.*]
AMAR.   And thus, then,
I bid you follow; catch me if you can!
                        Exit.
SULL. And, if I stay behind, I am no
    man!   [*Exit, running after her.*]

Enter Perigot.

PERI. Night, do not steal away; I woo
    thee yet
To hold a hard hand o'er the rusty bit

[2] "*I.e.*, of which masts are made" (Greg).
[3] From 1629 edn.

That guides thy lazy team. Go back
  again,
Boötes, thou that driv'st thy frozen
  wain
Round as a ring, and bring a second
  night   290
To hide my sorrows from the coming
  light;
Let not the eyes of men stare on my
  face
And read my falling; give me some black
  place,
Where never sunbeam shot his whole-
  some light,
That I may sit and pour out my sad
  sprite
Like running water, never to be known
After the forcéd fall and sound is gone.

Enter Amoret, looking of [1] Perigot.

AMO. This is the bottom.[2]—Speak, if
  thou be here,
My Perigot! Thy Amoret, thy dear,
Calls on thy lovéd name.
PERI.   What [art] [3] thou dare   300
  Tread these forbidden paths, where
  death and care
  Dwell on the face of darkness?
AMO.   'Tis thy friend,
Thy Amoret, come hither to give end
To these consumings. Look up, gentle
  boy;
I have forgot those pains and dear
  annoy
I suffered for thy sake, and am content
To be thy love again. Why hast thou
  rent
Those curléd locks where I have often
  hung
Ribands and damask-roses, and have
  flung
Waters distilled, to make thee fresh
  and gay,   310
Sweeter than nosegays on a bridal day?
Why dost thou cross thine arms, and
  hang thy face
Down to thy bosom, letting fall apace
From those two little heavens, upon the
  ground,
Showers of more price, more orient, and
  more round
Than those that hang upon the moon's
  pale brow?

Cease these complainings, shepherd; I
  am now
The same I ever was, as kind and free,
And can forgive before you ask of me;
Indeed, I can and will.
PERI.   So spoke my fair!   320
  O, you great working powers of earth
  and air,
Water and forming fire, why have you
  lent
Your hidden virtues of so ill intent?
Even such a face, so fair, so bright of
  hue,
Had Amoret; such words, so smooth
  and new,
Came flowing from her tongue; such
  was her eye,
And such the pointed sparkle that did
  fly
Forth like a bleeding shaft. All is the
  same,
The robe and buskins, painted hook,
  and frame
Of all her body. O me, Amoret!   330
AMO. Shepherd, what means this riddle?
  Who hath set
So strong a difference twixt myself and
  me
That I am grown another? Look, and see
The ring thou gav'st me, and about my
  wrist
That curious bracelet thou thyself didst
  twist
From those fair tresses. Know'st thou
  Amoret?
Hath not some newer love forced thee
  forget
Thy ancient faith?
PERI.   Still nearer to my love!
  These be the very words she oft did
  prove
Upon my temper; so she still would
  take   340
Wonder into her face, and silent make
Signs with her head and hand, as who
  would say,
"Shepherd, remember this another day."
AMO. Am I not Amoret? Where was I
  lost?
Can there be heaven and time and men,
  [and] [4] most
Of these unconstant?   Faith, where
  art thou fled?

[1] For.   [2] Dale.   [3] From 1629 edn.   [4] From 1629 edn.

Are all the vows and protestations
   dead,
The hands held up, the wishes and the
   heart?
Is there not one remaining, not a part
Of all these to be found? Why, then, I
   see   350
Men never knew that virtue, constancy.
PERI. Men ever were most blessed, till
   cross fate
Brought love and women forth, unfor-
   tunate
To all that ever tasted of their smiles;
Whose actions are all double, full of
   wiles,
Like to the subtle hare, that fore the
   hounds
Makes many turnings, leaps, and many
   rounds,
This way and that way, to deceive the
   scent
Of her pursuers.
AMO.   'Tis but to prevent
Their speedy coming on, that seek her
   fall;   360
The hands of cruel men, more bestial,
And of a nature more refusing good
Than beasts themselves, or fishes of the
   flood.
[PERI.] [1] Thou art all these, and more than
   nature meant
When she created all: frowns, joys,
   content;
Extreme fire for an hour, and presently
Colder than sleepy poison, or the sea
Upon whose face sits a continual frost;
Your actions ever driven to the most,
Then down again as low, that none can
   find   370
The rise or falling of a woman's mind.
AMO. Can there be any age or days or time
Or tongues of men guilty so great a crime
As wronging simple maid? O, Perigot,
Thou that wast yesterday without a
   blot,
Thou that wast every good and every-
   thing
That men call blessed, thou that wast the
   spring
From whence our looser grooms drew all
   their best,
Thou that wast always just and al-
   ways blessed

[1] From 1629 edn.

In faith and promise, thou that hadst
   the name   380
Of virtuous given thee, and made good
   the same
Ev'n from thy cradle, thou that wast
   that all
That men delighted in! O, what a fall
Is this, to have been so, and now to be
The only best in wrong and infamy!
And I to live to know this! And by me,
That loved thee dearer than mine eyes, or
   that
Which we esteem our honor, virgin
   state!
Dearer than swallows love the early
   morn,
Or dogs of chase the sound of merry
   horn;   390
Dearer than thou canst love thy new
   love, if thou hast
Another, and far dearer than the last;
Dearer than thou canst love thyself,
   though all
The self-love were within thee that did
   fall
With that coy swain that now is made
   a flower,
For whose dear sake Echo weeps many a
   shower!
And am I thus rewarded for my flame?
Loved worthily to get a wanton's name?
Come, thou forsaken willow, wind my
   head,
And noise it to the world, my love is
   dead!   400
I am forsaken, I am cast away,
And left for every lazy groom to say
I was unconstant, light, and sooner lost
Than the quick clouds we see, or the
   chill frost
When the hot sun beats on it! Tell me
   yet,
Canst thou not love again thy Amoret?
PERI. Thou art not worthy of that blessed
   name;
I must not know thee. Fling thy wanton
   flame
Upon some lighter blood that may be
   hot   409
With words and feignéd passions; Perigot
Was ever yet unstained, and shall not
   now
Stoop to the meltings of a borrowed
   brow.

Amo. Then hear me, heaven, to whom
    I call for right,
And you, fair twinkling stars, that crown
    the night;
And hear me, woods, and silence of this
    place,
And ye, sad hours, that move a sullen
    pace;
Hear me, ye shadows, that delight to
    dwell
In horrid darkness, and ye powers of
    hell,
Whilst I breathe out my last! I am that
    maid,   419
That yet-untainted Amoret, that played
The careless prodigal, and gave away
My soul to this young man that now
    dares say
I am a stranger, not the same, more
    wild;
And thus with much belief I was be-
    guiled.
I am that maid that have delayed,
    denied,
And almost scorned the loves of all
    that tried
To win me but this swain, and yet
    confess
I have been wooed by many with no
    less
Soul of affection, and have often had
Rings, belts, and cracknels sent me from
    the lad   430
That feeds his flocks down westward;
    lambs and doves
By young Alexis; Daphnis sent me
    gloves—
All which I gave to thee. Nor these
    nor they
That sent them did I smile on, or e'er
    lay
Up to my after-memory. But why
Do I resolve to grieve, and not to die?
Happy had been the stroke thou gav'st,
    if home,
By this time had I found a quiet room,
Where every slave is free, and every
    breast,
That living bred new care, now lies at
    rest;   440
And thither will poor Amoret.
Peri.   Thou must.
Was ever any man so loath to trust
His eyes as I? Or was there ever yet

Any so like as this to Amoret?
For whose dear sake I promise, if there
    be
A living soul within thee, thus to free
Thy body from it.   *He hurts her again.*
Amo. [*Falling.*]   So, this work hath end.
    Farewell, and live; be constant to thy
    friend
That loves thee next.

Enter Satyr; Perigot runs off.

Sat. See, the day begins to break,   450
    And the light shoots [1] like a streak
    Of subtle fire; the wind blows cold,
    Whilst the morning doth unfold;
    Now the birds begin to rouse,
    And the squirrel from the boughs
    Leaps to get him nuts and fruit.
    The early lark, that erst was mute,
    Carols to the rising day
    Many a note and many a lay;
    Therefore here I end my watch,   460
    Lest the wand'ring swain should catch
    Harm, or lose himself.
Amo.   Ah me!
Sat. Speak again, whate'er thou be.
    I am ready; speak, I say!
    By the dawning of the day,
    By the power of night and Pan,
    I enforce thee, speak again!
Amo. O, I am most unhappy!
Sat. Yet more blood!
    Sure, these wanton swains are wood.   470
    Can there be a hand or heart
    Dare commit so vild [2] a part
    As this murder? By the moon,
    That hid herself when this was done,
    Never was a sweeter face;
    I will bear her to the place
    Where my goddess keeps,[3] and crave
    Her to give her life or grave.   *Exeunt.*

Enter Clorin.

Clo. Here whilst one patient takes his
    rest secure,   479
I steal abroad to do another cure.—
Pardon, thou buried body of my love,
That from thy side I dare so soon re-
    move;
I will not prove unconstant, nor will leave
Thee for an hour alone. When I deceive

---

[1] From 1634 edn. Original reads *shutts.*
[2] Vile.   [3] Dwells.

My first-made vow, the wildest of the
   wood
Tear me, and o'er thy grave let out my
   blood!
I go by wit to cure a lover's pain,
Which no herb can; being done, I'll
   come again.   *Exit.*

Enter Thenot.

THE. Poor shepherd, in this shade forever lie
And, seeing thy fair Clorin's cabin,
   die!   [*Lies down.*]   490
O, hapless love, which being answered,
   ends!
And, as a little infant cries and bends
His tender brows, when, rolling of his
   eye,
He hath espied something that glisters
   nigh,
Which he would have, yet, give it him,
   away
He throws it straight, and cries afresh
   to play
With something else—such my affection,
   set
On that which I should loathe, if I could
   get.

Enter Clorin.

CLO. [*Aside.*] See, where he lies! Did
   ever man but he
Love any woman for her constancy 500
To her dead lover, which she needs
   must end
Before she can allow him for her friend,
And he himself must needs the cause
   destroy
For which he loves, before he can en-
   joy?
Poor shepherd, heaven grant I at once
   may free
Thee from thy pain, and keep my loy-
   alty!—
Shepherd, look up.
THE.   Thy brightness doth amaze;
So Phœbus may at noon bid mortals
   gaze.
Thy glorious constancy appears so bright,
I dare not meet the beams with my
   weak sight.   510
CLO. Why dost thou pine away thyself
   for me?

THE. Why dost thou keep such spotless
   constancy?
CLO. Thou holy shepherd, see what for
   thy sake
Clorin, thy Clorin, now dare undertake.
                 He starts up.
THE. Stay there, thou constant Clorin!
   If there be
Yet any part of woman left in thee,
To make thee light, think yet before
   thou speak.
CLO. See, what a holy vow for thee I
   break—
I, that already have my fame far spread
For being constant to my lover dead.
THE. Think yet, dear Clorin, of your love,
   how true,   521
If you had died, he would have been to
   you.
CLO. Yet, all I'll lose for thee—
THE.   Think but how blessed
A constant woman is above the rest!
CLO. And offer up myself, here on this
   ground,
To be disposed by thee.
THE.   Why dost thou wound
His heart with malice against women
   more,
That hated all the sex but thee before?
How much more pleasant had it been to
   me
To die than [to] [1] behold this change in
   thee!   530
Yet, yet return; let not the woman sway̨
CLO. Insult not on [2] her now, nor use de-
   lay,
Who for thy sake hath ventured all her
   fame.
THE. Thou hast not ventured, but bought
   certain shame.
Your sex's curse, foul falsehood, must
   and shall,
I see, once in your lives light on you all.
I hate thee now. Yet turn!
CLO.   Be just to me;
Shall I at once lose both my fame and
   thee?
THE. Thou hadst no fame; that which
   thou didst like good
Was but thy appetite that swayed thy
   blood   540
For that time to the best, for as a blast

---

[1] From 1634 edn.
[2] Do not behave insolently toward.

That through a house comes, usually
doth cast
Things out of order, yet by chance may
come
And blow some one thing to his proper
room,
So did thy appetite, and not thy zeal,
Sway thee by chance to do some one
thing well.
Yet turn!
CLO.   Thou dost but try me, if I would
Forsake thy dear embraces for my old
Love's, though he were alive; but do not
fear.
THE. I do contemn thee now, and dare
come near,   550
And gaze upon thee; for methinks that
grace,
Austerity, which sate upon that face,
Is gone, and thou like others. False
maid, see,
This is the gain of foul inconstancy!
                           Exit.
CLO. 'Tis done.—Great Pan, I give thee
thanks for it!—
What art could not have healed is cured
by wit.

Enter Thenot again.

THE. Will ye be constant yet? Will ye
remove
Into the cabin to your buried love?
CLO. No, let me die, but by thy side re-
main.
THE. There's none shall know that thou
didst ever stain   560
Thy worthy strictness, but shalt honored
be,
And I will lie again under this tree,
And pine and die for thee with more
delight
Than I have sorrow now to know thee
light.
CLO. Let me have thee, and I'll be where
thou wilt.
THE. Thou art of women's race, and full
of guilt.
Farewell all hope of that sex! Whilst I
thought
There was one good, I feared to find
one naught;
But, since their minds I all alike espy,
Henceforth I'll choose, as others, by
mine eye.   *[Exit.]*   570

CLO. Blessed be ye powers that gave such
quick redress,
And for my labors sent so good success!
I rather choose, though I a woman be,
He should speak ill of all than die for
me.   *[Exit.]* [1]

ACTUS QUINTUS. SCENA PRIMA.

[The same.]

Enter Priest and Old Shepherd.

PRIEST. Shepherds, rise, and shake off
sleep!
See, the blushing morn doth peep
Through the windows, whilst the sun
To the mountain tops is run,
Gilding all the vales below
With his rising flames, which grow
Greater by his climbing still.
Up, ye lazy grooms, and fill
Bag and bottle for the field!   9
Clasp your cloaks fast, lest they yield
To the bitter northeast wind.
Call the maidens up, and find
Who lay longest, that she may
Go without a friend all day;
Then reward your dogs, and pray
Pan to keep you from decay.
So unfold, and then away!—
What, not a shepherd stirring? Sure,
the grooms
Have found their beds too easy, or the
rooms
Filled with such new delight and heat
that they   20
Have both forgot their hungry sheep and
day.
Knock, that they may remember what
a shame
Sloth and neglect lays on a shepherd's
name.
OLD SHEP. It is to little purpose. Not a
swain
This night hath known his lodging here,
or lain
Within these cotes. The woods, or
some near town
That is a neighbor to the bordering down,
Hath drawn them thither 'bout some
lusty sport,
Or spicéd wassail bowl, to which resort
All the young men and maids of many
a cote,   30

---

[1] Original edn. here adds *Finis actus quartus.*

Whilst the trim minstrel strikes his
　　merry note.
PRIEST. God pardon sin!—Show me the
　　way that leads
To any of their haunts.
OLD SHEP.　　　　　This to the meads,
And that down to the woods.
PRIEST.　　　　　Then, this for me.
Come, shepherd, let me crave your
　　company.　　　　　*Exeunt.*

Enter Clorin in her cabin, Alexis with her.[1]

CLO. Now your thoughts are almost pure,
And your wound begins to cure.
Strive to banish all that's vain,
Lest it should break out again.
ALEX. Eternal thanks to thee, thou holy
　　maid!　　　　　　　　　　40
I find my former wand'ring thoughts
　　well stayed
Through thy wise precepts; and my
　　outward pain
By thy choice herbs is almost gone again.
Thy sex's vice and virtue are revealed
At once; for what one hurt another
　　healed.
CLO. May thy grief more appease!
Relapses are the worst disease.
Take heed how you in thought offend;
So mind and body both will mend.

Enter Satyr with Amoret.

AMO. Be'st thou the wildest creature of
　　the wood,　　　　　　　　50
That bear'st me thus away, drowned in
　　my blood,
And dying, know I cannot injured be;
I am a maid; let that name fight for me.
SAT. Fairest virgin, do not fear
Me, that doth thy body bear,
Not to hurt, but healed to be;
Men are ruder far than we.—
See, fair goddess, in the wood
They have let out yet more blood.
Some savage man hath struck her
　　breast,　　　　　　　　　60
So soft and white, that no wild beast
Durst 'a' touched, asleep or wake—
So sweet that adder, newt, or snake
Would have lain, from arm to arm,
On her bosom to be warm

[1] Early edns. here erroneously add *and Ama-rillis.*

All a night, and, being hot,
Gone away and stung her not.
Quickly clap herbs to her breast.
A man, sure, is a kind of beast.　　69
CLO. With spotless hand on spotless breast
I put these herbs, to give thee rest—
Which, till it heal thee, there will bide,
If both be pure; if not, off slide.—
See, it falls off from the wound!
Shepherdess, thou art not sound,
Full of lust.
SAT.　　　Who would have thought it?
　　So fair a face!
CLO.　　　　　Why, that hath brought it.
AMO. For aught I know or think, these
　　words my last,
Yet Pan so help me as my thoughts are
　　chaste!
CLO. And so may Pan bless this my
　　cure,　　　　　　　　　80
As all my thoughts are just and pure!
Some uncleanness nigh doth lurk,
That will not let my medicines work.—
Satyr, search if thou canst find it.
SAT. Here away methinks I wind[2] it.
Stronger yet!—O, here they be;
Here, here, in a hollow tree
Two fond mortals have I found.
CLO. Bring them out; they are unsound.

Enter Cloe and Daphnis.

SAT. By the fingers thus I wring ye;　90
To my goddess thus I bring ye;
Strife is vain; come gently in.—
I scented them; they're full of sin.
CLO. Hold, satyr; take this glass,
Sprinkle over all the place,
Purge the air from lustful breath,
To save this shepherdess from death,
And stand you still whilst I do dress
Her wound, for fear the pain increase.
SAT. From this glass I throw a drop　100
Of crystal water on the top
Of every grass, on flowers a pair.—
Send a fume, and keep the air
Pure and wholesome, sweet and blessed,
Till this virgin's wound be dressed.
CLO. Satyr, help to bring her in.
SAT. By Pan, I think she hath no sin,
　　[*Carries Amoret into the bower.*]
She is so light.—Lie on these leaves.
Sleep, that mortal sense deceives,

[2] *I.e.,* catch wind of.

Crown thine eyes and ease thy pain; 110
Mayst thou soon be well again!
CLO. Satyr, bring the shepherd near;
Try him, if his mind be clear.
SAT. Shepherd, come.
DAPH.   My thoughts are pure.
SAT. The better trial to endure.
CLO. In this flame his finger thrust,
Which will burn him if he lust;
But if not, away will turn,
As loath unspotted flesh to burn.
[*Satyr holds Daphnis' finger to the flame.*]
See, it gives back; let him go.   120
SAT.[1] Farewell, mortal; keep thee so.—
                          [*Exit Daphnis.*]
Stay, fair nymph; fly not so fast;
We must try if you be chaste.—
Here's a hand that quakes for fear;
Sure, she will not prove so clear.
CLO. Hold her finger to the flame;
That will yield her praise or shame.
SAT. To her doom she dares not stand,
       [*Holds Cloe's finger to the flame.*]
But plucks away her tender hand,
And the taper darting sends   130
His hot beams at her fingers' ends.—
O, thou art foul within, and hast
A mind, if nothing else, unchaste!
ALEX. Is not that Cloe? 'Tis my love,
   'tis she!
Cloe, fair Cloe!
CLOE.   My Alexis!
ALEX.   He.
CLOE. Let me embrace thee.
CLO.   Take her hence,
Lest her sight disturb his sense.
ALEX. Take not her; take my life first!
CLO. See, his wound again is burst!
Keep her near, here in the wood,   140
Till I have stopped these streams of
blood.   [*Exeunt Cloe and Satyr.*]
Soon again he ease shall find,
If I can but still his mind.
This curtain thus I do display,
To keep the piercing air away.
     [*Draws the traverse across the bower.*]

    Enter Old Shepherd and Priest.

PRIEST. Sure, they are lost forever; 'tis
   in vain
To find them out with trouble and
  much pain

That have a ripe desire and forward will
To fly the company of all but ill.
What shall be counseled now?   Shall
  we retire,   150
Or constant follow still that first desire
We had to find them?
OLD SHEP.   Stay a little while,
For, if the morning's mist do not be-
  guile
My sight with shadows, sure I see a
  swain;
One of this jolly troop's come back
  again.

        Enter Thenot.

PRIEST. Dost thou not blush, young
  shepherd, to be known
Thus without care leaving thy flocks
  alone,
And following what desire and present
  blood
Shapes out before thy burning sense
  for good,
Having forgot what tongue hereafter
  may   160
Tell to the world thy falling off, and say
Thou art regardless both of good and
  shame,
Spurning at virtue and a virtuous name?
And like a glorious,[2] desperate man that
  buys
A poison of much price, by which he
  dies,
Dost thou lay out for lust, whose only
  gain
Is foul disease, with present age and
  pain,
And then a grave? These be the fruits
  that grow
In such hot veins, that only beat to know
Where they may take most ease, and
  grow ambitious   170
Through their own wanton fire and
  pride delicious.
THE. Right holy sir, I have not known this
  night
What the smooth face of mirth was, or
  the sight
Of any looseness; music, joy, and ease
Have been to me as bitter drugs to
  please
A stomach lost with weakness, not a
  game

---

[1] In the original, this speech head has dropped
so that it precedes the next line.

[2] Boastful.

That I am skilled at throughly; nor a dame,
Went her tongue smoother than the feet of time,
Her beauty ever-living like the rime
Our blessed Tityrus [1] did sing of yore;
No, were she more enticing that the store   181
Of fruitful summer, when the loaden tree
Bids the faint traveler be bold and free;
'Twere but to me like thunder gainst the bay,
Whose lightning may inclose, but never stay
Upon his charméd branches; such am I
Against the catching flames of woman's eye.

PRIEST. Then, wherefore hast thou wandered?

THE.   'Twas a vow
That drew me out last night, which I have now
Strictly performed, and homewards go to give   190
Fresh pasture to my sheep, that they may live.

PRIEST. 'Tis good to hear ye, shepherd, if the heart
In this well-sounding music bear his part.
Where have you left the rest?

[THE.] [2]   I have not seen,
Since yesternight we met upon this green
To fold our flocks up, any of that train;
Yet have I walked these woods round, and have lain
All this long night under an aged tree;
Yet neither wand'ring shepherd did I see,   199
Or shepherdess; or drew into mine ear
The sound of living thing, unless it were
The nightingale, among the thick-leaved spring,
That sits alone in sorrow, and doth sing
Whole nights away in mourning; or the owl,
Or our great enemy,[3] that still doth howl
Against the moon's cold beams.

[1] Either Virgil or Chaucer.   [3] *I.e.*, the wolf.
[2] From 1629 edn.

PRIEST.   Go, and beware
Of after-falling.

THE.   Father, 'tis my care.
                                    Exit Thenot.

Enter Daphnis.

OLD SHEP. Here comes another straggler. Sure I see
A shame in this young shepherd.—Daphnis?

DAPH.   He.

PRIEST. Where hast left the rest, that should have been   210
Long before this grazing upon the green
Their yet-imprisoned flocks?

DAPH.   Thou holy man,
Give me a little breathing, till I can
Be able to unfold what I have seen—
Such horror, that the like hath never been
Known to the ear of shepherd. O, my heart
Labors a double motion to impart
So heavy tidings! You all know the bower
Where the chaste Clorin lives, by whose great power
Sick men and cattle have been often cured.   220
There lovely Amoret, that was assured [4]
To lusty Perigot, bleeds out her life,
Forced by some iron hand and fatal knife;
And, by her, young Alexis.

Enter Amarillis, running from her Sullen Shepherd.

AMAR.   If there be
Ever a neighbor brook or hollow tree,
Receive my body, close me up from lust
That follows at my heels! Be ever just,
Thou god of shepherds, Pan, for her dear sake
That loves the rivers' brinks, and still doth shake
In cold remembrance of thy quick pursuit.   230
Let me be made a reed, and, ever mute,
Nod to the waters' fall, whilst every blast
Sings through my slender leaves that I was chaste!

[4] Affianced.

PRIEST. This is a night of wonder.—
　Amarill,
Be comforted; the holy gods are still
Revengers of these wrongs.
AMAR.　　　　　Thou blessed man,
　Honored upon these plains, and loved
　　of Pan,
Hear me, and save from endless infamy
My yet unblasted flower, virginity!
By all the garlands that have crowned
　　that head,　　　　　　　　　240
By thy chaste office, and the marriage
　　bed
That still is blessed by thee, by all the
　　rites
Due to our god, and by those virgin
　　lights
That burn before his altar, let me not
Fall from my former state, to gain the
　　blot
That never shall be purged! I am not
　　now
That wanton Amarillis; here I vow
To heaven and thee, grave father, if I
　　may
Scape this unhappy night, to know the
　　day
A virgin, never after to endure　　250
The tongues or company of men un-
　　pure!
I hear him come; save me!
PRIEST.　　　　　Retire awhile
　Behind this bush, till we have known
　　that vile
Abuser of young maidens. [*They retire.*]

Enter Sullen.

SULL.　　　　　Stay thy pace,
　Most lovéd Amarillis; let the chase
Grow calm and milder; fly me not so
　　fast;
I fear the pointed brambles have unlaced
Thy golden buskins. Turn again, and see
Thy shepherd follow, that is strong and
　　free,　　　　　　　　　259
Able to give thee all content and ease.
I am not bashful, virgin; I can please
At first encounter, hug thee in mine
　　arm,
And give thee many kisses, soft and warm
As those the sun prints on the [1] smiling
　　cheek

Of plums or mellow peaches; I am sleek
And smooth as Neptune when stern
　　Æolus
Locks up his surly winds, and nimbly
　　thus
Can show my active youth. Why dost
　　thou fly?
Remember, Amarillis, it was I　　269
That killed Alexis for thy sake, and set
An everlasting hate twixt Amoret
And her beloved Perigot; 'twas I
That drowned her in the well, where she
　　must lie
Till time shall leave to be. Then, turn
　　again,
Turn with thy open arms, and clip the
　　swain
That hath performed all this; turn, turn,
　　I say;
I must not be deluded.
PRIEST. [*Coming forward.*]　　Monster,
　　stay!
Thou that art like a canker to the state
Thou liv'st and breath'st in, eating with
　　debate [2]
Through every honest bosom, forcing
　　still　　　　　　　　　280
The veins of any men may serve thy
　　will;
Thou that hast offered with a sinful hand
To seize upon this virgin that doth stand
Yet trembling here!
SULL.　　　　Good holiness, declare
　What had the danger been, if being bare
I had embraced her; tell me, by your
　　art,
What coming wonders would that sight
　　impart?
PRIEST. Lust and branded soul.
SULL.　　　　　Yet, tell me more;
　Hath not our mother Nature, for her
　　store
And great increase, said it is good and
　　just,　　　　　　　　　290
And willed that every living creature
　　must
Beget his like?
PRIEST.　　　Ye are better read than I,
　I must confess, in blood and lechery.—
Now to the bower, and bring this beast
　　along,
Where he may suffer penance for his
　　wrong.　　　　　　　[*Exeunt.*]

---

[1] From 1634 edn. Original has *thy.*

[2] Discord.

Enter Perigot, with his hand bloody.

PERI. Here will I wash it in the morning's
  dew,
  Which she on every little grass doth
  strew
  In silver drops against the sun's appear.[1]
  'Tis holy water, and will make me
  clear.—
  My hand will not be cleansed.—My
  wrongéd love,   300
  If thy chaste spirit in the air yet move,
  Look mildly down on him that yet doth
  stand
  All full of guilt, thy blood upon his hand.
  And, though I struck thee undeservedly,
  Let my revenge on her that injured thee
  Make less a fault which I intended not,
  And let these dewdrops wash away my
  spot!—
  It will not cleanse. O, to what sacred
  flood
  Shall I resort to wash away this blood?
  Amidst these trees the holy Clorin
  dwells   310
  In a low cabin of cut boughs, and heals
  All wounds; to her I will myself ad-
  dress,
  And my rash faults repentantly confess;
  Perhaps she'll find a means, by art or
  prayer,
  To make my hand, with chaste blood
  stainéd, fair.
  That done, not far hence, underneath
  some tree
  I'll have a little cabin built, since she
  Whom I adored is dead; there will I give
  Myself to strickness,[2] and, like Clorin,
  live.   *Exit.*

*The curtain is drawn; Clorin appears sitting
  in the cabin, Amoret sitting on the one
  side of her, Alexis and Cloe on the other,
  the Satyr standing by.*

CLO. Shepherd, once more your blood is
  stayed;   320
  Take example by this maid,
  Who is healed ere you be pure,
  So hard it is lewd lust to cure.
  Take heed, then, how you turn your eye
  On these other lustfully.—
  And, shepherdess, take heed lest you
  Move his willing eye thereto;

¹ Appearance.   ² Strictness.

Let no wring nor pinch nor smile
  Of yours his weaker sense beguile.—
  Is your love yet true and chaste, 330
  And forever so to last?
ALEX. I have forgot all vain desires,
  All looser thoughts, ill-tempered fires.
  True love I find a pleasant fume,
  Whose moderate heat can ne'er con-
  sume.
CLOE. And I a new fire feel in me,
  Whose chaste flame[3] is not quenched to
  be.
CLO. Join your hands with modest touch,
  And forever keep you such.

Enter Perigot.

PERI. [*Aside.*] Yon is her cabin; thus far
  off I'll stand,   340
  And call her forth; for my unhallowed
  hand
  I dare not bring so near yon sacred
  place.—
  Clorin, come forth, and do a timely
  grace
  To a poor swain.
CLO.   What art thou that dost call?
  Clorin is ready to do good to all.
  Come near.
PERI.   I dare not.
CLO.   Satyr, see
  Who it is that calls on me.
SAT. There, at hand,[4] some swain doth
  stand,
  Stretching out a bloody hand.
PERI. Come, Clorin, bring thy holy waters
  clear,   350
  To wash my hand.
CLO.   What wonders have been here
  Tonight! Stretch forth thy hand, young
  swain;
  Wash and rub it, whilst I rain
  Holy water.
PERI.   Still you pour,
  But my hand will never scour.
CLO. Satyr, bring him to the bower.
  We will try the sovereign power
  Of other waters.
SAT.   Mortal, sure,
  'Tis the blood of maiden pure
  That stains thee so.

³ From 1656 edn. Original reads *base end.*
⁴ From 1634 edn. Original reads *there's a*
hand.

The Satyr leadeth him to the bower, where
  he spieth Amoret, and kneeleth down;
                    she knoweth him.

PERI.   Whate'er thou be,   360
  Beest thou her sprite, or some divinity
  That in her shape thinks good to walk
    this grove,
  Pardon poor Perigot!
AMO.   I am thy love,
  Thy Amoret, forevermore thy love;
  Strike [1] once more on my naked breast,
    I'll prove
  As constant still. O, canst thou love me
    yet,
  How soon could I my former griefs forget!
PERI. So overgreat with joy that you live,
    now
  I am, that no desire of knowing how
  Doth seize me. Hast thou still power to
    forgive?   370
AMO. Whilst thou hast power to love, or I
    to live.
  More welcome now than hadst thou
    never gone
  Astray from me!
PERI.   And, when thou lov'st alone,
  And not I, death or some ling'ring pain
  That's worse, light on me!
CLO.   Now your stain
  Perhaps will cleanse thee [2] once again.
  See, the blood that erst did stay,
  With the water drops away.
  All the powers again are pleased,
  And with this new knot are appeased. 380
  Join your hands, and rise together;
  Pan be blessed that brought you hither!

        Enter Priest and Old Shepherd.

  Go back again, whate'er thou art; unless
  Smooth maiden thoughts possess thee,
    do not press
  This hallowed ground.—Go, satyr, take
    his hand,
  And give him present trial.
SAT.   Mortal, stand,
  Till by fire I have made known
  Whether thou be such a one
  That mayst freely tread this place.
  Hold thy hand up.—[*Holds the Priest's
    hand to the flame.*] Never was   390
  More untainted flesh than this.—
  Fairest, he is full of bliss.

[1] From 1634 edn. Original reads *stick*.
[2] *I.e.*, be cleansed for thee.

CLO. Then boldly speak; why dost thou
    seek this place?
PRIEST. First, honored virgin, to behold
    thy face,
  Where all good dwells that is; next, for
    to try
  The truth of late report was given to
    me—
  Those shepherds that have met with
    foul mischance
  Through much neglect and more ill
    governance,
  Whether the wounds they have may yet
    endure
  The open air, or stay a longer cure;   400
  And lastly, what the doom may be shall
    light
  Upon those guilty wretches, through
    whose spite
  All this confusion fell; [3] for to this place,
  Thou holy maiden, have I brought the
    race
  Of these offenders, who have freely told
  Both why and by what means they gave
    this bold
  Attempt upon their lives.
CLO.   Fume all the ground,
  And sprinkle holy water, for unsound
  And foul infection gins to fill the air;
  It gathers yet more strongly; [take a
    pair] [4]   410
  Of censers filled with frankincense and
    myrrh,
  Together with cold camphire; [5] quickly
    stir
  Thee, gentle satyr, for the place begins
  To sweat and labor with the abhorréd
    sins
  Of those offenders. Let them not come
    nigh,
  For full of itching flame and leprosy
  Their very souls are, that the ground
    goes back,
  And shrinks to feel the sullen weight of
    black
  And so unheard-of venom.—Hie thee
    fast,
  Thou holy man, and banish from the
    chaste   420
  These manlike monsters; let them never
    more

[3] From 1629 edn. Original reads *full*.
[4] From 1629 edn.
[5] Camphor, supposedly an antaphrodisiac.

Be known upon these downs, but, long
  before
The next sun's rising, put them from
  the sight
And memory of every honest wight.
Be quick in expedition, lest the sores
Of these weak patients break into new
  gores.   *Ex[it] Priest.*
PERI. My dear, dear Amoret, how happy
  are
Those blessed pairs, in whom a little jar
Hath bred an everlasting love, too
  strong   429
For time or steel or envy to do wrong!
How do you feel your hurts? Alas, poor
  heart,
How much I was abused! Give me the
  smart,
For it is justly mine.
AMO.   I do believe.
It is enough, dear friend; leave off to
  grieve,
And let us once more, in despite of ill,
Give hands and hearts again.
PERI.   With better will
Than e'er I went to find in hottest day
Cool crystal of the fountain, to allay
My eager thirst. May this band never
  break!
Hear us, O heaven!
AMO.   Be constant.
PERI.   Else Pan wreak   440
With double vengeance my disloyalty!
Let me not dare to know the company
Of men, or any more behold those eyes!
AMO. Thus, shepherd, with a kiss all envy [1]
  dies.

Enter Priest.

PRIEST. Bright maid, I have performed
  your will. The swain
In whom such heat and black rebellions
  reign
Hath undergone your sentence [and dis-
  grace]; [2]
Only the maid I have reserved,[3] whose
  face
Shows much amendment; many a tear
  doth fall
In sorrow of her fault. Great fair,
  recall   450
Your heavy doom, in hope of better
  days,

Which I dare promise; once again up-
  raise
Her heavy spirit, that near drownéd
  lies
In self-consuming care that never dies.
CLO. I am content to pardon; call her in.—
The air grows cool again, and doth be-
  gin
To purge itself. How bright the day
  doth show
After this stormy cloud!—Go, satyr, go,
And with this taper boldly try her hand.
If she be pure and good, and firmly
  stand   460
To be so still, we have performed a work
Worthy the gods themselves.
           Satyr brings Amarillis in.
SAT. Come forward, maiden; do not lurk,
Nor hide your face with grief and shame.
Now or never get a name
That may raise thee, and recure [4]
All thy life that was impure.
Hold your hand unto the flame.
If thou beest a perfect dame,
Or hast truly vowed to mend,   470
This pale fire will be thy friend.—
       [Holds her hand to the flame.]
See, the taper hurts her not!
Go thy ways; let never spot
Henceforth seize upon thy blood.
Thank the gods, and still be good.
CLO. Young shepherdess, now ye are
  brought again
To virgin state, be so, and so remain
To thy last day, unless the faithful love
Of some good shepherd force thee to
  remove;
Then labor to be true to him, and
  live   480
As such a one that ever strives to give
A blessed memory to aftertime;
Be famous for your good, not for your
  crime.—
Now, holy man, I offer up again
These patients, full of health and free
  from pain.
Keep them from after-ills; be ever near
Unto their actions; teach them how to
  clear
The tedious way they pass through from
  suspect;
Keep them from wrong in others, or neg-
  lect

---

[1] Ill will.   [2] From 1629 edn.   [3] Preserved.   [4] Recover, cure.

Of duty in themselves; correct the
blood   490
With thrifty bits [1] and labor; let the
flood
Or the next neighboring spring give
remedy
To greedy thirst and travail, not the
tree
That hangs with wanton clusters; let
not wine,
Unless in sacrifice or rites divine,
Be ever known of shepherds; have a care,
Thou man of holy life! Now do not spare
Their faults through much remissness,
nor forget
To cherish him whose many pains and
sweat
Hath giv'n increase and added to the
downs.   500
Sort all your shepherds from the lazy
clowns
That feed their heifers in the budded
brooms.
Teach the young maidens strictness,
that the grooms
May ever fear to tempt their blowing
youth.
Banish all compliment, but single truth,
From every tongue and every shepherd's
heart;
Let them use persuading, but no art.
Thus, holy priest, I wish to thee and
these
All the best goods and comforts that
may please.
ALL. And all those blessings heaven did
ever give,   510
We pray upon this bower may ever live.
PRIEST. Kneel, every shepherd, whilst with
powerful hand
I bless your after-labors, and the land
You feed your flocks upon. Great Pan
defend you
From misfortune, and amend you;
Keep you from those dangers still
That are followed by your will;
Give ye means to know at length
All your riches, all your strength,
Cannot keep your foot from falling   520
To lewd lust, that still is calling
At your cottage, till his power
Bring again that golden hour
Of peace and rest to every soul;

[1] Scanty fare.

May his care of you control
All diseases, sores, or pain
That in aftertime may reign
Either in your flocks or you;
Give ye all affections new,
New desires, and tempers new,   530
That ye may be ever true!
Now rise, and go; and, as ye pass away,
Sing to the God of Sheep that happy lay
That honest Dorus [2] taught ye—Dorus, he
That was the soul and god of melody.
They all sing [and strew flowers on the ground].

THE SONG

All ye woods and trees and bowers,
All ye virtues and ye powers
That inhabit in the lakes,
In the pleasant springs or brakes,
Move your feet   540
    To our sound,
Whilst we greet
    All this ground
With his honor and his name
That defends our flocks from blame. [3]

He is great, and he is just;
He is ever good, and must
Thus be honored. Daffadillies,
Roses, pinks, and lovéd lilies,
Let us fling,   550
Whilst we sing,
Ever holy,
Ever holy,
Ever honored, ever young!
Thus great Pan is ever sung!

Exeunt [all except Clorin and Satyr].

SAT. Thou divinest, fairest, brightest,
Thou most powerful maid and whitest,
Thou most virtuous and most blessed,
Eyes of stars, and golden-tresséd
Like Apollo, tell me, sweetest,   560
What new service now is meetest
For the satyr? Shall I stray
In the middle air, and stay
The sailing rack, or nimbly take
Hold by the moon, and gently make
Suit to the pale queen of the night
For a beam to give thee light?
Shall I dive into the sea,
And bring thee coral, making way
Through the rising waves that fall   570

[2] Probably a reference to Spenser and *The Shepherd's Calendar.*
[3] Harm.

In snowy fleeces? Dearest, shall
I catch thee wanton fauns, or flies
Whose woven wings the summer dyes
Of many colors, get thee fruit,
Or steal from heaven old Orpheus' lute?
All these I'll venter [1] for, and more,
To do her service all these woods adore.

CLO. No other service, satyr, but thy watch
About these thicks,[2] lest harmless people catch
Mischief or sad mischance. 580

SAT. Holy virgin, I will dance
Round about these woods as quick
As the breaking light, and prick [3]
Down the lawns and down the vales
Faster than the windmill-sails.
So I take my leave, and pray
All the comforts of the day,
Such as Phœbus' heat doth send
On the earth, may still befriend
Thee and this arbor!

CLO.   And to thee 590
All thy master's love be free! *Exeunt.*

[1] Venture.   [2] Thickets.   [3] Spur, speed.

FINIS. THE PASTORAL OF THE FAITHFUL SHEPHERDESS.

PHILASTER,
OR
LOVE LIES A-BLEEDING [1]

BY

FRANCIS BEAUMONT AND JOHN FLETCHER

[The scene being in Sicily.
The persons represented in the play are these, viz.:

THE KING.
PHILASTER, *heir to the crown.*
PHARAMOND, *Prince of Spain.*
DION, *a lord.*
CLEREMONT ⎱ *noble gentlemen,*
THRASILINE ⎰ *his associates.*
ARETHUSA, *the king's daughter.*
GALATEA, *a wise, modest lady attending the*
princess.
MEGRA, *a lascivious lady.*

AN OLD WANTON LADY, *or crone.*
ANOTHER LADY *attending the princess.*
EUPHRASIA, *daughter of Dion, but disguised*
like a page and called Bellario.
AN OLD CAPTAIN.
FIVE CITIZENS.
A COUNTRY FELLOW.
TWO WOODMEN.
THE KING'S GUARD AND TRAIN.] [2]

[TIME: Indefinite.]

ACTUS I. SCENA i.

[The presence chamber in the palace.]

Enter Dion, Cleremont, and Thrasiline. [3]

CLE. Here's nor lords nor ladies.

DI. Credit me, gentlemen, I wonder at it. They received strict charge from the king to attend here; besides, it was boldly published that no officer should forbid any gentleman that desired to attend and hear.

CLE. Can you guess the cause?

DI. Sir, it is plain—about the Spanish prince that's come to marry our king- [10] dom's heir and be our sovereign.

THRA. Many that will seem to know much say she looks not on him like a maid in love.

DI. Faith, sir, the multitude, that seldom know anything but their own opinions, speak that they would have; but the prince, before his own approach, received so many confident messages from the state that I think she's resolved to be ruled. 20

CLE. Sir, it is thought with her he shall enjoy both these kingdoms of Sicily and Calabria.

DI. Sir, it is without controversy so meant. But 'twill be a troublesome labor for him to enjoy both these kingdoms with safety, the right heir to one of them living, and living so virtuously—especially, the people admiring the bravery of his mind and lamenting his injuries. 30

CLE. Who? Philaster?

DI. Yes; whose father, we all know, was by our late King of Calabria unrighteously deposed from his fruitful Sicily. Myself drew some blood in those wars, which I would give my hand to be washed from.

CLE. Sir, my ignorance in state policy will not let me know why, Philaster being

[1] The title-page continues: "As It Hath Been Divers Times Acted at the Globe and Black-friars by His Majesty's Servants."
[2] From 1630 edn.
[3] So all other quartos. 1622 edn. reads *Trasiline.*

1180

heir to one of these kingdoms, the king should suffer him to walk abroad with [40 such free liberty.

DI. Sir, it seems your nature is more constant than to inquire after state news. But the king, of late, made a hazard of both the kingdoms, of Sicily and his own, with offering but to imprison Philaster, at which the city was in arms, not to be charmed down by any state order or proclamation, till they saw Philaster ride through the streets pleased and without a guard, [50 at which they threw their hats and their arms from them, some to make bonfires, some to drink, all for his deliverance— which wise men say is the cause the king labors to bring in the power of a foreign nation to awe his own with.

Enter Galatea, Megra, and a Lady.[1]

THRA. See, the ladies! What's the first?

DI. A wise and modest gentlewoman that attends the princess.

CLE. The second?　　　　　　60

DI. She is one that may stand still discreetly enough and ill-favoredly dance her measure, simper when she is courted by her friend, and slight her husband.

CLE. The last?

DI. Faith, I think she is one whom the state keeps for the agents of our confederate princes; she'll cog [2] and lie with a whole army, before the league shall break. Her name is common through the kingdom, [70 and the trophies of her dishonor advanced beyond Hercules' Pillars. She loves to try the several constitutions of men's bodies, and, indeed, has destroyed the worth of her own body by making experiment upon it for the good of the commonwealth.

CLE. She's a profitable member.

LA. Peace, if you love me! You shall see these gentlemen stand their ground and not court us.　　　　　　80

GAL. What if they should?

MEG. What if they should!

LA. [*To Galatea.*] Nay, let her alone.— What if they should? Why, if they should,

---

[1] The order of the last two characters has been transposed and the speech heads *La.* and *Meg.* reversed by all other modern editors in the dialogue preceding the entrance of the King. But the *Lady* is probably the "old wanton lady, or crone."

[2] Cheat.

I say they were never abroad. What foreigner would do so? It writes them directly untraveled.

GAL. Why, what if they be?

MEG. What if they be!

LA. [*To Galatea.*] Good madam, let [90 her go on.—What if they be? Why, if they be, I will justify, they cannot maintain discourse with a judicious lady, nor make a leg [3] nor say, "Excuse me."

GAL. Ha, ha, ha!

LA. Do you laugh, madam?

DI. Your desires upon you, ladies!

LA. Then you must sit beside us.

DI. I shall sit near you then, lady.

LA. Near me, perhaps; but there's a lady endures no stranger; and to me [101 you appear a very strange fellow.

MEG. Methinks he's not so strange; he would [4] quickly to be acquainted.

THRA. Peace, the king!

Enter King, Pharamond, Arethusa, and Train.

KING. To give a stronger testimony of love
Than sickly promises (which commonly
In princes find both birth and burial
In one breath), we have drawn you, worthy sir,
To make your fair endearments to our daughter,　　　　110
And worthy services known to our subjects,
Now loved and wondered at; next, our intent
To plant you deeply our immediate heir
Both to our blood and kingdoms. For this lady
(The best part of your life, as you confirm me,
And I believe), though her few years and sex
Yet teach her nothing but her fears and blushes,
Desires without desire, discourse and knowledge
Only of what herself is to herself,
Make her feel moderate health; and, when she sleeps,　　　　120
In making no ill day, knows no ill dreams.
Think not, dear sir, these undivided parts

---

[3] Bow.　　　　　　[4] Wishes.

That must mold up a virgin, are put on
To show her so, as borrowed ornaments
To talk of her perfect love to you, or add
An artificial shadow to her nature.
No, sir; I boldly dare proclaim her yet
No woman. But woo her still, and think
  her modesty
A sweeter mistress than the offered lan-
  guage
Of any dame, were she a queen, whose
  eye   130
Speaks common loves and comforts to
  her servants.[1]
Last, noble son (for so I now must call
  you),
What I have done thus public is not only
To add comfort in particular
To you or me, but all, and to confirm
The nobles and the gentry of these king-
  doms
By oath to your succession, which shall
  be
Within this month at most.
THRA. [*Aside.*] This will be hardly done.
CLE. [*Aside.*] It must be ill done, if it be
  done.   140
DI. [*Aside.*! When 'tis at best, 'twill be but
  half done, whilst [2]
So brave a gentleman is wronged and
  flung off.
THRA. [*Aside.*] I fear.
CLE. [*Aside.*] Who does not?
DI. [*Aside.*] I fear not for myself, and
  yet I fear too.
Well, we shall see, we shall see. No more.
PHA. Kissing your white hand, mistress, I
  take leave
To thank your royal father, and thus far
To be my own free trumpet. Under-
  stand,
Great king, and these your subjects, mine
  that must be   150
(For so deserving you have spoke me,
  sir,
And so deserving I dare speak myself),
To what a person, of what eminence,
Ripe expectation, of what faculties,
Manners, and virtues, you would wed
  your kingdoms;
You in me have your wishes. O, this
  country!

[1] Lovers.
[2] Here and in a few other passages the line
division has been regularized.

By more than all the gods, I hold it
  happy—
Happy in their dear memories that have
  been
Kings great and good; happy in yours
  that is;   159
And from you (as a chronicle to keep
Your noble name from eating age) do I
Open [3] myself most happy.   Gentle-
  men,
Believe me in a word, a prince's word,
There shall be nothing to make up a
  kingdom
Mighty and flourishing, defenséd, feared,
Equal to be commanded and obeyed,
But through the travails of my life I ll
  find it,
And tie it to this country.   By all the
  gods,
My reign shall be so easy to the subject
That every man shall be his prince him-
  self,   170
And his own law—yet I his prince and
  law.
And, dearest lady, to your dearest self
(Dear in the choice of him whose name
  and luster
Must make you more and mightier) let
  me say
You are the blessed'st living, for, sweet
  princess,
You shall enjoy a man of men to be
Your servant; you shall make him yours,
  for whom
Great queens must die,
THRA. [*Aside.*] [4] Miraculous!
CLE. [*Aside.*] This speech calls him   [180
Spaniard, being nothing but a large inven-
tory of his own commendations.

Ent[er] Philaster.

DI. [*Aside.*] I wonder what's his price,
for certainly he'll sell himself, he has so
praised his shape.—But here comes one
more worthy those large speeches than the
large speaker of them. Let me be swallowed
quick, if I can find, in all the anatomy of
yon man's virtues, one sinew sound enough
to promise for him he shall be con-   [190
stable. By this sun, he'll ne'er make king

[3] Reveal, declare.
[4] In several speeches, such as the following, although prose is used, it may be scanned as
rough iambics.

unless it be of trifles, in my poor judgment.

PHI. [*Kneeling.*] Right noble sir, as low as my obedience,

And with a heart as loyal as my knee,

I beg your favor.

KING.					Rise; you have it, sir.

					[*Philaster rises.*]

DI. Mark but the king, how pale he looks! He fears!

O, this same whoreson [1] conscience, how it jades us!

KING. Speak your intent, sir.

PHI.				Shall I speak um freely?

Be still my royal sovereign.

KING.					As a subject, 200

We give you freedom.

DI. [*Aside.*]			Now it heats.

PHI.					Then thus I turn

My language to you, prince—you, foreign man!

Ne'er stare nor put on wonder, for you must

Endure me, and you shall. This earth you tread upon

(A dowry, as you hope, with this fair princess),

By my dead father (O, I had a father,

Whose memory I bow to!) was not left [2]

To your inheritance, and I up and living—

Having myself about me and my sword,

The souls of all my name and memories,

These arms and some few friends beside the gods—				211

To part so calmly with it, and sit still

And say, "I might have been." I tell thee, Pharamond,

When thou art king, look I be dead and rotten,

And my name ashes, as I; for, hear me, Pharamond,

This very ground thou goest on, this fat earth

My father's friends made fertile with their faiths,

Before that day of shame shall gape and swallow

Thee and thy nation, like a hungry grave,

Into her hidden bowels. Prince, it shall.

By the just gods, it shall!

PHA. He's mad; beyond cure, mad. 221

DI. [*Aside.*] Here's a fellow has some fire in 's veins;

The outlandish [3] prince looks like a tooth-drawer.

PHI. Sir Prince of Poppingjays, [4] I'll make it well appear

To you I am not mad.

KING.					You displease us;

You are too bold.

PHI.				No, sir, I am too tame,

Too much a turtle, [5] a thing born without passion,

A faint shadow that every drunken cloud

Sails over, and makes nothing.

KING.				I do not fancy this.

Call our physicians; sure, he's somewhat tainted. [6]					230

THRA. [*Aside.*] I do not think 'twill prove so.

DI. [*Aside.*] H'as given him a general purge already, for all the right he has; and now he means to let him blood. Be constant, gentlemen; by heaven, I'll run his hazard, [7] although I run my name out of the kingdom!

CLE. [*Aside.*] Peace, we are all one soul.

PHA. What you have seen in me to stir offense					239

I cannot find, unless it be this lady,

Offered into mine arms with the succession,

Which I must keep (though it hath pleased your fury

To mutiny within you) without disputing

Your genealogies, or taking knowledge

Whose branch you are. The king will leave it me,

And I dare make it mine. You have your answer.

PHI. If thou wert sole inheritor to him

That made the world his, [8] and couldst see no sun

Shine upon anything but thine; were Pharamond

As truly valiant as I feel him cold, 250

And ringed amongst the choicest of his friends

(Such as would blush to talk such serious follies,

---

[1] Rascally.

[2] The order of this and the preceding line is reversed in the original.

[3] Foreign.
[4] Popinjays.
[5] Turtledove.

[6] Mentally unbalanced.
[7] *I.e.*, I'll run a risk for him.
[8] *I.e.*, Alexander the Great.

Or back such belied [1] commendations),
And from this presence, spite of [all] [2]
these bugs,[3]
You should hear further from me.

KING. Sir, you wrong the prince;
I gave you not this freedom to brave our
best friends.
You deserve our frown. Go to; be better
tempered.

PHI. It must be, sir, when I am nobler
used.

GAL. [Aside.] Ladies, 260
This would have been a pattern of suc-
cession,
Had he ne'er met this mischief. By my
life,
He is the worthiest the true name of
man
This day within my knowledge.

MEG. [Aside.] I cannot tell what you may
call your knowledge;
But the other is the man set in my eye.
O, 'tis a prince of wax! [4]

GAL. [Aside.] A dog it is.[5]

KING. Philaster, tell me
The injuries you aim at in your riddles.

PHI. If you had my eyes, sir, and sufferance,[6] 270
My griefs upon you, and my broken
fortunes,
My wants great, and now-nothing hopes
and fears,
My wrongs would make ill riddles to be
laughed at.
Dare you be still my king, and right me
[not]? [7]

KING. Give me your wrongs in private.

PHI. Take them,
And ease me of a load would bow strong
Atlas. *They whisper.*

CLE. [Aside.] He dares not stand the
shock.

DI. [Aside.] I cannot blame him; there's
danger in 't. Every man in this age [280
has not a soul of crystal for all men to read
their actions through; men's hearts and faces
are so far asunder that they hold no intelligence. Do but view yon stranger well, and
you shall see a fever through all his bravery,[8]

---

[1] Lying.
[2] Supplied from other quartos.
[3] Bugbears.
[4] *I.e.*, perfect like a wax model.
[5] "A dog of wax" was a cant phrase indicating contempt.
[6] Suffering. [7] From 1628 edn. [8] Insolence.

and feel him shake like a true tenant.[9] If he
give not back his crown again upon the report of an elder gun,[10] I have no augury.

KING. Go to;
Be more yourself, as you respect our
favor; 290
You'll stir us else. Sir, I must have you
know
That y' are and shall be, at our pleasure,
what fashion we
Will put upon you. Smooth your brow,
or by the gods—

PHI. I am dead, sir; y' are my fate. It was
not I
Said I was wronged. I carry all about
me
My weak stars lead me to, all my weak
fortunes.
Who dares in all this presence speak (that
is
But man [11] of flesh, and may be mortal),
tell me
I do not most entirely love this prince,
And honor his full virtues!

KING. Sure, he's possessed! 300

PHI. Yes, with my father's spirit. It's
here, O king,
A dangerous spirit! Now he tells me,
king,
I was a king's heir, bids me be a king,
And whispers to me these are all my
subjects.
'Tis strange he will not let me sleep, but
dives
Into my fancy, and there gives me shapes
That kneel and do me service, cry me
king.
But I'll suppress him; he's a factious
spirit,
And will undo me.—[To Pharamond.]
Noble sir, your hand;
I am your servant.

KING. Away! I do not like this. 310
I'll make you tamer, or I'll dispossess you
Both of life and spirit. For this time
I pardon your wild speech, without so
much
As your imprisonment.

*Exeunt K[ing], Pha[ramond], Are[thusa, and
Train].*

---

[9] *I.e.*, "one who has only temporary possession" (Dyce).
[10] Popgun.
[11] From 1620 edn. Original reads *men*.

Dɪ. I thank you, sir; you dare not for the people.

Gᴀʟ. Ladies, what think you now of this brave fellow?

Mᴇɢ. A pretty talking fellow, hot at hand. But eye yon stranger; is he not a fine complete gentleman? O, these strangers, I do affect[1] them strangely! [320 They do the rarest home-things, and please the fullest! As I live, I could love all the nation over and over for his sake.

Gᴀʟ. Gods comfort your poor head-piece, lady! 'Tis a weak one, and had need of a nightcap. *Exeunt*[2] *Ladies*.

Dɪ. [*Aside.*] See, how his fancy labors! Has he not spoke
Home and bravely? What a dangerous train
Did he give fire to! How he shook the king,
Made his soul melt within him, and his blood   330
Run into whey! It stood upon his brow
Like a cold, winter dew.

Pʜɪ.   Gentlemen,
You have no suit to me? I am no minion.
You stand, methinks, like men that would be courtiers,
If you[3] could well be flattered at a price
Not to undo your children. Y' are all honest.
Go, get you home again, and make your country
A virtuous court, to which your great ones may,
In their diseaséd age, retire and live re-cluse.

Cʟᴇ. How do you, worthy sir?

Pʜɪ.   Well, very well;   340
And so well that, if the king please, I find
I may live many years.

Dɪ.   The king must please,
Whilst we know what you are and who you are,
Your wrongs and injuries. Shrink not, worthy sir,
But add your father to you, in whose name
We'll waken all the gods, and conjure up
The rods of vengeance, the abuséd people,
Who, like to raging torrents, shall swell high,

And so begirt the dens of these male dragons
That, through the strongest safety, they shall beg   350
For mercy at your sword's point.

Pʜɪ.   Friends, no more;
Our ears may be corrupted. 'Tis an age
We dare not trust our wills to. Do you love me?

Tʜʀᴀ. Do we love heaven and honor?

Pʜɪ. My Lord Dion, you had
A virtuous gentlewoman called you father;
Is she yet alive?

Dɪ.   Most honored sir, she is,
And, for the penance but of an idle dream,
Has undertook a tedious pilgrimage.

Enter a Lady.

Pʜɪ. Is it to me, or any of these gentle-men, you come?   360

Lᴀ. To you, brave lord; the princess would entreat
Your present company.

Pʜɪ. The princess send for me! Y' are mis-taken.

Lᴀ. If you be called Philaster, 'tis to you.

Pʜɪ. Kiss her fair hand, and say I will attend her.   [*Exit Lady.*]

Dɪ. Do you know what you do?

Pʜɪ. Yes; go to see a woman.

Cʟᴇ. But do you weigh the danger you are in?

Pʜɪ. Danger in a sweet face?
By Jupiter, I must not fear a woman!   370

Tʜʀᴀ. But are you sure it was the princess sent?
It may be some foul train[4] to catch your life.

Pʜɪ. I do not think it, gentlemen; she's noble.
Her eye may shoot me dead, or those true red
And white friends in her face may steal my soul out;
There's all the danger in 't. But, be what may,
Her single[5] name hath arméd me.

                          Exit Phil[aster].

Dɪ.   Go on.
And be as truly happy as thou'rt fear-less!—

---

[1] Admire.   [3] Mason suggests *I*.
[2] Original reads *Exit*.

[4] Trick, plot.   [5] Mere.

Come, gentlemen, let's make our friends
acquainted,
Lest the king prove false.   380
Exeunt [1] *Gentlemen.*

[SCENA ii.

Arethusa's chambers in the palace.]

Enter Arethusa and a Lady.

ARE. Comes he not?
LA.   Madam?
ARE.   Will Philaster come?
LA. Dear madam, you were wont
To credit me at first.
ARE. But didst thou tell me so?
I am forgetful, and my woman's strength
Is so o'ercharged with dangers like to
grow
About my marriage that these under-
things
Dare not abide in such a troubled sea.
How looked he when he told thee he
would come?
LA. Why, well.   10
ARE. And not a little fearful?
LA. Fear, madam? Sure, he knows not
what it is.
ARE. You all are of his faction; the whole
court
Is bold in praise of him, whilst I
May live neglected, and do noble things,
As fools in strife throw gold into the sea,
Drowned in the doing. But I know he
fears.
LA. Fear, madam! Methought, his looks
hid more
Of love than fear.
ARE.   Of love? To whom? To you?
Did you deliver those plain words I sent,
With such a winning gesture and quick
look   21
That you have caught him?
LA.   Madam, I mean to you.
ARE. Of love to me! Alas, thy ignorance
Lets thee not see the crosses of our births!
Nature, that loves not to be questionéd
Why she did this or that, but has her
ends,
And knows she does well, never gave the
world
Two things so opposite, so contrary,
As he and I am. If a bowl of blood

Drawn from this arm of mine would poi-
son thee,   30
A draught of his would cure thee. Of
love to me!
LA. Madam, I think I hear him.
ARE.   Bring him in.—[*Exit Lady.*]
You gods, that would not have your
dooms withstood,
Whose holy wisdoms at this time it is
To make the passions of a feeble maid
The way unto your justice, I obey.

Enter Phil[*aster with Lady*].

LA. Here is my Lord Philaster.
ARE.   O, it is well.
Withdraw yourself.   [*Exit Lady.*]
PHI.   Madam, your messenger
Made me believe you wished to speak
with me.
ARE. 'Tis true, Philaster; but the words
are such   40
I have to say and do so ill beseem
The mouth of woman that I wish them
said,
And yet am loath to speak them. Have
you known
That I have aught detracted from your
worth?
Have I in person wronged you, or have
set
My baser instruments to throw disgrace
Upon your virtues?
PHI.   Never, madam, you.
ARE. Why, then, should you, in such a
public place,
Injure a princess, and a scandal lay   49
Upon my fortunes, famed to be so great,
Calling a great part of my dowry in ques-
tion?
PHI. Madam, this truth which I shall
speak will be
Foolish; but, for your fair and virtuous
self,
I could afford myself to have no right
To anything you wished.
ARE.   Philaster, know
I must enjoy these kingdoms.
PHI.   Madam, both?
ARE. Both, or I die; by heaven, I die, Phil-
aster,
If I not calmly may enjoy them both.
PHI. I would do much to save that noble
life,
Yet would be loath to have posterity 60

Find in our stories that Philaster gave
His right unto a scepter and a crown
To save a lady's longing.

ARE.   Nay, then, hear:
I must and will have them, and more—

PHI.   What more?

ARE. Or lose that little life the gods prepared
To trouble this poor piece of earth withal.

PHI. Madam, what more?

ARE.   Turn then away thy face.

PHI. No.

ARE. Do.

PHI. I can endure it. Turn away my
face?   70
I never yet saw enemy that looked
So dreadfully but that I thought myself
As great a basilisk[1] as he, or spake
So horrible but that I thought my tongue
Bore thunder underneath, as much as his,
Nor beast that I could turn from. Shall
I then
Begin to fear sweet sounds? A lady's
voice,
Whom I do love? Say you would have
my life.
Why, I will give it you, for it is of me
A thing so loathed, and unto you that
ask   80
Of so poor use, that I shall make no price.
If you entreat, I will unmovedly hear.

ARE. Yet, for my sake, a little bend thy
looks.

PHI. I do.

ARE.   Then know I must have them
and thee.

PHI. And me?

ARE.   Thy love—without which all
the land
Discovered yet will serve me for no use
But to be buried in.

PHI.   Is 't possible?

ARE. With it, it were too little to bestow
On thee. Now, though thy breath do
strike me dead
(Which, know, it may), I have unripped
my breast.   90

PHI. Madam, you are too full of noble
thoughts
To lay a train for this contemnéd life,
Which you may have for asking. To suspect

Were base, where I deserve no ill. Love
you!
By all my hopes, I do, above my life!
But how this passion should proceed
from you
So violently, would amaze a man
That would be jealous.[2]

ARE. Another soul into my body shot
Could not have filled me with more
strength and spirit   100
Than this thy breath. But spend not
hasty time
In seeking how I came thus. 'Tis the gods,
The gods, that make me so; and, sure,
our love
Will be the nobler and the better blessed,
In that the secret justice of the gods
Is mingled with it. Let us leave, and kiss,
Lest some unwelcome guest should fall
betwixt us,
And we should part without it.

PHI.   'Twill be ill
I should abide here long.

ARE.   'Tis true; and worse
You should come often. How shall we
devise   110
To hold intelligence,[3] that our true loves,
On any new occasion, may agree
What path is best to tread?

PHI.   I have a boy,
Sent by the gods, I hope, to this intent,
Not yet seen in the court. Hunting the
buck,
I found him sitting by a fountain's side,
Of which he borrowed some to quench his
thirst,
And paid the nymph again as much in
tears.
A garland lay him by, made by himself
Of many several flowers bred in the bay,[4]
Stuck in that mystic order that the rare-
ness   121
Delighted me; but ever when he turned
His tender eyes upon um, he would weep,
As if he meant to make um grow again.
Seeing such pretty, helpless innocence
Dwell in his face, I asked him all his
story.
He told me that his parents gentle died,
Leaving him to the mercy of the fields,

[1] A fabulous creature whose breath and look
were fatal.

[2] Suspicious.

[3] Communication.

[4] "An indentation, recess in a range of hills,
etc." (N.E.D.)

Which gave him roots; and of the crystal
    springs,
Which did not stop their courses; and the
    sun,   130
Which still, he thanked him, yielded him
    his light.
Then took he up his garland, and did
    show
What every flower, as country people
    hold,
Did signify, and how all, ordered thus,
Expressed his grief, and, to my thoughts,
    did read
The prettiest lecture of his country art
That could be wished, so that methought
    I could
Have studied it. I gladly entertained
Him, who was glad to follow, and have
    got
The trustiest, loving'st, and the gentlest
    boy   140
That ever master kept. Him will I send
To wait on you, and bear our hidden love.
ARE. 'Tis well; no more.

Enter Lady.

LA. Madam, the prince is come to do
    his service.
ARE. What will you do, Philaster, with
    yourself?
PHI. Why, that which all the gods have
    appointed out for me.
ARE. Dear, hide thyself!—
    Bring in the prince.   [*Exit Lady.*]
PHI.   Hide me from Pharamond!
    When thunder speaks, which is the voice
    of God,
    Though I do reverence, yet I hide me
    not;   150
    And shall a stranger prince have leave to
    brag
    Unto a foreign nation that he made
    Philaster hide himself?
ARE.   He cannot know it.
PHI. Though it should sleep forever to the
    world,
    It is a simple sin to hide myself,
    Which will forever on my conscience lie.
ARE. Then, good Philaster, give him scope
    and way
    In what he says, for he is apt to speak
    What you are loath to hear. For my
    sake, do.
PHI. I will.   160

Enter Pharamond [with Lady].

PHA. My princely mistress, as true lovers
    ought,   [*Exit Lady.*]
    I come to kiss these fair hands, and to
    show,
    In outward ceremonies, the dear love
    Writ in my heart.
PHI. If I shall have an answer no directlier,
    I am gone.
PHA.   To what would he have answer?
ARE. To his claim unto the kingdom.
PHA. Sirrah, I forbare [1] you before the
    king—
PHI. Good sir, do so still; I would not talk
    with you.
PHA. But now the time is fitter. Do but
    offer   170
    To make mention of right to any king-
    dom,
    Though it be scarce habitable—
PHI.   Good sir, let me go.
PHA. And, by the gods—
PHI.   Peace, Pharamond! If thou—
ARE. Leave us, Philaster.
PHI. I have done.
PHA. You are gone! By heaven, I'll fetch
    you back.
PHI. You shall not need.
PHA.   What now?
PHI.   Know, Pharamond,
    I loathe to brawl with such a blast as
    thou,
    Who art naught but a valiant voice, but,
    if
    Thou shalt provoke me further, men shall
    say   180
    Thou wert—and not lament it.
PHA.   Do you slight
    My greatness so, and in the chamber of
    the princess?
PHI. It is a place to which I must confess
    I owe a reverence; but, were 't the
    church,
    Ay, at the altar, there's no place so safe,
    Where thou dar'st injure me, but I dare
    kill thee.
    And for your greatness, know, sir, I can
    grasp
    You and your greatness thus, thus into
    nothing.
    Give not a word, not a word back! Fare-
    well.   *Exit.*

[1] Forbore.

PHA. 'Tis an odd fellow, madam; we must
    stop   190
His mouth with some office when we are
    married.
ARE. You were best make him your con-
    troller.
PHA. I think he would discharge it well.
    But, madam,
I hope our hearts are knit; but yet so slow
The ceremonies of state are that 'twill be
    long
Before our hands be so. If then you
    please,
Being agreed in heart, let us not wait
For dreaming form, but take a little
    stolen
Delights, and so prevent [1] our joys to
    come.
ARE. If you dare speak such thoughts, 200
    I must withdraw in honor.
                    Exit Are[thusa].
PHA. The constitution of my body will
never hold out till the wedding; I must seek
elsewhere.   *Exit Ph[aramond].*

ACTUS II. SCENA i.

[A hall in the palace.]

Enter Philaster and Bellario.

PHI. And thou shalt find her honorable,
    boy,
Full of regard unto thy tender youth,
For thine own modesty, and, for my sake,
Apter to give than thou wilt be to ask,
Ay, or deserve.
BEL.   Sir, you did take me up
When I was nothing, and only yet am
    something
By being yours. You trusted me un-
    known,
And that which you were apt to conster [2]
A simple innocence in me, perhaps
Might have been craft, the cunning of a
    boy   10
Hardened in lies and theft, yet ventured
    you
To part my miseries and me, for which
I never can expect to serve a lady
That bears more honor in her breast than
    you.
PHI. But, boy, it will prefer [3] thee. Thou
    art young,

[1] Anticipate.   [3] Advance.
[2] Construe, interpret.

And bearest a childish, overflowing love
To them that clap thy cheeks and speak
    thee fair yet;
But, when thy judgment comes to rule
    those passions,
Thou wilt remember best those careful
    friends
That placed thee in the noblest way of
    life.   20
She is a princess I prefer thee to.
BEL. In that small time that I have seen
    the world,
I never knew a man hasty to part
With a servant he thought trusty. I
    remember
My father would prefer the boys he kept
To greater men than he, but did it not
Till they were grown too saucy for him-
    self.
PHI. Why, gentle boy, I find no fault at all
    In thy behavior.
BEL.   Sir, if I have made   29
A fault of ignorance, instruct my youth;
I shall be willing, if not apt, to learn.
Age and experience will adorn my mind
With larger knowledge; and, if I have
    done
A willful fault, think me not past all hope
For once. What master holds so strict a
    hand
Over his boy that he will part with him
Without one warning? Let me be cor-
    rected
To break my stubbornness, if it be so,
Rather than turn me off; and I shall
    mend.
PHI. Thy love doth plead so prettily to
    stay   40
That, trust me, I could weep to part
    with thee.
Alas, I do not turn thee off! Thou
    knowest
It is my business that doth call thee hence;
And, when thou art with her, thou
    dwellest with me.
Think so, and 'tis so; and, when time is
    full,
That thou hast well discharged this
    heavy trust,
Laid on so weak a one, I will again
With joy receive thee. As I live, I will!
Nay, weep not, gentle boy. 'Tis more
    than time
Thou didst attend the princess.

BEL.   I am gone. 50
But, since I am to part with you, my
    lord,
And none knows whether I shall live to
    do
More service for you, take this little
    prayer:
Heaven bless your loves, your fights, all
    your designs!
May sick men, if they have your wish, be
    well,
And heaven hate those you curse, though
    I be one!   *Exit.*
PHI. The love of boys unto their lords is
    strange.
I have read wonders of it; yet this boy
For my sake (if a man may judge by
    looks
And speech) would outdo story. I may
    see   60
A day to pay him for his loyalty.
                          Exit Phi[laster].

Enter Pharamond.

PHA. Why should these ladies stay so
long? They must come this way. I know
the queen employs um not, for the reverend
mother [1] sent me word they would all be
for the garden. If they should all prove
honest [2] now, I were in a fair taking.[3] I
was never so long without sport in my life,
and, in my conscience, 'tis not my fault.
O, for our country ladies! [4]—Here's one [70
bolted; I'll hound at her.—[Madam!] [5]

Enter Galatea.

GAL. Your grace!
PHA. Shall I not be a trouble?
GAL. Not to me, sir.
PHA. Nay, nay, you are too quick. By
this sweet hand—
GAL. You'll be forsworn, sir; 'tis but
an old glove. If you will talk at distance,
I am for you; but, good prince, be not
bawdy, nor do not brag; these two I [80
bar; and then, I think, I shall have
sense enough to answer all the weighty
apothegms your royal blood shall manage.

---

[1] *I.e.,* the lady in charge of the maids of honor.
[2] Chaste.
[3] Dilemma.
[4] *I.e.,* ladies of our country (Spain).
[5] From 1620 edn.

PHA. Dear lady, can you love?
GAL. "Dear," prince? How dear? I
ne'er cost you a coach yet, nor put you to
the dear repentance of a banquet. Here's
no scarlet, sir, to blush the sin out it was
given for. This wire [6] mine own hair [90
covers; and this face has been so far from
being dear to any that it ne'er cost penny
painting; and, for the rest of my poor
wardrobe, such as you see, it leaves no
hand [7] behind it to make the jealous mercer's
wife curse our good doings.
PHA. You mistake me, lady.
GAL. Lord, I do so; would you or I
could help it!
PHA. Do ladies of this country use [100
to give no more respect to men of my
full being?
GAL. Full being! I understand you not,
unless your grace means growing to fatness;
and then your only remedy (upon my
knowledge, prince) is, in a morning, a cup
of neat white wine brewed with carduus,[8]
then fast till supper—about eight you may
eat; use exercise, and keep a sparrow
hawk; you can shoot in a tiller; [9] but, [110
of all, your grace must fly phlebotomy,
fresh pork, conger, and clarified whey; they
are all dullers of the vital spirits.
PHA. Lady, you talk of nothing all this
while.
GAL. 'Tis very true, sir; I talk of you.
PHA. [*Aside.*] This is a crafty wench; I
like her wit well; 'twill be rare to stir up a
leaden appetite. She's a Danaë, and must
be courted in a shower of gold.— [120
[*Shows her money.*] Madam, look here; all
these, and more than—
GAL. What have you there, my lord?
Gold? Now, as I live, 'tis fair gold! You
would have silver for it, to play with the
pages. You could not have taken me in a
worse time; but, if you have present use,
my lord, I'll send my man with silver and
keep your gold for you.
PHA. Lady, lady!   130
GAL. She's coming, sir, behind, will take
white money.[10] —[*Aside.*] Yet for all this
I'll match ye. [*Takes gold.*]
          Exit GAL[ATEA] *behind the hangings.*

---

[6] Used as a frame for the headdress.
[7] Record of indebtedness.
[8] A panacea made from a kind of thistle.
[9] With a crossbow.   [10] *I.e.,* silver.

PHA. If there be but two such more in this kingdom, and near the court, we may even hang up our harps. Ten such camphire [1] constitutions as this will call the golden age again in question, and teach the old way for every ill-faced husband to get his own children; and what a mis- [140 chief that will breed, let all consider!—

Enter Megra.

Here's another; if she be of the same last, the devil shall pluck her on.—Many fair mornings, lady!

MEG. As many mornings bring as many days,

Fair, sweet, and hopeful to your grace!

PHA. [*Aside.*] She gives good words yet; sure this wench is free.—

If your more serious business do not call you,

Let me hold quarter [2] with you; we'll talk

An hour out quickly.

MEG.   What would your grace talk of?

PHA. Of some such pretty subject as yourself.   151

I'll go no further than your eye, or lip;

There's theme enough for one man for an age.

MEG. Sir, they stand right, and my lips are yet even,

Smooth, young enough, ripe enough, and red enough,

Or my glass wrongs me.

PHA. O, they are two twinned cherries dyed in blushes,

Which those fair suns above with their bright beams

Reflect upon and ripen. Sweetest beauty,

Bow down those branches, that the long-ing taste   160

Of the faint looker-on may meet those blessings,

And taste and live.   [*They kiss.*] [3]

MEG. [*Aside.*]   O, delicate, sweet prince!

She that hath snow enough about her heart

To take the wanton spring of ten such lines off,

May be a nun without probation.—Sir,

[1] Camphor was formerly considered to possess the property of coldness.
[2] Friendly intercourse.
[3] From 1620 edn.

You have in such neat poetry gathered a kiss

That, if I had but five lines of that number,

Such pretty, begging blanks, [4] I should commend

Your forehead or your cheeks, and kiss you too.

PHA. Do it in prose; you cannot miss it, madam.   170

MEG. I shall, I shall.

PHA.   By my life, but you shall not;

I'll prompt you first. [*Kisses her.*] Can you do it now?

MEG. Methinks 'tis easy, now I ha' done 't before;

But yet I should stick at it. [*Kisses him.*]

PHA.   Stick till tomorrow;

I'll ne'er part you, sweetest. But we lose time.

Can you love me?

MEG. Love you, my lord? How would you have me love you?

PHA. I'll teach you in a short sentence, cause I will not load your memory. This is all: love me, and lie with me.   180

MEG. Was it "lie with you" that you said? 'Tis impossible.

PHA. Not to a willing mind, that will endeavor. If I do not teach you to do it as easily in one night as you'll go to bed, I'll lose my royal blood for 't.

MEG. Why, prince, you have a lady of your own that yet wants teaching.

PHA. I'll sooner teach a mare the old measures [5] than teach her anything [190 belonging to the function. She's afraid to lie with herself if she have but any masculine imaginations about her. I know, when we are married, I must ravish her.

MEG. By mine honor, that's a foul fault, indeed; but time and your good help will wear it out, sir.

PHA. And for any other I see, excepting your dear self, dearest lady, I had rather be Sir Tim the schoolmaster, and [200 leap a dairymaid, madam.

MEG. Has your grace seen the court star, Galatea?

PHA. Out upon her! She's as cold of her favor as an apoplex; [6] she sailed by but now.

MEG. And how do you hold her wit, sir?

[4] Blank verses.   [6] Apoplexy.
[5] Stately dances.

PHA. I hold her wit? The strength of all the guard cannot hold it, if they were tied to it; she would blow um out of the kingdom. They talk of Jupiter; he's but [210 a squib-cracker to her. Look well about you, and you may find a tongue-bolt.[1] But speak, sweet lady, shall I be freely welcome?

MEG. Whither?

PHA. To your bed. If you mistrust my faith, you do me the unnoblest wrong.

MEG. I dare not, prince, I dare not.

PHA. Make your own conditions, my purse shall seal um, and what you [220 dare imagine you can want, I'll furnish you withal. Give two hours to your thoughts every morning about it. Come, I know you are bashful. Speak in my ear; will you be mine? Keep this. [*Gives a ring.*] And, with it, me. Soon I will visit you.

MEG. My lord, my chamber's most unsafe; but, when 'tis night, I'll find some means to slip into your lodging; till [230 when—

PHA. Till when, this and my heart go with thee!   *Exeunt.*

Enter Galatea from behind the hangings.

GAL. O, thou pernicious petticoat prince, are these your virtues? Well, if I do not lay a train to blow your sport up, I am no woman; and, Lady Towsabel,[2] I'll fit you for 't.   *Exit Gal[atea].*

[SCENA ii.

Arethusa's chambers in the palace.]

Enter Arethusa and a Lady.

ARE. Where's the boy?

LA. Within, madam.

ARE. Gave you him gold to buy him clothes?

LA. I did.

ARE. And has he done 't?

LA. Yes, madam.

ARE. 'Tis a pretty, sad-talking[3] boy, is it not? Asked you his name?

LA. No, madam.   10

[1] With an allusion to Jupiter's thunderbolt.
[2] A contemptuous form of Dowsabell, a sweetheart.
[3] Serious-talking.

Enter Galatea.

ARE. O, you are welcome. What good news?

GAL. As good as anyone can tell your grace, That says she has done that you would have wished.

ARE. Hast thou discovered?

GAL. I have strained a point of modesty for you.

ARE. I prithee, how?

GAL. In listening after bawdry. I see, let a lady live never so modestly, she shall be sure to find a lawful time to hearken after bawdry. Your prince, brave Phara- [20 mond, was so hot on 't!

ARE. With whom?

GAL. Why, with the lady I suspected. I can tell the time and place.

ARE. O, when, and where?

GAL. Tonight, his lodging.

ARE. Run thyself into the presence;[4] mingle there again With other ladies; leave the rest to me.— [*Exit Galatea.*]

If destiny (to whom we dare not say, Why thou didst this) have not decreed it so,   30 In lasting leaves (whose smallest characters Were never altered), yet this match shall break.— Where's the boy?

LA. Here, madam.

Enter Bellario.

ARE. Sir, you are sad to change your service, is 't not so?

BEL. Madam, I have not changed; I wait on you, To do him service.

ARE.   Thou disclaim'st[5] in me. Tell me thy name.

BEL. Bellario.

ARE. Thou canst sing and play?   40

BEL. If grief will give me leave, madam, I can.

ARE. Alas, what kind of grief can thy years know? Hadst thou a curst[6] master when thou went'st to school? Thou art not capable of other grief; Thy brows and cheeks are smooth as waters be

[4] Presence chamber.   [6] Ill-tempered.
[5] Renouncest all share.

When no breath troubles them. Believe
  me, boy,
Care seeks out wrinkled brows and hol-
  low eyes,
And builds himself caves, to abide in
  them.
Come, sir, tell me truly, doth your lord
  love me?
BEL. Love, madam? I know not what
  it is.   50
ARE. Canst thou know grief, and never
  yet knew'st love?
  Thou art deceived, boy. Does he speak
  of me
As if he wished me well?
BEL.   If it be love
To forget all respect of his own friends
With thinking of your face; if it be love
To sit cross-armed and think away the
  day,
Mingled with starts, crying your name as
  loud
And hastily as men i' the streets do fire;
If it be love to weep himself away
When he but hears of any lady dead 60
Or killed, because it might have been
  your chance;
If, when he goes to rest (which will not
  be),
Twixt every prayer he says, to name you
  once,
As others drop a bead, be to be in love,
Then, madam, I dare swear he loves you.
ARE. O, y' are a cunning boy, and taught
  to lie
For your lord's credit! But thou knowest
  a lie
That bears this sound is welcomer to me
Than any truth that says he loves me
  not.
Lead the way, boy.—[*To Lady.*] Do you
  attend me too.—   70
'Tis thy lord's business hastes me thus.
  Away!   *Exeunt.*

[SCENA iii.

Before Pharamond's lodging in the palace
*   yard.*]

Enter Dion, Cleremont, Thrasiline, Megra,
*   Galatea.*

DI. Come, ladies, shall we talk a round?
  As men

Do walk a mile, women should talk an
  hour
After supper; 'tis their exercise.
GAL. 'Tis late.
MEG.   'Tis all
My eyes will do to lead me to my
  bed.
GAL. I fear they are so heavy they'll
  scarce find
The way to your own lodging with um
  tonight.

Enter Pharamond.

THRA. The prince!
PHA. Not abed, ladies? Y' are good sit-
  ters-up.   10
What think you of a pleasant dream, to
  last
Till morning?
MEG. I should choose, my lord, a pleasing
  wake before it.

Enter Arethusa and Bellario.

ARE. 'Tis well, my lord; y' are courting
  of these ladies.—
Is 't not late, gentlemen?
CLE. Yes, madam.
ARE. Wait you there.   *Exit Arethusa.*
MEG. [*Aside.*] She's jealous, as I live.—
  Look you, my lord,
The princess has a Hylas, an Adonis.
PHA. His form is angel-like.   20
MEG. Why, this is he must, when you are
  wed,
Sit by your pillow, like young Apollo,
  with
His hand and voice binding your
  thoughts in sleep;
The princess does provide him for you
  and for herself.
PHA. I find no music in these boys.
MEG.   Nor I.
They can do little, and that small they
  do,
They have not wit to hide.
DI.   Serves he the princess?
THRA. Yes.
DI.   'Tis a sweet boy; how brave [1] she
  keeps him!
PHA. Ladies all, good rest; I mean to kill a
  buck

[1] Richly dressed.

Tomorrow morning ere y'ave done your
dreams.   30
MEG. All happiness attend your grace!—
[*Exit Pharamond.*] Gentlemen, good
rest.—
Come, shall we to bed?
GAL.   Yes.—All, good night.
              Exit Gal[atea with] Meg[ra].
DI. May your dreams be true to you!—
What shall we do, gallants? 'Tis late.
The king
Is up still; see, he comes, a guard
along
With him.

Enter King, Arethusa, and Guard.

KING.   Look your intelligence be true.
ARE. Upon my life, it is; and I do hope
Your highness will not tie me to a
man
That in the heat of wooing throws me
off,
And takes another.   40
DI. What should this mean?
KING. If it be true,
That lady had been better have em-
braced
Cureless diseases. Get you to your rest.
              Ex[eunt] Are[thusa], Bell[ario].
You shall be righted.—Gentlemen, draw
near;
We shall employ you. Is young Phara-
mond
Come to his lodging?
DI.   I saw him enter there.
KING. Haste, some of you, and cunningly
discover
If Megra be in her lodging. [*Exit Dion.*]
CLE. Sir,   50
She parted hence but now, with other
ladies.
KING. If she be there, we shall not need to
make
A vain discovery of our suspicion.—
[*Aside.*] You gods, I see that who un-
righteously
Holds wealth or state from others shall
be cursed
In that which meaner men are blessed
withal;
Ages to come shall know no male of
him
Left to inherit, and his name shall be

Blotted from earth; if he have any child
It shall be crossly matched; the gods
themselves   60
Shall sow wild strife betwixt her lord and
her.
Yet, if it be your wills, forgive the sin
I have committed; let it not fall
Upon this understanding child of mine!
She has not broke your laws. But how
can I
Look to be heard of gods that must be
just,
Praying upon the ground I hold by
wrong?

Enter Dion.

DI. Sir, I have asked, and her women
swear she is within; but they, I think, are
bawds. I told um I must speak with   [70
her; they laughed, and said their lady lay
speechless. I said my business was important; they said their lady was about it.
I grew hot, and cried my business was a
matter that concerned life and death; they
answered, so was sleeping, at which their
lady was. I urged again, she had scarce
time to be so since last I saw her. They
smiled again, and seemed to instruct me
that sleeping was nothing but lying   [80
down and winking.[1] Answers more direct
I could not get; in short, sir, I think she is
not there.
KING. 'Tis then no time to dally.—You o'
th' guard,
Wait at the back door of the prince's
lodging,
And see that none pass thence, upon your
lives.—   [*Exeunt Guards.*]
Knock, gentlemen; knock loud; louder
yet.   [*They knock.*]
What, has their pleasure taken off their
hearing?—
I'll break your meditations.—Knock
again!—
Not yet? I do not think he sleeps, having
this   90
Larum[2] by him.—Once more.—Phara-
mond! Prince!

Pharamond above.

PHA. What saucy groom knocks at this
dead of night?

[1] Closing the eyes.   [2] Alarum.

Where be our waiters?[1] By my vexéd
    soul,
He meets his death that meets me, for
    this boldness.
KING. Prince, you wrong your thoughts;
    we are your friends.
Come down.
PHA.   The king?
KING.   The same, sir. Come down;
We have cause of present counsel with
    you.
PHA. If your grace please
To use me, I'll attend you to your
    chamber.

Pha[ramond] below.

KING. No, 'tis too late, prince; I'll make
    bold with yours.   100
PHA. I have some private reasons to my-
    self
Makes me unmannerly, and say you
    cannot.—
Nay, press not forward, gentlemen; he
    must come
Through my life that comes here.
KING. Sir, be resolved[2] I must and will
    come.—Enter!
PHA. I will not be dishonored.
He that enters, enters upon his
    death.
Sir, 'tis a sign you make no stranger of
    me,
To bring these renegadoes to my cham-
    ber
At these unseasoned hours.
KING.   Why do you   110
Chafe yourself so? You are not wronged
    nor shall be;
Only I'll search your lodging, for some
    cause
To ourself known.—Enter, I say.
PHA.   I say, no.

Meg[ra] above.

MEG. Let um enter, prince, let um en-
    ter;
I am up and ready.[3] I know their
    business;
'Tis the poor breaking of a lady's
    honor
They hunt so hotly after; let um enjoy
    it.—

[1] Attendants.   [2] Convinced.   [3] Dressed.

You have your business, gentlemen. I
    lay here.
O, my lord the king, this is not noble in
    you
To make public the weakness of a
    woman!   120
KING. Come down.
MEG. I dare, my lord. Your whootings[4]
    and your clamors,
Your private whispers and your broad
    fleerings,
Can no more vex my soul than this base
    carriage.[5]
But I have vengeance yet in store for
    some
Shall, in the most contempt you can
    have of me,
Be joy and nourishment.
KING.   Will you come down?
MEG. Yes, to laugh at your worst; but I
    shall wring you,
If my skill fail me not.   [*Exit above.*]
KING. Sir, I must dearly chide you for
    this looseness;   130
You have wronged a worthy lady; but
    no more.—
Conduct him to my lodging and to bed.
    [*Exeunt Pharamond and Attendants.*]
CLE. Get him another wench, and you
bring him to bed indeed.
DI. 'Tis strange a man cannot ride a
    stag[6]
Or two, to breathe himself, without a
    warrant.
If this gear[7] hold, that lodgings be
    searched thus,
Pray God we may lie with our own wives
    in safety,
That they be not by some trick of state
    mistaken!

Enter [Attendants] with Megra.

KING. Now, lady of honor, where's your
    honor now?   140
No man can fit your palate but the
    prince.
Thou most ill-shrouded rottenness, thou
    piece
Made by a painter and a pothe-
    cary,

[4] Hootings.   [6] A romping girl.
[5] Behavior.   [7] Matter.

Thou troubled sea of lust, thou wilderness
Inhabited by wild thoughts, thou swoln
cloud
Of infection, thou ripe mine of all dis-
eases,
Thou all-sin, all-hell, and, last, all-devils,
tell me,
Had you none to pull on with your
courtesies
But he that must be mine, and wrong my
daughter?
By all the gods, all these, and all the
pages,   150
And all the court shall hoot thee through
the court,
Fling rotten oranges, make ribald
rimes,
And sear thy name with candles upon
walls!
Do you laugh, Lady Venus?
MEG. Faith, sir, you must pardon me;
I cannot choose but laugh to see you
merry.
If you do this, O king, nay, if you dare
do it,
By all those gods you swore by, and as
many
More of my own, I will have fellows, and
such
Fellows in it as shall make noble
mirth!   160
The princess, your dear daughter, shall
stand by me
On walls, and sung in ballads, any-
thing.
Urge me no more; I know her and her
haunts,
Her lays,[1] leaps, and outlays, and will
discover all,
Nay, will dishonor her. I know the
boy
She keeps, a handsome boy, about
eighteen,
Know what she does with him, where,
and when.
Come, sir, you put me to a woman's madness,
The glory of a fury; and, if I do
not   169
Do it to the height—
KING.   What boy is this she raves
at?

[1] Hiding places.

MEG. Alas, good-minded prince, you know
not these things?
I am loath to reveal um. Keep this
fault
As you would keep your health from the
hot air
Of the corrupted people, or, by heaven,
I will not fall alone. What I have
known
Shall be as public as a print; all
tongues
Shall speak it as they do the language
they
Are born in, as free and commonly; I'll
set it,
Like a prodigious star,[2] for all to gaze
at,
And so high and glowing that other king-
doms far and foreign   180
Shall read it there, nay, travel with it,
till they find
No tongue to make it more, nor no more
people;
And then behold the fall of your fair
princess!
KING. Has she a boy?
CLE. So please your grace, I have seen a
boy wait
On her, a fair boy.
KING.   Go, get you to your quarter,
For this time I'll study to forget you.
MEG. Do you study to forget me, and I'll
study
To forget you.
           Ex[eunt] K[ing], Meg[ra], *Guard.*
CLE. Why, here's a male spirit fit   [190
for Hercules. If ever there be Nine Worthies of women, this wench shall ride astride
and be their captain.
DI. Sure, she has a garrison of devils in
her tongue, she uttered such balls of wildfire. She has so nettled[3] the king that all
the doctors in the country will scarce cure
him. That boy was a strange-found-out antidote to cure her infection; that boy, that
princess' boy; that brave, chaste, vir-   [200
tuous lady's boy! And a fair boy, a well-
spoken boy, all these considered, can make
nothing else—but there I leave you, gentlemen.
THRA. Nay, we'll go wander with you.
                                   Exeunt.

[2] Portentous comet.
[3] From 1620 edn. Original reads *metled.*

Actus III. Scena i.

[The court of the palace.]

Enter Cle[remont], Di[on], Thra[siline].

CLE. Nay, doubtless, 'tis true.

DI. Ay; and 'tis the gods
That raised this punishment to scourge
    the king
With his own issue. Is it not a shame
For us that should write noble [1] in the
    land,
For us that should be freemen, to behold
A man that is the bravery of his age,
Philaster, pressed down from his royal
    right
By this regardless [2] king, and only look
And see the scepter ready to be cast   10
Into the hands of that lascivious lady
That lives in lust with a smooth boy, now
    to be
Married to yon strange prince, who, but
    that people
Please to let him be a prince, is born a
    slave
In that which should be his most noble
    part,
His mind?

THRA.   That man that would not stir
    with you
To aid Philaster, let the gods forget
That such a creature walks upon the
    earth!

CLE. Philaster is too backward in 't him-
    self.   19
The gentry do await it, and the people
Against their nature are all bent for
    him,
And like a field of standing corn, that's
    moved
With a stiff gale, their heads bow all one
    way.

DI. The only cause that draws Philaster
    back
From this attempt is the fair princess'
    love,
Which he admires, and we can now con-
    fute.

THRA. Perhaps he'll not believe it.

DI. Why, gentlemen, 'tis without question
    so.

CLE. Ay, 'tis past speech she lives dis-
    honestly.

But how shall we, if he be curious,[3]
    work   30
Upon his faith?

THRA. We all are satisfied within our-
    selves.

DI. Since it is true, and tends to his own
    good,
I'll make this new report to be my knowl-
    edge;
I'll say I know it; nay, I'll swear I saw it.

CLE. It will be best.

THRA.   'Twill move him.

Enter Philas[ter].

DI.   Here he comes.
Good morrow to your honor; we have
    spent
Some time in seeking you.

PHI.   My worthy friends,
You that can keep your memories to
    know
Your friend in miseries, and cannot
    frown   40
On men disgraced for virtue, a good day
Attend you all! What service may I do
Worthy your acceptation?

DI.   My good lord,
We come to urge that virtue, which we
    know
Lives in your breast, forth. Rise, and
    make a head; [4]
The nobles and the people are all dulled
With this usurping king, and not a man
That ever heard the word, or knew such a
    thing
As virtue, but will second your attempts.

PHI. How honorable is this love in you   50
To me that have deserved none! Know,
    my friends
(You that were born to shame your poor
    Philaster
With too much courtesy), I could afford
To melt myself in thanks; but my designs
Are not yet ripe. Suffice it that ere long
I shall employ your loves; but yet the
    time
Is short of what I would.

DI. The time is fuller, sir, than you expect;
That which hereafter will not, perhaps,
    be reached
By violence, may now be caught. As for
    the king,   60

---

[1] *I.e.*, rank as nobles.   [2] Neglectful.   [3] Scrupulous, skeptical.   [4] Raise an army.

You know the people have long hated
　　him;
But now the princess, whom they
　　loved—
PHI. Why, what of her?
DI.　　　　　Is loathed as much as he.
PHI. By what strange means?
DI.　　　　　She's known a whore.
PHI.　　　　　　　　Thou liest!
DI. My lord—
PHI. Thou liest,
　　　　Offers to draw and is held.
And thou shalt feel it! I had thought
　　thy mind
Had been of honor. Thus to rob a lady
Of her good name is an infectious sin
Not to be pardoned.　Be it false as
　　hell,　　　　　　　　　　　70
'Twill never be redeemed, if it be sown
Amongst the people, fruitful to increase
All evil they shall hear.　Let me alone
That I may cut off falsehood whilst it
　　springs!
Set hills on hills betwixt me and the man
That utters this, and I will scale them all,
And from the utmost top fall on his neck,
Like thunder from a cloud.
DI.　　　　　This is most strange;
Sure, he does love her.
PHI.　　　I do love fair truth.　79
She is my mistress, and who injures her
Draws vengeance from me.　Sirs, let go
　　my arms.
THRA. Nay, good my lord, be patient.
CLE. Sir, remember this is your honored
　　friend
That comes to do his service, and will
　　show you
Why he uttered this.
PHI.　　　I ask your pardon, sir;
My zeal to truth made me unmannerly.
Should I have heard dishonor spoke of
　　you,
Behind your back, untruly, I had been
As much distempered and enraged as
　　now.
DI. But this, my lord, is truth.
PHI.　　　　　O, say not so!　90
　Good sir, forbear to say so.　'Tis then
　　truth
　That womankind is false.　Urge it no
　　more;
　It is impossible.　Why should you think
　The princess light!

DI.　　　　Why, she was taken at it.
PHI. 'Tis false! By heaven, 'tis false! It
　　cannot be!
　Can it? Speak, gentlemen; for God's
　　love, speak!
　Is 't possible? Can women all be damned?
DI. Why, no, my lord.
PHI.　　　　Why, then, it cannot be.
DI. And she was taken with her boy.
PHI.　　　　　　　What boy?
DI. A page, a boy that serves her.
PHI.　　　　O, good gods!　100
　A little boy?
DI.　　　Ay; know you him, my lord?
PHI. [*Aside.*] Hell and sin know him!—
　Sir, you are deceived;
I'll reason it a little coldly with you.
If she were lustful, would she take a
　　boy,
That knows not yet desire? She would
　　have one
Should meet her thoughts and know the
　　sin he acts,
Which is the great delight of wickedness.
You are abused,[1] and so is she, and I.
DI. How you, my lord?
PHI.　　　Why, all the world's abused
In an unjust report.
DI.　　　O, noble sir, your virtues　110
Cannot look into the subtle thoughts of
　　woman!
In short, my lord, I took them, I myself.
PHI. Now, all the devils, thou didst! Fly
　　from my rage!
Would thou hadst ta'en devils engend'-
　　ring plagues,
When thou didst take them! Hide thee
　　from mine eyes!
Would thou hadst ta'en thunder on thy
　　breast
When thou didst take them, or been
　　strucken dumb
Forever, that this foul deed might have
　　slept
In silence!
THRA. [*Aside.*]　Have you known him
　　so ill-tempered?
CLE. [*Aside.*] Never before.
PHI.　　The winds that are let loose　120
From the four several corners of the
　　earth,
And spread themselves all over sea and
　　land,
_____
[1] Deceived.

Kiss not a chaste one. What friend bears
  a sword
To run me through?
Di.   Why, my lord, are you
So moved at this?
Phi.   When any fall from virtue,
  I am distracted; I have an interest in 't.
Di. But, good my lord, recall yourself, and
  think
What's best to be done.
Phi.   I thank you; I will do it.
  Please you to leave me; I'll consider of it.
  Tomorrow I will find your lodging
  forth,   130
  And give you answer.
Di.   All the gods direct you
  The readiest way!
Thra. [*Aside.*]   He was extreme im-
  patient.
Cle. [*Aside.*] It was his virtue and his
  noble mind.
Exit Di[on, with] Cle[remont], Thra[siline].
Phi. I had forgot to ask him where he took
  them;
I'll follow him. O, that I had a sea
Within my breast to quench the fire I
  feel!
More circumstances will but fan this fire.
It more afflicts me now, to know by whom
This deed is done, than simply that 'tis
  done,   139
And he that tells me this is honorable,
As far from lies as she is far from truth.
O, that like beasts we could not grieve
  ourselves
With that we see not! Bulls and rams
  will fight
To keep their females, standing in their
  sight;
But take um from them, and you take
  at once
Their spleens away, and they will fall
  again
Unto their pastures, growing fresh and
  fat,
And taste the waters of the springs as
  sweet
As 'twas before, finding no start in sleep.
But miserable man—

Enter Bellario.

[*Aside.*]   See, see, you gods, 150
He walks still; and the face you let him
  wear

When he was innocent is still the same,
Not blasted! Is this justice? Do you
  mean
To entrap mortality, that you allow
Treason so smooth a brow? I cannot now
Think he is guilty.
Bel.   Health to you, my lord!
The princess doth commend her love,
  her life,
And this, unto you.   [*Gives a letter.*]
Phi.   O, Bellario,
Now I perceive she loves me; she does
  show it
In loving thee, my boy; she has made
  thee brave.   160
Bel. My lord, she has attired me past my
  wish,
Past my desert, more fit for her attend-
  ant,
Though far unfit for me who do attend.
Phi. Thou art grown courtly, boy.—
  [*Aside.*] O, let all women
That love black deeds, learn to dissemble
  here,
Here, by this paper! She does write to
  me
As if her heart were mines of adamant
To all the world besides; but, unto me,
A maiden snow that melted with my
  looks.—
Tell me, my boy, how doth the princess
  use thee?   170
For I shall guess her love to me by that.
Bel. Scarce like her servant, but as if I
  were
Something allied to her, or had pre-
  served
Her life three times by my fidelity;
As mothers fond do use their only sons,
As I'd use one that's left unto my trust,
For whom my life should pay if he met
  harm,
So she does use me.
Phi.   Why, this is wondrous well.
But what kind language does she feed
  thee with?
Bel. Why, she does tell me she will trust
  my youth   180
With all her loving secrets, and does call
  me
Her pretty servant; bids me weep no more
For leaving you; she'll see my services
Regarded; and such words of that soft
  strain

That I am nearer weeping when she ends
Than ere she spake.

PHI.   This is much better still.

BEL. Are you not ill, my lord?

PHI.   Ill? No, Bellario.

BEL. Methinks your words
Fall not from off your tongue so evenly,
Nor is there in your looks that quietness
That I was wont to see.

PHI.   Thou art deceived, boy.   191
And she strokes thy head?

BEL. Yes.

PHI. And she does clap thy cheeks?

BEL.   She does, my lord.

PHI. And she does kiss thee, boy? Ha!

BEL.   How, my lord?

PHI. She kisses thee?

BEL.   Never, my lord, by heaven.

PHI. That's strange; I know she does.

BEL.   No, by my life.

PHI. Why, then she does not love me.
Come, she does.
I bade her do it; I charged her, by all
    charms
Of love between us, by the hope of
    peace   200
We should enjoy, to yield thee all de-
    lights
Naked as to her bed; I took her oath
Thou shouldst enjoy her. Tell me, gentle
    boy,
Is she not parallelless? Is not her breath
Sweet as Arabian winds when fruits are
    ripe?
Are not her breasts two liquid ivory
    balls?
Is she not all a lasting mine of joy?

BEL. Ay, now I see why my disturbéd
    thoughts
Were so perplexed. When first I went to
    her,   209
My heart held augury. You are abused;
Some villain has abused you. I do
    see
Whereto you tend. Fall rocks upon his
    head
That put this to you! 'Tis some subtile
    train
To bring that noble frame of yours to
    naught.

PHI. Thou think'st I will be angry with
    thee. Come,
Thou shalt know all my drift. I hate her
    more

Than I love happiness, and placed thee
    there
To pry with narrow eyes into her deeds.
Hast thou discovered? Is she fall'n to
    lust,
As I would wish her? Speak some com-
    fort to me.   220

BEL. My lord, you did mistake the boy
    you sent.
Had she the lust of sparrows or of goats,
Had she a sin that way, hid from the
    world,
Beyond the name of lust, I would not aid
Her base desires; but what I came to
    know
As servant to her, I would not reveal
To make my life last ages.

PHI. [Aside.]   O, my heart!
This is a salve worse than the main
    disease.—
Tell me thy thoughts, for I will know the
    least
That dwells within thee, or will rip thy
    heart   230
To know it. I will see thy thoughts as
    plain
As I do now thy face.

BEL.   Why, so you do.
She is (for aught I know), by all the
    gods,
As chaste as ice! But, were she foul as
    hell,
And I did know it thus, the breath of
    kings,
The points of swords, tortures, nor bulls
    of brass [1]
Should draw it from me.

PHI.   Then 'tis no time
To dally with thee; I will take thy life,
For I do hate thee. I could curse thee
    now·

BEL. If you do hate, you could not curse
    me worse;   240
The gods have not a punishment in store
Greater for me than is your hate.

PHI.   Fie, fie,
So young and so dissembling! Tell me
    when
And where thou didst enjoy her, or let
    plagues
Fall on me, if I destroy thee not!
                    [Draws his sword.]

[1] An instrument of torture causing death by
roasting.

BEL. By heaven, I never did; and, when I lie
　To save my life, may I live long and loathed!
　Hew me asunder, and, whilst I can think,
　I'll love those pieces you have cut away
　Better than those that grow, and kiss those limbs　　　250
　Because you made um so.

PHI. 　　　　　　　Fear'st thou not death?
　Can boys contemn that?

BEL. 　　　　　　　O, what boy is he
　Can be content to live to be a man,
　That sees the best of men thus passionate,
　Thus without reason?

PHI. 　　　　　O, but thou dost not know
　What 'tis to die.

BEL. 　　　　　Yes, I do know, my lord.
　'Tis less than to be born, a lasting sleep,
　A quiet resting from all jealousy,
　A thing we all pursue. I know, besides,
　It is but giving over of a game　　　260
　That must be lost.

PHI. 　　　But there are pains, false boy,
　For perjured souls. Think but on those, and then
　Thy heart will melt, and thou wilt utter all.

BEL. May they fall all upon me whilst I live,
　If I be perjured, or have ever thought
　Of that you charge me with! If I be false,
　Send me to suffer in those punishments
　You speak of; kill me!

PHI. 　　　　　　　O, what should I do?
　Why, who can but believe him? He does swear
　So earnestly that, if it were not true,　270
　The gods would not endure him. Rise, Bellario;
　Thy protestations are so deep, and thou
　Dost look so truly when thou utter'st them
　That, though I know um false as were my hopes,
　I cannot urge thee further. But thou wert
　To blame to injure me, for I must love
　Thy honest looks, and take no revenge upon
　Thy tender youth. A love from me to thee
　Is firm, whate'er thou doest; it troubles me

That I have called the blood out of thy cheeks,　　　280
　That did so well become thee. But, good boy,
　Let me not see thee more; something is done
　That will distract me, that will make me mad,
　If I behold thee. If thou tender'st [1] me,
　Let me not see thee.

BEL. 　　　　　I will fly as far
　As there is morning, ere I give distaste
　To that most honored mind. But, through these tears
　Shed at my hopeless parting, I can see
　A world of treason practiced upon you,
　And her, and me. Farewell forevermore!
　If you shall hear that sorrow struck me dead,　　　291
　And after find me loyal, let there be
　A tear shed from you in my memory,
　And I shall rest at peace.
　　　　　　　　Exit Bell[ario].

PHI. 　　　　　Blessing be with thee,
　Whatever thou deserv'st! O, where shall I
　Go bathe this body? Nature too unkind,
　That made no medicine for a troubled mind! 　　　*Ex[it] Phi[laster].*

[SCENA ii.

Arethusa's chambers in the palace.]

Enter Arethusa.

ARE. I marvel my boy comes not back again;
　But that I know my love will question him
　Over and over—how I slept, waked, talked,
　How I remembered him when his dear name
　Was last spoke, and how, when I sighed, wept, sung,
　And ten thousand such—I should be angry at his stay.

Enter King.

KING. What, at your meditations? Who attends you?

ARE. None but my single self. I need no guard;
　I do no wrong, nor fear none.

[1] Regardest.

KING. Tell me, have you not a boy?

ARE.   Yes, sir.   10

KING. What kind of boy?

ARE.   A page, a waiting-boy.

KING. A handsome boy?

ARE.   I think he be not ugly;
Well qualified and dutiful I know him;
I took him not for beauty.

KING. He speaks and sings and plays?

ARE.   Yes, sir.

KING. About eighteen?

ARE.   I never asked his age.

KING. Is he full of service?

ARE. By your pardon, why do you ask?

KING. Put him away.

ARE.   Sir?

KING.   Put him away, I say.
H'as done you that good service shames
me to speak of.   20

ARE. Good sir, let me understand you.

KING.   If you fear me,
Show it in duty; put away that boy.

ARE. Let me have reason for it, sir, and
then
Your will is my command.

KING. Do not you blush to ask it? Cast
him off,
Or I shall do the same to you. Y' are one
Shame with me, and so near unto my-
self
That, by my life, I dare not tell myself
What you, myself, have done.

ARE. What I have done, my lord?   30

KING. 'Tis a new language, that all love
to learn;
The common people speak it well already;
They need no grammar. Understand
me well;
There be foul whispers stirring. Cast
him off,
And suddenly. Do it! Farewell.

                                   Exit King.

ARE. Where may a maiden live securely
free,
Keeping her honor fair? Not with the
living.
They feed upon opinions, errors, dreams,
And make um truths; they draw a
nourishment   39
Out of defamings, grow upon disgraces,
And, when they see a virtue fortified
Strongly above the battery of their
tongues,

O, how they cast [1] to sink it, and, defeated
(Soul-sick with poison), strike the monuments
Where noble names lie sleeping, till
they sweat,
And the cold marble melt.

                              Enter Philaster.

PHI. Peace to your fairest thoughts, dearest mistress!

ARE. O, my dearest servant, I have a war
within me!

PHI. He must be more than man that
makes these crystals
Run into rivers. Sweetest fair, the
cause?   50
And, as I am your slave, tied to your
goodness,
Your creature, made again from what
I was
And newly-spirited, I'll right your honor.

ARE. O, my best love, that boy!

PHI.   What boy?

ARE. The pretty boy you gave me—

PHI.   What of him?

ARE. Must be no more mine.

PHI.   Why?

ARE.   They are jealous of him.

PHI. Jealous! Who?

ARE.   The king.

PHI. [*Aside.*]   O, my misfortune!
Then 'tis no idle jealousy.—Let him go.

ARE. O, cruel!
Are you hard-hearted too? Who shall
now tell you   60
How much I loved you? Who shall
swear it to you,
And weep the tears I send? Who shall
now bring you
Letters, rings, bracelets? Lose his health
in service?
Wake tedious nights in stories of your
praise?
Who shall sing your crying elegies,
And strike a sad soul into senseless
pictures,
And make them mourn? Who shall
take up his lute,
And touch it till he crown a silent sleep
Upon my eyelids, making me dream
and cry,
"O, my dear, dear Philaster!"

[1] Plan.

PHI. [*Aside.*] O, my heart! 70
Would he had broken thee, that made
    thee know
This lady was not loyal!—Mistress,
Forget the boy; I'll get thee a far better.
ARE. O, never, never such a boy again
    As my Bellario!
PHI. 'Tis but your fond affection.
ARE. With thee, my boy, farewell forever
All secrecy in servants! Farewell, faith,
And all desire to do well for itself!
Let all that shall succeed thee for thy
    wrongs
Sell and betray chaste love! 80
PHI. And all this passion for a boy?
ARE. He was your boy, and you put him
    to me,
And the loss of such must have a mourn-
    ing for.
PHI. O, thou forgetful woman!
ARE. How, my lord?
PHI. False Arethusa!
Hast thou a medicine to restore my wits,
When I have lost um? If not, leave to
    talk
And do thus.
ARE. Do what, sir? Would you sleep?
PHI. Forever, Arethusa. O, you gods,
Give me a worthy patience! Have I
    stood, 90
Naked, alone, the shock of many for-
    tunes?
Have I seen mischiefs numberless and
    mighty
Grow like a sea upon me? Have I taken
Danger as stern as death into my
    bosom,
And laughed upon it, made it but a
    mirth,
And flung it by? Do I live now like him,
Under this tyrant king, that languish-
    ing
Hears his sad bell and sees his mourners?
    Do I
Bear all this bravely, and must sink
    at length
Under a woman's falsehood? O, that
    boy, 100
That cursed boy! None but a villain
    boy
To ease your lust?
ARE. Nay, then, I am betrayed.
I feel the plot cast for my overthrow.
O, I am wretched!

PHI. Now you may take that little right
    I have
To this poor kingdom. Give it to your
    joy,
For I have no joy in it. Some far place,
Where never womankind durst set her
    foot
For [1] bursting with her poisons, must
    I seek,
And live to curse you. 110
There dig a cave, and preach to birds
    and beasts
What woman is, and help to save them
    from you:
How heaven is in your eyes, but in
    your hearts
More hell than hell has; how your
    tongues, like scorpions,
Both heal and poison; how your thoughts
    are woven
With thousand changes in one subtle
    web,
And worn so by you; how that foolish
    man,
That reads the story of a woman's face
And dies believing it, is lost forever;
How all the good you have is but a
    shadow, 120
I' th' morning with you, and at night
    behind you,
Past and forgotten; how your vows are
    frosts,
Fast for a night, and with the next sun
    gone;
How you are, being taken all together,
A mere confusion, and so dead a chaos
That love cannot distinguish. These
    sad texts,
Till my last hour, I am bound to utter
    of you.
So, farewell all my woe, all my delight!
    Exit Phi[laster].
ARE. Be merciful, ye gods, and strike me
    dead!
What way have I deserved this? Make
    my breast 130
Transparent as pure crystal, that the
    world,
Jealous of me, may see the foulest
    thought
My heart holds. Where shall a woman
    turn her eyes
To find out constancy?

[1] For fear of.

Enter Bell[ario].

     Save me, how black
And guiltily, methinks, that boy looks
 now!—
O, thou dissembler, that, before thou
 spak'st,
Wert in thy cradle false, sent to make
 lies
And betray innocents! Thy lord and
 thou
May glory in the ashes of a maid
Fooled by her passion; but the con-
 quest is   140
Nothing so great as wicked. Fly away!
Let my command force thee to that
 which shame
Would do without it. If thou under-
 stood'st
The loathéd office thou hast undergone,
Why, thou wouldst hide thee under heaps
 of hills,
Lest men should dig and find thee.
BEL.   O, what god,
 Angry with men, hath sent this strange
  disease
Into the noblest minds? Madam, this
 grief
You add unto me is no more than drops
To seas, for which they are not seen to
 swell.   150
My lord hath struck his anger through
 my heart,
And let out all the hope of future joys.
You need not bid me fly; I came to part,
To take my latest leave. Farewell for-
 ever!
I durst not run away in honesty
From such a lady, like a boy that stole
Or made some grievous fault. The power
 of gods
Assist you in your sufferings! Hasty
 time
Reveal the truth to your abuséd lord
And mine, that he may know your worth,
 whilst I   160
Go seek out some forgotten place to
 die!   *Exit Bell[ario].*
ARE. Peace guide thee! Th'ast over-
 thrown me once;
Yet, if I had another Troy to lose,
Thou, or another villain with thy looks,
Might talk me out of it, and send me
 naked,

My hair disheveled, through the fiery
 streets.

Enter a Lady.

LA. Madam, the king would hunt, and
 calls for you
With earnestness.
ARE.   I am in tune to hunt!
Diana, if thou canst rage with a maid
As with a man,[1] let me discover thee 170
Bathing, and turn me to a fearful hind,
That I may die pursued by cruel hounds,
And have my story written in my
 wounds!   *Exeunt.*

ACTUS IV. SCENA i.

[Outside the palace.]

Enter King, Pharamond, Arethusa, Gala-
* tea, Megra, Dion, Cleremont, Thrasi-*
* line, and Attendants.*

KING. What, are the hounds before and
 all the woodmen?
Our horses ready and our bows bent?
DI.   All, sir.
KING. [*To Pharamond.*] Y' are cloudy,
 sir. Come, we have forgotten
Your venial trespass; let not that sit
 heavy
Upon your spirit; here's none dare utter it.
DI. [*Aside.*] He looks like an old surfeited stallion after his leaping, dull as a
dormouse. See how he sinks! The wench
has shot him between wind and water,
and, I hope, sprung a leak. 10
THRA. [*Aside.*] He needs no teaching;
he strikes sure enough. His greatest fault
is, he hunts too much in the purlieus;
would he would leave off poaching!
DI. [*Aside.*] And, for his horn, h'as left
it at the lodge where he lay late. O, he's
a precious limehound![2] Turn him loose
upon the pursue[3] of a lady, and, if he lose
her, hang him up i' th' slip.[4] When my
fox bitch, Beauty, grows proud,[5] I'll [20
borrow him.
KING. Is your boy turned away?

[1] *I.e.*, Actaeon.
[2] A hunting dog led by a lime, or leash.
[3] Pursuit.
[4] Noose by which hounds are held.
[5] Sexually excited.

ARE. You did command, sir, and I obeyed you.

KING. 'Tis well done. Hark ye further. [*All except Cleremont, Dion, and Thrasiline retire. The King and Arethusa talk apart.*]

CLE. Is 't possible this fellow should repent? Methinks that were not noble in him; and yet he looks like a mortified member, as if he had a sick man's salve [1] in 's mouth. If a worse man had done [30 this fault now, some physical justice [2] or other would presently (without the help of an almanac [3]) have opened the obstructions of his liver, and let him blood with a dog whip.

DI. See, see how modestly yon lady looks, as if she came from churching with her neighbors! Why, what a devil can a man see in her face but that she's honest?

THRA. Faith, no great matter to [40 speak of—a foolish twinkling with the eye, that spoils her coat; [4] but he must be a cunning herald that finds it.

DI. See how they muster [5] one another! O, there's a rank regiment where the devil carries the colors, and his dam drum major! Now the world and the flesh come behind with the carriage. [6]

CLE. Sure this lady has a good turn done her against her will; before, she [50 was common talk; now none dare say cantharides [7] can stir her. Her face looks like a warrant, willing and commanding all tongues, as they will answer it, to be tied up and bolted when this lady means to let herself loose. As I live, she has got her a goodly protection and a gracious, and may use her body discreetly for her health' sake, once a week, excepting Lent and dog days. O, if they were to be [60 got for money, what a large sum would come out of the city for these licenses!

KING. To horse, to horse! We lose the morning, gentlemen.   *Exeunt.*

[SCENA ii.

A forest.]

Enter two Woodmen.

1 WOOD. What, have you lodged [8] the deer?

2 WOOD. Yes, they are ready for the bow.

1 WOOD. Who shoots?

2 WOOD. The princess.

1 WOOD. No, she'll hunt.

2 WOOD. She'll take a stand, I say.

1 WOOD. Who else?

2 WOOD. Why, the young stranger [10 prince.

1 WOOD. He shall shoot in a stone-bow [9] for me. [10] I never loved his beyond-sea-ship since he forsook the say, for paying ten shillings. [11] Hew as there at the fall of a deer, and would needs (out of his mightiness) give ten groats for the dowcets; [12] marry, the steward would have the velvet-head, [13] into the bargain, to turf [14] his hat withal. I think he should love venery; [20 he is an old Sir Tristram; [15] for, if you be remembered, he forsook the stag once to strike a rascal milking [16] in a meadow, and her he killed in the eye. Who shoots else?

2 WOOD. The Lady Galatea.

1 WOOD. That's a good wench, and [17] she would not chide us for tumbling of her women in the brakes. She's liberal, and, by the gods, they say she's honest, and whether that be a fault, I have nothing [30 to do. There's all?

2 WOOD. No, one more—Megra.

1 WOOD. That's a firker, [18] i' faith, boy. There's a wench will ride her haunches as hard after a kennel of hounds as a hunting saddle, and, when she comes home, get um clapped, [19] and all is well again. I have known her lose herself three times in one afternoon (if the woods have been answerable [20]), and it has been work enough [40 for one man to find her, and he has sweat

---

[1] An allusion to such religious pamphlets as Thomas Becon's *The Sick Man's Salve* (1561) and William Perkins' *Salve for a Sick Man* (1595).

[2] *I.e.*, a justice acting as a physician.

[3] Almanacs gave directions for bloodletting.

[4] "The allusion is to mullets, or stars, introduced into coats of arms to distinguish the younger branches of a family, which of course denote inferiority" (Mason).

[5] Set off.   [6] Baggage.   [7] A provocative.

[8] Entrapped.

[9] With a crossbow for shooting stones.

[10] For all I care.

[11] Refused the assay, or slitting of the deer, to avoid paying the customary keeper's fee.

[12] Doucets.

[13] The down-covered horns of a young deer.

[14] Re-cover.   [17] If.   [18] A lively one.

[15] An expert huntsman.   [19] Rubbed.

[16] A lean doe feeding.   [20] Suitable.

for it. She rides well and she pays well.
Hark! Let's go.   *Exeunt.*

Enter Philaster.

PHI. O, that I had been nourished in these
    woods
With milk of goats and acorns, and not
    known
The right of crowns nor the dissembling
    trains
Of women's looks, but digged myself a
    cave
Where I, my fire, my cattle, and my
    bed
Might have been shut together in one
    shed,
And then had taken me some mountain
    girl,   50
Beaten with winds, chaste as the hard-
    ened rocks
Whereon she dwells, that might have
    strewed my bed
With leaves and reeds, and with the skins
    of beasts,
Our neighbors, and have borne at her big
    breasts
My large, coarse issue! This had been a
    life
Free from vexation.

Enter Bellario.

BEL. [*To himself.*]   O, wicked men!
An innocent may walk safe among
    beasts;
Nothing assaults me here. See, my
    grieved lord
Sits as his soul were searching out a way
To leave his body!—Pardon me, that
    must   60
Break thy last commandment, for I
    must speak.
You that are grieved can pity; hear,
    my lord!
PHI. Is there a creature yet so miserable
That I can pity?
BEL.   O, my noble lord,
View my strange fortune, and bestow
    on me,
According to your bounty (if my service
Can merit nothing), so much as may
    serve
To keep that little piece I hold of life
From cold and hunger!

PHI.   Is it thou? Begone!
Go, sell those misbeseeming clothes thou
    wear'st,   70
And feed thyself with them.
BEL. Alas, my lord, I can get nothing for
    them!
The silly country people think 'tis trea-
    son
To touch such gay things.
PHI.   Now, by the gods, this is
Unkindly done, to vex me with thy
    sight.
Th' art fall'n again to thy dissembling
    trade.
How shouldst thou think to cozen me
    again?
Remains there yet a plague untried for
    me?
Even so thou wep[t]'st, and look[ed]'st,
    and spok'st when first   79
I took thee up. Curse on the time! If thy
Commanding tears can work on any
    other,
Use thy art; I'll not betray it. Which
    way
Wilt thou take, that I may shun thee,
For thine eyes are poison to mine, and I
Am loath to grow in rage? This way, or
    that way?
BEL. Any will serve; but I will choose to
    have
That path in chase that leads unto my
    grave.
    Exit Phi[laster, with] Bel[lario], severally.

Enter Dion and the Woodmen.

DI. This is the strangest sudden chance!
    —You, woodmen!
1 WOOD. My lord Dion?
DI. Saw you a lady come this way   [90
on a sable horse studded with stars of
white?
2 WOOD. Was she not young and tall?
DI. Yes. Rode she to the wood or to the
    plain?
2 WOOD. Faith, my lord, we saw none.
               Exeunt [1] Woodmen.
DI. Pox of your questions then!—

Enter Cleremont.

             What, is she found?
CLE. Nor will be, I think.

[1] Original reads *Exit.*

Di. Let him seek his daughter himself.
She cannot stray about a little necessary
natural business, but the whole court   [100
must be in arms. When she has done, we
shall have peace.

CLE. There's already a thousand fatherless tales amongst us. Some say her horse
ran away with her; some, a wolf pursued
her; others, 'twas a plot to kill her, and
that armed men were seen in the wood; but
questionless she rode away willingly.

Enter King and Thrasiline.

KING. Where is she?
CLE.   Sir, I cannot tell.
KING.   How's that?
Answer me so again!
CLE.   Sir, shall I lie?   110
KING. Yes, lie and damn, rather than tell
me that.
I say again, where is she? Mutter not!—
Sir, speak you; where is she?
Di.   Sir, I do not know.
KING. Speak that again so boldly, and, by
heaven,
It is thy last!—You, fellows, answer me;
Where is she? Mark me, all; I am your
king.
I wish to see my daughter; show her me.
I do command you all, as you are sub-
jects,
To show her me! What! Am I not your
king?
If ay, then am I not to be obeyed?   120
Di. Yes, if you command things possible
and honest.
KING. Things possible and honest! Hear
me, thou,
Thou traitor, that dar'st confine thy
king to things
Possible and honest! Show her me,
Or, let me perish, if I cover not
All Sicily with blood!
Di.   Faith, I cannot,
Unless you tell me where she is.
KING. You have betrayed me; y' have let
me lose
The jewel of my life. Go, bring her
me,   129
And set her here before me. 'Tis the king
Will have it so, whose breath can still the
winds,
Uncloud the sun, charm down the swell-
ing sea,

And stop the floods of heaven. Speak,
can it not?
Di. No.
KING.   No? Cannot the breath of kings
do this?
Di. No; nor smell sweet itself, if once the
lungs
Be but corrupted.
KING.   Is it so? Take heed!
Di. Sir, take you heed how you dare the
powers
That must be just.
KING.   Alas! What are we kings?
Why do you gods place us above the
rest,
To be served, flattered, and adored, till
we   140
Believe we hold within our hands your
thunder?
And, when we come to try the power we
have,
There's not a leaf shakes at our threat'-
nings.
I have sinned, 'tis true, and here stand
to be punished;
Yet would not thus be punished. Let me
choose
My way, and lay it on!
Di. [*Aside.*] He articles [1] with the gods.
Would somebody would draw bonds for
the performance of covenants betwixt
them!   150

Enter Pha[ramond], Galatea, and Megra.

KING. What, is she found?
PHA.   No; we have ta'en her horse;
He galloped empty by. There's some
treason.
You, Galatea, rode with her into the
wood.
Why left you her?
GAL. She did command me.
KING. Command! You should not.
GAL. 'Twould ill become my fortunes and
my birth
To disobey the daughter of my king.
KING. Y' are all cunning to obey us for our
hurt;
But I will have her.
PHA.   If I have her not,   160
By this hand, there shall be no more
Sicily.

[1] Bargains.

Di. [*Aside.*] What, will he carry it to
Spain in 's pocket?

Pha. I will not leave one man alive but
the king,
A cook, and a tailor.

Di. [*Aside.*] Yes; you may do well to
spare your lady-bedfellow; and her you may
keep for a spawner.

King. [*Aside.*] I see the injuries I have
done must be revenged.

Di. Sir, this is not the way to find her
out.

King. Run all; disperse yourselves. The
man that finds her,   170
Or (if she be killed) the traitor, I'll make
him great.

Di. I know some would give five thousand
pounds to find her.

Pha. Come, let us seek.

King. Each man a several way; here I myself.

Di. Come, gentlemen, we here.

Cle. Lady, you must go search too.

Meg. I had rather be searched myself.
Exeunt[1] *omnes.*

[Scena iii.

Another part of the forest.]

Enter Arethusa.

Are. Where am I now? Feet, find me out
a way,
Without the counsel of my troubled head.
I'll follow you boldly about these woods,
O'er mountains, through brambles, pits,
and floods.
Heaven, I hope, will ease me. I am sick.
[*She sits down.*][2]

Enter Bellario.

Bel. [*Aside.*] Yonder's my lady. God
knows I want nothing,
Because I do not wish to live; yet I
Will try her charity.—O, hear, you that
have plenty!
From that flowing store drop some on
dry ground.—See,   9
The lively red is gone to guard her heart!
I fear she faints.—Madam, look up!—
She breathes not.—
Open once more those rosy twins, and
send

[1] Original reads *Exit.*   [2] From 1620 edn.

Unto my lord your latest farewell!—O,
she stirs.—
How is it, madam? Speak comfort.

Are. 'Tis not gently done,
To put me in a miserable life,
And hold me there. I prithee, let me
go.
I shall do best without thee; I am well.

Enter Philaster.

Phi. [*Aside.*] I am to blame to be so
much in rage.
I'll tell her coolly when and where I
heard   20
This killing truth. I will be temperate
In speaking, and as just in hearing.—
O, monstrous! Tempt me not, you gods!
Good gods,
Tempt not a frail man! What's he that
has a heart
But he must ease it here!

Bel. My lord, help, help! The princess!

Are. I am well; forbear.

Phi. [*Aside.*] Let me love lightning; let me
be embraced
And kissed by scorpions, or adore the
eyes   29
Of basilisks, rather than trust the tongues
Of hell-bred woman! Some good god
look down,
And shrink these veins up! Stick me
here a stone,
Lasting to ages in the memory
Of this damned act!—Hear me, you
wicked ones!
You have put hills of fire into this
breast,
Not to be quenched with tears, for which
may guilt
Sit on your bosoms! At your meals and
beds
Despair await you! What, before my
face?
Poison of asps between your lips! Dis-
eases
Be your best issues! Nature make a
curse,   40
And throw it on you!

Are.   Dear Philaster, leave
To be enraged, and hear me.

Phi.   I have done;
Forgive my passion. Not the calméd
sea,
When Aeolus locks up his windy brood,

Is less disturbed than I. I'll make you
    know 't.
Dear Arethusa, do but take this sword,
              [*Offers his drawn sword.*] [1]
And search how temperate a heart I
    have;
Then you and this your boy may live and
    reign
In lust without control.—Wilt thou,
    Bellario?
I prithee, kill me; thou art poor, and
    mayst   50
Nourish ambitious thoughts; when I am
    dead,
This way were freer. Am I raging now?
If I were mad, I should desire to live.
Sirs,[2] feel my pulse, whether you have
    known
A man in a more equal tune to die.
BEL. Alas, my lord, your pulse keeps mad-
    man's time!
So does your tongue.
PHI.   You will not kill me, then?
ARE. Kill you?
BEL.   Not for the world.
PHI.   I blame not thee,
    Bellario; thou has done but that which
    gods
Would have transformed themselves to
    do. Begone;   60
Leave me without reply. This is the
    last
Of all our meeting.—(*Exit Bell*[*ario*].)
    Kill me with this sword.
Be wise, or worse will follow; we are two
Earth cannot bear at once. Resolve to
    do,
Or suffer.
ARE. If my fortune be so good to let me
    fall
Upon [3] thy hand, I shall have peace in
    death.
Yet tell me this: will there be no slan-
    ders,
No jealousy in the other world, no ill
    there?
PHI. No.   70
ARE. Show me then the way.
PHI. Then guide my feeble hand,
    You that have power to do it, for I must
Perform a piece of justice!—If your
    youth

---

[1] From 1620 edn.   [3] At.
[2] Formerly applied to both sexes.

Have any way offended heaven, let
    prayers
Short and effectual reconcile you to it.
ARE. I am prepared.

Enter a Country Fellow.

COUN. [*Aside.*] I'll see the king, if he be
in the forest; I have hunted him these two
hours. If I should come home and not [80
see him, my sisters would laugh at me. I
can see nothing but people better horsed
than myself, that outride me; I can hear
nothing but shouting. These kings had
need of good brains; this whooping is able
to put a mean man out of his wits.—
There's a courtier with his sword drawn;
by this hand, upon a woman, I think!
PHI. Are you at peace?
ARE.   With heaven and earth. 89
PHI. May they divide thy soul and body!
                    [*Wounds her.*]
COUN. Hold, dastard! Strike a woman!
Th' art a craven. I warrant thee, thou
wouldst be loath to play half a dozen venies
at wasters [4] with a good fellow for a
broken head.
PHI. Leave us, good friend.
ARE. What ill-bred man art thou, to in-
    trude thyself
Upon our private sports, our recreations?
COUN. God 'uds [5] me, I understand you
not; but I know the rogue has hurt you.
PHI. Pursue thy own affairs. It will be ill
    To multiply blood upon my head, which
    thou   102
Wilt force me to.
COUN. I know not your rhetoric; but I
can lay it on, if you touch the woman.
                     They fight.
PHI. Slave, take what thou deservest!
ARE.   Heavens guard my lord!
COUN. O, do you breathe?
PHI. I hear the tread of people. I am hurt.
    The gods take part against me. Could
    this boor
Have held me thus else? I must shift
    for life,   110
Though I do loathe it. I would find a
    course
To lose it rather by my will than force.
                  Exit Philaster.
COUN. I cannot follow the rogue. I
pray thee, wench, come and kiss me now.

---

[4] Bouts at cudgels.   [5] God judge.

Enter Phara[mond], Dion, Cle[remont], Thra-
si[line], and Woodmen.

PHA. What art thou?

COUN. Almost killed I am for a foolish
woman; a knave has hurt her.

PHA. The princess, gentlemen! —Where's
the wound, madam?   Is it dangerous?

ARE. He has not hurt me.   120

COUN. By God, she lies; h'as hurt her in
the breast; look else.

PHA. O sacred spring of innocent blood!

DI. 'Tis above wonder!   Who should
dare this?

ARE. I felt it not.

PHA. Speak, villain, who has hurt the
princess?

COUN. Is it the princess?

DI. Ay.   130

COUN. Then I have seen something yet.

PHA. But who has hurt her?

COUN. I told you, a rogue; I ne'er saw
him before, I.

PHA. Madam, who did it?

ARE.   Some dishonest wretch;
Alas, I know him not, and do forgive him!

COUN. He's hurt too; he cannot go far;
I made my father's old fox [1] fly about his
ears.

PHA. How will you have me kill [140
him?

ARE. Not at all; 'tis some distracted fellow.

PHA. By this hand, I'll leave ne'er a
piece of him bigger than a nut, and bring
him all to you in my hat.

ARE. Nay, good sir,
If you do take him, bring him quick [2] to
me,
And I will study for a punishment
Great as his fault.   149

PHA. I will.

ARE.   But swear.

PHA.   By all my love, I will.—
Woodmen, conduct the princess to the
king,
And bear that wounded fellow to dressing.—
Come, gentlemen, we'll follow the chase
close.

Exeunt [3] *Are[thusa], Pha[ramond], Di[on],*
Cle[remont], Thra[siline], and 1 Wood-
man.

---

[1] Broad sword.   [3] Original reads *Exit.*
[2] Alive.

COUN. I pray you, friend, let me see the
king.

2 WOOD. That you shall, and receive
thanks.

COUN. If I get clear with this, I'll go to
see no more gay sights.   *Exeunt.* [4]

[SCENA iv.

Another part of the forest.]

Enter Bellario.

BEL. A heaviness near death sits on my
brow,
And I must sleep.   Bear me, thou gentle
bank,
Forever, if thou wilt.   You sweet ones
all,   [*Lies down.*]
Let me unworthy press you; I could wish
I rather were a corse strewed o'er with
you
Than quick above you.   Dullness shuts
mine eyes,
And I am giddy.   O, that I could take
So sound a sleep that I might never
wake!   [*Sleeps.*]

Enter Philaster.

PHI. I have done ill; my conscience calls
me false
To strike at her that would not strike at
me.   10
When I did fight, methought I heard her
pray
The gods to guard me.   She may be
abused,
And I a loathéd villain; if she be,
She will conceal who hurt her.   He has
wounds
And cannot follow; neither knows he me.
Who's this?   Bellario sleeping?   If thou
beest
Guilty, there is no justice that thy
sleep   *Cry within.*
Should be so sound, and mine, whom
thou hast wronged,
So broken.   Hark!   I am pursued.   You
gods,
I'll take this offered means of my
escape.   20
They have no mark to know me but my
wounds,

---

[4] In original, stage direction appears at end of
preceding speech.

If she be true; if false, let mischief light
On all the world at once! Sword, print
  my wounds
Upon this sleeping boy! I ha' none, I
  think,
Are mortal, nor would I lay greater on
  thee. *Wounds him.*
BEL. O, death, I hope, is come! Blessed
  be that hand!
It meant me well. Again, for pity's sake!
PHI. I have caught myself;
                  Phi[laster] falls.
The loss of blood hath stayed my flight.
  Here, here
Is he that stroke [1] thee. Take thy full
  revenge;   30
Use me, as I did mean thee, worse than
  death;
I'll teach thee to revenge. This luckless
  hand
Wounded the princess; tell my followers [2]
Thou didst receive these hurts in staying
  me,
And I will second thee. Get a reward.
BEL. Fly, fly, my lord, and save yourself!
PHI.   How's this?
Wouldst thou I should be safe?
BEL.   Else were it vain
For me to live. These little wounds I
  have
Ha' not bled much. Reach me that noble
  hand;
I'll help to cover you.
PHI.   Art thou true to me? 40
BEL. Or let me perish loathed! Come,
  my good lord,
Creep in among those bushes. Who does
  know
But that the gods may save your much-
  loved breath?
PHI. Then I shall die for grief, if not for
  this,
That I have wounded thee. What wilt
  thou do?
BEL. Shift for myself well. Peace! I hear
  um come. [*Philaster conceals himself.*]
[VOICES.] (*Within.*) Follow, follow, follow!
  That way they went.
BEL. With my own wounds I'll bloody
  my own sword.
I need not counterfeit to fall; heaven
  knows
That I can stand no longer. [*Falls.*] 50

[1] Struck.   [2] Pursuers.

Enter Pharamond, Dion, Cleremont, Thrasi-
                     line.

PHA. To this place we have tracked him
  by his blood.
CLE. Yonder, my lord, creeps one away.
DI. Stay, sir! What are you?
BEL. A wretched creature, wounded in
  these woods
By beasts. Relieve me, if your names
  be men,
Or I shall perish.
DI.   This is he, my lord,
Upon my soul, that hurt her. 'Tis the
  boy,
That wicked boy that served her.
PHA.   O, thou damned
In thy creation! What cause couldst
  thou shape
To hurt the princess?
BEL.   Then I am betrayed. 60
DI. Betrayed! No, apprehended.
BEL.   I confess
(Urge it no more) that, big with evil
  thoughts,
I set upon her, and did make my aim
Her death. For charity, let fall at once
The punishment you mean, and do not
  load
This weary flesh with tortures.
PHA.   I will know
Who hired thee to this deed.
BEL.   Mine own revenge.
PHA. Revenge! For what?
BEL.   It pleased her to receive
Me as her page and, when my fortunes
  ebbed,
That men strid [3] o'er them careless, she
  did shower   70
Her welcome graces on me, and did swell
My fortunes till they overflowed their
  banks,
Threat'ning the men that crossed um,
  when, as swift
As storms arise at sea, she turned her
  eyes
To burning suns upon me, and did dry
The streams she had bestowed, leaving
  me worse
And more contemned than other little
  brooks,
Because I had been great. In short, I
  knew

[3] Strode.

I could not live, and therefore did desire
To die revenged.

PHA.   If tortures can be found   80
Long as thy natural life, resolve to feel
The utmost rigor.

                Philaster creeps out of a bush.

CLE.   Help to lead him hence.

PHI. Turn back, you ravishers of innocence!
Know ye the price of that you bear away
So rudely?

PHA.   Who's that?

DI.   'Tis the Lord Philaster.

PHI. 'Tis not the treasure of all kings in
one,
The wealth of Tagus, nor the rocks of
pearl
That pave the court of Neptune, can
weigh down
That virtue. It was I that hurt the princess.
Place me, some god, upon a pyramis [1]   90
Higher than hills of earth, and lend a
voice
Loud as your thunder to me, that from
thence
I may discourse to all the underworld
The worth that dwells in him!

PHA.   How's this?

BEL.   My lord, some man
Weary of life, that would be glad to die.

PHI. Leave these untimely courtesies,
Bellario.

BEL. Alas, he's mad! Come, will you lead
me on?

PHI. By all the oaths that men ought
most to keep,
And gods do punish most when men do
break,
He touched her not.—Take heed, Bellario,   100
How thou dost drown the virtues thou
hast shown
With perjury.—By all that's good, 'twas
I!
You know she stood betwixt me and my
right.

PHA. Thy own tongue be thy judge!

CLE.   It was Philaster.

DI. Is 't not a brave boy?
Well, sirs, I fear me we were all deceived.

PHI. Have I no friend here?

[1] Pyramid.

DI.   Yes.

PHI.   Then show it. Some
Good body lend a hand to draw us
nearer.
Would you have tears shed for you when
you die?
Then lay me gently on his neck, that
there   110
I may weep floods and breathe forth my
spirit.
'Tis not the wealth of Plutus, nor the
gold   [*Embraces Bellario.*]
Locked in the heart of earth, can buy
away
This armful from me; this had been a
ransom
To have redeemed the great Augustus
Cæsar,
Had he been taken. You hard-hearted
men,
More stony than these mountains, can
you see
Such clear, pure blood drop, and not
cut your flesh
To stop his life, to bind whose bitter
wounds
Queens ought to tear their hair, and
with their tears   120
Bathe um?—Forgive me, thou that art
the wealth
Of poor Philaster!

Enter King, Arethusa, and a Guard.

KING.   Is the villain ta'en?

PHA. Sir, here be two confess the deed;
but say [2]
It was Philaster—

PHI.   Question it no more;
It was.

KING.   The fellow that did fight with him
Will tell us that.

ARE.   Ay me! I know he will.

KING. Did not you know him?

ARE.   Sir, if it was he,
He was disguised.

PHI.   I was so.—O, my stars,
That I should live still!

KING.   Thou ambitious fool,
Thou that hast laid a train for thy own
life!—   130
Now [3] I do mean to do, I'll leave to
talk.
Bear him to prison.

[2] Suppose.   [3] Now that.

ARE. Sir, they did plot together to take hence
This harmless life; should it pass un-
revenged,
I should to earth go weeping. Grant me,
then,
By all the love a father bears his child,
Their custodies, and that I may appoint
Their tortures and their deaths.
DI. Death? Soft; our law will not reach
that for this fault.
KING. 'Tis granted; take um to you with
a guard.—   140
Come, princely Pharamond, this busi-
ness past,
We may with more security go on
To your intended match.
CLE. [*Aside.*] I pray that this action lose
not Philaster the hearts of the people.
DI. [*Aside.*] Fear it not; their overwise
heads will think it but a trick.
Exeunt omnes.[1]

ACTUS V. SCENA i.

[*Outside the palace.*]

Enter Dion, Cleremont, Thrasiline.

THRA. Has the king sent for him to
death?
DI. Yes; but the king must know 'tis
not in his power to war with heaven.
CLE. We linger time; the king sent for
Philaster and the headsman an hour ago.
THRA. Are all his wounds well?
DI. All. They were but scratches, but
the loss of blood made him faint.
CLE. We dally, gentlemen.   10
THRA. Away!
DI. We'll scuffle hard before he perish.
Exeunt.

[SCENA ii.

A room in a prison.]

Enter Philaster, Arethusa, Bellario.

ARE. Nay, faith, Philaster, grieve not;
we are well.
BEL. Nay, good my lord, forbear; we're
wondrous well.
PHI. O, Arethusa, O, Bellario,
Leave to be kind!

---

[1] In the original *Finis actus quarti* is inserted
here.

I shall be shut [2] from heaven, as now
from earth,
If you continue so. I am a man
False to a pair of the most trusty ones
That ever earth bore; can it bear us
all?
Forgive, and leave me. But the king
hath sent
To call me to my death. O, show it me, 10
And then forget me! And for thee, my
boy,
I shall deliver words will mollify
The hearts of beasts to spare thy inno-
cence.
BEL. Alas, my lord, my life is not a thing
Worthy your noble thoughts! 'Tis not
a life;
'Tis but a piece of childhood thrown
away.
Should I outlive you, I should then out-
live
Virtue and honor; and, when that day
comes,
If ever I shall close these eyes but once,
May I live spotted for my perjury,   20
And waste my [3] limbs to nothing!
ARE. And I (the woeful'st maid that ever
was,
Forced with my hands to bring my lord
to death)
Do by the honor of a virgin swear
To tell no hours beyond it! [4]
PHI.   Make me not hated so.
ARE. Come from this prison all joyful to
our deaths!
PHI. People will tear me, when they find
you true
To such a wretch as I; I shall die loathed.
Enjoy your kingdoms peaceably, whilst
I   29
Forever sleep forgotten with my faults.
Every just servant, every maid in love,
Will have a piece of me, if you be
true.
ARE. My dear lord, say not so.
BEL.   A piece of you?
He was not born of women that can cut
It and look on.
PHI. Take me in tears betwixt you, for
my heart
Will break with shame and sorrow.

---

[2] From 1620 edn. Original reads *shot.*
[3] From 1630 edn. Original reads *by.*
[4] *I.e.*, to die.

ARE.   Why, 'tis well.
BEL. Lament no more.
PHI.   What would you have done
  If you had wronged me basely, and had
    found
  Your [1] life no price compared to mine?[1]
  For love, sirs,   40
  Deal with me truly.
BEL.   'Twas mistaken, sir.
PHI. Why, if it were?
BEL.   Then, sir, we would have asked
  Your pardon.
PHI.   And have hope to enjoy it?
ARE. Enjoy it? Ay.
PHI.   Would you indeed? Be plain.
BEL. We would, my lord.
PHI.   Forgive me, then.
ARE.   So, so.
BEL. 'Tis as it should be now.
PHI.   Lead to my death. *Exeunt.*

[SCENA iii.

A state room in the palace.]

Enter King, Dion, Cleremont, Thrasiline.

KING. Gentlemen, who saw the prince?
CLE. So please you, sir, he's gone to see
  the city
  And the new platform, with some gentle-
    men
  Attending on him.
KING.   Is the princess ready
  To bring her prisoner out?
THRA.   She waits your grace.
KING. Tell her we stay.
              [*Exit Thrasiline.*] [2]
DI. [*Aside.*]   King, you may be de-
  ceived yet.
  The head you aim at cost more setting
    on
  Than to be lost so lightly. If it must off,
  Like a wild overflow, that soops [3] be-
    fore him
  A golden stack, and with it shakes down
    bridges,   10
  Cracks the strong hearts of pines, whose
    cable-roots
  Held out a thousand storms, a thousand
    thunders,
  And, so made mightier, takes whole
    villages

[1] Mason's emendation for *my . . . yours* of
all early edns.
[2] From 1620 edn.   [3] Sweeps.

Upon his back, and in that heat of pride
Charges strong towns, towers, castles,
  palaces,
And lays them desolate, so shall thy
  head,
Thy noble head, bury the lives of thou-
  sands,
That must bleed with thee like a sacri-
  fice,
In thy red ruins.

*Enter Philaster, Arethusa, Bellario in a
  robe and garland* [*, and Thrasiline*].

KING.   How now? What masque is this?
BEL. Right royal sir, I should   20
  Sing you an epithalamion of these lovers,
  But having lost my best airs with my
    fortunes,
  And wanting a celestial harp to strike
  This blessed union on, thus in glad story
  I give you all. These two fair cedar
    branches,
  The noblest of the mountain where they
    grew,
  Straightest and tallest, under whose
    still shades
  The worthier beasts have made their
    lairs, and slept
  Free from [the fervor of] [4] the Sirian
    star
  And the fell thunderstroke, free from
    the clouds   30
  When they were big with humor,[5] and
    delivered
  In thousand spouts their issues to the
    earth
  (O, there was none but silent quiet
    there),
  Till never-pleaséd Fortune shot up
    shrubs,
  Base underbrambles, to divorce these
    branches;
  And for a while they did so, and did reign
  Over the mountain, and choke up his
    beauty
  With brakes, rude thorns, and thistles,
    till the sun
  Scorched them even to the roots and
    dried them there.   39
  And now a gentle gale hath blown again,
  That made these branches meet and
    twine together,
  Never to be divided. The god that sings

[4] From 1620 edn.   [5] Moisture.

His holy numbers [1] over marriage beds
Hath knit their noble hearts; and here
they stand,
Your children, mighty king; and I have
done.
KING. How, how?
ARE. Sir, if you love it in plain truth
(For now there is no masquing in 't),
this gentleman,
The prisoner that you gave me, is be-
come
My keeper, and through all the bitter
throes
Your jealousies and his ill fate have
wrought him, 50
Thus nobly hath he struggled, and at
length
Arrived here my dear husband.
KING. Your dear husband!—
Call in the Captain of the Citadel—
There you shall keep your wedding.
I'll provide
A masque shall make your Hymen turn
his saffron
Into a sullen coat, and sing sad requiems
To your departing souls.
Blood shall put out your torches; and,
instead
Of gaudy flowers about your wanton
necks,
An ax shall hang, like a prodigious
meteor, 60
Ready to crop your loves' sweets. Hear,
you gods!
From this time do I shake all title off
Of father to this woman, this base
woman;
And what there is of vengeance in a
lion
Chased among dogs or robbed of his
dear young,
The same, enforced more terrible, more
mighty,
Expect from me!
ARE. Sir, by that little life I have left to
swear by,
There's nothing that can stir me from
myself.
What I have done, I have done without
repentance, 70
For death can be no bugbear unto me,
So long as Pharamond is not my heads-
man.

___
[1] Verses.

DI. [*Aside.*] Sweet peace upon thy soul,
thou worthy maid,
Whene'er thou diest! For this time I'll
excuse thee,
Or be thy prologue. [2]
PHI. Sir, let me speak next,
And let my dying words be better with
you
Than my dull, living actions. If you aim
At the dear life of this sweet innocent,
Y' are a tyrant and a savage monster.
Your memory shall be as foul behind
you, 80
As you are living; all your better deeds
Shall be in water writ, but this in marble;
No chronicle shall speak you, though
your own,
But for the shame of men. No monu-
ment,
Though high and big as Pelion, shall be
able
To cover this base murther, make it
rich
With brass, with purest gold, and shin-
ing jasper,
Like the pyramidës; lay on epitaphs
Such as make great men gods; my little
marble,
That only clothes my ashes, not my
faults, 90
Shall far outshine it. And for after-
issues [3]
Think not so madly of the heavenly
wisdoms
That they will give you more for your
mad rage
To cut off, unless it be some snake, or
something
Like yourself, that in his birth shall
strangle you.
Remember my father, king! There was
a fault,
But I forgive it. Let that sin persuade
you
To love this lady; if you have a soul,
Think, save her, and be savéd. For my-
self, 99
I have so long expected [4] this glad hour,
So languished under you, and daily
withered,
That, by the gods, it is a joy to die;
I find a recreation in 't.

___
[2] *I.e.*, precede thee in death.   [4] Awaited.
[3] Future offspring.

Enter a Messenger.

MESS. Where's the king?

KING.   Here.

MESS.   Get you to your strength,
And rescue the Prince Pharamond from
     danger.
He's taken prisoner by the citizens,
Fearing [1] the Lord Philaster.

DI. [*Aside.*]   O, brave followers!
Mutiny, my fine, dear countrymen,
     mutiny!
Now, my brave, valiant foremen, show
     your weapons
In honor of your mistresses!   110

Enter another Messenger.

[2] MESS. Arm, arm, arm, arm!

KING. A thousand devils take um!

DI. [*Aside.*] A thousand blessings on um!

[2] MESS. Arm, O king! The city is in
     mutiny,
Led by an old gray ruffian, who comes
     on
In rescue of the Lord Philaster.

KING. Away to the citadel!—

Exit with Are[thusa], Phi[laster], Bellario.
          I'll see them safe,
And then cope with these burghers. Let
     the guard
And all the gentlemen give strong at-
     tendance.

Exit King; manent [2] *Dion, Cleremont,
          Thrasiline.*

CLE. The city up! This was above our
     wishes.   120

DI. Ay, and the marriage too. By my
life, this noble lady has deceived us all.
A plague upon myself, a thousand plagues,
for having such unworthy thoughts of her
dear honor! O, I could beat myself! Or
do you beat me, and I'll beat you, for we
had all one thought.

CLE. No, no, 'twill but lose time.

DI. You say true. Are your swords
sharp?—Well, my dear countrymen [130
What-ye-lacks,[3] if you continue, and fall
not back upon the first broken shin, I'll
have ye chronicled and chronicled, and
cut and chronicled, and all-to [4] bepraised
and sung in sonnets, and bathed [5] in new,

brave ballads, that all tongues shall troll
you *in sæcula sæculorum,*[6] my kind can-·
carriers.

THRA. What if a toy [7] take um i' th'
heels now, and they run all away, [140
and cry, "The devil take the hind-
most"?

DI. Then the same devil take the foremost too, and souse him for his breakfast!
If they all prove cowards, my curses fly
among them and be speeding! May they
have murrains [8] reign to keep the gentlemen at home unbound in easy frieze!
May the moths branch [9] their velvets, and
their silks only be worn before sore [150
eyes! May their false lights undo um, and
discover presses,[10] holes, stains, and old-
ness in their stuffs, and make them shop-
rid! May they keep whores and horses,
and break,[11] and live mewed up with necks
of beef and turnips! May they have many
children, and none like the father! May
they know no language but that gibberish they prattle to their parcels,[12] unless
it be the goatish [13] Latin they write in [160
their bonds—and may they write that false,
and lose their debts!

Enter the King.

KING. Now the vengeance of all the
gods confound them! How they swarm
together! What a hum they raise!—Devils
choke your wild throats!—If a man had
need to use their valors, he must pay a
brokage for it, and then bring um on, and
they will fight like sheep. 'Tis Philaster,
none but Philaster, must allay this [170
heat. They will not hear me speak, but
fling dirt at me and call me tyrant. O, run,
dear friend, and bring the Lord Philaster!
Speak him fair; call him prince; do him
all the courtesy you can; commend me to
him. O, my wits, my wits!

          Exit Cleremont.

DI. [*Aside.*]   O, my brave countrymen!
As I live, I will not buy a pin out of your
walls [14] for this. Nay, you shall cozen me,
and I'll thank you, and send you [180
brawn and bacon, and soil [15] you every long

---

[1] Fearing for.   [4] Completely.
[2] Remain.   [5] Heath suggests *bawled.*
[3] Shopkeepers, who used this cry.

[6] Forever and ever.   [11] "Go broke."
[7] Trifle, whim.   [12] Conveyances.
[8] Plagues.   [13] Foul.
[9] Eat patterns on.   [14] Outside of your shops.
[10] Creases.   [15] Fatten.

vacation a brace of foremen, [1] that at Michaelmas shall come up fat and kicking.

KING. What they will do with this poor prince, the gods know, and I fear.

DI. [*Aside.*] Why, sir, they'll flay him, and make church buckets [2] on 's skin, to quench rebellion; then clap a rivet in 's sconce, and hang him up for [a] [3] sign.

Enter Cleremont with Philaster.

KING. O, worthy sir, forgive me! Do not make 190
Your miseries and my faults meet together,
To bring a greater danger. Be yourself,
Still sound amongst diseases. I have wronged you;
And, though I find it last, and beaten to it,
Let first your goodness know it. Calm the people,
And be what you were born to. Take your love,
And with her my repentance, all my wishes,
And all my prayers. By the gods, my heart speaks this;
And, if the least fall from me not performed,
May I be strook with thunder!
PHI. Mighty sir, 200
I will not do your greatness so much wrong,
As not to make your word truth. Free the princess
And the poor boy, and let me stand the shock
Of this mad sea-breach, which I'll either turn,
Or perish with it.
KING. Let your own word free them.
PHI. Then thus I take my leave, kissing your hand,
And hanging on your royal word. Be kingly,
And be not moved, sir. I shall bring your peace
Or never bring myself back.
KING. All the gods go with thee.
Exeunt omnes.

[1] Geese.
[2] Leather buckets kept in the church in case of fire. [3] From 1620 edn.

[SCENA iv.

A street.]

Enter an old Captain and Citizens with Pharamond.

CAP. Come, my brave myrmidons, let's fall on. Let your [4] caps swarm, my boys, and your nimble tongues forget your mother-gibberish of "what do you lack?" And set your mouths up,[5] children, till your palates fall frighted half a fathom past the cure of bay salt and gross pepper, and then cry, "Philaster, brave Philaster!" Let Philaster be deeper in request, my dingdongs,[6] my pairs of dear indentures, [10 kings of clubs,[7] than your cold water chamblets [8] or your paintings spitted with copper.[9] Let not your hasty [10] silks, or your branched cloth of bodkin, [11] or your tissues, dearly beloved of spiced cake and custards, your Robin Hoods, Scarlets, and Johns, tie your affections in darkness to your shops. No, dainty duckers, [12] up with your three-piled spirits, your wrought valors; [13] and let your uncut cholers [14] make the king [20 feel the measure of your mightiness. Philaster! Cry, my rose-nobles,[15] cry!

ALL. Philaster! Philaster!

CAP. How do you like this, my lord prince? These are mad boys, I tell you; these are things that will not strike their topsails to a foist,[16] and let a man of war, an argosy, hull and cry "cockles." [17]

PHA. Why, you rude slave, do you know what you do?

CAP. My pretty prince of puppets, we do know, 30
And give your greatness warning that you talk
No more such bug's [18] words, or that soldered crown

[4] From 1620 edn. Original reads *our.*
[5] 1620 edn. has *ope.*
[6] Hearties.
[7] *I.e.,* apprentices, who were bound by indentures and preferred the club as a weapon.
[8] Camlets, a kind of watered cloth.
[9] Painted cloths interwoven with copper.
[10] Shoddy.
[11] Embroidered cloth of gold and silk.
[12] *I.e.,* those who bow before their customers.
[13] With a pun on *velours.*
[14] With a pun on *collars.*
[15] Name of a coin.
[16] A small pleasure boat.
[17] Lie idle and be meanly engaged.
[18] Bugbear's; *i.e.,* swaggering.

Shall be scratched with a musket. Dear
Prince Pippin,
Down with your noble blood, or, as I
live,
I'll have you coddled.—Let him loose,
my spirits;
Make us a round ring with your bills, my
Hectors,
And let me see what this trim man
dares do.
Now, sir, have at you! Here I lie,
And with this swashing [1] blow (do you
see, sweet prince?)
I could hulk [2] your grace, and hang you
up cross-legged,   40
Like a hare at a poulter's,[3] and do this
with this wiper.[4]

PHA. You will not see me murdered,
wicked villains?

1 CIT. Yes, indeed, will we, sir; we have
not seen one for a great while.

CAP. He would have weapons, would he?
Give him a broadside, my brave boys,
with your pikes; branch me his skin in
flowers like a satin, and between every
flower a mortal cut.—Your royalty shall
ravel!—Jag him, gentlemen; I'll have him
cut to the kell,[5] then down the seams. [50
O, for a whip to make him galloon-laces! [6]
I'll have a coachwhip.

PHA. O, spare me, gentlemen!

CAP. Hold, hold; the man begins to fear
and know himself. He shall for this time
only be seeled up,[7] with a feather through
his nose, that he may only see heaven, and
think whither he's going. Nay, my beyond-
sea sir, we will proclaim you. You would
be king! Thou tender heir apparent [60
to a church ale,[8] thou slight prince of
single sarcenet,[9] thou royal ringtail,[10] fit to
fly at nothing but poor men's poultry, and
have every boy beat thee from that too
with his bread and butter!

PHA. Gods keep me from these hell-
hounds!

1 CIT. Shall 's geld him, captain?

CAP. No, you shall spare his dowcets, my
dear donsels; [11]
As you respect the ladies, let them
flourish.   70
The curses of a longing woman kills
As speedy as a plague, boys.

1 CIT. I'll have a leg, that's certain.

2 CIT. I'll have an arm.

3 CIT. I'll have his nose, and at mine
own charge build a college and clap 't upon
the gate.[12]

4 CIT. I'll have his little gut to string a
kit [13] with; for certainly a royal gut will
sound like silver.   80

PHA. Would they were in thy belly, and
I past my pain once!

5 CIT. Good captain, let me have his
liver to feed ferrets.

CAP. Who will have parcels else? Speak.

PHA. Good gods, consider me! I shall
be tortured.

1 CIT. Captain, I'll give you the trimming of your two-hand sword, and let me
have his skin to make false scabbards. 90

2 CIT. He had no horns, sir, had he?

CAP. No, sir, he's a pollard.[14] What
wouldst thou do with horns?

2 CIT. O, if he had had, I would have
made rare hafts and whistles of um; but
his shin bones, if they be sound, shall
serve me.

Enter Philaster.

ALL. Long live Philaster, the brave
Prince Philaster!

PHI. I thank you, gentlemen. But why are
these
Rude weapons brought abroad, to teach
your hands   100
Uncivil trades?

CAP.   My royal Rosicleer,
We are thy myrmidons, thy guard, thy
roarers;
And, when thy noble body is in durance,
Thus do we clap our musty murrions [15]
on,
And trace [16] the streets in terror. Is it
peace,
Thou Mars of men? Is the king sociable,
And bids thee live? Art thou above thy
foemen,

---

[1] Slashing.
[2] Disembowel.
[3] Poulterer's.
[6] Tape used for trimming or binding.
[7] As a hawk's eyelids were temporarily sewed together.
[8] *I.e.*, a bastard child conceived at a church festivity.
[9] Thin silk.
[4] Ramrod.
[5] Caul.
[10] A sort of kite.
[11] Young dons, young fellows.
[12] In allusion to Brasenose College, Oxford.
[13] Cittern.
[14] Unhorned animal.
[15] Helmets.
[16] Walk.

And free as Phœbus? Speak. If not,
　　this stand [1]
Of royal blood shall be abroach, atilt,
And run even to the lees of honor.　　110
PHI. Hold, and be satisfied. I am myself,
　　Free as my thoughts are; by the gods,
　　I am!
CAP. Art thou the dainty darling of the
　　king?
Art thou the Hylas to our Hercules?
Do the lords bow, and the regarded
　　scarlets [2]
Kiss their gummed golls,[3] and cry, "We
　　are your servants"?
Is the court navigable and the presence
　　stuck
With flags of friendship? If not, we are
　　thy castle,
And this man sleeps.
PHI. I am what I do desire to be, your
　　friend;　　　　　　　　　　　　120
I am what I was born to be, your prince.
PHA. Sir, there is some humanity in you;
　　You have a noble soul. Forget my name,
And know my misery; set me safe
　　aboard
From these wild cannibals, and, as I
　　live,
I'll quit this land forever. There is
　　nothing—
Perpetual prisonment, cold, hunger,
　　sickness
Of all sorts, of all dangers, and al-
　　together
The worst company of the worst men,
　　madness, age,　　　　　　　　129
To be as many creatures as a woman,
And do as all they do, nay, to despair—
But I would rather make it a new na-
　　ture,
And live with all these, than endure one
　　hour
Amongst these wild dogs.
PHI. I do pity you.—Friends, discharge
　　your fears;
Deliver me the prince. I'll warrant you
I shall be old enough to find my safety.
3 CIT. Good sir, take heed he does not
　　hurt you;
He's a fierce man, I can tell you, sir.
CAP. Prince, by your leave, I'll have a
　　surcingle,[4]　　　　　　　　　140

[1] Cask, *i.e.*, Pharamond.　　[3] Perfumed hands.
[2] Courtiers clad in scarlet.　[4] Band.

And make [5] you like a hawk. (*He strives.*)[6]
PHI. Away, away, there is no danger in
　　him!
Alas, he had rather sleep to shake his
　　fit off!
Look you, friends, how gently he leads!
　　Upon my word,
He's tame enough; he need[s] no further
　　watching.
Good my friends, go to your houses,
And by me have your pardons and my
　　love;
And know there shall be nothing in my
　　power
You may deserve, but you shall have
　　your wishes.
To give you more thanks were to flatter
　　you.　　　　　　　　　　　　150
Continue still your love; and for an
　　earnest
Drink this.　　　　　　[*Gives money.*]
ALL. Long mayst thou live, brave prince,
　　brave prince, brave prince!
　　Exeunt [7] *Phi*[*laster*] *and Pharamond.*
CAP. Go thy ways, thou art the king of
　　courtesy!—
Fall off again, my sweet youths. Come,
And every man trace to his house again,
And hang his pewter up; then to the
　　tavern,
And bring your wives in muffs. We will
　　have music;
And the red grape shall make us dance
　　and rise, boys.　　　　　　*Exeunt.*

[SCENA v.]

An apartment in the palace.]

*Enter King, Arethusa, Galatea, Megra,
Cleremont, Dion, Thrasiline, Bellario, and
　　　　　　　　　　　　　　Attendants.*

KING. Is it appeased?
DI. Sir, all is quiet as this dead of night,
As peaceable as sleep. My Lord Philaster
Brings on the prince himself.
KING.　　　　　　　Kind gentlemen,
I will not break the least word I have
　　given
In promise to him. I have heaped a
　　world
Of grief upon his head, which yet I hope
To wash away.

[5] Train.　　　　　　　[7] Original reads *Exit.*
[6] *I.e.*, Pharamond tries to get away.

Enter Philaster and Pharamond.

CLE.   My lord is come.

KING.   My son!
Blessed be the time that I have leave to call
Such virtue mine!   Now thou art in mine arms,   10
Methinks I have a salve unto my breast
For all the stings that dwell there. Streams of grief
That I have wrought thee, and as much of joy
That I repent it, issue from mine eyes;
Let them appease thee. Take thy right. Take her
(She is thy right too), and forget to urge
My vexéd soul with that I did before.

PHI. Sir, it is blotted from my memory,
Past and forgotten.—For you, Prince of Spain,
Whom I have thus redeemed, you have full leave   20
To make an honorable voyage home.
And, if you would go furnished to your realm
With fair provision, I do see a lady,
Methinks, would gladly bear you company.
How like you this piece?

MEG.   Sir, he likes it well,
For he hath tried it, and hath found it worth
His princely liking. We were ta'en abed;
I know your meaning. I am not the first
That nature taught to seek a fellow forth.
Can shame remain perpetually in me,   30
And not in others?   Or have princes salves
To cure ill names, that meaner people want?

PHI. What mean you?

MEG.   You must get another ship,
To bear the princess and her boy together.

DI. How now!

MEG. Others took me, and I took her and him
At that all women may be ta'en sometime.
Ship us all four, my lord; we can endure
Weather and wind alike.

KING. Clear thou thyself, or know not me
for father.   40

ARE. This earth, how false it is! What means is left for me
To clear myself? It lies in your belief.
My lords, believe me; and let all things else
Struggle together to dishonor me.

BEL. O, stop your ears, great king, that I may speak
As freedom would! Then I will call this lady
As base as are her actions. Hear me, sir;
Believe your heated blood when it rebels
Against your reason, sooner than this lady.

MEG. By this good light, he bears it handsomely.   50

PHI. This lady? I will sooner trust the wind
With feathers, or the troubled sea with pearl,
Than her with anything. Believe her not.
Why, think you, if I did believe her words,
I would outlive 'em? Honor cannot take
Revenge on you. Then what were to be known
But death?

KING.   Forget her, sir, since all is knit
Between us. But I must request of you
One favor, and will sadly be denied.

PHI. Command, whate'er it be.

KING.   Swear to be true   60
To what you promise.

PHI.   By the powers above,
Let it not be the death of her or him,
And it is granted!

KING.   Bear away that boy
To torture; I will have her cleared or buried.

PHI. O, let me call my word back, worthy sir!
Ask something else; bury my life and right
In one poor grave; but do not take away
My life and fame at once.

KING. Away with him! It stands irrevocable.

PHI. Turn all your eyes on me. Here stands a man,   70
The falsest and the basest of this world.

Set swords against this breast, some
    honest man,
For I have lived till I am pitiéd!
My former deeds were hateful; but this
    last
Is pitiful, for I unwillingly
Have given the dear preserver of my
    life
Unto his torture. Is it in the power
Of flesh and blood to carry this, and live?
    Offers to kill himself.
ARE. Dear sir, be patient yet! O, stay
    that hand!
KING. Sirs, strip that boy.
DI.   Come, sir; your tender flesh   80
Will try [1] your constancy.
BEL.   O, kill me, gentlemen!
DI. No.—Help, sirs!
BEL.   Will you torture me?
KING.   Haste there.
    Why stay you?
BEL.   Then I shall not break my vow,
You know, just gods, though I discover
    all.
KING. How's that? Will he confess?
DI.   Sir, so he says.
KING. Speak then.
BEL.   Great king, if you command
    This lord to talk with me alone, my
    tongue
Urged by my heart, shall utter all the
    thoughts
My youth hath known; and stranger
    things than these
You hear not often.
KING.   Walk aside with him.   90
    [*Dion and Bellario walk apart.*]
DI. Why speak'st thou not?
BEL.   Know you this face, my lord?
DI. No.
BEL. Have you not seen it, nor the like?
DI. Yes, I have seen the like, but readily
I know not where.
BEL.   I have been often told
In court of one Euphrasia, a lady,
And daughter to you, betwixt whom
    and me
They that would flatter my bad face
    would swear
There was such strange resemblance
    that we two
Could not be known asunder, dressed
    alike.
[1] From 1620 edn. Original reads *tire.*

DI. By heaven, and so there is!
BEL.   For her fair sake,   100
Who now doth spend the springtime of
    her life
In holy pilgrimage, move to the king
That I may scape this torture.
DI.   But thou speak'st
As like Euphrasia as thou dost look.
How came it to thy knowledge that she
    lives
In pilgrimage?
BEL.   I know it not, my lord;
But I have heard it, and do scarce
    believe it.
DI. O, my shame! Is 't possible? Draw
    near
That I may gaze upon thee. Art thou
    she,
Or else her murderer? [2] Where wert
thou born?   110
BEL. In Syracusa.
DI.   What's thy name?
BEL.   Euphrasia.
DI. O, 'tis just, 'tis she!
Now I do know thee. O, that thou hadst
    died,
And I had never seen thee nor my
    shame!
How shall I own thee? Shall this tongue
    of mine
E'er call thee daughter more?
BEL. Would I had died indeed! I wish it
    too;
And so [I] [3] must have done by vow, ere
    published
What I have told, but that there was no
    means
To hide it longer. Yet I joy in this,   120
The princess is all clear.
KING.   What, have you done?
DI. All 's discovered.
PHI.   Why then hold you me?
All is discovered! Pray you, let me go.
    He offers to stab himself.
KING. Stay him!
ARE.   What is discovered?
DI.   Why, my shame.
It is a woman; let her speak the rest.
PHI. How? That again!
DI. It is a woman.

[2] Some barbarous peoples believed that the
murderer assumed the shape of the person he
murdered.
[3] From 1620 edn.

Phi. Blessed be you powers that favor
　innocence!

King. Lay hold upon that lady.

　　　　　　　　　[*Megra is seized.*]

Phi. It is a woman, sir!—Hark, gentle-
　men,　　　　　　　　　　　130
　It is a woman!—Arethusa, take
　My soul into thy breast, that would be
　gone
　With joy. It is a woman! Thou art fair,
　And virtuous still to ages, in despite
　Of malice.

King. Speak you, where lies his shame?

Bel.　　　　　　I am his daughter.

Phi. The gods are just.

Di. I dare accuse none; but, before you
　two,
　The virtue of our age, I bend my knee
　For mercy.　　　　　[*Kneels.*]

Phi. [*Raising him.*]　　Take it freely, for
　I know,　　　　　　　　140
　Though what thou didst were undis-
　creetly done,
　'Twas meant well.

Are.　　　　　And, for me,
　I have a power to pardon sins, as oft
　As any man has power to wrong me.

Cle. Noble and worthy!

Phi.　　　　　　But, Bellario
　(For I must call thee still so), tell me
　why
　Thou didst conceal thy sex. It was a
　fault,
　A fault, Bellario, though thy other deeds
　Of truth outweighed it.　All these
　jealousies　　　　　　　150
　Had flown to nothing if thou hadst dis-
　covered
　What now we know.

Bel.　　　　My father oft would speak
　Your worth and virtue; and, as I did
　grow
　More and more apprehensive,[1] I did
　thirst
　To see the man so raised. But yet all
　this
　Was but a maiden longing, to be lost
　As soon as found, till, sitting in my
　window,
　Printing my thoughts in lawn,[2] I saw a
　god,
　I thought (but it was you), enter our
　gates.

[1] Quick to understand.　[2] *I.e.*, embroidering.

My blood flew out and back again, as
　fast　　　　　　　　　160
As I had puffed it forth and sucked
　it in
Like breath. Then was I called away in
　haste
To entertain you.　Never was a man,
Heaved from a sheepcote to a scepter,
　raised
So high in thoughts as I. You left a kiss
Upon these lips then, which I mean to
　keep
From you forever. I did hear you talk,
Far above singing. After you were gone,
I grew acquainted with my heart, and
　searched　　　　　　　169
What stirred it so.　Alas, I found it love,
Yet far from lust, for, could I but have
　lived
In presence of you, I had had my end.
For this I did delude my noble father
With a feigned pilgrimage, and dressed
　myself
In habit of a boy; and, for I knew
My birth no match for you, I was past
　hope
Of having you; and, understanding well
That when I made discovery of my sex
I could not stay with you, I made a vow,
By all the most religious things a maid
Could call together, never to be known,
Whilst there was hope to hide me from
　men's eyes,　　　　　　182
For other than I seemed, that I might
　ever
Abide with you. Then sat I by the fount,
Where first you took me up.

King.　　　　　Search out a match
Within our kingdom, where and when
　thou wilt,
And I will pay thy dowry; and thyself
Wilt well deserve him.

Bel.　　　　　　Never, sir, will I
Marry; it is a thing within my vow.
But, if I may have leave to serve the
　princess,　　　　　　190
To see the virtues of her lord and her,
I shall have hope to live.

Are.　　　　　　I, Philaster,
Cannot be jealous, though you had a lady
Dressed like a page to serve you; nor
　will I
Suspect her living here.—Come, live
　with me;

Live free as I do. She that loves my
    lord,
Cursed be the wife that hates her!
PHI. I grieve such virtue should be laid in
    earth
  Without an heir.—Hear me, my royal
    father.
  Wrong not the freedom of our souls so
    much,   200
  To think to take revenge of that base
    woman;
  Her malice cannot hurt us. Set her free
  As she was born, saving from shame and
    sin.
KING. Set her at liberty.—But leave the
    court;
  This is no place for such.—You, Phara-
    mond,
  Shall have free passage, and a conduct
    home
  Worthy so great a prince. When you
    come there,

Remember 'twas your faults that lost
    you her,
And not my purposed will.
PHA.   I do confess,
  Renownéd sir.   210
KING. Last, join your hands in one. En-
    joy, Philaster,
  This kingdom, which is yours, and,
    after me,
  Whatever I call mine. My blessing on
    you!
  All happy hours be at your marriage
    joys,
  That you may grow yourselves over all
    lands,
  And live [1] to see your plenteous branches
    spring
  Wherever there is sun! Let princes learn
  By this to rule the passions of their blood;
  For what heaven wills can never be
    withstood.   *Exeunt omnes.*

[1] From 1620 edn. Original reads *like*.

FINIS.

THE MAID'S TRAGEDY[1]

[BY
FRANCIS BEAUMONT AND JOHN FLETCHER][2]

SPEAKERS

KING.
LYSIPPUS, *brother to the king.*
AMINTOR [, *a noble gentleman*].[3]
EVADNE, *wife to Amintor.*
MELANTIUS ⎱ *brothers to Evadne.*
DIPHILUS ⎰
ASPATIA, *troth-plight wife to Amintor.*
CALIANAX, *an old humorous* [4] *lord, and father
  to Aspatia.*
CLEON ⎱ *gentlemen.*
STRATO ⎰
DIAGORAS, *a servant.*

[LORDS, GENTLEMEN, SERVANTS, *etc.*]
ANTIPHILA ⎱ *waiting gentlewomen to As-*
OLYMPIAS ⎰ *patia.*
DULA, *a lady* [, *attendant on Evadne*].
[LADIES.]

NIGHT ⎫
CYNTHIA ⎪
NEPTUNE ⎬ *masquers.*
ÆOLUS ⎪
[SEA GODS] ⎪
[WINDS] ⎭

[SCENE: *Rhodes.*

TIME: *Indefinite.*]

ACTUS I. SCEN[A] i.

[*An apartment in the palace.*]

Enter Cleon, Strato, Lysippus, Diphilus.

CLE. The rest are making ready, sir.

LYS.[5] So let them; there's time enough.

DIPH. You are the brother to the king,
my lord; we'll take your word.

LYS. Strato, thou hast some skill in
poetry; what think'st [thou] [6] of the [7]
masque? Will it be well?

STRA. As well as masques can be.

LYS. As masques can be?

STRA. Yes; they must commend [10
their king, and speak in praise of the assembly, bless the bride and bridegroom in person of some god; they're tied to rules of
flattery.

CLE. See, good my lord, who is returned!

Enter Melantius.

LYS. Noble Melantius, the land by me
welcomes thy virtues home to Rhodes—
thou that with blood abroad buyest our
peace! The breath of kings is like the
breath of gods; my brother wished [20
thee here, and thou art here. He will be
too kind, and weary thee with often welcomes; but the time doth give thee a welcome above his or all the world's.

MEL. My lord, my thanks; but these
scratched limbs of mine have spoke my
love and truth unto my friends more than
my tongue e'er could. My mind's the same
it [8]
Ever was to you. Where I find worth,
I love the keeper till he let it go,   31
And then I follow it.

DIPH.   Hail, worthy brother!
He that rejoices not at your return
In safety is mine enemy forever.

MEL. I thank thee, Diphilus. But thou
  art faulty:

1233

I sent for thee to exercise thine arms
With me at Patria; thou cam'st not,
Diphilus;
'Twas ill.

DIPH.   My noble brother, my excuse
Is my king's strict command, which
you, my lord,
Can witness with me.

LYS.   'Tis true, Melantius; 40
He might not come till the solemnity
Of this great match were past.

DIPH.   Have you heard of it?

MEL. Yes, I have given cause to those
that
Envy my deeds abroad to call me gamesome.
I have no other business here at Rhodes.

LYS. We have a masque tonight, and you
must tread
A soldier's measure.

MEL. These soft and silken wars are not
for me;
The music must be shrill and all confused
That stirs my blood; and then I dance
with arms.   50
But is Amintor wed?

DIPH. This day.

MEL. All joys upon him, for he is my
friend.
Wonder not that I call a man so young
my friend.
His worth is great; valiant he is and
temperate,
And one that never thinks his life his
own,
If his friend need it. When he was a
boy,
As oft as I returned (as, without boast,
I brought home conquest), he would
gaze upon me
And view me round to find in what one
limb   60
The virtue lay to do these things he
heard;
Then would he wish to see my sword,
and feel
The quickness of the edge, and in his
hand
Weigh it. He oft would make me smile
at this.
His youth did promise much, and his
ripe years
Will see it all performed.—

Enter Aspatia, passing by.

                Hail, maid and wife!
Thou fair Aspatia, may the holy knot
That thou hast tied today last till the
hand
Of age undo 't! Mayst thou bring a
race   69
Unto Amintor that may fill the world
Successively with soldiers!

ASP.   My hard fortunes
Deserve not scorn, for I was never
proud
When they were good.   *Exit Aspatia.*

MEL.   How's this?

LYS.   You are mistaken,[1]
For she is not married.

MEL.   You said Amintor was.

DIPH. 'Tis true; but—

MEL.   Pardon me; I did receive
Letters at Patria from my Amintor,
That he should marry her.

DIPH.   And so it stood
In all opinion long; but your arrival
Made me imagine you had heard the
change.

MEL. Who hath he taken then?

LYS.   A lady, sir, 80
That bears the light about her, and
strikes dead
With flashes of her eye—the fair Evadne,
Your virtuous sister.

MEL.   Peace of heart betwixt them!
But this is strange.

LYS.   The king, my brother, did it
To honor you; and these solemnities
Are at his charge.

MEL. 'Tis royal, like himself. But I am
sad
My speech bears so unfortunate a sound
To beautiful Aspatia. There is rage
Hid in her father's breast. Calianax 90
Bent long against me, and he should
not think,
If I could call it back, that I would take
So base revenges as to scorn the state
Of his neglected daughter. Holds he still
His greatness with the king?

LYS.   Yes. But this lady
Walks discontented, with her wat'ry eyes
Bent on the earth. The unfrequented
woods

---

[1] Here and in a few other passages the line
division has been regularized.

Are her delight; and, when she sees a
bank
Stuck full of flowers, she with a sigh will
tell   99
Her servants what a pretty place it were
To bury lovers in, and make her maids
Pluck 'em, and strow her over like a
corse.
She carries with her an infectious grief
That strikes all her beholders; she will
sing
The mournful'st things that ever ear
hath heard,
And sigh, and sing again; and, when the
rest
Of our young ladies, in their wanton [1]
blood,
Tell mirthful tales in course,[2] that fill
the room
With laughter, she will with so sad a
look   109
Bring forth a story of the silent death
Of some forsaken virgin, which her grief
Will put in such a phrase that, ere she
end,
She'll send them weeping one by one
away.
MEL. She has a brother under my com-
mand,
Like her—a face as womanish as hers,
But with a spirit that hath much out-
grown
The number of his years.

Enter Amintor.

CLE.   My lord the bridegroom!
MEL. I might run fiercely, not more hast-
ily,
Upon my foe. I love thee well, Amintor.
My mouth is much too narrow for my
heart;   120
I joy to look upon those eyes of thine.
Thou art my friend, but my disordered
speech
Cuts off my love.
AMIN.   Thou art Melantius;
All love is spoke in that. A sacrifice,
To thank the gods Melantius is returned
In safety! Victory sits on his sword,
As she was wont. May she build there
and dwell,
And may thy armor be, as it hath been,

Only thy valor and thine innocence!
What endless treasures would our ene-
mies give   130
That I might hold thee still thus!
MEL.   I am poor
In words; but credit me, young man,
thy mother
Could no more but weep for joy to see
thee
After long absence. All the wounds I
have
Fetched not so much away, nor all the
cries
Of widowèd mothers. But this is peace,
And that was war.
AMIN.   Pardon, thou holy god
Of marriage bed, and frown not I am
forced,
In answer of such noble tears as those,
To weep upon my wedding day!   140
MEL. I fear thou art grown too fickle,
for I hear
A lady mourns for thee, men say, to
death,
Forsaken of thee, on what terms [3] I
know not.
AMIN. She had my promise; but the king
forbade it,
And made me make this worthy change,
thy sister,
Accompanied with graces about her,
With whom I long to lose my lusty
youth
And grow old in her arms.
MEL.   Be prosperous!

Enter Messenger.

MESS.[4] My lord, the masquers rage for
you.
LYS. We are gone. Cleon, Strato, Diphi-
lus!   150
AMIN. We'll all attend you.—
        [*Exeunt All but Amintor and Melantius.*]
                        We shall trouble you
With our solemnities.
MEL.   Not so, Amintor;
But, if you laugh at my rude carriage
In peace, I'll do as much for you in war,
When you come thither. Yet I have a
mistress
To bring to your delights; rough though
I am,

---

[1] Lively.   [2] Turn.

[3] Under what circumstances.
[4] Original reads *Serv.*

I have a mistress, and she has a heart,
She says; but, trust me, it is stone, no
   better.
There is no place that I can challenge.
But you stand still, and here my way
   lies.   *Exit* [*with Amintor*]. 160

[SCENA ii.

*A hall in the palace, with Spectators in a
balcony.*]

Enter Calianax with Diagoras.

CAL. Diagoras, look to the doors better,
for shame! You let in all the world, and
anon the king will rail at me. Why, very
well said.[1] By Jove, the king will have the
show i' th' court!

DIAG. Why do you swear so, my lord?
You know he'll have it here.

CAL. By this light, if he be wise, he
will not.

DIAG. And, if he will not be wise, [10
you are forsworn.

CAL. One may swear [2] his heart out
with swearing, and get thanks on no side.
I'll be gone, look to 't who will.

DIAG. My lord, I shall never keep
them out. Pray, stay; your looks will
terrify them.

CAL. My looks terrify them, you cox-
combly ass, you! I'll be judge[d] by all
the company whether thou hast not a [20
worse face than I.

DIAG. I mean, because they know you
and your office.

CAL. Office! I would I could put it
off! I am sure I sweat quite through my
office. I might have made room at my
daughter's wedding—they ha' near killed
her among them; and now I must do service for him that hath forsaken her. Serve [3]
that will!   *Exit Calianax.* 30

DIAG. He's so humorous since his daughter was forsaken! (*Knock within.*) Hark,
hark! There, there! So, so! Codes, codes![4]
What now?

MEL. (*Within.*) Open the door!

DIAG. Who's there?

MEL. Melantius.

DIAG. I hope your lordship brings no
troop with you, for, if you do, I must
return them.   [*Opens the door.*] 40

Enter Melantius and a Lady.

MEL. None but this lady, sir.

DIAG. The ladies are all placed above,
save those that come in the king's troop;
the best of Rhodes sit there, and there's
room.

MEL. I thank you, sir.—When I have
seen you placed, madam, I must attend
the king; but, the masque done, I'll wait
on you again.

     [*Exit Melantius, Lady, other door.*] [5]

DIAG. Stand back there!—Room for [50
my Lord Melantius!—Pray, bear back
—this is no place for such youths and
their trulls—let the doors shut again.—
Ay!—Do your heads itch? I'll scratch
them for you. [*Shuts door.*] So, now
thrust and hang.—[*Knocking within.*]
Again! Who is 't now?—I cannot blame
my Lord Calianax for going away. Would
he were here! He would run raging among
them, and break a dozen wiser heads [60
than his own in the twinkling of an eye.
—What's the news now?

[VOICE.] (*Within.*) I pray you, can
you help me to the speech of the master
cook?

DIAG. If I open the door, I'll cook some
of your calves' heads. Peace, rogues!—
[*Knocking within.*] Again! Who is 't?

MEL. (*Within.*) Melantius.

Enter Calianax to Melantius.

CAL. Let him not in.   70
DIAG. O, my lord, a [6] must.—

[*Opens door. Enter Melantius.*]

Make room there for my lord.—Is your
lady placed?
MEL. Yes, sir.
I thank you.—My Lord Calianax, well
   met.
Your causeless hate to me I hope is
   buried.
CAL. Yes, I do service for your sister here,
That brings my own poor child to time-
   less [7] death.
She loves your friend Amintor, such
   another
False-hearted lord as you.

---

[1] Done.   [3] Let him serve.
[2] Folio reads *wear.*   [4] Corruption of *God's* (?).
[5] From 1619 edn. Thus, Diagoras is guarding
two doors, one to the gallery, and one to the
outside.   [6] He.   [7] Untimely.

MEL.   You do me wrong, 80
A most unmanly one, and I am slow
In taking vengeance; but be well advised.
CAL. It may be so.—Who placed the lady
    there
So near the presence of the king?
MEL.   I did.
CAL. My lord, she must not sit there.
MEL.   Why?
CAL. The place is kept for women of more
    worth.
MEL. More worth than she? It mis-
    becomes your age
And place to be thus womanish. Forbear!
What you have spoke, I am content to
    think
The palsy shook your tongue to.
CAL.   Why, 'tis well, 90
If I stand here to place men's wenches.
MEL.   I
Shall forget this place, thy age, my
    safety,
And, through all, cut that poor sickly
    week
Thou hast to live away from thee.
CAL. Nay, I know you can fight for your
    whore.
MEL. Bate[1] the king, and, be he flesh and
    blood,
A lies that says it! Thy mother at
    fifteen
Was black and sinful to her.
DIAG.   Good my lord—
MEL. Some god pluck threescore years
    from that fond[2] man,
That I may kill him and not stain mine
    honor!   100
It is the curse of soldiers that in peace
They shall be braved by such ignoble
    men
As, if the land were troubled, would
    with tears
And knees beg succor from 'em. Would
    that blood,
That sea of blood, that I have lost in
    fight,
Were running in thy veins, that it might
    make thee
Apt to say less, or able to maintain,
Shouldst thou say more! This Rhodes,
    I see, is naught
But a place privileged to do men wrong.
CAL. Ay, you may say your pleasure.

Enter Amintor.

AMIN.   What vild[3] injury 110
Has stirred my worthy friend, who is
    as slow
To fight with words as he is quick of
    hand?
MEL. That heap of age, which I should
    reverence
If it were temperate—but testy years
Are most contemptible.
AMIN.   Good sir, forbear.
CAL. There is just such another as your-
    self.
AMIN. He will wrong you, or me, or any
    man,
And talk as if he had no life to
    lose,
Since this our match. The king is coming
    in;
I would not for more wealth than I
    enjoy   120
He should perceive you raging. He did
    hear
You were at difference now, which has-
    tened him.   *Hautboys play within.*
CAL. Make room there!

Enter King, Evadne, Aspatia, Lords, and
                                Ladies.

KING. Melantius, thou art welcome, and
    my love
Is with thee still; but this is not a
    place
To brabble[4] in.—Calianax, join hands.
CAL. He shall not have mine hand.
KING.   This is no time
To force you to 't. I do love you
    both.
Calianax, you look well to your office;
And you, Melantius, are welcome
    home.—   130
Begin the masque.
MEL. Sister, I joy to see you and your
    choice;
You looked with my eyes when you
    took that man.
Be happy in him!   *Recorders [play].*
EVAD.   O, my dearest brother,
Your presence is more joyful than this
    day
Can be unto me.

---

[1] Except.   [2] Foolish.   [3] Vile.   [4] Quarrel.

The Masque

Night rises in mists.

NIGHT. Our reign is come, for in the raging
　　sea
　The sun is drowned, and with him fell
　　the Day.
　Bright Cynthia, hear my voice! I am
　　the Night,
　For whom thou bear'st about thy bor-
　　rowed light.　　　　　　　　　　140
　Appear! No longer thy pale visage
　　shroud,
　But strike thy silver horns quite through
　　a cloud,
　And send a beam upon my swarthy
　　face,
　By which I may discover all the place
　And persons, and how many longing
　　eyes
　Are come to wait on our solemnities.

Enter Cynthia.

　How dull and black am I! I could not
　　find
　This beauty [1] without thee, I am so
　　blind;
　Methinks they show like to those east-
　　ern streaks
　That warn us hence before the morning
　　breaks.　　　　　　　　　　　　150
　Back, my pale servant, for these eyes
　　know how
　To shoot far more and quicker rays
　　than thou.
CYNTH. Great queen, they be a troop for
　　whom alone
　One of my clearest moons I have put on—
　A troop that looks as if thyself and I
　Had plucked our reins in and our whips
　　laid by,
　To gaze upon these mortals that appear
　Brighter than we.
NIGHT.　　　Then let us keep 'em here,
　And never more our chariots drive
　　away,
　But hold our places and outshine the
　　Day.　　　　　　　　　　　　160
CYNTH. Great queen of shadows, you are
　　pleased to speak
　Of more than may be done. We may not
　　break

[1] Referring to the ladies of the court.

The gods' decrees, but, when our time
　is come,
　Must drive away, and give the Day our
　　room.
　Yet, whilst our reign lasts, let us stretch
　　our power
　To give our servants one contented
　　hour,
　With such unwonted solemn grace and
　　state
　As may forever after force them hate
　Our brother's glorious beams, and wish
　　the Night
　Crowned with a thousand stars and our
　　cold light,　　　　　　　　　　170
　For almost all the world their service
　　bend
　To Phœbus, and in vain my light I
　　lend,
　Gazed on unto my setting from my rise
　Almost of none but of unquiet eyes.
NIGHT. Then shine at full, fair queen,
　　and by thy power
　Produce a birth—to crown this happy
　　hour—
　Of nymphs and shepherds; let their
　　songs discover,
　Easy and sweet, who is a happy lover;
　Or, if thou woot,[2] then call thine own
　　Endymion　　　　　　　　　　179
　From the sweet flow'ry bed he lies upon,
　On Latmus' top, thy pale beams drawn
　　away,
　And of this long night let him make
　　this day.
CYNTH. Thou dream'st, dark queen; that
　　fair boy was not mine,
　Nor went I down to kiss him. Ease and
　　wine
　Have bred these bold tales. Poets,
　　when they rage,
　Turn gods to men, and make an hour
　　an age.
　But I will give a greater state and
　　glory,
　And raise to time a noble memory
　Of what these lovers are.—Rise, rise, I
　　say,
　Thou power of deeps, thy surges laid
　　away,　　　　　　　　　　　　190
　Neptune, great king of waters, and by
　　me
　Be proud to be commanded!

[2] Wilt.

Neptune rises.

NEP.   Cynthia, see
  Thy word hath fetched me hither; let
    me know
  Why I ascend.
CYNTH.   Doth this majestic show
  Give thee no knowledge yet?
NEP.   Yes, now I see
  Something intended, Cynthia, worthy
    thee.
  Go on; I'll be a helper.
CYNTH.   Hie thee, then,
  And charge the Wind fly from his rocky
    den;
  Let loose thy subjects; only Boreas, 199
  Too foul for our intentions as he was,
  Still keep him fast chained. We must
    have none here
  But vernal blasts and gentle winds
    appear,
  Such as blow flowers, and through the
    glad boughs sing
  Many soft welcomes to the lusty spring.
  These are our music. Next, thy wat'ry
    race
  Bring on in couples (we are pleased to
    grace
  This noble night), each in their richest
    things
  Your own deeps or the broken vessel
    brings.
  Be prodigal, and I shall be as kind 209
  And shine at full upon you.
NEP.   O, the wind-
  Commanding Æolus!

Enter Æolus out of a rock.

ÆOL.   Great Neptune!
NEP.   He.
ÆOL. What is thy will?
NEP.   We do command thee free
  Favonius and thy milder winds, to wait
  Upon our Cynthia; but tie Boreas
    strait.
  He's too rebellious.
ÆOL.   I shall do it. [*Exit.*]
NEP.   Do.
[ÆOL. (*Within.*)] Great master of the flood
    and all below,
  Thy full command has taken.—O, the
    Main!
  Neptune!
NEP.   Here.

[*Enter Æolus with Favonius and other
                                Winds.*]

ÆOL.   Boreas has broke his chain,
  And, struggling with the rest, has got
    away.
NEP. Let him alone; I'll take him up at
    sea.   220
  He will not long be thence. Go once
    again,
  And call out of the bottoms of the main
  Blue Proteus and the rest; charge them
    put on
  Their greatest pearls, and the most
    sparkling stone
  The beaten rock breeds, till this night
    is done
  By me a solemn honor to the Moon.
  Fly, like a full sail.
ÆOL.   I am gone. [*Exit.*]
CYNTH.   Dark Night,
  Strike a full silence, do a thorough
    right
  To this great chorus, that our music
    may
  Touch high as heaven, and make the
    east break day   230
  At midnight.   *Music.*

[FIRST] SONG

[*During the song enter Proteus and other Sea
                                Deities.*]

    Cynthia, to thy power and thee
          We obey.
    Joy to this great company!
          And no day
    Come to steal this night away,
      Till the rites of love are ended,
    And the lusty bridegroom say,
      "Welcome, light, of all befriended!"

    Pace out, you wat'ry powers below; 240
          Let your feet,
    Like the galleys when they row,
          Even beat.
    Let your unknown measures, set
      To the still winds, tell to all
    That gods are come, immortal, great,
      To honor this great nuptial.
                        The measure.

SECOND SONG

  Hold back thy hours, dark Night, till we
    have done;
    The Day will come too soon.

Young maids will curse thee, if thou
    steal'st away, 250
And leav'st their blushes open to the day.
    Stay, stay, and hide
    The blushes of the bride.

Stay, gentle Night, and with thy darkness
    cover
    The kisses of her lover.
Stay, and confound her tears and her shrill
    cryings,
Her weak denials, vows, and often-dyings.
    Stay, and hide all.
    But help not, though she call.

NEP. Great queen of us and heaven, hear
    what I bring 260
To make this hour a full one.
           Another measure.[1]
CYNTH.   Speak, sea's king.
NEP. Thy tunes my Amphitrite joys to
    have,
When they will dance upon the rising
    wave,
And court me as the sails. My Tritons,
    play
Music to lead a storm! I'll lead the way.
           Measure.

[THIRD] SONG

To bed, to bed! Come, Hymen, lead the
    bride,
And lay her by her husband's side.
    Bring in the virgins every one,
    That grieve to lie alone,
That they may kiss while they may say, "A
    maid;" 270
Tomorrow 'twill be other[2] kissed and said.
    Hesperus, be long a-shining,
    Whilst these lovers are a-twining.

ÆOL. [*Within.*] Ho, Neptune!
NEP.   Æolus!

[*Enter Æolus.*]

ÆOL.   The sea goes high;
Boreas hath raised a storm. Go and
    apply
Thy trident; else, I prophesy, ere day
Many a tall ship will be cast away.
Descend with all the gods and all their
    power,
To strike a calm.

[1] Fleay's emendation for *if not her measure.*
[2] Otherwise.

CYNTH. A thanks to everyone and to
    gratulate 280
So great a service, done at my desire,
Ye shall have many floods, fuller and
    higher
Than you have wished for; no ebb shall
    dare
To let the Day see where your dwelling[s]
    are.
Now back unto your government in
    haste,
Lest your proud charge should swell
    above the waste,
And win upon the island.
NEP.   We obey.
Neptune descends and the Sea Gods. [*Exeunt*
        Favonius and other Winds.]
CYNTH. Hold up thy head, dead Night;
    see'st thou not Day?
The east begins to lighten. I must down,
And give my brother place.
NIGHT.   O, I could frown
To see the Day, the Day that flings his
    light 291
Upon my kingdoms and contemns old
    Night!
Let him go on and flame! I hope to see
Another wildfire in his axletree,
And all fall drenched. But I forget.—
    Speak, queen.
The Day grows on; I must no more be
    seen.
CYNTH. Heave up thy drowsy head again
    and see
A greater light, a greater majesty,
Between our set[3] and us! Whip up thy
    team.
The Day breaks here, and yon same
    flashing stream[4] 300
Shot from the south. Say, which way
    wilt thou go?
NIGHT. I'll vanish into mists.
CYNTH.   I into Day. *Exeunt.*

FINIS MASQUE

KING. Take lights there!—Ladies, get the
    bride to bed.—
We will not see you laid. Good night,
    Amintor.
We'll ease you of that tedious cere-
    mony.

[3] Seward's emendation for *sect.*
[4] The "effulgence of the court" (Thorndike).

Were it my case, I should think time
    run slow.
If thou beest noble, youth, get me a boy
That may defend my kingdoms from my
    foes.

AMIN. All happiness to you!

KING.   Good night, Melantius.
                                    Exeunt.

ACTUS II. [SCENA i.

Anteroom to Evadne's bedchamber.]

*Enter Evadne, Aspatia, Dula, and other
                                    Ladies.*

DUL. Madam, shall we undress you for
    this fight?
The wars are nak'd that you must make
    tonight.

EVAD. You are very merry, Dula.

DUL.   I should be
Far merrier, madam, if it were with me
As it is with you.

[EVAD.   How's that?

DUL.   That I might go
To bed with him wi' th' credit that you
    do.]¹

EVAD. Why, how now, wench?

DUL.   Come, ladies, will you help?

EVAD. I am soon undone.

DUL.   And as soon done;
Good store of clothes will trouble you at
    both.

EVAD. Art thou drunk, Dula?

DUL.   Why, here's none but we. 10

EVAD. Thou think'st belike ² there is no
    modesty
When we are alone.

DUL.   Ay, by my troth,
You hit my thoughts aright.

EVAD. You prick me, lady.

DUL.   'Tis against my will.
Anon you must endure more and lie still;
You're best to practice.

EVAD.   Sure, this wench is mad.

DUL. No, faith, this is a trick that I have
    had
Since I was fourteen.

EVAD.   'Tis high time to leave it.

DUL. Nay, now I'll keep it till the trick
    leave me.   19
A dozen wanton words put in your head
Will make you livelier in your husband's
    bed.

¹ From 1619 edn.   ² Perhaps.

EVAD. Nay, faith, then take it.³

DUL.   Take it, madam! Where?
We all, I hope, will take it that are here.

EVAD. Nay, then I'll give you o'er.

DUL.   So will I make
The ablest man in Rhodes, or his heart,
    ache.

EVAD. Wilt take my place tonight?

DUL.   I'll hold your cards
Against any two I know.

EVAD.   What wilt thou do?

DUL. Madam, we'll do 't, and make 'em
    leave play too.

EVAD. Aspatia, take her part.

DUL.   I will refuse it.
She will pluck down a side; ⁴ she does not
    use it.   30

EVAD. Do, I prithee.⁵

DUL.   You will find the play
Quickly, because your head lies well
    that way.

EVAD. I thank thee, Dula. Would thou
    couldst instill
Some of thy mirth into Aspatia!
Nothing but sad thoughts in her breast
    do dwell;
Methinks, a mean betwixt you would
    do well.

DUL. She is in love; hang me, if I were so,
But I could run ⁶ my country. I love too
To do those things that people in love
    do.

ASP. It were a timeless smile should prove
    my cheek.⁷   40
It were a fitter hour for me to laugh,
When at the altar the religious priest
Were pacifying the offended powers
With sacrifice than now. This should
    have been
My night; and all your hands have been
    employed
In giving me a spotless offering
To young Amintor's bed, as we are now
For you. Pardon, Evadne. Would my
    worth
Were great as yours, or that the king,
    or he,
Or both, thought so! Perhaps he found
    me worthless,   50
But till he did so, in these ears of mine,

³ *I.e.,* the trick.
⁴ Cause the loss of the game.
⁵ From 1619 edn. Original reads *Why, do.*
⁶ Ride at a hot pace.   ⁷ Audacity.

These credulous ears, he poured the
sweetest words
That art or love could frame. If he were
false,
Pardon it, heaven! And, if I did want
Virtue, you safely may forgive that too,
For I have lost none that I had from you.
EVAD. Nay, leave this sad talk, madam.
ASP. Would I could!
Then I should leave the cause.
EVAD. See, if you have not spoiled all
Dula's mirth!
ASP. Thou think'st thy heart hard; but,
if thou beest caught, 60
Remember me; thou shalt perceive a
fire
Shot suddenly into thee.
DUL. That's not so good;
Let 'em shoot anything but fire, I fear
'em not.
ASP. Well, wench, thou mayst be taken.
EVAD. Ladies, good night; I'll do the rest
myself.
DUL. Nay, let your lord do some.
ASP. [*Singing.*]

Lay a garland on my hearse
Of the dismal yew—

EVAD. That's one of your sad songs,
madam.
ASP. Believe me, 'tis a very pretty one. 70
EVAD. How is it, madam?

SONG

ASP. Lay a garland on my hearse
Of the dismal yew;
Maidens, willow branches bear;
Say I diéd true.

My love was false, but I was firm
From my hour of birth.
Upon my buried body lay
Lightly gentle earth!

EVAD. Fie on 't, madam! The words [80
are so strange, they are able to make one
dream of hobgoblins.—"I could never
have the power"—sing that, Dula.
DUL. [*Singing.*]

I could never have the power
To love one above an hour,
But my heart would prompt mine eye
On some other man to fly.

Venus, fix mine eyës fast,
Or, if not, give me all that I shall see at
last! 89

EVAD. So, leave me now.
DUL. Nay, we must see you laid.
ASP. Madam, good night. May all the
marriage joys
That longing maids imagine in their
beds
Prove so unto you! May no discontent
Grow twixt your love and you! But, if
there do,
Inquire of me, and I will guide your
moan,
Teach you an artificial [1] way to grieve,
To keep your sorrow waking. Love your
lord
No worse than I; but, if you love so
well,
Alas, you may displease him! So did I.
This is the last time you shall look on
me.— 100
Ladies, farewell. As soon as I am dead,
Come all and watch one night about
my hearse;
Bring each a mournful story and a tear,
To offer at it when I go to earth;
With flattering ivy clasp my coffin
round;
Write on my brow my fortune; let my
bier
Be borne by virgins that shall sing by
course
The truth of maids and perjuries of
men.
EVAD. Alas, I pity thee. *Exit Evadne.*
OMNES. Madam, good night.
1 LADY. Come, we'll let in the bride-
groom.
DUL. Where's my lord? 110
1 LADY. Here, take this light.

Enter Amintor.

DUL. You'll find her in the dark.
1 LADY. Your lady's scarce abed yet;
you must help her.
ASP. Go, and be happy in your lady's
love.
May all the wrongs that you have done
to me
Be utterly forgotten in my death!
I'll trouble you no more; yet I will take

[1] Artful.

A parting kiss, and will not be denied.
[*Kisses Amintor.*]
You'll come, my lord, and see the vir-
gins weep
When I am laid in earth, though you
yourself
Can know no pity. Thus I wind my-
self   120
Into this willow garland, and am prouder
That I was once your love, though now
refused,
Than to have had another true to me.
So with [my] [1] prayers I leave you, and
must try
Some yet unpracticed way to grieve and
die.   *Exit Aspatia.*
DUL. Come, ladies, will you go?
OMNES.   Good night, my lord.
AMIN. Much happiness unto you all!
                    Exeunt [Dula and] Ladies.
I did that lady wrong. Methinks, I feel
Her grief shoot suddenly through all
my veins;
Mine eyes run. This is strange at such
a time.   130
It was the king first moved me to 't; but
he
Has not my will in keeping. Why do I
Perplex myself thus? Something whis-
pers me,
"Go not to bed." My guilt is not so
great
As mine own conscience, too sensible,[2]
Would make me think; I only brake a
promise,
And 'twas the king that forced me.
Timorous flesh,
Why shak'st thou so? Away, my idle
fears!

Enter Evadne.

Yonder she is, the luster of whose eye
Can blot away the sad remembrance 140
Of all these things.--O, my Evadne,
spare
That tender body; let it not take cold!
The vapors of the night will not fall
here.
To bed, my love; Hymen will punish us
For being slack performers of his rites.
Cam'st thou to call me?
EVAD.   No.

AMIN.   Come, come, my love,
And let us lose ourselves to one another.
Why art thou up so long?
EVAD.   I am not well.
AMIN. To bed then; let me wind thee in
these arms
Till I have banished sickness.
EVAD.   Good my lord,   150
I cannot sleep.
AMIN.   Evadne, we'll watch;
I mean no sleeping.
EVAD.   I'll not go to bed.
AMIN. I prithee, do.
EVAD.   I will not for the world.
AMIN. Why, my dear love?
EVAD.   Why? I have sworn I will not.
AMIN. Sworn!
EVAD.   Ay.
AMIN.   How? Sworn, Evadne?
EVAD. Yes, sworn, Amintor—and will
swear again,
If you will wish to hear me.
AMIN. To whom have you sworn this?
EVAD. If I should name him, the matter
were not great.
AMIN. Come, this is but the coyness of
a bride.   160
EVAD. The coyness of a bride?
AMIN.   How prettily
That frown becomes thee!
EVAD.   Do you like it so?
AMIN. Thou canst not dress thy face in
such a look
But I shall like it.
EVAD.   What look likes [3] you best?
AMIN. Why do you ask?
EVAD. That I may show you one less
pleasing to you.
AMIN. How's that?
EVAD. That I may show you one less
pleasing to you.
AMIN. I prithee, put thy jests in milder
looks;
It shows as thou wert angry.
EVAD.   So perhaps   170
I am indeed.
AMIN.   Why, who has done thee wrong?
Name me the man, and by thyself I
swear,
Thy yet unconquered self, I will revenge
thee!
EVAD. Now I shall try thy truth. If thou
dost love me,

---

[1] From 1630 edn.   [2] Sensitive.   [3] Pleases.

Thou weigh'st not anything compared
　　with me.
Life, honor, joys eternal, all delights
This world can yield, or hopeful people
　　feign,
Or in the life to come, are light as air
To a true lover when his lady frowns,
And bids him, "Do this." Wilt thou
　　kill this man?　　　　　　　　180
Swear, my Amintor, and I'll kiss the sin
Off from thy lips.
AMIN.　　　　I wo' not swear, sweet love,
Till I do know the cause.
EVAD.　　　　　I would thou wouldst.
Why, it is thou that wrong'st me.　I
　　hate thee.
Thou shouldst have killed thyself.
AMIN. If I should know that, I should
　　quickly kill
The man you hated.
EVAD.　　　　Know it, then, and do 't.
AMIN. O, no!　What look soe'er thou
　　shalt put on
To try my faith, I shall not think thee
　　false;
I cannot find one blemish in thy face, 190
Where falsehood should abide.　Leave,
　　and to bed.
If you have sworn to any of the virgins
That were your old companions, to
　　preserve
Your maidenhead a night, it may be done
Without this means.
EVAD.　　　　A maidenhead, Amintor,
At my years?
AMIN.　　Sure she raves.　This cannot be
Thy natural temper.　Shall I call thy
　　maids?
Either thy healthful sleep hath left
　　thee long,
Or else some fever rages in thy blood.
EVAD. Neither, Amintor.　Think you I
　　am mad,　　　　　　　　　　200
Because I speak the truth?
AMIN.　　　　　[Is this the truth?] [1]
Will you not lie with me tonight?
EVAD.　　　　　　　　Tonight?
You talk as if [you thought] [1] I would
　　hereafter.
AMIN. Hereafter?　Yes, I do.
EVAD.　　　　　　You are deceived.
Put off amazement, and with patience
　　mark

[1] From 1619 edn.

What I shall utter, for the oracle
Knows nothing truer.　'Tis not for a
　　night
Or two that I forbear thy bed, but ever.
AMIN. I dream.　Awake, Amintor!
EVAD.　　　　　You hear right;　209
I sooner will find out the beds of snakes,
And with my youthful blood warm their
　　cold flesh,
Letting them curl themselves about
　　my limbs,
Than sleep one night with thee.　This is
　　not feigned,
Nor sounds it like the coyness of a bride.
AMIN. Is flesh so earthly to endure all
　　this?
Are these the joys of marriage?　Hymen,
　　keep
This story, that will make succeeding
　　youth
Neglect thy ceremonies, from all ears;
Let it not rise up for thy shame and
　　mine
To after ages; we will scorn thy laws, 220
If thou no better bless them.　Touch the
　　heart
Of her that thou hast sent me, or the
　　world
Shall know; there's not an altar that
　　will smoke
In praise of thee; we will adopt us sons;
Then virtue shall inherit, and not blood.
If we do lust, we'll take the next we
　　meet,
Serving ourselves as other creatures do,
And never take note of the female more,
Nor of her issue.—I do rage in vain;
She can but jest.—O, pardon me, my
　　love!　　　　　　　　　　230
So dear the thoughts are that I hold of
　　thee,
That I must break forth.　Satisfy my
　　fear;
It is a pain, beyond the hand of death,
To be in doubt.　Confirm it with an oath,
If this be true.
EVAD.　　　　Do you invent the form;
Let there be in it all the binding words
Devils and conjurers can put together,
And I will take it.　I have sworn be-
　　fore,
And here by all things holy do again,
Never to be acquainted with thy bed!
Is your doubt over now?　　　241

AMIN. I know too much; would I had
  doubted still!
Was ever such a marriage night as this!
You powers above, if you did ever mean
Man should be used thus, you have
  thought a way
How he may bear himself, and save
  his honor.
Instruct me in it, for to my dull eyes
There is no mean, no moderate course
  to run;
I must live scorned, or be a murderer.
Is there a third? Why is this night so
  calm?   250
Why does not heaven speak in thunder
  to us,
And drown her voice?
EVAD.   This rage will do no good.
AMIN. Evadne, hear me. Thou has ta'en
  an oath,
But such a rash one that to keep it
  were
Worse than to swear it. Call it back to
  thee;
Such vows as those never ascend to
  the heaven;
A tear or two will wash it quite away.
Have mercy on my youth, my hopeful
  youth,
If thou be pitiful, for, without boast,
This land was proud of me. What lady
  was there   260
That men called fair and virtuous in
  this isle,
That would have shunned my love? It
  is in thee
To make me hold this worth. O, we
  vain men,
That trust all our reputation
To rest upon the weak and yielding
  hand
Of feeble woman! But thou art not
  stone;
Thy flesh is soft, and in thine eyes doth
  dwell
The spirit of love; thy heart cannot be
  hard.
Come, lead me from the bottom of de-
  spair
To all the joys thou hast, I know thou
  wilt,   270
And make me careful lest the sudden
  change
O'ercome my spirits.

EVAD.   When I call back this oath,
The pains of hell environ me!
AMIN. I sleep, and am too temperate.
  Come to bed!
Or by those hairs, which, if thou hast
  a soul
Like to thy locks, were threads for kings
  to wear
About their arms——
EVAD.   Why, so perhaps they are.
AMIN. I'll drag thee to my bed, and make
  thy tongue
Undo this wicked oath, or on thy flesh
I'll print a thousand wounds to let out
  life!   280
EVAD. I fear thee not; do what thou
  dar'st to me!
Every ill-sounding word or threat'ning
  look
Thou show'st to me will be revenged at
  full.
AMIN. It will not, sure, Evadne.
EVAD. Do not you hazard that.
AMIN.   Ha' ye your champions?
EVAD. Alas, Amintor, think'st thou I
  forbear
To sleep with thee because I have put
  on
A maiden's strictness? Look upon
  these cheeks,
And thou shalt find the hot and rising
  blood   289
Unapt for such a vow. No; in this heart
There dwells as much desire and as
  much will
To put that wished act in practice as
  ever yet
Was known to woman; and they have
  been shown
Both. But it was the folly of thy youth
To think this beauty, to what land[1]
  soe'er
It shall be called, shall stoop to any
  second.
I do enjoy the best, and in that height
Have sworn to stand or die. You guess
  the man.
AMIN. No; let me know the man that
  wrongs me so,
That I may cut his body into motes, 300
And scatter it before the northern wind.
EVAD. You dare not strike him.

---

[1] Bullen suggests *hand*, to fit the figure of
falconry in the passage.

AMIN.   Do not wrong me so.
Yes, if his body were a poisonous plant
That it were death to touch, I have a
  soul
Will throw me on him.
EVAD.   Why, 'tis the king.
AMIN.   The king!
EVAD. What will you do now?
AMIN.   'Tis not the king!
EVAD. What did he make this match for,
  dull Amintor?
AMIN. O, thou hast named a word that
  wipes away
All thoughts revengeful! In that sacred
  name,
"The king," there lies a terror. What
  frail man   310
Dares lift his hand against it? Let the
  gods
Speak to him when they please; till
  when, let us
Suffer and wait.
EVAD. Why should you fill yourself so
  full of heat,
And haste so to my bed? I am no virgin.
AMIN. What devil put it in thy fancy,
  then,
To marry me?
EVAD.   Alas, I must have one
To father children, and to bear the name
Of husband to me, that my sin may be
More honorable!
AMIN.   What a strange thing am I! 320
EVAD. A miserable one; one that myself
Am sorry for.
AMIN.   Why, show it then in this:
If thou hast pity, though thy love be
  none,
Kill me; and all true lovers, that shall
  live
In after ages crossed in their desires,
Shall bless thy memory, and call thee
  good,
Because such mercy in thy heart was
  found,
To rid a ling'ring wretch.
EVAD.   I must have one
To fill thy room again, if thou wert
  dead;
Else, by this night, I would! I pity
  thee.   330
AMIN. These strange and sudden injuries
  have fall'n
So thick upon me that I lose all sense

Of what they are. Methinks, I am not
  wronged;
Nor is it aught, if from the censuring
  world
I can but hide it. Reputation,
Thou art a word, no more!—But thou
  hast shown
An impudence so high that to the world
I fear thou wilt betray or shame thy-
  self.
EVAD. To cover shame, I took thee;
  never fear
That I would blaze [1] myself.
AMIN.   Nor let the king 340
Know I conceive he wrongs me; then
  mine honor
Will thrust me into action; that my flesh
Could bear with patience. And it is
  some ease
To me in these extremes that I know
  this
Before I touched thee; else, had all the
  sins
Of mankind stood betwixt me and the
  king,
I had gone through 'em to his heart and
  thine.
I have lost one desire; 'tis not his crown
Shall buy me to thy bed, now I resolve [2]
He has dishonored thee. Give me thy
  hand.   350
Be careful of thy credit, and sin close; [3]
'Tis all I wish. Upon thy chamber floor
I'll rest tonight, that morning visitors
May think we did as married people
  use.
And, prithee, smile upon me when they
  come,
And seem to toy, as if thou hadst been
  pleased
With what we did.
EVAD.   Fear not; I will do this.
AMIN. Come, let us practice; and, as wan-
  tonly
As ever loving bride and bridegroom met,
Let's laugh and enter here.
EVAD.   I am content. 360
AMIN. Down all the swellings of my
  troubled heart!
When we walk thus entwined, let all
  eyes see
If ever lovers better did agree.
                  Exit [with Evadne].

[1] Proclaim.   [2] Am convinced.   [3] Privately.

[SCENA ii.

A room in the house of Calianax.]

Enter Aspatia, Antiphila, and Olympias.

ASP. Away, you are not sad! Force it no
further.
Good gods, how well you look! Such a
full color
Young bashful brides put on; sure, you
are new married!
ANT. Yes, madam, to your grief.
ASP.   Alas, poor wenches!
Go learn to love first; learn to lose your-
selves;
Learn to be flattered, and believe and
bless
The double tongue that did it; make a
faith
Out of the miracles of ancient lovers,
Such as speak truth and died in 't; and,
like me,
Believe all faithful, and be miserable. 10
Did you ne'er love yet, wenches? Speak,
Olympias; [1]
Thou hast an easy temper, fit for stamp.
OLYM. Never.
ASP.   Nor you, Antiphila?
ANT.   Nor I.
ASP. Then, my good girls, be more than
women, wise;
At least be more than I was; and be sure
You credit anything the light gives life
to,
Before a man. Rather believe the sea
Weeps for the ruined merchant, when he
roars;
Rather, the wind courts but the preg-
nant sails,
When the strong cordage cracks; rather,
the sun   20
Comes but to kiss the fruit in wealthy
autumn,
When all falls blasted. If you needs
must love
(Forced by ill fate), take to your maiden
bosoms
Two dead-cold aspics, and of them make
lovers.
They cannot flatter nor forswear; one
kiss
Makes a long peace for all. But man—

---

[1] This line follows l. 8 in original. Emended
by Theobald.

O, that beast man! Come, let's be sad,
my girls;
That down-cast of thine eye, Olympias,
Shows a fine sorrow.—Mark, Antiphila;
Just such another was the nymph
Oenone's,   30
When Paris brought home Helen.—
Now, a tear;
And then thou art a piece expressing
fully
The Carthage queen, when from a cold
sea rock,
Full with her sorrow, she tied fast her
eyes
To the fair Trojan ships, and, having
lost them,
Just as thine does, down stole a tear.—
Antiphila,
What would this wench do, if she were
Aspatia?
Here she would stand, till some more
pitying god
Turned her to marble!— 'Tis enough,
my wench!
Show me the piece of needlework you
wrought.   40
ANT. Of Ariadne, madam?
ASP. [*Examining the needlework.*]   Yes,
that piece.—
This should be Theseus; h'as a cozening
face.—
You meant him for a man?
ANT.   He was so, madam.
ASP. Why, then, 'tis well enough.—Never
look back;
You have a full wind and a false heart,
Theseus.—
Does not the story say his keel was
split,
Or his masts spent, or some kind rock
or other
Met with his vessel?
ANT.   Not as I remember.
ASP. It should ha' been so. Could the
gods know this,
And not, of all their number, raise a
storm?   50
But they are all as ill. This false smile
Was well expressed; just such another
caught me.—
[*To Theseus.*] You shall not go so.—
Antiphila, in this place work a quick-
sand,
And over it a shallow, smiling water,

And his ship plowing it, and then a
    Fear.
Do that Fear to the life, wench.

ANT.   'Twill wrong the story.

ASP. 'Twill make the story, wronged by
    wanton poets,
Live long and be believed. But where's
    the lady?

ANT. There, madam.   60

ASP. Fie, you have missed it here, Anti-
    phila;
You are much mistaken, wench.
These colors are not dull and pale
    enough
To show a soul so full of misery
As this sad lady's was. Do it by me,
Do it again by me, the lost Aspatia;
And you shall find all true but the wild
    island.
I stand upon the sea-breach now, and
    think
Mine arms thus, and mine hair blown
    with the wind,
Wild as that desert; and let all about
    me   70
Tell that I am forsaken. Do my face
(If thou hadst ever feeling of a sor-
    row)
Thus, thus, Antiphila: strive to make
    me look
Like Sorrow's monument; and the trees
    about me,
Let them be dry and leafless; let the
    rocks
Groan with continual surges; and, be-
    hind me,
Make all a desolation. Look, look,
    wenches,
A miserable life [1] of this poor picture!

OLYM. Dear madam!

ASP.   I have done. Sit down; and let us
Upon that point fix all our eyes, that
    point there.   80
Make a dull silence, till you feel a sudden
    sadness
Give us new souls.

Enter Calianax.

CAL. The king may do this, and he may
    not do it.
My child is wronged, disgraced.—Well,
    how now, huswives? [2]

What, at your ease? Is this a time to
    sit still?
Up, you young lazy whores, up, or I'll
    swenge [3] you!

OLYM. Nay, good my lord—

CAL. You'll lie down shortly. Get you in,
    and work!
What, are you grown so resty [4] you want
    heats?
We shall have some of the court boys do
    that office.   90

ANT. My lord, we do no more than we
    are charged.
It is the lady's pleasure we be thus
In grief; she is forsaken.

CAL.   There's a rogue too,
A young dissembling slave!—Well, get
    you in.—
I'll have a bout with that boy. 'Tis high
    time
Now to be valiant; I confess my youth
Was never prone that way. What, made
    an ass?
A court stale? [5] Well, I will be valiant,
And beat some dozen of these whelps; I
    will!
And there's another of 'em, a trim,
    cheating soldier;   100
I'll maul that rascal; has outbraved me
    twice;
But now, I thank the gods, I am val-
    iant.—
Go, get you in.—I'll take a course with
    all.   *Exeunt om[nes].*

ACTUS III. [SCENA i.

Anteroom to Evadne's bedchamber.]

Enter Cleon, Strato, and Diphilus.

CLE. Your sister is not up yet.

DIPH. O, brides must take their morning's rest; the night is troublesome.

STRA. But not tedious.

DIPH. What odds, he has not my
sister's maidenhead tonight?

STRA. No; it's odds against any bridegroom living, he ne'er gets it while he
lives.

DIPH. Y' are merry with my sister; [10
you'll please to allow me the same freedom
with your mother.

---

[1] Living representation.   [2] Hussies.
[3] Swinge, beat.   [5] Laughingstock.
[4] Restive, sluggish.

STRA. She's at your service.

DIPH. Then she's merry enough of herself; she needs no tickling.—Knock at the door.

STRA. We shall interrupt them.

DIPH. No matter; they have the year before them.—[*Strato knocks.*] Good morrow, sister. Spare yourself today; the [20 night will come again.

Enter Amintor.

AMIN. Who's there? My brother! I'm no readier yet. Your sister is but now up.

DIPH. You look as you had lost your eyes tonight; I think you ha' not slept.

AMIN. I' faith, I have not.

DIPH.   You have done better, then.

AMIN. We ventured for a boy; when he is twelve,
A shall command against the foes of Rhodes.
Shall we be merry?   29

STRA. You cannot; you want sleep.

AMIN. 'Tis true.—(*Aside.*) But she,
As if she had drunk Lethe, or had made
Even with heaven, did fetch so still a sleep,
So sweet and sound——

DIPH.   What's that?

AMIN.   Your sister frets
This morning, and does turn her eyes upon me,
As people on their headsman. She does chafe,
And kiss, and chafe again, and clap my cheeks.
She's in another world.

DIPH. Then I had lost; I was about to lay
You had not got her maidenhead to-night.[1]

AMIN. [*Aside.*] Ha! He does not mock me?
—Y'ad lost indeed;   40
I do not use to bungle.

CLE.   You do deserve her.

AMIN. (*Aside.*) I laid my lips to hers, and that wild breath,
That was so rude and rough to me last night,
Was sweet as April. I'll be guilty too,
If these be the effects.

[1] Last night.

Enter Melantius.

MEL. Good day, Amintor, for to me the name
Of brother is too distant; we are friends,
And that is nearer.

AMIN.   Dear Melantius!
Let me behold thee. Is it possible?

MEL. What sudden gaze is this?

AMIN.   'Tis wondrous strange! 50

MEL. Why does thine eye desire so strict a view
Of that it knows so well? There's nothing here
That is not thine.

AMIN.   I wonder much, Melantius,
To see those noble looks that make me think
How virtuous thou art; and, on the sudden,
'Tis strange to me thou shouldst have worth and honor,
Or not be base, and false, and treacherous,
And every ill. But——

MEL.   Stay, stay, my friend;
I fear this sound will not become our loves.
No more embrace me.

AMIN.   O, mistake me not! 60
I know thee to be full of all those deeds
That we frail men call good; but by the course
Of nature thou shouldst be as quickly changed
As are the winds, dissembling as the sea,
That now wears brows as smooth as virgins' be,
Tempting the merchant to invade his face,
And in an hour calls his billows up,
And shoots 'em at the sun, destroying all
A carries on him.—(*Aside.*) O, how near am I
To utter my sick thoughts!   70

MEL. But why, my friend, should I be so by nature?

AMIN. I have wed thy sister, who hath virtuous thoughts
Enough for one whole family; and it is strange
That you should feel no want.

MEL. Believe me, this is compliment too cunning for me.

DIPH. What should I be then by the course
 of nature,
 They having both robbed me of so much
  virtue?
 STRA. O, call the bride, my Lord Amin-
tor, that we may see her blush, and turn
her eyes down. It is the prettiest sport!
AMIN. Evadne!
EVAD. (*Within.*)   My lord?
AMIN.   Come forth, my love; 81
 Your brothers do attend to wish you joy.
EVAD. I am not ready yet.
AMIN.   Enough, enough.
EVAD. They'll mock me.
AMIN.   Faith, thou shalt come in.

Enter Evadne.

MEL. Good morrow, sister. He that under-
 stands
 Whom you have wed, need not to wish
  you joy.
 You have enough; take heed you be not
  proud.
DIPH. O, sister, what have you done?
EVAD. I done! Why, what have I done?
STRA. My Lord Amintor swears you are
 no maid now.   90
EVAD. Push!
STRA. I' faith, he does.
EVAD.   I knew I should be mocked.
DIPH. With a truth.
EVAD.   If 'twere to do again,
 In faith I would not marry.
AMIN. (*Aside.*)   Nor I, by heaven!
DIPH. Sister, Dula swears she heard you
 cry two rooms off.
EVAD. Fie, how you talk!
DIPH. Let's see you walk.
EVAD.   By my troth, y' are spoiled.
MEL.   Amintor!
AMIN. Ha!
MEL. Thou art sad.
AMIN. Who, I? I thank you for that.
 Shall Diphilus, thou, and I sing a catch?
MEL. How!   100
AMIN. Prithee, let's.
MEL. Nay, that's too much the other way.
AMIN. I am so lightened with my hap-
 piness!—
 How dost thou, love? Kiss me.
EVAD. I cannot love you; you tell tales of
 me.
AMIN. Nothing but what becomes us.—
 Gentlemen,

Would you had all such wives, and all
 the world,
 That I might be no wonder! Y' are all
  sad.
 What, do you envy me? I walk, me-
  thinks,   109
 On water, and ne'er sink, I am so light.
MEL. 'Tis well you are so.
AMIN.   Well! How can I be other,
 When she looks thus?—Is there no
  music there?
 Let's dance.
MEL.   Why, this is strange, Amintor!
AMIN. I do not know myself; yet I could
 wish
 My joy were less.
DIPH. I'll marry too, if it will make one
 thus.
EVAD. (*Aside.*) Amintor, hark.
AMIN. [*Aside.*] What says my love?—I
 must obey.
EVAD. [*Aside.*] You do it scurvily; 'twill
 be perceived.   119
CLE. My lord, the king is here.

Enter King and Lysip[pus].

AMIN.   Where?
STRA.   And his brother.
KING. Good morrow, all!—
 Amintor, joy on joy fall thick upon
  thee!—
 And, madam, you are altered since I
  saw you;
 I must salute you; you are now an-
  other's.
 How liked you your night's rest?
EVAD.   Ill, sir.
AMIN.   Indeed,
 She took but little.
LYS.   You'll let her take more,
 And thank her too, shortly.
KING. Amintor, wert thou truly honest [1] till
 Thou wert married?
AMIN. Yes, sir.
KING.   Tell me, then, how shows
 The sport unto thee?
AMIN. Why, well.
KING.   What did you do? 130
AMIN. No more, nor less, than other
 couples use;
 You know what 'tis; it has but a coarse
  name.

[1] Chaste.

KING. But, prithee, I should think, by her
    black eye,
And her red cheek, she should be quick
    and stirring
In this same business; ha?
AMIN.   I cannot tell;
I ne'er tried other, sir, but I perceive
She is as quick [1] as you deliveréd.
KING. Well, you'll trust me then, Amintor,
    to choose
A wife for you again?
AMIN.   No, never, sir.
KING. Why, like you this so ill?
AMIN.   So well I like her.   140
For this I bow my knee in thanks to
    you,
And unto heaven will pay my grateful
    tribute
Hourly, and do hope we shall draw out
A long contented life together here,
And die both, full of gray hairs, in one
    day,
For which the thanks is yours. But, if
    the powers
That rule us please to call her first
    away,
Without pride spoke, this world holds
    not a wife
Worthy to take her room.
KING. [*Aside.*]   I do not like this.—
All forbear the room but you, Amin-
    tor,   150
And your lady.
[*Exeunt All but the King, Amintor, and
                   Evadne.*]
          I have some speech with you,
That may concern your after living well.
AMIN. [*Aside.*] A will not tell me that he
    lies with her?
If he do, something heavenly stay my
    heart,
For I shall be apt to thrust this arm of
    mine
To acts unlawful!
KING.   You will suffer me
To talk with her, Amintor, and not have
A jealous pang?
AMIN.   Sir, I dare trust my wife
With whom she dares to talk, and not be
    jealous.   [*Retires.*]
KING. How do you like Amintor?
EVAD.   As I did, sir.   160
KING. How's that?

[1] *I.e.*, quickened with child.

EVAD. As one that, to fulfill your will and
    pleasure,
I have given leave to call me wife and
    love.
KING. I see there is no lasting faith in sin;
They that break word with heaven will
    break again
With all the world, and so dost thou
    with me.
EVAD. How, sir?
KING.   This subtle woman's ignorance
Will not excuse you; thou hast taken
    oaths,
So great that, methought, they did mis-
    become
A woman's mouth, that thou wouldst
    ne'er enjoy   170
A man but me.
EVAD.   I never did swear so;
You do me wrong.
KING.   Day and night have heard it.
EVAD. I swore indeed that I would never
    love
A man of lower place; but, if your for-
    tune
Should throw you from this height, I
    bade you trust
I would forsake you, and would bend to
    him
That won your throne. I love with my
    ambition,
Not with my eyes. But, if I ever yet
Touched any other, leprosy light here
Upon my face, which for your royalty
I would not stain!   181
KING. Why, thou dissemblest, and it is
    in me
To punish thee.
EVAD.   Why, it is in me, then,
Not to love you, which will more afflict
Your body than your punishment can
    mine.
KING. But thou hast let Amintor lie with
    thee.
EVAD. I ha' not.
KING.   Impudence! He says himself so.
EVAD. A lies.
KING.   A does not.
EVAD.   By this light, he does,
Strangely and basely, and I'll prove it
    so!
I did not only shun him for a night,   190
But told him I would never close with
    him.

King. Speak lower; 'tis false.

Evad.   I am no man
To answer with a blow, or, if I were,
  You are the king. But urge [me] [1] not;
  'tis most true.
King. Do not I know the uncontrolléd
    thoughts
That youth brings with him, when his
    blood is high
With expectation and desire of that
He long hath waited for? Is not his
    spirit,
Though he be temperate, of a valiant
    strain
As this our age hath known? What could
  he do,   200
If such a sudden speech had met his
    blood,
But ruin thee forever, if he had not killed
    thee?
He could not bear it thus; he is as we,
Or any other wronged man.
Evad.   It is dissembling.
King. Take him! Farewell; henceforth
    I am thy foe,
And what disgraces I can blot thee with
  look for.
Evad. Stay, sir!—Amintor!—You shall
  hear.—Amintor!
Amin. [Coming forward.] What, my love?
Evad. Amintor, thou hast an ingenious [2]
  look,
And shouldst be virtuous; it amazeth
  me   210
That thou canst make such base, mali-
    cious lies!
Amin. What, my dear wife?
Evad.   Dear wife! I do despise thee.
Why, nothing can be baser than to sow
Dissension amongst lovers.
Amin.   Lovers! Who?
Evad. The king and me—
Amin.   O, God!
Evad. Who should live long, and love
  without distaste,
Were it not for such pickthanks [3] as
  thyself.
Did you lie with me? Swear now, and be
  punished
In hell for this!
Amin.   The faithless sin I made
To fair Aspatia is not yet revenged;   220
It follows me.—I will not lose a word

[1] From 1630 edn.   [2] Ingenuous.   [3] Talebearers.

To this wild [4] woman; but to you, my
  king,
The anguish of my soul thrusts out this
    truth:
Y' are a tyrant!—and not so much to
    wrong
An honest man thus, as to take a pride
In talking with him of it.
Evad.   Now, sir, see
How loud this fellow lied!
Amin. You that can know to wrong, should
    know how men
Must right themselves—what punish-
    ment is due
From me to him that shall abuse my
  bed.   230
It is not death; nor can that satisfy,
Unless I send your lives [5] through all
    the land,
To show how nobly I have freed my-
    self.
King. Draw not thy sword; thou knowest
    I cannot fear
A subject's hand. But thou shalt feel
    the weight
Of this, if thou dost rage.
Amin.   The weight of that!
If you have any worth, for heaven's
    sake, think
I fear not swords; for, as you are mere
    man,
I dare as easily kill you for this deed   239
As you dare think to do it. But there is
Divinity about you that strikes dead
My rising passions; as you are my king,
I fall before you, and present my sword
To cut mine own flesh, if it be your will.
Alas, I am nothing but a multitude
Of walking [6] griefs! Yet, should I mur-
    der you,
I might before the world take the ex-
    cuse
Of madness; for, compare [7] my injuries,
And they will well appear too sad a
    weight   249
For reason to endure. But fall I [8] first
Amongst my sorrows, ere my treacher-
    ous hand
Touch holy things! But why (I know
    not what

[4] Dyce suggests vild, i.e., vile.
[5] Life histories.
[6] So all edns. except original, which reads
waking.
[7] Examine.   [8] I.e., may I fall.

I have to say), why did you choose out
me
To make thus wretched?   There were
thousands, fools
Easy to work on, and of state [1] enough,
Within the island.

EVAD.   I would not have a fool;
It were no credit for me.

AMIN.   Worse and worse!
Thou, that dar'st talk unto thy husband
thus,
Profess thyself a whore, and, more than
so,
Resolve to be so still!—It is my fate   260
To bear and bow beneath a thousand
griefs,
To keep that little credit with the
world!—
But there were wise ones too; you might
have ta'en
Another.

KING.   No; for I believe thee honest,
As thou wert valiant.

AMIN.   All the happiness [2]
Bestowed upon me turns into disgrace.
Gods, take your honesty again, for I
Am loaden with it!—Good my lord the
king,
Be private in it.

KING.   Thou mayst live, Amintor,
Free as thy king, if thou wilt wink at
this,   270
And be a means that we may meet in
secret.

AMIN. A bawd! Hold, hold, my breast! A
bitter curse
Seize me, if I forget not all respects
That are religious, on another word [3]
Sounded like that, and through a sea
of sins
Will wade to my revenge, though I should
call
Pains here and after life upon my soul!

KING. Well, I am resolute [4] you lay not
with her;
And so I leave you.   Exit King.

EVAD.   You must needs be prating;
And see what follows!

AMIN.   Prithee, vex me not.   280
Leave me; I am afraid some sudden start
Will pull a murther on me.

[1] Estate, position.   [4] Convinced.
[2] Good fortune.
[3] I.e., a repetition of bawd (?).

EVAD.   I am gone;
I love my life well.   Exit Evadne.

AMIN.   I hate mine as much.
This 'tis to break a troth! I should be
glad,
If all this tide of grief would make me
mad.   Exit.

[SCENA ii.

A room in the palace.]

Enter Melantius.

MEL. I'll know the cause of all Amintor's
griefs,
Or friendship shall be idle. [5]

Enter Calianax.

CAL.   O, Melantius,
My daughter will die!

MEL.   Trust me, I am sorry;
Would thou hadst ta'en her room!

CAL.   Thou art a slave,
A cutthroat slave, a bloody, treacherous slave!

MEL. Take heed, old man; thou wilt be
heard to rave,
And lose thine offices.

CAL.   I am valiant grown
At all these years, and thou art but a
slave!

MEL. Leave! Some company will come,
and I respect
Thy years, not thee, so much that I   10
could wish
To laugh at thee alone.

CAL.   I'll spoil your mirth.
I mean to fight with thee. There lie,
my cloak!
This was my father's sword, and he
durst fight.
Are you prepared?

MEL.   Why wilt thou dote thyself
Out of thy life? Hence, get thee to bed,
Have careful looking-to, and eat warm
things,
And trouble not me; my head is full of
thoughts
More weighty than thy life or death can
be.

CAL. You have a name in war, where
you stand safe
Amongst a multitude; but I will try   20

[5] Vain.

What you dare do unto a weak old man
In single fight. You'll give ground, I fear.
Come, draw!

MEL. I will not draw, unless thou pull'st
thy death
Upon thee with a stroke. There's no
one blow
That thou canst give hath strength
enough to kill me.
Tempt me not so far, then; the power
of earth
Shall not redeem thee.

CAL. [*Aside.*]　　I must let him alone;
He's stout and able; and, to say the
truth,
However I may set a face and talk,　30
I am not valiant. When I was a youth,
I kept my credit with a testy trick
I had amongst cowards, but durst never
fight.

MEL. I will not promise to preserve your
life,
If you do stay.

CAL. [*Aside.*]　　I would give half my land
That I durst fight with that proud man
a little.
If I had men to hold him, I would beat
him
Till he ask me mercy.

MEL.　　　　　Sir, will you be gone?

CAL. [*Aside.*] I dare not stay; but I will
go home, and beat my servants all　[40
over for this.　　　　*Exit Calianax.*

MEL. This old fellow haunts me.
But the distracted carriage of mine
Amintor
Takes deeply on me.[1] I will find the
cause;
I fear his conscience cries he wronged
Aspatia.

Enter Amintor.

AMIN. [*Aside.*] Men's eyes are not so
subtle to perceive
My inward misery; I bear my grief
Hid from the world. How art thou
wretched then?
For aught I know, all husbands are
like me;
And every one I talk with of his wife　50
Is but a well dissembler of his woes,
As I am. Would I knew it! For the
rareness

[1] Affects me deeply.

Afflicts me now.

MEL. Amintor, we have not enjoyed
our friendship of late, for we were wont
to charge [2] our souls in talk.

AMIN. Melantius, I can tell thee a
good jest of Strato and a lady the last day.

MEL. How was 't?

AMIN. Why, such an odd one!　60

MEL. I have longed to speak with you,
not of an idle jest, that's forced, but of
matter you are bound to utter to me.

AMIN. What is that, my friend?

MEL. I have observed your words fall
from your tongue
Wildly, and all your carriage
Like one that strove to show his merry
mood,
When he were ill disposed. You were
not wont
To put such scorn into your speech, or
wear
Upon your face ridiculous jollity.　70
Some sadness sits here, which your
cunning would
Cover o'er with smiles, and 'twill not
be.
What is it?

AMIN.　　　A sadness here! What cause
Can fate provide for me to make me so?
Am I not loved through all this isle?
The king
Rains greatness on me. Have I not
received
A lady to my bed, that in her eye
Keeps mounting fire, and on her tender
cheeks
Inevitable [3] color, in her heart　79
A prison for all virtue? Are not you,
Which is above all joys, my constant
friend?
What sadness can I have? No; I am
light,
And feel the courses of my blood more
warm
And stirring than they were. Faith,
marry too,
And you will feel so unexpressed [4] a joy
In chaste embraces that you will indeed
Appear another.

MEL.　　　　You may shape, Amintor,
Causes to cozen the whole world withal,
And yourself too; but 'tis not like a
friend

[2] Weigh down.　[3] Irresistible.　[4] Inexpressible.

To hide your soul from me. 'Tis not
  your nature   90
To be thus idle. I have seen you stand
As you were blasted midst of all your
  mirth,
Call thrice aloud, and then start, feign-
  ing joy
So coldly!—World, what do I here? A
  friend
Is nothing. Heaven, I would ha' told
  that man
My secret sins! I'll search [1] an unknown
  land,
And there plant friendship; all is with-
  ered here.
Come with a compliment! I would have
  fought,
Or told my friend a lied, ere soothed [2]
  him so.—
Out of my bosom!   100
AMIN. But there is nothing.
MEL.   Worse and worse! Farewell!
From this time have acquaintance, but
  no friend.
AMIN. Melantius, stay; you shall know
  what that is.
MEL. See how you played with friendship!
  Be advised
How you give cause unto yourself to say
You ha' lost a friend.
AMIN.   Forgive what I ha' done,
For I am so o'ergone with injuries
Unheard of, that I lose consideration
Of what I ought to do. O, O!
MEL.   Do not weep.
What is 't? May I once but know the
  man   110
Hath turned my friend thus!
AMIN.   I had spoke at first
But that—
MEL.   But what?
AMIN.   I held it most unfit
For you to know. Faith, do not know
  it yet.
MEL. Thou seest my love, that will keep
  company
With thee in tears; hide nothing, then,
  from me,
For, when I know the cause of thy dis-
  temper,
With mine old armor I'll adorn myself,
My resolution, and cut through thy
  foes,

[1] *I.e.*, search for.   [2] Flattered.

Unto thy quiet, till I place thy heart
As peaceable as spotless innocence. 120
What is it?
AMIN.   Why, 'tis this—it is too big
To get out—let my tears make way
  awhile.
MEL. Punish me strangely, heaven, if he
  escape
Of life or fame, that brought this youth
  to this!
AMIN. Your sister—
MEL.   Well said.
AMIN.   You'll wish't unknown,
When you have heard it.
MEL.   No.
AMIN.   —is much to blame,
And to the king has given her honor
  up,
And lives in whoredom with him.
MEL.   How's this?
Thou art run mad with injury indeed;
Thou couldst not utter this else. Speak
  again,   130
For I forgive it freely; tell thy griefs.
AMIN. She's wanton; I am loath to say
  "a whore,"
Though it be true.
MEL. Speak yet again, before mine anger
  grow
Up beyond throwing down. What are
  thy griefs?
AMIN. By all our friendship, these.
MEL.   What, am I tame?
After mine actions, shall the name of
  friend
Blot all our family, and strike the brand
Of whore upon my sister, unrevenged?
My shaking flesh, be thou a witness for
  me,   140
With what unwillingness I go to scourge
This railer, whom my folly hath called
  friend?
I will not take thee basely; thy sword
          [*Draws his sword.*]
Hangs near thy hand; draw it, that I
  may whip
Thy rashness to repentance. Draw thy
  sword!
AMIN. Not on thee, did thine anger go as
  high
As the wild surges. Thou shouldst do
  me ease
Here and eternally, if thy noble hand
Would cut me from my sorrows.

MEL. This is base
And fearful.[1] They that use to utter
lies 150
Provide not blows but words to qualify [2]
The men they wronged. Thou hast a
guilty cause.

AMIN. Thou pleasest me; for so much
more like this
Will raise my anger up above my griefs
(Which is a passion easier to be borne)
And I shall then be happy.

MEL. Take, then, more
To raise thine anger: 'tis mere coward-
ice
Makes thee not draw; and I will leave
thee dead,
However. But, if thou art so much
pressed
With guilt and fear as not to dare to
fight, 160
I'll make thy memory loathed, and fix
a scandal
Upon thy name forever.

AMIN. [Drawing his sword.] Then I
draw,
As justly as our magistrates their
swords
To cut offenders off. I knew before
'Twould grate your ears; but it was
base in you
To urge a weighty secret from your
friend,
And then rage at it. I shall be at ease,
If I be killed; and, if you fall by me,
I shall not long outlive you.

MEL. Stay awhile.— 169
The name of friend is more than family,
Or all the world besides; I was a fool.
Thou searching human nature, that
didst wake
To do me wrong, thou art inquisitive,
And thrusts me upon questions that
will take
My sleep away! Would I had died, ere
known
This sad dishonor!—Pardon me, my
friend! [Sheathes his sword.]
If thou wilt strike, here is a faithful
heart;
Pierce it, for I will never heave my
hand
To thine. Behold the power thou hast
in me!

I do believe my sister is a whore, 180
A leprous one. Put up thy sword, young
man.

AMIN. How should I bear it, then, she
being so?
I fear, my friend, that you will lose me
shortly; [Sheathes his sword.]
And I shall do a foul act on myself,
Through these disgraces.

MEL. Better half the land
Were buried quick [3] together. No,
Amintor;
Thou shalt have ease. O, this adulter-
ous king
That drew her to 't! Where got he the
spirit
To wrong me so?

AMIN. What is it, then, to me,
If it be wrong to you?

MEL. Why, not so much. 190
The credit of our house is thrown away.
But from his iron den I'll waken Death,
And hurl him on this king. My honesty
Shall steel my sword; and on my horrid
point
I'll wear my cause, that shall amaze
the eyes
Of this proud man, and be too glittering
For him to look on.

AMIN. I have quite undone my fame.

MEL. Dry up thy watery eyes, 199
And cast a manly look upon my face,
For nothing is so wild as I, thy friend,
Till I have freed thee. Still this swell-
ing breast.
I go thus from thee, and will never
cease
My vengeance till I find my heart at
peace.

AMIN. It must not be so. Stay. Mine
eyes would tell
How loath I am to this; but, love and
tears,
Leave me awhile, for I have hazarded
All that this world calls happy!—Thou
hast wrought
A secret from me, under name of friend,
Which art could ne'er have found, nor
torture wrung 210
From out my bosom. Give it me again,
For I will find it, wheresoe'er it lies,
Hid in the mortal'st part. Invent a way
To give it back.

[1] Cowardly. [2] Mollify. [3] Alive.

MEL.   Why would you have it back?
I will to death pursue him with revenge.
AMIN. Therefore I call it back from thee,
    for I know
Thy blood so high that thou wilt stir
    in this,
And shame me to posterity.   Take to
    thy weapon!   [*Draws his sword.*]
MEL. Hear thy friend, that bears more
    years than thou.
AMIN. I will not hear.   But draw, or I—
MEL.   Amintor!   220
AMIN. Draw, then; for I am full as reso-
    lute
As fame and honor can enforce me be.
I cannot linger.   Draw!
MEL. [*Drawing his sword.*]   I do.   But is
    not
My share of credit equal with thine,
If I do stir?
AMIN.   No; for it will be called
Honor in thee to spill thy sister's blood,
If she her birth abuse; and on the king
A brave revenge; but on me, that have
    walked
With patience in it, it will fix the name
Of fearful cuckold.   O, that word!   Be
    quick.   230
MEL. Then, join with me.
AMIN.   I dare not do a sin,
Or else I would.   Be speedy.
MEL. Then, dare not fight with me, for
    that's a sin.—
[*Aside.*] His grief distracts him.—Call
    thy thoughts again,
And to thyself pronounce the name of
    friend,
And see what that will work.   I will not
    fight.
AMIN. You must.
MEL. [*Sheathing his sword.*]   I will be
    killed first.   Though my passions
Offered the like to you, 'tis not this earth
Shall buy my reason to it.   Think awhile,
For you are (I must weep when I speak
    that)   240
Almost besides yourself.
AMIN. [*Sheathing his sword.*]   O, my soft
    temper!
So many sweet words from thy sister's
    mouth
I am afraid would make me take her to
Embrace, and pardon her.   I am mad
    indeed,

And know not what I do.   Yet have a
    care
Of me in what thou doest.
MEL.   Why, thinks my friend
I will forget his honor, or, to save
The bravery of our house, will lose his
    fame,
And fear to touch the throne of majesty?
AMIN. A curse will follow that; but rather
    live   250
And suffer with me.
MEL.   I will do what worth
Shall bid me, and no more.
AMIN.   Faith, I am sick,
And desperately I hope; yet, leaning
    thus,
I feel a kind of ease.
MEL.   Come, take again
Your mirth about you.
AMIN.   I shall never do 't.
MEL. I warrant you.   Look up; we'll
    walk together.
Put thine arm here; all shall be well
    again.
AMIN. Thy love (O, wretched!), ay, thy
    love, Melantius.
Why, I have nothing else.
MEL.   Be merry, then.   *Exeunt.*

Enter Melantius again.

MEL. This worthy young man may do
    violence   260
    Upon himself; but I have cherished
    him
To my best power, and sent him smil-
    ing from me,
To counterfeit again.   Sword, hold thine
    edge;
My heart will never fail me.—

Enter Diphilus.[1]

                           Diphilus!
Thou com'st as [2] sent.
DIPH.   Yonder has been such laughing.
MEL. Betwixt whom?
DIPH.   Why, our sister and the king.
    I thought their spleens would break;
    they laughed us all
Out of the room.
MEL. They must weep, Diphilus.
DIPH.   Must they?

---

[1] In original, direction appears a line later.
[2] As if.

MEL. They must.
Thou art my brother; and, if I did be-
lieve 270
Thou hadst a base thought, I would rip
it out,
Lie where it durst.

DIPH. You should not; I would first
Mangle myself and find it.

MEL. That was spoke
According to our strain. Come, join
thy hands to mine,
And swear a firmness to what project I
Shall lay before thee.

DIPH. You do wrong us both.
People hereafter shall not say there
passed
A bond, more than our loves, to tie our
lives
And deaths together. 279

MEL. It is as nobly said as I would wish.
Anon [1] I'll tell you wonders: we are
wronged.

DIPH. But I will tell you now, we'll right
ourselves.

MEL. Stay not; prepare the armor in my
house;
And what friends you can draw unto
our side,
Not knowing of the cause, make ready
too.
Haste, Diph[ilus]; the time requires it,
haste!— *Exit Diphilus.*
I hope my cause is just; I know my blood
Tells me it is; and I will credit it.
To take revenge, and lose myself withal,
Were idle, and to scape impossible 290
Without I had the fort, which (misery!)
Remaining in the hands of my old en-
emy,
Calianax—but I must have it. See

Enter Calianax.

Where he comes shaking by me!—Good
my lord,
Forget your spleen to me. I never
wronged you,
But would have peace with every man.

CAL. 'Tis well.
If I durst fight, your tongue would lie
at quiet.

MEL. Y' are touchy without all cause.

CAL. Do, mock me.

[1] At once.

MEL. By mine honor, I speak truth.

CAL. Honor? Where is 't?

MEL. See, what starts you make 300
Into your hatred, to my love
And freedom to you. I come with resolu-
tion
To obtain a suit of you.

CAL. A suit of me!
'Tis very like it should be granted, sir.

MEL. Nay, go not hence.
'Tis this: you have the keeping of the
fort,
And I would wish you, by the love you
ought
To bear unto me, to deliver it
Into my hands.

CAL. I am in hope thou art mad,
To talk to me thus.

MEL. But there is a reason 310
To move you to it: I would kill the king
That wronged you and your daughter.

CAL. Out, traitor!

MEL. Nay, but stay; I cannot scape, the
deed once done,
Without I have this fort.

CAL. And should I help thee?
Now thy treacherous mind betrays itself.

MEL. Come, delay me not.
Give me a sudden answer, or already
Thy last is spoke! Refuse not offered
love 318
When it comes clad in secrets.

CAL. [*Aside.*] If I say
I will not, he will kill me; I do see 't
Writ in his looks; and should I say I will,
He'll run and tell the king.—I do not
shun
Your friendship, dear Melantius; but
this cause
Is weighty. Give me but an hour to
think.

MEL. Take it.—[*Aside.*] I know this goes
unto the king;
But I am armed. *Exit Melantius.*

CAL. Methinks I feel myself
But twenty now again. This fighting
fool 327
Wants policy; I shall revenge my girl,
And make her red [2] again. I pray my legs
Will last that pace that I will carry them;
I shall want breath before I find the
king. *Exit.*

[2] *I.e.*, healthy.

Actus IV. [Scena i.

Evadne's apartment.]

Enter Melantius, Evadne, and Ladies.[1]

MEL. Save you!

EVAD.   Save you, sweet brother.

MEL. In my blunt eye, methinks, you
look [2] Evadne.

EVAD. Come, you would make me blush.

MEL.   I would, Evadne;
I shall displease my ends else.

EVAD.   You shall, if you
Commend [3] me; I am bashful.   Come,
sir, how do
I look?

MEL.   I would not have your women
hear me
Break into commendations of you; 'tis
not
Seemly.

EVAD. [*To Ladies.*]   Go wait me in
the gallery.—
Now speak.

MEL.   I'll lock the door first.
                              Exeunt Ladies.

EVAD.   Why?

MEL. I will not have your gilded things,
that dance   10
In visitation with their Milan skins,[4]
Choke up my business.

EVAD.   You are strangely disposed, sir.

MEL. Good madam, not to make you
merry.

EVAD. No; if you praise me, 'twill make
me sad.

MEL. Such a sad commendations I have
for you.

EVAD. Brother,
The court hath made you witty, and
learn to riddle.

MEL. I praise the court for 't; has it learned
you nothing?

EVAD. Me?

MEL.   Ay, Evadne; thou art young
and handsome,
A lady of a sweet complexion,   20
And such a flowing carriage that it can-
not
Choose but inflame a kingdom.

EVAD.   Gentle brother!

MEL. 'Tis yet in thy repentance, foolish
woman,
To make me gentle.

EVAD.   How is this?

MEL.   'Tis base;
And I could blush, at these years,
through all
My honored scars, to come to such a
parley.

EVAD. I understand you not.

MEL.   You dare not, fool!
They that commit thy faults fly the
remembrance.

EVAD. My faults, sir! I would have you
know I care not
If they were written here, here in my
forehead.   30

MEL. Thy body is too little for the story,
The lusts of which would fill another
woman,[5]
Though she had twins within her.

EVAD.   This is saucy.
Look you intrude no more!   There's
your way.

MEL. Thou art my way, and I will tread
upon thee
Till I find truth out.

EVAD.   What truth is that you look for?

MEL. Thy long-lost honor.   Would the
gods had set me
Rather to grapple with the plague, or
stand [6]
One of their loudest bolts!   Come, tell
me quickly,   39
Do it without enforcement, and take heed
You swell me not above my temper.

EVAD.   How, sir?
Where got you this report?

MEL.   Where there was people,
In every place.

EVAD.   They and the seconds of it
Are base people.   Believe them not;
they lied.

MEL. Do not play with mine anger; do
not, wretch!   [*Seizes her.*]
I come to know that desperate fool that
drew thee
From thy fair life.   Be wise, and lay him
open.

EVAD. Unhand me, and learn manners!
Such another
Forgetfulness forfeits your life.

[1] Original has *a Lady.*   [4] Gloves.
[2] *I.e.*, look like.
[3] Theobald's emendation for *Command.*

[5] The account of whose lusts would cover the
body of another woman.   [6] Withstand.

MEL. Quench me this mighty humor, and
  then tell me   50
  Whose whore you are; for you are one,
    I know it.
  Let all mine honors perish but I'll find
    him,
  Though he lie locked up in thy blood!
    Be sudden;
  There is no facing it;[1] and be not flattered.
  The burnt air, when the Dog reigns, is
    not fouler
  Than thy contagious name, till thy re-
    pentance
  (If the gods grant thee any) purge thy
    sickness.
EVAD. Begone! You are my brother;
    that's your safety.
MEL. I'll be a wolf first. 'Tis, to be thy
    brother,
  An infamy below the sin of coward. 60
  I am as far from being part of thee
  As thou art from thy virtue. Seek a
    kindred
  Mongst sensual beasts, and make a goat
    thy brother;
  A goat is cooler. Will you tell me yet?
EVAD. If you stay here and rail thus, I
    shall tell you
  I'll ha' you whipped! Get you to your
    command,
  And there preach to your sentinels, and
    tell them
  What a brave man you are. I shall laugh
    at you.
MEL. Y' are grown a glorious[2] whore!
    Where be your fighters?
  What mortal fool durst raise thee to
    this daring,   70
  And I alive! By my just sword, h'ad safer
  Bestride a billow when the angry North
  Plows up the sea, or made heaven's fire
    his food!
  Work me no higher. Will you discover
    yet?
EVAD. The fellow's mad. Sleep, and speak
    sense.
MEL. Force my swoln heart no further;
    I would save thee.
  Your great maintainers are not here—
    they dare not.
  Would they were all, and armed! I
    would speak loud;

Here's one should thunder to 'em! Will
    you tell me?
  Thou hast no hope to scape. He that
    dares most,   80
  And damns away his soul to do thee serv-
    ice,
  Will sooner snatch meat from a hungry
    lion
  Than come to rescue thee. Thou hast
    death about thee—
  Has undone thine honor, poisoned thy
    virtue,
  And, of a lovely rose, left thee a canker.[3]
EVAD. Let me consider.
MEL.   Do, whose child thou wert,
  Whose honor thou hast murdered, whose
    grave opened,
  And so pulled on[4] the gods that in their
    justice
  They must restore him flesh again and
    life,
  And raise his dry bones to revenge this
    scandal.   90
EVAD. The gods are not of my mind; they
    had better
  Let 'em lie sweet still in the earth; they'll
    stink here.
MEL. Do you raise mirth out of my easi-
    ness?
  Forsake me, then, all weaknesses of
    nature
  That make men women! [Draws his
    sword.] Speak, you whore, speak truth,
  Or, by the dear soul of thy sleeping
    father,
  This sword shall be thy lover! Tell,
    or I'll kill thee;
  And, when thou hast told all, thou wilt
    deserve it.
EVAD. You will not murther me?   99
MEL. No; 'tis a justice, and a noble one,
  To put the light out of such base of-
    fenders.
EVAD. Help!
MEL. By thy foul self, no human help
    shall help thee,
  If thou criest! When I have killed thee,
    as I
  Have vowed to do, if thou confess not,
    naked
  As thou hast left thine honor will I
    leave thee,

---

[1] I.e., there is nothing to be gained by main-
taining a false appearance.   [2] Boasting.

[3] Dog-rose; also a disease of plants.
[4] Provoked.

That on thy branded flesh the world
    may read
Thy black shame and my justice. Wilt
    thou bend yet?
EVAD. Yes.
MEL. Up, and begin your story.   110
EVAD. O, I am miserable!
MEL. 'Tis true, thou art. Speak truth
    still.
EVAD. I have offended; noble sir, forgive
    me!
MEL. With what secure [1] slave?
EVAD.   Do not ask me, sir;
    Mine own remembrance is a misery
    Too mighty for me.
MEL.   Do not fall back again;
    My sword's unsheathéd yet.
EVAD.   What shall I do?
MEL. Be true, and make your fault less.
EVAD.   I dare not tell.
MEL. Tell, or I'll be this day a-killing thee.
EVAD. Will you forgive me, then?   120
MEL. Stay; I must ask mine honor first.
    I have too much foolish nature in me.
    Speak.
EVAD. Is there none else here?
MEL. None but a fearful conscience;
    that's too many.
    Who is 't?
EVAD.   O, hear me gently! It was
    the king.
MEL. No more! My worthy father's and
    my services
    Are liberally rewarded! King, I thank
    thee!
    For all my dangers and my wounds thou
    hast paid me
    In my own metal: these are soldiers'
    thanks!—
    How long have you lived thus, Evadne?
EVAD.   Too long. 130
MEL. Too late you find it. Can you be
    sorry?
EVAD. Would I were half as blameless!
MEL. Evadne, thou wilt to thy trade
    again.
EVAD. First to my grave.
MEL.   Would gods thou
    hadst been so blessed!
    Dost thou not hate this king now?
    Prithee, hate him.
    Couldst thou not curse him? I com-
    mand thee, curse him;

[1] Overconfident.

Curse till the gods hear, and deliver
    him
To thy just wishes. Yet I fear, Evadne,
You had rather play your game out.
EVAD.   No; I feel
Too many sad confusions here, to let
    in   140
Any loose flame hereafter.
MEL. Dost thou not feel, amongst all
    those, one brave anger
    That breaks out nobly, and directs
    thine arm
    To kill this base king?
EVAD.   All the gods forbid it!
MEL. No, all the gods require it;
    They are dishonored in him.
EVAD.   'Tis too fearful.
MEL. Y' are valiant in his bed, and bold
    enough
    To be a stale whore, and have your
    madam's name
    Discourse for grooms and pages, and
    hereafter,
    When his cool majesty hath laid you
    by,   150
    To be at pension with some needy sir
    For meat and coarser clothes; thus far
    you know
    No fear. Come, you shall kill him.
EVAD.   Good sir!
MEL. An 'twere to kiss him dead, thou'dst
    smother him.
    Be wise, and kill him. Canst thou live,
    and know
    What noble minds shall make thee,
    see thyself
    Found out with every finger, made the
    shame
    Of all successions, and in this great
    ruin
    Thy brother and thy noble husband
    broken?
    Thou shalt not live thus. Kneel, and
    swear to help me,   160
    When I shall call thee to it; or, by
    all
    Holy in heaven and earth, thou shalt
    not live
    To breathe a full hour longer; not a
    thought!
    Come, 'tis a righteous oath. Give me
    thy hand[s],
    And, both to heaven held up, swear, by
    that wealth

This lustful thief stole from thee, when
I say it,
To let his foul soul out.

EVAD. 　　　　　　Here I swear it;
And, all you spirits of abuséd ladies,
Help me in this performance!

MEL. Enough.　This must be known to
none　　　　　　　　　　　　170
But you and I, Evadne—not to your
lord,
Though he be wise and noble, and a
fellow
Dares step as far into a worthy action
As the most daring, ay, as far as justice.
Ask me not why.　Farewell!

　　　　　　　　　Exit Mel[antius].

EVAD. Would I could say so to my black
disgrace!
O, where have I been all this time?
How friended,
That I should lose myself thus desper-
ately,
And none for pity show me how I
wandered?　　　　　　　　179
There is not in the compass of the light
A more unhappy creature; sure, I am
monstrous,
For I have done those follies, those mad
mischiefs,
Would dare [1] a woman.　O, my loaden
soul,
Be not so cruel to me; choke not up
The way to my repentance!—

　　　　　　Enter Amintor.

　　　　　　　　　　O, my lord!

AMIN. How now?

EVAD.　My much abuséd lord! [*Kneels.*]

AMIN.　　　　　　This cannot be!

EVAD. I do not kneel to live; I dare not
hope it.
The wrongs I did are greater.　Look
upon me,
Though I appear with all my faults.

AMIN.　　　　　　Stand up!　189
This is no new way to beget more sorrow!
Heaven knows I have too many.　Do
not mock me;
Though I am tame, and bred up with
my wrongs,
Which are my foster-brothers, I may
leap,

[1] Frighten.

Like a hand-wolf,[2] into my natural
wildness,
And do an outrage.　Prithee, do not
mock me.

EVAD. My whole life is so leprous, it
infects
All my repentance.　I would buy your
pardon,
Though at the highest set,[3] even with
my life,
That slight contrition—that's [4] no sacrifice
For what I have committed.

AMIN.　　　　　Sure, I dazzle;　200
There cannot be a faith in that foul
woman,
That knows no god more mighty than
her mischiefs.
Thou dost still worse, still number on
thy faults,
To press my poor heart thus.　Can I
believe
There's any seed of virtue in that woman
Left to shoot up, that dares go on in
sin
Known, and so known as thine is?　O,
Evadne!
Would there were any safety [5] in thy
sex
That I might put a thousand sorrows
off,
And credit thy repentance!　But I must
not.　　　　　　　　　210
Thou hast brought me to that dull
calamity,
To that strange misbelief of all the world
And all things that are in it, that I
fear
I shall fall like a tree, and find my grave,
Only rememb'ring that I grieve.

EVAD.　　　　　　　My lord,
Give me your griefs.　You are an inno-
cent,
A soul as white as heaven.　Let not my
sins
Perish [6] your noble youth.　I do not fall
here
To shadow by dissembling with my
tears　　　　　　　　　　219
(As all say women can) or to make less

[2] Hand-raised, tamed wolf.
[3] Stake.
[4] From 1630 edn.　Original reads *that*.
[5] Trustworthiness.　　　　　[6] Destroy.

What my hot will hath done, which
    heaven and you
Knows to be tougher than the hand of
    time
Can cut from man's remembrance. No,
    I do not.
I do appear the same, the same Evadne,
Dressed in the shames I lived in, the
    same monster.
But these are names of honor to what
    I am;
I do present myself the foulest creature,
Most poisonous, dangerous, and de-
    spised of men,
Lerna e'er bred or Nilus. I am hell,
Till you, my dear lord, shoot your light
    into me,   230
The beams of your forgiveness; I am
    soul-sick,
And wither with the fear of one con-
    demned,
Till I have got your pardon.
AMIN.   Rise, Evadne!
    Those heavenly powers that put this
        good into thee
Grant a continuance of it! I forgive thee.
Make thyself worthy of it, and take
    heed,
Take heed, Evadne, this be serious.
Mock not the powers above, that can
    and dare
Give thee a great example of their jus-
    tice
To all ensuing eyes, if thou play'st   240
With thy repentance, the best sacrifice.
EVAD. I have done nothing good to win
    belief,
My life hath been so faithless. All the
    creatures,
Made for heaven's honors, have their
    ends, and good ones,
All but the cozening crocodiles, false
    women.
They reign here like those plagues, those
    killing sores,
Men pray against; and, when they die,
    like tales
Ill told and unbelieved, they pass away,
And go to dust forgotten. But, my
    lord,
Those short days I shall number to my
    rest   250
(As many must not see me), shall—
    though too late.

Though in my evening—yet perceive
    a will
(Since I can do no good, because a
    woman)
Reach constantly at something that is
    near it.
I will redeem one minute of my age,
Or, like another Niobe, I'll weep
Till I am water.
AMIN.   I am now dissolved.
My frozen soul melts. May each sin
    thou hast,
Find a new mercy! Rise; I am at
    peace.
Hadst thou been thus, thus excellently
    good   260
Before that devil-king tempted thy
    frailty,
Sure thou hadst made a star. Give me
    thy hand;
From this time I will know thee; and,
    as far
As honor gives me leave, be thy Amintor.
When we meet next, I will salute thee
    fairly,
And pray the gods to give thee happy
    days.
My charity shall go along with thee,
Though my embraces must be far from
    thee.
I should ha' killed thee, but this sweet
    repentance
Locks up my vengeance, for which thus
    I kiss thee—   270
The last kiss we must take—and would
    to heaven
The holy priest that gave our hands to-
    gether
Had given us equal virtues! Go,
    Evadne;
The gods thus part our bodies. Have a
    care
My honor falls no farther. I am well,
    then.
EVAD. All the dear joys here, and above
    hereafter,
Crown thy fair soul! Thus I take leave,
    my lord;
And never shall you see the foul
    Evadne
Till she have tried all honored means
    that may
Set her in rest and wash her stains
    away.   *Exeunt.* 280

[SCENA ii.

A hall in the palace.]

*Banquet. Enter King, Calianax. Hautboys
play within.*

KING. I cannot tell how I should credit
this
From you, that are his enemy.

CAL.   I am sure
He said it to me; and I'll justify it
What way he dares oppose—but with
my sword.

KING. But did he break,[1] without all circumstance,[2]
To you, his foe, that he would have the
fort
To kill me, and then scape?

CAL.   If he deny it,
I'll make him blush.

KING.   It sounds incredibly.

CAL. Ay, so does everything I say of late.

KING. Not so, Calianax.

CAL.   Yes, I should sit   10
Mute, whilst a rogue with strong arms
cuts your throat.

KING. Well, I will try him; and, if this be
true,
I'll pawn my life I'll find it; if 't be false,
And that you clothe your hate in such
a lie,
You shall hereafter dote in your own
house,
Not in the court.

CAL.   Why, if it be a lie,
Mine ears are false, for I'll be sworn I
heard it.
Old men are good for nothing; you were
best
Put me to death for hearing, and free him
For meaning it. You would 'a' trusted
me   20
Once, but the time is altered.

KING.   And will still,
Where I may do with justice to the
world.
You have no witness.

CAL.   Yes, myself.

KING.   No more,
I mean, there were that heard it.

CAL.   How? No more?
Would you have more? Why, am not I
enough
To hang a thousand rogues?

KING   But so you may
Hang honest men too, if you please.

CAL.   I may!
'Tis like I will do so; there are a hun-
dred
Will swear it for a need too, if I say it.

KING. Such witnesses we need not.

CAL.   And 'tis hard   30
If my word cannot hang a boisterous
knave.

KING. Enough.—Where's Strato?

STRA. Sir?

Enter Strat[o].

KING. Why, where's all the company?
Call Amintor in;
Evadne. Where's my brother, and
Melant:us?
Bid him come too; and Diphilus. Call all
That are without there.—(*Exit Strat[o].*)
If he should desire
The combat of you, 'tis not in the power
Of all our laws to hinder it, unless
We mean to quit 'em.

CAL.   Why, if you do think   40
'Tis fit an old man and a councilor
To fight for what he says, then you may
grant it.

*Enter Amint[or], Evad[ne], Melant[ius],
Diph[ilus], Lysip[pus], Cle[on], Stra[to],
Diag[oras].*

KING. Come, sirs!—Amintor, thou art yet
a bridegroom,
And I will use thee so; thou shalt sit
down.—
Evadne, sit; and you, Amintor, too;
This banquet is for you, sir.—Who has
brought
A merry tale about him, to raise laughter
Amongst our wine? Why, Strato, where
art thou?
Thou wilt chop out with them[3] un-
seasonably,
When I desire 'em not.   50

STRA. 'Tis my ill luck, sir, so to spend
them, then.

KING. Reach me a bowl of wine.—
Melantius, thou
Art sad.

MEL.[4] I should be, sir, the merriest here,

---

[1] Impart.   [2] Without any ceremony.
[3] *I.e.*, blurt out tales.
[4] From 1619 edn. Original reads *Amint*.

But I ha' ne'er a story of mine own
Worth telling at this time.
KING.   Give me the wine.—
Melantius, I am now considering
How easy 'twere for any man we trust
To poison one of us in such a bowl.
MEL. I think it were not hard, sir, for a
    knave.
CAL. [*Aside.*] Such as you are.   60
KING. I' faith, 'twere easy. It becomes
    us well
To get plain-dealing men about our-
    selves,
Such as you all are here.—Amintor, to
    thee,
And to thy fair Evadne.   [*Drinks.*]
MEL. (*Aside.*)   Have you thought
Of this, Calianax?
CAL. [*Aside.*]   Yes, marry, have I.
MEL. [*Aside.*] And what's your resolu-
    tion?
CAL. [*Aside.*]   Ye shall have it—
    [*To himself.*] Soundly, I warrant you.
KING. Reach to Amintor, Strato.
AMIN.   Here, my love.
    [*Drinks and hands the cup to Evadne.*]
This wine will do thee wrong, for it will
    set
Blushes upon thy cheeks; and, till thou
    dost   70
A fault, 'twere pity.
KING.   Yet I wonder much
Of [1] the strange desperation of these
    men
That dare attempt such acts here in our
    state.
He could not scape that did it.
MEL.   Were he known,
Unpossible.
KING.   It would be known, Melantius.
MEL. It ought to be. If he got then away,
He must wear all our lives upon his
    sword.
He need not fly the island; he must
    leave
No one alive.
KING.   No; I should think no man
Could kill me, and scape clear, but that
    old man.   80
CAL. But I! Heaven bless me! I! Should
    I, my liege?
KING. I do not think thou wouldst; but
    yet thou mightst,
    [1] At.

For thou hast in thy hands the means
    to scape,
By keeping of the fort.—He has, Melan-
    tius,
And he has kept it well.
MEL.   From cobwebs, sir,
'Tis clean swept; I can find no other
    art
In keeping of it now.   'Twas ne'er be-
    sieged
Since he commanded.
CAL.   I shall be sure
Of your good word; but I have kept it
    safe
From such as you.
MEL.   Keep your ill temper in.   90
I speak no malice; had my brother kept
    it,
I should ha' said as much.
KING.   You are not merry.
Brother, drink wine. Sit you all still!—
    (*Aside.*) Calianax,
I cannot trust thus. I have thrown out
    words
That would have fetched warm blood
    upon the cheeks
Of guilty men, and he is never moved;
He knows no such thing.
CAL.   Impudence may scape,
When feeble virtue is accused.
KING.   A must,
If he were guilty, feel an alteration
At this our whisper, whilst we point
    at him.   100
You see he does not.
CAL.   Let him hang himself.
What care I what he does? This he did
    say.
KING. Melan[tius], you can easily con-
    ceive
What I have meant, for men that are
    in fault
Can subtly apprehend when others aim
At what they do amiss; but I forgive
Freely before this man. Heaven do so
    too!
I will not touch thee, so much as with
    shame
Of telling it.   Let it be so no more.
CAL. Why, this is very fine!
MEL.   I cannot tell   110
What 'tis you mean; but I am apt
    enough
Rudely to thrust into ignorant fault.

But let me know it. Happily [1] 'tis naught
But misconstruction; and, where I am clear,
I will not take forgiveness of the gods,
Much less of you.

KING.   Nay, if you stand so stiff,
I shall call back my mercy.

MEL.   I want smoothness
To thank a man for pardoning of a crime
I never knew.

KING. Not to instruct your knowledge, but to show you   120
My ears are everywhere; you meant to kill me,
And get the fort to scape.

MEL.   Pardon me, sir;
My bluntness will be pardoned. You preserve
A race of idle people here about you,
Eaters and talkers, to defame the worth
Of those that do things worthy. The man that uttered this
Had perished without food, be 't who it will,
But for this arm, that fenced him from the foe;
And, if I thought you gave a faith to this,
The plainness of my nature would speak more.   130
Give me a pardon (for you ought to do 't)
To kill him that spake this.

CAL. [Aside.]   Ay, that will be
The end of all; then I am fairly paid
For all my care and service.

MEL.   That old man,
Who calls me enemy, and of whom I
(Though I will never match my hate so low)
Have no good thought, would yet, I think, excuse me,
And swear he thought me wronged in this.

CAL.   Who, I?
Thou shameless fellow, didst thou not speak to me
Of it thyself?

MEL.   O, then it came from him! 140

CAL. From me! Who should it come from but from me?

MEL. Nay, I believe your malice is enough;

[1] Haply.

But I ha' lost my anger.—Sir, I hope
You are well satisfied.

KING.   Lysip[pus], cheer
Amintor and his lady.—There's no sound
Comes from you; I will come and do 't myself.

AMIN. [Aside.] You have done already, sir, for me, I thank you.

KING. Melantius, I do credit this from him,
How slight soe'er you make 't.

MEL.   'Tis strange you should.

CAL. 'Tis strange a should believe an old man's word   150
That never lied in 's life!

MEL.   I talk not to thee.—
Shall the wild words of this distempered man,
Frantic with age and sorrow, make a breach
Betwixt your majesty and me? 'Twas wrong
To hearken to him; but to credit him,
As much at least as I have power to bear—
But pardon me—whilst I speak only truth,
I may commend myself—I have bestowed
My careless blood with you, and should be loath
To think an action that would make me lose   160
That and my thanks too. When I was a boy,
I thrust myself into my country's cause,
And did a deed that plucked five years from time,
And styled me man then. And for you, my king,
Your subjects all have fed by virtue of
My arm. This sword of mine hath plowed the ground,
And reaped the fruit in peace;
And you yourself have lived at home in ease.
So terrible I grew that, without swords,
My name hath fetched you conquest; and my heart   170
And limbs are still the same; my will as great
To do you service. Let me not be paid
With such a strange distrust.

KING.   Melant[ius],
I held it great injustice to believe
Thine enemy, and did not; if I did,
I do not; let that satisfy.—What, struck
With sadness,[1] all? More wine!
CAL.   A few fine words
Have overthrown my truth. Ah, thou'rt
a villain!
MEL. (*Aside.*) Why, thou wert better
let me have the fort.
Dotard, I will disgrace thee thus for-
ever.   180
There shall no credit lie upon thy words.
Think better, and deliver it.
CAL.   My liege,
He's at me now again to do it.—Speak!
Deny it, if thou canst.—Examine him
Whilst he is hot, for, if he cool again,
He will forswear it.
KING.   This is lunacy,
I hope, Melantius.
MEL.   He hath lost himself
Much, since his daughter missed the
happiness
My sister gained; and, though he call
me foe,
I pity him.
CAL.   A pity! A pox upon you!   190
MEL. Mark his disordered words; and
at the masque
Diagoras knows he raged and railed
at me,
And called a lady "whore," so innocent
She understood him not. But it be-
comes
Both you and me too to forgive dis-
traction.[2]
Pardon him, as I do.
CAL.   I'll not speak for thee,
For all thy cunning.—If you will be
safe,
Chop off his head, for there was never
known
So impudent a rascal.
KING.   Some that love him
Get him to bed. Why, pity should not
let   200
Age make itself contemptible; we must
be
All old. Have him away.
MEL. [*Aside.*]   Calianax,
The king believes you. Come, you shall
go home,

And rest; you ha' done well. You'll
give it up,
When I have used you thus a month,
I hope.
CAL. Now, now, 'tis plain, sir; he does
move me still.
He says he knows I'll give him up the
fort,
When he has used me thus a month. I
am mad,
Am I not, still?
OMNES. Ha, ha, ha!   210
CAL. I shall be mad indeed, if you do
thus.
Why should you trust a sturdy fellow
there
(That has no virtue in him; all's in his
sword)
Before me? Do but take his weapons
from him,
And he's an ass; and I am a very fool,
Both with him and without him, as you
use me.
OMNES. Ha, ha, ha!
KING. 'Tis well, Cal[ianax]; but, if you
use
This once again, I shall entreat some
other
To see your offices be well discharged.—
Be merry, gentlemen.—It grows some-
what late.—   221
Amintor, thou wouldst be abed again.
AMIN. Yes, sir.
KING.   And you, Evadne.—Let me take
Thee in my arms, Melantius, and be-
lieve
Thou art, as thou deservest to be, my
friend
Still and forever.—Good Cal[ianax],
Sleep soundly; it will bring thee to
thyself.
Exeunt omnes.   Manent [3] *Mel[antius] and*
Cal[ianax].
CAL. Sleep soundly! I sleep soundly now,
I hope;
I could not be thus else.—How dar'st
thou stay
Alone with me, knowing how thou hast
used me?   230
MEL. You cannot blast me with your
tongue, and that's
The strongest part you have about you.
CAL.   I

Do look for some great punishment for
this,
For I begin to forget all my hate,
And take 't unkindly that mine enemy
Should use me so extraordinarily scur-
vily.
MEL. I shall melt too, if you begin to take
Unkindnesses; I never meant you hurt.
CAL. Thou'lt anger me again. Thou
wretched rogue,
"Meant me no hurt"! Disgrace me with
the king!   240
Lose all my offices! This is no hurt,
Is it? I prithee, what dost thou call
hurt?
MEL. To poison men, because they love
me not;
To call the credit of men's wives in ques-
tion;
To murder children betwixt me and
land—
This I call hurt.
CAL.   All this thou think'st is sport;
For mine is worse. But use thy will
with me;
For betwixt grief and anger I could cry.
MEL. Be wise, then, and be safe; thou
mayst revenge—
CAL. Ay, o' th' king! I would revenge of
thee.   250
MEL. That you must plot yourself.
CAL.   I'm a fine plotter.
MEL. The short is, I will hold thee with
the king
In this perplexity, till peevishness
And thy disgrace have laid thee in thy
grave.
But, if thou wilt deliver up the fort,
I'll take thy trembling body in my arms,
And bear thee over dangers. Thou
shalt hold
Thy wonted state.
CAL.   If I should tell the king,
Canst thou deny 't again?
MEL.   Try, and believe.
CAL. Nay, then, thou canst bring any-
thing about.   260
Thou shalt have the fort.
MEL. Why, well.
Here let our hate be buried; and this
hand
Shall right us both. Give me thy aged
breast
To compass.

CAL.   Nay, I do not love thee yet;
I cannot well endure to look on thee;
And, if I thought it were a courtesy,
Thou shouldst not have it. But I am
disgraced;
My offices are to be ta'en away;
And, if I did but hold this fort a day,
I do believe the king would take it from
me,   271
And give it thee, things are so strangely
carried.
Ne'er thank me for 't; but yet the king
shall know
There was some such thing in 't I told
him of,
And that I was an honest man.
MEL.   He'll buy
That knowledge very dearly.—

Enter Diphilus.

Diph[ilus],
What news with thee?
DIPH.   This were a night indeed
To do it in; the king hath sent for her.
MEL. She shall perform it then.—Go,
Diph[ilus],
And take from this good man, my
worthy friend,   280
The fort; he'll give it thee.
DIPH.   Ha' you got that?
CAL. Art thou of the same breed? Canst
thou deny
This to the king too?
DIPH.   With a confidence
As great as his.
CAL. Faith, like enough.
MEL. Away, and use him kindly.
CAL.   Touch not me;
I hate the whole strain. If thou follow
me
A great way off, I'll give thee up the
fort—
And hang yourselves!
MEL.   Begone.
DIPH.   He's finely wrought.[1]
Exeunt Cal[ianax], Diph[ilus].
MEL. This is a night, spite of astrono-
mers,[2]   290
To do the deed in. I will wash the stain
That rests upon our house off with his
blood.

[1] Wrought up, excited.
[2] Astrologers.

Enter Amintor.

AMIN. Melantius, now assist me. If thou
beest
 That which thou say'st, assist me. I
 have lost
 All my distempers, and have found a
 rage
 So pleasing! Help me.
MEL. [*Aside.*]   Who can see him thus,
 And not swear vengeance?—What's
 the matter, friend?
AMIN. Out with thy sword; and, hand in
 hand with me,
 Rush to the chamber of this hated king,
 And sink him with the weight of all his
 sins   300
 To hell forever.
MEL.   'Twere a rash attempt,
 Not to be done with safety. Let your
 reason
 Plot your revenge, and not your passion.
AMIN. If thou refusest me in these ex-
 tremes,
 Thou art no friend. He sent for her to
 me;
 By heaven, to me, myself! And, I must
 tell ye,
 I love her as a stranger; there is worth
 In that vild woman, worthy things,
 Melantius;
 And she repents. I'll do 't myself alone,
 Though I be slain. Farewell.
MEL. [*Aside.*]   He'll overthrow   310
 My whole design with madness.—
 Amintor,
 Think what thou doest. I dare as much
 as valor,
 But 'tis the king, the king, the king,
 Amintor,
 With whom thou fightest!—(*Aside.*) I
 know he's honest,[1]
 And this will work with him.
AMIN.   I cannot tell
 What thou hast said; but thou hast
 charmed my sword
 Out of my hand, and left me shaking
 here,
 Defenseless.
MEL.   I will take it up for thee.
AMIN. What a wild beast is uncollected [2]
 man!

[1] Loyal.
[2] Not self-controlled.

The thing that we call honor bears us all
Headlong unto sin, and yet itself is
 nothing.   321
MEL. Alas, how variable are thy thoughts!
AMIN. Just like my fortunes. I was run
 to [3] that
 I purposed to have chid thee for. Some
 plot
 I did distrust thou hadst against the
 king,
 By that old fellow's carriage. But take
 heed;
 There's not the least limb growing to
 a king
 But carries thunder in 't.
MEL.   I have none
 Against him.
AMIN.   Why, come, then; and still
 remember
 We may not think revenge.
MEL.   I will remember. *Exeunt.*   330

ACTUS V. [SCENA i.

An anteroom opening upon the king's bed-
 chamber curtained off on the inner
 stage.]
Enter Evadne and a Gentleman [of the bed-
 chamber].

EVAD. Sir, is the king abed?
GENT.   Madam, an hour ago.
EVAD. Give me the key, then, and let
 none be near;
 'Tis the king's pleasure.
GENT. I understand you, madam; would
 'twere mine!
 I must not wish good rest unto your
 ladyship.
EVAD. You talk, you talk.
GENT. 'Tis all I dare do, madam; but
 the king
 Will wake, and then—
EVAD. Saving your imagination, pray,
 good night, sir.
GENT. A good night be it, then, and a
 long one, madam.   10
 I am gone.   *Exit.*
EVAD. The night grows horrible, and all
 about me
 Like my black purpose. O, the con-
 science   *King abed.*
 Of a lost virgin, whither wilt thou pull
 me?

[3] *I.e.*, just on the point of doing.

To what things dismal as the depth of
hell
Wilt thou provoke me? Let no woman
dare
From this hour be disloyal, if her heart
be flesh,
If she have blood, and can fear. 'Tis a
daring
Above that desperate fool's that left
his peace,
And went to sea to fight; 'tis so many
sins,   20
An age cannot prevent [1] 'em, and so
great
The gods want mercy for. Yet I must
through 'em.
I have begun a slaughter on my honor,
And I must end it there.—A sleeps.
Good heavens!
Why give you peace to this untemperate
beast,
That hath so long transgressed you?
I must kill him,
And I will do 't bravely; the mere joy
Tells me, I merit in it. Yet I must not
Thus tamely do it as he sleeps—that
were
To rock him to another world. My
vengeance   30
Shall take him waking, and then lay be-
fore him
The number of his wrongs and punish-
ments.
I'll shape his sins like Furies, till I
waken
His evil angel, his sick conscience,
And then I'll strike him dead.—King,
by your leave!—

Ties his arms to the bed.

I dare not trust your strength; your
grace and I
Must grapple upon even terms no more.
So, if he rail me not from my resolu-
tion,
I shall be strong enough.—My lord the
king!
My lord!—A sleeps, as if he meant to
wake   40
No more.—My lord!—Is he not dead
already?—
Sir! My lord!
KING. Who's that?
EVAD. O, you sleep soundly, sir!

[1] Recount (?). 1619 edn. has *repent*.

KING.   My dear Evadne,
I have been dreaming of thee; come to
bed.
EVAD. I am come at length, sir; but how
welcome?
KING. What pretty new device is this,
Evadne?
What, do you tie me to you? By my love,
This is a quaint one. Come, my dear,
and kiss me.
I'll be thy Mars; to bed, my Queen of
Love.   50
Let us be caught together, that the
gods
May see and envy our embraces.
EVAD.   Stay, sir, stay;
You are too hot, and I have brought
you physic
To temper your high veins.
KING. Prithee, to bed then; let me take
it warm.
There thou shalt know the state of my
body better.
EVAD. I know you have a surfeited, foul
body,
And you must bleed. [*Draws a knife.*]
KING. Bleed!
EVAD. Ay, you shall bleed. Lie still; and,
if the devil,   60
Your lust, will give you leave, repent.
This steel
Comes to redeem the honor that you
stole,
King, my fair name, which nothing but
thy death
Can answer to the world.
KING.   How's this, Evadne?
EVAD. I am not she; nor bear I in this
breast
So much cold spirit to be called a woman.
I am a tiger; I am anything
That knows not pity. Stir not! If thou
dost,
I'll take thee unprepared, thy fears
upon thee,
That make thy sins look double, and
so send thee   70
(By my revenge, I will!) to look [2] those
torments
Prepared for such black souls.
KING. Thou dost not mean this; 'tis im-
possible.
Thou art too sweet and gentle.

[2] Behold.

EVAD.   No, I am not;
I am as foul as thou art, and can number
As many such hells here. I was once
    fair;
Once I was lovely, not a blowing rose
More chastely sweet, till thou, thou,
    thou, foul canker
(Stir not!), didst poison me. I was a
    world of virtue,
Till your cursed court and you (hell
    bless you for 't!)   80
With your temptations on temptations
Made me give up mine honor, for which,
    king,
I am come to kill thee.
KING.   No!
EVAD.   I am.
KING.   Thou art not!
I prithee, speak not these things. Thou
    art gentle,
And wert not meant thus rugged.
EVAD.   Peace, and hear me.
Stir nothing but your tongue, and that
    for mercy
To those above us, by whose lights I vow,
Those blessed fires [1] that shot to see
    our sin,
If thy hot soul had substance with thy
    blood,
I would kill that too; which, being past
    my steel,   90
My tongue shall reach. Thou art a
    shameless villain,
A thing out of the overcharge of nature,
Sent like a thick cloud to disperse a
    plague
Upon weak, catching [2] women—such
    a tyrant
That for his lust would sell away his
    subjects,
Ay, all his heaven hereafter!
KING.   Hear, Evadne,
Thou soul of sweetness, hear! I am thy
    king.
EVAD. Thou art my shame! Lie still;
    there's none about you,
Within your cries; all promises of safety
Are but deluding dreams. Thus, thus,
    thou foul man,   100
Thus I begin my vengeance! *Stabs him.*
KING.   Hold, Evadne!
I do command thee hold.
EVAD.   I do not mean, sir,

To part so fairly with you; we must
    change
More of these love tricks yet.
KING.   What bloody villain
Provoked thee to this murther?
EVAD.   Thou, thou monster!
KING. O!
EVAD. Thou kept'st me brave [3] at court,
    and whored me, king;
Then married me to a young, noble
    gentleman,
And whored me still.
KING.   Evadne, pity me!
EVAD. Hell take me, then! This for my
    lord, Amintor!   110
This for my noble brother! And this
    stroke
For the most wronged of women!
                            Kills him.
KING.   O, I die!
EVAD. Die all our faults together! I for-
    give thee.   *Exit.* [4]

Enter Two of the bedchamber.

1. Come, now she's gone, let's enter;
the king expects it, and will be angry.
2. 'Tis a fine wench; we'll have a snap
at her one of these nights, as she goes from
him.
1. Content. How quickly he had done
with her! I see kings can do no more   [120
that way than other mortal people.
2. How fast [5] he is! I cannot hear him
    breathe.
1. Either the tapers give a feeble light,
Or he looks very pale.
2.   And so he does.
Pray heaven he be well; let's look.—
    Alas!
He's stiff, wounded, and dead! Treason,
    treason!
1. Run forth and call! *Exit [2] Gent[leman].*
2. Treason, treason!
1.   This will be laid on us.
Who can believe a woman could do this?

Enter Cleon and Lysippus.

CLE. How now! Where's the traitor?
1. Fled, fled away; but there her woeful
    act   131
Lies still.

---

[1] Shooting stars.   [2] Easily infected.
[3] Well-dressed.   [5] Fast asleep.
[4] Original reads *Exeunt.*

CLE. Her act! A woman!

LYS. Where's the body?

1. There.

LYS. Farewell, thou worthy man! There
were two bonds
 That tied our loves, a brother and a
  king,
 The least of which might fetch a flood
  of tears;
 But such the misery of greatness is,
 They have no time to mourn. Then,
  pardon me!
 Sirs, which way went she?

Enter Strato.

STRA. Never follow her,
 For she, alas, was but the instrument.
 News is now brought in that Melantius
 Has got the fort, and stands upon the
  wall, 142
 And with a loud voice calls those few
  that pass
 At this dead time of night, delivering
 The innocence of this act.

LYS. Gentlemen,
 I am your king.

STRA. We do acknowledge it.

LYS. I would I were not! Follow, all;
 for this
 Must have a sudden stop. *Exeunt.*

[SCENA ii.

Before the fort.]

*Enter Melant[ius], Diph[ilus], Cal[ianax] on
the walls.*

MEL. If the dull people can believe I am
 armed
 (Be constant, Diph[ilus]), now we have
  time
 Either to bring our banished honors
  home,
 Or create new ones in our ends.

DIPH. I fear not;
 My spirit lies not that way.—Courage,
  Calianax!

CAL. Would I had any! You should
 quickly know it.

MEL. Speak to the people; thou art eloquent.

CAL. 'Tis a fine eloquence to come to the
 gallows.
 You were born to be my end; the devil
 take you!

Now must I hang for company? 'Tis
 strange 10
I should be old, and neither wise nor
 valiant.

*Enter Lysip[pus], Diag[oras], Cleon, Strat[o],
Guard.*

LYS. See where he stands, as boldly confident
 As if he had his full command about
  him.

STRA. He looks as if he had the better
 cause, sir;
 Under your gracious pardon, let me
  speak it!
 Though he be mighty-spirited, and for-
  ward
 To all great things, to all things of that
  danger
 Worse men shake at the telling of, yet
  certainly
 I do believe him noble, and this action
 Rather pulled on than sought. His
  mind was ever 20
 As worthy as his hand.

LYS. 'Tis my fear, too.
 Heaven forgive all!—Summon him,
  Lord Cleon.

CLE. Ho, from the walls there!

MEL. Worthy Cleon, welcome.
 We could 'a' wished you here, lord;
  you are honest.

CAL. (*Aside.*) Well, thou art as flattering a knave, though
 I dare not tell thee so—

LYS. Melantius!

MEL. Sir?

LYS. I am sorry that we meet thus; our
 old love
 Never required such distance. Pray
  heaven,
 You have not left yourself, and sought
  this safety
 More out of fear than honor! You have
  lost 30
 A noble master, which your faith, Melantius,
 Some think might have preserved; yet
  you know best.

CAL. [*Aside.*] When time was,[1] I was mad;
 some that dares fight
 I hope will pay this rascal.

[1] Once upon a time.

MEL. Royal young man, those tears look
    lovely on thee;
Had they been shed for a deserving one,
They had been lasting monuments. Thy
    brother,
Whilst he was good, I called him king,
    and served him
With that strong faith, that most un-
    wearied valor,
Pulled people from the farthest sun to
    seek him,   40
And buy his friendship. I was then his
    soldier.
But, since his hot pride drew him to
    disgrace me,
And brand my noble actions with his
    lust
(That never-cured dishonor of my sister,
Base stain of whore, and, which is worse,
    the joy
To make it still so), like myself, thus I
Have flung him off with my allegiance,
And stand here, mine own justice, to
    revenge
What I have suffered in him, and this
    old man
Wronged almost to lunacy.
CAL.   Who, I? 50
You would draw me in. I have had no
    wrong;
I do disclaim ye all.
MEL.   The short is this:
'Tis no ambition to lift up myself
Urgeth me thus; I do desire again
To be a subject, so I may be free.
If not, I know my strength, and will
    unbuild
This goodly town. Be speedy, and be
    wise,
In a reply.
STRA.   Be sudden, sir, to tie
All up again. What's done is past re-
    call,
And past you to revenge; and there are
    thousands 60
That wait for such a troubled hour as
    this.
Throw him the blank.
LYS.   Melantius, write in that
Thy choice; my seal is at it.
    [*Throws a paper to Melantius.*]
MEL. It was our honors drew us to this act,
    Not gain; and we will only work our
    pardons.

CAL. Put my name in too.
DIPH.   You disclaimed us all
    But now, Calianax.
CAL.   That's all one.
I'll not be hanged hereafter by a trick;
    I'll have it in.
MEL.   You shall, you shall.—
Come to the back gate, and we'll call
    you king, 70
And give you up the fort.
LYS.   Away, away!   *Exeunt omnes.*

[SCENA iii.

An anteroom to Amintor's apartment.]

Enter Aspatia in man's apparel [*and with
her face disguised with counterfeit scars*].

ASP. This is my fatal hour. Heaven
    may forgive
My rash attempt, that causelessly hath
    laid
Griefs on me that will never let me rest,
And put a woman's heart into my
    breast.
It is more honor for you that I die,
For she that can endure the misery
That I have on me, and be patient
    too,
May live and laugh at all that you can
    do.—

Enter Servant.

God save you, sir!
SER.   And you, sir! What's your
    business?
ASP. With you, sir, now; to do me the
    fair office 10
To help me to your lord.
SER.   What, would you serve him?
ASP. I'll do him any service; but, to haste,
For my affairs are earnest, I desire
To speak with him.
SER. Sir, because you are in such haste,
    I would
Be loath to delay you longer. You can
    not.
ASP. It shall become you, though, to tell
    your lord.
SER. Sir, he will speak with nobody.
ASP.   This is most strange.
Art thou gold-proof? There's for thee;
    help me to him.   [*Gives money.*]
SER. Pray be not angry, sir; I'll do my
    best.   *Exit.* 20

Asp. How stubbornly this fellow answered me!
There is a vild, dishonest trick in man,
More than in women. All the men I meet
Appear thus to me, are harsh and rude,
And have a subtilty in everything,
Which love could never know; but we fond women
Harbor the easiest and the smoothest thoughts,
And think all shall go so. It is unjust
That men and women should be matched together.

Enter Amintor and his Man.

Amin. Where is he?
Ser.   There, my lord.
Amin.   What would you, sir? 30
Asp. Please it your lordship to command your man
Out of the room, I shall deliver things
Worthy your hearing.
Amin.   Leave us. [*Exit Servant.*]
Asp. (*Aside.*)   O, that that shape
Should bury falsehood in it!
Amin.   Now your will, sir.
Asp. When you know me, my lord, you needs must guess
My business; and I am not hard to know;
For, till the chance of war marked this smooth face
With these few blemishes, people would call me
My sister's picture, and her mine. In short, 39
I am the brother to the wronged Aspatia.
Amin. The wronged Aspatia! Would thou wert so too
Unto the wronged Amintor! Let me kiss
That hand of thine, in honor that I bear
Unto the wronged Aspatia. Here I stand
That did it. Would he could not! Gentle youth,
Leave me, for there is something in thy looks
That calls my sins in a most hideous form
Into my mind; and I have grief enough
Without thy help.

Asp.   I would I could with credit!
Since I was twelve years old, I had not seen 50
My sister till this hour I now arrived;
She sent for me to see her marriage—
A woeful one! But they that are above
Have ends in everything. She used few words,
But yet enough to make me understand
The baseness of the injuries you did her.
That little training I have had is war;
I may behave myself rudely in peace;
I would not, though. I shall not need to tell you
I am but young, and would be loath to lose 60
Honor, that is not easily gained again.
Fairly I mean to deal; the age is strict
For [1] single combats; and we shall be stopped,
If it be published. If you like your sword,
Use it; if mine appear a better to you,
Change; for the ground is this, and this the time,
To end our difference.   [*Draws.*]
Amin.   Charitable youth,
If thou beest such, think not I will maintain
So strange a wrong; and, for thy sister's sake,
Know that I could not think that desperate thing 70
I durst not do; yet, to enjoy this world,
I would not see her, for, beholding thee,
I am I know not what. If I have aught
That may content thee, take it, and be-gone,
For death is not so terrible as thou;
Thine eyes shoot guilt into me.
Asp.   Thus, she swore
Thou wouldst behave thyself, and give me words
That would fetch tears into my eyes;
and so
Thou dost indeed. But yet she bade me watch
Lest I were cozened; and be sure to fight 80
Ere I returned.
Amin.   That must not be with me.
For her I'll die directly; but against her
Will never hazard it.

[1] Against.

Asp.   You must be urged.
I do not deal uncivilly with those
That dare to fight; but such a one as you
Must be used thus.   *She strikes him.*
Amin.   I prithee, youth, take heed.
Thy sister is a thing to me so much
Above mine honor that I can endure
All this—Good gods! A blow I can en-
    dure!
But stay not, lest thou draw a timeless
    death   90
Upon thyself.
Asp.   Thou art some prating fellow,
One that hath studied out a trick to
    talk,
And move soft-hearted people; to be
    kicked—   *She kicks him.*
Thus to be kicked!—(*Aside.*)   Why
    should he be so slow
In giving me my death?
Amin.   A man can bear
No more, and keep his flesh. Forgive
    me, then!
I would endure yet, if I could. Now
    show   [*Draws.*]
The spirit thou pretendest, and under-
    stand
Thou hast no hour to live.
    They fight [; Aspatia is wounded].
           What dost thou mean?
Thou canst not fight. The blows thou
    mak'st at me   100
Are quite besides;[1] and those I offer
    at thee,
Thou spread'st thine arms, and tak'st
    upon thy breast,
Alas, defenseless!
Asp.   I have got enough,
And my desire. There is no place so fit
For me to die as here.   [*Falls.*]

Enter Evadne, her hands bloody, with a
                     knife.

Evad. Amintor, I am loaden with events,
That fly to make thee happy; I have
    joys
That in a moment can call back thy
    wrongs,
And settle thee in thy free state again.
It is Evadne still that follows thee,   110
But not her mischiefs.
Amin. Thou canst not fool me to believe
    again;

[1] To one side.

But thou hast looks and things so full
    of news
That I am stayed.
Evad. Noble Amintor, put off thy amaze,
Let thine eyes loose, and speak. Am I
    not fair?
Looks not Evadne beauteous with these
    rites now?
Were those hours half so lovely in thine
    eyes
When our hands met before the holy
    man?
I was too foul within to look fair then; 120
Since I knew ill, I was not free till now.
Amin. There is presage of some impor-
    tant thing
About thee, which it seems thy tongue
    hath lost.
Thy hands are bloody, and thou hast
    a knife.
Evad. In this consists thy happiness and
    mine.
Joy to Amintor, for the king is dead!
Amin. Those have most power to hurt us
    that we love;
We lay our sleeping lives within their
    arms.
Why, thou hast raised up mischief to
    his height,
And found one to outname[2] thy other
    faults;   130
Thou hast no intermission of thy sins,
But all thy life is a continued ill.
Black is thy color now, disease thy na-
    ture.
"Joy to Amintor!" Thou hast touched
    a life,
The very name of which had power to
    chain
Up all my rage, and calm my wildest
    wrongs.
Evad. 'Tis done; and, since I could not
    find a way
To meet thy love so clear as through
    his life,
I cannot now repent it.
Amin. Couldst thou procure the gods to
    speak to me,   140
To bid me love this woman and forgive,
I think I should fall out with them. Be-
    hold,
Here lies a youth whose wounds bleed
    in my breast,

[2] Surpass.

Sent by a violent fate to fetch his death
From my slow hand! And, to augment
my woe,
You now are present, stained with a
king's blood
Violently shed. This keeps night here,
And throws an unknown wilderness [1]
about me.

ASP. O, O, O!

AMIN. No more; pursue me not.

EVAD.   Forgive me then, 150
And take me to thy bed; we may not
part.   [Kneels.]

AMIN. Forbear, be wise, and let my rage
go this way.

EVAD. 'Tis you that I would stay, not it.

AMIN.   Take heed;
It will return with me.

EVAD.   If it must be,
I shall not fear to meet it. Take me
home.

AMIN. Thou monster of cruelty, forbear!

EVAD. For heaven's sake, look more calm!
Thine eyes are sharper
Than thou canst make thy sword.

AMIN.   Away, away!
Thy knees are more to me than violence.
I am worse than sick to see knees fol-
low me   160
For that I must not grant. For God's
sake, stand.

EVAD. Receive me, then.

AMIN.   I dare not stay thy language.
In midst of all my anger and my grief,
Thou dost awake something that trou-
bles me,
And says I loved thee once. I dare not
stay;
There is no end of woman's reasoning.
                        Leaves her.

EVAD. [*Rising.*] Amintor, thou shalt love
me now again.
Go; I am calm. Farewell, and peace
forever!
Evadne, whom thou hat'st, will die
for thee.   *Kills herself.* 169

AMIN. I have a little human nature yet,
That's left for thee, that bids me stay
thy hand.   *Returns.*

EVAD. Thy hand was welcome, but it
came too late.
O, I am lost! The heavy sleep makes
haste.   *She dies.*

[1] Wildness.

ASP. O, O, O!

AMIN. This earth of mine doth tremble,
and I feel
A stark affrighted motion in my blood.
My soul grows weary of her house, and I
All over am a trouble to myself.
There is some hidden power in these
dead things   179
That calls my flesh into 'em; I am cold.
Be resolute and bear 'em company.
There's something yet, which I am loath
to leave.
There's man enough in me to meet the
fears
That death can bring; and yet would it
were done!
I can find nothing in the whole dis-
course
Of death I durst not meet the boldest
way;
Yet still, betwixt the reason and the act,
The wrong I to Aspatia did stands up;
I have not such another fault to answer.
Though she may justly arm herself
with scorn   190
And hate of me, my soul will part less
troubled,
When I have paid to her in tears my
sorrow.
I will not leave this act unsatisfied,
If all that's left in me can answer it.

ASP. Was it a dream? There stands Amintor still,
Or I dream still.

AMIN. How dost thou? Speak; receive
my love and help.
Thy blood climbs up to his old place
again;
There's hope of thy recovery.

ASP. Did you not name Aspatia?

AMIN.   I did. 200

ASP. And talked of tears and sorrow unto
her?

AMIN. 'Tis true; and, till these happy
signs in thee
Stayéd my course, 'twas thither I was
going.

ASP. Thou art there already, and these
wounds are hers.
Those threats I brought with me sought
not revenge,
But came to fetch this blessing from thy
hand.
I am Aspatia yet.

Amin. Dare my soul ever look abroad again?

Asp. I shall sure live, Amintor; I am well. A kind of healthful joy wanders within me.   210

Amin. The world wants lines to excuse thy loss;
Come, let me bear thee to some place of help.

Asp. Amintor, thou must stay; I must rest here;
My strength begins to disobey my will. How dost thou, my blessed soul? I would fain live
Now, if I could.   Wouldst thou have loved me, then?

Amin. Alas,
All that I am 's not worth a hair from thee!

Asp. Give me thy hand; mine hands grope up and down,
And cannot find thee; I am wondrous sick.   220
Have I thy hand, Amintor?

Amin. Thou greatest blessing of the world, thou hast.

Asp. I do believe thee better than my sense.
O, I must go! Farewell!   Dies.

Amin. She sounds.[1]—Aspatia!—Help! For God's sake, water,
Such as may chain life ever to this frame!—
Aspatia, speak!—What, no help? Yet I fool![2]
I'll chafe her temples. Yet there nothing stirs.
Some hidden power tell her Amintor calls,
And let her answer me!—Aspatia, speak!—   230
I have heard, if there be any life, but bow
The body thus, and it will show itself.
O, she is gone! I will not leave her yet.
Since out of justice we must challenge nothing,
I'll call it mercy, if you'll pity me,
You heavenly powers, and lend for some few years
The blessed soul to this fair seat again!
No comfort comes; the gods deny me too.

---

[1] Swounds, swoons.   [2] Act foolishly.

I'll bow the body once again.—Aspa-tia!—
The soul is fled forever, and I wrong   240
Myself, so long to lose her company.
Must I talk now? Here's to be with thee, love!   Kills himself.

Enter Servant.

Ser. This is a great grace to my lord, to have the new king come to him. I must tell him he is entering.—O, God!—Help, help!

*Enter Lysip[pus], Melant[ius], Cal[ianax],
Cleon, Diph[ilus], Strato.*

Lys. Where's Amintor?

Stra. O, there, there!

Lys. How strange is this!

Cal.   What should we do here?

Mel. These deaths are such acquainted things with me   250
That yet my heart dissolves not. May I stand
Stiff here forever! Eyes, call up your tears!
This is Amintor. Heart, he was my friend.
Melt! Now it flows.—Amintor, give a word
To call me to thee.

Amin. O!

Mel. Melantius calls his friend Amintor. O!
Thy arms are kinder to me than thy tongue!
Speak, speak!

Amin. What?   260

Mel. That little word was worth all the sounds
That ever I shall hear again.

Diph.   O, brother,
Here lies your sister slain! You lose yourself
In sorrow there.

Mel.   Why, Diphilus, it is
A thing to laugh at, in respect of this.
Here was my sister, father, brother, son—
All that I had.—Speak once again; what youth
Lies slain there by thee?

Amin.   'Tis Aspatia.

My last is said. Let me give up my soul
Into thy bosom.   [*Dies.*]   270
CAL. What's that? What's that? Aspatia!
MEL.   I never did
Repent the greatness of my heart till
   now;
It will not burst at need.
CAL. My daughter dead here too! And
you have all fine new tricks to grieve; but
I ne'er knew any but direct crying.
MEL. I am a prattler; but no more.
            [*Offers to stab himself.*]
DIPH.   Hold, brother!
LYS. Stop him.
DIPH. Fie, how unmanly was this offer
   in you!
Does this become our strain?   280
CAL. I know not what the matter
is, but I am grown very kind, and am
friends with you. You have given me that
among you will kill me quickly; but I'll
go home, and live as long as I can. [*Exit.*]

MEL. His spirit is but poor that can be
   kept
From death for want of weapons.
Is not my hands a weapon sharp enough
To stop my breath? Or, if you tie down
   those,
I vow, Amintor, I will never eat,   290
Or drink, or sleep, or have to do with
   that
That may preserve life! This I swear
   to keep.
LYS. Look to him, though, and bear those
   bodies in.
May this a fair example be to me
To rule with temper; [1] for, on lustful
   kings,
Unlooked-for, sudden deaths from God
   are sent,
But cursed is he that is their instrument.
                       [*Exeunt.*]

FINIS.

[1] Temperance, self-restraint.

THOMAS MIDDLETON AND WILLIAM ROWLEY

No partnership in the composition of Elizabethan plays was conducted with more success than that of Thomas Middleton and William Rowley, for their joint efforts resulted in better work than either dramatist produced independently. Thomas Middleton was christened son of William Middleton and Anne Snow at St. Lawrence in the Old Jewry on April 18, 1580. As a lad in his teens he published *The Wisdom of Solomon Paraphrased* (1597) and *Micro-Cynicon, Six Snarling Satires* (1599), but meanwhile, in April, 1598, had matriculated at Queen's College, Oxford. There is no record of his connection with the theater until May 22, 1602, when Henslowe records in his Diary a payment made to him together with Munday, Drayton, and Webster "in earnest of a book called *Cæsar's Fall.*" From this time almost to his death numerous references to his dramatic activity show that he sometimes wrote alone but more often with other well-known dramatists, notably Dekker and Rowley. Two satirical tales, *The Black Book* and *Father Hubbard's Tale*, published in 1604, reveal his early interest in the seamy side of London life, which he was to turn to good account in his comedies of manners written between 1604 and 1611. Among these may be mentioned *A Trick to Catch the Old One; A Mad World, My Masters;* and *Michaelmas Term*—all dealing with the duping of an unsuspecting victim by London sharpers; *Your Five Gallants*, which reveals the wiles of five different types of swindlers and ruffians; and that laughter-provoking farce, *A Chaste Maid in Cheapside.* Middleton's one unaided tragedy, *Women, Beware Women*, written about 1612, was followed in 1613 by his first masque, *The Triumphs of Truth;* and until his death he was in demand as a writer of this type of entertainment. The temporary amalgamation of the companies of Princess Elizabeth and Prince Charles in 1614 or 1615 brought Middleton and Rowley together, and their period of collaboration began shortly thereafter. Little is known of William Rowley's life. He was born about 1585, or perhaps earlier, and died in February, 1626. He was writing for the stage as early as 1607, and he not only achieved something of a reputation as an actor, but collaborated with a number of the best dramatists of the time. The best results of his collaboration with Middleton are *A Fair Quarrel, The Changeling*, and *The Spanish Gipsy.* From 1620 until his death Middleton held the office of city chronologer. He was buried in the Newington Butts Parish Church on July 4, 1627.

Middleton possesses no unusual poetic gifts, and his style is often uneven. His strength lies rather in his constructive skill, and in his fine dramatic sense, which enables him to give rapidity of movement and effectiveness to his scenes, and to make very real his pictures of low life in London. These features are well illustrated by *A Trick to Catch the Old One*, which was composed between 1604 and 1606, entered in the Stationers' Register October 7, 1607, and issued in two quartos dated 1608, and again in 1616. The plot, ingeniously contrived save for the lack of moral justice in the *dénouement*, is presumably of Middleton's own invention, and the materials of the play are drawn from the dramatist's experience in London life. The present text is based on photostats of the copy of the 1608 quarto, with readings from photostats of the 1616 quarto—both in the possession of the Huntington Library—with permission of the authorities of the library.

The Changeling, the best of Middleton and Rowley's joint efforts, although written between 1622 and the date of its performance at Whitehall on January 4, 1624, was not published until 1653. The story of Beatrice Joanna and Deflores is drawn from John Reynolds' *The Triumphs of God's Revenge against the Crying and Execrable Sin of Murther*, entered in the Stationers' Register June 7, 1621, and published later the same year; and one episode in the story is derived from Leonard Digges' translation of the Spanish novel of Cespedes, *Gerardo, the Unfortunate Spaniard* (1622). For the sub-plot, which gives the play its name, no source is known. According to Miss Pauline G. Wiggin (*An Inquiry into the Authorship of the Middleton-Rowley Plays*, Boston, 1897), "the first and last scenes, as well as the underplot," of the play are by Rowley. The play has been accorded high praise as a psychological tragedy and as one of the most successful plays written in collaboration in the whole range of Elizabethan drama. The present text is based on photostats of the copy of the 1653 quarto in the Harvard College Library, and reference has been made to the editions by Dyce and Bullen.

A TRICK TO CATCH THE OLD ONE

BY

T[HOMAS] M[IDDLETON]

[DRAMATIS PERSONÆ

THEODORUS WITGOOD.
PECUNIUS LUCRE, *his uncle.*
WALKADINE HOARD.
ONESIPHORUS HOARD, *his brother.*
LIMBER ⎤
KIX ⎥
LAMPREY ⎥ *friends of Hoard.*
SPICHCOCK ⎦
HARRY DAMPIT ⎤ *usurers.*
GULF ⎦
SAM FREEDOM, *son of Mistress Lucre.*
MONEYLOVE.

SIR LANCELOT.
HOST.
GEORGE, *Lucre's servant.*
ARTHUR, *Hoard's servant.*
CREDITORS, GENTLEMEN, DRAWER, BOY,
    SCRIVENER, SERVANTS, *etc.*

COURTESAN.
MISTRESS LUCRE.
JOYCE, *Hoard's niece.*
LADY FOXTONE.
AUDREY, *Dampit's servant.*

SCENE: *Leicestershire and London.*

TIME: *Contemporary.*

ACTUS I. SCENA i.

A street in a town in Leicestershire.]

Enter Witgood, a gentleman, solus.

WIT. All's gone! Still thou'rt a gentleman—that's all; but a poor one—that's nothing. What milk brings thy meadows forth now? Where are thy goodly uplands and thy downlands? All sunk into that little pit, lechery. Why should a gallant pay but two shillings for his ordinary that nourishes him, and twenty times two for his brothel that consumes him? But where's Longacre? [2] In my uncle's conscience, [10 which is three years' voyage about. He that sets out upon his conscience ne'er finds the way home again; he is either swallowed in the quicksands of law quillets, [3] or splits upon the piles of a præmunire. Yet these old fox-brained and ox-browed uncles have still defenses for their avarice, and apologies for their practices, and will thus greet our follies:

He that doth his youth expose   20
    To brothel, drink, and danger,
Let him that is his nearest kin
    Cheat him before a stranger—

and that's his uncle; 'tis a principle in usury. I dare not visit the city; there I should be too soon visited by that horrible plague, my debts, and by that means I lose a virgin's love, her portion, and her virtues. Well, how should a man live now that has no living—hum? Why, are there not [30 a million of men in the world that only sojourn upon their brain, and make their wits their mercers; and am I but one amongst that million, and cannot thrive upon 't? Any trick, out of the compass of law, now would come happily to me.

Enter Courtesan.

COUR. My love!
WIT. My loathing! Hast thou been the secret consumption of my purse, and now

123

com'st to undo my last means, my [40
wits? Wilt leave no virtue in me, and yet
thou ne'er the better?

Hence, courtesan, round-webbed tarantula,[1]
That dryest the roses in the cheeks of
youth!

Cour. I have been true unto your
pleasure; and all your lands thrice racked [2]
was never worth the jewel which I prodigally gave you, my virginity.

Lands mortgaged may return, and more
esteemed,
But honesty,[3] once pawned, is ne'er redeemed.   50

Wit. Forgive; I do thee wrong
To make thee sin, and then to chide thee
for 't.

Cour. I know I am your loathing now.
Farewell.

Wit. Stay, best invention,[4] stay!

Cour. I that have been the secret consumption of your purse, shall I stay now to
undo your last means, your wits? Hence,
courtesan, away!

Wit. I prithee, make me not mad at my
own weapon. Stay (a thing few [60
women can do, I know that, and therefore
they had need wear stays); be not contrary.
Dost love me? Fate has so cast [5] it that all
my means I must derive from thee.

Cour. From me? Be happy then;
What lies within the power of my per-
formance
Shall be commanded of thee.

Wit.   Spoke like
An honest drab, i' faith! It may prove
something.
What trick is not an embryon at first,
Until a perfect shape come over it?   70

Cour. Come, I must help you. Where-
abouts left you?
I'll proceed.
Though you beget, 'tis I must help to
breed.
Speak, what is 't? I'd fain conceive it.

Wit. So, so, so. Thou shalt presently
take the name and form upon thee of a rich

country widow, four hundred a year valiant [6] in woods, in bullocks, in barns, and
in rye stacks. We'll to London, and to my
covetous uncle.   80

Cour. I begin to applaud thee; our
states being both desperate, they are soon
resolute. But how for horses?

Wit. Mass, that's true; the jest will be
of some continuance. Let me see; horses
now, a bots [7] on 'em! Stay, I have acquaintance with a mad host, never yet
bawd to thee. I have rinsed the whoreson's
gums in mull-sack [8] many a time and often.
Put but a good tale into his ear now, [90
so it come off cleanly, and there's horse
and man for us, I dare warrant thee.

Cour. Arm your wits then speedily;
There shall want nothing in me, either in
behavior, discourse, or fashion,
That shall discredit your intended pur-
pose.
I will so artfully disguise my wants,
And set so good a courage on my state,
That I will be believed.

Wit. Why, then, all's furnished. [100
I shall go nigh to catch that old fox, mine
uncle, though he make but some amends
for my undoing. Yet there's some comfort
in 't: he cannot otherwise choose (though
it be but in hope to cozen me again) but
supply any hasty want that I bring to town
with me. The device well and cunningly
carried, the name of a rich widow and four
hundred a year in good earth will so conjure up a kind of usurer's love in him [110
to me that he will not only desire my
presence—which at first shall scarce be
granted him; I'll keep off a [9] purpose—but
I shall find him so officious to deserve, so
ready to supply! I know the state of an old
man's affection so well: if his nephew be
poor indeed, why, he lets God alone with
him; but, if he be once rich, then he'll be
the first man that helps him.

Cour. 'Tis right the world; [10] for, [120
in these days, an old man's love to his
kindred is like his kindness to his wife—
'tis always done before he comes at it.

Wit. I owe thee for that jest. Begone!
Here's all my wealth; prepare thyself.
Away! I'll to mine host with all possible

[1] Here and in a few other passages the original
prose has been changed into verse. Later, some
line divisions have also been regularized.
[2] Rented at excessively high rates.
[3] Chastity.
[4] Referring to her as the instrument for his
plan described below.   [5] Planned.

[6] Worth.   [9] On.
[7] Plague.   [10] Exactly the way of the world.
[8] Spiced and heated wine.

haste, and, with the best art and most profitable form, pour the sweet circumstance
into his ear, which shall have the gift to
turn all the wax to honey.—[*Exit* [130
Courtesan.] How now? O, the right worshipful seniors of our country!

[*Enter Onesiphorus Hoard, Limber, and
Kix.*] [1]

O. Hoa. Who's that?
Lim. O, the common rioter; take no note
of him.
Wit. [*Aside.*] You will not see me now;
   the comfort is,
Ere it be long you will scarce see your-
   selves.   [*Exit.*]
O. Hoa. I wonder how he breathes; h'as
   consumed all
Upon that courtesan.
Lim.   We have heard so much.
O. Hoa. You have heard all truth. His
   uncle and my brother   140
Have been these three years mortal adversaries.
Two old, tough spirits, they seldom meet
   but fight,
Or quarrel when 'tis calmest. I think
   their anger
Be the very fire that keeps their age alive.
Lim. What was the quarrel, sir?
O. Hoa. Faith, about a purchase,[2] fetching over a young heir. Master Hoard, my
brother, having wasted much time in beating the bargain, what did me old Lucre, but,
as his conscience moved him, knowing [150
the poor gentleman, stepped in between 'em
and cozened him himself.
Lim. And was this all, sir?
O. Hoa. This was e'en it, sir; yet for all
this I know no reason but the match might
go forward betwixt his wife's son and my
niece. What though there be a dissension
between the two old men? I see no reason
it should put a difference between the two
younger; 'tis as natural for old folks [160
to fall out as for young to fall in. A scholar
comes a-wooing to my niece; well, he's wise,
but he's poor. Her son comes a-wooing to
my niece; well, he's a fool, but he's rich.

---

[1] These characters, represented in the speech
heads of the original by the numbers 1, 2, and 3
only, were first identified by Dyce. The following speech heads have been altered accordingly.   [2] Booty.

Lim. Ay, marry, sir?
O. Hoa. Pray now, is not a rich fool
better than a poor philosopher?
Lim. One would think so, i' faith.
O. Hoa. She now remains at London
with my brother, her second uncle, [170
to learn fashions, practice music; the voice
between her lips, and the viol between her
legs, she'll be fit for a consort [3] very speedily. A thousand good pound is her portion;
if she marry, we'll ride up and be merry.
Kix. A match, if it be a match. *Exeunt.*

[Scena ii.

Another street in the same town.]

Enter at one door, Witgood; at the other, Host.

Wit. Mine host!
Host. Young Master Witgood.
Wit. I have been laying [4] all the town
for thee.
Host. Why, what's the news, bully
Hadland?
Wit. What geldings are in the house,
of thine own? Answer me to that first.
Host. Why, man, why?
Wit. Mark me what I say. I'll [10
tell thee such a tale in thine ear that thou
shalt trust me spite of thy teeth, furnish
me with some money willy-nilly, and ride
up with me thyself *contra voluntatem et
professionem.*[5]
Host. How? Let me see this trick,
and I'll say thou hast more art than a
conjuror.
Wit. Dost thou joy in my advancement?   20
Host. Do I love sack and ginger?
Wit. Comes my prosperity desiredly
to thee?
Host. Come forfeitures to a usurer,
fees to an officer, punks to an host, and
pigs to a parson desiredly? Why, then, la!
Wit. Will the report of a widow of four
hundred a year, boy, make thee leap and
sing and dance, and come to thy place
again?   30
Host. Wilt thou command me now?
I am thy spirit; conjure me into any shape.
Wit. I ha' brought her from her friends,
turned back the horses by a sleight; not

---

[3] With the double meaning, *concert* and *husband.*   [4] Searching.
[5] Contrary to your wish and profession.

so much as one amongst her six men, goodly, large, yeomanly fellows, will she trust with this her purpose—by this light, all unmanned,[1] regardless of her state, neglectful of vainglorious ceremony, all for my love. O, 'tis a fine little vol- [40 uble tongue, mine host, that wins a widow!

HOST. No, 'tis a tongue with a great T, my boy, that wins a widow.

WIT. Now, sir, the case stands thus. Good mine host, if thou lov'st my happiness, assist me.

HOST. Command all my beasts i' th' house.

WIT. Nay, that's not all neither. Prithee, take truce with thy joy, and listen to me. Thou know'st I have a wealthy [50 uncle i' th' city, somewhat the wealthier by my follies. The report of this fortune, well and cunningly carried, might be a means to draw some goodness from the usuring rascal, for I have put her in hope already of some estate that I have either in land or money. Now, if I be found true in neither, what may I expect but a sudden breach of our love, utter dissolution of the match, and confusion [60 of my fortunes forever?

HOST. Wilt thou but trust the managing of thy business with me?

WIT. With thee? Why, will I desire to thrive in my purpose? Will I hug four hundred a year, I that know the misery of nothing? Will that man wish a rich widow, that has ne'er a hole to put his head in? With thee, mine host? Why, believe it, sooner with thee than with a [70 covey of counselors.

HOST. Thank you for your good report, i' faith, sir; and, if I stand you not in stead, why, then, let an host come off *hic et hæc hostis*,[2] a deadly enemy to dice, drink, and venery. Come, where's this widow?

WIT. Hard at Park End.

HOST. I'll be her serving-man for once.

WIT. Why, there we let off together, keep full time; my thoughts were strik- [80 ing then just the same number.

HOST. I knew 't. Shall we then see our merry days again?

WIT. Our merry nights—[*Aside.*] which ne'er shall be more seen.   *Exeunt.*

---

[1] Without attendants.
[2] A pun on the meaning *host* and *enemy* is intended.

A street in London.]

Enter at several doors old Lucre and old Hoard, Gentlemen [, i.e., Lamprey, Spichcock, Freedom, and Moneylove,] coming between them to pacify 'em.

LAMP. Nay, good Master Lucre, and you, Master Hoard, anger is the wind which you're both too much troubled withal.

HOARD. Shall my adversary thus daily affront me, ripping up the old wound of our malice, which three summers could not close up, into which wound the very sight of him drops scalding lead instead of balsamum?   10

LUC. Why, Hoard, Hoard, Hoard, Hoard, Hoard! May I not pass in the state of quietness to mine own house? Answer me to that, before witness, and why? I'll refer the cause to honest, even-minded gentlemen, or require the mere indifferences [3] of the law to decide this matter. I got the purchase, true. Was 't not any man's case? Yes. Will a wise man stand as a bawd, whilst another wipes [20 his nose [4] of the bargain? No; I answer no in that case.

LAMP. Nay, sweet Master Lucre.

HOARD. Was it the part of a friend? No, rather of a Jew. Mark what I say— when I had beaten the bush to the last bird, or, as I may term it, the price to a pound, then, like a cunning usurer, to come in the evening of the bargain and glean all my hopes in a minute, to en- [30 ter, as it were, at the back door of the purchase? For thou ne'er cam'st the right way by it.

LUC. Hast thou the conscience to tell me so without any impeachment to thyself?

HOARD. Thou that canst defeat thy own nephew, Lucre, lap his lands into bonds, and take the extremity of thy kindred's forfeitures, because he's a [40 rioter, a wastethrift, a brothel-master, and so forth—what may a stranger expect from thee but *vulnera dilacerata*,[5] as the poet says, dilacerate dealing?

---

[3] Impartialities.   [5] Lacerated wounds.
[4] *I.e.*, cheats him.

Luc. Upbraidest thou me with nephew?
Is all imputation laid upon me? What
acquaintance have I with his follies? If
he riot, 'tis he must want it; if he surfeit,
'tis he must feel it; if he drab it, 'tis he
must lie by 't. What's this to me?　　50
　　Hoard. What's all to thee? Nothing,
nothing; such is the gulf of thy desire and
the wolf of thy conscience. But be assured,
old Pecunius Lucre, if ever fortune so
bless me that I may be at leisure to vex
thee, or any means so favor me that I
may have opportunity to mad thee, I will
pursue it with that flame of hate, spirit
of malice, unrepressed wrath, that I will
blast thy comforts.　　　　　　60
　　Luc. Ha, ha, ha!
　　Lamp. Nay, Master Hoard, you're a
wise gentleman—
　　Hoard. I will so cross thee—
　　Luc. And I thee.
　　Hoard. So without mercy fret thee—
　　Luc. So monstrously oppose thee—
　　Hoard. Dost scoff at my just anger?
O, that I had as much power as usury has
over thee!　　　　　　　　70
　　Luc. Then thou wouldst have as much
power as the devil has over thee.
　　Hoard. Toad!
　　Luc. Aspic!
　　Hoard. Serpent!
　　Luc. Viper!
　　Spi. Nay, gentlemen, then we must
divide you perforce.
　　Lamp. When the fire grows too un-
reasonable hot, there's no better way　[80
than to take off the wood.
Exeunt. Mane[n]t [1] *Sam [Freedom] and
Moneylove.*
　　Sam. A word, good signior.
　　Mon. How now, what's the news?
　　Sam. 'Tis given me to understand that
you are a rival of mine in the love of Mis-
tress Joyce, Master Hoard's niece. Say
me ay, say me no?
　　Mon. Yes, 'tis so.
　　Sam. Then look to yourself. You can-
not live long; I'm practicing every　[90
morning. A month hence I'll challenge
you.
　　Mon. Give me your hand upon 't;
there's my pledge I'll meet you.
　　　　　　　　Strikes him. Exit.

[1] Remain.

　　Sam. O, O! What reason had you for
that, sir, to strike before the month? You
knew I was not ready for you, and that
made you so crank.[2] I am not such a
coward to strike again, I warrant you. My
ear has the law of her side, for it burns　[100
horribly. I will teach him to strike a naked
face, the longest day of his life. 'Slid,[3] it
shall cost me some money, but I'll bring
this box into the chancery.　　　*Exit.*

[Scena iv.

Another street in London.]

Enter Witgood and the Host.

　　Host. Fear you nothing, sir; I have
lodged her in a house of credit, I warrant
you.
　　Wit. Hast thou the writings?
　　Host. Firm, sir.
　　Wit. Prithee, stay, and behold two
the most prodigious rascals that ever
slipped into the shape of men—Dampit,
sirrah, and young Gulf, his fellow cater-
pillar.　　　　　　　　　10
　　Host. Dampit? Sure, I have heard of
that Dampit.
　　Wit. Heard of him? Why, man, he
that has lost both his ears may hear of
him—a famous, infamous trampler of
time:[4] his own phrase. Note him well.
That Dampit, sirrah, he in the uneven
beard and the serge cloak, is the most
notorious, usuring, blasphemous, atheistical, brothel-vomiting rascal that we　[20
have in these latter times now extant,
whose first beginning was the stealing of
a masty[5] dog from a farmer's house.
　　Host. He looked as if he would obey
the commandment well, when he began
first with stealing.
　　Wit. True. The next town he came at,
he set the dogs together by th' ears.
　　Host. A sign he should follow the law,
by my faith.　　　　　　　30
　　Wit. So it followed, indeed; and, being destitute of all fortunes, staked his
masty against a noble,[6] and by great fortune his dog had the day. How he made
it up ten shillings, I know not, but his own
boast is that he came to town with but

[2] Lively.　　　[3] God's eyelid, a mild oath.
[4] Lawyer.　　　[5] Mastiff.　　　[6] Gold coin.

ten shillings in his purse, and now is credibly worth ten thousand pound.

Host. How the devil came he by it?

[*Enter Dampit and Gulf.*]

Wit. [*Aside.*] How the devil came [40
he not by it? If you put in the devil once,
riches come with a vengeance. H'as been
a trampler of the law, sir; and the devil
has a care of his footmen. The rogue has
spied me now; he nibbled me finely once,
too.—A pox search you!—[*Turns to Dampit.*] O, Master Dampit!—[*Aside.*] The very
loins of thee!—Cry you mercy,[1] Master
Gulf; you walk so low I promise you I
saw you not, sir.   50

Gulf. He that walks low walks safe,
the poets tell us.

Wit. [*Aside.*] And nigher hell by a foot
and a half than the rest of his fellows.—
But, my old Harry!

Damp. My sweet Theodorus!

Wit. 'Twas a merry world when thou
cam'st to town with ten shillings in thy
purse.

Damp. And now worth ten thou- [60
sand pound, my boy. Report it. Harry
Dampit, a trampler of time, say, he would
be up in a morning, and be here with his
serge gown, dashed up to the hams in a
cause, have his feet stink about Westminster Hall and come home again, see
the galleons, the galleasses. the great
armadoes[2] of the law; then there be hoys
and petty vessels, oars[3] and scullers of
the time. There be picklocks of the [70
time too. Then would I be here; I would
trample up and down like a mule. Now to
the judges: "May it please your reverend-
honorable fatherhoods!" Then to my
counselor: "May it please your worshipful patience!" Then to the examiner's
office: "May it please your mastership's
gentleness!" Then to one of the clerks:
"May it please your worshipful lousi-
ness!"—for I find him scrubbing in [80
his codpiece. Then to the hall again, then
to the chamber again—

Wit. And when to the cellar again?

Damp. E'en when thou wilt again.
Tramplers of time, motions[4] of Fleet

Street, and visions of Holborn! Here I
have fees of one, there I have fees of another; my clients come about me, the
fooliaminy[5] and coxcombry of the country. I still trashed[6] and trotted for [90
other men's causes. Thus was poor Harry
Dampit made rich by others' laziness,
who though they would not follow their
own suits, I made 'em follow me with
their purses.

Wit. Didst thou so, old Harry?

Damp. Ay, and I soused 'em with bills
of charges, i' faith; twenty pound a year
have I brought in for boat hire, and I
ne'er stepped into boat in my life.   100

Wit. Tramplers of time!

Damp. Ay, tramplers of time, rascals
of time, bull-beggars![7]

Wit. Ah, thou'rt a mad old Harry!—
Kind Master Gulf, I am bold to renew my
acquaintance.

Gulf. I embrace it, sir.   *Exeunt.*

MUSIC.

Incipit [8]

Act[us] II. [Scena i.

A room in Lucre's house.]

Enter Lucre.

Luc. My adversary evermore twits me
with my nephew, forsooth, my nephew.
Why may not a virtuous uncle have a dissolute nephew? What though he be a
brotheler, a wastethrift, a common surfeiter,
and, to conclude, a beggar? Must sin in
him call up shame in me? Since we have
no part in their follies, why should we have
part in their infamies? For my strict hand
toward his mortgage, that I deny not; [10
I confess I had an uncle's pen'worth. Let
me see, half in half; true. I saw neither
hope of his reclaiming nor comfort in his
being, and was it not then better bestowed
upon his uncle than upon one of his aunts?
—I need not say bawd, for everyone knows
what "aunt" stands for in the last translation.[9]—

---

[1] I beg your pardon.   [3] Rowboats.
[2] Armadas, large warships.   [4] Puppet shows.

[5] One of Dampit's coinages.
[6] Tramped.   [8] Begins.
[7] Hobgoblins.   [9] Tralation, metaphor.

[*Enter Servant.*]

Now, sir?

SER.[1] There's a country serving- [20
man, sir, attends to speak with your worship.

LUC. I'm at best leisure now; send him
in to me. [*Exit Servant.*]

Enter Host like a serving-man.

HOST. Bless your venerable worship.

LUC. Welcome, good fellow.

HOST. [*Aside.*] He calls me thief [2] at
first sight, yet he little thinks I am an host.

LUC. What's thy business with me?

HOST. Faith, sir, I am sent from [30
my mistress to any sufficient gentleman
indeed, to ask advice upon a doubtful
point. 'Tis indifferent, sir, to whom I come,
for I know none, nor did my mistress direct
me to any particular man, for she's as mere [3]
a stranger here as myself; only I found your
worship within, and 'tis a thing I ever
loved, sir, to be despatched as soon as I can.

LUC. [*Aside.*] A good, blunt honesty; I
like him well.—What is thy mistress? [40

HOST. Faith, a country gentlewoman,
and a widow, sir. Yesterday was the first
flight of us; but now she intends to stay till
a little term [4] business be ended.

LUC. Her name, I prithee?

HOST. It runs there in the writings, sir,
among her lands: Widow Medler.

LUC. Medler? Mass, have I ne'er heard
of that widow?

HOST. Yes, I warrant you, have [50
you, sir; not the rich widow in Staffordshire?

LUC. Cud's [5] me, there 'tis indeed; thou
hast put me into memory. There's a widow
indeed; ah, that I were a bachelor again!

HOST. No doubt your worship might do
much then; but she's fairly promised to a
bachelor already.

LUC. Ah, what is he, I prithee?

HOST. A country gentleman too, [60
one whom your worship knows not, I'm
sure; h'as spent some few follies in his
youth, but marriage, by my faith, begins
to call him home. My mistress loves him,

sir, and love covers faults, you know: one
Master Witgood, if ever you have heard of
the gentleman.

LUC. Ha! Witgood, say'st thou?

HOST. That's his name indeed, sir my
mistress is like to bring him to a goodly [70
seat yonder—four hundred a year, by my
faith.

LUC. But, I pray, take me with you.[6]

HOST. Ay, sir.

LUC. What countryman might this
young Witgood be?

HOST. A Leicestershire gentleman, sir.

LUC. [*Aside.*] My nephew, by th' Mass,
my nephew! I'll fetch out more of this, i'
faith. A simple country fellow! I'll [80
work 't out of him.—And is that gentleman,
say'st thou, presently [7] to marry her?

HOST. Faith, he brought her up to town,
sir; h'as the best card in all the bunch for 't,
her heart; and I know my mistress will be
married ere she go down.[8] Nay, I'll swear
that, for she's none of those widows that
will go down first, and be married after; she
hates that, I can tell you, sir.

LUC. By my faith, sir, she is like to [90
have a proper gentleman and a comely; I'll
give her that gift.

HOST. Why, does your worship know
him, sir?

LUC. I know him? Does not all the
world know him? Can a man of such exquisite qualities be hid under a bushel?

HOST. Then your worship may save me
a labor, for I had charge given me to inquire after him. 100

LUC. Inquire of him? If I might counsel thee, thou shouldst ne'er trouble thyself
further; inquire of him no more but of me;
I'll fit thee. I grant he has been youthful,
but is he not now reclaimed? Mark you
that, sir. Has not your mistress, think you,
been wanton in her youth? If men be wags,
are there not women wagtails?

HOST. No doubt, sir.

LUC. Does not he return wisest [110
that comes home whipped with his own
follies?

HOST. Why, very true, sir.

LUC. The worst report you can hear of
him, I can tell you, is that he has been a
kind gentleman, a liberal, and a worthy.

---

[1] Original reads *Ser. 2.*
[2] *Good fellow* was a cant phrase for *thief.*
[3] Absolute.　　　　　[5] God's.
[4] Pertaining to court sessions.
[6] Tell me your meaning.
[7] Immediately.　　　[8] *I.e.,* to the country.

Who but lusty Witgood, thrice-noble Witgood!

HOST. Since your worship has so much knowledge in him, can you resolve [120 me, sir, what his living might be? My duty binds me, sir, to have a care of my mistress' estate; she has been ever a good mistress to me, though I say it. Many wealthy suitors has she nonsuited for his sake; yet, though her love be so fixed, a man cannot tell whether his non-performance may help to remove it, sir; he makes us believe he has lands and living.

LUC. Who, young Master Wit- [130 good? Why, believe it, he has as goodly a fine living out yonder—what do you call the place?

HOST. Nay, I know not, i' faith.

LUC. Hum—see, like a beast, if I have not forgot the name—pooh! And out yonder again, goodly grown woods and fair meadows—pax [1] on 't, I can ne'er hit of that place neither. He? Why, he's Witgood of Witgood Hall. He an un- [140 known thing?

HOST. Is he so, sir? To see how rumor will alter! Trust me, sir, we heard once he had no lands, but all lay mortgaged to an uncle he has in town here.

LUC. Push! [2] 'Tis a tale, 'tis a tale.

HOST. I can assure you, sir, 'twas credibly reported to my mistress.

LUC. Why, do you think, i' faith, he was ever so simple to mortgage his lands [150 to his uncle, or his uncle so unnatural to take the extremity of such a mortgage?

HOST. That was my saying still, sir.

LUC. Pooh, ne'er think it.

HOST. Yet that report goes current.

LUC. Nay, then you urge me. Cannot I tell that best that am his uncle?

HOST. How, sir? What have I done!

LUC. Why, how now! In a sown, [3] man?

HOST. Is your worship his uncle, [160 sir?

LUC. Can that be any harm to you, sir?

HOST. I do beseech you, sir, do me the favor to conceal it. What a beast was I to utter so much! Pray, sir, do me the kindness to keep it in; I shall have my coat pulled o'er my ears, an 't [4] should be known; for the truth is, an 't please your worship, to prevent much rumor and many suitors,

[1] Pox.　　[2] Pish!　　[3] Swoon.　　[4] If it.

they intend to be married very sud- [170 denly and privately.

LUC. And dost thou think it stands with my judgment to do them injury? Must I needs say the knowledge of this marriage comes from thee? Am I a fool at fifty-four? Do I lack subtilty now, that have got all my wealth by it? There's a leash of angels [5] for thee. Come, let me woo thee; speak, where lie they?

HOST. So I might have no anger, [180 sir—

LUC. Passion of me, not a jot. Prithee, come.

HOST. I would not have it known it came by my means.

LUC. Why, am I a man of wisdom?

HOST. I dare trust your worship, sir; but I'm a stranger to your house; and to avoid all intelligencers, I desire your worship's ear.　　190

LUC. [Aside.] This fellow's worth a matter of trust.—Come, sir. [Host whispers to him.] Why, now, thou'rt an honest lad.— [Aside.] Ah, Sirrah Nephew!

HOST. Please you, sir, now I have begun with your worship, when shall I attend for your advice upon that doubtful point? I must come warily now.

LUC. Tut, fear thou nothing; tomorrow's evening shall resolve the doubt.　　200

HOST. The time shall cause my attendance.　　　　　　　　　　　Exit.

LUC. Fare thee well.—There's more true honesty in such a country serving-man than in a hundred of our cloak companions; [6] I may well call 'em companions, for, since blue coats [7] have been turned into cloaks, we can scarce know the man from the master.—George!

[Enter George.]

GEO. Anon, sir?　　　　　　　　210

LUC. List hither. [Whispers.] Keep the place secret. Commend me to my nephew; I know no cause, tell him, but he might see his uncle.

GEO. I will, sir.

LUC. And, do you hear, sir, take heed you use him with respect and duty.

GEO. [Aside.] Here's a strange alteration! One day he must be turned out like

[5] Three gold coins.
[6] Servants, knaves.　　[7] Servants' livery.

a beggar, and now he must be called [220
in like a knight.   *Exit.*

Luc. Ah, sirrah, that rich widow! Four
hundred a year! Beside, I hear she lays
claim to a title of a hundred more. This
falls unhappily that he should bear a
grudge to me now, being likely to prove so
rich. What is 't, trow, that he makes me a
stranger for? Hum—I hope he has not so
much wit to apprehend that I cozened him.
He deceives me then? Good heaven, [230
who would have thought it would ever
have come to this pass! Yet he's a proper
gentleman, i' faith, give him his due—
marry, that's his mortgage; but that I
ne'er mean to give him. I'll make him rich
enough in words, if that be good, and, if it
come to a piece of money, I will not greatly
stick for 't. There may be hope some of
the widow's lands, too, may one day fall
upon me, if things be carried wisely.—[240

[Enter George.]

Now, sir, where is he?

Geo. He desires your worship to hold
him excused; he has such weighty business it commands him wholly from all men.

Luc. Were those my nephew's words?

Geo. Yes, indeed, sir.

Luc. [*Aside.*] When men grow rich,
they grow proud too, I perceive that. He
would not have sent me such an answer
once within this twelvemonth. See [250
what 'tis when a man comes to his lands!—
Return to him again, sir; tell him his uncle
desires his company for an hour. I'll trouble him but an hour, say; 'tis for his own
good, tell him. And, do you hear, sir, put
"worship" upon him. Go to, do as I bid
you; he's like to be a gentleman of worship
very shortly.

Geo. [*Aside.*] This is good sport, i'
faith.   *Exit.* 260

Luc. Troth, he uses his uncle discour-
teously now. Can he tell what I may do
for him? Goodness may come from me
in a minute, that comes not in seven year
again. He knows my humor; I am not so
usually good. 'Tis no small thing that
draws kindness from me; he may know
that and [1] he will. The chief cause that
invites me to do him most good is the

[1] If.

sudden astonishing of old Hoard, [270
my adversary. How pale his malice will
look at my nephew's advancement! With
what a dejected spirit he will behold his
fortunes, whom but last day he proclaimed
rioter, penurious makeshift, despised brothel-master! Ha, ha! 'Twill do me more
secret joy than my last purchase, more
precious comfort than all these widow's
revenues.—Now, sir—

Enter Witgood [, shown in by George].

Geo. With much entreaty he's at [280
length come, sir.   [*Exit.*]

Luc. O, nephew, let me salute you, sir!
You're welcome, nephew.

Wit. Uncle, I thank you.

Luc. Y'ave a fault, nephew; you're a
stranger here. Well, heaven give you
joy!

Wit. Of what, sir?

Luc. Hah, we can hear!
You might have known your uncle's
    house, i' faith,   290
You and your widow. Go to, you were
    to blame,
If I may tell you so without offense.

Wit. How could you hear of that, sir?

Luc.   O, pardon me!
It was your will to have kept it from me,
    I perceive now.

Wit. Not for any defect of love, I protest, uncle.

Luc. O, 'twas unkindness,[2] nephew! Fie,
fie, fie!

Wit. I am sorry you take it in that
sense, sir.   300

Luc. Pooh, you cannot color it, i' faith,
nephew.

Wit. Will you but hear what I can say
in my just excuse, sir?

Luc. Yes, faith, will I, and welcome.

Wit. You that know my danger i' th'
city, sir, so well, how great my debts are,
and how extreme my creditors, could not
out of your pure judgment, sir, have
wished us hither.   310

Luc. Mass, a firm reason indeed.

Wit. Else, my uncle's house, why, 't 'ad
been the only make-match—

Luc. Nay, and thy credit.

Wit. My credit? Nay, my counte-

[2] Perhaps *unnaturalness*, forgetfulness of the
relationship due a relative.

nance. Push, nay, I know, uncle, you would
have wrought it so by your wit you would
have made her believe in time the whole
house had been mine.   319

Luc. Ay, and most of the goods too—

Wit. La, you there! Well, let 'em all
prate what they will, there's nothing like
the bringing of a widow to one's uncle's
house.

Luc. Nay, let nephews be ruled as they
list, they shall find their uncle's house the
most natural place when all's done.

Wit. There they may be bold.

Luc. Life, they may do anything there,
man, and fear neither beadle nor som-   [330
ner.[1] An uncle's house! A very Cole Harbor.[2] Sirrah, I'll touch thee near now. Hast
thou so much interest in thy widow that
by a token thou couldst presently send for
her?

Wit. Troth, I think I can, uncle.

Luc. Go to, let me see that.

Wit. Pray, command one of your men
hither, uncle.

Luc. George!   340

[Enter George.]

Geo. Here, sir.

Luc. Attend my nephew.—[Witgood
whispers to George, who goes out.—Aside.]
I love a' life[3] to prattle with a rich
widow; 'tis pretty, methinks, when our
tongues go together—and then to promise
much and perform little. I love that
sport a' life, i' faith; yet I am in the mood
now to do my nephew some good, if he
take me handsomely.—What, have you
despatched?   350

Wit. I ha' sent, sir.

Luc. Yet I must condemn you of unkindness, nephew.

Wit. Heaven forbid, uncle!

Luc. Yes, faith, must I. Say your debts
be many, your creditors importunate, yet
the kindness of a thing is all, nephew. You
might have sent me close [4] word on 't without the least danger or prejudice to your
fortunes.   360

Wit. Troth, I confess it, uncle; I was
to blame there; but, indeed, my intent
was to have clapped it up suddenly, and

so have broke forth like a joy to my friends,
and a wonder to the world. Beside, there's
a trifle of a forty pound matter toward the
setting of me forth; my friends should ne'er
have known on 't; I meant to make shift for
that myself.

Luc. How, nephew? Let me not   [370
hear such a word again, I beseech you.
Shall I be beholding [5] to you?

Wit. To me? Alas, what do you mean,
uncle?

Luc. I charge you, upon my love, you
trouble nobody but myself.

Wit. Y'ave no reason for that, uncle.

Luc. Troth, I'll ne'er be friends with
you while you live, and you do.

Wit. Nay, and you say so, uncle,   [380
here's my hand; I will not do 't—

Luc. Why, well said! There's some hope
in thee when thou wilt be ruled. I'll make
it up fifty, faith, because I see thee so reclaimed. Peace; here comes my wife with
Sam, her tother [6] husband's son.

[Enter Mistress Lucre and Sam Freedom.]

Wit. Good aunt—

Sam. Cousin Witgood! I rejoice in my
salute; you're most welcome to this noble
city, governed with the sword in the   [390
scabbard.

Wit. [Aside.] And the wit in the pom-
mel.[7]—Good Master Sam Freedom, I return the salute.

Luc. By the Mass, she's coming, wife;
let me see now how thou wilt entertain her.

Wife. I hope I am not to learn, sir, to
entertain a widow; 'tis not so long ago since
I was one myself.

[Enter Courtesan.]

Wit. Uncle—   400

Luc. She's come indeed.

Wit. My uncle was desirous to see you,
widow, and I presumed to invite you.

Cour. The presumption was nothing,
Master Witgood. Is this your uncle, sir?

Luc. Marry am I, sweet widow; and his
good uncle he shall find me; ay, by this
smack that I give thee [Kisses her.], thou'rt
welcome.—Wife, bid the widow welcome
the same way again.   410

---

[1] Summoner.
[2] Cold Harbor, where debtors found sanctuary.
[3] As life, dearly.   [4] Secret.

[5] Beholden.   [6] Other.
[7] The amount of wit in the knob on the hilt of
a sword; i.e., no wit at all.

SAM. [*Aside.*] I am a gentleman now too by my father's occupation, and I see no reason but I may kiss a widow by my father's copy;[1] truly, I think the charter [2] is not against it. Surely these are the words, "The son, once a gentleman, may revel it, though his father were a dauber" [3] —'tis about the fifteen page. I'll to her. [*Attempts to kiss the Courtesan, who rebuffs him.*]

LUC. Y' are not very busy now; a word with thee, sweet widow— 420

SAM. [*Aside.*] Coad's nigs![4] I was never so disgraced since the hour my mother whipped me.

LUC. Beside, I have no child of mine own to care for; she's my second wife, old, past bearing. Clap sure to him, widow; he's like to be my heir, I can tell you.

COUR. Is he so, sir?

LUC. He knows it already, and the knave's proud on 't; jolly rich widows [430 have been offered him here i' th' city, great merchants' wives; and do you think he will once look upon 'em? Forsooth, he'll none. You are beholding to him i' th' country, then, ere we could be; nay, I'll hold a wager, widow, if he were once known to be in town, he would be presently sought after; nay, and happy were they that could catch him first.

COUR. I think so. 440

LUC. O, there would be such running to and fro, widow! He should not pass the streets for 'em; he'd be took up in one great house or other presently. Fah! They know he has it, and must have it. You see this house here, widow; this house and all comes to him, goodly rooms, ready furnished, ceiled with plaster of Paris, and all hung about with cloth of arras.—Nephew!

WIT. Sir. 450

LUC. Show the widow your house; carry her into all the rooms, and bid her welcome.—You shall see, widow.—[*Aside to Witgood.*] Nephew, strike all sure above and thou beest a good boy—ah!

WIT. Alas, sir, I know not how she would take it!

LUC. The right way, I warrant t'ee. A pox, art an ass? Would I were in thy stead! Get you up; I am ashamed of you.— [460

[*Exeunt Witgood and Courtesan.*] So, let 'em agree as they will now. Many a match has been struck up in my house a [5] this fashion. Let 'em try all manner of ways, still there's nothing like an uncle's house to strike the stroke in. I'll hold my wife in talk a little. —Now, 'Ginny, your son there goes a-wooing to a poor gentlewoman but of a thousand portion. See my nephew, a lad of less hope, strikes at four hundred [470 a year in good rubbish.[6]

WIFE. Well, we must do as we may, sir.

LUC. I'll have his money ready told [7] for him again [8] he come down. Let me see, too. By th' Mass, I must present the widow with some jewel, a good piece a [9] plate, or such a device; 'twill hearten her on well. I have a very fair standing cup; and a good high standing cup will please a widow above all other pieces. *Exit.* 480

WIFE. Do you mock us with your nephew?—I have a plot in my head, son— i' faith, husband, to cross you.

SAM. Is it a tragedy plot, or a comedy plot, good mother?

WIFE. 'Tis a plot shall vex him. I charge you, of my blessing, son Sam, that you presently withdraw the action of your love from Master Hoard's niece.

SAM. How, mother! 490

WIFE. Nay, I have a plot in my head, i' faith. Here, take this chain of gold and this fair diamond. Dog me the widow home to her lodging, and at thy best opportunity fasten 'em both upon her. Nay, I have a reach; [10] I can tell you thou art known what thou art, son, among the right worshipful, all the twelve companies.[11]

SAM. Truly, I thank 'em for it.

WIFE. He? He's a scab to thee— [500 and so certify her thou hast two hundred a year of thyself, besides thy good parts—a proper person and a lovely. If I were a widow, I could find in my heart to have thee myself, son; ay, from 'em all.

SAM. Thank you for your good will, mother; but, indeed, I had rather have a stranger. And, if I woo her not in that violent fashion, that I will make her be glad to take these gifts ere I leave [510

---

[1] Example.   [2] *I.e.*, of a trade guild.
[3] Plasterer.   [4] God's nigs, a meaningless oath.
[5] In.   [9] Of.
[6] Money.   [10] Scheme.
[7] Counted.   [11] *I.e.*, of the trade guilds.
[8] Against, by the time that.

her, let me never be called the heir of your body.

WIFE. Nay, I know there's enough in you, son, if you once come to put it forth.

SAM. I'll quickly make a bolt or a shaft on 't.[1]   *Exeunt.*

[SCENA ii.

A street in London.]

Enter Hoard and Moneylove.

MON. Faith, Master Hoard, I have bestowed many months in the suit of your niece, such was the dear love I ever bore to her virtues; but, since she hath so extremely denied me, I am to lay out for my fortunes elsewhere.

HOARD. Heaven forbid but you should, sir! I ever told you my niece stood otherwise affected.[2]

MON. I must confess you did, sir; [10 yet, in regard of my great loss of time, and the zeal with which I sought your niece, shall I desire one favor of your worship.

HOARD. In regard of those two, 'tis hard but you shall, sir.

MON. I shall rest grateful. 'Tis not full three hours, sir, since the happy rumor of a rich country widow came to my hearing.

HOARD. How? A rich country widow?

MON. Four hundred a year landed.   20

HOARD. Yea?

MON. Most firm, sir; and I have learnt her lodging. Here my suit begins, sir; if I might but entreat your worship to be a countenance for me, and speak a good word (for your words will pass), I nothing doubt but I might set fair for the widow; nor shall your labor, sir, end altogether in thanks; two hundred angels—

HOARD. So, so. What suitors has [30 she?

MON. There lies the comfort, sir; the report of her is yet but a whisper, and only solicited by young riotous Witgood, nephew to your mortal adversary.

HOARD. Ha! Art certain he's her suitor?

MON. Most certain, sir; and his uncle very industrious to beguile the widow, and make up the match.

HOARD. So? Very good.   40

MON. Now, sir, you know this young

---

[1] A proverb meaning *to succeed or fail.*
[2] Was in love with another.

Witgood is a spendthrift, dissolute fellow.

HOARD. A very rascal.

MON. A midnight surfeiter.

HOARD. The spume of a brothel house.

MON. True, sir; which, being well told in your worship's phrase, may both heave him out of her mind, and drive a fair way for me to the widow's affections.

HOARD. Attend me about five.   50

MON. With my best care, sir.   *Exit.*

HOARD. Fool, thou hast left thy treasure with a thief,

To trust a widower with a suit in love! Happy revenge, I hug thee! I have not only the means laid before me, extremely to cross my adversary, and confound the last hopes of his nephew, but thereby to enrich my state, augment my revenues, and build mine own fortunes greater. Ha, ha!

I'll mar your phrase, o'erturn your flatteries,   60

Undo your windings, policies, and plots, Fall like a secret and despatchful plague On your securéd comforts. Why, I am able

To buy three of Lucre, thrice outbid him, Let my outmonies [3] be reckonéd and all.

Enter three Creditors.

1 [CRED.] I am glad of this news.

2 [CRED.] So are we, by my faith.

3 [CRED.] Young Witgood will be a gallant again now.

HOARD. [*Aside.*] Peace!   70

1 [CRED.] I promise you, Master Cockpit, she's a mighty rich widow.

2 [CRED.] Why, have you ever heard of her?

1 [CRED.] Who? Widow Medler? She lies open to much rumor.

3 [CRED.] Four hundred a year, they say, in very good land.

1 [CRED.] Nay, take 't of my word, if you believe that, you believe the least. [80

2 [CRED.] And to see how close he keeps it!

1 [CRED.] O, sir, there's policy in that to prevent better suitors.

3 [CRED.] He owes me a hundred pound, and I protest I ne'er looked for a penny.

1 [CRED.] He little dreams of our coming; he'll wonder to see his creditors upon him.   *Exeunt* [*Creditors*].

---

[3] Money put out in loans.

HOARD. Good! His creditors! I'll follow.
　This makes for me.　　　　　　　　90
All know the widow's wealth; and 'tis
　well known
I can estate her fairly, ay, and will.
In this one chance shines a twice happy
　fate;
I both deject my foe and raise my state.
　　　　　　　　　　　　　　　Exit.
　　　　　MUSIC.

　　　　　Incipit
　　ACT[US] III. [SCENA i.

　　Witgood's room.]

　Witgood with his Creditors.

WIT. Why, alas, my creditors, could you
find no other time to undo me but now?
Rather your malice appears in this than the
justness of the debt.
1 [CRED.] Master Witgood, I have forborne my money long.
WIT. I pray, speak low, sir. What do
you mean?
2 [CRED.] We hear you are to be married
suddenly to a rich country widow.　　10
WIT. What can be kept so close but you
creditors hear on 't! Well, 'tis a lamentable
state that our chiefest afflictors should first
hear of our fortunes. Why, this is no good
course, i' faith, sirs. If ever you have hope
to be satisfied, why do you seek to confound
the means that should work it? There's
neither piety, no, nor policy in that. Shine
favorably now, why, I may rise and spread
again to your great comforts.　　　20
1 [CRED.] He says true, i' faith.
WIT. Remove me now, and I consume for-
　ever.
2 [CRED.] Sweet gentleman!
WIT. How can it thrive which from the sun
　you sever?
3 [CRED.] It cannot, indeed.
WIT. O, then, show patience! I shall have
　enough
To satisfy you all.
1 [CRED.]　　　　　Ay, if we could
Be content, a shame take us!
WIT.　　　　　　For, look you,
I am but newly sure [1] yet to the widow,
And what a rend might this discredit
　make!　　　　　　　　　　30

　　¹ Engaged.

Within these three days will I bind you
　lands
For your securities.
1 [CRED.]　　　No, good Master Witgood.
Would 'twere as much as we dare trust
　you with!
WIT. I know you have been kind; how-
　ever, now,
Either by wrong report or false incite-
　ment
Your gentleness is injured. In such
A state as this a man cannot want
　foes.
If on the sudden he begin to rise,
No man that lives can count his enemies.
You had some intelligence, I warrant
　ye,　　　　　　　　　　　　40
From an ill-willer.
2 [CRED.] Faith, we heard you brought
up a rich widow, sir, and were suddenly to
marry her.
WIT. Ay, why, there it was; I knew 'twas
so; but, since you are so well resolved [2] of
my faith toward you, let me be so much
favored of you, I beseech you all—
ALL. O, it shall not need, i' faith,
sir!—　　　　　　　　　　　　50
WIT. As to lie still awhile, and bury my
debts in silence, till I be fully possessed of
the widow; for the truth is—I may tell you
as my friends—
ALL. O—O—O!—
WIT. I am to raise a little money in the
city, toward the setting forth of myself, for
my own credit and your comfort. Now, if
my former debts should be divulged, all
hope of my proceedings were quite [60
extinguished.
1 [CRED.] Do you hear, sir? I may deserve your custom hereafter. Pray, let my
money be accepted before a stranger's.
Here's forty pound I received as I came to
you. If that may stand you in any stead,
make use on 't. [*Offers money, which Witgood at first refuses.*] Nay, pray, sir; 'tis at
your service.
WIT. You do so ravish me with kindness
　that　　　　　　　　　　　　70
I'm constrained to play the maid, and
　take it.
1 [CRED. (*Aside to Witgood.*)] Let none
of them see it, I beseech you.
WIT. [*Taking money. (Aside.*)] Fah!

　　² Satisfied.

1 [CRED. (*Aside.*)] I hope I shall be first in your remembrance
After the marriage rites.
WIT. [*Aside.*] Believe it firmly.
1 [CRED.] So.—What, do you walk, sirs?
2 [CRED.] I go.—[*Aside to Witgood.*] Take no care, sir, for money to furnish you; within this hour I'll send you suffi- [80 cient.—Come, Master Cockpit, we both stay for you.
3 [CRED.] I ha' lost a ring, i' faith; I'll follow you presently.—[*Exeunt 1 and 2 Creditors.*] But you shall find it, sir. I know your youth and expenses have disfurnished you of all jewels. There's a ruby of twenty pound price, sir; bestow it upon your widow. [*Offers a ring, which Witgood at first refuses.*] What, man! 'Twill [90 call up her blood to you; beside, if I might so much work with you, I would not have you beholding to those bloodsuckers for any money.
WIT. [*Taking ring.*] Not I, believe it.
3 [CRED.] They're a brace of cutthroats.
WIT. I know 'em.
3 [CRED.] Send a note of all your wants to my shop, and I'll supply you instantly.
WIT. Say you so? Why, here's my [100 hand then; no man living shall do 't but thyself.
3 [CRED.] Shall I carry it away from 'em both, then?
WIT. I' faith, shalt thou.
3 [CRED.] Troth, then, I thank you, sir.
WIT. Welcome, good Master Cockpit. —(*Exit* [3 *Creditor*].) Ha, ha, ha! Why, is not this better now than lying abed? I perceive there's nothing conjures up wit [110 sooner than poverty, and nothing lays it down sooner than wealth and lechery! This has some savor yet. O, that I had the mortgage from mine uncle as sure in possession as these trifles! I would forswear brothel at noonday, and muscadine and eggs [1] at midnight.

Enter Courtesan.

COUR. Master Witgood, where are you?
WIT. Holla!
COUR. Rich news! 120
WIT. Would 'twere all in plate!
COUR. There's some in chains and jewels. I am so haunted with suitors, Master

[1] A concoction used as an aphrodisiac.

Witgood, I know not which to despatch first.
WIT. You have the better term,[2] by my faith.
COUR. Among the number one Master Hoard, an ancient gentleman.
WIT. Upon my life, my uncle's [130 adversary.
COUR. It may well hold so, for he rails on you,
Speaks shamefully of him.
WIT. As I could wish it.
COUR. I first denied him, but so cunningly It rather promised him assuréd hopes Than any loss of labor.
WIT. Excellent!
COUR. I expect him every hour with gentlemen,
With whom he labors to make good his words,
To approve [3] you riotous, your state consumed,
Your uncle— 140
WIT. Wench, make up thy own fortunes now; do thyself a good turn once in thy days. He's rich in money, movables, and lands. Marry him. He's an old, doting fool, and that's worth all. Marry him. 'Twould be a great comfort to me to see thee do well, i' faith. Marry him. 'Twould ease my conscience well to see thee well bestowed; I have a care of thee, i' faith.
COUR. Thanks, sweet Master Wit- [150 good.
WIT. I reach at farder happiness. First, I am sure it can be no harm to thee, and there may happen goodness to me by it. Prosecute it well; let's send up for our [4] wits, now we require their best and most pregnant assistance.
COUR. Step in; I think I hear 'em.
Exit [*with Witgood*].

Enter Hoard and Gentlemen with the Host [*as*] *serving-man.*

HOARD. Art thou the widow's man? By my faith, sh'as a company of proper [5] [160 men then.
HOST. I am the worst of six, sir; good enough for bluecoats.

[2] The time for lawsuits, at which many dissolute people came to London.
[3] Prove. [5] Handsome.
[4] From 1616 edn. Original reads *out*.

HOARD. Hark hither. I hear say thou art in most credit with her.

HOST. Not so, sir.

HOARD. Come, come, thou'rt modest. There's a brace of royals; [1] prithee, help me to th' speech of her. [*Gives him money.*]

HOST. I'll do what I may, sir, al- [170 ways saving myself harmless.

HOARD. Go to, do 't, I say; thou shalt hear better from me.

HOST. [*Aside.*] Is not this a better place than five mark a year standing wages? Say a man had but three such clients in a day, methinks he might make a poor living on 't. Beside, I was never brought up with so little honesty to refuse any man's money; never. What gulls there are a this side the [180 world! Now know I the widow's mind, none but my young master comes in her clutches. Ha, ha, ha! *Exit.*

HOARD. Now, my dear gentlemen, stand firmly to me;
You know his follies and my worth.

1 [GENT.] We do, sir.

2 [GENT.] But, Master Hoard, are you sure he is not i' th' house now?

HOARD. Upon my honesty, I chose this time
A purpose, fit; the spendthrift is abroad.
Assist me; here she comes.—

[*Enter Courtesan.*]

Now, my sweet widow. 190

COUR. Y' are welcome, Master Hoard.

HOARD. Despatch, sweet gentlemen, despatch.—
I am come, widow, to prove those my words
Neither of envy sprung nor of false tongues,
But such as their [2] deserts and actions
Do merit and bring forth, all which these gentlemen,
Well known and better reputed, will confess.

COUR. I cannot tell
How my affections may dispose of me;
But surely, if they find him so desertless, 200
They'll have that reason to withdraw themselves;

And therefore, gentlemen, I do entreat you,
As you are fair in reputation
And in appearing form, so shine in truth.
I am a widow, and, alas, you know,
Soon overthrown! 'Tis a very small thing
That we withstand, our weakness is so great.
Be partial unto neither, but deliver,
Without affection, [3] your opinion.

HOARD. And that will drive it home. 210

COUR. Nay, I beseech your silence, Master Hoard;
You are a party.

HOARD. Widow, not a word.

1 [GENT.] The better first to work you to belief,
Know neither of us owe him flattery,
Nor tother [4] malice, but unbribéd censure [5]—
So help us our best fortunes!

COUR. It suffices.

1 [GENT.] That Witgood is a riotous, undone man,
Imperfect both in fame and in estate,
His debts wealthier than he, and executions
In wait for his due body, we'll maintain 220
With our best credit and our dearest blood.

COUR. Nor land nor living, say you? Pray, take heed
You do not wrong the gentleman.

1 [GENT.] What we speak
Our lives and means are ready to make good.

COUR. Alas, how soon are we poor souls beguiled!

2 [GENT.] And for his uncle—

HOARD. Let that come to me.
His uncle, a severe extortioner;
A tyrant at a forfeiture; greedy of others' Miseries; one that would undo his brother, 229
Nay, swallow up his father, if he can,
Within the fadoms [6] of his conscience.

1 [GENT.] Nay, believe it, widow,
You had not only matched yourself to wants,
But in an evil and unnatural stock.

[1] Gold pieces.
[2] *I.e.*, Lucre's and Witgood's.
[3] Prejudice.
[4] *I.e.*, Witgood.
[5] Judgment.
[6] Fathoms.

HOARD. [*Aside to Gentlemen.*] Follow hard, gentlemen, follow hard.

COUR. Is my love so deceived? Before you all
I do renounce him; on my knees I vow
He ne'er shall marry me.

WIT. [*Looking in. (Aside.)*] Heaven knows he never meant it!

HOARD. [*Aside to Gentlemen.*] There take her at the bound.   240

1 [GENT.] Then, with a new and pure affection,
Behold yon gentleman, grave, kind, and rich,
A match worthy yourself; esteeming him,
You do regard your state.

HOARD. [*Aside to Gentlemen.*] I'll make her a jointure, say.

1 [GENT.] He can join land to land, and will possess you
Of what you can desire.

2 [GENT.]   Come, widow, come.

COUR. The world is so deceitful!

1 [GENT.]   There, 'tis deceitful
Where flattery, want, and imperfection lies;
But none of these in him. Push!

COUR.   Pray, sir—   250

1 [GENT.] Come, you widows are ever most backward when you should do yourselves most good; but, were it to marry a chin not worth a hair now, then you would be forward enough. Come, clap hands! A match!

HOARD. With all my heart, widow.— Thanks, gentlemen.
I will deserve[1] your labor and thy love.

COUR. Alas, you love not widows but for wealth!
I promise you I ha' nothing, sir.

HOARD.   Well said, widow,   260
Well said; thy love is all I seek, before These gentlemen.

COUR.   Now I must hope the best.

HOARD. My joys are such they want to be expressed.

COUR. But, Master Hoard, one thing I must remember you of, before these gentlemen, your friends: how shall I suddenly avoid the loathed soliciting of that perjured Witgood, and his tedious, dissembling uncle, who this very day hath appointed a meeting for the same   [270

[1] Reward.

purpose too, where, had not truth come forth, I had been undone, utterly undone?

HOARD. What think you of that, gentlemen?

1 [GENT.] 'Twas well devised.

HOARD. Hark thee, widow. Train[2] out young Witgood single; hasten him thither with thee, somewhat before the hour, where, at the place appointed, these gentlemen and myself will wait the oppor-   [280 tunity, when, by some slight removing him from thee, we'll suddenly enter and surprise thee, carry thee away by boat to Cole Harbor, have a priest ready, and there clap it up instantly. How lik'st it, widow?

COUR. In that it pleaseth you, it likes me well.

HOARD. I'll kiss thee for those words.
Come, gentlemen;
Still must I live a suitor to your favors,
Still to your aid beholding.

1 [GENT.]   We're engaged, sir;
'Tis for our credits now to see 't well ended.   290

HOARD. 'Tis for your honors, gentlemen; nay, look to 't.
Not only in joy, but I in wealth excel.
No more sweet widow, but, sweet wife, farewell.

COUR. Farewell, sir.

Exeunt [Hoard and Gentlemen].

Enter Witgood.

WIT. O, for more scope! I could laugh eternally!
Give you joy, Mistress Hoard. I promise your fortune was good, forsooth. Y'ave fell upon wealth enough, and there's young gentlemen enow can help you to the rest. Now it requires our wits. Carry thy-   [300 self but heedfully now, and we are both—

[Enter Host.]

HOST. Master Witgood, your uncle.

Enter Lucre.

WIT. [*Aside.*] Cud's me! Remove thyself awhile; I'll serve for him.

[Exeunt Courtesan and Host.]

LUC. Nephew, good morrow, nephew.

WIT. The same to you, kind uncle.

[2] Lure.

Luc. How fares the widow? Does the meeting hold?

Wit. O, no question of that, sir.

Luc. I'll strike the stroke, then, for thee; no more days.[1]   309

Wit. The sooner the better, uncle. O, she's mightily followed!

Luc. And yet so little rumored!

Wit. Mightily! Here comes one old gentleman, and he'll make her a jointure of three hundred a year, forsooth; another wealthy suitor will estate his son in his life-time, and make him weigh down the widow; here a merchant's son will possess her with no less than three goodly lordships[2] at once, which were all pawns to his father.   320

Luc. Peace, nephew, let me hear no more of 'em; it mads me. Thou shalt pre-vent[3] 'em all. No words to the widow of my coming hither. Let me see—'tis now upon nine. Before twelve, nephew, we will have the bargain struck, we will, faith, boy.

Wit. O, my precious uncle!

                          Exit [with Lucre].

[Scena ii.

A room in Hoard's house.]

Hoard and his Niece.

Hoard. Niece, sweet niece, prithee, have a care to my house; I leave all to thy discretion. Be content to dream awhile. I'll have a husband for thee shortly; put that care upon me, wench, for in choosing wives and husbands I am only fortunate; I have that gift given me.   *Exit.*

Niece. But 'tis not likely you should choose for me,

  Since nephew to your chiefest enemy   9
  Is he whom I affect. But, O, forgetful!
  Why dost thou flatter thy affections so,
  With name of him that for a widow's bed
  Neglects thy purer love? Can it be so,
  Or does report dissemble?—

[*Enter George.*]

                          How now, sir?

Geo. A letter, with which came a private charge.

Niece. Therein I thank your care.—

                          [*Exit George.*]

          I know this hand—(*Reads.*)
"Dearer than sight,

¹ Delays.   ² Manors.   ³ Anticipate.

What the world reports of me, yet believe not; rumor will alter shortly. Be thou con-stant; I am still the same that I was in   [20 love, and I hope to be the same in fortunes.

          Theodorus Witgood."

I am resolved. No more shall fear or doubt

Raise their pale powers to keep affection out.   *Exit.*

[Scena iii.

A room in a tavern.]

Enter, with a Drawer, Hoard and two Gentle-men.

Dra. You're very welcome, gentle-men.—Dick, show those gentlemen the Pomegranate[4] there.

Hoard. Hist!

Dra. Up those stairs, gentlemen.

Hoard. Pist,[5] drawer!

Dra. Anon, sir.

Hoard. Prithee, ask at the bar if a gentlewoman came not in lately.

Dra. William, at the bar, did you   [10 see any gentlewoman come in lately? Speak you ay, speak you no?

[William.] (*Within.*) No, none came in yet but Mistress Florence.

Dra. He says none came in yet, sir, but one Mistress Florence.

Hoard. What is that Florence?   A widow?

Dra. Yes, a Dutch widow.

Hoard. How?   20

Dra. That's an English drab, sir—give your worship good morrow.   [*Exit.*]

Hoard. A merry knave, i' faith! I shall remember a Dutch widow the longest day of my life.

1 [Gent.] Did not I use most art to win the widow?

2 [Gent.] You shall pardon me for that, sir; Master Hoard knows I took her at best vantage.   30

Hoard. What's that, sweet gentlemen, what's that?

2 [Gent.] He will needs bear me down, that his art only wrought with the widow most.

Hoard. O, you did both well, gentle-men, you did both well, I thank you.

1 [Gent.] I was the first that moved her.

⁴ The name of one of the rooms.   ⁵ Hist!

HOARD.   You were, i' faith.
2 [GENT.] But it was I that took her at
the bound.
HOARD. Ay, that was you. Faith, gentlemen, 'tis right.   40
1 ¹ [GENT.] I boasted least, but 'twas I
joined their hands.
HOARD. By th' Mass, I think he did. You
did all well,
Gentlemen, you did all well. Contend
no more.
1 [GENT.] Come, yon room's fittest.
HOARD.   True, 'tis next the door.
    Exit [with Gentlemen].

*Enter [Drawer,] Witg[ood], Court[esan], and
Host.*

DRA. You're very welcome. Please you
to walk upstairs; cloth's laid, sir.
COUR. Upstairs? Troth, I am weary,
Master Witgood.
WIT. Rest yourself here awhile, widow;
we'll have a cup of muscadine in this   [50
little room.
DRA. A cup of muscadine? You shall
have the best, sir.
WIT. But do you hear, sirrah?
DRA. Do you call? Anon, sir.
WIT. What is there provided for dinner?
DRA. I cannot readily tell you, sir. If
you please, you may go into the kitchen
and see yourself, sir; many gentlemen of
worship do use to do it, I assure you,   [60
sir.   [Exit.]
HOST. A pretty, familiar, priggin ² ras-
cal; he has his part without book.
WIT. Against you are ready to drink to
me, widow, I'll be present to pledge you.
COUR. Nay, I commend your care; 'tis
done well of you.—[*Exit Witgood.*] 'Las,³
what have I forgot!
HOST. What, mistress?
COUR. I slipped my wedding ring off   [70
when I washed, and left it at my lodging.
Prithee, run; I shall be sad without it.—
[*Exit Host.*] So, he's gone.—Boy!

[Enter Boy.]

BOY. Anon, forsooth.
COUR. Come hither, sirrah.   Learn

¹ Original reads *3*, but see III, i, 251–6.
² Prigging; usually *thieving*, here *smart*.
³ Emended by Bullen. Early edns. read *asse*,
but apparently a letter has dropped out.

secretly if one Master Hoard, an ancient
gentleman, be about house.
BOY. I heard such a one named.
COUR. Commend me to him.

Enter Hoard with Gentlemen.

HOARD.   I'll do thy commendations!
COUR. O, you come well. Away, to boat,
begone!   80
HOARD. Thus wise men are revenged, give
two for one.   *Exeunt.*

Enter Witgood and Vintner.

WIT. I must request
You, sir, to show extraordinary care.
My uncle comes with gentlemen, his
friends,
And 'tis upon a making.⁴
VIN.   Is it so?
I'll give a special charge, good Master
Witgood.
May I be bold to see her?
WIT.   Who? The widow?
With all my heart, i' faith; I'll bring you
to her.
VIN. If she be a Staffordshire gentle-
woman, 'tis much if I know her not.   90
WIT. How now? Boy! Drawer!
VIN. Hie!

[Enter Boy.]

BOY. Do you call, sir?
WIT. Went the gentlewoman up that
was here?
BOY. Up, sir? She went out, sir.
WIT. Out, sir?
BOY. Out, sir. One Master Hoard, with
a guard of gentlemen, carried her out at
back door, a pretty while since, sir.   100
WIT. Hoard? Death and darkness!
Hoard?

Enter Hoard.

HOST. The devil of ring I can find.
WIT. How now? What news? Where's
the widow?
HOST. My mistress? Is she not here, sir?
WIT. More madness yet!
HOST.   She sent me for a ring.
WIT. A plot, a plot!—To boat! She's stole
away.
HOST. What?   109

⁴ Mating.

Enter Lucre with Gentlemen.

WIT. Follow! Inquire! Old Hoard, my uncle's adversary—   [*Exit Host.*]

LUC. Nephew, what's that?

WIT.   Thrice-miserable wretch!

LUC. Why, what's the matter?

VIN.   The widow's borne away, sir.

LUC. Ha, passion of me!—A heavy welcome, gentlemen.

1 [GENT.] The widow gone?

LUC. Who durst attempt it?

WIT. Who but old Hoard, my uncle's adversary?

LUC. How?

WIT. With his confederates.

LUC. Hoard, my deadly enemy?—Gentlemen, stand to me;   120
I will not bear it; 'tis in hate of me;
That villain seeks my shame, nay, thirsts [1] my blood.
He owes me mortal malice.
I'll spend my wealth on this despiteful plot,
Ere he shall cross me and my nephew thus.

WIT. So maliciously!

Enter Host.

LUC. How now, you treacherous rascal?

HOST. That's none of my name, sir.

WIT. Poor soul, he knew not on 't!

LUC. I'm sorry. I see then 'twas a mere plot.   130

HOST. I traced 'em nearly—

LUC.   Well?

HOST.   And hear for certain
They have took Cole Harbor.

LUC.   The devil's sanctuary!
They shall not rest, I'll pluck her from his arms—
Kind and dear gentlemen,
If ever I had seat within your breasts—

1 [GENT.] No more, good sir; it is a wrong to us
To see you injured in a cause so just.
We'll spend our lives but we will right our friends.

LUC. Honest and kind! Come, we have delayed too long.   139
Nephew, take comfort; a just cause is strong.   *Exeunt* [*All but Witgood*].

---

[1] Early edns read *thrifts*.

WIT. That's all my comfort, uncle. Ha, ha, ha!
Now may events fall luckily and well;
He that ne'er strives, says wit, shall ne'er excel.   *Exit.*

[SCENA iv.

A room in Dampit's house.]

Enter Dampit, the usurer, drunk.

DAMP. When did I say my prayers? In *anno* '88, when the great armado was coming; and in *anno* '99, when the great thunder and lightning was, I prayed heartily then, i' faith, to overthrow Poovies' new buildings; I kneeled by my great iron chest, I remember.

[*Enter Audrey.*]

AUD. Master Dampit, one may hear you before they see you. You keep sweet hours, Master Dampit; we were all [10 abed three hours ago.

DAMP. Audrey?

AUD. O, y' are a fine gentleman!

DAMP. So I am, i' faith, and a fine scholar. Do you use to go to bed so early, Audrey?

AUD. Call you this early, Master Dampit?

DAMP. Why, is 't not one of clock i' th' morning? Is not that early enough? [20 Fetch me a glass of fresh beer.

AUD. Here, I have warmed your nightcap for you, Master Dampit.

DAMP. Draw it on then. I am very weak, truly. I have not eaten so much as the bulk of an egg these three days.

AUD. You have drunk the more, Master Dampit.

DAMP. What's that?

AUD. You mought,[2] and you would, [30 Master Dampit.

DAMP. I answer you, I cannot. Hold your prating; you prate too much, and understand too little. Are you answered? Give me a glass of beer.

AUD. May I ask you how you do, Master Dampit?

DAMP. How do I? I' faith, naught.

AUD. I ne'er knew you do otherwise.

DAMP. I eat not one pennort [3] of [40

---

[2] Might.   [3] Pennyworth.

bread these two years. Give me a glass of
fresh beer. I am not sick, nor I am not
well.

AUD. Take this warm napkin about
your neck, sir, whilst I help to make you
unready.[1]

DAMP. How now, Audrey-prater, with
your scurvy devices, what say you now?

AUD. What say I, Master Dampit? I
say nothing but that you are very weak. [50

DAMP. Faith, thou hast more cunny-
catching [2] devices than all London.

AUD. Why, Master Dampit, I never
deceived you in all my life.

DAMP. Why was that? Because I never
did trust thee.

AUD. I care not what you say, Master
Dampit.

DAMP. Hold thy prating. I answer thee,
thou art a beggar, a quean, and a bawd. [60
Are you answered?

AUD. Fie, Master Dampit! A gentleman, and have such words!

DAMP. Why, thou base drudge of in-
fortunity, thou kitchen-stuff drab of beggary, roguery, and coxcombry, thou cav-
ernesed [3] quean of foolery, knavery, and
bawdreaminy, I'll tell thee what, I will
not give a louse for thy fortunes.

AUD. No, Master Dampit? And [70
there's a gentleman comes a-wooing to
me, and he doubts [4] nothing but that you
will get me from him.

DAMP. I? If I would either have thee
or lie with thee for two thousand pound,
would I might be damned! Why, thou
base, impudent quean of foolery, flattery,
and coxcombry, are you answered?

AUD. Come, will you rise and go to
bed, sir?   80

DAMP. Rise, and go to bed too, Audrey?
How does Mistress Proserpine?

AUD. Fooh!

DAMP. She's as fine a philosopher of a
stinkard's wife as any within the liberties.[5]
Fah, fah, Audrey!

AUD. How now, Master Dampit?

DAMP. Fie, upon 't, what a choice of
stinks here is! What hast thou done, Au-

---

[1] Undress you.   [2] Cheating.
[3] Another of Dampit's coinages, of doubtful
meaning.   [4] Fears.
[5] The slum district just outside the walls of
the city.

drey? Fie upon 't, here's a choice of [90
stinks indeed! Give me a glass of fresh
beer, and then I will to bed.

AUD. It waits for you above, sir.

DAMP. Foh! I think they burn horns
in Barnard's Inn. If ever I smelt such an
abominable stink, usury forsake me. [Exit.]

AUD. They be the stinking nails of
his trampling feet, and he talks of burning horns.   Exit.

Incipit
ACT[US] IV. [SCENA i.]

*Enter at Cole Harbor, Hoard, the Widow,
[Lamprey, Spichcock,] and Gentlemen,
he married now.*

1 [GENT.] Join hearts, join hands,
    In wedlock's bands,
    Never to part
    Till death cleave your heart.
[*To Hoard.*] You shall forsake all other
    women;
[*To Courtesan.*] You lords, knights, gentle-
    men, and yeomen.
What my tongue slips
Make up with your lips.

HOARD. Give you joy, Mistress Hoard;
    let the kiss come about.—[*One knocks.*]
Who knocks?   Convey my little pig-
    eater [6] out.   10

LUC. [*Within.*] Hoard!

HOARD. Upon my life, my adversary,
    gentlemen!

LUC. [*Within.*] Hoard, open the door, or
    we will force it ope.

Give us the widow.

HOARD.   Gentlemen, keep 'em out.

LAMP. He comes upon his death that
    enters here.

LUC. [*Within.*] My friends, assist me!

HOARD. He has assistants, gentlemen.

LAMP. Tut, nor him nor them we in this
    action fear.

LUC. [*Within.*] Shall I, in peace, speak one
    word with the widow?

COUR. Husband and gentlemen, hear
    me but a word.

HOARD. Freely, sweet wife.

COUR.   Let him in peaceably; 20
You know we're sure from any act of
    his.

HOARD. Most true.

[6] Term of endearment.

COUR. [1] You may stand by and smile at
his old weakness.
Let me alone to answer him.

HOARD. Content;
'Twill be good mirth, i' faith. How
think you, gentlemen?

LAMP. Good gullery!

HOARD. Upon calm conditions let him in.

LUC. [*Within.*] All spite and malice!

LAMP. Hear me, Master Lucre.
So you will vow a peaceful entrance
With those your friends, and only exer-
cise
Calm conference with the widow, with-
out fury, 30
The passage shall receive you.

Enter Lucre [, Gentlemen, and Host].

LUC. I do vow it.

LAMP. Then enter and talk freely. Here
she stands.

LUC. O, Master Hoard, your spite has
watched [2] the hour!
You're excellent at vengeance, Master
Hoard.

HOARD. Ha, ha, ha!

LUC. I am the fool you laugh at.
You are wise, sir, and know the seasons
well.—
Come hither, widow. Why is it thus?
O, you have done me infinite disgrace,
And your own credit no small injury!
Suffer mine enemy so despitefully 40
To bear you from my nephew? O, I
had rather
Half my substance had been forfeit and
begged by some
Starved rascal!

COUR. Why, what would you
wish me do, sir?
I must not overthrow my state for love.
We have too many presidents [3] for that;
From thousands of our wealthy undone
widows
One may derive some wit. I do confess
I loved your nephew, nay, I did affect
him
Against the mind and liking of my
friends,[4]
Believed his promises, lay here in hope 50
Of flattered living and the boast of lands.

Coming to touch his wealth and state
indeed,
It appears dross; I find him not the
man,
Imperfect, mean, scarce furnished of
his needs—
In words, fair lordships; in performance,
hovels.
Can any woman love the thing that is
not?

LUC. Broke you for this?

COUR. Was it not cause too much?
Send to inquire his state; most part of
it
Lay two years mortgaged in his uncle's
hands.

LUC. Why, say it did; you might have
known my mind. 60
I could have soon restored it.

COUR. Ay, had I but seen any such thing
performed,
Why, 'twould have tied my affection,
and contained
Me in my first desires. Do you think,
i' faith,
That I could twine such a dry oak as
this,
Had promise in your nephew took effect?

LUC. Why, and there's no time past; and
rather than
My adversary should thus thwart my
hopes,
I would—

COUR. Tut, y'ave been ever full of golden
speech. 70
If words were lands, your nephew would
be rich.

LUC. Widow, believe it, I vow by my
best bliss,
Before these gentlemen, I will give in
The mortgage to my nephew instantly,
Before I sleep or eat.

1 [GENT.] [5] We'll pawn our
credits,
Widow, what he speaks shall be performed
In fullness.

LUC. Nay, more. I will estate him
In farther blessings; he shall be my
heir;
I have no son;
I'll bind myself to that condition. 80

---

[1] Early edns. read *Luc.*   [3] Precedents.
[2] Awaited.
[4] From 1616 edn. Original reads *friend.*
[5] Of Lucre's party.

Cour. When I shall hear this done, I
shall soon yield
  To reasonable terms.
Luc.   In the mean season,
  Will you protest, before these gentle-
  men,
  To keep yourself as you are now at this
  present?
Cour. I do protest, before these gentle-
  men,
  I will be as clear then as I am now.
Luc. I do believe you. Here's your own
  honest servant;
  I'll take him along with me.
Cour.   Ay, with all my heart.
Luc. He shall see all performed, and
  bring you word.
Cour. That's all I wait for.   90
Hoard. What, have you finished, Master
  Lucre? Ha, ha, ha, ha!
Luc. So laugh, Hoard, laugh at your
  poor enemy, do;
  The wind may turn; you may be laughed
  at too.
  Yes, marry, may you, sir.—Ha, ha, ha!
    Exeunt [Lucre, Gentlemen, and Host].
Hoard. Ha, ha, ha! If every man that
  swells in malice
  Could be revenged as happily as I,
  He would choose hate, and forswear
  amity.—
  What did he say, wife, prithee?
Cour. Faith, spoke to ease his mind.
Hoard. O—O—O!
Cour.   You know now, little to
  any purpose.   100
Hoard. True, true, true!
Cour.   He would do mountains now.
Hoard. Ay, ay, ay, ay.
Lamp.   Y'ave struck him dead, Master
  Hoard.
Spi. And his nephew desperate.
Hoard.   I know 't, sirs, I.
  Never did man so crush his enemy.
                        Exeunt.

[Scena ii.

A room in Lucre's house.]

*Enter Lucre with Gentlemen, [and Host,]
        meeting Sam Freedom.*

Luc. My   son-in-law,   Sam   Freedom,
  where's my nephew?
Sam. O, man in lamentation, father!

Luc.   How!
Sam. He thumps his breast like a gal-
lant dicer that has lost his doublet, and
stands in 's shirt to do penance.
Luc. Alas, poor gentleman!
Sam. I warrant you may hear him sigh
in a still evening to your house at High-
gate.
Luc. I prithee, send him in.   10
Sam. Were it to do a greater matter,
I will not stick with you, sir, in regard you
married my mother.   [*Exit.*]
Luc. Sweet gentlemen, cheer him up;
I will but fetch the mortgage and return
to you instantly.   *Exit.*
1 [Gent.] We'll do our best, sir.—See
  where he comes,
  E'en joyless and regardless of all form.

[*Enter Witgood.*]

2 [Gent.] Why, how now, Master Witgood? Fie! You a firm scholar, and [20
an understanding gentleman, and give
your best parts to passion?
1 [Gent.] Come, fie!
Wit. O, gentlemen—
1 [Gent.] Sorrow of me, what a sigh was
  there, sir!
  Nine such widows are not worth it.
Wit. To be borne from me by that lecher,
  Hoard!
1 [Gent.] That vengeance is your uncle's,
  being done
  More in despite to him than wrong to
  you.
  But we bring comfort now.
Wit.   I beseech you, gentlemen—   30
2 [Gent.] Cheer thyself, man; there's
  hope of her, i' faith.
Wit. Too gladsome to be true.

Enter Lucre.

Luc.   Nephew, what cheer?
  Alas, poor gentleman, how art thou
  changed!
  Call thy fresh blood into thy cheeks
  again.
  She comes.
Wit.   Nothing afflicts me so much,
  But that it is your adversary, uncle,
  And merely plotted in despite of you.
Luc. Ay, that's it mads me, spites me!
I'll spend my wealth ere he shall carry her

so, because I know 'tis only to spite me. [40
Ay, this is it.   Here, nephew.   [*Gives a
paper.*]   Before these kind gentlemen, I
deliver in your mortgage my promise to
the widow. See, 'tis done. Be wise; you're
once more master of your own. The widow
shall perceive now you are not altogether
such a beggar as the world reputes you;
you can make shift to bring her to three
hundred a year, sir.
1 [GENT.]   Berlady,[1] and that's no toy,
    sir.
LUC.   A word, nephew.   50
1 [GENT. (*To Host.*)]   Now you may certify
the widow.
LUC. You must conceive it aright, nephew,
    now;
    To do you good I am content to do this.
WIT. I know it, sir.
LUC. But your own conscience can tell I
    had it
    Dearly enough of you.
WIT.   Ay, that's most certain.
LUC. Much money laid out, beside many
    a journey
    To fetch the rent; I hope you'll think
    on 't, nephew.
WIT. I were worse than a beast else, i'
    faith.
LUC. Although to blind the widow and
    the world,   60
    I out of policy do 't, yet there's a con-
    science, nephew.
WIT. Heaven forbid else!
LUC.   When you are full possessed,
    'Tis nothing to return it.
WIT. Alas, a thing quickly done, uncle!
LUC. Well said! You know I give it you
    but in trust.
WIT. Pray, let me understand you rightly,
    uncle:
    You give it me but in trust?
LUC. No.
WIT. That is, you trust me with it?
LUC. True, true.   70
WIT. [*Aside.*] But, if ever I trust you with
    it again,
    Would I might be trussed up for my
    labor!
LUC. You can all witness, gentlemen,
and you, Sir Yeoman?
HOST. My life for yours, sir, now, I
know my mistress's mind too well toward

----
[1] By our Lady.

your nephew; let things be in preparation,
and I'll train her hither in most excellent
fashion.   *Exit.* 79
LUC. A good old boy!—Wife! 'Ginny!

Enter Wife.

WIFE. What's the news, sir?
LUC. The wedding day's at hand.
Prithee, sweet wife, express thy house-
wifery. Thou'rt a fine cook, I know 't;
thy first husband married thee out of an
alderman's kitchen; go to, he raised thee
for raising of paste. What! Here's none
but friends; most of our beginnings must
be winked at.—Gentlemen, I invite you
all to my nephew's wedding against [90
Thursday morning.
1 [GENT.] With all our hearts, and we
shall joy to see your enemy so mocked.
LUC. He laughed at me, gentlemen;
ha, ha, ha!   *Exeunt [All but Witgood].*
WIT. He has no conscience, faith,
would laugh at them. They laugh at one
another.
Who then can be so cruel? Troth,
    not I;
I rather pity now than aught envy.   100
I do conceive such joy in mine own
happiness I have no leisure yet to laugh
at their follies.—
    [*To the mortgage.*] Thou soul of my es-
        tate, I kiss thee!
I miss life's comfort when I miss thee.
O, never will we part again,
Until I leave the sight of men!
We'll ne'er trust conscience of our kin,
Since cozenage brings that title in. [*Exit.*]

[SCENA iii.

A street in London.]

Enter three Creditors.

1 [CRED.] I'll wait these seven hours but
I'll see him caught.
2 [CRED.] Faith, so will I.
3 [CRED.] Hang him, prodigal! He's
stripped of the widow.
1 [CRED.] A my troth, she's the wiser; she
has made the happier choice. And I wonder
of what stuff those widows' hearts are made
of, that will marry unfledged boys before
comely thrum-chinned [2] gentlemen.   10

----
[2] Rough-chinned.

Enter a Boy.

Boy. News, news, news!

1 [CRED.] What, boy?

Boy. The rioter is caught.

1 [CRED.] So, so, so, so! It warms me at the heart; I love a' life to see dogs upon men. O, here he comes.

Enter Witgood, with Serjeants.

WIT. My last joy was so great it took away the sense of all future afflictions. What a day is here o'ercast! How soon a black tempest rises! 20

1 [CRED.] O, we may speak with you now, sir! What's become of your rich widow? I think you may cast your cap at [1] the widow, may you not, sir?

2 [CRED.] He a rich widow? Who, a prodigal, a daily rioter, and a nightly vomiter? He a widow of account? He a hole i' th' Counter! [2]

WIT. You do well, my masters, to tyrannize over misery, to afflict the afflicted; [30 'tis a custom you have here amongst you. I would wish you never leave it, and I hope you'll do as I bid you.

1 [CRED.] Come, come, sir, what say you extempore now to your bill of a hundred pound? A sweet debt for froating [3] your doublets.

2 [CRED.] Here's mine of forty.

3 [CRED.] Here's mine of fifty. 39

WIT. Pray, sirs—you'll give me breath?

1 [CRED.] No, sir, we'll keep you out of breath still; then we shall be sure you will not run away from us.

WIT. Will you but hear me speak?

2 [CRED.] You shall pardon us for that, sir. We know you have too fair a tongue of your own. You overcame us too lately, a shame take you! We are like to lose all that for want of witnesses. We dealt in policy then; always when we strive to be [50 most politic we prove most coxcombs—*non plus ultra.*[4] I perceive by us we're not ordained to thrive by wisdom, and therefore we must be content to be tradesmen.

WIT. Give me but reasonable time, and I protest I'll make you ample satisfaction.

1 [CRED.] Do you talk of reasonable time to us?

WIT. 'Tis true, beasts know no reasonable time. 60

2 [CRED.] We must have either money or carcass.

WIT. Alas, what good will my carcass do you?

3 [CRED.] O, 'tis a secret delight we have amongst us! We that are used to keep birds in cages have the heart to keep men in prison, I warrant you.

WIT. [*Aside.*] I perceive I must crave a little more aid from my wits. Do but [70 make shift for me this once, and I'll forswear ever to trouble you in the like fashion hereafter; I'll have better employment for you, and I live.—You'll give me leave, my masters, to make trial of my friends, and raise all means I can?

1 [CRED.] That's our desires, sir.

Enter Host.

HOST. Master Witgood.

WIT. O, art thou come?

HOST. May I speak one word with [80 you in private, sir?

WIT. No, by my faith, canst thou; I am in hell here, and the devils will not let me come to thee.

CIT.[5] Do you call us devils? You shall find us Puritans.—Bear him away; let 'em talk as they go. We'll not stand to hear 'em.—Ah, sir, am I a devil? I shall think the better of myself as long as I live. A devil, i' faith! *Exeunt.* 90

[SCENA iv.

A room in Hoard's house.]

Enter Hoard.

HOARD. What a sweet blessing hast thou, Master Hoard, above a multitude! Wilt thou never be thankful? How dost thou think to be blessed another time? Or dost thou count this the full measure of thy happiness? By my troth, I think thou dost. Not only a wife large in possessions, but spacious in content; she's rich, she's young, she's fair, she's wise.[6] When I wake, I think of her lands—that revives me; [10

---

[1] Give up.

[2] London prison for debtors.

[3] Rubbing, probably with perfume.

[4] *I.e.*, go no further.

[5] Probably meaning *citizens, i.e., creditors.*

[6] From 1616 edn. Original reads *wife.*

when I go to bed, I dream of her beauty—
and that's enough for me. She's worth four
hundred a year in her very smock, if a man
knew how to use it. But the journey will
be all, in troth, into the country, to ride to
her lands in state and order following—my
brother and other worshipful gentlemen,
whose companies I ha' sent down for
already, to ride along with us in their goodly
decorum beards, their broad velvet [20
chashocks,[1] and chains of gold twice or
thrice double, against which time I'll entertain some ten men of mine own into liveries, all of occupations or qualities; I will
not keep an idle man about me, the sight
of which will so vex my adversary Lucre—
for we'll pass by his door a purpose, make
a little stand for [the][2] nonce, and have our
horses curvet before the window—certainly
he will never endure it, but run up [30
and hang himself presently.—

[Enter Servant.]

How now, sirrah, what news? Any that
offer their service to me yet?

SER. Yes, sir, there are some i' th' hall
that wait for your worship's liking, and
desire to be entertained.

HOARD. Are they of occupation?

SER. They are men fit for your worship,
sir. 39

HOARD. Say'st so? Send 'em all in.—
[Exit Servant.] To see ten men ride after
me in watchet[3] liveries, with orange-
tawny capes—'twill cut his comb, i' faith.

Enter All[4] [, i.e., Tailor, Barber, Perfumer,
Falconer, and Huntsman].

How now? Of what occupation are you,
sir?

TAIL. A tailor, an 't please your worship

HOARD. A tailor? O, very good. You
shall serve to make all the liveries.—What
are you, sir?

BAR. A barber, sir. 50

HOARD. A barber? Very needful. You
shall shave all the house, and, if need
require, stand for a reaper i' th' summer
time.—You, sir?

PER. A perfumer.

HOARD. I smelt you before. Perfumers,
of all men, had need carry themselves
uprightly; for if they were once knaves
they would be smelt out quickly.—To you,
sir? 60

FAL. A falc'ner, an 't please your worship.

HOARD. Sa ho, sa ho, sa ho![5]—And
you, sir?

HUNT. A huntsman, sir.

HOARD. There, boy, there, boy, there,
boy![6] I am not so old but I have pleasant
days to come. I promise you, my masters,
I take such a good liking to you that I entertain you all. I put you already [70
into my countenance, and you shall be
shortly in my livery. But especially you
two, my jolly falc'ner and my bonny huntsman, we shall have most need of you at my
wife's manor-houses i' th' country. There's
goodly parks and champion[7] grounds for
you; we shall have all our sports within ourselves; all the gentlemen a th' country shall
be beholding to us and our pastimes.

FAL. And we'll make your[8] worship [80
admire, sir.

HOARD. Say'st thou so? Do but make
me admire, and thou shall want for nothing.—My tailor.

TAIL. Anon, sir.

HOARD. Go presently in hand with the
liveries.

TAIL. I will, sir.

HOARD. My barber.

BAR. Here, sir. 90

HOARD. Make 'em all trim fellows,
louse 'em well—especially my huntsman—
and cut all their beards of the Polonian[9]
fashion.—My perfumer.

PER. Under your nose, sir.

HOARD. Cast a better savor upon the
knaves, to take away the scent of my
tailor's feet, and my barber's lotium
water.[10]

PER. It shall be carefully per- [100
formed, sir.

HOARD. But you, my falc'ner and
huntsman, the welcom'st men alive, i'
faith!

---

[1] Cassocks. [2] Added by Dyce. [3] Pale blue.
[4] This direction appears at the end of the speech
in the original.

[5] A hawking cry. [7] Champaign.
[6] A hunting cry.
[8] From 1616 edn. Original reads *you*.
[9] Polish.
[10] A preparation of urine used as a cosmetic.

HUNT. And we'll show you that, sir, shall deserve your worship's favor.

HOARD. I prithee, show me that.—Go, you knaves all, and wash your lungs i' th' buttery, go.—[*Exeunt Tailor, Barber, etc.*] By th' Mass, and well remembered! [110 I'll ask my wife that question.—Wife, Mistress Jane Hoard!

Enter Courtesan, altered in apparel.

COUR. Sir, would you with me?

HOARD. I would but know, sweet wife, which might stand best to thy liking, to have the wedding dinner kept here or i' th' country?

COUR. Hum! Faith, sir, 'twould like me better here; here you were married, here let all rites be ended.   120

HOARD. Could a marquesse [1] give a better answer? Hoard, bear thy head aloft; thou'st a wife will advance it.—

[*Enter Host with a letter.*]

What haste comes here now? Yea, a letter? Some dreg of my adversary's malice. Come hither; what's the news?

HOST. A thing that concerns my mistress, sir.   [*Gives letter to Courtesan.*]

HOARD. Why, then it concerns me, knave.   130

HOST. Ay, and you, knave, too (cry your worship mercy). You are both like to come into trouble, I promise you, sir; a precontract. [2]

HOARD. How? A precontract, say'st thou?

HOST. I fear they have too much proof on 't, sir. Old Lucre, he runs mad up and down, and will to law as fast as he can; young Witgood laid hold on [140 by his creditors, he exclaims upon you a tother side, says you have wrought his undoing by the injurious detaining of his contract.

HOARD. Body a me!

HOST. He will have utmost satisfaction; The law shall give him recompense, he says.

COUR. [*Aside.*] Alas, his creditors so

[1] Marchioness.
[2] "A pre-contract of marriage could not be set aside without the mutual consent of the parties" (Bullen).

merciless! My state being yet uncertain, I deem it not unconscionable to fur-   [150 der him.

HOST. True, sir.

HOARD. Wife, what says that letter? Let me construe it.

COUR. Cursed be my rash and unadviséd words!
    [*Tears and stamps upon the letter.*]
I'll set my foot upon my tongue,
And tread my inconsiderate grant to dust.

HOARD. Wife—

HOST. [*Aside.*] A pretty shift, i' faith! I commend a woman when she can [160 make away a letter from her husband handsomely, and this was cleanly done, by my troth.

COUR. I did, sir;
Some foolish words I must confess did pass,
Which now litigiously he fastens on me.

HOARD. Of what force? Let me examine 'em.

COUR. Too strong, I fear; would I were well freed of him!   170

HOARD. Shall I compound?

COUR. No, sir, I'd have it done some nobler way
Of your side; I'd have you come off with honor;
Let baseness keep with them. Why, have you not
The means, sir? The occasion's offered you.

HOARD. Where, how, dear wife?

COUR. He is now caught by his creditors; the slave's needy; his debts petty. He'll rather bind himself to all inconveniences than rot in prison; by this only [180 means you may get a release from him. 'Tis not yet come to his uncle's hearing. Send speedily for the creditors. By this time he's desperate; he'll set his hand to anything. Take order for his debts, or discharge 'em quite. A pax on him, let's be rid of a rascal!

HOARD. Excellent!
Thou dost astonish me.—Go, run, make haste;
Bring both the creditors and Witgood hither.   190

HOST. [*Aside.*] This will be some revenge yet.   [*Exit.*]

HOARD. In the mean space I'll have a release drawn.—
Within there!

[Enter Servant.]

SER. [1] Sir?

HOARD. Sirrah, come, take directions; go to my scrivener.

COUR. *[Aside.]* I'm yet like those whose riches lie in dreams;
If I be waked, they're false. Such is my fate,
Who ventures deeper than the desperate state.
Though I have sinned, yet could I become new,   199
For, where I once vow, I am ever true.

HOARD. Away, despatch! On my displeasure, quickly.—*[Exit Servant.]* Happy occasion! Pray heaven he be in the right vein now to set his hand to 't, that nothing alter him; grant that all his follies may meet in him at once, to besot him enough! I pray for him, i' faith, and here he comes.

[Enter Witgood and Creditors.]

WIT. What would you with me now, my uncle's spiteful adversary?   210

HOARD. Nay, I am friends.

WIT.   Ay, when your mischief's spent.

HOARD. I heard you were arrested.

WIT.   Well, what then?
You will pay none of my debts, I am sure.

HOARD. A wise man cannot tell;
There may be those conditions 'greed upon
May move me to do much.

WIT.   Ay, when?—'Tis thou,
Perjuréd woman! (O, no name is vild [2]
Enough to match thy treachery!) That art
The cause of my confusion.

COUR.   Out, you
Penurious slave!

HOARD.   Nay, wife, you are too forward;   220
Let him alone; give losers leave to talk.

WIT. Shall I remember thee of another promise
Far stronger than the first?

COUR.   I'd fain know that.

WIT. 'Twould call shame to thy cheeks.

COUR.   Shame!

WIT.   Hark in your ear.—
[Draws Courtesan aside.]
Will he come off, think'st thou, and pay my debts roundly?

COUR. Doubt nothing; there's a release a-drawing and all, to which you must set your hand.

WIT. Excellent!   230

COUR. But methinks, i' faith, you might have made some shift to discharge this yourself, having in the mortgage, and never have burdened my conscience with it.

WIT. A my troth, I could not, for my creditors' cruelties extend to the present.

COUR. No more.—*[Aloud.]* Why, do your worst for that. I defy you.

WIT. Y' are impudent. I'll call up witnesses.

COUR. Call up thy wits, for thou hast been devoted   240
To follies a long time.

HOARD.   Wife, y' are too bitter.—
Master Witgood, and you, my masters, you shall hear a mild speech come from me now, and this it is: 't 'as been my fortune, gentlemen, to have an extraordinary blessing poured upon me alate, and here she stands; I have wedded her, and bedded her, and yet she is little the worse. Some foolish words she hath passed to you in the country, and some peevish [3] debts you owe [250 here in the city. Set the hare's head to the goose-giblet [4]—release you her of her words, and I'll release you of your debts, sir.

WIT. Would you so? I thank you for that, sir; I cannot blame you, i' faith.

HOARD. Why, are not debts better than words, sir?

WIT. Are not words promises, and are not promises debts, sir?

HOARD. *[Aside.]* He plays at [260 backracket with me.[5]

1 [CRED.] Come hither, Master Witgood, come hither; be ruled by fools once.
[Creditors take Witgood aside.]

2 [CRED.] We are citizens, and know what belong to 't.

1 [CRED.] Take hold of his offer. Pax

[3] Small.
[4] *I.e.*, let equivalents balance each other.
[5] *I.e.*, he hits the ball back at me.

on her, let her go. If your debts were once discharged, I would help you to a widow myself worth ten of her.

3 [CRED.] Mass, partner, and now [270 you remember me on 't, there's Master Mulgrave's sister newly fallen a widow.

1 [CRED.] Cud's me, as pat as can be! There's a widow left for you, ten thousand in money, beside plate, jewels, *et cetera*. I warrant it a match; we can do all in all with her. Prithee, despatch; we'll carry thee to her presently.

WIT. My uncle will ne'er endure me when he shall hear I set my hand to a [280 release.

2 [CRED.] Hark, I'll tell thee a trick for that. I have spent five hundred pound in suits in my time; I should be wise. Thou'rt now a prisoner; make a release; take 't of my word, whatsoever a man makes as long as he is in durance, 'tis nothing in law, not thus much.

WIT. Say you so, sir?   289

3 [CRED.] I have paid for 't; I know 't.

WIT. Proceed then; I consent.

3 [CRED.] Why, well said.

HOARD. How now, my masters, what have you done with him?

1 [CRED.] With much ado, sir, we have got him to consent.

HOARD. Ah—a—a! And what came his debts to now?

1 [CRED.] Some eightscore odd pounds, sir.   300

HOARD. Naw, naw, naw, naw, naw! Tell me the second time; give me a lighter sum. They are but desperate debts, you know, ne'er called in but upon such an accident. A poor, needy knave, he would starve and rot in prison. Come, come, you shall have ten shillings in the pound, and the sum down roundly.

1 [CRED.] You must make it a mark, sir.

HOARD. Go to then; tell your money [310 in the meantime; you shall find little less there.—[*Gives money.*] Come, Master Witgood, you are so unwilling to do yourself good now!—

[*Enter Scrivener.*]

Welcome, honest scrivener.—Now you shall hear the release read.

SCRI. [*Reading.*] "Be it known to all men, by these presents, that I, Theodorus

Witgood, gentleman, sole nephew to Pecunius Lucre, having unjustly made [320 title and claim to one Jane Medler, late widow of Anthony Medler, and now wife to Walkadine Hoard, in consideration of a competent sum of money to discharge my debts, do forever hereafter disclaim any title, right, estate, or interest in or to the said widow, late in the occupation of the said Anthony Medler, and now in the occupation of Walkadine Hoard; as also neither to lay claim by virtue of any former [330 contract, grant, promise, or demise, to any of her manor[s], manor houses, parks, groves, meadow grounds, arable lands, barns, stacks, stables, dove holes, and cunny borrows,[1] together with all her cattle, money, plate, jewels, borders, chains, bracelets, furnitures, hangings, movables or immovables. In witness whereof, I, the said Theodorus Witgood, have interchangeably set to my hand and seal before [340 these presents, the day and date above written."

WIT. What a precious fortune hast thou slipped here, like a beast as thou art!

HOARD. Come, unwilling heart, come.

WIT. Well, Master Hoard, give me the pen; I see
'Tis vain to quarrel with our destiny.   [*Signs.*]

HOARD. O, as vain a thing as can be! You cannot commit a greater absurdity, sir. So, so; give me that hand now; before [350 all these presents, I am friends forever with thee.

WIT. Troth, and it were pity of my heart now, if I should bear you any grudge, i' faith.

HOARD. Content. I'll send for thy uncle against the wedding dinner; we will be friends once again.

WIT. I hope to bring it to pass myself, sir.

HOARD. How now? Is 't right, my [360 masters?

1 [CRED.] 'Tis something wanting, sir; yet it shall be sufficient.

HOARD. Why, well said; a good conscience makes a fine show nowadays. Come, my masters, you shall all taste of my wine ere you depart.

ALL. We follow you, sir.

[*Exeunt Hoard and Scrivener.*]

---

[1] Rabbit burrows.

WIT. [*Aside.*] I'll try these fellows now.
—A word, sir. What, will you carry [370 me to that widow now?

1 [CRED.] Why, do you think we were in earnest, i' faith? Carry you to a rich widow? We should get much credit by that. A noted rioter! A contemptible prodigal! 'Twas a trick we have amongst us to get in our money. Fare you well, sir.

                Exeunt [Creditors].

WIT. Farewell, and be hanged, you short pig-haired, ram-headed rascals! He that believes in you shall ne'er be saved, [380 I warrant him. By this new league I shall have some access unto my love.

         She [, i.e., Niece,] is above.

NIECE. Master Witgood!

WIT. My life!

NIECE. Meet me presently; that note directs you. [*Drops him a paper.*] I would not be suspected. Our happiness attends us. Farewell!

WIT. A word's enough.   *Exeunt.* [1]

[SCENA v.]

Dampit the usurer in his bed, Audrey spinning by. [Boy.]

SONG [*by Audrey*]

Let the usurer cram him, in interest that
    excel,
There's pits enow to damn him, before he
    comes to hell;
In Holborn some, in Fleet Street some,
Where'er he come there's some, there's
    some.

DAMP. *Trahe, trahito,* draw the curtain; give me a sip of sack more.

Enter Gentlemen [, i.e., Lamprey and Spichcock].

LAMP. Look you; did not I tell you he lay like the devil in chains, when he was bound for a thousand year?

SPI. But I think the devil had no [10 steel bedstaffs; [2] he goes beyond him for that.

LAMP. Nay, do but mark the conceit [3] of his drinking; one must wipe his mouth for him with a muckinder,[4] do you see, sir?

SPI. Is this the sick trampler? Why, he is only bedrid with drinking.

LAMP. True, sir. He spies us.

DAMP. What, Sir Tristram? You come and see a weak man here, a very weak man—   20

LAMP. If you be weak in body, you should be strong in prayer, sir.

DAMP. O, I have prayed too much, poor man!

LAMP. There's a taste of his soul for you!

SPI. Fah, loathsome!

LAMP. I come to borrow a hundred pound of you, sir.

DAMP. Alas, you come at an ill [30 time! I cannot spare it, i' faith; I ha' but two thousand i' th' house.

AUD. Ha, ha, ha!

DAMP. Out, you gernative [5] quean, the mullipoop [6] of villainy, the spinner of concupiscenty!

Enter other Gentleman [, i.e., Sir Lancelot].

LAN. Yea, gentlemen, are you here before us? How is he now?

LAMP. Faith, the same man still. The tavern bitch has bit him i' the head.[7]   40

LAN. We shall have the better sport with him. Peace!—And how cheers Master Dampit now?

DAMP. O, my bosom, Sir Lancelot, how cheer I? Thy presence is restorative.

LAN. But I hear a great complaint of you, Master Dampit, among gallants.

DAMP. I am glad of that, i' faith. Prithee, what?

LAN. They say you are waxed proud [50 alate, and, if a friend visit you in the afternoon, you'll scarce know him.

DAMP. Fie, fie! Proud? I cannot remember any such thing. Sure, I was drunk then.

LAN. Think you so, sir?

DAMP. There 'twas, i' faith; nothing but the pride of the sack; and so certify 'em.—Fetch sack, sirrah.

BOY. A vengeance sack you once!   60
     [*Exit Boy, who returns with sack.*]

AUD. Why, Master Dampit, if you hold on as you begin, and lie a little longer, you

---

[1] In original, stage direction appears after preceding line.

[2] For preparing a feather bed.

[3] Fancy, singularity.   [4] Handkerchief.

[5] Grinning, peevish.

[6] Another unintelligible coinage by Dampit.

[7] *I.e.,* he is drunk.

need not take care how to dispose your wealth; you'll make the vintner your heir.

DAMP. Out, you babliaminy, you un-feathered, cremitoried quean, you culli-sance of scabiosity!

AUD. Good words, Master Dampit, to speak before a maid and a virgin!   69

DAMP. Hang thy virginity upon the pole of carnality!

AUD. Sweet terms! My mistress shall know 'em.

LAMP. Note but the misery of this usur-ing slave. Here he lies, like a noisome dunghill, full of the poison of his drunken blasphemies; and they to whom he be-queaths all grudge him the very meat that feeds him, the very pillow that eases him. Here may a usurer behold his [80 end. What profits it to be a slave in this world, and a devil i' th' next?

DAMP. Sir Lancelot, let me buss thee, Sir Lancelot; thou art the only friend that I honor and respect.

LAN. I thank you for that, Master Dam-pit.

DAMP. Farewell, my bosom Sir Lance-lot.

LAN. Gentlemen, and you love me, [90 let me step behind you, and one of you fall a-talking of me to him.

LAMP. Content.—Master Dampit—

DAMP. So, sir.

LAMP. Here came Sir Lancelot to see you e'en now.

DAMP. Hang him, rascal!

LAMP. Who, Sir Lancelot?

DAMP. Pythagorical rascal!

LAMP. Pythagorical?   100

DAMP. Ay, he changes his cloak when he meets a serjeant.

LAN. What a rogue's this!

LAMP. I wonder you can rail at him, sir; he comes in love to see you.

DAMP. A louse for his love! His father was a comb maker; I have no need of his crawling love. He comes to have longer day, the superlative rascal!

LAN. 'Sfoot,[1] I can no longer en- [110 dure the rogue!—Master Dampit, I come to take my leave once again, sir.

DAMP. Who? My dear and kind Sir Lancelot, the only gentleman of England? Let me hug thee; farewell, and a thousand.

[1] God's foot, a mild oath.

LAMP. Composed of wrongs and slav-ish flatteries!

LAN. Nay, gentlemen, he shall show you more tricks yet; I'll give you another taste of him.   120

LAMP. Is 't possible?

LAN. His memory is upon departing.

DAMP. Another cup of sack!

LAN. Mass, then 'twill be quite gone! Before he drink that, tell him there's a country client come up, and here attends for his learned advice.

LAMP. Enough.

DAMP. One cup more, and then let the bell toll. I hope I shall be weak [130 enough by that time.

LAMP. Master Dampit—

DAMP. Is the sack spouting?

LAMP. 'Tis coming forward, sir. Here's a countryman, a client of yours, waits for your deep and profound advice, sir.

DAMP. A coxcombry? Where is he? Let him approach. Set me up a peg higher.

LAMP. [To Sir Lancelot.] You must draw near, sir.   140

DAMP. Now, good man fooliaminy, what say you to me now?

LAN. Please your good worship, I am a poor man, sir—

DAMP. What make [2] you in my chamber then?

LAN. I would entreat your worship's de-vice in a just and honest cause, sir.

DAMP. I meddle with no such matters; I refer 'em to Master No-man's office. [150

LAN. I had but one house left me in all the world, sir, which was my father's, my grandfather's, my great-grandfather's, and now a villain has unjustly wrung me out, and took possession on 't.

DAMP. Has he such feats? Thy best course is to bring thy *ejectione firmæ;* [3] and in seven year thou mayst shove him out by the law.

LAN. Alas, an 't please your wor- [160 ship, I have small friends and less money!

DAMP. Hoyday! This gear will fadge [4] well. Hast no money? Why, then, my advice is, thou must set fire a th' house, and so get him out.

LAMP. That will break strife, indeed.

LAN. I thank your worship for your hot counsel, sir.—Altering but my voice a little,

[2] Do.   [3] Writ of ejection.   [4] Work.

you see he knew me not. You may observe by this that a drunkard's mem- [170 ory holds longer in the voice than in the person. But, gentlemen, shall I show you a sight? Behold the little divedapper [1] of damnation, Gulf the usurer, for his time worse than tother.

Enter Hoard with Gulf.

LAMP. What's he comes with him?

LAN. Why, Hoard, that married lately the Widow Medler.

LAMP. O, I cry you mercy, sir.

HOARD. Now, gentlemen visitants, [180 how does Master Dampit?

LAN. Faith, here he lies, e'en drawing in, sir, good canary as fast as he can, sir; a very weak creature, truly, he is almost past memory.

HOARD. Fie, Master Dampit! You lie lazing abed here, and I come to invite you to my wedding dinner. Up, up, up!   189

DAMP. Who's this? Master Hoard? Who hast thou married, in the name of foolery?

HOARD. A rich widow.

DAMP. A Dutch widow?

HOARD. A rich widow; one Widow Medler.

DAMP. Medler? She keeps open house.

HOARD. She did, I can tell you, in her tother husband's days—open house for all comers; horse and man was welcome, [200 and room enough for 'em all.

DAMP. There's too much for thee, then; thou mayst let out some to thy neighbors.

GULF. What, hung alive in chains? O spectacle! Bedstaffs of steel? *"O monstrum horrendum, informe, ingens, cui lumen ademptum!"* [2] O Dampit, Dampit, here's a just judgment shown upon usury, extortion, and trampling villainy!   210

LAN. [*Aside.*] This exc'llent thief rails upon the thief!

GULF. Is this the end of cutthroat usury, brothel, and blasphemy? Now mayst thou see what race a usurer runs.

DAMP. Why, thou rogue of universal-

ity, do not I know thee? Thy sound is like the cuckoo, the Welsh ambassador; [3] thou cowardly slave, that offers to fight with a sick man when his weapon's [220 down! Rail upon me in my naked bed? Why, thou great Lucifer's little vicar, I am not so weak but I know a knave at first sight. Thou inconscionable rascal, thou that goest upon Middlesex juries, and will make haste to give up thy verdit [4] because thou wilt not lose thy dinner, are you answered?

GULF. An 't were not for shame— [22c
      Draws his dagger.

DAMP. Thou wouldst be hanged then.

LAMP. Nay, you must exercise patience, Master Gulf, always in a sick man's chamber.

LAN. He'll quarrel with none, I warrant you, but those that are bedrid.

DAMP. Let him come, gentlemen; I am armed. Reach my close-stool [5] hither.

LAN. Here will be a sweet fray anon. I'll leave you, gentlemen.

LAMP. Nay, we'll along with [240 you.—Master Gulf—

GULF. Hang him, usuring rascal!

LAN. Push, set your strength to his, your wit to his!

AUD. Pray, gentlemen, depart; his hour's come upon him.—Sleep in my bosom, sleep.

LAN. Nay, we have enough of him, i' faith; keep him for the house.

Now make your best.   250

For thrice his wealth I would not have his breast.

GULF. A little thing would make me beat him now he's asleep.

LAN. Mass, then 'twill be a pitiful day when he wakes. I would be loath to see that day come.

GULF. You overrule me, gentlemen, i' faith.   *Exeunt.*

ACTUS V. [SCENA i.

A room in Lucre's house.]

Enter Lucre and Witgood.

WIT. Nay, uncle, let me prevail with you so much. I' faith, go, now he has invited you.

---

[1] Didapper, dabchick.

[2] "O horrible monster, misshapen, huge, from whom sight is taken away!" (Virgil's *Æneid*, iii, 658).

[3] Nares conjectures that the cuckoo was so named because it migrated from the west.

[4] Verdict.   [5] Chamber pot.

Luc. I shall have great joy there when he has borne away the widow!

Wit. Why, la, I thought where I should find you presently. Uncle, a my troth, 'tis nothing so.

Luc. What's nothing so, sir? Is not he married to the widow?   10

Wit. No, by my troth, is he not, uncle.

Luc. How?

Wit. Will you have the truth on 't? He is married to a whore, i' faith.

Luc. I should laugh at that.

Wit. Uncle, let me perish in your favor if you find it not so, and that 'tis I that have married the honest woman.

Luc. Ha! I'd walk ten mile afoot to see that, i' faith.   20

Wit. And see 't you shall, or I'll ne'er see you again.

Luc. A quean, i' faith? Ha, ha, ha!
     Exeunt.

[Scena ii.

A room in Hoard's house.]

Enter Hoard, tasting wine, the Host following in a livery cloak.

Hoard. Pup, pup, pup, pup! I like not this wine. Is there never a better tierce [1] in the house?

Host. Yes, sir, there are as good tierce in the house as any are in England.

Hoard. Desire your mistress, you knave, to taste 'em all over; she has better skill.

Host. [*Aside.*] Has she so? The better for her, and the worse for you.   *Exit.*

Hoard. Arthur!   10

[*Enter Arthur.*]

Is the cupboard of plate set out?

Art. All's in order, sir.   [*Exit.*]

Hoard. I am in love with my liveries every time I think on 'em; they make a gallant show, by my troth.—Niece!

[*Enter Niece.*]

Niece. Do you call, sir?

Hoard. Prithee, show a little diligence, and overlook the knaves a little; they'll filch and steal today, and send whole pasties home to their wives; and thou beest [20 a good niece, do not see me purloined.

[1] A small cask.

Niece. Fear it not, sir.—[*Aside.*] I have cause; though the feast be prepared for you, yet it serves fit for my wedding dinner too.
     [*Exit.*]

Enter two Gentlemen [, i.e., Lamprey and Spichcock].

Hoard. Master Lamprey and Master Spichcock, two the most welcome gentlemen alive! Your fathers and mine were all free a th' fishmongers.[2]

Lamp. They were indeed, sir. You see bold guests, sir, soon entreated.   30

Hoard. And that's best, sir.—

[*Enter Servant.*]

How now, sirrah?

Ser. There's a coach come to th' door, sir.   [*Exit.*]

Hoard. My Lady Foxtone, a my life!— Mistress Jane Hoard! Wife!—Mass, 'tis her ladyship indeed!—

[*Enter Lady Foxtone.*]

Madam, you are welcome to an unfurnished house, dearth of cheer, scarcity of attendance.   40

Lad. You are pleased to make the worst, sir.

Hoard. Wife!

[*Enter Courtesan.*]

Lad. Is this your bride?

Hoard. Yes, madam.—Salute my Lady Foxtone.

Cour. Please you, madam, awhile to taste the air in the garden?

Lad. 'Twill please us well.
     Exeunt [*Lady and Courtesan*].

Hoard. Who would not wed? The most delicious life!   50

No joys are like the comforts of a wife.

Lamp. So we bachelors think, that are not troubled with them.

[*Enter Servant.*]

Ser. Your worship's brother with another ancient gentleman are newly alighted, sir.   [*Exit.*]

Hoard. Master Onesiphorus Hoard? Why, now our company begins to come in.—

[2] Members of the Company of Fishmongers.

[*Enter Onesiphorus Hoard, Limber, and Kix.*]

My dear and kind brother, welcome, i' faith.

O. HOA.[1] You see we are men at an   [60 hour, brother.

HOARD. Ay, I'll say that for you, brother; you keep as good an hour to come to a feast as any gentleman in the shire.— What, old Master Limber and Master Kix! Do we meet, i' faith, jolly gentlemen?

LIM. We hope you lack guess, [2] sir?

HOARD. O, welcome, welcome! We lack still such guess as your worships.

O. HOA. Ah, Sirrah Brother, have   [70 you catched up Widow Medler?

HOARD. From 'em all, brother; and I may tell you I had mighty enemies, those that stuck sore; old Lucre is a sore fox, I can tell you, brother.

O. HOA. Where is she? I'll go seek her out; I long to have a smack at her lips.

HOARD. And most wishfully,[3] brother, see where she comes.

[*Enter Courtesan and Lady.*]

Give her a smack [4] now we may hear   [80 it all the house over.

COUR. [*Aside.*] O heaven, I am betrayed! (*Both* [*, i.e., Courtesan and Onesiphorus Hoard,*] *turn back.*) I know that face.

HOARD. Ha, ha, ha! Why, how now? Are you both ashamed?—Come, gentlemen, we'll look another way

O. HOA. Nay, brother, hark you. Come, y' are disposed to be merry.   90

HOARD. Why do we meet else, man?

O. HOA. That's another matter. I was ne'er so fraid in my life but that you had been in earnest.

HOARD. How mean you, brother?

O. HOA. You said she was your wife?

HOARD. Did I so? By my troth, and so she is.

O. HOA. By your troth, brother?   99

HOARD. What reason have I to dissemble with my friends, brother? If marriage can make her mine, she is mine. Why—

O. HOA. Troth, I am not well of a sudden. I must crave pardon, brother; I came

to see you, but I cannot stay dinner, i' faith.

HOARD. I hope you will not serve me so, brother?

LIM. By your leave, Master Hoard—

HOARD. What now? What now? [110 Pray, gentlemen, you were wont to show yourselves wise men.

LIM. But you have shown your folly too much here.

HOARD. How?

KIX. Fie, fie! A man of your repute and name!

You'll feast your friends, but cloy 'em first with shame.

HOARD. This grows too deep; pray, let us reach the sense.

LIM. In your old age dote on a courtesan!

HOARD. Ha!

KIX. Marry a strumpet!   120

HOARD. Gentlemen!

O. HOA. And Witgood's quean!

HOARD. O! Nor lands nor living?

O. HOA. Living!

HOARD. [*To Courtesan.*]   Speak!

COUR.   Alas, you know, at first, sir, I told you I had nothing!

HOARD. Out, out! I am cheated; infinitely cozened!

LIM. Nay, Master Hoard—

Enter Witgood, [Niece,] and Lucre.

HOARD. A Dutch widow! A Dutch widow! A Dutch widow!

LUC. Why, nephew, shall I trace thee still a liar?

Wilt make me mad? Is not yon thing the widow?   130

WIT. Why, la, you are so hard a belief, uncle!

By my troth, she's a whore.

LUC.   Then thou'rt a knave.

WIT. *Negatur argumentum,*[5] uncle.

LUC. *Probo tibi,*[6] nephew. He that knows a woman to be a quean must needs be a knave; thou say'st thou know'st her to be one; *ergo,* if she be a quean, thou'rt a knave.

WIT. *Negatur sequela majoris,*[7] uncle. He that knows a woman to be a [140 quean must needs be a knave; I deny that.

---

[1] Through the rest of this scene in the original this speech head reads *Ony.* or *On.*

[2] Guests.   [4] Early edns. read *smerck.*

[3] Exactly on your wish.

[5] Proof is denied.   [6] I'll prove it to you.

[7] The conclusion of your major premise is denied.

HOARD. Lucre and Witgood, y' are both villains; get you out of my house!

LUC. Why, didst not invite me to thy wedding dinner?

WIT. And are not you and I sworn perpetual friends before witness, sir, and were both drunk upon 't?

HOARD. Daintily abused! Y'ave put a junt [1] upon me! 149

LUC. Ha, ha, ha!

HOARD.   A common strumpet!

WIT.   Nay, now
You wrong her, sir; if I were she, I'd have
The law on you for that; I durst depose
     for her
She ne'er had common use nor common
     thought.

COUR. Despise me, publish me, I am your
     wife.
What shame can I have now but you'll
     have part?
If in disgrace you share, I sought not
     you;
You pursuéd me, nay, forc[é]d me.
Had I friends would follow it,
Less than your action has been proved a
     rape.

O. HOA. Brother! 160

COUR. Nor did I ever boast of lands unto
     you,
Money, or goods; I took a plainer course,
And told you true, I'd nothing.
If error were committed, 'twas by you;
Thank your own folly. Nor has my sin
     been
So odious, but worse has been forgiven;
Nor am I so deformed, but I may chal-
     lenge
The utmost power of any old man's love.
She that tastes not sin before, twenty to one
but she'll taste it after. Most of you [170
old men are content to marry young virgins,
and take that which follows; where, marry-
ing one of us, you both save a sinner and are
quit from a cuckold forever.
"And more, in brief, let this your best
     thoughts win,
She that knows sin, knows best how to
     hate sin." [2]

HOARD. Cursed be all malice! Black are
the fruits of spite,

And poison first their owners. O, my
     friends,
I must embrace shame, to be rid of
     shame!
Concealed disgrace prevents a public
     name. 180
Ah, Witgood! Ah, Theodorus!

WIT. Alas, sir, I was pricked in conscience to see her well bestowed, and where
could I bestow her better than upon your
pitiful worship? Excepting but myself,
I dare swear she's a virgin; and now,
by marrying your niece, I have banished
myself forever from her. She's mine aunt
now, by my faith, and there's no meddling
with mine aunt, you know—a sin [190
against my nuncle. [3]

COUR. [Kneeling.] Lo, gentlemen, before
     you all
In true reclaiméd form I fall.
Henceforth forever I defy [4]
The glances of a sinful eye,
Waving of fans (which some suppose
Tricks of fancy [5]), treading of toes,
Wringing of fingers, biting the lip,
The wanton gait, th' alluring trip, 199
All secret friends and private meetings,
Close-borne letters and bawds' greetings,
Feigning excuse to women's labors
When we are sent for to th' next neigh-
     bor's,
Taking false physic, and ne'er start
To be let blood, though sign be at heart, [6]
Removing chambers, shifting beds,
To welcome friends in husbands' steads,
Them to enjoy, and you to marry,
They first served, while you must tarry,
They to spend, and you to gather, 210
They to get, and you to father—
These and thousand thousand more,
New reclaimed, I now abhor.

LUC. [To Witgood.] Ah, here's a lesson,
rioter, for you!

WIT. I must confess my follies; I'll down
     too.   [Kneels.]
And here forever I disclaim
The cause of youth's undoing, game,
Chiefly dice, those true outlanders,
That shake out beggars, thieves, and
     panders,
Soul-wasting surfeits, sinful riots, 220

---

[1] Fraud.
[2] Quotation marks were often used to call attention to sententious passages.

[3] Uncle.   [4] Renounce.   [5] Love.
[6] According to the almanacs a propitious time
for bloodletting.

Queans' evils, doctors' diets,
Pothecaries' drugs, surgeons' glisters,
Stabbing of arms [1] for a common mistress,
Riband favors, ribald speeches,
Dear perfumed jackets, penniless breeches,
Dutch flapdragons,[2] healths in urine,

[1] To drink off one's blood mixed with wine.
[2] Tidbits swallowed from burning brandy.

Drabs that keep a man too sure in—
I do defy you all.
Lend me each honest hand, for here I rise
A reclaimed man, loathing the general
      vice.   230
HOARD. So, so, all friends! The wedding
      dinner cools.
Who seem most crafty prove ofttimes
      most fools.   [*Exeunt.*]
                  FINIS.

THE CHANGELING[1]

BY

THOMAS MIDDLETON AND WILLIAM ROWLEY

DRAMATIS PERSONÆ

VERMANDERO, [governor of the castle of Alicant and] father to Beatrice.
TOMASO DE PIRACQUO, a noble lord.
ALONZO DE PIRACQUO, his brother, suitor to Beatrice.
ALSEMERO, a nobleman, afterwards married to Beatrice.
JASPERINO, his friend.
ALIBIUS, a jealous doctor.
LOLLIO, his man.
PEDRO, friend to Antonio.

ANTONIO, the changeling.
FRANCISCUS, the counterfeit madman.
DEFLORES, servant to Vermandero.
MADMEN.
SERVANTS.

BEATRICE [JOANNA], daughter to Vermandero.
DIAPHANTA, her waiting-woman.
ISABELLA, wife to Alibius.

THE SCENE: Alligant.[2]

[TIME: Contemporary.]

ACTUS PRIMUS. [SCENA PRIMA.

Outside a temple.]

Enter Alsemero.

[ALS.] 'Twas in the temple where I first beheld her,
And now again the same. What omen yet
Follows of that? None but imaginary.
Why should my hopes or fate be timorous?
The place is holy; so is my intent.
I love her beauties to the holy purpose;
And that, methinks, admits comparison
With man's first creation, the place blessed,
And is his right home back, if he achieve it.
The church hath first begun our interview,   10
And that's the place must join us into one;
So there's beginning and perfection too.

Enter Jasperino.

JAS. O sir, are you here? Come, the wind's fair with you;
Y' are like to have a swift and pleasant passage.
ALS. Sure, y' are deceived, friend; 'tis contrary,
In my best judgment.
JAS.   What, for Malta?
If you could buy a gale amongst the witches,
They could not serve you such a lucky pennyworth   18
As comes a[3] God's name.
ALS.   Even now I observed
The temple's vane to turn full in my face;
I know 'tis against me.
JAS.   Against you?
Then you know not where you are.
ALS.   Not well, indeed.
JAS. Are you not well, sir?
ALS.   Yes, Jasperino,
Unless there be some hidden malady
Within me that I understand not.

[1] The title continues: "As It Was Acted with Great Applause at the Private House in Drury Lane, and Salisbury Court."   [2] Alicant.

[3] In.

1317

JAS.   And that
I begin to doubt,[1] sir. I never knew
Your inclinations to travels at a pause
With any cause to hinder it, till now.
Ashore you were wont to call your serv-
    ants up,
And help to trap [2] your horses for the
    speed;   30
At sea I have seen you weigh the anchor
    with 'em,
Hoist sails for fear to lose the foremost
    breath,
Be in continual prayers for fair winds—
And have you changed your orisons? [3]
ALS.   No, friend;
I keep the same church, same devotion.
JAS. Lover I'm sure y' are none; the stoic
    was [4]
Found in you long ago; your mother nor
Best friends, who have set snares of
    beauty, ay,
And choice ones too, could never trap
    you that way.
What might be the cause?
ALS.   Lord, how violent   40
Thou art! I was but meditating of
Somewhat I heard within the temple.
JAS.   Is this
Violence? 'Tis but idleness compared
With your haste yesterday.
ALS.   I'm all this while
A-going, man.

Enter Servants.

JAS. Backwards, I think, sir. Look,
your servants.
1 SER. The seamen call. Shall we board
your trunks?
ALS. No, not today.   50
JAS. 'Tis the critical day, it seems, and
the sign in Aquarius.[5]
2 SER. We must not to sea today; this
smoke will bring forth fire.
ALS. Keep all on shore; I do not know the
    end,
Which needs I must do, of an affair in
    hand
Ere I can go to sea.

[1] Fear.   [2] Prepare.   [3] Prayers.
[4] In the original line ends with *stoic*. Other
instances of faulty line division later in the play
have been altered silently, and a few passages of
very rough verse have been printed as prose.
[5] *I.e.*, favorable for sailing.

1 SER.   Well, your pleasure.
2 SER. Let him e'en take his leisure too;
we are safer on land.
                  Exeunt Serv[ants].

*Enter Beatrice Joanna,[6] Diaphanta, and
    Servants. [Alsemero kisses Beatrice.]*

JAS. [*Aside.*] How now! The laws   [60
of the Medes are changed sure. Salute a
woman! He kisses too! Wonderful! Where
learnt he this? And does it perfectly too.
In my conscience,[7] he ne'er rehearsed it
before. Nay, go on; this will be stranger
and better news at Valencia than if he had
ransomed half Greece from the Turk.
BEA. You are a scholar, sir?
ALS.   A weak one, lady.
BEA. Which of the sciences is this love you
    speak of?
ALS. From your tongue I take it to be
    music.   70
BEA. You are skillful in 't; can sing at first
    sight.
ALS. And I have showed you all my skill
    at once;
I want more words to express me further,
And must be forced to repetition.
I love you dearly.
BEA.   Be better advised, sir.
Our eyes are sentinels unto our judg-
    ments,
And should give certain judgment what
    they see;
But they are rash sometimes, and tell us
    wonders
Of common things, which, when our
    judgments find,
They can then check the eyes, and call
    them blind.   80
ALS. But I am further, lady; yesterday
Was mine eyes' employment, and hither
    now
They brought my judgment, where are
    both agreed.
Both houses then consenting, 'tis agreed;
Only there wants the confirmation
By the hand royal. That's your part, lady.
BEA. O, there's one above me, sir.—
    [*Aside.*] For five days past
To be recalled! Sure mine eyes were
    mistaken;

[6] In the original *Joanna* appears after *Servants*.
[7] To my knowledge.

This was the man was meant me. That
   he should come
So near his time, and miss it!   90
JAS. We might have come by the carriers from Valencia, I see, and saved all our
sea-provision; we are at farthest sure. Methinks I should do something too; I meant
to be a venturer in this voyage. Yonder's
another vessel; I'll board her. If she be
lawful prize, down goes her topsail.

              [Goes to Diaphanta.]

        Enter Deflores.

DEF. Lady, your father—
BEA.   Is in health, I hope.
DEF. Your eye shall instantly instruct you,
   lady;
He's coming hitherward.
BEA.   What needed then   100
Your duteous preface? I had rather
He had come unexpected; you must stall [1]
A good presence with unnecessary blab-
   bing;
And how welcome for your part you are,
I'm sure you know.
DEF. [*Aside.*]   Will 't never mend,
   this scorn,
One side nor other? Must I be enjoined
To follow still [2] whilst she flies from me?
   Well,
Fates, do your worst, I'll please myself
   with sight
Of her at all opportunities,
If but to spite her anger. I know she had
Rather see me dead than living; and yet
She knows no cause for 't but a peevish
   will.   112
ALS. You seemed displeaséd, lady, on the
   sudden.
BEA. Your pardon, sir; 'tis my infirmity.
Nor can I other reason render you
Than his or hers, of [3] some particular thing
They must abandon as a deadly poison,
Which to a thousand other tastes were
   wholesome;
Such to mine eyes is that same fellow
   there,
The same that report speaks of the
   basilisk. [4]   120

ALS. This is a frequent frailty in our nature;
There's scarce a man amongst a thousand
   found
But hath his imperfection: one distastes
The scent of roses, which to infinites [5]
Most pleasing is and odoriferous;
One, oil, the enemy of poison;
Another, wine, the cheerer of the heart
And lively refresher of the countenance.
Indeed, this fault, if so it be, is general;
There's scarce a thing but is both loved
   and loathed.   130
Myself, I must confess, have the same
   frailty.
BEA. And what may be your poison, sir?
   I am bold with you.
ALS. And what might be your desire, per-
   haps—a cherry?
BEA. I am no enemy to any creature
My memory has, but yon gentleman.
ALS. He does ill to tempt your sight, if he
   knew it.
BEA. He cannot be ignorant of that, sir.
I have not spared to tell him so; and I
   want
To help myself, since he's a gentleman
In good respect [6] with my father, and
   follows him.   140
ALS. He's out of his place then now.
             [They walk aside.]
JAS. I am a mad wag, wench.
DIA. So methinks; but, for your comfort,
I can tell you we have a doctor in the city
that undertakes the cure of such.
JAS. Tush, I know what physic is best
for the state of mine own body.
DIA. 'Tis scarce a well-governed state, I
believe.
JAS. I could show thee such a [150
thing with an ingredian [7] that we two would
compound together, and, if it did not tame
the maddest blood i' th' town for two hours
after, I'll ne'er profess physic again.
DIA. A little poppy, sir, were good to
cause you sleep.
JAS. Poppy? I'll give thee a pop i' th'
lips for that first, and begin there. Poppy
is one simple indeed, and cuckoo [8] (what-
you-call 't) another. I'll discover no [160
more now; another time I'll show thee all.
               [Exit.]

---

[1] Forestall, anticipate.   [2] Always.
[3] Emended by Dyce. Original reads *or*.
[4] A fabulous creature whose look was supposed
to be fatal.

[5] Many people.   [6] Repute.
[7] Ingredience, mixture.
[8] The cuckoo-flower, with an obvious pun.

Enter Vermandero and Servants.

BEA. My father, sir.

VER. O Joanna, I came to meet thee. Your devotion's ended?

BEA. For this time, sir.—
[*Aside.*] I shall change my saint, I fear me; I find
A giddy turning in me.—Sir, this while
I am beholding to this gentleman,
Who left his own way to keep me company,
And in discourse I find him much desirous
To see your castle. He hath deserved it, sir,
If ye please to grant it.

VER. With all my heart, sir. 170
Yet there's an article between; I must know
Your country. We use not to give survey
Of our chief strengths to strangers; our citadels
Are placed conspicuous to outward view,
On promonts' tops, but within our secrets.

ALS. A Valencian, sir.

VER. A Valencian?
That's native, sir. Of what name, I beseech you?

ALS. Alsemero, sir.

VER. Alsemero? Not the son
Of John de Alsemero?

ALS. The same, sir.

VER. My best love bids you welcome.

BEA. He was wont 180
To call me so, and then he speaks a most
Unfeignéd truth.

VER. O sir, I knew your father;
We two were in acquaintance long ago,
Before our chins were worth iulan down,[1]
And so continued till the stamp of time
Had coined us into silver. Well, he's gone;
A good soldier went with him.

ALS. You went together in that, sir.

VER. No, by Saint Jacques, I came behind him;
Yet I have done somewhat too. An unhappy day 190
Swallowed him at last at Gibraltar,
In fight with those rebellious Hollanders.
Was it not so?

ALS. Whose death I had revenged,
Or followed him in fate, had not the late league [2]
Prevented me.

VER. Ay, ay, 'twas time to breathe.—
O Joanna, I should ha' told thee news;
I saw Piracquo lately.

BEA. [*Aside.*] That's ill news.

VER. He's hot preparing for this day of triumph;
Thou must be a bride within this sevennight.

ALS. [*Aside.*] Ha! 200

BEA. Nay, good sir, be not so violent; with speed
I cannot render satisfaction
Unto the dear companion of my soul,
Virginity, whom I thus long have lived with,
And part with it so rude and suddenly.
Can such friends divide, never to meet again,
Without a solemn farewell?

VER. Tush, tush! There's a toy.[3]

ALS. [*Aside.*] I must now part, and never meet again
With any joy on earth.—Sir, your pardon;
My affairs call on me.

VER. How, sir? By no means. 210
Not changed so soon, I hope? You must see my castle
And her best entertainment ere we part;
I shall think myself unkindly used else.
Come, come, let's on; I had good hope your stay
Had been awhile with us in Alligant.
I might have bid you to my daughter's wedding.

ALS. [*Aside.*] He means to feast me, and poisons me beforehand.—
I should be dearly glad to be there, sir,
Did my occasions suit as I could wish.

BEA. I shall be sorry if you be not there
When it is done, sir; but not so suddenly. 221

VER. I tell you, sir, the gentleman's complete,
A courtier and a gallant, enriched
With many fair and noble ornaments.
I would not change him for a son-in-law
For any he in Spain, the proudest he,
And we have great ones, that you know.

---

[1] The first growth of the beard.

[2] An armistice signed in 1609.   [3] Trifle.

ALS.   He's much
Bound to you, sir.
VER.   He shall be bound to me
As fast as this tie can hold him; I'll want
My will else.
BEA. [*Aside.*]   I shall want mine, if you
  do it.   230
VER. But come. By the way I'll tell you
more of him.
ALS. [*Aside.*] How shall I dare to venture
  in his castle,
When he discharges murderers[1] at the
  gate?
But I must on, for back I cannot go.
BEA. [*Aside.*] Not this serpent[2] gone yet?
                          [*Drops her glove.*]
VER.   Look, girl, thy glove's fall'n.
  Stay, stay. Deflores, help a little.
[*Exeunt Vermandero, Alsemero, and Serv-*
                                ants.]
DEF. [*Offering her her glove.*]   Here, lady.
BEA. Mischief on your officious forward-
  ness!
Who bade you stoop? They touch my
  hand no more.
There! For tother's[3] sake I part with
  this.   [*Throws down the other glove.*]
Take um, and draw thine own skin off
  with um!   240
Exeunt [*Beatrice, Diaphanta, and Attend-*
                                ants].
DEF. Here's a favor come with a mischief!
  Now I know
She had rather wear my pelt tanned in a
  pair
Of dancing pumps than I should thrust
  my fingers
Into her sockets here. I know she hates me,
Yet cannot choose but love her.
No matter! If but to vex her, I'll haunt
  her still;
Though I get nothing else, I'll have my
  will.   *Exit.*

[SCENA SECUNDA.

A room in the house of Alibius.]

Enter Alibius and Lollio.

ALIB. Lollio, I must trust thee with a
  secret,
But thou must keep it.
LOL. I was ever close to a secret, sir.

<hr>

[1] Cannon.   [2] Deflores.   [3] That other's.

ALIB. The diligence that I have found in
  thee,
The care and industry already past,
Assures me of thy good continuance.
Lollio, I have a wife.
LOL. Fie, sir, 'tis too late to keep her
secret; she's known to be married all the
town and country over.   10
ALIB. Thou goest too fast, my Lollio.
  That knowledge
I allow no man can be barred it;
But there is a knowledge which is
  nearer,
Deeper, and sweeter, Lollio.
LOL. Well, sir, let us handle that be-
tween you and I.
ALIB. 'Tis that I go about, man. Lollio,
  My wife is young.
LOL. So much the worse to be kept
secret, sir.   20
ALIB. Why, now thou meet'st the sub-
  stance of the point;
I am old, Lollio.
LOL. No, sir, 'tis I am old Lollio.
ALIB. Yet why may not this concord and
  sympathize?
Old trees and young plants often grow
  together,
Well enough agreeing.
LOL. Ay, sir, but the old trees raise
themselves higher and broader than the
young plants.
ALIB. Shrewd application! There's the
  fear, man;   30
I would wear my ring on my own finger;
Whilst it is borrowed, it is none of
  mine,
But his that useth it.
LOL. You must keep it on still then; if
it but lie by, one or other will be thrusting
into 't.
ALIB. Thou conceiv'st me, Lollio. Here
  thy watchful eye
Must have employment. I cannot al-
  ways be at home.
LOL. I dare swear you cannot.
ALIB. I must look out.   40
LOL. I know 't, you must look out; 'tis
every man's case.
ALIB. Here, I do say, must thy employ-
  ment be—
To watch her treadings, and in my ab-
  sence
Supply my place.

LOL. I'll do my best, sir; yet surely I
cannot see who you should have cause to be
jealous of.

ALIB. Thy reason for that, Lollio? 'Tis
a comfortable question.   50

LOL. We have but two sorts of people in
the house, and both under the whip—that's
fools and madmen; the one has not wit
enough to be knaves, and the other not
knavery enough to be fools.

ALIB. Ay, those are all my patients, Lollio.
I do profess the cure of either sort.
My trade, my living 'tis; I thrive
    by it.
But here's the care that mixes with my
    thrift:
The daily visitants, that come to see   60
My brainsick patients, I would not
    have
To see my wife. Gallants I do ob-
    serve
Of quick, enticing eyes, rich in habits,
Of stature and proportion very comely.
These are most shrewd temptations,
    Lollio.

LOL. They may be easily answered, sir.
If they come to see the fools and madmen,
you and I may serve the turn, and let my
mistress alone. She's of neither sort.

ALIB. 'Tis a good ward;[1] indeed, come they
    to see   70
Our madmen or our fools, let um see no
    more
Than what they come for. By that con-
    sequent
They must not see her; I'm sure she's no
    fool.

LOL. And I'm sure she's no madman.

ALIB. Hold that buckler fast. Lollio, my
    trust
Is on thee, and I account it firm and
    strong.
What hour is 't, Lollio?

LOL.   Towards belly hour, sir.

ALIB. Dinner time? Thou mean'st twelve
    a-clock?

LOL. Yes, sir, for every part has his hour:
we wake at six and look about us—   [80
that's eye hour; at seven we should pray—
that's knee hour; at eight walk—that's leg
hour; at nine gather flowers and pluck
a rose[2]—that's nose hour; at ten we

drink—that's mouth hour; at eleven lay
about us for victuals—that's hand hour; at
twelve go to dinner—that's belly hour.

ALIB. Profoundly, Lollio! It will be long
Ere all thy scholars learn this lesson, and
I did look to have a new one entered—
    stay,   90
I think my expectation is come home.

Enter Pedro, and Antonio like an idiot.

PED. Save you, sir. My business speaks
    itself;
This sight takes off the labor of my
    tongue.

ALIB. Ay, ay, sir, 'tis plain enough you
    mean him for my patient.

PED. And, if your pains prove but commodious, to give but some little strength to
his sick and weak part of nature in him,
these are [*Gives him money.*] but patterns to
show you of the whole pieces that will follow to you, beside the charge of diet, washing, and other necessaries, fully defrayed.

ALIB. Believe it, sir, there shall no care be
    wanting.   102

LOL. Sir, an officer in this place may
deserve something. The trouble will pass
through my hands.

PED. 'Tis fit something should come to
your hands then, sir.   [*Gives him money.*]

LOL. Yes, sir, 'tis I must keep him
sweet,[3] and read to him. What is his name?

PED. His name is Antonio; marry, we
use but half to him, only Tony.   111

LOL. Tony, Tony, 'tis enough, and
a very good name for a fool.—What's your
name, Tony?

ANT. He, he, he! Well, I thank you,
cousin. He, he, he!

LOL. Good boy, hold up your head.—He
can laugh; I perceive by that he is no beast.

PED. Well, sir,
If you can raise him but to any height,
Any degree of wit, might he attain,   121
As I might say, to creep but on all four
Towards the chair of wit, or walk on
    crutches,
'Twould add an honor to your worthy
    pains,
And a great family might pray for you,
To which he should be heir, had he dis-
    cretion

---

[1] Guard, defense.   [2] *I.e.*, relieve ourselves.   [3] Clean.

To claim and guide his own. Assure you, sir,
He is a gentleman.

Lol. Nay, there's nobody doubted that. At first sight I knew him for a gentleman; he looks no other yet.   131

Ped. Let him have good attendance and sweet lodging.

Lol. As good as my mistress lies in, sir; and, as you allow us time and means, we can raise him to the higher degree of discretion.

Ped. Nay, there shall no cost want, sir.

Lol. He will hardly be stretched up to the wit of a magnifico.

Ped. O, no, that's not to be expected; far shorter will be enough.   141

Lol. I'll warrant you [I'll] [1] make him fit to bear office in five weeks; I'll undertake to wind him up to the wit of constable.

Ped. If it be lower than that, it might serve turn.

Lol. No, fie; to level him with a headborough, [2] beadle, or watchman were but little better than he is. Constable I'll [150 able him; [3] if he do come to be a justice afterwards, let him thank the keeper. Or I'll go further with you. Say I do bring him up to my own pitch; say I make him as wise as myself.

Ped. Why, there I would have it.

Lol. Well, go to; either I'll be as errant a fool as he, or he shall be as wise as I, and then I think 'twill serve his turn.   159

Ped. Nay, I do like thy wit passing well.

Lol. Yes, you may; yet if I had not been a fool, I had had more wit than I have too. Remember what state [4] you find me in.

Ped. I will, and so leave you. Your best cares, I beseech you.   *Ex[it] Ped[ro].*

Alib. Take you none with you; leave um all with us.

Ant. O, my cousin's gone! Cousin, cousin, O!   170

Lol. Peace, peace, Tony! You must not cry, child; you must be whipped if you do. Your cousin is here still; I am your cousin, Tony.

Ant. He, he! Then I'll not cry, if thou beest my cousin. He, he, he!

Lol. I were best try his wit a little, that I may know what form [5] to place him in.

Alib. Ay, do, Lollio, do.

Lol. I must ask him easy ques- [180 tions at first.—Tony, how many true [6] fingers has a tailor on his right hand?

Ant. As many as on his left, cousin.

Lol. Good. And how many on both?

Ant. Two less than a deuce, cousin.

Lol. Very well answered. I come to you again, cousin Tony. How many fools goes to [7] a wise man?

Ant. Forty in a day sometimes, cousin.

Lol. Forty in a day? How prove [190 you that?

Ant. All that fall out amongst themselves, and go to a lawyer to be made friends.

Lol. A parlous fool! He must sit in the fourth form at least, I perceive that.—I come again, Tony. How many knaves make an honest man?

Ant. I know not that, cousin.

Lol. No, the question is too hard for you. I'll tell you, cousin. There's [200 three knaves may make an honest man—a serjeant, a jailor, and a beadle; the serjeant catches him, the jailor holds him, and the beadle lashes him; and, if he be not honest then, the hangman must cure him.

Ant. Ha, ha, ha! That's fine sport, cousin.

Alib. This was too deep a question for the fool, Lollio.

Lol. Yes, this might have served [210 yourself, though I say 't.—Once more and you shall go play, Tony.

Ant. Ay, play at pushpin, cousin. Ha, he!

Lol. So thou shalt. Say how many fools are here.

Ant. Two, cousin; thou and I.

Lol. Nay, y' are too forward there, Tony. Mark my question! How many fools and knaves are here: a fool before a knave, a fool behind a knave, between [220 every two fools a knave—how many fools, how many knaves?

Ant. I never learnt so far, cousin.

Alib. Thou putt'st too hard questions to him, Lollio.

Lol. I'll make him understand it easily. —Cousin, stand there.

Ant. Ay, cousin.

---

[1] Supplied by Dyce.   [2] Constable.
[3] *I.e.*, qualify him for.   [4] Position.

[5] Class.   [6] Honest.   [7] Make.

LOL. Master, stand you next the fool.

ALIB. Well, Lollio. 230

LOL. Here's my place. Mark now, Tony, there a fool before a knave.

ANT. That's I, cousin.

LOL. Here's a fool behind a knave—that's I; and between us two fools there is a knave—that's my master; 'tis but we three, that's all.

ANT. We three, we three, cousin.

Madmen within.

1 [MAD.] (*Within.*) Put's head i' th' pillory; the bread's too little. 240

2 [MAD.] (*Within.*) Fly, fly, and he catches the swallow.

3 [MAD.] (*Within.*) Give her more onion, or the devil put the rope about her crag.[1]

LOL. You may hear what time of day it is; the chimes of Bedlam goes.

ALIB. Peace, peace, or the wire [2] comes!

3 [MAD.] (*Within.*) Cat whore, cat [249 whore! Her parmasant, her parmasant! [3]

ALIB. Peace, I say!—Their hour's come; they must be fed, Lollio.

LOL. There's no hope of recovery of that Welsh madman; was undone by a mouse that spoiled him a parmasant; lost his wits for 't.

ALIB. Go to your charge, Lollio; I'll to mine.

LOL. Go you to your madmen's ward; let me alone with your fools. 260

ALIB. And remember my last charge, Lollio. *Exit.*

LOL. Of which your patients do you think I am? Come, Tony, you must amongst your schoolfellows now. There's pretty scholars amongst um, I can tell you; there's some of 'em at *stultus, stulta, stultum.*[4]

ANT. I would see the madmen, cousin, if they would not bite me. 270

LOL. No, they shall not bite thee, Tony.

ANT. They bite when they are at dinner, do they not, coz?

LOL. They bite at dinner, indeed, Tony. Well, I hope to get credit by thee; I like thee the best of all the scholars that ever I brought up, and thou shalt prove a wise man, or I'll prove a fool myself. *Exeunt.*

[1] Neck.   [2] Whip.   [3] Parmesan cheese.
[4] The beginning of the Latin declension of *stupid.*

ACTUS SECUNDUS. [SCENA PRIMA.

A room in the castle.]

Enter Beatrice and Jasperino severally.

BEA. O, sir, I'm ready now for that fair service
Which makes the name of friend sit glorious on you!
Good angels and this conduct be your guide! [*Gives a paper.*]
Fitness of time and place is there set down, sir.

JAS. The joy I shall return rewards my service. *Exit.*

BEA. How wise is Alsemero in his friend!
It is a sign he makes his choice with judgment.
Then I appear in nothing more approved
Than making choice of him, for, 'tis a principle,
He that can choose 10
That bosom well who of his thoughts partakes,
Proves most discreet in every choice he makes.
Methinks I love now with the eyes of judgment,
And see the way to merit, clearly see it.
A true deserver like a diamond sparkles;
In darkness you may see him—that's in absence,
Which is the greatest darkness falls on love;
Yet is he best discerned then
With intellectual eyesight. What's Piracquo
My father spends his breath for? And his blessing 20
Is only mine as I regard his name,
Else it goes from me, and turns head against me,
Transformed into a curse. Some speedy way
Must be remembered. He's so forward too,
So urgent that way, scarce allows me breath
To speak to my new comforts.

Enter Deflores.

DEF. [*Aside.*] Yonder's she;
Whatever ails me, now alate especially!
I can as well be hanged as refrain seeing her.

Some twenty times a day, nay, not so
little,
Do I force errands, frame ways and ex-
cuses,   30
To come into her sight; and I have small
reason for 't,
And less encouragement, for she baits
me still
Every time worse than other; does pro-
fess herself
The cruelest enemy to my face in town;
At no hand can abide the sight of me,
As if danger or ill luck hung in my
looks.
I must confess my face is bad enough,
But I know far worse has better fortune,
And not endured alone, but doted on;
And yet such pick-haired [1] faces, chins
like witches',   40
Here and there five hairs, whispering
in a corner
As if they grew in fear one of another,
Wrinkles like troughs, where swine-
deformity swills
The tears of perjury, that lie there like
wash
Fallen from the slimy and dishonest
eye—
Yet such a one plucks sweets without
restraint,
And has the grace of beauty to his sweet.
Though my hard fate has thrust me out
to servitude,
I tumbled into th' world a gentleman.
She turns her blessed eye upon me now,
And I'll endure all storms before I part
with 't.   51
BEA. [Aside.] Again?
This ominous ill-faced fellow more dis-
turbs me
Than all my other passions.
DEF. [Aside.]   Now 't begins again;
I'll stand this storm of hail, though the
stones pelt me.
BEA. Thy business? What's thy busi-
ness?
DEF. [Aside.]   Soft and fair!
I cannot part so soon now.
BEA. [Aside.]   The villain's fixed.—
Thou standing toad-pool—
DEF. [Aside.]   The shower falls
amain now.

[1] Thin-bearded.

BEA. Who sent thee? What's thy errand?
Leave my sight!
DEF. My lord your father charged me
to deliver   60
A message to you.
BEA.   What, another since?
Do 't, and be hanged then; let me be rid
of thee.
DEF. True service merits mercy.
BEA.   What's thy message?
DEF. Let beauty settle but in patience,
You shall hear all.
BEA.   A dallying, trifling torment!
DEF. Signior Alonzo de Piracquo, lady,
Sole brother to Tomaso de Piracquo—
BEA. Slave, when wilt make an end?
DEF.   Too soon I shall.
BEA. What all this while of him?
DEF.   The said Alonzo,
With the foresaid Tomaso—
BEA.   Yet again?   70
DEF. Is new alighted.
BEA.   Vengeance strike the news!
Thou thing most loathed, what cause
was there in this
To bring thee to my sight?
DEF.   My lord your father
Charged me to seek you out.
BEA.   Is there no other
To send his errand by?
DEF.   It seems 'tis my luck
To be i' th' way still.
BEA.   Get thee from me!
DEF.   So.—
[Aside.] Why, am not I an ass to devise
ways
Thus to be railed at? I must see her still!
I shall have a mad qualm within this
hour again,
I know 't; and, like a common Garden
bull, [2]   80
I do but take breath to be lugged [3] again.
What this may bode I know not; I'll
despair the less,
Because there's daily presidents [4] of
bad faces
Beloved beyond all reason. These foul
chops
May come into favor one day mongst
his fellows.
Wrangling has proved the mistress of
good pastime.

[2] Bulls were baited at Paris Garden.
[3] Pulled, baited.   [4] Precedents.

As children cry themselves asleep, I
  ha' seen
Women have chid themselves abed to
  men.   *Exit Def[lores].*
BEA. I never see this fellow but I think
Of some harm towards me; danger's
  in my mind still;   90
I scarce leave trembling of an hour after.
The next good mood I find my father in,
I'll get him quite discarded. O, I was
Lost in this small disturbance, and forgot
Affliction's fiercer torrent that now
  comes
To bear down all my comforts!

Enter Vermandero, Alonzo, Tomaso.

VER.   Y' are both welcome,
But an especial one belongs to you, sir,
To whose most noble name our love
  presents
The addition [1] of a son, our son Alonzo.
ALON. The treasury of honor cannot bring
  forth   100
A title I should more rejoice in, sir.
VER. You have improved it well.—Daugh-
  ter, prepare;
The day will steal upon thee suddenly.
BEA. [*Aside.*] Howe'er, I will be sure to
  keep the night,[2]
If it should come so near me.
          [*Beatrice takes Vermandero aside.*]
TOM.   Alonzo!
ALON.   Brother?
TOM. In troth, I see small welcome in her
  eye.
ALON. Fie, you are too severe a censurer [3]
Of love in all points. There's no bring-
  ing on [4] you.
If lovers should mark everything a
  fault,   109
Affection would be like an ill-set book,
Whose faults might prove as big as half
  the volume.
BEA. That's all I do entreat.
VER.   It is but reasonable;
I'll see what my son says to 't.—Son
  Alonzo,
Here's a motion made but to reprieve
A maidenhead three days longer; the
  request
Is not far out of reason, for indeed
The former time is pinching.

ALON.   Though my joys
Be set back so much time as I could
  wish
They had been forward, yet, since she
  desires it,
The time is set as pleasing as before.   120
I find no gladness wanting.
VER.   May I ever
Meet it in that point still! Y' are nobly
  welcome, sirs.
          Exeunt Ver[mandero] and Bea[trice].
TOM. So; did you mark the dullness of
  her parting now?
ALON. What dullness? Thou art so ex-
  ceptious [5] still!
TOM. Why, let it go then; I am but a fool
To mark your harms so heedfully.
ALON.   Where's the oversight?
TOM. Come, your faith's cozened in her,
  strongly cozened.
Unsettle your affection with all speed
Wisdom can bring it to; your peace is
  ruined else.
Think what a torment 'tis to marry
  one   130
Whose heart is leaped into another's
  bosom.
If ever pleasure she receive from thee,
It comes not in thy name, or of thy gift.
She lies but with another in thine arms,
He the half-father unto all thy children
In the conception; if he get 'em not,
She helps to get 'em for him in his [6]
  passions, and how dangerous
And shameful her restraint may go in
  time to,
It is not to be thought on without suf-
  ferings.
ALON. You speak as if she loved some
  other, then.   140
TOM. Do you apprehend so slowly?
ALON.   Nay, and that
Be your fear only, I am safe enough.
Preserve your friendship and your coun-
  sel, brother,
For times of more distress; I should de-
  part
An enemy, a dangerous, deadly one,
To any but thyself, that should but think
She knew the meaning of inconstancy,
Much less the use and practice; yet
  w' are friends.

----

[1] Title. [2] *I.e.*, watch. [3] Judge. [4] Persuading.

[5] Captions.   [6] *I.e.*, the husband's.

Pray, let no more be urged; I can endure
Much, till I meet an injury to her; 150
Then I am not myself. Farewell, sweet
  brother;
How much w' are bound to heaven to
  depart lovingly. *Exit.*
Tom. Why, here is love's tame madness;
  thus a man
Quickly steals into his vexation. *Exit.*

[Scena Secunda.

Another room in the castle.]

Enter Diaphanta and Alsemero.

Dia. The place is my charge; you have
  kept your hour,
And the reward of a just meeting bless
  you!
I hear my lady coming. Complete
  gentleman,
I dare not be too busy with my praises;
Th' are dangerous things to deal with.
  Exit.
Als. This goes well;
These women are the ladies' cabinets,
Things of most precious trust are lock[ed]
  into 'em.

Enter Beatrice.

Bea. I have within mine eye all my de-
  sires.
Requests that holy prayers ascend
  heaven for,
And brings 'em down to furnish our
  defects, 10
Come not more sweet to our necessities
Than thou unto my wishes.
Als. W' are so like
In our expressions, lady, that, unless I
  borrow
The same words, I shall never find their
  equals.
Bea. How happy were this meeting, this
  embrace,
If it were free from envy! This poor
  kiss
It has an enemy, a hateful one,
That wishes poison to 't. How well were
  I now,
If there were none such name known
  as Piracquo,
Nor no such tie as the command of
  parents! 20

I should be but too much blessed.
Als. One good service
Would strike off both your fears, and
  I'll go near it too,
Since you are so distressed. Remove
  the cause,
The command ceases; so there's two
  fears blown out
With one and the same blast.
Bea. Pray, let me find [1] you, sir.
What might that service be, so strangely
  happy?
Als. The honorablest piece 'bout man,
  valor.
I'll send a challenge to Piracquo in-
  stantly.
Bea. How? Call you that extinguishing
  of fear,
When 'tis the only way to keep it flam-
  ing? 30
Are not you ventured in the action,
That's all my joys and comforts?
Pray, no more, sir.
Say you prevailed; you're danger's and
  not mine then.
The law would claim you from me, or
  obscurity
Be made the grave to bury you alive.
I'm glad these thoughts come forth;
  O, keep not one
Of this condition, sir! Here was a course
Found to bring sorrow on her way to
  death;
The tears would ne'er 'a' dried, till dust
  had choked 'em.
Blood guiltiness becomes a fouler vis-
  age.— 40
[*Aside.*] And now I think on one; I was
  to blame—
I ha' marred so good a market with my
  scorn.
'T had been done questionless. The
  ugliest creature
Creation framed for some use! Yet to
  see
I could not mark so much where it should
  be!
Als. Lady—
Bea. [*Aside.*] Why, men of art make
  much of poison,
Keep one to expel another. Where was
  my art?
Als. Lady, you hear not me.

[1] Understand.

BEA.   I do especially, sir.
The present times are not so sure of our side
As those hereafter may be; we must
use 'em then   50
As thrifty folks their wealth, sparingly now,
Till the time opens.

ALS.   You teach wisdom, lady.

BEA. Within there, Diaphanta!

Enter Diaphanta.

DIA.   Do you call, madam?

BEA. Perfect your service, and conduct this gentleman
The private way you brought him.

DIA.   I shall, madam.

ALS. My love's as firm as love e'er built upon.

Ex[eunt] Dia[phanta] and Als[emero].

Enter Deflores.

DEF. [*Aside.*] I've watched this meeting, and do wonder much
What shall become of tother. I'm sure both
Cannot be served unless she transgress; happily[1]   59
Then I'll put in for one; for, if a woman
Fly from one point, from him she makes a husband,
She spreads and mounts then like arithmetic
(One, ten, a hundred, a thousand, ten thousand),
Proves in time sutler to an army royal.
Now do I look to be most richly railed at;
Yet I must see her.

BEA. [*Aside.*]   Why, put case[2] I loathed him
As much as youth and beauty hates a sepulcher,
Must I needs show it? Cannot I keep that secret,
And serve my turn upon him? See, he's here.—
Deflores!

DEF. [*Aside.*]   Ha, I shall run mad with joy!   70
She called me fairly by my name, Deflores,
And neither rogue nor rascal.

[1] Haply, perhaps.   [2] *I.e.*, suppose.

BEA.   What ha' you done
To your face alate? Y'ave met with some good physician;
Y'ave pruned[3] yourself, methinks. You were not wont
To look so amorously.[4]

DEF.   Not I.—[*Aside.*] 'Tis
The same physnomy,[5] to a hair and pimple,
Which she called scurvy scarce an hour ago.
How is this?

BEA.   Come hither; nearer, man.

DEF. [*Aside.*] I'm up to the chin in heaven!

BEA.   Turn, let me see.
Vaugh, 'tis but the heat of the liver, I perceive 't;   80
I thought it had been worse.

DEF. [*Aside.*]   Her fingers touched me!
She smells all amber.[6]

BEA. I'll make a water for you shall cleanse this
Within a fortnight.

DEF.   With your own hands, lady?

BEA. Yes, mine own, sir; in a work of cure
I'll trust no other.

DEF. [*Aside.*]   'Tis half an act of pleasure
To hear her talk thus to me.

BEA.   When w' are used
To a hard face, 'tis not so unpleasing;
It mends still in opinion, hourly mends;
I see it by experience.

DEF. [*Aside.*]   I was blessed 90
To light upon this minute; I'll make use on 't.

BEA. Hardness becomes the visage of a man well;
It argues service, resolution, manhood,
If cause were of employment.

DEF.   'Twould be soon seen
If e'er your ladyship had cause to use it;
I would but wish the honor of a service
So happy as that mounts to.

BEA.   We shall try you.—
O, my Deflores!

DEF. [*Aside.*] How's that? She calls me hers
Already! "My Deflores!"—You were about
To sigh out somewhat, madam?

[3] Preened.   [4] Like one to be loved.
[5] Physiognomy.   [6] Ambergris.

BEA.   No, was I? 100
I forgot—O!—
DEF.   There 'tis again, the very
    fellow on 't.
BEA. You are too quick, sir.
DEF. There's no excuse for 't now; I
    heard it twice, madam;
That sigh would fain have utterance.
    Take pity on 't,
And lend it a free word. 'Las, how it
    labors
For liberty! I hear the murmur yet
Beat at your bosom.
BEA.   Would creation—
DEF. Ay, well said, that's it.
BEA.   Had formed me man!
DEF. Nay, that's not it.
BEA.   O, 'tis the soul of freedom!
I should not then be forced to marry
    one   110
I hate beyond all depths; I should have
    power
Then to oppose my loathings, nay, re-
    move 'em
Forever from my sight.
DEF. [*Aside.*]   O blessed occasion!—
Without change to your sex you have
    your wishes;
Claim so much man in me.
BEA.   In thee, Deflores?
There's small cause for that.
DEF.   Put it not from me;
It's a service that I kneel for to you.
                            [*Kneels.*]
BEA. You are too violent to mean faith-
    fully.
There's horror in my service, blood and
    danger;
Can those be things to sue for?
DEF.   If you knew 120
How sweet it were to me to be employed
In any act of yours, you would say
    then
I failed, and used not reverence enough
When I receive the charge on 't.
BEA. [*Aside.*]   This is much,
Methinks; belike his wants are greedy;
    and,
To such, gold tastes like angel's food.
    Rise!
DEF. I'll have the work first.
BEA. [*Aside.*]   Possible his need
Is strong upon him.—There's to en-
    courage thee;   [*Gives money.*]

As thou art forward, and thy service
    dangerous,
Thy reward shall be precious.
DEF.   That I have thought on; 130
I have assured myself of that before-
    hand,
And know it will be precious; the thought
    ravishes!
BEA. Then take him to thy fury!
DEF.   I thirst for him.
BEA. Alonzo de Piracquo.
DEF. [*Rising.*]   His end's upon him;
He shall be seen no more.
BEA.   How lovely now
Dost thou appear to me! Never was
    man
Dearlier rewarded.
DEF.   I do think of that.
BEA. Be wondrous careful in the execu-
    tion.
DEF. Why, are not both our lives upon
    the cast?
BEA. Then I throw all my fears upon thy
    service.   140
DEF. They ne'er shall rise to hurt you.
BEA.   When the deed's done,
I'll furnish thee with all things for thy
    flight;
Thou mayst live bravely in another
    country.
DEF. Ay, ay;
We'll talk of that hereafter.
BEA. [*Aside.*]   I shall rid myself
Of two inveterate loathings at one
    time,
Piracquo, and his dog-face.   *Exit.*
DEF.   O my blood!
Methinks I feel her in mine arms already,
Her wanton fingers combing out this
    beard,
And, being pleased, praising this bad
    face.   150
Hunger and pleasure, they'll commend
    sometimes
Slovenly dishes, and feed heartily on
    'em—
Nay, which is stranger, refuse daintier
    for 'em.
Some women are odd feeders.—I'm too
    loud.
Here comes the man goes supperless
    to bed,
Yet shall not rise tomorrow to his din-
    ner.

Enter Alonzo.

ALON. Deflores.

DEF. My kind, honorable lord?

ALON. I am glad I ha' met with thee.

DEF. Sir?

ALON. Thou canst show me
The full strength of the castle?

DEF. That I can, sir.

ALON. I much desire it.

DEF. And if the ways and straits 160
Of some of the passages be not too tedious for you,
I will assure you, worth your time and
sight, my lord.

ALON. Puh, that shall be no hindrance.

DEF. I'm your servant, then.
'Tis now near dinner time; gainst [1]
your lordship's rising
I'll have the keys about me.

ALON. Thanks, kind Deflores.

DEF. [*Aside.*] He's safely thrust upon me
beyond hopes. *Exeunt.*

ACTUS TERTIUS. [SCENA PRIMA.

The top of a narrow stairway in the castle.]

*Enter Alonzo and Deflores. (In the act
time [2] Deflores hides a naked rapier.)*

DEF. Yes, here are all the keys. I was
afraid, my lord,
I'd wanted for the postern [3] —this
is it.
I've all, I've all, my lord. This for the
sconce. [4]

ALON. 'Tis a most spacious and impregnable fort.

DEF. You'll tell me more, my lord. This
descent
Is somewhat narrow; we shall never
pass
Well with our weapons. They'll but
trouble us.

ALON. Thou say[e]st true.

DEF. Pray, let me help your lordship.

ALON. 'Tis done. Thanks, kind Deflores.

DEF. Here are hooks, my lord,
To hang such things on purpose. 10
[*Hangs up the two swords.*]

ALON. Lead; I'll follow thee.

Ex[eunt] at one door and enter at the other.

[1] In anticipation of.
[2] *I.e.*, between the acts.
[3] Lacked the postern key.
[4] Isolated fortification.

[SCENA SECUNDA.

A landing place on the stairway.]

DEF. All this is nothing; you shall see
anon
A place you little dream on.

ALON. I am glad
I have this leisure; all your master's house
Imagine I ha' taken a gondola.

DEF. All but myself, sir—[*Aside.*] which
makes up my safety.—
My lord, I'll place you at a casement here
Will show you the full strength of all the
castle.
Look, spend your eye awhile upon that
object.

ALON. Here's rich variety, Deflores.

DEF. Yes, sir.

ALON. Goodly munition.

DEF. Ay, there's ordnance, sir— 10
No bastard metal, will ring you a peal
like bells
At great men's funerals. Keep your eye
straight, my lord.
Take special notice of that sconce before
you;
There you may dwell awhile.
[*Takes the rapier which he has hidden.*]

ALON. I am upon 't.

DEF. And so am I. [*Stabs him.*]

ALON. Deflores! O Deflores!
Whose malice hast thou put on?

DEF. Do you question
A work of secrecy? I must silence you.
[*Stabs him.*]

ALON. O, O, O!

DEF. I must silence you.—[*Stabs him.*]
So here's an undertaking well accom-
plished.
This vault serves to good use now. Ha,
what's that 20
Threw sparkles in my eye? O, 'tis a
diamond
He wears upon his finger. It was well
found;
This will approve [5] the work. What, so
fast on?
Not part in death? I'll take a speedy
course then.
Finger and all shall off. [*Cuts off the
finger.*] So, now I'll clear
The passages from all suspect [6] or fear.
Exit with body.

[5] Bear witness to. [6] Suspicion.

[SCENA TERTIA.

A room in the house of Alibius.]

Enter Isabella and Lollio.

ISA. Why, sirrah! Whence have you commission
To fetter the doors against me? If you
Keep me in a cage, pray, whistle to me;
Let me be doing something.

LOL. You shall be doing, if it please you;
I'll whistle to you, if you'll pipe after.

ISA. Is it your master's pleasure, or your own,
To keep me in this pinfold?

LOL. 'Tis for my master's pleasure, lest, being taken in another man's [10 corn, you might be pounded in another place.

ISA. 'Tis very well, and he'll prove very wise.

LOL. He says you have company enough in the house, if you please to be sociable, of all sorts of people.

ISA. Of all sorts? Why, here's none but fools and madmen.

LOL. Very well. And where will [20 you find any other, if you should go abroad? There's my master and I to boot, too.

ISA. Of either sort one, a madman and a fool.

LOL. I would ev'n participate of both then if I were as you. I know y' are half mad already; be half foolish too.

ISA. Y' are a brave, saucy rascal! Come on, sir;
Afford me then the pleasure of your bedlam.
You were commending once today to me   30
Your last-come lunatic—what a proper [1] Body there was without brains to guide it,
And what a pitiful delight appeared
In that defect, as if your wisdom had found
A mirth in madness. Pray, sir, let me partake,
If there be such a pleasure.

LOL. If I do not show you the handsomest, discreetest madman, one that I may call the understanding madman, then say I am a fool.   40

ISA. Well, a match,[2] I will say so.

¹ **Handsome.**   ² It is agreed.

LOL. When you have a taste of the madman, you shall, if you please, see Fool's College, o' th' side. I seldom lock there; 'tis but shooting a bolt or two, and you are amongst 'em. (*Ex[it]. Enter presently.*³)—Come on, sir; let me see how handsomely you'll behave yourself now.

Enter Loll[io], Franciscus.

FRAN. How sweetly she looks! O, but there's a wrinkle in her brow as deep as [50 philosophy. Anacreon, drink to my mistress' health; I'll pledge it. Stay, stay, there's a spider in the cup! No, 'tis but a grapestone. Swallow it; fear nothing, poet; so, so, lift higher.

ISA. Alack, alack, 'tis too full of pity
To be laughed at! How fell he mad?
Canst thou tell?

LOL. For love, mistress. He was a pretty poet, too, and that set him forwards first. The Muses then forsook him; [60 he ran mad for a chambermaid, yet she was but a dwarf neither.

FRAN. Hail, bright Titania!
Why stand'st thou idle on these flow'ry banks?
Oberon is dancing with his Dryads;
I'll gather daisies, primrose, violets,
And bind them in a verse of poesy.

LOL. [*Showing him a whip.*] Not too near! You see your danger.   69

FRAN. O, hold thy hand, great Diomede!
Thou feed'st thy horses well; they shall obey thee.
Get up! Bucephalus kneels.   [*Kneels.*]

LOL. You see how I awe my flock; a shepherd has not his dog at more obedience.

ISA. His conscience is unquiet; sure that was
The cause of this. A proper gentleman!

FRAN. Come hither, Aesculapius; hide the poison.

LOL. [*Hiding the whip.*] Well, 'tis hid. [79

FRAN. Didst thou never hear of one Tiresias, a famous poet?

LOL. Yes, that kept tame wild geese.

FRAN. That's he, I am the man.

LOL. No?

FRAN. Yes; but make no words on 't. I was a man seven years ago.

³ *I.e.*, after the following off-stage speech.

Lol. A stripling, I think, you might.

Fran. Now I'm a woman, all feminine.

Lol. I would I might see that!

Fran. Juno struck me blind. 90

Lol. I'll ne'er believe that; for a woman,
they say, has an eye more than a man.

Fran. I say she struck me blind.

Lol. And Luna made you mad; you
have two trades to beg with.

Fran. Luna is now big-bellied, and
there's room
For both of us to ride with Hecate.
I'll drag thee up into her silver sphere,
And there we'll kick the Dog—and beat
the bush—
That barks against the witches of the
night. 100
The swift *lycanthropi* [1] that walks the
round,
We'll tear their wolvish skins, and save
the sheep. [*Snatches at Lollio.*]

Lol. Is 't come to this? Nay, then, my
poison comes forth again. [*Shows the
whip.*] Mad slave, indeed, abuse your
keeper!

Isa. I prithee, hence with him, now he
grows dangerous.
[*Let Franciscus*] *sing.*

Fran. Sweet love, pity me;
Give me leave to lie with thee.

Lol. No, I'll see you wiser first. To
your own kennel! 111

Fran. No noise; she sleeps. Draw all the
curtains round;
Let no soft sound molest the pretty soul
But love, and love creeps in at a mouse-
hole.

Lol. I would you would get into your
hole! (*Exit Fra[nciscus].*)—Now, mistress, I
will bring you another sort; you shall be
fooled another while.—Tony, come hither,
Tony! Look who's yonder, Tony.

Enter Antonio.

Ant. Cousin, is it not my aunt? [2] 120

Lol. Yes, 'tis one of um, Tony.

Ant. He, he! How do you, uncle?

Lol. Fear him not, mistress; 'tis a
gentle nidget; [3] you may play with him—
as safely with him as with his bauble.

[1] Lycanthropes, werewolves.
[2] Slang term for *procuress.*
[3] Idiot.

Isa. How long hast thou been a fool?

Ant. Ever since I came hither, cousin.

Isa. Cousin? I'm none of thy cousins,
fool. 129

Lol. O, mistress, fools have always so
much wit as to claim their kindred.

Madman. (*Within.*) Bounce, bounce!
He falls, he falls!

Isa. Hark you, your scholars in the upper room are out of order.

Lol. Must I come amongst you there?—
Keep you the fool, mistress; I'll go up and
play left-handed Orlando amongst the
madmen. *Exit.*

Isa. Well, sir. 140

Ant. [*Revealing himself.*] 'Tis opportune-
ful now, sweet lady! Nay,
Cast no amazing [4] eye upon this change.

Isa. Ha!

Ant. This shape of folly shrouds your
dearest love,
The truest servant to your powerful
beauties,
Whose magic had this force thus to
transform me.

Isa. You are a fine fool indeed!

Ant. O, 'tis not strange!
Love has an intellect that runs through
all
The scrutinous sciences, and, like
A cunning poet, catches a quantity 150
Of every knowledge, yet brings all
home
Into one mystery, into one secret.
That he proceeds in.

Isa. Y' are a parlous fool.

Ant. No danger in me; I bring naught but
love
And his soft-wounding shafts to strike
you with.
Try but one arrow; if it hurt you,
I'll stand you twenty back in recompense. [*Kisses her.*]

Isa. A forward fool too!

Ant. This was Love's teaching.
A thousand ways he [5] fashioned out my
way,
And this I found the safest and the
nearest, 160
To tread the galaxia to my star.

Isa. Profound withal! Certain, you
dreamed of this;
Love never taught it waking.

[4] Wondering. [5] Original reads *she.*

ANT.   Take no acquaintance
Of these outward follies. There's within
A gentleman that loves you.

ISA.   When I see him,
I'll speak with him; so, in the meantime,
  keep
Your habit; it becomes you well enough.
As you are a gentleman, I'll not discover
  you.
That's all the favor that you must
  expect.
When you are weary, you may leave the
  school,   170
For all this while you have but played the
  fool.

Enter Lollio.

ANT. And must again.—He, he! I thank
  you, cousin;
I'll be your valentine tomorrow morning.
LOL. How do you like the fool, mistress?
ISA. Passing well, sir.
LOL. Is he not witty, pretty well, for a
fool?
ISA. If he hold on as he begins, he is
like to come to something.   179
LOL. Ay, thank a good tutor. You may
put him to 't; he begins to answer pretty
hard questions.—Tony, how many is five
times six?
ANT. Five times six is six times five.
LOL. What arithmetician could have
answered better? How many is one hun-
dred and seven?
ANT. One hundred and seven is seven
hundred and one, cousin.
LOL. This is no wit to speak on!—Will
you be rid of the fool now?   191
ISA. By no means; let him stay a little.
MADMAN. (*Within.*) Catch there, catch
the last couple in hell! [1]
LOL. Again must I come amongst you?
Would my master were come home! I am
not able to govern both these wards to-
gether.   *Exit.*
ANT. Why should a minute of love's hour
  be lost?   199
ISA. Fie, out again! I had rather you kept
Your other posture; you become not
  your tongue
When you speak from [2] your clothes.

[1] In the game of barleybreak the last couple
left in the center were said to be in hell.
[2] Out of keeping with.

ANT.   How can he freeze
Lives near so sweet a warmth? Shall I
  alone
Walk through the orchard of the Hes-
  perides,
And, cowardly, not dare to pull an apple?

Enter Lol[lio] above.

This with the red cheeks I must venter [3]
  for.   [*Attempts to kiss her.*]
ISA. Take heed; there's giants keep 'em.
LOL. [*Aside.*] How now, fool, are you
good at that? Have you read Lipsius? [4]
He's past *Ars Amandi*; [5] I believe I [210
must put harder questions to him, I per-
ceive that.
ISA. You are bold without fear too.
ANT.   What should I fear,
Having all joys about me? Do you smile,
And love shall play the wanton on your
  lip,
Meet and retire, retire and meet again;
Look you but cheerfully, and in your eyes
I shall behold mine own deformity,
And dress myself up fairer. I know this
  shape
Becomes me not, but in those bright
  mirrors   220
I shall array me handsomely.
LOL.   Cuckoo, cuckoo! *Exit.*
[*Cries of*] *Madmen above, some as birds,*
                            others as beasts.
ANT. What are these?
ISA.   ·   Of fear enough to part us;
Yet are they but our schools of lunatics,
That act their fantasies in any shapes,
Suiting their present thoughts: if sad,
  they cry;
If mirth be their conceit, they laugh
  again;
Sometimes they imitate the beasts and
  birds,
Singing or howling, braying, barking—all
As their wild fancies prompt um.

Enter Lollio.

ANT.   These are no fears.
ISA. But here's a large one, my man.
ANT. Ha, he! That's fine sport, indeed,
cousin.   232

[3] Venture.
[4] A humanist writer, with an obvious pun.
[5] Reference to Ovid's *Art of Love.*

LoL. I would my master were come
home! 'Tis too much for one shepherd
to govern two of these flocks; nor can I
believe that one churchman can instruct
two benefices at once. There will be some
incurable mad of the one side, and very
fools on the other.—Come, Tony.

ANT. Prithee, cousin, let me stay here
still.   241

LoL. No, you must to your book now;
you have played sufficiently.

ISA. Your fool has grown wondrous
witty.

LoL. Well, I'll say nothing; but I do not
think but he will put you down one of these
days.   *Exeunt Lol[lio] and Ant[onio].*

ISA. Here the restrainéd current might
      make breach,
  Spite of the watchful bankers.[1] Would a
      woman stray,   250
  She need not gad abroad to seek her sin;
  It would be brought home one ways or
      other.
  The needle's point will to the fixéd north;
  Such drawing artics [2] womens' beauties
      are.

Enter Lollio.

LoL. How dost thou, sweet rogue?

ISA. How now?

LoL. Come, there are degrees; one fool
may be better than another.

ISA. What's the matter?

LoL. Nay, if thou giv'st thy mind to
fool's flesh, have at thee!   261

ISA. You bold slave, you!

LoL. I could follow now as t'other fool
did.
  "What should I fear,
  Having all joys about me? Do you but
      smile,
  And love shall play the wanton on your
      lip,
  Meet and retire, retire and meet again;
  Look you but cheerfully, and in your
      eyes
  I shall behold my own deformity,   270
  And dress myself up fairer. I know this
      shape
  Becomes me not—"
And so as it follows. But is not this the
more foolish way? Come, sweet rogue;

kiss me, my little Lacedaemonian. Let
me feel how thy pulses beat. Thou hast a
thing about thee would do a man pleasure; I'll lay my hand on 't.

ISA. Sirrah, no more! I see you have dis-
      covered
  This love's knight errant, who hath made
      adventure   280
  For purchase of my love. Be silent,
      mute,
  Mute as a statue, or his injunction
  For me enjoying, shall be to cut thy
      throat;
  I'll do it, though for no other purpose;
      and
  Be sure he'll not refuse it.

LoL.   My share, that's all;
  I'll have my fool's part with you.

ISA.   No more! Your master.

Enter Alibius.

ALIB. Sweet, how dost thou?

ISA.   Your bounden servant, sir.

ALIB. Fie, fie, sweetheart, no more of that.

ISA. You were best lock me up.

ALIB. In my arms and bosom, my sweet
      Isabella,   290
  I'll lock thee up most nearly.—Lollio,
  We have employment, we have task in
      hand.
  At noble Vermandero's, our castle cap-
      tain,
  There is a nuptial to be solemnized—
  Beatrice Joanna, his fair daughter,
      bride—
  For which the gentleman hath bespoke
      our pains,
  A mixture of our madmen and our
      fools,
  To finish, as it were, and make the fag [3]
  Of all the revels, the third night from the
      first;
  Only an unexpected passage over,[4]   300
  To make a frightful pleasure, that is all,
  But not the all I aim at. Could we so act
      it,
  To teach it in a wild, distracted measure,
  Though out of form and figure, breaking
      time's head,
  It were no matter—'twould be healec
      again

[1] Dike builders. [2] *I.e.*, points of attraction.

[3] End.

[4] *I.e.*, of fools and madmen across the stage.

In one age or other, if not in this.
This, this, Lollio, there's a good reward
begun,
And will beget a bounty, be it known.

LOL. This is easy, sir, I'll warrant you.
You have about you fools and madmen
that can dance very well; and, 'tis no [311
wonder, your best dancers are not the wisest men; the reason is, with often jumping
they jolt their brains down into their feet,
that their wits lie more in their heels than
in their heads.

ALIB. Honest Lollio, thou giv'st me a good
reason,
And a comfort in it.

ISA.   Y'ave a fine trade on 't.
Madmen and fools are a staple commodity.

ALIB. O wife, we must eat, wear clothes,
and live.   320
Just at the lawyer's haven we arrive—
By madmen and by fools we both do
thrive.   *Exeunt.*

[SCENA QUARTA.

A room in the castle.]

Enter Vermandero, Alsemero, Jasperino, and
Beatrice.

VER. Valencia speaks so nobly of you, sir,
I wish I had a daughter now for you.

ALS. The fellow of this creature were a
partner
For a king's love.

VER.   I had her fellow once, sir,
But heaven has married her to joys
eternal;
'Twere sin to wish her in this vale again.
Come, sir, your friend and you shall see
the pleasures
Which my health chiefly joys in.

ALS. I hear the beauty of this seat largely.[1]

VER. It falls much short of that.
                Exeunt. Manet[2] Beatrice.

BEA.   So, here's one step   10
Into my father's favor; time will fix him.
I have got him now the liberty of the
house.
So wisdom, by degrees, works out her
freedom,
And if that eye be darkened that offends
me—

I wait but that eclipse—this gentleman
Shall soon shine glorious in my father's
liking,
Through the refulgent virtue of my love.

Enter Deflores.

DEF. [*Aside.*] My thoughts are at a banquet; for the deed,
I feel no weight in 't; 'tis but light and
cheap
For the sweet recompense that I set
down for 't.   20

BEA. Deflores!

DEF.   Lady!

BEA.   Thy looks promise cheerfully.

DEF. All things are answerable, time, circumstance,
Your wishes, and my service.

BEA.   Is it done, then?

DEF. Piracquo is no more.

BEA. My joys start at mine eyes; our
sweet'st delights
Are evermore born weeping.

DEF.   I've a token for you.

BEA. For me?

DEF. But it was sent somewhat unwillingly;
I could not get the ring without the finger.   [*Shows the finger and ring.*]

BEA. Bless me, what hast thou done?

DEF.   Why, is that more   30
Than killing the whole man? I cut his
heartstrings;
A greedy hand thrust in a dish at court
In a mistake hath had as much as this.

BEA. 'Tis the first token my father made
me send him.

DEF. And I made him send it back again
For his last token. I was loath to leave it,
And I'm sure dead men have no use of
jewels;
He was as loath to part with 't, for it stuck
As if the flesh and it were both one substance.

BEA. At the stag's fall, the keeper has his
fees.   40
'Tis soon applied; all dead men's fees are
yours, sir.
I pray, bury the finger, but the stone
You may make use on shortly; the true
value,
Take 't of my truth, is near three hundred
ducats.

---

[1] Widely   [2] Remains.

Def. 'Twill hardly buy a capcase [1] for
   one's conscience though,
   To keep it from the worm, as fine as 'tis.
   Well, being my fees, I'll take it;
   Great men have taught me that, or else
   my merit
   Would scorn the way on 't.

Bea.   It might justly, sir.
   Why, thou mistak'st, Deflores; 'tis not
   given   50
   In state [2] of recompense.

Def.   No, I hope so, lady;
   You should soon witness my contempt
   to 't then.

Bea. Prithee—thou look'st as if thou wert
   offended.

Def. That were strange, lady; 'tis not
   possible
   My service should draw such a cause
   from you.
   Offended? Could you think so? That
   were much
   For one of my performance, and so warm
   Yet in my service.

Bea. 'Twere misery in me to give you
   cause, sir.

Def. I know so much, it were so—
   misery   60
   In her most sharp condition.

Bea.   'Tis resolved then;
   Look you, sir, here's three thousand
   golden florins;
   I have not meanly thought upon thy
   merit.

Def. What! Salary? Now you move me.

Bea.   How, Deflores?

Def. Do you place me in the rank of ver-
   minous fellows,
   To destroy things for wages? Offer
   gold?
   The lifeblood of man? Is anything
   Valued too precious for my recompense?

Bea. I understand thee not.

Def.   I could ha' hired   69
   A journeyman in murder at this rate—
   And mine own conscience might have
   [slept at ease] [3] —
   And have had the work brought home.

Bea. [Aside.]   I'm in a labyrinth.
   What will content him? I would fain be
   rid of him.
   I'll double the sum, sir.

Def.   You take a course
   To double my vexation; that's the good
   you do.

Bea. [Aside]. Bless me, I am now in worse
   plight than I was;
   I know not what will please him.—For
   my fear's sake,
   I prithee, make away with all speed
   possible;
   And, if thou beest so modest not to name
   The sum that will content thee, paper
   blushes not.   80
   Send thy demand in writing; it shall
   follow thee.
   But, prithee, take thy flight.

Def.   You must fly too, then.

Bea. I?

Def.   I'll not stir a foot else.

Bea.   What's your meaning?

Def. Why, are not you as guilty? In, I'm
   sure,
   As deep as I? And we should stick to-
   gether.
   Come, your fears counsel you but ill;
   my absence
   Would draw suspect upon you instantly;
   There were no rescue for you.

Bea. [Aside.]   He speaks home!

Def. Nor is it fit we two, engaged so
   jointly,
   Should part and live asunder.

Bea.   How now, sir?   90
   This shows not well.

Def.   What makes your lip so strange?
   This must not be betwixt us.

Bea.   The man talks wildly!

Def. Come, kiss me with a zeal now.

Bea. [Aside.] Heaven, I doubt [4] him!

Def. I will not stand so long to beg 'em
   shortly.

Bea. Take heed, Deflores, of forgetfulness;
   'Twill soon betray us.

Def.   Take you heed first.
   Faith, y' are grown much forgetful; y' are
   to blame in 't.

Bea. [Aside.] He's bold, and I am blamed
   for 't.

Def.   I have eased
   You of your trouble; think on 't. I'm in
   pain,   100
   And must be eased of [5] you; 'tis a charity.
   Justice invites your blood to understand
   me.

---

[1] Bandbox.   [2] Place.
[3] Added by editor of 1816 edn.
[4] Fear.   [5] By.

BEA. I dare not.
DEF.   Quickly!
BEA.   O, I never shall!
Speak it yet further off, that I may lose
What has been spoken, and no sound
remain on 't.
I would not hear so much offense again
For such another deed.
DEF.   Soft, lady, soft!
The last is not yet paid for. O, this act
Has put me into spirit; I was as greedy
on 't
As the parched earth of moisture, when
the clouds weep.   110
Did you not mark, I wrought myself
into 't,
Nay, sued and kneeled for 't? Why was
all that pains took?
You see I have thrown contempt upon
your gold;
Not that I want it,[1] for I do piteously.
In order I will come unto 't, and make
use on 't,
But 'twas not held so precious to begin
with,
For I place wealth after the heels of
pleasure;
And, were not I resolved in my belief
That thy virginity were perfect in thee,
I should but take my recompense with
grudging,   120
As if I had but half my hopes I agreed
for.
BEA. Why, 'tis impossible thou canst be so
wicked,
Or shelter such a cunning cruelty,
To make his death the murderer of my
honor!
Thy language is so bold and vicious
I cannot see which way I can forgive it
With any modesty.
DEF.   Push![2] You forget yourself.
A woman dipped in blood, and talk of
modesty!
BEA. O misery of sin! Would I'd been
bound
Perpetually unto my living hate   130
In that Piracquo than to hear these
words!
Think but upon the distance that crea-
tion
Set twixt thy blood and mine, and keep
thee there.

DEF. Look but into your conscience; read
me there.
'Tis a true book; you'll find me there
your equal.
Push! Fly not to your birth, but settle
you
In what the act has made you; y' are no
more now.
You must forget your parentage[3] to me;
Y' are the deed's creature. By that name
You lost your first condition, and I
challenge you,   140
As peace and innocency has turned you
out,
And made you one with me.
BEA.   With thee, foul villain?
DEF. Yes, my fair murd'ress. Do you urge
me,
Though thou writ'st "maid," thou whore
in thy affection?
'Twas changed from thy first love, and
that's a kind
Of whoredom in thy heart; and he's
changed now
To bring thy second on, thy Alsemero,
Whom, by all sweets that ever darkness
tasted,
If I enjoy thee not, thou ne'er enjoy'st!
I'll blast the hopes and joys of mar-
riage;   150
I'll confess all. My life I rate at nothing.
BEA. Deflores!
DEF.   I shall rest from all lovers' plagues
then;
I live in pain now; that shooting eye
Will burn my heart to cinders.
BEA.   O, sir, hear me!
DEF. She that in life and love refuses me,
In death and shame my partner she shall
be.
BEA. [Kneeling.] Stay, hear me once for
all. I make thee master
Of all the wealth I have in gold and
jewels;
Let me go poor unto my bed with honor,
And I am rich in all things!
DEF.   Let this silence thee: 160
The wealth of all Valencia shall not
buy
My pleasure from me.
Can you weep Fate from its determined
purpose?
So soon may [you][4] weep me.

---

[1] I.e., want it not.   [2] Pish!

[3] Relationship.   [4] Added by Dyce.

BEA.   Vengeance begins.
Murder, I see, is followed by more sins.
Was my creation in the womb so cursted
It must engender with a viper first?
DEF. [*Raising her.*] Come, rise and shroud
    your blushes in my bosom;
Silence is one of pleasure's best receipts.
Thy peace is wrought forever in this
    yielding.   170
'Las! How the turtle pants! Thou'lt
    love anon
What thou so fear'st and faint'st to
    venture on.   *Exeunt.*

ACTUS QUARTUS.

[DUMB SHOW]

*Enter Gentlemen, Vermandero meeting them
with action of wonderment at the flight of
Piracquo. Enter Alsemero with Jasperino and Gallants; Vermandero points to
him, the Gentlemen seeming to applaud
the choice. Alsemero, Jasperino, and
Gentlemen; Beatrice the bride following
in great state, accompanied with Diaphanta, Isabella, and other Gentlewomen;
Deflores after All, smiling at the accident.[1] Alonzo's ghost appears to Deflores
in the midst of his smile, startles him,
showing him the hand whose finger he had
cut off. They pass over in great solemnity.*

[SCENA PRIMA.

Alsemero's chamber in the castle.]

Enter Beatrice.

BEA. This fellow has undone me endlessly;
Never was bride so fearfully distressed.
The more I think upon th' ensuing night,
And whom I am to cope with in em-
    braces,
One both ennobléd [2] in blood and mind,
So clear in understanding—that's my
    plague now—
Before whose judgment will my fault
    appear
Like malefactors' crimes before tri-
    bunals.
There is no hiding on 't, the more I dive
Into my own distress. How a wise
    man   10

Stands for [3] a great calamity! There's
    no venturing
Into his bed, what course soe'er I light
    upon,
Without my shame, which may grow up
    to danger.
He cannot but in justice strangle me
As I lie by him, as a cheater use me.
'Tis a precious craft to play with a false
    die
Before a cunning gamester. Here's his
    closet,
The key left in 't, and he abroad i' th'
    park!
Sure 'twas forgot; I'll be so bold as look
    in 't.   [*Passes to the inner stage.*]
Bless me! A right physician's closet 'tis,
Set round with vials, every one her mark
    too.   21
Sure he does practice physic for his own
    use,
Which may be safely called your great
    man's wisdom.
What manuscript lies here? *The Book of
    Experiment,*
Called Secrets in Nature. So 'tis; 'tis so.
[*Reads.*] "How to know whether a woman
    be with child or no."
I hope I am not yet; if he should try
    though!
Let me see. [*Reads.*] "Folio forty-five"—
    here 'tis,
The leaf tucked down upon 't, the place
    suspicious.   29
[*Reads.*] "If you would know whether a
woman be with child or not, give her two
spoonfuls of the white water in glass C——"
Where's that glass C? O yonder, I see 't
    now—
[*Reads.*] "and, if she be with child, she
sleeps full twelve hours after; if not, not."
None of that water comes into my belly;
I'll know you from a hundred. I could
    break you now,
Or turn you into milk, and so beguile
The master of the mystery; but I'll look
    to you.
Ha! That which is next is ten times
    worse: 40
[*Reads.*] "How to know whether a
woman be a maid or not."
If that should be applied, what would
    become of me?

---

[1] Event.   [2] Original repeats *both* here.   [3] Exposed to.

Belike he has a strong faith of my purity,
That never yet made proof; but this he calls
[*Reads*.] "A merry sleight, but true experiment; the author Antonius Mizaldus.
Give the party you suspect the quantity of
a spoonful of the water in the glass M,
which, upon her that is a maid, makes [50
three several effects: 'twill make her incontinently [1] gape, then fall into a sudden
sneezing, last into a violent laughing; else,
dull, heavy, and lumpish."
Where had I been?
I fear it; yet 'tis seven hours to bedtime.

Enter Diaphanta.

DIA. Cud's,[2] madam, are you here?
BEA. [*Aside*.]   Seeing that wench now,
A trick comes in my mind; 'tis a nice piece
Gold cannot purchase.—I come hither, wench,
To look [3] my lord.
DIA.   Would I had such a cause   60
To look him too!—Why, he's i' th' park, madam.
BEA. There let him be.
DIA.   Ay, madam, let him compass
Whole parks and forests, as great rangers do;
At roosting-time a little lodge can hold 'em.
Earth-conquering   Alexander,   that
thought the world
Too narrow for him, in the end had but
his pit-hole.
BEA. I fear thou art not modest, Diaphanta.
DIA. Your thoughts are so unwilling to be known, madam.
'Tis ever the bride's fashion, towards bedtime,
To set light by her joys, as if she owed [4]
'em not.   70
BEA. Her joys? Her fears thou wouldst say.
DIA.   Fear of what?
BEA. Art thou a maid, and talk'st so to a maid?
You leave a blushing business behind;
Beshrew your heart for 't!
DIA.   Do you mean good sooth, madam?
BEA. Well, if I'd thought upon the fear at first,
Man should have been unknown.

DIA.   Is 't possible?
BEA. I will give a thousand ducats to that woman
Would try what my fear were, and tell me true
Tomorrow, when she gets from 't; as she likes,
I might perhaps be drawn to 't.
DIA.   Are you in earnest?   80
BEA. Do you get the woman, then challenge me,
And see if I'll fly from 't; but, I must tell you
This by the way, she must be a true maid.
Else there's no trial; my fears are not hers else.
DIA. Nay, she that I would put into your hands, madam,
Shall be a maid.
BEA.   You know I should be shamed else,
Because she lies for me.
DIA.   'Tis a strange humor!
But are you serious still? Would you resign
Your first night's pleasure, and give money too?
BEA. As willingly as live.—[*Aside*.] Alas, the gold   90
Is but a by-bet to wedge in the honor!
DIA. I do not know how the world goes abroad
For faith or honesty; there's both required in this.
Madam, what say you to me, and stray no further?
I've a good mind, in troth, to earn your money.
BEA. Y' are too quick, I fear, to be a maid.
DIA. How? Not a maid? Nay, then you urge me, madam;
Your honorable self is not a truer,
With all your fears upon you—
BEA. [*Aside*.]   Bad enough then.
DIA. Than I with all my lightsome joys
about me.   100
BEA. I'm glad to hear 't. Then you dare put your honesty [5]
Upon an easy trial.
DIA.   Easy? Anything.
BEA. I'll come to you straight.
       [*Goes to the closet.*]

---

[1] Immediately.   [2] God's, part of a mild oath.
[3] Look for.   [4] Owned.   [5] Chastity.

DIA. She will not search me, will she,
Like the forewoman of a female jury?
BEA. Glass M. Ay, this is it. Look, Diaphanta;
You take no worse than I do. [*Drinks.*]
DIA. And, in so doing,
I will not question what 'tis, but take it.
[*Drinks.*]
BEA. [*Aside.*] Now if the experiment be
true, 'twill praise itself,
And give me noble ease. Begins already.
[*Diaphanta gapes.*]
There's the first symptom; and what
haste it makes 110
To fall into the second, there by this
time! [*Diaphanta sneezes.*]
Most admirable secret! On the contrary,
It stirs not me a whit, which most concerns it.
DIA. Ha, ha, ha!
BEA. [*Aside.*] Just in all things, and in
order
As if 'twere circumscribed; one accident [1]
Gives way unto another.
DIA. Ha, ha, ha!
BEA. How now, wench?
DIA. Ha, ha, ha! I'm so, so light
At heart—ha, ha, ha!—so pleasurable!
But one swig more, sweet madam.
BEA. Ay, tomorrow, 120
We shall have time to sit by 't.
DIA. Now I'm sad again.
BEA. [*Aside.*] It lays [2] itself so gently
too!—Come, wench.
Most honest Diaphanta I dare call thee
now.
DIA. Pray, tell me, madam, what trick call
you this?
BEA. I'll tell thee all hereafter; we must
study
The carriage of this business.
DIA. I shall carry 't well,
Because I love the burthen.
BEA. About midnight
You must not fail to steal forth gently,
That I may use the place.
DIA. O, fear not, madam,
I shall be cool by that time. The bride's
place, 130
And with a thousand ducats! I'm for a
justice now.
I bring a portion with me; I scorn small
fools. *Exeunt.*

[1] Effect, symptom.   [2] Allays.

[SCENA SECUNDA.

Another room in the castle.]

Enter Vermandero and Servant.

VER. I tell thee, knave, mine honor is in
question,
A thing till now free from suspicion,
Nor ever was there cause. Who of my
gentlemen
Are absent? Tell me, and truly, how
many, and who?
SER. Antonio, sir, and Franciscus.
VER. When did they leave the castle?
SER. Some ten days since, sir, the one
intending to
Briamata, th' other for Valencia.
VER. The time accuses um. A charge of
murder
Is brought within my castle gate, Piracquo's murder. 10
I dare not answer faithfully their absence.
A strict command of apprehension
Shall pursue um suddenly, and either
wipe
The stain off clear, or openly discover it.
Provide me wingéd warrants for the
purpose. *Exit Servant.*
See, I am set on again.

Enter Tomaso.

TOM. I claim a brother of you.
VER. Y' are too hot;
Seek him not here.
TOM. Yes, 'mongst your dearest bloods,
If my peace find no fairer satisfaction.
This is the place must yield account for
him, 20
For here I left him; and the hasty tie
Of this snatched marriage gives strong
testimony
Of his most certain ruin.
VER. Certain falsehood!
This is the place indeed. His breach of
faith
Has too much marred both my abuséd
love,
The honorable love I reserved for him,
And mocked my daughter's joy. The
prepared morning
Blushed at his infidelity; he left
Contempt and scorn to throw upon those
friends

Whose belief hurt 'em. O, 'twas most
  ignoble   30
To take his flight so unexpectedly,
And throw such public wrongs on those
  that loved him!

Tom. Then this is all your answer?

Ver.   'Tis too fair
For one of his alliance; and I warn you
That this place no more see you. *Exit.*

Enter Deflores.

Tom.   The best is
There is more ground to meet a man's
  revenge on.—
Honest Deflores?

Def.   That's my name indeed.
Saw you the bride? Good, sweet sir,
  which way took she?

Tom. I have blessed mine eyes from seeing
  such a false one.

Def. [*Aside.*] I'd fain get off; this man's
  not for my company.   40
I smell his brother's blood when I come
  near him.

Tom. Come hither, kind and true one; I
  remember
My brother loved thee well.

Def.   O, purely, dear sir!—
[*Aside.*] Methinks I am now again a-
  killing on him,
He brings it so fresh to me.

Tom.   Thou canst guess, sirrah—
One honest friend has an instinct of
  jealousy—
At some foul, guilty person.

Def. 'Las, sir, I am so charitable I think
  none
Worse than myself! You did not see the
  bride then?

Tom. I prithee, name her not. Is she not
  wicked?   50

Def. No, no; a pretty, easy, round-
  packed sinner,
As your most ladies are, else you might
  think
I flattered her; but, sir, at no hand wicked,
Till th' are so old their chins and noses [1]
  meet,
And they salute witches. I'm called, I
  think, sir.—
[*Aside.*] His company ev'n o'erlays my
  conscience.   *Exit.*

[1] Emended by Dyce. Original reads *sins and vices.*

Tom. That Deflores has a wondrous honest
  heart!
He'll bring it out in time, I'm assured on 't.
O, here's the glorious master of the day's
  joy!
'T [2] will not be long till he and I do
  reckon.—Sir!   60

Enter Alsemero.

Als. You are most welcome.

Tom.   You may call that word back;
I do not think I am, nor wish to be.

Als. 'Tis strange you found the way to
  this house, then.

Tom. Would I'd ne'er known the cause!
  I'm none of those, sir,
That come to give you joy, and swill
  your wine.
'Tis a more precious liquor that must lay
The fiery thirst I bring.

Als.   Your words and you
Appear to me great strangers.

Tom.   Time and our swords
May make us more acquainted. This the
  business:
I should have a brother in your place; 70
How treachery and malice have disposed
  of him,
I'm bound to inquire of him which holds
  his right,
Which never could come fairly.

Als.   You must look
To answer for that word, sir.

Tom.   Fear you not,
I'll have it ready drawn at our next meeting.
Keep your day solemn.[3] Farewell, I disturb it not;
I'll bear the smart with patience for a
  time.   *Exit.*

Als. 'Tis somewhat ominous this; a quarrel entered
Upon this day. My innocence relieves me;

Enter Jasperino.

I should be wondrous sad else.—Jasperino,   80
I have news to tell thee, strange news.

Jasp.   I ha' some too,
I think as strange as yours. Would I
  might keep

[2] Emended by Dyce. Original reads *I.*
[3] *I.e.,* celebrate your wedding day.

Mine, so my faith and friendship might
   be kept in 't!
Faith, sir, dispense a little with my zeal,
   And let it cool in this.
ALS.   This puts me on,
   And blames thee for thy slowness.
JAS.   All may prove nothing,
   Only a friendly fear that leaped from me,
   sir.
ALS. No question, it may prove nothing;
   let's partake it though.
JAS. 'Twas Diaphanta's chance—for to
   that wench
I pretend [1] honest love, and she deserves
   it—   90
To leave me in a back part of the house,
A place we chose for private conference.
She was no sooner gone but instantly
I heard your bride's voice in the next
   room to me,
And, lending more attention, found
   Deflores
Louder than she.
ALS.   Deflores? Thou art out now.
JAS. You'll tell me more anon.
ALS.   Still I'll prevent [2] thee.
The very sight of him is poison to her.
JAS. That made me stagger too; but Dia-
   phanta
At her return confirmed it.
ALS.   Diaphanta! 100
JAS. Then fell we both to listen, and words
   passed
Like those that challenge interest in a
   woman.
ALS. Peace! Quench thy zeal; 'tis dan-
   gerous to thy bosom.
JAS. Then truth is full of peril.
ALS.   Such truths are.
O, were she the sole glory of the earth,
Had eyes that could shoot fire into king's
   breasts,
And touched,[3] she sleeps not here! Yet I
   have time,
Though night be near, to be resolved [4]
   hereof.
And, prithee, do not weigh me by my
   passions.
JAS. I never weighed friend so.
ALS.   Done charitably! 110
That key will lead thee to a pretty secret,
                      [Gives key.]
By a Chaldean taught me, and I've
---
[1] Profess. [2] Anticipate. [3] Tainted. [4] Satisfied.

My study upon some. Bring from my
   closet
A glass inscribed there with the letter M,
And question not my purpose.
JAS.   It shall be done, sir. *Exit.*
ALS. How can this hang together? Not an
   hour since
Her woman came pleading her lady's fears,
Delivered her for the most timorous virgin
That ever shrunk at man's name, and
   so modest
She charged her weep out her request to
   me   120
That she might come obscurely to my
   bosom.

Enter Beatrice.

BEA. [*Aside.*] All things go well; my wo-
   man's preparing yonder
For her sweet voyage, which grieves me
   to lose.
Necessity compels it. I lose all, else.
ALS. [*Aside.*] Push! Modesty's shrine is
   set in yonder forehead.
I cannot be too sure though.—My Jo-
   anna!
BEA. Sir, I was bold to weep a message
   to you;
Pardon my modest fears.
ALS. [*Aside.*]   The dove's not meeker;
She's abused, questionless.—O, are you
   come, sir?

Enter Jasperino [with vial].

BEA. [*Aside.*] The glass, upon my life! I
   see the letter.   130
JAS. [*Giving vial.*] Sir, this is M.
ALS.   'T's it.
BEA. [*Aside.*]   I am suspected.
ALS. How fitly our bride comes to partake
   with us!
BEA. What is 't, my lord?
ALS.   No hurt.
BEA.   Sir, pardon me;
I seldom taste of any composition.
ALS. But this, upon my warrant, you shall
   venture on.
BEA. I fear 'twill make me ill.
ALS.   Heaven forbid that.
BEA. [*Aside.*] I'm put now to my cunning;
   th' effects I know,
If I can now but feign 'em handsomely.
                         [*Drinks.*]

ALS. It has that secret virtue, it ne'er
    missed, sir,
  Upon a virgin.
JAS.   Treble-qualitied?   140
            [*Beatrice gapes and sneezes.*]
ALS. By all that's virtuous it takes there—
    proceeds!
JAS. This is the strangest trick to know a
    maid by.
BEA. Ha, ha, ha!
  You have given me joy of heart to drink,
    my lord.
ALS. No, thou hast given me such joy of
    heart
  That never can be blasted.
BEA.   What's the matter, sir?
ALS. [*Aside.*] See now 'tis settled in a
    melancholy.
  Keep both the time and method.—My
    Joanna,
  Chaste as the breath of heaven, or
    morning's womb,
  That brings the day forth! Thus my love
  encloses thee.   *Exeunt.* 150

[SCENA TERTIA.

A room in the house of Alibius.]

Enter Isabella [with a letter,] and Lollio.

ISA. O heaven! Is this the waning [1] moon?
  Does love turn fool, run mad, and all at
    once?
  Sirrah, here's a madman, akin to the fool
    too,
  A lunatic lover.
LOL. No, no, not he I brought the letter
    from.
ISA. [*Giving him the letter.*] Compare his in-
    side with his out, and tell me.
LOL. The out's mad, I'm sure of that; I
    had a taste on 't. [*Reads letter.*] "To the
    bright Andromeda, chief chambermaid to
    the Knight of the Sun, at the sign of [10
    Scorpio, in the middle region, sent by the
    bellows-mender of Aeolus. Pay the post."
    This is stark madness!
ISA. Now mark the inside. [*Takes the
    letter and reads.*] "Sweet lady, having now
    cast off this counterfeit cover of a madman,
    I appear to your best judgment a true and
    faithful lover of your beauty."
LOL. He is mad still.

ISA. "If any fault you find, chide [20
    those perfections in you which have made
    me imperfect; 'tis the same sun that causeth
    to grow and enforceth to wither—"
LOL. O rogue!
ISA. "Shapes and transshapes, destroys
    and builds again. I come in winter to you,
    dismantled of my proper ornaments; by
    the sweet splendor of your cheerful smiles I
    spring and live a lover."
LOL. Mad rascal still!   30
ISA. "Tread him not under foot, that
    shall appear an honor to your bounties. I
    remain—mad till I speak with you, from
    whom I expect my cure,
        Yours all, or one beside himself,
                        FRANCISCUS."
LOL. You are like to have a fine time
    on 't. My master and I may give over our
    professions; I do not think but you can cure
    fools and madmen faster than we, with
    little pains too.   40
ISA. Very likely.
LOL. One thing I must tell you,[2] mis-
    tress: you perceive that I am privy to your
    skill;[3] if I find you minister once, and set up
    the trade, I put in for my thirds. I shall be
    mad or fool else.
ISA. The first place is thine, believe it,
    Lollio,
  If I do fall.
LOL.   I fall upon you.
ISA.   So.
LOL. Well, I stand to my venture.
ISA. But thy counsel now. How [50
    shall I deal with 'em?
LOL. Why,[4] do you mean to deal with um?
ISA. Nay, the fair understanding[5]—how to
    use um.
LOL. Abuse[6] um! That's the way to
    mad the fool, and make a fool of the mad-
    man, and then you use um kindly.[7]
ISA. 'Tis easy; I'll practice. Do thou ob-
    serve it.
  The key of thy wardrobe.
LOL. [*Giving key.*] There. Fit yourself
    for um, and I'll fit um both for you. [60
ISA. Take thou no further notice than the
    outside.   *Exit.*
LOL. Not an inch; I'll put you to the inside.

---

[1] Emended by editor of 1816. Original has
waiting.

[2] Original reads *your.*   [3] Profession.
[4] Emended by Dyce. Original reads *We.*
[5] *I.e.,* the proper meaning of my words.
[6] Deceive.   [7] According to their nature.

Enter Alibius.

ALIB. Lollio, art there? Will all be perfect,
think'st thou?
Tomorrow night, as if to close up the
Solemnity, Vermandero expects us.

LOL. I mistrust the madmen most. The
fools will do well enough; I have taken pains
with them.

ALIB. Tush! They cannot miss. The more
absurdity,
The more commends it, so [1] no rough
behaviors   70
Affright the ladies. They're nice [2] things,
thou know'st.

LOL. You need not fear, sir; so long as
we are there with our commanding peesles [3]
they'll be as tame as the ladies themselves.

ALIB. I will see them once more rehearse
before they go.

LOL. I was about it, sir. Look you to
the madmen's morris, and let me alone with
the other. There is one or two that I mistrust their fooling. I'll instruct them, and [80
then they shall rehearse the whole measure.

ALIB. Do so; I'll see the music prepared.
But, Lollio,
By the way, how does my wife brook her
restraint?
Does she not grudge at it?

LOL. So, so. She takes some pleasure in
the house; she would abroad else. You must
allow her a little more length; she's kept
too short.

ALIB. She shall along to Vermandero's
with us—   89
That will serve her for a month's liberty.

LOL. What's that on your face, sir?

ALIB. Where, Lollio? I see nothing.

LOL. Cry you mercy,[4] sir, 'tis your nose;
it showed like the trunk of a young elephant.[5]

ALIB. Away, rascal! I'll prepare the music,
Lollio.   *Ex[it] Ali[bius].*

LOL. Do, sir, and I'll dance the whilst.—
Tony, where art thou, Tony?

Enter Antonio.

ANT. Here, cousin. Where art thou?

LOL. Come, Tony, the footmanship [100
I taught you.

[1] Provided that.   [2] Fastidious.
[3] Pizzles, whips.   [4] I beg your pardon.
[5] A variation on the jest about the cuckold's
horns.

ANT. I had rather ride, cousin.

LOL. Ay, a whip take you! But I'll keep
you out. Vault in. Look you, Tony! Fa, la,
la, la, la.   [*Dances.*]

ANT. [*Dancing.*] Fa, la, la, la, la.

LOL. There, an honor.[6]

ANT. Is this an honor, coz?

LOL. Yes, and it please your worship. 109

ANT. Does honor bend in the hams, coz?

LOL. Marry, does it, as low as worship,
squireship, nay, yeomandry itself sometimes, from whence it first stiffened. There
rise, a caper.

ANT. Caper after an honor, coz?

LOL. Very proper, for honor is but a
caper, rise[s] as fast and high, has a knee or
two, and falls to th' ground again. You can
remember your figure,[7] Tony?   *Exit.*

ANT. Yes, cousin; when I see thy figure,
I can remember mine.   121

Enter Isabella [, dressed as a madwoman].

ISA. Hey, how she treads the air!
Shough, shough, tother way! He burns
his wings else. Here's wax enough below,
Icarus, more than will be canceled these
eighteen moons. He's down, he's down!
What a terrible fall he had!
Stand up, thou son of Cretan Daedalus,
And let us tread the lower labyrinth;
I'll bring thee to the clue.   130

ANT. Prithee, coz, let me alone.

ISA.   Art thou not drowned?
About thy head I saw a heap of clouds
Wrapped like a Turkish turbant; on thy
back
A crook'd chameleon-colored rainbow
hung
Like a tiara down unto thy hams.
Let me suck out those billows in thy
belly;
Hark, how they roar and rumble in the
streets!
Bless thee from the pirates!

ANT. Pox upon you, let me alone!

ISA. Why shouldst thou mount so high as
Mercury,   140
Unless thou hadst reversion of his place?
Stay in the moon with me, Endymion,
And we will rule these wild, rebellious
waves,
That would have drowned my love.

[6] Obeisance.   [7] Dance.

Ant. I'll kick thee, if again thou touch me,
  Thou wild unshapen antic; I am no fool,
  You bedlam!

Isa.   But you are, as sure as I am, mad.
              [*Reveals herself.*]
  Have I put on this habit of a frantic,
  With love as full of fury, to beguile   150
  The nimble eye of watchful jealousy,
  And am I thus rewarded?

Ant.   Ha! Dearest beauty!

Isa. No, I have no beauty now,
  Nor never had but what was in my gar-
    ments.
  You a quick-sighted lover!   Come not
    near me.
  Keep your caparisons; y' are aptly clad.
  I came a feigner, to return stark mad.
                        Exit.

Ant. Stay, or I shall change condition,
  And become as you are.   159

Enter Lollio.[1]

Lol. Why, Tony, whither now? Why, fool—

Ant. Whose fool, usher of idiots? You cox-
    comb!
  I have fooled too much.

Lol. You were best be mad another while
  then.

Ant. So I am, stark mad; I have cause
    enough.
  And I could throw the full effects on thee,
  And beat thee like a fury.

Lol. Do not, do not; I shall not forbear
  the gentleman under the fool, if you do.
  Alas! I saw through your foxskin before
  now! Come, I can give you comfort. [170
  My mistress loves you; and there is as
  arrant a madman i' th' house as you are a
  fool, your rival, whom she loves not. If
  after the masque we can rid her of him,
  you earn her love, she says, and the fool
  shall ride her.

Ant. May I believe thee?

Lol. Yes, or you may choose whether you
  will or no.

Ant. She's eased of him; I have a good
    quarrel on 't.

Lol. Well, keep your old station yet, and
    be quiet.   180

Ant. Tell her *I* will deserve her love.

Lol. And you are like to have your desire.
                  [*Exit Antonio.*]

Enter Franciscus.

Fran. [*Singing.*] "Down, down, down, a-
    down a-down—" and then with a
    horse trick [2]
  To kick Latona's forehead, and break
    her bowstring.

Lol. [*Aside.*] This is tother counterfeit;
  I'll put him out of his humor.—[*Reads Franciscus' letter.*] "Sweet lady, having now
  cast this counterfeit cover of a madman,
  I appear to your best judgment a   [189
  true and faithful lover of your beauty."
  This is pretty well for a madman.

Fran. Ha! What's that?

Lol. "Chide those perfections in you
  which [have] made me imperfect."

Fran. I am discovered to the fool.

Lol. I hope to discover the fool in you
  ere I have done with you. "Yours all, or one
  beside himself, Franciscus." This madman will mend sure.

Fran. What do you read, sirrah?   200

Lol. Your destiny, sir. You'll be hanged
  for this trick, and another that I know.

Fran. Art thou of counsel with thy
  mistress?

Lol. Next her apron strings.

Fran. Give me thy hand.

Lol. Stay, let me put yours in my pocket
  first. [*Puts the letter away.*] Your hand
  is true,[3] is it not? It will not pick? I   [209
  partly fear it, because I think it does lie.

Fran. Not in a syllable.

Lol. So if you love my mistress so well
  as you have handled the matter here, you
  are like to be cured of your madness.

Fran. And none but she can cure it.

Lol. Well, I'll give you over then, and
  she shall cast your water [4] next.

Fran. Take for thy pains past.   218
                    [*Gives money.*]

Lol. I shall deserve more, sir, I hope.
  My mistress loves you, but must have
  some proof of your love to her.

Fran. There I meet my wishes.

Lol. That will not serve; you must
  meet her enemy and yours.

Fran. He's dead already.

Lol. Will you tell me that, and I parted
  but now with him?

Fran. Show me the man.   228

LOL. Ay, that's a right course now. See him before you kill him, in any case; and yet it needs not go so far neither. 'Tis but a fool that haunts the house and my mistress in the shape of an idiot; bang but his fool's coat well-favoredly, and 'tis well.

FRAN. Soundly, soundly!

LOL. Only reserve him till the masque be past; and, if you find him not now in the dance yourself, I'll show you. In, in! My master!   [*Dances.*] [239

FRAN. He handles him like a feather. Hey!   [*Exit.*]

Enter Alibius.

ALIB. Well said.[1] In a readiness, Lollio?

LOL. Yes, sir.

ALIB. Away then, and guide them in, Lollio.
Entreat your mistress to see this sight.
Hark, is there not one incurable fool
That might be begged?[2] I have friends.

LOL. I have him for you, one that shall deserve it too.

ALIB. Good boy, Lollio!
    The Madmen and Fools dance.
'Tis perfect. Well, fit but once these strains,   250
We shall have coin and credit for our pains.   *Exeunt.*

ACTUS QUINTUS. [SCENA PRIMA.

A corridor in the castle.]

Enter Beatrice. A clock strikes one.

BEA. One struck, and yet she lies by 't!
O, my fears!
This strumpet serves her own ends, 'tis apparent now,
Devours the pleasure with a greedy appetite,
And never minds my honor or my peace,
Makes havoc of my right. But she pays dearly for 't;
No trusting of her life with such a secret
That cannot rule her blood to keep her promise.
Beside, I have some suspicion of her faith to me,
Because I was suspected of my lord,   9

And it must come from her. (*Strike two.*)[3]
Hark! By my horrors,
Another clock strikes two!

Enter Deflores.

DEF.   Pist! Where are you?

BEA. Deflores!

DEF. Ay. Is she not come from him yet?

BEA. As I am a living soul, not!

DEF.   Sure the devil
Hath sowed his itch within her. Who'd trust a waiting-woman?

BEA. I must trust somebody.

DEF.   Push! They're termagants,
Especially when they fall upon their masters
And have their ladies' first fruits. Th' are mad whelps;
You cannot stave 'em off from game royal. Then
You are so harsh[4] and hardy, ask no counsel;
And I could have helped you to a apothecary's daughter   20
Would have fall'n off before eleven, and thank you too.

BEA. O me, not yet! This whore forgets herself.

DEF. The rascal fares so well. Look, y' are undone;
The day-star, by this hand! See Phosphorus[5] plain yonder.

BEA. Advise me now to fall upon some ruin;
There is no counsel safe else.

DEF.   Peace! I ha 't now,
For we must force a rising; there's no remedy.

BEA. How? Take heed of that.

DEF. Tush! Be you quiet, or else give over all.   29

BEA. Prithee, I ha' done then.

DEF.   This is my reach:[6] I'll set
Some part afire of Diaphanta's chamber.

BEA. How? Fire, sir? That may endanger the whole house.

DEF. You talk of danger when your fame's on fire.

BEA. That's true; do what thou wilt now.

---

[1] Well done.
[2] Be appointed the fool's guardian to control and enjoy his estate.

[3] This stage direction in the original appears at the end of the speech.   [4] Rough, rude.
[5] Original reads *Bosphorus*.   [6] Trick.

DEF.   Push! I aim
At a most rich success strikes all dead
    sure.
The chimney being afire, and some light
    parcels
Of the least danger in her chamber only,
If Diaphanta should be met by chance
    then
Far from her lodging, which is now sus-
    picious,
It would be thought her fears and af-
    frights then   40
Drove her to seek for succor; if not seen
Or met at all, as that's the likeliest,
For her own shame she'll hasten towards
    her lodging.
I will be ready with a piece high-charged,
As 'twere to cleanse the chimney,
    there [1] 'tis proper now;
But she shall be the mark.
BEA.   I'm forced to love thee now,
Cause thou provid'st so carefully for
    my honor.
DEF. 'Slid, it concerns the safety of us
    both,
Our pleasure and continuance.
BEA.   One word now,
Prithee; how for the servants?
DEF.   I'll despatch them,   50
Some one way, some another in the
    hurry,
For buckets, hooks, ladders. Fear not you,
The deed shall find its time; and I've
    thought since
Upon a safe conveyance for the body
    too.
How this fire purifies wit! Watch you
    your minute.
BEA. Fear keeps my soul upon 't; I can-
    not stray from 't.

Enter Alonzo's Ghost.

DEF. Ha! What art thou that tak'st
    away the light
'Twixt that star and me? I dread thee
    not.—
'Twas but a mist of conscience; all's
    clear again.   [*Exit.*]
BEA. Who's that, Deflores? Bless me, it
    slides by!   [*Exit Ghost.*]   60
Some ill thing haunts the house; 't has
    left behind it

A shivering sweat upon me; I'm afraid
    now.
This night hath been so tedious!   O,
    this strumpet!
Had she a thousand lives, he should
    not leave her
Till he had destroyed the last.   List!
    O, my terrors!   *Struck three a-clock.*
Three struck by St. Sebastian's!
WITHIN.   Fire, fire, fire!
BEA. Already!   How rare is that man's
    speed!
How heartily he serves me!   His face
    loathes [2] one;
But, look upon his care, who would not
    love him?
The East is not more beauteous than
    his service.   70
WITHIN. Fire, fire, fire!

*Enter Deflores; Servants pass over.   Ring
    a bell.*

DEF. Away, despatch!   Hooks, buckets,
    ladders!   That's well said.
The fire bell rings; the chimney works.
    My charge!
The piece is ready.   *Exit.*

Enter Diaphanta.

BEA.   Here's a man worth loving!—
O, y' are a jewel!
DIA.   Pardon frailty, madam;
In troth, I was so well, I ev'n forgot myself.
BEA. Y' have made trim work!
DIA. What?
BEA.   Hie quickly to your chamber;
Your reward follows you.
DIA.   I never made
So sweet a bargain.   *Exit.*

Enter Alsemero.

ALS.   O, my dear Joanna!   80
Alas, art thou risen too?   I was coming,
My absolute treasure!
BEA.   When I missed you,
I could not choose but follow.
ALS.   Th'art all sweetness
The fire is not so dangerous.
BEA.   Think you so, sir?
ALS. I prithee, tremble not; believe me
    'tis not.

---

[1] Where.

[2] Repeis.

Enter Vermandero, Jasperino.

VER. O, bless my house and me!
ALS.   My lord your father.

Enter Deflores with a piece.

VER. Knave, whither goes that piece?
DEF.   To scour the chimney. *Exit.*
VER. O, well said, well said!
    That fellow's good on all occasions. 89
BEA. A wondrous necessary man, my lord.
VER. He hath a ready wit; he's worth 'em
    all, sir.
    Dog [1] at a house of fire; I ha' seen him
    singed ere now.— *The piece goes off.*
    Ha, there he goes!
BEA.   'Tis done!
ALS.   Come, sweet, to bed now;
    Alas, thou wilt get cold.
BEA.   Alas, the fear keeps that out!
    My heart will find no quiet till I hear
    How Diaphanta, my poor woman, fares;
    It is her chamber, sir, her lodging cham-
    ber.
VER. How should the fire come there?
BEA. As good a soul as ever lady coun-
    tenanced,   99
    But in her chamber negligent and heavy.
    She scaped a mine twice.
VER.   Twice?
BEA.   Strangely twice, sir.
VER. Those sleepy sluts are dangerous in
    a house,
    And they be ne'er so good.

Enter Deflores.

DEF.   O poor virginity,
    Thou hast paid dearly for 't!
VER.   Bless us, what's that?
DEF. A thing you all knew once—Dia-
    phanta's burnt.
BEA. My woman! O, my woman!
DEF.   Now the flames
    Are greedy of her; burnt, burnt, burnt
    to death, sir!
BEA. O, my presaging soul!
ALS.   Not a tear more!
    I charge you by the last embrace I gave
    you   109
    In bed before this raised us.
BEA.   Now you tie me;
    Were it my sister, now she gets no more.

[1] An adept.

Enter Servant.

VER. How now?
SER.   All danger's past; you may now
    take
    Your rests, my lords; the fire is throughly
    quenched.
    Ah, poor gentlewoman, how soon was
    she stifled!
BEA. Deflores, what is left of her inter,
    And we as mourners all will follow her.
    I will entreat that honor to my servant
    Ev'n of my lord himself.
ALS.   Command it, sweetness.
BEA. Which of you spied the fire first?
DEF.   'Twas I, madam.
BEA. And took such pains in 't too? A
    double goodness!   120
    'Twere well he were rewarded.
VER.   He shall be.—
    Deflores, call upon me.
ALS.   And upon me, sir.
            Exeunt [All but Deflores].
DEF. Rewarded? Precious! Here's a
    trick beyond me.
    I see in all bouts, both of sport and wit,
    Always a woman strives for the last
    hit.   *Exit.*

[SCENA SECUNDA.

A room in the castle].

Enter Tomaso.

TOM. I cannot taste the benefits of life
    With the same relish I was wont to do.
    Man I grow weary of, and hold his
    fellowship
    A treacherous, bloody friendship, and,
    because
    I am ignorant in whom my wrath should
    settle,
    I must think all men villains, and the
    next
    I meet, whoe'er he be, the murderer
    Of my most worthy brother. Ha!
    What's he?

Enter Deflores, passes over the stage.

    O, the fellow that some call honest
    Deflores—   9
    But methinks honesty was hard bestead
    To come there for a lodging; as if a
    queen

Should make her palace of a pesthouse.
I find a contrariety in nature
Betwixt that face and me.   The least
  occasion
Would give me game upon him; yet he's
  so foul
One would scarce touch [him] [1] with a
  sword he loved
And made account of—so most deadly
  venomous,
He would go near to poison any weapon
That should draw blood on him.   One
  must resolve
Never to use that sword again in fight   20
In way of honest manhood that strikes
  him.
Some river must devour 't; 'twere not fit
That any man should find it.   What,
  again?

Enter Deflores.

He walks a [2] purpose by, sure, to choke
  me up,
To infect my blood.
DEF.   My worthy, noble lord!
TOM. Dost offer to come near and breathe
  upon me?   [*Strikes him.*]
DEF. A blow!   [*Draws.*]
TOM.   Yea, are you so prepared?
I'll rather like a soldier die by th' sword
Than like a politician by thy poison.
                                   [*Draws.*]
DEF. Hold, my lord, as you are honorable!
TOM. All slaves that kill by poison are
  still cowards.   31
DEF. [*Aside.*] I cannot strike; I see his
  brother's wounds
Fresh-bleeding in his eye, as in a crys-
  tal.—
I will not question this; I know y' are
  noble.
I take my injury with thanks given, sir,
Like a wise lawyer, and as a favor
Will wear it for the worthy hand that
  gave it.—
[*Aside.*] Why this from him that yester-
  day appeared
So strangely loving to me?
O, but instinct is of a subtler strain!   40
Guilt must not walk so near his lodge
  again;
He came near me now.   *Exit.*

[1] Added by Dyce.   [2] On.

TOM. All league with mankind I renounce
  forever,
Till I find this murderer; not so much
As common courtesy but I'll lock up;
For, in the state of ignorance I live in,
A brother may salute his brother's
  murderer,
And wish good speed to th' villain in a
  greeting.

Enter Verman[dero], Ali[bius], and Isabella.

VER. Noble Piracquo!
TOM.   Pray, keep on your way, sir;
I've nothing to say to you.
VER.   Comforts bless you, sir.   50
TOM. I have forsworn compliment, in troth
  I have, sir;
As you are merely man, I have not left
A good wish for you, nor any here.
VER. Unless you be so far in love with
  grief,
You will not part from 't upon any
  terms.
We bring that news will make a welcome
  for us.
TOM. What news can that be?
VER.   Throw no scornful smile
Upon the zeal I bring you; 'tis worth
  more, sir.
Two of the chiefest men I kept about me
I hide not from the law or your just
  vengeance.   60
TOM. Ha!
VER. To give your peace more ample
  satisfaction,
Thank these discoverers.
TOM.   If you bring that calm,
Name but the manner I shall ask for-
  giveness in
For that contemptuous smile upon you;
I'll perfect it with reverence that belongs
Unto a sacred altar.   [*Kneels.*]
VER. [*Raising him.*]   Good sir, rise.
Why, now you overdo as much a this
  hand
As you fell short a tother.—Speak,
  Alibius.
ALIB. 'Twas my wife's fortune, as she is
  most lucky   70
At a discovery, to find out lately
Within our hospital of fools and madmen
Two counterfeits slipped into these
  disguises,

Their names Franciscus and Antonio.

VER. Both mine, sir, and I ask no favor
   for 'em.

ALIB. Now that which draws suspicion
   to their habits,
   The time of their disguisings, agrees
   justly
   With the day of the murder.

TOM.   O blessed revelation!

VER. Nay, more, nay, more, sir—I'll not
   spare mine own
   In way of justice—they both feigned
   a journey   80
   To Briamata, and so wrought out their
   leaves;
   My love was so abused in 't.

TOM.   Time's too precious
   To run in waste now; you have brought
   a peace
   The riches of five kingdoms could not
   purchase.
   Be my most happy conduct. I thirst for
   'em.
   Like subtile lightning will I wind about
   'em,
   And melt their marrow in 'em.   *Exeunt.*

[SCENA TERTIA.

Alsemero's apartment in the castle.]

Enter Alsemero and Jasperino.

JAS. Your confidence, I'm sure, is now of
   proof;
   The prospect from the garden has
   showed
   Enough for deep suspicion.

ALS.   The black mask
   That so continually was worn upon 't
   Condemns the face for ugly ere 't be seen,
   Her despite to him, and so seeming
   bottomless.

JAS. Touch it home then; 'tis not a shallow
   probe
   Can search this ulcer soundly; I fear
   you'll find it
   Full of corruption. 'Tis fit I leave you.
   She meets you opportunely from that
   walk;   10
   She took the back door at his parting
   with her.   *Ex[it] Jas[perino].*

ALS. Did my fate wait for this unhappy
   stroke
   At my first sight of woman?—She's here.

Enter Beatrice.

BEA. Alsemero!

ALS.   How do you?

BEA.   How do I?
   Alas, how do you? You look not well.

ALS. You read me well enough; I am not
   well.

BEA. Not well, sir? Is 't in my power to
   better you?

ALS. Yes.

BEA. Nay, then y' are cured again.   19

ALS. Pray, resolve [1] me one question, lady.

BEA. If I can.

ALS. None can so sure: are you honest?

BEA. Ha, ha, ha! That's a broad question,
   my lord.

ALS. But that's not a modest answer, my
   lady.
   Do you laugh? My doubts are strong
   upon me.

BEA. 'Tis innocence that smiles, and no
   rough brow
   Can take away the dimple in her cheek.
   Say I should strain a tear to fill the vault,
   Which would you give the better faith to?

ALS. 'Twere but hypocrisy of a sadder
   color,   30
   But the same stuff; neither your smiles
   nor tears
   Shall move or flatter me from my belief:
   You are a whore!

BEA.   What a horrid sound it hath!
   It blasts a beauty to deformity;
   Upon what face soever that breath falls,
   It strikes it ugly. O, you have ruined
   What you can ne'er repair again.

ALS. I'll all demolish, and seek out truth
   within you,
   If there be any left. Let your sweet
   tongue
   Prevent your heart's rifling; there I'll
   ransack   40
   And tear out my suspicion.

BEA.   You may, sir;
   'Tis an easy passage; yet, if you please,
   Show me the ground whereon you lost
   your love.
   My spotless virtue may but tread on that
   Before I perish.

ALS.   Unanswerable.
   A ground you cannot stand on. You fall
   down

[1] Answer.

Beneath all grace and goodness when you set
Your ticklish heel on 't. There was a visor
O'er that cunning face, and that became you;   49
Now Impudence in triumph rides upon 't.
How comes this tender reconcilement else
'Twixt you and your despite, your rancorous loathing,
Deflores? He that your eye was sore at sight of,
He's now become your arm's supporter, your
Lip's saint!
BEA.   Is there the cause?
ALS.   Worse, your lust's devil,
Your adultery!
BEA.   Would any but yourself say that,
'Twould turn him to a villain!
ALS.   'Twas witnessed
By the counsel of your bosom, Diaphanta.
BEA. Is your witness dead then?
ALS.   'Tis to be feared
It was the wages of her knowledge; poor soul,   60
She lived not long after the discovery.
BEA. Then hear a story of not much less horror
Than this your false suspicion is beguiled with;
To your bed's scandal I stand up innocence,
Which even the guilt of one black other deed
Will stand for proof of; your love has made me
A cruel murd'ress.
ALS.   Ha!
BEA.   A bloody one.
I have kissed poison for 't, stroked a serpent,
That thing of hate, worthy in my esteem
Of no better employment; and him, most worthy   70
To be so employed I caused to murder
That innocent Piracquo, having no
Better means than that worst to assure
Yourself to me.
ALS.   O, the place itself e'er since
Has crying been for vengeance, the temple,
Where blood and beauty first unlawfully

Fired their devotion and quenched the right one!
'Twas in my fears at first; 'twill have it now.
O, thou art all deformed!
BEA.   Forget not, sir,
It for your sake was done. Shall greater dangers   80
Make the less welcome?
ALS.   O, thou shouldst have gone
A thousand leagues about to have avoided
This dangerous bridge of blood! Here we are lost.
BEA. Remember, I am true unto your bed.
ALS. The bed itself's a charnel, the sheets shrouds
For murdered carcasses. It must ask pause
What I must do in this; meantime you shall   87
Be my prisoner only. Enter my closet.
                              Exit Beatrice.
I'll be your keeper yet. O, in what part
Of this sad story shall I first begin?—Ha!
This same fellow has put me in.[1]—
Deflores!

Enter Deflores.

DEF. Noble Alsemero!
ALS.   I can tell you
News, sir; my wife has her commended to you.
DEF. That's news indeed, my lord; I think she would
Commend me to the gallows if she could,
She ever loved me so well. I thank her.
ALS. What's this blood upon your band,[2] Deflores?
DEF. Blood? No, sure; 'twas washed since.
ALS.   Since when, man?
DEF. Since tother day I got a knock
In a sword-and-dagger school; I think 'tis out.   100
ALS. Yes, 'tis almost out, but 'tis perceived though.
I had forgot my message. This it is—
What price goes murder?
DEF.   How, sir?
ALS.   I ask you, sir.
My wife's behindhand with [3] you, she tells me,

---

[1] Given me the cue.   [2] Collar.
[3] In arrears of payment to.

For a brave, bloody blow you gave for
   her sake
Upon Piracquo.

DEF.   Upon? 'Twas quite through
   him sure.
Has she confessed it?

ALS.   As sure as death to both of you;
And much more than that.

DEF.   It could not be much more.
'Twas but one thing, and that—she is a
   whore.

ALS. I could not choose but follow. O cunning devils!   110
How should blind men know you from
   fair-faced saints?

BEA. (*Within.*) He lies! The villain does
   belie me!

DEF. Let me go to her, sir.

ALS.   Nay, you shall to her.—
Peace, crying crocodile, your sounds are
   heard.
Take your prey to you; get you into her,
   sir.   *Exit Def[lores].*
I'll be your pander now; rehearse again
Your scene of lust, that you may be
   perfect
When you shall come to act it to the
   black audience,
Where howls and gnashings shall be
   music to you.   119
Clip [1] your adult'ress freely; 'tis the pilot
Will guide you to the *mare mortuum,* [2]
Where you shall sink to fadoms [3] bottom-
   less.

Enter Vermandero, Alibius, Isabella, To-
   maso, Franciscus, and Antonio.

VER. O Alsemero! I have a wonder for
   you.

ALS. No, sir, 'tis I, I have a wonder for
   you.

VER. I have suspicion near as proof itself
For Piracquo's murder.

ALS.   Sir, I have proof
Beyond suspicion for Piracquo's murder.

VER. Beseech you, hear me; these two
   have been disguised
E'er since the deed was done.

ALS.   I have two other
That were more close disguised than
   your two could be   130
E'er since the deed was done.

VER. You'll hear me—these mine own
   servants—

ALS. Hear me—those nearer than your
   servants
That shall acquit them, and prove them
   guiltless.

FRAN. That may be done with easy truth,
   sir.

TOM. How is my cause bandied through
   your delays!
'Tis urgent in blood and calls for haste.
Give me a brother alive or dead—
Alive, a wife with him; if dead, for
   both   139
A recompense for murder and adultery.

BEA. (*Within.*) O, O, O!

ALS.   Hark! 'Tis coming to you.

DEF. (*Within.*) Nay, I'll along for company.

BEA. (*Within.*)   O, O!

VER. What horrid sounds are these?

ALS. Come forth, you twins of mischief!

Enter Deflores, bringing in Beatrice
   [wounded].

DEF. Here we are. If you have any more
To say to us, speak quickly. I shall not
Give you the hearing else; I am so stout
   yet,
And so, I think, that broken rib of man-
   kind.

VER. An host of enemies entered my
   citadel
Could not amaze like this! Joanna!
   Beatrice Joanna!   150

BEA. O, come not near me, sir; I shall
   defile you!
I am that of your blood [4] was taken
   from you
For your better health; look no more
   upon 't,
But cast it to the ground regardlessly.
Let the common sewer [5] take it from
   distinction.
Beneath the stars, upon yon meteor
         [Points to Deflores.]
Ever hung [6] my fate 'mongst things cor-
   ruptible;
I ne'er could pluck it from him; my
   loathing

---

[1] Embrace.   [2] Dead sea.   [3] Fathoms.

[4] That part of your blood which.
[5] Original reads *shewer.*
[6] Emended by Dyce. Original has *hang.*

Was prophet to the rest, but ne'er
believed.
Mine honor fell with him, and now my
life.—   160
Alsemero, I am a stranger to your bed;
Your bed was cozened on the nuptial
night—
For which your false bride died.

ALS.   Diaphanta!

DEF. Yes, and the while I coupled with
your mate
At barleybreak; now we are left in hell.

VER. We are all there; it circumscribes
[us] [1] here.

DEF. I loved this woman in spite of her
heart;
Her love I earned out of Piracquo's
murder.

TOM. Ha! My brother's murtherer?

DEF.   Yes, and her honor's prize 169
Was my reward. I thank life for nothing
But that pleasure; it was so sweet to me
That I have drunk up all, left none
behind
For any man to pledge me.

VER.   Horrid villain!
Keep life in him for further tortures.

DEF.   No!
I can prevent you; here's my penknife
still.
It is but one thread more [Stabs him-
self.]—and now 'tis cut.—
Make haste, Joanna, by that token to
thee,   177
Canst not forget, so lately put in mind;
I would not go to leave thee far behind.
                                     Dies.

BEA. Forgive me, Alsemero, all forgive!
'Tis time to die when 'tis a shame to live.
                                     Dies.

VER. O, my name is entered now in that
record
Where till this fatal hour 'twas never
read.

ALS. Let it be blotted out; let your heart
lose it,
And it can never look you in the face,
Nor tell a tale behind the back of life
To your dishonor. Justice hath so right
The guilty hit that innocence is quit
By proclamation, and may joy again.—
Sir, you are sensible of what truth hath
done;   190

[1] Added by Dyce.

'Tis the best comfort that your grief can
find.

TOM. Sir, I am satisfied; my injuries
Lie dead before me. I can exact no more,
Unless my soul were loose, and could
o'ertake
Those black fugitives that are fled from
thence,
To take a second vengeance; but there
are wraths
Deeper than mine, 'tis to be feared, about
'em.

ALS. What an opacous body had that
moon
That last changed on us! Here's beauty
changed
To ugly whoredom; here servant-obe-
dience   200
To a master-sin, imperious murder;
I, a supposed husband, changed embraces
With wantonness—but that was paid
before.
Your change is come too, from an igno-
rant wrath
To knowing friendship.—Are there any
more on's?

ANT. Yes, sir, I was changed too from a
little ass as I was to a great fool as I am; and
had like to ha' been changed to the gallows,
but that you know my innocence [2] always
excuses me.   210

FRAN. I was changed from a little wit to
be stark mad,
Almost for the same purpose.

ISA. [To Alibius.]   Your change is still
Behind, but deserve best your transformation.
You are a jealous coxcomb, keep schools
of folly,
And teach your scholars how to break
your own head.

ALIB. I see all apparent, wife, and will
change now
Into a better husband, and never keep
Scholars that shall be wiser than myself.

ALS. [To Vermandero.] Sir, you have yet
a son's duty living.
Please you, accept it. Let that your
sorrow,   220
As it goes from your eye, go from your
heart.
Man and his sorrow at the grave must
part.

[2] Idiocy.

EPILOGUE

ALS. All we can do to comfort one an-
other,
  To stay a brother's sorrow for a brother,
  To dry a child from the kind father's
  eyes,
  Is to no purpose—it rather multiplies.

Your only smiles have power to cause
relive
The dead again, or in their rooms to give
Brother a new brother, father a child;
If these appear, all griefs are reconciled.
                              Exeunt omnes.

                    FINIS.

PHILIP MASSINGER

Although Philip Massinger will never be estimated above the second rank of Elizabethan playwrights, he is becoming more and more admired by modern readers and critics because of his qualities of simplicity, saneness, and dramatic (rather than lyrical) effectiveness. He belongs to the third and last generation of Elizabethan writers for the stage, since he was born in 1584, established his contacts with the theater just as Shakespeare was beginning to bring his work to an end and as Beaumont and Fletcher were producing their most famous plays, and died in 1640, just before the closing of the theaters by the Puritans. Massinger's birth into a family of education, his early patronage by the Pembrokes, and his partial education at Oxford, all started his career under favorable auspices. When he left college for London without a degree, probably about 1606, he seems to have gradually won for himself the confidence of such men as Field, Tourneur, Dekker, and Fletcher, with all of whom he eventually collaborated. His work with Fletcher from 1613 to 1623 for the King's Men has given his own friends and contemporaries, such as Sir Aston Cockayne, as well as many later scholars, plenty of opportunities to claim for him large portions of plays generally attributed to the more famous member of the intimate partnership which succeeded that of Beaumont and Fletcher on the retirement and death of the former. With the exception of the two years from 1623 to 1625, when for some unknown reason Massinger transferred his talents to the Queen's Men, his characters were created for the King's Men during the remaining years of his life. But, although he wrote many plays, both alone and in collaboration with other dramatists, he was never prosperous, and is known to have borrowed money at least once from old Philip Henslowe.

The two plays here printed from Massinger's individual pen, *A New Way to Pay Old Debts* and *The Maid of Honor*, represent his work at its best and most characteristic, for his two fortes were comedy and tragi-comedy; tragedy he is known to have practiced rarely, in such plays as *The Duke of Milan* and *The Fatal Dowry*, although Bishop Warburton's unfortunate cook is reputed to have consumed the manuscripts of several of Massinger's unprinted plays in his culinary operations. *A New Way to Pay Old Debts*, which was printed in 1633 and perhaps acted about 1625 or 1626, is not only one of the few Elizabethan plays which could be successfully produced for a modern audience almost without alteration, but, because of its being founded directly on Middleton's *A Trick to Catch the Old One*, it also affords an extremely interesting comparison between the spirits of the two men as well as between those of their generations. For in this comedy, as well as in his tragi-comedy, *The Maid of Honor* (printed in 1632 and probably acted less than a decade before), Massinger reveals himself as close to the cleanest and most high-minded of the playwrights of his age, though unluckily the same statement cannot be made about all of his writings, some of which are gratuitously coarse. Not only morality but also religion often bear leading parts in his works, although there is no necessity for accusing him of turning Roman Catholic because he presents adherents of this church in a particularly heroic light in some of his plays. His women are especially attractive, and in fact offer more variety and interest than his men, who, like his plots, tend to lack originality. The story of *The Maid of Honor*, for instance, derives from Boccaccio's "Camiola and Rolande" through the intermediary of Painter's *Palace of Pleasure*.

The present text of *The Maid of Honor* is based on the careful critical edition (London, 1927) prepared by Eva A. W. Bryne for the Bryn Mawr series of dissertations editing Massinger's plays; her readings are drawn from a collation of nine copies of the first, and only early, quarto, all of which vary slightly among themselves, corrections having apparently been made by the printer as the pages were going through the press. Her text, however, has been checked with that of the 1632 quarto in the Newberry Library. The text of *A New Way to Pay Old Debts* is based on a copy of the 1633 edition in the Newberry Library at Chicago, compared with A. H. Cruikshank's edition (Oxford, 1926) and Brander Matthews' in volume three of Gayley's *Representative English Comedies*.

A NEW WAY TO PAY OLD DEBTS[1]

BY

PHILIP MASSINGER

DRAMATIS PERSONÆ

LOVELL, *an English lord.*
SIR GILES OVERREACH, *a cruel extortioner.*
[FRANK] WELLBORN, *a prodigal.*
[TOM] ALLWORTH, *a young gentleman, page
to Lord Lovell.*
GREEDY, *a hungry justice of peace.*
MARALL, *a term driver;*[2] *a creature of Sir
Giles Overreach.*
ORDER [, *a steward*] ⎫
AMBLE [, *an usher*] ⎪ *servants to the Lady*
FURNACE [, *a cook*] ⎬ *Allworth.*
WATCHALL [, *a porter*] ⎭

WILLDO, *a parson.*
TAPWELL, *an alehouse keeper.*
THREE CREDITORS [, SERVANTS, *etc.*]

THE LADY ALLWORTH, *a rich widow.*
MARGARET, *Overreach his daughter.*
WAITING-WOMAN.
CHAMBERMAID.
FROTH, *Tapwell's wife.*

[SCENE: *The country near Nottingham.*

TIME: *Contemporary.*]

ACTUS PRIMUS. SCENA PRIMA.

[*Before Tapwell's house.*]

Wellborn, Tapwell, Froth.

WELL. No booze? Nor no tobacco?
TAP.   Not a suck, sir,
  Nor the remainder of a single can
  Left by a drunken porter, all night
    palled[3] too.
FROTH. Not the dropping of the tap for
    your morning's draught, sir.
  'Tis verity, I assure you.
WELL.   Verity, you brach![4]
  The devil turned precisian?[5] Rogue,
    what am I?

[1] The title continues: "A Comedy. As It
Hath Been Often Acted at the Phœnix in Drury
Lane by the Queen's Majesty's Servants." On
the following pages appear the dedication to
the Earl of Carnarvon and two commendatory
poems by Sir Henry Moody and Sir Thomas
Jay.
[2] One who moves from court to court during
sessions.
[3] Paled, become flat.
[4] Bitch.   [5] Puritan.

TAP. Troth, durst I trust you with a look-
    ing-glass
  To let you see your trim shape, you
    would quit[6] me
  And take the name yourself.
WELL.   How, dog?
TAP.   Even so, sir.
  And I must tell you, if you but ad-
    vance   10
  Your Plimworth cloak[7] you shall be soon
    instructed
  There dwells, and within call, if it please
    your worship,
  A potent monarch called the constable,
  That does command a citadel called the
    stocks,
  Whose guards are certain files of rusty
    billmen[8]
  Such as with great dexterity will hale
  Your tattered, lousy—
WELL.   Rascal! Slave!
FROTH.   No rage, sir.

[6] Acquit.
[7] Plymouth cloak; *i.e.,* a cudgel.
[8] Watchmen armed with pikes.

1357

TAP. At his own peril. Do not put yourself
In too much heat, there being no water
   near
   To quench your thirst; and sure, for
     other liquor,   20
As mighty ale or beer, they are things, I
   take it,
You must no more remember—not in a
   dream, sir.
WELL. Why, thou unthankful villain,
   dar'st thou talk thus?
Is not thy house, and all thou hast, my
   gift?
TAP. I find it not in chalk; and Timothy
   Tapwell
Does keep no other register.
WELL.   Am not I he
   Whose riots fed and clothed thee? Wert
     thou not
Born on my father's land, and proud to
   be
A drudge in his house?
TAP.   What I was, sir, it skills [1] not;
What you are, is apparent. Now, for a
   farewell,   30
Since you talk of father, in my hope it
   will torment you,
I'll briefly tell your story. Your dead
   father,
My quondam master, was a man of wor-
   ship,
Old Sir John Wellborn, justice of peace
   and quorum,[2]
And stood fair to be *custos rotulorum;* [3]
Bare the whole sway of the shire, kept a
   great house,
Relieved the poor, and so forth; but, he
   dying,
And the twelve hundred a year coming
   to you,
Late Master Francis, but now forlorn
   Wellborn—
WELL. Slave, stop, or I shall lose my-
   self!
FROTH.   Very hardly;   40
   You cannot out of your way.
TAP.   But to my story.
You were then a lord of acres, the prime
   gallant,
And I your underbutler. Note the change
   now.

[1] Matters.
[2] One of the most eminent justices.
[3] Custodian of the records.

You had a merry time of 't—hawks and
   hounds,
With choice of running horses; mistresses
Of all sorts and all sizes, yet so hot
As their embraces made your lordships [4]
   melt,
Which your uncle, Sir Giles Overreach,
   observing,
Resolving not to lose a drop of 'em
On foolish mortgages, statutes, and
   bonds,   50
For a while supplied your looseness, and
   then left you.
WELL. Some curate hath penned this in-
   vective, mongrel,
And you have studied it.
TAP.   I have not done yet.
Your land gone, and your credit not
   worth a token,[5]
You grew the common borrower; no man
   scaped
Your paper pellets,[6] from the gentle-
   man
To the beggars on highways, that sold
   you switches
In your gallantry.
WELL.   I shall switch your brains out!
TAP. Where poor Tim Tapwell, with a
   little stock,
Some forty pounds or so, bought a small
   cottage,   60
Humbled myself to marriage with my
   Froth here,
Gave entertainment—
WELL.   Yes, to whores and canters,[7]
   Clubbers by night.
TAP.   True, but they brought in profit,
And had a gift to pay for what they
   called for,
And stuck [8] not like your mastership.
   The poor income
I gleaned from them hath made me in my
   parish
Thought worthy to be scavenger, and in
   time
May rise to be overseer of the poor,
Which if I do, on your petition, Wellborn,
I may allow you thirteenpence a quarter,
And you shall thank my worship.

[4] Estates.
[5] A counter used as a substitute for money.
[6] *I.e.,* I.O.U's.
[7] Users of thieves' cant.
[8] *I. e.,* delayed payment.

WELL.   Thus, you dogbolt,[1]   71
  And thus—   *Beats and kicks him.*
TAP. [*To Froth.*]   Cry out for help!
WELL.   Stir, and thou diest.
  Your potent prince, the constable, shall
    not save you.
  Hear me, ungrateful hellhound! Did
    not I
  Make purses for you? Then you licked
    my boots,
  And thought your holy day [2] cloak too
    coarse to clean 'em.
  'Twas I that, when I heard thee swear if
    ever
  Thou couldst arrive at forty pounds thou
    wouldst
  Live like an emperor, 'twas I that
    gave it
  In ready gold. Deny this, wretch!
TAP.   I must, sir,   80
  For, from the tavern to the taphouse, all,
  On forfeiture of their licenses, stand
    bound
  Never to remember who their best guests
    were,
  If they grew poor like you.
WELL.   They are well rewarded
  That beggar themselves to make such
    cuckolds rich.
  Thou viper, thankless viper! Impudent
    bawd!
  But, since you are grown forgetful, I will
    help
  Your memory, and tread thee into mor-
    tar,
  Not leave one bone unbroken.
                          [*Beats him again.*]
TAP.   O!
FROTH.   Ask mercy.

Enter Allworth.

WELL. 'Twill not be granted.
ALL.   Hold—for my sake, hold!   90
  Deny me, Frank? They are not worth
    your anger.
WELL. For once thou hast redeemed them
    from this scepter. [*Shows*] *his cudgel.*
  But let 'em vanish, creeping on their
    knees,
  And, if they grumble, I revoke my par-
    don.

[1] A worthless arrow, *i.e.*, a contemptible
fellow.   [2] Holiday.

FROTH. This comes of your prating, hus-
    band; you presumed
  On your ambling wit, and must use your
    glib tongue,
  Though you are beaten lame for 't.
TAP.   Patience, Froth;
  There's law to cure our bruises.
          They go off on their hands and knees.
WELL.   Sent to your mother?
ALL. My lady, Frank, my patroness, my
    all!
  She's such a mourner for my father's
    death,   100
  And, in her love to him, so favors me
  That I cannot pay too much observance
    to her.
  There are few such stepdames.
WELL.   'Tis a noble widow,
  And keeps her reputation pure and clear
  From the least taint of infamy; her life,
  With the splendor of her actions, leaves
    no tongue
  To envy or detraction. Prithee, tell me,
  Has she no suitors?
ALL.   Even the best of the shire, Frank,
  My lord excepted, such as sue and send,
  And send and sue again, but to no pur-
    pose.   110
  Their frequent visits have not gained her
    presence.
  Yet she's so far from sullenness and
    pride
  That I dare undertake you shall meet
    from her
  A liberal entertainment. I can give you
  A catalogue of her suitors' names.
WELL.   Forbear it,
  While I give you good counsel. I am
    bound to it;
  Thy father was my friend, and that
    affection
  I bore to him, in right descends to
    thee.
  Thou art a handsome and a hopeful
    youth,
  Nor will I have the least affront stick on
    thee,   120
  If I with any danger can prevent it.
ALL. I thank your noble care; but, pray
    you, in what
  Do I run the hazard?
WELL.   Art thou not in love?
  Put it not off with wonder.
ALL.   In love, at my years?

WELL. You think you walk in clouds, but are trans[pa]rent.
I have heard all, and the choice that you have made,
And with my finger can point out the north star
By which the loadstone of your folly's guided.
And, to confirm this true, what think you of   129
Fair Margaret, the only child and heir
Of cormorant Overreach? Does it blush and start,
To hear her only named? Blush at your want
Of wit and reason.
ALL.   You are too bitter, sir.
WELL. Wounds of this nature are not to be cured
With balms, but corrosives. I must be plain:
Art thou scarce manumised [1] from the porter's lodge [2]
And yet sworn servant to the pantofle,[3]
And dar'st thou dream of marriage? I fear
'Twill be concluded for impossible
That there is now, nor e'er shall be here-after,   140
A handsome page or player's boy of fourteen
But either loves a wench, or drabs love him—
Court-waiters [4] not exempted.
ALL.   This is madness.
Howe'er you have discovered my in-tents,
You know my aims are lawful; and, if ever
The queen of flowers, the glory of the spring,
The sweetest comfort to our smell, the rose,
Sprang from an envious brier, I may infer
There's such disparity in their condi-tions
Between the goddess of my soul, the daughter,   150
And the base churl of her father.

[1] Manumitted, freed.
[2] Where servants were punished.
[3] Slipper; *i.e.*, he is still a page.
[4] Pages at court.

WELL.   Grant this true,
As I believe it, canst thou ever hope
To enjoy a quiet bed with her whose father
Ruined thy state?
ALL.   And yours too.
WELL.   I confess it.
True, I must tell you as a friend, and freely,
That, where impossibilities are apparent,
'Tis indiscretion to nourish hopes.
Canst thou imagine (let not self-love blind thee)
That Sir Giles Overreach, that, to make her great
In swelling titles, without touch of con-science   160
Will cut his neighbor's throat, and I hope his own too,
Will e'er consent to make her thine? Give o'er,
And think of some course suitable to thy rank,
And prosper in it.
ALL.   You have well advised me.
But in the meantime you that are so studious
Of my affairs wholly neglect your own.
Remember yourself, and in what plight you are.
WELL. No matter, no matter.
ALL.   Yes, 'tis much material.[5]
You know my fortune and my means; yet something
I can spare from myself to help your wants.
WELL.   How's this?   170
ALL. Nay, be not angry; there's eight pieces
To put you in better fashion.
WELL.   Money from thee?
From a boy? A stipendary?[6] One that lives
At the devotion of a stepmother
And the uncertain favor of a lord?
I'll eat my arms first. Howsoe'er blind Fortune
Hath spent the utmost of her malice on me—
Though I am vomited out of an alehouse,
And, thus accoutered, know not where to eat,

[5] Very important.
[6] Stipendiary.

Or drink, or sleep, but underneath this
  canopy [1]—   180
Although I thank thee, I despise thy
  offer,
And, as I in my madness broke my state
Without th' assistance of another's brain,
In my right wits I'll piece it; at the worst,
Die thus and be forgotten.

ALL.   A strange humor! *Exeunt.*

ACTUS PRIMI SCENA SECUNDA.[2]

[*A room in Lady Allworth's house.*]

Order, Amble, Furnace, Watchall.

ORD. Set all things right, or, as my name is
  Order,
And by this staff of office that commands
  you,
This chain and double ruff, symbols of
  power,
Whoever misses in his function,
For one whole week makes forfeiture of
  his breakfast
And privilege in the wine cellar.

AMB.   You are merry,
  Good Master Steward.

FURN.   Let him; I'll be angry.

AMB. Why, fellow Furnace, 'tis not twelve
  a-clock yet,
Nor dinner taking up; then, 'tis allowed,
Cooks by their places may be choleric.

FURN. You think you have spoke wisely,
  Goodman Amble,   11
My lady's go-before! [3]

ORD.   Nay, nay, no wrangling.

FURN. Twit me with the authority of the
  kitchen?
At all hours and all places, I'll be angry;
And, thus provoked, when I am at my
  prayers,
I will be angry.

AMB.   There was no hurt meant.

FURN. I am friends with thee; and yet I
  will be angry.

ORD. With whom?

FURN.   No matter whom—yet, now I
  think on 't,
I am angry with my lady.

WATCH.   Heaven forbid, man!

ORD. What cause has she given thee?

FURN.   Cause enough, Master
  Steward.   20
I was entertained [4] by her to please her
  palate,
And, till she forswore eating, I performed
  it.
Now, since our master, noble Allworth,
  died,
Though I crack my brains to find out
  tempting sauces,
And raise fortifications in the pastry
Such as might serve for models in the
  Low Countries,
Which, if they had been practiced at
  Breda,
Spinola might have thrown his cap at it,[5]
  and ne'er took it—

AMB. But you had wanted matter there to
  work on.

FURN. Matter?   With six eggs and a
  strike [6] of rye meal   30
I had kept the town till doomsday, perhaps longer.

ORD. But what's this to your pet against
  my lady?

FURN. What's this? Marry, this: when I
  am three parts roasted
And the fourth part parboiled to prepare
  her viands,
She keeps her chamber, dines with a
  panada [7]
Or water gruel my sweat never thought
  on.

ORD. But your art is seen in the dining
  room.

FURN.   By whom?
By such as pretend love to her, but come
To feed upon her. Yet, of all the harpies
That do devour her, I am out of charity
With none so much as the thin-gutted
  squire   41
That's stolen into commission.

ORD.   Justice Greedy?

FURN. The same, the same. Meat's cast
  away upon him;
It never thrives. He holds this para-
  dox:
Who eats not well, can ne'er do justice
  well.

---

[4] Employed.
[5] Given it up as a bad job.
[6] A measure varying from one-half to four
bushels.
[7] A boiled bread pudding.

---

[1] *I.e.*, the sky.
[2] The second scene of the first act.
[3] *I.e.*, usher.

His stomach's as insatiate as the grave,
Or strumpets' ravenous appetites.
WATCH.　　　　　　　　　One knocks.

Allworth knocks, and enters.

ORD. Our late young master!
AMB.　　　　　　　　　Welcome, sir.
FURN.　　　　　　　　　Your hand.
　If you have a stomach, a cold bakemeat's
　ready.
ORD. His father's picture in little.
FURN.　　　We are all your servants. 50
AMB. In you he lives.
ALL.　　　　　　At once, my thanks to
　all;
　This is yet some comfort. Is my lady
　stirring?

Enter the Lady Allworth, Waiting-Woman,
　　　　　　　　　Chambermaid.
ORD.　　　　Her presence answer for us.
LADY.　　　　　　Sort those silks well.
　I'll take the air alone.
Exeunt Waiting-Woman and Chambermaid.
FURN.　　　　　　You air and air;
　But will you never taste but spoonmeat [1]
　more?
　To what use serve I?
LADY.　　　　Prithee, be not angry;
　I shall, ere long. I' the meantime, there
　is gold
　To buy thee aprons and a summer
　suit.
FURN. I am appeased, and Furnace now
　grows cook.
LADY. And, as I gave directions, if this
　morning　　　　　　　　　　　　60
　I am visited by any, entertain 'em
　As heretofore; but say, in my excuse,
　I am indisposed.
ORD.　　　　I shall, madam.
LADY.　　　　　　Do, and leave me.—
　Nay, stay you, Allworth.
Exeunt Order, Amble, Furnace, Watchall.
ALL.　　　　I shall gladly grow here,
　To wait on your commands.
LADY.　　　　So soon turned courtier!
ALL. Style not that courtship, madam,
　which is duty
　Purchased on your part.
LADY.　　　Well, you shall o'ercome;
　I'll not contend in words. How is it with
　Your noble master?

[1] Liquid diet.

ALL.　　　　　　Ever like himself,
　No scruple lessened in the full weight of
　honor.　　　　　　　　　　　　70
　He did command me, pardon my pre-
　sumption,
　As his unworthy deputy to kiss
　Your ladyship's fair hands.
LADY.　　　　I am honored in
　His favor to me. Does he hold his pur-
　pose
　For the Low Countries?
ALL.　　　Constantly, good madam;
　But he will in person first present his
　service.
LADY. And how approve you of his course?
　You are yet,
　Like virgin parchment, capable of any
　Inscription, vicious or honorable.
　I will not force your will, but leave you
　free　　　　　　　　　　　　80
　To your own election.
ALL.　　　　Any form you please
　I will put on; but, might I make my
　choice,
　With humble emulation I would follow
　The path my lord marks to me.
LADY.　　　　'Tis well answered,
　And I commend your spirit. You had a
　father—
　Blessed be his memory!—that some few
　hours
　Before the will of heaven took him from
　me,
　Who did commend you, by the dearest
　ties
　Of perfect love between us, to my charge;
　And therefore what I speak you are
　bound to hear　　　　　　　　　90
　With such respect as if he lived in me.
　He was my husband, and, howe'er you
　are not
　Son of my womb, you may be of my love,
　Provided you deserve it.
ALL.　　　　I have found you,
　Most honored madam, the best mother to
　me,
　And, with my utmost strengths of care
　and service,
　Will labor that you never may repent
　Your bounties showered upon me.
LADY.　　　　I much hope it.
　These were your father's words: "If e'er
　my son　　　　　　　　　　　　99
　Follow the war, tell him it is a school

Where all the principles tending to
honor
Are taught, if truly followed. But for
such
As repair thither as a place in which
They do presume they may with license
practice
Their lusts and riots, they shall never
merit
The noble name of soldiers. To dare
boldly
In a fair cause, and for the country's
safety
To run upon the cannon's mouth un-
daunted;
To obey their leaders, and shun muti-
nies; 109
To bear with patience the winter's
cold
And summer's scorching heat, and not to
faint,
When plenty of provision fails, with
hunger—
Are the essential parts make up a sol-
dier,
Not swearing, dice, or drinking."

ALL. There's no syllable
You speak but is to me an oracle,
Which but to doubt were impious.

LADY. To conclude:
Beware ill company, for often men
Are like to those with whom they do con-
verse;
And from one man I warned you, and
that's Wellborn,
Not cause he's poor—that rather claims
your pity— 120
But that he's in his manners so de-
bauched,
And hath to vicious courses sold him-
self.
'Tis true, your father loved him while he
was
Worthy the loving; but, if he had lived
To have seen him as he is, he had cast
him off,
As you must do.

ALL. I shall obey in all things.

LADY. You follow me to my chamber; you
shall have gold
To furnish you like my son, and still
supplied
As I hear from you.

ALL. I am still your creature. *Exeunt.*

ACTUS PRIMI SCENA TERTIA.

[*A hall in the same.*]

Overreach, Greedy, Order, Amble, Furnace,
Watchall, Marall.

GREEDY. Not to be seen?

OVER. Still cloistered up? Her reason,
I hope, assures her, though she make
herself
Close prisoner ever for her husband's
loss,
'Twill not recover him.

ORD. Sir, it is her will,
Which we that are her servants ought
to serve it
And not dispute. Howe'er, you are
nobly welcome;
And, if you please to stay, that you may
think so,
There came not six days since from
Hull a pipe
Of rich Canary, which shall spend itself
For my lady's honor.

GREEDY. Is it of the right race? 10

ORD. Yes, Master Greedy.

AMB. [*Aside.*] How his mouth runs
o'er!

FURN. [*Aside.*] I'll make it run, and run.—
Save your good worship!

GREEDY. Honest Master Cook, thy hand
again! How I love thee!
Are the good dishes still in being? Speak,
boy.

FURN. If you have a mind to feed, there
is a chine
Of beef, well seasoned.

GREEDY. Good!

FURN. A pheasant, larded.

GREEDY. That I might now give thanks
for 't!

FURN. Other kuckshaws.[1]
Besides, there came last night from the
forest of Sherwood
The fattest stag I ever cooked.

GREEDY. A stag, man?

FURN. A stag, sir—part of it prepared for
dinner, 20
And baked in puff paste.

GREEDY. Puff paste too, Sir Giles!
A ponderous chine of beef! A pheasant
larded!

[1] Kickshaws.

And red deer too, Sir Giles, and baked
in puff paste!
All business set aside, let us give thanks
here.

FURN. How the lean skeleton's raped![1]

OVER. You know we cannot.

MAR. Your worships are to sit on a commission,
And, if you fail to come, you lose the
cause.

GREEDY. Cause me no causes. I'll prove
't, for such a dinner
We may put off a commission: you shall
find it
Henrici decimo quarto [2] —

OVER. Fie, Master Greedy! 30
Will you lose me a thousand pounds
for a dinner?
No more, for shame! We must forget
the belly
When we think of profit.

GREEDY. Well, you shall o'errule me.
I could ev'n cry now.—Do you hear,
Master Cook?
Send but a corner of that immortal
pasty,
And I in thankfulness will by your boy
Send you—a brace of threepences.

FURN. Will you be so prodigal?

Enter Wellborn.

OVER. Remember me to your lady.—
Who have we here?

WELL. You know me.

OVER. I did once, but now I will not;
Thou art no blood of mine. Avaunt,
thou beggar! 40
If ever thou presume to own me more,
I'll have thee caged and whipped.

GREEDY. I'll grant the warrant.
Think of Pie Corner, Furnace!

Exeunt Overreach, Greedy, Marall.

WATCH. Will you out, sir?
I wonder how you durst creep in.

ORD. This is rudeness
And saucy impudence.

AMB. Cannot you stay
To be served, among your fellows, from
the basket,[3]
But you must press into the hall?

FURN. Prithee, vanish
Into some outhouse, though it be the
pigsty;
My scullion shall come to thee.

Enter Allworth.

WELL. This is rare.
O, here's Tom Allworth.—Tom!

ALL. We must be strangers; 50
Nor would I have you seen here for a
million. *Exit Allworth.*

WELL. Better and better. He contemns
me too!

Enter [Waiting-] Woman and Chambermaid.

WOMAN. Foh, what a smell's here! What
thing's this?

CHAM. A creature
Made out of the privy; let us hence,
for love's sake,
Or I shall sown.[4]

WOMAN. I begin to feel faint already.

*Exeunt [Waiting-] Woman and Chamber-
maid.*

WATCH. Will you know your way?

AMB. Or shall we teach it you
By the head and shoulders?

WELL. No; I will not stir.
Do you mark, I will not. Let me see
the wretch
That dares attempt to force me. Why,
you slaves, 59
Created only to make legs [5] and cringe,
To carry in a dish and shift a trencher,
That have not souls only to hope a
blessing
Beyond blackjacks [6] or flagons—you that
were born
Only to consume meat and drink, and
batten
Upon reversions!—Who advances? Who
Shows me the way?

ORD. My lady!

*Enter Lady, [Waiting-] Woman, Chamber-
maid.*

CHAM. Here's the monster.

WOMAN. Sweet madam, keep your glove
to your nose.

---

[1] Rapt, transported.
[2] In a law enacted in the fourteenth year of
Henry's reign.
[3] Of scraps.
[4] Sound, swoon.   [5] Bows.   [6] Leather jugs.

CHAM. 　　　　　Or let me
　Fetch some perfumes may be predominant;
　You wrong yourself else.
WELL. 　　　　Madam, my designs
　Bear me to you.
LADY. 　To me?
WELL. 　　And, though I have met with 70
　But ragged entertainment from your
　　grooms here,
　I hope from you to receive that noble
　　usage
　As may become the true friend of your
　　husband,
　And then I shall forget these.
LADY. 　　　　　I am amazed
　To see and hear this rudeness. Dar'st
　　thou think,
　Though sworn, that it can ever find belief
　That I, who to the best men of this
　　country
　Denied my presence since my husband's
　　death,
　Can fall so low as to change words with
　　thee? 　　　　　　　　　　79
　Thou son of infamy, forbear my house,
　And know and keep the distance that's
　　between us,
　Or, though it be against my gentler
　　temper,
　I shall take order you no more shall be
　An eyesore to me.
WELL. 　　　　Scorn me not, good lady;
　But, as in form you are angelical,
　Imitate the heavenly natures and vouch-
　　safe
　At the least awhile to hear me. You will
　　grant
　The blood that runs in this arm is as
　　noble
　As that which fills your veins; those
　　costly jewels,
　And those rich clothes you wear, your
　　men's observance 　　　　　　　　90
　And women's flattery are in you no
　　virtues,
　Nor these rags, with my poverty, in
　　me vices.
　You have a fair fame, and, I know, de-
　　serve it;
　Yet, lady, I must say, in nothing more
　Than in the pious sorrow you have
　　shown
　For your late noble husband.

ORD. [Aside.] 　　　　　How she starts!
FURN. [Aside.] And hardly can keep finger
　　from the eye
　To hear him named.
LADY. 　　Have you aught else to say?
WELL. That husband, madam, was once
　　in his fortune
　Almost as low as I; want, debts, and
　　quarrels 　　　　　　　　　　100
　Lay heavy on him. Let it not be thought
　A boast in me, though I say I relieved
　　him.
　'Twas I that gave him fashion; mine
　　the sword
　That did on all occasions second his;
　I brought him on and off with honor,
　　lady;
　And, when in all men's judgments he
　　was sunk
　And in his own hopes not to be bunged
　　up,
　I stepped unto him, took him by the
　　hand,
　And set him upright.
FURN. [Aside.] 　　Are not we base rogues,
　That could forget this?
WELL. 　　I confess, you made him 110
　Master of your estate; nor could your
　　friends,
　Though he brought no wealth with him,
　　blame you for 't,
　For he had a shape, and to that shape
　　a mind,
　Made up of all parts either great or
　　noble—
　So winning a behavior not to be
　Resisted, madam.
LADY. 　　　　　'Tis most true, he had.
WELL. For his sake, then, in that I was
　　his friend,
　Do not contemn me.
LADY. 　　　For what's past, excuse me;
　I will redeem it.—Order, give the gentle-
　　man
　A hundred pounds.
WELL. 　　No, madam, on no terms. 120
　I will nor beg nor borrow sixpence of
　　you,
　But be supplied elsewhere, or want
　　thus ever.
　Only one suit I make, which you deny
　　not
　To strangers; and 'tis this.
　　　　　　　　　　　　Whispers to her.

LADY.   Fie! Nothing else?

WELL. Nothing, unless you please to charge your servants
To throw away a little respect upon me.

LADY. What you demand is yours.

WELL.   I thank you, lady.
Now what can be wrought out of such a suit
Is yet in supposition. I have said all;
When you please, you may retire.—[*Exit Lady.*] Nay, all's forgotten;   130
And for a lucky omen to my project
Shake hands and end all quarrels in the cellar.

ORD. Agreed, agreed.

FURN.   Still merry Master Wellborn!
                     Exeunt.

ACTUS SECUNDI SCENA PRIMA.

[*A room in Overreach's house.*]

Overreach, Marall.

OVER. He's gone, I warrant thee; this commission crushed him.

MAR. Your worship have the way on 't,[1] and ne'er miss
To squeeze these unthrifts[2] into air; and yet
The chapfallen justice did his part, returning
For your advantage the certificate,
Against his conscience and his knowledge too
(With your good favor), to the utter ruin
Of the poor farmer.

OVER.   'Twas for these good ends
I made him a justice; he that bribes his belly
Is certain to command his soul.

MAR.   I wonder,   10
Still with your license, why your worship, having
The power to put this thin-gut in commission,
You are not in 't yourself?

OVER.   Thou art a fool.
In being out of office I am out of danger;
Where,[3] if I were a justice, besides the trouble,
I might or[4] out of willfulness or error

Run myself finely into a *præmunire*,[5]
And so become a prey to the informer.
No, I'll have none of 't. 'Tis enough I keep
Greedy at my devotion;[6] so he serve   20
My purposes, let him hang or damn, I care not.
Friendship is but a word.

MAR.   You are all wisdom.

OVER. I would be worldly wise; for the other wisdom,
That does prescribe as a well-governed life,
And to do right to others as ourselves,
I value not an atom.

MAR.   What course take you,
With your good patience, to hedge in the manor
Of your neighbor, Master Frugal, as 'tis said
He will nor sell nor borrow nor exchange?
And his land, lying in the midst of your many lordships,   30
Is a foul blemish.

OVER.   I have thought on 't, Marall,
And it shall take. I must have all men sellers,
And I the only purchaser.

MAR.   'Tis most fit, sir.

OVER. I'll therefore buy some cottage near his manor,
Which done, I'll make my men break ope his fences,
Ride o'er his standing corn, and in the night
Set fire on his barns, or break his cattle's legs.
These trespasses draw on suits and suits, expenses,
Which I can spare, but will soon beggar him.
When I have harried him thus two or three year,   40
Though he sue *in forma pauperis*,[7] in spite
Of all his thrift and care he'll grow behindhand.

MAR. The best I ever heard! I could adore you.

OVER. Then, with the favor of my man of law,

---

[1] Emended by Gifford. Original reads *out*.
[2] Spendthrifts.
[3] Whereas.   [4] Either.
[5] A legal writ; here a scrape or predicament.
[6] *I. e.*, interests.
[7] In the status of a pauper.

I will pretend some title. Want will
  force him
To put it to arbitrament; then, if he sell
For half the value, he shall have ready
  money,
And I possess his land.
MAR.   'Tis above wonder!
Wellborn was apt [1] to sell, and needed
  not
These fine arts, sir, to hook him in.
OVER.   Well thought on. 50
This varlet, Marall, lives too long to
  upbraid me
With my close cheat [2] put upon him.
  Will nor cold
Nor hunger kill him?
MAR.   I know not what to think on 't.
I have used all means, and the last
  night I caused
His host, the tapster, to turn him out
  of doors,
And have been since with all your
  friends and tenants
And on the forfeit of your favor charged
  them, [3]
Though a crust of moldy bread would
  keep him from starving,
Yet they should not relieve him. This
  is done, sir.
OVER. That was something, Marall; but
  thou must go further,   60
And suddenly, Marall.
MAR.   Where and when you please, sir.
OVER. I would have thee seek him out
  and, if thou canst,
Persuade him that 'tis better steal than
  beg;
Then, if I prove he has but robbed a
  henroost,
Not all the world shall save him from
  the gallows.
Do anything to work him to despair,
And 'tis thy masterpiece.
MAR.   I will do my best, sir.
OVER. I am now on my main work with
  the Lord Lovell,
The gallant-minded, popular Lord Lov-
  ell,
The minion of the people's love. I
  hear   70
He's come into the country, and my
  aims are

To insinuate myself into his knowledge,
And then invite him to my house.
MAR.   I have you;
This points at my young mistress.
OVER.   She must part with
That humble title, and write "honor-
  able,"
"Right honorable," Marall, my "right
  honorable" daughter,
If all I have, or e'er shall get, will
  do it.
I will have her well attended; there are
  ladies
Of errant knights decayed and brought
  so low
That for cast [4] clothes and meat will
  gladly serve her.   80
And 'tis my glory, though I come from
  the city,
To have their issue whom I have un-
  done,
To kneel to mine as bondslaves.
MAR.   'Tis fit state, sir.
OVER. And therefore I'll not have a cham-
  bermaid
That ties her shoes, or any meaner
  office,
But such whose fathers were right wor-
  shipful.
'Tis a rich man's pride, there having
  ever been
More than a feud, a strange antipathy,
Between us and true gentry.

Enter Wellborn.

MAR.   See who's here, sir.
OVER. Hence, monster! Prodigy!
WELL.   Sir, your wife's nephew; 90
She and my father tumbled in one belly.
OVER. Avoid my sight! Thy breath's
  infectious, rogue!
I shun thee as a leprosy or the plague.—
Come hither, Marall.—[*Aside.*] This is
  the time to work him.
MAR. I warrant you, sir.
                 Exit Over[*reach*].
WELL.   By this light, I think he's mad.
MAR. Mad? Had you took compassion
  on yourself,
You long since had been mad.
WELL.   You have took a course,
Between you and my venerable uncle,
To make me so.

---

[1] Prepared, willing.   [2] Secret trick.
[3] Matthews' reading; original reads *him*.
[4] Cast-off.

MAR.   The more pale-spirited you,
That would not be instructed. I swear
deeply—   100
WELL. By what?
MAR.   By my religion.
WELL. [*Aside.*]   Thy religion!
The devil's creed!—But what would
you have done?
MAR. Had there been but one tree in all
the shire,
Nor any hope to compass a penny
halter,
Before, like you, I had outlived my
fortunes,
A withe had served my turn to hang
myself.
I am zealous in your cause; pray you,
hang yourself,
And presently,[1] as you love your credit.
WELL.   I thank you.
MAR. Will you stay till you die in a ditch,
or lice devour you?
Or, if you dare not do the feat your-
self,   110
But that you'll put the state to charge
and trouble,
Is there no purse to be cut, house to be
broken,
Or market women with eggs, that you
may murther,
And so despatch the business?
WELL.   Here's variety,
I must confess; but I'll accept of
none
Of all your gentle offers, I assure you.
MAR. Why, have you hope ever to eat
again,
Or drink, or be the master of three
farthings?
If you like not hanging, drown your-
self! Take some course
For your reputation.
WELL.   'Twill not do, dear tempter, 120
With all the rhetoric the fiend hath
taught you.
I am as far as thou art from despair;
Nay, I have confidence, which is more
than hope,
To live, and suddenly, better than ever.
MAR. Ha, ha! These castles you build
in the air
Will not persuade me or to give or lend
A token to you.

[1] At once.

WELL.   I'll be more kind to thee.
Come, thou shalt dine with me.
MAR.   With you?
WELL.   Nay, more, dine gratis.
MAR. Under what hedge, I pray you?
Or at whose cost?
Are they padders[2] or Abram-men[3]
that are your consorts?   130
WELL. Thou art incredulous; but thou
shalt dine
Not alone at her house, but with a
gallant lady—
With me and with a lady.
MAR.   Lady? What lady?
With the Lady of the Lake,[4] or Queen
of Fairies?
For I know it must be an enchanted
dinner.
WELL. With the Lady Allworth, knave.
MAR.   Nay, now there's hope
Thy brain is cracked.
WELL.   Mark there, with what respect
I am entertained.
MAR.   With choice, no doubt, of dog
whips.
Why, dost thou ever hope to pass her
porter?
WELL. 'Tis not far off; go with me. Trust
thine own eyes.   140
MAR. Troth, in my hope, or my assurance
rather,
To see thee curvet and mount like a dog
in a blanket,
If ever thou presume to pass her thresh-
old,
I will endure thy company.
WELL.   Come along then. *Exeunt.*

ACTUS SECUNDI SCENA SECUNDA.

[*A room in Lady Allworth's house.*]

*Allworth, Waiting-Woman, Chambermaid,
Order, Amble, Furnace, Watchall.*

WOMAN. Could you not command your
leisure one hour longer?
CHAM. Or half an hour?
ALL. I have told you what my haste is.
Besides, being now another's, not mine
own,
Howe'er I much desire to enjoy you
longer,

[2] Footpads.
[3] Beggars who feigned insanity.
[4] In the *Morte d'Arthur.*

My duty suffers, if, to please myself,
I should neglect my lord.
WOMAN.   Pray you, do me the favor
To put these few quince cakes into your
pocket;
They are of mine own preserving.
CHAM.   And this marmulade;[1]
'Tis comfortable for your stomach.
WOMAN.   And, at parting,
Excuse me if I beg a farewell from you. 10
CHAM. You are still before me. I move the
same suit, sir.
    [*Allworth*] *kisses 'em severally.*
FURN. How greedy these chamberers are
of a beardless chin!
I think the tits [2] will ravish him.
ALL.   My service
To both.
WOMAN.   Ours waits on you.
CHAM.   And shall do ever.
ORD. You are my lady's charge; be there-
fore careful
That you sustain your parts.
WOMAN.   We can bear, I warrant you.
Exeunt [Waiting-] Woman and Chambermaid.
FURN. Here, drink it off. The ingredients
are cordial,
And this the true elixir; it hath boiled
Since midnight for you. 'Tis the quin-
tessence
Of five cocks of the game, ten dozen of
sparrows,   20
Knuckles of veal, potato roots and mar-
row,
Currall [3] and ambergris. Were you two
years elder,
And I had a wife or gamesome mistress,
I durst trust you with neither. You need
not bait [4]
After this, I warrant you, though your
journey's long;
You may ride on the strength of this till
tomorrow morning.
ALL. Your courtesies overwhelm me.   I
much grieve
To part from such true friends, and yet
find comfort—   28
My attendance on my honorable lord,
Whose resolution holds to visit my lady,
Will speedily bring me back.
*Knocking at the gate; Marall and Wellborn
within. [Exit Watchall.]*

MAR.   Dar'st thou venture further?
WELL. Yes, yes, and knock again.
ORD.   'Tis he; disperse!
AMB. Perform it bravely.
FURN.   I know my cue; ne'er doubt me.
*They go off several ways [, Allworth re-
maining.*

Enter Watchall with Wellborn and Marall.]

WATCH. Beast that I was, to make you
stay! Most welcome;
You were long since expected.
WELL.   Say so much
To my friend, I pray you.
WATCH.   For your sake, I will, sir.
MAR. [*Aside.*] For his sake!
WELL. [*Aside.*]   Mum; this is nothing.
MAR.   More than ever
I would have believed, though I had
found it in my primer.[5]
ALL. When I have given you reasons for
my late harshness,
You'll pardon and excuse me, for, be-
lieve me,   40
Though now I part abruptly, in my
service
I will deserve it.
MAR. [*Aside.*]   Service! With a ven-
geance!
WELL. I am satisfied. Farewell, Tom.
ALL.   All joy stay with you!
    Exit Allw[orth].

Enter Amble.

AMB. You are happily encountered; I yet
never
Presented one so welcome as I know
You will be to my lady.
MAR. [*Aside.*]   This is some vision,
Or, sure, these men are mad, to worship
a dunghill;
It cannot be a truth.
WELL.   Be still a pagan,
An unbelieving infidel; be so, miscreant,
And meditate on blankets and on dog
whips!   50

Enter Furnace.

FURN. I am glad you are come; until I
know your pleasure
I knew not how to serve up my lady's
dinner.

---

[1] Marmalade.
[2] Chits.
[3] Coral.
[4] Eat.

[5] "The original primers were books of prayers
for children" (Cruikshank).

MAR. [*Aside.*] His pleasure! Is it possible?

WELL. What's thy will?

FURN. Marry, sir, I have some grouse, and turkey chicken,
Some rails and quails, and my lady willed me ask you
What kind of sauces best affect your palate
That I may use my utmost skill to please it.

MAR. [*Aside.*] The devil's entered this cook. Sauce for his palate,
That, on my knowledge, for almost this twelvemonth
Durst wish but cheese parings, and brown bread on Sundays. 60

WELL. That way I like 'em best.

FURN. It shall be done, sir.
Exit Furnace.

WELL. What think you of "the hedge we shall dine under"?
Shall we feed gratis?

MAR. [*Aside.*] I know not what to think.
Pray you, make me not mad.

Enter Order.

ORD. This place becomes you not;
Pray you, walk, sir, to the dining room.

WELL. I am well here,
Till her ladyship quits her chamber.

MAR. [*Aside.*] Well here, say you?
'Tis a rare change! But yesterday you thought
Yourself well in a barn, wrapped up in peas-straw.

Enter [Waiting-] Woman and Chambermaid.

WOMAN. O, sir, you are wished for.

CHAM. My lady dreamt, sir, of you.

WOMAN. And the first command she gave, after she rose, 70
Was, her devotions done, to give her notice
When you approached here.

CHAM. Which is done, on my virtue.

MAR. [*Aside.*] I shall be converted; I begin to grow
Into a new belief, which saints nor angels
Could have won me to have faith in.

WOMAN. Sir, my lady!

Enter Lady [Allworth].

LADY. I come to meet you, and languished till I saw you.
This first kiss is for form; I allow a second
To such a friend. [*Kisses Wellborn.*]

MAR. [*Aside.*] To such a friend! Heaven bless me!

WELL. I am wholly yours; yet, madam, if you please
To grace this gentleman with a salute— 80

MAR. [*Aside.*] Salute me at his bidding!

WELL. I shall receive it
As a most high favor.

LADY. Sir, you may command me.
[*Advances to kiss Marall, who draws back.*]

WELL. Run backward from a lady? And such a lady?

MAR. To kiss her foot is to poor me a favor
I am unworthy of—
Offers to kiss her foot.

LADY. Nay, pray you, rise,
And, since you are so humble, I'll exalt you.
You shall dine with me today at mine own table.

MAR. Your ladyship's table? I am not good enough
To sit at your steward's board.

LADY. You are too modest;
I will not be denied.

Enter Furnace.

FURN. Will you still be babbling 90
Till your meat freeze on the table? The old trick still;
My art ne'er thought on!

LADY. Your arm, Master Wellborn.—
[*To Marall.*] Nay, keep us company.

MAR. I was never so graced.
Exeunt Wellborn, Lady [Allworth], Amble, Marall, [Waiting-] Woman [, and Chambermaid].

ORD. So we have played our parts, and are come off well;
But, if I know the mystery, why my lady
Consented to it, or why Master Wellborn
Desired it, may I perish!

Furn.   Would I had
The roasting of his heart that cheated
    him,
And forces the poor gentleman to these
    shifts!
By fire (for cooks are Persians, and
    swear by it),   100
Of all the griping and extorting tyrants
I ever heard or read of, I ne'er met
A match to Sir Giles Overreach.
Watch.   What will you take
To tell him so, fellow Furnace?
Furn.   Just as much
As my throat is worth, for that would be
    the price on 't.
To have a usurer that starves himself
And wears a cloak of one-and-twenty
    years
On a suit of fourteen groats, bought of
    the hangman,
To grow rich, and then purchase,[1] is too
    common;
But this Sir Giles feeds high, keeps many
    servants,   110
Who must at his command do any out-
    rage.
Rich in his habit, vast in his expenses,
Yet he to admiration [2] still increases
In wealth and lordships.
Ord.   He frights men out of their estates,
And breaks through all law nets, made
    to curb ill men,
As they were cobwebs. No man dares
    reprove him.
Such a spirit to dare and power to do
    were never
Lodged so unluckily.

Enter Amble.

Amb.   Ha, ha! I shall burst.
Ord. Contain thyself, man.
Furn.   Or make us partakers
Of your sudden mirth.
Amb.   Ha, ha! My lady has got 120
Such a guest at her table—this term
    driver, Marall,
This snip of an attorney!
Furn.   What of him, man?
Amb. The knave thinks still he's at the
    cook's shop in Ram Alley,[3]

[1] Acquire real estate by any other means than
inheritance.
[2] In a wonderful fashion.
[3] A street in London famous for its restaurants.

Where the clerks [4] divide, and the elder
    is to choose;[5]
And feeds so slovenly!
Furn.   Is this all?
Amb.   My lady
Drank to him for fashion' sake, or to
    please Master Wellborn.
As I live, he rises, and takes up a dish
In which there were some remnants of a
    boiled capon,
And pledges her in white broth!
Furn.   Nay, 'tis like 129
The rest of his tribe.
Amb.   And, when I brought him wine,
He leaves his stool and after a leg or two
Most humbly thanks my worship.
Ord.   Rose already!
Amb. I shall be chid.

Enter Lady [Allworth], Wellborn, Marall.

Furn. [*Aside.*]   My lady frowns.
Lady.   You wait well!
Let me have no more of this; I observed
    your jeering.
Sirrah, I'll have you know, whom I
    think worthy
To sit at my table, be he ne'er so mean,
When I am present, is not your com-
    panion.[6]
Ord. [*Aside.*] Nay, she'll preserve what's
    due to her.
Furn. [*Aside.*]   This refreshing
Follows your flux of laughter.
Lady. [*To Wellborn.*]   You are master
Of your own will. I know so much of
    manners   140
As not to inquire your purposes; in a
    word,
To me you are ever welcome, as to a
    house
That is your own.
Well. [*Aside to Marall.*]   Mark that.
Mar. [*Aside.*]   With reverence, sir,
And it like [7] your worship.
Well.   Trouble yourself no farther,
Dear madam; my heart's full of zeal and
    service,
However in my language I am sparing.—
Come, Master Marall.
Mar.   I attend your worship.
              Exeunt Wellb[orn], Mar[all].

[4] Lawyers.
[5] Have first choice of his portion.
[6] *I.e.*, kind.   [7] If it please.

LADY. I see in your looks you are sorry,
　and you know me
　An easy mistress. Be merry; I have for-
　got all.—
　Order and Furnace, come with me; I
　must give you　　　　　　　　　　150
　Further directions.
ORD. 　　　　　What you please.
FURN. 　　　　We are ready. [*Exeunt.*]

ACTUS SECUNDI SCENA TERTIA.

[*The country near Lady Allworth's house.*]

Wellborn, Marall.

WELL. I think I am in a good way.
MAR. 　　　　　　　Good sir, the best way,
　The certain best way.
WELL. 　　　　　　　There are casualties
　That men are subject to.
MAR. 　　　　　　　You are above 'em;
　And, as you are already worshipful,
　I hope ere long you will increase in wor-
　ship,
　And be right worshipful.
WELL. 　　　　　Prithee, do not flout me.
　What I shall be, I shall be. Is 't for your
　ease
　You keep your hat off?
MAR. 　　　Ease, and it like your worship?
　I hope Jack Marall shall not live so long,
　To prove himself such an unmannerly
　beast,　　　　　　　　　　　　10
　Though it hail hazelnuts, as to be covered
　When your worship's present.
WELL. (*Aside.*) 　Is not this a true rogue
　That, out of mere hope of a future
　coz'nage,[1]
　Can turn thus suddenly? 'Tis rank
　already.
MAR. I know your worship's wise, and
　needs no counsel;
　Yet, if in my desire to do you service
　I humbly offer my advice (but still
　Under correction), I hope I shall not
　Incur your high displeasure.
WELL. 　　　　　No; speak freely.
MAR. Then, in my judgment, sir, my
　simple judgment　　　　　　　20
　(Still with your worship's favor), I could
　wish you
　A better habit, for this cannot be
　But much distasteful to the noble lady

1 With a pun on *cousinage*, intimacy.

(I say no more) that loves you, for, this
　morning
　To me (and I am but a swine to her),
　Before th' assurance of her wealth
　perfumed you,
　You savored not of amber.[2]
WELL. 　　　　　　　I do now then?
[*Marall*] *kisses the end of his* [*Wellborn's*]
　　　　　　　　　　　　　cudgel.
MAR. This your batoon [3] hath got a touch
　of it.
　Yet, if you please, for change I have
　twenty pounds here
　Which out of my true love I presently 30
　Lay down at your worship's feet; 'twill
　serve to buy you
　A riding suit.
WELL. 　　But where's the horse?
MAR. 　　　　　　　My gelding
　Is at your service; nay, you shall ride me
　Before your worship shall be put to the
　trouble
　To walk afoot. Alas, when you are lord
　Of this lady's manor, as I know you will
　be,
　You may with the lease of glebe land,
　called Knave's Acre,
　A place I would manure,[4] requite your
　vassal.
WELL. I thank thy love, but must make no
　use of it.
　What's twenty pounds?
MAR. 　　'Tis all that I can make, sir. 40
WELL. Dost thou think, though I want
　clothes, I could not have 'em
　For one word to my lady?
MAR. 　　　　　As I know not that!
WELL. Come, I'll tell thee a secret, and so
　leave thee.
　I'll not give her the advantage, though
　she be
　A gallant-minded lady, after we are
　married
　(There being no woman but is sometimes
　froward),
　To hit me in the teeth, and say she was
　forced
　To buy my wedding clothes, and took
　me on
　With a plain riding suit and an ambling
　nag.

2 Ambergris.
3 Baton, stick.
4 Maneuver, operate, possess.

No, I'll be furnished something like
　　myself,　　　　　　　　　　　　　50
And so farewell. For thy suit touching
　　Knave's Acre,
When it is mine, 'tis thine.
MAR.　　　　　I thank your worship.—
　　　　　　　　　　Exit Wellb[orn].
How [I] [1] was cozened in the calcula-
　　tion
Of this man's fortune! My master
　　cozened too,
Whose pupil I am in the art of undoing
　　men,
For that is our profession! Well, well,
　　Master Wellborn,
You are of a sweet nature and fit again
　　to be cheated,
Which, if the Fates please, when you are
　　possessed
Of the land and lady, you, sans question,
　　shall be.
I'll presently think of the means.
　　　　　　　　　Walk by, musing. [2]

Enter Overreach.

OVER. [*To a Servant within.*]　　　Sirrah,
　　take my horse.　　　　　　　　　60
I'll walk to get me an appetite; 'tis but a
　　mile,
And exercise will keep me from being
　　pursy.
Ha! Marall! Is he conjuring? Perhaps
The knave has wrought the prodigal to
　　do
Some outrage on himself, and now he
　　feels
Compunction in his conscience for 't.
　　No matter,
So it be done.—Marall!
MAR.　　　　　Sir.
OVER.　　　　　　　How succeed we
　　In our plot on Wellborn?
MAR.　　　　　　　Never better, sir.
OVER. Has he hanged or drowned himself?
MAR.　　　　　　　No, sir, he lives—
　　Lives once more to be made a prey to
　　you,　　　　　　　　　　　　　70
A greater prey than ever.
OVER.　　　　　Art thou in thy wits?
If thou art, reveal this miracle, and
　　briefly.

---

[1] Added by Cruickshank.
[2] Matthews' reading; original reads *masing.*

MAR. A lady, sir, is fall'n in love with him.
OVER. With him? What lady?
MAR.　　　　　　The rich Lady Allworth.
OVER. Thou dolt! How dar'st thou speak
　　this?
MAR.　　I speak truth;
　　And I do so but once a year, unless
　　It be to you, sir. We dined with her
　　ladyship,
　I thank his worship.
OVER.　　　　　His worship!
MAR.　　　　　　　As I live, sir,
　I dined with him at the great lady's
　　table,
　Simple as I stand here, and saw when she
　　kissed him,　　　　　　　　　　80
And would at his request have kissed
　　me too;
But I was not so audacious as some
　　youths are,
And dare do anything, be it ne'er so
　　absurd,
And sad after performance.
OVER.　　　　　　Why, thou rascal,
　To tell me these impossibilities!
　Dine at her table? And kiss him? Or
　　thee?
　Impudent varlet, have not I myself,
　To whom great countesses' doors have
　　oft flew open,
　Ten times attempted, since her hus-
　　band's death,
　In vain to see her, though I came—a
　　suitor?　　　　　　　　　　　　90
　And yet your good solicitorship and
　　rogue Wellborn
　Were brought into her presence, feasted
　　with her!
　But that I know thee a dog that cannot
　　blush,
　This most incredible lie would call up
　　one
　On thy buttermilk cheeks.
MAR.　　　Shall I not trust my eyes, sir,
　Or taste? I feel her good cheer in my
　　belly.
OVER. You shall feel me, if you give not
　　over, sirrah.
　Recover your brains again, and be no
　　more gulled
　With a beggar's plot, assisted by the
　　aids
　Of serving-men and chambermaids, for
　　beyond these　　　　　　　　　100

Thou never saw'st a woman, or I'll quit [1]
you
From my employments.

MAR. Will you credit this yet?
On my confidence of their marriage, I
offered Wellborn—
(*Aside*.) I would give a crown now I
durst say "his worship"—
My nag and twenty pounds.

OVER. Did you so, idiot? [2]
Strikes him down.
Was this the way to work him to despair,
Or rather to cross me?

MAR. Will your worship kill me?

OVER. No, no; but drive the lying spirit
out of you.

MAR. He's gone.

OVER. I have done then. Now,
forgetting
Your late imaginary feast and lady, 110
Know my Lord Lovell dines with me
tomorrow.
Be careful naught be wanting to receive
him;
And bid my daughter's women trim her
up;
Though they paint her, so she catch the
lord I'll thank 'em.
There's a piece for my late blows.
[Gives money.]

MAR. (*Aside*.) I must yet suffer.
But there may be a time—

OVER. Do you grumble?

MAR. No, sir. *[Exeunt.]*

ACTUS TERTII SCENA PRIMA.

[*The country near Overreach's house.*]

Lovell, Allworth, Servants.

LOV. Walk the horses down the hill. Something in private
I must impart to Allworth. *Exeunt servi.* [3]

ALL. O, my lord,
What sacrifice of reverence, duty, watch-
ing,
Although I could put off the use of sleep,
And ever wait on your commands [to]
serve 'em,
What dangers, though ne'er so horrid
shapes,

Nay, death itself, though I should run
to meet it,
Can I, and with a thankful willingness,
suffer!
But still the retribution will fall short
Of your bounties showered upon me.

LOV. Loving youth, 10
Till what I purpose be put into act,
Do not o'erprize it. Since you have
trusted me
With your soul's nearest, nay, her
dearest secret,
Rest confident 'tis in a cabinet locked
Treachery shall never open. I have
found you
(For so much to your face I must profess,
Howe'er you guard [4] your modesty with a
blush for 't)
More zealous in your love and service
to me
Than I have been in my rewards.

ALL. Still great ones,
Above my merit.

LOV. Such your gratitude calls 'em; 20
Nor am I of that harsh and rugged tem-
per
As some great men are taxed with, who
imagine
They part from the respect due to their
honors
If they use not all such as follow 'em,
Without distinction of their births, like
slaves.
I am not so conditioned; I can make
A fitting difference between my footboy
And a gentleman by want compelled to
serve me.

ALL. 'Tis thankfully acknowledged. You
have been 29
More like a father to me than a master.
Pray you, pardon the comparison.

LOV. I allow it;
And, to give you assurance I am pleased
in 't,
My carriage and demeanor to your mis-
tress,
Fair Margaret, shall truly witness for me
I can command my passions.

ALL. 'Tis a conquest
Few lords can boast of when they are
tempted.—O!

LOV. Why do you sigh? Can you be
doubtful of me?

---

[1] Release, discharge.
[2] Emended by Coxeter. Original reads *I doe.*
Cf. V, i, 215.
[3] Servants.
[4] Adorn.

By that fair name I in the wars have
  purchased
And all my actions hitherto untainted,
I will not be more true to mine own
  honor   40
Than to my Allworth!

ALL.   As you are the brave Lord Lovell,
  Your bare word only given is an assur-
    ance
Of more validity and weight to me
Than all the oaths bound up with im-
  precations,
Which, when they would deceive, most
  courtiers practice;
Yet, being a man (for, sure, to style you
  more
Would relish of gross flattery), I am
  forced
Against my confidence of your worth and
  virtues
To doubt, nay, more, to fear.

LOV.   So young, and jealous?

ALL. Were you to encounter with a single
  foe,   50
The victory were certain; but to stand
The charge of two such potent enemies,
At once assaulting you, as wealth and
  beauty,
And those too seconded with power, is
  odds
Too great for Hercules.

LOV.   Speak your doubts and fears,
  Since you will nourish 'em, in plainer
    language
That I may understand 'em.

ALL.   What's your will,
  Though I lend arms against myself
    (provided
They may advantage [1] you), must be
  obeyed.
My much-loved lord, were Margaret
  only fair,   60
The cannon of her more than earthly
  form,
Though mounted high, commanding all
  beneath it,
And rammed with bullets of her sparkling
  eyes,
Of all the bulwarks that defend your
  senses
Could batter none [2] but that which
  guards your sight.

But, when the well-tuned accents of her
  tongue
Make music to you, and with numerous [3]
  sounds
Assault your hearing (such as if Ulysses
Now lived again, howe'er he stood the
  Sirens,
Could not resist), the combat must grow
  doubtful   70
Between your reason and rebellious
  passions.
Add this too: when you feel her touch,
  and breath
Like a soft western wind when it glides
  o'er
Arabia, creating gums and spices,
And, in the van, the nectar of her lips,
Which you must taste, bring the battalia [4]
  on,
Well armed, and strongly lined [5] with her
  discourse
And knowing manners, to give enter-
  tainment—
Hippolytus himself would leave Diana
To follow such a Venus.

LOV.   Love hath made you 80
Poetical, Allworth.

ALL.   Grant all these beat off
(Which, if it be in man to do, you'll do it),
Mammon, in Sir Giles Overreach, steps
  in
With heaps of ill-got gold, and so much
  land,
To make her more remarkable, as would
  tire
A falcon's wings in one day to fly over.
O my good lord! These powerful aids,
  which would
Make a misshapen negro beautiful
(Yet are but ornaments to give her
  luster,   89
That in herself is all perfection), must
Prevail for her. I here release your
  trust;
'Tis happiness enough for me to serve
  you
And sometimes with chaste eyes to look
  upon her.

LOV. Why, shall I swear?

ALL.   O, by no means, my lord;
  And wrong not so your judgment to the
    world

---

[1] Help.
[2] Emended by Gifford. Original reads *more*.

[3] Rhythmical.
[4] Army. [5] Strengthened. Original reads *liv'd*.

As from your fond indulgence to a boy,
Your page, your servant, to refuse a
    blessing
Divers great men are rivals for.

Lov.   Suspend
Your judgment till the trial. How far is it
To Overreach' house?

ALL.   At the most, some half hour's
    riding;   100
You'll soon be there.

Lov.   And you the sooner freed
From your jealous fears.

ALL.   O, that I durst but hope it!
                                Exeunt.

ACTUS TERTII SCENA SECUNDA.

[*A room in Overreach's house.*]

Overreach, Greedy, Marall.

OVER. Spare for no cost; let my dressers
    crack with the weight
Of curious viands.

GREEDY.   *Store indeed's no sore,*[1] sir.

OVER. That proverb fits your stomach,
    Master Greedy.
And let no plate be seen but what's pure
    gold,
Or such whose workmanship exceeds the
    matter
That it is made of; let my choicest linen
Perfume the room, and, when we wash,
    the water,
With precious powders mixed, so please
    my lord
That he may with envy wish to bathe so
    ever.

MAR. 'Twill be very chargeable.[2]

OVER.   Avaunt, you drudge!   10
Now all my labored ends are at the
    stake,
Is 't a time to think of thrift? Call in my
    daughter.—   [*Exit Marall.*]
And, Master Justice, since you love
    choice dishes,
And plenty of 'em—

GREEDY.   As I do, indeed, sir,
Almost as much as to give thanks for 'em.

OVER. I do confer that providence, with
    my power
Of absolute command to have abun-
    dance,
To your best care.

GREEDY.   I'll punctually discharge it
And give the best directions. Now am I
In mine own conceit[3] a monarch—at
    the least,   20
Archpresident of the boiled, the roast,
    the baked,
For which I will eat often and give
    thanks
When my belly's braced up like a drum—
    and that's pure justice.

OVER. I[t] must be so. Should the foolish
    girl prove modest,   *Exit Greedy.*
She may spoil all. She had it not from
    me,
But from her mother; I was ever forward,
As she must be, and therefore I'll pre-
    pare her.

[*Enter*] *Margaret.*

Alone—and let your women wait without.

MARG. Your pleasure, sir?

OVER.   Ha, this is a neat dressing!
These orient pearls and diamonds well
    placed too!   30
The gown affects[4] me not; it should have
    been
Embroidered o'er and o'er with flowers
    of gold;
But these rich jewels and quaint fashion
    help it.
And how below, since oft the wanton
    eye,
The face observed, descends unto the
    foot,
Which, being well proportioned, as
    yours is,
Invites as much as perfect white and red,
Though without art? How like you
    your new woman,
The Lady Downfall'n?

MARG.   Well, for a companion;
Not as a servant.

OVER.   Is she humble, Meg,   40
And careful too, her ladyship forgotten?

MARG. I pity her fortune.

OVER.   Pity her? Trample on her!
I took her up in an old tamine[5] gown
(Even starved for want of twopenny
    chops) to serve thee;
And, if I understand she but repines
To do thee any duty, though ne'er so
    servile,

---

[1] Harm. Sententious sayings are frequently
indicated by italics.   [2] Costly.

[3] Thought, opinion.
[4] Pleases.   [5] Thin woolen stuff.

I'll pack her to her knight, where I have
  lodged him,
Into the Counter [1] and there let 'em
  howl together.
MARG. You know your own ways; but, for
  me, I blush
When I command her that was once
  attended   50
With persons not inferior to myself
In birth.
OVER.   In birth? Why, art thou not
  my daughter,
The blessed child of my industry and
  wealth?
Why, foolish girl, was 't not to make thee
  great
That I have ran, and still pursue, those
  ways
That hale down curses on me, which I
  mind not?
Part with these humble thoughts, and
  apt [2] thyself
To the noble state I labor to advance
  thee,
Or, by my hopes to see thee honorable,
I will adopt a stranger to my heir,   60
And throw thee from my care. Do not
  provoke me.
MARG. I will not, sir; mold me which way
  you please.

Enter Greedy.

OVER. How! Interrupted?
GREEDY.   'Tis matter of importance.
The cook, sir, is self-willed, and will not
  learn
From my experience. There's a fawn
  brought in, sir,
And, for my life, I cannot make him
  roast it
With a Norfolk dumpling in the belly of
  it;
And, sir, we wise men know, without the
  dumpling
'Tis not worth threepence.
OVER.   Would it were whole in thy belly,
To stuff it out! Cook it any way; prithee,
  leave me.   70
GREEDY. Without order for the dumpling?
OVER.   Let it be dumpled
Which way thou wilt, or tell him I will
  scald him
In his own caldron.

GREEDY.   I had lost my stomach
Had I lost my Mistress Dumpling I'll
  give thanks for.
OVER. But to our business, Meg. You
  have heard who dines here?
                       Exit Greedy.
MARG. I have, sir.
OVER.   'Tis an honorable man;
A lord, Meg, and commands a regiment
Of soldiers, and, what's rare, is one
  himself,
A bold and understanding one; and to be
A lord and a good leader, in one volume,
Is granted unto few but such as rise [3]
  up   81
The kingdom's glory.

Enter Greedy.

GREEDY.   I'll resign my office,
If I be not better obeyed.
OVER.   'Slight, art thou frantic?
GREEDY. Frantic?   'Twould make me
  a frantic [4] and stark mad,
Were I not a justice of peace and coram [5]
  too,
Which this rebellious cook cares not a
  straw for.
There are a dozen of woodcocks—
OVER.   Make thyself
Thirteen, the baker's dozen.
GREEDY.   I am contented,
So they may be dressed to my mind. He
  has found out
A new device for sauce, and will not dish
  'em   90
With toasts and butter. My father was a
  tailor,
And my name, though a justice, Greedy
  Woodcock;
And, ere I'll see my linage [6] so abused,
I'll give up my commission.
OVER. [*To Cook within.*]   Cook! Rogue,
  obey him!
I have given the word; pray you, now
  remove yourself
To a collar of brawn,[7] and trouble me no
  farther.
GREEDY. I will, and meditate what to eat
  at dinner.   *Exit Greedy.*

[3] Raise.
[4] *I.e.*, an insane person.
[5] Obsolete corruption of *quorum.*
[6] Lineage.   [7] Neck of a boar.

---

[1] One of the London prisons.   [2] Fit.

OVER. And, as I said, Meg, when this gull disturbed us,
This honorable lord, this colonel,[1]
I would have thy husband.

MARG. There's too much disparity 100
Between his quality and mine to hope it.

OVER. I more than hope 't, and doubt not to effect it.
Be thou no enemy to thyself; my wealth
Shall weigh his titles down, and make you equals.
Now for the means to assure him thine, observe me:
Remember he's a courtier and a soldier,
And not to be trifled with; and, therefore, when
He comes to woo you, see you do not coy it.[2]
This mincing modesty hath spoiled many a match 109
By a first refusal, in vain after hoped for.

MARG. You'll have me, sir, preserve the distance that
Confines a virgin?

OVER. Virgin me no virgins!
I must have you lose that name, or you lose me.
I will have you private—start not—I say, private.
If thou art my true daughter, not a bastard,
Thou wilt venture alone with one man, though he came
Like Jupiter to Semele, and come off, too;
And therefore, when he kisses you, kiss close.

MARG. I have heard this is the strumpet's fashion, sir,
Which I must never learn.

OVER. Learn anything, 120
And from any creature that may make thee great—
From the devil himself.

MARG. [Aside.] This is but devilish doctrine!

OVER. Or, if his blood grow hot, suppose he offer
Beyond this, do not you stay till it cool,
But meet his ardor; if a couch be near,
Sit down on 't, and invite him.

MARG. In your house,
Your own house, sir? For heaven's sake, what are you then?
Or what shall I be, sir?

OVER. Stand not on form;
Words are no substances.

MARG. Though you could dispense
With your own honor, cast aside religion, 130
The hopes of heaven or fear of hell, excuse me.
In worldly policy this is not the way
To make me his wife; his whore, I grant it may do.
My maiden honor so soon yielded up,
Nay, prostituted, cannot but assure him
I, that am light to him, will not hold weight
When he is tempted by others; so, in judgment,
When to his lust I have given up my honor,
He must and will forsake me.

OVER. How? Forsake thee?
Do I wear a sword for fashion? Or is this arm 140
Shrunk up or withered? Does there live a man
Of that large list I have encountered with
Can truly say I e'er gave inch of ground
Not purchased with his blood that did oppose me?
Forsake thee when the thing is done? He dares not.
Give me but proof he has enjoyed thy person,
Though all his captains, echoes to his will,
Stood armed by his side to justify the wrong,
And he himself in the head of his bold troop, 149
Spite of his lordship and his colonelship,
Or the judge's favor, I will make him render
A bloody and a strict accompt,[3] and force him,
By marrying thee, to cure thy wounded honor!
I have said it.

[1] Trisyllabic here.　　　[2] Behave coyly.

[3] Account.

Enter Marall.

MAR.   Sir, the man of honor's come,
Newly alighted.
OVER.   In, without reply.
And do as I command, or thou art lost.
                  Exit Marg[aret].
Is the loud music I gave order for
Ready to receive him?
MAR.   'Tis, sir.
OVER.   Let 'em sound
A princely welcome.—[*Exit Marall.*]
Roughness, awhile leave me,
For fawning now, a stranger to my
nature,   160
Must make way for me.

*Loud music. Enter Lovell, Greed[y], All-
w[orth], Mar[all].*
LOV.   Sir, you meet your trouble.
OVER. What you are pleased to style so is
an honor
Above my worth and fortunes.
ALL. [*Aside.*]   Strange, so humble.
OVER. A justice of peace, my lord.
           Presents Greedy to him.
LOV.   Your hand, good sir.
GREEDY. [*Aside.*] This is a lord, and some
think this a favor;
But I had rather have my hand in my
dumpling.
OVER. Room for my lord.
LOV.   I miss, sir, your fair daughter
To crown my welcome.
OVER.   May it please my lord
To taste a glass of Greek wine first, and
suddenly
She shall attend my lord.
LOV.   You'll be obeyed, sir.   170
       Exeunt omnes præter [1] *Over[reach].*
OVER. 'Tis to my wish. As soon as come,
ask for her!—
Why, Meg! Meg Overreach!—

[*Enter Margaret.*]

       How! Tears in your eyes!
Ha! Dry 'em quickly, or I'll dig 'em
out.
Is this a time to whimper? Meet that
greatness
That flies into thy bosom; think what 'tis
For me to say, "My honorable daughter,"
_____
[1] All except.

And thou, when I stand bare, to say,
"Put on," [2]
Or, "Father, you forget yourself." No
more.
But be instructed, or expect—He
comes.—

Enter Lovell, Greedy, Allworth, Marall.
                 They salute.
A black-browed girl, my lord.
LOV. [*Kissing her.*]   As I live,
a rare one.   180
ALL. [*Aside.*] He's took already. I am
lost.
OVER. [*Aside.*]   That kiss
Came twanging off; I like it.—Quit the
room.—   *The Rest off.*
A little bashful, my good lord, but you,
I hope, will teach her boldness.
LOV.   I am happy
In such a scholar, but—
OVER.   I am past learning,
And therefore leave you to yourselves.—
(*To his Daughter.*) Remember!
                Exit Overreach.
LOV. You see, fair lady, your father is
solicitous
To have you change the barren name of
virgin
Into a hopeful wife.
MARG.   His [3] haste, my lord,
Holds no power o'er my will.
LOV.   But o'er your duty.   190
MARG. Which, forced too much, may
break.
LOV.   Bend rather, sweetest.
Think of your years.
MARG.   Too few to match with yours—
And choicest fruits, too soon plucked,
rot and wither.
LOV. Do you think I am old?
MARG.   I am sure I am too young.
LOV. I can advance you.
MARG.   To a hill of sorrow,
Where every hour I may expect to fall,
But never hope firm footing. You are
noble,
I of a low descent, however rich;
And tissues [4] matched with scarlet [5]
suit but ill.
_____
[2] *I.e.*, put on your hat.
[3] Emended by Gifford. Original reads *he.*
[4] Silk clothes.
[5] A scarlet gown, worn as a mark of dignity.

O, my good lord, I could say more, but
that   200
I dare not trust these walls.

Lov.   Pray you, trust my ear then.

Enter Over[reach behind], list'ning.

Over. Close at it! Whispering! This is
excellent!
And, by their postures, a consent on
both parts.

Enter Greed[y behind].

Greedy. Sir Giles, Sir Giles!

Over.   The great fiend stop
that clapper!

Greedy. It must ring out, sir, when my
belly rings noon.
The baked-meats are run out, the roast
turned powder.

Over. I shall powder you.

Greedy.   Beat me to dust, I care not;
In such a cause as this, I'll die a martyr.

Over. Marry, and shall, you barathrum
of the shambles! [1]   *Strikes him.*

Greedy. How! Strike a justice of peace?
'Tis petty treason,   210
Edwardi quinto.[2] But that you are my
friend,
I could commit you without bail or
mainprize.[3]

Over. Leave your bawling, sir, or I shall
commit you
Where you shall not dine today. Disturb my lord
When he is in discourse?

Greedy.   Is 't a time to talk
When we should be munching?

Lov.   Ha! I heard some noise.

Over. Mum, villain; vanish! Shall we
break a bargain
Almost made up?   *Thrust Greedy off.*

Lov.   Lady, I understand you,
And rest most happy in your choice,
believe it;
I'll be a careful pilot to direct   220
Your yet uncertain bark to a port of
safety.

Marg. So shall your honor save two lives,
and bind us
Your slaves forever.

[1] Gulf of the butcher shops; glutton.
[2] According to a law enacted in the fifth year
of Edward's reign.
[3] An undertaking of suretyship.

Lov.   I am in the act rewarded,
Since it is good; howe'er, you must put
on
An amorous carriage towards me to
delude
Your subtle father.

Marg.   I am prone to that.

Lov. Now break we off our conference.—
Sir Giles!
Where is Sir Giles?

Enter Overreach and the Rest.

Over.   My noble lord! And how
Does your lordship find her?

Lov.   Apt, Sir Giles, and coming,
And I like her the better.

Over.   So do I too.   230

Lov. Yet, should we take forts at the first
assault,
'Twere poor in the defendant; I must
confirm her
With a love letter or two, which I must
have
Delivered by my page, and you give way
to 't.

Over. With all my soul—a towardly gen-
tleman!—
Your hand, good Master Allworth.
Know my house
Is ever open to you.

All. (*Aside.*)   'Twas shut till now.

Over. Well done, well done, my honorable
daughter!
Th' art so already. Know this gentle
youth,
And cherish him, my honorable daughter.   240

Marg. I shall, with my best care.
          Noise within, as of a coach.

Over.   A coach!

Greedy.   More stops
Before we go to dinner! O my guts!

Enter Lady [Allworth] and Wellborn.

Lady.   If I find welcome,
You share in it; if not, I'll back again,
Now I know your ends, for I come armed
for all
Can be objected.

Lov.   How! The Lady Allworth!

Over. And thus attended!

*Lovell salutes the Lady; the Lady salutes
Margaret.*

MAR.   No, I am a dolt!
The spirit of lies had entered me!
OVER.   Peace, patch! [1]
'Tis more than wonder! An astonish-
ment
That does possess me wholly!
LOV.   Noble lady,
This is a favor, to prevent [2] my visit,   250
The service of my life can never equal.
LADY. My lord, I laid wait for you, and
much hoped
You would have made my poor house
your first inn;
And therefore, doubting that you might
forget me
Or too long dwell here, having such
ample cause
In this unequaled beauty for your stay,
And fearing to trust any but myself
With the relation of my service to
you,
I borrowed so much from my long re-
straint
And took the air in person to invite
you.   260
LOV. Your bounties are so great they rob
me, madam,
Of words to give you thanks.
LADY.   Good Sir Giles Overreach!—
                           Salutes him.
How doest thou, Marall? Liked you my
meat so ill
You'll dine no more with me?
GREEDY.   I will, when you please,
And it like your ladyship.
LADY.   When you please, Master
Greedy;
If meat can do it, you shall be satisfied.—
And now, my lord, pray take into your
knowledge
This gentleman; howe'er his outside's
coarse,   Presents Wellborn.
His inward linings are as fine and fair
As any man's. Wonder not I speak at
large. [3]   270
And howsoe'er his humor carries him
To be thus accoutered, or what taint
soever
For his wild life hath stuck upon his
fame, [4]
He may ere long with boldness rank
himself

With some that have contemned him.—
Sir Giles Overreach,
If I am welcome, bid him so.
OVER.   My nephew!
He has been too long a stranger. Faith,
you have;
Pray, let it be mended.
               Lovell conferring with Wellborn.
MAR.   Why, sir, what do you mean?
This is "rogue Wellborn, monster,
prodigy,
That should hang or drown himself;"
no man of worship,   280
Much less your nephew.
OVER.   Well, sirrah, we shall reckon
For this hereafter.
MAR. [Aside.]   I'll not lose my jeer,
Though I be beaten dead for 't.
WELL.   Let my silence plead
In my excuse, my lord, till better leisure
Offer itself to hear a full relation
Of my poor fortunes.
LOV.   I would hear, and help 'em.
OVER. Your dinner waits you.
LOV.   Pray you, lead; we follow.
LADY. Nay, you are my guest.—Come,
dear Master Wellborn.
                    Exeunt. Manet [5] Greedy.
GREEDY. "Dear Master Wellborn!" so
she said. Heaven! Heaven!
If my belly would give me leave, I could
ruminate   290
All day on this. I have granted twenty
warrants
To have him committed, from all prisons
in the shire,
To Nottingham jail. And now "Dear
Master Wellborn"!
And "My good nephew"!—but I play
the fool
To stand here prating, and forget my
dinner.—

                    Enter Marall.

Are they set, Marall?
MAR. Long since. Pray you, a word, sir.
GREEDY. No wording now.
MAR.   In troth, I must. My master,
Knowing you are his good friend, makes
bold with you
And does entreat you, more guests being
come in   299
Than he expected, especially his nephew,

[1] Fool.
[2] Anticipate.
[3] Freely.
[4] Reputation.
[5] Remains.

The table being full too, you would
　　excuse him
And sup with him on the cold meat.

GREEDY.　　　　　How! No dinner
After all my care?

MAR.　　　　　'Tis but a penance for
A meal; besides, you broke your fast.

GREEDY.　　　　　That was
But a bit to stay my stomach. A man
　　in commission
Give place to a tatterdemalion!

MAR.　　　　　No bug [1] words, sir;
Should his worship hear you—

GREEDY.　　　　Lose my dumpling too,
And buttered toasts, and woodcocks?

MAR.　　　　Come, have patience.
If you will dispense a little with your
　　worship,
And sit with the waiting-women, you
　　have dumpling,　　　　　310
Woodcock, and buttered toasts too.

GREEDY.　　　　This revives me;
I will gorge there sufficiently.

MAR.　　　This is the way, sir. *Exeunt.*

ACTUS TERTII SCENA TERTIA.

[*The same.*]

Overreach, as from dinner.

OVER. She's caught! O women! She
　　neglects my lord,
And all her compliments applied to
　　Wellborn!
The garments of her widowhood laid
　　by,
She now appears as glorious as the
　　spring.
Her eyes fixed on him, in the wine she
　　drinks,
He being her pledge, she sends him
　　burning kisses,
And sits on thorns till she be private
　　with him.
She leaves my meat to feed upon his
　　looks,
And, if in our discourse he be but named,
From her a deep sigh follows. But why
　　grieve I　　　　　10
At this? It makes for me; if she prove
　　his,
All that is hers is mine, as I will work
　　him.

[1] Pompous, conceited.

Enter Marall.

MAR. Sir, the whole board is troubled at
　　your rising.

OVER. No matter, I'll excuse it. Prithee,
　　Marall,
Watch an occasion to invite my nephew
To speak with me in private.

MAR.　　　　　Who? "The rogue
The lady scorned to look on"?

OVER.　　　　　You are a wag.

Enter Lady [Allworth] and Wellborn.

MAR. See, sir, she's come, and cannot
　　be without him.

LADY. With your favor, sir, after a plen-
　　teous dinner,　　　　　19
I shall make bold to walk a turn or two
In your rare garden.

OVER.　　　　There's an arbor too,
If your ladyship please to use it.

LADY.　　　　Come, Master Wellborn.
　　Exeunt Lady [Allworth] and Wellborn.

OVER. Grosser and grosser! Now I be-
　　lieve the poet
Feigned not, but was historical, when
　　he wrote
Pasiphaë was enamored of a bull.
This lady's lust's more monstrous.—
　　My good lord,

Enter Lord Lovell, Margaret, and the Rest.

Excuse my manners.

LOV.　　　　There needs none, Sir Giles—
I may ere long say father, when it
　　pleases
My dearest mistress to give warrant
　　to it.

OVER. She shall seal to it, my lord, and
　　make me happy.　　　　　30

Enter Wellb[orn] and the Lad[y].

MARG. My lady is returned.

LADY.　　　　Provide my coach;
I'll instantly away. My thanks, Sir
　　Giles,
For my entertainment.

OVER.　　　　'Tis your nobleness
To think it such.

LADY.　　　I must do you a further wrong
In taking away your honorable guest.

LOV. I wait on you, madam; farewell,
　　good Sir Giles.

LADY. Good Mistress Margaret!—Nay,
　come, Master Wellborn,
　I must not leave you behind; in sooth,
　　I must not.
OVER. Rob me not, madam, of all joys
　at once;
　Let my nephew stay behind. He shall
　have my coach,　　　　　　　　　40
　And, after some small conference be-
　　tween us,
　Soon overtake your ladyship.
LADY.　　　　　　Stay not long, sir.
LOV. This parting kiss! [*Kisses Margaret.*]
　You shall every day hear from me
　By my faithful page.
ALL.　　　　　'Tis a service I am proud of.
Exeunt Lovell, Lady [*Allworth*], *Allworth,*
　　　　　　Margaret, Marall.
OVER. Daughter, to your chamber.—
　You may wonder, nephew,
　After so long an enmity between us,
　I should desire your friendship.
WELL.　　　　　　So I do, sir;
　'Tis strange to me.
OVER.　　　But I'll make it no wonder;
　And, what is more, unfold my nature
　　to you.
　We worldly men, when we see friends
　　and kinsmen　　　　　　　　50
　Past hopes sunk in their fortunes, lend
　　no hand
　To lift 'em up, but rather set our feet
　Upon their heads to press 'em to the
　　bottom,
　As, I must yield, with you I practiced
　　it.
　But, now I see you in a way to rise,
　I can and will assist you. This rich lady
　(And I am glad of 't) is enamored of
　　you;
　'Tis too apparent, nephew.
WELL.　　　　　No such thing—
　Compassion rather, sir.
OVER.　　　　Well, in a word,
　Because your stay is short, I'll have
　　you seen　　　　　　　　　60
　No more in this base shape; nor shall
　　she say
　She married you like a beggar, or in
　　debt.
WELL. (*Aside.*) He'll run into the noose
　and save my labor.
OVER. You have a trunk of rich clothes
　not far hence

In pawn; I will redeem 'em. And, that
　no clamor
May taint your credit for your petty
　debts,
You shall have a thousand pounds to
　cut 'em off,
And go a free man to the wealthy
　lady.
WELL. This done, sir, out of love, and no
　ends else—
OVER. As it is, nephew.
WELL.　Binds me still your servant.　70
OVER. No compliments; you are stayed
　for. Ere y'ave supped,
　You shall hear from me.—My coach,
　knaves, for my nephew!—
　Tomorrow I will visit you.
WELL.　　　　　Here's an uncle
　In a man's extremes![1] How much they
　do belie you,
　That say you are hard-hearted!
OVER.　　　　My deeds, nephew,
　Shall speak my love; what men report
　I weigh not.　　　　　　　*Exeunt.*

FINIS ACTUS TERTII.

ACTUS QUARTI SCENA PRIMA.

[*A room in Lady Allworth's house.*]

Lovell, Allworth.

LOV. 'Tis well; give me my cloak; I now
　discharge you
　From further service. Mind your own
　　affairs;
　I hope they will prove successful.
ALL.　　　　　　What is blessed
　With your good wish, my lord, cannot
　　but prosper.
　Let aftertimes report, and to your
　　honor,
　How much I stand engaged,[2] for I want
　　language
　To speak my debt. Yet, if a tear or two
　Of joy for your much goodness can
　　supply
　My tongue's defects, I could—
LOV.　　　　　Nay, do not melt;
　This ceremonial thanks to me 's super-
　　fluous.　　　　　　　　　10
OVER. (*Within.*) Is my lord stirring?
LOV. 'Tis he! O, here's your letter. Let
　him in.

---

[1] Extremities.　　　　　[2] Indebted.

Enter Over[reach], Greed[y], Mar[all].

OVER. A good day to my lord!

LOV.   You are an early riser,
Sir Giles.

OVER.   And reason, to attend your
lordship.

LOV. And you too, Master Greedy, up
so soon?

GREEDY. In troth, my lord, after the sun
is up,
I cannot sleep, for I have a foolish stom-
ach
That croaks for breakfast. With your
lordship's favor,
I have a serious question to demand   19
Of my worthy friend Sir Giles.

LOV.   Pray you, use your pleasure.

GREEDY. How far, Sir Giles, and, pray
you, answer me
Upon your credit, hold you it to be
From your manor house to this of my
Lady Allsworth's?

OVER. Why, some four mile.

GREEDY.   How! Four mile? Good Sir
Giles,
Upon your reputation think better,
For, if you do abate but one half-quarter
Of five, you do yourself the greatest
wrong
That can be in the world; for four miles'
riding
Could not have raised so huge an appe-
tite   29
As I feel gnawing on me.

MAR.   Whether you ride
Or go afoot, you are that way still pro-
vided,
And it please your worship.

OVER.   How now, sirrah? Prating
Before my lord! No difference? Go to
my nephew,
See all his debts discharged, and help
his worship
To fit on his rich suit.

MAR. [*Aside.*]   I may fit you too.
Tossed like a dog still!   *Exit Marall.*

LOV.   I have writ this morning
A few lines to my mistress, your fair
daughter.

OVER. 'Twill fire her, for she's wholly
yours already.—
Sweet Master Allworth, take my ring.
'Twill carry you

To her presence, I dare warrant you;
and there plead   40
For my good lord, if you shall find occasion.
That done, pray ride to Nottingham;
get a license,
Still by this token. I'll have it despatched,
And suddenly, my lord, that I may
say
My "honorable," nay, "right honorable"
daughter.

GREEDY. Take my advice, young gentleman; get your breakfast.
'Tis unwholesome to ride fasting. I'll
eat with you
And eat to purpose.

OVER.   Some Fury's in that gut!
Hungry again! Did you not devour this
morning
A shield of brawn,[1] and a barrel of Colchester oysters?   50

GREEDY. Why, that was, sir, only to
scour my stomach,
A kind of a preparative. Come, gentleman,
I will not have you feed like the hangman of Vlushing [2]
Alone, while I am here.

LOV.   Haste your return.

ALL. I will not fail, my lord.

GREEDY.   Nor I, to line
My Christmas coffer.[3]
                Exeunt Greedy and Allworth.

OVER.   To my wish, we are private.
I come not to make offer with my daugh-
ter
A certain portion—that were poor and
trivial.
In one word, I pronounce all that is
mine,   59
In lands or leases, ready coin or goods,
With her, my lord, comes to you; nor
shall you have
One motive to induce you to believe
I live too long, since every year I'll
add
Something unto the heap, which shall
be yours too.

LOV. You are a right kind father.

---

[1] "The thick skin on the flanks of a boar: a
piece of this was filled up with meat and cooked
till soft" (Cruikshank).
[2] Flushing.   [3] *I.e.*, his stomach.

Over. You shall have reason
To think me such. How do you like
   this seat?
It is well wooded, and well watered, the
   acres
Fertile and rich. Would it not serve
   for change,
To entertain your friends in a summer
   progress?[1] 69
What thinks my noble lord?
Lov. 'Tis a wholesome air,
And well-built pile; and she that's mis-
   tress of it
Worthy the large revenue.
Over. She the mistress?
It may be so for a time, but, let my lord
Say only that he likes it, and would
   have it,
I say, ere long 'tis his.
Lov. Impossible.
Over. You do conclude too fast, not know-
   ing me,
Nor the engines[2] that I work by. 'Tis
   not alone
The Lady Allworth's lands, for those
   once Wellborn's
(As by her dotage on him I know they will
   be)
Shall soon be mine; but point out any
   man's 80
In all the shire, and say they lie con-
   venient
And useful for your lordship, and once
   more
I say aloud, they are yours.
Lov. I dare not own
What's by unjust and cruel means ex-
   torted;
My fame and credit are more dear to
   me
Than so to expose 'em to be censured by
The public voice.
Over. You run, my lord, no hazard.
Your reputation shall stand as fair
In all good men's opinions as now;
Nor can my actions, though condemned
   for ill, 90
Cast any foul aspersion upon yours,
For, though I do contemn report my-
   self
As a mere sound, I still will be so tender
Of what concerns you, in all points of
   honor,

That the immaculate whiteness of your
   fame
Nor your unquestioned integrity
Shall e'er be sullied with one taint or
   spot
That may take from your innocence and
   candor.[3]
All my ambition is to have my daugh-
   ter
Right honorable, which my lord can
   make her. 100
And, might I live to dance upon my
   knee
A young Lord Lovell, borne by her unto
   you,
I write *nil ultra*[4] to my proudest hopes.
As for possessions and annual rents,
Equivalent to maintain you in the port[5]
Your noble birth and present state re-
   quires,
I do remove that burthen from your
   shoulders
And take it on mine own, for, though
   I ruin
The country to supply your riotous
   waste,
The scourge of prodigals, want, shall
   never find you. 110
Lov. Are you not frighted with the im-
   precations
And curses of whole families, made
   wretched
By your sinister practices?
Over. Yes, as rocks are,
When foamy billows split themselves
   against
Their flinty ribs, or as the moon is moved
When wolves, with hunger pined, howl
   at her brightness.
I am of a solid temper and like these
Steer on a constant course. With mine
   own sword,
If called into the field, I can make that
   right
Which fearful enemies murmured at as
   wrong. 120
Now, for these other piddling com-
   plaints
Breathed out in bitterness, as when they
   call me
Extortioner, tyrant, cormorant, or in-
   truder

[1] Journey. [2] Devices.

[3] Immaculateness.
[4] Nothing beyond. [5] Style of living.

On my poor neighbor's right, or grand
    incloser
Of what was common, to my private
    use,
Nay, when my ears[1] are pierced with
    widows' cries,
And undone orphants[2] wash with tears
    my threshold,
I only think what 'tis to have my daugh-
    ter
Right honorable; and 'tis a powerful
    charm   129
Makes me insensible of remorse or pity
Or the least sting of conscience.

Lov.   I admire[3]
The toughness of your nature.

Over.   'Tis for you,
My lord, and for my daughter, I am
    marble;
Nay, more, if you will have my char-
    acter
In little, I enjoy more true delight
In my arrival to my wealth these dark
And crooked ways than you shall e'er
    take pleasure
In spending what my industry hath
    compassed.
My haste commands me hence. In one
    word, therefore,   139
Is it a match?

Lov.   I hope that is past doubt now.

Over. Then rest secure; not the hate of
    all mankind here,
Nor fear of what can fall on me here-
    after
Shall make me study aught but your
    advancement
One story higher. An earl, if gold can
    do it!
Dispute not my religion nor my faith.
Though I am borne thus headlong by
    my will,
You may make choice of what belief
    you please;
To me they are equal. So, my lord,
    good morrow.   *Exit.*

Lov. He's gone—I wonder how the earth
    can bear
Such a portent! I, that have lived a
    soldier,   150
And stood the enemy's violent charge
    undaunted,

To hear this blasphemous beast am
    bathed all over
In a cold sweat. Yet, like a mountain,
    he,
Confirmed in atheistical[4] assertions,
Is no more shaken than Olympus is
When angry Boreas loads his double
    head
With sudden drifts of snow.

Enter Amble, Lady [Allworth], [Waiting-]
                        Woman.

Lady.   Save you, my lord!
Disturb I not your privacy?

Lov.   No, good madam,
For your own sake I am glad you came
    no sooner,
Since this bold, bad man, Sir Giles
    Overreach,   160
Made such a plain discovery[5] of himself,
And read this morning such a devilish
    matins
That I should think it a sin next to his
But to repeat it.

Lady.   I ne'er pressed, my lord,
On others' privacies; yet, against my
    will,
Walking, for health' sake, in the gallery
Adjoining to your lodgings, I was made
(So vehement and loud he was) partaker
Of his tempting offers.

Lov.   Please you to command
Your servants hence, and I shall gladly
    hear   170
Your wiser counsel.

Lady.   'Tis, my lord, a woman's,
But true and hearty.—[*To Amble.*] Wait
    in the next room,
But be within call; yet not so near to
    force me
To whisper my intents.

Amb.   We are taught better
By you, good madam.

Woman.   And well know our distance.

Lady. Do so, and talk not; 'twill become
    your breeding.—
    Exeunt Amble and [Waiting-] Woman.
Now, my good lord, if I may use my
    freedom,
As to an honored friend—

Lov.   You lessen else
Your favor to me.

---

[1] Original read *cares*.
[2] Orphans.
[3] Wonder at.
[4] Godless.
[5] Revelation.

LADY.   I dare then say thus: 179
As you are noble (howe'er common men
Make sordid wealth the object and sole end
Of their industrious aims), 'twill not agree
With those of eminent blood, who are engaged
More to prefer [1] their honors than to increase
The state left to 'em by their ancestors,
To study large additions to their fortunes
And quite neglect their births—though I must grant
Riches, well got, to be a useful servant,
But a bad master.
LOV.   Madam, 'tis confessed. 189
But what infer you from it?
LADY.   This, my lord:
That as all wrongs, though thrust into one scale,
Slide of themselves off when right fills the other
And cannot bide the trial, so all wealth,
I mean if ill-acquired, cemented to honor
By virtuous ways achieved and bravely purchased,
Is but as rubbage [2] poured into a river
(Howe'er intended to make good the bank),
Rendering the water, that was pure before,
Polluted and unwholesome. I allow
The heir of Sir Giles Overreach, Margaret,   200
A maid well qualified and the richest match
Our north part can make boast of; yet she cannot,
With all that she brings with her, fill [3] their mouths,
That never will forget who was her father,
Or that my husband Allworth's lands and Wellborn's
(How wrung from both needs now no repetition)
Were real motive that more worked your lordship

To join your families than her form and virtues.
You may conceive the rest.
LOV.   I do, sweet madam,
And long since have considered it. I know,   210
The sum of all that makes a just man happy
Consists in the well choosing of his wife;
And there, well to discharge it, does require
Equality of years, of birth, of fortune,
For beauty, being poor and not cried up
By birth or wealth, can truly mix with neither.
And wealth, where there's such difference in years
And fair descent, must make the yoke uneasy.
But I come nearer.
LADY.   Pray you, do, my lord.
LOV. Were Overreach' states thrice centupled, his daughter   220
Millions of degrees much fairer than she is,
Howe'er I might urge presidents [4] to excuse me,
I would not so adulterate my blood
By marrying Margaret, and so leave my issue
Made up of several pieces, one part scarlet
And the other London blue. [5] In my own tomb
I will inter my name first.
LADY. (Aside.)   I am glad to hear this.—
Why then, my lord, pretend you marriage to her?
Dissimulation but ties false knots
On that straight line by which you hitherto   230
Have measured all your actions.
LOV.   I make answer,
And aptly, with a question. Wherefore have you
That, since your husband's death, have lived a strict
And chaste nun's life, on the sudden given yourself
To visits and entertainments? Think you, madam,

[1] Promote.
[2] Rubbish.   [3] I.e., stop.
[4] Precedents.
[5] Cloth symbolical of the servant class.

'Tis not grown public conference? Or
　the favors
Which you too prodigally have thrown
　on Wellborn,
Being too reserved before, incur not
　censure?

LADY. I am innocent here; and, on my
　life, I swear　　　　　　　　　　239
My ends are good.

LOV.　　　　On my soul, so are mine
To Margaret; but leave both to the
　event. [1]
And, since this friendly privacy does serve
But as an offered means unto ourselves
To search each other farther, you having
　shown
Your care of me, I my respect to you,
Deny me not, but still in chaste words,
　madam,
An afternoon's discourse.

LADY.　　　So I shall hear you. [*Exeunt.*]

ACTUS QUARTI SCENA SECUNDA.

[*Before Tapwell's house.*]

Tapwell, Froth.

TAP. Undone, undone! This was your
　counsel, Froth.

FROTH. Mine! I defy thee. Did not Master Marall
(He has marred all, I am sure) strictly
　command us,
On pain of Sir Giles Overreach' displeasure,
To turn the gentleman out of doors?

TAP.　　　　　　　　　　'Tis true;
But now he's his uncle's darling, and has
　got
Master Justice Greedy, since he filled
　his belly,
At his commandment, to do anything.
Woe, woe to us!

FROTH.　　　He may prove merciful.　9

TAP. Troth, we do not deserve it at his
　hands.
Though he knew all the passages [2] of our
　house,
As the receiving of stolen goods, and
　bawdry,
When he was rogue Wellborn no man
　would believe him,
And then his information could not hurt
　us;

But now he is "right worshipful" again,
Who dares but doubt [3] his testimony?
　Methinks,
I see thee, Froth, already in a cart,
For a close [4] bawd, thine eyes ev'n pelted
　out
With dirt and rotten eggs, and my hand
　hissing　　　　　　　　　　19
If I scape the halter, with the letter R [5]
Printed upon it.

FROTH.　　Would that were the worst!
That were but nine days' wonder. As
　for credit,
We have none to lose, but we shall lose
　the money
He owes us, and his custom—there's the
　hell on 't.

TAP. He has summoned all his creditors
　by the drum,
And they swarm about him like so many
　soldiers
On the pay day, and has found out such
　a new way
To pay his old debts as 'tis very likely
He shall be chronicled for it!

FROTH.　　　　　　　He deserves it
More than ten pageants. But are you
　sure his worship　　　　　　　30
Comes this way, to my lady's?
A cry within: "Brave Master Wellborn!"

TAP.　　　　　　Yes. I hear him.

FROTH. Be ready with your petition and
　present it
To his good grace.

*Enter Wellb[orn] in a rich habit, [Marall,]
　Greed[y], Ord[er], Furn[ace], three Creditors; Tapw[ell], kneeling, delivers his
　　　　　　　　　　　　　bill of debt.*

WELL.　　How's this? Petitioned, too?
But note what miracles the payment of
A little trash, and a rich suit of clothes,
Can work upon these rascals! I shall be,
I think, Prince Wellborn.

MAR.　　When your worship's married,
You may be—I know what I hope to
　see you.

WELL. Then look thou for advancement.

MAR.　　　　　　　To be known
Your worship's bailiff is the mark I shoot
　at.　　　　　　　　　　　　40

[1] Outcome.　　　　　　[2] Occurrences.
[3] Fear.
[4] Secret.　　　[5] Standing for "Rogue."

WELL. And thou shalt hit it.

MAR.   Pray you, sir, despatch
These needy followers, and for my ad-
    mittance,[1]
Provided you'll defend me from Sir Giles,
This interim, Tapwell and Froth flattering
          and bribing Justice Greedy.
Whose service I am weary of, I'll say
    som_ething
You shall give thanks for.

WELL.   Fear me not [2] Sir Giles.

GREEDY. Who? Tapwell? I remember
    thy wife brought me
Last New Year's tide a couple of fat
    turkeys.

TAP. And shall do every Christmas, let
    your worship
But stand my friend now.

GREEDY. How? With Master Wellborn?
I can do anything with him on such
    terms.—   50
[*To Wellborn.*] See you this honest cou-
    ple? They are good souls
As ever drew cut faucet. Have they
    not
A pair of honest faces?

WELL.   I o'erheard you,
And the bribe he promised. You are
    cozened in 'em,
For of all the scum that grew rich by my
    riots
This, for a most unthankful knave, and
    this,
For a base bawd and whore, have worst
    deserved me,[3]
And therefore speak not for 'em. By
    your place
You are rather to do me justice. Lend me
    your ear.—
[*Aside.*] Forget his turkeys, and call in
    his license,   60
And at the next fair I'll give you a yoke
    of oxen
Worth all his poultry.

GREEDY.   I am changed on the sudden
In my opinion!—Come near; nearer,
    rascal.
And, now I view him better, did you e'er
    see
One look so like an archknave? His very
    countenance,

Should an understanding judge but look
    upon him,
Would hang him, though he were inno-
    cent.

TAP. }
FROTH. }   Worshipful sir!

GREEDY. No, though the great Turk came,
    instead of turkeys,
To beg any favor, I am inexorable.
Thou hast an ill name; besides thy musty
    ale,   70
That hath destroyed many of the king's
    liege people,
Thou never hadst in thy house, to stay
    men's stomachs,
A piece of Suffolk cheese or gammon of
    bacon,
Or any esculent, as the learned call it,
For their emolument, but sheer drink
    only,
For which gross fault I here do damn thy
    license,
Forbidding thee ever to tap or draw;
For instantly I will in mine own person
Command the constable to pull down
    thy sign,
And do it before I eat.

FROTH.   No mercy?

GREEDY.   Vanish! 80
If I show any, may my promised oxen
    gore me!

TAP. Unthankful knaves are ever so re-
    warded.
          Exeunt Greedy, Tapwell, Froth.

WELL. Speak, what are you?

1 CRED.   A decayed vintner, sir,
That might have thrived, but that your
    worship broke me
With trusting you with muscadine and
    eggs,
And five-pound suppers, with your after-
    drinkings,
When you lodged upon the Bankside.

WELL.   [I] [4] remember.

1 CRED. I have not been hasty, nor e'er
    laid to arrest you;
And therefore, sir—

WELL.   Thou art an honest fellow. 89
I'll set thee up again; see his bill paid.—
What are you?

2 CRED.   A tailor once, but now
    mere botcher.[5]
I gave you credit for a suit of clothes,

---

[1] *I.e.*, admittance to his service.
[2] *I.e.*, fear not.
[3] Have deserved worst in respect to me.
[4] Supplied by Gifford.   [5] Mender.

Which was all my stock, but, you failing
in payment,
I was removed from the shopboard,[1] and
confined
Under a stall.[2]

WELL.　　　　　See him paid—and botch
no more.

2 CRED. I ask no interest, sir.

WELL.　　　　　　　　Such tailors need not;
If their bills are paid in one-and-twenty
year,
They are seldom losers.—[*To 3 Creditor.*]
O, I know thy face;
Thou wert my surgeon. You must tell
no tales;
Those days are done. I will pay you in
private.　　　　　　　　　　　　100

ORD. A royal gentleman!

FURN.　　　　　　　Royal as an emperor!
He'll prove a brave master; my good
lady knew
To choose a man.

WELL.　　See all men else discharged;
And, since *old debts are cleared by a new
way,*
A little bounty will not misbecome me.
There's something, honest cook, for thy
good breakfasts.—
[*To Order.*] And this, for your respect.
Take 't; 'tis good gold,
And I able to spare it.

ORD.　　　　　　　You are too munificent.

FURN. He was ever so.

WELL.　　　　　Pray you, on before.

3 CRED.　　　　　Heaven bless you!

MAR. At four a-clock the rest know where
to meet me.　　　　　　　　110
　　Exeunt Ord[er], Furn[ace], Credit[ors].

WELL. Now, Master Marall, what's the
weighty secret
You promised to impart?

MAR.　　　　　　　Sir, time nor place
Allow me to relate each circumstance.
This only, in a word: I know Sir Giles
Will come upon you for security
For his thousand pounds, which you
must not consent to.
As he grows in heat, as I am sure he
will,
Be you but rough, and say he's in your
debt
Ten times the sum, upon sale of your
land.

I had a hand in 't (I speak it to my
shame)　　　　　　　　　120
When you were defeated [3] of it.

WELL.　　　　　　　　That's forgiven.

MAR. I shall deserve 't then. Urge him to
produce
The deed in which you passed it over to
him,
Which I know he'll have about him, to
deliver
To the Lord Lovell with many other
writings
And present monies. I'll instruct you
further,
As I wait on your worship. If I play not
my price [4]
To your full content and your uncle's
much vexation,
Hang up Jack Marall.

WELL.　　　　I rely upon thee. *Exeunt.*

ACTUS QUARTI SCENA ULTIMA.[5]

[*A room in Overreach's house.*]

Allworth, Margaret.

ALL. Whether to yield the first praise to
my lord's
Unequaled temperance or your constant
sweetness
That I yet live, my weak hands fastened
on
Hope's anchor, spite of all storms of
despair,
I yet rest doubtful.

MARG.　　　　　　　Give it to Lord Lovell,
For what in him was bounty, in me's
duty.
I make but payment of a debt to which
My vows, in that high office[6] registered,
Are faithful witnesses.

ALL.　　　　　　　　'Tis true, my dearest;
Yet, when I call to mind how many fair
ones　　　　　　　　　　　　10
Make willful shipwrack of their faiths,
and oaths
To God and man, to fill the arms of greatness,
And you rise up [no] [7] less than a glorious
star,

---

[3] Defrauded.
[4] Prize (in a game); *i.e.*, part.
[5] The last scene of the fourth act.
[6] *I.e.*, heaven.　　　　　[7] Added by **Dodsley**.

[1] A tailor's workbench.　　　　[2] Bench.

To the amazement of the world, that hold
out
Against the stern authority of a father,
And spurn at honor when it comes to
court you,
I am so tender of your good that, faintly,[1]
With your wrong I can wish myself that
right
You yet are pleased to do me.
MARG. Yet and ever.
To me what's title, when content is want-
ing? 20
Or wealth, raked up together with much
care
And to be kept with more, when the
heart pines
In being dispossessed of what it longs for
Beyond the Indian [2] mines? Or the
smooth brow
Of a pleased sire, that slaves me to his
will,
And, so his ravenous humor may be
feasted
By my obedience, and he see me great,
Leaves to my soul nor faculties nor power
To make her own election?
ALL. But the dangers
That follow the repulse—
MARG. To me they are nothing. 30
Let Allworth love, I cannot be unhappy.
Suppose the worst, that in his rage he
kill me.
A tear or two, by you dropped on my
hearse
In sorrow for my fate, will call back life
So far as but to say that I die yours;
I then shall rest in peace. Or should he
prove
So cruel, as one death would not suffice
His thirst of vengeance, but with ling'ring
torments
In mind and body I must waste to air,
In poverty joined with banishment, so
you share 40
In my afflictions, which I dare not wish
you,
So high I prize you, I could undergo 'em
With such a patience as should look
down
With scorn on his worst malice.
ALL. Heaven avert
Such trials of your true affection to me!
Nor will it unto you, that are all mercy,

Show so much rigor. But, since we must
run
Such desperate hazards, let us do our best
To steer between 'em.
MARG. Your lord's ours, and sure;
And, though but a young actor, second
me 50
In doing to the life what he has plotted,

Enter Overreach [behind].

The end may yet prove happy. Now, my
Allworth— [*Sees her father.*]
ALL. [*Aside.*] To your letter, and put on a
seeming anger.
MARG. I'll pay my lord all debts due to his
title;
And when, with terms not taking from
his honor,
He does solicit me, I shall gladly hear
him.
But in this peremptory, nay, command-
ing way,
To appoint a meeting and, without my
knowledge,
A priest to tie the knot can ne'er be
undone
Till death unloose it, is a confidence [3] 60
In his lordship will deceive him.
ALL. I hope better,
Good lady.
MARG. Hope, sir, what you please.
For me
I must take a safe and secure course; I
have
A father, and without his full consent,
Though all lords of the land kneeled for
my favor,
I can grant nothing.
OVER. [*Coming forward.*] I like this obe-
dience.—
But whatsoever my lord writes must and
shall be
Accepted and embraced. Sweet Master
Allworth,
You show yourself a true and faithful
servant
To your good lord; he has a jewel of
you. 70
How? Frowning, Meg? Are these looks
to receive
A messenger from my lord? What's this?
Give me it.

[1] Half-heartedly.   [2] Of the Indes.   [3] Presumption.

MARG. A piece of arrogant paper, like th'
　inscriptions. *Overreach read[s] the letter.*
OVER. "Fair mistress, from your servant
　learn, all joys
That we can hope for, if deferred, prove
　toys;
Therefore this instant, and in private,
　meet
A husband, that will gladly at your
　feet
Lay down his honors, tend'ring them to
　you
With all content, the church being paid
　her due."—　　　　　　　　　　　79
Is this the arrogant piece of paper? Fool,
Will you still be one? In the name of
　madness what
Could his good honor write more to
　content you?
Is there aught else to be wished, after
　these two,
That are already offered: marriage first,
And lawful pleasure after? What would
　you more?
MARG. Why, sir, I would be married like
　your daughter,
Not hurried away i' th' night I know not
　whither,
Without all ceremony—no friends invited
To honor the solemnity.
ALL. 　　　　　　An 't please your honor,
For so before tomorrow I must style
　you,　　　　　　　　　　　　　90
My lord desire[s] this privacy, in respect
His honorable kinsmen are far off,
And his desires to have it done brook
　not
So long delay as to expect [1] their com-
　ing;
And yet he stands resolved, with all due
　pomp,
As running at the ring, plays, masques,
　and tilting,
To have his marriage at court celebrated,
When he has brought your honor up to
　London.
OVER. He tells you true; 'tis the fashion,
　on my knowledge.
Yet the good lord, to please your peevish-
　ness,　　　　　　　　　　　　100
Must put it off, forsooth, and lose a night,
In which perhaps he might get two boys
　on thee.

[1] Wait for.

Tempt me no farther; if you do, this
　goad [2]　　　　　[*Points to his sword.*]
Shall prick you to him.
MARG. 　　　　　　I could be contented,
Were you but by to do a father's part
And give me in the church.
OVER. 　　　　　　So my lord have you,
What do I care who gives you? Since
　my lord
Does purpose to be private, I'll not cross
　him.
I know not, Master Allworth, how my
　lord
May be provided, and therefore there's a
　purse　　　　　　　　　　　110
Of gold—'twill serve this night's expense;
　tomorrow
I'll furnish him with any sums. In the
　meantime,
Use my ring to my chaplain; he is
　beneficed
At my manor of Gotam,[3] and called
　Parson Willdo.
'Tis no matter for a license; I'll bear him
　out in 't.
MARG. With your favor, sir, what warrant
　is your ring?
He may suppose I got that twenty ways,
Without your knowledge; and then to be
　refused
Were such a stain upon me! If you
　pleased, sir,
Your presence would do better.
OVER. 　　　　　　Still perverse?　120
I say again, I will not cross my lord;
Yet I'll prevent you too.—Paper and
　ink there!
ALL. I can furnish you.
OVER. 　I thank you; I can write then.
　　　　　　　　　　Writes on his book.
ALL. You may, if you please, put out the
　name of my lord,
In respect he comes disguised, and only
　write,
"Marry her to this gentleman."
OVER. 　Well advised.—(*Margaret kneels.*)
'Tis done; away!—My blessing, girl?
　Thou hast it.
Nay, no reply; begone.—Good Master
　Allworth,
This shall be the best night's work you
　ever made.

[2] Emended by Gifford. Original reads *good*.
[3] Gotham.

ALL. I hope so, sir.   130

Exeunt Allworth and Margaret.

OVER. Farewell!—Now all's cocksure.

Methinks I hear already knights and
    ladies
Say, "Sir Giles Overreach, how is it with
Your honorable daughter?   Has her
    honor
Slept well tonight?" or, "Will her honor
    please
To accept this monkey?   Dog?   Or
    paraquit?" [1]
(This is state in ladies) "Or my eldest son
To be her page, and wait upon her
    trencher?"
My ends, my ends are compassed!   Then
    for Wellborn
And the lands.   Were he once married to
    the widow,   140
I have him here.   I can scarce contain
    myself,
I am so full of joy, nay, joy all over. *Exit.*

THE END OF THE FOURTH ACT

ACTUS QUINTI SCENA PRIMA.[2]

[*A room in Lady Allworth's house.*]

Lovell, Lady [Allworth], Amble.

LADY. By this you know how strong the
    motives were
That did, my lord, induce me to dispense
A little with my gravity to advance,
In personating some few favors to him,
The plots and projects of the downtrod
    Wellborn.
Nor shall I e'er repent, although I suffer
In some few men's opinions for 't, the
    action,
For he that ventured all for my dear
    husband
Might justly claim an obligation from
    me
To pay him such a courtesy, which
    had I   10
Coyly or overcuriously [3] denied,
It might have argued me of little love
To the deceased.

LOV.   What you intended, madam,
For the poor gentleman hath found good
    success,
For, as I understand, his debts are paid,

[1] Parakeet.
[2] Original reads *Quinta*.   [3] Overcarefully.

And he once more furnished for fair em-
    ployment.
But all the arts that I have used to raise
The fortunes of your joy and mine, young
    Allworth,
Stand yet in supposition, though I hope
    well,
For the young lovers are in wit more
    pregnant   20
Than their years can promise; and for
    their desires,
On my knowledge, they are equal.

LADY.   —As my wishes
Are with yours, my lord.   Yet give me
    leave to fear
The building, though well grounded.   To
    deceive
Sir Giles, that's both a lion and a fox
In his proceedings, were a work beyond
The strongest undertakers—not the trial
Of two weak innocents.

LOV.   Despair not, madam.

*Hard things are compassed oft by easy
    means;*
And judgment, being a gift derived from
    heaven,   30
Though sometimes lodged i' th' hearts of
    worldly men,
That ne'er consider from whom they re-
    ceive it,
Forsakes such as abuse the giver of it—
Which is the reason that the politic
And cunning statesman, that believes he
    fathoms
The counsels of all kingdoms on the
    earth,
Is by simplicity oft overreach[ed].[4]

LADY. May he be so!   Yet in his name to
    express it
Is a good omen.

LOV.   May it to myself   39
Prove so, good lady, in my suit to you!
What think you of the motion? [5]

LADY.   Troth, my lord,
My own unworthiness may answer for
    me,
For had you, when that I was in my
    prime
(My virgin flower uncropped), presented
    me
With this great favor, looking on my
    lowness
Not in a glass of self-love, but of truth,

[4] Added by Coxeter.   [5] Proposal.

I could not but have thought it as a blessing
Far, far beyond my merit.

Lov.   You are too modest,
And undervalue that which is above
My title, or whatever I call mine.   50
I grant, were I a Spaniard, to marry
A widow might disparage me; but, being
A true-born Englishman, I cannot find
How it can taint my honor. Nay, what's more,
That which you think a blemish is to me
The fairest luster. You already, madam,
Have given sure proofs how dearly you can cherish
A husband that deserves you, which confirms me
That, if I am not wanting in my care
To do you service, you'll be still the same   60
That you were to your Allworth. In a word,
Our years, our states, our births are not unequal,
You being descended nobly, and allied so;
If then you may be won to make me happy,
But join your lips to mine, and that shall be
A solemn contract.

Lady.   I were blind to my own good
Should I refuse it. [*Kisses him.*] Yet, my lord, receive me
As such a one, the study of whose whole life
Shall know no other object but to please you.

Lov. If I return not with all tenderness   70
Equal respect to you, may I die wretched!

Lady. There needs no protestation, my lord,
To her that cannot doubt.—

Enter Wellborn [handsomely appareled].[1]

                    You are welcome, sir.
Now you look like yourself.

Well.   And will continue
Such in my free acknowledgment that I am

Your creature, madam, and will never hold
My life mine own, when you please to command it.

Lov. It is a thankfulness that well becomes you.
You could not make choice of a better shape
To dress your mind in.

Lady.   For me, I am happy   80
That my endeavors prospered. Saw you of late
Sir Giles, your uncle?

Well.   I heard of him, madam,
By his minister, Marall; he's grown into strange passions
About his daughter. This last night he looked for
Your lordship at his house, but, missing you,
And she not yet appearing, his wisehead[2]
Is much perplexed and troubled.

Lov.   It may be,
Sweetheart, my project took.

Enter Over[reach], with distracted looks, driving in Marall before him [with a box].

Lady.   I strongly hope.

Over. Ha! Find her, booby, thou huge lump of nothing;
I'll bore thine eyes out else.

Well. [*Aside.*]   May it please your lordship,   90
For some ends of mine own but to withdraw
A little out of sight, though not of hearing,
You may perhaps have sport.

Lov.   You shall direct me. *Steps aside.*

Over. I shall *sol fa*[3] you, rogue!

Mar.   Sir, for what cause
Do you use me thus?

Over.   Cause, slave? Why, I am angry,
And thou a subject only fit for beating,
And so to cool my choler. Look to the writing;
Let but the seal be broke upon the box
That has slept in my cabinet these three years,
I'll rack thy soul for 't.

Mar. (*Aside.*)   I may yet cry quittance,   100
Though now I suffer, and dare not resist.

OVER. Lady, by your leave, did you see my
  daughter, lady?
  And the lord her husband? Are they in
  your house?
  If they are, discover, that I may bid 'em
  joy;
  And, as an entrance to her place of honor,
  See your ladyship on her left hand, and
  make curtseys
  When she nods on you, which you must
  receive
  As a special favor.
LADY.   When I know, Sir Giles,
  Her state requires such ceremony, I shall
  pay it;   109
  But in the meantime, as I am myself,
  I give you to understand I neither
  know
  Nor care where her honor is.
OVER.   When you once see her
  Supported and led by the lord her hus-
  band,
  You'll be taught better.—Nephew!
WELL.   Sir.
OVER.   No more?
WELL. 'Tis all I owe you.
OVER.   Have your redeemed rags
  Made you thus insolent?
WELL. (*In scorn.*)   Insolent to you?
  Why, what are you, sir, unless in your
  years,
  At the best, more than myself?
OVER. [*Aside.*]   His fortune swells him.
  'Tis rank [1] he's married.
LADY.   This is excellent!
OVER. Sir, in calm language, though I sel-
  dom use it,   120
  I am familiar with the cause that makes
  you
  Bear up thus bravely. There's a certain
  buzz
  Of a stol'n marriage—do you hear?—of a
  stol'n marriage,
  In which, 'tis said, there's somebody
  hath been cozened.
  I name no parties.
WELL.   Well, sir, and what follows?
OVER. Marry, this, since you are peremp-
  tory: remember,
  Upon mere hope of your great match, I
  lent you
  A thousand pounds. Put me in good
  security,

And suddenly, by [2] mortgage or by stat-
  ute,
  Of some of your new possessions, or I'll
  have you   130
  Dragged in your lavender [3] robes to the
  jail. You know me,
  And therefore do not trifle.
WELL.   Can you be
  So cruel to your nephew, now he's in
  The way to rise? Was this the courtesy
  You did me "in pure love, and no ends
  else"?
OVER. End me no ends! Engage the whole
  estate,
  And force your spouse to sign it, you
  shall have
  Three or four thousand more, to roar and
  swagger
  And revel in bawdy taverns.
WELL.   And beg after—   139
  Mean you not so?
OVER.   My thoughts are mine, and free.
  Shall I have security?
WELL.   No, indeed, you shall not,
  Nor bond, nor bill, nor bare acknowledg-
  ment;
  Your great looks fright not me.
OVER.   But my deeds shall.
  Outbraved?
      They both draw. The Servants enter.
LADY.   Help, murther! Murther!
WELL.   Let him come on,
  With all his wrongs and injuries about
  him,
  Armed with his cutthroat practices to
  guard him;
  The right that I bring with me will de-
  fend me,
  And punish his extortion.
OVER.   That I had thee
  But single in the field!
LADY.   You may; but make not
  My house your quarreling scene.
OVER.   Were 't in a church, 150
  By heaven and hell, I'll do 't!
MAR. [*Aside to Wellborn.*]   Now put
  him to
  The showing of the deed.
WELL.   This rage is vain, sir.
  For fighting, fear not, you shall have your
  hands full
  Upon the least incitement; and whereas

---

[1] Gross, plain.

[2] Emended by Coxeter. Original reads *my*.

[3] *I.e.*, pawned.

You charge me with a debt of a thousand
   pounds,
If there be law (howe'er you have no
   conscience),
Either restore my land or I'll recover
A debt that's truly due to me from you,
In value ten times more than what you
   challenge.[1]

OVER. I in thy debt! O impudence! Did
   I not purchase   160
The land left by thy father, that rich
   land
That had continuéd in Wellborn's name
Twenty descents, which, like a riotous
   fool,
Thou didst make sale of? Is not here
   inclosed
The deed that does confirm it mine?

MAR. [Aside.]   Now, now!

WELL. I do acknowledge none; I ne'er
   passed o'er
Any such land. I grant for a year or two
You had it in trust, which if you do
   discharge,
Surrend'ring the possession, you shall
   ease
Yourself and me of chargeable suits in
   law,   170
Which, if you prove not honest, as I
   doubt it,
Must of necessity follow.

LADY.   In my judgment
He does advise you well.

OVER.   Good! Good! Conspire
With your new husband, lady; second
   him
In his dishonest practices; but, when
This manor is extended [2] to my use,
You'll speak in an humbler key, and sue
   for favor.

LADY. Never; do not hope it.

WELL.   Let despair first seize me.

OVER. Yet, to shut up thy mouth, and
   make thee give
Thyself the lie, the loud lie, I draw
   out   180
The precious evidence; if thou canst for-
   swear
Thy hand and seal, and make a forfeit of
   Opens the box [and shows the document].
Thy ears to the pillory—see, here's that
   will make
My interest clear.—Ha!

[1] Claim.   [2] Seized for debt.

LADY.   A fair skin of parchment.

WELL. Indented, I confess, and labels
   too;
But neither wax nor words. How! Thunderstrook? [3]
Not a syllable to insult with? My wise
   uncle,
Is this your precious evidence? Is this
   that makes
Your interest clear?

OVER.   I am o'erwhelmed with wonder!
What prodigy is this? What subtle
   devil   190
Hath razed out the inscription, the wax
Turned into dust? The rest of my deeds
   whole
As when they were delivered, and this
   only
Made nothing! Do you deal with
   witches, rascal?
There is a statute for you, which will
   bring
Your neck in a hempen circle; yes, there
   is.
And now 'tis better thought, for, cheater,
   know
This juggling shall not save you.

WELL.   To save thee
Would beggar the stock of mercy.

OVER.   Marall!

MAR.   Sir.

OVER. (*Flattering him.*) Though the wit-
   nesses are dead, your testimony— 200
Help with an oath or two; and for thy
   master,
Thy liberal master, my good honest
   servant,
I know you will swear anything to dash
This cunning sleight. Besides, I know
   thou art
A public notary, and such stand in law
For a dozen witnesses. The deed, being
   drawn too
By thee, my careful Marall, and deliv-
   ered
When thou wert present, will make good
   my title.
Wilt thou not swear this?

MAR.   I? No, I assure you.
I have a conscience not seared up like
   yours;   210
I know no deeds.

OVER.   Wilt thou betray me?

[3] Thunderstruck.

MAR.   Keep him
From using of his hands, I'll use my
tongue
To his no little torment.
OVER.   Mine own varlet
Rebel against me?
MAR.   Yes, and uncase [1] you too.
The "idiot," the "patch," the "slave,"
the "booby,"
The property fit only to be beaten
For your morning exercise, your "foot-
ball," or
"Th' unprofitable lump of flesh," your
"drudge,"
Can now anatomize [2] you, and lay open
All your black plots, and level with the
earth   220
Your hill of pride, and, with these
gabions [3] guarded,
Unload my great artillery and shake,
Nay, pulverize the walls you think de-
fend you.
LADY. How he foams at the mouth with
rage!
WELL.   To him again.
OVER. O, that I had thee in my gripe; I
would tear thee
Joint after joint!
MAR.   I know you are a tearer,
But I'll have first your fangs pared off,
and then
Come nearer to you, when I have dis-
covered, [4]
And made it good before the judge, what
ways   229
And devilish practices you used to cozen
With an army of whole families, who yet
live,
And, but [5] enrolled for soldiers, were able
To take in [6] Dunkirk.
WELL.   All will come out.
LADY.   The better.
OVER. But that I will live, rogue, to torture
thee,
And make thee wish, and kneel in vain,
to die,
These swords that keep thee from me
should fix here,
Although they made my body but one
wound,

But I would reach thee.
LOV. (*Aside.*)   Heaven's hand is in this;
One bandog [7] worry the other!
OVER.   I play the fool,
And make my anger but ridiculous; 240
There will be a time and place, there will
be, cowards,
When you shall feel what I dare do.
WELL.   I think so.
You dare do any ill, yet want true valor
To be honest and repent.
OVER.   They are words I know not,
Nor e'er will learn. Patience, the beg-
gar's virtue,

Enter Greedy and Parson Willdo.

Shall find no harbor here.—After these
storms
At length a calm appears. Welcome,
most welcome!
There's comfort in thy looks. Is the deed
done?
Is my daughter married? Say but so, my
chaplain,   249
And I am tame.
WILLDO.   Married? Yes, I assure you.
OVER. Then vanish, all sad thoughts!
There's more gold for thee.
My doubts and fears are in the titles
drowned
Of my "right honorable," my "right
honorable" daughter.
GREEDY. Here will I be feasting! At least
for a month
I am provided. Empty guts, croak no
more.
You shall be stuffed like bagpipes, not
with wind,
But bearing [8] dishes.
OVER.   Instantly be here?
                    Whisp'ring to Willdo.
To my wish! To my wish! Now you that
plot against me,
And hoped to trip my heels up, that
contemned me,   *Loud music.*
Think on 't and tremble.—They come!
I hear the music.   260
A lane there for my lord!
WELL.   This sudden heat
May yet be cooled, sir.
OVER.   Make way there for my lord!

[1] Flay.
[2] Dissect.
[3] Cylinders filled with earth and used for
fortification.
[4] Revealed.
[5] If only.
[6] Capture.
[7] A ferocious dog kept chained.
[8] Substantial.

Enter Allworth and Margaret.

MARG. Sir, first your pardon, then your
blessing, with
Your full allowance of the choice I have
made,
As ever you could make use of your
reason.   *Kneeling.*
Grow not in passion, since you may as
well
Call back the day that's past, as untie
the knot
Which is too strongly fastened. Not to
dwell
Too long on words, this's my husband.

OVER.   How!

ALL. So I assure you; all the rites of marriage,   270
With every circumstance, are past. Alas,
sir,
Although I am no lord, but a lord's
page,
Your daughter and my loved wife mourns
not for it;
And, for "right honorable" son-in-law,
you may say,
Your "dutiful" daughter.

OVER.   Devil! Are they married?

WILLDO. Do a father's part, and say,
"Heaven give 'em joy!"

OVER. Confusion and ruin! Speak, and
speak quickly,
Or thou art dead.

WILLDO.   They are married.

OVER.   Thou hadst better
Have made a contract with the king of
fiends
Than these. My brain turns!

WILLDO.   Why this rage to me?   280
Is not this your letter, sir, and these the
words?
"Marry her to this gentleman."

OVER.   It cannot—
Nor will I e'er believe it—'sdeath, I will
not!—
That I, that in all passages I touched
At worldly profit have not left a print
Where I have trod for the most curious
search
To trace my footsteps, should be gulled
by children,
Baffled and fooled, and all my hopes and
labors
Defeated and made void.

WELL.   As it appears,
You are so, my grave uncle.

OVER.   Village nurses   290
Revenge their wrongs with curses; I'll
not waste
A syllable, but thus I take the life
Which, wretched, I gave to thee.
                    Offers to kill Margaret.

LOV. [*Rushing forward.*]   Hold, for
your own sake!
Though charity to your daughter hath
quite left you,
Will you do an act, though in your hopes
lost here,
Can leave no hope for peace or rest here-
after?
Consider; at the best you are but a man,
And cannot so create your aims but that
They may be crossed.

OVER.   Lord, thus I spit at thee   299
And at thy counsel, and again desire thee,
And as thou art a soldier, if thy valor
Dares show itself where multitude and
example
Lead not the way, let's quit the house,
and change
Six words in private.

LOV.   I am ready.

LADY.   Stay, sir.
Contest with one distracted?

WELL.   You'll grow like him,
Should you answer his vain challenge.

OVER.   Are you pale? [1]
Borrow his help; though Hercules call it
odds,
I'll stand against both, as I am hemmed
in thus.
Since, like Libyan lion in the toil,
My fury cannot reach the coward hun-
ters,   310
And only spends itself, I'll quit the place.
Alone I can do nothing; but I have
servants
And friends to second me; and, if I make
not
This house a heap of ashes (by my
wrongs,
What I have spoke I will make good!)
or leave [2]
One throat uncut—if it be possible,
Hell add to my afflictions!
                          Exit Overreach.

[1] Afraid.
[2] Emended by Gifford. Original reads *leav'd.*

MAR. Is 't not brave sport?

GREEDY. Brave sport? I am sure it has ta'en away my stomach;

I do not like the sauce.

ALL. Nay, weep not, dearest, Though it express your pity; what's decreed 320

Above, we cannot alter.

LADY. His threats move me No scruple, madam.

MAR. Was it not a rare trick, And it please your worship, to make the deed nothing?

I can do twenty neater, if you please

To purchase and grow rich, for I will be

Such a solicitor and steward for you

As never worshipful had.

WELL. I do believe thee. But first discover the quaint [1] means you used

To raze out the conveyance?

MAR. They are mysteries

Not to be spoke in public: certain minerals 330

Incorporated in the ink and wax.

Besides, he gave me nothing, but still fed me

With hopes and blows; and that was the inducement

To this conumbrum.[2] If it please your worship

To call to memory, this mad beast once caused me

To urge you or to drown or hang yourself;

I'll do the like to him, if you command me.

WELL. You are a rascal! He that dares be false

To a master, though unjust, will ne'er be true 339

To any other. Look not for reward

Or favor from me; I will shun thy sight

As I would do a basilisk's. Thank my pity

If thou keep thy ears; howe'er, I will take order

Your practice shall be silenced.

GREEDY. I'll commit him, If you'll have me, sir.

WELL. That were to little purpose;

His conscience be his prison. Not a word,

But instantly begone!

¹ Ingenious. ² Conundrum.

ORD. Take this kick with you.

AMB. And this.

FURN. If that I had my cleaver here, I would divide your knave's head.

MAR. This is the haven 349

False servants still arrive at.

Exit Mar[all].

Enter Over[reach].

LADY. Come again!

LOV. Fear not, I am your guard.

WELL. His looks are ghastly.

WILLDO. Some little time I have spent, under your favors,

In physical [3] studies, and, if my judgment err not,

He's mad beyond recovery. But observe him,

And look to yourselves.

OVER. Why, is not the whole world Included in myself? To what use then

Are friends and servants? Say there were a squadron

Of pikes, lined through with shot, [4] when I am mounted

Upon my injuries, shall I fear to charge 'em?

No; I'll through the battalia, and, that routed, 360

Flourishing his sword sheathed.[5]

I'll fall to execution. Ha! I am feeble;

Some undone widow sits upon mine arm,

And takes away the use of 't; and my sword,

Glued to my scabbard with wronged orphans' tears,

Will not be drawn. Ha! What are these? Sure, hangmen

That come to bind my hands, and then to drag me

Before the judgment seat. Now they are new shapes,

And do appear like Furies, with steel whips

To scourge my ulcerous soul. Shall I then fall

Ingloriously, and yield? No; spite of Fate, 370

I will be forced to hell like to myself.

³ Medical.
⁴ Interspersed with musketeers.
⁵ Emended by Gifford. Original reads *unsheathed.*

Though you were legions of accurséd
   spirits,
Thus would I fly among you.
> [*Runs forward and falls.*]

WELL.[1]   There's no help;
Disarm him first, then bind him.

GREEDY.   Take a *mittimus*,[2]
And carry him to Bedlam.

LOV.   How he foams!

WELL. And bites the earth!

WILLDO.   Carry him to some dark room;
   There try what art can do for his recovery.

MARG. O my dear father!
> *They force Overreach off.*

ALL.   You must be patient, mistress.

LOV. Here is a president to teach wicked
   men
That when they leave religion, and turn
   atheists,   380
Their own abilities leave 'em. Pray you,
   take comfort;
I will endeavor you shall be his guardians
In his distractions. And for your land,
   Master Wellborn,
Be it good or ill in law, I'll be an umpire
Between you and this, th' undoubted
   heir
Of Sir Giles Overreach. For me, here's
   the anchor
That I must fix on.

ALL.   What you shall determine,
My lord, I will allow of.[3]

---

[1] This speech head is placed before the preceding line in the original.
[2] A writ of committal.
[3] Agree to.

WELL.   'Tis the language
That I speak too; but there is something
   else
Beside the repossession of my land   390
And payment of my debts, that I must
   practice.
I had a reputation, but 'twas lost
In my loose course, and, till I redeem it
Some noble way, I am but half made up.
It is a time of action; if your lordship
Will please to confer a company upon me
In your command, I doubt not in my
   service
To my king and country but I shall do
   something
That may make me right again.

LOV.   Your suit is granted
And you loved for the motion.

WELL. [*To the audience.*]   Nothing
   wants then   400
But your allowance—

THE EPILOGUE

But your allowance, and in that our all
Is comprehended, it being known nor we
Nor he that wrote the comedy can be
   free
Without your manumission, which if you
Grant willingly, as a fair favor due
To the poet's and our labors (as you may,
For we despair not, gentlemen, of the
   play),
We jointly shall profess your grace hath
   might   409
To teach us action, and him how to write.
> [*Exeunt.*]

FINIS.

MAR.　　　　　　Is 't not brave sport?

GREEDY.　Brave sport?　I am sure it has
　ta'en away my stomach;
　I do not like the sauce.

ALL.　　　　　　Nay, weep not, dearest,
　Though it express your pity; what's
　　decreed　　　　　　　　　　　320
　Above, we cannot alter.

LADY.　　　　　His threats move me
　No scruple, madam.

MAR.　　　　Was it not a rare trick,
　And it please your worship, to make the
　　deed nothing?
　I can do twenty neater, if you please
　To purchase and grow rich, for I will be
　Such a solicitor and steward for you
　As never worshipful had.

WELL.　　　　　I do believe thee.
　But first discover the quaint [1] means you
　　used
　To raze out the conveyance?

MAR.　　　　　They are mysteries
　Not to be spoke in public: certain min-
　　erals　　　　　　　　　　　　330
　Incorporated in the ink and wax.
　Besides, he gave me nothing, but still
　　fed me
　With hopes and blows; and that was the
　　inducement
　To this conumbrum.[2]　If it please your
　　worship
　To call to memory, this mad beast once
　　caused me
　To urge you or to drown or hang your-
　　self;
　I'll do the like to him, if you command
　　me.

WELL.　You are a rascal!　He that dares be
　　false
　To a master, though unjust, will ne'er be
　　true　　　　　　　　　　　　339
　To any other.　Look not for reward
　Or favor from me; I will shun thy sight
　As I would do a basilisk's.　Thank my
　　pity
　If thou keep thy ears; howe'er, I will take
　　order
　Your practice shall be silenced.

GREEDY.　　　　　I'll commit him,
　If you'll have me, sir.

WELL.　　　That were to little purpose;
　His conscience be his prison.　Not a word,
　But instantly begone!

[1] Ingenious.　　　　　[2] Conundrum.

ORD.　　　　　Take this kick with you.

AMB.　And this.

FURN.　　If that I had my cleaver here,
　I would divide your knave's head.

MAR.　　　　　This is the haven　349
　False servants still arrive at.

　　　　　　　　　　Exit Mar[all].

　　　　Enter Over[reach].

LADY.　　　　　　　Come again!

Lov.　Fear not, I am your guard.

WELL.　　　　　His looks are ghastly.

WILLDO.　Some little time I have spent,
　under your favors,
　In physical [3] studies, and, if my judg-
　　ment err not,
　He's mad beyond recovery.　But observe
　　him,
　And look to yourselves.

OVER.　　Why, is not the whole world
　Included in myself?　To what use then
　Are friends and servants?　Say there were
　　a squadron
　Of pikes, lined through with shot, [4] when
　　I am mounted
　Upon my injuries, shall I fear to charge
　　'em?
　No; I'll through the battalia, and, that
　　routed,　　　　　　　　　　360
　　　Flourishing his sword sheathed.[5]
　I'll fall to execution.　Ha!　I am feeble;
　Some undone widow sits upon mine arm,
　And takes away the use of 't; and my
　　sword,
　Glued to my scabbard with wronged
　　orphans' tears,
　Will not be drawn.　Ha!　What are these?
　　Sure, hangmen
　That come to bind my hands, and then
　　to drag me
　Before the judgment seat.　Now they are
　　new shapes,
　And do appear like Furies, with steel
　　whips
　To scourge my ulcerous soul.　Shall I
　　then fall
　Ingloriously, and yield?　No; spite of
　　Fate,　　　　　　　　　　　370
　I will be forced to hell like to myself.

[3] Medical.
[4] Interspersed with musketeers.
[5] Emended by Gifford.　Original reads *unsheathed.*

Though you were legions of accursèd
spirits,
Thus would I fly among you.
[*Runs forward and falls.*]
WELL.[1] There's no help;
Disarm him first, then bind him.
GREEDY. Take a *mittimus*,[2]
And carry him to Bedlam.
LOV. How he foams!
WELL. And bites the earth!
WILLDO. Carry him to some dark room;
There try what art can do for his recov-
ery.
MARG. O my dear father!
They force Overreach off.
ALL. You must be patient, mistress.
LOV. Here is a president to teach wicked
men
That when they leave religion, and turn
atheists, 380
Their own abilities leave 'em. Pray you,
take comfort;
I will endeavor you shall be his guardians
In his distractions. And for your land,
Master Wellborn,
Be it good or ill in law, I'll be an umpire
Between you and this, th' undoubted
heir
Of Sir Giles Overreach. For me, here's
the anchor
That I must fix on.
ALL. What you shall determine,
My lord, I will allow of.[3]

[1] This speech head is placed before the preceding line in the original.
[2] A writ of committal.
[3] Agree to.

WELL. 'Tis the language
That I speak too; but there is something
else
Beside the repossession of my land 390
And payment of my debts, that I must
practice.
I had a reputation, but 'twas lost
In my loose course, and, till I redeem it
Some noble way, I am but half made up.
It is a time of action; if your lordship
Will please to confer a company upon me
In your command, I doubt not in my
service
To my king and country but I shall do
something
That may make me right again.
LOV. Your suit is granted
And you loved for the motion.
WELL. [*To the audience.*] Nothing
wants then 400
But your allowance—

THE EPILOGUE

But your allowance, and in that our all
Is comprehended, it being known nor we
Nor he that wrote the comedy can be
free
Without your manumission, which if you
Grant willingly, as a fair favor due
To the poet's and our labors (as you may,
For we despair not, gentlemen, of the
play),
We jointly shall profess your grace hath
might 409
To teach us action, and him how to write.
[*Exeunt.*]
FINIS.

To eat and sleep supinely is the end
Of human blessings. I must tell you, sir,
Virtue, if not in action, is a vice,
And, when we move not forward, we go
　backward.
Nor is this peace, the nurse of drones and
　cowards,
Our health, but a disease.
GASP.　　　　　　　Well urged, my lord.
ANT. Perfit [1] what is so well begun.
AMB.　　　　　　　And bind　190
My lord your servant.
ROB.　　　Hair-brained fool! What reason
Canst thou infer [2] to make this good?
BERT.　　　　　　　A thousand,
Not to be contradicted. But consider
Where your command lies. 'Tis not, sir,
　in France,
Spain, Germany, Portugal, but in Sicily,
An island, sir. Here are no mines of gold
Or silver to enrich you; no worm spins
Silk in her womb to make distinction
Between you and a peasant in your
　habits;
No fish lives near our shores, whose blood
　can dye　　　　　　　　　200
Scarlet or purple; all that we possess,
With beasts we have in common. Nature
　did
Design us to be warriors, and to break
　through
Our ring, the sea, by which we are en-
　vironed;
And we by force must fetch in what is
　wanting
Or precious to us. Add to this, we are
A populous nation, and increase so fast
That, if we by our providence are not
　sent
Abroad in colonies, or fall by the sword,
Not Sicily, though now it were more
　fruitful　　　　　　　　210
Than when 'twas styled the "granary of
　great Rome,"
Can yield our numerous fry bread. We
　must starve,
Or eat up one another.
ADOR.　　　　　　　The king hears
With much attention.
AST.　　　And seems moved with what
Bertoldo hath delivered.
BERT.　　　　May you live long, sir,
The king of peace, so you deny not us
[1] Perfect.　　　　　　[2] Bring forward.

The glory of the war; let not our nerves
Shrink up with sloth, nor for want of em-
　ployment
Make younger brothers thieves. 'Tis
　their swords, sir,
Must sow and reap their harvest. If
　examples　　　　　　　220
May move you more than arguments,
　look on England,
The empress of the European isles,
And unto whom alone ours yields prece-
　dence.
When did she flourish so as when she was
The mistress of the ocean? Her navies,
Putting a girdle round about the world
When the Iberian [3] quaked, her worthies
　named; [4]
And the fair flower-de-luce [5] grew pale,
　set by
The red rose and the white! Let not our
　armor
Hung up, or our unrigged armada, make
　us　　　　　　　　　230
Ridiculous to the late poor snakes our
　neighbors,
Warmed in our bosoms, and to whom
　again
We may be terrible, while we spend our
　hours
Without variety, confined to drink,
Dice, cards, or whores. Rouse us, sir,
　from the sleep
Of idleness, and redeem our mortgaged
　honors.
Your birth, and justly, claims my father's
　kingdom;
But his heroic mind descends to me.
I will confirm so much.
ADOR.　　　　　　In his looks he seems
To break ope Janus' temple.
AST.　　　　　How these younglings　240
Take fire from him!
ADOR.　　　　　It works an alteration
Upon the king.
ANT.　　　　　I can forbear no longer.
War, war, my sovereign!
FUL.　　　　　　The king appears
Resolved, and does prepare to speak.
ROB.　　　　　　　Think not
Our counsel's built upon so weak a base

[3] Spaniard, in reference to the Spanish
Armada.
[4] *I.e.,* England's navy made her great men.
[5] *I.e.,* France.

As to be overturned or shaken with
Tempestuous winds of words. As I, my
　　lord,
Before resolved you, I will not engage
My person in this quarrel, neither press
My subjects to maintain it; yet, to
　　show　　　　　　　　　　　　　　250
My rule is gentle and that I have feeling
Of your master's sufferings, since these
　　gallants, weary
Of the happiness of peace, desire to taste
The bitter sweets of war, we do con-
　　sent
That, as adventure[r]s and volunteers,
No way compelled by us, they may make
　　trial
Of their boasted valors.

Bert.　　　　　　　　We desire no more.

Rob. 'Tis well; and, but my grant in this,
　　expect not
Assistance from me.　　Govern as you
　　please
The province you make choice of, for I
　　vow,　　　　　　　　　　　　　　260
By all things sacred, if that thou mis-
　　carry
In this rash undertaking, I will hear it
No otherwise than as a sad disaster
Fallen on a stranger, nor will I esteem
That man my subject who in thy ex-
　　tremes
In purse or person aids thee. Take your
　　fortune.
You know me; I have said it. So, my
　　lord,
You have my absolute answer.

Amb.　　　　　　　　My prince pays
In me his duty.

Rob.　　　　　　　Follow me, Fulgentio,
And you, Astutio.

*Exeunt Roberto, Fulgentio, Astutio, Attend-
　　　　　　　　　　　　　　ants.*

Gasp.　　　What a frown he threw　270
At his departure on you!

Bert.　　　　　　　　Let him keep
His smiles for his state catamite; [1] I care
　　not.

Ant. Shall we aboard tonight?

Amb.　　　　　　Your speed, my lord,
Doubles the benefit.

Bert.　　　　　　　I have a business
Requires despatch; some two hours hence
I'll meet you.　　　　　　　*Exeunt.*

[1] Male prostitute.

[*A room in Camiola's house at Palermo.*]

*Signior Sylli, walking fantastically before,
　　followed by Camiola and Clarinda.*

Cam. Nay, signior, this is too much cere-
　　mony
In my own house.

Syl.　　　　　　　What's gracious abroad
Must be in private practiced.

Clar.　　　　　　For your mirth' sake
Let him alone; he has been all this morn-
　　ing
In practice with a peruged [2] gentleman
　　usher,
To teach him his true amble and his
　　postures

Sylli walking by and practicing his postures.
When he walks before a lady.

Syl.　　　　　　You may, madam,
Perhaps, believe that I in this use art
To make you dote upon me by exposing
My more than most rare features to
　　your view.　　　　　　　　　　　10
But I, as I have ever done, deal simply,
A mark of sweet simplicity ever noted
I' the family of the Syllis. Therefore,
　　lady,
Look not with too much contemplation
　　on me;
If you do, you are i' the suds. [3]

Cam.　　　　　　　You are no barber?

Syl. Fie, no! Not I. But my good parts
　　have drawn
More loving hearts out of fair ladies'
　　bellies
Than the whole trade have done teeth. [4]

Cam.　　　　　　　　　Is 't possible?

Syl. Yes, and they live too, marry, much
　　condoling [5]
The scorn of their Narcissus, as they
　　call me,　　　　　　　　　　　　20
Because I love myself—

Cam.　　　　　　　　Without a rival.
What philters or love powders do you
　　use
To force affection? I see nothing in
Your person but I dare look on, yet
　　keep
My own poor heart still.

[2] Peruked, bewigged.
[3] *I.e.*, in a pickle.
[4] The barber was also surgeon and dentist.
[5] Lamenting.

To eat and sleep supinely is the end
Of human blessings. I must tell you, sir,
Virtue, if not in action, is a vice,
And, when we move not forward, we go
  backward.
Nor is this peace, the nurse of drones and
  cowards,
Our health, but a disease.
GASP.   Well urged, my lord.
ANT. Perfit [1] what is so well begun.
AMB.   And bind 190
My lord your servant.
ROB.   Hair-brained fool! What reason
Canst thou infer [2] to make this good?
BERT.   A thousand,
Not to be contradicted. But consider
Where your command lies. 'Tis not, sir,
  in France,
Spain, Germany, Portugal, but in Sicily,
An island, sir. Here are no mines of gold
Or silver to enrich you; no worm spins
Silk in her womb to make distinction
Between you and a peasant in your
  habits;
No fish lives near our shores, whose blood
  can dye   200
Scarlet or purple; all that we possess,
With beasts we have in common. Nature
  did
Design us to be warriors, and to break
  through
Our ring, the sea, by which we are en-
  vironed;
And we by force must fetch in what is
  wanting
Or precious to us. Add to this, we are
A populous nation, and increase so fast
That, if we by our providence are not
  sent
Abroad in colonies, or fall by the sword,
Not Sicily, though now it were more
  fruitful   210
Than when 'twas styled the "granary of
  great Rome,"
Can yield our numerous fry bread. We
  must starve,
Or eat up one another.
ADOR.   The king hears
With much attention.
AST.   And seems moved with what
Bertoldo hath delivered.
BERT.   May you live long, sir,
The king of peace, so you deny not us

The glory of the war; let not our nerves
Shrink up with sloth, nor for want of em-
  ployment
Make younger brothers thieves. 'Tis
  their swords, sir,
Must sow and reap their harvest. If
  examples   220
May move you more than arguments,
  look on England,
The empress of the European isles,
And unto whom alone ours yields prece-
  dence.
When did she flourish so as when she was
The mistress of the ocean? Her navies,
Putting a girdle round about the world
When the Iberian [3] quaked, her worthies
  named; [4]
And the fair flower-de-luce [5] grew pale,
  set by
The red rose and the white! Let not our
  armor
Hung up, or our unrigged armada, make
  us   230
Ridiculous to the late poor snakes our
  neighbors,
Warmed in our bosoms, and to whom
  again
We may be terrible, while we spend our
  hours
Without variety, confined to drink,
Dice, cards, or whores. Rouse us, sir,
  from the sleep
Of idleness, and redeem our mortgaged
  honors.
Your birth, and justly, claims my father's
  kingdom;
But his heroic mind descends to me.
I will confirm so much.
ADOR.   In his looks he seems
To break ope Janus' temple.
AST.   How these younglings 240
Take fire from him!
ADOR.   It works an alteration
Upon the king.
ANT.   I can forbear no longer.
War, war, my sovereign!
FUL.   The king appears
Resolved, and does prepare to speak.
ROB.   Think not
Our counsel's built upon so weak a base

---

[1] Perfect.   [2] Bring forward.
[3] Spaniard, in reference to the Spanish
Armada.
[4] *I.e.*, England's navy made her great men.
[5] *I.e.*, France.

As to be overturned or shaken with
Tempestuous winds of words. As I, my
　　lord,
Before resolved you, I will not engage
My person in this quarrel, neither press
My subjects to maintain it; yet, to
　　show　　　　　　　　　　　　　　250
My rule is gentle and that I have feeling
Of your master's sufferings, since these
　　gallants, weary
Of the happiness of peace, desire to taste
The bitter sweets of war, we do con-
　　sent
That, as adventure[r]s and volunteers,
No way compelled by us, they may make
　　trial
Of their boasted valors.

BERT.　　　　　　　　We desire no more.

ROB. 'Tis well; and, but my grant in this,
　　expect not
Assistance from me.　　Govern as you
　　please
The province you make choice of, for I
　　vow,　　　　　　　　　　　　　　260
By all things sacred, if that thou mis-
　　carry
In this rash undertaking, I will hear it
No otherwise than as a sad disaster
Fallen on a stranger, nor will I esteem
That man my subject who in thy ex-
　　tremes
In purse or person aids thee. Take your
　　fortune.
You know me; I have said it. So, my
　　lord,
You have my absolute answer.

AMB.　　　　　　　　My prince pays
In me his duty.

ROB.　　　　　　Follow me, Fulgentio,
And you, Astutio.

Exeunt Roberto, Fulgentio, Astutio, Attend-
　　　　　　　　　　　　　　　　ants.

GASP.　　　What a frown he threw　270
At his departure on you!

BERT.　　　　　　　　Let him keep
His smiles for his state catamite; [1] I care
　　not.

ANT. Shall we aboard tonight?

AMB.　　　　　　Your speed, my lord,
Doubles the benefit.

BERT.　　　　　　I have a business
Requires despatch; some two hours hence
　　I'll meet you.　　　　　　*Exeunt.*

[1] Male prostitute.

ACT I. SCENE ii.

[*A room in Camiola's house at Palermo.*]

Signior Sylli, walking fantastically before,
　　　followed by Camiola and Clarinda.

CAM. Nay, signior, this is too much cere-
　　mony
In my own house.

SYL.　　　　　What's gracious abroad
Must be in private practiced.

CLAR.　　　　　　For your mirth' sake
Let him alone; he has been all this morn-
　　ing
In practice with a peruged [2] gentleman
　　usher,
To teach him his true amble and his
　　postures

Sylli walking by and practicing his postures.
When he walks before a lady.

SYL.　　　　　You may, madam,
Perhaps, believe that I in this use art
To make you dote upon me by exposing
My more than most rare features to
　　your view.　　　　　　　　　　10
But I, as I have ever done, deal simply,
A mark of sweet simplicity ever noted
I' the family of the Syllis. Therefore,
　　lady,
Look not with too much contemplation
　　on me;
If you do, you are i' the suds. [3]

CAM.　　　　　　You are no barber?

SYL. Fie, no! Not I. But my good parts
　　have drawn
More loving hearts out of fair ladies'
　　bellies
Than the whole trade have done teeth. [4]

CAM.　　　　　　　Is 't possible?

SYL. Yes, and they live too, marry, much
　　condoling [5]
The scorn of their Narcissus, as they
　　call me,　　　　　　　　　　　20
Because I love myself—

CAM.　　　　　　Without a rival.
What philters or love powders do you
　　use
To force affection? I see nothing in
Your person but I dare look on, yet
　　keep
My own poor heart still.

[2] Peruked, bewigged.
[3] *I.e.*, in a pickle.
[4] The barber was also surgeon and dentist.
[5] Lamenting.

Syl.   You are warned—be armed;
And do not lose the hope of such a hus-
    band
In being too soon enamored.
Clar.   Hold in your head,
Or you must have a martingale.
Syl.   I have sworn
Never to take a wife but such a
    one
(O, may your ladyship prove so strong!)
    as can   30
Hold out a month against me.
Cam.   Never fear it;
Though your best taking part, your
    wealth, were trebled,
I would not woo you. But, since in your
    pity
You please to give me caution, tell me
    what
Temptations I must fly from.
Syl.   The first is
That you never hear me sing, for I am
    a Syri.[1]
If you observe, when I warble, the dogs
    howl
As ravished with my ditties, and you
    will
Run mad to hear me.
Cam.   I will stop my ears,
And keep my little wits.
Syl.   Next, when I dance, 40
And come aloft thus [*Capers.*], cast not
    a sheep's eye
Upon the quivering of my calf.
Cam.   Proceed, sir.
Syl. But on no terms (for 'tis a main
    point) dream not
Of the strength of my back, though it
    will bear a burthen
With any porter.
Cam.   I mean not to ride you.
Syl. [2] Nor I your little ladyship, till you
    have
Performed the covenants. Be not taken
    with
My pretty spider-fingers, nor my
    eyes
That twinkle [3] on both sides.
Cam. [*Aside.*]   Was there ever such
    A piece of motley [4] heard of!—(*One*

knocks.)   Who's that? — You may
    spare
The catalogue of my dangers.
            Exit Clarinda.
Syl.   No, good madam;   51
I have not told you half.
Cam.   Enough, good signior;
If I eat more of such sweetmeats, I shall
    surfeit.—

Enter Clarinda.

Who is 't?
Clar.   The brother of the king.
Syl.   Nay, start not.
The brother of the king! Is he no more?
Were it the king himself, I'll give him
    leave
To speak his mind to you, for I am not
    jealous;
And, to assure your ladyship of so much,
I'll usher him in—[*Aside.*] and, that
    done, hide myself.   *Exit Syl[li].*
Cam. Camiola, if ever, now be constant. 60
This is indeed a suitor whose sweet
    presence,
Courtship,[5] and loving language would
    have staggered
The chaste Penelope; and, to increase
The wonder, did not modesty forbid it,
I should ask that from him he sues to
    me for.
And yet my reason, like a tyran,[6] tells
    me
I must nor give nor take it.

Enter Sylli and Bertoldo.

Syl.   I must tell you
You lose your labor. 'Tis enough to
    prove it,
Signior Sylli came before you; and you
    know
First come, first served; yet you shall
    have my countenance   70
To parley with her, and I'll take special
    care
That none shall interrupt you.
Bert.   You are courteous.
Syl. Come, wench, wilt thou hear wis-
    dom?
Clar.   Yes, from you, sir.
         Steps aside [with Sylli].

---

[1] A double pun on *Siren* and *Sirius*, the Dog
Star (Bryne).
[2] Original has *Cam.*
[3] Wink.   [4] *I.e.*, fool.
[5] Courtliness.   [6] Tyrant.

BERT. (*Kisseth her.*) If forcing this sweet favor from your lips,
Fair madam, argue me of too much boldness,
When you are pleased to understand I take
A parting kiss, if not excuse, at least
'Twill qualify, the offense.

CAM.   A parting kiss, sir?
What nation, envious of the happiness
Which Sicily enjoys in your sweet presence,   80
Can buy you from her, or what climate yield
Pleasures transcending those which you enjoy here,
Being both beloved and honored, the North Star
And guider of all hearts, and, to sum up
Your full accompt[1] of happiness in a word,
The brother of the king?

BERT.   Do you alone
And with an unexampled cruelty
Enforce my absence and deprive me of
Those blessings which you with a polished phrase
Seem to insinuate that I do possess,   90
And yet tax me as being guilty of
My willful exile? What are titles to me,
Or popular suffrage, or my nearness to
The king in blood, or fruitful Sicily,
Though it confessed no sovereign but myself,
When you, that are the essence of my being,
The anchor of my hopes, the real substance
Of my felicity, in your disdain
Turn all to fading and deceiving shadows?

CAM. You tax me without cause.

BERT.   You must confess it.   100
But, answer love with love, and seal the contract
In the uniting of our souls, how gladly
(Though now I were in action, and assured,
Following my fortune, that plumed Victory
Would make her glorious stand upon my tent)
Would I put off my armor in my heat

Of conquest and like Anthony pursue
My Cleopatra! Will you yet look on me
With an eye of favor?

CAM.   Truth bear witness for me
That in the judgment of my soul you are   110
A man so absolute and circular[2]
In all those wished-for rarities that may take
A virgin captive that, though at this instant
All sceptered monarchs of our western world
Were rivals with you, and Camiola worthy
Of such a competition, you alone
Should wear the garland.

BERT.   If so, what diverts
Your favor from me?

CAM.   No mulct[3] in yourself,
Or in your person, mind, or fortune.

BERT.   What then?

CAM. The consciousness of mine own wants. Alas, sir,   120
We are not parallels, but, like lines divided,
Can ne'er meet in one center. Your birth, sir,
Without addition, were an ample dowry
For one of fairer fortunes, and this shape,
Were you ignoble, far above all value;
To this, so clear a mind, so furnished with
Harmonious faculties molded from heaven,
That, though you were Thersites in your features,
Of no descent, and Irus in your fortunes,
Ulysses-like, you would force all eyes and ears   130
To love, but seen, and, when heard, wonder at
Your matchless story. But all these bound up
Together in one volume! Give me leave
With admiration to look upon 'em,
But not presume in my own flattering hopes
I may or can enjoy 'em.

BERT.   How you ruin
What you would seem to build up! I know no

---

[1] Account.

[2] Perfect, complete.   [3] Defect.

Ful.   Hear 't again:
  I love you honestly. Now you admire [1]
    me.
Cam. I do indeed, it being a word so sel-
    dom
  Heard from a courtier's mouth. But,
    pray you, deal plainly,   110
  Since you find me simple. What might
    be the motives
  Inducing you to leave the freedom of
  A bachelor's life, on your soft neck to
    wear
  The stubborn yoke of marriage? And,
    of all
  The beauties in Palermo, to choose me,
  Poor me? That is the main point you
    must treat of.
Ful. Why, I will tell you. Of a little
    thing
  You are a pretty peat,[2] indifferently [3]
    fair too,
  And, like a new-rigged ship, both tight
    and yare,[4]
  Well trussed to bear. Virgins of giant
    size   120
  Are sluggards at the sport, but for my
    pleasure
  Give me a neat, well-timbered gamester
    like you;
  Such need no spurs—the quickness of
    your eye
  Assures an active spirit.
Cam.   You are pleasant, sir;
  Yet I presume that there was one thing
    in me,
  Unmentioned yet, that took you more
    than all
  Those parts you have remembered.
Ful.   What?
Cam.   My wealth, sir.
Ful. You are i' the right; without that,
    beauty is
  A flower worn in the morning, at night
    trod on.
  But, beauty, youth, and fortune meet-
    ing in you,   130
  I will vouchsafe to marry you.
Cam.   You speak well;
  And in return excuse me, sir, if I
  Deliver reasons why upon no terms
  I'll marry you. I fable not.

[1] Wonder at.
[2] A term of endearment.
[3] Tolerably.   [4] Trim and lively.

Syl. [Aside.]   I am glad
  To hear this; I began to have an ague.
Ful. Come, your wise reasons.
Cam. Such as they are, pray you, take
    them:
  First, I am doubtful whether you are
    a man,
  Since, for your shape, trimmed up in a
    lady's dressing,
  You might pass for a woman; now I
    love   140
  To deal on certainties. And, for the
    fairness
  Of your complexion, which you think
    will take me,
  The color, I must tell you, in a man
  Is weak and faint, and never will hold
    out
  If put to labor—give me the lovely
    brown,
  A thick-curled hair of the same dye,
    broad shoulders,
  A brawny arm full of veins, a leg with-
    out
  An artificial calf. I suspect yours—
  But let that pass.
Syl. [Aside.]   She means me all this
    while,
  For I have every one of those good
    parts.   150
  O Sylli! Fortunate Sylli!
Cam.   You are moved, sir.
Ful. Fie! No; go on.
Cam.   Then, as you are a courtier,
  A graced one too, I fear you have been
    too forward.
  And so much for your person. Rich
    you are,
  Devilish rich, as 'tis reported, and sure
    have
  The aids of Satan's little fiends to get it;
  And what is got upon his back must be
  Spent, you know where—the proverb's
    stale. One word more,
  And I have done.
Ful.   I'll ease you of the trouble, 159
  Coy and disdainful!
Cam.   Save me, or else he'll beat me!
Ful. No, your own folly shall; and, since
    you put me
  To my last charm, look upon this and
    tremble.   *Shows the king's ring.*
Cam. At the sight of a fair ring? The
    king's, I take it.

I have seen him wear the like. If he
hath sent it
As a favor to me—

FUL.   Yes, 'tis very likely,
His dying mother's gift, prized at [1] his
crown!
By this he does command you to be
mine;
By his gift you are so. You may yet
redeem all.

CAM. You are in a wrong account still.
Though the king may
Dispose of my life and goods, my mind's
mine own,   170
And shall be never yours. The king—
heaven bless him!—
Is good and gracious, and,being in himself
Abstemious from base and goatish loose-
ness,
Will not compel, against their wills,
chaste maidens
To dance in his minions' circles. I be-
lieve,
Forgetting it when he washed his hands,
you stole it
With an intent to awe me. But you are
cozened;
I am still myself, and will be.

FUL.   A proud haggard,[2]
And not to be reclaimed! Which of
your grooms,
Your coachman, fool, or footman, min-
isters   180
Night-physic to you?

CAM.   You are foul-mouthed.

FUL.   Much fairer
Than thy black soul; and so I will proclaim thee.

CAM. Were I a man, thou durst not speak
this.

FUL.   Heaven
So prosper me, as I resolve to do it
To all men, and in every place. Scorned
by
A tit of tenpence![3]
                 Exeunt[4] *Fulgentio and his Page.*

SYL.   Now I begin to be valiant.
Nay, I will draw my sword. O, for a
brother![5]

---

[1] *I.e.,* at the value of.   [2] Wild female hawk.
[3] A girl not worth tenpence.
[4] Original reads *Exit.*
[5] *I.e.,* a sworn brother. Some copies of the
original read *butcher, i.e.,* bravo.

Do a friend's part; pray you, carry him
the length of 't.
I give him three years and a day to
match my Toledo,
And then we'll fight like dragons.

ADOR.   Pray, have patience.   190

CAM. I may live to have vengeance. My
Bertoldo
Would not have heard this.

ADOR.   Madam—

CAM.   Pray you, spare
Your language.—[*To Sylli.*] Prithee, fool
and make me merry.

SYL. That is my office ever.

ADOR.   I must do,
Not talk; this glorious gallant shall hear
from me.   *Exeunt.*

ACT II. SCENE iii.

[*Before the walls of Siena.*]

The chambers [6] *discharged; a flourish as
to an assault. Gonzaga, Pierio, Roderigo, Jacomo, Soldiers.*

GONZ. Is the breach made assaultable?

PIER.   Yes, and the moat
Filled up; the cannoneer hath done his
parts.
We may enter six abreast.

ROD.   There's not a man
Dares show himself upon the wall.

JAC.   Defeat not
The soldiers' hoped-for spoil.

PIER.   If you, sir,
Delay the assault, and the city be given
up
To your discretion, you in honor cannot
Use the extremity of war—but, in
Compassion to 'em, you to us prove
cruel.

JAC. And an enemy to yourself.

ROD.   A hindrance to   10
The brave revenge you have vowed.

GONZ.   Temper your heat
And lose not by too sudden rashness
that
Which, be but patient, will be offered
to you.
Security [7] ushers ruin; proud contempt
Of an enemy three parts vanquished,
with desire

---

[6] Small cannon used for theatrical purposes.
[7] Want of caution.

And greediness of spoil, have often
  wrested
A certain victory from the conqueror's
  gripe.
Discretion is the tutor of the war,
Valor the pupil; and, when we command
With lenity, and your direction's fol-
  lowed   20
With cheerfulness, a prosperous end
  must crown
Our works well undertaken.
Rod.   Ours are finished—
Pier. If we make use of fortune.
Gonz.   Her false smiles
Deprive you of your judgments. The
  condition
Of our affairs exacts a double care,
And, like bifronted Janus, we must look
Backward as forward. Though a flat-
  tering calm
Bids us urge on, a sudden tempest raised,
Not feared, much less expected, in our
  rear
May foully fall upon us, and distract[1]
  us   30
To our confusion.—

Enter Scout.

           Our scout! What brings
Thy ghastly looks and sudden speed?
Scout.   Th' assurance
Of a new enemy.
Gonz.   This I foresaw and feared.
What are they, know'st thou?
Scout.   They are by their colors
Sicilians, bravely mounted, and the
  brightness
Of their rich armors doubly gilded with
Reflection of the sun.
Gonz.   From Sicily?
The king in league! No war proclaimed!
  'Tis foul;
But this must be prevented, not dis-
  puted.
Ha, how is this? Your estridge[2] plumes,
  that but   40
E'en now like quills of porcupines seemed
  to threaten
The stars, drop at the rumor of a shower,
And like to captive colors sweep the
  earth!
Bear up; but, in great dangers, greater
  minds

[1] Draw apart, scatter.   [2] Ostrich.

Are never proud. Shall a few loose
  troops, untrained
But in a customary ostentation,
Presented as a sacrifice to your valors,
Cause a dejection in you?
Pier.   No dejection.
Rod. However startled, where you lead
  we'll follow.
Gonz. 'Tis bravely said. We will not
  stay their charge,   50
But meet 'em man to man, and horse
  to horse.
Pierio, in our absence hold our place,
And with our footmen[3] and those sickly
  troops
Prevent a sally. I in mine own person,
With part of the cavallerie,[4] will bid
These hunters welcome to a bloody
  breakfast.—
But I lose time.
Pier.   I'll to my charge. *Exit Pierio.*
Gonz.   And we
To ours. I'll bring you on.
Jac.   If we come off,
It is not amiss; if not, my state is set-
  tled.   *Exeunt. Alarm.*

Act II. Scene iv.

[The citadel of Siena.]

Ferdinand, Druso, Livio, above.[5]

Fer. No aids from Sicily? Hath hope
  forsook us,
And that vain comfort to affliction, pity,
By our vowed friend denied us? We
  can nor live
Nor die with honor. Like beasts in a
  toil,
We wait the leisure of the bloody hunter,
Who is not so far reconciled unto us,
As in one death to give a period
To our calamities; but in delaying
The fate we cannot fly from, starved
  with wants,   9
We die this night to live again tomorrow
And suffer greater torments.
Dru.   There is not
Three days' provision for every soldier,
At an ounce of bread a day, left in the
  city.
Liv. To die the beggar's death, with
  hunger made

[3] Foot soldiers.
[4] Cavalry.   [5] *I.e.*, on the walls.

Anatomies [1] while we live, cannot but
crack
Our heartstrings with vexation.

FER.   Would they would break,
Break altogether! How willingly, like
Cato,
Could I tear out my bowels rather than
Look on the conqueror's insulting face,
But that religion and the horrid dream
To be suffered in the other world de-
nies it!   21

Enter Soldier.

What news with thee?

SOLD.   From the turret of the fort,
By the rising clouds of dust, through
which, like lightning,
The splendor of bright arms sometimes
brake through,
I did descry some forces making towards
us;
And from the camp, as emulous of their
glory,
The general (for I know him by his
horse),
And bravely seconded, encountered 'em.
Their greetings were too rough for
friends, their swords
And not their tongues exchanging cour-
tesies.   30
By this the main battalias are joined,
And, if you please to be spectators of
The horrid issue, I will bring you where
As in a theater you may see their fates
In purple gore presented.

FER.   Heaven, if yet
Thou art appeased for my wrong done
to Aurelia,
Take pity of my miseries!—Lead the
way, friend.   [*Exeunt.*]

ACT II. SCENE V.

[*A plain near the walls.*]

*A long charge; after, a flourish for victory.
Gonzaga; Jacomo; Roderigo, wounded.
Bertoldo, Gasparo, Anthonio prisoners.*
     [*Officers and Soldiers.*]

GONZ. We have 'em yet, though they
cost us dear. This was
Charged home, and bravely followed.
(*To Jacomo and Roderigo.*) Be to
yourselves

True mirrors to each other's worth; and,
looking
With noble emulation on his [2] wounds,
The glorious livery of triumphant war,
Imagine these with equal grace appear
Upon yourself. [3] The bloody sweat you
have suffered
In this laborious, nay, toilsome harvest,
Yields a rich crop of conquest; and the
spoil,
Most precious balsam to a soldier's
hurts,   10
Will ease and cure 'em. Let me look
upon
The prisoners' faces.—(*To Gasparo and
Anthon[io].*) O, how much transformed
From what they were! O Mars! Were
these toys fashioned
To undergo the burthen of thy service?
The weight of their defensive armor
bruised
Their weak, effeminate limbs, and
would have forced 'em
In a hot day without a blow to yield.

ANT. This insultation [4] shows not manly
in you.

GONZ. To men I had forborne it; you are
women,
Or, at the best, loose carpet knights. [5]
What fury   20
Seduced you to exchange your ease in
court
For labor in the field? Perhaps you
thought
To charge through dust and blood an
arméd foe
Was but like graceful running at the
ring [6]
For a wanton mistress' glove, and the
encounter
A soft impression on her lips. But you
Are gaudy butterflies, and I wrong my-
self
In parling [7] with you.

GASP.   Væ victis! [8] Now we prove
it.

ROD. But here's one fashioned in another
mold,

---

[1] Skeletons.

[2] *I.e.*, Roderigo's.   [3] *I.e.*, Jacomo.
[4] Scornful exultation.
[5] Knights who have been created in court, not
on the battlefield.
[6] One of the favorite sports at a tournament.
[7] Parleying, speaking.
[8] Woe to the vanquished!

The brother of your king, whose worth
  disdains
Comparison with such as these, in irons?
If ransom may redeem them, I have
  lands,
A patrimony of mine own, assigned me
By my deceaséd sire, to satisfy
Whate'er can be demanded for my
  freedom.
AST. I wish you had, sir; but the king,
  who yields
No reason for his will, in his displeasure
Hath seized on all you had; nor will
  Gonzaga,   160
Whose prisoner now you are, accept of
  less
Than fifty thousand crowns.
BERT.   I find it now
That misery ne'er comes alone. But,
  grant
The king is yet inexorable, time
May work him to a feeling of my suffer-
  ings.
I have friends that swore their lives and
  fortunes were
At my devotion—and among the rest
Yourself, my lord, when, forfeited to the
  law
For a foul murther, and in cold blood
  done,
I made your life my gift, and reconciled
  you   170
To this incenséd king and got your par-
  don.
Beware ingratitude. I know you are rich,
And may pay down the sum.
AST.   I might, my lord;
But pardon me.
BERT.   And will Astutio prove then
(To please a passionate man—the king's
  no more)
False to his maker and his reason,
  which
Commands more than I ask? O summer
  friendship,
Whose flattering leaves, that shadowed
  us in our
Prosperity, with the least gust drop off
In th' autumn of adversity! How   180
  like
A prison is to a grave! When dead, we
  are
With solemn pomp brought thither, and
  our heirs.

Masking their joy in false, dissembled
  tears,
Weep o'er the hearse; but earth no
  sooner covers
The earth brought thither, but they turn
  away
With inward smiles, the dead no more
  remembered.
So, entered in a prison—
AST.   My occasions
Command me hence, my lord.
BERT.   Pray you, leave me, do;
And tell the cruel king that I will wear
These fetters till my flesh and they are
  one   190
Incorporated substance. In myself,
As in a glass, I'll look on human frailty,
And curse the height of royal blood,
  since I,
In being born near to Jove, am near his
  thunder.
Cedars once shaken with a storm, their
  own   *Exit Astutio.*
Weight grubs their roots out.—Lead me
  where you please;
I am his, not fortune's, martyr, and will
  die
The great example of his cruelty.
                           Exit cum suis.[1]

Act III. Scene ii.

[A grove near the palace near Palermo.]

Adorni.

ADOR. He undergoes my challenge and
  contemns it,
And threatens me with the late edict
  made
Gainst duelists—the [2] altar cowards fly to.
But I, that am engaged, and nourish in
  me
A higher aim than fair Camiola dreams
  of,
Must not sit down thus. In the court I
  dare not
Attempt him; and in public he's so
  guarded
With a herd of parasites, clients, fools,
  and suitors
That a musket cannot reach him. My
  designs

---

[1] With his attendants.
[2] Suggested by Davies. Original reads *then.*

Admit of no delay. This is her birth-
  day,   10
Which, with a fit and due solemnity,
Camiola celebrates; and on it all such
As love or serve her usually present
A tributary duty. I'll have something
To give, if my intelligence prove true,
Shall find acceptance. I am told, near
  this grove
Fulgentio every morning makes his
  markets [1]
With his petitioners; I may present him
With a sharp petition!—Ha, 'tis he!
  My fate
Be ever blessed for 't!   [Retires.]

Enter [2] Fulgen[tio and Page].

FUL.   Command such as wait me 20
  Not to presume, at the least for half an
    hour,
To press on my retirements.
PAGE.   I will say, sir,
  You are at your prayers.
FUL.   That will not find belief;
  Courtiers have something else to do.
  Begone, sir.—   [Exit Page.]
Challenged! 'Tis well! And by a groom!
  Still better!
Was this shape made to fight? I have a
  tongue yet,
Howe'er no sword, to kill him; and what
  way
This morning I'll resolve of.
               Exit Fulgentio.
ADOR.   I shall cross
  Your resolution, or suffer for you.
               Exit Adorni.

Act III. Scene iii.

[A room in Camiola's house.]

*Camiola, divers Servants with presents,
Sylli, Clarinda.*

SYL. What are all these?
CLAR.   Servants with several presents,
  And rich ones too.
1 SERV.   With her best wishes, madam,
  Of many such days to you, the Lady
    Petula
Presents you with this fan.
2 SERV.   This diamond
  From your aunt Honoria.

[1] Dealings.   [2] Original reads *Exit.*

3 SERV.   This piece of plate
  From your uncle, old Vincentio, with
    your arms
Graven upon it.
CAM.   Good friends they are too—
  Munificent in their love and favor to
    me.—
  [To Clarinda.] Out of my cabinet return
    such jewels   9
As this directs you.—[Gives Servants
    money.] For your pains; and yours;
Nor must you be forgotten.   Honor
    me
With the drinking of a health.
1 SERV.   Gold, on my life!
2 SERV. She scorns to give base silver.
3 SERV.   Would she had been
  Born every month in the year!
1 SERV.   Month? Every day.
2 SERV. Show such another maid.
3 [SERV.]   All happiness wait you!
SYLLI. I'll see your will done.
      Exeunt Sylli, Clarinda, Servants.

Enter Adorni, wounded.

CAM.   How, Adorni wounded?
ADOR. A scratch got in your service, else
    not worth
Your observation. I bring not, madam,
In honor of your birthday, antique plate
Or pearl for which the savage Indian
    dives   20
Into the bottom of the sea, nor diamonds
Hewn from steep rocks with danger.
    Such as give
To those that have what they themselves
    want, aim at
A glad return with profit. Yet despise
    not
My offering at the altar of your favor,
Nor let the lowness of the giver lessen
The height of what's presented, since it is
A precious jewel, almost forfeited,
And dimmed with clouds of infamy,
    redeemed
And in its natural splendor, with addi-
    tion,   30
Restored to the true owner.
CAM.   How is this?
ADOR. Not to hold you in suspense, I
  bring you, madam,
Your wounded reputation cured, the
    sting

The brother of your king, whose worth disdains
Comparison with such as these, in irons?
If ransom may redeem them, I have lands,
A patrimony of mine own, assigned me
By my deceaséd sire, to satisfy
Whate'er can be demanded for my freedom.

Ast. I wish you had, sir; but the king, who yields
No reason for his will, in his displeasure
Hath seized on all you had; nor will Gonzaga,　　　　　160
Whose prisoner now you are, accept of less
Than fifty thousand crowns.

Bert.　　　　　I find it now
That misery ne'er comes alone. But, grant
The king is yet inexorable, time
May work him to a feeling of my suffer-
ings.
I have friends that swore their lives and fortunes were
At my devotion—and among the rest
Yourself, my lord, when, forfeited to the law
For a foul murther, and in cold blood done,
I made your life my gift, and reconciled you　　　　　170
To this incenséd king and got your par-
don.
Beware ingratitude. I know you are rich,
And may pay down the sum.

Ast.　　　　　I might, my lord;
But pardon me.

Bert.　　　　　And will Astutio prove then
(To please a passionate man—the king's no more)
False to his maker and his reason, which
Commands more than I ask? O summer friendship,
Whose flattering leaves, that shadowed us in our
Prosperity, with the least gust drop off
In th' autumn of adversity! How　　　180
like
A prison is to a grave! When dead, we are
With solemn pomp brought thither, and our heirs.

Masking their joy in false, dissembled tears,
Weep o'er the hearse; but earth no sooner covers
The earth brought thither, but they turn away
With inward smiles, the dead no more remembered.
So, entered in a prison—

Ast.　　　　　My occasions
Command me hence, my lord.

Bert.　　　　　Pray you, leave me, do;
And tell the cruel king that I will wear
These fetters till my flesh and they are one　　　　　190
Incorporated substance. In myself,
As in a glass, I'll look on human frailty,
And curse the height of royal blood, since I,
In being born near to Jove, am near his thunder.
Cedars once shaken with a storm, their own　　　　　*Exit Astutio.*
Weight grubs their roots out.—Lead me where you please;
I am his, not fortune's, martyr, and will die
The great example of his cruelty.

　　　　　　　　　　Exit cum suis.[1]

Act III. Scene ii.

[*A grove near the palace near Palermo.*]

Adorni.

Ador. He undergoes my challenge and contemns it,
And threatens me with the late edict made
Gainst duelists—the [2] altar cowards fly to.
But I, that am engaged, and nourish in me
A higher aim than fair Camiola dreams of,
Must not sit down thus. In the court I dare not
Attempt him; and in public he's so guarded
With a herd of parasites, clients, fools, and suitors
That a musket cannot reach him. My designs

[1] With his attendants.
[2] Suggested by Davies. Original reads *then.*

Admit of no delay. This is her birth-
day,   10
Which, with a fit and due solemnity,
Camiola celebrates; and on it all such
As love or serve her usually present
A tributary duty. I'll have something
To give, if my intelligence prove true,
Shall find acceptance. I am told, near
    this grove
Fulgentio every morning makes his
    markets [1]
With his petitioners; I may present him
With a sharp petition!—Ha, 'tis he!
    My fate
Be ever blessed for 't!   [Retires.]

Enter [2] Fulgen[tio and Page].

FUL.   Command such as wait me   20
Not to presume, at the least for half an
    hour,
To press on my retirements.
PAGE.   I will say, sir,
You are at your prayers.
FUL.   That will not find belief;
Courtiers have something else to do.
    Begone, sir.—   [Exit Page.]
Challenged! 'Tis well! And by a groom!
    Still better!
Was this shape made to fight? I have a
    tongue yet,
Howe'er no sword, to kill him; and what
    way
This morning I'll resolve of.
                            Exit Fulgentio.
ADOR.   I shall cross
Your resolution, or suffer for you.
                            Exit Adorni.

ACT III. SCENE iii.

[A room in Camiola's house.]

*Camiola, divers Servants with presents,
        Sylli, Clarinda.*

SYL. What are all these?
CLAR.   Servants with several presents,
And rich ones too.
1 SERV.   With her best wishes, madam,
Of many such days to you, the Lady
    Petula
Presents you with this fan.
2 SERV.   This diamond
From your aunt Honoria.

---

[1] Dealings.   [2] Original reads *Exit.*

3 SERV.   This piece of plate
From your uncle, old Vincentio, with
    your arms
Graven upon it.
CAM.   Good friends they are too—
Munificent in their love and favor to
    me.—
[To Clarinda.] Out of my cabinet return
    such jewels   9
As this directs you.—[Gives Servants
    money.] For your pains; and yours;
Nor must you be forgotten. Honor
    me
With the drinking of a health.
1 SERV.   Gold, on my life!
2 SERV. She scorns to give base silver.
3 SERV.   Would she had been
Born every month in the year!
1 SERV.   Month? Every day.
2 SERV. Show such another maid.
3 [SERV.]   All happiness wait you!
SYLLI. I'll see your will done.
            Exeunt Sylli, Clarinda, Servants.

Enter Adorni, wounded.

CAM.   How, Adorni wounded?
ADOR. A scratch got in your service, else
    not worth
Your observation. I bring not, madam,
In honor of your birthday, antique plate
Or pearl for which the savage Indian
    dives   20
Into the bottom of the sea, nor diamonds
Hewn from steep rocks with danger.
    Such as give
To those that have what they themselves
    want, aim at
A glad return with profit. Yet despise
    not
My offering at the altar of your favor,
Nor let the lowness of the giver lessen
The height of what's presented, since it is
A precious jewel, almost forfeited,
And dimmed with clouds of infamy,
    redeemed
And in its natural splendor, with addi-
    tion,   30
Restored to the true owner.
CAM.   How is this?
ADOR. Not to hold you in suspense, I
    bring you, madam,
Your wounded reputation cured, the
    sting

Of virulent malice, festering your fair
name,
Plucked out and trod on. That proud
man, that was
Denied the honor of your bed, yet durst
With his untrue reports strumpet your
fame,
Compelled by me, hath given himself the
lie,
And in his own blood wrote it. [*Gives her
a paper.*] You may read
"Fulgentio" subscribed.
CAM.   I am amazed! 40
ADOR. It does deserve it, madam. Com-
mon service
Is fit for hinds, and the reward propor-
tioned
To their conditions. Therefore, look not
on me
As a follower of your father's fortunes, or
One that subsists on yours. You frown!
My service
Merits not this aspect.
CAM.   Which of my favors,
I might say bounties, hath begot and
nourished
This more than rude presumption?
Since you had
An itch to try your desperate valor,
wherefore
Went you not to the war? Couldst thou
suppose   50
My innocence could ever fall so low
As to have need of thy rash sword to
guard it
Against malicious slander? O, how much
Those ladies are deceived and cheated
when
The clearness and integrity of their
actions
Do not defend themselves, and stand
secure
On their own bases! Such as in a color [1]
Of seeming service give protection to 'em,
Betray their own strengths. Malice
scorned puts out   59
Itself, but argued gives a kind of credit
To a false accusation. In this, this your
Most memorable service, you believed
You did me right; but you have wronged
me more
In your defense of my undoubted honor
Than false Fulgentio could.

[1] Pretense.

ADOR.   I am sorry what was
So well intended is so ill received;
Yet, under your correction, you wished

Ente[r] Clarinda.

Bertoldo had been present.
CAM.   True, I did.
But he and you, sir, are not parallels,
Nor must you think yourself so.
ADOR.   I am what 70
You'll please to have me.
CAM.   If Bertoldo had
Punished Fulgentio's insolence, it had
shown
His love to her whom in his judgment he
Vouchsafed to make his wife—a height,
I hope,
Which you dare not aspire to. The same
actions
Suit not all men alike. But I perceive
Repentance in your looks. For this time,
leave me;
I may forgive, perhaps forget, your
folly.
Conceal yourself till this storm be blown
over.
You will be sought for, yet, for my
estate [2]   80
Can hinder it, shall not suffer in my
service.   *Gives him her hand to kiss.*
ADOR. [*Aside.*] This is something yet,
though I missed the mark I shot at.
                         Exit Adorni.
CAM. This gentleman is of a noble temper,
And I too harsh, perhaps, in my reproof.
Was I not, Clarinda?
CLAR.   I am not to censure [3]
Your actions, madam; but there are a
thousand
Ladies, and of good fame, in such a cause
Would be proud of such a servant.
CAM.   It may be.

Enter a Servant.

Let me offend in this kind.—Why,
uncalled for?
SERV. The signiors, madam, Gasparo and
Anthonio,   90
Selected friends of the renowned Ber-
toldo,
Put ashore this morning.
CAM.   Without him?

[2] Rank, position.   [3] Judge.

SERV. I think so.

CAM.   Never think more then.

SERV.   They have been at court,
Kissed the king's hand, and, their first
    duties done
To him, appear ambitious [1] to tender
To you their second service.

CAM.   Wait 'em hither. *Exit* [2] *Servant.*
Fear, do not rack me! Reason, now if
    ever,
Haste with thy aids and tell me such a
    wonder
As my Bertoldo is, with such care
    fashioned,
Must not, nay, cannot, in heaven's
    providence   100

Enter Anthonio, Gasparo, Serv[ant].

So soon miscarry!—Pray you, forbear;
    ere you
Take the privilege, as strangers, to
    salute me—
Excuse my manners—make me first
    understand
How it is with Bertoldo.

GASP. [3]   The relation
Will not, I fear, deserve your thanks.

ANT.   I wish
Some other should inform you.

CAM.   Is he dead?
You see, though with some fear, I dare
    inquire it.

GASP. Dead! Would that were the worst;
    a debt were paid then
Kings in their birth owe nature.

CAM.   Is there aught
More terrible than death?

ANT.   Yes, to a spirit   110
Like his: cruel imprisonment, and that
Without the hope of freedom.

CAM.   You abuse me.
The royal king cannot, in love to virtue,
Though all springs of affection were dried
    up,
But pay his ransom.

GASP.   When you know what 'tis,
You will think otherwise. No less will do
    it
Than fifty thousand crowns.

---

[1] Emended by Gifford. Original reads *am-bitions.*

[2] Original reads *Exeunt.*

[3] Original reads *Ber.*

CAM.   A pretty sum,
The price weighed with the purchase!
    Fifty thousand?
To the king 'tis nothing. He that can
    spare more
To his minion for a masque cannot but
    ransom   120
Such a brother at a million. You wrong
The king's magnificence.

ANT.   In your opinion;
But 'tis most certain. He does not alone
In himself refuse to pay it, but forbids
All other men.

CAM.   Are you sure of this?

GASP.   You may read
The edict to that purpose, published by
    him;
That will resolve you.

CAM.   Possible! Pray you, stand off.
If I do not mutter treason to myself,
My heart will break. Yet I will not curse
    him;
He is my king. The news you have de-
    livered   130
Makes me weary of your company; we'll
    salute
When we meet next. I'll bring you to the
    door.
Nay, pray you, no more compliments.

GASP.   One thing more,
And that's substantial: let your Adorni
Look to himself.

ANT.   The king is much incensed
Against him for Fulgentio.

CAM.   As I am,
For your slowness to depart.

BOTH.   Farewell, sweet lady.
    Exeunt Gaspa[ro], Antho[nio].

CAM. O more than impious times, when
    not alone
Subordinate ministers of justice are
Corrupted and seduced, but kings them-
    selves,   140
The greater wheels by which the lesser
    move,
Are broken or disjointed! Could it be,
    else,
A king, to soothe his politic ends, should
    so far
Forsake his honor as at once to break
Th' adamant chains of nature and
    religion
To bind up atheism [4] as a defense

---

[4] Godlessness, dishonor.

Ministered to me in a form more dread-
　　ful;
Set heaven and hell before me, I will take
　　'em.
False to Camiola? Never.—Shall I now
Begin my vows to you?
ADOR.　　　　　I am no churchman; 100
Such a one must file it on record. You
　　are free;
And, that you may appear like to your-
　　self,
For so she wished, there's [1] gold, with
　　which you may
Redeem your trunks and servants, and
　　whatever
Of late you lost. I have found out the
　　captain
Whose spoil they were; his name is Ro-
　　derigo.
BERT. I know him.
ADOR.　　　　　I have done my parts.
BERT.　　　　　　　　So much, sir,
As I am ever yours for 't. Now, me-
　　thinks,
I walk in air! Divine Camiola—
But words cannot express thee. I'll build
　　to thee　　　　　　　　　　110
An altar in my soul, on which I'll offer
A still-increasing sacrifice of duty.
　　　　　　　　　　　Exit Ber[toldo].
ADOR. What will become of me now is
　　apparent.
Whether a poniard or a halter be
The nearest way to hell (for I must
　　thither
After I have killed myself) is somewhat
　　doubtful.
This Roman resolution of self-murther
Will not hold water at the high tribunal
When it comes to be argued; my good
　　genius　　　　　　　　　　119
Prompts me to this consideration. He
That kills himself to avoid misery fears
　　it,
And, at the best, shows but a bastard
　　valor.
This life's a fort committed to my trust,
Which I must not yield up till it be
　　forced.
Nor will I. He's not valiant that dares
　　die,
But he that boldly bears calamity. *Exit.*

[1] Emended by Bryne. Different copies of the
quarto read *thee's* or *hee's*.

ACT IV. SCENE iv.

[The council chamber in the palace at Siena.]

*A flourish. Pierio, Roderigo, Jacomo, Gon-
　zaga, Aurelia, Ferdinand, Astutio,
　　　　　　　　　　　　Attendants.*

AUR. A seat here for the duke! It is our
　　glory
To overcome with courtesies, not rigor.
The lordly Roman, who held it the
　　height
Of human happiness to have kings and
　　queens
To wait by his triumphant chariot
　　wheels,
In his insulting pride, deprived himself
Of drawing near the nature of the gods,
Best known for such, in being merciful.
Yet give me leave, but still with gentle
　　language
And with the freedom of a friend, to
　　tell you　　　　　　　　　　10
To seek by force what courtship could
　　not win
Was harsh [2] and never taught in Love's
　　mild school.
Wise poets feign that Venus' coach is
　　drawn
By doves and sparrows, not by bears and
　　tigers.
I spare the application.
FER.　　　　　　　In my fortune,
Heaven's justice hath confirmed it; yet,
　　great lady,
Since my offense grew from excess of love,
And [3] not to be resisted, having paid too
With the loss of liberty the forfeiture
Of my presumption, in your clemency 20
It may find pardon.
AUR.　　　　　You shall have just cause
To say it hath. The charge of the long
　　siege
Defrayed, and the loss my subjects have
　　sustained
Made good, since so far I must deal with
　　caution,
You have your liberty.
FER.　　　　　　I could not hope for
Gentler conditions.
AUR.　　　　　　My Lord Gonzaga,

[2] Emended by Gifford. Original reads *not
harsh.*
[3] *I.e.,* and a love, etc.

Since my coming to Siena, I have heard
much
Of your prisoner, brave Bertoldo.

GONZ.   Such an one,
Madam, I had.

AST.   And have still, sir, I hope.

GONZ. Your hopes deceive you. He is ransomed, madam.   30

AST. By whom, I pray you, sir?

GONZ.   You had best inquire
Of your intelligencer. I am no informer.

AST. [*Aside.*] I like not this.

AUR.   He is, as 'tis reported,
A goodly gentleman, and of noble parts—
A brother of your order.

GONZ.   He was, madam,
Till he against his oath wronged you, a
princess,
Which his religion bound him from.

AUR.   Great minds
For trial of their valors oft maintain
Quarrels that are unjust, yet without
malice;
And such a fair construction I make of
him.   40
I would see that brave enemy.

GONZ.   My duty
Commands me to seek for him.

AUR.   Pray you, do,
And bring him to our presence.
                              Exit Gonzaga.

AST. [*Aside.*]   I must blast
His entertainment.—May it please your
excellency,
He is a man debauched, and, for his riots,
Cast off by the king my master; and that,
I hope, is
A crime sufficient.

FER.   To you, his subjects,
That like as your king likes.

*Enter Gonzaga, Bertoldo, richly habited;
                              Adorni.*

AUR.   But not to us;
We must weigh with our own scale.—
[*Aside.*] This is he, sure.
How soon mine eye had found him!
What a port   50
He bears! How well his bravery [1] be-
comes him!
A prisoner, nay, a princely suitor, rather!
But I am too sudden.

[1] Fine clothes.

GONZ.   Madam, 'twas his suit,
Unsent for, to present his service to you
Ere his departure.

AUR. [*Aside.*]   With what majesty
He bears himself!

AST.   The devil, I think, supplies him.
Ransomed, and thus rich too!
          Bertoldo,[2] kneeling, kisses her hand.

AUR.   You ill deserve
The favor of our hand—(We are not well;
Give us more air.)
                              She descends suddenly.

GONZ.   What sudden qualm is this?

AUR.—That lifted yours against me.

BERT. [*Kissing her hand.*]   Thus
once more   60
I sue for pardon.

AUR. (*Aside.*)   Sure his lips are poisoned
And through these veins force passage to
my heart,
Which is already seized upon.

BERT.   I wait, madam,
To know what your commands are; my
designs
Exact me in another place.

AUR.   Before
You have our license to depart? If man-
ners,
Civility of manners, cannot teach you
T' attend our leisure, I must tell you, sir,
That you are still our prisoner—[*To
Gonzaga.*] nor had you
Commission to free him.

GONZ.   How's this, madam?   70

AUR. You were my substitute and wanted
power
Without my warrant to dispose of him.
I will pay back his ransom ten times over
Rather than quit my interest.

BERT.   This is
Against the law of arms.

AUR. (*Aside.*)   But not of love.—
Why, hath your entertainment, sir, been
such,
In your restraint, that with the wings of
fear
You would fly from it?

BERT.   I know no man, madam,
Enamored of his fetters, or delighting
In cold or hunger, or that would in
reason   80
Prefer straw in a dungeon before
A down bed in a palace.

[2] Original reads *Ferdinand.*

Ministered to me in a form more dread-
ful;
Set heaven and hell before me, I will take
'em.
False to Camiola? Never.—Shall I now
Begin my vows to you?

ADOR. 　　　I am no churchman; 100
Such a one must file it on record. You
are free;
And, that you may appear like to yourself,
For so she wished, there's [1] gold, with
which you may
Redeem your trunks and servants, and
whatever
Of late you lost. I have found out the
captain
Whose spoil they were; his name is Roderigo.

BERT. I know him.

ADOR. 　　　I have done my parts.

BERT. 　　　　　So much, sir,
As I am ever yours for 't. Now, me-
thinks,
I walk in air! Divine Camiola—
But words cannot express thee. I'll build
to thee 　　　　　110
An altar in my soul, on which I'll offer
A still-increasing sacrifice of duty.
　　　　　　　Exit Ber[toldo].

ADOR. What will become of me now is
apparent.
Whether a poniard or a halter be
The nearest way to hell (for I must
thither
After I have killed myself) is somewhat
doubtful.
This Roman resolution of self-murther
Will not hold water at the high tribunal
When it comes to be argued; my good
genius 　　　　　119
Prompts me to this consideration. He
That kills himself to avoid misery fears
it,
And, at the best, shows but a bastard
valor.
This life's a fort committed to my trust,
Which I must not yield up till it be
forced.
Nor will I. He's not valiant that dares
die,
But he that boldly bears calamity. Exit.

----

[1] Emended by Bryne. Different copies of the
quarto read thee's or hee's.

ACT IV. SCENE iv.

[The council chamber in the palace at Siena.]

A flourish. Pierio, Roderigo, Jacomo, Gon-
　　zaga, Aurelia, Ferdinand, Astutio,
　　　　　　　　　　　　Attendants.

AUR. A seat here for the duke! It is our
glory
To overcome with courtesies, not rigor.
The lordly Roman, who held it the
height
Of human happiness to have kings and
queens
To wait by his triumphant chariot
wheels,
In his insulting pride, deprived himself
Of drawing near the nature of the gods,
Best known for such, in being merciful.
Yet give me leave, but still with gentle
language
And with the freedom of a friend, to
tell you 　　　　　10
To seek by force what courtship could
not win
Was harsh [2] and never taught in Love's
mild school.
Wise poets feign that Venus' coach is
drawn
By doves and sparrows, not by bears and
tigers.
I spare the application.

FER. 　　　　　In my fortune,
Heaven's justice hath confirmed it; yet,
great lady,
Since my offense grew from excess of love,
And [3] not to be resisted, having paid too
With the loss of liberty the forfeiture
Of my presumption, in your clemency 20
It may find pardon.

AUR. 　　　You shall have just cause
To say it hath. The charge of the long
siege
Defrayed, and the loss my subjects have
sustained
Made good, since so far I must deal with
caution,
You have your liberty.

FER. 　　　　I could not hope for
Gentler conditions.

AUR. 　　　　　My Lord Gonzaga,

----

[2] Emended by Gifford. Original reads not
harsh.

[3] I.e., and a love, etc.

Since my coming to Siena, I have heard
  much
Of your prisoner, brave Bertoldo.
GONZ.   Such an one,
Madam, I had.
AST.   And have still, sir, I hope.
GONZ. Your hopes deceive you. He is ran-
  somed, madam.   30
AST. By whom, I pray you, sir?
GONZ.   You had best inquire
Of your intelligencer. I am no informer.
AST. [*Aside.*] I like not this.
AUR.   He is, as 'tis reported,
A goodly gentleman, and of noble parts—
A brother of your order.
GONZ.   He was, madam,
Till he against his oath wronged you, a
  princess,
Which his religion bound him from.
AUR.   Great minds
For trial of their valors oft maintain
Quarrels that are unjust, yet without
  malice;
And such a fair construction I make of
  him.   40
I would see that brave enemy.
GONZ.   My duty
Commands me to seek for him.
AUR.   Pray you, do,
And bring him to our presence.
                      Exit Gonzaga.
AST. [*Aside.*]   I must blast
His entertainment.—May it please your
  excellency,
He is a man debauched, and, for his riots,
Cast off by the king my master; and that,
  I hope, is
A crime sufficient.
FER.   To you, his subjects,
That like as your king likes.

Enter Gonzaga, Bertoldo, richly habited;
           Adorni.

AUR.   But not to us!
We must weigh with our own scale.—
  [*Aside.*] This is he, sure.
How soon mine eye had found him!
  What a port   50
He bears! How well his bravery [1] be-
  comes him!
A prisoner, nay, a princely suitor, rather!
But I am too sudden.

[1] Fine clothes.

GONZ.   Madam, 'twas his suit,
Unsent for, to present his service to you
Ere his departure.
AUR. [*Aside.*]   With what majesty
He bears himself!
AST.   The devil, I think, supplies him.
Ransomed, and thus rich too!
     Bertoldo,[2] kneeling, kisses her hand.
AUR.   You ill deserve
The favor of our hand—(We are not well;
Give us more air.)
             She descends suddenly.
GONZ.   What sudden qualm is this?
AUR.—That lifted yours against me.
BERT. [*Kissing her hand.*]   Thus
  once more   60
I sue for pardon.
AUR. (*Aside.*)   Sure his lips are poisoned
And through these veins force passage to
  my heart,
Which is already seized upon.
BERT.   I wait, madam,
To know what your commands are; my
  designs
Exact me in another place.
AUR.   Before
You have our license to depart? If man-
  ners,
Civility of manners, cannot teach you
T' attend our leisure, I must tell you, sir,
That you are still our prisoner—[*To
Gonzaga.*] nor had you
Commission to free him.
GONZ.   How's this, madam?   70
AUR. You were my substitute and wanted
  power
Without my warrant to dispose of him.
I will pay back his ransom ten times over
Rather than quit my interest.
BERT.   This is
Against the law of arms.
AUR. (*Aside.*)   But not of love.—
Why, hath your entertainment, sir, been
  such,
In your restraint, that with the wings of
  fear
You would fly from it?
BERT.   I know no man, madam,
Enamored of his fetters, or delighting
In cold or hunger, or that would in
  reason   80
Prefer straw in a dungeon before
A down bed in a palace.

[2] Original reads *Ferdinand.*

AUR.   How!—[*To Gonzaga.*] Come
nearer.
   Was his usage such?
GONZ.   Yes; and it had been worse
Had I foreseen this.
AUR.   O thou misshaped monster!
In thee it is confirmed that such as
     have
No share in nature's bounties know no
     pity
To such as have 'em. Look on him with
     my eyes,
And answer, then, whether this were a
     man
Whose cheeks of lovely fullness should
     be made   89
A prey to meager famine? Or these eyes,
Whose every glance store Cupid's emp-
     tied quiver,
To be dimmed with tedious watching?
     Or these lips,
These ruddy lips, of whose fresh color
     cherries
And roses were but copies, should grow
     pale
For want of nectar? Or these legs, that
     bear
A burthen of more worth than is sup-
     ported
By Atlas' wearied shoulders, should be
     cramped
With the weight of iron? O, I could
     dwell ever
On this description!
BERT.   Is this in derision
   Or pity of me?
AUR.   In your charity   100
Believe me innocent. Now you are my
     prisoner,
You shall have fairer quarter. You will
     shame
The place where you have been, should
     you now leave it
Before you are recovered. I'll conduct
     you
To more convenient lodgings, and it shall
     be
My care to cherish you. Repine who
     dare;
It is our will. You'll follow me?
BERT.   To the center,
   Such a Sybilla guiding me.
Exeunt Aurelia, Bertoldo [, and Attendants].
GONZ.   Who speaks first?

FER. We stand as we had seen Medusa's
     head.   *All amazed.*
PIER. I know not what to think, I am so
     amazed.   110
ROD. Amazed! I am thunderstrook.
JAC.   We are enchanted,
   And this is some illusion.
ADOR. [*Aside.*]   Heaven forbid!
   In dark despair it shows a beam of hope.
   Contain thy joy, Adorni.
AST.   Such a princess,
And of so long-experienced reservedness,
Break forth, and on the sudden, into
     flashes
Of more than doubted [1] looseness!

[*Enter Aurelia and Bertoldo.*]

GONZ. [*Aside.*]   They come again,
   Smiling, as I live, his arm circling her
     waist!
I shall run mad. Some fury hath pos-
     sessed her.
If I speak, I may be blasted. Ha! I'll
     mumble   120
A prayer or two, and cross myself, and
     then,
Though the devil fart fire, have at him.
AUR.   Let not, sir,
   The violence of my passions nourish in
     you
An ill opinion; or, grant my carriage
Out of the road and garb of private
     women,
'Tis still done with decorum. As I am
A princess, what I do is above censure,
And to be imitated.
BERT.   Gracious madam,   128
Vouchsafe a little pause, for I am so rapt
Beyond myself that, till I have collected
My scattered faculties, I cannot tender
My resolution.
AUR.   Consider of it.
   I will not be long from you.
         Bertoldo walking by, musing.
GONZ. [*Aside.*]   Pray I cannot!
This cursèd object strangles my devotion.
I must speak, or I burst.—Pray you, fair
     lady,
If you can, in courtesy direct me to
The chaste Aurelia.
AUR.   Are you blind? Who are we?
GONZ. Another kind of thing. Her blood
     was governed

   [1] Suspected.

By her discretion, and not ruled her
reason.

The reverence and majesty of Juno 140
Shined in her looks, and, coming to the
camp,
Appeared a second Pallas. I can see
No such divinities in you. If I
Without offense may speak my thoughts,
you are,
As it were, a wanton Helen.

AUR.   Good! Ere long
You shall know me better.

GONZ.   Why, if you are Aurelia,
How shall I dispose of the soldier?

AST.   May it please you
To hasten my despatch?

AUR.   Prefer your suits
Unto Bertoldo; we will give him hearing,
And you'll find him your best advocate.
                     Exit Aurelia.

AST.   This is rare! 150
GONZ. What are we come to?

ROD.   Grown up in a moment
A favorite!

FERD.   He does take state already.

BERT. [*Aside.*] No, no, it cannot be. Yet
but [1] Camiola
There is no step between me and a crown.
Then my ingratitude—a sin in which
All sins are comprehended! Aid me,
virtue,
Or I am lost.

GONZ.   May it please your excellence—
Second me, sir.

BERT. [*Aside.*] Then my so horrid
oaths,
And hell-deep imprecations made against
it!

AST. The king, your brother, will thank
you for th' advancement   160
Of his affairs.

BERT. [*Aside.*] And yet who can hold
out
Against such batteries as her power and
greatness
Raise up against my weak defenses!

GONZ.   Sir,

Enter Aurelia.

Do you dream, waking?—'Slight,[2] she's
here again!

[1] Except for.
[2] By God's light, a mild oath.

BERT. Walks she on woolen feet!

AUR.   You dwell too long
In your deliberation, and come
With a cripple's pace to that which you
should fly to.

BERT. It is confessed. Yet why should I,
to win
From you that hazard all to my poor
nothing,
By false play send you off a loser from
me?   170
I am already too-too much engaged
To the king my brother's anger; and who
knows
But that his doubts and politic fears,
should you
Make me his equal, may draw war
upon
Your territories? Were that breach made
up,
I should with joy embrace what now I
fear
To touch but with due reverence.

AUR.   That hinderance
Is easily removed. I owe the king
For a royal visit, which I straight will
pay him;
And, having first reconciled you to his
favor,   180
A dispensation shall meet with us.

BERT. I am wholly yours.

AUR.   On this book seal it.

GONZ. [*Aside.*] What, hand and lip too!
Then the bargain's sure.—
You have no employment for me?

AUR.   Yes, Gonzaga;
Provide a royal ship.

GONZ.   A ship? Saint John,
Whither are we bound now?

AUR.   You shall know hereafter.
My lord, your pardon for my too much
trenching
Upon your patience.

ADOR. (*Whispers to Bertoldo.*) Camiola!

AUR. How do you?

BERT.   Indisposed; but I attend you.
                     Exeunt [All but Adorni].

ADOR. The heavy curse that waits on perjury   190
And foul ingratitude pursue thee ever!
Yet why from me this? In this breach of
faith
My loyalty finds reward! What poisons
him

Enter Sylli.

Syl.   If you ever will see brave sight,
    Lose it not now.   Bertoldo and the
    duchess
    Are presently to be married.   There's
    such pomp
    And preparation.
Cam.   If I marry, 'tis
    This day or never.
Syl.   Why, with all my heart;
    Though I break this, I'll keep the next
    oath I make,
    And then it is quit.
Cam.   Follow me to my cabinet.[1]
    You know my confessor, Father Paulo?
Syl.   Yes. Shall he
    Do the feat for us?
Cam.   I will give in writing
    Directions to him, and attire myself   130
    Like a virgin bride; and something I will
    do
    That shall deserve men's praise—and
    wonder too.
Syl.   And I, to make all know I am not
    shallow,
    Will have my points of cochineal and
    yellow.   *Exeunt.*

Act V. Scene ii.

[*The presence chamber in the palace at
Palermo.*]

*Loud music. Astutio, Gonzaga, Roderigo,
Jacomo, Pierio, Roberto, Bertoldo, Aurelia, [Ferdinand,] Bishop, with Attendants.*

Rob. Had our division been greater,
    madam,
    Your clemency, the wrong being done to
    you,
    In pardon of it, like the rod of concord,
    Must make a perfect union.—Once more
    With a brotherly affection we receive you
    Into our favor. Let it be your study
    Hereafter to deserve this blessing, far
    Beyond your merit.
Bert.   As the princess' grace
    To me is without limit, my endeavors
    With all obsequiousness to serve her
    pleasures   10
    Shall know no bounds; nor will I, being
    made

[1] Private room.

Her husband, e'er forget the duty that
    I owe her as a servant.
Aur.   I expect not
    But fair equality, since I well know,
    If that superiority be due,
    'Tis not to me. When you are made my
    consort,
    All the prerogatives of my high birth
    canceled,
    I'll practice the obedience of a wife,
    And freely pay it. Queens themselves,
    if they
    Make choice of their inferiors, only aim-
    ing   20
    To feed their sensual appetites, and to
    reign
    Over their husbands, in some kind com-
    mit
    Authorized whoredom; nor will I be
    guilty
    In my intent of such a crime.
Gonz.   This done,
    As it is promised, madam, may well
    stand for
    A president [2] to great women; but, when
    once
    The griping hunger of desire is cloyed,
    And the poor fool advanced, brought on
    his knees,
    Most of your eagle breed, I'll not say all,
    Ever excepting you, challenge [3] again   30
    What in hot blood they parted from.
Aur.   You are ever
    An enemy of our sex; but you, I hope,
    sir,
    Have better thoughts.
Bert.   I dare not entertain
    An ill one of your goodness.
Rob.   To my power
    I will enable [4] him, to prevent all danger
    Envy can raise against your choice. One
    word more
    Touching the articles.

Enter Fulgen[tio], Cam[iola], Syl[li], Ador[ni].

Ful.   In you alone
    Lie all my hopes; you can or kill or save
    me.
    But pity in you will become you better
    (Though I confess in justice 'tis denied
    me)   40
    Than too much rigor.

[2] Precedent.
[3] Lay claim to, demand.   [4] Elevate.

CAM.   I will make your peace
As far as it lies in me, but must first
Labor to right myself.

AUR. [*To Roberto.*]   Or add or alter
What you think fit. In him I have my all;
Heaven make me thankful for him!

ROB.   On to the temple.

CAM. Stay, royal sir; and, as you are a
    king,
Erect one here, in doing justice to
An injured maid.

AUR.   How's this?

BERT. [*Aside.*]   O, I am blasted!

ROB. I have given some proof, sweet lady,
    of my promptness
To do you right; you need not, therefore,
    doubt me.   50
And rest assured that, this great work
    despatched,
You shall have audience and satisfaction
To all you can demand.

CAM.   To do me justice
Exacts your present care, and can admit
Of no delay. If, ere my cause be heard,
In favor of your brother you go on, sir,
Your scepter cannot right me. He's the
    man,
The guilty man, whom I accuse; and you
Stand bound in duty, as you are supreme,
To be impartial. Since you are a judge,
As a delinquent look on him, and not 61
As on a brother. Justice painted blind
Infers her ministers are obliged to hear
The cause, and, truth the judge, deter-
    mine of it,
And, not swayed or by favor or affection,
By a false gloss or wrested comment, alter
The true intent and letter of the law.

ROB. Nor will I, madam.

AUR. [*To Bertoldo.*]   You seem trou-
    bled, sir.

GONZ. His color changes, too.

CAM.   The alteration
Grows from his guilt. The goodness of
    my cause   70
Begets such confidence in me that I bring
No hired tongue to plead for me, that
    with gay,
Rhetorical flourishes may palliate
That which, stripped naked, will appear
    deformed.
I stand here mine own advocate; and my
    truth,
Delivered in the plainest language, will

Make good itself; nor will I, if the king
Give suffrage to it, but admit of you,
My greatest enemy, and this stranger
    prince,
To sit assistants with him.

AUR.   I ne'er wronged you. 80

CAM. In your knowledge of the injury, I
    believe it;
Nor will you, in your justice, when you
    are
Acquainted with my interest in this man
Which I lay claim to.

ROB.   Let us take our seats.
What is your title to him?

CAM. [*Giving a paper to the King.*]   By
    this contract,
Sealed solemnly before a reverend man,
I challenge him for my husband.

SYL. [*Aside.*]   Ha! Was I
Sent for the friar for this? O Sylli!
    Sylli!—
Some cordial, or I faint.

ROB.   This writing is
Authentical.

AUR.   But, done in heat of blood, 90
Charmed by her flatteries as no doubt he
    was,
To be dispensed with.

FER.   Add this, if you please:
The distance and disparity between
Their births and fortunes.

CAM.   What can Innocence hope for,
When such as sit her judges are cor-
    rupted!
Disparity of birth or fortune, urge you?
Or Siren charms? Or, at his best, in me
Wants [1] to deserve him? Call some few
    days back
And, as he was, consider him, and you
Must grant him my inferior. Imagine
You saw him now in fetters, with his
    honor,   101
His liberty lost, with her black wings
    Despair
Circling his miseries, and this [2] Gonzaga
Trampling on his afflictions; the great
    sum
Proposed for his redemption; the king
Forbidding payment of it; this near kins-
    man,[3]

[1] Deficiencies.
[2] Emended by all editors. Original has *his.*
[3] The reading of the Princeton copy. Other
copies examined by Bryne read *kinsmen.*

With his protesting followers and friends,
Falling off from him; by the whole world
    forsaken;
Dead to all hope, and buried in the grave
Of his calamities; and then weigh duly
What she deserved, whose merits now
    are doubted,   111
That as his better angel in her bounties
Appeared unto him, his great ransom
    paid,
His wants, and with a prodigal hand,
    supplied—
Whether then, being my manumised [1]
    slave,
He owed not himself to me?

AUR.   Is this true?
ROB. In his silence 'tis acknowledged.
GONZ.   If you want
A witness to this purpose, I'll depose it.
CAM. If I have dwelt too long on my
    deservings
    To this unthankful man, pray you,
    pardon me;   120
The cause required it. And, though now
    I add
A little in my painting to the life
His barbarous ingratitude, to deter
Others from imitation, let it meet with
A fair interpretation. This serpent,
Frozen to numbness, was no sooner
    warmed
In the bosom of my pity and compassion,
But in return he ruined his preserver,
The prints the irons had made in his
    flesh   129
Still ulcerous; but all that I had done,
My benefits, in sand or water writ-
    ten,
As they had never been, no more re-
    membered!
And on what ground but his ambitious
    hopes
To gain this duchess' favor?

AUR.   Yes; the object—
Look on it better, lady—may excuse
The charge of [2] his affection.
CAM.   The object!
In what? Forgive me, modesty, if I say
You look upon your form in the false
    glass
Of flattery and self-love, and that de-
    ceives you.

That you were a duchess, as I take it, was
    not   140
Charactered on your face; and, that not
    seen,
For other feature, [3] make all these that are
Experienced in women judges of 'em,
And, if they are not parasites, they must
    grant, [4]
For beauty without art, though you
    storm at it,
I may take the right-hand file.
GONZ.   Well said, i' faith!
I see fair women on no terms will yield
Priority in beauty.
CAM.   Down, proud heart!
Why do I rise up in defense of that
Which, in my cherishing of it, hath un-
    done me?   150
No, madam, I recant—you are all
    beauty,
Goodness, and virtue, and poor I not
    worthy
As a foil to set you off. Enjoy your con-
    quest,
But do not tyrannize. Yet, as I am,
In my lowness, from your height you may
    look on me
And in your suffrage to me make him know
That, though to all men else I did appear
The shame and scorn of women, he
    stands bound
To hold me as her masterpiece.
ROB. [To Bertoldo.]   By my life,
You have shown yourself of such an
    abject temper,   160
So poor and low-conditioned, as I grieve
    for
Your nearness to me.
FER.   I am changed in my
Opinion of you, lady, and profess
The virtues of your mind an ample fortune
For an absolute monarch.
GONZ. [To Bertoldo.]   Since you
    are resolved
To damn yourself, in your forsaking of
Your noble order for a woman, do it
For this. You may search through the
    world, and meet not
With such another phœnix.
AUR.   On the sudden
I feel all fires of love quenched in the
    water   170

---

[1] Manumitted, freed.
[2] Accusation against.

[3] I.e., as far as other features are concerned.
[4] Supply that.

Of compassion.—Make your peace; you
have
My free consent; for here I do disclaim
All interest in you, and, to further your
Desires, fair maid, composed of worth
and honor,
The dispensation procured by me,
Freeing Bertoldo from his vow, makes
way
To your embraces.

BERT.   O, how have I strayed,
And willfully, out of the noble tract [1]
Marked me by virtue! Till now, I was
never
Truly a prisoner. To excuse my late   180
Captivity, I might allege the malice
Of fortune, you, that conquered me, con-
fessing
Courage in my defense was no way want-
ing.
But now I have surrendered up my
strengths
Into the power of vice, and on my fore-
head
Branded with mine own hand in capital
letters,
DISLOYAL and INGRATEFUL.   Though
barred from
Human society, and hissed into
Some desert ne'er yet haunted with the
curses   189
Of men and women, sitting as a judge
Upon my guilty self, I must confess
It justly falls upon me, and one tear,
Shed in compassion of my sufferings, more
Than I can hope for.

CAM.   This compunction
For the wrong that you have done me,
though you should
Fix here, and your true sorrow move no
further,
Will, in respect I loved once, make these
eyes
Two springs of sorrow for you.

BERT.   In your pity
My cruelty shows more monstrous; yet
I am not,
Though most ingrateful, grown to such a
height   200
Of impudence as in my wishes only
To ask your pardon. If, as now I fall
Prostrate before your feet, you will
vouchsafe

[1] Track, course.

To act your own revenge, treading upon
me
As a viper eating through the bowels of
Your benefits, to whom with liberty
I owe my being, 'twill take from the
burthen
That now is insupportable.

CAM.   Pray you, rise.
As I wish peace and quiet to my soul,
I do forgive you heartily. Yet, excuse
me,   210
Though I deny myself a blessing that,
By the favor of the duchess, seconded
With your submission, is offered to
me,
Let not the reason I allege for 't grieve
you:
You have been false once. I have done.
And if,
When I am married, as this day I will be,
As a perfit sign of your atonement [2] with
me,
You wish me joy, I will receive it for
Full satisfaction of all obligations
In which you stand bound to me.

BERT.   I will do it,   220
And, what's more, in despite of sorrow,
live
To see myself undone, beyond all hope
To be made up again.

SYL. [Aside.]   My blood begins
To come to my heart again.

CAM.   Pray you, Signior Syl,
Call in the holy friar. He's prepared
For finishing the work.

SYL.   I knew I was
The man. Heaven make me thankful!

ROB.   Who is this?

AST. His father was the banker of Palermo,
And this the heir of his great wealth; his
wisdom
Was not hereditary.

SYL.   Though you know me not,   230
Your majesty owes me a round sum; I
have
A seal or two to witness. Yet, if you please
To wear my colors and dance at my
wedding,
I'll never sue you.

ROB.   And I'll grant your suit.

SYL. Gracious madonna, noble general,
Brave captains, and my quondam rivals,
wear 'em,

[2] Reconciliation.

With his protesting followers and friends,
Falling off from him; by the whole world
    forsaken;
Dead to all hope, and buried in the grave
Of his calamities; and then weigh duly
What she deserved, whose merits now
    are doubted,   111
That as his better angel in her bounties
Appeared unto him, his great ransom
    paid,
His wants, and with a prodigal hand,
    supplied—
Whether then, being my manumised [1]
    slave,
He owed not himself to me?
AUR.   Is this true?
ROB. In his silence 'tis acknowledged.
GONZ.   If you want
A witness to this purpose, I'll depose it.
CAM. If I have dwelt too long on my
    deservings
    To this unthankful man, pray you,
        pardon me;   120
    The cause required it. And, though now
        I add
    A little in my painting to the life
    His barbarous ingratitude, to deter
    Others from imitation, let it meet with
    A fair interpretation. This serpent,
    Frozen to numbness, was no sooner
        warmed
    In the bosom of my pity and compassion,
    But in return he ruined his preserver,
    The prints the irons had made in his
        flesh   129
    Still ulcerous; but all that I had done,
    My benefits, in sand or water writ-
        ten,
    As they had never been, no more re-
        membered!
    And on what ground but his ambitious
        hopes
    To gain this duchess' favor?
AUR.   Yes; the object—
Look on it better, lady—may excuse
The charge of [2] his affection.
CAM.   The object!
In what? Forgive me, modesty, if I say
You look upon your form in the false
    glass
Of flattery and self-love, and that de-
    ceives you.

That you were a duchess, as I take it, was
    not   140
Charactered on your face; and, that not
    seen,
For other feature, [3] make all these that are
Experienced in women judges of 'em,
And, if they are not parasites, they must
    grant, [4]
For beauty without art, though you
    storm at it,
I may take the right-hand file.
GONZ.   Well said, i' faith!
I see fair women on no terms will yield
Priority in beauty.
CAM.   Down, proud heart!
Why do I rise up in defense of that
Which, in my cherishing of it, hath un-
    done me?   150
No, madam, I recant—you are all
    beauty,
Goodness, and virtue, and poor I not
    worthy
As a foil to set you off. Enjoy your con-
    quest,
But do not tyrannize. Yet, as I am,
In my lowness, from your height you may
    look on me
And in your suffrage to me make him know
That, though to all men else I did appear
The shame and scorn of women, he
    stands bound
To hold me as her masterpiece.
ROB. [To Bertoldo.]   By my life,
You have shown yourself of such an
    abject temper,   160
So poor and low-conditioned, as I grieve
    for
Your nearness to me.
FER.   I am changed in my
Opinion of you, lady, and profess
The virtues of your mind an ample fortune
For an absolute monarch.
GONZ. [To Bertoldo.]   Since you
    are resolved
To damn yourself, in your forsaking of
Your noble order for a woman, do it
For this. You may search through the
    world, and meet not
With such another phœnix.
AUR.   On the sudden
I feel all fires of love quenched in the
    water   170

---

[1] Manumitted, freed.
[2] Accusation against.

[3] I.e., as far as other features are concerned.
[4] Supply that.

Of compassion.—Make your peace; you have
My free consent; for here I do disclaim
All interest in you, and, to further your
Desires, fair maid, composed of worth and honor,
The dispensation procured by me,
Freeing Bertoldo from his vow, makes way
To your embraces.

BERT.   O, how have I strayed,
And willfully, out of the noble tract [1]
Marked me by virtue! Till now, I was never
Truly a prisoner. To excuse my late   180
Captivity, I might allege the malice
Of fortune, you, that conquered me, confessing
Courage in my defense was no way wanting.
But now I have surrendered up my strengths
Into the power of vice, and on my forehead
Branded with mine own hand in capital letters,
DISLOYAL and INGRATEFUL. Though barred from
Human society, and hissed into
Some desert ne'er yet haunted with the curses   189
Of men and women, sitting as a judge
Upon my guilty self, I must confess
It justly falls upon me, and one tear,
Shed in compassion of my sufferings, more
Than I can hope for.

CAM.   This compunction
For the wrong that you have done me, though you should
Fix here, and your true sorrow move no further,
Will, in respect I loved once, make these eyes
Two springs of sorrow for you.

BERT.   In your pity
My cruelty shows more monstrous; yet I am not,
Though most ingrateful, grown to such a height   200
Of impudence as in my wishes only
To ask your pardon. If, as now I fall
Prostrate before your feet, you will vouchsafe

[1] Track, course.

To act your own revenge, treading upon me
As a viper eating through the bowels of
Your benefits, to whom with liberty
I owe my being, 'twill take from the burthen
That now is insupportable.

CAM.   Pray you, rise.
As I wish peace and quiet to my soul,
I do forgive you heartily. Yet, excuse me,   210
Though I deny myself a blessing that,
By the favor of the duchess, seconded
With your submission, is offered to me,
Let not the reason I allege for 't grieve you:
You have been false once. I have done. And if,
When I am married, as this day I will be,
As a perfit sign of your atonement [2] with me,
You wish me joy, I will receive it for
Full satisfaction of all obligations
In which you stand bound to me.

BERT.   I will do it,   220
And, what's more, in despite of sorrow, live
To see myself undone, beyond all hope
To be made up again.

SYL. [Aside.]   My blood begins
To come to my heart again.

CAM.   Pray you, Signior Syl.
Call in the holy friar. He's prepared
For finishing the work.

SYL.   I knew I was
The man. Heaven make me thankful!

ROB.   Who is this?

AST. His father was the banker of Palermo,
And this the heir of his great wealth; his wisdom
Was not hereditary.

SYL.   Though you know me not,   230
Your majesty owes me a round sum; I have
A seal or two to witness. Yet, if you please
To wear my colors and dance at my wedding,
I'll never sue you.

ROB.   And I'll grant your suit.

SYL. Gracious madonna, noble general,
Brave captains, and my quondam rivals, wear 'em,

[2] Reconciliation.

THE WITCH OF EDMONTON [1]

BY

WILLIAM ROWLEY, THOMAS DEKKER, AND JOHN FORD

ACTORS' NAMES

SIR ARTHUR CLARINGTON.
OLD THORNEY, *a gentleman.*
OLD CARTER, *a rich yeoman.*
OLD BANKS, *a countryman.*
W. MAGO [2] } *two countrymen.*
W. HAMLUC [2] }
THREE OTHER COUNTRYMEN.
WARBECK } *suitors to Carter's daughters.*
SOMERTON }
FRANK, *Thorney's son.*
YOUNG CUDDY BANKS, *the clown.*
FOUR MORRIS DANCERS. [3]
OLD RATCLIFFE.
SAWGUT, *an old fiddler.*
POLDAVIS, *a barber's boy.* [4]

JUSTICE.
CONSTABLE.
OFFICERS.
SERVING-MEN.
DOG, *a familiar.* [5]
A SPIRIT.

WOMEN

MOTHER SAWYER, *the witch.*
ANN, *Ratcliffe's wife.*
SUSAN } *Carter's daughters.*
KATHERINE }
WINNIFRIDE, *Sir Arthur's maid.*
[JANE, *Carter's maid.*

SCENE: *Edmonton and its vicinity; London.*

TIME: *Early seventeenth century.*]

The whole argument is this distich.

Forced marriage, murder; murder, blood
　requires.
Reproach, revenge; revenge, hell's help
　desires.

PROLOGUE

The town of Edmonton hath lent the stage
A devil [6] and a witch, both in an age.
To make comparisons it were uncivil
Between so even a pair, a witch and devil;

But, as the year doth with his plenty bring
As well a latter as a former spring,
So has this witch enjoyed the first, and
　reason
Presumes she may partake the other season.
In acts deserving name, the proverb says,
"Once good, and ever." Why not so in
　plays?　　　　　　　　　　　　　　　10
Why not in this, since, gentlemen, we
　flatter
No expectation? Here is mirth and matter.
　　　　　　　　　　　　　　MR. BIRD. [7]

ACT[US] I. SCEN[A] i.

[*A room in Sir Arthur's House at Edmonton.*]

*Enter Frank Thorney; Winnifride, with
child.* [8]

FRANK. Come, wench. Why, here's a
　business soon despatched.
　Thy heart I know is now at ease; thou
　need'st not

---

[1] The title continues: "A Known True Story,
Composed into a Tragi-Comedy by Divers Well-
Esteemed Poets, William Rowley, Thomas
Dekker, John Ford, etc. Acted by the Prince's
Servants, Often at the Cockpit in Drury Lane,
Once at Court, with Singular Applause."
[2] These are the names of actual actors.
W. Mago, however, is not referred to by name
in the play itself.
[3] Who appear first as the above-mentioned
countrymen.
[4] Merely referred to in the play.
[5] *I.e.*, a familiar spirit.
[6] An allusion to *The Merry Devil of Edmonton,*
printed anonymously in 1608.
[7] Master Theophilus Bird.　[8] *I.e.*, pregnant.

Fear what the tattling gossips in their
cups
Can speak against thy fame. Thy child
shall know
Who to call dad now.

WIN.   You have discharged [1]
The true part of an honest man; I cannot
Request a fuller satisfaction
Than you have freely granted. Yet
methinks
'Tis an hard case, being lawful man and
wife,
We should not live together.

FRANK.   Had I failed   10
In promise of my truth to thee, we must
Have then been ever sundered; now the
longest
Of our forbearing either's company
Is only but to gain a little time
For our continuing thrift, that so here-
after
The heir that shall be born may not have
cause
To curse his hour of birth, which made
him feel
The misery of beggary and want—
Two devils that are occasions to enforce
A shameful end. My plots aim but to
keep   20
My father's love.

WIN.   And that will be as difficult
To be preserved, when he shall under-
stand
How you are married, as it will be now,
Should you confess it to him.

FRANK.   Fathers are
Won by degrees, not bluntly, as our
masters
Or wrongéd friends are; and besides I'll use
Such dutiful and ready means that ere
He can have notice of what's past, th'
inheritance
To which I am born heir shall be assured.
That done, why, let him know it; if he
like it not,   30
Yet he shall have no power in him left
To cross the thriving of it.

WIN.   You who had
The conquest of my maiden love may
easily

Conquer the fears of my distrust. And
whither
Must I be hurried?

FRANK.   Prithee, do not use
A word so much unsuitable to the con-
stant
Affections of thy husband. Thou shalt
live
Near Waltham Abbey with thy uncle
Selman.
I have acquainted him with all at large.[2]
He'll use thee kindly; thou shalt want
no pleasures   40
Nor any other fit supplies whatever
Thou canst in heart desire.

WIN.   All these are nothing
Without your company.

FRANK.   Which thou shalt have
Once every month at least.

WIN.   Once every month!
Is this to have an husband?

FRANK.   Perhaps oft'ner;
That's as occasion serves.

WIN.   Ay, ay; in case
No other beauty tempt your eye, whom
you
Like better, I may chance to be re-
membered,
And see you now and then. Faith, I did
hope
You'ld not have used me so; 'tis but
my fortune.   50
And yet, if not for my sake, have some
pity
Upon the child I go with, that's your own.
And, less you'll be a cruel-hearted father,
You cannot but remember that.
Heaven knows how—

FRANK.   To quit which fear at once,
As by the ceremony late performed
I plighted thee a faith as free from
challenge
As any double thought, once more, in
hearing
Of heaven and thee, I vow that never
henceforth
Disgrace, reproof, lawless affections,
threats,   60
Or what can be suggested gainst our
marriage,
Shall cause me falsify that bridal oath
That binds me thine. And, Winnifride,
whenever

---

[1] Here and in a few later passages the line
division has been regularized. Some passages
printed in the original as prose have been divided into verse.

[2] At length, fully.

THE WITCH OF EDMONTON[1]

BY

WILLIAM ROWLEY, THOMAS DEKKER, AND JOHN FORD

ACTORS' NAMES

SIR ARTHUR CLARINGTON.
OLD THORNEY, *a gentleman.*
OLD CARTER, *a rich yeoman.*
OLD BANKS, *a countryman.*
W. MAGO [2] ⎱ *two countrymen.*
W. HAMLUC [2] ⎰
THREE OTHER COUNTRYMEN.
WARBECK ⎱ *suitors to Carter's daughters.*
SOMERTON ⎰
FRANK, *Thorney's son.*
YOUNG CUDDY BANKS, *the clown.*
FOUR MORRIS DANCERS.[3]
OLD RATCLIFFE.
SAWGUT, *an old fiddler.*
POLDAVIS, *a barber's boy.*[4]

JUSTICE.
CONSTABLE.
OFFICERS.
SERVING-MEN.
DOG, *a familiar.*[5]
A SPIRIT.

WOMEN

MOTHER SAWYER, *the witch.*
ANN, *Ratcliffe's wife.*
SUSAN ⎱ *Carter's daughters.*
KATHERINE ⎰
WINNIFRIDE, *Sir Arthur's maid.*
[JANE, *Carter's maid.*

SCENE: *Edmonton and its vicinity; London.*

TIME: *Early seventeenth century.*]

The whole argument is this distich.

Forced marriage, murder; murder, blood requires.
Reproach, revenge; revenge, hell's help desires.

PROLOGUE

The town of Edmonton hath lent the stage
A devil [6] and a witch, both in an age.
To make comparisons it were uncivil
Between so even a pair, a witch and devil;
But, as the year doth with his plenty bring
As well a latter as a former spring,
So has this witch enjoyed the first, and reason
Presumes she may partake the other season.
In acts deserving name, the proverb says,
"Once good, and ever." Why not so in plays? 10
Why not in this, since, gentlemen, we flatter
No expectation? Here is mirth and matter.
MR. BIRD.[7]

ACT[US] I. SCEN[A] i.

[*A room in Sir Arthur's House at Edmonton.*]

Enter Frank Thorney; Winnifride, with child.[8]

FRANK. Come, wench. Why, here's a business soon despatched.
   Thy heart I know is now at ease; thou need'st not

---

[1] The title continues: "A Known True Story, Composed into a Tragi-Comedy by Divers Well-Esteemed Poets, William Rowley, Thomas Dekker, John Ford, etc. Acted by the Prince's Servants, Often at the Cockpit in Drury Lane, Once at Court, with Singular Applause."
[2] Probably the names of actual actors. W. Mago, however, is not referred to by name in the play itself.
[3] Who appear first as the above-mentioned countrymen.
[4] Merely referred to in the play.
[5] *I.e.*, a familiar spirit.
[6] An allusion to *The Merry Devil of Edmonton,* printed anonymously in 1608.
[7] Master Theophilus Bird. [8] *I.e.*, pregnant.

1445

Fear what the tattling gossips in their
cups
Can speak against thy fame. Thy child
shall know
Who to call dad now.

WIN.   You have discharged [1]
The true part of an honest man; I cannot
Request a fuller satisfaction
Than you have freely granted. Yet
methinks
'Tis an hard case, being lawful man and
wife,
We should not live together.

FRANK.   Had I failed 10
In promise of my truth to thee, we must
Have then been ever sundered; now the
longest
Of our forbearing either's company
Is only but to gain a little time
For our continuing thrift, that so here-
after
The heir that shall be born may not have
cause
To curse his hour of birth, which made
him feel
The misery of beggary and want—
Two devils that are occasions to enforce
A shameful end. My plots aim but to
keep   20
My father's love.

WIN.   And that will be as difficult
To be preserved, when he shall under-
stand
How you are married, as it will be now,
Should you confess it to him.

FRANK.   Fathers are
Won by degrees, not bluntly, as our
masters
Or wrongéd friends are; and besides I'll use
Such dutiful and ready means that ere
He can have notice of what's past, th'
inheritance
To which I am born heir shall be assured.
That done, why, let him know it; if he
like it not,   30
Yet he shall have no power in him left
To cross the thriving of it.

WIN.   You who had
The conquest of my maiden love may
easily

Conquer the fears of my distrust. And
whither
Must I be hurried?

FRANK.   Prithee, do not use
A word so much unsuitable to the con-
stant
Affections of thy husband. Thou shalt
live
Near Waltham Abbey with thy uncle
Selman.
I have acquainted him with all at large.[2]
He'll use thee kindly; thou shalt want
no pleasures   40
Nor any other fit supplies whatever
Thou canst in heart desire.

WIN.   All these are nothing
Without your company.

FRANK.   Which thou shalt have
Once every month at least.

WIN.   Once every month!
Is this to have an husband?

FRANK.   Perhaps oft'ner;
That's as occasion serves.

WIN.   Ay, ay; in case
No other beauty tempt your eye, whom
you
Like better, I may chance to be re-
membered,
And see you now and then. Faith, I did
hope
You'ld not have used me so; 'tis but
my fortune.   50
And yet, if not for my sake, have some
pity
Upon the child I go with, that's your own.
And, less you'll be a cruel-hearted father,
You cannot but remember that.
Heaven knows how—

FRANK.   To quit which fear at once,
As by the ceremony late performed
I plighted thee a faith as free from
challenge
As any double thought, once more, in
hearing
Of heaven and thee, I vow that never
henceforth
Disgrace, reproof, lawless affections,
threats,   60
Or what can be suggested gainst our
marriage,
Shall cause me falsify that bridal oath
That binds me thine. And, Winnifride,
whenever

_____
[1] Here and in a few later passages the line division has been regularized. Some passages printed in the original as prose have been divided into verse.

[2] At length, fully.

The wanton heat of youth, by subtle baits
Of beauty, or what woman's art can practice,[1]
Draw me from only loving thee, let heaven
Inflict upon my life some fearful ruin!
I hope thou dost believe me.

Win.   Swear no more;
I am confirmed, and will resolve to do
What you think most behooveful for us.

Frank.   Thus, then: 70
Make thyself ready; at the furthest house
Upon the green without the town your uncle
Expects you. For a little time, farewell!

Win.   Sweet,
We shall meet again as soon as thou canst possibly?

Frank. We shall. One kiss!—Away!
           [Exit Winnifride.]

Ent[er] Sir Art[hur] Clarington.

Sir Art.   Frank Thorney!
Frank.   Here, sir.
Sir Art. Alone? Then must I tell thee in plain terms
Thou hast wronged thy master's house basely and lewdly.
Frank. Your house, sir?
Sir Art. Yes, sir. If the nimble devil
That wantoned in your blood rebelled against 79
All rules of honest duty, you might, sir,
Have found out some more fitting place than here
To have built a stews in. All the country whispers
How shamefully thou hast undone a maid,
Approved for modest life, for civil carriage,
Till thy prevailing perjuries enticed her
To forfeit shame. Will you be honest yet,
Make her amends and marry her?
Frank.   So, sir,
I might bring both myself and her to beggary;
And that would be a shame worse than the other.
Sir Art. You should have thought on this before, and then 90

Your reason would have overswayed the passion
Of your unruly lust. But, that you may
Be left without excuse, to salve the infamy
Of my disgracéd house, and cause [2] you are
A gentleman, and both of you my servants,
I'll make the maid a portion.
Frank.   So you promised me
Before, in case I married her. I know
Sir Arthur Clarington deserves the credit
Report hath lent him, and presume you are
A debtor to your promise. But upon 100
What certainty shall I resolve? Excuse me
For being somewhat rude.
Sir Art.   'Tis but reason.
Well, Frank, what think'st thou of two hundred pounds
And a continual friend?
Frank.   Though my poor fortunes
Might happily [3] prefer me to a choice
Of a far greater portion, yet, to right
A wrongéd maid and to preserve your favor,
I am content to accept your proffer.
Sir Art.   Art thou?
Frank. Sir, we shall every day have need to employ
The use of what you please to give.
Sir Art.   Thou shalt have 't. 110
Frank. Then I claim your promise. We are man and wife.
Sir Art. Already?
Frank.   And more than so; I have promised her
Free entertainment in her uncle's house
Near Waltham Abbey, where she may securely
Sojourn, till time and my endeavors work
My father's love and liking.
Sir Art.   Honest Frank!
Frank. I hope, sir, you will think I cannot keep her
Without a daily charge.
Sir Art.   As for the money,
'Tis all thine own! And, though I cannot make thee
A present payment, yet thou shalt be sure 120
I will not fail thee.

[1] Scheme.

[2] Because.   [3] Haply, perhaps.

FRANK. But our occasions—

SIR ART. Nay, nay,
Talk not of your occasions. Trust my bounty;
It shall not sleep. Hast married her, i' faith, Frank?
'Tis well, 'tis passing well! Then, Winnifride,
Once more thou art an honest [1] woman. Frank,
Thou hast a jewel. Love her; she'll deserve it.
And when to Waltham?

FRANK. She is making ready;
Her uncle stays for her.

SIR ART. Most provident speed.
Frank, I will be [thy] [2] friend, and such a friend!
Thou'lt bring her thither?

FRANK. Sir, I cannot; newly 130
My father sent me word I should come to him.

SIR ART. Marry, and do; I know thou hast a wit
To handle him.

FRANK. I have a suit t' ye.

SIR ART. What is 't?
Anything, Frank; command it.

FRANK. That you'll please
By letters to assure my father that
I am not married.

SIR ART. How!

FRANK. Someone or other
Hath certainly informed him that I purposed
To marry Winnifride, on which he threatened
To disinherit me. To prevent it,
Lowly I crave your letters, which he, seeing, 140
Will credit; and I hope, ere I return,
On such conditions as I'll frame, his lands
Shall be assured.

SIR ART. But what is there [3] to quit [4]
My knowledge of the marriage?

FRANK. Why, you were not
A witness to it.

SIR ART. I conceive; and then—
His land confirmed, thou wilt acquaint him throughly
With all that's past.

FRANK. I mean no less.

SIR ART. Provided
I never was made privy to it.

FRANK. Alas, sir,
Am I a talker?

SIR ART. Draw thyself the letter;
I'll put my hand to it. I commend thy policy; 150
Th' art witty, witty Frank; nay, nay, 'tis fit.
Despatch it.

FRANK. I shall write effectually. *Exit.*

SIR ART. Go thy way, cuckoo. Have I caught the young man?
One trouble, then, is freed. He that will feast
At other's cost must be a bold-faced guest.

Enter Win[nifride] in a riding suit.

WIN. I have heard the news; all now is safe;
The worst is past.

SIR ART. Thy lip, wench! [*Kisses her.*]
I must bid
Farewell, for fashion's sake; but I will visit thee
Suddenly, girl. This was cleanly carried;
Ha! Was 't not, Win?

WIN. Then were my happiness, 160
That I in heart repent I did not bring him
The dower of a virginity. Sir, forgive me;
I have been much to blame. Had not my lewdness [5]
Given way to your immoderate waste of virtue,
You had not with such eagerness pursued
The error of your goodness.

SIR ART. Dear, dear Win,
I hug this art of thine; it shows how cleanly
Thou canst beguile, in case occasion serve
To practice; it becomes thee. Now we share
Free scope enough, without control or fear, 170
To interchange our pleasures; we will surfeit
In our embraces, wench. Come, tell me, when
Wilt thou appoint a meeting?

[1] Chaste. [2] Added in Gifford-Dyce edn.
[3] Emended by Gifford. Original reads *that.*
[4] *I.e.*, rid myself of.
[5] Suggested by Dyce. Original reads *laundress.*

The wanton heat of youth, by subtle baits
Of beauty, or what woman's art can practice,[1]
Draw me from only loving thee, let heaven
Inflict upon my life some fearful ruin!
I hope thou dost believe me.

WIN.   Swear no more;
I am confirmed, and will resolve to do
What you think most behooveful for us.

FRANK.   Thus, then: 70
Make thyself ready; at the furthest house
Upon the green without the town your uncle
Expects you. For a little time, farewell!

WIN.   Sweet,
We shall meet again as soon as thou canst possibly?

FRANK. We shall. One kiss!—Away!
                        [*Exit Winnifride.*]

Ent[er] Sir Art[hur] Clarington.

SIR ART.   Frank Thorney!
FRANK.   Here, sir.
SIR ART. Alone? Then must I tell thee in plain terms
Thou hast wronged thy master's house basely and lewdly.

FRANK. Your house, sir?
SIR ART.   Yes, sir. If the nimble devil
That wantoned in your blood rebelled against   79
All rules of honest duty, you might, sir,
Have found out some more fitting place than here
To have built a stews in. All the country whispers
How shamefully thou hast undone a maid,
Approved for modest life, for civil carriage,
Till thy prevailing perjuries enticed her
To forfeit shame. Will you be honest yet,
Make her amends and marry her?

FRANK.   So, sir,
I might bring both myself and her to beggary;
And that would be a shame worse than the other.

SIR ART. You should have thought on this before, and then   90

[1] Scheme.

Your reason would have overswayed the passion
Of your unruly lust. But, that you may
Be left without excuse, to salve the infamy
Of my disgracéd house, and cause[2] you are
A gentleman, and both of you my servants,
I'll make the maid a portion.

FRANK.   So you promised me
Before, in case I married her. I know
Sir Arthur Clarington deserves the credit
Report hath lent him, and presume you are
A debtor to your promise. But upon 100
What certainty shall I resolve? Excuse me
For being somewhat rude.

SIR ART.   'Tis but reason.
Well, Frank, what think'st thou of two hundred pounds
And a continual friend?

FRANK.   Though my poor fortunes
Might happily[3] prefer me to a choice
Of a far greater portion, yet, to right
A wrongéd maid and to preserve your favor,
I am content to accept your proffer.

SIR ART.   Art thou?
FRANK. Sir, we shall every day have need to employ
The use of what you please to give.

SIR ART.   Thou shalt have 't. 110
FRANK. Then I claim your promise. We are man and wife.

SIR ART. Already?
FRANK.   And more than so; I have promised her
Free entertainment in her uncle's house
Near Waltham Abbey, where she may securely
Sojourn, till time and my endeavors work
My father's love and liking.

SIR ART.   Honest Frank!
FRANK. I hope, sir, you will think I cannot keep her
Without a daily charge.

SIR ART.   As for the money,
'Tis all thine own! And, though I cannot make thee
A present payment, yet thou shalt be sure   120
I will not fail thee.

[2] Because.   [3] Haply, perhaps.

FRANK.　　　　　But our occasions—

SIR ART.　　　　　　　Nay, nay,
Talk not of your occasions. Trust my
　bounty;
It shall not sleep. Hast married her,
　i' faith, Frank?
'Tis well, 'tis passing well! Then, Winni-
　fride,
Once more thou art an honest [1] woman.
　Frank,
Thou hast a jewel. Love her; she'll
　deserve it.
And when to Waltham?

FRANK.　　　　　She is making ready;
Her uncle stays for her.

SIR ART.　　　　Most provident speed.
Frank, I will be [thy] [2] friend, and such a
　friend!
Thou'lt bring her thither?

FRANK.　　　　　Sir, I cannot; newly　130
My father sent me word I should come
　to him.

SIR ART. Marry, and do; I know thou
　hast a wit
To handle him.

FRANK.　　　　　I have a suit t' ye.

SIR ART.　　　　　　What is 't?
Anything, Frank; command it.

FRANK.　　　　　That you'll please
By letters to assure my father that
I am not married.

SIR ART.　　　　How!

FRANK.　　　　Someone or other
Hath certainly informed him that I
　purposed
To marry Winnifride, on which he
　threatened
To disinherit me. To prevent it,
Lowly I crave your letters, which he,
　seeing,　　　　　　　　　　　　140
Will credit; and I hope, ere I return,
On such conditions as I'll frame, his lands
Shall be assured.

SIR ART.　　But what is there [3] to quit [4]
My knowledge of the marriage?

FRANK.　　　　　Why, you were not
A witness to it.

SIR ART.　　　　I conceive; and then—
His land confirmed, thou wilt acquaint
　him throughly
With all that's past.

[1] Chaste.　　　[2] Added in Gifford-Dyce edn.
[3] Emended by Gifford. Original reads *that.*
[4] *I.e.,* rid myself of.

FRANK.　　　　　I mean no less.

SIR ART.　　　　　　Provided
I never was made privy to it.

FRANK.　　　　　　Alas, sir,
Am I a talker?

SIR ART.　　　Draw thyself the letter;
I'll put my hand to it. I commend thy
　policy;　　　　　　　　　　　　150
Th' art witty, witty Frank; nay, nay,
　'tis fit.
Despatch it.

FRANK.　　I shall write effectually. *Exit.*

SIR ART. Go thy way, cuckoo. Have I
　caught the young man?
One trouble, then, is freed. He that will
　feast
At other's cost must be a bold-faced
　guest.

Enter Win[nifride] in a riding suit.

WIN. I have heard the news; all now is
　safe;
The worst is past.

SIR ART.　　Thy lip, wench! [*Kisses her.*]
　I must bid
Farewell, for fashion's sake; but I will
　visit thee
Suddenly, girl. This was cleanly carried;
Ha! Was 't not, Win?

WIN.　　Then were my happiness,　160
That I in heart repent I did not bring him
The dower of a virginity. Sir, forgive me;
I have been much to blame. Had not
　my lewdness [5]
Given way to your immoderate waste of
　virtue,
You had not with such eagerness pur-
　sued
The error of your goodness.

SIR ART.　　　　Dear, dear Win,
I hug this art of thine; it shows how
　cleanly
Thou canst beguile, in case occasion
　serve
To practice; it becomes thee. Now we
　share
Free scope enough, without control or
　fear,　　　　　　　　　　　　　170
To interchange our pleasures; we will
　surfeit
In our embraces, wench. Come, tell me,
　when
Wilt thou appoint a meeting?

[5] Suggested by Dyce. Original reads *laundress.*

FRANK.　　　　　　　　Alas, I knew　230
Your rage and grief proceeded from your
　love
To me; so I conceived it.
O. THOR.　　　　　　My good son,
I'll bear with many faults in thee here-
　after;
Bear thou with mine.
FRANK.　　　　　　The peace is soon
　concluded.

Enter Old Carter [and Susan].

O. CART. Why, Mr. Thorney, d' ye mean
to talk out your dinner? The company
attends your coming. What must it be,
Mr. Frank, or son Frank? I am plain Dun-
stable.[1]
O. THOR. Son, brother, if your daughter
　like to have it so.　　　　　　　240
FRANK. I dare be confident she's not al-
　tered
From what I left her at our parting last.
Are you, fair maid?
SUS.　　　　　　You took too sure
　possession
Of an engagéd heart.
FRANK.　　　　Which now I challenge.
O. CART. Marry, and much good may
it do thee, son. Take her to thee. Get me a
brace of boys at a burthen, Frank; the nursing shall not stand thee in a penny-worth
of milk. Reach her home and spare not!
When's the day?　　　　　　　250
O. THOR. Tomorrow, if you please. To use
　ceremony
Of charge and custom were to little
　purpose;
Their loves are married fast enough
　already.
O. CART. A good motion. We'll e'en have
an household dinner, and let the fiddlers go
scrape. Let the bride and bridegroom dance
at night together; no matter for the guests.
Tomorrow, Sue, tomorrow.—Shall 's to
dinner now?
O. THOR. We are on all sides pleased, I
　hope.　　　　　　　　　260
SUS. Pray heaven I may deserve the bless-
　ing sent me.
Now my heart is settled.
FRANK.　　　　　　So is mine.
O. CART. Your marriage money shall be

[1] Proverbial for outspoken and honest.

received before your wedding shoes can
be pulled on. Blessing on you both!
FRANK. *[Aside.]* No man can hide his
　shame from heaven that views him;
In vain he flees whose destiny pursues
　him.　　　　　　　*Exeunt omnes.*

ACT[US] II. SCEN[A] i.

[A field near Edmonton.]

Enter Elizabeth Sawyer gathering sticks.

SAWY. And why on me? Why should the
　envious world
Throw all their scandalous malice upon
　me?
Cause I am poor, deformed, and igno-
　rant,
And like a bow buckled and bent to-
　gether
By some more strong in mischiefs than
　myself,
Must I for that be made a common
　sink
For all the filth and rubbish of men's
　tongues
To fall and run into? Some call me
　witch,
And, being ignorant of myself, they go
About to teach me how to be one, urg-
　ing　　　　　　　　　10
That my bad tongue—by their bad
　usage made so—
Forspeaks [2] their cattle, doth bewitch
　their corn,
Themselves, their servants, and their
　babes at nurse.
This they enforce upon me, and in part

Enter O[ld] Banks.

Make me to credit it. And here comes
　one
Of my chief adversaries.
O. BANK. Out, out upon thee, witch!
SAWY.　　　　　　Dost call me witch?
O. BANK. I do, witch, I do; and worse
I would, knew I a name more hateful.
What makest [3] thou upon my ground? [20
SAWY. Gather a few rotten sticks to
warm me.
O. BANK. Down with them when I bid
thee, quickly; I'll make thy bones rattle in
thy skin else.
[2] Bewitches.　　　　　　　[3] Doest.

SAWY. You won't, churl, cutthroat, miser! There they be. [*Throws them down.*] Would they stuck cross thy throat, thy bowels, thy maw, thy midriff!

O. BANK. Say'st thou me so? Hag, [30 out of my ground! [*Beats her.*]

SAWY. Dost strike me, slave, curmudgeon? Now, thy bones aches, thy joints cramps, and convulsions stretch and crack thy sinews!

O. BANK. Cursing, thou hag! Take that and that! [*Beats her and*] *exit*.

SAWY. Strike, do, and withered may that hand and arm
Whose blows have lamed me drop from the rotten trunk.
Abuse me! Beat me! Call me hag and witch! 40
What is the name, where and by what art learned,
What spells, what charms, or invocations,
May the thing called Familiar be purchased?

Enter Young Banks and three or four more [Countrymen].

Y. BANK. A new head for the tabor, and silver tipping for the pipe; remember that, and forget not five leash of new bells.

1 [COUNT.] Double bells! Crooked Lane[1] ye shall have 'em straight in. Crooked Lane! Double bells all, if it be possible.

Y. BANK. Double bells? Double [50 coxcombs! Trebles, buy me trebles, all trebles, for our purpose is to be in the altitudes.

2 [COUNT.] All trebles? Not a mean?[2]

Y. BANK. Not one. The morris is so cast we'll have neither mean nor bass in our company, fellow Rowland.

3 [COUNT.] What? Nor a counter?[3]

Y. BANK. By no means, no hunting counter;[4] leave that to Enfield[5] Chase [60 men. All trebles, all in the altitudes. Now for the disposing of parts in the morris, little or no labor will serve.

2 [COUNT.] If you that be minded to follow your leader know me—an ancient

honor belonging to our house—for a fore-horse [i' th'][6] team and fore-gallant[7] in a morris, my father's stable is not unfurnished.

3 [COUNT.] So much for the fore- [70 horse; but how for a good hobbyhorse?[8]

Y. BANK. For a hobbyhorse? Let me see an almanac. Midsummer moon, let me see ye. "When the moon's in the full, then's wit in the wane." No more. Use your best skill; your morris will suffer an eclipse.

1 [COUNT.] An eclipse?

Y. BANK. A strange one.

2 [COUNT.] Strange? 80

Y. BANK. Yes, and most sudden. Remember the fore-gallant, and forget the hobbyhorse! The whole body of your morris will be darkened.—There be of us—but 'tis no matter. Forget the hobbyhorse!

1 [COUNT.] Cuddy Banks, have you forgot since he paced it from Enfield Chase to Edmonton? Cuddy, honest Cuddy, cast thy stuff. 90

Y. BANK. Suffer may ye all! It shall be known, I can take mine ease as well as another man. Seek your hobbyhorse where you can get him.

1 [COUNT.] Cuddy, honest Cuddy, we confess, and are sorry for our neglect.

2 [COUNT.] The old horse shall have a new bridle.

3 [COUNT.] The caparisons new painted.

4 [COUNT.] The tail repaired. The [100 snaffle and the bosses new saffroned o'er.[9]

1 [COUNT.] Kind—

2 [COUNT.] Honest—

3 [COUNT.] Loving, ingenious—

4 [COUNT.] Affable Cuddy.

Y. BANK. To show I am not flint, but affable, as you say, very well stuffed, a kind of warm dough or puffpaste, I relent, I connive, most affable Jack. Let the hobbyhorse provide a strong back, [110 he shall not want a belly when I am in 'em—but [*Sees Sawyer.*]—'uds me,[10] Mother Sawyer!

---

[1] A shopping district in London.
[2] Tenor.   [3] Countertenor.
[4] Following the trail in the wrong direction.
[5] The original spelling, *Envile*, indicates the pronunciation.

[6] Added in Gifford-Dyce edn.
[7] Leader of the dancers.
[8] A performer in a morris.
[9] The original gives this sentence to the first countryman.
[10] God's me; a mild oath.

FRANK.   Alas, I knew   230
Your rage and grief proceeded from your
    love
To me; so I conceived it.
O. THOR.   My good son,
I'll bear with many faults in thee here-
    after;
Bear thou with mine.
FRANK.   The peace is soon
    concluded.

Enter Old Carter [and Susan].

O. CART. Why, Mr. Thorney, d' ye mean
to talk out your dinner? The company
attends your coming. What must it be,
Mr. Frank, or son Frank? I am plain Dun-
stable.[1]
O. THOR. Son, brother, if your daughter
    like to have it so.   240
FRANK. I dare be confident she's not al-
    tered
From what I left her at our parting last.
Are you, fair maid?
SUS.   You took too sure
    possession
Of an engagéd heart.
FRANK.   Which now I challenge.
O. CART. Marry, and much good may
it do thee, son. Take her to thee. Get me a
brace of boys at a burthen, Frank; the nurs-
ing shall not stand thee in a penny-worth
of milk. Reach her home and spare not!
When's the day?   250
O. THOR. Tomorrow, if you please. To use
    ceremony
Of charge and custom were to little
    purpose;
Their loves are married fast enough
    already.
O. CART. A good motion. We'll e'en have
an household dinner, and let the fiddlers go
scrape. Let the bride and bridegroom dance
at night together; no matter for the guests.
Tomorrow, Sue, tomorrow.—Shall 's to
dinner now?
O. THOR. We are on all sides pleased, I
    hope.   260
SUS. Pray heaven I may deserve the bless-
    ing sent me.
Now my heart is settled.
FRANK.   So is mine.
O. CART. Your marriage money shall be

[1] Proverbial for outspoken and honest.

received before your wedding shoes can
be pulled on. Blessing on you both!
FRANK. [*Aside.*] No man can hide his
    shame from heaven that views him;
In vain he flees whose destiny pursues
    him.   *Exeunt omnes.*

ACT[US] II. SCEN[A] i.

[A field near Edmonton.]

Enter Elizabeth Sawyer gathering sticks.

SAWY. And why on me? Why should the
    envious world
Throw all their scandalous malice upon
    me?
Cause I am poor, deformed, and igno-
    rant,
And like a bow buckled and bent to-
    gether
By some more strong in mischiefs than
    myself,
Must I for that be made a common
    sink
For all the filth and rubbish of men's
    tongues
To fall and run into? Some call me
    witch,
And, being ignorant of myself, they go
About to teach me how to be one, urg-
    ing   10
That my bad tongue—by their bad
    usage made so—
Forspeaks[2] their cattle, doth bewitch
    their corn,
Themselves, their servants, and their
    babes at nurse.
This they enforce upon me, and in part

Enter O[ld] Banks.

Make me to credit it. And here comes
    one
Of my chief adversaries.
O. BANK. Out, out upon thee, witch!
SAWY.   Dost call me witch?
O. BANK. I do, witch, I do; and worse
I would, knew I a name more hateful.
What makest[3] thou upon my ground? [20
SAWY. Gather a few rotten sticks to
warm me.
O. BANK. Down with them when I bid
thee, quickly; I'll make thy bones rattle in
thy skin else.

[2] Bewitches.   [3] Doest.

SAWY. You won't, churl, cutthroat, miser! There they be. [*Throws them down.*] Would they stuck cross thy throat, thy bowels, thy maw, thy midriff!

O. BANK. Say'st thou me so? Hag, [30 out of my ground!   [*Beats her.*]

SAWY. Dost strike me, slave, curmudgeon? Now, thy bones aches, thy joints cramps, and convulsions stretch and crack thy sinews!

O. BANK. Cursing, thou hag! Take that and that!   [*Beats her and*] exit.

SAWY. Strike, do, and withered may that hand and arm
Whose blows have lamed me drop from the rotten trunk.
Abuse me! Beat me! Call me hag and witch!   40
What is the name, where and by what art learned,
What spells, what charms, or invocations,
May the thing called Familiar be purchased?

Enter Young Banks and three or four more
          [*Countrymen*].

Y. BANK. A new head for the tabor, and silver tipping for the pipe; remember that, and forget not five leash of new bells.

1 [COUNT.] Double bells! Crooked Lane[1] ye shall have 'em straight in. Crooked Lane! Double bells all, if it be possible.

Y. BANK. Double bells? Double [50 coxcombs! Trebles, buy me trebles, all trebles, for our purpose is to be in the altitudes.

2 [COUNT.] All trebles? Not a mean?[2]

Y. BANK. Not one. The morris is so cast we'll have neither mean nor bass in our company, fellow Rowland.

3 [COUNT.] What? Nor a counter?[3]

Y. BANK. By no means, no hunting counter;[4] leave that to Enfield[5] Chase [60 men. All trebles, all in the altitudes. Now for the disposing of parts in the morris, little or no labor will serve.

2 [COUNT.] If you that be minded to follow your leader know me—an ancient

honor belonging to our house—for a forehorse [i' th'][6] team and fore-gallant[7] in a morris, my father's stable is not unfurnished.

3 [COUNT.] So much for the fore- [70 horse; but how for a good hobbyhorse?[8]

Y. BANK. For a hobbyhorse? Let me see an almanac. Midsummer moon, let me see ye. "When the moon's in the full, then's wit in the wane." No more. Use your best skill; your morris will suffer an eclipse.

1 [COUNT.] An eclipse?

Y. BANK. A strange one.

2 [COUNT.] Strange?   80

Y. BANK. Yes, and most sudden. Remember the fore-gallant, and forget the hobbyhorse! The whole body of your morris will be darkened.—There be of us—but 'tis no matter. Forget the hobbyhorse!

1 [COUNT.] Cuddy Banks, have you forgot since he paced it from Enfield Chase to Edmonton? Cuddy, honest Cuddy, cast thy stuff.   90

Y. BANK. Suffer may ye all! It shall be known, I can take mine ease as well as another man. Seek your hobbyhorse where you can get him.

1 [COUNT.] Cuddy, honest Cuddy, we confess, and are sorry for our neglect.

2 [COUNT.] The old horse shall have a new bridle.

3 [COUNT.] The caparisons new painted.

4 [COUNT.] The tail repaired. The [100 snaffle and the bosses new saffroned o'er.[9]

1 [COUNT.] Kind—

2 [COUNT.] Honest—

3 [COUNT.] Loving, ingenious—

4 [COUNT.] Affable Cuddy.

Y. BANK. To show I am not flint, but affable, as you say, very well stuffed, a kind of warm dough or puffpaste, I relent, I connive, most affable Jack. Let the hobbyhorse provide a strong back, [110 he shall not want a belly when I am in 'em—but [*Sees Sawyer.*]—'uds me,[10] Mother Sawyer!

---

[1] A shopping district in London.
[2] Tenor.   [3] Countertenor.
[4] Following the trail in the wrong direction.
[5] The original spelling, *Envile*, indicates the pronunciation.
[6] Added in Gifford-Dyce edn.
[7] Leader of the dancers.
[8] A performer in a morris.
[9] The original gives this sentence to the first countryman.
[10] God's me; a mild oath.

1 [COUNT.] The old witch of Edmonton!
If our mirth be not crossed—

2 [COUNT.] Bless us, Cuddy, and let her
curse her tother [1] eye out.—What dost
now?

Y. BANK. "Ungirt, unblessed," says
the proverb; but my girdle shall [120
serve [2] a riding knot; [3] and a fig for all the
witches in Christendom!—What wouldst
thou?

1 [COUNT.] The devil cannot abide to
be crossed.

2 [COUNT.] And scorns to come at any
man's whistle.

3 [COUNT.] Away—

4 [COUNT.] With the witch!

OMN[ES]. Away with the witch [130
of Edmonton! *Ex[eunt] in strange posture.*

SAWY. Still vexed? Still tortured? That
    curmudgeon Banks
Is ground of all my scandal; I am
    shunned
And hated like a sickness, made a scorn
To all degrees and sexes. I have heard
    old beldams
Talk of familiars in the shape of mice,
Rats, ferrets, weasels, and I wot not
    what,
That have appeared, and sucked, some
    say, their blood;
But by what means they came ac-
    quainted with them
I'm now ignorant. Would some power,
    good or bad,   140
Instruct me which way I might be re-
    venged
Upon this churl, I'd go out of myself,
And give this fury leave to dwell within
This ruined cottage ready to fall with
    age,
Abjure all goodness, be at hate with
    prayer,
And study curses, imprecations,
Blasphemous speeches, oaths, detested
    oaths,
Or anything that's ill, so I might work
Revenge upon this miser, this black
    cur,
That barks and bites, and sucks the
    very blood   150
Of me and of my credit. 'Tis all one

To be a witch as to be counted one.
Vengeance, shame, ruin light upon that
    canker!

Enter Dog.

DOG. Ho! Have I found thee cursing?
    Now thou art
    Mine own.

SAWY.   Thine? What art thou?

DOG.   He thou hast so often
Importuned to appear to thee, the devil.

SAWY. Bless me! The devil?

DOG. Come, do not fear; I love thee much
    too well
To hurt or fright thee; if I seem terrible,
It is to such as hate me. I have
    found   160
Thy love unfeigned, have seen and
    pitiéd
Thy open wrongs, and come, out of my
    love,
To give thee just revenge against thy foes.

SAWY. May I believe thee?

DOG.   To confirm 't, command me
Do any mischief unto man or beast,
And I'll effect it, on condition
That, uncompelled, thou make a deed
    of gift
Of soul and body to me.

SAWY.   Out, alas!
My soul and body?

DOG.   And that instantly,
And seal it with thy blood. If thou
    deniest,   170
I'll tear thy body in a thousand pieces.

SAWY. I know not where to seek relief.
    But shall I,
After such covenants sealed, see full
    revenge
On all that wrong me?

DOG.   Ha, ha! Silly woman!
The devil is no liar to such as he loves.
Didst ever know or hear the devil a liar
To such as he affects?

SAWY. Then [4] I am thine; at least so
    much of me
As I can call mine own.

DOG.   Equivocations?
Art mine or no? Speak, or I'll tear—

SAWY.   All thine. 180

DOG. Seal 't with thy blood.
    Sucks her arm. Thunder and lightning.
    See! Now I dare call thee mine!

---

[1] Other.   [2] *I.e.,* serve as.
[3] Running knot, slip knot, used for hanging.
Original reads *knit.*

[4] Emended by Dyce. Original reads *when.*

For proof, command me; instantly I'll
run
To any mischief; goodness can I none.
Sawy. And I desire as little. There's an
old churl,
One Banks—
Dog.   That wronged thee: he lamed
thee, called thee witch.
Sawy. The same; first upon him I'ld be
revenged.
Dog. Thou shalt; do but name how.
Sawy.   Go, touch his life.
Dog. I cannot.
Sawy. Hast thou not vowed?   Go, kill
the slave!
Dog.   I wonnot.
Sawy. I'll cancel, then, my gift.
Dog.   Ha, ha!
Sawy.   Dost laugh?   190
Why wilt not kill him?
Dog.   Fool, because I cannot.
Though we have power, know it is cir-
cumscribed
And tied in limits. Though he be cursed
to thee,
Yet of himself he is loving to the world,
And charitable to the poor. Now men
That, as he, love goodness, though in
smallest measure,
Live without compass of our reach. His
cattle
And corn I'll kill and mildew; but his
life—
Until I take him, as I late found thee,
Cursing and swearing—I have no power
to touch.   200
Sawy. Work on his corn and cattle, then.
Dog.   I shall.
The witch of Edmonton shall see his
fall,
If she at least put credit in my power,
And in mine only, make orisons to me,
And none but me.
Sawy.   Say how and in what manner.
Dog. I'll tell thee. When thou wishest
ill,
Corn, man, or beast wouldst spoil or
kill,
Turn thy back against the sun,
And mumble this short orison:
"If thou to death or shame pursue
'em,   210
Sanctibicetur nomen tuum." [1]

[1] Hallowed be thy name.

Sawy. "If thou to death or shame pur-
sue 'em,
Sanctibicetur nomen tuum."
Dog. Perfect! Farewell. Our first-made
promises
We'll put in execution against Banks.
                         Exit.
Sawy. *Contaminetur nomen tuum.*[2] I'm
an expert scholar,
Speak Latin, or I know not well what
language,
As well as the best of 'em. But who
comes here?

        Enter Y[oung] Ba[nks].

The son of my worst foe. "To death pur-
sue 'em,
Ei sanctibicetur nomen tuum."   220
Y. Bank. [*Aside.*] What's that she mum-
bles? The devil's paternoster? Would
it were else!—Mother Sawyer, good mor-
row.
Sawy. Ill morrow to thee, and all the
world that flout
A poor old woman! "To death pursue
'em,
And *sanctibicetur nomen tuum.*"
Y. Bank. Nay, good Gammer Sawyer,
whate'er it pleases
My father to call you, I know you are—
Sawy.   A witch.
Y. Bank. A witch? Would you were else,
i' faith!
Sawy.   Your father   230
Knows I am by this.[3]
Y. Bank.   I would he did.
Sawy. And so in time may you.
Y. Bank. I would I might else! But,
witch or no witch, you are a motherly
woman, and, though my father be a kind
of God-bless-us, as they say, I have an
earnest suit to you; and, if you'll be so
kind to ka me one good turn, I'll be so
courteous as to kob you another.[4]
Sawy. What's that? To spurn, beat me,
and call me witch,   240
As your kind father doth?
Y. Bank. My father? I am ashamed
to own him. If he has hurt the head of thy
credit, there's money to buy thee a plaster.
[*Gives money.*] And a small courtesy I
would require at thy hands.

[2] Cursed be thy name.   [3] *I.e.*, by this time.
[4] Serve me, and I'll serve you.

1 [Count.] The old witch of Edmonton!
If our mirth be not crossed—

2 [Count.] Bless us, Cuddy, and let her
curse her tother [1] eye out.—What dost
now?

Y. Bank. "Ungirt, unblessed," says
the proverb; but my girdle shall [120
serve [2] a riding knot; [3] and a fig for all the
witches in Christendom!—What wouldst
thou?

1 [Count.] The devil cannot abide to
be crossed.

2 [Count.] And scorns to come at any
man's whistle.

3 [Count.] Away—

4 [Count.] With the witch!

Omn[es]. Away with the witch [130
of Edmonton! *Ex[eunt] in strange posture.*

Sawy. Still vexed? Still tortured? That
     curmudgeon Banks
Is ground of all my scandal; I am
     shunned
And hated like a sickness, made a scorn
To all degrees and sexes. I have heard
     old beldams
Talk of familiars in the shape of mice,
Rats, ferrets, weasels, and I wot not
     what,
That have appeared, and sucked, some
     say, their blood;
But by what means they came ac-
     quainted with them
I'm now ignorant. Would some power,
     good or bad,   140
Instruct me which way I might be re-
     venged
Upon this churl, I'd go out of myself,
And give this fury leave to dwell within
This ruined cottage ready to fall with
     age,
Abjure all goodness, be at hate with
     prayer,
And study curses, imprecations,
Blasphemous speeches, oaths, detested
     oaths,
Or anything that's ill, so I might work
Revenge upon this miser, this black
     cur,
That barks and bites, and sucks the
     very blood   150
Of me and of my credit. 'Tis all one

[1] Other.   [2] *I.e.*, serve as.
[3] Running knot, slip knot, used for hanging.
Original reads *knit*.

To be a witch as to be counted one.
Vengeance, shame, ruin light upon that
     canker!

Enter Dog.

Dog. Ho! Have I found thee cursing?
     Now thou art
     Mine own.

Sawy.   Thine? What art thou?

Dog.   He thou hast so often
Importuned to appear to thee, the devil.

Sawy. Bless me! The devil?

Dog. Come, do not fear; I love thee much
     too well
To hurt or fright thee; if I seem terrible,
It is to such as hate me. I have
     found   160
Thy love unfeigned, have seen and
     pitiéd
Thy open wrongs, and come, out of my
     love,
To give thee just revenge against thy foes.

Sawy. May I believe thee?

Dog.   To confirm 't, command me
Do any mischief unto man or beast,
And I'll effect it, on condition
That, uncompelled, thou make a deed
     of gift
Of soul and body to me.

Sawy.   Out, alas!
     My soul and body?

Dog.   And that instantly,
And seal it with thy blood. If thou
     deniest,   170
I'll tear thy body in a thousand pieces.

Sawy. I know not where to seek relief.
     But shall I,
After such covenants sealed, see full
     revenge
On all that wrong me?

Dog.   Ha, ha! Silly woman!
The devil is no liar to such as he loves.
Didst ever know or hear the devil a liar
To such as he affects?

Sawy. Then [4] I am thine; at least so
     much of me
As I can call mine own.

Dog.   Equivocations?
Art mine or no? Speak, or I'll tear—

Sawy.   All thine.   180

Dog. Seal 't with thy blood.
     Sucks her arm. Thunder and lightning.
     See! Now I dare call thee mine!

[4] Emended by Dyce. Original reads *when.*

For proof, command me; instantly I'll run

To any mischief; goodness can I none.

Sawy. And I desire as little. There's an old churl,

One Banks—

Dog.   That wronged thee: he lamed thee, called thee witch.

Sawy. The same; first upon him I'ld be revenged.

Dog. Thou shalt; do but name how.

Sawy.   Go, touch his life.

Dog. I cannot.

Sawy. Hast thou not vowed?   Go, kill the slave!

Dog.   I wonnot.

Sawy. I'll cancel, then, my gift.

Dog.   Ha, ha!

Sawy.   Dost laugh?   190
Why wilt not kill him?

Dog.   Fool, because I cannot.
Though we have power, know it is circumscribed

And tied in limits. Though he be cursed to thee,

Yet of himself he is loving to the world,

And charitable to the poor. Now men

That, as he, love goodness, though in smallest measure,

Live without compass of our reach. His cattle

And corn I'll kill and mildew; but his life—

Until I take him, as I late found thee,

Cursing and swearing—I have no power to touch.   200

Sawy. Work on his corn and cattle, then.

Dog.   I shall.
The witch of Edmonton shall see his fall,

If she at least put credit in my power,

And in mine only, make orisons to me,

And none but me.

Sawy.   Say how and in what manner.

Dog. I'll tell thee. When thou wishest ill,

Corn, man, or beast wouldst spoil or kill,

Turn thy back against the sun,

And mumble this short orison:

"If thou to death or shame pursue 'em,   210

Sanctibicetur nomen tuum." [1]

[1] Hallowed be thy name.

Sawy. "If thou to death or shame pursue 'em,

Sanctibicetur nomen tuum."

Dog. Perfect! Farewell. Our first-made promises

We'll put in execution against Banks.

                              Exit.

Sawy. *Contaminetur nomen tuum.* [2] I'm an expert scholar,

Speak Latin, or I know not well what language,

As well as the best of 'em. But who comes here?

        Enter Y[oung] Ba[nks].

The son of my worst foe. "To death pursue 'em,

Ei sanctibicetur nomen tuum."   220

Y. Bank. [*Aside.*] What's that she mumbles?   The devil's paternoster?   Would it were else!—Mother Sawyer, good morrow.

Sawy. Ill morrow to thee, and all the world that flout

A poor old woman! "To death pursue 'em,

And *sanctibicetur nomen tuum.*"

Y. Bank. Nay, good Gammer Sawyer, whate'er it pleases

My father to call you, I know you are—

Sawy.   A witch.

Y. Bank. A witch? Would you were else, i' faith!

Sawy.   Your father   230
Knows I am by this. [3]

Y. Bank.   I would he did.

Sawy. And so in time may you.

Y. Bank. I would I might else! But, witch or no witch, you are a motherly woman, and, though my father be a kind of God-bless-us, as they say, I have an earnest suit to you; and, if you'll be so kind to ka me one good turn, I'll be so courteous as to kob you another. [4]

Sawy. What's that? To spurn, beat me, and call me witch,   240
As your kind father doth?

Y. Bank. My father? I am ashamed to own him. If he has hurt the head of thy credit, there's money to buy thee a plaster. [*Gives money.*] And a small courtesy I would require at thy hands.

[2] Cursed be thy name.   [3] *I.e.*, by this time.
[4] Serve me, and I'll serve you.

3 [Dan.] So would not I, for, if she comes, the devil and all comes along with her.

Clow. Well, I'll have a witch; I have loved a witch ever since I played at cherry pit.[1] Leave me, and get my horse dressed. Give him oats; but water him not till I come. Whither do we foot it first?　　30

2 [Dan.] To Sir Arthur Clarington's first; then whither thou wilt.

Clow. Well, I am content. But we must up to Carter's, the rich yeoman; I must be seen on hobbyhorse there.

1 [Dan.] O, I smell him now! I'll lay my ears Banks is in love, and that's the reason he would walk melancholy by himself.

Clow. Ha! Who was that said I　[40 was in love?

1 [Dan.] Not I.

2 [Dan.] Nor I.

Clow. Go to, no more of that. When I understand what you speak, I know what you say; believe that.

1 [Dan.] Well, 'twas I; I'll not deny it. I meant no hurt in 't. I have seen you walk up to Carter's of Chessum. Banks, were not you there last Shrovetide?　　50

Clow. Yes, I was ten days together there the last Shrovetide.

2 [Dan.] How could that be, when there are but seven days in the week?

Clow. Prithee, peace! I reckon *stila nova*[2] as a traveler; thou understandest as a freshwater farmer that never sawest a week beyond sea. Ask any soldier that ever received his pay but in the Low Countries, and he'll tell thee there are eight days　[60 in the week there hard by. How dost thou think they rise in High Germany, Italy, and those remoter places?

3 [Dan.] Ay, but simply there are but seven days in the week yet.

Clow. No, simply as thou understandest. Prithee, look but in the lover's almanac. When he has been but three days absent, "O," says he, "I have not seen my love these seven years." There's a long　[70 cut! When he comes to her again and embraces her, "O," says he, "now methinks I am in heaven." And that's a pretty step! He that can get up to heaven in ten days

need not repent his journey; you may ride a hundred days in a caroche,[3] and be further off than when you set forth. But, I pray you, good morris mates, now leave me. I will be with you by midnight.

1 [Dan.] Well, since he will be　[80 alone, we'll back again and trouble him no more.

Omn[es]. But remember, Banks.

Clow. The hobbyhorse shall be remembered. But hark you; get Poldavis, the barber's boy, for the witch, because he can show his art better than another.—
　　　　　　　Exeunt [All but Clown].
Well, now to my walk. I am near the place where I should meet—I know not what. Say I meet a thief, I must follow him,　[90 if to the gallows; say I meet a horse, or hare, or hound, still I must follow. Some slow-paced beast, I hope. Yet love is full of lightness in the heaviest lovers. Ha! My guide is come.

[Enter the Dog.]

A water dog! I am thy first man, sculler; I go with thee; ply no other but myself. Away with the boat! Land me but at Katherine's Dock, my sweet Katherine's Dock, and I'll be a fare to thee.　[100 That way? Nay, which way thou wilt; thou know'st the way better than I. Fine, gentle cur it is, and well brought up, I warrant him. We go a-ducking, spaniel; thou shalt fetch me the ducks, pretty, kind rascal.

*Enter Spirit in shape of Katherine, vizarded,
　　　　　　　　　　and takes it [4] off.*

Spir. [*Aside.*] Thus throw I off mine own
　　essential horror,
And take the shape of a sweet, lovely
　　maid
Whom this fool dotes on. We can meet
　　his folly,　　　　　　　　　　109
But from his virtues must be runaways.
We'll sport with him; but, when we
　　reckoning call,
We know where to receive; th' witch
　　pays for all.　　　　*Dog barks.*
Clow. Ay? Is that the watchword? She's come. Well, if ever we be married,

---

[1] A children's game.
[2] According to the new style of dating.
[3] Coach.
[4] *I.e.*, his vizard, or natural appearance.

it shall be at Barking Church, in memory
of thee. Now come behind, kind cur.

> And have I met thee, sweet Kate?
> I will teach thee to walk so late.

O, see, we meet in meter. [*The Spirit moves
away.*] What! Dost thou trip from [120
me? O, that I were upon my hobbyhorse; I
would mount after thee so nimble! "Stay,
nymph; stay, nymph," singed Apollo.

> " Tarry and kiss me. Sweet nymph, stay!
> Tarry and kiss me, sweet."

We will to Chessum Street, and then to the
house stands in the highway.—Nay, by
your leave, I must embrace you.
                    Ex[eunt] Spir[it] and Banks.
[*Within.*] O, help, help! I am drowned,
I am drowned!   *Enter wet.* [130
  Dog. Ha, ha, ha, ha!
  Clow. This was an ill night to go a-wooing in. I find it now in Pond's almanac.
Thinking to land at Katherine's Dock, I
was almost at Gravesend. I'll never go to a
wench in the dog days again; yet 'tis cool
enough.—Had you never a paw in this dog-
trick? A mangie [1] take that black hide of
yours! I'll throw you in at Limehouse in
some tanner's pit or other.   140
  Dog. Ha, ha, ha, ha!
  Clow. How now! Who's that laughs
at me? Hist to him!—(*Dog barks.*) Peace,
peace! Thou didst but thy kind [2] neither;
'twas my own fault.
  Dog. Take heed how thou trustest the
devil another time.
  Clow. How now! Who's that speaks?
I hope you have not your reading tongue
about you.   150
  Dog. Yes, I can speak.
  Clow. The devil you can! You have
read Æsop's fables, then; I have played one
of your parts then—the dog that catched
at the shadow in the water. Pray you, let
me catechize you a little. What might one
call your name, dog?
  Dog. My dame calls me Tom.
  Clow. 'Tis well, and she may call me
Ass; so there's an whole one betwixt [160
us, Tom-Ass. She said I should follow you,
indeed. Well, Tom, give me thy fist; we

----

are friends. You shall be mine ingle.[3] I love
you, but, I pray you, let's have no more of
these ducking devices.
  Dog. Not, if you love me. Dogs love
where they are beloved; cherish me, and
I'll do anything for thee.
  Clow. Well, you shall have jowls and
livers; I have butchers to my friends [170
that shall bestow 'em. And I will keep
crusts and bones for you, if you'll be a kind
dog, Tom.
  Dog. Anything; I'll help thee to thy
love.
  Clow. Wilt thou? That promise shall
cost me a brown loaf, though I steal it out
of my father's cupboard. You'll eat stolen
goods, Tom, will you not?
  Dog. O, best of all; the sweetest [180
bits those.
  Clow. You shall not starve, ningle [4]
Tom; believe that. If you love fish, I'll
help you to maids [5] and soles; I'm acquainted with a fishmonger.
  Dog. Maids and soles? O, sweet bits!
Banqueting stuff those.
  Clow. One thing I would request you,
ningle, as you have played the knavish
cur with me a little, that you would [190
mingle amongst our morris dancers in the
morning. You can dance?
  Dog. Yes, yes, anything; I'll be there,
but unseen to any but thyself. Get thee
gone before; fear not my presence. I have
work tonight; I serve more masters, more
dames, than one.
  Clow. He can serve Mammon and the
devil too.
  Dog. It shall concern thee and thy love's
      purchase.   200
> There's a gallant rival loves the maid,
> And likely is to have her. Mark what a
>   mischief,
> Before the morris ends, shall light on
>   him!
  Clow. O, sweet ningle, thy neuf [6] once
again; friends must part for a time. Farewell, with this remembrance; shalt have
bread too when we meet again. If ever there
were an honest devil, 'twill be the devil
of Edmonton, I see. Farewell, Tom; I
prithee, dog me as soon as thou canst. [210
                              Ex[it] Banks.

----

[1] Mange.   [2] *I.e.*, according to thy nature.

[3] Crony.   [5] Female skates.
[4] *I.e.*, mine ingle.   [6] Fist.

Dog. I'll not miss thee, and be merry with thee.

Those that are joys denied must take delight

In sins and mischiefs; 'tis the devil's right.   *Ex[it] Dog.*

[Scena ii.

The neighborhood of Edmonton.]

Enter Young Thorney, Winnifride as a boy.

Frank. Prithee, no more! Those tears give nourishment

To weeds and briers in me, which shortly will

O'ergrow and top my head; my shame will sit

And cover all that can be seen of me.

Win. I have not shown this cheek in company.

Pardon me now. Thus singled with yourself,

It calls a thousand sorrows round about,

Some going before, and some on either side,

But infinite behind, all chained together.

Your second adulterous marriage leads;

That's the sad eclipse—th' effects must follow,   11

As plagues of shame, spite, scorn, and obloquy.

Y. Thor. Why, hast thou not left one hour's patience

To add to all the rest? One hour bears us

Beyond the reach of all these enemies.

Are we not now set forward in the flight,

Provided with the dowry of my sin

To keep us in some other nation?

While we together are, we are at home

In any place.

Win.   'Tis foul, ill-gotten coin,   20

Far worse than usury or extortion.

Y. Thor. Let my father, then, make the restitution,

Who forced me take the bribe. It is his gift

And patrimony to me; so I receive it.

He would not bless, nor look a father on me,

Until I satisfied his angry will.

When I was sold, I sold myself again—

Some knaves have done 't in lands, and I in body—

For money, and I have the hire. But, sweet, no more;   29

'Tis hazard of discovery, our discourse;

And then prevention takes off all our hopes.

For only but to take her leave of me

My wife is coming.

Win.   Who coming? Your wife?

Y. Thor. No, no; thou art here. The woman—I knew

Not how to call her now; but after this day

She shall be quite forgot and have no name

In my remembrance. See, see! She's come.

Enter Susan.

Go lead

The horses to the hill's top; there I'll meet thee.

Sus. Nay, with your favor let him stay a little;

I would part with him too, because he is   40

Your sole companion; and I'll begin with him,

Reserving you the last.

Y. Thor.   Ay, with all my heart.

Sus. You may hear, if it please you, sir.

Y. Thor.   No, 'tis not fit.

Some rudiments, I conceive, they must be,

To overlook my slippery footings. And so—

Sus. No, indeed, sir.

Y. Thor.   Tush, I know it must be so,

And 'tis necessary. On! But be brief.

    [*Walks forward.*]

Win. What charge soe'er you lay upon me, mistress,

I shall support it faithfully—being honest—

To my best strength.

Sus.   Believe 't shall be no other.   50

I know you were commended to my husband

By a noble knight.

Win.   O, gods! O, mine eyes!

Sus. How now! What ail'st thou, lad?

Win. Something hit mine eye—it makes it water still—

Even as you said "commended to my husband."

Some dor [1] I think it was. I was, forsooth,
Commended to him by Sir Arthur Clarington.

Sus. Whose servant once my Thorney was
himself.
That title, methinks, should make you
almost fellows,
Or at the least much more than a ser-
vant;   60
And I am sure he will respect you so.
Your love to him, then, needs no spur
from me,
And what for my sake you will ever do,
'Tis fit it should be bought with some-
thing more
Than fair entreats. Look, here's a jewel
for thee,
A pretty, wanton label for thine ear;
And I would have it hang there, still to
whisper
These words to thee, "Thou hast my
jewel with thee."
It is but earnest of a larger bounty,
When thou return'st with praises of thy
service,   70
Which I am confident thou wilt deserve.
Why, thou art many now besides thyself:
Thou mayst be servant, friend, and wife
to him;
A good wife is, then, all. A friend can
play
The wife and servant's part, and shift
enough;
No less the servant can the friend and
wife.
'Tis all but sweet society, good counsel,
Interchanged loves, yes, and counsel-
keeping.

Y. Thor. Not done yet?

Sus. Even now, sir.   80

Win. Mistress, believe my vow; your
severe eye,
Were it present to command, your bounteous hand,
Were it then by to buy or bribe my
service,
Shall not make me more dear or near
unto him
Than I shall voluntary. I'll be all your
charge,
Servant, friend, wife to him.

Sus.   Wilt thou?

[1] Beetle.

Now blessings go with thee for 't! Courtesies
Shall meet thee coming home.

Win.   Pray you, say plainly,
Mistress, are you jealous of him? If you
be,
I'll look to him that way too.

Sus.   Say'st thou so?   90
I would thou hadst a woman's bosom
now;
We have weak thoughts within us. Alas,
There's nothing so strong in us as sus-
picion;
But I dare not, nay, I will not think
So hardly of my Thorney.

Win.   Believe it, mistress,
I'll be no pander to him; and, if I find
Any loose, lubric [2] scapes in him, I'll
watch him,
And at my return protest I'll show you
all.
He shall hardly offend without my
knowledge.   99

Sus. Thine own diligence is that I press,
And not the curious eye over his faults.
Farewell. If I should never see thee more,
Take it forever.

Y. Thor. (Gives his sword.) Prithee, take
that along with thee, and haste thee
To the hill's top; I'll be there instantly.
                                        Ex[it] Win[nifride].

Sus. No haste, I prithee; slowly as thou
canst.
Pray, let him obey me now; 'tis happily
His last service to me. My power is
e'en
A-going out of sight.

Y. Thor.   Why would you delay?
We have no other business now but to
part.   110

Sus. And will not that, sweetheart, ask a
long time?
Methinks it is the hardest piece of work
That e'er I took in hand.

Y. Thor.   Fie, fie! Why, look,
I'll make it plain and easy to you—
farewell!   Kisses.

Sus. Ah, 'las, I am not half perfect in it
yet;
I must have it read over an hundred
times.
Pray you, take some pains; I confess my
dullness.

[2] Lubricous, lascivious.

Y. Thor. [*Aside.*] What a thorn this rose
grows on! Parting were sweet;
But what a trouble 'twill be to obtain
it!—
Come, again and again, farewell!—
(*Kisses.*) Yet wilt return? 120
All questions of my journey, my stay,
employment,
And revisitation, fully I have answered
all.
There's nothing now behind but—
nothing.
Sus. And
That "nothing" is more hard than any-
thing,
Than all the everythings. This request—
Y. Thor. What is it?
Sus. That I may bring you through one
pasture more
Up to yon knot of trees; amongst those
shadows
I'll vanish from you—they shall teach
me how.
Y. Thor. Why, 'tis granted; come, walk,
then.
Sus. Nay, not too fast.
They say slow things have best perfec-
tion; 130
The gentle shower wets to fertility,
The churlish storm may mischief with
his bounty;
The baser beasts take strength even from
the womb,
But the lord lion's whelp is feeble long.
Exeunt.

[Scena iii.

A field with a small grove.]

Enter Dog.[1]

Dog. Now for an early mischief and a
sudden!
The mind's about it now; one touch from
me
Soon sets the body forward.

Enter Young Thorney, Susan.

Y. Thor. Your request is out; yet will you
leave me?
Sus. What? So churlishly? You'll make
me stay forever
Rather than part with such a sound from
you.

[1] The Dog is, of course, invisible to all but the
audience.

Y. Thor. Why, you almost anger me.
Pray you, begone.
You have no company, and 'tis very
early;
Some hurt may betide you homewards.
Sus. Tush! I fear none;
To leave you is the greatest hurt I can
suffer. 10
Besides, I expect your father and mine
own
To meet me back, or overtake me with
you.
They began to stir when I came after you.
I know they'll not be long.
Y. Thor. [*Aside.*] So! I shall have more
trouble. (*Dog rubs him.*) Thank you
for that.
Then I'll ease all at once. 'Tis done
now—
What I ne'er thought on.—You shall not
go back.
Sus. Why, shall I go along with thee?
Sweet music!
Y. Thor. No, to a better place.
Sus. Any place I;
I'm there at home where thou pleasest to
have me. 20
Y. Thor. At home? I'll leave you in your
last lodging;
I must kill you.
Sus. O, fine! You'ld fright me from
you.
Y. Thor. You see I had no purpose; I'm
unarmed;
'Tis this minute's decree, and it must be.
Look, this will serve your turn.
[*Draws a knife.*]
Sus. I'll not turn from it,
If you be ear[ne]st, sir; yet you may tell
me
Wherefore you'll kill me.
Y. Thor. Because you are a whore.
Sus. There's one deep wound already. A
whore!
'Twas ever further from me than the
thought
Of this black hour. A whore?
Y. Thor. Yes, I'll prove it, 30
And you shall confess it. You are my
whore—
No wife of mine; the word admits no
second.
I was before wedded to another, have her
still.

I do not lay the sin unto your charge;
'Tis all mine own. Your marriage was
  my theft,
For I espoused your dowry, and I have
  it.
I did not purpose to have added mur-
  ther;
The devil did not prompt me. Till this
  minute
You might have safe returned; now you
  cannot.
You have dogged your own death.
                              Stabs her.
Sus.   And I deserve it;   40
I'm glad my fate was so intelligent.[1]
'Twas some good spirit's motion. Die?
  O, 'twas time!
How many years might I have slept in
  sin,
Sin of my most hatred, too, adultery?
Y. Thor. Nay, sure, 'twas likely that the
  most was past,
For I meant never to return to you
After this parting.
Sus.   Why, then, I thank you more.
You have done lovingly, leaving yourself,
That you would thus bestow me on
  another.
Thou art my husband, Death, and I em-
  brace thee   50
With all the love I have. Forget the stain
Of my unwitting sin; and then I come
A crystal virgin to thee. My soul's purity
Shall with bold wings ascend the doors
  of Mercy,
For Innocence is ever her companion.
Y. Thor. Not yet mortal? I would not
  linger you,
Or leave you a tongue to blab.
                      [*Stabs her again.*]
Sus. Now heaven reward you ne'er the
  worse for me!
I did not think that Death had been so
  sweet,
Nor I so apt to love him. I could ne'er
  die better,   60
Had I stayed forty years for preparation,
For I'm in charity with all the world.
Let me for once be thine example,
  heaven;
Do to this man as I him free forgive,
And may he better die and better live.
                              Moritur.[2]

¹ Communicative.   ² She dies.

Y. Thor. 'Tis done; and I am in! Once
  past our height,
We scorn the deep'st abyss. This follows
  now,
To hele ³ her wounds by dressing of the
  weapon.
Arms, thighs, hands, any place; we must
  not fail   *Wounds himself.*
Light scratches, giving such deep ones.
  The best I can   70
To bind myself to this tree. Now's the
  storm,
Which if blown o'er, many fair days may
  follow.   *Dog ties him.*
So, so, I'm fast; I did not think I could
Have done so well behind me. How
  prosperous
And effectual mischief sometimes is!
  Help! Help!
Murther, murther, murther!

Enter Carter and Old Thorney.

[O.] Cart. Ha! Whom tolls the bell for?
Y. Thor.   O, O!
O. Thor.   Ah me!
The cause appears too soon. My child,
  my son!
[O.] Cart. Susan, girl, child! Not speak
  to thy father? Ha!
Y. Thor. O, lend me some assistance to
  o'ertake   80
This hapless woman.
O. Thor.   Let's o'ertake the murtherers.
Speak whilst thou canst; anon may be too
  late.
I fear thou hast death's mark upon thee
  too.
Y. Thor. I know them both; yet such an
  oath is passed
As pulls damnation up if it be broke.
I dare not name 'em. Think what forced
  men do.
O. Thor. Keep oath with murtherers?
  That were a conscience
To hold the devil in.
Y. Thor.   Nay, sir, I can describe 'em,
Shall show them as familiar as their
  names.   89
The taller of the two at this time wears
His satin doublet white, but crimson-
  lined,
Hose of black satin, cloak of scarlet—

³ *I.e.*, conceal the source of.

O. THOR.   Warbeck,
Warbeck, Warbeck!—Do you list to this,
    sir?

[O.] CART. Yes, yes, I listen you; here's
nothing to be heard.

Y. THOR. Th' other's cloak branched [1] velvet, black, velvet-lined his suit.

O. THOR. I have 'em already. Somerton,
    Somerton!

Binal [2] revenge all this. Come, sir, the
    first work
Is to pursue the murtherers, when we
    have
Removed these mangled bodies hence.

[O.] CART. Sir, take that carcass there,
and give me this.   100
I'll not own her now; she's none of mine.
Bob me off with a dumb show? No, I'll
    have life.
This is my son too, and, while there's life
    in him,
'Tis half mine; take you half that silence
    for 't.—
When I speak, I look to be spoken to.
Forgetful slut!

O. THOR.   Alas, what grief may do
    now!—
Look, sir, I'll take this load of sorrow
    with me.

[O.] CART. Ay, do, and I'll have this.—[Exit
Old Thorney, carrying Susan.] How do
you, sir?

Y. THOR. O, very ill, sir.

[O.] CART. Yes, I think so; but 'tis well
you can speak yet.   110
There's no music but in sound; sound it
    must be.
I have not wept these twenty years be-
    fore,
And that I guess was ere that girl was
    born;
Yet now methinks, if I but knew the way,
My heart's so full I could weep night and
    day.   Exeunt.

[SCENA iv.

Before Sir Arthur Clarington's house.]
Enter Sir Arthur Clarington, Warbeck,
                                Somerton.

SIR ART. Come, gentlemen, we must all
    help to grace
The nimble-footed youth of Edmonton,

[1] Embroidered with a figured pattern.
[2] Twofold.

That are so kind
To call us up today with an high morris.

WARB. I could wish it for the best it
were the worst now. Absurdity's in my
opinion ever the best dancer in a morris.

SOM. I could rather sleep than see 'em.

SIR ART. Not well, sir?

SOM. Faith, not ever thus leaden; [10
yet I know no cause for 't.

WARB. Now am I beyond mine own
condition highly disposed to mirth.

SIR ART. Well, you may have yet a morris
    to help both:
To strike you in a dump, and make him
    merry.

Enter Fiddler and Morris, all but Banks.

FIDDL. Come, will you set yourselves
in morris ray? [3] The fore-bell, second bell,
tenor, and great bell; Maid Marian for the
same bell. But where's the weathercock
now? The hobbyhorse?   20

1 [DAN.] Is not Banks come yet? What
a spite 'tis!

SIR ART. When set you forward, gentlemen?

1 [DAN.] We stay but for the hobbyhorse, sir; all our footmen are ready.

SOM. 'Tis marvel your horse should be
behind your foot.

2 [DAN.] Yes, sir, he goes further about;
we can come in at the wicket, but the [30
broad gate must be opened for him.

Enter Banks, Hobbyhorse, and Dog.

SIR ART. O, we stayed for you, sir.

CLOW. Only my horse wanted a shoe,
sir; but we shall make you amends ere we
part.

SIR ART. Ay? Well said. Make 'em drink
ere they begin.

Ent[er] Serv[ants] with beer.

CLOW. A bowl, I prithee, and a little for
my horse; he'll mount the better. Nay,
give me. I must drink to him; he'll not
pledge else.—[Drinks.] Here, hobby. [40
(Holds him the bowl.) I pray you. No? Not
drink?—You see, gentlemen, we can but
bring our horse to the water; he may
choose whether he'll drink or no.

[3] Array.

Som. A good moral made plain by history.

1 [Dan.] Strike up, Father Sawgut, strike up.

Fiddl. E'en when you will, children. Now in the name of the best foot for- [50 ward!—[*The fiddle makes no sound.*] How now! Not a word in thy guts? I think, children, my instrument has caught cold on the sudden.

Clow. [*Aside.*] My ningle's knavery; black Tom's doing.

Omn[es]. Why, what mean you, Father Sawgut?

Clow. Why, what would you have him do? You hear his fiddle is speechless. 60

Fiddl. I'll lay mine ear to my instrument that my poor fiddle is bewitched. I played "The Flowers in May" e'en now, as sweet as a violet; now 'twill not go against the hair. You see I can make no more music than a beetle of a cow turd.

Clow. Let me see, Father Sawgut. [*Takes the fiddle.*] Say once you had a brave hobbyhorse that you were beholding [1] to. I'll play and dance too.—Ningle, [70 away with it.

Dog plays the morris, which ended, enter a Constable and Officers.

Omn[es]. Ay, marry, sir!

Con. Away with jollity! 'Tis too sad an hour.—
Sir Arthur Clarington, your own assistance,
In the king's name, I charge, for apprehension
Of these two murderers, Warbeck and Somerton.

Sir Art. Ha! Flat murtherers?

Som. Ha, ha, ha! This has awakened my melancholy.

Warb. And struck my mirth down [80 flat.—Murtherers?

Con. The accusation is flat against you, gentlemen.—
Sir, you may be satisfied with this.—
[*Shows warrant.*]
I hope you'll quietly obey my power;
'Twill make your cause the fairer.

Ambo.[2] O, with all our hearts, sir.

---

[1] Beholden.
[2] *I.e.*, both Somerton and Warbeck.

Clow. There's my rival taken up for hangman's meat. Tom told me he was about a piece of villainy.—Mates and morris men, you see here's no longer [90 piping, no longer dancing; this news of murder has slain the morris. You that go the footway, fare ye well; I am for a gallop.—Come, ningle.

Exe[unt Banks and Dog].

Fiddl. (*Strikes his fiddle.*) Ay? Nay, and my fiddle be come to himself again, I care not. I think the devil has been abroad amongst us today; I'll keep thee out of thy fit now, if I can.

Exe[unt Fiddler and Morris].

Sir Art. These things are full of horror, full of pity. 100
But, if this time be constant to the proof,
The guilt of both these gentlemen I dare take
Upon mine own danger; yet, howsoever, sir,
Your power must be obeyed.

Warb.   O, most willingly, sir.
'Tis a most sweet affliction; I could not meet
A joy in the best shape with better will.
Come, fear not, sir; nor judge nor evidence
Can bind him o'er who's freed by conscience.

Som. Mine stands so upright to the middle zone 109
It takes no shadow to 't; it goes alone.

Exeunt.

Act[us] IV. Scen[a] i.

[*The village green in Edmonton.*]

Enter Old Banks and two or three Countrymen.

O. Bank. My horse this morning runs most piteously of the glanders, whose nose yesternight was as clean as any man's here now coming from the barber's; and this, I'll take my death upon 't, is long [3] of this jadish witch, Mother Sawyer.

1 [Count.] I took my wife and a servingman in our town of Edmonton, thrashing in my barn together such corn as country wenches carry to market, and, examin- [10 ing my polecat [4] why she did so, she swore

---

[3] Because.   [4] Harlot.

in her conscience she was bewitched. And what witch have we about us but Mother Sawyer?

2 [Count.] Rid the town of her, else all our wives will do nothing else but dance about other country Maypoles.

3 [Count.] Our cattle fall, our wives fall, our daughters fall, and maidservants fall; and we ourselves shall not be able to [20 stand, if this beast be suffered to graze amongst us.

Enter W. Hamluc with thatch and a link.[1]

HAML. Burn the witch, the witch, the witch, the witch!

OMN[ES]. What hast got there?

HAML. A handful of thatch plucked off a hovel of hers; and they say, when 'tis burning, if she be a witch, she'll come running in.

O. BANK. Fire it, fire it! I'll stand [30 between thee and home for any danger.

As that burns enter the Witch.

SAWY. Diseases, plagues, the curse of an old woman follow and fall upon you!

OMN[ES]. Are you come, you old trot?

O. BANK. You hot whore, must we fetch you with fire in your tail?

1 [Count.] This thatch is as good as a jury to prove she is a witch.

OMN[ES]. Out, witch! Beat her, kick her, set fire on her!   40

SAWY. Shall I be murthered by a bed of serpents? Help, help!

Enter Sir Arthur Clarington and a Justice.

OMN[ES]. Hang her, beat her, kill her!

JUST. How now? Forbear this violence!

SAWY. A crew of villains, a knot of bloody hangmen, set to torment me, I know not why.

JUST. Alas, neighbor Banks, are you a ringleader in mischief? Fie, to abuse an aged woman!   50

O. BANK. Woman? A she-hellcat, a witch! To prove her one, we no sooner set fire on the thatch of her house, but in she came running as if the devil had sent her in a barrel of gunpowder, which trick as surely proves her a witch as the pox in a snuffling nose is a sign a man is a whoremaster.

[1] Torch.

JUST. Come, come. Firing her thatch? Ridiculous!

Take heed, sirs, what you do; unless your proofs
Come better armed, instead of turning her   60
Into a witch, you'll prove yourselves stark fools.

OMN[ES]. Fools?

JUST. Arrant fools.

O. BANK. Pray, Mr. Justice What-do-you-call-'em, hear me but in one thing: this grumbling devil owes me I know no good will ever since I fell out with her.

SAWY. And breakedst my back with beating me.

O. BANK. I'll break it worse.   70

SAWY. Wilt thou?

JUST. You must not threaten her; 'tis against law. Go on.

O. BANK. So, sir, ever since, having a dun cow tied up in my backside,[2] let me go thither, or but cast mine eye at her, and, if I should be hanged, I cannot choose, though it be ten times in an hour, but run to the cow, and, taking up her tail, kiss—saving your worship's reverence—my cow [80 behind, that the whole town of Edmonton has been ready to bepiss themselves with laughing me to scorn.

JUST. And this is long of her?

O. BANK. Who the devil else? For is any man such an ass to be such a baby, if he were not bewitched?

SIR ART. Nay, if she be a witch, and the harms she does end in such sports, she may scape burning.   90

JUST. Go, go! Pray, vex her not; she is a subject,
And you must not be judges of the law
To strike her as you please.

OMN[ES]. No, no, we'll find cudgel enough to strike her.

O. BANK. Ay; no lips to kiss but my cow's—!

Exeunt [Old Banks and Countrymen].

SAWY. Rots and foul maladies eat up thee and thine!

JUST. Here's none now, Mother Sawyer, but this gentleman,
Myself, and you. Let us to some mild questions;   100
Have you mild answers. Tell us honestly

[3] Back yard.

And with a free confession—we'll do
    our best
To wean you from it—are you a witch,
    or no?
SAWY. I am none!
JUST.   Be not so furious.
SAWY.   I am none!
  None but base curs so bark at me. I'm
    none.
  Or would I were! If every poor old
    woman
  Be trod on thus by slaves, reviled,
    kicked, beaten,
  As I am daily, she to be revenged
  Had need turn witch.
SIR ART.   And you to be revenged
  Have sold your soul to th' devil.
SAWY.   Keep thine own from him.
JUST. You are too saucy and too bitter.
SAWY.   Saucy? 111
  By what commission can he send my soul
  On the devil's errand more than I can
    his?
  Is he a landlord of my soul, to thrust it,
  When he list, out of door?
JUST.   Know whom you speak to.
SAWY. A man; perhaps no man. Men in
    gay clothes,
  Whose backs are laden with titles and
    honors,
  Are within far more crooked than I am,
  And, if I be a witch, more witchlike.
SIR ART. Y' are a base hellhound.— 120
  And now, sir, let me tell you, far and near
  She's bruited for a woman that maintains
  A spirit that sucks her.
SAWY.   I defy thee.
SIR ART.   Go, go.
  I can, if need be, bring an hundred voices,
  E'en here in Edmonton, that shall loud
    proclaim
  Thee for a secret and pernicious witch.
SAWY. Ha, ha!
JUST.   Do you laugh? Why laugh you?
SAWY.   At my name,
  The brave name this knight gives me—
    witch.
JUST. Is the name of witch so pleasing to
    thine ear?
SIR ART. Pray, sir, give way, and let her
    tongue gallop on. 130
SAWY. A witch! Who is not?
  Hold not that universal name in scorn,
    then.

What are your painted things in princes'
    courts,
Upon whose eyelids lust sits, blowing
    fires
To burn men's souls in sensual hot de-
    sires,
Upon whose naked paps a lecher's
    thought
Acts sin in fouler shapes than can be
    wrought?
JUST. But those work not as you do.
SAWY.   No, but far worse.
  These by enchantments can whole lord-
    ships [1] change
  To trunks of rich attire, turn plows and
    teams 140
  To Flanders mares and coaches, and huge
    trains
  Of servitors to a French butterfly.
  Have you not city witches who can turn
  Their husbands' wares, whole standing
    shops of wares,
  To sumptuous tables, gardens of stol'n
    sin,
  In one year wasting what scarce twenty
    win?
  Are not these witches?
JUST.   Yes, yes: but the law
  Casts not an eye on these.
SAWY.   Why then on me,
  Or any lean old beldam? Reverence once
  Had wont to wait on age; now an old
    woman, 150
  Ill-favored grown with years, if she be
    poor,
  Must be called bawd or witch. Such so
    abused
  Are the coarse witches; tother are the
    fine,
  Spun for the devil's own wearing.
SIR ART.   And so is thine.
SAWY. She on whose tongue a whirlwind
    sits to blow
  A man out of himself, from his soft
    pillow
  To lean his head on rocks and fighting
    waves,
  Is not that scold a witch? The man of
    law
  Whose honeyed hopes the credulous
    client draws—
  As bees by tinkling basins—to swarm to
    him 160

[1] Estates.

From his own hive to work the wax in
 his—
He is no witch, not he!

SIR ART.   But these men-witches
 Are not in trading with hell's merchan-
  dise,
 Like such as you are, that for a word, a
  look,
 Denial of a coal of fire, kill men,
 Children, and cattle.

SAWY.   Tell them, sir, that do so.
 Am I accused for such an one?

SIR ART.   Yes; 'twill be sworn.

SAWY. Dare any swear I ever tempted
  maiden
 With golden hooks flung at her chastity
 To come and lose her honor; and, being
  lost,   170
 To pay not a denier [1] for 't? Some slaves
  have done it.
 Men-witches can, without the fangs of
  law
 Drawing once one drop of blood, put
  counterfeit pieces
 Away for true gold.

SIR ART. By one thing she speaks
 I know now she's a witch, and dare no
  longer
 Hold conference with the fury.

JUST.   Let's, then, away.—
 Old woman, mend thy life; get home and
  pray. *Exeunt [Sir Arthur and Justice].*

SAWY. For his confusion!—

Enter Dog.

   My dear Tom-boy, welcome!
I'm torn in pieces by a pack of curs
Clapped all upon me, and for want of
 thee.   180
Comfort me; thou shalt have the teat
 anon.

DOG. Bow, wow! I'll have it now.

SAWY.   I am dried up
 With cursing and with madness, and
  have yet
 No blood to moisten these sweet lips of
  thine.
 Stand on thy hind legs up—kiss me, my
  Tommy,
 And rub away some wrinkles on my
  brow
 By making my old ribs to shrug for joy

[1] Penny.

Of thy fine tricks. What has thou done?
 Let's tickle.
Hast thou struck the horse lame as I bid
 thee?

DOG. Yes;
 And nipped the sucking child.

SAWY.   Ho, ho, my dainty, 190
 My little pearl! No lady loves her hound,
 Monkey, or parrakeet, as I do thee.

DOG. The maid has been churning butter
nine hours, but it shall not come.

SAWY. Let 'em eat cheese and choke.

DOG.   I had rare sport
 Among the clowns i' th' morris.

SAWY.   I could dance
 Out of my skin to hear thee. But, my
  curl-pate,
 That jade, that foul-tongued whore, Nan
  Ratcliffe,
 Who, for a little soap licked by my sow,
 Struck and almost had lamed it, did not
  I charge thee   200
 To pinch that quean to th' heart?

DOG.   Bow, wow, wow! Look
 here else.

Enter Ann Ratcliffe mad.

RATC. See, see, see! The man i' th'
moon has built a new windmill; and what
running there's from all quarters of the
city to learn the art of grinding!

SAWY. Ho, ho, ho! I thank thee, my
sweet mongrel.

RATC. Hoyda! A pox of the devil's false
hopper! All the golden meal runs into the
rich knaves' purses, and the poor [210
have nothing but bran. Hey derry down!—
Are not you Mother Sawyer?

SAWY. No, I am a lawyer.

RATC. Art thou? I prithee, let me
scratch thy face, for thy pen has flayed off
a great many men's skins. You'll have
brave doings in the vacation, for knaves
and fools are at variance in every village.
I'll sue Mother Sawyer, and her own sow
shall give in evidence against her. 220

SAWY. *[To Dog.]* Touch her.

RATC. O, my ribs are made of a paned
hose,[2] and they break! There's a Lan-
cashire hornpipe in my throat; hark, how
it tickles it, with doodle, doodle, doodle,
doodle! Welcome, serjeants! Welcome,

[2] Hose made by sewing strips together.

devil!—Hands, hands! Hold hands, and dance around, around, around. [*Dances.*]

Enter Old Banks, his son the Clown, Old Ratcliffe, Country Fellows.

O. Ratc. She's here; alas, my poor wife is here! 230

O. Bank. Catch her fast, and have her into some close chamber, do, for she's, as many wives are, stark mad.

Clow. The witch! Mother Sawyer, the witch, the devil!

O. Ratc. O, my dear wife! Help, sirs!
Car[ry] her[1] *off.*[2]

O. Bank. You see your work, Mother Bumby.[3]

Sawy. My work? Should she and all you here run mad, is the work mine? [240

Clow. No, on my conscience, she would not hurt a devil of two years old.—

Enter Old Ratcliffe and the Rest.

How now? What's become of her?

O. Ratc. Nothing; she's become nothing but the miserable trunk of a wretched woman. We were in her hands as reeds in a mighty tempest. Spite of our strengths, away she brake; and nothing in her mouth being heard but "the devil, the witch, the witch, the devil!" she beat out her [250 own brains, and so died.

Clow. It's any man's case, be he never so wise, to die when his brains go a-wool-gathering.

O. Bank. Masters, be ruled by me; let's all to a justice.—Hag, thou hast done this, and thou shalt answer it.

Sawy. Banks, I defy thee.

O. Bank. Get a warrant first to examine her; then ship her to Newgate. Here's [260 enough, if all her other villainies were pardoned, to burn her for a witch.— You have a spirit, they say, comes to you in the likeness of a dog; we shall see your cur at one time or other. If we do, unless it be the devil himself, he shall go howling to the goal[4] in one chain, and thou in another.

Sawy. Be hanged thou in a third, and do thy worst!

Clow. How, father? You send the [270

poor dumb thing howling to th' goal? He that makes him howl makes me roar.

O. Bank. Why, foolish boy, dost thou know him?

Clow. No matter if I do or not. He's bailable, I am sure, by law. But, if the dog's word will not be taken, mine shall.

O. Bank. Thou bail for a dog?

Clow. Yes, or a bitch either, being my friend. I'll lie by the heels myself [280 before puppison[5] shall; his dog days are not come yet, I hope.

O. Bank. What manner of dog is it? Didst ever see him?

Clow. See him? Yes, and given him a bone to gnaw twenty times. The dog is no court foisting[6] hound that fills his belly full by base wagging his tail; neither is it a citizen's water spaniel, enticing his master to go a-ducking twice or thrice a week, [290 whilst his wife makes ducks and drakes at home. This is no Paris Garden ban-dog[7] neither, that keeps a bow-wow-wowing to have butchers bring their curs thither; and, when all comes to all, they run away like sheep. Neither is this the Black Dog of Newgate.[8]

O. Bank. No, Goodman Son-fool, but the dog of hellgate.

Clow. I say, Goodman Father- [300 fool, it's a lie.

Omn[es]. He's bewitched.

Clow. A gross lie, as big as myself. The devil in St. Dunstan's will as soon drink with this poor cur as with any Temple Bar laundress that washes and wrings lawyers.

Dog. Bow, wow, wow, wow!

Omn[es]. O, the dog's here, the dog's here. 309

O. Bank. It was the voice of a dog.

Clow. The voice of a dog? If that voice were a dog's, what voice had my mother? So am I a dog. Bow, wow, wow! It was I that barked so, father, to make coxcombs of these clowns.

O. Bank. However, we'll be coxcombed no longer. Away, therefore, to th' justice for a warrant; and then, Gammer Gurton, have at your needle of witchcraft!

---

[1] *I.e.*, Ann Ratcliffe.
[2] This stage direction follows the preceding line in the original.
[3] A reference to Lyly's *Mother Bombie*.
[4] Gaol, jail.

[5] Probably equivalent to *his puppyship*.
[6] Cheating; also stinking.
[7] Fierce dog used for bear baiting.
[8] A probable allusion to a lost play of a similar title.

SAWY. And prick thine own eyes out. Go,
　peevish fools!　　　　　　　　　　　320
Exe[unt Old Banks, Ratcliffe, and Coun-
　　　　　　　　　　　　　trymen].
　CLOW. Ningle, you had liked to have
spoiled all with your bow-ings. I was glad
to put 'em off with one of my dogtricks
on a sudden; I am bewitched, little Cost-
me-naught, to love thee.—A pox!—That
morris makes me spit in thy mouth. I
dare not stay. Farewell, ningle; you
whoreson [1] dog's nose!—Farewell, witch!
　　　　　　　　　　　　　　Exit.
　DOG. Bow, wow, wow, wow!
　SAWY. Mind him not; he's not　　[330
worth thy worrying. Run at a fairer
game, that foul-mouthed knight, scurvy Sir
Arthur. Fly at him, my Tommy, and pluck
out 's throat.
　DOG. No, there['s] a dog already biting 's
conscience.
　SAWY. That's a sure bloodhound. Come,
let's home and play;
　Our black work ended, we'll make holiday.　　　　　　　　　　　　*Exeunt.*

SCEN[A] ii.

[A bedroom in Carter's house.]

Enter Katherine. A bed thrust forth; on it
　　　　　　　　Frank in a slumber.

　KAT. Brother, brother! So sound asleep?
That's well.
　FRANK. *[Waking.]* No, not I, sister; he
　that's wounded here
As I am—all my other hurts are bitings
Of a poor flea—but he that here once
　bleeds
Is maimed incurably.
　KAT.　　　　　My good sweet brother—
For now my sister must grow up in you—
Though her loss strikes you through,
　and that I feel
The blow as deep, I pray thee, be not
　cruel
To kill me too, by seeing you cast away
In your own helpless sorrow. Good love,
　sit up;　　　　　　　　　　　10
And, if you can give physic to yourself,
I shall be well.
　FRANK.　　　　I'll do my best.
　KAT.　　　　　　　I thank you.
What do you look about for?

[1] Rascally.

FRANK.　　　　　　　Nothing, nothing;
　But I was thinking, sister—
　KAT.　　　　　　　Dear heart, what?
　FRANK. Who but a fool would thus be
　bound to a bed,
Having this room to walk in?
　KAT.　　　　　Why do you talk so?
Would you were fast asleep!
　FRANK.　　　No, no; I'm not idle. [2]
But here's my meaning: being robbed as
　I am,
Why should my soul, which married was
　to hers,
Live in divorce, and not fly after her?　20
Why should not I walk hand in hand
　with Death,
To find my love out?
　KAT.　　　　That were well indeed,
Your time being come; when Death is
　sent to call you,
No doubt you shall meet her.
　FRANK.　　　　Why should not I
Go without calling?
　KAT.　　　Yes, brother, so you might,
Were there no place to go when y' are
　gone
But only this.
　FRANK.　　Troth, sister, thou say'st true,
For, when a man has been an hundred
　years
Hard traveling o'er the tottering bridge
　of age,　　　　　　　　　　　29
He's not the thousand part upon his way.
All life is but a wand'ring to find hcme;
When we are gone, we are there. Happy
　were man,
Could here his voyage end; he should
　not, then,
Answer how well or ill he steered his soul
By heaven's or by hell's compass; how
　he put in—
Losing blessed goodness' shore—at such
　a sin;
Nor how life's dear provision he has
　spent;
Nor how far he in 's navigation went
Beyond commission. This were a fine
　reign,
To do ill and not hear of it again;　　40
Yet then were man more wretched than
　a beast;
For, sister, our dead pay [3] is sure the
　best.

[2] Light-headed.　　　　[3] Retribution.

KAT. 'Tis so, the best or worst; and I wish heaven

To pay—and so I know it will—that traitor,

That devil Somerton, who stood in mine eye

Once as an angel, home to his deservings.

What villain but himself, once loving me,

With Warbeck's soul would pawn his own to hell

To be revenged on my poor sister?

FRANK. Slaves!

A pair of merciless slaves! Speak no more of them. 50

KAT. I think this talking hurts you.

FRANK. Does me no good, I'm sure;

I pay for 't everywhere.

KAT. I have done, then.

Eat, if you cannot sleep; you have these two days

Not tasted any food.—[Calls.] Jane, is it ready?

FRANK. What's ready? What's ready?

KAT. I have made ready a roasted chicken for you.

[Enter Jane with chicken.]

Sweet, wilt thou eat?

FRANK. A pretty stomach on a sudden, yes.

There's one in the house can play upon a lute. 60

Good girl, let's hear him too.

KAT. You shall, dear brother.

[Exit Jane.]

Would I were a musician; you should hear Lute plays.

How I would feast your ear! Stay, mend your pillow,

And raise you higher.

FRANK. I am up too high,

Am I not, sister, now?

KAT. No, no; 'tis well.

Fall to, fall to.—A knife! Here's never a knife.

Brother, I'll look out yours.

[Picks up his coat.]

Enter Dog, shrugging as it were for joy, and dances.

FRANK. Sister, O sister,

I am ill upon a sudden, and can eat nothing.

KAT. In very deed you shall. The want of food

Makes you so faint. Ha! [Sees the bloody knife.] Here's none in your pocket; 70

I'll go fetch a knife. Exit.

FRANK. Will you? 'Tis well;

All's well.

She gone, he searches first one, then the other, pocket. Knife found. Dog runs off. He lies on one side. The Spirit of Susan, his second wife, comes to the bed's side. He stares at it, and, turning to the other side, it's there too. In the meantime, Winnifride as a page comes in, stands at his bed's feet sadly. He, frighted, sits upright. The Spirit vanishes.

FRANK. What art thou?

WIN. A lost creature.

FRANK. So am I too.—Win? Ah, my she-page!

WIN. For your sake I put on

A shape that's false; yet do I wear a heart

True to you as your own.

FRANK. Would mine and thine

Were fellows in one house! Kneel by me here.

On this side now? How dar'st thou come to mock me

On both sides of my bed?

WIN. When?

FRANK. But just now.

Outface me, stare upon me with strange postures, 80

Turn my soul wild by a face in which were drawn

A thousand ghosts leaped newly from their graves

To pluck me into a winding sheet!

WIN. Believe it,

I came no nearer to you than yon place

At your bed's feet, and of the house had leave,

Calling myself your horse boy, in to come

And visit my sick master.

FRANK. Then 'twas my fancy—

Some windmill in my brains for want of sleep.

WIN. Would I might never sleep, so you could rest!

But you have plucked a thunder on your
   head,   90
Whose noise cannot cease suddenly.
   Why should you
Dance at the wedding of a second
   wife,
When scarce the music which you heard
   at mine
Had ta'en a farewell of you? O, this was
   ill!
And they who thus can give both hands
   away
In th' end shall want their best limbs.
FRANK.   Winnifride—
   The chamber door fast?
WIN.   Yes.
FRANK.   Sit thee, then, down,
   And, when th'ast heard me speak, melt
   into tears.
Yet I, to save those eyes of thine from
   weeping,
Being to write a story of us two,   100
Instead of ink dipped my sad pen in
   blood.
When of thee I took leave, I went abroad
Only for pillage, as a freebooter,
What gold soe'er I got to make it
   thine.
To please a father, I have heaven dis-
   pleased;
Striving to cast two wedding rings in
   one,
Through my bad workmanship I now
   have none.
I have lost her and thee.
WIN.   I know she's dead;
   But you have me still.
FRANK.   Nay, her this hand
   Murdered; and so I lose thee too.
WIN.   O me!   110
FRANK. Be quiet, for thou my evidence
   art,
Jury, and judge. Sit quiet, and I'll tell all.

*As they whisper, enter at one end o' th' stage
   Old Carter and Katherine, Dog at th'
   other, pawing softly at Frank.*

KAT. I have run madding up and down to
   find you,
Being laden with the heaviest news that
   ever
Poor daughter carried.
[O.] CART.   Why? Is the boy dead?

KAT.   Dead, sir!
   O father, we are cozened. You are told
The murtherer sings in prison, and he
   laughs here.
This villain killed my sister. See else,
   see,
A bloody knife in 's pocket!
[O.] CART.   Bless me, patience!
FRANK. [*Seeing them.*] The knife, the knife,
   the knife!   120
KAT. What knife?   *Exit Dog.*
FRANK.   To cut my chicken up,
   my chicken!—
Be you my carver, father.
[O.] CART.   That I will.
KAT. [*Aside.*] How the devil steels our
   brows after doing ill!
FRANK. My stomach and my sight are
   taken from me;
All is not well within me.
[O.] CART. I believe thee, boy—I that
have seen so many moons clap their horns
on other men's foreheads to strike them
sick, yet mine to scape and be well; I that
never cast away a fee upon urinals,   [130
but am as sound as an honest man's conscience when he's dying, I should cry out
as thou dost, "All is not well within me,"
felt I but the bag of thy imposthumes.
Ah, poor villain! Ah, my wounded rascal!
All my grief is, I have now small hope of
thee.
FRANK. Do the surgeons say my wounds
are dangerous then?
[O.] CART. Yes, yes, and there's no   [140
way with thee but one.
FRANK. Would he were here to open
them!
[O.] CART. I'll go to fetch him; I'll make
an holiday to see thee as I wish.
                Exit to fetch Officers.
FRANK. A wondrous kind old man!
WIN. [*Aside to Frank.*] Your sin's the
blacker so to abuse his goodness.—Master,
how do you?
FRANK. Pretty well now, boy; I   [150
have such odd qualms come cross my
stomach. I'll fall to; boy, cut me.
WIN. [*Aside.*] You have cut me, I'm
sure.—A leg or wing, sir?
FRANK. No, no, no! A wing?—[*Aside.*]
Would I had wings but to soar up you
tower! But here's a clog that hinders me.—
What's that?

Father with her in a coffin.

[O.] CART. That? What? O, now I see
her; 'tis a young wench, my daughter, [160
sirrah, sick to the death; and, hearing thee to
be an excellent rascal for letting blood, she
looks out at a casement, and cries, "Help,
help! Stay that man! Him I must have or
none."

FRANK. For pity's sake, remove her! See,
she stares

With one broad open eye still in my face!

[O.] CART. Thou puttest both hers out,
like a villain as thou art; yet, see, she
is willing to lend thee one again to [170
find out the murtherer, and that's thyself.

FRANK. Old man, thou liest!

[O.] CART.   So shalt thou—
i' th' goal.

Run for officers!

KAT.   O, thou merciless slave!
She was—though yet above ground—in
her grave
To me; but thou hast torn it up
again.
Mine eyes, too much drowned, now
must feel more rain.

[O.] CART. Fetch officers.

Exit Katherine.

FRANK. For whom?

[O.] CART.   For thee, sirrah, sirrah!
Some knives have foolish posies[1] upon [180
them, but thine has a villainous one.
[*Takes knife from Frank's pocket.*] Look!
O, it is enameled with the heart blood of
thy hated wife, my beloved daughter!
What say'st thou to this evidence? Is 't
not sharp? Does 't not strike home? Thou
canst not answer honestly and without
a trembling heart to this one point, this
terrible, bloody point.

WIN. I beseech you, sir, strike [190
him no more; you see he's dead already.

[O.] CART. O, sir, you held his horses;
you are as arrant a rogue as he. Up go
you too.

FRANK. As y' are a man, throw not upon
that woman
Your loads of tyranny, for she's innocent.

[O.] CART. How? How? A woman?
Is 't grown to a fashion for women in all
countries to wear the breeches?

WIN. I am not as my disguise [200

[1] Inscriptions.

speaks me, sir, his page, but his first, only
wife, his lawful wife.

[O.] CART. How? How? More fire i'
th' bedstraw!

WIN. The wrongs which singly fell on
your daughter
On me are multiplied; she lost a life,
But I an husband and myself must lose
If you call him to a bar for what he has
done.

[O.] CART. He has done it, then?

WIN. Yes, 'tis confessed to me.

FRANK.   Dost thou betray me?   210

WIN. O, pardon me, dear heart! I am
mad to lose thee,
And know not what I speak; but, if thou
didst,
I must arraign this father for two sins,
Adultery and murther.

Enter Katherine.

KAT.   Sir, they are come.

[O.] CART. Arraign me for what thou
wilt, all Middlesex knows me better for an
honest man than the middle of a market
place knows thee for an honest woman.—
Rise, sirrah, and don your tacklings; rig
yourself for the gallows, or I'll carry [220
thee thither on my back. Your trull shall to
th' goal go with you. There be as fine
Newgate birds as she, that can draw him in.
Pox on 's wounds!

FRANK. I have served thee, and my wages
now are paid;
Yet my worst punishment shall, I hope,
be stayed.   *Exeunt.*

ACT[US] V. SCEN[A] i.

[*Mother Sawyer's hut.*]

Enter Mother Sawyer alone.

SAWY. Still wronged by every slave, and
not a dog
Bark in his dame's defense? I am called
witch,
Yet am myself bewitched from doing
harm.
Have I given up myself to thy black
lust
Thus to be scorned? Not see me in
three days?
I'm lost without my Tomalin. Prithee,
come;

Revenge to me is sweeter far than life.
Thou art my raven, on whose coal-
    black wings
Revenge comes flying to me. O, my
    best love!
I am on fire, even in the midst of ice,   10
Raking my blood up, till my shrunk
    knees feel
Thy curled head leaning on them. Come,
    then, my darling;
If in the air thou hover'st, fall upon me
In some dark cloud; and, as I oft have
    seen
Dragons and serpents in the elements,
Appear thou now so to me. Art thou i'
    th' sea?
Muster up all the monsters from the
    deep,
And be the ugliest of them, so that my
    bulch [1]
Show but his swarth cheek to me, let
    earth cleave
And break from hell, I care not! Could
    I run   20
Like a swift powder mine beneath the
    world,
Up would I blow it, all to find out thee,
Though I lay ruined in it.   Not yet
    come!
I must, then, fall to my old prayer:
Sanctibicetur nomen tuum.

Not yet come!   Worrying of wolves,
biting of mad dogs, the manges, and the—

Enter Dog [, now white].

Dog. How now! Whom art thou cursing?
Sawy. Thee! Ha! No, 'tis my black cur
    I am cursing
For not attending on me.
Dog.   I am that cur.   30
Sawy. Thou liest.   Hence!   Come not
    nigh me.
Dog.   Baw, waw!
Sawy. Why dost thou thus appear to me
    in white,
As if thou wert the ghost of my dear
    love?
Dog. I am dogged—list not to tell
thee; yet, to torment thee, my whiteness
puts thee in mind of thy winding sheet.[2]
Sawy. Am I near death?

[1] Bull calf, a term of endearment.
[2] Original reads *sweet*.

Dog. Yes, if the dog of hell be near
thee; when the devil comes to thee as a
lamb, have at thy throat!   40
Sawy. Off, cur!
Dog. He has the back of a sheep, but
the belly of an otter; devours by sea and
land. Why am I in white? Didst thou not
pray to me?
Sawy. Yes,   thou   dissembling   hellhound! Why now in white more than at
other times?
Dog. Be blasted with the news! Whiteness is day's footboy, a forerunner [50
to light, which shows thy old riveled [3]
face.   Villains are stripped naked; the
witch must be beaten out of her cockpit.
Sawy. Must she?   She shall not; thou
    art a lying spirit.
Why to mine eyes art thou a flag of
    truce?
I am at peace with none; 'tis the black
    color,
Or none, which I fight under. I do not like
Thy puritan paleness; glowing furnaces
Are far more hot than they which flame
    outright.
If thou my old dog art, go and bite
    such   60
As I shall set thee on.
Dog. I will not.
Sawy. I'll sell myself to twenty thou-
    sand fiends
To have thee torn in pieces, then.
Dog. Thou canst not; thou art so ripe
to fall into hell, that no more of my kennel
will so much as bark at him that hangs
thee.
Sawy. I shall run mad.
Dog. Do so; thy time is come to [70
curse, and rave, and die. The glass of thy
sins is full, and it must run out at gallows.
Sawy. It cannot, ugly cur.   I'll confess
    nothing;
And, not confessing, who dare come
    and swear
I have bewitched them? I'll not confess
    one mouthful.
Dog. Choose, and be hanged or burned.
Sawy. Spite of the devil and thee, I'll
    muzzle up
My tongue from telling tales.
Dog. Spite of thee and the devil, thou'lt
    be condemned.

[3] Shriveled.

SAWY. Yes, when?

DOG. And, ere the executioner 80
Catch thee full in 's claws, thou'lt confess all.

SAWY. Out, dog!

DOG. Out, witch! Thy trial is at hand.
Our prey being had, the devil does
laughing stand. *The Dog stands aloof.*

Enter Old Banks, Ratcliffe, and Countrymen.

O. BANK. She's here; attach her.—
Witch, you must go with us.
[They seize her.]

SAWY. Whither? To hell?

O. BANK. No, no, no, old crone; your
mittimus shall be made thither, but your
own jailors shall receive you.—Away with
her! 90

SAWY. My Tommy! My sweet Tom-boy!
O, thou dog!
Dost thou now fly to thy kennel and for-
sake me?
Plagues and consumptions—
Exeunt [All but Dog].

DOG. Ha, ha, ha, ha!
Let not the world witches or devils
condemn;
They follow us, and then we follow them.

[Enter] Young Banks to the Dog.

CLOW. I would fain meet with mine
ingle once more. He has had a claw
amongst um. My rival that loved my
wench is like to be hanged like an [100
innocent.[1] A kind cur where he takes,
but, where he takes not, a dogged rascal. I
know the villain loves me. No!—([*Dog*]
barks.) Art thou there? [*Sees Dog.*]—That's
Tom's voice, but 'tis not he; this is a dog
of another hair, this. Bark, and not speak
to me? Not Tom, then; there's as much
difference betwixt Tom and this as betwixt
white and black.

DOG. Hast thou forgot me? 110

CLOW. That's Tom again.—Prithee,
ningle, speak. Is thy name Tom?

DOG. Whilst I served my old Dame
Sawyer, 'twas; I'm gone from her now.

CLOW.[2] Gone? Away with the witch,
then, too! She'll never thrive if thou
leav'st her; she knows no more how to
kill a cow, or a horse, or a sow, without
thee, than she does to kill a goose.

[1] Fool, idiot. [2] Original reads *Dog.*

DOG. No, she has done killing now, [120
but must be killed for what she has done;
she's shortly to be hanged.

CLOW. Is she? In my conscience, if
she be, 'tis thou hast brought her to the
gallows, Tom.

DOG. Right. I served her to that purpose; 'twas part of my wages.

CLOW. This was no honest servant's
part, by your leave, Tom. This remember,
I pray you, between you and I; I [130
entertained you ever as a dog, not as a
devil.

DOG. True; and so I used thee doggedly,
not devilishly;
I have deluded thee for sport to laugh
at.
The wench thou seek'st after thou never
spakest with,
But a spirit in her form, habit, and
likeness.
Ha, ha!

CLOW. I do not, then, wonder at the
change of your garments, if you can enter
into shapes of women too. 140

DOG. Any shape, to blind such silly
eyes as thine; but chiefly those coarse
creatures, dog, or cat, hare, ferret, frog,
toad.

CLOW. Louse or flea?

DOG. Any poor vermin.

CLOW. It seems you devils have poor,
thin souls, that you can bestow yourselves
in such small bodies. But, pray you, Tom,
one question at parting—I think I [150
shall never see you more—where do you
borrow those bodies that are none of your
own? The garment-shape you may hire
at broker's.

DOG. Why wouldst thou know that?
Fool, it avails thee not.

CLOW. Only for my mind's sake, Tom,
and to tell some of my friends.

DOG. I'll thus much tell thee: thou never
art so distant 159
From an evil spirit but that thy oaths,
Curses, and blasphemies pull him to
thine elbow.
Thou never tell'st a lie but that a devil
Is within hearing it; thy evil purposes
Are ever haunted; but, when they come
to act—
As thy tongue slandering, bearing false
witness,

Thy hand stabbing, stealing, cozening,
   cheating—
He's then within thee. Thou play'st;
   he bets upon thy part.
Although thou lose, yet he will gain by
   thee.
CLOW. Ay? Then he comes in the shape
   of a rook.
DOG. The old cadaver of some self-
   strangled wretch   170
We sometimes borrow, and appear
   human;
The carcass of some disease-slain strumpet
We varnish fresh, and wear as her first
   beauty.
Didst never hear? If not, it has been
   done.
An hot, luxurious lecher in his twines,
When he has thought to clip his dalliance,
There has provided been for his embrace
A fine, hot, flaming devil in her place.
CLOW. Yes, I am partly a witness to
this, but I never could embrace her. [180
I thank thee for that, Tom. Well, again I
thank thee, Tom, for all this counsel;
without a fee too! There's few lawyers of
thy mind now. Certainly, Tom, I begin to
pity thee.
DOG. Pity me? For what?
CLOW. Were it not possible for thee to
become an honest dog yet? 'Tis a base
life that you lead, Tom, to serve witches,
to kill innocent children, to kill [190
harmless cattle, to stroy corn and fruit,
etc. 'Twere better yet to be a butcher and
kill for yourself.
DOG. Why, these are all my delights,
my pleasures, fool.
CLOW. Or, Tom, if you could give your
mind to ducking—I know you can swim,
fetch, and carry—some shopkeeper in
London would take great delight in you,
and be a tender master over you. Or [200
if you have a mind to the game either at
bull or bear, I think I could prefer you
to Moll Cutpurse.
DOG. Ha, ha! I should kill all the game
—bulls, bears, dogs, and all; not a cub to
be left.
CLOW. You could do, Tom; but you
must play fair; you should be staved off

else. Or, if your stomach did better like to
serve in some nobleman's, knight's, [210
or gentleman's kitchen, if you could brook
the wheel and turn the spit (your labor
could not be much) when they have roast
meat (that's but once or twice in the week
at most), here you might lick your own
toes very well. Or, if you could translate
yourself into a lady's arming puppy, there
you might lick sweet lips, and do many
pretty offices. But to creep under an old
witch's coats, and suck like a great [220
puppy! Fie upon 't! I have heard beastly
things of you, Tom.
DOG. Ha, ha!
The worse thou heard'st of me, the better 'tis.
Shall I serve thee, fool, at the selfsame
   rate?
CLOW. No, I'll see thee hanged; thou
shalt be damned first! I know thy qualities
too well; I'll give no suck to such whelps.
Therefore henceforth I defy thee. Out,
and avaunt!   230
DOG. Nor will I serve for such a silly
   soul.
I am for greatness now, corrupted great-
   ness;
There I'll shug [1] in, and get a noble
   countenance;
Serve some Briarean footcloth-strider, [2]
That has an hundred hands to catch at
   bribes,
But not a finger's nail of charity.
Such, like the dragon's tail, shall pull
   down hundreds
To drop and sink with him. I'll stretch
   myself,
And draw this bulk small as a silver
   wire,   239
Enter at the least pore tobacco fume
Can make a breach for. Hence, silly
   fool!
I scorn to prey on such an atom soul.
CLOW. Come out, come out, you cur!
I will beat thee out of the bounds of
Edmonton, and tomorrow we go in procession, and after thou shalt never come
in again. If thou goest to London, I'll
make thee go about by Tyburn, stealing
in by Thieving Lane. If thou canst rub
thy shoulder against a lawyer's gown, [250

---

[1] Crawl, sneak.
[2] A rider on a horse trapped for state occasions.

as thou passest by Westminster Hall, do;
if not, to the stairs amongst the bandogs;
take water, and the devil go with thee!
          Exeunt Y[oung] Banks, Dog barking.

[SCENA ii.

Near Tyburn.]

*Enter Justice, Sir Arthur, [Somerton,]
          Warbeck, Carter, Kate.*

JUST. Sir Arthur, though the bench
hath mildly censured your errors, yet you
have indeed been the instrument that
wrought all their misfortunes; I would
wish you paid down your fine speedily and
willingly.

SIR ART. I'll need no urging to it.

[O.] CART. If you should, 'twere a
shame to you, for, if I should speak my
conscience, you are worthier to be [10
hanged of the two, all things considered;
and now make what you can of it. But I
am glad these gentlemen are freed.

WARB. We knew our innocence.

SOM.   And therefore feared it not.

KAT. But I am glad that I have you safe.
          Noise within.

JUST. How now! What noise is that?

[O.] CART. Young Frank is going the
wrong way. Alas, poor youth! Now I
begin to pity him.   [*Exeunt.*]

[SCENA iii.

Another place near Tyburn.]

*Enter Y[oung] Thorney and Halberts. Enter,
as to see the execution, O[ld] Carter,
O[ld] Thorney, Katherine, Winnifride
          weeping.*

O. THOR. Here let our sorrows wait him; to
          press nearer
The place of his sad death, some appre-
          hensions
May tempt our grief too much, at height
          already.—
Daughter, be comforted.

WIN.   Comfort and I
Are too far separated to be joined,
But in eternity. I share too much
Of him that's going thither.

[O.] CART. Poor woman, 'twas not thy
          fault; I grieve to see
Thee weep for him that hath my pity too.

WIN. My fault was lust; my punishment
          was shame.   10
Yet I am happy that my soul is free
Both from consent, foreknowledge, and
          intent
Of any murther but of mine own honor,
Restored again by a fair satisfaction,
And since not to be wounded.

O. THOR.   Daughter, grieve not
For what necessity forceth; rather
          resolve
To conquer it with patience.—Alas,
          she faints!

WIN. My griefs are strong upon me; my
          weakness scarce
Can bear them.

[VOICES.] (*within.*) Away with her! Hang
          her, witch!

*Enter Sawyer to execution; Officers with
          Halberts; Country People.*

[O.] CART. The witch, that instru- [20
ment of mischief! Did not she witch the
devil into my son-in-law, when he killed
my poor daughter?—Do you hear, Mother
Sawyer?

SAWY. What would you have? Cannot a
          poor old woman
Have your leave to die without vexa-
          tion?

[O.] CART. Did not you bewitch Frank
to kill his wife? He could never have
done 't without the devil.

SAWY. Who doubts it? But is every devil
          mine?   30
Would I had one now whom I might
          command
To tear you all in pieces! Tom would
          have done 't
Before he left me.

[O.] CART. Thou didst bewitch Ann
Ratcliffe to kill herself.

SAWY. Churl, thou liest; I never did her
          hurt.
Would you were all as near your ends as
          I am,
That gave evidence against me for it!

[1] COUNT. I'll be sworn, Mr. Carter, she
bewitched Gammer Washbowl's sow to cast
her pigs a day before she would have [40
farried.[1] Yet they were sent up to London
and sold for as good Westminster dog pigs [2]

---

[1] Farrowed.   [2] Male pigs.

at Bartholomew Fair as ever great-bellied
alewife longed for.

SAWY. These dogs will mad me; I was
　well resolved
To die in my repentance. Though 'tis
　true
I would live longer if I might, yet since
I cannot, pray, torment me not; my
　conscience
　Is settled as it shall be. All take heed
How they believe the devil; at last he'll
　cheat you.　　　　　　　　　　　　50
[O.] CART. Th'adst best confess all truly.
SAWY.　　　　　　　　　　Yet again?
Have I scarce breath enough to say my
　prayers,
And would you force me to spend that
　in bawling?
Bear witness, I repent all former evil;
There is no damnéd conjuror like the
　devil.
OMN[ES]. Away with her, away!
　　　　　　　　　[She is led away.]

*Enter Frank to execution, Officers, Justice,
　　Sir Arthur, Warbeck, Somerton.*

O. THOR. Here's the sad object which I
　yet must meet
With hope of comfort, if a repentant end
Make him more happy than misfortune
　would
Suffer him here to be.
FRANK.　　Good sirs, turn from me.　60
You will revive affliction almost killed
With my continual sorrow.
O. THOR.　　　　　　O, Frank, Frank!
Would I had sunk in mine own wants,
　or died
But one bare minute ere thy fault was
　acted!
FRANK. To look upon your sorrows
　executes me
Before my execution.
WIN.　　　　　　Let me pray you, sir—
FRANK. Thou much-wronged woman, I
　must sigh for thee,
As he that's only loath to leave the
　world
For that he leaves thee in it unprovided,
Unfriended; and for me to beg a pity
From any man to thee when I am gone
Is more than I can hope; nor, to say
　truth,　　　　　　　　　　　　　72

Have I deserved it. But there is a pay-
　ment
Belongs to goodness from the great
　exchequer
Above; it will not fail thee, Winnifride.
Be that thy comfort.
O. THOR.　　　　Let it be thine too,
Untimely-lost young man.
FRANK.　　　　　　He is not lost
Who bears his peace within him. Had I
　spun
My web of life out at full length, and
　dreamed
Away my many years in lusts, in sur-
　feits,　　　　　　　　　　　　　80
Murthers of reputations, gallant sins
Commended or approved, then, though
　I had
Died easily, as great and rich men do,
Upon my own bed, not compelled by
　justice,
You might have mourned for me indeed;
　my miseries
Had been as everlasting as remediless.
But now the law hath not arraigned,
　condemned
With greater rigor my unhappy fact [1]
Than I myself have every little sin
My memory can reckon from my child-
　hood.　　　　　　　　　　　　90
A court hath been kept here, where I
　am found
Guilty; the difference is, my impartial
　judge
Is much more gracious than my faults
Are monstrous to be named; yet they
　are monstrous.
O. THOR. Here's comfort in this penitence.
WIN.　　　　　　　　　　It speaks
How truly you are reconciled, and
　quickens
My dying comfort, that was near expiring
With my last breath. Now this re-
　pentance makes thee
As white as innocence; and my first sin
　with thee,
Since which I knew none like it, by my
　sorrow　　　　　　　　　　　　100
Is clearly canceled. Might our souls
　together
Climb to the height of their eternity,
And there enjoy what earth denied us,
　happiness!
[1] Deed.

But, since I must survive, and be the
  monument
Of thy loved memory, I will preserve it
With a religious care, and pay thy
  ashes
A widow's duty, calling that end best
Which, though it stain the name, makes
  the soul blessed.

FRANK. Give me thy hand, poor woman;
  do not weep.
  Farewell! Thou dost forgive me?

WIN.   'Tis my part   110
To use that language.

FRANK.   O, that my example
Might teach the world hereafter what a
  curse
Hangs on their heads who rather choose
  to marry
A goodly portion than a dower of virtues!—
Are you there, gentlemen? There is not
  one
Amongst you whom I have not
  wronged.—[To Carter.] You most—
[I] [1] robbed you of a daughter; but
  she is
In heaven, and I must suffer for it
  willingly.

[O.] CART. Ay, ay, she's in heaven, and I
am glad to see thee so well prepared   [120
to follow her. I forgive thee with all my
heart; if thou hadst not had ill counsel, thou
wouldst not have done as thou didst—the
more shame for them.

SOM. Spare your excuse to me; I do conceive
What you would speak. I would you
  could as easily
Make satisfaction to the law as to my
  wrongs.
I am sorry for you.

WARB.   And so am I,
And heartily forgive you.

KAT.   I will pray for you
For her sake, who I am sure did love
  you dearly.   130

SIR ART. Let us part friendly too; I am
  ashamed
Of my part in thy wrongs.

FRANK.   You are all merciful,
And send me to my grave in peace. Sir
  Arthur,

Heavens send you a new heart!—[To Old
  Thorney.] Lastly, to you, sir;
And, though I have deserved not to be
  called
Your son, yet give me leave upon my
  knees
To beg a blessing.   [Kneels.]

O. THOR.   Take it; let me wet
Thy cheeks with the last tears my griefs
  have left me.
O, Frank, Frank, Frank!

FRANK.   Let me beseech you, gentlemen,
To comfort my old father, keep him with
  ye;   140
Love this distresséd widow, and, as
  often
As you remember what a graceless
  man
I was, remember likewise that these are
Both free, both worthy of a better
  fate
Than such a son or husband as I have
  been.
All help me with your prayers.—On,
  on; 'tis just
That law should purge the guilt of blood
  and lust.   Exit [with Officers].

[O.] CART. Go thy ways. I did not think
to have shed one tear for thee, but thou
hast made me water my plants spite   [150
of my heart.—M[aster] Thorney, cheer up,
man; whilst I can stand by you, you shall
not want help to keep you from falling.
We have lost our children, both on 's,[2] the
wrong way, but we cannot help it; better
or worse, 'tis now as 'tis.

O. THOR. I thank you, sir; you are more
  kind than I
Have cause to hope or look for.

[O.] CART. Mr. Somerton, is Kate yours
or no?   160

SOM. We are agreed.

KAT. And, but my faith is passed, I
should fear to be married, husbands are so
cruelly unkind. Excuse me that I am thus
troubled.

SOM. Thou shalt have no cause.

JUST.[3] Take comfort, Mistress Winnifride.
  —Sir Arthur,

---

[1] The spreading of the type in the original
shows that this word has obviously fallen out.

[2] Of us.
[3] The content of the following speech indicates that it should be assigned to the Justice
rather than to Old Carter, as in the original.

For his abuse to you and to your husband,
Is by the bench enjoined to pay you
down   169
A thousand marks.
SIR ART.   Which I will soon discharge.
WIN. Sir, 'tis too great a sum to be employed
Upon my funeral.
[O.] CART. Come, come! If luck had
served, Sir Arthur, and every man had his
due, somebody might have tottered ere
this, without paying fines, like it as you
list.—Come to me, Winnifride; shalt be welcome.—Make much of her, Kate, I charge
you. I do not think but she's a good wench,
and hath had wrong as well as we. [180
So let's every man home to Edmonton with
heavy hearts, yet as merry as we can, though
not as we would.

JUST. Join, friends, in sorrow; make of
all the best.
Harms past may be lamented, not
redressed.   *Exeunt.*

EPILOGUE
Win[nifride].

I am a widow still, and must not sort [1]
A second choice without a good report,
Which though some widows find, and
few deserve,
Yet I dare not presume, but will not
swerve
From modest hopes. All noble tongues
are free;   190
The gentle may speak one kind word for
me.
                                   PHEN.[2]
FINIS.

[1] Select.   [2] This author is unidentified.

THE BROKEN HEART[1]

BY

JOHN FORD[2]

THE SCENE: *Sparta.*

[THE TIME: *About the eighth century, B.C.*]

THE SPEAKERS' NAMES FITTED TO THEIR QUALITIES

AMYCLAS, *common* [3] *to the kings of Laconia.*
ITHOCLES, *Honor of Loveliness: a favorite.*
ORGILUS, *Angry: son to Crotolon.*
BASSANES, *Vexation: a jealous nobleman.*
ARMOSTES, *an Appeaser: a councilor of state.*
CROTOLON, *Noise: another councilor.*
PROPHILUS, *Dear: friend to Ithocles.*
NEARCHUS, *Young Prince: Prince of Argos.*
TECNICUS, *Artist: a philosopher.*
HEMOPHIL, *Glutton* ⎫ *two courtiers.*
GRONEAS, *Tavern Haunter* ⎭
AMELUS, *Trusty: friend to Nearchus.*
PHULAS, *Watchful: servant to Bassanes.*

CALANTHA, *Flower of Beauty: the king's daughter.*
PENTHEA, *Complaint: sister to Ithocles [and wife to Bassanes].*
EUPHRANEA, *Joy: a maid of honor [and daughter to Crotolon].*
CHRISTALLA, *Crystal* ⎫ *maids of honor.*
PHILEMA, *a Kiss* ⎭
GRAUSIS,[4] *Old Beldam: overseer of Penthea.*

PERSONS INCLUDED

THRASUS, *Fierceness: Father of Ithocles.*
APLOTES, *Simplicity: Orgilus so disguised.*
[COURTIERS, OFFICERS, ATTENDANTS, ETC.]

THE PROLOGUE

Our scene is Sparta. He whose best of art
Hath drawn this piece calls it *The Broken Heart.*
The title lends no expectation here
Of apish laughter, or of some lame jeer
At place or persons; no pretended clause [5]
Of jests, fit for a brothel, courts applause
From vulgar admiration; such low songs,
Tuned to unchaste ears, suit not modest tongues.
The Virgin Sisters then deserved fresh bays
When Innocence and Sweetness crowned their lays;   10
Then vices gasped for breath, whose whole commerce
Was whipped to exile by unblushing verse.
This law we keep in our presentment now,
Not to take freedom more than we allow; [6]
What may be here thought a fiction, when Time's youth
Wanted some riper years, was known a truth,
In which, if words have clothed the subject right,
You may partake a pity with delight.

[1] The title continues: "A Tragedy. Acted by the King's Majesty's Servants at the Private House in the Blackfriars. *Fide Honor.*"
[2] The author's name does not appear on the title-page, but is affixed to the adulatory dedication (here omitted) to William, Lord Craven, Baron of Hampsted Marshall. The Latin motto is also an anagram of Ford's name, used elsewhere instead of his signature.
[3] *I.e.*, a name common.
[4] Throughout the text of the original, almost invariably misprinted *Gransis.*
[5] Conclusion, *i.e.*, by substituting different words for those expected or implied.
[6] Sanction.

1485

ACTUS PRIMUS. SCENA PRIMA.

[A room in Crotolon's house.]

Enter Crotolon and Orgilus.

CROT. Dally not further; I will know the reason
That speeds thee to this journey.
ORG. 　　　　　　Reason? Good sir,
I can yield many.
CROT. 　　　　Give me one, a good one;
Such I expect, and ere we part must have.
Athens? Pray, why to Athens? You intend not
To kick against the world, turn cynic, stoic,
Or read the logic lecture, or become
An Areopagite,[1] and judge in causes
Touching the commonwealth? For, as I take it,
The budding of your chin cannot prognosticate 　　　　　　　　　　10
So grave an honor.
ORG. 　　　　　All this I acknowledge.
CROT. You do! Then, son, if books and love of knowledge
Inflame you to this travel, here in Sparta
You may as freely study.
ORG. 　　　　　'Tis not that, sir.
CROT. Not that, sir! As a father, I command thee
To acquaint me with the truth.
ORG. 　　　　　　Thus I obey 'e.
After so many quarrels as dissension,
Fury, and rage had broached in blood, and sometimes
With death to such confederates as sided
With now-dead Thrasus and yourself, my lord, 　　　　　　　　　20
Our present king, Amyclas, reconciled
Your eager swords and sealed a gentle peace.
Friends you professed yourselves, which to confirm,
A resolution for a lasting league
Betwixt your families was entertained,
By joining in a Hymenean bond
Me and the fair Penthea, only daughter
To Thrasus.
CROT. 　　　What of this?
ORG. 　　　　　Much, much, dear sir. 28
A freedom of converse, an interchange
Of holy and chaste love, so fixed our souls

In a firm growth of [2] union, that no time
Can eat into the pledge; we had enjoyed
The sweets our vows expected, had not cruelty
Prevented all those triumphs [3] we prepared for,
By Thrasus his untimely death.
CROT. 　　　　　　　Most certain.
ORG. From this time sprouted up that poisonous stalk
Of aconite, whose ripened fruit hath ravished
All health, all comfort of a happy life,
For Ithocles, her brother, proud of youth,
And prouder in his power, nourished closely 　　　　　　　　　40
The memory of former discontents,
To glory in revenge. By cunning partly,
Partly by threats, a [4] woos at once and forces
His virtuous sister to admit a marriage
With Bassanes, a nobleman, in honor
And riches, I confess, beyond my fortunes.
CROT. All this is no sound reason to importune
My leave for thy departure.
ORG. 　　　　　　Now it follows.
Beauteous Penthea, wedded to this torture 　　　　　　　　　49
By an insulting brother, being secretly
Compelled to yield her virgin freedom up
To him who never can usurp her heart,
Before contracted mine, is now so yoked
To a most barbarous thralldom, misery,
Affliction, that he savors not humanity,
Whose sorrow melts not into more than pity
In hearing but her name.
CROT. 　　　　　As how, pray?
ORG. 　　　　　　　Bassanes,
The man that calls her wife, considers truly
What heaven of perfections he is lord of
By thinking fair Penthea his; this thought 　　　　　　　　　60
Begets a kind of monster-love, which love
Is nurse unto a fear so strong and servile
As brands all dotage with a jealousy.
All eyes who gaze upon that shrine of beauty,

---

[1] A member of the highest Athenian court of justice.

[2] Some copies of the original insert *holy* here.
[3] Celebrations. 　　　　　　　　　　　[4] He.

He doth resolve,[1] do homage to the mira-
  cle;
Someone, he is assured, may now or then,
If opportunity but sort,[2] prevail.
So much, out of a self-unworthiness,
His fears transport him—not that he
  finds cause   69
In her obedience, but his own distrust.
CROT. You spin out your discourse.
ORG.   My griefs are violent;
For, knowing how the maid was hereto-
  fore
Courted by me, his jealousies grow wild
That I should steal again into her favors,
And undermine her virtues, which the
  gods
Know I nor dare nor dream of. Hence,
  from hence
I undertake a voluntary exile—
First, by my absence to take off the cares
Of jealous Bassanes; but chiefly, sir,
To free Penthea from a hell on earth; 80
Lastly, to lose the memory of some-
  thing
Her presence makes to live in me afresh.
CROT. Enough, my Orgilus, enough. To
  Athens
I give a full consent.—Alas, good lady!—
We shall hear from thee often?
ORG.   Often.
CROT.   See,
Thy sister comes to give a farewell.

Enter Euphranea.

EUPH.   Brother!
ORG. Euphranea, thus upon thy cheeks I
  print
A brother's kiss, more careful of thine
  honor,
Thy health, and thy well-doing than my
  life.   89
Before we part, in presence of our father,
I must prefer a suit to 'e.
EUPH.   You may style it,
My brother, a command.
ORG.   That you will promise
To pass never to any man, however [3]
Worthy, your faith, till, with our
  father's leave,
I give a free consent.

[1] Conclude.
[2] Occur.
[3] Here and in a few other passages the line
division has been regularized.

CROT.   An easy motion! [4]
I'll promise for her, Orgilus.
ORG.   Your pardon.
Euphranea's oath must yield me satis-
  faction.
EUPH. By Vesta's sacred fires I swear.
CROT.   And I
By great Apollo's beams join in the vow,
Not without thy allowance to bestow her
On any living.
ORG.   Dear Euphranea,   101
Mistake me not; far, far 'tis from my
  thought,
As far from any wish of mine, to hinder
Preferment to an honorable bed
Or fitting fortune. Thou art young and
  handsome,
And 'twere injustice—more, a tyranny—
Not to advance thy merit. Trust me,
  sister,
It shall be my first care to see thee
  matched
As may become thy choice and our con-
  tents.
I have your oath.
EUPH.   You have. But mean
  you, brother,   110
To leave us, as you say?
CROT.   Ay, ay, Euphranea;
He has just grounds direct him. I will
  prove
A father and a brother to thee.
EUPH.   Heaven
Does look into the secrets of all hearts.
Gods, you have mercy with 'e, else—
CROT.   Doubt nothing
Thy brother will return in safety to us.
ORG. Souls sunk in sorrows never are with-
  out 'em;
They change fresh airs, but bear their
  griefs about 'em.   *Exeunt omnes.*

SCENE ii.

[A room in the palace.]

*Flourish. Enter Amyclas the king, Armostes,
              Prophilus, and Attendants.*

AMY. The Spartan gods are gracious; our
  humility
Shall bend before their altars, and perfume
Their temples with abundant sacrifice.

[4] Proposal.

See, lords, Amyclas, your old king, is
  ent'ring
Into his youth again! I shall shake off
This silver badge of age, and change this
  snow
For hairs as gay as are Apollo's locks;
Our heart leaps in new vigor.
ARM.   May old time
  Run back to double your long life, great
    sir!
AMY. It will, it must, Armostes; thy bold
  nephew,   10
  Death-braving Ithocles, brings to our
    gates
  Triumphs and peace upon his conquering
    sword.
  Laconia is a monarchy at length,
  Hath in this latter war trod under
    foot
  Messene's pride; Messene bows her neck
  To Lacedemon's royalty. O, 'twas
  A glorious victory, and doth deserve
  More than a chronicle—a temple, lords,
  A temple to the name of Ithocles!—
  Where didst thou leave him, Prophilus?
PRO.   At Pephon, 20
  Most gracious sovereign; twenty of the
    noblest
  Of the Messenians there attend your
    pleasure
  For such conditions as you shall propose
  In settling peace and liberty of life.
AMY. When comes your friend, the gen-
  eral?
PRO.   He promised
  To follow with all speed convenient.

Enter Crotolon, Calantha, Christalla, Philema
    [with a garland], and Euphranea.

AMY. Our daughter!—Dear Calantha, the
  happy news,
  The conquest of Messene, hath already
  Enriched thy knowledge.
CAL.   With the circumstance
  And manner of the fight, related faith-
    fully   30
  By Prophilus himself.—But, pray, sir,
    tell me
  How doth the youthful general demean
  His actions in these fortunes?
PRO.   Excellent princess,
  Your own fair eyes may soon report a
    truth

Unto your judgment, with what modera-
  tion,
  Calmness of nature, measure, bounds,
    and limits
  Of thankfulness and joy, a doth digest
  Such amplitude of his success as would
  In others, molded of a spirit less clear,
  Advance 'em to comparison with heaven.
  But Ithocles—
CAL.   Your friend—
PRO.   He is so, madam, 41
  In which the period [1] of my fate consists;
  He, in this firmament of honor, stands
  Like a star fixed, not moved with any
    thunder
  Of popular applause or sudden lightning
  Of self-opinion; he hath served his coun-
    try,
  And thinks 'twas but his duty.
CROT.   You describe
  A miracle of man.
AMY.   Such, Crotolon,
  On forfeit of a king's word, thou wilt find
    him.—
  Hark, warning of his coming! All attend
    him.   *Flourish.* 50

Enter Ithocles, Hemophil, and Groneas, the
    rest of the Lords ushering him in.

AMY. Return into these arms, thy home,
  thy sanctuary,
  Delight of Sparta, treasure of my bosom,
  Mine own, own Ithocles!
ITH.   Your humblest subject.
ARM. Proud of the blood I claim an in-
  terest in,
  As brother to thy mother, I embrace
    thee,
  Right noble nephew.
ITH.   Sir, your love's too partial.
CROT. Our country speaks by me, who by
  thy valor,
  Wisdom, and service shares in this great
    action,
  Returning thee, in part [2] of thy due merits,
  A general welcome.
ITH.   You exceed in bounty. 60
CAL. Christalla, Philema, the chaplet.—
  [Takes the chaplet from them.] Ith-
    ocles,
  Upon the wings of Fame the singular
  And chosen fortune of an high attempt

---

[1] Summation.   [2] On behalf.

Is borne so past the view of common
  sight
That I myself with mine own hands have
  wrought,
To crown thy temples, this provincial
  garland.[1]
Accept, wear, and enjoy it as our gift
Deserved, not purchased.
ITH.   Y' are a royal maid.
AMY. She is in all our daughter.
ITH.   Let me blush,
Acknowledging how poorly I have
  served,   70
What nothings I have done, compared
  with th' honors
Heaped on the issue of a willing mind;
In that lay mine ability, that only.
For who is he so sluggish from his birth,
So little worthy of a name or country,
That owes not out of gratitude for life
A debt of service, in what kind soever
Safety or counsel of the commonwealth
Requires, for payment?
CAL.   A speaks truth.
ITH.   Whom heaven
Is pleased to style victorious, there, to
  such,   80
Applause runs madding, like the drunken
  priests
In Bacchus' sacrifices, without reason,
Voicing the leader-on a demigod,
Whenas, indeed, each common soldier's
  blood
Drops down as current coin in that hard
  purchase
As his whose much more delicate condi-
  tion
Hath sucked the milk of ease. Judgment
  commands,
But resolution executes. I use not,
Before this royal presence, these fit
  slights
As in contempt of such as can direct;   90
My speech hath other end—not to at-
  tribute
All praise to one man's fortune, which is
  strengthéd
By many hands. For instance, here is
  Prophilus,
A gentleman—I cannot flatter truth—
Of much desert; and, though in other
  rank,

Both Hemophil and Groneas were not
  missing
To wish their country's peace; for, in a
  word,
All there did strive their best, and 'twas
  our duty.
AMY. Courtiers turn soldiers?—We vouch-
  safe our hand.
      [Hemophil and Groneas kiss his hand.]
Observe [2] your great example.
HEM.   With all diligence. 100
GRO. Obsequiously and hourly.
AMY.   Some repose
After these toils are needful. We must
  think on
Conditions for the conquered; they ex-
  pect [3] 'em.
On!—Come, my Ithocles.
EUPH.   Sir, with your favor,
I need not a supporter.
PRO.   Fate instructs me.
Exeunt. Manent [4] Hemophil, Groneas, Chris-
      talla, et Philema.   Hemophil stays
          Christalla; Groneas, Philema.
CHRIS. With me?
PHIL.   Indeed, I dare not stay.
HEM.   Sweet lady,
Soldiers are blunt—your lip.
CHRIS.   Fie, this is rudeness;
You went not hence such creatures.
GRO.   Spirit of valor
Is of a mounting nature.
PHIL.   It appears so.— 109
Pray, in earnest, how many men apiece
Have you two been the death of?
GRO.   Faith, not many;
We were composed of mercy.
HEM.   For our daring,
You heard the general's approbation
Before the king.
CHRIS.   You "wished your country's
  peace;"
That showed your charity. Where are
  your spoils,
Such as the soldier fights for?
PHIL.   They are coming.
CHRIS. By the next carrier, are they not?
GRO.   Sweet Philema,
When I was in the thickest of mine
  enemies,
Slashing off one man's head, another's
  nose,
Another's arms and legs—

---

[1] I.e., one "conferred on those who . . . had
added a *Province* to the empire" (Gifford).

[2] Do homage to.   [3] Await.   [4] Remain.

PHIL. And all together [1]— 120
GRO. Then would I with a sigh remember thee,
And cry, "Dear Philema, 'tis for thy sake
I do these deeds of wonder!"—Dost not love me
With all thy heart now?
PHIL. Now as heretofore.
I have not put my love to use; [2] the principal
Will hardly yield an interest.
GRO. By Mars,
I'll marry thee!
PHIL. By Vulcan, y' are forsworn,
Except my mind do alter strangely.
GRO. One word.
CHRIS. You lie beyond all modesty. Forbear me! 129
HEM. I'll make thee mistress of a city; 'tis
Mine own by conquest.
CHRIS. By petition; sue for 't
In forma pauperis.[3] City? Kennel! [4] Gallants,
Off with your feathers; [5] put on aprons, gallants.
Learn to reel, thrum,[6] or trim a lady's dog,
And be good, quiet souls of peace, hob-goblins!
HEM. Christalla!
CHRIS. Practice to drill hogs, in hope
To share in the acorns. Soldiers? Corn-cutters,
But not so valiant; they ofttimes draw blood,
Which you durst never do. When you have practiced 139
More wit or more civility, we'll rank 'e
I' th' list of men; till then, brave things-at-arms,
Dare not to speak to us—most potent Groneas!—
PHIL. And Hemophil the hardy!—at your services.
GRO. They scorn us as they did before we went.
HEM. Hang 'em! Let us scorn them, and be revenged.
Exeunt Chri[stalla] et Philema.

[1] Gifford-Dyce reading. Original reads *altogether*.
[2] *I.e.*, lent it out for profit.
[3] In the status of a pauper. [4] Gutter!
[5] Gifford-Dyce reading. Original reads *fathers*.
[6] Provide with fringe.

GRO. Shall we?
HEM. We will; and, when we slight them thus,
Instead of following them, they'll follow us;
It is a woman's nature.
GRO. 'Tis a scurvy one. *Exeunt omnes.*

SCENE iii.

[*The palace gardens adjoining a grove.*]

*Enter Tecnicus, a philosopher, and Orgilus
disguised like a scholar of his.*

TEC. Tempt not the stars, young man; thou canst not play
With the severity of fate. This change
Of habit and disguise in outward view
Hides not the secrets of thy soul within thee
From their quick-piercing eyes, which dive at all times
Down to thy thoughts; in thy aspect I note
A consequence of danger.
ORG. Give me leave,
Grave Tecnicus, without foredooming destiny,
Under thy roof to ease my silent griefs,
By applying to my hidden wounds the balm 10
Of thy oraculous lectures. If my fortune
Run such a crooked byway as to wrest
My steps to ruin, yet thy learned precepts
Shall call me back and set my footings straight.
I will not court the world.
TEC. Ah, Orgilus,
Neglects in young men of delights and life
Run often to extremities; they care not
For harms to others who contemn their own.
ORG. But I, most learned artist, am not so much
At odds with nature that I grutch [7] the thrift 20
Of any true deserver; nor doth malice [8]
Of present hopes so check them with despair
As that I yield to thought of more affliction

[7] Grudge. [8] Misfortune.

Than what is incident to frailty; where-
fore
Impute not this retiréd course of living
Some little time to any other cause
Than what I justly render—the infor-
mation
Of an unsettled mind; as the effect
Must clearly witness.

Tec.　　　　　Spirit of truth inspire thee!
On these conditions I conceal thy
change,　　　　　　　　　　　　　　30
And willingly admit thee for an audi-
tor.—
I'll to my study.

Org.　　　　　I to contemplations
In these delightful walks.—
　　　　　　　　　　　　[*Exit Tecnicus.*]
　　　　　　　Thus metamorphized [1]
I may without suspicion hearken after
Penthea's usage and Euphranea's faith.
Love, thou art full of mystery! The
deities
Themselves are not secure [2] in search-
ing out
The secrets of those flames, which,
hidden, waste
A breast made tributary to the laws
Of beauty; physic yet hath never
found　　　　　　　　　　　　　　40
A remedy to cure a lover's wound.—
Ha! Who are those that cross yon
private walk
Into the shadowing grove in amorous
foldings?

*Prophilus passeth over, supporting Euphra-
nea, and whispering.*

My sister—O, my sister? 'Tis Euphra-
nea
With Prophilus! Supported too! I
would
It were an apparition! Prophilus
Is Ithocles his friend. It strangely
puzzles me.
Again? Help me, my book; this scholar's
habit
Must stand my privilege; [3] my mind is
busy,
Mine eyes and ears are open.
　　　　　　　　　Walk by, reading.

[1] Metamorphosed.
[2] Certain.
[3] *I.e.*, must become my right to walk here.

Enter again Prophilus and Euphranea.

Pro.　　　　　　　　　Do not waste　50
The span of this stol'n time, lent by the
gods
For precious use, in niceness. [4]　Bright
Euphranea,
Should I repeat old vows, or study new,
For purchase of belief to my desires—
Org. [*Aside.*] Desires?
Pro.　　　　　　My service, my integrity—
Org. [*Aside.*] That's better.
Pro.　　　　　I should but repeat a lesson
Oft conned without a prompter but
thine eyes.
My love is honorable.
Org. [*Aside.*]　　　　　　So was mine
To my Penthea—chastely honorable.
Pro. Nor wants there more addition to
my wish　　　　　　　　　　　　60
Of happiness than having thee a wife—
Already sure of Ithocles, a friend
Firm and unalterable.
Org. [*Aside.*]　　　　　But a brother
More cruel than the grave.
Euph.　　　　　What can you look for,
In answer to your noble protestations,
From an unskillful maid, but language
suited
To a divided mind?
Org. [*Aside.*]　　　Hold out, Euphranea!
Euph. Know, Prophilus, I never under-
valued,
From the first time you mentioned
worthy love,
Your merit, means, or person; it had
been　　　　　　　　　　　　　　70
A fault of judgment in me, and a dull-
ness
In my affections, not to weigh and thank
My better stars that offered me the
grace
Of so much blissfulness. For, to speak
truth,
The law of my desires kept equal pace
With yours, nor have I left that resolu-
tion;
But only, in a word, whatever choice
Lives nearest in my heart must first
procure
Consent both from my father and my
brother,
Ere he can own me his.

[4] Coyness.

Org. [*Aside.*]   She is forsworn else. 80

Pro. Leave me that task.

Euph.   My brother, ere he parted
To Athens, had my oath.

Org. [*Aside.*]   Yes, yes, a had, sure.

Pro. I doubt not, with the means the
   court supplies,
But to prevail at pleasure.

Org. [*Aside.*]   Very likely!

Pro. Meantime, best, dearest, I may
   build my hopes
On the foundation of thy constant
   suff'rance
In any opposition.

Euph.   Death shall sooner
Divorce life and the joys I have in living
Than my chaste vows from truth.

Pro.   On thy fair hand
I seal the like.

Org. [*Aside.*]   There is no faith in
   woman.   90
Passion, O, be contained! My very
   heartstrings
Are on the tenters.[1]

Euph.   Sir, we are overheard.
Cupid protect us! 'Twas a stirring, sir,
Of someone near.

Pro.   Your fears are needless, lady;
None have access into these private
   pleasures
Except some near in court, or bosom
   student
From Tecnicus his oratory,[2] granted
By special favor lately from the king
Unto the grave philosopher.

Euph.   Methinks
I hear one talking to himself—I see
   him.   100

Pro. 'Tis a poor scholar, as I told you,
   lady.

Org. [*Aside.*] I am discovered.—[*As if
   studying aloud.*] Say it: is it possible,
With a smooth tongue, a leering countenance,
Flattery, or force of reason—I come t'e,[3]
   sir—
To turn or to appease the raging sea?
Answer to that.—Your art? What art
   to catch
And hold fast in a net the sun's small
   atoms?

[1] Tenterhooks.
[2] Lecture hall.
[3] He addresses an imaginary opponent.

No, no; they'll out, they'll out; ye may
   as easily
Outrun a cloud driven by a northern
   blast
As fiddle-faddle so! Peace, or speak
   sense.   110

Euph. Call you this thing a scholar? 'Las,
he's lunatic.

Pro. Observe him, sweet; 'tis but his recreation.

Org. But will you hear a little! You are
   so tetchy.
You keep no rule in argument. Philoso-
   phy
Works not upon impossibilities,
But natural conclusions.—Mew!—Ab-
   surd!
The metaphysics are but speculations
Of the celestial bodies, or such accidents
As, not mixed perfectly, in the air en-
   gendered
Appear to us unnatural; that's all.   120
Prove it; yet, with a reverence to your
   gravity,
I'll balk illiterate sauciness, submitting
My sole opinion to the touch of writers.

Pro. Now let us fall in with him.
                [*They come forward.*]

Org.   Ha, ha, ha!
These apish boys, when they but taste
   the grammates [4]
And principles of theory, imagine
They can oppose their teachers. Con-
   fidence
Leads many into errors.

Pro.   By your leave, sir.

Euph. Are you a scholar, friend?

Org.   I am, gay creature,
With pardon of your deities, a mushroom   130
On whom the dew of heaven drops now
   and then;
The sun shines on me too, I thank his
   beams!
Sometime I feel their warmth; and eat
   and sleep.

Pro. Does Tecnicus read [5] to thee?

Org.   Yes, forsooth.
He is my master surely; yonder door
Opens upon his study.

Pro.   Happy creatures!
Such people toil not, sweet, in heats of
   state,

[4] Rudiments.   [5] Lecture.

Nor sink in thaws of greatness; their
affections
Keep order with the limits of their
modesty; [1]
Their love is love of virtue.—What's thy
name?　　　　　　　　　　　　140
ORG. Aplotes, sumptuous master, a poor
wretch.
EUPH. Dost thou want anything?
ORG.　　　　　　Books, Venus, books.
PRO. Lady, a new conceit [2] comes in my
thought,
And most available for both our com-
forts.
EUPH. My lord—
PRO.　　　　Whiles I endeavor to deserve
Your father's blessing to our loves, this
scholar
May daily at some certain hours attend [3]
What notice I can write of my success,
Here in this grove, and give it to your
hands;
The like from you to me. So can we
never,　　　　　　　　　　　　150
Barred of our mutual speech, want sure
intelligence,
And thus our hearts may talk when our
tongues cannot.
EUPH. Occasion is most favorable; use it.
PRO. Aplotes, wilt thou wait us twice a
day,
At nine i' the morning and at four at
night,
Here in this bower, to convey such letters
As each shall send to other? Do it
willingly,
Safely, and secretly, and I will furnish
Thy study, or what else thou canst
desire.
ORG. Jove, make me thankful, thankful,
I beseech thee,　　　　　　　　160
Propitious Jove! I will prove sure and
trusty.
You will not fail me books?
PRO.　　　　　　Nor aught besides
Thy heart can wish. This lady's name's
Euphranea,
Mine Prophilus.
ORG.　　　　I have a pretty memory;
It must prove my best friend. I will not
miss
One minute of the hours appointed.
PRO.　　　　　　　　　　　　Write

The books thou wouldst have bought
thee in a note,
Or take thyself some money.
ORG.　　　　　　　　No, no money;
Money to scholars is a spirit invisible;
We dare not finger it. Or [4] books or
nothing.　　　　　　　　　　　　170
PRO. Books of what sort thou wilt. Do
not forget
Our names.
ORG.　　　　I warrant 'e, I warrant 'e.
PRO. Smile, Hymen, on the growth of our
desires;
We'll feed thy torches with eternal fires!
　　　　　　　Exeunt. Manet Org[ilus].
ORG. Put out thy torches, Hymen, or their
light
Shall meet a darkness of eternal night!
Inspire me, Mercury, with swift deceits.
Ingenious Fate has leapt into mine
arms,
Beyond the compass of my brain. Mor-
tality
Creeps on the dung of earth, and cannot
reach　　　　　　　　　　　　180
The riddles which are purposed by the
gods.
Great arts best write themselves in their
own stories;
They die too basely who outlive their
glories.　　　　　　　　　　　Exit.

ACTUS SECUNDUS. SCENA PRIMA.

[A room in Bassanes' house.]

Enter Bassanes and Phulas.

BASS. I'll have that window next the
street dammed up;
It gives too full a prospect to tempta-
tion,
And courts a gazer's glances. There's a
lust
Committed by the eye, that sweats and
travails,
Plots, wakes, contrives, till the deformed
bear whelp,
Adultery, be licked into the act,
The very act. That light shall be dammed
up;
D'e hear, sir?
PHU.　　　　I do hear, my lord; a mason
Shall be provided suddenly. [5]

---

[1] Moderation.　　[2] Idea.　　[3] Await.　　　　[4] Either.　　　　[5] At once.

Bass. Some rogue, 9
Some rogue of your confederacy, factor [1]
For slaves and strumpets, to convey
    close [2] packets
From this spruce springal [3] and the
    tother [4] youngster,
That gaudy earwig, [5] or my lord your
    patron,
Whose pensioner you are! I'll tear thy
    throat out,
Son of a cat, ill-looking hound's head,
    rip up
Thy ulcerous maw, if I but scent a paper,
A scroll but half as big as what can
    cover
A wart upon thy nose, a spot, a pimple,
Directed to my lady; it may prove
A mystical preparative to lewdness. 20
Phu. Care shall be had. I will turn every
    thread
About me to an eye.—[Aside.] Here's a
    sweet life!
Bass. The city housewives, cunning in the
    traffic
Of chamber merchandise, set all at
    price
By wholesale; yet they wipe their
    mouths and simper,
Cull, [6] kiss, and cry "sweetheart," and
    stroke the head
Which they have branched; [7] and all is
    well again!
Dull clods of dirt, who dare not feel the
    rubs [8]
Stuck on the foreheads.
Phu. 'Tis a villainous world;
One cannot hold his own in 't.
Bass. Dames at court, 30
Who flaunt in riots, run another bias; [9]
Their pleasure heaves the patient ass that
    suffers
Up on the stilts of office, titles, in-
    comes;
Promotion justifies the shame, and sues
    for 't.
Poor Honor, thou art stabbed, and
    bleed'st to death
By such unlawful hire! The country
    mistress

[1] Agent.
[2] Secret.
[3] Youth.
[4] That other.
[5] Earwig.
[6] Coll, "neck," embrace.
[7] A conventional allusion to cuckoldry.
[8] Knobs, horns.
[9] Direction.

Is yet more wary, and in blushes hides
Whatever trespass draws her troth to
    guilt.
But all are false. On this truth I am
    bold:
No woman but can fall, and doth, or
    would.— 40
Now for the newest news about the
    city;
What blab the voices, sirrah?
Phu. O, my lord,
The rarest, quaintest, strangest, tickling
    news
That ever—
Bass. Heyday! Up and ride me, rascal!
    What is 't?
Phu. Forsooth, they say, the king has
    mewed [10]
All his gray beard, instead of which is
    budded
Another of a pure carnation color,
Speckled with green and russet.
Bass. Ignorant block!
Phu. Yes, truly; and 'tis talked about the
    streets
That, since Lord Ithocles came home,
    the lions 50
Never left roaring, at which noise the
    bears
Have danced their very hearts out.
Bass. Dance out thine too.
Phu. Besides, Lord Orgilus is fled to
    Athens
Upon a fiery dragon, and 'tis thought
A never can return.
Bass. Grant it, Apollo!
Phu. Moreover, please your lordship,
    'tis reported
For certain that whoever is found jealous
Without apparent proof that 's wife is
    wanton
Shall be divorced; but this is but she-
    news—
I had it from a midwife. I have more
    yet. 60
Bass. Antic, no more! Idiots and stupid
    fools
Grate my calamities. Why to be fair
Should yield presumption of a faulty
    soul? [11]
Look to the doors.

[10] Moulted.
[11] I.e., why should beauty arouse suspicion of a
faulty soul?

PHU. [*Aside.*]　　　The horn of plenty crest
　　him!　　　　　　　　*Exit Phul[as].*
BASS. Swarms of confusion huddle in my
　　thoughts
In rare distemper.—Beauty? O, it is
An unmatched blessing or a horrid curse.

Enter Penthea and Grausis, an old lady.

[*Aside.*] She comes, she comes! So shoots
　　the morning forth,
Spangled with pearls of transparent
　　dew.
The way to poverty is to be rich,　　70
As I in her am wealthy; but for her,
In all contents a bankrupt.—Loved
　　Penthea!
How fares my heart's best joy?
GRAU.　　　　　In sooth, not well.
　　She is so oversad.
BASS.　　　　Leave chattering, magpie.—
　　Thy brother is returned, sweet, safe and
　　honored
With a triumphant victory; thou shalt
　　visit him.
We will to court, where, if it be thy
　　pleasure,
Thou shalt appear in such a ravishing
　　luster
Of jewels above value that the dames
Who brave it there, in rage to be out-
　　shined,　　　　　　　　　　　80
Shall hide them in their closets, and un-
　　seen
Fret in their tears, whiles every won-
　　d'ring eye
Shall crave none other brightness but thy
　　presence.
Choose thine own recreations; be a
　　queen
Of what delights thou fanciest best, what
　　company,
What place, what times; do anything, do
　　all things
Youth can command, so thou wilt chase
　　these clouds
From the pure firmament of thy fair
　　looks.
GRAU. Now 'tis well said, my lord.—What,
　　lady! Laugh;
Be merry! Time is precious.
BASS. [*Aside.*]　　　Furies whip thee!　90
PEN. Alas, my lord, this language to your
　　handmaid

Sounds as would music to the deaf; I need
No braveries [1] nor cost of art to draw
The whiteness of my name into offense,
Let such, if any such there are, who covet
A curiosity of admiration,
By laying out their plenty to full view,
Appear in gaudy outsides; my attires
Shall suit the inward fashion of my
　　mind,
From which, if your opinion, nobly
　　placed,　　　　　　　　　　100
Change not the livery your words be-
　　stow,
My fortunes with my hopes are at the
　　highest.
BASS. This house, methinks, stands some-
　　what too much inward; [2]
It is too melancholy. We'll remove
Nearer the court. Or what thinks my
　　Penthea
Of the delightful island we command?
Rule me as thou canst wish.
PEN.　　　　　　　I am no mistress.
Whither you please, I must attend; all
　　ways
Are alike pleasant to me.
GRAU.　　　　　　　Island? Prison!
A prison is as gaysome; we'll no is-
　　lands.　　　　　　　　　　110
Marry, out upon 'em! Whom shall we
　　see there?
Seagulls, and porpoises, and water rats,
And crabs, and mews, and dogfish—
　　goodly gear
For a young lady's dealing—or an old
　　one's!
On no terms islands; I'll be stewed first.
BASS. [*Aside.*]　　　　　　Grausis,
You are a juggling bawd.—This sadness,
　　sweetest,
Becomes not youthful blood.—[*Aside.*]
　　I'll have you pounded. [3] —
For my sake put on a more cheerful
　　mirth;
Thou'lt mar thy cheeks, and make me old
　　in griefs.—
[*Aside.*] Damnable bitch fox!
GRAU.　　　　I am thick of hearing　120
Still, [4] when the wind blows southerly.—
　　What think 'e,
If your fresh lady breed young bones, my
　　lord?

---

[1] Fineries.　　　　　　　[3] Impounded.
[2] Secret, secluded.　　　　[4] Always.

Would not a chopping boy d'e good at
   heart?
But, as you said—
BASS. [*Aside.*]   I'll spit thee on a stake,
Or chop thee into collops!
GRAU.   Pray, speak louder.
Sure, sure the wind blows south still.
PEN.   Thou prat'st madly.
BASS. 'Tis very hot; I sweat extremely.—
Now?

Enter Phulas.

PHU. A herd of lords, sir.
BASS.   Ha?
PHU.   A flock of ladies.
BASS. Where?
PHU.   Shoalds ¹ of horses.
BASS.   Peasant, how?
PHU.   Caroches ²
In drifts; th' one enter, th' other stand
   without, sir.   130
And now I vanish.   *Exit Phulas.*

Enter Prophilus, Hemophil, Groneas, Chris-
talla, and Philema.

PRO.   Noble Bassanes!
BASS. Most welcome, Prophilus; ladies,
   gentlemen,
To all my heart is open; you all honor
   me—
[*Aside.*] A tympany ³ swells in my head al-
   ready—
Honor me bountifully.—[*Aside.*] How
   they flutter,
Wagtails and jays together!
PRO.   From your brother
By virtue of your love to him, I require
Your instant presence, fairest.
PEN.   He is well, sir?
PRO. The gods preserve him ever! Yet,
   dear beauty,
I find some alteration in him lately,   140
Since his return to Sparta.—My good
   lord,
I pray, use no delay.
BASS.   We had not needed
An invitation, if his sister's health
Had not fallen into question.—Haste,
   Penthea,
Slack not a minute.—Lead the way, good
   Prophilus;
I'll follow step by step.

¹ Shoals.   ² Coaches.   ³ Distension.

PRO.   Your arm, fair madam.
Exeunt omnes sed ⁴ Bass[anes] et Grau[sis].
BASS. One word with your old bawdship:
   th' hadst been better
Railed at the sins thou worshipp'st than
   have thwarted
My will. I'll use thee cursedly.
GRAU.   You dote;   149
You are beside yourself. A politician
In jealousy? No, y' are too gross, too
   vulgar.
Pish, teach not me my trade; I know my
   cue.
My crossing you sinks me into her trust,
By which I shall know all; my trade's a
   sure one.
BASS. Forgive me, Grausis; 'twas consid-
   eration
I relished ⁵ not; but have a care now.
GRAU.   Fear not,
I am no new-come-to 't.
BASS.   Thy life's upon it,
And so is mine. My agonies are infinite.
                     Exeunt omnes.

SCENE ii.

[*Ithocles' apartment in the palace.*]

Enter Ithocles, alone.

ITH. Ambition? 'Tis of vipers' breed; it
   gnaws
A passage through the womb that gave
   it motion.
Ambition, like a seeléd ⁶ dove, mounts
   upward,
Higher and higher still, to perch on
   clouds,
But tumbles headlong down with heavier
   ruin.
So squibs and crackers fly into the air;
Then, only breaking with a noise, they
   vanish
In stench and smoke. Morality,⁷ applied
To timely practice, keeps the soul in
   tune,
At whose sweet music all our actions
   dance.   10
But this is form of books and school-
   tradition; ⁸
It physics not the sickness of a mind

⁴ But.   ⁷ Moralization.
⁵ Understood.   ⁸ *I.e.*, pedantry.
⁶ With eyelids sewed together.

Broken with griefs. Strong fevers are
  not eased
With counsel, but with best receipts
  and means—
Means, speedy means and certain; that's
  the cure.

Enter Armostes and Crotolon.

ARM. You stick, Lord Crotolon, upon a
  point
Too nice and too unnecessary; Prophilus
Is every way desertful. I am confident
Your wisdom is too ripe to need instruc-
  tion
From your son's tutelage.
CROT.   Yet not so ripe, 20
My Lord Armostes, that it dares to dote
Upon the painted [1] meat of smooth
  persuasion,
Which tempts me to a breach of faith.
ITH.   Not yet
Resolved, my lord? Why, if your son's
  consent
Be so available,[2] we'll write to Athens
For his repair[3] to Sparta. The king's
  hand
Will join with our desires; he has been
  moved to 't.
ARM. Yes, and the king himself impor-
  tuned Crotolon
For a despatch.
CROT. Kings may command; their wills
Are laws not to be questioned.
ITH.   By this marriage 30
You knit an union so devout, so hearty,
Between your loves to me and mine to
  yours,
As if mine own blood had an interest in
  it;
For Prophilus is mine, and I am his.
CROT. My lord, my lord!—
ITH.   What, good sir? Speak your
  thought.
CROT. Had this sincerity been real once,
My Orgilus had not been now unwived,
Nor your lost sister buried in a bridebed.
Your uncle here, Armostes, knows this
  truth,
For, had your father Thrasus lived—
  but peace 40
Dwell in his grave! I have done.
ARM.   Y' are bold and bitter.

ITH. [*Aside.*] A presses home the injury;
  it smarts.—
No reprehensions, uncle; I deserve 'em.
Yet, gentle sir, consider what the heat
Of an unsteady youth, a giddy brain,
Green indiscretion, flattery of greatness,
Rawness of judgment, willfulness in
  folly,
Thoughts vagrant as the wind and as
  uncertain,
Might lead a boy in years to; 'twas a
  fault,
A capital fault, for then I could not
  dive   50
Into the secrets of commanding love,
Since when, experience, by the ex-
  tremities [4] (in others),
Hath forced me to collect.[5] And, trust
  me, Crotolon,
I will redeem those wrongs with any
  service
Your satisfaction can require for current.
ARM. Thy acknowledgment is satisfac-
  tion.
What would you more?
CROT.   I'm conquered; if Euphranea
Herself admit the motion, let it be so;
I doubt not my son's liking.
ITH.   Use my fortunes,
Life, power, sword, and heart—all are
  your own.   60

Enter Bassanes, Prophilus, Calantha, Pen-
  thea, Euphranea, Christalla, Philema,
        and Grausis.

ARM. The princess, with your sister.
CAL.   I present 'e
A stranger here in court, my lord, for,
  did not
Desire of seeing you draw her abroad,
We had not been made happy in her
  company.
ITH. You are a gracious princess.—Sister,
  wedlock
Holds too severe a passion in your na-
  ture,
Which can engross all duty to your hus-
  band,
Without attendance on so dear a mis-
  tress.—
[*To Bassanes.*] 'Tis not my brother's
  pleasure, I presume,
T' immure her in a chamber.

---

[1] Counterfeit.   [2] Serviceable.   [3] Return.

[4] Extremes.   [5] Understand.

BASS.   'Tis her will; 70
She governs her own hours.   Noble
  Ithocles,
We thank the gods for your success and
  welfare.
Our lady has of late been indisposed,
Else we had waited on you with the first.

ITH. How does Penthea now?

PEN.   You best know, brother,
From whom my health and comforts
  are derived.

BASS. [*Aside.*] I like the answer well; 'tis
  sad [1] and modest.
There may be tricks yet, tricks.—Have
  an eye, Grausis!

CAL. Now, Crotolon, the suit we joined in
  must not
Fall by too long demur.[2]

CROT.   'Tis granted, princess, 80
For my part.

ARM.   With condition that his son
Favor the contract.

CAL.   Such delay is easy.—
The joys of marriage make thee, Pro-
  philus,
A proud deserver of Euphranea's love,
And her of thy desert!

PRO.   Most sweetly gracious!

BASS. The joys of marriage are the heaven
  on earth,
Life's paradise, great princess, the soul's
  quiet,
Sinews of concord, earthly immortality,
Eternity of pleasures—no restoratives
Like to a constant woman!—[*Aside.*]
  But where is she?   90
'Twould puzzle all the gods but to create
Such a new monster.—I can speak by
  proof,
For I rest in Elysium; 'tis my happiness.

CROT. Euphranea, how are you resolved—
  speak freely—
In your affections to this gentleman?

EUPH. Nor more nor less than as his love
  assures me,
Which—if your liking with my brother's
  warrants—
I cannot but approve in all points
  worthy.

CROT. So, so!—[*To Prophilus.*] I know
  your answer.

ITH.   'T had been pity 99
To sunder hearts so equally concented.[3]

[1] Serious.   [2] Delay.   [3] Harmonized.

Enter Hemophil.

HEM. The king, Lord Ithocles, commands
  your presence—
And, fairest princess, yours.

CAL.   We will attend him.

Enter Groneas.

GRO. Where are the lords? All must unto
  the king
Without delay; the Prince of Argos—

CAL.   Well, sir?

GRO. Is coming to the court, sweet lady.

CAL.   How!
The Prince of Argos?

GRO.   'Twas my fortune, madam,
T' enjoy the honor of these happy tidings.

ITH. Penthea!—

PEN.   Brother?

ITH.   Let me an hour hence
Meet you alone within the palace grove;
I have some secret with you.—Prithee,
  friend,   110
Conduct her thither, and have special
  care
The walks be cleared of any to disturb us.

PRO. I shall.

BASS. [*Aside.*]   How's that?

ITH.   Alone, pray be alone.—
I am your creature, princess.—On, my
  lords!   *Exeunt [All but] Bassanes.*

BASS. Alone, alone?   What means that
  word "alone"?
Why might not I be there?—Hum!—
He's her brother.
Brothers and sisters are but flesh and
  blood,
And this same whoreson [4] court ease is
  temptation
To a rebellion in the veins; besides,
His fine friend Prophilus must be her
  guardian.   120
Why may not he despatch a business
  nimbly
Before the other come?—Or—pand'ring,
  pand'ring
For one another—be 't to sister, mother,
Wife, cousin, anything—'mongst youths
  of mettle
Is in request; it is so—stubborn fate!
But, if I be a cuckold, and can know it,
I will be fell,[5] and fell.

[4] Rascally.   [5] Ruthless.

Enter Groneas.

GRO. My lord, y' are called for.

BASS. Most heartily I thank ye. Where's my wife, pray?

GRO. Retired amongst the ladies.

BASS. Still I thank 'e. There's an old waiter [1] with her; saw you her too? 130

GRO. She sits i' th' presence lobby fast asleep, sir.

BASS. Asleep? Sleep, sir?

GRO. Is your lordship troubled? You will not to the king?

BASS. Your humblest vassal.

GRO. Your servant, my good lord.

BASS. I wait your footsteps.
Exeunt.

SCENE THE THIRD.

[*The palace gardens adjoining a grove.*]

[*Enter*] *Prophilus, Penthea.*

PRO. In this walk, lady, will your brother find you;
And, with your favor, give me leave a little
To work a preparation. In his fashion
I have observed of late some kind of slackness
To such alacrity as nature [once] [2]
And custom took delight in, sadness grows
Upon his recreations, which he hoards
In such a willing [3] silence that to question
The grounds will argue [little] [2] skill in friendship,
And less good manners.

PEN. Sir, I'm not inquisitive 10
Of secrecies without an invitation.

PRO. With pardon, lady, not a syllable
Of mine implies so rude a sense; the drift—

Enter Orgilus [*, disguised as before*].

[*To Orgilus.*] Do thy best
To make this lady merry for an hour.
Exit.

ORG. Your will shall be a law, sir.

PEN. Prithee, leave me;

[1] Attendant, watcher.
[2] Supplied by Gifford-Dyce.
[3] Resolute.

I have some private thoughts I would account with;
Use thou thine own.

ORG. Speak on, fair nymph; our souls
Can dance as well to music of the spheres
As any's who have feasted with the gods. 20

PEN. Your school terms [4] are too troublesome.

ORG. What heaven
Refines mortality from dross of earth
But such as uncompounded [5] beauty hallows
With glorified perfection?

PEN. Set thy wits
In a less wild proportion.

ORG. Time can never
On the white table of unguilty faith
Write counterfeit dishonor; turn those eyes,
The arrows of pure love, upon that fire,
Which once rose to a flame, perfumed with vows
As sweetly scented as the incense smoking 30
The holiest artars, virgin tears (like
On Vesta's odors), sprinkled dews to feed 'em [6]
And to increase their fervor.

PEN. Be not frantic!

ORG. All pleasures are but mere imagination,
Feeding the hungry appetite with steam
And sight of banquet, whilst the body pines,
Not relishing the real taste of food;
Such is the leanness of a heart divided
From intercourse of troth-contracted loves;
No horror should deface that precious figure 40
Sealed with the lively stamp of equal souls.

PEN. Away! Some Fury hath bewitched thy tongue.
The breath of ignorance, that flies from thence,
Ripens a knowledge in me of afflictions

[4] *I.e.*, rhetorical language.
[5] Unadorned, simple.
[6] This incoherency may be intentional, but Gifford emends as follows:
"On Vesta's altars . . .
. . . the holiest odors, virgins' tears,
. . . sprinkled, like dews, to feed them."

Above all suff'rance.—Thing of talk, begone!
Begone, without reply!

ORG.   Be just, Penthea,
In thy commands; when thou send'st forth a doom
Of banishment, know first on whom it lights.
Thus I take off the shroud, in which my cares
Are folded up from view of common eyes.   [*Discloses himself.*] 50
What is thy sentence next?

PEN.   Rash man! Thou layest
A blemish on mine honor, with the hazard
Of thy too desperate life; yet I profess,
By all the laws of ceremonious wedlock,
I have not given admittance to one thought
Of female change since cruelty enforced
Divorce betwixt my body and my heart.
Why would you fall from goodness thus?

ORG.   O, rather
Examine me, how I could live to say
I have been much, much wronged. 'Tis for thy sake   60
I put on this imposture; dear Penthea,
If thy soft bosom be not turned to marble,
Thou't [1] pity our calamities; my interest
Confirms me thou art mine still.

PEN.   Lend your hand;
With both of mine I clasp it thus, thus kiss it,
Thus kneel before ye.

ORG.   You instruct my duty.

PEN. We may stand up.—Have you aught else to urge
Of new demand? As for the old, forget it;
'Tis buried in an everlasting silence,
And shall be, shall be ever. What more would ye?   70

ORG. I would possess my wife; the equity
Of very reason bids me.

PEN.   Is that all?

ORG. Why, 'tis the all of me, myself.

PEN.   Remove
Your steps some distance from me.—At this space
A few words I dare change; but first put on
Your borrowed shape.

[1] Thou wilt.

ORG.   You are obeyed; 'tis done.
                       [*He resumes his disguise.*]

PEN. How, Orgilus, by promise I was thine
The heavens do witness; they can witness too
A rape done on my truth; [2] how I do love thee   79
Yet, Orgilus, and yet, must best appear
In tendering [3] thy freedom, for I find
The constant preservation of thy merit,
By thy not daring to attempt my fame
With injury of any loose conceit,
Which might give deeper wounds to discontents.
Continue this fair race; [4] then, though I cannot
Add to thy comfort, yet I shall more often
Remember from what fortune I am fallen,
And pity mine own ruin.—Live, live happy,
Happy in thy next choice, that thou mayst people   90
This barren age with virtues in thy issue!
And O, when thou art married, think on me
With mercy, not contempt! I hope thy wife,
Hearing my story, will not scorn my fall.—
Now let us part.

ORG.   Part! Yet advise thee better:
Penthea is the wife to Orgilus,
And ever shall be.

PEN.   Never shall nor will.

ORG. How!

PEN.   Hear me; in a word I'll tell thee why.
The virgin dowry which my birth bestowed   99
Is ravished by another; my true love
Abhors to think that Orgilus deserved
No better favors than a second bed.

ORG. I must not take this reason.

PEN.   To confirm it
Should I outlive my bondage, let me meet
Another worse than this and less desired,
If, of all men alive, thou shouldst but touch
My lip or hand again?

[2] Troth.   [4] Course.
[3] Having a care of.

Org.   Penthea, now
I tell 'e, you grow wanton in my suffer-
ance;
Come, sweet, th' art mine.
Pen.   Uncivil sir, forbear, 109
Or I can turn affection into vengeance!
Your reputation, if you value any,
Lies bleeding at my feet.   Unworthy
man,
If ever henceforth thou appear in lan-
guage,
Message, or letter to betray my frailty,
I'll call thy former protestations lust,
And curse my stars for forfeit of my
judgment.
Go thou, fit only for disguise and
walks,[1]
To hide thy shame.   This once I spare
thy life.
I laugh at mine own confidence; my
sorrows
By thee are made inferior to my for-
tunes.   120
If ever thou didst harbor worthy love,
Dare not to answer.   My good genius
guide me
That I may never see thee more!—Go
from me!
Org. I'll tear my veil of politic French[2]
off,
And stand up like a man resolved to
do;
Action, not words, shall show[3] me.—O
Penthea!   Exit Orgilus.
Pen. A sighed my name, sure, as he
parted from me;
I fear I was too rough.   Alas, poor
gentleman,
A looked not like the ruins of his
youth,   129
But like the ruins of those ruins. Honor,
How much we fight with weakness to
preserve thee!   [Walks aside.]

Enter Bassanes and Grausis.

Bass. Fie on thee!   Damn thee, rotten
maggot, damn thee!
Sleep? Sleep at court? And now? Aches,[4]
convulsions,

Imposthumes, rhemes,[5] gouts, palsies
clog thy bones
A dozen years more yet!
Grau.   Now y' are in hu-
mors.
Bass. She's by herself; there's hope of
that. She's sad too;
She's in strong contemplation; yes, and
fixed.
The signs are wholesome.
Grau.   Very wholesome, truly.
Bass. Hold   your   chops,[6]   nightmare!—
Lady, come; your brother
Is carried   to   his   closet;[7] you   must
thither.   140
Pen. Not well, my lord?
Bass.   A sudden fit; 'twill off!
Some surfeit or disorder.—How dost,
dearest?
Pen. Your news is none o' the best.

Enter Prophilus.

Pro.   The chief of men,
The excellentest Ithocles, desires
Your presence, madam.
Bass.   We are hasting to him.
Pen. In vain we labor in this course of
life
To piece our journey out at length, or
crave
Respite of breath; our home is in the
grave.
Bass. Perfect philosophy!
[Pen.][8]   Then let us care
To live so, that our reckonings may fall
even   150
When w' are to make account.
Pro.   He cannot fear
Who builds on noble grounds; sickness
or pain
Is the deserver's exercise;[9] and such
Your virtuous brother to the world is
known.
Speak comfort to him, lady; be all
gentle.
Stars fall but in the grossness of our
sight;
A good man dying, th' earth doth lose a
light.   Exeunt omnes.

---

[1] I.e., for secret meeting.
[2] A characteristic Elizabethan anachronism.
[3] Reveal.
[4] Pronounced aitches.

[5] Remes, rheums.   [6] Jaws.   [7] Chamber.
[8] Emended by Gifford-Dyce.   Original assigns
this speech to Bassanes.
[9] Discipline.

ACTUS TERTIUS. SCENA PRIMA.

[*The study of Tecnicus.*]

Enter Tecnicus, and Orgilus in his own shape.

TEC. Be well advised; let not a resolution
  Of giddy rashness choke the breath of
    reason.

ORG. It shall not, most sage master.

TEC.   I am jealous,[1]
  For, if the borrowed shape so late put on
  Inferred a consequence, we must con-
    clude
  Some violent design of sudden nature
  Hath shook that shadow off, to fly upon
  A new-hatched execution.[2] Orgilus,
  Take heed thou hast not, under our
    integrity,
  Shrouded unlawful plots; our mortal
    eyes   10
  Pierce not the secrets of your hearts;
    the gods
  Are only privy to them.

ORG.   Learned Tecnicus,
  Such doubts are causeless; and, to clear
    the truth
  From misconceit,[3] the present state com-
    mands me.
  The Prince of Argos comes himself in
    person
  In quest of great Calantha for his bride,
  Our kingdom's heir; besides, mine only
    sister,
  Euphranea, is disposed to Prophilus;
  Lastly, the king is sending letters for me
  To Athens, for my quick repair to
    court.   20
  Please to accept these reasons.

TEC.   Just ones, Orgilus,
  Not to be contradicted; yet beware
  Of an unsure foundation; no fair colors[4]
  Can fortify a building faintly jointed.
  I have observed a growth in thy aspect
  Of dangerous extent, sudden, and—
    look to 't—
  I might add, certain—

ORG.   My aspect? Could art
  Run through mine inmost thoughts, it
    should not sift
  An inclination there more than what
    suited
  With justice of mine honor.

TEC.   I believe it. 30
  But know then, Orgilus, what honor is.
  Honor consists not in a bare opinion
  By doing any act that feeds content,
  Brave in appearance, cause we think it
    brave;
  Such honor comes by accident, not
    nature,
  Proceeding from the vices of our passion,
  Which makes our reason drunk. But real
    honor
  Is the reward of virtue, and acquired
  By justice or by valor which for bases
  Hath justice to uphold it. He then
    fails   40
  In honor, who for lucer [or][5] revenge
  Commits thefts, murthers, treasons, and
    adulteries,
  With suchlike, by intrenching on just
    laws,
  Whose sovereignty is best preserved by
    justice.
  Thus, as you see how honor must be
    grounded
  On knowledge, not opinion—for opinion
  Relies on probability and accident,
  But knowledge on necessity and truth—
  I leave thee to the fit consideration
  Of what becomes the grace of real
    honor,   50
  Wishing success to all thy virtuous mean-
    ings.

ORG. The gods increase thy wisdom, rev-
    erend oracle,
  And in thy precepts make me ever
    thrifty!   *Exit Org[ilus].*

TEC. I thank thy wish.—Much mystery
    of fate
  Lies hid in that man's fortunes; curiosity
  May lead his actions into rare attempts.
  But let the gods be moderators still,
  No human power can prevent their
    will.—

Enter Armostes [with a casket].

  From whence come 'e?

ARM.   From King Amyclas—pardon
  My interruption of your studies. Here,
  In this sealed box, he sends a treasure
    dear   61
  To him as his crown. A prays your grav-
    ity

---

[1] Suspicious.   [2] Achievement, enterprise.
[3] Misconception.   [4] Reasons, excuses.

[5] Emended by Gifford. Original has *of.*

You would examine, ponder, sift, and
 bolt
The pith and circumstance of every tittle
The scroll within contains.
Tec.   What is 't, Armostes?
Arm. It is the health of Sparta, the king's
 life,
Sinews and safety of the common-
 wealth—
The sum of what the oracle delivered
When last he visited the prophetic
 temple
At Delphos. What his reasons are, for
 which,   70
After so long a silence, he requires
Your counsel now, grave man, his
 majesty
Will soon himself acquaint you with.
Tec. [*Taking the casket.*] Apollo
Inspire my intellect!—The Prince of
 Argos
Is entertained?
Arm.   He is, and has demanded
Our princess for his wife, which I con-
 ceive
One special cause the king importunes
 you
For resolution [1] of the oracle.
Tec. My duty to the king, good peace to
 Sparta,
And fair day to Armostes!
Arm. Like to Tecnicus! *Exeunt.* 80

[Scene ii.

Ithocles' apartment in the palace.]

Soft music.

A Song

Can you paint a thought, or number
Every fancy in a slumber?
Can you count soft minutes roving
From a dial's point by moving?
Can you grasp a sigh, or, lastly,
Rob a virgin's honor chastely?
 No, O, no! Yet you may
Sooner do both that and this,
This and that, and never miss,
 Than by any praise display 10
Beauty's beauty—such a glory,
As beyond all fate, all story,
  All arms, all arts,
  All loves, all hearts,
 Greater than those or they,
 Do, shall, and must obey.

[1] Interpretation.

*During which time enters Prophilus, Bas-
sanes, Penthea, Grausis, passing over
the stage; Bassanes and Grausis enter
again softly, stealing to several stands,*[2]
       and listen.

Bass. All silent, calm, secure.—Grausis,
 no creaking?
No noise? Dost hear nothing?
Grau.   Not a mouse,
Or whisper of the wind.
Bass.   The floor is matted;
The bedposts sure are steel or marble.—
 Soldiers   20
Should not affect, methinks, strains so
 effeminate;
Sounds of such delicacy are but fawn-
 ings
Upon the sloth of luxury;[3] they heighten
Cinders of covert lust up to a flame.
Grau. What do you mean, my lord?
 Speak low; that gabbling
Of yours will but undo us.
Bass.   Chamber combats
Are felt, not heard.
Pro. [*Within.*] A wakes.
Bass.   What's that?
Ith. [*Within.*]   Who's there?
Sister?—All quit the room else.
Bass.   'Tis consented!

Enter Prophilus.

Pro. Lord Bassanes, your brother would
 be private;
We must forbear; his sleep hath newly
 left him.   30
Please 'e withdraw.
Bass.   By any means; 'tis fit.
Pro. Pray, gentlewoman, walk too.
Grau.   Yes, I will, sir. *Exeunt omnes.*

Ithocles discovered [4] *in a chair, and Penthea.*
Ith. Sit nearer, sister, to me; nearer yet.
We had one father, in one womb took
 life,
Were brought up twins together, yet
 have lived
At distance, like two strangers. I could
 wish
That the first pillow whereon I was
 cradled
Had proved to me a grave.

[2] Different positions.   [3] Lust.
[4] By the drawing of the curtain from the inner
stage.

PEN.   You had been happy;
Then had you never known that sin
of life
Which blots all following glories with
a vengeance,   40
For forfeiting the last will of the dead,
From whom you had your being.
ITH.   Sad Penthea,
Thou canst not be too cruel; my rash
spleen
Hath with a violent hand plucked from
thy bosom
A lover-blessed heart, to grind it into dust
For which mine's now a-breaking.
PEN.   Not yet, heaven,
I do beseech thee! First let some wild
fires
Scorch, not consume it! May the heat
be cherished
With desires infinite, but hopes impos-
sible!
ITH. Wronged soul, thy prayers are heard.
PEN.   Here, lo, I breathe, 50
A miserable creature, led to ruin
By an unnatural brother!
ITH.   I consume
In languishing affections [1] for that tres-
pass,
Yet cannot die.
PEN.   The handmaid to the wages
Of country toil drinks the untroubled [2]
streams
With leaping kids and with the bleating
lambs,
And so allays her thirst secure,[3] whiles I
Quench my hot sighs with fleetings [4] of
my tears.
ITH. The laborer doth eat his coarsest
bread,
Earned with his sweat, and lies him
down to sleep,   60
Whiles [5] every bit I touch turns in di-
gestion
To gall as bitter as Penthea's curse.
Put me to any penance for my tyranny,
And I will call thee merciful.
PEN.   Pray, kill me;
Rid me from living with a jealous hus-
band.

Then we will join in friendship, be again
Brother and sister.—Kill me, pray; nay,
will 'e?
ITH. How does thy lord esteem thee?
PEN.   Such an one
As only you have made me: a faith-
breaker,
A spotted whore. Forgive me. I am
one   70
In art,[6] not in desires, the gods must wit-
ness.
ITH. Thou dost belie thy friend.
PEN.   I do not, Ithocles;
For she that's wife to Orgilus, and lives
In known adultery with Bassanes,
Is at the best a whore. Wilt kill me now?
The ashes of our parents will assume
Some dreadful figure, and appear to
charge
Thy bloody guilt, that hast betrayed
their name   78
To infamy in this reproachful match.
ITH. After my victories abroad, at home
I meet despair; ingratitude of nature
Hath made my actions monstrous.
Thou shalt stand
A deity, my sister, and be worshipped
For thy resolvéd martyrdom; wronged
maids
And married wives shall to thy hallowed
shrine
Offer their orisons, and sacrifice
Pure turtles,[7] crowned with myrtle, if
thy pity
Unto a yielding brother's pressure lend
One finger but to ease it.
PEN.   O, no more!
ITH. Death waits to waft me to the
Stygian banks,   90
And free me from this chaos of my
bondage;
And, till thou wilt forgive, I must en-
dure.
PEN. Who is the saint you serve?
ITH.   Friendship, or [nearness] [8]
Of birth to any but my sister, durst not
Have moved that question; as a secret,
sister,
I dare not murmur to myself—
PEN.   Let me,
By your new protestations I conjure 'e,
Partake her name.

[1] Emotions.
[2] The last two words are misplaced at the
head of the line in the original.
[3] Unmolested.
[4] Flowings, streams.
[5] Gifford-Dyce reading. Original reads *Which*.

[6] Act, practice (?).   [8] Supplied by Gifford.
[7] Turtledoves.

ITH.　　　　　Her name?—'Tis—'tis—
I dare not.

PEN. All your respects [1] are forged.

ITH.　　　　　They are not.—Peace!
Calantha is—the princess—the king's
daughter—　　　　　　　　　100
Sole heir of Sparta.—Me most miser-
able,
Do I now love thee? For my injuries,
Revenge thyself with bravery, and gos-
sip
My treasons to the king's ears; do.
Calantha
Knows it not yet, nor Prophilus, my
nearest.

PEN. Suppose you were contracted to her,
would it not
Split even your very soul to see her
father
Snatch her out of your arms against
her will,
And force her on the Prince of Argos?

ITH.　　　　　Trouble not
The fountains of mine eyes with thine
own story;　　　　　　　110
I sweat in blood for 't.

PEN.　　　　　We are reconciled.
Alas, sir, being children, but two
branches
Of one stock, 'tis not fit we should divide.
Have comfort; you may find it.

ITH.　　　　　Yes, in thee;
Only in thee, Penthea mine.

PEN.　　　　　If sorrows
Have not too much dulled my infected
brain,
I'll cheer invention for an active strain. [2]

ITH. Mad man! Why have I wronged a
maid so excellent?

Enter Bassanes with a poniard; Prophilus,
Groneas, Hemophil, and Grausis.

BASS. I can forbear no longer; more, I
will not.
Keep off your hands, or fall upon my
point.　　　　　　　　120
Patience is tired, for, like a slow-paced
ass,
Ye ride my easy nature, and proclaim
My sloth to vengeance a reproach and
property. [3]

[1] Supply *for me.*
[2] *I.e.,* I will try to contrive some plan.
[3] Characteristic condition.

ITH. The meaning of this rudeness?

PRO.　　　　　He's distracted.

PEN. O, my grieved lord!—

GRAU.　　　　　Sweet lady, come not near
him;
He holds his perilous weapon in his
hand
To prick a cares not whom nor where—
see, see, see!

BASS. My birth is noble. Though the
popular blast
Of vanity, as giddy as thy youth,
Hath reared thy name up to bestride
a cloud,　　　　　　　　130
Or progress in the chariot of the sun,
I am no clod of trade, to lackey pride,
Nor, like your slave of expectation, [4]
wait [5]
The bawdy hinges of your doors, or
whistle
For mystical conveyance to your bed
sports.

GRO. Fine humors! They become him.

HEM.　　　　　How a stares,
Struts, puffs, and sweats! Most admirable [6] lunacy!

ITH. But that I may conceive the spirit
of wine
Has took possession of your soberer
custom,
I'd say you were unmannerly.

PEN.　　　　　Dear brother!—　140

BASS. Unmannerly!—Mew,　kitling! [7]—
Smooth Formality
Is usher to the rankness of the blood,
But Impudence bears up the train. In-
deed, sir,
Your fiery mettle, or your springal [8]
blaze
Of huge renown, is no sufficient royalty [9]
To print upon my forehead the scorn,
"cuckold."

ITH. His jealousy has robbed him of his
wits;
A talks a knows not what.

BASS.　　　　　Yes, and a knows
To whom a talks—to one that franks [10]
his lust
In swine-security of bestial incest.　150

ITH. Ha, devil!

[4] Attendance.　　　[8] Youthful.
[5] Attend.　　　　[9] Right.
[6] Wonderful.　　　[10] Fattens.
[7] Kitten.

Bass. I will hallo [1] 't, though I blush
 more
To name the filthiness than thou to act
 it.
Ith. Monster!
Pro.   Sir, by our friendship—
Pen.   By our bloods—
Will you quite both undo us, brother?
Grau.   Out on him!
These are his megrims, firks,[2] and melan-
 cholies.
Hem. Well said, old touchhole!
Gro.   Kick him out at doors!
Pen. With favor, let me speak.—My
 lord, what slackness
In my obedience hath deserved this
 rage?
Except humility and silent duty
Have drawn on your unquiet, my sim-
 plicity   160
Ne'er studied your vexation.
Bass.   Light of beauty,
Deal not ungently with a desperate
 wound!
No breach of reason dares make war
 with her
Whose looks are sovereignty, whose
 breath is balm.
O, that I could preserve thee in fruition
As in devotion!
Pen.   Sir, may every evil
Locked in Pandora's box shower, in
 your presence,
On my unhappy head, if, since you
 made me
A partner in your bed, I have been
 faulty
In one unseemly thought against your
 honor!   170
Ith. Purge not his griefs, Penthea.
Bass.   Yes, say on,
Excellent creature!—[To Ithocles.] Good,
 be not a hinderance
To peace and praise of virtue.—O, my
 senses
Are charmed with sounds celestial!—
 On, dear, on;
I never gave you one ill word; say, did
 I?
Indeed, I did not.
Pen.   Nor, by Juno's forehead,
Was I e'er guilty of a wanton error.
Bass. A goddess! Let me kneel.

<hr>

[1] Proclaim.   [2] Freaks.

Grau.   Alas, kind animal!
Ith. No; but for penance—
Bass.   Noble sir, what is it?
With gladness I embrace it; yet, pray,
 let not   180
My rashness teach you to be too un-
 merciful.
Ith. When you shall show good proof
 that manly wisdom,
Not overswayed by passion or opinion,
Knows how to lead judgment, then this
 lady,
Your wife, my sister, shall return in
 safety
Home, to be guided by you; but, till
 first
I can out of clear evidence approve it,
She shall be my care.
Bass.   Rip my bosom up,
I'll stand the execution with a con-
 stancy;
This torture is unsufferable.
Ith.   Well, sir,   190
I dare not trust her to your fury.
Bass.   But
Penthea says not so.
Pen.   She needs no tongue
To plead excuse who never purposed
 wrong.
Hem. [To Grausis.] Virgin of reverence
 and antiquity,
Stay you behind.
Gro. [To Grausis.]   The court wants not
 your diligence.
   Exeunt omnes sed Bass[anes] et Graus[is].
Grau. What will you do, my lord? My
 lady's gone;
I am denied to follow.
Bass.   I may see her,
Or speak to her once more?
Grau.   And feel her too,
 man;
Be of good cheer, she's your own flesh
 and bone.
Bass. Diseases desperate must find cures
 alike.   200
She swore she has been true.
Grau.   True, on my modesty.
Bass. Let him want truth who credits
 not her vows!
Much wrong I did her, but her brother
 infinite;
Rumor will voice me the contempt of
 manhood,

Should I run on thus. Some way I must
   try
To outdo art, and cry [1] a jealousy.
             Exeunt omnes.

      [SCENE iii.

   A room in the palace.]

*Flourish. Enter Amyclas, Nearchus, lead-
   ing Calantha, Armostes, Crotolon, Euphranea, Christalla, Philema, and Am-
                    elus.*

AMY. Cousin of Argos, what the heavens
   have pleased
In their unchanging counsels to con-
   clude
For both our kingdoms' weal, we must
   submit to;
Nor can we be unthankful to their
   bounties,
Who, when we were even creeping to
   our graves,
Sent us a daughter, in whose birth our
   hope
Continues of succession. As you are
In title next, being grandchild to our
   aunt,
So we in heart desire you may sit near-
   est
Calantha's love, since we have ever
   vowed   10
Not to enforce affection by our will,
But by her own choice to confirm it
   gladly.
NEAR. You speak the nature of a right
   just father.
I come not hither roughly to demand
My cousin's thralldom, but to free
   mine own.
Report of great Calantha's beauty,
   virtue,
Sweetness, and singular perfections,
   courted
All ears to credit what I find was pub-
   lished
By constant truth, from which, if any
   service
Of my desert can purchase fair construc-
   tion,   20
This lady must command it.
CAL.   Princely sir,
So well you know how to profess ob-
   servance [2]

[1] Decry, disprove.   [2] Courtship.

That you instruct your hearers to be-
   come
Practitioners in duty, of which number
I'll study to be chief.
NEAR.   Chief, glorious virgin,
In my devotions, as in all men's wonder.
AMY. Excellent cousin, we deny no liberty;
Use thine own opportunities.—Armos-
   tes,
We must consult with the philosophers;
The business is of weight.
ARM.   Sir, at your pleasure. 30
AMY. You told me, Crotolon, your son's
   returned
From Athens? Wherefore comes a not
   to court
As we commanded?
CROT.   He shall soon attend
Your royal will, great sir.
AMY.   The marriage
Between young Prophilus and Eu-
   phranea
Tastes of too much delay.
CROT.   My lord—
AMY.   Some pleasures
At celebration of it would give life
To th' entertainment of the prince our
   kinsman;
Our court wears gravity more than we
   relish.
ARM. Yet the heavens smile on all your
   high attempts   40
Without a cloud.
CROT.   So may the gods protect us.
CAL. A prince a subject?
NEAR.   Yes, to beauty's scepter;
As all hearts kneel, so mine.
CAL.   You are too courtly.

To them, Ithocles, Orgilus, Prophilus.

ITH. Your safe return to Sparta is most
   welcome;
I joy to meet you here, and, as occasion
Shall grant us privacy, will yield you
   reasons
Why I should covet to deserve the title
Of your respected friend; for, without
   compliment,
Believe it, Orgilus, 'tis my ambition.
ORG. Your lordship may command me
   your poor servant.   50
ITH. [*Aside.*] So amorously close? So
   soon? My heart!

PRO. What sudden change is next?

ITH.   Life to the
        king,
    To whom I here present this noble
        gentleman,
    New come from Athens. Royal sir,
        vouchsafe
    Your gracious hand in favor of his
        merit.

CROT. [*Aside.*] My son preferred by Itho-
        cles!

AMY.   Our bounties
    Shall open to thee, Orgilus; for in-
        stance—
    Hark in thine ear—if, out of those in-
        ventions
    Which flow in Athens, thou hast there
        engrossed [1]
    Some rarity of wit, to grace the nup-
        tials   60
    Of thy fair sister, and renown our court
    In th' eyes of this young prince, we
        shall be debtor
    To thy conceit; think on 't.

ORG.   Your highness honors me.

NEAR. My tongue and heart are twins.

CAL.   A noble birth,
    Becoming such a father.—Worthy Or-
        gilus,
    You are a guest most wished for.

ORG.   May my duty
    Still rise in your opinion, sacred prin-
        cess!

ITH. Euphranea's brother, sir; a gentle-
        man
    Well worthy of your knowledge.

NEAR.   We embrace him,
    Proud of so dear acquaintance.

AMY.   All prepare   70
    For revels and disport; the joys of Hy-
        men,
    Like Phœbus in his luster, puts to
        flight
    All mists of dullness. Crown the hours
        with gladness.
    No sounds but music, no discourse but
        mirth!

CAL. Thine arm, I prithee, Ithocles.—
        Nay, good
    My lord, keep on your way; I am pro-
        vided.

NEAR. I dare not disobey.

ITH.   Most heavenly lady!   *Exeunt.*

[1] Acquired, learned.

[SCENE iv.

A room in Crotolon's house.]

Enter Crotolon, Orgilus.

CROT. The king hath spoke his mind.

ORG.   His will he hath;
    But, were it lawful to hold plea against
    The power of greatness, not the reason,
        haply
    Such undershrubs as subjects sometimes
        might
    Borrow of nature justice, to inform
    That license [2] sovereignty holds without
        check
    Over a meek obedience.

CROT.   How resolve you
    Touching your sister's marriage? Pro-
        philus
    Is a deserving and a hopeful youth.   9

ORG. I envy not his merit, but applaud it;
    Could wish [3] him thrift [4] in all his best
        desires,
    And with a willingness inleague our blood
    With his, for purchase of full growth in
        friendship.
    He never touched on any wrong that
        maliced [5]
    The honor of our house nor stirred our
        peace;
    Yet, with your favor, let me not forget
    Under whose wing he gathers warmth
        and comfort,
    Whose creature he is bound, made, and
        must live so.

CROT. Son, son, I find in thee a harsh con-
        dition; [6]
    No courtesy can win it; 'tis too ran-
        corous.   20

ORG. Good sir, be not severe in your con-
        struction.
    I am no stranger to such easy calms
    As sit in tender bosoms. Lordly Ithocles
    Hath graced my entertainment in abun-
        dance,
    Too humbly hath descended from that
        height
    Of arrogance and spleen which wrought
        the rape
    On grieved Penthea's purity; his scorn
    Of my untoward fortunes is reclaimed

[2] To control that authority.
[3] Suggested by Gifford-Dyce. Original reads
with.   [5] Sought to injure.
[4] Success.   [6] Disposition.

Unto a courtship, almost to a fawning.
I'll kiss his foot, since you will have it
    so.   30
CROT. Since I will have it so?   Friend, I
    will have it so,
Without our ruin by your politic plots,
Or wolf of hatred snarling in your breast.
You have a spirit, sir, have ye? A fa-
    miliar
That posts i' th' air for your intelligence?
Some such hobgoblin hurried you from
    Athens,
For yet you come unsent for.
ORG.   If unwelcome,
I might have found a grave there.
CROT.   Sure, your business
Was soon despatched, or your mind al-
    tered quickly.
ORG. 'Twas care, sir, of my health cut
    short my journey;   40
For there a general infection
Threatens a desolation.
CROT.   And I fear
Thou hast brought back a worse infection
    with thee—
Infection of thy mind, which, as thou
    say'st,
Threatens the desolation of our family.
ORG. Forbid it, our dear genius![1] I will
    rather
Be made a sacrifice on Thrasus' monu-
    ment,
Or kneel to Ithocles, his son, in dust,
Than woo a father's curse. My sister's
    marriage
With Prophilus is from my heart con-
    firmed.   50
May I live hated, may I die despised,
If I omit to further it in all
That can concern me!
CROT.   I have been too rough.
My duty to my king made me so earnest.
Excuse it, Orgilus.
ORG.   Dear sir!—

Enter to them, Prophilus, Euphranea, Itho-
        cles, Groneas, Hemophil.

CROT.   Here comes
Euphranea with Prophilus and Ithocles.
ORG. Most honored! Ever famous!
ITH.   Your true friend;
On earth not any truer.—With smooth[2]
    eyes

[1] Tutelary spirit.   [2] Kindly.

Look on this worthy couple; your consent
Can only make them one.
ORG.   They have it.—Sister, 60
Thou pawn'dst to me an oath, of which
    engagement
I never will release thee, if thou aim'st
At any other choice than this.
EUPH.   Dear brother
At him, or none.
CROT.   To which my blessing's added.
ORG. Which, till a greater ceremony per-
    fect—
Euphranea, lend thy hand. Here, take
    her, Prophilus;
Live long a happy man and wife; and
    further,
That these in presence may conclude an
    omen,
Thus for a bridal song I close my wishes:

Comforts lasting; loves increasing,   70
Like soft hours never ceasing;
Plenty's pleasure; peace complying,
Without jars, or tongues envying;
Hearts by holy union wedded
More than theirs by custom bedded;
Fruitful issues; life so gracéd,
Not by age to be defacéd,
Budding, as the year ensu'th,
Every spring another youth—
All what thought can add beside   80
Crown this bridegroom and this bride!

PRO. You have sealed joy close to my
    soul.—Euphranea,
Now I may call thee mine.
ITH.   I but exchange
One good friend for another.
ORG.   If these gallants
Will please to grace a poor invention
By joining with me in some slight device,
I'll venture on a strain my younger days
Have studied for delight.
HEM.   With thankful willingness
I offer my attendance.
GRO.   No endeavor
Of mine shall fail to show itself.
ITH.   We will 90
All join to wait on thy directions, Orgilus.
ORG. O, my good lord, your favors flow
    towards
A too unworthy worm—but as you
    please;
I am what you will shape me.
ITH.   A fast friend.

CROT. I thank thee, son, for this acknowl-
 edgment;
It is a sight of gladness.
ORG.   But my duty. *Exeunt omnes.*

[SCENE v.

Calantha's apartment in the palace.]

Enter Calantha, Penthea, Christalla, Phi-
           lema.

CAL. Whoe'er would speak with us, deny
 his entrance;
Be careful of our charge.
CHRIS.   We shall, madam.
CAL. Except the king himself, give none
 admittance;
Not any.
PHIL. Madam, it shall be our care.

  Exeunt [All but] Calantha, Penthea.
CAL. Being alone, Penthea, you have
 granted
The opportunity you sought, and might
At all times have commanded.
PEN.   'Tis a benefit
Which I shall owe your goodness even in
 death for.
My glass [1] of life, sweet princess, hath few
 minutes
Remaining to run down; the sands are
 spent,   10
For by an inward messenger I feel
The summons of departure short and
 certain.
CAL. You feed too much your melancholy.
PEN.   Glories
Of human greatness are but pleasing
 dreams
And shadows soon decaying; on the stage
Of my mortality my youth hath acted
Some scenes of vanity, drawn out at
 length
By varied pleasures, sweetened in the
 mixture,
But tragical in issue; beauty, pomp,
With every sensuality our giddiness 20
Doth frame an idol, are unconstant
 friends,
When any troubled passion makes as-
 sault
On the unguarded castle of the mind.
CAL. Contemn not your condition for the
 proof
 [1] Hourglass.

Of bare opinion only.[2] To what end
Reach all these moral texts?
PEN.   To place before 'e
A perfect mirror, wherein you may see
How weary I am of a ling'ring life,
Who count the best a misery.
CAL.   Indeed
You have no little cause; yet none so
 great   30
As to distrust a remedy.
PEN.   That remedy
Must be a winding sheet, a fold of lead,
And some untrod-on corner in the
 earth.—
Not to detain your expectation, princess,
I have an humble suit.
CAL.   Speak; I enjoy it.
PEN. Vouchsafe, then, to be my executrix,
And take that trouble on 'e to dispose
Such legacies as I bequeath, impartially.
I have not much to give—the pains are
 easy;
Heaven will reward your piety, and
 thank it   40
When I am dead. For sure I must not
 live;
I hope I cannot.
CAL.   Now, beshrew thy sadness;
Thou turn'st me too much woman.
         [*Weeps.*]
PEN. [*Aside.*]   Her fair eyes
Melt into passion. Then I have assurance
Encouraging my boldness.—In this paper
My will was charactered, which you, with
 pardon,
Shall now know from mine own mouth.
CAL.   Talk on, prithee;
It is a pretty earnest.[3]
PEN.   I have left me
But three poor jewels to bequeath. The
 first is
My youth, for, though I am much old in
 griefs,   50
In years I am a child.
CAL.   To whom that?
PEN. To virgin wives, such as abuse not
 wedlock
By freedom of desires, but covet chiefly
The pledges of chaste beds for ties of love,
Rather than ranging of their blood; and
 next

[2] On account of your experience from mere
public opinion.
 [3] A small advance payment, a foretaste.

To married maids, such as prefer the
        number
Of honorable issue in their virtues
Before the flattery of delights by mar-
        riage.
May those be ever young!
CAL.   A second jewel
You mean to part with?
PEN.   'Tis my fame, I trust 60
By scandal yet untouched; this I be-
        queath
To Memory, and Time's old daughter,
        Truth.
If ever my unhappy name find mention
When I am fall'n to dust, may it deserve
Beseeming charity without dishonor!
CAL. How handsomely thou play'st with
        harmless sport
Of mere imagination! Speak the last.
I strangely like thy will.
PEN.   This jewel, madam,
Is dearly precious to me; you must use
The best of your discretion to employ 70
This gift as I intend it.
CAL.   Do not doubt me.
PEN. 'Tis long agone since first I lost my
        heart;
Long I have lived without it, else for cer-
        tain
I should have given that too; but instead
Of it, to great Calantha, Sparta's heir,
By service bound and by affection vowed,
I do bequeath, in holiest rites of love,
Mine only brother, Ithocles.
CAL.   What said'st thou?
PEN. Impute not, heaven-blessed lady, to
        ambition   79
A faith as humbly perfect as the prayers
Of a devoted suppliant can endow it.
Look on him, princess, with an eye of
        pity.
How like the ghost of what he late ap-
        peared
A moves before you!
CAL.   Shall I answer here,
Or lend my ear too grossly?
PEN.   First his heart
Shall fall in cinders, scorched by your
        disdain,
Ere he will dare, poor man, to ope an eye
On these divine looks, but with low-bent
        thoughts
Accusing such presumption, as, for
        words,

A dares not utter any but of service.   90
Yet this lost creature loves 'e. Be a
        princess
In sweetness as in blood; give him his
        doom,
Or raise him up to comfort.
CAL.   What new change
Appears in my behavior, that thou dar'st
Tempt my displeasure?
PEN.   I must leave the world
To revel [in] [1] Elysium, and 'tis just
To wish my brother some advantage
        here;
Yet, by my best hopes, Ithocles is ig-
        norant
Of this pursuit. But, if you please to kill
        him,
Lend him one angry look or one harsh
        word,   100
And you shall soon conclude how strong
        a power
Your absolute authority holds over
His life and end.
CAL.   You have forgot, Penthea,
How still I have a father.
PEN.   But remember
I am a sister, though to me this brother
Hath been, you know, unkind, O, most
        unkind!
CAL. Christalla, Philema, where are 'e?—
        Lady,
Your check [2] lies in my silence.

Enter Christalla and Philema.

BOTH.   Madam, here.
CAL. I think 'e sleep, 'e drones! Wait on
        Penthea
Unto her lodging.—[*Aside.*] Ithocles?
        Wronged lady!   110
PEN. My reckonings are made even;
        death or fate
Can now nor strike too soon, nor force
        too late.   *Exeunt.*

ACTUS QUARTUS. SCENA PRIMA.

[*Ithocles' apartment in the palace.*]

Enter Ithocles and Armostes.

ITH. Forbear your inquisition; curiosity
Is of too subtle and too searching nature,
In fears of love too quick, too slow of
        credit.

_____
[1] Supplied by Gifford-Dyce.   [2] Censure.

I am not what you doubt [1] me.

ARM.   Nephew, be, then,
As I would wish.—[*Aside.*] All is not right.—Good heaven
Confirm your resolutions for dependence
On worthy ends, which may advance your quiet!

ITH. I did the noble Orgilus much injury,
But grieved Penthea more; I now repent it.
Now, uncle, now; this "now" is now too late.   10
So provident [2] is folly in sad issue
That after-wit, like bankrupts' debts, stand tallied [3]
Without all possibilities of payment.
Sure, he's an honest, very honest gentleman;
A man of single [4] meaning.

ARM.   I believe it;
Yet, nephew, 'tis the tongue informs our ears;
Our eyes can never pierce into the thoughts,
For they are lodged too inward. But I question
No truth in Orgilus.—The princess, sir.

ITH. The princess? Ha!

ARM.   With her the Prince of Argos.   20

Enter Nearchus, leading Calantha; Amelus,
                  Christalla, Philema.

NEAR. Great fair one, grace my hopes with any instance
Of livery,[5] from the allowance of your favor;
This little spark—
       [*Tries to take a ring from her finger.*]

CAL.   A toy!

NEAR.   Love feasts on toys,
For Cupid is a child. Vouchsafe this bounty;
It cannot be [de][6]nied.

CAL.   You shall not value,
Sweet cousin, at a price, what I count cheap,
So cheap that let him take it who dares stoop for 't,
And give it at next meeting to a mistress;

[1] Suspect.
[2] Productive.
[3] Reckoned up.
[4] Sincere.
[5] Badge of service.
[6] Supplied by Gifford-Dyce.

She'll thank him for 't, perhaps.
            Casts it to Ithocles.

AME.   The ring, sir, is 29
The princess's; I could have took it up.

ITH. Learn manners, prithee.—To the blessed owner,
Upon my knees—

NEAR.   Y' are saucy.

CAL.   This is pretty!
I am, belike, "a mistress." Wondrous pretty!
Let the man keep his fortune, since he found it;
He's worthy on 't.—On, cousin!

ITH. [*To Amelus.*]   Follow, spaniel;
I'll force 'e to a fawning else.

AME.   You dare not.
     Exeunt. Manent Itho[cles] et Armost[es].

ARM. My lord, you were too forward.

ITH.   Look 'e, uncle,
Some such there are whose liberal contents
Swarm without care in every sort of plenty,
Who after full repasts can lay them down   40
To sleep; and they sleep, uncle—in which silence
Their very dreams present 'em choice of pleasures,
Pleasures—observe me, uncle—of rare object;
Here heaps of gold, there increments of honors,
Now change of garments, then the votes of people,
Anon varieties of beauties, courting,
In flatteries of the night, exchange of dalliance.
Yet these are still but dreams. Give me felicity
Of which my senses waking are partakers,
A real, visible, material happiness;   50
And then, too, when I stagger in expectance
Of the least comfort that can cherish life—
I saw it, sir, I saw it, for it came
From her own hand.

ARM.   The princess threw it t'e.

ITH. True; and she said—well I remember what.
Her cousin prince would beg it.

ARM.   Yes, and parted
In anger at your taking on 't.
ITH.   Penthea,
O, thou hast pleaded with a powerful
    language!
I want a fee to gratify thy merit;
But I will do—
ARM.   What is 't you say?
ITH.   In anger, 60
In anger let him part, for could his
    breath,
Like whirlwinds, toss such servile slaves
    as lick
The dust his footsteps print into a vapor,
It durst not stir a hair of mine, it should
    not;
I'd rend it up by th' roots first. To be
    anything
Calantha smiles on is to be a blessing
More sacred than a petty prince of Argos
Can wish to equal, or in worth or title.
ARM. Contain yourself, my lord. Ixion,
    aiming   69
To embrace Juno, bosomed but a cloud,
And begat Centaurs; 'tis an useful
    moral.
Ambition hatched in clouds of mere opin-
    ion
Proves but in birth a prodigy.
ITH.   I thank 'e;
Yet, with your license, I should seem un-
    charitable
To gentler fate, if, relishing the dainties
Of a soul's settled peace, I were so feeble
Not to digest it.
ARM.   He deserves small trust
Who is not privy counselor to himself.

Enter Nearchus, Orgilus, and Amelus.

NEAR. Brave me?
ORG.   Your excellence mistakes
    his temper,
For Ithocles in fashion of his mind   80
Is beautiful, soft, gentle, the clear mirror
Of absolute perfection.
AME.   Was 't your modesty
Termed any of the prince his servants
    "spaniel"?
Your nurse, sure, taught you other lan-
    guage.
ITH.   Language!
NEAR. A gallant man-at-arms is here, a
    doctor

In feats of chivalry, blunt and rough-
    spoken,
Vouchsafing not the fustian of civility,
Which [less] [1] rash spirits style good man-
    ners!
ITH.   Manners!
ORG. No more, illustrious sir; 'tis match-
    less Ithocles.
NEAR. You might have understood who I
    am.
ITH.   Yes,   90
I did; else—but the presence [2] calmed
    th' affront—
Y' are cousin to the princess.
NEAR.   To the king, too;
A certain instrument that lent support-
    ance
To your colossic greatness—to that king
    too,
You might have added.
ITH.   There is more divinity
In beauty than in majesty.
ARM.   O, fie, fie!
NEAR. This odd youth's pride turns heretic
    in loyalty.
Sirrah, low mushrooms never rival ce-
    dars!   *Exeunt Nearchus et Amelus.*
ITH. Come back!—What pitiful dull thing
    am I
So to be tamely scolded at!   Come
    back!—   100
Let him come back, and echo once
    again
That scornful sound of "mushroom"!
    Painted colts—
Like heralds' coats gilt o'er with crowns
    and scepters—
May bait a muzzled lion.
ARM.   Cousin, cousin,
Thy tongue is not thy friend.
ORG.   In point of honor
Discretion knows no bounds.   Amelus
    told me
'Twas all about a little ring.
ITH.   A ring
The princess threw away, and I took up.
Admit she threw 't to me, what arm of
    brass
Can snatch it hence? No; could a grind
    the hoop   110
To powder, a might sooner reach my
    heart

[1] Supplied by Gifford.
[2] *I.e.*, of the princess.

Than steal and wear one dust [1] on 't.
Orgilus,
I am extremely wronged.

ORG. A lady's favor
Is not to be so slighted.

ITH. Slighted!

ARM. Quiet
These vain, unruly passions, which will
render ye
Into a madness.

ORG. Griefs will have their vent.

Enter Tecnicus [with a scroll].

ARM. Welcome; thou com'st in season, reverend man,
To pour the balsam of a suppling [2] patience
Into the festering wound of ill-spent fury.

ORG. [*Aside.*] What makes he here?

TEC. The hurts are yet but [3] mortal,
Which shortly will prove deadly. To
the king, 121
Armostes, see in safety thou deliver
This sealed-up counsel; bid him with a
constancy
Peruse the secrets of the gods.—O
Sparta,
O Lacedemon! Double-named, but one
In fate! When kingdoms reel—mark
well my saw—
Their heads must needs be giddy. Tell
the king
That henceforth he no more must inquire
after
My aged head; Apollo wills it so.
I am for Delphos.

ARM. Not without some conference
With our great master.

TEC. Never more to see him; 131
A greater prince commands me.—Ithocles,
*When youth is ripe, and age from time
doth part,
The lifeless trunk shall wed the broken
heart.*

ITH. What's this, if understood?

TEC List, Orgilus;
Remember what I told thee long before;
These tears shall be my witness.

[1] One particle.
[2] Healing. Suggested by Gifford-Dyce; original
reads *supplying.*
[3] Gifford-Dyce suggests *not* but retains original.

ARM. 'Las, good man!

TEC. *Let craft with courtesy awhile confer;
Revenge proves its own executioner.*

ORG. Dark sentences are for Apollo's
priests; 140
I am not Œdipus.

TEC. My hour is come.
Cheer up the king; farewell to all.—O
Sparta,
O Lacedemon! *Exit Tecn[icus].*

ARM. If prophetic fire
Have warmed this old man's bosom, we
might construe
His words to fatal sense.

ITH. Leave to the
powers
Above us the effects of their decrees;
My burthen lies within me. Servile
fears
Prevent no great effects.—Divine Calantha!

ARM. The gods be still propitious!
Exeunt. Manet Org[ilus].

ORG. Something oddly
The bookman prated, yet a talked it
weeping: 150
"*Let craft with courtesy awhile confer;
Revenge proves its own executioner.*"
Con it again.—For what? It shall not
puzzle me;
'Tis dotage of a withered brain.—Pen-
thea
Forbade me not her presence; I may see
her,
And gaze my fill. Why, see her, then, I
may,
When, if I faint to speak—I must be
silent. *Exit Org[ilus].*

[SCENE ii.

A room in Bassanes' house.]

Enter Bassanes, Grausis, and Phulas.

BASS. Pray, use your recreations; all the
service
I will expect is quietness amongst 'e;
Take liberty at home, abroad, at all
times,
And in your charities appease the gods,
Whom I, with my distractions, have
offended.

GRAU. Fair blessings on thy heart!

PHU. [*Aside.*] Here's a rare change!

My lord, to cure the itch, is surely
gelded;
The cuckold in conceit [1] hath cast his
horns.
Bass. Betake 'e to your several occasions;
And, wherein I have heretofore been
faulty,   10
Let your constructions mildly pass it
over.
Henceforth I'll study reformation; more
I have not for employment.
Grau.   O sweet man!
Thou art the very "Honeycomb of
Honesty."
Phu. The "Garland of Goodwill." [2] —Old
lady, hold up
Thy reverend snout, and trot behind me
softly,
As it becomes a moil [3] of ancient carriage.
        Exeunt. Manet Bass[anes].
Bass. Beasts, only capable of sense, enjoy
The benefit of food and ease with thank-
fulness;
Such silly creatures, with a grudging,
kick not   20
Against the portion nature hath be-
stowed;
But men, endowed with reason and the
use
Of reason, to distinguish from the chaff
Of abject scarcity the quintessence,
Soul, and elixir of the earth's abundance,
The treasures of the sea, the air, nay,
heaven,
Repining at these glories of creation,
Are verier beasts than beasts; and of
those beasts
The worst am I—I, who was made a
monarch
Of what a heart could wish for—a chaste
wife—   30
Endeavored what in me lay to pull down
That temple built for adoration only,
And level 't in the dust of causeless
scandal.
But, to redeem a sacrilege so impious,
Humility shall pour, before the deities
I have incensed, a largeness [4] of more pa-
tience
Than their displeaséd altars can require.

No tempests of commotion shall disquiet
The calms of my composure.

Enter Orgilus.

Org.   I have found thee,
Thou patron of more horrors than the
bulk   40
Of manhood, hooped about with ribs of
iron,
Can cram within thy breast. Penthea,
Bassanes,
Cursed by thy jealousies—more, by thy
dotage—
Is left a prey to words. [5]
Bass.   Exercise
Your trials for addition to my penance;
I am resolved.
Org.   Play not with misery
Past cure; some angry minister of fate
hath
Deposed the empress of her soul, her
reason,
From its most proper throne; but, what's
the miracle
More new, I, I have seen it, and yet
live!   50
Bass. You may delude my senses, not my
judgment;
'Tis anchored into a firm resolution;
Dalliance of mirth or wit can ne'er unfix
it.
Practice [6] yet further.
Org.   May thy death of love to her
Damn all thy comforts to a lasting fast
From every joy of life! Thou barren
rock,
By thee we have been split in ken [7] of
harbor.

*Enter Ithocles, Penthea, her hair about her
ears, [Armostes,] Philema, Christalla.*

Ith. Sister, look up; your Ithocles, your
brother,
Speaks t'e; why do you weep? Dear,
turn not from me.—
Here is a killing sight; lo, Bassanes,   60
A lamentable object!
Org.   Man, dost see 't?
Sports are more gamesome; am I yet in
merriment?
Why dost not laugh?

[1] Imagination.
[2] A popular miscellany of the time.
[3] Mule.
[4] Bounty, liberality.

[5] *I.e.*, scandal.   [6] Carry on.   [7] Sight.

Bass.   Divine and best of ladies,
Please to forget my outrage; mercy ever
Cannot but lodge under a roof [1] so ex-
cellent.
I have cast off that cruelty of frenzy
Which once appeared impostors, and then
     juggled
To cheat my sleeps of rest.
Org.   Was I in earnest?
Pen. Sure, if we were all Sirens, we should
     sing pitifully.
And 'twere a comely music, when in
     parts   70
One sung another's knell. The turtle
     sighs
When he hath lost his mate; and yet
     some say
A must be dead first. 'Tis a fine deceit
To pass away in a dream; indeed, I've
     slept
With mine eyes open a great while. No
     falsehood
Equals a broken faith; there's not a hair
Sticks on my head but, like a leaden
     plummet,
It sinks me to the grave. I must creep
     thither;
The journey is not long.
Ith.   But thou, Penthea,
Hast many years, I hope, to number
     yet,   80
Ere thou canst travel that way.
Bass.   Let the sun [2] first
Be wrapped up in an everlasting dark-
     ness,
Before the light of nature, chiefly formed
For the whole world's delight, feel an
     eclipse
So universal!
Org.   Wisdom, look 'e, begins
To rave!—Art thou mad too, antiquity?
Pen. Since I was first a wife, I might have
     been
Mother to many pretty, prattling babes;
They would have smiled when I smiled,
     and for certain
I should have cried when they cried.—
     Truly, brother,   90
My father would have picked me out a
     husband,

And then my little ones had been no
     bastards;
But 'tis too late for me to marry now—
I am past childbearing; 'tis not my fault.
Bass. Fall on me, if there be a burning
     Ætna,
And bury me in flames! Sweats hot as
     sulphur
Boil through my pores! Affliction hath
     in store
No torture like to this.
Org.   Behold a patience!
Lay by thy whining, gray dissimulation;
Do something worth a chronicle. Show
     justice   100
Upon the author of this mischief; dig out
The jealousies that hatched this thrall-
     dom first
With thine own poniard. Every antic
     rapture
Can roar as thine does.
Ith.   Orgilus, forbear.
Bass. Disturb him not; it is a talking
     motion [3]
Provided for my torment. What a fool
     am I
To bawdy passion! Ere I'll speak a word,
I will look on and burst.
Pen. [To Orgilus.]   I loved you once.
Org. Thou didst, wronged creature, in de-
     spite of malice;
For it I love thee ever.
Pen.   Spare your hand;   110
Believe me, I'll not hurt it.
Org.   Pain my heart too.
[Pen.] [4] Complain not though I wring it
     hard. I'll kiss it;
O, 'tis a fine soft palm!—Hark, in thine
     ear;
Like whom do I look, prithee?—Nay, no
     whispering.
Goodness! We had been happy; too
     much happiness
Will make folk proud, they say—but that
     is he—   Points at Ithocles.
And yet he paid for 't home. Alas, his
     heart
Is crept into the cabinet of the princess;
We shall have points [5] and bride laces.
     Remember,

---

[1] Emended by Gifford-Dyce; original reads
root.
[2] Emended by Gifford-Dyce; original reads
swan.

[3] Puppet.
[4] This speech is assigned to Orgilus in the
original.
[5] Tagged laces.

When we last gathered roses in the gar-
den,   120
I found my wits, but truly you lost yours.
That's he, and still 'tis he.
ITH.   Poor soul, how idly [1]
Her fancies guide her tongue!
BASS. [*Aside.*]   Keep in, vexation,
And break not into clamor.
ORG. [*Aside.*]   She has tutored me;
Some powerful inspiration checks my
laziness.[2]—
Now let me kiss your hand, grieved
beauty.
PEN.   Kiss it.—
Alack, alack, his lips be wondrous cold.
Dear soul, h'as lost his color; have 'e
seen
A straying heart? All crannies! Every
drop
Of blood is turn[é]d to an amethyst,   130
Which married bachelors hang in their
ears.
ORG. Peace usher her into Elysium!—
If this be madness, madness is an oracle.
                              Exit Org[ilus].
ITH. Christalla, Philema, when slept my
sister,
Her ravings are so wild?
CHRIS.   Sir, not these ten days.
PHIL. We watch by her continually; be-
sides,
We cannot any way pray her to eat.
BASS. O, misery of miseries!
PEN.   Take comfort;
You may live well, and die a good old
man.
By yea and nay, an oath not to be
broken,   140
If you had joined our hands once in the
temple—
'Twas since my father died, for had he
lived
He would have done 't—I must have
called you father.
O, my wracked honor, ruined by those
tyrants,
A cruel brother and a desperate dotage!
There is no peace left for a ravished
wife
Widowed by lawless marriage; to all
memory
Penthea's, poor Penthea's, name is
strumpeted.

But, since her blood was seasoned by
the forfeit
Of noble shame with mixtures of pollu-
tion,   150
Her blood—'tis just—be henceforth
never heightened
With taste of sustenance! Starve; let
that fullness
Whose plurisy [3] hath fevered faith and
modesty—
Forgive me; O, I faint!
        [*Falls into the arms of her Attendants.*]
ARM.   Be not so willful,
Sweet niece, to work thine own destruc-
tion.
ITH.   Nature
Will call her daughter monster!—What!
Not eat?
Refuse the only ordinary means
Which are ordained for life? Be not, my
sister,
A murth'ress to thyself.—Hear'st thou
this, Bassanes?
BASS. Foh! I am busy, for I have not
thoughts   160
Enow to think; all shall be well anon.
'Tis tumbling in my head; there is a
mastery
In art to fatten and keep smooth the
outside;
Yes, and to comfort up the vital spirits
Without the help of food, fumes or per-
fumes,
Perfumes or fumes. Let her alone; I'll
search out
The trick on 't.
PEN.   Lead me gently; heavens reward
ye.
Griefs are sure friends; they leave with-
out control
Nor cure nor comforts for a leprous soul.
        Exeunt the Maids supporting Penthea.
BASS. I grant 'e, and will put in practice
instantly   170
What you shall still admire.[4] 'Tis won-
derful;
'Tis super-singular, not to be matched;
Yet, when I've done 't, I've done 't.—Ye
shall all thank me.   *Exit Bassanes.*
ARM. The sight is full of terror.
ITH.   On my soul
Lies such an infinite clog of massy dull-
ness

---

[1] Madly.   [2] Procrastination.   [3] Superabundance.   [4] Wonder at.

As that I have not sense enough to feel
it.—

See, uncle, th' augury [1] thing returns
again;

Shall 's welcome him with thunder? We
are haunted,

And must use exorcism to conjure down

This spirit of malevolence.

ARM.　　　　　　　　Mildly, nephew. 180

Enter Nearchus and Amelus.

NEAR. I come not, sir, to chide your late
disorder,

Admitting that th' inurement to a roughness

In soldiers of your years and fortunes,
chiefly,

So lately prosperous, hath not yet shook
off

The custom of the war in hours of leisure;

Nor shall you need excuse, since y' are to
render

Account to that fair excellence, the
princess,

Who in her private gallery expects it

From your own mouth alone. I am a
messenger

But to her pleasure.

ITH.　　　　　　Excellent Nearchus, 190

Be prince still of my services, and conquer

Without the combat of dispute; I hon-
or 'e.

NEAR. The king is on a sudden indisposed;

Physicians are called for. 'Twere fit,
Armostes,

You should be near him.

ARM.　　　　　Sir, I kiss your hands.

Exeunt. Manent Nearchus et Amelus.

NEAR. Amelus, I perceive Calantha's
bosom

Is warmed with other fires than such as
can

Take strength from any fuel of the love

I might address to her. Young Ithocles,

Or ever I mistake, is lord ascendant 200

Of her devotions—one, to speak him
truly,

In every disposition nobly fashioned.

AME. But can your highness brook to be
so rivaled,

Considering th' inequality of the persons?

[1] Foreboding.

NEAR. I can, Amelus, for affections injured

By tyranny or rigor of compulsion,

Like tempest-threatened trees unfirmly
rooted,

Ne'er spring to timely growth. Observe,
for instance,

Life-spent Penthea and unhappy Orgilus.

AME. How does your grace determine?

NEAR.　　　　　　　To be jealous 210

In public of what privately I'll further;

And, though they shall not know, yet
they shall find it.　　　*Exeunt omnes.*

[SCENE iii.

An apartment in the palace.]

*Enter Hemophil and Groneas leading Amy-
clas, and placing him in a chair; followed
by Armostes [with a box], Crotolon, and
Prophilus.*

AMY. Our daughter is not near?

ARM.　　　　　　　She is retired, sir,

Into her gallery.

AMY.　　　Where's the prince our cousin?

PRO. New walked into the grove, my lord.

AMY.　　　　　　　All leave us

Except Armostes, and you, Crotolon;

We would be private.

PRO.　　　　Health unto your majesty!

Exeunt Prophilus, Hemophil, et Groneas.

AMY. What! Tecnicus is gone?

ARM.　　　　　　He is to Delphos,

And to your royal hands presents this
box.

AMY. Unseal it, good Armostes; therein
lies

The secrets of the oracle. Out with it.

　　　[*Armostes removes the scroll.*]

Apollo live our patron! Read, Armostes.　　　　　　　　　10

ARM. "*The plot in which the vine takes root
Begins to dry from head to foot;
The stock soon withering, want of sap
Doth cause to quail [2] the budding grape;
But from the neighboring elm a dew
Shall drop, and feed the plot anew.*"

AMY.　　That is the oracle. What exposi-
tion

Makes the philosopher?

ARM.　　　　　This brief one only.

"*The plot is Sparta; the dried vine the king;*

[2] Die.

The quailing grape his daughter; but the thing　　　20
Of most importance, not to be revealed,
Is a near prince, the elm—the rest concealed.

TECNICUS."

AMY. Enough; although the opening [1] of this riddle
Be but itself a riddle, yet we construe
How near our laboring age draws to a rest.
But must Calantha quail too? That young grape
Untimely budded! I could mourn for her;
Her tenderness hath yet deserved no rigor
So to be crossed by fate.

ARM. 　　　　　You misapply, sir.　29
With favor let me speak it—what Apollo
Hath clouded in hid sense. I here conjecture
Her marriage with some neighb'ring prince, the dew
Of which befriending elm shall ever strengthen
Your subjects with a sovereignty of power.

CROT. Besides, most gracious lord, the pith of oracles
Is to be then digested when th' events
Expound their truth, not brought as soon to light
As uttered. Truth is child of Time; and herein
I find no scruple, rather cause of comfort,
With unity of kingdoms.

AMY. 　　　　　May it prove so,　40
For weal of this dear nation!—Where is Ithocles?—
Armostes, Crotolon, when this withered vine
Of my frail carcass, on the funeral pile
Is fired into its ashes, let that young man
Be hedged about still with your cares and loves.
Much owe I to his worth, much to his service.—
Let such as wait come in now.

ARM. 　　　　　　　All attend here!

Enter Ithocles, Calantha, Prophilus, Orgilus,
　　Euphranea, Hemophil, and Groneas.

CAL. Dear sir! King! Father!
ITH. 　　　　　O my royal master!

[1] *I.e.*, interpretation.

AMY. Cleave not my heart, sweet twins of my life's solace,
With your forejudging fears; there is no physic　50
So cunningly restorative to cherish
The fall of age, or call back youth and vigor,
As your consents in duty. I will shake off
This languishing disease of time, to quicken
Fresh pleasures in these drooping hours of sadness.
Is fair Euphranea married yet to Prophilus?

CROT. This morning, gracious lord.
ORG. 　　　　　This very morning,
Which, with your highness' leave, you may observe too.
Our sister looks, methinks, mirthful and sprightly,
As if her chaster fancy could already　60
Expound the riddle of her gain in losing
A trifle maids know only that they know not.
Pish! Prithee, blush not; 'tis but honest change
Of fashion in the garment, loose for strait,
And so the modest maid is made a wife.
Shrewd business—is 't not, sister?

EUPH. 　　　　　You are pleasant.
AMY. We thank thee, Orgilus; this mirth becomes thee.
But wherefore sits the court in such a silence?
A wedding without revels is not seemly.

CAL. Your late indisposition, sir, forbade it.　70
AMY. Be it thy charge, Calantha, to set forward
The bridal sports, to which I will be present;
If not, at least consenting.—Mine own Ithocles,
I have done little for thee yet.

ITH. 　　　　　Y' have built me
To the full height I stand in.
CAL. [*Aside.*] 　　　　Now or never!—
May I propose a suit?
AMY. 　　　　　Demand, and have it.
CAL. Pray, sir, give me this young man,
and no further
Account him yours than he deserves in all things

To be thought worthy mine; I will
      esteem him
According to his merit.

AMY.   Still th' art my daughter,   80
Still grow'st upon my heart.—[*To
Ithocles.*] Give me thine hand.—
Calantha, take thine own.   In noble
      actions
Thou'lt find him firm and absolute.—I
      would not
Have parted with thee, Ithocles, to any
But to a mistress who is all what I am.

ITH. A change, great king, most wished
      for, cause the same!

CAL. [*Aside to Ithocles.*] Th' art mine. Have
      I now kept my word?

ITH. [*Aside to Calantha.*]   Divinely.

ORG. Rich fortunes guard, the [1] favor of a
      princess
Rock thee, brave man, in ever-crownéd
      plenty!
Y' are minion of the time; be thankful for
      it.—   90
[*Aside.*] Ho! Here's a swinge [2] in destiny.
      Apparent,
The youth is up on tiptoe, yet may stum-
      ble.

AMY. On to your recreations.—Now con-
      vey me
Unto my bedchamber.   None on his fore-
      head
Wear a distempered look.

OMNES.   The gods preserve 'e!

CAL. [*Aside to Ithocles.*]   Sweet, be not
      from my sight.

ITH. [*Aside to Calantha.*]   My whole
      felicity!

*Exeunt, carrying out of the King; Orgilus
                          stays Ithocles.*

ORG. Shall I be bold, my lord?

ITH.   Thou canst not, Orgilus.
Call me thine own, for Prophilus must
      henceforth
Be all thy sister's.   Friendship, though it
      cease not   99
In marriage, yet is oft at less command
Than when a single freedom can dispose
      it.

ORG. Most right, my most good lord, my
      most great lord,
My gracious, princely lord, I might add,
      royal.

---

[1] Emended by Gifford-Dyce; original reads *to*.
[2] Sway.

ITH. Royal! A subject royal?

ORG.   Why not, pray, sir?
The sovereignty of kingdoms in their
      nonage
Stooped to desert, not birth; there's as
      much merit
In clearness of affection [3] as in puddle
Of generation.[4] You have conquered love
Even in the loveliest; if I greatly err
      not,
The son of Venus hath bequeathed his
      quiver   110
To Ithocles his manage,[5] by whose
      arrows
Calantha's breast is opened.

ITH.   Can 't be possible?

ORG. I was myself a piece of suitor once,
And forward in preferment too—so for-
      ward
That, speaking truth, I may without
      offense, sir,
Presume to whisper that my hopes and
      —hark 'e—
My certainty of marriage stood assured
With as firm footing—by your leave—as
      any's
Now at this very instant—but—

ITH.   'Tis granted;
And, for a league of privacy between
      us,   120
Read o'er my bosom and partake a
      secret:
The princess is contracted mine.

ORG.   Still, why not?
I now applaud her wisdom; when your
      kingdom
Stands seated in your will, secure and
      settled,
I dare pronounce you will be a just mon-
      arch;
Greece must admire and tremble.

ITH.   Then the sweetness
Of so imparadised a comfort, Orgilus!
It is to banquet with the gods.

ORG.   The glory
Of numerous children, potency of nobles,
Bent knees, hearts paved to tread on!

ITH.   With a friendship   130
So dear, so fast as thine.

ORG.   I am unfitting
For office; but for service—

---

[3] Nobility of mental tendencies.
[4] Birth.
[5] To Ithocles' management.

ITH.   We'll distinguish
Our fortunes merely in the title; partners
In all respects else but the bed.

ORG.   The bed?
Forfend it, Jove's own jealousy, till
        lastly
We slip down in the common earth to-
        gether,
And there our beds are equal, save some
        monument
To show this was the king, and this the
        subject.—
List, what sad sounds are these?—Ex-
        tremely sad ones!

ITH. Sure, from Penthea's lodgings.

ORG.   Hark! A voice too. 140

Soft, sad music.

A SONG

O, no more, no more, too late
        Sighs are spent; the burning tapers
Of a life as chaste as fate,
        Pure as are unwritten papers,
Are burnt out. No heat, no light
Now remains; 'tis ever night.

Love is dead; let lovers' eyes,
        Locked in endless dreams,
Th' extremes of all extremes,
Ope no more, for now Love dies,   150
        Now Love dies, implying
Love's martyrs must be ever, ever dying.

ITH. O, my misgiving heart!

ORG.   A horrid stillness
Succeeds this deathful air; let's know the
        reason.
Tread softly; there is mystery in mourn-
        ing.   *Exeunt.*

[SCENE iv.

Penthea's apartment in the palace.]

Enter Christalla and Philema, bringing in
        Penthea in a chair, veiled; two other
        Servants placing two chairs, one on the
        one side, and the other with an engine [1]
        on the other. The Maids sit down at her
        feet, mourning. The Servants go out;
        meet them Ithocles and Orgilus.

SERV. [*Aside to Orgilus.*] 'Tis done; that on
        her right hand.

_____
[1] Mechanical contrivance.

ORG.   Good; begone!
                    [*Exeunt Servants.*]

ITH. Soft peace enrich this room!

ORG.   How fares the lady?

PHIL. Dead!

CHRIS.   Dead!

PHIL.   Starved!

CHRIS.   Starved!

ITH.   Me miserable!

ORG.   Tell us
How parted she from life.

PHIL.   She called for music,
And begged some gentle voice to tune a
        farewell
To life and griefs. Christalla touched the
        lute;
I wept the funeral song.

CHRIS.   Which scarce was ended
But her last breath sealed up these hollow
        sounds,
"O, cruel Ithocles and injured Orgilus!"
So down she drew her veil, so died.

ITH.   So died! 10

ORG. Up! You are messengers of death; go
        from us;
Here's woe enough to court without a
        prompter!
Away; and—hark ye—till you see us
        next,
No syllable that she is dead.—Away;
                    Exeunt Phil[ema] et Chri[stalla].
Keep a smooth brow.—My lord—

ITH.   Mine only sister!
Another is not left me.

ORG.   Take that chair;
I'll seat me here in this. Between us sits
The object of our sorrows; some few
        tears
We'll part among us; I perhaps can mix
One lamentable story to prepare 'em.—
There, there; sit there, my lord.

ITH.   Yes, as you please. 21

Ithocles sits down, and is catched in the
                                engine.
What means this treachery?

ORG.   Caught! You are caught,
Young master; 'tis thy throne of corona-
        tion,
Thou fool of greatness! See, I take this
        veil off;
Survey a beauty withered by the flames
Of an insulting Phaëton, her brother.

ITH. Thou mean'st to kill me basely.

ORG.   I foreknew

The last act of her life, and trained [1] thee
  hither
To sacrifice a tyrant to a turtle.
You dreamt of kingdoms, did 'e? How to
  bosom   30
The delicacies of a youngling princess,
How with this nod to grace that subtle
  courtier,
How with that frown to make this noble
  tremble,
And so forth, whiles Penthea's groans and
  tortures,
Her agonies, her miseries, afflictions
Ne'er touched upon your thought? As
  for my injuries,
Alas, they were beneath your royal
  pity;
But yet they lived, thou proud man, to
  confound thee.
Behold thy fate, this steel!
                          [Draws a dagger.]
ITH.   Strike home! A courage
As keen as thy revenge shall give it wel-
  come.   40
But, prithee, faint not; if the wound
  close up,
Tent [2] it with double force, and search it
  deeply.
Thou look'st that I should whine and beg
  compassion,
As loath to leave the vainness of my
  glories.
A statelier resolution arms my confidence,
To cozen thee of honor; neither could I
With equal trial of unequal fortune
By hazard of a duel; 'twere a bravery
Too mighty for a slave intending mur-
  ther.
On to the execution, and inherit   50
A conflict with thy horrors!
ORG.   By Apollo,
Thou talk'st a goodly language! For
  requital
I will report thee to thy mistress richly.
And take this peace along: some few
  short minutes
Determined,[3] my resolves shall quickly
  follow
Thy wrathful ghost; then, if we tug for
  mastery,
Penthea's sacred eyes shall lend new
  courage.

Give me thy hand; be healthful in thy
  parting
From lost mortality! Thus, thus I free it!
                              Kills him.
ITH. Yet, yet, I scorn to shrink.
ORG.   Keep up thy spirit. 60
I will be gentle even in blood; to linger [4]
Pain, which I strive to cure, were to be
  cruel.   [Stabs him again.]
ITH. Nimble in vengeance, I forgive thee.
  Follow
Safety, with best success. O, may it
  prosper!—
Penthea, by thy side thy brother
  bleeds—
The earnest of his wrongs to thy forced
  faith.
Thoughts of ambition, or delicious ban-
  quet,
With beauty, youth, and love, together
  perish
In my last breath, which on the sacred
  altar
Of a long-looked-for peace—now—moves
  —to heaven.   Moritur.[5] 70
ORG. Farewell, fair spring of manhood.
  Henceforth welcome
Best expectation of a noble suff'rance.
I'll lock the bodies safe, till what must
  follow
Shall be approved.—Sweet twins, shine
  stars forever!—
In vain they build their hopes whose life
  is shame;
No monument lasts but a happy name.
                              Exit Orgilus.

ACTUS QUINTUS. SCENA PRIMA.

[A room in Bassanes' house.]

Enter Bassanes, alone.

BASS. Athens!—To Athens I have sent,
  the nursery
Of Greece for learning and the fount of
  knowledge,
For here in Sparta there's not left
  amongst us
One wise man to direct; we're all turned
  madcaps.
'Tis said Apollo is the god of herbs;
Then certainly he knows the virtue of
  'em.

---

[1] Lured.   [3] Brought to a termination.
[2] Probe.

[4] Prolong.   [5] He dies.

To Delphos I have sent too. If there
can be
A help for nature, we are sure yet.

Enter Orgilus.

ORG.   Honor
Attend thy counsels ever!
BASS.   I beseech thee
With all my heart, let me go from thee
quietly;   10
I will not aught to do with thee of all
men.
The doubles [1] of a hare—or, in a morning,
Salutes from a splay-footed witch—to
drop
Three drops of blood at th' nose just
and no more—
Croaking of ravens, or the screech of
owls—
Are not so boding mischief as thy cross-
ing
My private meditations.   Shun me,
prithee;
And, if I cannot love thee heartily,
I'll love thee as well as I can.
ORG.   Noble Bassanes,
Mistake me not.
BASS.   Phew!   Then we shall be
troubled.   20
Thou wert ordained my plague—heaven
make me thankful,
And give me patience too, heaven, I
beseech thee.
ORG. Accept a league of amity, for hence-
forth
I vow by my best genius, in a syllable,
Never to speak vexation. I will study
Service and friendship, with a zealous
sorrow
For my past incivility towards 'e.
BASS. Heyday, good words, good words! I
must believe 'em,
And be a coxcomb for my labor.
ORG.   Use not
So hard a language; your misdoubt is
causeless.   30
For instance, if you promise to put on
A constancy of patience, such a patience
As chronicle or history ne'er mentioned,
As follows not example, but shall stand
A wonder and a theme for imitation,

---

[1] Doublings. Reading of Gifford-Dyce; original
reads *doublers.*

The first, the index pointing to a second,
I will acquaint 'e with an unmatched
secret,
Whose knowledge to your griefs shall
set a period.
BASS. Thou canst not, Orgilus; 'tis in the
power   39
Of the gods only; yet, for satisfaction,
Because I note an earnest in thine
utterance,
Unforced and naturally free, be resolute [2]
The virgin bays shall not withstand the
lightning
With a more careless [3] danger than my
constancy
The full of thy relation. Could it move
Distraction in a senseless marble statue,
It should find me a rock. I do expect
now
Some truth of unheard moment.
ORG.   To your patience
You must add privacy, as strong in
silence
As mysteries locked up in Jove's own
bosom.   50
BASS. A skull hid in the earth a treble age
Shall sooner prate.
ORG.   Lastly, to such direction
As the severity of a glorious action
Deserves to lead your wisdom and your
judgment,
You ought to yield obedience.
BASS.   With assurance
Of will and thankfulness.
ORG.   With manly courage
Please then to follow me.
BASS.   Where'er, I fear not.
                              Exeunt omnes.

SCENE ii.

[A room of state in the palace.]

*Loud music. Enter Groneas and Hemophil,
    leading Euphranea; Christalla and
    Philema, leading Prophilus; Nearchus
    supporting Calantha; Crotolon and
    Amelus. Cease loud music; All make a
                                        stand.*

CAL. We miss our servant Ithocles and
Orgilus;
On whom attend they?
CROT.   My son, gracious princess,

---

[2] Certain.   [3] *I.e.*, heedlessness of.

Whispered some new device, to which
these revels
Should be but usher, wherein 1 conceive
Lord Ithocles and he himself are actors.

CAL. A fair excuse for absence. As for
Bassanes,
Delights to him are troublesome.
Armostes
Is with the king?

CROT.   He is.

CAL.   On to the dance!—
Dear cousin, hand you the bride; the
bridegroom must be
Intrusted to my courtship. Be not
jealous,   10
Euphranea; I shall scarcely prove a
temptress.—
Fall to our dance.   *Music.*

*Nearchus dance with Euphranea, Prophilus
with Calantha, Christalla with Hemophil, Philema with Groneas. Dance
the first change,[1] during which enter
Armostes.*

ARM. (*In Calantha's ear.*)   The king
your father's dead.

CAL. To the other change.

ARM.   Is 't possible?   *Dance again.*

Enter Bassanes.

BASS. [*In Calantha's ear.*]   O, madam!
Penthea, poor Penthea's starved.

CAL.   Beshrew thee!—
Lead to the next.

BASS.   Amazement dulls my senses.
         Dance again.

Enter Orgilus.

ORG. [*In Calantha's ear.*] Brave Ithocles
is murthered, murthered cruelly.

CAL. How dull this music sounds! Strike
up more sprightly;
Our footings are not active like our heart,
Which treads the nimbler measure.

ORG.   I am thunderstrook.
         Last change. Cease music.

CAL. So! Let us breathe awhile.—Hath
not this motion   20
Raised fresher color on your cheeks?

[1] Figure of the dance.

NEAR.   Sweet princess,
A perfect purity of blood enamels
The beauty of your white.

CAL.   We all look cheerfully;
And, cousin, 'tis, methinks, a rare pre-
sumption
In any who prefers our lawful pleasures
Before their own sour censure, to in-
terrupt
The custom of this ceremony bluntly.

NEAR. None dares, lady.

CAL. Yes, yes; some hollow voice delivered
to me
How that the king was dead.

ARM.   The king is dead.   30
That fatal news was mine; for in mine
arms
He breathed his last, and with his crown
bequeathed 'e
Your mother's wedding ring, which here
I tender.

CROT. Most strange!

CAL.   Peace crown his ashes! We are
queen, then.

NEAR. Long live Calantha! Sparta's sovereign queen!

OMNES. Long live the queen!

CAL.   What whispered Bassanes?

BASS. That my Penthea, miserable soul,
Was starved to death.

CAL.   She's happy; she hath finished
A long and painful progress.—A third
murmur
Pierced mine unwilling ears.

ORG.   That Ithocles   40
Was murthered—rather butchered—had
not bravery
Of an undaunted spirit, conquering terror,
Proclaimed his last act triumph over
ruin.

ARM. How? Murthered!

CAL.   By whose hand?

ORG.   By mine; this weapon
Was instrument to my revenge. The
reasons
Are just, and known; quit him of these,
and then
Never lived gentleman of greater merit,
Hope, or abiliment[2] to steer a kingdom.

CROT. Fie, Orgilus!

EUPH.   Fie, brother!

CAL.   You have done it?

[2] Ability.

BASS. How it was done let him report,
the forfeit   50
Of whose allegiance to our laws doth
covet
Rigor of justice; but that done it is,
Mine eyes have been an evidence of
credit
Too sure to be convinced.[1] Armostes,
rent [2] not
Thine arteries with hearing the bare
circumstances
Of these calamities. Thou 'st lost a
nephew,
A niece, and I a wife. Continue man
still;
Make me the pattern of digesting [3]
evils,
Who can outlive my mighty ones, not
shrinking   59
At such a pressure as would sink a soul
Into what 's most of death, the worst of
horrors.
But I have sealed a covenant with sad-
ness,
And entered into bonds without condi-
tion,
To stand these tempests calmly. Mark
me, nobles,
I do not shed a tear, not for Penthea!
Excellent misery!
CAL.   We begin our reign
With a first act of justice: thy confession,
Unhappy Orgilus, dooms thee a sen-
tence;
But yet thy father's or thy sister's
presence
Shall be excused.—Give, Crotolon, a
blessing   70
To thy lost son; Euphranea, take a
farewell;
And both be gone.
CROT. [To Orgilus.]   Confirm thee,
noble sorrow,
In worthy resolution!
EUPH.   Could my tears speak,
My griefs were slight.
ORG.   All goodness dwell amongst ye!
Enjoy my sister, Prophilus; my ven-
geance
Aimed never at thy prejudice.
CAL.   Now withdraw.
Exeunt Crotolon, Prophilus, et Euphranea.

---

[1] Confuted.   [3] Stomaching, enduring.
[2] Rend.

Bloody relater of thy stains in blood,
For that thou hast reported him, whose
fortunes
And life by thee are both at once
snatched from him,
With honorable mention, make thy
choice   80
Of what death likes thee best; there's
all our bounty.—
But, to excuse delays, let me, dear
cousin,
Entreat you and these lords see execution
Instant before 'e part.
NEAR.   Your will commands us.
ORG. One suit, just queen, my last:
vouchsafe your clemency
That by no common hand I be divided
From this my humble frailty.
CAL.   To their wisdoms
Who are to be spectators of thine end
I make the reference. Those that are
dead
Are dead; had they not now died, of
necessity   90
They must have paid the debt they owed
to nature
One time or other.—Use despatch, my
lords;
We'll suddenly prepare our coronation.
Exeunt Calantha, Philema, Christalla.
ARM. 'Tis strange these tragedies should
never touch on
Her female pity.
BASS.   She has a masculine spirit;
And wherefore should I pule, and, like
a girl,
Put finger in the eye?   Let's be all
toughness,
Without distinction betwixt sex and sex.
NEAR. Now, Orgilus, thy choice?
ORG.   To bleed to death.
ARM. The executioner?
ORG.   Myself, no surgeon;   100
I am well skilled in letting blood. Bind
fast
This arm, that so the pipes may from
their conduits
Convey a full stream; here's a skillful
instrument.   [*Shows his dagger.*]
Only I am a beggar to some charity
To speed me in this execution
By lending th' other prick to th' tother
arm,
When this is bubbling life out.

BASS.   I am for 'e;
It most concerns my art, my care, my
    credit.—
Quick, fillet both his [1] arms.
ORG.   Gramercy, friendship!
Such courtesies are real which flow
    cheerfully   110
Without an expec[ta]tion of requital.
Reach me a staff in this hand.
                [*They give him a staff.*]
                        If a proneness
Or custom in my nature from my
    cradle
Had been inclined to fierce and eager
    bloodshed,
A coward guilt, hid in a coward quaking,
Would have betrayed fame to ignoble
    flight
And vagabond pursuit of dreadful safety;
But look upon my steadiness, and scorn
    not
The sickness of my fortune, which,
    since Bassanes
Was husband to Penthea, had lain
    bedrid.   120
We trifle time in words. Thus I show
    cunning
In opening of a vein too full, too lively.
                    [*Opens the vein.*]
ARM. Desperate courage!
ORG.   Honorable infamy!
HEM. I tremble at the sight.
GRO.   Would I were loose!
BASS. It sparkles like a lusty wine new
    broached;
The vessel must be sound from which it
    issues.
Grasp hard this other stick; I'll be as
    nimble—
But, prithee, look not pale. Have at
    'e! Stretch out
Thine arm with vigor and unshook
    virtue.   [*Opens the other vein.*]
Good! O, I envy not a rival, fitted   130
To conquer in extremities. This pastime
Appears majestical; some high-tuned
    poem
Hereafter shall deliver to posterity
The writer's glory and his subject's
    triumph.
How is 't, man? Droop not yet.
ORG.   I feel no palsies.

On a pair-royal [2] do I wait in death:
My sovereign, as his liegeman; on my
    mistress,
As a devoted servant; and on Ithocles,
As if no brave, yet no unworthy enemy.
Nor did I use an engine to entrap   140
His life out of a slavish fear to combat
Youth, strength, or cunning, [3] but for
    that I durst not
Engage [4] the goodness of a cause on for-
    tune,
By which his name might have outfaced
    my vengeance.
O Tecnicus, inspired with Phœbus' fire!
I call to mind thy augury; 'twas per-
    fect:
"*Revenge proves its own executioner.*"
When feeble man is bending to his
    mother,
The dust a was first framed on, thus he
    totters.
BASS. Life's fountain is dried up.
ORG.   So falls the standards   150
Of my prerogative in being a creature!
A mist hangs o'er mine eyes; the sun's
    bright splendor
Is clouded in an everlasting shadow.
Welcome, thou ice, that sitt'st about my
    heart;
No heat can ever thaw thee.   *Dies.*
NEAR.   Speech hath left him.
BASS. A has shook hands with time; his
    funeral urn
Shall be my charge. Remove the blood-
    less body.
The coronation must require attendance;
That past, my few days can be but one
    mourning.   *Exeunt.*

[SCENE iii.

A temple.]

*An altar covered with white; two lights of
    virgin wax, during which music of
    recorders. Enter Four bearing Ithocles
    on a hearse, or in a chair, in a rich
    robe, and a crown on his head; place
    him on one side of the altar. After
    him enter Calantha in a white robe
    and crowned; Euphranea, Philema,
    Christalla, in white; Nearchus, Armostes
    Crotolon, Prophilus, Amelus, Bassanes*

---

[1] Emended by Gifford-Dyce; original reads
this.

[2] In cards, three of the same denomination.
[3] Skill.   [4] Stake.

*Hemophil, and Groneas.   Calantha
goes and kneels before the altar;   the
Rest stand off, the women kneeling behind.   Cease recorders during her devotions.   Soft music.   Calantha and the
Rest rise, doing obeisance to the altar.*

CAL. Our orisons are heard; the gods are
 merciful.—

Now tell me, you whose loyalties pays
 tribute
To us your lawful sovereign, how un-
 skillful
Your duties or obedience is to render
Subjection to the scepter of a virgin,
Who have been ever fortunate in princes
Of masculine and stirring composi-
 tion.
A woman has enough to govern wisely
Her own demeanors, passions, and di-
 visions.[1]
A nation warlike and inured to prac-
 tice   10
Of policy and labor cannot brook
A feminate authority; we therefore
Command your counsel how you may
 advise us
In choosing of a husband whose abili-
 ties
Can better guide this kingdom.
NEAR.   Royal lady,
 Your law is in your will.
ARM.   We have seen tokens
Of constancy too lately to mistrust it.
CROT. Yet, if your highness settle on a
 choice
By your own judgment both allowed and
 liked of,
Sparta may grow in power, and pro-
 ceed   20
To an increasing height.
CAL.   Hold you the same
 mind?
BASS. Alas, great mistress, reason is so
 clouded
With the thick darkness of my infinite
 woes
That I forecast nor dangers, hopes, or
 safety.
Give me some corner of the world to wear
 out
The remnant of the minutes I must
 number,

[1] Uncertainties.

Where I may hear no sounds but sad
 complaints
Of virgins who have lost contracted
 partners;
Of husbands howling that their wives
 were ravished
By some untimely fate; of friends
 divided   30
By churlish opposition; or of fathers
Weeping upon their children's slaugh-
 tered carcasses;
Or daughters groaning o'er their fathers'
 hearses;
And I can dwell there, and with these
 keep consort [2]
As musical as theirs.   What can you
 look for
From an old, foolish, peevish, doting man
But craziness of age?
CAL. Cousin of Argos!
NEAR.   Madam?
CAL.   Were I presently
To choose you for my lord, I'll open
 freely
What articles I would propose to treat
 on   40
Before our marriage.
NEAR.   Name them, virtuous lady.
CAL. I would presume you would retain
 the royalty
Of Sparta in her own bounds; then in
 Argos
Armostes might be viceroy; in Messene
Might Crotolon bear sway; and Bas-
 sanes—
BASS. I, queen?   Alas, what I?
CAL.   Be Sparta's mar-
 shal.
The multitudes of high employments
 could not
But set a peace to private griefs.   These
 gentlemen,
Groneas and Hemophil, with worthy
 pensions,
Should wait upon your person in your
 chamber.   50
I would bestow Christalla on Amelus;
She'll prove a constant wife.   And
 Philema
Should into Vesta's temple.
BASS.   This is a testament!
It sounds not like conditions on a
 marriage.

[2] Harmony.

NEAR. All this should be performed.

CAL.   Lastly, for Prophilus,
He should be, cousin, solemnly invested
In all those honors, titles, and prefer-
   ments
Which his dear friend and my neglected
   husband
Too short a time enjoyed.

PRO.   I am unworthy
To live in your remembrance.

EUPH.   Excellent lady! 60

NEAR. Madam, what means that word,
   "neglected husband"?

CAL. Forgive me.—Now I turn to thee,
   thou shadow
Of my contracted lord! Bear witness
   all,
I put my mother's [1] wedding ring upon
His finger; 'twas my father's last be-
   quest.

[*Places a ring on the finger of Ithocles.*]
Thus I new-marry him whose wife I
   am;
Death shall not separate us. O my
   lords,
I but deceived your eyes with antic
   gesture,
When one news straight came huddling
   on another
Of death, and death, and death! Still
   I danced forward;   70
But it strook home, and here, and in an
   instant.
Be [2] such mere women, who with shrieks
   and outcries
Can vow a present end to all their sor-
   rows,
Yet live to vow new pleasures, and out-
   live them.
They are the silent griefs which cut the
   heartstrings;
Let me die smiling.

NEAR.   'Tis a truth too ominous.

CAL. One kiss on these cold lips, my last!—
[*Kisses Ithocles.*] Crack, crack!—
Argos now's Sparta's king.—Command
   the voices
Which wait at th' altar now to sing the
   song
I fitted for my end.

NEAR.   Sirs, the song! 80

---

[1] Original reads *mother*, perhaps a survival of
an old genitive.
[2] *I.e.*, there be.

A SONG

ALL. Glories, pleasures, pomps, delights,
     and ease
     Can but please
[Th']³ outward senses when the mind
Is [4] untroubled or by peace refined.

1 [VOICE.] Crowns may flourish and decay;
     Beauties shine, but fade away.

2 [VOICE.] Youth may revel, yet it must
     Lie down in a bed of dust.

3 [VOICE.] Earthly honors flow and waste;
     Time alone doth change and
     last.   90

ALL. Sorrows mingled with contents pre-
     pare
     Rest for care;
Love only reigns in death, though art
Can find no comfort for a broken
     heart.

               [*Calantha dies.*]

ARM. Look to the queen!

BASS.   Her heart is broke, indeed.
O, royal maid, would thou hadst missed
   this part;
Yet 'twas a brave one. I must weep
   to see
Her smile in death.

ARM.   Wise Tecnicus! Thus said he:
"*When youth is ripe, and age from time
   doth part,
The lifeless trunk shall wed the broken
   heart.*"   100
'Tis here fulfilled.

NEAR.   I am your king.

OMNES.   Long live
Nearchus, King of Sparta!

NEAR.   Her last will
Shall never be digressed from; wait in
   order
Upon these faithful lovers, as becomes
   us.—
The counsels of the gods are never known
Till men can call th' effects of them
   their own.   [*Exeunt.*]

FINIS.

THE EPILOGUE

WHERE noble judgments and clear eyes
   are fixed
To grace endeavor, there sits Truth,
   not mixed

---

[3] A space here indicates that something has
dropped out.
[4] Original reads *Is not*.

With ignorance; those censures [1] may command
Belief which talk not till they understand.
Let some say, "This was flat;" some, "Here the scene
Fell from its height;" another, that the mean
Was "ill observed" in such a growing passion
As it transcended either state or fashion.

[1] Opinions.

Some few may cry, "'Twas pretty well," or so,
"But—" and there shrug in silence; yet we know   10
Our writer's aim was in the whole addressed
Well to deserve of *all*, but please the *best*,
Which granted, by th' allowance of this strain,
The *Broken Heart* may be pieced up again.

FINIS.

THE CHRONICLE HISTORY OF
PERKIN WARBECK [1]

[BY

JOHN FORD]

THE SCENE: *The continent of Great Britain.*

[THE TIME: *1499 and the years preceding.*]

THE PERSONS PRESENTED

HENRY THE SEVENTH.
[LORD] DAWBNEY.[2]
SIR WILLIAM STANLEY.
[EARL OF] OXFORD.
[EARL OF] SURREY.
[FOX,] *Bishop of Durham.*
URSWICK, *chaplain to King Henry.*
SIR ROBERT CLIFFORD.
LAMBERT SIMNEL.
HIALAS,[3] *a Spanish agent.*
CONSTABLE, OFFICERS, [POST,] [4] SERVING-
MEN *and* SOLDIERS.

JAMES THE FOURTH, *King of Scotland.*
EARL OF HUNTLEY.

EARL OF CRAWFORD.
LORD DALIELL.
MARCHMOUNT, *a herald.*

PERKIN WARBECK.
[STEPHEN] FRION, *his secretary.*
[JOHN A WATER,] *Mayor of Cork.*
HERON, *a mercer.*
SKETON, *a tailor.*
ASTLEY, *a scrivener.*

WOMEN

LADY KATHERINE GORDON, *wife to Perkin.*
COUNTESS OF CRAWFORD.
JANE DOUGLAS, *Lady Kath[erine's] maid* ·

PROLOGUE

Studies have of this nature been of late
So out of fashion, so unfollowed, that
It is become more justice [6] to revive
The antic [7] follies of the times than strive
To countenance wise industry. No want
Of art doth render wit or [8] lame or scant
Or slothful in the purchase of fresh bays,
But want of truth in them who give the
  praise
To their self-love, presuming to outdo
The writer, or—for need—the actors too. 10
But such this author's silence best befits,
Who bids them be in love with their own
  wits.
From him to clearer judgments we can
  say
He shows a history couched in a play—
A history of noble mention, known
Famous and true; most noble, cause [9] our
  own;
Not forged from Italy, from France, from
  Spain,
But chronicled at home; as rich in strain
Of brave attempts as ever fertile rage [10]
In action could beget to grace the stage. 20

[1] The title continues· "A Strange Truth. Acted (Sometimes) by the Queen's Majesty's Servants at the Phœnix in Drury Lane. *Fide Honor.*" The Latin motto is an anagram of Ford's name used elsewhere instead of his signature.
[2] *I.e.*, Giles, Baron Daubeney.
[3] *I.e.*, Don Pedro Ayala.   [4] Messenger.
[5] Here follow the dedicatory epistle to William Cavendish, Earl of Newcastle, signed by John Ford, and five commendatory poems.
[6] Judiciousness, wisdom.
[7] Antique, ancient.   [8] Either.
[9] Because.   [10] Poetic inspiration.

1531

We cannot limit scenes, for the whole land
Itself appeared too narrow to withstand
Competitors for kingdoms; nor is here
Unnecessary mirth forced, to endear
A multitude. On these two rests the fate
Of worthy expectation—truth and state.

ACTUS PRIMUS. SCENA PRIMA.

[*The presence chamber at Westminster.*]

Enter King Henry, Durham, Oxford, Sur-
rey, Sir William Stanley, Lord Cham-
berlain, Lord Dawbney; the King
supported to his throne by Stanley and
Durham. A Guard.

KING. Still[1] to be haunted, still to be
    pursued,
Still to be frighted with false appari-
    tions
Of pageant majesty and new-coined
    greatness,
As if we were a mockery king in state,
Only ordained to lavish sweat and blood
In scorn and laughter to the ghosts of
    York,[2]
Is all below our merits; yet, my lords,
My friends and counselors, yet we sit
    fast
In our own royal birthright. The rent
    face
And bleeding wounds of England's
    slaughtered people   10
Have been by us as by the best physi-
    cian
At last both throughly cured and set in
    safety;
And yet for all this glorious work of
    peace
Ourself is scarce secure.
DUR.   The rage of malice
Conjures fresh spirits with the spells of
    York.
For ninety years ten English kings and
    princes,
Threescore great dukes and earls, a
    thousand lords
And valiant knights, two hundred fifty
    thousand
Of English subjects have in civil wars
Been sacrificed to an uncivil thirst   20

Of discord and ambition.   This hot
    vengeance
Of the just powers above to utter ruin
And desolation had reigned on, but that
Mercy did gently sheathe the sword
    of justice
In lending to this blood-shrunk common-
    wealth
A new soul, new birth, in your sacred
    person.
DAW. Edward the Fourth, after a doubt-
    ful fortune,
Yielded to nature, leaving to his sons,
Edward and Richard, the inheritance
Of a most bloody purchase.[3]   These
    young princes,   30
Richard the tyrant,[4] their unnatural
    uncle,
Forced to a violent grave, so just is
    heaven.
Him hath your majesty by your own
    arm,
Divinely strengthened, pulled from his
    boar's sty[5]
And struck the black usurper to a car-
    cass.
Nor doth the house of York decay in
    honors,
Though Lancaster doth repossess his
    right,
For Edward's daughter is King Henry's
    queen,
A blessed union, and a lasting blessing
For this poor panting island, if some
    shreds,   40
Some useless remnant of the house of
    York,
Grudge not at this content.
OX.   Margaret of Burgundy
Blows fresh coals of division.
SUR.   Painted fires,
Without or heat to[6] scorch or light to
    cherish.
DAW. York's headless trunk, her father;
    Edward's fate,
Her brother king; the smothering of her
    nephews
By tyrant Gloucester,[7] brother to her
    nature;

---

[1] Always.
[2] *I.e.*, Simnel and Warbeck, pretenders to the
throne, who were supported by the Yorkist
faction.

[3] Acquisition.   [4] *I.e.*, Richard III.
[5] A reference to the arms of Richard III.
[6] Emended by Gifford-Dyce. Original reads *ta*
heat or.
[7] *I.e.*, Richard III.

Nor Gloucester's own confusion (all
    decrees
Sacred in heaven) can move this woman-
    monster,
But that she still from the unbottomed
    mine   50
Of devilish policies doth vent the ore
Of troubles and sedition.
Ox.   In her age—
    Great sir, observe the wonder—she
      grows fruitful,
Who in her strength of youth was always
    barren,
Nor are her births as other mothers'
    are,
At nine or ten months' end—she has been
    with child
Eight or seven years at least; whose
    twins [1] being born—
A prodigy in nature—even the youngest
Is fifteen years of age at his first entrance
As soon as known i' th' world, tall strip-
    lings, strong   60
And able to give battle unto kings,
Idols of Yorkish malice.
Daw.[2]   And but idols!
A steely hammer crushes 'em to pieces.
King. Lambert, the eldest, lords, is in
    our service,
Preferred by an officious care of duty
From the scullery to a falc'ner—strange
    example!—
Which shows the difference between
    noble natures
And the baseborn. But for the upstart
    duke,
The new revived York, Edward's sec-
    ond son,
Murdered long since i' th' Tower, he
    lives again   70
And vows to be your king.
Stan.   The throne is filled, sir.
King. True, Stanley; and the lawful heir
    sits on it.
A guard of angels and the holy prayers
Of loyal subjects are a sure defense
Against all force and counsel of intru-
    sion.
But now, my lords, put case [3] some of
    our nobles,

Our great ones, should give counte-
    nance and courage
To trim Duke Perkin. You will all con-
    fess
Our bounties have unthriftily been
    scattered
Amongst unthankful men.
Daw.   Unthankful beasts, 80
Dogs, villains, traitors!
King.   Dawbney, let the guilty
Keep silence; I accuse none, though I
    know
Foreign attempts against a state and
    kingdom
Are seldom without some great friends
    at home.
Stan. Sir, if no other abler reasons else
Of duty or allegiance could divert
A headstrong resolution, yet the dangers
So lately passed by men of blood and
    fortunes
In Lambert Simnel's party must com-
    mand
More than a fear, a terror, to conspir-
    acy.   90
The highborn Lincoln, son to De la
    Pole,
The Earl of Kildare, [the][4] Lord Ger-
    aldine,
Francis, Lord Lovell, and the German
    baron
Bold Martin Swart, with Broughton
    and the rest—
Most spectacles of ruin, some of mercy—
Are presidents [5] sufficient to forewarn
The present times, or any that live in
    them,
What folly, nay, what madness, 'twere
    to lift
A finger up in all defense but yours,
Which can be but impostorous in a
    title.   100
King. Stanley, we know thou lov'st us,
    and thy heart
Is figured on thy tongue; nor think we
    less
Of any's here.—How closely we have
    hunted
This cub, since he unlodged, from hole
    to hole,
Your knowledge is our chronicle. First
    Ireland,
The common stage of novelty, presented

---

[1] These youths were not actually her sons, but
were impostors put forward by her.
[2] Gifford-Dyce's emendation for *Ox.*
[3] Suppose.
[4] Supplied by Gifford-Dyce.   [5] Precedents.

This gewgaw to oppose us; there the
  Geraldines
And Butlers once again stood in sup-
  port
Of this colossic statue.   Charles of
  France   109
Thence called him into his protection,
Dissembled him the lawful heir of Eng-
  land;
Yet this was all but French dissimula-
  tion,
Aiming at peace with us, which being
  granted
On honorable terms on our part, sud-
  denly
This smoke of straw was packed from
  France again
T' infect some grosser air. And now we
  learn—
Mauger the malice of the bastard Nevill,
Sir Taylor, and a hundred English
  rebels—
They're all retired to Flanders, to the
  dam
That nursed this eager whelp, Margaret
  of Burgundy.   120
But we will hunt him there too; we will
  hunt him,
Hunt him to death, even in the beldam's
  closet,
Though the archduke were his buckler.
SUR. She has styled him "the fair white
  rose of England."
DAW. Jolly gentleman, more fit to be a
  swabber
To the Flemish after a drunken surfeit.

Enter Urswick.

UR. Gracious sovereign, please you pe-
  ruse this paper.   [*The King reads.*]
DUR. The king's countenance gathers a
  sprightly blood.
DAW. Good news, believe it.
KING.   Urswick, thine ear.
  Th'ast lodged [1] him?
UR.   Strongly safe, sir.   130
KING. Enough. Is Barley come too?
UR.   No, my lord.
KING. No matter—phew, he's but a run-
  ning weed,
  At pleasure to be plucked up by the
    roots!

[1] Thou hast entrapped.

But more of this anon.—I have be-
  thought me.
My lords, for reasons which you shall
  partake,
It is our pleasure to remove our court
From Westminster to th' Tower. We
  will lodge
This very night there; give, Lord Cham-
  berlain,
A present order for it.
STAN. [*Aside.*]   The Tower!—I shall, sir.
KING. Come, my true, best, fast friends.
  These clouds will vanish;   140
The sun will shine at full; the heavens
  are clearing.   *Exeunt. Flourish.*

[SCENA SECUNDA.

A room in Huntley's house at Edinburgh.]

Enter Huntley and Daliell.

HUNT. You trifle time, sir.
DAL.   O, my noble lord,
  You conster [2] my griefs to so hard a sense
  That where the text is argument [3] of pity,
  Matter of earnest love, your gloss cor-
    rupts it
  With too much ill-placed mirth.
HUNT.   Much mirth, Lord Daliell?
  Not so, I vow. Observe me, sprightly
    gallant.
  I know thou art a noble lad, a handsome,
  Descended from an honorable ancestry,
  Forward and active, dost resolve to
    wrestle
  And ruffle in the world by noble ac-
    tions   10
  For a brave mention to posterity.
  I scorn not thy affection to my daughter,
  Not I, by good St. Andrew; but this bug-
    bear,
  This whoresome [4] tale of honor—honor,
    Daliell!—
  So hourly chats and tattles in mine ear
  The piece of royalty that is stitched up
  In my Kate's blood [5] that 'tis as danger-
    ous
  For thee, young lord, to perch so near an
    eaglet
  As foolish for my gravity to admit it.
  I have spoke all at once.

[2] Construe, interpret.
[3] Evidence.   [4] Whoreson, rascally.
[5] Huntley had married Annabella, daughter
of James I of Scotland.

DAL.   Sir, with this truth 20
  You mix such wormwood that you leave
    no hope
For my disordered palate e'er to relish
A wholesome taste again. Alas, I know,
  sir,
What an unequal distance lies between
Great Huntley's daughter's birth and
  Daliell's fortunes.
She's the king's kinswoman, placed near
  the crown,
A princess of the blood, and I a subject.
HUNT. Right; but a noble subject—put in
  that too.
DAL. I could add more, and in the rightest
  line   29
Derive my pedigree from Adam Mure,
A Scottish knight, whose daughter was
  the mother
To him who first begot the race of
  Jameses
That sway the scepter to this very day.
But kindreds are not ours when once the
  date
Of many years have swallowed up the
  memory
Of their originals; so pasture fields
Neighboring too near the ocean are
  sooped [1] up
And known no more; for, stood I in my
  first
And native [2] greatness, if my princely
  mistress
Voutsafed [3] me not her servant,[4] 'twere
  as good   40
I were reduced to clownery,[5] to nothing,
As to a throne of wonder.
HUNT. [*Aside.*]   Now, by Saint Andrew,
A spark of mettle! [6] A [7] has a brave fire
  in him.
I would a had my daughter, so I knew 't
  not.
But must not be so, must not.—Well,
  young lord,
This will not do yet. If the girl be head-
  strong
And will not hearken to good counsel,
  steal her
And run away with her; dance galliards,[8]
  do,

And frisk about the world to learn the
  languages.
'Twill be a thriving trade; you may set up
  by 't.   50
DAL. With pardon, noble Gordon, this disdain
Suits not your daughter's virtue or my
  constancy.
HUNT. You are angry.—[*Aside.*] Would a
  would beat me; I deserve it.—
Daliell, thy hand; w' are friends. Follow
  thy courtship.
Take thine own time and speak; if thou
  prevail'st
With passion more than I can with my
  counsel,
She's thine. Nay, she is thine; 'tis a fair
  match,
Free and allowed. I'll only use my
  tongue,
Without a father's power; use thou thine.
Self do, self have. No more words; win
  and wear her.   60
DAL. You bless me; I am now too poor
  in thanks
To pay the debt I owe you.
HUNT.   Nay, th' art poor [9]
Enough.—[*Aside.*] I love his spirit in-
  finitely.—
Look ye, she comes. To her now, to her,
  to her!

Enter Katherine and Jane.

KATH. The king commands your presence,
  sir.
HUNT.   The gallant—
This—this—this lord—this servant,
  Kate, of yours—
Desires to be your master.
KATH.   I acknowledge him
A worthy friend of mine.
DAL.   Your humblest creature.
HUNT. [*Aside.*] So, so, the game's afoot!
  I'm in cold hunting;
The hare and hounds are parties.[10]
DAL.   Princely lady, 70
How most unworthy I am to employ
My services in honor of your virtues,
How hopeless my desires are to enjoy

---

[1] Supped.
[2] Inherited.
[3] Vouchsafed.
[4] Suitor.
[5] Base birth.
[6] A high-spirited young man.
[7] He.
[8] Lively dances.

[9] Here, as in many other passages throughout the play, lines which have obviously been wrongly divided by the printer have been silently regularized.
[10] Confederates.

Your fair opinion, and much more your
    love,
Are only matter of despair, unless
Your goodness give large warrant to my
    boldness,
My feeble-winged ambition.
Hunt. [*Aside.*]   This is scurvy.[1]
Kath. My lord, I interrupt you not.
Hunt. [*Aside.*]   Indeed!
    Now, on my life, she'll court him.—Nay,
    nay, on, sir.
Dal. Oft have I tuned the lesson of my
    sorrows   80
To sweeten discord and enrich your pity;
But all in vain. Here had my comforts
    sunk,
And never risen again to tell a story
Of the despairing lover, had not now,
Even now, the earl your father—
Hunt. [*Aside.*]   A means me, sure.
Dal. After some fit disputes of your con-
    dition,
Your highness and my lowness, given a
    license
Which did not more embolden than en-
    courage
My faulting [2] tongue.
Hunt.   How, how? How's that?
    Embolden?
Encourage? I encourage ye? D'e [3] hear,
    sir?   90
A subtle trick, a quaint one! Will you
    hear, man?
What did I say to you? Come, come, to
    th' point.
Kate. It shall not need, my lord.
Hunt.   Then hear me, Kate.—
    Keep you on that hand of her, I on
    this.—
Thou stand'st between a father and a
    suitor,
Both striving for an interest in thy heart.
He courts thee for affection, I for duty;
He as a servant pleads; but, by the
    privilege
Of nature though I might command, my
    care   99
Shall only counsel what it shall not force.
Thou canst but make one choice; the
    ties of marriage
Are tenures not at will, but during life.
Consider whose thou art, and who—a
    princess,

A princess of the royal blood of Scotland,
In the full spring of youth and fresh in
    beauty.
The king that sits upon the throne is
    young,
And yet unmarried, forward in attempts
On any least occasion to endanger
His person; wherefore, Kate, as I am
    confident
Thou dar'st not wrong thy birth and
    education   110
By yielding to a common servile rage
Of female wantonness, so I am confident
Thou wilt proportion all thy thoughts to
    side [4]
Thy equals, if not equal thy superiors.
My Lord of Daliell, young in years, is
    old
In honors, but nor eminent in titles
Or in estate that may support or add to
The expectation of thy fortunes. Settle
Thy will and reason by a strength of
    judgment,
For, in a word, I give thee freedom; take
    it.   120
If equal fates have not ordained to pitch
Thy hopes above my height, let not thy
    passion
Lead thee to shrink mine honor in ob-
    livion.
Thou art thine own; I have done.
Dal.   O, y' are all oracle,
The living stock and root of truth and
    wisdom!
Kath. My worthiest lord and father, the
    indulgence
Of your sweet composition [5] thus com-
    mands
The lowest of obedience. You have
    granted
A liberty so large that I want skill   129
To choose without direction of example,
From which I daily learn by how much
    more
You take off from the roughness of a
    father,
By so much more I am engaged to tender
The duty of a daughter. For respects
Of birth, degrees of title, and advance-
    ment,
I nor admire nor slight them; all my
    studies
Shall ever aim at this perfection only—

---

[1] Wretched.   [2] Failing.   [3] Do ye.   [4] Match.   [5] Nature.

To live and die so, that you may not
blush
In any course of mine to own me yours.
HUNT. Kate, Kate, thou grow'st upon my
heart like peace,   140
Creating every other hour a jubilee.
KATE. To you, my Lord of Daliell, I ad-
dress
Some few remaining words. The general
fame,
That speaks your merit even in vulgar
tongues,
Proclaims it clear; but in the best, a
president.[1]
HUNT. Good wench, good girl, i' faith!
KATH.   For my part, trust me,
I value mine own worth at higher rate
Cause you are pleased to prize it. If the
stream
Of your protested service—as you term
it—
Run in a constancy more than a compli-
ment,   150
It shall be my delight that worthy love
Leads you to worthy actions, and these
guide ye
Richly to wed an honorable name.[2]
So every virtuous praise in after ages
Shall be your heir, and I in your brave
mention
Be chronicled the mother of that issue,
That glorious issue.
HUNT.   O, that I were young again!
She'd make me court proud danger, and
suck spirit
From reputation.
KATH.   To the present motion [3]
Here's all that I dare answer: when a
ripeness   160
Of more experience, and some use of
time,
Resolves to treat the freedom of my
youth
Upon exchange of troths, I shall desire
No surer credit of a match with virtue
Than such as lives in you. Meantime my
hopes are
Preserved secure in having you a friend.
DAL. You are a blessed lady, and instruct
Ambition not to soar a farther flight
Than in the perfumed air of your soft
voice.—

My noble Lord of Huntley, you have
lent   170
A full extent of bounty to this parley,
And for it shall command your humblest
servant.
HUNT. Enough. We are still friends, and
will continue
A hearty love.—O, Kate, thou art mine
own!—
No more. My Lord of Crawford!

Enter Crawford.

CRAW.   From the king
I come, my Lord of Huntley, who in
council
Requires your present aid.
HUNT.   Some weighty business!
CRAW. A secretary from a Duke of York,
The second son to the late English
Edward,
Concealed I know not where these four-
teen years,   180
Craves audience from our master; and
'tis said
The duke himself is following to the
court.
HUNT. Duke upon duke! 'Tis well, 'tis
well; here's bustling
For majesty. My lord, I will along with
ye.
CRAW. My service, noble lady!
KATH.   Please ye walk, sir?
DAL. [*Aside.*] "Times have their changes;
sorrow makes men wise;
The sun itself must set as well as rise." [4]
Then, why not I?—Fair madam, I wait
on ye.   *Exeunt omnes.*

[SCENA TERTIA.

A room in the Tower of London.]

*Enter Durham, Sir Robert Clifford, and
Urswick. Lights.*

DUR. You find, Sir Robert Clifford, how
securely
King Henry, our great master, doth com-
mit
His person to your loyalty; you taste
His bounty and his mercy even in this,
That at a time of night so late, a place
So private as his closet, he is pleased

---

[1] Model, pattern.
[2] Reputation, career.   [3] Proposal.

[4] Quotation marks were often used to attention to sententious passages.

To admit you to his favor. Do not falter
In your discovery;[1] but, as you covet
A liberal grace and pardon for your
  follies,
So labor to deserve it by laying open   10
All plots, all persons that contrive against
  it.

URS. Remember not the witchcraft or the
  magic,
The charms and incantations, which the
  sorceress
Of Burgundy hath cast upon your reason.
Sir Robert, be your own friend now; discharge
Your conscience freely. All of such as
  love you
Stand sureties for your honesty and
  truth.
Take heed you do not dally with the
  king;
He is wise as he is gentle.

CLIF.   I am miserable,
If Henry be not merciful.

URS.   The king comes.   20

Enter King Henry.

KING. Clifford!
CLIF. [*Kneeling.*]   Let my weak knees
  rot on the earth,
If I appear as leap'rous[2] in my treach-
  eries
Before your royal eyes, as to mine own
I seem a monster by my breach of truth.

KING. Clifford, stand up; for instance[3] of
  thy safety,
I offer thee my hand.

CLIF.   A sovereign balm
For my bruised soul, I kiss it with a
  greediness.   [*Rises.*]
Sir, you are a just master, but I—

KING.   Tell me,
Is every circumstance thou hast set down
With thine own hand within this paper
  true?   30
Is it a sure intelligence of all
The progress of our enemies' intents
Without corruption?

CLIF.   True, as I wish heaven,
Or my infected honor white again.

KING. We know all, Clifford, fully, since
  this meteor,

This airy apparition, first discradled[4]
From Tournay into Portugal, and thence
Advanced his fiery blaze for adoration
To th' superstitious Irish; since the
  beard   39
Of this wild comet, conjured into France,
Sparkled in antic flames in Charles his
  court,
But shrunk again from thence, and, hid
  in darkness,
Stole out of[5] Flanders, flourishing the
  rags
Of painted power on the shore of Kent.
Whence he was beaten back with shame
  and scorn,
Contempt, and slaughter of some naked
  outlaws.
But tell me what new course now shapes
  Duke Perkin?

CLIF. For Ireland, mighty Henry; so in-
  structed
By Stephen Frion, sometimes[6] secretary
In the French tongue unto your sacred
  excellence,   50
But Perkin's tutor now.

KING.   A subtle villain,
That Frion, Frion. You, my Lord of Dur-
  ham,
Knew well the man.

DUR.   French both in heart and actions.

KING. Some Irish heads work in this mine
  of treason;
Speak[7] 'em.

CLIF.   Not any of the best; your fortune
Hath dulled their spleens. Never had
  counterfeit
Such a confuséd rabble of lost bank-
  routs[8]
For counselors: first Heron, a broken
  mercer;
Then John a Water, sometimes Major[9] of
  Cork;
Sketon, a tailor; and a scrivener   60
Called Astley. And whate'er these list[10]
  to treat of,
Perkin must hearken to; but Frion, cun-
  ning
Above these dull capacities, still prompts
  him

---

[4] Left its cradle, emerged.
[5] Suggested by Struble. Original reads *into.*
[6] Sometime, formerly.
[7] Reveal.   [9] Mayor.
[8] Bankrupts.   [10] Please.

[1] Disclosure.   [2] Leprous.   [3] Proof.

To fly to Scotland to young James the
    Fourth,
And sue for aid to him. This is the latest
Of all their resolutions.
KING.   Still more Frion!
    Pestilent adder, he will hiss out poison
As dang'rous as infectious. We must
    match 'em.
Clifford, thou hast spoke home; we give
    thee life.
But, Clifford, there are people of our
    own   70
Remain behind untold; who are they,
    Clifford?
Name those, and we are friends, and will
    to rest.
'Tis thy last task.
CLIF.   O, sir, here I must break
    A most unlawful oath to keep a just one.
KING. Well, well, be brief, be brief.
CLIF.   The first in rank
    Shall be John Ratcliffe, Lord Fitzwater,
    then
Sir Simon Mountford and Sir Thomas
    Thwaites,
With William Dawbney, Cressoner, Ast-
    wood,
Worsley the Dean of Paul's, two other
    friars,   79
And Robert Ratcliffe.
KING.   Churchmen are turned devils.
    These are the principal?
CLIFF.   One more remains
    Unnamed, whom I could willingly forget.
KING. Ha, Clifford! One more?
CLIF.   Great sir, do not hear him;
    For, when Sir William Stanley, your lord
    chamberlain,
Shall come into the list, as he is chief,
I shall lose credit with ye; yet this lord
Last named is first against you.
KING.   Urswick, the light!
    View well my face, sirs; is there blood
    left in it?
DUR. You alter strangely, sir.
KING.   Alter, Lord Bishop?
    Why, Clifford stabbed me, or I dreamed
    a stabbed me.—   90
    Sirrah, it is a custom with the guilty
To think they set their own stains off by
    laying
Aspersions on some nobler than them-
    selves.
Lies wait on treasons, as I find it here.

Thy life again is forfeit; I recall
My word of mercy, for I know thou
    dar'st
Repeat the name no more.
CLIF.   I dare, and once more,
    Upon my knowledge, name Sir William
    Stanley
Both in his counsel and his purse the
    chief   99
Assistant to the feign[é]d Duke of York.
DUR. Most strange!
URS.   Most wicked!
KING.   Yet again, once more.
CLIF. Sir William Stanley is your secret
    enemy,
And, if time fit, will openly profess it.
KING. Sir William Stanley! Who? Sir
    William Stanley?
My chamberlain, my counselor, the love,
The pleasure of my court, my bosom
    friend,
The charge and the controlment of my
    person,
The keys and secrets of my treasury,
The all of all I am! I am unhappy.   109
Misery of confidence—let me turn traitor
To mine own person, yield my scepter up
To Edward's sister and her bastard duke!
DUR. You lose your constant temper.
KING.   Sir William Stanley!
    O, do not blame me; he, 'twas only he,
Who, having rescued me in Bosworth
    Field
From Richard's bloody sword, snatched
    from his head
The kingly crown, and placed it first on
    mine.
He never failed me. What have I de-
    served
To lose this good man's heart, or he his
    own?
URS. The night doth waste. This passion
    ill becomes ye;   120
Provide against your danger.
KING.   Let it be so.
    Urswick, command straight Stanley to
    his chamber;
'Tis well we are i' th' Tower; set a guard
    on him.
Clifford, to bed; you must lodge here to-
    night.
We'll talk with you tomorrow. My sad
    soul
Divines strange troubles.

DAW. [*Within.*]   Ho! The king, the king!
I must have entrance.
KING.   Dawbney's voice! Admit him.
What new combustions huddle next, to
   keep
Our eyes from rest?—The news?

Enter Dawbney.

DAW.   Ten thousand Cornish,
   Grudging to pay your subsidies, have
   gathered   130
A head.[1] Led by a blacksmith and a
   lawyer,
They make for London, and to them is
   joined
Lord Audley. As they march, their num-
   ber daily
Increases; they are—
KING.   Rascals!—Talk no more;
   Such are not worthy of my thoughts to-
   night.
And, if I cannot sleep, I'll wake.—To bed.
When counsels fail, and there's in man no
   trust,
Even then an arm from heaven fights for
   the just.   *Exeunt.*

FINIS ACTUS PRIMI.

ACTUS SECUNDUS. SCENA PRIMA.

[*The presence chamber in the palace at
   Edinburgh.*]

*Enter above, Countess of Crawford, Kath-
   erine, Jane, with other Ladies.*

COUN. Come, ladies, here's a solemn prep-
   aration
For entertainment of this English prince;
The king intends grace more than
   ordinary.
'Twere pity now if a should prove a
   counterfeit.
KATH. Bless the young man, our nation
   would be laughed at
For honest[2] souls through Christendom.
   My father
Hath a weak stomach to the business,
   madam,
But that the king must not be crossed.
COUN.   A brings
A goodly troop, they say, of gallants with
   him,

But very modest people, for they strive
   not   10
To fame[3] their names too much; their
   godfathers
May be beholding[4] to them, but their
   fathers
Scarce owe them thanks.   They are
   disguiséd princes,
Brought up, it seems, to honest trades.
   No matter,
They will break forth in season.
JANE.   Or break out;[5]
For most of 'em are broken, by report.—
   The king!
KATH. Let us observe 'em and be silent.
   Flourish.

*Enter [below] King James, Huntley, Craw-
   ford, and Daliell [, with other Noblemen].*

K. JA. The right of kings, my lords, ex-
   tends not only
To the safe conservation of their own,
But also to the aid of such allies   20
As change of time and state hath often-
   times
Hurled down from careful crowns to
   undergo
An exercise of sufferance in both for-
   tunes.
So English Richard, surnamed Cœur-de-
   Lion,
So Robert Bruce, our royal ancestor,
Forced by the trial of the wrongs they
   felt,
Both sought and found supplies from
   foreign kings
To repossess their own.   Then grudge
   not,[6] lords,
A much distresséd prince. King Charles
   of France
And Maximilian of Bohemia both   30
Have ratified his credit by their letters.
Shall we then be distrustful? No, com-
   passion
Is one rich jewel that shines in our
   crown,
And we will have it shine there.
HUNT.   Do your will, sir.
K. JA. The young duke is at hand. Daliell,
   from us
First greet him, and conduct him on;
   then Crawford

---

[1] Armed force.   [2] Trusting, simple.
[3] Boast.   [5] *I.e.*, rebel.
[4] Beholden.   [6] Do not begrudge aid to.

Shall meet him next; and Huntley, last
  of all,
Present him to our arms. Sound sprightly
  music,
Whilst majesty encounters majesty.
                              Hautboys.

*Daliell goes out, brings in Perkin at the
  door, where Crawford entertains him,
  and from Crawford, Huntley salutes him
  and presents him to the King. They
  embrace; Perkin in state retires some
  few paces back, during which ceremony
  the noblemen slightly salute Frion,
  Heron, a mercer, Sketon, a tailor,
  Astley, a scrivener, with John a Water,*[1]
  *all Perkin's followers. Salutations
                              ended, cease music.*

WAR. Most high, most mighty king! That
  now there stands   40
Before your eyes, in presence of your
  peers,
A subject of the rarest kind of pity
That hath in any age touched noble
  hearts,
The vulgar [2] story of a prince's ruin
Hath made it too apparent. Europe
  knows,
And all the western world, what per-
  secution
Hath raged in malice against us, sole
  heir
To the great throne of old Plantagenets.
How from our nursery we have been
  hurried
Unto the sanctuary, from the sanctu-
  ary   50
Forced to the prison, from the prison
  haled
By cruel hands to the tormentor's fury
Is registered already in the volume
Of all men's tongues, whose true rela-
  tion draws
Compassion, melted into weeping eyes
And bleeding souls. But our misfortunes
  since
Have ranged a larger progress through
  strange lands,
Protected in our innocence by heaven.
Edward the Fift, our brother, in his
  tragedy
Quenched their hot thirst of blood,
  whose hire to murther   60

Paid them their wages of despair and
  horror.
The softness of my childhood smiled
  upon
The roughness of their task, and robbed
  them farther
Of hearts to dare, or hands to execute.
Great king, they spared my life, the
  butchers spared it,
Returned the tyrant, my unnatural
  uncle,
A truth [3] of my despatch. I was con-
  veyed
With secrecy and speed to Tournay,
  fostered
By obscure means, taught to unlearn
  myself.   69
But, as I grew in years, I grew in sense
Of fear and of disdain—fear of the
  tyrant
Whose power swayed the throne then,
  when disdain
Of living so unknown, in such a servile
And abject lowness, prompted me to
  thoughts
Of recollecting who I was. I shook off
My bondage, and made haste to let my
  aunt
Of Burgundy acknowledge me her kins-
  man,
Heir to the crown of England, snatched
  by Henry
From Richard's head—a thing scarce
  known i' th' world.
K. JA. My lord, it stands not with your
  counsel now   80
To fly upon invectives. If you can
Make this apparent what you have
  discoursed
In every circumstance, we will not
  study
An answer, but are ready in your cause.
WAR. You are a wise and just king, by the
  powers
Above reserved beyond all other aids
To plant me in mine own inheritance,
To marry these two kingdoms in a love
Never to be divorced while time is
  time.
As for the manner, first of my escape, 90
Of my conveyance next, of my life since,
The means and persons who were instru-
  ments,

---

[1] Original reads *Watring.*   [2] Common.   [3] Pledge.

Great sir, 'tis fit I overpass in silence,
Reserving the relation to the secrecy
Of your own princely ear, since it con-
cerns
Some great ones living yet, and others
dead,
Whose issue might be questioned. For
your bounty,
Royal magnificence to him that seeks it,
We vow hereafter to demean ourself
As if we were your own and natural
brother, 100
Omitting no occasion in our person
To express a gratitude beyond example.
K. JA. He must be more than subject
who can utter
The language of a king, and such is
thine.
Take this for answer: be whate'er thou
art,
Thou never shalt repent that thou hast
put
Thy cause and person into my protection.
Cousin of York, thus once more we em-
brace thee.
Welcome to James of Scotland! For thy
safety,
Know such as love thee not shall never
wrong thee. 110
Come, we will taste awhile our court de-
lights,
Dream hence afflictions past, and then
proceed
To high attempts of honor. On, lead on!
Both thou and thine are ours, and we will
guard ye.
Lead on! *Exeunt. Manent* [1] *Ladies above.*
COUN. I have not seen a gentleman
Of a more brave aspect or goodlier car-
riage;
His fortunes move not him.—Madam,
y' are passionate.[2]
KATH. Beshrew me,[3] but his words have
touched me home,
As if his cause concerned me. I should
pity him 119
If a should prove another than he seems.

Enter Crawford.

CRAW. Ladies, the king commands your
presence instantly
For entertainment of the duke.

[1] Remain.
[2] Compassionate, moved.
[3] A mild oath.

KATH. The duke
Must then be entertained, the king
obeyed;
It is our duty.
COUN. We will all wait on him.
Exeunt.

[SCENA SECUNDA.

A room in the Tower of London.]

*Flourish. Enter King Henry [and his
Train]; Oxford, Durham, Surrey.*

KING. Have ye condemned my chamber-
lain?
DUR. His treasons
Condemned him, sir, which were as
clear and manifest
As foul and dangerous. Besides, the guilt
Of his conspiracy pressed him so nearly [4]
That it drew from him free confession
Without an importunity.
KING. O, lord bishop,
This argued shame and sorrow for his
folly,
And must not stand in evidence against
Our mercy and the softness of our na-
ture.
The rigor and extremity of law 10
Is sometimes too-too bitter, but we
carry
A chancery [5] of pity in our bosom.
I hope we may reprieve him from the sen-
tence
Of death; I hope we may.
DUR. You may, you may,
And so persuade your subjects that the
title
Of York is better, nay, more just and
lawful,
Than yours of Lancaster! So Stanley
holds—
Which if it be not treason in the highest,
Then we are traitors all, perjured and
false,
Who have took oath to Henry and the
justice 20
Of Henry's title: Oxford, Surrey, Dawb-
ney,
With all your other peers of state and
church,

[4] Closely.
[5] A chancellorship, whose holder could lighten
sentences.

Forsworn, and Stanley true alone to
   heaven
And England's lawful heir!
Ox.   By Vere's old honors,
   I'll cut his throat dares speak it.
Sur.   'Tis a quarrel
   To engage a soul in.
King.   What a coil [1] is here
   To keep my gratitude sincere and per-
      fect!
   Stanley was once my friend, and came
      in time
   To save my life; yet, to say truth, my
      lords,
   The man stayed long enough t' endan-
      ger it.   30
   But I could see no more into his heart
   Than what his outward actions did
      present,
   And for 'em have rewarded 'em so fully
   As that there wanted nothing in our
      gift
   To gratify his merit, as I thought,
   Unless I should divide my crown with
      him,
   And give him half—though now I well
      perceive
   'Twould scarce have served his turn
      without the whole.
   But I am charitable, lords; let justice
   Proceed in execution, whiles I mourn 40
   The loss of one whom I esteemed a
      friend.
Dur. Sir, he is coming this way.
King.   If a speak to me,
   I could deny him nothing; to prevent it,
   I must withdraw. Pray, lords, commend
      my favors
   To his last peace, which I with him will
      pray for.
   That done, it doth concern us to consult
   Of other following troubles.
      Exeunt [King Henry with his Train].
Ox.   I am glad
   He's gone. Upon my life, he would have
      pardoned
   The traitor, had a seen him.
Sur.   'Tis a king
   Composed of gentleness.
Dur.   Rare and unheard of! 50
   But every man is nearest to [2] himself;
   And that the king observes. 'Tis fit a
      should.

[1] Tumult.   [2] Closest to most concerned for.

Enter Stanley, Executioner, Urswick, and
                                    Dawbney.

Stan. May I not speak with Clifford ere
   I shake
   This piece of frailty off?
Daw.   You shall; he's sent for.
Stan. I must not see the king?
Dur.   From him, Sir William,
   These lords and I am sent; he bade us
      say
   That he commends his mercy to your
      thoughts,
   Wishing the laws of England could
      remit
   The forfeit of your life as willingly
   As he would in the sweetness of his
      nature   60
   Forget your trespass. But howe'er your
      body
   Fall into dust, he vows, the king him-
      self
   Doth vow to keep a requiem for your
      soul,
   As for a friend close treasured in his
      bosom.
Ox. Without remembrance of your errors
      past,
   I come to take my leave, and wish you
      heaven.
Sur. And I. Good angels guard ye!
Stan.   O, the king,
   Next to my soul, shall be the nearest
      subject
   Of my last prayers. My grave Lord of
      Durham,
   My Lords of Oxford, Surrey, Dawbney,
      all,   70
   Accept from a poor dying man a fare-
      well.
   I was as you are, once—great, and stood
      hopeful
   Of many flourishing years; but fate and
      time
   Have wheeled about to turn me into
      nothing.

Enter Clifford.

Daw. Sir Robert Clifford comes—the
   man, Sir William,
   You so desire to speak with.
Dur.   Mark their meeting.
Clif. Sir William Stanley, I am glad your
   conscience

Before your end hath emptied every
burthen
Which charged it, as that [1] you can
clearly witness
How far I have proceeded in a duty   80
That both concerned my truth and the
state's safety.

STAN. Mercy, how dear is life to such as
hug it!
Come hither; by this token think on me!
*Makes a cross on Clifford's face with his
finger.*

CLIF. This token? What? I am abused!

STAN.   You are not.
I wet upon your cheeks a holy sign,
The cross, the Christian's badge, the
traitor's infamy.
Wear, Clifford, to thy grave this painted
emblem;
Water shall never wash it off; all eyes
That gaze upon thy face shall read there
written   89
A state-informer's character, more ugly
Stamped on a noble name than on a
base.
The heavens forgive thee! Pray, my
lords, no change [2]
Of words; this man and I have used too
many.

CLIF. Shall I be disgraced
Without reply?

DUR.   Give losers leave to talk;
His loss is irrecoverable.

STAN.   Once more,
To all a long farewell! The best of great-
ness
Preserve the king! My next suit is, my
lords,
To be remembered to my noble brother,
Derby, my much-grieved brother. O,
persuade him   100
That I shall stand no blemish to his
house
In chronicles writ in another age.
My heart doth bleed for him and for his
sighs.
Tell him, he must not think the style [3]
of Derby,
Nor being husband to King Henry's
mother,
The league with peers, the smiles of for-
tune, can
Secure his peace above the state of man.

I take my leave, to travel to my dust.
"Subjects deserve their deaths whose
kings are just."—
[*To Urswick.*] Come, confessor.—[*To
Executioner.*] On with thy ax, friend,
on!   110
Exeunt [Urswick, Stanley, and Executioner].

CLIF. Was I called hither by a traitor's
breath
To be upbraided? Lords, the king shall
know it.

Enter King Henry with a white staff.[4]

KING. The king doth know it, sir; the
king hath heard
What he or you could say. We have
given credit
To every point of Clifford's information,
The only evidence gainst Stanley's
head.
A dies for 't; are you pleased?

CLIF.   I pleased, my lord!

KING. No echoes. For your service we
dismiss
Your more attendance on the court.
Take ease,
And live at home; but, as you love your
life,   120
Stir not from London without leave
from us.
We'll think on your reward. Away!

CLIF.   I go, sir. *Exit Clifford.*

KING. Die all our griefs with Stanley!
Take this staff
Of office, Dawbney; henceforth be our
chamberlain.

DAW. I am your humblest servant.

KING.   We are followed
By enemies at home, that will not cease
To seek their own confusion. 'Tis most
true
The Cornish under Audley are marched
on
As far as Winchester. But let them
come;
Our forces are in readiness; we'll catch
'em   130
In their own toils.

DAW.   Your army, being mustered,
Consists in all, of horse and foot, at least
In number six-and-twenty thousand—
men

---

[1] So that.   [2] Exchange.   [3] Title.

[4] Emblematic of the Lord Chamberlain's office.

Daring and able, resolute to fight,
And loyal in their truths.
KING.   We know it, Dawbney.
For them we order thus: Oxford in
chief,
Assisted by bold Essex and the Earl
Of Suffolk, shall lead on the first bat-
talia.[1] —
Be that your charge.
Ox.   I humbly thank your majesty.
KING. The next division we assign to
Dawbney.   140
These must be men of action, for on
those
The fortune of our fortunes must rely.
The last and main ourself commands in
person,
As ready to restore the fight at all
times
As to consummate an assuréd victory.
DAW. The king is still oraculous.[2]
KING.   But, Surrey,
We have employment of more toil for
thee,
For our intelligence comes swiftly to
us
That James of Scotland late hath enter-
tained
Perkin the counterfeit with more than
common   150
Grace and respect, nay, courts him with
rare favors.
The Scot is young and forward; we must
look for
A sudden storm to England from the
north,
Which to withstand, Durham shall post
to Norham
To fortify the castle and secure
The frontiers against an invasion
there.
Surrey shall follow soon, with such an
army
As may relieve the bishop and en-
counter
On all occasions the death-daring
Scots.
You know your charges all; 'tis now a
time   160
To execute, not talk. Heaven is our
guard still.
War must breed peace; such is the fate
of kings.   *Exeunt.*

[1] Division.   [2] Oracular, wise.

[SCENA TERTIA.

A room in the palace at Edinburgh.]

Enter Crawford and Daliell.

CRAW. 'Tis more than strange; my reason
cannot answer
Such argument of fine imposture,
couched
In witchcraft of persuasion, that it fash-
ions
Impossibilities, as if appearance
Could cozen truth itself. This dukeling
mushroom
Hath doubtless charmed the king.
DAL.   A courts the ladies
As if his strength of language chained
attention
By power of prerogative.
CRAW.   It madded
My very soul to hear our master's mo-
tion.   9
What surety both of amity and honor
Must of necessity ensue upon
A match betwixt some noble of our nation
And this brave prince, forsooth!
DAL.   'Twill prove too fatal;
Wise Huntley fears the threat'ning.
Bless the lady
From such a ruin.
CRAW.   How the council privy
Of this young Phaëton do screw their
faces
Into a gravity their trades, good people,
Were never guilty of! The meanest of
'em
Dreams of at least an office in the state.
DAL. Sure, not the hangman's; 'tis be-
spoke already   20
For service to their rogueships.—Silence!

Enter King James and Huntley.

K. JA.   Do not
Argue against our will; we have de-
scended
Somewhat—as we may term it—too
familiarly
From justice of our birthright to examine
The force of your allegiance—sir, we
have—
But find it short of duty.
HUNT.   Break my heart,
Do, do, king! Have my services, my
loyalty—

Heaven knows untainted ever—drawn
upon me
Contempt now in mine age, when I but
wanted [1]   29
A minute of a peace not to be troubled,
My last, my long one? Let me be a
dotard,
A bedlam,[2] a poor sot,[3] or what you
please
To have me, so you will not stain your
blood,
Your own blood, royal sir, though mixed
with mine,
By marriage of this girl to a straggler!
Take, take my head, sir; whilst my
tongue can wag,
It cannot name him other.

K. Ja.   Kings are counterfeits
In your repute, grave oracle, not pres-
ently [4]
Set on their thrones with scepters in their
fists.
But use your own detraction; [5] 'tis our
pleasure   40
To give our cousin York for wife our
kinswoman,
The Lady Katherine. Instinct of sover-
eignty
Designs the honor, though her peevish
father
Usurps our resolution.[6]

Hunt.   O, 'tis well,
Exceeding well. I never was ambitious
Of using congees to my daughter-queen—
A queen? Perhaps a quean! Forgive me,
Daliell,
Thou honorable gentleman. None here
Dare speak one word of comfort?

Dal.   Cruel misery!

Craw. The lady, gracious prince, maybe
hath settled   50
Affection on some former choice.

Dal.   Enforcement
Would prove but tyranny.

Hunt.   I thank 'e heartily.
Let any yeoman of our nation challenge
An interest in the girl, then the king
May add a jointure of ascent in titles,
Worthy a free consent; now a pulls down
What old desert hath builded.

[1] Lacked.   [3] Fool.
[2] Lunatic.   [4] I.e., if not actually.
[5] I.e., speak to your own injury.
[6] Power of decision.

K. Ja.   Cease persuasions.
I violate no pawns of faiths, intrude
not
On private loves. That I have played
the orator
For kingly York to virtuous Kate, her
grant   60
Can justify, referring her contents
To our provision.[7] The Welsh Harry [8]
henceforth
Shall therefore know, and tremble to
acknowledge,
That not the painted idol of his policy
Shall fright the lawful owner from a
kingdom.
We are resolved.

Hunt.   Some of thy subjects' hearts,
King James, will bleed for this.

K. Ja.   Then shall their bloods
Be nobly spent. No more disputes; he is
not
Our friend who contradicts us.

Hunt.   Farewell, daughter!
My care by one is lessened: thank the
king for 't.[9]   70
I and my griefs will dance now.—Look,
lords, look;
Here's hand in hand already!

K. Ja.   Peace, old frenzy!—

*Enter Warbeck, leading Katherine, com-
plimenting; Countess of Crawford, Jane,
Frion, Major of Cork, Astley, Heron,
and Sketon.*

How like a king a looks! Lords, but observe
The confidence of his aspect. Dross
cannot
Cleave to so pure a metal. Royal
youth!
Plantagenet undoubted!

Hunt. [*Aside.*]   Ho, brave lady!
But no Plantagenet, by'r Lady, yet,
By red rose or by white.

War.   An union this way
Settles possession in a monarchy
Established rightly, as is my inherit-
ance.   80
Acknowledge me but sovereign of this
kingdom,

[7] Oversight.
[8] Henry VII's grandfather was a Welshman.
[9] Original has *Enter* in the margin.

Your heart, fair princess, and the hand
  of providence
Shall crown you queen of me and my
  best fortunes.
KATH. Where my obedience is, my lord, a
    duty,
Love owes true service.
WAR.   Shall I—
K. JA.   Cousin, yes,
Enjoy her; from my hand accept your
  bride;   [*He joins their hands.*]
And may they live at enmity with com-
  fort
Who grieve at such an equal pledge of
  troths!
Y' are the prince's wife now.
KATH.   By your gift, sir.
WAR. Thus I take seizure of mine own.
KATH.   I miss yet 90
A father's blessing. Let me find it.
  [*Kneels.*] Humbly
Upon my knees I seek it.
HUNT.   I am Huntley,
Old Alexander Gordon, a plain subject,
Nor more nor less; and, lady, if you
  wish for
A blessing, you must bend your knees to
  heaven,
For heaven did give me you. Alas, alas,
What would you have me say? May all
  the happiness
My prayers ever sued to fall upon
  you
Preserve you in your virtues!—Prithee,
  Daliell,
Come with me, for I feel thy griefs as
  full   100
As mine. Let's steal away and cry
  together.
DAL. My hopes are in their ruins.
                    Exeunt Huntley and Daliell.
K. JA.   Good, kind Huntley
Is overjoyed. A fit solemnity
Shall perfit [1] these delights.—Crawford,
  attend
Our order for the preparation.
Exeunt. Manent Frion, Major, Astley,
                    Heron, et Sketon.
FRI. Now, worthy gentlemen, have I not
  followed
My undertakings with success? Here's
  entrance
Into a certainty above a hope.

[1] Perfect.

HER. Hopes are but hopes; I was ever
confident, when I traded but in rem- [110
nants, that my stars had reserved me to
the title of a viscount at least. Honor is
honor, though cut out of any stuffs.
SKE. My brother Heron hath right
wisely delivered his opinion; for he that
threads his needle with the sharp eyes of
industry shall in time go through-stitch [2]
with the new suit of preferment.
AST. Spoken to the purpose, my fine-
witted brother Sketon; for as no in- [120
denture but has its counterpawn, [3] no
noverint [4] but his [5] condition or defeasance;
so no right but may have claim, no claim
but may have possession, any act of parliament to the contrary notwithstanding.
FRI. You are all read in mysteries of state,
  And quick of apprehension, deep in judg-
    ment,
  Active in resolution; and 'tis pity
  Such counsel should lie buried in ob-
    scurity.
  But why, in such a time and cause of
    triumph,   130
  Stands the judicious Major of Cork so
    silent?
  Believe it, sir, as English Richard pros-
    pers,
  You must not miss employment of high
    nature.
MAJ. If men may be credited in their
  mortality, which I dare not peremptorily
  aver but they may or not be, presumptions
  by this marriage are then, in sooth, of
  fruitful expectation. Or else I must not
  justify other men's belief more than other
  should rely on mine.   140
FRI. Pith of experience! Those that have
  borne office
  Weigh every word before it can drop
    from them.
  But, noble counselors, since now the
    present
  Requires in point of honor—pray, mis-
    take not—
  Some service to our lord, 'tis fit the Scots
  Should not engross all glory to them-
    selves
  At this so grand and eminent solemnity.

[2] Finish thoroughly.
[3] Indentures were torn in two, each person
keeping half.
[4] Writ, deed, bond.   [5] Its.

SKE. The Scots? The motion is defied. I had rather, for my part, without trial of my country, suffer persecution under [150 the pressing iron of reproach, or let my skin be punched [1] full of oilet-holes [2] with the bodkin of derision.

AST. I will sooner lose both my ears on the pillory of forgery.

HER. Let me first live a bankrout, and die in the lousy Hole [3] of hunger, without compounding for sixpence in the pound.

MAJ. If men fail not in their expectations, there may be spirits also that [160 disgest [4] no rude affronts, Master Secretary Frion, or I am cozened—which is possible, I grant.

FRI. Resolved like men of knowledge! At this feast then,
In honor of the bride, the Scots, I know,
Will in some show, some masque, or some device
Prefer their duties. Now it were uncomely
That we be found less forward for our prince
Than they are for their lady; and by how much   169
We outshine them in persons of account,
By so much more will our endeavors meet with
A livelier applause. Great emperors
Have for their recreations undertook
Such kind of pastimes; as for the conceit, [5]
Refer it to my study. The performance
You all shall share a thanks in. 'Twill be grateful.

HER. The motion is allowed. I have stole to a dancing school when I was a prentice.

AST. There have been Irish hub-   [180 bubs, [6] when I have made one too.

SKE. For fashioning of shapes and cutting a cross caper, [7] turn me off to my trade again.

MAJ. Surely there is, if I be not deceived, a kind of gravity in merriment, as there is, or perhaps ought to be, respect of persons in the quality of carriage, which is, as it is construed, either so or so.

[Demonstrates.]

FRI. Still you come home to me; upon occasion   190
I find you relish courtship [8] with discretion,
And such are fit for statesmen of your merits.
Pray 'e wait [9] the prince, and in his ear acquaint him
With this design.   I'll follow and direct 'e.   Exeunt; mane[t] Frion.
O, the toil
Of humoring this abject scum of mankind,
Muddy-brained peasants!   Princes feel a misery
Beyond impartial sufferance, whose extremes
Must yield to such abettors. Yet [10] our tide
Runs smoothly without adverse winds. Run on!   200
Flow to a full sea! Time alone debates
Quarrels forewritten in the book of fates.
Exit.

ACTUS TERTIUS. SCENA PRIMA.

[The presence chamber at Westminster.]

Enter King Henry, his gorget [11] on, his sword, plume of feathers, leading staff; [12] and Urswick.

KING. How runs the time of day?
URS.   Past ten, my lord.
KING. A bloody hour will it prove to some,
Whose disobedience, like the sons o' th' Earth, [13]
Throw a defiance gainst the face of heaven.
Oxford, with Essex and stout De la Pole,
Have quieted the Londoners, I hope,
And set them safe from fear.
URS.   They are all silent.
KING. From their own battlements they may behold
Saint George's Fields o'erspread with arméd men,

---

[1] Suggested by Gifford-Dyce. Original reads *pincht*.   [2] Eyelet-holes.
[3] One of the worst cells in the Counter Prison.
[4] Digest.   [6] Celebrations.
[5] Idea.   [7] A movement in dancing.

[8] Court behavior.   [9] Await.   [10] Thus far.
[11] A piece of armor for the throat.
[12] A baton borne by a commanding officer.
[13] *I.e.*, the Titans.

Amongst whom our own royal standard
    threatens   10
Confusion to opposers. We must learn
To practice war again in time of peace,
Or lay our crown before our subjects'
    feet—
Ha, Urswick, must we not?

URS.   The powers who seated
King Henry on his lawful throne will ever
Rise up in his defense.

KING.   Rage shall not fright
The bosom of our confidence. In Kent
Our Cornish rebels, cozened of their
    hopes,
Met brave resistance by that country's [1]
    earl,
George Abergeny,[2] Cobham, Poynings,
    Guilford,   20
And other loyal hearts; now, if Black-
    heath
Must be reserved the fatal tomb to
    swallow
Such stiff-necked abjects as with weary
    marches
Have traveled from their homes, their
    wives and children,
To pay, instead of subsidies, their lives,
We may continue sovereign. Yet, Urs-
    wick,
We'll not abate one penny what in parlia-
    ment
Hath freely been contributed; we must
    not.
Money gives soul to action. Our competi-
    tor,
The Flemish counterfeit, with James of
    Scotland,   30
Will prove what courage need and want
    can nourish,
Without the food of fit supplies. But,
    Urswick,
I have a charm in secret that shall loose
The witchcraft wherewith young King
    James is bound,
And free it at my pleasure without blood-
    shed.

URS. Your majesty's a wise king, sent from
    heaven,
Protector of the just.

KING.   Let dinner cheerfully
Be served in; this day of the week is
    ours,
Our day of providence; for Saturday

Yet never failed in all my undertak-
    ings   40
To yield me rest at night. (*A flourish.*)
What means this warning?
Good fate, speak peace to Henry!

Enter Dawbney, Oxford, and Attendants.

DAW.   Live the king,
Triumphant in the ruin of his enemies!

OX. The head of strong rebellion is cut off,
The body hewed in pieces.

KING.   Dawbney, Oxford,
Minions to noblest fortunes, how yet
    stands
The comfort of your wishes?

DAW.   Briefly thus:
The Cornish under Audley, disappointed
Of flattered expectation, from the Kent-
    ish
(Your majesty's right trusty liegemen)
    flew,   50
Feathered by rage and heartened by
    presumption,
To take the field even at your palace
    gates,
And face you in your chamber royal.
    Arrogance
Improved their ignorance, for they, sup-
    posing,
Misled by rumor, that the day of battle
Should fall on Monday, rather braved
    your forces
Than doubted [3] any onset; yet this morn-
    ing,
When in the dawning I by your direc-
    tion
Strove to get Dartford Strand bridge,
    there I found
Such a resistance as might show what
    strength   60
Could make. Here arrows hailed in
    showers upon us
A full yard long at least, but we pre-
    vailed.
My Lord of Oxford, with his fellow peers
Environing the hill, fell fiercely on them
On the one side, I on the other, till great
    sir
(Pardon the oversight), eager of doing
Some memorable act, I was engaged
Almost a prisoner, but was freed as soon
As sensible of danger. Now the fight

---

[1] County's.   [2] Abergavenny.   [3] Feared.

Began in heat, which, quenched in the
blood of   70
Two thousand rebels, and as many more
Reserved to try your mercy, have re-
turned
A victory with safety.

KING.   Have we lost
An equal number with them?

Ox.   In the total
Scarcely four hundred. Audley, Flam-
mock, Joseph,
The ringleaders of this commotion,
Railed [1] in ropes, fit ornaments for trai-
tors,
Wait your determinations.

KING.   We must pay
Our thanks where they are only due. O,
lords,   79
Here is no victory, nor shall our people
Conceive that we can triumph in their
falls.
Alas, poor souls! Let such as are escaped
Steal to the country back without pur-
suit.
There's not a drop of blood spilt but hath
drawn
As much of mine. Their swords could
have wrought wonders
On their king's part, who faintly were un-
sheathed
Against their prince, but wounded their
own breasts.
Lords, we are debtors to your care; our
payment
Shall be both sure and fitting your
deserts.

DAW. Sir, will you please to see those
rebels, heads   90
Of this wild monster-multitude?

KING.   Dear friend,
My faithful Dawbney, no. On them our
justice
Must frown in terror; I will not vouchsafe
An eye of pity to them. Let false Audley
Be drawn upon an hurdle from the New-
gate
To Tower Hill in his own coat of arms,
Painted on paper, with the arms re-
versed,
Defaced, and torn; there let him lose his
head.
The lawyer and the blacksmith shall be
hanged,

Quartered, their quarters into Cornwall
sent   100
Examples to the rest, whom we are
pleased
To pardon and dismiss from further
quest.[2]
My Lord of Oxford, see it done.

Ox.   I shall, sir.

KING. Urswick!

URS.   My lord?

KING.   To Dinham, our high treas-
urer,
Say we command commissions be new
granted
For the collection of our subsidies
Through all the west, and that speedily.
Lords, we acknowledge our engagements
due
For your most constant services.

DAW.   Your soldiers   109
Have manfully and faithfully acquitted
Their several duties.

KING.   For it we will throw
A largess free amongst them, which shall
hearten
And cherish up [3] their loyalties. More yet
Remains of like employment; not a man
Can be dismissed till enemies abroad,
More dangerous than these at home,
have felt
The puissance of our arms. O happy
kings
Whose thrones are raiséd in their sub-
jects' hearts!   *Exeunt omnes.*

[SCENA SECUNDA.

A room in the palace at Edinburgh.]

Enter Huntley and Daliell.

HUNT. Now, sir, a modest [4] word with
you, sad gentleman.
Is not this fine, I trow,[5] to see the gam-
bolds,[6]
To hear the jigs,[7] observe the frisks, b'
enchanted
With the rare discord of bells, pipes,
and tabors,
Hotchpotch of Scotch and Irish twingle-
twangles,

[1] Tied in a row.

[2] Inquest, inquiry.   [4] Quiet.
[3] Cheer, encourage.
[5] Here merely an expression of contempt.
[6] Gambols.   [7] Lively songs or ballads.

Like to so many quiristers [1] of Bedlam
Trolling a catch! [2] The feasts, the manly
   stomachs,
The healths in usquebaugh [3] and bonny-
   clabber, [4]
The ale in dishes never fetched from
   China,
The hundred thousand knacks [5] not to
   be spoken of—   10
And all this for King Oberon and Queen
   Mab—
Should put a soul int'e. Look 'e, good
   man,
How youthful I am grown. But, by
   your leave,
This new queen-bride must henceforth
   be no more
My daughter; no, bur [6] Lady, 'tis unfit.
And yet you see how I do bear this
   change,
Methinks courageously, then shake off
   care
In such a time of jollity.
DAL.   Alas, sir,
How can you cast a mist upon your
   griefs,
Which, howsoe'er you shadow, but pre-
   sent   20
To any judging eye the perfect sub-
   stance,
Of which mine are but counterfeits?
HUNT.   Foh, Daliell!
Thou interrupts the part I bear in
   music
To this rare bridal feast. Let us be
   merry,
Whilst flattering calms secure us against
   storms.
Tempests, when they begin to roar, put
   out
The light of peace, and cloud the sun's
   bright eye
In darkness of despair; yet we are safe.
DAL. I wish you could as easily forget
The justice of your sorrows as my
   hopes   30
Can yield to destiny.
HUNT.   Pish! Then I see
Thou dost not know the flexible condi-
   tion

[1] Choristers.
[2] Singing a round song.
[4] Coagulated sour milk.
[5] Knickknacks, trifles.
[3] Whiskey.
[6] By our.

Of my apt nature. I can laugh, laugh
   heartily,
When the gout cramps my joints; let
   but the stone
Stop in my bladder, I am straight a-
   singing;
The quartan-fever, shrinking every limb,
Sets me a-capering straight. Do but
   betray me,
And bind me a friend ever. What! I
   trust
The losing of a daughter, though I
   doted
On every hair that grew to trim her
   head,   40
Admits not any pain like one of these.
Come, th' art deceived in me. Give me
   a blow,
A sound blow on the face, I'll thank thee
   for 't.
I love my wrongs. Still th' art deceived
   in me.
DAL. Deceived? O, noble Huntley, my
   few years
Have learnt experience of too ripe an
   age
To forfeit fit credulity. Forgive
My rudeness; I am bold.
HUNT.   Forgive me first
A madness of ambition; by example
Teach me humility, for patience scorns
Lectures, which schoolmen use to read
   to boys   51
Uncapable of injuries. Though old,
I could grow tough in fury, and disclaim
Allegiance to my king, could fall at odds
With all my fellow peers that durst not
   stand
Defendants gainst the rape done on
   mine honor.
But kings are earthly gods; there is no
   meddling
With their anointed bodies; for their
   actions
They only are accountable to heaven.
Yet in the puzzle of my troubled brain
One antidote's reserved against the
   poison   61
Of my distractions; 'tis in thee t' apply
   it.
DAL. Name it; O, name it quickly, sir!
HUNT.   A pardon
For my most foolish slighting thy de-
   serts;

I have culled out this time to beg it.
    Prithee,
Be gentle. Had I been so, thou hadst
    owned
A happy bride, but now a castaway,
And never child of mine more.
DAL.   Say not so, sir;
It is not fault in her.
HUNT.   The world would prate
How she was handsome; young I know
    she was,   70
Tender and sweet in her obedience—
But lost now. What a bankrupt am I
    made
Of [1] a full stock of blessings! Must I
    hope
A mercy from thy heart?
DAL.   A love, a service,
A friendship to posterity. [2]
HUNT.   Good angels
Reward thy charity! I have no more
But prayers left me now.
DAL.   I'll lend you mirth, sir,
If you will be in consort. [3]
HUNT.   Thank ye truly.
I must; yes, yes, I must. Here's yet
    some ease,
A partner in affliction; look not angry. 80
DAL. Good, noble sir!   [Flourish.]
HUNT.   O, hark! We may be quiet;
The king and all the others come, a
    meeting
Of gaudy sights. This day's the last of
    revels;
Tomorrow sounds of war; then new ex-
    change.
Fiddles must turn to swords. Unhappy
    marriage!

Flourish.   Enter King James; Warbeck
    leading Katherine; Crawford, Countess,
    and Jane [, with other Ladies]. Huntley
    and Daliell fall among them.

K. JA. Cousin of York, you and your
    princely bride
Have liberally enjoyed such soft de-
    lights
As a new-married couple could forethink;
Nor has our bounty shortened [4] expecta-
    tion.
But after all those pleasures of repose, 90

Or amorous safety, we must rouse the
    ease
Of dalliance with achievements of more
    glory
Than sloth and sleep can furnish. Yet,
    for farewell,
Gladly we entertain a truce with time
To grace the joint endeavors of our
    servants.
WAR. My royal cousin, in your princely
    favor
The extent of bounty hath been so un-
    limited
As only an acknowledgment in words
Would breed suspicion in [5] our state
    and quality.
When we shall, in the fullness of our
    fate,   100
Whose minister, necessity, will perfit, [6]
Sit on our own throne; then our arms,
    laid open
To gratitude, in sacred memory
Of these large benefits, shall twine them
    close,
Even to our thoughts and heart, without
    distinction.
Then James and Richard, being in effect
One person, shall unite and rule one
    people,
Divisible in titles only.
K. JA.   Seat ye.
Are the presenters ready?
CRAW.   All are entering.
HUNT. Dainty sport toward, Daliell! Sit;
    come, sit,   110
Sit and be quiet. Here are kingly bug's
    words! [7]

Enter at one door four Scotch Antics, [8] ac-
    cordingly habited; enter at another
    four Wild Irish in trowses, [9] long-
    haired and accordingly habited. Music.
                    The Masquers dance.

K. JA. To all a general thanks!
WAR.   In the next room
Take your own shapes again; you shall
    receive
Particular acknowledgment.
                    [Exeunt Masquers.]

[5] As to.
[6] I.e., bring our destiny to perfection.
[7] Words of a bug, or bogey; swaggering
language.
[8] Burlesque performers. [9] Close-fitting trousers.

[1] From.
[2] i.e., remembered by posterity.
[3] Harmony.   [4] Come short of.

K. JA.   Enough
Of merriments.—Crawford, how far's
  our army
Upon the march?
CRAW.   At Hedonhall, great king;
Twelve thousand, well prepared.
K. JA.   Crawford, tonight
Post thither. We in person with the
  prince
By four a-clock tomorrow after dinner
Will be w'e.[1] Speed away!
CRAW.   I fly, my lord. [*Exit.*] 120
K. JA. Our business grows to head now.
  Where's your secretary,
That he attends 'e not to serve?
WAR.   With Marchmount,
Your herald.
K. JA.   Good! The proclamation's
  ready;
By that it will appear how the English
  stand
Affected to your title. Huntley, com-
  fort
Your daughter in her husband's ab-
  sence; fight
With prayers at home for us, who for
  your honors
Must toil in fight abroad.
HUNT.   Prayers are the weapons
Which men so near their graves as I
  do use.
I've little else to do.
K. JA.   To rest, young beauties! 130
We must be early stirring; quickly part.
"A kingdom's rescue craves both speed
  and art."
Cousins, good night.   *Flourish.*
WAR.   Rest to our cousin king.
KATH. Your blessing, sir.
HUNT. Fair blessings on your highness!
  Sure, you need 'em.
*Exeunt omnes; manent Warb[eck, Jane,]
          et Katherine.*
WAR. Jane, set the lights down, and from
  us return
To those in the next room this little
  purse;
Say we'll deserve [2] their loves.
JANE.   It shall be done, sir. [*Exit.*]
WAR. Now, dearest, ere sweet sleep shall
  seal those eyes,
Love's precious tapers, give me leave to
  use   140

A parting ceremony, for tomorrow
It would be sacrilege to intrude upon
The temple of thy peace. Swift as the
  morning
Must I break from the down of thy em-
  braces,
To put on steel, and trace the paths
  which lead
Through various hazards to a careful [3]
  throne.
KATH. My lord, I would fain go w'e;
  there's small fortune
In staying here behind.
WAR.   The churlish brow
Of war, fair dearest, is a sight of horror
For ladies' entertainment. If thou
  hear'st   150
A truth of my sad ending by the hand
Of some unnatural subject, thou withal
Shalt hear how I died worthy of my
  right,
By falling like a king; and in the close,
Which my last breath shall sound, thy
  name, thou fairest,
Shall sing a requiem to my soul, unwill-
  ing
Only of greater glory, cause [4] divided
From such a heaven on earth as life
  with thee.
But these are chimes for funerals. My
  business
Attends on fortune of a sprightlier
  triumph,   160
For love and majesty are reconciled,
And vow to crown thee empress of the
  west.
KATH. You have a noble language, sir;
  your right
In me is without question, and how-
  ever
Events of time may shorten my deserts
In others' pity, yet it shall not stagger
Or constancy or duty in a wife.
You must be king of me; and my poor
  heart
Is all I can call mine.
WAR.   But we will live,
Live, beauteous virtue, by the lively
  test   170
Of our own blood to let the "counter-
  feit"
Be known the world's contempt.
KATH.   Pray, do not use

[1] With ye.   [2] Reward.   [3] Full of care.   [4] Because.

That word; it carries fate in 't. The first
　suit
I ever made, I trust your love will grant.
WAR. Without denial, dearest.
KATH.　　　　　　That hereafter,
If you return with safety, no adventure
May sever us in tasting any fortune.
I ne'er can stay behind again.
WAR.　　　　　　Y' are lady
Of your desires, and shall command
　your will;
Yet 'tis too hard a promise.
KATH.　　　　What our destinies 180
Have ruled out in their books we must
　not search,
But kneel to.
WAR.　　　　Then to fear when hope is
　fruitless,
Were to be desperately miserable,
Which poverty our greatness dares not
　dream of,
And much more scorns to stoop to.
Some few minutes
Remain yet; let's be thrifty in our hopes.
　　　　　　　　　　　　　　Exeunt.

[SCENA TERTIA.

The presence chamber in the palace at
　　　　　　　　Westminster.]

Enter King Henry, Hialas, and Urswick.

KING. Your name is Pedro Hialas, a
　Spaniard?
HIAL. Sir, a Castilian born.
KING.　　　　　King Ferdinand,
With wise Queen Isabel, his royal con-
　sort,
Write 'e [1] a man of worthy trust and
　candor.
Princes are dear to heaven who meet
　with subjects
Sincere in their employments; such I
　find
Your commendation, sir. Let me de-
　liver
How joyful I repute the amity
With your most fortunate master, who
　almost
Comes near a miracle in his success 10
Against the Moors, who had devoured
　his country
Entire now to his scepter. We for our
　part

[1] Report ye.

Will imitate his providence, [2] in hope
Of partage [3] in the use on .'t. We
　repute
The privacy of his advisement to us
By you, intended an ambassador
To Scotland for a peace between our
　kingdoms,
A policy of love which well becomes
His wisdom and our care.
HIAL.　　　　　　Your majesty
Doth understand him rightly.
KING.　　　　　　　Else 20
Your knowledge can instruct me;
　wherein, sir,
To fall on ceremony would seem use-
　less,
Which shall not need, for I will be as
　studious
Of your concealment in our conference
As any council shall advise.
HIAL.　　　　　　Then, sir,
My chief request is that, on notice
　given,
At my despatch in Scotland you will
　send
Some learned man of power and ex-
　perience
To join entreaty with me.
KING.　　　　　I shall do it,
Being that way well provided by [4] a
　servant 30
Which may attend 'e ever.
HIAL.　　　　If King James
By any indirection should perceive
My coming near your court, I doubt
　the issue
Of my employment.
KING.　　　Be not your own herald;
I learn sometimes without a teacher.
HIAL.　　　　　　Good days
Guard all your princely thoughts!
KING.　　　　　Urswick, no further
Than the next open gallery attend him.
A hearty love go with you!
HIAL.　　　　Your vowed beadsman. [5]
　　　　　Ex[eunt] Ursw[ick] and Hialas.
KING. King Ferdinand is not so much a
　fox
But that a cunning huntsman may in
　time 40
Fall on the scent. In honorable actions
Safe imitation best deserves a praise.—

[2] Foresight.　　　　[4] With.
[3] Share.　　　　　[5] Devoted servant.

Enter Urswick.

What, the Castilian's passed away?

Urs.   He is,
And undiscovered. The two hundred
    marks
Your majesty conveyed,[1] a gently
    pursed
With a right modest gravity.

King.   What was 't
A muttered in the earnest [2] of his wis-
    dom?
A spoke not to be heard. 'Twas
    about—

Urs.   Warbeck:
How if King Henry were but sure of
    subjects,
Such a wild runagate might soon be
    caged,   50
No great ado withstanding.

King.   Nay, nay; something
About my son Prince Arthur's match.

Urs.   Right, right, sir.
A hummed it out, how that King Ferdi-
    nand
Swore that the marriage twixt the Lady
    Katherine,
His daughter, and the Prince of Wales,
    your son,
Should never be consummated as
    long
As any Earl of Warwick lived in Eng-
    land,
Except by new creation.

King.   I remember
'Twas so, indeed. The king his master
    swore it?

Urs. Directly, as he said.

King.   An Earl of Warwick! 60
Provide a messenger for letters in-
    stantly
To Bishop Fox. Our news from Scot-
    land creeps,
It comes so slow. We must have airy
    spirits;
Our time requires depatch.—[*Aside.*]
    The Earl of Warwick!
Let him be son to Clarence, younger
    brother
To Edward! Edward's daughter is, I
    think,
Mother to our Prince Arthur.—Get a
    messenger.   *Exeunt.*

Before the castle of Norham.]

*Enter King James, Warbeck, Crawford,
    Daliell, Heron, Astley, Major, Sketon,
                            and Soldiers.*

K. Ja. We trifle time against these castle
    walls;
The English prelate will not yield.
    Once more
Give him a summons.   *Parley.*

*Enter above, Durham, armed, a truncheon
    in his hand, and Soldiers.*

War.   See, the jolly clerk [3]
Appears, trimmed [4] like a ruffian!

K. Ja.   Bishop, yet
Set ope the ports, and to your lawful
    sovereign,
Richard of York, surrender up this
    castle,
And he will take thee to his grace; else
    Tweed
Shall overflow his banks with English
    blood,
And wash the sand that cements those
    hard stones,
From their foundation.

Dur.   Warlike King of Scotland, 10
Vouchsafe a few words from a man en-
    forced
To lay his book aside and clap on arms
Unsuitable to my age or my profession.
Courageous prince, consider on what
    grounds
You rend the face of peace, and break a
    league
With a confederate king that courts
    your amity.
For whom too? For a vagabond, a
    straggler,
Not noted in the world by birth or name,
An obscure peasant, by the rage of hell
Loosed from his chains to set great kings
    at strife.   20
What nobleman, what common man of
    note,
What ordinary subject hath come in,
Since first you footed on our territories,
To only feign a welcome? Children
    laugh at
Your proclamations, and the wiser pity

---

[1] Sent.   [2] Soberness.
[3] Ecclesiastic.   [4] Armed.

So great a potentate's abuse by one
Who juggles merely with the fawns [1]
  and youth
Of an instructed compliment.   Such
  spoils,
Such slaughters as the rapine of your
  soldiers
Already have committed, is enough   30
To show your zeal in a conceited jus-
  tice.[2]
Yet, great king, wake not yet my mas-
  ter's vengeance,
But shake that viper off which gnaws
  your entrails.
I and my fellow subjects are resolved,
If you persist, to stand your utmost fury
Till our last blood drop from us.
WAR.   O, sir, lend
Me ear to this seducer of my honor!—
What shall I call thee, thou gray-bearded
  scandal,
That kick'st against the sovereignty to
  which
Thou owest allegiance?—Treason is
  boldfaced   40
And eloquent in mischief.   Sacred king,
Be deaf to his known malice.
DUR.   Rather yield
Unto those holy motions which inspire
The sacred heart of an anointed body.
It is the surest policy in princes
To govern well their own than [3] seek en-
  croachment
Upon another's right.
CRAW. [Aside.]   The king is serious,
Deep in his meditation[s]. [4]
DAL. [Aside.]   Lift them up
To heaven, his better genius!
WAR.   Can you study
While such a devil raves?   O, sir!
K. JA.   Well, bishop,   50
You'll not be drawn to mercy?
DUR.   Conster me
In like case by a subject of your own.
My resolution's fixed.   King James, be
  counseled.
A greater fate waits on thee.
          Exit Durham cum suis.[5]
K. JA.   Forage through
The country; spare no prey of life or
  goods.

WAR. O, sir, then give me leave to yield
  to nature;
I am most miserable.   Had I been
Born what this clergyman would by
  defame [6]
Baffle belief with, I had never sought
The truth of mine inheritance with rapes
Of women or of infants murthered,
  virgins   61
Deflowered, old men butchered, dwell-
  ings fired,
My land depopulated, and my people
Afflicted with a kingdom's devastation.
Show more remorse,[7] great king, or I
  shall never
Endure to see such havoc with dry eyes.
Spare, spare my dear, dear England!
K. JA.   You fool [8] your piety,
Ridiculously careful of an interest
Another man possesseth.   Where's your
  faction?
Shrewdly the bishop guessed of your
  adherents,   70
When not a petty burgess of some town,
No, not a villager, hath yet appeared
In your assistance.   That should make
  'e whine,
And not your country's sufferance,[9]
  as you term it.
DAL. [Aside.]   The king is angry.
CRAW. [Aside.]   And the
  passionate duke
Effeminately dolent.[10]
WAR.   The experience
In former trials, sir, both of mine own
Or other princes cast out of their thrones,
Have so acquainted me how misery
Is destitute of friends or of relief   80
That I can easily submit to taste
Lowest reproof without contempt or
  words.

          Enter Frion.

K. JA. An humble-minded man!—Now,
  what intelligence
Speaks Master Secretary Frion?
FRI.   Henry
Of England hath in open field o'erthrown
The armies who opposed him in the
  right
Of this young prince.

---

[1] Fawnings.   [2] Imagined act of justice.
[3] Rather than. [4] Added by Gifford-Dyce.
[5] With his men.

[6] Defamation.   [9] Suffering.
[7] Pity.   [10] Doleful.
[8] Make foolish.

K. JA.   His subsidies,[1] you mean.
More, if you have it?
FRI.   Howard, Earl of Surrey,
Backed by twelve earls and barons of
the north,
An hundred knights and gentlemen of
name,   90
And twenty thousand soldiers, is at
hand
To raise your siege. Brooke, with a
goodly navy,
Is admiral at sea; and Dawbney follows
With an unbroken army for a second.
WAR. 'Tis false! They come to side with
us.
K. JA.   Retreat!
We snall not find them stones and walls
to cope with.
Yet, Duke of York, for such thou sayest
thou art,
I'll try thy fortune to the height. To
Surrey,
By Marchmount, I will send a brave
defiance
For single combat. Once [2] a king will
venter [3]   100
His person to an earl, with condition
Of spilling lesser blood.[4] Surrey is bold,
And James resolved.[5]
WAR.   O, rather, gracious sir,
Create me [6] to this glory, since my cause
Doth interest [7] this fair quarrel; valued
least,
I am his equal.
K. JA.   I will be the man.—
March softly off. "Where victory can
reap
A harvest crowned with triumph, toil is
cheap."   *Exeunt omnes.*

ACTUS QUARTUS. SCENA PRIMA.

[*The English camp near Ayton, on the
border.*]

*Enter Surrey, Durham, Soldiers, with drums
and colors.*

SUR. Are all our braving enemies shrunk
back,
Hid in the fogs of their distempered [8]
climate,

[1] Auxiliaries.   [2] For once.   [3] Venture.
[4] With the intention of spilling less blood.
[5] Resolute.   [7] Is concerned in.
[6] *I.e.*, advance me.   [8] Intemperate.

Not daring to behold our colors wave
In spite of this infected air? Can they
Look on the strength of Cundrestine
defaced,
The glory of Hedonhall devasted,[9] that
Of Edington cast down, the pile of
Fulden
O'erthrown, and this the strongest of
their forts,
Old Ayton Castle, yielded and demol-
ished,
And yet not peep abroad? The Scots
are bold,   10
Hardy in battle; but it seems the cause
They undertake, considered, appears
Unjointed in the frame on 't.
DUR.   Noble Surrey,
Our royal master's wisdom is at all times
His fortune's harbinger, for when he
draws
His sword to threaten war, his provi-
dence
Settles on peace, the crowning of an
empire.   *Trumpet.*
SUR. Rank all in order; 'tis a herald's
sound,
Some message from King James. Keep a
fixed station.

*Enter Marchmount and another Herald in
their coats.*

MARCH. From Scotland's awful majesty
we come   20
Unto the English general.
SUR.   To me?
Say on.
MARCH.   Thus then: the waste and
prodigal
Effusion of so much guiltless blood
As in two potent armies of necessity
Must glut the earth's dry womb, his
sweet compassion
Hath studied to prevent, for which to
thee,
Great Earl of Surrey, in a single fight
He offers his own royal person, fairly
Proposing these conditions only, that,
If victory conclude our master's right, 30
The earl shall deliver for his ransom
The town of Berwick to him, with the
fishgarths; [10]
If Surrey shall prevail, the king will pay

[9] Devastated.   [10] Weirs.

A thousand pounds down present for his
freedom,
And silence further arms. So speaks
King James.
Sur. So speaks King James! So like a
king a speaks.
Heralds, the English general returns
A sensible devotion from his heart,
His very soul, to this unfellowed [1] grace.
For let the king know, gentle heralds,
truly,   40
How his descent from his great throne to
honor
A stranger subject with so high a title
As his compeer in arms, hath conquered
more
Than any sword could do, for which—
my loyalty
Respected—I will serve his virtues ever
In all humility. But Berwick, say,
Is none of mine to part with. "In affairs
Of princes, subjects cannot traffic rights
Inherent to the crown." My life is mine;
That I dare freely hazard· and—with
pardon   50
To some unbribed vainglory—if his
majesty
Shall taste a change of fate, his liberty
Shall meet no articles.[2] If I fall, falling
So bravely, I refer me to his pleasure
Without condition; and for this dear
favor,
Say, if not countermanded, I will cease
Hostility, unless provoked.
March.   This answer
We shall relate unpartially.
Dur.   With favor,
Pray have a little patience.—[Aside to
Surrey.] Sir, you find
By these gay flourishes how wearied
travail   60
Inclines to willing rest; here's but a
prologue,
However confidently uttered, meant
For some ensuing acts of peace. Consider
The time of year, unseasonableness of
weather,
Charge, barrenness of profit; and occa-
sion
Presents itself for honorable treaty,
Which we may make good use of. I will
back,

<hr>

[1] Unique.
[2] *I.e.*, no conditions shall be imposed.

As sent from you in point of noble grati-
tude,
Unto King James, with these his heralds.
You
Shall shortly hear from me, my lord, for
order   70
Of breathing or proceeding; and King
Henry,
Doubt not, will thank the service.
Sur. [*Aside to Durham.*]   To your
wisdom,
Lord Bishop, I refer it.
Dur. [*Aside to Surrey.*]   Be it so, then.
Sur. Heralds, accept this chain and these
few crowns.
March. Our duty, noble general.
Dur.   In part
Of retribution [3] for such princely love,
My lord the general is pleased to show
The king your master his sincerest zeal,
By further treaty, by no common man.
I will myself return with you.
Sur.   Y' oblige 80
My faithfullest affections t'e, Lord
Bishop.
March. All happiness attend your lord-
ship!
Sur.   Come, friends
And fellow soldiers! We, I doubt, shall
meet
No enemies but woods and hills to fight
with.
Then 'twere as good to feed and sleep at
home.
We may be free from danger, not secure.
                                   Exeunt omnes.

[Scena Secunda.

The Scottish camp.]

Enter Warbeck and Frion.

War. Frion, O Frion, all my hopes of
glory
Are at a stand! The Scottish king grows
dull,
Frosty, and wayward, since this Spanish
agent
Hath mixed discourses with him. They
are private;
I am not called to council now. Confu-
sion
On all his crafty shrugs! I feel the fabric
Of my designs are tottering.

<hr>

[3] In partial payment.

FRI.   Henry's policies
Stir with too many engines.[1]
WAR.   Let his mines,
Shaped in the bowels of the earth, blow
    up
Works raised for my defense, yet can
    they never   10
Toss into air the freedom of my birth,
Or disavow my blood Plantagenet's.
I am my father's son still. But, O, Frion,
When I bring into count with my dis-
    asters
My wife's compartnership,[2] my Kate's,
    my life's,
Then, then my frailty feels an earth-
    quake. Mischief
Damn Henry's plots! I will be England's
    king,
Or let my aunt of Burgundy report
My fall in the attempt deserved[3] our
    ancestors!
FRI. You grow too wild in passion. If you
    will   20
Appear a prince indeed, confine your
    will
To moderation.
WAR.   What a saucy rudeness
Prompts this distrust! If? If I will
    appear?
Appear a prince? Death throttle such
    deceits
Even in their birth of utterance! Cursèd
    cozenage
Of trust! Ye make me mad. 'Twere
    best, it seems,
That I should turn impostor to myself,
Be mine own counterfeit, belie the truth
Of my dear mother's womb, the sacred
    bed
Of a prince murthered and a living
    baffled.   30
FRI. Nay, if you have no ears to hear, I
    have
No breath to spend in vain.
WAR.   Sir, sir, take heed!
Gold and the promise of promotion
    rarely
Fail in temptation.
FRI.   Why to me this?
WAR.   Nothing.
Speak what you will; we are not sunk so
    low

But your advice may piece again the
    heart
Which many cares have broken. You
    were wont
In all extremities to talk of comfort;
Have ye none left now? I'll not interrupt
    ye.
Good, bear with my distractions. If
    King James   40
Deny us dwelling here, next whither
    must I?
I prithee, be not angry.
FRI.   Sir, I told ye
Of letters come from Ireland—how the
    Cornish
Stomach their last defeat, and humbly
    sue
That with such forces as you could par-
    take[4]
You would in person land in Cornwall,
    where
Thousands will entertain your title
    gladly.
WAR. Let me embrace thee, hug thee.
    Th'ast revived
My comforts; if my cousin king will fail,
Our cause will never.—Welcome, my tried
    friends!   50

Enter Major, Heron, Astley, Sketon.

You keep your brains awake in our
    defense.
Frion, advise with them of these affairs,
In which be wondrous secret; I will listen
What else concerns us here. Be quick
    and wary.   *Ex[it] Warbeck.*
AST. Ah, sweet young prince!—Secretary, my fellow counselors and I have consulted, and jump[5] all in one opinion
directly: that, if this Scotch garboils[6] do
not fadge[7] to our minds, we will pell-mell
run amongst the Cornish choughs[8] [60
presently and in a trice.
SKE. 'Tis but going to sea and, leaping
ashore, cut ten or twelve thousand unnecessary throats, fire seven or eight
towns, take half a dozen cities, get into the
market place, crown him Richard the
Fourth, and the business is finished.
MAJ. I grant ye, quoth I, so far forth
as men may do, no more than men may

---

[1] Contrivances.   [3] Was worthy of.
[2] Copartnership.

[4] Bring together.   [6] Tumults.   [8] Crows.
[5] Agree.   [7] Succeed.

do. For it is good to consider when [70
consideration may be to the purpose;
otherwise—still you shall pardon me—
little said is soon amended.

FRI. Then you conclude the Cornish
action surest?

HER. We do so, and doubt not but to
thrive abundantly. Ho, my masters, had
we known of the commotion when we set
sail out of Ireland, the land had been ours
ere this time.   80

SKE. Pish, pish! 'Tis but forbearing
being an earl or a duke a month or two
longer. I say, and say it again, if the work
go not on apace, let me never see new
fashion more. I warrant ye, I warrant ye;
we will have it so, and so it shall be.

AST. This is but a cold, phlegmatic
country, not stirring enough for men of
spirit. Give me the heart of England for
my money!   90

SKE. A man may batten there in a week
only, with hot loaves and butter, and a
lusty cup of muscadine [1] and sugar at
breakfast, though he make never a meal
all the month after.

MAJ. Surely, when I bore office, I found
by experience that to be much troublesome was to be much wise and busy. I
have observed how filching and bragging has
been the best service in these last [100
wars, and therefore conclude peremptorily
on the design in England. If things and
things may fall out, as who can tell what
or how—but the end will show it.

FRI. Resolved like men of judgment.
    Here to linger [2]
More time is but to lose it. Cheer the
    prince
And haste him on to this; on this de-
    pends
Fame in success, or glory in our ends.
                            Exeunt omnes.

[SCENA TERTIA.

Another part of the same.]

*Enter King James, Durham, and Hialas on
                            either side.*

HIAL. France, Spain, and Germany com-
    bine a league
Of amity with England. Nothing wants

For settling peace through Christen-
    dom but love
Between the British monarchs, James
    and Henry.

DUR. The English merchants, sir, have
    been received
With general procession into Antwerp;
The emperor confirms the combination.

HIAL. The King of Spain resolves a
    marriage
For Katherine his daughter with Prince
    Arthur.

DUR. France courts this holy contract.

HIAL.   What can hinder 10
A quietness in England—

DUR.   But your suffrage
To such a silly creature, mighty sir,
As is but in effect an apparition,
A shadow, a mere trifle?

HIAL.   To this union
The good of both the church and com-
    monwealth
Invite 'e—

DUR.   To this unity, a mystery
Of providence points out a greater
    blessing
For both these nations than our human
    reason
Can search into. King Henry hath a
    daughter,
The Princess Margaret; I need not
    urge   20
What honor, what felicity can follow
On such affinity twixt two Christian
    kings
Inleagued by ties of blood. But sure I
    am,
If you, sir, ratify the peace proposed,
I dare both motion [3] and effect this mar-
    riage
For weal of both the kingdoms.

K. JA.   Dar'st thou, Lord Bishop?

DUR. Put it to trial, royal James, by
    sending
Some noble personage to the English
    court
By way of embassy.

HIAL.   Part of the business
Shall suit my mediation.

K. JA.   Well; what heaven 30
Hath pointed out to be, must be. You
    two
Are ministers, I hope, of blessed fate.

[1] A sweet wine.   [2] Delay.   [3] Move, propose.

But herein only I will stand acquitted—
No blood of innocents shall buy my
  peace.
For Warbeck, as you nick [1] him, came to
  me
Commended by the states of Christen-
  dom,
A prince, though in distress. His fair
  demeanor,
Lovely behavior, unappalléd spirit,
Spoke him not base in blood, however
  clouded.
The brute beasts have both rocks and
  caves to fly to,   40
And men the altars of the church; to
  us
He came for refuge. "Kings come near
  in nature
Unto the gods in being touched with
  pity."
Yet, noble friends, his mixture with our
  blood,
Even with our own, shall no way inter-
  rupt
A general peace. Only I will dismiss
  him
From my protection, throughout my
  dominions
In safety, but not ever to return.
HIAL. You are a just king.
DUR.   Wise, and herein happy.
K. JA. Nor will we dally in affairs of
  weight.   50
Huntley, lord bishop, shall with you to
  England
Ambassador from us. We will throw
  down
Our weapons. Peace on all sides now.
  Repair
Unto our council; we will soon be with
  you.
HIAL. Delay shall question no despatch;
  heaven crown it.
          Exeunt Durham and Hialas.
K. JA. A league with Ferdinand? A mar-
  riage
With English Margaret? A free re-
  lease
From restitution for the late affronts?
Cessation from hostility? And all
For Warbeck, not delivered, but dis-
  missed.   60
We could not wish it better.—Daliell!

[1] Nickname.

          Enter Daliell.

DAL.   Here, sir.
K. JA. Are Huntley and his daughter sent
  for?
DAL.   Sent for
And come, my lord.
K. JA.   Say to the English prince
We want his company.
DAL.   He is at hand, sir.

*Enter Warbeck, Katherine, Jane, Frion,
     Heron, Sketon, Major, Astley.*

K. JA. Cousin, our bounty, favors, gentle-
  ness,
Our benefits, the hazard of our person,
Our people's lives, our land hath evi-
  denced
How much we have engaged on your
  behalf.
How trivial and how dangerous our
  hopes
Appear, how fruitless our attempts in
  war,   70
How windy, rather smoky, your assur-
  ance
Of party [2] shows, we might in vain
  repeat!
But now obedience to the mother church,
A father's care upon his country's weal,
The dignity of state, directs our wis-
  dom
To seal an oath of peace through Chris-
  tendom,
To which we are sworn already. 'Tis
  you
Must only seek new fortunes in the
  world,
And find an harbor elsewhere. As I
  promised   79
On your arrival, you have met no usage
Deserves repentance in your being here;
But yet I must live master of mine own.
However, what is necessary for you
At your departure, I am well content
You be accommodated with, provided
Delay prove not my enemy.
WAR.   It shall not,
Most glorious prince. The fame of my
  designs
Soars higher than report of ease and
  sloth
Can aim at. I acknowledge all your
  favors

[2] Support.

Boundless and singular, am only
wretched   90
In words as well as means to thank the
grace
That flowed so liberally. Two empires
firmly
You're lord of—Scotland and Duke
Richard's heart.
My claim to mine inheritance shall
sooner
Fail than my life to serve you, best of
kings.
And, witness Edward's blood in me, I am
More loath to part with such a great
example
Of virtue than all other mere respects.
But, sir, my last suit is, you will not
force
From me what you have given—this
chaste lady,   100
Resolved on all extremes.[1]

KATH.   I am your wife;
No human power can or shall divorce
My faith from duty.

WAR.   Such another treasure
The earth is bankrout of.

K. JA.   I gave her, cousin,
And must avow the gift, will add withal
A furniture [2] becoming her high birth
And unsuspected [3] constancy, provide
For your attendance. We will part good
friends.   *Exeunt [4] King and Daliell.*

WAR. The Tudor hath been cunning in
his plots.   109
His Fox of Durham would not fail at last.
But what! Our cause and courage are
our own.
Be men, my friends, and let our cousin
king
See how we follow fate as willingly
As malice follows us. Y' are all resolved
For the west parts of England?

OMNES.   Cornwall, Cornwall!

FRI. The inhabitants expect you daily.

WAR.   Cheerfully
Draw all our ships out of the harbor,
friends;
Our time of stay doth seem too long.
We must
Prevent [5] intelligence. About it sud-
denly!

---

[1] Extremities.
[2] Portion.
[3] Not distrusted.
[4] Original reads *Exit.*
[5] Forestall.

OMNES. A prince, a prince, a prince!   120
Exeunt Counselors.

WAR. Dearest, admit not into thy pure
thoughts
The least of scruples, which may charge
their softness
With burden of distrust. Should I prove
wanting
To noblest courage now, here were the
trial.
But I am perfect, sweet; I fear no change
More than thy being partner in my
sufferance.

KATH. My fortunes, sir, have armed me
to encounter
What chance soe'er they meet with —
Jane, 'tis fit
Thou stay behind, for whither wilt thou
wander?

JANE. Never till death will I forsake my
mistress,   130
Nor then, in wishing to die with 'e
gladly.

KATH. Alas, good soul!

FRI.   Sir, to your aunt of Burgundy
I will relate your present undertakings.
From her expect on all occasions wel-
come.
You cannot find me idle in your services.

WAR. Go, Frion, go! Wise men know how
to soothe
Adversity, not serve it. Thou hast
waited
Too long on expectation. "Never yet
Was any nation read of so besotted
In reason as to adore the setting sun."
Fly to the archduke's court; say to the
duchess   141
Her nephew, with fair Katherine his
wife,
Are on their expectation to begin
The raising of an empire. If they fail,
Yet the report will never. Farewell,
Frion.—   *Exit Frion.*
This man, Kate, has been true, though
now of late
I fear too much familiar with the Fox.

Enter Huntley and Daliell.

HUNT. I come to take my leave. You need
not doubt
My interest in this sometime child of
mine.

She's all yours now, good sir. O, poor
   lost creature,   150
Heaven guard thee with much patience!
   If thou canst
Forget thy title to old Huntley's family,
As much of peace will settle in thy mind
As thou canst wish to taste but in thy
   grave.
Accept my tears yet, prithee; they are
   tokens
Of charity as true as of affection.

KATH. This is the cruel'st farewell!

HUNT.   Love, young gentleman,
This model of my griefs. She calls you
   husband.
Then be not jealous of a parting kiss;
It is a father's, not a lover's offering.   160
Take it, my last.—[*Kisses her.*] I am too
   much a child.
Exchange of passion is to little use;
So [1] I should grow too foolish. Goodness
   guide thee!   *Exit Hunt[ley].*

KATH. Most miserable daughter!—Have
   you aught
To add, sir, to our sorrows?

DAL.   I resolve,
Fair lady, with your leave, to wait on all
Your fortunes in my person, if your lord
Vouchsafe me entertainment.

WAR. We will be bosom friends, most
   noble Daliell,
For I accept this tender of your love   170
Beyond ability of thanks to speak it.
Clear thy drowned eyes, my fairest;
   time and industry
Will show us better days, or end the
   worst.   *Exeunt omnes.*

[SCENA QUARTA.

The presence chamber at Westminster.]

Enter Oxford and Dawbney.

OX. No news from Scotland yet, my lord?

DAW.   Not any
But what King Henry knows himself. I
   thought
Our armies should have marched that
   way; his mind,
It seems, is altered.

OX.   Victory attends
His standard everywhere.

DAW.   Wise princes, Oxford,
Fight not alone with forces. Providence

[1] Thus.

Directs and tutors strength; else ele-
   phants
And barbéd [2] horses might as well prevail
As the most subtile stratagems of war.

OX. The Scottish king showed more than
   common bravery   10
In proffer of a combat hand to hand
With Surrey.

DAW.   And but showed it. Northern bloods
Are gallant, being fired, but the cold
   climate,
Without good store of fuel, quickly
   freezeth
The glowing flames.

OX.   Surrey, upon my life,
Would not have shrunk an hair's
   breadth.

DAW.   May a forfeit
The honor of an English name and
   nature,
Who would not have embraced it with a
   greediness
As violent as hunger runs to food!   19
'Twas an addition [3] any worthy spirit
Would covet, next to immortality,
Above all joys of life. We all missed
   shares
In that great opportunity.

Enter King Henry and Urswick, whispering.

OX.   The king!
See, a comes smiling.

DAW.   O, the game runs smooth
On his side, then, believe it. Cards, well
   shuffled
And dealt with cunning, bring some
   gamester thrift,
But others must rise losers.

KING.   The train [4] takes?

URS. Most prosperously.

KING.   I knew it should not miss.
He fondly [5] angles who will hurl his bait
Into the water cause the fish at first   30
Plays round about the line and dares not
   bite.
Lords, we may reign your king yet.
   Dawbney, Oxford,
Urswick, must Perkin wear the crown?

DAW.   A slave!

OX. A vagabond!

[2] Barded, armored.   [4] Plot.
[3] Honor.   [5] Foolishly

URS. A glowworm!

KING. Now, if Frion,
His practiced politician, wear a brain
Of proof, King Perkin will in progress ride
Through all his large dominions. Let us
  meet him,
And tender homage. Ha, sirs? Liegemen
  ought
To pay their fealty.

DAW. Would the rascal were, 39
With all his rabble, within twenty miles
Of London.

KING. Farther off is near enough
To lodge him in his home. I'll wager odds
Surrey and all his men are either idle
Or hasting back. They have not work, I
  doubt,
To keep them busy.

DAW. 'Tis a strange conceit, sir.

KING. Such voluntary favors as our people
In duty aid us with, we never scattered
On cobweb parasites, or lavished out
In riot or a needless hospitality.
No undeserving favorite doth boast 50
His issues [1] from our treasury; our charge
Flows through all Europe, proving us but
  steward
Of every contribution which provides
Against the creeping canker of disturb-
  ance.
Is it not rare, then, in this toil of state
Wherein we are embarked, with breach
  of sleep,
Cares, and the noise of trouble, that our
  mercy
Returns nor thanks nor comfort? Still
  the west
Murmur and threaten innovation,[2]
Whisper our government tyrannical, 60
Deny us what is ours, nay, spurn their
  lives,
Of which they are but owners by our gift.
It must not be.

Ox. It must not, should not.

Enter a Post.[3]

KING. So then—
To whom?

POST. This packet to your sacred
  majesty.

KING. Sirrah, attend without. [*Exit Post.*]

Ox. News from the north, upon my life.

DAW. Wise Henry
Divines aforehand of events; with him
Attempts and execution are one act.

KING. Urswick, thine ear: Frion is caught;
  the man
Of cunning is outreached. We must be
  safe. 70
Should reverend Morton, our archbishop,
  move
To a translation higher yet,[4] I tell thee
My Durham owns a brain deserves that
  see.[5]
He's nimble in his industry, and mount-
  ing.[6]
Thou hear'st me?

URS. And conceive your highness fitly.

KING. Dawbney and Oxford, since our
  army stands
Entire, it were a weakness to admit
The rust of laziness to eat amongst them.
Set forward toward Salisbury; the plains
Are most commodious for their exer-
  cise. 80
Ourself will take a muster of them there,
And or disband them with reward or else
Dispose as best concerns us.

DAW. Salisbury?
Sir, all is peace at Salisbury.

KING. Dear friend,
The charge must be our own; we would a
  little
Partake the pleasure with our subjects'
  ease.—
Shall I entreat your loves?

Ox. Command our lives.

KING. Y' are men know how to do, not to
  forethink.
My bishop is a jewel tried and perfect;
A jewel, lords. The post who brought
  these letters 90
Must speed another to the Mayor of
  Exeter.
Urswick, dismiss him not.

URS. He waits your pleasure.

KING. Perkin a king? A king?

URS. My gracious lord.

KING. Thoughts busied in the sphere of
  royalty
Fix not on creeping worms, without their
  stings

---

[1] Monetary grants. [2] Revolution.
[3] This stage direction follows the King's speech
in the original.
[4] *I.e.*, die. [6] Ambitious.
[5] *I.e.*, of Canterbury.

Mere excrements of earth. The use of
  time
Is thriving safety and a wise prevention
Of ills expected. W' are resolved for Salisbury.   *Exe[unt] omnes.*

[SCENA QUINTA.

The coast of Cornwall.]

*A general shout within.   Enter Warbeck,
    Daliell, Katherine, and Jane.*

WAR. After so many storms as wind and
  seas
Have threatened to our weather-beaten
  ships,
At last, sweet fairest, we are safe arrived
On our dear mother earth, ingrateful only
To heaven and us in yielding sustenance
To sly usurpers of our throne and right.
These general acclamations are an omen
Of happy process [1] to their welcome lord.
They flock in troops, and from all parts
  with wings   9
Of duty fly to lay their hearts before us.
Unequaled pattern of a matchless wife,
How fares my dearest yet?
KATH.   Confirmed in health,
By which I may the better undergo
The roughest face of change; but I shall
  learn
Patience to hope, since silence courts
  affliction
For comforts, to this truly noble gentle-
  man,
Rare unexampled pattern of a friend,
And my beloved Jane, the willing fol-
  lower
Of all misfortunes.
DAL.   Lady, I return   19
But barren crops of early protestations,
Frost-bitten in the spring of fruitless
  hopes.
JANE. I wait but as the shadow to the
  body;
For, madam, without you, let me be
  nothing.
WAR. None talk of sadness; we are on the
  way
Which leads to victory. Keep cowards'
  thoughts
With desperate sullenness.   The lion
  faints not,

----

[1] Progress.

Locked in a grate,[2] but loose disdains all
  force
Which bars his prey—and we are lion-
  hearted—
Or else no king of beasts. (*Another shout
  [within].*) Hark, how they shout,
Triumphant in our cause! Bold confidence   30
Marches on bravely, cannot quake at
  danger.

Enter Sketon.

SKE. Save King Richard the Fourth!
Save thee, king of hearts! The Cornish
blades are men of mettle, have proclaimed,
through Bodnam and the whole county,
my sweet prince monarch of England. Four
thousand tall yeomen, with bow and sword,
already vow to live and die at the foot of
King Richard.

Enter Astley.

AST. The mayor, our fellow coun-   [40
selor, is servant for an emperor. Exeter is
appointed for the rendezvous, and nothing
wants to victory but courage and resolution. *Sigillatum et datum decimo Septem-
bris, anno regni regis primo, et cætera; con-
firmatum est.*[3] All's cocksure.[4]
WAR. To Exeter! To Exeter, march on!
Commend us to our people. We in person
Will lend them double spirits; tell them
  so.
SKE. AND AST.   King Richard!   King
  Richard!   50
WAR. A thousand blessings guard our law-
  ful arms!
A thousand horrors pierce our enemies'
  souls!
Pale fear unedge their weapons' sharpest
  points
And, when they draw their arrows to the
  head,
Numbness shall strike their sinews! Such
  advantage
Hath majesty in its pursuit of justice
That on the proppers-up of Truth's old
  throne
It both enlightens counsel and gives heart

----

[2] Cage.
[3] Sealed and dated on the tenth of September, in the first year of the king's reign, etc.
Confirmed.   [4] Perfectly safe.

To execution, whiles [1] the throats of
   traitors
Lie bare before our mercy. O, divin-
   ity   60
Of royal birth! How it strikes dumb the
   tongues
Whose prodigality of breath is bribed
By trains to greatness! Princes are but
   men
Distinguished in the fineness of their
   frailty,
Yet not so gross in beauty of the mind,
For there's a fire more sacred purifies
The dross of mixture. Herein stand the
   odds:
"Subjects are men on earth; kings, men
   and gods."   *Exeunt omnes.*

ACTUS QUINTUS. SCENA PRIMA.

[*St. Michael's Mount, Cornwall.*]

Enter Katherine and Jane in riding suits,
*   with one Servant.*

KATH. It is decreed; and we must yield to
   fate,
Whose angry justice, though it threaten
   ruin,
Contempt, and poverty, is all but trial
Of a weak woman's constancy in suffer-
   ing.
Here, in a stranger's and an enemy's
   land,
Forsaken and unfurnished of all hopes
But such as wait on misery, I range
To meet affliction wheresoe'er I tread.
My train and pomp of servants is reduced
To one kind gentlewoman and this
   groom.   10
Sweet Jane, now whither must we?
JANE.   To your ships,
Dear lady, and turn home.
KATH.   Home! I have none.
Fly thou to Scotland; thou hast friends
   will weep
For joy to bid thee welcome. But, O,
   Jane,
My Jane, my friends are desperate of
   comfort,
As I must be of them. The common
   charity,
Good people's alms and prayers of the
   gentle,

[1] While

Is the revenue must support my state.
As for my native country, since it once
Saw me a princess in the height of great-
   ness   20
My birth allowed me, here I make a vow
Scotland shall never see me, being fallen
Or lessened in my fortunes. Never, Jane,
Never to Scotland more will I return.
Could I be England's queen—a glory,
   Jane,
I never fawned on—yet the king who
   gave me
Hath sent me with my husband from his
   presence,
Delivered us suspected to his [2] nation,
Rendered us spectacles to time and pity.
And is it fit I should return to such   30
As only listen after our descent
From happiness enjoyed, to misery
Expected, though uncertain? Never,
   never!
Alas, why dost thou weep, and that poor
   creature
Wipe his wet cheeks too? Let me feel
   alone
Extremities, who know [3] to give them
   harbor.
Nor thou nor he has cause. You may
   live safely.
JANE. There is no safety whiles your dan-
   gers, madam,
Are every way apparent.
SERV.   Pardon, lady
I cannot choose but show my honest
   heart—   40
You were ever my good lady.
KATH.   O, dear souls,
Your shares in grief are too-too much!

Enter Daliell.

DAL.   I bring,
Fair princess, news of further sadness yet
Than your sweet youth hath been ac-
   quainted with.
KATH. Not more, my lord, than I can
   welcome. Speak it;
The worst, the worst I look for.
DAL.   All the Cornish
At Exeter were by the citizens
Repulsed, encountered by the Earl of
   Devonshire
And other worthy gentlemen of the coun-
   try.

[2] Perkin's.   [3] Know how.

Your husband marched to Taunton, and
　　was there　　　　　　　　　　　50
Affronted [1] by King Henry's chamber-
　　lain,
The king himself in person with his army
Advancing nearer to renew the fight
On all occasions. But the night before
The battles [2] were to join, your husband
　　privately,
Accompanied with some few horse, de-
　　parted
From out the camp, and posted none
　　knows whither.

KATH. Fled without battle given?

DAL. 　　　　　　　　　Fled, but followed
By Dawbney, all his parties [3] left to taste
King Henry's mercy—for to that they
　　yielded—　　　　　　　　　　60
Victorious without bloodshed.

KATH. 　　　　　　　　　O, my sorrows!
If both our lives had proved the sacrifice
To Henry's tyranny, we had fallen like
　　princes,
And robbed him of the glory of his pride.

DAL. Impute it not to faintness or to
　　weakness
Of noble courage, lady, but foresight;
For by some secret friend he had in-
　　telligence
Of being bought and sold by his base fol-
　　lowers.
Worse yet remains untold.

KATH. 　　　　　　　　　No, no, it cannot.

DAL. I fear y' are betrayed: the Earl of
　　Oxford　　　　　　　　　　　70
Runs hot in your pursuit.

KATH. 　　　　　　　　　A shall not need;
We'll run as hot in resolution gladly
To make the earl our jailor.

JANE. 　　　　　　　　　Madam, madam,
They come, they come!

Enter Oxford with Followers.

DAL. 　　Keep back! Or he who dares
Rudely to violate the law of honor
Runs on my sword.

KATH. 　　　　　　　Most noble sir, forbear.
What reason draws you hither, gentle-
　　men?
Whom seek 'e?

OX. 　　All stand off!—With favor, lady,
From Henry, England's king, I would
　　present

---

[1] Confronted.　　　[2] Armies.　　　[3] Allies.

Unto the beauteous princess, Katherine
　　Gordon,　　　　　　　　　　80
The tender of a gracious entertainment.

KATH. We are that princess, whom your
　　master king
Pursues with reaching arms to draw into
His power. Let him use his tyranny;
We shall not be his subjects.

OX. 　　　　　　　　　My commission
Extends no further, excellentest lady,
Than to a service; 'tis King Henry's
　　pleasure
That you, and all that have relation t'e,
Be guarded as becomes your birth and
　　greatness,
For, rest assured, sweet princess, that
　　not aught　　　　　　　　　　90
Of what you do call yours shall find dis-
　　turbance,
Or any welcome other than what suits
Your high condition.

KATH. 　　　　　　　　　By what title, sir,
May I acknowledge you?

OX. 　　　　　　　　　Your servant, lady,
Descended from the line of Oxford's earls,
Inherits what his ancestors before him
Were owners of.

KATH. 　　　　　　Your king is herein royal,
That by a peer so ancient in desert
As well as blood commands us to his
　　presence.

OX. Invites 'e, princess, not commands.

KATH. 　　　　　　　　　Pray, use　100
Your own phrase as you list. To your
　　protection
Both I and mine submit.

OX. 　　　　　　　　　There's in your number
A nobleman whom fame hath bravely
　　spoken.
To him the king my master bade me
　　say
How willingly he courts his friendship; far
From an enforcement, more than what in
　　terms
Of courtesy so great a prince may hope
　　for.

DAL. My name is Daliell.

OX. 　　　　　　　　　'Tis a name hath won
Both thanks and wonder from report, my
　　lord.
The court of England emulates your
　　merit,　　　　　　　　　　110
And covets to embrace 'e.

DAL.   I must wait on
The princess in her fortunes.

OX.   Will you please,
Great lady, to set forward?

KATH.   Being driven
By fate, it were in vain to strive with
    heaven.   *Exeunt omnes.*

[SCENA SECUNDA.

Salisbury.]

*Enter King Henry, Surrey, Urswick, and a
                        guard of Soldiers.*

KING. The counterfeit, King Perkin, is
    escaped—
Escape, so let him; he is hedged too fast
Within the circuit of our English pale
To steal out of our ports, or leap the walls
Which guard our land. The seas are
    rough and wider
Than his weak arms can tug with.—Sur-
    rey, henceforth
Your king may reign in quiet; turmoils
    past,
Like some unquiet dream, have rather
    busied
Our fancy than affrighted rest of state.
But, Surrey, why, in articling a peace   10
With James of Scotland, was not restitu-
    tion
Of losses which our subjects did sustain
By the Scotch inroads questioned?

SUR.   Both demanded
And urged, my lord, to which the king
    replied,
In modest merriment, but smiling ear-
    nest,
How that our master Henry was much
    abler
To bear the detriments than he repay
    them.

KING. The young man, I believe, spake
    honest truth;
A studies to be wise betimes.[1]—Has, Urs-
    wick,
Sir Rice ap Thomas and Lord Brooke our
    steward   20
Returned the Western gentlemen full
    thanks
From us for their tried loyalties?

URS.[2]   They have—

Which, as if health and life had reigned
    amongst 'em,
With open hearts they joyfully received.

KING. Young Buckingham is a fair-
    natured prince,
Lovely in hopes, and worthy of his
    father.
Attended by an hundred knights and
    squires
Of special name, he tendered humble
    service,
Which we must ne'er forget; and Devon-
    shire's wounds,
Though slight, shall find sound cure in
    our respect.[3]   30

Enter Dawbney with [*a Guard, conducting*]
    *Warbeck, Heron, John a Water, Astley,
                        Sketon.*

DAW. Life to the king, and safety fix his
    throne!
I here present you, royal sir, a shadow
Of majesty, but in effect a substance
Of pity—a young man, in nothing grown
To ripeness but th' ambition of your
    mercy,
Perkin, the Christian world's strange
    wonder.

KING.   Dawbney,
We observe no wonder. I behold, 'tis
    true,
An ornament of nature, fine and polished,
A handsome youth indeed, but not ad-
    mire [4] him.
How came he to thy hands?

DAW.   From sanctuary   40
At Bewley, near Southampton, regis-
    tered,
With these few followers, for persons
    privileged.

KING. I must not thank you, sir; you were
    to blame
To infringe the liberty of houses sacred.
Dare we be irreligious?

DAW.   Gracious lord,
They voluntarily resigned themselves
Without compulsion.

KING.   So? 'Twas very well;
'Twas very, very well.—Turn now thine
    eyes,
Young man, upon thyself and thy past
    actions.

---

[1] Early.
[2] Suggested by Weber. Original has *Sur.*

[3] In respect to us, at our hands.
[4] Wonder at.

What revels in combustion through our
   kingdom   50
A frenzy of aspiring youth hath danced,
Till, wanting breath, thy feet of pride
   have slipped
To break thy neck!
WAR.   But not my heart; my heart
   Will mount till every drop of blood be
   frozen
By death's perpetual winter. If the sun
Of majesty be darkened, let the sun
Of life be hid from me in an eclipse
Lasting and universal. Sir, remember
There was a shooting in of light when
   Richmond,
Not aiming at a crown, retired, and
   gladly,   60
For comfort to the Duke of Britain's [1]
   court.
Richard, who swayed the scepter, was re-
   puted
A tyrant then; yet then a dawning glim-
   mered
To some few wandering remnants, prom-
   ising day
When first they ventured on a frightful
   shore
At Milford Haven—
DAW.   Whither speeds his boldness?
   Check his rude tongue, great sir.
KING.   O, let him range.
   The player's on the stage still; 'tis his part;
A does but act.—What followed?
WAR.   Bosworth Field,
   Where, at an instant, to the world's
   amazement,   70
A morn to Richmond and a night to
   Richard
Appeared at once. The tale is soon
   applied:
Fate, which crowned these attempts
   when least assured,
Might have befriended others like re-
   solved.
KING. A pretty gallant! Thus your aunt
   of Burgundy,
Your   duchess-aunt,   informed   her
   nephew; so
The lesson, prompted and well conned,
   was molded
Into familiar dialogue, oft rehearsed,
Till, learnt by heart, 'tis now received for
   truth.

[1] Bretagne's.

WAR. Truth, in her pure simplicity, wants
   art   80
To put a feignéd blush on. Scorn wears
   only
Such fashion as commends to gazers' eyes
Sad ulcerated novelty, far beneath
The sphere of majesty. In such a court
Wisdom and gravity are proper robes,
By which the sovereign is best distin-
   guished
From zanies [2] to his greatness.
KING.   Sirrah, shift
   Your antic [3] pageantry, and now appear
In your own nature, or you'll taste the
   danger
Of fooling out of season.
WAR.   I expect 90
   No less than what severity calls justice,
And politicians safety. Let such beg
As feed on alms, but, if there can be
   mercy
In a protested enemy, then may it
Descend to these poor creatures, whose
   engagements,
To th' bettering of their fortunes, have
   incurred
A loss of all. To them if any charity
Flow from some noble orator, in death
I owe the fee of thankfulness.
KING.   So brave!
   What a bold knave is this!—Which of
   these rebels   100
Has been the Mayor of Cork?
DAW.   This wise formality.
   Kneel to the king, 'e rascals!
KING.   Canst thou hope
   A pardon where thy guilt is so apparent?
MAYOR. Under your good favors, as men
are men, they may err; for I confess, re-
spectively, in taking great parts, the one
side prevailing, the other side must go
down. Herein the point is clear, if the
proverb hold, that hanging goes by destiny,
that it is to little purpose to say this [110
thing or that shall be thus or thus; for, as
the Fates will have it, so it must be; and
who can help it?
DAW. O, blockhead! Thou a privy-coun-
   selor?
   Beg life, and cry aloud, "Heaven save
   King Henry!"
MAYOR. Every man knows what is best,
as it happens; for my own part, I believe it

[2] Clownish imitators.   [3] Fantastic, fanciful.

is true, if I be not deceived, that kings must
be kings and subjects subjects; but which
is which, you shall pardon me for that. [120
Whether we speak or hold our peace, all are
mortal; no man knows his end.

KING. We trifle time with follies.

OMNES.　　　　　　　　　　Mercy, mercy!

KING. Urswick, command the dukeling
and these fellows

　To Digby, the lieftenant [1] of the Tower;
　With safety let them be conveyed to
　　London.
　It is our pleasure no uncivil outrage,
　Taunts, or abuse be suffered to their
　　persons;
　They shall meet fairer law than they de-
　　serve.
　Time may restore their wits, whom vain
　　ambition　　　　　　　　　　　　130
　Hath many years distracted.

WAR.　　　　　　　　　　Noble thoughts
　Meet freedom in captivity. The Tower?
　Our childhood's dreadful nursery!

KING.　　　　　　　　　　　　No more.

URS. Come, come, you shall have leisure
　to bethink 'e.

Exit Ursw[ick] with Perkin and his [Follow-
　　　　　　　　　　　　　　　　ers].

KING. Was ever so much impudence in
　forgery?
　The custom, sure, of being styled a king
　Hath fastened in his thought that he is
　　such;
　But we shall teach the lad another lan-
　　guage.
　'Tis good we have him fast.

DAW.　　　　　　　The hangman's physic
　Will purge this saucy humor.

KING.　　　　　　　　　Very likely;　140
　Yet we could temper mercy with ex-
　　tremity,
　Being not too far provoked.

Enter Oxford, Katherine in her richest attire,
　　　　　[*Daliell,*] *Jane, and Attendants.*

OX.　　　　　　　　　Great sir, be pleased,
　With your accustomed grace to enter-
　　tain
　The Princess Katherine Gordon.

KING.　　　　　　　　　Oxford, herein
　We must beshrew [2] thy knowledge of our
　　nature.

　[1] Lieutenant.　　　　　　　　[2] Deprecate.

A lady of her birth and virtues could not
Have found us so unfurnished of good
　manners
As not, on notice given, to have met her
Half way in point of love.—Excuse, fair
　cousin,
The oversight. O, fie! You may not
　kneel;　　　　　　　　　　　　150
'Tis most unfitting. First, vouchsafe this
　welcome,
A welcome to your own, for you shall
　find us
But guardian to your fortune and your
　honors.

KATH. My fortunes and mine honors are
　weak champions,
　As both are now befriended, sir. How-
　　ever,
　Both bow before your clemency.

KING.　　　　　　　　　　Our arms
Shall circle them from malice.—A sweet
　lady!
Beauty incomparable!—Here lives maj-
　esty
At league with love.

KATH.　　　　　O, sir, I have a husband.

KING. We'll prove your father, husband,
　friend, and servant.　　　　　　160
　Prove what you wish to grant us.—
　　Lords, be careful
　A patent presently be drawn for issuing
　A thousand pounds from our exchequer
　　yearly
　During our cousin's life.—Our queen
　　shall be
　Your chief companion, our own court
　　your home,
　Our subjects all your servants.

KATH.　　　　　　　But my husband?

KING. [*To Daliell.*] By all descriptions,
　you are noble Daliell,
　Whose generous truth hath famed a rare
　　observance.
　We thank 'e; 'tis a goodness gives addi-
　　tion
　To every title boasted from your an-
　　cestry,　　　　　　　　　　　170
　In all most worthy.

DAL.　　　　　Worthier than your praises,
　Right princely sir, I need not glory in.

KING. Embrace him, lords.—[*To Kath-
　erine.*] Whoever calls you mistress
　Is lifted in our charge. A goodlier beauty
　Mine eyes yet ne'er encountered.

KATH.　　　　　　　　　　Cruel misery
　　Of fate! What rests [1] to hope for?
KING.　　　　　　　　　Forward, lords,
　　To London.—Fair, ere long I shall pre-
　　sent 'e
　　With a glad object, peace, and Huntley's
　　blessing.　　　　　　*Exeunt omnes.*

　　　　　　　[SCENA TERTIA.

　　　　The Tower Hill, London.]

*Enter Constable and Officers; Warbeck,
　Urswick, and Lambert Simnel like a
　falconer [, followed by a Mob]. A pair
　　　　　　　　　　　　　of stocks.*

CONST. Make room there! Keep off,
　I require 'e; and none come within twelve
　foot of his majesty's new stocks, upon
　pain of displeasure.—Bring forward the
　malefactors.—Friend, you must to this
　gear [2]—no remedy.—Open the hole, and
　in with his legs, just in the middle hole;
　there, that hole.—[*Warbeck is put in the
　stocks.*] Keep off, or I'll commit you all.
　Shall not a man in authority be　[10
　obeyed?—So, so, there; 'tis as it should be.
　Put on the padlock, and give me the key.—
　Off, I say, keep off!
URS. Yet, Warbeck, clear thy conscience.
　　Thou hast tasted
　King Henry's mercy liberally; the law
　Has forfeited thy life; an equal [3] jury
　Have doomed thee to the gallows, twice,
　　most wickedly,
　Most desperately, hast thou escaped
　　the Tower,
　Inveigling to thy party with thy witch-
　　craft
　Young Edward, Earl of Warwick, son
　　to Clarence,　　　　　　　　　20
　Whose head must pay the price of that
　　attempt.
　Poor gentleman, unhappy in his fate,
　And ruined by thy cunning! So a mon-
　　grel
　May pluck the true stag down. Yet,
　　yet confess
　Thy parentage; for yet the king has
　　mercy.
LAM. You would be Dick the Fourth;
　　very likely!
　Your pedigree is published; you are
　　known

For Osbeck's son of Tournay, a loose
　runagate,
A landloper; [4] your father was a Jew,
Turned Christian merely to repair his
　miseries.　　　　　　　　　　30
Where's now your kingship?
WAR.　　　　　　Baited to my death?
　Intolerable cruelty! I laugh at
　The Duke of Richmond's practice on
　my fortunes.
"Possession of a crown ne'er wanted
　heralds."
LAM. You will not know who I am?
URS.　　　　　　　Lambert Simnel,
　Your predecessor in a dangerous uproar,
　But, on submission, not alone received
　To grace, but by the king vouchsafed
　his service.
LAM. I would be Earl of Warwick, toiled
　and ruffled
Against my master, leaped to catch the
　moon,　　　　　　　　　　　　40
Vaunted my name Plantagenet, as you
　do;
An earl, forsooth, whenas in truth I
　was,
As you are, a mere rascal! Yet his maj-
　esty,
A prince composed of sweetness—heaven
　protect him!—
Forgave me all my villainies, reprived [5]
The sentence of a shameful end, ad-
　mitted
My surety [6] of obedience to his service;
And I am now his falconer, live plen-
　teously,
Eat from the king's purse, and enjoy
　the sweetness
Of liberty and favor, sleep securely.　50
And is not this, now, better than to
　buffet
The hangman's clutches, or to brave
　the cordage
Of a tough halter which will break your
　neck?
So, then, the gallant totters!—Prithee,
　Perkin,
Let my example lead thee; be no longer
A counterfeit. Confess and hope for
　pardon.
WAR. For pardon? Hold, my heart-
　strings, whiles contempt

---

[1] Remains.　　[2] Business.　　[3] Impartial.
[4] Vagabond.　　　　[6] Accepted my oath.
[5] Reprieved.

Of injuries, in scorn, may bid defiance
To this base man's foul language!—
Thou poor vermin,
How dar'st thou creep so near me? Thou
an earl?   60
Why, thou enjoy'st as much of happi-
ness
As all the swinge [1] of slight ambition
flew at.
A dunghill was thy cradle. So a puddle,
By virtue of the sunbeams, breathes
a vapor
To infect the purer air, which drops
again
Into the muddy womb that first ex-
haled it.
Bread and a slavish ease, with some as-
surance
From the base beadle's whip, crowned
all thy hopes.
But, sirrah, ran there in thy veins one
drop   69
Of such a royal blood as flows in mine,
Thou wouldst not change condition to
be second
In England's state, without the crown
itself.
Coarse creatures are incapable of ex-
cellence.
But let the world, as all to whom I am
This day a spectacle, to time deliver,[2]
And by tradition fix [3] posterity,
Without another chronicle than truth,
How constantly my resolution suffered
A martyrdom of majesty.
LAM.   He's past
Recovery; a Bedlam cannot cure him. 80
URS. Away, inform the king of his be-
havior.
LAM. Perkin, beware the rope!   The
hangman's coming.
URS. If yet thou hast no pity of thy
body,
Pity thy soul!   *Exit Simnel.*

Enter Katherine, Jane, Daliell, and Ox-
                                ford.

JANE.   Dear lady!
OX.   Whither will 'e,
Without respect of shame?
KATH.   Forbear me,[4] sir,

And trouble not the current of my
duty.—
O, my loved lord! Can any scorn be
yours
In which I have no interest?—Some
kind hand
Lend me assistance that I may partake
Th' infliction of this penance.—My
life's dearest,   90
Forgive me. I have stayed too long from
tendering
Attendance on reproach; yet bid me
welcome.
WAR. Great miracle of constancy! My
miseries
Were never bankrout of their confi-
dence
In worst afflictions, till this. Now I feel
them.
Report and thy deserts, thou best of
creatures,
Might to eternity have stood a pattern
For every virtuous wife without this
conquest.
Thou hast outdone belief; yet may
their ruin
In after-marriages be never pitied, 100
To whom thy story shall appear a fable!
Why wouldst thou prove so much un-
kind to greatness
To glorify thy vows by such a servitude?
I cannot weep; but trust me, dear, my
heart
Is liberal of passion.—Harry Richmond,
A woman's faith hath robbed thy fame
of triumph!
OX. Sirrah, leave off your juggling, and
tie up
The devil that ranges in your tongue.
URS.   Thus witches,
Possessed, even [to] [5] their deaths de-
luded, say
They have been wolves and dogs, and
sailed in eggshells   110
Over the sea, and rid on fiery dragons,
Passed in the air more than a thousand
miles
All in a night. The enemy of mankind
Is powerful, but false; and falsehood
confident.
OX. Remember, lady, who you are; come
from
That impudent impostor.

---

[1] Sway.   [3] Assure.
[2] Proclaim.   [4] Let me alone.
                            [5] Supplied by Gifford-Dyce.

Kath. You abuse us,
For, when the holy churchman joined
    our hands,
Our vows were real then; the ceremony
Was not in apparition,[1] but in act.—
Be what these people term thee, I am
    certain   120
Thou art my husband; no divorce in
    heaven
Has been sued out between us; 'tis in-
    justice
For any earthly power to divide us.
Or we will live or let us die together.
There is a cruel mercy.
War.   Spite of tyranny
We reign in our affections, blessed
    woman!
Read in my destiny the wrack of honor;
Point out, in my contempt of death, to
    memory
Some miserable happiness, since herein,
Even when I fell, I stood enthroned a
    monarch   130
Of one chaste wife's troth, pure and
    uncorrupted.
Fair angel of perfection, immortality
Shall raise thy name up to an adora-
    tion,
Court every rich opinion of true merit,
And saint it in the calendar of Virtue,
When I am turned into the selfsame
    dust
Of which I was first formed.
Ox.   The Lord Ambassador
Huntley, your father, madam, should
    a look on
Your strange subjection in a gaze so
    public,
Would blush on your behalf, and wish
    his country   140
Unleft for entertainment to such sorrow.
Kath. Why art thou angry, Oxford? I
    must be
More peremptory in my duty. Sir,
Impute it not unto immodesty
That I presume to press you to[2] a
    legacy
Before we part forever.
War.   Let it be, then,
My heart, the rich remains of all my
    fortunes.
Kath. Confirm it with a kiss, pray.
War. [*Kissing her.*]   O, with that

I wish to breathe my last! Upon thy
    lips,
Those equal twins of comeliness, I
    seal   150
The testament of honorable vows.
Whoever be that man that shall un-
    kiss
This sacred print next, may he prove
    more thrifty
In this world's just applause, not more
    desertful!
Kath. By this sweet pledge of both our
    souls, I swear
To die a faithful widow to thy bed,
Not to be forced or won. O, never,
    never!

Enter Surrey, Dawbney, Huntley, and
        Crawford.

Daw. Free the condemnéd person;
    quickly free him!
What has a yet confessed?
    [*Warbeck is released from the stocks.*]
Urs.   Nothing to purpose;
But still a will be king.
Sur.   Prepare your journey 160
To a new kingdom, then.—Unhappy
    madam,
Willfully foolish!—See, my lord am-
    bassador,
Your lady daughter will not leave the
    counterfeit
In this disgrace of fate.
Hunt.   I never pointed[3]
Thy marriage, girl; but yet, being mar-
    ried,
Enjoy thy duty to a husband freely.
The griefs are mine. I glory in thy con-
    stancy,
And must not say I wished that I had
    missed
Some partage in these trials of a patience.
Kath. You will forgive me, noble sir?
Hunt.   Yes, yes; 170
In every duty of a wife and daughter
I dare not disavow thee. To your hus-
    band—
For such you are, sir—I impart a fare-
    well
Of manly pity. What your life has
    passed through,
The dangers of your end will make ap-
    parent.

---

[1] Appearance.   [2] For.

[3] Appointed.

And I can add, for comfort to your sufferance,
No cordial but the wonder of your
frailty,
Which keeps so firm a station. We are
parted.

WAR. We are. A crown of peace renew
thy age,
Most honorable Huntley.—Worthy
Crawford,   180
We may embrace; I never thought thee
injury.

CRAW. Nor was I ever guilty of neglect
Which might procure such thought. I
take my leave, sir.

WAR. To you, Lord Daliell—what? Accept a sigh;
'Tis hearty and in earnest.

DAL.   I want utterance.
My silence is my farewell.

KATH.   O, O!

JANE.   Sweet madam,
What do you mean?—[To Daliell.] My
lord, your hand.

DAL.   Dear lady,
Be pleased that I may wait [1] 'e to your
lodging.
                Exeunt Daliell, Katherine, Jane.

*Enter Sheriff and Officers, Sketon, Astley,
Heron, and Mayor, with halters about
their necks.*

Ox. Look 'e; behold your followers, appointed
To wait on 'e in death!

WAR.   Why, peers of England, 190
We'll lead 'em on courageously. I read
A triumph over tyranny upon
Their several foreheads. Faint not in
the moment
Of victory! Our ends, and Warwick's
head,
Innocent Warwick's head—for we are
prologue
But to his tragedy—conclude the wonder
Of Henry's fears; and then the glorious
race
Of fourteen kings, Plantagenets, de-
termines [2]
In this last issue male. Heaven be obeyed!
Impoverish time of its amazement,
friends,   200

[1] Attend.   [2] Terminates.

And we will prove as trusty in our pay-
ments
As prodigal to nature in our debts.
Death? Pish! 'Tis but a sound; a name
of air;
A minute's storm, or not so much. To
tumble
From bed to bed, be massacred alive
By some physicians for a month or two,
In hope of freedom from a fever's tor-
ments,
Might stagger manhood. Here the pain
is past
Ere sensibly 'tis felt. Be men of spirit!
Spurn coward passion! So illustrious
mention   210
Shall blaze our names, and style us
kings o'er death.

DAW. Away, impostor beyond president!
No chronicle records his fellow.
                Ex[eunt] all Officers and Prisoners.

HUNT.   I have
Not thoughts left; 'tis sufficient in such
cases
Just laws ought to proceed.

Enter King Henry, Durham, and Hialas.

KING.   We are resolved.
Your business, noble lords, shall find
success
Such as your king importunes.

HUNT.   You are gracious.

KING. Perkin, we are informed, is armed
to die;
In that we'll honor him. Our lords shall
follow
To see the execution; and from hence 220
We gather this fit use: that "public
states,
As our particular bodies, taste most
good
In health when purgéd of corrupted
blood."   *Exeunt omnes.*

FINIS.

EPILOGUE

Here has appeared, though in a several [3]
fashion,
The threats of majesty, the strength of
passion,
Hopes of an empire, change of fortunes—
all

[3] Separate.

What can to theaters of greatness fall,
Proving their weak foundations. Who will please,
Amongst such several sights, to censure [1] these
No births abortive, nor a bastard brood

[1] Judge.

(Shame to a parentage or fosterhood),
May warrant,[2] by their loves, all just excuses,[3]   9
And often find a welcome to the Muses.

FINIS.

[2] Authorize, sanction.   [3] Deserved defenses (?)

JAMES SHIRLEY

Shirley has been called "the last of the Elizabethans" partly because he was actually the last of the dramatists of his age to be born (in 1596, in London) and the last to die (in 1666, from exposure in the Great Fire), but even more because his work bears an extremely close and interesting relationship to that of his fellows while at the same time, especially in comedy, it anticipates much of the material and characters of the Restoration, if not its spirit. After attending the Merchant Tailors' School, Oxford, and Cambridge as an Anglican, he was converted to Roman Catholicism and abandoned what might have been a career in the church for school-teaching at St. Albans Grammar School, in Hertfordshire. In 1624, however, he gave up his head-mastership, and took up his residence at Gray's Inn, London, although there is no evidence that he ever actually became a lawyer. But in the following year his first play, *Love Tricks*, was licensed, and he continued to write voluminously for the stage, first for the Queen's Men and later for the King's. Not one of the least significant phases of his life was his four-year sojourn in Ireland, where the production of several of his plays in his friend John Ogilby's new Dublin theater marks one of the earliest signs of dramatic activity in that country. During the first days of the Civil War Shirley attended his patron, the Duke of Newcastle, on some of the Royalist campaigns, but after the defeat at Marston Moor he returned to his former profession of school-teaching, the closing of the theaters in 1642 precluding his earning a living in the manner he would have preferred. Nevertheless, he continued to write for the reading public, and saw that his plays as well as his poems and some pot-boiling works were put into print. He also edited the first collected edition of Beaumont and Fletcher, and according to tradition essayed to write for the stage once more after the Restoration, but if so none of his attempts struck the popular taste sufficiently to be known today as his.

It was both an advantage and a handicap to Shirley to have had before him the examples of his great predecessors; in fact, the playwright was so steeped in his study of these men that scarcely one of his scenes but has its parallels which have gone before. At the same time, however, so great was Shirley's ingenuity and dramatic sense that out of this material he was able to construct plays of considerable effectiveness and even originality—plays which in general read with naturalness and ease even though they fall sadly short in the usual Elizabethan poetry. He can claim to have written successfully in four different fields: masques, such as the lavishly produced *The Triumph of Peace* (1634); comedies of manners, such as *Hyde Park* (1632) and *The Lady of Pleasure* (1635), all dealing with the lower levels of fashionable society in the time of Charles I; tragi-comedies, such as *The Young Admiral* (1633) and *The Politician* (1639); and pure tragedies, the best of which are clearly *The Traitor* (1631) and *The Cardinal* (1641), decadent as these are in their excessive ingenuity, their reminiscences of other plays, their horrors, and their use of the old motives of lust, madness, and revenge.

The basis of the present text of *The Lady of Pleasure* is the copy of the first quarto (1637) in the Newberry Library at Chicago; that of *The Cardinal* the Library of Congress copy, dated 1652, in the 1653 collection, entitled *Six New Plays*. In both cases reference has sometimes been made to the not overreliable six-volume edition of *The Dramatic Works and Poems of James Shirley* (1833) by Alexander Dyce, which used many notes left by William Gifford.

THE LADY OF PLEASURE[1]

BY

JAMES SHIRLEY

PERSONS OF THE COMEDY

LORD.
SIR THOMAS BORNWELL.
SIR WILLIAM SCENTLOVE.
MR.[2] ALEX[ANDER] KICKSHAW.
MR. JOHN LITTLEWORTH.
MR. HAIRCUT [, a barber].
MR. FREDERICK [, Lady Bornwell's nephew].
STEWARD to the Lady Aretina.
STEWARD to the Lady Celestina.

SECRETARY [to Lord].
SERVANTS, etc.

ARETINA, Sir Thomas Bornwell's lady.
CELESTINA, a young widow.
ISABELLA [NOVICE] ⎱ [Kinswomen of Ce-
MARIANA [NOVICE] ⎰ lestina].
MADAM DECOY [, a procuress].
[GENTLEWOMAN.]

SCENE: The Strand.

[TIME: Contemporary.][3]

THE FIRST ACT. [SCENE i.

A room in Bornwell's house.]

Enter Aretina and her Steward.

STEW. Be patient, madam; you may have
your pleasure.
ARE. 'Tis that I came to town for. I
would not
Endure again the country conversation,[4]
To be the lady of six shires! The men,
So near the primitive making they re-
tain
A sense of nothing but the earth, their
brains
And barren heads standing as much in
want
Of plowing as their ground! To hear
a fellow
Make himself merry and his horse, with
whistling
"Sellinger's Round"![5] To observe with
what solemnity   10

They keep their wakes,[6] and throw for
pewter candlesticks!
How they become the morris,[7] with
whose bells
They ring all in to Whitsun ales,[8] and
sweat
Through twenty scarfs and napkins,
till the hobbyhorse
Tire, and the Maid Marian, dissolved
to a jelly,
Be kept for spoon meat![9]
STEW. These, with your pardon, are no
argument
To make the country life appear so
hateful,
At least to your particular,[10] who en-
joyed
A blessing in that calm, would you be
pleased   20
To think so, and the pleasure of a kingdom.
While your own will commanded what
should move
Delights, your husband's love and power
joined

[1] The title continues: "A Comedy, As It Was
Acted by Her Majesty's Servants at the Private
House in Drury Lane."
[2] I.e., Master
[3] Here follows a brief dedication to Richard,
Lord Lovelace of Hurley.
[4] Association.
[5] An old-fashioned country dance tune.
[6] Annual parish festivals.
[7] A dance in which the hobbyhorse and Maid
Marian were characters.
[8] Parish festivals held at Whitsuntide.
[9] Liquid food eaten with a spoon.
[10] In your case.

To give your life more harmony. You
  lived there
Secure and innocent, beloved of all,
Praised for your hospitality, and prayed
  for;
You might be enviéd, but malice knew
Not where you dwelt. I would not
  prophesy,
But leave to your own apprehension
What may succeed your change.

ARE.   You do imagine, 30
  No doubt, you have talked wisely, and
  confuted
London past all defense. Your master
  should
Do well to send you back into the coun-
  try,
With title of superintendent-baily.[1]

STEW.   How, madam!
ARE. Even so, sir.
STEW.   I am a gentleman,
  Though now your servant.[2]
ARE.   A country gentleman,
  By your affection to converse with stub-
  ble.
His tenants will advance your wit, and
  plump it so
With beef and bag pudding!
STEW.   You may say your pleasure;
  It becomes not me dispute.
ARE.   Complain to the 40
  Lord of the soil, your master.
STEW.   Y' are a woman
  Of an ungoverned passion, and I pity
  you.

Enter Sir Thomas Bornwell.

BORN. How now![3] What's the matter?
STEW.   Nothing, sir. [*Exit.*]
BORN. Angry, sweetheart?
ARE.   I am angry with myself,
To be so miserably restrained in things
Wherein it doth concern your love and
  honor
To see me satisfied.
BORN.   In what, Aretina?
Dost thou accuse me? Have I not
  obeyed

All thy desires? Against mine own
  opinion
Quitted the country, and removed the
  hope 50
Of our return, by sale of that fair lord-
  ship[4]
We lived in? Changed a calm and re-
  tire[d] life
For this wild town, composed of noise
  and charge?[5]
ARE. What charge more than is neces-
  sary for
A lady of my birth and education?
BORN. I am not ignorant how much no-
  bility
Flows in your blood—your kinsmen great
  and powerful
I' th' state; but with this lose not your
  memory
Of being my wife. I shall be studious,
Madam, to give the dignity of your
  birth 60
All the best ornaments which become
  my fortune,
But would not flatter it to ruin both,
And be the fable of the town, to teach
Other men loss of wit by mine, employed
To serve your vast expenses.
ARE.   Am I then
Brought in the balance? So, sir!
BORN.   Though you weigh
Me in a partial[6] scale, my heart is
  honest,
And must take liberty to think you have
Obeyed no modest counsel, to effect,[7]
Nay, study, ways of pride and costly
  ceremony: 70
Your change of gaudy furniture, and
  pictures
Of this Italian master and that Dutch-
  man's;
Your mighty looking-glasses, like ar-
  tillery,
Brought home[8] on engines; the super-
  fluous plate,
Antique and novel; vanities of tires;[9]
Fourscore-pound suppers for my lord,
  your kinsman,
Banquets for tother[10] lady aunt, and
  cousins,

---

[1] Bailiff.
[2] Here and in several other passages the line
division has been somewhat regularized, although
much of the original meter is rather rough.
[3] Gifford-Dyce's reading. Original reads *how.*

[4] Estate
[5] Expense.
[6] Prejudiced.
[7] Affect, desire.
[8] Gifford-Dyce's reading. Original reads *whom.*
[9] Headdresses.
[10] The other.

And perfumes that exceed all; train of
   servants
To stifle us at home and show abroad
More motley than the French or the
   Venetian,   80
About your coach, whose rude postil-
   lion
Must pester [1] every narrow lane, till
   passengers [2]
And tradesmen curse your choking up
   their stalls,
And common cries pursue your lady-
   ship,
For hind'ring o' their market.
ARE.   Have you done, sir?
BORN. I could accuse the gaiety of your
   wardrobe
And prodigal embroideries,[3] under which
Rich satins, plushes, cloth of silver,
   dare
Not show their own complexions; your
   jewels,
Able to burn out the spectators' eyes, 90
And show like bonefires [4] on you by the
   tapers.
Something might here be spared, with
   safety [5] of
Your birth and honor, since the truest
   wealth
Shines from the soul, and draws up
   just admirers.
I could urge something more.
ARE.   Pray do; I like
   Your homily of thrift.
BORN.   I could wish, madam,
   You would not game so much.
ARE.   A gamester too?
BORN. But are not come to that acquaint-
   ance [6] yet
Should teach you skill enough to raise
   your profit.
You look not through the subtilty of
   cards   100
And mysteries of dice, nor can you save
Charge with the box,[7] buy petticoats
   and pearls,
And keep your family by the precious
   income.

Nor do I wish you should. My poorest
   servant
Shall not upbraid my tables nor his hire,
Purchased beneath my honor. You
   make play
Not a pastime but a tyranny, and vex
Yourself and my estate by 't.
ARE.   Good! Proceed.
BORN. Another game you have, which
   consumes more
Your fame than purse—your revels in
   the night,   110
Your meetings called the "Ball," [8] to
   which appear,
As to the Court of Pleasure, all your
   gallants
And ladies, thither bound by a subpœna
Of Venus, and small Cupid's high dis-
   pleasure;
'Tis but the Family of Love [9] translated
Into more costly sin! There was a play
   on 't,
And, had the poet not been bribed to
   a modest
Expression of your antic gambols in 't,
Some darks [10] had been discovered, and
   the deeds too.
In time he may repent, and make some
   blush   120
To see the second part danced on the
   stage.
My thoughts acquit you for dishonor-
   ing me
By any foul act; but the virtuous know
'Tis not enough to clear ourselves, but
   the
Suspicions of our shame.
ARE.   Have you concluded
   Your lecture?
BORN.   I ha' done; and, howsoever
My language may appear to you, it
   carries
No other than my fair and just intent
To your delights, without curb to their
   modest [11]
And noble freedom.
ARE.   I'll not be so tedious 130
   In my reply, but, without art or ele-
   gance,

---

[1] Obstruct.
[2] Passer-by
[3] Embroideries.
[4] Bonfires.
[5] Gifford-Dyce's reading. Original reads *which safely*.
[6] Emended by Gifford-Dyce. Original reads *repentance*.
[7] Dice box.
[8] The newly invented subscription dance, upon which Shirley wrote a play.
[9] A religious sect, object of scandalous charges; also the title of a play by Middleton.
[10] Secrets.   [11] Moderate.

Assure you I keep still my first opinion;
And, though you veil your avaricious
  meaning
With handsome names of modesty and
  thrift,
I find you would intrench and wound
  the liberty
I was born with. Were my desires un-
  privileged
By example, while my judgment thought
  'em fit,
You ought not to oppose; but, when
  the practice
And tract [1] of every honorable lady 139
Authorize me, I take it great injustice
To have my pleasures circumscribed
  and taught me.
A narrow-minded husband is a thief
To his own fame, and his preferment
  too;
He shuts his parts and fortunes from
  the world,
While, from the popular vote and knowl-
  edge, men
Rise to employment in the state.
BORN.   I have
No great ambition to buy preferment
At so dear rate.
ARE.   Nor I to sell my honor
By living poor and sparingly. I was not
Bred in that ebb of fortune, and my
  fate   150
Shall not compel me to 't.
BORN.   I know not,
Madam; but you pursue these ways—
ARE.   What ways?
BORN. In the strict sense of honesty, I
  dare
Make oath they are innocent.
ARE.   Do not divert,
By busy troubling of your brain, those
  thoughts
That should preserve 'em.
BORN.   How was that?
ARE.   'Tis English.
BORN. But carries some unkind sense.

Enter Madam Decoy.

DEC. Good morrow, my sweet madam.
ARE.   Decoy, welcome!
This visit is a favor.
DEC.   Alas, sweet madam,
I cannot stay. I came but to present 160

[1] Course of action.

My service to your ladyship; I could
  not
Pass by your door but I must take the
  boldness
To tender my respects.
ARE.   You oblige me, madam;
But I must not dispense so with your
  absence.
DEC. Alas, the coach, madam, stays for
  me at the door.
ARE. Thou sha't command mine; prithee,
  sweet Decoy—
DEC. I would wait on you, madam, but
  I have many
Visits to make this morning; I beseech—
ARE. So you will promise to dine with
  me.
DEC.   I shall
Present a guest.
ARE.   Why, then good morrow,
  madam.   170
DEC. A happy day shine on your ladyship!
                    Exit.

Enter Steward.

ARE. What's your news, sir?
STEW.   Madam, two gentlemen.
ARE. What gentlemen? Have they no
  names?
STEW.   They are
The gentleman with his own head of
  hair,
Whom you commended for his horse-
  ship
In Hyde Park, and becoming the saddle,
The tother day.
ARE.   What circumstance is this
To know him by?
STEW.   His name's at my tongue's end—
He liked the fashion of your pearl chain,
  madam,
And borrowed it for his jeweler to
  take   180
A copy by it.
BORN. [*Aside.*] What cheating gallant's
  this?
STEW. That never walks without a lady's
  busk,[2]
And plays with fans—Mr. Alexander
  Kickshaw—
I thought I should remember him.
ARE.   What's the other?
STEW. What an unlucky memory I have!

[2] Corset.

The gallant that still [1] danceth in the
  street,
And wears a gross of ribbon in his hat;
That carries oringado [2] in his pocket,
And sugarplums to sweeten his dis-
  course;   189
That studies compliment, defies all wit
On black, [3] and censures plays that are
  not bawdy—
Mr. John Littleworth.

ARE.   They are welcome; but
  Pray, entertain them a small time, lest I
  Be unprovided.

BORN.   Did they ask for me?

STEW. No, sir.

BORN.   It matters not; they must be
  welcome.

ARE. Fie! How's this hair disordered?
  Here's a curl
  Straddle[s] [4] most impiously. I must to
  my closet.   *Exit.*

BORN. Wait on 'em; my lady will return
  again.—   [*Exit Steward.*]
  I have to such a height fulfilled her
  humor,
  All application's [5] dangerous. These
  gallants   200
  Must be received, or she will fall into
  A tempest, and the house be shook with
  names
  Of all her kindred. 'Tis a servitude
  I may in time shake off.

*Enter Alexander [Kickshaw] and Little-
                                       worth.*

AL. }
LIT. }   Save you, Sir Thomas!

BORN. Save you, gentlemen!

AL.   I kiss your hand.

BORN. What day [6] is it abroad?

LIT. The morning rises from your lady's
  eye;
  If she look clear, we take the happy
  omen
  Of a fair day.

BORN.   She'll instantly appear,
  To the discredit of your compliment; 210
  But you express your wit thus.

AL.   And you, modesty,
  Not to affect [7] the praises of your own.

[1] Always.   [2] Candied orange peel.
[3] In black, in print.
[4] Supplied by Gifford-Dyce.
[5] *I.e*, all pleading to be reasonable is.
[6] Weather.   [7] Appear to be pleased with.

BORN. Leaving this subject, what game's
  now on foot?
  What exercise carries the general vote? [8]
  O' th' town now, nothing moves without your knowledge.

AL. The cocking [9] now has all the noise;
  I'll have
  A hundred pieces of one battle. O,
  These birds of Mars!

LIT.   Venus is Mars his bird too.

AL. Why, and the pretty doves are
  Venus's,
  To show that kisses draw the chariot. 220

LIT. I am for that skirmish.

BORN.   When shall we have
  More booths and bagpipes upon Ban-
  stead Downs?
  No mighty race is expected?—But my
  lady
  Returns!

Enter Aretina.

ARE.   Fair morning to you, gentlemen!
  You went not late to bed by your early
  visit.
  You do me honor.

AL.   It becomes our service.

ARE. What news abroad? You hold precious intelligence.

LIT. All tongues are so much busy with
  your praise
  They have not time to frame other discourse.
  Will please you, madam, taste a sugar-
  plum?   230

BORN. What does the goldsmith think
  the pearl is worth
  You borrowed of my lady?

AL.   'Tis a rich one.

BORN. She has many other toys, whose
  fashion you
  Will like extremely. You have no intention
  To buy any of her jewels?

AL.   Understand me—

BORN. You had rather sell, perhaps. But,
  leaving this,
  I hope you'll dine with us.

AL.   I came a-purpose.

ARE. And where were you last night?

AL.   I, madam? Where
  I slept not; it had been sin, where so
  much

[8] Approval.   [9] Cockfighting.

Delight and beauty was to keep me wak-
ing.   240
There is a lady, madam, will be worth
Your free society; my conversation
Ne'er knew so elegant and brave [1] a
  soul,
With most incomparable flesh and blood,
So spirited, so courtly, speaks the lan-
  guages,
Sings, dances, plays o' th' lute to ad-
  miration,
Is fair and paints not, games too, keeps
  a table,
And talks most witty satire, has a wit
Of a clean [2] Mercury—

LIT.   Is she married?

AL.   No. 249

ARE. A virgin?

AL.   Neither.

LIT.   What! A widow? Something
Of this wide commendation might have
  been
Excused. This such a prodigy?

AL.   Repent,
Before I name her. She did never see
Yet full sixteen, an age, in the opinion
Of wise men, not contemptible. She
  has
Mourned out her year, too, for the
  honest knight
That had compassion of her youth, and
  died
So timely. Such a widow is not com-
  mon;
And now she shines more fresh and
  tempting
Than any natural virgin.

ARE.   What's her name? 260

AL. She was christened Celestina; by her
  husband,
The Lady Bellamour. This ring was
  hers.

BORN. You borrowed it to copy out the
  posy. [3]

AL. Are they not pretty rubies? 'Twas
  a grace
She was pleased to show me, that I
  might have one
Made of the same fashion, for I love
All pretty forms.

ARE.   And is she glorious?

AL. She is full of jewels, madam; but I am

Most taken with the bravery [4] of her
  mind,
Although her garments have all grace
  and ornament. 270

ARE. You have been high in praises.

AL.   I come short;
No flattery can reach her.

BORN. [Aside.]   Now my lady
Is troubled, as she feared to be eclipsed;
This news will cost me somewhat.

ARE.   You deserve
Her favor, for this noble character.

AL. And I possess it, by my star's benevo-
  lence.

ARE. You must bring us acquainted.

BORN.   I pray, do, sir;
I long to see her too.—Madam, I have
Thought upon 't, and corrected my
  opinion.
Pursue what ways of pleasure your
  desires 280
Incline you to, not only with my state,
But with my person; I will follow
  you.
I see the folly of my thrift, and will
Repent in sack and prodigality,
To your own heart's content.

ARE.   But do not mock.

BORN. Take me to your embraces, gentlemen,
And tutor me.

LIT.   And will you kiss the ladies?

BORN. And sing and dance. I long to see
  this beauty.
I would fain lose a hundred pounds at
  dice now.
Thou sha't have another gown and petticoat 290
Tomorrow. Will you sell my running
  horses?
We have no Greek wine in the house, I
  think;
Pray, send one of our footmen to the
  merchant,
And throw the hogsheads of Marchbeer [5] into
The kennel, [6] to make room for sacks and
  claret.
What think you to be drunk yet before
  dinner?
We will have constant music, and maintain

---

[1] Fine.
[2] Veritable.
[3] Inscription in a ring.
[4] Finery, excellence.
[5] Bock beer.
[6] Channel, gutter.

Them and their fiddles in fantastic
    liveries;
I'll tune my voice to catches. I must
    have
My dining room enlarged, to invite am-
    bassadors.   300
We'll feast the parish in the fields, and
    teach
The military men new discipline,
Who shall charge all their new artillery
With oranges and lemonds,[1] boy, to play
All dinner upon our capons.
AL.   He's exalted!
BORN. I will do anything to please my
    lady—
Let that suffice—and kiss o' th' same
    condition.
I am converted; do not you dispute,
But patiently allow the miracle.

Enter Servant.

ARE. I am glad to hear you, sir, in so good
    tune.   310
SER. Madam, the painter.
ARE.   I am to sit this morning.
BORN. Do, while I give new directions to
    my steward.
AL. With your favor, we'll wait on you;
    sitting's but
A melancholy exercise without
Some company to discourse.
ARE.   It does conclude
A lady's morning work. We rise, make
    fine,
Sit for our picture, and 'tis time to dine.
LIT. Praying's forgot.
AL.   'Tis out of fashion. *Exeunt.*

[SCENE ii.

A room in Celestina's house.]

Enter Celestina and her Steward.

CEL. Fie, what an air this room has!
STEW.   'Tis perfumed.
CEL. With some cheap stuff. Is it your
    wisdom's thrift
To infect my nostrils thus? Or is 't to
    favor
The gout in your worship's hand, you are
    afraid
To exercise your pen in your account
    book?

[1] Lemons.

Or do you doubt my credit to discharge
Your bills?
STEW.   Madam, I hope you have not
    found
My duty, with the guilt of sloth or
    jealousy,
Unapt to your command.
CEL.   You can extenuate
Your faults with language, sir; but I
    expect   10
To be obeyed. What hangings have we
    here?
STEW. They are arras, madam.
CEL.   Impudence! I know 't.
I will have fresher and more rich, not
    wrought
With faces that may scandalize a Chris-
    tian,
With Jewish stories stuffed with corn and
    camels.
You had best wrap all my chambers in
    wild Irish,
And make a nursery of monsters here,
To fright the ladies comes to visit me.
STEW. Madam, I hope—
CEL.   I say I will have other,   19
Good Master Steward, of a finer loom—
Some silk and silver, if your worship
    please
To let me be at so much cost. I'll have
Stories to fit the seasons of the year,
And change as often as I please.
STEW.   You shall, madam.
CEL. I am bound to your consent, for-
    sooth! And is
My coach brought home?
STEW.   This morning I expect it.
CEL. The inside, as I gave direction,
Of crimson plush?
STEW.   Of crimson camel plush.
CEL. Ten thousand moths consume 't!
    Shall I ride through
The streets in penance, wrapped up
    round in haircloth?   30
Sell 't to an alderman; 'twill serve his
    wife
To go a-feasting to their country house,
Or fetch a merchant's nurse child, and
    come home
Laden with fruit and cheesecakes. I
    despise it!
STEW. The nails adorn it, madam, set in
    method
And pretty forms.

CEL. But single gilt, I warrant.

STEW. No, madam.

CEL. Another solecism! O, fie!
This fellow will bring me to a consump-
tion
With fretting at his ignorance. Some
lady
Had rather never pray than go to church
in 't.　　　　40
The nails not double gilt? To market
wo't? [1]
'Twill hackney out to Mile End, or con-
vey
Your city tumblers [2] to be drunk with
cream
And prunes at Islington.

STEW. Good madam, hear me.

CEL. I'll rather be beholding [3] to my aunt,
The countess, for her mourning coach
than be
Disparaged so. Shall any juggling trades-
man
Be at charge to shoe his running horse
with gold,
And shall my coach nails be but single
gilt?
How dare these knaves abuse me so?

STEW. Vouchsafe 50
To hear me speak.

CEL. Is my sedan yet finished,
And liveries for my men-mules, [4] accord-
ing
As I gave charge?

STEW. Yes, madam, it is finished,
But without tilting-plumes [5] at the four
corners;
The scarlet's pure, but not embroideréd.

CEL. What mischief were it to your con-
science
Were my coach lined with tissue, [6] and
my harness
Covered with needlework? If my sedan
Had all the story of the prodigal
Embroderéd with pearl?

STEW. Alas, good madam, 60
I know 'tis your own cost; I am but your
steward,
And would discharge my duty the best
way.
You have been pleased to hear me; 'tis
not for

My profit that I manage your estate
And save expense, but for your honor,
madam.

CEL. How, sir, my honor?

STEW. Though you hear it not,
Men's tongues are liberal in your char-
acter,
Since you began to live thus high. I know
Your fame [7] is precious to you.

CEL. I were best
Make you my governor, audacious var-
let!　　　　70
How dare you interpose your doting
counsel?
Mind your affairs with more obedience,
Or I shall ease you of an office, sir.
Must I be limited to please your honor,
Or, for the vulgar breath, confine my
pleasures?
I will pursue 'em in what shapes I fancy,
Here and abroad; my entertainments
shall
Be oft'ner and more rich. Who shall con-
trol me?
I live i' th' Strand, whither few ladies
come
To live, and purchase more than fame. I
will　　　　80
Be hospitable then, and spare no cost
That may engage all generous report
To trumpet forth my bounty and my
bravery,
Till the court envy, and remove. I'll have
My house the academy of wits, who shall
Exalt [their genius] [8] with rich sack and
sturgeon,
Write panegyrics of my feasts, and
praise
The method of my witty superfluities.
The horses shall be taught, with frequent
waiting　　　　89
Upon my gates, to stop in their career
Toward Charing Cross, spite of the
coachman's fury;
And not a tilter [9] but shall strike his
plume
When he sails by my window; my bal-
cony
Shall be the courtier's idol, and more
gazed at
Than all the pageantry at Temple Bar
By country clients.

---

[1] With it.
[2] Prostitutes.
[3] Beholden.
[4] Chairmen.
[5] Plumes for a canopy.
[6] Fine silk cloth.
[7] Reputation.　　[8] Supplied by Gifford-Dyce.
[9] One riding to the tilting grounds.

STEW.   Sure, my lady's mad.
CEL. [*Striking him.*] Take that for your ill
    manners.
STEW.   Thank you, madam.
    I would there were less quicksilver in
    your fingers.   *Exit.*
CEL. There's more than simple honesty in
    a servant
    Required to his full duty; none should
    dare   100
    But with a look, much less a saucy lan-
    guage,
    Check at their mistress' pleasure. I'm
    resolved
    To pay for some delight; my estate will
    bear it;
    I'll rein it shorter when I please.

Enter Steward.

STEW.   A gentleman
    Desires to speak with your ladyship.
CEL.   His name?
STEW. He says you know him not; he
    seems to be
    Of quality.
CEL.   Admit him.—[*Exit Steward.*]

Enter Haircut.[1]

                            Sir, with me?
HAIR. Madam, I know not how you may
    receive
    This boldness from me; but my fair in-
    tents,   109
    Known, will incline you to be charitable.
CEL. No doubt, sir.
HAIR.   He must live obscurely, madam,
    That hath not heard what virtues you
    possess;
    And I, a poor admirer of your fame,
    Am come to kiss your hand.
CEL.   That all your business?
HAIR. Though it were worth much travel,
    I have more
    In my ambition.
CEL.   Speak it freely, sir.
HAIR. You are a widow.
CEL.   So.
HAIR.   And I a bachelor.
CEL. You come a-wooing, sir, and would
    perhaps
    Show me a way to reconcile these two.

[1] In the original this stage direction appears
at the end of Celestina's speech.

HAIR. And bless my stars for such a happi-
    ness.   120
CEL. I like you, sir, the better, that you do
    not
    Wander about, but shoot home to the
    meaning;
    'Tis a confidence will make a man
    Know sooner what to trust to; but I
    never
    Saw you before, and I believe you come
    not
    With hope to find me desperate upon
    marriage.
    If maids, out of their ignorance of what
    Men are, refuse these offers, widows may,
    Out of their knowledge, be allowed some
    coyness.
    And yet I know not how much happi-
    ness   130
    A peremptory answer may deprive me of;
    You may be some young lord, and,
    though I see not
    Your footmen and your groom, they may
    not be
    Far off, in conference with your horse.
    Please you
    To instruct me with your title, against
    which
    I would not willingly offend.
HAIR.   I am
    A gentleman; my name is Haircut,
    madam.
CEL. Sweet Mr. Haircut, are you a court-
    ier?
HAIR. Yes.
CEL.   I did think so, by your confidence.
    Not to detain you, sir, with circum-
    stance,[2]   140
    I was not so unhappy in my husband
    But that 'tis possible I may be a wife
    Again; but I must tell you he that wins
    My affection shall deserve me.
HAIR.   I will hope,
    If you can love, I sha' not present,
    madam,
    An object to displease you in my person;
    And, when time and your patience shall
    possess you
    With further knowledge of me, and the
    truth
    Of my devotion, you will not repent
    The offer of my service.
CEL.   You say well. 150

[2] Detailed narration.

How long do you imagine you can love,
sir?
Is it a quotidian,[1] or will it hold
But every other day?

HAIR.   You are pleasant,[2] madam.

CEL. Does 't take you with a burning at
the first,
Or with a cold fit? For you gentlemen
Have both your summer and your winter
service.

HAIR. I am ignorant what you mean; but
I shall never
Be cold in my affection to such beauty.

CEL. And 'twill be somewhat long ere I be
warm in 't.

HAIR. If you vouchsafe me so much honor,
madam,   160
That I may wait on you sometimes, I sha'
not
Despair to see a change.

CEL.   But now I know
Your mind, you shall not need to tell it
when
You come again; I shall remember it.

HAIR. You make me fortunate.

Enter Steward.

STEW.   Madam, your kinswomen,
The Lady Novice and her sister, are
New lighted from their coach.

CEL.   I did expect 'em;
They partly are my pupils. I'll attend
'em.   [*Exit Steward.*]

HAIR. Madam, I have been too great a
trespasser   169
Upon your patience; I'll take my leave.
You have affairs, and I have some em-
ployment
Calls me to court; I shall present again
A servant[3] to you.   *Exit Ha[ircut].*

CEL.   Sir, you may present,
But not give fire, I hope.—Now to the
ladies.
This recreation's past; the next must
be
To read to them some court philosophy.
       Exit.[4]

[1] Something of daily occurrence.
[2] Facetious.
[3] *I.e.*, present myself as a servant, with a pun
on the meaning *lover*.
[4] Original reads *Exeunt*.

THE SECOND ACT. [SCENE i.

A room in Bornwell's house.]

Enter Sir Thomas Bornwell.

[BORN.] 'Tis a strange humor I have under-
taken,
To dance, and play, and spend as fast as
she does;
But I am resolved. It may do good upon
her,
And fright her into thrift. Nay, I'll en-
deavor
To make her jealous too; if this do not
Allay her gamboling, she's past a woman,
And only a miracle must tame her.

Enter Steward.

STEW. 'Tis Mr. Frederick, my lady's
nephew.

BORN.   What of him?

STEW. Is come from the university.

BORN.   By whose directions?

STEW. It seems, my lady's.

BORN.   Let me speak with him   10
Before he see his aunt.—[*Exit Steward.*]
I do not like it.—

Enter [Steward, with] Mr. Frederick.

Mr. Frederick, welcome! I expected not
So soon your presence. What's the hasty
cause?

FRED. These letters from my tutor will acquaint you. [*Gives Bornwell letters.*]

STEW. Welcome home, sweet Mr. Frederick!

FRED.   Where's my aunt?

STEW. She's busy about her painting in
her closet;[5]
The outlandish[6] man of art is copying
out
Her countenance.

FRED.   She is sitting for her picture?

STEW. Yes, sir; and when 'tis drawn she
will be hanged
Next the French cardinal in the dining
room.   20
But, when she hears you're come, she
will dismiss
The Belgic gentleman, to entertain
Your worship.

FRED.   Change of air has made you
witty.   [*Exit Steward.*]

[5] Chamber   [6] Foreign.

Born. Your tutor gives you a handsome
    character,
Frederick, and is sorry your aunt's
    pleasure
Commands you from your studies; but I
    hope
You have no quarrel to the liberal arts.
Learning is an addition [1] beyond
Nobility of birth. Honor of blood,
Without the ornament of knowledge,
    is   30
A glorious [2] ignorance.
Fred. I never knew more sweet and happy
    hours
Than I employed upon my books. I
    heard
A part of my philosophy, and was so
Delighted with the harmony of nature
I could have wasted my whole life
    upon 't.
Born. [Aside.] 'Tis pity a rash indulgence
    should corrupt
So fair a genius! She's here; I'll observe.

*Enter Aretina, Alexander, Littleworth, Stew-
    ard.*

Fred. My most loved aunt!
Are.   Support me; I shall faint.
Lit. What ails your ladyship?
Are.   Is that Frederick,   40
    In black?
Al.   Yes, madam; but the doublet's
    satin.
Are. The boy's undone!
Fred.   Madam, you appear troubled.
Are. Have I not cause? Was not I trusted
    with
Thy education, boy, and have they sent
    thee
Home like a very scholar?
Al.   'Twas ill done,
Howe'er they used him in the university,
To send him to his friends thus.
Fred.   Why, sir, black
(For 'tis the color that offends your eye-
    sight)
Is not, within my reading, any blemish;
Sables are no disgrace in heraldry.   50
Al. 'Tis coming from the college thus that
    makes it
Dishonorable. While you ware [3] it for

Your father, it was commendable; or,
    were
Your aunt dead, you might mourn, and
    justify.
Are. What luck [4] I did not send him into
    France!
They would have given him generous
    education,
Taught him another garb, to wear his
    lock
And shape as gaudy as the summer, how
To dance, and wag his feather *à la mode*,
To compliment and cringe,[5] to talk not
    modestly,   60
Like, "ay, forsooth," and "no, forsooth,"
    to blush,
And look so like a chaplain! There he
    might
Have learned a brazen confidence, and
    observed
So well the custom of the country that
He might by this time have invented
    fashions
For us, and been a benefit to the king-
    dom,
Preserved our tailors in their wits, and
    saved
The charge of sending into foreign courts
For pride and antic fashions. Observe
In what a posture he does hold his hat
    now!   70
Fred. Madam, with your pardon, you
    have practiced
Another dialect than was taught me
    when
I was commended to your care and breed-
    ing.
I understand not this. Latin or Greek
Are more familiar to my apprehension;
Logic was not so hard in my first lectures
As your strange language.
Are.   Some strong waters—O!
Lit. [*Offering a box.*] Comfits will be as
    comfortable to your stomach, madam.
Are. I fear he's spoiled forever! He did
    name
Logic, and may, for aught I know, be
    gone   80
So far to understand it. I did always
Suspect they would corrupt him in the
    college.—
Will your Greek saws and sentences dis-
    charge

---

[1] Title, ornament.
[2] Vainglorious.   [3] Wore.
[4] *I.e.*, bad luck.   [5] Bow.

The mercer? Or is Latin a fit language
To court a mistress in?—Mr. Alexander,
If you have any charity, let me
Commend him to your breeding. I sus-
　pect
I must employ my doctor first, to purge
The university that lies in 's head;
It alters his complexion.[1]

AL. 　　　　　　　　If you dare 90
Trust me to serve him—

ARE. 　　　　　　Mr. Littleworth,
Be you joined in commission.

LIT. 　　　　　　I will teach him
Postures and rudiments.

ARE. 　　　　　I have no patience
To see him in this shape; it turns my
　stomach.
When he has cast his academic skin,
He shall be yours. I am bound in con-
　science
To see him bred; his own state shall
　maintain
The charge, while he's my ward.—Come
hither, sir.

FRED. What does my aunt mean to do
with me?

STEW. To make you a fine gentleman, and
　translate you　　　　　　100
Out of your learned language, sir, into
The present Goth and Vandal, which is
　French.

BORN. [Aside.] Into what mischief will
　this humor ebb?
She will undo the boy; I see him ruined.
My patience is not manly, but I must
Use stratagem to reduce her—open ways
Give me no hope. 　　　　　Exit.

STEW. 　　　You shall be obeyed, madam.
Exeunt [All but Frederick and Steward].

FRED. Mr. Steward, are you sure we do
not dream?
Was 't not my aunt you talked to?

STEW. 　　　　　One that loves you
Dear as her life. These clothes do not be-
come you;　　　　　　110
You must have better, sir—

FRED. 　　　　　These are not old.

STEW. More suitable to the town and time;
we keep
No Lent here, nor is 't my lady's pleasure
you
Should fast from anything you have a
mind to—

[1] Disposition.

Unless it be your learning, which she
would have you
Forget with all convenient speed that
may be,
For the credit of your noble family.
The case is altered since we lived i' th'
country;
We do not invite the poor o' th' parish
To dinner, keep a table for the tenants;
Our kitchen does not smell of beef; the
cellar　　　　　　121
Defies the price of malt and hops; the
footmen
And coachdrivers may be drunk like
gentlemen
With wine, nor will three fiddlers upon
holidays,
With aid of bagpipes, that called in the
country
To dance and plow the hall up with their
hobnails
Now make my lady merry. We do feed
Like princes, and feast nothing but
princes;
And are these robes fit to be seen amongst
'em?

FRED. My lady keeps a court then! Is Sir
Thomas　　　　　　130
Affected with this state and cost?

STEW. 　　　　　　He was not,
But is converted; and I hope you wo' not
Persist in heresy, but take a course
Of riot, to content your friends; you shall
Want nothing, if you can be proud, and
spend it
For my lady's honor. Here are a hun-
dred
Pieces will serve you till you have new
clothes;
I will present you with a nag of mine,
Poor tender of my service—please you
accept.
My lady's smile more than rewards me
for it.　　　　　　140
I must provide fit servants to attend you,
Monsieurs, for horse and foot.

FRED. 　　　　　I shall submit,
If this be my aunt's pleasure, and be
ruled;
My eyes are opened with this purse already,
And sack will help to inspire me. I must
spend it?

STEW. What else, sir?

FRED.   I'll begin with you. To encourage
You to have still a special care of me,
There is five pieces—not for your nag.
STEW. No, sir; I hope it is not.
FRED.   Buy a beaver [1]
For thy own block; I shall be ruled. Who does   150
Command the wine cellar?
STEW.   Who command but you, sir?
FRED. I'll try to drink a health or two, my aunt's,
Or anybody's; and, if that foundation
Stagger me not too much, I will commence
In all the arts of London.
STEW.   If you find, sir,
The operation of the wine exalt
Your blood to the desire of any female
Delight, I know your aunt wo' not deny
Any of her chambermaids to practice on;
She loves you but too well.
FRED.   I know not how   160
I may be for that exercise.—Farewell, Aristotle!
Prithee, commend me to the library
At Westminster; my bones I bequeath thither,
And to the learned worms that mean to visit 'em.
I will compose myself; I begin to think
I have lost time indeed.—Come, to the wine cellar.   *Exit [with Steward].*

[SCENE ii.

A room in Celestina's house.]

Enter Celestina, Mariana, Isabella.

MAR. But shall we not, madam, expose ourselves
To censure for this freedom?
CEL.   Let them answer
That dare mistake us. Shall we be so much
Cowards, to be frighted from our pleasure,
Because men have malicious tongues, and show
What miserable souls they have? No, cousin,
We hold our life and fortunes upon no
Man's charity; if they dare show so little

[1] Beaver hat.

Discretion to traduce our fames, we will
Be guilty of so much wit to laugh at 'em.
ISA. 'Tis a becoming fortitude.
CEL.   My stars   11
Are yet kind to me; for, in a happy minute
Be 't spoke, I'm not in love, and men shall never
Make my heart lean with sighing, nor with tears
Draw on my eyes the infamy of spectacles.
'Tis the chief principle to keep your heart
Under your own obedience; jest, but love not.
I say my prayers, yet can wear good clothes,
And only satisfy my tailor for 'em.
I wo' not lose my privilege.   20
MAR. And yet they say your entertainments are—
Give me your pardon, madam—to proclaim
Yourself a widow, and to get a husband.
CEL. As if a lady of my years, some beauty,
Left by her husband rich, that had mourned for him
A twelvemonth too, could live so obscure i' th' town
That gallants would not know her, and invite
Themselves, without her chargeable [2] proclamations!
Then we are worse than citizens.[3] No widow
Left wealthy can be throughly warm in mourning,   30
But some one noble blood or lusty kindred
Claps in with his gilt coach and Flandrian trotters,
And hurries her away to be a countess.
Courtiers have spies, and great ones with large [4] titles,
Cold in their own estates, would warm themselves
At a rich city bonefire.
ISA.   Most true, madam.

[2] Expensive.
[3] Dwellers in the city, *i.e.*, middle-class persons.
[4] Gifford-Dyce's reading. Original reads *charge.*

Cel. No matter for corruption of the
blood—
Some undone courtier made her husband
rich,
And this new lord receives it back again.
Admit it were my policy, and that   40
My entertainments pointed to acquaint
me
With many suitors, that I might be safe
And make the best election, could you
blame me?
Mar. Madam, 'tis wisdom.
Cel.   But I should be
In my thoughts miserable, to be fond [1]
Of leaving the sweet freedom I possess,
And court myself into new marriage
fetters.
I now observe men's several wits and
windings,
And can laugh at their follies.
Mar.   You have given
A most ingenious satisfaction.   50
Cel. One thing I'll tell you more, and this
I give you
Worthy your imitation, from my prac-
tice:
You see me merry, full of song and danc-
ing,
Pleasant in language, apt to all delights
That crown a public meeting; but you
cannot
Accuse me of being prodigal of my favors
To any of my guests. I do not summon,
By any wink, a gentleman to follow me
To my withdrawing chamber; I hear all
Their pleas in court, nor can they boast
abroad   60
(And do me justice [2]) after a salute
They have much conversation with my
lip.
I hold the kissing of my hand a courtesy,
And he that loves me must, upon the
strength
Of that, expect [3] till I renew his favor.
Some ladies are so expensive in their
graces
To those that honor 'em, and so prodigal,
That in a little time they have nothing
but
The naked sin left to reward their serv-
ants,

Whereas a thrift in our rewards will
keep   70
Men long in their devotion, and preserve
Ourselves in stock, to encourage those
that honor us.
Isa. This is an art worthy a lady's practice.
Cel. It takes not from the freedom of our
mirth,
But seems to advance it, when we can
possess
Our pleasures with security of our honor;
And, that preserved, I welcome all the
joys
My fancy can let in. In this I have given
The copy of my mind, nor do I blush
You understand it.

Enter Celestina's Gentlewoman.

Isa.   You have honored us.   80
Gen. Madam, Sir William Scentlove's
come to wait on you.
Cel. There's one would be a client.—Make
excuse
For a few minutes.   [*Exit Gentlewoman.*]
Mar.   One that comes a-wooing?
Cel. Such a thing he would seem, but in
his guiltiness
Of little land, his expectation is not
So valiant as it might be. He wears [rich] [4]
clothes,
And feeds with noblemen; to some, I
hear,
No better than a wanton emissary
Or scout for Venus' wild fowl, which
made tame,
He thinks no shame to stand court
sentinel,   90
In hope of the reversion.
Mar.   I have heard
That some of them are often my lord's
tasters;
The first fruits they condition for and will
Exact as fees, for the promotion.
Cel. Let them agree; there's no account
shall lie
For me among their traffic.

Enter Gentlewo[man].

Gen.   Mr. Haircut, madam,
Is new come in, to tender you his service.
Cel. Let him discourse a little with Sir
William.   *Exit [Gentlewoman].*

---

[1] Foolishly desirous.
[2] Gifford-Dyce's reading.   Original reads
justifie.   [3] Wait.
[4] Supplied by Gifford-Dyce.

MAR. What is this gentleman, Mr. Hair-
cut, madam?
I note him very gallant, and much
courted   100
By gentlemen of quality.
CEL.   I know not,
More than a trim, gay man; he has some
great office,
Sure, by his confident behavior.
He would be entertained under the title
Of servant to me, and I must confess
He is the sweetest of all men that visit
me.
ISA. How mean you, madam?
CEL.   He is full of powder;
He will save much in perfume for my
chamber,
Were he but constant here.—Give 'em
access.

Enter Sir Will[iam] Scentlove, Mr. Haircut.

SCENT. Madam, the humblest of your
servants is   110
Exalted to a happiness, if you smile
Upon my visit.
HAIR.   I must beg your charity
Upon my rudeness, madam; I shall
give
That day up lost to any happiness,
When I forget to tender you my serv-
ice.
CEL. You practice courtship, gentlemen.
SCENT.   But cannot
Find where with more desert to exercise
it.—
What lady's this, I pray?
CEL.   A kinswoman
Of mine, Sir William.
SCENT.   I am more her servant.
                         [*Takes Mariana aside.*]
CEL. You came from court, now, I pre-
sume.
HAIR.   'Tis, madam,   120
The sphere I move in, and my destiny
Was kind to place me there, where I
enjoy
All blessings that a mortal can possess,
That lives not in your presence; and I
should
Fix my ambition, when you would vouch-
safe
Me so much honor to accept from me
An humble entertainment there.

CEL.   But by
What name shall I be known? In what
degree
Shall I be of kinred [1] to you?
HAIR.   How mean you, madam?
CEL. Perhaps you'll call me sister—I shall
take it   130
A special preferment; or it may be
I may pass under title of your mistress,
If I seem rich and fair enough to engage
Your confidence to own me.
HAIR.   I would hope—
CEL. But 'tis not come to that yet; you
will, sir,
Excuse my mirth.
HAIR.   Sweet madam!
CEL.   Shall I take
Boldness to ask what place you hold in
court?
'Tis an uncivil curiosity,
But you'll have mercy to a woman's
question.
HAIR. My present condition, madam, car-
ries   140
Honor and profit, though not to be named
With that employment I expect i' th'
state,
Which shall discharge the first maturity
Upon your knowledge; until then, I beg
You allow a modest silence.
CEL.   I am charmed, sir;
And, if you scape ambassador, you can-
not
Reach a preferment wherein I'm against
you.
But where's Sir William Scentlove?
HAIR.   Give him leave
To follow his nose, madam; while he
hunts
In view, he'll soon be at a fault.[2]
CEL.   You know him?   150
HAIR. Know Scentlove? Not a page but
can decipher him;
The waiting-women know him to a
scruple.
He's called the blister-maker of the town.
CEL. What's that?
HAIR.[3]   The laundry ladies can
resolve [4] you,

---

[1] Kindred.
[2] *I.e.*, while now he can see the quarry, he'll
soon lose the scent.
[3] Emended by Gifford-Dyce. Original reads
Isa.   [4] Inform.

And you may guess—an arrant epicure
As this day lives, born to a pretty wit,
A knight, but no gentleman. I must
Be plain to you; your ladyship may have
Use of this knowledge, but conceal the
    author.
SCENT. I kiss your fairest hand.
MAR.   You make a difference; 160
    Pray reconcile 'em to an equal whiteness.
SCENT. You wound my meaning, lady.
CEL.   Nay, Sir William
    Has the art of compliment.
SCENT.   Madam, you honor me
    'Bove my desert of language.
CEL.   Will you please
    To enrich me with your knowledge of
    that gentleman?
SCENT. Do you not know him, madam?
CEL.   What is he?
SCENT. A camphire [1] ball. You shall know
    more hereafter;
He shall tell you himself, and save my
    character.
Till then—you see he's proud.
CEL.   One thing, gentlemen,
    I observe in your behavior, which is
    rare   170
In two that court one mistress: you pre-
    serve
A noble friendship. There's no gum
    within
Your hearts; you cannot fret,[2] or show an
    envy
Of one another's hope. Some would not
    govern
Their passions with that temper!
SCENT.   The whole world
    Sha' not divorce our friendship.—Mr.
    Haircut!
Would I had lives to serve him! He is
    lost
To goodness does not honor him.
HAIR.   My knight!
CEL. [Aside.] This is right playing at
    court shuttlecock.

Enter Gentlew[oman].

GEN. Madam, there is a gentleman de-
    sires   180
To speak wi'e, one Sir Thomas Born-
    well.

[1] Camphor.
[2] Gum was used to stiffen velvet, which thereafter fretted easily.

CEL.   Bornwell?
GEN. He says he is a stranger to your lady-
    ship.
SCENT. I know him.
HAIR.   Your neighbor, madam.
SCENT.   Husband to
    The lady that so revels in the Strand.
HAIR. He has good parts, they say, but
    cannot help
    His lady's bias.
CEL.   They have both much fame
    I' th' town, for several merits. Pray, ad-
    mit him.   [Exit Gentlewoman.]
HAIR. [Aside.] What comes he for?

Enter Sir Thomas.

BORN. Your pardon, noble lady, that I
    have
Presumed, a stranger to your knowl-
    edge—   [Kisses Celestina.]
CEL.   Sir,   190
Your worth was here before you, and
    your person
Cannot be here ingrateful.
BORN.   'Tis the bounty
Of your sweet disposition, madam.—[To
    Isabella.] Make me
Your servant, lady, by her fair example,
To favor me.—[Offers to kiss Isabella, who
    turns her cheek. Aside.] I never knew
    one turn
Her cheek to a gentleman that came to
    kiss her,
But sh'ad a stinking breath.—Your serv-
    ant, gentlemen.
Will Scentlove, how is 't?
CEL.   I am sorry, coz,
To accuse you; we in nothing more be-
    tray   199
Ourselves to censure of ridiculous pride
Than answering a fair salute too rudely.
O, it shows ill upon a gentlewoman
Not to return the modest lip, if she
Would have the world believe her breath
    is not
Offensive.
BORN.   Madam, I have business
    With you.   [The Rest step aside.]
SCENT.   His looks are pleasant.
CEL.   With me, sir?
BORN. I hear you have an ex'llent wit,
    madam;
I see you're fair.

CEL.   The first is but report;
And do not trust your eyesight for the
    last,
Cause I presume y' are mortal, and may
    err.   210
HAIR. He is very gamesome.
BORN.   Y'ave an ex'llent voice
(They say you catched it from a dying
    swan),
Which, joined to the sweet harmony of
    your lute,
You ravish all mankind.
CEL.   Ravish mankind?
BORN. With their consent.
CEL.   It were the stranger rape;
But there's the less indictment lies
    against it,
And there is hope your little honesties [1]
Cannot be much the worse, for men do
    rather
Believe they had a maidenhead than put
Themselves to th' rack of memory how
    long   220
'Tis since they left the burden of their
    innocence.
BORN. Why, you are bitter, madam!
CEL.   So is physic;
I do not know your constitution.
BORN. You shall, if please you, madam.
CEL.   Y' are too hasty;
I must examine what certificate
You have first, to prefer you.
BORN.   Fine! Certificate?
CEL. Under your lady's hand and seal.
BORN.   Go to.
I see you are a wag.
CEL.   But take heed how
You trust to 't.
BORN.   I can love you in my wedlock
As well as that young gallant o' th' first
    hair   230
Or the knight bachelor, and can return
As amorous delight to thy soft bosom.
CEL. Your person and your language are
    both strangers.
BORN. But may be more familiar; I have
    those
That dare make affidavit for my body.
CEL. D'e mean your surgeon?
BORN.   My surgeon, madam?
I know not how you value my abilities,
But I dare undertake as much, to express
My service to your ladyship, and with

[1] Chastities.

As fierce ambition fly to your commands
As the most valiant of these lay siege to
    you.   241
CEL. You dare not, sir.
BORN.   How, madam?
CEL.   I will justify 't.
You dare not marry me; and I imagine
Some here, should I consent, would
    fetch a priest
Out of the fire.
BORN.   I have a wife indeed.
CEL. And there's a statute not repealed, I
    take it.
BORN. Y' are in the right; I must confess
    y'ave hit
And bled me in a master vein.
CEL.   You think
I took you on the advantage; use your
    best
Skill at defense, I'll come up to your
    valor,   250
And show another work you dare not do:
You dare not, sir, be virtuous.
BORN.   I dare,
By this fair hand I dare, and ask a par-
    don
If my rude words offend thy innocence,
Which, in a form so beautiful, would
    shine
To force a blush in them suspected it,
And from the rest draw wonder.
HAIR.   I like not
Their secret parley; shall I interrupt 'em?
ISA. By no means, sir.
SCENT.   Sir Thomas was not wont
To show so much a courtier.
MAR.   He cannot   260
Be prejudicial to you. Suspect not
Your own deserts so much; he's married.
BORN. I have other business, madam.
    You keep music;
I came to try how you can dance.
CEL. You did?—[Aside.] I'll try his humor
    out of breath.—
Although I boast no cunning, sir, in
    revels,
If you desire to show your art that way,
I can wait on you.
BORN.   You much honor me;
Nay, all must join to make a harmony.
                                    They dance.
BORN. I have nothing now, madam, but
    to beseech,   270
After a pardon for my boldness, you

Would give occasion to pay my gratitude.
I have a house will be much honor[é]d,
If you vouchsafe your presence, and a wife
Desires to present herself your servant.
I came with the ambition to invite you;
Deny me not. Your person you shall trust
On fair security.

CEL.   Sir, although I use not
This freedom with a stranger, you shall have
No cause to hold me obstinate.

BORN.   You grace me. 280
Sir William Scentlove—

HAIR.   I must take my leave.
You will excuse me, madam; court attendances—

CEL. By any means.

BORN.   Ladies, you will vouchsafe
Your company?

ISA. ⎱
MAR. ⎰   We wait upon you, sir.

Exeunt.

THE THIRD ACT. [SCENE i.

A dressing room.]

Enter Lord, unready; [1] *Haircut preparing
his periwig; table and looking-glass.*

LORD. What hour is 't?

HAIR.   'Bout three a-clock, my lord.

LORD.[2] 'Tis time to rise.

HAIR.   Your lordship went but late
To bed last night.

LORD.   'Twas early in the morning.

Enter Secre[tary].

SEC. [*Calling back.*] Expect awhile.—My
lord is busy?

LORD. What's the matter?

SEC.   Here is a lady
Desires access to you upon some affairs
She says may specially concern your
lordship.

LORD. A lady? What her name?

SEC.   Madam Decoy.

LORD. Decoy? Prithee, admit her.—

Enter Decoy.

      Have you business, madam, 9
With me?

DEC.   And such, I hope, as will not be
Offensive to your lordship.

[1] Partly dressed.   [2] Original reads *Bor.*

LORD.   I pray, speak it.

DEC. I would desire your lordship's ear
more private.

LORD. [*To Secretary and Haircut.*] Wait i'
th' next chamber till I call.—(*Exeunt
*[*Haircut and Secretary*].) Now, madam.

DEC. Although I am a stranger to your
lordship,
I would not lose a fair occasion offered
To show how much I honor and would
serve you.

LORD. Please you to give me the particular,
That I may know the extent of my engagement.
I am ignorant by what desert you should
Be encouraged to have care of me.

DEC.   My lord, 20
I will take boldness to be plain; beside
Your other excellent parts, you have
much fame
For your sweet inclination to our sex.

LORD. How d'e mean, madam?

DEC.   I' that way your lordship
Hath honorably practiced upon some
Not to be named, your noble constancy
To a mistress hath deserved our general
vote,
And I, a part of womankind, have
thought
How to express my duty.

LORD.   In what, madam?

DEC. Be not so strange, my lord. I
know the beauty 30
And pleasures of your eyes—that handsome creature
With whose fair life all your delight took
leave,
And to whose memory you have paid
too much
Sad tribute.

LORD.   What's all this?

DEC.   This: if your lo[rd]s[hip]
Accept my service, in pure zeal to cure
Your melancholy, I could point where
you might
Repair your loss.

LORD.   Your ladyship, I conceive,
Doth traffic in flesh merchandise.

DEC.   To men
Of honor, like yourself. I am well known
To some in court, and come not with ambition 40
Now to supplant your officer.

LORD.   What is
  The lady of pleasure you prefer?
DEC.   A lady
  Of birth and fortune, one upon whose
    virtue
  I may presume, the Lady Aretina.
LORD. Wife to Sir Thomas Bornwell?
DEC.   The same, sir.
LORD. Have you prepared her?
DEC. Not for your lordship, till I have
    found your pulse.
  I am acquainted with her disposition;
  She has a very appliable [1] nature.
LORD. And, madam, when expect you to
    be whipped   50
  For doing these fine favors?
DEC.   How, my lord?
  Your lordship does but jest, I hope; you
    make
  A difference between a lady that
  Does honorable offices, and one
  They call a bawd. Your lordship was not
    wont
  To have such coarse opinion of our prac-
    tice.
LORD. The Lady Aretina is my kins-
    woman.
DEC. What if she be, my lord? The nearer
    blood,
  The dearer sympathy.
LORD.   I'll have thee carted.[2]
DEC. Your lordship wo' not so much stain
    your honor   60
  And education to use a woman
  Of my quality—
LORD.   'Tis possible you may
  Be sent off with an honorable convoy
  Of halberdiers.
DEC.   O, my good lord!
LORD. Your ladyship [3] shall be no protec-
    tion,
  If thou but stay'st three minutes.
DEC.   I am gone.—
  When next you find rebellion in your
    blood,
  May all within ten mile o' th' court turn
    honest! [4]   *Exit.*
LORD. I do not find that proneness, since
    the fair
  Bella Maria died; my blood is cold,   70

Nor is there beauty enough surviving
To heighten me to wantonness.—Who
  waits?

Enter Haircut.

And what said my lady?
HAIR. The silent language of her face, my
    lord,
  Was not so pleasant as it showed upon
  Her entrance.
LORD.   Would any man that meets
  This lady take her for a bawd?
HAIR.   She does
  The trade an honor, credit to the pro-
    fession.
  We may in time see baldness, quarter
    noses,
  And rotten legs to take the wall of [5]
    footcloths.[6]   80
LORD. I ha' thought better.—[*To Secretary
    within.*] Call the lady back.
  I wo' not lose this opportunity.
  Bid her not fear. The favor is not com-
    mon,
  And I'll reward it.—I do wonder much
  Will Scentlove was not here today.
HAIR. I heard him say this morning he
    would wait
  Upon your lordship.—She is returned,
    sir.

Enter Secre[tary] and Decoy.

SEC. Madam, be confident; my lord's not
    angry.
LORD. You return welcome, madam; you
    are better
  Read in your art, I hope, than to be
    frighted   90
  With any shape of anger, when you bring
  Such news to gentlemen. Madam, you
    shall
  Soon understand how I accept the office.
DEC. You are the first lord, since I studied
    carriage,[7]
  That showed such infidelity and fury
  Upon so kind a message. Every gentle-
    man
  Will show some breeding, but if one right
    honorable
  Should not have noble blood—

---

[1] Pliable, compliant.
[2] Bawds were punished by being whipped
through the streets at the tail of a cart.
[3] Station as a lady.   [4] Chaste

[5] Take precedence over.
[6] The caparison of a horse.
[7] Acting as a go-between.

LORD. You shall return
My compliment in a letter to my Lady
Aretina. Favor me with a little pa-
tience.— 100
Show her that chamber.

DEC. I'll attend your lordship.

[*Exeunt Decoy and Haircut. Secretary prepares to write.*]

LORD. Write—"Madam, where your honor
is in danger,
My love must not be silent."—

Enter Scentlove and Kickshaw.

Scentlove and Kickshaw!

KICK. Your lordship's busy.

LORD. Writing a letter.—Nay, it sha' not
bar
Any discourse.

SEC. "—silent."

LORD. "Though I be no physician, I may
Prevent a fever in your blood."—And
where
Have you spent the morning's conversation?

SCENT. Where you would have given the
best Barbary 110
In your stable to have met on honorable
terms.

LORD. What new beauty? You acquaint
yourselves
With none but wonders.

SCENT. 'Tis too low—a miracle.

LORD. 'Twill require a strong faith.

SEC. "—your blood."

LORD. "If you be innocent, preserve your
fame, lest this Decoy,
Madam, betray it, to your repentance."—
By what name is she known?

SCENT. Ask Alexander;
He knows her.

AL. Whom?

SCENT. The Lady Celestina.

LORD. He has a vast knowledge of ladies.
'Las, poor Alexander!
When dost thou mean thy body shall lie
fallow? 120

AL. When there is mercy in a petticoat.
I must turn pilgrim for some breath.

LORD. I think
'Twere cooler travel, if you examine it,
Upon the hoof through Spain.

SCENT. Through Ethiopia.

LORD. Nay, less laborious to serve a pren-
ticeship
In Peru, and dig gold out of the mine,
Where all the year is dog days.

SEC. "— to repentance."

LORD. "In brief, this lady, could you fall
from virtue,
Within my knowledge, will not blush to
be a bawd."

SCENT. But, hang 't, 'tis honorable journey-
work; 130
Thou art famous by 't, and thy name's
up.

AL. So, sir!
Let me ask you a question, my dear
knight:
Which is less servile, to bring up the
pheasant
And wait, or sit at table uncontrolled
And carve to my own appetite?

SCENT. No more;
Th' art witty, as I am.

SEC. "— a bawd."

SCENT. How's that?

AL. O, you are famous by 't, and your
name's up, sir.

LORD. "Be wise, and reward my caution
with
Timely care of yourself, so I shall not
repent
To be known your loving kinsman and
servant"— 140
Gentlemen, the Lady Celestina,
Is she so rare a thing?

AL. If you'll have my
Opinion, my lord, I never saw
So sweet, so fair, so rich a piece of nature.

LORD. I'll show thee a fairer presently, to
shame
Thy eyes and judgment; look o' that.—
[*Shows him a picture.*] So, I'll subscribe. [*Signs his name.*]
Seal it; I'll excuse your pen for the direction.

AL. Bella Maria's picture! She was handsome.

SCENT. But not to be compared—

LORD. Your patience, gentlemen; I'll return instantly. *Exit.* 150

AL. Whither is my lord gone?

SEC. To a lady i' th' next chamber.

SCENT. What is she?

SEC. You shall pardon me; I am his secretary.

Scent. I was wont to be of his counsel. A
 new officer,
And I not know 't? I am resolved to
 batter
All other with the praise of Celestina.
I must retain him.

Enter Lord.

Lord.   Has not that object—
Convinced your erring judgments?
Al.   What, this picture?
Lord. Were but your thoughts as capable
 as mine   159
Of your idea, you would wish no thought
That were not active in her praise, above
All worth and memory of her sex.
Scent.   She was fair,
I must confess; but, had your lordship
 looked
With eyes more narrow and some less
 affection
Upon her face—
Al. I do not love the copies
Of any dead; they make me dream of
 goblins.
Give me a living mistress, with but half
The beauty of Celestina. Come, my lord,
'Tis pity that a lord of so much flesh
Should waste upon a ghost, when they
 are living   170
Can give you a more honorable consump-
 tion.
Scent. Why, do you mean, my lord, to
 live an infidel?
Do, and see what will come on 't; observe
 still
And dote upon your vigils; build a cham-
 ber
Within a rock, a tomb among the worms,
Not far off, where you may in proof
 apocryphal
Court 'em not devour the pretty pile
Of flesh your mistress carried to the
 grave.
There are no women in the world; all eyes
And tongue and lips are buried in her
 coffin!   180
Lord. Why, do you think yourselves com-
 petent judges
Of beauty, gentlemen?
Both.   What should hinder us?
Al. I have seen and tried as many as an-
 other
With a mortal back.

Lord.   Your eyes are bribed,
And your hearts chained to some desires;
 you cannot
Enjoy the freedom of a sense.
Al.   Your lordship
Has a clear eyesight, and can judge and
 penetrate.
Lord. I can, and give a perfect censure[1] of
Each line and point; distinguish beauty
 from
A thousand forms, which your corrupted
 optics   190
Would pass for natural.
Scent.   I desire no other
Judge should determine[2] us, and, if your
 lordship
Dare venture but your eyes upon this
 lady,
I'll stand their justice, and be confident
You shall give Celestina victory
And triumph o'er all beauties past and
 living.
Al. I dare, my lord, venture a suit of
 clothes
You will be o'ercome.
Lord. You do not know my fortitude.
Scent. Nor frailty; you dare not trust
 yourself to see her.
Lord. Think you so, gentlemen? I dare
 see this creature   200
To make you know your errors, and the
 difference
Of her whose memory is my saint. Not
 trust
My senses? I dare see and speak with
 her.
Which holds the best acquaintance to
 prepare
My visit to her?
Scent.   I will do 't, my lord.
Al. She is a lady free in entertainments.
Lord. I would give this advantage to your
 cause.
Bid her [3] appear in all the ornaments
Did ever wait on beauty, all the riches
Pride can put on, and teach her face more
 charm   210
Than ever poet dressed up Venus in;
Bid her be all the Graces and the Queen
Of Love in one, I'll see her, Scentlove,
 and

---

[1] Judgment.   [2] Decide for.
[3] Emended by Gifford-Dyce. Original reads
him.

Bring off my heart, armed but [with a] [1]
  single thought
Of one that is dead, without a wound,
  and, when
I have made your folly prisoner, I'll
  laugh at you.
SCENT. She shall expect you; trust to me
  for knowledge.
LORD. I'm for the present somewhere else
  engaged;
Let me hear from you.   [*Exit.*]
SCENT.   So! I am glad he's yet
So near conversion.
AL.   I am for Aretina.   220
SCENT. No mention of my lord.
AL.   Prepare his lady;
'Tis time he were reduced [2] to the old
  sport.
One lord like him more would undo the
  court.   *Exit* [*with Scentlove*].

[SCENE ii.

A room in Bornwell's house.]

Enter Aretina with a letter; Decoy.

DEC. He is the ornament of your blood,
  madam;
I am much bound to his lordship.
ARE.   He gives you
A noble character.
DEC.   'Tis his goodness, madam.
ARE. [*Aside.*] I wanted such an engine.[3]
  My lord has
Done me a courtesy to disclose her na-
  ture;
I now know one to trust, and will employ
  her.—
Touching my lord, for reasons which I
  shall
Offer to your ladyship hereafter, I
Desire you would be silent; but, to
  show
How much I dare be confident in your
  secrecy,   10
I pour my bosom forth. I love a gentle-
  man,
On whom there wo' not need [4] much con-
  juration
To meet.—Your ear.   [*Whispers to her.*]
DEC.   I apprehend you, and I shall
Be happy to be serviceable. I am sorry

[1] Supplied by Gifford-Dyce.
[2] Brought back.   [3] Device.
[4] Gifford-Dyce's reading. Original reads *meet*.

Your ladyship did not know me before
  now.
I have done offices, and not a few
Of the nobility but have done feats
Within my house, which is convenient
For situation and artful chambers
And pretty pictures to provoke the
  fancy.   20

Enter Littleworth.

LIT. Madam, all pleasures languish in your
  absence.
ARE. Your pardon a few minutes, sir.—
  [*Walks aside with Decoy.*] You must
Contrive it thus.
LIT.   I attend, and shall account it
Honor to wait on your return.
ARE.   He must not
Have the least knowledge of my name or
  person.
DEC. I have practiced that already for
  some great ones,
And dare again, to satisfy you, madam;
I have a thousand ways to do sweet
  offices.
LIT. [*To himself.*] If this Lady Aretina
  should be honest,   29
I ha' lost time. She's free as air; I must
Have closer conference, and, if I have art,
Make her affect me in revenge.
DEC.   This evening?
Leave me to manage things.
ARE.   You will oblige me.
DEC. You shall commend my art, and
  thank me after.   *Ex*[*it*].
ARE. I hope the revels are maintained
  within.
LIT. By Sir Thomas and his mistress.
ARE.   How? His mistress?
LIT. The Lady Celestina; I ne'er saw
Eyes shoot more amorous interchange.
ARE.   Is 't so?
LIT. He wears her favor with o'er-pride[5] —
ARE.   Her favor?
LIT. A feather that he ravished from her
  fan—   40
And is so full of courtship, which she
  smiles on.
ARE. 'Tis well.
LIT.   And praises her beyond all poetry.
ARE. I'm glad he has so much wit.
LIT. [*Aside.*]   Not jealous!

[5] Immense pride.

ARE. [*Aside*.] This secures me. What
　would make other ladies pale
With jealousy, gives but a license to my
　wand'rings.
Let him now tax me, if he dare; and
　yet
Her beauty's worth my envy, and I wish
Revenge upon it, not because he loves,
But that it shines above my own.

Enter Alex[ander].

AL.　　　　　　　　　Dear madam!
ARE. [*Aside*.] I have it.—You two gentle-
　men profess　　　　　　　　　　50
Much service to me; if I have a way
To employ your wit and secrecy—
BOTH.　　　　　　　You'll honor us.
ARE. You gave a high and worthy char-
　acter
Of Celestina.
AL.　　　　　　　I remember, madam.
ARE. Do either of you love her?
AL.　　　　　　　　　Not I, madam.
LIT. I would not, if I might.
ARE.　　　　　　　She's now my guest
And, by a trick, invited by my husband
To disgrace me. You, gentlemen, are
　held
Wits of the town, the consuls that do
　govern
The senate here, whose jeers are all
　authentic.　　　　　　　　　　60
The taverns and the ordinaries are
Made academies, where you come, and
　all
Your sins and surfeits made the time's
　example.
Your very nods can quell a theater;
No speech or poem good without your
　seal;
You can protect scurrility, and publish;
By your authority believed, no rapture
Ought to have honest meaning.
AL.　　　　　　　Leave our characters.
LIT. And name the employment.
ARE.　　　　　　　You must exercise
The strength of both your wits upon this
　lady,　　　　　　　　　　　　70
And talk her into humbleness or anger,
Both which are equal, to my thought. If
　you
Dare undertake this slight thing for my
　sake,

My favor shall reward it; but be faith-
　ful,
And seem to let all spring from your own
　freedom.
AL. This all? We can defame her. If you
　please,
My friend shall call her whore, or any-
　thing,
And never be endangered to a duel.
ARE. How's that?
AL. He can endure a cudgeling, and no
　man　　　　　　　　　　　　　80
Will fight after so fair a satisfaction.
But leave us to our art, and do not limit
　us.
ARE. They are here; begin not till I whis-
　per you.

Enter Sir Thomas, Celestina, Mariana, Isa-
*　　　　　　　　　　　　　　bella.*

ARE.[1] *Je vous prie, madame, d'excuser*
l'importunité de mes affaires, qui m'ont fait
offenser, par mon absence, une dame de
laquelle j'ai reçu tant d'obligation.
　CEL. *Pardonnez-moi, madame; vous me*
faites trop d'honneur.　　　　　　89
　ARE. *C'est bien de la douceur de votre na-*
turel, que vous tenez cette langage. Mais
j'espère que mon mari n'a pas manqué de
vous entretenir en mon absence.
　CEL. *En vérité, monsieur nous a fort*
obligé.
　ARE. *Il eût trop failli, s'il n'eût taché de*
tout son pouvoir à vous rendre toutes sortes de
services.
　CEL. *C'est de sa bonté qu'il nous a tant*
favorisé.　　　　　　　　　　100
　ARE. *De la vôtre plutôt, madame, que*
vous fait donner d'interprétation si bénigne
à ses efforts.
　CEL. *Je vois bien que la victoire sera tou-*
jours à madame, et de langage et de la
courtesie.
　ARE. *Vraiment, madame, que jamais per-*
sonne a plus désiré l'honneur de votre
compagnie que moi.
　CEL. *Laissons-en, je vous supplie,* [110
des compliments, et permettez à votre servante
de vous baiser les mains.

[1] The French as well as some of the English
which follows has been printed as prose, although in the original an unsuccessful attempt
at line division has been made.

ARE. *Vous m'obligez trop.*[1]

BORN. I have no more patience; let's be merry again

In our own language. Madam, our mirth cools.—

Enter Frederick [, intoxicated, and Steward].

Our nephew!

ARE. Passion of my brain!

FRED. Save you, gentlemen! Save you, ladies!

ARE. I am undone!   120

FRED. I must salute, no matter at which end I begin.   [*Kisses Celestina.*]

ARE. There's a compliment!

CEL. Is this your nephew, madam?

ARE. *Je vous prie, madame, d'excuser les habits et le rude comportement de mon cousin. Il est tout fraîchement venu de l'université, où on l'a tout gâté.*

CEL. *Excusez-moi, madame; il est bien accompli.*[2]   130

FRED. This language should be French by the motions of your heads and the mirth of your faces.

[1] ARE. I beg you, madam, to pardon the importunity of my affairs, which have made me offend, by my absence, a lady from whom I have received so much obligation.
CEL. Pardon me, madam; you do me too much honor.
ARE. It is indeed from the kindness of your good nature that you use such language. But I hope that my husband has not failed to entertain you in my absence.
CEL. In truth, your husband has been very kind.
ARE. He would have been too remiss if he hadn't tried with all his might to render you all kinds of services.
CEL. It is out of his good nature that he has been so good to us.
ARE. It is your good nature rather that makes you give such a gracious interpretation to his efforts.
CEL. I see indeed that the victory will always be madam's both in language and in courtesy.
ARE. Truly, madam, no one ever more desired the honor of your company than I.
CEL. Leave compliments, I pray you, and permit your servant to kiss your hand.
ARE. You are too kind.
[2] ARE. I beg you, madam, to excuse the dress and the rude behavior of my kinsman. He has but lately come from the university, where they completely corrupted him.
CEL. Excuse me, madam; he is indeed accomplished.

ARE. I am dishonored.

FRED. 'Tis one of the finest tongues for ladies to show their teeth in. If you'll Latin, I am for you, or Greek it; my tailor has not put me into French yet. *Mille basia, basia mille.*[3]   139

CEL. *Je ne vous entends pas, monsieur—* I understand you not, sir.

FRED. Why, so?

You and I then shall be in charity,

For, though we should be abusive, we ha' the benefit

Not to understand one another. Where's my aunt?

I did hear music somewhere, and my brains,

Tuned with a bottle of your capering claret,

Made haste to show their dancing.

LIT. [*Offering sweetmeats to Celestina.*]
                         Please you, madam,

They are very comfortable.[4]

STEW.   Alas, madam,

How would you have me help it? I did use   150

All means I could, after he heard the music,

To make him drunk, in hope so to contain him;

But the wine made him lighter, and his head

Flew hither, ere I missed his heels.

AL. Nay, he spoke Latin to the lady.

ARE. O, most unpardonable! Get him off

Quickly, and discreetly; or, if I live—

STEW. 'Tis not in my power; he swears I am

An absurd, sober fellow, and, if you keep

A servant in his house to cross his humor,   160

When the rich sword and belt comes home, he'll kill him.

ARE. What shall I do? Try your skill, Master Littleworth.

LIT. He has ne'er a sword.—Sweet Mr. Frederick—

BORN. 'Tis pity, madam, such a scion should

Be lost. But you are clouded.

CEL.   Not I, sir;

I never found myself more clear at heart.

[3] A thousand kisses, kisses a thousand.
[4] Comforting.

BORN. I could play with a feather; your fan, lady.—

Gentlemen, Aretina, ta, ra, ra, ra! Come, madam.

FRED. Why, my good tutor in election? You might have been a scholar.

LIT.   But I thank 170
My friends they brought me up a little better.

Give me the town wits, that deliver jests
Clean from the bow, that whistle in the air,
And cleave the pin at twelvescore! Ladies do
But laugh at a gentleman that has any learning;
'Tis sin enough to have your clothes suspected.
Leave us, and I will find a time to instruct you.
Come, here are sugarplums. 'Tis a good Frederick.

FRED. Why, is not this my aunt's house in the Strand?
The noble rendezvous? Who laughs at me?   180
Go, I will root here if I list,[1] and talk
Of rhetoric, logic, Latin, Greek, or anything,
And understand 'em too. Who says the contrary?
Yet, in a fair way, I contemn all learning,
And will be as ignorant as he, or he,
Or any taffeta, satin, scarlet, plush,
Tissue, or cloth-a-bodkin[2] gentleman,
Whose manners are most gloriously infected.—
Did you laugh at me, lady?

CEL.   Not I, sir;
But, if I did show mirth upon your question,   190
I hope you would not beat me, little gentleman.

FRED. How, "little gentleman"? You dare not say
These words to my new clothes and fighting sword.

ARE. Nephew Frederick!

FRED.   "Little gentleman"!
This an affront both to my blood and person!

¹ Please.
² Baudekin was a rich gold and silk cloth.

I am a gentleman of as tall [3] a birth
As any boast nobility; though my clothes
Smell o' the lamp, my coat [4] is honorable,
Right honorable, full of or and argent.—
A "little gentleman"!

BORN.   Coz, you must be patient;
My lady meant you no dishonor, and
You must remember she's a woman.   202

FRED. Is she a woman? That's another matter.—
D'e hear? My uncle tells me what you are.

CEL. So, sir.

FRED.   You called me "little gentleman."

CEL. I did, sir.

FRED. A little pink [5] has made a lusty ship
Strike her topsail. The Crow [6] may beard the Elephant; [6]
A whelp [7] may tame the Tiger,[6] spite of all
False decks [8] and murderers; [9] and a "little gentleman"   210
Be hard enough to grapple with your ladyship,
Top and topgallant.—Will you go drink, uncle,
Tother enchanted bottle? You and I
Will tipple, and talk philosophy.

BORN.   Come, nephew.—
You will excuse a minute's absence, madam.—
Wait you on us.

STEW.   My duty, sir.

*Ex[eunt] All but [Aretina and] Cel[estina] and
                Alex[ander] and Little[worth].*

ARE.   Now, gentlemen.

AL. Madam, I had rather you accuse my language
For speaking truth than virtue suffer in
My further silence; and it is my wonder
That you, whose noble carriage hath deserved   220
All honor and opinion, should now
Be guilty of ill manners.

CEL.   What was that
You told me, sir?

LIT.   Do you not blush, madam,
To ask that question?

³ High.   ⁴ Coat of arms.
⁵ A small coasting vessel.
⁶ Probably the name of a ship of war.
⁷ A small ship.
⁸ Barricades raised against boarders.
⁹ Cannon discharging grapeshot.

CEL. You amaze rather
My cheek to paleness. What mean you
  by this?
I am not troubled with the hiccup, gen-
  tlemen,
[1] You should bestow this fright upon me.[2]
LIT. Then
Pride and ill memory go together.
CEL. How, sir?
AL. The gentleman on whom you exercise
Your thin wit was a nephew to the lady
Whose guest you are, and, though her
  modesty 231
Look calm on the abuse of one so near
Her blood, the affront was impious.
LIT. I am ashamed on 't.
You an ingenious lady, and well man-
  nered?
I'll teach a bear as much civility.
CEL. You may be master of the college,
  sir,
For aught I know.
LIT. What college?
CEL.[3] Of the bears.
Have you a plot upon me? D'e possess
Your wits, or know me, gentlemen?

Enter Bornwell [behind].

BORN. How's this?
AL. [*Aside.*] Know you? Yes, we do know
  you to an atom. 240
LIT. Madam, we know what stuff your
  soul is made on.
CEL. But do not bark so like a mastive,[4]
  pray.—
[*Aside.*] Sure they are mad.—Let your
  brains stand awhile
And settle, gentlemen. You know not
  me.
What am I?
LIT. Th' art a puppet, a thing made
Of clothes and painting, and not half so
  handsome
As that which played Susanna in the fair.
CEL. I heard you visited those canvas
  tragedies,
One of their constant audience, and so
  taken

With Susan that you wished yourself a
  rival 250
With the two wicked elders.
AL. You think this
Is wit now. Come, you are—
CEL. What, I beseech you?
Your character will be full of salt and
  satire,
No doubt. What am I?
AL. Why, you are a woman—
CEL. And that's at least a bow [5] wide of
  your knowledge.
AL. Would be thought handsome, and
  might pass i' th' country
Upon a market day, but miserably
Forfeit to pride and fashions, that if
  heaven
Were a new gown, you'd not stay in 't a
  fortnight.
CEL. It must be miserably out of fashion
  then. 260
Have I no sin but pride?
AL. Hast any virtue,
Or but a good face, to excuse that want?
CEL. You praised it yesterday.
AL. That made you proud.
CEL. More pride?
AL. You need not to close up the
  praise;
I have seen a better countenance in a
  sybil.
CEL. When you wore spectacles of sack,[6]
  mistook
The painted cloth,[7] and kissed it for your
  mistress.
AL. Let me ask you a question: how much
Have you consumed in expectation
That I would love you?
CEL. Why, I think as much 270
As you have paid away in honest debts
This seven year. 'Tis a pretty impu-
  dence,
But cannot make me angry.
LIT. Is there any
Man that will cast away his limbs upon
  her?
AL. You do not sing so well as I im-
  agined,
Nor dance; you reel in your coranto,[8]
  and pinch

---

[1] Supply *so that.*
[2] A reference to the belief that fright cured
the hiccups.
[3] In the original this speech head appears at
the beginning of the next line.
[4] Mastiff.
[5] Bowshot.
[6] *I.e.*, had drunk too much sack.
[7] Cheap wall hangings.
[8] A lively dance.

Your petticoat too hard; y'ave no good
   ear
To th' music, and incline too much one
   shoulder,
As you were dancing on the rope, and
   falling.   279
You speak abominable French, and make
A curtsy like a dairymaid.—[*Aside.*] Not
   mad?
LIT. [*Aside.*] Do we not sting her hand-
   somely?
BORN. [*Aside.*]   A conspiracy!
AL. Your state is not so much as 'tis re-
   ported.
When you confer[1] notes, all your hus-
   band's debts
And your own reconciled—but that's
   not it
Will so much spoil your marriage.
CEL.   As what, sir?
Let me know all my faults.
AL.   Some men do whisper
You are not overhonest.
CEL.   All this shall not
Move me to more than laughter, and
   some pity,
Because you have the shapes of gentle-
   men,   290
And, though you have been insolent
   upon me,
I will engage no friend to kick or cudgel
   you,
To spoil your living and your limbs to-
   gether.
I leave that to diseases that offend you,
And spare my curse, poor silken vermin,
   and
Hereafter shall distinguish men from
   monkeys.
BORN. [*Coming forward.*] Brave soul!—
   You brace of horseleeches!—I have
   heard
Their barbarous language, madam; y' are
   too merciful.
They shall be silent to your tongue; pray,
   punish 'em.
CEL. They are things not worth my char-
   acter,[2] nor mention   300
Of any clean breath, so lost in honesty
They cannot satisfy for wrongs enough,
Though they should steal out of the
   world at Tyburn.[3]

LIT. We are hanged already.
CEL. Yet I will talk a little to the pil-
   chards.[4]—
   You two, that have not twixt you both
   the hundred
Part of a soul, coarse woolen-witted
   fellows,
Without a nap, with bodies made for
   burdens,
You, that are only stuffings for apparel,
As you were made but engines[5] for your
   tailors   310
To frame their clothes upon, and get
   them custom,
Until men see you move, yet then you
   dare not,
Out of your guilt of being the ignobler
   beast,
But give a horse the wall, whom you excel
Only in dancing of the brawls,[6] because
The horse was not taught the French
   way! Your two faces,
One fat, like Christmas, tother lean, like
   Candlemas
And prologue to a Lent, both bound to-
   gether,
Would figure Janus, and do many cures
On agues and the green disease[7] by
   frighting;   320
But neither can, with all the characters
And conjuring circles, charm a woman,
   though
Sh'ad fourscore years upon her and but
   one
Tooth in her head, to love or think well
   of you;
And I were miserable to be at cost
To court such a complexion[8] as your
   malice
Did impudently insinuate. But I waste
   time,
And stain my breath in talking to such
   tadpoles.
Go home and wash your tongues in bar-
   ley water,
Drink[9] clean tobacco, be not hot i' th'
   mouth,   330
And you may scape the beadle; so I leave
   you

----

[1] Compare.   [2] Characterizing.
[3] Place of execution.

[4] A term of contempt, perhaps *sardines.*
[5] *I.e.,* manikins.
[6] A French dance like a cotillion.
[7] Greensickness, chlorosis (?).
[8] Disposition.   [9] Smoke.

To shame, and your own garters! [1] —
Sir, I must
Entreat you, for my honor, do not pen-
　ance 'em—
They are not worth your anger. How I
　shall
Acquit your lady's silence!

BORN.　　　　　　　　　Madam, I
Am sorry to suspect, and dare revenge—

CEL. No cause of mine.

BORN. It must become me to attend you
　home.

CEL. You are noble.—Farewell, mush-
　rooms!　　　　[Exit with Bornwell.]

ARE.　　　Is she gone?

LIT. I think we peppered her.

AL.　　　I am glad 'tis over;　340
But I repent no service for you,
　madam.—

Enter Servant, with a letter [and a jewel].

To me? From whence?—A jewel! A
　good preface.
Be happy the conclusion.

ARE.　　Some love letter. *He*[2] *smiles
　upon 't.*

LIT. He has a hundred mistresses. You
　may
Be charitable, madam; I ha' none.
He surfeits, and I fall away i' th' kidneys.

AL. I'll meet.—　　　[*Exit Servant.
Aside.*] 'Tis some great lady, question-
　less, that has
Taken notice, and would satisfy her
　appetite.

ARE. Now, Mr. Alexander, you look bright
　o' the sudden;　　　　　　　　350
Another spirit's in your eye.

AL.　　　　　　Not mine, madam;
Only a summons to meet a friend.

ARE. What friend?

AL.[3]　　By this jewel, I know her not.

ARE. 'Tis a she-friend. I'll follow, gentle-
　men;
We may have a game at sant [4] before
　you go.

AL. I shall attend you, madam.

LIT.　　　　　　　　'Tis our duty.
　　　　　[*Exit with Alexander.*]

ARE. I blush while I converse with my
　own thoughts.

---

[1] *I.e.,* for hanging themselves.
[2] *I.e.,* Alexander.　　[3] Original reads *Lit.*
[4] Cent, a game at cards.

Some strange fate governs me, but I must
　on;
The ways are cast already, and we thrive
When our sin fears no eye nor perspec-
　tive.[5]　　　　　　　　*Exit.*　360

THE FOURTH ACT. [SCENE i.

A room in Decoy's house.]

*Enter two Men leading Alexander, blinded,[6]
　　　and go off suddenly.*

AL. I am not hurt; my patience to obey
　'em,
Not without fear to ha' my throat cut
　else,
Did me a courtesy. Whither ha' they
　brought me?　　[*Pulls off bandage.*]
'Tis devilish dark; the bottom of a well
At midnight, with but two stars on the
　top,
Were broad day to this darkness. I but
　think
How like a whirlwind these rogues caught
　me up,
And smotheréd [7] my eyesight. Let me
　see.
These may be spirits, and, for aught I
　know,
Have brought me hither over twenty
　steeples.　　　　　　　　10
Pray heaven they were not bailiffs (that's
　more worth
My fear) and this a prison! All my debts
Reek in my nostril, and my bones begin
To ache with fear to be made dice; and
　yet
This is too calm and quiet for a prison.
What if the riddle prove I am robbed?
　And yet
I did not feel 'em search me. [*Music
within.*] How now? Music?

Enter Decoy, like an old woman, with a light.

And a light? What beldam's this? I
　cannot pray.—
What art?

DEC.　　　　A friend. Fear not, young
　man; I am
No spirit.

AL. Off!

DEC.　　　Despise me not for age,　20
Or this coarse outside, which I wear not
　out

---

[5] Telescope.　[6] Blindfolded.　[7] Smothered.

Of poverty. Thy eyes be witness, 'tis
No cave or beggar's cell th' art brought
  to; let
That gold speak here's no want, which
  thou mayst spend,
And find a spring to tire even prodigality,
If thou beest wise. [*Gives him a purse.*]

AL.   The devil was a coiner
From the beginning; yet the gold looks
  current.

DEC. Th' art still in wonder. Know, I am
  mistress of
This house, and of a fortune that shall
  serve
And feed thee with delights. 'Twas I sent
  for thee;   30
The jewel and the letter came from me.
It was my art thus to contrive our meeting,
Because I would not trust thee with my
  fame,
Until I found thee worth a woman's
  honor.

AL. [*Aside.*] Honor and fame? The devil
  means to have
A care on 's credit. Though she sent for
  me,
I hope she has another customer
To do the trick withal; I would not turn
Familiar [1] to a witch.

DEC.   What say'st? Canst thou
Dwell in my arms tonight? Shall we
  change kisses,   40
And entertain the silent hours with pleas-
  ure,
Such as old Time shall be delighted with,
And blame the too swift motion of his
  wings,
While we embrace?

AL. [*Aside.*]   Embrace? She has had no
  teeth
This twenty years, and the next violent
  cough
Brings up her tongue; it cannot possibly
Be sound at root. I do not think but one
Strong sneeze upon her, and well meant,
  would make
Her quarters fall away; one kick would
  blow
Her up like gunpowder, and loose all her
  limbs.   50
She is so cold an incubus would not heat
  her;

[1] Familiar spirit.

Her phlegm would quench a furnace, and
  her breath
Would damp a musket bullet.

DEC.   Have you, sir,
  Considered?

AL.   What?

DEC.   My proposition.
Canst love?

AL.   I could have done. Whom do you
  mean?
I know you are pleased but to make
  sport.

DEC.   Thou art not
So dull of soul as thou appear'st.

AL. [*Aside.*]   This is
But some device; my grannam has some
  trick in 't.—
Yes, I can love.

DEC.   But canst thou affect [2] me?

AL. Although to reverence so grave a matron   60
Were an ambitious word in me, yet
  since
You give me boldness, I do love you.

DEC.   Then
Thou art my own.

AL. [*Aside.*]   Has she no cloven foot?

DEC. And I am thine, and all that I command
Thy servants; from this minute thou art
  happy,
And fate in thee will crown all my de-
  sires.
I grieved a proper [3] man should be com-
  pelled
To bring his body to the common mar-
  ket.
My wealth shall make thee glorious; and,
  the more
To encourage thee, howe'er this form
  may fright   70
Thy youthful eyes, yet thou wo't find,
  by light
Of thy own sense, for other light is ban-
  ished
My chamber, when our arms tie lovers'
  knots,
And kisses seal the welcome of our lips,
I shall not there affright thee, nor seem
  old,
With riveled [4] veins; my skin is smooth
  and soft
As ermines, with a spirit to meet thine,

[2] Fancy, love.   [3] Handsome.   [4] Shriveled.

Active and equal to the Queen of Love's
When she did court Adonis.

AL. [*Aside.*]   This doth more
Confirm she is a devil, and I am   80
Within his own dominions. I must on,
Or else be torn a-pieces. I have heard
These succubae must not be crossed.

DEC.   We trifle
Too precious time away; I'll show you a
  prospect
Of the next chamber, and then out the
  candle.

AL. Have you no sack i' th' house?   I
  would go armed
Upon this breach.

DEC.   It sha' not need.

AL.   One word,
Mother—have not you been a cat in
  your days?

DEC. I am glad you are so merry, sir. You
  observe
That bed?   [*Opens a door.*]

AL.   A very brave one.

DEC.   When you are   90
Disrobed, you can come thither in the
  dark.
You sha' not stay for me. Come, as you
  wish
For happiness.   *Exit.*

AL.   I am preferred, if I
Be modest and obey. She cannot have
The heart to do me harm, and [1] she were
  Hecate
Herself. I will have a strong faith, and
  think
I march upon a mistress, the less evil.
If I scape fire now, I defy the devil. *Exit.*

[SCENE ii.

A room in Bornwell's house.]

Enter Fred[erick], Little[worth], Steward.

FRED. And how d'e like me now?
STEW.   Most excellent.
FRED. Your opinion, Mr. Littlewor[th].
LIT.   Your French tailor
Has made you a perfect gentleman; I
  may
Converse now with you, and preserve my
  credit.
D'e find no alteration in your body
With these new clothes?

[1] If.

FRED.   My body altered? No.
LIT. You are not yet in fashion then. That
  must
Have a new motion, garb, and posture
  too,
Or all your pride is cast away; it is not
The cut of your apparel makes a gallant,
But the geometrical wearing of your
  clothes.   11

STEW. Mr. Littleworth tells you right; you
  wear your hat
Too like a citizen.

LIT.   'Tis like a midwife.
Place it with best advantage of your hair.
Is half your feather molted? This does
  make
No show; it should spread over, like a
  canopy.
Your hot-reined monsieur wears it for a
  shade
And cooler to his back. Your doublet
  must
Be more unbuttoned hereabouts; you'll
  not
Be a sloven else. A foul shirt is no blem-
  ish;   20
You must be confident, and outface clean
  linen.
Your doublet and your breeches must be
  allowed
No private meeting here; your cloak's
  too long.
It reaches to your buttock, and doth
  smell
Too much of Spanish gravity; the
  fashion
Is to wear nothing but a cape; a coat
May be allowed a covering for one elbow,
And some, to avoid the trouble, choose
  to walk
In *quirpo*,[2] thus.

STEW. [*Aside.*]   Your coat and
  cloak's a-brushing
In Long Lane, Lumbard.[3]

FRED.   But what if it rain?   30

LIT. Your belt about your shoulder is suffi-
  cient
To keep off any storm; beside, a reed
But waved discreetly has so many pores
It sucks up all the rain that falls about
  one.

[2] *Cuérpo* (Span.); *i.e.*, in your shirt.
[3] The Lombard district was famous for pawn-
shops.

With this defense, when other men have
    been
Wet to the skin through all their cloaks,
    I have
Defied a tempest, and walked by the
    taverns
Dry as a bone.
STEW. [*Aside.*]   Because he had no
    money
To call for wine.
FRED.   Why, you do walk enchanted.
Have you such pretty charms in town?
    But stay.   40
Who must I have to attend me?
LIT.   Is not that
Yet thought upon?
STEW.   I have laid out [1] for servants.
LIT. They are everywhere.
STEW.   I cannot yet be furnished
With such as I would put into his
    hands.
FRED. Of what condition must they be,
    and how
Many in number, sir?
LIT.   Beside your fencing,
    Your singing, dancing, riding, and
      French master,
    Two may serve domestic, to be constant
      waiters
Upon a gentleman: a fool, a pimp.
STEW. For these two officers I have in-
    quired,   50
And I am promised a convenient
    whiskin. [2]
I could save charges, and employ the pie-
    wench,
That carries her intelligence in white-
    pots; [3]
Or 'tis but taking order with the woman
That holds the ballads—she could fit him
    with
A concubine to any tune; but I
Have a design to place a fellow with
    him
That has read all Sir Pandarus' works, a
    Trojan [4]
That lies concealed, and is acquainted
    with
Both city and suburbian fripperies, [5]   60
Can fetch 'em with a spell at midnight to
    him,

And warrant which are for his turn; can,
    for
A need, supply the surgeon too.
FRED.   I like
Thy providence; [6] such a one deserves a
    livery twice a year.
STEW. It sha' not need; a cast [7] suit of your
    worship's
Will serve; he'll find a cloak to cover it,
Out of his share with those he brings to
    bed to you.
FRED. But must I call this fellow pimp?
LIT.   It is
Not necessary—or [8] Jack or Harry,
Or what he's known abroad by, will
    sound better,   70
That men may think he is a Christian.
FRED. But hear you, Mr. Littleworth: is
    there not
A method and degrees of title in
Men of this art?
LIT.   According to the honor
Of men that do employ 'em. An emperor
May give this office to a duke; a king
May have his viceroy to negotiate for
    him;
A duke may use a lord; the lord a knight;
A knight may trust a gentleman; and,
    when   79
They are abroad and merry, gentlemen
May pimp to one another.
FRED.   Good, good fellowship!
But for the fool now, that should wait on
    me,
And break me jests?
LIT.   A fool is necessary.
STEW. By any [9] means.
FRED.   But which of these two servants
Must now take place? [10]
LIT.   That question, Mr. Frederick,
The school of heraldry should conclude
    upon;
But, if my judgment may be heard, the
    fool
Is your first man; and it is known a
    point
Of state to have a fool.
STEW.   But, sir, the other
Is held the finer servant; his employ-
    ments   90
Are full of trust, his person clean and
    nimble,

---

[1] Been on the lookout.
[2] Go-between.   [4] Sly rascal.
[3] Milkpuddings.   [5] Suburban prostitutes.

[6] Foresight.   [8] Either.
[7] Discarded.   [9] All.   [10] Precedence.

And none so soon can leap into preferment,
Where fools are poor.

LIT.   Not all; there's story for 't:
Princes have been no wiser than they
should be.
Would any nobleman, that were no fool,
Spend all in hope of the philosophers'
stone,
To buy new lordships in another coun-
try?
Would knights build colleges, or gentle-
men
Of good estates challenge the field, and
fight,
Because a whore wo' not be honest?
Come,   100
Fools are a family over all the world;
We do affect one naturally; indeed
The fool is lieger [1] with us.

STEW.   Then the pimp
Is extraordinary.

FRED.   Do not you fall out
About their places.—Here's my noble
aunt!

Enter Aretina.

LIT. How do you like your nephew, madam,
now?

ARE. Well!—Turn about, Frederick.—
Very well!

FRED.[2] Am I not now a proper gentleman?
The virtue of rich clothes! Now could I
take
The wall of Julius Cæsar, affront   110
Great Pompey's upper lip, and defy the
senate.
Nay, I can be as proud as your own heart,
madam;
You may take that for your comfort. I
put on
That virtue with my clothes, and I doubt
not
But in a little time I shall be impudent
As any page, or player's boy. I am
Beholding to this gentleman's good disci-
pline;
But I shall do him credit in my practice.
Your steward has some pretty notions,
too,
In moral mischief.

ARE.   Your desert in this   120
Exceeds all other service, and shall bind
me
Both to acknowledge and reward.

LIT.   Sweet madam,
Think me but worth your favor; I would
creep
Upon my knees to honor you, and, for
every
Minute you lend to my reward, I'll pay
A year of serviceable tribute.

ARE.   You
Can compliment.

LIT. [*Aside.*]   Thus still she puts me off;
Unless I speak the downright word, she'll
never
Understand me. A man would think that
creeping
Upon one's knees were English to a
lady.   130

Enter Alex[ander].

AL. How is 't, Jack?—Pleasures attend
you, madam!
How does my plant of honor?

ARE.   Who is this?

AL. 'Tis Alexander.

ARE.   Rich and glorious!

LIT. 'Tis Alexander the Great.

AL.   And my Bucephalus
Waits at the door.

ARE.   Your case is altered, sir.

AL. I cannot help these things. The Fates
will have it.
'Tis not my land does this.

LIT.   But thou hast a plow
That brings it in.

ARE.   Now he looks brave and lovely.

FRED. Welcome, my gallant Macedonian.

AL. Madam, you gave your nephew for my
pupil.   140
I read [3] but in a tavern; if you'll honor us,
The Bear at the bridge foot shall enter-
tain you.
A drawer [4] is my Ganymede; he shall
skink [5]
Brisk nectar to us. We will only have
A dozen partridge in a dish; as many
pheasants,
Quails, cocks, and godwits [6] shall come
marching up

---

[1] Ledger, resident, as an ordinary ambassador.
[2] Original reads *Are*.

[3] Lecture, teach.
[4] Waiter.

[5] Draw.
[6] Snipe.

Like the trained-band;[1] a fort of sturgeon
Shall give most bold defiance to an army,
And triumph o'er the table.

ARE.   Sir, it will
But dull the appetite to hear more, and
    mine   150
Must be excused. Another time I may
Be your guest.

AL.   'Tis grown in fashion
    now with ladies.
When you please, I'll attend you. Little-
    worth!—
Come, Frederick.

FRED.   We'll have music; I love noise.
We will outroar the Thames, and shake
    the bridge, boy. *Ex[it with Alexander]*.

LIT. Madam, I kiss your hand; would you
    would think
Of your poor servant. Flesh and blood is
    frail,
And troublesome to carry without help.

ARE. A coach will easily convey it, or
You may take water at Strand Bridge.

LIT.   But I   160
Have taken fire.

ARE.   The Thames will cool—

LIT. But never quench my heart; your
    charity
Can only do that.

ARE.   I will keep it cold
Of purpose.

LIT.   Now you bless me, and I dare
Be drunk in expectation.   [*Exit.*]

ARE.   I am confident
He knows me not, and I were worse than
    mad
To be my own betrayer.—Here's my
    husband.

Enter Born[well].

BORN. Why, how now, Aretina? What!
    Alone?
The mystery of this solitude? My house
Turn desert o' the sudden? All the game-
    sters   170
Blown up? Why is the music put to
    silence?
Or ha' their instruments caught a cold,
    since we
Gave 'em the last heat? I must know thy
    ground
Of melancholy.

[1] London militia.

ARE.   You are merry, as
You came from kissing Celestina.

BORN.   I
Feel her yet warm upon my lip; she is
Most excellent company. I did not think
There was that sweetness in her sex. I
    must
Acknowledge 'twas thy cure to disen-
    chant me   179
From a dull husband to an active lover.
With such a lady I could spend more
    years
Than since my birth my glass hath run
    soft minutes,
And yet be young. Her presence has a
    spell
To keep off age; she has an eye would
    strike
Fire through an adamant.

ARE.   I have heard as much
Bestowed upon a dull-faced chamber-
    maid,
Whom love and wit would thus com-
    mend. True beauty
Is mocked when we compare thus, itself
    being
Above what can be fetched to make it
    lovely,
Or could our thoughts reach something
    to declare   190
The glories of a face, or body's elegance
(That touches but our sense), when
    beauty spreads
Over the soul, and calls up understanding
To look what[2] thence is offered, and ad-
    mire!
In both I must acknowledge Celestina
Most excellently fair, fair above all
The beauties I ha' seen, and one most
    worthy
Man's love and wonder.

BORN.   Do you speak, Aretina,
This with a pure sense to commend? Or
    is 't
The mockery of my praise?

ARE.   Although it shame 200
Myself, I must be just, and give her all
The excellency of women; and, were I
A man—

BORN.   What then?

ARE.   I know not with what loss
I should attempt her love. She is a piece
So angelically moving, I should think

[2] Gifford-Dyce's reading. Original reads *when*.

Frailty excused to dote upon her form,
And almost virtue to be wicked with her.
　　　　　　　　　　　　　　　　　Exit.
BORN. What should this mean? This is no
　jealousy,
Or she believes I counterfeit. I feel
Something within me, like a heat, to
　give　　　　　　　　　　　　　　210
Her cause, would Celestina but consent.
What a frail thing is man! It is not worth
Our glory to be chaste, while we deny
Mirth and converse with women. He is
　good
That dares the tempter, yet corrects his
　blood.　　　　　　　　　　　　*Exit.*

[SCENE iii.

A room in Celestina's house.

Enter] Celestina, Mariana, Isabella.

CEL. I have told you all my knowledge;
　since he is pleased
To invite himself, he shall be entertained,
And you shall be my witnesses.
MAR.　　　　　　　Who comes with him?
CEL. Sir William Scentlove, that prepared
　me for
The honorable encounter. I expect
His lordship every minute.

Enter Scentlove.

SCENT.　　　　　　　My lord is come.

Enter Lord, Haircut.

CEL. He has honored me.
SCENT.　　My lord, your periwig is awry!
LORD. You, sir—
While Haircut is busy about his hair, Scent-
　　　　　love goes to Celestina.
SCENT. You may guess at the gentleman
　that's with him.　　　　　　　9
It is his barber, madam, d'e observe,
And your ladyship wants a shaver.
HAIR.　　　　　　　She is here, sir.
I am betrayed.—Scentlove, your plot. I
　may
Have opportunity to be revenged. *Exit.*
SCENT. She in the midst.
LORD.　　　　She's fair, I must confess;
But does she keep this distance out of
　state?
CEL. Though I am poor in language to
　express

How much your lordship honors me, my
　heart
Is rich and proud in such a guest. I shall
Be out of love with every air abroad,
And, for his grace done my unworthy
　house,　　　　　　　　　　　　20
Be a fond prisoner, become anchorite,
And spend my hours in prayer, to reward
The blessing and the bounty of this
　presence.
LORD. Though you could turn each place
　you move in, to
A temple, rather than a wall should hide
So rich a beauty from the world, it were
Less want to lose our piety and your
　prayer.
A throne were fitter to present you to
Our wonder, whence your eyes, more
　worth than all
They look on, should chain every heart
　a prisoner.　　　　　　　　　　30
SCENT. [*Aside.*] 'Twas pretty well come
　off.
LORD.　　By your example
I shall know how to compliment; in this,
You more confirm my welcome.
CEL.　　　　　　　　I shall love
My lips the better, if their silent lan-
　guage
Persuade your lordship but to think so
　truly.
LORD. You make me smile, madam.
CEL.　　　　　　I hope you came not
With fear that any sadness here should
　shake
One blossom from your eye. I should be
　miserable
To present any object should displease
　you.
LORD. You do not, madam.
CEL.　　　　　As I should account　40
It no less sorrow, if your lordship should
Lay too severe a censure on my free-
　dom.
I wo' not court a prince against his jus-
　tice,
Nor bribe him with a smile to think me
　honest.
Pardon, my lord, this boldness and the
　mirth
That may flow from me. I believe my
　father
Thought of no winding sheet when he
　begot me.

LORD. [*Aside.*] She has a merry soul.—It will become
Me ask your pardon, madam, for my rude
Approach, so much a stranger to your knowledge.　　　50
CEL. Not, my lord, so much stranger to my knowledge;
Though I have but seen your person afar off,
I am acquainted with your character,
Which I have heard so often I can speak it.
LORD. You shall do me an honor.
CEL.　　　　　　If your lordship will
Be patient.
LORD.　　　　And glad to hear my faults.
CEL. That, as your conscience can agree upon 'em.
However, if your lordship give me privilege,
I'll tell you what's the opinion of the world.
LORD. You cannot please me better.
CEL.　　　　　　Y' are a lord　60
Born with as much nobility as would,
Divided, serve to make ten noblemen
Without a herald, but with so much spirit
And height of soul as well might furnish twenty.
You are learned, a thing not compatible now
With native honor, and are master of
A language that doth chain all ears,[1] and charm
All hearts, where you persuade; a wit so flowing,
And prudence to correct it, that all men
Believe they only meet in you, which, with　　　70
A spacious memory, make up the full wonders.
To these, you have known valor, and upon
A noble cause know how to use a sword
To honor's best advantage, though you wear none.
You are as bountiful as the showers that fall
Into the Spring's green bosom, as you were
Created lord of Fortune, not her steward;

So constant to tne cause in which you make
Yourself an advocate, you dare all dangers;
And men had rather you should be their friend　　　80
Than justice or the bench bound up together.
LORD. But did you hear all this?
CEL.　　　　　　And more, my lord.
LORD. Pray, let me have it, madam.
CEL. To all these virtues there is added one
(Your lordship will remember, when I name it,
I speak but what I gather from the voice
Of others)—it is grown to a full fame [2]
That you have loved a woman.
LORD.　　　　　　But one, madam?
CEL. Yes, many. Give me leave to smile, my lord;
I shall not need to interpret in what sense.　　　90
But you have showed yourself right honorable,
And, for your love to ladies, have deserved,
If their vote might prevail, a marble statue.
I make no comment on the people's text.
My lord, I should be sorry to offend.
LORD. You cannot, madam; these are things we owe
To nature for.
CEL.　　　　And honest men will pay
Their debts.
LORD.　　　If they be able, or compound.
CEL. She had a hard heart would be unmerciful,　　　99
And not give day [3] to men so promising;
But you owed women nothing.
LORD.　　　　　　Yes, I am
Still in their debt, and I must owe them love;
It was part of my character.
CEL.　　　　　　With your lordship's
Pardon, I only said you had a fame
For loving women; but of late men say
You have, against the imperial laws of love,
Restrained the active flowings of your blood,

[1] Gifford-Dyce reading. Original reads *years.*
[2] Report.
[3] "Good day," *i.e.*, notice, attention.

And with a mistress buried all that is
Hoped for in love's succession, as all
　beauty
Had died with her, and left the world be-
　nighted!　　　　　　　　　　　　110
In this you more dishonor all our sex
Than you did grace a part, when every-
　where
Love tempts your eye to admire a glori-
　ous harvest,
And everywhere as full-blown ears sub-
　mit
Their golden heads, the laden trees bow
　down
Their willing fruit, and court your
　amorous tasting.
LORD. I see men would dissect me to a
　fiber.
But do you believe this?
CEL.　　　　　　　　　　It is my wonder,
I must confess, a man of nobler earth
Than goes to vulgar composition　　120
(Born and bred high, so unconfined, so
　rich
In fortunes, and so read in all that
　sum
Up human knowledge, to feed gloriously,
And live at court, the only sphere where-
　in
True beauty moves, nature's most
　wealthy garden,
Where every blossom is more worth than
　all
The Hesperian fruit by jealous dragon
　watched,
Where all delights do circle appetite,
And pleasures multiply by being tasted)
Should be so lost with thought of one,
　turn ashes.　　　　　　　　　　130
There's nothing left, my lord, that can
　excuse you,
Unless you plead what I am ashamed to
　prompt
Your wisdom to.
LORD　　　　　What's that?
CEL.　　　　　　　　That you have played
The surgeon with yourself.
LORD.　　　　　　And am made eunuch?
CEL. It were much pity.
LORD.　　　　　　　Trouble not yourself;
I could convince your fears with demon-
　stration
That I am man enough, but knew not
　where,

Until this meeting, beauty dwelt. The
　court
You talked of must be where the Queen
　of Love is,
Which moves but with your person; in
　your eye　　　　　　　　　　　　140
Her glory shines, and only at that flame
Her wanton boy doth light his quick'ning
　torch.
CEL. Nay, now you compliment; I would
　it did,
My lord, for your own sake.
LORD.　　　　　　　You would be kind,
And love me then?
CEL.　　　　　My lord, I should be loving
Where I found worth to invite it, and
　should cherish
A constant man.
LORD.　　　Then you should me, madam.
CEL. But is the ice about your heart fallen
　off?
Can you return to do what love com-
　mands?—　　　　　　　　　　　149
Cupid, thou shalt have instant sacrifice,
And I dare be the priest.
LORD.　　　　　Your hand, your lip.
　　　　　　　　　　　　　[Kisses her.]
Now I am proof gainst all temptation.
CEL. Your meaning, my good lord?
LORD.　　　　　　　I, that have strength
Against thy voice and beauty, after
　this
May dare the charms of womankind.—
　Thou art,
Bella Maria, unprofanéd yet;
This magic has no power upon my
　blood.—
Farewell, madam! If you durst be the
　example
Of chaste as well as fair, thou wert a
　brave one.
CEL. I hope your lordship means not this
　for earnest;　　　　　　　　　　160
Be pleased to grace a banquet.
LORD.　　　　　　Pardon, madam.—
Will Scentlove, follow; I must laugh at
　you.
CEL. My lord, I must beseech you stay,
　for honor
For her whose memory you love best.
LORD.　　　　　　　　Your pleasure.
CEL. And, by that virtue you have now
　professed,
I charge you to believe me too; I can

Now glory that you have been worth my
　trial,
Which, I beseech you, pardon. Had not
　you
So valiantly recovered in this conflict,
You had been my triumph, without hope
　of more　　　　　　　　　　　　170
Than my just scorn upon your wanton
　flame;
Nor will I think these noble thoughts
　grew first
From melancholy for some female loss,
As the fantastic world believes, but from
Truth and your love of innocence, which
　shine
So bright in the two royal luminaries
At court,[1] you cannot lose your way to
　chastity.
Proceed, and speak of me as honor guides
　you.　　　　　　　　　　　*Exit Lord.*
I am almost tired.—Come, ladies, we'll
　beguile
Dull time, and take the air another while.
　　　　　　　　　　　　　　Exeunt.

The Fifth Act. [Scene i.

A room in Bornwell's house.]

Enter Aretina and Servant [with a purse].

Are. But hath Sir Thomas lost five hun-
　dred pounds
　Already?
Ser.　　And five hundred more he bor-
　rowed.
The dice are notable devourers, madam;
They make no more of pieces than of
　pebbles,
But thrust their heaps together to en-
　gender.
"Two hundred more!" the caster [2] cries
　this [3] gentleman.
"I am w'e. I ha' that to nothing, sir."
　The caster
Again: " 'Tis covered!"—and the table
　too,
With sums that frighted me. Here one
　sneaks out,　　　　　　　　　　　9
And with a martyr's patience smiles upon
His money's executioner, the dice,
Commands a pipe of good tobacco, and
I' th' smoke on 't vanishes. Another
　makes

The bones vault o'er his head, swears
　that ill-throwing
Has put his shoulder out of joint, calls for
A bonesetter, that looks to th' box, to bid
His master send him some more hundred
　pounds,
Which lost, he takes tobacco, and is
　quiet.
Here a strong arm throws in and in, with
　which
He brusheth all the table,[4] pays the
　rooks [5]　　　　　　　　　　　20
That went their smelts [6] apiece upon his
　hand,
Yet swears he has not drawn a stake this
　seven year.
But I was bid make haste; my master
　may
Lose this five hundred pounds ere I come
　thither.　　　　　　　　　　　*Exit.*
Are. If we both waste so fast, we shall
　soon find
Our state is not immortal. Something in
His other ways appear not well already.

Enter Sir Thomas [with Servants].

Born. Ye tortoises, why make you no
　more haste?
Go pay to th' master of the house that
　money,
And tell the noble gamesters I have an-
　other　　　　　　　　　　　　30
Superfluous thousand pound; at night I'll
　visit 'em.
D'e hear?
Ser.　　Yes, and please you.
Born.　　　　　Do 't, ye drudges.—
　　　　　　　　　　[Exeunt Servants.]
Ta, ra, ra!—Aretina!
Are.　You have a pleasant humor, sir.
Born. What, should a gentleman be sad?
Are.　　　　　You have lost—
Born. A transitory sum; as good that
　way
As another.
Are.　　Do you not vex within for 't?
Born. I had rather lose a thousand more
　than one
Sad thought come near my heart for 't.
　Vex for trash?
Although it go from other men like drops

---

[1] Charles I and Queen Henrietta Maria.
[2] Thrower of dice.　　　　[3] *I.e.,* to this.
[4] Wins all the stakes.
[5] Gulls, fools.　　　[6] Bet their half-guineas.

Of their life blood, we lose with the
    alacrity   40
We drink a cup of sack, or kiss a mistress.
No money is considerable with a game-
    ster;
They have souls more spacious than
    kings. Did two
Gamesters divide the empire of the world,
They'd make one throw for 't all, and he
    that lost
Be no more melancholy than to have
    played for
A morning's draught. Vex a rich soul for
    dirt,
The quiet of whose every thought is
    worth
A province!

ARE.   But, when dice have consumed
    all,
Your patience will not pawn for as much
    more.   50

BORN. Hang pawning! Sell outright, and
    the fear's over.

ARE. Say you so? I'll have another coach
    tomorrow
If there be rich above ground.

BORN.   I forgot
To bid the fellow ask my jeweler
Whether the chain of diamonds be made
    up;
I will present it to my Lady Bellamour,
Fair Celestina.

ARE.   This gown I have worn
Six days already; it looks dull. I'll give it
My waiting-woman, and have one of
    cloth
Of gold embrodered; shoes and pant-
    ables [1]   60
Will show well of the same.

BORN.   I have invited
A covey of ladies, and as many gentlemen
Tomorrow, to the Italian ordinary;
I shall have rarities and regalias [2]
To pay for, madam; music, wanton
    songs,
And tunes of silken petticoats to dance
    to.

ARE. And tomorrow have I invited half
    the court
To dine here. What misfortune 'tis your
    company
And ours should be divided! After dinner
I entertain 'em with a play.

BORN.   By that time 70
Your play inclines to the epilogue, shall
    we
Quit our Italian host, and whirl in
    coaches
To the Dutch magazine of sauce, [3] the
    Stillyard, [4]
Where deal, [5] and backrag, [6] and what
    strange wine else
They dare but give a name to in the
    reckoning,
Shall flow into our room, and drown
    Westphalias, [7]
Tongues, and anchovies, like some little
    town
Endangered by a sluice, through whose
    fierce ebb
We wade, and wash ourselves into a boat,
And bid our coachmen drive their
    leather tenements   80
By land, while we sail home with a fresh
    tide
To some new rendezvous.

ARE.   If you have not
Pointed [8] the place, pray, bring your
    ladies hither;
I mean to have a ball tomorrow night,
And a rich banquet for 'em, where we'll
    dance
Till morning rise and blush to interrupt
    us.

BORN. Have you no ladies i' th' next room
    to advance
A present mirth? What a dull house you
    govern!
Farewell! A wife's no company.—Are-
    tina,
I've summed up my estate, and find we
    may have   90
A month good yet.

ARE.   What mean you?

BORN.   And I'd rather
Be lord one month of pleasures, to the
    height
And rapture of our senses, than be years
Consuming what we have in foolish tem-
    perance,
Live in the dark, and no fame wait upon
    us!

[1] Slippers.   [2] Regalos, delicacies.

[3] Storehouse of sauce, tavern.
[4] The Steelyard, in the former German trading
district of the same name.
[5] An unidentified kind of German wine.
[6] Baccarach, a Rhenish wine.
[7] Westphalian hams.   [8] Appointed.

I will live so posterity shall stand
At gaze when I am mentioned.

ARE.   A month good!
And what shall be done then?

BORN.   I'll over sea,
And trail a pike. With watching, march-
  ing, lying
In trenches, with enduring cold and
  hunger,   100
And, taking here and there a musket shot,
I can earn every week four shillings,
  madam;
And, if the bullets favor me to snatch
Any superfluous limb, when I return
With good friends, I despair not to be
  enrolled
Poor Knight of Windsor.[1] For your
  course, madam,
No doubt you may do well; your friends
  are great;
Or, if your poverty and their pride can-
  not
Agree, you need not trouble much in-
  vention
To find a trade to live by; there are cus-
  tomers.   110
Farewell; be frolic, madam! If I live,
I will feast all my senses, and not fall
Less than a Phaëton from my throne of
  pleasure,
Though my estate flame like the world
  about me.

ARE. 'Tis very pretty!—

Enter Decoy.

Madam Decoy! *Exit [Bornwell].*

DEC.   What! Melancholy
After so sweet a night's work? Have
  not I
Showed myself mistress of my art?

ARE.   A lady.

DEC. That title makes the credit of the
  act
A story higher. Y'ave not seen him yet?
I wonder what he'll say.

ARE.   He's here.

Enter Alexander and Frederick

AL.   Bear up,   120
My little myrmidon; does not Jack
  Littleworth
Follow?

[1] A pensioned knight who had quarters in
Windsor Castle.

FRED.   Follow? He fell into the Thames
At landing.

AL.   The devil shall dive for him,
Ere I endanger my silk stockings for
  him.
Let the watermen alone; they have drags
  and engines.
When he has drunk his julep, I shall
  laugh
To see him come in pickled the next tide.

FRED. He'll never sink, he has such a cork
  brain.

AL. Let him be hanged or drowned, all's
  one to me;   129
Yet he deserves to die by water, cannot [2]
Bear his wine credibly.

FRED.   Is not this my aunt?

AL. And another handsome lady; I must
  know her.   [*Takes Decoy aside.*]

FRED. [*Aside.*] My blood is rampant too;
  I must court somebody—
As good my aunt as any other body.

ARE. Where have you been, cousin?

FRED.   At the bridge
At the Bear's foot, where our first health
  began
To the fair Aretina, whose sweet com-
  pany
Was wished by all. We could not get a
  lay,
A tumbler, a device, a *bona roba* [3]
For any money; drawers were grown
  dull.   140
We wanted our true firks [4] and our
  vagaries.—
When were you in drink, aunt?

ARE.   How?

FRED.   Do not ladies
Play the good fellows too? There's no
  true mirth
Without 'em. I have now such tickling
  fancies!
That doctor of the chair of wit has read
A precious lecture, how I should behave
Myself to ladies; as now, for example—

ARE. Would you practice upon me?

FRED.   I first salute you. [*Kisses her.*]
You have a soft hand, madam; are you so
All over?

ARE. Nephew!

FRED.   Nay, you should but smile.   150
                    [*Kisses her again.*]

[2] *I.e.*, who cannot.
[3] Four synonyms for *courtesan*.   [4] Tricks.

And then again I kiss you, and thus draw
Off your white glove, and start, to see
   your hand
More excellently white. I grace my own
Lip with this touch, and, turning gently
   thus,
Prepare you for my skill in palmistry,
Which, out of curiosity, no lady
But easily applies [1] to. The first line
I look [2] with most ambition to find out,
Is Venus' girdle, a fair semicircle,
Enclosing both the mount of Sol and
   Saturn;   160
If that appear, she's for my turn—a lady
Whom nature has prepared for the ca-
   reer;
And, Cupid at my elbow, I put forward.
You have this very line, aunt.

ARE.   The boy's frantic!

FRED. You have a couch or pallet; I can
   shut
The chamber door. Enrich a stranger,
   when
Your nephew's coming into play!

ARE.   No more.

FRED. Are you so coy to your own flesh
   and blood?

AL. [*Coming forward.*] Here, take your
   playfellow; I talk of sport,
And she would have me marry her.   170

FRED. Here's Littleworth.—

Enter Littleworth, wet.

Why, how now, tutor?

LIT.   I ha' been fishing.

FRED. And what ha' you caught?

LIT.   My belly full of water.

AL. Ha, ha! Where's thy rapier?

LIT.   My rapier is drowned,
And I am little better. I was up by th'
   heels,
And out came a tun of water, beside
   wine.

AL. 'T has made thee sober.

LIT.   Would you have me drunk
   With water?

ARE.   I hope your fire is quenched by
   this time.

FRED. It is not now, as when your worship
   "walked   179
By all the taverns, Jack, dry as a bone."

<hr>

[1] Yields.
[2] Emended by Gifford-Dyce. Original reads
look.

AL. You had store of fish under water,
   Jack.

LIT. It has made a poor John [3] of me.

FRED. I do not think but if we cast an
   angle
Into his belly, we might find some pil-
   chards.

LIT. And boiled, by this time.—Dear
   madam, a bed.

AL. Carry but the water spaniel to a grass
   plot,
Where he may roll himself; let him but
   shake
His ears twice in the sun, and you may
   grind him
Into a posset.

FRED.   Come, thou shalt to my bed,
   Poor pickerel.

DEC.   Alas, sweet gentleman!   190

LIT. I have ill luck and I should smell by
   this time;
I am but new ta'en, I am sure.—Sweet
   gentlewoman!

DEC. Your servant.

LIT.   Pray, do not pluck off my skin;
It is so wet, unless you have good eyes,
You'll hardly know it from a shirt.

DEC.   Fear nothing.
   Exeunt [All but Aretina and Alexander]. [4]

ARE. [*Aside.*] He has sack enough, and I
   may find his humor.

AL. And how is 't with your ladyship? You
   look
Without a sunshine in your face.

ARE.   You are glorious
   In mind and habit.

AL.   Ends of gold and silver!

ARE. Your other clothes were not so rich.
   Who was   200
Your tailor, sir?

AL.   They were made for me long since;
They have known but two bright days
   upon my back.
I had a humor, madam, to lay things by;
They will serve two days more. I think
   I ha' gold enough
To go to th' mercer. I'll now allow myself
A suit a week, as this, with necessary
Dependences, beaver, silk stockings, gar-
   ters,
And roses, [5] in their due conformity;

<hr>

[3] A poor John was a small dried fish.
[4] This stage direction follows the next line in the
original.   [5] Rosettes.

Boots are forbid a clean leg but to ride
in.   209
My linen every morning comes in new;
The old goes to great bellies.
ARE.   You are charitable.
AL. I may dine w'e sometime, or at the
court,
To meet good company, not for the table.
My clerk o' th' kitchen's here, a witty
epicure,
A spirit, that, to please me with what's
rare,
Can fly a hundred mile a day to market,
And make me Lord of Fish and Fowl. I
shall
Forget there is a butcher; and to make
My footman nimble he shall feed on
nothing
But wings of wild fowl.
ARE.   These ways are costly. 220
AL. Therefore I'll have it so; I ha' sprung
a mine.
ARE. You make me wonder, sir, to see
this change
Of fortune; your revenue was not late
So plentiful.
AL.   Hang dirty land and lordships!
I wo' not change one lodging I ha' got
For the Chamber of London.
ARE.   Strange, of such a sudden
To rise to this estate! No fortunate hand
At dice could lift you up so, for 'tis since
Last night; yesterday you were no such
monarch.
AL. There be more games than dice.
ARE.   It cannot be   230
A mistress, though your person is worth
love;
None possibly are rich enough to feed
As you have cast the method of your
riots.
A princess, after all her jewels, must
Be forced to sell her provinces.
AL. [Showing a jewel.]   Now you talk
Of jewels, what do you think of this?
ARE.   A rich one.
AL. You'll honor me to wear 't.   This
other toy
I had from you. This chain I borrowed
of you;
A friend had it in keeping. [Gives her the
jewely.] If your ladyship
Want any sum, you know your friend,
and Alexander.   240

ARE. Dare you trust my security?
AL.   There's gold;
I shall have more tomorrow.
ARE.   You astonish me.
Who can supply these?
AL.   A dear friend I have.
She promised we should meet again i' th'
morning.
ARE. Not that I wish to know
More of your happiness than I have a
ready
Heart to congratulate, be pleased to lay
My wonder.
AL.   'Tis a secret—
ARE.   Which I'll die
Ere I'll betray.
AL.   You have always wished me well;
But you shall swear not to reveal the
party.   250
ARE. I'll lose the benefit of my tongue.
AL.   Nor be
Afraid at what I say. What think you
first
Of an old witch, a strange, ill-favored
hag,
That, for my company last night, has
wrought
This cure upon my fortune? I do sweat
To think upon her name.
ARE.   How, sir, a witch?
AL. I would not fright your ladyship too
much
At first, but witches are akin to spirits.
The truth is—nay, if you look pale al-
ready,   259
I ha' done.
ARE.   Sir, I beseech you.
AL.   If you have
But courage then to know the truth, I'll
tell you
In one word: my chief friend is—the
devil!
ARE. What devil? How I tremble!
AL.   Have a heart;
'Twas a she-devil too, a most insatiate,
Abominable devil, with a tail
Thus long.
ARE.   Goodness defend me! Did you see
her?
AL. No, 'twas i' th' dark; but she appeared
first to me
I' th' likeness of a beldam,[1] and was
brought,

[1] Original reads bedlam.

I know not how nor whither, by two
  goblins,   269
More hooded than a hawk.

ARE.   But would you venter [1]
Upon a devil?

AL.   Ay, for means.

ARE. [*Aside.*]   How black
An impudence is this!—But are you sure
It was the devil you enjoyed?

AL.   Say nothing;
I did the best to please her; but, as
  sure
As you live, 'twas a hell-cat.

ARE.   D'e not quake?

AL. I found myself in the very room [2] i' th'
  morning,
Where two of her familiars had left me.

Enter Servant.

SER. My lord is come to visit you.

AL.   No words,
As you respect my safety. I ha' told
  tales
Out of the devil's school; if it be
  known,   280
I lose a friend. 'Tis now about the
  time
I promised her to meet again; at my
Return I'll tell you wonders. Not a
  word!   *Exit.*

ARE. [*Looking in a mirror.*] 'Tis a false
glass; sure I am more deformed.
What have I done? My soul is miserable.

Enter Lord.

LORD. I sent you a letter, madam.

ARE.   You expressed
Your noble care of me, my lord.

Enter Bornwell, Celestina.

BORN.   Your lordship
Does me an honor.

LORD.   Madam, I am glad
To see you here; I meant to have kissed
  your hand   289
Ere my return to court.

CEL.   Sir Thomas has
Prevailed to bring me, to his trouble,
  hither.

LORD. You do him grace.

---

[1] Venture.
[2] Emended by Gifford-Dyce. Original reads
the very same in.

BORN.   Why, what's the matter,
  madam?
Your eyes are tuning "Lachrimæ." [3]

ARE.   As you
Do hope for heaven, withdraw, and give
  me but
The patience of ten minutes.

BORN.   Wonderful!
I wo' not hear you above that proportion.
She talks of heaven.—Come, where must
we to counsel?

ARE. You shall conclude [4] me when you
  please.   [*Exit.*]

BORN.   I follow.

LORD. [*Aside.*] What alteration is this? I,
  that so late   299
Stood the temptation of her eye and voice,
Boasted a heart 'bove all licentious flame,
At second view turn renegade, and think
I was too superstitious, and full
Of phlegm, not to reward her amorous
  courtship
With manly freedom.

CEL.   I obey you, sir.

BORN. I'll wait upon your lordship presently.   [*Exit.*]

LORD. [*Aside.*] She could not want a cun-
  ning to seem honest
When I neglected her. I am resolved.—
You still look pleasant, madam.

CEL.   I have cause,
My lord, the rather for your presence,
  which   310
Hath power to charm all trouble in my
  thoughts.

LORD. I must translate that compliment,
  and owe
All that is cheerful in myself to these
All-quick'ning smiles; and, rather than
  such bright
Eyes should repent their influence upon
  me,
I would release the aspects, and quit the
  bounty
Of all the other stars. Did you not think
  me
A strange and melancholy gentleman
To use you so unkindly?

CEL.   Me, my lord?

LORD. I hope you made no loud complaint;
  I would not   320
Be tried by a jury of ladies.

---

[3] *I.e.*, beginning to weep. "Lachrimæ" was a
melancholy song.   [4] Stop.

CEL.   For what, my lord?
LORD. I did not meet that noble entertain-
    ment
  You were late pleased to show me.
CEL.   I observed
  No such defect in your lordship, but a
    brave
  And noble fortitude.
LORD.   A noble folly;
  I bring repentance for 't. I know you
    have,
  Madam, a gentle faith, and wo' not ruin
  What you have built to honor you.
CEL.   What's that?
LORD. If you can love, I'll tell your lady-
  ship.   329
CEL. I have a stubborn soul else.
LORD.   You are all
  Composed of harmony.
CEL.   What love d'e mean?
LORD. That which doth perfect both. Ma-
  dam, you have heard
  I can be constant, and, if you consent
  To grace it so, there is a spacious dwelling
  Prepared within my heart for such a mis-
    tress.
CEL. Your mistress, my good lord?
LORD.   Why, my good lady,
  Your sex doth hold it no dishonor
  To become mistress to a noble servant
  In the now court Platonic way. Consider
  Who 'tis that pleads to you; my birth and
    present   340
  Value can be no stain to your embrace.
  But these are shadows when my love ap-
    pears,
  Which shall in his first miracle return
  Me in my bloom of youth, and thee a
    virgin,
  When I, within some new Elysium,
  Of purpose made and meant for us, shall
    be
  In everything Adonis but in his
  Contempt of love, and court thee from a
    Daphne
  Hid in the cold rind of a bashful tree,
  With such warm language and delight,
    till thou   350
  Leap from that bays into the Queen of
    Love,
  And pay my conquest with composing
    garlands
  Of thy own myrtle for me.
CEL.   What's all this?

LORD. Consent to be my mistress, Celes-
  tina,
  And we will have it springtime all the
    year,
  Upon whose invitations, when we walk,
  The winds shall play soft descant [1] to our
    feet,
  And breathe rich odors to re-pure the air;
  Green bowers on every side shall tempt
    our stay,
  And violets stoop to have us tread upon
    'em.   360
  The red rose shall grow pale, being near
    thy cheek,
  And the white blush, o'ercome with such
    a forehead.
  Here laid, and measuring with ourselves
    some bank,
  A thousand birds shall from the woods
    repair,
  And place themselves so cunningly be-
    hind
  The leaves of every tree that, while they
    pay
  Us [2] tribute of their songs, thou sha't
    imagine
  The very trees bear music, and sweet
    voices
  Do grow in every arbor. Here can we
  Embrace and kiss, tell tales, and kiss
    again,   370
  And none but heaven our rival.
CEL.   When we are
  Weary of these, what if we shift our para-
    dise,
  And through a grove of tall and even pine
  Descend into a valley, that shall shame
  All the delights of Tempe, upon whose
  Green plush the Graces shall be called to
    dance
  To please us, and maintain their fairy
    revels
  To the harmonious murmurs of a stream
  That gently falls upon a rock of pearl.
  Here doth the nymph, forsaken Echo,
    dwell,   380
  To whom we'll tell the story of our love,
  Till at our surfeit and her want of joy
  We break her heart with envy. Not far
    off,
  A grove shall call us to a wanton river
  To see a dying swan give up the ghost,

---

[1] Melody.

[2] Gifford-Dyce's reading. Original reads **As.**

The fishes shooting up their tears in bubbles
That they must lose the genius of their waves—
And such love linsey-woolsey, to no purpose!
LORD. You chide me handsomely; pray, tell me how   389
You like this language.
CEL.   Good my lord, forbear.
LORD. You need not fly out of this circle, madam;
These widows so are full of circumstance!
I'll undertake, in this time I ha' courted
Your ladyship for the toy, to ha' broken ten,
Nay, twenty colts—virgins, I mean—and taught 'em
The amble, or what pace I most affected.
CEL. Y' are not my lord again—the lord I thought you;
And I must tell you now you do forget
Yourself and me.
LORD.   You'll not be angry, madam?
CEL. Nor rude (though gay men have a privilege)   400
It shall appear. There is a man, my lord,
Within my acquaintance, rich in worldly fortunes,
But cannot boast any descent of blood,
Would buy a coat of arms.
LORD.   He may, and legs
Booted and spurred, to ride into the country.
CEL. But these will want antiquity, my lord,
The seal of honor. What's a coat cut out
But yesterday, to make a man a gentleman?   408
Your family, as old as the first virtue
That merited an escutcheon, doth owe [1]
A glorious coat of arms; if you will sell now
All that your name doth challenge in that ensign,
I'll help you to a chapman [2] that shall pay,
And pour down wealth enough for 't.
LORD.   Sell my arms?
I cannot, madam.
CEL.   Give but your consent,
You know not how the state may be inclined
To dispensation; we may prevail
Upon the Herald's office afterward.

[1] Own.   [2] Merchant.

LORD. I'll sooner give these arms to th' hangman's ax,
My head, my heart, to twenty executions,   420
Than sell one atom from my name.
CEL.   Change that,
And answer him would buy my honor from me—
Honor, that is not worn upon a flag
Or pennon that without the owner's dangers
An enemy may ravish and bear from me,
But that which grows and withers with my soul,
Beside the body's stain. Think, think, my lord,
To what you would unworthily betray me,
If you would not, for price of gold or pleasure
(If that be more your idol) lose the glory   430
And painted honor of your house. I ha' done.
LORD. Enough to rectify a satyr's blood.
Obscure my blushes here.

Enter Scentlove and Haircut [behind].

HAIR.   Or this or fight with me.
It shall be no exception that I wait
Upon my lord. I am a gentleman;
You may be less and be a knight. The office
I do my lord is honest, sir. How many
Such you have been guilty of, heaven knows.
SCENT. 'Tis no fear of your sword, but that I would not
Break the good laws established against duels.   440
HAIR. Off with your periwig, and stand bare.   [*Scentlove removes his wig.*]
LORD.   From this
Minute I'll be a servant to thy goodness.
A mistress in the wanton sense is common;
I'll honor you with chaste thoughts, and call you so.
CEL. I'll study to be worth your fair opinion.
LORD. Scentlove, your head was used to a covering
Beside a hat; when went the hair away?

SCENT. I laid a wager, my lord, with Hair-
　　cut,
　　Who thinks I shall catch cold, that I'll
　　　stand bare　　　　　　　　　　449
　　This half hour.
HAIR.　　　　　　　Pardon my ambition,
　　Madam. I told you truth; I am a gen-
　　　tleman,
　　And cannot fear that name is drowned in
　　　my
　　Relation to my lord.
CEL.　　　　　　　I dare not think so.
HAIR. From henceforth call my service
　　duty, madam.
　　That pig's head, that betrayed me to
　　　your mirth,
　　Is doing penance for 't.
SCENT.　　　　　　Why may not I,
　　My lord, begin a fashion of no hair?
CEL. Do you sweat, Sir William?
SCENT.　　　Not with store of nightcaps.

Enter Aretina, Bornwell.

ARE. Heaven has dissolved the clouds that
　　hung upon
　　My eyes, and, if you can with mercy
　　　meet　　　　　　　　　　　460
　　A penitent, I throw my own will off,
　　And now in all things obey yours. My
　　　nephew
　　Send back again to th' college, and my-
　　　self
　　To what place you'll confine me.
BORN.　　　　　　　Dearer now
　　Than ever to my bosom, thou sha't
　　　please
　　Me best to live at thy own choice. I did
　　But fright thee with a noise of my
　　　expenses;
　　The sums are safe, and we have wealth
　　　enough,　　　　　　　　　468
　　If yet we use it nobly. My lord—madam,
　　Pray, honor [us] [1] tonight.
ARE.　　　　　I beg your presence
　　And pardon.
BORN.　　　I know not how my Aretina
　　May be disposed tomorrow for the coun-
　　　try.
CEL. You must not go before you both
　　have done
　　Me honor to accept an entertainment
　　Where I have power; on those terms I'm
　　　your guest.

[1] Supplied by Gifford-Dyce.

BORN. You grace us, madam.
ARE. [*Aside.*] Already
　　I feel a cure upon my soul, and promise
　　My after-life to virtue. Pardon, heaven,
　　My shame, yet hid from the world's eye.

Enter Decoy. [2]

DEC.　　　　　　　Sweet madam!　480
ARE. Not for the world be seen here! We
　　are lost.
　　I'll visit you at home.—[*Aside.*] But not
　　　to practice
　　What she expects; my counsel may re-
　　　cover her.　　　　[*Exit Decoy.*]

Enter Alexander.

AL. Where's madam?—Pray, lend me a
　　little money;
　　My spirit has deceived me. Proserpine
　　Has broke her word.
ARE.　　　　　Do you expect to find
　　The devil true to you?
AL.　　　　　　Not too loud!
ARE.　　　　　　I'll voice it
　　Louder, to all the world, your horrid sin,
　　Unless you promise me religiously
　　To purge your foul blood by repentance,
　　　sir.　　　　　　　　　490
AL. Then I'm undone.
ARE.　　　　Not while I have power
　　To encourage you to virtue. I'll endeavor
　　To find you out some nobler way at court
　　To thrive in.
AL.　　　Do 't, and I'll forsake the devil
　　And bring my flesh to obedience. You
　　　shall steer me.—
　　My lord, your servant.
LORD.　　　　You are brave again.
AL. Madam, your pardon.
BORN.　　　　Your offense requires
　　Humility.
AL.　　　Low as my heart.—Sir Thomas,
　　I'll sup with you, a part of satisfaction.
BORN. Our pleasures cool. Music! And,
　　when our ladies　　　　　500
　　Are tired with active motion, to give
　　Them rest, in some new rapture to ad-
　　　vance
　　Full mirth, our souls shall leap into a
　　　dance.　　　　　　*Exeunt.*

FINIS.

[2] This stage direction follows the next line in the
original.

THE CARDINAL[1]

BY

JAMES SHIRLEY

PERSONS

KING OF NAVARRE.
CARDINAL.
COLUMBO, *the cardinal's nephew.*
[COUNT D']ALVAREZ.
HERNANDO, *a colonel.*
ALPHONSO [, *a captain*].
LORDS.
[ANTONIO,] *secretary to the duchess.*
COLONELS.
ANTONELLI, *the cardinal's servant.*

SURGEON.
GUARD.
ATTENDANTS, *etc.*

DUCHESS ROSAURA.
VALERIA ⎫ *ladies.*
CELINDA ⎭
PLACENTIA, *a lady that waits upon the duchess.*

SCENE: *Navarre.*

[TIME: *Contemporary.*]

PROLOGUE[2]

The Cardinal! Cause[3] we express no scene,
We do believe most of you gentlemen
Are at this hour in France,[3] and busy there,
Though you vouchsafe to lend your bodies
here;
But keep your fancy active, till you know,
By th' progress of our play, 'tis nothing so.
A poet's art is to lead on your thought
Through subtle paths and workings of a
plot,
And, where your expectation does not
thrive,   9
If things fall better, yet you may forgive.
I will say nothing positive; you may
Think what you please; we call it but a
"play."
Whether the comic Muse, or ladies' love,
Romance, or direful tragedy it prove,
The bill determines not; and, would you be
Persuaded, I would have 't a comedy,

For all the purple in the name and state
Of him that owns it;[4] but 'tis left to fate.
Yet I will tell you, ere you see it played,
What the author—and he blushed too, when
he said,   20
Comparing with his own (for 't had been
pride,
He thought, to build his wit a pyramide
Upon another's wounded fame), this play
Might rival with his best, and dared to
say—
Troth, I am out. He said no more. You,
then,
When 'tis done, may say your pleasures,
gentlemen.[5]

ACT I. [SCENE i.

A room in the king's palace.]

*Enter two Lords at one door; Secretary at the
other.*

1 Lo. Who is that?
2 Lo.   The duchess' secretary.
1 Lo. Signior!
SEC.   Your lordship's servant.
1 Lo. How does her grace since she left
her mourning

---

[1] The title continues: "A Tragedy As It Was
Acted at the Private House in Blackfriars."
The unimportant dedication, "To My Worthily
Honored Friend, G. B., Esq.," is omitted.

[2] The prologue appears before the cast in
the original.

[3] Because we hang out no placard, "The Cardinal" recalls Richelieu in France.

[4] Alluding to the cardinal himself.

[5] Here follows a complimentary poem by Hall

For the young Duke Mendoza, whose
   timeless [1] death
At sea left her a virgin and a widow?

2 Lo. She's now inclining to a second
   bride.[2] —
When is the day of mighty marriage
To our great cardinal's nephew, Don
   Columbo?

SEC. When they agree. They wo' not steal
   to church.
I guess the ceremonies will be loud and
   public.   10
Your lordships will excuse me.   *Exit.*

1 Lo. When they agree? Alas, poor lady,
   she
Dotes not upon Columbo when she
   thinks
Of the young Count d'Alvarez, divorced
   from her
By the king's power.

2 Lo. And counsel of the cardinal to advance
His nephew to the duchess' bed. 'Tis
   not well.

1 Lo. Take heed; the cardinal holds intelligence [3]
With every bird i' th' air.

2 Lo.   Death on his purple pride!
He governs all, and yet Columbo is   20
A gallant gentleman.

1 Lo. The darling of the war, whom vic-
   tory
Hath often courted; a man of daring
And most exalted spirit. Pride in him
Dwells like an ornament, where so much
   honor
Secures his praise.

2 Lo.   This is no argument
He should usurp and wear Alvarez' title
To the fair duchess; men of coarser
   blood
Would not so tamely give this treasure
   up.

1 Lo. Although Columbo's name is great
   in war,   30
Whose glorious art and practice is above
The greatness of Alvarez, yet he can-
   not
Want soul, in whom alone survives the
   virtue
Of many noble ancestors, being the last
Of his great family.

2 Lo.   'Tis not safe, you'll say.
To wrastle with the king.[4]

1 Lo. More danger if the cardinal be dis-
   pleased,
Who sits at helm of state. Count d'Al-
   varez
Is wiser to obey the stream than, by
Insisting on his privilege to her love,   40
Put both their fates upon a storm.

2 Lo. If wisdom, not inborn fear, make
   him compose,[5]
I like it. How does the duchess bear
   herself?

1 Lo. She moves by the rapture [6] of an-
   other wheel [7]
That must be obeyed, like some sad
   passenger,
That looks upon the coast his wishes fly
   to,
But is transported by an adverse wind,
Sometimes a churlish pilot.

2 Lo. She has a sweet and noble nature.

1 Lo.   That   49
Commends Alvarez; Hymen cannot tie
A knot of two more equal hearts and
   blood.

Enter Alphonso.

2 Lo. Alphonso!

ALPH.   My good lord.

1 Lo.   What great affair
Hath brought you from the confines?

ALPH.   Such as will
Be worth your counsels, when the king
   hath read
My letters from the governor. The
   Aragonians,
Violating their confederate oath and
   league,
Are now in arms; they have not yet
   marched towards us,
But 'tis not safe to expect,[8] if we may
   timely
Prevent invasion.

2 Lo.   Dare they be so insolent?

1 Lo. This storm I did foresee.   60

2 Lo. What have they but the sweetness of
   the king
To make a crime?

---

[1] Untimely.
[2] Bridegroom.   [3] Communication.

[4] Here and in several other passages the line
division has been regularized.
[5] Agree.   [7] *I.e.*, steering wheel.
[6] Energy, force.   [8] Wait.

1 Lo.   But how appears the cardinal
At this news?
Alph.   Not pale, although
He knows they have no cause to think
     him innocent,
As by whose counsel they were once sur-
     prised.
1 Lo.   There is more
Than all our present art can fathom in
This story, and I fear I may conclude
This flame has breath at home to cherish
     it.
There's treason in some hearts, whose
     faces are   70
Smooth to the state.
Alph.   My lords, I take my leave.
2 Lo.   Your friends, good captain. *Exeunt.*

[Scene ii.

A room in the duchess' palace.]

Enter Duchess, Valeria, Celinda.

Val. Sweet madam, be less thoughtful;
     this obedience
To passion will destroy the noblest
     frame
Of beauty that this kingdom ever
     boasted.
Cel. This sadness might become your
     other habit
And ceremonies black for him that died.
The times of sorrow are expired; and all
The joys that wait upon the court, your
     birth,
And a new Hymen, that is coming to-
     wards you,
Invite a change.
Duch.   Ladies, I thank you both.
I pray, excuse a little melancholy   10
That is behind; my year of mourning
     hath not
So cleared my account with sorrow but
     there may
Some dark thoughts stay, with sad re-
     flections,
Upon my heart for him I lost. Even this
New dress and smiling garment, meant
     to show
A peace concluded twixt my grief and
     me,
Is but a sad remembrance. But I resolve
To entertain more pleasing thoughts;
     and, if

You wish me heartily to smile, you
     must
Not mention grief, not in advice to
     leave it.   20
Such counsels open but afresh the
     wounds
Ye would close up, and keep alive the
     cause,
Whose bleeding you would cure. Let's
     talk of something
That may delight. You two are read in
     all
The histories of our court. Tell me,
     Valeria,
Who has thy vote for the most handsome
     man?—
[*Aside.*] Thus I must counterfeit a peace,
     when all
Within me is at mutiny.
Val.   I have examined
All that are candidates for the praise of
     ladies,
But find—may I speak boldly to your
     grace?   30
And will you not return it in your mirth
To make me blush?
Duch.   No, no; speak freely.
Val. I wo' not rack your patience,
     madam; but
Were I a princess, I should think Count
     d'Alvarez
Had sweetness to deserve[1] me from the
     world.
Duch. [*Aside.*] Alvarez! She's a spy upon
     my heart.
Val. He's young and active, and composed
     most sweetly.
Duch. I have seen a face more tempting.
Val.   It had then
Too much of woman in 't. His eyes speak
     movingly,
Which may excuse his voice, and lead
     away   40
All female pride his captive; his hair,
     black,
Which, naturally falling into curls—
Duch. Prithee, no more; thou art in love
     with him.—
The man in your esteem, Celinda, now?
Cel. Alvarez is, I must confess, a gentle-
     man
Of handsome composition; but with
His mind, the greater excellence, I think

[1] Be worthy of.

Another may delight a lady more,
If man be well considered. That's
  Columbo,
Now, madam, voted to be yours.

DUCH. [*Aside.*]   My torment! 50

VAL. [*Aside.*] She affects [1] him not.

CEL. He has person, and a bravery beyond
All men that I observe.

VAL.   He is a soldier,
A rough-hewn man, and may show well
  at distance.
His talk will fright a lady; War and
  grim-
Faced Honor are his mistresses; he raves
To hear a lute; Love meant him not his
  priest.—
Again your pardon, madam. We may
  talk,
But you have art to choose, and crown
  affection. [*Celinda and Valeria retire.*]

DUCH. What is it to be born above these
  ladies, 60
And want their freedom! They are not
  constrained,
Nor slaved by their own greatness, or
  the king's,
But let their free hearts look abroad and
  choose
By their own eyes to love. I must repair
My poor afflicted bosom, and assume
The privilege I was born with, which now
  prompts me
To tell the king he hath no power nor art
To steer a lover's soul.—

Enter Secretary.

      What says Count d'Alvarez?

SEC. Madam, he'll attend you.

DUCH. Wait you, as I directed. When he
  comes, 70
Acquaint me privately.

SEC.   Madam, I have news;
'Tis now arrived the court we shall have
  wars.

DUCH. [*Aside.*] I find an army here of
  killing thoughts.

SEC. The king has chosen Don Columbo
  general,
Who is immediately to take his leave.

DUCH. [*Aside.*] What flood is let into my
  heart!—How far
  Is he to go?

[1] Likes.

SEC.   To Aragon.

DUCH.   That's well
At first. He should not want a pilgrimage
To the unknown world, if my thoughts
  might convey him. 79

SEC. 'Tis not impossible he may go thither.

DUCH. How?

SEC. To the unknown other world. He
  goes to fight;
That's in his way. Such stories are in
  nature.

DUCH. Conceal this news.

SEC.   He wo' not be long absent;
The affair will make him swift to kiss
  your grace's hand.   [*Exit.*]

DUCH. He cannot fly
With too much wing to take his leave.—
  [*To the Ladies.*] I must
Be admitted to your conference. Ye have
Enlarged my spirits; they shall droop no
  more.

CEL. We are happy if we may advance
  one thought 90
To your grace's pleasure.

VAL. Your eye before was in eclipse; these
  smiles
Become you, madam.

DUCH. [*Aside.*] I have not skill to contain
  myself.

Enter Placentia.

PLA. The cardinal's nephew, madam, Don
  Columbo.

DUCH. Already? Attend him.
        Ex[it] Plac[*entia*].

VAL.   Shall we take our leave?

DUCH. He shall not know, Celinda, [2] how
  you praised him.

CEL.[3] If he did, madam, I should have the
  confidence
To tell him my free thoughts.

Enter Columbo.

DUCH. My lord, while I'm in study to
  requite 100
The favor you ha' done me, you increase
My debt to such a sum, still by a new
  honoring
Your servant, I despair of my own freedom.

[2] Original reads *Valeria*, but *cf.* ll. 45ff. The
reversing of the two names here and later in the
scene was first suggested by Gifford.

[3] Original reads *Val.*

Col. Madam, he kisseth your white hand,
  that must
  Not surfeit in this happiness—and, la-
  dies,
  I take your smiles for my encouragement!
  I have not long to practice these court
  tactics.   [*Kisses them.*]
Cel. [*Aside.*] He has been taught to kiss.
Duch.   There's something, sir,
  Upon your brow I did not read before.
Col. Does the character please you,
  madam?
Duch.   More,   110
  Because it speaks you cheerful.
Col.   'Tis for such
  Access of honor as must make Columbo
  Worth all your love; the king is pleased
  to think
  Me fit to lead his army.
Duch.   How, an army?
Col. We must not use the priest, till I
  bring home
  Another triumph that now stays for me
  To reap it in the purple field of glory.
Duch. But do you mean to leave me, and
  expose
  Yourself to the devouring war? No
  enemy
  Should divide us; the king is not so
  cruel.   120
Col. The king is honorable; and this grace
  More answers my ambition than his gift
  Of thee and all thy beauty, which I can
  Love, as becomes thy soldier, and fight
                    She weeps.
  To come again, a conqueror of thee.
  Then I must chide this fondness.[1]

                Enter Secretary.

Sec. Madam, the king and my Lord Cardinal.   [*Exit.*]

  Enter King, Cardinal, and Lords.

King. Madam, I come to call a servant[2]
  from you,
  And strengthen his excuse; the public
  cause
  Will plead for your consent. At his
  return   130
  Your marriage shall receive triumphant
  ceremonies;
  Till then you must dispense.
                [*He walks aside with the Duchess.*]

[1] Foolishness.   [2] Lover.

Car. [*Walking aside with Columbo.*]   She
  appears sad
  To part with him.—I like it fairly,
  nephew.
Cel.[3] Is not the general a gallant man?
  What lady would deny him a small
  courtesy?
Val. Thou hast converted me, and I begin
  To wish it were no sin.
Cel. Leave that to narrow consciences.
Val.   You are pleasant.
Cel. But he would please one better. Do
  such men
  Lie with their pages?
Val.   Wouldst thou make a shift?   140
Cel. He is going to a bloody business;
  'Tis pity he should die without some heir.
  That lady were hard-hearted now that
  would
  Not help posterity, for the mere good
  O' th' king and commonwealth.
Val. Thou art wild; we may be observed.
Duch. Your will must guide me; happiness
  and conquest
  Be ever waiting on his sword!
Col.   Farewell.
Ex[eunt] K[ing], Col[umbo], Card[inal], and
                    Lo[rds].
Duch. Pray, give leave to examine a few
  thoughts;   149
  Expect me in the garden.
Ladies.   We attend. *Ex[eunt] Ladies.*
Duch. This is above all expectation
  happy.
  Forgive me, Virtue, that I have dis-
  sembled,
  And witness with me I have not a
  thought
  To tempt or to betray him, but secure
  The promise I first made to love and
  honor.

                Enter Secretary.

Sec. The Count d'Alvarez, madam.
Duch.   Admit him,
  And let none interrupt us.—[*Exit Secre-
  tary.*] How shall I
  Behave[4] my looks? The guilt of my neg-
  lect,
  Which had no seal from hence, will call
  up blood

[3] The original reverses the names of *Cel.* and
Val. throughout this dialogue.
[4] Control.

To write upon my cheeks the shame and
story 160
In some red letter.

Enter d'Alvarez.

D'ALV. Madam, I present
One that was glad to obey your grace,
and come
To know what your commands are.
DUCH. Where I once
Did promise love, a love that had the
power
And office of a priest to chain my heart
To yours, it were injustice to command.
D'ALV. But I can look upon you, madam,
as
Becomes a servant; with as much humil-
ity,
In tenderness of[1] your honor and great
fortune,
Give up, when you call back your bounty,
all that 170
Was mine, as I had pride to think them
favors.
DUCH. Hath love taught thee no more
assurance in
Our mutual vows thou canst suspect it
possible
I should revoke a promise made to
heaven
And thee so soon? This must arise from
some
Distrust of thy own faith.
D'ALV. Your grace's pardon;
To speak with freedom, I am not so old
In cunning to betray, nor young in time,
Not to see when and where I am at loss,
And how to bear my fortune and my
wounds, 180
Which, if I look for health, must still
bleed inward,
A hard and desperate condition.
I am not ignorant your birth and great-
ness
Have placed you to grow up with the
king's grace
And jealousy, which to remove, his
power
Hath chosen a fit object for your beauty
To shine upon, Columbo, his great favor-
ite.
I am a man on whom but late the king

[1] Regard for.

Has pleased to cast a beam, which was
not meant 189
To make me proud, but wisely to direct
And light me to my safety. O, dear
madam,
I will not call more witness of my love
(If you will let me still give it that name)
Than this, that I dare make myself a
loser,
And to your will give all my blessings up.
Preserve your greatness, and forget a
trifle
That shall at best, when you have drawn
me up,
But hang about you like a cloud, and dim
The glories you are born to.
DUCH. Misery
Of birth and state! That I could shift
into 200
A meaner blood, or find some art to purge
That part which makes my veins un-
equal! Yet
Those nice distinctions have no place in
us;
There's but a shadow difference, a title.
Thy stock partakes as much of noble sap
As that which feeds the root of kings; and
he
That writes a lord hath all the essence of
Nobility.
D'ALV. 'Tis not a name that makes
Our separation; the king's displeasure
Hangs a portent to fright us, and the
matter 210
That feeds this exhalation[2] is the car-
dinal's
Plot to advance his nephew; then Co-
lumbo,
A man made up for some prodigious act,
Is fit to be considered. In all three
There is no character you fix upon
But has a form of ruin to us both.
DUCH. Then you do look on these with
fear?
D'ALV. With eyes
That should think tears a duty, to lament
Your least unkind fate; but my youth
dares boldly
Meet all the tyranny o' th' stars, whose
black 220
Malevolence but shoot my single tragedy.
You are above the value of many worlds
Peopled with such as I am.

[2] Meteor.

Duch.   What if Columbo,
  Engaged to war, in his hot thirst of
    honor
  Find out the way to death?
D'Alv.   'Tis possible.
Duch. Or say (no matter by what art or
    motive)
  He gives his title up, and leave me to
  My own election?
D'Alv.   If I then be happy
  To have a name within your thought,
    there can
  Be nothing left to crown me with new
    blessing.   230
  But I dream thus of heaven, and wake
    to find
  My amorous soul a mockery. When the
    priest
  Shall tie you to another, and the joys
  Of marriage leave no thought at leisure to
  Look back upon Alvarez, that must
    wither
  For loss of you, yet then I cannot lose
  So much of what I was once in your
    favor,
  But in a sigh pray still you may live
    happy.   *Exit.*
Duch. My heart is in a mist; some good
    star smile
  Upon my resolution, and direct   240
  Two lovers in their chaste embrace to
    meet!
  Columbo's bed contains my winding
    sheet.   *Exit.*

ACT II. [Scene i.

*Columbo's tent outside the walls of a frontier
city.*]

*Enter General Columbo, Hernando, two Colo-
nels, Alphonso, two Captains, and other
Officers, as at a council of war.*

Col. I see no face in all this council that
  Hath one pale fear upon 't, though we
    arrived not
  So timely to secure the town, which gives
  Our enemy such triumph.
1 Col.   'Twas betrayed.
Alph. The wealth of that one city
  Will make the enemy glorious.[1]
1 Col.   They dare
  Not plunder it.

[1] Boastful.

Alph.   They give fair quarter yet;
  They only seal up men's estates, and
    keep
  Possession for the city's use; they take up
  No wares without security, and he   10
  Whose single credit will not pass puts in
  Two lean comrades, upon whose bonds
    'tis not
  Religion to deny 'em.
Col.   To repair this
  With honor, gentlemen?
Her.   My opinion is
  To expect awhile.
Col.   Your reason?
Her.   Till their own
  Surfeit betray 'em, for their soldier[s],
  Bred up with coarse and common bread,
    will show
  Such appetites on the rich cates they find,
  They will spare our swords a victory,
    when their own
  Riot and luxury destroys 'em.
1 Col.   That   20
  Will show our patience too like a fear.
  With favor of his excellence, I think
  The spoil of cities takes not off the cour-
    age,
  But doubles it on soldiers; besides,
  While we have tameness to expect, the
    noise
  Of their success and plenty will increase
  Their army.
Her.   ''Tis considerable; we do not
  Exceed in foot or horse, our muster not
  'Bove sixteen thousand both, and the
    infantry
  Raw, and not disciplined to act.
Alph.   Their hearts,   30
  But with a brave thought of their coun-
    try's honor,
  Will teach 'em how to fight, had they not
    seen
  A sword. But we decline [2] our own too
    much;
  The men are forward in their arms, and
    take
  The use with avarice of fame.
                They rise, and talk privately.
Col.   Colonel,
  I do suspect you are a coward.
Her.   Sir!
Col. Or else a traitor; take your choice.
  No more.

[2] Undervalue.

I called you to a council, sir, of war;
Yet keep your place.
HER.   I have worn other names.
COL. Deserve 'em. Such   40
Another were enough to unsoul an army.
Ignobly talk of patience, till they drink
And reel to death? We came to fight, and
    force 'em
To mend their pace; thou hast no honor
    in thee,
Not enough noble blood to make a blush
For thy tame eloquence.
HER.   My lord, I know
My duty to a general; yet there are
Some that have known me here. Sir, I
    desire
To quit my regiment.
COL.   You shall have license.—
Ink and paper!   50

Enter with paper and standish.[1]

1 COL. The general's displeased.
2 COL.   How is 't, Hernando?
HER. The general has found out em-
    ployment for me;
He is writing letters back.
ALPH. }
1]CAP. }   To his mistress?
HER. Pray, do not trouble me; yet, prithee,
    speak,
And flatter not thy friend. Dost think I
    dare
Not draw my sword, and use it, when
    cause
With honor calls to action?
ALPH. }
[1]COL. } With the most valiant man alive.
HER. You'll do me some displeasure in
    your loves.
Pray, to your places.   60
COL. So; bear those letters to the king;
It speaks my resolution, before
Another sun decline, to charge the
    enemy.
HER. [*Aside.*] A pretty court way
Of dismissing an officer.—I obey; success
Attend your counsels!   *Exit.*
COL. If here be any dare not look on dan-
    ger,
And meet it like a man, with scorn of
    death,
I beg his absence; and a coward's fear
Consume him to a ghost!

[1] A stand for writing.

1 COL.   None such here. 70
COL. Or, if in all your regiments you find
One man that does not ask to bleed with
    honor,
Give him a double pay to leave the army;
There's service to be done will call the
    spirits
And aid of men.
1 COL.   You give us all new flame.
COL. I am confirmed, and you must lose no
    time;
The soldier that was took last night, to
    me
Discovered[2] their whole strength, and
    that we have
A party in the town, the river that   79
Opens the city to the west unguarded.
We must this night use art and resolu-
    tions.
We cannot fall ingloriously.
1 CAP. That voice is every man's.

Enter Soldier and Secretary with a letter.

COL. What now?
SOL. Letters.
COL. Whence?
SOL. From the duchess.
COL. They are welcome.—[*Takes the let-
    ter.*]
Meet at my tent again this evening;
Yet stay, some wine.—The duchess'
    health!   90
See it go round.   [*Opens the letter.*]
SEC.   It wo' not please his excellence.
1 COL. The duchess' health!   [*Drinks.*]
2 CAP. To me! More wine.
SEC. The clouds are gathering, and his eyes
    shoot fire;
Observe what thunder follows.
2 CAP. The general has but ill news. I
    suspect
The duchess sick, or else the king.
1 CAP.   May be
The cardinal.
2 CAP.   His soul has long been looked
    for.
COL. [*Aside.*] She dares not be so insolent.
    It is
The duchess' hand. How am I shrunk in
    fame   100
To be thus played withal! She writes,
    and counsels,

[2] Revealed.

Under my hand, to send her back a free
Resign of all my interest to her person,
Promise, or love; that there's no other way,
With safety of my honor, to revisit her.
The woman is possessed with some bold devil,
And wants an exorcism; or I am grown
A cheap, dull, phlegmatic fool, a post that's carved
I' th' common street, and holding out my forehead
To every scurril wit to pin disgrace   110
And libels on 't.—Did you bring this to me, sir?
My thanks shall warm your heart.
                       Draws a pistol.
SEC.   Hold, hold, my lord!
I know not what provokes this tempest, but
Her grace ne'er showed more freedom from a storm
When I received this paper. If you have
A will to do an execution,
Your looks, without that engine, sir, may serve.
I did not like the employment.
COL.   Ha! Had she
No symptom, in her eye or face, of anger,
When she gave this in charge?
SEC.   Serene as I   120
Have seen the morning rise upon the spring;
No trouble in her breath, but such a wind
As came to kiss and fan the smiling flowers.
COL. No poetry.
SEC.   By all the truth in prose,
By honesty and your own honor, sir,
I never saw her look more calm and gentle.
COL. I am too passionate; you must forgive me.
I have found it out; the duchess loves me dearly.
She expressed a trouble in her when I took   129
My leave, and chid me with a sullen eye.
'Tis a device to hasten my return;
Love has a thousand arts. I'll answer it
Beyond her expectation, and put
Her soul to a noble test.—Your patience, gentlemen;
The king's health will deserve a sacrifice
of wine.   [*Sits at the table and writes.*]

SEC. [*Aside.*] I am glad to see this change, and thank my wit
For my redemption.
1 COL. Sir, the soldier's curse on him loves not our master!
2 COL. And they curse loud enough to be heard.
2 CAP. Their curse has the nature of gunpowder.   140
SEC. They do not pray with half the noise.
1 COL. Our general is not well mixed;
He has too great a portion of fire.
2 COL. His mistress cool him (her complexion [1]
Carries some phlegm) when they two meet in bed!
2 CAP. A third may follow.
1 CAP. 'Tis much pity
The young duke lived not to take the virgin off.
1 COL. 'Twas the king's act to match two rabbit-suckers. [2]
2 COL. A common trick of state;   150
The little great man marries, travels then
Till both grow up, and dies when he should do
The feat. These things are still unlucky
On the male side.
COL. This to the duchess' fair hand.
                  [*Gives Secretary a letter.*]
SEC.   She will think
Time hath no wing, till I return.   [*Exit.*]
COL.   Gentlemen,
Now each man to his quarter, and encourage
The soldier. I shall take a pride to know
Your diligence, when I visit all your
Several commands.
OMNES.   We shall expect.
2 COL.   And move   160
By your directions.
COL.   Y' are all noble.   *Exeunt.*

[SCENE ii.

A room in the duchess' palace.]

Enter Cardinal, Duchess, Placentia.

CAR. I shall perform a visit daily, madam,
In th' absence of my nephew, and be happy
If you accept my care.
DUCH.   You have honored me
_____
[1] Temperament.   [2] Sucking rabbits, children

And, if your entertainment have not been
Worthy your grace's person, 'tis because
Nothing can reach it in my power; but,
  where
There is no want of zeal, other defect
Is only a fault to exercise your mercy.
CAR. You are bounteous in all. I take my
  leave,
My fair niece, shortly, when Columbo
  has   10
Purchased more honors to prefer [1] his
  name
And value to your noble thoughts; mean-
  time,
Be confident you have a friend, whose
  office
And favor with the king shall be effectual
To serve your grace.
DUCH.   Your own good deeds reward
  you,
Till mine rise equal to deserve their bene-
  fit.—   *Exit Cardinal.*
Leave me awhile.—   *Exit Placen[tia].*
Do not I walk upon the teeth of serpents,
And, as I had a charm against their poi-
  son,
Play with their stings? The cardinal is
  subtle,   20
Whom 'tis not wisdom to incense, till I
Hear to what destiny Columbo leaves
  me.
May be the greatness of his soul will
  scorn
To own what comes with murmur, if he
  can
Interpret me so happily.—Art come?

Enter Secretary with a letter.

SEC. His excellence salutes your grace.
DUCH.   Thou hast
A melancholy brow. How did he take my
  letter?
SEC. As he would take a blow; with so
  much sense
Of anger his whole soul boiled in his face,
And such prodigious flame in both his
  eyes   30
As they'd been th' only seat of fire, and at
Each look a salamander leaping forth,
Not able to endure the furnace.
DUCH.   Ha! Thou dost
Describe him with some horror.

[1] Advance.

SEC.   Soon as he
Had read again, and understood your
  meaning,
His rage had shot me with a pistol, had
  not
I used some soft and penitential language
To charm the bullet.
DUCH.   Wait at some more distance.—
My soul doth bath itself in a cold dew.
Imagine I am opening of a tomb.   40
                   [Opens the letter.]
Thus I throw off the marble, to discover
What antic posture death presents in this
Pale monument to fright me. (*Reads.*)
  Ha!
My heart, that called my blood and
  spirits to
Defend it from the invasion of my fears,
Must keep a guard about it still, lest this
Strange and too mighty joy crush it to
  nothing.—
Antonio.
SEC.   Madam.
DUCH.   Bid my steward give thee
Two thousand ducats. Art sure I am
  awake?   49
SEC. I shall be able to resolve [2] you, madam,
When he has paid the money.
DUCH. Columbo now is noble.
                     Exit Duch[ess].
SEC.   This is better
Than I expected—if my lady be
Not mad, and live to justify her bounty.
                         Exit.

[SCENE iii.

A room in the king's palace.]

Enter King, Alvarez, Hernando, Lords.

KING. The war is left to him, but we must
  have
You reconciled, if that be all your dif-
  ference.
His rage flows like a torrent, when he
  meets
With opposition. Leave to wrastle with
  him,
And his hot blood retreats into a calm,
And then he chides his passion. You shall
  back
With letters from us.
HER.   Your commands are not
  To be disputed.

[2] Inform.

KING.   Alvarez. [*Takes him aside.*]
1 LO.   Lose not
   Yourself by cool submission; he will find
   His error, and the want of such a soldier.
2 LO. Have you seen the cardinal?
HER.   Not yet.   11
1 LO. He wants no plot—
HER.   The king I must obey;
   But let the purple gownman place his
     engines[1]
   I' th' dark, that wounds me.
2 LO.   Be assured
   Of what we can to friend you; and the
     king
   Cannot forget your service.
HER.   I am sorry
   For that poor gentleman.
D'ALV.   I must confess, sir,
   The duchess has been pleased to think
     me worthy
   Her favors, and in that degree of honor
   That has obliged my life to make the
     best   20
   Return of service, which is not, with bold
   Affiance in her love, to interpose
   Against her happiness and your election.
   I love so much her honor I have quitted
   All my desires, yet would not shrink to
     bleed
   Out my warm stock of life, so the last
     drop
   Might benefit her wishes.
KING.   I shall find
   A compensation for this act, Alvarez;
   It hath much pleased us.

Enter Duchess with a letter; Gentleman Usher.

DUCH.   Sir, you are the king,
   And in that sacred title it were sin   30
   To doubt a justice. A'l that does concern
   My essence in this world, and a great part
   Of the other bliss, lives in your breath.
KING. What intends the duchess?
DUCH. That will instruct you, sir.—[*Gives
     him the letter.*] Columbo has,
   Upon some better choice or discontent,
   Set my poor soul at freedom.
KING.   'Tis his character.[2]   *Reads.*[3]
"Madam, I easily discharge all my preten-
sions to your love and person; I leave you to
your own choice; and, in what you have [40

obliged yourself to me, resume a power to
cancel, if you please.
                     COLUMBO."
   This is strange!
DUCH.   Now do an act to make
   Your chronicle beloved and read forever.
KING. Express yourself.
DUCH.   Since by divine infusion,
   For 'tis no art could force the general to
   This change, second this justice, and
     bestow
   The heart you would have given from
     me, by
   Your strict commands to love Columbo,
     where   50
   'Twas meant by heaven; and let your
     breath return
   Whom you divorced, Alvarez, mine.
LORDS.   This is
   But justice, sir.
KING.   It was decreed above;
   And, since Columbo has released his
     interest,
   Which we had wrought him, not without
     some force
   Upon your will, I give you your own
     wishes.
   Receive your own Alvarez. When you
     please
   To celebrate your nuptial, I invite
   Myself your guest.
DUCH.   Eternal blessings crown you!
OMNES. And every joy your marriage! 60
Exit King, who meets the Cardinal; they confer.
D'ALV. I know not whether I shall wonder
     most
   Or joy to meet this happiness.
DUCH.   Now the king
   Hath planted us, methinks we grow
     already,
   And twist our loving souls, above the
     wrath
   Of thunder to divide us.
D'ALV.   Ha! The cardinal
   Has met the king! I do not like this con-
     ference;
   He looks with anger this way. I expect
   A tempest.
DUCH.   Take no notice of his presence;
   Leave me to meet, and answer it. If the
     king
   Be firm in 's royal word, I fear no light-
     ning.   70
   Expect me in the garden.

D'ALV.   I obey,
But fear a shipwrack on the coast. *Exit.*
CAR.   Madam.
DUCH. My lord.
CAR. The king speaks of a letter that has
    brought
A riddle in 't.
DUCH.   'Tis easy to interpret.
CAR. From my nephew? May I deserve
    the favor?
        [*Duchess hands him the letter.*]
DUCH. [*Aside.*] He looks as though his
    eyes would fire the paper.
They are a pair of burning glasses, and
His envious blood doth give 'em flame.
CAR. [*Aside.*] What lethargy could thus
    unspirit him?   80
I am all wonder.—Do not believe,
    madam,
But that Columbo's love is yet more
    sacred
To honor and yourself than thus to for-
    feit
What I have heard him call the glorious
    wreath
To all his merits, given him by the king,
From whom he took you with more pride
    than ever
He came from victory. His kisses hang
Yet panting on your lips; and he but now
Exchanged religious farewell to return,
But with more triumph, to be yours.
DUCH.   My lord,
You do believe your nephew's hand was
    not   91
Surprised or strained[1] to this?
CAR. Strange arts and windings in the
    world! Most dark
And subtle progresses! Who brought this
    letter?
DUCH. I inquired not his name; I thought
    it not
Considerable[2] to take such narrow
    knowledge.
CAR. Desert and honor urged it here, nor
    can
I blame you to be angry; yet his person
Obliged you should have given a nobler
    pause
Before you made your faith and change
    so violent   100
From his known worth into the arms of
    one,

[1] Compelled.   [2] Weighty, important.

However fashioned to your amorous
    wish,
Not equal to his cheapest fame,[3] with all
The gloss of blood and merit.
DUCH.   This comparison,
My good lord cardinal, I cannot think
Flows from an even justice; it betrays
You partial where your blood runs.
CAR.   I fear, madam,
Your own takes too much license, and
    will soon
Fall to the censure of unruly tongues.
Because Alvarez has a softer cheek,   110
Can like a woman trim his wanton hair,
Spend half a day with looking in the
    glass
To find a posture to present himself,
And bring more effeminacy than man
Or honor to your bed, must he supplant
    him?
Take heed, the common murmur, when
    it catches
The scent of a lost fame—
DUCH.   My fame, Lord Cardinal?
It stands upon an innocence as clear
As the devotions you pay to heaven.
I shall not urge, my lord, your soft in-
    dulgence   120
At my next shrift.
CAR.   You are a fine court lady!
DUCH. And you should be a reverend
    churchman.
CAR.   One
That, if you have not thrown off mod-
    esty,
Would counsel you to leave Alvarez.
DUCH.   Cause
You dare do worse than marriage, must
    not I
Be admitted what the church and law
    allows me?
CAR. Insolent! Then you dare marry him?
DUCH.   Dare?
Let your contracted flame and malice,
    with
Columbo's rage, higher than that, meet
    us
When we approach the holy place,
    clasped hand   130
In hand we'll break through all your
    force, and fix
Our sacred vows together there.
CAR.   I knew

[3] Reputation.

When, with as chaste a brow, you promised fair
To another. You are no dissembling lady!
DUCH. Would all your actions had no falser lights
About 'em!
CAR. Ha!
DUCH. The people would not talk and curse so loud.
CAR. I'll have you chid into a blush for this.
DUCH. Begin at home, great man; there's cause enough.   140
You turn the wrong end of the perspective [1]
Upon your crimes, to drive them to a far
And lesser sight; but let your eyes look right,
What giants would your pride and surfeit seem!
How gross your avarice, eating up whole families!
How vast are your corruptions and abuse
Of the king's ear, at which you hang a pendant,
Not to adorn, but ulcerate, while the honest
Nobility, like pictures in the arras,
Serve only for court ornament. If they speak,   150
'Tis when you set their tongues, which you wind up
Like clocks, to strike at the just [2] hour you please.
Leave, leave, my lord, these usurpations,
And be what you were meant, a man to cure,
Not let in, agues to religion.
Look on the church's wounds.
CAR.   You dare presume,
In your rude spleen to me, to abuse the church?
DUCH. Alas, you give false aim, my lord; 'tis your
Ambition and scarlet sins that rob   159
Her altar of the glory and leave wounds
Upon her brow, which fetches grief and paleness
Into her cheeks, making her troubled bosom

Pant with her groans, and shroud her holy blushes
Within your reverend purples.
CAR.   Will you now take breath?
DUCH. In hope, my lord, you will behold yourself
In a true glass, and see those injust acts
That so deform you, and by timely cure
Prevent a shame, before the short-haired men [3]
Do crowd and call for justice. I take leave.   *Exit.*
CAR. This woman has a spirit that may rise   170
To tame the devil's. There's no dealing with
Her angry tongue; 'tis action and revenge
Must calm her fury. Were Columbo here,
I could resolve; but letters shall be sent
To th' army, which may wake him into sense
Of his rash folly, or direct his spirit
Some way to snatch his honor from this flame.
All great men know, "The soul of life is fame."   *Exit.*

ACT III. [SCENE i.

An apartment in the king's palace.]

Enter Valeria, Celinda.

VAL. I did not think, Celinda, when I praised
Alvarez to the duchess, that things thus
Would come about. What does your ladyship
Think of Columbo now? It staggers all
The court he should forsake his mistress; I
Am lost with wonder yet.
CEL.   'Tis very strange,
Without a spell; but there's a fate in love.
I like him ne'er the worse.

Enter two Lords.

1 LO. Nothing but marriages and triumph now!
VAL. What new access of joy makes you, my lord,   10
So pleasant?
1 LO.   There's a packet come to court

---

[1] Telescope.   [2] Exact.   [3] Perhaps an allusion to the Puritans.

Makes the king merry; we are all concerned in 't.

Columbo hath given the enemy a great
And glorious defeat, and is already
Preparing to march home.

CEL. He thrived the better for my prayers.

2 LO. 　　　　　　　　　You have been
His great admirer, madam.

1 LO. 　　　　　　　　The king longs
To see him.

VAL. 　This news exalts the cardinal.

Enter Cardinal.

1 LO. [*Aside.*] 　　　　　　He's here.
He appears with discontent; the mar-
riage 　　　　　　　　　　　　　19
With Count d'Alvarez hath a bitter taste,
And not worn off his palate. But let us
leave him.

LADIES. [*Aside.*] We'll to the duchess.
　　　　Exeunt. Manet [1] *Car[dinal].*

CAR. He has not won so much upon the
Aragon
As he has lost at home; and his neglect
Of what my studies had contrived to add
More luster to our family by the access
Of the great duchess' fortune, cools his
triumph,
And makes me wild.

Enter Hernando.

HER. 　　　　　My good Lord Cardinal!

CAR. You made complaint to th' king
about your general.

HER. Not a complaint, my lord; I did but
satisfy 　　　　　　　　　　　　30
Some questions o' the king's.

CAR. 　　　　　　　You see he thrives
Without your personal valor or advice,
Most grave and learned in the wars.

HER. 　　　　　　　　　　My lord,
I envy not his fortune.

CAR. 　　　　　　　　'Tis above
Your malice, and your noise not worth
his anger;
'Tis barking gainst the moon.

HER. 　　　　　　More temper would
Become that habit.

CAR. The military thing would show some
spleen.
I'll blow an army of such wasps about
The world. Go look [2] your sting you left
i' th' camp, sir. 　　　　　　　　40

[1] Remains. 　　　　　　　[2] Look for.

Enter King and Lords.

HER. The king!—This may be one day
counted [3] for. 　　　　　　　*Exit.*

KING. All things conspire, my lord, to
make you fortunate.
Your nephew's glory—

CAR. 　　　　'Twas your cause and justice
Made him victorious; had he been so
valiant
At home, he had had another conquest
to
Invite, and bid her welcome to new wars.

KING. You must be reconciled to provi-
dence, my lord.
I heard you had a controversy with
The duchess; I will have you friends.

CAR. I am not angry.

KING. 　　　　　　For my sake, then, 50
You shall be pleased, and with me grace
the marriage.
A churchman must show charity, and
shine
With first example: she's a woman.

CAR. You shall prescribe in all things, sir.
You cannot
Accuse my love, if I still wish my
nephew
Had been so happy, to be constant to
Your own and my election; yet my brain
Cannot reach how this comes about; I
know
My nephew loved her with a near affec-
tion.

Enter Hernando.

KING. He'll give you fair account at his
return.— 　　　　　　　　　　60
Colonel, your letters may be spared; the
general
Has finished, and is coming home. [*Exit.*]

HER. I am glad on 't, sir.—My good Lord
Cardinal,
'Tis not impossible but some man pro-
voked
May have a precious mind to cut your
throat.

CAR. You shall command me, noble colonel; [4]
I know you wo' not fail to be at th'
wedding.

HER. 'Tis not Columbo that is married,
sir.

[3] Accounted. 　　　　　　　[4] Trisyllabic.

CAR. Go teach the postures of the pike and
　　musket;　　　　　　　　　　　　69
Then drill your myrmidons into a ditch,
　Where starve,[1] and stink in pickle.—You
　　shall find
Me reasonable. You see the king expects
　me.
IER. So does the devil.
Some desperate hand may help you on
　your journey.　　　　　　　　*Exeunt.*

[SCENE ii.

A room in the duchess' palace.]

Enter Secretary and Servants.

SEC. Here, this; ay, this will fit your
part: you shall wear the slashes, because
you are a soldier. Here's for the blue [2]
mute.
1 [SERV.] This doublet will never fit me;
pox on 't![3] Are these breeches good
enough for a prince too? Pedro plays but a
lord, and he has two laces more in a seam.
SEC. You must consider Pedro is a foolish lord; he may wear what lace he [10
please.
2 [SERV.] Does my beard fit my clothes
well, gentlemen?
SEC. Pox o' your beard!
3 [SERV.] That will fright away the hair.
1 [SERV.] This fellow plays but a mute,
and he is so troublesome, and talks.
3 [SERV.] Mr.[4] Secretary might have let
Jaques play the soldier; he has a black
patch already.　　　　　　　　　20
2 [SERV.] By your favor, Mr. Secretary,
I was asked who writ this play for us.
SEC. For us? Why, art thou any more
than a blue mute?
2 [SERV.] And, by my troth, I said I
thought it was all your own.
SEC. Away, you coxcomb!
4 [SERV.] Dost think he has no more wit
than to write a comedy? My lady's chaplain made the play, though he is con- [30
tent, for the honor and trouble of the business, to be seen in 't.

Enter Fifth Servant.

5 [SERV.] Did anybody see my head,
gentlemen? 'Twas here but now. I shall
have never a head to play my part in.

SEC. Is thy head gone? 'Tis well thy
part was not in 't. Look, look about; has
not Jaques it?
4 [SERV.] I his head? 'T wo' not come
on upon my shoulders.　　　　　40
SEC. Make haste, gentlemen; I'll see
whether the king has supped. Look every
man to his wardrope [5] and his part.
　　　　　　Exit [with Fifth Servant].
2 [SERV.] Is he gone? In my mind, a
masque had been fitter for a marriage.
4 [SERV.] Why, mute? There was no
time for 't, and the scenes are troublesome.
2 [SERV.] Half a score deal tacked together in the clouds.[6] What's that? A
throne, to come down and dance; all [50
the properties have been paid forty times
over, and are in the court stock, but the
secretary must have a play to show his wit.
4 [SERV.] Did not I tell thee 'twas the
chaplain's? Hold your tongue, mute.
1 [SERV.] Under the rose, and would
this cloth of silver doublet might never
come off again, if there be any more plot
than you see in the back of my hand.
2 [SERV.] You talk of a plot! I'll [60
not give this for the best poet's plot in the
world, and if it be not well carried.
4 [SERV.] Well said, mute.
3 [SERV.] Ha, ha! Pedro, since he put on
his doublet, has repeated but three lines,
and he has broke five buttons.
2 [SERV.] I know not; but, by this false
beard, and here's hair enough to hang a
reasonable honest man, I do not remember,
to say, a strong line indeed in the [70
whole comedy but when the chambermaid
kisses the captain.
3 [SERV.] Excellent, mute!

Enter another Servant.

5 [SERV.] They have almost supped, and
I cannot find my head yet.
4 [SERV.] Play in thine own.
5 [SERV.] Thank you for that! So I may
have it made a property! If I have not a
head found me, let Mr. Secretary play my
part himself without it.　　　　80

Enter Secretary.

SEC. Are you all ready, my masters?
The king is coming through the gallery.

[1] Die.
[2] Color worn by servants.
[3] A plague on it!
[4] *I.e.*, Master.
[5] Wardrobe.
[6] Ten planks nailed together under the roof of
the stage.

Are the women dressed?

1 [Serv.] Rogero wants a head.

Sec. Here, with a pox to you, take mine! You a player? You a puppy dog! Is the music ready?

Enter Gentleman Usher.

Gent. Gentlemen, it is my lady's pleasure that you expect till she call for you. There are a company of cavaliers in [90 gallant equipage, newly alighted, have offered to present their revels in honor of this Hymen; and 'tis her grace's command that you be silent till their entertainment be over.

1 [Serv.] Gentlemen?

2 [Serv.] Affronted?

5 [Serv.] Mr. Secretary, there's your head again; a man's a man. Have I broken my sleep to study fifteen lines for an [100 ambassador, and after that a constable, and is it come to this?

Sec. Patience, gentlemen, be not so hot; 'tis but deferred, and the play may do well enough cold.

4 [Serv.] If it be not presented, the chaplain will have the greatest loss; he loses his wits. *Hautboys.*

Sec. This music speaks the king upon entrance. Retire, retire, and grumble [110 not. *Exeunt [All but Secretary].*

Enter King, Cardinal, Alvarez, Duchess, Celinda, Valeria, Placentia, Lords, Hernando. They being set, enter Columbo and five more, in rich habits, vizarded; between every two a Torchbearer. They dance, and after beckon to Alvarez, as desirous to speak with him.

D'Alv. With me!
They embrace and whisper.

King. Do you know the masquers, madam?

Duch. Not I, sir.

Car. There's one—but that my nephew is abroad,
And has more soul than thus to jig upon
Their hymeneal night, I should suspect
'Twere he.
The Masquers lead in Alvarez.

Duch. Where's my Lord Alvarez?
Recorders.

King. Call in the bridegroom.

Enter Columbo. Four Masquers bring in Alvarez dead, in one of their habits, and, having laid him down, exeunt [the four Masquers].

Duch. What mystery is this?

Car. We want the bridegroom still.

King. Where is Alvarez? 119
Columbo points to the body; they unvizard it, and find Alvar[ez] bleeding.

Duch. O, 'tis my lord! He's murdered!

King. Who durst commit this horrid act?

Col. [*Removing his mask.*] I, sir.

King. Columbo? Ha!

Col. Yes; Columbo, that dares stay
To justify that act.

Her. Most barbarous!

Duch. O, my dearest lord!

King. Our guard seize on them all. This sight doth shake
All that is man within me.—Poor Alvarez,
Is this thy wedding day?

Enter Guard.

Duch. If you do think there is a heaven, or pains
To punish such black crimes i' th' other world,
Let me have swift and such exemplar[1] justice 130
As shall become this great assassinate.
You will take off our faith else, and, if here
Such innocence must bleed, and you look on,
Poor men, that call you gods on earth. will doubt
To obey your laws, nay, practice to be devils,
As fearing, if such monstrous sins go on,
The saints will not be safe in heaven.

King. You shall,
You shall have justice.

Car. [*Aside.*] Now to come off[2] were brave.[3]

Enter Servant.

Serv. The masquers, sir, are fled; their horse, prepared 139
At gate, expected to receive 'em, where

[1] Exemplary.
[2] Escape, get clear.   [3] Fine.

They quickly mounted. Coming so like
    friends,
None could suspect their haste, which is
    secured
By advantage of the night.
COL. I answer for 'em all; 'tis stake
    enough
For many lives. But, if that poniard
Had voice, it would convince they were
    but all
Spectators of my act. And now, if you
Will give your judgments leave, though
    at the first
Face of this object your cool bloods were
    frighted,   149
I can excuse this deed, and call it justice,
An act your honors and your office, sir,
Is bound to build a law upon for others
To imitate. I have but took his life,
And punished her with mercy, who had
    both
Conspired to kill the soul of all my fame.
Read there—and read an injury as deep
In my dishonor as the devil knew
A woman had capacity or malice
To execute. Read there how you were
    cozened, sir,
    [*Gives the King the duchess' letter.*]
Your power affronted, and my faith; her
    smiles,   160
A juggling witchcraft to betray, and
    make
My love her horse to stalk withal, and
    catch
Her curléd minion.
CAR.   Is it possible
The duchess could dissemble so, and for-
    feit
Her modesty with you, and to us all?
Yet I must pity her. My nephew has
Been too severe, though this affront
    would call
A dying man from prayers, and turn him
    tiger,
There being nothing dearer than our
    fame,
Which, if a common man, whose blood
    has no   170
Ingredient of honor, labor to
Preserve, a soldier (by his nearest tie
To glory) is, above all others, bound
To vindicate. And yet it might have
    been less bloody.
HER. [*Aside.*] Charitable devil!

KING. (*Reads.*) "I pray, my lord, release under your hand what you dare challenge in my love or person, as a just forfeit
to myself. This act will speak you honor-
able to my thoughts, and, when you   [180
have conquered thus yourself, you may
proceed to many victories, and after, with
safety of your fame, visit again
                 The lost ROSAURA."
To this your answer was a free resign?
COL. Flattered with great opinion of her
    faith,
And my desert of her (with thought that
    she,
Who seemed to weep and chide my easy
    will
To part with her, could not be guilty of
A treason or apostasy so soon,   190
But rather meant this a device to make
Me expedite the affairs of war), I sent
That paper, which her wickedness, not
    justice,
Applied [1] (what I meant trial) her di-
    vorce.
I loved her so, I dare call heaven to wit-
    ness,
I knew not whether [2] I loved most, while
    she
With him whose crimson penitence I pro-
    voked [3]
Conspired my everlasting infamy.
Examine but the circumstance.
CAR.   'Tis clear.
This match was made at home, before
    she sent   200
That cunning writ, in hope to take him
    off,
As knowing his impatient soul would
    scorn
To own a blessing came on crutches to
    him.
It was not well to raise his expectation
(Had you, sir, no affront?) to ruin him
With so much scandal and contempt.
KING.   We have
Too plentiful a circumstance to accuse
You, madam, as the cause of your own
    sorrows,
But not without an accessary more
Than young Alvarez.
CAR.   Any other instrument?   210
KING. Yes; I am guilty, with herself, and
    Don

---

[1] Considered as.   [2] Which.   [3] Caused.

Columbo, though our acts looked several
　ways,
That thought a lover might so soon be
　ransomed,
And did exceed the office of a king
To exercise dominion over hearts
That owe to the prerogative of heaven
Their choice or separation; you must,
　therefore,
When you do kneel for justice and re-
　venge,
Madam, consider me a lateral agent
In poor Alvarez' tragedy.　　　　220
1 Lo. It was your love to Don Columbo,
　sir.
Her. [*Aside*.] So, so! The king is charmed.
　Do you observe
How, to acquit Columbo, he would draw
Himself into the plot. Heaven, is this
　justice?
Car. Your judgment is divine in this.
King.　　　　　　　　　　And yet
Columbo cannot be secure, and we
Just in his pardon, that durst make so
　great
And insolent a breach of law and duty.
2 Lo. [*Aside*.] Ha! Will he turn again?
King.　　　　　　　And should we leave
This guilt of blood to heaven, which cries,
　and strikes　　　　　　　　　230
With loud appeals the palace of eternity?
Yet here is more to charge Columbo
　than
Alvarez' blood, and bids me punish it,
Or be no king.
Her. [*Aside*.]　　　　'Tis come about,
　my lords.
King. And, if I should forgive
His timeless death, I cannot the offense,
That with such boldness struck at me.
　Has my
Indulgence to your merits, which are
　great,
Made me so cheap your rage could meet
　no time
Nor place for your revenge but where
　my eyes　　　　　　　　　　240
Must be affrighted, and affronted with
The bloody execution? This contempt
Of majesty transcends my power to par-
　don,
And you shall feel my anger, sir.
Her. Thou shalt have one short prayer
　more for that.

Col. Have I, i' th' progress of my life,
No actions to plead me up deserving
Against this ceremony?
Car.　　　　　　　　Contain yourself.
Col. I must be dumb then. Where is
　honor
And gratitude of kings, when they for-
　get　　　　　　　　　　　　250
Whose hand secured their greatness?
　Take my head off;
Examine then which of your silken lords,
As I have done, will throw himself on
　dangers;
Like to a floating island move in blood;
And, where your great defense calls him
　to stand
A bulwark, upon his bold breast to
　take
In death, that you may live. But soldiers
　are
Your valiant fools, whom, when your
　own securities
Are bleeding, you can cherish, but, when
　once
Your state and nerves are knit, not think-
　ing when　　　　　　　　　260
To use their surgery again, you cast
Them off, and let them hang in dusty
　armories,
Or make it death to ask for pay.
King.　　　　　　　　　　No more.
We thought to have put your victory
　and merits
In balance with Alvarez' death, which,
　while
Our mercy was to judge, had been your
　safety;
But the affront to us, made greater by
This boldness to upbraid our royal
　bounty,
Shall tame, or make you nothing.
[2] Lo. [*Aside*.]　　　　　　Excellent!
Her. [*Aside*.] The cardinal is not pleased.
Car.　　　　　　　Humble yourself　270
To th' king.
Col.　　　And beg my life? Let cowards
　do 't
That dare not die; I'll rather have no
　head
Than owe it to his charity.
King.　　　　　To th' Castle with him!—
　　　　[*The Guard take Columbo away.*]
Madam, I leave you to your grief, and
　what

The king can recompense to your tears, or honor
Of your dead lord, expect.

Duch. This shows like justice. *Exeunt.*

ACT IV. [SCENE i.

A room in the king's palace.]

Enter two Lords, Hernando.

1 Lo. This is the age of wonders.

2 Lo.   Wondrous mischiefs!

Her. Among those guards, which some call tutelar angels,
Whose office is to govern provinces,
Is there not one will undertake Navarre?
Hath heaven forsook us quite?

1 [Lo.]   Columbo at large!

2 [Lo.] And graced now more than ever.

1 [Lo.]   He was not pardoned;
That word was prejudicial to his fame.

Her. But, as the murder done had been a dream
Vanished to memory, he's courted as
Preserver of his country. With what chains   10
Of magic does this cardinal hold the king?

2 [Lo.] What will you say, my lord, if they enchant
The duchess now and by some impudent art
Advance a marriage to Columbo yet?

Her. Say! I'll say no woman can be saved; nor is 't
Fit, indeed, any should pretend to heaven
After one such impiety in their sex.
And yet my faith has been so staggered, since
The king restored Columbo, I'll be now
Of no religion.

1 [Lo.]   'Tis not possible   20
She can forgive the murder; I observed
Her tears.

Her.   Why, so did I, my lord;
And, if they be not honest, 'tis to be
Half damned to look upon a woman weeping.
When do you think the cardinal said his prayers?

2 [Lo.] I know not.

Her.   Heaven forgive my want of charity,

But, if I were to kill him, he should have
No time to pray; his life could be no sacrifice,
Unless his soul went too.

1 [Lo.]   That were too much.

Her. When you mean to despatch him, you may give   30
Time for confession. They have injured me
After another rate.

2 [Lo]. You are too passionate, cousin.

Enter Columbo, Colonels, Alphonso, Court-
iers. They pass over the stage.

Her. How the gay men do flutter to congratulate
His goal [1] delivery! There's one honest man.
What pity 'tis a gallant fellow should
Depend on knaves for his preferment!

1 [Lo.] Except this cruelty upon Alvarez,
Columbo has no mighty stain upon him;
But for his uncle—

Her.   If I had a son   40
Of twelve years old that would not fight with him,
And stake his soul against his cardinal's cap,
I would disinherit him. Time has took a lease
But for three lives, I hope; a fourth may see
Honesty walk without a crutch.

2 [Lo.]   This is
But air and wildness.

Her.   I'll see the duchess.

1 [Lo.] [2] You may do well to comfort her;
We must attend the king.

Her.   Your pleasures.
Exit Her[nando].

Enter King and Cardinal.

1 [Lo. *Aside.*] A man of a brave soul.

2 [Lo. *Aside.*]   The less his safety.
The king and cardinal in consult!   50

King. Commend us to the duchess, and employ
What language you think fit and powerful

---

[1] Gaol, jail.
[2] In the original this speech head introduces the following line.

To reconcile her to some peace.—My lords.

CAR. Sir, I possess all for your sacred uses.

Exeunt severally.

[SCENE ii.

A room in the duchess' palace.]

Enter Secretary and Celinda.

SEC. Madam, you are the welcom'st lady living.

CEL. To whom, Mr. Secretary?

SEC.   If you have mercy
To pardon so much boldness, I durst say,
To me—I am a gentleman.

CEL.   And handsome.

SEC. But my lady has much wanted you.

CEL. Why, Mr. Secretary?

SEC. You are the prettiest—

CEL. So!

SEC. The wittiest—

CEL. So!   10

SEC. The merriest lady i' th' court.

CEL. And I was wished to make the duchess pleasant?

SEC. She never had so deep a cause of sorrow;
Her chamber's but a coffin of a larger
Volume, wherein she walks so like a ghost,
'Twould make you pale to see her.

CEL.   Tell her grace
I attend here.

SEC.   I shall most willingly.—
[*Aside.*] A spirited lady! Would I had
her in my closet!
She is excellent company among the lords.
Sure she has an admirable treble.—
Madam.   *Exit.* 20

CEL. I do suspect this fellow would be nibbling,
Like some whose narrow fortunes will not rise
To wear things when the invention's rare and new,
But, treading on the heel of pride, they hunt
The fashion when 'tis crippled, like fell tyrants.
I hope I am not old yet. I had the honor
To be saluted by our cardinal's nephew
This morning. There's a man!

Enter Secretary.

SEC.   I have prevailed.
Sweet madam, use what eloquence you can
Upon her, and, if ever I be useful   30
To your ladyship's service, your least
breath commands me.   [*Exit.*]

Enter Duchess.

DUCH. Madam, I come to ask you but one question:
If you were in my state, my state of grief,
I mean an exile from all happiness
Of this world, and almost of heaven (for my
Affliction is finding out despair),
What would you think of Don Columbo?

CEL.   Madam?

DUCH. Whose bloody hand wrought all this misery.
Would you not weep as I do, and wish rather   39
An everlasting spring of tears to drown
Your sight than let your eyes be cursed to see
The murderer again, and glorious?
So careless of his sin that he is made
Fit for new parricide, even while his soul
Is purpled o'er, and reeks with innocent blood?
But do not, do not answer me; I know
You have so great a spirit (which I want,
The horror of his fact [1] surprising all
My faculties), you would not let him live.
But I, poor I, must suffer more. There's not   50
One little star in heaven will look on me,
Unless to choose me out the mark, on whom
It may shoot down some angry influence.

Enter Placentia.

PLA. Madam, here's Don Columbo says he must
Speak with your grace.

DUCH.   But he must not, I charge you.—
         [*Exit Placentia.*]
None else wait?—Is this well done,
To triumph in his tyranny? Speak, madam,
Speak but your conscience.

[1] Deed.

Enter Columbo and Secretary.

SEC.   Sir, you must not see her.
COL. Not see her? Were she cabled up
    above
The search of bullet or of fire, were
    she   60
Within her grave, and that the toughest
    mine
That ever nature teemed and groaned
    withal,
I would force some way to see her.—[*Exit
    Secretary.*] Do not fear
I come to court you, madam; y' are not
    worth
The humblest of my kinder thoughts. I
    come
To show the man you have provoked,
    and lost,
And tell you what remains of my re-
    venge.
Live, but never presume again to marry;
I'll kill the next at th' altar, and quench
    all
The smiling tapers with his blood. If,
    after,   70
You dare provoke the priest and heaven
    so much
To take another, in thy bed I'll cut him
    from
Thy warm embrace, and throw his heart
    to ravens.
CEL. This will appear an unexampled
    cruelty.
COL. Your pardon, madam. Rage and my
    revenge,
Not perfect, took away my eyes. You are
A noble lady—this not worth your eye-
    beam—
One of so slight a making and so thin
An autumn leaf is of too great a value
To play, which shall be soonest lost i' th'
    air.   80
Be pleased to own me by some name in
    your
Assurance; I despise to be received
There. Let her witness that I call you
    mistress;
Honor me to make these pearls your
    carcanet.   [*Gives her a necklace.*]
CEL. My lord, you are too humble in your
    thoughts.
COL. [*Aside.*] There's no vexation too
    great to punish her.   *Exit.*

Enter Secretary.

SEC. Now, madam?
CEL. Away, you saucy fellow!—Madam, I
    Must be excused, if I do think more hon-
    orably
Than you have cause, of this great lord.
DUCH.   Why, is not 90
All womankind concerned to hate what's
    impious?
CEL. For my part—
DUCH.   Antonio, is this a woman?
SEC. I know not whether she be man or
    woman;
    I should be nimble to find out the experi-
    ment.
    She looked with less state when Columbo
    came.
DUCH. Let me entreat your absence.—
    [*Aside.*] I am cozened in her.—
    I took you for a modest, honest [1] lady.
CEL. Madam, I scorn any accuser; and,
    Deducting the great title of a duchess,
    I shall not need one grain of your dear
    honor   100
To me make full weight. If your grace be
    jealous,
I can remove.   *Exit.*
SEC.   She is gone.
DUCH.   Prithee, remove
My fears of her return.—(*Ex[it] Sec-
    [retary].*) She is not worth
Considering; my anger's mounted higher.
He need not put in caution for my next
Marriage. Alvarez, I must come to thee,
Thy virgin, wife, and widow; but not till
I ha' paid those tragic duties to thy
    hearse
Become [2] my piety and love. But how?
Who shall instruct a way?

Enter Placentia.

PLA.   Madam, Don 110
Hernando much desires to speak with
    you.
DUCH. Will not thy own discretion think I
    am
Unfit for visit?
PLA.   Please your grace, he brings
Something he says imports your ear, and
    love
Of the dead Lord Alvarez.
DUCH.   Then admit him.
    ¹ Chaste.   ² *I.e.*, which become.

Enter Hernando.

HER. I would speak, madam, to yourself.

DUCH.   Your absence. [*Exit Placentia.*]

HER. I know not how your grace will censure so

Much boldness, when you know the affairs I come for.

DUCH. My servant has prepared me to receive it,

If it concern my dead lord.

HER.   Can you name   120

So much of your Alvarez in a breath,

Without one word of your revenge? O, madam,

I come to chide you, and repent my great

Opinion of your virtue, that can walk,

And spend so many hours in naked solitude,

As if you thought that no arrears were due

To his death, when you had paid his funeral charges,

Made your eyes red, and wept a handkercher.

I come to tell you that I saw him bleed;

I, that can challenge nothing in his name   130

And honor, saw his murdered body warm

And panting with the labor of his spirits,

Till my amazed soul shrunk and hid itself,

While barbarous Columbo, grinning, stood

And mocked the weeping wounds. It is too much

That you should keep your heart alive so long

After this spectacle, and not revenge it.

DUCH. You do not know the business of my heart,

That censure me so rashly; yet I thank you.   139

And, if you be Alvarez' friend, dare tell

Your confidence that I despise my life,

But know not how to use it in a service

To speak me his revenger. This will need

No other proof than that to you, who may

Be sent with cunning to betray me, I

Have made this bold confession. I so much

Desire to sacrifice to that hovering ghost

Columbo's life that I am not ambitious

To keep my own two minutes after it.

HER. If you will call me coward, which is equal   150

To think I am a traitor, I forgive it

For this brave resolution, which time

And all the destinies must aid. I beg

That I may kiss your hand for this, and may

The soul of angry honor guide it.

DUCH.   Whither?

HER. To Don Columbo's heart.

DUCH. It is too weak, I fear, alone.

HER. Alone? Are you in earnest? Why, will it not   158

Be a dishonor to your justice, madam,

Another arm should interpose? But that

It were a saucy act to mingle with you,

I durst, nay, I am bound in the revenge

Of him that's dead (since the whole world has interest

In every good man's loss) to offer it.

Dare you command me, madam?

DUCH.   Not command;

But I should more than honor such a truth

In man, that durst, against so mighty odds,

Appear Alvarez' friend and mine. The cardinal—

HER. Is for the second course. Columbo must

Be first cut up; his ghost must lead the dance.   170

Let him die first.

DUCH. But how?

HER. How? With a sword; and, if I undertake it,

I wo' not lose so much of my own honor

To kill him basely.

DUCH.   How shall I reward

This infinite service? 'Tis not modesty

While now my husband groans beneath his tomb,

And calls me to his marble bed, to promise

What this great act might well deserve, myself,   179

If you survive the victor; but, if thus

Alvarez' ashes be appeased, it must

Deserve an honorable memory;

And, though Columbo (as he had all power,

And grasped the fates) has vowed to kill the man

That shall succeed Alvarez—

HER.   Tyranny!
DUCH. Yet, if ever
I entertain a thought of love hereafter,
Hernando from the world shall challenge
  it,
Till when, my prayers and fortune shall
  wait on you.
HER. This is too mighty recompense.
DUCH.   'Tis all just. 190
HER. If I outlive Columbo, I must not
Expect security at home.
DUCH.   Thou canst
Not fly where all my fortunes and my
  love
Shall not attend to guard thee.
HER.   If I die—
DUCH. Thy memory
Shall have a shrine, the next within my
  heart,
To my Alvarez.
HER.   Once again your hand.
Your cause is so religious you need not
Strengthen it with your prayers; trust it
to me.

Enter Placentia and Cardinal.

PLA. Madam, the cardinal.
DUCH.   Will you appear? 200
HER. And [1] he had all the horror of the
  devil
In 's face, I would not balk him.
He stares upon the Cardinal in his exit.
CAR. [*Aside.*] What makes [2] Hernando
  here? I do not like
They should consult; I'll take no note.—
  The king
Fairly salutes your grace, by whose com-
  mand
I am to tell you, though his will and
  actions,
Illimited, stoop not to satisfy
The vulgar inquisition, he is
Yet willing to retain a just opinion
With those that are placed near him;
and, although   210
You look with nature's eye upon your-
  self,
Which needs no perspective to reach, nor
  art
Of any optic [3] to make greater what
Your narrow sense applies [4] an injury

(Ourselves still nearest to ourselves),
  but there's
Another eye that looks abroad, and walks
In search of reason and the weight of
  things,
With which, if you look on him, you will
  find
His pardon to Columbo cannot be 219
So much against his justice as your erring
Faith would persuade your anger.
DUCH.   Good my lord,
Your phrase has too much landshape,[5]
  and I cannot
Distinguish at this distance; you present
The figure perfect, but indeed my eyes
May pray your lordship find excuse, for
  tears
Have almost made them blind.
CAR.   Fair, peace restore 'em!
To bring the object nearer, the king says
He could not be severe to Don Columbo
Without injustice to his other merits,
Which call more loud for their reward
  and honor   230
Than you for your revenge; the kingdom
  made
Happy by those, you only, by the last,
Unfortunate; nor was it rational
(I speak the king's own language) he
  should die
For taking one man's breath, without
  whose valor
None now had been alive without dis-
  honor.
DUCH. In my poor understanding, 'tis the
  crown
Of virtue to proceed in its own tract,[6]
Not deviate from honor. If you acquit
A man of murder, cause he has done
  brave   240
Things in the war, you will bring down
  his valor
To a crime, nay, to a bawd, if it secure
A rape, and but teach those that deserve
  well
To sin with greater license. But dispute
Is now too late, my lord; 'tis done; and
  you,
By the good king, in tender [7] of my sor-
  rows,
Sent to persuade me 'tis unreasonable
That justice should repair me.

[1] If.   [3] Magnifying glass.
[2] Does.   [4] Interprets as.
[5] Landscape.
[6] Track.   [7] Consideration.

Car.　　　　　　　　　　　　　You mistake,
For, if Columbo's death could make
　　Alvarez　　　　　　　　　　　　　　249
Live, the king had given him up to law,
Your bleeding sacrifice, but, when his
　　life
Was but another treasure thrown away
To obey a clamorous statute, it was wis-
　　dom
To himself, and common safety, to take
　　off
This killing edge of law, and keep
　　Columbo
To recompense the crime by noble acts
And sorrow, that in time might draw
　　your pity.
Duch. This is a greater tyranny than that
Columbo exercised; he killed my lord,
And you have not the charity to let　260
Me think it worth a punishment.
Car.　　　　　　　　　　　　　To that,
In my own name, I answer: I condemn
And urge the bloody guilt against my
　　nephew;
'Twas violent and cruel, a black deed,
A deed whose memory doth make me
　　shudder,
An act that did betray a tyrannous
　　nature,
Which he took up in war, the school of
　　vengeance,
And, though the king's compassion spare
　　him here,
Unless his heart
Weep itself out in penitent tears here-
　　after—　　　　　　　　　　　　　　270
Duch. This sounds
As you were now a good man.
Car.　　　　　　　　　　　　Does your grace
Think I have conscience to allow the
　　murder?
Although, when it was done, I did obey
The stream of nature, as he was my kins-
　　man,
To plead he might not pay his forfeit life,
Could I do less for one so near my blood?
Consider, madam, and be charitable;
Let not this wild injustice make me
　　lose　　　　　　　　　　　　　　　　279
The character I bear, and reverend habit.
To make you full acquainted with my
　　innocence,
I challenge here my soul and heaven to
　　witness.

If I had any thought or knowledge with
My nephew's plot, or person, when he
　　came
Under the smooth pretense of friend to
　　violate
Your hospitable laws, and do that act
Whose frequent mention draws this tear,
　　a whirlwind
Snatch me to endless flames!
Duch.　　　　　　　　　　　I must believe,
And ask your grace's pardon. I confess
I ha' not loved you since Alvarez' death,
Though we were reconciled.
Car.　　　　　　　　　　　I do not blame　291
Your jealousy,[1] nor any zeal you had
To prosecute revenge against me, ma-
　　dam,
As I then stood suspected, nor can yet
Implore your mercy to Columbo. All
I have to say is, to retain my first
Opinion and credit with your grace,
Which you may think I urge not out of
　　fear
Or ends[2] upon you (since, I thank the
　　king,　　　　　　　　　　　　　　　299
I stand firm on the base of royal favor),
But for your own sake, and to show I
　　have
Compassion of your sufferings.
Duch.　　　　　　　　　　You have cleared
A doubt, my lord, and by this fair remon-
　　strance
Given my sorrow so much truce, to think
That we may meet again and yet be
　　friends.
But be not angry, if I still remember
By whom Alvarez died, and weep, and
　　wake
Another justice with my prayers.
Car.　　　　　　　　　　　　All thoughts
That may advance a better peace dwell
　　with you!　　　　　　　　　　　　Exit.
Duch. How would this cozening statesman
　　bribe my faith　　　　　　　　　　310
With flatteries to think him innocent!
No; if his nephew die, this cardinal must
　　not
Be long-lived. All the prayers of a
　　wronged widow
Make firm Hernando's sword, and my
　　own hand
Shall have some glory in the next re-
　　venge.

---

[1] Mistrust.　　　　　　　　　　　[2] Designs.

I will pretend my brain with grief dis-
tracted;
It may gain easy credit, and, beside
The taking off examination
For great Columbo's death, it makes
    what act   319
I do, in that believed want of my reason,
Appear no crime, but my defense. Look
    down,
Soul of my lord, from thy eternal shade,
And unto all thy blessed companions
    boast
Thy duchess busy to revenge thy ghost!
                     Exit.

[SCENE iii.

A lonely spot outside the city.]

Enter Columbo, Hernando, Alphonso, Colo-
                  nel.

COL. Hernando, now I love thee, and do
    half
  Repent the affront my passion threw
    upon thee.
HER. You wo' not be too prodigal o' your
    penitence.
COL. This makes good thy nobility of
    birth;
  Thou mayst be worth my anger and my
    sword,
  If thou dost execute as daringly
  As thou provok'st a quarrel. I did think
  Thy soul a starve'ing, or asleep.
HER.   You'll find it
  Active enough to keep your spirit wak-
    ing,
  Which, to exasperate, for yet I think   10
  It is not high enough to meet my rage—
  D'e smile?
COL.   This noise is worth it.—Gentle-
    men,
  I'm sorry this great soldier has engaged
  Your travail; all his business is to talk.
HER. A little of your lordship's patience.
  You shall have other sport, and swords
    that will
  Be as nimble 'bout your heart as you can
    wish.
  'Tis pity more than our two single lives
  Should be at stake.
COLONEL.   Make that no scruple, sir.
HER. To him then that survives, if fate
    allow   20

That difference, I speak, that he may tell
The world I came not hither on slight
    anger,
But to revenge my honor, stained and
    trampled on
By this proud man. When general, he
    commanded
My absence from the field.
COL.   I do remember,
  And I'll give your soul now a discharge.
HER.   I come
  To meet it, if your courage be so fortu-
    nate.
  But there is more than my own injury
  You must account for, sir, if my sword
    prosper,
  Whose point and every edge is made more
    keen   30
  With young Alvarez' blood, in which I
    had
  A noble interest. Does not that sin be-
    numb
  Thy arteries, and turn the guilty flowings
  To trembling jelly in thy veins? Canst
    hear
  Me name that murder, and thy spirits
    not
  Struck into air, as thou wert shot by
    some
  Engine from heaven?
COL.   You are the duchess' champion!
  Thou hast given me a quarrel now. I
    grieve
  It is determined all must fight, and I
  Shall lose much honor in his fall.
HER.   That duchess 40
  (Whom but to mention with thy breath
    is sacrilege),
  An orphan of thy making, and con-
    demned
  By thee to eternal solitude, I come
  To vindicate; and, while I am killing
    thee,
  By virtue of her prayers sent up for
    justice,
  At the same time in heaven I am par-
    doned for 't.
COL. I cannot hear the bravo.
HER.   Two words more,
  And take your chance. Before you all I
    must
  Pronounce that noble lady without
    knowledge   49
  Or thought of what I undertake for her.

Poor soul, she's now at her devotions,
Busy with heaven, and wearing out the
    earth
With her stiff knees, and bribing her
    good angel
With treasures of her eyes, to tell her
    lord
How much she longs to see him. My
    attempt
Needs no commission from her. Were I
A stranger in Navarre, the inborn right
Of every gentleman to Alvarez' loss
Is reason to engage their swords and
    lives   59
Against the common enemy of virtue.
Col. Now have you finished? I have an
    instrument
Shall cure this noise, and fly up to thy
    tongue
To murder all thy words.
Her.   One little knot
Of phlegm, that clogs my stomach, and
    I ha' done:
You have an uncle, called a cardinal.
Would he were lurking now about thy
    heart,
That the same wounds might reach you
    both, and send
Your reeling souls together! Now have
    at you!
Alph. We must not, sir, be idle.
        They fight; Columbo's Second slain.
Her. What think you now of praying?
Col.   Time enough. 70
        He kills Hernando's Second.
Commend me to my friend; the scales
    are even.
I would be merciful, and give you time
Now to consider of the other world;
You'll find your soul benighted pres-
    ently.
Her. I'll find my way i' th' dark.
*They fight, and close; Columbo gets both the
    swords, and Hernando takes up the Sec-
        ond's weapon.*
Col.   A stumble's dangerous.
Now ask thy life. Ha!
Her.   I despise to wear it,
A gift from any but the first bestower.
Col. I scorn a base advantage. Ha!
*Columbo throws away one of the swords.
    They fight; Hernando wounds Columbo.*
Her.   I am now
Out of your debt.

Col.   Th'ast done 't and I forgive thee.
Give me thy hand. When shall we meet
    again?   80
Her. Never, I hope.
Col. I feel life ebb apace, yet I'll look
    upwards,
And show my face to heaven.   [*Dies.*]
Her.   The matter's done;
I must not stay to bury him.   *Exit.*

Act V. [Scene i.

A garden.]

Enter two Lords.

1 Lo. Columbo's death doth much afflict
    the king.
2 Lo. I thought the cardinal would have
    lost his wits
At first, for 's nephew; it drowns all the
    talk
Of the other that were slain.
1 [Lo.]   We are friends.
I do suspect Hernando had some interest,
And knew how their wounds came.
2 [Lo.]   His flight confirms it,
For whom the cardinal has spread his
    nets.
1 [Lo.] He is not so weak to trust himself
    at home
To his enemy's gripe.
2 [Lo.]   All strikes not me so much
As that the duchess, most oppresséd
    lady,   10
Should be distracted, and before Co-
    lumbo
Was slain.
1 [Lo.]   But that the cardinal should be
    made
Her guardian is to me above that wonder.
2 [Lo.] So it pleased the king; and she,
    with that small stock
Of reason left her, is so kind and smooth
Upon him.
1 [Lo.]   She's turned a child again. A
    madness,
That would ha' made her brain and blood
    boil high,
In which distemper she might ha'
    wrought something—
2 [Lo.] Had been to purpose.
1 [Lo.] The cardinal is cunning, and, how-
    e'er   20

His brow does smile, he does suspect
    Hernando
Took fire from her, and waits a time to
    punish it.
2 [Lo.] But what a subject of disgrace and
    mirth
Hath poor Celinda made herself by pride,
In her belief Columbo was her servant! [1]
Her head hath stooped much since he
    died, and she
Almost ridiculous at court.

Enter Cardinal, Antonelli, Servant.

1 [Lo.]   The cardinal
Is come into the garden, now—
CAR.   Walk off.—[*Exeunt Lords.*]
It troubles me the duchess by her loss
Of brain is now beneath my great re-
    venge.   30
She is not capable to feel my anger,
Which, like to unregarded thunder spent
In woods, and lightning aimed at sense-
    less trees,
Must idly fall, and hurt her not, not to
That sense her guilt deserves. A fatal
    stroke,
Without the knowledge for what crime,
    to fright her
When she takes leave, and make her tug
    with death,
Until her soul sweat, is a pigeon's tor-
    ment,
And she is sent a babe to the other world.
Columbo's death will not be satisfied, 40
And I but wound her with a two-edged
    feather.
I must do more. I have all opportunity
(She by the king now made my charge),
    but she's
So much a turtle [2] I shall lose by killing
    her,
Perhaps do her a pleasure and prefer-
    ment;
That must not be.

Enter Celinda with a parchment.

ANT. [*Stopping her.*] Is not this she that
    would be thought to have been
Columbo's mistress? Madam, his grace
    is private,
And would not be disturbed; you may
    displease him.

----

[1] Admirer.   [2] Turtledove.

CEL. What will your worship wager that
    he shall   50
Be pleased again before we part?
ANT. I'll lay this diamond, madam, gainst
    a kiss,
And trust yourself to keep the stakes.
CEL.   'Tis done.
            [*Approaches the Cardinal.*]
ANT. [*Aside.*] I have long had an appe-
    tite to this lady;
But the lords keep her up so high—this
    toy
May bring her on.
CAR. This interruption tastes not of good
    manners.
CEL. But where necessity, my lord, com-
    pels,
    The boldness may meet pardon, and,
        when you
    Have found my purpose, I may less ap-
        pear   60
    Unmannerly.
CAR.   To th' business.
CEL.   It did please
    Your nephew, sir, before his death, to
        credit me
With so much honorable favor, I
Am come to tender to his near'st of blood,
Yourself, what does remain a debt to him.
Not to delay your grace with circum-
    stance,
That deed, if you accept, makes you my
    heir
Of no contemptible estate.   *He reads.*
    —[*Aside.*] This way
Is only left to tie up scurrile tongues
And saucy men, that since Columbo's
    death   70
Venture to libel on my pride and folly;
His greatness and this gift, which I enjoy
Still for my life (beyond which term a
    kingdom's
Nothing), will curb the giddy spleens of
    men
That live on impudent rime, and railing at
Each wandering fame [3] they catch.
CAR.   Madam, this bounty
Will bind my gratitude, and care to serve
    you.
CEL. I am your grace's servant.
CAR.   Antonelli! *Whisper.*
And, when this noble lady visits me,
Let her not wait.   80

----

[3] Rumor.

CEL. [*Aside.*]   What think you, my offi-
cious sir? His grace
Is pleased, you may conjecture. I may keep
Your gem; the kiss was never yours.
ANT. [*Aside.*]   Sweet madam—
CEL. [*Aside.*]   Talk if you dare; you know
I must not wait.
And so, farewell for this time.   [*Exit.*]
CAR. 'Tis in my brain already, and it forms
Apace—good, excellent revenge, and
pleasant!
She's now within my talons; 'tis too
cheap
A satisfaction for Columbo's death,   89
Only to kill her by soft charm or force.
I'll rifle first her darling chastity;
'Twill be after time enough to poison her,
And she to th' world be thought her own
destroyer.
As I will frame the circumstance, this
night
All may be finished; for the colonel,
Her agent in my nephew's death (whom I
Disturbed at counsel with her), I may
reach him
Hereafter, and be master of his fate.
*We starve our conscience when we thrive in
   state.*   *Exeunt.*

[SCENE ii.

A room in the duchess' palace.]

Enter Secretary and Placentia.

SEC. Placentia, we two are only left
Of my lady's servants; let us be true
To her and one another, and be sure,
When we are at prayers, to curse the
cardinal.
PLA. I pity my sweet lady.
SEC. I pity her too, but am a little angry;
She might have found another time to
lose
Her wits.
PLA.   That I were a man!
SEC.   What wouldst thou do,
Placentia?
PLA.   I would revenge my lady.
SEC. 'Tis better being a woman; thou
mayst do   10
Things that may prosper better, and the
fruit
Be thy own another day.

PLA.   Your wit still loves
To play the wanton.
SEC.   'Tis a sad time, Placentia;
Some pleasure would do well. The truth
is, I
Am weary of my life, and I would have
One fit of mirth before I leave the world.
PLA. Do not you blush to talk thus wildly?
SEC. 'Tis good manners
To be a little mad after my lady.   19
But I ha' done. Who is with her now?
PLA. Madam Valeria.
SEC. Not Celinda? There's a lady for my
humor!
A pretty book of flesh and blood, and well
Bound up, in a fair letter too. Would I
Had her with all the errata!
PLA.   She has not
An honorable fame.
SEC.   Her fame? That's nothing;
A little stain; her wealth will fetch again
The color, and bring honor into her
cheeks
As fresh. If she were mine, and I had
her
Exchequer, I know the way to make her
honest—   30
Honest to th' touch, the test, and the
last trial.
PLA. How, prithee?
SEC. Why, first I would marry her—that's
a verb material;
Then I would print her with an *index
Expurgatorius*, a table drawn
Of her court heresies; and, when she's
read
Cum privilegio,[1] who dares call her whore?
PLA. I'll leave you, if you talk thus.
SEC.   I ha' done.
Placentia, thou mayst be better com-
pany
After another progress; and now, tell
me,   40
Didst ever hear of such a patient mad-
ness
As my lady is possessed with? She has
raved
But twice; and she would fright the
cardinal,
Or at a supper if she did but poison
him,
It were a frenzy I could bear withal.
She calls him her dear governor—
[1] With license.

Enter Hernando disguised, having a letter.

PLA.   Who is this?

HER. Her secretary!—Sir,
Here is a letter, if it may have so
Much happiness to kiss her grace's hand.

SEC. From whom?

HER.   That's not in your commission, sir,   50
To ask, or mine to satisfy; she will
   want
No understanding when she reads.

SEC.   Alas!
Under your favor, sir, you are mistaken;
Her grace did never more want under-
   standing.

HER. How?

SEC. Have you not heard? Her skull is
   broken, sir,
And many pieces taken out; she's mad.

HER. The sad fame of her distraction
Has too much truth, it seems.

PLA.   If please you, sir,
To expect awhile, I will present the
   letter.   60

HER. Pray, do.—   *Exit Placen[tia].*
How long has she been thus distempered,
   sir?

SEC. Before the cardinal came to govern
   here,
Who, for that reason, by the king was
   made
Her guardian. We are now at his devotion.[1]

HER. A lamb given up to a tiger! May
   diseases
Soon eat him through his heart!

SEC.   Your pardon, sir.
I love that voice; I know it too a little.
Are not you—be not angry, noble sir;
I can with ease be ignorant again,   70
And think you are another man; but, if
You be that valiant gentleman they
   call—

HER. Whom? What?

SEC. That killed—I would not name him,
   if I thought
You were not pleased to be that very
   gentleman.

HER. Am I betrayed?

SEC. The devil sha' not
Betray you here. Kill me, and I will take
My death you are the noble colonel.

[1] Power of disposal.

We are all bound to you for the general's
   death,   80
Valiant Hernando! When my lady knows
You are here, I hope 'twill fetch her
   wits again.
But do not talk too loud; we are not all
Honest[2] i' th' house; some are the car-
   dinal's creatures.

HER. Thou wert faithful to thy lady. I
   am glad
'Tis night. But tell me how the churchman uses
The duchess.

Enter Antonelli.

SEC. He carries angels in his tongue and
   face, but I
Suspect his heart. This is one of his
   spawns.—
Signior Artonelli.

ANT.   Honest Antonio!   90

SEC. And how, and how—a friend of mine
   —where is
The cardinal's grace?

HER. [*Aside.*]   That will be never answered.

ANT. He means to sup here with the duchess.

SEC.   Will he?

ANT. We'll have the charming bottles at
   my chamber.
Bring that gentleman; we'll be mighty
   merry.

HER. [*Aside.*] I may disturb your jollity.

ANT.   Farewell, sweet—[*Exit.*]

SEC. Dear Antonelli!—[*Aside.*]   A round
   pox confound you!
This is court rhetoric at the back stairs.

Enter Placentia.

PLA. Do you know this gentleman?

SEC.   Not I.

PLA. My lady presently dismissed Va-
   leria,   100
And bade me bring him to her bed-
   chamber.

SEC. The gentleman has an honest face.

PLA.   Her words
Fell from her with some evenness and
   joy.—
Her grace desires your presence.

[2] Loyal.

Her.　　　　　　　　　　　I'll attend her.

Exit [*with Placentia*].

Sec. I would this soldier had the cardinal
Upon a promontory. With what a spring
The churchman would leap down! It
　　were a spectacle
Most rare to see him topple from the
　　precipice,
And souse in the salt water with a noise
To stun the fishes; and, if he fell into　　110
A net, what wonder would the simple
　　sea gulls
Have, to draw up the o'ergrown lobster,[1]
So ready boiled! He shall have my good
　　wishes.
This colonel's coming may be lucky; I
Will be sure none shall interrupt 'em.

Enter Celinda.

Cel.　　　　　　　　　　　　　　Is
Her grace at opportunity?
Sec.　　　　　　No, sweet madam;
She is asleep, her gentlewoman says.
Cel. My business is but visit. I'll expect.
Sec. That must not be, although I like
　　your company.　　　　　　　　119
Cel. You are grown rich, Mr. Secretary.
Sec. I, madam? Alas!
Cel. I hear you are upon another pur-
　　chase.
Sec. I upon a purchase?
Cel.　　　　　　If you want any sum—
Sec. If I could purchase your sweet favor,
　　madam?
Cel. You shall command me, and my
　　fortune, sir.
Sec. [*Aside.*] How's this?
Cel.　　　　I have observed you, sir, a staid
And prudent gentleman—and I shall
　　want—
Sec. Not me?
Cel. (*Aside.*) A father for some infant.
　　He has credit
I' th' world. I am not the first cast
　　lady　　　　　　　　　　　　130
Has married a secretary.
Sec. Shall I wait upon you?
Cel.　　　　　　　　　　Whither?
Sec.　　　　　　　　　　Any whither.
Cel. I may chance lead you then—
Sec. I shall be honored to obey. My blood
Is up, and in this humor I'm for any-
　　thing.

[1] An allusion to the color of the cardinal's robes.

Cel. Well, sir, I'll try your manhood.
Sec.　　　　　　　　'Tis my happiness;
You cannot please me better.
Cel. [*Aside.*]　　　　　This was struck
I' th' opportunity.
Sec.　　　　　I am made forever.

[*Exeunt.*]

[Scene iii.

Another room in the same.]

Enter Hernando and Duchess.

Her. Dear madam, do not weep.
Duch.　　　　　Y' are very welcome.
I ha' done; I wo' not shed a tear more
Till I meet Alvarez; then I'll weep for
　　joy.
He was a fine young gentleman, and sung
　　sweetly;
And you had heard him but the night
　　before
We were married, you would ha' sworn
　　he had been
A swan, and sung his own sad epitaph.
But we'll talk o' the cardinal.
Her.　　　　　　　Would his death
Might ransom your fair sense! He should
　　not live
To triumph in the loss. Beshrow[2] my
　　manhood,　　　　　　　　　　10
But I begin to melt.
Duch.　　　　　I pray, sir, tell me,
For I can understand, although they say
I have lost my wits; but they are safe
　　enough,
And I shall have 'em when the cardinal
　　dies,
Who had a letter from his nephew, too,
Since he was slain.
Her.　　　　　　　From whence?
Duch. I know not where he is. But in
　　some bower
Within a garden he is making chaplets,
And means to send me one; but I'll not
　　take it;
I have flowers enough, I thank him,
　　while I live.　　　　　　　　　20
Her. But do you love your governor?
Duch. Yes, but I'll never marry him; I am
　　promised
Already.
Her.　　　　To whom, madam?

[2] Beshrew, curse

Duch. Do not you
Blush when you ask me that? Must not
you be
My husband? I know why, but that's a
secret.
Indeed, if you believe me, I do love
No man alive so well as you. The cardi-
nal
Shall never know 't; he'll kill us both; and
yet
He says he loves me dearly, and has
promised   29
To make me well again. But I'm afraid
One time or other he will give me poison.
Her. Prevent him, madam, and take
nothing from him.
Duch. Why, do you think 'twill hurt me?
Her.   It will kill you.
Duch. I shall but die, and meet my dear-
loved lord,
Whom, when I have kissed, I'll come
again and work
A bracelet of my hair for you to carry
him,
When you are going to heaven; the
poesy [1] shall
Be my own name, in little tears, that I
Will weep next winter, which, congealed
i' th' frost,
Will show like seed pearl. You'll deliver
it?   40
I know he'll love and wear it for my sake.
Her. She is quite lost.
Duch.   I pray, give me, sir, your
pardon.
I know I talk not wisely; but, if you
had
The burthen of my sorrow, you would
miss
Sometimes your better reason. Now I'm
well.
What will you do when the cardinal
comes?
He must not see you for the world.
Her.   He sha' not;
I'll take my leave before he come.
Duch.   Nay, stay;
I shall have no friend left me when you
go.
He will but sup; he sha' not stay to lie
wi' me.   50
I have the picture of my lord abed;
Three are too much this weather.

1 Posy, inscription.

Enter Placentia.

Pla.   Madam, the cardinal.
Her. He shall sup with the devil.
Duch.   I dare not stay;
The red cock [2] will be angry. I'll come
again. *Exeunt [Duchess and Placentia].*
Her. This sorrow is no fable. Now I find
My curiosity is sadly satisfied.—
Ha! If the duchess in her straggled wits
Let fall words to betray me to the car-
dinal,
The panther will not leap more fierce to
meet
His prey, when a long want of food hath
parchèd   60
His starvèd maw, than he to print his
rage,
And tear my heartstrings. Everything
is fatal;
And yet she talked sometimes with chain
of sense,
And said she loved me. Ha! They come
not yet.
I have a sword about me, and I left
My own security to visit death.
Yet I may pause a little, and consider
Which way does lead me to 't most hon-
orably.
Does not the chamber that I walk in
tremble?   69
What will become of her, and me, and all
The world in one small hour? I do not
think
Ever to see the day again; the wings
Of night spread o'er me like a sable
hearsecloth;
The stars are all close mourners too; but I
Must not alone to the cold, silent grave,
I must not.—If thou canst, Alvarez, open
That ebon curtain, and behold the man,
When the world's justice fails, shall right
thy ashes,
And feed their thirst with blood! Thy
duchess is   79
Almost a ghost already, and doth wear
Her body like a useless upper garment,
The trim and fashion of it lost.—Ha!

Enter Placentia.

Pla. You need not doubt me, sir. My lady
prays
You would not think it long; she in my
ear

2 *I.e.,* the cardinal.

Commanded me to tell you that, when last
She drank, she had happy wishes to your health.

HER. And did the cardinal pledge it?

PLA.   He was not
Invited to 't, nor must he know you are here.

HER. What do they talk of, prithee?

PLA. His grace is very pleasant   90
         A lute is heard.
And kind to her; but her returns [1] are after
The sad condition of her sense, sometimes Unjointed.

HER.   They have music.

PLA.   A lute only.
His grace prepared, they say, the best of Italy,
That waits upon my lord.

HER.   He thinks the duchess
Is stung with a tarantula.

PLA.   Your pardon;
My duty is expected.   *Exit.*

HER.   Gentle lady!—
A voice too?

SONG (*within*)

STRE. Come, my Daphne, come away;
     We do waste the crystal day.   100
     'Tis Strephon calls.

DA.   What says my love?

STRE. Come, follow to the myrtle grove,
     Where Venus shall prepare
     New chaplets for thy hair.

DA.   Were I shut up within a tree,
     I'd rend my bark to follow thee.

STRE. My shepherdess, make haste;
     The minutes slide too fast.

DA.   In those cooler shades will I,
     Blind as Cupid, kiss thine eye.   110

STRE. In thy bosom then I'll stay;
     In such warm snow who would not
        lose his way?

CHOR. We'll laugh, and leave the world
        behind,
     And gods themselves that see,
     Shall envy thee and me,
     But never find
     Such joys, when they embrace a
        deity.

[HER.] If at this distance I distinguish, 'tis not
Church music; and the air's wanton, and no anthem

[1] Replies.

Sung to 't, but some strange ode of love
and kisses.   120
What should this mean?—Ha, he is coming hither.
I am betrayed; he marches in her hand.
I'll trust a little more; mute as the arras,
My sword and I here.
       [With drawn sword] he observes.

*Enter Cardinal, Duchess, Antonelli, and
Attendants.*

CAR. Wait you in the first chamber, and let none   .
Presume to interrupt us.—
          Ex[eunt] Serv[ants].
          [Aside.] She is pleasant;
Now for some art to poison all her innocence.

DUCH. *[Aside.]* I do not like the cardinal's humor; he
Little suspects what guest is in my chamber.   129

CAR. Now, madam, you are safe.
          [Embraces her.]

DUCH.   How means your lordship?

CAR. Safe in my arms, sweet duchess.

DUCH.   Do not hurt me.

CAR. Not for the treasures of the world!
     You are
My pretty charge. Had I as many lives
As I have careful thoughts to do you service,
I should think all a happy forfeit to
Delight your grace one minute; 'tis a heaven
To see you smile.

DUCH.   What kindness call you this?

CAR. It cannot want a name while you preserve
So plentiful a sweetness; it is love.

DUCH. Of me? How shall I know 't, my lord?   140

CAR. By this, and this, swift messengers to whisper
Our hearts to one another.   *Kisses.*

DUCH. Pray, do you come a-wooing?

CAR.   Yes, sweet madam;
You cannot be so cruel to deny me.

DUCH. What, my lord?

CAR.   Another kiss.

DUCH.   Can you
Dispense with this, my lord?—*(Aside.)*
Alas, I fear
Hernando is asleep, or vanished from me.

CAR. [*Aside*.] I have mocked my blood into a flame; and what
My angry soul had formed for my revenge   149
Is now the object of my amorous sense.
I have took a strong enchantment from her lips,
And fear I shall forgive Columbo's death,
If she consent to my embrace.—Come, madam.

DUCH. Whither, my lord?

CAR.   But to your bed or couch,
Where, if you will be kind, and but allow
Yourself a knowledge, Love, whose shape and raptures
Wise poets have but glorified in dreams,
Shall make your chamber his eternal palace,
And with such active and essential streams
Of new delights glide o'er your bosom, you   160
Shall wonder to what unknown world you are
By some blessed change translated. Why d'e pause,
And look so wild? Will you deny your governor?

DUCH. How came you by that cloven foot?

CAR.   Your fancy
Would turn a traitor to your happiness.
I am your friend; you must be kind.

DUCH.   Unhand me,
Or I'll cry out a rape.

CAR.   You wo' not, sure?

DUCH. I have been cozened with Hernando's shadow;
Here's none but heaven to hear me.—
Help! A rape!

CAR. Are you so good at understanding? Then,   170
I must use other argument.
He forces her. [*Hernando rushes forth.*]

HER. Go to, cardinal!
Strikes him. Ex[*it*] *Duch*[*ess*].

CAR. Hernando? Murder! Treason! Help!

HER. An army sha' not rescue thee. Your blood
Is much inflamed; I have brought a lancet wi' me
Shall open your hot veins, and cool your fever.

To vex thy parting soul, it was the same
Engine that pierced [1] Columbo's heart.

CAR.   Help! Murder!
[*Hernando stabs him.*]

Enter Antonelli and Servants.

ANT. Some ring the bell; 'twill raise the court.   179
My lord is murdered! 'Tis Hernando!
The bell rings.

HER. I'll make you all some sport.—[*Stabs himself.*] So; now we are even.
Where is the duchess? I would take my leave
Of her, and then bequeath my curse among you.   *Her*[*nando*] *falls.*

Enter King, Duchess, Valeria, Lords, Guard.

KING. How come these bloody objects?

HER. With a trick my sword found out. I hope he's paid.

1 LO. [*Aside*.] I hope so too.—A surgeon for my Lord Cardinal!

KING. Hernando?

DUCH. Justice! O, justice, sir, against a ravisher!

HER. Sir, I ha' done you service.

KING.   A bloody service.

HER. 'Tis pure scarlet.   190

Enter Surgeon.

CAR. [*Aside*.] After such care to perfect my revenge,
Thus banded [2] out o' th' world by a woman's plot!

HER. I have preserved the duchess from a rape.
Good night to me and all the world forever.   *Dies.*

KING. So impious!

DUCH.   'Tis most true; Alvarez' blood
Is now revenged; I find my brain return,
And every straggling sense repairing home.

CAR. I have deserved you should turn from me, sir.
My life hath been prodigiously wicked;
My blood is now the kingdom's balm.
O, sir,   200

[1] Emended by Gifford-Dyce. Original reads *pinc'd*.
[2] Bandied.

I have abused your ear, your trust, your people,
And my own sacred office; my conscience
Feels now the sting. O, show your char-
ity,
And with your pardon, like a cool, soft
- gale,
Fan my poor sweating soul, that wanders
through
Unhabitable climes and parchéd deserts.
But I am lost, if the great world forgive
me,
Unless I find your mercy for a crime
You know not, madam, yet, against your
life,
I must confess, more than my black in-
tents   210
Upon your honor; y' are already poi-
soned.
KING. By whom?
CAR. By me,
In the revenge I owed Columbo's loss.
With your last meat was mixed a poison
that
By subtle and by sure degrees must let
In death.
KING.   Look to the duchess, our physi-
cians!
CAR. Stay! I will deserve her mercy,
though I cannot
Call back the deed. In proof of my re-
pentance,   219
If the last breath of a now dying man
May gain your charity and belief, re-
ceive
This ivory box; in it an antidote
'Bove that they boast the great magis-
tral [1] medicine.
That powder, mixed with wine, by a most
rare
And quick access to the heart, will for-
tify it
Against the rage of the most nimble
poison.
I am not worthy to present her with it.
O, take it, and preserve her innocent life.
1 Lo. Strange, he should have a good thing
in such readiness.
CAR. 'Tis that, which in my jealousy and
state,   230
Trusting to false predictions of my
birth,
That I should die by poison, I preserved

[1] Sovereign, effectual.

For my own safety. Wonder not I made
That my companion was to be my refuge.

Enter Servant with a bowl of wine.

1 Lo. Here's some touch of grace.
CAR. In greater proof of my pure thoughts,
I take
This first, and with my dying breath
confirm
My penitence; it may benefit her life,
But not my wounds. [*He drinks.*] O,
hasten to preserve her;
And, though I merit not her pardon, let
not   240
Her fair soul be divorced.
                          [*The Duchess drinks.*]
KING. This is some charity; may it pros-
per, madam!
VAL. How does your grace?
DUCH. And must I owe my life to him
whose death
Was my ambition? Take this free ac-
knowledgment;
I had intent this night with my own hand
To be Alvarez' justicer.
KING.   You were mad,
And thought past apprehension of re-
venge.
DUCH. That shape I did usurp, great sir, to
give
My art more freedom and defense; but,
when   250
Hernando came to visit me, I thought
I might defer my execution,
Which his owe [2] rage supplied without
my guilt,
And, when his lust grew high, met with
his blood.
1 Lo. The cardinal smiles.
CAR.   Now my revenge has met
With you, my nimble duchess! I have
took
A shape [3] to give my act more freedom
too,
And now I am sure she's poisoned with
that dose
I gave her last.
KING.   Th' art not so horrid?
DUCH. Ha, some cordial!
CAR.   Alas, no preservative 260
Hath wings to overtake it. Were her
heart

[2] Own.   [3] Disguise, trick.

Locked in a quarry, it would search and kill
Before the aids can reach it. I am sure
You sha' not now laugh at me.
KING. How came you by that poison?
CAR.   I prepared it,
Resolving, when I had enjoyed her, which
The colonel prevented, by some art
To make her take it, and by death conclude
My last revenge. You have the fatal story.
KING. This is so great a wickedness it will   270
Exceed belief.
CAR.   I knew I could not live.
SURG. Your wounds, sir, were not desperate.
CAR.   Not mortal?
Ha, were they not mortal?
SURG.   If I have skill in surgery.
CAR. Then I have caught myself in my own engine.
2 Lo. It was your fate, you said, to die by poison.
CAR. That was my own prediction to abuse
Your faith. No human art can now resist it;
I feel it knocking at the seat of life;
It must come in. I have wracked all my own
To try your charities. Now it would be rare   280
If you but waft me with a little prayer;
My wings that flag may catch the wind, but 'tis
In vain; the mist is risen, and there's none
To steer my wand'ring bark.   Dies.
1 Lo.   He's dead.
KING.   With him
Die all deceivéd trust.
2 Lo. This was a strange impiety.
KING.   When men
Of gifts and sacred function once decline
From virtue, their ill deeds transcend example.
DUCH. The minute's come that I must take my leave, too.
Your hand, great sir; and, though you be a king,   290

We may exchange forgiveness. Heaven forgive,
And all the world! I come, I come, Alvarez!   Dies.
KING. Dispose their bodies for becoming funeral.
How much are kings abused by those they take
To royal grace, whom, when they cherish most
By nice indulgence, they do often arm
Against themselves, from whence this maxim springs:
None have more need of perspectives than kings.   *Exeunt.*

EPILOGUE

[VOICE.] (*Within.*) Mr. Pollard! Where's Mr. Pollard, for the epilogue?
    He is thrust upon the stage, and falls.
EPI. [*Rising.*] I am coming to you, gentlemen; the poet
Has helped me thus far on my way, but I'll
Be even with him: the play is a tragedy,
The first that ever he composed for us,
Wherein he thinks he has done prettily,

Enter Servant.

And I am sensible.[1] —I prithee, look.
Is nothing out of joint? Has he broke nothing?
SERV. No, sir, I hope.
EPI. Yes, he has broke his epilogue all to pieces.   10
Canst thou put it together again?
SERV.   Not I, sir.
EPI. Nor I. Prithee, begone!—[*Exit Servant.*] Hum!—Mr. Poet,
I have a teeming mind to be revenged.—
[*To audience.*] You may assist, and not be seen in 't now,
If you please, gentlemen, for I do know
He listens to the issue of his cause;
But blister not your hands in his applause,
Your private smile, your nod, or hum, to tell
My fellows that you like the business well.   19
And, when without a clap you go away,

[1] Satisfied.

I'll drink a small beer health to his
   second day,
And break his heart, or make him swear
   and rage
He'll write no more for the unhappy
   stage.

But that's too much; so we should lose.
   Faith, shew it,
And, if you like his play, 't 's as well he
   knew it.

FINIS.